Tax Formula for Individuals

Income (broadly defined)...	$xx,xxx
Less: Exclusions..	(x,xxx)
Gross income...	$xx,xxx
Less: Deductions *for* adjusted gross income...........................	(x,xxx)
Adjusted gross income...	$xx,xxx
Less: The greater of—	
Total itemized deductions	
or standard deduction...	(x,xxx)
Less: Personal and dependency exemptions*.............................	(x,xxx)
Deduction for qualified business income**.......................	(x,xxx)
Taxable income...	$xx,xxx
Tax on taxable income..	$ x,xxx
Less: Tax credits (including Federal income tax	
withheld and prepaid)..	(xxx)
Tax due (or refund)..	$ xxx

*Exemption deductions are not allowed from 2018 through 2025.
**Only applies from 2018 through 2025.

Basic Standard Deduction Amounts

Filing Status	2019	2020
Single	$12,200	$12,400
Married, filing jointly	24,400	24,800
Surviving spouse	24,400	24,800
Head of household	18,350	18,650
Married, filing separately	12,200	12,400

Amount of Each Additional Standard Deduction

Filing Status	2019	2020
Single	$1,650	$1,650
Married, filing jointly	1,300	1,300
Surviving spouse	1,300	1,300
Head of household	1,650	1,650
Married, filing separately	1,300	1,300

Personal and Dependency Exemption*

2019	2020
$4,200	$4,300

*Note: Exemption deductions have been
suspended from 2018 through 2025.
However, the personal and dependency
exemption amount is used for other purposes
(including determining whether a "qualifying
relative" is a taxpayer's dependent).

Intuit proconnect™

ProConnect™ Tax Online

Work like a pro.

Get the #1 cloud-based professional tax software for free.[1,2]

Go beyond the basics and connect with the modern tools you need to work efficiently.

- **Work with confidence.**
  Get returns done right the first time with access to all the forms you need, backed by industry-leading calculations and diagnostics.

- **Work smarter.**
  Save time with logical data-entry worksheets instead of traditional forms-based methods. Plus, get quick training resources so it's easy to stay up to speed.

- **Work from anywhere.**
  It's all online, so there's nothing to install or maintain. And whether you're on your mobile phone or laptop, PC or Mac — you're always good to go.

Visit TaxEducation.Intuit.com to get started.

Only one sign-up per student. No special code required. If you have trouble accessing or using the software, reach out to us at taxeducation_support@intuit.com anytime for help.

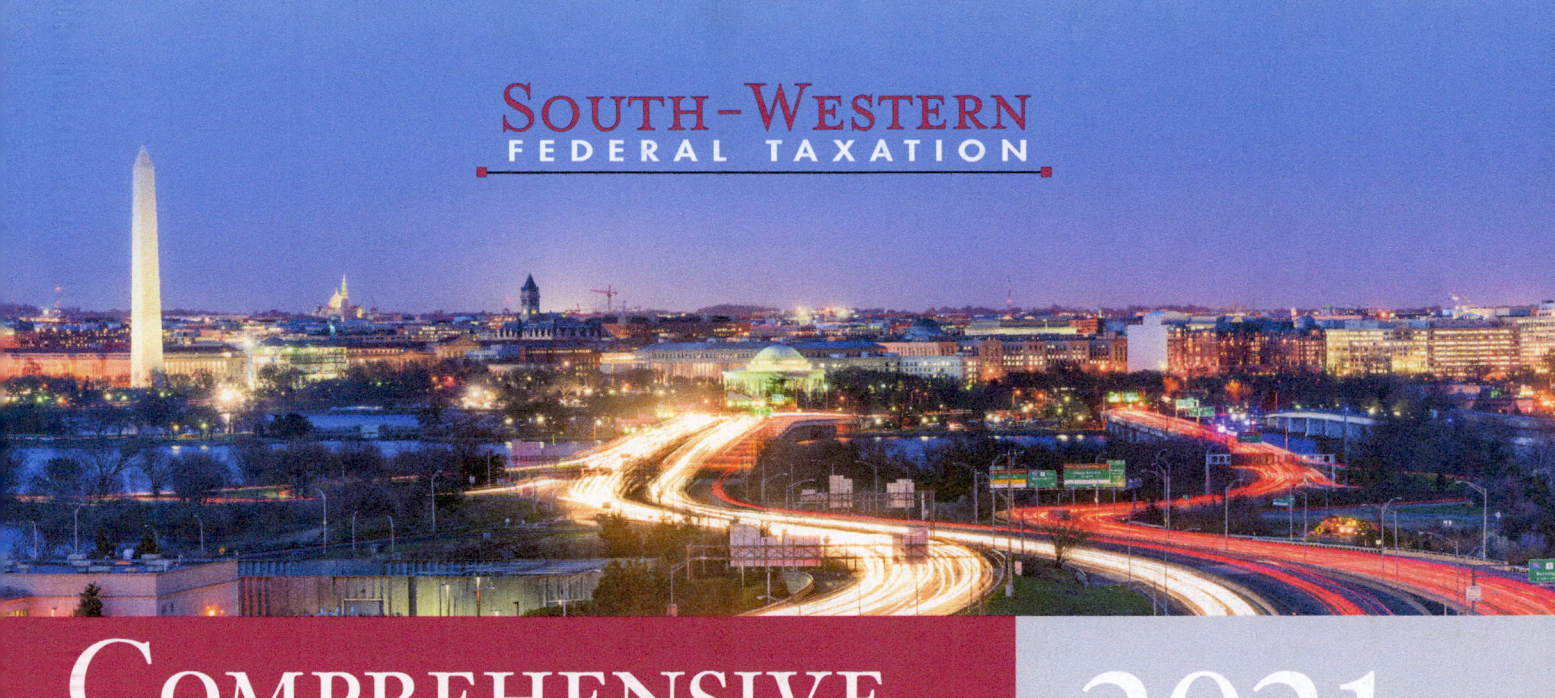

SOUTH-WESTERN
FEDERAL TAXATION

COMPREHENSIVE VOLUME

2021

General Editors

David M. Maloney
Ph.D., CPA

James C. Young
Ph.D., CPA

Annette Nellen
J.D., CPA, CGMA

Mark B. Persellin
Ph.D., CPA, CFP®

Contributing Authors

James H. Boyd
Ph.D., CPA
Arizona State University

Bradrick M. Cripe
Ph.D., CPA
Northern Illinois University

D. Larry Crumbley
Ph.D., CPA
Texas A&M University -
Corpus Christi

Andrew D. Cuccia
Ph.D., CPA
University of Oklahoma

Steven C. Dilley
J.D., Ph.D., CPA
Michigan State University

William H. Hoffman, Jr.
J.D., Ph.D., CPA
University of Houston

David M. Maloney
Ph.D., CPA
University of Virginia

Annette Nellen
J.D., CPA, CGMA
San Jose State University

Mark B. Persellin
Ph.D., CPA, CFP®
St. Mary's University

William A. Raabe
Ph.D., CPA
Madison, Wisconsin

Toby Stock
Ph.D., CPA
Ohio University

James C. Young
Ph.D., CPA
Northern Illinois University

Kristina Zvinakis
Ph.D.
The University of Texas
at Austin

CENGAGE

Australia • Brazil • Mexico • Singapore • United Kingdom • United States

South-Western Federal Taxation: Comprehensive Volume, 2021 Edition

David M. Maloney, James C. Young, Annette Nellen, Mark B. Persellin

Senior Vice President, Higher Ed Product, Content, and Market Development: Erin Joyner

Product Director: Jason Fremder

Assoc. Product Manager: Jonathan Gross

Sr. Content Manager: Nadia Saloom

Learning Designer: Emily S. Lehmann

Marketing Manager: Chris Walz

Marketing Coordinator: Sean D. Messer

Sr. Digital Delivery Lead: Tim Richison

Production Service: SPi Global

Designer: Chris A. Doughman

Text Designer: Red Hangar Design

Cover Image: iStock.com/Sean Pavone

Cover Designer: Bethany Bourgeois

Intellectual Property:
   Analyst: Ashley Maynard
   Project Manager: Carly Belcher

Design Images:
   Concept Summary: iStock.com/enot-poloskun
   Global Tax Issues: enot-poloskun/
   E+/Getty Images
   Ethics & Equity: iStock.com/LdF
   Cumulative Problems/Tax Return Problems:
   iStock.com/peepo
   Financial Disclosure Insights: Vyaseleva Elena/
   Shutterstock.com
   Framework 1040: Concept Photo/
   Shutterstock.com

For product information and technology assistance, contact us at **Cengage Customer & Sales Support, 1-800-354-9706** or **support.cengage.com.**

For permission to use material from this text or product, submit all requests online at **www.cengage.com/permissions**.

All tax forms within the text are: Source: Internal Revenue Service
Tax software: Source: Intuit ProConnect
Becker CPA Review: Source: Becker CPA
Excel screenshots: Source: Used with permissions from Microsoft
Intuit Proconnect, Becker, Microsoft and Checkpoint and all Intuit Proconnect, Becker, Microsoft and Checkpoint-based trademarks and logos are registered trademarks of Intuit Proconnect, Becker, Microsoft and Checkpoint in the United States and other countries.

ISSN: 0741-5184
2021 Annual Edition

Student Edition with Intuit ProConnect + RIA Checkpoint
ISBN: 978-0-357-35931-0
Loose Leaf Edition with Intuit Proconnect + RIA Checkpoint
ISBN: 978-0-357-35939-6

Cengage
200 Pier 4 Boulevard
Boston, MA 02210
USA

Cengage is a leading provider of customized learning solutions with employees residing in nearly 40 different countries and sales in more than 125 countries around the world. Find your local representative at **www.cengage.com**.

Cengage products are represented in Canada by Nelson Education, Ltd.

To learn more about Cengage platforms and services, register or access your online learning solution, or purchase materials for your course, visit **www.cengage.com**.

Printed in the United States of America
Print Number: 01   Print Year: 2020

Preface

COMMITTED TO EDUCATIONAL SUCCESS

South-Western Federal Taxation (SWFT) is the most trusted and best-selling series in college taxation. We are focused exclusively on providing the most useful, comprehensive, and up-to-date tax texts, online study aids, tax preparation tools, and research tools to help instructors and students succeed in their tax courses and beyond.

SWFT is a comprehensive package of teaching and learning materials, significantly enhanced with each edition to meet instructor and student needs and to add overall value to learning taxation.

The *SWFT Comprehensive Volume,* 2021 Edition provides a dynamic learning experience inside and outside of the classroom. Built with resources and tools that have been identified as the most important, our complete learning system provides options for students to achieve success.

In addition, the *SWFT Comprehensive Volume,* 2021 Edition provides accessible, comprehensive, and authoritative coverage of the relevant tax code and regulations as they pertain to the individual and business taxpayer, as well as coverage of all major developments in Federal Taxation.

In revising the 2021 Edition, we focused on:

- *Accessibility. Clarity. Substance.* The text authors and editors made this their mantra as they revised the 2021 Edition. Coverage has been streamlined to make it more accessible to students, and difficult concepts have been clarified, all without losing the substance that makes up the *South-Western Federal Taxation* series.

- *Developing professional skills.* SWFT excels in bringing students to a professional level in their tax knowledge and skills, to prepare them for immediate success in their careers. In this regard, we include development of speaking and writing communications skills, the use of tax preparation and tax research software, orientation toward success on the CPA Exam, consideration of the time value of money in the tax planning process, and facility with advanced spreadsheet applications and data analytics.

- *CengageNOWv2 as a complete learning system.* Cengage Learning understands that digital learning solutions are central to the classroom. Through sustained research, we continually refine our learning solutions in CengageNOWv2 to meet evolving student and instructor needs. CengageNOWv2 fulfills learning and course management needs by offering a personalized study plan, video lectures, auto-graded homework, auto-graded tests, and a full eBook with features and advantages that address common challenges.

Learning Tools and Features to Help Students Make the Connection

FULL-COLOR DESIGN: We understand that students struggle with learning difficult tax law concepts and applying them to real-world scenarios. The 2021 Edition uses color to bring the text to life, capture student attention, and present the tax law in an understandable and logical format.

❑ Selected **content is streamlined** to guide students in focusing on the most important concepts for the CPA Exam while still providing in-depth coverage of topics.

❑ Examples are clearly labeled and directly follow concepts to assist with student application. An **average of over 40 examples in each chapter** use realistic situations to illustrate the complexities of the tax law and allow students to integrate chapter concepts with illustrations and examples.

COMPUTATIONAL EXERCISES: Students need to learn to apply the concepts covered in each chapter. These exercises, many of which mirror text examples, allow students to practice and apply what they are learning.

❏ Found in the end-of-chapter sections of the textbook

❏ CengageNOWv2 provides algorithmic versions of these problems

26. **LO.1** Melba purchases land from Adrian. Melba gives Adrian $225,000 in cash and agrees to pay Adrian an additional $400,000 one year later plus interest at 5%.
   a. What is Melba's adjusted basis for the land at the acquisition date?
   b. What is Melba's adjusted basis for the land one year later?

27. **LO.1** On July 1, 2020, Katrina purchased tax-exempt bonds (face value of $75,000) for $82,000. The bonds mature in five years, and the annual interest rate is 3%.
   a. How much interest income and/or interest expense must Katrina report in 2020, assuming that straight-line amortization is appropriate?
   b. What is Katrina's adjusted basis for the bonds on January 1, 2021?

RESEARCH AND DATA ANALYTICS PROBLEMS:

❏ Research problems provide students with vital practice in an increasingly demanded skill area. Some of these end-of-chapter items ask students to analyze tax data, helping them to understand the application of this information in various scenarios. These essential features prepare students for professional tax environments.

BECKER PROFESSIONAL EDUCATION REVIEW QUESTIONS: End-of-Chapter CPA Review Questions from Becker PREPARE STUDENTS FOR SUCCESS. Students review key concepts using proven questions from Becker Professional Education®—one of the industry's most effective tools to prepare for the CPA Exam.

❏ Located in select end-of-chapter sections

❏ Tagged by concept in CengageNOWv2

❏ Questions similar to what students would actually find on the CPA Exam

Becker CPA Review Questions

1. Jasmin purchased 100 shares of Pinkstey Corporation (publicly traded company) on January 1 of year 1 for $5,000. The FMV of the shares at the end of year 1 was $6,000. On January 1 of year 4, Pinkstey Corporation declared a 2-for-1 stock split when the fair market value of the stock was $65 per share. On January 1 of year 5, Jasmin sold all of her Pinkstey Corporation stock when the fair market value was $40 per share. Which of the following statements is true?

   a. Jasmin reports $6,500 in gross income for the 2-for-1 stock split in year 4.
   b. Jasmin's basis in the Pinkstey Corporation stock at the end of year 4 is $65 per share.
   c. Jasmin has no taxable income for the Pinkstey Corporation stock in year 4.
   d. Jasmin owns 100 shares in Pinkstey Corporation stock at the end of year 4.

Becker.

See how the SWFT series helps students understand the big picture and the relevancy behind what they are learning.

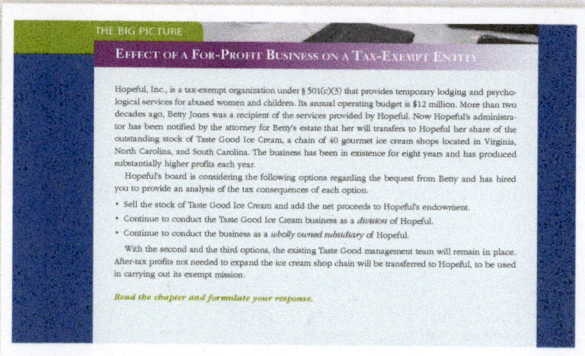

THE BIG PICTURE: Tax Solutions for the Real World. Taxation comes alive at the start of each chapter as The Big Picture examples give a glimpse into the lives, families, careers, and tax situations of typical filers. Students will follow a family, individual, or other taxpayer throughout the chapter, to discover how the concepts they are learning apply in the real world.

Finally, to solidify student comprehension, each chapter concludes with a **Refocus on the Big Picture** summary and tax planning scenario. These scenarios re-emphasize the concepts and topics from the chapter and allow students to confirm their understanding of the material.

FRAMEWORK 1040:

Fitting It All Together.
This chapter-opening feature demonstrates how individual income tax topics fit together, using the Income Tax Formula for Individuals as the framework. The framework helps students organize their understanding of the chapters and topics to see how they relate to the basic tax formula and then identify where these items are reported on Form 1040. Framework 1040 helps students navigate topics by explaining how tax concepts are organized.

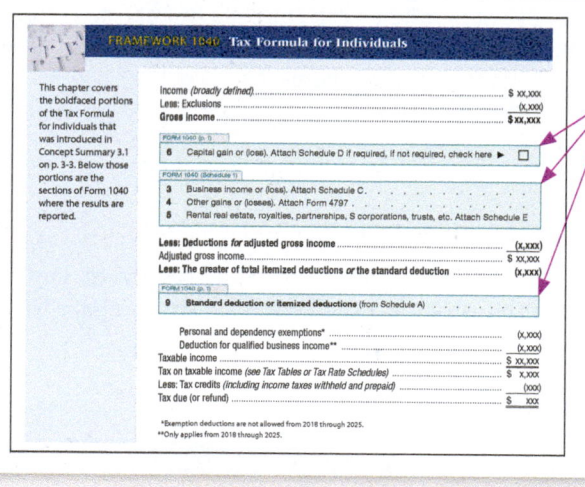

Use this chapter-opening **Framework 1040**, which shows the topics as they appear in the individual tax formula, to understand where on Form 1040 these chapter topics would appear.

vi

FINANCIAL DISCLOSURE INSIGHTS: Tax professionals need to understand how taxes affect financial statements. **Financial Disclosure Insights**, appearing throughout the text, use current information about existing taxpayers to highlight book-tax reporting differences, effective tax rates, and trends in reporting conventions.

> **FINANCIAL DISCLOSURE INSIGHTS** **Tax and Book Depreciation**
>
> A common book-tax difference relates to the depreciation amounts that are reported for GAAP and Federal income tax purposes. Typically, tax depreciation deductions are accelerated; that is, they are claimed in earlier reporting periods than is the case for financial accounting purposes.
>
> Almost every tax law change since 1980 has included depreciation provisions that accelerate the related deductions relative to the expenses allowed under GAAP. Accelerated cost recovery deductions represent a means by which the taxing jurisdiction infuses the business with cash flow created by the reduction in the year's tax liabilities.
>
> For instance, recently, about one-quarter of General Electric's deferred tax liabilities related to depreciation differences. For Toyota's and Ford's depreciation differences, that amount was about one-third. And for the trucking firm Ryder Systems, depreciation differences accounted for all but 1 percent of the deferred tax liabilities.

> **ETHICS & EQUITY** **Punching the Time Clock at Year-End**
>
> As the end of the tax year approaches, Julie, a successful full-time real estate developer and investor, recognizes that her income tax situation for the year could be bleak. Unless she and her spouse, Ralph, are able to generate more hours of participation in one of her real estate rental activities, they will not reach the material participation threshold. Consequently, the tax losses from the venture will not be deductible. To ensure deductibility, Julie suggests the following plan:
>
> - She will document the time she spends "thinking" about her rental activities.
> - During the week, Ralph will visit the apartment building to oversee (in a management role) the operations of the rentals.
>
> - On weekends, she and Ralph will visit the same units to further evaluate the operations.
> - Also on the weekends, while they are doing their routine household shopping, they will be on the lookout for other rental properties to buy. Julie plans to count both her and Ralph's weekend hours toward the tally of total participation.
>
> Julie contends that the law clearly allows the efforts of one's spouse to count for purposes of the material participation tests. Likewise, nothing in the tax law requires taxpayers to be efficient in their hours of participation. How do you react?

ETHICS & EQUITY: Some tax issues do not have just one correct answer. **Ethics & Equity** features will spark critical thinking and invite classroom discussion, enticing students to evaluate their own value system. Suggested answers to Ethics & Equity scenarios appear in the Solutions Manual.

TAX PLANNING: Chapters include a separate section calling attention to how taxpayers can use the law to reach financial and other goals. Tax planning applications and suggestions also appear throughout each chapter.

> **27-5 TAX PLANNING**
>
> **27-5a The Federal Gift Tax**
>
> For gifts that generate a tax, consideration must be given to the present value to the donor of the gift taxes paid. Because the donor loses the use of these funds, the expected interval between a gift (the imposition of the gift tax) and death (the imposition of the estate tax) may make the gift less attractive from an economic standpoint. On the plus side, however, are the estate tax savings that result from any gift tax paid. Because these funds are no longer in the gross estate of the donor (except for certain gifts within three years of death), the estate tax thereon is avoided.

> **GLOBAL TAX ISSUES** **Tracking Down Tax Dollars**
>
> Non-U.S. persons who earn income within the United States may need to file a Federal income tax return, but they may not have a Social Security number for filing purposes. If not, they can use a nine-digit Individual Tax Identification Number (ITIN) instead. The IRS issues ITINs upon the submission of an application and proof of identification (e.g., a driver's license). As the IRS does not require an applicant to show that he or she is in the United States legally, the ITINs are freely available to undocumented persons (i.e., illegal immigrants). The use of an ITIN also can enable the holder to carry out other financial transactions (e.g., establish a bank account, secure a credit card, and obtain a loan).
>
> The position of the IRS is that the current ITIN procedure brings in revenue that otherwise would not be forthcoming. Some undocumented workers want to comply with the law and pay the income taxes they owe. This practice should not be discouraged, as the tax law applies with equal force to legal and illegal residents of the United States.
>
> However, ITINs have been criticized for their use by illegal immigrants and undocumented workers. A recent report found that individuals who are not authorized to work in the United States were paid $4.2 billion in refundable tax credits, such as the child tax credit, because they were able to file tax returns using an ITIN.

GLOBAL TAX ISSUES: The **Global Tax Issues** feature gives insight into the ways in which taxation is affected by international concerns and illustrates the effects of various events on tax liabilities across the globe.

MASTERY
APPLICATION
MOTIVATION

CengageNOWv2 is a powerful course management tool and online homework resource that elevates student thinking by providing superior content designed with the entire student workflow in mind.

❏ **MOTIVATION:** engage students and better prepare them for class

❏ **APPLICATION:** help students learn problem-solving behavior and skills to guide them to complete taxation problems on their own

❏ **MASTERY:** help students make the leap from memorizing concepts to actual critical thinking

Motivation —

Many instructors find that students come to class unmotivated and unprepared. To help with engagement and preparedness, CengageNOWv2 for SWFT offers:

❏ **"Tax Drills" test students on key concepts and applications.** With three to five questions per learning objective, these "quick-hit" questions help students prepare for class lectures or review prior to an exam.

Application —

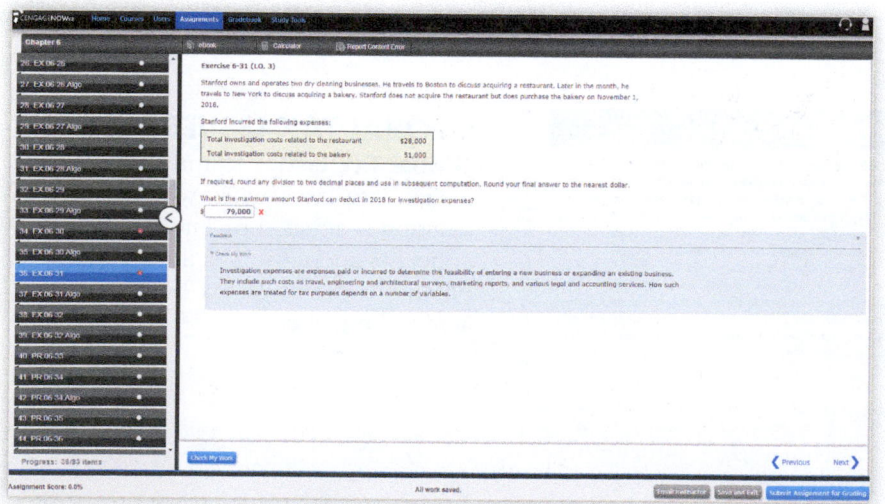

Students need to learn problem-solving behavior and skills, to guide them to complete taxation problems on their own. However, as students try to work through homework problems, sometimes they become stuck and need extra help. To reinforce concepts and keep students on the right track, CengageNOWv2 for SWFT offers the following.

❏ **End-of-chapter homework from the text** is expanded and enhanced to follow the workflow a professional would use to solve various client scenarios. These enhancements better engage students and encourage them to think like a tax professional.

- ❏ **Algorithmic versions** of end-of-chapter homework are available for computational exercises and at least 15 problems per chapter.

- ❏ **"Check My Work" Feedback.** Homework questions include immediate feedback so students can learn as they go. Levels of feedback include an option for "check my work" prior to submission of an assignment.

- ❏ **Post-Submission Feedback.** After submitting an assignment, students receive even more extensive feedback explaining why their answers were incorrect. Instructors can decide how much feedback their students receive and when, including the full solution.

- ❏ **Built-in Test Bank** for online assessment.

Mastery —

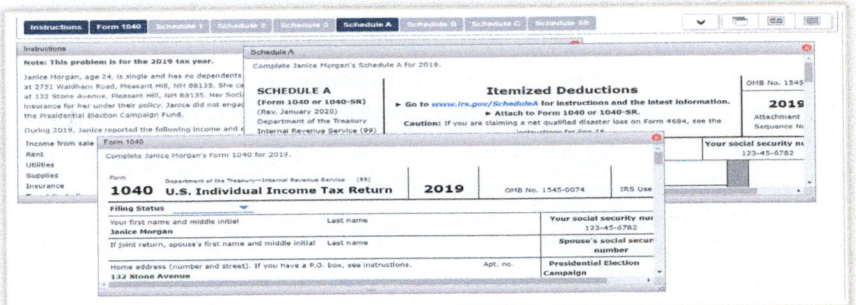

- ❏ **Tax Form Problems** give students the option to complete the Cumulative Intuit ProConnect Problems and other homework items found in the end-of-chapter manually or in a digital environment.

- ❏ **"What-If" Questions** allow students to develop a deeper understanding of the material as they are challenged to use their prior knowledge of the tax situations and critically think through new attributes to determine how the outcome will change.

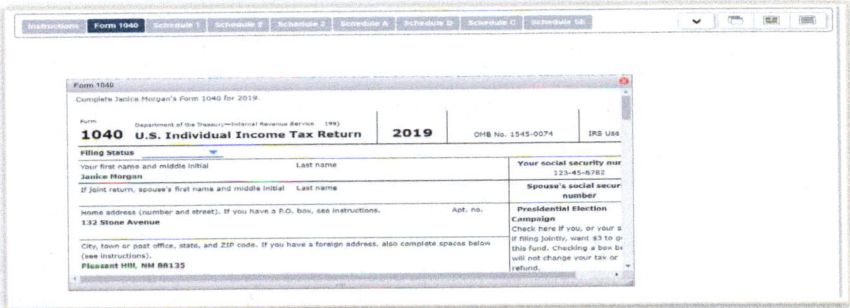

- ❏ **An Adaptive Study Plan** comes complete with an eBook, practice quizzes, crossword puzzle, glossary, and flashcards. It is designed to help give students additional support and prepare them for the exam.

CengageNOWv2 Instant Access Code ISBN: 978-0-357-35947-1 (two-semester access)

Contact your Cengage Learning Consultant about different bundle options.

EXTENSIVELY REVISED. DEFINITIVELY UP TO DATE.

Each year the **South-Western Federal Taxation** series is updated with thousands of changes to each text. Some of these changes result from the feedback we receive from instructors and students in the form of reviews, focus groups, web surveys, and personal e-mail correspondence with our authors and team members. Other changes come from our careful analysis of the evolving tax environment. **We make sure that every tax law change relevant to the introductory taxation course was considered, summarized, and fully integrated into the revision of text and supplementary materials.**

The **South-Western Federal Taxation** authors have made every effort to keep all materials up to date and accurate. All chapters contain the following general changes for the 2021 Edition.

- Updated materials to reflect changes made by Congress through legislative action (including the tax provisions contained in the Consolidated Appropriations Act of 2020).
- Streamlined chapter content (where applicable) to clarify material and make it easier for students to understand.
- Revised numerous materials as the result of changes caused by indexing of statutory amounts.
- Revised Problem Materials, Computational Exercises, and CPA Exam problems.
- Updated Chapter Outlines to provide an overview of the material and to make it easier to locate specific topics.
- Revised *Financial Disclosure Insights* and *Global Tax Issues* as to current developments.

In addition, the following materials are available online.

- An appendix that helps instructors broaden and customize coverage of important tax provisions of the Affordable Care Act. (Instructor Companion Website at **www.cengage.com/login**)
- The Depreciation and the Accelerated Cost Recovery System (ACRS) appendix. (Instructor Companion Website at **www.cengage.com/login**)
- An appendix that has comprehensive tax return problems for the 2019 tax filing year (Appendix E). (Instructor Companion Website at **www.cengage.com/login**)

- The *Taxation in the Real World* weekly blog posts for instructors. (**tinyurl.com/swft-blog**)

Chapter 1

- Clarified the wording for several learning objectives.
- Clarified the terms *progressive, regressive,* and *proportional* using new examples. These terms are used in the context of how a tax affects low-income taxpayers relative to high-income taxpayers.
- Added a new question to encourage students to review the text to identify features that can help them in learning about taxes (e.g., the glossary and list of key terms in each chapter).

Chapter 2

- Made minor changes to Exhibit 2.4 and Concept Summary 2.1.
- Updated references and citations throughout the chapter.
- Updated discussion on changes to the CPA Exam.

Chapter 3

- Updated chapter materials to reflect revised Form 1040 and related schedules.
- Added exhibit summarizing when Form 1040 Schedules 1 through 3 are used.
- Updated the exhibit summarizing the 0, 15, and 20 percent break points for the alternative tax on net capital gains.
- Added new material on the taxation of virtual currency (text Section 3-7e).
- Updated chapter materials to reflect 2020 inflation adjustments.
- Revised and clarified materials as needed throughout the chapter.

Chapter 4

- Combined former text Sections 4-1d and 4-1e discussing the differences between economic, accounting, and taxable income.
- Moved discussion of group term life insurance to Chapter 5 with other employment-related fringe benefits.

- Added the recognition of unrealized gains on marketable securities for financial reporting purposes as an example of a financial accounting income versus taxable income difference.
- Deleted discussion of Rev.Proc. 2004–34 dealing with the treatment of unearned income prior to the passage of IRC § 451(c).
- Expanded the examples related to imputed interest to include the deemed retransfer from the lender to the borrower required in § 7872(a)(1)(A).

Chapter 5

- Added group term life insurance to discussion of employee fringe benefits (new text Section 5-8e; previously covered in Chapter 4).
- Added a discussion of Rev.Rul. 2019–11 on how the tax benefit rule applies in light of the $10,000 SALT cap added by the TCJA of 2017.
- Updated text materials for 2020 inflation adjustments; revised other materials as needed.
- Added an additional problem on the tax benefit rule with the $10,000 SALT cap.

Chapter 6

- Revised and updated chapter materials as needed; clarified chapter materials when necessary.
- Updated Exhibit 6.2 to reflect revised Form 1040 (and Schedules).
- Updated Exhibit 6.3, summarizing the limitations that may reduce or eliminate the QBI deduction.
- Updated the Ethics & Equity item on marijuana to reflect both medical and nonmedical adult use activities.
- Updated text and end-of-chapter materials as needed to reflect revised inflation-adjusted items and revised Form 1040 (and Schedules).

Chapter 7

- Revised and clarified chapter materials as needed.
- Updated text and end-of-chapter materials to reflect annual inflation adjustments.

- Revised a Research Problem to include implications of states not conforming to TCJA of 2017 changes [e.g., personal casualty losses, excess business loss limitation, net operating loss limitations (carryforward only; 80 percent of taxable income limitation)].

Chapter 8

- Removed discussion of pre-MACRS depreciation systems at beginning of chapter; directed readers to online appendix summarizing these pre-1987 rules.
- Updated chapter materials to reflect various inflation adjustments.
- Updated in-chapter example illustrating Form 4562 and Schedule C (Form 1040) to 2019 forms.
- Selectively removed some overemphasized content.

Chapter 9

- Revised and clarified chapter materials based on adopter feedback.
- Updated text and end-of-chapter materials to reflect revised standard mileage amounts.
- Updated content related to § 401(k) plans, self-employed retirement plans, IRA and Roth IRA, and rollovers.
- Updated balance of end-of-chapter materials as needed.

Chapter 10

- Revised and clarified text as needed.
- Updated text and end-of-chapter materials for annual inflation adjustments.

Chapter 11

- Clarified special rule for real estate professionals, specifically, that if the requirements are met, they can apply a material participation test to their rental real estate (i.e., not *per se* a passive activity).
- Revised and clarified materials as needed throughout the chapter.
- Updated text and end-of-chapter materials to reflect annual inflation adjustments.

Chapter 12

- Updated chapter materials as needed for new law and inflation adjustments.

Chapter 13

- Clarified rules on basis of inherited property.
- Clarified and expanded wash sale rule coverage.

Chapter 14

- Updated text materials for 2020 inflation adjustments to Tax Rate Schedules and alternative tax rate brackets (for net capital gains).
- Added new exhibit on the alternative Tax Rate Schedule for net capital gains.

Chapter 15

- Changed title to better reflect chapter content.
- Revised and clarified materials based on feedback from adopters.
- Updated chapter materials to reflect inflation adjustments to threshold amounts for the QBI deduction.
- Expanded an end-of-chapter problem to include a computation of the taxpayer's marginal tax rate when the taxpayer is in the QBI deduction phaseout range.
- Updated end-of-chapter materials as needed (including revisions for inflation adjustments to threshold amounts).

Chapter 16

- Simplified the explanation of the possible limitation on the salary deduction for a personal service corporation using a special tax year per § 444.
- Removed questions on the salary reduction calculation for a personal service corporation making a § 444 election to use a year other than the required calendar year.

Chapter 17

- Updated chapter materials as needed for new rulings and inflation adjustments.

- Significantly revised chapter materials on accounting for income taxes, emphasizing and illustrating the balance sheet approach adopted by ASC 740.
- Updated end-of-chapter materials as needed.
- Added a new Research Problem focused on the donation of inventory items to local food banks or shelters.

Chapter 18

- Streamlined writing to reduce passive voice and increase clarity.
- Added a new planning section comparing a corporation to proprietorships that do/do not qualify for the § 199A qualified business income deduction.
- Added a new problem that asks students to use Microsoft Excel to compare a corporation to proprietorships that do/do not qualify for the § 199A qualified business income deduction.

Chapter 19

- Revised and updated chapter materials as needed; clarified chapter materials when necessary.
- Created a new Research Problem on Qualified Opportunity Zones (established by the TCJA of 2017).
- Updated end-of-chapter materials as needed.

Chapter 20

- Updated and clarified text and end-of-chapter materials as needed.
- Revised introductory paragraphs in the reorganization discussion.
- Replaced the Financial Disclosure discussion about M&A deals that do not succeed.
- Replaced internet Research Problem 5.

Chapter 21

- Revised LO 7 to focus on the partner's perspective, which now reads as "Describe the information provided on a partner's Schedule K–1 and how the partner reports that information."

- Split old text Section 21-3 into partnership and partner reporting sections.
  - Section 21-3, Partnership Operations and Reporting
  - Section 21-4, Partner Calculations and Reporting
- Revised and renamed text Section 21-5, Other Taxes on Partnership Income.
  - Simplified related-party transactions content and incorporated it into the corresponding section of the Tax Planning materials (text Section 21-9).
  - Covered (only) self-employment tax and the net investment income tax.
- Replaced old Exhibit 21.1 with a chart summarizing partnership taxable year options.
- Added a new Financial Disclosure Insights item to introduce special features of GAAP-basis financial statements issued by partnerships.
- Replaced Research Problem 3.

Chapter 22

- Revised introductory discussion and added Exhibit 22.1 comparing business entities.
- Reduced materials concerning the QBI regime and straight debt.
- Added two new Microsoft Excel problems.
- Added a new Research Problem.

Chapter 23

- Updated statistics relative to the exempt economy, private foundations, and UBIT.
- Added discussion of the effects of tax exemptions on state and local governments.
- Revised and reorganized material on determining exempt status.
- Added material about the investment income tax on universities.
- Added material on filing the Form 990, including potential penalties and loss of exempt status.
- Added one more Microsoft Excel problem.

Chapter 24

- Updated statistics about state/local tax collections.
- Clarified the role of the Multistate Tax Compact, the MTC, and the UDITPA.
- Updated financial statement data for the state/local tax expenses of selected corporations.
- Added definitional material for the use tax and illustrated it in new Exhibit 24.4.
- Added material as to economic sales/use tax nexus and nexus by marketplace facilitators.
- Added material on minimum income taxes by states for flow-through entities.
- Expanded the discussion of how § 118 may generate gross income from government incentives for retention or expansion of a business; added a related planning discussion to the Refocus on the Big Picture feature.
- Added economic nexus items to two Research Problems.

Chapter 25

- Combined income sourcing rules into a single section (text Section 25-3a).
- Updated and added statistics about the global economy, worldwide tax rates, treaty withholding rates, advance pricing agreements, FTC deferrals, and CFCs.
- Added explanation of withholding taxes for payments to non-U.S. persons.
- Added definition of a foreign branch.
- Clarified the makeup of the foreign tax credit general income basket.
- Clarified the application of § 367 to cross-border transfers.
- Reduced discussion of the 2017 one-time transition tax on unrepatriated profits.
- Added comments about tax planning for multinationals.
- Added a Microsoft Excel feature to one problem.

Chapter 26

- Updated statistics about IRS budget and audit rates.
- Updated IRS organizational chart to show the new Independent Office of Appeals.
- Updated statistics about the informant and whistleblower programs.
- Updated various penalty and interest amounts and statistics.
- Updated statistics for offers in compromise.
- Added two more internet Research Problems.

Chapter 27

- Incorporated indexed amounts for deductions, exclusions, and credits.
- Added a cross reference to text Exhibit 28.2 to illustrate the terms and operations of a trust in defining present and future interests.

- Clarified language defining the incidents of ownership for a life insurance policy.
- Clarified the discussion involving the optimal use of the bypass amount.
- Added another Microsoft Excel requirement.

Chapter 28

- Updated statistics as to Form 1041 filings and income sources.
- Updated comparison of Federal income tax liabilities among types of filing entity, showing the high marginal rates on fiduciaries.
- Updated amounts pertaining to AMT and the NIIT for fiduciary entities and clarification of the application of the NIIT to trusts.
- Added and updated examples of entity deductions and their limitations.
- Expanded computations in Example 13.
- Expanded Concept Summary 28.3.

TAX LAW OUTLOOK

From your SWFT Series Editors

Although Congress continues to discuss technical corrections to the Tax Cuts and Jobs Act of 2017 (TCJA), the 2020 election likely will put most legislative tax changes on hold. Nonetheless, we anticipate that Treasury and the IRS will continue to issue guidance on the TCJA throughout 2020 and beyond. With any additional guidance forthcoming, taxpayers and their advisers will continue to evaluate how TCJA changes affect their financial and tax planning strategies and will adjust their plans appropriately. In addition, as candidates prepare for the 2020 presidential election, many tax ideas will be suggested. They present opportunities for students and researchers to analyze how they work and how they measure up against principles of good tax policy.

The SWFT editors will be monitoring these activities and provide updates to adopters as needed, including via the SWFT blog *Taxation in the Real World* (**tinyurl.com/swft-blog**).

SUPPLEMENTS SUPPORT STUDENTS AND INSTRUCTORS

Built around the areas students and instructors have identified as the most important, our integrated supplements package offers more flexibility than ever before to suit the way instructors teach and students learn.

Online and Digital Resources for Students

CengageNOWv2 is a powerful course management and online homework tool that provides robust instructor control and customization to optimize the student learning experience and meet desired outcomes.

CengageNOWv2 Instant Access Code ISBN:
978-0-357-35947-1 (two-semester access)

Contact your Cengage Learning Consultant about different bundle options.

 Thomson Reuters Checkpoint™ is the leading online tax research database used by professionals. There are three simple ways Checkpoint™ helps introduce students to tax research:

- Intuitive web-based design makes it fast and simple to find what you need.
- Checkpoint™ provides a comprehensive collection of primary tax law, cases, and rulings along with analytical insight you simply can't find anywhere else.
- Checkpoint™ has built-in productivity tools such as calculators to make research more efficient—a resource more tax pros use than any other.

Six months' access to Checkpoint™ (after activation) is packaged automatically with every NEW copy of the textbook.*

 More than software: Put the experience of ProConnect™ Tax Online on your side.

- Get returns done right the first time with access to all the forms you need, backed by industry-leading calculations and diagnostics.
- Save time with logical data-entry worksheets instead of traditional forms-based methods.
- It's all online, so there's nothing to install or maintain.

Online access to ProConnect™ Tax Online software is offered with each NEW copy of the textbook—at no additional cost to students.*

www.cengage.com Students can use **www.cengage.com** to select this textbook and access Cengage Learning content, empowering them to choose the most suitable format and giving them a better chance of success in the course. Buy printed materials, eBooks, and digital resources directly through Cengage Learning and save at **www.cengage.com**.

Online Student Resources

Students can go to **www.cengage.com** for free resources to help them study as well as the opportunity to purchase additional study aids. These valuable free study resources will help students earn a better grade:

- Flashcards use chapter terms and definitions to aid students in learning tax terminology for each chapter.
- Online glossary for each chapter provides terms and definitions from the text in alphabetical order for easy reference.
- Learning objectives can be downloaded for each chapter to help keep students on track.
- Tax tables used in the textbook are downloadable for reference.

CENGAGE UNLIMITED The first-of-its-kind digital subscription designed specially to lower costs.

Students get total access to everything Cengage has to offer on demand—in one place. That's 20,000 eBooks, 2,300 digital learning products, and dozens of study tools across 70 disciplines and over 675 courses. **www.cengage.com/unlimited**

Printed Resources for Students

Looseleaf Edition (978-0-357-35939-6)

This version provides all the pages of the text in an unbound, three-hole punched format for portability and ease of use. Online access to ProConnect™ Tax Online software is included with every NEW textbook as well as Checkpoint™ from Thomson Reuters.*

*NEW printed copies of the textbook are automatically packaged with access to Checkpoint™ and ProConnect™ Tax Online tax software. If students purchase the eBook, they will not automatically receive access to Checkpoint™ and ProConnect™ Tax Online software.

Comprehensive Supplements Support Instructors' Needs

CengageNOWv2 is a powerful course management and online homework tool that provides robust instructor control and customization to optimize the student learning experience and meet desired outcomes. In addition to the features and benefits mentioned earlier for students, CengageNOWv2 includes these features for instructors:

- **Learning Outcomes Reporting** and the ability to analyze student work from the gradebook. Each exercise and problem is tagged by topic, learning objective, level of difficulty, estimated completion time, and business program standards to allow greater guidance in developing assessments and evaluating student progress.

- **Built-in Test Bank for online assessment.** The Test Bank files are included in CengageNOWv2 so that they may be used as additional homework or tests.

Solutions Manual

Written by the **South-Western Federal Taxation** editors and authors, the Solutions Manual features solutions arranged in accordance with the sequence of chapter material.

Solutions to all homework items are tagged with their Estimated Time to Complete, Level of Difficulty, and Learning Objective(s), as well as the AACSB's and AICPA's core competencies—giving instructors more control than ever in selecting homework to match the topics covered. The Solutions Manual also contains the solutions to Appendix E: Comprehensive Tax Return Problems and answers with explanations to the end-of-chapter Becker CPA Review Questions. **Available on the Instructor Companion Website at www.cengage.com/login.**

PowerPoint® Lectures with Notes

The Instructor PowerPoint® Lectures contain more than 30 slides per chapter, including outlines and instructor guides, concept definitions, and key points. **Available on the Instructor Companion Website at www.cengage. com/login.**

Test Bank

Written by the **South-Western Federal Taxation** editors and authors, the Test Bank contains approximately 2,200 items and solutions arranged in accordance with the sequence of chapter material.

Each test item is tagged with its Estimated Time to Complete, Level of Difficulty, and Learning Objective(s), as well as the AACSB's and AICPA's core competencies— for easier instructor planning and test item selection. The 2021 Test Bank is available in Cengage's test generator software, Cognero.

Cengage Learning Testing Powered by Cognero is a flexible, online system that allows you to:

- author, edit, and manage Test Bank content from multiple Cengage Learning solutions

- create multiple test versions in an instant

- deliver tests from your LMS, your classroom, or wherever you want

- create tests from school, home, the coffee shop— anywhere with internet access (No special installs or downloads needed.)

Test Bank files in Word format as well as versions to import into your LMS are available on the Instructor Companion Website. **Cognero Test Banks available via single sign-on (SSO) account at www.cengage.com/ login.**

Other Instructor Resources

All of the following instructor course materials are available online at www.cengage.com/login. Once logged into the site, instructors should select this textbook to access the online Instructor Resources.

- Instructor Guide

- Edition-to-edition correlation grids by chapter

- An appendix that helps instructors broaden and customize coverage of important tax provisions of the Affordable Care Act

- The Depreciation and the Accelerated Cost Recovery System (ACRS) appendix

- Comprehensive Tax Return Problems appendix

Custom Solutions

Cengage Learning Custom Solutions develops personalized solutions to meet your taxation education needs. Consider the following for your adoption of **South-Western Federal Taxation 2021 Edition.**

- Remove chapters you do not cover or rearrange their order to create a streamlined and efficient text.

- Add your own material to cover additional topics or information.

- Add relevance by including sections from Sawyers/Gill's *Federal Tax Research* or your state's tax laws and regulations.

ACKNOWLEDGMENTS

We want to thank all the adopters and others who participated in numerous online surveys as well as the following individuals who provided content reviews and feedback in the development of the **South-Western Federal Taxation** 2021 titles.

David M. Maloney / James C. Young / Annette Nellen / Mark B. Persellin

Lindsay G. Acker, *University of Wisconsin-Madison*

Deborah S. Adkins, *Nperspective, LLC*

Mark P. Altieri, *Kent State University*

Susan E. Anderson, *Elon University*

Henry M. Anding, *Woodbury University*

Jennifer A. Bagwell, *Ohio University*

George Barbi, *Lanier Technical College*

Terry W. Bechtel, *Texas A&M University – Texarkana*

Chris Becker, *LeMoyne College*

Tamara Berges, *UCLA*

Ellen Best, *University of North Georgia*

Tim Biggart, *Berry College*

Rachel Birkey, *Illinois State University*

Patrick M. Borja, *Citrus College / California State University, Los Angeles*

Dianne H. Boseman, *Nash Community College*

Cathalene Bowler, *University of Northern Iowa*

Madeline Brogan, *Lone Star College – Montgomery*

Darryl L. Brown, *Illinois Wesleyan University*

Timothy G. Bryan, *University of Southern Indiana*

Robert S. Burdette, *Salt Lake Community College*

Ryan L. Burger, *Concordia University Nebraska*

Lisa Busto, *William Rainey Harper College*

Julia M. Camp, *Providence College*

Al Case, *Southern Oregon University*

Machiavelli W. Chao, *Merage School of Business, University of California, Irvine*

Eric Chen, *University of Saint Joseph*

Christine Cheng, *Louisiana State University*

James Milton Christianson, *Southwestern University and Austin Community College*

Wayne Clark, *Southwest Baptist University*

Ann Burstein Cohen, *University at Buffalo, The State University of New York*

Ciril Cohen, *Fairleigh Dickinson University*

Seth Colwell, *University of Texas - Rio Grande Valley*

Dixon H. Cooper, *University of Arkansas*

Rick L. Crosser, *Metropolitan State University of Denver*

John P. Crowley, *Castleton University*

Susan E. M. Davis, *South University*

Dwight E. Denman, *Newman University*

James M. DeSimpelare, *Ross School of Business at the University of Michigan*

John Dexter, *Northwood University*

James Doering, *University of Wisconsin – Green Bay*

Michael P. Donohoe, *University of Illinois at Urbana Champaign*

Deborah A. Doonan, *Johnson & Wales University*

Monique O. Durant, *Central Connecticut State University*

Wayne L. Edmunds, *Virginia Commonwealth University*

Rafi Efrat, *California State University, Northridge*

Frank J. Faber, *St. Joseph's College*

A. Anthony Falgiani, *University of South Carolina, Beaufort*

Jason Fiske, *Thomas Jefferson School of Law*

John Forsythe, *Eagle Gate College*

Alexander L. Frazin, *University of Redlands*

Carl J. Gabrini, *College of Coastal Georgia*

Kenneth W. Gaines, *East-West University, Chicago, Illinois*

Carolyn Galantine, *Pepperdine University*

Sheri Geddes, *Hope College*

Alexander Gelardi, *University of St. Thomas*

Daniel J. Gibbons, *Waubonsee Community College*

Martie Gillen, *University of Florida*

Charles Gnizak, *Fort Hays State University*

J. David Golub, *Northeastern University*

George G. Goodrich, *John Carroll University*

Marina Grau, *Houston Community College – Houston, TX*

Vicki Greshik, *University of Jamestown College*

Jeffrey S. Haig, *Santa Monica College*

Marcye S. Hampton, *University of Central Florida*

June Hanson, *Upper Iowa University*

Donald Henschel, *Benedictine University*

Susanne Holloway, *Salisbury University*

Susan A. Honig, *Herbert H. Lehman College*

Jeffrey L. Hoopes, *University of North Carolina*

Christopher R. Hoyt, *University of Missouri (Kansas City) School of Law*

Marsha M. Huber, *Youngstown State University*

Carol Hughes, *Asheville-Buncombe Technical Community College*

Helen Hurwitz, *Saint Louis University*

Richard R. Hutaff, *Wingate University*

Zite Hutton, *Western Washington University*

Steven L. Jager, *Cal State Northridge*

Janeé M. Johnson, *University of Arizona*

Brad Van Kalsbeek, *University of Sioux Falls*

John E. Karayan, *Woodbury University*

Carl Keller, *Missouri State University*

Cynthia Khanlarian, *Concord University*

Bob G. Kilpatrick, *Northern Arizona University*

Gordon Klein, *UCLA Anderson School*

Taylor Klett, *Sam Houston State University*

Aaron P. Knape, *Peru State College*

Cedric Knott, *Colorado State University – Global Campus*

Ausher M. B. Kofsky, *Western New England University*

Emil Koren, *Saint Leo University*

Jack Lachman, *Brooklyn College – CUNY*

Richard S. Leaman, *University of Denver*

Adena LeJeune, *Louisiana College*

Gene Levitt, *Mayville State University*

Teresa Lightner, *University of North Texas*

Sara Linton, *Roosevelt University*

Roger Lirely, *The University of Texas at Tyler*

Jane Livingstone, *Western Carolina University*

Heather Lynch, *Northeast Iowa Community College*

Michael J. MacDonald, *University of Wisconsin-Whitewater*

Mabel Machin, *Florida Institute of Technology*

Maria Alaina Mackin, *ECPI University*

Anne M. Magro, *George Mason University*

Richard B. Malamud, *California State University, Dominguez Hills*

Harold J. Manasa, *Winthrop University*

Barry R. Marks, *University of Houston – Clear Lake*

Dewey Martin, *Husson University*

Anthony Masino, *East Tennessee State University*

Norman Massel, *Louisiana State University*

Bruce W. McClain, *Cleveland State University*

Jeff McGowan, *Trine University*

Allison M. McLeod, *University of North Texas*

Meredith A. Menden, *Southern New Hampshire University*

Robert H. Meyers, *University of Wisconsin-Whitewater*

John G. Miller, *Skyline College*

Tracie L. Miller-Nobles, *Austin Community College*
Jonathan G. Mitchell, *Stark State College*
Richard Mole, *Hiram College*
David Morack, *Lakeland University*
Lisa Nash, *University of North Georgia*
Mary E. Netzler, *Eastern Florida State College*
Joseph Malino Nicassio, *Westmoreland County Community College*
Mark R. Nixon, *Bentley University*
Garth Novack, *Pantheon Heavy Industries & Foundry*
Claude R. Oakley, *DeVry University, Georgia*
Al Oddo, *Niagara University*
Sandra Owen, *Indiana University – Bloomington*
Vivian J. Paige, *Old Dominion University*
Carolyn Payne, *University of La Verne*
Ronald Pearson, *Bay College*
Thomas Pearson, *University of Hawaii at Manoa*
Nichole L. Pendleton, *Friends University*
Chuck Pier, *Angelo State University*
Lincoln M. Pinto, *DeVry University*
Sonja Pippin, *University of Nevada – Reno*
Steve Platau, *The University of Tampa*
Walfyette Powell, *Strayer University*
Darlene Pulliam, *West Texas A&M University*
Thomas J. Purcell, *Creighton University*
John S. Repsis, *University of Texas at Arlington*
John D. Rice, *Trinity University*

Jennifer Hardwick Robinson, *Trident Technical College*
Shani N. Robinson, *Sam Houston State University*
Donald Roth, *Dordt College*
Richard L. Russell, *Jackson State University*
Robert L. Salyer, *Northern Kentucky University*
Rhoda Sautner, *University of Mary*
Bunney L. Schmidt, *Keiser University*
Allen Schuldenfrei, *University of Baltimore*
Eric D. Schwartz, *LaRoche College*
Tony L. Scott, *Norwalk Community College*
Cheryl Sears
Randy Serrett, *University of Houston – Downtown*
Wayne Shaw, *Southern Methodist University*
Paul A. Shoemaker, *University of Nebraska – Lincoln*
Kimberly Sipes, *Kentucky State University*
Georgi Smatrakalev, *Florida Atlantic University*
Randy Smit, *Dordt College*
Leslie S. Sobol, *California State University Northridge*
Marc Spiegel, *University of California, Irvine*
Teresa Stephenson, *University of Wyoming*
Beth Stetson, *Oklahoma City University*
Debra Stone, *Eastern New Mexico University*
Frances A. Stott, *Bowling Green State University*
Todd S. Stowe, *Southwest Florida College*
Julie Straus, *Culver-Stockton College*

Martin Stub, *DeVry University*
James Sundberg, *Eastern Michigan University*
Kent Swift, *University of Montana*
Robert L. Taylor, *Lees-McRae College*
Francis C. Thomas, *Richard Stockton College of New Jersey*
Randall R. Thomas, *Upper Iowa University*
Ronald R. Tidd, *Central Washington University*
MaryBeth Tobin, *Bridgewater State University*
James P. Trebby, *Marquette University*
Heidi Tribunella, *University of Rochester*
James M. Turner, *Georgia Institute of Technology*
Anthony W. Varnon, *Southeast Missouri State University*
Adria Palacios Vasquez, *Texas A&M University – Kingsville*
Terri Walsh, *Seminole State College of Florida*
Marie Wang
Natasha R. Ware, *Southeastern University*
Mark Washburn, *Sam Houston State University*
Bill Weispfenning, *University of Jamestown (ND)*
Kent Williams, *Indiana Wesleyan University*
Candace Witherspoon, *Valdosta State University*
Sheila Woods, *DeVry University, Houston, TX*
Xinmei Xie, *Woodbury University*
Thomas Young, *Lone Star College – Tomball*

SPECIAL THANKS

We are grateful to the faculty members who have diligently worked through the problems and test questions to ensure the accuracy of the ***South-Western Federal Taxation*** homework, solutions manuals, test banks, and comprehensive tax form problems. Their comments and corrections helped us focus on clarity as well as accuracy and tax law currency. We also thank Thomson Reuters for its permission to use Checkpoint™ with the text.

Sandra A. Augustine, *Hilbert College*
Robyn Dawn Jarnagin, *University of Arkansas*
Kate Mantzke, *Northern Illinois University*
Ray Rodriguez, *Murray State University*

Miles Romney, *Florida State University*
George R. Starbuck, *McMurry University*
Lisa Swallow, *Missoula College University of Montana*
Donald R. Trippeer, *State University of New York College at Oneonta*

Raymond Wacker, *Southern Illinois University, Carbondale*
Michael Weissenfluh, *Tillamook Bay Community College*
Marvin Williams, *University of Houston-Downtown*

The South-Western Federal Taxation Series

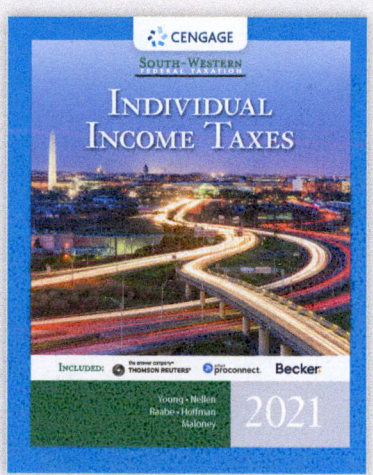

INDIVIDUAL INCOME TAXES, 2021 EDITION

(YOUNG, NELLEN, RAABE, HOFFMAN, MALONEY, Editors) provides accessible, comprehensive, and authoritative coverage of the relevant tax code and regulations as they pertain to the individual taxpayer, as well as coverage of all major developments in Federal taxation.

(ISBN 978-0-357-35932-7)

CORPORATIONS, PARTNERSHIPS, ESTATES & TRUSTS, 2021 EDITION

(RAABE, YOUNG, NELLEN, HOFFMAN, MALONEY, Editors) covers tax concepts as they affect corporations, partnerships, estates, and trusts. The authors provide accessible, comprehensive, and authoritative coverage of relevant tax code and regulations, as well as all major developments in Federal income taxation. This market-leading text is intended for students who have had a previous course in tax.

(ISBN 978-0-357-35933-4)

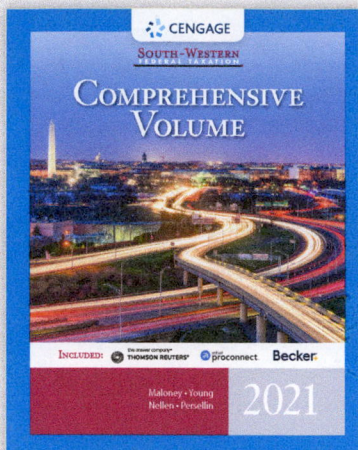

COMPREHENSIVE VOLUME, 2021 EDITION

(MALONEY, YOUNG, NELLEN, PERSELLIN Editors)
Combining the number one individual tax text with the number one corporations text, *Comprehensive Volume, 2021 Edition* is a true winner. An edited version of the first two **South-Western Federal Taxation** textbooks, this book is ideal for undergraduate or graduate levels. This text works for either a one-semester course in which an instructor wants to integrate coverage of individual and corporate taxation or for a two-semester sequence in which the use of only one book is desired.

(ISBN 978-0-357-35931-0)

ESSENTIALS OF TAXATION: INDIVIDUALS AND BUSINESS ENTITIES, 2021 EDITION

(NELLEN, CUCCIA, PERSELLIN, YOUNG, MALONEY, Editors) emphasizes tax planning and the multidisciplinary aspects of taxation. This text is designed with the AICPA Model Tax Curriculum in mind, presenting the introductory Federal taxation course from a business entity perspective. Its **Tax Planning Framework** helps users fit tax planning strategies into an innovative pedagogical framework. The text is an ideal fit for programs that offer only one course in taxation where users need to be exposed to individual taxation, as well as corporate and other business entity taxation. This text assumes no prior course in taxation has been taken.

(ISBN 978-0-357-35934-1)

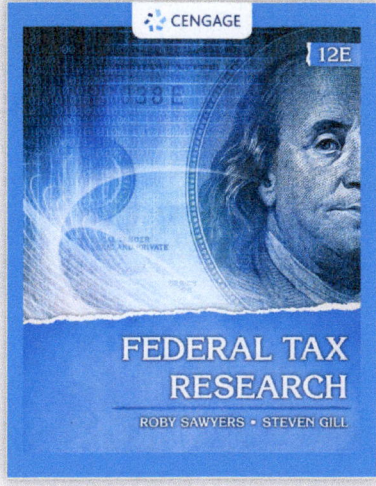

FEDERAL TAX RESEARCH, 12E

(SAWYERS AND GILL). *Federal Tax Research*, Twelfth Edition, offers hands-on tax research analysis and fully covers computer-oriented tax research tools. Also included in this edition is coverage on international tax research, a review of tax ethics, and many new real-life cases to help foster a true understanding of Federal tax law.

(ISBN 978-0-357-36638-7)

ABOUT THE EDITORS

David M. Maloney, Ph.D., CPA, is the Carman G. Blough Professor of Accounting Emeritus at the University of Virginia's McIntire School of Commerce. He completed his undergraduate work at the University of Richmond and his graduate work at the University of Illinois at Urbana-Champaign. Upon joining the Virginia faculty in January 1984, Dr. Maloney taught Federal taxation in the graduate and undergraduate programs and was a recipient of major research grants from the Ernst & Young and KPMG Foundations. Dr. Maloney has published work in numerous professional journals, including *Journal of Taxation, The Tax Adviser, Tax Notes, Corporate Taxation, Accounting Horizons, Journal of Taxation of Investments, and Journal of Accountancy.*

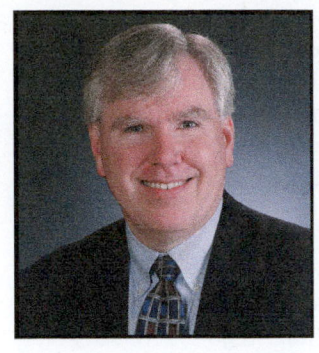

James C. Young is the PwC Professor of Accountancy at Northern Illinois University. A graduate of Ferris State University (B.S.) and Michigan State University (M.B.A. and Ph.D.), Jim's research focuses on taxpayer responses to the income tax using archival data. His dissertation received the PricewaterhouseCoopers/ American Taxation Association Dissertation Award, and his subsequent research has received funding from a number of organizations, including the Ernst & Young Foundation Tax Research Grant Program. His work has been published in a variety of academic and professional journals, including the *National Tax Journal, The Journal of the American Taxation Association,* and *Tax Notes.* Jim is a Northern Illinois University Distinguished Professor, received the Illinois CPA Society Outstanding Accounting Educator Award in 2012, and has received university teaching awards from Northern Illinois University, George Mason University, and Michigan State University.

Annette Nellen, J.D., CPA, CGMA, directs San José State University's graduate tax program (MST) and teaches courses in tax research, tax fundamentals, accounting methods, property transactions, employment tax, ethics, leadership, and tax policy. Professor Nellen is a graduate of CSU Northridge, Pepperdine (MBA), and Loyola Law School. Prior to joining SJSU in 1990, she was with a Big 4 firm and the IRS. At SJSU, Professor Nellen is a recipient of the Outstanding Professor and Distinguished Service Awards. Professor Nellen is an active member of the tax sections of the AICPA and American Bar Association. In 2013, she received the AICPA Arthur J. Dixon Memorial Award, the highest award given by the accounting profession in the area of taxation. Professor Nellen is the author of BloombergBNA Tax Portfolio, *Amortization of Intangibles.* She has published numerous articles in the *AICPA Tax Insider, Tax Adviser, State Tax Notes,* and *The Journal of Accountancy.* She has testified before the House Ways & Means and Senate Finance Committees and other committees on Federal and state tax reform. Professor Nellen maintains the 21st Century Taxation website and blog (21stcenturytaxation .com) as well as websites on tax policy and reform, virtual currency, and state tax issues (sjsu.edu/people/ annette.nellen/).

Mark B. Persellin, Ph.D., CPA, CFP®, is a Professor of Accounting at St. Mary's University. He is a graduate of the University of Arizona (B.S.), the University of Texas at Austin (M.P.A. in Taxation), and the University of Houston (Ph.D.). He teaches Personal Income Tax, Business Income Tax, and Research in Federal Taxation. Prior to joining St. Mary's University in 1991, Professor Persellin taught at Florida Atlantic University and Southwest Texas University (Texas State University) and worked on the tax staff of a Big 4 firm. His research has been published in numerous academic and professional journals including *The Journal of the American Taxation Association, The Accounting Educators' Journal, The Tax Adviser, The CPA Journal, Journal of Taxation, Corporate Taxation, The Tax Executive, TAXES—The Tax Magazine, Journal of International Taxation,* and *Practical Tax Strategies.* In 2003, Professor Persellin established the St. Mary's University Volunteer Income Tax Assistance (VITA) site, and he continues to serve as a trainer and reviewer at the site.

Brief Contents

PART 1: INTRODUCTION AND BASIC TAX MODEL

CHAPTER 1	AN INTRODUCTION TO TAXATION AND UNDERSTANDING THE FEDERAL TAX LAW	1-1
CHAPTER 2	WORKING WITH THE TAX LAW	2-1
CHAPTER 3	COMPUTING THE TAX	3-1

PART 2: GROSS INCOME

| CHAPTER 4 | GROSS INCOME: CONCEPTS AND INCLUSIONS | 4-1 |
| CHAPTER 5 | GROSS INCOME: EXCLUSIONS | 5-1 |

PART 3: DEDUCTIONS AND CREDITS

CHAPTER 6	DEDUCTIONS AND LOSSES: IN GENERAL	6-1
CHAPTER 7	DEDUCTIONS AND LOSSES: CERTAIN BUSINESS EXPENSES AND LOSSES	7-1
CHAPTER 8	DEPRECIATION, COST RECOVERY, AMORTIZATION, AND DEPLETION	8-1
CHAPTER 9	DEDUCTIONS: EMPLOYEE AND SELF-EMPLOYED-RELATED EXPENSES	9-1
CHAPTER 10	DEDUCTIONS AND LOSSES: CERTAIN ITEMIZED DEDUCTIONS	10-1
CHAPTER 11	INVESTOR LOSSES	11-1
CHAPTER 12	TAX CREDITS AND PAYMENTS	12-1

PART 4: PROPERTY TRANSACTIONS

| CHAPTER 13 | PROPERTY TRANSACTIONS: DETERMINATION OF GAIN OR LOSS, BASIS CONSIDERATIONS, AND NONTAXABLE EXCHANGES | 13-1 |
| CHAPTER 14 | PROPERTY TRANSACTIONS: CAPITAL GAINS AND LOSSES, § 1231, AND RECAPTURE PROVISIONS | 14-1 |

PART 5: SPECIAL TAX COMPUTATIONS AND ACCOUNTING PERIODS AND METHODS

CHAPTER 15   THE DEDUCTION FOR QUALIFIED BUSINESS INCOME FOR NONCORPORATE TAXPAYERS   15-1

CHAPTER 16   ACCOUNTING PERIODS AND METHODS   16-1

PART 6: CORPORATIONS

CHAPTER 17   CORPORATIONS: INTRODUCTION AND OPERATING RULES   17-1

CHAPTER 18   CORPORATIONS: ORGANIZATION AND CAPITAL STRUCTURE   18-1

CHAPTER 19   CORPORATIONS: DISTRIBUTIONS NOT IN COMPLETE LIQUIDATION   19-1

CHAPTER 20   CORPORATIONS: DISTRIBUTIONS IN COMPLETE LIQUIDATION AND AN OVERVIEW OF REORGANIZATIONS   20-1

PART 7: FLOW-THROUGH ENTITIES

CHAPTER 21   PARTNERSHIPS   21-1

CHAPTER 22   S CORPORATIONS   22-1

PART 8: ADVANCED TAX PRACTICE CONSIDERATIONS

CHAPTER 23   EXEMPT ENTITIES   23-1

CHAPTER 24   MULTISTATE CORPORATE TAXATION   24-1

CHAPTER 25   TAXATION OF INTERNATIONAL TRANSACTIONS   25-1

CHAPTER 26   TAX PRACTICE AND ETHICS   26-1

PART 9: FAMILY TAX PLANNING

CHAPTER 27   THE FEDERAL GIFT AND ESTATE TAXES   27-1

CHAPTER 28   INCOME TAXATION OF TRUSTS AND ESTATES   28-1

Contents

Part 1: Introduction and Basic Tax Model

CHAPTER 1
AN INTRODUCTION TO TAXATION AND UNDERSTANDING THE FEDERAL TAX LAW   1-1
The Big Picture: *Family and Taxes—A Typical Year*   *1-1*

APPROACHING THE STUDY OF TAXATION   **1-2**
What Is Taxation?   1-2
Taxation in Our Lives   1-2
The Relevance of Taxation to Accounting and Finance Professionals   1-3
How to Study Taxation   1-4

A BRIEF HISTORY OF U.S. TAXATION   **1-4**
Early Periods   1-4
Concept Summary: *Individuals and Taxes*   *1-5*
Revenue Acts   1-5
Trends   1-6

TAX SYSTEM DESIGN   **1-6**
Legal Foundation   1-6
The Basic Tax Formula   1-7
Tax Principles   1-8

MAJOR TYPES OF TAXES   **1-8**
Property Taxes   1-10
Transaction Taxes   1-11
Ethics & Equity: *Making Good Use of Out-of-State Relatives*   *1-12*
Taxes on Transfers at Death   1-13
Gift Taxes   1-14
Income Taxes   1-15
Employment Taxes   1-17
Other U.S. Taxes   1-18
Concept Summary: *Overview of Taxes in the United States*   *1-19*
Proposed U.S. Taxes   1-20
Global Tax Issues: *VAT in USA?*   *1-21*

TAX ADMINISTRATION   **1-21**
Internal Revenue Service   1-21
The Audit Process   1-21
Statute of Limitations   1-24
Interest and Penalties   1-24

Tax Practice   1-25
Global Tax Issues: *Outsourcing of Tax Return Preparation*   *1-26*

UNDERSTANDING THE FEDERAL TAX LAW   **1-27**
Revenue Needs   1-27
Economic Considerations   1-27
Social Considerations   1-28
Equity Considerations   1-29
Political Considerations   1-31
Influence of the Internal Revenue Service   1-32
Influence of the Courts   1-33
Summary   1-34
Refocus on the Big Picture: *Family and Taxes—A Typical Year*   *1-35*

CHAPTER 2
WORKING WITH THE TAX LAW   2-1
The Big Picture: *Importance of Tax Research*   *2-1*

TAX SOURCES   **2-2**
Statutory Sources of the Tax Law   2-2
Administrative Sources of the Tax Law   2-6
Ethics & Equity: *Reporting Tax Fraud*   *2-7*
Judicial Sources of the Tax Law   2-10
Concept Summary: *Federal Judicial System: Trial Courts*   *2-12*
Concept Summary: *Judicial Sources*   *2-15*
Other Sources of the Tax Law   2-17

WORKING WITH THE TAX LAW— TAX RESEARCH TOOLS   **2-18**
Commercial Tax Services   2-18
Using Electronic (Online) Tax Services   2-19
Noncommercial Electronic (Online) Tax Services   2-19

WORKING WITH THE TAX LAW— TAX RESEARCH   **2-20**
Identifying the Problem   2-22
Refining the Problem   2-22
Locating the Appropriate Tax Law Sources   2-23
Assessing the Validity of Tax Law Sources   2-23
Arriving at the Solution or at Alternative Solutions   2-25
Financial Disclosure Insights: *Where Does GAAP Come From?*   *2-26*
Communicating Tax Research   2-26

**WORKING WITH THE TAX LAW—
TAX PLANNING**   **2-28**
Nontax Considerations   2-29
Components of Tax Planning   2-29
Tax Avoidance and Tax Evasion   2-30
Follow-Up Procedures   2-30
Tax Planning   2-31

TAXATION ON THE CPA EXAMINATION   **2-31**
Preparation Blueprints   2-31
Regulation Section   2-31

**CHAPTER 3
COMPUTING THE TAX**   **3-1**
The Big Picture: *A Divided Household*   *3-1*

TAX FORMULA   **3-2**
Components of the Tax Formula   3-2
Concept Summary: *Tax Formula for Individuals*   *3-3*
Global Tax Issues: *Citizenship Is Not Tax-Free*   *3-5*
Standard Deduction   3-6
Application of the Tax Formula   3-9

EXEMPTIONS   **3-9**

DEPENDENTS   **3-9**
Qualifying Child   3-9
Qualifying Relative   3-11
Other Rules for Determining Dependents   3-14
Comparison of Dependent Categories   3-15
Concept Summary: *Tests to Identify a Dependent*   *3-15*
Child and Dependent Tax Credits   3-15

FILING THE RETURN   **3-17**
Filing Status   3-17
Ethics & Equity: *Abandoned Spouse?*   *3-20*
Filing the Return   3-21
Global Tax Issues: *Tracking Down Tax Dollars*   *3-23*

TAX COMPUTATIONS   **3-24**
Tax Rates   3-24
Tax Table Method   3-24
Tax Rate Schedule Method   3-24
Computation of Net Taxes Payable or Refund Due   3-25
Kiddie Tax—Unearned Income of Dependent Children   3-26

**GAINS AND LOSSES FROM PROPERTY
TRANSACTIONS—IN GENERAL**   **3-28**

**GAINS AND LOSSES FROM PROPERTY
TRANSACTIONS—CAPITAL GAINS AND LOSSES**   **3-29**
Capital Assets   3-29
Taxation of Net Capital Gain   3-29
Determination of Net Capital Gain   3-30
Treatment of Net Capital Loss   3-31
Taxation of Virtual Currency   3-31

TAX PLANNING   **3-32**
Optimizing the Use of the Standard Deduction   3-32
Taking Advantage of Tax Rate Differentials   3-32
Unearned Income of Children   3-33
Refocus on the Big Picture: *A Divided Household*   *3-33*

Part 2: Gross Income

**CHAPTER 4
GROSS INCOME: CONCEPTS AND
INCLUSIONS**   **4-1**
The Big Picture: *Calculation of Gross Income*   *4-1*
Global Tax Issues: *From "All Sources" Is a Broad Definition* *4-3*

GROSS INCOME   **4-3**
Definition   4-3
Recovery of Capital Doctrine   4-3
Economic and Accounting Concepts of Income   4-4
Financial Accounting Income versus Taxable Income   4-4
Form of Receipt   4-5

TIMING OF INCOME RECOGNITION   **4-6**
Taxable Year   4-6
Accounting Methods   4-6
Special Rules Applicable to Cash Basis Taxpayers   4-9
Ethics & Equity: *Should the Tax Treatment of
    Government Bonds and Corporate Bonds Be Different?* *4-11*
Exceptions Applicable to Accrual Basis Taxpayers   4-12

**GENERAL SOURCES OF INCOME AND TO WHOM
THEY ARE TAXED**   **4-13**
Personal Services   4-13
Income from Property   4-13
Income Received by an Agent   4-16
Income from Partnerships, S Corporations, Trusts, and Estates 4-16
Concept Summary: *Taxation of Income and Distributions* *4-17*
Income in Community Property States   4-17

**ITEMS SPECIFICALLY INCLUDED IN
GROSS INCOME**   **4-19**
Alimony and Separate Maintenance Payments   4-19
Concept Summary: *Tax Treatment of Payments and
    Transfers Pursuant to Divorce Agreements and Decrees* *4-21*
Imputed Interest on Below-Market Loans   4-21
Concept Summary: *Effect of Certain Below-Market Loans on the
    Lender and Borrower*   *4-22*
Concept Summary: *Exceptions to the Imputed Interest Rules for
    Below-Market Loans*   *4-24*
Ethics & Equity: *Taxing "Made-Up" Income*   *4-24*
Income from Annuities   4-24
Prizes and Awards   4-27
Unemployment Compensation   4-27
Social Security Benefits   4-28
Income Earned from Foreign Bank and Financial Accounts and
    FBAR Rules   4-29

TAX PLANNING **4-29**
Minimize Income Included in Gross Income 4-30
Tax Deferral 4-30
Shifting Income to Other Taxpayers 4-32
Refocus on the Big Picture: *Calculation of Gross Income* *4-33*

CHAPTER 5
GROSS INCOME: EXCLUSIONS **5-1**
The Big Picture: *Exclusions* *5-1*

STATUTORY AUTHORITY **5-2**

GIFTS AND INHERITANCES **5-3**
Legislative Intent 5-3
Employer Payments to Employees 5-3
Employee Death Benefits 5-4

LIFE INSURANCE PROCEEDS **5-4**
General Rule 5-4
Accelerated Death Benefits 5-5
Ethics & Equity: *Should the Terminally Ill Pay Social Security Taxes?* *5-6*
Transfer for Valuable Consideration 5-6

SCHOLARSHIPS **5-7**
General Information 5-7
Timing Issues 5-8

COMPENSATION FOR INJURIES AND SICKNESS **5-8**
Damages 5-8
Ethics & Equity: *Tax Treatment of Damages Not Related to Physical Personal Injury* *5-9*
Concept Summary: *Taxation of Damages* *5-9*
Ethics & Equity: *Classifying the Amount of the Claim* *5-10*
Wrongful Incarceration 5-10
Workers' Compensation 5-10
Accident and Health Insurance Benefits 5-10

EMPLOYER-SPONSORED ACCIDENT AND HEALTH PLANS **5-11**
Medical Reimbursement Plans 5-11
Long-Term Care Insurance Benefits 5-12

MEALS AND LODGING **5-13**
General Rules for the Exclusion 5-13
Other Housing Exclusions 5-14

EMPLOYEE FRINGE BENEFITS **5-14**
Specific Benefits 5-15
Cafeteria Plans 5-15
Flexible Spending Plans 5-16
General Classes of Excluded Benefits 5-16
Ethics & Equity: *Fringe Benefits* *5-20*
Group Term Life Insurance 5-20

FOREIGN EARNED INCOME **5-21**
Concept Summary: *Employee Fringe Benefits* *5-22*

Global Tax Issues: *Benefits of the Earned Income Exclusion Are Questioned* *5-23*

INTEREST ON CERTAIN STATE AND LOCAL GOVERNMENT OBLIGATIONS **5-23**

CORPORATE DISTRIBUTIONS TO SHAREHOLDERS **5-24**
General Information 5-24
Stock Dividends 5-25

EDUCATIONAL SAVINGS BONDS **5-25**

EDUCATION SAVINGS PROGRAMS (§ 529 AND § 530 PLANS) **5-26**
Qualified Tuition Program 5-26
Coverdell Education Savings Account 5-27

QUALIFIED ABLE PROGRAMS (§ 529A PLANS) **5-27**

TAX BENEFIT RULE **5-27**

INCOME FROM DISCHARGE OF INDEBTEDNESS **5-29**

TAX PLANNING **5-30**
Life Insurance 5-30
Employee Fringe Benefits 5-30
Investment Income 5-31
Refocus on the Big Picture: *Exclusions* *5-32*

Part 3: Deductions and Credits

CHAPTER 6
DEDUCTIONS AND LOSSES: IN GENERAL **6-1**
The Big Picture: *Calculation of Deductible Expenses* *6-1*

CLASSIFICATION OF DEDUCTIBLE EXPENSES **6-2**
Classifying Deductions 6-3
Authority for Deductions 6-3
Deduction Criteria for § 162 and § 212 6-5
Personal Expenses 6-6
Business and Nonbusiness Losses 6-6
Deduction for Qualified Business Income 6-7
Reporting Procedures 6-8

DEDUCTIONS AND LOSSES—TIMING OF EXPENSE RECOGNITION **6-9**
Importance of Taxpayer's Method of Accounting 6-9
Cash Method Requirements 6-10
Accrual Method Requirements 6-10
Prepaid Expenses—The "12-Month Rule" 6-12
Time Value of Tax Deductions 6-12

DISALLOWANCE POSSIBILITIES **6-13**
Public Policy Limitation 6-13
Global Tax Issues: *Overseas Gun Sales Result in Large Fines* *6-14*

Ethics & Equity: *State Allowed Marijuana Activity: Do Regular Business Deduction Rules Apply (or Those for Drug Dealers)?* 6-15

Political Contributions and Lobbying Activities 6-15

Excessive Executive Compensation 6-16

Investigation of a Business 6-17

Concept Summary: *Costs of Investigating a Business* 6-18

Hobby Losses 6-18

Concept Summary: *Common Questions from the IRS Concerning Hobbies/Businesses with Losses* 6-20

Rental of Vacation Homes 6-21

Concept Summary: *Vacation/Rental Home* 6-22

Expenditures Incurred for Taxpayer's Benefit or Taxpayer's Obligation 6-25

Disallowance of Personal Expenditures 6-26

Ethics & Equity: *Personal or Business Expenses?* 6-26

Disallowance of Deductions for Capital Expenditures 6-26

Transactions between Related Parties 6-28

Substantiation Requirements 6-29

Expenses and Interest Relating to Tax-Exempt Income 6-29

Other Disallowances 6-30

TAX PLANNING **6-30**

Vacation Homes 6-30

Concept Summary: *Classification of Expenses* 6-31

Hobby Losses 6-32

Do Deduction Limits Affect Executive Compensation? 6-33

Refocus on the Big Picture: *Calculation of Deductible Business Expenses and Tax Planning* 6-33

CHAPTER 7
DEDUCTIONS AND LOSSES: CERTAIN BUSINESS EXPENSES AND LOSSES   **7-1**

The Big Picture: *Losses* 7-1

BAD DEBTS **7-2**

Specific Charge-Off Method 7-3

Concept Summary: *The Tax Treatment of Bad Debts Using the Specific Charge-Off Method* 7-4

Business versus Nonbusiness Bad Debts 7-4

Loans between Related Parties 7-5

Concept Summary: *Bad Debt Deductions* 7-5

WORTHLESS SECURITIES AND SMALL BUSINESS STOCK LOSSES **7-6**

Worthless Securities 7-6

Small Business Stock (§ 1244 Stock) Losses 7-6

LOSSES OF INDIVIDUALS **7-7**

Events That Are Not Casualties 7-7

Theft Losses 7-8

When to Deduct Casualty Losses 7-8

Measuring the Amount of Loss 7-9

Ethics & Equity: *Is Policy Cancellation an Escape Hatch?* 7-10

Personal Casualty Gains and Losses 7-12

Concept Summary: *Casualty Gains and Losses* 7-14

Statutory Framework for Deducting Losses of Individuals 7-14

Concept Summary: *Statutory Framework for Deducting Losses of Individuals* 7-15

RESEARCH AND EXPERIMENTAL EXPENDITURES **7-15**

Expense Method 7-16

Deferral and Amortization Method 7-16

EXCESS BUSINESS LOSSES **7-17**

Excess Business Loss Defined 7-17

Losses from Partnerships or S Corporations 7-18

Other Rules 7-19

NET OPERATING LOSSES **7-19**

General Rules 7-20

TAX PLANNING **7-21**

Small Business Stock (§ 1244 Stock) Losses 7-21

Casualty Losses 7-21

Refocus on the Big Picture: *Losses* 7-21

CHAPTER 8
DEPRECIATION, COST RECOVERY, AMORTIZATION, AND DEPLETION   **8-1**

The Big Picture: *Calculating Cost Recovery Deductions* 8-1

DEPRECIATION AND COST RECOVERY **8-2**

Nature of Property 8-2

Placed in Service Requirement 8-3

Cost Recovery Allowed or Allowable 8-3

Cost Recovery Basis for Personal Use Assets Converted to Business or Income-Producing Use 8-4

MODIFIED ACCELERATED COST RECOVERY SYSTEM (MACRS): GENERAL RULES **8-4**

Concept Summary: *MACRS: Class Lives, Methods, and Conventions* 8-4

Personalty (and Certain Realty): Recovery Periods and Methods 8-5

Financial Disclosure Insights: *Tax and Book Depreciation* 8-6

Concept Summary: *MACRS Conventions (by Property Type)* 8-6

Concept Summary: *Straight-Line Cost Recovery under MACRS (Personalty vs. Realty)* 8-9

Realty: Recovery Periods and Methods 8-9

MODIFIED ACCELERATED COST RECOVERY SYSTEM (MACRS): SPECIAL RULES **8-10**

Election to Expense Assets (§ 179) 8-10

Ethics & Equity: *Section 179 Limitation* 8-14

Additional First-Year Depreciation (Bonus Depreciation) 8-14

Using § 179 and Bonus Depreciation Effectively 8-15

Concept Summary: *Using § 179 and Bonus Depreciation in 2020* 8-17

Business and Personal Use of Automobiles and Other Listed Property 8-18

Alternative Depreciation System (ADS) 8-23

REPORTING PROCEDURES **8-24**

AMORTIZATION **8-25**

DEPLETION	**8-28**
Intangible Drilling and Development Costs (IDCs)	8-29
Depletion Methods	8-29
TAX PLANNING	**8-31**
Cost Recovery	8-31
Amortization	8-32
Cost Recovery Tables	8-32
Refocus on the Big Picture: *Calculating Cost Recovery Deductions*	*8-36*

CHAPTER 9
DEDUCTIONS: EMPLOYEE AND SELF-EMPLOYED-RELATED EXPENSES   9-1

The Big Picture: *The First Job*	*9-1*
EMPLOYEE VERSUS INDEPENDENT CONTRACTOR	**9-2**
Concept Summary: *Employee versus Independent Contractor*	*9-4*
SELF-EMPLOYED AND EMPLOYEE-RELATED EXPENSES—IN GENERAL	**9-5**
TRANSPORTATION EXPENSES	**9-5**
Qualified Expenses	9-5
Computation of Automobile Expenses	9-6
TRAVEL EXPENSES	**9-9**
Definition of Travel Expenses	9-9
Away-from-Home Requirement	9-10
Restrictions on Travel Expenses	9-11
Combined Business and Pleasure Travel	9-12
EDUCATION EXPENSES	**9-14**
General Requirements	9-14
Legal Requirements to Keep a Job	9-14
Maintaining or Improving Existing Skills	9-15
Concept Summary: *Conditions for Deducting Regular Education Expenses*	*9-15*
What Expenses Are Allowed?	9-15
Deduction for Qualified Tuition and Related Expenses	9-16
Other Provisions Dealing with Education	9-17
Concept Summary: *Tax Consequences of Provisions Dealing with Education*	*9-17*
OTHER BUSINESS EXPENSES	**9-18**
Office in the Home	9-18
Moving Expenses	9-22
Entertainment and Meal Expenses	9-22
Ethics & Equity: *Your Turn or Mine?*	*9-23*
Miscellaneous Employee Expenses	9-24
CONTRIBUTIONS TO RETIREMENT ACCOUNTS	**9-25**
§ 401(k) Plans	9-25
INDIVIDUAL RETIREMENT ACCOUNTS (IRAs)	**9-26**
General Rules	9-26
Taxation of Benefits	9-29

Rollovers and Conversions	9-30
Concept Summary: *Comparison of IRAs*	*9-30*
RETIREMENT PLANS FOR SELF-EMPLOYED INDIVIDUALS	**9-31**
Keogh (H.R. 10) Plans	9-31
Solo § 401(k) Plans	9-31
Savings Incentive Match Plan for Employees (SIMPLE Plans)	9-32
Simplified Employee Pension Plans (SEPs)	9-32
CLASSIFICATION OF EMPLOYEE EXPENSES	**9-33**
Accountable Plans	9-33
Nonaccountable Plans	9-34
LIMITATIONS ON ITEMIZED DEDUCTIONS	**9-35**
Miscellaneous Itemized Deductions Subject to the 2%-of-AGI Floor	9-35
Miscellaneous Itemized Deductions Not Subject to the 2%-of-AGI Floor	9-35
TAX PLANNING	**9-36**
Employment Status	9-36
Implications of Misclassifying Workers	9-36
Transportation and Travel Expenses	9-37
Education Expenses	9-37
Refocus on the Big Picture: *The First Job*	*9-38*

CHAPTER 10
DEDUCTIONS AND LOSSES: CERTAIN ITEMIZED DEDUCTIONS   10-1

The Big Picture: *Impact of Itemized Deductions on Major Purchases*	*10-1*
MEDICAL EXPENSES	**10-3**
Medical Expenses Defined	10-3
Capital Expenditures for Medical Purposes	10-4
Medical Expenses Incurred for Spouse and Dependents	10-5
Transportation, Meal, and Lodging Expenses for Medical Treatment	10-6
Amounts Paid for Medical Insurance Premiums	10-6
Year of Deduction	10-7
Reimbursements	10-7
Health Savings Accounts	10-8
Affordable Care Act Provisions	10-10
TAXES	**10-10**
Deductibility as a Tax	10-10
Property Taxes	10-11
State and Local Income Taxes and Sales Taxes	10-13
INTEREST	**10-14**
Allowed and Disallowed Items	10-14
Restrictions on Deductibility and Timing Considerations	10-17
Classification of Interest Expense	10-17
Concept Summary: *Deductibility of Personal, Student Loan, Mortgage, and Investment Interest*	*10-18*

CHARITABLE CONTRIBUTIONS — **10-18**
Criteria for a Gift — 10-18
Qualified Organizations — 10-20
Ethics & Equity: *An Indirect Route to a Contribution Deduction* — *10-20*
Time of Deduction — 10-20
Record-Keeping and Valuation Requirements — 10-21
Concept Summary : *Documentation and Substantiation Requirements for Charitable Contributions* — *10-21*
Global Tax Issues: *Choose the Charity Wisely* — *10-22*
Limitations on Charitable Contribution Deduction — 10-22
Concept Summary: *Determining the Deduction for Contributions of Appreciated Property by Individuals* — *10-25*

TIMING OF PAYMENTS TO MAXIMIZE DEDUCTIONS — **10-26**

OTHER ITEMIZED DEDUCTIONS — **10-27**

COMPREHENSIVE EXAMPLE OF SCHEDULE A — **10-27**

TAX PLANNING — **10-29**
Maximizing the Medical Deduction — 10-29
Ensuring the Charitable Contribution Deduction — 10-29
Planning to Avoid Nondeductible Treatment — 10-31
Refocus on the Big Picture: *Impact of Itemized Deductions on Major Purchases* — *10-31*

CHAPTER 11
INVESTOR LOSSES — **11-1**
The Big Picture: *Investor Loss Limitations Affect the Viability of Certain Investment Opportunities* — *11-1*

THE TAX SHELTER PROBLEM — **11-2**

AT-RISK LIMITS — **11-4**
Concept Summary: *Calculation of At-Risk Amount* — *11-5*

PASSIVE ACTIVITY LOSS LIMITS — **11-5**
Classification and Impact of Passive Activity Income and Losses — 11-5
Taxpayers Subject to the Passive Activity Loss Rules — 11-9
Rules for Determining Passive Activities — 11-10
Concept Summary: *Tests to Determine Material Participation* — *11-14*
Interaction of the At-Risk and Passive Activity Loss Limits — 11-15
Special Passive Activity Rules for Real Estate Activities — 11-16
Concept Summary : *Treatment of Losses Subject to the At-Risk and Passive Activity Loss Limitations* — *11-17*
Ethics & Equity: *Punching the Time Clock at Year-End* — *11-18*
Dispositions of Passive Interests — 11-20

INVESTMENT INTEREST LIMITATION — **11-21**
Limitation Imposed — 11-21
Concept Summary : *Passive Activity Loss Rules: Key Issues and Answers* — *11-22*
Computation of Allowable Deduction — 11-23

OTHER INVESTMENT LOSSES — **11-23**
Concept Summary: *Common Investment Loss Limitation Rules* — *11-24*

TAX PLANNING — **11-24**
Using Passive Activity Losses — 11-24
Planning with the Investment Interest Limitation — 11-26
Effect of the Additional Tax on Net Investment Income — 11-26
Refocus on the Big Picture: *Investor Loss Limitations Affect the Viability of Certain Investment Opportunities* — *11-27*

CHAPTER 12
TAX CREDITS AND PAYMENTS — **12-1**
The Big Picture: *Education Tax Credits* — *12-1*

TAX POLICY CONSIDERATIONS — **12-3**

TAX CREDITS — **12-3**
Refundable versus Nonrefundable Credits — 12-3
General Business Credit — 12-5
Treatment of Unused General Business Credits — 12-5

SPECIFIC BUSINESS-RELATED TAX CREDITS — **12-6**
Tax Credit for Rehabilitation Expenditures — 12-6
Ethics & Equity: *The Rehabilitation Tax Credit* — *12-7*
Work Opportunity Tax Credit — 12-7
Credit for Increasing Research Activities — 12-8
Low-Income Housing Credit — 12-9
Disabled Access Credit — 12-10
Credit for Small Employer Pension Plan Startup Costs — 12-10
Credit for Employer-Provided Child Care — 12-11
Credit for Employer-Provided Family and Medical Leave — 12-11

OTHER TAX CREDITS — **12-12**
Earned Income Credit — 12-12
Ethics & Equity: *Holding on to the Earned Income Credit with the Aid of a Transient Child* — *12-13*
Foreign Tax Credit — 12-13
Global Tax Issues: *Sourcing Income in Cyberspace— Getting It Right When Calculating the Foreign Tax Credit* — *12-13*
Child and Dependent Tax Credits — 12-14
Credit for Child and Dependent Care Expenses — 12-14
Education Tax Credits — 12-16
Ethics & Equity: *Is This the Right Way to Use the Credit for Child and Dependent Care Expenses?* — *12-16*
Energy Credits — 12-18
Credit for Certain Retirement Plan Contributions — 12-18

TAX PAYMENTS — **12-19**
Concept Summary: *Major Tax Credits* — *12-20*
Payments by Employers — 12-22
Payments by Self-Employed Persons — 12-22
Affordable Care Act Provisions — 12-24
Alternative Minimum Tax — 12-25

TAX PLANNING   **12-27**
Credit for Child and Dependent Care Expenses   12-27
Refocus on the Big Picture: *Education Tax Credits*   *12-28*

Part 4: Property Transactions

CHAPTER 13
PROPERTY TRANSACTIONS: DETERMINATION OF GAIN OR LOSS, BASIS CONSIDERATIONS, AND NONTAXABLE EXCHANGES   13-1

The Big Picture: *Sale or Gift of Inherited House and Other Property Transactions*   *13-1*

DETERMINATION OF GAIN OR LOSS   **13-2**
Realized Gain or Loss   13-2
Concept Summary: *Realized Gain or Loss*   *13-3*
Recognized Gain or Loss   13-8
Concept Summary: *Realized and Recognized Gain or Loss*   *13-9*
Nonrecognition of Gain or Loss   13-9

BASIS CONSIDERATIONS   **13-10**
Determination of Cost Basis   13-10
Gift Basis   13-12
Inherited Property   13-14
Disallowed Losses   13-16
Concept Summary: *Wash Sale Rules*   *13-18*
Ethics & Equity: *Washing a Loss Using an IRA*   *13-19*
Conversion of Property from Personal Use to Business or Income-Producing Use   13-19
Summary of Basis Adjustments   13-20
Concept Summary: *Adjustments to Basis*   *13-21*

NONTAXABLE EXCHANGES   **13-22**

LIKE-KIND EXCHANGES—§ 1031   **13-22**
Like-Kind Property   13-23
Exchange Requirement   13-24
Concept Summary: *Delayed § 1031 Exchange*   *13-25*
Boot   13-25
Basis and Holding Period of Property Received   13-26
Reporting Considerations   13-29

INVOLUNTARY CONVERSIONS—§ 1033   **13-29**
Involuntary Conversion Defined   13-31
Computing the Amount Realized   13-31
Replacement Property   13-32
Concept Summary: *Involuntary Conversions: Replacement Property Tests*   *13-33*
Time Limitation on Replacement   13-33
Nonrecognition of Gain   13-34
Reporting Considerations   13-35

SALE OF A RESIDENCE—§ 121   **13-35**
Principal Residence   13-36
Requirements for Exclusion Treatment   13-36
Calculating the Exclusion   13-38
Exceptions to the Two-Year Rules   13-39

TAX PLANNING   **13-41**
Cost Identification and Documentation Considerations   13-41
Selection of Property for Making Gifts   13-41
Selection of Property to Pass at Death   13-42
Disallowed Losses   13-42
Like-Kind Exchanges   13-43
Involuntary Conversions   13-43
Sale of a Principal Residence   13-44
Refocus on the Big Picture: *Sale or Gift of Inherited House and Other Property Transactions*   *13-45*

CHAPTER 14
PROPERTY TRANSACTIONS: CAPITAL GAINS AND LOSSES, § 1231, AND RECAPTURE PROVISIONS   14-1

The Big Picture: *Managing Capital Asset Transactions*   *14-1*

GENERAL SCHEME OF TAXATION   **14-3**

CAPITAL ASSETS   **14-3**
Definition of a Capital Asset (§ 1221)   14-4
Ethics & Equity: *Sculpture as a Capital Asset*   *14-6*
Effect of Judicial Action   14-6
Statutory Expansions   14-7

SALE OR EXCHANGE   **14-8**
Worthless Securities and § 1244 Stock   14-8
Retirement of Corporate Obligations   14-9
Options   14-9
Concept Summary: *Options: Consequences to the Grantor and Grantee*   *14-11*
Patents   14-11
Franchises, Trademarks, and Trade Names (§ 1253)   14-12
Concept Summary: *Franchises: Consequences to the Franchisor and Franchisee*   *14-14*
Lease Cancellation Payments   14-14

HOLDING PERIOD   **14-15**
General Rules   14-15
Special Holding Period Rules   14-15
Special Rules for Short Sales   14-16
Concept Summary: *Short Sales of Securities*   *14-18*

TAX TREATMENT OF CAPITAL GAINS AND LOSSES OF NONCORPORATE TAXPAYERS   **14-19**
Capital Gain and Loss Netting Process   14-19
Qualified Dividend Income   14-22
Alternative Tax on Net Capital Gain and Qualified Dividend Income   14-22

Concept Summary: *Income Layers for Alternative Tax on Capital Gain Computation*   *14-24*

Treatment of Net Capital Losses   14-26

Concept Summary: *Final Results of the Capital Gain and Loss Netting Process and How They Are Taxed*   *14-27*

TAX TREATMENT OF CAPITAL GAINS AND LOSSES OF CORPORATE TAXPAYERS   **14-27**

OVERVIEW OF § 1231 AND THE RECAPTURE PROVISIONS   **14-28**

SECTION 1231 ASSETS   **14-28**

Relationship to Capital Assets   14-28

Property Included   14-29

Property Excluded   14-30

Section 1231 Assets Disposed of by Casualty or Theft   14-30

Concept Summary: *Section 1231 Netting Procedure (Discussed in Section 14-8e)*   *14-31*

General Procedure for § 1231 Computation   14-32

SECTION 1245 RECAPTURE   **14-35**

Section 1245 Property   14-37

Observations on § 1245   14-38

SECTION 1250 RECAPTURE   **14-38**

Section 1250 Recapture Situations   14-39

Concept Summary: *Comparison of § 1245 and § 1250 Depreciation Recapture*   *14-39*

Unrecaptured § 1250 Gain (Real Estate 25% Gain)   14-39

Ethics & Equity: *The Sale of a "Cost-Segregated" Building*   *14-41*

CONSIDERATIONS COMMON TO §§ 1245 AND 1250   **14-41**

Exceptions   14-41

Global Tax Issues: *Depreciation Recapture in Other Countries*   *14-42*

Other Applications   14-43

Concept Summary: *Depreciation Recapture and § 1231 Netting Procedure*   *14-44*

SPECIAL RECAPTURE PROVISIONS   **14-44**

Special Recapture for Corporations   14-44

Gain from Sale of Depreciable Property between Certain Related Parties   14-45

Intangible Drilling Costs   14-45

REPORTING PROCEDURES   **14-45**

Ethics & Equity: *Incorrect Depreciation and Recognized Gain*   *14-45*

TAX PLANNING   **14-46**

Importance of Capital Asset Status   14-46

Planning for Capital Asset Status   14-46

Global Tax Issues: *Capital Gain Treatment in the United States and Other Countries*   *14-47*

Effect of Capital Asset Status in Transactions Other Than Sales   14-47

Stock Sales   14-48

Maximizing Benefits   14-48

Year-End Planning   14-48

Timing of § 1231 Gain   14-48

Timing of Recapture   14-49

Postponing and Shifting Recapture   14-49

Avoiding Recapture   14-50

Refocus on the Big Picture: *Managing Capital Asset Transactions*   *14-50*

Part 5: Special Tax Computations and Accounting Periods and Methods

CHAPTER 15
THE DEDUCTION FOR QUALIFIED BUSINESS INCOME FOR NONCORPORATE TAXPAYERS   15-1

The Big Picture: *Entrepreneurial Pursuits*   *15-1*

TAX TREATMENT OF VARIOUS BUSINESS FORMS   **15-2**

Sole Proprietorships   15-2

Partnerships   15-3

Corporations   15-3

Concept Summary: *Tax Treatment of Business Forms Compared*   *15-6*

Global Tax Issues: *U.S. Corporate Taxes and International Business Competitiveness*   *15-7*

Limited Liability Companies   15-7

THE TAX CUTS AND JOBS ACT (TCJA) OF 2017 AND ENTITY TAX RATES   **15-8**

Challenges of Lowering Tax Rates   15-8

Lowering Tax Rates for Different Business Forms   15-9

THE DEDUCTION FOR QUALIFIED BUSINESS INCOME   **15-9**

General Rule   15-10

The Overall Limitation: Modified Taxable Income   15-10

Definition of Qualified Business Income   15-10

Definition of a Qualified Trade or Business   15-11

Limitations on the QBI Deduction   15-12

Concept Summary: *An Overview of the 2020 Qualified Business Income Deduction*   *15-13*

Limitation Based on Wages and Capital Investment   15-14

Limitation for "Specified Services" Businesses   15-17

Treatment of Losses   15-21

Coordination with Other Rules   15-22

Considerations for Partnerships and S Corporations   15-22

Other Issues   15-22

TAX PLANNING   **15-23**

Corporate versus Noncorporate Forms of Business Organization   15-23

Optimizing the Deduction for Qualified Business Income   15-24

Refocus on the Big Picture: *Entrepreneurial Pursuits*   *15-24*

CHAPTER 16
ACCOUNTING PERIODS AND METHODS   16-1
The Big Picture: *Accounting Period and Method*   *16-1*

ACCOUNTING PERIODS   16-2
Specific Provisions for Partnerships, S Corporations, and
    Personal Service Corporations   16-3
Ethics & Equity: *Who Benefits from the Change in Tax Year?*   *16-5*
Selecting the Tax Year   16-6
Changes in the Accounting Period   16-6
Taxable Periods of Less Than One Year   16-7
Mitigation of the Annual Accounting Period Concept   16-8
Ethics & Equity: *Special Tax Relief*   *16-10*

ACCOUNTING METHODS   16-10
Permissible Methods   16-10
Cash Receipts and Disbursements Method   16-11
Accrual Method   16-13
Concept Summary: *Accruals Under the Economic
    Performance Test*   *16-14*
Financial Disclosure Insights: *Tax Deferrals from Reserves*   *16-16*
Hybrid Method   16-16
Change of Method   16-17
Ethics & Equity: *Change in Accounting Method*   *16-19*

SPECIAL ACCOUNTING METHODS   16-19
Installment Method   16-19
Concept Summary: *Interest on Installment Sales*   *16-24*
Long-Term Contracts   16-27

INVENTORIES   16-30
Determining Inventory Cost   16-31
Ethics & Equity: *Preserving the LIFO Reserve*   *16-35*
The LIFO Election   16-35
Special Inventory Methods Relating to Farming and Ranching   16-36
Inventory of Small Taxpayers   16-36

TAX PLANNING   16-37
Taxable Year   16-37
Cash Method of Accounting   16-37
Installment Method   16-37
Inventories   16-38
Refocus on the Big Picture: *Accounting Period and Method*   *16-38*

Part 6: Corporations

CHAPTER 17
CORPORATIONS: INTRODUCTION AND OPERATING RULES   17-1
The Big Picture: *A Half-Baked Idea?*   *17-1*

AN INTRODUCTION TO THE INCOME TAXATION OF CORPORATIONS   17-2
An Overview of Corporate versus Individual Income
    Tax Treatment   17-2
Specific Provisions Compared   17-3
Accounting Periods and Methods   17-4
Capital Gains and Losses   17-5
Recapture of Depreciation   17-6
Business Interest Expense Limitation   17-6
Passive Activity Losses   17-8
Concept Summary: *Special Rules Applicable to Personal
    Service Corporations (PSCs)*   *17-9*
Charitable Contributions   17-9
Excessive Executive Compensation   17-11
Net Operating Losses   17-12
Deductions Available Only to Corporations   17-12
Ethics & Equity: *Pushing the Envelope on Year-End Planning*   *17-15*
Concept Summary: *Income Taxation of Individuals and
    Corporations Compared*   *17-17*

DETERMINING THE CORPORATE INCOME TAX LIABILITY   17-18
Corporate Income Tax Rates   17-18
Alternative Minimum Tax   17-19
Restrictions on Corporate Accumulations   17-19
Consolidated Returns   17-20
Financial Disclosure Insights: *GAAP and Tax Treatment
    of Consolidations*   *17-22*

PROCEDURAL MATTERS   17-23
Filing Requirements for Corporations   17-23
Estimated Tax Payments   17-24
Schedule M–1—Reconciliation of Income
    (Loss) per Books with Income per Return   17-24
Schedule M–2—Analysis of Unappropriated Retained
    Earnings per Books   17-25
Concept Summary: *Conceptual Diagram of Schedule M–1
    (Form 1120)*   *17-26*
Schedule M–3—Net Income (Loss) Reconciliation
    for Corporations with Total Assets of $10 Million or
    More   17-26
Income Taxes in the Financial Statements   17-28

TAX PLANNING   17-34
Corporate versus Noncorporate Forms of
    Business Organization   17-34
Operating the Corporation   17-35
Refocus on the Big Picture: *Cooked to Perfection*   *17-37*

CHAPTER 18
CORPORATIONS: ORGANIZATION AND CAPITAL STRUCTURE   18-1
The Big Picture: *The Vehicle for Business Growth Is the
    Corporate Form*   *18-1*

ORGANIZATION OF AND TRANSFERS TO CONTROLLED CORPORATIONS   18-2
Section 351 Rationale and General Rules   18-2
Global Tax Issues: *Tax Reform Adds a New Wrinkle to the
    Choice of Organizational Form When Operating Overseas*   *18-3*
Concept Summary: *Shareholder Consequences: Taxable
    Corporate Formation versus Tax-Deferred § 351 Transaction*   *18-5*

Property Defined   18-5
Stock Transferred   18-6
Control of the Corporation   18-6
Assumption of Liabilities—§ 357   18-10
Basis Determination and Related Issues   18-12
Concept Summary: *Tax Consequences of Liability
    Assumption*   *18-13*
Concept Summary: *Tax Consequences to the Shareholders and
    Corporation: With and Without the Application of
    § 351 (Based on the Facts of Example 22)*   *18-15*

CAPITAL STRUCTURE OF A CORPORATION   **18-18**
Capital Contributions   18-18
Debt in the Capital Structure   18-18

INVESTOR LOSSES   **18-21**
Stock and Security Losses   18-21
Business versus Nonbusiness Bad Debts   18-21
Ethics & Equity: *Can a Loss Produce a Double Benefit?*   *18-21*
Section 1244 Stock   18-23

**GAIN FROM QUALIFIED SMALL
BUSINESS STOCK**   **18-24**

TAX PLANNING   **18-24**
Working with § 351   18-24
Selecting Assets to Transfer   18-26
Debt in the Capital Structure   18-26
Investor Losses   18-27
Corporations versus Flow-Through Entities   18-28
Refocus on the Big Picture: *The Vehicle for Business Growth
    Is the Corporate Form*   *18-29*

CHAPTER 19
**CORPORATIONS: DISTRIBUTIONS
NOT IN COMPLETE LIQUIDATION**   **19-1**
The Big Picture: *Taxing Corporate Distributions*   *19-1*

CORPORATE DISTRIBUTIONS—OVERVIEW   **19-2**

EARNINGS AND PROFITS (E & P)   **19-3**
Computation of E & P   19-3
Summary of E & P Adjustments   19-6
Concept Summary: *E & P Adjustments*   *19-7*
Current versus Accumulated E & P   19-8
Allocating E & P to Distributions   19-8
Concept Summary: *Allocating E & P to Distributions*   *19-9*
Ethics & Equity: *Shifting E & P*   *19-12*

DIVIDENDS   **19-12**
Rationale for Reduced Tax Rates on Dividends   19-12
Qualified Dividends   19-13
Property Dividends   19-14
Concept Summary: *Noncash Property Distributions*   *19-16*
Constructive Dividends   19-16
Stock Dividends and Stock Rights   19-19

STOCK REDEMPTIONS   **19-21**
Overview   19-21
Global Tax Issues: *Foreign Shareholders Prefer Sale or
    Exchange Treatment in Stock Redemptions*   *19-23*
Historical Background   19-24
Concept Summary: *Summary of the Qualifying Stock
    Redemption Rules*   *19-24*
Stock Attribution Rules   19-25
Concept Summary: *Tax Consequences of Stock Redemptions to
    Shareholders*   *19-26*
Not Essentially Equivalent Redemptions   19-26
Disproportionate Redemptions   19-27
Complete Termination Redemptions   19-28
Redemptions to Pay Death Taxes   19-28

**STOCK REDEMPTIONS—EFFECT ON
THE CORPORATION**   **19-29**
Recognition of Gain or Loss   19-29
Effect on Earnings and Profits   19-30
Redemption Expenditures   19-30

OTHER CORPORATE DISTRIBUTIONS   **19-30**

TAX PLANNING   **19-30**
Corporate Distributions   19-30
Concept Summary: *Corporate Distributions*   *19-31*
Planning for Qualified Dividends   19-32
Constructive Dividends   19-33
Stock Redemptions   19-33
Refocus on the Big Picture: *Taxing Corporate Distributions*   *19-34*

CHAPTER 20
**CORPORATIONS: DISTRIBUTIONS IN
COMPLETE LIQUIDATION AND AN
OVERVIEW OF REORGANIZATIONS**   **20-1**
The Big Picture: *The Options for Transitioning to Retirement*   *20-1*

LIQUIDATIONS—IN GENERAL   **20-2**
The Liquidation Process   20-2
Liquidating and Nonliquidating Distributions Compared   20-2

**LIQUIDATIONS—EFFECT ON THE
DISTRIBUTING CORPORATION**   **20-3**
The General Rule   20-3
Antistuffing Rules   20-4
Concept Summary: *Summary of Antistuffing Loss
    Disallowance Rules*   *20-8*

LIQUIDATIONS—EFFECT ON THE SHAREHOLDER   **20-8**
Ethics & Equity: *Transferee Liability for Tax Deficiency of
    Liquidated Corporation*   *20-9*

LIQUIDATIONS—PARENT-SUBSIDIARY SITUATIONS   **20-9**
Concept Summary: *Summary of Liquidation Rules*   *20-10*
Minority Shareholder Interests   20-10
Indebtedness of the Subsidiary to the Parent   20-11

Global Tax Issues: *Basis Rules for Liquidations of Foreign Subsidiaries* 20-11

Basis of Property Received by the Parent Corporation— The General Rule 20-12

Basis of Property Received by the Parent Corporation— § 338 Election 20-12

CORPORATE REORGANIZATIONS **20-14**

In General 20-15

Summary of the Different Types of Reorganizations 20-15

Summary of the Tax Consequences in a Tax-Free Reorganization 20-15

Financial Disclosure Insights: *Acquisitions Can Have Negative Consequences* 20-16

Concept Summary: *Gain and Basis Rules for Nontaxable Exchanges* 20-16

Concept Summary: *Basis to Acquiring Corporation of Property Received* 20-18

TAX PLANNING **20-19**

Effect of a Liquidating Distribution on the Corporation 20-19

Effect of a Liquidating Distribution on the Shareholder 20-19

Parent-Subsidiary Liquidations 20-20

Asset Purchase versus Stock Purchase 20-20

Refocus on the Big Picture: *The Transition to Retirement Is Subject to Double Taxation* 20-21

Part 7: Flow-Through Entities

CHAPTER 21
PARTNERSHIPS **21-1**

The Big Picture: *Why Use a Partnership, Anyway?* *21-1*

OVERVIEW OF PARTNERSHIP TAXATION **21-2**

What Is a Partnership? 21-2

Concept Summary: *Comparison of Partnership Types* *21-3*

Key Concepts in Taxation of Partnership Income 21-4

FORMATION OF A PARTNERSHIP: TAX EFFECTS **21-6**

Contributions to the Partnership 21-6

Exceptions to the General Rule of § 721 21-7

Other Issues Related to Contributed Property 21-9

Concept Summary: *Partnership Formation and Initial Basis Computations* *21-11*

Tax Accounting Elections 21-11

Initial Costs of a Partnership 21-12

Method of Accounting 21-12

Taxable Year of the Partnership 21-13

PARTNERSHIP OPERATIONS AND REPORTING **21-15**

Partnership Reporting, In General 21-15

Measuring Partnership Income 21-16

Form 1065 Example 21-18

Financial Disclosure Insights: *Financial Reporting for Partnerships* *21-24*

PARTNER CALCULATIONS AND REPORTING **21-24**

Partner Reporting of Partnership Income 21-24

Partner Allocations 21-26

Schedule K–1 Example 21-28

Concept Summary: *Tax Reporting of Partnership Items* *21-30*

Partner's Basis 21-31

Effect of Partnership Liabilities on Partner's Basis 21-31

Partner's Capital Account 21-35

Loss Limitations 21-36

Global Tax Issues: *Withholding Requirements for non-U.S. Partners* *21-38*

OTHER TAXES ON PARTNERSHIP INCOME **21-38**

Self-Employment Tax 21-38

Net Investment Income Tax 21-39

DISTRIBUTIONS FROM THE PARTNERSHIP **21-40**

Distributions in General 21-40

Proportionate Current Distributions 21-41

Proportionate Liquidating Distributions 21-43

Concept Summary: *Proportionate Current Distributions (General Rules)* *21-44*

SALE OF A PARTNERSHIP INTEREST **21-46**

General Rules 21-46

Hot Assets and Carried Interests 21-48

LIMITED LIABILITY ENTITIES **21-49**

Limited Liability Companies 21-49

Limited Liability Partnerships 21-49

TAX PLANNING **21-50**

Choosing Partnership Taxation 21-50

Concept Summary: *Major Advantages and Disadvantages of the Partnership Form* *21-51*

Formation and Operation of a Partnership 21-51

Basis Considerations and Loss Deduction Limitations 21-51

Transactions between Partners and Partnerships 21-51

Drafting the Partnership Agreement 21-52

Refocus on the Big Picture: *Why Use a Partnership, Anyway?* *21-52*

CHAPTER 22
S CORPORATIONS **22-1**

The Big Picture: *Deductibility of Losses and the Choice of Business Entity* *22-1*

CHOICE OF BUSINESS ENTITY **22-2**

An Overview of S Corporations 22-2

QUALIFYING FOR S CORPORATION STATUS **22-3**

Definition of a Small Business Corporation 22-3

Making the Election 22-5

Shareholder Consent 22-6

Loss of the Election 22-7

OPERATIONAL RULES — **22-9**

Computation of Taxable Income — 22-9

Qualified Business Income Deduction — 22-12

Allocation of Income and Loss — 22-12

Tax Treatment of Distributions to Shareholders — 22-13

Concept Summary: *Classification Procedures for Distributions from an S Corporation* — *22-14*

Tax Treatment of Noncash Property Distributions by the Corporation — 22-18

Concept Summary: *Consequences of Noncash Distributions* — *22-18*

Shareholder's Basis in S Stock — 22-19

Treatment of Losses — 22-21

Tax on Pre-Election Built-In Gain — 22-23

LIFO Recapture Tax — 22-24

Passive Investment Income Penalty Tax — 22-24

Other Operational Rules — 22-25

TAX PLANNING — **22-26**

When the Election Is Advisable — 22-26

Concept Summary: *Making an S Election* — *22-26*

Making a Proper Election — 22-26

Operation of the S Corporation — 22-27

OVERALL COMPARISON OF FORMS OF DOING BUSINESS — **22-28**

Concept Summary: *Tax Attributes of Different Forms of Business (Assume That Partners and Shareholders Are All Individuals)* — *22-29*

Refocus on the Big Picture: *Deductibility of Losses and the Choice of Business Entity* — *22-33*

Part 8: Advanced Tax Practice Considerations

CHAPTER 23
EXEMPT ENTITIES — 23-1

The Big Picture: *Effect of a For-Profit Business on a Tax-Exempt Entity* — *23-1*

TYPES OF EXEMPT ORGANIZATIONS — **23-3**

CHARACTERISTICS OF EXEMPT ENTITIES — **23-3**

Serving the Common Good — 23-3

Not-for-Profit Entity — 23-3

Net Earnings and Members of the Organization — 23-3

Concept Summary: *Consequences of Exempt Status* — *23-5*

TAXES ON EXEMPT ENTITIES — **23-5**

Taxable Transactions — 23-5

Feeder Organizations — 23-8

PRIVATE FOUNDATIONS — **23-8**

Tax Consequences of Private Foundation Status — 23-8

Concept Summary: *Exempt Organizations: Classification* — *23-10*

Taxes Imposed on Private Foundations — 23-11

UNRELATED BUSINESS INCOME TAX — **23-12**

Unrelated Trade or Business — 23-13

Unrelated Business Taxable Income — 23-16

Concept Summary: *Unrelated Business Income Tax* — *23-18*

REPORTING REQUIREMENTS — **23-19**

Obtaining Exempt Organization Status — 23-19

Annual Filing Requirements — 23-19

Disclosure Requirements — 23-21

TAX PLANNING — **23-21**

General Considerations — 23-21

Maintaining Exempt Status — 23-21

Private Foundation Status — 23-22

Unrelated Business Income Tax — 23-22

Refocus on the Big Picture: *Effect of a For-Profit Business on a Tax-Exempt Entity* — *23-23*

CHAPTER 24
MULTISTATE CORPORATE TAXATION — 24-1

The Big Picture: *Making a Multistate Location Decision* — *24-1*

CORPORATE STATE INCOME TAXATION — **24-2**

Computing State Income Tax — 24-3

State Modifications — 24-3

The UDITPA and the Multistate Tax Commission — 24-6

Jurisdiction to Impose Tax: Nexus and Public Law 86–272 — 24-6

Nexus in Today's Economy — 24-6

Concept Summary: *Multistate Taxation* — *24-8*

APPORTIONMENT AND ALLOCATION OF INCOME — **24-8**

The Apportionment Procedure — 24-9

Apportionable Income — 24-9

Apportionment Factors: Elements and Planning — 24-11

Concept Summary: *Apportionable Income* — *24-12*

The Sales Factor — 24-13

The Payroll Factor — 24-14

The Property Factor — 24-16

Financial Disclosure Insights: *State/Local Taxes and the Tax Expense* — *24-17*

THE UNITARY THEORY — **24-18**

What Is a Unitary Business? — 24-19

Tax Effects of the Unitary Theory — 24-19

Consolidated and Combined Returns — 24-21

Global Tax Issues: *Water's Edge Is Not a Day at the Beach* — *24-21*

Concept Summary: *Using Apportionment Formulas* — *24-22*

TAXATION OF S CORPORATIONS — **24-22**

Eligibility — 24-22

State Tax Filing Requirements — 24-22

TAXATION OF PARTNERSHIPS AND LLCS — **24-23**

OTHER STATE AND LOCAL TAXES — **24-23**

State and Local Sales and Use Taxes — 24-23

Local Property Taxes 24-25
Other Taxes 24-26
Ethics & Equity: *Encouraging Economic Development through Tax Concessions* 24-27

TAX PLANNING **24-28**
Selecting the Optimal State in Which to Operate 24-28
Restructuring Corporate Entities 24-29
Subjecting the Corporation's Income to Apportionment 24-31
Ethics & Equity: *Can You Be a Nowhere Adviser?* 24-32
Planning with Apportionment Factors 24-32
Sales/Use Tax Compliance 24-33
Capital Stock Taxation 24-33
Refocus on the Big Picture: *Making a Multistate Location Decision* 24-33

CHAPTER 25
TAXATION OF INTERNATIONAL TRANSACTIONS 25-1
The Big Picture: *Going International* 25-1

OVERVIEW OF INTERNATIONAL TAXATION **25-3**
Global Tax Issues: *Tax Reform Can Make Strange Bedfellows* 25-4

TAX TREATIES **25-5**

SOURCING OF INCOME AND DEDUCTIONS **25-6**
Income Sourcing Rules 25-6
Allocation and Apportionment of Deductions 25-9
Concept Summary: *The Sourcing Rules* 25-10
Transfer Pricing 25-10
Ethics & Equity: *The Costs of Good Tax Planning* 25-11

FOREIGN CURRENCY GAIN/LOSS **25-14**

U.S. PERSONS WITH OFFSHORE INCOME **25-15**
Export Property, Licenses, Foreign Branches 25-15
Financial Disclosure Insights: *Overseas Operations and Book-Tax Differences* 25-17
Concept Summary: *The Foreign Tax Credit* 25-17
Creating a Cross-Border Business Entity 25-18
Tax Havens 25-19
Offshore (Foreign) Corporations Controlled by U.S. Persons 25-20
Concept Summary : *Subpart F Income and a CFC* 25-22
Movement Toward a Territorial System 25-23
Concept Summary : *Income of a CFC That Is Included in Gross Income of a U.S. Shareholder, Selected* 25-24

U.S. TAXATION OF NONRESIDENT ALIENS AND FOREIGN CORPORATIONS **25-26**
Nonresident Alien Individuals 25-26
Foreign Corporations 25-28
Foreign Investment in Real Property Tax Act 25-28
Expatriation to Avoid U.S. Taxation 25-28

TAX PLANNING **25-29**
The Foreign Tax Credit Limitation and Sourcing Provisions 25-30
Transfer Pricing 25-30
Refocus on the Big Picture: *Going International* 25-31

CHAPTER 26
TAX PRACTICE AND ETHICS 26-1
The Big Picture: *A Tax Adviser's Dilemma* 26-1

TAX ADMINISTRATION **26-2**
Organizational Structure of the IRS 26-3
IRS Procedure—Letter Rulings 26-4
IRS Procedure—Other Issuances 26-4
Ethics & Equity: *Tax Compliance Costs* 26-5
Administrative Powers of the IRS 26-5
The Audit Process 26-6
Ethics & Equity: *Can the IRS Pretend to Be Your Friend?* 26-7
The Taxpayer Appeal Process 26-9
Offers in Compromise and Closing Agreements 26-10
Ethics & Equity: *Our Taxing System of Self-Assessment* 26-11
Interest 26-12
Concept Summary: *Working with the IRS* 26-13
Taxpayer Penalties 26-13
Ethics & Equity: *First-Time Tax Violators Can Get Off with Just a Warning* 26-18
Statute of Limitations 26-21

THE TAX PROFESSION AND TAX ETHICS **26-22**
The Tax Professional 26-22
Regulating Tax Preparers 26-23
IRS Rules Governing Tax Practice 26-23
Preparer Penalties 26-24
Privileged Communications 26-26
AICPA Statements on Standards for Tax Services 26-27
Concept Summary: *Tax Profession and Ethics* 26-30

TAX PLANNING **26-30**
Strategies in Seeking a Letter Ruling 26-30
Considerations in Handling an IRS Audit 26-30
Statute of Limitations 26-31
Litigation Considerations 26-32
Penalties 26-32
Privileged Communications 26-33
Refocus on the Big Picture: *A Tax Adviser's Dilemma* 26-33

Part 9: Family Tax Planning

CHAPTER 27
THE FEDERAL GIFT AND ESTATE TAXES 27-1
The Big Picture: *An Eventful and Final Year* 27-1

TRANSFER TAXES—IN GENERAL **27-2**
Nature of the Taxes 27-2
Global Tax Issues: *U.S. Transfer Taxes and NRAs* 27-3

Concept Summary: *Gift Tax Formula*   *27-3*
Concept Summary: *Estate Tax Formula*   *27-4*
Valuation for Federal Transfer Tax Purposes   27-5
Key Property Concepts   27-6

THE FEDERAL GIFT TAX   **27-7**
General Considerations   27-7
Ethics & Equity: *It's the Thought That Counts*   *27-7*
Transfers Subject to the Gift Tax   27-9
Annual Gift Tax Exclusion   27-10
Deductions   27-11
Computing the Federal Gift Tax   27-11
Procedural Matters   27-12
Concept Summary: *Federal Gift Tax Provisions*   *27-13*

THE FEDERAL ESTATE TAX   **27-13**
Gross Estate   27-13
Concept Summary: *Federal Estate Tax Provisions—Gross Estate* *27-18*
Taxable Estate   27-19
Estate Tax Credits   27-22
Global Tax Issues: *Treaty Relief Is Not Abundant!*   *27-23*
Procedural Matters   27-23
Concept Summary: *Federal Estate Tax Provisions—
   Taxable Estate and Procedural Matters*   *27-24*

THE GENERATION-SKIPPING TRANSFER TAX   **27-24**
Inter-Generational Transfers   27-24
The Tax on Generation-Skipping Transfers   27-24

TAX PLANNING   **27-25**
The Federal Gift Tax   27-25
The Federal Estate Tax   27-26
Refocus on the Big Picture: *An Eventful and Final Year*   *27-28*

CHAPTER 28
**INCOME TAXATION OF TRUSTS AND
ESTATES**   **28-1**
The Big Picture: *Setting Up a Trust to Protect a Family*   *28-1*

AN OVERVIEW OF FIDUCIARY TAXATION   **28-2**
What Is a Trust?   28-2
What Is an Estate?   28-5

NATURE OF TRUST AND ESTATE TAXATION   **28-5**
Concept Summary: *Tax Characteristics of Major
   Pass-Through Entities*   *28-6*
Tax Accounting Periods and Methods   28-6
Tax Rates and Personal Exemption   28-6
Alternative Minimum Tax   28-7
Additional Tax on Net Investment Income   28-8

TAXABLE INCOME OF TRUSTS AND ESTATES   **28-8**
Entity Accounting Income   28-8
Gross Income   28-11
Ethics & Equity: *To Whom Can I Trust My Pet?*   *28-13*
Ordinary Deductions   28-13

Deductions for Losses   28-15
Charitable Contributions   28-15
Deduction for Distributions to Beneficiaries   28-16
Concept Summary: *Uses of the DNI Amount*   *28-17*
Tax Credits   28-19
Concept Summary: *Principles of Fiduciary Income Taxation* *28-20*

TAXATION OF BENEFICIARIES   **28-20**
Distributions by Simple Trusts   28-20
Distributions by Estates and Complex Trusts   28-20
Character of Income   28-22

PROCEDURAL MATTERS   **28-23**

TAX PLANNING   **28-24**
A Trust or an Estate as an Income-Shifting Device   28-24
Income Tax Planning for Estates   28-24
Distributions of In-Kind Property   28-25
Ethics & Equity: *Who Should Be a Trustee?*   *28-26*
Additional Taxes on Capital Gains and Net
   Investment Income   28-26
Refocus on the Big Picture: *Setting Up a Trust to Protect a Family* *28-27*

APPENDICES

TAX RATE SCHEDULES AND TABLES   A-1

TAX FORMS   B-1

GLOSSARY   C-1

TABLE OF CODE SECTIONS CITED   D-1

TABLE OF REGULATIONS CITED   D-13

TABLE OF REVENUE PROCEDURES AND
REVENUE RULINGS CITED   D-17

PRACTICE SET ASSIGNMENTS—
COMPREHENSIVE TAX RETURN PROBLEMS   E-1

TAX FORMULAS   F-1

PRESENT VALUE AND FUTURE VALUE TABLES   G-1

INDEX   I-1

Online Appendices

DEPRECIATION AND THE ACCELERATED COST
RECOVERY SYSTEM (ACRS)

AFFORDABLE CARE ACT PROVISIONS

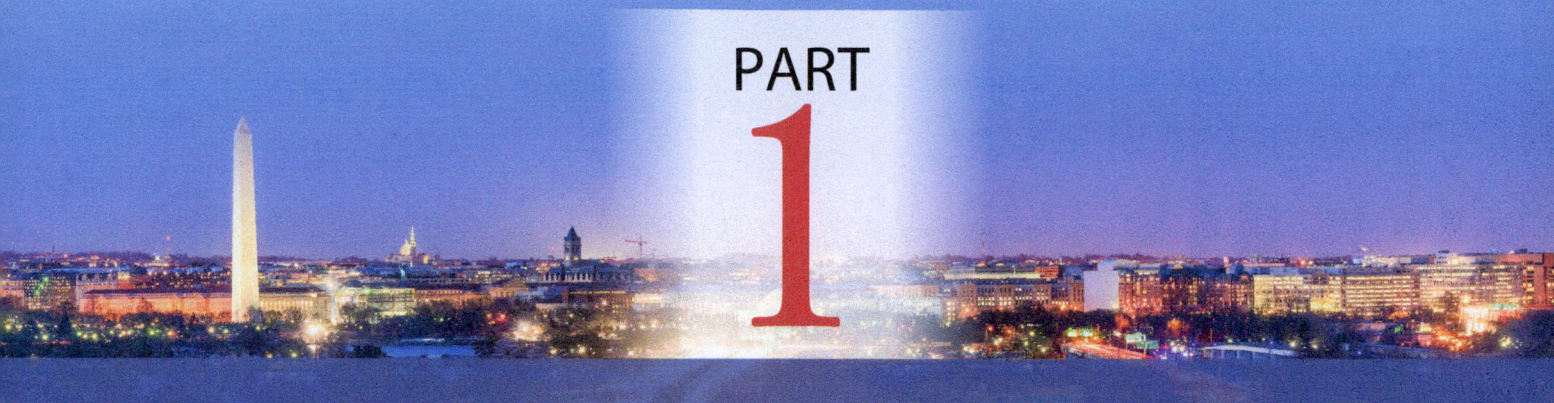

PART

1

INTRODUCTION AND BASIC TAX MODEL

CHAPTER **1**

An Introduction to Taxation and Understanding the Federal Tax Law

CHAPTER **2**

Working with the Tax Law

CHAPTER **3**

Computing the Tax

Part 1 provides an introduction to taxation in the United States. Although this text focuses on income taxation, other types of taxes also are briefly discussed. The purposes of the Federal tax law are examined, and the legislative, administrative, and judicial sources of Federal tax law, including their application to the tax research process, are analyzed. Part 1 concludes by introducing the basic tax model for the individual taxpayer and providing an overview of property transactions.

CHAPTER

1

An Introduction to Taxation and Understanding the Federal Tax Law

LEARNING OBJECTIVES: *After completing Chapter 1, you should be able to:*

LO.1 Explain the importance of taxation and apply methods for studying this topic.

LO.2 Describe some of the history and trends of the Federal income tax.

LO.3 Describe and apply principles and terminology relevant to the design of a tax system.

LO.4 Identify the different taxes imposed in the United States at the Federal, state, and local levels.

LO.5 Explain the administration of the tax law, including the audit process utilized by the IRS.

LO.6 Evaluate some of the ethical guidelines involved in tax practice.

LO.7 Classify tax rules based on their possible economic, social, equity, and political reasons for inclusion in a particular tax system.

LO.8 Explain the role played by the IRS and the courts in the evolution of the Federal tax system.

CHAPTER OUTLINE

1-1 Approaching the Study of Taxation, 1-2
  1-1a What Is Taxation? 1-2
  1-1b Taxation in Our Lives, 1-2
  1-1c The Relevance of Taxation to Accounting and Finance Professionals, 1-3
  1-1d How to Study Taxation, 1-4

1-2 A Brief History of U.S. Taxation, 1-4
  1-2a Early Periods, 1-4
  1-2b Revenue Acts, 1-5
  1-2c Trends, 1-6

1-3 Tax System Design, 1-6
  1-3a Legal Foundation, 1-6
  1-3b The Basic Tax Formula, 1-7
  1-3c Tax Principles, 1-8

1-4 Major Types of Taxes, 1-8
  1-4a Property Taxes, 1-10
  1-4b Transaction Taxes, 1-11
  1-4c Taxes on Transfers at Death, 1-13
  1-4d Gift Taxes, 1-14

  1-4e Income Taxes, 1-15
  1-4f Employment Taxes, 1-17
  1-4g Other U.S. Taxes, 1-18
  1-4h Proposed U.S. Taxes, 1-20

1-5 Tax Administration, 1-21
  1-5a Internal Revenue Service, 1-21
  1-5b The Audit Process, 1-21
  1-5c Statute of Limitations, 1-24
  1-5d Interest and Penalties, 1-24
  1-5e Tax Practice, 1-25

1-6 Understanding the Federal Tax Law, 1-27
  1-6a Revenue Needs, 1-27
  1-6b Economic Considerations, 1-27
  1-6c Social Considerations, 1-28
  1-6d Equity Considerations, 1-29
  1-6e Political Considerations, 1-31
  1-6f Influence of the Internal Revenue Service, 1-32
  1-6g Influence of the Courts, 1-33
  1-6h Summary, 1-34

CORBIS/SUPERSTOCK

FAMILY AND TAXES—A TYPICAL YEAR

Travis and Amy Carter are married and live in a state that imposes both a sales tax and an income tax. They have two children, April (age 17) and Martin (age 18). Travis is a mining engineer who specializes in land reclamation. After several years with a mining corporation, Travis established a consulting practice that involves a considerable amount of travel due to work he performs in other states. Amy is a registered nurse who, until recently, was a homemaker. In November of this year, she decided to reenter the job market and accepted a position with a medical clinic. The Carters live only a few blocks from Ernest and Mary Walker, Amy Carter's parents. The Walkers are retired and live on interest, dividends, and Social Security benefits.

Activities during the year with possible tax ramifications are summarized below.

- The ad valorem property taxes on the Carters' residence are increased, whereas those on the Walkers' residence are lowered.

- When Travis registers an automobile purchased last year in another state, he is required to pay a sales tax to his home state.

- As an anniversary present, the Carters gave the Walkers a recreational vehicle (RV).

- Travis employs his children to draft blueprints and prepare scale models for use in his work. Both April and Martin have had training in drafting and topography.

- Early in the year, the Carters are audited by the state on an income tax return filed a few years ago. Later in the year, they are audited by the IRS on a Form 1040 they filed for the same year. In each case, a tax deficiency and interest were assessed.

- The Walkers are audited by the IRS. Unlike the Carters, they did not have to deal with an agent, but settled the matter by mail.

Explain these developments, and resolve the issues raised.

Read the chapter and formulate your response.

This chapter provides an overview of the Federal tax system. Among the topics discussed:

- The importance and relevance of taxation and how to study taxation.
- A brief history of the Federal income tax.
- The types of taxes imposed at the Federal, state, and local levels.
- Some highlights of tax law administration.
- Tax concepts that help explain the reasons for various tax provisions.
- The influence the Internal Revenue Service (IRS) and the courts have had in the evolution of current tax law.

LO.1

Explain the importance of taxation and apply methods for studying this topic.

1-1 APPROACHING THE STUDY OF TAXATION

1-1a What Is Taxation?

"Taxes are what we pay for civilized society."

This is a famous quote from U.S. Supreme Court Justice Oliver Wendell Holmes, Jr. (1841 to 1935).[1] It is engraved on the government building at 1111 Constitution Avenue in Washington, D.C.—headquarters of the Internal Revenue Service (IRS). This quote eloquently sums up the primary purpose of taxation—to raise revenue for government operations. Governments at all levels—national, state, and local—require funds for defense, protection (police and fire), education, roads, the court system, social services, and more. Various types of taxes provide the resources to pay for government services.

In addition, taxation is often used as a tool to influence the behavior of individuals and businesses. For example, an income tax credit (which reduces a taxpayer's tax bill) may be designed to *encourage* people to purchase a fuel-efficient car. A tobacco excise tax may *discourage* individuals from smoking by increasing the cost of tobacco products. The tax system can also be used to provide direct benefits to taxpayers, such as to help pay for health insurance.

1-1b Taxation in Our Lives

"Nothing is certain, except death and taxes."

Most people attribute this quote to Benjamin Franklin (1706 to 1790). Taxes permeate our society. Various types of taxes, such as income, sales, property, and excise taxes (discussed in text Section 1-4), come into play in many of the activities of individuals, businesses, nonprofit entities (e.g., charitable organizations), and even governments.

Most directly, individuals are affected by taxes by paying them. Taxes may be paid directly or indirectly. A direct tax is paid to the government by the person who pays the tax. Examples include the personal income tax, which is paid by filing a personal income tax return (Form 1040 at the Federal level), and property taxes on one's home (paid to the local government). Individuals also pay many taxes indirectly. For example, most states impose sales tax on the purchase of tangible goods such as clothes. While this tax is collected and remitted to the government by the seller, the buyer is charged the tax along with the purchase price of the goods or services. Taxes also can be imposed indirectly when embedded in the prices charged by the seller. For example, when you buy gasoline for your car, the price you pay likely includes some of the income taxes and the gasoline excise taxes owed by the oil company.

Ultimately, all taxes are paid by individuals. The corporate income tax, for example, is paid directly by the corporation but is really paid indirectly by individuals in their capacity as customers, investors (owners), or employees. Economists and others often study this topic to estimate the percentage of the corporate income tax borne by individuals in these different capacities. It is not easy to measure, but it is known that taxes are passed along to individuals through higher prices, lower dividends, and/or lower wages.

Taxes also affect the lives of individuals via the ballot box. Federal, state, and local elections often include initiatives that deal with taxation, such as whether state income taxes should be raised (or lowered), whether a new tax should be imposed on soda,

---

[1] *Compania General De Tabacos De Filipinas v. Collector of Internal Revenue,* 275 U.S. 87, 100 (1927), dissenting opinion.

or whether the sales tax rate should be changed. Candidates running for office often have positions on tax changes they would like to make if elected.

Given the pervasiveness of taxation—in our roles as both direct and indirect payers of taxes as well as citizens/voters—it is important that we understand how the tax system operates.

1-1c The Relevance of Taxation to Accounting and Finance Professionals

The U.S. corporate income tax rate is 21 percent. State income taxes can easily constitute, on average, an additional 5 percent. So a large corporation such as a Fortune 500 company may have to devote 26 percent or more of its net income to pay income taxes. In addition, businesses are subject to employment taxes, property taxes, sales taxes, and various excise taxes. Corporations with international operations are subject to taxation in other countries. Small businesses are also subject to a variety of taxes that affect profits and cash flows.

Given its significance, taxation is a crucial topic for accounting and finance professionals. They must understand the various types of business taxes to assist effectively with the following:

- *Compliance:* Ensure that the business files all tax returns and makes all tax payments on time. Mistakes and missed due dates will lead to penalties and interest expense.

- *Planning:* Help a business apply favorable tax rules, such as income deferral and tax credits, to minimize tax liability (and maximize owner wealth). The time value of money concept is also important here, as is coordinating tax planning with other business goals to maximize earnings per share.

- *Financial reporting:* Financial statements include a variety of tax information, including income tax expense on the income statement and deferred tax assets and liabilities on the balance sheet. Footnotes to the financial statements report various tax details including the company's effective tax rate. Computation and proper reporting of this information require knowledge of both tax and financial reporting rules [including the Financial Accounting Standards Board's Accounting Standards Codification (ASC) 740, *Income Taxes*].

- *Controversy:* This term refers to interaction a taxpayer may have with a tax agency such as the IRS. The IRS and state and local tax agencies regularly audit tax returns that have been filed to verify that taxes were properly computed and paid.

- *Cash management:* Taxes must be paid on time to avoid penalties and interest. Income and self-employment taxes must be estimated and paid quarterly and reconciled on the annual return. Other taxes may be due weekly, monthly, or semiannually. Businesses must be sure they have the funds ready when the taxes are due and have procedures to track due dates.

- *Data analysis:* With a majority, if not all, of a company's records maintained in digital form, there are opportunities to use this information to enhance profits, better understand the customer base, and improve and understand the information from a tax perspective. Tax practitioners often need skills in data analysis and visualization to identify samples for both internal and external audits, find ways to identify the products and services subject to sales tax in different states, and extract tax data to help inform other business functions such as where to locate a new sales office.

These tasks are also relevant to professionals such as CPAs who advise business and individual clients.

The level and depth of tax knowledge needed for any accounting or tax professional depends on his or her specific job. The vice president of tax for a company clearly needs thorough knowledge in all areas of taxation; the same is true of a partner in a CPA firm. In contrast, the corporate treasurer likely focuses more on cash management, while working closely with the company's tax advisers.

Ultimately, much of taxation is transaction-based. How a transaction is structured (e.g., as a sale or a lease) has varying tax consequences that must be considered. Even the purchase of a home can result in significant change—the new mortgage interest and property tax deductions may mean that an individual itemizes her deductions (using Schedule A of Form 1040) rather than using the standard deduction. And life events such as marriage (and divorce) will change an individual's tax situation. Similar "life events" can also affect a corporation (e.g., acquiring a different corporation or spinning off a subsidiary).

It is essential in working with taxation to maintain a balanced perspective. A corporation that is deciding where to locate a new factory does not automatically select the city or state that offers the most generous tax benefits. Nor does the person who is retiring to a warmer climate pick Belize over Arizona because the former has no income tax but the latter does. Tax considerations should not control decisions, but they remain one of many factors to be considered (and often one of the most significant).

1-1d How to Study Taxation

The goal of studying taxation is to be able to recognize issues (or transactions) that have tax implications and, when possible, try to understand the justification for them. Suppose, for example, that you come upon a situation that involves a discharge of indebtedness. If you know that forgiveness of debt results in income but there are exceptions to this rule, the battle is won! The issue has been identified, and the outcome (i.e., when an exception applies) can be resolved through research. A variety of commercial and free tools and resources are available to help you research and reach a conclusion.

You may have heard that tax is a difficult subject because of the many rules, exceptions, and definitions. You even may have heard that taxation is boring. Taxation is a challenging topic, but it is certainly not boring. Taxation is an important and exciting topic due to constant change by the three branches of our Federal government (as well as changes by state and local governments), the significance of taxes to the bottom line of a company and an individual's finances, and the impact on our economy and society.

Tax professionals tend to find enjoyment in their chosen field due to the intellectual challenge of dealing with tax rules for compliance and planning purposes, the opportunity to interact with colleagues or clients to help them understand the effect of taxes, and the knowledge that their work affects the financial well-being of individuals and businesses.

In studying taxation, focus on understanding the rules and the why(s) behind them (rather than memorizing the many isolated or disconnected rules and terms). The rules become more meaningful by thinking about why they exist for the particular type of tax. For example, why does the Federal income tax allow for a casualty loss deduction in certain situations? Why is tax depreciation different from that used for financial reporting? Also consider how the rules apply to different types of taxpayers (like employees, sole proprietors, corporations, investors, children, and retirees). Also think about how the rules apply to taxpayers of varying income levels and sophistication of transactions (a homeowner versus someone who owns assets in several countries). Aiming for understanding rather than memorization will make your journey into the world of taxation interesting and meaningful and will prepare you well for dealing with taxation in your accounting or finance career.

For tax professionals, the study of taxation is an ongoing and intriguing process. When Congress changes the tax law, tax professionals must review the new rules in order to understand how they affect clients or their employer. In addition, decisions rendered by the courts in tax disputes and guidance issued by the Treasury Department and Internal Revenue Service must be understood to ensure correct compliance with the law as well as identification of updated and proper tax planning ideas.

Concept Summary 1.1 illustrates the various ways that individuals deal with, and are affected by, taxes.

1-2 A BRIEF HISTORY OF U.S. TAXATION

LO.2

Describe some of the history and trends of the Federal income tax.

1-2a Early Periods

An income tax was first enacted in 1634 by the English colonists in the Massachusetts Bay Colony, but the Federal government did not adopt an income tax until 1861. In fact, both the Federal Union and the Confederate States of America used the income tax to raise funds to finance the Civil War.

When the Civil War ended, the need for additional revenue disappeared and the income tax was repealed. Once again the Federal government was able to finance its operations almost exclusively from customs duties (tariffs).

When a new Federal income tax on individuals was enacted in 1894, its opponents were prepared to successfully challenge its constitutionality. In *Pollock v. Farmers' Loan*

Concept Summary 1.1

Individuals and Taxes

The diagram to the right illustrates the many ways individuals interact with taxes. For example, as shown in the outer circle, individuals pay taxes and file tax returns (tax compliance). They also engage in tax planning as part of their desire to maximize after-tax wealth. If their tax return is audited or they do not pay their taxes, taxpayers will deal with the IRS or their state tax agency (tax controversy). Individuals deal with tax rules and planning in their roles as consumers, employees, investors, and business owners. Tax law is designed around these various tax-payer activities. Finally, as shown by the inner circle, individuals have a personal responsibility to comply with tax laws and pay any taxes due. Individuals also have a civic responsibility to under-stand taxes in their role as citizens and voters. And individuals need to understand how taxes affect their personal cash flows, consumption, and savings.

Use this diagram as you study the materials in this text, consid-ering where in the circle various rules fit.

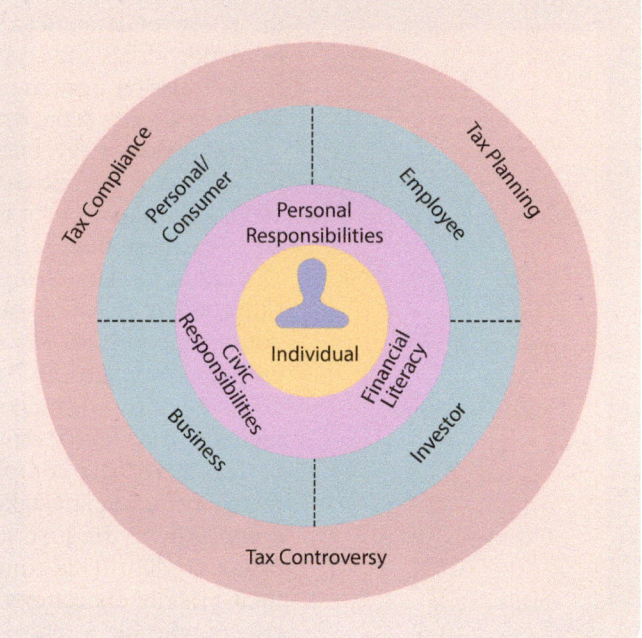

and Trust Co., the U.S. Supreme Court found that taxes on the income of real and per-sonal property were the legal equivalent of a tax on the property involved and, there-fore, required apportionment based on the population of the United States, as required by Article I, Section 8 of the Constitution.[2]

A Federal corporate income tax, enacted by Congress in 1909, fared better in the judicial system. The U.S. Supreme Court found this tax to be constitutional because it was treated as an excise tax.[3] In essence, it was a tax on the right to do business in the corporate form. So it was viewed as a form of the franchise tax.[4] Since the corporate form of doing business had been developed in the late nineteenth century, it was unknown to the framers of the U.S. Constitution. Because a corporation is an entity created under law, jurisdictions possess the right to tax its creation and operation. Using this rationale, many states still impose franchise taxes on corporations.

The ratification of the Sixteenth Amendment to the U.S. Constitution in 1913 sanc-tioned both the Federal individual and corporate income taxes and, as a consequence, neutralized the continuing effect of the *Pollock* decision.

1-2b Revenue Acts

After the Sixteenth Amendment was ratified by the states, Congress enacted the Revenue Act of 1913. Under this Act, the first Form 1040 was due on March 1, 1914. The law allowed various deductions and personal exemptions of $3,000 for a single individual and $4,000 for married taxpayers. These large exemptions excluded all but the more wealthy taxpayers from the new income tax.[5] Rates ranged from a low of 1 percent to a high of 6 percent. The 6 percent rate applied only to taxable income in excess of $500,000![6]

Various revenue acts were passed between 1913 and 1939. In 1939, all of these rev-enue laws were codified (arranged in a systematic manner) into the Internal Revenue Code of 1939. In 1954, a similar codification took place. The Internal Revenue Code of 1986, which largely carries over the provisions of the 1954 Code, is our current law. Tax law changes occur almost every year (how this happens is discussed in Chapter 2).

---

[2]3 AFTR 2602, 15 S.Ct. 912 (USSC, 1895). See Chapter 2 for an explanation of the citations of judicial decisions.

[3]*Flint v. Stone Tracy Co.*, 3 AFTR 2834, 31 S.Ct. 342 (USSC, 1911).

[4]See the discussion of state franchise taxes later in text Section 1-4g.

[5]A $3,000 exemption in 1913 would be about $79,000 today, while a $4,000 exemption would be about $105,000.

[6]This should be contrasted with the highest 2020 tax rate of 37%, which applies once taxable income exceeds $518,400 for single taxpayers and $622,050 for married taxpayers filing a joint return.

1-2c **Trends**

The income tax is a major source of revenue for the Federal government. Exhibit 1.1 shows the tax revenue sources[7] and the importance of the income tax. Income tax collections from individuals and corporations amount to 59 percent of the total receipts. One revenue source missing from the Exhibit 1.1 pie chart is borrowing to cover the deficit, which in recent years has represented between 10 to 40 percent of total government revenues.

The need for revenues to finance the war effort during World War II converted the income tax from one that applied mostly to high-income individuals to a *mass tax*. In 1939, less than 6 percent of the U.S. population was subject to the Federal income tax. By 1945, more than 74 percent of the population was subject to the Federal income tax.[8]

Certain tax law changes are important to understand. In 1943, Congress passed the Current Tax Payment Act, which provided for a pay-as-you-go tax system. A pay-as-you-go income tax system requires employers to withhold a specified portion of an employee's wages and remit them to the government to cover the worker's income taxes. Persons with income from other than wages may have to make quarterly payments to the IRS for estimated taxes due for the year.

The increasing complexity of the Federal income tax laws causes concern among many, including lawmakers, taxpayers, and tax practitioners. Congress has added to this complexity by frequently changing the tax laws (e.g., by adding or deleting deductions or tax credits). This complexity forces many taxpayers to seek assistance in preparing their income tax returns. According to estimates, more than one-half of individual taxpayers who file a return pay a preparer and one-third purchase tax software.[9]

New ways of doing business and living often require changes to the tax law. For example, increased longevity requires a need for more revenues from Social Security taxes (and/or an increase in retirement age). Increased global business activity means modifying a country's tax system to be more in line with other countries to make sure businesses are not impeded when entering the global marketplace. Ideally, lawmakers should review tax systems periodically to ensure that they continue to be efficient in light of changes in how businesses and individuals function.

1-3 **TAX SYSTEM DESIGN**

LO.3

Describe and apply principles and terminology relevant to the design of a tax system.

1-3a **Legal Foundation**

Article I, Section 8 of the U.S. Constitution states in part: "The Congress shall have power to lay and collect taxes." The Constitution also provided some limits on this taxing power, which led to the enactment of the Sixteenth Amendment to allow for an income

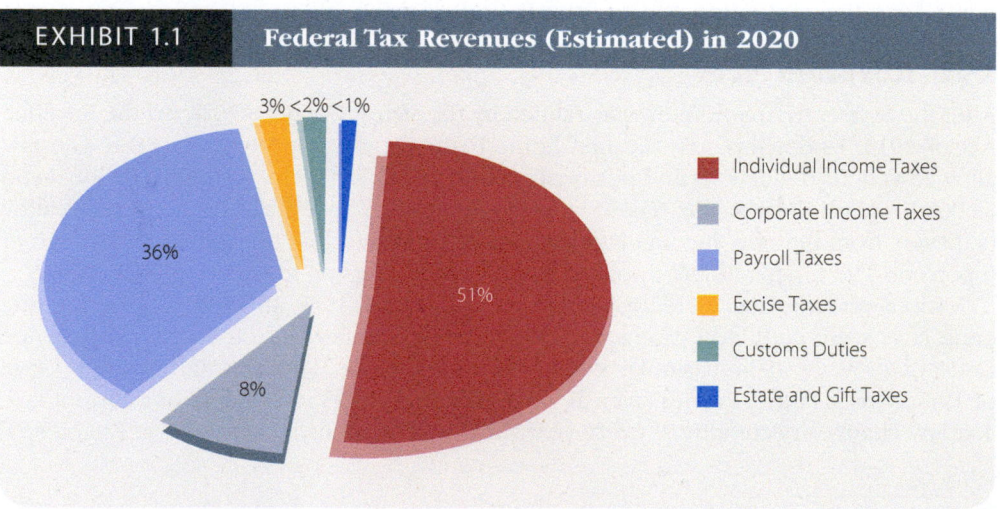

EXHIBIT 1.1	Federal Tax Revenues (Estimated) in 2020

3% <2% <1%
36%
51%
8%

- Individual Income Taxes
- Corporate Income Taxes
- Payroll Taxes
- Excise Taxes
- Customs Duties
- Estate and Gift Taxes

[7]Revenue data can be found at **cbo.gov** and **whitehouse.gov/omb**. The instruction booklet for Form 1040 includes a revenue pie chart that includes borrowing to cover the deficit, as well as a pie chart that shows government spending in broad categories.

[8]Richard Goode, *The Individual Income Tax* (Washington, D.C.: The Brookings Institution, 1964), pp. 2–4.

[9]The Tax Foundation estimates that individual taxpayers spend over $20 billion and devote about 1.35 billion hours in preparing their tax returns.

tax (discussed in text Section 1-2a). This history lesson is important for a legislature or an electorate that wants to change a tax system. The jurisdiction's underlying governing documents (whether a country, state, or city) must be reviewed to determine whether they impose any restrictions relevant to taxation.

For example, the California Constitution (Article 13A) states that the maximum tax rate for real property taxation is 1 percent. The Florida Constitution (Section 5) specifies limits on the imposition of income taxes on natural persons. Also, state law may impose limitations on the types or amounts of taxes that cities and counties can impose.

Thus, the governing documents of a jurisdiction must be considered as part of any effort to modify that jurisdiction's tax system to make sure the change is permissible. If a change is not permissible but desired, then the governing document must be amended, as was done with the addition of the Sixteenth Amendment to the U.S. Constitution.

1-3b The Basic Tax Formula

The basic formula for any tax is:

Tax Base

A tax base is the amount to which the tax rate is applied. In the case of the Federal income tax, the tax base is *taxable income*. As noted later in the chapter (Exhibit 1.3), taxable income is gross income reduced by certain deductions (both business and personal).

Tax Rates

Tax rates are applied to the tax base to determine a taxpayer's liability. Some taxes, like the sales tax and the gasoline excise tax, apply a fixed tax rate to all transactions.

Kansas applies a sales tax rate of 6.5% to all taxable items. In contrast, Illinois applies a sales tax rate of 6.25% for most taxable items but applies a rate of 1% when the tax base consists of food or prescription drugs.

Alternatively, for some taxes, tax rates may vary depending on the details of the tax base. Income taxes tend to use a *progressive* tax rate structure where a higher rate of tax applies as the tax base increases.

Bill and Cora, a married couple filing jointly, have taxable income of $15,000. Their Federal income tax rate for 2020 is 10%, which is the rate that applies to the first $19,750 of taxable income for a married couple filing jointly.

If, however, their taxable income is $85,000, their Federal income tax rates progress from 10% to 12% to 22% as their taxable income increases. In this case, their 2020 Federal income tax liability is $10,280. The Federal income tax uses a *progressive* rate structure that applies higher rates to taxable income (the tax base) as that income increases (see Appendix A to confirm these calculations, and note how progressivity is built into the rate structure of the Federal income tax).

The basic tax formula (shown above) is relevant for both computing taxes and planning, as well as for reforming a tax system. For example, if a legislator wants to lower tax rates but generate the same amount of tax revenues, the tax base must be increased. However, if she wants to increase tax revenues, the tax base can be increased *or* tax rates can be increased (or both can be increased). Changes to the tax base will depend on how it is constructed. For example, the income tax base is taxable income (income minus income exclusions minus deductions). To increase this tax base, income exclusions could be eliminated or deductions could be limited. The details of the income tax base are discussed in later chapters. Tax system changes also involve canons (or principles) of taxation, discussed next.

1-3c Tax Principles

In the late 1700s, Adam Smith identified the following *canons (or principles) of taxation*, which are still considered today when evaluating a particular tax structure:[10]

- *Equity.* Each taxpayer enjoys fair or equitable treatment by paying taxes in proportion to his or her income level. Ability to pay a tax is one of the measures of how equitably a tax is distributed among taxpayers.
- *Certainty.* A tax should be certain rather than arbitrary. Taxpayers need to be able to understand how tax rules work so that they understand the effect of the rules on various transactions and can comply.
- *Convenience of payment.* Taxes should be imposed in a manner that involves a convenient time for payment. An advantage of the existing withholding system (pay-as-you-go) is its convenience for taxpayers.
- *Economy in collection.* A *good* tax system involves only nominal collection costs by the government and minimal compliance costs on the part of the taxpayer.

The American Institute of Certified Public Accountants (AICPA) has issued suggestions to guide tax reform and policy activities. Titled *Guiding Principles of Good Tax Policy: A Framework for Evaluating Tax Proposals*, the monograph identifies 12 principles that are commonly used as indicators of desirable tax policy. The first four principles are adapted from Adam Smith's *The Wealth of Nations*. The complete list follows:[11]

1. *Equity and Fairness.* Similarly situated taxpayers should be taxed in a similar manner.
2. *Certainty.* Taxpayers should have certainty rather than ambiguity as to when and how a tax is paid as well as how to calculate it.
3. *Convenience of Payment.* A tax should be due at a time and manner that is most convenient for the taxpayer.
4. *Effective Tax Administration.* Tax compliance and administrative costs should be kept to a minimum.
5. *Information Security.* Taxpayer information must be protected from improper disclosure.
6. *Simplicity.* Tax rules should be simple so that taxpayers understand them and can follow them in a cost-efficient manner.
7. *Neutrality.* The effect of tax rules on taxpayer decision making should be kept to a minimum.
8. *Economic Growth and Efficiency.* The tax system should not harm economic growth or distort economic effects among different activities and investments.
9. *Transparency and Visibility.* Taxpayers should know that a tax exists and how and when it applies to them.
10. *Minimum Tax Gap.* A tax should be structured to minimize noncompliance.
11. *Accountability to Taxpayers.* Taxpayers should have access to information on taxes as well as proposed law changes and their rationale.
12. *Appropriate Government Revenues.* Tax rules should enable the government to predict the amount and timing of revenue production.

Exhibit 1.2 provides an application of these principles to a proposed tax law change.

LO.4

Identify the different taxes imposed in the United States at the Federal, state, and local levels.

1-4 MAJOR TYPES OF TAXES

Why does a text devoted primarily to the Federal income tax discuss state and local taxes? A simple illustration demonstrates the importance of non-Federal taxes.

---

[10]*The Wealth of Nations* (New York: Dutton, 1910), Book V, Chapter II, Part II.

[11]AICPA, *Guiding Principles of Good Tax Policy: A Framework for Evaluating Tax Proposals*, 2017. Similarly, see GAO, *Understanding the Tax Reform Debate: Background, Criteria, & Questions*, 2005. As "long-standing criteria," the GAO lists "equity; economic efficiency; and a combination of simplicity, transparency, and administrability."

Rick is employed by Flamingo Corporation in San Antonio, Texas, at a salary of $74,000. Rick's employer offers him a chance to transfer to its New York City office at a salary of $94,000.

Although Rick must consider many nontax factors before he decides on a job change, he should also evaluate the tax climate. How do state and local taxes compare? For example, neither Texas nor San Antonio imposes an income tax, but New York State and New York City do. A quick computation indicates that the additional income taxes (Federal, state, and local) involve approximately $12,000.

Consequently, what appears to be a $20,000 pay increase is actually only about $8,000 when the additional $12,000 of income taxes are taken into account. Other taxes and costs (e.g., sales taxes, property taxes, food, utilities, transportation) will also have to be factored into a decision.

EXAMPLE

3

EXHIBIT 1.2	Application of the *Guiding Principles of Good Tax Policy*

The *Guiding Principles of Good Tax Policy* can be applied to evaluate an existing tax rule or a proposed change. Here is an example of how the principles apply to a state's proposal to exempt college textbooks from sales tax.

Principle	Application	Result
Equity and fairness	Although all college students would pay no sales tax on their textbooks, the effect varies among students based on their ability to pay. This proposal provides tax savings not only to lower-income students but also to higher-income students who may not need the tax break to cover school costs. Also, higher-income students might buy full-price new books rather than lower-cost used books, resulting in larger tax savings.	Not fully met
Certainty	College textbooks can be identified, such as by looking at what is listed on a course syllabus.	Met
Convenience of payment	A sales tax exemption generally means that the tax is not owed at the time of purchase. If, instead, the exemption is structured for the student to pay the sales tax and apply for a refund later, convenience of payment would not be met.	Met
Effective tax administration	Sellers will have additional record keeping and reporting requirements to separate tax-exempt textbook sales from taxable sales. Some type of system is needed to prove that the buyer is a student purchasing a book for a college class. The state tax agency will incur additional time and costs in writing rules, modifying tax forms, and auditing compliance with the new rule.	Not met
Information security	If obtaining the exemption requires that students show proof to retailers that they are a student, there should be no need to provide a Social Security number. If students are required to claim the exemption with the state tax agency after purchasing the textbooks, the agency might request a student's Social Security number, which could increase the risk of identity theft.	Likely met
Simplicity	"Textbook" needs to be defined. The intent of the exemption is to benefit students. The seller needs to verify that the book is for use by a student for a class. For example, both students and nonstudents might buy a copy of *Romeo and Juliet*. Only the student purchasing it for a college class is entitled to the sales tax exemption. Complexity exists in the procedures needed to ensure that the exemption is used properly.	Not met
Neutrality	Students purchase textbooks because they are needed for class. The exemption is unlikely to change a student's behavior.	Met
Economic growth and efficiency	The exemption will reduce costs of attending college by a small amount. As a result, the change is unlikely to result in a greater number of college graduates (which might benefit the economy). Savings from not paying sales tax might be spent on other consumables. The impact on the economy is likely minor.	Met
Transparency and visibility	Students and textbook sellers are likely to be aware of the exemption because colleges will promote it as a reduction in the cost of attending college.	Met
Minimum tax gap	Students may abuse the rule by using the exemption for books that are not for class use. Nonstudents may abuse this rule by claiming they are college students.	Not met
Accountability to taxpayers	Were students and universities, particularly those funded by the state, aware of the textbook sales tax exemption proposal? Students and universities could provide information to legislators on whether there is a need for a sales tax exemption or if other financial support would be more helpful. Bookstores would want an opportunity to provide information on the compliance costs and challenges of the exemption.	More information needed
Appropriate government revenue	Existing data on how many textbooks are purchased enable the government to estimate how much tax revenues will decrease due to the new exemption.	Met

Conclusion: Although the majority of the principles are met, the ones that are not met (effective tax administration, simplicity, and minimum tax gap) are significant. If lawmakers believe this tax exemption is necessary to help lower costs for college students, they should consider alternative means of achieving the goal that are less complex. For example, grants could be offered or increased for college students in need of financial assistance.

1-4a **Property Taxes**

Correctly referred to as   ad valorem taxes   because they are based on value, property taxes are a tax on wealth, or capital. As a result, they have much in common with estate taxes and gift taxes discussed later in the chapter. Although property taxes do not tax income, the income actually derived from the property (or the potential for any income) may be relevant if it affects the value of the property being taxed.

Property taxes fall into *two* categories: those imposed on real property (land and buildings) and those imposed on personal property (assets other than land and buildings). Both have added importance because they often generate a deduction for Federal income tax purposes (see Chapter 10).

Ad Valorem Taxes on Real Property

Property taxes on real property are used exclusively by states and their local subdivisions (such as cities, counties, and school districts). They represent a major source of revenue for *local* governments (and school districts).

How real property is defined can have an important bearing on which assets are subject to tax. This is especially true in jurisdictions that do not impose ad valorem taxes on personal property. Real property, or   realty , generally includes real estate and any fixtures. A *fixture* is something so permanently attached to the real estate that its removal will cause irreparable damage. A built-in bookcase is likely a fixture, whereas a movable bookcase is not. Electrical wiring and plumbing become realty when they are installed in a building.

Here are some of the characteristics of ad valorem taxes on real property:

- Property owned by the Federal government is exempt from tax. In general, the same is true for property owned by state and local governments and by charitable organizations.

- Some states provide for lower valuations on property used for agriculture or other special uses (e.g., wildlife sanctuaries).

- States may have a homestead exemption, which makes some portion of the value of a personal residence exempt from tax.

- Lower taxes may apply to a residence owned by a taxpayer aged 65 or older.

- When non-income-producing property (e.g., a personal residence) is converted to income-producing property (e.g., a rental house), the appraised value may be increased.

The Big Picture

EXAMPLE 4

Return to the facts of *The Big Picture* on p. 1-1. Why did the Walkers' property taxes decrease but those of the Carters increase?

A likely explanation is that one (or both) of the Walkers achieved senior citizen status, leading to a reduction of their property taxes. In the case of the Carters, the assessed value of their property might have increased due to property values increasing in their location. Or perhaps they made significant home improvements (e.g., kitchen/bathroom renovation or addition of a deck) that increased the value (tax base) of the home.

Ad Valorem Taxes on Personal Property

Personal property, or   personalty , can be defined as all property that is not realty. There is a difference between how property is *classified* (realty or personalty) and how it is *used*. Both realty and personalty can be either business use or personal use property. Examples include a residence (realty that is personal use), an office building (realty that is business use), surgical instruments (personalty that is business use), and home furniture (personalty that is personal use).[12]

---

[12]The distinction, important for ad valorem and for Federal income tax purposes, often becomes confusing when personalty is referred to as "personal" property to distinguish it from "real" property. This designation does not give a complete picture of what is involved. The description "personal" residence, however, is clearer, because a residence can be identified as being realty. What is meant in this case is realty that is personal use property.

Personal property can also be classified as tangible property or intangible property. For ad valorem tax purposes, intangible personalty includes stocks, bonds, and various other securities (e.g., bank shares).

Here are some general rules related to ad valorem taxes on personal property:

- Generally, for individuals, vehicles (e.g., cars and boats) are the only non-realty personal use assets subject to property tax. The value of a vehicle is typically established by a schedule based on its age and make/model (a high-priced car versus a low-priced car). Usually, any vehicle property tax is assessed and collected along with vehicle license or registration fees.
- Generally, businesses are assessed property taxes on equipment and other tangible property, although many states do not tax inventory.
- A few states levy an ad valorem tax on intangibles such as stocks and bonds.

1-4b Transaction Taxes

Transaction taxes, imposed at the manufacturer's, wholesaler's, or retailer's level, cover a wide range of transfers. Transaction taxes can be assessed by any taxing authority (Federal, state, or local government). As the description implies, these taxes cover transfers of property and normally are determined by multiplying the value by a percentage rate.

Federal Excise Taxes

In general, Federal excise taxes cover fewer items than in the past. Congress has focused (and substantially increased) the Federal excise taxes on items such as tobacco products, fuel and gasoline sales, and air travel. Other Federal excise taxes include:

- Manufacturers' excise taxes on trucks, trailers, tires, firearms, sporting equipment, and coal and the gas guzzler tax on automobiles.[13]
- Alcohol taxes.
- Miscellaneous taxes (e.g., the tax on wagering and the tax on investment income of certain private colleges and universities).

When reviewing the list of both Federal and state excise taxes, recognize that these taxes may be trying to influence social behavior. For example, the gas guzzler tax is intended as an incentive for an individual to buy (and for the automobile companies to build) fuel-efficient cars.

State and Local Excise Taxes

Many state and local excise taxes parallel the Federal version. For example, all states tax the sale of gasoline, liquor, and tobacco products. However, the rates vary significantly. For gasoline products, for example, compare the 58.7 cents per gallon imposed by the Commonwealth of Pennsylvania with the 19.0 cents per gallon levied by the state of Arizona. For tobacco sales, contrast the 17.0 cents per pack of 20 cigarettes in effect in Missouri with the $4.35 per pack in the state of New York.

Other excise taxes found at some state and local levels include those on admission to amusement facilities, on the sale of playing cards, and on prepared foods. Some counties impose a transaction tax on the transfer of property that requires the recording of documents (e.g., real estate sales).

Over the last few years, two types of excise taxes imposed at the local level have become increasingly popular: the hotel occupancy tax and the rental car "surcharge." The hotel occupancy tax is called a transient occupancy tax (TOT) in some areas. This tax can also apply to short-term rentals of one's home or a room in the home (such as via Airbnb). Because they tax the visitor who cannot vote, they are a political windfall and are often used to finance special projects that generate civic pride (e.g., convention centers and state-of-the-art sports arenas). These levies can be significant, as demonstrated by Houston's hotel tax of 17 percent [6 percent (state) + 7 percent (city) + 2 percent (county) + 2 percent (sports authority)].

---

[13]The gas guzzler tax is imposed on the manufacturers of automobiles (both domestic and foreign) with fuel economy under 22.5 miles per gallon (mpg). For example, a 2020 Bentley Mulsanne manages about 18 mpg in combined city/highway driving and costs over $300,000. The gas guzzler tax on this vehicle is $2,600. The highest gas guzzler tax is $7,700 imposed on vehicles achieving less than 12.5 mpg. § 4064.

General Sales Taxes

The distinction between an excise tax and a general **sales tax** is easy to make. One is restricted to a particular transaction (e.g., the 18.4 cents per gallon Federal excise tax on the sale of gasoline), whereas the other covers a multitude of transactions (e.g., a 5 percent tax on *all* retail sales). In actual practice, however, the distinction is not always that clear. Some states exempt certain items from the general sales taxes (e.g., groceries, medicines, and drugs). Also, sales tax rates can vary. Many states, for example, allow lower rates for the sale of agricultural equipment or prescription drugs or apply different rates (either higher or lower than the general rate) to the sale of automobiles.

A **use tax** is a complement to the sales tax and is assessed at the same rate as the sales tax. A use tax is owed on property purchased outside the state but used in the state. The purpose of a use tax is to prevent the avoidance of a sales tax. For example, if you purchase clothes online and are not charged sales tax but clothes are subject to sales tax in your state, you owe use tax on the purchase. State rules vary on how use tax is collected. Many states allow individuals to pay it along with their state income tax. Alaska, Delaware, Montana, New Hampshire, and Oregon do not impose sales or use taxes. There is no Federal general sales or use tax.

The Big Picture

EXAMPLE

5

Return to the facts of *The Big Picture* on p. 1-1. The payment Travis made when he registered the car is probably a use tax.

When the car was purchased in another state, likely no (or a lesser) sales tax was levied. The current payment makes up for the amount of sales tax he would have paid had the car been purchased in his home state.

ETHICS & EQUITY   **Making Good Use of Out-of-State Relatives**

Marcus, a resident of Austin, Texas, has found the ideal gift for his wife in celebration of their upcoming wedding anniversary—a $22,000 diamond bracelet. However, Marcus is appalled at the prospect of paying the state and local sales tax of $1,815 (combined rate of 8.25 percent). Therefore, he asks his aunt, a resident of Montana, to purchase the bracelet. The jewelry store lists the aunt as the buyer and ships the bracelet to her, with no sales tax owed on the transaction. Prior to the anniversary, Marcus receives the bracelet from his aunt. Is Marcus able to save $1,815 on the present for his wife? What can go wrong?

Local general sales taxes, over and above state sales taxes, are common. It is not unusual to find taxpayers living in the same state but paying different general sales taxes due to the location of their residence.

EXAMPLE

6

Pete and Sam both live in a state that has a general sales tax of 3%. Sam, however, resides in a city that imposes an additional general sales tax of 2%. Even though Pete and Sam live in the same state, one is subject to a rate of 3%, whereas the other pays a tax of 5%.

For various reasons, some jurisdictions will suspend the application of a general sales tax for a specified, brief time period. For example, a state may have a "sales tax holiday" in late summer for back-to-school clothing and supplies. Some states use sales tax holidays to encourage the purchase of energy-conserving appliances and hurricane preparedness items.

Severance Taxes

Severance taxes are transaction taxes that are based on the notion that the state has an interest in its natural resources (e.g., oil, gas, iron ore, or coal). Therefore, a tax is imposed when the natural resources are extracted. For some states, severance taxes can be a significant source of revenue.

1-4c Taxes on Transfers at Death

The right to transfer property or to receive property upon the death of the owner may be subject to estate and/or inheritance taxes. Consequently, such taxes fall into the category of excise taxes. An **estate tax** is levied on the estate of the decedent (it is a tax on the right to pass property at death). An **inheritance tax** is levied on the person receiving the property (the heir). The value of the property transferred provides the base for determining the amount of the tax.

The Federal government imposes only an estate tax. Some state governments, however, levy inheritance taxes, estate taxes, or both. Some states (e.g., Florida and Texas) levy neither tax.

At the time of her death, Cari lived in a state that imposes an inheritance tax but not an estate tax. Amy, one of Cari's heirs, lives in the same state. Cari's estate is subject to the Federal estate tax, and Amy is subject to the state inheritance tax.

EXAMPLE 7

The Federal Estate Tax

The Revenue Act of 1916 incorporated the estate tax into the tax law. The tax was originally intended to prevent large concentrations of wealth from being kept in a family for many generations. Whether this objective has been accomplished is debatable. Like the income tax, estate taxes can be reduced through various planning procedures.

The gross estate includes property the decedent owned at the time of death.[14] It also includes property interests, such as life insurance proceeds paid to the estate. All property included in the gross estate is valued as of the date of death or, if the alternate valuation date is elected, six months later.[15]

Deductions from the gross estate in arriving at the taxable estate include funeral and administration expenses; certain taxes; debts of the decedent; casualty losses[16] incurred during the administration of the estate; transfers to charitable organizations; and, in some cases, the marital deduction. The *marital deduction* is available for amounts actually passing to a surviving spouse (a widow or widower).

Once the taxable estate has been determined and certain taxable gifts made by the decedent during life have been added to it, the estate tax can be computed. From this amount, various credits are subtracted to arrive at the tax, if any, that is due.[17] The most significant credit is the *unified transfer tax credit*. The main reason for this credit is to eliminate or reduce the estate tax liability for certain estates. For 2020, the credit exempts a tax base of up to $11,580,000, meaning that the vast majority of estates pass tax-free to the heirs.

Jason made no taxable gifts before his death in 2020. If Jason's taxable estate amounts to $11,580,000 or less, no Federal estate tax is due because of the application of the unified transfer tax credit.

EXAMPLE 8

State Taxes on Transfers at Death

As noted earlier, some states levy an inheritance tax, an estate tax, or both. Typically, a state inheritance tax divides the heirs into classes based on their relationship to the decedent. The more closely related the heir, the lower the rates imposed and/or the greater the exemption allowed. Some states allow amounts passing to a surviving spouse to escape taxation.

---

[14]For further information on these matters, see Chapter 27.

[15]See the discussion of the alternate valuation date in Chapter 13.

[16]For a definition of *casualty losses*, see the Glossary in Appendix C.

[17]For tax purposes, it is crucial to appreciate the difference between a deduction and a credit. A *credit* is a dollar-for-dollar reduction of tax liability.

A *deduction*, however, benefits the taxpayer only to the extent of his or her tax bracket. A taxpayer in a 50% tax bracket, for example, would need $2 of deductions to prevent $1 of tax liability. In contrast, $1 of credit neutralizes $1 of tax liability.

1-4d Gift Taxes

Like taxes on transfers at death, a <mark>gift tax</mark> is an excise tax levied on property transfers made during the owner's life and not at death. If the recipient pays the donor for the property (but at an amount less than its fair market value), the difference is a gift.

Carl sells property worth $50,000 to his daughter for $1,000. Although property worth $50,000 has been transferred, only $49,000 represents a gift because this is the portion that was not paid for.

The Federal Gift Tax

First enacted in 1932, the Federal gift tax was intended to complement the estate tax. If lifetime transfers by gift were not taxed, it would be possible to avoid the estate tax and escape taxation entirely.

Only taxable gifts are subject to the gift tax. For this purpose, a taxable gift is measured by the fair market value of the property on the date of transfer less the *annual exclusion per donee* and, in some cases, less the *marital deduction*, which allows tax-free transfers between spouses. In 2020, each donor is allowed an annual exclusion of $15,000 for each donee (the same as in 2019).[18]

On December 31, 2019, Louise (a widow) gives $15,000 to each of her four married children, their spouses, and her eight grandchildren. On January 2, 2020, she repeats the procedure.

Due to the annual exclusion, Louise has not made a taxable gift, although she transferred $240,000 [$15,000 (annual exclusion) × 16 (donees)] in 2019 and another $240,000 in 2020, for a total of $480,000 ($240,000 + $240,000).

A married couple may make a special election that allows one-half of the gift made by the donor-spouse to a third party to be treated as being made by the non-donor-spouse. This *gift splitting* effectively allows the annual exclusion to double.

The Big Picture

Return to the facts of *The Big Picture* on p. 1-1. Although the value of the RV is not stated, it is likely to exceed the annual exclusion allowed of $60,000 [$15,000 (annual exclusion) × two donees (the Walkers) × two donors (the Carters)].

As a result, a taxable gift results, and a Form 709 (Gift Tax Return) must be filed. Whether any gift tax is due depends on what past taxable gifts the Carters have made and how much of their unified transfer tax credit (see the following discussion) is still available.

The gift tax and estate tax rate schedules are the same. The schedule is commonly referred to as the *unified transfer tax rate schedule*.

The Federal gift tax is *cumulative* in effect. What this means is that the tax base for current taxable gifts includes past taxable gifts. Although a credit is allowed for prior gift taxes, the result of adding past taxable gifts to current taxable gifts could force the donor into a higher tax bracket.[19] Like the Federal estate tax rates, the Federal gift tax rates are progressive (see Example 2 earlier in this chapter).

The unified transfer tax credit is available for all taxable gifts. As was the case with the Federal estate tax, the credit for 2020 is $4,577,800 (which covers taxable gifts up to $11,580,000) and for 2019 is $4,505,800 (which covers taxable gifts up to $11,400,000). There is, however, only one unified transfer tax credit, and it applies to both taxable

---

[18]The purpose of the annual exclusion is to avoid the need to report and pay a tax on *modest* gifts. Without the exclusion, the IRS could face a real problem of taxpayer noncompliance. The annual exclusion is indexed as the level of inflation warrants. The exclusion was $14,000 from 2013 to 2017 and $13,000 from 2009 through 2012.

[19]For further information on the Federal gift tax, see Chapter 27.

gifts and the Federal estate tax. Once the unified transfer tax credit has been used up for Federal gift tax purposes, any transfers at death will be subject to the Federal estate tax.

Making lifetime gifts of property carries several tax advantages over passing the property at death. If income-producing property is involved (e.g., marketable securities and rental real estate), a gift may shift subsequent income to donees in a lower income tax bracket. If the gift involves property that is expected to appreciate in value (e.g., life insurance policies, real estate, and artwork), future increases in value will be assigned to the donee and will not be included in the donor's estate. And due to the annual exclusion ($15,000 per donee in 2020 and 2019), some of the gift can escape tax (with gift splitting, married donors can double the annual exclusion).

Neither the actual receipt of a gift nor an inheritance will cause income tax consequences to the donee or heir.

1-4e Income Taxes

Income taxes are levied by the Federal government, most states, and some local governments. Income taxes generally are imposed on individuals, corporations, and certain fiduciaries (estates and trusts). Most jurisdictions attempt to ensure the collection of income taxes by requiring pay-as-you-go procedures, including withholding requirements for employees and estimated tax payments for all taxpayers.

Federal Income Taxes

Exhibit 1.3 illustrates the formula for the Federal income tax imposed on individuals. This formula provides a framework for part of the text. Beginning with Chapter 3, each component of the formula is illustrated and explained.

Unlike its individual counterpart, the Federal corporate income tax is not progressive, but instead uses a flat tax rate of 21 percent. Also, it does not include the computation of adjusted gross income (AGI) and does not provide for the standard deduction or the deduction for qualified business income. As a result, a corporation's taxable income is the

EXHIBIT 1.3	Formula for Federal Income Tax on Individuals	
Income (broadly defined)		$xx,xxx
Less: Exclusions (income that is not subject to tax)		(x,xxx)
Gross income (income that is subject to tax)		$xx,xxx
Less: Certain deductions (usually referred to as deductions *for* adjusted gross income)		(x,xxx)
Adjusted gross income		$xx,xxx
Less: The greater of:		
Certain personal and investment deductions (referred to as *itemized deductions*)		
or		
The standard deduction (including any additional standard deduction)		(x,xxx)
Less: Personal and dependency exemptions*		(x,xxx)
Deduction for qualified business income**		(x,xxx)
Taxable income		$xx,xxx
Tax on taxable income (see the Tax Tables and Tax Rate Schedules in Appendix A)		$ x,xxx
Less: Tax credits (including Federal income tax withheld and other prepayments of Federal income taxes)		(xxx)
Tax due (or refund)		$ xxx

*Exemption deductions are not allowed from 2018 through 2025.
**Only applies from 2018 through 2025.

difference between gross income and deductions. Chapter 17 discusses the rules relating to the determination of the Federal income tax on corporations.[20]

State Income Taxes

Almost all states impose an income tax on individuals.[21]

Here are some of the characteristics of state income taxes:

- With few exceptions, all states require some form of withholding procedures.

- Most states use as the tax base the income determination made for Federal income tax purposes. This is often referred to as the piggyback approach to state income taxation. Although the term *piggyback* does not lend itself to a precise definition, in this context, it means making use, for state income tax purposes, of what was done for Federal income tax purposes.

- Some states "decouple" from selected Federal tax changes passed by Congress. The purpose of the decoupling is to retain state revenue that would otherwise be lost. For example, some states do not allow "bonus depreciation" allowed for Federal tax purposes.

- Because of the tie-ins to the Federal return, a state may be notified of any changes made by the IRS upon audit of a Federal return (or vice versa).

- Most states allow a deduction for personal and dependency exemptions. Some states substitute a tax credit for a deduction.

- Many state income tax returns provide checkoff boxes for donations to various causes. Many are dedicated to medical research and wildlife programs, but special projects are not uncommon. For example, Wisconsin uses one for maintenance and operating costs of Lambeau Field (home of the Green Bay Packers). These checkoff boxes have been criticized as adding complexity to the returns and misleading taxpayers.[22]

- The objective of most states is to tax the income of residents and those who conduct business in the state (e.g., employees sent to the state to help a client or a professional athlete playing a game in the state).

- Most states allow their residents some form of tax credit for income taxes paid to other states.

The Big Picture

EXAMPLE 12

Return to the facts of *The Big Picture* on p. 1-1. Travis will need to review the state income tax laws in each state he has clients to determine if he is subject to that state's tax on his consulting income earned in that state. If the income is subject to tax in another state as well as his home state, the home state might provide a credit to negate the double taxation.

- The due date for filing generally is the same as for the Federal income tax (for individuals, the fifteenth day of the fourth month following the close of the tax year; usually April 15 for calendar year taxpayers).

- Some states have occasionally instituted amnesty programs that allow taxpayers to pay back taxes (and interest) on unreported income with no (or reduced) penalty. In many cases, the tax amnesty has generated enough revenue to warrant the authorization of follow-up programs covering future years.[23] Amnesties usually include other taxes as well (e.g., sales, franchise, and severance).

---

[20]For an in-depth treatment of the Federal income tax as it affects corporations, partnerships, estates, and trusts, and owners or beneficiaries of these entities as well as sole proprietors, see Chapters 17 through 22 and 28. See Chapters 6, 9, and 15 for additional discussion of the deduction for qualified business income.

[21]Alaska, Florida, Nevada, South Dakota, Texas, Washington, and Wyoming do not have an individual income tax. New Hampshire and Tennessee impose an individual income tax only on interest and dividends.

[22]Many taxpayers do not realize they are paying for the checkoff donation (usually with some of their income tax refund). Unlike the presidential election campaign fund available for Federal income tax purposes ($3 in this case), the contribution is *not made* by the government.

[23]Although the suggestion has been made, no comparable amnesty program has been offered for the Federal income tax. The IRS has, however, offered exemption from certain penalties for taxpayers who disclose offshore bank accounts and participation in certain tax shelters.

- Because many consumers do not pay state and local sales taxes on out-of-state purchases, state income tax returns in some states include a separate line for reporting any use tax that is due. As a result, the income tax return serves as a means of collecting use taxes.

Nearly all states have an income tax applicable to corporations. Other states have a franchise tax (discussed later in the chapter) that can be based in part on corporate income.

Local Income Taxes

Cities imposing an income tax include Baltimore, Cincinnati, Cleveland, Detroit, Kansas City (Missouri), New York, Philadelphia, and St. Louis. The application of a city income tax is not limited to local residents.

1-4f Employment Taxes

Employment taxes are a type of income tax imposed on employers and employees. We concentrate on the two major employment taxes: FICA (Federal Insurance Contributions Act—commonly referred to as the Social Security tax) and FUTA (Federal Unemployment Tax Act). Both taxes can be justified by social and public welfare considerations: FICA offers some measure of retirement security, and FUTA provides a modest source of income in the event of loss of employment.

These employment taxes come into play for employees (*not self-employed* individuals) if the particular work is covered under FICA or FUTA or both.[24]

FICA Taxes

The FICA tax rates and wage base have increased steadily over the years. It is difficult to imagine that the initial rate in 1937 was only 1 percent of the first $3,000 of covered wages. Thus, the maximum tax due was only $30.

The FICA tax has two components: Social Security tax (old age, survivors, and disability insurance) *and* Medicare tax (hospital insurance). The Social Security tax rate is 6.2 percent and generally does not change. The base amount usually increases each year. For 2020, the base amount is $137,700 ($132,900 for 2019).

The Medicare portion of FICA is applied at a rate of 1.45 percent and, unlike Social Security, is not subject to any dollar limitation. The Affordable Care Act (ObamaCare) imposes an additional 0.9 percent tax on earned income (including self-employment income) *above* $200,000 (single filers) or $250,000 (married filing jointly). Unlike the Social Security tax of 6.2 percent and the regular Medicare portion of 1.45 percent, an employer does not have to match the employees' 0.9 percent tax.

A spouse employed by another spouse is subject to FICA. However, children under the age of 18 who are employed in a parent's unincorporated trade or business are exempted.

> **The Big Picture**
>
> **EXAMPLE 13**
>
> Return to the facts of *The Big Picture* on p. 1-1. Presuming that April and Martin perform meaningful services for Travis (which the facts seem to imply), they are legitimate employees. April is not subject to Social Security tax because she is under the age of 18. However, Martin is 18 and needs to be covered. Furthermore, recall that Amy Carter is now working at a medical clinic and will likewise be subject to Social Security tax. Travis, as an independent contractor, is subject to self-employment tax.

---

[24]Chapter 12 includes additional coverage of employment taxes for employees, employers, and self-employed persons. See also Circular E, *Employer's Tax Guide*, issued by the IRS as Publication 15.

Taxpayers who are not employees (e.g., sole proprietors and independent contractors) may also be subject to Social Security taxes. Known as the self-employment tax, the rates are 12.4 percent for Social Security and 2.9 percent for Medicare, or twice that applicable to an employee. The additional 0.9 percent Medicare tax also covers situations involving high net income from self-employment. The Social Security tax is imposed on net self-employment income up to the annual base amount ($137,700 for 2020; $132,900 for 2019). The Medicare portion of the self-employment tax is not subject to any dollar limitation.

To help cover the government's cost of medical care, Congress enacted a special tax on investment income.[25] For this purpose, "investment income" is often referred to as "unearned income" because it is not generated by the performance of services. A tax of 3.8 percent is imposed on net investment income when a taxpayer's modified adjusted gross income (MAGI) exceeds certain threshold amounts.[26] The threshold amounts are $250,000 for married taxpayers and $200,000 for single taxpayers. Investment income generally includes passive-type income (e.g., rents, taxable interest, dividends, and capital gains). For further discussion, see Chapter 12 and the online appendix on the Affordable Care Act.

FUTA Taxes

The purpose of the **FUTA tax** is to provide funds the states can use to administer unemployment benefits. This leads to the somewhat unusual situation of one tax being handled by both Federal and state governments. This joint administration means that the employer must observe two sets of rules. State and Federal returns must be filed and payments made to both governmental units.

In 2020, FUTA is 6 percent on the first $7,000 of covered wages paid during the year to each employee. The Federal government allows a credit for FUTA paid (or allowed under a merit rating system) to the state. The credit cannot exceed 5.4 percent of the covered wages. Thus, the amount required to be paid to the Federal government could be as low as 0.6 percent (6.0% − 5.4%).

States reduce the unemployment tax on employers who experience stable employment, since the state pays less unemployment benefits. Thus, an employer with little or no employee turnover might find that the state rate drops to as low as 0.1 percent or, in some states, even to zero.

FUTA, unlike FICA, is paid entirely by the employer. A few states, however, levy a special tax on employees to provide either disability benefits or supplemental unemployment compensation or both.

1-4g Other U.S. Taxes

To complete the overview of the U.S. tax system, some missing links need to be covered that do not fit into the classifications discussed elsewhere in this chapter.

Federal Customs Duties

The tariff on imported goods,[27] also known as customs duties, together with excise taxes, provided most of the revenues needed by the Federal government during the nineteenth century. In view of present times, it is remarkable that tariffs and excise taxes alone paid off the national debt in 1835 and enabled the U.S. Treasury to pay a surplus of $28 million to the states.

In recent years, tariffs have served both as an instrument for carrying out protectionist policies and to generate revenue. By imposing customs duties on the importation of foreign goods that can be sold at lower prices, protectionists contend that the tariff thereby neutralizes the competitive edge held by the producer of the foreign goods. However, history shows that tariffs often lead to retaliatory action on the part of the nation or nations affected.

---

[25]Enacted as part of the Health Care and Education Reconciliation Act of 2010.

[26]MAGI is adjusted gross income (see Exhibit 1.3 and page 2 of Form 1040) plus any foreign income or excluded foreign housing costs. An online appendix covers the net investment income tax (NIIT) and other Affordable Care Act tax provisions.

[27]Less-developed countries that rely principally on one or more major commodities (e.g., oil or coffee) are prone to favor *export* duties.

Miscellaneous State and Local Taxes

Most states impose a <mark>franchise tax</mark> on corporations for the right to do business in the state.[28] The tax base used varies from state to state but most often is based on the capitalization of the corporation (either with or without certain long-term indebtedness).

Similar to the franchise tax are <mark>occupational fees</mark> that apply to various trades or businesses (e.g., a liquor store license; a taxicab permit; or a fee to practice a profession such as law, medicine, or accounting). Most of these are not significant revenue producers, and the fees are used to fund the costs of regulating the business or profession in the interest of the public good.

The Big Picture

EXAMPLE

14

Return to the facts of *The Big Picture* on p. 1-1. Although the facts do not mention the matter, both Travis and Amy might owe occupation or license fees—Travis for engineering and Amy for nursing.

Concept Summary 1.2 provides an overview of the major taxes existing in the United States and specifies which political jurisdiction imposes them.

Concept Summary 1.2

Overview of Taxes in the United States

Type of Tax	Imposed by Jurisdiction		
	Federal	**State**	**Local**
Property taxes:			
Ad valorem on realty	No	Yes	Yes
Ad valorem on personalty	No	Yes	Yes
Transaction taxes:			
Excise	Yes	Yes	Few*
General sales	No	Most	Some
Severance	Yes**	Most	No
Estate	Yes	Some	No
Inheritance	No	Some	No
Gift	Yes	Few	No
Income taxes:			
Corporations	Yes	Most	Few
Individuals	Yes	Most	Few
Employment taxes:			
FICA	Yes	No	No
FUTA	Yes	Yes	No
Customs duties	Yes	No	No
Franchise taxes	No	Yes	No
Occupational taxes or fees***	Yes	Yes	Yes

  * An example of a local excise tax is a tax on hotel occupancy, typically referred to as a transient occupancy tax (TOT).

  ** For Federal public lands and continental-shelf areas.

  *** An example is a fee to operate a beauty salon or barbershop.

---

[28]Only five states do not impose a franchise tax (Michigan, Nevada, South Dakota, Washington, and Wyoming).

1-4h Proposed U.S. Taxes

The last two major reforms to the U.S. tax system were in 2017 [the Tax Cuts and Jobs Act (TCJA) of 2017] and in 1986 (the Tax Reform Act of 1986). Tax reform discussions over the past few decades also have included use of a consumption tax to replace all or a portion of the income tax or as a new additional tax. Consumption taxes considered include the flat tax, a national sales tax, and a value added tax. Federal tax reform discussions have also included adding a carbon tax or a financial transactions tax. A brief description of these types of taxes follows.

Flat Tax

The flat tax, as introduced in 1981 by economists Robert Hall and Alvin Rabushka of the Hoover Institution, is a form of a consumption tax. Their proposal achieves some of the administrative advantages of a value added tax (VAT) relative to a sales tax while also partially addressing concerns that consumption taxes impose a relatively heavier tax burden on lower-income taxpayers. It assesses a "flat" 19 percent tax on all businesses (corporate or otherwise)—identical to the VAT, except that wages, pension contributions, materials costs, and capital investments are deducted from the tax base. Individuals (or households) are assessed a 19 percent flat-rate tax on wages and pension benefits above an exemption of $25,500 for a family of four. No other income is taxable, and no other deductions are allowed. Over the past 35 years, the Hall-Rabushka proposal has served as the blueprint for a number of proposals to reform the Federal tax system.[29]

National Sales Tax

A national sales tax would operate similarly to most state sales taxes although the tax base would be larger. The rate would also be higher to generate the revenues needed to replace the Federal income tax.

A frequent proposal for a national sales tax, called the "Fair Tax," would tax all purchases, including food and medicine, real property, and many types of services, at approximately 23 percent. Exempt items include business expenses, used goods, and the costs of education. The Fair Tax would replace the income tax (both individual and corporate), payroll taxes (including the self-employment tax), and the gift and estate taxes. To help address the regressivity of the tax, many individuals would receive a monthly rebate to offset a portion of sales tax paid.

Value Added Tax

A value added tax (VAT) is imposed on the value added by each party in a production cycle. For example, a furniture maker is charged VAT on wood purchased to make the furniture. Customers are charged VAT when they buy the furniture. A system of credits results in the VAT ultimately only being paid by the final consumer. This form of VAT—a credit invoice VAT—is similar to a sales tax. It is viewed as more efficient than a sales tax because assessment throughout the production process better ensures collection of the tax. The credit invoice VAT is widely used throughout the world.

A VAT has been considered in the United States various times since the 1960s. In 1984, the Treasury Department released a three-volume tax reform report, with one volume devoted to the VAT.[30] In 2016, Congressman James Renacci (R-OH) introduced a proposal to replace the corporate income tax with a credit invoice VAT as part of his Simplifying America's Tax System (SATS) proposal.[31]

[29]Usually, the tax bill carries the number H.R. 1040. See R. E. Hall and A. Rabushka, *The Flat Tax*, Hoover Institution (2007).

[30]U.S. Treasury Department, *Tax Reform for Fairness, Simplicity, and Economic Growth: The Treasury Department Report to the President*, Volume 3, 1984.

[31]Tax Foundation, *Details and Analysis of Rep. Jim Renacci's Tax Reform Proposal*, July 14, 2016.

GLOBAL TAX ISSUES   VAT in USA?

The United States is the only country in the OECD (Organization of Economic Cooperation and Development) that does not have a value added tax (VAT). Over 140 countries around the world use a VAT, with rates ranging from 5 percent to 27 percent.

Is the United States out of sync with most other countries by not having a VAT? One advantage of a VAT is that it provides a significant revenue source, allowing for lower individual and corporate income tax rates. Also, unlike the income tax, a VAT is "border-adjustable," meaning that a country can impose it on imports but not exports. These are some considerations for U.S. lawmakers in evaluating the economic effects of the U.S. tax system and tax reform options in a global perspective.

One challenge of implementing a VAT in the United States is that it is a regressive tax (it has a greater impact on lower-income taxpayers relative to higher-income taxpayers). As a result, adjustments need to be implemented to protect lower-income taxpayers (e.g., expanding the earned income tax credit and/or child tax credit; both occur in the SATS proposal). Another challenge is that the Treasury Department (and IRS) will have to learn how to implement and enforce the VAT.

Carbon Tax

A **carbon tax** aims to help reduce carbon emissions (i.e., greenhouse gases). The tax could be applied to fossil fuels based on their level of greenhouse gas emissions. Because a significant fossil fuel is gasoline, some people suggest a higher gasoline excise tax as a simple form of a carbon tax.

Financial Transaction Tax

A **financial transaction tax** can take many forms. For example, it could be imposed on the value of financial instruments purchased (e.g., stocks and bonds). It could be restricted in some way (e.g., only applying to high-frequency trading). It could be imposed on the value of bank assets. Because the tax base is quite large, the tax rate would likely be low, perhaps even less than 1 percent. The primary concern with this type of tax is the possible adverse effects on financial markets.

1-5 TAX ADMINISTRATION

LO.5

Explain the administration of the tax law, including the audit process utilized by the IRS.

1-5a Internal Revenue Service

The responsibility for administering the Federal tax laws rests with the Treasury Department. The IRS is part of the Department of the Treasury and is responsible for enforcing the tax laws. The Commissioner of Internal Revenue is appointed by the President with the advice and consent of the Senate. The Commissioner is responsible for establishing policy and supervising the activities of the IRS. Here is the mission statement of the IRS:

> *Provide America's taxpayers top quality service by helping them understand and meet their tax responsibilities and enforce the law with integrity and fairness to all.*

1-5b The Audit Process

Selection of Returns for Audit

Only a small number of tax returns are audited each year. The overall audit rate for individuals is 0.6 percent. The audit rate for corporations is 0.9 percent. Keep in mind, however, that the probability for audit increases for higher-income taxpayers.[32]

---

[32]Internal Revenue Service, *Data Book 2018*, Table 9a. Examination Coverage: Recommended and Average Recommended Additional Tax After Examination, by Type and Size of Return, Fiscal Year 2018.

Tax returns are selected for audit in different ways. A common technique for individuals is called information matching. For example, the IRS compares information returns it receives (e.g., a Form 1099 interest income statement from a bank related to an individual) to an individual's tax return. If the information is not reported correctly, the IRS sends a notice to the taxpayer indicating the problem and the additional tax owed. Another approach is done through computer scoring. This approach uses mathematical formulas and statistical sampling techniques to select tax returns that are most likely to contain errors and to provide significant amounts of additional tax revenues when audited. The mathematical formula produces what is called a Discriminant Index Formula (DIF) score. It is the DIF score given to a particular return that may lead to its selection for audit. Periodically, the IRS updates the DIF components by auditing a random cross section of returns to determine the most likely areas of taxpayer noncompliance.

Although the IRS does not openly disclose the details of all of its audit selection techniques, here are some general comments about audit selection:

- Certain groups of taxpayers are subject to audit much more frequently than others. These groups include individuals with large amounts of gross income, self-employed individuals with substantial deductions, and taxpayers with prior tax deficiencies. The same is true for businesses that receive a large proportion of their receipts in cash (e.g., cafés and small service businesses) and thus have a high potential for tax avoidance.

EXAMPLE 15

Jack owns and operates a liquor store on a cash-and-carry basis. Because all of Jack's sales are for cash, he might be a prime candidate for an audit by the IRS. Cash transactions are easier to conceal than those made on credit.

- If information returns (e.g., Form 1099 or Form W–2) are not in substantial agreement with reported income, an audit can be anticipated.
- If an individual's itemized deductions are in excess of averages established for various income levels, the probability of an audit is increased.
- Filing of a refund claim by the taxpayer may prompt an audit of the return.
- Information obtained from other sources (e.g., informants and news items) may lead to an audit.

The IRS pays rewards to persons who provide information leading to the discovery and punishment of those who violate the tax laws. The rewards may not exceed 30 percent of the taxes, fines, and penalties recovered.

Information Leading to an IRS Audit

EXAMPLE 16

After 15 years of service, Rita is discharged by her employer, Dr. Benjamin Smith. Shortly thereafter, the IRS receives an anonymous letter stating that Dr. Smith keeps two separate sets of books and that the one used for tax reporting substantially understates his cash receipts.

EXAMPLE 17

During a divorce proceeding, it is revealed that Leo, a public official, kept large amounts of cash in a shoe box at home. This information is widely disseminated by the news media and comes to the attention of the IRS. Needless to say, the IRS is interested in knowing whether these funds originated from a taxable source and, if so, whether they were reported on Leo's income tax returns.

Types of Audits

Once a return is selected for audit, the taxpayer is notified by mail. If the issue involved is minor, the matter often can be resolved simply by correspondence (a **correspondence audit**) between the IRS and the taxpayer. Approximately 81 percent of individual audits are handled via correspondence, whereas only about 3 percent of corporate audits are handled this way.[33]

Other examinations are generally classified as either office audits or field audits. An **office audit** usually is restricted in scope and is conducted in IRS offices. In contrast, a **field audit** involves an examination of numerous items reported on the return and is conducted at the taxpayer's location (or that of the taxpayer's representative). Exhibit 1.4 illustrates the types of audits pursued by the IRS for all tax returns filed during 2017 (individual, corporate, partnership, and exempt organizations).

The Big Picture

EXAMPLE 18

Return to the facts of *The Big Picture* on p. 1-1. The audit of the Walkers by the IRS obviously was a correspondence type. The reason for the audit was probably triggered by a minor oversight by the Walkers, such as the omission of some interest or dividend income. The audit of the Carters, however, was more serious—probably a field or office type. Because the Federal audit followed a state audit that was productive (i.e., led to the assessment of a deficiency), there may have been an exchange of information between the two taxing authorities—see p. 1-16 in this chapter.

At the end of an audit, the examining agent issues a Revenue Agent's Report (RAR) that summarizes the findings. The RAR will result in a refund (the tax was overpaid), a deficiency (the tax was underpaid), or a no change (the tax was correct) finding. If during the course of an audit a special agent accompanies (or takes over from) the regular auditor, this means the IRS suspects fraud. In this case, the taxpayer should retain competent legal counsel.

Settlement Procedures

If an audit results in an assessment of additional tax and no settlement is reached with the IRS agent, the taxpayer may request an appeal within the IRS. The Appeals Division of the IRS is authorized to settle all disputes based on the *hazards of litigation* (the probability of favorable resolution of the disputed issue or issues if litigated). In some

EXHIBIT 1.4   IRS Audit Types and Rates (all returns)

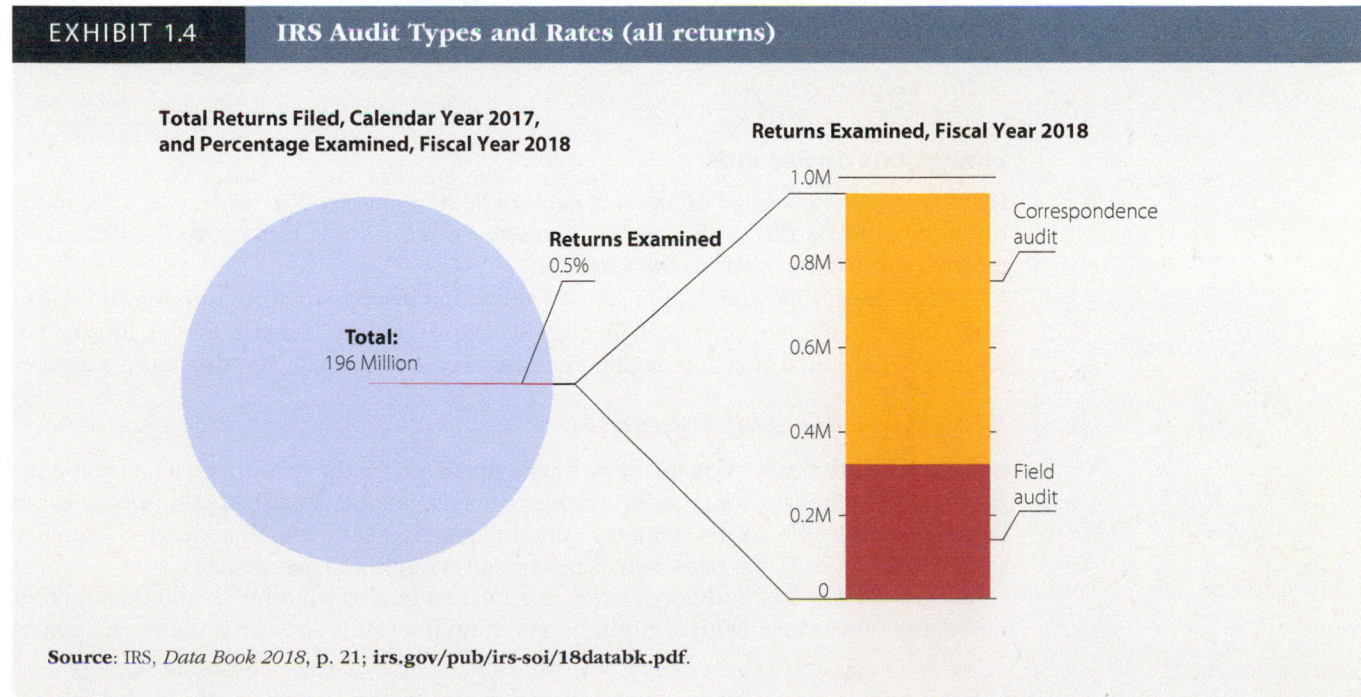

Source: IRS, *Data Book 2018*, p. 21; **irs.gov/pub/irs-soi/18databk.pdf**.

[33]Internal Revenue Service, *Data Book, 2018*. Table 9a.

cases, a taxpayer may be able to obtain an overall reduction of the assessment or a favorable settlement of one or more disputed issues.

If a satisfactory settlement is not reached within the IRS, the taxpayer can litigate the case in the Tax Court, a Federal District Court, or the Court of Federal Claims. However, litigation is normally discouraged because of the legal costs involved and the uncertainty of the final outcome. Tax litigation considerations are discussed more fully in Chapter 2.

1-5c Statute of Limitations

A statute of limitations is a provision that requires any lawsuit to be brought within a reasonable period of time. Found at the state and Federal levels, such statutes cover a multitude of suits, both civil and criminal.

For the Federal income tax, two categories are involved, which cover time limits on the assessment of additional tax deficiencies by the IRS and time limits related to refund claims by taxpayers.

Assessment by the IRS

In general, the IRS may assess an additional tax liability against a taxpayer within *three years* of the filing of the income tax return. If the return is filed early, the three-year period begins to run from the due date of the return (usually April 15 for a calendar year individual taxpayer). If the taxpayer files the return late (i.e., beyond the due date), the three-year period begins to run on the date filed.

If a taxpayer omits an amount of gross income in excess of 25 percent of the gross income reported on the return, the statute of limitations is increased to six years.

EXAMPLE 19

For 2020, Mark, a calendar year taxpayer, reported gross income of $400,000 on a timely filed income tax return. If Mark omitted more than $100,000 (25% × $400,000), the six-year statute of limitations would apply to the 2020 tax year.

The six-year provision on assessments by the IRS applies only to the omission of income; it does not cover other factors that might lead to an understatement of tax liability, such as overstatement of deductions and credits.

There is *no* statute of limitations on assessments of tax if *no return* is filed or if a *fraudulent* return is filed.

Limitations on Refunds

If a taxpayer believes that an overpayment of Federal income tax was made, a claim for refund should be filed with the IRS. A *claim for refund* is a request to the IRS that it return a tax overpayment to the taxpayer.[34]

A claim for refund generally must be filed within *three years* from the date the return was filed *or* within *two years* from the date the tax was paid, whichever is later. Income tax returns that are filed early are deemed to have been filed on the date the return was due.

1-5d Interest and Penalties

Interest rates are determined quarterly by the IRS based on the existing Federal short-term rate. Currently, the rates for tax refunds (overpayments) for individual taxpayers are the same as those applicable to assessments (underpayments). For the first quarter (January 1–March 31) of 2020, the rates were 5 percent for refunds and assessments.[35]

For assessments of additional taxes, the interest begins running on the unextended due date of the return. With refunds, however, no interest is allowed if the overpayment

---

[34]Generally, an individual filing a claim for refund should use Form 1040X.   [35]Rev.Rul. 2019–28, 2019–52 I.R.B. 1401; the rates for the remainder of 2020 were not available when the text went to press.

is refunded to the taxpayer within 45 days of the date the return is filed. For this purpose, returns filed early are deemed to have been filed on the due date.

In addition to interest, the tax law provides various penalties for lack of compliance by taxpayers. Some of these penalties are summarized as follows:

- For *failure to file* a tax return by the due date (including extension—see Chapter 3), a penalty of 5 percent per month up to a maximum of 25 percent is imposed on the amount of tax shown as due on the return. Any fraction of a month counts as a full month.

- A penalty for *failure to pay* the tax due as shown on the return is imposed in the amount of 0.5 percent per month up to a maximum of 25 percent. Again, any fraction of a month counts as a full month. During any month in which both the failure to file penalty and the failure to pay penalty apply, the failure to file penalty is reduced by the amount of the failure to pay penalty.

EXAMPLE 20

Adam files his tax return 18 days after the due date of the return. Along with the return, he remits a check for $1,000, which is the balance of the tax he owed. Disregarding the interest element, Adam's total penalties are as follows:

Failure to pay penalty (0.5% × $1,000)		$ 5
Plus:		
Failure to file penalty (5% × $1,000)	$50	
Less failure to pay penalty for the same period	(5)	
Failure to file penalty		45
Total penalties		$50

Note that the penalties for one full month are imposed even though Adam was delinquent by only 18 days. Unlike the method used to compute interest, any part of a month is treated as a whole month.

- A *negligence* penalty of 20 percent is imposed if any of the underpayment was for intentional disregard of rules and Regulations without intent to defraud. The penalty applies to just that portion attributable to the negligence.

EXAMPLE 21

Cindy underpaid her taxes in the amount of $20,000, of which $15,000 is attributable to negligence. Cindy's negligence penalty is $3,000 (20% × $15,000).

- Various penalties may be imposed in the case of *fraud*. Fraud involves specific intent on the part of the taxpayer to evade a tax. In the case of *civil* fraud, the penalty is 75 percent of the underpayment attributable to fraud. In the case of *criminal* fraud, the penalties can include large fines as well as prison sentences. The difference between civil and criminal fraud is one of degree. Criminal fraud involves the presence of willfulness on the part of the taxpayer. Also, the burden of proof, which is on the IRS in both situations, is more stringent for criminal fraud than for civil fraud. The negligence penalty is not imposed when the fraud penalty applies. For possible fraud situations, refer to Examples 16 and 17.

1-5e **Tax Practice**

If a practitioner is a member of a profession (e.g., public accounting or law), he or she must abide by certain ethical standards. Furthermore, the Internal Revenue Code imposes penalties on Federal tax return preparers who violate identified acts and procedures.

GLOBAL TAX ISSUES   Outsourcing of Tax Return Preparation

The use of foreign nationals to carry out certain job assignments for U.S. businesses is an increasingly popular practice. Outsourcing such activities as telemarketing to India, for example, can produce the same satisfactory result as having the work done in the United States but at a lower cost.

Outsourcing is also being applied to the preparation of tax returns. This practice not only can be expected to continue but also is likely to increase in volume. Outsourcing tax return preparation does not violate Federal law and is compatible with accounting ethical guidelines as long as three safeguards are followed: First, the practitioner must make sure client confidentiality is maintained. Second, the practitioner must verify the accuracy of the work that has been outsourced. Third, the practitioner must inform clients, preferably in writing, when any third-party contractor is used to provide professional services.

Practitioners justify outsourcing as a means of conserving time and effort that can be applied toward more meaningful tax planning on behalf of their clients.

LO.6

Evaluate some of the ethical guidelines involved in tax practice.

Ethical Guidelines

The American Institute of CPAs has issued its "Statements on Standards for Tax Services," dealing with CPAs engaged in tax practice. These pronouncements are *enforceable* as part of its Code of Professional Conduct. They include the following summarized provisions:

- Do not take questionable positions on a client's tax return in the hope the return will not be selected for audit by the IRS. Any positions taken should be supported by a good-faith belief that they have a realistic possibility of being sustained if challenged. The client should be fully advised of the risks involved and of the penalties that will result if the position taken is not successful.

- A practitioner can use a client's estimates if they are reasonable under the circumstances. If the tax law requires receipts or other verification, the client should be so advised. In no event should an estimate be given the appearance of greater accuracy than is the case. For example, an estimate of $1,000 should not be deducted on a return as $999.

- Every effort should be made to answer questions appearing on tax returns. A question need not be answered if the information requested is not readily available, the answer is voluminous, or the question's meaning is uncertain. The failure to answer a question on a return cannot be justified on the grounds that the answer could prove disadvantageous to the taxpayer.

- Upon learning of an error on a past tax return, advise the client to correct it. Do not, however, inform the IRS of the error. If the error is material and the client refuses to correct it, consider withdrawing from the engagement. This will be necessary if the error has a carryover effect and prevents the current year's tax liability from being determined correctly.

Statutory Penalties Imposed on Tax Return Preparers

In addition to ethical constraints, a tax return preparer may be subject to specific penalties, including the following:

- Various penalties involving procedural matters. Examples include failing to furnish the taxpayer with a copy of the return, endorsing a taxpayer's refund check, failing to sign the return as a preparer, failing to furnish one's identification number, and failing to keep copies of returns or maintain a client list.

- Penalty for understatement of a tax liability based on a position that lacks substantial authority. If the position has a reasonable basis, the penalty can be avoided by disclosing it on the return.

- Penalty for any willful attempt to understate taxes. This usually results when a preparer disregards or makes no effort to obtain pertinent information from a client.

- Penalty for failure to exercise due diligence in determining eligibility for, or the amount of, an earned income tax credit, the child tax credit, or the American opportunity tax credit.

1-6 UNDERSTANDING THE FEDERAL TAX LAW

LO.7

Classify tax rules based on their possible economic, social, equity, and political reasons for inclusion in a particular tax system.

The Federal tax law reflects the three branches of our Federal government. It is a mixture of laws passed by Congress, explanations provided by the Treasury Department and the Internal Revenue Service (IRS), and interpretation of the law by the courts. Anyone who has attempted to work with this vast amount of information is familiar with its complexity. For the person who has to sift through this information to find the solution to a tax problem, it is good to know that there are reasons behind the law. Knowing these reasons is the first step toward understanding the Federal tax law.

The *primary objective* of any tax system is the raising of revenue to fund government operations. Although the fiscal needs of the government are important, other considerations (economic, social, equity, and political factors) also play a significant role. The Treasury Department, the IRS, and the courts also have significant impacts on the evolution of Federal tax law. The remainder of the chapter focuses on these topics. While the discussion focuses on the Federal tax system, it also applies to any level of government that imposes taxes.

1-6a Revenue Needs

Raising revenues to fund the cost of government operations is the key factor in structuring a tax system. In a perfect world, taxes raised by the government would equal the expenses incurred by government operations. However, this goal is rarely achieved by the U.S. government, but is typically achieved by state and local governments that may face restrictions on borrowing.

When enacting tax legislation, a deficit-conscious Congress often has been guided by the concept of revenue neutrality so that changes neither increase nor decrease the net revenues received by the government. With revenue-neutral legislation, there are likely to be both "winners" (taxpayers who see a reduction in taxes paid) and "losers" (taxpayers who see an increase in taxes paid).

In addition to making revenue-neutral changes in the tax law, several other procedures can be taken to mitigate any revenue loss. When tax reductions are involved, the full impact of the legislation can be phased in over a period of years. Or as an alternative, the tax reduction can be limited to a period of years. When the period expires, the prior law is reinstated through a sunset provision. For example, at times, Congress has allowed more rapid depreciation treatment for a specified number of years. These sunset (or temporary) provisions move legislation toward revenue neutrality (even though it is not achieved).

1-6b Economic Considerations

Sometimes tax legislation is designed to help control the economy or encourage certain activities and businesses.

Control of the Economy

Congress has used the tax depreciation rules as a means of controlling the economy. Theoretically, shorter asset lives and accelerated methods should encourage additional investment in depreciable property acquired for business use. On the other hand, longer asset lives and use of straight-line depreciation should discourage capital outlays. Congress also uses incentives such as bonus depreciation to stimulate the economy when needed.

A change in tax rates has a more immediate impact on the economy. With lower tax rates, taxpayers retain money that can be used for other purposes (e.g., purchases or savings). If, however, Congress is using the concept of revenue neutrality, these rate reductions may be offset by a reduction or elimination of deductions or credits. As a result, lower tax rates do not always mean lower taxes.

Encouragement of Certain Activities

Congress uses the tax law to encourage certain types of economic activity or segments of the economy. For example, research and development expenditures can be either deducted in the year incurred or capitalized and amortized over a period of 60 months or more. Inventions are also encouraged by tax law. Under certain conditions, the sale of a patent results in long-term capital gain treatment.

Part of the tax law addresses the nation's energy policy—in terms of both our reliance on carbon-based fuels and the need to ease the problem of climate change. For example, a tax credit is available for installation of solar and small wind energy equipment. Residential energy credits are available for home improvements that conserve energy or make its use more efficient (e.g., solar water heaters). Ecological considerations explain why pollution control facilities can be amortized over 60 months (rather than over the 39-year period for most buildings).

Is saving desirable for the economy? Saving can lead to capital formation, making funds available to finance home construction and industrial expansion. The tax law encourages saving by giving private retirement plans preferential treatment. Besides contributions to certain Individual Retirement Accounts (IRAs) and Keogh (H.R. 10) plans being deductible, income from the contributions accumulates tax-free until it is withdrawn.

Encouragement of Certain Industries

Historically, agricultural activities have been favored under Federal tax law. Among the benefits are the election to expense rather than capitalize certain soil and water conservation expenditures and fertilizers and the election to defer the recognition of gain on the receipt of crop insurance proceeds.

The tax law favors the development of natural resources by permitting the use of percentage depletion and a write-off (rather than a capitalization) of certain exploration costs. The railroad and banking industries also receive special tax treatment under Federal tax law.

Encouragement of Small Business

Small business development is also encouraged under the tax law. For example, the shareholders of a small business corporation can make an election that allows the profits (or losses) of the corporation to flow through to its shareholders, avoiding the corporate income tax.[36] Another provision allows a shareholder in a small business corporation to take an ordinary deduction (rather than a capital loss) for any loss recognized on the stock investment.

1-6c Social Considerations

Some provisions of the Federal tax law, particularly those dealing with individuals, can be explained by social considerations. Here are some notable examples:

- Certain benefits provided to employees through accident and health plans financed by employers are nontaxable to employees. It is socially desirable to encourage these plans because they provide medical benefits in the event of an employee's illness or injury. In addition, insurance companies are paying for these benefits (rather than the government).

- Most premiums paid by an employer for group term insurance covering the life of the employee are nontaxable to the employee. Life insurance proceeds (which are also nontaxable) provide funds to help the family unit adjust to the loss of wages caused by the employee's death.

- A contribution made by an employer to a qualified pension or profit sharing plan for an employee may receive special treatment. The contribution and any income it generates are not taxed to the employee until the funds are distributed. This arrangement also benefits the employer by allowing a tax deduction for the contribution to the qualified plan. Private retirement plans are encouraged to supplement any Social Security payments.[37]

---

[36]Known as the S election, it is discussed in Chapter 22.

[37]The same rationale explains the availability of similar arrangements for self-employed persons (e.g., the H.R. 10, or Keogh, plan).

- A deduction is allowed for contributions to qualified charities. The deduction shifts some of the financial and administrative burden of socially desirable programs from the public (the government) to the private sector.

- A tax credit is allowed for amounts spent to furnish care for dependents to enable the taxpayer to work. A credit for employers who incur certain child care expenses assists employees indirectly.

- To encourage taxpayers to join the workforce even though their wages may be low, an earned income tax credit can be claimed. The credit varies depending on the number of qualifying children and the level of wages earned.

- Certain credits are made available to elderly and disabled persons. Credits also are allowed to businesses that incur expenditures to make their facilities more accessible to the disabled.

- Various tax credits, deductions, and exclusions are designed to encourage taxpayers to obtain additional education.[38]

- A tax deduction is not allowed for certain expenses deemed to be contrary to public policy. Expenses not allowed include items such as fines, penalties, illegal kickbacks, bribes to government officials, and gambling losses in excess of gains. The TCJA of 2017 denies any business deduction (including attorney fees) related to sexual harassment or abuse if the settlement or payment is subject to a nondisclosure agreement.

1-6d **Equity Considerations**

The concept of equity (or fairness) is relative. One measure of equity is whether a tax is *regressive or progressive*. The determination is made by calculating the percentage of a taxpayer's income that is used to pay a tax. As noted earlier, the Federal income tax is progressive. In contrast, the gasoline excise tax is regressive.

Hanna and Lori are single taxpayers living in the same state. Hanna has income of $100,000 and Lori has income of $10,000. Assume that Hanna pays $5,000 in state income taxes while Lori pays only $100. The state income tax represents 5% of Hanna's income but only 1% of Lori's income. Because the higher-income taxpayer (Hanna) devotes a larger percentage of her income to pay the tax relative to a lower-income taxpayer (Lori), this state income tax is *progressive* in its effect on taxpayers.

Alternatively, assume that Hanna and Lori each purchase the same quantity of gasoline during the year and each pays gasoline excise tax of $200. This tax represents less than 0.1% of Hanna's income but 2% of Lori's income. Because the lower-income taxpayer (Lori) devotes a larger percentage of her income to pay the tax relative to a higher-income taxpayer (Hanna), the gasoline excise tax is *regressive* in its effect on taxpayers.

EXAMPLE 22

Lawmakers and others often consider whether a tax change is progressive or regressive to understand its impact on taxpayers and whether the change should be made. If a tax represents the same percentage of the income of all taxpayers, it is a *proportional* tax.

Eduardo and Sanjay are single taxpayers living in the same state. Eduardo has income of $50,000 and pays $1,500 in state taxes. Sanjay has income of $20,000 and pays $600 in state taxes. In this case, Eduardo and Sanjay are devoting the same percentage of their income to the state tax (3%), making the tax *proportional* in terms of the effect it has on taxpayers.

EXAMPLE 23

The concept of equity also appears in tax provisions that alleviate the effect of multiple taxation and postpone the recognition of gain when the taxpayer lacks the ability or wherewithal to pay the tax. Provisions that mitigate the effect of the application of the annual accounting period concept and help taxpayers cope with the eroding results of inflation also reflect equity considerations.

---

[38]These provisions can also be justified under the category of economic considerations because a better-educated workforce carries a positive economic impact.

Alleviating the Effect of Multiple Taxation

Equity considerations can explain the Federal tax treatment of certain income from foreign sources. Because double taxation results when the same income is subject to both foreign and U.S. income taxes, the tax law permits the taxpayer to choose between a credit and a deduction for the foreign taxes paid.

The Wherewithal to Pay Concept

The ==wherewithal to pay== concept recognizes the inequity of taxing a transaction when the taxpayer lacks the means (i.e., funds) to pay the tax. This concept is typically applied to transactions where the taxpayer's economic position has not changed significantly.

An illustration of the wherewithal to pay concept is the tax treatment of an involuntary conversion. An involuntary conversion occurs when property is destroyed by a casualty (e.g, a fire or hurricane) or taken by a public authority through condemnation (e.g., taking land to build a new road). If gain results from the conversion, it is deferred if the taxpayer replaces the property within a specified period of time.

Some of the pasture land belonging to Ron, a rancher, is condemned by the state for use as a game preserve. The condemned pasture land cost Ron $120,000, but the state pays him $150,000 (its fair market value). Shortly thereafter, Ron buys more pasture land for $150,000.

In Example 24, Ron has a realized gain of $30,000 [$150,000 (condemnation award) − $120,000 (cost of land)]. It would be inequitable to force Ron to pay a tax on this gain for two reasons. First, without selling the property acquired (the new land), Ron does not have the funds to pay the tax. Second, his economic position has not changed (i.e., he still owns pasture land worth $150,000). If, however, the taxpayer's economic position changes in any way, tax consequences may result.

Assume the same facts as in Example 24, except that Ron reinvests only $140,000 of the award in new pasture land. Now Ron has a taxable gain of $10,000. Instead of ending up with only replacement property, Ron has $10,000 in cash.

Mitigating the Effect of the Annual Accounting Period Concept

All taxpayers must report their taxable income to the Federal government at regular intervals. The accounting period used to report taxable income (and settle any tax liability) is one year. Referred to as the annual accounting period concept, its effect is to divide each taxpayer's life, for tax purposes, into equal annual intervals.

The annual accounting period concept can lead to different tax treatment for taxpayers who are in the same economic position. Consider the following example.

José and Alicia, both sole proprietors, showed the following results during the past three years:

	Profit (or Loss)	
Year	**José**	**Alicia**
2018	$50,000	$150,000
2019	60,000	60,000
2020	60,000	(40,000)

Although José and Alicia have the same total profit of $170,000 over the three-year period, the annual accounting period concept places Alicia at a definite disadvantage for tax purposes. The net operating loss (NOL) deduction offers Alicia some relief by allowing her to carry forward (but not back) some or all of her 2020 loss to future years. With a net operating loss carryforward, Alicia may apply her 2020 loss to future years' profits (with certain limitations; see Chapter 7).

The reasoning used to support the net operating loss deduction also can explain the special treatment the tax law accords to excess capital losses and excess charitable contributions.[39] Carryback and carryover procedures help mitigate the effect of limiting a loss or a deduction to the accounting period in which it was realized. Using these procedures, a taxpayer can salvage a loss or a deduction that might otherwise be lost.

The installment method of recognizing gain on the sale of property allows a taxpayer to spread tax consequences over the payout period.[40] The installment method is supported by the wherewithal to pay concept; recognition of gain corresponds to the collection of the cash received from the sale of the property. The tax consequences match the seller's ability to pay the tax.

Coping with Inflation

Because of the progressive nature of the income tax, a wage adjustment to compensate for inflation could place the employee in a higher income tax bracket. Known as *bracket creep*, its overall impact is an erosion of purchasing power. Congress recognizes this problem and adjusts various income tax components, such as tax brackets, standard deduction amounts, and a wide variety of other items, through an indexation procedure. <mark>Indexation</mark> is based on the change in the chained consumer price index over the prior year.

1-6e Political Considerations

A large segment of the Federal tax law is made up of statutory provisions. Because these statutes are enacted by Congress, political considerations often influence tax law. The effect of political considerations on the tax law includes special interest legislation, political expediency situations, and state and local government influences.

Special Interest Legislation

There is no doubt that certain provisions of the tax law can largely be explained by the political influence some groups have had on Congress. For example, prepaid subscription and dues income is not taxed until earned, whereas prepaid rents are taxed to the landlord in the year received. This exception was created because certain organizations (e.g., the American Automobile Association) convinced Congress that special tax treatment was needed for multi-year dues and subscriptions.

Another provision, sponsored by a senator from Georgia, suspended the import duties on ceiling fans. The nation's largest seller of ceiling fans is Atlanta-based Home Depot.

Although some special interest legislation can be justified on economic or social grounds, in most cases, it cannot. It is, however, an inevitable product of our political system.

Political Expediency Situations

Various tax changes can be tied to the shifting moods of the American public. That Congress is sensitive to popular feelings is an accepted fact. Therefore, certain provisions of the tax law can be explained by the political climate at the time they were enacted.

Measures that deter more affluent taxpayers from obtaining so-called preferential tax treatment have always had popular appeal and, consequently, the support of Congress. Tax provisions such as the imputed interest rules and the limitations on the deductibility of interest on investment indebtedness affect affluent taxpayers directly. More subtle are provisions that phase out tax breaks as income rises. These phaseouts are often called *stealth taxes* because the effects are *indirect* (and the taxpayer might not be aware of

---

[39]The tax treatment of these items is discussed in Chapters 7, 10, and 14.

[40]Under the installment method, each payment received by the seller represents both a recovery of capital (the nontaxable portion) and profit from the sale (the taxable portion). The tax rules governing the installment method are discussed in Chapter 16.

them). The tax law contains several of these phaseout rules. Examples include the phaseout of the child tax credit and education tax credits.

State and Local Government Influences

Political considerations played a major role in the nontaxability of interest received on state and local obligations. Somewhat less apparent has been the influence state law has had in shaping our present Federal tax law. Such was the case with community property systems. The nine states with community property systems are Arizona, California, Idaho, Louisiana, Nevada, New Mexico, Texas, Washington, and Wisconsin. The rest of the states are common law jurisdictions.[41] The difference between common law and community property systems centers around the property rights possessed by married persons. In a common law system, each spouse owns whatever he or she earns. Under a community property system, one-half of the earnings of each spouse is considered owned by the other spouse.

EXAMPLE 27

Adam and Fran are married, and their only income is the $80,000 annual salary Adam receives. If they live in New Jersey (a common law state), the $80,000 salary belongs to Adam. If, however, they live in Arizona (a community property state), the $80,000 is divided equally, in terms of ownership, between Adam and Fran.

At one time, the tax position of the residents of community property states was so advantageous that many common law states adopted community property systems. Needless to say, the political pressure placed on Congress to correct the disparity in tax treatment was considerable. To a large extent, this was accomplished in the Revenue Act of 1948, which extended many of the community property tax advantages to residents of common law jurisdictions.

Congress accomplished this by allowing married taxpayers to file joint returns and compute their tax liability as if one-half of the income had been earned by each spouse. This result is automatic in a community property state because half of the income earned by one spouse belongs to the other spouse. The income-splitting benefits of a joint return are now incorporated as part of the tax rates applicable to married taxpayers. See Chapter 3.

1-6f **Influence of the Internal Revenue Service**

LO.8

Explain the role played by the IRS and the courts in the evolution of the Federal tax system.

The IRS has exerted its influence in many areas of the tax law. As the protector of the national revenue, the IRS has been instrumental in securing the passage of legislation designed to curtail aggressive tax avoidance practices (i.e., closing *tax loopholes*). In addition, the IRS has sought and obtained law changes to make its job easier (to attain administrative feasibility).

The IRS as Protector of the Revenue

Many provisions in the tax law resulted from the direct efforts of the IRS to prevent taxpayers from exploiting a tax loophole. Working within the letter of existing laws, ingenious taxpayers and their advisers devise techniques that accomplish indirectly what cannot be accomplished directly. As a result, Congress passes laws to close the loopholes that taxpayers have located and exploited.

In addition, Congress has passed laws that enable the IRS to make adjustments based on the substance of a transaction (rather than the form chosen by the taxpayer). For example, the IRS can make adjustments to a taxpayer's method of accounting when the method used by the taxpayer does not *clearly reflect income*.[42]

---

[41]In Alaska, spouses can choose to have the community property rules apply. Otherwise, property rights are determined under common law rules.

[42]See Chapter 16.

Tran owns and operates a clothing distribution business with over $26,000,000 of annual gross receipts. The merchandise acquired is charged to the purchases account and written off (expensed) for tax purposes in the year of acquisition. Since this procedure does not clearly reflect income, it would be appropriate for the IRS to require that Tran establish and maintain an ending inventory account.

EXAMPLE
28

Administrative Feasibility

Some tax laws are created to simplify the task of the IRS in collecting the revenue and administering the law. As to collecting revenue, the IRS long ago realized the importance of placing taxpayers on a pay-as-you-go basis. Withholding procedures apply to wages, but the tax on other types of income may have to be paid via quarterly estimated payments. The IRS has been instrumental in convincing the courts that accrual basis taxpayers should, in most cases, pay taxes on prepaid income in the year received and not when earned. The approach may be contrary to generally accepted accounting principles, but prepayment is consistent with the wherewithal to pay concept.

To help the IRS collect revenues when due, Congress has passed many provisions that impose interest and penalties on taxpayers if they don't comply with the tax law. Provisions such as the penalties for failure to pay a tax or to file a return that is due, the negligence penalty for intentional disregard of rules and Regulations, and various penalties for civil and criminal fraud are intended to encourage taxpayers to comply with the tax law.

The audit process conducted by the IRS is key to an effective administration of our tax system. To carry out this function, the IRS is aided by provisions that reduce the chance of taxpayer error or manipulation, thus simplifying the audit effort. For example, by increasing the standard deduction amount, the audit function is simplified because fewer returns with itemized deductions need to be checked.[43]

1-6g **Influence of the Courts**

In addition to interpreting statutory provisions and the administrative pronouncements issued by the Treasury Department and the IRS, the Federal courts have influenced tax law in two other ways.[44] First, the courts have developed a number of judicial concepts that help guide how tax provisions are applied. Second, certain key decisions have led to changes in the Internal Revenue Code.

Judicial Concepts Relating to Tax

A leading tax concept developed by the courts deals with the interpretation of statutory tax provisions that operate to benefit taxpayers. The courts have decided that these relief provisions are to be applied narrowly. If a taxpayer wants a relief provision to apply, the taxpayer has the responsibility to meet the provision's requirements (i.e., no exceptions).

The *arm's length* concept is important here. Particularly in dealings between related parties, transactions may be tested by asking this question: Would unrelated parties have handled the transaction in the same way?

Matt, the sole shareholder of Silver Corporation, leases property to the corporation for a yearly rent of $60,000. To test whether the corporation should be allowed a rent deduction for this amount, the IRS and the courts will apply the arm's length concept. Would Silver Corporation have paid $60,000 a year in rent if it had leased the same property from an unrelated party (rather than from Matt)?

EXAMPLE
29

continued

---

[43]For a discussion of the standard deduction, see Chapter 3. The same justification was given by the IRS when it proposed to Congress the $100 limitation on personal casualty and theft losses. Imposition of the limitation eliminated many casualty and theft loss deductions and, as a consequence, saved the IRS considerable audit time. Later legislation, in addition to retaining the $100 feature, generally limits deductible losses to those in Federally declared disaster areas. In addition, only losses in excess of 10% of a taxpayer's adjusted gross income are allowed. See Chapter 7.

[44]A great deal of case law is devoted to ascertaining congressional intent. The courts, in effect, ask: What did Congress have in mind when it enacted a particular tax provision?

Suppose it is determined that an unrelated third party would have charged an annual rent for the property of only $50,000. Under these circumstances, Silver Corporation will be allowed a deduction of only $50,000. The other $10,000 it paid for the use of the property represents a nondeductible dividend. Accordingly, Matt will be treated as having received rent income of $50,000 and dividend income of $10,000.

Judicial Influence on Statutory Provisions

Some court decisions have been so important that Congress incorporated them into the Internal Revenue Code. For example, many years ago the courts found that stock dividends distributed to the shareholders of a corporation were not taxable as income. This result was largely accepted by Congress, and the Code was modified to reflect the court's position.

On occasion, however, Congress reacts negatively to judicial interpretations of the tax law.

EXAMPLE 30

Nora leases unimproved real estate to Wade for 20 years. At a cost of $400,000, Wade erects a building on the land. The building is worth $150,000 when the lease terminates and Nora takes possession of the property.

Does Nora have any income either when the improvements are made or when the lease terminates? In a landmark decision, a court held that Nora must recognize income of $150,000 upon the termination of the lease.

Congress believed that the result reached in Example 30 was not consistent with the wherewithal to pay concept. As a result, the tax law was changed to provide that a landlord does not recognize any income either when the improvements are made (unless made in lieu of rent) or when the lease terminates.[45]

1-6h **Summary**

In addition to raising revenues, other factors have influenced the development of Federal tax law:

- *Economic considerations.* Congress uses the tax law to help regulate the economy and encourage certain activities and types of businesses.

- *Social considerations.* The tax law has been used to encourage (or discourage) certain socially desirable (or undesirable) practices.

- *Equity considerations.* The tax law can be designed to alleviate the effect of multiple taxation, recognize the wherewithal to pay concept, mitigate the effect of the annual accounting period concept, and recognize the eroding effect of inflation.

- *Political considerations.* Some tax law represents special interest legislation, reflects political expediency, or illustrates the effect of state and local law.

- *Influence of the IRS.* Laws are enacted to aid the IRS in the collection of revenue and the administration of the tax law.

- *Influence of the courts.* Court decisions have established a body of judicial concepts relating to tax law and have, on occasion, led Congress to enact laws to either clarify or negate their effect.

These factors help us understand how tax law develops (and why some provisions exist). We also must learn to work with the tax law, which is the subject of Chapter 2.

---

[45]*M.E. Blatt Co. v. U.S.*, 305 U.S. 267 (1938) and § 109.

FAMILY AND TAXES—A TYPICAL YEAR

The explanation given for the difference in the ad valorem property taxes—the Carters' increase and the Walkers' decrease—seems reasonable (see Example 4). It is not likely that the Carters' increase was solely due to a *general* upward assessment in valuation, because the Walkers' taxes on their residence (located nearby) dropped. More business use of the Carters' residence (presuming that Travis conducts his consulting practice from his home) might be responsible for the increase, but capital improvements appear to be a more likely cause.

The imposition of the use tax when Travis registered the new automobile illustrates one of the means by which a state can preclude the avoidance of its sales tax (see Example 5).

When gifts between family members are material in amount (e.g., an RV) and exceed the annual exclusion, a gift tax return needs to be filed (see Example 11). Even though no gift tax may be due because of the availability of the unified transfer tax credit, the filing of a return starts the running of the statute of limitations.

The Carters must recognize that some of their income is subject to income taxes in more than one state and take advantage of whatever relief is available to mitigate the result of double taxation (see Example 12).

Employment within and by the family group (e.g., children, other relatives, and domestics) has become a priority item in the enforcement of Social Security tax and income tax withholdings. Thus, the Carters must be aware of the need to cover their son, Martin (see Example 13).

Because of the double audit (i.e., both state and Federal) and the deficiency assessed, the Carters need to make sure that future returns do not contain similar errors (see Example 18). As the text suggests, taxpayers with prior deficiencies are among those whose returns may be selected for audit.

Key Terms

Ad valorem taxes, 1-10

Carbon tax, 1-21

Correspondence audit, 1-22

Employment taxes, 1-17

Estate tax, 1-13

Excise taxes, 1-11

FICA tax, 1-17

Field audit, 1-23

Financial transaction tax, 1-21

Flat tax, 1-20

Franchise tax, 1-19

FUTA tax, 1-18

Gift tax, 1-14

Indexation, 1-31

Inheritance tax, 1-13

National sales tax, 1-20

Occupational fees, 1-19

Office audit, 1-23

Personalty, 1-10

Realty, 1-10

Revenue neutrality, 1-27

Sales tax, 1-12

Severance taxes, 1-12

Statute of limitations, 1-24

Sunset provision, 1-27

Use tax, 1-12

Value added tax (VAT), 1-20

Wherewithal to pay, 1-30

Discussion Questions

1. **LO.1** This textbook includes many features beyond the text materials in each chapter. For example, a glossary is included in the appendices and the end of each chapter contains a list of key terms. Skim through the chapters, appendices, and any other supplemental materials required for your course, and identify two special features. For each, explain what it is and how it can help you understand taxation in this tax course.

2. **LO.1, 4** In the following independent situations, is the tax position of the taxpayer likely to change? Explain why or why not.

   a. John started renting out a spare room in his home.

   b. Theresa quit her job as a staff accountant and established her own practice as a CPA.

   c. Paul's employer transferred him from its California office to an office in Florida.

Critical Thinking 3. **LO.1, 4** Marvin is the executor and sole heir of his aunt's estate. The estate includes her furnished home, which Marvin is considering converting to rental property to generate additional cash flow. What are some of the tax considerations Marvin may confront?

4. **LO.2** World War II converted the Federal income tax into a *mass tax*. Explain.

5. **LO.2** How does the pay-as-you-go procedure apply to wage earners? To persons who have income from sources other than wages?

6. **LO.3** Jane, a tax practitioner, has reviewed the law on how State X's income tax applies to a client's web-based consulting business but is unable to reach a conclusion for which she has a high level of confidence. Assuming that Jane is a knowledgeable and experienced tax professional, which *Guiding Principles of Good Tax Policy* might not be followed by State X?

7. **LO.3** Distinguish between taxes that are *regressive* and those that are *progressive*.

Critical Thinking 8. **LO.4** Several years ago Ethan purchased the former parsonage of St. James Church to use as a personal residence. To date, Ethan has not received any ad valorem property tax bills from either the city or the county tax authorities.

   a. What is a reasonable explanation for this oversight?

   b. What should Ethan do?

Critical Thinking 9. **LO.4** The Adams Independent School District wants to sell a parcel of unimproved land that it does not need. Its three best offers are as follows: from the state's Department of Public Safety (DPS), $2,300,000; from the Second Baptist Church, $2,200,000; and from Baker Motors, $2,100,000. DPS would use the property for a new state highway patrol barracks, Second Baptist would start a church school, and Baker would open a car dealership. If you are the financial adviser for the school district, which offer would you prefer? Why?

10. **LO.4** The commissioners for Walker County are actively negotiating with Falcon Industries regarding the location of a new manufacturing plant in the area. Since Falcon is considering several other sites, a "generous tax holiday" may be needed to influence the final choice. The local school district is opposed to any "generous tax holiday."

   a. What would probably be involved in a generous tax holiday?

   b. Why would the school district be opposed?

11. **LO.4** Sophia lives several blocks from her parents in the same residential subdivision. Sophia is surprised to learn that her ad valorem property taxes for the year were raised but those of her parents were lowered. What is a possible explanation for the difference?

12. **LO.4** The Morgan family lives in Massachusetts. They moor their sailboat in Rhode Island. What might be a plausible reason for this?

13. **LO.4** Is the breadth and number of Federal excise taxes increasing or decreasing? Explain.

14. **LO.4** After her first business trip to a major city, Ginger is alarmed when she reviews her credit card receipts. Both the hotel bill and the car rental charge are in

excess of the price she was quoted. Was Ginger overcharged, or is there an explanation for the excess amounts?

15. **LO.4** What is the difference between an excise tax and a general sales tax?
    a. Do all states impose a general sales tax?
    b. Does the Federal government impose a general sales tax?

16. **LO.4** The Grays live in Clay County, which is adjacent to Jackson County. Although the retail stores in both counties are comparable, the Grays usually drive a few extra miles to shop in Jackson County. As to why the Grays might do this, consider the following:
    a. Clay County is in a different state than Jackson County.
    b. Clay County and Jackson County are in the same state.

17. **LO.4** During a social event, Muriel and Ben are discussing the home computer each recently purchased. Although the computers are identical makes and models, Muriel is surprised to learn that she paid a sales tax but Ben did not. Comment as to why this could happen.   *Critical Thinking*

18. **LO.4** Distinguish between an estate tax and an inheritance tax.
    a. Do some states impose both? Neither?
    b. Which, if either, does the Federal government impose?

19. **LO.4** Jake (age 72) and Jessica (age 28) were recently married. To avoid any transfer taxes, Jake has promised to leave Jessica all of his wealth when he dies. Is Jake under some misconception about the operation of the Federal gift and estate taxes? Explain.

20. **LO.4** Address the following issues:
    a. What is the purpose of the unified transfer tax credit?
    b. Is the same amount available for both the Federal gift tax and the estate tax? Explain.
    c. Does the use of the credit for a gift affect the amount of credit available for the estate tax? Explain.

21. **LO.4** Elijah and Anastasia are married and have five married children and nine minor grandchildren. For 2020, what is the maximum amount they can give to their family (including the sons- and daughters-in-law) without using any of their unified transfer tax credit?

22. **LO.4** What is the difference between the Federal income tax on individuals and that imposed on corporations?

23. **LO.4** As to those states that impose an income tax, comment on the following:
    a. "Piggyback" approach and possible "decoupling" from this approach.
    b. Use of IRS audit results as part of a state tax audit.
    c. Credit for taxes paid to other states.

24. **LO.4** In May 2020, Hernando, a resident of California, has his 2018 Federal income tax return audited by the IRS. An assessment of additional tax is made because he inadvertently omitted some rental income. In October 2020, California audits his state return for the same year. Explain the coincidence.

25. **LO.4** Mike Barr was an outstanding football player in college and expects to be drafted by the NFL in the first few rounds. Mike has let it be known that he would prefer to sign with a club located in Florida, Texas, or Washington. Mike sees no reason why he should have to pay state income tax on his player's salary. Is Mike under any delusions? Explain.   *Critical Thinking*

Critical Thinking

26. **LO.4, 5** A question on a state income tax return asks the taxpayer if he or she made any out-of-state internet or mail-order catalog purchases during the year. The question requires a yes or no answer, and if the taxpayer answers yes, the total dollar amount of these purchases is to be provided.

    a. Does this inquiry have any relevance to the state income tax? If not, why is it being asked?

    b. Your client, Harriet, wants to leave the question unanswered. As the preparer of her return, how do you respond?

27. **LO.4** Many state income tax returns contain checkoff boxes that allow taxpayers to make donations to a multitude of local charitable causes. On what grounds has this procedure been criticized?

28. **LO.4** Many states have occasionally adopted amnesty programs that allow taxpayers to pay back taxes with reduced penalties.

    a. Besides the revenue generated, how are these programs advantageous?

    b. Could an amnesty program be used by a state that does not levy an income tax?

    c. Does the IRS utilize this approach?

29. **LO.4** Contrast FICA and FUTA as to the following:

    a. Purpose of the tax.

    b. Upon whom imposed.

    c. Governmental administration of the tax.

    d. Reduction of tax based on a merit rating system.

30. **LO.4** In connection with the Medicare component of FICA, comment on the following:

    a. Any dollar limitation imposed.

    b. The applicability of the 0.9% increase in the 1.45% regular tax rate.

31. **LO.4** One of the tax advantages of hiring family members to work in your business is that FICA taxes are avoided. Do you agree with this statement? Explain.

32. **LO.4** Describe the nature and purpose of the following taxes:

    a. Severance taxes.

    b. Franchise taxes.

    c. Occupational fees.

    d. Customs duties.

    e. Export duties.

33. **LO.4** Regarding the value added tax (VAT), comment on the following:

    a. Popularity of this type of tax.

    b. Nature of the tax.

    c. Effect on government spending.

34. **LO.4** Both a value added tax (VAT) and a national sales tax have been criticized as *regressive* in their effect.

    a. Explain.

    b. How could this shortcoming be remedied?

35. **LO.4, 5** Serena operates a gift shop. To reduce costs of credit card transactions, she offers customers a discount if they pay in cash. For the holiday rush, she hires some short-term workers but pays them cash and does not add them to the payroll.

    a. What are some of the tax problems Serena might have?

    b. Assess Serena's chances of audit by the IRS.

36. **LO.5** With regard to the IRS audit process, comment on the following:
    a. The audit is resolved by mail.
    b. The audit is conducted at the office of the IRS.
    c. A "no change" RAR results.
    d. A special agent joins the audit team.

37. **LO.5** Aldo has just been audited by the IRS. He does not agree with the agent's findings but believes that he has only two choices: pay the proposed deficiency or resort to the courts. Do you agree with Aldo's conclusion? Why or why not?

38. **LO.5** What purpose is served by a statute of limitations? How is it relevant in the case of tax controversies?

39. **LO.5** Regarding the statute of limitations on additional assessments of tax by the IRS, determine the applicable period in each of the following situations. Assume a calendar year individual with no fraud or substantial omission involved.
    a. The income tax return for 2019 was filed on February 19, 2020.
    b. The income tax return for 2019 was filed on June 25, 2020.
    c. The income tax return for 2019 was prepared on April 4, 2020, but was never filed. Through some misunderstanding between the preparer and the taxpayer, each expected the other to file the return.
    d. The income tax return for 2019 was never filed because the taxpayer thought no additional tax was due.

40. **LO.5** Brianna, a calendar year taxpayer, files her income tax return for 2019 on February 3, 2020. Although she makes repeated inquiries, she does not receive her refund from the IRS until May 28, 2020. Is Brianna entitled to interest on the refund? Explain.

41. **LO.5, 6** On a Federal income tax return filed five years ago, Andy inadvertently omitted a large amount of gross income.
    a. Andy seeks your advice as to whether the IRS is barred from assessing additional income tax in the event he is audited. What is your advice?
    b. Would your advice differ if you were the person who prepared the return in question? Explain.
    c. Suppose Andy asks you to prepare his current year's return. Would you do so? Explain.

42. **LO.5** Rita files her income tax return 35 days after the due date of the return without obtaining an extension from the IRS. Along with the return, she remits a check for $40,000, which is the balance of the tax she owes. Disregarding the interest element, what are Rita's penalties for failure to file and for failure to pay?

43. **LO.5** For tax year 2017, the IRS assesses a deficiency against David for $500,000. Disregarding the interest component, what is David's penalty if the deficiency is attributable to:
    a. Negligence?
    b. Fraud?

44. **LO.5, 6** In March 2020, Jim asks you to prepare his Federal income tax returns for tax years 2017, 2018, and 2019. In discussing this matter with him, you discover that he also has not filed for tax year 2016. When you mention this fact, Jim tells you that the statute of limitations precludes the IRS from taking any action as to this year.

   a. Is Jim correct about the application of the statute of limitations? Why or why not?

   b. If Jim refuses to file for 2016, should you prepare returns for 2017 through 2019? Explain.

45. **LO.5, 6** The Benson CPA firm is considering utilizing an offshore service provider to prepare many of its tax returns. In this regard, what ethical considerations must be taken into account?

46. **LO.7** In terms of tax policy, what do the following mean?

   a. Revenue neutrality.

   b. Sunset provision.

   c. Indexation.

47. **LO.7** Some tax rules can be justified on multiple grounds (e.g., economic and social). In this connection, comment on the possible justification for the rules governing the following:

   a. Pension plans.

   b. Education.

   c. Home ownership.

Critical Thinking   48. **LO.7, 8** Discuss the probable justification for each of the following aspects of the tax law. Be sure to use concepts and terminology covered in this chapter.

   a. A tax credit is allowed for amounts spent to furnish care for minor children while the parent works.

   b. Deductions for interest on home mortgage and property taxes on a personal residence.

   c. The income-splitting benefits of filing a joint return.

   d. Fines and penalties are not deductible.

   e. Net operating losses of a current year can be carried forward to profitable years.

   f. A taxpayer who sells property on an installment basis can recognize gain on the sale over the period the payments are received.

   g. The exclusion from Federal tax of certain interest income from state and local bonds.

   h. Prepaid income is taxed to the recipient in the year received and not in the year earned.

49. **LO.7** Mia owns a warehouse that has a cost basis to her of $80,000. The city condemns the warehouse to make room for a new fire station. It pays Mia $400,000 for the property, its agreed-to fair market value. Shortly after the condemnation, Mia purchases another warehouse as a replacement. What is her recognized gain if the new property cost:

   a. $280,000?

   b. $444,000?

   c. $80,000?

   d. What, if any, is the justification for deferring the recognition of gain on the involuntary conversion?

50. **LO.8** A mother sells a valuable collection of antiques to her son for $1,000. What judicial concept might the IRS invoke to question this transaction?

Research Problems

Use internet tax resources to address the following questions. Look for reliable websites and blogs of the IRS and other government agencies, media outlets, businesses, tax professionals, academics, think tanks, and political outlets.

Research Problem 1. Using information from this chapter as well as information from the tax agency in your state (likely called the Department of Revenue) and your local government, find all of the taxes to which a sole proprietor is subject. Create a table that lists all of these taxes, the rate(s), and the level(s) of government that imposes each tax.

Research Problem 2. Use **congress.gov** or another reliable website to find a proposal for a carbon tax or a financial transactions tax. Draft a summary of the tax, and analyze it against five of the AICPA's principles of good tax policy.

Critical Thinking

Research Problem 3. Find a Federal or state proposal for a soda tax or sweetened beverage tax. Provide the bill number and a brief explanation. Also apply the AICPA's principles of good tax policy to support your recommendation for or against the bill.

Critical Thinking

Research Problem 4. Visit the websites of a few public accounting firms to learn how they are using data analytics and visualization in the tax function. In an e-mail to your instructor, explain what you found, provide the source(s) you used, and explain how you think the data analysis helps businesses engage in tax compliance and planning.

Data Analytics

Communications

CHAPTER

2

Working with the Tax Law

LEARNING OBJECTIVES: *After completing Chapter 2, you should be able to:*

LO.1 Distinguish between the statutory, administrative, and judicial sources of the tax law and understand the purpose of each source.

LO.2 Locate and work with the appropriate tax law sources.

LO.3 Develop an awareness of tax research tools.

LO.4 Describe the tax research process.

LO.5 Communicate the results of the tax research process in a client letter and a tax file memorandum.

LO.6 Apply tax research techniques and planning procedures.

LO.7 Be aware of taxation on the CPA examination.

CHAPTER OUTLINE

2-1 Tax Sources, 2-2
    2-1a Statutory Sources of the Tax Law, 2-2
    2-1b Administrative Sources of the Tax Law, 2-6
    2-1c Judicial Sources of the Tax Law, 2-10
    2-1d Other Sources of the Tax Law, 2-17

2-2 Working with the Tax Law—Tax Research Tools, 2-18
    2-2a Commercial Tax Services, 2-18
    2-2b Using Electronic (Online) Tax Services, 2-19
    2-2c Noncommercial Electronic (Online) Tax Services, 2-19

2-3 Working with the Tax Law—Tax Research, 2-20
    2-3a Identifying the Problem, 2-22
    2-3b Refining the Problem, 2-22
    2-3c Locating the Appropriate Tax Law Sources, 2-23

    2-3d Assessing the Validity of Tax Law Sources, 2-23
    2-3e Arriving at the Solution or at Alternative Solutions, 2-25
    2-3f Communicating Tax Research, 2-26

2-4 Working with the Tax Law—Tax Planning, 2-28
    2-4a Nontax Considerations, 2-29
    2-4b Components of Tax Planning, 2-29
    2-4c Tax Avoidance and Tax Evasion, 2-30
    2-4d Follow-Up Procedures, 2-30
    2-4e Tax Planning, 2-31

2-5 Taxation on the CPA Examination, 2-31
    2-5a Preparation Blueprints, 2-31
    2-5b Regulation Section, 2-31

IMPORTANCE OF TAX RESEARCH

Early in November 2020, Fred and Megan Martel scheduled a meeting with you to discuss a potential tax problem. Fred and Megan purchased a 40-acre parcel of property in 2015 for $195,000. On it, they built their "dream home" in 2016. In March 2020, while walking on a remote part of their property, they spotted something shiny on the ground. They started digging and eventually unearthed eight metal cans containing more than 1,400 rare gold coins in $5, $10, and $20 denominations dated from 1846 to 1895. The face value of the gold coins is about $28,000, and the coins are in mint condition. Their delay in coming to you for tax advice was due to a state law that required their discovery to be turned over to the state for disposition. The state, for a period of six months, was required to publicize the find and ask if anyone could prove ownership. When no one came forward, the coins were returned to the Martels in October 2020. Since they are now the rightful owners of the coins, they want to know the tax implications (if any) of their discovery.

Read the chapter and formulate your responses.

2-2 **PART 1** Introduction and Basic Tax Model

Federal tax law reflects the three branches of our Federal government. It is a mixture of laws passed by Congress, explanations provided by the Treasury Department and the Internal Revenue Service (IRS), and court decisions. Anyone who has attempted to work with this vast amount of information is familiar with its complexity. The tax research process allows us to understand, evaluate, and apply the tax law to questions that are raised by taxpayers and tax practitioners.

In addition to being able to locate and interpret tax law, a tax professional also must understand the relative *weight of authority* that each source carries. The tax law is of little significance, however, until it is applied to a set of facts and circumstances. This chapter introduces the statutory, administrative, and judicial sources of tax law and explains how the law is applied to individual and business transactions. It also explains how to apply research techniques and use planning procedures effectively. A large part of tax research focuses on determining the intent of Congress.

Frequently, uncertainty in the tax law causes disputes between the Internal Revenue Service (IRS) and taxpayers. Due to these *gray areas* and the complexity of the tax law, a taxpayer may have more than one alternative for structuring a financial transaction. In structuring financial transactions and engaging in other tax planning activities, the tax adviser must be cognizant that the objective of tax planning is not necessarily to minimize the tax liability. Instead, a taxpayer should maximize his or her after-tax wealth, which may include maximizing nontax as well as noneconomic benefits.

2-1 TAX SOURCES

LO.1

Distinguish between the statutory, administrative, and judicial sources of the tax law and understand the purpose of each source.

Understanding taxation requires a mastery of the sources of tax law. These sources include laws passed by Congress, which are contained in the Internal Revenue Code and congressional Committee Reports, Treasury Department Regulations, other Treasury Department and IRS pronouncements, and court decisions. Thus, the *primary sources* of tax law include information from all three branches of government: legislative (or statutory), executive, and judicial.[1]

2-1a Statutory Sources of the Tax Law

Statutory sources of law include the Constitution (Article I, Sections 7, 8, and 10), the Internal Revenue Code, and tax treaties (agreements between countries to mitigate the double taxation of taxpayers subject to the tax laws of those countries). The Constitution grants Congress the power to impose and collect taxes and authorizes the creation of treaties with other countries. The power of Congress to implement and collect taxes is reflected in the Internal Revenue Code, the official title of U.S. tax law, and the Code is the basis for arriving at solutions to all tax questions.

Origin of the Internal Revenue Code

Before 1939, the statutory provisions relating to Federal taxation were contained in the individual revenue acts enacted by Congress. Because dealing with many separate acts was inconvenient and confusing, Congress codified all of the Federal tax laws in 1939. Known as the Internal Revenue Code of 1939, the codification arranged all Federal tax provisions in a logical sequence and placed them in a separate part of the Federal statutes. A further rearrangement took place in 1954 and resulted in the Internal Revenue Code of 1954, which continued in effect until 1986, when it was replaced by the Internal Revenue Code of 1986. Although Congress did not recodify the law in the Tax Reform Act (TRA) of 1986, the magnitude of the changes made by TRA of 1986 did provide some rationale for renaming the Federal tax law the Internal Revenue Code of 1986.[2]

---

[1] *Secondary sources* also are used by tax practitioners. These sources are not part of the tax law and include items like tax articles from professional tax journals, newsletters, and textbooks. Commentary contained in various tax research services (such as Thomson Reuters *Checkpoint*) also are secondary sources.

[2] This point is important in assessing judicial decisions interpreting provisions of the Internal Revenue Code of 1939 and the Internal Revenue Code of 1954. If a provision from the 1939 or 1954 Code was included in the Internal Revenue Code of 1986 and has not been subsequently amended, the provision and the related judicial decisions have continuing validity.

The Legislative Process

Exhibit 2.1 illustrates the legislative process for enacting changes to the Internal Revenue Code of 1986. Federal tax legislation generally originates in the House of Representatives, where it is first considered by the House Ways and Means Committee.[3] Once approved by the House Ways and Means Committee, the proposed bill is referred to the entire House of Representatives for approval or disapproval. Approved bills are sent to the Senate, where they are considered by the Senate Finance Committee.[4]

After approval by the Senate Finance Committee, the bill is sent to the entire Senate. Assuming no disagreement between the House and Senate, passage by the Senate results in referral to the President for approval or veto. If the bill is approved or if

EXHIBIT 2.1	Legislative Process for Tax Bills

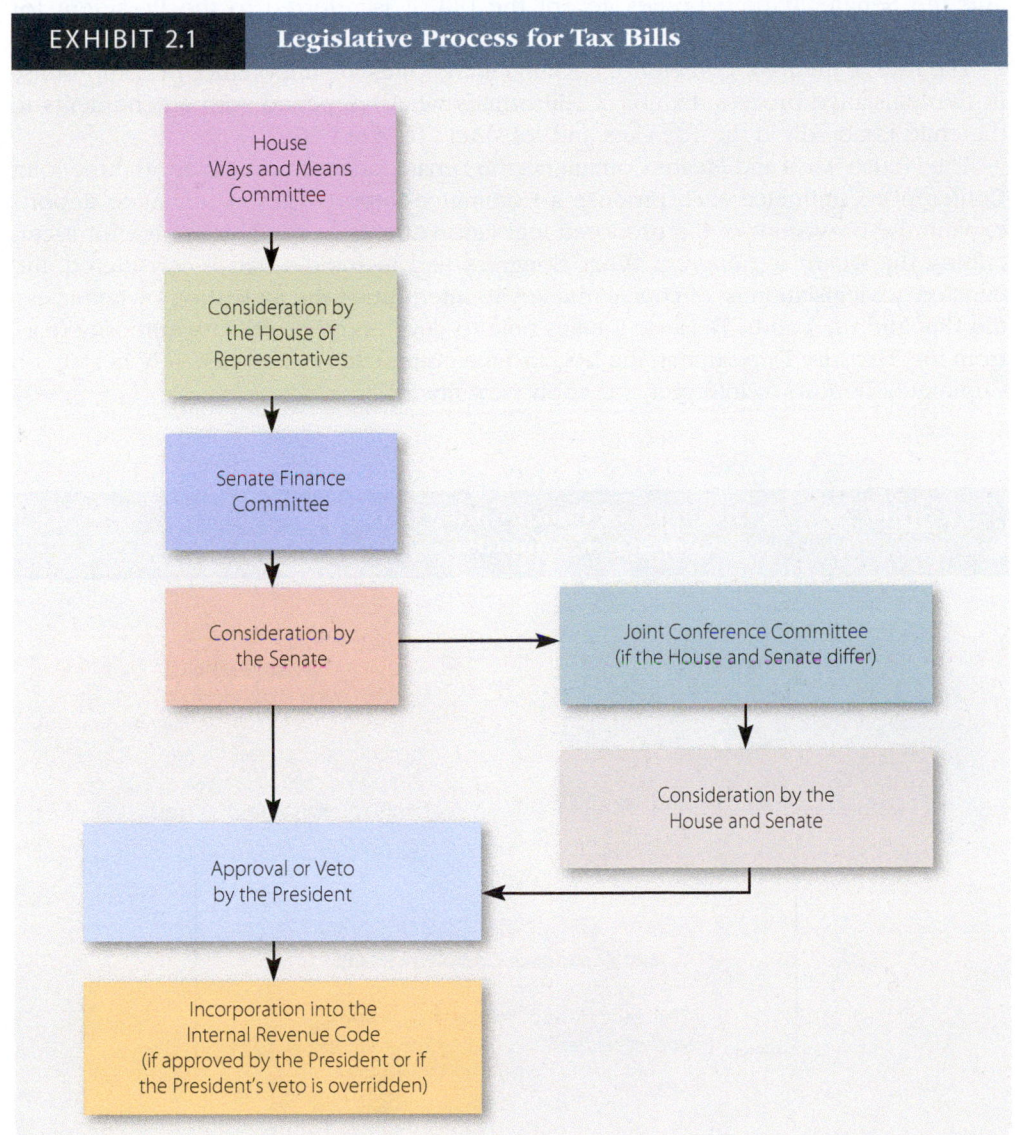

---

[3]Congress enacts tax legislation virtually every year, and each piece of legislation contains changes to the Internal Revenue Code of 1986.

[4]Although rare, a tax bill can originate in the Senate when it is attached as a rider to a different legislative proposal. The Tax Equity and Fiscal Responsibility Act of 1982 originated in the Senate, and its constitutionality was upheld by the courts.

the President's veto is overridden, the bill becomes law and part of the Internal Revenue Code of 1986.

House and Senate versions of major tax bills frequently differ. One reason bills are often changed in the Senate is that each senator has considerable latitude to make amendments when the Senate as a whole is voting on a bill referred to it by the Senate Finance Committee.[5] In contrast, the entire House of Representatives either accepts or rejects what is proposed by the House Ways and Means Committee, and changes from the floor are rare. When the Senate version of the bill differs from that passed by the House, the Joint Conference Committee, which includes members of both the House Ways and Means Committee and the Senate Finance Committee, resolves the differences. The deliberations of the Joint Conference Committee usually produce a compromise between the two versions, which then is voted on by both the House and the Senate. If both bodies accept the bill, it is referred to the President for approval or veto.

The role of the Joint Conference Committee indicates the importance of compromise in the legislative process. Exhibit 2.2 illustrates what happened with amendments to the child tax credit in the Tax Cuts and Jobs Act (TCJA) of 2017.

The House Ways and Means Committee, the Senate Finance Committee, and the Joint Conference Committee each produce a Committee Report. These Committee Reports explain the provisions of the proposed legislation and are a valuable source for ascertaining the *intent of Congress*. What Congress had in mind when it considered and enacted tax legislation is, of course, the key to interpreting the legislation by taxpayers, the IRS, and the courts. Because it takes time to develop other primary authority (e.g., from the Treasury Department, the IRS, and the courts), tax researchers rely heavily on Committee Reports to interpret and apply new tax laws.

EXHIBIT 2.2   Example of Compromise in the Joint Conference Committee

House Version
Replaces the child tax credit with an expanded family tax credit, allowing a tax credit of $1,600 per child and $300 for the taxpayer, spouse, and other dependents. Credit is partially refundable ($1,000 per child).

Senate Version
Increases the child tax credit to $2,000 per child and allows a $500 tax credit for other dependents. Increases the age limit of a qualified child by one year. Credit is partially refundable ($1,000 per child).

Joint Conference Committee Result
Increases the child tax credit to $2,000 per child and allows a $500 tax credit for other dependents. No change in the age limit of a qualified child. Credit is partially refundable ($1,400 per child).

---

[5]During the passage of the Tax Reform Act of 1986, Senate leaders tried to make the bill *amendment proof* to avoid the normal amendment process.

Arrangement of the Internal Revenue Code

The Internal Revenue Code of 1986 is found in Title 26 of the U.S. Code. In working with the Internal Revenue Code, it helps to understand the format. Here is a partial table of contents:

> Subtitle A. Income Taxes
> > Chapter 11. Normal Taxes and Surtaxes
> > > Subchapter A. Determination of Tax Liability
> > > > Part I. Tax on Individuals
> > > > > Sections 1–5
> > > > Part II. Tax on Corporations
> > > > > Sections 11–12

In referring to a provision of the Code, the *key* is usually the Section number. In citing a Section number, identifying the related Subtitle, Chapter, Subchapter, and Part is not necessary. Merely mentioning the Section is sufficient because the Section numbers run consecutively and do not begin again with each new Subtitle, Chapter, Subchapter, or Part.[6]

Tax researchers often refer to specific areas of income tax law by their Subchapters. Some of the more common Subchapter designations include Subchapter C ("Corporate Distributions and Adjustments"), Subchapter K ("Partners and Partnerships"), and Subchapter S ("Tax Treatment of S Corporations and Their Shareholders").

Citing the Code

Code Sections often are broken down into subparts.[7] Section 2(a)(1)(A) serves as an example.

Broken down by content, § 2(a)(1)(A) becomes:

Throughout the text, references to the Code Sections are in the form given above. The symbols "§" and "§§" are used in place of "Section" and "Sections," respectively. The following table summarizes the format that we use:

---

[6]When the 1954 Code was drafted, some Section numbers were intentionally omitted so that later changes could be incorporated into the Code without disrupting its organization. When Congress does not leave enough space, subsequent Code Sections are given A, B, C, etc., designations. A good example is the treatment of §§ 280A through 280H.

[7]Some Code Sections do not require subparts. See, for example, §§ 211 and 241.

[8]Some Code Sections omit the subsection designation and use the paragraph designation as the first subpart. See, for example, §§ 212(1) and 1222(1).

Complete Reference	Text Reference
Section 2(a)(1)(A) of the Internal Revenue Code of 1986	§ 2(a)(1)(A)
Sections 1 and 2 of the Internal Revenue Code of 1986	§§ 1 and 2
Section 2 of the Internal Revenue Code of 1954	§ 2 of the Internal Revenue Code of 1954
Section 12(d) of the Internal Revenue Code of 1939[9]	§ 12(d) of the Internal Revenue Code of 1939

2-1b Administrative Sources of the Tax Law

The administrative sources of the Federal tax law include Treasury Department Regulations, Revenue Rulings and Revenue Procedures, and various other administrative pronouncements (see Exhibit 2.3). All are issued by either the U.S. Treasury Department or the IRS.

Treasury Department Regulations

Regulations are issued by the U.S. Treasury Department under authority granted by Congress.[10] Interpretive by nature, they provide taxpayers with considerable guidance on the meaning and application of the Code. Regulations, which carry considerable authority as the official interpretation of tax law, may be issued in *proposed*, *temporary*, or *final* form.

Because Regulations interpret the Code, they are arranged in the same sequence as the Code. A number is added at the beginning, however, to indicate the type of tax or administrative, procedural, or definitional matter to which they relate.[11] For example,

EXHIBIT 2.3	Administrative Sources	

Source	Location	Authority
Regulations	*Federal Register*	Force and effect of law.
Temporary Regulations	*Federal Register* *Internal Revenue Bulletin* *Cumulative Bulletin**	May be cited as a precedent.
Proposed Regulations	*Federal Register* *Internal Revenue Bulletin* *Cumulative Bulletin**	Preview of Final Regulations.
Revenue Rulings Revenue Procedures Treasury Decisions Actions on Decisions	*Internal Revenue Bulletin* *Cumulative Bulletin**	Do not have the force and effect of law.
General Counsel Memoranda Technical Advice Memoranda	Tax Analysts' *Tax Notes;* Thomson Reuters *Checkpoint***; Commerce Clearing House *IntelliConnect*	May not be cited as a precedent.
Letter Rulings	Thomson Reuters and Commerce Clearing House tax services	Applicable only to taxpayer addressed. No precedential force.

*Through 2008, the contents of *Internal Revenue Bulletins* were consolidated semiannually into a *Cumulative Bulletin*. Beginning in 2009, the IRS stopped producing a *Cumulative Bulletin* because all *Internal Revenue Bulletins* are available electronically on the IRS website (**irs.gov**).

**Thomson Reuters *Checkpoint* includes a wide variety of tax resources. The most significant are materials produced by the Research Institute of America (RIA), including the *Federal Tax Coordinator 2d*.

[9]Section 12(d) of the Internal Revenue Code of 1939 is the predecessor to § 2 of the Internal Revenue Code of 1954 and the Internal Revenue Code of 1986. Keep in mind that the 1954 Code superseded the 1939 Code and the 1986 Code superseded the 1954 Code. Footnote 2 explains why references to the 1939 or 1954 Code are included.

[10]§ 7805.

[11]The prefix 20 designates estate tax Regulations, 25 covers gift tax Regulations, 31 relates to employment taxes, and 301 refers to procedure and administration.

the prefix 1 designates the Regulations under the income tax law. Thus, the Regulations under Code § 2 are cited as Reg. § 1.2, with subparts added for further identification. The numbering patterns of these subparts often have no correlation with the Code subsections.

ETHICS & EQUITY Reporting Tax Fraud

Maybe someone in your extended family is driving a luxury car and comments that only fools pay all of their taxes. Or maybe a contractor demands payment in cash. Or perhaps someone at work is not reporting all of his or her income. If cheating on taxes bothers you, the IRS wants to hear from you (and may make it worthwhile). The IRS has two whistleblower programs. The small-awards program is for situations involving less than $2 million of tax, and the award can be as high as 15% of collections, although it often is less. The large-awards program covers situations involving $2 million or more of tax. Here, the reward can go as high as 30%. The IRS's tip line is 1-800-829-0433, and the appropriate form to report tax fraud is Form 3949–A (Information Referral). Would you turn in someone?

New Regulations and changes to existing Regulations are usually issued in proposed form before they are finalized. The interval between the proposal of a Regulation and its finalization permits taxpayers and other interested parties to comment on the propriety of the proposal. **Proposed Regulations** under Code § 2, for example, are cited as Prop.Reg. § 1.2. The Tax Court indicates that Proposed Regulations carry little weight.[12] **Final Regulations** have the force and effect of law.

Sometimes the Treasury Department issues **Temporary Regulations** where immediate guidance is important. These Regulations are issued without the comment period required for Proposed Regulations. Temporary Regulations, cited as Temp.Reg. §, have the same authoritative value as Final Regulations and may be cited as precedents. However, Temporary Regulations also must be issued as Proposed Regulations and automatically expire within three years after the date of issuance.[13]

Proposed, Temporary, and Final Regulations are published in the *Federal Register*, in the *Internal Revenue Bulletin* (I.R.B.), and by major tax services. Final Regulations are issued as Treasury Decisions (TDs).

Regulations also may be classified as *legislative, interpretive,* or *procedural*. These classifications are discussed in text Section 2-3d (Assessing the Validity of Tax Law Sources) later in the chapter.

Revenue Rulings and Revenue Procedures

Revenue Rulings are official pronouncements of the National Office of the IRS.[14] They typically provide one or more examples of how the IRS would apply a law to *specific fact situations*. Like Regulations, Revenue Rulings are designed to provide interpretation of the tax law. Although they do not carry the same legal force and effect as Regulations, because they are focused on a specific fact pattern, they provide a more detailed analysis of the law.

Although letter rulings (discussed below) are not the same as Revenue Rulings, a Revenue Ruling often results from a specific taxpayer's request for a letter ruling. If the IRS believes that a letter ruling request has widespread impact, the letter ruling will be converted into a Revenue Ruling and issued. Revenue Rulings also can be issued in response to technical advice to District Offices of the IRS, court decisions, and suggestions from tax practitioner groups.

Revenue Procedures deal with the internal management practices and procedures of the IRS. For example, Rev.Proc. 2020–1 (2020–1 I.R.B. 1) provides general instructions

---

[12]*F. W. Woolworth Co.*, 54 T.C. 1233 (1970); *Harris M. Miller*, 70 T.C. 448 (1978); and *James O. Tomerlin Trust*, 87 T.C. 876 (1986).

[13]§ 7805(e).

[14]§ 7805(a).

for taxpayers requesting letter rulings or determination letters from the IRS. A taxpayer's failure to follow a Revenue Procedure can result in unnecessary delay or, in a discretionary situation, can cause the IRS to decline to act.

Both Revenue Rulings and Revenue Procedures serve an important function by providing *guidance* to IRS personnel and taxpayers in handling routine tax matters. Revenue Rulings and Revenue Procedures generally apply retroactively and are binding on the IRS until revoked or modified by subsequent rulings or procedures, Regulations, legislation, or court decisions.

Revenue Rulings and Revenue Procedures are published weekly by the U.S. Government in the *Internal Revenue Bulletin* (I.R.B.).

The proper form for citing Revenue Rulings is as follows. Revenue Procedures are cited in the same manner, except that "Rev.Proc." is substituted for "Rev.Rul."

Rev.Rul. 2019–13, 2019–20 I.R.B. 1179.

Explanation: Revenue Ruling Number 13, appearing on page 1179 of the 20th weekly issue of the *Internal Revenue Bulletin* for 2019.

Revenue Rulings and other tax resources may be found at the IRS website: **irs.gov**.[15]

Letter Rulings

Letter rulings are issued for a fee upon a taxpayer's request and describe how the IRS will treat a *proposed* transaction for tax purposes. Issued by the National Office of the IRS, they apply only to the taxpayer who asks for and obtains the ruling.[16] Letter rulings can be useful to taxpayers who want to be certain of how a transaction will be taxed before proceeding with it. Letter rulings also allow taxpayers to avoid unexpected tax costs and may be the most effective way to carry out tax planning. However, the IRS limits the issuance of individual rulings to restricted, preannounced areas of taxation.[17] The IRS issues more than 2,500 letter rulings each year.

The IRS must make individual rulings available for public inspection after identifying details are deleted.[18] Published digests of private letter rulings can be found in a variety of sources, including *IRS Letter Rulings Reports* (published by CCH), Bloomberg BNA's *Daily Tax Reports*, Tax Analysts' *Tax Notes*, and electronic (online) tax research services (such as Thomson Reuters *Checkpoint*).

Letter rulings are issued multi-digit file numbers that indicate the year and week of issuance as well as the number of the ruling during that week. For example, Ltr.Rul. 201933005 holds that a portion of the fee paid for a DNA test kit for ancestry and health testing qualifies as a deductible medical expense.

2019	33	005
Year 2019	33rd week of 2019	5th ruling issued during the 33rd week

Other Administrative Pronouncements

Treasury Decisions (TDs) are issued by the Treasury Department to announce new Regulations, amend or change existing Regulations, or announce the position of the

---

[15]Commercial sources for Revenue Rulings and Revenue Procedures are available, usually requiring a subscription fee. Older Revenue Rulings and Revenue Procedures are often cited as being published in the *Cumulative Bulletin* (C.B.) rather than in the *Internal Revenue Bulletin* (I.R.B.).

[16]Post-1984 letter rulings may be substantial authority for purposes of the accuracy-related penalty; see pp. 2-24 and 2-25; Notice 90–20, 1990–1 C.B. 328. In this regard, letter rulings differ from Revenue Rulings, which are applicable to *all* taxpayers. A letter ruling may later lead to the issuance of a Revenue Ruling if the holding affects many taxpayers. In its Internal Revenue Manual, the IRS indicates that letter rulings may be used as a

guide with other research materials in formulating a District Office position on an issue. The IRS is required to charge a taxpayer a fee for letter rulings, determination letters, etc.

[17]Rev.Proc. 2020–3, 2020–1 I.R.B. 131 contains a list of areas in which the IRS will not issue advance rulings. According to the IRS, the main reason it will not rule in certain areas is that specific fact-oriented situations are involved. Thus, a ruling may not be obtained on many of the problems that are particularly troublesome for taxpayers.

[18]§ 6110.

Government on selected court decisions. Like Revenue Rulings and Revenue Procedures, TDs are published in the *Internal Revenue Bulletin*.

The IRS also publishes other administrative communications in the *Internal Revenue Bulletin*, such as Announcements, Notices, IRs (News Releases), Internal Legal Memoranda (ILMs), Chief Counsel Notices (CC), and Prohibited Transaction Exemptions.

Like letter rulings, determination letters are issued at the request of taxpayers and provide guidance on the application of the tax law. They differ from letter rulings in that the issuing source is an IRS Area Director (rather than the National Office of the IRS). Also, determination letters usually involve *completed* (as opposed to proposed) transactions. Determination letters are not published and are made known only to the party making the request.

The following examples illustrate the distinction between letter rulings and determination letters.

Difference between Letter Rulings and Determination Letters

The shareholders of Red Corporation and Green Corporation want assurance that the consolidation of the corporations into Blue Corporation will be a nontaxable reorganization. The proper approach is to request that the National Office of the IRS issue a letter ruling concerning the income tax effect of the proposed transaction.

Chris operates a barbershop in which he employs eight barbers. To comply with the rules governing income tax and payroll tax withholdings, Chris wants to know whether the barbers working for him are employees or independent contractors. The proper procedure is to request a determination letter on their status from the appropriate Area Director.

A variety of internal memoranda that constitute the working law of the IRS also are released. These General Counsel Memoranda (GCMs), Technical Advice Memoranda (TAMs), Internal Legal Memoranda (ILMs), and Field Service Advice Memoranda (FSAs) are not officially published, and the IRS indicates that they may not be cited as precedents by taxpayers.[19] However, these working documents do explain the IRS's position on various issues.

The National Office of the IRS releases Technical Advice Memoranda (TAMs) weekly. TAMs resemble letter rulings in that they give the IRS's determination of an issue. However, they differ in several respects. Letter rulings deal with proposed transactions and are issued to taxpayers at their request. In contrast, TAMs deal with completed (rather than proposed) transactions. TAMs are issued by the National Office of the IRS in response to questions raised by taxpayers or IRS field personnel during audits. TAMs are not officially published and may not be cited or used as precedent.[20] They are assigned file numbers according to the same procedure used for letter rulings. For example, TAM 201929019 refers to the 19th TAM issued during the 29th week of 2019.

The Office of Chief Counsel prepares Field Service Advice Memoranda (FSAs) to help IRS employees. These are issued in response to requests for advice, guidance, and analysis on difficult or significant tax issues and are not binding on either the taxpayer to whom they pertain or the IRS. Some FSAs are being replaced by another form of field guidance called Technical Expedited Advice Memoranda (TEAMs). The purpose of TEAMs is to expedite legal guidance to field agents as disputes are developing. FSAs are reverting to their original purpose of case-specific development of facts.[21]

---

[19]These are made available by the publishers listed in Exhibit 2.3. These internal memoranda may be substantial authority for purposes of the accuracy-related penalty for post-1984 transactions (see pp. 2-24 and 2-25; Notice 90–20, 1990–1 C.B. 328).

[20]§ 6110(k)(3). Post-1984 TAMs may be substantial authority for purposes of avoiding the accuracy-related penalty. Notice 90–20, 1990–1 C.B. 328.

[21]A TEAM guidance differs from a TAM in several ways, including a mandatory presubmission conference involving the taxpayer. In the event of a tentatively adverse conclusion for the taxpayer or the field agent, a conference of right is offered to the taxpayer and to the field agent; once the conference of right is held, no further conferences are offered.

2-1c Judicial Sources of the Tax Law

Five Federal courts have jurisdiction over tax disputes between the IRS and taxpayers: the U.S. Tax Court, the U.S. District Court, the U.S. Court of Federal Claims, the U.S. Court of Appeals, and the U.S. Supreme Court.

The Judicial Process in General

Once a taxpayer has exhausted the remedies available within the IRS (i.e., no satisfactory settlement has been reached at the agent or at the Appeals Division level), the dispute can be taken to the Federal courts. The trial and appellate court system for Federal tax litigation is illustrated in Exhibit 2.4.

A trial court, also known as a court of original jurisdiction, initially hears the case. Appeals (either by the taxpayer or the IRS) are heard by the appropriate appellate court. A taxpayer has a choice of *three trial courts:* a U.S. District Court, the U.S. Court of Federal Claims, or the U.S. Tax Court.

The U.S. Tax Court contains a Small Cases Division that only hears cases involving amounts of $50,000 or less. The ruling of the judge is final (no appeal is available), and these rulings are not precedent for any other cases (i.e., they are not primary authority and are not citable as substantial authority). Proceedings of the Small Cases Division are informal, and because there is no requirement that a taxpayer be represented by an attorney, they can be less costly for a taxpayer (the filing fee is only $60). The typical small case lasts one to two hours, and the taxpayer only needs to tell the judge his or her story and present any supporting evidence. Special trial judges, rather than Tax Court judges, often preside over these hearings. Some of these cases can be found on the U.S. Tax Court website.

American law, following English law, is frequently *created* by judicial decisions. Under the doctrine of *stare decisis* ("let the decision stand"), each case has precedential value for future cases with the same set of facts. Judges are not required to follow judicial precedent beyond their own jurisdiction. For example, the decisions of an appellate court are binding only on the trial courts within its jurisdiction and not on other trial courts. Different appellate courts may reach different opinions about the same issue. Further, the doctrine of *precedential authority* requires a court to follow prior cases only when the issues and material facts of the current case are essentially the same as those involved in the prior decisions.

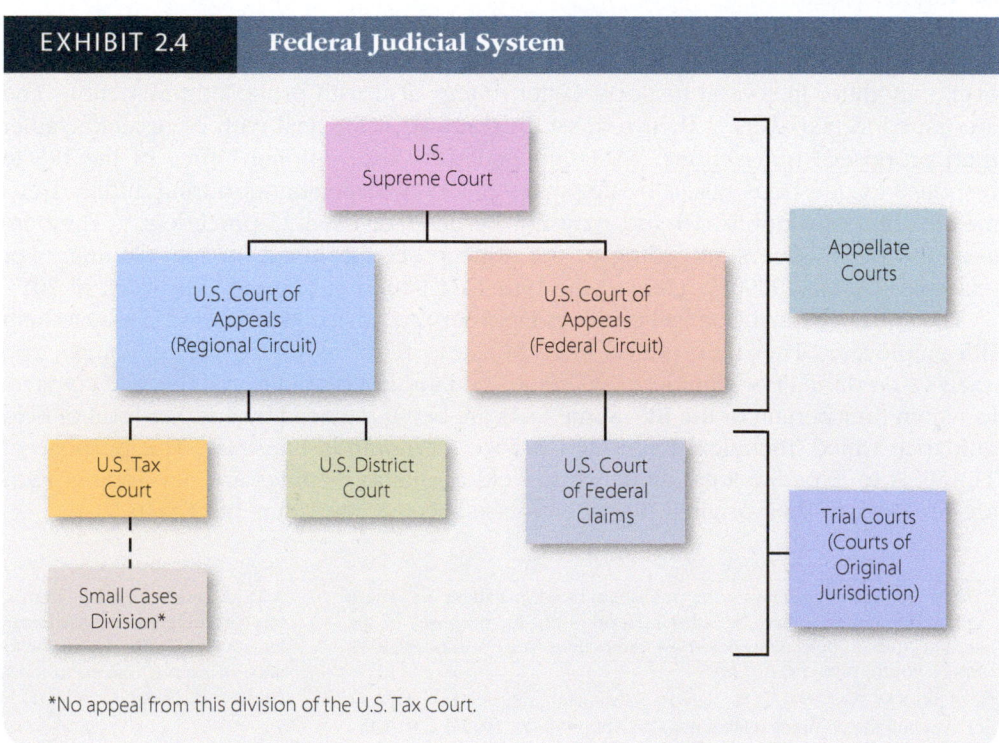

EXHIBIT 2.4   Federal Judicial System

U.S. Supreme Court

U.S. Court of Appeals (Regional Circuit)

U.S. Court of Appeals (Federal Circuit)

Appellate Courts

U.S. Tax Court

U.S. District Court

U.S. Court of Federal Claims

Trial Courts (Courts of Original Jurisdiction)

Small Cases Division*

*No appeal from this division of the U.S. Tax Court.

Most Federal and state appellate court decisions and some decisions of trial courts are published. Published court decisions are organized by jurisdiction (Federal or state) and level of court (trial or appellate).[22]

Several other terms are important to understand. The *plaintiff* is the party requesting a hearing, and the *defendant* is the party being challenged. Sometimes a court uses the terms *petitioner* and *respondent* (rather than *plaintiff* and *defendant*). At the trial court level, a taxpayer is normally the plaintiff (or petitioner), and the Government is the defendant (or respondent). If the taxpayer wins and the Government appeals, the Government becomes the petitioner (or appellant), and the taxpayer becomes the respondent.

Trial Courts

Here are some differences between the various trial courts (courts of original jurisdiction):

- *Number of courts.* There is only one Court of Federal Claims and only one Tax Court, but there are many U.S. District Courts. District Courts hear cases based on where the taxpayer lives (so a taxpayer in Atlanta would have her case heard by the Atlanta U.S. District Court).

- *Number of judges.* District Courts have a number of judges, but only one judge hears a case. The Court of Federal Claims has 16 judges, and the Tax Court has 19 regular judges. Typically, Tax Court cases are heard and decided by only one of the 19 regular judges. However, if the case is viewed as important or novel tax issues are raised, the entire Tax Court might hear the case. If a case is reviewed by the full Tax Court, such an *en banc* decision has compelling authority.

- *Location.* The Court of Federal Claims meets most often in Washington, D.C. Each state has at least one District Court, and many of the more populous states have more than one. Although the Tax Court is officially based in Washington, D.C., the various judges travel to different parts of the country and hear cases at predetermined locations and dates.

- *Jurisdiction of the Tax Court and District Courts.* The Tax Court hears only tax cases and is the most popular forum for tax cases since its judges have more tax expertise; many had careers in the IRS or Treasury Department before being appointed to the Tax Court. The District Courts hear a wide variety of nontax cases as well as tax cases. As a result, District Court judges are viewed as generalists (rather than specialists) in tax law.

- *Jurisdiction of the Court of Federal Claims.* The Court of Federal Claims has jurisdiction over any claim against the United States. As a result, the Court of Federal Claims hears nontax litigation as well as tax cases. Court of Federal Claims judges are tax law generalists. This court is viewed as a stronger option when equity is an issue (as opposed to purely technical issues) or when the case requires extensive discovery of evidence. In addition, it has a pro-business orientation.[23]

- *Jury trial.* A jury trial is available only in a District Court. However, because juries can decide only questions of fact (and not questions of law), taxpayers who choose a District Court often do not request a jury trial. In that event, the judge decides all issues in a bench trial. A District Court decision carries precedential value only in its district.

- *Payment of deficiency.* Before the Court of Federal Claims or a District Court will hear a case, the taxpayer must pay any taxes assessed by the IRS and sue for a refund. This is not the case with the Tax Court. Here, a taxpayer may request a hearing without making any payments to the IRS. As a result, whether to pay the

---

[22]A decision of a particular court is called its holding. Sometimes a decision includes *dicta*, or incidental opinions beyond the current facts. Such passing remarks, illustrations, or analogies are not essential to the current holding. Although the holding has precedential value under *stare decisis*, dicta are not binding on a future court.

[23]T. D. Peyser, "The Case for Selecting the Claims Court to Litigate a Federal Tax Liability," *Tax Executive* (Winter 1988): 149.

tax in advance (and limit further interest and penalties) or wait to pay the tax (and risk additional interest and penalties) becomes part of the decision-making process of selecting a venue.

- *Appeals.* Appeals from a District Court or a Tax Court decision are to the U.S. Court of Appeals for the circuit where the taxpayer lives. Appeals from the Court of Federal Claims go to the Court of Appeals for the Federal Circuit.

- *Bankruptcy.* When a taxpayer files a bankruptcy petition, the IRS, like other creditors, is prevented from taking action against the taxpayer. Sometimes a bankruptcy court may settle a tax claim.

- *Gray areas.* Because there are "gray areas" in the tax laws, courts may disagree as to the proper tax treatment of an item. With these differences in judicial authority, a taxpayer may have some flexibility to choose the most favorable forum to hear the case.

See Concept Summary 2.1 for a summary of various attributes of the Federal trial courts.

Concept Summary 2.1

Federal Judicial System: Trial Courts

Issue	U.S. Tax Court	U.S. District Court	U.S. Court of Federal Claims
Number of judges per court	19*	Varies	16
Payment of deficiency before trial	No	Yes	Yes
Jury trial available	No	Yes	No
Types of disputes	Tax cases only	Most criminal and civil issues	Claims against the United States
Jurisdiction	Nationwide	Location of taxpayer	Nationwide
IRS acquiescence policy	Yes	Yes	Yes
Appeal route	U.S. Court of Appeals	U.S. Court of Appeals	U.S. Court of Appeals for the Federal Circuit

*Currently, there are only 15 regular judges. They are assisted by 11 senior judges (whose terms have ended but return to hear cases as needed) and 4 special trial judges (who are appointed by the Senior Judge of the U.S. Tax Court rather than by the President) (January 2020).

Appellate Courts

A trial court decision can be appealed to the appropriate **Circuit Court of Appeals** . The 11 geographic circuits, the circuit for the District of Columbia, and the Federal Circuit[24] appear in Exhibit 2.5. Generally, a three-judge panel hears a Court of Appeals case, but occasionally the *full* court decides more controversial cases.

If the Government loses at the trial court level (District Court, Tax Court, or Court of Federal Claims), it may decide not to appeal. However, the fact that the IRS does not appeal does not mean that the IRS agrees with the result (and it may litigate similar issues in the future).

The IRS may decide not to appeal for a number of reasons. First, the IRS may decide that available personnel should be assigned to other more important cases. Second, the IRS may decide that the taxpayer has a sympathetic position or the facts are particularly strong in his or her favor. In that event, the IRS may wait to test the legal issues with a different taxpayer (who might have a weaker case). Third, the Court of Appeals jurisdiction might matter. Based on past experience and precedent, the IRS may decide that the chance for success on a particular issue might be more promising in a different Court of Appeals.

The Federal Circuit provides the taxpayer with an alternative forum. When a particular Circuit Court of Appeals has issued an adverse decision in a similar case, the taxpayer may prefer the Court of Federal Claims route because any appeal is to the Federal Circuit.

---

[24]The Court of Appeals for the Federal Circuit was created effective October 1, 1982, by P.L. 97-64 (4/2/82) to hear decisions appealed from the Claims Court (now the Court of Federal Claims).

EXHIBIT 2.5	The Federal Courts of Appeals

ADMINISTRATIVE OFFICE OF THE UNITED STATES SUPREME COURT

APRIL 1988

The Appellate Process

The *role* of the appellate court is usually limited to a review of whether the trial court applied the proper law in arriving at its decision. Rarely does an appellate court question a lower court's fact-finding determination. Both the Code and the Supreme Court indicate that Federal appellate courts are bound by findings of facts unless they are clearly erroneous.[25]

An appeal can have a number of possible outcomes. The appellate court may approve (affirm) or disapprove (reverse) the lower court's finding, or it may send the case back to the trial court for further consideration (remand). When many issues are involved, a mixed result is not unusual. Thus, the lower court may be affirmed (*aff'd*) on Issue A and reversed (*rev'd*) on Issue B and Issue C is remanded (*rem'd*) for additional fact finding.

When more than one judge is involved in the decision-making process, disagreements are common. In addition to the majority view, one or more judges may concur (agree with the result reached but not with some or all of the reasoning) or dissent (disagree with the result). In any decision, of course, the majority controls. But concurring and dissenting views can have an influence on future cases or other courts.

Appellate Precedents and the Tax Court District Courts, the Tax Court, and the Court of Federal Claims must abide by the precedents set by a Court of Appeals jurisdiction. A particular Court of Appeals need not follow the decisions of another Court of Appeals. All courts, however, must follow the decisions of the U.S. Supreme Court.

This pattern of appellate precedents raises an issue for the Tax Court. Because the Tax Court is a national court, it decides cases from all parts of the country. Under a

---

[25]§§ 7482(a) and (c). *Comm. v. Duberstein,* 60–2 USTC ¶9515, 5 AFTR 2d 1626, 80 S.Ct. 1190 (USSC, 1960). See Rule 52(a) of the Federal Rules of Civil Procedure.

policy known as the *Golsen* rule, the Tax Court decides a case as it believes the law should be applied *only* if the Court of Appeals of appropriate jurisdiction has not yet ruled on the issue or has previously affirmed the Tax Court's rationale. If the Court of Appeals has ruled on a case similar to the one being heard by the Tax Court, the Tax Court will conform to the Appeals Court decision under the *Golsen* rule even though it disagrees with the decision.[26]

Emily lives in Texas and sues in the Tax Court on Issue A. The Fifth Circuit Court of Appeals is the appropriate appellate court for Texas. The Fifth Circuit has already decided, in a case involving similar facts but a different taxpayer, that Issue A should be resolved in favor of the taxpayer. Although the Tax Court believes that the Fifth Circuit Court of Appeals is wrong, under its *Golsen* policy, the trial court will rule in favor of Emily.

Shortly thereafter, Rashad, a resident of New York, in a comparable case, sues in the Tax Court on Issue A. The Second Circuit Court of Appeals, the appellate court that would hear a Tax Court appeal from New York, has never expressed itself on Issue A. As a result, the Tax Court will decide against Rashad.

As a result, it is possible for two taxpayers, both having their cases heard by the Tax Court, to end up with opposite results merely because they live in different parts of the country.

Appeal to the U.S. Supreme Court Appeal to the U.S. Supreme Court is by ==Writ of Certiorari==. If the Court agrees to hear the case, it will grant the Writ (*Cert. granted*). Since the Supreme Court rarely hears tax cases, most often, it denies jurisdiction (*Cert. denied*). The Court usually grants certiorari to resolve a conflict among the Courts of Appeals (e.g., two or more appellate courts have assumed opposing positions on a particular issue) or where the tax issue is extremely important. The granting of a Writ of Certiorari indicates that at least four of the nine members of the Supreme Court believe that the issue is of sufficient importance to be heard by the full Court.

Judicial Citations

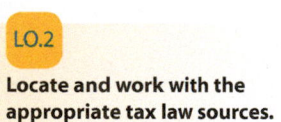

Locate and work with the appropriate tax law sources.

Court decisions are an important source of tax law, and the ability to cite and locate a case is a critical skill when working with the tax law. Judicial citations usually follow a standard pattern: case name, volume number, reporter series, page or paragraph number, court (where necessary), and year of the decision (see Concept Summary 2.2).

Judicial Citations—The U.S. Tax Court The U.S. Tax Court issues two types of decisions: Regular and Memorandum, based on the Chief Judge's determination. They differ in both substance and form. In terms of substance, *Memorandum* decisions deal with cases that involve only the application of established principles of law. *Regular* decisions involve novel issues not previously resolved by the Tax Court. In actual practice, however, both *Regular* and *Memorandum* represent the position of the Tax Court and, as such, can be relied on.[27]

The Regular and Memorandum decisions issued by the Tax Court also differ in form. Regular decisions are published by the U.S. Government in a series entitled *Tax Court of the United States Reports* (T.C.). Each volume of these *Reports* covers a six-month period (January 1 through June 30 and July 1 through December 31) and is given a succeeding volume number. Usually there is a time lag between the date a decision is rendered and the date it is published. A temporary citation may be necessary to help the researcher locate a recent Regular decision. Consider, for example, the temporary and permanent citations for *Renee Vento, et al.*, a decision filed on February 4, 2019.

---

[26]*Jack E. Golsen*, 54 T.C. 742 (1970).

[27]In contrast, U.S. Tax Court Small Cases Division Summary Opinions carry no precedential value. Summary Opinions issued after January 9, 2001, are available on the U.S. Tax Court website.

Concept Summary 2.2

Judicial Sources

Court	Location	Authority
U.S. Supreme Court	S.Ct. Series (West)	Highest authority
	U.S. Series (U.S. Gov't.)	
	L.Ed.2d (Lawyer's Co-op.)	
	AFTR (RIA)	
	USTC (CCH)	
U.S. Courts of Appeal	Federal 3d (West)	Next highest appellate court
	AFTR (RIA)	
	USTC (CCH)	
Tax Court (Regular decisions)	U.S. Gov't. Printing Office	Highest trial court*
	RIA/CCH separate services	
Tax Court (Memorandum decisions)	RIA T.C.Memo. (RIA)	Less authority than Regular T.C. decision
	TCM (CCH)	
U.S. Court of Federal Claims**	Federal Claims Reporter (West)	Similar authority as Tax Court
	AFTR (RIA)	
	USTC (CCH)	
U.S. District Courts	F.Supp.2d Series (West)	Lowest trial court
	AFTR (RIA)	
	USTC (CCH)	
Small Cases Division of Tax Court	U.S. Tax Court website***	No precedent value

*Theoretically, the Tax Court, Court of Federal Claims, and District Courts are on the same level of authority. But some people believe that because the Tax Court hears and decides tax cases from all parts of the country (i.e., a national court), its decisions may be more authoritative than a Court of Federal Claims or District Court decision.

**Before October 29, 1992, the U.S. Claims Court.

***Starting in 2001.

Temporary Citation
$\begin{cases}\textit{Renee Vento, et al.}, 152\ \text{T.C.} \underline{\quad}, \text{No. 1 (2019).} \\ \textit{Explanation:}\ \text{Page number left blank because not yet known.}\end{cases}$

Permanent Citation
$\begin{cases}\textit{Renee Vento, et al.}, 152\ \text{T.C. 1 (2019).} \\ \textit{Explanation:}\ \text{Page number now available.}\end{cases}$

Both citations tell us that the case will ultimately appear in Volume 152 of the *Tax Court of the United States Reports*. But until this volume is made available, the page number must be left blank. Instead, the temporary citation identifies the decision as being the first Regular decision issued by the Tax Court since Volume 151 ended. With this information, the decision can easily be located in the special Tax Court services published by Commerce Clearing House (CCH) and Research Institute of America (RIA). Once Volume 152 is released, the permanent citation can be substituted and the number of the case dropped. Starting in 1995, both Regular decisions and Memorandum decisions are published on the U.S. Tax Court website (**ustaxcourt.gov**). Memorandum decisions, although available on the U.S. Tax Court website, are not published by the U.S. Government.

Before 1943, the Tax Court was called the Board of Tax Appeals, and its decisions were published as the *United States Board of Tax Appeals Reports* (B.T.A.). These 47 volumes cover the period from 1924 to 1942. For example, the citation *Karl Pauli*, 11 B.T.A. 784 (1928), refers to the 11th volume of the *Board of Tax Appeals Reports*, page 784, issued in 1928.

Memorandum decisions are published by both CCH and RIA. Consider, for example, the three different ways the *Nick R. Hughes* case can be cited:

Nick R. Hughes, T.C.Memo. 2009–94
  Explanation: The 94th Memorandum decision issued by the Tax Court in 2009.

Nick R. Hughes, 97 TCM 1488
  Explanation: Page 1488 of Vol. 97 of the CCH *Tax Court Memorandum Decisions*.

Nick R. Hughes, 2009 RIA T.C.Memo. ¶2009,094
  Explanation: Paragraph 2009,094 of the RIA *T.C. Memorandum Decisions*.

Note that the third citation contains the same information as the first. Thus, ¶2009,094 indicates both the year and decision number of the case.[28]

U.S. Tax Court Summary Opinions relate to decisions of the Tax Court's Small Cases Division.[29] These opinions may not be treated as precedent for any other case. For example, *Joel H. Arseo*, filed on May 2, 2019, is cited as follows:

Joel H. Arseo, T.C. Summary Opinion 2019–8.

If the IRS loses a decision, it may indicate whether it agrees or disagrees with the results reached by the court by publishing an ==acquiescence== ("A" or "*Acq.*") or ==nonacquiescence== ("NA" or "*Nonacq.*"), respectively. Until 1991, acquiescences and non-acquiescences were published only for certain Regular decisions of the Tax Court, but the IRS expanded its acquiescence program to include other tax cases. The acquiescence or nonacquiescence is published in the *Internal Revenue Bulletin* as an *Action on Decision*. The IRS can retroactively revoke an acquiescence.

Most often, the IRS issues nonacquiescences to adverse decisions that are not appealed. In this manner, the Government indicates that it disagrees with the result reached, despite its decision not to seek review of the matter in an appellate court. A nonacquiescence provides a warning to taxpayers that a similar case cannot be settled administratively. A taxpayer will incur fees and expenses while the case moves through the IRS even though the IRS may be unwilling to litigate a fact pattern similar to a nonacquiescence decision.[30]

Judicial Citations—The U.S. District Court, Court of Federal Claims, and Courts of Appeals District Court, Court of Federal Claims, Court of Appeals, and Supreme Court decisions dealing with Federal tax matters are reported in both the CCH *U.S. Tax Cases* (USTC) and the RIA *American Federal Tax Reports* (AFTR) series. U.S. District Court decisions, dealing with *both* tax and nontax issues, also are published by West in its *Federal Supplement Second Series* (F.Supp.2d).[31] The following examples illustrate three different ways of citing a District Court case:

Turner v. U.S., 2004–1 USTC ¶60,478 (D.Ct. Tex., 2004).
  Explanation: Reported in the first volume of the *U.S. Tax Cases*, published by Commerce Clearing House, for calendar year 2004 (2004–1) and located at paragraph 60,478 (¶60,478).

Turner v. U.S., 93 AFTR 2d 2004–686 (D.Ct. Tex., 2004).
  Explanation: Reported in the 93rd volume of the second series of the *American Federal Tax Reports* (AFTR 2d), published by RIA, and beginning on page 686.

Turner v. U.S., 306 F.Supp.2d 668 (D.Ct. Tex., 2004).
  Explanation: Reported in the 306th volume of the *Federal Supplement Second Series* (F.Supp.2d), published by West, and beginning on page 668.

---

[28]In this text, the RIA citation for Memorandum decisions of the U.S. Tax Court is omitted. Thus, *Nick R. Hughes* is cited as 97 TCM 1488, T.C. Memo. 2009–94.

[29]In 2005, the U.S. Supreme Court held that decisions of the Small Cases Division must be made public.

[30]G. W. Carter, "Nonacquiescence: Winning by Losing," *Tax Notes* (September 19, 1988): 1301–1307.

[31]Cases prior to 1999 are found in West's *Federal Supplement Series* (F.Supp.).

The case name, the reference to the U.S. District Court of Texas (D.Ct. Tex.), and the year the decision was rendered (2004) appear in each of the citations.[32]

Decisions of the Court of Federal Claims[33] and the Courts of Appeals are published in the USTCs, the AFTRs, and two West reporters. The *Federal Third Series* (F.3d) reports Courts of Appeals decisions, whereas the *Federal Claims Reporter* (abbreviated as Fed.Cl.) reports Court of Federal Claims decisions.[34] The following examples illustrate the different forms:

Estate of Gribauskas v. Comm.   (CA–2, 2003)

- 2003–2 USTC ¶60,466 (CCH citation)
- 92 AFTR 2d 2003–5914 (RIA citation)
- 342 F.3d 85 (West citation)

Apollo Computer, Inc. v. U.S.   (Fed.Cl., 1994)

- 95–1 USTC ¶50,015 (CCH citation)
- 74 AFTR 2d 94–7172 (RIA citation)
- 32 Fed.Cl. 334 (West citation)

Estate of Gribauskas v. Comm. is a decision rendered by the Second Circuit Court of Appeals in 2003 (CA–2, 2003), and *Apollo Computer, Inc.,* was issued by the Court of Federal Claims in 1994 (Fed.Cl., 1994).

Judicial Citations—The U.S. Supreme Court Supreme Court decisions are published by CCH in the USTCs and by RIA in the AFTRs. The U.S. Government Printing Office also publishes these decisions in the *United States Supreme Court Reports* (U.S.), as does West in its *Supreme Court Reporter* (S.Ct.), and the Lawyer's Co-operative Publishing Company in its *United States Reports, Lawyer's Edition* (L.Ed.). The following illustrates the different ways the same decision can be cited:

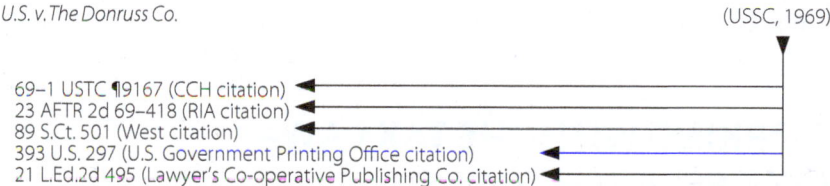

U.S. v. The Donruss Co.   (USSC, 1969)

- 69–1 USTC ¶9167 (CCH citation)
- 23 AFTR 2d 69–418 (RIA citation)
- 89 S.Ct. 501 (West citation)
- 393 U.S. 297 (U.S. Government Printing Office citation)
- 21 L.Ed.2d 495 (Lawyer's Co-operative Publishing Co. citation)

The parenthetical reference (USSC, 1969) identifies the decision as having been rendered by the U.S. Supreme Court in 1969. In this text, Supreme Court decision citations are limited to the CCH (USTC), RIA (AFTR), and West (S.Ct.) versions.

2-1d Other Sources of the Tax Law

Other sources of tax information that a tax professional may need to consult include tax treaties and tax periodicals.

Tax Treaties

The United States signs certain tax treaties (sometimes called tax conventions) with foreign countries to assist in tax enforcement and to avoid double taxation. Since 1988, when there is a direct conflict between the Code and a treaty, the most recent item takes precedence. A taxpayer must disclose on the tax return any position where a treaty overrides a tax law.[35]

---

[32]In this text, the case is cited in the following form: *Turner v. U.S.,* 2004–1 USTC ¶60,478, 93 AFTR 2d 2004–686, 306 F.Supp.2d 668 (D.Ct. Tex., 2004).

[33]Before October 29, 1992, the Court of Federal Claims was called the Claims Court. Before October 1, 1982, the Court of Federal Claims was called the Court of Claims.

[34]West's *Federal Second Series* (F.2d) contains cases prior to 1994. Beginning in October 1982, the Court of Federal Claims decisions were published in a different West reporter called the *Claims Court Reporter* (abbreviated Cl.Ct.).

[35]§ 7852(d); there is a $1,000 penalty per failure to disclose for individuals and a $10,000 per failure penalty for corporations. See Reg. §§ 301.6114–1, 301.6712–1, and 301.7701(b)(7).

Tax Periodicals

The use of tax periodicals can often shorten the research time needed to resolve a tax issue. An article relevant to the issue at hand may provide the references needed to locate the primary sources of the tax law that apply (e.g., citations to judicial decisions, Regulations, and other IRS pronouncements).

Several indexes are available for locating tax articles, including CCH's *Federal Tax Articles* (which includes a subject index, a Code Section number index, and an author's index) and the *Index to Federal Tax Articles* (published by Thomson Reuters). Both of these indexes are available by subscription.

Here are some of the more useful tax periodicals:

Journal of Taxation
Journal of International Taxation
Practical Tax Strategies
Estate Planning
Corporate Taxation
Business Entities
Taxation of Exempts
Real Estate Taxation
ria.thomsonreuters.com/
journals

The Tax Executive
tei.org

The Tax Adviser
thetaxadviser.com

Tax Law Review
law.nyu.edu/tax/taxlawreview/

Journal of the American Taxation Association
aaajournals.org/loi/atax

The ATA Journal of Legal Tax Research
aaajournals.org/loi/jltr

Oil, Gas & Energy Quarterly
bus.lsu.edu/accounting/faculty/
lcrumbley/oilgas.html

Trusts and Estates
wealthmanagement.com/
trusts-estates

Journal of Passthrough Entities
TAXES—The Tax Magazine
taxna.wolterskluwer.com

Tax Notes
taxnotes.com

Develop an awareness of tax research tools.

2-2 WORKING WITH THE TAX LAW— TAX RESEARCH TOOLS

Tax law consists of a body of legislative (e.g., Code Sections and tax treaties), administrative (e.g., Regulations and Rulings), and judicial (e.g., court cases) pronouncements. Working with the tax law requires being able to locate and use these sources effectively. A major consideration is the time required to find relevant information related to the issues identified.

Unless the problem is simple (e.g., the Code Section is known and there is a Regulation on point), the research process begins with a tax service.

2-2a Commercial Tax Services

In the past, commercial tax services could be classified as *annotated* (i.e., organized by Internal Revenue Code) or *topical* (i.e., organized by major topics). However, as tax research has become electronic, this classification system is no longer appropriate. For example, Thomson Reuters *Checkpoint* includes both the *Federal Tax Coordinator 2d* (topical) and the *United States Tax Reporter* (annotated).

Here is a partial list of the available commercial tax services:

- *Standard Federal Tax Reporter*, Commerce Clearing House.

- *CCH IntelliConnect*, Commerce Clearing House—the online version of the *Standard Federal Tax Reporter* (along with other CCH materials).

- *United States Tax Reporter*, Research Institute of America, Thomson Reuters.

- Thomson Reuters *Checkpoint*, Research Institute of America—the online versions of RIA's *Federal Tax Coordinator 2d* and *United States Tax Reporter*.

- *Practical Tax Expert*, CCH/Wolters Kluwer.
- *Tax Management Portfolios*, Bloomberg BNA.
- *Mertens Law of Federal Income Taxation*, Thomson Reuters.
- Thomson Reuters *Westlaw* and *WestlawNext*—compilations include access to *Tax Management Portfolios*, *Federal Tax Coordinator 2d*, and *Mertens*.
- LexisNexis *TaxCenter*—a compilation of primary sources and various materials taken from CCH, Matthew Bender, Kleinrock, and Bloomberg BNA.

2-2b Using Electronic (Online) Tax Services

A competent tax professional must become familiar and proficient with electronic research services and be able to use them to complete research projects efficiently. Following certain general procedures can simplify the research process. The following suggestions may be helpful:[36]

- Carefully choose keywords for the search. Words with a broad usage, such as *income*, are of limited value. If the researcher is interested in a specific type of dividend income, the search phrase *dividend income* is too broad because it finds a variety of topics including stock dividends, constructive dividends, and liquidating dividends (drawing about 2,000 hits in Thomson Reuters *Checkpoint*). Searching for *qualified dividend income* obtains 728 items, whereas *stock dividend income* obtains 100 items, *cash dividend income* finds 89 items, and *property dividend income* finds 20 items.
- Take advantage of *connectors* such as "+" and quotation marks to place parameters on the search and further restrict the output. Although each tax service has its own set of connectors, many are similar. Thus, quotation marks around a phrase mean "exact phrase" in both Thomson Reuters *Checkpoint* and CCH *IntelliConnect* (e.g., "personal service corporation").
- Be selective in choosing the data to search. For example, if the research project does not involve case law, do not include judicial decisions in the search.
- Use a table of contents, an index, or a citation when appropriate. Although the keyword approach is most frequently used, electronic databases can be searched in other ways. Using the table of contents or index may narrow the information that needs to be examined. Tax law (including annotations) also can be accessed by a citation: statutory (e.g., Code Section), administrative (e.g., Rev.Rul.), or judicial (e.g., Tax Court).

2-2c Noncommercial Electronic (Online) Tax Services

The internet provides a wealth of tax information in several popular forms, sometimes at no cost to the researcher. A tax professional can access a significant amount of information that can assist in the research process.

- *Websites* are provided by accounting and consulting firms, publishers, tax academics, libraries, and governmental bodies as a means of making information widely available. One of the best sites available to the tax professional is the Internal Revenue Service's home page, illustrated in Exhibit 2.6. This site offers downloadable forms and instructions, interpretations of Regulations, and news update items. Exhibit 2.7 lists some of the websites that may be most useful to tax researchers. Particularly useful is the directory at **taxsites.com**, which provides links to accounting and tax sources (including international, state, and payroll tax sources).

---

[36]For a more complete discussion of the use of Thomson Reuters *Checkpoint* and CCH *IntelliConnect* and internet research in taxation, see Sawyer and Gill, *Federal Tax Research*, 11th ed. (Cengage Learning, 2018), Chapters 6 and 7.

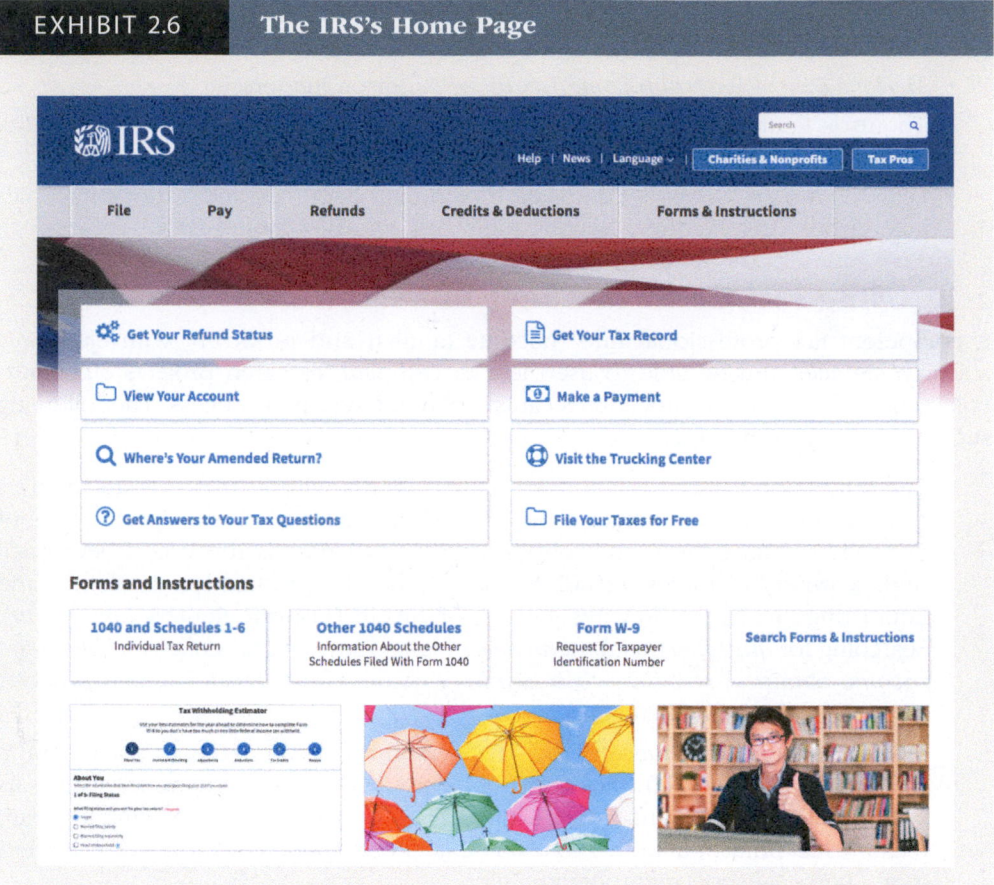

EXHIBIT 2.6   The IRS's Home Page

- *Blogs and RSS sites* provide a means by which information related to the tax law can be exchanged among taxpayers, tax professionals, and others who subscribe to the group's services. Individuals can read the exchanges and offer replies and suggestions to inquiries. Discussions address the interpretation and application of existing law, analysis of proposals and new pronouncements, and reviews of tax software.

Although tax information on the internet is plentiful, information in the public domain should not be relied upon without referring to other sources. Anyone can set up a website, and the quality of the information can be difficult for a tax professional to ascertain.

LO.4

Describe the tax research process.

2-3 WORKING WITH THE TAX LAW— TAX RESEARCH

Tax research is the process of finding a competent and professional conclusion to a tax problem. The problem may originate from completed or proposed transactions. In the case of a completed transaction, the objective of the research is to determine the tax result of what has already taken place. For example, is a taxpayer expense deductible? When dealing with proposed transactions, tax research has a different objective: effective tax planning by determining the tax consequences of various alternatives. A large part of a tax professional's career is spent on this type of tax research.

EXHIBIT 2.7	Tax-Related Websites

Website	Web Address	Description
Accounting firms and professional organizations	For instance, the AICPA's page is at **aicpa.org**, Ernst & Young is at **ey.com**, and KPMG is at **kpmg.com**	Tax planning newsletters, descriptions of services offered and career opportunities, and exchange of data with clients and subscribers
Cengage Learning	**cengage.com**	Informational updates, newsletters, support materials for students and adopters, and continuing education
Commercial tax publishers	For instance, **taxnotes.com**, **taxna.wolterskluwer.com**, **tax.thomsonreuters.com**, and **bna.com**	Information about products and services available for subscription and newsletter excerpts
Court opinions	The site at **law.justia.com** covers state, Federal, and Supreme Court decisions (but not Tax Court)	A synopsis of results reached by the court
Internal Revenue Service	**irs.gov**	News releases, downloadable forms and instructions, tables, Circular 230, and e-mail
Tax Almanac	**taxalmanac.org**	Smorgasbord of tax research resources
Tax Analysts	**taxanalysts.org**	Policy-oriented readings on the tax law and proposals to change it, moderated bulletins on various tax subjects
Tax Foundation	**taxfoundation.org**	Nonprofit educational organization that promotes sound tax policy and measures tax burdens
Tax laws online	Regulations are at **law.cornell.edu/cfr**, and the Code is at **uscode.house.gov** and **law.cornell.edu/uscode**	
Tax Sites Directory	**taxsites.com**	References and links to tax sites on the internet, including state and Federal tax sites, academic and professional pages, tax forms, and software
U.S. Tax Court decisions	**ustaxcourt.gov**	Recent U.S. Tax Court decisions

Caution: Web addresses change frequently.

Tax research involves the following steps:

- Identifying and refining the problem.
- Locating the appropriate tax law sources.
- Assessing the validity of the tax law sources.
- Arriving at the solution or at alternative solutions (including consideration of nontax factors).
- Effectively communicating the solution to the taxpayer.
- Updating the solution (where appropriate) in light of new developments.

The tax research process is illustrated in Exhibit 2.8. The broken lines reflect the steps of particular interest when tax research is directed toward proposed, rather than completed, transactions.

EXHIBIT 2.8	**Tax Research Process**

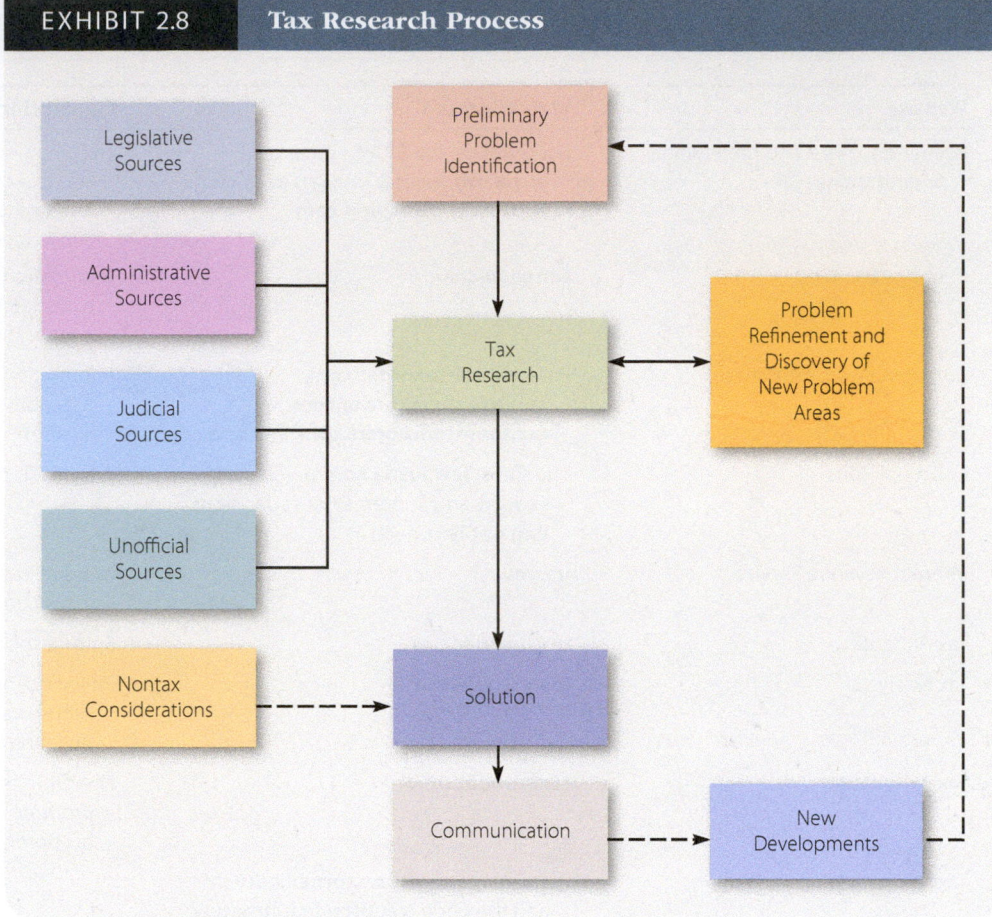

2-3a Identifying the Problem

Problem identification starts by documenting the relevant facts involved with the issue.[37] *All* of the facts that may have a bearing on the problem must be gathered; if any facts are omitted, the solution provided will likely change. To illustrate, return to the facts of *The Big Picture* on p. 2-1 and consider the tax implications of the gold coins discovered by Fred and Megan Martel.

2-3b Refining the Problem

In the facts of *The Big Picture* on p. 2-1, the question of the tax implications of the Martels' discovery can be determined with some basic research. Internal Revenue Code § 61 defines gross income as "all income from whatever source derived."[38] Further, Treasury Regulation § 1.61–14(a) states that "a treasure trove, to the extent of its value in United States currency, constitutes gross income for the taxable year in which it is reduced to undisputed possession."

Given that the Martels discovered the coins on their property in March 2020 and the state returned the coins to them in October 2020 ("undisputed possession"), their gross income in 2020 will include the "value in United States currency" of the coins. The question of "value" is key to the Martels' situation.

---

[37]For an excellent discussion of the critical role of facts in carrying out tax research, see Gardner, Stewart, and Worsham, *Tax Research Techniques*, 10th ed. (New York: The American Institute of Certified Public Accountants, 2017), Chapter 2.

[38]See the related discussion in Chapter 3.

2-3c Locating the Appropriate Tax Law Sources

Once a problem is clearly defined, what is the next step? Although the next step is a matter of individual judgment, most tax research begins with a keyword search using an electronic tax service. If the problem is not complex, the researcher may turn directly to the Internal Revenue Code and Treasury Regulations. The Code and Regulations are accessible electronically (and also available in print from a number of publishers).[39]

2-3d Assessing the Validity of Tax Law Sources

Once a source has been located, the next step is to assess it in light of the problem at hand. Proper assessment involves careful interpretation of the tax law with consideration given to its relevance and validity. In connection with validity, an important step is to check for recent changes in the tax law.

Interpreting the Internal Revenue Code

The language of the Code can be extremely difficult to comprehend. Some of this difficulty is due to its structure (the Code follows the structure of all U.S. law), so getting used to reading (and interpreting) the Code can take time.

The Code must be read carefully for restrictive language such as "*at least* 80 percent" and "*more than* 80 percent" or "*less than* 50 percent" and "*exceeds* 50 percent." Whether two or more clauses are connected by *or* or by *and* makes a great deal of difference.

Sometimes the Code directs the researcher elsewhere for the answer. For example, § 162(c) refers to the Foreign Corrupt Practices Act for purposes of determining when payments to foreign officials are deductible.

Definitions vary from one Code Section to another. For example, § 267 disallows losses between related parties. Brothers and sisters are included in this definition of related parties. This is not the case with § 318, which deals with the definition of related parties for certain stock redemptions. Research has shown that in one-third of the conflicts reaching the Tax Court, the court could not discern the intent of Congress by simply reading the statute (the Court had to look to Committee Reports to understand intent).[40]

If an answer is not in the Code, it may be necessary to look to other tax law, including Regulations and judicial decisions.

Assessing the Validity of a Treasury Regulation

Treasury Regulations are the official interpretation of the Code and are entitled to great deference. Occasionally, however, a court invalidates a Regulation (or a portion of it) because the Regulation is contrary to the intent of Congress. Usually, courts do not question the validity of Regulations. Courts believe that "the first administrative interpretation of a provision as it appears in a new act often expresses the general understanding of the times or the actual understanding of those who played an important part when the statute was drafted."[41]

Keep the following things in mind when you assess the validity of a Regulation:

- IRS agents must give the Code and any related Regulations equal weight when dealing with taxpayers and their representatives.

- Proposed Regulations provide a preview of future Final Regulations, but they are not binding on the IRS or taxpayers.

- Taxpayers have the burden of proof to show that a Regulation varies from the language of the statute and is not supported by the related Committee Reports.

---

[39]The Internal Revenue Service provides a gateway to the Internal Revenue Code, Treasury Department Regulations, and other items at **irs.gov/ tax-professionals/tax-code-regulations-and-official-guidance**.

[40]T. L. Kirkpatrick and W. B. Pollard, "Reliance by the Tax Court on the Legislative Intent of Congress," *The Tax Executive* (Summer 1986): 358–359.

[41]*Augustus v. Comm.*, 41–1 USTC ¶9255, 26 AFTR 612, 118 F.2d 38 (CA–6, 1941).

- If the taxpayer challenges a Regulation and loses, a 20 percent negligence penalty may apply.[42]

- Final Regulations can be classified as procedural, interpretive, or legislative. <mark>Procedural Regulations</mark> are *housekeeping-type instructions* indicating information that taxpayers should provide the IRS, as well as information about the internal management and conduct of the IRS itself.

- Some <mark>interpretive Regulations</mark> rephrase or elaborate what Congress stated in the Committee Reports that were issued when the tax legislation was enacted. These Regulations are almost impossible to overturn because they clearly reflect the intent of Congress. Historically, an interpretive Regulation has been given less deference than a legislative Regulation.[43] The Supreme Court has told lower courts to analyze Treasury Regulations carefully before accepting the Treasury's interpretation.[44]

- In some Code Sections, Congress has given the *Treasury Secretary or his delegate* the authority to prescribe Regulations to carry out the details of administration or to otherwise complete the operating rules. In these cases, Congress is delegating its legislative powers to the Treasury Department. Regulations issued under this type of authority possess the force and effect of law and are often called <mark>legislative Regulations</mark>.

- Courts tend to apply a legislative reenactment doctrine. A particular Regulation is assumed to have received congressional approval if the Regulation was finalized many years earlier and Congress has not amended the related Code Section.

Assessing the Validity of Other Administrative Sources of the Tax Law

Revenue Rulings issued by the IRS carry less weight than Treasury Department Regulations. Revenue Rulings are important, however, in that they reflect the position of the IRS on tax matters. IRS agents will follow the results reached in a Revenue Ruling that relates to the research question (or the tax return). A 1986 Tax Court decision, however, indicated that Revenue Rulings "typically do not constitute substantive authority for a position."[45] Most Revenue Rulings apply retroactively unless the ruling indicates otherwise.[46]

Actions on Decisions document the IRS's reaction to certain court decisions. The IRS follows a practice of either acquiescing (agreeing) or nonacquiescing (not agreeing) with selected judicial decisions.

Assessing the Validity of Judicial Sources of the Tax Law

How much reliance can be placed on a particular decision depends on the following variables:

- *The level of court.* A decision rendered by a trial court (e.g., a U.S. District Court) carries less weight than one issued by an appellate court (e.g., the Fifth Circuit Court of Appeals). Unless Congress changes the Code, decisions by the U.S. Supreme Court represent the last word on any tax issue.

- *Residence of the taxpayer.* A decision of the appellate court in the taxpayer's circuit carries more weight than one rendered by an appellate court in a different circuit. If, for example, a taxpayer lives in Texas, a decision of the Fifth Circuit Court of Appeals (which would hear an appeal from a Texas trial court) means more than one rendered by the Second Circuit Court of Appeals.[47]

---

[42]§§ 6662(a) and (b)(1). This accuracy-related penalty applies to any failure to make a reasonable attempt to comply with the tax law and any disregard of rules and Regulations [§ 6662(c)]. The term *reasonable* is not defined in the Code; the IRS looks at all of the facts and circumstances surrounding the effort of the taxpayer to report the correct tax liability.

[43]However, see *Mayo Foundation for Medical Education and Research*, 2011–1 USTC ¶50,143, 107 AFTR 2d 2011–341, 103 S.Ct. 704 (USSC, 2011), where the Supreme Court provided greater deference to interpretive Regulations (and appeared to blur the line between legislative and interpretive Regulations).

[44]*U.S. v. Vogel Fertilizer Co.*, 82–1 USTC ¶9134, 49 AFTR 2d 82–491, 102 S.Ct. 821 (USSC, 1982); *National Muffler Dealers Assn., Inc.*, 79–1 USTC ¶9264, 43 AFTR 2d 79–828, 99 S.Ct. 1304 (USSC, 1979).

[45]*Nelda C. Stark*, 86 T.C. 243 (1986). See also *Ann R. Neuhoff*, 75 T.C. 36 (1980). For a different opinion, however, see *Industrial Valley Bank & Trust Co.*, 66 T.C. 272 (1976).

[46]Rev.Proc. 87–1, 1987–1 C.B. 503.

[47]Before October 1, 1982, an appeal from the then-named U.S. Court of Claims (the other trial court) was directly to the U.S. Supreme Court.

- *Regular or Memorandum decision.* A Tax Court Regular decision carries more weight than a Memorandum decision because the Tax Court does not consider Memorandum decisions to be binding precedents.[48] A Tax Court *reviewed* decision (where *all* of the Tax Court judges participate) carries even more weight.

- *Supreme Court certiorari.* A Circuit Court decision where *certiorari* has been requested and denied by the U.S. Supreme Court carries more weight than a Circuit Court decision that was not appealed. A Circuit Court decision heard *en banc* (all of the judges participate) carries more weight than a normal Circuit Court case.

- *Other courts' support.* A decision that is supported by cases from other courts carries more weight than a decision that is not supported by other cases.

- *Status on appeal.* The weight of a decision also can be affected by its status on appeal. For example, was the decision affirmed or overruled?

In connection with the last three variables, the use of a citator is invaluable to tax research.[49] A citator provides the history of a case, including the authority relied on (e.g., other judicial decisions) in reaching the result. Reviewing the references listed in the citator discloses whether the decision was appealed and, if so, with what result (e.g., affirmed, reversed, or remanded). This tool also shows other cases with the same or similar issues and how they were decided. As a result, a citator reflects on the validity of a case and may lead to other relevant judicial material.[50] If one intends to rely on a judicial decision, "citating" the case is imperative.

Assessing the Validity of Other Sources

Primary sources of tax law include the Constitution, legislative history materials, statutes, treaties, Treasury Regulations, IRS pronouncements, and judicial decisions. The IRS considers only primary sources to constitute substantial authority. However, reference to *secondary sources* such as legal periodicals, treatises, legal opinions, IRS publications, and other materials can be useful. In general, secondary sources are not authority.

Although the statement that the IRS regards only primary sources as substantial authority generally is true, there is one exception. For purposes of the accuracy-related penalty in § 6662, the IRS expands the list of substantial authority to include a number of secondary sources (e.g., letter rulings, General Counsel Memoranda, and the Bluebook).[51] "Authority" does not include conclusions reached in treatises, legal periodicals, and opinions rendered by tax professionals.

A letter ruling or determination letter is substantial authority *only* for the taxpayer to whom it is issued, except for the accuracy-related penalty.

Once major tax legislation is completed, the staff of the Joint Committee on Taxation (in consultation with the staffs of the House Ways and Means and Senate Finance Committees) often prepares a General Explanation of the Act, commonly known as the Bluebook (because of the color of its cover). The IRS does not accept this detailed explanation as having legal effect, except for the accuracy-related penalty. The Bluebook does, however, provide valuable guidance to tax advisers and taxpayers until Regulations are issued.

2-3e Arriving at the Solution or at Alternative Solutions

The Big Picture on p. 2-1 raises the question of how a "treasure trove" should be taxed. Based on Reg. § 1.61–14(a), the Martels must include in their gross income the "value in United States currency" of the coins once they have "undisputed possession" of the coins.

Does it make any difference that the couple paid $195,000 for the land where the coins were buried? Since the taxpayers found the gold coins on their own property, they could argue that they purchased the coins when they purchased the land. This argument is similar to an individual discovering oil or natural gas on her property. And with

---

[48]*Severino R. Nico, Jr.,* 67 T.C. 647 (1977).
[49]The major citators are published by CCH, RIA, Westlaw, and Shepard's.
[50]The CCH citator is available online through the CCH *IntelliConnect* service; RIA's citator can be found in Thomson Reuters *Checkpoint.* Westlaw's citator (KeyCite) is part of its online service. Shepard's citator is part of LexisNexis.
[51]Notice 90–20, 1990–1 C.B. 328; see also Reg. § 1.6661–3(b)(2).

FINANCIAL DISCLOSURE INSIGHTS Where Does GAAP Come From?

Tax law is developed by many entities, including Congress, and the legislators of other countries, the courts, and the IRS. Accounting principles also have many sources. Consequently, in reconciling the tax and financial accounting reporting of a transaction, the tax professional needs to know the hierarchy of authority of accounting principles—in particular, the level of importance to assign to a specific GAAP document. The diagram below presents the sources of GAAP arranged in a general order of authority from highest to lowest.

Professional research is conducted to find and analyze the sources of accounting reporting standards in much the same way a tax professional conducts research on an open tax question. In fact, many of the publishers that provide tax research materials also can be used to find GAAP and International Financial Reporting Standards (IFRS) documents. The Financial Accounting Standards Board (FASB) also makes its standards and interpretations available by subscription.

Highest Authority
- Financial Accounting Standards and Interpretations of the FASB.
- Pronouncements of bodies that preceded the FASB, such as the Accounting Principles Board (APB).

- FASB Technical Bulletins.
- Audit and Accounting Guides, prepared by the American Institute of CPAs (AICPA) and cleared by the FASB.
- Practice Bulletins, prepared by the American Institute of CPAs (AICPA) and cleared by the FASB.

- Interpretation Guides of the FASB Staff.
- Accounting Interpretations of the AICPA.
- IASB Accounting Standards.
- FASB Concepts Standards.
- Widely accepted accounting practices, professional journals, accounting textbooks, and treatises.

natural resources, there must be a realization event (e.g., a sale or exchange) before there is income. Would this notion work for this couple? Unfortunately, no. A decision affirmed by the Sixth Circuit Court of Appeals indicates that the *entire value* of the couple's discovery would be included in their income in the year of discovery.[52] In *Cesarini*, the taxpayer purchased a piano that happened to conceal cash. The courts allocated the entire purchase price to the piano, so the "windfall" currency was wholly taxable in the year of discovery. Although the Martels might want to argue that there is no "income" until the coins are sold (i.e., the coins have a zero basis on discovery), Reg. § 1.61–14(a) and *Cesarini* indicate that the treasure trove's value should be included in gross income as soon as the couple has "undisputed possession."

Finally, the "value" is *not* the $28,000 face value of the coins. Rather, it is the *fair market* value of the coins. But how does one *value* the coins? It will likely depend on the appraisal of the coins (and, as you might suspect, there could be differences in appraisals). If the Martels sell any of the coins, they could argue that the best "value" would be the sales price of the coins. But an appraisal will be required to determine the fair market value of the coins, and this amount must be included in the Martels' 2020 gross income.[53]

LO.5

Communicate the results of the tax research process in a client letter and a tax file memorandum.

2-3f **Communicating Tax Research**

Once the research process has been completed, the researcher will need to prepare a memo, a letter, or an oral presentation. The form of communication depends on a number of factors. For example, most firms document the results of a tax research project in a memorandum. Although the format of this memorandum can vary, certain

---

[52]*Cesarini v. U.S.*, 69–1 USTC ¶9270, 23 AFTR 2d 69–997, 296 F.Supp. 3 (D.Ct. N.Oh., 1969), *aff'd* 70–2 USTC ¶9509, 26 AFTR 2d 70–5107, 428 F.2d 812 (CA–6, 1970).

[53]This *Big Picture* example is based on a 2013 discovery made in California; see **en.wikipedia.org/wiki/Saddle_Ridge_Hoard**. For more detail on the tax implications of this discovery, see M. Morris, C. Cheng, and

D. L. Crumbley, "The Saddle Ridge Gold Coin Discovery: How the U.S. Should Tax U.S. Currency Under the Treasure Trove Regulations," *Houston Business and Tax Law Journal*, Vol. 17, Issue 2 (2017), pp. 120–145.

elements appear in all memos. In addition, virtually all memos are reviewed by senior tax professionals to ensure accuracy.

How are results communicated to the client (does the client receive the tax research memo, a letter, or some other form of communication)? If an oral presentation is required, who will be the audience? Whatever form it takes, the following elements will be part of the communication:

- A clear statement of the issue.
- In more complex situations, a short review of the facts that raised the issue.
- A review of the relevant tax law sources (e.g., Code, Regulations, Revenue Rulings, and judicial authority).
- Any assumptions made in arriving at the solution.
- The solution recommended and the logic or reasoning supporting it.
- The references consulted in the research process.

A good tax research communication should tell the audience what was researched, the results of that research, and the justification for any recommendations.[54]

Exhibits 2.9 and 2.10 present the tax file memorandum (internal to the firm) and the client letter associated with the facts of *The Big Picture*.

EXHIBIT 2.9	Tax File Memorandum

November 11, 2020

TAX FILE MEMORANDUM

FROM: John J. Jones
SUBJECT: Fred and Megan Martel
          Income from Coin Discovery

Today I met with Fred and Megan Martel related to a request for tax assistance. In 2015, the Martels purchased 40 acres of land for $195,000; they built their current residence on the property in 2016. In March 2020, while walking on a remote part of their property, they spotted something shiny on the ground. They started digging and eventually unearthed eight metal cans containing more than 1,400 rare gold coins in $5, $10, and $20 denominations dated from 1846 to 1895. The face value of the gold coins is about $28,000, and the coins are in mint condition. As required by state law, the Martels turned over the coins to the state for disposition. For a period of six months, the state was required to publicize the find and ask if anyone could prove ownership. When no one came forward, the coins were returned to the Martels in October 2020.

ISSUE: What are the tax implications of the Martels' coin discovery?

FINDINGS: Internal Revenue Code § 61 defines gross income as "all income from whatever source derived." Further, Treasury Regulation § 1.61–14(a) states that "a treasure trove, to the extent of its value in United States currency, constitutes gross income for the taxable year in which it is reduced to undisputed possession." The fact that the state returned the coins to the Martels in October 2020 appears to indicate "undisputed possession" as required by Reg. § 1.61–14(a). As a result, their gross income will include "value in United States currency" of the coins. The question of "value" is key to the Martels' situation.

Since the Martels found the gold coins on their own property, the taxpayers could argue that they purchased the coins when they purchased the land. This argument is similar to an individual discovering oil or natural gas on her property. With natural resources, there must be a realization event (e.g., a sale or exchange) before there is income.

Given the findings in *Cesarini* [70–2 USTC ¶9509, 26 AFTR 2d 70–5107, 428 F.2d 812 (CA–6, 1970)], this notion would not appear to work for the Martels. In *Cesarini*, the taxpayer purchased a piano that happened to conceal cash. The court allocated the entire purchase price to the piano, so the "windfall" currency was wholly taxable in the year of discovery. As a result, this decision by the Sixth Circuit Court of Appeals would indicate that the *entire value* of the couple's discovery is to be included in their income in the year of discovery.

Although the Martels might want to argue that there is no "income" until the coins are sold (i.e., the coins have a zero basis on discovery), Reg. § 1.61–14(a) and *Cesarini* indicate that the treasure trove's value should be included in gross income as soon as the couple has "undisputed possession."

Finally, the "value" is *not* the $28,000 face value of the coins. Rather, it is the *fair market value* of the coins. The Martels should engage a qualified appraiser (or appraisers) to value the coins appropriately. Then the appraised value of the coins will be included in their 2020 gross income.

---

[54]See Chapter 7 of the AICPA publication cited in Footnote 37. For oral presentations, see W. A. Raabe and G. E. Whittenburg, "Talking Tax: How to Make a Tax Presentation," *Tax Adviser* (March 1997): 179–182.

EXHIBIT 2.10	Client Letter

Maloney, Young, Nellen, & Persellin, CPAs
5191 Natorp Boulevard
Mason, OH 45040

November 18, 2020

Mr. and Mrs. Fred Martel
111 Saddle Ridge Road
Williamsburg, VA 23185

Dear Mr. and Mrs. Martel:

This letter is in response to your request for advice related to your discovery of gold coins on your property in March 2020. Our conclusions are based on the facts discussed during our meeting with you on November 11, 2020. Any change in the facts may affect our conclusions.

In general, the fair market value of the coins you discovered must be included in your 2020 gross income. This conclusion is based on your "undisputed possession" of the coins (as of October 2020) and opinions expressed in U.S. Treasury Department Regulations and court cases (including one from the Sixth Circuit Court of Appeals).

Given the potential value of your discovery, I would encourage you to seek a competent appraiser (or appraisers) to assess the value of the coins. Once a determination of value is made, we can work on a plan to pay the related Federal and state income taxes.

Should you need more information or want to clarify our conclusions, do not hesitate to contact me.

Sincerely yours,

John J. Jones, CPA
Partner

LO.6

Apply tax research techniques and planning procedures.

2-4 WORKING WITH THE TAX LAW—TAX PLANNING

Tax research and tax planning are inseparable. The *primary* purpose of effective *tax planning* is to maximize the taxpayer's after-tax wealth. The course of action selected might not produce the lowest possible tax under the circumstances. The minimization of tax liability must be considered in context with the nontax goals of the taxpayer.

A *secondary* objective of effective tax planning is to reduce or defer the tax in the current tax year. Specifically, this objective aims to accomplish one or more of the following:

- Eliminating the tax entirely.
- Eliminating the tax in the current year.
- Deferring the receipt of income.
- Converting ordinary income into capital gains.
- Converting active income to passive activity income.
- Converting passive activity expense to active expense.
- Increasing the number of taxpayers (i.e., forming partnerships and corporations or making lifetime gifts to family members).
- Eluding double taxation.
- Avoiding ordinary income.
- Creating, increasing, or accelerating deductions.

However, this objective should be approached with caution. For example, a tax election in one year may reduce taxes currently but cause future years to have disadvantageous tax positions.

2-4a Nontax Considerations

There is a danger that tax considerations may impair the exercise of sound financial planning or business judgment by the taxpayer. Thus, the tax planning process can lead to ends that are economically (or socially) incorrect. Unfortunately, a tendency exists for planning to move toward the opposing extremes of placing either too little or too much emphasis on tax considerations. The goal should be a balance that recognizes the significance of taxes, but not beyond the point where planning detracts from the exercise of good business judgment. In general, if the only reason for pursuing a specific course of action is because of the tax benefits, then one should rethink that decision.

2-4b Components of Tax Planning

The popular perception of tax planning often is restricted to the adage "defer income and accelerate deductions." Although this timing approach does hold true and is important, meaningful tax planning involves considerably more.

Preferable to deferring taxable income is complete *avoidance* of taxation. Consider, for example, the employee who chooses nontaxable fringe benefits (e.g., group term life insurance and health insurance coverage) over a fully taxable future pay increase.[55] Complete avoidance of gain recognition also occurs when the owner of appreciated property transfers it by death. Here, the "step-up" (appreciation) in basis to fair market value completely escapes the income tax.[56]

If the recognition of income cannot be avoided, its deferral will postpone income tax consequences. A tax paid in the future costs less than a tax paid today because of the time value of money. *Deferral* of income can take many forms. Besides like-kind exchanges and involuntary conversions, most retirement plans postpone income tax consequences until the benefits are paid. Deferral of gain recognition also can occur when appreciated property is transferred to a newly formed corporation or partnership.[57]

A corollary to the deferral of income is the acceleration of deductions. For example, if an accrual basis, calendar year corporation authorizes a charitable contribution in 2020 and pays it on or before the due date of its tax return in 2021, the deduction can be claimed for 2020.[58] Taxes also can be saved by *shifting* income to lower-bracket taxpayers. Gifts of appreciated property to lower-bracket family members can reduce the related capital gain tax rate on a later sale by 15 percentage points (from 15 percent to 0 percent).[59] For certain high-income taxpayers, the reduction is 20 percentage points.

If income cannot be avoided, deferred, or shifted, the nature of the gain can be *converted*. By changing the classification of property, income taxes can be reduced. Thus, a taxpayer who transfers appreciated inventory to a controlled corporation has converted ordinary income property (the inventory) to a capital asset (stock in the corporation). When the taxpayer's stock is later sold, preferential capital gain rates apply.

The conversion approach also can work in tax planning for losses. Properly structured, a loan to a corporation that becomes worthless can be an ordinary loss rather than a capital loss. Likewise, via § 1244, an investor in qualified small business stock can convert what would be a capital loss into an ordinary loss.[60]

Effective tax planning requires that careful consideration be given to the *choice of entity* used for conducting a business. The corporate form results in double taxation but permits shareholder-employees to be covered by fringe benefit programs. Partnerships and S corporations allow a pass-through of losses and other tax attributes, but transferring ownership interests as gifts to family members may be difficult.[61]

Although the substance of a transaction rather than its form generally controls, this rule is not always the case with tax planning. *Preserving formalities*, with particularly

---

[55]See text Sections 5-6 and 5-8 and Examples 19 and 40 in Chapter 5.

[56]See Example 24 in Chapter 13.

[57]See Chapters 18 and 21.

[58]See Chapter 17.

[59]See text Section 13-2b in Chapter 13.

[60]See Example 9 in Chapter 7.

[61]See Chapters 21 and 22.

clear documentation, often is crucial to the result. Is an advance to a corporation a loan or a contribution to capital? The answer may depend on the existence of a note.

Along with preserving formalities, the taxpayer should keep records that support how a transaction is treated. Returning to the issue of loan versus contribution to capital, how is the advance listed on the books of the borrower? What do the corporate minutes say about the advance?

Finally, effective tax planning requires *consistency* on the part of taxpayers. A shareholder who treats a corporate distribution as a return of capital cannot later avoid a stock basis adjustment by contending that the distribution was really a dividend.

In summary, the key components of tax planning include the following:

- *Avoid* the recognition of income (usually by resorting to a nontaxable source or nontaxable event).
- *Defer* the recognition of income (or accelerate deductions).
- *Convert* the classification of income (or deductions) to a more advantageous form (e.g., ordinary income into capital gain).
- *Choose* the business *entity* with the desired tax attributes.
- Preserve *formalities* by generating and maintaining supporting documentation.
- Act in a manner *consistent* with the intended objective.

2-4c   Tax Avoidance and Tax Evasion

A fine line exists between legal tax planning and illegal tax planning—tax avoidance versus tax evasion. **Tax avoidance** is merely tax minimization through legal techniques, which is the proper objective of all tax planning. Tax evasion, although also aimed at the elimination or reduction of taxes, connotes the use of subterfuge and fraud as a means to an end. Popular usage—probably because of the common goals involved—has so linked these two concepts that many individuals are no longer aware of the true distinctions between them. Consequently, some taxpayers may not take advantage of planning possibilities. The now classic words of Judge Learned Hand in *Commissioner v. Newman* reflect the true values the taxpayer should have:

> Over and over again courts have said that there is nothing sinister in so arranging one's affairs as to keep taxes as low as possible. Everybody does so, rich or poor; and all do right, for nobody owes any public duty to pay more than the law demands: taxes are enforced extractions, not voluntary contributions. To demand more in the name of morals is mere cant.[62]

As Denis Healy, a former British Chancellor, once said, "The difference between tax avoidance and tax evasion is the thickness of a prison wall."

U.S. taxpayers spent over 8.9 billion hours (or more than 1 million years) preparing and filing tax returns in 2016. Considering individual, business, and employment taxes, this time amounts to about $409 billion annually in compliance costs.[63] For example, the Treasury Department's Final Regulations related to the qualified business income deduction are 248 pages long, and the IRS estimates that they could increase compliance costs by $1.3 billion over the next 10 years. Of course, additional time is spent filing state tax returns each year.

2-4d   Follow-Up Procedures

Because tax planning usually involves a proposed (rather than a completed) transaction, being aware of if or when the law changes is critical to the tax planning process. A change in the tax law (legislative, administrative, or judicial) could alter the original conclusion. Additional research may be necessary to test the solution in light of current developments (refer to the broken lines at the right in Exhibit 2.8).

---

[62]*Comm. v. Newman*, 47–1 USTC ¶9175, 35 AFTR 857, 159 F.2d 848 (CA–2, 1947).

[63]Scott A. Hodge, "The Compliance Costs of IRS Regulations," Tax Foundation, June 15, 2016.

2-4e Tax Planning

Throughout this text, each chapter concludes with observations on Tax Planning. These observations are not all-inclusive, but they are intended to illustrate some of the ways in which the material covered in the chapter can be effectively utilized to minimize taxes.

2-5 TAXATION ON THE CPA EXAMINATION

LO.7

Be aware of taxation on the CPA examination.

The CPA exam continues to test in the familiar four sections—Auditing and Attestation (AUD), Business Environment and Concepts (BEC), Financial Accounting and Reporting (FAR), and Regulation (REG). However, the exam continues to evolve, placing less emphasis on remembering-and-understanding skills, and greater focus on higher-level analysis and evaluation skills.

- Task-based simulations, a highly effective way to assess higher-order skills, are part of each section of the CPA exam. Four task-based simulations appear on the BEC section, and eight task-based simulations appear on the AUD, FAR, and REG sections.

- Total testing time is 16 hours (4 hours per section).

- Multiple-choice questions and task-based simulations each contribute about 50 percent toward the candidate's score in the AUD, FAR, and REG sections. In the BEC section, multiple-choice questions contribute about 50 percent of the scoring, with 35 percent coming from task-based simulations and 15 percent from written communication.

- Using Bloom's taxonomy, the CPA exam tests remembering and understanding, application, analysis, and evaluation. In prior years, the CPA exam only tested for the first two of these items.

2-5a Preparation Blueprints

To prepare for the CPA exam, candidates are able to use AICPA-developed blueprints that replaced the Content Specification Outline (CSO) and Skill Specification Outline (SSO).[64]

The blueprints provide candidates with more detail about what to expect on the exam. They contain about 600 representative tasks, which are aligned with the skills required of newly licensed CPAs, across the four exam sections. The blueprints are designed to provide candidates with clearer information on the material the exam tests and show educators what knowledge and skills candidates need as newly licensed CPAs. In addition, the blueprints provide candidates with sample tasks that align with both the content and skill level at which the content will be tested.

2-5b Regulation Section

Taxation continues to be tested within the REG section of the CPA exam. Testing within REG is administered in five blocks called testlets, which feature multiple-choice questions (MCQs) and task-based simulations (TBSs). Candidates receive at least one research question (research-oriented TBS) that requires the candidate to search the applicable authoritative literature and find an appropriate reference.

Each of the five topics in REG includes one or more representative tasks that are not necessarily questions on the exam. For example, the exam does not specifically ask

---

[64]The blueprints can be accessed at **aicpa.org/content/dam/aicpa/becomeacpa/cpaexam/examinationcontent/downloadabledocuments/cpa-exam-blueprints-effective-july-2019.pdf**; a summary of changes made to the previous blueprints can be accessed at **aicpa.org/content/dam/aicpa/becomeacpa/cpaexam/examinationcontent/downloadabledocuments/summary-of-changes-to-exam-blueprints-effective-july-2019.pdf**.

a candidate to "Calculate taxpayer penalties relating to Federal tax returns." However, identifying *situations* where a taxpayer penalty might apply would be appropriate. In addition, tasks are to be inclusive, not exclusive, of exam content. For example, the task "Calculate tax depreciation for a tangible business property..." could include the calculation of additional first-year (bonus) depreciation.

Task-based simulations are case studies that allow candidates to demonstrate their knowledge and skills by generating responses to questions rather than simply selecting an answer. They typically require candidates to use spreadsheets and/or to research authoritative literature provided in the CPA exam (e.g., Internal Revenue Code, Treasury Department Regulations, IRS publications, and Federal tax forms).

There are five content areas in the REG section of the CPA exam:

- Area 1: Ethics, professional responsibilities, and Federal tax procedures (weight: 10 to 20 percent).
- Area 2: Business law (weight: 10 to 20 percent).
- Area 3: Federal taxation of property transactions (weight: 12 to 22 percent).
- Area 4: Federal taxation of individuals (weight: 15 to 25 percent).
- Area 5: Federal taxation of entities (weight: 28 to 38 percent).

Area 1 covers ethics and responsibilities in tax practice, licensing and disciplinary systems, Federal tax procedures, and legal duties and responsibilities of a CPA.

Area 3 covers Federal taxation of property transactions and Federal estate and gift taxation.

Area 4 covers the Federal income taxation of individuals from both a tax preparation and tax planning perspective (e.g., income, exclusions, deductions, and retirement plans).

Area 5 covers the Federal income taxation of entities, including sole proprietorships, partnerships, limited liability companies, C corporations, S corporations, joint ventures, trusts, estates, and tax-exempt organizations from both a tax preparation and tax planning perspective.

Accounting methods and periods and tax elections are included in Areas 3, 4, and 5. Only Area 2 does not involve taxation.

Remembering-and-understanding skills are tested mainly in Areas 1 and 2. Application and analysis skills are tested primarily in Areas 3, 4, and 5. These three areas contain more of the day-to-day tasks that newly licensed CPAs are expected to perform. As a result, they are tested at the higher end of the skill level continuum. Overall, the REG section tests skills in the following way: remembering and learning (25 to 35 percent), application (35 to 45 percent), and analysis (25 to 35 percent). The REG section does not test any content at the evaluation skill level since newly licensed CPAs are not expected to demonstrate that level of skill in regard to the REG content.

The REG section has 76 multiple-choice questions and 8 task-based simulations (TBSs). The TBSs are used by the AICPA to assess the candidate's higher-order skills. In addition, TBSs on the CPA exam provide increased background material and data that require candidates to determine what information is or is not relevant to the question. The scoring weight of multiple-choice questions and TBSs is about 50 percent each on the REG section of the CPA exam.

Depending on the skill level being assessed, well-prepared candidates likely will spend 15 to 20 minutes for each TBS. Certain analysis and/or evaluation-level TBSs could take a well-prepared candidate up to 30 minutes to complete. Several illustrations of task-based simulations are shown in the examples that follow.

CPA Exam Simulation Examples

The *tax citation type* simulation requires the candidate to research the Internal Revenue Code and enter a Code Section and subsection.

For example, Amber Company is considering using the simplified dollar-value method of pricing its inventory for purposes of the LIFO method that is available to certain small businesses. What Code Section is the relevant authority in the Internal Revenue Code you should use to determine whether the taxpayer is eligible to use this method? To be successful, the candidate must find § 474.

EXAMPLE 4

A *tax form completion* simulation requires the candidate to fill out a portion of a tax form. For example, Red Company is a limited liability company (LLC) for tax purposes. Complete the income section of Form 1065 for Red Company using the values found and calculated on previous tabs along with the following data:

Ordinary income from other partnerships	$ 5,200
Net gain (loss) from Form 4797	2,400
Management fee income	12,000

The candidate is provided with page 1 of Form 1065 on which to record the appropriate amounts.

Any field that requires an entry is a shaded rectangular cell. Some white rectangular cells will automatically calculate based on the entries in the shaded cells.

EXAMPLE 5

Candidates can learn more about the CPA examination at **aicpa.org/becomeacpa/cpaexam.html**. In addition to accessing the Uniform CPA Examination Blueprints, candidates will find tutorials related to the exam, have the ability to take sample exams, learn how the exam is graded, and discover the requirements needed to sit for the CPA exam in each licensing jurisdiction. Content related to the TCJA of 2017 is now being tested on the CPA exam.

Key Terms

Acquiescence, 2-16

Circuit Court of Appeals, 2-12

Citator, 2-25

Court of original jurisdiction, 2-10

Determination letters, 2-9

Final Regulations, 2-7

Interpretive Regulations, 2-24

Legislative Regulations, 2-24

Letter rulings, 2-8

Nonacquiescence, 2-16

Precedents, 2-13

Procedural Regulations, 2-24

Proposed Regulations, 2-7

Revenue Procedures, 2-7

Revenue Rulings, 2-7

Small Cases Division, 2-10

Tax avoidance, 2-30

Tax research, 2-20

Technical Advice Memoranda (TAMs), 2-9

Temporary Regulations, 2-7

U.S. Court of Federal Claims, 2-10

U.S. District Court, 2-10

U.S. Supreme Court, 2-13

U.S. Tax Court, 2-10

Writ of Certiorari, 2-14

Discussion Questions

1. **LO.1** A large part of tax research consists of determining what?

2. **LO.1** Why do taxpayers often have more than one alternative for structuring a business transaction?

3. **LO.1** Where does Federal tax legislation generally originate?

Communications 4. **LO.2, 5** Sonja Bishop operates a small international firm named Tile, Inc. A new treaty between the United States and Spain conflicts with a Section of the Internal Revenue Code. Sonja asks you for advice. If she follows the treaty position, does she need to disclose this on her tax return? If she is required to disclose, are there any penalties for failure to disclose? Prepare a letter in which you respond to Sonja. Tile's address is 100 International Drive, Tampa, FL 33620.

5. **LO.1, 2** Interpret this Regulation citation: Reg. § 1.163–10(a)(2).

6. **LO.1** In the citation Notice 90–20, 1990–1 C.B. 328, to what do the 20 and the 328 refer?

7. **LO.1, 4** Rank the following items from the lowest to highest authority in the Federal tax law system:
   a. Interpretive Regulation.
   b. Legislative Regulation.
   c. Letter ruling.
   d. Revenue Ruling.
   e. Internal Revenue Code.
   f. Proposed Regulation.

8. **LO.1** Interpret each of the following citations:
   a. Temp.Reg. § 1.956–2T.
   b. Rev.Rul. 2012–15, 2012–23 I.R.B. 975.
   c. Ltr.Rul. 200204051.

Communications 9. **LO.1, 5** Sally Andrews calls you on the phone. She says that she has found a 2014 letter ruling that agrees with a position she wants to take on her tax return. She asks you about the precedential value of a letter ruling. Draft a memo for the tax files, outlining what you told Sally.

10. **LO.1** Where may private letter rulings be found?

Critical Thinking 11. **LO.1** Sanjay receives a settlement letter from the IRS after his discussion with an IRS appeals officer. He is not satisfied with the $101,000 settlement offer. Identify the relevant issues facing Sanjay if he chooses to contest the settlement offer.

12. **LO.1** List an advantage and a disadvantage of using the U.S. Court of Federal Claims as the trial court for Federal tax litigation.

Communications 13. **LO.1, 5** Eddy Falls is considering litigating a tax deficiency of approximately $229,030 in the court system. He asks you to provide him with a short description of his alternatives, indicating the advantages and disadvantages of each. Prepare your response to Eddy in the form of a letter. His address is 200 Mesa Drive, Tucson, AZ 85714.

14. **LO.1** List an advantage and a disadvantage of using the U.S. Tax Court as the trial court for Federal tax litigation.

15. **LO.1** A taxpayer lives in Michigan. In a controversy with the IRS, the taxpayer loses at the trial court level. Describe the appeal procedure under the following different assumptions:
    a. The trial court was the Small Cases Division of the U.S. Tax Court.
    b. The trial court was the U.S. Tax Court.
    c. The trial court was a U.S. District Court.
    d. The trial court was the U.S. Court of Federal Claims.

16. **LO.1** What is meant by the term *petitioner*?

17. **LO.1** A taxpayer living in the following states would appeal a decision of the U.S. District Court to which Court of Appeals?
    a. Wyoming.
    b. Nebraska.
    c. Idaho.
    d. Louisiana.
    e. Illinois.

18. **LO.1** What precedents must each of these courts follow?
    a. U.S. Tax Court.
    b. U.S. Court of Federal Claims.
    c. U.S. District Court.

19. **LO.1** What determines the appropriate Circuit Court of Appeals for a particular taxpayer?

20. **LO.1, 4** In assessing the validity of a prior court decision, discuss the significance of the following on the taxpayer's issue:
    a. The decision was rendered by the U.S. District Court of Wyoming. Taxpayer lives in Wyoming.
    b. The decision was rendered by the U.S. Court of Federal Claims. Taxpayer lives in Wyoming.
    c. The decision was rendered by the Second Circuit Court of Appeals. Taxpayer lives in California.
    d. The decision was rendered by the U.S. Supreme Court.
    e. The decision was rendered by the U.S. Tax Court. The IRS has acquiesced in the result.
    f. Same as part (e) except that the IRS has issued a nonacquiescence as to the result.

21. **LO.2** In the citation *Schuster's Express, Inc.*, 66 T.C. 588 (1976), *aff'd* 562 F.2d 39 (CA–2, 1977), *nonacq.*, to what do the 66, 39, and *nonacq.* refer?

22. **LO.2** Is there an automatic right to appeal to the U.S. Supreme Court? If so, what is the process?

23. **LO.2** Referring to the citation only, determine which court issued these decisions.
    a. 716 F.2d 693 (CA–9, 1983).
    b. 92 T.C. 400 (1998).
    c. 70 U.S. 224 (1935).
    d. 3 B.T.A. 1042 (1926).
    e. T.C.Memo. 1957–169.

    f.   50 AFTR2d 92–6000 (Ct. Cl., 1992).

    g.   Ltr.Rul. 9046036.

    h.   111 F.Supp.2d 1294 (S.D.N.Y., 2000).

    i.   98–50, 1998–1 C.B. 10.

24. **LO.2** Interpret each of the following citations:

    a.   14 T.C. 74 (1950).

    b.   592 F.2d 1251 (CA–5, 1979).

    c.   95–1 USTC ¶50,104 (CA–6, 1995).

    d.   75 AFTR2d 95–110 (CA–6, 1995).

    e.   223 F.Supp. 663 (W.D. Tex., 1963).

    f.   491 F.3d 53 (CA–1, 2007).

    g.   775 F.Supp.2d 765 (D.Ct. V.I., 2011).

25. **LO.2** Give the Commerce Clearing House citation for the following courts:

    a.   Small Cases Division of the Tax Court.

    b.   U.S. District Court.

    c.   U.S. Supreme Court.

    d.   U.S. Court of Federal Claims.

    e.   Tax Court Memorandum decision.

26. **LO.2** Where can you locate a published decision of the U.S. Court of Federal Claims?

Critical Thinking   27. **LO.3** For her tax class, Yvonne must prepare a research paper discussing the tax aspects of qualified stock options. Explain to Yvonne how she can research this topic using various tax research resources.

28. **LO.4** Where can a researcher find the current Internal Revenue Code of 1986?

Decision Making   29. **LO.2, 3, 4** You inherit a tax problem that was researched five months ago. You believe the answer is correct, but you are unfamiliar with the general
Critical Thinking   area. How would you find recent articles dealing with the subject area? How do you evaluate the reliability of the authority cited in the research report? How do you determine the latest developments pertaining to the research problem?

30. **LO.6** What is the primary purpose of effective tax planning? Explain.

31. **LO.7** Describe the task-based simulations that are part of the CPA exam.

Problems

32. **LO.1** In which Subchapter of the Internal Revenue Code would one find information about corporate distributions?

    a.   Subchapter S.

    b.   Subchapter C.

    c.   Subchapter P.

    d.   Subchapter K.

    e.   Subchapter M.

Decision Making   33. **LO.1, 4** Rank the items below from most reliable to least reliable.

    a.   Letter Ruling.

    b.   Legislative Regulation.

    c.   Code Section.

   d.   Revenue Ruling.

   e.   Proposed Regulation.

   f.   Interpretive Regulation.

   g.   Recent Temporary Regulation.

34. **LO.4** Using the legend provided, classify each of the following tax sources:

Legend
P = Primary tax source
S = Secondary tax source
B = Both
N = Neither

   a.   Sixteenth Amendment to the U.S. Constitution.

   b.   Tax treaty between the United States and India.

   c.   Revenue Procedure.

   d.   An IRS publication.

   e.   U.S. District Court decision.

   f.   *Yale Law Journal* article.

   g.   Temporary Regulations (issued 2018).

   h.   U.S. Tax Court Memorandum decision.

   i.   Small Cases Division of the U.S. Tax Court decision.

   j.   House Ways and Means Committee report.

35. **LO.1, 2** Using the legend provided, classify each of the following citations as to publisher:

Legend
RIA = Research Institute of America
CCH = Commerce Clearing House
W = West
U.S. = U.S. Government
O = Others

   a.   83–2 USTC ¶9600.

   b.   52 AFTR 2d 83–5954.

   c.   67 T.C. 293 (1976).

   d.   39 TCM 32 (1979).

   e.   416 U.S. 938.

   f.   RIA T.C. Memo. ¶80,582.

   g.   89 S.Ct. 501.

   h.   40 Fed.Cl. 172.

   i.   415 F.2d 488.

   j.   592 F.Supp. 18.

   k.   77–37, 1977–2 C.B. 568.

   l.   S. Rep. No. 1622, 83rd Cong., 2d Sess. 42 (1954).

36. **LO.6** Using the legend provided, classify each of the following statements:

Legend
A = Tax avoidance
E = Tax evasion
N = Neither

a. Sue writes a $707 check for a charitable contribution on December 26, 2020, but does not mail the check to the charitable organization until January 10, 2021. She takes a deduction in 2020.

b. Sam decides not to report interest income from a bank because the amount is only $19.75.

c. Harry pays property taxes on his home in December 2020 rather than waiting until February 2021.

d. Variet switches her investments from taxable corporate bonds to tax-exempt municipal bonds.

e. Mel encourages his mother to save most of her Social Security benefits so that he will be able to claim her as a dependent.

Research Problems

Note: Solutions to the Research Problems can be prepared by using the Thomson Reuters Checkpoint™ online tax research database, which accompanies this textbook. Solutions can also be prepared by using research materials found in a typical tax library.

Research Problem 1. Determine the missing data in these court decisions and rulings.

a. *Higgens v. Comm.*, 312 U.S. _____ (1941).
b. *Talen v. U.S.*, 355 F.Supp.2d 22 (D.Ct. D.C., _____).
c. Rev.Rul. 2008–18, 2008–13 I.R.B. _____.
d. *Pahl v. Comm.*, 150 F.3d 1124 (CA–9, _____).
e. *Veterinary Surgical Consultants PC*, 117 T.C. _____ (2001).
f. *Yeagle Drywall Co.*, T.C.Memo. 2001_____.

Decision Making   **Research Problem 2.** When Oprah gave away Pontiac G6 sedans to her TV audience, was the value of the cars taxable? On Labor Day weekend in 2006, World Furniture Mall in Plano, Illinois, gave away $275,000 of furniture because the Chicago Bears shut out the Green Bay Packers in the team's football season opener at Lambeau Field in Green Bay (26–0). Was the free furniture in the form of a discount or rebate taxable, or should the furniture company have handed the customers a Form 1099–MISC?

Decision Making   **Research Problem 3.** You are interviewing a client before preparing his tax return. He indicates that he did not list as income $96,000 received as a recovery for false imprisonment. What should you do with respect to this significant recovery?

Partial list of research aids:
CCA 200809001.
Daniel and Brenda Stadnyk, T.C.Memo. 2008–289.
Rev.Rul. 2007–14, 2007–1 C.B. 747.
§ 104.

Use internet tax resources to address the following questions. Look for reliable web-sites and blogs of the IRS and other government agencies, media outlets, businesses, tax professionals, academics, think tanks, and political outlets.

Research Problem 4. (1) Use an internet search engine (e.g., Google) to find Internal Revenue Code § 61(a). What is defined in this Code Section? Is the definition broad or narrow? (2) Go to **legalbitstream.com**, and find the U.S Tax Court case in which Mark Spitz, the former Olympic gold medalist, is the petitioner. Answer the following questions about the case:

a. What tax years are at issue in the case?

b. In what year was the case decided?

c. Did the court decide in favor of Mr. Spitz or the IRS?

d. Were any penalties imposed on Mr. Spitz? Why or why not?

Research Problem 5. Go to the U.S. Tax Court website (**ustaxcourt.gov**).   Communications

a. What different types of cases can be found on the site?

b. What is a Summary Opinion? Find one.

c. What is a Memorandum Opinion? Find one.

d. Find the "Rules of Practice and Procedure."

e. Summarize your responses in a brief e-mail to your instructor.

CHAPTER

3

Computing the Tax

LEARNING OBJECTIVES: *After completing Chapter 3, you should be able to:*

LO.1 Recognize and apply the components of the Federal income tax formula.

LO.2 Explain the use of the standard deduction in computing taxable income.

LO.3 Describe the current status of the exemption deduction.

LO.4 Apply the rules for determining whether someone is a dependent.

LO.5 Choose the proper filing status and identify the related filing requirements.

LO.6 Use the proper method for determining the tax liability.

LO.7 Identify and report the unearned income of dependent children (the kiddie tax).

LO.8 Describe the tax treatment of property transactions.

LO.9 Identify tax planning opportunities associated with the individual tax formula.

CHAPTER OUTLINE

3-1 Tax Formula, 3-2
  3-1a Components of the Tax Formula, 3-2
  3-1b Standard Deduction, 3-6
  3-1c Application of the Tax Formula, 3-9

3-2 Exemptions, 3-9

3-3 Dependents, 3-9
  3-3a Qualifying Child, 3-9
  3-3b Qualifying Relative, 3-11
  3-3c Other Rules for Determining Dependents, 3-14
  3-3d Comparison of Dependent Categories, 3-15
  3-3e Child and Dependent Tax Credits, 3-15

3-4 Filing the Return, 3-17
  3-4a Filing Status, 3-17
  3-4b Filing the Return, 3-21

3-5 Tax Computations, 3-24
  3-5a Tax Rates, 3-24
  3-5b Tax Table Method, 3-24
  3-5c Tax Rate Schedule Method, 3-24

  3-5d Computation of Net Taxes Payable or Refund Due, 3-25
  3-5e Kiddie Tax—Unearned Income of Dependent Children, 3-26

3-6 Gains and Losses from Property Transactions—In General, 3-28

3-7 Gains and Losses from Property Transactions—Capital Gains and Losses, 3-29
  3-7a Capital Assets, 3-29
  3-7b Taxation of Net Capital Gain, 3-29
  3-7c Determination of Net Capital Gain, 3-30
  3-7d Treatment of Net Capital Loss, 3-31
  3-7e Taxation of Virtual Currency, 3-31

3-8 Tax Planning, 3-32
  3-8a Optimizing the Use of the Standard Deduction, 3-32
  3-8b Taking Advantage of Tax Rate Differentials, 3-32
  3-8c Unearned Income of Children, 3-33

THE BIG PICTURE

A DIVIDED HOUSEHOLD

Aleha maintains a household in which she lives with her unemployed spouse (Trevor), stepdaughter (Paige), and a family friend (Terrah). Aleha provides more than half of the support for both Paige and Terrah. Terrah was fatally injured in an automobile accident in February, and Aleha paid for Terrah's hospitalization and funeral expenses. Paige, an accomplished gymnast, graduated from high school last year. Paige has a part-time job but spends most of her time training and looking for an athletic scholarship to the "right" college. In March, Trevor left for parts unknown and has not been seen or heard from since. Aleha was more surprised than distressed over Trevor's unexpected departure. One reaction, however, was to sell her wedding rings to a cousin who was getting married. The rings cost $11,800 and were sold for their approximate value of $9,000.

Based on these facts, what are Aleha's income tax concerns for the current year?

Read the chapter and formulate your response.

This chapter covers the boldfaced portions of the Tax Formula for Individuals that is introduced in Concept Summary 3.1 on p. 3-3. Below those portions are the sections of Form 1040 where the results are reported.

Income (*broadly defined*)	$ xx,xxx
Less: Exclusions	(x,xxx)
Gross income	**$xx,xxx**
Less: Deductions *for* adjusted gross income	**(x,xxx)**
Adjusted gross income..	$ xx,xxx

FORM 1040 (p. 1)

Filing Status	☐ Single ☐ Married filing jointly ☐ Married filing separately (MFS) ☐ Head of household (HOH) ☐ Qualifying widow(er) (QW)
Check only one box.	If you checked the MFS box, enter the name of spouse. If you checked the HOH or QW box, enter the child's name if the qualifying person is a child but not your dependent. ▶

FORM 1040 (p. 1)

Standard Deduction	Someone can claim: ☐ You as a dependent ☐ Your spouse as a dependent
	☐ Spouse itemizes on a separate return or you were a dual-status alien

Age/Blindness	You: ☐ Were born before January 2, 1955 ☐ Are blind **Spouse:** ☐ Was born before January 2, 1955 ☐ Is blind

Dependents (see instructions):		(2) Social security number	(3) Relationship to you	(4) ✓ If qualifies for (see instructions):
(1) First name	Last name			Child tax credit Credit for other dependents

FORM 1040 (p. 1)

9	**Standard deduction or itemized deductions** (from Schedule A). . . . .
10	**Qualified business income deduction.**** (Attach Form 8995 or Form 8995-A) . . . . . .

Personal and dependency exemptions*	(x,xxx)
Taxable income..	**$ xx,xxx**
Tax on taxable income *(see Tax Tables or Tax Rate Schedules)*	**$ x,xxx**
Less: Tax credits *(including income taxes withheld and prepaid)*	(xxx)
Tax due (or refund)	$ xxx

* Exemption deductions are not allowed from 2018 through 2025.
** Only applies from 2018 through 2025.

The tax formula provides a framework for applying the Federal income tax to individuals. The tax formula is an integral part of our U.S. tax system (i.e., local, state, and Federal), and Chapter 3 provides a summary of its components. In addition, several of its key components are discussed at length.[1]

The chapter also introduces the computation of gain and loss when a taxpayer disposes of an asset in a *property transaction*. The tax formula and its effect on the chapters to follow are reflected in Concept Summary 3.1.

LO.1

Recognize and apply the components of the Federal income tax formula.

3-1 TAX FORMULA

3-1a Components of the Tax Formula

Income (Broadly Defined)

In the tax formula, "income" is thought of in very broad terms; it includes all of the taxpayer's income, both taxable and nontaxable. In general, the courts have defined "income" as any increase in wealth.[2] As a result, income under the tax rules does not include a return of capital or the receipt of borrowed funds.

---

[1] Variations of the framework apply to other taxpayers (e.g., corporations and trusts).

[2] *Comm. v. Glenshaw Glass Co.,* 55–1 USTC ¶9308, 47 AFTR 162, 348 U.S. 426 (USSC, 1955).

Concept Summary 3.1

Tax Formula for Individuals

		Text Discussion
Income (broadly defined)	$xx,xxx	Chs. 3, 4
Less: **Exclusions**	(x,xxx)	Ch. 5
Gross income	$xx,xxx	Chs. 4, 13, 14
Less: **Deductions** *for* adjusted gross income	(x,xxx)	Chs. 6–11, 13, 14
Adjusted gross income	$xx,xxx	
Less: The greater of—		
Total **itemized deductions**	(x,xxx)	Chs. 6, 9, 10, 11
or **standard deduction**		Ch. 3
Less: **Personal and dependency exemptions***	(x,xxx)	
Less: **Deduction for qualified business income****	(x,xxx)	Chs. 6, 9
Taxable income	$xx,xxx	Chs. 3, 12, 15
Tax on taxable income	$ x,xxx	Chs. 3, 12, 15
Less: **Tax credits**	(xxx)	Ch. 12
Tax due (or refund)	$ xxx	Chs. 3, 12

(handwritten annotation: "You and your spouse" next to standard deduction)

* Exemption deductions are not allowed from 2018 through 2025.
** Only applies from 2018 through 2025.

Dan decides to quit renting and buy a new house. Consequently, the owner of the apartment building returns to Dan the $600 damage deposit that Dan previously paid. To make a down payment on the house, Dan sells stock for $50,000 (original cost of $28,000) and borrows $200,000 from a bank.

Only the $22,000 gain from the sale of the stock constitutes gross income to Dan. The $600 damage deposit and the $28,000 cost of the stock are a return of capital. The $200,000 bank loan is not income, since Dan has an obligation to repay that amount.

EXAMPLE 1

Exclusions

For various reasons, Congress excludes certain types of income from the income tax base. The principal income exclusions are discussed in Chapter 5. A partial list of these exclusions is shown in Exhibit 3.1.

Gross Income

The Internal Revenue Code defines gross income broadly as "except as otherwise provided …, all income from whatever source derived."[3] The "except as otherwise provided" phrase refers to exclusions. A partial list of items included in gross income

EXHIBIT 3.1	Partial List of Exclusions from Gross Income
Accident and health insurance proceeds	Life insurance paid upon death
Alimony received (divorces after 2018)	Meals and lodging (if furnished for employer's convenience)
Annuities (cost element)	Military allowances
Bequests	Minister's dwelling rental value or allowance *(handwritten: Parsonage)*
Child support payments	Railroad retirement benefits (to a limited extent)
Cost-of-living allowance (for military)	Scholarship grants (to a limited extent)
Damages for personal injury or sickness	Social Security benefits (to a limited extent)
Gifts received	Veterans' benefits
Group term life insurance, premium paid by employer (for coverage up to $50,000)	Welfare payments
	Workers' compensation benefits
Inheritances	
Interest from state and local (i.e., municipal) bonds	

---

[3]§ 61(a).

appears in Exhibit 3.2. Gross income does not include unrealized gains, such as appreciation in the value of an asset that the taxpayer has not yet sold. Gross income is discussed in Chapters 4, 13, and 14.

EXAMPLE 2

Beth received the following amounts during the year.

Salary	$30,000
Interest on savings account	900
Gift from her aunt	10,000
Prize won in state lottery	1,000
Alimony from ex-husband (divorce finalized in 2015)	12,000
Child support from ex-husband	6,000
Damages for injury in auto accident	25,000
Ten $50 bills in an unmarked envelope found in an airport lounge (airport authorities could not locate anyone who claimed ownership)	500
Federal income tax refund for last year's tax overpayment	120
Increase in the value of stock held for investment	5,000

Review Exhibits 3.1 and 3.2 to determine the amount Beth must include in the computation of taxable income and the amount she may exclude.[4]

EXHIBIT 3.2   Partial List of Gross Income Items

Alimony (divorces before 2019)	Group term life insurance, premium paid by employer (for coverage over $50,000)
Annuities (income element)	Hobby income
Awards	Interest
Back pay	Jury duty fees
Bargain purchase from employer	Living quarters, meals (unless furnished for employer's convenience)
Bonuses	Mileage allowance
Breach of contract damages	Military pay (unless combat pay)
Business income	Partnership income KI
Clergy fees	Pension distributions
Commissions	Prizes
Compensation for services	Professional fees
Death benefits	Punitive damages
Debts forgiven	Rents
Director's fees	Rewards
Dividends	Royalties
Embezzled funds *stolen*	Salaries
Employee awards (in certain cases)	Severance pay
Employee benefits (except certain fringe benefits)	Strike and lockout benefits
Estate and trust income *Form 1041*	Tips and gratuities
Farm income	Travel allowance (in certain cases)
Fees	Treasure trove (found property)
Gains from illegal activities	Unemployment benefits
Gains from sale of property	Wages
Gambling winnings	

---

[4]Beth includes $44,400 in computing taxable income ($30,000 salary + $900 interest + $1,000 lottery prize + $12,000 alimony + $500 found property). She excludes $41,000 ($10,000 gift from aunt + $6,000 child support + $25,000 damages). The $120 Federal income tax refund is excluded because it represents a refund of a nondeductible expenditure made in the previous year. The unrealized gain on the stock held for investment is not included in gross income. Such gain is included in gross income only when it is realized upon a disposition of the stock; see text Sections 3-6 and 3-7.

Deductions *for* Adjusted Gross Income

Individual taxpayers have available two categories of deductions: deductions *for* adjusted gross income (i.e., items subtracted from gross income to arrive at adjusted gross income) and deductions *from* adjusted gross income.

Deductions *for* adjusted gross income (AGI) are sometimes called *above-the-line* deductions because on the tax return, they are taken before the "line" designating AGI. Deductions *for* AGI include the following.[5] Many of these items are subject to computational limitations.

- Expenses incurred in a trade or business.
- Part of any Federal self-employment tax paid.
- Certain contributions to traditional Individual Retirement Accounts (IRAs) and other retirement plans.
- College tuition and related expenses.
- Contributions to Health Savings Accounts (HSAs).
- Interest on student loans.
- Excess capital losses.   *Stocks, real estate*
- Certain alimony payments.

The principal deductions *for* AGI are discussed in Chapters 6 through 11, 13, and 14.

EXAMPLE 3

Mason, age 45, earned a salary of $78,000 in the current year. He contributed $4,000 to his traditional Individual Retirement Account (IRA), sold stock held as an investment for a short-term capital loss of $2,000, and paid $4,600 in alimony to his ex-wife under a 2017 divorce. Mason's AGI is determined as follows.

Gross income		
Salary		$ 78,000
Less: Deductions *for* AGI		
IRA contribution	$4,000	
Capital loss	2,000	
Alimony paid	4,600	(10,600)
AGI		$ 67,400

---

[5]§ 62.

Deductions *from* Adjusted Gross Income

As a general rule, personal expenses are not allowed as deductions in computing taxable income. However, Congress allows some personal expenses as deductions *from* AGI.

AGI is an important subtotal that is the basis for computing percentage limitations on certain itemized deductions, such as medical expenses, charitable contributions, and certain casualty losses.[6] For example, medical expenses are deductible only to the extent they exceed 7.5 percent of AGI, and deductions for gifts to public charities may not exceed 50 percent of AGI (60 percent for cash contributions to public charities). These limitations often are described as a *floor* under the medical expense deduction and a *ceiling* on the charitable contribution deduction.

EXAMPLE 4

Assume the same facts as in Example 3. Mason also incurred medical expenses of $8,000. Medical expenses are included in Mason's itemized deductions to the extent they exceed 7.5% of AGI. In computing his itemized deductions, Mason claims medical expenses of $2,945 [$8,000 medical expenses − $5,055 (7.5% × $67,400 AGI)].

==Itemized deductions== include medical expenses, certain taxes and interest, and charitable contributions. Itemized deductions are discussed in Chapter 10. Exhibit 3.3 provides a partial list of itemized deductions.

Many expenses are not deductible and, therefore, provide no direct income tax benefit. Examples include, but are not limited to, the following. Most of the nondeductible items in this list are discussed further in Chapter 6.

- Personal living expenses.
- Losses on the sale of personal use property.
- Hobby expenses.
- Life insurance premiums.
- Gambling losses (in excess of winnings).
- Child support payments.
- Fines and penalties.
- Political contributions.
- Unreimbursed employee business expenses.
- Capital expenditures.

A deduction for qualified business income is allowed *from* AGI. In general, this deduction relates to business income generated by *noncorporate* businesses (e.g., proprietorships, S corporations, partnerships, and LLCs). This deduction is discussed in Chapter 6.

EXHIBIT 3.3	Partial List of Itemized Deductions

Medical expenses in excess of 7.5% of AGI
State and local income or sales taxes
Real estate taxes ⎫
Personal property taxes ⎬ Maximum $10,000
Interest on home mortgage (subject to certain limitations)
Investment interest (to a limited extent)
Charitable contributions (within specified percentage limitations)
Casualty and theft losses in excess of 10% of AGI

LO.2

Explain the use of the standard deduction in computing taxable income.

3-1b **Standard Deduction**

The ==standard deduction== is specified by Congress and depends on the filing status of the taxpayer. The effect of the standard deduction is to exempt a taxpayer's income, up to the specified amount, from Federal income tax liability, to add to the progressivity of the income tax system, and to exempt from tax amounts used to meet the necessities of life.[7]

---

[6]§ 62.

[7]S.Rep. No. 92–437, 92nd Cong., 1st Sess., 1971, p. 54.

Basic and Additional Standard Deduction

The standard deduction is the sum of two components: the *basic* standard deduction and the *additional* standard deduction.[8] Exhibit 3.4 lists the basic standard deduction allowed for taxpayers in each filing status. The standard deduction amounts are subject to adjustment for inflation each year.

Certain taxpayers are not allowed to claim *any* standard deduction, and the standard deduction is *limited* for others. These provisions are discussed later in the chapter.

A taxpayer who is age 65 or over *or* blind qualifies for an *additional standard deduction* of $1,300 or $1,650, depending on filing status (see amounts in Exhibit 3.5). Two additional standard deductions are allowed for a taxpayer who is age 65 or over *and* blind. The additional standard deduction provisions also apply for a qualifying spouse who is age 65 or over or blind, but not for a dependent.

To determine whether it is best to itemize, the taxpayer compares the *total* standard deduction (the sum of the basic standard deduction and any additional standard deductions) with total itemized deductions. Taxpayers usually elect to deduct the *greater* of itemized deductions or the standard deduction. Over 80 percent of individual tax returns employ the standard deduction every year.

The taxpayer chooses whether to itemize or claim the standard deduction. This is an annual election; the default choice is to use the standard deduction. A taxpayer is not bound by choices made in prior tax years. For example, many taxpayers who previously have claimed the standard deduction switch to itemizing after purchasing a home (because of the mortgage interest and property tax deductions). In other circumstances, a taxpayer may switch from itemizing to the standard deduction.

> Sara, who is single, always had chosen to itemize her tax deductions. In 2020, however, Sara reaches age 65. Her itemized deductions for the tax year are $12,500, but Sara's total standard deduction is $14,050 [$12,400 (basic standard deduction) + $1,650 (additional standard deduction)].
>
> Sara should compute her taxable income using the standard deduction, because it exceeds her itemized deductions.

EXAMPLE 5

EXHIBIT 3.4	Basic Standard Deduction Amounts	
Filing Status	**2019**	**2020**
Single	$12,200	$12,400
Married, filing jointly	24,400	24,800
Surviving spouse	24,400	24,800
Head of household	18,350	18,650
Married, filing separately	12,200	12,400

For 2 years Only if there is a dependent

EXHIBIT 3.5	Additional Standard Deduction Amounts	
Filing Status	**2019**	**2020**
Single	$1,650	$1,650
Married, filing jointly	1,300	1,300
Surviving spouse	1,300	1,300
Head of household	1,650	1,650
Married, filing separately	1,300	1,300

---

[8]§ 63(c)(1).

Individuals Not Eligible for the Standard Deduction

The following individual taxpayers cannot use the standard deduction and therefore must itemize their deductions.[9]

- A married individual filing a separate return where either spouse itemizes deductions.
- A nonresident alien (i.e., an individual who is neither a U.S. citizen nor a U.S. resident).

If an individual dies during a year, a full standard deduction is available for the final tax return; the deduction is not reduced because the return only covers a portion of the calendar year. If, for example, Sandy (age 80 and single) died on January 14, 2020, her executor computes a standard deduction of $14,050 [$12,400 (basic standard deduction) + $1,650 (additional standard deduction for age)] on Sandy's final income tax return (covering the period from January 1 to January 14, 2020).

Limitations on the Standard Deduction for Individuals Who Can Be Claimed as Dependents

Special rules apply to the standard deduction of an individual who can be claimed as a dependent on another person's tax return.

When filing his or her own tax return, a dependent's basic standard deduction for 2020 is limited to the greater of $1,100 or the sum of the individual's *earned income* for the year plus $350.[10] However, this amount cannot exceed the appropriate amount shown in Exhibit 3.4. "Earned income" includes items such as wages, while unearned income often is in the form of interest, dividends, and capital gains.

These limitations apply only to the basic standard deduction. A dependent who is 65 or over or blind or both also is allowed the additional standard deduction amount on his or her own return (refer to Exhibit 3.5).

Dependent Standard Deduction

Susan, who is 17 years old and single, is a dependent of her parents. During 2020, she received $1,200 interest (unearned income) on a savings account. She also earned $400 from a part-time job. When Susan files her own tax return, her standard deduction is $1,100 [the greater of $1,100 or the sum of earned income plus $350 ($400 + $350 = $750)].

Assume the same facts as in Example 6, except that Susan is 67 years old and is a dependent of her son. When Susan files her own tax return, her standard deduction is $2,750 [$1,100 (the amount as computed in Example 6) + $1,650 (the additional standard deduction allowed because Susan is age 65 or older)].

Aleisha, who is 16 years old and single, earned $800 from a summer job and no unearned income during 2020. She is a dependent of her parents. Aleisha's standard deduction is $1,150 [the greater of $1,100 or $1,150 (the sum of $800 earned income plus $350)].

Javiera, a 20-year-old, single, full-time college student, is a dependent of his parents. He worked as a musician during the summer of 2020, earning $12,750. Javiera's standard deduction is $12,400 [the greater of $1,100 or $12,400 (the sum of $12,750 earned income plus $350, but limited to the $12,400 standard deduction amount for a single taxpayer)].

---

[9]§ 63(c)(6).

[10]§ 63(c)(5). Both the $1,100 and the $350 amounts are subject to adjustment for inflation each year. For 2019, the amounts also were $1,100 and $350.

3-1c **Application of the Tax Formula**

The structure of the individual income tax return (Form 1040) parallels the tax formula in Concept Summary 3.1. Like the formula, the tax return places major emphasis on the adjusted gross income (AGI) and taxable income (TI) subtotals. In arriving at AGI, however, most exclusions are not reported on the tax return.

EXAMPLE 10

Grace, age 25, is single. She lives with her disabled and dependent mother. This qualifies Grace for head-of-household filing status and a standard deduction of $18,650 for 2020.

Grace earned a $62,000 salary. Her other income consisted of $1,100 interest from a bank account and $500 interest on municipal bonds that she previously had received as a graduation gift. In addition, she sustained a deductible capital loss of $1,000 from the sale of stock. Her itemized deductions amount to $11,000. Grace's taxable income is computed as follows.

Salary	$62,000
Interest from bank account	1,100
Interest on municipal bonds	500
Income (broadly defined)	$63,600
Less: Exclusion—Interest on municipal bonds	(500)
Gross income	$63,100
Less: Deduction *for* adjusted gross income—capital loss	(1,000)
Adjusted gross income	$62,100
Less: The greater of total itemized deductions ($11,000) *or* the standard deduction for a head of household ($18,650)	(18,650)
Deduction for qualified business income	(–0–)
Taxable income	$43,450

3-2 **EXEMPTIONS**

At one time, tax exemptions were allowed in computing taxable income. Exemptions allowed for the taxpayer and spouse were designated as ==personal exemptions==.[11] Those exemptions allowed for the care and maintenance of other persons were called ==dependency exemptions==.[12]

Deductions for exemptions no longer are allowed under the Federal income tax law, but *pro forma* exemption amounts ($4,300 for 2020 and $4,200 for 2019) still are used by various provisions of the Code. Similarly, certain rules turn on whether one person is the dependent of another. We now examine the use of the rules that determine who is a dependent of another person.

LO.3

Describe the current status of the exemption deduction.

3-3 **DEPENDENTS**

A dependent taxpayer must be either a *qualifying child* or a *qualifying relative*.

LO.4

Apply the rules for determining whether someone is a dependent.

3-3a **Qualifying Child**

The term *qualifying child* is used in several Code provisions, including those relating to:

- Head-of-household filing status.
- Credit for child and dependent care expenses.
- Earned income tax credit.
- Child tax credit.

---

[11]§ 151(b).   [12]§ 151(c).

A qualifying child must meet the relationship, residence, age, and support tests (discussed below).[13] A qualifying child also must satisfy the joint return test and the citizenship or residency test, both discussed in text Section 3-3c.

Relationship Test

The relationship test is met by a taxpayer's child (son, daughter), adopted child, stepchild, eligible foster child, brother, sister, half brother, half sister, stepbrother, stepsister, or a *descendant* of any of these parties (e.g., grandchild, nephew, and niece). *Ancestors* of any of these parties (e.g., uncle and aunt) and in-laws (e.g., son-in-law and brother-in-law) are not included.

An adopted child includes a child placed with the taxpayer even though the adoption is not final. An eligible foster child is one who is placed with the taxpayer by an authorized placement agency or by a court order.[14]

EXAMPLE 11

Maureen's household includes her mother, grandson, stepbrother, stepbrother's daughter, uncle, and sister. All meet the relationship test for a qualifying child except the mother and uncle.

Residence Test

A qualifying child must live with the taxpayer for more than half of the year. For this purpose, temporary absences (e.g., school, vacation, medical care, military service, detention in a juvenile facility) are ignored. Special rules apply in the case of certain kidnapped children.[15]

Age Test

At the end of the tax year, a qualifying child must be under age 19 (age 24 in the case of a full-time student). A full-time student is the taxpayer's child who was in school for any part of five months of the year.[16] An individual cannot be older than the taxpayer claiming him or her as a qualifying child (e.g., a brother cannot claim his older sister as a qualifying child). The age test does not apply to a child who is disabled during any part of the year.

The Big Picture

EXAMPLE 12

Return to the facts of *The Big Picture* on p. 3-1. Does Paige meet the requirements of a qualifying child as to Aleha? Paige satisfies the relationship and residence tests, but the application of the age test remains unclear under the facts as given; because Paige is not a full-time student or disabled, she must be under 19 to meet the age test.

Support Test

A qualifying child cannot be self-supporting (i.e., provide more than half of his or her own support). Support includes food, shelter, clothing, medical and dental care, education, recreation, transportation, and similar items. In the case of the taxpayer's child who is a full-time student, scholarships are not considered to be support.[17]

---

[13]§ 152(c).
[14]§ 152(f)(1)(A)(ii).
[15]§ 152(f)(6).

[16]§ 152(f)(2).
[17]§ 152(f)(5).

Shawn, age 23, is a full-time student who lives with his parents and an older cousin. Shawn receives his support from the following sources: 30% from a part-time job, 30% from a scholarship, 20% from his parents, and 20% from the cousin. Shawn is not self-supporting, so he is a dependent of his parents, even though the parents contribute only 20% of Shawn's support. (Note: Shawn cannot be his cousin's qualifying child, due to the relationship test.)

Tiebreaker Rules

In some situations, a child may be a qualifying child for more than one person. In this event, the tax law specifies which person has priority in claiming the child as a dependent.[18] Called "tiebreaker rules," these rules are summarized in Exhibit 3.6 and are illustrated in the examples that follow.

Tiebreaker Rules for Qualifying Child

Tim, age 15, lives in the same household with his mother and grandmother. As the parent, the mother has priority as to the dependency exemption.

Jennifer, age 17, lives in the same household with her parents during the entire year. If her parents file separate returns, the one with the higher AGI has priority as to the dependency exemption.

Carlos, age 12, lives in the same household with his two aunts. The aunt with the higher AGI has priority as to the dependency exemption.

3-3b Qualifying Relative

A **qualifying relative** must meet the relationship, gross income, and support tests.[19] Qualifying relative status also requires that the joint return and nonresident alien tests be met (discussion of both is found in text Section 3-3c). One who does not satisfy the qualifying child definition still may be a qualifying relative.

EXHIBIT 3.6	Tiebreaker Rules for Claiming a Qualifying Child
Persons Eligible to Claim Qualifying Child as Dependent	**Person Prevailing**
One of the persons is the parent.	Parent
Both persons are the parents, and the child lives with one parent for a longer period.	Parent with the longer period of residence
Both persons are the parents, and the child lives with each the same period of time.	Parent with the higher adjusted gross income (AGI)
None of the persons is the parent.	Person with highest AGI

---

[18]§ 152(c)(4).   [19]§ 152(d).

Inez provides more than half of the support of her son Manuel, age 20, who is neither disabled nor a full-time student. Manuel is not a qualifying child due to the age test, but he is a qualifying relative if the gross income test is met.

Relationship Test

The relationship test for a qualifying relative is more expansive than for a qualifying child. Also included are:

- Lineal ascendants (e.g., parents and grandparents).
- Collateral ascendants (e.g., uncles and aunts).
- Certain in-laws (e.g., son-, daughter-, father-, mother-, brother-, and sister-in-law).[20]

The relationship test also includes parties who live with the taxpayer for the entire tax year (i.e., they are members of the same household). Member-of-the-household status is not available for anyone whose relationship with the taxpayer violates an enforced local law or for anyone who was a spouse during any part of the year.[21] However, an ex-spouse can qualify as a member of the household in a year following that of the divorce.

As the relationship test indicates, the term *qualifying relative* is somewhat misleading. Persons other than relatives can qualify as dependents, and not all relatives qualify.

The Big Picture

Return to the facts of *The Big Picture* on p. 3-1. Although Terrah is unrelated to Aleha, Terrah qualifies as Aleha's dependent by being a member of the household. Because Terrah is a dependent, Aleha can claim the medical expenses she paid on Terrah's behalf. The funeral expenses are not deductible.

Gross Income Test

A qualifying relative's gross income must be *less* than the exemption amount—$4,300 for 2020 and $4,200 for 2019. Gross income is the amount that the tax law counts as taxable. In the case of scholarships, for example, include the taxable portion (e.g., amounts received for room and board) and exclude the nontaxable portion (e.g., amounts received for books and tuition). In contrast, the qualifying child rule does not contain a gross income test.

Gross Income Test

Haylie provides more than half of the support of her son, Tom, who does not live with her. Tom, age 26, is a full-time student in medical school, earns $3,000 from a part-time job, and receives a $62,000 scholarship covering his tuition.

Tom is Haylie's dependent because he meets the gross income test and is a qualifying relative. (Tom is *not* a qualifying child; he fails both the residence and age tests.)

Aaron provides more than half of the support of his widowed aunt, Myrtle, who does not live with him. Myrtle's income for the year is as follows: dividend income of $1,100, earnings from pet sitting of $1,200, nontaxable Social Security benefits of $10,000, and $4,000 nontaxable interest from City of Milwaukee bonds.

Because Myrtle's gross income is only $2,300 ($1,100 + $1,200), she meets the gross income test and is Aaron's dependent.

---

[20]Once established by marriage, in-law status continues to exist and survives divorce.

[21]§§ 152(d)(2)(H) and (f)(3).

The Big Picture

Return to the facts of *The Big Picture* on p. 3-1. Assuming that Paige is not a qualifying child (see Example 12), can she be a qualifying relative? Paige meets the relationship and support tests, but what about the gross income test?

If the income from her part-time job is less than $4,300 (the 2020 exemption amount), she does qualify and is Aleha's dependent.

EXAMPLE
21

Support Test   *You have to actually support your dependent*

The taxpayer must furnish more than one-half of the qualifying relative's support. Support includes food, shelter, clothing, medical and dental care, education, recreation, transportation, and similar items. If a child is being evaluated as a qualifying relative (and is a full-time student), a scholarship received by the child is *not included* for purposes of computing whether the taxpayer furnished more than half of the child's support. Any other relative being evaluated must include a scholarship as support in making this determination.

Hal contributed $3,400 (consisting of food, clothing, and medical care) toward the support of his nephew, Sam, who lives with him. Sam earned $1,300 from a part-time job and used a $2,000 student loan to attend a local university. Assuming that the other dependency tests are met, Sam is Hal's dependent because Hal provided more than half of Sam's support ($3,400 Hal's support > $3,300 self-support).

EXAMPLE
22

Capital expenditures for items such as furniture, appliances, and automobiles are included in total support if the item does, in fact, constitute support.[22]

Ajit purchased a television set costing $1,950 and gave it to his mother, Vera, who lives with him. The television set was placed in Vera's bedroom and was used exclusively by her. Ajit includes the cost of the television set in determining Vera's support.

EXAMPLE
23

Multiple Support Agreements An exception to the support test involves a <mark>multiple support agreement</mark>. A multiple support agreement permits one person in a group of taxpayers who furnish support for a qualifying relative to claim the relative as a dependent, even if no one person provides more than 50 percent of the support.[23] Collectively, the group must provide more than 50 percent of the support.

Any person who contributed *more than 10 percent* of the support is entitled to identify the other person as dependent; each person in the group who contributed more than 10 percent must consent in writing to the designation of the party who supports the dependent. This provision frequently enables one of the children of aged dependent parents to identify a dependent when none of the children individually meets the 50 percent support test.

Each person who is involved in a multiple support agreement must meet all other tests (i.e., except the support requirement) for identifying the dependent. A person who does not meet the relationship or member-of-the-household requirement, for instance, cannot have a dependent, even under a multiple support agreement.

---

[22]Rev.Rul. 77–282, 1977–2 C.B. 52.   [23]§ 152(d)(3).

Wanda, who resides with her son, Adam, received $24,000 from various sources during the year. This constituted her entire support for the year.

	Support Received	Percentage of Total
Adam, son	$10,000	42%
Bob, son	1,200	5
Carol, daughter	9,200	38
Diane, friend	3,600	15
	$24,000	100%

If Adam and Carol file a multiple support agreement, either may name Wanda as a dependent. Bob may not claim Wanda because he did not contribute more than 10% of her support. Bob's consent is not required for Adam and Carol to file a multiple support agreement. Diane does not meet the relationship or member-of-the-household test and cannot be a party to the agreement.

The decision as to who claims Wanda as a dependent rests with Adam and Carol. If Adam agrees, Carol can claim Wanda even though Adam furnished more of Wanda's support.

The individual who supports the dependent must complete Form 2120 (Multiple Support Declaration) and file it with his or her tax return. In addition, every other person who qualifies under the more-than-10 percent rule must submit a signed statement agreeing not to claim the individual as a dependent.

Children of Divorced or Separated Parents Another exception to the support test applies when parents with children are divorced or legally separated. Generally, the parent having custody of the child (children) for the greater part of the year (i.e., the custodial parent) claims the child as a dependent. A special rule applies if the now-unmarried parents live apart for the last six months of the year and:[24]

• They would have been entitled to identify the dependent had they been married and filed a joint return.

• They have custody (jointly or singly) of the child (children) for more than half of the year.

The special rule allows the noncustodial parent to claim the dependent if the divorce (or separation) decree so specifies or if the custodial parent signs a waiver on Form 8332.[25]

If the special rule does not apply (i.e., the divorce decree is silent or the custodial parent does not sign Form 8332), the child (children) is a dependent under the qualifying child or qualifying relative rules.

3-3c Other Rules for Determining Dependents

In addition to fitting into either the qualifying child or the qualifying relative category, a dependent must meet the joint return and the citizenship tests.

Joint Return Test

If a dependent is married, the supporting taxpayer (e.g., the parent of a married child) generally cannot claim the individual as a dependent if the potential dependent files a joint return with his or her spouse.[26] The joint return rule does not apply, however, if the reason for filing is to claim a refund for tax withheld.

Paul provides over half of the support of his son Quinn. He also provides over half of the support of Lina, who is Quinn's spouse. During the year, both Quinn and Lina hold part-time jobs. To recover the taxes withheld, they file a joint return. Both Quinn and Lina are dependents of Paul.

Citizenship Test

To be a dependent, the individual must be a U.S. citizen, a U.S. resident, or a resident of Canada or Mexico for some part of the calendar year in which the taxpayer's tax year begins.[27]

3-3d Comparison of Dependent Categories

Concept Summary 3.2 sets forth the tests for the two ways to identify a dependent. In contrasting the two categories, several observations can be made.

- As to the relationship tests, the qualifying relative category is considerably more expansive. Besides including those prescribed under the qualifying child grouping, other relatives are added. Nonrelated persons who are members of the household are also included.
- The support tests are entirely different. In the case of a qualifying child, the key is that the child is not self-supporting.
- The qualifying child category has no gross income limitation, whereas the qualifying relative category has no age restriction.

Concept Summary 3.2

Tests to Identify a Dependent

Test	Qualifying Child	Qualifying Relative
Relationship		
• Children (natural, step, or adopted) and their *descendants*, and siblings and stepsiblings and their *descendants*.	X	
• Children (natural, step, or adopted) and their *descendants*, siblings and their children, parents and their *ascendants*, uncles and aunts, stepparents and stepsiblings, and certain in-laws.		X
• Member of the household (live with taxpayer for *entire* year; relative or non-relative)		X
Residence	X	
Age	X	
Support		
• Not self-supporting ("child" furnishes one-half or less of his or her support)	X	
• Taxpayer furnishes over one-half of the support of potential dependent		X
Gross income is *less* than the exemption amount		X
Joint return (potential dependent cannot file joint return)	X	X
Citizenship (potential dependent must meet test)	X	X

3-3e Child and Dependent Tax Credits

The child tax credit and the dependent tax credit are provided to individual taxpayers based on the *number* of their qualifying children and dependents.[28]

A $2,000 tax credit is allowed for each qualifying child (including stepchildren and foster children). To be eligible for the credit, the child must be under age 17, a U.S. citizen, and a dependent of the taxpayer.[29] A Social Security number must be provided for any qualifying child.[30]

In addition, a $500 tax credit is allowed for each dependent of the taxpayer (other than a qualifying child).[31] Examples of qualifying relatives for purposes of the

[27]§ 152(b)(3).
[28]§ 24(h).
[29]§ 24(c).
[30]§ 24(h)(4)(7).
[31]§ 24(h)(4).

dependent tax credit include children over age 16 (including full-time students under age 24), children without a Social Security number, parents of the taxpayer, and "members of the household" (see text Section 3-3b). For purposes of the dependent tax credit, these qualifying relatives must be a U.S. citizen, a U.S. national, or a U.S. resident.[32]

The child and dependent tax credits are subject to a phaseout based on a taxpayer's adjusted gross income.

Child and Dependent Tax Credits Phaseout

The available child and dependent tax credits begin to phase out when AGI reaches $400,000 for married taxpayers filing jointly ($200,000 for all other taxpayers). The credit is phased out by $50 for each $1,000 (or part thereof) of AGI above the $400,000 (or $200,000) amounts.[33] Because the maximum credit amount depends on the *number* of qualifying children and dependents, the income level at which these credits are phased out completely also depends on the *number* of qualifying children and dependents.

If married taxpayers filing a joint return have one qualifying child, the child tax credit is completely phased out if their AGI exceeds $440,000. If those taxpayers have two qualifying children, the child tax credit is completely phased out if their AGI exceeds $480,000. For all other taxpayers, these amounts would be $240,000 and $280,000, respectively. The allowed tax credit can be determined using the following steps.

1. AGI − Threshold amount = Excess amount.
2. Excess amount ÷ $1,000 = Reduction factor (round up to next whole number; for example, 18.2 = 19).
3. Reduction factor × $50 = Child and dependent tax credit reduction.
4. Maximum child and dependent tax credit amount − Child and dependent tax credit reduction = Child and dependent tax credit allowed.

Child and Dependent Tax Credit

EXAMPLE 26

In 2020, Juanita and Alberto are married and file a joint tax return. They have two dependent children, ages 6 and 8. Their AGI is $85,400. Juanita and Alberto's maximum child tax credit is $4,000 ($2,000 × 2 children).

Because Juanita and Alberto's AGI is less than the $400,000 threshold, they are allowed a child tax credit of $4,000.

EXAMPLE 27

Assume the same facts as Example 26, except that Juanita and Alberto's AGI is $412,400. Since their AGI is over the $400,000 threshold, the maximum child tax credit ($4,000) must be reduced by $50 for every $1,000 (or portion of $1,000) above the $400,000 threshold. The child tax credit allowed is $3,350, computed as follows.

1. $412,400 (AGI) − $400,000 (Threshold amount) = $12,400 (Excess amount).
2. $12,400 (Excess amount) ÷ $1,000 = Reduction factor (12.4, rounded up to 13).
3. 13 (Reduction factor) × $50 = $650 (Child and dependent tax credit reduction).
4. $4,000 (Maximum child and dependent tax credit amount) − $650 (Child and dependent tax credit reduction) = $3,350 (Child and dependent tax credit allowed).

EXAMPLE 28

Assume the same facts as Example 27, but also assume that Juanita's mother (age 88) is living with Juanita and Alberto and is a qualifying relative.

Since Juanita's mother is a qualifying relative, Juanita and Alberto will receive a $500 dependent tax credit. Their maximum combined child and dependent tax credit is $4,500 ($4,000 child tax credit + $500 dependent tax credit). This maximum amount is reduced by $650 (the child and dependent tax credit reduction; see Example 27). So their allowed child and dependent tax credit is $3,850 ($4,500 − $650).

---

[32]§ 24(h)(4)(B).

[33]§ 24(b), as modified by § 24(h)(3). AGI is modified for this purpose; the threshold amounts are *not* indexed for inflation.

If the tax credit amounts to more than what is owed as tax

Refundable Portion of Child Tax Credit

For all taxpayers with qualifying children (regardless of how many), the <u>child tax credit</u> is refundable to the extent of the *lesser* of:

1. $1,400 of the child tax credit for each qualifying child, or
2. 15 percent of the taxpayer's earned income in excess of $2,500.

The $1,400 amount is adjusted for inflation each year; the $2,500 amount is not inflation adjusted. The dependent tax credit is *nonrefundable*.

Return to the facts of Example 26. Assume that Juanita and Alberto have $82,000 of earned income. The refundable portion of their child tax credit is $2,800, computed as follows.

1. $2,800 (2 qualifying children × $1,400), or
2. $11,925 [15% × ($82,000 − $2,500)].

EXAMPLE 29

3-4 FILING THE RETURN

3-4a Filing Status

The amount of tax varies considerably depending on which **filing status**[34] the taxpayer uses. One's filing status is determined for every tax year. The taxpayer's filing status is used to determine:

LO.5

Choose the proper filing status and identify the related filing requirements.

- The taxpayer's standard deduction (see Exhibits 3.4 and 3.5).
- Whether the taxpayer must file a tax return.
- The taxpayer's tax liability.
- Reductions of itemized deductions and certain tax credits.
- Eligibility for certain provisions (e.g., some credits are not available when the married, filing separately status is used).

There are five filing statuses, and all taxpayers will file a return based on the filing status selected.

- Single.
- Married, filing jointly.
- Married, filing separately.
- Surviving spouse (qualifying widow or widower).
- Head of household. *with any dependent*

The following amounts of Federal income tax are computed using the 2020 Tax Rate Schedules for a taxpayer (or taxpayers in the case of a joint return) with $60,000 of taxable income (see Appendix A). This illustrates the differences in tax liability that arise due to the filing status that is used.

Filing Status	Amount of Tax
Single	$8,990
Married, filing joint return	6,805
Married, filing separate return	8,990
Head of household	7,548

EXAMPLE 30

---

[34]§§ 1 and 2.

Single Taxpayers

State law governs whether a taxpayer is considered married, divorced, or legally separated. A taxpayer who is unmarried, divorced, or legally separated from his or her spouse and does not qualify for another filing status must file as a single taxpayer. Marital status is determined as of the last day of the tax year, except when a spouse dies during the year. In that case, marital status is determined as of the "date" of death. See Exhibit 3.7.   *Surviving Status starts the following year*

Married Taxpayers

The *joint return* results in equity between married taxpayers in community property states and those in common law states. Before the joint filing status was created, taxpayers in community property states had an advantage relative to taxpayers in common law states because community property law allowed them to split their income between two tax returns. For instance, if one spouse earned $100,000 and the other spouse was not employed, each spouse could report $50,000 of income. Splitting the income in this manner caused the total income to be subject to lower marginal tax rates, under the progressive income tax rate system of the United States.

Taxpayers in common law states did not have this income-splitting option, so their taxable income potentially was subject to higher marginal rates. This inconsistency in treatment was remedied by the joint filing status. The joint return Tax Rate Schedule is constructed assuming that income is earned equally by the two spouses.

If married individuals elect to file *separate returns*, each reports only his or her own income, deductions, and credits, and each must use the tax rates for those married, filing separately.

Most married couples file a joint return, because the combined amount of tax is lower. However, special circumstances (e.g., significant medical expenses incurred by one spouse subject to the AGI limitation) may lead a couple to file separate returns. Usually, tax filing software computes the tax under both assumptions to determine which filing status produces the lower tax liability.

Once a joint return has been filed and the due date has passed, the spouses cannot switch to separate returns for that year. However, if married persons file separately, they can change later to a joint return.

Additional limitations apply to married persons who file separate returns. Examples of these limitations are listed below. In such cases, filing as a single individual is preferable to being married and filing separately.

- If either spouse itemizes deductions, the other spouse must also itemize.
- The earned income credit and the credit for child and dependent care expenses cannot be claimed (see text Section 12-4).
- No deduction is allowed for interest paid on qualified education loans (see text Section 10-3a).
- Only $1,500 of excess capital losses can be claimed by each spouse for the tax year (see text Section 14-5d).

EXHIBIT 3.7	Marital Status for Filing Status Purposes

Taxpayers	Marital Status at Year-End
Walt is the widower of Helen, who died on January 3.	Walt and Helen are married.
Bill and Jane entered into a divorce decree that is effective on December 31.	Bill and Jane are unmarried.

Duke and Carla are in the process of divorcing. They qualify this year for a $4,000 earned income credit. If the taxpayers stay married but file separate returns this year, neither party can claim the credit. If instead a joint return is filed, the credit is available, presumably to be divided with the couple's other assets. If the divorce is finalized this year, both parties will file Forms 1040 using single filing status, and either of them can claim the credit.

EXAMPLE 31

A married same-sex couple is treated as married for Federal tax purposes. To the contrary, registered domestic partners are not "spouses" under Federal law, nor are those who are part of a civil union. Therefore, those parties must file Federal tax returns as single individuals.

Surviving Spouse

Joint filing status is available for two years following the death of one spouse, if the surviving spouse maintains a household for a dependent child. The child must be a son, stepson, daughter, or stepdaughter who qualifies as a dependent of the taxpayer. This is referred to as **surviving spouse** status.[35]

Fred dies in 2020, leaving Ethel with a dependent child. For 2020, Ethel files a joint return with Fred (presuming that the consent of Fred's executor is obtained). For the next two tax years (2021 and 2022), Ethel, filing as a surviving spouse, may use the joint return rates. In subsequent years, Ethel uses the head-of-household rates if she continues to maintain a household as her home that is the domicile of the child.

EXAMPLE 32

Head of Household

An unmarried individual who maintains a household for one or more dependents may qualify to use the **head-of-household** filing status.[36] The tax liability using the head-of-household rates falls between the tax liabilities for married taxpayers filing jointly and single taxpayers.

To qualify for head-of-household rates, a taxpayer must pay more than half the cost of maintaining a household as his or her home. The household also must be the principal home of a dependent. That dependent must be either a qualifying child or a qualifying relative who meets the relationship test.[37]

Except for temporary absences (e.g., school, hospitalization), the dependent must live in the taxpayer's household for more than half the year. Head-of-household status is allowed if the taxpayer maintains a *separate home* for his or her *parent or parents*, if at least one parent qualifies as a dependent of the taxpayer.[38]

The Big Picture

Return to the facts of *The Big Picture* on p. 3-1. Assuming that Aleha can be treated as single (i.e., not married), can Terrah qualify Aleha for head-of-household filing status? The answer is no. Even though Terrah can be claimed as Aleha's dependent (see Example 18), she does not meet the relationship test and is not a qualifying relative.

EXAMPLE 33

Head-of-Household Rules

Nisha, a widow, maintains a household in which she and her aunt live. If the aunt qualifies as a dependent, Nisha may file as head of household. An aunt meets the relationship test.

EXAMPLE 34

---

[35]§ 2(a). The IRS term for surviving spouse status is "Qualifying Widow(er) with Dependent Child."

[36]§ 2(b).

[37]§ 2(b)(3)(B). The member-of-the-household test cannot be used for this purpose.

[38]§ 2(b)(1)(B).

Head-of-Household Rules

EXAMPLE 35

Nancy maintains a household in which she and her daughter, Renata, live. Renata, age 27, is single and earns $9,000 from a part-time job. Nancy does not qualify for head-of-household filing status, as she cannot claim Renata as a dependent (due to the gross income test).[39]

EXAMPLE 36

Raza, an unmarried individual, lives in New York City and maintains a household in Arizona for his dependent parents. Raza may use the head-of-household rates, even though his parents do not reside in his New York home.

Abandoned Spouse Rules

When married individuals file separate returns, several unfavorable tax consequences result. For example, the taxpayer likely must use the higher married, filing separately tax rates. To mitigate such harsh treatment for some individuals, Congress enacted provisions commonly referred to as the **abandoned spouse** rules. These rules allow a married taxpayer to file as *not married*, and thus as head of household, if all of the following conditions are met.[40]

- The taxpayer does not file a joint return.
- The taxpayer paid more than half the cost of maintaining his or her home for the tax year.
- The taxpayer's spouse did not live in the home during the last six months of the tax year.
- The home was the principal residence of the taxpayer's son, daughter, stepson, stepdaughter, foster child, or adopted child for more than half the year, and the child can be claimed as a dependent.[41]

The Big Picture

EXAMPLE 37

Return to the facts of *The Big Picture* on p. 3-1. Can Aleha qualify as an abandoned spouse? Yes, if she can claim Paige as a dependent—either as a qualifying child (see Example 12) or as a qualifying relative (see Example 21). If so, Aleha can use head-of-household filing status. If not, her filing status is married filing separately.

ETHICS & EQUITY   **Abandoned Spouse?**

Bob and Carol have been in and out of marital counseling for the past few years. Early in the current tax year, they decide to separate. However, because they are barely able to get by on their current incomes, they cannot afford separate housing or the legal costs of a divorce. So Bob moves out of their house in March and takes up residence in their detached garage (which has an enclosed workshop and bathroom). Carol stays in the house with their two children and pays more than half of the costs of maintaining their residence. Bob does not enter the house for the remainder of the year.

Can Carol qualify as an abandoned spouse when filing her Federal income tax return for the year?

---

[39]Can Renata be a dependent under the qualifying child rules? Even though the gross income test does not apply for a qualifying child, Renata fails the age test.

[40]§ 7703(b).

[41]§ 152(f)(1).

3-4b **Filing the Return**

General Rules

Generally, an individual must file a tax return if gross income equals or exceeds the applicable standard deduction.[42] A married taxpayer filing a separate return is required to file a return if he or she reports *any* amount of gross income.

For example, a single taxpayer under age 65 must file a tax return for 2020 if gross income equals or exceeds $12,400 (the amount of the standard deduction). Exhibit 3.8 lists the income levels[43] that require the filing of tax returns.

The additional standard deduction for those age 65 or older is considered in applying the gross income filing requirements. The additional standard deduction for blindness is not taken into account for this purpose.

A self-employed individual with net earnings of $400 or more from a business or profession must file a Federal income tax return regardless of the amount of gross income.

Even though an individual records gross income below the filing level amounts and therefore does not owe any tax, he or she must file a return to obtain a tax refund of amounts withheld. Filing a return also is necessary to obtain the benefits of the earned income credit allowed to taxpayers with little or no tax liability. Text Section 12-4a discusses the earned income credit.

Filing Requirements for Dependents

The gross income filing requirement for an individual who can be claimed as a dependent on another person's tax return is tied to the amount of a dependent's standard deduction (see text Section 3-1b). For 2020, a dependent must file a return for the year if he or she has *any* of the following.

- Earned income only and gross income that is more than the total standard deduction (including any additional standard deduction).

EXHIBIT 3.8	Income Levels When a Form 1040 Must Be Filed	
Filing Status	**2019 Gross Income**	**2020 Gross Income**
Single		
Under 65 and not blind	$12,200	$12,400
65 or older	13,850	14,050
Married, filing joint return		
Both spouses under 65	$24,400	$24,800
One spouse 65 or older	25,700	26,100
Both spouses 65 or older	27,000	27,400
Married, filing separate return		
All	Any	Any
Head of household		
Under 65	$18,350	$18,650
65 or older	20,000	20,300
Qualifying widow(er)		
Under 65	$24,400	$24,800
65 or older	25,700	26,100

---

[42]The gross income amounts for determining whether a tax return must be filed are adjusted for inflation each year, because the standard deduction amounts similarly are indexed.

[43]§ 6012(a)(1).

- Unearned income only and gross income of more than $1,100 plus any additional standard deduction.
- Both earned and unearned income and gross income of more than the larger of $1,100 or the sum of earned income plus $350 (but limited to the basic standard deduction), plus any additional standard deduction.

Thus, the filing requirement for a dependent who has no unearned income is the total of the *basic* standard deduction plus any *additional* standard deduction, which includes both the additional deduction for blindness and the deduction for being age 65 or older. For example, the 2020 filing requirement for a single dependent who is under age 65 is $12,400, the amount of the basic standard deduction.

Selecting the Proper Form

Because the 2020 tax forms had not been released when this text was published, the following comments apply to the 2019 forms.[44]

All taxpayers use Form 1040 as a starting point. Then depending on their various activities (e.g., business, investment, personal), supplemental schedules may be required.

If the taxpayer:	File:
Has additional income to report (e.g., business income or loss, unemployment compensation, prize or award money, or gambling winnings). OR Has any deductions to claim (e.g., student loan interest, self-employment tax, individual retirement account contributions, or educator expenses).	Schedule 1 (Form 1040)
Owes the alternative minimum tax or needs to make an excess advance premium tax credit repayment. OR Owes other taxes (e.g., the self-employment tax, household employment taxes, or additional taxes on IRAs or other qualified retirement plans and tax-favored accounts).	Schedule 2 (Form 1040)
Can claim a nonrefundable credit other than the child tax credit or the dependent credit (e.g., the foreign tax credit, education credits, or the general business credit). OR Can claim a refundable credit other than the earned income credit, American Opportunity credit, or additional child tax credit (e.g., the net premium tax credit or health coverage credit). OR Has other payments to report (e.g., an amount paid with an extension to file or excess Social Security tax withheld).	Schedule 3 (Form 1040)

The schedules are available on the IRS website (**irs.gov**). Other forms and schedules may be needed to supplement Form 1040 and Schedules 1 through 3. For example, a self-employed taxpayer will need to complete Schedule C (Form 1040) as a supplement to Schedule 1 while also computing his or her self-employment tax liability by completing Schedule SE (Form 1040) as a supplement to Schedule 2. Taxpayers who want to itemize deductions *from* AGI need to complete Schedule A (Form 1040) to document those deductions.

As required by a 2018 law change, the IRS has developed a tax return (Form 1040SR) for taxpayers who are age 65 by the last day of the year. Form 1040SR is mostly similar to Form 1040.[45]

E-Filing

The **e-file** program is the means by which almost 90 percent of individual taxpayers file their Federal income tax returns. Most tax preparers are required to file their clients' returns in this manner as well.

When e-filing is used, the required tax information is transmitted to the IRS electronically either directly from the taxpayer (i.e., an "e-file online return") or indirectly

---

[44]Draft tax forms are available from the IRS at **apps.irs.gov/app/picklist/ list/draftTaxForms.html**.

[45]Created by Sec. 41106 of P.L. 115–123, the Bipartisan Budget Act of 2018.

GLOBAL TAX ISSUES **Tracking Down Tax Dollars**

Non-U.S. persons who earn income within the United States may need to file a Federal income tax return, but they may not have a Social Security number for filing purposes. If not, they can use a nine-digit Individual Tax Identification Number (ITIN) instead. The IRS issues ITINs upon the submission of an application and proof of identification (e.g., a driver's license). As the IRS does not require an applicant to show that he or she is in the United States legally, the ITINs are freely available to undocumented persons (i.e., illegal immigrants). The use of an ITIN also can enable the holder to carry out other financial transactions (e.g., establish a bank account, secure a credit card, and obtain a loan).

The position of the IRS is that the current ITIN procedure brings in revenue that otherwise would not be forthcoming. Some undocumented workers want to comply with the law and pay the income taxes they owe. This practice should not be discouraged, as the tax law applies with equal force to legal and illegal residents of the United States.

However, ITINs have been criticized for their use by illegal immigrants and undocumented workers. A recent report found that individuals who are not authorized to work in the United States were paid $4.2 billion in refundable tax credits, such as the child tax credit, because they were able to file tax returns using an ITIN.

---

through tax professionals who have been accepted into the electronic filing program by the IRS. Such parties often hold themselves out to the general public as "authorized IRS e-file providers."

For direct e-filing, a taxpayer uses a personal computer, laptop, phone, or tablet, employing tax preparation software with the capability of conveying the information online to an electronic return transmitter. A taxpayer then can use the free smartphone app "IRS2Go" to check the status of a refund.

Through an arrangement with the IRS, designated software providers offer free e-filing services. These services are available only to lower-income taxpayers. A list of these "Free-File" providers and their eligibility requirements can be obtained at **irs.gov/filing/e-file-options**.

All e-filing taxpayers and tax return preparers must attest to the returns they file. For most taxpayers, this attesting can be done through an electronic return signature using a personal identification number.

E-filing has two major advantages. First, compliance with the format required by the IRS eliminates many math and clerical errors that would otherwise occur. Second, the time required for processing a refund usually is reduced.

When and Where to File

Tax returns of individuals are due on or before the fifteenth day of the fourth month following the close of the tax year. For the calendar year taxpayer, the usual filing date is on or before April 15 of the following year.[46] When the due date falls on a Saturday, Sunday, or legal holiday, the filing deadline is the next business day. The return should be e-filed or sent to an IRS Service Center.[47]

If the return is mailed to the proper address with sufficient postage and is postmarked on or before the due date, it is deemed timely filed. The IRS has issued rules governing the filing of returns using various private delivery services (e.g., FedEx and UPS).[48]

If a taxpayer is unable to file the return by the specified due date, a six-month extension of time is obtained by filing Form 4868 by no later that the due date of the return.[49] Some military personnel are allowed extra time to file their Forms 1040.

Although an extension provides additional time to file a return, it does not extend the deadline for paying any tax due. If more tax is owed, it should be paid when the Form 4868 is filed.

---

[46] § 6072(a). State and local holidays can alter these dates; see Rev.Rul. 2015–13, 2015–22 I.R.B. 1011.

[47] Filing addresses can be determined at **irs.gov/filing/where-to-file-tax-returns-addresses-listed-by-return-type**.

[48] § 7502(f); Notice 2016–30, 2016–18 I.R.B. 676.

[49] Reg. § 1.6081–4.

If an individual taxpayer needs to file an amended return (e.g., because of a failure to report income or to claim an additional deduction or tax credit), Form 1040X is filed. The form generally is filed within three years of the filing date of the original return or within two years from the time the tax was paid, whichever is later.

Mode of Payment

A Federal tax payment can be made by check, made out to "United States Treasury." More commonly, the taxpayer elects on the Form 1040 a direct payment of the amount due, or a direct deposit of a refund receivable, using an indicated bank account. Payments by debit or credit card or through an electronic fund transfer also are allowed; the credit card providers typically assess a processing fee.

3-5 TAX COMPUTATIONS

LO.6

Use the proper method for determining the tax liability.

The computation of income tax due (or refund) involves applying the proper set of tax rates to taxable income and then subtracting available credits.

3-5a Tax Rates

The basic Federal income tax rate structure is progressive, with current rates ranging from 10 percent to 37 percent. By way of comparison, the lowest Federal income tax rates, in effect in 1913–1915, ranged from 1 to 7 percent; the highest, in effect during 1944–1945, ranged from 23 to 94 percent.

3-5b Tax Table Method

The tax liability is computed using either the Tax Table method or the Tax Rate Schedule method. Most taxpayers compute their tax using the `Tax Table`. Eligible taxpayers compute taxable income (as shown in Concept Summary 3.1) and *must* determine their tax by reference to the Tax Table. Taxpayers, however, may not use the Tax Table method when taxable income exceeds $100,000.

The IRS does not release the Tax Tables until late in the year to which they apply. However, the Tax Rate Schedules for a given tax year are released at the end of the preceding year.[50] For purposes of estimating tax liability and making quarterly prepayments, the Tax Rate Schedules usually are consulted.

3-5c Tax Rate Schedule Method

The 2020 Tax Rate Schedule for single taxpayers is reproduced in Exhibit 3.9.[51]

EXHIBIT 3.9	2020 Tax Rate Schedule for Single Taxpayers		
If Taxable Income Is			
Over	**But Not Over**	**The Tax Is:**	**Of the Amount Over**
$ –0–	$ 9,875	10%	$ –0–
9,875	40,125	$ 987.50 + 12%	9,875
40,125	85,525	4,617.50 + 22%	40,125
85,525	163,300	14,605.50 + 24%	85,525
163,300	207,350	33,271.50 + 32%	163,300
207,350	518,400	47,367.50 + 35%	207,350
518,400		156,235.00 + 37%	518,400

[50]The 2019 Tax Table and the 2019 and 2020 Tax Rate Schedules are reproduced in Appendix A. For quick reference, the Tax Rate Schedules also are reproduced inside the front cover of this text.

[51]§ 1(i).

Darpak is single and reported $5,810 of taxable income in 2020. His Federal income tax liability per the Tax Rate Schedule is $581 ($5,810 × 10%).

Darpak's tax liability based on the Tax Table is $583. This amount is based on taxable income of $5,825 (the midpoint between $5,800 and $5,850). Darpak must use the Tax Table because his taxable income does not exceed $100,000.

Several terms are used to describe tax rates. The rates in the Tax Rate Schedules often are referred to as *statutory* (or nominal) rates. The *marginal* rate is the highest rate that is applied in the tax computation for a particular taxpayer. In Example 38, both the statutory rate and the marginal rate are 10 percent.

Angelita is single and recorded taxable income of $102,000 in 2020. Her tax is $18,559.50 [$14,605.50 + 24%($102,000 − $85,525)].

One's *average* rate is equal to the tax liability divided by taxable income. In Example 39, Angelita is subject to progressive statutory rates of 10 percent, 12 percent, 22 percent, and 24 percent. Her marginal income tax rate is 24 percent. Angelita's average rate is 18.2 percent ($18,559.50 tax liability ÷ $102,000 taxable income).

A special computation limits the statutory tax rate for qualified dividends (see text Section 4-3b) and net long-term capital gains (see text Section 14-5c).

3-5d Computation of Net Taxes Payable or Refund Due

The pay-as-you-go feature of the Federal income tax system requires payment of all or part of the taxpayer's income tax liability during the year. These payments take the form of Federal income tax withheld by employers and estimated tax paid by the taxpayer.[52] The payments are applied against the tax liability to determine whether the taxpayer will receive a refund or pay additional tax.

Employers are required to withhold income tax on compensation paid to their employees and to pay this tax to the government. The employer must provide each employee a Form W–2 (Wage and Tax Statement), which details the wages and withheld taxes. The employee should receive this form by January 31 after the year in which the income tax is withheld.

If taxpayers receive income that is not subject to withholding or income from which not enough tax is withheld, they may need to pay estimated tax. These individuals file Form 1040–ES (Estimated Tax for Individuals) and pay in quarterly installments the income tax and self-employment tax estimated to be due.

Tax Credits

Gail is a taxpayer in the 24% Federal income tax bracket. As a result of incurring $1,000 in child care expenses (see text Section 12-4d), she is entitled to a $200 child care credit ($1,000 child care expenses × 20% credit rate). She also contributed $1,000 to the American Cancer Society and included this amount in her itemized deductions.

The child care credit results in a $200 reduction of Gail's tax liability for the year. The contribution to the American Cancer Society reduces taxable income by $1,000 and results in a $240 reduction in Gail's tax liability ($1,000 reduction in taxable income × 24% tax rate).

Return to the facts of Example 10. Grace's taxable income is $43,450. Now further assume that Grace reports the following: income tax withheld, $2,300; estimated tax payments, $3,000; and a credit for child care expenses, $200. Grace's net tax liability is computed as follows.

continued

---

[52]§ 3402 for withholding; § 6654 for estimated payments.

Income tax on taxable income (from 2020 Tax Rate Schedule for Head of Household, Appendix A, rounded)		$ 4,932
Less: Tax credits and prepayments—		
Credit for dependent care expenses	$ 200	
Income tax withheld	2,300	
Estimated tax payments	3,000	(5,500)
Net taxes payable (or refund due, if negative)		($ 568)

One's income tax liability is reduced by any available tax credits. There is an important distinction between tax credits and tax deductions. Tax credits reduce the tax liability dollar for dollar. Tax deductions reduce taxable income on which the tax liability is based. Tax credits are discussed in Chapter 12.

LO.7

Identify and work with kiddie tax situations.

3-5e **Kiddie Tax—Unearned Income of Dependent Children**

At one time, a dependent child could claim an exemption deduction (along with a standard deduction) on his or her own return even if claimed as a dependent by the parents. This enabled a parent to shift investment income (like interest and dividends) to a child by transferring income-producing assets. The child would pay no tax on the income to the extent that it was sheltered by the child's exemption and standard deduction amounts. And if the child did pay any tax, that tax was at the child's (lower) rates rather than the parents' (higher) rates.

To reduce the tax savings that result from shifting income from parents to children, the net **unearned income**[53] (commonly called investment income) of certain children is taxed using special rules. This provision, commonly referred to as the **kiddie tax**, applies to any child who is under age 19 (or under age 24 if a full-time student) and has unearned income of more than $2,200 (in 2020 and 2019).[54]

Net Unearned Income

In 2020, net unearned income of a dependent child is computed as follows:[55]

Unearned income

Less: $1,100

Less: The greater of:
- $1,100 of the standard deduction, *or*
- The amount of allowable itemized deductions directly connected with the production of the unearned income

Equals: Net unearned income

If net unearned income is zero (or negative), the child's tax is computed using the appropriate Tax Rate Schedule (likely single). If net unearned income is positive, this amount is taxed at the parents' rate. The child's remaining taxable income (known as nonparental source income) is taxed at the child's rate.[56]

---

[53]Unearned income includes taxable interest, dividends, capital gains, rents, royalties, the taxable portion of scholarships, pension and annuity income, and income (other than earned income) received as the beneficiary of a trust.

[54]§ 1(g)(2). The kiddie tax does not apply if the child has earned income that exceeds half of his or her support, if the child is married and files a joint return, or if both parents are deceased.

[55]The $1,100 amounts in the net unearned income computation are adjusted each year for inflation. The amounts were the same in 2019.

[56]For 2018 and 2019, taxpayers are allowed to use an alternative method for determining the tax on net unearned income. In general, the alternative method [former § 1(j)(4)] requires the use of a modified Single Tax Rate Schedule (incorporating the Estate and Trust Tax Rate Schedule) and the determination of "earned taxable income." Since this method only applies to 2018 and 2019 tax years, we have chosen not to include a discussion of the alternative method in the text. However, a discussion of the alternative method, along with several examples, is available in the 2020 edition of *South-Western Federal Taxation: Comprehensive Volume* (see text Section 3–5e).

Tax Determination

If a child is subject to the kiddie tax, there are two options for computing the tax on the income. A separate return may be filed for the child, or the parents may elect to report the child's income on their own return.

If a separate return is filed for the child, the tax on net unearned income (referred to as the *allocable parental tax*) is computed as though the income had been included on the parents' return. Form 8615 is used to compute the tax. The steps required in this computation are illustrated in Example 42.

Kiddie Tax Computations

EXAMPLE 42

Olaf and Olga have a child, Hans (age 10). In 2020, Hans received $3,300 of interest income and had no earned income. Olaf and Olga had $70,000 of taxable income, not including their child's investment income. The parents have no qualified dividends or capital gains. Olaf and Olga do not make the parental election (discussed below).

1. Determine Hans's net unearned income

Gross income (unearned)	$ 3,300
Less: $1,050	(1,100)
Less: The greater of	
• $1,050 or	
• Investment expense ($200)	(1,100)
Equals: Net unearned income	$ 1,100

2. Determine allocable parental tax

Parents' taxable income	$70,000
Plus: Hans's net unearned income	1,100
Equals: Revised taxable income	$71,100
Tax on revised taxable income	$ 8,137
Less: Tax on parents' taxable income	(8,005)
Allocable parental tax	$ 132

3. Determine Hans's nonparental source tax

Hans's AGI	$ 3,300
Less: Standard deduction	(1,100)
Less: Personal exemption	(–0–)
Equals: Taxable income	$ 2,200
Less: Net unearned income	(1,100)
Nonparental source taxable income	$ 1,100
Nonparental source tax ($1,100 × 10% rate)	$ 110

4. Determine Hans's total tax liability

Nonparental source tax (step 3)	$ 110
Allocable parental tax (step 2)	132
Total tax	$ 242

Election to Claim Certain Unearned Income on Parent's Return

A parent may elect to report the child's unearned income that exceeds $2,200 (the same in 2019) on the parent's own tax return if the child meets *all* of the following requirements:

- Gross income is from interest and dividends only.
- Gross income is more than $1,100 but less than $11,000 (for 2019, these amounts are the same).
- No estimated tax has been paid in the name and Social Security number of the child, and the child is not subject to backup withholding.

If this election is made, the child is treated as having no gross income and is not required to file a tax return. In this case, Form 8814 (Parents' Election to Report Child's Interest and Dividends) must be filed as part of the parents' tax return. The parent(s) must also pay an additional tax equal to the smaller of $110 or 10 percent of the child's gross income over $1,100.[57]

Other Rules

Here are a few other rules that apply to the kiddie tax:[58]

- If parents have more than one child subject to the tax on net unearned income, the tax for the children is computed as shown in Example 42 and then allocated to the children based on their relative amounts of income.
- For children of divorced parents, the taxable income of the custodial parent is used to determine the allocable parental tax. This parent is the one who may elect to report the child's unearned income.
- For married individuals filing separate returns, the individual with the greater taxable income is the applicable parent.

LO.8

Describe the tax treatment of property transactions.

3-6 GAINS AND LOSSES FROM PROPERTY TRANSACTIONS—IN GENERAL

Gains and losses from property transactions are included in gross income. These items are discussed in detail in Chapters 13 and 14. Because of their importance in the tax system, however, they are introduced briefly at this point.

When property is sold or otherwise disposed of, gain or loss may result. Such gain or loss has an effect on the income tax position of the seller when the *realized* gain or loss is *recognized* for tax purposes. Without realized gain or loss, there generally can be no recognized gain or loss.

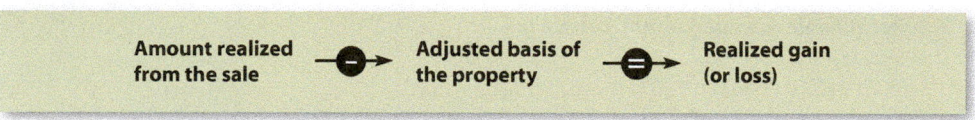

The amount realized is the selling price of the property less any costs of disposition (e.g., brokerage commissions) incurred by the seller. The adjusted basis of the property is determined as follows.

Cost (or other original basis) at date of acquisition
Add: **Capital additions**
Subtract: **Depreciation (if appropriate) and other capital recoveries (see Chapter 8)**
Equals: **Adjusted basis at date of sale or other disposition**

All realized gains are recognized (taxable) unless some specific part of the tax law provides otherwise (e.g., see Chapter 13 dealing with certain nontaxable exchanges). Realized losses may or may not be recognized (deductible) for tax purposes. Generally, losses realized from the disposition of personal use property (e.g., a residence, home furnishings, clothing, sports equipment) are not recognized.

---

[57]Parents who have substantial itemized deductions based on AGI (see Chapter 10) may find that making the parental election increases total taxes for the family unit. Taxes should be calculated both with and without the parental election to determine the appropriate choice.

[58]See *Your Federal Income Tax* (IRS Publication 17) and Form 8615 (Tax for Certain Children Who Have Unearned Income).

Ted sells his sailboat (adjusted basis of $4,000) for $5,500. Ted also sells one of his personal auto-mobiles (adjusted basis of $8,000) for $5,000. Ted's realized gain of $1,500 from the sale of the sailboat is recognized. On the other hand, the $3,000 realized loss on the sale of the automobile is not recognized and does not provide Ted with any deductible tax benefit.

EXAMPLE 43

Once it has been determined that the disposition of property results in a recognized gain or loss, the next step is to classify the gain or loss as capital or ordinary. Although ordinary gain is fully taxable and ordinary loss is fully deductible, the same may not hold true for capital gains and capital losses.

3-7 GAINS AND LOSSES FROM PROPERTY TRANSACTIONS—CAPITAL GAINS AND LOSSES

Capital gains and losses can generate unique tax consequences, as summarized in this section. For in-depth treatment of property transactions (including capital gains and losses), refer to Chapters 13 and 14.

3-7a Capital Assets

Capital assets include any property held by the taxpayer *other than* inventory, accounts receivable, and depreciable property or real estate used in a business. Thus, the sale or exchange of assets in these categories usually results in ordinary income or loss treatment (see Chapter 14).

The principal capital assets held by an individual taxpayer include assets held for personal (rather than business) use (e.g., a personal residence or an automobile) and assets held for investment purposes (e.g., corporate securities and land). Capital assets also include collectibles, which include art, antiques, gems, metals, stamps, some coins and bullion, and alcoholic beverages that are held as investments.

When an individual sells a capital asset, a capital gain or loss results. Capital gains are taxable, and capital losses are netted against them, resulting in a net capital gain or loss. Special tax rates apply to most capital asset sales, but an individual cannot deduct a capital loss that results from the sale of a personal use asset.

Sima owns a pizza parlor. During the current year, she sells two automobiles. The first automobile, which had been used as a pizza delivery car for three years, was sold at a loss of $1,000. Because this automobile is an asset used in her business, Sima claims an ordinary loss deduction of $1,000 rather than a capital loss deduction. The second automobile, which Sima had owned for two years, was her personal use car. It was sold for a gain of $800. The personal use car is a capital asset. Therefore, Sima recognizes a capital gain of $800.

EXAMPLE 44

3-7b Taxation of Net Capital Gain

Net capital gains are classified and subject to Federal income tax rates as follows.

Classification	Maximum Rate
Short-term gains (held for one year or less)	Applicable rate for ordinary income (e.g., 37%)
Long-term gains (held for more than one year)—	
Certain depreciable realty used in a trade or business	25%
Collectibles	28% *unless regular income tax rates are lower*
All other long-term capital gains	20%, 15%, or 0%

The special tax rates for long-term capital gains (called the alternative tax computation) are used when the taxpayer's regular tax rate *exceeds* the alternative tax rate. When tax liability is determined, long-term capital gains are taxed last. As a result, the tax rate applied to a long-term capital gain will depend on the taxpayer's regular tax rate on other income and the size of the long-term capital gain (a large long-term capital gain may cross marginal rates brackets and, theoretically, could be taxed at 0%, 15%, and 20% rates). The alternative rates are applied based on the taxpayer's filing status and taxable income (see Exhibit 3.10). Special rates apply to collectibles and certain types of depreciable realty. If losses are used to offset gains, the losses are first used to offset gains with the *highest* tax rates. These special tax rates also apply to qualified dividend income (see Chapter 4). Chapter 14 provides a detailed discussion of these tax computations.[59]

Tax on Net Capital Gain

EXAMPLE 45

Polly is single and reports taxable income of $35,000. She also reports the following capital gains.

Robin Corporation stock (held for 6 months)	$1,000
Crow Corporation stock (held for 13 months)	1,000

Polly's tax on these transactions is $120 ($1,000 × 12%) as to Robin and $0 ($1,000 × 0%) as to Crow.

EXAMPLE 46

Assume the same facts as in Example 45, except that Polly's taxable income for the year is $170,000 (rather than $35,000). Polly's taxable income puts her in the 32% tax bracket. Polly's tax on these transactions becomes $320 ($1,000 × 32%) as to Robin and $150 ($1,000 × 15%) as to Crow.

EXHIBIT 3.10	2020 Alternative Tax Rates on Net Capital Gains (NCG) (Based on Filing Status and Taxable Income)

	FILING STATUS								
	Single		Married, Filing Jointly		Married, Filing Separately		Head of Household		NCG Tax Rate
	Taxable Income		Taxable Income		Taxable Income		Taxable Income		
	Greater Than	No More Than	Greater Than	No More Than	Greater Than	No More Than	Greater Than	No More Than	
	$ –0–	$ 40,000	$ –0–	$ 80,000	$ –0–	$ 40,000	$ –0–	$ 53,600	0%
	40,000	441,450	80,000	496,600	40,000	248,300	53,600	469,050	15%
	441,450		496,600		248,300		469,050		20%

3-7c **Determination of Net Capital Gain**

To arrive at a *net* capital gain, capital losses are taken into account. The capital losses are aggregated by holding period (short- and long-term) and applied against the gains in that category. If excess losses result, they are shifted to the category carrying the *highest* tax rate. A *net capital gain* occurs if the net long-term capital gain (NLTCG) exceeds the net short-term capital loss (NSTCL).   *Net long-term − Net short term*

---

[59]§ 1(h)(1). In 2019, the 0% rate applies when taxable income does not exceed $78,750 (married, filing jointly), $52,750 (head of household), or $39,375 (single and married, filing separately). The 20% rate applies only when the taxpayer's taxable income exceeds $488,850 (married, filing jointly), $244,425 (married, filing separately), $461,700 (head of household), or $434,550 (single).

In the current year, Colin is single, has taxable income of $195,000, and has the following capital transactions and resulting gains (losses).

Penguin Corporation stock (held for 8 months)	$ 1,000
Owl Corporation stock (held for 10 months)	(3,000)
Stamp collection (held for 5 years)	2,000
Land (held as an investment for 3 years)	4,000

The Penguin short-term capital gain (STCG) of $1,000 is offset by the Owl short-term capital loss (STCL) of $3,000. The remaining STCL of $2,000 then is applied against the collectible gain of $2,000, as that is the capital gain that is subject to the highest tax rate. The end result is a net long-term capital gain of $4,000 from the land sale, taxed at a 15% rate.

3-7d Treatment of Net Capital Loss

For individual taxpayers, net capital loss can be used to offset ordinary income of up to $3,000 ($1,500 for married persons filing separate returns). If a taxpayer reports both short- and long-term capital losses, the short-term category is used first to arrive at the $3,000. Any remaining net capital loss is carried forward indefinitely until it is used up. When carried forward, the excess capital loss retains its classification as short or long term.

Tina reports a short-term capital loss of $2,000, a long-term capital loss of $2,500, and no capital gains. She can deduct $3,000 ($2,000 short-term + $1,000 long-term) of this amount as an ordinary loss. The remaining $1,500 is carried forward to future tax years as a long-term capital loss.

The Big Picture

Return to the facts of *The Big Picture* on p. 3-1. Aleha's sale of her wedding rings resulted in a realized capital loss of $2,800 [$9,000 (selling price) − $11,800 (cost basis)]. However, because they were personal use property, Aleha cannot deduct any part of the loss.

3-7e Taxation of Virtual Currency

Over 2,000 types of virtual currency exist. The first and best-known virtual currency is bitcoin, which had its first real-world transaction in 2010 (to purchase two pizzas).[60] In 2014, the IRS issued guidance on the tax treatment of convertible virtual currency used to pay for goods or services.[61] Convertible means that the virtual currency can be exchanged for real (sovereign) currency in that it acts as a substitute for real currency, such as the U.S. dollar. The key point of this IRS guidance is that virtual currency is treated as *property* rather than as a *foreign currency*. As a result, if an employee is paid in bitcoin, her wages are equal to the value of the bitcoin when received. When a holder of virtual currency uses it to acquire goods or services, the transaction is treated as a barter transaction with tax consequences to the holder.

Neha acquired $500 of bitcoin from a virtual currency exchange in 2018 to hold for investment. In 2020, when its value was $650, Neha used all of her bitcoin to pay for repairs to her car.

Neha must report a long-term capital gain of $150 ($650 fair market value less $500 basis; her holding period is more than one year). She is treated as having sold her bitcoin for $650 when she exchanged it for services worth $650.

---

[60]**en.bitcoinwiki.org/wiki/Bitcoin_history**. Other virtual currencies include Ethereum and Litecoin.

[61]Notice 2014–21, 2014–16 I.R.B. 938.

The 2019 Schedule 1 (Form 1040) includes a specific question about virtual currency.

SCHEDULE 1 (Form 1040 or 1040-SR) Department of the Treasury Internal Revenue Service	**Additional Income and Adjustments to Income** ▶ **Attach to Form 1040 or 1040-SR.** ▶ **Go to** *www.irs.gov/Form1040* **for instructions and the latest information.**	OMB No. 1545-0074 20**19** Attachment Sequence No. **01**
Name(s) shown on Form 1040 or 1040-SR		Your social security number

At any time during 2019, did you receive, sell, send, exchange, or otherwise acquire any financial interest in any virtual currency? . . . . ☐ Yes ☐ No

As most individuals do not own virtual currency, most filers of Schedule 1 will answer "no." And if a Schedule 1 is not otherwise required and the answer to the virtual currency question is "no," then the taxpayer need not file a Schedule 1.

However, individuals not otherwise required to file Schedule 1 must do so if the answer to the question is "yes." It appears that a purpose of the question is to remind taxpayers about the need to report taxable virtual currency transactions, like the sale of virtual currency for cash or other virtual currency, or the use of virtual currency to buy goods or services. To assist taxpayers in complying with these rules, the IRS also maintains a comprehensive "*frequently asked questions*" page on its website.[62]

LO.9

Identify tax planning opportunities associated with the individual tax formula.

3-8 TAX PLANNING

3-8a Optimizing the Use of the Standard Deduction

In most cases, the choice between using the standard deduction and itemizing deductions *from* AGI is a simple matter—pick whichever yields the larger tax benefit. Families in the early years of home ownership, for example, likely will itemize, due to their substantial mortgage interest and property tax payments. Older taxpayers, however, may have repaid the mortgage debt on their homes and, in some states, qualify for reduced property taxes due to senior exemptions. For them, the more attractive choice may be the standard deduction, including any additional amounts based on their age.

In some cases, the difference between using the standard deduction and itemizing may not be a significant amount. Here, taxes might be saved by alternating between the two options. The taxpayer does this by using the cash method to concentrate multiple years' deductions in a single year (e.g., paying off a five-year church pledge in one year). Then the standard deduction is used in alternate years.

3-8b Taking Advantage of Tax Rate Differentials

It is natural for taxpayers to be concerned about the taxes they are paying. How does a tax professional communicate information about tax rates to clients? There are several possibilities.

The *marginal tax rate* (refer to Examples 38 and 39) provides information that can help a taxpayer evaluate a particular course of action or structure a transaction in the most advantageous manner. For example, a taxpayer who is in the 12 percent bracket this year and expects to be in the 24 percent bracket next year should, if possible, defer payment of deductible expenses until next year, to maximize the tax benefit of the deduction.

---

[62]irs.gov/individuals/international-taxpayers/frequently-asked-questions-on-virtual-currency-transactions.

A taxpayer's *effective rate* can be an informative measure of the effectiveness of tax planning. The effective rate is computed by dividing the taxpayer's tax liability by the total amount of income. A low effective rate can be considered an indication of effective tax planning.

One way of lowering the effective rate is to exclude income from the tax base. For example, a taxpayer might consider investing in tax-free municipal bonds rather than taxable corporate bonds. Although pretax income from corporate bonds is usually higher, after-tax income may be higher if the taxpayer invests in tax-free municipal bonds.

3-8c Unearned Income of Children

Taxpayers can use several strategies to avoid or minimize the effect of the kiddie tax rules. Parents should consider giving a younger child assets that defer taxable income until the child is free of the kiddie tax. For example, U.S. government Series EE savings bonds can be used to defer income until the bonds are cashed in (see text Section 4-2c).

Growth stocks typically pay little in the way of dividend income. However, the capital gain on an astute investment may more than offset the lack of dividends. The stock can be held and then sold only when the child's own tax rates apply.

Taxpayers who own a business can employ their children in their business and pay them a reasonable wage for the work they actually perform (e.g., light office help such as data entry). The child's earned income is sheltered by the standard deduction, and the parents' business is allowed a deduction for the wages. The kiddie tax rules have no effect on earned income, and the income can be sheltered further if it is contributed to a retirement plan.

REFOCUS ON THE BIG PICTURE

A DIVIDED HOUSEHOLD

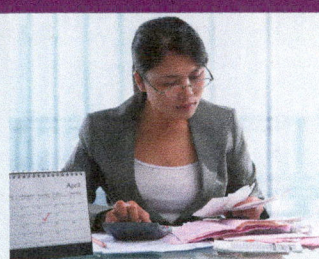
ATNOYDUR/ISTOCK/GETTY IMAGES

Of major concern to Aleha is her filing status. If she qualifies as an abandoned spouse, she is entitled to file as head of household. If not, she is considered to be a married person filing separately. Moreover, to be an abandoned spouse, Aleha must be able to claim Paige as a dependent. To be a dependent, Paige must meet the requirements of a qualifying child *or* a qualifying relative.

Does Terrah qualify Aleha for head-of-household filing status? Although Terrah is Aleha's dependent, Terrah does not meet the relationship test (see Example 33).

The sale of the wedding rings results in a capital loss of $2,800 ($9,000 − $11,800). Because the loss is for personal use property, it cannot be deducted for tax purposes.

What If?

Assume that Trevor left for parts unknown in August (not March). Now Aleha cannot qualify as an abandoned spouse. Her husband lived in the home during part of the last six months of the year. Consequently, Aleha is treated as married and cannot qualify for head-of-household filing status. She is a married person filing separately. This likely is a costly tax result. When Trevor left does not affect the dependency issue regarding Paige, however.

ATNOYDUR/ISTOCK/GETTY IMAGES

Key Terms

Abandoned spouse, 3-20

Child tax credit, 3-15

Collectibles, 3-29

Dependency exemptions, 3-9

Dependent tax credit, 3-15

E-file, 3-22

Filing status, 3-17

Head of household, 3-19

Itemized deductions, 3-6

Kiddie tax, 3-26

Multiple support agreement, 3-13

Personal exemptions, 3-9

Qualifying child, 3-10

Qualifying relative, 3-11

Standard deduction, 3-6

Surviving spouse, 3-19

Tax Table, 3-24

Unearned income, 3-26

Discussion Questions

Critical Thinking

1. **LO.1, 5, 8, 9** During the year, Addison is involved in the following transactions:
   a. Lost money gambling on a recent trip to a casino.
   b. Helped pay for her neighbor's dental bills. The neighbor is a good friend who is unemployed.
   c. Received from the IRS a tax refund due to Addison's overpayment of last year's Federal income taxes.
   d. Paid a traffic ticket received while double parking to attend a business meeting.
   e. Contributed to the mayor's reelection campaign. The mayor had promised Addison to have some of her land rezoned. The mayor was reelected and got Addison's land rezoned.
   f. Borrowed money from a bank to make a down payment on an automobile.
   g. Sold a houseboat and a camper on eBay. Both were personal use items, and the gain from one offset the loss from the other.
   h. Paid for dependent grandfather's funeral expenses.
   i. Paid premiums on her dependent son's life insurance policy.

   What are the possible income tax ramifications of these transactions?

2. **LO.1** Which of the following items are *inclusions* in gross income?
   a. During the year, stock that the taxpayer purchased as an investment doubled in value.
   b. Amount an off-duty motorcycle police officer received for escorting a funeral procession.
   c. While his mother was in the hospital, the taxpayer sold some of her jewelry to help pay for the hospital bills.
   d. Child support payments received.
   e. A damage deposit the taxpayer recovered when he vacated the apartment he had rented.
   f. Interest received by the taxpayer on an investment in general purpose bonds issued by IBM.
   g. Amounts received by the taxpayer, a baseball "Hall of Famer," for autographing sports equipment (e.g., balls and gloves).
   h. Tips received by a bartender from patrons. (Taxpayer is paid a regular salary by the cocktail lounge that employs him.)
   i. Taxpayer sells his Super Bowl tickets for three times what he paid for them.
   j. Taxpayer receives a new BMW from his grandmother when he passes the CPA exam.

3. **LO.1** Which of the following items are *exclusions* from gross income?
   a. Alimony payments received (relates to a divorce settlement in 2016).
   b. Damages award received by the taxpayer for personal physical injury—none were for punitive damages.
   c. A new golf cart won in a church raffle.
   d. Amount collected on a loan previously made to a college friend.
   e. Insurance proceeds paid to the taxpayer on the death of her uncle—she was the designated beneficiary under the policy.
   f. Interest income on City of Chicago bonds.
   g. Jury duty fees.
   h. Stolen funds the taxpayer had collected for a local food bank drive.
   i. Reward paid by the IRS for information provided that led to the conviction of the taxpayer's former employer for tax evasion.
   j. An envelope containing $8,000 found (and unclaimed) by the taxpayer in a bus station.

4. **LO.1, 8, 9** In late 2020, the Polks come to you for tax advice. They are considering selling some stock investments for a loss and making a contribution to a traditional IRA. In reviewing their situation, you note that they have large medical expenses and a casualty loss (in a Federally declared disaster area), neither of which is covered by insurance. What advice would you give the Polks?

   Decision Making
   Critical Thinking

5. **LO.2** In choosing between taking the standard deduction and itemizing deductions *from* AGI, what effect, if any, does each of the following have?

   Critical Thinking
   a. The age of the taxpayer(s).
   b. The health (i.e., physical condition) of the taxpayer.
   c. Whether taxpayers rent or own their residence.
   d. Taxpayer's filing status (e.g., single, married, filing jointly).
   e. Whether married taxpayers decide to file separate returns.
   f. The taxpayer's uninsured personal residence that was recently destroyed by a wildfire (the region was declared a disaster area by the Federal government).
   g. The number of dependents the taxpayer can claim.

6. **LO.2, 3, 5** In 2020, David is age 78, is a widower, and is being claimed as a dependent by his son. How does this situation affect the following?
   a. David's own individual filing requirement.
   b. The standard deduction allowed to David.
   c. The availability of any additional standard deduction.

7. **LO.4** Magda maintains a household that includes a son (age 30) and a cousin (age 28). She can claim the cousin as a dependent but not her son. Explain.

   Critical Thinking

8. **LO.4** Heather, age 12, lives in the same household with her mother, grandmother, and uncle.
   a. Who can claim Heather as a dependent?
   b. Who takes precedence?

9. **LO.4** Caden and Lily are divorced on March 3, 2019. For financial reasons, however, Lily continues to live in Caden's apartment and receives her support from him. Caden does not claim Lily as a dependent on his 2019 Federal income tax return but does so on his 2020 return. Explain.

10. **LO.4** Isabella, Emma, and Jacob share equally in the support of their parents. Jacob tells his sisters to each claim one of their parents as a dependent. Explain what Jacob means.

Critical Thinking 11. **LO.4** Mark and Lisa were divorced in 2019. In 2020, Mark has custody of their children, but Lisa provides nearly all of their support. Who is entitled to claim the children as dependents?

Critical Thinking 12. **LO.4** Mario, who is single, is a U.S. citizen and resident. He provides almost all of the support of his parents and two aunts, who are citizens and residents of Guatemala. Mario's parents and aunts are seriously considering moving to and becoming residents of Mexico. Would such a move have any impact on Mario? Why or why not?

13. **LO.4, 5** Comment on the availability of head-of-household filing status for 2020 in each of the following independent situations:

a. Taxpayer lives alone but maintains the household of his parents. In July 2020, the parents use their savings to purchase a new BMW for $62,000.

b. Taxpayer maintains a home in which she and her dependent father live. The father enters a nursing facility for treatment of a mental disorder.

c. Taxpayer, a single parent, maintains a home in which she and her unmarried son live. The son, age 18, earns $5,000 from a part-time job.

d. Assume the same facts as in part (c), except that the son is age 19, not 18.

e. Taxpayer is married and maintains a household in which he and his dependent stepson live.

f. Taxpayer lives alone but maintains the household where her dependent daughter lives.

g. Taxpayer maintains a household that includes an unrelated friend who qualifies as his dependent.

14. **LO.6** Jayden calculates his 2020 income tax by using both the Tax Tables and the Tax Rate Schedules. Because the Tax Rate Schedules yield a slightly lower tax liability, he plans to pay this amount.

a. Why is there a difference?

b. Is Jayden's approach permissible? Why or why not?

15. **LO.7** In connection with the application of the kiddie tax, comment on the following:

a. The child has only earned income.

b. The child has a modest amount of unearned income.

c. The child is age 20, is not a student, and is not disabled.

d. The child is married.

e. Effect of the parental election.

f. The result when the parental election is made and the married parents file separate returns.

16. **LO.8** During the year, Hernando has the following transactions:

• Gain on the sale of stock held as an investment for 10 months.

• Gain on the sale of land held as an investment for 4 years.

• Gain on the sale of a houseboat owned for 2 years and used for family vacations.

• Loss on the sale of a reconditioned motorcycle owned for 3 years and used for recreational purposes.

How should Hernando treat these transactions for income tax purposes?

Computational Exercises

Critical Thinking 17. **LO.2** Sam and Abby are dependents of their parents, and each has income of $2,100 for the year. Sam's standard deduction for the year is $1,100, and Abby's is $2,450. Because their income is the same, what causes the difference in the amount of the standard deduction?

18. **LO.2** Compute the 2020 standard deduction for the following taxpayers.

    a.   Ellie is 15 and claimed as a dependent by her parents. She has $800 in dividends income and $1,400 in wages from a part-time job.

    b.   Ruby and Woody are married and file a joint tax return. Ruby is age 66, and Woody is 69. Their taxable retirement income is $10,000.

    c.   Shonda is age 68 and single. She is claimed by her daughter as a dependent. Her earned income is $500, and her interest income is $125.

    d.   Frazier, age 55, is married but is filing a separate return. His wife itemizes her deductions.

19. **LO.5, 9** Paul and Sonja, who are married, had itemized deductions of $13,200 and   Critical Thinking $400, respectively, during 2020. Paul suggests that they file separately—he will itemize his deductions *from* AGI, and she will claim the standard deduction.

    a.   Evaluate Paul's suggestion.

    b.   What should they do?

20. **LO.6** Compute the 2020 tax liability and the marginal and average tax rates for the following taxpayers (use the 2020 Tax Rate Schedules in Appendix A for this purpose):

    a.   Chandler, who files as a single taxpayer, has taxable income of $94,800.

    b.   Lazare, who files as a head of household, has taxable income of $57,050.

21. **LO.7** In 2020, Simon, age 12, has interest income of $4,900 on funds he inherited from his grandmother, and no earned income. He has no investment expenses. His parents have taxable income of $82,250 and file a joint return. Assume that no parental election is made. Determine Simon's net unearned income, allocable parental tax, and total tax liability.

22. **LO.8** Rebecca sells her personal scooter for $550. She purchased the scooter for $700 three years ago. She also sells a painting for $1,200 that she acquired five years ago for $900. What are the tax implications of these sales?

23. **LO.8** During the year, Tamara had capital transactions resulting in gains (losses) as follows:

Sold stock in ABC Company (acquired two years ago)	($1,500)
Sold collectible coins (held for more than one year)	2,000
Sold stock in XYZ Company (acquired six months ago)	(4,100)
Sold stock in LMN Company (acquired three years ago)	500

Determine Tamara's net capital gain or loss as a result of these transactions.

Problems

24. **LO.1** Compute the taxable income for 2020 in each of the following independent situations:

    a.   Drew and Meg, ages 40 and 41, respectively, are married and file a joint return. In addition to four dependent children, they have AGI of $125,000 and itemized deductions of $27,000.

    b.   Sybil, age 40, is single and supports her dependent parents who live with her, as well as her grandfather who is in a nursing home. She has AGI of $80,000 and itemized deductions of $8,000.

    c.   Scott, age 49, is a surviving spouse. His household includes two unmarried stepsons who qualify as his dependents. He has AGI of $75,000 and itemized deductions of $10,100.

d. Amelia, age 33, is an abandoned spouse who maintains a household for her three dependent children. She has AGI of $58,000 and itemized deductions of $10,650.

e. Dale, age 42, is divorced but maintains the home in which he and his daughter, Jill, live. Jill is single and qualifies as Dale's dependent. Dale has AGI of $64,000 and itemized deductions of $9,900.

Note: *Problems 25 and 26 can be solved by referring to* Concept Summary 3.1, Exhibits 3.1 through 3.5, *and the discussion under* Deductions *for* Adjusted Gross Income *in this chapter.*

25. **LO.1, 8** Compute the taxable income for 2020 for Emily on the basis of the following information. Her filing status is single.

Salary	$85,000
Interest income from bonds issued by Xerox	1,100
Alimony payments received (divorce occurred in 2014)	6,000
Contribution to traditional IRA	6,000
Gift from parents	25,000
Short-term capital gain from stock investment	2,500
Amount lost in football office pool	500
Age	40

26. **LO.1** Compute the taxable income for 2020 for Aiden on the basis of the following information. Aiden is married but has not seen or heard from his wife since 2018.

Salary	$ 80,000
Interest on bonds issued by City of Boston	3,000
Interest on CD issued by Wells Fargo Bank	2,000
Cash dividend received on Chevron common stock	2,200
Life insurance proceeds paid upon death of aunt (Aiden was the designated beneficiary of the policy)	200,000
Inheritance received upon death of aunt	100,000
Jackson (a cousin) repaid a loan Aiden made to him in 2014 (no interest was provided for)	5,000
Itemized deductions (state income tax, property taxes on residence, interest on home mortgage, and charitable contributions)	9,700
Number of dependents (children, ages 17 and 18, and mother-in-law, age 70)	3
Age	43

27. **LO.2** Determine the amount of the standard deduction allowed for 2020 in the following independent situations. In each case, assume that the taxpayer is claimed as another person's dependent.

a. Curtis, age 18, has income as follows: $700 interest from a certificate of deposit and $12,600 from repairing cars.

b. Mattie, age 18, has income as follows: $600 cash dividends from a stock investment and $4,700 from handling a paper route.

c. Jason, age 16, has income as follows: $675 interest on a bank savings account and $800 for painting a neighbor's fence.

d. Ayla, age 15, has income as follows: $400 cash dividends from a stock investment and $500 from grooming pets.

e. Sarah, age 67 and a widow, has income as follows: $500 from a bank savings account and $3,200 from babysitting.

28. **LO.4** Analyze each of the characteristics in considering the indicated test for dependency as a qualifying child or qualifying relative. In the last two columns, after each listed test (e.g., gross income), state whether the particular test is Met, Not Met, or Not Applicable (NA).

	Characteristic	Qualifying Child Test	Qualifying Relative Test
a.	Taxpayer's son has gross income of $7,000.	Gross income	Gross income
b.	Taxpayer's niece has gross income of $3,000.	Gross income	Gross income
c.	Taxpayer's uncle lives with him.	Relationship	Relationship
d.	Taxpayer's daughter is 25 and disabled.	Age	Age
e.	Taxpayer's daughter is age 18, has gross income of $8,000, and does not live with him.	Residence Gross income	Gross income
f.	Taxpayer's cousin does not live with her.	Relationship Residence	Relationship
g.	Taxpayer's brother does not live with her.	Residence	Relationship
h.	Taxpayer's sister has dropped out of school, is age 17, and lives with him.	Relationship Residence Age	Relationship
i.	Taxpayer's older nephew is age 23 and a full-time student.	Relationship Age	Relationship
j.	Taxpayer's grandson lives with her and has gross income of $7,000.	Relationship Residence	Relationship Gross income

29. **LO.3, 4** For tax year 2020, determine the number of dependents in each of the following independent situations:

   a. Leo and Amanda (ages 48 and 46, respectively) are husband and wife and furnish more than 50% of the support of their two children, Elton (age 18) and Trista (age 24). During the year, Elton earns $4,500 providing transportation for elderly persons with disabilities, and Trista receives a $5,000 scholarship for tuition at the law school she attends.

   b. Audry (age 45) was divorced this year. She maintains a household in which she, her ex-husband (Clint), and his mother (Olive) live and furnishes more than 50% of their support. Olive is age 91 and blind.

   c. Crystal, age 45, furnishes more than 50% of the support of her married son, Andy (age 18), and his wife, Paige (age 19), who live with her. During the year, Andy earned $8,700 from a part-time job. All parties live in Iowa (a common law state).

   d. Assume the same facts as in part (c), except that all parties live in Washington (a community property state).

30. **LO.3, 4** Determine the number of dependents in each of the following independent situations, and identify whether the dependent is a qualifying child or a qualifying relative.

   a. Andy maintains a household that includes a cousin (age 12), a niece (age 18), and a son (age 26). All are full-time students. Andy furnishes all of their support, and all are "members of the household."

   b. Mandeep provides all of the support of a family friend's son (age 20) who lives with her. She also furnishes most of the support of her stepmother, who does not live with her.

   c. Raul, a U.S. citizen, lives in Costa Rica. Raul's household includes a friend, Mariana, who is age 19 and a citizen of Costa Rica. Raul provides all of Mariana's support.

   d. Karen maintains a household that includes her ex-husband, her mother-in-law, and her brother-in-law (age 23 and not a full-time student). Karen provides more than half of all of their support. Karen is single and was divorced last year.

31. **LO.4** During 2020, Jenny, age 14, lives in a household with her father, uncle, and grandmother. The household is maintained by the uncle. The parties, all of whom file separate returns, have AGI as follows: father ($30,000), uncle ($50,000), and grandmother ($40,000).

    a. Who is eligible to claim Jenny as a dependent?

    b. Who has precedence to claim Jenny as a dependent?

32. **LO.4, 9** Wesley and Camilla (ages 90 and 88, respectively) live in an assisted care facility and for 2019 and 2020 received their support from the following sources:

	Percentage of Support
Social Security benefits	16%
Son	20
Niece	29
Cousin	12
Brother	11
Family friend (not related)	12

    a. Which persons are eligible to claim Wesley and Camilla as dependents under a multiple support agreement?

    b. Must Wesley and Camilla be claimed as dependents by the same person(s) for both 2019 and 2020? Explain.

    c. Who, if anyone, can claim their medical expenses?

33. **LO.5** In each of the following independent situations, determine Winston's filing status for 2020. Winston is not married.

    a. Winston lives alone, but he maintains a household in which his parents live. The mother qualifies as Winston's dependent, but the father does not.

    b. Winston lives alone but maintains a household in which his married daughter, Karin, lives. Both Karin and her husband (Winston's son-in-law) qualify as Winston's dependents.

    c. Winston maintains a household in which he and a family friend, Ward, live. Ward qualifies as Winston's dependent.

    d. Winston maintains a household in which he and his mother-in-law live. Winston's wife died in 2019.

    e. Same as part (d), except that Winston's wife disappeared (i.e., she did not die) in 2018.

34. **LO.4, 5** Christopher died in 2018 and is survived by his wife, Chloe, and their 18-year-old son, Dylan. Chloe is the executor of Christopher's estate and maintains the household in which she and Dylan live. All of their support is furnished by Chloe, and Dylan saves his earnings. Dylan's earnings and student status for 2018 to 2020 are as follows:

Year	Earnings	Student Status
2018	$5,000	Yes
2019	7,000	No
2020	6,000	Yes

    What is Chloe's filing status for:

    a. 2018?

    b. 2019?

    c. 2020?

35. **LO.4, 9** Walter and Nancy provide 60% of the support of their daughter (age 18) and son-in-law (age 22). The son-in-law (John) is a full-time student at a local university, and the daughter (Stella) holds various part-time jobs from which she earns $11,000. Walter and Nancy engage you to prepare their tax return for 2020. During a meeting with them in late March 2021, you learn that John and Stella have filed a joint return. What tax advice would you give based on the following assumptions?

    a.   All parties live in Louisiana (a community property state).

    b.   All parties live in New Jersey (a common law state).

Decision Making
Critical Thinking

36. **LO.1, 2, 3, 4, 5, 6** Charlotte (age 40) is a surviving spouse and provides all of the support of her four minor children who live with her (all are under age 16). She also maintains the household in which her parents live and furnished 60% of their support. Besides interest on City of Miami bonds in the amount of $5,500, Charlotte's father received $2,400 from a part-time job. Charlotte has a salary of $80,000, a short-term capital loss of $2,000, a cash prize of $4,000 from a church raffle, and itemized deductions of $10,500. Using the Tax Rate Schedules, compute Charlotte's 2020 tax liability.

37. **LO.1, 2, 3, 4, 5, 6** Morgan (age 45) is single and provides more than 50% of the support of Tammy (a family friend), Jen (a niece, age 18), and Jerold (a nephew, age 18). Both Tammy and Jen live with Morgan, but Jerold (a French citizen) lives in Canada. Morgan earns a salary of $95,000, contributes $5,000 to a traditional IRA, and receives sales proceeds of $15,000 for an RV that cost $60,000 and was used for vacations. She has $8,200 in itemized deductions. Using the Tax Rate Schedules, compute Morgan's 2020 tax liability.

38. **LO.5** Which of the following individuals are required to file a tax return for 2020? Should any of these individuals file a return even if filing is not required? Why or why not?

    a.   Patricia, age 19, is a self-employed single individual with gross income of $5,200 from an unincorporated business. Business expenses amounted to $4,900.

    b.   Mike is single and is 67 years old. His gross income from wages was $12,750.

    c.   Ronald is a dependent child under age 19 who received $6,800 in wages from a part-time job.

    d.   Sam is married and files a joint return with his spouse, Lana. Both Sam and Lana are 67 years old. Their combined gross income was $24,250.

    e.   Quinn, age 20, is a full-time college student who is claimed as a dependent by his parents. For 2020, Quinn has taxable interest and dividends of $2,500.

39. **LO.5, 6, 9** Roy and Brandi are engaged and plan to get married. During 2020, Roy is a full-time student and earns $9,000 from a part-time job. With this income, student loans, savings, and nontaxable scholarships, he is self-supporting. For the year, Brandi is employed and has wages of $61,000. How much income tax, if any, can Brandi save if she and Roy marry in 2020 and file a joint return?

Decision Making
Critical Thinking

40. **LO.3, 7** Taylor, age 18, is claimed as a dependent by her parents. For 2020, she has the following income: $4,000 wages from a summer job, $1,800 interest from a money market account, and $2,000 interest from City of Chicago bonds.

    a.   What is Taylor's taxable income for 2020?

    b.   What is Taylor's tax for 2020? [Her parents file a joint return and have taxable income of $135,000 (no dividends or capital gains).]

41. **LO.1, 3, 7** Paige, age 17, is a dependent of her parents. Her parents report taxable income of $120,000 on their joint return (no qualified dividends or capital gains). During 2020, Paige earned $3,900 pet sitting and $4,300 in interest on a savings account. What are Paige's taxable income and tax liability for 2020?

42. **LO.8** During 2020, Inez (a single taxpayer) had the following transactions involving capital assets:

Gain on the sale of unimproved land (held as an investment for 3 years)	$ 6,000
Loss on the sale of a camper (purchased 2 years ago and used for family vacations)	(5,000)
Gain on the sale of ADM stock (purchased 9 months ago as an investment)	2,450
Gain on the sale of a fishing boat and trailer (acquired 18 months ago at an auction and used for recreational purposes)	1,000

    a.   If Inez has taxable income of $188,450, how much income tax results?

    b.   If Inez has taxable income of $32,250, how much income tax results?

Decision Making

Critical Thinking

Communications

43. **LO.9** Each year, Tom and Cindy Bates normally have itemized deductions of $22,000 (which includes a $4,000 pledge payment to their church). On the advice of a friend, they do the following: in early January 2020, they pay their pledge for 2019; during 2020, they pay their pledge for 2020; and in late December 2020, they prepay their pledge for 2021.

    a.   Explain what the Bateses are trying to accomplish.

    b.   What will be the tax saving if their marginal tax bracket is 24% for all three years? (Assume that the standard deduction amounts for 2020 and 2021 are the same.)

    c.   Write a letter to Tom and Cindy Bates (8212 Bridle Court, Reston, VA 20194) summarizing your analysis.

Tax Return Problems

Tax Forms Problem

44. Lance H. and Wanda B. Dean are married and live at 431 Yucca Drive, Santa Fe, NM 87501. Lance works for the convention bureau of the local Chamber of Commerce, and Wanda is employed part-time as a paralegal for a law firm.

During 2019, the Deans had the following receipts:

Salaries ($60,000 for Lance, $41,000 for Wanda)		$101,000
Interest income—		
City of Albuquerque general purpose bonds	$1,000	
Ford Motor company bonds	1,100	
Ally Bank certificate of deposit	400	2,500
Child support payments from John Allen		7,200
Annual gifts from parents		26,000
Settlement from Roadrunner Touring Company		90,000
Lottery winnings		600
Federal income tax refund (for tax year 2018)		400

Wanda was previously married to John Allen. When they divorced several years ago, Wanda was awarded custody of their two children, Penny and Kyle. (Note: Wanda has never issued a Form 8332 waiver.) Under the divorce decree, John was obligated to pay alimony and child support—the alimony payments were to terminate if Wanda remarried.

In July, while going to lunch in downtown Santa Fe, Wanda was injured by a tour bus. Because the driver was clearly at fault, the owner of the bus, Roadrunner Touring Company, paid her medical expenses (including a one-week stay in a hospital). To avoid a lawsuit, Roadrunner also transferred $90,000 to her in settlement of the personal injuries she sustained.

The Deans had the following expenditures for 2019:

Medical expenses (not covered by insurance)		$7,200
Taxes—		
Property taxes on personal residence	$3,600	
State of New Mexico income tax (includes		
amount withheld from wages during 2019)	4,200	7,800
Interest on home mortgage (First National Bank)		6,000
Charitable contributions		3,600
Life insurance premiums (policy on Lance's life)		1,200
Contribution to traditional IRA (on Wanda's behalf)		5,000
Traffic fines		300
Contribution to the reelection campaign fund of the		
mayor of Santa Fe		500
Funeral expenses for Wayne Boyle		6,300

The life insurance policy was taken out by Lance several years ago and designates Wanda as the beneficiary. As a part-time employee, Wanda is excluded from coverage under her employer's pension plan. Consequently, she provides for her own retirement with a traditional IRA obtained at a local trust company. Because the mayor is a member of the local Chamber of Commerce, Lance felt compelled to make the political contribution.

The Deans' household includes the following, for whom they provide more than half of the support:

	Social Security Number	Birth Date
Lance Dean (age 42)	123-45-6786	12/16/1977
Wanda Dean (age 40)	123-45-6787	08/08/1979
Penny Allen (age 19)	123-45-6788	10/09/2000
Kyle Allen (age 16)	123-45-6780	05/03/2003
Wayne Boyle (age 75)	123-45-6785	06/15/1944

Penny graduated from high school on May 9, 2019, and is undecided about college. During 2019, she earned $8,500 (placed in a savings account) playing a harp in the lobby of a local hotel. Wayne is Wanda's widower father who died on December 20, 2019. For the past few years, Wayne qualified as a dependent of the Deans.

Federal income tax withheld is $3,900 (Lance) and $1,800 (Wanda). The proper amount of Social Security and Medicare tax was withheld.

Determine the Federal income tax for 2019 for the Deans on a joint return by completing the appropriate forms. They do not own and did not use any virtual currency during the year, and they do not want to contribute to the Presidential Election Campaign Fund. If an overpayment results, it is to be refunded to them. Suggested software: ProConnect Tax Online.

45. Logan B. Taylor is a widower whose wife, Sara, died on June 6, 2017. He lives at 4680 Dogwood Lane, Springfield, MO 65801. He is employed as a paralegal by a local law firm. During 2019, he had the following receipts:

Tax Forms Problem

Decision Making

Communications

Salary		$ 80,000
Interest income—		
Money market account at Omni Bank	$ 300	
Savings account at Boone State Bank	1,100	
City of Springfield general purpose bonds	3,000	4,400
Inheritance from Daniel		60,000
Life insurance proceeds		200,000
Amount from sale of St. Louis lot		80,000
Proceeds from estate sale		9,000
Federal income tax refund (for 2018 tax overpayment)		700

Logan inherited securities worth $60,000 from his uncle, Daniel, who died in 2019. Logan also was the designated beneficiary of an insurance policy on Daniel's life with a maturity value of $200,000. The lot in St. Louis was purchased on May 2, 2014, for $85,000 and held as an investment. Because the neighborhood has deteriorated, Logan decided to cut his losses and sold the lot on January 5, 2019, for $80,000. The estate sale consisted largely of items belonging to Sara and Daniel (e.g., camper, boat, furniture, and fishing and hunting equipment). Logan estimates that the property sold originally cost at least twice the $9,000 he received and has declined or stayed the same in value since Sara and Daniel died.

Logan's expenditures for 2019 include the following:

Medical expenses (including $10,500 for dental)		$11,500
Taxes—		
State of Missouri income tax (includes withholdings during 2019)	$4,200	
Property taxes on personal residence	4,500	8,700
Interest on home mortgage (Boone State Bank)		5,600
Contribution to church (paid pledges for 2019 and 2020)		4,800

While Logan and his dependents are covered by his employer's health insurance policy, he is subject to a deductible, and dental care is not included. The $10,500 dental charge was for Helen's implants. Helen is Logan's widowed mother, who lives with him (see below). Logan normally pledges $2,400 ($200 per month) each year to his church. On December 5, 2019, upon the advice of his pastor, he prepaid his pledge for 2020.

Logan's household, all of whom he supports, includes the following:

	Social Security Number	Birth Date
Logan Taylor (age 48)	123-45-6787	08/30/1971
Helen Taylor (age 70)	123-45-6780	01/13/1949
Asher Taylor (age 23)	123-45-6783	07/18/1996
Mia Taylor (age 22)	123-45-6784	02/16/1997

Helen receives a modest Social Security benefit. Asher, a son, is a full-time student in dental school and earns $4,500 as a part-time dental assistant. Mia, a daughter, does not work and is engaged to be married.

Part 1—Tax Computation
Using the appropriate forms and schedules, compute Logan's income tax for 2019. Federal income tax of $4,500 was withheld from his wages. If Logan has any overpayment on his income tax, he wants the refund sent to him. Assume that the proper amounts of Social Security and Medicare taxes were withheld. Logan does not own and did not use any virtual currency during the year, and he does not want to contribute to the Presidential Election Campaign Fund. Suggested software: ProConnect Tax Online.

Part 2—Follow-Up Advice
In early 2020, the following take place:

- Helen decides that she wants to live with one of her daughters and moves to Arizona.
- Asher graduates from dental school and joins an existing practice in St. Louis.
- Mia marries, and she and her husband move in with his parents.
- Using the insurance proceeds he received on Daniel's death, Logan pays off the mortgage on his personal residence.

Logan believes that these events may have an effect on his tax position for 2020. Therefore, he requests your advice.

Write a letter to Logan explaining in general terms the changes that will occur for tax purposes. Assume that Logan's salary and other factors not mentioned (e.g., property and state income taxes) will remain the same.

Research Problems

Note: Solutions to the Research Problems can be prepared by using the Thomson Reuters Checkpoint™ online tax research database, which accompanies this textbook. Solutions can also be prepared by using research materials found in a typical tax library.

Research Problem 1. John and Janet Baker are married and maintain a household in which the following persons live: Calvin and Florence Carter and Darin, Andrea, and Morgan Baker.

Decision Making

- Calvin and Florence are Janet's parents, who are retired. During the year, they receive $19,000 in nontaxable funds (e.g., disability income, interest on municipal bonds, and Social Security benefits). Of this amount, $8,000 is spent equally between them for clothing, transportation, and recreation (e.g., gym fees and travel), and the balance of $11,000 is invested in tax-exempt securities. Janet paid $1,000 for her mother's dental work, and she paid the $1,200 premium on an insurance policy that her father owned on his own life. Calvin also incurred medical expenses, but he insisted on paying for them with his own funds.

- Darin is the Bakers' 18-year-old son, who is not a student but operates a pool-cleaning service on a part-time basis. During the year, he earns $14,000 from the business, which he places in a savings account for later college expenses.

- Andrea is the Bakers' 19-year-old daughter, who does not work or go to school. Tired of the inconvenience of borrowing and sharing the family car, she purchased a Camaro for $21,000 during the year. Andrea used funds from a savings account that she had established several years ago with an inheritance from her paternal grandfather.

- Morgan is the Bakers' 23-year-old daughter. To attend graduate school at a local university, she applied for and obtained a student loan of $20,000. She uses the full amount of the loan to pay her college tuition.

The Bakers' fair rental value of their residence, including utilities, is $14,000, and their total food expense for the household is $10,500.

a. Who can the Bakers claim as Federal income tax dependents for the year? Explain your answer.

b. From an income tax planning standpoint, how might the Bakers have improved the tax result?

Partial list of research aids:
Reg. §§ 1.152–1(a) and –1(c).

Research Problem 2. Kathy and Brett Ouray married in 2002. They began to experience marital difficulties in 2016 and, in the current year, although they are not legally separated, the couple considers themselves completely estranged. They have contemplated getting a divorce. However, because of financial concerns and because they both want to remain involved in the lives of their three sons, they have not yet filed for divorce. In addition, the Ourays' financial difficulties have meant that Kathy and Brett cannot afford to live in separate residences. So Kathy, Brett, and their three sons all reside in a single-family home in Chicago.

Decision Making

Communications

Although Brett earns significantly more annual income than does Kathy, both parties contribute financially to maintaining their home and supporting their teenage sons. In one of their few, brief conversations this year, they determined that Brett had contributed far more consideration than had Kathy to the maintenance of their home and the support of their sons.

Thus, Brett has decided that for the current tax year, he and Kathy will file separate Federal income tax returns and he will claim head-of-household filing status.

Even though they live under the same roof, Brett believes that he and Kathy should "maintain separate households." Therefore, Brett believes that he is eligible for head-of-household filing status.

Advise Brett on which filing status is most appropriate for him in the current year in a letter to him at 16 Lahinch Parkway, Chicago, IL 60608.

Use internet tax resources to address the following questions. Look for reliable websites and blogs of the IRS and other government agencies, media outlets, businesses, tax professionals, academics, think tanks, and political outlets.

Communications

Research Problem 3. When taxpayers pay Federal income taxes by means of a credit or debit card, they are charged "convenience fees" by the issuer of the card. How are these fees determined? Are these fees themselves deductible? Explain. Summarize your findings in a memo for the tax research file.

Data Analytics

Communications

Research Problem 4. How do U.S. individuals generate their income? Does it vary by size of income (AGI)? Go to the IRS tax statistics website (**irs.gov/statistics**), and download a recent tax year's information on "sources of income." Compare the following types of income by size of AGI: (1) wages, (2) capital gain distributions, (3) sales of capital assets, and (4) sales of property other than capital assets. Cluster the data into no more than six AGI categories. Present your findings in a visual (e.g., bar chart), and summarize your findings in a one-page memo to your instructor.

Research Problem 5. Locate IRS Form 2120 (at **irs.gov**), and answer the following questions.

a.   Who must sign the form?

b.   Who must file the form?

c.   Can it be used for someone who is not related to the taxpayer? Explain.

Research Problem 6. A nonresident alien earns money in the United States that is subject to Federal income tax. What guidance does the IRS provide about what tax form needs to be used and when it should be filed? In terms of the proper filing date, does it matter whether the earnings were subject to income tax withholding? Explain.

Research Problem 7. Research the following questions regarding virtual currency and write your answers in the form of a set of "frequently asked questions" (FAQs) suitable for the website of your CPA firm. As part of your research, consider the IRS's FAQs on virtual currency transactions (**irs.gov/individuals/international-taxpayers/frequently-asked-questions-on-virtual-currency-transactions**) and Rev.Rul. 2019–24 (2019–44 I.R.B. 1004).

a.   Since taxpayers want to easily track virtual currency and use it to acquire goods and services, how do taxpayers typically "hold" their virtual currency?

b.   Janice acquired bitcoin in 2014 and 2016. This year, she used a portion of her bitcoin holdings to acquire 50 litecoin. What are the tax implications of this transaction? What do you recommend Janice do to help track her acquisition and use of virtual currency (in order to have records readily available about these investments and their tax consequences)?

c.   Rajiv acquired $20 worth of bitcoin in 2015 using an automatic teller machine that converted cash to bitcoin. He has never used any of this currency. How should Rajiv answer the virtual currency question on Schedule 1 this year? Why? Consider the possibility that there was a "hard fork" or an "airdrop" associated with Rajiv's bitcoin (also explain these terms in your FAQs).

Becker CPA Review Questions

Becker.

1. Bob provides more than half of his mother's support. His mother earns $6,000 per year as a hairdresser. She lives in an apartment across town. Bob is unmarried and has no children. What is Bob's most advantageous filing status?

   a. Single

   b. Head of household

   c. Qualifying single

   d. Supporting single

2. Jane is 20 years old and is a sophomore at Lake University. She is a full-time student and does not have any gross income. Jane spends the holidays and summers at home with her parents. Her total support for the current tax year is $30,000, including a scholarship for $5,000 to cover her tuition. Jane used $12,000 of her savings, and her grandparents provided $13,000. Which of the following statements regarding the dependency rules for Jane is true?

   a. If Jane's parents (rather than her grandparents) provided the $13,000, then they would not be able to claim Jane as a dependent because Jane provided more than half of her own support.

   b. Jane's grandparents can claim her as a dependent because Jane did not provide more than half of her own support.

   c. Jane's grandparents cannot claim her as a dependent because Jane provided more than half of her own support.

   d. Jane does not qualify as a dependent for either her parents or grandparents.

3. In the current tax year, Blake Smith provided more than half of the support for his cousin Nico, his niece Summer, and Marilyn, a close family friend. Blake lives alone and sends a monthly support check to each person. None of the individuals whom Blake supports has any income or files a tax return. All three individuals are U.S. citizens. Which of the three people Blake supports qualifies as a dependent on his Federal income tax return?

   a. Nico

   b. Summer

   c. Marilyn

   d. None of the three parties is Blake's dependent.

4. Jeff and Rhonda are married and have two children, Max and Jen. Max is 20, attends college in the Los Angeles area full-time, and works as a stunt double for a television show while he is in school. Max earns $15,000 per year as a stunt double and lives at home when school is not in session. Jeff and Rhonda pay for Max's tuition and all of his living expenses. Jen, who lives at home, is 18 years old and makes $18,000 per year working full-time as an office administrator. Jeff and Rhonda pay for 65% of Jen's living expenses. In addition, Rhonda's mother, Joanne (a widow), resides with the family, earns $3,000 per year in interest and dividends from her investments, and receives $9,000 per year in Social Security benefits. Jeff and Rhonda receive no rent from Joanne and provide all the support she needs for the year. Everyone mentioned is a U.S. citizen. How many people qualify as dependents for Jeff and Rhonda's income tax return?

   a. Two

   b. Three

   c. Four

   d. Five

5. Katherine and Bill Grant have two children. Kelly is 22 years old and is a full-time student. She lives on campus at an out-of-state university but will return home for the summer. Kelly earns $5,000 a year working part-time. Her parents provide her with $15,000 of support, and her grandparents provide her with $15,000 of support. Jake is 15 years old and lives at home. He is fully supported by his parents. Jake's friend Luke also lives with the Grants. Luke is 15 years old and moved into the Grant home in April. The Grants pay all of Luke's support. How many total dependents may Katherine and Bill Grant claim for the current year?

   a. One

   b. Three

   c. Two

   d. Zero

6. Bill and Anne Chambers are married and file a joint return. They have no children. Their college friend Ryan lived with them for the entire current tax year. Ryan is 40 years old and earned $2,000 at a part-time job and received $25,000 in municipal bond interest. Ryan is a citizen of the United States and is unmarried. Which of the following statements is true regarding claiming Ryan as a dependent on the Chamberses' tax return?

   a. If Ryan earns $15,000 in self-employment income in addition to the part-time job and municipal bond interest, he will qualify as a dependent on the Chamberses' tax return.

   b. Ryan qualifies as a dependent for the Chamberses under the qualifying child rules.

   c. As long as Ryan does not provide more than half of his own support, he qualifies as a dependent for the Chamberses under the qualifying relative rules because he lived with them for the entire year.

   d. As long as the Chamberses provide more than half of Ryan's support, he qualifies as a dependent for the Chamberses under the qualifying relative rules.

7. Susie, John, Luke, and Will provide support for their 80-year-old mother, Joyce. Joyce lives by herself in an apartment in Miami, Florida. Joyce earned $5,000 this year working at her church. Joyce provides 5% of her own support. Susie provides 30% of Joyce's support, John provides 10% of Joyce's support, Luke provides 15% of Joyce's support, and Will provides 40% of Joyce's support. Under a multiple support agreement, who may claim Joyce as a dependent?

   a. Susie, Luke, John, and Will

   b. Susie, Luke, and Will

   c. Susie and Will

   d. Will

8. Heather is single and has one son, Rhett, who is 19 years old. Rhett lived at home for four months of the current tax year before moving away to take a full-time job in another city. Heather provided more than half of Rhett's support for the taxable year. Rhett earned $20,000 in gross income and is unmarried. Which of the following statements regarding the dependency rules for Rhett is true?

   a. Heather may claim Rhett as a dependent because he is a qualifying child.

   b. Heather may claim Rhett as a dependent because he is a qualifying relative.

   c. Rhett fails the age limit test for a qualifying child.

   d. Rhett must live with Heather for the entire year to meet the qualifying relative test.

9. Jonathan Jones is a 19-year-old full-time college student at the local community college. He lives in an apartment near campus during the school year and returns home for the summer break and holidays. Jonathan earned $5,000 this year working at the campus bookstore. His parents gave him $20,000 and his grandparents gave him $10,000 this year in support. Which of the following statements is true?

    a. Jonathan does not qualify as a dependent for his parents because his gross income is too high.

    b. Jonathan does not meet the residency test for a qualifying child.

    c. Jonathan's grandparents can claim him as a dependent.

    d. Jonathan's parents can claim him as a dependent.

10. Madison and Nick Koz have two children, ages 8 and 10. Both children meet the definition of qualifying child. The Koz family has adjusted gross income of $300,000. What is the amount of the child tax credit on the couple's income tax return?

    a. $1,000

    b. $2,000

    c. $3,000

    d. $4,000

11. The Tiller family has an adjusted gross income of $200,000. The Tillers have two children, ages 12 and 13, who qualify as dependents. All of the Tillers' income is from wages. What is the Tillers' child tax credit, and what portion of their child tax credit is refundable?

	Child Tax Credit	Refundable Portion
a.	$4,000	$0
b.	$4,000	$1,400
c.	$2,000	$1,400
d.	$2,000	$0

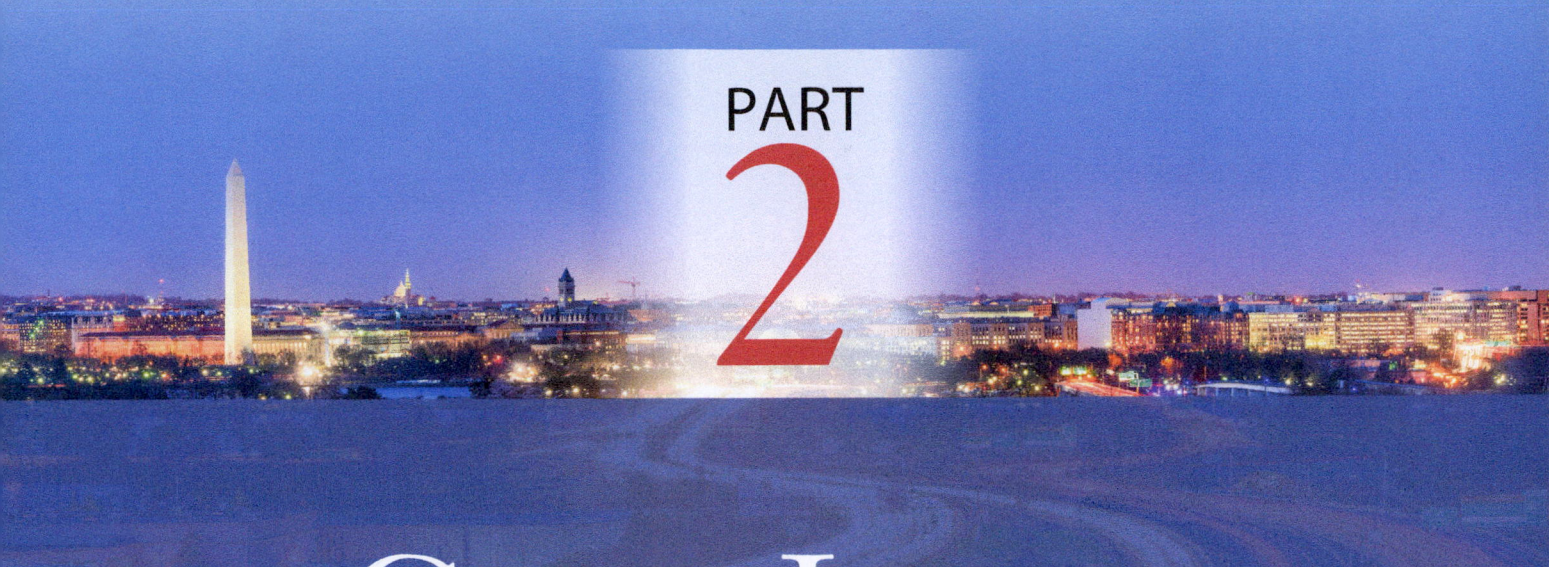

PART 2

GROSS INCOME

CHAPTER **4**

Gross Income: Concepts and Inclusions

CHAPTER **5**

Gross Income: Exclusions

Part 2 presents the income component of the basic tax model. The determination of what is income and the statutory exclusions that are permitted in calculating gross income are discussed. Because the taxpayer's accounting method and accounting period affect when income is reported, a basic discussion of these topics is also included.

Gross Income: Concepts and Inclusions

LEARNING OBJECTIVES: *After completing Chapter 4, you should be able to:*

LO.1 Explain the differences between the economic, accounting, and tax concepts of gross income.

LO.2 Describe the taxable years and tax accounting methods generally available to taxpayers and other tax reporting entities.

LO.3 Identify the general sources of income and to whom they are taxable.

LO.4 Apply the tax rules on alimony, loans made at below-market interest rates, annuities, prizes and awards, unemployment compensation, Social Security benefits, and foreign bank accounts.

LO.5 Identify tax planning strategies for minimizing gross income and the present value of the related tax.

CHAPTER OUTLINE

4-1 Gross Income, 4-3
4-1a Definition, 4-3
4-1b Recovery of Capital Doctrine, 4-3
4-1c Economic and Accounting Concepts of Income, 4-4
4-1d Financial Accounting Income versus Taxable Income, 4-4
4-1e Form of Receipt, 4-5

4-2 Timing of Income Recognition, 4-6
4-2a Taxable Year, 4-6
4-2b Accounting Methods, 4-6
4-2c Special Rules Applicable to Cash Basis Taxpayers, 4-9
4-2d Exceptions Applicable to Accrual Basis Taxpayers, 4-12

4-3 General Sources of Income and to Whom They Are Taxed, 4-13
4-3a Personal Services, 4-13
4-3b Income from Property, 4-13
4-3c Income Received by an Agent, 4-16
4-3d Income from Partnerships, S Corporations, Trusts, and Estates, 4-16
4-3e Income in Community Property States, 4-17

4-4 Items Specifically Included in Gross Income, 4-19
4-4a Alimony and Separate Maintenance Payments, 4-19
4-4b Imputed Interest on Below-Market Loans, 4-21
4-4c Income from Annuities, 4-24
4-4d Prizes and Awards, 4-27
4-4e Unemployment Compensation, 4-27
4-4f Social Security Benefits, 4-28
4-4g Income Earned from Foreign Bank and Financial Accounts and FBAR Rules, 4-29

4-5 Tax Planning, 4-29
4-5a Minimize Income Included in Gross Income, 4-30
4-5b Tax Deferral, 4-30
4-5c Shifting Income to Other Taxpayers, 4-32

Bob Daemmrich/Alamy Stock Photo

CALCULATION OF GROSS INCOME

In 2020, Dr. Cliff Payne, age 27, opened his dental practice as a sole proprietorship with a December 31 year-end. By the beginning of February, construction on his medical building was completed. He also leased a separate office building and entered into a contract to make improvements to it. In addition, early in the year, he invested $12,000 in the stock of an unrelated corporation.

The following financial information shows the results of Dr. Payne's first year of operation:

Revenues (amounts billed patients for dental services throughout the year)	$385,000
Accounts receivable: January 1	–0–
Accounts receivable: December 31	52,000

During the year, Sam Jones, a contractor who owed Dr. Payne $4,000 for dental services, satisfied his account by installing solar panels on the roof of Dr. Payne's new medical building.

As an undergraduate student, Dr. Payne took an accounting course in which he learned that the accrual method of accounting provides a good measure of the income and expenses of a business. Based on this knowledge and the above financial information, Dr. Payne concludes that the gross income for Federal income tax purposes is the $385,000 he billed his patients for the dental services rendered.

Has Dr. Payne correctly calculated the gross income of his dental practice in its first year of operations? Is there an alternative method of accounting that would result in less taxable income in this first year?

Read the chapter and formulate your response.

FRAMEWORK 1040 Tax Formula for Individuals

This chapter covers the boldfaced portions of the Tax Formula for Individuals that was introduced in Concept Summary 3.1 on p. 3-3. Below those portions are the sections of Form 1040 where the results are reported.

Income *(broadly defined)* .... $xx,xxx
Less: Exclusions .... (x,xxx)
Gross income .... $xx,xxx

FORM 1040 (p. 1)

1	Wages, salaries, tips, etc. Attach Form(s) W-2		1	
2a	Tax-exempt interest	2a		b	Taxable interest. Attach Sch. B if required	2b	
3a	Qualified dividends	3a		b	Ordinary dividends. Attach Sch. B if required	3b	
4a	IRA distributions	4a		b	Taxable amount	4b	
c	Pensions and annuities . . .	4c		d	Taxable amount	4d	
5a	Social security benefits . . .	5a		b	Taxable amount	5b	

FORM 1040 (Schedule 1)

2a	Alimony received . . . .
b	Date of original divorce or separation agreement (see instructions) ▶ _____
3	Business income or (loss). Attach Schedule C. . . . .
8	Other income. List type and amount ▶ _____

Less: Deductions *for* adjusted gross income .... (x,xxx)
Adjusted gross income .... $xx,xxx
Less: The greater of total itemized deductions *or* the standard deduction .... (x,xxx)
  Personal and dependency exemptions* .... (x,xxx)
  Deduction for qualified business income** .... (x,xxx)
Taxable income .... $xx,xxx
Tax on taxable income *(see Tax Tables or Tax Rate Schedules)* .... $ x,xxx
Less: Tax credits *(including income taxes withheld and prepaid)* .... (xxx)
Tax due (or refund) .... $ xxx

* Exemption deductions are not allowed from 2018 through 2025.
** Only applies from 2018 through 2025.

This chapter addresses the first step in the computation of taxable income—the determination of gross income. Questions that are addressed include the following:

- What is income?
- When is the income recognized?
- To whom is the income taxable?

As you will see, the Code starts with an all-inclusive definition of gross income that includes any increase in a taxpayer's wealth. However, as discussed in Chapter 5, it goes on to identify several items of income that are specifically excluded from gross income (exclusions). *When* gross income is taxable is determined by the tax period and tax accounting method used by a taxpayer. Finally, income is generally taxable to the taxpayer who has the legal right to the income, although exceptions and special rules may sometimes apply. These issues are addressed in more depth below.

GLOBAL TAX ISSUES From "All Sources" Is a Broad Definition

When § 61 refers to "income from whatever source derived," the taxing authorities are reaching far beyond the borders of the United States. Although one interpretation of "source" in this context is type of income (e.g., wages and interest), a broader interpretation revolves around the place where the income is generated. In this context, citizens and residents of the United States are subject to taxation on income earned from sources both inside and outside the country. This "worldwide income" tax base can cause potential double taxation problems, with other countries also taxing income earned within their borders. However, mechanisms such as the foreign tax credit can alleviate these tax burdens.

Over the years, a number of individuals have relocated to other countries and renounced their U.S. citizenship to avoid high U.S. tax rates. Others who have already relocated may renounce their U.S. citizenship to avoid complicated filing and reporting requirements. In 2017, after five years of annual increases, the number of expatriations reached 5,411. Once per quarter, the Department of State publishes the names of U.S. citizens who have renounced their citizenship. Some of these individuals may owe Federal taxes upon renouncing. See § 877A.

See "Americans Renouncing Citizenship? Not What You Might Think" by Robert Wood at **forbes.com/sites/robertwood/2018/12/03/americans-renouncing-citizenship-not-what-you-might-think/#665aa5397d22**.

4-1 GROSS INCOME

LO.1

Explain the differences between the economic, accounting, and tax concepts of gross income.

4-1a Definition

Section 61(a) of the Internal Revenue Code defines the term **gross income** as follows:

> Except as otherwise provided in this subtitle, gross income means all income from whatever source derived.

This definition is taken straight from the Sixteenth Amendment to the Constitution. It provides perhaps the broadest definition of gross income possible, clearly requiring that all income be included in a taxpayer's gross income unless it is explicitly excluded. All income is taxable unless the Internal Revenue Code says it is not. However, the amendment provides no definition of income itself. Nor is such a definition provided elsewhere in the Code. Rather, Congress left it to the judicial and administrative branches to specifically determine the meaning of *income*. Some of the most important issues are discussed below.

4-1b Recovery of Capital Doctrine

Although gross income is clearly defined to include all income, the Supreme Court has held that gross income is not synonymous with gross receipts. Rather, a taxpayer does not have income until recovering any amount of capital that might have been invested in the item sold.[1] This concept, known as the **recovery of capital doctrine**, prevents income from being taxed more than once. The rationale is that "capital" is the accumulation of previously taxed income.

In its simplest application, this doctrine means that sellers can reduce their gross receipts (selling price) by the adjusted basis of the property sold to determine the amount of gross income.[2]

The Big Picture

Return to the facts of *The Big Picture* on p. 4-1. Assume that Dr. Payne receives $15,000 when he sells the common stock he had purchased for $12,000. Although he has $15,000 of gross receipts, $12,000 represent a recovery of capital, leaving him with $3,000 of gross income.

EXAMPLE

1

---

[1]*Doyle v. Mitchell Bros. Co.*, 1 USTC ¶17, 3 AFTR 2979, 38 S.Ct. 467 (USSC, 1916).   [2]Reg. § 1.61–3. For a definition of *adjusted basis*, see the Glossary in Appendix C.

4-1c   Economic and Accounting Concepts of Income

Even after clarifying that income did not include recoveries of capital, the courts were nonetheless required to interpret "the commonly understood meaning of the term which must have been in the minds of the people when they adopted the Sixteenth Amendment to the Constitution."[3] Early in the development of the income tax law, a choice had to be made between two competing models: economic income and accounting income. The Supreme Court rejected the economic concept of income in favor of accounting income.

Economists measure income (economic income) as the sum of (1) the value of goods and services consumed during a period and (2) the change in the value of net assets (assets minus liabilities) from the beginning to the end of the period. Notice that the change in the value of net assets is not dependent on the sale or exchange of those assets: economic income can be derived by a mere change in the value of assets held. Similarly, economic income includes in consumption the imputed value of personally provided items such as as the rental value of an owner-occupied home and the value of food grown for personal consumption.[4]

Sharon has economic income as follows:

Consumption			
Food, clothing, and other personal expenditures	$ 25,000		
Imputed rental value of the home Sharon owns and occupies	12,000		
Total consumption			$37,000
Fair market value of Sharon's assets on December 31, 2020	$220,000		
Less liabilities on December 31, 2020	(40,000)		
Net worth on December 31, 2020		$180,000	
Fair market value of Sharon's assets on January 1, 2020	$200,000		
Less liabilities on January 1, 2020	(80,000)		
Net worth on January 1, 2020		(120,000)	
Increase in net worth			60,000
Economic income for 2020			$97,000

The need to value assets annually would make compliance with the tax law burdensome and would cause numerous controversies between the taxpayer and the IRS over valuation. In addition, using market values to determine income for tax purposes could result in liquidity problems. The taxpayer's assets may increase in value even though they are not readily convertible into the cash needed to pay the tax (e.g., commercial real estate). As a result, the courts have rejected the economic concept of income as impractical.[5]

In contrast, the accounting concept of income is founded on the realization principle.[6] According to this principle, accounting income is not recognized until it is realized. Realization requires (1) an exchange of goods or services to take place between the accounting entity and some independent, external party and (2) the accounting entity to receive in the exchange assets that are capable of being objectively valued. For example, income is not recognized merely due to the appreciation of assets held by the taxpayer, or when an individual or a business creates an asset for its own use. Income is realized, however, whenever a taxpayer enters into any transaction that results in an accession to wealth.[7]

4-1d   Financial Accounting Income versus Taxable Income

The measurement of taxable income is much closer to financial accounting income than it is to economic income. For example, unlike economic income, taxable income relies

---

[3]*Merchants Loan and Trust Co. v. Smietanka*, 1 USTC ¶42, 3 AFTR 3102, 41 S.Ct. 386 (USSC, 1921).

[4]See Henry C. Simons, *Personal Income Taxation* (Chicago: University of Chicago Press, 1933), Chapters 2–3.

[5]*Eisner v. Macomber*, 1 USTC ¶32, 3 AFTR 3020, 40 S.Ct. 189 (USSC, 1920).

[6]See the American Accounting Association Committee Report on the "Realization Concept," *The Accounting Review* (April 1965): 312–322.

[7]*Glenshaw Glass Co.*, 348 U.S. 426, 429–430, 75 S.Ct. 473, 99 L.Ed. 483 (1955); Reg. § 1.61–14.

heavily on the realization principle. However, due to the different purposes they serve, several differences exist between accounting and taxable income. The purpose of financial reporting is to provide information to investors and creditors relevant to predicting a business's future cash flows. Taxable income is primarily intended to capture taxpayers' relative abilities to pay tax. To better predict future cash flows, some assets are valued at their net realizable value for financial accounting purposes with any appreciation in value recognized as income even without realization. For example, an increase in the value of marketable securities is recognized as income for financial accounting purposes. Conversely, the determination of taxable income seldom strays from the realization principle. Therefore, the same appreciation of marketable securities will not result in taxable income. Similarly, to better predict future cash flows and to better match expenses with the revenues they generate, financial accounting is amenable to the use of estimates. For example, estimates of receivables that will not be collected and future costs that will be incurred to honor warranties on products sold during the current period reduce financial accounting income but have no impact on taxable income.

The Supreme Court provided an explanation for some of the variations between accounting and taxable income in a decision involving inventory and bad debt adjustments:

> The primary goal of financial accounting is to provide useful information to management, shareholders, creditors, and others properly interested; the major responsibility of the accountant is to protect these parties from being misled. The primary goal of the income tax system, in contrast, is the equitable collection of revenue.... Consistently with its goals and responsibilities, financial accounting has as its foundation the principle of conservatism, with its corollary that 'possible errors in measurement [should] be in the direction of understatement rather than overstatement of net income and net assets.' In view of the Treasury's markedly different goals and responsibilities, understatement of income is not destined to be its guiding light.
>
> ... Financial accounting, in short, is hospitable to estimates, probabilities, and reasonable certainties; the tax law, with its mandate to preserve the revenue, can give no quarter to uncertainty.[8]

Finally, because the tax law is used by the government to achieve several social and economic goals, taxable income is impacted by several things that do not impact accounting income and vice versa. For example, although income earned by foreign subsidiaries, the appreciation of property donated to charity, and the payment of fines and penalties all impact financial accounting income, none are included in the determination of taxable income. Conversely, although taxable income may be reduced for a portion of income earned on sales to customers in foreign countries, there is no corresponding reduction of financial accounting income. For these reasons, the taxable income reported by corporations in their financial statements may differ significantly from their taxable income (see text Section 17-3c). Many of these differences between accounting and taxable income will be discussed in greater detail throughout this text.

4-1e Form of Receipt

As discussed above, income is not taxable until it is realized. Realization, however, does not require the (eventual) receipt of cash. "Gross income includes income realized in any form, whether in money, property, or services. Income may be realized [and recognized], therefore, in the form of services, meals, accommodations, stock or other property, as well as in cash."[9]

[8]*Thor Power Tool Co. v. Comm.*, 79–1 USTC ¶9139, 43 AFTR 2d 79–362, 99 S.Ct. 773 (USSC, 1979).   [9]Reg. § 1.61–1(a).

Form of Receipt

Ostrich Corporation allows Bill, an employee, to use a company car for his vacation. Bill realizes income equal to the rental value of the car for the time and mileage.

Terry owes $10,000 on a mortgage. The creditor accepts $8,000 in full satisfaction of the debt. Terry realizes income of $2,000 from retiring the debt, the amount of his increase in net worth.[10]

Sam, a practicing attorney, owns a personal residence in need of repairs. Sam decided to list his services on a barter exchange. He offered to provide an hour of legal services in exchange for home repairs.

A qualified carpenter performed the repairs in eight hours. The carpenter normally charges $50 an hour. Sam formed a corporation for the carpenter in exchange for the carpenter's services. Sam realized $400 (8 hours × $50) in gross income for his services.

4-2 TIMING OF INCOME RECOGNITION

LO.2

Describe the taxable years and tax accounting methods generally available to taxpayers and other tax reporting entities.

4-2a Taxable Year

The annual accounting period, or **taxable year**, is a basic component of our tax system. As a general rule, a taxpayer may use as a taxable year either a calendar year or a fiscal year (a period of 12 months ending on the last day of any month other than December) as long as adequate books and records based on that year are maintained.[11] Although it is not required, most individuals use a calendar year as their taxable year. The fiscal year option generally is not available to partnerships, S corporations, and personal service corporations, as discussed in Chapter 16.[12]

It is important that income be recognized in the proper year for several reasons. For example, a taxpayer's tax rate may vary across years. This may occur for the following reasons:

• With a progressive rate system, a taxpayer's marginal tax rate can change from year to year.
• Congress may change the tax rates.
• The relevant rates may change because of a change in the taxpayer's status (e.g., a person may marry or a business may be incorporated).

Even when the rates do not change between tax years, the longer the tax payment can be postponed, the lower the present value of the tax. Finally, several provisions in the Code are dependent on the taxpayer's gross income for the year (e.g., a deduction or credit might not be available if the taxpayer's income exceeds a specified amount). Therefore, the proper determination of several items of income and deduction will depend on other items being recognized in the proper year.

4-2b Accounting Methods

The year an item of income is recognized depends upon which acceptable **accounting method** the taxpayer regularly employs.[13] The two primary methods of accounting allowed are (1) the cash receipts and disbursements method and (2) the accrual method. Most individuals and many small businesses may use either of these allowable methods, although most choose to use the cash method. In general, large corporations are required to use the accrual method. Generally, the tax law also requires use of the accrual method for determining purchases and sales when inventory is an income-producing factor.[14] Taxpayers

---

[10]Reg. § 1.61–12. See *U.S. v. Kirby Lumber Co.*, 2 USTC ¶814, 10 AFTR 458, 52 S.Ct. 4 (USSC, 1931). Exceptions to this general rule are discussed in Chapter 5.
[11]§ 441.

[12]§§ 441(i), 706, and 1378.
[13]See Accounting Methods in Chapter 16.
[14]Reg. § 1.446–1(c)(2)(i) and § 471(c). Other circumstances in which the accrual method must be used are presented in Chapter 16.

may also use a hybrid method that is a combination of the cash and accrual methods of accounting (e.g., the accrual method for sales and cost of goods sold and the cash method for all other items of income and expenses).

In addition to these overall accounting methods, taxpayers may use special accounting methods in specific situations. For example, a taxpayer may choose to spread the gain from a sale of eligible property over the collection period by using the *installment method* of income recognition. Taxpayers with certain long-term contracts may either spread the profits from the contract over the periods in which the work is done (the *percentage of completion method*) or defer all profit until the year in which the project is completed (the *completed contract method*, which can be used only in limited circumstances).[15]

The ability to use any accounting method is dependent on its ability to clearly reflect the taxpayer's income. Section 446(b) grants the IRS broad powers to determine whether a taxpayer's accounting method *clearly reflects income*:

> If no method of accounting has been regularly used by the taxpayer, or *if the method used does not clearly reflect income, the computation of taxable income shall be made under such method as, in the opinion of the Secretary . . . does clearly reflect income.*

A change in method of accounting requires the advance consent of the IRS.[16]

Cash Receipts Method

Under the cash receipts method, income is recognized in the year of actual or constructive receipt by the taxpayer or the taxpayer's agent, regardless of whether the income was earned in that year.[17] Further, in spite of the method's name, the taxpayer need not receive cash to be required to recognize income under the cash receipts method. Rather, the receipt of anything with a fair market value, or a cash equivalent, is taxable under the cash receipts method.[18] As a result, a cash basis taxpayer who receives a note in payment for services has income equal to the fair market value of the note in the year the note is received. However, a creditor's mere promise to pay (e.g., an account receivable), with no supporting note, usually is not considered to have a fair market value and therefore is not a cash equivalent.[19] As a result, a cash basis taxpayer who receives an account receivable in return for goods or services defers income recognition until the receivable is collected.

EXAMPLE 6

Dana, an accountant, reports her income using the cash method. In 2020, she performed an audit for Orange Corporation and billed the client for $5,000, which was collected in 2021. In 2020, Dana also performed an audit for Blue Corporation. Because of Blue's precarious financial position, Dana required Blue to issue an $8,000 secured negotiable note in payment of the fee. The note had a fair market value of $6,000. Dana collected $8,000 on the note in 2021. Dana's gross income for the two years is as follows:

	2020	2021
Fair market value of note received from Blue	$6,000	
Cash received		
From Orange on account receivable		$ 5,000
From Blue on note receivable		8,000
Less: Recovery of capital (Blue's note receivable)		(6,000)
Total gross income	$6,000	$ 7,000

Generally, a check is considered a cash equivalent and must be recognized as income upon receipt by a cash basis taxpayer. An exception to this rule is if the person paying with the check requests that the check not be cashed until a subsequent date, the income is deferred until that later date.[20]

---

[15]§§ 453 and 460. See Chapter 16 for limitations on the use of the installment method and the completed contract method. See the Glossary in Appendix C for definitions of *installment method* and *completed contract method*.

[16]§ 446(e).

[17]*Julia A. Strauss*, 2 B.T.A. 598 (1925). See the Glossary in Appendix C for a discussion of the terms *cash equivalent doctrine* and *constructive receipt*.

[18]Reg. §§ 1.446–1(a)(3) and (c)(1)(i).

[19]*Bedell v. Comm.*, 1 USTC ¶359, 7 AFTR 8469, 30 F.2d 622 (CA–2, 1929).

[20]*Charles F. Kahler*, 18 T.C. 31 (1952); *Bright v. U.S.*, 91–1 USTC ¶50,142, 67 AFTR 2d 91–673, 926 F.2d 383 (CA–5, 1991).

The cash receipts method could distort taxable income, as income and expenses from the same activity may be recognized in different tax years. Moreover, a taxpayer using the cash receipts method has some degree of control over when income is recognized, such as by delaying the sending of invoices to customers. As a result, the tax law restricts the availability of the cash receipts method. For example, most corporations with average annual gross receipts greater than $26 million over the preceding three-year period must use the accrual method. Other businesses with average annual gross receipts in excess of $26 million, whether or not they are corporations, are required to account for their inventory under the accrual method.[21]

Accrual Method

Under the **accrual method**, an item is generally included in gross income for the year in which it is earned, regardless of when it is collected. Income is earned when (1) all events have occurred that fix the right to receive such income and (2) the amount to be received can be determined with reasonable accuracy. However, regardless of when these tests are actually met, they are treated as satisfied no later than when the revenue is included in the taxpayer's financial statements.[22]

Generally, a taxpayer's right to income accrues when title to property being sold passes to the buyer or services are performed for the customer or client.[23] If the rights to the income have accrued but are subject to a potential refund claim (e.g., under a product warranty), the income is reported in the year of sale and a deduction is allowed in subsequent years when actual claims accrue.[24]

Where a taxpayer's right to income is contested (e.g., when a customer claims that a contractor has failed to meet the specifications of a construction contract), the year in which the income is subject to tax depends upon whether payment has been received. If payment has not been received, no income is recognized until the claim is settled. Only then is the right to the income established.[25] However, if the payment is received before the dispute is settled, a **claim of right doctrine** requires the taxpayer to recognize the income in the year of receipt.[26]

The Big Picture

EXAMPLE 7

Return to the facts of *The Big Picture* on p. 4-1. Assume that upon completing the construction improvements to Dr. Payne's medical office building in 2020, the contractor, who uses the accrual method, submitted a bill. Dr. Payne refused to pay the bill, however, claiming that the contractor had not met specifications. The contractor did not reach a settlement with Dr. Payne until 2021. No income is taxable to the contractor until 2021. If Dr. Payne had paid for the work and then filed suit for damages, the contractor could not defer the income (the income would be taxable in 2020).

Under the accrual method, the amount of income that must be included in gross income is the amount the taxpayer has earned and, therefore, has the right to receive. Unlike the cash basis, the fair market value of a customer's obligation is irrelevant in measuring accrual basis income. The ability to defer income that is earned but not yet received is a distinct advantage of the cash method over the accrual method. However, as discussed above, most larger corporations are required to use the accrual method.[27]

EXAMPLE 8

Assume the same facts as in Example 6, except that Dana is an accrual basis taxpayer. Dana must recognize $13,000 ($8,000 + $5,000) of gross income in 2020, the year her rights to the income accrued.

---

[21]§§ 448, 471(c), and 263A(i). Section 448, which requires certain taxpayers to use the accrual method, does not apply to individuals, partnerships without a C corporation partner, S corporations, estates, and trusts. In general, these types of taxpayers may use the cash receipts method regardless of their gross receipts level. Additional analysis as to accounting methods is required if these taxpayers have inventory as well as gross receipts above the $26 million threshold. See further discussion in Chapter 16.

[22]§ 451(b).

[23]*Lucas v. North Texas Lumber Co.*, 2 USTC ¶484, 8 AFTR 10276, 50 S.Ct. 184 (USSC, 1930). See also Rev.Rul. 84–31, 1984–1 C.B. 127.

[24]*Brown v. Helvering*, 4 USTC ¶1222, 13 AFTR 851, 54 S.Ct. 356 (USSC, 1933).

[25]*Burnet v. Sanford and Brooks*, 2 USTC ¶636, 9 AFTR 603, 51 S.Ct. 150 (USSC, 1931).

[26]*North American Oil Consolidated Co. v. Burnet*, 3 USTC ¶943, 11 AFTR 16, 52 S.Ct. 613 (USSC, 1932).

[27]§§ 448(c) and 471(c) and Reg. § 1.446–1(c)(2).

Hybrid Method

The hybrid method is a combination of the accrual method and the cash method. Generally, a taxpayer using the hybrid method is in the business of buying and selling inventory but not otherwise required to use the accrual method. As a result, a taxpayer using the hybrid method would account for the sale of goods and cost of goods sold using the accrual method and use the cash method for other income and expense items (e.g., services and interest income). Since, beginning in 2018, more types of businesses can use the cash method and not account for inventory, the hybrid method is not likely to be commonly used.

4-2c Special Rules Applicable to Cash Basis Taxpayers

Constructive Receipt

In general, a cash basis taxpayer does not recognize income until it is received. Income that has not actually been received by the taxpayer is nonetheless taxed as though it had been received—the income is considered constructively received, if the amount is made readily available to the taxpayer and not subject to substantial limitations or restrictions.[28] For example, if an employee receives a paycheck on December 31 that is dated for January 8, it is not constructively received in December due to the date limitation. It would be considered taxable income in January.

The purpose of the constructive receipt doctrine is to prevent a cash basis taxpayer from deferring the recognition of income that, although not yet received, has been made practically available to the taxpayer. For instance, a taxpayer is not permitted to defer income earned in December simply by refusing to accept payment until January. Conversely, if an employee receives a paycheck on December 31 that is dated for January 8, the constructive receipt doctrine would allow the employee to defer recognizing the income until January. Determining whether income is *readily available* and whether *substantial limitations or restrictions exist* necessitates a factual inquiry.[29] Following are some examples of the application of the constructive receipt doctrine.

Constructive Receipt

Ted is a member of a barter club. In 2020, Ted performed services for other club members and earned 1,000 points. Each point entitles him to $1 in goods and services provided by other members of the club; the points can be used at any time. In 2021, Ted exchanged his points for a new high-definition TV. Ted must recognize $1,000 gross income in 2020 when the 1,000 points were credited to his account.[30]

EXAMPLE 9

Rick has a savings account with Eagle Savings and Loan Association. Under the terms of the account, interest accrues monthly and the depositor can withdraw the funds (including accrued interest) at any time. The interest accrued during the year is constructively received by Rick even though he does not withdraw the funds.[31]

EXAMPLE 10

The Big Picture

Return to the facts of *The Big Picture* on p. 4-1. On December 31, Dr. Payne has $10,000 in patients' checks that have not been deposited. They include a check for $3,000 from a patient who asked Dr. Payne not to deposit the check until after January 4 of next year because her account did not contain sufficient funds to pay the debt.

Under the cash method, Dr. Payne must recognize $7,000 of income from the $7,000 in checks on hand in the current year because the checks are a cash equivalent that is actually received. The income from the $3,000 check is neither actually nor constructively received in the current year because an insufficient account means that the funds are not available.[32]

EXAMPLE 11

---

[28]Reg. § 1.451–2(a).

[29]*Baxter v. Comm.*, 87–1 USTC ¶9315, 59 AFTR 2d 87–1068, 816 F.2d 493 (CA–9, 1987).

[30]Rev.Rul. 80–52, 1980–1 C.B. 100.

[31]Reg. § 1.451–2(a).

[32]*L. M. Fischer*, 14 T.C. 792 (1950).

The constructive receipt doctrine does not apply to income the taxpayer is not yet entitled to receive even though the taxpayer could have contracted to receive the income at an earlier date.[33]

The Big Picture

Return to the facts of *The Big Picture*. Assume that Dr. Payne adopted the cash basis of accounting. On December 15, Dr. Payne sees a new patient in need of extensive dental work at a cost of $2,000. The patient indicates she may be willing to pay for the services before they are performed. However, before the services are performed, the patient agrees to a payment plan that requires payment to be made within 30 days after services are performed. The services are performed December 28, and the patient pays on January 15.

Dr. Payne is not in constructive receipt of the $2,000 at the end of the year. Although Dr. Payne could have collected the fee prior to year-end, he was not yet entitled to the fee when he contracted to receive payment at a later date.[34]

Even income set apart or made available to the taxpayer is not constructively received if the ultimate right to it is subject to *substantial restrictions*. The life insurance industry has used substantial restrictions as a cornerstone for designing life insurance contracts with favorable tax features. Ordinary life insurance policies provide (1) current protection—an amount payable in the event of death—and (2) a savings feature—a cash surrender value payable to the policyholder if the policy is terminated during the policyholder's life. The annual increase in cash surrender value is not taxable because the policyholder must cancel the policy to actually receive the increase in value. Because the cancellation requirement is a substantial restriction, the policyholder does not constructively receive the annual increase in cash surrender value.[35] Employees sometimes receive from their employers property subject to substantial restrictions, such as stock options. Generally, no income is recognized until the restrictions lapse.[36]

Carlos is a key employee of Red, Inc. The corporation gives stock with a value of $10,000 to Carlos. The stock cannot be sold, however, for five years. Carlos is not required to recognize income until the restrictions lapse at the end of five years.

Original Issue Discount

Lenders frequently make loans that require a payment at maturity of more than the amount of the original loan. The difference between the original amount of the loan and the amount due at maturity, or the **original issue discount**, is actually interest. In such an arrangement, the original issue discount must be reported as it is earned, regardless of the taxpayer's accounting method.[37] The interest "earned" is calculated using the effective interest rate method.

EXAMPLE 14

On January 1, 2020, Mark, a cash basis taxpayer, pays $90,703 for a 24-month certificate of deposit. The certificate is priced to yield 5% (the effective interest rate) with interest compounded annually. No interest is paid until maturity, when Mark receives $100,000.

As a result, Mark's gross income from the certificate is $9,297 ($100,000 − $90,703). Mark's income earned each year is calculated as follows:

2020 (5% × $90,703)	$4,535
2021 [5% × ($90,703 + $4,535)]	4,762
	$9,297

---

[33]*Baxter v. Comm.*, 816 F.2d 493, 59 AFTR 2d 87–1068, 87–1 USTC ¶9315 (CA–9, 1997).

[34]*Cowden v. Comm.*, 61–1 USTC ¶9382, 7 AFTR 2d 1160, 289 F.2d 20 (CA–5, 1961).

[35]*Theodore H. Cohen*, 39 T.C. 1055 (1963).

[36]§ 83(a).

[37]§§ 1272(a)(3) and 1273(a).

The original issue discount rules do not apply to U.S. savings bonds (discussed in the following paragraphs) or to obligations with a maturity date of one year or less from the date of issue.[38] See Chapter 14 for additional discussion of the tax treatment of original issue discount.

Series E and Series EE Bonds

Certain U.S. government savings bonds (Series E before 1980 and Series EE after 1979) are issued at a discount and are redeemable for fixed amounts that increase at stated intervals. No interest payments are actually made. The difference between the purchase price and the amount received on redemption is the bondholder's interest income from the investment.

In general, the income from these savings bonds is deferred until the bonds are redeemed or mature. As discussed above, these bonds are not subject to the rules generally applicable to original issue discount. So U.S. savings bonds have attractive income deferral features not available with corporate bonds and certificates of deposit issued by financial institutions.

Of course, the deferral feature of government bonds issued at a discount is not an advantage if the investor has insufficient income to be subject to tax as the income accrues. In fact, the deferral may work to the investor's disadvantage if the bunching of the bond interest into one tax year moves the investor to a higher tax bracket than in prior years. Fortunately, U.S. government bonds have a provision for these investors. A cash basis taxpayer can elect to include in gross income the annual increment in redemption value.[39] These savings bond features can be relevant in planning with respect to reducing the kiddie tax (see text Section 3-5e).

EXAMPLE

15

Kate purchases Series EE U.S. savings bonds for $500 (face value of $1,000) on January 2 of the current year. If the bonds are redeemed during the first six months, no interest is paid. At December 31, the redemption value is $519.60.

If Kate elects to report the interest income annually, she must report interest income of $19.60 for the current year. If she does not make the election, she will report no interest income for the current year. When the bond matures, Kate may receive a Form 1099 from the bank for all of the interest. She should keep good records to prove that she paid the tax on the interest income over the life of the bond.

When a taxpayer elects to report the income from the bonds on an annual basis, the election applies to all such bonds the taxpayer owns at the time of the election and to all such securities acquired subsequent to the election. A change in the method of reporting the income from the bonds requires permission from the IRS.

ETHICS & EQUITY   Should the Tax Treatment of Government Bonds and Corporate Bonds Be Different?

Taxpayers are permitted to defer the original issue discount earned on U.S. Government Series EE bonds until the bonds mature, but the original issue discount on a corporate bond must be taken into gross income each year the bond is held. Is

this difference in the tax treatment of income earned on government and corporate bonds defensible in terms of equity? Why or why not?

---

[38]§ 1272(a)(2).

[39]§ 454(a).

Amounts Received under an Obligation to Repay

The receipt of funds with an obligation to repay those funds in the future is the essence of borrowing. Because the taxpayer's assets and liabilities increase by the same amount, no income is realized when the borrowed funds are received. This same concept extends to the receipt by a taxpayer of any funds that carry an obligation for repayment.

EXAMPLE 16

A landlord receives a damage deposit from a tenant. The landlord does not recognize income until the deposit is forfeited because the landlord has an obligation to repay the deposit if no damage occurs.[40] However, if the deposit is in fact a prepayment of rent, it is taxed in the year of receipt.

4-2d Exceptions Applicable to Accrual Basis Taxpayers

Unearned Income

For financial reporting purposes, advance payments received from customers are initially reflected in the financial statements of the seller as a liability and recognized as income over the period in which the income is earned. However, for tax purposes, unearned income generally is taxed in the year of receipt.

EXAMPLE 17

In December 2020, a tenant pays his January 2021 rent of $1,000. The accrual basis landlord must include the $1,000 in her 2020 gross income for tax purposes, although the unearned rent income is reported as a liability on the landlord's December 31, 2020 financial accounting balance sheet.

However, accrual basis taxpayers who receive advance payments may elect to include in gross income in the year of receipt only the amount that would be recognized as income in their financial statements with the remaining amount recognized in the subsequent year.[41] The special deferral rule for accrual method taxpayers is a method of accounting that must be properly adopted (discussed further in Chapter 16). This special method will result in differences in the timing of the reporting of revenue when financial reporting rules require the revenue to be reported over three or more years, as illustrated in the following example.

EXAMPLE 18

Yellow Corporation, an accrual basis calendar year taxpayer, sells its services under 12-month, 24-month, and 36-month contracts. The corporation provides services to each customer every month. On May 1, 2020, Yellow Corporation sold the following customer contracts:

Length of Contract	Total Proceeds
12 months	$3,000
24 months	4,800
36 months	7,200

Yellow may defer until 2021 all of the income that will be earned after 2020.

Length of Contract	Income Recorded in 2020	Income Recorded in 2021
12 months	$2,000 ($3,000 × 8/12)	$1,000 ($3,000 × 4/12)
24 months	1,600 ($4,800 × 8/24)	3,200 ($4,800 × 16/24)
36 months	1,600 ($7,200 × 8/36)	5,600 ($7,200 × 28/36)

The special election generally is available for advance payments for goods and services. It is not available, however, for unearned rent, interest, insurance premiums, and certain other advance payments. Advance payments for these items are taxed in the year of receipt.

---

[40] *John Mantell*, 17 T.C. 1143 (1952) and *Indianapolis Power & Light Co.*, 90–1 USTC ¶50,007, 65 AFTR2d 90–394, 110 S.Ct. 589 (USSC, 1990).

[41] § 451(c).

4-3 GENERAL SOURCES OF INCOME AND TO WHOM THEY ARE TAXED

LO.3

Identify the general sources of income and to whom they are taxable.

Gross income is often described as including that coming from labor (i.e., personal services) and capital (i.e., property). This section examines several issues generally related to income from personal services and property, including when and to whom such income is taxable.

4-3a Personal Services

It is a well-established principle of taxation that income from personal services must be included in the gross income of the person who performs the services. This principle was first established in a Supreme Court decision, *Lucas v. Earl*.[42] Mr. Earl entered into a binding agreement with his wife under which Mrs. Earl was to receive one-half of Mr. Earl's salary. Justice Holmes used the celebrated fruit and tree metaphor to explain that the fruit (income) must be attributed to the tree from which it came (Mr. Earl). A mere assignment of income does not shift the liability for the tax.

Services of an Employee

As discussed above, the income from personal services generally is taxable to the person performing the services. However, services performed by an employee for an employer's customers or clients are considered performed by the employer. So the employer is taxed on the income from the services provided, and the employee is taxed on any compensation received from the employer.[43]

The Big Picture

EXAMPLE 19

Return to the facts of *The Big Picture* on p. 4-1. Assume that instead of operating his dental practice as a sole proprietorship, Dr. Payne incorporated his dental practice in an attempt to limit his liability. He entered into an employment contract with his corporation and was to receive a salary. All patients contract to receive their services from the corporation, and those services are provided through the corporation's employee, Dr. Payne.

As a result, the corporation earned the income from patients' services and must include the patients' fees in its gross income. Dr. Payne must include his salary in his gross income. The corporation is allowed a deduction for the reasonable salary paid to Dr. Payne. (See the discussion of unreasonable compensation in Chapters 6 and 19.)

Services of a Child

In the case of a child, the Code specifically provides that amounts earned from personal services must be included in the child's gross income. This result applies even though the income may be paid to other persons (e.g., the child's parents).[44]

4-3b Income from Property

The courts have used the fruit and tree metaphor also to determine who should pay the tax on the income from property. In this context, the "tree" is the property and income is its "fruit." The owner of the tree has control over the fruit; therefore, the owner of the property should pay tax on the income the property produces. For example, if a father gives his daughter the right to collect the rent from his rental property, the father will nonetheless be taxed on the rent because he retains ownership of the property.[45] The fact that he can grant the right to the income to his daughter is evidence that he has control over the income. On the other hand, if a father gives his daughter the property, she is taxed on all the income earned after ownership of the property is transfered to her.

---

[42]2 USTC ¶496, 8 AFTR 10287, 50 S.Ct. 241 (USSC, 1930).

[43]*Sargent v. Comm.*, 91–1 USTC ¶50,168, 67 AFTR 2d 91–718, 929 F.2d 1252 (CA–8, 1991).

[44]§ 73. For treatment of the child's unearned income, see Kiddie Tax— Unearned Income of Dependent Children in text Section 3–5e.

[45]*Galt v. Comm.*, 54–2 USTC ¶9457, 46 AFTR 633, 216 F.2d 41 (CA–7, 1954); *Helvering v. Horst*, 40–2 USTC ¶9787, 24 AFTR 1058, 61 S.Ct. 144 (USSC, 1940).

Interest

Because income from property is taxable to the owner of the property when the income is generated, it is important to determine when that income is deemed generated, especially when ownership of the property may be transferred during the year. Interest is considered to accrue daily. Therefore, the interest on an obligation for the period that includes a transfer of ownership is allocated between the transferor and transferee based on the number of days during the period that each owned the obligation.

EXAMPLE 20

Floyd, a cash basis taxpayer, gave his son, Ethan, corporate bonds with a face amount of $12,000 and a 5% stated annual interest rate. The gift was made on February 28, 2020, and the interest was paid on the last day of each quarter. Floyd must recognize $100 of interest income (5% × $12,000 × 3/12 × 2/3) accrued at the time of the gift.

For the transferor, the timing of the recognition of the income from the property depends upon the accounting method and the manner in which the property was transferred. In the case of a gift of income-producing property, the donor must recognize his or her share of the accrued income at the time it would have been recognized had the donor continued to own the property.[46]

EXAMPLE 21

Return to the facts of Example 20. Assume that Floyd is a cash basis taxpayer. Because he transferred the bonds to his son as a gift, he must recognize the $100 of interest income as of March 31, the date he would have received the interest had he retained ownership of the bonds.

If the property transfer is a sale, the transferor must recognize the accrued income at the time of the sale. This results because the accrued interest will be included in the sales proceeds.

EXAMPLE 22

Mia purchased a corporate bond at its face amount of $10,000 on July 1, 2020. The bond pays 5% interest on each June 30. On September 30, 2020, Mia sold the bond for $10,600. Mia must recognize $125 of interest income in 2020 (5% × $10,000 × 3/12). She must also recognize a $475 capital gain from the sale of the bond:

Amount received from sale	$ 10,600
Less accrued interest income	(125)
Selling price of bond less interest	$ 10,475
Less cost of the bond	(10,000)
Capital gain on sale	$ 475

Dividends

As a separate taxable entity, a corporation is taxed on its earnings, with those earnings taxed again as dividends when distributed to shareholders. Therefore, corporate earnings distributed as dividends are subject to double taxation. Partial relief from this double taxation is provided by taxing qualified dividends received by individuals at the same rate as capital gains.[47] Depending on the individual's taxable income, capital gain tax rates of 0 percent, 15 percent, and 20 percent apply (see text Section 3-7b).

A holding period requirement must be satisfied for the special rates to apply: the stock must have been held for more than 60 days during the 121-day period beginning 60 days before the ex-dividend date.[48] The purpose of this requirement is to prevent the taxpayer from buying the stock shortly before the dividend is paid, receiving the dividend, and then selling the stock at a loss (a short-term capital loss) after the stock goes ex-dividend. A stock's price often declines after the stock goes ex-dividend.

---

[46]Rev.Rul. 72–312, 1972–1 C.B. 22.

[47]§§ 1(h)(11) and (j).

[48]The ex-dividend date is the date before the record date on which the corporation finalizes the list of shareholders who will receive the dividends.

Note that qualified dividends are not included as capital gains in the gains and losses netting process; as a result, they are *not* reduced by capital losses. Qualified dividend income is merely taxed at the rates that would apply to the taxpayer if he or she had an excess of net long-term capital gain over net short-term capital loss.

Stock Holding Period

In June 2020, Green Corporation pays a dividend of $1.50 on each share of its common stock. Madison and Daniel, two unrelated shareholders, each own 1,000 shares of the stock. Consequently, each receives a dividend of $1,500 (1,000 shares × $1.50). Assume that Daniel satisfies the 60/121-day holding period rule but Madison does not.

The $1,500 that Daniel receives is subject to preferential 0%/15%/20% treatment in 2020. The $1,500 that Madison receives, however, is not. Because Madison did not comply with the holding period rule, her dividend is not a *qualified dividend* and is taxed at ordinary income rates.

Assume that both Madison and Daniel in Example 23 are in the 32% tax bracket. Consequently, Madison pays a tax of $480 (32% × $1,500) on her dividend, whereas Daniel pays a tax of $225 (15% × $1,500) on his. The $255 savings that Daniel enjoys underscores the advantages of qualified dividend treatment.

Unlike individuals, corporations are not granted special tax rates for capital gains or dividends. However, corporations are permitted a dividends received deduction ranging from 50 percent to 100 percent of the dividends received from another domestic corporation. This deduction is discussed in text Section 17-1k.

Although interest generally accrues on a daily basis, dividends do not because the declaration of a dividend is at the discretion of the corporation's board of directors. Generally, dividends are taxed to the person who is entitled to receive them—the shareholder of record as of the corporation's record date.[49] As a result, if a taxpayer sells stock after a dividend has been declared but before the record date, the dividend generally will be taxed to the purchaser.

This rule differs in the case of a gift of stock. If a donor makes a gift of stock to someone (e.g., a family member) after the declaration date but before the record date, the Tax Court has held that the donor does not shift the dividend income to the donee. The *fruit* has sufficiently ripened as of the declaration date to tax the dividend income to the donor of the stock.[50] However, where a taxpayer gave stock to a qualified charity (a charitable contribution) after the declaration date and before the record date, the Fifth Circuit Court of Appeals concluded that the dividend income should be included in the gross income of the donee (the owner at the record date).[51] As a result, dividends declared on stock gifted to a charity and stock gifted to family members are treated differently.

On June 20, the board of directors of Black Corporation declares a $10 per share dividend. The dividend is payable on June 30 to shareholders of record on June 25. As of June 20, Maria owned 200 shares of Black Corporation's stock. On June 21, Maria sold 100 of the shares to Norm for their fair market value and gave 100 of the shares to Sam (her son). Both Norm and Sam are shareholders of record as of June 25.

Norm (the purchaser) will be taxed on $1,000 because he is entitled to receive the dividend. However, Maria (the donor) will be taxed on the $1,000 received by Sam (the donee) because the gift was made after the declaration date but before the record date of the dividend.

---

[49]Reg. § 1.61–9(c). The record date is the cutoff for determining the shareholders who are entitled to receive the dividend.

[50]*M. G. Anton*, 34 T.C. 842 (1960).

[51]*Caruth Corp. v. U.S.*, 89–1 USTC ¶9172, 63 AFTR 2d 89–716, 865 F.2d 644 (CA–5, 1989).

4-3c Income Received by an Agent

Income received by the taxpayer's agent is considered to be received by the taxpayer. Therefore, a cash basis principal must recognize the income at the time it is received by the agent.[52]

EXAMPLE 26

Jack, a cash basis taxpayer, delivered cattle to the auction barn in late December. The auctioneer, acting as Jack's agent, sold the cattle and collected the proceeds in December. The auctioneer did not pay Jack until the following January. Jack must include the sales proceeds in his gross income for the year the auctioneer received the funds.

4-3d Income from Partnerships, S Corporations, Trusts, and Estates

A **partnership** is not a separate taxpaying entity for Federal income tax purposes. Rather, the income of a partnership is included in the taxable income of its partners. A partnership merely files an information return (Form 1065) that serves to provide the data necessary for determining the amount and character of each partner's distributive share of the partnership's income and deductions. Each partner must then report his or her distributive share of the partnership's income and deductions for the partnership's tax year ending in or with the partner's tax year. The income must be reported by each partner in the year it is recognized by the partnership, even if such amounts are not actually distributed to the partners. Because a partner pays tax on partnership income as the partnership earns it, a distribution by the partnership to the partner is treated as a tax-free recovery of capital.[53]

EXAMPLE 27

Tara owns a one-half interest in the capital and profits of T & S Company (a calendar year partnership). For tax year 2020, the partnership earned revenue of $150,000 and had operating expenses of $80,000. During the year, Tara withdrew from her capital account $2,500 per month (for a total of $30,000).

For 2020, Tara must report $35,000 as her share of the partnership's profits [½ × ($150,000 − $80,000)] even though she received distributions of only $30,000.

Contrary to the general rule that a corporation must pay tax on its income, a *small business corporation* may elect to be taxed, under Subchapter S of the Internal Revenue Code, similarly to a partnership. As a result, the shareholders rather than the corporation pay the tax on the corporation's income.[54] The electing corporation is commonly referred to as an **S corporation**. Similar to partners in a partnership, the shareholders report their proportionate shares of the corporation's income and deductions for the year, regardless of whether the corporation actually makes any distributions to the shareholders.

Unlike partnerships and S corporations, estates and trusts generally are not business entities. Rather, they are intended to care for assets on the behalf of their beneficiaries until those assets are distributed to the beneficiaries. However, because those assets are often income-generating (e.g., investments), estates and trusts often earn income while caring for and administering their assets. The *beneficiaries of estates and trusts* generally are taxed on the income earned by the estates or trusts that is actually distributed or required to be distributed to them.[55] Any income not taxed to the beneficiaries is taxable to the estate or trust.

The taxation of income and distributions of partnerships, S corporations, and estates and trusts is compared in Concept Summary 4.1.

---

[52]Rev.Rul. 79–379, 1979–2 C.B. 204.

[53]§ 706(a) and Reg. § 1.706–1(a)(1). For further discussion, see Chapter 21.

[54]§§ 1361(a) and 1366. For further discussion, see Chapter 21.

[55]§§ 652(a) and 662(a). For further discussion of the taxation of income from partnerships, S corporations, trusts, and estates, see Chapters 21, 22, and 28.

Concept Summary 4.1

Taxation of Income and Distributions

	Partnership	S Corporation	Estate or Trust
Share of the income for the year	Partner's share taxed when earned by the partnership.	Stockholder's share taxed when earned by the S corporation.	Undistributed income taxed to the estate or trust.
Distributions	Recovery of capital, which reduces basis in the partnership.	Recovery of capital, which reduces basis in the stock.	Beneficiary's income taxed when distributed.

4-3e Income in Community Property States

General

State law in Arizona, California, Idaho, Louisiana, Nevada, New Mexico, Texas, Washington, and Wisconsin is based on a community property system. In Alaska, spouses can choose to have the community property rules apply. All other states have a common law property system. The basic difference between common law and community property systems centers around the property rights of married persons. Questions about the taxation of income from community property most frequently arise when spouses file separate returns.

Under a community property system, all property owned by a married individual is deemed either to be separately owned by one spouse or to belong to the marital community. Property may be held separately by a spouse if it was acquired before marriage or received by gift or inheritance following marriage. Otherwise, property is deemed to be community property.

The Federal income taxation of income generated by property in community property states generally is based on who has the right to the income. Any income generated by community property is taxable equally to each spouse regardless of the state in which the property is held. The taxation of income from separate property, however, differs across states. The laws of Idaho, Louisiana, Texas, and Wisconsin distinguish between separate property and the income it produces. In these states, the income from separate property belongs to the community. Accordingly, for Federal income tax purposes, each spouse is taxed on one-half of the income. In the remaining community property states, separate property produces separate income that the owner-spouse must report on his or her Federal income tax return.

What appears to be income, however, may really represent a recovery of capital. A recovery of capital and gain realized on separate property retain their identity as separate property. Items such as nontaxable stock dividends, royalties from mineral interests, and gains and losses from the sale of property take on the same classification as the assets to which they relate.

EXAMPLE 28

Bob and Jane are married and reside in California. Among other transactions during the year, the following occurred:

- A nontaxable stock dividend was received by Jane on stock that was given to her by her mother after Jane's marriage.
- A gain of $10,000 was realized on the sale of unimproved land purchased by Bob before the marriage.
- Oil royalties of $15,000 were received from a lease Jane acquired with her separate funds after the marriage.

Because the stock dividend was distributed on stock held by Jane as separate property, it also is her separate property. The same result occurs for the oil royalties Jane receives. All of the proceeds from the sale of the unimproved land (including the gain of $10,000) are Bob's separate property.

In all community property states, income from personal services (e.g., salaries, wages, and income from a professional partnership) is generally treated as if one-half is earned by each spouse.

EXAMPLE 29

Fred and Wilma are married but file separate returns. Fred received $25,000 of salary and $300 of taxable interest on a savings account he established in his name. All deposits to the savings account were made from Fred's salary that he earned since the marriage. Wilma collected $2,000 taxable dividends on stock she inherited from her father. Wilma's gross income is computed as follows under three assumptions as to the state of residency of the couple:

	California	Texas	Common Law States
Dividends	$ 2,000	$ 1,000	$2,000
Salary	12,500	12,500	–0–
Interest	150	150	–0–
	$14,650	$13,650	$2,000

Note that the savings account is a community asset because it was created with community funds (i.e., Fred's salary).

Because they have community property income and are filing separately, each spouse must include Form 8958, Allocation of Tax Amounts Between Certain Individuals in Community Property States, on his or her Form 1040.

Community property should not be confused with jointly owned property. There are several differences between the two. For example:

- Jointly owned property (i.e., property owned by tenants in common or joint tenants) is not limited to married couples.

- More than two owners can own property jointly. As a result, three siblings or two or more unrelated individuals can be joint owners of a tract of land.

- Ownership interests in jointly owned property need not be equal. For example, one sibling can hold a one-half interest while two others own a one-quarter interest each.

Community Property Spouses Living Apart

The general rules for taxing the income from services performed by residents of community property states can create complications and even inequities for spouses who are living apart.

EXAMPLE 30

Mason and Lily, a married couple, have always lived in a community property state. After a bitter argument in December 2019, Lily moves in with her parents, where she remains for all of 2020. During 2020, Lily receives none of Mason's income. Nor is she sure how much income he earned. When Lily files her separate return for 2020, must she include one-half of Mason's salary?

Congress has developed a simple solution to this problem. A spouse (or former spouse) is taxed only on his or her actual earnings from personal services if all of the following conditions are met:[56]

- The spouses (or former spouses) live apart for the entire year.
- They do not file a joint return with each other.
- No portion of the earned income is transferred between the individuals.

---

[56]§ 66. See Form 8958.

4-4 ITEMS SPECIFICALLY INCLUDED IN GROSS INCOME

LO.4

Apply the tax rules on alimony, loans made at below-market interest rates, annuities, prizes and awards, unemployment compensation, Social Security benefits, and foreign bank accounts.

Although § 61 makes it clear that all income is taxable unless explicitly excluded, Congress has deemed it necessary to clarify and provide specific rules for several types of income. Some of these special rules appear in §§ 71–91 of the Code.

4-4a Alimony and Separate Maintenance Payments

When a married couple divorce or become legally separated, state law generally requires a division of the property accumulated during the marriage. In addition, one spouse may have a legal obligation to support the other spouse. The Code distinguishes between the support payments (alimony or separate maintenance) and the property division in terms of the tax consequences.

==Alimony and separate maintenance payments== made under a divorce agreement executed after 2018 are neither taxable to the recipient nor deductible by the payor.[57] Payments made under an agreement entered into on or before December 31, 2018, are *includible* in the gross income of the party receiving the payments and *deductible* by the party making the payments. For payments related to these pre-2019 agreements, income is shifted from the income earner to the income beneficiary, who has a legal right to the income and is better able to pay the tax on the amount received.

EXAMPLE 31

Pete and Tina were divorced in 2018. Pete is required to pay Tina $15,000 of alimony each year. Pete earns $61,000 a year. Tina has the ultimate legal right to the $15,000 and is better able than Pete to pay the tax on it. Therefore, Tina must include the $15,000 in her gross income. Pete is required to include the $61,000 in his gross income but is allowed to deduct $15,000 from his gross income.

If the divorce occurred in 2020, Tina would not be required to include the alimony in her income and Pete would not be allowed a deduction for the alimony paid.

Property Settlements

A transfer of property *other than cash* to a former spouse under a divorce decree or agreement is not a taxable event. The transferor is not entitled to a deduction and does not recognize gain or loss on the transfer. The transferee does not recognize income and has a basis equal to the transferor's basis.[58]

EXAMPLE 32

Paul transfers stock to Rosa as part of a divorce settlement. The cost of the stock to Paul is $12,000, and the stock's value at the time of the transfer is $15,000. Rosa later sells the stock for $16,000. Neither Paul nor Rosa recognizes any gain or income from the transfer of the stock to Rosa. Rosa has a realized and recognized gain of $4,000 ($16,000 − $12,000) when she sells the stock.

Requirements for Alimony

Because a payor may face a higher marginal tax rate than a payee, parties entering into divorce agreements before 2019 may have had an incentive to have payments treated as support obligation (alimony) rather than as part of a property settlement. To clarify the appropriate treatment of payments between former spouses subsequent

---

[57]§§ 71 and 215.

[58]§ 1041, added to the Code in 1984 to repeal the rule of *U.S. v. Davis*, 62–2 USTC ¶9509, 9 AFTR 2d 1625, 82 S.Ct. 1190 (USSC, 1962). Under the *Davis* rule, which applied to pre-1985 divorces, a property transfer incident to divorce was a taxable event.

to a divorce, Congress developed the following objective rules. Payments made under pre-2019 agreements and decrees are *classified as alimony* only if the following conditions are satisfied:

- The payments are in cash. (This clearly distinguishes alimony from a property division.)
- The agreement or decree does not specify that the payments are not alimony. (This allows the parties to determine by agreement whether the payments will be alimony.)
- The payor and payee are not members of the same household at the time the payments are made. (This ensures that the payments are for maintaining two households.)
- There is no liability to make the payments for any period after the death of the payee. (Payments due after death would be a property interest that could be transferred to the heirs.)

Front-Loading

As an additional safeguard against a pre-2019 property settlement being disguised as alimony, special rules apply if payments in the first or second year of the arrangement exceed $15,000. If the payments meet the requirements laid out above, they are treated as alimony during the first two years of the agreement. However, if the annual payments decrease after the second year of the agreement by more than a statutory amount, the <mark>alimony recapture</mark> rules require that the payor include the excess payments made in years 1 and 2 as income to the the extent they were deducted previously. Similarly, the payee may deduct in year 3 the excess payments from years 1 and 2 that were included in income previously. The mechanics involved in computing recapture are complex and beyond the scope of this text. Worksheets for computing the recapture are provided in *Divorced or Separated Individuals* (IRS Publication 504).

Child Support

A taxpayer does not realize income from the receipt of child support payments made by his or her former spouse. Child support payments are not treated as income because the money is received subject to the duty to use the money for the child's benefit. Similarly, the payor is not allowed to deduct the child support payments because the payments are made to satisfy the payor's legal obligation to support the child.

In many cases, it may be difficult to determine whether payments subject to pre-2019 agreements are intended to be alimony or child support. The tax law generally treats any payments that would be reduced upon the happening of a contingency related to a child (e.g., the child attains age 21 or dies) as child support. In addition, if the total payments for the year are less than legally required, they are considered to first cover the required child support with any excess treated as the required alimony payments. These rules are applied even though the divorce agreement specifies other amounts for the support of the child.[59]

EXAMPLE 33

Under a divorce agreement entered into in 2017, Matt is required to make periodic alimony payments of $500 per month to Grace. However, when Matt and Grace's child reaches age 21, marries, or dies (whichever occurs first), the payments will be reduced to $300 per month. Grace has custody of the child. Because the required payments will be reduced by $200 per month due to the relevant contingencies, $200 of the monthly payments will be considered child support for Federal tax purposes regardless of how they are labeled. Only $300 of the monthly payment will be considered alimony.

If Matt makes payments of only $350 per month, the first $200 is treated as child support with the remaining $150 considered alimony.

[59]§§ 71(c)(2) and (3), and *Allen H. Johnson*, 107 TCM 1358, T.C.Memo. 2014–67.

The tax rules relating to divorce settlements are reviewed in Concept Summary 4.2.

Concept Summary 4.2

Tax Treatment of Payments and Transfers Pursuant to Divorce Agreements and Decrees

	Payor	Recipient
Alimony*	Deduction from gross income.	Included in gross income.
Alimony recapture*	Included in gross income of the third year.	Deducted from gross income of the third year.
Child support	Not deductible.	Not includible in gross income.
Property settlement	No income or deduction.	No income or deduction; basis for the property is the same as the transferor's basis.

*These alimony rules apply for agreements entered into before 2019.

4-4b Imputed Interest on Below-Market Loans

The tax on income can be reduced if the income can be shifted to a taxpayer in a lower tax bracket. As discussed above, shifting the taxation of income from services is difficult given the assignment of income doctrine. Although shifting the taxation of the income from property can be accomplished by shifting the ownership of the property, this might be a high price to pay. However, lending income-producing property to another taxpayer without charging interest on the loan, as illustrated in Example 34, could allow such shifting without requiring the taxpayer to give up ownership of the income-producing property.

Kareem is in the 50% (combined Federal and state) marginal tax bracket, while his daughter, Veneia, is in the 20% marginal tax bracket. Kareem has $400,000 available to invest. He plans to use the income from the investment to help support Veneia. Rather than invest the money himself, Kareem decides to loan the money to Veneia in exchange for a non-interest-bearing demand note. Veneia could invest the cash, and the income would be taxed at her 20% tax rate. As a result, the income that Kareem could have earned on the $400,000 and that would have been taxed at 50% becomes Veneia's income, potentially taxed at 20%. In addition, Kareem retains control over the principal because he could demand payment on the note at any time.

Although this was a common tax planning technique at one time, the imputed interest rules now prevent the income shifting illustrated in Example 34. Even when no interest is charged on a loan, the lender and borrower may be required to calculate their income as if it had been. If the rules are applicable, a lender will be treated as if he or she had earned interest on the loan and be required to recognize this <mark>imputed interest</mark> in his or her gross income. Likewise, the borrower will be treated as if he or she had incurred interest expense, although whether the interest expense is deductible will depend on several factors (see Chapters 10 and 11).[60]

Returning to Example 34, Kareem would be treated as if he had earned interest on the loan and be required to recognize the imputed interest in his gross income. Veneia would be treated as if she had incurred interest expense. Veneia's interest may be deductible as investment interest if she itemizes her deductions.

Imputed interest is calculated using the rate the Federal government pays on new borrowings, compounded semiannually. This Federal rate is adjusted monthly and is published by the IRS.[61] There are three Federal rates: short-term (not over three years and including demand loans), mid-term (over three years but not over nine years), and long-term (over nine years).[62]

---

[60]§ 7872(a)(1).

[61]§§ 7872(b)(2) and (f)(2).

[62]§ 1274(d).

EXAMPLE 36

Assume that the Federal rate applicable to the loan in Example 34 is 3.5% through June 30 and 4% from July 1 through December 31. Kareem makes the loan on January 1, and the loan is still outstanding on December 31. Kareem must recognize interest income of $15,140, and Veneia has interest expense of $15,140.

Imputed interest calculations:	
January 1–June 30: 3.5% × $400,000 × ½ year	$ 7,000
July 1–December 31: 4% × ($400,000 + $7,000) × ½ year	8,140
	$15,140

If interest is charged on the loan but is less than the Federal rate, the imputed interest is the difference between the amount that would have been charged at the Federal rate and the amount actually charged.

EXAMPLE 37

Assume the same facts as in Example 36, except that Kareem charged 3% interest, compounded annually.

Interest at the Federal rate	$ 15,140
Less interest charged (3% × $400,000)	(12,000)
Imputed interest	$ 3,140

Although a lender may be required to recognize imputed interest as income for tax purposes, the lender nonetheless has realized no economic benefit. To better capture the economic positions of the parties involved, the lender is deemed to transfer back to the borrower an amount of money equal to the imputed interest. The nature of this transfer (and its Federal tax consequences) is determined by the relation of the parties to each other.

EXAMPLE 38

Return to Example 36. Kareem is deemed to transfer back to Veneia $15,140, the same amount he is deemed to have received in interest. Assuming that Kareem's only relation to Veneia is as a family member, the transfer from Kareem to Veneia is deemed to be a gift. Since gifts are not subject to income taxes (see Chapter 5), this transfer has no income tax consequences for either Kareem or Veneia. However, it may have gift tax consequences for Kareem (see Chapters 1 and 27).

The imputed interest rules apply to most below-market rate loans including the following:[63]

- Gift loans (loans made out of love, affection, or generosity, as in Example 34).
- Compensation-related loans (loans made by an employer to an employee).
- Corporation-shareholder loans (loans made by a corporation to a shareholder).

The effects of these loans on the borrower and lender are summarized in Concept Summary 4.3.

Concept Summary 4.3

Effect of Certain Below-Market Loans on the Lender and Borrower

Type of Loan	Lender	Borrower
Gift	Interest income	Interest expense
	Gift made	Gift received
Compensation-related	Interest income	Interest expense
	Compensation expense	Compensation income
Corporation to shareholder	Interest income	Interest expense
	Dividend paid	Dividend income

[63]§ 7872(c).

Exceptions and Limitations

No interest is imputed on total outstanding *gift loans* of $10,000 or less between individuals unless the loan proceeds are used to purchase income-producing property.[64] This exemption eliminates immaterial amounts that do not result in apparent shifts of income. However, if total gift loans between individuals exceed $10,000 or the proceeds of such a loan are used to purchase income-producing property, this exception does not apply.

On loans of $100,000 or less between individuals, the imputed interest cannot exceed the borrower's net investment income for the year (gross income from all investments less the related expenses).[65] As a result, the income imputed to the lender is limited to the borrower's net investment income. In addition, if the borrower's net investment income for the year does not exceed $1,000, no interest is imputed on loans of $100,000 or less. However, these limitations for loans of $100,000 or less do not apply if a principal purpose of a loan is tax avoidance.[66]

EXAMPLE

39

Vicki made interest-free gift loans as follows:

Borrower	Amount	Borrower's Net Investment Income	Purpose
Susan	$ 8,000	$ –0–	Education
Dan	9,000	500	Purchase of stock
Bonnie	25,000	–0–	Purchase of a business
Megan	90,000	15,000	Purchase of a residence
Olaf	120,000	–0–	Purchase of a residence

Assume that tax avoidance is not a principal purpose of any of the loans. The loan to Susan is not subject to the imputed interest rules because the $10,000 exception applies. The $10,000 exception does not apply to the loan to Dan because the proceeds were used to purchase income-producing assets. However, under the $100,000 exception, the imputed interest is limited to Dan's investment income ($500). Because the $1,000 threshold also applies to this loan, no interest is imputed.

No interest is imputed on the loan to Bonnie because the $100,000 exception applies. Interest is imputed on the loan to Megan based on the lesser of (1) the borrower's $15,000 net investment income or (2) the interest as calculated by applying the Federal rate to the outstanding loan. None of the exceptions apply to the loan to Olaf because the loan was for more than $100,000.

Assume that the relevant Federal rate is 5% and that the loans were outstanding for the entire year. Vicki would recognize interest income, compounded semiannually, as follows:

Loan to Megan:	
First 6 months (5% × $90,000 × ½ year)	$ 2,250
Second 6 months (5% × $94,500 × ½ year)	2,362
	$ 4,612
Loan to Olaf:	
First 6 months (5% × $120,000 × ½ year)	$ 3,000
Second 6 months (5% × $126,000 × ½ year)	3,150
	$ 6,150
Total imputed interest ($4,612 + $6,150)	$10,762

As with gift loans, there is a $10,000 exemption for *compensation-related loans* and *corporation-shareholder loans*. However, the $10,000 exception does not apply to compensation-related or corporation-shareholder loans if tax avoidance is one of the principal purposes of the loan.[67] This vague tax avoidance standard makes practically all compensation-related and corporation-shareholder loans suspect. Nevertheless, the $10,000 exception should apply when an employee's borrowing was necessitated by personal needs (e.g., to meet unexpected expenses) rather than tax considerations.

---

[64]§ 7872(c)(2).

[65]§ 7872(d).

[66]*Deficit Reduction Tax Act of 1984: Explanation of the Senate Finance Committee* (April 2, 1984), p. 484.

[67]§ 7872(c)(3).

These exceptions to the imputed interest rules are summarized in Concept Summary 4.4.

Concept Summary 4.4

Exceptions to the Imputed Interest Rules for Below-Market Loans

Exception	Eligible Loans	Ineligible Loans and Limitations
De minimis—aggregate loans of $10,000 or less	Gift loans	Proceeds are used to purchase income-producing assets.
	Employer-employee	Principal purpose is tax avoidance.
	Corporation-shareholder	Principal purpose is tax avoidance.
Aggregate loans of $100,000 or less	Between individuals	Principal purpose is tax avoidance. For all other loans, interest is imputed to the extent of the borrower's net investment income if that income exceeds $1,000.

ETHICS & EQUITY   Taxing "Made-Up" Income

Under the imputed interest rules, the taxpayer who makes a below-market loan may be required to recognize income he or she did not actually receive. For example, assume that Christiana loans $200,000 to Max, her son, to start a business (income-producing property).

Christiana does not charge interest because Max needs the funds to operate a struggling startup business. Why should Christiana be required to pay tax on interest she did not collect? On one hand, she received no interest income. On the other hand, interest would have been charged by Christiana in an arm's length loan made to any other borrower or by any other lender on a loan to Max. Christiana's choice not to charge interest is really an indirect gift to Max. Should Christiana be able to avoid tax on the income she assigned to Max? This type of income is sometimes referred to as "phantom" income.

4-4c Income from Annuities

Annuity contracts generally involve a purchaser (the annuitant) paying a fixed amount for the right to receive a future stream of payments. Typically, the issuer of the contract is an insurance company and will pay the annuitant a cash value if the annuitant cancels the contract. The insurance company invests the amounts received from the annuitant, and the income earned serves to increase the cash value of the annuity. Generally, the increase in the cash value of the contract is not immediately taxable because it is subject to substantial restrictions (the contract must be canceled to realize the benefit). However, if the contract is canceled early, the amount received over the cost of the contract must be recognized as income.

EXAMPLE 40

Jean, age 50, pays $30,000 for an annuity contract that is to pay her $500 per month beginning when she reaches age 65 and continuing until her death. A year after purchasing the contract, its cash value increases to $30,200. If Jean should cancel the policy after one year, she would include $200 ($30,200 − $30,000) in her gross income. However, if she does not cancel the policy, the $200 increase in value is not includible in her gross income.

The tax accounting problem associated with receiving periodic payments under an annuity contract is one of apportioning the amounts received between recovery of capital (the original investment in the contract) and income.

Computing the Exclusion Amount

The annuitant can exclude from income (as a recovery of capital) the proportion of each payment that the investment in the contract bears to the expected return under the contract. The *exclusion amount* is calculated as follows:

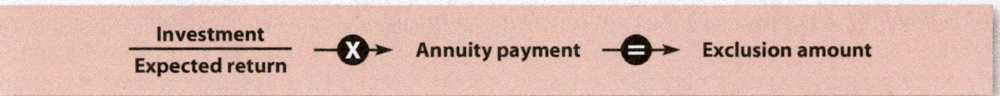

The *expected return* is the annual amount to be paid to the annuitant multiplied by the number of years the payments will be received. The payment period may be fixed (a *term certain*) or may be for the life of one or more individuals. When payments are for life, the taxpayer generally must use an annuity table published by the IRS to determine the expected return (see Exhibit 4.1).[68] The expected return is calculated by multiplying the appropriate multiple (life expectancy) by the annual payment.

EXHIBIT 4.1	Ordinary Life Annuities: One Life—Expected Return Multiples				

Age	Multiple	Age	Multiple	Age	Multiple
5	76.6	42	40.6	79	10.0
6	75.6	43	39.6	80	9.5
7	74.7	44	38.7	81	8.9
8	73.7	45	37.7	82	8.4
9	72.7	46	36.8	83	7.9
10	71.7	47	35.9	84	7.4
11	70.7	48	34.9	85	6.9
12	69.7	49	34.0	86	6.5
13	68.8	50	33.1	87	6.1
14	67.8	51	32.2	88	5.7
15	66.8	52	31.3	89	5.3
16	65.8	53	30.4	90	5.0
17	64.8	54	29.5	91	4.7
18	63.9	55	28.6	92	4.4
19	62.9	56	27.7	93	4.1
20	61.9	57	26.8	94	3.9
21	60.9	58	25.9	95	3.7
22	59.9	59	25.0	96	3.4
23	59.0	60	24.2	97	3.2
24	58.0	61	23.3	98	3.0
25	57.0	62	22.5	99	2.8
26	56.0	63	21.6	100	2.7
27	55.1	64	20.8	101	2.5
28	54.1	65	20.0	102	2.3
29	53.1	66	19.2	103	2.1
30	52.2	67	18.4	104	1.9
31	51.2	68	17.6	105	1.8
32	50.2	69	16.8	106	1.6
33	49.3	70	16.0	107	1.4
34	48.3	71	15.3	108	1.3
35	47.3	72	14.6	109	1.1
36	46.4	73	13.9	110	1.0
37	45.4	74	13.2	111	0.9
38	44.4	75	12.5	112	0.8
39	43.5	76	11.9	113	0.7
40	42.5	77	11.2	114	0.6
41	41.5	78	10.6	115	0.5

---

[68]The life expectancies in Exhibit 4.1 apply for annuity investments made on or after July 1, 1986. See *General Rules for Pensions and Annuities*, IRS Publication 939 (Rev. April 2003), p. 25. See also *Pension and Annuity Income*, IRS Publication 575.

EXAMPLE 41

A taxpayer, age 60, purchases an annuity from an insurance company for $90,000. She is to receive $500 per month for life. Her life expectancy (from Exhibit 4.1) is 24.2 years from the annuity starting date. As a result, her expected return is $500 × 12 × 24.2 = $145,200, and the exclusion amount is $3,719 [($90,000 investment ÷ $145,200 expected return) × $6,000 annual payment]. On an annual basis, the $3,719 is a nontaxable return of capital, and $2,281 ($6,000 − $3,719) is included in gross income.

The *exclusion ratio* (investment ÷ expected return) applies until the annuitant has recovered his or her investment in the contract. Once the investment is recovered, the entire amount of subsequent payments is taxable. If the annuitant dies before recovering the investment, the unrecovered cost (adjusted basis) is deductible in the year the payments cease (usually the year of death).[69]

EXAMPLE 42

Assume that the taxpayer in Example 41 receives annuity payments for 25.2 years (302 months). For the last 12 months [302 − (12 × 24.2) = 12], the taxpayer will include $500 (the total amount received) each month in gross income. If instead the taxpayer dies after 36 months, she is eligible for a $78,843 deduction on her final tax return.

Cost of the contract	$ 90,000
Cost previously recovered [$90,000 ÷ $145,200 × 36($500)]	(11,157)
Deduction	$ 78,843

Simplified Method for Annuity Distributions from Qualified Retirement Plans

A simplified method is required for allocating basis to the annuity payments received under a qualified retirement plan. The portion of each annuity payment that is excluded as a return of capital is the employee's investment in the contract divided by the number of anticipated monthly payments determined in accordance with Exhibit 4.2 rather than the annuity table illustrated in Exhibit 4.1.[70]

EXAMPLE 43

Andrea, age 62, receives an annuity distribution of $500 per month for life from her qualified retirement plan beginning in January 2019. Her investment in the contract is $100,100. The excludible amount of each payment is $385 ($100,100 investment ÷ 260 monthly payments). As a result, $115 ($500 − $385) of each annuity payment is included in Andrea's gross income.

The rules for annuity payments received after the basis has been recovered by the annuitant and for the annuitant who dies before the basis is recovered are the same as under the exclusion ratio method discussed earlier.

EXHIBIT 4.2	Number of Anticipated Monthly Annuity Payments under the Simplified Method

Age	Number of Anticipated Monthly Payments
55 and under	360
56–60	310
61–65	260
66–70	210
71 and over	160

---

[69]§ 72(b).   [70]§ 72(d).

4-4d Prizes and Awards

Gross income includes the fair market value of any prizes and awards received by a taxpayer (other than scholarships exempted under § 117, to be discussed subsequently).[71] For example, TV giveaway prizes, magazine publisher prizes, door prizes, and awards from an employer to an employee in recognition of performance are fully taxable to the recipient.

A narrow exception permits a prize or an award to be excluded from gross income if *all* of the following requirements are satisfied:

- The prize or award is received in recognition of religious, charitable, scientific, educational, artistic, literary, or civic achievement (e.g., Nobel Prize, Pulitzer Prize, or faculty teaching award).
- The recipient transfers the prize or award to a qualified governmental unit or nonprofit organization.
- The recipient was selected without any action on his or her part to enter the contest or proceeding.
- The recipient is not required to render substantial future services as a condition for receiving the prize or award.[72]

The transfer of the property to a qualified governmental unit or nonprofit organization ordinarily would be a deductible charitable contribution (an itemized deduction as explained in Chapter 10). The exclusion produces beneficial tax consequences in the following situations:

- The taxpayer does not itemize deductions and so would receive no tax benefit from the charitable contribution.
- The taxpayer's charitable contributions exceed the annual statutory ceiling on the deduction.
- Including the prize or award in gross income would reduce the amount of deductions for which the taxpayer would otherwise qualify because of gross income limitations (e.g., the adjusted gross income limitation in calculating the medical expense deduction).

The taxpayer can avoid including prizes and awards in gross income by refusing to accept the prize or award.[73]

Another exception allows an exclusion for certain *employee achievement awards* made in the form of tangible personal property (e.g., a gold watch) but not cash or cash equivalents (e.g., gift certificates, meals, lodging, or tickets to theater or sporting events). To qualify for the exclusion, the award must be made in recognition of an employee's length of service or safety achievement. Generally, the ceiling on the excludible amount for an employee is $400 per taxable year. However, if the award is made as a part of a tax qualified plan, the ceiling on the exclusion is $1,600 per taxable year.[74]

A final exception allows certain participants in the Olympic and Paralympic Games to exclude the value of any medal and cash award received. The exclusion is only available to those with income of $1 million or less. The rationale offered for this tax preference is that the athletes "perform a valuable patriotic service."[75]

4-4e Unemployment Compensation

The unemployment compensation program is sponsored and operated by the states and Federal government to provide a source of income for people who have been employed and are temporarily (hopefully) out of work. In a series of rulings over a

[71]§ 74.
[72]§ 74(b).
[73]See Rev.Rul. 57–374, 1957–2 C.B. 69 and Rev.Proc. 87–54, 1987–2 C.B. 669.
[74]§ 74(c). Qualified plan awards are defined in § 274(j) and explained in *Business Expenses*, Chapter 2 (IRS Publication 535).
[75]P.L. 114–239 (10/7/16), adding § 74(d) effective for awards received after 2015. Also see H.R. Rep. No. 114–762 (9/20/16).

period of 40 years, the IRS exempted unemployment benefits from tax. These payments were considered social benefit programs for the promotion of the general welfare. After experiencing dissatisfaction with the IRS's treatment of unemployment compensation, Congress amended the Code to make the benefits taxable.[76]

4-4f **Social Security Benefits**

The amount of Social Security benefits included in a taxpayer's gross income is based on two factors: (1) the taxpayer's ability to pay and (2) the amount of benefits considered to be a recovery of the taxpayer's contributions, or a recovery of capital. In this context, ability to pay is based on modified adjusted gross income (MAGI). MAGI is equal to the taxpayer's adjusted gross income from all sources other than Social Security benefits, increased by the foreign earned income exclusion and any tax-exempt income. Regardless of ability to pay, at least 15 percent of the benefits received are considered a recovery of capital.[77]

If a taxpayer's MAGI plus 50 percent of his or her Social Security benefits, often referred to as *provisional income*, does *not exceed* a threshold amount ($32,000 for married taxpayers filing a joint return or $25,000 for single taxpayers), the taxpayer need not include any Social Security benefits in gross income. If provisional income *exceeds* this threshold, the taxpayer must include a portion of the Social Security benefits in gross income, determined as follows:

1. The amount included in gross income is equal to 50 percent of the amount by which the provisional income exceeds the threshold, limited to 50 percent of the benefits themselves.
2. If the taxpayer's provisional income also exceeds a second threshold ($44,000 for a married couple filing a joint return or $34,000 for a single taxpayer), the amount included in gross income is equal to 85 percent of the amount that provisional income exceeds the higher threshold, plus the *smaller* of the following:
   - The amount determined in 1, above, or
   - 50 percent of the difference between the two threshold amounts (i.e., $6,000 for a married taxpayer filing jointly or $4,500 for a single taxpayer).

The total amount included in gross income is limited to 85 percent of the benefits themselves.

In general, the threshold amounts for married taxpayers filing separately are set at zero.

EXAMPLE 44

Taxation of Social Security Benefits

A married couple with adjusted gross income of $30,000, no tax-exempt interest, and $11,000 of Social Security benefits who file jointly must include $1,750 of the benefits in gross income. This is determined as follows:

1. $50\% \times [\$30,000 + \frac{1}{2}(\$11,000) - \$32,000] = \$1,750$
2. Limited to $50\% \times \$11,000 = \$5,500$

If instead the couple had adjusted gross income of $15,000, none of the benefits would be taxable because provisional income [$15,000 + (50\% \times \$11,000)$] does not exceed $32,000.

---

[76]§ 85.

[77]§ 86. The rationale for taxing 85% of the Social Security benefits is as follows: For the average Social Security recipient, 15% of the amount received is a recovery of amounts that the individual paid into the program, and the remainder of the benefits is financed by the employer's contribution and interest earned by the Social Security trust fund.

Taxation of Social Security Benefits

A married couple who file jointly have adjusted gross income of $72,000, no tax-exempt interest, and $12,000 of Social Security benefits. Their includible Social Security benefits will be $10,200, determined as follows:

EXAMPLE 45

1. $85\% \times [\$72,000 + \frac{1}{2}(\$12,000) - \$44,000] = \$28,900$

    Plus the lesser of:

    $50\% \times [\$72,000 + \frac{1}{2}(\$12,000) - \$32,000] = \$23,000$

    $50\% \times (\$44,000 - \$32,000) = \$6,000$

2. All limited to $85\% \times \$12,000 = \$10,200$

Because 85% of the Social Security benefits received is less than $34,900 ($28,900 + $6,000), $10,200 is included in the couple's gross income.[78]

4-4g Income Earned from Foreign Bank and Financial Accounts and FBAR Rules

Given the broad definition of gross income, income earned outside the United States is included in gross income (although limited exclusions are available, as discussed in Chapter 5). Taxpayers with a foreign bank account, brokerage account, or similar financial account also may be required to file an annual report with the Treasury Department. If the aggregate value of their foreign accounts exceeds $10,000 at any time during the calendar year, FinCEN Form 114, **Report of Foreign Bank and Financial Accounts (FBAR)**, must be filed electronically with the Treasury Department. This form is due by April 15 (with an automatic extension until October 15) for the preceding tax year. The form is filed separately from the account holder's income tax return. Schedule B of Form 1040 includes questions that also must be answered for individuals with foreign accounts. The penalty for failure to comply with the FBAR reporting requirements can be substantial: as much as 50 percent of the value of the foreign accounts.[79]

Jane, an employee of Maple Corporation, travels frequently for her work. She learned that it is easier to handle rent and other payments while working abroad if she has banking arrangements in these countries. In June and July of this year, during her trips, she opened an account in Canada and an account in France. Each started with a deposit of $6,000. Because on at least one day this year Jane had over $10,000 in foreign financial accounts, she must file FinCEN Form 114 (FBAR) to report the accounts. In addition, any interest earned on the accounts is included in calculating her Federal income tax liability.

EXAMPLE 46

4-5 TAX PLANNING

The topics covered in this chapter have focused on the following questions:

- What is income?
- When is the income recognized?
- To whom is the income taxable?

Planning strategies suggested by these questions include the following:

- Minimize economic benefits that are included in gross income.
- Defer the recognition of income.
- Shift income to taxpayers who are in a lower marginal tax bracket.

Some specific techniques for accomplishing these strategies are discussed in the following paragraphs.

LO.5

Identify tax planning strategies for minimizing gross income and the present value of the related tax.

---

[78]To help taxpayers compute taxable benefits, a worksheet is provided in the instructions to Form 1040, as well as in *Social Security and Equivalent Railroad Retirement Benefits* (IRS Publication 915).

[79]See **fincen.gov/resources/filing-information**. FinCEN is the Financial Crimes Enforcement Network and is part of the U.S. Department of the Treasury.

4-5a **Minimize Income Included in Gross Income**

Given the broad definition of gross income included in the Code, most items of income are included in gross income. However, a taxpayer may be able to restructure a transaction so that an item is not considered income. For example, a lessor may be able to structure a lease such that some amounts received under the contract are considered deposits. Given the requirement that the amount be repaid under certain circumstances, the receipt would not be considered income.[80] Conversely, in situations in which more than one taxpayer is involved, taxpayers may find it advantageous to have transfers between the parties considered income. For example, before 2019, it was often advantageous to structure divorce agreements such that payments between former spouses would qualify as taxable alimony rather than child support or a property settlement. Assuming that the payer was in a higher tax bracket than the recipient, alimony payments could reduce the joint tax liability of the parties.

In spite of the broad general definition of gross income, several types of income are specifically excluded from gross income. Several of these are discussed in Chapter 5.

4-5b **Tax Deferral**

General

Because deferring the recognition of income and the payment of the related taxes reduces the net present value of the tax liability, the deferral of taxes is a primary goal of the tax planner. In fact, a significant amount of tax planning deals with when taxes are owed rather than how much is owed. As discussed in text Section 4-2, the timing of income recognition generally is determined by the taxpayer's accounting method. The cash method provides the taxpayer with more deferral opportunities than does the accrual method. For example, under the cash method, income derived from services can be deferred until it is collected rather than recognized when the services are provided as required under the accrual method. Although taxpayers are somewhat constrained by the constructive receipt doctrine (they cannot turn their backs on income), seldom will customers and clients offer to pay before they are asked. The usual lag between billings and collections (e.g., December's billings collected in January) will result in a continuous deferring of some income until the last year of operations.

Regardless of a taxpayer's method of accounting, no income is recognized and no tax is due on a property transaction until a gain has been realized. Therefore, the law favors investments that appreciate in value over ones that provide regular cash payments.

EXAMPLE 47

Vera can buy a corporate bond or an acre of land for $10,000. The bond pays $600 of interest (6%) each year, and Vera expects the land to increase in value 6% each year for the next 10 years. She is in the 40% (combined Federal and state) tax bracket for ordinary income and 26% for qualifying capital gains. Assuming that the bond would mature or the land would be sold in 10 years and Vera would reinvest the interest at a 6% before-tax return, she would accumulate the following amount at the end of 10 years:

		Bond	Land
Original investment		$10,000	$10,000
Annual income	$ 600		
Less tax	(240)		
	$ 360		
Compound amount reinvested for 10 years at 6%	× 13.18	4,745	
		$14,745	
Compound amount, 10 years at 6%			× 1.79
			$17,900
Less tax on sale:			
26%($17,900 − $10,000)			(2,054)
			$15,846

Therefore, the value of the deferral that results from investing in the land rather than in the bond, combined with the lower tax rate, is $1,101 ($15,846 − $14,745).

---

[80]See *Commissioner v. Indianapolis Power and Light*, 90–1 USTC ¶50,007, 65 AFTR 2d 90–394, 110 S.Ct. 589 (USSC, 1990).

Of course, a taxpayer can often defer the recognition of income from appreciated property by postponing the event triggering realization (the final closing on a sale or exchange of property). If the taxpayer needs cash, obtaining a loan by using the appreciated property as collateral may be a less costly alternative than selling the property. The need to sell an appreciated asset to purchase a new investment will practically increase the return available on the new asset necessary to make it preferable to the old.

EXAMPLE
48

Ira owns 100 shares of Pigeon Company common stock with a cost of $20,000 and a fair market value of $50,000. Although the stock's value has increased substantially in the past three years, Ira thinks future appreciation will be much less. Ira is considering selling the Pigeon stock and investing the proceeds from the sale in other common stock. Assuming that Ira's marginal tax rate on the sale is 15%, he will have only $45,500 [$50,000 − 15%($50,000 − $20,000)] to reinvest. Therefore, if considered as competing alternatives, Ira will have to earn approximately 10% more ($50,000/$45,500) on a new investment to make it as profitable as his current investment in the Pigeon stock.

As discussed in text Section 4-2c, Series EE bonds offer taxpayers the unusual opportunity of long-term deferral of interest income until the maturity of the bond. In situations where the taxpayer's goal is merely to shift income one year into the future, bank certificates of deposit are useful tools. If the maturity period is one year or less, all interest is reported in the year of maturity. Bank certificates of deposit are especially useful for a taxpayer who finds himself or herself in an unusually high tax bracket in one year (perhaps due to a nonrecurring gain on the sale of property) but expects his or her gross income to be less the following year.

Generally, the timing of income recognition under the accrual method is not impacted by when cash is received. However, even accrual basis taxpayers may be able to defer the recognition of income by deferring when payment is received. Recall that an accrual basis taxpayer who receives unearned income need only recognize for tax purposes in the year of receipt what is recognized in his or her financial statements, but cannot defer recognition of the remainder beyond the year following the year of receipt. In some cases, deferring receipt from a year prior to when income would first be recognized to a subsequent year may result in a valuable tax deferral.

EXAMPLE
49

NerdSquad, Inc., sells three-year computer service agreements for $15,000, requiring the customer to prepay for the service when a contract is signed. In December 2020, NerdSquad will sell several three-year contracts covering the period from January 2021 to December 2023. It is considering whether to require customers to pay in December 2020 or January 2021. As illustrated below, Nerd-Squad will recognize in its financial statements $5,000 of income from each contract in each year from 2021 through 2023. However, by deferring receipt of the revenue for only a short period, the company will defer the tax on a significant portion of it.

	Financial Statement Income	Taxable Income	
		If payments are made December 30, 2020	If payments are made January 2, 2021
2020	$ –0–	$ –0–	$ –0–
2021	5,000	15,000	5,000
2022	5,000		10,000
2023	5,000		

Of course, the tax planner must also consider the tax rates for the years the income is shifted from and to. For example, a one-year deferral of income from a year in which the taxpayer's tax rate is 24 percent to a year in which the tax rate will be 35 percent would not be advisable unless the taxpayer could earn an after-tax return of approximately 45 percent on the deferred tax.

4-5c Shifting Income to Other Taxpayers

The benefits of income are often shared among multiple individuals regardless of who earns it. The tax liability of a family who may be directly or indirectly sharing income can be minimized by shifting the taxability of that income from higher- to lower-bracket family members. This can be accomplished through gifts of income-producing property. Furthermore, in many cases, income can be shifted with no negative effect on the family's spending or investment plans.

Adam, who is in the 24% tax bracket, would like to save for his children's education. All of the children are under 19 years of age and are dependents of Adam. Adam could transfer income-producing properties to the children, and the children could each receive up to $1,050 of income each year with no tax liability. Adam needs to determine whether it is advantageous to give additional assets, considering the high income tax rate applicable to unearned income of children of certain ages (see text Section 3-5e).

The Uniform Gifts to Minors Act, a model law adopted by all states (but with some variations among the states), facilitates such income shifting. Under the Act, a gift of intangibles (e.g., bank accounts, stocks, bonds, and life insurance contracts) can be made to a minor but with an adult serving as custodian. Usually, the parent who makes the gift is also named as custodian. State laws allow the custodian to sell or redeem and reinvest the principal and to accumulate or distribute the income, practically at the custodian's discretion provided there is no commingling of the child's income with the parent's property. By giving appreciated securities to the child, and having the donor custodian sell the securities and reinvest the proceeds, the parent shifts both the gain and the annual income to the child. Such planning is limited by the kiddie tax (refer to text Section 3-5e).

U.S. savings bonds provide another opportunity for income shifting. As discussed above, taxpayers may defer the interest (original issue discount) earned on U.S. government (Series EE) bonds. However, if and when this income is shifted to children, it may be beneficial to elect to recognize the interest early while the child has little or no other income. When this is done, the children generally should file a return and elect to report the income on the accrual basis.

Abby pays $7,500 for Series EE bonds in 2020 and registers them in her son's name. The son, Wade, will enter college the year of original maturity of the bonds. The bonds have a maturity value of $10,000. Wade elects to report the annual increment in redemption value as income for each year the bonds are held. The first year the increase is $250, and Wade includes that amount in his gross income. If Wade has no other income, no tax will be due on the $250 bond interest because such an amount will be more than offset by his available standard deduction. The following year the increment is $260, and Wade includes this amount in income. As a result, over the life of the bonds, Wade will include $2,500 in income ($10,000 − $7,500), none of which will result in a tax liability, assuming that he has no other income.

However, if the election had not been made, Wade would have been required to include $2,500 in income on the bonds in the year of original maturity if they had been redeemed as planned. This amount of income might result in a tax liability.

REFOCUS ON THE BIG PICTURE

CALCULATION OF GROSS INCOME

Using the accrual method of accounting, Dr. Cliff Payne has correctly calculated the gross income of his sole proprietorship. He will report the $385,000 amount on his tax return (Schedule C of Form 1040).

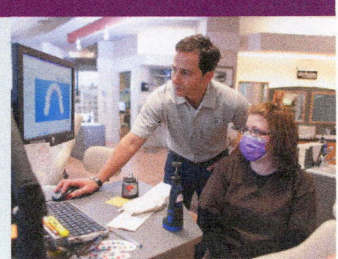

What If?

From a tax planning perspective, what can Dr. Payne do to decrease his gross income from the first year of operating his dental practice and thereby produce better financial results for him?

Rather than adopt the accrual method of accounting, Dr. Payne should adopt the cash method of accounting because his dental practice is a service entity rather than a merchandising entity. His gross income for Federal income tax purposes under the cash method is calculated as follows:

Revenues	$385,000
Plus: Accounts receivable: January 1	–0–
Less: Accounts receivable: December 31	(52,000)
Gross income	$333,000

The cash method of accounting enables Dr. Payne to defer paying Federal income taxes on the unpaid accounts receivable. Furthermore, each year that Dr. Payne has accounts receivable at the end of the tax year, that income is continuously deferred. As a result, if his accounts receivable remain at $52,000 at the end of each tax year, by using the cash method of accounting rather than the accrual method, he will defer that amount of income until he terminates his practice.

Bob Daemmrich/Alamy Stock Photo

Key Terms

Accounting income, 4-4
Accounting method, 4-6
Accrual method, 4-8
Alimony and separate maintenance payments, 4-19
Alimony recapture, 4-20
Annuity, 4-24
Assignment of income, 4-13
Cash receipts method, 4-7

Claim of right doctrine, 4-8
Community property, 4-17
Constructive receipt, 4-9
Economic income, 4-4
Fruit and tree metaphor, 4-13
Gross income, 4-3
Hybrid method, 4-9
Imputed interest, 4-21
Income, 4-4

Original issue discount, 4-10
Partnership, 4-16
Recovery of capital doctrine, 4-3
Report of Foreign Bank and Financial Accounts (FBAR), 4-29
S corporation, 4-16
Taxable year, 4-6

Discussion Questions

1. **LO.1** According to the Supreme Court, would it be good tax policy to use income as computed by financial accounting principles as the correct measure of income for Federal income tax purposes? Explain.

2. **LO.1** Compare and contrast the economist's concept used to recognize income with the concept employed in measuring taxable income.

Critical Thinking   3.   **LO.1** Allen visits Reno, Nevada, once a year to gamble. This year his gambling loss was $25,000. He commented to you, "At least I didn't have to pay for my airfare and hotel room. The casino paid that because I am such a good customer. That was worth at least $3,000." What are the relevant tax issues for Allen?

4.   **LO.1** Ben lost his job when his employer moved its plant. During the year, he collected unemployment benefits for three months, a total of $1,800. While he was waiting to hear from prospective employers, he painted his house. If Ben had paid someone else to paint his house, the cost would have been $3,000. The cost of the paint Ben used was $800. What is Ben's gross income for tax purposes from the above events?

Critical Thinking   5.   **LO.1** Howard buys wrecked cars and stores them on his property. Recently, he purchased a 1991 Ford Taurus for $400. If he can sell all of the usable parts, his total proceeds from the Taurus will be over $2,500. As of the end of the year, he has sold only the radio for $75 and he does not know how many, if any, of the remaining parts will ever be sold. What are Howard's income recognition issues?

6.   **LO.2, 3** On December 29, 2020, an employee received a $5,000 check from her employer's client. The check was payable to the employer. The employee did not remit the funds to the employer until December 30, 2020. The employer deposited the check on December 31, 2020, but the bank did not credit the employer's bank account until January 2, 2021. When is the cash basis employer required to include the $5,000 in gross income?

7.   **LO.2** What is the purpose of the constructive receipt doctrine?

8.   **LO.2** A Series EE U.S. government savings bond accrues 3.5% interest each year. The bond matures in three years, at which time the principal and interest will be paid. The bank will pay the taxpayer at a 3.5% interest rate each year if he agrees to leave money on deposit for three years. What tax advantage does the Series EE bond offer that is not available with the bank deposit?

9.   **LO.2** The taxpayer performs services with payment due from the customer within 30 days. All customers pay within the time limit. What would be the benefit to the taxpayer using the cash method of accounting rather than the accrual method?

10.   **LO.3, 5** Wade paid $7,000 for an automobile that needed substantial repairs. He worked nights and weekends to restore the car and spent $2,400 on parts for it. He knows that he can sell the car for $13,000, but he is very wealthy and does not need the money. On the other hand, his daughter, who has very little income, needs money to make the down payment on a house.

   a.   Would it matter, after taxes, whether Wade sells the car and gives the money to his daughter or whether he gives the car to his daughter and she sells it for $13,000? Explain.

   b.   Assume that Wade gave the car to his daughter after he had arranged for another person to buy it from his daughter. The daughter then transferred the car to the buyer and received $13,000. Who is taxed on the gain?

11.   **LO.3** Anita, a cash basis taxpayer, sued her former employer for wage discrimination. Her attorney agreed to pursue the case on a contingent fee basis—the attorney would receive one-third of any settlement or court award. The parties reached a settlement, and the attorney for Anita's former employer wrote a check payable to Anita for $320,000 and a check payable to her attorney for $160,000. Anita reasons that she and the attorney were partners in the lawsuit who shared profits two-thirds and one-third, respectively. Therefore, she includes $320,000 in her gross income. Is Anita's analysis correct? Explain.

12.   **LO.3** Rex purchased a 30% interest in a partnership for $200,000. In 2020, the partnership generated $400,000 of taxable income and Rex withdrew $100,000. In 2021, the partnership earned $600,000 of taxable income and Rex withdrew $200,000. What is Rex's gross income from the partnership in 2020 and 2021?

13. **LO.4** A divorce agreement entered into in 2017 requires Alice to pay her former spouse $50,000 a year for the next 10 years. Will the payments qualify as alimony? Why or why not?

14. **LO.4, 5** William and Abigail, who live in San Francisco, have been experiencing problems with their marriage. They have a three-year-old daughter, April, who stays with William's parents during the day because both William and Abigail are employed. Abigail worked to support William while he attended medical school, and now she has been accepted by a medical school in Mexico. Abigail has decided to divorce William and attend medical school. April will stay in San Francisco because of her strong attachment to her grandparents and because they can provide her with excellent day care. Abigail knows that William will expect her to contribute to the cost of raising April. Abigail also believes that to finance her education, she must receive cash for her share of the property they accumulated during their marriage. In addition, she believes that she should receive some reimbursement for her contribution to William's support while he was in medical school. She expects the divorce proceedings to take several months. Identify the relevant tax issues for Abigail. *Critical Thinking*

15. **LO.4, 5** Patrick and Eva are planning to divorce in 2020. Patrick has offered to pay Eva $12,000 each year until their 11-year-old daughter reaches age 21. Alternatively, Patrick will transfer to Eva common stock that he owns with a fair market value of $100,000. What factors should Eva and Patrick consider in deciding between these two options? *Decision Making*

16. **LO.4** In the current year, Rose Corporation made a $400,000 interest-free loan to John Rose, the corporation's controlling shareholder. Mr. Rose is also the corporation's chief executive officer and receives a salary of $300,000 a year. What are the tax consequences of classifying the loan as a compensation-related loan rather than as a corporation-shareholder loan?

17. **LO.4** Connor purchased an annuity that was to pay him a fixed amount each month for the remainder of his life. He began receiving payments in 2003, when he was 65 years old. In 2020, Connor was killed in an automobile accident. What are the effects of the annuity on Connor's final tax return?

18. **LO.4** For a person who receives Social Security benefits, what effect, if any, can an increase in other income have on that person's taxable income? *Critical Thinking*

19. **LO.4** In January 2020, Sonja deposited $20,000 in a bank in the Bahamas. She earned $500 interest income. She closed the account in December 2020.
    a. Is Sonja subject to the FBAR reporting requirement? Explain.
    b. Is the interest income taxable in the United States? Explain.

Computational Exercises

20. **LO.2** On January 1, 2020, Kunto, a cash basis taxpayer, pays $46,228 for a 24-month certificate. The certificate is priced to yield 4% (the effective interest rate) with interest compounded annually. No interest is paid until maturity, when Kunto receives $50,000. In your computations:
    a. Compute Kunto's gross income from the certificate for 2020.
    b. Compute Kunto's gross income from the certificate for 2021.

    Round any amounts to the nearest dollar.

21. **LO.2** Bigham Corporation, an accrual basis calendar year taxpayer, sells its services under 12- and 24-month contracts. The corporation provides services to each customer every month. On July 1, 2020, Bigham sold the following customer contracts:

Length of Contract	Total Proceeds
12 months	$14,000
24 months	$24,000

Determine the income to be recognized in taxable income in 2020 and 2021.

Length of Contract	2020 Income	2021 Income
12 months	a. _____	c. _____
24 months	b. _____	d. _____

22. **LO.3** Simba and Zola are married but file separate returns. Simba received $80,000 of salary and $1,200 of taxable dividends on stock he purchased in his name and paid from the salary he earned since the marriage. Zola collected $900 in taxable interest on a certificate of deposit she inherited from her aunt. Compute Zola's gross income under two assumptions as to the state of residency of the couple. If an amount is zero, enter "$0."

	Idaho (Community Property State)	South Carolina (Common Law State)
Dividends	a. _____	d. _____
Interest	b. _____	e. _____
Salary	c. _____	f. _____

23. **LO.4** Casper and Cecile divorced in 2018. As part of the divorce settlement, Casper transferred stock to Cecile. Casper purchased the stock for $25,000, and it had a market value of $43,000 on the date of the transfer. Cecile sold the stock for $40,000 a month after receiving it. In addition, Casper is required to pay Cecile $1,500 a month in alimony. He made five payments to her during the year. What are the tax consequences for Casper and Cecile regarding these transactions?

   a.   How much gain or loss does Casper recognize on the transfer of the stock?

   b.   Does Casper receive a deduction for the $7,500 alimony paid?

   c.   How much income does Cecile have from the $7,500 alimony received?

   d.   When Cecile sells the stock, how much does she report?

24. **LO.4** Elizabeth made the following interest-free loans during the year. Assume that tax avoidance is not a principal purpose of any of the loans. Assume that the relevant Federal rate is 5% and that the loans were outstanding for the last six months of the year.

Borrower	Amount	Borrower's Net Investment Income	Purpose of Loan
Richard	$ 5,000	$800	Gift
Woody	8,000	600	Purchase stock
Irene	105,000	–0–	Purchase residence

What are the effects of the imputed interest rules on these transactions? Compute Elizabeth's gross income from each loan.

   a.   Richard

   b.   Woody

   c.   Irene

25. **LO.4** A taxpayer, age 64, purchases an annuity from an insurance company for $50,000. She is to receive $300 per month for life. Her life expectancy is 20.8 years from the annuity starting date. Assuming that she receives $3,600 this year, what is the exclusion percentage, and how much is included in her gross income? Round the exclusion percentage to two decimal places. Round the final answer for the income to the nearest dollar.

26. **LO.4** Compute the taxable Social Security benefits in each of the following situations:
    a. Erwin and Eleanor are married and file a joint tax return. They have adjusted gross income of $46,000, no tax-exempt interest, and $12,400 of Social Security benefits.
    b. Erwin and Eleanor have adjusted gross income of $12,000, no tax-exempt interest, and $16,000 of Social Security benefits.
    c. Erwin and Eleanor have adjusted gross income of $85,000, no tax-exempt interest, and $15,000 of Social Security benefits.

Problems

27. **LO.1** Determine the taxpayer's current-year (1) economic income and (2) gross income for tax purposes from the following events:
    a. Ja-ron's employment contract as chief executive of a large corporation was terminated, and he was paid $500,000 not to work for a competitor of the corporation for five years.
    b. Elliot, a six-year-old child, was paid $5,000 for appearing in a television commercial. His parents put the funds in a savings account for the child's education.
    c. Valery found a suitcase that contained $100,000. She could not determine who the owner was.
    d. Winn purchased a lottery ticket for $5 and won $750,000.
    e. Larry spent $1,000 to raise vegetables that he and his family consumed. The cost of the vegetables in a store would have been $2,400.
    f. Dawn purchased an automobile for $1,500 that was worth $3,500. The seller was in desperate need of cash.

28. **LO.1, 2, 5** Harper is considering three alternative investments of $10,000. Assume that the taxpayer is in the 24% marginal tax bracket for ordinary income and 15% for qualifying capital gains in all tax years. The selected investment will be liquidated at the end of five years. The alternatives are: *Decision Making*
    • A taxable corporate bond yielding 5.333% before tax and the interest can be reinvested at 5.333% before tax.
    • A Series EE bond that will have a maturity value of $12,200 (a 4% before-tax rate of return).
    • Land that will increase in value.

    The gain on the land is classified and taxed as a long-term capital gain. The income from the bonds is taxed as ordinary income. How much must the land increase in value to yield a greater after-tax return than either of the bonds?

    Use the future value tables in Appendix G as needed for your calculations and comparisons. Present your answers using spreadsheet software such as Microsoft Excel.

29. **LO.2** Determine the taxpayer's gross income for tax purposes in each of the following situations:

   a.   Deb, a cash basis taxpayer, traded a corporate bond with accrued interest of $300 for corporate stock with a fair market value of $12,000 at the time of the exchange. Deb's cost of the bond was $10,000. The value of the stock had decreased to $11,000 by the end of the year.

   b.   Deb needed $10,000 to make a down payment on her house. She instructed her broker to sell some stock to raise the $10,000. Deb's cost of the stock was $3,000. Based on her broker's advice, instead of selling the stock, she borrowed the $10,000 using the stock as collateral for the debt.

   c.   Deb's boss gave her two tickets to the Rabid Rabbits rock concert because she met her sales quota. At the time she received the tickets, each ticket had a face price of $200 and was selling on eBay for $300. On the date of the concert, the tickets were selling for $250 each. Deb and her son attended the concert.

30. **LO.1, 2** Determine Amos's gross income in each of the following cases:

   a.   In the current year, Amos purchased an automobile for $25,000. As part of the transaction, Amos received a $1,500 rebate from the manufacturer.

   b.   Amos sold his business. In addition to the selling price of the stock, he received $50,000 for a covenant not to compete—an agreement that he will not compete with his former business for five years.

   c.   Amos owned some land he held as an investment. As a result of a change in the zoning rules, the property increased in value by $20,000.

Decision Making   31. **LO.2, 5** Al is a medical doctor who conducts his practice as a sole proprietor. During 2020, he received cash of $280,000 for medical services. Of the amount collected, $40,000 was for services provided in 2019. At the end of 2020, Al had accounts receivable of $60,000, all for services rendered in 2020. In addition, at the end of the year, Al received $12,000 as an advance payment from a health maintenance organization (HMO) for services to be rendered in 2021. Compute Al's gross income for 2020:

   a.   Using the cash basis of accounting.

   b.   Using the accrual basis of accounting.

   c.   Advise Al on which method of accounting he should use.

32. **LO.2** Selma operates a contractor's supply store. She maintains her books using the cash method. At the end of 2020, her accountant computes her accrual basis income that is used on her tax return. For 2020, Selma had cash receipts of $1,400,000, which included $200,000 collected on accounts receivable from 2019 sales. It also included the proceeds of a $100,000 bank loan. At the end of 2020, she had $250,000 in accounts receivable from customers, all from 2020 sales.

   a.   Compute Selma's accrual basis gross receipts for 2020.

   b.   Selma paid cash for all of the purchases. The total amount paid for merchandise in 2020 was $1,300,000. At the end of 2019, she had merchandise on hand with a cost of $150,000. At the end of 2020, the cost of merchandise on hand was $300,000. Compute Selma's gross income from merchandise sales for 2020.

Decision Making   33. **LO.2, 3, 5** Your client is a partnership, ARP Associates, which is an engineering
Communications   consulting firm. Generally, ARP bills clients for services at the end of each month. Client billings are about $50,000 each month. On average, it takes 45 days to collect the receivables. ARP's expenses are primarily for salary and rent. Salaries are paid on the last day of each month, and rent is paid on the first day of each month. The partnership has a line of credit with a bank, which requires monthly financial statements. These must be prepared using the accrual method. ARP's managing partner, Amanda Sims, has suggested that the firm also use the accrual method for

tax purposes and thus reduce accounting fees by $600. Assume that the partners are in the 35% (combined Federal and state) marginal tax bracket. Write a letter to your client explaining why you believe it would be worthwhile for ARP to file its tax return on the cash basis even though its financial statements are prepared on the accrual basis. ARP's address is 100 James Tower, Denver, CO 80208.

34. **LO.2** Trip Garage, Inc. (459 Ellis Avenue, Harrisburg, PA 17111), is an accrual basis taxpayer that repairs automobiles. In late December 2020, the company repaired Samuel Mosley's car and charged him $1,000. Samuel did not think the problem had been fixed and refused to pay; as a result, Trip refused to release the automobile. In early January 2021, Trip made a few adjustments and convinced Samuel that the automobile was working properly. At that time, Samuel agreed to pay only $900 because he did not have the use of the car for a week. Trip said "fine," accepted the $900, and released the automobile to Samuel. An IRS agent thinks Trip, as an accrual basis taxpayer, should report $1,000 of income in 2020, when the work was done, and then deduct a $100 loss in 2021. Prepare a memo to Susan Apple, the treasurer of Trip, with the recommended treatment for the disputed income. *Communications*

35. **LO.2** Determine the effects of the following on a cash basis taxpayer's gross income for 2020 and 2021:
    a. On the morning of December 31, 2020, the taxpayer received a $1,500 check from a customer. The taxpayer did not cash the check until January 3, 2021.
    b. The same as part (a), except that the customer asked the taxpayer not to cash the check until January 3, 2021, after the customer's salary check could be deposited.
    c. The same as part (a), except that the check was not received until after the bank had closed on December 31, 2020.

36. **LO.2** Marlene, a cash basis taxpayer, invests in Series EE U.S. government savings bonds and bank certificates of deposit (CDs). Determine the tax consequences of the following on her 2020 gross income:
    a. On September 30, 2020, she cashed in Series EE bonds for $10,000. She purchased the bonds in 2010 for $7,090. The yield to maturity on the bonds was 3.5%.
    b. On July 1, 2019, she purchased a CD for $10,000. The CD matures on June 30, 2021, and will pay $10,816, yielding a 4% annual return.
    c. On July 1, 2020, she purchased a CD for $10,000. The maturity date on the CD was June 30, 2021, when Marlene would receive $10,300.

37. **LO.2** Drake Appliance Company, an accrual basis taxpayer, sells home appliances and service contracts. Determine the effect of each of the following transactions on the company's 2020 gross income assuming that the company uses any available options to defer its taxes.
    a. In December 2019, the company received a $1,200 advance payment from a customer for an appliance that Drake special-ordered from the manufacturer. The appliance did not arrive from the manufacturer until January 2020, and Drake immediately delivered it to the customer. The sale was reported in 2020 for financial accounting purposes.
    b. In October 2020, the company sold a 6-month service contract for $240. The company also sold a 36-month service contract for $1,260 in July 2020.
    c. On December 31, 2020, the company sold an appliance for $1,200. The company received $500 cash and a note from the customer for $700 and $260 interest, to be paid at the rate of $40 a month for 24 months. Because of the customer's poor credit record, the fair market value of the note was only $600. The cost of the appliance was $750.

38. **LO.2, 5** Freda is a cash basis taxpayer. In 2019, she negotiated her salary for 2021. Her employer offered to pay her $21,000 per month in 2021 for a total of $252,000. Freda countered that she would accept $10,000 each month for the 12 months in 2021 and the remaining $132,000 in January 2022. The employer accepted Freda's terms for 2021 and 2022.

    a. Did Freda actually or constructively receive $252,000 in 2021?

    b. What could explain Freda's willingness to spread her salary over a longer period of time?

Decision Making

39. **LO.2, 5** The Bluejay Apartments, a new development, is in the process of structuring its lease agreements. The company would like to set the damage deposits high enough that tenants will keep the apartments in good condition. The company is actually more concerned about damage than about tenants not paying their rent.

    a. Discuss the tax effects of the following alternatives:
       • $1,000 damage deposit with no rent prepayment.
       • $500 damage deposit and $500 rent for the final month of the lease.
       • $1,000 rent for the final two months of the lease and no damage deposit.

    b. Which option do you recommend? Why?

40. **LO.3** Rusty has been experiencing serious financial problems. His annual salary was $100,000, but a creditor garnished his salary for $20,000; so the employer paid the creditor (rather than Rusty) the $20,000. To prevent creditors from attaching his investments, Rusty gave his investments to his 21-year-old daughter, Rebecca. Rebecca received $5,000 in dividends and interest from the investments during the year. Rusty transferred some cash to a Swiss bank account that paid him $6,000 interest during the year. Rusty did not withdraw the interest from the Swiss bank account. Rusty also hid some of his assets in his wholly owned corporation that received $150,000 rent income but had $160,000 in related expenses, including a $20,000 salary paid to Rusty. Rusty reasons that his gross income should be computed as follows:

Salary received	$ 80,000
Loss from rental property ($150,000 − $160,000)	(10,000)
Gross income	$ 70,000

Compute Rusty's correct gross income for the year, and explain any differences between your calculation and Rusty's.

41. **LO.2, 3** Troy, a cash basis taxpayer, is employed by Eagle Corporation, also a cash basis taxpayer. Troy is a full-time employee of the corporation and receives a salary of $60,000 per year. He also receives a bonus equal to 10% of all collections from clients he serviced during the year. Determine the tax consequences of the following events to the corporation and to Troy:

    a. On December 31, 2020, Troy was visiting a customer. The customer gave Troy a $10,000 check payable to the corporation for appraisal services Troy performed during 2020. Troy did not deliver the check to the corporation until January 2021.

    b. The facts are the same as in part (a), except that the corporation is an accrual basis taxpayer and Troy deposited the check on December 31, but the bank did not add the deposit to the corporation's account until January 2021.

    c. The facts are the same as in part (a), except that the customer told Troy to hold the check until January 2021 when the customer could make a bank deposit that would cover the check.

42. **LO.3, 4** Faye, Gary, and Heidi each have a one-third interest in the capital and profits of the FGH Partnership. Each partner had a capital account of $50,000 at
the beginning of the tax year. The partnership profits for the tax year were $270,000.
Changes in their capital accounts during the tax year were as follows:

	Faye	Gary	Heidi	Total
Beginning balance	$ 50,000	$ 50,000	$ 50,000	$150,000
Withdrawals	(20,000)	(35,000)	(10,000)	(65,000)
Additional contributions	–0–	–0–	5,000	5,000
Allocation of profits	90,000	90,000	90,000	270,000
Ending balance	$120,000	$105,000	$135,000	$360,000

Compute each partner's gross income from the partnership for the tax year.

43. **LO.3, 5** During the year, Alva received dividends on her stocks as follows:

Amur Corporation (a French corporation whose stock is traded on an established U.S. securities market)	$60,000
Blaze, Inc., a Delaware corporation	40,000
Grape, Inc., a Virginia corporation	22,000

a. Alva purchased the Grape stock three years ago, and she purchased the Amur stock two years ago. She purchased the Blaze stock 18 days before it went ex-dividend and sold it 20 days later at a $5,000 loss. Alva had no other capital gains and losses for the year. She is in the 32% marginal tax bracket. Compute Alva's tax on her dividend income for the year.

b. Alva's daughter, who is 25 and not Alva's dependent, had taxable income of $6,000, which included $1,000 of dividends on Grape, Inc. stock. The daughter had purchased the stock two years ago. Compute the daughter's tax liability on the dividends.

c. Alva can earn 4.5% before-tax interest on a corporate bond or a 4% dividend on a preferred stock. Assuming that the appreciation in value is the same, which investment produces the greater after-tax income?

d. The same as part (c), except that Alva's daughter is to make the investment.

44. **LO.3** Liz and Doug were divorced on December 31, 2020, after 10 years of marriage. Their current year's income received before the divorce was as follows:

Doug's salary	$41,000
Liz's salary	55,000
Rent on apartments purchased by Liz 15 years ago	8,000
Dividends on stock Doug inherited from his mother 4 years ago	1,900
Interest on a savings account in Liz's name funded with her salary	2,400

Allocate the income to Liz and Doug assuming that they live in:
a. California.
b. Texas.

45. **LO.4** Nell and Kirby are in the process of negotiating their divorce agreement, to be finalized in 2020. What should be the tax consequences to Nell and Kirby if the following, considered individually, became part of the agreement?

a. In consideration for her one-half interest in their personal residence, Kirby will transfer to Nell stock with a value of $200,000 and $50,000 of cash. Kirby's cost of the stock was $150,000, and the value of the personal residence is $500,000. They purchased the residence three years ago for $300,000.

b. Nell will receive $1,000 per month for 120 months. If she dies before receiving all 120 payments, the remaining payments will be made to her estate.

c. Nell is to have custody of their 12-year-old son, Bobby. She is to receive $1,200 per month until Bobby (1) dies or (2) attains age 21 (whichever occurs first). After either of these events occurs, Nell will receive only $300 per month for the remainder of her life.

Decision Making   46. **LO.4** Alicia and Rafel are in the process of negotiating a divorce agreement to be finalized in 2020. They both worked during the marriage and contributed an equal amount to the marital assets. They own a home with a fair market value of $400,000 (cost of $300,000) that is subject to a mortgage of $250,000. They have lived in the home for 12 years. They also have investment assets with a cost of $160,000 and a fair market value of $410,000. As a result, the net worth of the couple is $560,000 ($400,000 − $250,000 + $410,000). The holding period for the investments is longer than one year. Alicia would like to continue to live in the house. Therefore, she has proposed that she receive the residence subject to the mortgage, a net value of $150,000. In addition, she would receive $17,600 each year for the next 10 years, which has a present value (at 6% interest) of $130,000. Rafel would receive the investment assets. If Rafel accepts this plan, he must sell one-half of the investments so that he can purchase a home. Assume that you are counseling Alicia. Explain to Alicia whether the proposed agreement would be "fair" on an after-tax basis.

Decision Making   47. **LO.4, 5** Roy decides to buy a personal residence and goes to the bank for a $150,000 loan. The bank tells him that he can borrow the funds at 4% if his father will guarantee the debt. Roy's father, Hal, owns a $150,000 CD currently yielding 3.5%. The Federal rate is 3%. Hal agrees to either of the following:

- Roy borrows from the bank with Hal's guarantee to the bank.
- Hal cashes in the CD (with no penalty) and lends Roy the funds at 2% interest.

Hal is in the 32% marginal tax bracket. Roy, whose only source of income is his salary, is in the 12% marginal tax bracket. The interest Roy pays on the mortgage will be deductible by him. Which option will maximize the family's after-tax wealth?

48. **LO.2, 4** Ridge is a generous individual. During the year, he made interest-free loans to various family members when the Federal rate was 3%. What are the tax consequences of the following loans by Ridge:

a. On June 30, 2019, Ridge loaned $12,000 to his cousin, Jim, to buy a used truck. Jim's only source of income was his wages on various construction jobs during the year.

b. On August 1, 2019, Ridge loaned $8,000 to his niece, Sonja. The loan was to enable her to pay her college tuition. Sonja had $1,200 interest income from CDs her parents had given her.

c. On September 1, 2019, Ridge loaned $25,000 to his brother, Al, to start a business. Al had $220 of dividends and interest for the year.

d. On September 30, 2019, Ridge loaned $150,000 to his mother so that she could enter a nursing home. His mother's only income was $9,000 of Social Security benefits and $500 of interest income.

49. **LO.4** Indicate whether the imputed interest rules should apply in the following situations. Assume that all of the loans were made at the beginning of the tax year unless otherwise indicated.

a. Mike loaned his sister $90,000 to buy a new home. Mike did not charge interest on the loan. The Federal rate was 5%. Mike's sister had $900 of investment income for the year.

b. Nico's employer maintains an emergency loan fund for its employees. During the year, Nico's wife was very ill and he incurred unusually large medical expenses. He borrowed $8,500 from his employer's emergency loan fund for six months. The Federal rate was 5.5%. Nico and his wife had no investment income for the year.

c. Jody borrowed $25,000 from her controlled corporation for six months. She used the funds to pay her daughter's college tuition. The corporation charged Jody 4% interest. The Federal rate was 5%. Jody had $3,500 of investment income for the year.

d. Kait loaned her son, Jake, $60,000 for six months. Jake used the $60,000 to pay off college loans. The Federal rate was 5%, and Kait did not charge Jake any interest. Jake had dividend and interest income of $2,100 for the tax year.

50. **LO.4** Vito is the sole shareholder of Vito, Inc. He is also employed by the corporation. On June 30, 2020, Vito borrowed $8,000 from Vito, Inc., and on July 1, 2021, he borrowed an additional $10,000. Both loans were due on demand. No interest was charged on the loans, and the Federal rate was 4% for all relevant dates. Vito used the money to purchase a boat, and he had $2,500 of investment income. Determine the tax consequences to Vito and Vito, Inc., in each of the following situations:

a. The loans are considered employer-employee loans.

b. The loans are considered corporation-shareholder loans.

51. **LO.4** Pam retires after 28 years of service with her employer. She is 66 years old and has contributed $42,000 to her employer's qualified pension fund, all of which was taxable when earned. She elects to receive her retirement benefits as an annuity of $3,000 per month for the remainder of her life.

a. Assume that Pam retired in June 2019 and collected six annuity payments that year. What is her gross income from the annuity payments in the first year?

b. Assume that Pam lives 25 years after retiring. What is her gross income from the annuity payments in the twenty-fourth year?

c. Assume that Pam dies after collecting 160 payments. She collected eight payments in the year of her death. What are Pam's gross income and deductions from the annuity contract in the year of her death?

52. **LO.4** For each of the following, determine the amount that should be included in gross income:

a. Peyton was selected the most valuable player in the Super Bowl. In recognition of this, he was awarded an automobile with a value of $60,000. Peyton did not need the automobile, so he asked that the title be put in his parents' names.

b. Jacob was awarded the Nobel Peace Prize. When he was presented the check for $1,400,000, Jacob said, "I do not need the money. Give it to the United Nations to use toward the goal of world peace."

c. Linda appeared on a television game show during the year, winning $6,000 of cash and $4,000 of furniture and appliances.

53. **LO.2, 4** Herbert was employed for the first six months of 2020 and earned $90,000 in salary. During the next six months, he collected $8,800 of unemployment compensation, borrowed $12,000 (using his personal residence as collateral), and withdrew $2,000 from his savings account (including $60 of interest). He received dividends of $550. His luck was not all bad; in December, he won $1,500 in the lottery on a $5 ticket. Calculate Herbert's gross income.

Decision Making   54. **LO.4, 5** Linda and Don are married and file a joint return. In 2020, they received $12,000 in Social Security benefits and $35,000 in taxable pension benefits and interest.

a.   Compute the couple's adjusted gross income on a joint return.

b.   Don would like to know whether they should sell for $100,000 (at no gain or loss) a corporate bond that pays 8% in interest each year and use the proceeds to buy a $100,000 nontaxable State of Virginia bond that will pay $6,000 in interest each year. Assume that their marginal tax rate is 12%.

c.   If Linda in part (a) works part-time and earns $30,000, how much will Linda and Don's adjusted gross income increase?

55. **LO.4** Charles E. Bennett, age 64, will retire next year and is trying to decide whether to begin collecting his Social Security benefits at that time. His monthly benefits will increase if he defers his starting date for the benefits. He has asked you to estimate how much his income tax will increase as a result of collecting Social Security. Charles and his wife Bernice B., file a joint return, have no other dependents, and claim the standard deduction. Their only income other than the Social Security benefits are:

Interest and dividends	$ 6,000
Taxable pension	40,000

The Social Security benefits for the year would be $12,000.

a.   Complete Worksheet 1, Figuring Your Taxable Benefits, included in IRS Publication 915 to determine the taxable portion of this couple's taxable Social Security benefits (the publication includes a blank worksheet).

b.   What is the taxable portion of the $12,000 in Social Security benefits?

56. **LO.3, 4, 5** Donna does not think she has an income tax problem but would like to discuss her situation with you just to make sure there is no unexpected tax liability. Base your suggestions on the following relevant financial information:

a.   Donna's share of the SAT Partnership income is $150,000, but none of the income can be distributed because the partnership needs the cash for operations.

b.   Donna's Social Security benefits totaled $8,400, but Donna loaned the cash received to her nephew.

c.   Donna assigned to a creditor the right to collect $1,200 of interest on some bonds she owned.

d.   Donna and her husband lived together in California until September, when they separated. Donna has heard rumors that her husband had substantial gambling winnings since they separated.

Tax Return Problems

Tax Forms Problem
Decision Making
Communications

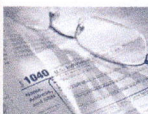
proconnect

57. Daniel B. Butler and Freida C. Butler, husband and wife, file a joint return. The Butlers live at 625 Oak Street in Corbin, KY 40701. Dan's Social Security number is 111-11-1112, and Freida's is 123-45-6780. Dan was born on January 15, 1968, and Freida was born on August 20, 1969.

During 2019, Dan and Freida furnished over half of the total support of each of the following individuals, all of whom still live at home:

a. Gina, their daughter, age 22, a full-time student, who married on December 21, has no income of her own and did not file a joint return with her husband, Casey, who earned $10,600 during 2019. Gina's Social Security number is 123-45-6788.

b. Willie, their son, age 19, graduated high school in May 2019. He is taking a leap year and will not begin college until 2020. He had gross income of $6,300 in 2019. Willie's Social Security number is 123-45-6787.

c. Ben, their oldest son, age 26, is a full-time graduate student with gross income of $5,200. Ben's Social Security number is 123-45-6786.

Dan was employed as a manager by WJJJ, Inc. (employer identification number 11-1111111, 604 Franklin Street, Corbin, KY 40702), and Freida was employed as a salesperson for Corbin Realty, Inc. (employer identification number 98-7654321, 899 Central Street, Corbin, Ky 40701). Selected information from the W–2 forms provided by the employers is presented below. Dan and Freida use the cash method.

Line	Description	Dan	Freida
1	Wages, tips, other compensation	$74,000	$86,000
2	Federal income tax withheld	11,000	12,400
17	State income tax withheld	2,960	3,440

Freida sold a house on December 30, 2019, and will be paid a commission of $3,100 (not included in the $86,000 reported on the W–2) on the January 10, 2020, closing date.

Other income (as reported on 1099 forms) for 2019 consisted of the following:

Dividends on CSX stock (qualified)	$4,200
Interest on savings at Second Bank	1,600
Interest on City of Corbin bonds	900
Interest on First Bank CD	382

The $382 from First Bank was an original issue discount. Dan and Freida collected $16,000 on the First Bank CD that matured on September 30, 2019. The CD was purchased on October 1, 2017, for $14,995, and the yield to maturity was 3.3%. Dan participated on a game show and won a cash prize of $7,000.

In addition to the above information, Dan and Freida's itemized deductions included the following:

Paid on 2019 Kentucky income tax	$ 700
Personal property tax paid	600
Real estate taxes paid	1,800
Interest on home mortgage (Corbin S&L)	4,900
Cash contributions to the United Way	800

Sales tax from the sales tax table is $1,860. Dan and Freida made Federal estimated tax payments of $8,000. They have never owned or used any virtual currency, and they do not wish to contribute to the Presidential Election Campaign. The Kentucky income tax rate is 4%.

Part 1—Tax Computation
Compute Dan and Freida's 2019 Federal income tax payable (or refund due). If you use tax forms for your computations, you will need Form 1040 and Schedules 1, 3, and B. Suggested software: ProConnect Tax Online.

Part 2—Tax Planning
Dan plans to reduce his work schedule and work only half-time for WJJJ in 2020. He has been writing songs for several years and wants to devote more time to developing a career as a songwriter. Because of the uncertainty in the music business, however, he would like you to make all computations assuming that he will have no income from songwriting in 2020. To make up for the loss of income, Freida plans to increase the amount of time she spends selling real estate. She estimates that she will be able to earn $90,000 in 2020. Assume that all other income and expense

items will be approximately the same as they were in 2019 (including the prize winnings). Assume that Willie will be enrolled in college as a full-time student for the summer and fall semesters. Will the Butlers have more or less disposable income (after Federal income tax) in 2020? Write a letter to the Butlers that contains your advice, and prepare a memo for the tax files.

Tax Computation Problem   58. Cecil C. Seymour is a 64-year-old widower. He had income for 2020 as follows:

Pension from former employer	$39,850
Interest income from Alto National Bank	5,500
Interest income on City of Alto bonds	4,500
Dividends received from IBM stock held for over one year	2,000
Collections on annuity contract he purchased from Great Life Insurance	5,400
Social Security benefits	14,000
Rent income on townhouse	9,000

The cost of the annuity was $46,800, and Cecil was expected to receive a total of 260 monthly payments of $450. Cecil has received 22 payments through 2020.

Cecil's 40-year-old daughter, Sarah C. Seymour, borrowed $60,000 from Cecil on January 2, 2020. She used the money to start a new business. Cecil does not charge her interest because she could not afford to pay it, but he does expect to collect the principal eventually. Sarah is living with Cecil until the business becomes profitable. Except for housing, Sarah provides her own support from her business and $1,600 in dividends on stocks that she inherited from her mother.

Other relevant information is presented below.

- Expenses on rental townhouse:

Utilities	$2,800
Maintenance	1,000
Depreciation	2,000
Real estate taxes	750
Insurance	700

- State income taxes paid: $3,500
- County personal property taxes paid: $3,100
- Payments on estimated 2020 Federal income tax: $5,900
- Charitable contributions of cash to Alto Baptist Church: $7,400
- Federal interest rate: 6%
- Sales taxes paid: $912

Compute Cecil's 2020 Federal income tax payable (or refund due).

Research Problems

Note: Solutions to the Research Problems can be prepared by using the Thomson Reuters Checkpoint™ online tax research database, which accompanies this textbook. Solutions can also be prepared by using research materials found in a typical tax library.

Communications   **Research Problem 1.** Tranquility Funeral Home, Inc., your client, is an accrual basis taxpayer that sells preneed funeral contracts. Under these contracts, the customer pays in advance for goods and services to be provided at the contract beneficiary's death. These payments are refundable at the contract purchaser's request, pursuant to state law, anytime until the goods and services are furnished. Tranquility, consistent with its financial accounting reporting, includes the payments in income for the year the funeral service is provided. The IRS agent insists that the payments be prepaid income subject to tax in the year of receipt. Your client believes that the amounts involved are customer deposits. Write a letter to Tranquility that contains your advice about how the issue should be resolved. The client's address is 400 Rock Street, Memphis, TN 38152.

Research Problem 2. Your client was the beneficiary of an annuity contract purchased by her stepmother. When the stepmother died, the insurance company paid the client $400,000 and sent her a Form 1099 indicating that the taxable portion (i.e., the amount in excess of the investment in the contract) was $50,000. However, according to the client, her father fraudulently convinced her that he was the intended beneficiary. She gave her father a check equal to the amount she had received from the insurance company. She did not report any of the annuity proceeds in her income tax return. She later discovered the fraud and filed a lawsuit to collect from her father. The IRS has examined your client's return and has taken the position that she must include the $50,000 in her gross income.

   Evaluate the IRS's position.

Research Problem 3. Your client owns a life insurance policy on his life. He has paid $6,800 in premiums, and the cash surrender value of the policy is $30,000. He borrowed $30,000 from the insurance company, using the cash surrender value as collateral. He is considering canceling the policy in payment of the loan. He would like to know the tax consequences of canceling his policy.

Use internet tax resources to address the following questions. Look for reliable websites and blogs of the IRS and other government agencies, media outlets, businesses, tax professionals, academics, think tanks, and political outlets.

Research Problem 4. Lottery winnings are taxable for Federal income tax purposes. What many lottery hopefuls forget to factor into their tax considerations are that lottery winnings are also taxable in many states. Search the internet to see whether you can determine whether lottery winnings are taxable for California residents.

Research Problem 5. Go to the web page of a consulting firm that offers counseling services to individuals as they negotiate the terms of a divorce. What specific tax-related services do these firms offer? Suggest a new tax-related service the consulting firm could offer.

Communications

Becker CPA Review Questions

Becker.

1. Which of the following statements is true regarding the taxation of Social Security benefits?
    a. 85% is the maximum amount of taxable Social Security benefits.
    b. 50% is the maximum amount of taxable Social Security benefits.
    c. If a taxpayer's only source of income is $10,000 of Social Security benefits, then 50% of the benefits are taxable.
    d. If a taxpayer's only source of income is $10,000 of Social Security benefits, then 85% of the benefits are taxable.

2. Fred and Wilma were divorced in year 1 (before 2019). Fred is required to pay Wilma $12,000 of alimony each year until their child turns 18. At that time, the payment will be reduced to $10,000 per year. In year 3, in accordance with the divorce agreement, Fred paid $6,000 directly to Wilma and $6,000 directly to the law school Wilma is attending. What amount of the payments received in year 3 is income to Wilma?
    a. $6,000
    b. $10,000
    c. $12,000
    d. $0

3. Bill and Jane Jones were divorced on January 1, 2018. They have no children. In accordance with the divorce decree, Bill transferred the title of their house over to Jane. The home had a fair market value of $250,000 and was subject to a $100,000 mortgage. Under the divorce agreement, Bill is to make $1,000 monthly mortgage payments on the home for the remainder of the mortgage. In the current year, Bill made 12 mortgage payments. What amount is taxable to Jane in the current year?

   a. $12,000   c. $100,000
   b. $250,000   d. $0

4. Jake pays the following amounts to his former spouse during the current year:

Regular alimony payments	$ 12,000
Child support	10,000
Residence as part of a property settlement	115,000

   What amount can Jake deduct as alimony for the current year? Assume that the divorce occurred before 2019.

   a. $0   c. $22,000
   b. $12,000   d. $137,000

5. Mary purchased an annuity that pays her $500 per month for the rest of her life. She paid $70,000 for the annuity. Based on IRS annuity tables, Mary's life expectancy is 16 years. How much of the first $500 payment will Mary include in her gross income (round to two decimals)?

   a. $0   c. $364.58
   b. $135.42   d. $500.00

6. Which of the following is taxable as gross income?

   a. Child support received based on a divorce agreement executed in 2015.
   b. Alimony received based on a divorce agreement executed in 2015.
   c. Child support received based on a divorce agreement executed in 2019.
   d. Alimony received based on a divorce agreement executed in 2019.

CHAPTER 5

Gross Income: Exclusions

LEARNING OBJECTIVES: *After completing Chapter 5, you should be able to:*

LO.1 Recognize that statutory authority is required to exclude an item from gross income.

LO.2 Identify the circumstances under which various items are excludible from gross income.

LO.3 Determine the extent to which receipts can be excluded under the tax benefit rule.

LO.4 Describe the circumstances under which income must be reported from the discharge of indebtedness.

LO.5 Identify tax planning strategies for obtaining the maximum benefit from allowable exclusions.

CHAPTER OUTLINE

5-1 Statutory Authority, 5-2

5-2 Gifts and Inheritances, 5-3
5-2a   Legislative Intent, 5-3
5-2b   Employer Payments to Employees, 5-3
5-2c   Employee Death Benefits, 5-4

5-3 Life Insurance Proceeds, 5-4
5-3a   General Rule, 5-4
5-3b   Accelerated Death Benefits, 5-5
5-3c   Transfer for Valuable Consideration, 5-6

5-4 Scholarships, 5-7
5-4a   General Information, 5-7
5-4b   Timing Issues, 5-8

5-5 Compensation for Injuries and Sickness, 5-8
5-5a   Damages, 5-8
5-5b   Wrongful Incarceration, 5-10
5-5c   Workers' Compensation, 5-10
5-5d   Accident and Health Insurance Benefits, 5-10

5-6 Employer-Sponsored Accident and Health Plans, 5-11
5-6a   Medical Reimbursement Plans, 5-11
5-6b   Long-Term Care Insurance Benefits, 5-12

5-7 Meals and Lodging, 5-13
5-7a   General Rules for the Exclusion, 5-13
5-7b   Other Housing Exclusions, 5-14

5-8 Employee Fringe Benefits, 5-14
5-8a   Specific Benefits, 5-15
5-8b   Cafeteria Plans, 5-15
5-8c   Flexible Spending Plans, 5-16
5-8d   General Classes of Excluded Benefits, 5-16
5-8e   Group Term Life Insurance 5-20

5-9 Foreign Earned Income, 5-21

5-10 Interest on Certain State and Local Government Obligations, 5-23

5-11 Corporate Distributions to Shareholders, 5-24
5-11a   General Information, 5-24
5-11b   Stock Dividends, 5-25

5-12 Educational Savings Bonds, 5-25

5-13 Education Savings Programs (§ 529 and § 530 Plans), 5-26
5-13a   Qualified Tuition Program, 5-26
5-13b   Coverdell Education Savings Account, 5-27

5-14 Qualified ABLE Programs (§ 529A Plans), 5-27

5-15 Tax Benefit Rule, 5-27

5-16 Income from Discharge of Indebtedness, 5-29

5-17 Tax Planning, 5-30
5-17a   Life Insurance, 5-30
5-17b   Employee Fringe Benefits, 5-30
5-17c   Investment Income, 5-31

VM/E+/GETTY IMAGES

EXCLUSIONS

Paul is a graduate student in the last semester of the accounting program at State University. This past summer he was an intern with a CPA firm, working in the compliance area. Paul was paid well enough for his work as an intern that he was able to pay for his meals and lodging and to save some for school. The CPA firm was so pleased with Paul's work that at the conclusion of his internship, he was given a bonus of $1,500 more than the firm had agreed to pay him. The extra amount was intended to help with his graduate school expenses. The CPA firm offered him a full-time job after he completes his graduate program in December.

Because of his excellent academic record, the university awarded Paul a graduate assistantship that waives his tuition of $6,000 per semester and pays him $400 per month. Paul is required to teach a principles of accounting course each semester. Paul has used the $400 per month for books and for room and board.

In November, Paul was crossing a street in the pedestrian crosswalk when a delivery van struck him. The driver of the truck was found to be driving under the influence of alcohol. Paul suffered a severe injury to his right arm that delayed his starting date for work by three months. The delivery company's insurance company settled the case by paying the following damages:

Compensatory damages:	
Medical expenses	$ 30,000
Injury to Paul's right arm	100,000
Pain and suffering	50,000
Loss of income	15,000
Legal fees	25,000
Punitive damages	160,000
	$380,000

Paul's mother was with him in the crosswalk. Fortunately, the van did not hit her, and she was not physically injured. But she did suffer emotional distress and received $25,000 in the settlement.

Besides being Paul's friend, you also are a senior accounting major and have a keen interest in taxation. You tell Paul that you will look into the tax consequences of the various payments he has received.

Read the chapter and formulate your response.

FRAMEWORK 1040   Tax Formula for Individuals

This chapter covers the boldfaced portions of the Tax Formula for Individuals that was introduced in Concept Summary 3.1 on p. 3-3. Below those portions are the sections of Form 1040 where the results are reported.

Income *(broadly defined)*	$xx,xxx
Less: Exclusions	**(x,xxx)**

FORM 1040 (p. 1)

2a Tax-exempt interest . . .	**2a** [ ]	**b** Taxable interest. Attach Sch. B if required	**2b** [ ]

Gross income	**$xx,xxx**

FORM 1040 (Schedule 1)

1	Taxable refunds, credits, or offsets of state and local income taxes	
7	Unemployment compensation	
8	Other income. List type and amount ▶ _____	

Less: Deductions *for* adjusted gross income	(x,xxx)
Adjusted gross income	$ xx,xxx
Less: The greater of total itemized deductions *or* the standard deduction............................	(x,xxx)
Personal and dependency exemptions*	(x,xxx)
Deduction for qualified business income**	(x,xxx)
Taxable income	$ xx,xxx
Tax on taxable income *(see Tax Tables or Tax Rate Schedules)*	$ x,xxx
Less: Tax credits *(including income taxes withheld and prepaid)*....................................	(xxx)
Tax due (or refund)	$ xxx

 * Exemption deductions are not allowed from 2018 through 2025.
** Only applies from 2018 through 2025.

C hapter 4 discussed the concepts and judicial doctrines that affect the determination of gross income. If an income item is within the all-inclusive definition of gross income, the item can be excluded only if the taxpayer can locate specific authority for doing so. Chapter 5 focuses on the exclusions Congress has authorized.

5-1 STATUTORY AUTHORITY

Sections 101 through 140 provide the authority for excluding specific items from gross income. Each exclusion has its own reason for enactment.

Some exclusions are intended as tax relief measures, such as the exclusion on up to $500,000 of gain from sale of a principal residence.[1] Others are to encourage and support certain activities, such as higher education. Some exclusions relate to design of the income tax. For example, damages received for physical injury are excluded under the premise that they are restoring damage to one's body rather than increasing one's personal wealth.[2]

At times, Congress responds to specific events. For example, in 2001, Congress enacted § 139, Disaster Relief Payment, to ensure that victims of a *qualified disaster*

---

[1]§ 121. See Chapter 13.

[2]Other examples include § 117 on certain scholarships and § 104 on physical injury; each is discussed in more detail later in this chapter.

(disaster resulting from a terrorist attack, Presidentially declared disaster, or common carrier accident of a catastrophic nature) could exclude from gross income payments received for living expenses, funeral expenses, and property damage resulting from the disaster.

For some types of transactions, the IRS does not tax what is in fact income because the revenue involved is not worth the collection effort or it is too difficult to measure the income. For example, the IRS has decided that it will not attempt to tax the value of frequent flier miles earned on airline tickets purchased for business use.

5-2 GIFTS AND INHERITANCES

Identify the circumstances under which various items are excludible from gross income.

5-2a Legislative Intent

From the beginning of the Federal income tax in 1913, Congress has allowed the recipient of a gift to exclude its value from gross income. The exclusion applies to gifts made during the life of the donor (*inter vivos* gifts) and transfers that take effect upon the death of the donor (bequests and inheritances).[3] However, as discussed in Chapter 4, when income-producing property is gifted, the recipient is subject to tax on the income subsequently earned from the property. Also, as discussed in Chapters 1 and 27, gift or estate taxes on the transfer might apply.

In many cases, gifts are made in a business setting. For example, a salesperson gives a purchasing agent free samples, an employee receives cash from his or her employer upon retirement, or a corporation makes payments to employees who were victims of a natural disaster. In these and similar instances, it is frequently unclear whether the payment was a gift or represents compensation for past, present, or future services.

The courts have defined a gift as "a voluntary transfer of property by one to another without adequate [valuable] consideration or compensation therefrom."[4] If the payment is intended to be for services rendered, it is *not* a gift, even though the payment is made without legal or moral obligation and the payor receives no economic benefit from the transfer. To qualify as a gift, the payment must be made "out of affection, respect, admiration, charity or like impulses."[5] As a result, these cases have been decided by looking at the donor's intent.

In a landmark case, *Comm. v. Duberstein*,[6] the taxpayer (Duberstein) received a Cadillac from a business acquaintance. Duberstein had supplied the businessman with the names of potential customers with no expectation of compensation. The Supreme Court concluded:

> … despite the characterization of the transfer of the Cadillac by the parties [as a gift] and the absence of any obligation, even of a moral nature, to make it, it was at the bottom a recompense for Duberstein's past service, or an inducement for him to be of further service in the future.

As a result, Duberstein was required to include the fair market value of the car in gross income.

5-2b Employer Payments to Employees

In the case of cash or other property *received by an employee* from his or her employer, Congress has eliminated any ambiguity. Transfers from an employer to an employee cannot be excluded as a gift.[7]

---

[3]§ 102.

[4]*Estate of D. R. Daly*, 3 B.T.A. 1042 (1926).

[5]*Robertson v. U.S.*, 52–1 USTC ¶9343, 41 AFTR 1053, 72 S.Ct. 994 (USSC, 1952).

[6]60–2 USTC ¶9515, 5 AFTR 2d 1626, 80 S.Ct. 1190 (USSC, 1960).

[7]§ 102(c). But see § 139 for qualified disaster situations.

The Big Picture

EXAMPLE 1

Return to the facts of *The Big Picture* on p. 5-1. The $1,500 bonus paid to Paul by his summer employer was compensation for his services rather than a gift, even though the employer had not contracted to pay this additional amount. This results because the payment was most likely not motivated by the employer's generosity, but rather was made as a result of business considerations. Even if the payment had been made out of generosity, because the payment was received from his employer, Paul could not exclude the "gift."

5-2c Employee Death Benefits

Frequently, an employer makes payments (death benefits) to a deceased employee's surviving spouse, children, or other beneficiaries. If the decedent had a nonforfeitable right to the payments (e.g., the decedent's accrued salary), the amounts are generally taxable to the recipient as if the employee had lived and collected the payments. But when the employer makes voluntary payments to the family of the deceased employee, the gift issue arises. Generally, the IRS considers these payments to be compensation.[8] However, some courts have held that these payments are gifts if all of the following are true:[9]

- The payments were made to the surviving spouse and children rather than to the employee's estate.
- The employer derived no benefit from the payments.
- The surviving spouse and children performed no services for the employer.
- The decedent had been fully compensated for services rendered.
- Payments were made pursuant to a board of directors' resolution that followed a general company policy of providing payments for families of deceased employees (but not exclusively for families of shareholder-employees).

If all of these conditions are satisfied, the payment is presumed to have been made *as an act of affection or charity*. When one or more of these conditions is *not* satisfied, the surviving spouse and children may still be deemed the recipients of a gift if the payment is made in light of the survivors' financial needs.[10]

Income earned by an employee that was not received by the employee prior to his or her death is not an employee death benefit. These earnings are referred to as "income in respect of a decedent"[11] and are generally taxable income to the decedent's beneficiary. This is another rare instance where the beneficiary of the income, rather than the person who earned the income, is subject to tax.

5-3 LIFE INSURANCE PROCEEDS

5-3a General Rule

Life insurance proceeds paid to the beneficiary because of the death of the insured are excluded from gross income.[12]

EXAMPLE 2

Linda purchases an insurance policy on her life and names her husband, Mark, as the beneficiary. Linda pays $45,000 in premiums. When she dies, Mark collects the insurance proceeds of $200,000. The $200,000 is excluded from Mark's gross income (and exempt from Federal income tax).

---

[8]Rev.Rul. 62–102, 1962–2 C.B. 37.

[9]*Estate of Sydney J. Carter v. Comm.*, 72–1 USTC ¶9129, 29 AFTR 2d 332, 453 F.2d 61 (CA–2, 1972), and the cases cited there.

[10]*Simpson v. U.S.*, 58–2 USTC ¶9923, 2 AFTR 2d 6036, 261 F.2d 497 (CA–7, 1958), *cert. denied* 79 S.Ct. 724 (USSC, 1958).

[11]§ 691.

[12]§ 101(a).

Congress believed it was good tax policy to exclude life insurance proceeds for the following reasons:

- For family members, life insurance proceeds serve much the same purpose as a nontaxable inheritance.
- In a business context (as well as in a family situation), life insurance proceeds replace an economic loss suffered by the business.

Gold Corporation purchases a life insurance policy to cover its CEO (a key employee). If the proceeds were taxable, the corporation would require more insurance coverage to pay the tax as well as to cover the economic loss of the employee.

EXAMPLE 3

5-3b Accelerated Death Benefits

Generally, if the owner of a life insurance policy cancels the policy and receives the cash surrender value, the taxpayer must recognize gain equal to the excess of the amount received over premiums paid on the policy (a loss is not deductible). The gain is recognized because the proceeds were *not* paid on the death of the insured. If the taxpayer cancels the policy and receives the cash surrender value, the life insurance policy is treated as an investment by the insured.

In a limited circumstance, however, the insured is permitted to receive the benefits of the life insurance contract without having to include the gain in gross income. Under the **accelerated death benefits** rules, an exclusion is available for insured taxpayers who are either terminally ill or chronically ill.[13] A terminally ill taxpayer can collect the cash surrender value of the policy from the insurance company or assign the policy proceeds to a qualified third party. The resulting gain, if any, is excluded from the insured's gross income. A person is *terminally ill* if a medical doctor certifies that death is likely to occur within 24 months.

In the case of a chronically ill patient, no gain is recognized if the proceeds of the policy are used for the patient's long-term care. A person is *chronically ill* if he or she is certified as needing assistance to perform certain activities of daily living. These exclusions for the terminally ill and the chronically ill are available only to the insured. A person who purchases a life insurance policy from the insured does not qualify.

Accelerated Death Benefits

Tom owned a term life insurance policy at the time he was diagnosed as having a terminal illness. After paying $5,200 in premiums, he sold the policy to Amber Benefits, Inc., a company that is authorized by the state of Virginia to purchase such policies. Amber paid Tom $50,000. When Tom died six months later, Amber collected the face amount of the policy, $75,000. Tom is not required to include the $44,800 gain ($50,000 − $5,200) on the sale of the policy in his gross income.

EXAMPLE 4

Assume that Amber Benefits, Inc., in Example 4 paid additional premiums of $4,000 during the six months it owned the policy. When Amber collects the life insurance proceeds of $75,000, it must include the $21,000 gain [$75,000 proceeds − ($50,000 cost + $4,000 additional premiums paid)] in gross income.

EXAMPLE 5

---

[13]§ 101(g); reporting may be required per § 6050Y.

5-3c Transfer for Valuable Consideration

A life insurance policy (other than one associated with accelerated death benefits) may be transferred after it is issued by the insurance company. If the policy is *transferred for valuable consideration*, the insurance proceeds are includible in the gross income of the purchaser to the extent the proceeds received exceed the amount paid for the policy plus any subsequent premiums paid.

EXAMPLE 6

Adam pays premiums of $4,000 for an insurance policy that has a face amount of $10,000 on the life of Beth and subsequently transfers the policy to Carol for $6,000. Upon Beth's death, Carol receives the proceeds of $10,000.

The amount Carol can exclude from gross income is limited to $6,000 plus any premiums she paid subsequent to the transfer.

The Code, however, provides five exceptions to the rule illustrated in Example 6. Exclusion treatment is allowed for transfers to the following:

1. The insured under the policy.
2. A partner of the insured.
3. A partnership in which the insured is a partner.
4. A corporation in which the insured is an officer or a shareholder.
5. A transferee whose basis in the policy is determined by reference to the transferor's basis.

The fifth exception applies to policies that were transferred in a tax-free exchange or were received by gift.[14]

EXAMPLE 7

When Logan's daughter Emily was born, he purchased an insurance policy on her life. Twenty-four years later after Emily graduated from college and married, Logan sold her the policy for its fair value. When Emily dies, the transfer for consideration rules will not apply.

Because the transfer was to the insured, the policy proceeds paid to Emily's beneficiaries will be excluded from the recipient's gross income. The results would be the same if Logan gave (rather than sold) the policy to Emily.

Investment earnings arising from the reinvestment of life insurance proceeds are generally subject to income tax. Often the beneficiary will elect to collect the insurance proceeds in installments. The annuity rules (discussed in text Section 4-4c) are used to apportion the installment payment between the principal element (excludible) and the interest element (includible).[15]

---

[14]See the discussion of gifts in Chapter 13 and tax-free exchanges in Chapters 13, 18, and 21. In the case of a gift, the donor's basis becomes the donee's basis.

[15]Reg. § 1.72–7(c)(1) and Temp.Reg. § 1.101–7T.

5-4 **SCHOLARSHIPS**

5-4a General Information

Payments or benefits received by a student at an educational institution may be (1) compensation for services, (2) a gift, or (3) a scholarship. If the payments or benefits are received as compensation for services (past or present), the fact that the recipient is a student generally does not render the amounts received nontaxable.[16] A university teaching or research assistant is generally considered an employee, and his or her stipend is taxable compensation. On the other hand, athletic scholarships generally are nontaxable when the individual is expected (but not required) to participate in the sport.[17] Unless received from family members, amounts received for educational purposes cannot be excluded as gifts because conditions usually attached to the funds mean that the payments were not made out of "detached generosity."

The scholarship rules are intended to provide exclusion treatment for education-related benefits that cannot qualify as gifts but are not compensation for services. To be excluded from income, the scholarship must be used for qualified tuition and related expenses (e.g., books and supplies).[18] The recipient must be a candidate for a degree at an educational institution.[19]

Terry enters a contest sponsored by a local newspaper. Each contestant is required to submit an essay on local environmental issues. The prize is one year's tuition at State University. Terry wins the contest. The newspaper has a legal obligation to Terry (as contest winner). As a result, the benefits are not a gift. However, because the tuition payment aids Terry in pursuing her studies, the payment is a scholarship.

If a nonprofit educational institution provides tuition reductions for its employees, the employees can exclude these amounts from their gross income. The exclusion also applies to tuition reductions granted to the employee's spouse and the employee's dependent children. In general, the exclusion applies only to education below the graduate level. However, tuition reductions for graduate students who are engaged in teaching or research activities at the educational institution also qualify for the exclusion.[20]

The Big Picture

Return to the facts of *The Big Picture* on p. 5-1. Paul was paid $400 a month by the university for teaching. This is reasonable compensation for his services. Although he received the assistantship because of his excellent academic record, the monthly payment of $400 must be included in his gross income because it is compensation for his services. However, the $6,000 graduate tuition reduction can be excluded from gross income.

The exclusion for qualified scholarships does not apply to room and board.[21] The NCAA allows athletic scholarships to include a "cost of attendance" amount. In addition to tuition, fees, books, and room and board, an athletic scholarship can include expenses like academic-related supplies, transportation, and other similar items. The value of these benefits may differ from campus to campus. However, only the amounts received for tuition, books, and supplies can be excluded from gross income.

---

[16]Reg. § 1.117–2(a). See *C. P. Bhalla*, 35 T.C. 13 (1960), for a discussion of the distinction between a scholarship and compensation. See also *Bingler v. Johnson*, 69–1 USTC ¶9348, 23 AFTR 2d 1212, 89 S.Ct. 1439 (USSC, 1969). For potential exclusion treatment, see the subsequent discussion of qualified tuition reductions.

[17]Rev.Rul. 77–263, 1977–2 C.B. 47.

[18]§ 117(b).

[19]§ 117(a).

[20]§ 117(d).

[21]§ 117(b). See also **irs.gov/newsroom/tax-benefits-for-education-information-center**.

Kelly received an athletic scholarship from State University. The scholarship pays her tuition of $9,000, and books and supplies of $2,400. She also receives $4,500 a year for costs of attendance, which she uses to pay for housing, food, laundry, and transportation.

The tuition and the cost of books and supplies are excluded from gross income as a qualified scholarship. The $4,500 received as costs of attendance does not qualify for the scholarship exclusion, and Kelly must include that amount in her gross income.

Some employers make scholarships available solely to the children of key employees. The tax objective of these plans is to provide a nontaxable fringe benefit to the executives by making the payment to the child in the form of an excludible scholarship. However, the IRS has ruled that the payments are generally includible in the gross income of the parent-employee.[22]

5-4b Timing Issues

Frequently, the scholarship recipient is a cash basis taxpayer who receives the money in one tax year but pays the educational expenses in a subsequent year. The amount eligible for exclusion may not be known at the time the money is received. In that case, the transaction is held *open* until the educational expenses are paid.[23]

In August 2020, Sanjay received a $10,000 scholarship for the 2020–2021 academic year. Sanjay's expenditures for tuition, books, and supplies were as follows:

August–December 2020	$3,000
January–May 2021	4,500
	$7,500

Sanjay's gross income for 2021 includes $2,500 ($10,000 − $7,500) that is not excludible as a scholarship. None of the scholarship is included in his gross income in 2020.

5-5 COMPENSATION FOR INJURIES AND SICKNESS

5-5a Damages

A person who suffers harm caused by another is often entitled to compensatory damages. The tax consequences of the damages awarded depend on the type of harm the taxpayer experienced. The taxpayer may seek recovery for (1) a loss of income, (2) expenses incurred, (3) property destroyed, or (4) personal injury.

Generally, reimbursement for a loss of income is taxed the same as the income replaced (see the exception under Personal Injury below). The recovery of an expense is not income unless the expense was deducted; if the expense was deducted, the damages generally are taxable under the tax benefit rule, discussed later in this chapter.

A payment for damaged or destroyed property is treated as an amount received in a sale or exchange of the property. As a result, the taxpayer has a realized gain if the damages received exceed the property's basis. Damages for personal injuries receive special treatment under the Code.

Personal Injury

The legal theory of personal injury damages is that the amount received is intended "to make the plaintiff [the injured party] whole as before the injury."[24] It follows that if the

---

[22]Rev.Rul. 75–448, 1975–2 C.B. 55; *Richard T. Armantrout*, 67 T.C. 996 (1977).   [24]*C. A. Hawkins*, 6 B.T.A. 1023 (1928).

[23]Prop.Reg. § 1.117–6(b)(2).

damages payments received were subject to tax, the after-tax amount received would be less than the actual damages incurred and the injured party would not be "whole as before the injury." In terms of personal injury damages, a distinction is made between compensatory damages and punitive damages.

ETHICS & EQUITY Tax Treatment of Damages Not Related to Physical Personal Injury

An individual who prevails in a personal injury claim for something other than a physical injury or sickness must include the amount of the award or settlement in gross income. In contrast, an award or a settlement for a physical personal injury or sickness can be excluded (except for punitive damages) from gross income. Should damages awarded for a physical personal injury or sickness be treated more favorably than damages awarded for emotional distress or other nonphysical personal injuries such as age and sex discrimination?

Compensatory damages are intended to compensate the taxpayer for the damages incurred. Only those compensatory damages received for *physical personal injury or physical sickness* can be excluded from gross income.[25] This includes amounts received for loss of income associated with the physical personal injury or physical sickness. Compensatory damages awarded for emotional distress cannot be excluded (except to the extent of any amount received for medical care) from gross income. Likewise, any amounts received for age discrimination or injury to one's reputation cannot be excluded.

Punitive damages are amounts the person who caused the harm must pay to the victim as punishment for the bad conduct. Punitive damages are not intended to compensate the victim, but rather to punish the party who caused the harm. So amounts received as punitive damages may actually place the victim in a better economic position than before the harm was experienced. As a result, punitive damages are included in gross income.

These rules are summarized in Concept Summary 5.1.

Concept Summary 5.1

Taxation of Damages

Type of Claim	Taxation of Award or Settlement
Breach of contract (generally loss of income)	Taxable.
Property damages	Gain to the extent damages received exceed basis. A loss is deductible for business property and investment property to the extent of basis over the amount realized. In certain cases, a loss may be deductible for personal use property (see discussion of casualty losses in Chapter 7).
Personal injury	
Physical	All compensatory amounts are excluded unless previously deducted (e.g., medical expenses). Amounts received as punitive damages are included in gross income.
Nonphysical	Compensatory damages and punitive damages are included in gross income.

---

[25]§ 104(a)(2).

The Big Picture

EXAMPLE 12

Return to the facts of *The Big Picture* on p. 5-1. The damages Paul received were awarded as a result of a physical personal injury. As a result, all of the compensatory damages can be excluded. Note that even the compensation for the loss of income of $15,000 can be excluded. The punitive damages Paul received, however, must be included in his gross income.

Paul's mother did not suffer a personal physical injury or sickness. So the $25,000 she received must be included in her gross income.

ETHICS & EQUITY   Classifying the Amount of the Claim

Lee was injured in an automobile accident caused by a negligent driver of a commercial vehicle. Lee threatened to file a lawsuit against the company for $100,000 in damages for his physical injury and $100,000 for punitive damages. The company's insurer would not pay punitive damages. As a result, the company advised Lee to revise his claim for $150,000 in physical damages and no punitive damages. Should Lee accept the offer?

5-5b Wrongful Incarceration

Section 139F exempts amounts received as damages for being wrongfully incarcerated. The exclusion applies to an individual convicted of a Federal or state crime who is later exonerated.

5-5c Workers' Compensation

State workers' compensation laws require the employer to pay fixed amounts for specific job-related injuries. The state laws were enacted to allow the employee to recover the damages without suing the employer. Although the payments are intended, in part, to compensate for a loss of future income, Congress has specifically excluded workers' compensation benefits from gross income.[26]

5-5d Accident and Health Insurance Benefits

The income tax treatment of accident and health insurance benefits depends on whether the policy providing the benefits was purchased by the taxpayer or the taxpayer's employer. Benefits collected under an accident and health insurance policy *purchased by the taxpayer* are excludible even though the payments are a substitute for income.[27]

Tax-Exempt Benefits

EXAMPLE 13

Quynh purchases a medical and disability insurance policy. The insurance company pays Quynh $1,000 per week to replace wages she loses while in the hospital. Although the payments serve as a substitute for income, the amounts received are tax-exempt benefits collected under Quynh's insurance policy.

EXAMPLE 14

Joe's injury results in a partial paralysis of his left foot. He receives $20,000 for the injury from his accident insurance company under a policy he had purchased. The $20,000 accident insurance proceeds are tax-exempt.

---

[26]§ 104(a)(1).   [27]§ 104(a)(3).

A different set of rules applies if the accident and health insurance protection was *purchased by the individual's employer*, as discussed in the following section.

5-6 EMPLOYER-SPONSORED ACCIDENT AND HEALTH PLANS

Congress encourages employers to provide employees, retired former employees, and their dependents with accident and health benefits, disability insurance, and long-term care plans. The *premiums* are deductible by the employer and excluded from the employee's income.[28] Although § 105(a) provides the general rule that the employee has includible income when he or she collects the insurance *benefits*, two exceptions are provided.

Section 105(b) generally excludes payments received for medical care of the employee, spouse, and dependents. However, if the payments are for expenses that do not meet the Code's definition of medical care,[29] the amount received must be included in gross income. In addition, the taxpayer must include in gross income any amounts received for medical expenses that were deducted by the taxpayer on a prior return.

In 2020, Branden's employer-sponsored health insurance plan pays $4,000 for hair transplants that do not meet the Code's definition of medical care. Branden must include the $4,000 in his gross income for 2020.

EXAMPLE 15

Section 105(c) excludes payments for the permanent loss or the loss of the use of a member or function of the body or the permanent disfigurement of the employee, the spouse, or a dependent. Payments that are a substitute for salary (e.g., related to the period of time absent) are includible.

Jill loses an eye in an automobile accident unrelated to her work. As a result of the accident, Jill incurs $2,000 of medical expenses, which she deducts on her return. She collects $100,000 from an accident insurance policy carried by her employer. The benefits are paid according to a schedule of amounts that vary with the part of the body injured (e.g., $100,000 for loss of an eye and $150,000 for loss of a hand).

Because the payment is for loss of a *member or function of the body*, the $100,000 is excluded from gross income. Jill is absent from work for several weeks as a result of the accident. Her employer provides her with insurance for the loss of income due to illness or injury. Jill collects $7,500, and this amount is includible in her gross income.

EXAMPLE 16

5-6a Medical Reimbursement Plans

As discussed above, amounts received through the insurance coverage (insured plan benefits) are excluded from income under § 105 or § 106. Instead of providing the employee with insurance coverage for hospital and medical expenses, the employer may agree to reimburse the employee for these expenses (a self-insured arrangement). Generally, the benefits received under a self-insured plan can be excluded from the employee's income if the plan does not discriminate in favor of highly compensated employees.[30]

---

[28]§ 106, Reg. § 1.106–1, and Rev.Rul. 82–196, 1982–1 C.B. 106.

[29]See the discussion of medical care in Chapter 10.

[30]§ 105(h). Also see § 106 and Rev.Rul. 61–146, 1961–2 C.B. 25. Employers should make sure such reimbursement plans fall within the requirements of the Affordable Care Act to avoid an excise tax. See § 4980D, Notice

2013–54, 2013–40 I.R.B. 287 and Notice 2015–17, 2015–10 I.R.B. 845. Also see rules on Qualified Small Employer Health Reimbursement Arrangements (QSEHRA) at § 9831(d), enacted by P.L. 114–255 (12/13/16), and Notice 2017–67, 2017–47 I.R.B. 517.

There is also an alternative means of accomplishing a medical reimbursement plan. The employer can purchase a medical insurance plan with a high deductible (e.g., the employee is responsible for the first $2,800 of the family's medical expenses) and then make contributions to the employee's **Health Savings Account (HSA)**.[31] The employer can make contributions each month up to the maximum contribution of 100 percent of the deductible amount. The monthly deductible amount is limited to one-twelfth of $3,550 under a high-deductible plan for self-only coverage. The monthly amount for an individual who has family coverage is limited to one-twelfth of $7,100 under a high-deductible plan. Withdrawals from the HSA must be used to reimburse the employee for the medical expenses paid by the employee that are not covered under the high-deductible plan. The employee is not taxed on the employer's contributions to the HSA, the earnings on the funds in the account, or the withdrawals made for medical expenses.[32]

5-6b Long-Term Care Insurance Benefits

Generally, **long-term care insurance**, which covers expenses such as the cost of care in a nursing home, is treated the same as accident and health insurance benefits. As a result, the employee does not recognize income when the employer pays the premiums. Also, the individual who purchases his or her own policy can exclude the benefits from gross income. However, the Code specifies limits (annually indexed for inflation) for the following amounts:

- Premiums paid by the employer.
- Benefits collected under the employer's plan.
- Benefits collected from the individual's policy.

The employer or insurance company generally provides the employee with information on the amount of his or her taxable benefits. The maximum amount excluded must be reduced by any amount received from third parties (e.g., Medicare, Medicaid).[33]

EXAMPLE 17

Hazel, who suffers from Alzheimer's disease, is a patient in a nursing home for the last 30 days of 2020. While in the nursing home, she incurs total costs of $7,900. Medicare pays $3,800 of the costs. Hazel receives $7,900 from her long-term care insurance policy, which pays benefits while she is in the nursing home. In 2020, $380 per day of long-term care benefits is excludible from gross income. The amount Hazel may exclude is calculated as follows:

Greater of:		
Daily excludible amount in 2020 ($380 × 30 days)	$11,400	
Actual cost of the care	7,900	$11,400
Less: Amount received from Medicare		(3,800)
Available exclusion amount		$ 7,600

As a result, Hazel must include $300 ($7,900 − $7,600) of the long-term care benefits received in her gross income.

The exclusion for long-term care insurance is not available if it is provided as part of a cafeteria plan or a flexible spending plan (explained later in the chapter).

---

[31] §§ 106(d) and 223. See additional coverage in Chapter 10.

[32] §§ 106(d), 223(b), and 223(d). The 2020 inflation-adjusted amounts are published in Rev.Proc. 2019–25 (2019–22 I.R.B. 1261). The amounts for 2019 were $3,500 and $7,000.

[33] §§ 7702B and 213(d)(10). See IRS Publication 525 for the taxable and nontaxable amounts that the employer is required to report on the employee's W–2.

5-7 MEALS AND LODGING

5-7a General Rules for the Exclusion

As discussed in Chapter 4, income can take any form, including meals and lodging. However, § 119 excludes from income the value of meals and lodging provided to the employee and the employee's spouse and dependents under the following conditions:[34]

- The meals and/or lodging are *furnished* by the employer on the employer's *business premises* for the *convenience of the employer*. From 2018 through 2025, the employer may only deduct 50 percent of the cost of the meals provided. After 2025, employers may not claim any deduction for these meals. If the employer continues to provide such meals, their value remains as an exclusion for the employees.

- In the case of lodging, the *employee is required* to accept the lodging as a condition of employment.

The courts have interpreted these requirements strictly.

Furnished by the Employer

The following two questions have been raised with regard to the *furnished by the employer* requirement:

- Who is considered an *employee*?
- What is meant by *furnished*?

The IRS and some courts have reasoned that because a partner is not an employee, the exclusion does not apply to a partner. However, the Tax Court and the Fifth Circuit Court of Appeals disagree with this conclusion.[35]

The Supreme Court held that a cash meal allowance was ineligible for the exclusion because the employer did not actually furnish the meals.[36] Similarly, one court denied the exclusion where the employer paid for the food and supplied the cooking facilities but the employee prepared the meal.[37]

On the Employer's Business Premises

The *on the employer's business premises* requirement, applicable to both meals and lodging, has resulted in much litigation. The Regulations define business premises as simply "the place of employment of the employee."[38] The Sixth Circuit Court of Appeals held that a residence, owned by the employer and occupied by an employee, two blocks from the motel that the employee managed was *not* part of the business premises.[39] However, the Tax Court considered an employer-owned house across the street from the hotel that was managed by the taxpayer to be on the business premises of the employer.[40] Apparently, the closer the lodging is to the business operations, the more likely the convenience of the employer is served.

---

[34]§ 119(a). The value of the meals and lodging is also excluded from FICA and FUTA tax. *Rowan Companies, Inc. v. U.S.*, 81–1 USTC ¶9479, 48 AFTR 2d 81–5115, 101 S.Ct. 2288 (USSC, 1981).

[35]Rev.Rul. 80, 1953–1 C.B. 62; *Comm. v. Doak*, 56–2 USTC ¶9708, 49 AFTR 1491, 234 F.2d 704 (CA–4, 1956); but see *G. A. Papineau*, 16 T.C. 130 (1951); *Armstrong v. Phinney*, 68–1 USTC ¶9355, 21 AFTR 2d 1260, 394 F.2d 661 (CA–5, 1968).

[36]*Comm. v. Kowalski*, 77–2 USTC ¶9748, 40 AFTR 2d 6128, 98 S.Ct. 315 (USSC, 1977).

[37]*Tougher v. Comm.*, 71–1 USTC ¶9398, 27 AFTR 2d 1301, 441 F.2d 1148 (CA–9, 1971).

[38]Reg. § 1.119–1(c)(1).

[39]*Comm. v. Anderson*, 67–1 USTC ¶9136, 19 AFTR 2d 318, 371 F.2d 59 (CA–6, 1966).

[40]*J. B. Lindeman*, 60 T.C. 609 (1973).

For the Convenience of the Employer

The *convenience of the employer* test is intended to focus on the employer's motivation for furnishing the meals and lodging rather than on the benefits received by the employee. If the employer furnishes the meals and lodging primarily to enable the employee to perform his or her duties properly, the "convenience" test is met.

The Regulations give the following examples where the "convenience" test is met:[41]

- A restaurant requires its service staff to eat their meals on the premises during the busy lunch and breakfast hours.
- A bank furnishes meals on the premises for its tellers to limit the time the employees are away from their booths during the busy hours.
- A worker is employed at a construction site in a remote part of Alaska. The employer must furnish meals and lodging due to the inaccessibility of other facilities.

Required as a Condition of Employment

The *required as a condition of employment* test applies only to lodging. If the employee's use of the housing would serve the convenience of the employer but the employee is not required to use the housing, the exclusion is not available.

EXAMPLE 18

Khalid is the manager of a large apartment complex. The employer requires Khalid to live on the premises but does not charge him rent. The rental value of his apartment is $9,600 a year. Although Khalid considers the rent-free housing a significant benefit, he is not required to include the value of the housing in his gross income.

5-7b Other Housing Exclusions

An employee of an educational institution may be able to exclude the value of campus housing provided by the employer. If the employee pays annual rents equal to or greater than 5 percent of the appraised value of the facility, the housing benefit may be excluded. If the rent payments are less than 5 percent of the value of the facility, the deficiency must be included in gross income.[42]

Ministers of the gospel and other religious leaders can exclude (1) the rental value of a home furnished as compensation; (2) a rental allowance paid to them as compensation, to the extent the allowance is used to rent, buy, or provide a home; or (3) the rental value of a home owned by the minister.[43] The housing or housing allowance must be provided as compensation for the conduct of religious worship, the administration and maintenance of religious organizations, or the performance of teaching and administrative duties at theological seminaries.

Military personnel are allowed housing exclusions under various circumstances. Authority for these exclusions generally is found in Federal laws that are not part of the Internal Revenue Code.[44]

5-8 EMPLOYEE FRINGE BENEFITS

Benefits other than wages and salary that are provided to employees by the employer are often referred to as **fringe benefits**. Generally, Congress decided that the availability of these benefits serves social goals. In addition, providing an income tax

---

[41]Reg. § 1.119–1(f).
[42]§ 119(d).

[43]§ 107 and Reg. § 1.107–1.
[44]H. Rep. No. 99–841, 99th Cong., 2d Sess., p. 548 (1986). See § 134 and *Armed Forces Tax Guide* (IRS Publication 3).

exclusion provides an incentive for employees to bargain for these nontaxable fringe benefits instead of taxable compensation. For example, if the employee is in the 22 percent marginal tax bracket, $100 of nontaxable fringe benefits is equivalent to $128 [$100/(1 − 0.22) = $128] in taxable compensation. From the employer's perspective then, it costs only $100 to provide $128 in value to that employee in the form of a tax-favored fringe benefit.

In Chapter 4 and earlier in this chapter, various fringe benefits were discussed (e.g., accident and health insurance and meals and lodging). Other employee benefits are discussed below.

5-8a Specific Benefits

Congress has dealt specifically with some other fringe benefits, which are summarized below.

- An employee does not have to include in gross income the value of child and dependent care services paid for by the employer and incurred to enable the employee to work. The exclusion cannot exceed $5,000 per year ($2,500 if married and filing separately). For a married couple, the annual exclusion cannot exceed the earned income of the spouse with the smaller amount of earned income. For an unmarried taxpayer, the exclusion cannot exceed the taxpayer's earned income.[45]

- The value of the use of a gymnasium or other athletic facilities by employees, their spouses, and their dependent children may be excluded from an employee's gross income. The facilities must be on the employer's premises, and substantially all of the use of the facilities must be by employees and their family members.[46]

- Qualified employer-provided educational assistance (tuition, fees, books, and supplies) at the undergraduate and graduate levels is excludible from gross income. An employee can exclude a maximum of $5,250 per year.[47] The exclusion does not cover meals, lodging, and transportation costs. In addition, it does not cover educational payments for courses involving sports, games, or hobbies.

- If an employer has a qualified adoption assistance program, an employee can exclude up to $14,300 of adoption expenses that are paid or reimbursed by the employer.[48] If the child has special needs (is not physically or mentally capable of caring for himself or herself), the $14,300 exclusion from gross income applies even if the actual adoption expenses are less than that amount. For 2020, the exclusion is phased out as adjusted gross income increases from $214,520 to $254,520.

5-8b Cafeteria Plans

Generally, if an employee is offered a choice between cash and some other form of compensation, the employee is deemed to have constructively received the cash even when the noncash option is elected. As a result, the employee has gross income regardless of the option chosen.

An exception to this constructive receipt treatment is provided under the cafeteria plan rules. Under these plans, the employee can choose between cash and nontaxable benefits (e.g., group term life insurance, health and accident protection, child care). If the employee chooses nontaxable benefits, the cafeteria plan rules enable the benefits

---

[45]§ 129. The exclusion applies to the same types of expenses that, if paid by the employee (and not reimbursed by the employer), would be eligible for the credit for child and dependent care expense discussed in Chapter 12.

[46]§ 132(j)(4).

[47]§ 127.

[48]§ 137. A credit is also available under § 23, as discussed in Chapter 12.

to remain nontaxable.[49] Cafeteria plans provide tremendous flexibility in tailoring the employee pay package to fit individual needs. Some employees (usually younger employees) prefer cash, while others (usually older employees) will opt for the fringe benefit program.

EXAMPLE 19

Hawk Corporation offers its employees (on a nondiscriminatory basis) a choice of any one or all of the following benefits:

Benefit	Cost
Group term life insurance	$ 200
Hospitalization insurance for family members	2,400
Child care payments	1,800
	$4,400

If a benefit is not selected, the employee receives cash equal to the cost of the benefit. Kay, an employee, has a spouse who works for another employer that provides hospitalization insurance but no child care payments. Kay elects to receive the group term life insurance, the child care payments, and $2,400 of cash. Only the $2,400 must be included in Kay's gross income.

5-8c Flexible Spending Plans

Flexible spending plans (often referred to as flexible benefit plans) operate much like cafeteria plans. Under these plans, the employee accepts lower cash compensation in return for the employer agreeing to pay certain costs that would normally be excludible from the employee's income. An annual inflation-adjusted cap applies to these plans ($2,750 in 2020).

For example, assume that the employer's health insurance policy does not cover dental expenses. Under a flexible spending plan, an employee estimates his or her dental expenses for the upcoming year and agrees to a salary reduction equal to the estimated dental expenses. The employer then pays or reimburses the employee for the actual dental expenses incurred, with a ceiling of the amount of the salary reduction. If the employee's actual dental expenses are less than the reduction in cash compensation, the employee cannot recover the difference. As a result, these plans are often called *use or lose* plans. To avoid the loss of unpaid amounts, the IRS allows a payment until two and a half months after the end of the plan year to count (March 15 for calendar year plans). As is the case for cafeteria plans, flexible spending plans cannot be used to pay long-term care insurance premiums.

5-8d General Classes of Excluded Benefits

An employer can provide many forms and types of economic benefits to employees. Under the all-inclusive concept of income, the benefits are taxable unless the Code specifically excludes the item from gross income. The amount of the income is the fair market value of the benefit.

EXAMPLE 20

Ryan is employed in New York as a ticket clerk for Trans National Airlines. He has a sick mother in Miami, Florida, but has no money for plane tickets. Trans National has daily flights from New York to Miami that often leave with empty seats. The cost of a round-trip ticket is $400.

In general, if Trans National allows Ryan to fly without charge to Miami, Ryan has income equal to the value of a ticket ($400). However, as discussed below, this is one of several classes of excluded benefits allowed under the tax law.

---

[49]§ 125.

Because Congress believed that taxing fringe benefits often yielded harsh results, § 132 was enacted to provide gross income exclusions for eight broad classes of employee benefits:[50]

- No-additional-cost services.
- Qualified employee discounts.
- Working condition fringes.
- *De minimis* fringes.
- Qualified transportation fringes.
- Qualified moving expense reimbursements.
- Qualified retirement planning services.
- Qualified military base realignment and closure fringes.

No-Additional-Cost Services

The value of the services that the employer provides its employees is nontaxable under certain circumstances. Example 20 above illustrates the reason for the **no-additional-cost service** type of fringe benefit. The services are excludible from the employee's gross income if all of the following conditions are satisfied:

- The employee receives services, as opposed to property.
- The employer does not incur substantial additional cost, including forgone revenue, in providing the services to the employee.
- The services are offered to customers in the ordinary course of the business in which the employee works.[51]

EXAMPLE 21

In Example 20, although the airplane may burn slightly more fuel because Ryan is on board and he may receive the same snacks as paying customers, the additional costs to the airline are *not* substantial. As a result, the flight qualifies as a no-additional-cost service, and the value of Ryan's flight is excluded from his gross income.

The no-additional-cost exclusion extends to the employee's spouse and dependent children and to retired and disabled former employees.[52] However, the exclusion is not allowed to highly compensated employees unless the benefit is available on a nondiscriminatory basis.

Qualified Employee Discounts

When the employer sells goods or services (other than no-additional-cost benefits just discussed) to the employee for a price that is less than the price charged regular customers, the employee realizes income equal to the discount. However, the discount, referred to as a **qualified employee discount**, can be excluded from the employee's gross income, subject to the following conditions and limitations:

- The exclusion is not available for real property (e.g., a house) or for personal property commonly held for investment (e.g., common stock).
- The property or services must be from the same line of business in which the employee works.
- In the case of *property*, the exclusion is limited to the *gross profit component* of the customer price.
- In the case of *services*, the exclusion is limited to 20 percent of the customer price.

---

[50]See, generally, § 132.
[51]Reg. § 1.132–2.

[52]Reg. § 1.132–1(b).

EXAMPLE 22

Silver Corporation, which operates a department store, sells a television to a store employee for $300. The regular customer price is $500, and the gross profit rate is 25%. The corporation also sells the employee a service contract for $120; the regular customer price for the contract is $150. The employee must include $75 in gross income ($75 for the television; $0 for the service contract).

Customer price for property (television)	$ 500
Less: Gross profit (25%)	(125)
	$ 375
Employee price	(300)
Income	$ 75
Customer price for service contract	$ 150
Less: 20% (maximum exclusion)	(30)
	$ 120
Employee price	(120)
Income	$ –0–

As in the case of no-additional-cost benefits, the exclusion applies to employees (including service partners), employees' spouses and dependent children, and retired and disabled former employees.

Working Condition Fringes

Generally, an employee is not required to include in gross income the cost of property or services provided by the employer if the employee could deduct the cost of those items if he or she had actually paid for them. These benefits are called ==working condition fringes==.

EXAMPLE 23

Mitch is a CPA employed by an accounting firm. The employer pays Mitch's annual dues to professional organizations. Mitch is not required to include the payment of the dues in gross income because it is an allowable business expense to Mitch (as discussed in text Section 9-10).[53]

Unlike the other fringe benefits discussed previously, working condition fringes can be made available on a discriminatory basis and still qualify for the exclusion.

De Minimis Fringes

As the term suggests, ==*de minimis* fringe== benefits are so small that accounting for them is impractical. The House Report contains the following examples of *de minimis* fringes:

- Occasional personal use of a company copying machine, occasional company cocktail parties or picnics for employees, occasional supper money or taxi fare for employees because of overtime work, and certain holiday gifts of property with a low fair market value are excluded.

- Subsidized eating facilities (e.g., an employees' cafeteria) operated by the employer are excluded if located on or near the employer's business premises, if revenue equals or exceeds direct operating costs, and if nondiscrimination requirements are met. This exclusion applies regardless of whether the employer can deduct any of the facility's costs.

When taxpayers venture beyond the specific examples contained in the House Report and the Regulations, there can be room for disagreement as to what is *de minimis*. According to the IRS, cash or gift cards are not considered *de minimis*.[54]

In Notice 2011–72, the IRS provided that the value of a cell phone can be excluded if it is provided for business reasons (e.g., to enable the employee to be in contact with clients when the employee is away from the office). When the primary purpose test is satisfied, any personal use of the employer-provided cell phone will be excluded as a *de minimis* fringe benefit.

---

[53]In many cases, this exclusion merely avoids reporting income and using an off-setting deduction. The TCJA of 2017 suspends the deduction for unreimbursed employee business expenses for 2018 through 2025. So if Mitch had paid the dues on his own, he could not deduct them. IRS Publication

15B (2019), *Employer's Tax Guide to Fringe Benefits*, states that the payment continues to be a nontaxable fringe benefit for the employee.

[54]TAM 200437030 (9/10/04) and IRS Publication 15B (2019), *Employer's Tax Guide to Fringe Benefits*, p. 9.

Qualified Transportation Fringes

The exclusion for <mark>qualified transportation fringes</mark> is intended to encourage the use of mass transit for commuting to and from work. Qualified transportation fringes include the following benefits provided by the employer to the employee:

1. Transportation in a commuter highway vehicle between the employee's residence and the place of employment.
2. A transit pass.
3. Qualified parking.

These exclusions have annual limits. For 2020, the inflation adjusted limit for items 1 and 2 combined, as well as for item 3, is $270 per month ($265 in 2019).[55]

A *commuter highway vehicle* is any highway vehicle with a seating capacity of at least six adults (excluding the driver). In addition, at least 80 percent of the vehicle's use must be for transporting employees between their residences and place of employment.

Qualified parking includes the following:

- Parking provided to an employee on or near the employer's business premises.
- Parking provided to an employee on or near a location from which the employee commutes to work via mass transit, in a commuter highway vehicle, or in a carpool.

Qualified transportation fringes may be provided directly by the employer or may be in the form of cash reimbursements.

Gray Corporation's offices are located in the center of a large city. The company pays for parking spaces to be used by the company officers. Steve, a vice president, receives $300 of such benefits each month during 2020. The parking space rental qualifies as a qualified transportation fringe. Of the $300 benefit received each month by Steve, $270 is excludible from gross income. The balance of $30 is included in his gross income. The same result would occur if Steve paid for the parking and was reimbursed by his employer.

EXAMPLE 24

The TCJA of 2017 prohibits employers from *deducting* qualified transportation fringe benefits provided to employees [§ 274(a)(4)]. If the employer provides the benefit, though, the employee may exclude it from income within the limits stated above.

Qualified Moving Expense Reimbursements

Prior to the TCJA of 2017, qualified moving expenses reimbursed or paid by the employer were excludible from gross income. A qualified moving expense would be deductible under § 217. For 2018 through 2025, the exclusion only applies to members of the Armed Forces on active duty. See the discussion of moving expenses in text Section 9-6b.

Qualified Retirement Planning Services

Qualified retirement planning services include any retirement planning advice or information that an employer who maintains a qualified retirement plan provides to an employee or the employee's spouse. Congress decided to exclude the value of these services from gross income because they are a key part of retirement income planning, and they may serve as motivation for more employers to provide retirement planning services to their employees.

Qualified Military Base Realignment and Closure Fringe

Payments made under the Demonstration Cities and Metropolitan Development Act of 1966 are generally excluded from income.

---

[55]Prior to 2018, qualified transportation fringes included qualified bicycle commuting reimbursement up to $20 per month. For 2018 through 2025, this benefit is not treated as a qualified transportation fringe benefit. As a result, if an employer provides this benefit, it is taxable to the employee and deductible by the employer.

The TCJA of 2017 changed the tax treatment of certain fringe benefits to better tie an employer's deduction for employee compensation with the amount employees report as wage income. The approach taken, such as for meals provided for the convenience of the employer and qualified transportation fringe benefits, was to retain the exclusion for the employee receiving these benefits but to repeal or reduce the deduction for the employer. Did Congress take the right approach? Or should Congress instead have allowed employers to deduct the cost of the benefits provided to employees with the employees including the benefits in wage income?

Nondiscrimination Provisions

For no-additional-cost services, qualified employee discounts, and qualified retirement planning services that are discriminatory in favor of highly compensated employees, exclusion treatment is denied. However, for the discriminatory plans, the exclusion treatment for non-highly compensated employees remains.[56]

EXAMPLE 25

Dove Company's officers are allowed to purchase goods from the company at a 25% discount. All other employees are allowed only a 15% discount. The company's gross profit margin on these goods is 30%. Because the officers receive more favorable discounts, the plan is discriminatory in favor of the officers. In regard to all other employees, the discount is "qualified" because it is available to all employees (other than the officers who receive a more favorable discount) and the discount is less than the company's gross profit.

Peggy, an officer in the company, purchased goods from the company for $750 when the price charged to customers was $1,000. Peggy must include $250 in gross income because the plan is discriminatory.

Mason, an employee of the company who is not an officer, purchased goods for $850 when the customer price was $1,000. Mason is not required to recognize gross income because he received a qualified employee discount.

De minimis (except in the case of subsidized eating facilities) and working condition fringe benefits can be provided on a discriminatory basis. The *de minimis* benefits are not subject to tax because the accounting problems that would be created are out of proportion to the amount of additional tax that would result.

A review of employee fringe benefits is provided in Concept Summary 5.2.

5-8e Group Term Life Insurance

For many years, the IRS did not attempt to tax the value of life insurance protection provided to an employee or former employee by the employer. Some companies took undue advantage of the exclusion by providing large amounts of insurance protection for executives. As a result, Congress enacted § 79, which created a limited exclusion for **group term life insurance**. The premiums on the first $50,000 of group term life insurance protection are excludible from the employee's and former employee's gross income.

The benefits of this exclusion are available only to employees. Proprietors and partners are not considered employees. The Regulations generally require broad-scale coverage of employees to satisfy the *group* requirement (e.g., shareholder-employees would not constitute a qualified group). The exclusion applies only to term insurance (protection for a period of time but with no cash surrender value) and not to ordinary life insurance (lifetime protection plus a cash surrender value that can be drawn upon before death).

As mentioned, the exclusion applies to the first $50,000 of group term life insurance protection. For each $1,000 of coverage in excess of $50,000, the employee must include the amounts indicated in Exhibit 5.1 in gross income.[57]

---

[56]§§ 132(j)(1) and (m)(2).

[57]Reg. § 1.79–3(d)(2).

Finch Corporation has a group term life insurance policy with coverage equal to the employee's annual salary. Keith, age 52, is president of the corporation and receives an annual salary of $350,000. Keith must include $828 in gross income from the insurance protection for the year.

$$\frac{\$350,000 - \$50,000}{\$1,000} \times \$0.23 \times 12 \text{ months} = \$828$$

Generally, the amount that must be included in gross income, computed from Exhibit 5.1, is much less than the price an individual would pay an insurance company for the same amount of protection. As a result, even the excess coverage provides some tax-favored income for employees when group term life insurance coverage exceeds $50,000.

If the plan discriminates in favor of certain key employees (e.g., officers), the key employees are not eligible for the exclusion. In such a case, the key employees must include in gross income the *greater* of actual premiums paid by the employer or the amount calculated from the Uniform Premiums in Exhibit 5.1. The other employees are still eligible for the $50,000 exclusion and continue to use the Uniform Premiums table to compute the income from excess insurance protection.[58]

5-9 FOREIGN EARNED INCOME

For individuals, the United States uses a global tax system as opposed to a territorial system. Under this global system, a U.S. citizen is generally subject to tax on his or her income regardless of its economic origin. Some other countries use a territorial system; that is, a person's income is taxed only in the country in which the income was earned. Under this global system, a U.S. citizen who earns income in another country could experience double taxation—the same income would be taxed in the United States and in the foreign country. Out of a sense of fairness and to encourage U.S. citizens to work abroad (so that exports might be increased), Congress has provided alternative forms of relief from taxes on foreign earned income. The taxpayer can elect *either* (1) to include the foreign earned income in his or her taxable income and then claim a credit for foreign taxes paid or (2) to exclude up to $107,600 of foreign earned income from his or her U.S. gross income (the **foreign earned income exclusion**).[59] As will be apparent from the following discussion, most taxpayers choose the exclusion.

EXHIBIT 5.1	Uniform Premiums for $1,000 of Group Term Life Insurance Protection
Attained Age on Last Day of Employee's Tax Year	**Cost per $1,000 of Protection for One-Month Period***
Under 25	$0.05
25–29	0.06
30–34	0.08
35–39	0.09
40–44	0.10
45–49	0.15
50–54	0.23
55–59	0.43
60–64	0.66
65–69	1.27
70 and above	2.06

*Reg. § 1.79–3, effective for coverage after June 30, 1999.

---

[58]§ 79(d).   [59]§ 911(a). The exclusion for 2019 was $105,900.

Concept Summary 5.2

Employee Fringe Benefits

Type of Benefit	Exclusion
Group term life insurance (§ 79)	Premiums on up to $50,000 of protection
Employee achievement awards (§ 74)	Up to $1,600 in a year
Accident, health, and long-term care insurance and medical reimbursement (§§ 105 and 106)	Insurance premiums paid by the employer and benefits collected
High-deductible health insurance and contributions to employee's Health Savings Account (§§ 106 and 223)	Employer premiums on high-deductible medical insurance plus contributions to Health Savings Account (statutory limits, indexed for inflation)
Meals and lodging furnished for the convenience of the employer (§ 119)	Value of meals and lodging on the employer's premises
Child care provided by the employer or reimbursement for employee's cost (§ 129)	Services provided or reimbursement of expenses up to $5,000 a year
Athletic facilities on the employer's premises (§ 132)	Value of services
Educational assistance for tuition, fees, books, and supplies (§ 127)	Limited to $5,250 per year
No-additional-cost services [e.g., use of employer's facilities (§ 132)]	Value of the use
Employee discount on purchase of goods from employer at employer's cost (§ 132)	Employer's normal profit margin
Employee discount for purchases of employer's services (§ 132)	Maximum of 20% of employer's normal price
Working condition fringes [e.g., a mechanic's tools (§ 132)]	Employer's cost
De minimis items so small that the accounting effort is not warranted [e.g., use of employer telephone (§ 132)]	Value of the goods or services
Qualified transportation [e.g., transit passes and parking (§ 132)]	Statutory amounts, adjusted for inflation
Moving expense reimbursement for members of the Armed Forces on active duty (§ 132)	Reimbursement to the extent otherwise deductible by employee
Retirement planning services (§ 132)	Reasonable cost of services

Foreign earned income consists of the earnings from the individual's personal services rendered in a foreign country (other than as an employee of the U.S. government). To qualify for the exclusion, the taxpayer must be either:

- A bona fide resident of the foreign country (or countries), or
- Present in a foreign country (or countries) for at least 330 days during any 12 consecutive months.[60]

The following rules apply in calculating the exclusion and tax owed:

- The exclusion must be computed on a daily basis when the exclusion period straddles two years.
- The tax on the income in excess of the excluded amount is taxed at the marginal rate that would apply without the exclusion (i.e., as though the excluded income were included in taxable income).

Calculating the Exclusion and Tax

EXAMPLE 27

Sandra's trips to and from a foreign country in connection with her work were as follows:

Arrived in Foreign Country	Returned to United States
March 10, 2019	February 16, 2020

During the 12 consecutive months ending on March 10, 2020, Sandra was present in the foreign country for at least 330 days (366 days less the 13 days remaining in February 2020 and 10 days in March 2020). As a result, the income earned in the foreign country through March 10, 2020, is eligible for the exclusion.

---

[60]§ 911(d). For the definition of *resident*, see Reg. § 1.871–2(b). Under the Regulations, a taxpayer is not a resident if he or she is there for a definite period (e.g., until completion of a construction contract).

GLOBAL TAX ISSUES   Benefits of the Earned Income Exclusion Are Questioned

The foreign earned income exclusion is intended to be a means to increase exports. But a GAO study questioned whether the $6 billion of lost revenue is money well spent. The report was inconclusive. It is clear that repealing the exclusion would make it more costly for U.S. companies to send their employees abroad, but there is no evidence that the benefits to the United States, in general, are worth the cost.

Source: Economic Benefits of Income Exclusion for U.S. Citizens Working Abroad Are Uncertain GAO-14-387: Published: May 20, 2014, available at **gao.gov/products/GAO-14-387**.

Calculating the Exclusion and Tax

Keith qualifies for the foreign earned income exclusion. He was present in France for all of 2020. Keith's salary for 2020 is $120,000. Because all of the days in 2020 are qualifying days, Keith can exclude $107,600 of his $120,000 salary.

Assume instead that only 342 days were qualifying days. Then Keith's exclusion is limited to $100,544, computed as follows:

$$\$107,600 \times \frac{342 \text{ days in foreign country}}{366 \text{ days in the year}} = \$100,544$$

EXAMPLE 28

In 2020, Carol, who is not married, had taxable income of $30,000 after excluding $107,600 of foreign earned income. Without the benefit of the exclusion, Carol's taxable income would have been $137,600 ($30,000 + $107,600). The tax on the taxable income of $30,000 is calculated using the marginal rate applicable to income between $107,600 and $137,600, which is 24%. As a result, Carol's tax liability is $7,200 ($30,000 × 24%).

EXAMPLE 29

As previously mentioned, the taxpayer may elect to include the foreign earned income in gross income and claim a credit (an offset against U.S. tax) for the foreign tax paid. The credit alternative may be advantageous if the individual's foreign earned income *far exceeds* the excludible amount so that the foreign taxes paid exceed the U.S. tax on the amount excluded. However, once an election is made, it applies to all subsequent years unless affirmatively revoked. A revocation is effective for the year of the change and the four subsequent years.

5-10 INTEREST ON CERTAIN STATE AND LOCAL GOVERNMENT OBLIGATIONS

At the time the Sixteenth Amendment was ratified by the states, there was some question as to whether the Federal government possessed the constitutional authority to tax interest on state and local government obligations. Taxing this interest was thought to violate the doctrine of intergovernmental immunity in that the tax would impair the state and local governments' ability to finance their operations.[61] As a result, interest on state and local government obligations was specifically exempted from Federal income taxation.[62] However, the Supreme Court has concluded that there is no constitutional prohibition against levying a nondiscriminatory Federal income tax on state and local government obligations.[63] Congress, however, has shown no inclination to eliminate this exclusion.

Obviously, the exclusion of the interest reduces the cost of borrowing for state and local governments. A taxpayer in the 35 percent tax bracket requires only a 3.9 percent

---

[61]*Pollock v. Farmer's Loan & Trust Co.*, 3 AFTR 2602, 15 S.Ct. 912 (USSC, 1895).

[62]§ 103(a).

[63]*South Carolina v. Baker III*, 88–1 USTC ¶9284, 61 AFTR 2d 88–995, 108 S.Ct. 1355 (USSC, 1988).

yield on a tax-exempt bond to obtain the same after-tax income as a taxable bond paying 6 percent interest [$3.9\% \div (1-0.35) = 6\%$].

The current exempt status applies solely to state and local government bonds. Income received from the accrual of interest on a condemnation award or an overpayment of state income tax is fully taxable.[64] In addition, the exemption does not apply to gains on the sale of tax-exempt securities.

EXAMPLE 30

Megan purchases State of Virginia bonds for $10,000 on July 1, 2019. The bonds pay $300 interest each June 30 and December 31. On March 31, 2020, Megan sells the bonds for $10,500 plus $150 for accrued interest. Megan must recognize a $500 gain ($10,500 − $10,000), but the $150 accrued interest is exempt from taxation.

Although the Internal Revenue Code excludes from Federal gross income the interest on state and local government bonds, the interest on U.S. government bonds is *not* excluded from the Federal tax base. Congress decided, however, that if the Federal government does not tax state and local bond interest, state and local governments should not tax interest on U.S. government bonds.[65] However, state and local governments are free to tax each other's obligations. As a result, some states exempt the interest on the bonds they issue but tax the interest on bonds issued by other states.[66]

5-11 CORPORATE DISTRIBUTIONS TO SHAREHOLDERS

5-11a General Information

A corporate distribution is a payment to a shareholder with respect to his or her stock (see Chapter 4).

- Distributions are taxed as dividends to shareholders only to the extent the payments are made from *either* the corporation's *current earnings and profits* (similar to net income per books) or its *accumulated earnings and profits* (similar to retained earnings per books).[67]

- Distributions that exceed earnings and profits are treated as a nontaxable recovery of capital and reduce the shareholder's basis in the stock.

- Once the shareholder's basis is reduced to zero, any subsequent distributions are taxed as capital gains (see Chapters 13 and 19).[68]

Some payments are frequently referred to as dividends but are *not* considered dividends for tax purposes:

- Dividends received on deposits with savings and loan associations, credit unions, and banks are actually interest (an amount paid for the use of money).

- Patronage dividends paid by cooperatives (e.g., for farmers) are rebates made to the users and are considered reductions in the cost of items purchased from the association. The rebates are usually made after year-end (after the cooperative has determined whether it has met its expenses) and are apportioned among members on the basis of their purchases.

- Mutual insurance companies pay dividends on unmatured life insurance policies that are considered rebates of premiums.

---

[64]*Kieselbach v. Comm.*, 43–1 USTC ¶9220, 30 AFTR 370, 63 S.Ct. 303 (USSC, 1943); *U.S. Trust Co. of New York v. Anderson*, 3 USTC ¶1125, 12 AFTR 836, 65 F.2d 575 (CA–2, 1933).

[65]31 U.S.C.A. § 742.

[66]The practice of a state exempting interest on its bonds from tax but taxing the interest on bonds issued by other states has been upheld by the Supreme Court. See *Department of Revenue of Kentucky v. Davis*, 128 S.Ct. 1801 (USSC, 2008).

[67]§ 316(a). Refer to the discussion of the beneficial tax rates for qualified dividends in Chapter 4.

[68]§ 301(c). See Chapter 19 for a detailed discussion of corporate distributions.

- Shareholders in a mutual investment fund are allowed to report as capital gains their proportionate share of the fund's gains realized and distributed. The capital gain and ordinary income portions are reported on the Form 1099 that the fund supplies its shareholders each year.

5-11b Stock Dividends

When a corporation issues a simple stock dividend (e.g., common stock issued to common shareholders), the shareholder has received additional shares but maintains the same total investment. As a result, the shareholder does not realize income; instead, the per share basis is reduced.[69]

However, if the shareholder has the *option* of receiving either cash or stock in the corporation, the individual realizes gross income whether he or she receives stock or cash.[70] A taxpayer who elects to receive the stock values the stock dividend by determining the value of the stock received (which could be different from the cash rejected).[71] See Chapters 13 and 19 for a discussion of stock dividends.

5-12 EDUCATIONAL SAVINGS BONDS

The cost of a college education has risen dramatically during the past few decades. According to U.S. Department of Education estimates, the cost of attending a publicly supported university for four years now commonly exceeds $60,000. For a private university, the cost often exceeds $200,000. Consequently, Congress has attempted to assist low- to middle-income parents in saving for their children's college education.

One of the ways Congress assists such families is through an interest income exclusion on **educational savings bonds**.[72] The interest on Series EE U.S. government savings bonds may be excluded from gross income if the bond proceeds are used to pay qualified higher education expenses. The bonds must be issued to a taxpayer age 24 or older.

Qualified higher education expenses consist of tuition and fees paid to an eligible educational institution for the taxpayer, spouse, or dependent. If the redemption proceeds (both principal and interest) exceed the qualified higher education expenses, only a pro rata portion of the interest will qualify for exclusion treatment.

EXAMPLE
31

Tracy's redemption proceeds from qualified savings bonds during the taxable year are $6,000 (principal of $4,000 and interest of $2,000). Tracy's qualified higher education expenses are $5,000. Because the redemption proceeds exceed the qualified higher education expenses, only $1,667 [($5,000/$6,000) × $2,000] of the interest is excludible.

Once a taxpayer's modified adjusted gross income exceeds a threshold amount, the exclusion is phased out. *Modified adjusted gross income (MAGI)* is adjusted gross income prior to the foreign earned income exclusion and the educational savings bond exclusion. The threshold amounts are adjusted for inflation each year. For 2020, the phaseout begins at $82,350 ($123,550 on a joint return).[73] The phaseout is completed when MAGI exceeds the threshold amount by more than $15,000 ($30,000 on a joint return). The otherwise excludible interest is reduced by the amount calculated as follows:

$$\frac{\text{MAGI} - \$82,350}{\$15,000} \quad \times \quad \begin{array}{c}\text{Excludible interest} \\ \text{before phaseout}\end{array} \quad = \quad \begin{array}{c}\text{Reduction in} \\ \text{excludible interest}\end{array}$$

On a joint return, $123,550 is substituted for $82,350 (in 2020) and $30,000 is substituted for $15,000.

---

[69]*Eisner v. Macomber*, 1 USTC ¶32, 3 AFTR 3020, 40 S.Ct. 189 (USSC, 1920); § 305(a).

[70]§ 305(b).

[71]Refer to the discussion of constructive receipt in Chapter 4.

[72]§ 135.

[73]The indexed amounts for 2019 were $81,100 and $121,600.

EXAMPLE 32

Assume the same facts as in Example 31, except that Tracy's MAGI for 2020 is $86,000. The phaseout results in Tracy's interest exclusion being reduced by $406 {[($86,000 − $82,350)/$15,000] × $1,667}. As a result, Tracy's exclusion is $1,261 ($1,667 − $406).

5-13 EDUCATION SAVINGS PROGRAMS (§ 529 AND § 530 PLANS)

The Federal tax law provides two types of programs to help individuals and families save for education costs. These savings programs are referred to as the qualified tuition program (§ 529 plans) and Coverdell education savings accounts (§ 530 plans). Earnings in these accounts are not taxable if distributions are used for qualified education expenses. Also, rules govern the type of account that can be used for these savings programs, and specific rules exist regarding contributions, distributions, rollovers, and other transfers. In addition, the benefits of these plans must be coordinated with other educational tax provisions, such as nontaxable scholarships. Distributions from these accounts are reported on Form 1099–Q, Payments from Qualified Education Programs. Taxable distributions (generally those not used for qualified purposes) may be subject to an additional 10 percent tax [reported on Form 5329, Additional Taxes on Qualified Plans (Including IRAs) and Other Tax-Favored Accounts].

There are income limits on contributions to Coverdell accounts as well as a dollar limit on the annual contribution per beneficiary. A beneficiary may have both § 529 and § 530 plans.

5-13a Qualified Tuition Program

Nearly all states have created programs whereby parents can in effect prepay their child's college tuition. The prepayment serves as a hedge against future increases in tuition. Generally, if the child does not attend college, the parents are refunded their payments plus interest. Although these prepaid tuition programs resemble the below-market loans (discussed in text Section 4-4b), Congress has created an exclusion provision for these programs.

Under a **qualified tuition program (§ 529 plan)**, the amounts contributed must be used for qualified higher education expenses. These expenses include tuition, fees, books, supplies, room and board, and equipment required for enrollment or attendance at a college, a university, or certain vocational schools. Allowable expenses also include computers and peripheral equipment, software, and internet access used primarily by the beneficiary while enrolled at an eligible educational institution. Qualified higher education expenses also include the expenses for special needs services that are incurred in connection with the enrollment and attendance of special needs students. Tuition paid to public, private, and religious K–12 schools, as well as certain apprenticeship programs, are also allowable expenses. In addition, a lifetime maximum of $10,000 of funds in a § 529 account may be used to pay principal or interest on a qualified education loan.

The earnings of the contributed funds, including the discount on tuition charged to participants, are not included in Federal gross income provided the contributions and earnings are used for qualified higher education expenses. Some states also exclude these educational benefits from state gross income.

EXAMPLE 33

Angie paid $20,000 into a qualified tuition program to be used for her son's college tuition. When her son graduated from high school, the fund balance had increased to $30,000 as a result of interest credited to the account. The interest was not included in Angie's gross income. During the current year, $7,500 of the balance in the fund was used to pay the son's tuition and fees. None of this amount is included in either Angie's or the son's gross income.

If the parent receives a refund (e.g., child does not attend college), the excess of the amount refunded over the amount contributed by the parent is included in the parent's gross income. A special rule applies to refunded amounts recontributed to a qualified tuition program of the beneficiary.

5-13b Coverdell Education Savings Account

A **Coverdell education savings account (§ 530 plan)** may be used to save for K–12 education as well as postsecondary education expenses. The contributions to the plan are limited to $2,000 in any year, and the beneficiary must be under 18 or must be a special needs beneficiary in the year the contribution is made. As with the § 529 plan, contributions are nondeductible, but the income to the beneficiary is nontaxable provided the funds are used for qualified education expenses.

5-14 QUALIFIED ABLE PROGRAMS (§ 529A PLANS)

The **qualified ABLE program** was created to assist individuals who become blind or disabled before age 26. The program allows for § 529A plans, or ABLE (Achieving a Better Life Experience) plans, similar in concept to § 529 plans described earlier. The program must be established by a state. The ABLE account must be for the benefit of a designated beneficiary's disability expenses, and the beneficiary must have a disability certification from the government.

Contributions to the account must be in cash and may not, in total, exceed the annual gift tax exclusion for the year ($15,000 for 2020 and 2019). Contributions to the account are not deductible. The tax benefit of an ABLE account is that its earnings are not taxable. Distributions from the account also are not taxable provided they do not exceed the qualified disability expenses of the designated beneficiary. The TCJA of 2017 permits certain rollovers from a § 529 account to an ABLE account (for 2018 through 2025).

5-15 TAX BENEFIT RULE

LO.3

Determine the extent to which receipts can be excluded under the tax benefit rule.

Often a person will incur a cost or an expense in one year but receive a refund or recovery in a subsequent year. Effectively, this refund or recovery reduces the original cost. For example, the taxpayer may purchase an item from a retailer and then receive a rebate from the manufacturer. The rebate is generally a purchase price adjustment. If the item purchased did not result in a tax deduction (e.g., the purchase of a personal automobile), the rebate does not affect taxable income. However, if the original payment resulted in a tax deduction in one year and the rebate is received in a subsequent year, the tax benefit rule will apply. Generally, if a taxpayer claims a deduction for an item in one year and in a later year recovers all or a portion of the prior deduction, the recovery is included in gross income in the year received.[74]

EXAMPLE

34

An accrual basis taxpayer deducted as a loss a $1,000 receivable from a customer when it appeared the amount would never be collected. The following year, the customer paid $800 on the receivable. The taxpayer must report the $800 as gross income in the year it is received.

However, the § 111 **tax benefit rule** provides that no income is recognized upon the recovery of a deduction, or the portion of a deduction, that did not yield a tax benefit in the year it was taken. If the taxpayer in Example 34 had no tax liability in the year of the deduction (e.g., itemized deductions exceeded adjusted gross income), the recovery would be partially or totally excluded from gross income in the year of the recovery.[75]

---

[74]§ 111(a).

[75]Itemized deductions are discussed in Chapter 10.

A common situation that leads to consideration of the tax benefit rule occurs when individuals who itemize their deductions (on Schedule A of Form 1040) get part of their state income tax back as a refund the next year. The TCJA of 2017 added a new wrinkle to this situation. For 2018 through 2025, individuals may only deduct up to $10,000 of state and local taxes as part of their itemized deductions. This is often referred to as the "SALT" deduction. This new limitation raises the question of how the tax benefit rule works when individuals who itemize their deductions (1) paid state and local taxes (SALT) greater than the $10,000 allowable deduction and (2) receive a state income tax refund the next year.

In early 2019, the IRS issued guidance on how the tax benefit rule applies to state income tax refunds in light of the new $10,000 SALT cap.[76] Basically, the taxpayer needs to determine what his or her tax return would have looked like if he or she had known the actual state income tax amount when the return was prepared (factoring in the later refund). This analysis leads to one of the following:

1. *All or part of the refund is taxable:* If the amount of the refund causes the actual SALT amount for the year to drop below $10,000, then the individual obtained a tax benefit from the SALT deduction and all or part of that refund is taxable under the tax benefit rule. The individual must also determine if the refund results in total itemized deductions totaling less than the standard deduction amount. See Example 35.
2. *The refund is not taxable:* If the individual had a SALT amount greater than $10,000 and the SALT amount equals or exceeds $10,000 even when considering the refund, then no income results under the tax benefit rule. See Example 36.

Tax Benefit Rule and the SALT Cap

EXAMPLE 35

Ali filed his 2019 income tax return as a single individual. His AGI for 2019 was $78,000. He had $12,800 in itemized deductions, including $6,200 in state income tax and no other state or local taxes. In 2020, he received a $700 refund of the state income taxes that he paid in 2019.

Because the standard deduction in 2019 was $12,200, the $6,200 of state income taxes Ali paid in 2019 yielded a tax benefit from only $600 of the state income tax deduction ($12,800 itemized deductions − $12,200 standard deduction). Under the tax benefit rule, only $600 of the state income tax refund is included in gross income in 2020.

EXAMPLE 36

Julie filed her 2019 return as a single individual. Her AGI for 2019 was $170,000, and she reported $22,000 of itemized deductions. In 2019, Julie paid property taxes on her home of $8,000 and state income taxes of $15,000, for total SALT of $23,000. Due to the SALT cap, she could only deduct $10,000 of this amount on her 2019 return.

After filing her 2019 state income tax return in early 2020, Julie received a state income tax refund of $1,250. Under the tax benefit rule and IRS guidance on the TCJA of 2017, none of this refund is includible in Julie's 2020 gross income; even if the refund was received in 2019, Julie would still be subject to the SALT cap of $10,000. As a result, she received no tax benefit from the $1,250 state income taxes paid in 2019 that were refunded to her in 2020.

---

[76]Rev.Rul. 2019–11, 2019–17 I.R.B. 1041.

5-16 **INCOME FROM DISCHARGE OF INDEBTEDNESS**

When a person is relieved of a debt for less than the amount owed, the debtor's net worth increases. This increase in net worth is taxable income unless one of the exceptions discussed below applies.[77]

LO.4

Describe the circumstances under which income must be reported from the discharge of indebtedness.

Kayla is unable to make her credit card payments and has negotiated a settlement with the credit card issuer. Her $40,000 debt will be settled for $25,000. Kayla must recognize income of $15,000 from the discharge of debt.

EXAMPLE 37

When property serves as security for debt, the creditor may foreclose on the property. The foreclosure is treated as a sale.[78]

Juan owns land that serves as security for a $60,000 mortgage held by State Bank. Juan does not have personal liability for the mortgage (it is nonrecourse debt). When Juan's basis in the land is $20,000 and the land's fair market value is $50,000, the bank forecloses on the loan and takes title to the land. Juan must recognize a $40,000 gain on the foreclosure, as though he sold the land for $60,000 (the amount of the nonrecourse debt). No income from discharge of indebtedness is generated in this transaction.

EXAMPLE 38

If property serves as security for the debt and the taxpayer is personally liable for the difference between the value of the property and the amount of the debt (i.e., the debt is "with recourse"), the taxpayer may have income from the discharge of the debt in addition to gain or loss from the foreclosure.

Assume the same facts in Example 38, except that Juan's debt is recourse. Juan is treated as selling the property for its fair market value ($50,000) resulting in a gain or loss. His gain is $30,000 ($50,000 sales price − $20,000 basis). In addition, Juan has $10,000 of income from discharge of indebtedness because the lender accepted the $50,000 sales price in discharging the $60,000 debt. Juan will want to determine whether any exclusion applies to his income from discharge of indebtedness (discussed next).

EXAMPLE 39

The following discharge of indebtedness situations are subject to special exclusion treatment:[79]

1. Creditors' gifts.
2. Discharges under Federal bankruptcy law.
3. Discharges that occur when the debtor is insolvent (the exclusion is limited to the amount of insolvency).
4. Discharge of the farm debt of a solvent taxpayer.
5. Discharge of **qualified real property business indebtedness**.
6. A seller's cancellation of the buyer's indebtedness.
7. A shareholder's cancellation of the corporation's indebtedness.
8. Forgiveness of certain loans to students.

---

[77]§ 61(a)(12) and Reg. § 1.1001–2(a).

[78]*Estate of Delman*, 73 T.C. 15 (1979).

[79]§§ 108 and 1017. See Rev.Proc. 2018–39, 2018–34 I.R.B. 319, for a special debt discharge exclusion under the U.S. Department of Education's "Defense to Repayment" program.

9. Discharge of indebtedness on the taxpayer's principal residence that occurs between January 1, 2007, and January 1, 2021, and is the result of the financial condition of the debtor.

If the creditor reduces the debt as an act of *love*, *affection*, or *generosity*, the debtor has simply received a nontaxable gift (situation 1). Rarely will a gift be found to have occurred in a business context. A businessperson may settle a debt for less than the amount due, but as a matter of business expediency (e.g., high collection costs or disputes as to contract terms) rather than generosity.[80]

In situations 2, 3, 4, 5, and 9, the Code allows the debtor to reduce his or her basis in the assets by the realized income from the discharge.[81] As a result, the realized income is merely deferred until the assets are sold (or depreciated). Similarly, in situation 6 (a price reduction), the debtor reduces the basis in the specific assets financed by the seller.[82]

A shareholder's cancellation of the corporation's indebtedness to him or her (situation 7) usually is considered a tax-free contribution of capital to the corporation by the shareholder. As a result, the corporation's paid-in capital is increased, and its liabilities are decreased by the same amount.[83]

Many states make loans to students on the condition that the loan will be forgiven if the student practices a profession in the state upon completing his or her studies. The amount of the loan that is forgiven (situation 8) is excluded from gross income.[84]

5-17 **TAX PLANNING**

LO.5

Identify tax planning strategies for obtaining the maximum benefit from allowable exclusions.

The present law excludes certain types of economic gains from taxation. As a result, taxpayers may find tax planning techniques helpful in obtaining the maximum benefits from the exclusion of such gains. Following are some of the tax planning opportunities made available by the exclusions described in this chapter.

5-17a **Life Insurance**

Life insurance offers several favorable tax attributes. As discussed in Chapter 4, the annual increase in the cash surrender value of the policy is not taxable (because no income has been actually or constructively received). By borrowing on the policy's cash surrender value, the owner can actually receive the policy's increase in value in cash without recognizing income.

5-17b **Employee Fringe Benefits**

Generally, employees view accident and health insurance, as well as life insurance, as necessities. Employees can obtain group coverage at much lower rates than individuals would have to pay for the same protection. Premiums paid by the employer can be excluded from the employees' gross income. Because of the exclusion, employees will have a greater after-tax and after-insurance income if the employer pays a lower salary but also pays the insurance premiums.

EXAMPLE

40

Pat receives a salary of $30,000. The company has group insurance benefits, but Pat is required to pay his own premiums as follows:

Hospitalization and medical insurance	$1,400
Term life insurance ($30,000 coverage)	200
Disability insurance	400
	$2,000

continued

---

[80]*Comm. v. Jacobson*, 49–1 USTC ¶9133, 37 AFTR 516, 69 S.Ct. 358 (USSC, 1949).

[81]§§ 108(a), (c), (e), and (g). Note that § 108(b) provides that other tax attributes (e.g., net operating loss) will be reduced by the realized gain from the debt discharge prior to the basis adjustment unless the taxpayer elects to apply the basis adjustment first.

[82]§ 108(e)(5).

[83]§ 108(e)(6).

[84]§ 108(f).

To simplify the analysis, assume that Pat's tax rate on income is 24%. After paying taxes of $7,200 ($30,000 × 24%) and $2,000 for insurance, Pat has $20,800 remaining ($30,000 − $7,200 − $2,000) for his other living needs.

If Pat's employer reduced Pat's salary by $2,000 (to $28,000) but paid his insurance premiums, Pat's tax liability would be only $6,720 ($28,000 × 24%). As a result, Pat would have $21,280 ($28,000 − $6,720) to meet his other living needs. The change in the compensation plan would save Pat $480 ($21,280 − $20,800).

Similarly, employees often incur expenses for child care and parking. The employee can have more income for other uses if the employer pays these costs but reduces the employee's salary by the cost of the benefits.

The use of cafeteria plans has increased dramatically in recent years. These plans allow employees to tailor their benefits to meet their individual situations. As a result, where both spouses are working, duplication of benefits can be avoided and other needed benefits can often be added. If less than all of the employee's allowance is spent, the employee can receive cash.

The meals and lodging exclusion enables employees to receive from their employer what they ordinarily must purchase with after-tax dollars. Although the employee must live on the employer's premises in order to exclude the value of the lodging, the exclusion is an important factor in the employee's compensation in certain situations (e.g., hotels, motels, restaurants, farms, and ranches). The meals and lodging are clearly a benefit to the employee but are also for the convenience of the employer; as a result, they are excluded from income.

The employees' discount provision is especially important for manufacturers and wholesalers. Employees of manufacturers can avoid tax on the manufacturer's, wholesaler's, and retailer's markups. The wholesaler's employees can avoid tax on an amount equal to the wholesale and retail markups.

The exclusion of benefits is generally available only to employees. Proprietors and partners must pay tax on the same benefits their employees receive tax-free. By incorporating and becoming an employee of the corporation, the former proprietor or partner can also receive these tax-exempt benefits. As a result, the availability of employee benefits is a consideration in the decision to incorporate.

5-17c **Investment Income**

Tax-exempt state and local government bonds are logical investments for high-income taxpayers, who may be subject to a 37 percent regular tax rate plus a 3.8 percent rate on their net investment income. To realize the maximum benefit from the exemption, the investor can purchase zero-coupon bonds. Like Series EE U.S. government savings bonds, these investments pay interest only at maturity. The advantage of the zero-coupon feature for a tax-exempt bond is that the investor can earn tax-exempt interest on the accumulated principal and interest. If the investor purchases a bond that pays the interest each year, the interest received may be such a small amount that an additional tax-exempt investment cannot be made. In addition, reinvesting the interest may entail transaction costs (brokers' fees). The zero-coupon feature avoids these problems.

Series EE U.S. government savings bonds can earn tax-exempt interest if the bond proceeds are used for qualified higher education expenses. Many taxpayers can foresee these expenditures being made for their children's educations. In deciding whether to invest in the bonds, however, the investor must take into account the income limitations for excluding the interest from gross income.

REFOCUS ON THE BIG PICTURE

EXCLUSIONS

You have looked into Paul's tax situation and have the following information for him:

- *Compensation.* The amount Paul was paid for his internship is compensation for services rendered and must be included in his gross income. This includes both his base pay and the $1,500 bonus (Example 1).
- *Graduate assistantship.* The tuition waiver of $6,000 is excluded from Paul's gross income. The related payments of $400 per month are intended as a form of compensation. So Paul must include the $400 per month in his gross income (Example 9).
- *Damages.* Damages awards that relate to personal physical injury or sickness can be excluded from gross income if the payments are for compensatory damages. So all of the compensatory damages of $220,000 can be excluded from gross income. The punitive damages of $160,000 must be included in Paul's gross income. Likewise, the compensatory damages of $25,000 received by Paul's mother must be included in her gross income because emotional distress does not qualify as personal physical injury or sickness (Example 12).

What If?

From a tax planning perspective, can Paul do anything to reduce the amount of the punitive damages settlement that he must include in his gross income?

As things now stand (i.e., a completed settlement), Paul cannot reduce the $160,000 punitive damages amount he must include in gross income. However, proper tax planning might have enabled Paul to reduce the amount includible in gross income. Note that both the amount of the damages and the labels attached to the damages are negotiated. If a larger portion of the settlement had been assigned to compensatory damages rather than punitive damages, Paul could have reduced the amount he must include in his gross income.

VM/E+/GETTY IMAGES

Key Terms

Accelerated death benefits, 5-5

Accident and health benefits, 5-11

Cafeteria plan, 5-15

Compensatory damages, 5-9

Coverdell education savings account (§ 530 plan), 5-27

De minimis fringe, 5-18

Death benefits, 5-4

Educational savings bonds, 5-25

Flexible spending plans, 5-16

Foreign earned income exclusion, 5-21

Fringe benefits, 5-14

Group term life insurance, 5-20

Health Savings Account (HSA), 5-12

Life insurance proceeds, 5-4

Long-term care insurance, 5-12

No-additional-cost service, 5-17

Punitive damages, 5-9

Qualified ABLE program, 5-27

Qualified employee discount, 5-17

Qualified real property business indebtedness, 5-29

Qualified transportation fringes, 5-19

Qualified tuition program (§ 529 plan), 5-26

Scholarship, 5-7

Tax benefit rule, 5-27

Working condition fringes, 5-18

Discussion Questions

1. **LO.2** Fred specified in his will that his nephew John should serve as executor of Fred's estate. John received $10,000 for serving as executor. Can John exclude the $10,000 from his gross income? Explain.

2. **LO.2** Leonard's home was damaged by a fire. He also had to be absent from work for several days to make his home habitable. Leonard's employer paid Leonard his regular salary, $2,500, while he was absent from work. In Leonard's pay envelope was the following note from the employer: To help you in your time of need. Leonard's fellow employees also took up a collection and gave him $900. Leonard spent over $4,000 repairing the fire damage.

    Based on the above information, how much is Leonard required to include in his gross income?

3. **LO.2** Megan is a college student who works as a part-time server in a restaurant. Her usual tip is 20% of the price of the meal. A customer ordered a piece of pie and said that he would appreciate prompt service. Megan abided by the customer's request. The customer's bill was $8, but the customer left a $100 bill on the table and did not ask for a receipt. Megan gave the cashier $8 and pocketed the $100 bill. Megan concludes that the customer thought that he had left a $10 bill, although the customer did not return to correct the apparent mistake. The customer had commented about how much he appreciated Megan's prompt service. Megan thinks that a $2 tip would be sufficient and that the other $98 is like "found money." How much should Megan include in her gross income?

4. **LO.2** Carey is a waiter at a restaurant that pays a small hourly amount plus tips. Customers are not required to tip the waiter. Carey is especially attentive and friendly, and her tips average 25% of the restaurant charges. Is Carey required to include any of her tips in gross income when the customer has no legal obligation to make the payment? Explain the basis for your conclusion.

5. **LO.2** Lime Finance Company requires its customers to purchase a credit life insurance policy associated with the loans it makes. Lime is the beneficiary of the policy to the extent of the remaining balance on the loan at the time of the customer's death. In 2019, Lime wrote off as uncollectible a $5,000 account receivable from Wally, which included $1,500 of accrued interest. When Wally died in 2020, the life insurance policy was still in force and Lime received $3,500. Is the $3,500 of life insurance proceeds received by Lime included in its gross income? Explain.

6. **LO.2** Billy fell off a bar stool and hurt his back. As a result, he was unable to work for three months. He sued the bar owner and collected $100,000 for the physical injury and $50,000 for the loss of income. Billy also collected $15,000 from an income replacement insurance policy he purchased. Amber was away from work for three months following heart bypass surgery. Amber collected $30,000 under an income replacement insurance policy purchased by her employer. Are the amounts received by Billy and Amber treated the same under the tax law? Explain.

7. **LO.2** Wes was a major league baseball pitcher who earned $10,000,000 for his 20 wins this year. Sam was also a major league baseball pitcher before a career-ending injury caused by a negligent driver. Sam sued the driver and collected $6,000,000 as compensation for lost estimated future income as a pitcher and $4,000,000 as punitive damages. Do the amounts that Wes and Sam receive have the same effect on their gross income? Explain.

8. **LO.2** Holly was injured while working in a factory and received $12,000 as workers' compensation while she was unable to work because of the injury. Jill, who was self-employed, was also injured and unable to work. Jill collected $12,000 on an

insurance policy she had purchased to replace her loss of income while she was unable to work. How much are Holly and Jill each required to include in their gross income?

Decision Making   9. **LO.2, 5** Casey is in the 12% marginal tax bracket, and Jean is in the 35% marginal tax bracket. Their employer is experiencing financial difficulties and cannot continue to pay for the company's health insurance plan. The annual premiums are approximately $8,000 per employee. The employer has proposed to either (1) require the employee to pay the premiums or (2) reduce each employee's pay by $10,000 per year with the employer paying the premium. Which option is less objectionable to Casey, and which is less objectionable to Jean?

10. **LO.2** What is the difference between a cafeteria plan and an employee flexible spending plan?

11. **LO.2** Ted works for Azure Motors, an automobile dealership. All employees can buy a car at the company's cost plus 2%. The company does not charge employees the $300 dealer preparation fee that nonemployees must pay. Ted purchased an automobile for $29,580 ($29,000 + $580). The company's cost was $29,000. The price for a nonemployee would have been $33,900 ($33,600 + $300 preparation fee). What is Ted's gross income from the purchase of the automobile?

12. **LO.2, 5** Wilbur has been offered a job at a salary that would put him in the 24% marginal tax bracket. In addition to his salary, he would receive health insurance coverage. Another potential employer does not offer health insurance but has agreed to match the first offer on an after-tax and insurance basis. The cost of health insurance comparable to that provided by the other potential employer is $9,000 per year. How much more in salary must the second potential employer pay so that Wilbur's financial status will be the same under both offers?

13. **LO.2, 5** Eagle Life Insurance Company pays its employees $0.30 per mile for driving their personal automobiles to and from work. The company reimburses each employee who rides the bus $100 a month for the cost of a pass. Tom collected $100 for his automobile mileage, and Mason received $100 as reimbursement for the cost of a bus pass.

   a.   What are the effects of the above on Tom's and Mason's gross income?

   b.   Assume that Tom and Mason are in the 24% marginal tax bracket and the actual before-tax cost for Tom to drive to and from work is $0.30 per mile. What are Tom's and Mason's after-tax costs of commuting to and from work?

Critical Thinking   14. **LO.2** Several of Egret Company's employees have asked the company to create a hiking trail that employees could use during their lunch hours. The company owns vacant land that is being held for future expansion but would have to spend approximately $50,000 if it were to make a trail. Nonemployees would be allowed to use the facility as part of the company's effort to build strong community support. What are the relevant tax issues for the employees?

15. **LO.2** The Sage Company has the opportunity to purchase a building located next to its office. Sage would use the building as a day care center for the children of its employees and an exercise facility for the employees. Occasionally, portions of the building could be used for employees' family events such as reunions, birthday parties, and anniversaries. The company would like to know if the planned uses of the building would fit into a beneficially taxed employee compensation plan.

Decision Making   16. **LO.2, 5** Tammy, a resident of Virginia, is considering purchasing a North Carolina bond that yields 4.6% before tax. She is in the 35% Federal marginal tax bracket and the 5% state marginal tax bracket. She is aware that State of Virginia bonds of comparable risk are yielding 4.5%. However, the Virginia bonds are exempt from Virginia tax, but the North Carolina bond interest is taxable in Virginia. Which of the two options will provide the greater after-tax return to Tammy? Tammy can deduct any state taxes paid on her Federal income tax return. In your analysis, assume that the bond amount is $100,000.

17. **LO.2** Andrea entered into a § 529 qualified tuition program for the benefit of her daughter, Joanna. Andrea contributed $15,000 to the fund. The fund balance had accumulated to $25,000 by the time Joanna was ready to enter college. However, Joanna received a scholarship that paid for her tuition, fees, books, supplies, and room and board. So Andrea withdrew the funds from the § 529 plan and bought Joanna a new car.

    a. What are the tax consequences to Andrea of withdrawing the funds?

    b. Assume instead that Joanna's scholarship did not cover her room and board, which cost $7,500 per academic year. During the current year, $7,500 of the fund balance was used to pay for Joanna's room and board. The remaining amount was left in the § 529 plan to cover her room and board for future academic years. What are the tax consequences to Andrea and to Joanna of using the $7,500 to pay for the room and board?

18. **LO.3** Dolly is a cash basis taxpayer. In 2020, she filed her 2019 South Carolina income tax return and received a $2,200 refund. Dolly took the standard deduction on her 2019 Federal income tax return but will itemize her deductions in 2020. Molly, a cash basis taxpayer, also filed her 2019 South Carolina income tax return in 2020 and received a $600 refund. She deducted no other state or local taxes. Molly had $16,000 in itemized deductions on her 2019 Federal income tax return but will take the standard deduction in 2020. How does the tax benefit rule apply to Dolly's and Molly's situations? Explain.

19. **LO.4** Ralph has experienced financial difficulties as a result of his struggling business. He has been behind on his mortgage payments for the last six months. The mortgage holder, who is a friend of Ralph's, has offered to accept $80,000 in full payment of the $100,000 owed on the mortgage and payable over the next 10 years. The interest rate of the mortgage is 7%, and the market rate is now 8%. What tax issues are raised by the creditor's offer?

Critical Thinking

Computational Exercises

20. **LO.2** Valentino is a patient in a nursing home for 45 days of 2020. While in the nursing home, he incurs total costs of $13,500. Medicare pays $8,000 of the costs. Valentino receives $15,000 from his long-term care insurance policy, which pays while he is in the facility. Assume that the Federal daily excludible amount for Valentino is $380.

    Of the $15,000, what amount may Valentino exclude from his gross income?

21. **LO.2** Mio was transferred from New York to Germany. He lived and worked in Germany for 340 days in 2020. Mio's salary for 2020 is $190,000. In your computation, round any division to four decimal places before converting to a percentage. For example, 0.473938 would be rounded to 47.39%.

    What is Mio's foreign earned income exclusion?

22. **LO.2** Ellie purchases an insurance policy on her life and names her brother, Jason, as the beneficiary. Ellie pays $32,000 in premiums for the policy during her life. When she dies, Jason collects the insurance proceeds of $500,000.

    As a result, how much gross income does Jason report?

23. **LO.2** Alfred owned a term life insurance policy at the time he was diagnosed with a terminal illness. After paying $18,300 in premiums, he sold the policy to a company that is authorized by the state of South Carolina to purchase such policies. The company paid Alfred $125,000. When Alfred died 18 months later, the company collected the face amount of the policy, $150,000.

    As a result of the sale of the policy, how much is Alfred required to include in his gross income?

24. **LO.1, 2** Leland pays premiums of $5,000 for an insurance policy in the face amount of $25,000 upon the life of Caleb and subsequently transfers the policy to Tyler for $7,500. Over the years, Tyler pays subsequent premiums of $1,500 on the policy. Upon Caleb's death, Tyler receives the proceeds of $25,000.

As a result, what amount is Tyler required to include in his gross income?

25. **LO.1, 2** Jarrod receives a scholarship of $18,500 from East State University to be used to pursue a bachelor's degree. He spends $12,000 on tuition, $1,500 on books and supplies, $4,000 for room and board, and $1,000 for personal expenses. How much may Jarrod exclude from his gross income?

26. **LO.3** Apply the tax benefit rule to determine the amount of the state income tax refund included in gross income in 2020.

a. Myrna and Geoffrey filed a joint tax return in 2019. Their AGI was $85,000, and itemized deductions were $25,100, which included $7,000 in state income tax and no other state or local taxes. In 2020, they received a $1,800 refund of the state income taxes they paid in 2019. The standard deduction for married filing jointly in 2019 was $24,400.

b. Veronica filed as a single taxpayer in 2019. Her AGI was $230,000, and itemized deductions were $42,000. Her local property taxes were $13,000 and her state income taxes were $17,000. In 2020, Veronica received a $2,100 refund of the state income taxes she paid in 2019. The standard deduction for single filers in 2019 was $12,200.

Problems

27. **LO.2** Ed, an employee of the Natural Color Company, suffered from a rare disease that was very expensive to treat. The local media ran several stories about Ed's problems, and the family created a website that generated more than $10,000 in gifts from individuals to help pay the medical bills. Ed's employer provided hospital and medical insurance for its employees, but the policy did not cover Ed's illness. When it became apparent that Ed could not pay all of his medical expenses, the hospital canceled the $25,000 Ed owed at the time of his death. After Ed's death, his former employer paid Ed's widow $12,000 in "her time of need." Ed's widow also collected $50,000 on a group term life insurance policy paid for by Ed's employer. What are Ed's and his widow's gross income?

28. **LO.2** Determine the gross income of the beneficiaries in the following cases:

a. Justin's employer was downsizing and offered employees an amount equal to one year's salary if the employee would voluntarily retire.

b. Trina contracted a disease and was unable to work for six months. Because of her dire circumstances, her employer paid her one-half of her regular salary while she was away from work.

c. Coral Corporation collected $1,000,000 on a key person life insurance policy when its chief executive died. The corporation had paid the premiums on the policy of $77,000, which were not deductible by the corporation.

d. Juan collected $40,000 on a life insurance policy when his wife, Leona, died in 2020. The insurance policy was provided by Leona's employer, and the premiums were excluded from Leona's gross income as group term life insurance. In 2020, Juan also collected the $3,500 accrued salary owed to Leona at the time of her death.

Decision Making 29. **LO.2, 5** As a result of a cancer diagnosis in early 2020, Laura has begun chemotherapy treatments. A cancer specialist has stated that Laura has less than one year to live. She has incurred many medical bills and other general living expenses and is in need of cash. So she is considering selling stock that cost $35,000 and has a fair market value of $50,000. This amount would be sufficient to pay her medical bills. However, she has read about a company (the Vital Benefits Company) that would purchase her life insurance policy for $50,000. She has paid $30,000 in premiums on the policy.

a. Considering only the tax effects, would selling the stock or selling the life insurance policy result in more beneficial tax treatment?

b. Assume that Laura is a dependent child and that her mother owns the stock and the life insurance policy, which is on the mother's life. Which of the alternative means of raising the cash would result in more beneficial tax treatment?

30. **LO.2** What is the taxpayer's gross income in each of the following situations?

a. Darrin received a salary of $50,000 from his employer, Green Construction.

b. In July, Green gave Darrin an all-expense-paid trip to Las Vegas (value of $3,000) for exceeding his sales quota.

c. Marta received $10,000 from her employer to help her pay medical expenses not covered by insurance.

d. Blake received $15,000 from his deceased wife's employer "to help him in his time of greatest need."

e. Clint collected $50,000 as the beneficiary of a group term life insurance policy when his wife died. The premiums on the policy were paid by his deceased wife's employer.

31. **LO.2** Donald was killed in an accident while he was on the job. Darlene, Donald's wife, received several payments as a result of Donald's death. What is Darlene's gross income from the items listed below?

a. Donald's employer paid Darlene an amount equal to Donald's three months' salary ($60,000), which is what the employer does for all widows and widowers of deceased employees.

b. Donald had $20,000 in accrued salary that was paid to Darlene.

c. Donald's employer had provided Donald with group term life insurance of $480,000 (twice his annual salary), which was payable to his widow in a lump sum. Premiums on this policy totaling $12,500 had been included in Donald's gross income under § 79.

d. Donald had purchased a life insurance policy (premiums totaled $250,000) that paid $600,000 in the event of accidental death. The proceeds were payable to Darlene, who elected to receive installment payments as an annuity of $30,000 each year for a 25-year period. She received her first installment this year.

32. **LO.2** Ray and Carin are partners in an accounting firm. The partners have entered into an arm's length agreement requiring Ray to purchase Carin's partnership interest from Carin's estate if she dies before Ray. The price is set at 120% of the book value of Carin's partnership interest at the time of her death. Ray purchased an insurance policy on Carin's life to fund this agreement. After Ray had paid $45,000 in premiums, Carin was killed in an automobile accident and Ray collected $800,000 of life insurance proceeds. Ray used the life insurance proceeds to purchase Carin's partnership interest.

a. What amount should Ray include in his gross income from receiving the life insurance proceeds?

b. The insurance company paid Ray $16,000 interest on the life insurance proceeds during the period Carin's estate was in administration. During this period, Ray had left the insurance proceeds with the insurance company. Is this interest taxable?

c. When Ray paid $800,000 for Carin's partnership interest, priced as specified in the agreement, the fair market value of Carin's interest was $1,000,000. How much should Ray include in his gross income from this bargain purchase?

33. **LO.2** Sally was an all-state soccer player during her junior and senior years in high school. She accepted an athletic scholarship from State University. The scholarship provided the following:

Tuition and fees	$15,000
Housing and meals	6,000
Books and supplies	1,500
Transportation	1,200

   a. Determine the effect of the scholarship on Sally's gross income.
   b. Sally's brother, Willy, was not a gifted athlete, but he received $8,000 from their father's employer as a scholarship during the year. The employer grants the children of all executives a scholarship equal to one-half of annual tuition, fees, books, and supplies. Willy also received a $6,000 scholarship (to be used for tuition) as the winner of an essay contest related to bioengineering, his intended field of study. Determine the effect of the scholarships on Willy's and his father's gross income.

34. **LO.2** Adrian was awarded an academic scholarship to State University for the 2020–2021 academic year. He received $6,500 in August and $7,200 in December 2020. Adrian had enough personal savings to pay all expenses as they came due. Adrian's expenditures for the relevant period were as follows:

Tuition, August 2020	$3,700
Tuition, January 2021	3,750
Room and board	
August–December 2020	2,800
January–May 2021	2,500
Books and educational supplies	
August–December 2020	1,000
January–May 2021	1,200

Determine the effect on Adrian's gross income for 2020 and 2021.

35. **LO.2** Leigh sued an overzealous bill collector and received the following settlement:

Damage to her automobile that the collector attempted to repossess	$ 3,300
Physical damage to her arm caused by the collector	15,000
Loss of income while her arm was healing	6,000
Punitive damages	80,000

   a. What effect does the settlement have on Leigh's gross income?
   b. Assume that Leigh also collected $25,000 of damages for slander to her personal reputation caused by the bill collector misrepresenting the facts to Leigh's employer and other creditors. Is this $25,000 included in Leigh's gross income? Explain.

36. **LO.2** Determine the effect on gross income in each of the following cases:
   a. Eloise received $150,000 in settlement of a sex discrimination case against her former employer.
   b. Nell received $10,000 for damages to her personal reputation. She also received $40,000 in punitive damages.
   c. Orange Corporation, an accrual basis taxpayer, received $50,000 from a lawsuit filed against its auditor who overcharged for services rendered in a previous year.
   d. Beth received $10,000 in compensatory damages and $30,000 in punitive damages in a lawsuit she filed against a tanning parlor for severe burns she received from using its tanning equipment.
   e. Joanne received compensatory damages of $75,000 and punitive damages of $300,000 from a cosmetic surgeon who botched her nose job.

37. **LO.2** Rex, age 55, is an officer of Blue Company, which provides him with the following nondiscriminatory fringe benefits in 2020:

    - Hospitalization insurance premiums for Rex and his dependents. The cost of the coverage for Rex is $2,900 per year, and the additional cost for his dependents is $3,800 per year. The plan has a $2,000 deductible, but his employer contributed $1,500 to Rex's Health Savings Account (HSA). Rex withdrew only $800 from the HSA, and the account earned $50 of interest during the year.
    - Insurance premiums of $840 for salary continuation payments. Under the plan, Rex will receive his regular salary in the event he is unable to work due to illness. Rex collected $4,500 on the policy to replace lost wages while he was ill during the year.
    - Rex is a part-time student working on his bachelor's degree in engineering. His employer reimbursed his $5,200 tuition under a plan available to all full-time employees.

    Determine the amount Rex must include in gross income.

38. **LO.2** The UVW Union and HON Corporation are negotiating contract terms. **Communications** Assume that the union members are in the 24% marginal tax bracket and that all benefits are provided on a nondiscriminatory basis. Write a letter to the UVW Union members, explaining the tax consequences of the options discussed below. The union's address is 905 Spruce Street, Washington, DC 20227.
    a. The company would eliminate the $250 deductible on medical insurance benefits. Most employees incur more than $250 each year in medical expenses.
    b. Employees would get an additional paid holiday with the same annual income (the same pay but less work).
    c. An employee who did not need health insurance (because the employee's spouse works and receives family coverage) would be allowed to receive the cash value of the coverage.

39. **LO.2, 5** Mauve Corporation has a group hospitalization insurance plan that has a **Decision Making** $200 deductible amount for hospital visits and a $15 deductible for doctor visits and prescriptions. The deductible portion paid by employees who have children has become substantial for some employees. The company is considering adopting a medical reimbursement plan or a flexible benefits plan to cover the deductible amounts. Either of these plans can be tailored to meet the needs of the employees. What are the cost considerations to the employer that should be considered in choosing between these plans?

40. **LO.2** Belinda spent the last 60 days of 2020 in a nursing home. The cost of the services provided to her was $18,000 ($300 per day). Medicare paid $8,500 toward the cost of her stay. Belinda also received $5,500 of benefits under a long-term care insurance policy she purchased. Assume that the Federal daily excludible amount is $380. What is the effect on Belinda's gross income?

41. **LO.2** Tim is the vice president of western operations for Maroon Oil Company and is stationed in San Francisco. He is required to live in an employer-owned home, which is three blocks from his company office. The company-provided home is equipped with high-speed internet access and several telephone lines. Tim receives telephone calls and e-mails that require immediate attention any time of day or night because the company's business is spread all over the world. A full-time administrative assistant resides in the house to assist Tim with the urgent business matters. Tim often uses the home for entertaining customers, suppliers, and employees. The fair market value of comparable housing is $9,000 per month. Tim is also provided with free parking at his company's office. The value of the parking is $360 per month. Calculate the amount associated with the company-provided housing and free parking that Tim must include in his gross income for 2020.

42. **LO.2** Does the taxpayer recognize gross income in the following situations?

    a. Ava is a filing clerk at a large insurance company. She is permitted to leave the premises for lunch, but she usually eats in the company's cafeteria because it is quick and she is on a tight schedule. On average, she pays $2 for a lunch that would cost $12 at a restaurant and it cost her employer $10 to prepare. However, if the prices in the cafeteria were not so low and the food was not so delicious, she would probably bring her lunch at a cost of $3 per day.

    b. Scott is an executive for an international corporation located in New York City. Often he works late, taking telephone calls from the company's European branch. Scott often stays in a company-owned condominium when he has a late-night work session. The condominium is across the street from the company office and has the technology needed to communicate with employees and customers throughout the world.

    c. Ira recently moved to take a job. For the first month on the new job, Ira was searching for a home to purchase or rent. During this time, his employer permitted Ira to live in an apartment the company maintains for customers during the buying season. The month that Ira occupied the apartment was not during the buying season, and the apartment would not otherwise have been occupied.

Decision Making   43. **LO.2, 5** Bertha is considering taking an early retirement offered by her employer. She would receive $3,000 per month, indexed for inflation. However, she would no longer be able to use the company's health facilities, and she would be required to pay her hospitalization insurance premiums of $8,000 each year. Bertha and her husband will file a joint return and take the standard deduction. She currently receives a salary of $55,000 a year. If she retires, she will spend approximately $300 less each month for commuting and clothing. Bertha and her husband have other sources of income and are in and will remain in the 22% marginal tax bracket. Her income tax for the current year was $8,875. She currently pays Social Security and Medicare taxes of 7.65% on her salary, but her retirement pay would not be subject to this tax. According to Bertha, she and her husband could live well if her after-tax retirement income was at least 50% of her current income. Provide Bertha with information she will need to make her decision.

Communications   44. **LO.2, 5** Finch Construction Company provides the carpenters it employs with all of the required tools. However, the company believes that this practice has led to some employees not taking care of the tools and to the mysterious disappearance of some tools. The company is considering requiring all of its employees to provide their own tools. Each employee's salary would be increased by $1,500 to compensate for the additional cost. Write a letter to Finch's management explaining the tax consequences of this plan to the carpenters. Finch's address is 300 Harbor Drive, Vermillion, SD 57069.

45. **LO.2, 5** Bluebird, Inc., does not provide its employees with any tax-exempt fringe benefits. The company is considering adopting a hospital and medical benefits insurance plan that will cost approximately $9,000 per employee. To adopt this plan, the company may have to reduce salaries and/or lower future salary increases. Bluebird is in the 25% (combined Federal and state rates) bracket. Bluebird is also responsible for matching the Social Security and Medicare taxes withheld on employees' salaries (at the full 7.65% rate). The hospital and medical benefits insurance plan will not be subject to the Social Security and Medicare taxes, and the company is not eligible for the small business credit for health insurance. The employees generally fall into two marginal tax rate groups:

Income Tax	Social Security and Medicare Tax	Total
12%	7.65%	19.65%
24%	1.45%	25.45%

The company has asked you to assist in its financial planning for the hospital and medical benefits insurance plan by computing the following:

a.   How much taxable compensation is the equivalent of $9,000 of exempt compensation for each of the two classes of employees?

b.   What is the company's after-tax cost of the taxable compensation computed in part (a)?

c.   What is the company's after-tax cost of the exempt compensation?

d.   Briefly explain your conclusions from the preceding analysis.

46. **LO.2, 5** Rosa's employer has instituted a flexible benefits program. Rosa will use   Decision Making
the plan to pay for her daughter's dental expenses and other medical expenses that are not covered by health insurance. Rosa is in the 24% marginal tax bracket and estimates that the medical and dental expenses not covered by health insurance will be within the range of $4,000 to $5,000. Her employer's plan permits her to set aside as much as $5,000 in the flexible benefits account. Rosa does not itemize her deductions.

a.   Rosa puts $4,000 into her flexible benefits account, and her actual expenses are $5,000. What is her cost of underestimating the expenses?

b.   Rosa puts $5,000 into her flexible benefits account, and her actual expenses are only $4,000. What is her cost of overestimating her expenses?

c.   What is Rosa's cost of underfunding as compared with the cost of overfunding the flexible benefits account?

d.   Does your answer in part (c) suggest that Rosa should fund the account closer to the low end or to the high end of her estimates?

47. **LO.2** Sparrow Corporation would like you to review its employee fringe benefits program with regard to the tax consequences of the plan for the company's president (Polly), who is also the majority shareholder.

a.   The company has a qualified retirement plan. The company pays the cost of employees attending a retirement planning seminar. The employee must be within 10 years of retirement, and the cost of the seminar is $1,500 per attendee.

b.   The company owns a parking garage that is used by customers, employees, and the general public. Only the general public is required to pay for parking. The charge to the general public for Polly's parking for the year would have been $3,600 (a $300 monthly rate).

c.   All employees are allowed to use the company's fixed charge long-distance telephone services, as long as the privilege is not abused. Although no one has kept track of the actual calls, Polly's use of the telephone had a value (what she would have paid on her personal telephone) of approximately $600.

d.   The company owns a condominium at the beach, which it uses to entertain customers. Employees are allowed to use the facility without charge when the company has no scheduled events. Polly used the facility 10 days during the year. Her use had a rental value of $1,000.

e.   The company is in the household moving business. Employees are allowed to ship goods without charge whenever there is excess space on a truck. Polly purchased a dining room suite for her daughter. Company trucks delivered the furniture to the daughter. Normal freight charges would have been $750.

f.   The company has a storage facility for household goods. Officers are allowed a 20% discount on charges for storing their goods. All other employees are allowed a 10% discount. Polly's discounts for the year totaled $900.

48. **LO.2** George is a U.S. citizen who is employed by Hawk Enterprises, a global company. Beginning on June 1, 2020, George began working in London. He worked there until January 31, 2021, when he transferred to Paris. He worked in Paris the remainder of 2021. His salary for the first five months of 2020 was

$100,000, and it was earned in the United States. His salary for the remainder of 2020 was $175,000, and it was earned in London. George's 2021 salary from Hawk was $300,000, with part being earned in London and part being earned in Paris. What is George's gross income in 2020 and 2021? (Assume that the foreign earned income exclusion amount is the same in both 2020 and 2021.)

49. **LO.2, 3** Determine Hazel's gross income from the following receipts for the year:

Gain on sale of Augusta County bonds	$800
Interest on U.S. government savings bonds	400
Interest on state income tax refund	200
Interest on Augusta County bonds	700
Patronage dividend from Potato Growers Cooperative	350

The patronage dividend was received in March of the current year for amounts paid for her (nondeductible) garden and lawn supplies.

50. **LO.2** In January 2020, Ezra purchased 2,000 shares of Gold Utility Mutual Fund for $20,000. In June, Ezra received an additional 100 shares as a dividend, in lieu of receiving $1,000 in cash dividends. In December, the company declared a two-for-one stock split. Ezra received an additional 2,100 shares, but there was no option to receive cash. At the time of the stock dividend in December and at the end of the year, the fund shares were trading for $5 per share. Also, at the end of the year, the fund offered to buy outstanding shares for $4.50. Ezra did not sell any shares during the year.

a. What is Ezra's gross income from the 100 shares received in June?

b. What is Ezra's gross income from the receipt of the 2,100 shares as a two-for-one stock split in December?

c. Should Ezra be required to recognize gross income in 2020 even though the fair market value of his investment at the end of the year was less than the fair market value at the beginning of the year? Explain.

Decision Making 51. **LO.2** Tonya, who lives in California, inherited a $100,000 State of California bond in 2020. Her marginal Federal tax rate is 35%, and her marginal state tax rate is 5%. The California bond pays 3.3% interest, which is not subject to California income tax. She can purchase a corporate bond of comparable risk that will yield 5.2% or a U.S. government bond that pays 4.6% interest. Which investment will provide the greatest after-tax yield?

Decision Making 52. **LO.2** Lynn Swartz's husband died three years ago. Her parents have income of
Communications over $200,000 a year and want to ensure that funds will be available for the education of Lynn's eight-year-old son, Eric. Lynn is currently earning $45,000 a year. Lynn's parents have suggested that they start a savings account for Eric. They have calculated that if they invest $4,000 a year for the next 8 years, at the end of 10 years, sufficient funds will be available for Eric's college expenses. Lynn realizes that the tax treatment of the investments could significantly affect the amount of funds available for Eric's education. She asked you to write a letter to her advising about options available to her parents and to her for Eric's college education. Lynn's address is 100 Myrtle Cove, Fairfield, CT 06824.

53. **LO.2** Starting in 2009, Chuck and Luane have been purchasing Series EE bonds in their name to use for the higher education of their daughter Susie, who currently is age 18. During the year, they cash in $12,000 of the bonds to use for freshman year tuition, fees, and room and board. Of this amount, $5,000 represents interest. Of the $12,000, $8,000 is used for tuition and fees and $4,000 is used for room and board. Chuck and Luane's AGI, before the educational savings bond exclusion, is $126,950. Review § 135, and answer the following questions.

a. Determine the tax consequences for Chuck and Luane, who will file a joint return, and for Susie.

b. Assume that Chuck and Luane purchased the bonds in Susie's name. Determine the tax consequences for Chuck and Luane and for Susie.

54. **LO.2** Albert established a qualified tuition program for each of his twins, Kim and Jim. He started each fund with $20,000 when the children were five years old. Albert made no further contributions to his children's plans. Thirteen years later, both children have graduated from high school. Kim's fund has accumulated to $45,000, and Jim's has accumulated to $42,000. Kim decides to attend a state university, which will cost $60,000 for four years (tuition, fees, room and board, and books). Jim decides to go to work instead of going to college. During the current year, $7,500 is used from Kim's plan to pay the cost of her first semester in college. Because Jim is not going to college now or in the future, Albert withdraws the $42,000 plan balance and gives it to Jim to start his new life after high school.

    a. During the period since the plans were established, should Albert or the twins have been including the annual plan earnings in gross income? Explain.

    b. What are the tax consequences to Kim and Albert of the $7,500 being used for the first semester's higher education costs?

    c. Because of her participation in the qualified tuition program, Kim received a 10% reduction in tuition charges; so less than $7,500 was withdrawn from her account. Is either Albert or Kim required to include the value of this discount in gross income? Explain.

    d. What are the tax consequences to Albert and Jim of Jim's qualified tuition program being closed?

55. **LO.3** How does the tax benefit rule apply in the following cases?

    a. In 2018, the Orange Furniture Store, an accrual method sole proprietorship, sold furniture on credit for $1,000 to Sammy. The cost of the furniture was $600. In 2019, Orange took a bad debt deduction for the $1,000. In 2020, Sammy inherited some money and paid Orange the $1,000 he owed. Orange's owner was in the 35% marginal tax bracket in 2018, the 12% marginal tax bracket in 2019, and the 35% marginal tax bracket in 2020.

    b. In 2019, Marvin, a cash basis taxpayer, took a $2,000 itemized deduction for state income taxes paid; the deduction was not limited by the SALT cap. This increased his itemized deductions to a total that was $800 more than the standard deduction. In 2020, Marvin received a $1,500 refund when he filed his 2019 state income tax return. Marvin was in the 12% marginal tax bracket in 2019 but was in the 35% marginal tax bracket in 2020.

    c. In 2019, Barb, a cash basis taxpayer, was in an accident and incurred $8,000 in medical expenses, which she claimed as an itemized deduction for medical expenses. Because of the 7.5%-of-AGI reduction, the expense reduced her taxable income by only $3,000. In 2020, Barb successfully sued the person who caused the physical injury and collected $8,000 to reimburse her for the cost of her medical expenses. Barb was in the 22% marginal tax bracket in 2019, 12% in 2020.

56. **LO.4** Vic, who was experiencing financial difficulties, was able to adjust his debts as follows:

    a. Vic is an attorney. Vic owed his uncle $25,000. The uncle told Vic that if he serves as the executor of the uncle's estate, Vic's debt will be canceled in the uncle's will.

    b. Vic borrowed $80,000 from First Bank. The debt was secured by land that Vic purchased for $100,000. Vic was unable to pay, and the bank foreclosed when the liability was $80,000, which was also the fair market value of the property.

    c. The Land Company, which had sold land to Vic for $80,000, reduced the mortgage on the land by $12,000.

    Determine the tax consequences to Vic.

Tax Return Problems

Tax Forms Problem

Decision Making

Critical Thinking

57. Alfred E. Old and Beulah A. Crane, each age 42, married on September 7, 2017. Alfred and Beulah will file a joint return for 2019. Alfred's Social Security number is 111-11-1109. Beulah's Social Security number is 123-45-6780, and she adopted "Old" as her married name. They live at 211 Brickstone Drive, Atlanta, GA 30304.

 Alfred was divorced from Sarah Old in March 2016. Under the divorce agreement, Alfred is to pay Sarah $1,250 per month for the next 10 years or until Sarah's death, whichever occurs first. Alfred pays Sarah $15,000 in 2019. In addition, in January 2019, Alfred pays Sarah $50,000, which is designated as being for her share of the marital property. Also, Alfred is responsible for all prior years' income taxes. Sarah's Social Security number is 123-45-6788.

 Alfred's salary for 2019 is $150,000. He is an executive working for Cherry, Inc. (Federal I.D. No. 98-7654321). As part of his compensation package, Cherry provides him with group term life insurance equal to twice his annual salary. His employer withheld $24,900 for Federal income taxes and $8,000 for state income taxes. The proper amounts were withheld for FICA taxes.

 Beulah recently graduated from law school and is employed by Legal Aid Society, Inc. (Federal I.D. No. 11-1111111), as a public defender. She receives a salary of $42,000 in 2019. Her employer withheld $7,500 for Federal income taxes and $2,400 for state income taxes. The proper amounts were withheld for FICA taxes.

 Alfred and Beulah had interest income of $500. They receive a $1,900 refund on their 2018 state income taxes. They claimed the standard deduction on their 2018 Federal income tax return. Alfred and Beulah pay $4,500 interest and $1,450 property taxes on their personal residence in 2019. Their charitable contributions total $2,400 (all to their church). They paid sales taxes of $1,400, for which they maintain the receipts. Alfred and Beulah have never owned or used any virtual currency, and they do not want to contribute to the Presidential Election Campaign.

 Compute the Olds' net tax payable (or refund due) for 2019. Suggested software: ProConnect Tax Online.

Tax Computation Problem

Decision Making

Communications

58. Martin S. Albert (Social Security number 111-11-1111) is 39 years old and is married to Michele R. Albert (Social Security number 123-45-6789). The Alberts live at 512 Ferry Road, Newport News, VA 23601. They file a joint return and have two dependent children, Charlene, age 17, and Jordan, age 18. Charlene's Social Security number is 123-45-6788, and Jordan's Social Security number is 123-45-6787. In 2020, Martin and Michele had the following transactions:

 a. Martin received $120,000 in salary from Red Steel Corporation, where he is a construction engineer. Withholding for Federal income tax was $10,750. The amounts withheld for FICA taxes were as follows: $7,049 ($113,700 × 6.2%) for Social Security and $1,740 ($120,000 × 1.45%) for Medicare. Martin worked in Mexico from January 1, 2019, until February 15, 2020. His $120,000 salary for 2020 includes $18,000 he earned for January and one-half of February 2020 while working in Mexico.

 b. Martin and Michele received $400 interest on Montgomery County (Virginia) school bonds.

 c. Martin received $2,300 interest from a Bahamian bank account.

 d. Michele received 50 shares of Applegate Corporation common stock as a stock dividend. The shares had a fair market value of $2,500 at the time Michele received them, and she did not have the option of receiving cash.

 e. Martin and Michele received a $1,200 refund on their 2019 Virginia income taxes. Their itemized deductions in 2019 totaled $34,000 and included state taxes of $7,400.

f. Martin paid $6,600 alimony to his former wife, Rose T. Morgan (Social Security number 123-45-6786). The divorce was finalized in 2016.

g. Martin and Michele kept the receipts for their sales taxes paid of $1,100.

h. Martin and Michele's itemized deductions were as follows:
- State income tax paid and withheld totaled $5,100.
- Real estate taxes on their principal residence were $3,700.
- Mortgage interest on their principal residence was $2,500.
- Cash contributions to the church totaled $2,800.

Part 1—Tax Computation

Compute the Alberts' net tax payable (or refund due) for 2020.

Part 2—Tax Planning

The Alberts are considering buying another house. Their house mortgage payments would increase by $500 (to $1,500) per month, which includes a $250 increase in interest and a $100 increase in property tax. The Alberts would like to know how much the mortgage payments would increase net of any change in their income tax. Write a letter to the Alberts that contains your advice.

Research Problems

Note: Solutions to the Research Problems can be prepared by using the Thomson Reuters Checkpoint™ online tax research database, which accompanies this textbook. Solutions can also be prepared by using research materials found in a typical tax library.

the answer company™
THOMSON REUTERS

Research Problem 1. Murray reported to the Environmental Protection Agency that his employer was illegally dumping chemicals into a river. His charges were true, and Murray's employer was fined. In retaliation, Murray's employer fired him and made deliberate efforts to prevent Murray from obtaining other employment. Murray sued the employer, claiming that his reputation had been damaged. Murray won his lawsuit and received an award for "damages to his personal and professional reputation and for his mental suffering." Now he would like to know whether the award is taxable. He argues that he was awarded damages as a recovery of his human capital and that a recovery of capital is not income. Is Murray's logic correct?

Research Problem 2. Your client, John Butler, is an avid Houston Astros fan. Last March at the Astros' home opener, as a result of a random drawing of those in attendance at the game, John won 300 Shipley Do-Nut coupons. Each coupon entitled him to a cup of coffee and a free doughnut or a dozen doughnut holes.

John used some of the coupons (approximately 20), but he found that eating so many doughnuts directly conflicted with his goal of losing weight. The unused coupons expired on January 1, 2020. Thus, John was surprised when he received a Form 1099 in February 2020 that valued his prize at $900. John would like to know whether the value of the doughnut coupons should be included in income and asks you to research his question. If you conclude that their value should be included in income, John also would like to know if he can reduce his gross income by including in income only the value of the coupons that he used. He has the unused coupons as documentation that neither he nor anyone else used them.

Research Problem 3. Aubrey Brown is a decorated veteran of the Vietnam War. As a result of his exposure to Agent Orange during the war, Aubrey developed lung cancer and is unable to work. He received $12,000 of Social Security disability payments in the current year. He reasons that the payments should be excluded from his gross income because the payments are compensation for the physical injury he suffered as a result of his service in the armed forces. Is Aubrey correct? Explain.

Partial list of research aids:
Rev.Rul. 77–318, 1977–2 C.B. 45.
Reimels v. Comm., 2006–1 USTC ¶50,147, 97 AFTR 2d 2006–820, 436 F.3d 344 (CA–2, 2006).

Use internet tax resources to address the following questions. Look for reliable websites and blogs of the IRS and other government agencies, media outlets, businesses, tax professionals, academics, think tanks, and political outlets.

Data Analytics
Communications

Research Problem 4. Use information about individual income tax returns available at the IRS Tax Stats website (**irs.gov/statistics/soi-tax-stats-individual-income-tax-returns**) to find data on the number of individuals who report tax-exempt interest income on their tax return and the amount of that exempt income. The data you find should show this information for individuals at different ranges of adjusted gross income (AGI). Use the data to create pie charts (or similar visuals) of the percent of AGI represented by the tax-exempt interest income exclusion as well as the number of individuals claiming this exclusion at different AGI levels. Analyze the IRS data, draw conclusions from it, and summarize your findings in a two- to three-paragraph e-mail sent to your instructor. Be sure your conclusions are explained and supported by the data.

Research Problem 5. Employers often use the internet as a means of attracting applications from potential employees. Locate an internet site offering employment opportunities, ideally one provided by a well-known corporation. How does the employer promote its fringe benefit and cafeteria plan packages? Compare and contrast several such sites.

Research Problem 6. One income exclusion that some states allow but the Federal government does not is for lottery winnings. Does your state have an exclusion for lottery winnings? If so, how does it work? Why do you think a state might allow winnings from its own state lottery to be excluded from state income taxes?

Becker CPA Review Questions

Becker.

1. Stephen is a graduate student at West University. He works part-time at the campus coffee shop earning $5,000 this year. Stephen also receives a $25,000 scholarship that pays for his tuition, fees, and books. What amount does Stephen include in his gross income?

   a. $25,000   c. $30,000
   b. $5,000   d. $0

2. Jeffrey Dean, a Master's Degree candidate at North State Central University, was awarded a $15,000 scholarship from North State Central in the current year. During the current year, he paid the following expenses:

Tuition	$12,000
Books	1,000
Fees	500
Room and board	1,500

   In addition, he received $6,000 for teaching two undergraduate accounting courses. What amount must be included in Dean's gross income?

   a. $0   c. $7,500
   b. $6,000   d. $21,000

3. Linda is an employee of JRH Corporation. Which of the following would be included in Linda's gross income?

    a. Premiums paid by JRH Corporation for a group term life insurance policy for $50,000 of coverage for Linda.

    b. $1,000 of tuition paid by JRH Corporation to State University for Linda's master's degree program.

    c. A $2,000 trip given to Linda by JRH Corporation for meeting sales goals.

    d. $1,200 paid by JRH Corporation for an annual parking pass for Linda.

4. Kim was seriously injured at her job. As a result of her injury, she received the following payments:

    - $5,000 reimbursement from employer-provided health insurance for medical expenses paid by Kim. The premiums this year paid by Kim's employer totaled $6,000.

    - $15,000 disability pay. Kim has disability insurance provided by her employer as a nontaxable fringe benefit. Kim's employer paid $6,000 in disability premiums this year on behalf of Kim.

    - $10,000 received for damages for personal physical injury.

    - $200,000 for punitive damages.

    What amount is taxable to Kim?

    a. $215,000   c. $236,000

    b. $225,000   d. $0

5. Danny received the following interest and dividend payments this year. What amount should Danny include in his gross income?

Source	Amount
City of Atlanta bond interest	$1,200
U.S. Treasury bond interest	500
State of Georgia bond interest	1,000
Ellis Company common stock dividend	400
Row Corporation bond interest	600

    a. $2,500   c. $3,700

    b. $1,500   d. $2,200

6. Elizabeth received the following sources of income in the current year:

U.S. Treasury bond certificates interest	$500
Interest on state tax refund (paid by state government for late payment of tax refund to Elizabeth)	200
Corporate bond interest	600
Amount received for opening a new savings account at a local bank	50
Puerto Rico bond interest	350

    What amount must Elizabeth include in gross income on her Federal income tax return?

    a. $650   c. $1,350

    b. $1,150   d. $1,700

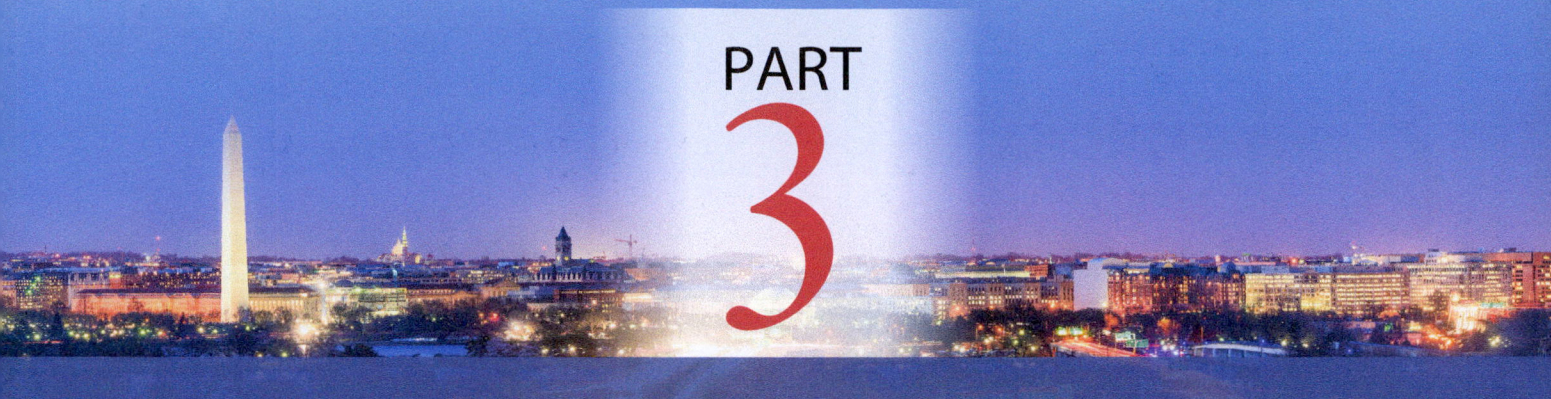

PART 3

DEDUCTIONS AND CREDITS

CHAPTER **6**

Deductions and Losses: In General

CHAPTER **7**

Deductions and Losses: Certain Business Expenses and Losses

CHAPTER **8**

Depreciation, Cost Recovery, Amortization, and Depletion

CHAPTER **9**

Deductions: Employee and Self-Employed-Related Expenses

CHAPTER **10**

Deductions and Losses: Certain Itemized Deductions

CHAPTER **11**

Investor Losses

CHAPTER **12**

Tax Credits and Payments

Part 3 presents the deduction component of the basic tax model. Deductions are classified as business versus nonbusiness, "for" AGI versus "from" AGI, employee versus employer, active versus passive, and reimbursed versus unreimbursed. The effect of each of these classifications is analyzed. Deduction limitations, disallowances, and the deduction for qualified business income are also discussed. A separate chapter examines the special tax treatment affecting losses from investment activities. After deductions offset the income subject to tax in the basic tax model and the tax is computed, a wide variety of tax credits can be used to reduce the calculated tax liability. However, these credits are not always available and are subject to various limitations. The general procedures related to payment of the tax liability are also covered. Part 3 concludes with a discussion of two tax provisions that are part of the Affordable Care Act: the premium tax credit available to defray health care insurance costs and additional Medicare taxes imposed on high-income individuals.

CHAPTER

6

Deductions and Losses: In General

LEARNING OBJECTIVES: *After completing Chapter 6, you should be able to:*

LO.1 Differentiate between deductions *for* and *from* adjusted gross income and describe the relevance of the differentiation.

LO.2 Describe the cash and accrual methods of accounting with emphasis on the deduction aspects.

LO.3 Apply the Internal Revenue Code deduction disallowance provisions associated with the following: public policy limitations, political activities, excessive executive compensation, investigation of

business opportunities, hobby losses, vacation home rentals, payment of others' expenses, personal expenditures, capital expenditures, related-party transactions, business interest expense, and expenses related to tax-exempt income.

LO.4 Identify tax planning opportunities for maximizing deductions and minimizing the disallowance of deductions.

CHAPTER OUTLINE

6-1   Classification of Deductible Expenses, 6-2
  6-1a   Classifying Deductions, 6-3
  6-1b   Authority for Deductions, 6-3
  6-1c   Deduction Criteria for § 162 and § 212, 6-5
  6-1d   Personal Expenses, 6-6
  6-1e   Business and Nonbusiness Losses, 6-6
  6-1f   Deduction for Qualified Business Income, 6-7
  6-1g   Reporting Procedures, 6-8

6-2   Deductions and Losses—Timing of Expense Recognition, 6-9
  6-2a   Importance of Taxpayer's Method of Accounting, 6-9
  6-2b   Cash Method Requirements, 6-10
  6-2c   Accrual Method Requirements, 6-10
  6-2d   Prepaid Expenses—The "12-Month Rule," 6-12
  6-2e   Time Value of Tax Deductions, 6-12

6-3   Disallowance Possibilities, 6-13
  6-3a   Public Policy Limitation, 6-13
  6-3b   Political Contributions and Lobbying Activities, 6-15

  6-3c   Excessive Executive Compensation, 6-16
  6-3d   Investigation of a Business, 6-17
  6-3e   Hobby Losses, 6-18
  6-3f   Rental of Vacation Homes, 6-21
  6-3g   Expenditures Incurred for Taxpayer's Benefit or Taxpayer's Obligation, 6-25
  6-3h   Disallowance of Personal Expenditures, 6-26
  6-3i   Disallowance of Deductions for Capital Expenditures, 6-26
  6-3j   Transactions between Related Parties, 6-28
  6-3k   Substantiation Requirements, 6-29
  6-3l   Expenses and Interest Relating to Tax-Exempt Income, 6-29
  6-3m   Other Disallowances, 6-30

6-4   Tax Planning, 6-30
  6-4a   Vacation Homes, 6-30
  6-4b   Hobby Losses, 6-32
  6-4c   Do Deduction Limits Affect Executive Compensation? 6-33

CALCULATION OF DEDUCTIBLE EXPENSES

Dr. Cliff Payne determines that the deductible expenses associated with his dental practice (a sole proprietorship) are as follows:

Salaries including FICA ($5,000 are unpaid at year-end)	$120,000
Building rent	24,000
Depreciation of dental equipment and office furnishings and equipment	52,000
Insurance (malpractice, dental equipment, and office furnishings and equipment)	22,000
Dental supplies	16,000
Office supplies	3,000
Investigation expenses	6,000
Contribution to the State Senate campaign fund of Tom Smith	1,000
Contribution to the State Senate campaign fund of Virginia White	1,000
Legal expenses associated with patient lawsuit	4,000
Fine imposed by city for improper disposal of medical waste	3,000
Dues paid to The Dental Society	10,000
Draw by Dr. Payne for living expenses ($5,000 monthly)	60,000

Has Dr. Payne correctly calculated the deductible business expenses for his dental practice?

Read the chapter and formulate your response.

FRAMEWORK 1040 Tax Formula for Individuals

This chapter covers the boldfaced portions of the Tax Formula for Individuals that was introduced in Concept Summary 3.1 on p. 3-3. Below those portions are the sections of Form 1040 where the results are reported.

Income *(broadly defined)*	$ xx,xxx
Less: Exclusions	(x,xxx)
Gross income	**$xx,xxx**
Less: Deductions *for* adjusted gross income	**(x,xxx)**

FORM 1040 (Schedule 1)

3	Business income or (loss). Attach Schedule C	. . . .

Adjusted gross income	$ xx,xxx
Less: The greater of total itemized deductions *or* the standard deduction	(x,xxx)

FORM 1040 (p. 1)

9	**Standard deduction or itemized deductions** (from Schedule A)	. . . .

Personal and dependency exemptions*	(x,xxx)
Deduction for qualified business income**	(x,xxx)
Taxable income	$ xx,xxx
Tax on taxable income *(see Tax Tables or Tax Rate Schedules)*	$ x,xxx
Less: Tax credits *(including income taxes withheld and prepaid)*	(xxx)
Tax due (or refund)	$ xxx

* Exemption deductions are not allowed from 2018 through 2025.
** Only applies from 2018 through 2025.

The tax law has an all-inclusive definition of income; that is, income from whatever source derived is includible in gross income. Income cannot be excluded unless there is a specific statement to that effect in the tax law.

The opposite approach is used for deductions. A deduction is allowed only if there is a specific provision in the tax law that permits it. The inclusive definition of income and the exclusive definition of deductions may not seem fair to taxpayers, but it is the structure of the tax law. The courts agree with this structure, holding that any exclusions from income and all deductions are gifts from Congress.[1]

LO.1

Differentiate between deductions *for* and *from* adjusted gross income and describe the relevance of the differentiation.

6-1 CLASSIFICATION OF DEDUCTIBLE EXPENSES

It is important to classify deductible expenses as **deductions *for* adjusted gross income** (AGI) or **deductions *from* adjusted gross income**. Deductions *for* AGI can be claimed whether or not the taxpayer itemizes. Deductions *from* AGI result in a tax benefit only if, collectively, they exceed the taxpayer's standard deduction. If itemized deductions (*from* AGI) are less than the standard deduction, they provide no tax benefit. As Example 1 illustrates, whether a deduction is classified as *for* AGI or *from* AGI can affect the benefit the taxpayer receives from the deduction.

---

[1]The courts refer to this as "legislative grace"; see *New Colonial Ice Co. v. Helvering*, 4 USTC ¶1292, 13 AFTR 1180, 54 S.Ct. 788 (USSC, 1934).

Steve is a self-employed CPA. Ralph is one of Steve's employees. During the year, Steve and Ralph incur the following expenses:

EXAMPLE
1

	Steve	Ralph
Dues to American Institute of CPAs and State Society of CPAs	$ 400	$ 300
Subscriptions to professional journals	500	200
Registration fees for tax conferences	800	800
	$1,700	$1,300

Steve does not reimburse any of his employees for dues, subscriptions, or educational programs.
Steve's expenses are classified as deductions *for* AGI because they are considered business expenses since he is a sole proprietor. Therefore, he can deduct the $1,700 on his Federal income tax return. Ralph's unreimbursed employee business expenses are classified as deductions *from* AGI. However, these expenses are miscellaneous itemized deductions and, from 2018 through 2025, are not deductible.

Deductions *for* AGI may directly affect the *amount* of itemized deductions because some itemized deductions are limited to amounts in excess of specified percentages of AGI. Itemized deductions that have AGI limitations include medical expenses and personal casualty losses.

Tina, age 36, earns a salary of $90,000 and has no other income. She itemizes her deductions during 2020. Unreimbursed medical expenses for the year are $12,000. Tina's medical expense deduction is $5,250, as computed below.
Alternatively, assume that Tina receives a $10,000 bonus from her employer in 2020. Her AGI would then be $100,000 ($90,000 + $10,000), and her medical expense is reduced by $750 to $4,500.

EXAMPLE
2

	Without Bonus	With Bonus
Qualified medical expenses	$12,000	$12,000
Reduction: AGI × 7.5%	(6,750)	(7,500)
Deductible medical expenses	$ 5,250	$ 4,500

When Tina's income increased by $10,000, this reduced her medical expense deduction by $750; so the total effect on taxable income is an increase of $10,750.[2]

6-1a Classifying Deductions

Two key issues must be resolved for any potential deduction. First, it must be determined whether the item is deductible, as discussed in text Section 6-1b. If the item is deductible, then the second issue is to determine if the deduction is classified as *for* AGI or *from* AGI. Deductions *for* AGI are listed in § 62. If a deduction is not listed in § 62, it is an itemized deduction. Exhibit 6.1 provides a partial list of the items classified as deductions *for* AGI.

6-1b Authority for Deductions

The specific authority for deductions is provided in many different Code sections. However, two of the most important are § 212 and § 162. To determine the proper authority for claiming a deduction, first determine what type of activity the expenditure relates to. All activities can be divided into one of the following mutually exclusive categories:

1. Investment/production of income (§ 212).
2. Trade or business (§ 162).
3. Personal (various Code sections).

---

[2]Example 4 in Chapter 3 illustrates this same point. See Chapter 10 for additional discussion of medical expenses.

EXHIBIT 6.1	Common Deductions *for* Adjusted Gross Income	
Deduction		**Chapter**
Alimony payments (divorce decrees before 2019)		4
Expenses attributable to property held for the production of rents and royalties		6
Expenses attributable to a trade or business		9
Employee business expenses (reimbursed)		9
Professional development and supplies (up to $250) for elementary and secondary school teachers		9
Student loan interest		9 and 10
Contributions to retirement plans		9
Medical insurance premiums paid by a self-employed taxpayer		10
Self-employment taxes		12
Losses on the sale or exchange of property		13 and 14

For example, are legal expenses deductible? To make that determination, first determine whether the legal expense relates to an investment, a trade or business, or a personal activity.

EXAMPLE 3

Darryl pays $400 to an attorney for her advice. If this payment relates to his business, it is a § 162 business expense. If the payment relates to the purchase of land that he intends to hold for profit, it is a § 212 investment/production of income expense. If the payment relates to the development of an estate plan, it is a nondeductible personal expense (§ 262).

Section 212 Expenses

Section 212 allows deductions for ordinary and necessary expenses paid or incurred for:

- The production or collection of income.
- The management, conservation, or maintenance of property held for the production of income.
- Expenses paid in connection with the determination, collection, or refund of any tax.

Most § 212 expenses are deductible *for* AGI. Common examples of deductions *for* AGI are expenses related to rent and royalty income (reported on Schedule E) and professional fees paid by a sole proprietor (reported on Schedule C) or a farmer (reported on Schedule F).

All other § 212 expenses are itemized deductions (deductions *from* AGI). For example, investment interest expense is a *from* AGI deduction. All other investment-related expenses (e.g., safe deposit box rentals) are miscellaneous itemized deductions and, from 2018 through 2025, are not deductible.[3]

Section 162 Trade or Business Expenses

Section 162(a) permits a deduction for all ordinary and necessary expenses paid or incurred in carrying on a trade or business. These include reasonable salaries paid for services, expenses for the use of business property, and one-half of self-employment taxes paid (see Chapter 12). These expenses are deducted *for* AGI.

It is sometimes difficult to determine whether an expense is deductible as a trade or business expense. The term *trade or business* is not defined in the Code or Regulations, and the courts have not provided a satisfactory definition. One key determination is to ensure that the activity is not a hobby. If the taxpayer's operations are not extensive enough to indicate that a trade or business exists, expenses related to the activity are deductible only to the extent of the activity's income (discussed further in text Section 6-3e).

[3]§ 62(a)(4) and Reg. § 1.212–1(g).

Section 162 *excludes* the following items from classification as trade or business expenses:

- Charitable contributions or gifts.
- Illegal bribes and kickbacks and certain treble damage payments.
- Fines and penalties.

6-1c Deduction Criteria for § 162 and § 212

Expenses under § 162 and § 212 must be ordinary and necessary to be deductible. In addition, compensation for services must be "reasonable" in amount.

An expense is *necessary* if a prudent businessperson would incur the same expense and the expense is expected to be appropriate and helpful in the taxpayer's business.[4] An expense is *ordinary* if it is normal, usual, or customary in the type of business conducted by the taxpayer and is not capital in nature.[5] However, an expense need not be recurring to be deductible as ordinary. For example, a business may be in a situation that is a very rare occurrence and incur an expense. If other businesses in a similar situation are likely to incur a similar expense, then the expense can be ordinary even though it is not recurring.

Nisha engaged in a mail-order business. The post office judged that her advertisements were false and misleading. Under a fraud order, the post office stamped "fraudulent" on all letters addressed to Nisha's business and returned them to the senders. Nisha spent $30,000 on legal fees in an unsuccessful attempt to force the post office to stop.

The legal fees (although not recurring) were ordinary business expenses because they were normal, usual, or customary in the circumstances.[6]

To be deductible, an expense must be both ordinary *and* necessary.

Pat purchased a business that had just been adjudged bankrupt. Because the business had a poor financial rating, Pat wanted to restore its financial reputation. Consequently, he paid off some of the debts owed by the former owners that had been canceled by the bankruptcy court.

Because Pat had no legal obligation to make these payments, the U.S. Supreme Court found that he was trying to generate goodwill. Although the payments were necessary (i.e., appropriate and helpful), they were *not* ordinary and their deduction *was not* allowed.[7]

The Code refers to reasonableness solely with respect to salaries and other compensation for services.[8] But the courts have held that for any business expense to be ordinary and necessary, it must also be reasonable in amount.[9] Example 6 illustrates the reasonableness concept for an investment expense.

Debbye is a retired pilot who owns a small portfolio of investments, including 10 shares of Robin, Inc., a publicly traded company, worth $1,000. She incurred $350 in travel expenses to attend the annual shareholders' meeting where she voted her 10 shares against the current management group.

No deduction is permitted because a 10-share investment is insignificant in value in relation to the travel expenses incurred.[10]

What constitutes reasonableness is a question of fact. If an expense is unreasonable, the excess amount is not allowed as a deduction.

The question of reasonableness generally arises with respect to closely held corporations since there is no separation of ownership and management. Transactions between the shareholders and the closely held company may result in the disallowance of deductions for excessive salaries and rent expense paid by the corporation to the shareholders. An unusually large salary will often be challenged by the IRS, but the courts may

---

[4]*Welch v. Helvering*, 3 USTC ¶1164, 12 AFTR 1456, 54 S.Ct. 8 (USSC, 1933).

[5]*Deputy v. DuPont*, 40–1 USTC ¶9161, 23 AFTR 808, 60 S.Ct. 363 (USSC, 1940).

[6]*Comm. v. Heininger*, 44–1 USTC ¶9109, 31 AFTR 783, 64 S.Ct. 249 (USSC, 1943).

[7]*Welch v. Helvering*, cited in Footnote 4.

[8]§ 162(a)(1).

[9]*Comm. v. Lincoln Electric Co.*, 49–2 USTC ¶9388, 38 AFTR 411, 176 F.2d 815 (CA–6, 1949).

[10]*J. Raymond Dyer*, 36 T.C. 456 (1961).

conclude that it is reasonable given the facts that surround a particular business.[11] If excessive payments for salaries and rents are closely related to the percentage of stock owned by the recipients, the payments are generally treated as dividends.[12] Because dividends are not deductible by the corporation, the disallowance results in an increase in the corporate taxable income.

EXAMPLE 7

Sparrow Corporation, a closely held corporation, is owned equally by Lupe, Carlos, and Ramon. The company has been highly profitable for several years and has not paid dividends. Lupe, Carlos, and Ramon are key officers of the company, and each receives a salary of $200,000. Salaries for similar positions in comparable companies average only $100,000.

Amounts paid to the owners in excess of $100,000 may be deemed unreasonable; if so, a total of $300,000 in salary deductions by Sparrow is disallowed. The disallowed amounts are treated as dividends rather than salary to Lupe, Carlos, and Ramon because the payments are proportional to stock ownership. Salaries are deductible by the corporation, but dividends are not.

Note that the shareholders may benefit from this reclassification. Salaries would be taxed at ordinary income rates and are subject to payroll taxes. However, dividend income would be taxed at long-term capital gains rates if qualified and would not be subject to payroll taxes.

6-1d **Personal Expenses**

Expenditures that are incurred in one's personal life are deductible only if a specific Code section authorizes the deduction. These expenses are usually deductions *from* AGI. Some of the more common deductions in this category include the following:

- Contributions to qualified charitable organizations.
- Mortgage interest expense.
- State and local taxes.
- Medical expenses.
- Personal casualty losses.

Many of these deductions are limited in some way (e.g., only amounts in excess of a specific percentage of AGI; a specific cap on the deduction). Casualty losses are discussed in Chapter 7; itemized deductions are discussed in Chapter 10.

EXAMPLE 8

Yolanda paid her doctor $650 for a medical procedure this year. She also made a charitable contribution to the United Way for $1,000. She spent $400 on uniforms for her children to wear to school.

The Internal Revenue Code specifically provides for deducting medical expenses and qualified charitable contributions, so these are deductible. Since the Code does not provide a deduction for clothing worn for personal use, the uniforms are not deductible.

6-1e **Business and Nonbusiness Losses**

Section 165 provides for a deduction for losses not compensated for by insurance. As a general rule, deductible losses of individual taxpayers are limited to those incurred in a trade or business or in a transaction entered into for profit. Individuals also are allowed to deduct losses that are the result of a casualty, but only if the casualty occurs in a Federally declared disaster area. Casualty losses include, but are not limited to, those caused by fire, storm, shipwreck, and theft (see Chapter 7). A deductible personal casualty loss is an itemized deduction (i.e., *from* AGI).

EXAMPLE 9

During the current year, Kareem encountered a series of unfortunate events. A tornado hit his personal residence in March, and he incurred a loss of $30,000; due to the widespread damage, his county was declared a Federal disaster area. In June, he sold his car to generate cash to pay his bills. The loss on the car sale was $3,500. In October, he sold 100 shares of stock in MMM Company at a loss of $2,000.

continued

---

[11]*Kennedy, Jr. v. Comm.*, 82–1 USTC ¶9186, 49 AFTR 2d 82–628, 671 F.2d 167 (CA–6, 1982), *rev'g* 72 T.C. 793 (1979).

[12]Reg. § 1.162–8.

Since the tornado is a casualty that occurred in a Federal disaster area, the $30,000 loss is potentially deductible on Schedule A (but subject to limitations). The car is a personal use asset, and the loss was not caused by a casualty, so the $3,500 loss is not deductible. The $2,000 stock loss is from an investment activity, so this is deductible as a capital loss.

6-1f Deduction for Qualified Business Income

An individual can deduct up to 20 percent of qualified business income (QBI) from a sole proprietorship, a partnership, or an S corporation. This *from* AGI deduction reduces the tax on income from proprietorships and flow-through businesses.[13] The deduction does *not* reduce self-employment income. The QBI deduction is discussed in detail in text Section 9-7 and Chapter 15; a brief overview is provided here.

In general, the deduction for QBI is the *lesser of* 20 percent of:

1. Qualified business income, or
2. Modified taxable income (taxable income before the QBI deduction, reduced by any net capital gain).[14]

Qualified business income[15] is defined as the ordinary income less ordinary deductions a taxpayer earns from a "qualified trade or business" (e.g., from a sole proprietorship, an S corporation, or a partnership). QBI does not include any wages earned as an employee, any capital gains or losses, any dividend income, or any interest income. If a taxpayer has a qualified business loss in one year, no QBI deduction is allowed and the loss is carried over to the next year to reduce QBI (but not below zero).

Simone, a married taxpayer, operates a business as a sole proprietor. The business has one employee, who is paid $80,000 during 2020. Assume that the business has no significant assets. During 2020, the net income of Simone's business [as reported on Schedule C (Form 1040)] amounts to $230,000 and her modified taxable income is $250,000.

Simone's QBI deduction is $46,000 ($230,000 × 20%).

Limit on the QBI Deduction Based on Wages and Capital Investment

In 2020, if taxable income before the QBI deduction is greater than $326,600 (married, filing jointly) or $163,300 (single and head of household), the QBI deduction cannot exceed (i.e., is limited to) the *greater of*:[16]

1. 50 percent of the W–2 wages relating to the qualified trade or business, or
2. The sum of:
   a. 25 percent of the W–2 wages relating to the qualified trade or business, and
   b. 2.5 percent of the unadjusted basis (immediately after acquisition) of all qualified property.

This limit is phased in over $100,000 (married, filing jointly) or $50,000 (all other taxpayers) of taxable income. Once a married couple has taxable income in 2020 over $426,600 ($213,300 for singles and heads of household), the W–2 wages and capital investment limitation will be completely in play. Exhibit 6.2 summarizes the limitations that may reduce or eliminate the QBI deduction.

QBI Deduction Limitation

Assume the same facts as in Example 10, except that the net income from Simone's proprietorship amounts to $500,000 and her taxable income before the QBI deduction is $600,000. Because $600,000 exceeds $426,600, her QBI deduction is $40,000, the lower of:

- $100,000 (20% × $500,000), or
- $40,000 (50% of W–2 wages of $80,000).

[13]§ 199A.
[14]§ 199A(a).
[15]§ 199A(c).

[16]In 2020, married taxpayers filing separately have a threshold amount of $163,300. In 2019, the threshold amounts were $321,400 (married taxpayers filing a joint return) and $160,700 (all other taxpayers).

EXHIBIT 6.2	2020 QBI Limitations		
Filing Status*	**Taxable Income Before the QBI Deduction**		
Married, Filing Jointly	$326,600 or less	More than $326,600 and less than $426,600	$426,600 or more
Single and Head of Household	$163,300 or less	More than $163,300 and less than $213,300	$213,300 or more
Wage/Asset Limitation	Does not apply	Limitation phased in	Limitation applies in full
Specified Services Limitation	Does not apply	QBI deduction partially allowed	QBI deduction not allowed
Does 20% of Modified Taxable Income Limitation Apply?	Yes	Yes	Yes

* In 2020, married taxpayers filing separately have a threshold amount of $163,300.

QBI Deduction Limitation

EXAMPLE 12

Assume the same facts as in Example 11, except that Simone's taxable income before the QBI deduction is $366,600.

Because Simone's taxable income before the QBI deduction exceeds $326,600 but is less than $426,600, the W–2 limit is partially phased in. Her taxable income before the QBI deduction exceeds $326,600 by $40,000. So Simone must reduce her "normal" QBI deduction ($100,000) by 40% ($40,000/$100,000) of the difference between the "normal" QBI deduction and the "limited" QBI deduction (based on W–2 wages; $40,000). As a result, Simone's QBI deduction is $76,000, computed as follows:

Normal QBI deduction	$100,000
Less: 40% × $60,000 ($100,000 − $40,000)	(24,000)
QBI deduction	$ 76,000

Qualified Trade or Business

A qualified trade or business means any trade or business *other than* a "specified service trade or business."[17] Specified services include the following:

- Health.
- Law.
- Accounting.
- Actuarial Science.
- Performing Arts.
- Consulting.
- Athletics.
- Financial Services.
- Brokerage Services.

Special rules apply to specified service businesses. In general, a trade or business is *not* a specified service trade or business if the trade or business has gross receipts of $25 million or less in a taxable year and *less than 10 percent* of its gross receipts relates to a "specified service." For a trade or business with gross receipts greater than $25 million in a taxable year, the test is *less than 5 percent* (rather than less than 10 percent).[18] And if taxable income is below the thresholds identified, a taxpayer is still allowed a partial (or full) QBI deduction. These rules are discussed in more depth in Chapter 9.

6-1g Reporting Procedures

All deductions *for* AGI are ultimately reported on Schedule 1 (Form 1040). Most of the deductions *for* AGI originate on supporting schedules. Examples include business

---

[17]§§ 199A(d)(1) and (2).   [18]Prop.Reg. § 1.199A–5(c)(1).

expenses (Schedule C); rent, royalty, partnership, and fiduciary deductions (Schedule E); and farming expenses (Schedule F). Other deductions *for* AGI, such as contributions to traditional IRAs and Keogh retirement plans and alimony payments, are entered directly on Schedule 1 (Form 1040).

Adjusted gross income appears on page 1 of Form 1040. Deductions *from* AGI (itemized deductions) are reported on Schedule A (Form 1040). The total of all itemized deductions is subtracted *from* AGI (unless the standard deduction is greater). Then the qualified business income deduction is subtracted to arrive at taxable income.

Exhibit 6.3 summarizes the reporting and flow of deductions on the taxpayer's return (Form 1040). See Concept Summary 6.4 later in the chapter for the classification of deductions as *for* AGI or *from* AGI.

EXHIBIT 6.3 Format of Form 1040

*Deductions subject to the 2%-of-AGI floor are suspended from 2018 through 2025.

6-2 DEDUCTIONS AND LOSSES—TIMING OF EXPENSE RECOGNITION

LO.2

Describe the cash and accrual methods of accounting with emphasis on the deduction aspects.

6-2a Importance of Taxpayer's Method of Accounting

A taxpayer's **accounting method** is a major factor in determining taxable income. The method used determines when an item is includible in income and when an item is deductible on the tax return. Usually, the taxpayer's normal method of record keeping is used for income tax purposes.[19] The taxing authorities require that the method used clearly reflect income and that items be handled consistently.[20] The most common methods of accounting are the cash method and the accrual method. If a taxpayer owns multiple businesses, it may be possible to use the cash method for some and the accrual method for others.

Throughout the portions of the Code dealing with deductions, the phrase *paid or incurred* is used. *Paid* refers to the cash basis taxpayer who gets a deduction only in the year of payment. *Incurred* concerns the accrual basis taxpayer who obtains the deduction in the year in which the liability for the expense becomes certain (refer to Chapter 4).

6-2b Cash Method Requirements

The expenses of cash basis taxpayers are deductible only when they are actually paid with cash or other property. Promising to pay or issuing a note does *not* satisfy the actually paid requirement.[21] However, the payment can be made with borrowed funds. At the time taxpayers charge expenses on their credit cards, they are allowed to claim the deduction. They borrowed money from the credit card issuer and simultaneously paid the expenses.[22]

A cash basis taxpayer must have actually or constructively paid the expense. A current deduction is not allowed for capital expenditures except through amortization, depletion, or depreciation over the life of the asset. An expenditure that creates an asset having a useful life that extends substantially beyond the end of the tax year must be capitalized.[23]

As Chapter 16 explains, not all taxpayers are allowed to use the cash method.[24] For example, in some cases, the taxpayer is required to use the accrual method for sales and cost of goods sold if inventories are an income-producing factor of the business. In 2020, corporations can use the cash method if average gross receipts for the prior three years do not exceed $26 million (the same as in 2019). Exceptions to the inventory reporting rules also are provided for taxpayers meeting the average gross receipts test.

6-2c Accrual Method Requirements

The period in which an accrual basis taxpayer can deduct an expense is determined by applying the *all events test* and the *economic performance test*. That is, a deduction cannot be claimed until (1) all of the events have occurred to create the taxpayer's liability and (2) the amount of the liability can be determined with reasonable accuracy. Once these requirements are satisfied, the deduction is permitted only if economic performance has occurred. The economic performance test is met only when the service, property, or use of property giving rise to the liability is actually performed for, provided to, or used by the taxpayer.[25]

EXAMPLE 13

Greg's entertainment business sponsored a jazz festival in a rented auditorium at a local college. His business is responsible for cleaning up after the festival, which took place on December 22, 2020, and reinstalling the auditorium seats. Because the college is closed over the Christmas holidays, the company hired by Greg to perform the work did not begin these activities until January 3, 2021. Greg's business cannot deduct the related costs until 2021, when the services are performed.

---

[19]§ 446(a).

[20]§§ 446(b) and (e); Reg. § 1.446–1(a)(2).

[21]*Page v. Rhode Island Trust Co., Exr.*, 37–1 USTC ¶9138, 19 AFTR 105, 88 F.2d 192 (CA–1, 1937).

[22]Rev.Rul. 78–39, 1978–1 C.B. 73. See also Rev.Rul. 80–335, 1980–2 C.B. 170, which applies to pay-by-phone arrangements.

[23]Reg. § 1.461–1(a).

[24]§§ 448 and 448(c)(1).

[25]§ 461(h).

An exception to the economic performance requirements allows certain *recurring items* to be deducted immediately if all of the following conditions are met:

- The item is recurring in nature and is treated consistently by the taxpayer.
- Either the accrued item is not material or accruing it in the current period results in better matching of income and expenses.
- All of the events have occurred that determine the existence of the liability, and the amount of the liability can be determined with reasonable accuracy.
- Economic performance occurs within a reasonable period (but not later than 8½ months after the close of the taxable year).[26]

The Third Circuit Court of Appeals has ruled that accrual basis taxpayers who award points to customers to use for future purchases can deduct the value of the points when awarded to the customers.[27] The IRS and Tax Court had taken the position that the deduction could not be recorded until the points were redeemed and used. In addition, the court noted that the points are recurring items and can qualify for this exception to the economic performance test if the requirements listed above have been met.

Exceptions to Economic Performance Rules

Marco, an accrual basis, calendar year taxpayer, entered into a monthly maintenance contract during the year. He makes a monthly accrual at the end of every month for this service and pays the fee sometime between the first and fifteenth of the following month when services are performed. The amount involved is immaterial, and all of the other tests are met.

The December 2020 accrual is deductible in 2020 even though the service is performed on January 12, 2021.

EXAMPLE 14

Rita, an accrual basis, calendar year taxpayer, shipped merchandise sold on December 30, 2020, via Greyhound Van Lines on January 3, 2021, and paid the freight charges at that time.

Because Rita reported the sale of the merchandise in 2020, the shipping charge should also be deductible in 2020. This procedure results in a better matching of income and expenses.

EXAMPLE 15

Reserves for estimated expenses such as warranties and bad debts are often deducted for financial accounting purposes before the specific expense is identified. Generally, these reserves are not allowed for tax purposes because the economic performance test cannot be satisfied.

Blackbird Airlines is required by Federal law to test its engines after 3,000 flying hours. Aircraft cannot return to flight until the tests have been conducted. An unrelated aircraft maintenance company does all of the company's tests for $1,500 per engine.

For financial reporting purposes, the company accrues an expense based upon $0.50 per hour of flight and credits an allowance account. The actual amounts paid for maintenance are offset against the allowance account.

For tax purposes, the economic performance test is not satisfied until the work has been done. Therefore, the reserve method cannot be used for tax purposes.

EXAMPLE 16

---

[26]§ 461(h)(3)(A).

[27]*Giant Eagle, Inc.*, 822 F.3d 666 117 AFTR 2d 2016–1476 (CA–3, 2016), *rev'g* T.C.Memo. 2014–146. Also see IRS Action on Decision 2016–03.

6-2d Prepaid Expenses—The "12-Month Rule"

A taxpayer doesn't have to capitalize amounts paid to create a benefit that doesn't extend beyond the earlier of (1) 12 months after the first date on which the taxpayer realized the benefit or (2) the end of the tax year following the tax year in which the payment was made (the "12-month rule").[28] Although this rule applies to both cash and accrual method taxpayers, accrual method taxpayers cannot claim a deduction unless economic performance has occurred.[29]

"12-Month Rule"

On November 1, 2020, Nada, a calendar year and cash basis taxpayer, pays $6,000 for a one-year premium on a catastrophic liability policy that takes effect December 15, 2020. Nada will receive a benefit from this policy from December 15, 2020, through December 14, 2021. Her benefit does not extend beyond 12 months after the benefit begins on December 15. It also does not extend beyond the end of 2021. Therefore, this payment satisfies the requirements of the 12-month rule and Nada can deduct the $6,000 in 2020.

Assume the same facts as in Example 17, except that the benefit from the policy runs from February 1, 2021, through January 31, 2022. Nada's benefit now extends beyond the end of the tax year following the tax year in which the payment was made (December 31, 2021), so the 12-month rule requirements are not met. Nada must capitalize the $6,000 payment in 2020 and amortize it over the benefit period.

6-2e Time Value of Tax Deductions

Both the time value of money and marginal tax rate changes must be considered when an expense can be paid and deducted in either of two years. Cash basis taxpayers often have the choice to pay expenses at the end of the current year or at the beginning of the following year. In view of the time value of money, a tax deduction this year may be worth more than the same deduction next year. However, accelerating the payment may not be advantageous if the taxpayer's marginal tax rate is higher in the following year. Before accelerating a payment, the taxpayer also needs to forecast future cash flow to ensure that an early payment makes sense.

Rita pledged $50,000 to her church's special building fund. She can make the contribution on December 31, 2020, or January 1, 2021. Rita is in the 24% tax bracket in 2020 and in the 35% bracket in 2021. She itemizes her deductions in both years. Assume that Rita's discount rate is 5%. If she takes the deduction in 2021, she saves $4,667 ($16,667 − $12,000). Even though the tax savings from a January 1, 2021 contribution won't be realized until her 2021 tax return is filed, the increase in her deduction due to her increased marginal tax rates overcomes the time value of money consequences. See Table G-2 in Appendix G.

	2020	2021
Contribution	$50,000	$50,000
Tax bracket	× 0.24	× 0.35
Tax savings	$12,000	$17,500
Discounted @ 5%	×1.0000	×0.9524
Savings in present value	$12,000	$16,667

If tax rates are changing between two years, there are several areas in which taxpayers may have discretion as to which year to make a payment to achieve tax savings. Examples include certain alimony payments (see Chapter 4), assets purchased and expensed under § 179 or additional first-year (bonus) depreciation (see Chapter 8), home mortgage interest, and charitable contributions (see Chapter 10). Always remember to consider the time value of money in the analysis.

---

[28]Reg. § 1.263(a)–4(f).   [29]Reg. § 1.263(a)–4(f)(6).

6-3 **DISALLOWANCE POSSIBILITIES**

Certain types of expenses are disallowed by the tax law. Without these restrictions, taxpayers might attempt to deduct items that, in reality, are personal expenditures. For example, specific tax rules are provided to determine whether an expense is for trade or business purposes or is related to a personal hobby.

6-3a **Public Policy Limitation**

Payments considered to be in violation of public policy are not deductible. In addition, any payment to a governmental entity is not deductible. This provision does not apply to payments that are restitution for damage caused by the taxpayer or payments for taxes paid.[30]

Justification for Denying Deductions

The courts developed the principle that a payment in violation of public policy is not a necessary expense and is not deductible.[31] Allowing a deduction would, in effect, be indirectly subsidizing a taxpayer's wrongdoing. The following expenses, which are considered contrary to public policy, are not deductible:

- Bribes and kickbacks, including those associated with Medicare or Medicaid (in the case of foreign bribes and kickbacks, only if the payments violate the U.S. Foreign Corrupt Practices Act of 1977).
- Fines and penalties paid to a government for violation of law.
- Two-thirds of the treble damage payments made to claimants resulting from violation of the antitrust law.[32]

LO.3

Apply the Internal Revenue Code deduction disallowance provisions associated with the following: public policy limitations, political activities, excessive executive compensation, investigation of business opportunities, hobby losses, vacation home rentals, payment of others' expenses, personal expenditures, capital expenditures, related-party transactions, business interest expense, and expenses related to tax-exempt income.

The Big Picture

EXAMPLE 20

Refer to the facts of *The Big Picture* on p. 6-1. Dr. Payne had not instituted proper procedures for disposing of medical waste from his laboratory. During the current tax year, he was fined $3,000 by the city. Dr. Payne believes the fine should be deducted as an ordinary business expense.

However, because the fine was due to a violation of public policy and fines are disallowed, the $3,000 is not deductible.

To be disallowed, a bribe or kickback must be illegal under either Federal or state law and must also subject the payor to a criminal penalty or the loss of a license or privilege to engage in a trade or business. For a bribe or kickback that is illegal under state law, a deduction is denied if the state law is generally enforced.

EXAMPLE 21

During the year, Jean-Paul, an insurance salesperson, paid $5,000 to Karen, a real estate broker. The payment represented 20% of the commissions Jean-Paul earned from customers referred by Karen. Under state law, the splitting of commissions by an insurance salesperson is an act of misconduct that could warrant a revocation of the salesperson's license.

Jean-Paul's $5,000 payments to Karen are not deductible if the state law is generally enforced.

Legal Expenses Incurred in Defense of Civil or Criminal Penalties

To deduct legal expenses, the taxpayer must be able to show that the origin and character of the claim are directly related to (1) a trade or business or (2) an income-producing activity. Personal legal expenses are not deductible. As a result, legal fees incurred in connection with a criminal defense are deductible only if the crime is associated with the taxpayer's trade or business or income-producing activity.[33]

---

[30]§ 162(f)(1).

[31]*Tank Truck Rentals, Inc. v. Comm.*, 58–1 USTC ¶9366, 1 AFTR 2d 1154, 78 S.Ct. 507 (USSC, 1958).

[32]§§ 162(c), (f), and (g).

[33]*Comm. v. Tellier*, 66–1 USTC ¶9319, 17 AFTR 2d 633, 86 S.Ct. 1118 (USSC, 1966).

GLOBAL TAX ISSUES Overseas Gun Sales Result in Large Fines

The Foreign Corrupt Practices Act (FCPA) is intended to punish taxpayers who make illegal payments to foreign officials to obtain economic advantages. Besides such payments (usually improperly recorded as business expenses) being nondeductible for income tax purposes, serious and consistent violations can lead to the imposition of fines. Severe consequences can result from violating the bribery provisions of the FCPA, as Smith & Wesson recently discovered.

Smith & Wesson is a Massachusetts-based firearms manufacturer that wanted to begin selling firearms in India, Pakistan, and other foreign countries. As a small player in this international market, company officials decided to provide gifts to government officials in these countries to encourage them to do business with Smith & Wesson. This turned out to be a costly mistake. Smith & Wesson had profits of only $100,000 from this scheme before it was uncovered, and in 2014, it agreed to pay the Securities and Exchange Commission fines of more than $2 million. Of course, the fines are not deductible because they are a violation of public policy and disallowed under § 162(f).

Source: sec.gov/News/PressRelease/Detail/PressRelease/1370542384677#.

EXAMPLE 22

Debra, a financial officer of Blue Corporation, incurs legal expenses in connection with her defense in a criminal indictment for evasion of Blue's income taxes.

Debra's legal expenses relate to her role as an employee because she is deemed to be in the trade or business of being an executive. The legal action impairs her ability to conduct this business activity.[34] However, since these legal expenses are employee business expenses, they are classified as a miscellaneous itemized deduction (and not deductible from 2018 through 2025).

The following legal expenses are deductible *for* AGI:

- Ordinary and necessary expenses incurred in connection with a trade or business.
- Ordinary and necessary expenses incurred in conjunction with rental or royalty property held for the production of income.

Legal expenses for tax advice relative to the preparation of an individual's income tax return are a miscellaneous itemized deduction (and not deductible from 2018 through 2025). On the other hand, legal fees for tax advice relative to the preparation of the portion of the tax return for a sole proprietor's trade or business (Schedule C) or an individual's rental or royalty income (Schedule E) are a *for* AGI deduction.

EXAMPLE 23

Gabriela received an invoice from MJY LLC (a law firm) for $5,000 for the following services performed in 2020:

- $1,200 (advising on a lawsuit filed against her sole proprietorship)
- $800 (advising on a dispute with a tenant who lives in a duplex she owns and rents)
- $1,300 (fees related to preparing and filing her Form 1040)
- $1,700 (fees for preparing a will)

The $1,700 in fees for preparing her will is a personal expense and is not deductible. The $1,300 for preparing and filing her Form 1040 is a miscellaneous itemized deduction (and currently is not deductible). The balance of the legal fees ($2,000) is deductible when paid.

The $1,200 for the sole proprietorship is deducted on Schedule C (Form 1040) as a *for* AGI deduction. The $800 related to the duplex is a rental expense and is deducted on Schedule E as a *for* AGI deduction.

Expenses Relating to an Illegal Business

The ordinary and necessary expenses of operating an illegal business (e.g., a gambling operation) are deductible.[35] Although allowing deductions for illegal activity may seem inappropriate, this is necessary because the law taxes net income from a business

---

[34]Rev.Rul. 68–662, 1968–2 C.B. 69.

[35]*Comm. v. Sullivan*, 58–1 USTC ¶9368, 1 AFTR 2d 1158, 78 S.Ct. 512 (USSC, 1958).

operation, not gross revenue. However, § 162 disallows a deduction for fines, bribes to public officials, illegal kickbacks, and other illegal payments whether these payments are part of a legal or illegal business.

EXAMPLE 24

Sam owns and operates an illegal gambling establishment. In connection with this activity, he has the following expenses during the year:

Rent	$ 60,000
Payoffs to the police	40,000
Depreciation on equipment	100,000
Wages	140,000
Interest	30,000
Criminal fines	50,000
Illegal kickbacks	10,000
Total	$430,000

All of the usual expenses (rent, depreciation, wages, and interest) are deductible; payoffs, fines, and kickbacks are not deductible. Of the $430,000 spent, $330,000 is deductible and $100,000 is not.

An exception applies to expenses incurred in illegal trafficking in drugs.[36] *Drug dealers* are not allowed a deduction for ordinary and necessary business expenses incurred in their business, except for cost of goods sold.[37]

EXAMPLE 25

Assume in Example 24 that instead of an illegal gambling business, Sam was operating an illegal drug business. Also assume that the $100,000 was not for depreciation, but for the cost of the drugs sold.

Of the $430,000 spent, only $100,000 (the cost of goods sold) is deductible. Also note that to claim the cost of goods sold as a deduction, Sam will need documentation supporting the purchases—something that is not likely to exist.

ETHICS & EQUITY **State Allowed Marijuana Activity: Do Regular Business Deduction Rules Apply (or Those for Drug Dealers)?**

Cole England operates Herbal Center in Sacramento, California, as a sole proprietorship. The distribution of marijuana for medical purposes as well as nonmedical use by adults is legal in California.

This is Cole's first year of business operations, and he reports the following tax information:

Revenues	$200,000
Cost of goods sold	120,000
Other business expenses	50,000

Cole reported $30,000 of net income on Schedule C this year for Herbal Center. Is this reporting appropriate?

6-3b Political Contributions and Lobbying Activities

Generally, no business deduction is allowed for direct or indirect payments for political purposes.[38] The government has been reluctant to allow these deductions since it might encourage abuses and enable businesses to have undue influence on the political process.

---

[36]§ 280E.

[37]Reg. § 1.61–3(a). Gross income is defined as sales minus cost of goods sold. Thus, although § 280E prohibits any deductions for drug dealers, it does not modify the normal definition of gross income.

[38]§ 276.

The Big Picture

EXAMPLE 26

Refer to the facts of *The Big Picture* on p. 6-1. Dr. Payne had made political contributions to the State Senate campaigns of Tom Smith and Virginia White. Dr. Payne made these contributions to encourage these senators to support a new bill that is beneficial to the state's dental profession. Therefore, he assumed that these would be deductible business expenses.

However, political contributions are not deductible, so he will receive no tax benefit from them.

Lobbying expenses incurred in attempting to influence local, state, or Federal legislation or the actions of certain high-ranking public officials are not deductible.[39] The disallowance also applies to a pro rata portion of the membership dues of trade associations and other groups that are involved in lobbying activities.

The Big Picture

EXAMPLE 27

Refer to the facts of *The Big Picture* on p. 6-1. Dr. Payne had made contributions to The Dental Society, a trade association for dentists. The trade association estimates that 70% of its dues are allocated to lobbying activities. As a result, his deduction on Schedule C is limited to $3,000 ($10,000 × 30%).

There are two exceptions to the disallowance of lobbying expenses. First, the disallowance provision does not apply to activities devoted solely to monitoring legislation. Second, a *de minimis* exception is provided for annual in-house expenditures (lobbying expenses other than those paid to professional lobbyists or any portion of dues used by associations for lobbying) if such expenditures do not exceed $2,000. If the in-house expenditures exceed $2,000, none of the in-house expenditures can be deducted.

EXAMPLE 28

The city of Florence, Tennessee, is considering spending $1,000,000 to build a sports complex that will host youth baseball and softball tournaments. Julie, who owns a local hotel, spends $1,500 on lobbying (not paid to a professional lobbyist) to persuade the five members of the Florence City Council to support the project.

The $1,500 is deductible as a lobbying expense since it meets the *de minimis* exception.

6-3c Excessive Executive Compensation

The deduction of executive compensation normally is subject to two limitations. As discussed earlier, the compensation of shareholder-employees of closely held corporations is subject to the reasonableness requirement. The second limitation, known as the millionaires' provision, applies to publicly held corporations, including foreign corporations traded on U.S. exchanges.[40]

The millionaires' provision does not limit the amount of compensation that can be paid to an employee. Instead, it limits the amount the employer can deduct for the taxable compensation of a covered executive to $1 million annually. Covered employees are the chief executive officer (CEO), the chief financial officer (CFO), and the three other most highly compensated executives. Any individual who is a covered employee after 2016 will be subject to this rule for all future years. Compensation paid to all individuals who held the title of CEO or CFO during the tax year are subject to this limitation.

In general, the $1 million maximum applies to compensation, commissions based on individual performance, and performance-based compensation tied to overall company performance. Before 2018, the $1 million limit *excluded* commissions and performance-based compensation. Contracts in place on November 2, 2017, are grandfathered into pre-2018 law as long as there are no material changes to the contract.

---

[39]§ 162(e). Before 2018, an exception was provided for influencing local legislation (e.g., city and county governments).

[40]§ 162(m).

EXAMPLE 29

Yvette became CEO of Lowe's Depot, a home supply store and a publicly traded corporation on May 1, 2020 (the date her contract was signed by Yvette and the Board of Lowe's Depot). For 2020, her compensation package consists of the following:

Cash compensation	$1,800,000
Taxable fringe benefits	100,000
Bonus from a qualified bonus plan tied to company performance	5,000,000

Lowe's Depot can deduct only $1,000,000 of her compensation.

6-3d Investigation of a Business

Investigation expenses are expenses paid or incurred to determine the feasibility of entering a new business or expanding an existing business. They include such costs as travel, engineering and architectural surveys, marketing reports, and various legal and accounting services. How such expenses are treated for tax purposes depends on a number of variables, including the following:

- The current business, if any, of the taxpayer.
- The nature of the business being investigated.
- The extent to which the investigation has proceeded.
- Whether the acquisition actually takes place.

If the taxpayer is in a business that is the *same as or similar to* that being investigated, all investigation expenses are deductible in the year paid or incurred. The tax result is the same whether or not the taxpayer acquires the business being investigated.[41]

The Big Picture

EXAMPLE 30

Refer to the facts of *The Big Picture* on p. 6-1. Dr. Payne believes that his administrative and business skills can be used to turn around dental practices whose revenues have been declining. He investigates Teeth Restoration LLC, a local dental practice that is for sale. Expenses paid to consultants and accountants as part of this investigation totaled $6,000. He determined that Teeth Restoration would not be a good investment, so he did not buy it.

The $6,000 spent to investigate this business is deductible as a business expense because Dr. Payne is already in the dental business. Expenses incurred to investigate new business opportunities in one's current trade or business are deductible as ordinary and necessary business expenses.

When the taxpayer is *not* in a business that is the same as or similar to the one being investigated, the tax result depends on whether the new business is acquired. If the business is not acquired, all investigation expenses generally are nondeductible.[42]

EXAMPLE 31

Lynn, a retired merchant, incurs expenses in traveling from Rochester, New York, to California to investigate the feasibility of acquiring several auto care centers.

If no acquisition takes place, none of the expenses are deductible.

If the taxpayer is *not* in a business that is the same as or similar to the one being investigated and actually acquires the new business, the expenses must be capitalized as **startup expenditures**. Startup expenses are not deductible under § 162 because they are incurred *before* a business begins rather than in the course of carrying on a trade or business. The first $5,000 of the expenses is immediately deducted. Any excess over $5,000 is amortized over a period of 180 months (15 years). In arriving at the $5,000

---

[41]§ 195. *York v. Comm.*, 58–2 USTC ¶9952, 2 AFTR 2d 6178, 261 F.2d 421 (CA–4, 1958).

[42]Rev.Rul. 57–418, 1957–2 C.B. 143; *Morton Frank*, 20 T.C. 511 (1953); and *Dwight A. Ward*, 20 T.C. 332 (1953).

immediate deduction allowed, a dollar-for-dollar reduction must be made for those expenses in excess of $50,000.[43] An election can be made by the taxpayer not to deduct or amortize any portion of the startup costs. In that case, this intangible asset will remain on the balance sheet until the business is sold.

EXAMPLE

32

Dasha owns and operates 10 restaurants located in various cities throughout the Southeast. She travels to Atlanta to discuss the acquisition of an auto dealership. In addition, she incurs legal and accounting costs associated with the potential acquisition. After incurring total investigation costs of $52,000, she acquires the auto dealership on October 1, 2020.

Dasha may immediately deduct $3,000 [$5,000 − ($52,000 − $50,000)] and amortize the balance of $49,000 ($52,000 − $3,000) over a period of 180 months. For calendar year 2020, therefore, Dasha can deduct $3,817 [$3,000 + ($49,000 × 3/180)].

Concept Summary 6.1 depicts the tax rules related to the costs involved in investigating a business.

Concept Summary 6.1

Costs of Investigating a Business

Are the investigation expenses for a business that the taxpayer either acquires or commences?

Yes → Is the taxpayer already in the same or a similar business?
- Yes → Deduct
- No → Deduct up to $5,000 (amortize portion not deducted over a 180-month period)

No → Is the taxpayer already in the same or a similar business?
- Yes → Deduct
- No → Not deductible

6-3e **Hobby Losses**

Business or investment expenses are deductible only if the taxpayer can show that the activity was entered into for the purpose of making a profit. Certain activities can have attributes that make it difficult to determine if the primary motivation for the activity is to make a profit or is for personal pleasure. Examples include raising horses and operating a farm used as a weekend residence.

Although personal losses are not deductible, losses attributable to profit-seeking activities may be deducted and used to offset a taxpayer's other income. Activities that have both personal and profit-seeking motives are classified as hobbies, and the tax law limits the deductibility of hobby losses.

The income and deductions from a hobby are reported separately on the tax return. The revenue for the hobby is always reported as other income [line 8 of Schedule 1 (Form 1040)]. The deductions (and how they are reported) are discussed in more detail below.

[43]§ 195(b).

General Rules

If an individual can show that an activity has been conducted with the intent to earn a profit, losses from the activity are fully deductible (and reported, along with any income, on Schedule C). The hobby loss rules apply only if the activity is *not* engaged in for profit. Hobby expenses are deductible only to the extent of hobby income.[44]

The Regulations indicate that the following nine factors should be considered in determining whether an activity is profit-seeking or is a hobby:[45]

- Whether the activity is conducted in a businesslike manner.
- The expertise of the taxpayers or their advisers.
- The time and effort expended.
- The expectation that the assets of the activity will appreciate in value.
- The taxpayer's previous success in conducting similar activities.
- The history of income or losses from the activity.
- The relationship of profits earned to losses incurred.
- The financial status of the taxpayer (e.g., if the taxpayer does not have substantial amounts of other income, this may indicate that the activity is engaged in for profit).
- Elements of personal pleasure or recreation in the activity.

Whether an activity is profit-seeking or a hobby does not depend on the presence or absence of one of these factors. Rather, the decision is a subjective one that is based on an analysis of all of the facts and circumstances. Exhibit 6.4 provides a list of the common activities that may likely be treated as hobbies. Concept Summary 6.2 provides more details on the nature of the nine factors identified in the Regulations.

Presumptive Rule of § 183

The Code provides a rebuttable presumption that an activity is profit-seeking if the activity shows a profit in at least three of the previous five tax years.[46] If the activity involves horses, a profit in at least two of the previous seven tax years meets the presumptive rule. If these profitability tests are met, the activity is presumed to be a trade or business rather than a personal hobby. If this is the case, the IRS must prove that the activity is personal rather than trade- or business-related. In all circumstances, the history of profits and losses is just one of the factors used in determining whether the activity is a hobby or business.

EXAMPLE 33

Camille and Walter are married taxpayers who enjoy a busy lifestyle. Camille, who is an executive for a large corporation, is paid a salary of $800,000. Walter is a collector of antiques. Several years ago he opened an antique shop in a local shopping center and spends most of his time buying and selling antiques. He occasionally earns a small profit from this activity but more frequently incurs substantial losses. If Walter's losses are business-related, they are fully deductible against Camille's salary income on a joint return. In resolving this issue, consider the following:

- Initially determine whether Walter's antique activity has met the three-out-of-five years profit test.

- If the presumption is not met, the activity may nevertheless qualify as a business if Walter can show that the intent is to engage in a profit-seeking activity. It is not necessary to show actual profits.

- Determine if the operation is for profit, using the nine criteria prescribed in the Regulations listed previously.

---

[44]§ 183(b)(2).

[45]Reg. §§ 1.183–2(b)(1) through (9).

[46]§ 183(d).

EXHIBIT 6.4	Common Activities Classified as Hobbies

Airplane Charter	Entertainers	Photography
Artists	Farming	Rentals
Auto Racing	Fishing	Stamp Collecting
Bowling	Gambling	Writing
Craft Sales	Horse Breeding	Yacht Charter
Direct Sales	Horse Racing	
Dog Breeding	Motorcross Racing	

Source: Internal Revenue Service Audit Technique Guide: IRC § 183: Activities Not Engaged in For Profit (Revised June 2009).

Concept Summary 6.2

Common Questions from the IRS Concerning Hobbies/Businesses with Losses

Whether the activity is conducted in a businesslike manner.

- Is there a written business plan?
- Is there business insurance? Is it covered in the company name?
- Are books and records maintained for the business?
- Is there a business license to operate?

The expertise of the taxpayers or their advisers.

- Does the taxpayer have any relevant education?
- Did the taxpayer prepare for the activity by conducting research or an extensive study of its accepted business, economic, and scientific practices?

The time and effort expended.

- How many hours are spent on this activity per week? Per month? Per year? Per season?
- Who is involved with the day-to-day business operations?

The expectation that the assets of the activity will appreciate in value.

- Were the assets held prior to starting the business?
- Has anyone ever offered to buy any of the assets?

The taxpayer's previous success in conducting similar activities.

- In what other activities has the taxpayer had previous success?
- Was the business ultimately profitable?

The history of income or losses from the activity.

- Is there a trend toward profitability?
- Did the taxpayer change operating methods, adopt new techniques, or abandon nonprofitable methods in a manner consistent with intent to improve profitability?

The relationship of profits earned to losses incurred.

- Is this a highly speculative business?
- What amount of investment has the taxpayer made in the business?

The financial status of the taxpayer.

- Does the taxpayer have substantial income or capital (e.g., investments) from other sources?
- Are there other economic reasons for the taxpayer to be engaged in the activity (e.g., reduced property taxes for farmland, low-interest loans, or federal grants)?

Elements of personal pleasure or recreation in the activity.

- Are elements of fun or recreation generally associated with it by the taxpayer, by members of the taxpayer's family, or by the taxpayer's friends?
- If there are any personal benefits to being in this business, are they substantial?

Source: Internal Revenue Service Audit Technique Guide: IRC § 183: Activities Not Engaged in For Profit (Revised June 2009).

Determining the Amount of the Deduction

If an activity is a hobby, the expenses are deductible only to the extent of the gross income from the hobby. These expenses must be deducted in the following order:

1. Amounts deductible under other Code sections without regard to the nature of the activity, such as property taxes and home mortgage interest.

2. Amounts deductible under other Code sections if the activity had been engaged in for profit, but only if those amounts do not affect adjusted basis (e.g., maintenance, utilities, and supplies).
3. Amounts for depreciation, amortization, and depletion.[47]

From 2018 through 2025, *miscellaneous itemized deductions are not deductible.* Since property taxes and mortgage interest are deductible without the hobby revenue, the net effect is that the taxpayer is taxed on all of the revenue from the hobby.

EXAMPLE 34

Stefan, the vice president of an oil company, has AGI of $80,000. He decides to pursue painting in his spare time. He uses a home studio comprising 10% of the home's square footage. During 2020, Stefan incurs the following expenses:

Frames	$ 1,800
Art supplies	900
Fees paid to models	4,000
Home studio expenses:	
Total home property taxes	2,000
Total home mortgage interest	10,000
Total home maintenance and utilities	4,600
Calculated depreciation on 10% of home	500

During the year, Stefan sold paintings for a total of $8,660. If the activity is held to be a hobby, Stefan would determine his potential deductions under the hobby loss rules as follows:

Gross income		$ 8,660
Deduct: Property taxes and mortgage interest (10% of $12,000)		(1,200)
Remainder		$ 7,460
Deduct: Frames	$1,800	
Art supplies	900	
Models' fees	4,000	
Maintenance and utilities (10%)	460	(7,160)
Remainder		$ 300
Deduct: Depreciation ($500, but limited to $300)		(300)
Net income		$ –0–

Outcome: Stefan includes the $8,660 of income in AGI, making his AGI $88,660. The taxes and interest are itemized deductions, deductible in full. The remaining $7,460 of expenses are *miscellaneous itemized deductions and currently not deductible.*

Because the property taxes and home mortgage interest are deductible even without the hobby and no deduction is allowed for the other expenses, Stefan is taxed on his $8,660 of gross income.

6-3f Rental of Vacation Homes

Restrictions on the deductions allowed for part-year rentals of personal vacation homes prevent taxpayers from deducting essentially personal expenses as rental losses. Many taxpayers who own vacation homes use the property for personal use during a portion of the year and rent the property at other times. For example, assume that a summer cabin is rented for two months per year, used for a family vacation for one month, and left vacant the rest of the year. The issue is how to treat expenses during the nine months the cabin is vacant. If these expenses are allowed as rental expenses, a rental loss is likely to result (otherwise, personal expenses have been converted to rental expenses). Section 280A

---

[47]Reg. § 1.183–1(b)(1).

eliminates this treatment by not allowing a loss for property that is not used primarily for rental purposes. Deductions are only allowed to the extent of income received.

There are three possible tax treatments for residences used for both personal and rental purposes. The treatment depends upon the *relative time* the residence is used for personal purposes versus rental use. These rules are summarized in Concept Summary 6.3.

Primarily Personal Use

If the residence is *rented* for *fewer than 15 days* in a year, it is treated as a personal residence. The rent income is excluded from gross income, and mortgage interest and real estate taxes are allowed as itemized deductions, as with any personal residence.[48] No other expenses (e.g., depreciation, utilities, and maintenance) are deductible.

Concept Summary 6.3

Vacation/Rental Home

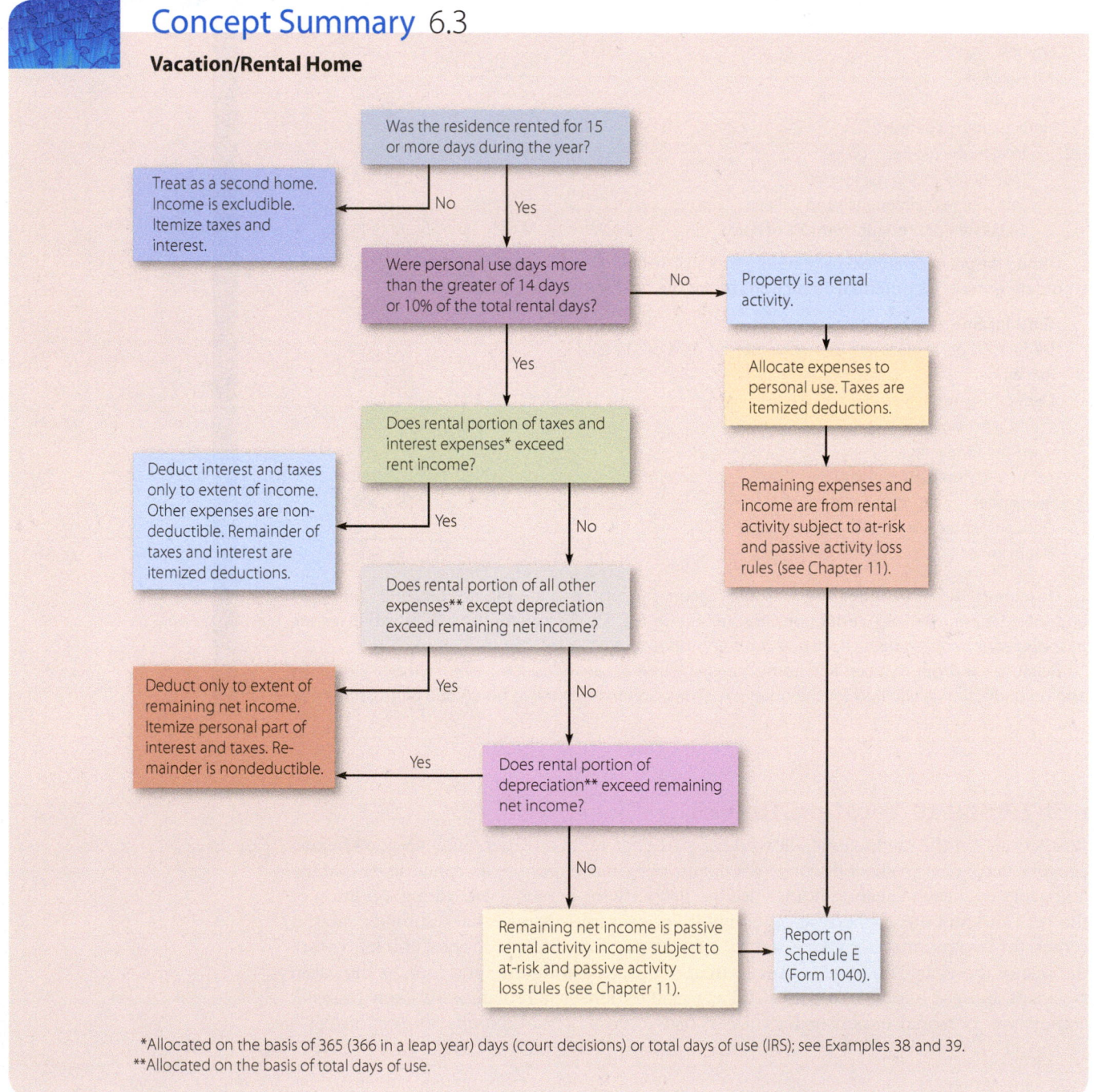

*Allocated on the basis of 365 (366 in a leap year) days (court decisions) or total days of use (IRS); see Examples 38 and 39.
**Allocated on the basis of total days of use.

[48]§ 280A(g).

EXAMPLE

35

Catherine owns a vacation cottage on the lake. During the current year, she rented it for $1,600 for two weeks, lived in it two months, and left it vacant the remainder of the year. The year's expenses amounted to $6,000 mortgage interest expense, $500 property taxes, $1,500 utilities and maintenance, and $2,400 depreciation.

Because the property was not rented for at least 15 days, the income is excluded, the mortgage interest and property tax expenses are itemized deductions, and the remaining expenses are nondeductible personal expenses.

Primarily Rental Use

If the residence is *rented* for 15 days or more in a year and is *not used* for personal purposes for more than the greater of (1) 14 days or (2) 10 percent of the total days rented, the residence is treated as rental property.[49] The expenses must be allocated between personal and rental days if there are any personal use days during the year. The real estate taxes allocated to the personal days are deductible as an itemized deduction. However, the mortgage interest allocated to the personal days cannot be deducted because the property is not a qualified residence. The deduction of the expenses allocated to rental days can exceed rent income and result in a rental loss. The loss may be deductible, subject to the at-risk and passive activity loss rules (discussed in Chapter 11).

EXAMPLE

36

Assume instead that Catherine in Example 35 used the cottage for 12 days and rented it for 48 days for $4,800. The threshold for personal use is 14 days—the greater of (1) 14 days or (2) 4.8 days (10% × 48 rental days). Because she rented the cottage for 15 days or more but did not use it for more than 14 days, the cottage is treated as rental property. The expenses must be allocated between personal and rental days.

	Percentage of Use	
	Rental 80%	**Personal 20%**
Income	$4,800	$ –0–
Expenses		
Mortgage interest ($6,000)	($4,800)	($1,200)
Property taxes ($500)	(400)	(100)
Utilities and maintenance ($1,500)	(1,200)	(300)
Depreciation ($2,400)	(1,920)	(480)
Total expenses	($8,320)	($2,080)
Rental loss	($3,520)	$ –0–

Catherine deducts the $3,520 rental loss *for* AGI on Schedule E (assuming that she satisfies the at-risk and passive activity loss rules, discussed in Chapter 11). She also has an itemized deduction for property taxes of $100 associated with the personal use. The mortgage interest of $1,200 associated with the personal use is not deductible as an itemized deduction because the cottage is not a qualified residence (qualified residence interest) for this purpose (see Chapter 10). The portion of utilities and maintenance and depreciation attributable to personal use is not deductible.

Personal/Rental Use

If the residence is rented for 15 days or more in a year *and* is used for personal purposes for more than the greater of (1) 14 days or (2) 10 percent of the total days rented, it is treated as a personal/rental use residence. The expenses must be allocated between personal days and rental days. Expenses are allowed only to the extent of rent income.[50]

---

[49]§ 280A(d) and Prop.Reg. § 1.280A–3(c).

[50]A related issue is whether a taxpayer's primary residence is subject to the preceding rules if it is converted to rental property. If the vacation home rules apply, a taxpayer who converts a personal residence to rental property during the tax year, without any tax-avoidance motive, could have the allowable deductions limited to the rent income. To prevent this from occurring, the personal use days will not cause the property to be treated as personal/rental if once the rental period begins, the property is rented for at least 12 consecutive months at a fair rental price (a qualified rental period).

EXAMPLE
37

Assume instead that Catherine in Example 35 rented the property for 30 days and lived in it for 30 days. The threshold for personal use is 14 days—the greater of (1) 14 days or (2) 3 days (10% × 30 rental days).

The residence is classified as personal/rental use property because she used it more than 14 days and rented it for 15 days or more. The expenses must be allocated between rental use and personal use, and the rental expenses are allowed only to the extent of rent income.

If a residence is classified as personal/rental use property, the expenses that are deductible anyway (e.g., real estate taxes and mortgage interest) must be deducted first. If a positive net income results, expenses, other than depreciation, that are deductible for rental property (e.g., maintenance, utilities, and insurance) are allowed next. Finally, if any positive balance remains, depreciation is allowed. Any disallowed expenses allocable to rental use are carried forward and used in future years subject to the same limitations. Note that these ordering rules for deductions are the same as for hobby expenses.

Expenses must be allocated between personal and rental days before the limits are applied. The courts have held that real estate taxes and mortgage interest, which accrue ratably over the year, are allocated on the basis of 365 days (366 days in a leap year).[51] The IRS, however, disagrees and allocates real estate taxes and mortgage interest on the basis of total days of use.[52] Other expenses (e.g., utilities, maintenance, depreciation) are allocated on the basis of total days used.

Personal/Rental: IRS vs. Courts

EXAMPLE
38

Jason rents his vacation home for 60 days and lives in the home for 30 days. The property is classified as personal/rental because it is rented for 15 days or more, and personal use (30 days) is greater than 14 [greater of 14 days or 6 days (10% × 60 rental days)]. Jason's gross rent income is $10,000. For the entire year, the real estate taxes are $2,190, his mortgage interest expense is $10,220, utilities and maintenance expense equals $2,400, and depreciation is $9,000.

Using the IRS approach, these amounts are deductible in this specific order:

Gross income	$10,000
Deduct: Taxes and interest ($\frac{60}{90}$ × $12,410)	(8,273)
Remainder to apply to rental operating expenses and depreciation	$ 1,727
Deduct: Utilities and maintenance ($\frac{60}{90}$ × $2,400)	(1,600)
Balance	$ 127
Deduct: Depreciation ($\frac{60}{90}$ × $9,000 = $6,000 but limited to above balance)	(127)
Net rent income	$ –0–

The nonrental use portion of real estate taxes and mortgage interest ($4,137 in this case) is deductible if the taxpayer elects to itemize (see Chapter 10). The personal use portion of utilities, maintenance, and depreciation is not deductible in any case.

Jason has a carryover of $5,873 ($6,000 − $127) of the unused depreciation, which he may be able to deduct in future years. Also note that the basis of the property is only reduced by the $127 depreciation allowed because of the above limitation. (See Chapter 13 for a discussion of the reduction in basis for depreciation allowed or allowable.)

[51]*Bolton v. Comm.*, 82–2 USTC ¶9699, 51 AFTR 2d 83–305, 694 F.2d 556   [52]Prop.Reg. § 1.280A–3(d)(4).
(CA–9, 1982).

Personal/Rental: IRS vs. Courts

EXAMPLE 39

Using the court's approach in allocating real estate taxes and mortgage interest, Jason, in Example 38, would have this result:

Gross income	$10,000
Deduct: Taxes and interest ($\frac{60}{365} \times \$12,410$)	(2,040)
Remainder to apply to rental operating expenses and depreciation	$ 7,960
Deduct: Utilities and maintenance ($\frac{60}{90} \times \$2,400$)	(1,600)
Balance	$ 6,360
Deduct: Depreciation ($\frac{60}{90} \times \$9,000$ but limited to above balance)	(6,000)
Net rent income	$ 360

Jason can deduct $10,370 ($12,410 paid − $2,040 deducted as expense in computing net rent income) of personal use mortgage interest and real estate taxes as itemized deductions.

Note the contrasting results in Examples 38 and 39. The IRS's approach (Example 38) results in no rental gain or loss and an itemized deduction for real estate taxes and mortgage interest of $4,137. In Example 39, Jason has net rent income of $360 and $10,370 of itemized deductions. The court's approach decreases his taxable income by $10,010 ($10,370 itemized deductions less $360 net rent income). The IRS's approach reduces his taxable income by only $4,137.

6-3g Expenditures Incurred for Taxpayer's Benefit or Taxpayer's Obligation

To be deductible, an expense must be incurred for the taxpayer's benefit or arise from the taxpayer's obligation. An individual cannot claim a tax deduction for the payment of the expenses of another individual.

EXAMPLE 40

During the current year, Carlos pays the property taxes on his son Jayden's home. Neither Carlos nor Jayden can take a deduction for the amount paid for Jayden's property taxes. Carlos is not entitled to a deduction because the property taxes are not his obligation. Jayden cannot claim a deduction because he did not pay the property taxes.

The tax result would have been more favorable had Carlos made a cash gift to Jayden and let him pay the property taxes. Then Jayden could have deducted the property taxes.

One exception to this disallowance rule is the payment of medical expenses for a dependent. These expenses are deductible by the payor subject to the normal rules that limit the deductibility of medical expenses (see Chapters 3 and 10).[53] The Tax Court has provided a different exception to this disallowance rule in the case of a mother who paid medical expenses and property taxes for her adult daughter, who was not her dependent.[54] The mother, who was not legally obligated to do so, paid medical providers and the city government directly on behalf of her daughter. The Tax Court ruled that the mother had, in substance, made a gift to her daughter in the amounts of the payments and deemed that the daughter had then paid the related medical expenses and property taxes. As a result, the daughter was permitted to take a deduction for these expenses on her return. Although this case provides substantial authority for these deductions, when planning with taxpayers, it is better to have the donor make the gift directly to the donee and then have the donee pay the expenses.

---

[53] § 213(a).

[54] *Judith F. Lang*, T.C.Memo. 2010–286, Dec. 30, 2010.

6-3h **Disallowance of Personal Expenditures**

No deduction is allowed for personal, living, or family expenses.[55] To justify a deduction, an individual must be able to identify a particular section of the Code that permits the deduction (e.g., charitable contributions and medical expenses).

ETHICS & EQUITY   **Personal or Business Expenses?**

For the last eight years, Jaynice and her family have lived in a large Victorian house in New England. In the current year, Jaynice and her husband decide to convert the home into a bed-and-breakfast. The family (including the two children and the dog) moves into the basement, which accounts for 30 percent of the square footage of the house. The basement has two bedrooms, two baths, a den, and a small kitchen. The upper two floors of the house are used for the bed-and-breakfast, which is operated as a sole proprietorship.

Jaynice hires two employees to help her run the business. Total expenses for the first year of operation are as follows:

Mortgage interest	$18,000
Real estate taxes	3,000
Salaries for two employees	40,000
Groceries for breakfast and snacks	7,000
Depreciation	10,000

For breakfast, all of the family members eat the same food that is prepared for the guests. They usually also share in the homemade cookies and cakes in the evening.

On Jaynice's Schedule C for the business, she deducts $78,000 of expenses for the current tax year. Discuss whether these deductions are appropriate.

6-3i **Disallowance of Deductions for Capital Expenditures**

A deduction is not allowed for amounts paid for new buildings or for permanent improvements or betterments that increase the value of any property.[56] Incidental repairs and maintenance of the property are not capital expenditures and can be deducted as ordinary and necessary business expenses. Repairing a roof is a deductible expense, but replacing a roof is a capital expenditure subject to depreciation deductions over its recovery period. The tune-up of a delivery truck is an expense; a complete engine overhaul probably is a capital expenditure. Adding new gravel to a gravel parking lot is a repair, but paving the parking lot is a capital expenditure because this is doing more than restoring the asset to its original condition.

All costs incurred in acquiring or producing a unit of property (UOP) are included in its cost, except for employee compensation and overhead costs. The taxpayer can elect to capitalize employee compensation and overhead costs (can elect separately or both). The cost includes all related expenditures incurred before the date the asset is placed in service, even if these expenditures would be repairs if incurred after the asset was placed in service. The cost of a UOP includes costs incurred to obtain a clean title and investigation costs.[57] Material or supplies that cost $200 or less can generally be deducted in the first tax year they are used or consumed.[58]

Capitalize or Expense

EXAMPLE 41

In year 1, Corporation Biz purchases 100 cell phones for its employees to use, each phone costing $130. Each cell phone is considered to be a unit of property. During year 1, 60 of the phones are put into use. The remaining phones are not used until year 2.

Since the cell phones cost less than $200, they are considered to be material and supplies. Therefore, 60 of the phones can be expensed in year 1 ($7,800). The remaining 40 phones cannot be expensed until they are put into use in year 2.

---

[55]§ 262.
[56]§ 263(a)(1).

[57]Reg. § 1.263(a)–3(e)(1).
[58]Reg. § 1.162–3(a)(1).

Capitalize or Expense

Jared owns a building that has 10 apartments. During the current year, one of the apartments needed a new stove. Jared paid $800 for the stove, including $75 of sales tax. He also paid $50 for the stove to be delivered and an extra $60 for it to be installed.

The stove is considered to be a unit of property, and all of these costs are included in its basis. Therefore, $910 ($800 + $50 + $60) is capitalized for the stove and this amount will be depreciated.

A single UOP includes all components that are functionally interdependent. Thus, a building includes, for example, the walls, floors, ceilings, roof, windows, doors, electrical systems, plumbing, and heating and air systems. The major exception to this rule is that if a component is treated separately for depreciation purposes, it will not be grouped into another UOP.[59]

Taxpayers can elect under the *de minimis* safe harbor election to expense outlays for lower-cost items. The election is irrevocable. This safe harbor applies if the taxpayer:

- Has written procedures in place at the beginning of the tax year that provide for the expensing of amounts below a specified dollar amount or that have a useful life of 12 months or less,

- Also expenses the items for its accounting/book records, and

- Ensures that items costing more than $5,000 are capitalized [$2,500 if the company does not have acceptable (generally meaning audited) financial statements].

The *de minimis* safe harbor election cannot be made for inventory, land, and certain types of spare parts.[60]

Freight Car Unlimited builds railroad cars and has adopted a written policy providing that any item purchased for $5,000 or less will be expensed for both financial reporting and tax purposes. Freight Car has audited financial statements.

During the current tax year, Freight Car purchases 120 laptop computers that cost $2,700 each. These computers do not have to be capitalized and will be expensed in Freight Car's current-year tax return.

Routine maintenance to keep UOPs operating efficiently is expensed, such as testing, cleaning, inspecting, and replacing parts. To be routine, the expectation is that the expenditure will be needed more than once during the asset's life. An expense cannot be treated as routine maintenance if it improves a UOP (treated as a betterment). A cost is treated as a betterment if it:

- Enlarges or increases the capacity of a UOP, or

- Materially increases the productivity, efficiency, or quality of the UOP.[61]

Qualifying small taxpayers (those with $10 million or less of average annual gross receipts in the three preceding tax years) can deduct improvements made to an eligible building property (one with an unadjusted basis of $1 million or less). The safe harbor election applies only if the total amount paid during the tax year for repairs, maintenance, improvements, and similar activities performed on the eligible building does not exceed the lesser of $10,000 or 2 percent of the building's unadjusted basis.[62]

Capitalization versus Expense

When an expenditure is for a tangible asset that has an ascertainable life, it is capitalized and may be deducted as depreciation (or cost recovery) over its depreciable life. Land is not subject to depreciation (or cost recovery) because it does not have an ascertainable life. [See Chapter 8 for a discussion of depreciation (cost recovery).]

---

[59]Reg. § 1.263(a)–3(e)(6).
[60]Reg. § 1.263(a)–1(f)(1).

[61]Reg. § 1.263(a)–3(i)(1).
[62]Reg. § 1.263(a)–3(h)(1); Rev.Proc. 2015–14, 2015–5 I.R.B. 450.

EXAMPLE 44

Stan purchased a prime piece of land located in an apartment-zoned area. Stan paid $500,000 for the property, which had an old but usable apartment building on it. He immediately had the building demolished at a cost of $100,000.

The $500,000 purchase price and the $100,000 demolition costs must be capitalized, and the basis of the land is $600,000. Because land is a nondepreciable asset, no deduction is allowed.

If the expenditure is for an intangible asset (e.g., copyright, patent, covenant not to compete, and goodwill), the capitalized expenditure can be amortized regardless of whether the intangible asset has an ascertainable life. Intangible assets, referred to as § 197 intangibles, are amortized over a 15-year statutory period using the straight-line method. See Chapter 8 for additional discussion of the amortization of intangibles.

EXAMPLE 45

Elite Fireworks purchased all of the assets of Interstate Fireworks for $2,000,000. The fair market value of Interstate's assets is $1,400,000.

The additional $600,000 paid is allocated to goodwill. The goodwill is a § 197 intangible asset and will be amortized over 15 years.

6-3j Transactions between Related Parties

The Code places restrictions on the recognition of losses from related-party transactions. Without these restrictions, relationships created by birth, marriage, and business would provide endless possibilities for engaging in financial transactions that produce tax savings with no real economic substance or change. For example, to create an artificial loss, a wife could sell investment property to her husband at a loss and deduct the loss on their joint return. Her husband could then hold the asset indefinitely, and the family would sustain no real economic loss. A complex set of rules has been designed to eliminate these possibilities.

Relationships and Constructive Ownership

Before reviewing the tax consequences of related-party sales, it is important to know the individuals and business entities that are considered to be related parties. *Related parties* include the following:

- Brothers and sisters (whether whole, half, or adopted), spouse, ancestors (parents and grandparents), and lineal descendants (children and grandchildren) of the taxpayer.
- A corporation that is owned more than 50 percent (directly or indirectly) by the taxpayer.
- Two corporations that are members of a controlled group.
- A series of other complex relationships between trusts, corporations, partnerships, and individual taxpayers.

Constructive ownership provisions are applied to determine whether the taxpayers are related. Under these provisions, stock owned by certain relatives or related entities is *deemed* to be owned by the taxpayer for purposes of applying the loss and expense deduction disallowance provisions. For example, a taxpayer is deemed to own not only his or her stock but also the stock owned by lineal descendants, ancestors, brothers and sisters or half-brothers and half-sisters, and spouse.

EXAMPLE 46

The stock of Sparrow Corporation is owned 20% by Ted, 30% by Ted's father, 30% by Ted's mother, and 20% by Ted's sister. Although Ted actually owns only 20% of Sparrow Corporation, he is *deemed* to own the stock owned by his father (30%), mother (30%), and sister (20%).

As a result, Ted directly and indirectly owns 100% of Sparrow Corporation, and Ted and Sparrow are related parties. The same outcome (100% direct and indirect ownership) results for all of the shareholders in this example.

Losses

Losses are disallowed from sales or exchanges of property between related parties.[63] A right of offset is created equal to the disallowed loss. When the property is subsequently sold to a nonrelated party, any gain recognized is reduced by the right of offset. However, the right of offset cannot create or increase a loss. Any right of offset is permanently lost if it is not used by the related-party buyer to offset some or all of the recognized gain on a subsequent sale or exchange to an unrelated party.

Use of Right of Offset

EXAMPLE 47

Ming sells common stock with a basis of $10,000 to her son, Jin, for its fair market value of $8,000. The $2,000 realized loss is not recognized, which creates a $2,000 right of offset. Jin sells the stock several years later for $11,000.

Ming's $2,000 loss is disallowed on the sale to Jin, and only $1,000 of gain ($11,000 selling price − $8,000 basis − $2,000 right of offset) is recognized by Jin on the subsequent sale.

EXAMPLE 48

Assume the same facts as in Example 47, except that Jin sells the stock for $9,500. Jin's gain of $1,500 ($9,500 selling price − $8,000 basis) is not recognized because of the right of offset of $2,000 from Ming's sale. The remaining $500 right of offset is permanently lost.

Note that the offset may result in only partial tax benefit on the subsequent sale (as in this case). If Ming had sold the stock to an unrelated party rather than to Jin, she could have recognized a $2,000 loss. However, as a family unit, Ming and Jin recognized only $1,500 of loss.

6-3k Substantiation Requirements

The tax law is built on a voluntary compliance system. Taxpayers file their tax returns, report income and take deductions to which they are entitled, and pay their taxes through withholding or estimated tax payments during the year. The taxpayer has the burden of proof for substantiating expenses deducted on the returns and must retain adequate records. Upon audit, the IRS can disallow any undocumented or unsubstantiated deductions. These requirements have resulted in numerous conflicts between taxpayers and the IRS.

For example, *specific* and *more stringent* rules apply for deducting travel, entertainment, and gift expenses, which are discussed in Chapter 9. Certain mixed-use (both personal and business use) assets are also subject to more stringent documentation rules (see Chapter 8).

Substantiation is also important for establishing the basis of an asset (see Chapter 13). An asset's basis includes all costs incurred to place an asset in service, which includes transportation, sales tax, setup, testing, unpaid property taxes of the previous owner, and other purchase costs. Basis is used to determine gain or loss on a sale of the asset and to compute depreciation for depreciable assets. The taxpayer must document all expenses included in basis.

6-3l Expenses and Interest Relating to Tax-Exempt Income

Certain income, such as interest on municipal bonds, is tax-exempt.[64] The law also allows the taxpayer to deduct expenses incurred for the production of income.[65] However, expenses related to the production of tax-exempt income are not deductible.[66] Interest on debt used to purchase or hold tax-exempt financial instruments also is disallowed.

[63]§ 267(a)(1).
[64]§ 103.
[65]§ 212.
[66]§ 265.

Expenses Related to Tax-Exempt Income

EXAMPLE 49

Sandy, a taxpayer in the 35% bracket, purchased $100,000 of 6% municipal bonds. At the same time, she used the bonds as collateral on a bank loan of $100,000 at 8% interest. A positive cash flow would result from the tax benefit as follows:

Cash paid for interest expense on loan	($8,000)
Cash received as interest income from bonds	6,000
Net negative cash flow	($2,000)

Had the deduction of $8,000 been allowed for interest expense, this would have resulted in a tax benefit of $2,800 (35% × $8,000). In that case, a positive cash flow of $800 ($6,000 + $2,800 − $8,000) would have resulted.

EXAMPLE 50

In January of the current year, Alan borrowed $100,000 at 8% interest. He used the loan proceeds to purchase 5,000 shares of stock in White Corporation. In July, he sold the stock for $120,000 and reinvested the proceeds in City of Denver bonds, the income from which is tax-exempt.

Assuming that the $100,000 loan remained outstanding throughout the entire year, Alan cannot deduct the interest attributable to the period in which he held the tax-exempt bonds.

6-3m Other Disallowances

The following expenditures also are disallowed:

- Settlements or payments, including attorney's fees, related to sexual harassment or sexual abuse if subject to a nondisclosure disagreement.[67]
- Payments for qualified transportation fringe benefits, including mass transit and qualified parking.[68]
- Net interest expense, which is limited to business interest income plus 30 percent of adjusted taxable income. Any disallowed interest is carried forward indefinitely. The limitation does not apply to businesses that have annual average gross receipts of $26 million or less during the prior three taxable years.[69]

EXAMPLE 51

For 2020, Corporation NFL has $50,000,000 of adjusted taxable income, $1,000,000 of business interest income, and $20,000,000 of business interest expense. Interest expense is limited to $16,000,000, the sum of its $1,000,000 of business interest income plus 30% of its adjusted taxable income (30% × $50,000,000 = $15,000,000). The $4,000,000 of disallowed interest expense is carried forward to future tax years.

The classification of various expenses in terms of their deductibility and nondeductibility is reflected in Concept Summary 6.4.

LO.4

Identify tax planning opportunities for maximizing deductions and minimizing the disallowance of deductions.

6-4 TAX PLANNING

6-4a Vacation Homes

As previously discussed in this chapter, homes that are used for both personal and rental use can fall into one of three categories, all of which have different tax consequences. Therefore, careful tax planning often ensures that the home is classified into the category that provides the optimal tax result. For example, if a taxpayer is

---

[67] § 162(q).
[68] § 274(a)(4).

[69] § 163(j); § 448(c).

Concept Summary 6.4

Classification of Expenses

Expense Item	Deductible		Not Deductible	Applicable Code Section
	For AGI	**From AGI**		
Investment expenses				
Rent and royalty	X			§ 62(a)(4)
All other investments			X[4]	§ 212
Employee expenses				
Commuting expenses			X	§ 262
Travel and transportation[1]			X[4,5]	§ 162(a)(2)
Reimbursed expenses[1]	X			§ 62(a)(2)(A)
Moving expenses			X	§ 62(a)(15)
Entertainment[1]			X[4,5]	§ 162(a)
Teacher professional development and supplies	X[11]		X[4]	§ 62(a)(2)(D)
All other employee expenses[1]			X[4,5]	§ 162(a)
Certain expenses of performing artists	X			§ 62(a)(2)(B)
Trade or business				
Entertainment			X	§ 274(a)(1)(A)
Meals	X[5]			§ 274(n)
Other	X			§§ 162 and 62(a)(1)
Qualified business income		X		§ 199A
Casualty losses				
Business	X			§ 165(c)(1)
Personal		X[6]		§ 165(c)(3)
Tax determination				
Collection or refund expenses	X[8]		X	§§ 212 and 62(a)(1) or (4)
Bad debts	X			§§ 166 and 62(a)(1) or (3)
Medical expenses		X[7]		§ 213
Charitable contributions		X		§ 170
Taxes				
Trade or business	X			§§ 162, 164, and 62(a)(1)
Personal taxes				
Real property		X[12]		§ 164(a)(1)
Personal property		X[12]		§ 164(a)(2)
State and local income *or* sales tax		X[12]		§§ 164(a)(3) and (b)(5)
Investigation of a business[2]	X			§§ 162 and 62(a)(1)
Interest				
Business	X[13]			§§ 162, 163, and 62(a)(1)
Personal	X[9]	X[3]	X[10]	§§ 163(a), (d), and (h)
Qualified tuition and related expenses	X			§§ 62(a)(18) and 222
All other personal expenses			X	§ 262

[1]Deduction *for* AGI if reimbursed, an adequate accounting is made, and employee is required to repay excess reimbursements.
[2]Provided certain criteria are met.
[3]Subject to the excess investment interest and the qualified residence interest provisions.
[4]From 2018 through 2025, miscellaneous itemized deductions are not deductible.
[5]50% of meals related to employee travel and other business-related activities are deductible.
[6]Subject to a $100 floor per event and a 10%-of-AGI floor per tax year. Must be part of Presidentially declared disaster.
[7]Subject to a 7.5%-of-AGI floor (10% in 2021).
[8]Only the portion relating to business, rental, or royalty income or losses.
[9]Only the portion relating to student loans.
[10]Other personal interest is disallowed.
[11]Subject to a statutory limit of $250.
[12]From 2018 through 2025, total personal state and local taxes are limited to $10,000.
[13]Subject to 30% of adjusted taxable income limitation.

planning to rent a home for 15 or more days, this will subject the net income from the rental activity to taxation. If the homeowner could rent the home for 14 days or less (possibly just one less day), then all of the rental income received would escape taxation. This strategy is particularly attractive to individuals who live in areas where major sporting or entertainment events are held if there is a lack of hotel accommodations in the area.

In addition, assume that a taxpayer intends to use a home for 150 rental days and 16 personal days. Because the personal days exceed 15 (the greater of 14 days or 10% × the number of rental days), the property will be classified as *rental/personal* and a rental loss will not be allowed. However, if the owner can reduce the personal use days by only one day to 15, then the property will be classified as *rental*, and a rental loss can be allowed (subject to the passive activity loss rules).

6-4b Hobby Losses

To demonstrate that an activity has been entered into for the purpose of making a profit, a taxpayer should treat the activity as a business. The business should engage in advertising, use business letterhead stationery, and maintain a business phone.

If a taxpayer's activity earns a profit in three out of five consecutive years, the presumption is that the activity is engaged in for profit. It may be possible for a cash basis taxpayer to meet these requirements by timing the payment of expenses or the receipt of revenues. The payment of certain expenses incurred before the end of the year might be made in the following year. The billing of year-end sales might be delayed so that collections are received in the following year.

Keep in mind that the three-out-of-five-years rule under § 183 is not absolute. All it does is shift the burden of proof. If a profit is not made in three out of five years, the losses may still be allowed if the taxpayer can show that they are due to the nature of the business. For example, success in artistic or literary endeavors can take a long time, so losses for several years in a row could occur even for a legitimate business. Also, depending on the state of the economy, full-time farmers and ranchers may have losses for several consecutive years.

Merely satisfying the three-out-of-five-years rule does not guarantee that a taxpayer is automatically home free. If the three years of profits are insignificant relative to the losses of other years or if the profits are not from the ordinary operation of the business, the taxpayer is vulnerable. The IRS may still be able to establish that the taxpayer is not engaged in an activity for profit.

EXAMPLE 52

Ashley had the following gains and losses in an artistic endeavor:

2016	($50,000)
2017	(65,000)
2018	400
2019	200
2020	125

Under these circumstances, the IRS might try to overcome the presumption that this is a business because it has profits in three of the last five years. To do this, the IRS would focus on the nine factors from the Regulations discussed in text Section 6-3e.

On the other hand, if Ashley could show conformity with the factors enumerated in the Regulations or could show evidence of business hardships (e.g., injury, death, or illness), the government might have difficulty overriding the presumption.[70]

---

[70]*Faulconer, Sr. v. Comm.*, 84–2 USTC ¶9955, 55 AFTR 2d 85–302, 748 F.2d 890 (CA–4, 1984), *rev'g* 45 TCM 1084, T.C.Memo. 1983–165.

6-4c Do Deduction Limits Affect Executive Compensation?

Only $1 million of compensation can be deducted for the CEO, the CFO, and the three other highest compensated executives of publicly traded companies. However, this limitation did not apply to performance-based compensation before 2018. This exception was removed because it was broad enough to allow publicly traded companies to pay substantial compensation to executives and still receive a tax deduction.

For example, in 2014, the CEO of Microsoft received a base salary of $918,917, which was just under the $1 million limitation. However, he received bonuses and stock incentives of over $80 million, which qualify to be deducted under the performance-based exception.

Fortune magazine recently reported that cash salaries account for only 10 percent of CEO compensation.[71] The remaining 90 percent consists primarily of performance incentives. This indicates that the $1 million limit does have an influence on the base salary of CEOs. However, because of the performance-based exception, prior law appeared to have had very little impact on the escalation of executives' salaries. It will be interesting to observe how the removal of the exception for performance-based compensation influences the type and amount of executive compensation in the future.

REFOCUS ON THE BIG PICTURE

CALCULATION OF DEDUCTIBLE BUSINESS EXPENSES AND TAX PLANNING

Of the expenses incurred by Dr. Payne, several comments need to be made. Being personal in nature, none of the $5,000 monthly draw is deductible. Nor is the amount involved subject to the reasonableness test (see Example 7). Dr. Payne is a sole proprietor and not in an employment relationship. The fine paid for violating waste control rules comes under the public policy limitations (see Example 20) and is specifically made nondeductible by § 162(f). Along the same line, the political contributions (Example 26) are made nondeductible by § 162(e). However, Dr. Payne's investigation of the practice of another dental firm (Example 30) appears reasonable and the expense incurred is deductible. The dues paid to The Dental Society are not 100 percent deductible because 70 percent of the Society's efforts relate to lobbying activities (Example 27). Although not specifically discussed in the text, his legal fees incurred in connection with a lawsuit filed by a patient appear related to his practice (Example 22). As a result, they are deductible because they are ordinary and necessary to his trade or business.

What If?

From a tax planning perspective, should Dr. Payne calculate his deductible business expenses using the accrual method of accounting or the cash method?

In Chapter 4, we concluded that Dr. Payne could minimize his Federal income tax liability if he used the cash method of accounting. If the cash method is used for reporting the gross income of a Schedule C business, the cash method also must be used for reporting the deductible business expenses that will appear on Schedule C of Form 1040.

ISTOCK.COM/DLEWIS33

---

[71]Laura Lorenzetti, "Salaries for These CEOs Make Pay for Big Bank Bosses Look Modest," *Fortune*, September 2, 2015, **http://fortune.com/2015/09/02/pay-ratio-retail-ceos-banks/**.

Key Terms

Accounting method, 6-9

Deductions *for* adjusted
gross income, 6-2

Deductions *from* adjusted
gross income, 6-2

Hobby losses, 6-18

Ordinary and necessary, 6-5

Qualified business income (QBI), 6-7

Reasonableness, 6-5

Related-party transactions, 6-28

Startup expenditures, 6-17

Vacation homes, 6-21

Discussion Questions

1. **LO.1** "All income must be reported, and all deductions are allowed unless specifically disallowed in the Code." Discuss.

2. **LO.1** Michael earned $20,000 at the K-M Resort Golf Club during the summer prior to his senior year in college. He wants to make a contribution to a traditional IRA, but the amount is dependent on whether it reduces his taxable income. If Michael is going to claim the standard deduction, will a contribution to a traditional IRA reduce his taxable income? Explain.

3. **LO.1** Classify each of the following expenditures paid in 2020 as a deduction *for* AGI, a deduction *from* AGI, or not deductible:
   a. Roberto gives cash to his father as a birthday gift.
   b. Sandra gives cash to her church.
   c. Albert pays Dr. Dafashy for medical services rendered.
   d. Mia pays alimony to Bill.
   e. Rex, who is self-employed, contributes to his pension plan.
   f. Bonita pays expenses associated with her rental property.

4. **LO.1** Classify each of the following expenditures paid in 2020 as a deduction *for* AGI, a deduction *from* AGI, or not deductible:
   a. Barak contributes to his H.R. 10 plan (i.e., a retirement plan for a self-employed individual).
   b. Keith pays child support to his former wife, Renee, for the support of their son, Chris.
   c. Judy pays professional dues that are *not* reimbursed by her employer.
   d. Ted pays $500 as the monthly mortgage payment on his personal residence. Of this amount, $100 represents a payment on principal and $400 represents an interest payment.
   e. Oni pays a moving company for moving her household goods to Detroit, where she is starting a new job. She is not reimbursed by her employer.
   f. Ralph pays $6,000 of property taxes on his personal residence and $5,000 of state income taxes.

Critical Thinking 5. **LO.1** In 2020, Larry and Susan each invest $10,000 in separate investment activities. They each incur deductible expenses of $800 associated with their respective investments. Explain why Larry's expenses might not be deductible and Susan's expenses might be appropriately classified as deductions *for* AGI.

6. **LO.1** Nanette, a single taxpayer, is a first-grade teacher. Potential deductions are charitable contributions of $800, personal property taxes on her car of $240,

and various supplies purchased for use in her classroom of $225 (none reimbursed by her school). How will these items affect Nanette's Federal income tax return for 2020?

7. **LO.1** In the determination of whether a business expense is deductible, the reasonableness requirement applies only to salaries. Evaluate this statement.

8. **LO.1** Dave uses the second floor of a building for his residence and the first floor for his business. The uninsured building is destroyed by fire. Are the tax consequences the same for each part of the building? Explain.   *Critical Thinking*

9. **LO.1** Monique owns a building that she leases to an individual who operates a grocery store. Rent income is $10,000, and rental expenses are $6,000. On what Form 1040 schedule or schedules are the income and expenses reported?

10. **LO.2** What is the "actually paid" requirement for the deduction of an expense by a cash basis taxpayer? Does actual payment ensure a deduction? Explain.

11. **LO.2** Aubry, a cash basis and calendar year taxpayer, decides to reduce his taxable income for 2020 by buying $65,000 worth of supplies for his business on December 27, 2020. The supplies will be used up in 2021.
    a. Can Aubry deduct the expenditure for 2020? Explain.
    b. Would your answer in part (a) change if Aubry bought the supplies because the seller was going out of business and offered a large discount on the price? Explain.

12. **LO.3** Clear, Inc., is a bottled water distributor. Clear's delivery trucks frequently are required to park in no-parking zones to make their deliveries. If the trucks are occasionally ticketed, can Clear deduct the fines that it pays? Explain.

13. **LO.3** Angelo, an agent for an airline manufacturer, is negotiating a sale with a representative of the U.S. government and with a representative of a developing country. Angelo's company has sufficient capacity to handle only one of the orders. Both orders will have the same contract price. Angelo believes that if his employer authorizes a $500,000 payment to the representative of the foreign country, he can guarantee the sale. He is not sure that he can obtain the same result with the U.S. government. Identify the relevant tax issues for Angelo.   *Critical Thinking*

14. **LO.3** Stuart, an insurance salesperson, is arrested for allegedly robbing a convenience store. He hires an attorney who is successful in getting the charges dropped. Is the attorney's fee deductible? Explain.

15. **LO.3** Linda operates an illegal gambling operation. Which of the following expenses that she incurs can reduce taxable income?
    a. Bribes paid to city employees.
    b. Salaries to employees.
    c. Security cameras.
    d. Kickbacks to police.
    e. Rent on an office.
    f. Depreciation on office furniture and equipment.
    g. Tenant's casualty insurance.
    h. Utilities.

16. **LO.3** Gordon anticipates that being positively perceived by the individual who is elected mayor will be beneficial for his business. Therefore, he contributes to the campaigns of both the Democratic and Republican candidates. The Republican candidate is elected mayor. Can Gordon deduct any of the political contributions he made?

Critical Thinking   17. **LO.3** Melissa, the owner of a sole proprietorship, does not provide health insurance for her 20 employees. She plans to spend $1,500 lobbying in opposition to legislation that would require her to provide such insurance. Discuss the tax advantages and disadvantages of paying the $1,500 to a professional lobbyist rather than spending the $1,500 on in-house lobbying expenditures.

18. **LO.3** What limits exist on the deductibility of executive compensation? Do the limits apply to all types of business entities? Are there any exceptions to the limitations? Explain.

Critical Thinking   19. **LO.3** Blaze operates a restaurant in Cleveland. He travels to Columbus to investigate acquiring a business. He incurs expenses as follows: $1,500 for travel, $2,000 for legal advice, and $3,500 for a market analysis. Based on the different tax consequences listed below, describe the circumstances that were involved in Blaze's investigation of the business.

a.   Blaze deducts the $7,000 of expenses.
b.   Blaze cannot deduct any of the $7,000 of expenses.
c.   Blaze deducts $5,000 of the expenses and amortizes the $2,000 balance over a period of 180 months.

Critical Thinking   20. **LO.3** Karen and Andy own a beach house. They have an agreement with a rental agent to rent it up to 200 days per year. For the past three years, the agent has been successful in renting it for 200 days. Karen and Andy use the beach house for one week during the summer and one week during Thanksgiving. Their daughter, Sarah, a college student, has asked if she and some friends can use the beach house for the week of spring break. Advise Karen and Andy on how they should respond, and identify any relevant tax issues.

21. **LO.3** Hank was transferred from Arizona to North Dakota on March 1 of the current year. He immediately put his home in Phoenix up for rent. The home was rented May 1 to November 30 and was vacant during the month of December. It was rented again on January 1 for six months. What expenses related to the home, if any, can Hank deduct on his return? Which deductions are *for* AGI, and which ones are *from* AGI?

Decision Making
Critical Thinking   22. **LO.3** Ray loses his job as a result of a corporate downsizing. Consequently, he falls behind on the mortgage payments on his personal residence. His friend Ted would like to make the delinquent mortgage payments for him.

a.   Could the payments be structured so that Ray can deduct the mortgage interest?
b.   Could the payment arrangement deny both Ray and Ted a mortgage interest deduction?
c.   Could the payments be structured so that Ted can deduct the mortgage interest?

23. **LO.3** Lavinia incurs various legal fees in obtaining a divorce. Which types of expenses associated with the divorce are deductible by Lavinia, and which are not?

Critical Thinking   24. **LO.3** Ella owns 60% of the stock of Peach, Inc. The stock has declined in value since she purchased it five years ago. She is going to sell 5% of the stock to a relative. Ella is also going to make a gift of 10% of the stock to another relative. Identify the relevant tax issues for Ella.

25. **LO.3** Jarret owns City of Charleston bonds with an adjusted basis of $190,000. During the year, he receives interest payments of $3,800. Jarret partially financed the purchase of the bonds by borrowing $100,000 at 5% interest. Jarret's interest payments on the loan this year are $4,900, and his principal payments are $1,100.

a.   Should Jarret report any interest income this year? Explain.
b.   Can Jarret deduct any interest expense this year? Explain.

26. **LO.2** Shanna, a calendar year and cash basis taxpayer, rents property to be used in her business from Janice. As part of the rental agreement, Shanna pays $8,400 rent on April 1, 2020, for the 12 months ending March 31, 2021.
    a. How much is Shanna's deduction for rent expense in 2020?
    b. Assume the same facts, except that the $8,400 is for 24 months' rent ending March 31, 2022. How much is Shanna's deduction for rent expense in 2020?

27. **LO.2** Falcon, Inc., paid salaries of $500,000 to its employees during its first year of operations. At the end of the year, Falcon had unpaid salaries of $45,000.
    a. Calculate the salary deduction if Falcon is a cash basis taxpayer.
    b. Calculate the salary deduction if Falcon is an accrual basis taxpayer.

28. **LO.2** Meghan, a calendar year taxpayer, is the owner of a sole proprietorship that uses the cash method. On February 1, 2020, she leases an office building to use in her business for $120,000 for an 18-month period. To obtain this favorable lease rate, she pays the $120,000 at the inception of the lease. How much rent expense may Meghan deduct on her 2020 tax return?

29. **LO.3** Vella owns and operates an illegal gambling establishment. In connection with this activity, he has the following expenses during the year:

Rent	$ 24,000
Bribes	40,000
Travel expenses	4,000
Utilities	18,000
Wages	230,000
Payroll taxes	13,800
Property insurance	1,600
Illegal kickbacks	22,000

    What are Vella's total deductible expenses for tax purposes?

30. **LO.3** Printer Company pays a $25,000 annual membership fee to a trade association for paper wholesalers. The trade association estimates that 60% of its dues are allocated to lobbying activities.
    a. What are Printer's total deductible expenses for tax purposes?
    b. Assume the same facts as above, except that the $25,000 was incurred for in-house lobbying expenses. What are Printer's total deductible expenses for tax purposes?

31. **LO.3** Stanford owns and operates two dry cleaning businesses. He travels to Boston to discuss acquiring a restaurant. Later in the month, he travels to New York to discuss acquiring a bakery. Stanford does not acquire the restaurant but does purchase the bakery on November 1, 2020.
    Stanford incurred the following expenses:

Total investigation costs related to the restaurant	$28,000
Total investigation costs related to the bakery	51,000

    What is the maximum amount Stanford can deduct in 2020 for investigation expenses?

32. **LO.3** Tobias has a brokerage account and buys on the margin, which resulted in an interest expense of $20,000 during the year. Income generated through the brokerage account was as follows:

Municipal interest	$ 50,000
Taxable dividends and interest	350,000

    How much investment interest can Tobias deduct?

Problems

33. **LO.1** Amos is a self-employed tax attorney. He and Monica, his employee, attend a tax conference in Dallas sponsored by the American Institute of CPAs. The following expenses are incurred during the trip:

	Amos	Monica
Conference registration	$ 900	$900
Airfare	1,200	700
Taxi fares	100	–0–
Lodging in Dallas	750	300

a. Amos pays for all of these expenses. Calculate the effect of these expenses on Amos's AGI.

b. Would your answer to part (a) change if the American Bar Association had sponsored the conference? Explain.

Decision Making

Critical Thinking

34. **LO.1** Daniel, age 38, is single and has the following income and expenses in 2020:

Salary income	$60,000
Net rent income	6,000
Dividend income	3,500
Payment of alimony (divorce finalized in March 2019)	12,000
Mortgage interest on residence	9,900
Property tax on residence	1,200
Contribution to traditional IRA	5,000
Contribution to United Church	2,100
Loss on the sale of real estate (held for investment)	2,000
Medical expenses	3,250
State income tax	300
Federal income tax	7,000

a. Calculate Daniel's AGI.

b. Should Daniel itemize his deductions *from* AGI or take the standard deduction? Explain.

Critical Thinking

35. **LO.1** Janice, age 32, earns $50,000 working in 2020. She has no other income. Her medical expenses for the year total $4,000. During the year, she suffers a casualty loss of $7,500 when her apartment is damaged by flood waters (part of a Federally declared disaster area). Janice contributes $10,000 to her church. On the advice of her friend, Janice is trying to decide whether to contribute $1,000 to a traditional IRA. What effect would the IRA contribution have on Janice's itemized deductions?

36. **LO.1** A list of the items that Faith sold and the losses she incurred during the current tax year is as follows:

Yellow, Inc. stock	$ 1,600
Faith's personal use SUV	8,000
Faith's personal residence	10,000
City of Newburyport bonds	900

She also had a theft loss of $1,500 on her uninsured business use car. Calculate Faith's deductible losses.

37. **LO.1** Suzanne, a single taxpayer, operates a printing business as a sole proprietor. The business has two employees who are paid a total of $90,000 during 2020.

Assume that the business has no significant assets. During 2020, the business generates $150,000 of income and Suzanne's taxable income before the QBI deduction is $155,000.

a. What is Suzanne's qualified business income deduction?

b. What is Suzanne's qualified business income deduction if the facts are the same except that the business income is $250,000 and Suzanne's taxable income before the QBI deduction is $270,000?

38. **LO.2** Duck, an accrual basis corporation, sponsored a rock concert on December 29, 2020. Gross receipts were $300,000. The following expenses were incurred and paid as indicated:

Critical Thinking

Expense		Payment Date
Rental of coliseum	$ 25,000	December 21, 2020
Cost of goods sold:		
Food	30,000	December 30, 2020
Souvenirs	60,000	December 30, 2020
Performers	100,000	January 5, 2021
Cleaning of coliseum	10,000	February 1, 2021

Because the coliseum was not scheduled to be used again until January 15, the company with which Duck had contracted did not perform the cleanup until January 8–10, 2021.

a. Calculate Duck's net income from the concert for tax purposes for 2020.

b. Using the present value tables in Appendix G, what is the true cost to Duck if it had to defer the $100,000 deduction for the performers until 2021? Assume a 5% discount rate and a 21% marginal tax rate in 2020 and 2021.

39. **LO.3** Fynn incurred and paid the following expenses during 2020:

• $50 for a ticket for running a red light while he was commuting to work.
• $100 for a ticket for parking in a handicapped parking space.
• $200 to an attorney to represent him in traffic court as to the two tickets.
• $500 to an attorney to draft an agreement with a tenant for a one-year lease on an apartment that Fynn owns.
• $1,000 to an attorney to negotiate a reduction in his child support payments.
• $2,500 to an attorney to negotiate a reduction in his qualified alimony payments to a former spouse.

Calculate the amount of Fynn's deductible expenses.

40. **LO.3** Trevor, a friend of yours from high school, works as a server at the ST Café. He asks you to help him prepare his Federal income tax return. When you inquire about why his bank deposits substantially exceed his tip income, he confides to you that he is a bookie on the side. Trevor then provides you with the following documented income and expenses for the year:

Tip income	$16,000
Gambling income	52,000
Gambling expenses	
Payouts to winners	29,000
Employee compensation	8,000
Bribe to police officer who is aware of Trevor's bookie activity	7,500

a. How will these items affect Trevor's AGI (ignore the impact of self-employment taxes)?

b. His taxable income (ignore the impact of self-employment taxes)?

Decision Making
Critical Thinking
Communications

41. **LO.3, 4** Amber, a publicly held corporation, currently pays its president an annual salary of $900,000. As a means of increasing company profitability, the board of directors increased the president's compensation effective January 1, 2017, with a performance-based compensation program. This program increased the president's compensation by $300,000 in 2017 and $350,000 in 2018 and 2019. Her compensation under this performance-based compensation program is expected to remain at $350,000 in 2020. Prepare a letter to Amber's board of directors that identifies the amount of compensation that will be deductible by Amber in 2020 and explains whether any changes should be made to the president's compensation plan in 2020. Address the letter to the board chairperson, Angela Riddle, whose address is 100 James Tower, Cleveland, OH 44106.

42. **LO.3** Henrietta, the owner of a very successful hotel chain in the Southeast, is exploring the possibility of expanding the chain into a city in the Northeast. She incurs $35,000 of expenses associated with this investigation. Based on the regulatory environment for hotels in the city, she decides not to expand. During the year, she also investigates opening a restaurant that will be part of a national restaurant chain. Her expenses for this are $53,000. She proceeds with opening the restaurant, and it begins operations on September 1. Determine the amount that Henrietta can deduct in the current year for investigating these two businesses.

43. **LO.3** Terry traveled to a neighboring state to investigate the purchase of two hardware stores. His expenses included travel, legal, accounting, and miscellaneous expenses. The total was $52,000. He incurred the expenses in June and July 2020. Under the following circumstances, what can Terry deduct in 2020?

    a.   Terry was in the hardware store business and did not acquire the two hardware stores.

    b.   Terry was in the hardware store business and acquired the two hardware stores and began operating them on October 1, 2020.

    c.   Terry did not acquire the two hardware stores and was not in the hardware store business.

    d.   Terry acquired the two hardware stores but was not in the hardware store business when he acquired them. Operations began on October 1, 2020.

44. **LO.3** Jamari Peters (Social Security number 123-45-6789) conducts a business with the following results in 2020:

Revenue	$20,000
Depreciation on car	3,960
Operating expenses of car	3,100
Rent	6,000
Wages	8,200
Amortization of intangibles	680

    Jamari estimates that due to a depressed real estate market, the value of land owned by the business declined by $5,200.

    a.   Calculate the effect of Jamari's business on his AGI.

    b.   How would your answer in part (a) change if the activity was a hobby?

45. **LO.3** Alex, who is single, conducts an activity in 2020 that is appropriately classified as a hobby. The activity produces the following revenues and expenses:

Revenue	$18,000
Property taxes	3,000
Materials and supplies	4,500
Utilities	2,000
Advertising	5,000
Insurance	750
Depreciation	4,000

Without regard to this activity, Alex's AGI is $42,000. Determine the amount of income Alex must report and the amount of the expenses he is permitted to deduct.

46. **LO.3** Piper owns a vacation cabin in the Tennessee mountains. Without considering the cabin, she has gross income of $65,000. During the year, she rents the cabin for two weeks for $2,500 and uses it herself for four weeks. The total expenses for the year are $10,000 mortgage interest; $1,500 property tax; $2,000 utilities, insurance, and maintenance; and $3,200 depreciation.

   a.   What effect does the rental of the vacation cabin have on Piper's AGI?

   b.   What expenses can Piper deduct, and how are they classified (i.e., *for* or *from* AGI)?

47. **LO.3** Adelene, who lives in a winter resort area, rented her personal residence for 14 days while she was visiting Brussels. Rent income was $5,000. Related expenses for the year were as follows:

Real property taxes	$ 3,800
Mortgage interest	7,500
Utilities	3,700
Insurance	2,500
Repairs	2,100
Depreciation	15,000

Determine the effect on Adelene's AGI.

48. **LO.3** During the year (not a leap year), Anna rented her vacation home for 30 days, used it personally for 20 days, and left it vacant for 315 days. She had the following income and expenses:

Rent income	$ 7,000
Expenses	
Real estate taxes	2,500
Interest on mortgage	9,000
Utilities	2,400
Repairs	1,000
Roof replacement (a capital expenditure)	12,000
Depreciation	7,500

   a.   Compute Anna's net rent income or loss and the amounts she can itemize on her tax return, using the court's approach to allocating property taxes and interest.

   b.   How would your answer in part (a) differ using the IRS's method of allocating property taxes and interest?

49. **LO.3** How would your answer to Problem 48 differ if Anna had rented the house for 87 days and had used it personally for 13 days?

50. **LO.1, 3** Chee, single, age 40, had the following income and expenses during 2020:   Critical Thinking

Income	
Salary	$43,000
Rental of vacation home (rented 60 days, used personally 60 days, vacant 245 days)	4,000
Municipal bond interest	2,000
Dividend from General Electric	400
Expenses	
Interest on home mortgage	8,400
Interest on vacation home	4,758
Interest on loan used to buy municipal bonds	3,100

Property tax on home	$2,200
Property tax on vacation home	1,098
State income tax	3,300
State sales tax	900
Charitable contributions	1,100
Tax return preparation fee	300
Utilities and maintenance on vacation home	2,600
Depreciation on rental portion of vacation home	3,500

Calculate Chee's taxable income for the year. If Chee has any options, choose the method that maximizes his deductions.

Decision Making
Critical Thinking

51. **LO.1, 3, 4** Elisa and Clyde operate a retail sports memorabilia shop. For the current year, sales revenue is $55,000 and expenses are as follows:

Cost of goods sold	$21,000
Advertising	1,000
Utilities	2,000
Rent	4,500
Insurance	1,500
Wages to Boyd	8,000

Elisa and Clyde pay $8,000 in wages to Boyd, a part-time employee. Because this amount is $1,000 below the minimum wage, Boyd threatens to file a complaint with the appropriate Federal agency. Although Elisa and Clyde pay no attention to Boyd's threat, Chelsie (Elisa's mother) gives Boyd a check for $1,000 for the disputed wages. The retail shop is the only source of income for Elisa and Clyde.

a. Calculate Elisa and Clyde's AGI.
b. Can Chelsie deduct the $1,000 payment on her tax return? Explain.
c. How could the tax position of the parties be improved?

Decision Making
Communications

52. **LO.3, 4** Brittany Callihan sold stock (basis of $184,000) to her son, Ridge, for $160,000, the fair market value.

a. What are the tax consequences to Brittany?
b. What are the tax consequences to Ridge if he later sells the stock for $190,000? For $152,000? For $174,000?
c. Prepare your solution using spreadsheet software such as Microsoft Excel. The spreadsheet should compute the gain or loss for Ridge for all scenarios. Use the IF function to compute the right of offset.
d. Write a letter to Brittany in which you inform her of the tax consequences if she sells the stock to Ridge for $160,000. Explain how a sales transaction could be structured that would produce better tax consequences for her. Brittany's address is 32 Country Lane, Lawrence, KS 66045.

53. **LO.3** Robin Corporation is owned as follows:

Isabelle	26%
Peter, Isabelle's husband	19%
Sonya, Isabelle's mother	15%
Reggie, Isabelle's father	25%
Quinn, an unrelated party	15%

Robin is on the accrual basis, and Isabelle and Peter are on the cash basis. Isabelle and Peter each loaned Robin Corporation $40,000 out of their separate funds. On December 31, 2020, Robin accrued interest at 7% on both loans. The interest was paid on February 4, 2021. What is the tax treatment of this interest expense/income to Isabelle, Peter, and Robin?

54. **LO.3** For each of the following independent transactions, calculate the recognized gain or loss to the seller and the adjusted basis to the buyer.

a. Kiera sells Parchment, Inc. stock (adjusted basis $17,000) to Phillip, her brother, for its fair market value of $12,000.

b. Amos sells land (adjusted basis $85,000) to his nephew, Boyd, for its fair market value of $70,000.

c. Susan sells a tax-exempt bond (adjusted basis $20,000) to her wholly owned corporation for its fair market value of $19,000.

d. Sinbad sells a business truck (adjusted basis $20,000) that he uses in his sole proprietorship to his cousin, Agnes, for its fair market value of $18,500.

e. Martha sells her partnership interest (adjusted basis $175,000) in Pearl Partnership to her adult daughter, Kim, for $220,000.

55. **LO.1, 3, 4** During the current year, Robert pays the following amounts associated with his own residence:

Property taxes	$3,000
Mortgage interest	8,000
Repairs	1,200
Utilities	2,700
Replacement of roof	4,000

Decision Making
Critical Thinking
Communications

In addition, Robert paid $1,500 of property taxes on the home that is owned and used by Anne, his daughter.

a. Which of these expenses can Robert deduct?

b. Can Anne deduct the $1,500 of property taxes?

c. Are the deductions *for* AGI or *from* AGI (itemized)?

d. How could the tax consequences be improved? Summarize your recommendation in an e-mail, and send it to your instructor.

56. **LO.3** For 2020, MSU Corporation has $500,000 of adjusted taxable income, $22,000 of business interest income, and $120,000 of business interest expense. It has average annual gross receipts of more than $25,000,000 over the prior three taxable years.

a. What is MSU's interest expense deduction?

b. How much interest expense can be deducted if MSU's adjusted taxable income is $300,000?

Tax Return Problems

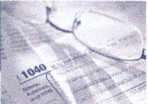

57. Roberta Santos, age 41, is single and lives at 120 Sanborne Avenue, Springfield, IL 60781. Her Social Security number is 123-45-6780. Roberta has been divorced from her former husband, Wayne, for three years. She has a son, Jason, who is 17, and a daughter, June, who is 18. Jason's Social Security number is 111-11-1112, and June's is 123-45-6788. Roberta has never owned or used any virtual currency. She does not want to contribute $3 to the Presidential Election Campaign Fund.

Tax Forms Problem

Roberta, an advertising executive, earned a salary from ABC Advertising of $80,000 in 2019. Her employer withheld $9,000 in Federal income tax and $3,100 in state income tax.

Roberta has legal custody of Jason and June. The divorce decree provides that Roberta is to receive the dependency deductions for the children. Jason lives with his father during summer vacation. Wayne indicates that his expenses for Jason are $5,500. Roberta can document that she spent $6,500 for Jason's support during 2019. In prior years, Roberta gave a signed Form 8332 to Wayne regarding Jason. For 2019, she has decided not to do so. Roberta provides all of June's support.

Roberta's mother died on January 7, 2019. Roberta inherited assets worth $625,000 from her mother. As the sole beneficiary of her mother's life insurance policy,

Roberta received insurance proceeds of $300,000. Her mother's cost basis for the life insurance policy was $120,000. Roberta's favorite aunt gave her $13,000 for her birthday in October.

On November 8, 2019, Roberta sells for $22,000 Amber stock that she had purchased for $24,000 from her first cousin, Walt, on December 5, 2013. Walt's cost basis for the stock was $26,000, and the stock was worth $23,000 on December 5, 2015. On December 1, 2019, Roberta sold Falcon stock for $13,500. She had acquired the stock on July 2, 2015, for $8,000.

An examination of Roberta's records reveals that she received the following:

- Interest income of $2,500 from First Savings Bank.
- Groceries valued at $750 from Kroger Groceries for being the 100,000th customer.
- Qualified dividend income of $1,800 from Amber.
- Interest income of $3,750 on City of Springfield school bonds.
- Alimony of $16,000 from Wayne; divorce finalized in May 2015.
- Distribution of $4,800 from ST Partnership. Her distributive share of the partnership passive taxable income was $5,300. She had no prior passive activity losses. Assume that the qualified business income deduction applies and the W–2 wage limitation does not.

From her checkbook records, she determines that she made the following payments during 2019:

- Charitable contributions of $4,500 to First Presbyterian Church and $1,500 to the American Red Cross (proper receipts obtained).
- Paid $5,000 to ECM Hospital for the medical expenses of a friend from work.
- Mortgage interest on her residence of $7,800 to Peoples Bank.
- Property taxes of $3,200 on her residence and $1,100 (ad valorem) on her car. $800 for landscaping expenses for residence.
- Estimated Federal income taxes of $2,800 and estimated state income taxes of $1,000.
- Medical expenses of $5,000 for her and $800 for Jason. In December, her medical insurance policy reimbursed $1,500 of her medical expenses.
- A $1,000 ticket for parking in a handicapped space.
- Attorney's fees of $500 associated with unsuccessfully contesting the parking ticket.
- Contribution of $250 to the campaign of a candidate for governor.

Because she did not maintain records of the sales tax she paid, she calculates the amount from the sales tax table to be $994.

Calculate Roberta's net tax payable or refund due for 2019. Use the appropriate forms and schedules. Suggested software: ProConnect Tax Online.

Tax Computation Problem
Decision Making
Critical Thinking
Communications

58. John and Mary Jane Diaz are married, filing jointly. Their address is 204 Shoe Lane, Blacksburg, VA 24061. John is age 35, and Mary Jane is age 30. They are expecting their first child in early 2021. John's salary in 2020 was $105,000, from which $20,800 of Federal income tax and $4,700 of state income tax were withheld. Mary Jane made $52,000 and had $3,000 of Federal income tax and $3,100 of state income tax withheld. The appropriate amounts of FICA tax and Medicare tax were withheld for John and for Mary Jane. John's Social Security number is 111-11-1111, and Mary Jane's Social Security number is 123-45-6789.

Both John and Mary Jane are covered by their employer's medical insurance policies with 80% of the premiums being paid by their employers. The total premiums were $10,000 for John and $6,200 for Mary Jane. Mary Jane received medical benefits of $7,300 under the plan. John was not ill during 2020. Mary Jane paid noncovered medical expenses of $1,300.

John makes child support payments of $15,000 for his son, Rod, who lives with Jill, John's former spouse, except for two months in the summer when he visits John and Mary Jane. At the time of the divorce, John worked for a Fortune 500 company and received a salary of $225,000. As a result of corporate downsizing, he lost his job.

Mary Jane's father lived with them until his death in November. His only sources of income were salary of $2,800, unemployment compensation benefits of $3,500, and Social Security benefits of $4,100. Of this amount, he deposited $6,000 in a savings account. The remainder of his support of $9,500, which included funeral expenses of $4,500, was provided by John and Mary Jane.

Other income received by the Diazes was as follows:

Interest on certificates of deposit	$3,500
Share of S corporation taxable income (distributions from the S corporation to Mary Jane were $1,100; assume no wage limitation for qualified business income deduction)	1,500
Award received by Mary Jane from employer for an outstanding suggestion for cutting costs	4,000

John has always wanted to operate his own business. In October 2020, he incurred expenses of $15,000 in investigating the establishment of a retail computer franchise. With the birth of their child expected next year, however, he decides to forgo self-employment for at least a couple of years.

John and Mary Jane made charitable contributions of $8,700 during the year and paid an additional $1,800 in state income taxes in 2020 upon filing their 2019 state income tax return. Their deductible home mortgage interest was $8,200, and their property taxes came to $4,800. They paid sales taxes of $2,000, for which they have receipts. They paid a ticket of $150 that Mary Jane received for running a red light (detected by a red light camera).

Part 1—Tax Computation
Calculate John and Mary Jane's tax (or refund) due for 2020.

Part 2—Tax Planning
Assume that the Diazes come to you for advice in December 2020. John has learned that he will receive a $40,000 bonus. He wants to know if he should take it in December 2020 or in January 2021. Mary Jane will quit work on December 31 to stay home with the baby. Their itemized deductions will decrease by $3,100 because Mary Jane will not have state income taxes withheld. Mary Jane will not receive the employee award in 2021. She expects the medical benefits received to be $9,000. The Diazes expect all of their other income items to remain the same in 2021. Write a letter to John and Mary Jane that contains your advice, and prepare a memo for the tax files.

Research Problems

Note: Solutions to the Research Problems can be prepared by using the Thomson Reuters Checkpoint™ online tax research database, which accompanies this textbook. Solutions can also be prepared by using research materials found in a typical tax library.

the answer company™
THOMSON REUTERS®

Research Problem 1. Gray Chemical Company manufactured pesticides that were toxic. Over the course of several years, the toxic waste contaminated the air and water around the company's plant. Several employees suffered toxic poisoning, and the Environmental Protection Agency cited the company for violations. In court, the judge found Gray guilty and imposed fines of $15 million. The company voluntarily set up a charitable fund for the purpose of bettering the environment and funded it with $8 million. The company incurred legal expenses in setting up the foundation and defending itself in court. The court reduced the fine from $15 million to $7 million.

Critical Thinking
Communications

Gray Chemical Company deducted the $8 million paid to the foundation and the legal expenses incurred. The IRS disallowed both deductions on the grounds that the payment was, in fact, a fine and in violation of public policy.

Gray's president, Ted Jones, has contacted you regarding the deductibility of the $7 million fine, the $8 million payment to the foundation, and the legal fees. Write a letter to Mr. Jones that contains your advice, and prepare a memo for the tax files. Gray's address is 200 Lincoln Center, Omaha, NE 68182.

Partial list of research aids:
§§ 162(a) and (f).
Reg. § 1.162–21(b).

Critical Thinking   **Research Problem 2.** Rex and Agnes Harrell purchased a beach house at Duck, North Carolina, in early 2020. Although they intended to use the beach house occasionally for recreational purposes, to help pay the mortgage payments, property taxes, and maintenance costs, they also planned to rent it through the realty agency that had handled the purchase. Rex is a surgeon, and Agnes is a counselor.

The beach house was in need of substantial repairs. Rather than hiring a contractor, Rex and Agnes decided they would make the repairs themselves. During both high school and college, Rex had worked summers in construction. In addition, he had taken an advanced course in woodworking and related subjects from a local community college several years ago.

During 2020, according to a log maintained by the Harrells, they occupied the beach house 38 days and rented it 49 days. The log also indicated that on 24 of the 38 days they occupied the beach house, one or both of them were engaged in work on the beach house. Their two teenage children were with them on all of these days but did not help with the work being done. On their 2020 income tax return, Rex and Agnes, who filed a joint return, treated the beach house as a rental property and deducted a pro rata share of the property taxes, mortgage interest, utilities, maintenance and repairs, and depreciation in determining their net loss from the beach home. In the current year, after examining their return, an IRS agent has limited the deductions to the rent income. He contends that the 14-day personal use provision was exceeded and that many of the alleged repairs were capital expenditures. Advise the Harrells on how they should respond to the IRS.

Critical Thinking   **Research Problem 3.** Mona viewed herself as a creative individual who had chosen to go to law school for economic reasons. Mona's undergraduate majors were creative writing and American Indian studies.

Mona was very successful as an attorney and eventually was admitted to partnership in her law firm, having an expertise in negotiating settlements involving Indian water rights.

While practicing law, Mona continued her interest in the arts. She had directed plays in high school and maintained her involvement in the theater, even during law school. She belonged to local theater organizations while she practiced law. She took several courses in filmmaking and read extensively in the area. She even took several months off from her legal practice to enroll in NYU's filmmaking program. Her enrollment in the program provided her with hands-on experience and taught her about the technical aspects of filmmaking and allowed her to meet individuals who would later work with her on her documentary.

When she discovered that her husband had similar interests, she decided to create a documentary about Way to Sing America. After acquiring the rights to all of the archival footage of Way to Sing America, she hired a video production company to film interviews that she conducted with Way to Sing America alumni (over 400 hours of such interviews). She spent weekends and nights over a three-year period working on the documentary.

Once the documentary was completed, Mona began marketing it at film festivals. At some of these festivals, her documentary received awards. At the same time, she developed a business plan, hired a bookkeeper to manage the finances, and hired an accounting firm to provide tax advice.

During this three-year period, she reported the following losses:

2017	$ 30,000
2018	400,000
2019	200,000

On her tax returns for the three-year period, in each year, she offset these amounts against her law firm income of approximately $1,000,000.

Upon audit by the IRS, the agent concluded that her filmmaking activity is a hobby and therefore the losses cannot be deducted except to the extent of the income generated.

Who is correct? Explain.

Use internet tax resources to address the following questions. Look for reliable websites and blogs of the IRS and other government agencies, media outlets, businesses, tax professionals, academics, think tanks, and political outlets.

Research Problem 4. Sarah was contemplating making a contribution to her traditional IRA in 2019. She determined that she would contribute $5,000 in December 2019, but forgot about making the contribution until she was preparing her 2019 tax return in February 2020. Use the website of any well-known IRA provider (e.g., Fidelity, Vanguard, T. Rowe Price) to determine if Sarah can make a 2019 contribution to her IRA after the tax year has ended.

Research Problem 5. The $1 million maximum compensation deduction does not seem to have deterred large corporations from remunerating their executives at very high levels. What techniques are being used to work around the millionaires' provision? Are executives taking pay cuts, or are their salaries being deferred or changed in nature due to § 162(m)? How do you think companies should respond to the changes made to this area by the TCJA of 2017?

Research Problem 6. A qualified expense is not deductible unless there is appropriate substantiation to document it. Find two websites and/or articles that provide (1) guidance on the types of substantiation required for business expenses and (2) suggestions for taxpayers on how to collect this information and organize it.

Becker CPA Review Questions

1. Which of the following is a deduction *for* AGI?

    a. Charitable contributions.

    b. Alimony paid for a divorce finalized in 2015.

    c. Tax preparation fees.

    d. Mortgage interest paid on your primary residence.

2. Which of the following is *not* a deduction *for* AGI?

    a. Alimony paid for a divorce finalized in 2018.

    b. Business rent on a self-employed business.

    c. Property taxes paid on your primary residence.

    d. One half of self-employment tax.

3. David is a CPA and enjoys playing the lottery. This year David won $10,000 in lottery scratch-off tickets. He spent $200 purchasing the tickets. Which statement is true regarding David's winnings?

    a. David must include $9,800 in gross income.

    b. David must include the $10,000 in gross income and can deduct $200 as an itemized deduction not subject to the 2%-of-AGI limitation.

    c. David must include $10,000 in gross income and can deduct $200 as an adjustment to AGI.

    d. David's winnings are not taxable.

4. Bob is a farmer and is required to use the accrual method. At the beginning of the year, Bob has inventory, including livestock held for resale, amounting to $10,000. During the year, Bob purchased livestock totaling $3,000. Bob's ending inventory was $4,000. Bob's net sales for the year totaled $17,000. What is Bob's gross profit for the current year?

   a. $9,000   c. $8,000
   b. $17,000   d. $13,000

5. The Griffins own a mountain cabin that is used for both personal and rental purposes. In the current year, the Griffins rented the cabin out for 150 days and used it personally for 50 days. Assume that the Griffins itemize their deductions. Which of the following statements regarding the treatment of the mountain cabin on the Griffins' tax return is true?

   a. 100% of the utilities for the mountain cabin for the entire year are deductible.
   b. Depreciation is deductible under all rental circumstances.
   c. Real estate taxes are deductible under all rental circumstances.
   d. The rental income received is not included in gross income.

6. The Groves own a beach house as a second home. This year, the Groves used the beach house personally for 4 months. For 14 days during the summer, the Groves rented out their beach house for $5,000 total to friends. Which statement is true regarding the taxability of the Groves' beach house?

   a. $5,000 is included in gross income.
   b. Mortgage interest paid on the beach house is deductible.
   c. All repair expenses on the beach house are deductible.
   d. Depreciation expense on the beach house is deductible.

CHAPTER 7

Deductions and Losses: Certain Business Expenses and Losses

LEARNING OBJECTIVES: *After completing Chapter 7, you should be able to:*

LO.1 Determine the amount, classification, and timing of the bad debt deduction.

LO.2 State and illustrate the tax treatment of worthless securities, including § 1244 stock.

LO.3 Distinguish between deductible and nondeductible losses of individuals.

LO.4 Identify a casualty and determine the amount, classification, and timing of casualty and theft losses.

LO.5 State and apply the alternative tax treatments for research and experimental expenditures.

LO.6 Apply the excess business loss limitation rules.

LO.7 Describe the tax impact of a net operating loss and review the effect of the carryback and carryover provisions on previous and subsequent years' taxable income.

LO.8 Identify tax planning opportunities in deducting certain business expenses, business losses, and personal losses.

CHAPTER OUTLINE

7-1 Bad Debts, 7-2
7-1a Specific Charge-Off Method, 7-3
7-1b Business versus Nonbusiness Bad Debts, 7-4
7-1c Loans between Related Parties, 7-5

7-2 Worthless Securities and Small Business Stock Losses, 7-6
7-2a Worthless Securities, 7-6
7-2b Small Business Stock (§ 1244 Stock) Losses, 7-6

7-3 Losses of Individuals, 7-7
7-3a Events That Are Not Casualties, 7-7
7-3b Theft Losses, 7-8
7-3c When to Deduct Casualty Losses, 7-8
7-3d Measuring the Amount of Loss, 7-9
7-3e Personal Casualty Gains and Losses, 7-12
7-3f Statutory Framework for Deducting Losses of Individuals, 7-14

7-4 Research and Experimental Expenditures, 7-15
7-4a Expense Method, 7-16
7-4b Deferral and Amortization Method, 7-16

7-5 Excess Business Losses, 7-17
7-5a Excess Business Loss Defined, 7-17
7-5b Losses from Partnerships or S Corporations, 7-18
7-5c Other Rules, 7-19

7-6 Net Operating Losses, 7-19
7-6a General Rules, 7-20

7-7 Tax Planning, 7-21
7-7a Small Business Stock (§ 1244 Stock) Losses, 7-21
7-7b Casualty Losses, 7-21

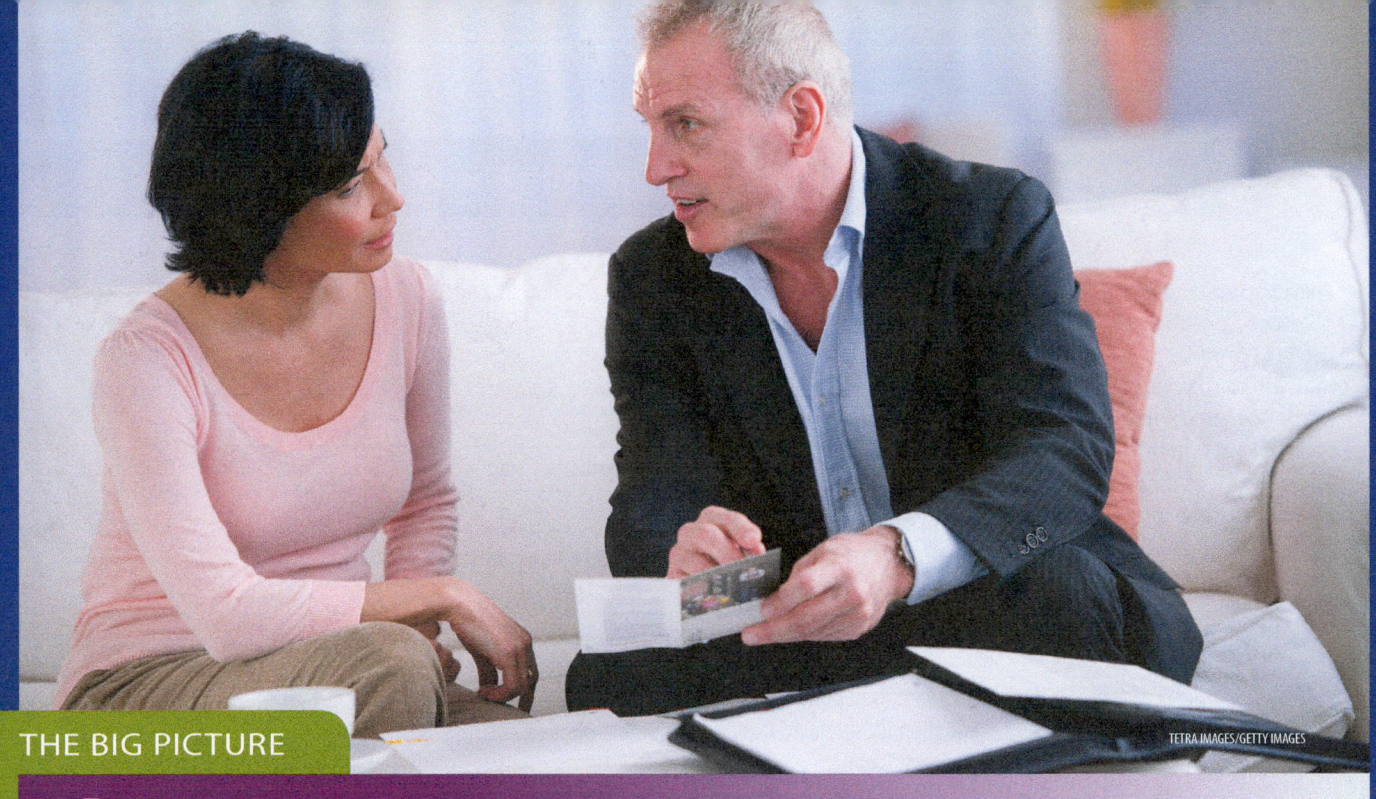

THE BIG PICTURE

LOSSES

Martha, a cash basis and calendar year taxpayer, is nearing the end of a year she would like to forget. Several years ago she loaned $25,000 to her friend Janice to enable her to start a business. Janice had made scheduled payments of $7,000 ($1,000 of this was interest) when she unexpectedly died in January. At the time of her death, Janice was insolvent. Martha's attempts to collect on the debt were fruitless.

On October 1, 2019, Martha invested $50,000 in the stock of a pharmaceutical company that previously had been profitable. However, as a result of losing a patent infringement suit, the company declared bankruptcy on May 31, 2020. The bankruptcy trustee has informed shareholders that they should not expect to receive anything from the company.

Martha has owned and operated a bookstore as a sole proprietorship for the past 10 years. The bookstore previously produced annual profits of about $75,000. Due to the continued growth of online vendors and e-books, Martha's bookstore sustained a net loss of $180,000 this year.

On September 28, 2020, a hurricane caused a large oak tree to blow over onto Martha's house. In the aftermath of the hurricane, Martha's county was designated a Federal disaster area by the President. The cost of removing the tree and making repairs was $32,000. Martha received a check for $25,000 from her insurance company in final settlement of the claim. Her adjusted basis for the house was $280,000.

On March 8, 2019, Martha purchased what she believed to be "small business stock" (§ 1244 stock) from her friend Peter for $20,000. The stock's value began to decline significantly soon after its purchase. On November 2, 2020, Martha sold the stock for $12,000.

Can you help relieve Martha's feeling of despair by making her aware of beneficial loss provisions in the tax law?

Read the chapter and formulate your response.

FRAMEWORK 1040 Tax Formula for Individuals

This chapter covers the boldfaced portions of the Tax Formula for Individuals that was introduced in Concept Summary 3.1 on p. 3-3. Below those portions are the sections of Form 1040 where the results are reported.

Income *(broadly defined)*...	$ xx,xxx
Less: Exclusions	(x,xxx)
Gross income	$ xx,xxx
Less: Deductions *for* adjusted gross income	**(x,xxx)**

FORM 1040 (Schedule 1)

> 3   Business income or (loss). Attach Schedule C .   .   .   .

Adjusted gross income...	$ xx,xxx
Less: The greater of total itemized deductions *or* the standard deduction	**(x,xxx)**

FORM 1040 (p. 1)

> 9   **Standard deduction or itemized deductions** (from Schedule A) .   .   .   .

Personal and dependency exemptions*	(x,xxx)
Deduction for qualified business income**	(x,xxx)
Taxable income	$ xx,xxx
Tax on taxable income *(see Tax Tables or Tax Rate Schedules)*......................................	$ x,xxx
Less: Tax credits *(including income taxes withheld and prepaid)*...................................	(xxx)
Tax due (or refund)	$ xxx

  * Exemption deductions are not allowed from 2018 through 2025.
** Only applies from 2018 through 2025.

ndividual deductions must be properly classified as either *for* adjusted gross income (AGI) or *from* AGI (e.g., itemized deductions). Business expenses and losses, along with expenses and losses related to rent and royalty activities (entered into for profit), are deducted *for* AGI. Most other investment expenses are deducted *from* AGI. The determination of the taxpayer's activity (i.e., whether the taxpayer is engaged in a trade or business, an investment, or a personal activity) is crucial in this classification process.[1]

Deductible losses on personal use property are deductions *from* AGI (as itemized deductions). Casualty and theft losses on personal use property are discussed in this chapter; other itemized deductions are discussed in Chapter 10.

In determining the amount and timing of the deduction for bad debts, proper classification is again important. A business bad debt is classified as a deduction *for* AGI, and a nonbusiness bad debt is classified as a short-term capital loss.

Other topics discussed in Chapter 7 are research and experimental expenditures, the limitation on excess business losses, and the net operating loss deduction.

LO.1

Determine the amount, classification, and timing of the bad debt deduction.

7-1 BAD DEBTS

If a taxpayer sells goods or provides services on credit and, later, the account receivable becomes worthless, a **bad debt** deduction is allowed only if the income related to the account receivable was previously included in income.[2] No deduction is allowed, for example, for a bad debt related to the sale of a product or service when the taxpayer is on the cash basis because no income is reported until the cash has been collected.

---

[1]See, for example, *Groetzinger v. Comm.*, 85–2 USTC ¶9622, 56 AFTR 2d 85–5683, 771 F.2d 269 (CA–7, 1985), *aff'd* in 87–1 USTC ¶9191, 59 AFTR 2d 87–532, 107 S.Ct. 980 (USSC, 1987).

[2]Reg. § 1.166–1(e).

EXAMPLE 1

Tracy, a sole proprietor, operates a business named Executive Accounting and Tax Services. Last year Pat hired Tracy to help him with the accounting for his small business. Tracy also prepared the S corporation income tax return for the business and Pat's personal income tax return. Tracy billed Pat $8,000 for the services she performed. Pat has never paid the bill, his business no longer exists, and his whereabouts are unknown.

If Tracy is an *accrual basis taxpayer*, she includes the $8,000 in income when the services are performed. When she determines that Pat's account will not be collected, she deducts the $8,000 as a bad debt expense.

If Tracy is a *cash basis taxpayer*, she does not include the $8,000 in income until payment is received. When she determines that Pat's account will not be collected, she cannot deduct the $8,000 as a bad debt expense because it was never recognized as income.

The Big Picture

EXAMPLE 2

Return to the facts of *The Big Picture* on p. 7-1. Because Martha is a cash basis taxpayer, she cannot take a bad debt deduction for any unpaid accrued interest on the loan to Janice (her friend) because the interest was never recognized as income.

A bad debt can also result from the nonrepayment of a loan made by the taxpayer or from purchased debt instruments.

7-1a Specific Charge-Off Method

In general, the specific charge-off method must be used for tax purposes when accounting for bad debts. Certain financial institutions are allowed to use the reserve method for computing deductions for bad debts.

A taxpayer using the specific charge-off method may claim a deduction in the year when a specific business debt becomes either partially or wholly worthless. A nonbusiness debt must be wholly worthless to claim a deduction.[3] The taxpayer must be able to document the fact that the debt is either partially or completely worthless. This is one of the more difficult tasks facing a taxpayer. Legal proceedings against the debtor are not required as long as the taxpayer can demonstrate that collection is unlikely.

In the case of a business debt, partial worthlessness can result in a deduction. If, in a later year, the balance of the debt is deemed uncollectible, it can be deducted. In the case of a nonbusiness debt, a deduction is only allowed in the year the debt becomes completely worthless.

EXAMPLE 3

In 2018, Ross loaned $1,000 to Josh, who agreed to repay the loan in two years. In 2020, Josh disappeared after the note became delinquent. If a reasonable investigation by Ross indicates that he cannot find Josh or that a suit against Josh would not result in collection, Ross can deduct the $1,000 in 2020.

Bankruptcy is generally an indication of at least partial worthlessness of a debt. Bankruptcy may create worthlessness before the settlement date. If this is the case, the deduction may be taken in the year of worthlessness.

EXAMPLE 4

In Example 3, assume that Josh filed for personal bankruptcy in 2019 and that the debt is a business debt. At that time, Ross learned that unsecured creditors (including Ross) were ultimately expected to receive 20 cents on the dollar.

In 2020, settlement is made, and Ross receives only $150. He should deduct $800 ($1,000 loan − $200 expected settlement) in 2019 and $50 in 2020 ($200 balance − $150 proceeds).

---

[3]§ 166(a).

If a receivable is written off (deducted) as uncollectible and then collected in a later tax year, income will result if the deduction yielded a tax benefit in the year it was taken. See the discussion and examples in text Section 5-15.

Concept Summary 7.1 provides a summary of the tax treatment of bad debts using the specific charge-off method.

Concept Summary 7.1

The Tax Treatment of Bad Debts Using the Specific Charge-Off Method

	Business Bad Debts	**Nonbusiness Bad Debts**
Timing of deduction	A deduction is allowed when the debt becomes either partially or wholly worthless.	A deduction is allowed *only* when the debt becomes wholly worthless.
Character of deduction	The bad debt is deducted as an ordinary loss.	The bad debt is classified as a short-term capital loss, subject to the $3,000 net capital loss limitation for individuals.
Recovery of amounts previously deducted	If the account recovered was written off during the current tax year, the write-off entry is reversed. If the account was written off in a previous tax year, income is created subject to the tax benefit rule.	If the account recovered was written off during the current tax year, the write-off entry is reversed. If the account was written off in a previous tax year, income is created subject to the tax benefit rule.

7-1b Business versus Nonbusiness Bad Debts

Whether a debt is business or nonbusiness depends on the role of the lender. How the borrower uses the funds is of no consequence. A <mark>nonbusiness bad debt</mark> is unrelated to the lender's trade or business either when it was created or when it became worthless. Loans to relatives or friends are the most common type of nonbusiness bad debt.

The Big Picture

EXAMPLE 5

Return to the facts of *The Big Picture* on p. 7-1. Martha loaned her friend Janice $25,000. Janice used the money to start a business, which subsequently failed. When Janice died after having made payments of $7,000 on the loan, she was insolvent.

Even though the proceeds of the loan were used in a business, the loan is a nonbusiness bad debt because the business was Janice's, not Martha's, and Martha is not in the business of lending money.

The distinction between a business bad debt and a nonbusiness bad debt is important. A <mark>business bad debt</mark> is treated as an ordinary deduction in the year incurred. In contrast, a nonbusiness bad debt is always treated as a short-term capital loss. Since net capital loss deductions are limited to no more than $3,000 per year, a taxpayer's nonbusiness bad debt deduction could have a limited benefit (see Chapter 14 for a detailed discussion). It is assumed that any loans made by a business are related to its trade or business. Credit sales to customers are a common example. Any bad debts that occur from these transactions are business bad debts.

The following example is an illustration of business bad debts adapted from the Regulations.[4]

EXAMPLE 6

In 2019, Leif sold his business but retained a claim (note or account receivable) against Bob. The claim became worthless in 2020.

Leif's loss is treated as a business bad debt because the debt was created in the conduct of his former trade or business. Leif is accorded business bad debt treatment even though he was holding the note as an investor and was no longer in a trade or business when the claim became worthless.

[4]Reg. § 1.166–5(d).

7-1c **Loans between Related Parties**

Loans between related parties (especially family members) raise the issue of whether the transaction was a *bona fide* loan or a gift. The Regulations indicate that individual circumstances must be examined to determine whether advances between related parties are gifts or loans. Some considerations are these:

- Was a note properly executed?
- Was there a reasonable rate of interest?
- Was collateral provided?
- What collection efforts were made?
- What was the intent of the parties?

EXAMPLE

7

Lana loans $2,000 to her widowed mother for an operation. Lana's mother owns no property and is not employed, and her only income consists of Social Security benefits. No note is issued for the loan, no provision for interest is made, and no repayment date is mentioned. In the current year, Lana's mother dies, leaving no estate.

Assuming that the loan is not repaid, Lana cannot take a deduction for a nonbusiness bad debt because the facts indicate that no debtor-creditor relationship existed.

See Concept Summary 7.2 for a review of the bad debt deduction rules.

Concept Summary 7.2

Bad Debt Deductions

```
                    ┌─────────────────────────────────┐
   No deduction ◄── │ Does a valid debt exist          │
   allowed      No  │ (a debtor-creditor relationship)?│
                    └─────────────────────────────────┘
                                  │ Yes
                                  ▼
                    ┌─────────────────────────────────┐
   No deduction ◄── │ Is the debt really              │
   allowed      No  │ worthless?                       │
                    └─────────────────────────────────┘
                                  │ Yes
                                  ▼
                    ┌─────────────────────┐   Yes   ┌──────────────────────────┐
                    │ Is the debt evidenced│ ──────► │ See § 165(g) dealing with│
                    │ by a security?       │         │ worthless securities     │
                    └─────────────────────┘         │ (discussed on p. 7-6)    │
                                  │ No               └──────────────────────────┘
                                  ▼
                    ┌─────────────────────┐   Yes   ┌──────────────────────────┐
                    │ Is the creditor a    │ ──────► │ Business bad debt        │
                    │ corporation?         │         │ (treated as an           │
                    └─────────────────────┘         │ ordinary deduction)      │
                                  │ No               └──────────────────────────┘
                                  ▼
                    ┌─────────────────────────────┐  No  ┌──────────────────────────┐
                    │ Is the debt created or       │────► │ Nonbusiness bad          │
                    │ incurred in connection with  │      │ debt (treated as a       │
                    │ the creditor's trade or      │      │ short-term capital loss) │
                    │ business?                    │      └──────────────────────────┘
                    └─────────────────────────────┘
                                  │ Yes
                                  ▼
                    ┌─────────────────────┐
                    │ Business bad debt    │
                    │ (treated as an       │
                    │ ordinary deduction)  │
                    └─────────────────────┘
```

State and illustrate the tax treatment of worthless securities, including § 1244 stock.

7-2 WORTHLESS SECURITIES AND SMALL BUSINESS STOCK LOSSES

7-2a Worthless Securities

A loss is allowed for securities that become *completely* worthless during the year (**worthless securities**).[5] Such securities are shares of stock, bonds, notes, or other evidence of indebtedness issued by a corporation or government. The losses generated are treated as capital losses deemed to have occurred on the *last day* of the taxable year. By treating the loss as having occurred on the last day of the taxable year, a loss that would otherwise have been classified as short term (if the date of worthlessness was used) may be classified as a long-term capital loss. Capital losses may be of limited benefit due to the $3,000 net capital loss limitation.[6]

The Big Picture

EXAMPLE 8

Return to the facts of *The Big Picture* on p. 7-1. Martha owned stock in a pharmaceutical company that she acquired as an investment on October 1, 2019, at a cost of $50,000. On May 31, 2020, the stock became worthless when the company declared bankruptcy.

Because the stock is deemed to have become worthless as of December 31, 2020, Martha has a capital loss from an asset held for 15 months (a long-term capital loss).

7-2b Small Business Stock (§ 1244 Stock) Losses

In general, shareholders receive capital gain or loss treatment when they sell stock. However, it is possible to receive an ordinary loss deduction if the loss relates to **small business stock (§ 1244 stock)**. Only *individuals*[7] who acquired the stock *from* the corporation are eligible to receive ordinary loss treatment under § 1244. The ordinary loss is limited to $50,000 ($100,000 for married individuals filing jointly) per year. Losses in excess of these limits receive capital loss treatment.

The corporation issuing the stock must be a "small business corporation."[8] A corporation meets this definition if the total amount of money and other property received by the corporation for stock as a contribution to capital (or paid-in surplus) does not exceed $1 million. The $1 million test is made at the time the stock is issued. Section 1244 stock can be common or preferred stock. Section 1244 applies only to losses. If § 1244 stock is sold at a gain, the provision is not applicable and the gain is capital gain.

EXAMPLE 9

Paulina, a single individual, was looking for an investment that would give some diversity to her stock portfolio. A friend suggested that she acquire some stock in Eagle Corporation, a new startup company. On July 1, 2018, Paulina purchased 100 shares of Eagle Corporation for $100,000. At the time Paulina acquired her stock from Eagle Corporation, the corporation had $700,000 of paid-in capital. As a result, the stock qualified as § 1244 stock. On June 20, 2020, Paulina sold all of her Eagle stock for $20,000.

Because the Eagle stock is § 1244 stock, Paulina has a $50,000 ordinary loss and a $30,000 long-term capital loss.

The Big Picture

EXAMPLE 10

Return to the facts of *The Big Picture* on p. 7-1. On March 8, 2020, Martha purchases what she believes is "small business stock" (§ 1244 stock) from her friend Peter for $20,000. On November 2, 2020, she sells the stock in the marketplace for $12,000.

Because Martha did not acquire the stock from the corporation, the stock is *not* § 1244 stock to Martha. As a result, Martha has an $8,000 short-term capital loss.

---

[5]§ 165(g).
[6]§ 1211(b).

[7]The term *individuals* for this purpose does not include a trust or an estate (but could include a partnership or an LLC).
[8]§ 1244(c)(3).

7-3 LOSSES OF INDIVIDUALS

An individual may deduct the following losses under § 165(c):

- Losses incurred in a trade or business (e.g., business loss of a sole proprietor or sale of a business asset at a loss).

- Losses incurred in a transaction entered into for profit (e.g., sale of an asset used in a rental activity at a loss).

- Losses caused by fire, storm, shipwreck, or other casualty or by theft (e.g., a residence damaged in a hurricane).

Although the terms *fire, storm, shipwreck,* and *theft* are easy to understand, what is meant by *other casualty*? First, it means that events similar to a fire, storm, or shipwreck qualify. In addition, accidental losses also qualify.

Overall, the loss must result from an event that is (1) identifiable; (2) damaging to property; and (3) sudden, unexpected, and unusual in nature.[9] Examples include auto accidents, mine cave-ins, sonic booms, and vandalism. Weather that causes damage (e.g., drought) must be unusual and severe for the particular region. Damage must be to the taxpayer's property to qualify as a casualty loss.

In general, losses on personal use property (e.g., a car, furniture, or a residence) are not deductible. The casualty loss rules are an exception. However, from 2018 through 2025, a taxpayer can take a deduction for a *personal* casualty or theft loss only if the loss occurs in a Federally declared disaster area.[10]

LO.3

Distinguish between deductible and nondeductible losses of individuals.

> **EXAMPLE 11**
>
> In May 2020, due to significant rainstorms, the river behind Jiawen's house overflows its banks and floods the basement. After receiving an insurance settlement, Jiawen's remaining loss is $10,000. Although this event results in a casualty loss, Jiawen's loss will not be deductible unless the event is part of a Federally declared disaster.
>
> Assume instead that the flooding affects a rental home owned by Jiawen. Because the rental home is *not* a personal use asset, the loss is deductible.

See text Section 7-3e for an exception to this rule when there are personal casualty gains during the year.

7-3a Events That Are Not Casualties

Not all acts of nature are treated as casualty losses for income tax purposes. Because a casualty must be sudden, unexpected, and unusual, progressive deterioration (e.g., erosion due to wind or rain) is not a casualty because it does not meet the suddenness test.

Examples of nonsudden events that generally do not qualify as casualties include disease and insect damage. When the damage was caused by termites over a period of several years, some courts have disallowed a casualty loss deduction.[11] Other examples of events that are not casualties are losses resulting from a decline in value rather than an actual loss of the property. No loss was allowed where the taxpayer's home declined in value as a result of a landslide that destroyed neighboring homes but did no actual damage to the taxpayer's home.[12] Similarly, a taxpayer was allowed a loss for the actual flood damage to his property but not for the decline in market value due to the property being flood-prone.[13]

LO.4

Identify a casualty and determine the amount, classification, and timing of casualty and theft losses.

---

[9]Rev.Rul. 72–592, 1972–2 C.B. 101.

[10]§ 165(h)(5). A Federally declared disaster is a disaster determined by the President of the United States to warrant assistance by the Federal government under the Stafford Disaster Relief and Emergency Assistance Act [§ 165(i)(5)].

[11]*Fay v. Helvering,* 41–2 USTC ¶9494, 27 AFTR 432, 120 F.2d 253 (CA–2, 1941); *U.S. v. Rogers,* 41–1 USTC ¶9442, 27 AFTR 423, 120 F.2d 244

(CA–9, 1941). The current position of the IRS is that termite damage is not deductible (Rev.Rul. 63–232, 1963 C.B. 97).

[12]*H. Pulvers v. Comm.,* 69–1 USTC ¶9222, 23 AFTR 2d 69–678, 407 F.2d 838 (CA–9, 1969).

[13]*S. L. Solomon,* 39 TCM 1282, T.C.Memo. 1980–87.

7-3b **Theft Losses**

Theft includes, but is not necessarily limited to, larceny, embezzlement, and robbery.[14] Theft does not include misplaced items.[15]

Theft losses are deducted in the year of *discovery*, which may not be the same as the year of the theft. If an insurance claim exists and there is a reasonable expectation of recovering the adjusted basis of the asset from the insurance company, no deduction is permitted.[16] If in the year of settlement the recovery is less than the asset's adjusted basis, a partial deduction may be available. If the recovery is greater than the asset's adjusted basis, gain may be recognized.

Keith's new sailboat, which he uses for business purposes, was stolen from the storage marina in May 2020. He discovered the loss on June 3, 2020, and filed a claim with his insurance company that was settled on January 30, 2021.

Assuming that there is a reasonable expectation of full recovery, no deduction is allowed in 2020 (the year of discovery). A partial deduction may be available in 2021 if the actual insurance proceeds are less than the lower of the fair market value or the adjusted basis of the asset.

If Keith used his sailboat personally (i.e., not for business), no deduction would be allowed. In general, only personal casualty losses in Federally declared disaster areas are deductible.

7-3c **When to Deduct Casualty Losses**

General Rule

Generally, a casualty loss is deducted in the year the loss occurs. However, no casualty loss is permitted if an insurance claim with a *reasonable prospect of full recovery* exists.[17] If the taxpayer has a partial claim, only part of the loss can be claimed in the year of the casualty, and the remainder is deducted in the year the claim is settled.

Brian's new fishing boat, which he uses in his charter fishing business, was completely destroyed by fire in 2020. Its cost and fair market value were $15,000. Brian's only claim against the insurance company was on a $10,000 policy, which was not settled by year-end. The following year, 2021, Brian settled with the insurance company for $8,000.

Brian is entitled to a $5,000 deduction in 2020 ($10,000 − $15,000) and a $2,000 deduction in 2021.

If a taxpayer receives reimbursement for a casualty loss sustained and deducted in a previous year, an amended return is *not* filed. Instead, the taxpayer includes the reimbursement in gross income when it is received to the extent the previous deduction resulted in a tax benefit.

Selena had a deductible casualty loss of $4,000 on her 2019 tax return. Selena's taxable income for 2019 was $60,000. In June 2020, Selena is reimbursed $2,750 for the prior year's casualty loss.

Selena includes the entire $2,750 in gross income for 2020 because the deduction in 2019 produced a tax benefit.

Disaster Area Losses

An exception to the general rule for the time of deduction is allowed for **disaster area losses**, which are casualties sustained in an area designated as a disaster area by the President of the United States.[18] In these cases, a taxpayer may *elect* to treat the loss as

---

[14]Reg. § 1.165–8(d).

[15]*Mary Francis Allen*, 16 T.C. 163 (1951).

[16]Reg. §§ 1.165–1(d)(2) and 1.165–8(a)(2).

[17]Reg. § 1.165–1(d)(2)(i).

[18]§ 165(i) refers to Federally declared disasters. Disaster loss treatment also applies if a residence has been rendered unsafe as the result of a disaster within 120 days of the disaster loss designation [§ 165(k)].

having occurred in the taxable year immediately *preceding* the taxable year in which the disaster actually occurred. The rationale for this exception is to provide immediate relief to disaster victims by accelerating the tax refunds related to the loss.

The Big Picture

EXAMPLE 15

Return to the facts of *The Big Picture* on p. 7-1. On September 28, 2020, Martha's personal residence was damaged when a hurricane caused an oak tree to fall onto the house. The amount of her uninsured loss was $7,000 ($25,000 insurance settlement − $32,000 damages incurred). Because of the extent of the damage in the area, the President of the United States designated the area a disaster area.

Because Martha's loss is a disaster area loss, she may elect to file an amended return for 2019 and take the loss in that year. Alternatively, she may take the loss on her 2020 income tax return.

7-3d Measuring the Amount of Loss

Amount of Loss

The rules for determining the amount of a loss depend in part on whether business use, income-producing use, or personal use property was involved. Another factor that must be considered is whether the property was partially or completely destroyed.

If business or rental property is *completely destroyed*, the loss is equal to the adjusted basis of the property at the time of destruction.

EXAMPLE 16

Vicki's business equipment was destroyed by flood. Vicki had no flood insurance on her business. The fair market value of the equipment was $9,000 at the time of the flood, and its adjusted basis was $10,000.

Vicki is allowed a loss deduction of $10,000 (the basis of the equipment). The $10,000 loss is a deduction *for* AGI.

A different measurement rule applies for *partial destruction* of business or rental property and for *partial* or *complete destruction* of personal use property. In these situations, the loss is the *lesser* of the following:

- The adjusted basis of the property.
- The difference between the fair market value of the property before the event and the fair market value immediately after the event.

EXAMPLE 17

Wan's uninsured automobile, which was used only for business purposes, was damaged in an accident. On the date of the accident, the fair market value of the automobile was $12,000, and its adjusted basis was $9,000. After the accident, the automobile was appraised at $4,000.

Wan's loss deduction is $8,000 (the lesser of the adjusted basis or the decrease in fair market value). The $8,000 loss is a deduction *for* AGI.

If the property is used for both personal and business/rental use, the loss deduction must be computed separately for the business portion and the personal portion. If a taxpayer has insurance coverage on *personal use* property, an insurance claim must be filed to claim a casualty loss.[19]

Generally, an appraisal before and after the casualty is needed to measure the amount of the loss. However, the *cost of repairs* can be used if the following criteria are met:

- The repairs are necessary to restore the property to its condition immediately before the casualty.
- The amount spent for repairs is not excessive.

---

[19]§ 165(h)(4)(E).

- The repairs do not extend beyond the damage suffered.
- The value of the property after the repairs does not, as a result of the repairs, exceed the value of the property immediately before the casualty.[20]

ETHICS & EQUITY   Is Policy Cancellation an Escape Hatch?

Noah's house is flooded for the third time, and he knows that if he files a claim, the insurance company will cancel his homeowner's policy or impose a prohibitive premium. Noah does not file a claim, yet he deducts the loss on his tax return. Is his loss allowed?

Personal Use Loss Reductions: The $100-per-Event and 10%-of-AGI Floors

The amount of the allowed loss for *personal use* property must be further reduced by a $100-*per-event* floor and a 10%-of-AGI *aggregate* floor.[21] The $100 floor applies separately to each casualty and applies to the entire loss from each casualty (e.g., if a storm damages both a taxpayer's residence and automobile, only $100 is subtracted from the total amount of the loss). The losses are then added together, and the total is reduced by 10 percent of the taxpayer's AGI. The resulting loss is the taxpayer's itemized deduction for casualty and theft losses.

EXAMPLE 18

Nick, who had AGI of $30,000, lost all the furniture in his apartment as a result of a flood in a Federally declared disaster area in 2020. His furniture had a fair market value of $12,000 and an adjusted basis of $9,000 and was completely destroyed. He received $5,000 from his insurance company.

Nick's casualty loss deduction is $900 [$9,000 basis − $5,000 insurance recovery − $100 floor − $3,000 (10% × $30,000 AGI)]. The $900 casualty loss is an itemized deduction (*from* AGI).

When a nonbusiness casualty loss is spread between two taxable years because of an outstanding insurance claim, the loss in the second year is not reduced by the $100 floor (the "$100-per-event" reduction occurred in the first year). However, the loss in the second year is still subject to the 10 percent floor based upon the taxpayer's second-year AGI. For taxpayers who suffer qualified disaster area losses, the 10%-of-AGI floor is determined by using the AGI of the year the deduction is claimed.[22]

EXAMPLE 19

Brian's new *personal use* sailboat was completely destroyed by a hurricane in 2020 (a Federally declared disaster area). The boat had a $15,000 cost and fair market value, but Brian only had $10,000 of insurance coverage for the boat. He filed an insurance claim and settled with the insurance company in 2021 for $8,000.

Brian is entitled to a $5,000 deduction in 2020 ($10,000 − $15,000) and a $2,000 deduction in 2021. Brian's $5,000 casualty loss deduction in 2020 is reduced first by $100 and then by 10% of his 2020 AGI. The $2,000 deduction in 2021 is reduced by 10% of his 2021 AGI.

Multiple Losses

The rules for computing loss deductions where multiple losses have occurred are explained in Examples 20 and 21.

---

[20]Reg. § 1.165–7(a)(2)(ii).
[21]§ 165(h).

[22]§ 165(i).

Multiple Casualty Losses

During the year, Kien had the following casualty losses related to assets used in his business:

EXAMPLE 20

		Fair Market Value of Asset		
Asset	Adjusted Basis	Before the Casualty	After the Casualty	Insurance Recovery
A	$900	$600	$ —0—	$400
B	300	800	250	100

The following losses are allowed:

Asset A: $500. The complete destruction of a business asset results in a deduction of the adjusted basis of the property (reduced by any insurance recovery), regardless of the asset's fair market value.

Asset B: $200. The partial destruction of a business (or personal use) asset results in a deduction equal to the lesser of the adjusted basis ($300) or the decline in value ($550), reduced by any insurance recovery ($100).

Both the Asset A and Asset B losses are deductions *for* AGI. The $100 floor and the 10%-of-AGI floor do not apply because the assets are business assets.

During the year, Emily had AGI of $20,000 and the following personal casualty losses related to a flood in a Federally declared disaster area:

EXAMPLE 21

		Fair Market Value of Asset		
Asset	Adjusted Basis	Before the Casualty	After the Casualty	Insurance Recovery
A	$1,900	$1,400	$ —0—	$200
B	2,500	4,000	1,000	—0—
C	800	400	100	250

The loss for each asset is computed as follows:

Asset A: $1,200. The lesser of the adjusted basis of $1,900 or the $1,400 decline in value, reduced by the insurance recovery of $200.

Asset B: $2,500. The lesser of the adjusted basis of $2,500 or the $3,000 decline in value.

Asset C: $50. The lesser of the adjusted basis of $800 or the $300 decline in value, reduced by the insurance recovery of $250.

Since the losses all related to a single casualty, Emily must reduce the sum of the losses by $100 and then apply the 10%-of-AGI floor. Emily's itemized casualty loss deduction for the year is $1,650:

Asset A loss	$ 1,200
Asset B loss	2,500
Asset C loss	50
Total loss	$ 3,750
Less: $100-per-event reduction	(100)
Less: 10% of AGI (10% × $20,000)	(2,000)
Itemized casualty loss deduction	$ 1,650

7-3e Personal Casualty Gains and Losses

If a taxpayer has personal casualty and theft gains as well as losses, a special set of rules applies for determining the tax consequences. Here, an exception to the rule that disallows a deduction for personal casualty losses other than those in Federally declared disaster areas applies.[23] In this case, the taxpayer may use a personal casualty loss (or losses) *not* attributable to a Federally declared disaster to offset any personal casualty gains. After this netting process, if any loss remains, it is not deductible (since it relates to a non-Federally declared disaster area casualty). If, however, a net personal casualty gain remains, it is offset by any Federally declared disaster area casualty losses.

Calculating Personal Casualty Gains and Losses

EXAMPLE 22

During 2020, Emmanuel has AGI of $50,000 and the following personal casualty gains and losses (after deducting the $100 floor):

Asset	Item	Gain or (Loss)
A	Personal casualty gain	$ 2,500
B	Personal casualty loss (non-Federally declared disaster area)	(2,000)
C	Personal casualty loss (Federally declared disaster area)	(9,000)

Emmanuel first offsets the non-Federally declared disaster area losses against the personal casualty gain, resulting in an excess personal casualty gain of $500, computed as follows:

Personal casualty gain	$ 2,500
Personal casualty loss (non-Federally declared disaster area)	(2,000)
Excess personal casualty gain	$ 500

Next, the excess personal casualty gain offsets the Federally declared disaster area loss. Emmanuel's overall net personal casualty loss is $8,500, computed as follows:

Personal casualty loss (Federally declared disaster area)	($ 9,000)
Less: Excess personal casualty gain	500
Overall net personal casualty loss	($ 8,500)

After this second netting process, because a net personal casualty loss remains, it will be deductible to the extent of the 10%-of-AGI floor. Emmanuel's itemized deduction for casualty losses is $3,500, computed as follows:

Net personal casualty loss	$ 8,500
Less: 10% of AGI (10% × $50,000)	(5,000)
Itemized deduction for casualty loss	$ 3,500

EXAMPLE 23

Refer back to the facts of Example 22. How would your answer change if the casualty loss related to Asset B was $4,000 (rather than $2,000)?

Emmanuel would begin by offsetting the non-Federally declared disaster area losses against the personal casualty gain, resulting in an excess personal casualty loss of $1,500, computed as follows:

Personal casualty gain	$ 2,500
Personal casualty loss (non-Federally declared disaster area)	(4,000)
Excess personal casualty loss	($ 1,500)

continued

---

[23]§ 165(h)(5)(B); personal casualty gains and losses are defined at § 165(h)(3).

Since this net loss relates to a non-Federally declared disaster area, the loss is *not* deductible. Emmanuel's itemized deduction for casualty losses is $4,000, computed as follows:

Personal casualty loss (Federally declared disaster area)	$ 9,000
Less: 10% of AGI (10% × $50,000)	(5,000)
Itemized deduction for casualty loss	$ 4,000

One further complication exists—determining the character of the casualty gains and losses. If the gains exceed the losses, the gains and losses are treated as gains and losses from the sale of capital assets.[24] The capital gains and losses are short term or long term, depending on how long the taxpayer held each of the assets (assets held more than one year are long term). In the netting process, personal casualty and theft gains and losses are not netted with the gains and losses on business and income-producing property.

EXAMPLE 24

During the year, Cliff had the following personal casualty gains and losses (after deducting the $100 floor):

Asset	Holding Period	Gain or (Loss)
A	Three months	($ 300)
B	Three years	(2,400)
C	Two years	3,200

Cliff computes the tax consequences as follows:

Personal casualty gain	$ 3,200
Personal casualty loss ($300 + $2,400)	(2,700)
Net personal casualty gain	$ 500

Cliff treats all of the gains and losses as capital gains and losses:

Short-term capital loss (Asset A)	$ 300
Long-term capital loss (Asset B)	2,400
Long-term capital gain (Asset C)	3,200

If personal casualty losses exceed personal casualty gains, all gains and losses are treated as ordinary items. The gains—and the losses to the extent of gains—are treated as ordinary income and ordinary loss in computing AGI. Losses in excess of gains are deducted as itemized deductions and are deductible only if related to a Federally declared disaster.[25]

[24]§ 165(h)(2)(B). [25]§ 165(h).

EXAMPLE 25

During the year, Hazel had AGI of $20,000 and the following personal casualty gain and loss (after deducting the $100 floor). Neither are related to a Federally declared disaster:

Asset	Holding Period	Gain or (Loss)
A	Three years	($2,700)
B	Four months	200

Hazel computes the tax consequences as follows:

Personal casualty loss	($2,700)
Personal casualty gain	200
Net personal casualty loss	($2,500)

Hazel treats the gain and the loss as ordinary items. The $200 gain and $200 of the loss are included in computing AGI. The remaining net personal casualty loss is not deductible (it is not related to a Federally declared disaster area).

See Concept Summary 7.3 for a review of the tax treatment of casualty gains and losses.

Concept Summary 7.3

Casualty Gains and Losses

	Business Use or Income-Producing Property	Personal Use Property*
Event creating the loss	Any event.	Casualty or theft.
Amount	The lesser of the decline in fair market value or the adjusted basis, but always the adjusted basis if the property is totally destroyed.	The lesser of the decline in fair market value or the adjusted basis.
Insurance	Insurance proceeds received reduce the amount of the loss.	Insurance proceeds received (or for which there is an unfiled claim) reduce the amount of the loss.
$100 floor	Not applicable.	Applicable per event.
Gains and losses	Gains and losses are netted (see detailed discussion in Chapter 14).	Personal casualty and theft gains and losses are netted.
Gains exceeding losses	See Chapter 14.	The gains and losses are treated as gains and losses from the sale of capital assets.
Losses exceeding gains	See Chapter 14.	The gains—and the losses to the extent of gains—are treated as ordinary items in computing AGI. The losses in excess of gains, to the extent they exceed 10% of AGI, are itemized deductions.

*In general, from 2018 through 2025, losses are allowed only if the event is related to a Federally declared disaster; if there are both casualty gains and losses, non-Federally declared casualty losses can be used to offset casualty gains.

7-3f Statutory Framework for Deducting Losses of Individuals

Concept Summary 7.4 provides a summary of the statutory framework of deducting losses of individuals.

Concept Summary 7.4
Statutory Framework for Deducting Losses of Individuals

	Personal Casualty/Theft Losses*		Employee Casualty/Theft Losses	Production of Income Casualty/Theft Losses	Trade or Business Casualty/Theft Losses
	$100-per-Event Rule	10%-of-AGI Rule	Reimbursed Expenses and 2%-of-AGI Rule		
General Application	Reduce each casualty or theft loss by $100 when figuring the potential casualty loss deduction. Apply this rule to personal use property after the amount of the loss has been determined.	Reduce the *total* casualty or theft loss by 10% of adjusted gross income. Apply this rule to personal use property after each loss is reduced by $100 (the "$100-per-event rule").	Casualty and theft losses incurred by an employee in connection with a trade or business are deductible *for* AGI if the loss is reimbursed by the employer (with the net loss being deductible). If the loss is *not* reimbursed, the loss is deductible *from* AGI as an employee business expense (a miscellaneous itemized deduction). Although these losses are not subject to the $100-per-event rule or the 10%-of-AGI rule, miscellaneous itemized deductions are currently not deductible.[26]	Casualty and theft losses incurred by an individual in a transaction entered into for profit are not subject to the $100-per-event and the 10%-of-AGI limitations. If these losses are attributable to rents or royalties, the deduction is *for* AGI.[27] If not, they are deductions *from* AGI (and are *not* a miscellaneous itemized deduction).[28]	Casualty and theft losses incurred by an individual in connection with a trade or business are deductible *for* AGI.[29] These losses are not subject to the $100-per-event and the 10%-of-AGI limitations.
Single Event	Apply this rule only once to each casualty or theft event, even if many pieces of property are affected by the event.	Apply this rule only once, even if many pieces of property are affected.	Apply this rule only once, even if many pieces of property are affected.		
More Than One Event	Apply to the loss from each event.	Apply to the total of all losses from all events.	Apply to the total of all losses from all events.		

*From 2018 through 2025, only personal casualty or theft losses occurring in Federally declared disaster areas are allowed.

7-4 RESEARCH AND EXPERIMENTAL EXPENDITURES

Section 174 covers the treatment of research and experimental expenditures. The Regulations define ==research and experimental expenditures== as follows:

> all such costs incident to the development or improvement of a product (including an experimental or pilot model, a plant process, a product, a formula, an invention, or similar property). The term includes the costs of obtaining a patent, such as attorneys' fees expended in making and perfecting a patent application. Expenditures represent research and development costs in the experimental or laboratory sense if they are for activities

LO.5

State and apply the alternative tax treatments for research and experimental expenditures.

---

[26]§ 67(b)(3). No deduction is allowed for miscellaneous itemized deductions from 2018 through 2025.

[27]§ 62(a)(4).

[28]§ 67(b)(3).

[29]§ 62(a)(1).

intended to discover information that would eliminate uncertainty concerning the development or improvement of a product. The term does not include expenditures such as those for the ordinary testing or inspection of materials or products for quality control or those for efficiency surveys, management studies, consumer surveys, advertising, or promotions.[30]

The law permits the following *three alternatives* for the handling of research and experimental expenditures:

- Expensed in the year paid or incurred.
- Deferred and amortized.
- Capitalized.

If the costs are capitalized, a deduction may not be available until the research project is abandoned or is deemed worthless. Because many products resulting from research projects do not have a definite and limited useful life, most taxpayers choose to write off the expenditures immediately or to defer and amortize them.[31]

7-4a Expense Method

A taxpayer can expense all of the research and experimental expenditures incurred provided this method is adopted for the first taxable year in which these expenditures were paid or incurred.[32] Once this method is adopted, the taxpayer must continue to expense all qualifying expenditures unless a request for a change is made to, and approved by, the IRS. As discussed below, the expense method will not be available in taxable years beginning after December 31, 2021.

7-4b Deferral and Amortization Method

Taxable Years Beginning before January 1, 2022

If elected by the taxpayer, research and experimental expenditures may be deferred and amortized ratably over a period of not less than 60 months.[33] A deduction is allowed beginning with the month in which the taxpayer first realizes benefits from the experimental expenditure. The election is binding, and a change requires permission from the IRS.

EXAMPLE 26

Gold Corporation decides to develop a new line of adhesives. The project begins in 2019. Gold incurs the following expenses in 2019 and 2020 in connection with the project:

	2019	2020
Salaries	$25,000	$18,000
Materials	8,000	2,000
Depreciation on machinery	6,500	5,700

The benefits from the project will be realized starting in March 2021. If Gold Corporation elects a 60-month deferral and amortization period, there is no deduction prior to March 2021, the month benefits from the project begin to be realized. The deduction for 2021 is $10,867, computed as follows:

Salaries ($25,000 + $18,000)	$43,000	
Materials ($8,000 + $2,000)	10,000	
Depreciation ($6,500 + $5,700)	12,200	
Total	$65,200	
Research and experimentation expense in 2021	$10,867	[$65,200 × (10 months/60 months)]

---

[30]Reg. §§ 1.174–2(a)(1), (2), and (3). Expenses in connection with the acquisition or improvement of land or depreciable property are not research and experimental expenditures. Rather, they increase the basis of the land or depreciable property. However, depreciation on an asset used for research may be a research and experimental expense.

[31]A credit for increasing research expenditures is also available; § 41. See Chapter 12 for a more detailed discussion of this credit.

[32]Deductions are even allowed if incurred before carrying on a trade or business activity as long as incurred in connection with a trade or business; *Snow v. Comm.*, 74–1 USTC ¶9432, 33 AFTR 2d 74–1251, 94 S.Ct. 1876 (USSC, 1974).

[33]§ 174(b)(2).

The option to defer and amortize research and experimental expenditures is usually employed when a company does not have sufficient income to offset the expenses.[34] The deferral of research and experimental expenditures should also be considered if the taxpayer expects higher tax rates in the future.

Taxable Years Beginning after December 31, 2021

Research and experimental expenditures paid or incurred in taxable years beginning after December 31, 2021, must be capitalized and amortized (i.e., the expense method discussed in text Section 7-4a, above, will not be available). Two other changes also occur. First, amortization begins at the midpoint of the year the expenses are paid or incurred, rather than the month in which the taxpayer first realizes benefits. Second, the expenditures are amortized ratably over a five-year period (15 years for foreign research expenses), rather than ratably over a period of not less than 60 months.[35]

7-5 EXCESS BUSINESS LOSSES

LO.6

Apply the excess business loss limitation rules.

If a noncorporate taxpayer has an **excess business loss** for the year, it is not allowed.[36] Instead, it is carried forward and treated as part of the taxpayer's net operating loss (NOL) carryforward in subsequent years (NOLs are discussed in text Section 7-6).

7-5a Excess Business Loss Defined

An *excess business loss* is defined as:[37]

	The aggregate deductions for the year attributable to the taxpayer's businesses
Less:	The sum of aggregate gross income or gains of the taxpayer
Less:	A threshold amount (in 2020, $518,000 for married taxpayers filing a joint return; $259,000 for all other taxpayers)

The threshold amounts are adjusted for inflation each year.[38]

At its core, the purpose of the excess business loss limitation is to limit the amount of nonbusiness income (e.g., salaries, interest, dividends, and capital gains) that can be "sheltered" from tax as a result of business losses.

Calculating an Excess Business Loss

EXAMPLE 27

In 2020, Tonya, a single taxpayer, operates a sole proprietorship in which she materially participates. Her proprietorship generates gross income of $320,000 and deductions of $600,000, resulting in a loss of $280,000. The large deductions are due to the acquisition of equipment and the use of immediate expense and additional first-year depreciation to deduct all of the costs associated with the acquisitions. Tonya's excess business loss is $21,000, computed as follows:

Aggregate business deductions	$ 600,000
Less: Aggregate business gross income and gains	(320,000)
Less: Threshold amount	(259,000)
Excess business loss	$ 21,000

So of Tonya's $280,000 proprietorship loss, $259,000 can be used to offset nonbusiness income. The $21,000 excess business loss is treated as part of Tonya's net operating loss carryforward in subsequent years.

---

[34]Another option is to deduct these expenses for regular tax purposes, but elect in any year where helpful, to capitalize and amortize the expenses over 10 years for both regular tax and alternative minimum tax purposes [§ 59(e)].

[35]§ 174(a)(2).

[36]§ 461(l).

[37]§ 461(l)(3). Due to a drafting error, § 461 treats wages as business income (although this is not what Congress intended). This error is expected to be corrected in subsequent legislation. The 2019 Form 461 follows the statute and treats wages as business income, resulting in smaller disallowed losses.

[38]In 2019, the threshold amounts were $510,000 and $255,000, respectively.

> ### Calculating an Excess Business Loss
>
> **EXAMPLE 28**
>
> Assume the same facts as Example 27, except that Tonya is married and files a joint return. In this case, Tonya does not have an excess business loss due to the increased threshold amount.
>
> | | |
> |---|---:|
> | Aggregate business deductions | $ 600,000 |
> | Less: Aggregate business gross income and gains | (320,000) |
> | Less: Threshold amount | (518,000) |
> | Excess business loss | $　None |
>
> As a result, Tonya's $280,000 sole proprietorship loss is fully deductible and can be used to offset nonbusiness income (e.g., her spouse's wages and their interest and dividend income).

The excess business loss limitation applies to the aggregate gross income and deductions from all of a taxpayer's trades or businesses.[39] So if a married couple files a joint return, information from all of the couple's trades or businesses must be consolidated. Further, as noted in Example 28, if married taxpayers file a joint return, the losses of one spouse can be used to offset the other spouse's nonbusiness income (up to the $518,000 limit in 2020).

7-5b Losses from Partnerships or S Corporations

For a partnership or an S corporation, the excess business loss limitation applies at the partner or shareholder level.[40] Each partner's or S corporation shareholder's share of items of income, gain, deduction, or loss of the partnership or S corporation is taken into account in applying the limitation for the tax year of the partner or S corporation shareholder.

> **EXAMPLE 29**
>
> Jayson, a single taxpayer, is an S corporation shareholder and materially participates in the grocery store business. During 2020, the store had a large depreciation deduction causing a substantial loss. Jayson has a flow-through loss of $345,000 from the S corporation. He also received a $78,000 salary from the corporation. At the beginning of the year, Jayson had a $520,000 basis in his S corporation shares—enough to absorb the S corporation loss. Because he materially participates in the business, it is not a passive activity (see Chapter 11 for a discussion of passive activity losses).
>
> However, Jayson's flow-through loss exceeds the $259,000 excess business loss threshold by $86,000 ($345,000 − $259,000). So Jayson can deduct $259,000 (and use it to offset his salary and other nonbusiness income). The $86,000 excess is not deductible in 2020 but carries forward as a net operating loss.
>
> Assume that in 2021, the grocery store business generates a profit and flows through $210,000 of income to Jayson. Jayson can deduct the 2020 excess business loss of $86,000 against this flow-through income.

The excess business loss rules also treat similarly situated owners differently (based on their filing status).

> **EXAMPLE 30**
>
> Margie leaves her job in 2020 to pursue her dream, a technology startup. Margie is single and invests $500,000 of capital, as does her business partner Janice, who is married. Together they form TechStart LLC (which reports as a partnership for Federal tax purposes); both materially participate in the business. In 2020, the LLC reports a net loss of $700,000. Each LLC member receives a Schedule K–1 from the LLC indicating a $350,000 ordinary loss; each will report this loss on her 2020 individual income tax return [on Form 1040 (Schedule E)].
>
> *continued*

---

[39]§ 461(l)(3)(A)(i).

[40]§ 461(l)(4)(A).

Margie has an excess business loss of $91,000 ($350,000 minus the $259,000 threshold for single taxpayers). This excess business loss is an NOL carryforward for Margie.[41] Janice can use the full $350,000 loss in 2020 since it is less than the $518,000 threshold that applies to married taxpayers who file jointly.

7-5c Other Rules

The excess business loss limitation is applied *after* the application of the § 469 passive activity loss rules (see Chapter 11 for a discussion of these rules).[42] Given this requirement, losses from *passive* trades or businesses (e.g., a business in which the taxpayer does not materially participate) are limited first by the § 469 passive activity loss rules, and once the losses are allowed under § 469, they are subject to these rules.

The Treasury Department and IRS are to specify reporting requirements necessary to implement these rules.[43] Form 461 (Limitation on Business Losses) is used to calculate and report the loss limitation.

7-6 NET OPERATING LOSSES

LO.7

Describe the tax impact of a net operating loss and review the effect of the carryback and carryover provisions on previous and subsequent years' taxable income.

The requirement that every taxpayer file an annual income tax return may result in inequities for taxpayers who experience income fluctuations (and losses in certain tax years) versus taxpayers with stable income levels. A loss in a particular tax year would produce no tax benefit if the Code did not provide for the use of these losses in profitable years.

EXAMPLE 31

Juanita has a business and realizes $300,000 of taxable income or loss over a five-year period as follows: year 1, $50,000; year 2, ($30,000); year 3, $100,000; year 4, ($200,000); and year 5, $380,000. She is married and files a joint return. Sean also has a business and has a taxable income pattern of $60,000 every year ($300,000 over the five-year period). He, too, is married and files a joint return. Assuming that there is no provision for carryback or carryover of net operating losses (NOLs), Juanita and Sean would pay the following taxes over the five-year period:

Year	Juanita's Tax	Sean's Tax
1	$ 5,605	$ 6,805
2	–0–	6,805
3	13,580	6,805
4	–0–	6,805
5	83,631	6,805
	$102,816	$34,025

The 2020 Tax Rate Schedules are used to compute the tax.

Even though Juanita and Sean realized the same total taxable income over the five-year period, Juanita had to pay taxes of $102,816, while Sean paid taxes of only $34,025.

To provide partial relief from this inequitable tax treatment, a **net operating loss (NOL)** deduction is allowed.[44] NOLs for any one year can be offset against taxable income of other years. In general, only losses from the operation of a trade or business and casualty and theft losses can create an NOL.

---

[41]Prior to 2018, NOLs could be carried back two years and used to offset income in those years. This carryback allowed taxpayers to immediately "monetize" an NOL by using the NOL to generate an income tax refund in those years. Beginning in 2018, NOL carrybacks are no longer allowed; NOLs can only be carried forward. Thus, in addition to treating similarly

situated owners differently based on filing status, the inability to carry back these losses also is detrimental to business owners.

[42]§ 461(l)(6).

[43]§ 461(l)(5).

[44]§ 172.

7-6a **General Rules**

Carryforward Only

In general, an NOL can be carried forward indefinitely. In taxable years prior to 2018, an NOL could be carried back 2 tax years and forward 20 years. The two-year carryback provided a way for businesses to receive a tax refund for taxes paid in prior profitable years. Beginning in 2018, taxpayers must wait at least one year to receive a tax benefit from the loss.[45]

EXAMPLE 32

For 2020, the taxpayer and spouse have an NOL of $50,000. The NOL can be carried forward indefinitely (beginning with 2021).

NOL Deduction Limit

In general, an NOL deduction is limited to 80 percent of taxable income, determined without regard to the NOL deduction itself.[46] If the NOL carryover is less than the computed limitation, the entire carryover is allowed as a deduction.

In taxable years prior to 2018, there was no limit on the utilization of NOLs. As a result, the 80 percent of taxable income limit may extend the time over which an NOL is used, making taxpayers wait longer to receive a tax benefit from the NOL (and reducing the present value of the related tax benefit).

EXAMPLE 33

For 2020, taxpayer and spouse have an NOL of $25,000 (and no other NOL carryovers exist). The NOL is carried forward to 2021. In 2021, the taxpayers have taxable income of $80,000 before considering the 2020 NOL carryover. The taxpayers' 2021 NOL deduction can be no more than $64,000 ($80,000 × 80%). Since the NOL carryover from 2020 is only $25,000, the entire 2020 NOL carryover can be used to reduce their 2021 taxable income. As a result, their 2021 taxable income is $55,000 ($80,000 − $25,000).

If, instead, the taxpayers had taxable income of $30,000 before considering the 2020 NOL carryover, only $24,000 ($30,000 × 80%) of the carryover could be used. In this case, their 2021 taxable income would be $6,000 ($30,000 − $24,000), and the remaining $1,000 of the 2020 NOL carryover would be carried forward to 2022.

NOLs and the Deduction for Qualified Business Income

The deduction for qualified business income will not create or increase a net operating loss.[47] Losses from qualified businesses are carried over separately and will offset future income from qualified businesses, reducing the related deduction for qualified business income.[48]

NOLs and Self-Employment Taxes

An NOL *cannot* be used to reduce self-employment income. As a result, a taxpayer's self-employment tax liability will not change as the result of an NOL deduction.[49]

---

[45]A two-year carryback period is available for any NOL resulting from a farming business; § 172(b)(1)(B)(i).

[46]§ 172(a).

[47]§ 172(d)(8).

[48]§ 199A(c)(2).

[49]§ 1402(a).

7-7 TAX PLANNING

LO.8

Identify tax planning opportunities in deducting certain business expenses, business losses, and personal losses.

7-7a Small Business Stock (§ 1244 Stock) Losses

Because § 1244 limits the amount of loss classified as ordinary loss on a yearly basis, a taxpayer might maximize the benefits of § 1244 by selling the stock in more than one taxable year. The result could be that the losses in any one taxable year would not exceed the § 1244 limits on ordinary loss.

EXAMPLE 34

Mitch, a single individual, purchased small business stock in 2018 for $150,000 (150 shares at $1,000 per share). On December 20, 2020, the stock is worth $60,000 (150 shares at $400 per share). Mitch wants to sell the stock at this time. Mitch earns a salary of $80,000 a year, has no other capital transactions, and does not expect any in the future.

If Mitch sells all of the small business stock in 2020, his recognized loss will be $90,000 ($60,000 − $150,000). The loss will be characterized as a $50,000 ordinary loss and a $40,000 long-term capital loss. In computing taxable income for 2020, Mitch could deduct the $50,000 ordinary loss but could deduct only $3,000 of the capital loss. The remainder of the capital loss could be carried over and used in future years subject to the $3,000 limitation if Mitch has no capital gains.

Instead, if Mitch sells 82 shares in 2020, he will recognize an ordinary loss of $49,200 [82 × ($1,000 − $400)]. If Mitch then sells the remainder of the shares in 2021, he will recognize an ordinary loss of $40,800 [68 × ($1,000 − $400)]. Mitch could deduct the $49,200 ordinary loss in computing 2020 taxable income and the $40,800 ordinary loss in computing 2021 taxable income.

7-7b Casualty Losses

A special election is available for taxpayers who sustain casualty losses in an area designated by the President as a disaster area. This election affects only the *timing*, not the calculation, of the deduction. The benefit, of course, is a faster refund (or reduction in tax). It will also be advantageous to carry the loss back if the taxpayer's tax rate in the carryback year is higher than the tax rate in the year of the loss.

To find out if an event qualifies as a disaster area loss, one can look in any of the major tax services, the Compilation of Presidential Documents (released by the U.S. Government Publishing Office), or the *Internal Revenue Bulletin*.

REFOCUS ON THE BIG PICTURE

LOSSES

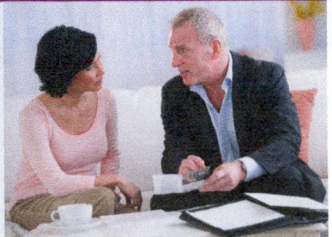

Martha can receive tax benefits associated with her unfortunate occurrences during the current tax year. Some of the losses, however, will provide a greater tax benefit than others as a result of different tax provisions governing the amount and the classification of the losses.

Bad Debt

Based on the facts provided, it appears that Martha's loan to her friend Janice was a bona fide debt. Otherwise, nothing would be deductible. The amount of the deduction is the unpaid principal balance of $19,000 ($25,000 − $6,000). Unfortunately, because the bad debt is a nonbusiness bad debt, it is classified as a short-term capital loss (see Example 5).

continued

Investment Losses

The $50,000 loss from the pharmaceutical company stock is deductible. However, it appears that the loss should be classified as a long-term capital loss rather than as a short-term capital loss. Although the actual holding period was not greater than one year (October through May), the disposal date for the stock (which qualifies as a worthless security) is deemed to be the last day of the tax year (October of last year through end of December of the current year). Further, the loss does not appear to qualify for ordinary loss treatment under § 1244 (see Example 8).

The stock she purchased from her friend Peter results in an $8,000 short-term capital loss (and does not qualify under § 1244; see Example 10).

Loss from Bookstore

The $180,000 loss from Martha's sole proprietorship (her bookstore) is reported on Schedule C of Form 1040. It is an ordinary loss, and it qualifies for NOL treatment. Martha can carry forward any net loss and offset it against future taxable income. However, the NOL carryforward will be limited (each year) to the lesser of the NOL or 80 percent of taxable income (computed without regard to the NOL carryforward).

Casualty Loss

The loss from the damage to Martha's personal residence is classified as a personal casualty loss. Using the cost of repairs method, the amount of the casualty loss is $7,000 ($25,000 − $32,000). However, this amount must be reduced by the $100-per-event floor and the 10%-of-AGI floor.

Because the President classified the county in which Martha's house is located as a Federal disaster area, Martha has the option of deducting the casualty loss on the prior year's tax return (see Example 15).

Key Terms

Bad debt, 7-2
Business bad debt, 7-4
Casualty loss, 7-7
Disaster area losses, 7-8
Excess business loss, 7-17

Net operating loss (NOL), 7-19
Nonbusiness bad debt, 7-4
Research and experimental expenditures, 7-15
Reserve method, 7-3

Small business stock (§ 1244 stock), 7-6
Specific charge-off method, 7-3
Theft losses, 7-8
Worthless securities, 7-6

Discussion Questions

1. **LO.1** Explain how an account receivable can give rise to a bad debt deduction.

2. **LO.1** Ron, a cash basis taxpayer, sells his business accounts receivable of $100,000 to Felicia for $70,000 (70% of the actual accounts receivable). Discuss the amount and classification of Ron's bad debt deduction.

3. **LO.1** Discuss when a bad debt deduction can be taken for a nonbusiness debt.

4. **LO.1** Discuss the treatment of a business bad debt when the business also has long-term capital gains.

5. **LO.1, 2, 3, 4, 5** Many years ago, Jack purchased 400 shares of Canary stock. During the current year, the stock became worthless. It was determined that the company "went under" because several corporate officers embezzled a large amount of company funds. Identify the relevant tax issues for Jack.   *Critical Thinking*

6. **LO.2** Sean is in the business of buying and selling stocks and bonds. He has a bond of Green Corporation for which he paid $200,000. The bond is currently worth only $50,000. Discuss whether Sean can take a $150,000 loss for a business bad debt or for a worthless security.

7. **LO.2** Discuss the tax treatment of the sale of § 1244 stock at a gain.

8. **LO.3, 4** Jim discovers that his residence has extensive termite damage. Discuss whether he may take a deduction for the damage to his residence.

9. **LO.3, 4** The value of Terrah's personal residence has declined significantly because of a recent forest fire in the area where she lives. The fire was a Federally declared disaster. Terrah's house suffered no actual damage during the fire, but because much of the surrounding area was destroyed, the value of all of the homes in the area declined substantially. Discuss whether Terrah can take a casualty loss for the decline in value of her residence caused by the fire.

10. **LO.4** Discuss at what point in time a theft loss generally is recognized.

11. **LO.4** Discuss the circumstances under which the cost of repairs to the damaged property can be used to measure the amount of a casualty loss.

12. **LO.4** In 2020, Kelsey sustained a loss on the theft of a painting. She had paid $20,000 for the painting, but it was worth $40,000 at the time of the theft. Evaluate the tax consequences of treating the painting as investment property or as personal use property.

13. **LO.4** Kelly decided to invest in Lime, Inc. common stock after reviewing Lime's public disclosures, including recent financial statements and a number of press releases issued by Lime. On August 7, 2018, Kelly purchased 60,000 shares of Lime for $210,000. In May 2019, Lime entered into a joint venture with Cherry, Inc. In November 2019, the joint venture failed, and Lime's stock began to decline in value. In December 2019, Cherry filed a lawsuit against Lime for theft of corporate opportunity and breach of fiduciary responsibility. In February 2020, Lime filed a countersuit against Cherry for fraud and misappropriation of funds. At the end of December 2020, Kelly's stock in Lime was worth $15,000. Identify the relevant tax issues for Kelly.   *Critical Thinking*

14. **LO.3, 4** In 2017, John opened an investment account with Randy Hansen, who held himself out to the public as an investment adviser and securities broker. John contributed $200,000 to the account in 2017. John provided Randy with a power of attorney to use the $200,000 to purchase and sell securities on John's behalf. John instructed Randy to reinvest any gains and income earned. In 2017, 2018, and 2019, John received statements of the amount of income earned by his account and included these amounts in his gross income for these years. In 2020, it was discovered that Randy's purported investment advisory and brokerage activity was in fact a fraudulent investment arrangement known as a Ponzi scheme. In reality, John's account balance was zero, the money having been used by Randy in his scheme. Identify the relevant tax issues for John.   *Critical Thinking*

15. **LO.5** Discuss under what circumstances a company would elect to amortize research and experimental expenditures rather than use the expense method.

Critical Thinking   16. **LO.6, 7** Amos began a business, Silver LLC (a single-member LLC), on July 1, 2017. The business extracts and processes silver ore. During 2020, as a result of a decline in demand for silver ore, Amos expects to generate a large loss. Identify the relevant tax issues for Amos.

17. **LO.6** Discuss the rationale behind the excess business loss provision.

18. **LO.7** Discuss whether deductions *for* AGI can be treated as nonbusiness deductions in computing an individual's NOL.

Computational Exercises

19. **LO.1** Last year Aleshia identified $15,000 as a nonbusiness bad debt. In that tax year, before considering the tax implications of the nonbusiness bad debt, Aleshia had $100,000 of taxable income, of which $12,000 consisted of short-term capital gains. This year Aleshia collected $8,000 of the amount she had previously identified as a bad debt. Determine Aleshia's tax treatment of the $8,000 received in the current tax year.

20. **LO.1** Bob owns a collection agency. He purchases uncollected accounts receivable from other businesses at 60% of their face value and then attempts to collect these accounts. During the current year, Bob collected $60,000 on an account with a face value of $80,000. Determine the amount of Bob's bad debt deduction.

21. **LO.2** On May 9, 2018, Calvin acquired 250 shares of stock in Hobbes Corporation, a new startup company, for $68,750. Calvin acquired the stock directly from Hobbes, and it is classified as § 1244 stock (at the time Calvin acquired his stock, the corporation had $900,000 of paid-in capital). On January 15, 2020, Calvin sold all of his Hobbes stock for $7,000. Assuming that Calvin is single, determine his tax consequences as a result of this sale.

22. **LO.4** Noelle's diamond ring was stolen in November 2017. She originally paid $8,000 for the ring, but it was worth considerably more at the time of the theft. Noelle filed an insurance claim for the stolen ring, but the claim was denied. Because the insurance claim was denied, Noelle took a casualty loss for the stolen ring on her 2017 tax return. In 2017, Noelle had AGI of $40,000. After Noelle threatened legal action, in early 2020, the insurance company had a "change of heart" and sent Noelle a check for $5,000 for the stolen ring. Determine the proper tax treatment of the $5,000 Noelle received from the insurance company in 2020.

23. **LO.4** Determine the treatment of a loss on rental property under the following facts:

Basis	$650,000
FMV before the loss	800,000
FMV after the loss	200,000

24. **LO.4** Belinda was involved in a boating accident in 2020. Her speedboat, which was used only for personal use and had a fair market value of $28,000 and an adjusted basis of $14,000, was completely destroyed. She received $10,000 from her insurance company. Her AGI for 2020 is $37,000. What is Belinda's casualty loss deduction (after any limitations)?

25. **LO.4** During the current year, Tucker had the following personal casualty gains and losses (after deducting the $100 floor):

Asset	Holding Period	Gain or (Loss)
Asset 1	18 months	($1,200)
Asset 2	2 months	750
Asset 3	3 years	1,500

What are the tax consequences of these items to Tucker?

26. **LO.5** Sandstorm Corporation decides to develop a new line of paints. The project begins in 2020. Sandstorm incurs the following expenses in 2020 in connection with the project:

Salaries	$85,000
Materials	30,000
Depreciation on equipment	12,500

The benefits from the project will be realized starting in July 2021. If Sandstorm Corporation chooses to defer and amortize its research and experimental expenditures over a period of 60 months, what are its related deductions in 2020 and 2021?

27. **LO.6** Tim, a single taxpayer, operates a business as a single-member LLC. In 2020, his LLC reports business income of $225,000 and business deductions of $584,000, resulting in a loss of $359,000. What are the implications of this business loss? Can this business loss be used to offset other income that Tim reports? If so, how much? If not, what happens to the loss?

Problems

28. **LO.1** Several years ago John Johnson, who is in the lending business, loaned Sara $30,000 to purchase an automobile to be used for personal purposes. In August of the current year, Sara filed for bankruptcy, after paying back $1,000 of the loan to John. John was notified by the bankruptcy court that he could not expect to receive more than an additional $4,000. John has contacted you about the possibility of taking a bad debt deduction for the current year.

    Write a letter to John that contains your advice as to whether he can claim a bad debt deduction for the current year. Also prepare a memo for the tax files. John's address is 100 Tyler Lane, Erie, PA 16563.

Communications

29. **LO.1** Monty loaned his friend Ned $20,000 three years ago. Ned signed a note and made payments on the loan. Last year, when the remaining balance was $11,000, Ned filed for bankruptcy and notified Monty that he would be unable to pay the balance on the loan. Monty treated the $11,000 as a nonbusiness bad debt. Last year, before considering the tax implications of the nonbusiness bad debt, Monty had capital gains of $9,000 and taxable income of $45,000. During the current year, Ned paid Monty $10,000 in satisfaction of the debt. Determine Monty's tax treatment for the $10,000 received in the current year.

30. **LO.1** Sally is in the business of purchasing accounts receivable. Last year Sally purchased an account receivable with a face value of $80,000 for $60,000. During the current year, Sally settled the account, receiving $65,000. Determine the maximum amount of the bad debt deduction for Sally for the current year.

31. **LO.1, 2** Jocelyn and Esteban file a joint return. For the current year, they had the following items:

Salaries	$120,000
Loss on sale of § 1244 stock acquired two years ago	105,000
Gain on sale of § 1244 stock acquired six months ago	20,000
Nonbusiness bad debt	19,000

Determine their AGI for the current year.

Decision Making
Critical Thinking

32. **LO.2, 8** Abby, a single taxpayer, purchased 10,000 shares of § 1244 stock several years ago at a cost of $20 per share. In November of the current year, Abby received an offer to sell the stock for $12 per share. She has the option of either selling all of the stock now or selling half of the stock now and half of the stock in January of next year. Abby will receive a salary of $80,000 for the current year and $90,000 next year. Abby will have long-term capital gains of $8,000 for the current year and $10,000 next year. If Abby's goal is to minimize her AGI for the two years, determine whether she should sell all of her stock this year or half of her stock this year and half next year.

Decision Making
Critical Thinking

33. **LO.3, 4, 8** Olaf lives in the state of Minnesota. In 2020, a tornado hit the area and damaged his home and automobile. Applicable information is as follows:

Item	Adjusted Basis	FMV before	FMV after	Insurance Proceeds
Home	$350,000	$500,000	$100,000	$280,000
Auto	60,000	40,000	10,000	20,000

Because of the extensive damage caused by the tornado, the President designated the area a Federal disaster area.

Olaf and his wife, Anna, always file a joint return. Their 2019 tax return shows AGI of $180,000 and taxable income of $145,000. In 2020, their return shows AGI of $300,000 and taxable income (exclusive of the casualty loss deduction) of $225,000.

Determine the amount of Olaf and Anna's loss and the year in which they should take the loss.

34. **LO.3, 4** Heather owns a two-story building. The building is used 40% for business use and 60% for personal use. During 2020, a fire caused major damage to the building and its contents. Heather purchased the building for $800,000 and has taken depreciation of $100,000 on the business portion. At the time of the fire, the building had a fair market value of $900,000. Immediately after the fire, the fair market value was $200,000. The insurance recovery on the building was $600,000. The contents of the building were insured for any loss at fair market value. The business assets had an adjusted basis of $220,000 and a fair market value of $175,000. These assets were totally destroyed. The personal use assets had an adjusted basis of $50,000 and a fair market value of $65,000. These assets were also totally destroyed. If Heather's AGI is $100,000 before considering the effects of the fire, determine her itemized deduction as a result of the fire. Also determine Heather's AGI.

Decision Making
Communications

35. **LO.3, 4** On July 24 of the current year, Sam Smith was involved in an accident with his business use automobile. Sam had purchased the car for $30,000. The automobile had a fair market value of $20,000 before the accident and $8,000 immediately after the accident. Sam has taken $20,000 of depreciation on the car. The car is insured for the fair market value of any loss. Because of Sam's history, he is afraid that if he submits a claim, his policy will be canceled. Therefore, he is considering not filing a claim. Sam believes that the tax loss deduction will help mitigate the loss of the insurance reimbursement. Sam's current marginal tax rate is 35%.

Write a letter to Sam that contains your advice with respect to the tax and cash-flow consequences of filing versus not filing a claim for the insurance reimbursement for the damage to his car. Also prepare a memo for the tax files. Sam's address is 450 Colonel's Way, Warrensburg, MO 64093.

36. **LO.5** Blue Corporation, a manufacturing company, decided to develop a new line of merchandise. The project began in 2019. Blue had the following expenses in connection with the project:

	2019	2020
Salaries	$500,000	$600,000
Materials	90,000	70,000
Insurance	8,000	11,000
Utilities	6,000	8,000
Cost of inspection of materials for quality control	7,000	6,000
Promotion expenses	11,000	18,000
Advertising	–0–	20,000
Equipment depreciation	15,000	14,000
Cost of market survey	8,000	–0–

The new product will be introduced for sale beginning in July 2021. Determine the amount of the deduction for research and experimental expenditures for 2019, 2020, and 2021 if:

a. Blue Corporation elects to expense the research and experimental expenditures.

b. Blue Corporation elects to amortize the research and experimental expenditures over 60 months.

37. **LO.6** During 2020, Leisel, a single taxpayer, operates a sole proprietorship in which she materially participates. Her proprietorship generates gross income of $142,000 and deductions of $420,000, resulting in a loss of $278,000. The large deductions are due to the acquisition of equipment and the use of immediate expense and additional first-year depreciation to deduct all of the acquisitions. Can Leisel use all of this loss to offset other income she has? Explain.

38. **LO.6** Timothy Gates and Prada Singh decide to form a new company, TGPS LLC (a multimember LLC that will report its operations as a partnership). Timothy is married, and Prada is single. Each contributes $400,000 of capital to begin the business, and both materially participate in the business. In 2020, TGPS reports a net loss of $580,000. What are the implications of this loss for Timothy and Prada?

Tax Return Problems

39. Jane Smith, age 40, is single and has no dependents. She is employed as a legal secretary by Legal Services, Inc. She owns and operates Typing Services located near the campus of Florida Atlantic University at 1986 Campus Drive, Boca Raton, FL 33434. Jane is a material participant in the business. She is a cash basis taxpayer. Jane lives at 2020 Oakcrest Road, Boca Raton, FL 33431. Jane's Social Security number is 123-45-6781. Jane indicates that she wants to designate $3 to the Presidential Election Campaign Fund. Jane has never owned or used any virtual currency. During 2019, Jane had the following income and expense items:

a. $100,000 salary from Legal Services, Inc.

b. $20,000 gross receipts from her typing services business.

c. $700 interest income from Third National Bank.

Tax Forms Problem

Decision Making

Critical Thinking

Communications

d. $1,000 Christmas bonus from Legal Services, Inc.

e. $60,000 life insurance proceeds on the death of her sister.

f. $5,000 check given to her by her wealthy aunt.

g. $100 won in a bingo game.

h. Expenses connected with the typing service:

Office rent	$7,000
Supplies	4,400
Utilities and telephone	4,680
Wages to part-time typists	5,000
Payroll taxes	500
Equipment rentals	3,000

i. $9,500 interest expense on a home mortgage (paid to San Jose Savings and Loan).

j. $15,000 fair market value of silverware stolen from her home by a burglar on October 12, 2019. Jane had paid $14,000 for the silverware on July 1, 2009. She was reimbursed $10,000 by her insurance company.

k. Jane had loaned $2,100 to a friend, Joan Jensen, on June 3, 2015. Joan declared bankruptcy on August 14, 2019, and was unable to repay the loan. Assume that the loan is a bona fide debt.

l. Legal Services, Inc., withheld Federal income tax of $15,000 and the appropriate amount of FICA tax from her wages.

m. Alimony of $10,000 received from her former husband, Ted Smith; divorce was finalized on December 2, 2013, and no changes have been made to the divorce decree since that time.

n. Interest income of $800 on City of Boca Raton bonds.

o. Jane made estimated Federal tax payments of $2,000.

p. Sales taxes from the sales tax table of $953.

q. Property taxes on her residence of $3,200.

r. Charitable contribution of $2,500 to her alma mater, Citrus State College.

s. On November 1, 2019, Jane was involved in an automobile accident. At the time of the accident, Jane's automobile had an FMV of $45,000. After the accident, the automobile's FMV was $38,000. Jane acquired the car on May 2, 2018, at a cost of $52,000. Jane's car was covered by insurance, but because the policy had a $5,000 deduction clause, Jane decided not to file a claim for the damage.

Part 1—Tax Computation

Compute Jane Smith's 2019 Federal income tax payable (or refund due). If you use tax forms for your computations, at a minimum, you will need Form 1040, Schedule 1 (Form 1040), and Schedules A, C, and D. Suggested software: ProConnect Tax Online.

Part 2—Tax Planning

In 2020, Jane plans to continue her job with Legal Services, Inc. Therefore, items a, d, and l will recur in 2020. Jane plans to continue her typing services business (refer to item b) and expects gross receipts of $34,000. She projects that all business expenses (refer to item h) will increase by 10%, except for office rent, which, under the terms of her lease, will remain the same as in 2019. Items e, f, g, j, k, and s will not recur in 2020. Items c, i, m, n, p, q, and r will be approximately the same as in 2019.

Based on this information, Jane would like you to provide a tentative computation of her 2020 taxable income. Prepare a memo to her tax files that details this computation.

40. Mason Phillips, age 45, and his wife, Ruth, live at 230 Wood Lane, Salt Lake City,
    UT 84101. Mason's Social Security number is 111-11-1111. Ruth's Social Security
    number is 123-45-6789. Mason and Ruth are cash basis taxpayers and had the fol-
    lowing items for 2020:

    Tax Computation Problem

    - Salary of $140,000.
    - Bad debt of $30,000 from uncollected rent.
    - Collection of unpaid rent from a prior year of $6,000.
    - Sale of § 1244 stock resulting in a loss of $105,000. The stock was acquired eight
      months ago.
    - Rental income of $60,000 (property is managed by Mason and Ruth).
    - Rental expenses of $33,000.
    - Casualty loss on rental property of $10,000.
    - Personal casualty loss (from one event) of $3,000; not in a Federally declared
      disaster area.
    - Theft loss of $8,000 on a painting held for investment.
    - Other itemized deductions of $21,000.
    - Federal income tax withheld of $3,000.

    Compute Mason and Ruth's 2020 Federal income tax payable (or refund due).

Research Problems

**Note: Solutions to the Research Problems can be prepared by using the Thomson
Reuters Checkpoint™ online tax research database, which accompanies this
textbook. Solutions can also be prepared by using research materials found in a
typical tax library.**

Research Problem 1. During 2020, John was the chief executive officer and a shareholder of Maze, Inc. He owned 60% of the outstanding stock of Maze. In 2017, John
and Maze, as co-borrowers, obtained a $100,000 loan from United National Bank.
This loan was secured by John's personal residence. Although Maze was listed as a
co-borrower, John repaid the loan in full in 2020. On Maze's Form 1120 tax returns,
no loans from shareholders were reported. Discuss whether John is entitled to a bad
debt deduction for the amount of the payment on the loan.

Partial list of research aids:
U.S. v. Generes, 405 U.S. 93 (1972).
Dale H. Sundby, T.C.Memo. 2003–204.
Arrigoni v. Comm., 73 T.C. 792 (1980).
Estate of Herbert M. Rapoport, T.C.Memo. 1982–584.
Clifford L. Brody and Barbara J. DeClerk, T.C. Summary Opinion, 2004–149.

Research Problem 2. Esther owns a large home on the Southeast Coast. Her home
is surrounded by large, mature oak trees that significantly increase the value of her
home. In September 2019, a hurricane damaged many of the trees surrounding her
home; her region was declared a Federal disaster area as a result of the hurricane's
damage. In October 2019, Esther engaged a local arborist to evaluate and treat the
trees, but five of the largest trees were seriously weakened by the storm. These trees
died from disease in 2020. Esther has ascertained that the amount of the casualty
loss from the death of the five trees is $25,000; however, she is uncertain in which
year to deduct this loss. Discuss whether the casualty loss should be deducted in the
calculation of Esther's 2019 or 2020 taxable income.

Partial list of research aids:
Reg. § 1.165–1.
Oregon Mesabi Corporation, 39 B.T.A. 1033 (1939).

Use internet tax resources to address the following questions. Look for reliable websites and blogs of the IRS and other government agencies, media outlets, businesses, tax professionals, academics, think tanks, and political outlets.

Research Problem 3. Find a newspaper article that discusses tax planning for casualty losses when a Federal disaster area designation is made. Does the article convey the pertinent tax rules correctly? Then list all of the locations identified by the President as Federal disaster areas in the last two years.

Data Analytics

Communications

Research Problem 4. How many U.S. individuals claim a deduction for casualties? Does it vary by size of income (AGI)? How do casualty loss deductions compare to the amounts of other itemized deductions claimed by taxpayers? Go to the IRS tax statistics website (**irs.gov/statistics**), and download a recent tax year's information on "Individual Income Tax Returns with Itemized Deductions." Cluster the data into no more than six AGI categories. Present your findings in a visual (e.g., a bar chart), and summarize your findings in a one-page memo to your instructor.

Communications

Research Problem 5. Many states have their income tax calculations "piggyback" the Federal income tax calculation. In other words, these states' income tax calculations incorporate many of the Federal calculations and deductions to make both compliance and verification of tax liability easier. However, given the significant changes implemented via the TCJA of 2017, some state legislatures have passed laws modifying some of these rules for state purposes. Determine how states are reacting to the TCJA of 2017. Specifically, how are states reacting to the TCJA of 2017 changes to personal casualty losses, the excess business loss limitation, and the net operating loss changes (no carryback and 80% of taxable income limitation)? Be sure to state the sources for your answer.

Becker CPA Review Questions

Becker.

1. Mark and Lucy owned two stocks, Tinker, Inc. and Chance, Inc., that became worthless during year 8. The adjusted basis in Tinker was $300,000. Tinker was incorporated in year 2, and Mark and Lucy purchased their stock in year 4. Their adjusted basis in Chance was $200,000. Chance was incorporated in year 2, and Mark and Lucy were original stockholders. Both stocks were purchased for cash, and each corporation had total capital of $500,000. How much ordinary loss can Mark and Lucy deduct on their joint year 8 tax return as a result of these transactions?

    a. $0
    b. $100,000
    c. $200,000
    d. $300,000

2. Mark and Lucy owned two stocks, Tinker, Inc. and Chance, Inc., that became worthless during year 8. The adjusted basis in Tinker was $80,000. Tinker was incorporated in year 2, and Mark and Lucy purchased their stock in year 4. Their adjusted basis in Chance was $20,000. Chance was incorporated in year 2, and Mark and Lucy were original stockholders. Both stocks were purchased for cash, and each corporation had total capital of $500,000. How much ordinary loss can Mark and Lucy deduct on their joint year 8 tax return as a result of these transactions?

    a. $0
    b. $20,000
    c. $80,000
    d. $100,000

3. Chad owned an office building that was destroyed in a tornado. The area was declared a Federal disaster area. The adjusted basis of the building at the time was $890,000. After the deductible, Chad received an insurance check for $850,000. He used the $850,000 to purchase a new building that same year. How much is Chad's recognized loss, and what is his basis in the new building?

	Recognized Loss	**New Basis**
a.	$0	$850,000
b.	$0	$890,000
c.	$40,000	$850,000
d.	$40,000	$890,000

4. Hunter has a loss of $50,000 from his landscaping business in the current year. He reports the loss on Schedule C of his Form 1040. After deducting the loss against his other sources of income, he has a remaining business loss of $10,000. What are Hunter's options regarding the remaining $10,000 business loss?

   a. He can carry the loss back 4 years and forward 20 years.

   b. He can carry the loss back 2 years and forward 20 years.

   c. He can choose to only carry the loss forward 20 years.

   d. He can carry the loss forward indefinitely.

CHAPTER

8

Depreciation, Cost Recovery, Amortization, and Depletion

LEARNING OBJECTIVES: *After completing Chapter 8, you should be able to:*

LO.1 State the rationale for allowing the cost recovery of an asset and identify when the various tax systems (depreciation, ACRS, and MACRS) apply.

LO.2 Determine the amount of cost recovery under MACRS.

LO.3 Recognize when and how to make the § 179 expensing election and use additional first-year depreciation and calculate the amount of these deductions as part of the MACRS calculation.

LO.4 Identify listed property and apply the deduction limitations on listed property and on luxury automobiles.

LO.5 Determine when and how to use the alternative depreciation system (ADS).

LO.6 Report cost recovery deductions appropriately.

LO.7 Identify intangible assets that are eligible for amortization and calculate the amount of the deduction.

LO.8 Determine the amount of depletion expense, including being able to apply the alternative tax treatments for intangible drilling and development costs.

LO.9 Identify tax planning opportunities for cost recovery, amortization, and depletion.

CHAPTER OUTLINE

8-1 Depreciation and Cost Recovery, 8-2
    8-1a Nature of Property, 8-2
    8-1b Placed in Service Requirement, 8-3
    8-1c Cost Recovery Allowed or Allowable, 8-3
    8-1d Cost Recovery Basis for Personal Use Assets Converted to Business or Income-Producing Use, 8-4

8-2 Modified Accelerated Cost Recovery System (MACRS): General Rules, 8-4
    8-2a Personalty (and Certain Realty): Recovery Periods and Methods, 8-5
    8-2b Realty: Recovery Periods and Methods, 8-9

8-3 Modified Accelerated Cost Recovery System (MACRS): Special Rules, 8-10
    8-3a Election to Expense Assets (§ 179), 8-10
    8-3b Additional First-Year Depreciation (Bonus Depreciation), 8-14

    8-3c Using § 179 and Bonus Depreciation Effectively, 8-15
    8-3d Business and Personal Use of Automobiles and Other Listed Property, 8-18
    8-3e Alternative Depreciation System (ADS), 8-23

8-4 Reporting Procedures, 8-24

8-5 Amortization, 8-25

8-6 Depletion, 8-28
    8-6a Intangible Drilling and Development Costs (IDCs), 8-29
    8-6b Depletion Methods, 8-29

8-7 Tax Planning, 8-31
    8-7a Cost Recovery, 8-31
    8-7b Amortization, 8-32
    8-7c Cost Recovery Tables, 8-32

THE BIG PICTURE

CALCULATING COST RECOVERY DEDUCTIONS

Dr. Cliff Payne purchased and placed in service $612,085 of new fixed assets in his dental practice during the current year.

Office furniture and fixtures	$ 70,000
Computers and peripheral equipment	67,085
Dental equipment	475,000

Using his financial reporting system, he concludes that the depreciation expense on Schedule C of Form 1040 is $91,298.

Office furniture and fixtures ($70,000 × 14.29%)	$10,003
Computers and peripheral equipment ($67,085 × 20%)	13,417
Dental equipment ($475,000 × 14.29%)	67,878
	$91,298

In addition, this year Dr. Payne purchased another personal residence for $480,000 and converted his original residence to a rental property.

Has Dr. Payne correctly calculated the depreciation expense for his dental practice? Will he be able to deduct any depreciation expense for his rental properties?

Read the chapter and formulate your response.

FRAMEWORK 1040 Tax Formula for Individuals

This chapter covers the boldfaced portions of the Tax Formula for Individuals that was introduced in Concept Summary 3.1 on p. 3-3. Below those portions are the sections of Form 1040 where the results are reported.

Income *(broadly defined)*	$ xx,xxx
Less: Exclusions	(x,xxx)
Gross income	**$ xx,xxx**
Less: Deductions *for* adjusted gross income	**(x,xxx)**

FORM 1040 (Schedule 1)

3	Business income or (loss). Attach Schedule C.	

Adjusted gross income	$ xx,xxx
Less: The greater of total itemized deductions *or* the standard deduction	(x,xxx)
Personal and dependency exemptions*	(x,xxx)
Deduction for qualified business income**	(x,xxx)
Taxable income	$ xx,xxx
Tax on taxable income *(see Tax Tables or Tax Rate Schedules)*	$ x,xxx
Less: Tax credits *(including income taxes withheld and prepaid)*	(xxx)
Tax due (or refund)	$ xxx

  * Exemption deductions are not allowed from 2018 through 2025.
** Only applies from 2018 through 2025.

The Internal Revenue Code allows a depreciation, cost recovery, amortization, or depletion deduction based on an asset's cost. These deductions reflect the recovery of capital doctrine (see text Section 4-1b). Cost recovery deductions are based on the idea that the asset acquired (or improvement made) benefits more than one accounting period. If not, the expenditure is deducted in the year incurred.[1]

Taxpayers may "write off" (deduct) the cost of certain assets that are used in a trade or business or held for the production of income. The deduction may take the form of depreciation (or cost recovery), depletion, or amortization. Tangible assets, other than natural resources, are *depreciated*. Natural resources, such as oil, gas, coal, and timber, are *depleted*. Intangible assets, such as copyrights and patents, are *amortized*. Generally, a deduction is allowed for an asset only if it has a determinable useful life.

Congress completely revised the tax <mark>depreciation</mark> rules in 1981 by creating the <mark>accelerated cost recovery system (ACRS)</mark>, which shortened depreciable lives and allowed accelerated depreciation methods. In 1986, Congress made substantial modifications to ACRS, which resulted in the <mark>modified accelerated cost recovery system (MACRS)</mark>, which is the focus of this chapter. Although the terms *depreciation* and <mark>cost recovery</mark> often are used interchangeably, the former normally refers to the allocation of costs to the appropriate period for financial reporting purposes whereas the latter refers to an equivalent concept for tax purposes.[2] A brief discussion of the amortization of intangible property and startup expenditures and the depletion of natural resources concludes the chapter.

8-1 DEPRECIATION AND COST RECOVERY

8-1a Nature of Property

Property includes both realty (real property) and personality (personal property). *Realty* generally includes land and buildings permanently affixed to the land. *Personalty* is

---

[1] See the discussion of capitalization versus expense in text Section 6-3i.

[2] § 168. The terms *depreciation* and *cost recovery* are used interchangeably in the text and in § 168. Pre-1986 depreciation rules are covered in the online appendix *Depreciation and the Accelerated Cost Recovery System (ACRS)*.

defined as any asset that is not realty.[3] Personalty includes furniture, machinery, equipment, and any other asset that is movable or not permanently affixed to land. Personalty (or personal property) should not be confused with *personal use* property. Personal use property is any property (realty or personalty) that is held for personal use rather than for use in a trade or business or an income-producing activity. Cost recovery deductions are not allowed for personal use assets.

 LO.1

State the rationale for allowing the cost recovery of an asset and identify when the various tax systems (depreciation, ACRS, and MACRS) apply.

In summary, both realty and personalty can be either business use/income-producing property or personal use property. Examples include:

- A residence (realty that is personal use),
- An office building (realty that is business use),
- A dump truck (personalty that is business use), and
- Common clothing (personalty that is personal use).

It is critical that the distinction between the *classification* of an asset (realty or personalty) and the *use* to which the asset is put (business/income-producing or personal) be understood.

Assets used in a trade or business or for the production of income are eligible for cost recovery if they are subject to wear and tear, decay or decline from natural causes, or obsolescence (e.g., equipment the taxpayer rents to third parties). Assets that do not decline in value on a predictable basis or that do not have a determinable useful life (e.g., land, stock, and antiques) are not eligible for cost recovery.

8-1b Placed in Service Requirement

Cost recovery begins on the date an asset is placed in service (ready and available for use), *not* the date of purchase. This distinction is particularly important for an asset that is purchased near the end of the tax year, but not placed in service until the following tax year.

8-1c Cost Recovery Allowed or Allowable

To prevent the recovery of the same cost more than once (i.e., through periodic cost recovery during the asset's life and via its basis the sale of the asset), the basis of property is reduced by any cost recovery deducted on a tax return (this is the *allowed* cost recovery). However, the property's basis is reduced by at least the amount of cost recovery that could have been taken using the appropriate cost recovery method (this is the *allowable* cost recovery). As a result, even if the taxpayer does not claim any cost recovery on property during a particular year, the basis of the property still is reduced by the amount of cost recovery that should have been deducted (the allowable cost recovery).

EXAMPLE

1

On March 15, year 1, Jack purchased a copier, to use in his business, for $10,000. The copier is 5-year property, and Jack elected to use the straight-line method of cost recovery. Jack made the election because the business was a new undertaking and he reasoned that in the first few years of the business, a large cost recovery deduction was not needed.

Because the business was doing poorly, Jack did not deduct any cost recovery in years 3 and 4. In years 5 and 6, Jack deducted the proper amount of cost recovery. The *allowed* cost recovery (cost recovery actually deducted) and the *allowable* cost recovery are computed as follows:

	Cost Recovery Allowed	Cost Recovery Allowable
Year 1	$1,000	$1,000
Year 2	2,000	2,000
Year 3	–0–	2,000
Year 4	–0–	2,000
Year 5	2,000	2,000
Year 6	1,000	1,000

continued

---
[3]Refer to text Section 1-4a for further discussion.

If Jack sold the copier for $800 in year 7, he would recognize an $800 gain ($800 amount realized − $0 adjusted basis); the adjusted basis of the copier is zero ($10,000 cost − $10,000 total *allowable* cost recovery in years 1 through 6).

8-1d Cost Recovery Basis for Personal Use Assets Converted to Business or Income-Producing Use

If personal use assets are converted to business or income-producing use, the basis for cost recovery and for loss is the *lower* of the adjusted basis or the fair market value at the time the property was converted. This rule ensures that any decline in value that occurred while the property was a personal use asset is not eligible for cost recovery.

The Big Picture

EXAMPLE

2

Return to the facts of *The Big Picture* on p. 8-1. In 2007, Dr. Payne purchased a personal residence for $250,000. In the current year, Dr. Payne found a larger home that he acquired for his personal residence. Because of the downturn in the housing market, however, he was not able to sell his original residence and recover his purchase price of $250,000. The residence was appraised at $180,000.

Instead of continuing to try to sell the original residence, Dr. Payne converted it to rental property. The basis for cost recovery of the rental property is $180,000 because the fair market value is less than the adjusted basis. The $70,000 decline in value is deemed to be personal (because it occurred while the property was held for personal use by Dr. Payne) and therefore nondeductible.

LO.2

Determine the amount of cost recovery under MACRS.

8-2 MODIFIED ACCELERATED COST RECOVERY SYSTEM (MACRS): GENERAL RULES

Under the modified accelerated cost recovery system (MACRS), the cost of an asset is recovered over a time period that generally is shorter than the economic life of an asset. The MACRS rules were designed to encourage investment, improve productivity, and simplify the tax law and its administration.

MACRS provides separate cost recovery systems for realty and personalty. Based on cost recovery periods (called class lives), methods, and conventions specified in the Internal Revenue Code, the IRS provides tables that identify cost recovery allowances for personalty and for realty. Excerpts from the IRS tables are provided in text Section 8-7c.

Concept Summary 8.1 provides an overview of the class lives, methods, and conventions that apply to personalty and realty under MACRS.

Concept Summary 8.1

MACRS: Class Lives, Methods, and Conventions

	Personalty	Realty
Class lives	3 to 20 years	Residential: 27.5 years Nonresidential: 39 years
Method	200% declining balance for property with class lives less than 15 years 150% declining balance for property with 15- or 20-year class lives	Straight-line
Convention	Half-year or mid-quarter	Mid-month

8-2a Personalty (and Certain Realty): Recovery Periods and Methods

Classification of Property

MACRS provides that the basis of eligible personalty (and certain realty) is recovered over 3, 5, 7, 10, 15, or 20 years. An asset's MACRS recovery period is determined by identifying its Asset Depreciation Range (ADR) midpoint life (determined by the IRS).[4] See Exhibit 8.1 for examples of assets in each class.[5]

Double declining balance is used for the 3-, 5-, 7-, and 10-year classes, with a switchover to straight-line depreciation when appropriate. Cost recovery for the 15- and 20-year classes is based on the 150 percent declining-balance method, with an appropriate straight-line switchover.[6] These methods and conventions are built into the IRS tables. As a result, it is generally not necessary to make these calculations.

To determine an asset's cost recovery deduction for a year, you identify the asset's MACRS class, find the cost recovery percentage for the year using the appropriate IRS table, and multiply this percentage by the asset's cost. The MACRS percentages for personalty appear in Exhibit 8.3 (see text Section 8-7c). Concept Summary 8.2 provides an overview of the various conventions that apply under the regular MACRS method.

EXHIBIT 8.1	Cost Recovery Periods: MACRS Personalty (and Certain Realty)	

Property Class	Generally Includes Assets with the Following ADR Lives	Examples
3-year	4 years or less	Tractor units for use over the road
		A racehorse that is more than 2 years old, or any other horse that is more than 12 years old, at the time it is placed in service
		Special tools used in the manufacturing of motor vehicles, such as dies, fixtures, molds, and patterns
5-year	More than 4 years and less than 10 years	Automobiles and taxis
		Light and heavy general-purpose trucks
		Calculators and copiers
		Computers and peripheral equipment
		Rental appliances, furniture, carpets
7-year	10 years or more and less than 16 years	Office furniture, fixtures, and equipment
		Agricultural machinery and equipment
10-year	16 years or more and less than 20 years	Vessels, barges, tugs, and similar water transportation equipment
		Assets used for petroleum refining or for the manufacture of grain and grain mill products, sugar and sugar products, or vegetable oils and vegetable oil products
		Single-purpose agricultural or horticultural structures
15-year	20 years or more and less than 25 years	Land improvements
		Qualified improvement property
		Assets used for industrial steam and electric generation and/or distribution systems
		Assets used in the manufacture of cement
20-year	25 years or more	Farm buildings except single-purpose agricultural and horticultural structures
		Water utilities

[4]Personalty is assigned to recovery classes based on Asset Depreciation Range (ADR) midpoint lives (Rev.Proc. 87–56, 1987–2 C.B. 674). ADR lives generally represent estimates of an asset's useful economic life.

[5]§ 168(e).
[6]§ 168(b).

FINANCIAL DISCLOSURE INSIGHTS   Tax and Book Depreciation

A common book-tax difference relates to the depreciation amounts that are reported for GAAP and Federal income tax purposes. Typically, tax depreciation deductions are accelerated; that is, they are claimed in earlier reporting periods than is the case for financial accounting purposes.

Almost every tax law change since 1980 has included depreciation provisions that accelerate the related deductions relative to the expenses allowed under GAAP. Accelerated cost recovery deductions represent a means by which the taxing jurisdiction infuses the business with cash flow created by the reduction in the year's tax liabilities.

For instance, recently, about one-quarter of General Electric's deferred tax liabilities related to depreciation differences. For Toyota's and Ford's depreciation differences, that amount was about one-third. And for the trucking firm Ryder Systems, depreciation differences accounted for all but 1 percent of the deferred tax liabilities.

Concept Summary 8.2

MACRS Conventions (by Property Type)

	Personal Property	Real Property*
Convention	Half-year or mid-quarter	Mid-month
Cost recovery deduction in the year of disposition**	Half-year for year of sale or half-quarter for quarter of sale	Half-month for month of sale

*Straight-line method must be used.

**A disposition can include a sale, exchange, abandonment, or retirement. For simplicity, we will assume a sale in this chapter.

Taxpayers may *elect* the straight-line method to compute cost recovery allowances for each of these classes of property. Certain property is not eligible for accelerated cost recovery and must be depreciated under an alternative depreciation system (ADS). Both the straight-line election and ADS are discussed later in the chapter.

Cost recovery for personalty generally incorporates the <mark>half-year convention</mark>; that is, cost recovery in the year the asset is placed in service, as well as the year it is removed from service, is based on the assumption that the asset was used for exactly one half of the year, allowing a half-year of cost recovery.[7] For example, the regular MACRS recovery period for property with a life of three years begins in the middle of the year an asset is placed in service and ends three years later, in the fourth taxable year. In practical terms, this means that an asset's cost is actually recovered over 4, 6, 8, 11, 16, or 21 years.

MACRS Personalty; Half-Year Convention

EXAMPLE 3

Kareem acquires a 5-year class asset on April 10, 2020, for $30,000. Kareem's cost recovery deduction for 2020 is computed as follows.

MACRS cost recovery [$30,000 × 0.20 (Exhibit 8.3)]   <u>$6,000</u>

EXAMPLE 4

Assume the same facts as in Example 3. Kareem sells the asset on March 5, 2022. Kareem's cost recovery deduction for 2022 is $2,880 [$30,000 × 0.192 (Exhibit 8.3) × ½].

---

[7]§ 168(d)(4)(A).

Mid-Quarter Convention

The half-year convention is based on the simplifying presumption that assets generally are acquired at an even pace throughout the tax year. However, Congress was concerned that taxpayers might defeat that presumption by placing large amounts of property in service toward the end of the taxable year (and by doing so, receive a half-year's depreciation on those large end-of-year acquisitions).

To inhibit this behavior, Congress added the **mid-quarter convention** that applies if more than 40 percent of the cost of property other than real estate (see text Section 8-2b) is placed in service during the last quarter of the year.[8] If the mid-quarter convention applies, property acquisitions are grouped by the quarter of acquisition. Acquisitions made during the first quarter are allowed 10.5 months (three and one-half quarters) of cost recovery in the first year; the second quarter, 7.5 months (two and one-half quarters); the third quarter, 4.5 months (one and one-half quarters); and the fourth quarter, 1.5 months (one-half quarter). The percentages are shown in Exhibit 8.4.

EXAMPLE
5

Silver Corporation acquires the following new 5-year class property in 2020.

Property Acquisition Dates	Cost
February 15	$ 200,000
July 10	400,000
December 5	600,000
Total	$1,200,000

Because more than 40% ($600,000/$1,200,000 = 50\%$) of the acquisitions are in the last quarter, the mid-quarter convention applies. Silver's cost recovery allowances for the first two years are computed below.

2020

	Mid-Quarter Convention Depreciation (Exhibit 8.4)	Total Depreciation
February 15	$200,000 × 0.35	$ 70,000
July 10	$400,000 × 0.15	60,000
December 5	$600,000 × 0.05	30,000
		$160,000

2021

	Mid-Quarter Convention Depreciation (Exhibit 8.4)	Total Depreciation
February 15	$200,000 × 0.26	$ 52,000
July 10	$400,000 × 0.34	136,000
December 5	$600,000 × 0.38	228,000
		$416,000

Without the mid-quarter convention, Silver's 2020 cost recovery deduction would have been $240,000 [$1,200,000 × 0.20 (Exhibit 8.3)]. As a result, the mid-quarter convention reduces the taxpayer's available cost recovery deductions in the acquisition year (and defers those deductions to later years).

When "mid-quarter" property is sold, the property is treated as though it were sold at the midpoint of the quarter. So in the quarter when sold, cost recovery is allowed for one-half of the quarter.

[8]§ 168(d)(3).

EXAMPLE 6

Assume the same facts as in Example 5, except that Silver Corporation sells the $400,000 asset on November 30, 2021. The cost recovery deduction for 2021 is computed as follows (using Exhibit 8.4).

February 15	$200,000 × 0.26	$ 52,000
July 10	$400,000 × 0.34 × (3.5/4)	119,000
December 5	$600,000 × 0.38	228,000
Total cost recovery deduction		$399,000

The tax adjusted basis of the $400,000 asset when sold is $221,000 [$400,000 (cost) − $60,000 (2020 cost recovery) − $119,000 (2021 cost recovery)].

The Big Picture

EXAMPLE 7

Return to the facts of *The Big Picture* on p. 8-1. If the placed-in-service date for the office furniture and fixtures and computers and peripheral equipment is September 29 and the placed-in-service date for the dental equipment is October 3, Dr. Payne's total cost recovery deduction is computed as follows.

Office furniture and fixtures:	
MACRS cost recovery $70,000 × 0.1071 (Exhibit 8.4)	$ 7,497
Computers and peripheral equipment:	
MACRS cost recovery $67,085 × 0.15 (Exhibit 8.4)	10,063
Dental equipment:	
MACRS cost recovery $475,000 × 0.357 (Exhibit 8.4)	16,958
Total cost recovery deduction	$34,518

Note the implications of the mid-quarter convention. If the dental equipment had been placed in service before October 1 (the beginning of the fourth quarter), the total cost recovery deduction would have been $91,298 (as detailed on p. 8-1).

Qualified Improvement Property

Nonresidential realty has a 39-year life, and any improvements made to this property would normally have a 39-year life. An exception to this general rule is provided for ==qualified improvement property==. Qualified improvement property is recovered over a 15-year life using the half-year convention and the straight-line method.[9]

Qualified improvement property is any improvement to an interior portion of nonresidential real property made after the property is placed in service, including leasehold improvements. However, it does not include the costs of an elevator or escalator or improvements that enlarge a building or modify its internal framework.

EXAMPLE 8

Redbud, Inc., finishes construction of an office building in July 2019. It plans to lease the third floor of the building to a tenant. In January 2020, Crimson Enterprises leases the third floor and immediately builds out the rental space to meet its needs. It spends $50,000 on cubicles, shelving, and other non-permanent additions. These improvements are qualified improvement property and will be recovered over 15 years using the half-year convention and straight-line method.

In 2020, Crimson's cost recovery deduction is $1,667 ($50,000 × 0.03333; see Exhibit 8.5 for cost recovery percentages).

Straight-Line Election

A taxpayer may *elect* to use the straight-line method for personal property.[10] If elected, the property is depreciated using the MACRS life of the asset with a half-year convention

---

[9]§ 168(e)(6). Due to a drafting error, the TCJA of 2017 classifies qualified improvement property as having a 39-year life. This error is expected to be corrected in subsequent legislation.

[10]§ 168(b)(5).

or a mid-quarter convention, whichever applies. The election is available on a class-by-class and year-by-year basis (see Concept Summary 8.3). So, for example, a taxpayer could elect the straight-line method for 5-year MACRS assets placed in service during the current year; 5-year MACRS assets placed in service the following year are not bound by this choice. And the choice of having 5-year MACRS assets on the straight-line method would not apply to other personalty (e.g., the 3-year and 7-year MACRS classes) unless elected by the taxpayer. The percentages for the straight-line election with a half-year convention appear in Exhibit 8.5.

Concept Summary 8.3

Straight-Line Cost Recovery under MACRS (Personalty vs. Realty)

	Personalty	Realty*
Convention	Half-year or mid-quarter	Mid-month
Cost recovery deduction in the year of disposition**	Half-year for year of sale or half-quarter for quarter of sale	Half-month for month of sale
Elective or mandatory	Elective	Mandatory
Breadth of election	Class by class	

*Straight-line method must be used.

**A disposition can include a sale, exchange, abandonment, or retirement. For simplicity, we will assume a sale in this chapter.

The Big Picture

EXAMPLE
9

Return to the facts of *The Big Picture* on p. 8-1. If Dr. Payne elects the straight-line method of cost recovery, his total cost recovery deduction is computed as follows.

Office furniture and fixtures	
($70,000 × 0.0714) (Exhibit 8.5)	$ 4,998
Computers and peripheral equipment	
($67,085 × 0.10) (Exhibit 8.5)	6,709
Dental equipment	
($475,000 × 0.0714) (Exhibit 8.5)	33,915
Total cost recovery deduction	$45,622

If Dr. Payne does not elect the straight-line cost recovery method, his cost recovery deduction is $91,298 (as detailed on p. 8-1).

The Big Picture

EXAMPLE
10

Assume the same facts as in Example 9, except that Dr. Payne sells the computers and peripheral equipment on November 21, 2021. His cost recovery deduction for 2021 is $6,709 ($67,085 × 0.20 × $\frac{1}{2}$) (Exhibit 8.5).

8-2b Realty: Recovery Periods and Methods

Under MACRS, the cost of most real property is recovered using the straight-line method. The recovery period for residential rental real estate is 27.5 years. Residential rental real estate includes property where 80 percent or more of the gross rental revenues are from residential units (e.g., an apartment building). Hotels, motels, and similar establishments are not residential rental property. Nonresidential real estate is recovered over 39 years.[11]

[11]§§ 168(b), (c), and (e). A 31.5-year life is used for nonresidential real estate placed in service before May 13, 1993.

Some items of real property are not treated as real estate under MACRS. For example, single-purpose agricultural structures are in the 10-year MACRS class. Land improvements are in the 15-year MACRS class.

All MACRS real estate is depreciated using the **mid-month convention**.[12] Under this convention, one-half month's cost recovery is allowed for the month the property is placed in service. So if a calendar year taxpayer places MACRS real estate in service on June 2 of the current tax year, it will be able to deduct six and one-half months of cost recovery (June 15 to December 31). If the property is sold before the end of the recovery period, one-half month's cost recovery is allowed for the month of sale (no matter when the property is sold).

As with personalty, the IRS provides tables to assist taxpayers in computing cost recovery on realty. Cost recovery is computed by multiplying the applicable rate (Exhibit 8.8) by the cost recovery basis.

Real Estate Cost Recovery

EXAMPLE 11

Alec acquired a building on April 1, 2003, for $800,000. If the building is classified as residential rental real estate, the cost recovery deduction for 2020 is $29,088 (0.03636 × $800,000).

If, instead, the building is sold on October 7, 2020, the cost recovery deduction for 2020 is $23,028 [0.03636 (Exhibit 8.8) × (9.5/12) × $800,000].

EXAMPLE 12

Jane acquired a building on March 2, 1993, for $1,000,000. If the building is classified as nonresidential real estate, the cost recovery deduction for 2020 is $31,740 (0.03174 × $1,000,000).

If, instead, the building is sold on January 5, 2020, the cost recovery deduction for 2020 is $1,323 [0.03174 (Exhibit 8.8) × (0.5/12) × $1,000,000].

EXAMPLE 13

Mark acquired a building on November 19, 2020, for $1,200,000. If the building is classified as non-residential real estate, the cost recovery deduction for 2020 is $3,852 [0.00321 (Exhibit 8.8) × $1,200,000]. The cost recovery deduction for 2021 is $30,768 [0.02564 (Exhibit 8.8) × $1,200,000].

If, instead, the building is sold on May 21, 2021, the cost recovery deduction for 2021 is $11,538 [0.02564 (Exhibit 8.8) × (4.5/12) × $1,200,000].

8-3 MODIFIED ACCELERATED COST RECOVERY SYSTEM (MACRS): SPECIAL RULES

LO.3

Recognize when and how to make the § 179 expensing election and use additional first-year depreciation and calculate the amount of these deductions as part of the MACRS calculation.

A number of special rules apply under MACRS. To encourage investment in capital assets and reduce the related compliance costs, Congress has implemented two rules: immediate expensing (§ 179) and additional first-year depreciation (also called bonus depreciation). To curb potential taxpayer abuses of certain assets—particularly when the assets are used for both business and personal purposes—Congress established specific rules for "listed property." Finally, Congress also created an alternative depreciation system (ADS) that taxpayers can use instead of MACRS. The ADS must be used in certain settings (e.g., for the alternative minimum tax).

8-3a Election to Expense Assets (§ 179)

Section 179 (Election to Expense Certain Depreciable Business Assets) permits the taxpayer to deduct up to $1,040,000 in 2020 ($1,020,000 in 2019) of the acquisition cost of specific types of *trade or business* property. Amounts that are expensed under § 179 reduce the asset's basis for additional first-year depreciation (see text Section 8-3b) and MACRS cost recovery (see text Section 8-2a).

---

[12]§ 168(d)(1).

The §179 expensing election (also known as the immediate expense election) applies to the acquisition cost of property placed in service during a year. Property to which § 179 applies includes tangible personal property, computer software, qualified improvement property, and certain real property (roofs; heating, ventilation, and air conditioning units; fire protection and alarm systems; security systems). In general, the immediate expense election is not available for real property or for property used for the production of income.[13]

Any elected § 179 expense is taken *before* additional first-year depreciation is computed (see text Section 8-3b). Any MACRS deduction is calculated on the basis of the asset net of the § 179 expense and any additional first-year depreciation.

§ 179 Election and Basis

EXAMPLE 14

Allison acquires and places in service business equipment (a 5-year class asset) on February 1, 2020, at a cost of $80,000. It is the only asset she places in service in 2020. If Allison elects § 179, she can deduct the asset's entire cost in 2020. If not, she will use MACRS to cost recover the asset's cost over six years.

- If Allison elects § 179:

2020	§ 179 deduction	$80,000

- If Allison uses MACRS (see Exhibit 8.3):

2020	$80,000 × 0.20	$16,000
2021	$80,000 × 0.32	25,600
2022	$80,000 × 0.192	15,360
2023	$80,000 × 0.1152	9,216
2024	$80,000 × 0.1152	9,216
2025	$80,000 × 0.0576	4,608
		$80,000

EXAMPLE 15

Assume the same facts as in Example 14. Allison sells the asset in 2022 for $50,000.

- If Allison elects § 179, the asset's adjusted basis is zero ($80,000 − $80,000) and she has a realized gain of $50,000.

- If Allison uses MACRS, the asset's adjusted basis is $30,720 and she has a realized gain of $19,280.

Selling price			$ 50,000
Cost		$ 80,000	
Less: Cost recovery			
2020 MACRS	$16,000		
2021 MACRS	25,600		
2022 MACRS ($15,360 × ½)	7,680	(49,280)	(30,720)
Realized gain			$ 19,280

Deduction Limitations

The § 179 expense deduction is subject to three limitations, applied in this order.

1. **Ceiling Amount.** A taxpayer's § 179 deduction cannot exceed an annual ceiling amount ($1,040,000 in 2020; $1,020,000 in 2019).

2. **Property Placed in Service Maximum.** The § 179 deduction ceiling amount ($1,040,000 in 2020) is reduced dollar for dollar when § 179 property placed in

---

[13]The § 179 amount allowed is per taxpayer, per year. On a joint return, the statutory amount applies to the couple. If the taxpayers are married and file separate returns, each spouse is eligible for 50% of the statutory amount.

The annual expense and phaseout amounts in § 179 ($1,000,000 and $2,500,000, respectively) are adjusted for inflation each year and rounded to the nearest $10,000 multiple.

service during the taxable year exceeds a specified maximum amount ($2,590,000 in 2020; $2,550,000 in 2019). In 2020, a taxpayer who places in service $3,630,000 or more of qualifying property ($1,040,000 + $2,590,000) cannot claim a § 179 deduction.

3. **Business Income Limitation.** The § 179 deduction allowed for a taxable year cannot exceed the taxpayer's business income for the year.

Ceiling Amount. A taxpayer can choose to use *all, part, or none* of the annual § 179 amount. If a business expects its marginal tax rate to increase in the future, it may decide *not* to use the § 179 deduction. In such a situation, it may be better to defer deductions to those later years. As discussed below, the business income limitation may also lead a business owner to choose not to expense assets.

EXAMPLE 16

In 2020, Sonya Peters places in service $450,000 of 7-year MACRS assets. Although she could immediately expense all of these assets, she would prefer to use § 179 on just $275,000 of the assets. She knows that combining this expense with regular MACRS depreciation effectively reduces her business income to zero, and she wants to defer the remaining deductions to future years when her marginal tax rate will be higher. As a result, Sonya's total cost recovery deduction for 2020 is calculated as:

§ 179 expense	$275,000
MACRS depreciation [($450,000 − $275,000) × 0.1429 (Exhibit 8.3)]	25,008
Total cost recovery deduction	$300,008

Property Placed in Service Maximum. This rule effectively restricts the application of the § 179 deduction to smaller businesses. In 2020, a business that places in service more than $2,590,000 of qualifying property will have its § 179 deduction reduced. A business that places in service $3,630,000 or more of qualifying property will have its § 179 deduction eliminated.

§ 179: Property Placed in Service Maximum

EXAMPLE 17

During 2020, Madison Sanders places $1,245,000 of § 179 property in service for use in her engineering consultancy. Madison can take a $1,040,000 § 179 expense election; there is no reduction in the § 179 amount; the property placed in service maximum ($2,590,000) was not reached.

EXAMPLE 18

During 2020, George Krull places $3,150,000 of § 179 property in service for use in his manufacturing business (all assets are 7-year MACRS assets). Because George placed in service more than the $2,590,000 maximum, he must reduce his § 179 deduction ($3,150,000 − $2,590,000 = $560,000).

As a result, George's maximum § 179 deduction is $480,000 ($1,040,000 − $560,000). This reduction cannot be reclaimed in any way; it is permanently lost. George's total cost recovery deduction for 2020 is calculated as follows.

§ 179 expense	$480,000
MACRS depreciation [($3,150,000 − $480,000) × 0.1429 (Exhibit 8.3)]	381,543
Total cost recovery deduction	$861,543

George also places in service a $1,500,000 office building during 2020. Will this have any effect on the calculation above? No. The building is MACRS *realty*. Only *§ 179 property* is used to determine whether the § 179 ceiling amount ($1,040,000 in 2020) is reduced.

Note: George can also take additional first-year (bonus) depreciation on the 7-year MACRS assets. We will revisit this example after discussing bonus depreciation.

Business Income Limitation. The §179 deduction allowed for a taxable year cannot exceed the taxpayer's business income for the year. For this purpose, business income is calculated by deducting all business expenses except the § 179 deduction. As a result, a taxpayer's § 179 deduction cannot create (or increase) a net operating loss. A taxpayer's "business income" includes income not only from a sole proprietorship but also from wages and any allocated business income from a partnership or an S corporation.

During 2020, Lance Smith has a sole proprietorship through which he provides accounting and tax services that generated net income of $68,000. In addition, Lance is a 40% shareholder in a management consultancy operated as an S corporation. The S corporation pays Lance a salary of $40,000, and it recorded taxable income of $50,000. In this case, Lance's business income is $128,000 [$68,000 + $40,000 + $20,000 ($50,000 × 40%)].

Any § 179 amount in excess of taxable income is carried forward to future taxable years and added to other amounts eligible for expensing. Then the various limitations for that carryforward year are applied (i.e., the ceiling amount, the placed in service maximum amount, and the business income limitation).

Jill owns a computer service and operates it as a sole proprietorship. In 2020, taxable income is $138,000 before considering any § 179 deduction. If Jill spends $2,730,000 on new equipment, her § 179 expense deduction for the year is computed as follows.

§ 179 deduction before adjustment	$1,040,000
Less: Dollar limitation reduction ($2,730,000 − $2,590,000)	(140,000)
Remaining § 179 deduction	$ 900,000
Business income limitation	$ 138,000
§ 179 deduction allowed	$ 138,000
§ 179 deduction carryforward ($900,000 − $138,000)	$ 762,000

Additional first-year (bonus) depreciation is *not* limited by a taxpayer's taxable income. Taxpayers who make large capital investments with limited taxable income may choose *not* to make a § 179 election and only take bonus depreciation on these items.

Effect on Basis

The basis of the property for cost recovery purposes is reduced by the § 179 amount after accounting for the current-year amount of property placed in service in excess of the specified maximum amount ($2,590,000 for 2020). This adjusted amount does not reflect any business income limitation.

Assume the same facts as in Example 20. Jill's adjusted basis in the equipment for cost recovery purposes is $1,830,000 ($2,730,000 cost less the $900,000 § 179 expense amount before the business income limitation). If any portion of the $762,000 carryover (due to the business income limitation) is not deducted before the equipment is sold, this amount may be added back to the basis of the equipment in determining its adjusted basis.

Section 179 and the Mid-Quarter Convention

The mid-quarter convention generally results in smaller depreciation deductions in the asset's acquisition year. However, the basis of property used to determine whether the mid-quarter convention applies is derived *after* any § 179 immediate expense election.[14] As a result, a taxpayer may be able to avoid the mid-quarter convention by designating § 179 treatment for assets placed in service during the last quarter of the taxable year.

---

[14]Reg. § 1.168(d)–1(b)(4).

EXAMPLE 22

Dimond Manufacturing places the following assets in service during 2020. All are 5-year class assets, and they are the only assets Dimond placed in service during the year.

Asset 1 (April 3, 2020)	$ 873,000
Asset 2 (July 17, 2020)	232,000
Asset 3 (October 22, 2020)	1,085,000
Total	$2,190,000

As Dimond has placed more than 40% of the assets in service during the last quarter of the taxable year, the mid-quarter convention applies ($1,085,000/$2,190,000= 49.5%). As a result, Dimond's cost recovery deduction for the year is computed as follows (see Exhibit 8.4).

Asset 1	$873,000 × 0.25	$ 218,250
Asset 2	$232,000 × 0.15	34,800
Asset 3	$1,085,000 × 0.05	54,250
Total		$ 307,300

However, if Dimond elects to expense $1,040,000 of the October 22 acquisition under § 179, the mid-quarter convention would not apply.

Asset 1 (April 3, 2020)	$ 873,000
Asset 2 (July 17, 2020)	232,000
Asset 3 (October 22, 2020; $1,085,000 − $1,040,000)	45,000
Total	$1,150,000

Now Dimond has placed only 3.9% ($45,000/$1,150,000) of the assets in service during the last quarter of the taxable year. As a result, the mid-quarter convention does not apply, and Dimond's cost recovery deduction for the year (including the § 179 expense election) is as follows.

MACRS depreciation ($1,150,000 × 0.20; Exhibit 8.3)	$ 230,000
Section 179 expense (Asset 3)	1,040,000
Total cost recovery deduction	$1,270,000

As a result of its effective use of § 179, Dimond has increased its 2020 cost recovery deduction and simplified its reporting and record keeping related to these assets.

Conversion to Personal Use

Conversion of the expensed property to personal use at any time results in recapture income (see text Section 14-9). A property is converted to personal use if it is not used predominantly in a trade or business.[15]

ETHICS & EQUITY   Section 179 Limitation

Joe Moran worked in the construction business throughout most of his career. In June of the current year, he sold his interest in Ajax Enterprises LLC for a profit of $300,000. Shortly thereafter, Joe started his own business, which involves the redevelopment of distressed residential real estate.

In connection with his new business venture, Joe purchased a dump truck at a cost of $70,000. The new business struggled and showed a net operating loss for the year. Joe is considering expensing the $70,000 cost of the truck under § 179 on this year's tax return. Evaluate Joe's plan.

8-3b Additional First-Year Depreciation (Bonus Depreciation)

Congress often uses the tax system to stimulate the economy. An example is ==additional first-year depreciation== (also referred to as bonus depreciation). In a significant expansion

---

[15]See Reg. § 1.179–1(e) and related examples.

of this provision, the TCJA of 2017 allows taxpayers to deduct 100 percent cost recovery in the year *qualified property* is placed in service.[16]

The term *qualified property* includes most depreciable assets other than buildings with a recovery period of 20 years or less.[17] Bonus depreciation applies to both new *and* used property.[18]

The additional first-year depreciation is taken in the year in which the qualifying property is placed in service; it is computed after any immediate expense (§ 179) deduction is claimed. After the additional first-year depreciation is determined, the regular MACRS cost recovery deduction is calculated by multiplying the remaining cost recovery basis (original cost recovery basis less § 179 expense and additional first-year depreciation) by the appropriate MACRS percentage. A taxpayer may elect *not* to take additional first-year depreciation.

Kelly acquires equipment (a 5-year class asset) on February 1, 2020, at a cost of $1,345,000 and elects to expense $1,040,000 under § 179. Kelly also chooses to take bonus depreciation. As a result, her total cost recovery deduction for the year is calculated as follows:

§ 179 expense	$1,040,000
Additional first-year depreciation [($1,345,000 − $1,040,000) × 100%]	305,000
Total cost recovery deduction	$1,345,000

Alternatively, Kelly could choose *not* to elect § 179 on the equipment and completely deduct the cost of the equipment using bonus depreciation.

8-3c Using § 179 and Bonus Depreciation Effectively

With 100 percent bonus depreciation available from 2018 through 2022, the majority of taxpayers will be able to completely deduct the cost of any MACRS personalty. However, there may be times when the taxpayer will find it better to defer some of these deductions to future years. This might be the case if the taxpayer expects marginal tax rates to increase over time. In addition, the limitations on excess business losses (see text Section 7-5) or the 80 percent of taxable income limit on net operating losses (see text Section 7-6) might lead a taxpayer not to use § 179 and/or bonus depreciation. In addition, certain assets might not qualify for § 179 expensing or bonus depreciation. If any of these conditions applies, then other considerations come into play.

Deferring MACRS Deductions to Future Years

Taxpayers may find it better not to use § 179 expensing and/or bonus depreciation to completely write off asset acquisitions. If taxpayers expect their marginal tax rates to increase over time (and in some instances, remain the same), it might be best, in present value terms, to defer some MACRS deductions to future years.

---

[16]§ 168(k). Additional first-year depreciation is allowed for qualified property placed in service after 2011 and before 2027. The additional first-year depreciation percentage (100% from 2018 to 2022) decreases to 80% in 2023, 60% in 2024, 40% in 2025, and 20% in 2026. No bonus depreciation is scheduled for tax years after 2026. Different rules applied between 2008 and 2017 (in general, the bonus depreciation percentage was no more than 50%).

[17]Bonus depreciation is available for both "qualified film or television productions" and "qualified live theatrical productions." Bonus depreciation is *not* available to (1) any business that has floor-plan financing (e.g., an auto dealer) if the related interest is deducted in full or (2) regulated public utilities. In addition, bonus depreciation is *not* available on any asset that is required to use ADS depreciation.

[18]Effective for property placed in service after September 27, 2017. Used property will qualify as long as it is the taxpayer's first use of the property. § 168(k)(2)(E)(ii)(I).

EXAMPLE

24

Aditi Moore is married and operates a small business in Fairfax, Virginia. During the year, she purchases $550,000 of equipment (5-year MACRS assets) for use in her business. Aditi and her spouse report $569,700 of taxable income before considering any cost recovery related to the equipment. Their marginal tax rate is 35%.

Aditi is confident that her business will grow significantly over the next few years and expects her marginal tax rate to remain at least 35% during that time. As a result, she is wondering whether to use bonus depreciation on the entire 2020 purchase or spread her MACRS deductions over the next few years.

If Aditi takes $550,000 of bonus depreciation in 2020, she and her spouse will have tax savings of $147,015.* However, much of the bonus depreciation will offset income that would have been taxed at rates lower than 35%.

Another option is to take just enough cost recovery (both bonus depreciation and regular MACRS) to reduce the couple's taxable income from $569,700 to $414,700 (the bottom of the 35% rate bracket). We can determine this combined amount using the following formula.

$$\text{Bonus depreciation} + [(\$550,000 - \text{Bonus depreciation}) \times 20\% \text{ (first-year MACRS)}] = \$155,000$$

Solving for bonus depreciation yields $56,250. So we can reduce the couple's taxable income to $414,700 by taking bonus depreciation of $56,250 and the usual MACRS of $98,750 [($550,000 − $56,250) × 20%].

If we assume a 5% discount rate on future tax savings, Aditi and her spouse will save $178,386 in taxes by deferring some of the available cost recovery deductions and using it to offset future income that would otherwise be subject to a 35% tax rate.

	2020	2021	2022	2023	2024	2025
Normal MACRS	$493,750	$493,750	$493,750	$493,750	$493,750	$493,750
MACRS factor	× 0.2000	× 0.3200	× 0.1920	× 0.1152	× 0.1152	× 0.0576
MACRS depreciation	$ 98,750	$158,000	$ 94,800	$ 56,880	$ 56,880	$ 28,440
Bonus depreciation	56,250	—0—	—0—	—0—	—0—	—0—
Total MACRS deduction	$155,000	$158,000	$ 94,800	$ 56,880	$ 56,880	$ 28,440
Marginal tax rate	× 35%	× 35%	× 35%	× 35%	× 35%	× 35%
Tax savings	$ 54,250	$ 55,300	$ 33,180	$ 19,908	$ 19,908	$ 9,954
PV factors @ 5% (Appendix G)	× 1.0000	× 0.9524	× 0.9070	× 0.8638	× 0.8227	× 0.7835
	$ 54,250	$ 52,668	$ 30,094	$ 17,197	$ 16,378	$ 7,799
Net present value	$178,386					

Overall, the combination of $56,250 bonus depreciation in 2020 plus MACRS depreciation in 2020 through 2025 provides a better outcome for Aditi and her spouse, generating $31,371 of tax savings in present value terms over the next six years ($178,386 tax savings by deferring MACRS deductions *less* $147,015 tax savings by using $550,000 of bonus depreciation in 2020).

* Tax on $569,700 = $148,985 {$94,735 + [($569,700 − $414,700) × 35%]}; tax on $19,700 = $1,970 ($19,700 × 10%).

Choosing Assets for Immediate Expensing

The § 179 deduction can be allocated to reduce the basis of qualifying assets in any manner the taxpayer chooses. This allows the deduction to be allocated proportionally across all assets acquired during the year or to specific assets identified by the taxpayer. This flexibility is important.

Two general rules might affect this choice. First, taxpayers generally should *not* use the § 179 election on automobiles. Automobiles are subject to special cost recovery rules (and annual limits), which we discuss later in this chapter. Second, given the time value of money, taxpayers should accelerate deductions to the earliest year possible. This is accomplished by expensing the assets with the *longest* MACRS lives first.

During 2020, Dexter purchases manufacturing equipment (a 7-year MACRS asset) costing $685,000 and a computer system costing $480,000 (a 5-year MACRS asset). As the total amount of MACRS assets placed in service for the year ($1,165,000; $685,000 + $480,000) is less than $2,590,000, there is no reduction in the $1,040,000 § 179 deduction.

EXAMPLE
25

Dexter chooses not to take bonus depreciation. How should Dexter allocate his $1,040,000 § 179 expense election?

Dexter should expense the longest-lived MACRS asset first (the equipment; the 7-year MACRS asset). If he makes this choice, Dexter's total cost recovery deduction in 2020 is:

Equipment (7-year MACRS asset)	
§ 179 expense	$ 685,000
Computer system (5-year MACRS asset)	
§ 179 expense ($1,040,000 − $685,000)	355,000
MACRS cost recovery [($480,000 − $355,000) × 0.20 (Exhibit 8.3)]	25,000
Total cost recovery deduction	$1,065,000

If Dexter were to allocate the § 179 expense election to the machinery (MACRS 5-year asset), his total cost recovery deduction in 2020 would be only $1,057,863.

Computer system (5-year MACRS asset)	
§ 179 expense	$ 480,000
Equipment (7-year MACRS asset)	
§ 179 expense ($1,040,000 − $480,000)	560,000
MACRS cost recovery [($685,000 − $560,000) × 0.1429 (Exhibit 8.3)]	17,863
Total cost recovery deduction	$1,057,863

No matter which asset is expensed, after using both § 179 and bonus depreciation, $125,000 is subject to MACRS cost recovery. However, if the 7-year MACRS asset is expensed, this $125,000 is cost recovered over six tax years (here, the $125,000 relates to the 5-year MACRS asset). If the 5-year MACRS asset is expensed, the $125,000 will be recovered over eight tax years (here, the $125,000 relates to the 7-year MACRS asset).

Using the § 179 expense election on the longest-lived asset accelerates overall cost recovery deductions to earlier years, gaining a time-value-of-money advantage for the taxpayer.

Using Both § 179 and Bonus Depreciation

In general, in 2020, a business that places in service $1,040,000 or less of qualifying § 179 property will exclusively use § 179 to immediately expense all of those assets, while a business placing in service $3,630,000 or more of qualifying assets (the point at which the § 179 amount is completely phased out; $1,040,000 + $2,590,000) will qualify only for bonus depreciation. Any business placing in service between $1,040,000 and $3,630,000 of qualifying § 179 property will be able to use a combination of both § 179 and bonus depreciation (see Concept Summary 8.4).[19]

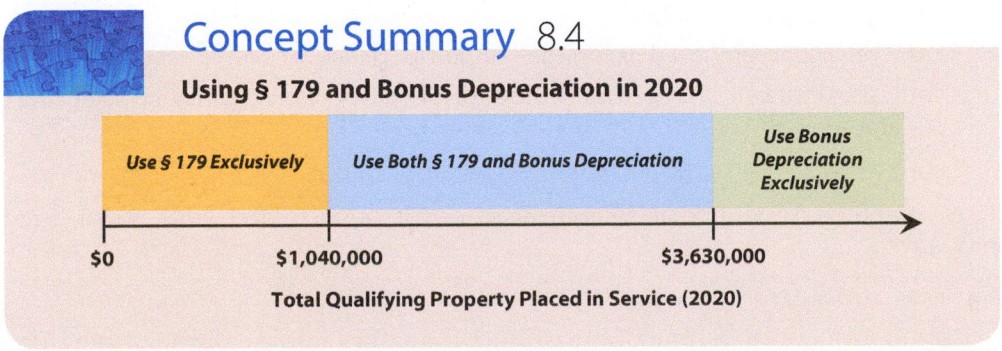

Concept Summary 8.4

Using § 179 and Bonus Depreciation in 2020

Use § 179 Exclusively	Use Both § 179 and Bonus Depreciation	Use Bonus Depreciation Exclusively

$0 — $1,040,000 — $3,630,000

Total Qualifying Property Placed in Service (2020)

[19]This general rule applies to the vast majority of taxpayers. However, it would not apply if the § 179 taxable income limitation applies or the taxpayer chooses to defer deductions to later tax years (e.g., if the taxpayer expects marginal tax rates to increase) to gain a time value of money advantage.

Automobiles and Other Listed Property Used Predominantly in Business

For listed property to be *predominantly used in business*, its *business use* must exceed 50 percent.[22] The use of listed property for production of income does not qualify as business use for purposes of the more-than-50% test. However, both production of income and business use percentages are used to compute the cost recovery deduction.

EXAMPLE 28

On September 1, 2020, Emma places in service listed property (MACRS 5-year property). The property cost $10,000. She elects not to take any available additional first-year depreciation.

If Emma uses the property 40% for business and 25% for the production of income, the property is not considered as predominantly used for business. The cost is recovered using straight-line cost recovery. Emma's cost recovery allowance for the year is $650 ($10,000 × 0.10 × 65%).

If, however, Emma uses the property 60% for business and 25% for the production of income, the property is considered as used predominantly for business. As a result, she may use the regular MACRS method. Emma's cost recovery allowance for the year is $1,700 ($10,000 × 0.20 × 85%).

In determining the percentage of business use of listed property, a mileage-based percentage is used for automobiles. For other listed property, one employs the most appropriate unit of time (e.g., hours) for which the property actually is used (rather than its availability for use).[23]

Limits on Cost Recovery for Automobiles

The law places further limits on the annual cost recovery deductions for passenger automobiles. These dollar limits were imposed because of the belief that the tax system was being used to underwrite automobiles whose cost and luxury far exceeded what was needed for the taxpayer's business use.

A *passenger automobile* is any four-wheeled vehicle manufactured for use on public streets, roads, and highways with an unloaded gross vehicle weight (GVW) rating of 6,000 pounds or less.[24] This definition specifically excludes vehicles used directly in the business of transporting people or property for compensation [e.g., taxicabs (including autos used for Uber or Lyft), ambulances, hearses, and trucks and vans].

The following "luxury auto" depreciation limits apply.[25]

Date Placed in Service	First Year	Second Year	Third Year	Fourth and Later Years
2019*	$10,100	$16,100	$9,700	$5,760
2018	$10,000	$16,000	$9,600	$5,760
2017	$ 3,160	$ 5,100	$3,050	$1,875

*The TCJA of 2017 significantly increased the annual limitations beginning in 2018. Because the 2020 indexed amounts were not available when we published, the 2019 amounts are used in the Examples and end-of-chapter problem materials.

In the event a passenger automobile used predominantly for business qualifies for additional first-year depreciation, the first-year recovery limitation is increased by $8,000 for automobiles placed in service before 2027.[26] As a result, for acquisitions made in 2019, the initial-year cost recovery limitation increases from $10,100 to $18,100 ($10,100 + $8,000).[27]

The luxury auto limits must be reduced proportionally for any personal use of the auto. In addition, the limitation in the first year includes any amount the taxpayer elects

---

[22]§ 280F(b)(3).

[23]Reg. § 1.280F–6T(e).

[24]§ 280F(d)(5).

[25]§ 280F(a)(1); Rev.Proc. 2019–26, 2019–24 I.R.B. 1323. Cost recovery limitations for years prior to 2017 are found in IRS Publication 463.

[26]§ 168(k)(2)(F)(i).

[27]Different cost recovery limitations apply to trucks and vans and to electric automobiles.

to expense under § 179.[28] If the passenger automobile is used partly for personal use, the personal use percentage is ignored for the purpose of determining the unrecovered cost available for deduction in later years.

EXAMPLE 29

On July 1, 2020, Dan places in service a new automobile that cost $55,000. He does not elect § 179 expensing, and he elects not to take any available additional first-year depreciation. The car is used 80% for business and 20% for personal use in each tax year. Dan chooses the MACRS 200% declining-balance method of cost recovery (the auto is a 5-year asset).

The depreciation computation for 2020 through 2025 is summarized in the table below. The cost recovery allowed is the lesser of the MACRS amount or the recovery limitation.

Year	MACRS Amount	Recovery Limitation	Depreciation Allowed
2020	$8,800 ($55,000 × 0.2000 × 80%)	$8,080 ($10,100 × 80%)	$ 8,080
2021	$14,080 ($55,000 × 0.3200 × 80%)	$12,880 ($16,100 × 80%)	$12,880
2022	$8,448 ($55,000 × 0.1920 × 80%)	$7,760 ($9,700 × 80%)	$ 7,760
2023	$5,069 ($55,000 × 0.1152 × 80%)	$4,608 ($5,760 × 80%)	$ 4,608
2024	$5,069 ($55,000 × 0.1152 × 80%)	$4,608 ($5,760 × 80%)	$ 4,608
2025	$2,534 ($55,000 × 0.0576 × 80%)	$4,608 ($5,760 × 80%)	$ 2,534

If Dan continues to use the car after 2025, his cost recovery is limited to the lesser of the recoverable basis or the recovery limitation (i.e., $5,760 × business use percentage). For this purpose, the recoverable basis is computed as if the full recovery limitation was allowed even if it was not. As a result, the recoverable basis as of January 1, 2026, is $4,412 ($55,000 − $10,100 − $16,100 − $9,700 − $5,760 − $5,760 − $3,168*).

If Dan takes additional first-year depreciation, the calculated amount of additional first-year depreciation is $44,000 ($55,000 × 100% × 80%). However, the deduction would be limited to $14,480 [($8,000 + $10,100) × 80%].

* $55,000 × 0.0576 × 100%; this is the full 2025 MACRS amount (which is less than the $5,760 recovery limitation for the year).

The cost recovery limitations are maximum amounts. If the regular MACRS calculation produces a smaller amount of cost recovery, the smaller amount is used.

EXAMPLE 30

On April 2, 2020, Gail places in service a used automobile that cost $10,000. The car is used 70% for business and 30% for personal use. The cost recovery allowance for 2020 is $1,400 ($10,000 × 0.20 MACRS table factor × 70%), not $7,000 ($10,000 passenger auto maximum × 70%).

Special Limitation for Sport-Utility Vehicles (SUVs)

Some sport-utility vehicles (SUVs) are not considered passenger automobiles and, therefore, are not subject to the luxury automobile limitations. However, in 2020, a $25,900 limit applies for the § 179 deduction when the luxury auto limits do not apply ($25,500 in 2019). The limit is in effect for SUVs with an unloaded GVW rating of more than 6,000 pounds and not more than 14,000 pounds.[29]

---

[28]§ 280F(d)(1).

[29]§ 179(b)(5).

During 2020, Jay acquires and places in service a new SUV that cost $70,400 and has a GVW of 8,000 pounds. Jay uses the vehicle 100% of the time for business use and elects not to use bonus depreciation. The total cost recovery deduction for 2020 with respect to the SUV is:

§ 179 expense	$25,900
Regular MACRS calculation [($70,400 − $25,900) × 0.20 (Exhibit 8.3)]	8,900
Total cost recovery deduction	$34,800

If Jay chooses to use bonus depreciation on the SUV, then the entire $70,400 cost will be recovered in 2020 ($25,900 § 179 and $44,500 bonus depreciation).

Automobiles and Other Listed Property Not Used Predominantly in Business

For automobiles and other listed property not used predominantly in business in the year of acquisition (i.e., 50 percent or less), the straight-line method under the alternative depreciation system is required (see text Section 8-3e).[30] Under this system, the straight-line recovery period for automobiles is five years. However, the cost recovery deduction for any passenger automobile cannot exceed the luxury auto limit.

Auto Not Predominantly Used in Business

On July 27, 2020, Fred places in service an automobile that cost $20,000. The auto is used 40% for business and 60% for personal use. The cost recovery allowance for 2020 is $800 [$20,000 × 0.10 (Exhibit 8.7) × 40%].

Assume the same facts as in Example 32, except that the automobile cost $50,000. The cost recovery allowance for 2020 is $2,000 [$50,000 × 0.10 (Exhibit 8.7) × 40%; $2,000 is less than 40% of the $10,000 first-year limit].

The straight-line method is used even if, at some later date, the business use of the property increases to more than 50 percent (although the cost recovery allowed will reflect the increase in business use).

Assume the same facts as in Example 32, except that in 2021, Fred uses the automobile 70% for business and 30% for personal use. Fred's cost recovery allowance for 2021 is $2,800 [$20,000 × 0.20 (Exhibit 8.7) × 70%], which is less than 70% of the second-year limit.

Change from Predominantly Business Use

If the business use percentage of listed property falls to 50 percent or less after the year the property is placed in service, the property is subject to *cost recovery recapture*. The amount required to be recaptured and included in the taxpayer's ordinary income is the *excess cost recovery*.

Excess cost recovery is the excess of the cost recovery deduction taken in prior years using the regular MACRS method over the amount that would have been allowed if the straight-line method had been used since the property was placed in service.[31]

---

[30]§ 280F(b)(1). [31]§ 280F(b)(2).

EXAMPLE 35

Seth purchased a new car on January 22, 2020, at a cost of $40,000. Business use was 80% in 2020, 70% in 2021, 40% in 2022, and 60% in 2023. Seth elects not to take any available additional first-year depreciation. Seth's excess cost recovery to be recaptured as ordinary income in 2022 is as follows.

2020	
MACRS ($40,000 × 0.20 × 80%, limited to $10,100 × 80%)	$ 6,400
Straight-line ($40,000 × 0.10 × 80%, limited to $10,100 × 80%)	(3,200)
Excess	$ 3,200

2021	
MACRS ($40,000 × 0.32 × 70%, limited to $16,100 × 70%)	$ 8,960
Straight-line ($40,000 × 0.20 × 70%, limited to $16,100 × 70%)	(5,600)
Excess	$ 3,360

2022	
2020 excess	$ 3,200
2021 excess	3,360
Ordinary income recapture	$ 6,560

After the business use of the listed property drops below the more-than-50% level, the straight-line method is used for the remaining life of the property.

EXAMPLE 36

Assume the same facts as in Example 35. Seth's cost recovery deductions for 2022 and 2023 are:

2022 $3,200 [$40,000 × 0.20 × 40% ($3,200), limited to $9,700 × 40% ($3,880)]
2023 $3,456 [$40,000 × 0.20 × 60% ($4,800), limited to $5,760 × 60% ($3,456)]

Leased Automobiles

Taxpayers who lease rather than purchase a passenger automobile for business purposes are not subject to the luxury auto limits. To prevent taxpayers from circumventing the luxury auto limits by deducting the full amount of rental payments associated with a luxury automobile leased for business, the law requires these taxpayers to report an *inclusion amount* in gross income.

The inclusion amount (determined from an IRS table) is based on the fair market value of the automobile. It must be computed for each taxable year the automobile is leased. Once determined, the inclusion amount is prorated for the number of days the auto is used during the taxable year. The prorated dollar amount then is multiplied by the business and income-producing use percentage.[32] The taxpayer deducts the lease payments, multiplied by the business and income-producing use percentage. In effect, the taxpayer's annual deduction for the lease payment is reduced by the inclusion amount.

[32]Reg. § 1.280F–7(a).

On April 1, 2020, Jim leases and places in service a passenger automobile worth $72,400. The lease is to be for a period of five years. During the taxable years 2020 and 2021, Jim uses the automobile 70% for business and 30% for personal use.

Assuming that the dollar amounts from the IRS table for 2020 and 2021 are $98 and $217, respectively, Jim includes in gross income:

2020	$98 × (275/366) × 70% = $52
2021	$217 × (365/365) × 70% = $152

In each year, Jim still can deduct 70% of the lease payments made (i.e., the amount related to his business use of the auto).

Substantiation Requirements

The substantiation requirements of § 274 apply to listed property. A taxpayer must be able to prove for any business use the amount of expense or use, the time and place of use, the business purpose for the use, and the business relationship to the taxpayer of persons using the property.

Substantiation requires adequate records or sufficient evidence corroborating the taxpayer's statement. For example, to document business use of an automobile, it is expected that a taxpayer maintain a contemporaneous record of business miles driven (versus other miles), any expenses incurred (e.g., fuel, repairs, business tolls, parking), and the business reason for the auto's use.[33]

8-3e **Alternative Depreciation System (ADS)**

The **alternative depreciation system (ADS)** must be used:[34]

- To calculate the portion of depreciation treated as an alternative minimum tax (AMT) adjustment for purposes of the individual AMT (see text Section 12-5d).[35]

- For residential and nonresidential real estate and any qualified improvement property placed in service after 2017 by a "real property trade or business" that opts out of the interest expense limitations of § 163(j). In general, these interest expense limitation rules only apply to businesses with annual gross receipts in excess of $26 million (in 2019 and 2020).

- To compute depreciation allowances for earnings and profits purposes (see text Section 19-2a).

In general, ADS depreciation is computed using the straight-line method. However, for AMT, depreciation of personal property is computed using the 150 percent declining-balance method with a switch to the straight-line method when appropriate.

The taxpayer must use the half-year or the mid-quarter convention, whichever is applicable, for all property other than real estate. The mid-month convention is used for real estate. Under ADS, personal property (other than qualified improvement property) is depreciated using the appropriate asset class life (e.g., 5- or 7-year) and the 150 percent declining-balance method (see Exhibits 8.6 and 8.7). Under ADS, qualified improvement property has a 20-year life, residential rental real estate has a 30-year life, and nonresidential real estate has a 40-year life; all are depreciated using the straight-line method (see Exhibits 8.5 and 8.9).[36]

LO.5

Determine when and how to use the alternative depreciation system (ADS).

---

[33]§§ 274(d) and (i). These substantiation requirements do not apply to vehicles that, by reason of their nature, are not likely to be used more than a *de minimis* amount for personal purposes.

[34]§ 168(g). ADS must also be used to compute cost recovery for property used predominantly outside the United States, by a tax-exempt entity, and in several other situations.

[35]This AMT adjustment applies for real and personal property placed in service before 1999. However, it also applies for personal property placed in service after 1998 if the taxpayer uses the 200% declining-balance method for regular income tax purposes.

[36]Residential rental real estate placed in service before 2018 uses an ADS life of 40 years. The class life for certain properties described in § 168(e)(3) is specially determined under § 168(g)(3)(B).

To simplify reporting, taxpayers may *elect* to use the 150 percent declining-balance method to compute cost recovery for the regular income tax (rather than the 200 percent declining-balance method that is available for personal property). If this election is made, there is no difference between the regular income tax and AMT cost recovery.[37]

EXAMPLE 38

On March 1, 2020, Abby purchases computer-based telephone central office switching equipment for $80,000. Abby elects not to take any available additional first-year depreciation. If Abby uses regular MACRS cost recovery (assuming no § 179 election), her deduction for 2020 is $16,000 [$80,000 × 0.20 (Exhibit 8.3, 5-year class property)].

If Abby elects to use ADS 150% declining-balance cost recovery for the regular income tax (assuming no § 179 election), the cost recovery allowance for 2020 is $12,000 [$80,000 × 0.15 (Exhibit 8.6, 5-year class property)].

Rather than determining depreciation under the regular MACRS method, taxpayers may *elect* straight-line under ADS. One reason for making this election is to defer cost recovery deductions to later years (presuming that marginal tax rates will be higher in those years). Another reason is to simplify record keeping, since the cost recovery deduction will be the same as earnings and profits depreciation.[38]

EXAMPLE 39

Palladium, Inc., acquires an office building on March 17, 2020, for $1,700,000. It takes the maximum cost recovery allowance for determining taxable income. For 2020, Palladium deducts $34,561 [$1,700,000 × 0.02033 (Exhibit 8.8)].

However, Palladium's cost recovery for computing its earnings and profits is only $33,643 [$1,700,000 × 0.01979 (Exhibit 8.9)].

LO.6

Report cost recovery deductions appropriately.

8-4 **REPORTING PROCEDURES**

Sole proprietors engaged in a business file a Schedule C, Profit or Loss from Business, to accompany Form 1040. A 2019 Schedule C is illustrated; the 2020 Schedule C was not available when this text was printed.

The top part of page 1 requests certain key information about the taxpayer (e.g., name, address, Social Security number, principal business activity, and accounting method used). Part I provides for the reporting of items of income. If the business requires the use of inventories and the computation of cost of goods sold (see text Section 16-2 for when this is necessary), Part III must be completed and the cost of goods sold amount transferred to line 4 of Part I.

Part II allows for the reporting of deductions. Some of the deductions discussed in this chapter and their location on the form are depletion (line 12) and depreciation (line 13). Other expenses (line 27) include those items not already covered (see lines 8–26). An example is research and experimental expenditures.

If depreciation is claimed, it should be supported by completing Form 4562. A 2019 Form 4562 is illustrated; the 2020 Form 4562 was not available when this text was published. The amount listed on line 22 of Form 4562 is transferred to line 13 of Part II of Schedule C.

---

[37]For personal property placed in service before 1999, taxpayers making the election use the ADS recovery periods in computing cost recovery for the regular income tax. The ADS recovery periods generally are longer than the regular recovery periods under MACRS.

[38]This straight-line election is made on a year-by-year basis. For property other than real estate, the election is made by MACRS class and applies to all assets in that MACRS class. So, for example, the election could be made for 7-year MACRS property and not for 5-year MACRS property placed in service during the same year. For real estate, the election is made on a property-by-property basis.

Thomas Andrews, Social Security number 111-11-1111, was employed as an accountant until May 2019, when he opened his own practice. His address is 279 Mountain View, Ogden, UT 84201. Andrews keeps his books on the cash basis and reported the following revenue and business expenses in 2019.

a. Revenue from accounting practice, $192,000.
b. Insurance, $5,000.
c. Office supplies, $4,000.
d. Office rent, $16,000.
e. Copier lease payments, $3,000.
f. Licenses, $2,000.
g. New furniture and fixtures were acquired on May 10 for $142,000. Thomas elects § 179 expensing and uses the regular MACRS cost recovery method.

Andrews reports the above information on Schedule C and Form 4562 as illustrated on the following pages.

EXAMPLE
40

8-5 AMORTIZATION

LO.7

Identify intangible assets that are eligible for amortization and calculate the amount of the deduction.

Taxpayers can recover the costs of certain intangible assets through an **amortization** deduction. The amount of the deduction is determined by amortizing the adjusted basis of these intangibles ratably over a 15-year period beginning in the month in which the intangible is acquired.[39]

Section 197 covers the amortization of most intangibles. *Amortizable § 197 intangibles* include most intangibles acquired after August 10, 1993, and acquired in connection with the acquisition of a business, including goodwill, going-concern value, franchises, trademarks, copyrights, patents, and covenants not to compete. Generally, self-created intangibles are *not* § 197 intangibles.

The 15-year amortization period applies regardless of the actual useful life of an amortizable § 197 intangible. No other depreciation or amortization deduction is permitted for these intangibles.

On June 1, 2020, Neil purchased and began operating the Falcon Café. Of the purchase price, $90,000 is allocated to goodwill. The 2020 § 197 amortization deduction is $3,500 [($90,000/15) × (7/12)].

EXAMPLE
41

Startup expenditures are partially amortizable by election.[40] A taxpayer must make this election no later than the due date of the return for the taxable year in which the trade or business begins.[41] If no election is made, the startup expenditures are capitalized.[42]

The amortization election for startup expenditures allows the taxpayer to deduct the smaller of (1) the startup expenditures related to the trade or business or (2) $5,000. The $5,000 maximum is reduced dollar for dollar by the amount of startup expenditures in excess of $50,000. As a result, if startup expenditures equal or exceed $55,000, no immediate deduction is allowed. Any startup expenditures not deducted are amortized ratably over a 180-month period, beginning in the month in which the trade or business begins.[43]

---

[39]§ 197(a).
[40]§§ 195(a) and (b).
[41]§ 195(d).

[42]§ 195(a).
[43]§§ 195(b)(1)(A) and (B).

Form **4562**

Department of the Treasury
Internal Revenue Service   (99)

Depreciation and Amortization
(Including Information on Listed Property)
▶ Attach to your tax return.
▶ Go to *www.irs.gov/Form4562* for instructions and the latest information.

OMB No. 1545-0172

20**19**

Attachment
Sequence No. **179**

Name(s) shown on return	Business or activity to which this form relates	Identifying number
Thomas Andrews	*Andrews Accounting Services*	*111-11-1111*

Part I Election To Expense Certain Property Under Section 179
Note: If you have any listed property, complete Part V before you complete Part I.

1	Maximum amount (see instructions)	**1**	*1,020,000*
2	Total cost of section 179 property placed in service (see instructions)	**2**	*142,000*
3	Threshold cost of section 179 property before reduction in limitation (see instructions)	**3**	*2,550,000*
4	Reduction in limitation. Subtract line 3 from line 2. If zero or less, enter -0-	**4**	*-0-*
5	Dollar limitation for tax year. Subtract line 4 from line 1. If zero or less, enter -0-. If married filing separately, see instructions	**5**	*142,000*

6	**(a)** Description of property	**(b)** Cost (business use only)	**(c)** Elected cost	
	Furniture and Fixtures	*142,000*	*142,000*	

7	Listed property. Enter the amount from line 29 . . . . **7**		
8	Total elected cost of section 179 property. Add amounts in column (c), lines 6 and 7	**8**	*142,000*
9	Tentative deduction. Enter the **smaller** of line 5 or line 8	**9**	*142,000*
10	Carryover of disallowed deduction from line 13 of your 2018 Form 4562	**10**	*-0-*
11	Business income limitation. Enter the smaller of business income (not less than zero) or line 5. See instructions	**11**	*142,000*
12	Section 179 expense deduction. Add lines 9 and 10, but don't enter more than line 11 . . .	**12**	*142,000*
13	Carryover of disallowed deduction to 2020. Add lines 9 and 10, less line 12 ▶ **13**		

Note: Don't use Part II or Part III below for listed property. Instead, use Part V.

Part II Special Depreciation Allowance and Other Depreciation (Don't include listed property. See instructions.)

14	Special depreciation allowance for qualified property (other than listed property) placed in service during the tax year. See instructions	**14**	
15	Property subject to section 168(f)(1) election	**15**	
16	Other depreciation (including ACRS)	**16**	

Part III MACRS Depreciation (Don't include listed property. See instructions.)

Section A

17	MACRS deductions for assets placed in service in tax years beginning before 2019	**17**	
18	If you are electing to group any assets placed in service during the tax year into one or more general asset accounts, check here . . . . ▶ ☐		

Section B—Assets Placed in Service During 2019 Tax Year Using the General Depreciation System

(a) Classification of property	(b) Month and year placed in service	(c) Basis for depreciation (business/investment use only—see instructions)	(d) Recovery period	(e) Convention	(f) Method	(g) Depreciation deduction
19a 3-year property						
b 5-year property						
c 7-year property						
d 10-year property						
e 15-year property						
f 20-year property						
g 25-year property			25 yrs.		S/L	
h Residential rental property			27.5 yrs.	MM	S/L	
			27.5 yrs.	MM	S/L	
i Nonresidential real property			39 yrs.	MM	S/L	
				MM	S/L	

Section C—Assets Placed in Service During 2019 Tax Year Using the Alternative Depreciation System

20a Class life					S/L	
b 12-year			12 yrs.		S/L	
c 30-year			30 yrs.	MM	S/L	
d 40-year			40 yrs.	MM	S/L	

Part IV Summary (See instructions.)

21	Listed property. Enter amount from line 28	**21**	
22	**Total.** Add amounts from line 12, lines 14 through 17, lines 19 and 20 in column (g), and line 21. Enter here and on the appropriate lines of your return. Partnerships and S corporations—see instructions .	**22**	*142,000*
23	For assets shown above and placed in service during the current year, enter the portion of the basis attributable to section 263A costs **23**		

For Paperwork Reduction Act Notice, see separate instructions.   Cat. No. 12906N   Form **4562** (2019)

SCHEDULE C (Form 1040 or 1040-SR) Department of the Treasury Internal Revenue Service (99)	**Profit or Loss From Business** (Sole Proprietorship) ▶ Go to *www.irs.gov/ScheduleC* for instructions and the latest information. ▶ **Attach to Form 1040, 1040-SR, 1040-NR, or 1041; partnerships generally must file Form 1065.**	OMB No. 1545-0074 20**19** Attachment Sequence No. **09**

Name of proprietor *Thomas Andrews*	Social security number (SSN) *111–11–1111*

A	Principal business or profession, including product or service (see instructions)	**B** Enter code from instructions ▶				

C	Business name. If no separate business name, leave blank. *Andrews Accounting Services*	**D** Employer ID number (EIN) (see instr.)							

E Business address (including suite or room no.) ▶ *279 Mountain View*
City, town or post office, state, and ZIP code   *Ogden, UT 84201*

F Accounting method: **(1)** ☑ Cash   **(2)** ☐ Accrual   **(3)** ☐ Other (specify) ▶ _____

G Did you "materially participate" in the operation of this business during 2019? If "No," see instructions for limit on losses . ☑ Yes ☐ No

H If you started or acquired this business during 2019, check here . . . . ▶ ☐

I Did you make any payments in 2019 that would require you to file Form(s) 1099? (see instructions) . . . . ☐ Yes ☐ No

J If "Yes," did you or will you file required Forms 1099? . . . . ☐ Yes ☐ No

Part I Income

1	Gross receipts or sales. See instructions for line 1 and check the box if this income was reported to you on Form W-2 and the "Statutory employee" box on that form was checked . . . . ▶ ☐	**1**	192,000
2	Returns and allowances	**2**	
3	Subtract line 2 from line 1	**3**	192,000
4	Cost of goods sold (from line 42)	**4**	
5	**Gross profit.** Subtract line 4 from line 3	**5**	192,000
6	Other income, including federal and state gasoline or fuel tax credit or refund (see instructions)	**6**	
7	**Gross income.** Add lines 5 and 6 . . . . ▶	**7**	192,000

Part II Expenses. Enter expenses for business use of your home **only** on line 30.

8	Advertising	**8**		18	Office expense (see instructions)	**18**	4,000
9	Car and truck expenses (see instructions)	**9**		19	Pension and profit-sharing plans .	**19**	
10	Commissions and fees .	**10**		20	Rent or lease (see instructions):		
11	Contract labor (see instructions)	**11**		a	Vehicles, machinery, and equipment	**20a**	3,000
12	Depletion	**12**		b	Other business property . . .	**20b**	16,000
13	Depreciation and section 179 expense deduction (not included in Part III) (see instructions)	**13**	142,000	21	Repairs and maintenance . .	**21**	
				22	Supplies (not included in Part III) .	**22**	
				23	Taxes and licenses	**23**	2,000
				24	Travel and meals:		
14	Employee benefit programs (other than on line 19) . .	**14**	5,000	a	Travel	**24a**	
				b	Deductible meals (see instructions)	**24b**	
15	Insurance (other than health)	**15**		25	Utilities	**25**	
16	Interest (see instructions):			26	Wages (less employment credits) .	**26**	
a	Mortgage (paid to banks, etc.)	**16a**		27a	Other expenses (from line 48) . .	**27a**	
b	Other	**16b**		b	**Reserved for future use** . . .	**27b**	
17	Legal and professional services	**17**					

28	**Total expenses** before expenses for business use of home. Add lines 8 through 27a . . . . . . ▶	**28**	172,000
29	Tentative profit or (loss). Subtract line 28 from line 7	**29**	20,000
30	Expenses for business use of your home. Do not report these expenses elsewhere. Attach Form 8829 unless using the simplified method (see instructions). **Simplified method filers only:** enter the total square footage of: (a) your home: _____ and (b) the part of your home used for business: _____ . Use the Simplified Method Worksheet in the instructions to figure the amount to enter on line 30	**30**	
31	**Net profit or (loss).** Subtract line 30 from line 29. • If a profit, enter on both **Schedule 1 (Form 1040 or 1040-SR), line 3** (or **Form 1040-NR, line 13**) and on **Schedule SE, line 2.** (If you checked the box on line 1, see instructions). Estates and trusts, enter on **Form 1041, line 3.** • If a loss, you **must** go to line 32.	**31**	20,000
32	If you have a loss, check the box that describes your investment in this activity (see instructions). • If you checked 32a, enter the loss on both **Schedule 1 (Form 1040 or 1040-SR), line 3** (or **Form 1040-NR, line 13**) and on **Schedule SE, line 2.** (If you checked the box on line 1, see the line 31 instructions). Estates and trusts, enter on **Form 1041, line 3.** • If you checked 32b, you **must** attach **Form 6198.** Your loss may be limited.	**32a** ☐ All investment is at risk. **32b** ☐ Some investment is not at risk.	

For Paperwork Reduction Act Notice, see the separate instructions.   Cat. No. 11334P   Schedule C (Form 1040 or 1040-SR) 2019

Startup Expenditures

EXAMPLE 42

Green Corporation begins business on August 1, 2020. The corporation incurs startup expenditures of $47,000. If Green elects amortization under § 195, the total startup expenditures that Green may deduct in 2020 are computed as follows.

Deductible amount	$5,000
Amortizable amount {[($47,000 − $5,000)/180] × 5 months}	1,167
Total deduction	$6,167

EXAMPLE 43

Assume the same facts as in Example 42, except that the startup expenditures total $53,000. The 2020 deduction is computed as follows.

Deductible amount [$5,000 − ($53,000 − $50,000)]	$2,000
Amortizable amount {[($53,000 − $2,000)/180] × 5 months}	1,417
Total deduction	$3,417

Amortizable startup expenditures generally must satisfy two requirements.[44] First, the expenses must be paid or incurred in connection with:

- Creating a business,
- Investigating the creation or acquisition of a business, or
- Anticipating an activity becoming a business.

Second, the expenses must reflect those that could be deducted in an existing trade or business in the same field (see Investigation of a Business, text Section 6-3d).

The startup costs of creating a new active trade or business could include advertising; salaries and wages; travel and other expenses incurred in lining up prospective distributors, suppliers, or customers; and salaries and fees for executives, consultants, and professional services. Costs that relate to either created or acquired businesses could include expenses incurred for the analysis or survey of potential markets, products, labor supply, transportation facilities, and the like. Startup expenditures do not include allowable deductions for interest, taxes, and research and experimental costs.[45]

Amortization deductions also can be claimed for organizational expenses (see text Section 17-1k) and research and experimental expenditures (see text Section 7-4).

8-6 DEPLETION

LO.8

Determine the amount of depletion expense, including being able to apply the alternative tax treatments for intangible drilling and development costs.

Natural resources (e.g., oil, gas, coal, gravel, and timber) are subject to **depletion**, a form of cost recovery that applies to natural resources. Land generally cannot be depleted.

Although all natural resources are subject to depletion, oil and gas wells are used as an example in the following paragraphs to illustrate the related costs and issues.

In developing an oil or gas well, the producer typically makes four types of expenditures.

- Natural resource costs.
- Intangible drilling and development costs.
- Tangible asset costs.
- Operating costs.

Natural resources are physically limited, and the costs to acquire them (e.g., oil under the ground) are, therefore, recovered through depletion. Costs incurred in making the

---

[44]§§ 195(c)(1)(A) and (B).   [45]§ 195(c).

property ready for drilling, such as the cost of labor in clearing the property, erecting derricks, and drilling the hole, are intangible drilling and development costs (IDCs). These costs generally have no salvage value and are a lost cost if the well is dry.

Costs for tangible assets such as tools, pipes, and engines are capitalized and recovered through depreciation (cost recovery). Costs incurred after the well is producing are operating costs. These costs include expenditures for such items as labor, fuel, and supplies. Operating costs are deductible as trade or business expenses. Depletable costs and intangible drilling and development costs receive different treatment.

8-6a Intangible Drilling and Development Costs (IDCs)

Intangible drilling and development costs can be handled in one of two ways at the option of the taxpayer. They can be *either* charged off as an expense in the year in which they are incurred *or* capitalized and written off through depletion. The taxpayer makes the election in the first year such expenditures are incurred, either by taking a deduction on the return or by adding them to the depletable basis.

Once made, the election is binding on both the taxpayer and the IRS for all such expenditures in the future. If the taxpayer fails to elect to expense IDCs on the original timely filed return for the first year in which such expenditures are incurred, an irrevocable election to capitalize them has been made.

As a general rule, it is more advantageous to expense IDCs. The obvious benefit of an immediate write-off (as opposed to a deferred write-off through depletion) is not the only advantage. Because a taxpayer can use percentage depletion, which is calculated without reference to basis (see Example 47), the IDCs may be completely lost as a deduction if they are capitalized.

8-6b Depletion Methods

There are two methods of calculating depletion. *Cost depletion* can be used on any wasting asset (and is the only method allowed for timber). *Percentage depletion* is subject to a number of limitations, particularly for oil and gas deposits. Depletion should be calculated both ways, and the method that results in the larger deduction should be used. The choice between cost depletion and percentage depletion is an annual decision; the taxpayer can use cost depletion in one year and percentage depletion in the following year.

Cost Depletion

Cost depletion resembles units-of-production depreciation.[46] The basis is divided by the estimated recoverable units of the asset (e.g., barrels and tons) to arrive at the depletion per unit. This amount then is multiplied by the number of units sold (*not* the units produced) during the year to arrive at the cost depletion allowed.

EXAMPLE 44

On January 1, 2020, Pablo purchases the rights to a mineral interest for $1,000,000. At that time, the remaining recoverable units in the mineral interest are estimated to be 200,000. The depletion per unit is $5 ($1,000,000 adjusted basis ÷ 200,000 estimated recoverable units).

If 60,000 units are mined and 25,000 are sold this year, the cost depletion is $125,000 ($5 depletion per unit × 25,000 units sold).

If the taxpayer later discovers that the original estimate was incorrect, the depletion per unit for future calculations is redetermined using the revised estimate.[47]

---

[46]§ 612.   [47]§ 611(a).

EXAMPLE 45

Assume the same facts as in Example 44. In 2021, Pablo realizes that an incorrect estimate was made as to the capacity of the mine. The remaining recoverable units now are determined to be 400,000. Based on this new information, the revised depletion per unit is $2.1875 ($875,000 adjusted basis ÷ 400,000 estimated recoverable units). The $875,000 adjusted basis is the original cost ($1,000,000) reduced by the depletion claimed in 2020 ($125,000).

If 30,000 units are sold in 2021, the depletion for the year is $65,625 ($2.1875 depletion per unit × 30,000 units sold).

Percentage Depletion

Percentage depletion uses a specified percentage provided by the Code. The percentage varies according to the type of mineral interest involved. A sample of these percentages is shown in Exhibit 8.2. The rate is applied to the gross income from the property, but in no event may percentage depletion exceed 50 percent of the taxable income from the property before the allowance for depletion.[48]

EXAMPLE 46

CarrollCo reports gross income of $100,000 and other property-related expenses of $60,000 and uses a depletion rate of 22%. CarrollCo's depletion allowance is determined as follows.

Gross income	$100,000
Less: Other expenses	(60,000)
Taxable income before depletion	$ 40,000
Depletion allowance [the lesser of $22,000 (22% × $100,000) or $20,000 (50% × $40,000)]	(20,000)
Taxable income after depletion	$ 20,000

The adjusted basis of CarrollCo's property is reduced by $20,000, the depletion deduction allowed. If the other expenses had been only $55,000, the full $22,000 could have been deducted, and the adjusted basis would have been reduced by $22,000.

EXHIBIT 8.2	Selected Percentage Depletion Rates	
22% Depletion		
Cobalt		Sulfur
Lead		Tin
15% Depletion		
Copper		Oil, gas, oil shale
Gold		Silver
14% Depletion		
Granite		Marble
Limestone		Potash
10% Depletion		
Coal		Sodium chloride
5% Depletion		
Gravel		Sand

---

[48]§ 613(a). Special rules apply for certain oil and gas wells (e.g., the 50% ceiling is replaced with a 100% ceiling and the percentage depletion may not exceed 65% of the taxpayer's taxable income from all sources before the allowance for depletion). § 613A.

Note that percentage depletion is based on a percentage of the gross income from the property and makes no reference to cost. All other deductions detailed in this chapter are a function of the adjusted basis (cost) of the property. Thus, when percentage depletion is used, it is possible to claim aggregate depletion deductions that exceed the original cost of the property. If percentage depletion is used, however, the adjusted basis of the property (for computing cost depletion in a future tax year) is reduced by any depletion deducted until the basis reaches zero.

EXAMPLE
47

Melissa reports the following related to her sulfur mine.

Remaining depletable basis	$ 11,000
Gross income (10,000 units)	100,000
Expenses (other than depletion)	30,000

Because cost depletion is limited to the remaining depletable basis of $11,000, Melissa would choose percentage depletion of $22,000 (a 22% depletion rate is used for sulfur). Her basis in the mine then becomes zero. In future years, however, she can continue to take percentage depletion; percentage depletion is computed without reference to the remaining basis.

8-7 TAX PLANNING

LO.9

Identify tax planning opportunities for cost recovery, amortization, and depletion.

8-7a Cost Recovery

Cost recovery schedules should be reviewed annually for possible retirements, abandonments, and obsolescence.

EXAMPLE
48

An examination of the cost recovery schedule of Eagle Company reveals the following.

- Asset A was abandoned when it was discovered that the cost of repairs would be in excess of the cost of replacement. Asset A had an adjusted basis of $3,000.
- Asset J became obsolete this year, at which point its adjusted basis was $8,000.

Assets A and J should be written off, resulting in deductions of $11,000.

Another consideration when making decisions related to cost recovery is whether faster (or slower) cost recovery will be more beneficial for the taxpayer. If the taxpayer's goal is to recover the cost of fixed assets as quickly as possible, then using § 179 or additional first-year depreciation is preferable.

If, however, a taxpayer has a new business with little income or a business with a net operating loss carryover, the taxpayer's goal may be to slow down cost recovery. In this situation, the taxpayer generally should do the following.

- Elect not to take additional first-year depreciation, if available.
- Choose the straight-line cost recovery method.
- Not elect to expense assets under § 179.
- Defer placing assets in service in the current tax year or postpone capital outlays until future tax years.

8-7b **Amortization**

When a business is purchased, goodwill and covenants not to compete are both subject to an amortization period of 15 years. Given that goodwill and covenants not to compete are treated the same from a tax perspective, bargaining for a covenant should be based on legal rather than tax reasons. The seller, however, may have different motives because goodwill is a capital asset whereas a covenant is an ordinary income asset.

Because the amortization period for both goodwill and a covenant is 15 years, the purchaser may want to assign purchase costs to assets with shorter lives (e.g., inventory, receivables, and personalty). If, however, the purchase price will be assigned to assets with longer recovery periods (e.g., realty) or to assets not eligible for cost recovery (e.g., land), the purchaser would likely prefer costs to be assigned to goodwill or a covenant.

8-7c **Cost Recovery Tables**

Summary of Tables

Exhibit 8.3   Regular MACRS table for personalty.
   Depreciation methods: 200 or 150 percent declining-balance switching to straight-line.
   Recovery periods: 3, 5, 7, 10, 15, 20 years.
   Convention: half-year.

Exhibit 8.4   Regular MACRS table for personalty.
   Depreciation method: 200 percent declining-balance switching to straight-line.
   Recovery periods: 3, 5, 7 years.
   Convention: mid-quarter.

Exhibit 8.5   MACRS optional straight-line table for personalty.
   Depreciation method: straight-line.
   Recovery periods: 3, 5, 7, 10, 15, 20 years.
   Convention: half-year.

Exhibit 8.6   Alternative minimum tax declining-balance table for personalty.
   Depreciation method: 150 percent declining-balance switching to straight-line.
   Recovery periods: 3, 5, 7, 9.5, 10, 12 years.
   Convention: half-year.

Exhibit 8.7   Alternative depreciation system straight-line table for personalty.
   Depreciation method: straight-line.
   Recovery periods: 5, 10, 12 years.
   Convention: half-year.

Exhibit 8.8   Regular MACRS straight-line table for realty.
   Depreciation method: straight-line.
   Recovery periods: 27.5, 31.5, 39 years.
   Convention: mid-month.

Exhibit 8.9   Alternative depreciation system straight-line table for realty.
   Depreciation method: straight-line.
   Recovery period: 30, 40 years.
   Convention: mid-month.

EXHIBIT 8.3	MACRS Accelerated Depreciation for Personal Property Assuming Half-Year Convention (Percentage Rates)

For Property Placed in Service after December 31, 1986

Recovery Year	3-Year (200% DB)	5-Year (200% DB)	7-Year (200% DB)	10-Year (200% DB)	15-Year (150% DB)	20-Year (150% DB)
1	33.33	20.00	14.29	10.00	5.00	3.750
2	44.45	32.00	24.49	18.00	9.50	7.219
3	14.81*	19.20	17.49	14.40	8.55	6.677
4	7.41	11.52*	12.49	11.52	7.70	6.177
5		11.52	8.93*	9.22	6.93	5.713
6		5.76	8.92	7.37	6.23	5.285
7			8.93	6.55*	5.90*	4.888
8			4.46	6.55	5.90	4.522
9				6.56	5.91	4.462*
10				6.55	5.90	4.461
11				3.28	5.91	4.462
12					5.90	4.461
13					5.91	4.462
14					5.90	4.461
15					5.91	4.462
16					2.95	4.461
17						4.462
18						4.461
19						4.462
20						4.461
21						2.231

*Switchover to straight-line depreciation.

EXHIBIT 8.4	MACRS Accelerated Depreciation for Personal Property Assuming Mid-Quarter Convention (Percentage Rates)

For Property Placed in Service after December 31, 1986 (Partial Table*)

3-Year

Recovery Year	First Quarter	Second Quarter	Third Quarter	Fourth Quarter
1	58.33	41.67	25.00	8.33
2	27.78	38.89	50.00	61.11

5-Year

Recovery Year	First Quarter	Second Quarter	Third Quarter	Fourth Quarter
1	35.00	25.00	15.00	5.00
2	26.00	30.00	34.00	38.00

7-Year

Recovery Year	First Quarter	Second Quarter	Third Quarter	Fourth Quarter
1	25.00	17.85	10.71	3.57
2	21.43	23.47	25.51	27.55

*The figures in this table are taken from the official tables that appear in Rev.Proc. 87–57, 1987–2 C.B. 687. Because of their length, the complete tables are not presented.

EXHIBIT 8.5	MACRS Straight-Line Depreciation for Personal Property Assuming Half-Year Convention*

For Property Placed in Service after December 31, 1986

MACRS Class	% First Recovery Year	Other Recovery Years		Last Recovery Year	
		Years	%	Year	%
3-year	16.67	2–3	33.33	4	16.67
5-year	10.00	2–5	20.00	6	10.00
7-year	7.14	2–7	14.29	8	7.14
10-year	5.00	2–10	10.00	11	5.00
15-year	3.33	2–15	6.67	16	3.33
20-year	2.50	2–20	5.00	21	2.50

*The official table contains a separate row for each year. For ease of presentation, certain years are grouped in this table. In some instances, this will produce a difference of .01 for the last digit when compared with the official table.

Note: The last two rows of this table are used for qualified improvement property (15-year normal MACRS; 20-year ADS).

EXHIBIT 8.6	Alternative Minimum Tax: 150% Declining-Balance Assuming Half-Year Convention (Percentage Rates)

For Property Placed in Service after December 31, 1986 (Partial Table*)

Recovery Year	3-Year 150%	5-Year 150%	7-Year 150%	9.5-Year 150%	10-Year 150%	12-Year 150%
1	25.00	15.00	10.71	7.89	7.50	6.25
2	37.50	25.50	19.13	14.54	13.88	11.72
3	25.00**	17.85	15.03	12.25	11.79	10.25
4	12.50	16.66**	12.25**	10.31	10.02	8.97
5		16.66	12.25	9.17**	8.74**	7.85
6		8.33	12.25	9.17	8.74	7.33**
7			12.25	9.17	8.74	7.33
8			6.13	9.17	8.74	7.33
9				9.17	8.74	7.33
10				9.16	8.74	7.33
11					4.37	7.32
12						7.33
13						3.66

*The figures in this table are taken from the official table that appears in Rev.Proc. 87–57, 1987–2 C.B. 687. Because of its length, the complete table is not presented.

**Switchover to straight-line depreciation.

EXHIBIT 8.7	ADS Straight-Line for Personal Property Assuming Half-Year Convention (Percentage Rates)

For Property Placed in Service after December 31, 1986 (Partial Table)*

Recovery Year	5-Year Class	10-Year Class	12-Year Class
1	10.00	5.00	4.17
2	20.00	10.00	8.33
3	20.00	10.00	8.33
4	20.00	10.00	8.33
5	20.00	10.00	8.33
6	10.00	10.00	8.33
7		10.00	8.34
8		10.00	8.33
9		10.00	8.34
10		10.00	8.33
11		5.00	8.34
12			8.33
13			4.17

*The figures in this table are taken from the official table that appears in Rev.Proc. 87–57, 1987–2 C.B. 687. Because of its length, the complete table is not presented. The tables for the mid-quarter convention also appear in Rev.Proc. 87–57.

EXHIBIT 8.8	MACRS Straight-Line Depreciation for Real Property Assuming Mid-Month Convention* (Percentage Rates)

For Property Placed in Service after December 31, 1986: 27.5-Year Residential Real Property

Recovery Year(s)	The Applicable Percentage Is (Use the Column for the Month in the First Year the Property Is Placed in Service):											
	1	2	3	4	5	6	7	8	9	10	11	12
1	3.485	3.182	2.879	2.576	2.273	1.970	1.667	1.364	1.061	0.758	0.455	0.152
2–18	3.636	3.636	3.636	3.636	3.636	3.636	3.636	3.636	3.636	3.636	3.636	3.636
19–27	3.637	3.637	3.637	3.637	3.637	3.637	3.637	3.637	3.637	3.637	3.637	3.637
28	1.970	2.273	2.576	2.879	3.182	3.485	3.636	3.636	3.636	3.636	3.636	3.636
29	0.000	0.000	0.000	0.000	0.000	0.000	0.152	0.455	0.758	1.061	1.364	1.667

For Property Placed in Service after December 31, 1986, and before May 13, 1993: 31.5-Year Nonresidential Real Property

Recovery Year(s)	The Applicable Percentage Is (Use the Column for the Month in the First Year the Property Is Placed in Service):											
	1	2	3	4	5	6	7	8	9	10	11	12
1	3.042	2.778	2.513	2.249	1.984	1.720	1.455	1.190	0.926	0.661	0.397	0.132
2–19	3.175	3.175	3.175	3.175	3.175	3.175	3.175	3.175	3.175	3.175	3.175	3.175
20–31	3.174	3.174	3.174	3.174	3.174	3.174	3.174	3.174	3.174	3.174	3.174	3.174
32	1.720	1.984	2.249	2.513	2.778	3.042	3.175	3.175	3.175	3.175	3.175	3.175
33	0.000	0.000	0.000	0.000	0.000	0.000	0.132	0.397	0.661	0.926	1.190	1.455

For Property Placed in Service after May 12, 1993: 39-Year Nonresidential Real Property

Recovery Year(s)	The Applicable Percentage Is (Use the Column for the Month in the First Year the Property Is Placed in Service):											
	1	2	3	4	5	6	7	8	9	10	11	12
1	2.461	2.247	2.033	1.819	1.605	1.391	1.177	0.963	0.749	0.535	0.321	0.107
2–39	2.564	2.564	2.564	2.564	2.564	2.564	2.564	2.564	2.564	2.564	2.564	2.564
40	0.107	0.321	0.535	0.749	0.963	1.177	1.391	1.605	1.819	2.033	2.247	2.461

*The official tables contain a separate row for each year. For ease of presentation, certain years are grouped in these tables. In some instances, this will produce a difference of .001 for the last digit when compared with the official tables.

EXHIBIT 8.9	ADS Straight-Line for Real Property Assuming Mid-Month Convention (Percentage Rates)

For Property Placed in Service after December 31, 2017; 30-Year Residential Rental Property

Recovery Year	Month Placed in Service											
	1	2	3	4	5	6	7	8	9	10	11	12
1	3.194	2.917	2.639	2.361	2.083	1.806	1.528	1.250	0.972	0.694	0.417	0.139
2–30	3.333	3.333	3.333	3.333	3.333	3.333	3.333	3.333	3.333	3.333	3.333	3.333
31	0.139	0.417	0.694	0.972	1.250	1.528	1.806	2.083	2.361	2.639	2.917	3.194

For Property Placed in Service after December 31, 1986; 40-Year Nonresidential Real Property*

Recovery Year	Month Placed in Service											
	1	2	3	4	5	6	7	8	9	10	11	12
1	2.396	2.188	1.979	1.771	1.563	1.354	1.146	0.938	0.729	0.521	0.313	0.104
2–40	2.500	2.500	2.500	2.500	2.500	2.500	2.500	2.500	2.500	2.500	2.500	2.500
41	0.104	0.312	0.521	0.729	0.937	1.146	1.354	1.562	1.771	1.979	2.187	2.396

* Also used for residential rental property placed in service before 2018.

REFOCUS ON THE BIG PICTURE

CALCULATING COST RECOVERY DEDUCTIONS

Regardless of whether the accrual or cash method of accounting is used, MACRS must be used to calculate the cost recovery of fixed assets for tax purposes. Evidently, Dr. Payne's financial reporting system uses MACRS because $91,298 is the correct amount of cost recovery. The computers and peripheral equipment are 5-year property. The office furniture and fixtures and the dental equipment are 7-year property.

Based on the IRS cost recovery tables, the following percentages are used in calculating depreciation expense for the first year of each asset's life.

5-year property	20.00%
7-year property	14.29%

Dr. Payne can deduct depreciation on the house he converted from personal use to rental use and on the rental house he purchased.

What If?

From a tax planning perspective, Dr. Payne can increase the cost recovery deductions associated with the purchase of these fixed assets and reduce the amount of the business net income reported on Schedule C of Form 1040 for his dental practice by using the § 179 immediate expense election or additional first-year (bonus) depreciation.

Section 179 applies to personalty, but does not apply to realty (e.g., buildings). The maximum amount that can be deducted under § 179 is subject to several limitations. First, the total amount deducted cannot exceed $1,040,000. Second, the maximum amount is reduced dollar for dollar for any § 179 assets placed in service in excess of $2,590,000. Finally, the § 179 deduction cannot exceed the taxable income from the business. Additional first-year (bonus) depreciation allows 100 percent of qualified property to be deducted.

The sequence of calculating the cost recovery deduction is, in order:

1. § 179 immediate expensing.
2. Additional first-year depreciation.
3. Regular MACRS cost recovery.

continued

If Dr. Payne reports sufficient business income to avoid the § 179 business income limitation, he can use § 179 to expense all of the assets placed in service in 2020 ($612,085).

If § 179's business income limitation comes into play, Dr. Payne can elect out of § 179 and deduct $612,085 using additional first-year depreciation (which has no income limitation). In this case, however, other limitations might affect his decision (including the excess business loss limitation; see text Section 7-5). Or he can apply § 179 or additional first-year depreciation to selected assets, reducing his taxable income this year and deferring some deductions to future years.

Key Terms

Accelerated cost recovery system (ACRS), 8-2

Additional first-year depreciation, 8-14

Alternative depreciation system (ADS), 8-23

Amortization, 8-25

Cost depletion, 8-29

Cost recovery, 8-2

Depletion, 8-28

Depreciation, 8-2

Half-year convention, 8-6

Intangible drilling and development costs (IDCs), 8-29

Listed property, 8-18

Mid-month convention, 8-10

Mid-quarter convention, 8-7

Modified accelerated cost recovery system (MACRS), 8-2

Percentage depletion, 8-30

Qualified improvement property, 8-8

Residential rental real estate, 8-9

Section 179 expensing, 8-11

Startup expenditures, 8-25

Discussion Questions

1. **LO.1** Discuss whether property that is classified as personal use is subject to cost recovery.

2. **LO.1** Discuss the difference between personal property and personal use property.

3. **LO.1** Discuss whether land improvements used in a trade or business are eligible for cost recovery.

4. **LO.2** At the beginning of the current year, Henry purchased a ski resort for $10,000,000. Henry does not own the land on which the resort is located. The Federal government owns the land, and Henry has the right to operate the resort on the land pursuant to Special Use Permits, which are terminable at will by the Federal government, and Term Special Use Permits, which allow the land to be used for a fixed number of years.

   Critical Thinking

   In preparing the income tax return for the current year, Henry properly allocated $2,000,000 of the purchase price to the costs of constructing mountain roads, slopes, and trails. Since the acquisition, Henry has spent an additional $2,000,000 on maintaining the mountain roads, slopes, and trails. Identify the relevant tax issues for Henry.

5. **LO.2** Identify the three factors reflected in the MACRS tables when the amount of cost recovery is determined.

6. **LO.2** Discuss the computation of cost recovery in the year an asset is placed in service when the mid-quarter convention is being used.

7. **LO.2** Discuss the computation of cost recovery in the year of sale of an asset when the mid-quarter convention is being used.

Critical Thinking   8.   **LO.2** Robert purchased and placed in service $100,000 of 7-year class assets on August 10 of the current year. He also purchased and placed in service $500,000 of 5-year class assets on November 15 of the current year. He does not claim any available additional first-year depreciation. If Robert elects to use the MACRS straight-line method of cost recovery on the 7-year class assets, discuss the calculation of cost recovery for the 5-year class assets.

9.   **LO.3** Discuss when § 179 expense must be recaptured.

10.   **LO.3** Explain how the § 179 immediate expensing deduction affects the computation of MACRS cost recovery.

11.   **LO.3** Discuss the treatment of a § 179 expensing carryforward.

12.   **LO.3** Discuss the definition of *business income* as it is used in limiting the § 179 expensing amount.

Critical Thinking   13.   **LO.2, 3** A professional consulting business sells professional tools and equipment and provides associated services, such as repair and maintenance, to its customer base. The company's employees include technicians who are required to provide and maintain their own tools and equipment for performing the repairs and maintenance work. The company will reimburse a technician for amounts spent to purchase tools and equipment eligible for a § 179 deduction up to a set amount each year. Any costs for tools and equipment that exceed the set amount will not be reimbursed.

   John is a technician for the company. During the current year, he purchased equipment that qualifies for the § 179 deduction. John paid $50,000 for the equipment and was reimbursed the set amount of $40,000. Identify the relevant tax issues for John with respect to § 179 and the computation of his taxable income.

14.   **LO.4** Discuss how the limits on cost recovery apply to listed property.

15.   **LO.4** Discuss the tax consequences if the business use percentage of listed property falls to 50% or lower after the year the property is placed in service.

Critical Thinking   16.   **LO.7** Harold and Bart own 75% of the stock of Orange Motors. The other 25% of the stock is owned by Jeb. Orange Motors entered into an agreement with Harold and Bart to acquire all of their Orange stock.

   In addition, Harold and Bart signed a noncompete agreement with Orange Motors. Under the terms of the noncompete agreement, Orange will pay Harold and Bart $15,000 each per year for four years. Identify the relevant tax issues for Orange Motors.

Critical Thinking   17.   **LO.4, 7** In May 2020, Gwen began searching for a trade or business to acquire. In anticipation of finding a suitable acquisition, Gwen hired an investment banker to evaluate three potential businesses. She also hired a law firm to begin drafting regulatory approval documents for a target company. Eventually, Gwen decided to purchase all of the assets of Brash Corporation. Brash and Gwen entered into an acquisition agreement on December 1, 2020. Identify the relevant tax issues for Gwen.

18.   **LO.8** Discuss how the cost of mineral rights enters into the calculation of cost depletion.

Computational Exercises

19. **LO.2** Euclid acquires a 7-year class asset on May 9, 2020, for $80,000 (the only asset acquired during the year). Euclid does not elect immediate expensing under § 179. She does not claim any available additional first-year depreciation. Calculate Euclid's cost recovery deduction for 2020 and 2021.

20. **LO.2** Hamlet acquires a 7-year class asset on November 23, 2020, for $100,000 (the only asset acquired during the year). Hamlet does not elect immediate expensing under § 179. He does not claim any available additional first-year depreciation. Calculate Hamlet's cost recovery deductions for 2020 and 2021.

21. **LO.2** Lopez acquired a building on June 1, 2015, for $1,000,000. Calculate Lopez's cost recovery deduction for 2020 if the building is:
    a. Classified as residential rental real estate.
    b. Classified as nonresidential real estate.

22. **LO.2** Andre acquired a computer on March 3, 2020, for $2,800. He elects the straight-line method for cost recovery. Andre does not elect immediate expensing under § 179. He does not claim any available additional first-year depreciation. Calculate Andre's cost recovery deduction for the computer for tax years 2020 and 2021.

23. **LO.2, 3** Diana acquires, for $65,000, and places in service a 5-year class asset on December 19, 2020. It is the only asset that Diana acquires during 2020. Diana does not elect immediate expensing under § 179. She elects additional first-year deprecation. Calculate Diana's total cost recovery deduction for 2020.

24. **LO.3** McKenzie purchased qualifying equipment for his business that cost $212,000 in 2020. The taxable income of the business for the year is $5,600 before consideration of any § 179 deduction.
    a. Calculate McKenzie's § 179 expense deduction for 2020 and any carryover to 2021.
    b. How would your answer change if McKenzie decided to use additional first-year (bonus) depreciation on the equipment instead of using § 179 expensing?

25. **LO.4** On April 5, 2020, Kinsey places in service a new automobile that cost $60,000. He does not elect § 179 expensing, and he elects not to take any available additional first-year depreciation. The car is used 70% for business and 30% for personal use in each tax year.
    Kinsey chooses the MACRS 200% declining-balance method of cost recovery (the auto is a 5-year asset). Assume the following luxury automobile limitations: year 1: $10,100; year 2: $16,100. Compute the total depreciation allowed for 2020 and 2021.

26. **LO.7** On October 1, 2020, Priscilla purchased a business. Of the purchase price, $60,000 is allocated to a patent and $375,000 is allocated to goodwill. Calculate Priscilla's 2020 § 197 amortization deduction.

27. **LO.8** On March 25, Parscale Company purchases the rights to a mineral interest for $8,000,000. At that time, the remaining recoverable units in the mineral interest are estimated to be 500,000 tons. If 80,000 tons are mined and 75,000 tons are sold this year, calculate Parscale's cost depletion for the year.

28. **LO.8** Jebali Company reports gross income of $340,000 and other property-related expenses of $229,000 and uses a depletion rate of 14%. Calculate Jebali's depletion allowance for the current year.

Problems

29. **LO.1, 2** On November 4, 2018, Blue Company acquired an asset (27.5-year residential real property) for $200,000 for use in its business. In 2018 and 2019, respectively, Blue deducted $642 and $5,128 of cost recovery. These amounts were incorrect; Blue applied the wrong percentages (i.e., those for 39-year rather than 27.5-year assets). Blue should have taken $910 and $7,272 cost recovery in 2018 and 2019, respectively.

    On January 1, 2020, the asset was sold for $180,000. Calculate the gain or loss on the sale of the asset for that year.

30. **LO.1, 2** In 2017, José purchased a house for $325,000 ($300,000 relates to the house; $25,000 relates to the land). He used the house as his personal residence. In March 2020, when the fair market value of the house was $400,000, he converted the house to rental property. What is José's cost recovery for 2020?

31. **LO.2, 3** Orange Corporation acquired new office furniture on August 15, 2020, for $130,000. Orange does not elect immediate expensing under § 179. Orange claims any available additional first-year depreciation.
    a. Determine Orange's cost recovery for 2020.
    b. How would your answer change if Orange decided to use $52,000 of bonus depreciation and use normal MACRS on the balance of the acquisition cost?

32. **LO.2** Juan acquires a new 5-year class asset on March 14, 2020, for $200,000. This is the only asset Juan acquired during the year. He does not elect immediate expensing under § 179. He does not claim any available additional first-year depreciation. On July 15, 2021, Juan sells the asset.
    a. Determine Juan's cost recovery for 2020.
    b. Determine Juan's cost recovery for 2021.

33. **LO.2** Debra acquired the following new assets during 2020.

Date	Asset	Cost
April 11	Furniture	$40,000
July 28	Trucks	40,000
November 3	Computers	70,000

    Determine Debra's cost recovery deductions for the current year. Debra does not elect immediate expensing under § 179. She does not claim any available additional first-year depreciation.

34. **LO.2** On August 2, 2020, Wendy purchased a new office building for $3,800,000. On October 1, 2020, she began to rent out office space in the building. On July 15, 2024, Wendy sold the office building.
    a. Determine Wendy's cost recovery deduction for 2020.
    b. Determine Wendy's cost recovery deduction for 2024.

35. **LO.2** On April 3, 2020, Terry purchased and placed in service a building that cost $2,000,000. An appraisal determined that 25% of the total cost was attributed to the value of the land. The bottom floor of the building is leased to a retail business for $32,000. The other floors of the building are rental apartments with an annual rent of $160,000. Determine Terry's cost recovery deduction for 2020.

36. **LO.2** On May 5, 2020, Christy purchased and placed in service a hotel. The hotel cost $10,800,000, and the land cost $1,200,000 ($12,000,000 in total). Calculate Christy's cost recovery deductions for 2020 and for 2030.

37. **LO.2** Janice acquired an apartment building on June 4, 2020, for $1,600,000. The value of the land is $300,000. Janice sold the apartment building on November 29, 2026.

    a. Determine Janice's cost recovery deduction for 2020.

    b. Determine Janice's cost recovery deduction for 2026.

38. **LO.2, 3, 9** Lori, who is single, purchased 5-year class property for $200,000 and 7-year class property for $420,000 on May 20, 2020. Lori expects the taxable income derived from her business (before considering any amount expensed under § 179) to be about $550,000. Lori has determined that she should elect immediate § 179 expensing in the amount of $520,000, but she doesn't know which asset she should completely expense under § 179. She does not claim any available additional first-year depreciation.

    Decision Making
    Critical Thinking
    Communications

    a. Determine Lori's total cost recovery deduction if the § 179 expense is first taken with respect to the 5-year class asset.

    b. Determine Lori's total cost recovery deduction if the § 179 expense is first taken with respect to the 7-year class asset.

    c. What is your advice to Lori?

    d. Assume that Lori is in the 24% marginal tax state and Federal income bracket and that she elects § 179 for the 7-year asset. Determine the present value of the tax savings from the cost recovery deductions for both assets. See Appendix G for present value factors, and assume a 6% discount rate.

    e. Assume the same facts as in part (d), except that Lori decides not to use § 179 on either asset. Determine the present value of the tax savings under this choice. In addition, determine which option Lori should choose.

    f. Present your solution to parts (d) and (e) of the problem in a spreadsheet using appropriate Microsoft Excel formulas. E-mail your spreadsheet to your instructor with a two-paragraph summary of your findings.

39. **LO.2, 3** Olga is the proprietor of a small business. In 2020, the business's income, before consideration of any cost recovery or § 179 deduction, is $250,000. Olga spends $620,000 on new 7-year class assets and elects to take the § 179 deduction on them. She does not claim any available additional first-year depreciation. Olga's cost recovery deduction for 2020, except for the cost recovery with respect to the new 7-year assets, is $95,000. Determine Olga's total cost recovery for 2020 with respect to the 7-year class assets and the amount of any § 179 carryforward.

    Critical Thinking

40. **LO.2, 3, 9** On June 5, 2019, Javier Sanchez purchased and placed in service a new 7-year class asset costing $560,000 for use in his landscaping business, which he operates as a single member LLC (Sanchez Landscaping LLC). During 2019, his business generated a net income of $945,780 before any § 179 immediate expense election.

    a. Rather than using bonus depreciation, Javier would like to use § 179 to expense $200,000 of this asset and then use regular MACRS to cost recover the remaining cost. Given this information, determine the cost recovery deductions that Javier can claim with respect to this asset in 2019 and 2020.

    b. Complete Javier's Form 4562 (page 1) for 2019. His Social Security number is 123-45-6789.

41. **LO.2, 4** On October 15, 2020, Jon purchased and placed in service a used car. The purchase price was $38,000. This was the only business use asset Jon acquired in 2020. He used the car 80% of the time for business and 20% for personal use. Jon used the regular MACRS method. Calculate the total cost recovery deduction Jon may take for 2020 with respect to the car.

42. **LO.4** On June 5, 2019, Leo purchased and placed in service a new car that cost $75,000. The business use percentage for the car is always 100%. Leo does not claim any available additional first-year depreciation. Compute Leo's cost recovery deductions for 2019 and 2020.

43. **LO.2, 3, 4** On March 15, 2020, Helen purchased and placed in service a new Escalade. The purchase price was $62,000, and the vehicle had a rating of 6,500 GVW. The vehicle was used 100% for business.

    a. Assuming that Helen does not use additional first-year depreciation, calculate the total depreciation deduction that she can take on the vehicle for 2020.

    b. What would your answer be if Helen decided to take additional first-year depreciation?

44. **LO.2, 4** On May 28, 2020, Mary purchased and placed in service a new $60,000 car. The car was used 60% for business, 20% for production of income, and 20% for personal use in 2020. In 2021, the usage changed to 40% for business, 30% for production of income, and 30% for personal use. Mary did not elect immediate expensing under § 179. She did not claim any available additional first-year depreciation. Compute Mary's cost recovery deduction and any cost recovery recapture for 2021.

Decision Making   45. **LO.2, 4, 9** Sally purchased a new computer (5-year property) on June 1, 2020, for $4,000. Sally could use the computer 100% of the time in her business, or she could allow her family to use the computer as well. Sally estimates that if her family uses the computer, the business use will be 45% and the personal use will be 55%.

    Determine the tax cost to Sally, in the year of acquisition, of allowing her family to use the computer. Assume that Sally would not elect § 179 immediate expensing and that her marginal income tax rate is 32%. She does not claim any available additional first-year depreciation.

Decision Making   46. **LO.2, 4, 9** Dennis Harding is considering acquiring a new automobile that he will
Critical Thinking   use 100% for business. The purchase price of the automobile would
Communications   be $64,500. If Dennis leased the car for five years, the lease payments would be $875 per month. Dennis will acquire the car on January 1, 2020. The inclusion dollar amounts from the IRS table for the next five years are $63, $140, $208, $251, and $289.

    Dennis wants to know the effect on his adjusted gross income of purchasing versus leasing the car for the next five years. He does not claim any available additional first-year depreciation. Write a letter to Dennis, and present your calculations. Then prepare a memo for the tax files on these matters. Dennis's address is 150 Avenue I, Memphis, TN 38112.

47. **LO.2, 5** In 2020, Muhammad purchased a new computer for $16,000. The computer is used 100% for business. Muhammad did not make a § 179 election with respect to the computer. He does not claim any available additional first-year depreciation. If Muhammad uses the regular MACRS method, determine his cost recovery deduction for 2020 for computing taxable income and for computing his alternative minimum tax.

Decision Making   48. **LO.2, 5, 9** Jamie purchased $100,000 of new office furniture for her business in
Critical Thinking   June of the current year. Jamie understands that if she elects to use ADS
Communications   to compute her regular income tax, there will be no difference between the cost recovery for computing the regular income tax and the AMT.

    a. Jamie wants to know the present value of the *tax cost*, after three years, of using ADS rather than MACRS. Assume that Jamie does not elect § 179 expensing, she does not claim any additional first-year depreciation, and her combined state and Federal income marginal tax rate is 32%. See Appendix G for present value factors, and assume a 6% discount rate.

b. What is the present value of the tax savings/costs that result over the life of the asset if Jamie uses MACRS rather than ADS?

c. Present your solution to part (b) of the problem in a spreadsheet using appropriate Microsoft Excel formulas. E-mail your spreadsheet to your instructor with a one-paragraph explanation.

49. **LO.2, 7, 9** Mike Saxon is negotiating the purchase of a business. The final purchase price ($2,000,000) has been agreed upon, but the allocation of the purchase price to the assets is still being discussed. Appraisals on a warehouse range from $1,200,000 to $1,500,000. If a value of $1,200,000 is used for the warehouse, the remainder of the purchase price, $800,000, will be allocated to goodwill. If $1,500,000 is allocated to the warehouse, goodwill will be $500,000.

    Mike wants to know what effect each alternative will have on cost recovery and amortization during the first year. Under the agreement, Mike will take over the business on January 1 of next year.

    Write a letter to Mike in which you present your calculations and recommendation. Then prepare a memo for the tax files, addressing these matters. Mike's address is 200 Rolling Hills Drive, Shavertown, PA 18708.

Decision Making
Critical Thinking
Communications

50. **LO.7** Oleander Corporation, a calendar year entity, begins business on March 1, 2020. The corporation incurs startup expenditures of $64,000. If Oleander elects § 195 treatment, determine the total amount of startup expenditures that it may deduct for 2020.

51. **LO.7** Martha was considering starting a new business. During her preliminary investigations related to the new venture, she incurred the following expenditures.

Salaries	$22,000
Travel	18,000
Interest on short-term note	4,000
Professional fees	13,000

Martha begins the business on July 1 of the current year. If Martha elects § 195 treatment, determine her startup expenditure deduction for the current year.

52. **LO.8** Wes acquired a mineral interest during the year for $10,000,000. A geological survey estimated that 250,000 tons of the mineral remained in the deposit. During the year, 80,000 tons were mined and 45,000 tons were sold for $12,000,000. Other related expenses amounted to $5,000,000. Assuming that the mineral depletion rate is 22%, calculate Wes's lowest taxable income after any depletion deductions.

Tax Return Problems

53. Janice Morgan, age 24, is single and has no dependents. She is a freelance writer. In January 2019, Janice opened her own office located at 2751 Waldham Road, Pleasant Hill, NM 88135. She called her business Writers Anonymous. Janice is a cash basis taxpayer. She lives at 132 Stone Avenue, Pleasant Hill, NM 88135. Her Social Security number is 123-45-6782. Janice's parents continue to provide health insurance for her under their policy. Janice did not engage in any virtual currency transactions during the year and wants to contribute to the Presidential Election Campaign Fund.

Tax Forms Problem

    During 2019, Janice reported the following income and expense items connected with her business.

Income from sale of articles	$85,000
Rent	16,500
Utilities	7,900
Supplies	1,800
Insurance	5,000
Travel (including meals of $1,200)	3,500

Janice purchased and placed in service the following fixed assets for her business. Janice wants to elect immediate expensing under § 179, if possible.

- Furniture and fixtures (new) costing $21,000 on January 10
- Computer equipment (new) costing $12,400 on July 28

Janice's itemized deductions include:

State income tax	$2,950
Home mortgage interest paid to First National Bank	6,000
Property taxes on home	2,500
Charitable contribution to her alma mater, State College	1,200

Janice did not keep a record of the sales tax she paid. The amount allowed by the sales tax table is $437.

Janice reports interest income of $4,000 on certificates of deposit at Second National Bank. Janice makes estimated tax payments of $3,000 for 2019.

Compute Janice Morgan's 2019 Federal income tax payable (or refund due). If you use tax forms for your computations, you will need Forms 1040, 4562, 8995, and Schedules 1, 2, 3, A, B, C, and SE. Suggested software: ProConnect Tax Online.

Tax Computation Problem

Decision Making

Communications

54. John Smith, age 31, is single and has no dependents. At the beginning of 2020, John started his own excavation business and named it Earth Movers. John lives at 1045 Center Street, Lindon, UT, and his business is located at 381 State Street, Lindon, UT. The Zip Code for both addresses is 84042. John's Social Security number is 111-11-1111, and the business identification number is 11-1111111. John is a cash basis taxpayer. During 2020, John reports the following items in connection with his business.

Fee income for services rendered	$912,000
Building rental expense	36,000
Office furniture and equipment rental expense	9,000
Office supplies	2,500
Utilities	4,000
Salary for secretary	34,000
Salary for equipment operators	42,000
Payroll taxes	7,000
Fuel and oil for the equipment	21,000
Purchase of three new front-end loaders on January 15, 2020	560,000
Purchase of a new dump truck on January 18, 2020	80,000

During 2020, John recorded the following additional items.

Interest income from First National Bank	$10,000
Dividends from ExxonMobil	9,500
Quarterly estimated tax payments	11,500

John wants to maximize his cost recovery deductions (including taking any § 179 expense and any available additional first-year depreciation).

On October 8, 2020, John inherited IBM stock from his Aunt Mildred. John had been her favorite nephew. According to the data provided by the executor of Aunt Mildred's estate, the stock was valued for estate tax purposes at $110,000. John is considering selling the IBM stock for $125,000 on December 29, 2020, and using $75,000 of the proceeds to purchase an Acura ZDX. He would use the car 100% for business. John wants to know what effect these transactions would have on his 2020 adjusted gross income.

Write a letter to John in which you present your calculations. Ignore any Federal self-employment tax implications.

Research Problems

Note: Solutions to the Research Problems can be prepared by using the Thomson Reuters Checkpoint™ online tax research database, which accompanies this textbook. Solutions can also be prepared by using research materials found in a typical tax library.

Research Problem 1. Your client, Dave's Sport Shop, sells sports equipment and clothing in three retail outlets in New York City. During 2020, the CFO decided that keeping track of inventory using a combination of QuickBooks and spreadsheets was not an efficient way to manage the stores' inventories. So Dave's purchased an inventory management system for $9,000 that allowed the entity to keep track of inventory, as well as automate ordering and purchasing, without replacing QuickBooks for its accounting function.

Communications

The CFO would like to know whether the cost of the inventory management program can be expensed in the year of purchase. Write a letter to the CFO, Cassandra Martin, that addresses the tax treatment of purchased software. Cassandra's mailing address is 867 Broadway, New York, NY 10003.

Research Problem 2. In 2015, Jed James began planting a vineyard. The costs of the land preparation, labor, rootstock, and planting were capitalized. The land preparation costs do not include any nondepreciable land costs. In 2020, when the plants became viable, Jed placed the vineyard in service. Jed wants to know whether he can claim a deduction under § 179 on his 2020 income tax return for the 2015 costs for planting the vineyard.

Research Problem 3. Juan owns a business that acquires exotic automobiles that are high-tech, state-of-the-art vehicles with unique design features or equipment. The exotic automobiles are not licensed or set up to be used on the road. Rather, the cars are used exclusively for car shows or related promotional photography. With respect to the exotic automobiles, Juan would like to know whether he can take a cost recovery deduction on his Federal income tax return.

Partial list of research aids:
Bruce Selig, 70 TCM 1125, T.C.Memo. 1995–519.

Use internet tax resources to address the following questions. Look for reliable websites and blogs of the IRS and other government agencies, media outlets, businesses, tax professionals, academics, think tanks, and political outlets.

Research Problem 4. Locate a financial calculator app or program that assesses the wisdom of buying versus leasing a new car. Use it to work through Problem 46 in this chapter.

Research Problem 5. There are significant tax planning opportunities related to fixed asset acquisition (and depreciation). Search out how large public accounting firms are assisting clients in this area. Summarize your findings in an e-mail to your instructor.

Communications

Research Problem 6. Do depreciation deductions vary by entity type or by industry? Go to the IRS Tax Statistics page (**irs.gov/statistics**) and review the spreadsheets containing data for corporations, partnerships, and nonfarm proprietorships by sector or industry. You can find these in the Business Tax Statistics section of the IRS site.

Data Analytics

Critical Thinking

Communications

Evaluate the depreciation deductions by sector (19 sectors are identified in the IRS spreadsheets) and by entity using Microsoft Excel. E-mail the spreadsheet to your instructor along with a brief summary of your findings.

Becker CPA Review Questions

Becker.

1. Michael Sima, a sole proprietor craftsman, purchased an amount of equipment in the current year that exceeded the maximum allowable § 179 depreciation election limit by $20,000. Sima's total purchases of property placed in service in the current year did not exceed the limit imposed by § 179. All of the property (including the equipment) was purchased in November of the current year, and Sima elected to depreciate the maximum amount of equipment under § 179. Sima had bottom-line Schedule C income of $50,000 in the current year. Which method may Sima use to depreciate the remaining equipment in the current year?

   a. Sima may not depreciate any additional equipment other than the § 179 maximum in the current year and must carry forward the excess amount to use in the following taxable year.

   b. MACRS half-year convention for personal property.

   c. MACRS mid-quarter convention for personal property.

   d. Straight-line, mid-month convention over 27.5 years for real property.

2. Cox Construction, a company in its 10th year of business, purchased a piece of equipment on April 1, year 9, for $20,000. Cox has used it for business purposes since the initial purchase date. The company depreciated the equipment using the MACRS half-year table for 5-year assets. For tax purposes, what is the amount of accumulated depreciation expense for the equipment as of December 31, year 10?

   a. $6,000   c. $11,600
   b. $10,400   d. $12,800

3. Stem Corp. bought a machine in February of year 7 for $20,000. Then Stem bought furniture in November of year 7 for $30,000. Both machines were placed in service for business purposes immediately after purchase. No other assets were purchased during year 7. What depreciation convention must Stem use for the machine purchased in February year 7?

   a. Mid-month   c. Mid-quarter
   b. Half-year   d. Full-year

4. Data, Inc., purchased and placed in service $5,000 of office furniture on August 24, year 3. This is the only asset purchase during the year. Section 179 expensing and bonus depreciation were not elected. Using the excerpt of the MACRS half-year convention table below, what is the MACRS depreciation in year 3 for the office furniture?

Recovery Period	5-Year	7-Year	10-Year
1	20%	14.29%	10%
2	32%	24.49%	18%
3	19.2%	17.49%	14.4%

   a. $500   c. $875
   b. $715   d. $1,000

5. Which statement below is correct?

   a. Real property is depreciated using the half-year convention.

   b. Residential real estate is depreciated over a 39-year life.

   c. One-half month of depreciation is taken for the month real property is disposed of.

   d. Salvage value is considered in MACRS depreciation.

6. Charlie purchased an apartment building on November 16, year 1, for $1,000,000. Determine the cost recovery for year 20.

   a. $36,360   c. $45,500
   b. $32,100   d. $331,850

CHAPTER

9

Deductions: Employee and Self-Employed-Related Expenses

LEARNING OBJECTIVES: *After completing Chapter 9, you should be able to:*

LO.1 Distinguish between employee and self-employed (independent contractor) status.

LO.2 Recognize deductible transportation expenses.

LO.3 Describe how travel expenses are treated.

LO.4 Differentiate between deductible and nondeductible education expenses.

LO.5 Identify other business expenses.

LO.6 Compare various deductions for contributions to retirement accounts.

LO.7 Demonstrate the difference between accountable and nonaccountable employee plans.

LO.8 Understand the limitations on miscellaneous itemized deductions.

LO.9 List and evaluate tax planning ideas related to employee and self-employed business expenses.

CHAPTER OUTLINE

9-1 Employee versus Independent Contractor, 9-2

9-2 Self-Employed and Employee-Related Expenses— In General, 9-5

9-3 Transportation Expenses, 9-5
9-3a Qualified Expenses, 9-5
9-3b Computation of Automobile Expenses, 9-6

9-4 Travel Expenses, 9-9
9-4a Definition of Travel Expenses, 9-9
9-4b Away-from-Home Requirement, 9-10
9-4c Restrictions on Travel Expenses, 9-11
9-4d Combined Business and Pleasure Travel, 9-12

9-5 Education Expenses, 9-14
9-5a General Requirements, 9-14
9-5b Legal Requirements to Keep a Job, 9-14
9-5c Maintaining or Improving Existing Skills, 9-15
9-5d What Expenses Are Allowed?, 9-15
9-5e Deduction for Qualified Tuition and Related Expenses, 9-16
9-5f Other Provisions Dealing with Education, 9-17

9-6 Other Business Expenses, 9-18
9-6a Office in the Home, 9-18
9-6b Moving Expenses, 9-22
9-6c Entertainment and Meal Expenses, 9-22
9-6d Miscellaneous Employee Expenses, 9-24

9-7 Contributions to Retirement Accounts, 9-25
9-7a § 401(k) Plans, 9-25

9-8 Individual Retirement Accounts (IRAs), 9-26
9-8a General Rules, 9-26
9-8b Taxation of Benefits, 9-29
9-8c Rollovers and Conversions, 9-30

9-9 Retirement Plans for Self-Employed Individuals, 9-31
9-9a Keogh (H.R. 10) Plans, 9-31
9-9b Solo § 401(k) Plans, 9-31
9-9c Savings Incentive Match Plan for Employees (SIMPLE Plans), 9-32
9-9d Simplified Employee Pension Plans (SEPs), 9-32

9-10 Classification of Employee Expenses, 9-33
9-10a Accountable Plans, 9-33
9-10b Nonaccountable Plans, 9-34

9-11 Limitations on Itemized Deductions, 9-35
9-11a Miscellaneous Itemized Deductions Subject to the 2%-of-AGI Floor, 9-35
9-11b Miscellaneous Itemized Deductions Not Subject to the 2%-of-AGI Floor, 9-35

9-12 Tax Planning, 9-36
9-12a Employment Status, 9-36
9-12b Implications of Misclassifying Workers, 9-36
9-12c Transportation and Travel Expenses, 9-37
9-12d Education Expenses, 9-37

ISTOCK.COM/SVETIKD

THE FIRST JOB

After an extensive search, Morgan, a recent college graduate with a major in child development, has accepted a job with Enrichment Child Care Center (ECCC) in a neighboring state. ECCC is located in the western suburbs of a large metropolitan city, roughly 30 miles from the center of the city. Morgan will be moving into a two-bedroom apartment about two miles from ECCC. At ECCC, Morgan will work with preschool children Monday to Friday from 7 A.M. to 3 P.M. One of the reasons she accepted the position at ECCC is the flexibility it provides. Because she is eager to pay off her student loans and save to buy a house, she has decided to freelance in the late afternoons and evenings and on weekends—joining the "gig economy."

She finds two ways to freelance: (1) transporting people, packages, and meals for a few companies where she finds work through an "app" (like driving for Uber) and (2) tutoring elementary school students in English and math. Her tutoring can take place online or in person (either in her apartment or at the child's home). She has dedicated the second bedroom in her apartment for freelancing. She has a large table and several chairs in this bedroom that allow her to meet her tutoring students or connect with them via her laptop. She keeps all of her freelancing records in a file cabinet, which she keeps in a closet in the bedroom. She also purchases and keeps various supplies for her tutoring activities in the closet. Although there are some freelance driving options in the suburbs, most often Morgan heads for the city, where there are more passengers and higher fares.

What are some of the income tax problems presented by this situation?

Read the chapter and formulate your response.

FRAMEWORK 1040 Tax Formula for Individuals

This chapter covers the boldfaced portions of the Tax Formula for Individuals that was introduced in Concept Summary 3.1 on p. 3-3. Below those portions are the sections of Form 1040 where the results are reported.

Income *(broadly defined)*	$ xx,xxx
Less: Exclusions	(x,xxx)
Gross income..	$ xx,xxx
Less: Deductions *for* adjusted gross income	**(x,xxx)**

FORM 1040 (Schedule 1)

3	Business income or (loss). Attach Schedule C.	
10	Educator expenses	
11	Certain business expenses of reservists, performing artists, and fee-basis government officials. Attach Form 2106	
14	Deductible part of self-employment tax. Attach Schedule SE	
15	Self-employed SEP, SIMPLE, and qualified plans	
16	Self-employed health insurance deduction	
19	IRA deduction	

Adjusted gross income..	$ xx,xxx
Less: The greater of total itemized deductions *or* the standard deduction	(x,xxx)

FORM 1040 (p. 1)

9	**Standard deduction or itemized deductions** (from Schedule A)	

Personal and dependency exemptions*	(x,xxx)
Deduction for qualified business income**	(x,xxx)
Taxable income	$ xx,xxx
Tax on taxable income *(see Tax Tables or Tax Rate Schedules)*	$ x,xxx
Less: Tax credits *(including income taxes withheld and prepaid)*	(xxx)
Tax due (or refund)	$ xxx

 * Exemption deductions are not allowed from 2018 through 2025.
** Only applies from 2018 through 2025.

Considering the large number of taxpayers affected, the tax treatment of job-related expenses is somewhat complex. To resolve this complexity, a number of key questions must be asked:

- Is the taxpayer an *employee* or *self-employed*?
- What expenses *qualify* as deductions?
- How are the deductible expenses *classified* for tax purposes (*for* AGI or *from* AGI)?
- To the extent the expenses are classified as deductions *from* AGI, are they subject to any *limitation*?

In addition to answering these questions, the chapter also discusses contributions to retirement accounts and provides some tax planning ideas.

LO.1

Distinguish between employee and self-employed (independent contractor) status.

9-1 EMPLOYEE VERSUS INDEPENDENT CONTRACTOR

When one person performs services for another, the person performing the service either is an employee or is self-employed (an **independent contractor**). Failure to recognize a person's work status correctly can have serious tax consequences (in addition to Federal and state labor law consequences). Tax deficiencies as well as interest and penalties may result from improper classification.

Unlike employees, self-employed individuals do not have to be included in various fringe benefit programs (e.g., group term life insurance and retirement plans). Because self-employed individuals are not covered by FICA and FUTA (see Chapter 1), a business also avoids these payroll costs. The IRS is aware of the tendency of some businesses to attempt to classify workers as self-employed rather than as employees.

Employment status also makes a great deal of difference to the person who performs the services. Expenses of self-employed individuals, if deductible, are classified as deductions *for* AGI and are reported on Schedule C (Profit or Loss From Business) of Form 1040.[1] Unless reimbursed under an accountable plan (discussed later in the chapter), employee business expenses are deductions *from* AGI as miscellaneous itemized deductions. However, from 2018 through 2025, the deduction for miscellaneous itemized deductions is suspended. As a result, there is no tax benefit from these deductions during this period.[2]

Most persons classified as employees are common law employees. The common law employee classification originated in the courts and is summarized in various IRS pronouncements.[3] Revenue Ruling 87–41, for example, lists 20 factors to determine whether a worker is a common law employee or an independent contractor (and, thus, self-employed).[4] The IRS has indicated that these 20 factors can be grouped into three broad categories: behavioral control, financial control, and the relationship of the parties.

An employee-employer relationship exists when the employer has the right to control what is to be done and the ways and means by which results are to be attained.[5] In general, this means that a worker is classified as an employee if the employer identifies *what* should be done and *how* it should be done. If an individual is told *what* to do but is allowed to independently determine how to do it, an employee-employer relationship likely does not exist.

If a business provides the following items to a worker, a common law employee-employer relationship likely exists:

- Furnishing tools or equipment and a place to work.
- Providing support services, including the hiring of assistants to help do the work.
- Training the worker for needed job skills.
- Allowing participation in various workplace fringe benefits (e.g., accident and health plans, group life insurance, and retirement plans).
- Paying for services based on time rather than the task performed.

Alternatively, independent contractors are more likely to have unreimbursed business expenses, a significant investment in tools and work facilities, and less permanency in their business relationships. Independent contractors anticipate a profit from their work, make their services available to the relevant marketplace, and are likely to be paid a flat fee on a per-job basis.

In resolving employment status, each case must be tested on its own merits. But the key test is whether the business (service recipient) has the *right to control* the means and methods of accomplishment (both what must be done *and* how it should be done). If this is the case, an employer-employee relationship exists. Concept Summary 9.1 provides an overview of the current IRS position in this area.

Employee *versus* Independent Contractor

Arnold is a lawyer whose major client accounts for 60% of his billings. He does the routine legal work and income tax returns at the client's request. He is paid a monthly retainer in addition to amounts charged for extra work. Arnold is a self-employed individual. Even though most of his income comes from one client, he still has the right to determine how the end result of his work is attained.

EXAMPLE 1

---

[1]In simple situations, a Schedule C–EZ can be used. Also, a Schedule SE (Self-Employment Tax) must be filed.

[2]§ 67(g); added by the Tax Cuts and Jobs Act (TCJA) of 2017.

[3]See, for example, IRS Publication 15–A (*Employer's Supplemental Tax Guide*).

[4]1987–1 C.B. 296. Also see IRS Publication 1779 (*Independent Contractor or Employee*).

[5]Reg. § 31.3401(c)–(1)(b).

Concept Summary 9.1

Employee versus Independent Contractor

Although the 20 factors identified by the Internal Revenue Service in Revenue Ruling 87–41 remain relevant, the IRS has grouped these factors into three broad categories in order to provide some clarity to a difficult area, while acknowledging that the 20 factors are not all-inclusive.

Behavioral Control	Financial Control	The Relationship of the Parties

• Does the business control (or have the right to control) what the worker does and how the worker does his or her job?
• Facts that show whether the business has **behavioral control** include:
  ➤ *Instructions.* An employee is generally told:
    1. When, where, and how to work.
    2. What equipment, tools, or processes to use.
    3. What workers can be hired to assist with the work.
    4. Where to purchase supplies and services.
    5. What work must be performed by a specified individual.
    6. What order or sequence to follow in performing the work.
  ➤ *Training.* An employee normally receives training to perform work in a particular manner.
	• Are the business aspects of the worker's job controlled by the payer?
	• Facts that show whether the business has **financial control** include:
	  ➤ The extent to which the worker has unreimbursed business expenses.
	  ➤ The extent of the worker's investment.
	  ➤ The extent to which the worker makes services available to a larger market (e.g., is the worker marketing his or her services to multiple businesses?).
	  ➤ How the business pays the worker (is it the same or different from how employees are paid?).
	  ➤ The extent to which the worker can realize a profit or loss.
		• A variety of facts and documents can show the **relationship of the parties**:
		  ➤ Written contracts describing the relationship the parties intended to create.
		  ➤ Whether the worker is provided with employee-type fringe benefits.
		  ➤ The permanency of the relationship (e.g., is the work for a specified period of time or indefinite?).
		  ➤ How integral the services are to the principal activity of the business.

Summary

1. Businesses must weigh all factors when determining whether a worker is an employee or independent contractor. Some factors might indicate that the worker is an employee, and other factors might indicate that the worker is an independent contractor.

2. No set number of factors "makes" the worker an employee or an independent contractor, and no one factor controls in making this determination. Also, factors that are relevant in one setting may not be relevant in a different setting.

3. Overall, one must look at the entirety of the relationship, consider the degree or extent of the right to direct and control, and document each of the factors used in coming to a decision.

Employee *versus* Independent Contractor

Ellen is a lawyer hired by Arnold to assist him in the performance of services for the client mentioned in Example 1. Ellen is under Arnold's supervision; he reviews her work and pays her an hourly fee. Ellen is an employee of Arnold.

When one taxpayer holds multiple jobs, it is possible to have dual status as both an employee and an independent contractor (i.e., self-employed).

Dr. Stephanie Davis, DDS, is a full-time employee at the Robin University Health Center. In the evenings and on weekends, she shares a practice with another dentist who works the Monday through Friday day-time shifts. Dr. Davis is both employed and self-employed.

Certain workers who *are not* common law employees are treated as employees for employment tax purposes. Known as <mark>statutory employees</mark>, this group includes certain drivers (e.g., nondairy beverage distributors and laundry and dry cleaning pickup service), life insurance sales agents, home workers, and other salespersons. These employees are allowed to claim their business-related expenses as deductions *for* AGI by using Schedule C. The wages or commissions paid to statutory employees are not subject to Federal income tax withholding but are subject to Social Security tax.[6]

To avoid the confusion that might otherwise result in their classification, the tax law categorically treats certain categories of workers as independent contractors. Included in this group are licensed real estate agents and direct sellers. These individuals are treated as self-employed for all Federal purposes, including income and employment taxes.[7]

If a taxpayer wants to know whether employee or independent contractor status exists, the IRS will make a determination if the taxpayer files a Form SS–8 (Determination of Worker Status for Purposes of Federal Employment Taxes and Income Tax Withholding).

9-2 SELF-EMPLOYED AND EMPLOYEE-RELATED EXPENSES—IN GENERAL

Self-employed and employee expenses fall into one of the following categories:

- Transportation.
- Travel.
- Moving.
- Education.
- Entertainment.
- Other (including office in the home and miscellaneous expenses).

Self-employed deductions are allowed *for* AGI; most employee business expenses are miscellaneous itemized deductions (a *from* AGI deduction and subject to a 2%-of-AGI floor). The Tax Cuts and Jobs Act (TCJA) of 2017 made a significant change in this area by suspending the deduction for miscellaneous itemized deductions (including unreimbursed employee business expenses) from 2018 through 2025. As a result, the only employee business expenses that are currently deductible are those that are *reimbursed by an employer* (and these expenses, once reimbursed, have no effect on an employee's taxable income).

Given the TCJA of 2017 changes to the status of employee business expenses, the materials that follow are focused on the self-employed taxpayer. However, employees incurring these expenses in employer-related activities might be able to seek reimbursement for them. In addition, an employee might also have a separate business (e.g., consulting, rentals, etc.) that would allow these business expenses to be deducted in that activity.

9-3 TRANSPORTATION EXPENSES

LO.2

Recognize deductible transportation expenses.

9-3a Qualified Expenses

A deduction is allowed for business transportation expenses. <mark>Transportation expenses</mark> include only the cost of transporting the self-employed taxpayer (or employee) from one place to another in the course of business when the taxpayer is *not in travel status* (discussed in text Section 9-4). Transportation costs include taxi fares, automobile expenses, tolls, and parking.

---

[6]§ 3121(d)(3). See Circular E, *Employer's Tax Guide* (IRS Publication 15), for further discussion of statutory employees.

[7]§ 3508. Also see *Employer's Supplemental Tax Guide* (IRS Publication 15–A).

Commuting Expenses

Commuting between home and one's place of employment is a personal, nondeductible expense. The fact that one employee drives 30 miles to work and another employee walks six blocks to work does not matter.

Geraldo is employed by Sparrow Corporation. He drives 22 miles each way to work. The 44 miles he drives each workday are nondeductible commuting expenses.

If a taxpayer has a home office that qualifies as a principal place of business, the transportation costs between home and various work locations are deductible (i.e., the costs are *not* a commuting expense).

The Big Picture

Return to the facts of *The Big Picture* on p. 9-1. Because Morgan will have an office in her home for her two freelancing businesses, the apartment will be her principal place of business. As a result, any transportation from her home to freelancing sites (e.g., driving to a child's home for tutoring) is *not* a commuting expense.[8] However, Morgan will have commuting expenses for the mileage between her apartment and her job at Enrichment Child Care Center.

9-3b Computation of Automobile Expenses

A taxpayer has two choices in determining automobile expenses: the automatic mileage method and the actual cost method. If an automobile is used for both business and personal purposes (mixed use), only the expenses related to the business use are deductible. The percentage of business use is usually arrived at by comparing the business mileage with total mileage—both business and personal.

Automatic Mileage Method

Also called the standard mileage method, the ==automatic mileage method== is convenient in that it simplifies record keeping. The rate allowed per mile takes into account average operating expenses (such as gas and oil, repairs, and depreciation). Consequently, the taxpayer only has to multiply the automatic mileage rate by the business miles driven to compute the deduction.

For 2020, the deduction is based on 57.5 cents per mile for business miles.[9] This represents a one-half cent decrease from the rate of 58 cents that applied in 2019. Although the mileage rate usually remains constant for an entire year, the IRS occasionally makes mid-year changes to the rate, usually when there is a large change in the cost of fuel. As a result, it is important that the taxpayer keep records to identify when the driving took place.

Chad drove his car 20,000 miles for business during 2020. To determine his standard mileage deduction, he simply multiplies his business miles by the appropriate standard mileage rate (57.5 cents per mile in 2020). So his total standard mileage deduction for the year is $11,500 (20,000 miles × 57.5 cents per mile).

The automatic mileage rate for deductible education expenses is the same as for business; 17 cents per mile is allowed for medical purposes, and the rate for the charitable contribution deduction is 14 cents a mile (see Chapter 10 for a discussion of medical expenses

---

[8]*Walter K. Strohmalter*, 113 T.C. 106 (1999).

[9]Notice 2020–5, 2020–4 I.R.B. 380 and Rev.Proc. 2019–46, 2019–49 I.R.B. 1301.

and charitable contributions). Parking fees and tolls are allowed in addition to the deduction computed using the automatic mileage method.

Generally, a taxpayer may elect either method for any particular year. However, the following restrictions apply to the standard mileage method:

- The vehicle must be owned or leased by the taxpayer.
- If five or more vehicles are in use (for business purposes) at the *same* time (not alternately), a taxpayer may not use the automatic mileage method.
- A basis adjustment for depreciation is required if the taxpayer changes from the automatic mileage method to the actual operating cost method. The depreciation adjustment for the business miles is determined using the following schedule:

Year	Rate per Mile
2020	27 cents
2019	26 cents
2018	25 cents
2017	25 cents
2016	24 cents

EXAMPLE

7

Tim purchased his automobile in 2017 for $36,000. It is used 90% for business purposes. Tim drove the automobile for 10,000 business miles in 2019, 8,500 business miles in 2018, and 6,000 business miles in 2017. At the beginning of 2020, the basis of the business portion of his car is $26,175.

Depreciable basis ($36,000 × 90%)	$32,400
Less depreciation:	
2019 (10,000 miles × 26 cents)	(2,600)
2018 (8,500 miles × 25 cents)	(2,125)
2017 (6,000 miles × 25 cents)	(1,500)
Adjusted business basis 1/1/2020	$26,175

- Use of the automatic mileage method in the first year an auto is placed in service is considered an election to exclude the auto from MACRS cost recovery (discussed in Chapter 8).
- A taxpayer may not switch to the automatic mileage method if the MACRS statutory percentage method or a § 179 expense election has been used.

Actual Cost Method

Under this method, the actual cost of operating the automobile is used to compute the deduction. Actual costs include the following expenses:

- Gas and oil, lubrication.
- Depreciation (or lease payments).   — *if you bought the car*
- Insurance.
- Dues to auto clubs.
- Repairs.
- Tires and other parts.
- Licenses and registration fees.
- Parking and tolls.

EXAMPLE 8

Return to the facts of Example 6. Chad drove his car a total of 25,000 miles in 2020 (20,000 for business and 5,000 for personal use). He incurred the following automobile costs (he has receipts for all of these expenses):

Lease payments ($350 per month)	$ 4,200
Fuel	2,300
Insurance	2,800
Repairs and maintenance	1,200
State registration fee	150
Total expenses	$ 10,650
× Business use percentage (20,000 ÷ 25,000)	× 80%
Actual cost method deduction	$ 8,520

As a result, Chad is better off using the automatic mileage method. Chad's true cost of operating the vehicle is 42.6 cents per mile ($10,650 ÷ 25,000 miles), yet the government is allowing him to deduct 57.5 cents per mile.

As noted in Chapter 8, deductions for depreciation (or lease payments) are subject to limitations when a "mixed use" vehicle is involved (e.g., a vehicle used in both business and personal activities). Interest on a car loan is not deductible if the taxpayer is an employee, but it can qualify as a business expense if the taxpayer is self-employed. Sales taxes paid on the purchase of a car are added to the cost of the car and recovered via the MACRS deduction. In mixed use situations, the portion of the sales tax attributable to personal use may, in some cases, be claimed as a deduction *from* AGI (see Chapter 10 and the choice required between state and local income and sales taxes).

Except for parking and tolls, none of the expenses noted previously can be separately claimed under the automatic mileage method. A deduction for parking tickets and other traffic violations is not allowed under either method because it is a violation of public policy [§ 162(f); see Chapter 6].

The Big Picture

EXAMPLE 9

Return to the facts of *The Big Picture* on p. 9-1. During Morgan's senior year in college, her parents gave her one of the family cars—a 2016 Toyota Camry. Morgan has no idea as to the car's original cost or the odometer reading at the time the car was registered in her name. She has, however, kept track of the miles driven for business since she accepted her new job. Morgan should use the automatic mileage method in claiming business use of the car.

Which Method Is Best?

Every year the American Automobile Association estimates how much it costs per mile to drive a car in the United States. Its most recent report shows that it costs, on average, anywhere from 47.4 cents to 69.4 cents per mile to drive a sedan for 15,000 miles. Driving a minivan for 15,000 miles costs an average of 66.9 cents per mile, and an all-wheel drive SUV costs 68.4 cents per mile.[10]

The difference depends on the size (and cost) of the car and the number of miles driven during the year—the more miles driven, the less one's cost per mile.

In general, taxpayers are better off using the standard mileage rate if they drive a smaller car, particularly if they drive many business miles. And a taxpayer is likely to benefit from using the standard mileage rate if an old or inexpensive car is used. Why? Because the same fixed deduction rate applies no matter how much the car is worth. Because the standard mileage rate factors in depreciation (which does not vary), an inexpensive car might benefit more from using this method than would an expensive vehicle.

---

[10]American Automobile Association, *Your Driving Costs*, 2019 edition.

The actual cost method will likely provide a larger deduction if the taxpayer drives a more expensive car, an SUV, or a minivan. In addition, the actual cost method will normally result in a larger deduction if fewer business miles are driven.

Yet, the only way to know for sure which method is best is to keep careful track of the actual costs and the business mileage driven. Then calculations can be done under both methods, and the larger deduction can be taken.

The Big Picture

EXAMPLE

10

Return to the facts of *The Big Picture* on p. 9-1. Morgan wants to make sure she documents her business miles appropriately. She knows that the IRS expects her to keep track of her business miles on a regular basis, including where she drove and the business reason for the trip. She wonders whether there are some mobile apps that can help.

Actually, a number of mileage tracking apps are available that would allow Morgan to begin logging miles automatically every time she started a trip. Some use Bluetooth and begin as soon as the car starts moving; others (usually free) require the user to input locations. All of the apps create detailed records of all trips; the user just needs to identify the purpose of the trip. Here are a few apps that are available (with information from the developer's website):

- **MileIQ (mileiq.com)** tracks every trip you take automatically. Then it lets you quickly categorize a trip as business, personal, medical, charity, or a custom category you create. It also lets you log any additional information (like freeway tolls or parking fees). Trip information is backed up automatically using MileIQ's cloud servers, and its data integrates with a number of accounting/tax software programs (including QuickBooks). MileIQ is free if you track fewer than 40 trips per month and about $60 per year with unlimited trip tracking.

- **TripLog (triplogmileage.com)** monitors your mileage via GPS; tracks any parking, tolls, or other expenses; records fuel costs; generates IRS-ready reports; and integrates with Quick-Books. As with MileIQ, you have the option of specifying the nature of the trip (business, charity, medical, etc.), entering notes, and adding any applicable parking or toll costs. TripLog's basic features are free. Advanced features, such as Bluetooth "autostart" and automatic daily cloud backup, cost about $50 per year. You can also use TripLog to estimate your gas mileage and find the best gas prices.

- **QuickBooks Self-Employed (quickbooks.intuit.com/self-employed/)** automatically tracks mileage using your phone's GPS and groups the information into trips (allowing you to categorize them as business or personal). This feature, combined with easy expense categorization (via swiping on the phone) and the ability to organize receipts by taking a picture, lets you easily compare whether you should use the standard mileage or actual cost method. And it integrates seamlessly with TurboTax when it is time to file a tax return. The app costs $15 per month ($25 per month when combined with TurboTax).

- **Stride Drive (stridehealth.com/drive)** is a free mileage and expense tracking app that records your mileage by running in the background as you drive. You can start and stop recording your mileage for each trip by tapping the start button when you leave home, or in some versions of the app, you can set it up to record automatically. You can also use Stride Drive to log your receipts and expense records, so all your business deductions are in one place at tax time. The app includes preloaded categories and explanations (many geared toward rideshare drivers) that help identify which expenses to log (and what percentage of them you can deduct).

9-4 TRAVEL EXPENSES

LO.3

Describe how travel expenses are treated.

9-4a Definition of Travel Expenses

A deduction is allowed for business travel expenses. Travel expenses include transportation expenses, meals and lodging, and incidental expenses while working away from home. In general, the reason for allowing a travel expense deduction is to alleviate the duplication of living expenses (where the taxpayer incurs expenses while at home and while working away from home).

Transportation expenses (discussed previously) are deductible even if the taxpayer is *not* away from home. Meals cannot be lavish or extravagant. Examples of incidental expenses include laundry, baggage fees and/or tips, and ATM fees. A deduction for travel expenses, however, is only allowed if the taxpayer is away from his or her tax home.

9-4b Away-from-Home Requirement

The crucial test for the deductibility of travel expenses is whether the taxpayer is away from home overnight. "Overnight" need not be a 24-hour period, but it must be a period substantially longer than an ordinary day's work and must require rest, sleep, or a relief-from-work period.[11] A one-day business trip normally does not warrant travel status; therefore, meals and lodging for such a trip are not deductible.

Temporary Assignments

The taxpayer must be away from home for a temporary period. If a taxpayer relocates to a new area for an indefinite period of time, that new location becomes his or her tax home. *Temporary* indicates that the assignment's termination is expected within a reasonably short period of time. The position of the IRS is that the tax home is the business location of the taxpayer. As a result, travel expenses are not deductible if a taxpayer is reassigned for an indefinite period and does not move his or her place of residence to the new location.

Temporary Becomes Permanent

EXAMPLE 11

Malcolm maintains a consulting practice in Los Angeles. Due to new client responsibilities, Malcolm decided to open a new office in San Diego. Malcolm worked out of the new office for three months to train a new manager and to assist in setting up the new office. He tried commuting from his home in Los Angeles for a week and decided that he could not continue driving several hours a day. He rented an apartment in San Diego, where he lived during the week. He spent weekends with his wife and children at their home in Los Angeles.

Malcolm's rent, meals, laundry, incidentals, and automobile expenses in San Diego are deductible. To the extent that Malcolm's transportation expense related to his weekend trips home exceeds what his cost of meals and lodging would have been, the excess is personal and nondeductible.

EXAMPLE 12

Assume that Malcolm in Example 11 decided that he was the best person to manage the new office in San Diego and so decided to move there permanently. His wife and children continued to live in Los Angeles until the end of the school year.

Malcolm is no longer "away from home" because the assignment is not temporary. His travel expenses are not deductible.

To curtail controversy in this area, the Code specifies that a taxpayer "*shall not* be treated as *temporarily* away from home during any period of employment if such period exceeds 1 year."[12]

Determining the Tax Home

In most situations, determining the location of a taxpayer's tax home is not difficult. The tax home is the area in which the taxpayer works.

It is possible for a taxpayer never to be away from his or her tax home. In other words, the tax home follows the taxpayer. In this situation, all meals and lodging remain personal and are not deductible.

---

[11]*U.S. v. Correll*, 68–1 USTC ¶9101, 20 AFTR 2d 5845, 88 S.Ct. 445 (USSC, 1967); Rev.Rul. 75–168, 1975–1 C.B. 58.

[12]§ 162(a).

Jim is single and works full-time as a long-haul truck driver. He lists his mother's home as his address and stays there during holidays. However, he contributes nothing toward its maintenance.

Because Jim has no regular place of duty or place where he regularly lives, his tax home is where he works (i.e., on the road). As an itinerant (transient), he is never away from home, and all of his meals and lodging while on the road are personal and not deductible.

EXAMPLE 13

The result reached in Example 13 is justified on the grounds that there is no duplication of living expenses in the case of itinerant taxpayers.[13]

When a taxpayer has more than one place of business or work, the main one is considered to be the tax home. This is determined by considering the time spent, the level of activity involved, and the income earned at each job.

Art, a physical therapist, lives with his family in Lancaster, Pennsylvania. For seven months each year, he is employed by the New Orleans Saints football team at a salary of $150,000. During this period, he rents an apartment in New Orleans. In the off-season, he works for the Lancaster YMCA at a salary of $15,000.

Art's tax home is clearly New Orleans and not Lancaster. Consequently, his living expenses while in New Orleans (i.e., food and lodging) are not deductible.

EXAMPLE 14

9-4c Restrictions on Travel Expenses

The possibility always exists that taxpayers will attempt to treat vacation or pleasure travel as deductible business travel. To prevent such practices, the law contains restrictions on certain travel expenses.

Conventions

For travel expenses to be deductible, a convention must be directly related to the taxpayer's trade or business.[14] Compare Examples 15 and 16.

Type of Convention

Dr. Hill, a pathologist who works for a hospital in Ohio, travels to Las Vegas to attend a two-day session on recent developments in estate planning. No deduction is allowed for Dr. Hill's travel expenses.

EXAMPLE 15

Assume the same facts as in Example 15, except that the convention deals entirely with recent developments in pathology. Now a travel deduction is allowed.

EXAMPLE 16

The taxpayer must attend convention sessions along with other participants in order to claim a deduction. Attendance does not include watching or listening to sessions at a later date that are recorded (e.g., a taxpayer cannot vacation during the convention sessions and watch the videos later). However, a deduction will be allowed for costs (other than travel, meals, and entertainment) of renting or using recorded materials related to business.

---

[13]Rev.Rul. 73–529, 1973–2 C.B. 37 and *James O. Henderson*, 70 TCM 1407, T.C.Memo. 1995–559, *aff'd* by 98–1 USTC ¶50,375, 81 AFTR 2d 98–1748, 143 F.3d 497 (CA–9, 1998).

[14]§ 274(h)(1).

EXAMPLE 17

A CPA is unable to attend a convention at which current developments in taxation are discussed. She pays $300 to stream the recorded sessions and views them at home later. The $300 is a deduction *for* AGI if the CPA is self-employed. If the CPA is an employee, the $300 is a miscellaneous itemized deduction (and not allowed from 2018 through 2025).

The Code places stringent restrictions on the deductibility of travel expenses of the taxpayer's spouse or dependent.[15] Generally, there must be a business reason for the spouse or dependent to attend, and the expenses must be otherwise deductible.

EXAMPLE 18

Assume the same facts as in Example 16 with the additional fact that Dr. Hill is accompanied by her husband, Mr. Hill. Mr. Hill is not employed, but possesses secretarial skills and takes notes during the proceedings. No deduction is allowed for Mr. Hill's travel expenses.

If, however, Mr. Hill is a medical professional trained in pathology and is employed by Dr. Hill as her assistant, his travel expenses become deductible.

Education

Travel as a form of education is not deductible.[16] If, however, the education qualifies as a deduction, the travel involved is allowed. Compare Examples 19 and 20.

Education Travel

EXAMPLE 19

Greta, a German teacher, travels to Germany to maintain general familiarity with the language and culture. No travel expense deduction is allowed.

EXAMPLE 20

Jean-Claude, a scholar of French literature, travels to Paris to do specific library research that cannot be done elsewhere and to take courses that are offered only at the Sorbonne. The travel costs are deductible, assuming that the other requirements for deducting education expenses (discussed later in the chapter) are met.

9-4d Combined Business and Pleasure Travel

To be deductible, travel expenses need not be incurred in the performance of specific job functions.

Domestic Travel for Business and Pleasure

In order to limit the possibility of a taxpayer claiming a tax deduction for what is essentially a personal vacation, several rules were created to handle deductions associated with combined business and pleasure trips. If the business/pleasure trip is entirely within the United States, the transportation expenses are deductible only if the trip is *primarily for business*.[17] Meals, lodging, and other expenses are allocated between business and personal days. If the trip is primarily for pleasure, no transportation expenses qualify as a deduction. Compare Examples 21 and 22.

---

[15]§ 274(m)(3).

[16]§ 274(m)(2).

[17]Reg. § 1.162–2(b)(1).

Meeting the Primary Business Purpose Requirement

In the current year, Hana travels from Seattle to New York primarily for business. She spends five days conducting business and three days sightseeing and attending shows. Her plane and taxi fare amounts to $1,160. Her meals amount to $200 per day, and lodging and incidental expenses are $350 per day.

   She can deduct the transportation charges of $1,160, because the trip is primarily for business (five days of business versus three days of sightseeing). Meals are limited to five days and are subject to a 50% reduction (see text Section 9-6c), for a total of $500 [5 days × ($200 × 50%)], and other expenses are limited to $1,750 (5 days × $350).

EXAMPLE 21

Assume that Hana goes to New York for a two-week vacation. While there, she spends several hours renewing acquaintances with people in her company's New York office. Her transportation expenses are not deductible.

EXAMPLE 22

Foreign Travel for Business and Pleasure

When the trip is *outside the United States*, different rules apply. Transportation expenses must be allocated between business and personal unless:

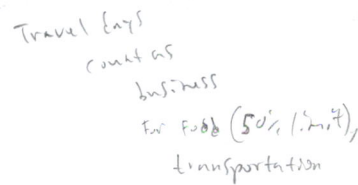

1. The taxpayer is away from home for seven days or less, *or*
2. Less than 25 percent of the time was for personal purposes.

   No allocation is required if the taxpayer has no substantial control over arrangements for the trip or the desire for a vacation is not a major factor in taking the trip. If the trip is primarily for pleasure, no transportation charges are deductible. Days devoted to travel are considered business days. Weekends, legal holidays, and intervening days are considered business days, provided both the day before and the day after were business days.[18] Compare Examples 23 and 24.

The Amount of Nonbusiness Time Permitted

In the current year, Robert takes a trip from New York to Japan primarily for business purposes. He is away from home from June 10 through June 19. He spends three days vacationing and seven days (including two travel days) conducting business. His airfare is $4,000, his meals amount to $200 per day, and lodging and incidental expenses are $300 per day. Because Robert is away from home for more than seven days and more than 25% of his time is devoted to personal purposes, only 70% (7 days business/10 days total) of the transportation is deductible. His deductions are as follows:

EXAMPLE 23

Transportation (70% × 4,000)		$2,800
Lodging ($300 × 7)		2,100
Meals ($200 × 7)	$1,400	
Less: 50% reduction (see text Section 9-6c)	(700)	700
Total		$5,600

Assume the same facts as in Example 23. Robert is gone the same period of time but spends only two days (rather than three) vacationing.

   Now no allocation of transportation is required. Because the pleasure portion of the trip is less than 25% of the total, all of the airfare qualifies for the travel deduction.

EXAMPLE 24

---

[18]§ 274(c) and Reg. § 1.274–4. For purposes of the seven-days-or-less exception, the departure travel day is not counted.

Record-Keeping Requirements

Distinguishing between business and personal expenses can be difficult (and somewhat subjective). As a result, the tax law includes specific provisions that require the taxpayer to maintain specific, written, contemporaneous records for travel expenses.[19] These records, which assist the IRS and courts in reaching a fair determination of the legitimacy of the expenses, must include the amount, time (or dates), place, and business purpose behind the expenses.

Differentiate between deductible and nondeductible education expenses.

9-5 EDUCATION EXPENSES

9-5a General Requirements

In general, a self-employed taxpayer can deduct education expenses provided the expenses are:

- To meet the specific legal requirements to keep his or her job, or
- To maintain or improve existing skills required in the present job.

Education expenses are *not* deductible if the education is:

getting abgreefrom Cope

- To meet the minimum educational standards for qualification in the taxpayer's existing job.
- To qualify the taxpayer for a new trade or business.[20]

From 2018 through 2025, employees incurring education expenses that are not reimbursed by the employer may not deduct these expenses (they are employee business expenses and miscellaneous itemized deductions). As discussed in text Section 9-5e (Deduction for Qualified Tuition and Related Expenses), a limited deduction for higher education costs is allowed, even if the related education is to meet the minimum standards required for a job. The deduction still can be taken as long as the education maintained and improved existing skills and did not qualify a person for a new trade or business. A deduction is generally allowed for education related to new duties if the new duties involve the same general work. For example, the IRS has ruled that a practicing dentist's education expenses incurred to become an orthodontist are deductible.[21] Fees incurred for professional qualification exams (the bar exam, for example) and fees for review courses (such as a CPA review course) are not deductible.[22]

9-5b Legal Requirements to Keep a Job

Taxpayers can deduct education expenses if the education is required by law. If, however, the required education is the minimum degree required for the job, no deduction is allowed. So a taxpayer classified as a staff accountant who went back to school to obtain a bachelor's degree in accounting was not allowed to deduct the expenses, since a bachelor's degree was the minimum requirement for his job.[23] Education required by law for various professions also qualifies for a deduction.

To satisfy the State Board of Public Accountancy rules for maintaining her CPA license, Nancy takes an auditing course sponsored by a local college. The cost of the education is deductible.

Improving skills

---

[19]§ 274(d). Corroborating evidence (e.g., receipt from a hotel or an airline ticket) is also required. In general, approximations and estimates are not sufficient. If a taxpayer is unable to substantiate expenses, courts use the Cohan rule to estimate the deductible amount [*Cohan v. Commissioner*, 39 F.2d 540 (CA–2, 1930)].

[20]Reg. §§ 1.162–5(b)(2) and (3).

[21]Rev.Rul. 74–78, 1974–1 C.B. 44.

[22]Reg. § 1.212–1(f) and Rev.Rul. 69–292, 1969–1 C.B. 84.

[23]Reg. § 1.162–5(b)(2)(iii) Example (2); *Collin J. Davidson*, 43 TCM 743, T.C.Memo. 1982–119. But see the subsequent discussion of § 222 (i.e., the deduction for higher education qualified tuition and related expenses).

9-5c Maintaining or Improving Existing Skills

The "maintaining or improving existing skills" requirement has been difficult for both taxpayers and the courts to interpret. For example, a business consultant may be permitted to deduct the costs of obtaining an advanced degree on the grounds that the advanced management education is undertaken to maintain and improve existing management skills. The consultant can also deduct the costs of specialized, nondegree management courses that maintain or improve existing skills. Expenses incurred by a self-employed accountant to obtain a law degree are not deductible, however, because the education constitutes training for a new trade or business.[24] *If you become a lawyer, you don't have to be a tax lawyer; you can be any type of lawyer w/ your law degree.*

* But deduction for Qualified Tuition up to $4,000 allowed

The conditions required for the regular education expense deduction are summarized in Concept Summary 9.2.

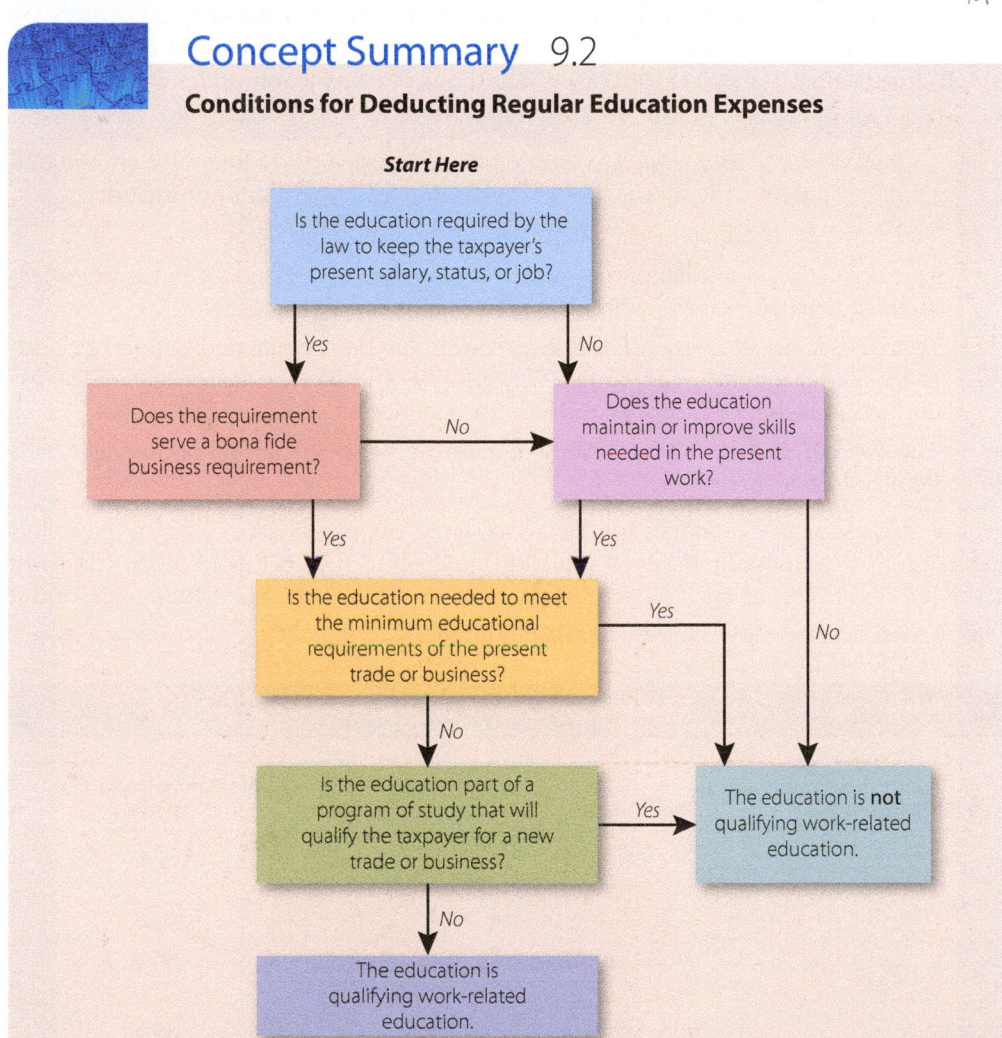

Concept Summary 9.2

Conditions for Deducting Regular Education Expenses

Start Here

Is the education required by the law to keep the taxpayer's present salary, status, or job?
— Yes → Does the requirement serve a bona fide business requirement?
— No → Does the education maintain or improve skills needed in the present work?

Does the requirement serve a bona fide business requirement?
— No → Does the education maintain or improve skills needed in the present work?
— Yes → Is the education needed to meet the minimum educational requirements of the present trade or business?

Does the education maintain or improve skills needed in the present work?
— Yes → Is the education needed to meet the minimum educational requirements of the present trade or business?
— No → The education is **not** qualifying work-related education.

Is the education needed to meet the minimum educational requirements of the present trade or business?
— Yes → The education is **not** qualifying work-related education.
— No → Is the education part of a program of study that will qualify the taxpayer for a new trade or business?

Is the education part of a program of study that will qualify the taxpayer for a new trade or business?
— Yes → The education is **not** qualifying work-related education.
— No → The education is qualifying work-related education.

9-5d What Expenses Are Allowed?

Education expenses include tuition, books and supplies, and transportation (e.g., from the office to school) and travel (e.g., meals and lodging while away from home at an executive education training program).

---

[24]Reg. § 1.162–5(b)(3)(ii) Example (1).

9-5e **Deduction for Qualified Tuition and Related Expenses**

[handwritten: Going for higher education even a diff. trade]

One of the major shortcomings of the education deduction, previously discussed, is that it is unavailable for taxpayers obtaining a basic skill (i.e., to meet the minimum standards required for a job). This shortcoming has been partly resolved with the ==deduction for qualified tuition and related expenses==.

A deduction *for* AGI is allowed for qualified tuition and related expenses involving higher education. The deduction allowed depends on the taxpayer's modified AGI (MAGI) and filing status (see Exhibit 9.1).[25]

In general, single taxpayers with MAGI of $65,000 or less (or married taxpayers with MAGI of $130,000 or less) are allowed a maximum deduction of $4,000. A two-step phaseout applies if MAGI exceeds these amounts. The maximum deduction decreases to $2,000 for single taxpayers with MAGI between $65,001 and $80,000 and married taxpayers with MAGI between $130,001 and $160,000. The benefit of § 222 *disappears completely* with the second step. As a result, a single taxpayer (married couple) with MAGI greater than $80,000 ($160,000) is not allowed a deduction under § 222.[26]

Various aspects of the higher education tuition deduction are summarized below.

- *Qualified tuition and related expenses* include whatever is required for enrollment. Usually, student activity fees, books, and room and board are not included.[27]

- The expense need not be employment related, although it can be.

- The deduction is available for a taxpayer's spouse or dependent but is not available for married persons who file separate returns.

- To avoid a "double benefit," the deduction must be coordinated with other education provisions (e.g., American Opportunity and lifetime learning credits). No deduction is allowed for a taxpayer who qualifies as another's dependent.[28]

- The *for* AGI deduction classification avoids the nondeductibility of miscellaneous itemized deductions.

The deduction for qualified tuition and related expenses is claimed by completing Form 8917 (Tuition and Fees Deduction) and filing it with a Form 1040 (or Form 1040–A). The taxpayer must have received a Form 1098–T (Tuition Statement) from a higher education institution in order to claim a deduction.

EXHIBIT 9.1	Limitations for Qualified Tuition Deduction	
Filing Status	**Modified AGI**	**Maximum Deduction Allowed**
Single	$65,000 or less	$4,000
	More than $65,000 and less than or equal to $80,000	$2,000
	More than $80,000	None
Married	$130,000 or less	$4,000
	More than $130,000 and less than or equal to $160,000	$2,000
	More than $160,000	None

---

[25]MAGI is modified adjusted gross income as defined in § 222(b)(2)(C). Various items are added to regular AGI in determining MAGI. One example is the foreign earned income exclusion. See IRS Publication 970 (*Tax Benefits for Education*).

[26]Section 222 expires on December 31, 2020. The various § 222 dollar amounts are not adjusted for inflation.

[27]Section 222(d) refers to § 25A(f), which deals with the American Opportunity and lifetime learning credits (see Chapter 12). Student activity fees and prescribed course-related books may be allowed if they are a condition for enrollment.

[28]§ 222(c).

The Big Picture

Return to the facts of *The Big Picture* on p. 9-1. After starting her new job, Morgan enrolls in the evening master's degree program in child development at a local university and begins attending classes.

Although Morgan believes that the master's degree would be useful, it is not a requirement of ECCC and it is not needed to maintain or improve existing skills in her current job. As a result, except for the deduction allowed by § 222, none of her education expenses are deductible.[29]

9-5f Other Provisions Dealing with Education

Although this chapter deals with employment-related expenses, a wide variety of tax provisions deal with education. Because the encouragement of education is a desirable social goal, Congress continues to enact laws that provide tax incentives. The incentives come in the form of income exclusions, deductions (both *for* AGI and *from* AGI), and various credits.

Concept Summary 9.3 reviews the tax consequences of the various provisions dealing with education and indicates where they are discussed in the text.

Concept Summary 9.3

Tax Consequences of Provisions Dealing with Education

Provision	Tax Effect	Income Phaseout[a]	Reference Code	Reference Text
Educational savings bonds	*Exclusion* for interest on U.S. Series EE bonds used for higher education	Yes	§ 135	Ch. 5, p. 5-25
Qualified tuition program	No deduction; *exclusion* for distributions	No	§ 529	Ch. 5, p. 5-26
Educational assistance plans	*Exclusion* of up to $5,250 for employer-provided assistance	No[b]	§ 127	Ch. 5, p. 5-15
Scholarships	*Exclusion* allowed for education costs (excluding room and board)	No	§ 117	Ch. 5, p. 5-7
Qualified tuition reduction plan	*Exclusion* as to tuition waivers for employees (and dependents) of nonprofit educational institutions	No[b]	§ 117(d)	Ch. 5, p. 5-7
Coverdell education savings account (CESA)	No deduction ($2,000 maximum annual contribution); *exclusion* for distributions	Yes[c]	§ 530	Ch. 5, p. 5-27
Early distributions from IRAs	If used for qualified higher education, income recognized but penalty waived	—	§ 72(t)	Ch. 9, p. 9-29
Qualified tuition and related expenses[d]	*Deduction for* AGI; up to $4,000	Yes	§ 222	Ch. 9, p. 9-16
Educator expenses	*Deduction for* AGI; up to $250	No	§ 62(a)(2)(D)	Ch. 9, p. 9-24
Interest on student loans	*Deduction for* AGI; up to $2,500 per year	Yes	§ 221	Ch. 10, p. 10-14
Job-related education expenses	*Deduction for* AGI for self-employed taxpayer; *no deduction* for employees through 2025	No	§ 162	Ch. 9, p. 9-24
American Opportunity credit	Allowed for the first four years of postsecondary education; up to $2,500 per year	Yes	§ 25A(i)	Ch. 12, p. 12-16
Lifetime learning credit	20% of qualifying expenses (not to exceed $10,000 per year)	Yes	§ 25(A)(c)	Ch. 12, p. 12-16

[a]The phaseout of benefits occurs when income reaches a certain level. The phaseout amounts vary widely, depend on filing status (i.e., single or married filing jointly), and are based on MAGI (modified AGI).

[b]The availability of the benefit cannot be discriminatory (i.e., cannot favor higher-income taxpayers).

[c]The phaseout begins once AGI reaches $190,000 (married taxpayers) or $95,000 (unmarried taxpayers).

[d]Expires on December 31, 2020.

---

[29]*Steven Galligan*, 83 TCM 1859, T.C.Memo. 2002–150.

9-6 OTHER BUSINESS EXPENSES

9-6a Office in the Home

Most expenses for personal use assets are not deductible. Except for certain expenses (primarily interest and taxes), this is the case with a personal residence. However, self-employed individuals are allowed a deduction for <mark>office in the home expenses</mark> if a portion of the residence is used *exclusively* on a *regular basis* as either:

- The principal place of business for any trade or business of the taxpayer, or
- A place of business used by clients, patients, or customers.

From 2018 through 2025, employees are not allowed an office in the home deduction because these expenses are employee business expenses (and miscellaneous itemized deductions).

The term *principal place of business* includes a place of business that satisfies the following requirements:[30]

- The office is used by the taxpayer to conduct administrative or management activities of a trade or business, and
- There is no other fixed location of the trade or business where the taxpayer conducts these activities.

EXAMPLE 27

Josh Butler is a self-employed anesthesiologist. During the year, he spends 30 to 35 hours per week administering anesthesia and postoperative care to patients in three hospitals, none of which provides him with an office. He also spends two or three hours per day in a room in his home that he uses exclusively as an office. He does not meet patients there, but he performs a variety of tasks related to his medical practice (e.g., contacting surgeons, doing bookkeeping, and reading medical journals).

A deduction will be allowed because Dr. Butler uses the office in the home to conduct administrative or management activities of his trade or business and there is no other fixed location where these activities can be carried out.

The exclusive use requirement means that part of the home must be used *solely* for business purposes. An "exception" allows mixed use (both business and personal) of the home if a licensed day-care business is involved.

Exclusive Use Requirement

EXAMPLE 28

Trisha is self-employed and maintains an office in her home for business purposes. The office is also used by her spouse to pay the family bills and by their children to do homework assignments. The exclusive use requirement is not met, and no office in the home deduction is allowed.

EXAMPLE 29

Muriel operates a licensed day-care center in her home. The children use the living room as a play area during the day, and Muriel and her family use it for personal purposes in the evening and on weekends. Even though the living room is used for both business and personal purposes, Muriel can claim an office in the home deduction.

The office in the home deduction can be determined in either of two ways: the Regular (actual expense) Method or the Simplified (safe harbor) Method.

---

[30]§ 280A(c)(1) as modified by the Tax Reform Act of 1997.

Regular Method

When using the Regular Method, relevant expenses must be categorized as direct or indirect. Direct expenses benefit only the business part of the home (e.g., repainting the office) and are deducted in full. Indirect expenses are for maintaining and operating the home (e.g., utilities and insurance). Because indirect expenses benefit both business and personal use, an allocation between the two is necessary. The allocation is made based on the floor space involved, dividing the business area by the total home area to arrive at the business percentage.

The allowable home office expenses cannot exceed the gross income from the business less all other business expenses (i.e., this deduction cannot create a loss). And the home office expenses that are allowed as itemized deductions anyway (e.g., mortgage interest and real estate taxes) must be deducted first.

Home office expenses of a self-employed individual are trade or business expenses and are deductible *for* AGI. Any disallowed home office expenses are *carried forward* and used in future years subject to the same limitations.

EXAMPLE 30

Rick is a certified public accountant employed by a regional CPA firm as a tax manager. He operates a separate furniture refinishing business that he operates out of his home. For this business, he uses two rooms in the basement exclusively and regularly. The floor space of the two rooms is 240 square feet, which is 10% of the total floor space of his 2,400-square-foot residence. Gross income from the business totals $8,000. Expenses of the business (other than home office expenses) are $6,500. Rick incurs the following home office expenses:

Real property taxes on residence	$ 4,000
Interest expense on residence	7,500
Operating expenses of residence (including homeowners insurance)	2,000
MACRS cost recovery on residence (based on 10% business use)	350

Rick's deductions are determined as follows:

Business income		$ 8,000
Less: Other business expenses		(6,500)
Net income from the business (before the office in the home deduction)		$ 1,500
Less: Allocable taxes ($4,000 × 10%)	$400	
Allocable interest ($7,500 × 10%)	750	(1,150)
		$ 350
Allocable operating expenses of the residence ($2,000 × 10%)		(200)
		$ 150
Allocable MACRS cost recovery ($350, limited to remaining income)		(150)
		$ –0–

Rick has a carryover of $200 (the unused excess MACRS cost recovery). Because he is self-employed, the allocable taxes and interest ($1,150), the other deductible office expenses ($200 + $150), and $6,500 of other business expenses are deductible *for* AGI.

As noted in Example 30, the office in the home deduction includes an allocable portion of the cost recovery on the personal residence. To arrive at this cost recovery, taxpayers use the MACRS percentage for 39-year nonresidential real property (see Chapter 8). Except for the first and last years (i.e., 1 and 40), the applicable percentage is 2.564 percent—see Exhibit 8.8. Cost recovery for office equipment and furnishings is computed using the MACRS rules for personal property—see Exhibits 8.1 and 8.3. These assets can also be expensed under § 179; bonus depreciation is also available.

An office in the home deduction is also available to those who rent (rather than own) their home. In this case, the business use percentage is applied to the rent being paid.

If the Regular Method is used, the office in the home deduction is claimed using Form 8829 (Expenses for Business Use of Your Home).

Simplified Method

Because of the record keeping and calculations involved in using the Regular Method, the IRS established an optional Simplified Method for the office in the home deduction.[31] If the Simplified Method is used, Form 8829 is not required. Taxpayers using the Simplified Method are allowed a deduction of $5 per square foot of space devoted to the office. However, since no more than 300 square feet can be counted, the maximum deduction is limited to $1,500.

The various rules governing the use of the Simplified Method are summarized below.

- No depreciation on the residence can be claimed.
- Actual expenses of maintaining and operating the home (e.g., qualified residence interest, property taxes, homeowners insurance, utilities) are ignored. Expenses that are deductible elsewhere on the tax return (e.g., qualified residence interest, property taxes) can be claimed in full without any reduction due to a home office deduction being claimed.
- Office in the home deductions in excess of the net income from the business *cannot* be carried over to a future year. An unused Regular Method deduction from a prior year *cannot* be carried to a Simplified Method year.

Taxpayers can choose between the Regular Method and the Simplified Method each year. However, once a choice is made, that choice cannot be changed for that year. Care should be taken in making the choice because the Simplified Method may yield a smaller deduction.

EXAMPLE 31

Assume the same facts as in Example 30, except that Rick chooses the Simplified Method. This choice results in the following deduction:

Net income from the business (before the office in the home deduction)	$ 1,500
Simplified Method office in the home deduction ($5 × 240 square feet)	(1,200)
Net income from the business	$ 300

In comparing the results of Examples 30 and 31, note that the use of the Simplified Method left Rick with $500 less in deductions (counting the $200 unused carryover). However, Rick can now use the property taxes ($400) and interest ($750) allocated to the office in the home deduction under the Regular Method as itemized deductions on Schedule A.

Which Method to Use

The availability of the Simplified Method presents an annual decision for the taxpayer. In choosing which method to use, here are some factors to consider:

- Both methods require exclusive and regular use of the home office.
- The Simplified Method requires fewer calculations and less record keeping.
- Because no depreciation is allowed, the Simplified Method will avoid the 25 percent tax on real estate gains when the home is sold (see Chapter 14).
- Even though the Simplified Method frees up certain home-related expenses (e.g., qualified residence interest, property taxes, homeowners insurance, utilities), not all of these expenses are deductible. Some are (property taxes), and some are not (homeowners insurance). But even the expenses that are deductible (property taxes) may be subject to other itemized deduction limitations (see Chapter 10).
- With a maximum deduction of $1,500, the Simplified Method, in most cases, will result in a smaller deduction than the Regular Method.

- Under the Simplified Method, a taxpayer is not allowed to carry over unused deductions.
- Once a taxpayer has made a choice for a year, the choice cannot be changed.

EXAMPLE 32

Tyler, a calendar year taxpayer, prepared and filed his own tax return for 2019. Being in a hurry, he decided to use the Simplified Method of computing his home office deduction. In March 2021, Tyler seeks tax advice and learns how much he could have saved by using the Regular Method. Tyler cannot file an amended return for 2019, but he can switch to the Regular Method for 2020.

The Big Picture

EXAMPLE 33

Return to the facts of *The Big Picture* on p. 9-1. Morgan is using her apartment's second bedroom as a home office. Her apartment has 1,200 square feet; the second bedroom has 200 square feet. Her home office is, therefore, one-sixth of her apartment (200 square feet ÷ 1,200 square feet). During 2020, her apartment expenses include:

Rent ($1,250 per month)	$15,000
Utilities	2,600
Renter's insurance	1,100
Total	$18,700

In addition, she purchases various supplies and software for her tutoring ($700) and freelance driving ($75), as well as office furniture ($100 for a file cabinet to store her business records, $400 for a table, $250 for chairs, and $50 for a lamp; $800 total). The office furniture, which she can expense immediately under § 179, will be allocated to her freelance businesses based on total revenues.

Income from her tutoring amounts to $6,795, and she earned $8,305 from her freelance driving. She also has documented her business mileage for the year (630 for tutoring and 5,400 for freelance driving) and has receipts for freeway tolls of $175 (all related to her freelance driving). Morgan uses the automatic mileage method for her business miles (see Example 9).

Using the Simplified Method, Morgan's home office deduction would be $1,000 (200 square feet × $5 per square foot). Morgan will be better off using the Actual Cost Method, where her deduction will be $3,117 ($18,700 total apartment expenses × $\frac{1}{6}$). This deduction will be allocated to her freelance businesses (tutoring and freelance driving), based on total revenues.

	Tutoring	Freelance Driving	Total
Revenues	$ 6,795	$ 8,305	$15,100
Expenses:			
Business mileage:			
630 × $0.575/mile	(362)		(362)
5,400 × $0.575/mile		(3,105)	(3,105)
Business tolls		(175)	(175)
Supplies/Software	(700)	(75)	(775)
Office furniture ($800)	(360)	(440)	(800)
Home office	(1,403)	(1,714)	(3,117)
Net income	$ 3,970	$ 2,796	$ 6,766

Note: This example assumes that Morgan meets the "exclusive use" requirement for her home office (see text Section 9-6a and Examples 27, 28, and 29). As discussed there, the "exclusive use" requirement is a significant constraint. What would happen if on *one day* during the year Morgan went into the home office, opened her laptop computer, and spent *one hour* responding to her personal e-mails?

Answer: The "exclusive use" test would not be met, and Morgan would lose the home office deduction. Further, proving a negative is difficult (how does one document that the home office was *never* used for personal purposes?). But Morgan needs to understand the standard and ensure that she complies with it. In our example, that means when she wants to use her laptop for personal purposes, she needs to use it somewhere other than the office.

9-6b **Moving Expenses**

The TCJA of 2017 suspended the deduction for moving expenses from 2018 through 2025. However, during this period, the moving expense deduction is retained for members of the Armed Forces (or their spouse or dependents) on active duty who move because of a military order that relates to a permanent change of station.[32] The rules providing for exclusions of amounts attributable to in-kind moving and storage expenses (and reimbursements or allowances for these expenses) also remain in place for these individuals.

9-6c **Entertainment and Meal Expenses**

Many businesses incur entertainment and meal expenses. Although such expenses can help build business activity, a personal element also is involved in these activities. As a result, Congress decided to limit these deductions. *No deduction* is allowed with respect to:

1. An activity generally considered to be entertainment, amusement, or recreation;
2. Membership dues with respect to any club organized for business, pleasure, recreation, or other social purposes; or
3. A facility (or portion thereof) used in connection with any of the above items.

However, taxpayers still may deduct *50 percent of the food and beverage expenses* associated with operating their trade or business (e.g., a business meal with a current or potential client, or meals consumed by employees on work travel).[33]

Subsidized Eating Facilities and *De Minimis* Fringe Benefits

Prior to 2018, additional exceptions to the 50% rule applied to meals and entertainment in a subsidized eating facility or where the *de minimis* fringe benefit rule applied to food and beverages provided to employees (see Chapter 5). The TCJA of 2017 applies the 50 percent limitation to these items from 2018 through 2025 and then eliminates the deduction for these items beginning in 2026.

Subsidized Eating Facilities and *De Minimis* Fringe Benefits

EXAMPLE 34

General Hospital has an employee cafeteria on the premises for its doctors, nurses, and other employees. The cafeteria operates at cost. The 50% rule applies to the employee cafeteria costs of General Hospital.

EXAMPLE 35

Canary Corporation provides coffee and sometimes donuts to employees in the breakroom. This is a *de minimis* fringe benefit that is not taxable to the employees. Canary may deduct only 50% of the cost of this food.

Exceptions to the 50% Rule

The 50% rule has a number of exceptions.[34] One exception covers the case where the full value of the meals is included in the compensation of the employee (or independent contractor). Expenses directly related to business meetings of employees also are not subject to the 50% rule (and are fully deductible). A similar exception applies to employer-paid recreational or social activities for employees (e.g., the annual holiday

---

[32]§ 217(k).

[33]§ 274.

[34]§§ 274(e) and (n).

party or spring picnic). In addition, businesses that have retreats and/or other off-site training events are generally allowed to deduct 100 percent of the meals provided to participants at those sites.[35]

Myrtle wins an all-expense-paid trip to Europe for selling the most insurance for her company during the year. Her employer treats this trip as additional compensation to Myrtle. The 50% rule does not apply to the employer.

EXAMPLE 36

Business Meals

A business meal is deductible only if all of the following conditions are met:[36]

- The meal is business-related.
- The expense is reasonable (i.e., not lavish or extravagant).
- The taxpayer (or an employee) is present at the meal.
- The food and beverages are provided to a current or potential business customer or client.
- If combined with entertainment, the meal and beverages cost is separately itemized on the bill or receipt.

Business Meals

Lance Smith has submitted a proposed consulting contract to a local business. He invites the two business owners to dinner to discuss the contract and pays for the meal, during which Lance answers questions about the proposed contract. Lance can deduct 50% of this qualified business meal.

EXAMPLE 37

Assume the same facts as Example 37, except that Lance buys dinner for the two business owners but does not attend the dinner. Since Lance was not present at the meal, no deduction is allowed.

EXAMPLE 38

If the taxpayer is in travel status, his or her meals expense can be deducted, subject to the 50% rule.

Lacy travels to San Francisco for a business convention. She pays for her meals and is reimbursed by her employer. Lacy's employer can deduct 50% of the cost of her meals.

EXAMPLE 39

ETHICS & EQUITY   Your Turn or Mine?

Natalie (a CPA), Mathew (an attorney), Jacob (a banker), and Avery (an insurance agent) all live and work in the same community. They have been friends since college. Every Friday, they have lunch together and make it a point to discuss some business matters. They take turns paying for the group's lunches, and each deducts the amount he or she paid for the lunch as an entertainment expense. Presuming that one of the four is audited, do you anticipate any difficulty with the IRS? Explain.

---

[35]*Jacobs*, 148 T.C. No. 4 (6/26/17).

[36]§ 274(k); Notice 2018–76 (2018–42 I.R.B. 599).

Business Gifts

Although not subject to the 50 percent limit on meals, business gifts are deductible only to the extent of $25 per donee per year.[37] Incidental costs such as engraving, gift-wrapping, mailing, and delivery are also allowed (in addition to the $25 maximum). Gifts costing $4 or less (e.g., pens with the employee's or company's name on them) or promotional materials are not subject to the $25 limit. Records must be maintained to substantiate business gifts.

Business Gifts

EXAMPLE 40

In December, Prism Associates purchases framed prints from a local artist and mails one to each of its clients. Each print costs $70; packaging and shipping costs are $10 per print. Prism may deduct $35 for each print sent ($25 gift maximum plus $10 for packaging and shipping).

EXAMPLE 41

Assume the same facts as Example 40. In addition to the framed prints, Prism also encloses a coffee mug imprinted with its name and logo. Each mug costs $3.

The coffee mug is considered a promotional item, and its cost is also allowed as a deduction.

Record-Keeping/Documentation Requirements

Proper documentation of meal expenses is essential because of the strict record-keeping requirements that must be met. For example, documentation that consists solely of credit card receipts and canceled checks may be inadequate to substantiate the business purpose and business relationship.[38] Taxpayers should maintain detailed records of amounts, time, place, business purpose, and business relationships. A credit card receipt details the place, date, and amount of the expense. A notation made on the receipt of the names of the person(s) attending, the business relationship, and the topic of discussion should be sufficient.

9-6d Miscellaneous Employee Expenses

Miscellaneous employee expenses include costs that are job-related, not reimbursed by the employer, and not covered elsewhere in the tax law. Expenses related to maintaining job status make up a significant category of miscellaneous expenses. They include union dues; membership dues to professional organizations; subscriptions to trade publications and professional journals; special clothing (e.g., uniforms, protective shoes, and safety glasses); and various license fees paid to government agencies and other regulatory bodies. As previously mentioned, the TCJA of 2017 suspends the deduction for miscellaneous itemized deductions (including employee business expenses) from 2018 through 2025.

Educator Expenses

Many teachers pay for professional development courses or purchase school supplies for classroom use and are not reimbursed by their employer. These expenses are miscellaneous itemized deductions (i.e., *from* AGI deductions) and are not deductible from 2018 through 2025 (see text Section 9-11a).

Modest relief is provided though for elementary and secondary school educators, allowing them to claim up to $250 of these expenses as a deduction *for* AGI.[39] Eligible educators must work at least 900 hours during a school year as a teacher, an instructor,

---

[37]§ 274(b)(1). Multiple gifts to members of the same customer's family are consolidated (so there will be only one $25 deduction allowed). Gifts to an employer (or an employee's superior) are not deductible.

[38]*Kenneth W. Guenther*, 54 TCM 382, T.C.Memo. 1987–440.
[39]§ 62(a)(2)(D).

a counselor, a principal, or an aide. Covered costs include unreimbursed expenses for professional development courses, books, supplies, computer and other equipment, and supplementary materials used in the classroom.

Ron is a full-time teacher at Hoover Elementary. During the year, he spends $1,200 for school supplies for his fourth-grade class. Under an accountable plan (see text Section 9-10a), Hoover reimburses him for $400 of these supplies. As to the $800 balance, Ron may claim $250 as a deduction *for* AGI. The remaining expenses ($550) are miscellaneous itemized deductions (and not allowed from 2018 through 2025).

EXAMPLE 42

9-7 CONTRIBUTIONS TO RETIREMENT ACCOUNTS

LO.6
Compare various deductions for contributions to retirement accounts.

Pension considerations are an essential feature of any compensation arrangement. From a tax policy perspective, providing retirement security for employees can be justified on both economic and social grounds. Because the public sector (i.e., Social Security) will not provide sufficient retirement security for recipients, the private sector must fill the need. Congress has given the private sector the necessary incentive by enacting various measures that provide significant tax advantages for retirement plans. Although amounts that may be deferred under these plans are limited, the tax advantages are substantive and include (1) the deductibility of contributions (individuals are not taxed on these contributions until they are distributed), (2) income earned on the contributions is not subject to tax until distributed (thus growing at a tax-free rate of return), and (3) employer contributions to and benefits payable under qualified plans generally are not subject to FICA and FUTA taxes.

Although a wide variety of retirement plans exist, we will focus on some typical qualified retirement plans: (1) § 401(k) plans (a defined contribution plan[40] typically offered to employees); (2) Individual Retirement Accounts (available to any person who has earned income); and (3) plans available to self-employed individuals, including Keogh plans (also known as H.R. 10 plans), Solo § 401(k) plans, Saving Incentive Match for Employees (SIMPLE) plans, and Simplified Employee Pension (SEP) plans.

9-7a § 401(k) Plans

In General

A **§ 401(k) plan** allows participants to elect either to receive up to $19,500 in 2020[41] in cash (taxed currently) or to have a contribution made on their behalf to a profit sharing or stock bonus plan. The § 401(k) plan is often in the form of a salary-reduction agreement under which a contribution will be made only if the participant elects to reduce his or her compensation or to forgo an increase in compensation.

Any employee-elected § 401(k) plan contributions are pretax amounts that are excluded from gross income in the year of the deferral; they are 100 percent vested on behalf of the employee. Like employer plan contributions, employee contributions are tax-deferred until distributed, as are earnings on those contributions.

Sam participates in a § 401(k) plan of his employer. The plan permits the participants to choose between a full salary or a reduced salary where the reduction becomes a pretax contribution to a retirement plan. Sam elects to contribute 10% of his annual compensation of $40,000 to the plan. Income taxes are paid on only $36,000. No income taxes are paid on the $4,000—or on any earnings—until it is distributed from the plan to Sam. The main benefit of a § 401(k) plan is that Sam can shift a portion of his income to a later taxable year.

EXAMPLE 43

---

[40]There are two types of qualified pension plans: defined benefit plans and defined contribution plans. A defined benefit plan includes a formula that defines the *benefits* employees are to receive. A defined contribution plan defines the amount of the *contribution* to the plan. The majority of employer pension plans today are defined contribution plans.

[41]§§ 402(g)(1) and (4). The amount was $19,000 in 2019, $18,500 in 2018, and $18,000 in 2015 through 2017.

The maximum annual elective contribution to a § 401(k) plan is reduced dollar for dollar by other salary-reduction contributions to tax-sheltered annuities, simplified employee pension plans, and § 401(k) plans. Elective contributions in excess of the maximum limitation are taxable in the year of deferral. These amounts may be refunded from the plan tax-free before April 15 of the following year. Excess amounts not timely distributed will be double-taxed because they will be taxable in the year of distribution, even though they were included in income in the year of deferral. Annual elective contributions are also limited by complicated nondiscrimination requirements designed to encourage participation by non-highly compensated employees and by the general defined contribution plan limitations.

A person who has attained age 50 by the end of 2020 can make catch-up contributions of $6,500.[42]

9-8 INDIVIDUAL RETIREMENT ACCOUNTS (IRAs)

9-8a General Rules

Employees not covered by another qualified plan can establish their own tax-deductible **Individual Retirement Accounts (IRAs)**. For 2020, the contribution ceiling is the smaller of $6,000 ($12,000 for spousal IRAs, discussed later) or 100 percent of compensation.[43] The contribution ceiling applies to all types of IRAs (traditional deductible, traditional nondeductible, and Roth). An individual who attains the age of 50 by the end of the tax year can make an additional catch-up IRA contribution of $1,000 for the year.

The amount accumulated in an IRA can be substantial. For example, if each spouse of a married couple contributes just $4,000 annually to an IRA from ages 25–65 and earns an average of 6 percent annually on the investment, the two account balances will approximate $1.4 million at age 65.

If the taxpayer is an *active participant* in another qualified plan, the traditional IRA deduction limitation is phased out *proportionately* between certain AGI ranges, as shown in Exhibit 9.2.[44] If AGI is above the phaseout range, no IRA deduction is allowed. There is a $200 floor on the IRA deduction for individuals whose AGI is not above the phaseout range.

IRA Deduction Calculation

EXAMPLE 44

Dan, who is single and age 45, earns compensation income of $71,000 in 2020 and is an active participant in his employer's qualified retirement plan. Dan contributes $6,000 to a traditional IRA. The deductible amount is reduced by $3,600 because of the phaseout.

$$\frac{\$6{,}000 \text{ amount into phaseout range}}{\$10{,}000 \text{ phaseout range}} \times \$6{,}000 \text{ contribution} = \$3{,}600 \text{ reduction}$$

As a result of the $6,000 contribution, Dan can deduct only $2,400 ($6,000 – $3,600).

---

[42]The catch-up contribution amount is indexed in $500 increments. The catch-up contribution amount was $6,000 from 2015 through 2019.

[43]§§ 219(b)(1) and (c)(2). The limit is adjusted annually for inflation in $500 increments.

[44]§ 219(g).

EXHIBIT 9.2	Phaseout of IRS Deduction of an Active Participant in 2020	
Filing Status (AGI Phaseout)	**Phaseout Begins***	**Phaseout Ends**
Single and head of household	$ 65,000	$ 75,000
Married, filing joint return	104,000	124,000
Married, filing separate return	–0–	10,000

*These amounts are indexed annually for inflation.

IRA Deduction Calculation

Aaron, an unmarried individual who is age 45, is an active participant in his employer's qualified retirement plan in 2020. With AGI of $74,800, he normally would have an IRA deduction limit of $120 {$6,000 − [($74,800 − $65,000)/$10,000 × $6,000]}. However, because of the floor amount, Aaron is allowed a $200 IRA deduction. $200

EXAMPLE 45

An individual is not considered an active participant in a qualified plan merely because the individual's spouse is an active participant in such a plan for any part of a plan year. Thus, even when filing jointly, the nonparticipating individual may take a full $6,000 deduction regardless of the participation status of his or her spouse unless the couple has AGI above $196,000. If their AGI is above $196,000, the phaseout of the deduction begins at $196,000 and ends at $206,000 (phaseout over the $10,000 range) rather than beginning and ending at the phaseout amounts in Exhibit 9.2.[45]

Nell is covered by a qualified employer retirement plan at work. Her husband, Nick, is not an active participant in a qualified plan. If Nell and Nick's combined AGI is $135,000, Nell cannot make a deductible IRA contribution because she exceeds the income threshold for an active participant in Exhibit 9.2.

However, because Nick is not an active participant and their combined AGI does not exceed $196,000, he can make a deductible contribution of $6,000 to his own IRA.

EXAMPLE 46

To the extent that an individual is ineligible to make a deductible contribution to an IRA, *nondeductible contributions* can be made to the account.[46] The nondeductible contributions are subject to the same dollar limits as deductible contributions ($6,000 of earned income, $12,000 for a spousal IRA). Income in the account accumulates tax-free until distributed. Only the account earnings are taxed upon distribution; the individual's account basis equals the contributions made.

A taxpayer may be entitled to a nonrefundable credit for contributions to an IRA or elective deferrals for a § 401(k) plan (see text Section 13-4f). Distributions to a traditional IRA holder must begin no later than April 1 of the calendar year following the year in which the IRA holder reaches 72.[47]

Roth IRAs

A **Roth IRA** is a *nondeductible* alternative to the traditional deductible IRA. Earnings inside a Roth IRA are not taxable, and all qualified distributions from a Roth IRA are tax-free.[48] The maximum allowable annual contribution to a Roth IRA for 2020 is the smaller of $6,000 ($12,000 for spousal IRAs) or 100 percent of the individual's compensation for

---

[45]§ 219(g)(7).
[46]§ 408(o).

[47]§ 401(a)(9).
[48]§ 408A.

the year. Contributions to a Roth IRA must be made by the due date (excluding extensions) of the taxpayer's tax return. Roth IRAs are not subject to the minimum distribution rules that apply to traditional IRAs.

A taxpayer can make tax-free withdrawals from a Roth IRA after an initial five-year holding period if any one of the following requirements is satisfied.

- The distribution is made on or after the date on which the participant attains age 59 ½.
- The distribution is made to a beneficiary (or the participant's estate) on or after the participant's death.
- The participant becomes disabled.
- The distribution is used to pay for qualified first-time homebuyer's expenses (statutory ceiling of $10,000).

Amy establishes a Roth IRA at age 42 and contributes $5,000 per year for 20 years. The account is now worth $149,400, consisting of $100,000 of nondeductible contributions and $49,400 in accumulated earnings that have not been taxed. Amy may withdraw the $149,400 tax-free from the Roth IRA because she is over age 59 ½ and has met the five-year holding period requirement.

If the taxpayer receives a distribution from a Roth IRA and does not satisfy the aforementioned requirements, the distribution may be taxable to the extent of the plan's accumulated earnings. Distributions are treated as first made from the individual's contributions (i.e., as a return of capital).

Assume the same facts as in the previous example, except that Amy is age 50 and receives a distribution of $55,000. Because her adjusted basis for the Roth IRA is $100,000 (contributions made), the distribution is tax-free, and her adjusted basis is reduced to $45,000 ($100,000 − $55,000).

Roth IRAs are subject to income limits. In 2020, the maximum annual contribution of $6,000 is phased out beginning at AGI of $124,000 for single taxpayers and $196,000 for married couples who file a joint return. The phaseout range is $10,000 for married filing jointly and $15,000 for single taxpayers. For a married taxpayer filing separately, the phaseout begins with AGI of $0 and is phased out over a $10,000 range.[49]

Ben, a gig worker who is single, would like to contribute $6,000 to his Roth IRA in 2020. However, his AGI is $134,000, so his contribution is limited to $2,000 ($6,000 − $4,000).

$$\frac{\$10,000 \text{ amount into phaseout range}}{\$15,000 \text{ phaseout range}} \times \$6,000 \text{ contribution} = \$4,000 \text{ reduction}$$

Spousal IRAs

For a married couple, each spouse may establish an IRA individually and deduct contributions of up to $6,000 if the combined compensation of the spouses is at least equal to the total contributed amount. Thus, if only one spouse is employed or if both are

---

[49]The income limits for Roth IRA contributions are indexed annually for inflation.

employed but one has compensation of less than $6,000, each of them may contribute a maximum of $6,000 if their combined compensation is at least $12,000.

For the spousal IRA provision to apply, a joint return must be filed.[50] The spousal IRA deduction is reduced proportionately for active participants whose AGI exceeds the above target ranges.

Spousal IRAs

EXAMPLE 50

Tony, who is married, is eligible to establish an IRA. He received $30,000 in compensation in 2020, and his spouse Lita does not work outside the home. Tony can contribute up to $12,000 to two IRAs to be divided in any manner between the two spouses, with no more than $6,000 allocated to either spouse.

EXAMPLE 51

Assume the same facts as in the previous example, except that Lita has compensation income of $2,200. Without the spousal IRA provision, Tony could contribute $6,000 to his IRA, and Lita could contribute only $2,200 to her IRA. With the spousal IRA provision, they both can contribute $6,000 to their IRAs.

Timing of Contributions

Contributions (both deductible and nondeductible) can be made to an IRA anytime before the due date of the individual's tax return.[51] For example, an individual can establish and contribute to an IRA through April 15, 2021 (the 2020 individual tax return due date), and deduct this amount on his or her 2020 tax return. IRA contributions that are made during a tax return extension period do not satisfy the requirement of being made by the return due date.[52]

9-8b **Taxation of Benefits**

A participant has a zero basis in the *deductible* contributions of a traditional IRA because the contributions were deducted.[53] Therefore, all withdrawals from a deductible IRA are taxed as ordinary income in the year of receipt. They are not eligible for the 10-year averaging allowed for certain lump-sum distributions.

A participant has a basis equal to the contributions made for a *nondeductible* traditional IRA. As a result, only the earnings component of withdrawals is included in gross income. Such amounts are taxed as ordinary income in the year of receipt.

In addition to being included in gross income, payments from IRAs made to a participant before age 59½ are subject to a nondeductible 10 percent penalty tax on such payments.[54] However, an individual may make penalty-free withdrawals to pay for medical expenses in excess of 10 percent of AGI, to pay for qualified higher-education expenses, and to pay for qualified first-time homebuyer expenses (up to $10,000). Further, an individual who has received unemployment compensation for at least 12 consecutive weeks may use IRA withdrawals to pay for health insurance for himself or herself, a spouse, and dependents without incurring the 10 percent penalty tax.[55]

---

[50]§ 219(c).

[51]§ 219(f)(3).

[52]§ 404(h)(1)(B).

[53]§ 408(d)(1).

[54]§ 72(t). There are limited exceptions to the penalty on early distributions.

[55]§§ 72(t)(2)(B), (D), (E), and (F). For purposes of the unemployment provision, a self-employed individual who otherwise would have been eligible for unemployment compensation qualifies.

9-8c **Rollovers and Conversions**

An IRA may be the recipient of a rollover from another qualified plan, including another IRA. Such a distribution from a qualified plan is not included in gross income if it is transferred within 60 days of receipt to an IRA or to another qualified plan.

EXAMPLE 52

Ruth Sanchez withdraws $15,000 from a traditional IRA on May 2, 2020 (closing the account). She deposits these funds into a different traditional IRA on June 5, 2020. This situation is a qualified rollover and will not result in any gross income for Ruth during 2020.

Taxpayers are allowed only one traditional IRA rollover per 12-month period regardless of how many IRAs they have.[56] A Roth IRA may be rolled over tax-free into another Roth IRA.[57]

Unlike a traditional IRA, which requires withdrawals at age 72, there are no required withdrawals from a Roth IRA.[58] Such savings can be accumulated over the taxpayer's lifetime and then passed to heirs without incurring Federal income or estate taxes.[59]

EXAMPLE 53

Frank has both traditional IRAs and Roth IRAs. A rollover between his traditional IRA to a Roth IRA (a conversion) is not subject to the one-per-year rule. However, a rollover between his Roth IRAs will preclude a separate rollover within the one-year period between his traditional IRAs (including SEP and SIMPLE IRAs) and vice versa. The aggregation rule (which takes into account all distributions and rollovers among Frank's individual IRAs) applies to distributions from different IRAs if each of the distributions occurs after 2014.

Concept Summary 9.4 provides a comparison of the key features of IRAs.

Concept Summary 9.4

Comparison of IRAs

	Traditional		
	Deductible IRA	**Nondeductible IRA**	**Roth IRA**
Maximum contribution (per year)	$6,000*	$6,000*	$6,000*
Tax-deductible contribution	Yes	No	No
Tax-free growth of income	Yes	Yes	Yes
Beginning of AGI phaseout for active participant (2020)	$65,000 single, $104,000 joint	N/A	$124,000 single, $196,000 joint
Income tax on distributions	Yes, for entire distribution	Yes, for the earnings portion	No, if satisfy 5-year holding period**
50% excise tax: age 72 insufficient distributions	Yes	Yes	No
10% early withdrawal penalty (before age 59½)	Yes, with exceptions†	Yes, with exceptions†	Yes, with exceptions†

*The total of deductible, nondeductible, and Roth IRA contributions may not exceed $6,000 per year.

**In addition, the distribution must satisfy one of the following: made after age 59½, used for qualified first-time homebuyer expenses, made to participant who is disabled, or made to a beneficiary on or after the participant's death.

†Qualified education and first-time homebuyer costs (up to $10,000) avoid the 10% penalty.

[56]*Bobrow v. Commissioner,* 107 TCM 110, T.C.Memo. 2014–21; IRS Announcement 2014–15, 2014–16 I.R.B. 973; IRS Announcement 2013–32, 2014–48 I.R.B. 907.
[57]§ 408A(c)(3)(B).
[58]§ 408A(c)(4).
[59]Additional details on traditional and Roth IRAs can be found in IRS Publication 590, *Individual Retirement Accounts (IRAs).*

9-9 RETIREMENT PLANS FOR SELF-EMPLOYED INDIVIDUALS

A wide variety of retirement plans are available to self-employed individuals. In addition to Individual Retirement Accounts (discussed previously), self-employed individuals can establish a Keogh plan (also known as an H.R. 10 plan), a Solo § 401(k) plan, a Saving Incentive Match for Employees (SIMPLE) plan, or a Simplified Employee Pension plan (SEP).

9-9a Keogh (H.R. 10) Plans

Keogh plans are the self-employed equivalent of corporate pension plans. A Keogh plan covers the self-employed party, and it can extend to other employees of the business. These plans must be administered by an independent trustee, but if an individual elects to make all investment decisions for the plan, a *self-directed Keogh plan* is established. In such a case, the individual may prefer to invest the funds with a financial institution such as a broker, bank, or mutual fund. Investment in most collectibles is not allowed in a self-directed Keogh plan.

Contribution Limitations

A self-employed individual may contribute annually to a *defined contribution* Keogh plan the smaller of $57,000 in 2020 ($56,000 in 2019) or 100 percent of earned income.[60] Under a *defined benefit* Keogh plan, the annual benefit payable to an employee or a self-employed person is limited to the smaller of $230,000 in 2020 ($225,000 in 2019) or 100 percent of the individual's average compensation for the three highest years of employment.[61]

Earned income equals one's net earnings from self-employment[62] (i.e., the gross income derived from a trade or business less appropriate deductions).[63] Earned income is reduced by contributions to a Keogh plan on the individual's behalf and by 50 percent of any self-employment tax.[64]

Pat, a sole proprietor, has earned income of $150,000 in 2020 (after the deduction for one-half of self-employment tax). The maximum contribution Pat may make to a defined contribution Keogh plan is $57,000, the lesser of $150,000 or $57,000.

EXAMPLE 54

Although a Keogh plan must be established before the end of the year in question, contributions may be made up to the tax return filing date for that year. Self-employed individuals who hire employees may want to choose a different retirement plan, since a Keogh plan must provide retirement benefits to all employees on a nondiscriminatory basis (i.e., the sole proprietor's employees must also be covered by the Keogh plan). This requirement could be a substantial cost to the owner. Thus, a sole proprietor with few or no employees is an ideal candidate for a Keogh plan.

9-9b Solo § 401(k) Plans

A Solo § 401(k) plan is designed for self-employed individuals with no employees. Because the compensation deferred as part of a § 401(k) plan does not count toward the 20 percent limit for Keogh plans, the proprietor can defer the maximum amount of compensation under the § 401(k) plan and contribute an additional 20 percent of self-employment income to the Keogh plan.[65]

---

[60]§ 415(c)(1).
[61]§ 415(b)(1). This amount is indexed annually.
[62]§ 401(c)(2).

[63]§ 1402(a).
[64]§§ 401(c)(2)(A)(v) and 164(f).
[65]Reg. § 1.401(k)–1(a)(6)(ii).

Dan is 35 years old and is a sole proprietor. His net earnings from self-employment in 2020 are $100,000. Dan sets up a Solo § 401(k) plan for his retirement. Dan can contribute $20,000 (20% of $100,000) to a Keogh plan and make a § 401(k) elective deferral contribution up to $19,500 for 2020. As a result, Dan can make total retirement contributions of $39,500 ($20,000 + $19,500, which is less than the maximum allowed of $57,000).

9-9c   Savings Incentive Match Plan for Employees (SIMPLE Plans)

Employers with 100 or fewer employees who do not maintain another qualified retirement plan may establish a *savings incentive match plan for employees* (SIMPLE plan).[66] The plan can be in the form of a § 401(k) plan or an IRA. A SIMPLE § 401(k) plan is not subject to the nondiscrimination rules that usually apply to § 401(k) plans.

All employees who received at least $5,000 in compensation from the employer during any two preceding years and who reasonably expect to receive at least $5,000 in compensation during the current year must be eligible to participate in the plan. The decision to participate is up to the employee.

The contributions made by the employee (a salary-reduction approach) must be expressed as a percentage of compensation, not as a fixed dollar amount. The SIMPLE plan must not permit the SIMPLE elective employee contribution for the year to exceed $13,500 in 2020 ($13,000 in 2019).[67] The SIMPLE elective deferral limit is increased under the catch-up provision for employees age 50 and over. The catch-up amount is $3,000 in 2020 (the same as in 2019).[68]

Generally, the employer must either match elective employee contributions up to 3 percent of the employee's compensation or provide nonmatching contributions of 2 percent of compensation.

No other contributions may be made to the plan other than the employee elective contribution and the required employer matching contribution (or nonmatching contribution under the 2 percent rule). All contributions are fully vested on behalf of the employee.

9-9d   Simplified Employee Pension Plans (SEPs)

Simplified Employee Pensions—referred to as SEPs or SEP-IRAs—are retirement plans that allow the proprietor to deduct up to 20 percent of self-employment income.[69]

As with Keogh and Solo § 401(k) plans, the maximum deduction allowed is $57,000 in 2020 ($56,000 in 2019). SEPs are simple to establish and administer, and costs are minimal. Overall, SEPs are as easy to administer as deductible IRAs but have a higher annual contribution limit.

---

[66]§ 408(p).

[67]The $13,500 statutory amount is indexed for inflation in $500 increments; § 408(p)(2)(E)(i). As a result, the maximum amount that may be contributed to the plan for an employee under age 50 for 2020 is $22,050 [$13,500 employee contributions + $8,550 ($285,000 compensation ceiling × 3%) employer match].

[68]The catch-up amount is indexed for inflation in $500 increments.

[69]§ 408; employees can contribute 25% of earned income up to the annual maximum.

9-10 **CLASSIFICATION OF EMPLOYEE EXPENSES**

The classification of employee expenses depends on whether the expenses are reimbursed by the employer under an accountable plan. If so, neither the reimbursement nor the expense is reported by the employee. In effect, this result is equivalent to treating the expenses as deductions *for* AGI. If the expenses are reimbursed under a <u>nonaccountable</u> plan or are not reimbursed at all, then they are classified as deductions *from* AGI and are classified as miscellaneous itemized deductions.[70] Given that the TCJA of 2017 suspends the deduction of miscellaneous itemized deductions from 2018 through 2025, understanding the difference between accountable and nonaccountable plans is important.

> **LO.7**
> Demonstrate the difference between accountable and nonaccountable employee plans.

9-10a **Accountable Plans**

An **accountable plan** requires the employee to satisfy these two requirements:

- *Substantiate the Expenses.* An employee provides an *adequate accounting* by submitting a record (e.g., completing an employer-provided travel expense reimbursement form), with receipts and other substantiation, to the employer.[71]
- *Return Any Excess Reimbursement or Allowance.* An "excess reimbursement or allowance" is any amount the employee does *not* adequately account for as an ordinary and necessary business expense.

Substantiation

No deduction is allowed for any travel, entertainment, business gift, or listed property (e.g., automobiles and computers) expenses unless properly substantiated by adequate records. The records should contain the following information:[72]

- The amount of the expense.
- The time and place of travel or entertainment (or date of gift).
- The business purpose of the expense.
- The business relationship of the taxpayer to the person entertained (or receiving the gift).

As a result, the taxpayer must keep records (e.g., in a calendar or by other means) to document these expenses. Documentary evidence, such as itemized receipts, is required to support any lodging expenses while traveling away from home and for any other expenditure of $75 or more. If a taxpayer fails to keep adequate records, a written or oral statement of the exact details of the expense will be required, along with other corroborating evidence.[73]

Inadequate Substantiation

Ben has travel expenses substantiated only by canceled checks. The checks establish the date, place, and amount of the expenditure. Because neither the business relationship nor the business purpose is established, the deduction is disallowed.[74]

EXAMPLE
56

---

[70]The employment-related expenses of performing artists are allowed as *for* AGI deductions; § 62(b).

[71]Reg. § 1.162–17(b)(4).

[72]§ 274(d).

[73]Reg. § 1.274–5T(c)(3).

[74]*William T. Whitaker*, 56 TCM 47, T.C.Memo. 1988–418.

Inadequate Substantiation

EXAMPLE 57

Justin has travel and entertainment expenses substantiated by a digital diary showing the time, place, and amount of the expenditure. He is able to provide information about the business relationship and business purpose orally. However, because he has no receipts, any expenditures of $75 or more are disallowed.[75]

Deemed Substantiation

Instead of reimbursing actual expenses for travel away from home, many employers reduce their paperwork by adopting a policy of reimbursing employees with a *per diem* allowance, a flat dollar amount per day of business travel. Of the substantiation requirements listed previously, the *amount* of the expense is proved, or *deemed substantiated*, by using such a per diem allowance or reimbursement procedure. The amount of expenses that is deemed substantiated is equal to the lesser of the per diem allowance or the amount of the Federal per diem rate.

The regular Federal per diem rate is the highest amount the Federal government will pay to its employees for lodging, meals, and incidental expenses[76] while traveling. The rates are different for different locations.[77]

The use of the standard Federal per diem rates for meals and incidental expenses also constitutes an adequate accounting. Employees and self-employed persons can use these standard allowances instead of deducting the actual cost of daily meals and incidental expenses, even if not reimbursed.

Only the amount of the expense is considered substantiated under the deemed substantiated method. Records must be maintained for the other items: place, date, business purpose of the expense, and the business relationship of the parties involved.

9-10b Nonaccountable Plans

A nonaccountable plan is a plan where an adequate accounting or return of excess amounts, or both, is not required. All expense reimbursements are included as wages on the employee's Form W–2. Any allowable expenses are deductible in the same manner as unreimbursed expenses.

Unreimbursed Employee Expenses

Unreimbursed employee business expenses (including 50 percent of any meals) are treated as miscellaneous itemized deductions and not deductible from 2018 through 2025 (see text Section 9-11). If the employee could have received but did not seek reimbursement for whatever reason, none of the employment-related expenses are deductible.

Failure to Comply with Accountable Plan Requirements

An employer may have an accountable plan and require employees to return excess reimbursements or allowances, but an employee may fail to follow the rules of the plan. In that case, the expenses and reimbursements are subject to nonaccountable plan treatment.

---

[75]*W. David Tyler*, 43 TCM 927, T.C.Memo. 1982–160.

[76]For this purpose, incidental expenses include tips and fees to porters, bellhops, hotel maids, etc. These expenses are expected to be relatively small and typically paid out in cash.

[77]*Per Diem Rates* (IRS Publication 1542) contains the list and amounts for the year. This publication is available only on the internet at **irs.gov**. Links to per diem rates can also be found at **gsa.gov**.

9-11 LIMITATIONS ON ITEMIZED DEDUCTIONS

LO.8

Understand the limitations on miscellaneous itemized deductions.

Many itemized deductions (*from* AGI deductions) are subject to limitations based on a taxpayer's AGI. For example, only those medical expenses in excess of 7.5 percent of AGI are deductible (this is often called a "floor") and charitable contributions made in cash are limited to a maximum of 60 percent of a taxpayer's AGI (this is often called a "ceiling"). These limitations are discussed in Chapter 10.

Miscellaneous itemized deductions (including employee business expenses) are also subject to limitations. From 2018 through 2025, the deduction for miscellaneous itemized deductions subject to the 2%-of-AGI floor has been suspended (these items are discussed in text Section 9-11a). Other miscellaneous itemized deductions are not subject to the 2%-of-AGI floor and remain deductible as a *from* AGI deduction (these items are discussed in text Section 9-11b).

9-11a Miscellaneous Itemized Deductions Subject to the 2%-of-AGI Floor

Certain miscellaneous itemized deductions, including most *unreimbursed employee business expenses*, are subject to a 2%-of-AGI floor. These expenses, which are listed below, are not deductible from 2018 through 2025.[78]

- All § 212 expenses, except expenses of producing rent and royalty income (see Chapter 6).
- All unreimbursed employee business expenses, after the 50 percent limit for meals, if applicable.
- Professional dues and subscriptions.
- Union dues and work uniforms.
- Employment-related education expenses (except § 222 qualified tuition and related expenses).
- Expenses of job hunting (including employment agency fees and résumé-writing expenses).
- Home office expenses of an employee or outside salesperson.
- Legal, accounting, and tax return preparation fees.
- Hobby expenses, up to hobby income (see Chapter 6).
- Investment expenses, including investment counsel fees, subscriptions, and safe deposit box rental.
- Custodial fees relating to income-producing property or a traditional IRA or a Keogh plan.
- Appraisal fees paid to determine a casualty loss or charitable contribution.

9-11b Miscellaneous Itemized Deductions Not Subject to the 2%-of-AGI Floor

Certain miscellaneous itemized deductions, including the following, are *not* subject to the 2%-of-AGI floor and remain deductible *from* AGI:

- Impairment-related work expenses of individuals with a disability.
- Amortizable premium on taxable bonds.
- Losses from Ponzi-type investment schemes.
- Gambling losses to the extent of gambling winnings.
- Unrecovered investment in an annuity.

---

[78]§ 67(g).

List and evaluate tax planning ideas related to employee and self-employed business expenses.

9-12 **TAX PLANNING**

9-12a **Employment Status**

When considering the merits of employee or independent contractor status, much depends on which party is involved. Earlier in the chapter, we discussed some of the employer implications of this choice. If it is the worker, being self-employed carries the obvious advantage of a deduction *for* AGI category of work-related expenses and the avoidance of the limitations related to employee business expenses.

However, a self-employed individual may have other costs, such as local gross receipts taxes, license fees, franchise fees, personal property taxes, and occupation taxes. In addition, the record-keeping and filing requirements can be quite burdensome.

One of the most expensive considerations is the Social Security tax versus the self-employment tax. For an employee in 2020, for example, the Social Security tax applies at a rate of 6.2 percent on a base amount of wages of $137,700 ($132,900 in 2019) and the Medicare tax applies at a rate of 1.45 percent with no limit on the base amount. Further, a 0.9 percent additional Medicare tax applies to certain high earners. For self-employed persons, the Social Security and Medicare tax rates *double* (to 12.4 percent and 2.9 percent, respectively). Even though a deduction *for* AGI is allowed for part of the self-employment tax paid, an employee and a self-employed individual are not in the same tax position on equal amounts of earnings. The self-employment tax is explained in Chapter 12. For the applicability of these taxes to employees, see Chapter 1.

9-12b **Implications of Misclassifying Workers**

The Affordable Care Act (ACA) places specific compliance burdens (both financial and reporting) on employers regarding the provision of health care coverage for their employees. The rules are complex and vary according to the size of the employer (large or small) and the status of the employee (full- or part-time).[79] Because the ACA does not apply to independent contractors and part-time employees, employers may be more likely to misclassify workers. To discourage this from happening, penalties are levied on those employers who wrongfully categorize workers as independent contractors.

There are many reasons to favor classifying workers as independent contractors rather than as employees. Besides avoiding payroll taxes and income tax withholdings, the employer circumvents a myriad of state and local laws. Examples include vacation pay obligations, unemployment tax and workers' compensation requirements, and overtime and minimum wage restrictions. Because complying with these rules is costly and burdensome, some employers are motivated to misclassify their workers as independent contractors.

In the event of misclassification, two remedies are available regarding Federal employment taxes—one legislative and one administrative. The legislative option, known as Section 530 relief, absolves the employer of the employment taxes that should have been paid.[80] To obtain Section 530 relief, *all* three of the following requirements must be met:

1. The employer has a reasonable basis for *not* treating the workers as employees. Reasonable basis means reliance on any of the following:

   - A court case, a published IRS ruling, or IRS technical advice.
   - A past IRS audit that resulted in no employment tax assessment.
   - A long-standing practice of independent contractor status in the same industry.

---

[79]Large employers are those with 50 or more full-time or full-time equivalent employees. Part-time employees work less than 30 hours per week.

[80]This safe harbor for withholding purposes originated in Section 530 of the Revenue Act of 1978. See IRS *Headliner*, vol. 152 (March 27, 2006). Section 530 relief does not absolve an employer of any Affordable Care Act (ObamaCare) penalties.

2. The employer has consistently treated the workers as independent contractors.
3. The employer filed a Form 1099–MISC (Miscellaneous Income) for each worker (when required).

A Federal administrative remedy for employers who are misclassifying workers is the Voluntary Classification Settlement Program (VCSP).[81] A type of amnesty arrangement, the VCSP allows the applicant to be absolved from all employment taxes that should have been paid plus any interest and penalties that would be due. To be accepted, Form 8952 [Application for Voluntary Classification Settlement Program (VCSP)] must be filed with the IRS and certain conditions met.[82] A major condition is the payment of 10 percent of the employment taxes that are usually due when workers are reclassified.

9-12c Transportation and Travel Expenses

Adequate detailed records of all transportation and travel expenses should be kept. Because the automatic (standard) mileage method applies to all automobiles in the same manner, a new, expensive automobile used primarily for business may generate a higher deduction using the actual cost method. Once a method is chosen, a later change may be possible. Switching from the automatic mileage method to the actual cost method is allowed if a basis adjustment is made for depreciation deemed taken (see Example 7). Switching from the actual cost method to the automatic mileage method is possible only if the taxpayer has not used the MACRS statutory percentage method and has not claimed § 179 limited expensing.

If an automobile has mixed use (i.e., both personal and business), maintaining a record of business miles driven is critical. Further, the business use portion should be realistic under the circumstances. Although a 95 percent business use allocation for a one-car family living in the suburbs is possible, the IRS might question this allocation (i.e., does the 5 percent allocated to personal use reasonably account for commuting to work, trips to the grocery store and mall, soccer practice, and dance lessons?).

If a taxpayer wants to sightsee or vacation on a business trip, scheduling business on both the Friday and Monday surrounding the weekend turns the weekend into business days for allocation purposes. It is especially crucial to schedule appropriate business days when foreign travel is involved.

9-12d Education Expenses

The deduction for qualified tuition and related expenses (§ 222) provides some relief from the current restrictions on the deduction of education expenses by employees. First, the education expense does not have to be work-related. Second, it is a deduction *for* (not *from*) AGI. Unfortunately, the annual amount allowed as a deduction not only is quite modest (a maximum of $4,000) but also may be unavailable to certain taxpayers. It is not available, for example, to those whose income exceeds a modified AGI ceiling ($80,000 for singles; $160,000 for marrieds) or to someone who can be claimed as a dependent.

Before selecting this deduction, however, taxpayers should consider the American Opportunity credit or the lifetime learning credit under § 25A.[83] As credits provide a dollar-for-dollar reduction of tax liability, these credits could yield a greater tax benefit than deductions *for* AGI. But these credits also have limits that apply to higher-income taxpayers.

---

[81]Announcement 2011–64, 2011–4 I.R.B. 503.

[82]The conditions to be met are identified in the instructions for Form 8952. Many of these conditions are the same as those required for Section 530 relief.

[83]These credits are discussed at greater length in Chapter 12.

REFOCUS ON THE BIG PICTURE

THE FIRST JOB

The first issue that might arise as a result of Morgan's new job is the dependency exemption possibility. If Morgan was living at home and accepted the job late in the year, she could qualify as a dependent of her parents. If so, they might also be able to claim the qualified tuition deduction (or the lifetime learning credit). If, however, her employment began early in the year, she could not be a qualifying child (due to the self-supporting limitation) or a qualifying relative (due to the gross income limitation)—see Chapter 3.

Morgan can claim an office in the home deduction because she is using her second bedroom exclusively for her tutoring and freelance driving businesses. She can use either the Regular (actual expense) Method or the Simplified (safe harbor) Method. Under the Regular Method, the deduction would include a portion of the rent, utilities, and insurance paid. The Simplified Method would allow Morgan $5 per square foot for business space, but not more than 300 square feet, or $1,500. Since her second bedroom is 200 square feet, the Simplified Method produces a $1,000 deduction (see Example 33). Under either method, she would also be allowed to deduct other business expenses, including her software, supplies, and depreciation (or expensing) of office equipment and furnishings (e.g., computer, copier, desk, file cabinet). She must be careful, however, not to violate the "exclusive use" restriction (see Examples 28, 30, and 31) regardless of which method she uses. Morgan will use the Regular Method, since it results in a larger deduction ($3,117; see Example 33).

In addition to commuting between her apartment and her job at ECCC, Morgan also will use her car for her freelance businesses (see Example 5). Normally, she would need to make a choice between the automatic mileage method and the actual cost method. However, because she is using a car given to her by her parents (see Example 9), she will use the automatic mileage method.

In addition to her automobile expenses, Morgan should document any meal expenses she incurs while driving for Uber and other companies. However, any meals are subject to the 50 percent limitation. These expenses will be *for* AGI deductions.

Any expenses she incurs related to her job with Enrichment Child Care Center will be classified as employee business expenses. The total of all employment-related expenses is a miscellaneous itemized deduction (a *from* AGI deduction) and not deductible in 2020 (and through 2025).

Morgan must maintain adequate records regarding all of these transactions. Detailed records are particularly important in arriving at her office in the home deduction (if the Regular Method is used) and the business use of her car (for her freelancing jobs).

Key Terms

Accountable plan, 9-33

Automatic mileage method, 9-6

Deduction for qualified tuition and related expenses, 9-16

Education expenses, 9-14

Independent contractor, 9-2

Individual Retirement Accounts (IRAs), 9-26

Keogh plans, 9-31

Nonaccountable plan, 9-34

Office in the home expenses, 9-18

Roth IRA, 9-27

Section 401(k) plan, 9-25

Statutory employees, 9-5

Transportation expenses, 9-5

Travel expenses, 9-9

Discussion Questions

1. **LO.1** Mason performs services for Isabella. In determining whether Mason is an employee or an independent contractor, comment on the relevance of each of the factors listed below.
   a. Mason performs services only for Isabella and does not work for anyone else.
   b. Mason sets his own work schedule.
   c. Mason reports his job-related expenses on a Schedule C.
   d. Mason obtained his job skills from Isabella's training program.
   e. Mason performs the services at Isabella's business location.
   f. Mason is paid based on time worked rather than on task performed.

2. **LO.2** Milton is a resident of Mobile (Alabama) and is employed by Scaup Corpora-   *Critical Thinking*
   tion. Because Scaup closed its Mobile office, Milton no longer has any nonde-
   ductible commuting expenses although he continues to work for Scaup. Explain why.

3. **LO.2** In 2018, Emma purchased an automobile, which she uses for both business   *Critical Thinking*
   and personal purposes. Although Emma does not keep records as to operat-
   ing expenses (e.g., gas, oil, and repairs), she can prove the percentage of business
   use and the miles driven each year. In March 2020, Emma seeks your advice as to
   what income tax benefit, if any, she can derive from the use of her automobile. What
   would you suggest?

4. **LO.3** Dr. Werner is a full-time professor of accounting at Pelican University. During   *Critical Thinking*
   the year, he teaches continuing education programs for CPA groups in several
   cities. He also serves as an expert witness in numerous lawsuits involving accounting
   fraud. Comment on the possible tax treatment of Dr. Werner's job-related expenses.

5. **LO.4, 8** Jamie has an undergraduate degree in finance and is employed full-time by
   a bank. She is taking courses at a local university leading to an MBA degree.
   a. Is the full cost of this education deductible to her?
   b. If so, what limitations are imposed on the deduction?

6. **LO.4, 8** In connection with § 222 (deduction for qualified tuition and related
   expenses), comment on the relevance of the following:
   a. The standard deduction is claimed.
   b. Enrollment at a college does not require the payment of a student activity fee.
   c. Miscellaneous itemized deductions are not allowed.
   d. The taxpayer is married and files a separate return.

e. A father pays the tuition on behalf of a daughter who does not qualify as his dependent.

f. The taxpayer is single and has MAGI of $80,001.

g. The lifetime learning credit is claimed.

h. The taxpayer, a CPA, pays for tuition and course materials to attend law school.

7. **LO.5** In each of the following situations, indicate whether the 50% reduction for meals applies.

a. Each year, the employer awards its top salesperson an all-expense-paid trip to Jamaica.

b. The employer has a cafeteria for its employees where meals are furnished at cost.

c. The employer sponsors an annual Labor Day picnic for its employees.

d. Every Christmas, the employer gives each employee a fruitcake.

e. The taxpayer gives business gifts to her clients at Christmas.

8. **LO.5** In connection with the office in the home deduction, comment on the following:

a. The exclusive use requirement.

b. The distinction between *direct* and *indirect* expenses.

c. The effect of the taxpayer's work status (i.e., employed or self-employed) on the deduction.

d. The ownership status of the residence (i.e., owned or rented).

e. The tax treatment of office furnishings (e.g., desk, chairs, and file cabinets).

f. The treatment of expenses that exceed the gross income from the business.

9. **LO.5** Review the advantages and disadvantages of the Simplified Method for determining the office in the home deduction. Create a brief summary of your findings, and e-mail it to your instructor.

10. **LO.6** Regarding the tax implications of various retirement plans, comment on the following:

a. The difference between Keogh (H.R. 10) and traditional deductible IRA plans.

b. The difference between traditional IRA and Roth IRA plans.

11. **LO.6** Joey, who is single, is not covered by another qualified plan and earns $126,000 at his job in 2020. How much can he contribute to a traditional IRA or to a Roth IRA in 2020?

12. **LO.7** What tax return reporting procedures must be followed by an employee under the following circumstances?

a. Expenses and reimbursements are equal under an accountable plan.

b. Reimbursements at the appropriate Federal per diem rate exceed expenses, and an adequate accounting is made to the employer.

c. Expenses exceed reimbursements under a nonaccountable plan.

Computational Exercises

13. **LO.2** Lara uses the standard mileage method for determining auto expenses. During 2020, she used her car as follows: 9,000 miles for business, 2,000 miles for personal use, 2,500 miles for a move to a new job, 1,000 miles for charitable purposes, and 500 miles for medical visits. Presuming that all the mileage expenses are allowable (i.e., not subject to percentage limitations), what is Lara's deduction for:

a. Business?

b. Charitable?

c. Medical?

14. **LO.3** Fred, a self-employed taxpayer, travels from Denver to Miami primarily on business. He spends five days conducting business and two days sightseeing. His expenses are $400 (airfare), $150 per day (meals), and $300 per night (lodging). What are Fred's deductible expenses?

15. **LO.3** Brenda, a self-employed taxpayer, travels from Chicago to Barcelona (Spain) on business. She is gone 10 days (including 2 days of travel) during which time she spends 5 days conducting business and 3 days sightseeing. Her expenses are $1,500 (airfare), $200 per day (meals), and $400 per night (lodging). Because Brenda stayed with relatives while sightseeing, she only paid for 5 nights of lodging. What is Brenda's deduction for:
    a. Airfare?
    b. Meals?
    c. Lodging?

16. **LO.4** Samantha was recently employed by an accounting firm. During the year, she spends $2,500 for a CPA exam review course and begins working on a law degree in night school. Her law school expenses were $4,200 for tuition and $450 for books (which are not a requirement for enrollment in the course). Assuming no reimbursement, how much can Samantha deduct for the:
    a. CPA exam review course?
    b. Law school expenses?

17. **LO.5** In 2020, Robert takes four key clients and their spouses out to dinner. Business discussions occurred over dinner. Expenses were $700 (drinks and dinner) and $140 (tips to servers). If Robert is self-employed, how much can he deduct for this event?

18. **LO.5** In 2020, the CEO of Crimson, Inc., entertains seven clients at a skybox in Memorial Stadium for a single athletic event during the year. Substantive business discussions occurred at various times during the event. The box costs $2,000 per event and seats 10 people. (The cost of a regular seat at Memorial ranges from $55 to $100.) Refreshments served during the event cost $700 (and were separately itemized on the bill Crimson received). How much of these costs may Crimson deduct?

19. **LO.5** Andrew sends Godiva chocolates to 10 of his key clients at Christmas. The chocolates cost $50 a box not including $4 for gift wrapping and shipping. How much can Andrew deduct?

20. **LO.5** Cindy maintains an office in her home that comprises 8% (200 square feet) of total floor space. Gross income for her business is $42,000, and her residence expenses are as follows:

Real property taxes	$2,400
Interest on mortgage	4,000
Operating expenses	2,200
Depreciation (based on 8% business use)	450

What is Cindy's office in the home deduction based on:
    a. The Regular Method?
    b. The Simplified Method?

21. **LO.8** In 2020, Ava, an employee, has AGI of $58,000 and the following itemized deductions:

Home office expenses	$1,200
Union dues and work uniforms	350
Unreimbursed employee expenses	415
Gambling losses to the extent of gambling winnings	890

What is Ava's total itemized deduction related to these items?

Problems

22. **LO.2** Jackson, a self-employed taxpayer, uses his automobile 90% for business and during 2020 drove a total of 14,000 business miles. Information regarding his car expenses is listed below.

Business parking	$ 140
Auto insurance	1,300
Auto club dues (includes towing service)	180
Toll road charges (business-related)	200
Oil changes and engine tune-ups	210
Repairs	160
Depreciation allowable	2,850
Fines for traffic violations (incurred during business use)	320
Gasoline purchases	2,800

What is Jackson's deduction in 2020 for the use of his car if he uses:

a. The actual cost method?

b. The automatic mileage method?

c. What records must Jackson maintain?

23. **LO.2** On July 1, 2016, Rex purchases a new automobile for $40,000. He uses the car 80% for business and drives the car as follows: 8,000 miles in 2016, 19,000 miles in 2017, 20,000 miles in 2018, and 15,000 miles in 2019. Determine Rex's basis in the business portion of the auto as of January 1, 2020, under the following assumptions:

a. Rex uses the automatic mileage method.

b. Rex uses the actual cost method. [Assume that no § 179 expensing is claimed and that 200% declining-balance cost recovery with the half-year convention is used—see Chapter 8. The recovery limitation for an auto placed in service in 2016 is as follows: $3,160 (first year), $5,100 (second year), $3,050 (third year), and $1,875 (fourth year).]

24. **LO.3** Kristen, an independent management consultant, is based in Atlanta. During March and April of 2020, she is contracted by a national hardware chain to help implement revised human resource policies in Jackson (Mississippi) temporarily. During this period, Kristen flies to Jackson on Sunday night, spends the week at the district office, and returns home to Atlanta on Friday afternoon. The cost of returning home is $550, and the cost of spending the weekend in Jackson would have been $490.

a. Presuming no reimbursement for these expenses, how much, if any, of these weekend expenses may Kristen deduct?

b. Would your answer in part (a) change if the amounts involved were reversed (i.e., the trip home would have cost $490; staying in Jackson would have been $550)? Explain.

25. **LO.3, 5** In June of this year, Dr. and Mrs. Bret Spencer traveled to Denver to attend a three-day conference sponsored by the American Society of Implant Dentistry. Bret, a self-employed practicing oral surgeon, participated in scheduled technical sessions dealing with the latest developments in surgical procedures. On two days, Mrs. Spencer attended group meetings where various aspects of family tax planning were discussed. On the other day, she went sightseeing. Mrs. Spencer does not work for her husband, but she prepares their tax returns and handles

the family investments. Expenses incurred in connection with the conference are summarized below.

Airfare (two tickets)	$2,000
Lodging (single and double occupancy are the same rate—$250 each day)	750
Meals ($200 × 3 days)*	600
Conference registration fee (includes $120 for Family Tax Planning sessions)	620
Car rental	300

*Split equally between Dr. and Mrs. Spencer.

How much, if any, of these expenses can the Spencers deduct?

26. **LO.1, 3, 5** Kim works for a clothing manufacturer as a dress designer. During 2020, she travels to New York City to attend five days of fashion shows and then spends three days sightseeing. Her expenses are as follows:

Airfare	$1,500
Lodging (8 nights)	1,920
Meals (8 days)	1,440
Airport transportation	120

[Assume that lodging/meals are the same amount for the business and personal portion of the trip ($240 per day for lodging and $180 per day for meals).]
   a. Presuming no reimbursement, how much can Kim deduct as to the trip?
   b. Would the tax treatment of Kim's deduction differ if she was an independent contractor (rather than an employee)? Explain.

27. **LO.3** On Thursday, Justin flies from Baltimore (where the office for his sole proprietorship is located) to Cadiz (Spain). He conducts business on Friday and Tuesday; vacations on Saturday, Sunday, and Monday (a legal holiday in Spain); and returns to Baltimore on Thursday. Justin was scheduled to return home on Wednesday, but all flights were canceled due to bad weather. As a result, he spent Wednesday watching floor shows at a local casino.
   a. For tax purposes, what portion of Justin's trip is regarded as being for business?
   b. Suppose Monday was not a legal holiday. Would this change your answer to part (a)? Explain.
   c. Under either part (a) or (b), how much of Justin's airfare qualifies as a deductible business expense?

28. **LO.3** Monica, a self-employed taxpayer, travels from her office in Boston to Lisbon, Portugal, on business. Her absence of 13 days was spent as follows:

Critical Thinking

Decision Making

Thursday	Depart for and arrive at Lisbon
Friday	Business transacted
Saturday and Sunday	Vacationing
Monday through Friday	Business transacted
Saturday and Sunday	Vacationing
Monday	Business transacted
Tuesday	Depart Lisbon and return to office in Boston

   a. For tax purposes, how many days has Monica spent on business?
   b. What difference does it make?
   c. Could Monica have spent more time than she did vacationing on the trip without loss of existing tax benefits? Explain.

29. **LO.4** Elijah is employed as a full-time high school teacher. The school district where he works recently instituted a policy requiring all of its teachers to start working on a master's degree. Pursuant to this new rule, Elijah spent most of the summer of 2020 taking graduate courses at an out-of-town university. His expenses are as follows:

Tuition	$6,600
Books and course materials	1,500
Lodging	1,700
Meals	2,200
Laundry and dry cleaning	200
Campus parking	300

In addition, Elijah drove his personal automobile 2,200 miles in connection with the education. He uses the automatic mileage method.
   a. How much, if any, of these expenses might qualify as deductions *for* AGI?
   b. How much, if any, of these expenses might qualify as deductions *from* AGI?

30. **LO.4** In each of the following independent situations, determine how much, if any, qualifies as a deduction *for* AGI under § 222 (qualified tuition and related expenses):
   a. Lily is single and is employed as an architect. During 2020, she spends $4,100 in tuition to attend law school at night. Her modified AGI (MAGI) is $64,000.
   b. Liam is single and is employed as a pharmacist. During 2020, he spends $2,400 ($2,100 for tuition and $300 for books) to take a course in herbal supplements at a local university. His MAGI is $81,000.
   c. Hailey is married and is employed as a bookkeeper. She spends $5,200 for tuition and $900 for books and supplies pursuing a bachelor's degree in accounting. Her MAGI is $40,000 on the separate return she files.
   d. John spends $6,500 of his savings on tuition to attend Carmine State College. John is claimed as a dependent by his parents.

31. **LO.5** Stork Associates paid $60,000 for a 20-seat skybox at Veterans Stadium for eight professional football games. Regular seats to these games range from $80 to $250 each. At one game, an employee of Stork entertained 18 clients. Stork furnished food and beverages for the event at a cost of $1,300. The game was preceded by a bona fide business discussion, and all expenses are adequately substantiated. How much may Stork deduct for this event?

32. **LO.5** During the current year, Paul, the vice president of a bank, made gifts in the following amounts:

To Sarah (Paul's personal assistant) at Christmas	$36
To Darryl (a key client)—$3 was for gift wrapping	53
To Darryl's wife (a homemaker) on her birthday	20
To Veronica (Paul's boss) at Christmas	30

In addition, on professional assistants' day, Paul takes Sarah to lunch at a cost of $82. Presuming that Paul has adequate substantiation and is not reimbursed, how much can he deduct?

33. **LO.5** Melanie is employed full-time as an accountant for a national hardware chain. She recently started a private consulting practice, which provides tax advice and financial planning to the general public. For this purpose, she maintains an office in her home. Expenses relating to her home for 2020 are as follows:

Real property taxes	$3,600
Interest on home mortgage	3,800
Operating expenses of home	900

Melanie's residence cost $350,000 (excluding land) and has living space of 2,000 square feet, of which 20% (400 square feet) is devoted to business. The office was placed in service in February 2019, and under the Regular Method, Melanie had an unused office in the home deduction of $800 for 2019. Presuming sufficient net income from her consulting practice, what is Melanie's office in the home deduction under the:

a. Regular Method?

b. Simplified Method?

34. **LO.5** Christine is a full-time fourth-grade teacher at Vireo Academy. During the current year, she spends $1,400 for classroom supplies. On the submission of adequate substantiation, Vireo reimburses her for $500 of these expenses—the maximum reimbursement allowed for supplies under school policy. [The reimbursement is not shown as income (Box 1) of Form W–2 given to Christine by Vireo.] What are the income tax consequences of the $1,400 if Christine:

a. Itemizes her deductions *from* AGI?

b. Chooses the standard deduction?

35. **LO.6** Amber's employer, Lavender, Inc., has a § 401(k) plan that permits salary deferral elections by its employees. Amber's salary is $99,000, her marginal tax rate is 24%, and she is 42 years old.   *Decision Making*

a. What is the maximum amount Amber can elect for salary deferral treatment for 2020?

b. If Amber elects salary deferral treatment for the amount in part (a), how much can she save in taxes?

c. What amount would you recommend that Amber elect for salary deferral treatment for 2020?

36. **LO.6** Shyam is a participant in a SIMPLE § 401(k) plan. He elects to contribute 4% of his $40,000 compensation to the account, and his employer contributes 3%. What amount will not vest immediately, if any?

37. **LO.6** Harvey is a self-employed accountant with earned income from the business of $120,000 (after the deduction for one-half of his self-employment tax). He uses a defined contribution Keogh plan. What is the maximum amount Harvey can contribute to his retirement plan in 2020?

38. **LO.6** Answer the following independent questions with respect to traditional IRA contributions for 2020.

a. Juan, age 41, earns a salary of $28,000 and is not an active participant in any other qualified plan. His wife, Agnes, has no earned income. What is the maximum total deductible contribution to their IRAs? Juan wants to contribute as much as possible to his own IRA.

b. Abby, age 29, reports earned income of $25,000, and her husband, Sam, has earned income of $2,600. They are not active participants in any other qualified plan. What is the maximum contribution to their IRAs?

c. Leo's employer makes a contribution of $3,500 to Leo's simplified employee pension plan. If Leo is single, has earned income of $32,000, and has AGI of $29,000, what amount, if any, can he contribute to an IRA?

39. **LO.6** Jimmy establishes a Roth IRA at age 47 and contributes a total of $89,600 over 18 years. The account is now worth $112,000. How much of these funds may Jimmy withdraw tax-free?

40. **LO.6** Carri and Dane, ages 34 and 32, respectively, have been married for 11 years, and both are active participants in employer qualified retirement plans. Their total AGI in 2020 is $199,000, and they earn salaries of $87,000 and $95,000, respectively. What amount may Carri and Dane:

a. Contribute to regular IRAs?

b. Deduct for their contributions in part (a)?

c. Contribute to Roth IRAs?

d. Deduct for their contributions in part (c)?

Critical Thinking
Decision Making

41. **LO.5, 7, 8, 9** Ava recently graduated from college and is interviewing for a position in marketing. Gull Corporation has offered her a job as a sales representative that will require extensive travel and entertainment but provide valuable experience. Under the offer, she has two options: she receives a salary of $53,000, and she absorbs all expenses; she receives a salary of $39,000, and Gull reimburses for all expenses. Gull assures Ava that the $14,000 difference in the two options will be adequate to cover the expenses incurred. What issues should have an impact on Ava's choice?

42. **LO.1, 2, 5, 8** Complete the following table by classifying each of the independent expenditures (assume that no reimbursement takes place and that employee business expenses are not deductible).

Expense Item	Deductible *for* AGI	Deductible *from* AGI	Not Deductible
a. Tax return preparation fee incurred by an employed plumber	_____	_____	_____
b. Safety glasses purchased by an employed pipefitter	_____	_____	_____
c. Dues to auto club (e.g., AAA) for taxpayer who uses the automatic mileage method	_____	_____	_____
d. Nursing refresher course for taxpayer who retired from nursing five years ago	_____	_____	_____
e. Gambling loss not in excess of gambling gain by a self-employed architect	_____	_____	_____
f. Contribution to Roth IRA by a self-employed attorney	_____	_____	_____
g. Business travel expenses by a statutory employee	_____	_____	_____
h. Job hunting expense by an elementary school teacher seeking a position as an elementary school principal	_____	_____	_____
i. Cost of bar exam review course taken by a recent law school graduate	_____	_____	_____

Tax Return Problems

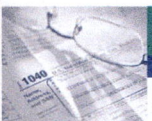

Tax Forms Problem
Critical Thinking
Communications

43. David R. and Ella M. Cole (ages 39 and 38, respectively) are husband and wife who live at 1820 Elk Avenue, Denver, CO 80202. David is a self-employed consultant specializing in retail management, and Ella is a dental hygienist for a chain of dental clinics.

- David earned consulting fees of $145,000 in 2019. He maintains his own office and pays for all business expenses. The Coles are adequately covered by the medical plan provided by Ella's employer but have chosen not to participate in its § 401(k) retirement plan.

   David's employment-related expenses for 2019 are summarized below.

Airfare	$8,800
Lodging	4,615
Meals (during travel status)	4,800
Entertainment	3,600
Ground transportation (e.g., limos, rental cars, and taxis)	800
Business gifts	900
Office supplies (includes postage, overnight delivery, and copying)	1,500

The entertainment involved taking clients to sporting and musical events. The business gifts consisted of $50 gift certificates to a national restaurant. These were sent by David during the Christmas holidays to 18 of his major clients.

In addition, David drove his 2017 Ford Expedition 11,000 miles for business and 3,000 for personal use during 2019. He purchased the Expedition on August 15, 2016, and has always used the automatic (standard) mileage method for tax purposes. Parking and tolls relating to business use total $340 in 2019.

- When the Coles purchased their present residence in April 2016, they devoted 450 of the 3,000 square feet of living space to an office for David. The property cost $440,000 ($40,000 of which is attributable to the land) and has since appreciated in value. Expenses relating to the residence in 2019 (except for mortgage interest and property taxes; see below) are as follows:

Insurance	$2,600
Repairs and maintenance	900
Utilities	4,700
Painting office area; area rugs and plants (in the office)	1,800

In terms of depreciation, the Coles use the MACRS percentage tables applicable to 39-year nonresidential real property. As to depreciable property (e.g., office furniture), David tries to avoid capitalization and uses whatever method provides the fastest write-off for tax purposes.

- Ella works at a variety of offices as a substitute when a hygienist is ill or on vacation or when one of the clinics is particularly busy (e.g., prior to the beginning of the school year). Besides her transportation, she must provide and maintain her own uniforms. Her expenses for 2019 appear below.

Uniforms	$690
State and city occupational licenses	380
Professional journals and membership dues in the American Dental Hygiene Association	340
Correspondence study course (taken online) dealing with teeth whitening procedures	420

Ella's salary for the year is $42,000, and her Form W–2 for the year shows income tax withholdings of $4,000 (Federal) and $1,000 (state) and the proper amount of Social Security and Medicare taxes.

- Besides the items already mentioned, the Coles had the following receipts during 2019.

Interest income—		
State of Colorado general purpose bonds	$2,500	
IBM bonds	800	
Wells Fargo Bank	1,200	$ 4,500
Federal income tax refund for year 2018		510
Life insurance proceeds paid by Eagle Assurance Corporation		200,000
Inheritance of savings account from Sarah Cole		50,000
Sales proceeds from two ATVs		9,000

For several years, the Coles' household has included David's divorced mother, Sarah, who has been claimed as their dependent. In late December 2018, Sarah unexpectedly died of cardiac arrest in her sleep. Unknown to Ella and David, Sarah had a life insurance policy and a savings account (with David as the designated beneficiary of each). In 2018, the Coles purchased two ATVs for $14,000. After several near mishaps, they decided that the sport was too dangerous. In 2019, they sold the ATVs to their neighbor.

- Additional expenditures for 2019 include:

Funeral expenses for Sarah		$ 4,500
Taxes—		
Real property taxes on personal residence	$6,400	
Colorado state income tax due (paid in April 2019 for tax year 2018)	310	6,710
Mortgage interest on personal residence (Rocky Mountain Bank)		6,600
Paid church pledge		2,400
Contributions to traditional IRAs for Ella and David ($6,000 + $6,000)		12,000

In 2019, the Coles made quarterly estimated tax payments of $6,000 (Federal) and $500 (state) for a total of $24,000 (Federal) and $2,000 (state).

Using the appropriate forms and schedules, compute the Coles' Federal income tax for 2019. Disregard the alternative minimum tax (AMT) and various education credits since these items are not discussed until later in the text (Chapter 12). Relevant Social Security numbers are:

David Cole	123-45-6788
Ella Cole	123-45-6787

The Coles have never owned or used any virtual currency. They do not want to contribute to the Presidential Election Campaign Fund. Also, they want any overpayment of tax refunded to them and *not* applied toward next year's tax liability. David will have a self-employment tax liability; refer to Chapter 12 to compute this liability. Suggested software: ProConnect Tax Online.

Tax Computation Problem 44. Addison Parker (Social Security number 123-45-6785), single and age 32, lives at 3218 Columbia Drive, Spokane, WA 99210. She is employed as a regional sales manager by VITA Corporation, a manufacturer and distributor of vitamins and food supplements. Addison is paid an annual salary of $83,000 and a separate travel allowance of $30,000. In order to access the travel allowance, VITA requires adequate accounting by Addison.

- Addison participates in VITA's contributory health and § 401(k) plans. During 2020, she paid $4,500 for her share of the medical insurance and contributed $11,000 to the § 401(k) retirement plan.

- Addison uses her automobile 70% for business and 30% for personal. The automobile, a Toyota Avalon, was purchased new on June 30, 2018, for $37,000 (no trade-in was involved). Depreciation has been claimed using the MACRS 200% declining-balance method, and no § 179 election was made in the year of purchase. (For depreciation information, see text Section 8-3d.) During 2020, Addison drove 15,000 miles and incurred and paid the following expenses relating to the automobile:

Gasoline	$3,100
Insurance	2,900
Auto club dues	240
Interest on car loan	1,100
Repairs and maintenance	1,200
Parking (during business use)	600
Traffic fines (during business use)	500

- Because VITA does not have an office in Spokane, the company expects Addison to maintain one in her home. Out of 1,500 square feet of living space in her apartment, Addison has set aside 300 square feet as an office. Expenses for 2020 relating to the office are listed below.

Rent	$18,000
Utilities	4,000
Insurance (renter's casualty and theft coverage)	1,600
Carpet replacement (office area only)	1,200

- Addison's employment-related expenses (except for the trip to Korea) for 2020 are summarized below.

Airfare	$4,100
Lodging	3,200
Meals	2,800
Transportation (taxis and airport limos)	300
Business gifts	540
Continuing education	400
Professional journals	140

Most of Addison's business trips involve visits to retail outlets in her region. Store managers and their key employees, as well as some suppliers, were the parties entertained. The business gifts were boxes of candy costing $30 ($25 each plus $5 for wrapping and shipping) sent to 18 store managers at Christmas. The continuing education was a noncredit course dealing with improving management skills that Addison took online.

- In July 2020, Addison traveled to Korea to investigate a new process that is being developed to convert fish parts to a solid consumable tablet form. She spent one week checking out the process and then took a one-week vacation tour of the country. The round-trip airfare was $3,600, and her expenses relating to business were $2,100 for lodging ($300 each night), $1,470 for meals, and $350 for transportation. Upon returning to the United States, Addison sent her findings about the process to her employer. VITA was so pleased with her report that it gave her an employee achievement award of $10,000. The award was sent to Addison in January 2021.

- Besides the items already mentioned, Addison had the following receipts in 2020:

Interest income—		
City of Tacoma general purpose bonds	$ 350	
Olympia State Bank	400	$ 750
Proceeds from property sales—		
City lot	$13,000	
Sailboat	18,000	31,000
Cash found at airport		5,000

Regarding the city lot (located in Vancouver), Addison purchased the property in 2005 for $16,000 and held it as an investment. Unfortunately, the neighborhood where the lot was located deteriorated, and property values declined. In 2020, Addison decided to cut her losses and sold the property for $13,000. The sailboat was used for pleasure and was purchased in 2016 for $16,500. Addison sold the boat because she purchased a new and larger model (see below). While at the Spokane airport, Addison found an unmarked envelope containing $5,000 in $50 bills. Because no mention of any lost funds was noted in the media, Addison kept the money.

- Addison's expenditures for 2020 (not previously noted) are summarized below.

Medical (not covered by insurance)	$6,000
State and local general sales tax	3,300
Church pledge (2020 and 2021)	5,600
Fee paid for preparation of 2019 income tax return	500
Contribution to mayor's reelection campaign fund	200
Contribution to a Coverdell education savings account (on behalf of a favorite nephew)	2,000

Addison keeps careful records regarding sales taxes. In 2020, the sales tax total was unusually high due to the purchase of a new sailboat. In 2020, Addison decided to pay her church pledge for both 2020 and 2021. The insurance premium was on a policy covering her father's life. (Addison is the designated beneficiary under the policy.)

Addison's employer withheld $8,600 for Federal income tax purposes, and she applied her $800 overpayment for 2019 toward the 2020 tax liability.

Compute Addison's Federal income tax payable (or refund) for 2020. In making the calculation, use the Tax Rate Schedule and disregard the application of the alternative minimum tax (AMT), which is not discussed until Chapter 12.

Research Problems

Note: Solutions to the Research Problems can be prepared by using the Thomson Reuters Checkpoint™ online tax research database, which accompanies this textbook. Solutions can also be prepared by using research materials found in a typical tax library.

Research Problem 1. Aaron, a resident of Minnesota, has been a driver for Green Delivery Service for the past six years. For this purpose, he leases a truck from Green, and his compensation is based on a percentage of the income resulting from his pickup and delivery services. Green allows its drivers to choose their 10-hour shifts and does not exercise any control on how these services are carried out (e.g., the route to be taken or the order in which parcels are delivered or picked up). Under Green's operating agreement with its drivers, Green can terminate the arrangement after 30 days' notice. In practice, however, Green allows its truckers to quit immediately without giving advance notice. The agreement also identifies the drivers as independent contractors. Green maintains no health or retirement plans for its drivers, and each year it reports their income by issuing Forms 1099–MISC (and not Forms W–2). Green requires its drivers to maintain a commercial driver's license and be in good standing with the state highway law enforcement division.

Citing the employment tax Regulations in §§ 31.3121(d)–1(c)(2) and 31.3306(i)–1(b), an IRS agent contends that Aaron is an independent contractor and, therefore, is subject to the self-employment tax. Based on *Peno Trucking, Inc.* (93 TCM 1027, T.C.Memo. 2007–66), Aaron disagrees and contends that he is an employee (i.e., not self-employed). Who is correct? Why?

Research Problem 2. Your client, a large construction firm organized as a C corporation, allows certain employees (including the president of the corporation) to use its company-owned airplane for nonbusiness flights. The employees include the value of the flights in their income. Your client is uncertain about how to treat the expenses related to these nonbusiness flights. In certain situations, the expenses of operating the plane are more than the income imputed to the employees, and in certain circumstances, the expenses are less. In doing some of its own research, your client found *Sutherland Lumber-Southwest, Inc.* [114 T.C. 197 (2000)], which suggests that as long as the employee imputes income, the full amount of the related expenses can be deducted. [The decision in the case was affirmed on appeal, *Sutherland Lumber-Southwest, Inc. v. Comm.*, 2001–2 USTC ¶50,503, 88 AFTR 2d 2001–5026, 255 F.3d 495 (CA–8, 2001).] Should your client follow the approach in *Sutherland*? Explain.

Use internet tax resources to address the following questions. Look for reliable websites and blogs of the IRS and other government agencies, media outlets, businesses, tax professionals, academics, think tanks, and political outlets.

Research Problem 3. Prepare a blog post for the "Online Tutor Match Company" to explain to its freelancers the tax implications of their work. Topics should include (1) what records to keep (both for income and expenses), (2) what unique situations freelancers face (e.g., home office deductions; self-employment status), and (3) what tax forms must be filed and (briefly) how to prepare those forms [e.g., Schedule C (Form 1040)]. — *Communications*

Research Problem 4. Download IRS Form 1099–K and its instructions from the IRS website. What is the purpose of the form, and when is it used? Go to the Square, Inc. website (**squareup.com**) and search for information about this form. Summarize what you discover in an e-mail to your instructor. — *Communications*

Research Problem 5. Analyze S. 700 (116th Congress) introduced by Senator John Thune to provide a new approach to provide freelance ("gig") workers independent contractor status. Also see his press release of March 7, 2019, at **thune.senate.gov/public/index.cfm/2019/3/thune-reintroduces-bill-to-add-certainty-to-worker-classification-rules**.

Compare the legislation against the current IRS rules (discussed in text Section 9-1 and Concept Summary 9.1) and against the AICPA's *Guiding Principles of Good Tax Policy* (discussed in text Section 1-3c).

Becker CPA Review Questions

1. In the current year, Barlow moved from Chicago to Miami to start a new job, incurring costs of $1,200 to move household goods and $2,500 in temporary living expenses. Barlow was not reimbursed for any of these expenses. What amount should Barlow deduct as an itemized deduction for moving expense?

   a. $0
   b. $1,200
   c. $2,500
   d. $3,700

2. Bob and Nancy are married and file a joint return in 2020. They are both under age 50 and employed, with wages of $50,000 each. Their total AGI is $110,000. Neither of them is an active participant in a qualified plan. What is the maximum traditional IRA deduction they can take for the current year?

   a. $0
   b. $6,000
   c. $8,400
   d. $12,000

3. Ryan is 39 years old and works as a real estate agent. Ryan's marginal tax rate is 24%. Ryan has a traditional IRA with a current balance of $80,000. The IRA consists of $60,000 of contributions that Ryan made and deducted on his tax return and $20,000 of account earnings. In the current year, Ryan receives a distribution of the entire $80,000. He contributes $60,000 of the distribution to a Roth IRA and keeps the remaining $20,000 for personal expenditures. What is Ryan's total income tax and penalty on the transactions?

   a. $0 income tax, $0 penalty
   b. $20,000 income tax, $8,000 penalty
   c. $5,000 income tax, $2,000 penalty
   d. $19,200 income tax, $2,000 penalty

CHAPTER

10

Deductions and Losses: Certain Itemized Deductions

LEARNING OBJECTIVES: *After completing Chapter 10, you should be able to:*

LO.1 Distinguish between deductible and nondeductible personal expenses.

LO.2 Define medical expenses and compute the medical expense deduction.

LO.3 Contrast deductible taxes with nondeductible fees, licenses, and other charges.

LO.4 Explain the Federal income tax treatment of property taxes, state and local income taxes, and sales taxes.

LO.5 Distinguish between deductible and nondeductible interest and apply the appropriate limitations to deductible interest.

LO.6 Recognize charitable contributions and identify their related measurement problems and percentage limitations.

LO.7 List the expenses that are deductible as other itemized deductions.

LO.8 Identify tax planning strategies that can maximize the benefit of itemized deductions.

CHAPTER OUTLINE

10-1 Medical Expenses, 10-3
10-1a Medical Expenses Defined, 10-3
10-1b Capital Expenditures for Medical Purposes, 10-4
10-1c Medical Expenses Incurred for Spouse and Dependents, 10-5
10-1d Transportation, Meal, and Lodging Expenses for Medical Treatment, 10-6
10-1e Amounts Paid for Medical Insurance Premiums, 10-6
10-1f Year of Deduction, 10-7
10-1g Reimbursements, 10-7
10-1h Health Savings Accounts, 10-8
10-1i Affordable Care Act Provisions, 10-10

10-2 Taxes, 10-10
10-2a Deductibility as a Tax, 10-10
10-2b Property Taxes, 10-11
10-2c State and Local Income Taxes and Sales Taxes, 10-13

10-3 Interest, 10-14
10-3a Allowed and Disallowed Items, 10-14
10-3b Restrictions on Deductibility and Timing Considerations, 10-17
10-3c Classification of Interest Expense, 10-17

10-4 Charitable Contributions, 10-18
10-4a Criteria for a Gift, 10-18
10-4b Qualified Organizations, 10-20
10-4c Time of Deduction, 10-20
10-4d Record-Keeping and Valuation Requirements, 10-21
10-4e Limitations on Charitable Contribution Deduction, 10-22

10-5 Timing of Payments to Maximize Deductions, 10-26

10-6 Other Itemized Deductions, 10-27

10-7 Comprehensive Example of Schedule A, 10-27

10-8 Tax Planning, 10-29
10-8a Maximizing the Medical Deduction, 10-29
10-8b Ensuring the Charitable Contribution Deduction, 10-29
10-8c Planning to Avoid Nondeductible Treatment, 10-31

IMPACT OF ITEMIZED DEDUCTIONS ON MAJOR PURCHASES

John and Susan Williamson, a young professional couple, have been renting an apartment in Atlanta, Georgia, since they were married. Their income has grown as they've become more established in their careers, and they now believe the time has come to purchase their own home. In addition, their desire to buy a home now may be coming at a good time, because John's mother, Martha, needs to move in with them due to her declining health and their current apartment is too small to accommodate her. John and Susan's current monthly rent is $2,000, but they are willing to spend up to $2,600 per month on an after-tax basis for their first home.

After months of house hunting, they have found the perfect home, but they are concerned it may be too expensive. If they acquire a standard mortgage to finance the purchase of the home, the total cash outlay during the first year of ownership will be $43,000 ($2,000 principal payments, $37,000 interest payments, and $4,000 real estate taxes). Alternatively, if they use their retirement and taxable investments to secure the home financing, they can qualify for a lower interest rate and thereby reduce the interest charge from $37,000 to $35,000. They expect their Federal AGI to be about $200,000 and their taxable income to range between $170,000 and $185,000 for the year. John and Susan have not itemized their deductions in prior years because the amount of their qualifying expenses has been just below the standard deduction amount. Assume that the Williamsons' marginal income tax rate under Georgia law is 6 percent.

Can John and Susan Williamson afford to pursue their dream of home ownership?

Read the chapter and formulate your response.

FRAMEWORK 1040   Tax Formula for Individuals

This chapter covers the boldfaced portions of the Tax Formula for Individuals that was introduced in Concept Summary 3.1 on p. 3-3. Below those portions are the sections of Form 1040 where the results are reported.

Income *(broadly defined)*	\$xx,xxx
Less: Exclusions	(x,xxx)
Gross income	\$xx,xxx
Less: Deductions *for* adjusted gross income	**(x,xxx)**

FORM 1040 (Schedule 1)

12	Health savings account deduction. Attach Form 8889	**12**
16	Self-employed health insurance deduction	**16**
20	Student loan interest deduction	**20**

Adjusted gross income	\$xx,xxx
Less: The greater of total itemized deductions *or* the standard deduction	**(x,xxx)**

FORM 1040 (p. 1)

9	**Standard deduction or itemized deductions** (from Schedule A)

Personal and dependency exemptions*	(x,xxx)
Deduction for qualified business income**	(x,xxx)
Taxable income	\$xx,xxx
Tax on taxable income *(see Tax Tables or Tax Rate Schedules)*	\$ x,xxx
Less: Tax credits *(including income taxes withheld and prepaid)*	(xxx)
Tax due (or refund)	\$ xxx

* Exemption deductions are not allowed from 2018 through 2025.
** Only applies from 2018 through 2025.

LO.1

Distinguish between deductible and nondeductible personal expenses.

As a general rule, personal expenses are not deductible (see § 262 of the Code). However, Congress has chosen to allow certain personal expenses to be deducted as itemized deductions. Personal expenses that are deductible as itemized deductions include medical expenses, certain taxes, mortgage interest, and charitable contributions. These (and other) personal expenses allowed as itemized deductions are covered in this chapter. Although certain exceptions exist (e.g., certain alimony and traditional IRA contributions are deductible *for* AGI), personal expenses not specifically allowed as itemized deductions by the tax law are nondeductible.

Certain business and investment expenses are also deductible, like interest expense on loans to acquire investment assets (e.g., publicly traded securities) and state income taxes on business and investment income. These rules are covered in this chapter and Chapter 11.

Allowable itemized deductions are deductible *from* AGI in arriving at taxable income if the taxpayer *elects* to itemize. A taxpayer will elect to itemize when total itemized deductions exceed the standard deduction based on the taxpayer's filing status.[1]

Itemized deductions are reported on Schedule A (Form 1040) and filed with an individual's Federal income tax return (Form 1040).

The Big Picture

EXAMPLE

1

Return to the facts of *The Big Picture* on p. 10-1. John and Susan Williamson will discover that with the purchase of a home, they will be able to itemize their deductions for the first time instead of claiming the standard deduction. Assuming that the home mortgage interest expense and real estate taxes meet the requirements discussed in this chapter, they can be deducted *from* AGI because their total would exceed the amount of the standard deduction for a married couple filing a joint return. Other qualifying expenses, including up to \$10,000 of state and local taxes as well as charitable contributions, also will be deductible as itemized deductions. All of these items provide a tax benefit to the Williamsons.

[1]See §§ 63(c) and (d), respectively, for the definitions of the terms *standard deduction* and *itemized deductions*.

10-1 MEDICAL EXPENSES

Medical expenses paid for the care of the taxpayer, spouse, and dependents are allowed as an itemized deduction to the extent the expenses are not reimbursed. The <mark>medical expense</mark> deduction is limited to the amount by which these expenses *exceed* 7.5 percent of the taxpayer's AGI.[2]

The threshold percentage, sometimes referred to as a "floor," is used to restrict deductions, because expenses below the floor are not deductible. Here, the floor is significant. Only medical expenses *in excess* of the "7.5%-of-AGI floor" are deductible. As a result, a medical expense deduction is rare (especially for high-income taxpayers).

> **LO.2**
> **Define medical expenses and compute the medical expense deduction.**

The Big Picture

EXAMPLE 2

Return to the facts of *The Big Picture* on p. 10-1. If, as expected, the Williamsons' AGI for the year is $200,000, to receive a tax benefit from any unreimbursed medical expenses, they must itemize their deductions and have more than $15,000 ($200,000 × 7.5%) of those expenses. If they paid $17,000 of unreimbursed medical expenses during the year and itemize their deductions, their total itemized deductions increase by $2,000 ($17,000 unreimbursed medical expenses − $15,000 AGI floor).

10-1a Medical Expenses Defined

The term *medical care* includes expenses incurred for the "diagnosis, cure, mitigation, treatment, or prevention of disease, or for the purpose of affecting any structure or function of the body."[3] A *partial* list of deductible and nondeductible medical items appears in Exhibit 10.1.

[handwritten margin note: One is included in medical deduction. If the only reason they can't be claimed is b/c gross income and/or joint return tests]

EXHIBIT 10.1	Examples of Deductible and Nondeductible Medical Expenses Paid by Taxpayer
Deductible	**Nondeductible**
Medical (including dental, mental, and hospital) care	Funeral, burial, or cremation expenses
	Over-the-counter medicines (except insulin)
Prescription drugs and insulin	Bottled water
Special equipment:	Toiletries, cosmetics
• Wheelchairs	Diaper service, maternity clothes
• Crutches	Programs for the *general* improvement of health:
• Artificial limbs	• Weight reduction
• Eyeglasses (including contact lenses)	• Health spas
• Hearing aids	• Social activities (e.g., dancing and swimming lessons)
Transportation for medical care	
Medical and hospital insurance premiums	Unnecessary cosmetic surgery
Long-term care insurance premiums (subject to limitations)	
Cost of alcohol and drug rehabilitation	
Certain costs to stop smoking	
Weight reduction programs related to obesity	

---

[2]From 2017 through 2020, the threshold is 7.5% of AGI for all individuals. Unless changed by Congress, the threshold will increase to 10% of AGI beginning in 2021.

[3]§ 213(d)(1)(A).

A medical expense does not have to relate to a particular ailment to be deductible. Because the definition of medical care is broad enough to cover preventive measures, the cost of periodic physical and dental exams qualifies even for a taxpayer in good health.

Amounts paid for unnecessary *cosmetic surgery* are not deductible medical expenses. Cosmetic surgery is necessary—and, therefore, deductible—when it improves the effects of (1) a deformity arising from a congenital abnormality, (2) a personal injury, or (3) a disfiguring disease.[4]

Jacob, age 75, paid $21,000 to a plastic surgeon for a face-lift. Jacob merely wanted to improve his appearance. The $21,000 does not qualify as a medical expense because the surgery was unnecessary.

In contrast, Marge's face is disfigured as a result of a serious automobile accident. Here, the cost of restorative cosmetic surgery is deductible as a medical expense.

The cost of care in a *nursing home or home for the aged*, including meals and lodging, is a deductible medical expense if the primary reason for being in the home is to get medical care. If the primary reason for being there is personal, any costs for medical or nursing care are deductible medical expenses, but the cost of meals and lodging must be excluded.[5]

Norman has a chronic heart ailment. In October, his family decides to place Norman in a nursing home equipped to provide medical and nursing care. Total nursing home expenses amount to $80,000 during the year. Of this amount, $50,000 is directly attributable to medical and nursing care.

Because Norman is in need of significant medical and nursing care and is placed in the facility primarily for this purpose, all $80,000 of the nursing home costs are deductible (subject to the AGI floor, explained earlier).

Tuition expenses of a dependent at a special school for a mentally or physically handicapped individual may be deductible as a medical expense. The deduction is allowed if a principal reason for sending the individual to the school is the school's special resources for alleviating the infirmities. In this case, the cost of meals and lodging, in addition to the tuition, is a proper medical expense deduction.[6]

Jason's daughter Jasmine attended public school through the seventh grade. Because Jasmine was a poor student, she was examined by a psychiatrist who concluded that Jasmine has dyslexia. Acting on the psychiatrist's recommendation, Jason enrolls Jasmine in a private school so that she can receive individual attention. The school specializes in students with learning disabilities and has a program of study designed to help students with dyslexia (including a staff of educational and psychological professionals who have developed the specialized curriculum).

The expense related to Jasmine's attendance is deductible as a medical expense. The cost of any psychiatric care also qualifies as a medical expense.[7]

10-1b Capital Expenditures for Medical Purposes

When capital expenditures are incurred for medical purposes, they must be deemed medically necessary by a physician and used primarily by the patient. In addition, their costs must be reasonable. Examples include dust elimination systems,[8] elevators,[9] and vans specially designed for wheelchair-bound taxpayers. Other expenditures that may qualify

---

[4]§ 213(d)(9)(A).

[5]Reg. § 1.213–1(e)(1)(v). In general, medical care is required if a taxpayer is deemed to be chronically ill and under a prescribed plan of care. A taxpayer is chronically ill if he or she cannot perform at least two daily living tasks (dressing, eating, bathing, toileting, moving from one place to another, continence) for 90 days or more (§ 7702B).

[6]Reg. § 1.213–1(e)(1)(v)(a). See *Donald R. Pfeifer*, 37 TCM 816, T.C.Memo. 1978–189. Also see Rev.Rul. 78–340, 1978–2 C.B. 124. Based on recent rulings, the IRS is allowing a deduction where there is a diagnosis of a neurologically

based learning disability or other handicap, leading to a recommendation of and attendance at an institution specially equipped to help the student overcome the handicap.

[7]Ltr.Rul. 200521003.

[8]Ltr.Rul. 7948029.

[9]*Riach v. Frank*, 62–1 USTC ¶9419, 9 AFTR 2d 1263, 302 F.2d 374 (CA–9, 1962).

are swimming pools (if the taxpayer does not have access to a neighborhood pool) and air conditioners if they do not become permanent improvements (e.g., window units).[10]

Both a capital expenditure for a permanent improvement and related operating and maintenance costs may qualify as medical expenses. The allowable costs are deductible in the year incurred. Although depreciation is required for most other capital expenditures, it is not required for those qualifying for medical purposes (in other words, the entire cost of a qualifying capital expenditure is immediately deductible).

A permanent capital improvement that ordinarily would not have a medical purpose qualifies as a medical expense if it is directly related to prescribed medical care (e.g., an elevator in a personal residence). Here, the cost is deductible to the extent it *exceeds* the increase in value of the related property. Appraisal costs related to capital improvements are not medical expenses. Instead, these costs are classified as miscellaneous itemized deductions (expenses incurred in the determination of the taxpayer's tax liability).[11] However, the deduction for miscellaneous itemized deductions has been suspended from 2018 through 2025 (see text Section 10-6).

EXAMPLE 6

Fred is afflicted with heart disease. His physician advises him to install an elevator in his residence so that he will not be required to climb the stairs. The cost of installing the elevator is $10,000, and the increase in the value of the residence is determined to be only $4,000.

Therefore, $6,000 ($10,000 − $4,000) is treated as a medical expense. Additional utility costs to operate the elevator and maintenance costs are also medical expenses as long as the medical reason for the capital expenditure continues to exist.

The full cost of certain home-related capital expenditures incurred to enable a *physically handicapped* individual to live independently and productively qualifies as a medical expense. Qualifying costs include expenditures for constructing entrance and exit ramps to the residence, widening hallways and doorways to accommodate wheelchairs, installing support bars and railings in bathrooms and other rooms, and adjusting electrical outlets and fixtures.[12] These expenditures are only subject to the AGI floor; the increase in the home's value is deemed to be zero.

10-1c Medical Expenses Incurred for Spouse and Dependents

In computing the medical expense deduction, a taxpayer may include medical expenses for a spouse and for a person who was a dependent at the time the expenses were paid or incurred. Of the requirements that normally apply in determining dependency status,[13] neither the gross income nor the joint return test applies in determining dependency status for medical expense deduction purposes.

EXAMPLE 7

William (age 22) is married and a full-time student at a university. During the year, William incurred medical expenses that were paid by Karen (William's mother). She provided more than half of William's support for the year.

Even if William files a joint return with his wife, Karen may claim the medical expenses she paid for him. Karen would combine William's expenses with her own before applying the AGI floor.

For *divorced persons* with children, a special rule applies to the noncustodial parent. The noncustodial parent may claim any medical expenses he or she pays even though the children are not the noncustodial parent's dependents.

EXAMPLE 8

Sam and Joan were divorced last year, and Joan was awarded custody of their child, Keith. During the current year, Sam pays $2,500 of Keith's medical bills. Together, Sam and Joan provide more than half of Keith's support.

Even though Keith is Joan's dependent, Sam can combine the $2,500 of medical expenses that he pays for Keith with his own when calculating his medical expense deduction.

---

[10]Reg. § 1.213–1(e)(1)(iii).

[11]§ 212(3).

[12]For a complete list of the items that qualify, see Rev.Rul. 87–106, 1987–2 C.B. 67.

[13]Refer to text Section 3-3 for discussion of these requirements.

10-1d Transportation, Meal, and Lodging Expenses for Medical Treatment

Payments for transportation to and from a point of treatment for medical care are deductible as medical expenses (subject to the AGI floor). These costs include bus, taxi, train, or plane fare; charges for ambulance service; and out-of-pocket expenses for the use of an automobile. A mileage allowance of 17 cents per mile for 2020 may be used instead of actual out-of-pocket automobile expenses.[14] Whether the taxpayer chooses to claim out-of-pocket automobile expenses or the 17 cents per mile automatic mileage option, related parking fees and tolls can also be deducted. Also included are transportation expenditures for someone like a family member or nurse who must accompany the patient. The cost of meals while en route to obtain medical care is not deductible.

A deduction is allowable for lodging while away from home for medical care if the following requirements are met:[15]

- The lodging is primarily for and essential to medical care.
- Medical care is provided by a physician in a licensed hospital or a similar medical facility (e.g., a clinic).
- The lodging is not lavish or extravagant.
- There is no significant element of personal pleasure in the travel.

The deduction for lodging expenses cannot exceed $50 *per* night for *each* person. The lodging deduction is allowed not only for the patient but also for anyone who must travel with the patient.

The Big Picture

EXAMPLE 9

Return to the facts of *The Big Picture* on p. 10-1. John's mother, Martha, eventually moves in with the Williamsons because of her declining health, and she becomes their dependent. Later, John is advised by Martha's physician that she needs specialized treatment for her heart condition. Consequently, John and Martha fly to Cleveland, Ohio, where Martha receives the therapy at a heart clinic on an outpatient basis. Expenses in connection with the trip are as follows:

Round-trip airfare ($250 each)	$500
Lodging in Cleveland for two nights ($120 each per night)	480

Assuming that the Williamsons itemize their deductions (including medical expenses), the medical expense deduction for transportation is $500 and the medical expense deduction for lodging is $200 ($50 per night per person). Because of the severity of Martha's health condition, it is assumed that John's accompanying her is justified.

No deduction is allowed for the cost of meals unless they are part of the medical care and are furnished at a medical facility. If deductible, these meals are not subject to the 50 percent limit applicable to business meals (see text Section 9-6).

10-1e Amounts Paid for Medical Insurance Premiums

Medical insurance premiums (including Medicare insurance costs withheld from a Social Security recipient's monthly benefits) are included with other medical expenses subject to the AGI floor. Premiums paid by the taxpayer under a group plan or an individual plan are included as medical expenses. If an employer pays all or part of the taxpayer's medical insurance premiums, the amount paid by the employer is not included in the employee's gross income (and these amounts are not deductible by the employee). However, the medical insurance premiums paid by the employer are deductible as business expenses on the employer's tax return.

an employee can only itemize

---

[14]This amount is adjusted periodically; see Notice 2020–5, 2020–4 I.R.B. 380. In 2019, the allowance was 20 cents per mile.   [15]§ 213(d)(2).

If a taxpayer is *self-employed*, insurance premiums paid for medical coverage are deductible as a *business* expense (*for* AGI).[16] The deduction *for* AGI is allowed for premiums paid for the taxpayer, the taxpayer's spouse, and dependents of the taxpayer. However, this deduction is not allowed if the taxpayer (or taxpayer's spouse) is eligible to participate in an employer-provided health plan.

The Big Picture

EXAMPLE 10

Return to the facts of *The Big Picture* on p. 10-1. John Williamson is the sole practitioner in his unincorporated accounting practice. During the year, he paid health insurance premiums of $12,000 for his own coverage and $8,000 for coverage for his wife, Susan. John can deduct $20,000 as a business deduction (*for* AGI) in computing their taxable income.

Taxpayers may also include premiums paid on qualified long-term care insurance contracts in medical expenses, subject to limitations based on the age of the insured. For 2020, the per-person limits range from $430 for taxpayers age 40 and under to $5,430 for taxpayers over age 70.[17]

10-1f Year of Deduction

Regardless of a taxpayer's method of accounting, medical expenses are deductible only in the year *paid*. In effect, individual taxpayers are on a cash basis for the medical expense deduction. One exception, however, is allowed for deceased taxpayers. If the medical expenses are paid within one year from the day following the day of death, they can be treated as being paid at the time they were *incurred*. As a result, these expenses may be reported on the final income tax return of the decedent or on earlier returns if incurred before the year of death.

No current deduction is allowed for payment for medical care to be rendered in the future unless the taxpayer is under an obligation to make the payment. Whether an obligation to make the payment exists depends on the policy of the physician or the institution furnishing the medical care.

EXAMPLE 11

Upon the recommendation of his regular dentist, in December 2020, Gary consults Dr. Smith, a prosthodontist, who specializes in crown and bridge work. Dr. Smith tells Gary that he can do the necessary restorative work for $12,000 and that he requires all new patients to prepay 40% of the total cost of the procedure. Accordingly, Gary pays $4,800 in December 2020. The balance of $7,200 is paid when the work is completed in January 2021.

Under these circumstances, the qualifying medical expense deductions are $4,800 for 2020 and $7,200 in 2021. The result would be the same even if Gary prepaid the full $12,000 in 2020.

10-1g Reimbursements

If medical expenses are reimbursed in the same year as paid, no problem arises. The reimbursement merely reduces the amount that would otherwise qualify for the medical expense deduction. But what happens if the reimbursement occurs in a later year than the expenditure? In computing "casualty losses," any reasonable prospect of recovery must be considered (refer to text Section 7-3). For medical expenses, however, any expected reimbursement is disregarded in measuring the amount of the deduction. Instead, the reimbursement is accounted for separately in the year in which it occurs.

Under the *tax benefit rule*, a taxpayer who receives an insurance reimbursement for medical expenses deducted in a previous year must include the reimbursement in income up to the amount of the deductions that decreased taxable income in the earlier

---

[16]§ 162(l).

[17]The amounts for 2019 were $420 for taxpayers age 40 and under and $5,270 for taxpayers over age 70. See IRS Publication 502 for details relating to requirements for deducting costs associated with qualified long-term care insurance contracts.

year. A taxpayer who did not itemize deductions in the year the expenses were paid did not receive a tax benefit and is *not* required to include a reimbursement in gross income.

Daniel had AGI of $45,000 for 2020. He was injured in a car accident and paid $4,300 for hospital expenses and $1,700 for doctor bills. Daniel also incurred medical expenses of $600 for his dependent child. In 2021, Daniel was reimbursed $950 by his insurance company for the medical expenses attributable to the car accident. His deduction for medical expenses in 2020 is computed as follows:

Hospitalization	$ 4,300
Bills for doctor's services	1,700
Medical expenses for dependent	600
Total	$ 6,600
Less: Medical expense floor (7.5% of $45,000)	(3,375)
Medical expense deduction (assuming that Daniel itemizes his deductions)	$ 3,225

Assume that Daniel would have elected to itemize his deductions even if he had no medical expenses in 2020. If the reimbursement for medical care had occurred in 2020, the medical expense deduction would have been only $2,275 [$6,600 (total medical expenses) − $950 (reimbursement) − $3,375 (floor)] and Daniel would have paid more income tax.

Because the reimbursement was made in a subsequent year, Daniel will include $950 in gross income for 2021. If Daniel had not itemized in 2020, he would *not* have included the $950 reimbursement in 2021 gross income because he would have received no tax benefit for the medical expenses in 2020.

10-1h Health Savings Accounts

Qualifying individuals may make deductible contributions to a **Health Savings Account (HSA)**.[18] A taxpayer can use an HSA in conjunction with a high-deductible medical insurance policy to help reduce the overall cost of medical coverage. Converting from a low-deductible to a high-deductible plan can generally save an individual a considerable amount in premiums. The high-deductible policy provides coverage for extraordinary medical expenses (in excess of the deductible), and expenses not covered by the policy can be paid with funds withdrawn tax-free from the HSA.

Sanchez, who is married and has three dependent children, carries a high-deductible medical insurance policy with a deductible of $4,400. He establishes an HSA and contributes the maximum allowable amount to the HSA in 2020.

During 2020, the Sanchez family incurs medical expenses of $7,000. The high-deductible policy covers $2,600 of the expenses ($7,000 expenses − $4,400 deductible). Sanchez may withdraw $4,400 from the HSA to pay the medical expenses not covered by the high-deductible policy.

High-Deductible Plans

High-deductible policies are less expensive than low-deductible policies, so taxpayers with low medical costs can benefit from the lower premiums and use funds from the HSA to pay costs not covered by the high-deductible policy. A plan must meet two requirements to qualify as a high-deductible plan.[19]

1. The annual deductible in 2020 is not less than $1,400 for self-only coverage ($2,800 for family coverage).
2. The annual limit in 2020 on total out-of-pocket costs (excluding premiums) under the plan does not exceed $6,900 for self-only coverage ($13,800 for family coverage).

---

[18]§ 223. An HSA is a qualified trust or custodial account administered by a qualified HSA trustee, which can be a bank, an insurance company, or another IRS-approved trustee.

[19]§ 223(c)(2). In 2019, the annual deductible limits were $1,350 (self-only coverage) and $2,700 (family coverage), and the annual out-of-pocket costs limits were $6,750 (self-only coverage) and $13,500 (family coverage).

Tax Treatment of HSA Contributions and Distributions

To establish an HSA, a taxpayer contributes funds to a custodial account.[20] As illustrated in the preceding example, funds can be withdrawn from an HSA to pay medical expenses that are not covered by the high-deductible policy. The following general tax rules apply to HSAs:

1. Contributions made by the taxpayer to an HSA are a deduction *for* AGI (i.e., the contributions reduce gross income in arriving at AGI). As a result, the taxpayer does not need to itemize to take the deduction.

2. Earnings on HSAs are not subject to taxation unless distributed, in which case taxability depends on the way the funds are used.[21]

   - Distributions from HSAs are excluded from gross income if they are used to pay for medical expenses not covered by the high-deductible policy.

   - Distributions that are not used to pay for medical expenses are included in gross income and are subject to an additional 20 percent penalty if made before age 65, death, or disability. Any distributions made by reason of death or disability and distributions made after the HSA beneficiary becomes eligible for Medicare are taxed but not penalized.

HSAs have at least two other attractive features. First, an HSA is portable. Taxpayers who switch jobs can take their HSAs with them. Second, anyone under age 65 who has a high-deductible plan and is not covered by another policy that is not a high-deductible plan can establish an HSA.

Deductible Amount

The annual deduction for contributions to an HSA is limited to an amount that depends on whether the taxpayer has self-only coverage or family coverage. The annual limit for an individual who has self-only coverage in 2020 is $3,550, and the annual limit for an individual who has family coverage in 2020 is $7,100. These amounts are subject to annual cost-of-living adjustments.[22] An eligible taxpayer who has attained age 55 by the end of the tax year may make an additional annual contribution in 2020 of up to $1,000. This additional amount is referred to as a *catch-up* contribution. A deduction is not allowed after the individual becomes eligible for Medicare coverage.

Determining the Maximum HSA Contribution Deduction

Liu (age 45), who is married and self-employed, carries a high-deductible medical insurance policy with family coverage and an annual deductible of $4,000. In addition, he has established an HSA. Liu's maximum annual deductible contribution to the HSA in 2020 is $7,100.

EXAMPLE 14

During 2020, Adam, who is self-employed, made 12 monthly payments of $1,200 for an HSA contract that provides medical insurance coverage with a $3,600 deductible. The plan covers Adam, his wife, and two children. Of the $1,200 monthly fee, $675 was for the high-deductible policy and $525 was deposited into an HSA.

Because Adam is *self-employed*, he can deduct $8,100 of the amount paid for the high-deductible policy ($675 per month × 12 months) as a deduction *for* AGI (refer to Example 10 and related discussion). In addition, he can deduct the $6,300 ($525 × 12) paid to the HSA as a deduction *for* AGI. Note that the $6,300 HSA deduction does not exceed the $7,100 annual ceiling.

EXAMPLE 15

---

[20]§ 223(d).
[21]§ 223(f).

[22]§ 223(b)(2). See Rev.Proc. 2019–25 (2019–22 I.R.B. 1261). The annual limits were $3,500 and $7,000 in 2019.

10-1i **Affordable Care Act Provisions**

Information about the tax provisions of the Affordable Care Act can be found in an online appendix to the text.

LO.3

Contrast deductible taxes with nondeductible fees, licenses, and other charges.

10-2 **TAXES**

A deduction is allowed for *certain* state and local taxes paid or accrued by a taxpayer.[23]

10-2a **Deductibility as a Tax**

It is important to understand the difference between a tax and a fee, because fees are not deductible unless incurred as a business expense or as an expense in the production of income. Here is the IRS definition of a tax:

> The word *taxes* has been defined as an enforced contribution, exacted pursuant to legislative authority in the exercise of taxing power, and imposed and collected for the purpose of raising revenue to be used for public or governmental purposes and not as payment for some special privilege granted or service rendered.[24]

As a result, fees for dog licenses, automobile inspections, automobile titles and registration, hunting and fishing licenses, bridge and highway tolls, driver's licenses, parking meter deposits, and postage are not taxes.

Not all taxes are deductible. For example, Federal income taxes are not deductible. Other taxes are not deductible by individuals if they relate to personal activities (rather than business activities). An example is excise taxes included in the cost of purchasing gasoline. Deductible and nondeductible taxes are summarized in Exhibit 10.2.

State and Local Taxes—*For* AGI versus *From* AGI

State and local taxes imposed directly on business or rental or royalty property are deductible *for* AGI. For example, real property taxes imposed on the buildings or personal property taxes imposed on the equipment used by a sole proprietor are deductible as a business expense [*for* AGI; reported on Schedule C (Form 1040)]. Real property taxes imposed on an individual's rental property are also deductible *for* AGI.

In contrast, real property taxes imposed on an individual's personal residence are only deductible if the individual itemizes his or her deductions [i.e., *from* AGI; reported on Schedule A (Form 1040)]. Additionally, real property taxes imposed on investment property (e.g., undeveloped land held for investment) are deductible as an itemized deduction (and not subject to the annual cap on state and local taxes discussed below).

Generally, state and local *income* taxes are considered to be only indirectly imposed on an individual's business and investment activity. Consider a sole proprietor with income who is operating in a state that imposes an income tax. This business owner pays state income taxes on this business income. The calculation of this state income tax, though, depends on other income and deductions of the sole proprietor as well as filing status and tax credits. As a result, the income tax is *not* directly imposed on the sole proprietorship business income (unlike property taxes that *are* directly imposed on the property used by the business). Since the income tax is *not* directly imposed on the business income, the state income tax is only deductible *from* AGI.

Changes made by Congress in 2017 make more relevant the distinction between state and local taxes *directly* imposed on a business versus those taxes *indirectly* imposed, as explained next.[25]

[handwritten note in margin: Cap of $10,000 from AGI except for taxes on Investment Property]

---

[23]Most deductible taxes are listed in § 164, and nondeductible items are included in § 275.

[24]Rev.Rul. 81–191, 1981–2 C.B. 49.

[25]Rev.Rul. 58–25, 1958–1 C.B. 95 and Rev.Rul. 81–288, 1981–2 C.B. 17.

EXHIBIT 10.2	Deductible and Nondeductible Taxes

Deductible	Nondeductible
State, local, and foreign real property taxes	Federal income taxes
	FICA taxes imposed on employees
State and local personal property taxes	Employer FICA taxes paid on domestic household workers
State and local income taxes *or* sales/use taxes	Estate, inheritance, and gift taxes
	Federal, state, and local excise taxes (e.g., gasoline, tobacco, and spirits)
Foreign income taxes	Foreign income taxes if the taxpayer chooses the foreign tax credit option
	Taxes on real property to the extent these taxes are to be apportioned and treated as imposed on another taxpayer

Overall Limit on State and Local Taxes

From 2018 through 2025, the deduction for state and local taxes (including property taxes and either income taxes or sales taxes) is limited to a maximum of $10,000 per year ($5,000 if married filing separately).[26] This limit applies to the taxes deductible *from* AGI that are *not directly imposed* on business and investment activity or property.

> **EXAMPLE 16**
>
> Adam owns and operates a dry cleaning business as a sole proprietorship. During 2020, Adam paid $7,000 of real property taxes on the building used in the business and $1,200 of personal property taxes on the equipment used in the business. In calculating and paying estimated state income taxes of $5,600 for 2020, Adam included the profit from his sole proprietorship, his investment income, and his itemized deductions and claimed a state tax credit for solar panels he installed on his home.
>
> The $8,200 of property taxes imposed on his business ($7,000 + $1,200) is deductible *for* AGI [on Schedule C (Form 1040)], but his state income taxes are deductible *from* AGI [on Schedule A (Form 1040)]. Only the $5,600 of state income taxes is subject to the $10,000 limit on state and local taxes, not the $8,200.
>
> Now assume that in addition to his state income taxes, Adam paid $6,000 of property taxes on his personal residence in 2020. His total state and local taxes are $11,600 ($5,600 + $6,000), and his Federal itemized deduction for state and local taxes is limited to $10,000.

10-2b Property Taxes

LO.4

Explain the Federal income tax treatment of property taxes, state and local income taxes, and sales taxes.

State, local, and foreign taxes on real property are generally deductible only by the person upon whom the tax is imposed. Foreign real property taxes are not deductible from 2018 through 2025 unless the taxes relate to an individual's business or investment property. Deductible personal property taxes must be *ad valorem* (assessed in relation to the value of the property). So a motor vehicle tax based on weight, model, year, and horsepower is not deductible. However, a tax based on value and other criteria will be partially deductible.

---

[26]§ 164(b)(6). Foreign income taxes are also included in this limit. This limitation is sometimes referred to as the "SALT cap." SALT is an acronym for *state and local taxes*.

The Big Picture

EXAMPLE 17

Return to the facts of *The Big Picture* on p. 10-1. Assuming that the Williamsons proceed with the purchase of a home, the real estate taxes they pay will be deductible *from* AGI (subject to the aggregate $10,000 limit) because they qualify to itemize their deductions. They should also review their annual registration statement for their car because a portion of it may represent personal property tax (if based on the value of the car).

For example, assume that in their state, the government imposes a motor vehicle registration tax on 2% of the value of the vehicle plus 40 cents per hundredweight. The Williamsons own a car having a value of $20,000 and weighing 3,000 pounds. They pay an annual registration fee of $412. Of this amount, $400 (2% × $20,000 of value) is deductible as a personal property tax (subject to the aggregate $10,000 annual limit). The remaining $12, based on the weight of the car, is not deductible. Any other amount included in the annual fee (e.g., processing charges) is not a tax.

Assessments for Local Benefits

As a general rule, real property taxes do not include taxes assessed for local benefits if the assessments increase the value of the property (e.g., special assessments for streets, sidewalks, curbing, and other similar improvements).[27] Instead of being deductible, these assessments are added to the basis of the taxpayer's property. Assessments included for personal benefit (e.g., trash removal and tree trimming) are not deductible and do not affect the basis of the property.

Apportionment of Real Property Taxes between Seller and Purchaser

Real estate taxes for the entire year are apportioned between the buyer and seller on the basis of the number of days the property was held by each during the real property tax year. This apportionment is required whether the tax is paid by the buyer or the seller or is prorated according to the purchase agreement. The apportionment determines who is entitled to deduct the real estate taxes in the year of sale. The required apportionment prevents the shifting of the deduction for real estate taxes from the buyer to the seller or vice versa. In making the apportionment, the assessment date and the lien date are disregarded.[28]

EXAMPLE 18

A county's real property tax year runs from January 1 to December 31. Sara, the owner on January 1 of real property located in the county, sells the real property to Bob on June 30. Bob owns the real property from June 30 through December 31. The tax for the real property tax year, January 1 through December 31, is $3,650.

Assuming that this is not a leap year, the portion of the real property tax treated as imposed upon Sara, the seller, is $1,800 [(180/365) × $3,650, January 1 through June 29], and $1,850 of the tax [(185/365) × $3,650, June 30 through December 31] is treated as imposed upon Bob, the buyer.

If the actual real estate taxes are not prorated between the buyer and seller as part of the purchase agreement, adjustments are required. The adjustments are necessary to determine the amount realized by the seller and the basis of the property to the buyer. If the buyer pays the entire amount of the tax, he or she has, in effect, paid the seller's portion of the real estate tax and has therefore paid more for the property than the

[27]Reg. § 1.164–4(a); see *Erie H. Rose*, 31 TCM 142, T.C.Memo. 1972–39, where a taxpayer was denied a deduction for the cost of a new sidewalk in front of his personal residence, even though the construction was required by the city and the sidewalk may have provided an incidental benefit to public welfare.

[28]For most years, the apportionment is based on a 365-day year. However, in a leap year (i.e., a year that is evenly divisible by 4, like 2020), the taxes are prorated over 366 days. In making the apportionment, the date of sale counts as a day the property is owned by the buyer.

actual purchase price. As a result, the amount of real estate tax that is apportioned to the seller (for Federal income tax purposes) and paid by the buyer is added to the buyer's basis. The seller must increase the amount realized on the sale by the same amount.

> **EXAMPLE 19**
>
> Seth sells real estate on October 3 for $400,000. The buyer, Barbara, pays the real estate taxes of $3,650 for the calendar year, which is the real estate property tax year.
>
> Assuming that this is not a leap year, $2,750 (for 275 days) of the real estate taxes is apportioned to and is deductible by the seller, Seth, and $900 (for 90 days) of the taxes is deductible by Barbara.
>
> Barbara has, in effect, paid Seth's real estate taxes of $2,750 and has therefore paid $402,750 for the property. Barbara's basis is increased to $402,750, and the amount realized by Seth from the sale is increased to $402,750.

The opposite result occurs if the seller (rather than the buyer) pays the real estate taxes. In this case, the seller reduces the amount realized from the sale by the amount that has been apportioned to the buyer. The buyer is required to reduce his or her basis by a corresponding amount.

10-2c State and Local Income Taxes and Sales Taxes

The position of the IRS is that state and local income taxes imposed upon an individual are deductible only as itemized deductions, even if the taxpayer's sole source of income is from a business, rents, or royalties.

Cash basis taxpayers are entitled to deduct state income taxes in the year *payment is made*. This includes taxes withheld by the employer, amounts paid with the state income tax return when filed, and estimated state income tax payments.[29] If the taxpayer overpays state income taxes, any refund received is included in gross income in the year received to the extent the deduction reduced taxable income in the prior year. See text Section 5-15 for a discussion of how the tax benefit rule applies to state income tax refunds when the overall $10,000 limit on state and local taxes applied in the prior year.

> **EXAMPLE 20**
>
> Leona, a cash basis, unmarried taxpayer, had $800 of state income tax withheld from her paychecks during 2020. Also in 2020, Leona paid $100 that was due when she filed her 2019 state income tax return and made estimated payments of $300 toward her 2020 state income tax liability. When Leona files her 2020 Federal income tax return in April 2021, she elects to itemize deductions, which amount to $15,500, including the $1,200 of state income tax payments and withholdings, all of which reduce her taxable income.
>
> As a result of overpaying her 2020 state income tax, Leona receives a refund of $200 early in 2021. She will include this amount in her 2021 gross income in computing her Federal income tax. It does not matter whether Leona received a check from the state for $200 or applied the $200 toward her 2021 state income tax.

Individuals can elect to deduct *either* their state and local income taxes *or* their sales/use taxes paid as an itemized deduction. This election is intended to provide equity to taxpayers living in states that do not impose a state income tax (but do have sales taxes). Taxpayers making this election can either deduct actual sales/use tax payments *or* an amount from an IRS table (available on the IRS website). The IRS table amount can be increased by sales tax paid on the purchase of motor vehicles, boats, and other specified items.

---

[29]Rev.Rul. 71–190, 1971–1 C.B. 70. See also Rev.Rul. 82–208, 1982–2 C.B. 58, where a deduction is not allowed when the taxpayer cannot, in good faith, reasonably determine that there is additional state income tax liability.

Schedule A

LO.5

Distinguish between deductible and nondeductible interest and apply the appropriate limitations to deductible interest.

10-3 INTEREST

A deduction for interest has been allowed since the income tax law was enacted in 1913. However, despite its long history, the interest deduction has been a controversial area for tax policy. Should all interest be allowed as a deduction? If not, what limits should apply? Should an interest deduction be allowed for only the taxpayer's principal residence (or all residences)? What about interest on credit cards and student loans? Lawmakers and taxpayers continue to raise these questions (and others).

Personal (consumer) interest is not deductible. This includes credit card interest, interest on car loans, and other types of personal interest. However, interest on qualified student loans, qualified residence (home mortgage) interest, and investment interest are deductible, subject to the limits discussed on the following pages.[30]

10-3a Allowed and Disallowed Items

The Supreme Court has defined *interest* as compensation for the use of money.[31] The general rule permits a deduction for interest paid or accrued within the taxable year on indebtedness.

Interest on Qualified Student Loans

Taxpayers who pay interest on a qualified student loan may be able to deduct the interest as a deduction *for* AGI. The deduction is allowed if the proceeds of the loan are used to pay qualified education expenses. These payments must be made to qualified educational institutions.[32]

The maximum annual deduction for qualified student loan interest is $2,500. However, in 2020, the deduction is phased out for taxpayers with modified AGI (MAGI) between $70,000 and $85,000 ($140,000 and $170,000 on joint returns). The interest expense deduction is phased out by applying the following formula:

If less than 70,000 or $140,000 - you can deduct the full $2,500. If it's over, you get nothing

$$\text{Education interest expense} \times \frac{\text{Modified AGI} - \text{AGI phaseout floor}}{\$15{,}000\ (\$30{,}000\ \text{for married filing jointly})}$$

The deduction is not allowed for taxpayers who are claimed as dependents or for married taxpayers filing separately.[33]

EXAMPLE 21

In 2020, Curt and Rita, who are married and file a joint return, paid $3,000 of interest on a qualified student loan. Their MAGI was $147,500. Their maximum potential deduction for qualified student loan interest is $2,500, but it must be reduced by $625 as a result of the phaseout rules.

$$\$2{,}500\ \text{interest} \times \frac{\$147{,}500\ (\text{MAGI}) - \$140{,}000\ (\text{AGI phaseout floor})}{\$30{,}000\ (\text{phaseout range})} = \$625\ \text{reduction}$$

Curt and Rita are allowed a student loan interest deduction of $1,875 ($2,500 maximum deduction − $625 reduction = $1,875 deduction *for* AGI).

Qualified Residence Interest

From AGI

Qualified residence interest is interest paid or accrued during the taxable year on indebtedness (subject to limitations) *secured* by a qualified residence of the taxpayer. Qualified residence interest falls into two categories: (1) interest on acquisition indebtedness and (2) interest on home equity loans.[34]

---

[30]As discussed in Chapter 6, interest expense paid or incurred in a trade or business is also deductible (§ 162; a *for* AGI deduction).

[31]*Old Colony Railroad Co. v. Comm.*, 3 USTC ¶880, 10 AFTR 786, 52 S.Ct. 211 (USSC, 1932).

[32]See IRS Publication 970, *Tax Benefits for Education*, for details.

[33]§ 221. See § 221(b)(2)(C) for the definition of MAGI. The 2019 MAGI threshold amounts were the same as the 2020 amounts [$70,000 and $85,000 ($140,000 and $170,000 on joint returns)].

[34]§ 163(h)(3)(F).

A *qualified residence* includes the taxpayer's principal residence and one other residence of the taxpayer or spouse. The *principal residence* meets the requirement for non-recognition of gain upon sale under § 121 (see text Section 13-6). The *one other residence*, or second residence, is used as a residence if not rented or, if rented, meets the requirements for a personal residence under the rental of vacation home rules (refer to Chapter 6). A taxpayer who has more than one second residence can choose the qualified second residence each year (i.e., the taxpayer can select a different second residence each year). A residence includes a house, a cooperative apartment, a condominium, and mobile homes and boats that have living quarters (sleeping, bathroom, and cooking facilities).

Although in most cases interest paid on a home mortgage is fully deductible, there are limitations.[35] A deduction is allowed for interest paid or accrued during the tax year on aggregate `acquisition indebtedness`. *Acquisition indebtedness* refers to amounts incurred in acquiring, constructing, or substantially improving the taxpayer's qualified residence that serves as security for that indebtedness. The amount of acquisition indebtedness is limited based on when the debt was incurred. If the debt is incurred after December 15, 2017, and before January 1, 2026, acquisition indebtedness is limited to $750,000 ($375,000 for married taxpayers filing separate returns). Debt incurred on or before December 15, 2017, is limited to $1 million ($500,000 for married taxpayers filing separate returns). These higher debt limits will apply to all homeowners after 2025, regardless of the date of borrowing.

The Big Picture

EXAMPLE 22

Return to the facts of *The Big Picture* on p. 10-1. Given that John and Susan Williamson will need to borrow at least a portion of the purchase price of a new home, a standard mortgage likely will qualify as acquisition indebtedness because the borrowed funds are used to acquire a principal residence. However, the interest on the acquisition indebtedness will be fully deductible only if the amount of the mortgage is $750,000 or less (assuming that John and Susan file a joint return) and the mortgage is secured by the home, which is the typical case.

Recall that the Williamsons are also considering what appears to be a less expensive route of using their retirement and taxable investments to secure the debt. If they choose this alternative, the interest will not be deductible as qualified residence interest because the loan would not be acquisition indebtedness (i.e., the loan would not be secured by the home).

From 2018 through 2025, interest on `home equity loans` is not deductible unless the funds are used to improve the principal residence (and the total acquisition debt and home equity debt is $750,000 or less). Home equity loans utilize the personal residence of the taxpayer as security, typically in the form of a second mortgage. If the funds from home equity loans are used for personal purposes (e.g., auto purchases, vacations, medical expenses), the related interest expense is not deductible.[36]

EXAMPLE 23

Larry owns a personal residence with a fair market value of $600,000 and an outstanding first mortgage of $420,000. Therefore, his equity in his home is $180,000 ($600,000 − $420,000). Larry borrows $75,000 that is secured by a second mortgage on his home to put an addition on his home.

All of Larry's interest is deductible; both loans are secured by his residence, and the total of the loans ($420,000 + $75,000) does not exceed $750,000 or the value of his residence. If Larry used the home equity loan proceeds to buy a new car and boat, the home equity loan interest would not be deductible.

---

[35]§ 163(h)(3).

[36]Interest on home equity loans prior to 2018 was deductible only on the portion of a home equity loan that did not exceed the lesser of (1) the fair market value of the residence reduced by any acquisition indebtedness, or (2) $100,000 ($50,000 for married persons filing separate returns). Proceeds from these home equity loans could be used for any purpose without impairing the interest deductibility. From 2018 through 2025, the treatment of interest expense on an equity debt that was not used to improve the home is determined using the interest tracing rules of Temp.Reg. 1.163–8T and Notice 89–35, 1989–1 C.B. 675.

For tax years prior to 2021, mortgage insurance premiums paid by the taxpayer on a qualified residence are deductible subject to a phaseout based on AGI. The amount allowed is treated as qualified residence interest.[37]

Interest Paid for Services

Mortgage loan companies commonly charge a fee, often called a loan origination fee, for finding, placing, or processing a mortgage loan. Loan origination fees are typically nondeductible amounts included in the basis of the acquired property. Other fees, sometimes called points and expressed as a percentage of the loan amount, are paid to reduce the interest rate charged over the term of the loan. Essentially, the payment of points is a prepayment of interest and is considered compensation to a lender for the use of money.[38]

In general, points are capitalized and are amortized and deductible ratably over the life of the loan. However, the purchaser of a principal residence can deduct qualifying points in the year of payment.[39] This exception also covers points paid to obtain funds for home improvements.

Points paid to *refinance* acquisition indebtedness (i.e., an existing home mortgage) must be capitalized and amortized as an interest deduction over the life of the new loan.[40]

EXAMPLE 24

Sandra purchased her residence many years ago, obtaining a 30-year mortgage at an annual interest rate of 6%. In the current year, Sandra refinances the mortgage to reduce the interest rate to 4%. To obtain the refinancing, she has to pay points of $2,600.

The $2,600, which is considered prepayment of interest, must be capitalized and amortized over the life of the mortgage.

Points paid by the seller for a buyer are, in effect, treated as an adjustment to the price of the residence, and the buyer is treated as having used cash to pay the points that were paid by the seller. A buyer may deduct seller-paid points in the tax year in which they are paid if certain conditions are met.[41]

Prepayment Penalty

When a mortgage or loan is paid off in full in a lump sum before its term (early), the lending institution may require an additional payment (normally, a specific percentage of the loan balance). This is known as a prepayment penalty and is considered to be interest (e.g., personal, qualified residence, or investment) in the year paid. The general rules for deductibility of interest also apply to prepayment penalties.

Investment Interest

Taxpayers sometimes borrow funds to acquire investment assets (e.g., stock). Congress, however, has limited the deductibility of interest on funds borrowed to purchase or hold investment property. The deduction for investment interest expense is limited to the net investment income for the year and is only deductible if the taxpayer itemizes deductions. A complete discussion of investment interest occurs in text Section 11-4.

Tax-Exempt Securities

No deduction is allowed for interest on debt incurred to purchase or hold tax-exempt securities.[42] Refer to text Section 6-3 for further discussion of this topic.

---

[37]§§ 163(h)(3)(E)(i) and (ii). The deduction begins to phase out for taxpayers with AGI in excess of $100,000 ($50,000 for married taxpayers filing separately). The deduction is fully phased out when AGI exceeds $109,000 ($54,500 for married taxpayers filing separately).

[38]Rev.Rul. 69–188, 1969–1 C.B. 54. To be deductible, points must be in the nature of interest and cannot be a form of service charge or payment for specific services.

[39]§ 461(g)(2).

[40]Rev.Rul. 87–22, 1987–1 C.B. 146.

[41]Refer to Revenue Procedure 94–27 for a complete list of these conditions and additional aspects of this arrangement. Rev.Proc. 94–27, 1994–1 C.B. 613.

[42]§ 265(a)(2).

10-3b Restrictions on Deductibility and Timing Considerations

Even if interest expense is deductible (e.g., qualified residence interest), a current deduction still may not be available unless certain additional conditions described below are met.

Taxpayer's Obligation

Allowed interest is deductible if the related debt represents a bona fide obligation of the taxpayer.[43] For interest to be deductible, both the debtor and the creditor must intend for the loan to be repaid. Intent of the parties can be especially crucial between related parties (e.g., family members or a shareholder and a closely held corporation).

In addition, an individual may not deduct interest paid on behalf of another taxpayer. For example, a shareholder may not deduct interest paid by the corporation on his or her behalf.[44] Likewise, a husband may not deduct interest paid on his wife's property if he files a separate return, except in the case of qualified residence interest. If both husband and wife consent in writing, either the husband or the wife may deduct the allowed interest on the principal residence and one other residence.

Time of Deduction

Under the cash method, interest must be paid to secure a deduction. Under the accrual method, interest is deductible ratably over the life of the loan.

On November 1, 2020, Ramon borrows $2,000 to purchase computers for his consulting business. The loan is payable in 90 days at 6% interest. On the due date in late January 2021, Ramon pays the $2,000 note and interest amounting to $30. $P \times R \times T$

Ramon can deduct the accrued portion ($\frac{2}{3} \times \$30 = \$20$) of the interest in 2020 only if he is an accrual basis taxpayer. Otherwise, the entire amount of interest ($30) is deductible in 2021.

EXAMPLE
25

Prepaid Interest

The accrual method treatment must be used by cash basis taxpayers for interest prepayments that extend beyond the end of the taxable year.[45] These payments must be allocated to the tax years to which the interest payments relate. This provision prevents cash basis taxpayers from creating tax deductions before the end of the year by prepaying interest.

10-3c Classification of Interest Expense

Whether interest is deductible *for* AGI or as an itemized deduction (*from* AGI) depends on whether the indebtedness has a business, investment, or personal purpose. If the debt proceeds are used for a business expense (other than performing services as an employee) or for an expense for an activity for the production of rent or royalty income, the interest is deductible *for* AGI. Business expenses appear on Schedule C of Form 1040, and expenses related to rents or royalties are reported on Schedule E.

If the indebtedness produces qualified residence interest, any deduction allowed is taken *from* AGI and is reported on Schedule A of Form 1040 (the taxpayer must itemize deductions to get any benefit). Recall, however, that interest on a limited amount of student loans is a deduction *for* AGI. If the taxpayer is an employee who incurs debt in relation to his or her employment, the interest is considered to be personal, or consumer, interest and is not deductible. Debt proceeds used for personal purposes (e.g., to pay for a vacation or personal credit card bills) produce nondeductible personal interest expense.

See Concept Summary 10.1 for a summary of the interest deduction rules.

---

[43]*Arcade Realty Co.*, 35 T.C. 256 (1960).
[44]*Continental Trust Co.*, 7 B.T.A. 539 (1927).

[45]§ 461(g)(1).

Concept Summary 10.1

Deductibility of Personal, Student Loan, Mortgage, and Investment Interest

Type	Deductible	Comments
Personal (consumer) interest	No	Includes any interest that is not qualified residence interest, qualified student loan interest, investment interest, or business interest. Examples include interest on car loans and credit card debt.*
Qualified student loan interest	Yes	Deduction *for* AGI; subject to limitations.
Qualified residence interest (acquisition indebtedness)	Yes	Deductible as an itemized deduction; limited to indebtedness of $750,000 (up to $1 million if incurred on or before December 15, 2017).
Qualified residence interest (home equity indebtedness)	No	In general, not deductible from 2018 through 2025.* Prior to 2018 and after 2025, deductible as an itemized deduction; limited to indebtedness equal to the lesser of $100,000 or the FMV of residence minus acquisition indebtedness.
Investment interest (*not* related to rental or royalty property)	Yes	Itemized deduction; limited to net investment income for the year; disallowed interest can be carried over to future years (see text Section 11-4).*
Investment interest (related to rental or royalty property)	Yes	Deduction *for* AGI; limited to net investment income for the year; disallowed interest can be carried over to future years (see text Section 11-4).*

*The classification rules for interest expense are provided by Temp.Reg. § 1.163–8T and Notice 89–35, 1989–1 C.B. 675.

LO.6

Recognize charitable contributions and identify their related measurement problems and percentage limitations.

10-4 CHARITABLE CONTRIBUTIONS

Section 170 allows individuals and corporations to deduct contributions made to qualified *domestic* organizations. Contributions to qualified charitable organizations serve certain social welfare needs and thus relieve the government of the cost of providing these needed services to the community.

The charitable contribution provisions are among the most complex in the tax law. To determine the amount deductible as a charitable contribution, several important questions must be answered:

- What constitutes a charitable contribution?
- Was the contribution made to a qualified organization?
- When is the contribution deductible?
- What record-keeping and reporting requirements apply to charitable contributions?
- How is the value of donated property determined?
- What special rules apply to contributions of property that has increased in value?
- What percentage limitations apply to the charitable contribution deduction?
- What rules apply to amounts in excess of percentage limitations (carryovers)?

These questions are addressed in the sections that follow.

10-4a Criteria for a Gift

or cash

A *charitable contribution* is defined as a gift of property made to a qualified organization. The major elements needed to qualify a contribution as a gift are a donative intent, the absence of consideration, and acceptance by the donee. Consequently, the taxpayer has the burden of establishing that the transfer was made from motives of *disinterested generosity* as established by the courts.[46] This test is quite subjective and has led to problems of interpretation (refer to the discussion of gifts in text Section 5-2).

Benefit Received Rule

When a donor derives a tangible benefit from a contribution, he or she cannot deduct the value of the benefit.

---

[46]*Comm. v. Duberstein*, 60–2 USTC ¶9515, 5 AFTR 2d 1626, 80 S.Ct. 1190 (USSC, 1960).

Jacob purchases a ticket at $100 for a special performance of the local symphony (a qualified charity). If the price of a ticket to a symphony concert is normally $35, Jacob is allowed only $65 as a charitable contribution. Even if Jacob does not attend the concert, the deduction is limited to $65.

If, however, Jacob does *not* accept the ticket from the symphony (or returns it prior to the event), he can deduct the full $100.

EXAMPLE
26

Contributions in Exchange for State and Local Tax Credits

Several states provide a state or local tax credit to taxpayers who donate to specified state or local funds or public charities. Primarily due to concerns that state and local governments might expand the availability of these programs to help taxpayers "work around" the $10,000 state and local tax deduction limit, the IRS issued proposed rules limiting the Federal tax benefits of these "contributions." Under these rules, if taxpayers receive a state or local tax credit greater than 15 percent of the payments made, the taxpayers must reduce their charitable contribution deduction by the amount of that credit.[47]

In 2020, Jane, a resident of State G, donated $5,000 to State G's Scholar Program. This donation provides Jane with a 60% state income tax credit [$3,000 ($5,000 × 60%)] that can be used to reduce her overall state income tax liability. By making this contribution, Jane is attempting to convert a state income tax payment (with an overall limit of $10,000 per year) into a charitable contribution (with a 50%-of-AGI limit).

On Jane's 2020 Federal return, she must reduce this charitable contribution by $3,000 because the credit she received was more than 15% of the payment made. As a result, Jane's charitable contribution deduction for this $5,000 donation is reduced to only $2,000 ($5,000 payment − $3,000 state income tax credit).

EXAMPLE
27

Contribution of Services

No deduction is allowed for a contribution of one's services to a qualified charitable organization. However, unreimbursed expenses related to the services rendered may be deductible. For example, the cost of a uniform (without general utility) that is required to be worn while performing services may be deductible. In addition, deductions are permitted for out-of-pocket transportation costs, reasonable expenses for lodging, and the cost of meals while away from home that are incurred in performing the donated services. In lieu of these out-of-pocket costs for an automobile, a standard mileage rate of 14 cents per mile is allowed.[48] The travel expenses are not deductible if the travel involves a significant element of personal pleasure, recreation, or vacation.[49]

Grace, a delegate representing her church in Miami, Florida, travels to a two-day national meeting in Denver, Colorado, in February. After the meeting, Grace spends two weeks at a nearby ski resort.

Under these circumstances, none of the transportation, meals, or lodging is deductible because the travel involved a significant element of personal pleasure, recreation, or vacation.

EXAMPLE
28

Nondeductible Items

In addition to the benefit received rule and the restrictions placed on contributions of services, the following items may *not* be deducted as charitable contributions:

- Dues, fees, or bills paid to country clubs, lodges, fraternal orders, or similar groups.
- Cost of raffle, bingo, or lottery tickets.
- Cost of tuition.
- Payment for the right to purchase tickets for seating at an athletic event in a university stadium.[50]

---

[47]Reg. § 1.170A–1(h)(3). Rev.Proc. 2019–12, 2019-4 I.R.B. 401, allows a *business* making contributions to such funds to treat the portion of the contribution for which a credit is earned as a business expense (§ 162) if the credit applies to a tax imposed directly on the business (e.g., a property tax). In such a situation, the business owner is able to "work around" the $10,000 state and local tax limit to the extent of the credit generated. Generally though, the rule of Rev.Proc. 2019–12 won't apply to state and local credits that reduce an *individual's* state and local income taxes.

Notice 2019–12, 2019–27 I.R.B. 57, allows an individual with state and local taxes below the $10,000 cap to treat the disallowed charitable contribution amount as a state tax deduction (but not to exceed the $10,000 cap).

[48]§ 170(i).

[49]§ 170(j).

[50]§ 170(l). Prior to 2018, 80% of these payments were allowed as a charitable contribution.

- Value of blood given to a blood bank.
- Donations to homeowners associations.
- Gifts to individuals.
- Rental value of property used by a qualified charity.

10-4b Qualified Organizations

To be deductible, a contribution must be made to one of the following organizations:[51]

- A state or possession of the United States (or any subdivision).
- A corporation, trust, community chest, fund, or foundation located in the United States and organized and operated exclusively for religious, charitable, scientific, literary, or educational purposes or for the prevention of cruelty to children or animals.
- A veterans' organization.
- A fraternal organization operating under the lodge system.
- A cemetery company.

It is commonly understood that contributions to a church, synagogue, or other religious organization are allowed. But for less well-known recipients, taxpayers can consult an IRS list of organizations that have applied for and received tax-exempt status under § 501 of the Code.[52]

Gifts made to needy individuals are not deductible (e.g., a needy family or a homeless individual). A deduction is allowed only if the gift is made to a qualified organization.

EXAMPLE 29

Sarah's neighbor is very ill and has been in the hospital for several weeks. Her insurance won't cover all of her medical bills. A neighborhood friend set up a crowdfunding website, allowing people to contribute money to help Sarah's neighbor with her medical bills. Sarah transfers $700 to this crowdfunding campaign.

Sarah may not treat the $700 as a charitable contribution because it is a nondeductible gift [i.e., for the benefit of an individual rather than a charitable (qualified) organization].

ETHICS & EQUITY   An Indirect Route to a Contribution Deduction

In July, a plane crashed into a residential community in Middleboro, destroying and damaging many homes. Chloe's church, a qualified charitable organization, initiated a fund-raising drive to help the Middleboro citizens whose homes had been affected. Chloe donated $50,000 to First Middleboro Church and suggested to the pastor that $25,000 of her contribution should be given to her sister, Rebecca, whose home had suffered extensive damage. The pastor appointed a committee to award funds to needy citizens. The committee solicited applications from the community and awarded Rebecca $15,000. Discuss whether Chloe is justified in deducting $50,000 as a charitable contribution.

10-4c Time of Deduction

A charitable contribution generally is deducted in the year the payment is made. This rule applies to both cash and accrual basis individuals. A contribution is ordinarily deemed to have been made on the delivery of the property to the donee. For example, if a gift of common stock is made to a qualified charitable organization, the gift is considered complete on the day of delivery or mailing. However, if the donor delivers the stock certificate to his or her bank or broker or to the issuing corporation, the gift is considered complete on the date the stock is transferred on the books of the corporation.

A contribution made by check is considered delivered on the date of mailing. Thus, a check mailed on December 31, 2020, is deductible on the taxpayer's 2020 tax return. If the contribution is charged on a credit card, the date the charge is made determines the year of deduction.

---

[51]§ 170(c).

[52]Although this *Cumulative List of Organizations*, IRS Publication 78, may be helpful, not all organizations that qualify are listed in this publication.

The IRS maintains a searchable database at **irs.gov/charities-non-profits/tax-exempt-organization-search**.

10-4d Record-Keeping and Valuation Requirements

Recall that income tax deductions allowed by law are a matter of legislative grace, but a taxpayer still bears the burden of showing that he or she is entitled to claim the deduction. Not surprisingly, the tax law provides specific documentation requirements that must be met to claim a charitable contribution deduction.

Record-Keeping Requirements

In order to claim a charitable contribution deduction, the taxpayer must have appropriate documentation. The specific type of documentation required depends on the amount of the contribution and whether the contribution is made in cash or noncash property.[53] In addition, special rules may apply to gifts of certain types of property (e.g., used cars or boats) where Congress noted taxpayer abuse in the past. In addition, for certain gifts of noncash property, Form 8283 (Noncash Charitable Contributions) must be attached to the taxpayer's return.

The taxpayer must have the required documentation by the date the tax return is filed for the year the contribution is claimed (and no later than the due date, including extensions, of that tax return). Failure to comply with the reporting rules typically results in disallowance of the charitable contribution deduction. In addition, substantial penalties may apply if the taxpayer significantly overvalues any contributed property.

Common documentation and substantiation requirements are summarized in Concept Summary 10.2.

Concept Summary 10.2

Documentation and Substantiation Requirements for Charitable Contributions

Cash gifts	• A deduction is allowed only if the taxpayer has a proper receipt (e.g., a canceled check or written statement from the charity) showing the name of the charitable organization and the date and amount of the contribution.
	• A written statement from the charity is required if a payment is for more than $75 and is partly a contribution and partly for goods or services. The statement must provide an estimate of the value of the goods and services received by the donor.
Noncash gifts (e.g., household items)	• A receipt from the charity must be kept for any gift of property other than money. Clothes or other household items are deductible if they are in "good used condition or better" at the time of the gift.
	• If an item is not in good used condition or better and its value exceeds $500, a deduction is allowed if a "qualified appraisal" is included with the return.
Used cars, boats, or airplanes	• The deduction is generally limited to the amount the charity receives on the sale of the car, boat, or airplane. The taxpayer should obtain a statement from the charity documenting the sales price. Form 1098–C (Contributions of Motor Vehicles, Boats, and Airplanes) must be attached to the return if the taxpayer claims a deduction in excess of $500.
Cash or noncash gifts (including out-of-pocket expenses) of $250 or more	• A contemporaneous written acknowledgment (CWA) from the charity (as well as certain payroll records in the case of gifts made by payroll deductions) is required to deduct a single cash or property contribution of $250 or more. A CWA is also required for a donation of $250 or more of out-of-pocket expenses a donor might incur in providing services to a charity. The CWA must include the amount of money and a description of any other property contributed, whether the charity provided any goods or services in return for the contribution, and a description and estimated value of the goods or services provided. Contemporaneous means that the donor must have the CWA by the earlier of (1) the date the tax return is filed for the year of the donation or (2) the due date (including extensions) for the tax return.
Noncash gifts of more than $500	• Additional substantiation (e.g., how the property was acquired and its basis) is required on the tax return if donated noncash property is valued at more than $500. Qualified appraisals may be required if noncash contributions exceed $5,000 in value.
Antiques, paintings, jewelry, and other "tangible personal property"	• The deduction is equal to the property's appreciated FMV only if the charity puts the property to "a use related to its tax-exempt purpose." Otherwise, the deduction is limited to the property's cost. The taxpayer should obtain a statement from the charity documenting the property's use.

---

[53]The specific documentation thresholds and requirements are provided in § 170(f).

Valuation Requirements

Property donated to a charity is generally valued at fair market value at the time the gift is made. The Code and Regulations give very little guidance on the measurement of the fair market value. Revenue Ruling 68–69 provides this definition:[54] "The fair market value is the price at which the property would change hands between a willing buyer and a willing seller, neither being under any compulsion to buy or sell and both having reasonable knowledge of relevant facts."

Generally, charitable organizations do not provide the fair market value of the donated property. Nevertheless, as noted in Concept Summary 10.2, the taxpayer must obtain written evidence of the donation from the charity and value the donation appropriately.

10-4e Limitations on Charitable Contribution Deduction

The charitable contribution deduction is the total of all donations made during the year, both money and property. However, the charitable contribution deduction is subject to a number of limitations (based on the taxpayer's AGI, the type of property contributed, and the charity receiving the property). In general:

- If the qualifying contributions for the year total 20 percent or less of AGI, they are fully deductible.

- If the qualifying contributions are more than 20 percent of AGI, the deductible amount may be limited to 20 percent, 30 percent, 50 percent, or 60 percent of AGI, depending on the type of property given and the type of organization to which the donation is made.

- In any case, the maximum charitable contribution deduction may not exceed 60 percent of AGI for the tax year.

If a taxpayer's contributions for the year exceed the limitations, the excess contributions may be carried forward and deducted during a five-year carryover period.

To understand the complex rules for computing the amount of a charitable contribution deduction, it is necessary to understand the distinction between ordinary income property and capital gain property. In addition, it is necessary to understand when the various limitations apply. These topics are discussed in the sections that follow.

Ordinary Income Property

Ordinary income property is any property that, if sold, will result in the recognition of ordinary income. The term includes inventory for sale in the taxpayer's trade or business, a work of art created by the donor, and a manuscript prepared by the donor. It also includes, *for purposes of the charitable contribution calculation*, a capital asset held by the donor for a year or less (this is the holding period for short-term capital gain treatment; see text Section 14-4). If a business contributes depreciable property, it is ordinary income property to the extent of any depreciation recapture that would have been recognized had the

---

[54]1968–1 C.B. 80.

property been sold. Ordinary income property also includes personal use and investment assets that have declined in value (i.e., the fair market value is *less than* the taxpayer's basis). Used clothing contributed to the Salvation Army would fit this description.[55]

If ordinary income property is contributed, the deduction is equal to the fair market value of the property less the amount of ordinary income that would have been reported if the property were sold. In most instances, the deduction is limited to the basis of the property to the donor.

EXAMPLE 30

Tim donates stock in White Corporation to a university on May 1, 2020. Tim had purchased the stock for $2,500 on March 3, 2020, and the stock had a value of $3,600 when he made the donation. Because he had not held the property long enough to meet the long-term capital gain requirement, Tim would have recognized a short-term capital gain of $1,100 if he had sold the property.

Because short-term capital gain property is treated as ordinary income property for charitable contribution purposes, Tim's charitable contribution deduction is limited to the property's basis of $2,500 ($3,600 − $1,100).

Assume, instead, that the stock had a fair market value of $2,300 (rather than $3,600) when Tim donated it to the university. Because the fair market value now is less than the basis, the charitable contribution deduction is $2,300.

Capital Gain Property

Capital gain property is any property that would have resulted in the recognition of long-term capital gain or § 1231 gain if the property had been sold by the donor.[56] As a general rule, the deduction for a contribution of capital gain property is equal to the fair market value of the property.

Two common exceptions disallow the deductibility of the appreciation on capital gain property. The first exception relates to the contribution of *tangible personalty*. Tangible personalty is all property that is not realty (land and buildings) and does not include intangible property (e.g., stock or securities). If tangible personalty is contributed to a public charity (e.g., a museum, church, or university) and the property is put to an *unrelated use*, the charitable deduction is limited to the property's basis (rather than its fair market value). The term *unrelated use* means a use that is unrelated to the exempt purpose or function of the charitable organization. For example, artwork donated to the American Red Cross is unlikely to be put to a related use. Instead, the Red Cross would likely sell the art to generate funds that would then be used to support its mission of providing assistance to individuals who have been struck by disasters.

Knowing this, taxpayers usually specify how their contributed property will be used and target donors appropriately (i.e., giving artwork to a museum rather than the Red Cross). As a result, this reduction will not apply if the property is put to a related use or if, at the time of the contribution, it was reasonable to anticipate that the property would not be put to an unrelated use by the donee.[57]

EXAMPLE 31

Emma contributes a Picasso painting, for which she paid $20,000, to a local museum. She had owned the painting for four years. It had a value of $30,000 at the time of the donation. The museum displays the painting for five years and subsequently sells it for $50,000.

The charitable contribution is $30,000. It is not reduced by the unrealized appreciation because the painting is not put to an unrelated use even though it is later sold by the museum.

The second exception relates to certain private foundations. Private foundations are organizations that traditionally do not receive their funding from the general public (e.g., the Bill and Melinda Gates Foundation). Generally, foundations fall into two categories: operating and nonoperating. A private *operating* foundation spends substantially all of its income in the active conduct of its charitable purposes. Other private foundations are

---

[55]Depreciation recapture rules are discussed in Chapter 14. For a more complete discussion of the difference between ordinary income and capital gain property, see Chapter 14.

[56]See text Section 14-4 for a discussion of holding periods.
[57]§ 170(e)(1)(B)(i) and Reg. § 1.170A–4(b)(3)(ii)(b).

nonoperating foundations. Often, only the private foundation knows its status (operating or nonoperating) for sure, and the status can change from year to year.

If capital gain property is contributed to a private *nonoperating* foundation, the taxpayer must reduce the contribution by the long-term capital gain that would have been recognized if the property had been sold at its fair market value. The effect of this provision is to limit the deduction to the property's basis.[58]

EXAMPLE 32

Ten years ago, Walter purchased land for $8,000 and has held it as an investment since then. This year, when the land is worth $20,000, he donates it to a private *nonoperating* foundation. Walter's charitable contribution is $8,000 ($20,000 − $12,000), the land's basis.

If, instead, Walter had donated the land to either a public charity or a private *operating* foundation, his charitable contribution would have been $20,000, the fair market value of the land.

Fifty Percent Ceiling

Contributions made to public charities may not exceed 50 percent of an individual's AGI for the year. Given that this ceiling is quite high, most taxpayers making contributions never have their charitable contributions limited. The 50 percent ceiling on contributions applies to public charities (e.g., churches; schools; hospitals; and Federal, state, or local governmental units). The 50 percent ceiling also applies to contributions to private operating foundations and certain private nonoperating foundations.

In the remaining discussion of charitable contributions, public charities and private foundations (both operating and nonoperating) that qualify for the 50 percent ceiling will be referred to as *50 percent organizations.*

EXAMPLE 33

During the year, Tom and Emma Waters contribute $8,000 to their church, donate $500 to the Salvation Army, and give used clothes to Goodwill Industries (cost of $1,000; fair market value of $200). The clothes are ordinary income property, and the charitable contribution deduction is limited to the fair market value. Their AGI for the year is $125,000.

Tom and Emma's charitable contribution deduction is $8,700 ($8,000 + $500 + $200). Their charitable contribution deduction is not limited, since $8,700 is less than 50% of their AGI ($62,500; $125,000 × 50%).

Temporary Sixty Percent Ceiling

From 2018 through 2025, the deduction limit for *cash donations* to 50 percent organizations is 60 percent of AGI (rather than 50 percent of AGI). Congress was concerned that the combination of the increased standard deduction and the scaling back of many individual itemized deductions during this period would reduce the tax incentive to make charitable contributions. Most policy organizations believe that the increased ceiling will have little, if any, effect on the expected decline in individual donations to charities.

Thirty Percent Ceiling

A 30 percent ceiling applies to contributions of cash and ordinary income property to private nonoperating foundations that are not 50 percent organizations. The 30 percent ceiling also applies to contributions of appreciated capital gain property to 50 percent organizations.[59]

---

[58]§ 170(e)(1)(B)(ii).

[59]Under a special election, a taxpayer may choose to permanently forgo a deduction of the appreciation on capital gain property. Referred to as the reduced deduction election, this enables the taxpayer to move from the 30% limitation to the 50% limitation. See § 170(b)(1)(C)(iii).

In the event the contributions for any one tax year involve both 50 percent and 30 percent property, the allowable deduction comes first from the 50 percent property.

During the year, Lisa makes the following donations to her church: cash of $2,000 and unimproved land worth $30,000. Lisa had purchased the land four years ago for $22,000 and held it as an investment. Therefore, it is capital gain property. Lisa's AGI for the year is $60,000. Disregarding percentage limitations, Lisa's potential deduction is $32,000 [$2,000 (cash) + $30,000 (fair market value of land)].

In applying the percentage limitations, however, the *current* deduction for the land is limited to $18,000 [30% (limitation applicable to capital gain property) × $60,000 (AGI)]. Thus, the total current deduction is $20,000 ($2,000 cash + $18,000 land). Note that the total deduction does not exceed $30,000, which is 50% of Lisa's AGI.

EXAMPLE 34

Twenty Percent Ceiling

A 20 percent ceiling applies to contributions of appreciated capital gain property to private nonoperating foundations that are not 50 percent organizations.

Concept Summary 10.3 summarizes limitations on the deductibility of charitable gifts.

Concept Summary 10.3

Determining the Deduction for Contributions of Appreciated Property by Individuals

If the Type of Property Contributed Is:	And the Property Is Contributed to:	The Contribution Is Measured by:	But the Deduction Is Limited to:
1. Capital gain property (see Example 34)	A 50% organization	Fair market value of the property	30% of AGI
2. Ordinary income property (see Example 30)	A 50% organization	The basis of the property*	50% of AGI
3. Capital gain property (and the property is tangible personal property put to an unrelated use by the donee; see Example 31)	A 50% organization	The basis of the property*	50% of AGI
4. Capital gain property (see Example 32)	A private nonoperating foundation that is not a 50% organization	The basis of the property*	The lesser of: 1. 20% of AGI 2. 50% of AGI minus other contributions to 50% organizations
5. Cash	A 50% organization	Amount of cash	60% of AGI

*If the fair market value of the property is less than the basis (i.e., the property has declined in value instead of appreciating), the fair market value is used.

Contribution Carryovers

Contributions that exceed the percentage limitations for the current year can be carried over for five years. In the carryover process, these contributions do not lose their identity for limitation purposes. Thus, if the contribution originally involved 30 percent property, the carryover will continue to be classified as 30 percent property in the carryover year.

Assume the same facts as in Example 34. Because only $18,000 of the $30,000 value of the land is deducted in the current year, the balance of $12,000 may be carried over to the following year. But the carryover will still be treated as capital gain property and is subject to the 30%-of-AGI limitation in the carryover year.

EXAMPLE 35

In applying the percentage limitations, current charitable contributions must be claimed first before any carryovers can be considered. If carryovers involve more than one year, they are utilized in a first-in, first-out order.

10-5 TIMING OF PAYMENTS TO MAXIMIZE DEDUCTIONS

Because an individual may use the standard deduction in one year and itemize deductions in another year, maximum benefits can be obtained by shifting itemized deductions from one year to another. For example, if a taxpayer's itemized deductions and the standard deduction are approximately the same for each year of a two-year period, the taxpayer should use the standard deduction in one year and shift itemized deductions (to the extent permitted by law) to the other year. The individual could, for example, prepay a church pledge for a particular year to shift the deduction to the current year or avoid paying end-of-the-year medical expenses to shift the deduction to the following year.

It is sometimes possible to defer or accelerate the payment of certain deductible items (e.g., state taxes and charitable contributions) to maximize deductions when itemized deductions are close to the standard deduction. For instance, the final installment of estimated state income tax is generally due in mid-January (after the end of a given tax year). Accelerating the payment of the final installment to December could result in larger itemized deductions for the current year.

Timing to Maximize Deductions

EXAMPLE 36

Jenny, who is single, expects to have itemized deductions of $11,200 in 2020 and $8,000 in 2021. She needs to pay $1,900 as the final installment on her 2020 estimated state income tax, which is due on January 15, 2021. The standard deduction for 2020 is $12,400 for single taxpayers. If Jenny pays the final installment of her 2020 state taxes in 2020, she increases her itemized deductions. If instead she pays it in January 2021 when she knows she will be claiming the standard deduction in 2021, she obtains no tax benefit for that payment.

As a result, making the final installment payment in 2020 is good tax planning. If Jenny pays the final installment in December 2020, and assuming that her state and local tax deduction is not limited, her itemized deductions will be $13,100 ($11,200 + $1,900) in 2020 and she will benefit from itemizing.

EXAMPLE 37

Juan and Lisa Green are married and file a joint tax return. Their state income and real estate taxes are greater than $10,000 each year. They do not have a mortgage, and their health insurance typically covers all of their medical expenses. They usually make charitable contributions of about $10,000 each year. With these facts, the Greens will claim the standard deduction ($24,800 in 2020) rather than itemize their deductions.

If the Greens change the timing of their charitable contributions to make them every other year (or every third year), they can increase their deductions over that period of time. For example, if they opt to make no charitable contributions in 2020, they will claim the $24,800 standard deduction. If in 2021 they make $20,000 of charitable contributions, representing what they otherwise would have contributed in 2020 and 2021, they will claim itemized deductions of $30,000 (which will likely exceed their 2021 standard deduction). They can repeat this pattern to maximize their *from AGI* deductions over time.

10-6 **OTHER ITEMIZED DEDUCTIONS**

LO.7

List the expenses that are deductible as other itemized deductions.

In general, no deduction is allowed for personal, living, or family expenses.[60] However, a number of other expenses and losses are allowed as itemized deductions on Schedule A (Form 1040):

- Gambling losses up to the amount of gambling winnings.
- Impairment-related work expenses of a handicapped person.
- Federal estate tax on income in respect of a decedent.
- Deduction for repayment of amounts under a claim of right (but only if more than $3,000; discussed in text Section 16-1).
- The unrecovered investment in an annuity contract when the annuity ceases by reason of death, discussed in text Section 4-4.

Prior to 2018, certain other personal expenses were deductible to the extent, in total, they exceeded 2 percent of the taxpayer's AGI (and only if the taxpayer itemized deductions instead of claiming the standard deduction). These ==miscellaneous itemized deductions== included unreimbursed employee business expenses, certain investment expenses, tax return preparation fees (other than for portions of the return related to business), and expenses related to hobby income (refer to text Section 6-3). From 2018 through 2025, these expenses are not deductible.

10-7 **COMPREHENSIVE EXAMPLE OF SCHEDULE A**

Jean Brown is single and had the following transactions for 2019:

Medicines that required a prescription	$ 830
Doctor and dentist bills paid and not reimbursed	3,120
Medical insurance premium payments	9,200
Contact lenses	370
Transportation for medical purposes on March 1, 2019 (310 miles × 20 cents/mile + $10.00 parking)	72
State income tax withheld (This amount exceeds the sales tax from the sales tax table.)	7,900
Real estate taxes	6,580
Interest paid on qualified residence mortgage (acquisition indebtedness)	4,340
Qualifying charitable contributions paid by check; proper documentation exists	2,160
Transportation in performing charitable services (800 miles × 14 cents/mile + $7.00 parking and tolls)	119
Unreimbursed employee expenses	1,870
Tax return preparation	450
Safe deposit box (used for keeping investment documents and tax records)	170

Jean's AGI is $120,000. The total of her itemized deductions is $21,211 (see the completed 2019 Schedule A on the following page). This amount is greater than her standard deduction of $12,400.[61]

---

[60]§ 262.

[61]Jean's unreimbursed employee expenses, tax return preparation fee, and safe deposit box rental cost are miscellaneous itemized deductions. From

2018 through 2025, the deduction for these items has been suspended. In 2017, the total of these expenses ($2,490) would have been deductible to the extent they exceeded 2% of Jean's AGI.

SCHEDULE A
(Form 1040 or 1040-SR)
(Rev. January 2020)
Department of the Treasury
Internal Revenue Service (99)

Itemized Deductions

▶ Go to *www.irs.gov/ScheduleA* for instructions and the latest information.
▶ Attach to Form 1040 or 1040-SR.

Caution: If you are claiming a net qualified disaster loss on Form 4684, see the instructions for line 16.

OMB No. 1545-0074

2019

Attachment
Sequence No. **07**

Name(s) shown on Form 1040 or 1040-SR
Jean Brown

Your social security number
123-45-6789

Medical and Dental Expenses	**Caution:** Do not include expenses reimbursed or paid by others.		
	1 Medical and dental expenses (see instructions)	**1** 13,592	
	2 Enter amount from Form 1040 or 1040-SR, line 8b **2** 120,000		
	3 Multiply line 2 by 7.5% (0.075)	**3** 9,000	
	4 Subtract line 3 from line 1. If line 3 is more than line 1, enter -0-	**4**	4,592
Taxes You Paid	5 State and local taxes.		
	a State and local income taxes or general sales taxes. You may include either income taxes or general sales taxes on line 5a, but not both. If you elect to include general sales taxes instead of income taxes, check this box ▶ ☐	**5a** 7,900	
	b State and local real estate taxes (see instructions)	**5b** 6,580	
	c State and local personal property taxes	**5c**	
	d Add lines 5a through 5c	**5d** 14,480	
	e Enter the smaller of line 5d or $10,000 ($5,000 if married filing separately)	**5e** 10,000	
	6 Other taxes. List type and amount ▶ _____	**6**	
	7 Add lines 5e and 6	**7**	10,000
Interest You Paid **Caution:** Your mortgage interest deduction may be limited (see instructions).	8 Home mortgage interest and points. If you didn't use all of your home mortgage loan(s) to buy, build, or improve your home, see instructions and check this box ▶ ☐		
	a Home mortgage interest and points reported to you on Form 1098. See instructions if limited	**8a** 4,340	
	b Home mortgage interest not reported to you on Form 1098. See instructions if limited. If paid to the person from whom you bought the home, see instructions and show that person's name, identifying no., and address ▶ _____	**8b**	
	c Points not reported to you on Form 1098. See instructions for special rules	**8c**	
	d Mortgage insurance premiums (see instructions)	**8d**	
	e Add lines 8a through 8d	**8e**	
	9 Investment interest. Attach Form 4952 if required. See instructions	**9**	
	10 Add lines 8e and 9	**10**	4,340
Gifts to Charity **Caution:** If you made a gift and got a benefit for it, see instructions.	11 Gifts by cash or check. If you made any gift of $250 or more, see instructions	**11** 2,160	
	12 Other than by cash or check. If you made any gift of $250 or more, see instructions. You **must** attach Form 8283 if over $500.	**12** 119	
	13 Carryover from prior year	**13**	
	14 Add lines 11 through 13	**14**	2,279
Casualty and Theft Losses	15 Casualty and theft loss(es) from a federally declared disaster (other than net qualified disaster losses). Attach Form 4684 and enter the amount from line 18 of that form. See instructions	**15**	
Other Itemized Deductions	16 Other—from list in instructions. List type and amount ▶ _____	**16**	
Total Itemized Deductions	17 Add the amounts in the far right column for lines 4 through 16. Also, enter this amount on Form 1040 or 1040-SR, line 9	**17**	21,211
	18 If you elect to itemize deductions even though they are less than your standard deduction, check this box ▶ ☐		

For Paperwork Reduction Act Notice, see the Instructions for Forms 1040 and 1040-SR.   Cat. No. 17145C   Schedule A (Form 1040 or 1040-SR) 2019

10-8 **TAX PLANNING**

LO.8

Identify tax planning strategies that can maximize the benefit of itemized deductions.

10-8a **Maximizing the Medical Deduction**

When a taxpayer anticipates that medical expenses will be close to the percentage floor for a year, the taxpayer should consider accelerating other medical expenses into the year. Any of the following techniques can help build a deduction by the end of the year:

- Incur the obligation for needed dental work or have needed work carried out.[62]
- Have elective remedial surgery that may have been postponed from prior years.
- Incur the obligation for capital improvements to the taxpayer's personal residence recommended by a physician (e.g., an air filtration system to alleviate a respiratory disorder).

The use of credit cards is deemed to be payment for purposes of timing the deductibility of charitable and medical expenses.

On December 13, 2020, Mary (a calendar year taxpayer) purchases two pairs of prescription contact lenses and one pair of prescribed orthopedic shoes for a total of $850. These purchases are charged separately to Mary's credit card. On January 6, 2021, Mary receives her statement containing these charges and makes payment shortly thereafter.

The purchases are deductible as medical expenses in the year charged (2020) rather than in the year the account is settled (2021).

EXAMPLE 38

Recognizing which expenses qualify for the medical deduction also may be crucial to exceeding the percentage limitations.

Ethan employs Leah (an unrelated party) to care for his incapacitated and dependent mother. Leah is not a trained nurse but spends approximately one-half of the time performing nursing duties (e.g., administering injections and providing physical therapy) and the rest of the time doing household chores. An allocable portion of Leah's wages that Ethan pays (including the employer's portion of FICA taxes) qualifies as a medical expense.

EXAMPLE 39

10-8b **Ensuring the Charitable Contribution Deduction**

For a charitable contribution deduction to be available, the recipient must be a qualified charitable organization. Sometimes the mechanics of how the contribution is carried out can determine whether a deduction results.

Fumiko wants to donate $5,000 to her church's mission in Kobe, Japan. In this regard, she considers three alternatives:

1. Send the money directly to the mission.
2. Give the money to her church in Charlotte with the understanding that it is to be passed on to the mission.
3. Give the money directly to the missionary in charge of the mission who is currently in the United States on a fund-raising trip.

If Fumiko wants to obtain a deduction for the contribution, she should choose alternative 2. A direct donation to the mission (alternative 1) is not deductible because the mission is a foreign charity. A direct gift to the missionary (alternative 3) does not comply because an individual cannot be a qualified charity for income tax purposes.[63]

EXAMPLE 40

---

[62]Prepayment of medical expenses does not generate a current deduction unless the taxpayer is under an obligation to make the payment.

[63]*Thomas E. Lesslie*, 36 TCM 495, T.C.Memo. 1977–111.

When making noncash donations, the type of property chosen can have significant implications in determining the amount, if any, of the deduction.

Sam wants to give $60,000 in value to his church in some form other than cash. In this connection, he considers four alternatives:

1. Stock held for two years as an investment with a basis of $100,000 and a fair market value of $60,000.
2. Stock held for five years as an investment with a basis of $10,000 and a fair market value of $60,000.
3. The rent-free use for a year of a building that normally leases for $5,000 a month.
4. A valuable stamp collection held as an investment and owned for 10 years with a basis of $10,000 and a fair market value of $60,000. The church plans to sell the collection if and when it is donated.

Alternative 1 is ill-advised as the subject of the gift. Even though Sam would obtain a deduction of $60,000, he would forgo the potential loss of $40,000 that would be recognized if the property were sold.[64]

Alternative 2 makes good sense because the deduction still is $60,000 and none of the $50,000 of appreciation that has occurred must be recognized as income.

Alternative 3 yields no deduction at all and is not a wise choice.

Alternative 4 involves tangible personalty that the recipient does not plan to use. As a result, the amount of the deduction is limited to $10,000, the stamp collection's basis.[65]

For property transfers (particularly real estate), the ceiling limitations on the amount of the deduction allowed in any one year (50 percent, 30 percent, or 20 percent of AGI, as the case may be) could be a factor to take into account. With proper planning, donations can be controlled to stay within the limitations and avoid the need for a carryover of unused charitable contributions.

Andrew wants to donate to Eastern University (a qualified charitable organization) a tract of unimproved land held as an investment. The land has been held for six years and has a current fair market value of $300,000 and a basis to Andrew of $50,000. Andrew's AGI for the current year is estimated to be $200,000, and he expects much the same for the next few years. In the current year, he deeds (transfers) an undivided one-fifth interest in the real estate to the university.

What has Andrew in Example 42 accomplished for income tax purposes? In the current year, he will be allowed a charitable contribution deduction of $60,000 ($\frac{1}{5} \times \$300,000$), which will be within the applicable AGI limitation ($30\% \times \$200,000$). Presuming no other charitable contributions for the year, Andrew has avoided the possibility of a carryover. In future years, Andrew can follow the same pattern. The only difficulty with this approach is the need to revalue the real estate each year before the donation, because the amount of the deduction is based on the fair market value of the interest contributed at the time of the donation.

The rules on documenting charitable contributions are crucial to the deduction. Thus, it is important for individuals who itemize their deductions to have and retain this documentation.

Karen made several charitable contributions this year. She wrote 10 checks of $500 each to different charitable organizations. In addition, she donated some of her furniture with an estimated value of $1,200.

Karen may only claim the $5,000 of cash donations if she has the canceled checks (or other proof of payment). In addition, because each donation was $250 or more, she must have a contemporaneous written acknowledgment from the charity before she files her return.

continued

---

[64]*LaVar M. Withers*, 69 T.C. 900 (1978).

[65]No reduction of appreciation is necessary in alternative 2 because stock is intangible property and not tangible personalty.

Because Karen donated noncash items valued at over $500, she must complete a Form 8283, documenting the date each item was acquired, how it was acquired, the basis (generally, cost) and fair market value of each item, and how that value was determined. A contemporaneous written acknowledgment is also required for these items (since the donation was valued at $250 or more).

Karen can only claim a charitable contribution deduction for those items for which she has the required documentation.

10-8c Planning to Avoid Nondeductible Treatment

Many personal expenditures are not deductible (e.g., tax return preparation fees and unreimbursed employee business expenses). Consideration should be given to whether any of these nondeductible items can become deductible with planning and knowledge of the tax law. For example, if an individual has a sole proprietor business, the tax return preparation fees can be split between the nondeductible personal portion and the deductible portion related to the business and reported on Schedule C (Form 1040).[66]

Employees who must incur expenses for work (e.g., continuing education classes and uniform cleaning) should encourage their employer to reimburse them for these expenses. If the employer establishes an accountable plan, the expenses are deductible by the employer and not treated as income to the employee.[67]

REFOCUS ON THE BIG PICTURE

IMPACT OF ITEMIZED DEDUCTIONS ON MAJOR PURCHASES

Because the Federal tax law provides that qualified residence interest and real estate taxes are deductible by individual taxpayers, the after-tax cost of a home purchase will be reduced by the tax savings associated with these itemized tax deductions (see Example 1). Given the Williamsons' projected taxable income, they are in the 24 percent Federal income tax bracket and the 6 percent state income tax bracket (i.e., aggregate marginal tax bracket of 30 percent). As a result, the after-tax cost of financing the purchase of the home will be:

Nondeductible principal payments	$ 2,000
Deductible qualified residence interest and real estate taxes	
[($37,000 + $4,000) × (1 − 0.30)]	28,700
Total	$30,700
After-tax monthly cost ($30,700 ÷ 12)	$ 2,558

Because the Williamsons will be able to itemize their deductions if they purchase a new home and will be able to deduct most of their monthly house payment, the home purchase will be affordable (see Examples 17 and 22).

What If?

What if the Williamsons use the less expensive route to finance the purchase of their home by using their retirement and taxable portfolio as security for the loan? What may at first appear to be a cost-effective approach ends up being more costly when considering the impact of the tax law. With this approach, the interest expense is not deductible because it is not qualified residence interest (see Example 22); further, it is not deductible as investment interest (see text Section 11-4). Therefore, the after-tax cost of financing the home using this approach makes the home more expensive, and perhaps unaffordable, for the Williamsons.

Nondeductible principal and interest payments ($2,000 + $35,000)	$37,000
Deductible real estate taxes [$4,000 × (1 − 0.30)]	2,800
Total	$39,800
After-tax monthly cost ($39,800 ÷ 12)	$ 3,317

---

[66]Rev.Rul. 92–29, 1992–1 C.B. 20.   [67]Reg. § 1.62–2.

Key Terms

Acquisition indebtedness, 10-15

Capital gain property, 10-23

Charitable contribution, 10-18

Health Savings Account (HSA), 10-8

Home equity loans, 10-15

Medical expense, 10-3

Miscellaneous itemized deductions, 10-27

Ordinary income property, 10-22

Points, 10-16

Qualified residence interest, 10-14

Discussion Questions

1. **LO.1, 2** Dan, a self-employed individual taxpayer, prepared his own income tax return for the past year and has asked you to check it for accuracy. Your review indicates that Dan failed to claim certain business meals expenses. Will the correction of this omission affect the amount of medical expenses Dan can deduct? Explain.

2. **LO.2** Joe was in an accident and required cosmetic surgery for injuries to his nose. He also had the doctor do additional surgery to reshape his chin, which had not been injured. Will the cosmetic surgery to Joe's nose qualify as a medical expense? Will the cosmetic surgery to Joe's chin qualify as a medical expense? Explain.

3. **LO.2, 8** Jerry and Ernie are comparing their tax situations. Both are paying all of the nursing home expenses of their parents. Jerry can include the expenses in computing his medical expense deduction, but Ernie cannot. What explanation can you offer for the difference?

Critical Thinking   4. **LO.2** Cheryl incurred $8,700 of medical expenses in November 2020. On December 5, the clinic where she was treated mailed her the insurance claim form it had prepared for her with a suggestion that she sign and return the form immediately to receive her reimbursement from the insurance company by December 31. What tax issues should Cheryl consider in deciding whether to sign and return the form in December 2020 or January 2021?

5. **LO.2** David, a sole proprietor of a bookstore, pays a $7,500 premium for medical insurance for him and his family. Joan, an employee of a small firm that doesn't provide her with medical insurance, pays medical insurance premiums of $8,000 for herself. How does the tax treatment differ for David and Joan?

6. **LO.2** Jayden, a calendar year taxpayer, paid $16,000 in medical expenses and sustained a $20,000 casualty loss in 2020 (the loss occurred in a Federally declared disaster area). He expects $12,000 of the medical expenses and $14,000 of the casualty loss to be reimbursed by insurance companies in 2021. Before considering any limitations on these deductions, how much can Jayden include in determining his itemized deductions for 2020?

7. **LO.2** Jacob, a self-employed taxpayer, is married and has two children. He has asked you to explain the tax and nontax advantages of creating a Health Savings Account (HSA) for him and his family.

Decision Making   8. **LO.5, 8** Diane owns a principal residence in Georgia, a townhouse in San Francisco, and a yacht in Cape Cod. All of the properties have mortgages on which
Critical Thinking   Diane pays interest. What are the limitations on Diane's mortgage interest deduction? What strategy should Diane consider to maximize her mortgage interest deduction?

9. **LO.5, 8** Mason Gregg's car was destroyed by a flood that occurred in a Federally   Critical Thinking
declared disaster area. Unfortunately, his insurance had lapsed two days before he incurred the loss. Mason uses his car for both business and personal use. Mason, who is self-employed, does not have adequate savings to replace the car and must borrow money to purchase a new car. He is considering using his credit card, at a 12% interest rate, to obtain funds for the purchase. Margaret, his wife, would prefer to sell some of their stock in Bluebird, Inc., to raise funds to purchase the new car. Mason does not want to sell the stock because it has declined in value since they purchased it and he is convinced that its price will increase in the next two years. Mason has suggested that they obtain conventional financing for the purchase from their bank, which charges 7% interest on car loans. Identify the tax issues related to each of the three alternatives Mason and Margaret are considering.

10. **LO.5** Commercial Bank has initiated an advertising campaign that encourages customers to take out loans secured by their home to pay for purchases of automobiles. Are there any tax advantages related to this type of borrowing? Explain.

11. **LO.5** Thomas purchased a personal residence from Rachel. To sell the residence, Rachel agreed to pay $5,500 in points related to Thomas's mortgage. Discuss the deductibility of the points.

12. **LO.6** The city of Lawrence recently was hit by a tornado, leaving many families in need of food, clothing, shelter, and other necessities. Betty contributed $500 to a family whose home was completely destroyed by the tornado. Jack contributed $700 to the family's church, which gave the money to the family. Discuss the deductibility of these contributions.

13. **LO.6** Mike purchased four $100 tickets to a fund-raising dinner and dance sponsored by the public library, a qualified charitable organization. In its advertising for the event, the library indicated that the cost of the tickets would be deductible for Federal income tax purposes. Comment on the library's assertion.

14. **LO.6, 8** William, a high school teacher, earns about $50,000 each year. In December   Critical Thinking
2020, he won $1,000,000 in the state lottery. William plans to donate $100,000 to his church. He has asked you, his tax adviser, whether he should donate the $100,000 in 2020 or 2021. Identify the tax issues related to William's decision.

Computational Exercises

15. **LO.2** Barbara incurred the following expenses during 2020: $840 dues at a health club she joined at the suggestion of her physician to improve her general physical condition, $240 for multiple vitamins and antioxidant vitamins, $3,500 for a smoking cessation program, $250 for nonprescription nicotine gum, $2,600 for insulin, and $7,200 for funeral expenses for her mother who passed away in June. Barbara's AGI for 2020 is $54,000. What is Barbara's medical expense deduction for 2020?

16. **LO.3, 4** Tabitha sells real estate on March 2 for $260,000. The buyer, Ramona, pays the real estate taxes of $5,200 for the calendar year, which is the real estate property tax year. Assume that this is *not* a leap year.
    a. Determine the real estate taxes apportioned to and deductible by the seller, Tabitha, and the amount of taxes deductible by Ramona.
    b. Calculate Ramona's basis in the property and the amount realized by Tabitha from the sale.

17. **LO.4** Pierre, a cash basis, unmarried taxpayer, had $1,400 of state income tax withheld during 2020. Also in 2020, Pierre paid $455 that was due when he filed his 2019 state income tax return and made estimated payments of $975 toward his 2020 state income tax liability. When Pierre files his 2020 Federal income tax return in April 2021, he elects to itemize deductions, which amount to $15,650, including the state income tax payments and withholdings, all of which reduce his taxable income.

   a. What is Pierre's 2020 state income tax deduction?

   b. As a result of overpaying his 2020 state income tax, Pierre receives a refund of $630 early in 2021. The standard deduction for single taxpayers for 2020 was $12,400. How much of the $630 will Pierre include in his 2021 gross income?

18. **LO.4** Derek, a cash basis, unmarried taxpayer, had $610 of state income tax withheld during 2020. Also in 2020, Derek paid $50 that was due when he filed his 2019 state income tax return and made estimated payments of $100 toward his 2020 state income tax liability. When Derek files his 2020 Federal income tax return in April 2021, he elects to take the standard deduction, which reduced his taxable income. As a result of overpaying his 2020 state income tax, Derek receives a refund of $435 early in 2021. How much of the $435 will Derek include in his 2021 gross income?

19. **LO.5** Miller owns a personal residence with a fair market value of $195,000 and an outstanding first mortgage of $157,500, which was used entirely to acquire the residence. This year, Miller gets a home equity loan of $10,000 to purchase a new fishing boat. How much of this mortgage debt is treated as qualified residence indebtedness?

20. **LO.6** Donna donates stock in Chipper Corporation to the American Red Cross on September 10, 2020. She purchased the stock for $18,100 on December 28, 2019, and it had a fair market value of $27,000 when she made the donation.

   a. What is Donna's charitable contribution deduction?

   b. Assume instead that the stock had a fair market value of $15,000 (rather than $27,000) when it was donated to the American Red Cross. What is Donna's charitable contribution deduction?

21. **LO. 5, 8** The Wilmoths plan to purchase a house but want to determine the after-tax cost of financing its purchase. Given their projected taxable income, the Wilmoths are in the 24% Federal income tax bracket and the 8% state income tax bracket (i.e., an aggregate marginal tax bracket of 32%). Assume that the Wilmoths will benefit from itemizing their deductions for both Federal and state purposes. The total cash outlay during the first year of ownership will be $23,400 ($1,200 principal payments, $22,200 qualified residence interest payments). Determine the initial year after-tax cost of financing the purchase of the home.

Problems

Communications   22. **LO.2** Emma Doyle is employed as a corporate attorney. For calendar year 2020, she had AGI of $75,000 and paid the following medical expenses:

Medical insurance premiums	$3,700
Doctor and dentist bills for Bob and April (Emma's parents)	6,800
Doctor and dentist bills for Emma	5,200
Prescription medicines for Emma	400
Nonprescription insulin for Emma	350

Bob and April would qualify as Emma's dependents except that they file a joint return. Emma's medical insurance policy does not cover them. Emma filed a claim for reimbursement of $2,800 of her own expenses with her insurance company in

December 2020 and received the reimbursement in January 2021. What is Emma's maximum allowable medical expense deduction for 2020? Prepare a memo for your firm's tax files in which you document your conclusions.

23. **LO.2** Reba is a single taxpayer. Lawrence, Reba's 84-year-old dependent grandfather, lived with Reba until this year, when he moved to Lakeside Nursing Home because he needs specialized medical and nursing care. During the year, Reba made the following payments on behalf of Lawrence:

Room at Lakeside	$11,000
Meals for Lawrence at Lakeside	2,200
Doctor and nurse fees at Lakeside	1,700
Cable TV service for Lawrence's room at Lakeside	380
Total	$15,280

Lakeside has medical staff in residence. Disregarding the AGI floor, how much, if any, of these expenses qualifies for a medical expense deduction by Reba?

24. **LO.2** Paul suffers from emphysema and severe allergies and, upon the recommendation of his physician, has a dust elimination system installed in his personal residence. In connection with the system, Paul incurs and pays the following amounts during 2020:

Doctor and hospital bills	$ 4,500
Dust elimination system	10,000
Increase in utility bills due to the system	450
Cost of certified appraisal	300

In addition, Paul pays $750 for prescribed medicines.

The system has an estimated useful life of 20 years. The appraisal was to determine the value of Paul's residence with and without the system. The appraisal states that his residence was worth $350,000 before the system was installed and $356,000 after the installation. Paul's AGI for the year was $50,000. How much of the medical expenses qualify for the medical expense deduction in 2020?

25. **LO.2** For calendar year 2020, Jean was a self-employed consultant with no employees. She had $80,000 of net profit from consulting and paid $7,000 in medical insurance premiums on her policy covering 2020. How much of these premiums may Jean deduct as a deduction *for* AGI? How much may she deduct as an itemized deduction (subject to the AGI floor)?

26. **LO.2** During 2020, Susan incurred and paid the following expenses for Beth (her daughter), Ed (her father), and herself:

Surgery for Beth	$4,500
Red River Academy charges for Beth:	
Tuition	5,100
Room, board, and other expenses	4,800
Psychiatric treatment	5,100
Doctor bills for Ed	2,200
Prescription drugs for Susan, Beth, and Ed	780
Insulin for Ed	540
Nonprescription drugs for Susan, Beth, and Ed	570
Charges at Heartland Nursing Home for Ed:	
Medical care	5,000
Lodging	2,700
Meals	2,650

Beth qualifies as Susan's dependent, and Ed would also qualify except that he receives $7,400 of taxable retirement benefits from his former employer. Beth's psychiatrist recommended Red River Academy because of its small classes and specialized psychiatric treatment program that is needed to treat Beth's illness. Ed, who is a paraplegic and diabetic, entered Heartland in October. Heartland offers the type of care that he requires.

Upon the recommendation of a physician, Susan has an air filtration system installed in her personal residence. She suffers from severe allergies. In connection with this equipment, Susan incurs and pays the following amounts during the year:

Filtration system and cost of installation	$6,500
Increase in utility bills due to the system	700
Cost of certified appraisal	360

The system has an estimated useful life of 10 years. The appraisal was to determine the value of Susan's residence with and without the system. The appraisal states that the system increased the value of Susan's residence by $2,200. Ignoring the AGI floor, what is the total of Susan's expenses that qualifies for the medical expense deduction?

Critical Thinking

27. **LO.2** In May, Rebecca's daughter, Isabella, sustained a serious injury that made it impossible for her to continue living alone. Isabella, who is a novelist, moved back into Rebecca's home after the accident. Isabella has begun writing a novel based on her recent experiences. To accommodate Isabella, Rebecca incurred significant remodeling expenses (widening hallways, building a separate bedroom and bathroom, and making kitchen appliances accessible to Isabella). In addition, Rebecca had an indoor swimming pool constructed so that Isabella could do rehabilitation exercises prescribed by her physician.

In September, Isabella underwent major reconstructive surgery in Denver. The surgery was performed by Dr. Rama Patel, who specializes in treating injuries of the type Isabella sustained. Rebecca drove Isabella from Champaign, Illinois, to Denver, a total of 1,100 miles, in Isabella's specially equipped van. They left Champaign on Tuesday morning and arrived in Denver on Thursday afternoon. Rebecca incurred expenses for gasoline, highway tolls, meals, and lodging while traveling to Denver. Rebecca stayed in a motel near the clinic for eight days while Isabella was hospitalized. Identify the relevant tax issues based on this information, and prepare a list of questions you would need to ask Rebecca and Isabella to advise them as to the resolution of any issues you have identified.

28. **LO.2** In the current year, Roger pays a $3,000 premium for high-deductible medical insurance for him and his family. In addition, he contributed $2,600 to a Health Savings Account.

a. How much may Roger deduct if he is self-employed? Is the deduction *for* AGI or *from* AGI?

b. How much may Roger deduct if he is an employee? Is the deduction *for* AGI or *from* AGI?

29. **LO.3, 4** Alicia sold her personal residence to Rick on June 30 for $300,000. Before the sale, Alicia paid the real estate tax of $4,380 for the calendar year. For income tax purposes, the deduction is apportioned as follows: $2,160 to Alicia and $2,220 to Rick. What is Rick's basis in the residence?

30. **LO.4** Norma, who is single and uses the cash method of accounting, lives in a state that imposes an income tax. In April 2020, she files her state income tax return for 2019 and pays an additional $1,000 in state income taxes. During 2020, her withholdings for state income tax purposes amount to $7,400, and she pays estimated

state income tax of $700. In April 2021, she files her state income tax return for 2020, claiming a refund of $1,800. Norma receives the refund in August 2021. Norma has no other state or local tax expenses.

a. Assuming that Norma itemized deductions in 2020, how much may she claim as a deduction for state income taxes on her Federal return for calendar year 2020 (filed April 2021)?

b. Assuming that Norma itemized deductions in 2020 (which totaled $20,000), how will the refund of $1,800 that she received in 2021 be treated for Federal income tax purposes?

c. Assume that Norma itemized deductions in 2020 (which totaled $20,000) and that she elects to have the $1,800 refund applied toward her 2021 state income tax liability. How will the $1,800 be treated for Federal income tax purposes?

d. Assuming that Norma did not itemize deductions in 2020, how will the refund of $1,800 received in 2021 be treated for Federal income tax purposes?

31. **LO.5** This year, Amy purchased a personal residence at a cost of $1,000,000. She borrowed $800,000 secured by the home to make the purchase. This year, she paid interest expense on this mortgage of $12,000. How much may she deduct?

32. **LO.6** This year, Nadia donates $4,000 to Eastern University's athletic department. The payment guarantees that Nadia will have preferred seating at football games near the 50-yard line. Assume that Nadia subsequently buys four $100 game tickets. How much can she deduct as a charitable contribution to the university's athletic department?

33. **LO.6** Liz had AGI of $130,000 in 2020. She donated Bluebird Corporation stock with a basis of $10,000 to a qualified charitable organization on July 5, 2020.

a. What is the amount of Liz's deduction assuming that she purchased the stock on December 3, 2019, and the stock had a fair market value of $17,000 when she made the donation?

b. Assume the same facts as in part (a), except that Liz purchased the stock on July 1, 2017.

c. Assume the same facts as in part (a), except that the stock had a fair market value of $7,500 (rather than $17,000) when Liz donated it to the charity.

34. **LO.6, 8** Ramon had AGI of $180,000 in 2020. He is considering making a charitable contribution this year to the American Heart Association, a qualified charitable organization. Determine the current allowable charitable contribution deduction in each of the following independent situations, and indicate the treatment for any amount that is not deductible currently. Identify any planning ideas to minimize Ramon's tax liability. *Decision Making* *Critical Thinking*

a. A cash gift of $95,000.

b. A gift of OakCo stock worth $95,000 on the contribution date. Ramon had acquired the stock as an investment two years ago at a cost of $84,000.

c. A gift of a painting worth $95,000 that Ramon purchased three years ago for $60,000. The charity has indicated that it would sell the painting to generate cash to fund medical research.

d. Ramon has decided to make a cash gift to the American Heart Association of $113,000. However, he is considering delaying his gift until next year when his AGI will increase to $300,000 and he will be in the 32% income tax bracket, an increase from his current-year income tax bracket of 24%. Ramon asks you to determine the tax savings from the tax deduction in present value terms if he were to make the gift this year rather than delay the gift until next year. See Appendix G for the present value factors, and assume a 6% discount rate.

35. **LO.6** On December 27, 2020, Roberta purchased four tickets to a charity ball sponsored by the city of San Diego for the benefit of underprivileged children. Each ticket cost $200 and had a fair market value of $35. On the same day as the purchase, Roberta gave the tickets to the minister of her church for personal use by his family. At the time of the gift of the tickets, Roberta pledged $4,000 to the building fund of her church. The pledge was satisfied by a check dated December 31, 2020, but not mailed until January 3, 2021.

   a. Presuming that Roberta is a cash basis and calendar year taxpayer, how much can she deduct as a charitable contribution for 2020?

   b. Would the amount of the deduction be any different if Roberta was an accrual basis taxpayer? Explain.

Critical Thinking
Communications

36. **LO.6, 8** In December of each year, Eleanor Young contributes 10% of her gross income to the United Way (a 50% organization). Eleanor, who is in the 24% marginal tax bracket, is considering the following alternatives for satisfying the contribution.

	Fair Market Value
(1) Cash donation	$23,000
(2) Unimproved land held for six years ($3,000 basis)	23,000
(3) Blue Corporation stock held for eight months ($3,000 basis)	23,000
(4) Gold Corporation stock held for two years ($28,000 basis)	23,000

Eleanor has asked you to help her decide which of the potential contributions listed above will be most advantageous taxwise. Evaluate the four alternatives, and write a letter to Eleanor to communicate your advice to her. Her address is 2622 Bayshore Drive, Berkeley, CA 94709.

Critical Thinking
Communications

37. **LO.2, 3, 4, 5, 7, 8** Bart and Elizabeth Forrest are married and have no dependents. They have asked you to advise them whether they should file jointly or separately in 2020. Bart incurred some significant medical expenses during the year related to an unexpected surgery. They present you with the following information:

	Bart	Elizabeth	Joint
Salary (Bart)	$38,000		
Salary (Elizabeth)		$110,000	
Interest income	400	1,200	$2,200
Deductions *for* AGI	2,400	14,000	
Medical expenses	10,427	3,358	
State income tax	900	11,800	
Real estate tax			5,800
Mortgage interest			4,200
Unreimbursed employee expenses	1,200		

If they file separately, Bart and Elizabeth will split the real estate tax and mortgage interest deductions equally. Write Bart and Elizabeth a letter in which you make and explain a recommendation on filing status for 2020. Bart and Elizabeth reside at 2003 Highland Drive, Durham, NC 27707.

38. **LO.2, 3, 4, 5, 6, 7** Evan is single and has AGI of $277,300 in 2020. His potential itemized deductions before any limitations for the year total $52,300 and consist of the following:

Medical expenses (before the AGI limitation)	$29,000
Interest on home mortgage	8,700
State income taxes	9,500
Real estate taxes	3,600
Charitable contributions	2,500

After all necessary adjustments are made, what is the amount of itemized deductions Evan may claim?

39. **LO.2, 3, 4, 5, 6, 7** Linda, who files as a single taxpayer, had AGI of $280,000 for 2020. She incurred the following expenses and losses during the year:

Medical expenses (before the 7.5%-of-AGI limitation)	$33,000
State and local income taxes	4,800
State sales tax	1,300
Real estate taxes	6,000
Home mortgage interest	5,000
Automobile loan interest	750
Credit card interest	1,000
Charitable contributions	7,000
Casualty loss (before 10% limitation but after $100 floor; not in a Federally declared disaster area)	34,000
Unreimbursed employee business expenses	7,600

Calculate Linda's allowable itemized deductions for the year.

40. **LO.2, 3, 4, 5, 6, 7** For calendar year 2020, Stuart and Pamela Gibson file a joint return reflecting AGI of $350,000. Their itemized deductions are as follows:

Casualty loss in a Federally declared disaster area after $100 floor (not covered by insurance)	$48,600
Home mortgage interest (loan qualifies as acquisition indebtedness)	19,000
Credit card interest	800
Property taxes on home	16,300
Charitable contributions	28,700
State income tax	18,000
Tax return preparation fees	1,200

Calculate the amount of itemized deductions the Gibsons may claim for the year.

Tax Return Problems

41. Alice J. and Bruce M. Byrd are married taxpayers who file a joint return. Their Social Security numbers are 123-45-6784 and 111-11-1113, respectively. Alice's birthday is September 21, 1972, and Bruce's is June 27, 1971. They live at 473 Revere Avenue, Lowell, MA 01850. Alice is the office manager for Lowell Dental Clinic, 433 Broad Street, Lowell, MA 01850 (Employer Identification Number 98-7654321). Bruce is the manager of a Super Burgers fast-food outlet owned and operated by Plymouth Corporation, 1247 Central Avenue, Hauppauge, NY 11788 (Employer Identification Number 11-1111111).

Tax Forms Problem

Decision Making

The following information is shown on their Wage and Tax Statements (Form W–2) for 2019.

Line	Description	Alice	Bruce
1	Wages, tips, other compensation	$58,000	$62,100
2	Federal income tax withheld	4,500	5,300
3	Social Security wages	58,000	62,100
4	Social Security tax withheld	3,596	3,850
5	Medicare wages and tips	58,000	62,100
6	Medicare tax withheld	841	900
15	State	Massachusetts	Massachusetts
16	State wages, tips, etc.	58,000	62,100
17	State income tax withheld	2,950	3,100

The Byrds provide over half of the support of their two children, Cynthia (born January 25, 1995, Social Security number 123-45-6788) and John (born February 7, 1999, Social Security number 123-45-6780). Both children are full-time students and live with the Byrds except when they are away at college. Cynthia earned $6,200 from a summer internship in 2019, and John earned $3,800 from a part-time job. Both children received scholarships covering tuition and materials.

During 2019, the Byrds provided 60% of the total support of Bruce's widower father, Sam Byrd (born March 6, 1943, Social Security number 123-45-6787). Sam lived alone and covered the rest of his support with his Social Security benefits. Sam died in November, and Bruce, the beneficiary of a policy on Sam's life, received life insurance proceeds of $1,600,000 on December 28.

The Byrds had the following expenses relating to their personal residence during 2019:

Property taxes	$5,000
Qualified interest on home mortgage (acquisition indebtedness)	8,700
Repairs to roof	5,750
Utilities	4,100
Fire and theft insurance	1,900

The Byrds had the following medical expenses for 2019:

Medical insurance premiums	$4,500
Doctor bill for Sam incurred in 2018 and not paid until 2019	7,600
Operation for Sam	8,500
Prescription medicines for Sam	900
Hospital expenses for Sam	3,500
Reimbursement from insurance company, received in 2019	3,600

The medical expenses for Sam represent most of the 60% that Bruce contributed toward his father's support.

Other relevant information follows:

- When they filed their 2018 state return in 2019, the Byrds paid additional state income tax of $900.

- During 2019, Alice and Bruce attended a dinner dance sponsored by the Lowell Police Disability Association (a qualified charitable organization). The Byrds paid $300 for the tickets. The cost of comparable entertainment would normally be $50.

- The Byrds contributed $5,000 to Lowell Presbyterian Church and gave used clothing (cost of $1,200 and fair market value of $350) to the Salvation Army. All donations are supported by receipts, and the clothing is in very good condition.

- Via a crowdfunding site (gofundme.com), Alice and Bruce made a gift to a needy family who lost their home in a fire ($400). In addition, they made several cash gifts to homeless individuals downtown (estimated to be $65).

- In 2019, the Byrds received interest income of $2,750, which was reported on a Form 1099–INT from Second National Bank, 125 Oak Street, Lowell, MA 01850 (Employer Identification Number 98-7654322).

- The home mortgage interest was reported on Form 1098 by Lowell Commercial Bank, P.O. Box 1000, Lowell, MA 01850 (Employer Identification Number 98-7654323). The mortgage (outstanding balance of $425,000 as of January 1, 2019) was taken out by the Byrds on May 1, 2015.

- Alice's employer requires that all employees wear uniforms to work. During 2019, Alice spent $850 on new uniforms and $566 on laundry charges.

- Bruce paid $400 for an annual subscription to the *Journal of Franchise Management* and $741 for annual membership dues to his professional association.
- Neither Alice's nor Bruce's employer reimburses for employee expenses.
- The Byrds do not keep the receipts for the sales taxes they paid and had no major purchases subject to sales tax.
- This year the Byrds gave each of their children $2,000, which was then deposited into their Roth IRAs.
- Alice and Bruce paid no estimated Federal income tax, and they did not engage in any virtual currency transactions during the year. Neither Alice nor Bruce wants to designate $3 to the Presidential Election Campaign Fund.

Part 1—Tax Computation

Compute net tax payable or refund due for Alice and Bruce Byrd for 2019. If they have overpaid, they want the amount to be refunded to them. If you use tax forms for your computations, you will need Form 1040 and its Schedules A and B. Suggested software: ProConnect Tax Online.

Part 2—Tax Planning

Alice and Bruce are planning some significant changes for 2020. They have provided you with the following information and asked you to project their taxable income and tax liability for 2020.

The Byrds will invest the $1,600,000 of life insurance proceeds in short-term certificates of deposit (CDs) and use the interest for living expenses during 2020. They expect to earn total interest of $32,000 on the CDs.

Bruce has been promoted to regional manager, and his salary for 2020 will be $88,000. He estimates that state income tax withheld will increase by $4,000 and the Social Security tax withheld will be $5,456.

Alice, who has been diagnosed with a serious illness, will take a leave of absence from work during 2020, so she will not receive a salary or incur any work-related expenses during the year. The estimated cost for her medical treatment is $15,400, of which $6,400 will be reimbursed by their insurance company in 2020. Their medical insurance premiums will increase to $9,769. Property taxes on their residence are expected to increase to $5,100. The Byrds' home mortgage interest expense and charitable contributions are expected to be unchanged from 2019.

John will graduate from college in December 2019 and will take a job in New York City in January 2020. His starting salary will be $46,000.

Assume that all of the information reported in 2019 will be the same in 2020 unless other information has been presented above.

42. Paul and Donna Decker are married taxpayers, ages 44 and 42, respectively, who file a joint return for 2020. The Deckers live at 1121 College Avenue, Carmel, IN 46032. Paul is an assistant manager at Carmel Motor Inn, and Donna is a teacher at Carmel Elementary School. They present you with W–2 forms that reflect the following information:

Tax Computation Problem

	Paul	**Donna**
Salary	$68,000	$56,000
Federal tax withheld	6,770	6,630
State income tax withheld	1,400	1,100
FICA (Social Security and Medicare) withheld	5,202	4,284
Social Security numbers	111-11-1112	123-45-6789

Donna is the custodial parent of two children from a previous marriage who reside with the Deckers throughout the school year. The children, Larry and Jane Parker, reside with their father, Bob, during the summer. Relevant information for the children follows:

	Larry	Jane
Age	17	18
Social Security numbers	123-45-6788	123-45-6787
Months spent with Deckers	9	9

Under the divorce decree, Bob pays child support of $150 per month per child during the nine months the children live with the Deckers. Bob says that he spends $200 per month per child during the three summer months they reside with him. Donna and Paul can document that they provide $2,000 support per child per year. The divorce decree is silent as to which parent can claim the exemptions for the children.

In August, Paul and Donna added a suite to their home to provide more comfortable accommodations for Hannah Snyder (123-45-6786), Donna's mother, who had moved in with them in February 2019 after the death of Donna's father. Not wanting to borrow money for this addition, Paul sold 300 shares of Acme Corporation stock for $50 per share on May 3, 2020, and used the proceeds of $15,000 to cover construction costs. The Deckers had purchased the stock on April 29, 2015, for $25 per share. They received dividends of $750 on the jointly owned stock a month before the sale.

Hannah, who is 66 years old, received $7,500 in Social Security benefits during the year, of which she gave the Deckers $2,000 to use toward household expenses and deposited the remainder in her personal savings account. The Deckers determine that they have spent $2,500 of their own money for food, clothing, medical expenses, and other items for Hannah. They do not know what the rental value of Hannah's suite would be, but they estimate it would be at least $300 per month.

Interest paid during the year included the following:

Home mortgage interest (paid to Carmel Federal Savings & Loan)	$7,890
Interest on an automobile loan (paid to Carmel National Bank)	1,660
Interest on Citibank Visa card	620

In July, Paul hit a submerged rock while boating. Fortunately, he was uninjured after being thrown from the boat and landing in deep water. However, the boat, which was uninsured, was destroyed. Paul had paid $25,000 for the boat in June 2019, and its value was appraised at $18,000 on the date of the accident.

The Deckers paid doctor and hospital bills of $12,700 and were reimbursed $2,000 by their insurance company. They spent $640 for prescription drugs and medicines and $5,904 for premiums on their health insurance policy. They have filed additional claims of $1,200 with their insurance company and have been told they will receive payment for that amount in January 2021. Included in the amounts paid for doctor and hospital bills were payments of $380 for Hannah and $850 for the children.

Additional information of potential tax consequence follows:

Real estate taxes paid	$6,850
Sales taxes paid (per table)	1,379
Contributions to church	4,600
Appraised value of books donated to public library	740
Refund of state income tax for 2019 (the Deckers itemized on their 2019 Federal tax return, and their total state and local taxes were less than $10,000)	1,520

Compute net tax payable or refund due for the Deckers for 2020. If the Deckers have overpaid, the amount is to be credited toward their taxes for 2021.

Research Problems

Note: Solutions to the Research Problems can be prepared by using the Thomson Reuters Checkpoint™ online tax research database, which accompanies this textbook. Solutions can also be prepared by using research materials found in a typical tax library.

Research Problem 1. Jane suffers from a degenerative spinal disorder. Her physician said that swimming could help prevent the onset of permanent paralysis and recommended the installation of a swimming pool at her residence for her use. Jane's residence had a market value of approximately $500,000 before the swimming pool was installed. The swimming pool was built, and an appraiser estimated that the value of Jane's home increased by $98,000 because of the addition.

The pool cost $194,000, and Jane claimed a medical expense deduction of $96,000 ($194,000 − $98,000) on her tax return. Upon audit of the return, the IRS determined that an adequate pool should have cost $70,000 and would increase the value of her home by only $31,000. Thus, the IRS claims that Jane is entitled to a deduction of only $39,000 ($70,000 − $31,000).

a. Is there any ceiling limitation on the amount deductible as a medical expense? Explain.

b. Can capital expenditures be deductible as medical expenses? Explain.

c. What is the significance of a "minimum adequate facility"? Should aesthetic or architectural qualities be considered in the determination? Why or why not?

Research Problem 2. Ken and Mary Jane Blough, your neighbors, have asked you for advice after receiving correspondence in the mail from the IRS. You learn that the IRS is asking for documentation in support of the itemized deductions the Bloughs claimed on a recent tax return. The Bloughs tell you that their income in the year of question was $75,000. Because their record-keeping habits are poor, they felt justified in claiming itemized deductions equal to the amounts that represent the average claimed by other taxpayers in their income bracket. These averages are calculated and reported by the IRS annually based on actual returns filed in an earlier year. Accordingly, they claimed medical expenses of $7,102, taxes of $6,050, interest of $10,659, and charitable contributions of $2,693. What advice do you give the Bloughs?

Partial list of research aids:
Cheryl L. de Werff, T.C. Summary Opinion, 2011–29.

Research Problem 3. Marcia, a shareholder in a corporation with stores in five states, donated stock with a basis of $10,000 to a qualified charitable organization in 2019. Although the stock of the corporation was not traded on a public stock exchange, many shares had been sold over the past several years. Based on the average selling price for the stock in 2019, Marcia deducted $95,000 on her 2019 tax return. Marcia received a notice from the IRS that the $95,000 deduction had been reduced to $10,000 because she had not obtained a qualified appraisal or attached a summary of her appraisal to her tax return. Marcia has asked you to advise her on this matter. Write a letter containing your conclusions to Ms. Marcia Meyer, 1311 Santos Court, San Bruno, CA 94066.

Communications

Partial list of research aids:
Reg. § 1.170A–13(c)(2).

Research Problem 4. On March 5, 2016, Mr. and Mrs. Horton borrowed $100,000 against the equity in their personal residence with the loan secured by that home. For 2016 and 2017, they were able to deduct the interest expense on this loan as home equity interest expense [an itemized deduction on Schedule A (Form 1040)]. The Tax Cuts and Jobs Act of 2017 disallows this interest expense deduction for 2018 through 2025. The Hortons' CPA has asked them to review their financial records for February and March of 2016. They discover that they sold Disney stock on February 20, 2016, and used the proceeds to purchase Microsoft stock. Why is their CPA asking them for this information? How might this stock purchase in March 2016 help them obtain a deduction for all or part of the interest paid in 2018 and later on this home equity loan?

Partial list of research aids:
Reg. § 1.163–8T.
Notice 89–35, 1989–1 C.B. 675.

Use internet tax resources to address the following questions. Look for reliable websites and blogs of the IRS and other government agencies, media outlets, businesses, tax professionals, academics, think tanks, and political outlets.

Research Problem 5. The Federal government incurs a cost for every item that is deductible in the computation of taxable income. These costs, which take the form of forgone tax revenue, are often referred to as "tax expenditures." The Joint Committee on Taxation regularly estimates the current and projected tax expenditures associated with a long list of provisions in the tax law. Locate the Joint Committee on Taxation's most recent analysis, and identify the current tax expenditure associated with the deductions for medical expenses, interest on student loans, mortgage interest, and charitable contributions. How are these costs expected to change over the next five years? How is the concept of tax expenditures helpful to tax policy analysts?

Research Problem 6. Look for reliable data on how many individuals are affected by the $10,000 SALT cap. Use that data to make an argument for or against the cap.

Becker CPA Review Questions

Becker.

1. In the current year, Wells paid the following expenses:

Premiums on an insurance policy against loss of earnings due to sickness or accident	$3,000
Physical therapy after spinal surgery	2,000
Premium on an insurance policy that covers reimbursement for the cost of prescription drugs	500

    In the current year, Wells recovered $1,500 of the $2,000 that she paid for physical therapy through insurance reimbursement from a group medical policy paid for by her employer. Disregarding the adjusted gross income percentage threshold, what amount could be claimed on Wells's current-year income tax return for medical expenses?

    a. $4,000   c. $1,000
    b. $3,500   d. $500

2. Jordan Johnson is single and has adjusted gross income of $50,000 in the current year. Additional information is as follows:

State income taxes paid	$ 2,000
Mortgage interest on her personal residence	9,000
Points paid on purchase of her personal residence	1,000
Deductible contributions to her IRA	3,000
Uninsured realized casualty loss (in a Federal disaster area)	6,000
Tax preparation fees for her prior year income tax return	400

What amount may Jordan claim as itemized deductions on her current-year income tax return?

a. $12,000

c. $13,300

b. $12,900

d. $15,900

3. Sydney, a single taxpayer, had $80,000 in adjusted gross income in year 2. During the year, she contributed $15,000 to her church. She also had a $17,000 contribution carryover from her year 1 church contributions. What is the maximum amount of charitable deduction that Sydney may claim on her year 2 income tax return?

a. $40,000

c. $19,200

b. $32,000

d. $15,000

4. Kurstie received an $800 state income tax refund this year. Kurstie deducted $3,000 of state income taxes paid in the prior year as part of her itemized deductions. Which of the following statements regarding the taxability of Kurstie's refund is true?

a. If Kurstie's itemized deductions exceeded the standard deduction by $200, then the $800 refund is included in gross income.

b. If Kurstie's itemized deductions exceeded the standard deduction by $200, then $200 of the refund is included in gross income.

c. If Kurstie claimed the standard deduction instead, then the $800 refund is taxable.

d. Kurstie must include $3,000 in gross income in the current year.

5. Which of the following would preclude a taxpayer from deducting student loan interest expense?

a. The total amount paid is $1,000.

b. The taxpayer is single with AGI of $55,000.

c. The taxpayer is married filing jointly with AGI of $120,000.

d. The taxpayer is taken as a dependent of another taxpayer.

6. Which of the following may *not* be claimed as a deduction by a taxpayer who claims the standard deduction?

a. Interest penalty on early withdrawal of savings

b. Self-employed health insurance

c. State income tax paid

d. IRA contribution

Investor Losses

LEARNING OBJECTIVES: *After completing Chapter 11, you should be able to:*

LO.1 Explain the tax shelter problem and the reasons for at-risk and passive activity loss limitations.

LO.2 Discuss the at-risk limitation.

LO.3 Describe how the passive activity loss rules limit deductions for losses and identify the taxpayers subject to these restrictions.

LO.4 Explain the elements required for an activity to be treated as passive and review the rules for identifying an activity.

LO.5 Identify the tests for material participation.

LO.6 Describe the nature of rental activities under the passive activity loss rules.

LO.7 Determine the relationship between the at-risk and passive activity loss limitations.

LO.8 Recognize the special treatment available to certain real estate activities.

LO.9 Determine the proper tax treatment on the disposition of a passive activity.

LO.10 Identify restrictions placed on the deductibility of other investor losses and deductions, including those that apply to investment interest.

LO.11 Suggest tax planning strategies to minimize the effect of the passive activity loss and investment interest limitations and recognize the general impact of the additional tax on net investment income.

CHAPTER OUTLINE

11-1 The Tax Shelter Problem, 11-2

11-2 At-Risk Limits, 11-4

11-3 Passive Activity Loss Limits, 11-5
    11-3a Classification and Impact of Passive Activity Income and Losses, 11-5
    11-3b Taxpayers Subject to the Passive Activity Loss Rules, 11-9
    11-3c Rules for Determining Passive Activities, 11-10
    11-3d Interaction of the At-Risk and Passive Activity Loss Limits, 11-15
    11-3e Special Passive Activity Rules for Real Estate Activities, 11-16
    11-3f Dispositions of Passive Interests, 11-20

11-4 Investment Interest Limitation, 11-21
    11-4a Limitation Imposed, 11-21
    11-4b Computation of Allowable Deduction, 11-23

11-5 Other Investment Losses, 11-23

11-6 Tax Planning, 11-24
    11-6a Using Passive Activity Losses, 11-24
    11-6b Planning with the Investment Interest Limitation, 11-26
    11-6c Effect of the Additional Tax on Net Investment Income, 11-26

INVESTOR LOSS LIMITATIONS AFFECT THE VIABILITY OF CERTAIN INVESTMENT OPPORTUNITIES

Trudy and Jim Reswick are considering ways to enhance their financial security. In fact, they are willing to borrow a substantial sum so that they can make an appropriate investment.

Currently, Trudy and Jim's sole sources of income are their salaries, totaling $140,000, from their full-time jobs. Their most significant asset is their personal residence (fair market value of $500,000 with a mortgage of $350,000). The Reswicks' financial planner suggests that they borrow $100,000 at 4 percent and use the proceeds to make *one* of the following investments:

- A high-growth, low-yield portfolio of marketable securities. The portfolio's value is expected to grow 8 percent each year.
- An interest in a limited partnership that owns and operates orange groves in Florida. The limited partnership interest is expected to generate tax losses of $25,000 in each of the next five years, after which profits are expected. Their financial planner predicts that after taking into account the tax benefit from the losses, the Reswicks would average an annual 8 percent return over a 10-year period.
- An interest in a local limited partnership that owns and rents apartments to college students. This limited partnership interest also would generate losses of $25,000 per year for five years, after which profits would follow. These expected profits and losses would produce an average annual total return of 8 percent over a 10-year period.

Trudy and Jim want to choose the alternative that produces the best after-tax return over a 10-year planning horizon. They are aware, however, that tax restrictions may limit the advantages of some of these investment options. In this connection, evaluate each option.

Read the chapter and formulate your response.

FRAMEWORK 1040 Tax Formula for Individuals

This chapter covers the boldfaced portions of the Tax Formula for Individuals that was introduced in Concept Summary 3.1 on p. 3-3. Below those portions are the sections of Form 1040 where the results are reported.

Income *(broadly defined)*..	$ xx,xxx
Less: Exclusions	(x,xxx)
Gross income	**$ xx,xxx**

FORM 1040 (p. 1)

6 Capital gain or (loss). Attach Schedule D if required, If not required, check here ▶ ☐

FORM 1040 (Schedule 1)

3 Business income or (loss). Attach Schedule C. . . . .
4 Other gains or (losses). Attach Form 4797 . . . .
5 Rental real estate, royalties, partnerships, S corporations, trusts, etc. Attach Schedule E

Less: Deductions *for* adjusted gross income	(x,xxx)
Adjusted gross income..	$ xx,xxx
Less: The greater of total itemized deductions *or* the standard deduction	(x,xxx)

FORM 1040 (p. 1)

9 **Standard deduction or itemized deductions** (from Schedule A) . . . .

Personal and dependency exemptions*	(x,xxx)
Deduction for qualified business income**	(x,xxx)
Taxable income	$ xx,xxx
Tax on taxable income *(see Tax Tables or Tax Rate Schedules)*	$ x,xxx
Less: Tax credits *(including income taxes withheld and prepaid)*	(xxx)
Tax due (or refund)	$ xxx

  *Exemption deductions are not allowed from 2018 through 2025.
**Only applies from 2018 through 2025.

A s discussed in Chapter 6, a tax deduction for an expense or a loss is not allowed unless specifically permitted by Congress. For example, losses can be recognized and deducted in the case of certain unprofitable investments only because the Code allows them. These losses can arise from the operation of an activity *or* on its sale. For most individual taxpayers, deductible investor losses come within the scope of § 165(c)(2) relating to transactions entered into for profit.[1] But what happens if the investment is mostly motivated by the tax loss it generates rather than the profits it might create? Or what if the investment generates expenses that offset ordinary income and it later is expected to produce appreciation taxed at capital gain rates? This chapter addresses these tax minimization strategies and the rules put in place to restrict their use.

LO.1

Explain the tax shelter problem and the reasons for at-risk and passive activity loss limitations.

11-1 **THE TAX SHELTER PROBLEM**

Before Congress passed laws to reduce their effectiveness, tax shelters provided a popular way to avoid or defer taxes, since they could generate deductions and other benefits to offset income from other sources. Because of the tax avoidance potential of many tax shelters, they were attractive to wealthy taxpayers in high income tax brackets. Many tax shelters merely provided an opportunity for "investors" to obtain deductions and credits in ventures that were not expected to generate a profit, even in the long run.

---

[1] If the losses are incurred in connection with a trade or business, § 165(c)(1) applies.

Although it may seem odd that a taxpayer would intentionally invest in an activity designed to produce losses, there is a logical explanation. The typical tax shelter operated as a partnership and relied heavily on nonrecourse financing.[2] Accelerated depreciation and interest expense deductions generated large losses in the early years of the activity. At the very least, the tax shelter deductions deferred the recognition of any net income until the activity was sold. In the best of situations, the investor could realize additional tax savings by offsetting other income (e.g., salary, interest, dividends) with deductions flowing from the tax shelter. Ultimately, the sale of the investment would result in capital gain. The following example illustrates what was possible *before* Congress stepped in to curb tax shelter abuses in the 1980s.

> **EXAMPLE 1**
>
> Bob, who earned a salary of $400,000 as a business executive and dividend income of $15,000, invested $20,000 for a 10% interest in a cattle-breeding tax shelter. Through the use of $800,000 of nonrecourse financing and available cash of $200,000, the partnership acquired a herd of an exotic breed of cattle costing $1,000,000. Depreciation, interest, and other deductions related to the activity resulted in a loss of $400,000, of which Bob's share was $40,000. Bob was allowed to deduct the $40,000 loss even though he had invested and stood to lose only $20,000 if the investment became worthless.
>
> The net effect of the $40,000 deduction from the partnership was that a portion of Bob's salary and dividend income was "sheltered" (i.e., offset or neutralized by the deduction), and as a result, he was required to calculate his tax liability on only $375,000 of income [$415,000 (salary and dividends) − $40,000 (deduction)] rather than $415,000. If this deduction were available under current law and if Bob was in a combined Federal and state income tax bracket of 40%, this deduction would generate a tax savings of $16,000 ($40,000 × 40%) in the first year alone!

A review of Example 1 shows that the taxpayer took a *two-for-one* write-off ($40,000 deduction, $20,000 investment). Tax shelter promoters often promised tax deductions for the investor well in excess of the amount invested.

The first major law change aimed at tax shelters was the **at-risk limitation**. Its objective is to limit a taxpayer's deductions to the amount "at risk," which is the amount the taxpayer stands to lose if the investment becomes worthless. So in Example 1, the at-risk rule limits Bob's deductible loss to $20,000—the amount he invested.

The second major attack on tax shelters came with the passage of the **passive activity loss** rules. The passive activity loss rules require the taxpayer to segregate all income and losses into three categories: active, portfolio, and passive (these categories are defined in text Section 11-3). In general, the passive activity loss rules disallow the deduction of passive activity losses against *active or portfolio income* even when the taxpayer is at risk to the extent of the loss. In general, passive activity losses can only offset passive activity income.

So in Example 1, the passive activity loss rules disallow a current deduction for any of the loss. The loss from the tax shelter is a passive activity loss because Bob does not "materially participate" in the activity (see text Section 11-3c). As a result, the $20,000 loss that is allowed under the at-risk rules is disallowed under the passive activity loss rules. Why? Because Bob does not report any passive activity income for the year—he reports only active and portfolio income. Consequently, Bob's current-year income only includes his nonpassive activity income of $415,000. As explained later in the chapter, the disallowed $20,000 passive activity loss is suspended and may be deducted in a future year under certain conditions.

The nature of the at-risk limits and the passive activity loss rules and their impact on investors are discussed in the pages that follow. Because of these rules, investors now

[2]Nonrecourse debt is an obligation for which the borrower is not personally liable. An example of nonrecourse debt is a liability on real estate acquired by a partnership without the partnership or any of the partners assuming any liability for the mortgage. The acquired property generally is pledged as collateral for the loan.

focus primarily on the economics of the investment instead of the tax benefits or tax avoidance possibilities that an investment may generate.

Discuss the at-risk limitation.

11-2 AT-RISK LIMITS

The at-risk rules limit the deductibility of losses from business and income-producing activities. These rules, which apply to individuals and closely held corporations, are designed to prevent taxpayers from deducting losses in excess of their actual economic investment in an activity. In the case of an S corporation or a partnership, the at-risk limits apply at the owner level. Under the at-risk rules, a taxpayer's deductible loss from an activity for any taxable year is limited to the amount the taxpayer has at risk at the end of the taxable year (the amount the taxpayer could actually lose in the activity).

Although the amount at risk usually changes over time, the initial "at-risk" amount includes the following:[3]

- The amount of cash and the adjusted basis of property contributed to the activity by the taxpayer, and
- Any amounts borrowed for use in the activity for which the taxpayer is personally liable or has pledged as security property not used in the activity.

This amount generally is increased each year by the taxpayer's share of income and is decreased by the taxpayer's share of deductible losses and withdrawals from the activity. In addition, because general partners are jointly and severally liable for recourse debts of the partnership, their at-risk amounts are increased when the partnership increases its debt and are decreased when the partnership reduces its debt. However, a taxpayer generally is *not* considered at risk with respect to borrowed amounts if:

- The taxpayer is not personally liable for repayment of the debt (e.g., nonrecourse debt), or
- The lender has an interest (other than as a creditor) in the activity.

An important exception provides that in the case of an activity that holds real property, a taxpayer is considered at risk for his or her share of any *qualified nonrecourse financing* that is secured by real property used in the activity.[4]

A taxpayer may deduct a loss as long as the at-risk amount is positive (but the passive activity loss rules still may apply to limit the deduction). However, once the at-risk amount is exhausted, any remaining loss cannot be deducted until a later year. Any losses disallowed for any given taxable year by the at-risk rules may be deducted when there is, and to the extent of, a positive at-risk amount.

The Big Picture

EXAMPLE

2

Return to the facts of *The Big Picture* on p. 11-1. In addition to the three investment options presented to the Reswicks, in 2020, they invest $40,000 in an oil partnership that incurs a first-year net loss, of which $60,000 is their share. Assume that the Reswicks' interest in the partnership is subject to the at-risk limits but is not subject to the passive activity loss limits.

Because the Reswicks have only $40,000 of capital at risk, they cannot deduct more than $40,000 against their other income and must reduce their at-risk amount to zero ($40,000 at-risk amount − $40,000 loss deducted). The nondeductible loss of $20,000 ($60,000 loss generated − $40,000 loss allowed) can be carried over to 2021.

---

[3]§ 465(b)(1).   [4]Section 465(b)(6) defines *qualified nonrecourse financing*.

Continue with the facts of the previous example. In 2021, the Reswicks have taxable income of $15,000 from the oil partnership and invest an additional $10,000 in the venture. Their at-risk amount is now $25,000 ($0 beginning balance + $15,000 taxable income + $10,000 additional investment). This enables them to deduct the carryover loss and requires them to reduce their at-risk amount to $5,000 ($25,000 at-risk amount − $20,000 carryover loss allowed).

Complicating the at-risk rule is the fact that previously allowed losses must be recaptured to the extent the at-risk amount falls below zero.[5] Under this rule, taxpayers must recognize income to bring the at-risk amount up to zero. Typically, this rule is triggered when the taxpayer receives a distribution or when the status of indebtedness changes from recourse to nonrecourse.

Calculation of at-risk amount is reviewed in Concept Summary 11.1.

Concept Summary 11.1

Calculation of At-Risk Amount

Increases to a taxpayer's at-risk amount:

- Cash and the adjusted basis of property contributed to the activity.
- Amounts borrowed for use in the activity for which the taxpayer is personally liable or has pledged as security property not used in the activity.
- Taxpayer's share of amounts borrowed for use in the activity that are qualified nonrecourse financing.
- Taxpayer's share of the activity's income.

Decreases to a taxpayer's at-risk amount:

- Withdrawals from the activity.
- Taxpayer's share of the activity's deductible loss.
- Taxpayer's share of any reductions of debt for which recourse against the taxpayer exists or any reductions of qualified nonrecourse debt.

11-3 PASSIVE ACTIVITY LOSS LIMITS

LO.3

Describe how the passive activity loss rules limit deductions for losses and identify the taxpayers subject to these restrictions.

This section identifies and explains the key issues that apply to the passive activity loss limits. Here are some key points:

- The limits apply only to passive activity losses incurred by certain types of taxpayers.
- Losses are limited under these rules only if they are generated by a passive activity.
- Special rules exist for interests in real estate activities.
- Any suspended losses are generally allowed when a passive activity is sold.

11-3a Classification and Impact of Passive Activity Income and Losses

The passive activity loss rules (§ 469) operate by requiring taxpayers to classify their income and losses into three categories: active, portfolio, or passive. Then the rules limit the extent to which losses in the passive category can be used to offset income in the other categories.

---

[5]§ 465(e).

Classification

The passive activity loss rules require income and losses to be classified as active, portfolio, or passive.

Active income includes:

- Wages, salary, commissions, bonuses, and other payments for services rendered by the taxpayer.
- Profit from a trade or business in which the taxpayer is a material participant (material participation is described in text Section 11-3c).
- Gain on the sale or other disposition of assets used in an active trade or business.
- Income from intangible property if the taxpayer's personal efforts significantly contributed to the creation of the property.

Portfolio income includes:

- Interest, dividends, annuities, and royalties not derived in the ordinary course of a trade or business.
- Gain or loss from the disposition of property that produces portfolio income or is held for investment purposes.

Passive activity income or loss arises from activities that are treated as passive, which include:

- Any trade or business or income-producing activity in which the taxpayer does not materially participate.
- Subject to certain exceptions (discussed in text Section 11-3e), all rental activities whether the taxpayer materially participates or not.

General Impact

Losses or expenses generated by passive activities can be deducted only to the extent of income from the taxpayer's passive activities. Any excess passive activity loss may not be used to offset active income or portfolio income. Instead, any unused passive activity losses are suspended and carried forward to future years to offset passive activity income generated in those years. Any remaining suspended losses may be used only when a taxpayer disposes of his or her *entire interest* in an activity. When that occurs, generally all current and suspended passive activity losses related to the activity may offset active and portfolio income.

The Big Picture

EXAMPLE 4

Return to the facts of *The Big Picture* on p. 11-1. In addition to their salaries of $140,000 from full-time jobs, assume that the Reswicks receive $12,000 in dividends and interest from various portfolio investments. Further, assume that they decide to invest $100,000 in the orange grove limited partnership, which is a passive activity that produces a $25,000 loss for the Reswicks this year.

Because their at-risk basis in the partnership is $100,000, the current $25,000 loss is not limited by the at-risk rules. However, because the loss is a passive activity loss, it is not deductible against their other income. The loss is suspended and carried over to the future.

If the Reswicks have passive activity income from this investment or from other passive activities in the future, they can offset the suspended loss against that passive activity income. If they do not have passive activity income to offset this suspended loss in the future, they will be allowed to offset the loss against other types of income when they eventually dispose of their investment in the passive activity.

Impact of Suspended Passive Activity Losses

When a taxpayer disposes of his or her entire interest in a passive activity, the actual economic gain or loss from the investment, including any suspended losses, can finally be determined. As a result, under the passive activity loss rules, when a fully taxable disposition occurs, any overall loss realized from the taxpayer's activity is recognized and can offset any income.

A *fully taxable disposition* generally involves a sale of the property to a third party at arm's length. This would imply that the sales price is equal to the property's fair market value. As presented in the following example, a gain recognized on the sale of a passive activity generally is treated as passive and is first offset by the suspended passive activity losses from that activity.

EXAMPLE
5

Cindy sells an apartment building, a passive activity, with an adjusted basis of $500,000 for $580,000. In addition, she has suspended passive activity losses of $60,000 associated with the building. Her total gain, $80,000, and her taxable gain, $20,000, are calculated as follows:

Net sales price	$ 580,000
Less: Adjusted basis	(500,000)
Total gain	$ 80,000
Less: Suspended passive activity losses	(60,000)
Taxable gain (passive)	$ 20,000

As highlighted in Example 5, gain recognized on the sale of a passive activity generally is treated as passive and is first offset by any suspended passive activity losses from that activity. This accomplishes the purpose of determining the true economic gain or loss from the activity.

But what happens if the suspended losses exceed the gain recognized or the sale results in a loss? In this case, the excess loss is allowed to offset other income in the following order:

1. Net passive activity income or gains (if any), and
2. Nonpassive income or gains (active or portfolio).

EXAMPLE
6

Dean sells an apartment building, a passive activity, with an adjusted basis of $600,000 for $650,000. In addition, he has current and suspended passive activity losses of $60,000 associated with the building and has no other passive activities. His total gain of $50,000 and his deductible loss of $10,000 are calculated as follows:

Net sales price	$ 650,000
Less: Adjusted basis	(600,000)
Total gain	$ 50,000
Less: Suspended passive activity losses	(60,000)
Deductible loss (not passive)	($ 10,000)

The $10,000 deductible loss offsets Dean's active and portfolio income.

What would be the outcome if Dean sold the building for $590,000? In this case, there would be a loss on the sale of $10,000 and an overall deductible loss of $70,000. This total loss, including the suspended passive activity losses, is deductible as a nonpassive activity loss.

Carryovers of Suspended Passive Activity Losses

The preceding examples assumed that the taxpayer had an interest in only one passive activity; as a result, the suspended loss was related exclusively to the activity that was sold. However, taxpayers often own interests in more than one activity, in which case any suspended losses must be allocated among those passive activities that generated losses. The allocation to an activity is made by multiplying the disallowed passive activity loss from all activities using the following fraction:

$$\frac{\text{Loss from one passive activity}}{\text{Sum of losses for taxable year from all passive activities having losses}}$$

Diego has investments in three passive activities with the following income and losses for 2019:

Activity A	($30,000)
Activity B	(20,000)
Activity C	25,000
Net passive activity loss	($25,000)
Net passive activity loss of $25,000 allocated to:	
Activity A ($25,000 × $30,000/$50,000)	($15,000)
Activity B ($25,000 × $20,000/$50,000)	(10,000)
Total suspended passive activity losses	($25,000)

Suspended losses are carried over indefinitely and are offset in the future first against any passive activity income from the activities to which they relate and then against passive activity income from other passive activities.[6] Taxpayers subject to the passive activity loss limitation rule must maintain records to track the suspended losses and the activities to which they belong.

Assume that the facts are the same as in Example 7 and that in 2020, Activity A produces $10,000 of income. Diego may use $10,000 of Activity A's suspended loss of $15,000 from 2019 to offset the $10,000 income from this activity.

If Diego sells Activity A in early 2021, the remaining $5,000 suspended loss is used to offset any income from the activity reported by Diego in 2021 and to determine his final gain or loss.

Passive Activity Credits

Credits (such as the low-income housing credit and rehabilitation credit—discussed in Chapter 12) that arise from passive activities are limited in much the same way as passive activity losses. Passive activity credits can be used only against regular tax attributable to passive activity income,[7] which is calculated by comparing the tax on all income (including passive activity income) with the tax on income excluding passive activity income.

Sam owes $50,000 of tax, disregarding net passive activity income, and $80,000 of tax, considering both net passive activity and other taxable income (disregarding the credits in both cases). The amount of tax attributable to the passive activity income is $30,000.

In the preceding example, Sam can claim a maximum of $30,000 of passive activity credits; the excess credits are carried over. These passive activity credits can be used only against the *regular* tax attributable to passive activity income. If a taxpayer has a net loss from passive activities during a given year, no credits can be used.

Carryovers of Passive Activity Credits

Tax credits related to passive activities can be carried forward indefinitely much like suspended passive activity losses. Unlike passive activity losses, however, passive activity credits are permanently lost when the activity is disposed of in a taxable transaction where a *loss* is recognized. Credits are allowed on dispositions only when there is sufficient tax on passive activity income to absorb them.

Use of Passive Activity Credits on Disposition of an Activity

Alicia sells a passive activity for a gain of $10,000. The activity had suspended losses of $40,000 and suspended credits of $15,000. The $10,000 gain is offset by $10,000 of the suspended losses, and the remaining $30,000 of suspended losses is deductible against Alicia's active and portfolio income. The suspended credits are permanently lost because the sale of the activity did not generate any tax.

---

[6]§ 469(b).

[7]§ 469(d)(2).

Use of Passive Activity Credits on Disposition of an Activity

If Alicia in Example 10 had realized a $100,000 gain on the sale of the passive activity, the suspended credits could have been used to the extent of the regular tax related to the net passive activity income.

Gain on sale	$100,000
Less: Suspended passive activity losses	(40,000)
Taxable gain	$ 60,000

If the tax related to the taxable gain of $60,000 is $15,000 or more, the entire $15,000 of suspended credits can be used. If the tax related to the gain is less than $15,000, the excess of the suspended credits over the tax related to the gain is lost.

EXAMPLE 11

When a taxpayer has a sufficient regular tax liability from passive activities to trigger the use of suspended credits, the credits lose their character as passive activity credits. They are reclassified as regular tax credits and made subject to the same limits as other credits (discussed in Chapter 12).

Passive Activity Changes to Active

If a passive activity becomes an active one, suspended passive activity losses are allowed to the extent of income from the now active business.[8] If any of the suspended loss remains, it continues to be treated as a loss from a passive activity. The excess suspended loss can be deducted from passive activity income or carried over to the next tax year and deducted to the extent of income from the now active business in the succeeding year(s). The activity must continue to be the same activity.

For several years, Rebecca has owned an interest in a passive activity that has produced losses of $80,000 during that period. Because she did not have passive activity income from other sources, she could not deduct any of the activity's passive activity losses.

In the current year, she has become a material participant in the activity (i.e., the passive activity is now an active business) and her share of the business profits total $25,000. As a result, she may use $25,000 of the suspended passive activity loss to offset the current business profits. Rebecca's remaining suspended passive activity loss from the activity is $55,000 ($80,000 − $25,000), which is carried over to future years and used to offset income from the formerly passive activity or income from other passive activities.

EXAMPLE 12

11-3b Taxpayers Subject to the Passive Activity Loss Rules

The passive activity loss rules apply to individuals, estates, trusts, personal service corporations, and closely held C corporations.[9] Passive activity income or loss from investments in partnerships or S corporations (see Chapters 21 and 22) flows through to the owners, and the passive activity loss rules are applied at the owner level.

Personal Service Corporations

Application of the passive activity loss limitations to personal service corporations is intended to prevent taxpayers from sheltering personal service income by creating personal service corporations and acquiring passive activities at the corporate level.

Two tax accountants who earn an aggregate of $200,000 a year in their individual practices agree to work together in a newly formed personal service corporation. Shortly after its formation, the corporation invests in a passive activity that produces a $200,000 loss during the year. Because the passive activity loss rules apply to personal service corporations, the corporation may not deduct the $200,000 passive activity loss against the $200,000 of active income.

EXAMPLE 13

---

[8]§ 469(f).

[9]§ 469(a).

Determination of whether a corporation is a <mark>personal service corporation</mark> is based on rather broad definitions. A personal service corporation is a regular (or C) corporation that meets *both* of the following conditions:

- The principal activity is the performance of personal services.
- Such services are substantially performed by employee-owners.

Generally, personal service corporations include those in the fields of health, law, engineering, architecture, accounting, actuarial science, performing arts, and consulting.[10] A corporation is treated as a personal service corporation if more than 10 percent of the stock (by value) is held by employee-owners.[11] An employee is treated as an employee-owner if he or she owns stock on *any day* during the taxable year.[12] For these purposes, shareholder status and employee status do not have to occur on the same day.

Closely Held C Corporations

Application of the passive activity loss rules to closely held (nonpersonal service) C corporations is also intended to prevent individuals from incorporating to avoid the passive activity loss limitations. A corporation is classified as a <mark>closely held corporation</mark> if at any time during the taxable year more than 50 percent of the value of its outstanding stock is owned, directly or indirectly, by or for five or fewer individuals. Closely held C corporations (other than personal service corporations) may use passive activity losses to offset *active* income but not portfolio income.

EXAMPLE 14

Silver Corporation, a closely held (nonpersonal service) C corporation, has $475,000 of passive activity losses from a rental activity, $400,000 of active income, and $100,000 of portfolio income. The corporation may offset $400,000 of the $475,000 passive activity loss against the $400,000 of active business income but may not offset the remainder against the $100,000 of portfolio income. As a result, $75,000 of the passive activity loss is suspended ($475,000 passive activity loss − $400,000 offset against active income).

Applying the passive activity loss limitations to closely held C corporations eliminates a benefit to taxpayers from transferring their portfolio investments (e.g., stocks and bonds) to these corporations.

LO.4

Explain the elements required for an activity to be treated as passive and review the rules for identifying an activity.

11-3c Rules for Determining Passive Activities

As noted earlier, the following types of activities are treated as passive:

- Any trade or business or income-producing activity in which the taxpayer does not materially participate.
- All rental activities, subject to certain exceptions pertaining to real estate (discussed in text Section 11-3e).

To understand the meaning of the term *passive activity* and the impact of the rules, one must address the following issues, each of which is the subject of statutory or administrative guidance:

- What constitutes an *activity?*
- What is meant by *material participation?*
- When is an activity a *rental activity?*

Even though guidance is available to help the taxpayer deal with these issues, their resolution is anything but simple.

---

[10]§ 448(d)(2)(A).

[11]§ 469(j)(2).

[12]§ 269A(b)(2).

Identification of an Activity

Identifying what constitutes an activity is the first step in applying the passive activity loss rules. Taxpayers who are involved in complex business operations need to determine whether a given segment of their overall business operations constitutes a separate activity or is to be treated as part of a larger activity. Proper treatment is necessary to determine whether income or loss from an activity is active or passive.

Treatment as a Component of an Activity or as a Separate Activity

Ben owns a business with two separate departments. Department A generates net income of $120,000, and Department B generates a net loss of $95,000. Ben participates 700 hours in the operations of Department A and 100 hours in Department B. If Ben is allowed to treat the departments as components of a single activity, he can offset the $95,000 loss from Department B against the $120,000 of income from Department A.

EXAMPLE 15

Assume the same facts as in the previous example. If Ben is required to treat each department as a separate activity, the tax result is not as favorable. Because he is a material participant in Department A (having devoted 700 hours to it), the $120,000 profit is active income. Assuming that Ben is not considered a material participant in Department B (100 hours), the $95,000 loss is a passive activity loss. As a result, Ben cannot offset the $95,000 passive activity loss from Department B against the $120,000 of active income from Department A. (A discussion of the material participation rules follows.)

EXAMPLE 16

On the disposition of a passive activity, a taxpayer is allowed to offset suspended losses from the activity against other types of income. As illustrated in the next example, identifying what constitutes an activity is of crucial importance for this purpose too.

Linda owns a business with two departments. Department A has a net loss of $125,000 in the current year, and Department B has a $70,000 net loss. She sells Department B at the end of the year.

Assuming that Linda is allowed to treat the two departments as separate passive activities, she can offset the passive activity loss from Department B against other types of income in the following order: gain from disposition of the passive activity, other passive activity income, and nonpassive activity income. This treatment leaves her with a suspended loss of $125,000 from Department A.

If, however, Departments A and B are treated as components of the same activity, when Department B is sold, its $70,000 net loss would be suspended along with the other $125,000 of suspended loss of the activity (from Department A).

EXAMPLE 17

Treasury Regulations have provided guidelines to be used in identifying activities subject to the passive activity loss rules.[13] These guidelines indicate, in general, that a taxpayer can treat one or more trade or business activities or rental activities as a single activity if those activities form an *appropriate economic unit* for measuring gain or loss. In making this decision, all of the relevant facts and circumstances must be considered. Taxpayers may use any reasonable method in applying the facts and circumstances. The following example, adapted from the Regulations, illustrates the application of the general rules for grouping activities.[14]

George owns a men's clothing store and a brewpub in Chicago. He also owns a men's clothing store and a brewpub in Milwaukee. Reasonable methods of applying the facts and circumstances test may result in any of the following groupings:

- All four activities may be grouped into a single activity because of common ownership and control.

continued

EXAMPLE 18

---

[13]Reg. § 1.469–4.　　　　　　　　　　　　　　　　[14]Reg. § 1.469–4(c)(3).

- The clothing stores may be grouped into an activity, and the brewpubs may be grouped into a separate activity.
- The Chicago activities may be grouped into an activity, and the Milwaukee activities may be grouped into a separate activity.
- Each of the four activities may be treated as a separate activity.

Regrouping of Activities Taxpayers should carefully consider all tax factors when deciding how to group their activities. Once activities have been grouped, they cannot be regrouped unless the original grouping was clearly inappropriate or there has been a material change in the facts and circumstances. The Regulations allow the IRS to regroup activities when *both* of the following conditions exist:[15]

- The taxpayer's grouping fails to reflect one or more appropriate economic units.
- One of the primary purposes of the taxpayer's grouping is to avoid the passive activity loss limitations.

Special Grouping Rules for Rental Activities Two rules deal specifically with the grouping of rental activities. These rules are designed to prevent taxpayers from grouping rental activities, which are generally passive, with other businesses in a way that would result in a tax advantage.

First, a rental activity may be grouped with a trade or business activity only if one activity is insubstantial in relation to the other. That is, the rental activity must be insubstantial in relation to the trade or business activity, or the trade or business activity must be insubstantial in relation to the rental activity. The Regulations provide no clear guidelines as to the meaning of "insubstantial."[16]

EXAMPLE 19

Schemers, a CPA firm, owns a building in Washington, D.C., in which it conducts its public accounting practice. The firm also rents space on the street level of the building to several retail establishments, which generally is considered a passive activity. Of the total revenue generated by the firm, 95% is associated with the public accounting practice and 5% is related to the rental operation.

It is likely that the rental activity would be considered insubstantial relative to the accounting practice and the two ventures could be grouped as one nonrental activity. This grouping could be advantageous to the firm, particularly if the rental operation generates a loss, since the rental loss could be used to offset any income from the public accounting practice.

Alternatively, treating the rental operation as a *separate* activity may be advantageous if this operation produces (passive activity) income. The passive activity income could then be used to absorb otherwise nondeductible passive activity losses.

Second, taxpayers generally may not treat an activity involving the rental of real property and an activity involving the rental of personal property as a single activity.

Material Participation

LO.5

Identify the tests for material participation.

If an individual taxpayer *materially participates* in a nonrental trade or business activity, any loss from that activity is treated as an active loss that can offset active or portfolio income. If a taxpayer does not materially participate, the loss is treated as a passive activity loss, which can only offset passive activity income. As a result, controlling whether a particular activity is treated as active or passive is an important part of the tax strategy of a taxpayer who owns an interest in one or more businesses. Consider the following examples.

---

[15]Reg. § 1.469–4(f).   [16]Reg. § 1.469–4(d).

Implications of Material Participation Status

Noah, a corporate executive, earns a salary of $600,000 per year. In addition, he owns a separate business in which he participates. The business produces a loss of $100,000 during the year. If Noah materially participates in the business, the $100,000 loss is an active loss that may offset his active income from his corporate employer.

If he does not materially participate, the loss is passive and is suspended unless he has other passive activity income. Noah may use the suspended passive activity loss in the future only when he has passive activity income or disposes of the activity.

Junghee, an attorney, earns $350,000 a year in her law practice. In addition, she owns interests in two activities, A and B, in which she participates. Activity A, in which she does *not* materially participate, produces a loss of $50,000. Activity B produces income of $80,000. However, Junghee has not yet met the material participation standard, described below, for Activity B. But Junghee can meet the material participation standard if she spends an additional 50 hours in Activity B during the year. Should Junghee attempt to meet the material participation standard for Activity B?

If she continues working in Activity B and becomes a material participant, the $80,000 of income from the activity is *active*, and the $50,000 passive activity loss from Activity A must be suspended. A more favorable tax strategy is for Junghee *not to meet* the material participation standard for Activity B, thus making the income from that activity passive. This enables her to offset the $50,000 passive activity loss from Activity A against most of the passive activity income from Activity B.

It is possible to devise numerous scenarios in which the taxpayer could control the tax outcome by increasing or decreasing his or her participation in different activities. Examples 20 and 21 demonstrate some of the possibilities. In most analyses of this type, taxpayers will benefit by having profitable activities classified as passive so that any passive activity losses can be used to offset that passive activity income. If the activity produces a loss, however, the taxpayer will benefit if it is classified as active so that the loss is not subject to the passive activity loss limitations.

A nonrental trade or business in which a taxpayer owns an interest must be treated as a passive activity unless the taxpayer materially participates. A material participant is one who has "a significant nontax economic profit motive" for taking on activities and selects them for their economic value.[17] In contrast, a passive investor mainly seeks a return from a capital investment (including a possible reduction in taxes) as a supplement to an ongoing source of livelihood.

Even if the concept of being a material participant is clear, the precise meaning of the term **material participation** can be vague. As enacted, § 469 requires a taxpayer to participate on a *regular*, *continuous*, and *substantial* basis to be a material participant. In many situations, however, it is difficult or impossible to gain any assurance that this nebulous standard is met.

In response to this dilemma, Temporary Regulations[18] provide seven tests that serve to determine when material participation is achieved. Material participation is achieved by meeting any *one* of the tests. These tests are listed in Concept Summary 11.2 and can be divided into the following three categories:

- Tests based on current participation.
- Tests based on prior participation.
- Test based on facts and circumstances.

---

[17]*General Explanation of the Tax Reform Act of 1986* ("Blue Book"), prepared by The Staff of the Joint Committee on Taxation, May 4, 1987, H.R. 3838, 99th Cong., p. 212.

[18]Temp.Reg. § 1.469–5T(a). The Temporary Regulations are also Proposed Regulations. Temporary Regulations have the same effect as Final Regulations. Refer to Chapter 2 for a discussion of the different categories of Regulations.

Concept Summary 11.2

Tests to Determine Material Participation

Tests Based on Current Participation

1. The individual participates in the activity for more than 500 hours during the year.

2. The individual's participation in the activity for the taxable year constitutes substantially all of the participation in the activity of all individuals (including nonowner employees) for the year.

3. The individual participates in the activity for more than 100 hours during the year, and this participation is not less than that participation of any other individual (including nonowner employees) for the year.

4. The activity is a ==significant participation activity== (where the person's participation *exceeds* 100 hours during the year), and the hours for all significant participation activities during the year is more than 500 hours.

Tests Based on Prior Participation

5. The individual materially participated in the activity for any 5 taxable years during the 10 taxable years that immediately precede the current taxable year.

6. The activity is a personal service activity, and the individual materially participated in the activity for any 3 preceding taxable years.

Test Based on Facts and Circumstances

7. Based on all of the facts and circumstances, the individual participates in the activity on a regular, continuous, and substantial basis during the year.

Participation Defined Participation generally includes any work done by an individual in an activity that he or she owns. Participation does not include work if it is of a type not customarily done by owners *and* if one of its principal purposes is to avoid the disallowance of passive activity losses or credits. Also, work done in an individual's capacity as an investor (e.g., reviewing financial reports in a nonmanagerial capacity) is not counted in applying the material participation tests. However, participation by an owner's spouse counts as participation by the owner.[19]

EXAMPLE 22

Emma, who is a partner in a CPA firm, owns a computer store that operated at a loss during the year. To offset this loss against the income from her CPA practice, Emma would like to avoid having the computer business classified as a passive activity. During the year, she worked 480 hours in the business participating in management and sales activities and 30 hours doing janitorial chores. In addition, Emma's spouse participated 40 hours as a salesperson.

It is likely that Emma's 480 hours of participation in management and sales activities will count as participation in work customarily done by owners, but the 30 hours spent doing janitorial chores will not. In addition, the 40 hours of participation by her spouse will also count.

Assuming that none of the participation's principal purposes is to avoid the disallowance of passive activity losses or credits, Emma will qualify as a material participant under the more-than-500-hour rule (480 + 40 = 520).

Limited Partners A *limited* partner is a partner whose liability to third-party creditors of the partnership is limited to the amount the partner has invested in the partnership. Such a partnership must have at least one *general* partner who is fully liable in an individual capacity for the debts of the partnership to third parties.

Generally, a *limited partner* is not considered a material participant unless he or she qualifies under Test 1, 5, or 6 as shown in Concept Summary 11.2. However, a *general partner* may qualify as a material participant by meeting any of the seven tests. If a general partner also owns a limited interest in the same limited partnership, all interests are treated as a general interest.[20]

---

[19]§ 469(h)(5) and Temp.Reg. § 1.469–5T(f)(3).

[20]§ 469(h)(2) and Temp.Reg. § 1.469–5T(e)(3)(ii). Under Prop.Reg. § 1.469–5, however, material participation status for owners of LLCs and LLPs is dependent on the taxpayer's general involvement in the business.

Rental Activities Defined

Subject to certain exceptions, all rental activities are treated as passive activities.[21] A <mark>rental activity</mark> is defined as any activity where payments are received principally for the use of tangible (real or personal) property.[22] Importantly, an activity that is classified as a rental activity is subject to the passive activity loss rules even if the taxpayer involved is a material participant.

LO.6

Describe the nature of rental activities under the passive activity loss rules.

Sarah owns a fleet of automobiles that are held for rent, and she spends an average of 60 hours a week in the activity. Assuming that her automobile business is classified as a rental activity, it is *automatically* subject to the passive activity rules even though Sarah spends more than 500 hours a year in its operation.

EXAMPLE 23

Certain rentals of real and personal property might be classified under the passive activity loss rules as *nonrental* activities.[23] In these situations, assuming that the activity is a trade or business, the material participation tests shown in Concept Summary 11.2 must be applied to determine whether the activity is a passive activity. Consider the following example.

Arturo owns a bicycle rental business at a nearby resort. Because the average period of customer use is seven days or less, Arturo's business is not treated as a rental activity.

EXAMPLE 24

Example 24 illustrates an exception to the definition of a rental activity. This exception is based on the presumption that a person who rents property for seven days or less is generally required to provide significant services to the customer. Providing these services supports a conclusion that the person is engaged in a service business rather than a rental business. Other examples of this exception include most hotels or motels and businesses that rent tools, tuxedos, or cars.[24]

This result, however, does not mean that Arturo's business is a nonpassive activity. Instead, it is treated as a trade or business activity subject to the material participation standards listed in Concept Summary 11.2. If Arturo is a material participant, the business is treated as active. If he is not a material participant, it is treated as a passive activity.

11-3d Interaction of the At-Risk and Passive Activity Loss Limits

LO.7

Determine the relationship between the at-risk and passive activity loss limitations.

The determination of whether a loss is suspended under the passive activity loss rules is made *after* application of the at-risk rules, as well as other rules relating to the measurement of taxable income. A loss that is not allowed for the year because of the at-risk rules is suspended under those rules, not under the passive activity loss rules. Further, a taxpayer's at-risk basis is reduced by the losses (but not below zero) even if the deductions are not currently usable because of the passive activity loss rules. The following examples illustrate these points.

At-Risk and Passive Activity Loss Interactions

Jack's adjusted basis in a passive activity is $10,000 at the beginning of 2018. His loss from the activity in 2018 is $4,000. Because Jack has no passive activity income, the $4,000 cannot be deducted. At year-end, Jack has an adjusted basis and an at-risk amount of $6,000 in the activity and a suspended passive activity loss of $4,000.

EXAMPLE 25

---

[21]§ 469(c)(2).

[22]§ 469(j)(8).

[23]Temp.Reg. § 1.469–1T(e)(3).

[24]For additional discussion of the rental exceptions, see IRS Publication 925 (*Passive Activity and At-Risk Rules*).

At-Risk and Passive Activity Loss Interactions

EXAMPLE 26

Jack in Example 25 has a loss of $9,000 in the activity in 2019. Because the $9,000 exceeds his at-risk amount ($6,000) by $3,000, that $3,000 loss is disallowed by the at-risk rules. If Jack has no passive activity income, the remaining $6,000 is suspended under the passive activity rules. At year-end, he has:

- A $3,000 loss suspended under the at-risk rules.
- $10,000 of suspended passive activity losses ($4,000 from 2018 and $6,000 from 2019).
- An adjusted basis and an at-risk amount in the activity of zero.

EXAMPLE 27

Jack in Example 26 realizes $1,000 of passive activity income from the activity in 2020. Because the $1,000 increases his at-risk amount, $1,000 of the $3,000 unused loss from 2019 is reclassified as a passive activity loss. If he has no other passive activity income, the $1,000 income is offset by $1,000 of suspended passive activity losses. At the end of 2020, Jack has:

- No taxable passive activity income.
- $2,000 ($3,000 − $1,000) of suspended losses under the at-risk rules.
- $10,000 of (reclassified) suspended passive activity losses ($10,000 + $1,000 of reclassified suspended at-risk losses − $1,000 of passive activity losses offset against passive activity income).
- An adjusted basis and an at-risk amount in the activity of zero.

EXAMPLE 28

In 2021, Jack has no gain or loss from the activity in Example 27. He contributes $5,000 more to the passive activity. Because the $5,000 increases his at-risk amount, the $2,000 of losses suspended under the at-risk rules is reclassified as passive. Jack gets no passive activity loss deduction in 2021. At year-end, he has:

- No suspended losses under the at-risk rules.
- $12,000 of suspended passive activity losses ($10,000 + $2,000 of reclassified suspended at-risk losses).
- An adjusted basis and an at-risk amount of $3,000 ($5,000 additional investment − $2,000 of reclassified losses).

The Big Picture

EXAMPLE 29

Return to the facts of *The Big Picture* on p. 11-1. If the Reswicks invest in the orange grove limited partnership, the at-risk rules will not limit the deductibility of the $25,000 losses until after year 4. Ample at-risk basis will exist until the close of that year (i.e., the at-risk basis is reduced from $100,000 by $25,000 over each of the first four years of the investment).

However, the passive activity loss rules prohibit deductions for the losses in the first four years of the investment (assuming that the Reswicks do not have passive activity income from other sources). Based on the facts provided, none of the suspended losses would be deductible until year 6, when the orange grove is expected to begin producing profits.

Concept Summary 11.3 illustrates the interactions of the at-risk and passive activity limits.

LO.8

Recognize the special treatment available to certain real estate activities.

11-3e **Special Passive Activity Rules for Real Estate Activities**

The passive activity loss limits contain two exceptions related to real estate activities. These exceptions allow all or part of real estate rental losses to offset active or portfolio income even though the activity otherwise is defined as a passive activity.

Concept Summary 11.3

Treatment of Losses Subject to the At-Risk and Passive Activity Loss Limitations

Material Participation in a Real Property Rental Trade or Business

The first exception to the passive activity loss rules provides relief to real estate professionals.[25] Under this exception, taxpayers meeting specific requirements are allowed to apply one of the seven material participation tests to their rental real estate activities (i.e., these *rental activities* are *not* automatically treated as passive activities). To qualify for this exception, a taxpayer must satisfy *both* of the following requirements:

- More than half of the personal services that the taxpayer performs in trades or businesses are performed in real property trades or businesses in which the taxpayer materially participates.

- The taxpayer performs more than 750 hours of services in real property trades or businesses in which the taxpayer materially participates.

Taxpayers who do not satisfy the above requirements must continue to treat income and losses from real estate rental activities as passive activity income and losses.

> **EXAMPLE 30**
>
> During the current year, Della performs personal service activities as follows: 900 hours as a personal financial planner, 550 hours in a real estate development business, and 600 hours in a rental real estate activity. Any loss Della incurs in either real estate activity will not be subject to the passive activity loss rules.
>
> - Being a nonrental business, the real estate development business is deemed active under the more-than-500-hour material participation test.
> - Della may apply a material participation test to the real estate rental activity because (1) more than 50% of Della's personal services are devoted to real property trades or businesses (i.e., the development and rental businesses) in which she materially participates, *and* (2) she has over 750 hours in real property trades or businesses in which she materially participates.
> - As a result, any loss from Della's rental real estate activity can offset active and portfolio sources of income because she meets the over-500-hour material participation test for that rental activity and she qualifies as a real estate professional. Likewise, any income from this activity would be nonpassive (active) income.

As discussed earlier, a spouse's work is taken into consideration in satisfying the material participation requirement. However, the hours worked by a spouse are *not* taken into account when evaluating whether a taxpayer spent more than 50 percent of his or her personal services in real property trades or businesses in which he or she

---

[25]§ 469(c)(7).

materially participates or has worked for more than 750 hours in these real property trades or businesses during the year.[26] Services performed by an employee are not treated as being related to a real property trade or business unless the employee performing the services owns more than a 5 percent interest in the employer. In addition, a closely held C corporation may also qualify for the passive activity loss relief if more than 50 percent of its gross receipts for the year are derived from real property trades or businesses in which it materially participates.

ETHICS & EQUITY   Punching the Time Clock at Year-End

As the end of the tax year approaches, Julie, a successful full-time real estate developer and investor, recognizes that her income tax situation for the year could be bleak. Unless she and her spouse, Ralph, are able to generate more hours of participation in one of her real estate rental activities, they will not reach the material participation threshold. Consequently, the tax losses from the venture will not be deductible. To ensure deductibility, Julie suggests the following plan:

- She will document the time she spends "thinking" about her rental activities.

- During the week, Ralph will visit the apartment building to oversee (in a management role) the operations of the rentals.

- On weekends, she and Ralph will visit the same units to further evaluate the operations.

- Also on the weekends, while they are doing their routine household shopping, they will be on the lookout for other rental properties to buy. Julie plans to count both her and Ralph's weekend hours toward the tally of total participation.

Julie contends that the law clearly allows the efforts of one's spouse to count for purposes of the material participation tests. Likewise, nothing in the tax law requires taxpayers to be efficient in their hours of participation. How do you react?

Real Estate Rental Activities with Active Participation

The second exception to the passive activity loss limits is more significant in that it is *not* restricted to real estate professionals. This exception allows individuals to deduct up to $25,000 of losses from real estate rental activities against active and portfolio income each year.[27] The potential annual $25,000 deduction is reduced by 50 percent of the taxpayer's AGI in excess of $100,000. As a result, the entire deduction is phased out at $150,000 of AGI. If married individuals file separately, the $25,000 deduction is reduced to zero unless they lived apart for the entire year. In this case, the loss amount is $12,500 each and the phaseout begins at $50,000 of AGI.[28]

To qualify for the $25,000 exception, a taxpayer must meet *both* of the following requirements:[29]

- *Actively participate* in the real estate rental activity, and

- Own 10 percent or more (in value) of all interests in the activity during the entire taxable year (or shorter period during which the taxpayer held an interest in the activity).

The difference between *active participation* and *material participation* is that the active participation threshold can be satisfied *without* regular, continuous, and substantial involvement in operations. The active participation standard is met if the taxpayer participates in making management decisions in a significant and bona fide sense. Approving new tenants, deciding on rental terms, and approving capital or repair expenditures meet this test.

---

[26]§ 469(c)(7)(B) and Reg. § 1.469–9. In *Frank Aragona Trust*, 142 T.C. 165 (2014), the Tax Court found that a trust also could qualify for the real estate professional rule.

[27]§ 469(i).

[28]In general, AGI for purposes of the phaseout is calculated without regard to IRA deductions, Social Security benefits, interest deductions on education loans, and net losses from passive activities. See § 469(i)(3)(F).

[29]§ 469(i)(6).

The Big Picture

Return to the facts of *The Big Picture* on p. 11-1. If the Reswicks invest in the apartment rental limited partnership, which is a passive activity, a portion (or all) of their $25,000 loss will be deductible under the real estate rental activities exception (the deductible loss will depend on their AGI and the loss phaseout that applies once AGI exceeds $100,000). This also assumes that they actively participate and own at least a 10% interest in the partnership.

The loss will be deductible in each of the first four years of their investment before their at-risk basis has been exhausted (as explained earlier, the Reswicks' original at-risk basis of $100,000 will be reduced to $0 over four years) even if they do not have passive activity income from other sources.

EXAMPLE 31

The $25,000 allowance is available after all active participation rental losses and gains are netted and applied to other passive activity income. If a taxpayer has a real estate rental loss in excess of the amount that can be deducted under the real estate rental exception, that excess is treated as a passive activity loss, usable in future years.

Brad has $90,000 of AGI before considering rental activities. Brad also has $85,000 of losses from a real estate rental activity in which he actively participates. He also actively participates in another real estate rental activity from which he has $30,000 of income. He has other passive activity income of $36,000.

Of the net rental loss of $55,000 ($30,000 − $85,000), $36,000 offsets the passive activity income, leaving $19,000 that can be deducted against active or portfolio income because of the availability of the $25,000 allowance.

EXAMPLE 32

The $25,000 allowance is an aggregate of both deductions and the "deduction equivalent" of tax credits. The deduction equivalent of a passive activity credit is the amount of deductions that reduces the tax liability for the taxable year by an amount equal to the credit.[30] A taxpayer with $2,200 of credits and a tax bracket of 22 percent would have a deduction equivalent of $10,000 ($2,200 ÷ 22%).

If the total deduction and deduction equivalent exceed $25,000, the taxpayer must allocate the allowance on a pro rata basis, first among the losses (including real estate rental activity losses suspended in prior years) and then to credits in the following order: (1) credits other than rehabilitation and low-income housing credits, (2) rehabilitation credits, and (3) low-income housing credits.

Deduction Equivalent Considerations

Kevin is an active participant in a real estate rental activity that produces $8,000 of income, $26,000 of deductions, and $1,500 of credits. Kevin is a single taxpayer with $98,000 of AGI before considering this rental activity and is in the 22% tax bracket. As a result, he may deduct the net passive activity loss of $18,000 ($8,000 − $26,000).

After deducting the loss, he has an available deduction equivalent of $7,000 ($25,000 − $18,000 passive activity loss). Because the actual credits produce a $6,818 deduction equivalent ($1,500 ÷ 22% = $6,818) and this amount is less than $7,000, Kevin may claim the entire $1,500 credit.

EXAMPLE 33

Kelly is an active participant in three separate real estate rental activities. Kelly is a single taxpayer with $92,000 of AGI before considering these rental activities and is in the 22% tax bracket. The relevant tax results for each activity are as follows:

- Activity A: $20,000 of losses.
- Activity B: $10,000 of losses.
- Activity C: $1,100 of credits.

continued

EXAMPLE 34

[30]§ 469(j)(5).

Kelly's deduction equivalent from the credits is $5,000 ($1,100 ÷ 22%). As a result, the total passive activity losses and deduction equivalents are $35,000 ($20,000 + $10,000 + $5,000), which exceeds the maximum allowable amount of $25,000. Consequently, Kelly must allocate the $25,000 allowance on a pro rata basis, first from among losses and then from among credits. Deductions from losses are limited as follows:

- Activity A {$25,000 × [$20,000 ÷ ($20,000 + $10,000)]} = $16,667

- Activity B {$25,000 × [$10,000 ÷ ($20,000 + $10,000)]} = $8,333

Because the amount of passive activity losses exceeds the $25,000 maximum, the remaining losses of $5,000 and passive activity credits of $1,100 must be carried forward. Kelly's suspended losses and credits by activity are as follows:

| | Total | Activity | | |
		A	B	C
Allocated losses	$ 30,000	$ 20,000	$10,000	$ –0–
Allocated credits	1,100	–0–	–0–	1,100
Utilized losses	(25,000)	(16,667)	(8,333)	–0–
Suspended losses	5,000	3,333	1,667	–0–
Suspended credits	1,100	–0–	–0–	1,100

 LO.9

Determine the proper tax treatment on the disposition of a passive activity.

11-3f **Dispositions of Passive Interests**

If a taxpayer disposes of an entire interest in a passive activity, any suspended losses (and in certain cases, suspended credits) may be used when calculating the final economic gain or loss on the investment. In addition, if there is an overall loss from the disposition, that loss can offset other types of income. However, the tax consequences may be different if the activity is disposed of in transactions that are not fully taxable (e.g., a transfer at death or by gift or an installment sale). The following sections discuss these types of dispositions.

Disposition of a Passive Activity at Death

When a transfer of a taxpayer's interest occurs because of a taxpayer's death, suspended losses are allowed (to the decedent) to the extent they exceed the amount, if any, of the allowed increase (step-up) in basis.[31] Suspended losses that are equal to or less than the amount of the basis increase are, however, lost. The losses allowed generally are reported on the final return of the deceased taxpayer.

Disposition of Suspended Passive Activity Losses at Death

 EXAMPLE 35

Alyson dies with passive activity property having an adjusted basis of $40,000, suspended losses of $10,000, and a fair market value at the date of her death of $75,000. The increase (step-up) in basis is $35,000 (fair market value at date of death in excess of adjusted basis).

None of the $10,000 suspended loss is deductible on Alyson's final return or by the beneficiary. The suspended losses ($10,000) are lost because they do not exceed the step-up in basis ($35,000).

 EXAMPLE 36

Assume the same facts as in the previous example, except that the property's fair market value at the date of Alyson's death is $47,000.

Because the step-up in basis is only $7,000 ($47,000 − $40,000), the suspended losses allowed are limited to $3,000 ($10,000 suspended loss at time of death − $7,000 increase in basis). The $3,000 loss available to Alyson is reported on her final income tax return.

---

[31]§ 469(g)(2); the basis of inherited property is generally the fair market value on the date of death (see Chapter 13).

Disposition of a Passive Activity by Gift

If a taxpayer's interest in a passive activity is transferred by gift, the suspended losses are added to the donee's basis of the property.[32] As a result, the donor will see no benefit from any suspended losses. However, a tax *benefit* may be available to the donee. Due to the increase in the property's basis, greater depreciation deductions can result, and there will be less gain (or more loss) on a subsequent sale of the property. The benefits of increased basis do not materialize if the recipient is a charity, as such organizations generally are not subject to income taxation.

EXAMPLE 37

Carlton makes a gift to Emma of passive activity property having an adjusted basis of $40,000, suspended losses of $10,000, and a fair market value at the date of the gift of $100,000. Carlton cannot deduct the suspended losses in the year of the disposition. However, the suspended losses transfer with the property and are added to the adjusted basis of the property, which becomes $50,000 in Emma's hands.

Assuming that Emma is able to sell the property for $105,000 soon after she receives the gift, her taxable gain would be $55,000 ($105,000 − $50,000), which reflects the benefit from the increased basis.

Installment Sale of a Passive Activity

An installment sale of a taxpayer's entire interest in a passive activity triggers recognition of the suspended losses.[33] The losses are allowed each year as payments are received on the installment obligation in the ratio that the gain recognized in each year bears to the total gain on the sale.

EXAMPLE 38

Lucas sells his entire interest in a passive activity for $100,000. His adjusted basis in the property is $60,000. If he uses the installment method, his gross profit ratio is 40% ($40,000 gross profit/$100,000 sales proceeds). If Lucas receives a $20,000 down payment, he will recognize a gain of $8,000 (40% of $20,000). If the activity has a suspended loss of $25,000, Lucas will deduct $5,000 [($8,000 ÷ $40,000) × $25,000] of the suspended loss in the first year.

This pattern will continue as Lucas receives installment payments. So, for example, if Lucas receives a $10,000 installment payment in the following year, he will recognize gain of $4,000 and can deduct $2,500 of the suspended loss in that year.

The general rules relating to passive activity losses are reviewed in Concept Summary 11.4.

11-4 INVESTMENT INTEREST LIMITATION

LO.10

Identify restrictions placed on the deductibility of other investor losses and deductions, including those that apply to investment interest.

Another way investors used the tax law to create wealth involved the use of the interest deduction. By borrowing to purchase investments that would appreciate over time, the interest on the debt was claimed as an ordinary deduction when paid. Later, when the asset was sold at a gain, only a capital gains tax was due on the appreciation. In addition to the "mismatch" of ordinary deductions leading to capital gains, the time value of money also played a role in these decisions (current deductions leading to lower taxes today; capital gains at lower rates at some point in the future).

11-4a Limitation Imposed

In response, Congress has limited the deductibility of <mark>investment interest</mark>, which is interest paid on debt borrowed for the purpose of purchasing or continuing to hold

[32]§ 469(j)(6).   [33]§ 469(g)(3).

Concept Summary 11.4

Passive Activity Loss Rules: Key Issues and Answers

What is the fundamental passive activity rule?	Passive activity losses may be deducted only against passive activity income and gains. Losses not allowed are suspended and used in future years.
Who is subject to the passive activity rules?	Individuals.
	Estates.
	Trusts.
	Personal service corporations.
	Closely held C corporations.
What is a passive activity?	Trade or business or income-producing activity in which the taxpayer does not materially participate during the year or rental activities, subject to certain exceptions, regardless of the taxpayer's level of participation.
What is an activity?	One or more trade or business or rental activities that comprise an appropriate economic unit.
How is an appropriate economic unit determined?	Based on a reasonable application of the relevant facts and circumstances.
What is material participation?	In general, the taxpayer participates on a regular, continuous, and substantial basis. More specifically, when the taxpayer meets the conditions of one of the seven tests provided in the Regulations.
What is a rental activity?	In general, an activity where payments are received for the use of tangible property. Special rules apply to rental real estate.

investment property. The deduction for investment interest allowed during the tax year is limited to the lesser of the investment interest paid or net investment income.[34]

The Big Picture

EXAMPLE 39

Return to the facts of *The Big Picture* on p. 11-1. If the Reswicks invest in the high-growth, low-yield portfolio of marketable securities, most of the investment return will consist of appreciation, which will not be taxed until the securities are sold. Relatively little of the current return will consist of currently taxable interest and dividend income.

Assume that the interest and dividend income for the year from these securities equals $1,500 and that all of it is treated as investment income. If the investment interest expense on the $100,000 loan is $4,000, only $1,500 of this interest will be deductible this year (i.e., the deduction for the investment interest is limited to the $1,500 of net investment income).

Investment Income and Expenses

Net investment income, which serves as the ceiling on the deductibility of investment interest, is the excess of investment income over investment expenses. **Investment income** includes gross income from interest, annuities, and royalties not derived in the ordinary course of a trade or business.[35] However, investment income does not include any income taken into account when calculating income or loss from a passive activity.

Investment expenses are those deductible expenses directly connected with the production of investment income, such as property taxes on investment holdings. Investment expenses do not include interest expense and, from 2018 through 2025, any expenses that are miscellaneous itemized deductions (e.g., brokerage charges and investment counsel fees).

---

[34]§ 163(d)(1).   [35]§ 163(d)(4)(B).

11-4b Computation of Allowable Deduction

After net investment income is determined, the allowable deductible investment interest expense is calculated.

EXAMPLE 40

Ethan's financial records for the year reflect the following:

Interest income from bank savings account	$10,000
Taxable annuity receipts	5,500
Local ad valorem property tax on investments	200
Investment interest expense	17,000

Ethan's investment income amounts to $15,500 ($10,000 + $5,500), and investment expenses total $200. As a result, his net investment income is $15,300 ($15,500 − $200). Consequently, the investment interest deduction is limited to $15,300 (the lesser of investment interest expense or net investment income).

The amount of investment interest disallowed is carried over to future years. In Example 40, the amount that is carried over to the following year is $1,700 ($17,000 investment interest expense − $15,300 deduction allowed). No limit is placed on the length of the carryover period.[36] The investment interest expense deduction is determined by completing Form 4952 (Investment Interest Deduction).

11-5 OTHER INVESTMENT LOSSES

The investment activities summarized below are discussed elsewhere in this text as shown in Concept Summary 11.5.

- Sales of securities held as investments for less than basis result in capital losses. These losses can offset capital gains. In the case of individual taxpayers, excess losses are applied against ordinary income up to $3,000 per year (§ 1211). Any remaining excess capital losses are carried over for use in future years (§ 1212).

- When an activity is classified as a hobby, any losses resulting are limited to the income from the activity [§ 183(b)(2)]. If the activity is not a hobby (i.e., a profit motive controls), however, full deduction of the losses is allowed [§§ 162 and 212(2)].

- Losses on small business stock (i.e., stock that qualifies under § 1244) are treated as ordinary losses up to a maximum of $100,000. As a result, the limitations placed on capital losses (see above) are avoided.

- Vacation homes that are rented for part of the year may generate investment losses depending on the extent of the rental period as compared to time devoted to personal use (§ 280A). If sufficient rental activity takes place, the vacation home may be treated as rental property. As a result, any losses could be subject to the passive activity loss rules.

- Securities held as an investment that become worthless produce capital losses. The losses are usually long term because they are treated as occurring on the last day of the year in which the securities become worthless [§ 165(g)(1)]. Because the securities must be completely worthless, determining the year when this takes place is often difficult.

[36]§ 163(d)(2).

Concept Summary 11.5

Common Investment Loss Limitation Rules

Item	Refer to Chapter	General Nature of Limitation
At-risk rules	11	Losses in excess of the at-risk basis are not deducted in the current year. Losses not deducted are suspended and used in future years when the at-risk basis increases.
Capital losses	14	Individuals may offset capital gains by capital losses realized. Up to $3,000 of realized net capital losses may offset ordinary income per year. Remaining excess capital losses are carried over to future years.
Hobby losses	6	Losses from hobby activities may be deducted to the extent of income from hobby activities. Excess hobby losses are carried forward to future years.
Investment interest	11	The deduction of investment interest is limited to the taxpayer's net investment income. Excess investment interest is deductible in future years.
Passive activity loss limitations	11	Generally, passive activity losses are deducted only to the extent of passive activity income. Excess passive activity losses are suspended and used in future years.
Small business (§ 1244) stock	7	Losses from the disposition of small business stock are given ordinary treatment up to a maximum of $100,000 per year.
Vacation homes	6	The deductibility of losses from vacation homes may be limited depending on the relative number of rental use days and personal use days of the property.
Worthless securities	7	Losses arising from investment securities that become worthless are treated as occurring on the last day of the tax year.

LO.11

Suggest tax planning strategies to minimize the effect of the passive activity loss and investment interest limitations and recognize the general impact of the additional tax on net investment income.

11-6 TAX PLANNING

11-6a Using Passive Activity Losses

Perhaps the biggest challenge individuals face with the passive activity loss rules is to recognize the potential impact of the rules and then to structure their affairs to minimize this impact. If a taxpayer does invest in an activity that produces losses subject to the passive activity loss rules, the following discussion describes strategies that may help minimize the loss of current deductions.

Taxpayers who have passive activity losses should adopt a strategy of buying an interest in an activity that is generating passive activity income that can be offset (or sheltered) by the existing passive activity losses. From a tax perspective, it would be foolish to buy a loss-generating passive activity unless (1) the taxpayer has other passive activity income to shelter, (2) the activity is rental real estate that can qualify for the $25,000 exception, or (3) the activity qualifies for the exception available to real estate professionals.

If money is borrowed to finance the purchase of a passive activity, the associated interest expense is generally treated as part of any passive activity loss. Consequently, by using more available (i.e., not borrowed) cash to purchase the passive investment, the investor will need less debt and will incur less interest expense. By incurring less interest expense, a possible suspended passive activity loss deduction is reduced.

As explained earlier, unusable passive activity losses often accumulate and provide no current tax benefit because the taxpayer has no passive activity income. When the taxpayer disposes of the entire interest in a passive activity, however, any suspended losses from that activity are used to reduce the taxable gain. If any taxable gain still remains, it can be offset by losses from other passive activities. As a result, the taxpayer should carefully select the year in which to dispose of a passive activity. It is to the taxpayer's advantage to wait until sufficient passive activity losses have accumulated to offset any gain recognized on the asset's disposition.

EXAMPLE 41

Bill, a calendar year taxpayer, owns interests in two passive activities: Activity A, which he plans to sell in December of this year at a gain of $100,000, and Activity B, which he plans to keep indefinitely. Current and suspended passive activity losses associated with Activity B total $60,000, and Bill expects losses from the activity to be $40,000 next year.

If Bill sells Activity A this year, the $100,000 gain can be offset by the current and suspended losses of $60,000 from Activity B, producing a net taxable gain of $40,000. However, if Bill delays the sale of Activity A until January of next year, the $100,000 gain will be fully offset by the $100,000 of losses generated by Activity B ($60,000 current and prior losses + $40,000 next year's loss). Consequently, by postponing the sale by one month, he could avoid recognizing $40,000 of gain that would otherwise result.

Taxpayers with passive activity losses should consider the level of their involvement in all other trades or businesses in which they have an interest. If they do not materially participate in a profitable activity, the activity becomes a passive activity. Any income generated by the profitable business then could be sheltered by current and suspended passive activity losses. Family partnerships in which certain members do not materially participate would qualify. The silent partner in any general partnership engaged in a trade or business also would qualify.

EXAMPLE 42

Gail has an investment in a limited partnership that produces annual passive activity losses of approximately $25,000. She also owns a newly acquired interest in a convenience store where she works. Her share of the store's income is $35,000. If she works enough to be classified as a material participant, her $35,000 share of income is treated as active income. This results in $35,000 being subject to tax every year, whereas her $25,000 loss is suspended.

However, if Gail reduces her involvement at the store so that she is not a material participant, the $35,000 of income receives passive activity treatment. Consequently, the $35,000 of passive activity income can be offset by the $25,000 passive activity loss, resulting in only $10,000 being subject to tax. By reducing her involvement, Gail ensures that the income from the profitable trade or business receives passive activity treatment and can then be used to absorb passive activity losses from other passive activities.

The impact of the passive activity loss rules often extends to other seemingly unrelated Code sections. For example, because of the restrictive nature of the passive activity loss rules, it may be advantageous for a taxpayer to use a vacation home enough to convert it to a second residence. This would enable qualified interest and real estate taxes to be deducted (subject to the limitations discussed in Chapter 10). However, this strategy would lead to the loss of other deductions, such as repairs, maintenance, and insurance. See Examples 36 and 38 and the related discussion in Chapter 6.

The passive activity loss rules can have a dramatic effect on a taxpayer's ability to claim passive activity losses currently. As a result, it is important to keep accurate records of all sources of income and losses, particularly any suspended passive activity losses and credits and the activities to which they relate, so that their potential tax benefit will not be lost.

11-6b Planning with the Investment Interest Limitation

The term *investment income* includes net capital gain and qualified dividend income only if the taxpayer *elects* to treat them as such. For this purpose:

- Net capital gain includes gain attributable to property held for investment.
- Qualified dividend income includes dividends that are taxed at the same marginal rate that is applicable to a net capital gain.

By electing to include net capital gain and qualified dividend income as components of investment income, the amount of investment interest deductible in a particular year likewise increases. Form 4952 is used to make such an election. However, the election comes with a cost and is available only if the taxpayer agrees to reduce amounts qualifying for the preferential tax rates that otherwise apply to net capital gain (see Chapter 14) and qualified dividends (refer to Chapter 4) by an equivalent amount.[37]

EXAMPLE 43

Olivia incurred $13,000 of interest expense related to her investments during the year. Her investment income included $4,000 of interest, $2,000 of qualified dividends, and a $5,000 net capital gain on the sale of investment securities.

If Olivia does not make the election to include the net capital gain and qualified dividends in investment income, her investment income for purposes of computing the investment income limitation is $4,000 (interest income). If she does make the election, her investment income is $11,000 ($4,000 interest + $2,000 qualified dividends + $5,000 net capital gain). In that case, $11,000 of her interest expense, rather than $4,000, is deductible currently.

Should Olivia in the previous example make the election to include the additional $7,000 of qualified dividends and net capital gain as investment income? By doing so, the current-year investment interest deduction increases by $7,000, and the investment interest deduction potentially carried forward to future years is reduced by the same amount. That is, the election allows for an acceleration of the investment interest deduction. As Olivia evaluates her decision, she should consider the following points:

- The election would make sense only if her marginal ordinary income tax rate exceeds the applicable capital gains rate.
- Using present value concepts, she should compare the tax cost of postponing the interest deduction to a subsequent year with the impact of losing the benefit from the preferential capital gains rate. In performing this analysis, consideration should be given to the length of the deferral of the investment interest deduction and the current and future years' tax brackets.

11-6c Effect of the Additional Tax on Net Investment Income

As if the passive activity loss and investment interest limitations are not complicated enough, individuals, estates, and trusts also are subject to an additional 3.8 percent tax on net investment income.[38] Net investment income *for this purpose* generally includes amounts such as interest, dividends, long- and short-term capital gains, royalties, rents, and income from passive activities.

The tax is levied at the flat 3.8 percent rate on the lesser of the taxpayer's net investment income or the excess of modified AGI over a threshold amount. The threshold amounts for individuals are $250,000 for surviving spouses and taxpayers filing a joint return, $125,000 for married taxpayers filing separate returns, and $200,000 for all other individual taxpayers. As a result, this tax is aimed at higher-income taxpayers and can potentially increase the marginal capital gain tax rate to 23.8 percent (from 20 percent) and the marginal ordinary income tax rate to 40.8 percent (from 37 percent). See text Section 12-5c for a discussion of this tax.

---

[37]Reg. § 1.163(d)–1.   [38]§ 1411.

REFOCUS ON THE BIG PICTURE

INVESTOR LOSS LIMITATIONS AFFECT THE VIABILITY OF CERTAIN INVESTMENT OPPORTUNITIES

The objective for most investors should be to maximize after-tax wealth from among investment alternatives. This requires an understanding of the relevant tax restrictions that apply to certain expenses and losses arising from various investment choices. The after-tax returns from the three alternatives the Reswicks are considering may be affected by the at-risk, passive activity, and investment interest limitations.

The high-growth, low-yield portfolio is expected to generate very little, if any, current interest and dividend income (i.e., investment income). Nonetheless, if the financial planner's prediction is correct, the market value of the securities will grow by approximately 8 percent a year. However, the annual $4,000 of interest expense on the debt incurred to purchase the securities is not deductible as investment interest to the extent there is no investment income. Unless investment income is generated from this or some other source, the interest will not be deductible until the securities are sold (see Example 39). In addition, to the extent that any capital gain from the portfolio's sale is treated as investment income, the gain will not be subject to preferential capital gains rates (see Example 43). As a result, the net after-tax return will be impaired because of the investment interest limitation.

The net returns from the other two investment choices will be diminished by the at-risk and passive activity loss rules in addition to the investment interest limitation. The projected 8 percent return is apparently contingent on the investors being able to use the current tax losses as they arise. These benefits will be deferred because the at-risk and passive activity loss rules delay the timing of the deductions. For example, in the case of the orange grove investment, none of the passive activity losses are deductible until year 6, when the investment is expected to produce passive activity income (see Example 29). In the real estate rental venture, however, the Reswicks possibly could deduct the $25,000 passive activity loss under the exception for rental real estate for the first four years, depending on their AGI and the related loss phaseout once AGI exceeds $100,000 (see Example 31); the at-risk rules would limit any additional losses in year 5 to the at-risk amount. Consequently, because the at-risk and passive activity loss rules limit the tax losses flowing to the Reswicks, the after-tax return will not be nearly as high as their financial planner predicts.

What If?

If the Reswicks decide that the investment in marketable securities is their best option, could they modify their plan so that they avoid the restriction imposed by the investment interest limitation? The Reswicks' net after-tax return would improve if the interest cost of financing their investment could be deducted as incurred. A viable strategy prior to 2018 would have been to finance their investment by borrowing up to $100,000 against the equity in their home. Using this strategy would have made the interest on the home equity loan fully deductible and increased the after-tax return from their investment. However, beginning in 2018, home equity loan interest generally is not deductible. As a result, the investment interest limitation continues to negatively impact the after-tax return from an investment in marketable securities.

Key Terms

Active income, 11-6

At-risk limitation, 11-3

Closely held corporation, 11-10

Investment income, 11-22

Investment interest, 11-21

Material participation, 11-13

Net investment income, 11-22

Passive activity loss, 11-3

Personal service corporation, 11-10

Portfolio income, 11-6

Rental activity, 11-15

Significant participation activity, 11-14

Tax shelters, 11-2

Discussion Questions

Communications

1. **LO.1, 2, 3** Identify two rules designed to limit the tax benefits a taxpayer may obtain from a tax shelter investment. In an e-mail to your instructor, describe how these rules reduce or defer the recognition of tax losses.

2. **LO.2** List some events that increase or decrease an investor's at-risk amount. What are some strategies that a taxpayer can employ to increase the at-risk amount to claim a higher deduction for losses?

3. **LO.2, 3** Roberto invested $18,000 in a chicken production operation. Using nonrecourse notes, the business purchases $120,000 worth of grain to feed the chickens. If Roberto's share of the expense is $26,000, how much can he deduct?

4. **LO.3** Explain the meaning of the terms *active income, portfolio income,* and *passive activity income.*

5. **LO.3** Carlos owns an interest in an activity that produces a $100,000 loss during the year. Would he prefer to have the activity classified as active or passive? Explain.

6. **LO.3** Kim owns an interest in an activity that produces $100,000 of income during the year. Would Kim prefer to have the activity classified as active or passive? Discuss.

7. **LO.3** On a taxable disposition of a passive activity, the taxpayer can use any suspended losses and credits related to that activity. Do you agree? Explain.

8. **LO.3** Discuss whether the passive activity loss rules apply to the following: individuals, closely held C corporations, S corporations, partnerships, and personal service corporations.

9. **LO.3** Bronze Corporation has $100,000 of active income, $55,000 of portfolio income, and a $55,000 passive activity loss. Under what circumstances is Bronze prohibited from deducting the loss? Allowed to deduct the loss?

10. **LO.4** Discuss what constitutes a passive activity.

11. **LO.5** What is the significance of the term *material participation*? Why is the extent of a taxpayer's participation in an activity important in determining whether a loss from the activity is deductible or nondeductible?

12. **LO.5** How many hours must a participant work in a nonrental activity to be guaranteed material participation status?

Decision Making

13. **LO.5** Suzanne owns interests in a bagel shop, a lawn and garden store, and a convenience store. Several full-time employees work at each of the enterprises. As of the end of November of the current year, Suzanne has worked 150 hours in the bagel shop, 250 hours at the lawn and garden store, and 70 hours at the convenience store. In reviewing her financial records, you learn that she has no passive

investments that are generating income and that she expects these three ventures collectively to produce a loss. What recommendation would you offer Suzanne as she plans her activities for the remainder of the year?

14. **LO.5, 11** John, an engineer, operates a separate business that he acquired eight years ago. If he participates 85 hours in the business and it incurs a loss of $34,000, under what circumstances can John claim an active loss?

15. **LO.2, 3, 5** Rita retired from public accounting after a long and successful career of 45 years. As part of her retirement package, she continues to share in the profits and losses of the firm, albeit at a lower rate than when she was working full-time. Because Rita wants to stay busy during her retirement years, she has invested and works in a local hardware business, operated as a partnership. Unfortunately, the business has recently gone through a slump and has not been generating profits. Identify relevant tax issues for Rita.   *Critical Thinking*

16. **LO.5** Some types of work are counted in applying the material participation standards, and some types are not counted. Discuss and give examples of each type.

17. **LO.5** Last year Alan's accountant informed him that he could not claim any of his passive activity losses on his income tax return because of his lack of material participation. To circumvent the tax problem this year, Alan tells his spouse that she may have to put in some time at the various businesses. Identify the tax issues that Alan faces.   *Critical Thinking*

18. **LO.5** Sean, a limited partner in Ivy Nursery, is informed that his portion of the entity's current loss is $18,000. As a limited partner, can Sean assume that his share of the partnership loss is a passive activity loss? Explain.

19. **LO.6** Explain why some rental activities may not be *treated* as such under the passive activity loss rules.

20. **LO.3, 4, 5, 6** How is *passive activity* defined in the Code? What aspects of the definition have been clarified by Final or Temporary Regulations?

21. **LO.8** What is a *real estate professional?* Why could qualifying for this status be beneficial under the passive activity loss rules?

22. **LO.8** Caroline owns a real estate rental activity that produces a loss of $65,000 during the current year. Under what circumstances can Caroline treat the entire loss as nonpassive?

23. **LO.8** Since his college days, Charles has developed an entrepreneurial streak. After working in his family's grocery business, he starts several ventures on his own. Even though Charles is independently wealthy, he is looking forward to working in each of the ventures. He plans to "drop in" on the businesses from time to time between personal trips to Europe and the Caribbean. As of the end of the year, he has established computer software stores in Dayton (Ohio), Austin, and Seattle; bagel bakeries in Albany, Athens (Georgia), and Tallahassee; and mountain bike and ski rental shops in small towns in Vermont, West Virginia, Colorado, and California. Identify the tax issues facing Charles.   *Critical Thinking*

24. **LO.8** Brad owns a small townhouse complex that generates a loss during the year. Under what circumstances can Brad deduct a loss from the rental activity? What limitations apply?

25. **LO.8** In connection with passive activities, what is a *deduction equivalent* and how is it computed?

26. **LO.10** What is *investment interest expense?* Describe the basic rules that may limit its deductibility.

Computational Exercises

27. **LO.2** In the current year, Ed invests $30,000 in an oil partnership. He has taxable income for the current year of $2,000 from the oil partnership and withdraws $10,000. What is Ed's at-risk amount at the end of the year?

28. **LO.3** Lucy sells her partnership interest, a passive activity, with an adjusted basis of $305,000 for $330,000. In addition, she has current and suspended losses of $28,000 associated with the partnership and has no other passive activities. Calculate Lucy's total gain and her current deductible loss. Describe the type of income that the deductible loss may offset.

29. **LO.4, 5** Zhou owns a nonrental business with two separate departments. Department A generates net income of $70,000, and Department B generates a net loss of $58,000. Zhou participates 800 hours in the operations of Department A and 300 hours in the operations of Department B. If Zhou is allowed to treat the departments as components of a single activity, calculate the amount of the Department B loss that can be offset against the income from Department A in the current year.

30. **LO.7** Rhonda has an adjusted basis and an at-risk amount of $7,500 in a passive activity at the beginning of the year. She also has a suspended passive activity loss of $1,500 carried over from the prior year. During the current year, she has a loss of $12,000 from the passive activity. Rhonda has no passive activity income from other sources this year. Determine the following items relating to Rhonda's passive activity as of the end of the year.
    a. Adjusted basis and at-risk amount in the passive activity.
    b. Loss suspended under the at-risk rules.
    c. Suspended passive activity loss.

31. **LO.8** Noah Yobs, who has $62,000 of AGI (solely from wages) before considering rental activities, has $70,000 of losses from a real estate rental activity in which he actively participates. He also actively participates in another real estate rental activity from which he has $33,000 of income. He has other passive activity income of $20,000.
    a. What amount of rental loss can Noah use to offset active or portfolio income in the current year?
    b. Compute Noah's AGI on Form 1040 [pages 1 and 2; also complete Schedule 1 (Form 1040)] for the current year. His Social Security number is 123-45-6789.

32. **LO.9** Rose dies with passive activity property having an adjusted basis of $65,000, suspended losses of $13,000, and a fair market value at the date of her death of $90,000. Of the $13,000 suspended loss existing at the time of Rose's death, how much is deductible on her final return or by the beneficiary?

33. **LO.10** Troy's financial records for the year reflect the following:

Interest income from bank savings account	$ 900
Taxable annuity receipts	1,800
City ad valorem property tax on investments	125
Investment interest expense	3,200

Calculate Troy's net investment income and his current investment interest deduction. How is a deduction for any potential excess investment interest treated?

Problems

34. **LO.2** In 2019, Fred invested $50,000 in a general partnership. Fred's interest is not considered to be a passive activity. If his share of the partnership losses is $35,000 in 2019 and $25,000 in 2020, how much can he deduct in each year?

35. **LO.2** In the current year, Bill Parker (54 Oak Drive, St. Paul, MN 55164) is considering making an investment of $60,000 in Best Choice Partnership. The prospectus provided by Bill's financial planner indicates that the partnership investment is not a passive activity and that Bill's share of the entity's loss in the current year will likely be $40,000, whereas his share of the partnership loss next year will probably be $25,000. Write a letter to Bill in which you indicate how the losses would be treated for tax purposes in the current year and the following year.

Communications

36. **LO.2, 11** Heather wants to invest $40,000 in a relatively safe venture and has discovered two alternatives that would produce the following reportable ordinary income and loss over the next three years:

Decision Making

Critical Thinking

Year	Alternative 1 Income (Loss)	Alternative 2 Income (Loss)
1	($20,000)	($48,000)
2	(28,000)	32,000
3	72,000	40,000

She is interested in the after-tax effects of these alternatives over a three-year horizon. Assume that Heather's investment portfolio produces sufficient passive activity income to offset any potential passive activity loss that may arise from these alternatives, that her cost of capital is 6%, that she is in the 24% tax bracket, that each investment alternative possesses equal growth potential, and that each alternative exposes her to comparable financial risk. In addition, assume that in the loss years for each alternative, there is no cash flow from or to the investment (i.e., the loss is due to depreciation), whereas in those years when the income is positive, cash flows to Heather equal the amount of the income.

   a. Based on these facts, compute the present value of these two investment alternatives and determine which option Heather should choose. Refer to Appendix G for the present value factors.

   b. Prepare your solution using spreadsheet software such as Microsoft Excel.

37. **LO.1, 3** Dorothy acquired a 100% interest in two passive activities: Activity A in January 2015 and Activity B in 2016. Through 2018, Activity A was profitable, but it produced losses of $200,000 in 2019 and $100,000 in 2020. Dorothy has passive activity income from Activity B of $20,000 in 2019 and $40,000 in 2020. After offsetting passive activity income, how much of the net losses may she deduct?

38. **LO.1, 3** A number of years ago, Kay acquired an interest in a partnership in which she is not a material participant. Kay's basis in her partnership interest at the beginning of 2019 is $40,000. Kay's share of the partnership loss is $35,000 in 2019, and her share of the partnership income is $15,000 in 2020. How much may Kay deduct in 2019 and 2020, assuming that she owns no other passive activities?

39. **LO.3** Mike, an attorney, earns $200,000 from his law practice and receives $45,000 in dividends and interest during the year. In addition, he incurs a loss of $50,000 from an investment in a passive activity acquired three years ago. What is Mike's net income for the current year after considering the passive investment?

40. **LO.3, 11** Emily has $100,000 that she wants to invest and is considering the following two options:

Decision Making

Critical Thinking

   • Option A: Investment in Redbird Mutual Fund, which is expected to produce interest income of $8,000 per year.

- Option B: Investment in Cardinal Limited Partnership (buys, sells, and operates wine vineyards). Emily's share of the partnership's ordinary income and loss over the next three years will be as follows:

Year	Income (Loss)
1	($ 8,000)
2	(2,000)
3	34,000

Emily is interested in the after-tax effects of these alternatives over a three-year horizon. Assume that Emily's investment portfolio produces ample passive activity income to offset any passive activity losses that may be generated. Her cost of capital is 8%, and she is in the 32% tax bracket. The two investment alternatives possess equal growth potential and comparable financial risk.

a. Based on these facts, compute the present value of these two investment alternatives and determine which option Emily should choose. Refer to Appendix G for the present value factors.

b. Prepare your solution using spreadsheet software such as Microsoft Excel.

41. **LO.3** Seojun acquired an activity several years ago, and in the current year, it generates a loss of $50,000. Seojun has AGI of $140,000 before considering the loss from the activity. If the activity is a bakery and Seojun is not a material participant, what is his AGI?

Decision Making   42. **LO.3, 9, 11** Jorge owns two passive investments, Activity A and Activity B. He plans to sell Activity A in the current year or next year. Juanita has offered to buy Activity A this year for an amount that would produce a taxable passive activity gain to Jorge of $115,000. However, if the sale, for whatever reason, is not made to Juanita, Jorge believes that he could find a buyer who would pay about $7,000 less than Juanita. Passive activity losses and gains generated (and expected to be generated) by Activity B follow:

Two years ago	($35,000)
Last year	(35,000)
This year	(8,000)
Next year	(30,000)
Future years	Minimal profits

All of Activity B's losses are suspended. Should Jorge close the sale of Activity A with Juanita this year, or should he wait until next year and sell to another buyer? Jorge is in the 32% tax bracket.

43. **LO.3, 9** Sarah has investments in four passive activity partnerships purchased several years ago. Last year the income and losses were as follows:

Activity	Income (Loss)
A	$ 30,000
B	(30,000)
C	(15,000)
D	(5,000)

In the current year, she sold her interest in Activity D for a $10,000 gain. Activity D, which had been profitable until last year, had a current loss of $1,500. How will the sale of Activity D affect Sarah's taxable income in the current year?

44. **LO.3, 9** Leon sells his interest in a passive activity for $100,000. Determine the tax effect of the sale based on each of the following independent facts:

a. Adjusted basis in this investment is $35,000. Losses from prior years that were not deductible due to the passive activity loss restrictions total $40,000.

b. Adjusted basis in this investment is $75,000. Losses from prior years that were not deductible due to the passive activity loss restrictions total $40,000.

c. Adjusted basis in this investment is $75,000. Losses from prior years that were not deductible due to the passive activity loss restrictions total $40,000. In addition, suspended credits total $10,000.

45. **LO.3** Ash, Inc., a closely held personal service corporation, has $100,000 of passive activity losses. In addition, Ash has $80,000 of active business income and $20,000 of portfolio income. How much of the passive activity loss may Ash use to offset the other types of income?

46. **LO.3** In the current year, White, Inc., earns $400,000 from operations and receives $36,000 of interest income from various portfolio investments. White also pays $150,000 to acquire a 20% interest in a passive activity that produces a $200,000 loss.

a. Assuming that White is a personal service corporation, how will these transactions affect its taxable income?

b. Same as part (a), except that White is closely held but not a personal service corporation.

47. **LO.2, 3, 7, 11** Kristin Graf (123 Baskerville Mill Road, Jamison, PA 18929) is trying to decide how to invest a $10,000 inheritance. One option is to make an additional investment in Rocky Road Excursions in which she has an at-risk basis of $0, suspended losses under the at-risk rules of $7,000, and suspended passive activity losses of $1,000. If Kristin makes this investment, her share of the expected profits this year will be $8,000. If her investment stays the same, her share of profits from Rocky Road Excursions will be $1,000. Another option is to invest $10,000 as a limited partner in the Ragged Mountain Winery; this investment will produce passive activity income of $9,000. Write a letter to Kristin to review the tax consequences of each alternative. Kristin is in the 24% tax bracket.

Decision Making

Communications

Critical Thinking

48. **LO.2, 3, 7, 11** The end of the year is approaching, and Maxine has begun to focus on ways of minimizing her income tax liability. Several years ago she purchased an investment in Teal Limited Partnership, which is subject to the at-risk and the passive activity loss rules. (Last year Maxine sold a different investment that was subject to these rules and that produced passive activity income.) She believes that her investment in Teal has good long-term economic prospects. However, it has been generating tax losses for several years in a row. In fact, when she was discussing last year's income tax return with her tax accountant, he said that unless "things change" with respect to her investments, she would not be able to deduct losses this year.

Decision Making

a. What was the accountant referring to in his comment?

b. You learn that Maxine's current at-risk basis in her investment is $1,000 and that her share of the current loss is expected to be $13,000. Based on these facts, how will her loss be treated?

c. After reviewing her situation, Maxine's financial adviser suggests that she invest at least an additional $12,000 in Teal to ensure a full loss deduction in the current year. How do you react to his suggestion?

d. What would you suggest Maxine consider as she attempts to maximize her current-year deductible loss?

49. **LO.2, 3, 7** A number of years ago, Lee acquired a 20% interest in the BlueSky Partnership for $60,000. The partnership was profitable through 2019, and Lee's amount at risk in the partnership interest was $120,000 at the beginning of 2020. BlueSky incurred a loss of $400,000 in 2020 and reported income of $200,000 in 2021. Assuming that Lee is not a material participant, how much of his loss from BlueSky Partnership is deductible in 2020 and 2021? Consider the at-risk and passive activity loss rules, and assume that Lee owns no other passive investments.

50. **LO.2, 3, 5, 7** Grace acquired an activity four years ago. The loss from the activity is $50,000 in the current year (at-risk basis of $40,000 as of the beginning of the year). Without considering the loss from the activity, she has gross income of $140,000. If the activity is a convenience store and Grace is a material participant, what is the effect of the activity on her taxable income?

51. **LO.2, 3, 5, 7** Jonathan, a physician, earns $200,000 from his practice. He also receives $18,000 in dividends and interest from various portfolio investments. During the year, he pays $45,000 to acquire a 20% interest in a partnership that produces a $300,000 loss. Compute Jonathan's AGI assuming that:
    a. He does not participate in the operations of the partnership.
    b. He is a material participant in the operations of the partnership.

52. **LO.2, 3, 7** Five years ago Gerald invested $150,000 in a passive activity, his sole investment venture. On January 1, 2019, his amount at risk in the activity was $30,000. His shares of the income and losses were as follows:

Year	Income (Loss)
2019	($40,000)
2020	(30,000)
2021	50,000

Gerald holds no suspended at-risk or passive activity losses at the beginning of 2019. How much can Gerald deduct in 2019 and 2020? What is his taxable income from the activity in 2021? Consider the at-risk rules as well as the passive activity loss rules.

Communications 53. **LO.3, 8** Several years ago Benny Jackson (125 Hill Street, Charleston, WV 25311) acquired an apartment building that currently generates a loss of $60,000. Benny's AGI is $130,000 before considering the loss. The apartment building is in an exclusive part of the city, and Benny is an active participant. Write a letter to Benny explaining what effect the loss will have on his AGI.

54. **LO.3, 5, 8** This year Maria works 1,200 hours as a computer consultant, 320 hours in a real estate development business, and 400 hours in real estate rental activities. Juan, her spouse, works 250 hours in the real estate development business and 180 hours in the real estate rental business. Maria earns $60,000 as a computer consultant, and she and Juan lost $18,000 in the real estate development business and $26,000 in the real estate rental business. How should they treat the losses?

Decision Making 55. **LO.3, 8, 11** Bonnie and Jake (ages 35 and 36, respectively) are married with no dependents and live in Montana (not a community property state). Because Jake has large medical expenses, they seek your advice about filing separately to save taxes. Their income and expenses for 2020 are as follows:

Bonnie's salary	$ 42,500
Jake's salary	26,000
Interest income (joint)	1,500
Rental loss from actively managed rental property	(23,000)
Jake's unreimbursed medical expenses	8,500
All other itemized deductions:*	
Bonnie	19,000
Jake	6,400

*None subject to limitations

Determine whether Bonnie and Jake should file jointly or separately for 2020.

Decision Making 56. **LO.3, 8, 11** Mary and Charles have owned a beach cottage on the New Jersey shore for several years and have always used it as a family retreat. When they acquired the property, they had no intentions of renting it. Because family circumstances have changed, they are considering using the cottage for only one week a year and renting it for the remainder of the year. Their AGI approximates $100,000 per year, they are in the 30% tax bracket (combined Federal and state), and their total itemized deductions exceed the standard deduction amount. Interest and real estate taxes total $8,000 per year and are expected to continue at this level in the foreseeable future. If Mary and Charles rent the property, their *incremental* revenue and expenses are projected to be:

Rent income	$ 22,000
Rental commissions	(4,000)
Maintenance expenses	(9,000)
Depreciation expense	(10,000)

If the cottage is converted to rental property, they plan to be actively involved in key rental and maintenance decisions. Given the tax effects of converting the property to rental use, would the cash flow from renting the property be enough to meet the $12,000 annual mortgage payment? Explain.

57. **LO.3, 8** During the current year, Gene, a CPA, performs services as follows: 1,800 hours in his tax practice and 50 hours in an apartment leasing operation in which he has a 15% interest. Because of his oversight duties, Gene is considered to be an active participant. He expects that his share of the loss realized from the apartment leasing operation will be $30,000 and that his tax practice will show a profit of approximately $80,000. Gene is single and has no other income. Discuss the character and treatment of the income and losses generated by these activities.

58. **LO.3, 8** Mandy, who has AGI of $80,000 before considering rental activities, is active in three separate real estate rental activities and is in the 22% tax bracket. She has $12,000 of losses from Activity A, $18,000 of losses from Activity B, and income of $10,000 from Activity C. She also has $2,100 of tax credits from Activity A. Calculate the deductions and credits that she is allowed and the suspended losses and credits.

59. **LO.8** Jiu has $105,000 of losses from a real estate rental activity in which she actively participates. She has other rental income of $25,000 and other passive activity income of $32,000. Her AGI before considering these items of income and loss is $95,000. How much rental loss can Jiu deduct against active and portfolio income (ignoring the at-risk rules)? Does she have any suspended losses to carry over? Explain.

60. **LO.9** At death, Francine owns an interest in a passive activity property (adjusted basis of $160,000, suspended losses of $16,000, and fair market value of $170,000). What is deductible on Francine's final income tax return?

61. **LO.9** In the current year, Abe gives an interest in a passive activity to his daughter, Andrea. The value of the interest at the date of the gift is $25,000, and its adjusted basis to Abe is $13,000. During the time that Abe owned the investment, losses of $3,000 could not be deducted because of the passive activity loss limitations. What is the tax treatment of the suspended passive activity losses to Abe and Andrea?

62. **LO.9** Tonya sells a passive activity in the current year for $150,000. Her adjusted basis in the activity is $50,000, and she uses the installment method of reporting the gain. The activity has suspended losses of $12,000. Tonya receives $60,000 in the year of sale. What is her gain? How much of the suspended losses can she deduct?

63. **LO.10, 11** In 2020, Kathleen Tweardy incurs $30,000 of interest expense related to her investments. Her investment income includes $7,500 of interest, $6,000 of qualified dividends, and a $12,000 net capital gain on the sale of securities. Kathleen asks you to compute the amount of her deduction for investment interest, taking into consideration any options she might have. In addition, she wants your

Decision Making

Communications

suggestions as to any tax planning alternatives that are available. Write a letter to her that contains your advice. Kathleen lives at 11934 Briarpatch Drive, Midlothian, VA 23113.

64. **LO.10** Helen Derby borrowed $150,000 to acquire a parcel of land to be held for investment purposes. During the current year, she reported AGI of $90,000 and paid interest of $12,000 on the loan. Other items related to Helen's investments include the following:

Interest and annuity income	$11,000
Long-term capital gain on sale of stock	3,500
Real estate tax on the investment land	800

a. Determine Helen's investment interest deduction for the current year.

b. Discuss the treatment of the portion of Helen's investment interest that is disallowed for the current year.

c. Complete Helen's Form 4952 for the current year. For this purpose, assume that she chooses not to include the long-term capital gain as investment income. Her Social Security number is 123-45-6789.

Research Problems

Note: Solutions to the Research Problems can be prepared by using the Thomson Reuters Checkpoint™ online tax research database, which accompanies this textbook. Solutions can also be prepared by using research materials found in a typical tax library.

Research Problem 1. Carol is a successful physician who owns 100% of her incorporated medical practice. She and her spouse, Dick, are considering the purchase of a commercial office building located near the local community hospital. If they purchase the building, Carol will move her medical practice to the new location and rent space for an arm's length price. The rent income Carol and Dick receive will be available to absorb passive activity losses generated by other passive activities they own. The net effect of this arrangement is a reduction in their income tax liability. Will Carol and Dick's plan work? Why or why not?

Research Problem 2. Five years ago Bridget decided to purchase a limited partnership interest in a fast-food restaurant conveniently located near the campus of Southeast State University. The general partner of the restaurant venture promised her that the investment would prove to be a winner. During the process of capitalizing the business, $2,000,000 was borrowed from Northside Bank; however, each of the partners was required to pledge personal assets as collateral to satisfy the bank loan in the event that the restaurant defaulted. Bridget pledged shares of publicly traded stock (worth $200,000, basis of $75,000) to satisfy the bank's requirement.

The restaurant did a good business until just recently, when flagrant health code violations were discovered and widely publicized by the media. As a result, business has declined to a point where the restaurant's continued existence is doubtful. In addition, the $2,000,000 loan is now due for payment. Because the restaurant cannot pay, the bank has called for the collateral provided by the partners to be used to satisfy the debt. Bridget sells the pledged stock for $200,000 and forwards the proceeds to the bank. Bridget believes that her share of the restaurant's current and suspended passive activity losses can offset the $125,000 gain from the stock sale. As a result, after netting the passive activity losses against the gain, none of the gain is subject to tax.

How do you react to Bridget's position?

Research Problem 3. Ida Ross has decided to purchase a new home in a retirement community for $400,000. She has $50,000 in cash for the down payment but needs to borrow the remaining $350,000 to finance the purchase. Her financial adviser, Marc, suggests that rather than seeking a conventional mortgage, she should borrow the funds from State Bank using her portfolio of appreciated securities as collateral. Selling the securities to generate $350,000 in cash would lead to a substantial tax on the capital gain recognized. As a result, a better strategy would be to borrow against her securities and then claim a deduction for the interest paid on the loan. How do you react to the financial adviser's strategy?

Partial list of research aids:
Temp.Reg. § 1.163–8T(c).

Use internet tax resources to address the following questions. Look for reliable websites and blogs of the IRS and other government agencies, media outlets, businesses, tax professionals, academics, think tanks, and political outlets.

Research Problem 4. Investment advisers and tax professionals are continuously striving to create sophisticated transactions and investment vehicles (i.e., tax-advantaged investments) that are designed to provide economic benefits to investors by reducing their taxes. These professionals might like to patent such schemes. Identify whether patenting a tax strategy is a legal possibility.

Research Problem 5. Scan the materials offered in several newsgroups frequented by tax advisers and consultants. In what context are "tax shelters" discussed by these professionals? Do these advisers and consultants adequately take into account the rules of §§ 465 and 469? Explain.

Research Problem 6. Investment interest is incurred when taxpayers borrow money that is used to purchase investment property. Using *IRS Tax Statistics* for the most recent year available, determine (a) the number of taxpayers who claimed a deduction for investment interest expense, (b) the aggregate amount deducted by all taxpayers, and (c) the amount not deducted because of the net investment income limitation. Also determine the percentage of the total investment interest deduction claimed across various ranges of AGI.

Data Analytics

Becker CPA Review Questions

1. Which of the following statements regarding passive activity losses is true?
    a. A net passive activity loss may be deducted against wages.
    b. Losses on rental property are always considered passive.
    c. A passive activity is one in which the taxpayer does not materially participate.
    d. Expenses related to passive activities may be deducted from passive activity income and portfolio income.

2. Michael owns a rental house that generated a $10,000 loss this year. Michael manages the rental property but does not meet the standards for material participation. Michael is a college professor and has wages of $60,000 and $5,000 in dividend income. How is the $10,000 rental real estate loss treated on Michael's tax return?
    a. $5,000 of the loss is deductible against the passive dividend income.
    b. The rental loss is not deductible because Michael does not have any passive income.
    c. $10,000 loss is not deductible because Michael does not materially participate in the rental activity.
    d. $10,000 loss is deductible under the rental real estate exception because Michael actively participates in the rental activity.

3. What is the correct order of applying the loss limitation rules?
   a. Passive loss limits, tax basis, at-risk amount
   b. Tax basis, at-risk amount, passive loss limits
   c. At-risk amount, tax basis, passive loss limits
   d. Passive loss limits, at-risk amount, tax basis

4. Sam rents his second home. During the current year, he reported a $40,000 net loss from the rental. Assume that Sam actively participates in the rental activity and no phaseout limitations apply. What is the greatest amount of the rental loss that Sam can deduct against ordinary income in the current year?
   a. $25,000
   b. $40,000
   c. $0
   d. $5,000

5. Sally recently invested $10,000 (tax basis) in a limited partnership interest. Her at-risk amount is also $10,000. The partnership lost $6,000 this year, and Sally's share of the loss is $2,000. Sally has $40,000 in wage income and $2,000 of dividend income. In addition, Sally's share of income from a different limited partnership is $1,000. Sally does not meet the tests for material participation for either of her partnership interests. How much of Sally's $2,000 loss from the limited partnership can she deduct this year?
   a. $2,000
   b. $0
   c. $1,000 because she has $2,000 of dividend income
   d. $1,000 because she has $1,000 income from another limited partnership

CHAPTER

12

Tax Credits and Payments

LEARNING OBJECTIVES: *After completing Chapter 12, you should be able to:*

LO.1 Explain how tax credits are used as a tool of Federal tax policy.

LO.2 Distinguish between refundable and nonrefundable credits and understand the order in which they can be used by taxpayers.

LO.3 Identify various business-related tax credits.

LO.4 Determine various tax credits that are available primarily to individual taxpayers.

LO.5 Apply the tax withholding and payment procedures used by employers.

LO.6 Execute the tax payment procedures used by self-employed persons.

LO.7 Identify tax planning opportunities related to tax credits and payments.

CHAPTER OUTLINE

12-1 Tax Policy Considerations, 12-3

12-2 Tax Credits, 12-3
12-2a Refundable versus Nonrefundable Credits, 12-3
12-2b General Business Credit, 12-5
12-2c Treatment of Unused General Business Credits, 12-5

12-3 Specific Business-Related Tax Credits, 12-6
12-3a Tax Credit for Rehabilitation Expenditures, 12-6
12-3b Work Opportunity Tax Credit, 12-7
12-3c Credit for Increasing Research Activities, 12-8
12-3d Low-Income Housing Credit, 12-9
12-3e Disabled Access Credit, 12-10
12-3f Credit for Small Employer Pension Plan Startup Costs, 12-10
12-3g Credit for Employer-Provided Child Care, 12-11
12-3h Credit for Employer-Provided Family and Medical Leave, 12-11

12-4 Other Tax Credits, 12-12
12-4a Earned Income Credit, 12-12
12-4b Foreign Tax Credit, 12-13
12-4c Child and Dependent Tax Credits, 12-14
12-4d Credit for Child and Dependent Care Expenses, 12-14
12-4e Education Tax Credits, 12-16
12-4f Energy Credits, 12-18
12-4g Credit for Certain Retirement Plan Contributions, 12-18

12-5 Tax Payments, 12-19
12-5a Payments by Employers, 12-22
12-5b Payments by Self-Employed Persons, 12-22
12-5c Affordable Care Act Provisions, 12-24
12-5d Alternative Minimum Tax, 12-25

12-6 Tax Planning, 12-27
12-6a Credit for Child and Dependent Care Expenses, 12-27

YELLOW DOG PRODUCTIONS/GETTY IMAGES

EDUCATION TAX CREDITS

Tom and Jennifer Snyder have two children in college. Lora is a freshman, and her tuition and required fees for 2020 total $14,000. Lora has a partial scholarship amounting to $6,500, and the Snyders paid the balance of her tuition ($7,500), plus room and board of $8,500. Sam is a junior, and the Snyders paid $8,100 for his tuition, plus $7,200 for his room and board. Both students qualify as Tom and Jennifer's dependents.

The Snyders report AGI of $158,000. They would like to know what tax options are available to them related to these education expenses. They have heard about various education-related deductions and credits, but they believe that their income is too high for them to get any benefit. Are they correct?

Read the chapter and formulate your response.

FRAMEWORK 1040 Tax Formula for Individuals

This chapter covers the boldfaced portions of the Tax Formula for Individuals that was introduced in Concept Summary 3.1 on p. 3-3. Below those portions are the sections of Form 1040 where the results are reported.

Income *(broadly defined)*	$xx,xxx
Less: Exclusions	(x,xxx)
Gross income	$xx,xxx
Less: Deductions *for* adjusted gross income	**(x,xxx)**
Adjusted gross income..	$xx,xxx
Less: The greater of total itemized deductions *or* the standard deduction	(x,xxx)
Personal and dependency exemptions*	(x,xxx)
Deduction for qualified business income**	(x,xxx)
Taxable income	$xx,xxx
Tax on taxable income *(see Tax Tables or Tax Rate Schedules)*	$ x,xxx
Less: Tax credits *(including income taxes withheld and prepaid)*	**(xxx)**

FORM 1040 (p. 2)

12a	**Tax** (see inst.) Check if any from Form(s): **1** ☐ 8814 **2** ☐ 4972 **3** ☐		12a	
b	Add Schedule 2, line 3, and line 12a and enter the total	▶	12b	
13a	Child tax credit or credit for other dependents	13a		
b	Add Schedule 3, line 7, and line 13a and enter the total	▶	13b	
14	Subtract line 13b from line 12b. If zero or less, enter -0-		14	
15	Other taxes, including self-employment tax, from Schedule 2, line 10		15	
16	Add lines 14 and 15. This is your **total tax**	▶	16	
17	Federal income tax withheld from Forms W-2 and 1099		17	
18	Other payments and refundable credits:			
a	Earned income credit (EIC)	18a		
b	Additional child tax credit. Attach Schedule 8812	18b		
c	American opportunity credit from Form 8863, line 8	18c		
d	Schedule 3, line 14	18d		
e	Add lines 18a through 18d. These are your **total other payments and refundable credits**	▶	18e	
19	Add lines 17 and 18e. These are your **total payments**	▶	19	

Tax due (or refund) .... $ xxx

* Exemption deductions are not allowed from 2018 through 2025.
** Only applies from 2018 through 2025.

ederal tax law often serves purposes other than merely raising revenue for the government. Evidence of equity, social, and economic considerations is found throughout the tax law, including in the area of <mark>tax credits</mark>. Consider the following examples.

EXAMPLE 1

Paul and Peggy, husband and wife, are both employed outside the home. Their combined salaries are $50,000. However, after paying for child care expenses of $2,000 on behalf of their daughter, Polly, the pretax economic benefit from both spouses working is $48,000. The child care expenses are, in a sense, business-related, because they would not have been incurred if both spouses did not work outside the home. If no tax benefits are associated with the child care expenses, $50,000 is subject to tax.

Another couple, Alicia and Diego, also have a child, John. Diego stays at home to care for John (the value of those services is $2,000) while Alicia earns a $48,000 salary. Because the value of Diego's services rendered is not subject to tax, only Alicia's earnings of $48,000 are subject to tax.

The *credit for child and dependent care expenses* mitigates the inequity felt by working taxpayers who must pay for child care services to work outside the home.

EXAMPLE 2

Jane is a single parent who depends on the government's "safety net" for survival—she receives benefits under the Temporary Assistance to Needy Families program in the amount of $15,000 per year. However, she very much wants to work. Jane has located a job that will pay $15,500 per year and has found an individual to care for her child at no cost. But with the $1,185.75 ($15,500 × 7.65%) withholding for Social Security and Medicare taxes, the economic benefit from working is less than remaining reliant on the government ($14,314.25 net pay versus $15,000 assistance payment).

To help offset the effect of Social Security and Medicare taxes on wages of the working poor and to provide an incentive to work, the *earned income credit* increases the after-tax earnings of qualified individuals. This credit helps to offset the regressive nature of certain Federal taxes, such as the Social Security and Medicare taxes, which impose a relatively greater burden on low-income taxpayers than on higher-income taxpayers.

These and many of the other tax credits available to individuals and other taxpayers are a major focus of this chapter. Also addressed are the procedures individuals use to pay their tax liabilities to the U.S. Treasury. The self-employment tax, alternative minimum tax (AMT), and additional taxes that support the Federal Medicare system are also explained.

12-1 TAX POLICY CONSIDERATIONS

LO.1

Explain how tax credits are used as a tool of Federal tax policy.

Congress generally uses tax credits to achieve social or economic objectives or to promote equity among different types of taxpayers. For example, the disabled access credit was enacted to accomplish a social objective: to encourage taxpayers to renovate older buildings so that they would be in compliance with the Americans with Disabilities Act. In addition, the foreign tax credit mitigates the burden of multiple taxation on a single stream of income that is generated in more than one country.

A tax credit is much different from an income tax deduction. Income tax deductions reduce a taxpayer's tax *base*; tax credits reduce a taxpayer's tax *liability*. While the tax benefit received from a tax deduction depends on the tax rate, a tax credit is not affected by the tax rate of the taxpayer.

EXAMPLE 3

Assume that Congress wants to encourage a certain type of activity. One way to accomplish this objective is to allow a tax credit of 25% for any expenses paid related to this activity. Another way is to allow an itemized deduction for the expenses. Abby's tax rate is 12%, while Bill's tax rate is 35%, and both itemize deductions. Carmen does not incur enough qualifying expenditures to itemize deductions. The following tax benefits are available to each taxpayer for a $1,000 expenditure.

	Abby	Bill	Carmen
Tax benefit if a 25% credit is allowed	$250	$250	$250
Tax benefit if an itemized deduction is allowed	120	350	–0–

As these results indicate, tax credits provide benefits on a more equitable basis than do tax deductions. Equally apparent is that the deduction approach in this case benefits only taxpayers who itemize deductions, while the credit approach benefits all taxpayers who make the specified payments.

12-2 TAX CREDITS

LO.2

Distinguish between refundable and nonrefundable credits and understand the order in which they can be used by taxpayers.

12-2a Refundable versus Nonrefundable Credits

Exhibit 12.1 identifies some of the more common refundable and nonrefundable tax credits. Refundable credits are paid to the taxpayer even if the amount of the credit (or credits) exceeds the taxpayer's tax liability.

EXHIBIT 12.1	Partial Listing of Refundable and Nonrefundable Credits

Refundable Credits

Taxes withheld on wages

Earned income credit

Affordable Care Act premium tax credit

Nonrefundable Credits

General business credit, which includes:

- Tax credit for rehabilitation expenditures
- Work opportunity tax credit
- Credit for increasing research activities
- Low-income housing credit
- Disabled access credit
- Credit for small employer pension plan startup costs
- Credit for employer-provided child care
- Credit for employer-provided family and medical leave

Credit for elderly or disabled

Foreign tax credit

Adoption expenses credit

Child and dependent tax credits*

Credit for child and dependent care expenses

Education tax credits**

Energy credits

Credit for certain retirement plan contributions

Small employer health insurance credit

*The child tax credit is refundable to the extent of 15% of the taxpayer's earned income in excess of $2,500, limited to a $1,400 maximum. Parents with three or more qualifying children may compute the refundable portion using an alternative method. The dependent tax credit is not refundable.

**Forty percent of the American Opportunity credit is refundable.

Ted, who is single, reported taxable income of $21,000 in 2020. His income tax liability is $2,323. Ted's employer withheld income tax of $3,200. Ted is entitled to a refund of $877; the credit for tax withheld on wages is a refundable credit.

Nonrefundable credits are not paid if they exceed the taxpayer's tax liability.

Tina is single, age 67. Her taxable income is $1,320, and the tax on this amount is $132. Tina's tax credit for the elderly is $225. This credit can be used to reduce her net tax liability to zero, but it will not result in a refund, even though the credit ($225) exceeds Tina's tax liability ($132). The credit for the elderly is nonrefundable.

Some nonrefundable credits, such as the foreign tax credit, can be "carried over" to another tax year if they exceed the credit allowed for a given year. Other nonrefundable credits, such as the credit for the elderly (refer to Example 5), are not subject to carryover provisions and are lost to the extent that they exceed the limitations. Because some credits are refundable and others are not, and because some credits are subject to carryover provisions while others are not, the order in which credits are offset against the tax liability is important.

EXAMPLE 6

Elijah's tax liability before credits is $1,000. He qualifies for two tax credits: a $400 Credit A (non-refundable) and an $800 Credit B (refundable). The order in which the credits are applied affects Elijah's tax refund for the year.

If Refundable Credit Is Applied First		If Nonrefundable Credit Is Applied First	
Precredit tax liability	$1,000	Precredit tax liability	$1,000
Credit B	(800)	Credit A	(400)
Remaining tax due	$ 200	Remaining tax due	$ 600
Credit A (as limited)	(200)	Credit B	(800)
Tax due/(Refund)	**$ –0–**	**Tax due/(Refund)**	**($ 200)**

12-2b General Business Credit

The general business credit is composed of a number of other credits, each of which is computed separately under its own set of rules.[1] The general business credit combines these credits into one amount to limit the amount of business credits that can be used to offset a taxpayer's income tax liability.

Two special rules apply to the general business credit. First, any unused credit must be carried back 1 year, then forward 20 years. Second, for any tax year, the general business credit is limited to the taxpayer's *net income tax* reduced by the greater of:[2]

- The *tentative minimum tax*. This amount relates to the alternative minimum tax. See text Section 12-5d.

- 25 percent of *net regular tax liability* that exceeds $25,000.[3]

Net regular tax liability is the regular tax liability reduced by certain nonrefundable credits (e.g., credit for child and dependent care expenses, foreign tax credit).

EXAMPLE 7

Alesia's general business credit for the current year is $70,000. Her net income tax is $150,000, the tentative minimum tax is $130,000, and Alesia's net regular tax liability is $150,000. She generates no other tax credits. Alesia's general business credit allowed for the tax year is computed as follows.

Net income tax	$ 150,000
Less: The greater of	
• $130,000 (tentative minimum tax)	
• $31,250 [25% × ($150,000 − $25,000)]	(130,000)
Amount of general business credit allowed for tax year	$ 20,000

Alesia now has $50,000 ($70,000 − $20,000) of unused general business credits that may be carried back or forward to other tax years as discussed below.

12-2c Treatment of Unused General Business Credits

Unused general business credits initially are carried back one tax year, to reduce the tax liability during that year. As a result, the taxpayer may receive a tax refund as a result of the carryback. Any remaining unused credits then are carried forward for up to 20 tax years.[4]

A FIFO method is applied to the carrybacks, carryovers, and utilization of credits earned during a tax year. By using the oldest credits first, the FIFO method minimizes the potential for loss of a general business credit benefit due to the expiration of credit carryovers.

---

[1]The separate credits are listed in § 38(b).
[2]§ 38(c).

[3]This amount is $12,500 for married taxpayers filing separately, unless one of the spouses is not entitled to the general business credit.
[4]§ 39(a)(1).

This example illustrates the use of general business credit carryovers.

General business credit carryovers		
2017	$ 4,000	
2018	6,000	
2019	2,000	
Total carryovers	$12,000	
2020 general business credit		$ 40,000
Total credit allowed in 2020 (based on tax liability)	$50,000	
Less: Utilization of carryovers		
2017	(4,000)	
2018	(6,000)	
2019	(2,000)	
Remaining credit allowed in 2020	$38,000	
Applied against 2020 general business credit		(38,000)
2020 unused amount carried forward to 2021		$ 2,000

LO.3

Identify various business-related tax credits.

12-3 SPECIFIC BUSINESS-RELATED TAX CREDITS

Each component of the general business credit is determined separately under its own set of rules. Some of the more important credits that make up the general business credit are explained here in the order listed in Exhibit 12.1.

12-3a Tax Credit for Rehabilitation Expenditures

Taxpayers are allowed a tax credit for expenditures incurred to rehabilitate industrial and commercial buildings and certified historic structures. The **rehabilitation expenditures credit** is intended to discourage businesses from moving from older, economically distressed areas (e.g., inner cities) to newer locations, while encouraging the preservation of historic structures.[5] The 20 percent credit is taken ratably over a five-year period starting with the year the rehabilitated building is placed in service.

When taking the credit, the basis of a rehabilitated building is reduced by the full rehabilitation credit allowed.[6]

In the current year, Juan spent $100,000 to rehabilitate a certified historic structure (adjusted basis of $40,000). He is allowed a $20,000 (20% × $100,000) credit for rehabilitation expenditures. The credit is claimed equally over five years, $4,000 per year.

Juan then increases the basis of the building by a net amount of $80,000 [an increase of $100,000 (rehabilitation expenditures) and a decrease of $20,000 (credit allowed)]. Stated otherwise, the $100,000 increases the basis of the building but the tax law requires that basis to be reduced by the amount of the credit for rehabilitation expenses.

To qualify for the credit, *certified historic structures* must be substantially rehabilitated during a 24-month period. A building has been *substantially rehabilitated* if qualified rehabilitation expenditures exceed the greater of:

- The adjusted basis of the property before the rehabilitation expenditures, or
- $5,000.

Qualified rehabilitation expenditures do not include the cost of acquiring a building, the cost of facilities related to a building (such as a parking lot), and the cost of enlarging an existing building.

---

[5]§ 47.   [6]§ 50(c).

Your brother—who buys, modernizes, and sells buildings in a large metropolitan city—has come to you for advice. Given the recent credit market conditions, business has been tough, and he has sold only a few buildings. One of your brother's buildings is a certified historic structure that would qualify for the 20 percent rehabilitation tax credit. Based on several recent appraisals, the building currently is worth $400,000. The expenditures needed to rehabilitate the building would be about $250,000, all of which would qualify for the rehabilitation tax credit.

Your brother has been approached by an individual who is interested in buying the building. The customer has offered to pay your brother $300,000 for the building and $350,000 for the rehabilitation work. This approach would provide the customer with a larger tax credit ($350,000 × 20% versus $250,000 × 20%) and provide a needed sale for your brother's business. How do you respond?

12-3b Work Opportunity Tax Credit

The **work opportunity tax credit** encourages employers to hire individuals from one or more of a number of targeted and economically disadvantaged groups.[7] Examples include long-term unemployed individuals (those unemployed for at least 27 weeks), qualified ex-felons, high-risk youths, food stamp recipients, veterans, summer youth employees, and long-term family assistance recipients.[8]

Work Opportunity Tax Credit: General

The credit generally is equal to 40 percent of the first $6,000 of wages (per eligible employee) for the first 12 months of employment. If the credit is taken, the employer's tax deduction for wages is reduced by the amount of the credit.

For an employer to qualify for the 40 percent credit, the employee must (1) be certified by a designated local agency as being a member of one of the targeted groups and (2) have completed at least 400 hours of service to the employer. If an employee meets the first condition but not the second, the credit rate is reduced to 25 percent provided the employee has completed a minimum of 120 hours of service to the employer.

Work Opportunity Credit Calculation

In January 2020, Green Company hires four individuals who are certified to be members of a qualifying targeted group. Each employee works 800 hours and is paid wages of $8,000 during the year. Green Company's work opportunity credit is $9,600 [($6,000 × 40%) × 4 employees]. If the tax credit is taken, Green must reduce its deduction for wages paid by $9,600. No credit is available for wages paid to these employees after their first year of employment.

EXAMPLE 10

On June 1, 2020, Maria, a calendar year taxpayer, hires Joe, a certified member of a targeted group. During the last seven months of 2020, Joe is paid $3,500 for 500 hours of work. Maria is allowed a credit of $1,400 ($3,500 × 40%) for 2020. Joe continues to work for Maria throughout 2021 and is paid $7,000 through May 31, 2021.

Because up to $6,000 of first-year wages are eligible for the credit, Maria is allowed a 40% credit on $2,500 [$6,000 − $3,500 (wages paid in 2020)] of wages paid in 2021. The credit equals $1,000 ($2,500 × 40%).

EXAMPLE 11

Continue with the facts of Example 11. Joe continues to work for Maria for five more years. None of Joe's wages paid after May 31, 2021, the end of the first year of Joe's employment, are eligible for the credit.

EXAMPLE 12

---

[7]§ 51. Note: The credit is only available if qualifying employees start work before 2021.

[8]§ 51(d).

12-3c Credit for Increasing Research Activities

To encourage business-related research and experimentation, also termed research and development (R&D), a credit is allowed for certain qualifying expenditures paid or incurred by a taxpayer. The **research activities credit** is the *sum* of three components: an incremental research activities credit, a basic research credit, and an energy research credit.[9]

Credit for Incremental Research Activities

The incremental research activities credit is 20 percent of the *excess* of qualified research expenses for the taxable year over the base amount.[10]

In general, *research expenditures* qualify if the research relates to discovering technological information that is intended for use in the development of a new or improved business component of the taxpayer. All such expenses qualify if the research is performed in-house (by the taxpayer or employees). If the research is contracted to others outside the taxpayer's business, only 65 percent of the amount paid qualifies for the credit.[11]

Javiera incurs the following research expenditures.

In-house wages, supplies, computer time	$50,000
Paid to Cutting Edge Scientific, a contractor	30,000

Javiera's qualified research expenditures are $69,500 [$50,000 + ($30,000 × 65%)].

The incremental research credit is *not* allowed for:[12]

- Research conducted once commercial production begins.
- Surveys and studies such as market research, testing, or routine data collection.
- Research conducted *outside* the United States, Puerto Rico, and U.S. possessions.
- Research in the social sciences, arts, or humanities.

Determining the *base amount* involves a complex series of computations, meant to approximate historical levels of research activity by the taxpayer. As a result, the credit is allowed only for increases in research expenses.

Jack, a calendar year taxpayer, incurs qualifying research expenditures of $200,000 at the beginning of the year. If Jack's base amount is $100,000, the incremental research activities credit is $20,000 [($200,000 − $100,000) × 20%].

Qualified expenditures are eligible for the 20 percent credit, and they can be *deducted* in the year incurred.[13] The taxpayer chooses among three options.[14]

1. Use the full credit and reduce the expense deduction for research expenses by 100 percent of the credit, or
2. Retain the full expense deduction and reduce the credit by the product of the full credit times the Federal corporate income tax rate (21 percent), or
3. Use the full credit, *capitalize* the research expenses, and *amortize* them over 60 months or more.

---

[9]§ 41. An eligible small business ($50 million or less in gross receipts) can use the credit to reduce its alternative minimum tax (AMT) liability. In addition, a qualified startup company (less than $5 million in gross receipts) can offset the credit against its payroll tax liability.

[10]An alternative simplified credit procedure is available. See §§ 41(c)(4) and (5).

[11]In the case of payments to a qualified research consortium, § 41(b)(3)(A) provides that 75% of the amount paid qualifies for the credit. In contrast,

for amounts paid to an energy research consortium, § 41(b)(3)(D) allows the full amount to qualify for the credit.

[12]§ 41(d). Reg. §§ 1.41–1 through 1.41–7.

[13]§ 174. Refer to the discussion of rules for deducting research and experimental expenditures in text Section 7-4.

[14]§ 280C(c). For option (3), the amount capitalized and subject to amortization is reduced by the full amount of the credit *only* if the credit exceeds the amount allowable as a deduction.

Assume the same facts as in Example 14, which shows that the potential incremental research activities credit is $20,000. The current-year deduction and corresponding credit are computed as follows.

EXAMPLE 15

	Credit Amount	Deduction Amount
Full credit and reduced deduction		
$20,000 − $0	$20,000	
$200,000 − $20,000		$180,000
Reduced credit and full deduction		
$20,000 − [(100% × $20,000) × 21%]	15,800	
$200,000 − $0		200,000
Full credit and capitalize and elect to amortize costs over 60 months		
$20,000 − $0	20,000	
($200,000/60) × 12		40,000

Credit for Basic Research

Corporations (other than S corporations or personal service corporations) are allowed an additional 20 percent credit for basic research payments made in *excess* of a base amount. This credit is not available to individual taxpayers. Basic research payments are amounts paid in cash to a qualified basic research organization, such as a college or university, or a tax-exempt organization operated primarily to conduct scientific research.

Basic research is any original investigation for the advancement of scientific knowledge not having a specific commercial objective. Basic research conducted outside the United States and basic research in the social sciences, arts, or humanities does not qualify. This reflects the intent of Congress to use the credit to encourage domestic high-tech research.

The basic research credit computation is based on expenditures in excess of a specially defined base amount. The basic research expenditures not in excess of the base amount still could qualify for the credit for incremental research activities.

Orange Corporation pays $75,000 to a university for basic research. Orange's base amount for the basic research credit is $50,000. The basic research activities credit allowed is $5,000 [($75,000 − $50,000) × 20%]. The $50,000 base amount for basic research also can be treated as research expenses for purposes of the incremental research activities credit.

EXAMPLE 16

Energy Research Credit

This credit was designed to stimulate additional energy research. The credit is 20 percent of the amounts paid to or incurred by a taxpayer for energy research through an energy research consortium.

12-3d Low-Income Housing Credit

To encourage building owners to make available affordable housing for low-income individuals, a credit is available for owners of qualified housing projects.[15]

More than any other credit, the low-income housing credit is influenced by nontax factors. For example, the property must be certified by an appropriate state or local agency. These credits are issued based on a nationwide allocation of congressional funding.

The credit amount depends on the number of units rented to low-income tenants. Occupants are low-income tenants if their income does not exceed a specified percentage of the area median gross income. The credit is determined by multiplying the qualified basis by a credit rate. The credit is claimed over a 10-year period, as long as the property continues to meet the required conditions.

---

[15]§ 42.

EXAMPLE 17

Sarah spends $1,000,000 to build a qualified low-income housing project that is completed on January 1 of the current year. The entire project is rented to low-income families. The credit rate for property placed in service during January is 7.25%.[16] Sarah claims a credit of $72,500 ($1,000,000 × 7.25%) in the current year and in each of the following nine years.

If Sarah only made 75% of the project's units available to low-income families, her credit would be $54,375 [($1,000,000 × 75%) × 7.25%].

Recapture of a portion of the credit may be required if the number of units set aside for low-income tenants falls below a minimum threshold, or if the taxpayer sells the property.

12-3e Disabled Access Credit

The disabled access credit encourages eligible small businesses to retrofit their existing facilities to make them more accessible to disabled individuals. The credit is 50 percent of the eligible expenditures that exceed $250 but do not exceed $10,250. Thus, the maximum amount for the credit is $5,000 ($10,000 × 50%).[17]

An *eligible small business* is one that during the previous year either had gross receipts of $1 million or less or had no more than 30 full-time employees. An eligible business can be a sole proprietorship, a partnership, a C corporation, or an S corporation.

Eligible expenditures include reasonable and necessary amounts that are paid or incurred to make certain changes to older facilities. Qualifying projects include installing ramps, widening doorways, and adding raised markings on elevator control buttons. Improvements also qualify if they assist hearing or visually impaired employees or customers who interact with the business.

The tax basis of the asset is reduced by the amount of the credit. Eligible expenditures do *not* include amounts incurred in connection with any facility that first was placed in service after November 5, 1990.

EXAMPLE 18

This year, Red, Inc., an eligible small business, makes $11,000 of capital improvements to a building that had been placed in service in June 1990. The improvements make Red's business more accessible to the disabled and constitute eligible expenditures for purposes of the disabled access credit. The amount of the credit is $5,000 [($10,250 − $250) × 50%].

Although $11,000 of eligible expenditures are incurred, only the excess of $10,250 over $250 qualifies for the credit. The adjusted basis of the capital improvement is $6,000 [$11,000 (cost) − $5,000 (amount of the credit)].

12-3f Credit for Small Employer Pension Plan Startup Costs

Small businesses are entitled to a nonrefundable credit for administrative costs associated with establishing and maintaining certain qualified retirement plans (primarily, plans for non-highly compensated employees).[18] Although such costs (e.g., payroll system changes, retirement-related education programs, consulting fees)[19] generally are deductible as ordinary and necessary business expenses, the credit lowers the after-tax cost of establishing a qualified retirement program and thereby encourages qualifying businesses to offer retirement plans for their employees.

The credit for small employer pension plan startup costs is 50 percent of qualified startup costs. An eligible employer is one with fewer than 100 employees who have earned at least $5,000 of compensation.

In general, the maximum credit is the lesser of (1) $5,000 or (2) $250 times the number of non-highly compensated employees. However, the minimum credit is $500. The deduction for the startup costs incurred is reduced by the amount of the credit. The credit can be claimed for qualifying costs incurred in each of the three years beginning with the tax year in which the retirement plan becomes effective.

---

[16]The rate is subject to a monthly adjustment by the IRS.

[17]§ 44.

[18]§ 45E. A highly compensated employee is one who owns 5% of the business in the current or prior year, or in the prior year earned more than

$125,000 (if 2019 is the prior year) or $130,000 (if 2020 is the prior year). Starting with tax years beginning after 2019, a $500 credit was added in late 2019 at § 45T to encourage small employers to include an automatic enrollment provision in retirement plans they offer.

[19]§§ 45E(c)(1) and (d)(1).

Maple Company decides to establish a qualified retirement plan for its non-highly compensated employees. In the process, it pays consulting fees of $21,200 to a firm that provides educational seminars to Maple's eligible employees and assists the payroll department in making necessary changes to the payroll system. Maple has 65 non-highly compensated employees who are eligible to participate in the plan.

Maple claims a credit for the pension plan startup costs of $5,000 [the lesser of $5,000 or $16,250 ($250 × 65 non-highly compensated employees)]. Its deduction for these expenses is reduced to $16,200 ($21,200 − $5,000).

12-3g Credit for Employer-Provided Child Care

An employer's expenditures incurred to provide for the care of children of employees can be deducted as ordinary and necessary business expenses. Alternatively, employers may claim a credit for providing child care facilities to their employees during normal working hours.[20] The **credit for employer-provided child care**, limited annually to $150,000, is composed of the aggregate of two components: 25 percent of qualified child care expenses and 10 percent of qualified child care resource and referral services.

Qualified child care expenses include the costs of acquiring, constructing, rehabilitating, expanding, and operating a child care facility. *Child care resource and referral services* include amounts paid or incurred under a contract to provide child care resource and referral services to an employee.

Any qualifying expenses otherwise deductible by the taxpayer are reduced by the amount of the credit. In addition, the taxpayer's basis for any property acquired or constructed and used for qualifying purposes is reduced by the amount of the credit. If, within 10 years of being placed in service, a child care facility ceases to be used in providing child care for employees, the taxpayer must recapture a portion of the credit previously claimed.[21] Such a rule, often referred to as a *clawback*, is an accountability measure to help ensure that tax incentives are used as intended.

During the year, Tan Company constructed a child care facility for $400,000 to be used by its employees who have preschool-aged children in need of child care services while their parents are at work. In addition, Tan incurred salaries for child care workers and other administrative costs associated with the facility of $100,000.

As a result, Tan's credit for employer-provided child care is $125,000 [($400,000 + $100,000) × 25%]. Correspondingly, the basis of the facility is reduced to $300,000 ($400,000 − $100,000), and Tan's deduction for salaries and administrative costs is reduced to $75,000 ($100,000 − $25,000).

12-3h Credit for Employer-Provided Family and Medical Leave

Employers can claim a general business credit equal to 12.5 percent of the wages paid to qualifying employees while they are on family and medical leave.[22] To claim the **credit for employer-provided family and medical leave**, employers must pay a minimum of 50 percent of the wages normally paid to an employee during the leave. If the wages paid during the leave *exceed* 50 percent of normal wages, the credit is increased by 0.25 percentage point for each percentage point above 50 percent. For example, if the employer pays 60 percent of the usual wages, then the credit is 15 percent [12.5 percent + (0.25 × 10)].

The credit is capped at 25 percent of wages paid (this would be allowed if the employer paid 100 percent of the employee's wages during the leave). The credit is limited to 12 weeks of leave per employee during any taxable year.

An employer must have a written policy in place that allows all qualifying full-time employees no less than two weeks of annual paid family and medical leave (non-full-time employees must be offered leave on a pro rata basis). Wages paid as vacation

---

[20]§ 45F.

[21]§ 45F(d).

[22]§ 45S; added by the Tax Cuts and Jobs Act (TCJA) of 2017, "family and medical leave" is as defined by the Family and Medical Leave Act of 1993.

leave, personal leave, or other medical or sick leave are not considered to be family and medical leave. The credit applies to wages paid in taxable years 2018 through 2020.

12-4 OTHER TAX CREDITS

LO.4

Determine various tax credits that are available primarily to individual taxpayers.

If you have no tax liability, they'll give you money = Negative Tax Liability!

refundable

12-4a Earned Income Credit

The `earned income credit` provides income tax equity to the working poor. Roughly, the credit has been designed to eliminate the Federal income tax and reimburse the taxpayer for certain other Federal taxes, such as the gasoline and Social Security taxes. In this way, the credit is intended to encourage economically disadvantaged individuals to become members of the workforce.

The earned income credit is determined by multiplying a maximum amount of earned income by the appropriate credit percentage. Generally, earned income includes employee compensation and net earnings from self-employment; it excludes items such as interest, dividends, retirement benefits, nontaxable employee compensation, and alimony/child support.[23] If a taxpayer has children, the credit percentage used in the calculation depends on the number of qualifying children.

Eligibility Requirements

Eligibility for the credit depends not only on the taxpayer meeting the earned income and AGI thresholds (shown in IRS tables), but also on whether he or she has a qualifying child. The term *qualifying child* generally has the same meaning here as it does for purposes of determining who qualifies as a dependent (see text Section 3-3a).

In addition to being available for taxpayers with qualifying children, the earned income credit is available to certain *workers without children*.[24] However, this provision is available only to taxpayers ages 25 through 64 who cannot be claimed as a dependent on another taxpayer's return.

Qualification for Credit

EXAMPLE 21

Maria, age 30, reports earned income for the year of $6,000. She is single and has no children. Maria can qualify for an earned income credit.

EXAMPLE 22

Willa, age 20, reports earned income for the year of $6,000. She is single and has no children. Willa does not qualify for an earned income credit until she reaches age 25.

Computing the Credit

For 2020, the maximum earned income credit is $3,584 ($10,540 × 34%) for a taxpayer with one qualifying child, $5,920 ($14,800 × 40%) for a taxpayer with two qualifying children, and $6,660 ($14,800 × 45%) for a taxpayer with three or more qualifying children. A taxpayer with no qualifying children can qualify for an earned income credit up to a maximum of $538.

The credit is available for a taxpayer who is married filing jointly, is single, or is filing as a head of household. The credit for those filing a joint return with qualifying children phases out to zero as earned income increases from about $25,000 to about $57,000.[25] Amounts in the IRS table are indexed annually for inflation.

---

[23]§ 32. The earned income credit is not available if the taxpayer's unearned income (e.g., interest, dividends) exceeds $3,650 in 2020 ($3,600 in 2019). See § 32(i).

[24]§ 32(c)(1)(A)(ii).
[25]§ 32(a)(2)(B).

ETHICS & EQUITY **Holding on to the Earned Income Credit with the Aid of a Transient Child**

For many years, Loretta Johnson, a single mother of three children, has been struggling to make ends meet by working two jobs that barely pay the minimum wage and together provide just over $10,000. Fortunately, her housing and food costs have been partially subsidized through various government programs. In addition, she has been able to take advantage of the earned income credit, which has provided almost $3,000 annually to help her with living expenses.

The credit truly has made a difference in the lives of Loretta and her family by helping them keep their creditors at bay. Loretta is proud that she has worked hard and provided for her family for many years without having to accept government assistance.

Now, however, Loretta faces a problem as her children have grown up and moved out of her home. With no qualifying children in her household, she no longer qualifies for a significant earned income credit. Although she will continue working her two jobs, such a significant loss to her household budget cuts into her ability to be self-reliant.

As a survival strategy and as a way of keeping the earned income credit, Loretta arranges to have one of her grandchildren live with her for just over six months every year. This enables almost 30 percent of her household budget to be secure. How do you react to Loretta's tax strategy?

To simplify the compliance process, the IRS issues an Earned Income Credit Table for the determination of the appropriate amount of the credit. This table and a worksheet are included in IRS Publication 596 at **irs.gov/forms-pubs/about-publication-596**.

12-4b Foreign Tax Credit

Individual taxpayers and corporations may claim a tax credit for foreign income tax paid on income earned and subject to tax in another country or a U.S. possession.[26] Alternatively, a taxpayer may claim a deduction instead of a credit.[27] In most instances, the **foreign tax credit (FTC)** is more advantageous because it provides a direct offset against the U.S. tax liability.

The FTC is designed to mitigate double taxation because income earned in another country by a U.S. person is subject to both U.S. and foreign income taxes. However, the FTC ceiling still may result in some form of double taxation when the effective foreign tax rates are higher than the applicable U.S. rates.

GLOBAL TAX ISSUES **Sourcing Income in Cyberspace—Getting It Right When Calculating the Foreign Tax Credit**

The limitation on the foreign tax credit (FTC) plays a critical role in restricting the amount of the credit available to a taxpayer. In the FTC formula, the taxpayer characterizes the year's taxable income as either earned (or sourced) inside the United States or earned from sources outside the United States. As a general rule, a greater percentage of foreign-source income in the formula leads to a larger FTC. Therefore, determining the source of various types of income is critical in calculating the credit. However, classifying income as either foreign or U.S. source is not always a simple matter. See text Section 25-3.

Consumers and businesses use the internet to conduct commerce involving both products and services. But the existing income-sourcing rules were developed long before the existence of the internet, and taxing authorities are finding it challenging to apply these rules to internet transactions. Where does a sale take place when the web server is in Scotland, the seller is in India, and the customer is in Illinois? Where is a service performed when all activities take place online?

---

[26]Section 27 provides for the credit, but the qualifications and calculation procedure for the credit are contained in §§ 901–908.

[27]§ 164.

Unused FTCs are carried back 1 year and forward 10 years.[28] The FTC is discussed in greater detail in text Section 25-5a.

Computation

The FTC allowed is the *lesser* of the foreign taxes incurred or the FTC *overall limitation*, which is equal to the Federal income tax paid on the double-taxed income.[29]

not refundable

> **Foreign Tax Credit and Its Limitations**
>
> **EXAMPLE 23**
>
> Yellow, based in the United States, sells widgets in Peru. Profits for the year in that country total $2,000,000. Yellow is subject to a 32% U.S. income tax rate, and a 20% marginal income tax rate applies to Yellow in Peru. Thus, attributable income taxes for this double-taxed income are $640,000 for the U.S. tax and $400,000 for the Peru tax.
>
> Yellow pays the full $400,000 tax to Peru. Its U.S. tax on this income is $640,000 minus the $400,000 foreign tax credit (lesser of $400,000 foreign tax paid or $640,000 attributable U.S. tax), or $240,000. The FTC allows a full recovery of the $400,000 tax paid to Peru.

> **EXAMPLE 24**
>
> Continue with the facts of Example 23, except that the applicable Peru tax rate is 40%, for an $800,000 liability. Yellow pays the full $800,000 tax to Peru. Its U.S. tax on this income is $640,000 minus the $640,000 foreign tax credit (lesser of $800,000 foreign tax paid or $640,000 attributable U.S. tax), or $0.
>
> The FTC overall limitation did not allow a full recovery of the $800,000 Peru liability. The widget profits are subject to a $160,000 double tax this year, even after the FTC is applied. The $160,000 excess amount is carried back 1 tax year and then forward 10 years.

If you paid $800,000 in taxes last year, you can get back $160,000

Only income taxes qualify for the credit.[30] Thus, value added taxes (VAT), severance taxes, property taxes, and sales taxes do not qualify because they are not regarded as taxes on income. Uncredited taxes still can be deducted by the taxpayer, however.

12-4c Child and Dependent Tax Credits

The **child tax credit** and **dependent tax credit** provisions allow individual taxpayers to take a tax credit based solely on the *number* of their qualifying children and dependents. These credits are two of several "family-friendly" provisions that currently are part of the Federal income tax law. To be eligible for the child tax credit, the child must be under age 17, a U.S. citizen, and a dependent of the taxpayer. The dependent tax credit is available for each dependent of the taxpayer (other than a qualifying child).

The child tax credit is $2,000 per child, and the dependent tax credit is $500 per non-child dependent. The child tax credit phases out as AGI exceeds $400,000 (married filing joint) or $200,000 (other taxpayers). The child tax credit is partially refundable (up to $1,400 per child, but no more than 15 percent of earned income in excess of $2,500). The dependent tax credit is subject to a phaseout and is not refundable.

12-4d Credit for Child and Dependent Care Expenses

The **credit for child and dependent care expenses** mitigates the inequity felt by working taxpayers who must pay for child care services to work outside the home.[31] This credit is a specified percentage of expenses incurred to enable the taxpayer to work or to seek employment. The credit is claimed by completing and filing Form 2441, Credit for Child and Dependent Care Expenses.

20% on up to $6,000 or 2 or more kids
$3,000 for one kid
not refundable

---

[28]§ 904(c) and Reg. § 1.904–2(g), Example 1.
[29]§ 904.

[30]Reg. § 1.901–1(a)(3)(i).
[31]§ 21.

Eligibility

To be eligible for the credit, an individual must have either of the following.

- A dependent under age 13.
- A dependent or spouse who is physically or mentally incapacitated and who lives with the taxpayer for more than one-half of the year.

Generally, married taxpayers must file a joint return to claim the credit.

Eligible Employment-Related Expenses

Eligible expenses include amounts paid for household services and care of a qualifying individual that are incurred to enable the taxpayer to be employed. The care can be provided in the home (e.g., by a nanny) or outside the home (e.g., at a day-care center).

Out-of-the-home expenses incurred for an older dependent or spouse who is physically or mentally incapacitated qualify for the credit if that person regularly spends at least eight hours each day in the taxpayer's household. This makes the credit available to taxpayers with handicapped older children and elderly relatives in their home. Out-of-the-home expenses incurred for services provided by a dependent care center qualify only if the center complies with all applicable laws and regulations of a state or unit of local government.

Child care payments to a relative are eligible for the credit unless the relative is a child (under age 19) of the taxpayer.

Wilma is an employed mother of an eight-year-old child. She pays her mother, Rita, $1,500 per year to care for the child after school. Wilma pays her daughter Eleanor, age 17, $900 for the child's care during the summer. Of these amounts, only the $1,500 paid to Rita qualifies as employment-related child care expenses.

EXAMPLE 25

Earned Income Ceiling

Qualifying employment-related expenses are limited in amount to an individual's earned income. For married taxpayers, this limitation applies to the spouse with the *lesser* amount of earned income.

Special rules are provided for taxpayers with nonworking spouses who are disabled or are full-time students. Here, the nonworking spouse is *deemed* to have earned income of $250 per month if there is one qualifying individual in the household or $500 per month if there are two or more qualifying individuals in the household. In the case of a student-spouse, only months for which the student is enrolled on a full-time basis are counted.[32]

Calculating the Credit

In general, the credit is equal to a percentage of *unreimbursed* employment-related expenses up to $3,000 for one qualifying individual and $6,000 for two or more individuals. The credit rate varies between 20 percent and 35 percent, depending on the taxpayer's AGI, as indicated in Exhibit 12.2.

Nancy, who has two children under age 13, worked full-time while her husband, Raji, was attending college for 10 months during the year. Nancy earned $22,000 and incurred $6,200 of child care expenses. Raji is deemed to have earned $500 for each of the 10 months (or a total of $5,000) that he was in school. Because Nancy and Raji report AGI of $22,000, they are allowed a credit rate of 31%.

Nancy and Raji are limited to $5,000 in qualified child care expenses ($6,000 maximum expenses, limited to Raji's $5,000 earned income). Therefore, the couple is entitled to a tax credit of $1,550 (31% × $5,000) for the year.

EXAMPLE 26

---

[32]§ 21(d).

EXHIBIT 12.2	Computing the Child and Dependent Care Credit	

Adjusted Gross Income		Applicable Rate of Credit
Over	**But Not Over**	
$ 0	$15,000	35%
15,000	17,000	34%
17,000	19,000	33%
19,000	21,000	32%
21,000	23,000	31%
23,000	25,000	30%
25,000	27,000	29%
27,000	29,000	28%
29,000	31,000	27%
31,000	33,000	26%
33,000	35,000	25%
35,000	37,000	24%
37,000	39,000	23%
39,000	41,000	22%
41,000	43,000	21%
43,000	No limit	20%

12-4e Education Tax Credits

40% refundable

The **American Opportunity credit** and the **lifetime learning credit** [33] are available to help qualifying low- and middle-income individuals defray the cost of higher education. The credits are available for qualifying tuition and related expenses incurred by students pursuing undergraduate or graduate degrees or vocational training. Books and other course materials are eligible for the American Opportunity credit (but not the lifetime learning credit). Room and board are ineligible for both credits.

ETHICS & EQUITY	Is This the Right Way to Use the Credit for Child and Dependent Care Expenses?

Your friends, Tim and Shia, have hired a child care provider (Rebecca) to come into their home for three hours a day to care for their two children while they both are at work. Rebecca charges $4,500 for her services for the year.

Tim and Shia have learned that up to $6,000 of qualifying expenditures will generate a credit for child and dependent care expenses and that qualifying expenditures can include payments for housecleaning services. As a result, they ask Rebecca whether she would be interested in working several hours more per week, after Tim returns from work, for the sole purpose of cleaning the house.

Tim and Shia offer to pay $1,500 for the additional work, and Rebecca seems interested. For Tim and Shia, the net cost of the additional services would be $1,200 [$1,500 − ($1,500 × 20%)] due to the availability of the credit for child and dependent care expenses.

You learn of Tim and Shia's opportunity, but you think it is unfair. If you hired someone to perform similar housecleaning services, your net cost would be $1,500, not $1,200, because you do not qualify for the credit. You are troubled by this apparent inequity. Is your intuition correct?

Maximum Credit

The American Opportunity credit permits a maximum credit of $2,500 per year (100 percent of the first $2,000 of tuition expenses plus 25 percent of the next $2,000 of tuition expenses) for each of the *first four years* of postsecondary education.[34] The lifetime learning credit permits a credit of 20 percent of qualifying expenses (up to $10,000 per year) incurred in a year in which the American Opportunity credit is not claimed.[35] Generally, the lifetime learning credit is used for individuals who are beyond the first four years of postsecondary education.

Eligible Individuals

Both education credits are available for qualified expenses incurred by a taxpayer, taxpayer's spouse, or taxpayer's dependent. The American Opportunity credit is available for each eligible student, while the lifetime learning credit is calculated per taxpayer. To be eligible for the American Opportunity credit, a student must take at least one-half of the full-time course load for at least one academic term at a qualifying educational institution. No comparable requirement exists for the lifetime learning credit. Therefore, taxpayers who take graduate training or continuing education are eligible for the lifetime learning credit. Taxpayers who are married must file joint returns to claim either education credit.

Income Limitations and Refundability

The education credits are subject to different income limitations. Forty percent of the American Opportunity credit is refundable, and it can offset a taxpayer's alternative minimum tax (AMT) liability. The lifetime learning credit is neither refundable nor an AMT liability offset.[36]

The American Opportunity credit amount is phased out, beginning when the taxpayer's AGI (modified for this purpose) reaches $80,000 ($160,000 for married taxpayers filing jointly). The credit is phased out proportionately over a $10,000 ($20,000 for married taxpayers filing jointly) range. As a result, the credit is eliminated completely when modified AGI reaches $90,000 ($180,000 for married taxpayers filing jointly).

For 2020, the lifetime learning credit amount is phased out, beginning when the taxpayer's AGI (modified for this purpose) reaches $59,000 ($118,000 for married taxpayers filing jointly).[37] After the phaseout, the credit equals zero when AGI reaches $69,000 (or $138,000).

The Big Picture

EXAMPLE 27

Return to the facts of *The Big Picture* on p. 12-1. Recall that Tom and Jennifer Snyder are married and file a joint tax return. The Snyders report modified AGI of $158,000. They have two children, Lora and Sam. The Snyders paid $7,500 of tuition and $8,500 for room and board for Lora (a freshman) and $8,100 of tuition plus $7,200 for room and board for Sam (a junior).

Lora and Sam are full-time students and are Tom and Jennifer's dependents. Lora's tuition and Sam's tuition are qualified expenses for the American Opportunity credit. For 2020, Tom and Jennifer may claim a $2,500 American Opportunity credit each for Lora's and Sam's expenses [(100% × $2,000) + (25% × $2,000)]. This totals to a $5,000 American Opportunity credit on the Snyders' return.

---

[34]§ 25A(i)(1).

[35]§ 25A(c).

[36]If the credit is claimed for a taxpayer subject to § 1(g) (the "kiddie tax"), the credit is not refundable.

[37]§ 25A(d). The phaseout amounts are indexed annually. For 2019, the AGI limits were $58,000 and $116,000.

The Big Picture

EXAMPLE

28

Return to the facts of *The Big Picture* on p. 12-1. Assume that Tom and Jennifer's 2020 modified AGI is $172,000, instead of $158,000. The Snyders can claim a $2,000 (rather than $5,000) American Opportunity credit. The taxpayers' available credit is reduced because modified AGI exceeds the $160,000 limit for married taxpayers.

The reduction is the amount by which modified AGI exceeds the limit, expressed as a percentage of the phaseout range. In this case, the reduction is 60% [($172,000 − $160,000)/$20,000]. Therefore, the maximum available credit is $2,000 ($5,000 × 40% allowable portion).

The Big Picture

EXAMPLE

29

Return to the facts of *The Big Picture* on p. 12-1. Now assume that Tom and Jennifer's modified AGI is $132,000. In addition, assume that Tom is going to school on a part-time basis to complete a graduate degree and pays qualifying tuition and fees of $4,000. Because the Snyders' modified AGI is below $160,000, a $5,000 American Opportunity credit is available to them relative to the two children (i.e., $2,500 each for Lora and Sam).

In addition, Tom's qualifying expenses are eligible for the lifetime learning credit. The potential lifetime learning credit of $800 ($4,000 × 20%) is reduced because modified AGI exceeds the $118,000 limit for married taxpayers. As modified AGI exceeds the limit by $14,000 and the phaseout range is $20,000, the couple's lifetime learning credit is reduced by 70%.

As a result, the Snyders' lifetime learning credit is $240 ($800 × 30% after the phaseout), and total education credits amount to $5,240 ($5,000 American Opportunity credit + $240 lifetime learning credit).

Restrictions on Double Tax Benefit

Taxpayers are prohibited from receiving a double tax benefit associated with qualifying educational expenses. As a result, taxpayers who claim an education credit may not deduct the expenses, nor may they claim the credit for amounts that are otherwise excluded from gross income (e.g., scholarships, employer-paid educational assistance).

12-4f Energy Credits

not depreciate →

The Internal Revenue Code contains a variety of credits for businesses and individuals to encourage the conservation of natural resources and the development of energy sources other than oil and gas. The **energy tax credits** include incentives to:

- Install energy-efficient windows, insulation, and heating and cooling equipment;
- Purchase solar and other energy-efficient water heaters; and
- Install equipment in a business to produce electricity using solar, wind, or geo-thermal sources.

Credit amounts and expiration dates differ for the various provisions.

12-4g Credit for Certain Retirement Plan Contributions

not refundable

Taxpayers may claim a nonrefundable **credit for certain retirement plan contributions** based on eligible contributions of up to $2,000 to certain qualified retirement plans, such as traditional and Roth IRAs and § 401(k) plans.[38] This credit, sometimes referred to as the "saver's credit," encourages lower- and middle-income taxpayers to contribute to qualified retirement plans. The benefit provided by this credit is in addition to any deduction or exclusion that otherwise is available due to the qualifying contribution.

---

[38]§§ 25B(a) through (d). In calculating the credit, the qualifying contributions are reduced by taxable distributions from any of the qualifying plans received by the taxpayer and spouse during the tax year, during the two previous tax years, and during the period prior to the due date of the current year's return.

EXHIBIT 12.3	"Saver's" Credit Rate and AGI Thresholds (2020)						

Joint Return		Head of Household		All Other Cases		Applicable Percentage
Over	Not Over	Over	Not Over	Over	Not Over	
$ 0	$39,000	$ 0	$29,250	$ 0	$19,500	50%
39,000	42,500	29,250	31,875	19,500	21,250	20%
42,500	65,000	31,875	48,750	21,250	32,500	10%
65,000		48,750		32,500		0%

The credit rate applied to the eligible contributions depends on the taxpayer's AGI[39] and filing status, as shown in Exhibit 12.3. However, the maximum credit allowed to an individual is $1,000 ($2,000 × 50%). Once AGI exceeds the upper end of the applicable range, no credit is available. To qualify for the credit, the taxpayer must be at least 18 years of age and cannot be a dependent of another taxpayer or a full-time student.

EXAMPLE 30

Earl and Josephine, married taxpayers, each contribute $2,500 to § 401(k) plans. The AGI reported on their joint return is $45,000.

The eligible retirement contributions for purposes of the credit are limited to $2,000 for Earl and $2,000 for Josephine. As a result, Earl and Josephine may claim a credit for their retirement plan contributions of $400 [($2,000 × 2) × 10%]. They would not qualify for the credit if their AGI had exceeded $65,000.

The various tax credits discussed in this chapter are summarized in Concept Summary 12.1.

12-5 TAX PAYMENTS

LO.5

Apply the tax withholding and payment procedures used by employers.

Taxes generally are remitted to the Treasury with the tax return. Withholdings are required, though, as to wages and a few other income items received by individuals. For example, employers must directly transfer a portion of an employee's pay to the Federal government. Using a Form W–4, the employee instructs the employer as to how much of the wages should be withheld, so that the taxes on the wages are remitted to the government on a "pay as you go" basis.

Corporations and other taxpayers, including sole proprietors, make quarterly payments to the Treasury of the estimated taxes that relate to their taxable income for the period. Taxpayers then claim a credit against the tax due for the withholdings and estimated payments that have been prepaid in this manner.

In addition, employers must withhold a portion of each wage payment that relates to <mark>employment taxes</mark>, that is, the Social Security and Medicare tax liabilities that relate to the employee's wages for the period.

Self-employed taxpayers (sole proprietors) do not have employers, so no withholding occurs, but income and employment taxes are prepaid nonetheless. Self-employeds are responsible for remitting their own income and employment taxes, in the form of quarterly estimated tax payments.

---

[39]The AGI thresholds are indexed annually for inflation. For purposes of this credit, the AGI thresholds are modified to include certain income exclusions. See § 25B(e).

Concept Summary 12.1

Major Tax Credits

Credit	Computation	Comments
Tax withheld on wages (§ 31)	Amount is reported to employee on Form W–2.	Refundable credit.
Earned income (§ 32)	Amount is determined by reference to Earned Income Credit Table published by IRS.	Refundable credit. A form of negative income tax to assist low-income taxpayers. Earned income and AGI must be less than certain threshold amounts. Generally, one or more qualifying children must reside with the taxpayer.
Child and dependent care (§ 21)	Rate ranges from 20% to 35% depending on AGI. Maximum base for credit is $3,000 for one qualifying individual, $6,000 for two or more.	Nonrefundable personal credit. No carryback or carryforward. Benefits taxpayers who incur employment-related child or dependent care expenses in order to work or seek employment. Eligible taxpayers must have a dependent under age 13 or a dependent (any age) or spouse who is physically or mentally incapacitated.
Elderly or disabled (§ 22)	Usually taken from an IRS table.	Nonrefundable personal credit. No carryback or carryforward. Provides relief for taxpayers not receiving substantial tax-free retirement benefits.
Adoption expenses (§ 23)	Up to $14,300 of costs incurred to adopt an eligible child qualify for the credit. Taxpayer claims the credit in the year qualified expenses were paid or incurred if they were paid or incurred during or after year in which adoption was finalized. For expenses paid or incurred in a year prior to when adoption was finalized, credit must be claimed in tax year following the tax year during which the expenses are paid or incurred.	Nonrefundable credit subject to a phaseout. Unused credit may be carried forward five years. Purpose is to assist taxpayers who incur nonrecurring costs associated with the adoption process.
Child and dependent (§ 24)	Credit is based on *number* of qualifying children under age 17 and dependents. Maximum credit is $2,000 per child and $500 per dependent. Credits are phased out for higher-income taxpayers.	Child tax credit is partially refundable (up to $1,400), but limited to 15% of earned income in excess of $2,500. Dependent tax credit is not refundable. Purpose is to assist families with children or dependents.
Education (§ 25A)	American Opportunity credit is available for qualifying education expenses of students in first four years of postsecondary education. Maximum credit is $2,500 per year per eligible student. Credit is phased out for higher-income taxpayers.	Credit is designed to help low- to middle-income families defray costs of the first four years of higher education. The credit is partially refundable.
	Lifetime learning credit permits a credit of 20% of qualifying expenses (up to $10,000 per year) provided American Opportunity credit is not claimed with respect to those expenses. Credit is calculated per taxpayer, not per student, and is phased out for higher-income taxpayers.	Nonrefundable credit. Credit is designed to help low- to middle-income taxpayers defray costs of higher education beyond the first four years.
Certain retirement plan contributions (§ 25B)	Calculation is based on amount of contribution multiplied by a percentage that depends on the taxpayer's filing status and AGI.	Nonrefundable credit. Purpose is to encourage contributions to qualified retirement plans by low- and middle-income taxpayers.

continued

Major Tax Credits—(Continued)

Credit	Computation	Comments
Foreign taxes paid (§ 27)	Foreign-source taxable income/total worldwide taxable income × U.S. tax = overall limitation. Lesser of foreign taxes imposed or overall limitation.	Nonrefundable credit. Unused credits may be carried back 1 year and forward 10 years. Purpose is to prevent double taxation of offshore income.
Energy credits	Various items to encourage individuals and businesses to "go green."	The credits are subject to various expiration dates.
General business (§ 38)	May not exceed net income tax minus the greater of tentative minimum tax or 25% of net regular tax liability that exceeds $25,000.	Nonrefundable credit. Components include tax credit for rehabilitation expenditures, work opportunity tax credit, research activities credit, low-income housing credit, disabled access credit, credit for small employer pension plan startup costs, and credit for employer-provided child care. Unused credit may be carried back 1 year and forward 20 years. FIFO method applies to carrybacks, carryovers, and credits earned during current year.
Rehabilitation expenditures (§ 47)	Qualifying expenditures times 20%.	Nonrefundable credit. Part of general business credit and therefore subject to same carryback, carryover, and FIFO rules. Purpose is to discourage businesses from moving from economically distressed areas to newer locations.
Credit for increasing research activities (§ 41)	Incremental credit is 20% of excess of computation year expenditures over the base amount. Basic research credit is allowed to certain corporations for 20% of cash payments to qualified organizations that exceed a specially calculated base amount. An energy research credit is allowed for 20% of qualifying payments made to an energy research consortium.	Nonrefundable credit. Part of general business credit and therefore subject to same carryback, carryover, and FIFO rules. Purpose is to encourage high-tech and energy research in the United States.
Low-income housing (§ 42)	Appropriate rate times eligible basis (portion of project attributable to low-income units). Credit is available each year for 10 years. Recapture may apply.	Nonrefundable credit. Part of general business credit and therefore subject to same carryback, carryover, and FIFO rules. Purpose is to encourage construction of housing for low-income individuals.
Disabled access (§ 44)	Credit is 50% of eligible access expenditures that exceed $250 but do not exceed $10,250. Maximum credit is $5,000. Available only to eligible small businesses.	Nonrefundable credit. Part of general business credit and therefore subject to same carryback, carryover, and FIFO rules. Purpose is to encourage small businesses to become more accessible to disabled individuals.
Small employer pension plan startup costs (§ 45E)	Credit equals 50% of qualified startup costs incurred by eligible employers. Maximum annual credit is $500. Deduction for related expenses is reduced by the amount of the credit.	Nonrefundable credit. Part of general business credit and therefore subject to same carryback, carryover, and FIFO rules. Purpose is to encourage small employers to establish qualified retirement plans for their employees.
Employer-provided child care (§ 45F)	Credit is equal to 25% of qualified child care expenses plus 10% of qualified expenses for child care resource and referral services. Maximum credit is $150,000. Deduction for related expenses or basis must be reduced by the amount of the credit.	Nonrefundable credit. Part of general business credit and therefore subject to same carryback, carryover, and FIFO rules. Purpose is to encourage employers to provide child care for their employees' children during normal working hours.

continued

Major Tax Credits—(Continued)

Credit	Computation	Comments
Credit for employer-provided family and medical leave (§ 45S)	Credit is equal to 12.5% of wages paid to qualifying employees while they are on family and medical leave (limited to 12 weeks per employee per year). Employers must pay a minimum of 50% of the wages normally paid; if wages paid during the leave *exceed* 50% of normal wages, the credit is increased by 0.25% for each percentage point above 50% to a maximum credit of 25%.	Nonrefundable credit. Part of general business credit and therefore subject to same carryback, carryover, and FIFO rules. Purpose is to encourage employers to provide leave to their employees for family and medical purposes (e.g,, birth of a child; care for a sick child, spouse, or parent).
Work opportunity (§ 51)	Credit is limited to 40% of the first $6,000 of wages paid to each eligible employee.	Nonrefundable credit. Part of the general business credit and therefore subject to the same carryback, carryover, and FIFO rules. Purpose is to encourage employment of individuals in specified groups.

12-5a Payments by Employers

The employer is responsible for withholding the employee's share of FICA (commonly referred to as the Social Security tax) and appropriate amounts for income taxes. In addition, the employer matches the FICA portion withheld, and it pays the full cost of FUTA. The sum of the employment taxes and the income tax withholdings is paid to the IRS at specified intervals.

Amount of FICA Taxes

The FICA tax has two components: Social Security tax (old age, survivors, and disability insurance; rate 6.2 percent) *and* Medicare tax (hospital insurance; rate 1.45 percent). Both the employer and the employee pay the tax at these rates.

The tax rates and wage base under FICA have increased substantially over the years. The base amount is adjusted each year for inflation.

Withholdings from employees continue until the maximum base amount is reached. For 2020, for example, FICA withholding for the Social Security portion (6.2 percent) ends once the employee has earned FICA wages of $137,700. No wage limit applies for the Medicare portion (1.45 percent) of the tax.

EXAMPLE 31

In 2020, Keshia earned a salary of $140,000 from her employer. Therefore, FICA taxes withheld from her salary are $8,537.40 ($137,700 × 6.2%) plus $2,030.00 ($140,000 × 1.45%) for a total of $10,567.40. In addition to remitting the amount withheld from Keshia's salary to the Federal government, her employer pays its own tax of $10,567.40 relative to her salary.

A spouse employed by another spouse is subject to FICA tax payments. However, children under the age of 18 who are employed in a parent's trade or business are exempted.

12-5b Payments by Self-Employed Persons

LO.6

Execute the tax payment procedures used by self-employed persons.

Although the following discussion largely centers on self-employed taxpayers, estimated tax may be required from some employees. An employee may be required to pay estimated tax for income other than wages that is not subject to withholding (e.g., investment income). Further, the taxpayer may conduct a second trade or business (e.g., as a sole proprietor), and these profits may require the payment of income and self-employment tax.

Estimated Tax

Estimated tax is the amount of tax (including any AMT and self-employment tax) an individual expects to owe for the year after subtracting tax credits and income tax withheld. Any individual who has estimated tax for the year of $1,000 or more in excess of withholdings must make quarterly estimated tax payments.[40] No penalty applies if the taxpayer had a zero tax liability for the preceding tax year *and* the preceding tax year was a taxable year of 12 months *and* the taxpayer was a U.S. citizen or resident for the entire preceding tax year.

First, the *required annual payment* is computed. This is the *smaller* of:

- 90 percent of the tax shown on the current year's return.
- 100 percent of the tax shown on the preceding year's return (the return must cover the full 12 months of the preceding year). If the AGI on the preceding year's return exceeds $150,000 ($75,000 if married filing separately), the 100 percent requirement is increased to 110 percent.

In general, one-fourth of this required annual payment is due on each of April 15, June 15, and September 15 of the tax year and January 15 of the following year.

An equal part of withholding is deemed paid on each due date. Thus, the estimated tax due on each date is the quarterly installment of the required annual payment, reduced by the quarter's share of the year's withholdings for the individual. Payments are accompanied by the payment voucher, Form 1040–ES.

Self-Employment Tax

The tax on self-employment income is levied to provide Social Security and Medicare benefits (old age, survivors, and disability insurance and hospital insurance) for self-employed individuals. Individuals with net earnings of $400 or more from self-employment are subject to the **self-employment tax**.[41] For 2020, the self-employment tax is 12.4 percent of self-employment earnings up to $137,700 (for the Social Security portion) *plus* 2.9 percent of the total amount of self-employment earnings (the Medicare portion).

Net earnings from self-employment includes gross income from a trade or business less allowable trade or business deductions, the distributive share of any partnership income or loss derived from a trade or business activity, and net income from rendering personal services as an independent contractor.

Self-employed taxpayers deduct a portion of the self-employment tax in determining the self-employment tax itself, *and* in computing AGI (normally, one-half of the self-employment tax liability).[42]

If an individual also receives wages subject to FICA tax, the ceiling amount of the Social Security portion on which the self-employment tax is computed is reduced. Thus, the self-employment tax may be reduced to zero if a self-employed individual also receives FICA wages in excess of the ceiling amount.

EXAMPLE 32

In 2020, Kelly reported $86,000 of net earnings from a data transfer services business that she owns. During the year, Kelly also received $67,500 in wages as an employee of an accounting firm.

Kelly's self-employment income subject to the Social Security portion (12.4%) is $70,200 ($137,700 − $67,500), not $86,000. This produces a Social Security portion of the self-employment tax of $8,704.80 ($70,200 × 12.4%). All of Kelly's net self-employment earnings are subject to the Medicare portion of the self-employment tax of 2.9%; no income limit applies for that tax.

[40]§§ 6654(c)(1) and 6654(e)(1).

[41]§ 6017.

[42]§§ 164(f) and 1402(a)(12).

12-5c **Affordable Care Act Provisions**

Several individual tax provisions support the Federal health insurance system, Medicare, with additional taxes on certain high-income individuals. Other ACA provisions are reviewed in the text's online appendix (Affordable Care Act Provisions).

Additional Medicare Tax on Wages

An additional 0.9 percent Medicare tax is imposed on wages received in excess of $250,000 for married taxpayers filing a joint return ($125,000 if married filing separately) and $200,000 for all other taxpayers.[43] Unlike the general 1.45 percent Medicare tax on wages, the additional tax on a joint return is computed on the *combined* wages of the employee and the employee's spouse. As a result, the Medicare tax rate is:

1. 1.45 percent on the first $200,000 of wages ($125,000 on a married filing separate return; $250,000 of combined wages on a married filing joint return), and
2. 2.35 percent (1.45% + 0.9%) on wages in excess of $200,000 ($125,000 on a married filing separate return; $250,000 of combined wages on a married filing joint return).

Additional Medicare Tax on Wages

EXAMPLE 33

Singh, who is single, earns wages of $500,000. Singh pays $2,900 of Medicare taxes on the first $200,000 of her wages ($200,000 × 1.45%) and $7,050 of Medicare taxes on her wages in excess of $200,000 ($300,000 × 2.35%). In total, her Medicare tax is $9,950. Singh's additional Medicare tax totals $2,700.

EXAMPLE 34

Patrick and Paula file a joint return. During the year, Patrick earns wages of $125,000, and Paula earns wages of $175,000—their total wages are $300,000. Patrick and Paula pay total Medicare taxes of $4,800 [($250,000 × 1.45%) + ($50,000 × 2.35%)]. The couple's additional Medicare tax is $450.

The additional Medicare tax also applies to self-employed individuals; net earnings from self-employment are used for the threshold computations. As a result, the tax rate for the Medicare tax on self-employment income is:

1. 2.9 percent on the first $200,000 of net earnings from self-employment ($125,000 on a married filing separate return; $250,000 on a married filing joint return), and
2. 3.8 percent (2.9% + 0.9%) on net earnings from self-employment in excess of $200,000 ($125,000 on a married filing separate return; $250,000 on a married filing joint return).

Additional Medicare Tax on Unearned Income (Net Investment Income Tax or NIIT)

An additional 3.8 percent Medicare tax is imposed on the unearned income of individuals, estates, and trusts.[44] For individuals, the tax is 3.8 percent of the lesser of:

1. Net investment income, or
2. The excess of modified adjusted gross income over $250,000 for married taxpayers filing a joint return ($125,000 if married filing separately) and $200,000 for all other taxpayers.[45]

---

[43]§ 3101(b)(2). The base amounts are not indexed for inflation.
[44]§ 1411.

[45]§ 1411(b). AGI is modified by adding back any foreign earned income exclusion. The base amounts are not indexed for inflation.

In general, "net investment income" includes interest, dividends, annuities, royalties, rents, income from passive activities, and net gains from the sale of investment property less deductions allowed in generating that income.[46]

Additional Medicare Tax on Unearned Income

Xinran records net investment income of $50,000 and MAGI of $180,000, and she files as a single taxpayer. As Xinran's MAGI does not exceed $200,000, Xinran need not pay the additional Medicare tax on unearned income.

EXAMPLE 35

Assume the same facts as in Example 35, except that Xinran reports net investment income of $85,000 and MAGI of $220,000. Now Xinran pays a Medicare tax on the lesser of (1) $85,000 (net investment income) or (2) $20,000 (the amount by which MAGI exceeds $200,000). Xinran's additional Medicare tax on unearned income is $760 ($20,000 × 3.8%).

EXAMPLE 36

Assume the same facts as in Example 36, except that Xinran's MAGI is $290,000. Because her MAGI exceeds the threshold amount by $90,000, she pays a Medicare tax on the entire $85,000 of net investment income. As a result, Xinran's additional Medicare tax on unearned income is $3,230 ($85,000 × 3.8%).

EXAMPLE 37

The 3.8 percent additional Medicare tax on unearned income is *in addition to* the additional 0.9 percent Medicare tax on wages or self-employment income. Taxpayers who generate both high wages (or self-employment income) *and* high investment income may be subject to both taxes.

Assume the same facts as in Example 37, except that Xinran records MAGI of $325,000 (including $240,000 of wages and $85,000 of net investment income).

In this case, Xinran also is subject to an additional Medicare tax of $360 ($40,000 × 0.9%, her wages in excess of $200,000). In total, Xinran pays $3,590 in additional Medicare taxes ($3,230 on unearned income and $360 on wages).

EXAMPLE 38

12-5d Alternative Minimum Tax Don't Need to Know

A small number of individual taxpayers pay an additional Federal income tax, known as the **alternative minimum tax** (AMT).[47] Congress designed the AMT to assure that all individuals paid a "fair share" into the income tax system; it had appeared that some taxpayers were taking advantage of "too many" of the Code's exclusions, deductions, exemptions, and credits, and that it was possible for some to pay little or no Federal income tax in certain tax years. The 2017 tax revisions drastically reduced the number of taxpayers who might be subject to the AMT, chiefly by increasing the annual exemption from the tax and eliminating some of the deductions previously available. The 2017 revisions repealed the AMT for C corporations. AMT also applies to trusts and estates (not addressed in this chapter).

The AMT works as a "shadow" tax system, such that all taxpayers are required to compute both the regular tax and the AMT, and then to *pay whichever liability is higher.* As most taxpayers now complete their income tax filings by using tax software and/or a tax professional, this typically does not present a compliance burden for the individual. However, additional record keeping is required.

---

[46]§1411(c). Certain types of income, including qualified retirement plan distributions, tax-exempt income, and any untaxed gain from the sale of a principal residence, are excluded from this definition.

[47]§ 55.

The AMT Tax Base

The AMT tax base is designed to allow fewer tax deductions and exclusions, and to make some items available in a manner that is slower than applies for the regular tax. Similarly, income items are identified in the AMT base that are included more quickly than is the case for regular tax purposes, and a few additional income items are subject to tax only under the AMT rules. The result is a form of income tax with lower rates and a broader tax base. In addition, most tax credits are not allowed to reduce AMT.

Here are some examples of items that are treated differently under the AMT rules, in deriving the tax base that is used to compute the AMT.

- Most cost recovery computations allow deductions that are taken over a longer time period. When a depreciable asset is sold, then, the AMT gain typically is smaller than the corresponding regular tax gain, as the AMT basis for the asset is larger.

- For an individual who itemizes deductions on the Form 1040, the limited deduction for taxes paid is not allowed for AMT purposes.

- For AMT purposes, only the percentage of completion method of accounting can be used for long-term contracts, and not the completed contract method.

- The AMT includes in the tax base the "spread" related to an incentive stock option (i.e., the excess of the stock's fair market value over the exercise price on the date of the option's exercise). This affects the AMT gain that is recognized when the shares obtained with the option later are sold in the market.

- Percentage depletion deductions can be taken under the AMT only until the basis of the productive property reaches zero.

- Municipal bond interest is included in the AMT tax base if the bond proceeds were used to benefit the "private activity" of a commercial business (e.g., in building a factory).

Individuals who are especially vulnerable to the AMT are those who claim large amounts of accelerated cost recovery deductions. One also might be subject to the AMT in a year when a large volume of profitable incentive stock options is exercised, or when large investments in private activity municipal bonds are made.

Computing and Paying the AMT

When the AMT tax base is computed, an annual exemption is allowed, and a two-bracket tax schedule is used (26 percent and 28 percent). AMT liabilities must be included in the taxpayer's estimated tax payments. Form 6251 is used by individuals to report the tax.

An annual AMT exemption is allowed. As the AMT tax base increases, the exemption phases out, potentially to zero, at a rate of 25 cents for each dollar of AMT tax base in the phaseout range.

Taxpayer's Filing Status	Exemption Amount (2020)	Exemption Phaseout Begins at	Exemption Phaseout Ends (Exemption = $0) at
Married, joint; Surviving spouse	$113,400	$1,036,800	$1,490,400
Single, Head of household	72,900	518,400	810,000
Married, separate	56,700	518,400	745,200

The 2020 AMT tax base for Harry, who files as a single individual on his Form 1040, is $680,000. Harry's AMT exemption phased out to the extent of [($680,000 − $518,400) × 25%], or $40,400. Harry's AMT exemption amount is $32,500 ($72,900 exemption − $40,400 reduction).

EXAMPLE
39

AMT liabilities for 2020 are computed as follows.

Tax Rate (%)	On the AMT tax base up to (Married Filing Separate)	On the AMT tax base up to (any other filing status)
26	$98,950	$197,900
28	Above $98,950	Above $197,900
0/15/20	On net long-term capital gains and qualified dividend income	

EXAMPLE
40

Anna's 2020 AMT liability is computed as follows. She is a single individual. She is subject to the AMT for this tax year, as the AMT liability exceeds her regular income tax liability. Anna owes a total of $115,630 consisting of regular tax of $79,795 and $35,835 which is the excess of the AMT liability over the regular tax ($115,630 − $79,795).

Regular taxable income	$300,000
"Spread" on an incentive stock option exercised this year	200,000
AMT exemption	(72,900)
AMT tax base	$427,100
Regular tax liability	$ 79,795
AMT liability [($197,900 × 26%) + ($229,200 × 28%)]	$115,630

12-6 TAX PLANNING

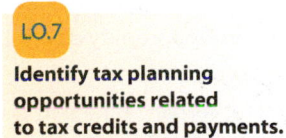
LO.7
Identify tax planning opportunities related to tax credits and payments.

12-6a Credit for Child and Dependent Care Expenses

Payments to certain relatives for the care of qualifying dependents and children qualify for the credit if the care provider is not a child (under age 19) of the taxpayer. Thus, if the care provider is in a lower tax bracket than the taxpayer, the following benefits result.

- Income is shifted to a lower-bracket family member.
- The taxpayer qualifies for the credit for child and dependent care expenses.

In addition, to the extent that child care payments can be shifted to future tax years, the benefit from the credit may be preserved on these excess expenditures.

Andre, a calendar year and cash basis taxpayer, spent $3,000 by December 1 on qualifying child care expenses for his dependent 11-year-old son. The $250 that is due the care provider for child care services rendered in December does not generate a tax credit benefit if the amount is paid in the current year because the $3,000 ceiling has been reached. However, if the payment can be delayed until the next year, the total credit over the two-year period for which Andre is eligible may be increased.

EXAMPLE
41

A similar shifting of expenditures to a subsequent year may be wise if this nonrefundable credit otherwise generated would exceed the tax liability available to absorb the credit.

REFOCUS ON THE BIG PICTURE

EDUCATION TAX CREDITS

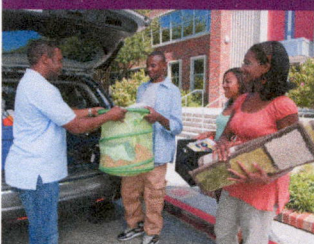

YELLOW DOG PRODUCTIONS/GETTY IMAGES

Lora and Sam qualify for the American Opportunity credit because they are both in their first four years of postsecondary education. Lora and Sam both qualify for a $2,500 credit (100 percent of the first $2,000 and 25 percent of the next $2,000 of qualified expenses).

These credits phase out over an income range of $20,000 once married taxpayers' AGI exceeds $160,000. The total education credits available to the Snyders amount to $5,240 (see Example 29), and they may claim this amount as a credit on their Form 1040. Further, the education credits may be used to offset any AMT liability, and a portion of the credits is refundable to the Snyders.

What If?

What if the Snyders' AGI is $188,000? In that case, the Snyders would not qualify for any education credits (their income exceeds the limits for both the American Opportunity and the lifetime learning credits). Although a deduction *for* AGI is allowed for qualified tuition and related expenses involving higher education, the taxpayers' AGI exceeds the $160,000 maximum allowed for a deduction (see text Section 9-5e for additional details).[48]

Key Terms

Alternative minimum tax, 12-25

American Opportunity credit, 12-16

Child tax credit, 12-14

Credit for certain retirement plan contributions, 12-18

Credit for child and dependent care expenses, 12-14

Credit for employer-provided child care, 12-11

Credit for employer-provided family and medical leave, 12-11

Credit for small employer pension plan startup costs, 12-10

Dependent tax credit, 12-14

Disabled access credit, 12-10

Earned income credit, 12-12

Employment taxes, 12-19

Energy tax credits, 12-18

Estimated tax, 12-23

Foreign tax credit (FTC), 12-13

General business credit, 12-5

Lifetime learning credit, 12-16

Low-income housing credit, 12-9

Nonrefundable credits, 12-4

Refundable credits, 12-3

Rehabilitation expenditures credit, 12-6

Research activities credit, 12-8

Self-employment tax, 12-23

Tax credits, 12-2

Work opportunity tax credit, 12-7

Discussion Questions

1. **LO.1** Would an individual taxpayer receive greater benefit from deducting an expense or from taking a credit equal to 25% of the expense? How would your response change if the item would only be deductible *from* AGI?

Critical Thinking   2. **LO.3** Clint, a self-employed engineering consultant, is contemplating purchasing an old building for renovation. After the work is completed, Clint plans to rent out two-thirds of the floor space to businesses; he would live and work in the remaining portion. Identify the relevant tax issues for Clint.

---

[48]This deduction under § 222 *for* AGI expires at the end of 2020; however, Congress may extend it.

3. **LO.3** Sonja is considering the purchase and renovation of an old building. She has Critical Thinking
heard about the tax credit for rehabilitation expenditures, but Sonja does not
know the specific rules applicable to the credit. Explain the most important and
relevant provisions for her.

4. **LO.4** Is the earned income credit a form of negative income tax? Why or why not?

5. **LO.4, 7** Ava and her husband, Leo, file a joint return and are in the 24% Federal Decision Making
income tax bracket in 2020. Ava's salary is $75,000. Her employer offers a
child and dependent care reimbursement plan that allows up to $5,000 of qualifying
expenses to be reimbursed in exchange for a $5,000 reduction in the employee's
salary. Because Ava and Leo have two minor children requiring child care that costs
$5,800 each year, Ava is wondering if she should sign up for the program instead
of taking advantage of the credit for child and dependent care expenses.
    Analyze the effect of the two alternatives. How would your answer differ if Ava's
salary was $30,000, the couple's AGI was $25,000, and their marginal tax rate was 10%.

6. **LO.4** Mark and Lisa are approaching an exciting time in their lives as their oldest Critical Thinking
son, Austin, graduates from high school and moves on to college. What are
some of the tax issues that Mark and Lisa should consider as they think about paying for Austin's college education?

7. **LO.5** Kathy owns and operates a grocery store as a sole proprietor. She pays wages
to her husband Joe and their 16-year-old daughter Marla, both of whom work
at the store. Should Kathy withhold FICA taxes from the wages paid to Joe and
Marla? Explain.

8. **LO.6** Describe the exposure (i.e., wage base and tax rate) of a self-employed
individual to the self-employment tax for 2020.

9. **LO.6** Kelly was promoted and received a substantial raise that includes compensation in the form of incentive stock options. She talks to her tax adviser about
potential tax ramifications. After making some projections, her adviser welcomes
her to the AMT club. Kelly is surprised to learn that her promotion will be rewarded
with an additional tax in the form of the AMT. Explain to Kelly the purpose of the
AMT and why it applies to her.

Computational Exercises

10. **LO.2** Carlson's general business credit (before limitations) for the current year is
$84,000. His net income tax is $190,000, tentative minimum tax is $175,000,
and net regular tax liability is $185,000. He reports no other Federal income tax
credits for the year. Compute Carlson's general business credit allowed for the year,
and any amounts that can be carried back and forward.

11. **LO.3** Emily spent $135,000 to rehabilitate a certified historic building (adjusted
basis of $90,000) that originally had been placed in service in 1935. Compute
Emily's credit for rehabilitation expenditures.

12. **LO.3** During 2020, Lincoln Company hires seven individuals who are certified to
be members of a qualifying targeted group. Each employee works in excess
of 600 hours and is paid wages of $7,500 during the year. Determine the amount of
Lincoln's work opportunity credit.

13. **LO.3** Alison incurs the following research expenditures.

In-house wages	$60,000
In-house supplies	5,000
Paid to ABC, Inc., for research services	80,000

  a. Determine the amount of Alison's qualified research expenditures for the tax year.

  b. If the taxpayer's base amount is $50,000, what is Alison's incremental research activities credit?

14. **LO.4** Santiago and Amy are married and file a joint tax return. They have three children, ages 12, 14, and 18. All parties are U.S. citizens. Their AGI is $140,000. Determine any available child tax credit and dependent tax credit.

15. **LO.4** Ivanna, who has three children under age 13, worked full-time while her husband, Sergio, was attending college for nine months during the year. Ivanna earned $28,000 and incurred $9,100 of child care expenses. Determine the amount of Ivanna and Sergio's child and dependent care credit.

16. **LO.4** Paola and Isadora Shaw are married, file a joint tax return, and have one dependent child, Dante. The Shaws report modified AGI of $148,000. The couple paid $12,000 of tuition and $10,000 for room and board for Dante, a full-time first-year student at Serene College. Determine the amount of the Shaws' American Opportunity credit for the year.

17. **LO.4** Rafael and Lucy Gonzalez, married taxpayers, each contribute $2,900 to their respective § 401(k) plans offered through their employers. The AGI reported on the couple's joint return is $39,000. Determine their credit for retirement plan contributions (the Saver's Credit).

18. **LO.5** In 2020, Bianca earned a salary of $164,000 from her employer. How much in FICA and Medicare taxes will be withheld from Bianca's salary?

19. **LO.7** Determine the additional Medicare taxes for these individuals.

  a. Mario, who is single, earns wages of $440,000.

  b. George and Shirley are married and file a joint return. During the year, George earns wages of $138,000, and Shirley earns wages of $210,000.

  c. Simon has net investment income of $38,000 and MAGI of $223,000 and files as a single taxpayer.

Problems

20. **LO.2** Adelyn generated a tentative general business credit of $42,000 for the current year. Her net regular tax liability before the general business credit is $107,000, and her tentative minimum tax is $88,000. Compute Adelyn's allowable general business credit for the year.

21. **LO.2** Oak Corporation holds the following general business credit carryovers.

2016	$ 5,000
2017	15,000
2018	6,000
2019	19,000
Total carryovers	$45,000

If Oak's general business credit generated by 2020 activities equals $36,000 and the total credit allowed during the current year is $60,000 (based on tax liability), what amounts of the current general business credit and carryovers are utilized against the 2020 income tax liability? What is the amount of unused credit carried forward to 2021?

22. **LO.3, 7** Paul Chaing (4522 Fargo Street, Geneva, IL 60134) acquires a qualifying   Critical Thinking
    historic structure for $350,000 (excluding the cost of the land) and plans to   Communications
    substantially rehabilitate the structure. He is planning to spend either $320,000 or
    $380,000 on rehabilitation expenditures. Write a letter to Paul and a memo for the
    tax research files explaining the following for the two alternative expenditures.
    a. The computation that determines the rehabilitation expenditures tax credit
        available.
    b. The effect of the credit on Paul's adjusted basis in the property.
    c. The cash-flow differences as a result of the tax consequences related to his
        expenditure choice.

23. **LO.3** Green Corporation hires six individuals on January 4, 2020, all of whom
    qualify for the work opportunity credit. Three of these individuals receive
    wages of $8,500 during 2020, and each individual works more than 400 hours dur-
    ing the year. The other three individuals each work 300 hours and receive wages of
    $5,000 during the year.
    a. Calculate the amount of Green's work opportunity credit.
    b. If Green pays total wages of $140,000 to its employees during the year, how
        much of this amount can Green deduct, assuming that the work opportunity
        credit is taken?

24. **LO.3, 7** Tom, a calendar year taxpayer, informs you that during the year, he incurs   Decision Making
    expenditures of $40,000 that qualify for the incremental research activities
    credit. In addition, Tom's research-credit base amount for the year is $32,800.
    a. Determine Tom's incremental research activities credit for the year.
    b. Tom is in the 24% tax bracket. Determine which approach to the research
        expenditures and the research activities credit (other than capitalization and
        subsequent amortization) would provide the greater tax benefit.

25. **LO.3** Ahmed Zinna (16 Southside Drive, Charlotte, NC 28204), one of your clients,   Communications
    owns two retail establishments in downtown Charlotte and has come to you
    seeking advice concerning the tax consequences of complying with the Americans
    with Disabilities Act. He understands that he needs to install various features at his
    stores (e.g., ramps, doorways, and restrooms that are handicap accessible) to make
    them more accessible to disabled individuals. He asks whether any tax credits are
    available to help offset the cost of the necessary changes. He estimates the cost of
    the planned changes to his facilities as follows.

Location	Projected Cost
Calvin Street	$22,000
Stowe Avenue	8,500

Ahmed reminds you that the Calvin Street store was constructed in 2004 and that
the Stowe Avenue store is in a building that was constructed in 1947. Ahmed operates his business as a sole proprietorship and has approximately eight employees
at each location. Write a letter to Ahmed in which you summarize your conclusions
concerning the tax consequences of his proposed capital improvements.

26. **LO.4** Which of the following individuals qualify for the earned income credit   Decision Making
    for 2020?
    a. Thomas is single, is 21 years old, and has no qualifying children. His income
        consists of $9,000 in wages.
    b. Shannon, who is 27 years old, maintains a household for a dependent 11-year-
        old son and is eligible for head-of-household tax rates. Her income consists of
        $16,050 of salary and $50 of taxable interest (Shannon's AGI is $16,100).

c.   Keith and Susan, both age 30, are married and file a joint return. Keith and Susan have no dependents. Their combined income consists of $28,500 of salary and $100 of taxable interest (i.e., their AGI is $28,600).

d.   Colin is a 26-year-old, self-supporting, single taxpayer. He has no qualifying children and generates earnings of $9,000.

27.   **LO.4, 7** Cooper National is incorporated in Alabama. It generated a $5,000,000 profit on its overseas operations this year. Cooper paid the following to various other countries.

- $1,000,000 in income taxes.
- $1,500,000 in value added taxes.

What are Cooper's alternatives as to the treatment of these tax payments on its U.S. Federal income tax returns?

28.   **LO.4** Jimenez Enterprises is incorporated in Arkansas. It generated a $5,000,000 profit on its overseas operations this year. Jimenez paid $1,000,000 in income taxes to various countries on these profits. Jimenez's marginal Federal income tax rate is 21%. Compute the Jimenez foreign tax credit and carryovers for the year.

29.   **LO.4** Same as Problem 28, except that Jimenez paid $2,000,000 in income taxes to other countries.

30.   **LO.4** Joshua and Ellen are married and file a joint return. Three individuals qualify as their dependents: their two children, ages 5 years and 6 months, and Ellen's 18-year-old son from a previous marriage. All parties are U.S. citizens. Joshua and Ellen's combined AGI is $68,000. Compute Joshua and Ellen's child tax credit and dependent tax credit.

31.   **LO.4** Paul and Karen Kent are married, and both are employed (Paul earned $44,000 and Karen earned $9,000 in 2020). Paul and Karen have two dependent children, Samuel and Joy, both under the age of 13. Paul and Karen pay $3,800 ($1,900 for each child) to Sunnyside Day Care Center (422 Sycamore Road, Ft. Worth, TX 76028; Employer Identification Number 11-2345678), to care for their children while they are working.

a.   Assuming that Paul and Karen file a joint return, what, if any, is their tax credit for child and dependent care expenses?

b.   Complete Form 2441 for Paul and Karen; their AGI is $53,750, and their tax liability before any available child care credit is $2,825. Relevant Social Security numbers are: Paul (123-45-6789); Sam (123-45-6788); Joy (123-45-6787). Neither Paul nor Karen received any child care benefits from their employers.

32.   **LO.4** Jim and Mary Jean are married and have two dependent children under the age of 13. Both parents are gainfully employed and earn salaries in 2020 as follows: $16,000 (Jim) and $5,200 (Mary Jean).

To care for their children while they work, Jim and Mary Jean pay Eleanor (Jim's mother) $5,600. Eleanor does not qualify as a dependent of Jim and Mary Jean. Jim and Mary Jean file a joint Federal income tax return. Compute their credit for child and dependent care expenses.

Communications   33.   **LO.4, 7** Jenna Rosen, a longtime client of yours, is an architect and the president of the local Rotary chapter. To keep up to date with the latest developments in her profession, she attends continuing education seminars offered by the architecture school at State University. This year, Jenna spends $2,000 on course tuition to attend these seminars. She spends another $400 on architecture books during the year.

Jenna's dependent daughter Caitlin is a senior majoring in engineering at the University of the Midwest. During the calendar year, Caitlin incurs the following expenses: $8,200 for tuition ($4,100 per semester) and $750 for books and course materials. Caitlin lives at home while attending school full-time.

Jenna is married, files a joint return, and reports a combined AGI with her husband Morrie of $120,000.

a. Calculate Jenna's education tax credits for these items.

b. In her capacity as president of the local Rotary chapter, Jenna has asked you to present a 20- to 30-minute speech outlining the different ways the tax law helps defray (1) the cost of higher education and (2) the cost of continuing education once someone is in the workforce. Prepare an outline of possible topics for presentation. A tentative title for your presentation is "How Can the Tax Law Help Pay for College and Continuing Professional Education?"

34. **LO.4** Kathleen and Glenn decide that this is the year to begin getting serious about saving for their retirement by participating in their employers' § 401(k) plans. As a result, they each have $3,000 of their salary set aside in their qualified plans.

a. Calculate the credit for certain retirement plan contributions available to Kathleen and Glenn if the AGI on their joint return is $35,000.

b. Kathleen and Glenn persuade their dependent 15-year-old son, Joel, to put $500 of his part-time earnings into a Roth IRA during the year. What is the credit for certain retirement plan contributions available to Joel? His AGI is $7,000.

Tax Return Problems

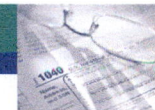

35. Beth R. Jordan lives at 2322 Skyview Road, Mesa, AZ 85201. She is a tax accountant with Mesa Manufacturing Company, 1203 Western Avenue, Mesa, AZ 85201 (employer identification number 11-1111111). She also writes computer software programs for tax practitioners and has a part-time tax practice. Beth is single and has no dependents. Beth was born on July 4, 1973, and her Social Security number is 123-45-6785. She wants to contribute $3 to the Presidential Election Campaign Fund.

Tax Forms Problem

The following information is shown on Beth's Wage and Tax Statement (Form W–2) for 2019.

Line	Description	Amount
1	Wages, tips, other compensation	$65,000.00
2	Federal income tax withheld	9,500.00
3	Social Security wages	65,000.00
4	Social Security tax withheld	4,030.00
5	Medicare wages and tips	65,000.00
6	Medicare tax withheld	942.50
15	State	Arizona
16	State wages, tips, etc.	65,000.00
17	State income tax withheld	1,954.00

During the year, Beth received interest of $1,300 from Arizona Federal Savings and Loan and $400 from Arizona State Bank. Each financial institution reported the interest income on a Form 1099–INT. She received qualified dividends of $800 from Blue Corporation, $750 from Green Corporation, and $650 from Orange Corporation. Each corporation reported Beth's dividend payments on a Form 1099–DIV.

Beth received a $1,100 income tax refund from the state of Arizona on April 29, 2019. On her 2018 Federal income tax return, she claimed the standard deduction.

Fees earned from her part-time tax practice in 2019 totaled $3,800. She paid $600 to have the tax returns processed by a computerized tax return service.

On February 8, 2019, Beth bought 500 shares of Gray Corporation common stock for $17.60 a share. On September 12, 2019, Beth sold the stock for $14 a share.

Beth bought a used sport utility vehicle for $6,000 on June 5, 2019. She purchased the vehicle from her brother-in-law, who was unemployed and was in need of cash. On November 2, 2019, she sold the vehicle to a friend for $6,500.

On January 2, 2019, Beth acquired 100 shares of Blue Corporation common stock for $30 a share. She sold the stock on December 19, 2019, for $55 a share.

During the year, Beth records revenues of $16,000 from the sale of a software program she developed. Beth incurred the following expenses in connection with her software development business.

Cost of personal computer	$7,000
Cost of printer	2,000
Furniture	3,000
Supplies	650
Fee paid to computer consultant	3,500

Beth elected to expense the maximum portion of the cost of the computer, printer, and furniture allowed under the provisions of § 179. These items were placed in service on January 15, 2019, and used 100% in her business.

Although her employer suggested that Beth attend a convention on current developments in corporate taxation, Beth was not reimbursed for the travel expenses of $1,420 she incurred in attending the convention. The $1,420 included $200 for the cost of meals.

During the year, Beth paid $300 for prescription medicines and $2,875 for doctor bills and hospital bills. Medical insurance premiums were paid for her by her employer. Beth paid real property taxes of $1,766 on her home. Interest on her home mortgage (Valley National Bank) was $3,845, and interest to credit card companies was $320. Beth contributed $2,080 to various qualifying charities during the year. Professional dues and subscriptions totaled $350.

Beth paid estimated taxes of $1,000. Beth does not own or use any virtual currency.

Part 1—Tax Computation

Compute the net tax payable or refund due for Beth R. Jordan for 2019. If you use tax forms for your solution, you will need Form 1040 (and its Schedules 1, 2, 3, B, C, D, and SE) and Forms 4562, 8949, and 8995. Suggested software: ProConnect Tax Online.

Part 2—Tax Planning

Beth is anticipating significant changes in her life in 2020, and she has asked you to estimate her taxable income and tax liability for 2020.

Beth just received word that she has been qualified to adopt a two-year-old daughter. Beth expects that the adoption will be finalized in 2020 and that she will incur approximately $2,000 of adoption expenses. In addition, she expects to incur approximately $3,500 of child and dependent care expenses relating to the care of her new daughter, which will enable her to keep her job at Mesa Manufacturing Company. However, with the additional demands on her time because of her daughter, she has decided to discontinue her two part-time jobs (i.e., the part-time tax practice and her software business), and she will cease making estimated income tax payments.

In your computations, assume that all other 2020 income and expenses will be the same as 2019 amounts.

36. Tim and Sarah Lawrence are married and file a joint return. Tim's Social Security number is 123-45-6789, and Sarah's Social Security number is 111-11-1112. They reside at 100 Olive Lane, Covington, LA 70434. They have two dependent children, Sean and Debra, ages 12 and 16, respectively. Sean's Social Security number is 123-45-6788, and Debra's Social Security number is 123-45-6787.

    Tax Computation Problem

    Tim is self-employed as the sole proprietor of an unincorporated business, and Sarah is a corporate executive. Tim reports the following 2020 income and expenses from his business.

Gross income	$325,000
Business expenses	201,000

    Other records related to Sarah's employment provide the following information.

Salary	$130,000
Unreimbursed travel expenses (including $200 of meals)	1,600

    Other pertinent information for the tax year follows.

Proceeds from sale of stock acquired on July 15, 2020 (cost of $12,000), and sold on August 1, 2020	$ 9,800
Proceeds from sale of stock acquired on September 18, 2019 (cost of $5,000), and sold on October 5, 2020	3,800
Wages paid to full-time domestic worker for housekeeping and child supervision	10,000
Interest income received	7,000
Total itemized deductions (not including any potential deductions above)	27,900
Federal income tax withheld	28,850
Estimated payments, Federal income tax	20,000

    Compute the 2020 net tax payable or refund due for Tim and Sarah Lawrence.

Research Problems

Note: Solutions to the Research Problems can be prepared by using the Thomson Reuters Checkpoint™ online tax research database, which accompanies this textbook. Solutions can also be prepared by using research materials found in a typical tax library.

the answer company™
THOMSON REUTERS®

Research Problem 1. Ashby and Curtis, married professionals, have a two-year-old son, Jason. Curtis works full-time as an electrical engineer, but Ashby has not worked outside the home since Jason was born. Because Jason is getting older, Ashby thinks that he would benefit from attending nursery school several times a week, which would give her an opportunity to reinvigorate her love of painting at a nearby art studio. Ashby thinks that if she is lucky, the proceeds from the sale of her paintings will pay for the nursery school tuition.

Ashby also is planning to claim the credit for child and dependent care expenses, because the care provided Jason at the nursery school is required for her to pursue her art career. Can Ashby and Curtis claim the credit for child and dependent care expenses for the nursery school expenditure? Why or why not?

Research Problem 2. During a recent Sunday afternoon excursion, Miriam, an admirer of early twentieth-century architecture, discovers a 1920s-era house in the countryside outside Mobile, Alabama. She wants to purchase and renovate this house, and to move the structure into Mobile so that her community can enjoy its architectural features.

Decision Making

Being aware of the availability of the tax credit for rehabilitation expenditures, Miriam wants to maximize her use of the provision, if it is available in this case, once the renovation work begins in Mobile. Miriam informs you that she will pursue the purchase, relocation, and renovation of the house only if the tax credit is available.

Comment on Miriam's decision and on whether any renovation expenditures incurred qualify for the tax credit for rehabilitation expenditures.

Partial list of research aids:
George S. Nalle III v. Comm., 72 AFTR 2d 93–5705, 93-2 USTC ¶50,468, 997 F.2d 1134 (CA–5).

Research Problem 3. The IRS provides a web-based tool to help taxpayers determine whether they are eligible for the earned income credit. Locate this tool at the IRS website; then apply the facts related to at least three hypothetical taxpayers, and determine whether the earned income credit is available.

Communications
Data Analytics

Research Problem 4. For your state and three of its neighbors, determine how many tax returns claimed an earned income credit. On a line or bar chart, track these data for the last five years, using **irs.gov**. Send your results in an e-mail to your instructor.

Communications

Research Problem 5. Some observers believe that the earned income tax credit is riddled with fraud, including claims involving nonexistent relatives and misreported income amounts. Others believe that the credit is too complex to compute and that it should provide more generous aid to low-income families. Find three articles or postings discussing the operation of the credit and addressing the issue of fraud concerning its application. Summarize the articles in no more than four PowerPoint slides designed to help you present to your classmates.

Communications
Data Analytics

Research Problem 6. What are the most significant credits claimed by individual taxpayers? How do the credits claimed differ by income class? To answer these questions, go to the IRS Tax Statistics page (**irs.gov/uac/tax-stats**) and download the Microsoft Excel spreadsheet that documents tax liability, tax credits, and tax payments. You can find this in the Individual Income Tax Return (Form 1040) Statistics section of the site; click on the "by Size of Adjusted Gross Income" link. Evaluate the credits claimed (both nonrefundable and refundable) by size of AGI. Group the data into the following AGI classes: $25,000 or less; $25,000 to $50,000; $50,000 to $100,000; $100,000 to $500,000; $500,000 or more. E-mail the spreadsheet to your instructor along with a brief summary of your findings.

Becker CPA Review Questions

Becker.

1. Which of the following statements regarding the self-employment tax is true?
   a. Income and expenses from self-employment are reported on Schedule D (Form 1040).
   b. Self-employment income is subject to both Federal income tax and self-employment tax.
   c. One half of self-employment tax is deductible as an itemized deduction.
   d. All self-employment income is subject to both Medicare and Social Security tax.

2. Which of the following credits is considered "refundable"?
   a. Child and dependent care credit
   b. Retirement plan contribution credit
   c. Child tax credit
   d. Credit for elderly

3. Jim spent four years earning his undergraduate degree at a local university. He began his first year of law school in January of the current year. Assuming he is under the phaseout limitation, what education tax credit is Jim eligible for in the current year?

   a. American Opportunity credit

   b. Earned income credit

   c. Lifetime learning credit

   d. Professional education and training credit

4. Disregarding any small business exceptions, for the current year, which of the following situations will result in a taxpayer owing a penalty for underpayment of taxes?

   a. A married filing joint taxpayer had AGI of $160,000 and total tax of $35,000 in the prior year. For the current year, AGI is $175,000 and total tax is $40,000. He had no withholding in the current year and paid a total of $35,000 in estimated taxes.

   b. The taxpayer owes $950 in taxes after his withholding was applied to his current year's tax return.

   c. The taxpayer had AGI of $75,000 and total tax of $15,000 in the prior year. For the current year, his AGI is $62,000 and total tax is $12,500. He had no withholding in the current year and paid a total of $11,500 in estimated taxes.

   d. The taxpayer had AGI of $100,000 and total tax of $20,000 in the prior year. For the current year, his AGI is also $100,000, but his total tax is $15,000. His withholding amounted to $10,000, and he paid $6,000 in estimated taxes.

5. Madison and Nick Koz have two children, ages 8 and 10. Both children meet the definition of qualifying child. The Koz family has adjusted gross income of $300,000. What is the amount of the child tax credit on the couple's income tax return?

   a. $1,000   c. $3,000

   b. $2,000   d. $4,000

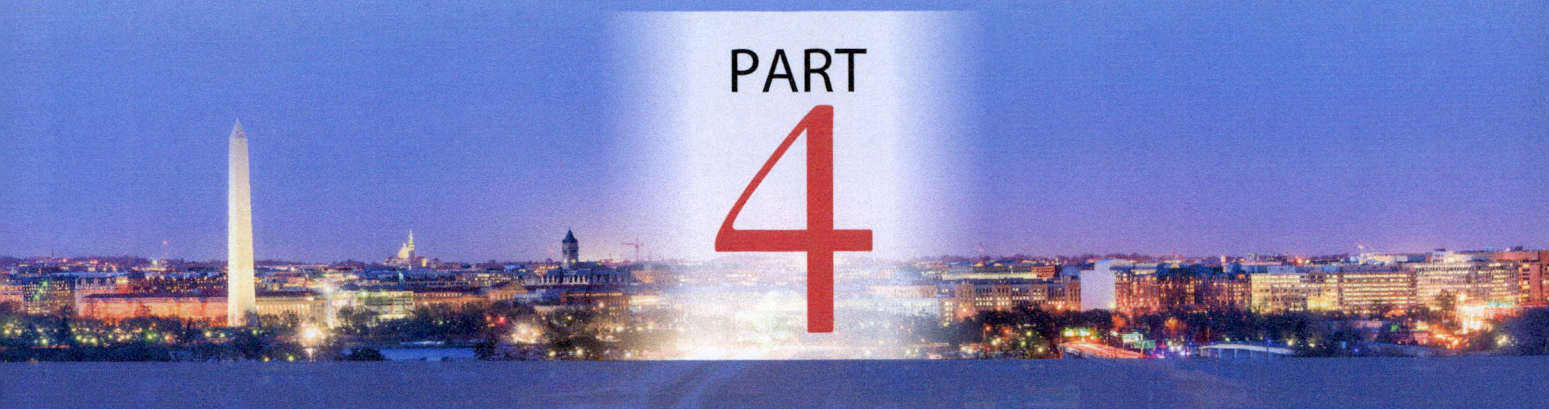

PART 4

PROPERTY TRANSACTIONS

CHAPTER **13**

Property Transactions: Determination of Gain or Loss, Basis Considerations, and Nontaxable Exchanges

CHAPTER **14**

Property Transactions: Capital Gains and Losses, § 1231, and Recapture Provisions

Part 4 covers the tax treatment of sales, exchanges, and other dispositions of property. Included here are the rules used to determine the realized gain or loss and recognized gain or loss, along with the classification of any recognized gain or loss as capital or ordinary. The topic of basis is evaluated both in terms of its effect on the calculation of the gain or loss and in terms of the determination of the basis of any property acquired as part of the transaction.

CHAPTER

13

Property Transactions: Determination of Gain or Loss, Basis Considerations, and Nontaxable Exchanges

LEARNING OBJECTIVES: *After completing Chapter 13, you should be able to:*

LO.1 Perform the computation of realized gain or loss on property dispositions.

LO.2 Distinguish between realized and recognized gain or loss.

LO.3 Review and illustrate how basis is determined for various methods of asset acquisition.

LO.4 Describe various loss disallowance provisions.

LO.5 State and explain the rationale for nonrecognition (postponement) of gain or loss in certain property transactions.

LO.6 Apply the nonrecognition provisions and basis determination rules for like-kind exchanges.

LO.7 Explain the nonrecognition provisions available on the involuntary conversion of property.

LO.8 Describe the provision for the permanent exclusion of gain on the sale of a personal residence.

LO.9 Review and apply various tax planning opportunities related to selected property transactions.

CHAPTER OUTLINE

13-1 Determination of Gain or Loss, 13-2
　13-1a Realized Gain or Loss, 13-2
　13-1b Recognized Gain or Loss, 13-8
　13-1c Nonrecognition of Gain or Loss, 13-9

13-2 Basis Considerations, 13-10
　13-2a Determination of Cost Basis, 13-10
　13-2b Gift Basis, 13-12
　13-2c Inherited Property, 13-14
　13-2d Disallowed Losses, 13-16
　13-2e Conversion of Property from Personal Use to Business or Income-Producing Use, 13-19
　13-2f Summary of Basis Adjustments, 13-20

13-3 Nontaxable Exchanges, 13-22

13-4 Like-Kind Exchanges—§ 1031, 13-22
　13-4a Like-Kind Property, 13-23
　13-4b Exchange Requirement, 13-24
　13-4c Boot, 13-25
　13-4d Basis and Holding Period of Property Received, 13-26
　13-4e Reporting Considerations, 13-29

13-5 Involuntary Conversions—§ 1033, 13-29
　13-5a Involuntary Conversion Defined, 13-31
　13-5b Computing the Amount Realized, 13-31
　13-5c Replacement Property, 13-32
　13-5d Time Limitation on Replacement, 13-33
　13-5e Nonrecognition of Gain, 13-34
　13-5f Reporting Considerations, 13-35

13-6 Sale of a Residence—§121, 13-35
　13-6a Principal Residence, 13-36
　13-6b Requirements for Exclusion Treatment, 13-36
　13-6c Calculating the Exclusion, 13-38
　13-6d Exceptions to the Two-Year Rules, 13-39

13-7 Tax Planning, 13-41
　13-7a Cost Identification and Documentation Considerations, 13-41
　13-7b Selection of Property for Making Gifts, 13-41
　13-7c Selection of Property to Pass at Death, 13-42
　13-7d Disallowed Losses, 13-42
　13-7e Like-Kind Exchanges, 13-43
　13-7f Involuntary Conversions, 13-43
　13-7g Sale of a Principal Residence, 13-44

IStockPhoto.com/Michael Courtney

SALE OR GIFT OF INHERITED HOUSE AND OTHER PROPERTY TRANSACTIONS

Alice owns a house that she inherited from her grandmother, Paula, seven months ago. Paula lived in the house for over 50 years. Alice has many fond memories associated with the house, because she spent many summer vacations there. This has caused her to delay making a decision regarding what she is going to do with the house.

Based on the estate tax return, the fair market value of the house at the date of Paula's death was $475,000. According to Paula's attorney, she paid $275,000 for the house. The real estate market for residential housing currently is robust in the city in which the house is located. So based on a recent appraisal, the house is worth $800,000. Alice is considering two options. The first is to give the house to her son, Michael. Michael, his wife Sandra, and their daughter Peggy would live in the house. The second option is to sell the house. Projected selling expenses would be about 7 percent of the selling price.

Alice would also like to know the tax consequences of selling her boat, which she purchased for $22,000 four months ago. She has been using it exclusively for personal use but is disappointed with its layout and capacity. Because it is a new model, there is significant demand for the boat, and based on listings in her area, she anticipates that she can sell it for $20,000 to $23,000.

While you are talking, Alice mentions that earlier this year, she sold some Green Corporation stock at a loss. A few days later, after hearing Green Corporation's quarterly earnings report, she decided to buy back the shares. You ask her to provide additional information to determine the tax effects of these transactions.

Alice also has owned a building (adjusted basis $50,000) that was used in her business. The building was recently destroyed by a fire, but fortunately, it was fully insured. The insurance company paid Alice $100,000 to compensate her for the loss. Now she is looking to acquire suitable replacement property for her business. If possible, she would like to claim a casualty loss, but certainly does not want to recognize any taxable gain from this event as she needs the funds for replacement property.

Alice has come to you for advice regarding the tax consequences of these various transactions. Alice's objectives are to minimize the recognition of any realized gain and to maximize the recognition of any realized loss.

Read the chapter and formulate your response.

FRAMEWORK 1040 Tax Formula for Individuals

This chapter covers the boldfaced portions of the Tax Formula for Individuals that was introduced in Concept Summary 3.1 on p. 3-3. Below those portions are the sections of Form 1040 where the results are reported.

Income *(broadly defined)*	$ xx,xxx
Less: Exclusions	(x,xxx)
Gross income	**$xx,xxx**

FORM 1040 (p. 1)

6	Capital gain or (loss). Attach Schedule D if required. If not required, check here ▶	☐

FORM 1040 (Schedule 1)

3	Business income or (loss). Attach Schedule C.	
4	Other gains or (losses). Attach Form 4797	

Less: Deductions *for* adjusted gross income	(x,xxx)
Adjusted gross income	$ xx,xxx
Less: The greater of total itemized deductions *or* the standard deduction	(x,xxx)
Personal and dependency exemptions*	(x,xxx)
Deduction for qualified business income**	(x,xxx)
Taxable income	$ xx,xxx
Tax on taxable income (*see Tax Tables or Tax Rate Schedules*)	$ x,xxx
Less: Tax credits (*including income taxes withheld and prepaid*)	(xxx)
Tax due (or refund)	$ xxx

  * Exemption deductions are not allowed from 2018 through 2025.
** Only applies from 2018 through 2025.

This chapter and Chapter 14 explain the income tax consequences of property transactions (the sale or other disposition of property).

- Is there a realized gain or loss?
- If so, is the gain or loss recognized?
- If the gain or loss is recognized, is it ordinary or capital?
- What is the basis of any replacement property that is acquired?

This chapter discusses the determination of realized and recognized gain or loss and the basis of property. Chapter 14 covers the classification of the recognized gain or loss as ordinary or capital.

LO.1

Perform the computation of realized gain or loss on property dispositions.

13-1 DETERMINATION OF GAIN OR LOSS

Gains and losses result from "realization events" such as sales, exchanges, or other dispositions of property. Very few gains and losses are recognized without first being realized. Realization events involve a significant change in ownership rights, and once a realization event has occurred, a realized gain or loss can be determined. Many, but not all, realized gains and losses also are recognized (i.e., included in the determination of taxable income) at the time of the realization event.

13-1a Realized Gain or Loss

Sale or Other Disposition

The term *sale or other disposition* is defined broadly in the tax law and includes virtually any disposition of property. Transactions such as trade-ins, casualties, condemnations, thefts, and bond retirements all are treated as property dispositions. Sales or exchanges are the most common property dispositions. Identifying a specific economic event (e.g., a sale) is a key factor in determining whether a disposition has occurred.[1] A change in the value of the property is *not* sufficient.[2]

Lori owns Tan Corporation stock that she bought for $3,000. The stock has appreciated in value and is now worth $5,000. Lori has no realized gain because a change in value is not an identifiable event for tax purposes. Here, Lori has an *unrealized gain* of $2,000 ($5,000 − $3,000).

The same is true if the stock had declined in value to $1,000. Because there was no identifiable event, there is no realized loss. Here, Lori would have an *unrealized loss* of $2,000 ($1,000 − $3,000).

Computation of Realized Gain or Loss

Realized gain or loss is the difference between the amount realized from the sale or other disposition of property and the property's adjusted basis on the disposition date. If the amount realized exceeds the property's adjusted basis, the result is a **realized gain**. On the other hand, if the property's adjusted basis exceeds the amount realized, the result is a **realized loss**.[3]

Carl sells Swan Corporation stock with an adjusted basis of $3,000 for $5,400. Carl's realized gain is $2,400 ($5,400 − $3,000). If Carl had sold the stock for $1,750, he would have had a realized loss of $1,250 ($1,750 − $3,000).

Concept Summary 13.1 summarizes this calculation. The various terms used in Concept Summary 13.1 are discussed on the following pages.

Concept Summary 13.1

Realized Gain or Loss

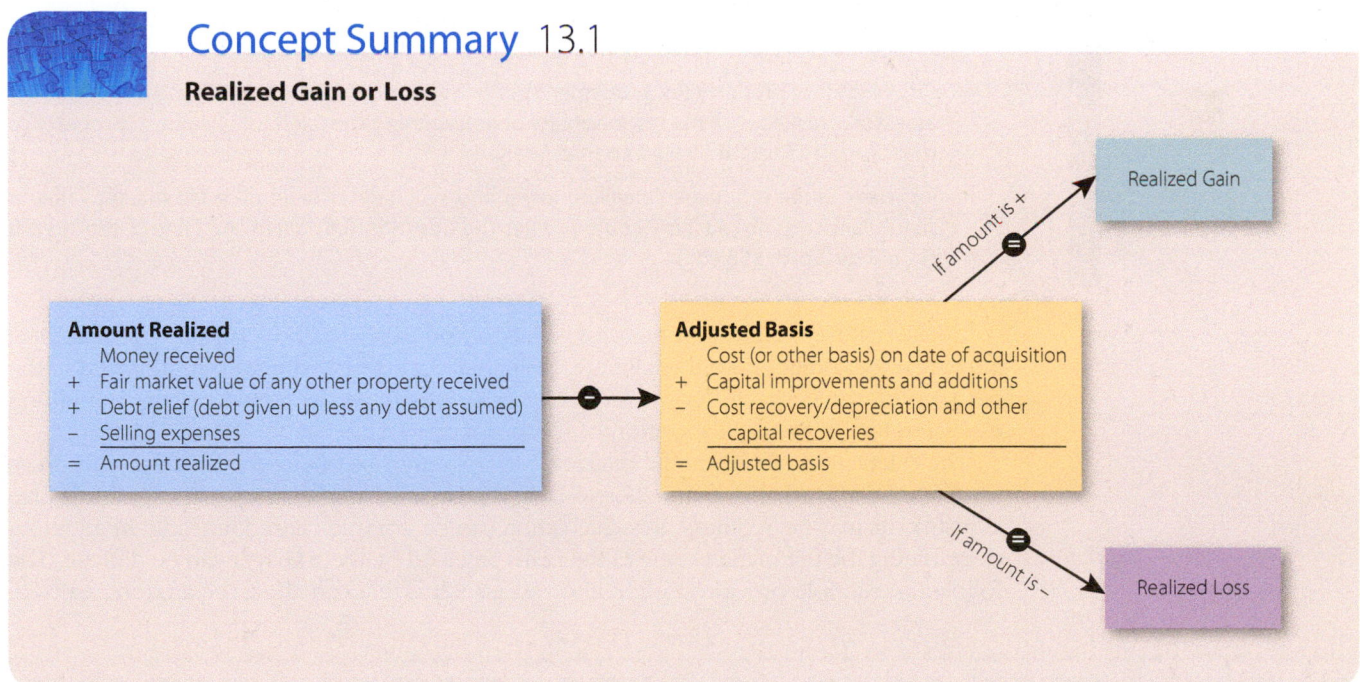

---

[1]Reg. § 1.1001–1(c)(1).

[2]*Lynch v. Turrish*, 1 USTC ¶18, 3 AFTR 2986, 38 S.Ct. 537 (USSC, 1918).

[3]§ 1001(a) and Reg. § 1.1001–1(a).

Amount Realized

The **amount realized** from a sale or other disposition of property is a measure of the economic value received for property given up. In general, it is the sum of any money received (which includes any debt relief) plus the fair market value of other property received.[4]

Debt relief includes any liability (e.g., a mortgage) assumed by the buyer when the property is sold. Debt relief also occurs if property is sold subject to the mortgage (i.e., the seller remains liable for the debt even though the buyer will be making the payments). In addition, debt relief is not limited by the fair market value of the property.[5]

Amount Realized

EXAMPLE 3

Juan sells a machine used in his landscaping business to Peter for $20,000 cash plus four acres of property that Peter owns in a nearby town with a fair market value of $36,000. Juan's amount realized on this sale is $56,000 ($20,000 cash + $36,000 land).

EXAMPLE 4

Barry owns property on which there is a mortgage of $20,000. He sells the property to Cole for $50,000 cash and Cole's agreement to assume the mortgage. Barry's amount realized from the sale is $70,000 ($50,000 cash + $20,000 debt relief).

In a property transaction, the **fair market value** of property received is the price determined by a willing seller and a willing buyer when neither is compelled to sell or buy and both have reasonable knowledge of relevant facts.[6] All of the relevant factors must be considered,[7] and if the fair market value of the property received cannot be determined, the value of the property given up by the taxpayer may be used.[8]

EXAMPLE 5

Return to the facts of Example 3. There are several ways one can determine the fair market value of the land Juan is receiving.

- An appraiser can be paid to provide an appraisal of the land.

- City or county property tax assessment information may also be helpful; the city or county assessor is tasked with the responsibility of determining the fair market value of property so that property taxes are levied appropriately.

- If the exchange is between a willing buyer and seller, determining the fair market value of Juan's landscaping machine could answer the question (i.e., given the facts of the case, it should be worth $56,000).

In calculating the amount realized, selling expenses (e.g., advertising, commissions, and legal fees) relating to the sale are deducted. As a result, the amount realized is the net amount the taxpayer received directly or indirectly, in the form of cash or anything else of value, from the disposition of the property.

The calculation of the amount realized may appear to be one of the least complex areas associated with property transactions. However, because numerous positive and negative adjustments may be required, this calculation can be complex and confusing. In addition, determining the fair market value of the items received by the taxpayer can be difficult. The following example provides insight into various items that can affect the amount realized.

---

[4]§ 1001(b) and Reg. § 1.1001–1(b). The amount realized also includes any real property taxes treated as imposed on the seller that are actually paid by the buyer. The reason for including these taxes in the amount realized is that by paying the taxes, the purchaser is, in effect, paying an additional amount to the seller of the property. Refer to text Section 10-2b for a discussion of this subject.

[5]*Crane v. Comm.*, 47–1 USTC ¶9217, 35 AFTR 776, 67 S.Ct. 1047 (USSC, 1947) and *Comm. v. Tufts*, 83–1 USTC ¶9328, 51 AFTR 2d 83–1132, 103 S.Ct. 1826 (USSC, 1983). Although a legal distinction exists between the direct assumption

of a mortgage and the taking of property subject to a mortgage, the Federal income tax consequences in calculating the amount realized are the same.

[6]*Comm. v. Marshman*, 60–2 USTC ¶9484, 5 AFTR 2d 1528, 279 F.2d 27 (CA–6, 1960) and Reg. §§ 1.737–1(b), 20.2031–1(b), and 25.2512–3(a).

[7]*O'Malley v. Ames*, 52–1 USTC ¶9361, 42 AFTR 19, 197 F.2d 256 (CA–8, 1952) and *Alan Baer Revocable Trust v. U.S.*, 2010–1 USTC ¶60,590, 105 AFTR 2d 2010–1544.

[8]*U.S. v. Davis*, 62–2 USTC ¶9509, 9 AFTR 2d 1625, 82 S.Ct. 1190 (USSC, 1962).

EXAMPLE

6

Ridge sells an office building and the associated land on October 1, 2020. Under the terms of the sales contract, Ridge is to receive $600,000 in cash. The purchaser is to assume Ridge's mortgage of $300,000 on the property. To assist the purchaser, Ridge agrees to pay $15,000 of the purchaser's closing costs (a "closing cost credit"). The broker's commission on the sale is $45,000. The amount realized by Ridge is calculated as follows:

Selling price:		
Cash	$600,000	
Mortgage assumed by purchaser	300,000	$900,000
Less:		
Broker's commission	$ 45,000	
Closing cost credit provided by Ridge	15,000	(60,000)
Amount realized		$840,000

Adjusted Basis

The ==adjusted basis== of property disposed of is the property's original basis adjusted to the date of disposition.[9] Original basis is the cost or other basis of the property on the date acquired by the taxpayer. Many assets are acquired without purchasing them (e.g., via gift or inheritance). We'll discuss how to determine basis for these acquisitions later in the chapter. *Capital additions* increase and *capital recoveries* decrease the original basis.[10] As a result, adjusted basis is determined as follows:

> Cost (or other adjusted basis) on date of acquisition
> + Capital additions
> − Capital recoveries
> = Adjusted basis on date of disposition

Capital Additions

Capital additions include the cost of improvements made to the property that lengthen its useful life or increase its production capacity or efficiency. These costs are different from repair and maintenance expenses, which are neither capitalized nor added to the original basis (refer to text Section 6-3i). As a result, repair and maintenance expenses are deductible in the current taxable year if they are related to business or income-producing property. Any liability on property that is assumed by the buyer also is included in the buyer's original basis of the property. The same rule applies if property is acquired subject to a liability. Amortization of the discount on bonds increases the adjusted basis of the bonds.[11]

Capital Recoveries

Capital recoveries decrease the adjusted basis of property. The prominent types of capital recoveries are discussed below.

Depreciation and Cost Recovery The original basis of depreciable property is reduced by any cost recovery or depreciation allowed while the property is held by the taxpayer. The amount subtracted annually from the original basis is the greater of the *allowed* or *allowable* cost recovery or depreciation.[12]

---

[9] § 1011(a) and Reg. § 1.1011–1.

[10] § 1016(a) and Reg. § 1.1016–1.

[11] See text Section 14-3b for a discussion of bond discount and the related amortization.

[12] § 1016(a)(2) and Reg. § 1.1016–3(a)(1)(i). In most cases, these amounts are the same (refer to text Section 8-1c).

EXAMPLE 7

Refer back to Example 3. The machine Juan sold was acquired four years ago for $100,000. It was 7-year MACRS property, and Juan did not take either an immediate expense deduction (§ 179) or bonus depreciation on the property. Juan's adjusted basis is computed as follows:

Original cost		$100,000
Cost recovery:		
Year 1 ($100,000 × 0.1429)	$14,290	
Year 2 ($100,000 × 0.2449)	24,490	
Year 3 ($100,000 × 0.1749)	17,490	
Year 4 ($100,000 × 0.1249 × ½)	6,245	
Total cost recovery		(62,515)
Adjusted basis		$ 37,485

Since Juan's amount realized on the sale was $56,000, his realized gain is $18,515.

Amount realized	$ 56,000
− Adjusted basis	(37,485)
Realized gain (loss)	$ 18,515

Casualties and Thefts A casualty or theft may result in the reduction of the adjusted basis of property.[13] The adjusted basis is reduced by the amount of the *deductible* loss. In addition, the adjusted basis is reduced by the amount of insurance proceeds received. However, the receipt of insurance proceeds may result in a recognized gain rather than a deductible loss. The gain increases the adjusted basis of the property.[14]

Capital Recoveries: Casualties and Thefts

EXAMPLE 8

An insured truck that Marvin used in his trade or business is destroyed in an accident. At the time of the accident, the adjusted basis of the truck was $8,000, and its fair market value was $6,500. Marvin receives insurance proceeds of $6,500.

The amount of the casualty loss is $1,500 ($6,500 insurance proceeds − $8,000 adjusted basis). The truck's adjusted basis is reduced by the $1,500 casualty loss and the $6,500 of insurance proceeds received ($8,000 basis before casualty − $1,500 casualty loss − $6,500 insurance proceeds = $0 adjusted basis).

EXAMPLE 9

How would your answer to Example 8 change if the basis of the truck was $6,000, its fair market value was $9,000, and Marvin received a $9,000 insurance settlement?

Now Marvin has a casualty gain of $3,000 ($9,000 insurance proceeds − $6,000 adjusted basis). The truck's adjusted basis is increased by the $3,000 casualty gain and is reduced by the $9,000 of insurance proceeds received ($6,000 basis before casualty + $3,000 casualty gain − $9,000 insurance proceeds = $0 adjusted basis).

Certain Corporate Distributions A nontaxable corporate distribution is treated as a return of capital, and it reduces the shareholder's stock basis.[15] Corporations typically disclose this information to shareholders. Once the basis of the stock is reduced to zero, the amount of any subsequent distributions is recorded as a capital gain if the stock is a capital asset. These rules are illustrated in text Section 19-2d.

---

[13]Refer to text Section 7-3 for a discussion of casualties and thefts. In general, personal casualty losses are deductible only if in a Federally declared disaster area; personal thefts are not deductible.

[14]Reg. § 1.1016–6(a).

[15]§ 1016(a)(4) and Reg. § 1.1016–5(a).

Amortizable Bond Premium The basis in a bond purchased at a premium is reduced by the amortizable portion of the bond premium.[16] Investors in taxable bonds may *elect* to amortize the bond premium, with an interest deduction allowed for the amount of the amortized premium.[17] So the election enables the taxpayer to take an annual interest deduction to offset ordinary income in exchange for a larger capital gain or smaller capital loss on the disposition of the bond. The amortization deduction is allowed for taxable bonds because the premium is viewed as a cost of earning the taxable interest from the bonds.

Unlike taxable bonds, the premium on tax-exempt bonds *must be* amortized (and the basis is reduced even though the amortization is not allowed as a deduction). No amortization deduction is permitted on tax-exempt bonds because the interest income is exempt from tax and the amortization of the bond premium merely represents an adjustment of the tax-exempt income earned on the bond.

EXAMPLE
10

Antonio purchases Eagle Corporation taxable bonds with a face value of $100,000 for $110,000, thus paying a premium of $10,000. The annual interest rate is 7%, and the bonds mature 10 years from the date of purchase. The annual interest income is $7,000 (7% × $100,000).

If Antonio elects to amortize the bond premium, the $10,000 premium is deducted over the 10-year period. Antonio's basis for the bonds is reduced each year by the amount of the amortization deduction.

If the bonds were tax-exempt, amortization of the bond premium and the basis adjustment would be mandatory. However, no deduction would be allowed for the amortization.

Easements An easement is the legal right to use another's land for a special purpose. Easements typically are used to obtain rights-of-way for utility lines, roads, and pipelines. In recent years, grants of conservation easements have become a popular means of obtaining charitable contribution deductions and reducing the value of real estate for transfer tax (i.e., estate and gift) purposes. For example, a conservation easement on property containing a rare wildlife habitat might prohibit any development; one on a farm might allow continued farming and the building of additional agricultural structures but no other development. Although a conservation easement can be sold, typically it is donated to a charitable organization (like the Nature Conservancy). If donated, the difference between the value of the land with and without the easement would be a charitable contribution. Likewise, scenic easements (granted to protect open spaces or scenic views) are used to reduce the value of land as assessed for property tax purposes.

The amount received for granting an easement is subtracted from the basis of the property. If the taxpayer does not retain any right to the use of the land, all of the basis is assigned to the easement. However, if the use of the land is only partially restricted, an allocation of some of the basis to the easement is appropriate. If, however, it is impossible or impractical to separate the basis of the part of the property on which the easement is granted, the basis of the whole property is reduced by the amount received. If the amount received for the easement exceeds the basis, a taxable gain results.[18]

Additional Complexities

Three types of issues tend to complicate the determination of adjusted basis. First, the tax provisions used to calculate the adjusted basis depend on how the property

---

[16]§ 1016(a)(5) and Reg. § 1.1016–5(b). The accounting treatment of bond premium amortization is the same as for tax purposes. The amortization results in a decrease in the bond investment account.

[17]§ 171(c).

[18]See Rev.Rul. 68–291, 1968–1 C.B. 351 and Rev.Rul. 77–414, 1977–2 C.B. 299.

was acquired (e.g., purchase, taxable exchange, nontaxable exchange, gift, or inheritance). These complications are discussed in text Section 13-2. Second, if the asset is subject to depreciation, cost recovery, amortization, or depletion, adjustments must be made to the basis during the time period the asset is held by the taxpayer. When the asset is sold, the taxpayer's records for both acquisition basis and adjustments to basis may not be complete. For example, the donee may not know the amount of the donor's basis. Third, the complex positive and negative adjustments encountered in calculating the amount realized are also involved in calculating the adjusted basis.

EXAMPLE 11

Jane purchased a personal residence. The purchase price and the related closing costs were:

Purchase price	$325,000
Recording costs	140
Title fees and title insurance	815
Survey costs	225
Attorney's fees	750
Appraisal fee	250

Other relevant tax information for the house during the time Jane owned it includes:

- Constructed a swimming pool for medical reasons. The cost was $20,000, of which $5,000 was deducted as a medical expense.
- Added a solar heating system. The cost was $18,000.
- Deducted home office expenses of $6,000. Of this amount, $5,200 was for depreciation.

The adjusted basis of the house is $354,980.

Purchase price	$325,000
Recording costs	140
Title fees and title insurance	815
Survey costs	225
Attorney's fees	750
Appraisal fee	250
Swimming pool ($20,000 − $5,000)	15,000
Solar heating system	18,000
Less: Depreciation deducted on home office	(5,200)
Adjusted basis	$354,980

LO.2

Distinguish between realized and recognized gain or loss.

13-1b Recognized Gain or Loss

Recognized gain is the amount of the realized gain that is included in the taxpayer's gross income.[19] A **recognized loss**, on the other hand, is the amount of a realized loss that is deductible for tax purposes.[20] As a general rule, the entire amount of a realized gain or loss is recognized.[21]

Concept Summary 13.2 summarizes the realized gain or loss and recognized gain or loss concepts.

---

[19]§ 61(a)(3) and Reg. § 1.61–6(a).
[20]§ 165(a) and Reg. § 1.165–1(a).
[21]§ 1001(c) and Reg. § 1.1002–1(a).

Concept Summary 13.2

Realized and Recognized Gain or Loss

13-1c Nonrecognition of Gain or Loss

In certain cases, a realized gain or loss on a property disposition is not recognized. Nontaxable exchanges, some of which are covered later in this chapter, are examples. Others include losses realized on the sale, exchange, or condemnation of personal use assets (as opposed to business or income-producing property) and gains realized on the sale of a residence. In addition, realized losses from the sale or exchange of business or income-producing property between certain related parties are not recognized.[22]

Sale, Exchange, or Condemnation of Personal Use Assets

A realized loss from the sale, exchange, or condemnation of personal use assets (e.g., a personal residence or an automobile used only for personal purposes) is not recognized for Federal income tax purposes. An exception exists for certain casualty or theft losses from personal use assets (see text Section 7-3). On the other hand, any gain realized from the sale or other disposition of personal use assets is, generally, fully taxable.

The Big Picture

Return to the facts of *The Big Picture* on p. 13-1. Assume that Alice sells the boat, which she has held exclusively for personal use, for $23,000. Recall that her adjusted basis for the boat is $22,000. Alice records a realized and recognized gain of $1,000 ($23,000 − $22,000).

EXAMPLE 12

The Big Picture

Return to the facts of *The Big Picture* on p. 13-1. Assume that Alice sells the boat in Example 12 for $20,000. She records a realized loss of $2,000 ($20,000 − $22,000), but the loss is not recognized because the boat is a personal use asset.

EXAMPLE 13

---

[22]§ 267(a)(1).

LO.3

Review and illustrate how basis is determined for various methods of asset acquisition.

13-2 **BASIS CONSIDERATIONS**

A key element in calculating gain or loss from a property transaction is the asset's basis at the time of the transaction. Various methods for determining basis apply, depending on how the asset was acquired.

13-2a **Determination of Cost Basis**

As noted earlier, the basis of property generally equals the property's cost. Cost is the amount paid for the property in cash or other property.[23]

A *bargain purchase* of property is an exception to the general rule for determining basis. A bargain purchase results when an employer transfers property to an employee at less than the property's fair market value (as compensation) or when a corporation transfers property to a shareholder at less than the property's fair market value (a dividend).

The amount included in gross income as either compensation for services or dividend income is the difference between the bargain purchase price and the property's fair market value. The basis of property acquired in a bargain purchase is the property's fair market value.[24] If the basis of the property were not increased by the bargain amount, the taxpayer would be taxed on this amount again at disposition.

Wade buys land from his employer for $10,000 on December 30. The fair market value of the land is $15,000.

In the year of purchase, Wade must include in his gross income the $5,000 difference between the cost and the fair market value of the land. The bargain element represents additional compensation to Wade. His basis for the land is $15,000, the land's fair market value.

Identification Problems

Cost identification problems are frequently encountered in securities transactions. For example, the Regulations require that the taxpayer identify the particular stock that has been sold (specific identification).[25] A problem arises when the taxpayer has purchased separate lots of stock on different dates or at different prices and cannot adequately identify the lot from which a particular sale takes place. In the typical case, the stock is presumed to come from the first lot or lots purchased (a FIFO presumption).[26] Brokers must provide investors with an annual report on the cost basis of stock sold during the year (this information is included on Form 1099–B and reported to the IRS).

Polly purchases 100 shares of Olive Corporation stock on July 1, 2018, for $5,000 ($50 a share) and another 100 shares of Olive stock on July 1, 2019, for $6,000 ($60 a share). She sells 50 shares of the stock on January 2, 2020.

The cost of the stock sold, assuming that Polly cannot adequately identify the shares, is $50 a share, or $2,500. If Polly was able to specifically identify the shares sold as the shares purchased in 2019, the cost basis would be $60 a share and the holding period (see text Section 14-4) would be short term.

Allocation Problems

When a taxpayer acquires *multiple assets in a lump-sum purchase*, the total cost must be allocated among the individual assets.[27] Allocation is necessary for several reasons.

- Some of the assets acquired may be depreciable (e.g., buildings), but others are not (e.g., land).

---

[23]§ 1012 and Reg. § 1.1012–1(a).

[24]Reg. §§ 1.61–2(d)(2)(i) and 1.301–1(j). See text Section 5-8d for a discussion of the circumstances under which what appears to be a taxable bargain purchase is an excludible qualified employee discount.

[25]Reg. § 1.1012–1(c)(1).

[26]*Kluger Associates, Inc.*, 69 T.C. 925 (1978).

[27]Reg. § 1.61–6(a).

- If one of the assets acquired is sold, its basis must be known to compute realized gain or loss.
- Some of the assets may be capital or § 1231 assets that receive special tax treatment when sold in the future.

The lump-sum cost is allocated on the basis of the fair market values of the individual assets acquired.

Harry purchases a building and land for $800,000. Because of the depressed nature of the industry in which the seller was operating, Harry was able to negotiate a favorable purchase price. Appraisals of the individual assets indicate that the fair market value of the building is $600,000, and that of the land is $400,000.

Harry's basis for the building is $480,000 [($600,000/$1,000,000) × $800,000], and his basis for the land is $320,000 [($400,000/$1,000,000) × $800,000].

If a business is purchased and **goodwill** is involved, a special allocation rule applies. Initially, the purchase price is allocated among the assets acquired, other than goodwill, based on their fair market value. Goodwill is then assigned the residual amount of the purchase price. This allocation applies to both the buyer and the seller.[28]

Rocky sells his business to Renata. An independent appraisal indicates that the business assets, other than goodwill, have the following fair market values:

Inventory	$ 50,000
Building	500,000
Land	200,000

After negotiations, Rocky and Renata agree on a sales price of $1,000,000. Applying the residual method with respect to goodwill results in the following allocation of the $1,000,000 purchase price:

Inventory	$ 50,000
Building	500,000
Land	200,000
Goodwill	250,000

The residual method requires that the excess of the purchase price over the fair market value of the assets other than goodwill ($1,000,000 − $750,000 = $250,000) be allocated to goodwill.

In the case of *nontaxable stock dividends*, the allocation depends on whether the dividend is a common stock dividend on common stock or a preferred stock dividend on common stock. If the stock dividend is common stock on common, the cost of the original common shares is allocated to the total shares owned after the dividend.[29]

Susan owns 100 shares of Sparrow Corporation common stock for which she paid $1,100. She receives a 10% common stock dividend, giving her a new total of 110 shares. Before the stock dividend, Susan's basis was $11 per share ($1,100 ÷ 100 shares). The basis of each share after the stock dividend is $10 ($1,100 ÷ 110 shares).

---

[28]§ 1060. The classification of the seller's recognized gain associated with the goodwill is discussed in text Section 14-14b.

[29]§§ 305(a) and 307(a).

If the nontaxable stock dividend is preferred stock on common, the cost of the original common shares is allocated between the common and preferred shares on the basis of their relative fair market values on the date of distribution.[30]

EXAMPLE 19

Fran owns 100 shares of Cardinal Corporation common stock for which she paid $1,000. She receives a nontaxable stock dividend of 50 shares of preferred stock on her common stock. The fair market values on the date of distribution of the preferred stock dividend are $30 a share for common stock and $40 a share for preferred stock.

Fair market value of common ($30 × 100 shares)	$3,000
Fair market value of preferred ($40 × 50 shares)	2,000
	$5,000
Basis of common: ⅗ × $1,000	$ 600
Basis of preferred: ⅖ × $1,000	$ 400

The basis per share for the common stock is $6 ($600/100 shares). The basis per share for the preferred stock is $8 ($400/50 shares).

The holding period for a nontaxable stock dividend, whether received in the form of common stock or preferred stock, includes the holding period of the original shares.[31] The significance of the holding period for capital assets is discussed in text Section 14-4.

13-2b Gift Basis

When a taxpayer receives property as a gift, the donee (recipient) of the gift has paid nothing to take ownership of the asset. Thus, under the cost basis provision, the donee's basis would be zero. However, this would violate the statutory intent that gifts not be subject to Federal income tax.[32] With a zero basis, if the donee sold the property, all of the amount realized would be treated as realized gain. As a result, a basis is assigned to the property received depending on:

- The date of the gift.
- The basis of the property to the donor.
- The amount of the gift tax paid.
- The fair market value of the property.

Gift Basis Rules, in General

The basis rules for gifts of property are as follows:

- If the fair market value of the property on the date of the gift exceeds (or is equal to) the donor's basis, then the recipient's (donee's) basis is the same as the donor's (i.e., a carryover basis).[33]

EXAMPLE 20

Melissa purchased stock in 2019 for $10,000. In 2020, she gave the stock to her son, Joe, when the fair market value was $15,000. Joe subsequently sells the property for $18,000. Joe's basis is $10,000, and he has a realized gain of $8,000 ($18,000 − $10,000).

If Joe sold the stock for $12,000, he would have a realized gain of $2,000 ($12,000 − $10,000). If Joe sold the stock for $7,000, he would have a realized loss of $3,000 ($7,000 − $10,000).

---

[30]Reg. § 1.307–1(a).
[31]§ 1223(5) and Reg. § 1.1223–1(e).
[32]§ 102(a).

[33]§ 1015(a) and Reg. § 1.1015–1(a)(1). See Reg. § 1.1015–1(a)(3) for cases in which the facts necessary to determine the donor's adjusted basis are unknown. Refer to Example 23 for the effect of depreciation deductions by the donee.

- If the fair market value of the property on the date of the gift is less than the donor's basis, then special *dual basis* rules apply. Here, the donee has one basis for measuring a gain and a different basis for measuring a loss. This special rule is in place to prevent the shifting of losses (typically among family members) to the individual who would receive the greatest benefit. Under this rule, the donee's *gain basis* is the donor's adjusted basis; the donee's *loss basis* is the fair market value of the property.

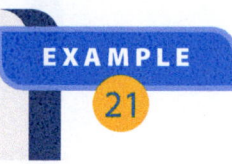

Burt purchased stock in 2018 for $10,000. In 2019, he gave the stock to his son, Cliff, when the fair market value was $7,000. Cliff later sells the stock for $6,000.

Cliff's basis is $7,000 (fair market value is less than donor's adjusted basis of $10,000), and the realized loss from the sale is $1,000 ($6,000 amount realized − $7,000 basis).

The amount of the loss basis will *differ* from the amount of the gain basis only if, at the date of the gift, the adjusted basis of the property exceeds the property's fair market value. The loss basis rule prevents the donee from receiving a tax benefit from a decline in value that occurred while the donor held the property.

So, in Example 21, Cliff records a loss of only $1,000 rather than a loss of $4,000 ($6,000 − $10,000). The $3,000 difference represents the decline in value that occurred while Burt held the property. In contrast, however, the donee may be subject to income tax on the appreciation that occurred while the donor held the property, as illustrated in Example 20.

If the amount realized from a sale is *between* the donee's loss basis and gain basis, no gain or loss is realized; here, the basis is deemed to be the same as the amount realized.

Assume the same facts as in Example 21, except that Cliff sells the stock for $8,000. Application of the gain basis rule produces a loss of $2,000 ($8,000 − $10,000). Application of the loss basis rule produces a gain of $1,000 ($8,000 − $7,000).

Because the amount realized is between the gain basis and the loss basis, Cliff recognizes neither a gain nor a loss.

Adjustment for Gift Tax

If Federal gift taxes are paid by the donor, the portion of the gift tax paid that is related to any appreciation is taken into account in determining the donee's gain basis.[34]

Holding Period

The **holding period** for property acquired by gift begins on the date the donor acquired the property if the gain basis rule applies.[35] The holding period starts on the date of the gift if the loss basis rule applies.[36]

Basis for Depreciation

The basis for depreciation on depreciable gift property is the donee's gain basis.[37] This rule is applicable even if the donee later sells the property at a loss and uses the loss basis rule in calculating the amount of the realized loss.

---

[34]§ 1015(d)(6) and Reg. § 1.1015–5(c)(2). Examples illustrating these rules can be found in Reg. § 1.1015–5(c)(5) and IRS Publication 551 (*Basis of Assets*), p. 9.

[35]§ 1223(2) and Reg. § 1.1223–1(b).

[36]Rev.Rul. 59–86, 1959–1 C.B. 209.

[37]§ 1011 and Reg. §§ 1.1011–1 and 1.167(g)–1.

EXAMPLE 23

Vito gave a machine (a MACRS 5-year asset) to Tina in 2020. At that time, the adjusted basis was $32,000 (cost of $40,000 − accumulated depreciation of $8,000), and the fair market value was $26,000. No Federal gift tax was paid. Tina's gain basis at the date of the gift is $32,000, and her loss basis is $26,000. During 2020, Tina deducts depreciation (cost recovery) of $6,400 ($32,000 × 20%). At the end of 2020, Tina's gain basis and loss basis are:

	Gain Basis	Loss Basis
Donor's basis or fair market value	$32,000	$26,000
Less: Depreciation (cost recovery)	(6,400)	(6,400)
	$25,600	$19,600

13-2c **Inherited Property**

Special basis rules apply for inherited property (property acquired from a decedent). Typically, these rules are favorable to the taxpayer receiving this property.

General Rules

The basis of inherited property almost always is the property's fair market value at the date of death.[38]

The Big Picture

EXAMPLE 24

Return to the facts of *The Big Picture* on p. 13-1. Alice inherited property from Paula, who died recently. At the date of death, Paula's basis for the property Alice inherited was $275,000. The house's fair market value at the date of death was $475,000.

Alice's basis for income tax purposes is $475,000. This commonly is referred to as a *stepped-up basis*.

The Big Picture

EXAMPLE 25

Return to the facts of *The Big Picture* on p. 13-1. Assume the same facts as in Example 24, except that the house's fair market value at the date of Paula's death was $260,000.

Alice's basis for income tax purposes is $260,000. This is commonly referred to as a *stepped-down basis*.

An *alternate valuation amount* is available to estates for which a Federal estate tax return must be filed [generally, estates with a valuation in excess of $11.58 million in 2020 ($11.4 million in 2019)]. If elected by the estate's executor, the property's basis is the fair market value six months after the date of death.[39] The alternate valuation date can be elected *only if*, as a result of the election, both the value of the gross estate and the estate tax liability are lower than they would have been if the primary valuation date had been used.[40]

Income in Respect of a Decedent

Income in respect of a decedent (IRD) usually exists when a cash basis taxpayer dies and, on the date of death, is entitled to some form of income (e.g., compensation, interest, or dividends) but has yet to receive it. IRD includes most post-death distributions from retirement plans, including traditional IRAs and § 401(k) plans.

---

[38]§§ 1014(a) and 1022. See Chapter 27 for additional information.

[39]§ 2032(a)(1) and Rev.Rul. 56–60, 1956–1 C.B. 443. For any property distributed by the executor during the six-month period preceding the alternate valuation date, the adjusted basis to the beneficiary is the fair market value on the date of distribution.

[40]§ 2032(c). This provision prevents the alternate valuation election from being used to increase the basis of the property to the beneficiary for income tax purposes without simultaneously increasing the estate tax liability (because of estate tax deductions or credits).

IRD is included in the estate at its fair market value (on the appropriate valuation date). Because IRD is not subject to the step-up or step-down rules applicable to property passed by death, the income tax basis of the decedent transfers to the estate or heirs.[41] Furthermore, the recipient of IRD must classify it in the same manner (e.g., ordinary income or capital gain) as the decedent would have.[42]

EXAMPLE

26

George, age 58, was entitled to a salary payment of $18,000 and a bonus of $20,000 at the time of his death. In addition, George had been contributing to a traditional IRA for over 20 years. The IRA has a basis of $83,000 (due to some nondeductible contributions over the years) and a current value of $560,000. George's estate collects the salary and bonus payments, and George's wife (his only beneficiary) cashes in the IRA.

Both the estate and George's wife have income in respect of a decedent (IRD) and must include ordinary income in their computation of taxable income for the year. The estate has IRD of $38,000 (salary of $18,000 + bonus of $20,000), and George's wife has IRD of $477,000 ($560,000 proceeds − $83,000 basis).[43]

Survivor's Share of Property

Both the decedent's share and the survivor's share of *community property* have a basis equal to the fair market value on the date of the decedent's death.[44] This occurs because the decedent's share of the community property is included in the estate and assumes a fair market value basis, whereas the surviving spouse's share is treated as if it were received from the decedent at its fair market value.

EXAMPLE

27

Andrew and LaTonya own, as community property, 200 shares of Biltmore Company stock acquired in 1991 for $100,000. Andrew dies in 2020, when the securities are valued at $300,000. One-half of the Biltmore stock is included in Andrew's estate. If LaTonya inherits Andrew's share of the community property, the basis for gain or loss is $300,000:

LaTonya's one-half of the community property (stepped up from $50,000 to $150,000 due to Andrew's death)	$150,000
Andrew's one-half of the community property (stepped up from $50,000 to $150,000 due to inclusion in his gross estate)	150,000
LaTonya's new basis	$300,000

In a *common law* state, only one-half of jointly held property of spouses (tenants by the entirety or joint tenants with rights of survivorship) is included in the estate.[45] In such a case, no adjustment of the basis is permitted for the surviving spouse's share of the asset.

EXAMPLE

28

Assume the same facts as in the previous example, except that the property is jointly held by Andrew and La Tonya, who reside in a common law state. Andrew purchased the property and made a gift of one-half of the property to LaTonya when the stock was acquired. No Federal gift tax was paid. Only one-half of the Biltmore stock is included in Andrew's estate. LaTonya's basis for determining gain or loss in the excluded half is not adjusted upward for the increase in value to date of death. As a result, LaTonya's basis is $200,000:

LaTonya's one-half of the jointly held property (carryover basis of $50,000)	$ 50,000
Andrew's one-half of the jointly held property (stepped up from $50,000 to $150,000 due to inclusion in his gross estate)	150,000
LaTonya's new basis	$200,000

---

[41]§ 1014(c).

[42]§ 691(a)(3).

[43]See Chapter 27 for additional information.

[44]§ 1014(b)(6). The community property states are listed in text Section 4-3e.

[45]§ 2040(b).

Holding Period of Inherited Property

The holding period of inherited property is *deemed to be long term* (held for the required long-term holding period). This rule applies regardless of whether the property is disposed of at a gain or at a loss.[46]

LO.4

Describe various loss disallowance provisions.

13-2d **Disallowed Losses**

In certain situations, realized losses are not recognized. Transactions between related parties and wash sales are two of these situations.

Related Taxpayers

Realized losses from sales or exchanges of property, directly or indirectly, between certain related parties are not recognized. This loss disallowance rule applies to several types of related-party transactions. The most common involve (1) members of a family and (2) an individual and a corporation (where the individual owns, directly or indirectly, more than 50 percent in value of the corporation's outstanding stock).[47]

The loss disallowance rules (1) prevent a taxpayer from directly transferring an unrealized loss to a related taxpayer in a higher tax bracket who could receive a greater tax benefit from recognition of the loss and (2) eliminate a substantial administrative burden on the IRS (there is no need to determine whether the selling price is equal to the asset's fair market value). The rules governing these relationships are discussed in text Section 6-3j.

If income-producing or business property is transferred to a related taxpayer and a loss is disallowed, the related-party buyer's basis is equal to the amount paid (i.e., its cost). However, if the related-party buyer later sells the property and realizes a gain, the gain is reduced by the loss that previously was disallowed.[48] This *right of offset* is not applicable if the original sale involved the sale of a personal use asset (e.g., the sale of a personal residence between related taxpayers). Furthermore, the right of offset is available only to the original transferee (the related-party buyer).[49]

EXAMPLE 29

Pedro sells business property with an adjusted basis of $50,000 to his daughter, Josefina, for its fair market value of $40,000. Pedro's realized loss of $10,000 ($40,000 − $50,000) is not recognized.

- How much gain does Josefina recognize if she sells the property for $52,000? Josefina recognizes a $2,000 gain. Her realized gain is $12,000 ($52,000 less her basis of $40,000), but she can offset Pedro's $10,000 loss against the gain.

- How much gain does Josefina recognize if she sells the property for $48,000? Josefina recognizes no gain or loss. Her realized gain is $8,000 ($48,000 less her basis of $40,000), but she can offset $8,000 of Pedro's $10,000 loss against the gain. The balance of Pedro's disallowed loss ($2,000) disappears and cannot be used. Note that Pedro's loss can only offset Josefina's gain. It cannot create a loss for Josefina.

- How much loss does Josefina recognize if she sells the property for $38,000? Josefina recognizes a $2,000 loss, the same as her realized loss ($38,000 less $40,000 basis). Pedro's loss does not increase Josefina's loss. His loss only can offset a gain. Because Josefina has no realized gain, Pedro's loss cannot be used and never is recognized. Note that if the property was a personal use asset (not business), her $2,000 loss would be personal and would not be recognized.

The holding period of the buyer for the property is not affected by the holding period of the seller; the buyer's *holding period* includes only the period of time he or she has held the property.[50]

Wash Sales

The **wash sale** rules are designed to eliminate the opportunity to sell stock at a loss, recognize the loss for tax purposes, but replace the stock sold by buying identical shares shortly before or after the sale. If the wash sale rule applies, a realized loss on the sale or

---

[46]§ 1223(9).

[47]Section 707 provides a similar disallowance provision where the related parties are a partner and a partnership in which the partner owns, directly or indirectly, more than 50% of the capital interests or profits interests in the partnership.

[48]§ 267(d) and Reg. § 1.267(d)–1(a).

[49]The loss disallowance rules are applicable even when the selling price is equal to the fair market value and can be validated (e.g., listed stocks).

[50]§§ 267(d) and 1223(2) and Reg. § 1.267(d)–1(c)(3).

exchange of stock or securities is not recognized. Recognition of the loss is disallowed because the taxpayer is considered to be in substantially the same economic position after the sale and repurchase as before the sale and repurchase.

The wash sale rule applies if a taxpayer sells or exchanges stock or securities at a loss and within 30 days before *or* after the date of the sale or exchange acquires substantially identical stock or securities.[51] Concept Summary 13.3 provides an overview of these rules.

Wash sale rules are triggered only when the investor buys a "substantially identical" investment to the one that was sold for a loss. According to the IRS, "stocks or securities of one corporation are not considered substantially identical to stocks or securities of another corporation."[52] However, an option to purchase substantially identical securities is treated the same as actually buying the stock. So, for instance, selling Ford and buying back Ford (or Ford call options) would trigger the wash sale rules, but selling Ford and buying General Motors, or selling Dell and buying Hewlett-Packard (in the same industry, but clearly a different company) would avoid the wash sale rules. Corporate bonds and preferred stock normally are not considered substantially identical to the corporation's common stock.[53]

Although the application of the "substantially identical" rule is fairly settled when dealing with individual stocks or bonds, there is more uncertainty when dealing with mutual funds or exchange-traded funds. For example, Vanguard's Windsor fund and Fidelity's Value Discovery fund have similar investment objectives (both are large cap, value funds). Not surprisingly, there is some overlap in their stock holdings. So, would the "substantially identical" rule apply if 30 percent of their holdings were identical? 50 percent? Unfortunately, there is little authoritative guidance on this issue. The lack of clear direction from the Treasury Department and the courts has led many investment advisers to develop a working list of transactions that are generally considered to be acceptable under the wash sale rules.[54]

For example, a tax-loss swap from one S&P 500 Index fund to another S&P 500 Index fund managed by a different fund company may result in scrutiny from the IRS. However, if the new fund tracks another large capitalization index, such as the Russell 1000, the tax loss should be allowed. These mutual fund transactions generally fall outside of the wash sale rules, despite the lack of a concrete definition of what is a "substantially identical" security.

1. Sell one index fund and buy another index fund, provided that the indexes of the two funds differ (e.g., S&P 500 for the Russell 1000).
2. Sell one actively managed fund and buy a fund at another company with different portfolio managers.
3. Sell an index fund and buy an actively managed fund regardless of the fund company.
4. Sell an actively managed fund and buy an index fund regardless of the fund company.

Attempts to avoid the application of the wash sales rules by having a related taxpayer repurchase the securities have been unsuccessful.[55]

Realized loss that is not recognized under the wash sale rule is added to the *basis* of the substantially identical stock or securities whose acquisition resulted in the nonrecognition of loss.[56] In other words, the basis of the replacement stock or securities is increased by the amount of the unrecognized loss. If the loss were not added to the basis of the newly acquired stock or securities, the taxpayer never would recover the entire basis of the old stock or securities.

The basis of the new stock or securities includes the unrecovered portion of the basis of the formerly held stock or securities. As a result, the *holding period* of the new stock or securities begins on the date of acquisition of the old stock or securities.[57]

---

[51]§ 1091(a) and Reg. §§ 1.1091–1(a) and (f).

[52]IRS Publication 550 (Investment Income and Expenses), p. 56.

[53]Rev.Rul. 56–406, 1956–2 C.B. 523. However, if the bonds and preferred stock are convertible into common stock, they may be considered substantially identical.

[54]See, for example, "Keeping Transactions Clean from the Wash Sale Rules," Kevin Trout, *Journal of the American Association of Independent Investors*

(December 2014) and "Tax Loss Harvesting: The Re-Balancing Act," Lee C. McGowen, *Journal of Financial Planning* (December 2008).

[55]*McWilliams v. Comm.*, 47–1 USTC ¶9289, 35 AFTR 1184, 67 S.Ct. 1477 (USSC, 1947).

[56]§ 1091(d) and Reg. § 1.1091–2(a).

[57]§ 1223(3) and Reg. § 1.1223–1(d).

The Big Picture

EXAMPLE

30

Return to the facts of *The Big Picture* on p. 13-1. Alice owned 100 shares of Green Corporation stock (basis of $20,000). She sold 50 shares for $8,000. Ten days later, she purchased 50 shares of the same stock for $7,000.

Alice's realized loss of $2,000 ($8,000 amount realized − $10,000 basis of 50 shares) is not recognized because it resulted from a wash sale. Alice's basis in the newly acquired stock is $9,000 ($7,000 purchase price + $2,000 unrecognized loss from the wash sale).

A taxpayer may acquire fewer shares than the number sold in a wash sale. In this case, the loss from the sale is prorated between recognized and unrecognized loss on the basis of the ratio of the number of shares acquired to the number of shares sold.[58]

Concept Summary 13.3

Wash Sale Rules

The Big Picture

EXAMPLE

31

Assume the same facts as Example 30, except that instead of purchasing 50 shares of Green Corporation stock for $7,000 ($140 per share), Alice purchased only 40 shares of the stock for $5,600 (40 shares × $140 per share).

Because Alice replaced only 40 of the 50 shares previously sold at a loss, only 80% (40 ÷ 50) of the $2,000 realized loss is disallowed ($1,600; 80% × $2,000). As a result, Alice will recognize a $400 loss ($2,000 × 20%) and will have a basis of $7,200 in the 40 shares of Green Corporation she purchased ($5,600 purchase price + $1,600 disallowed loss).

---

[58]§ 1091(b) and Reg. § 1.1091–1(c).

ETHICS & EQUITY Washing a Loss Using an IRA

Ajit owns 1,500 shares of Eagle, Inc. stock that he purchased over 10 years ago for $80,000. Although the stock has a current market value of $52,000, Ajit still views the stock as a solid long-term investment. He has sold other stock during the year with overall gains of $30,000, so he would like to sell the Eagle stock and offset the $28,000 loss against these gains, but somehow keep his Eagle investment. He has devised a plan to keep his Eagle investment by using funds in his traditional IRA to purchase 1,500 Eagle shares immediately after selling the shares he currently owns. Evaluate Ajit's treatment of these stock transactions. Can his plan work?

The wash sale rules do *not* apply to taxpayers engaged in the business of buying and selling securities.[59] In addition, the wash sales provisions do *not* apply to gains. As a result, taxpayers with capital losses (or capital loss carryovers from prior years) can sell an appreciated asset and then reacquire it, using the gain to offset the capital losses. Because the basis of the replacement stock will be the purchase price, the taxpayer gets an increased basis for the stock while using the capital gain to offset otherwise nondeductible capital losses.

13-2e Conversion of Property from Personal Use to Business or Income-Producing Use

As discussed previously, losses from the sale of personal use assets are not recognized for tax purposes, but losses from the sale of business and income-producing assets are deductible. Can a taxpayer convert a personal use asset that has declined in value to business or income-producing use and then sell the asset to recognize a business or income-producing loss?

The tax law prevents this practice by specifying that the *original basis for loss* on personal use assets converted to business or producing use is the *lower* of the property's adjusted basis or fair market value on the date of conversion.[60] The *gain basis* for converted property is the property's adjusted basis on the date of conversion. The tax law is not concerned with gains on converted property because gains are recognized regardless of whether property is business, income-producing, or personal use.

Diane's personal residence has an adjusted basis of $175,000 and a fair market value of $160,000. Diane converts the personal residence to rental property. Her basis for loss is $160,000 (lower of $175,000 adjusted basis and fair market value of $160,000). The $15,000 decline in value is a personal loss and can never be recognized for tax purposes. Diane's basis for gain is $175,000.

EXAMPLE 32

The basis for loss is also the *basis for depreciating* the converted property.[61] This is an exception to the general rule that the basis for depreciation is the gain basis (e.g., property received by gift). This exception prevents the taxpayer from recovering a personal loss indirectly through depreciation of the higher original basis. After the property is converted, both its basis for loss and its basis for gain are adjusted for depreciation deductions from the date of conversion to the date of disposition. These rules apply only if a conversion from personal to business or income-producing use has actually occurred.

At a time when his personal residence (adjusted basis of $140,000) is worth $150,000, Keith converts one-half of it to rental use. For simplicity, assume that the property is not covered by MACRS, will be depreciated using the straight-line method, has an estimated useful life of 20 years, and has no salvage value. As a result, annual depreciation will be $3,500 ($70,000 ÷ 20 years).

continued

EXAMPLE 33

---

[59]Reg. § 1.1091–1(a).

[60]Reg. § 1.165–9(b)(2).

[61]Reg. § 1.167(g)–1.

After renting the converted portion for five years, Keith sells the property for $144,000. All amounts relate only to the building; assume that the land has been accounted for separately. Keith has a $2,000 realized gain from the sale of the personal use portion of the residence and a $19,500 realized gain from the sale of the rental portion.

	Personal Use	Rental
Original basis for gain and loss—adjusted basis on date of conversion (fair market value is *greater than* the adjusted basis)	$70,000	$ 70,000
Depreciation—five years	(–0–)	(17,500)
Adjusted basis—date of sale	$70,000	$ 52,500
Amount realized	72,000	72,000
Realized gain	$ 2,000	$ 19,500

Keith may be able to exclude the $2,000 realized gain from the sale of the personal use portion of the residence (see text Section 13-6). If the exclusion applies, only $17,500 (equal to the depreciation deducted) of the $19,500 realized gain from the rental portion is recognized.

EXAMPLE
34

Assume the same facts as in the previous example, except that the fair market value on the date of conversion is $130,000 and the sales proceeds are $90,000. Keith has a $25,000 realized loss from the sale of the personal use portion of the residence and a $3,750 realized loss from the sale of the rental portion. These losses are computed as follows:

	Personal Use	Rental
Original basis for loss—fair market value on date of conversion (fair market value is *less than* the adjusted basis)	$70,000*	$ 65,000
Depreciation—five years	(–0–)	(16,250)**
Adjusted basis—date of sale	$70,000	$ 48,750
Amount realized	45,000	45,000
Realized loss	($25,000)	($ 3,750)

*Not applicable; use one-half of adjusted basis ($140,000 × 50%).
**($65,000 ÷ 20) × 5.

The $25,000 loss from the sale of the personal use portion of the residence is not recognized. The $3,750 loss from the rental portion is recognized.

13-2f **Summary of Basis Adjustments**

Some of the more common items that either increase or decrease the basis of an asset appear in Concept Summary 13.4.

There are a number of techniques for determining basis for tax purposes, with the method dependent on the manner in which the asset was acquired. In summary, the basis of an asset can be determined by reference to any of the following:

- The asset's cost.
- The basis of another asset.
- The asset's fair market value.
- The basis of the asset to another taxpayer.

Concept Summary 13.4

Adjustments to Basis

Item	Effect	Refer to Chapter	Explanation
Amortization of bond discount	Increase	14	Amortization is mandatory for certain taxable bonds and elective for tax-exempt bonds.
Amortization of bond premium	Decrease	13	Amortization is mandatory for tax-exempt bonds and elective for taxable bonds.
Amortization of covenant not to compete	Decrease	8	Covenant must be for a definite and limited time period. The amortization period is a statutory period of 15 years.
Amortization of intangibles	Decrease	8	Intangibles are amortized over a 15-year period.
Assessment for local benefits	Increase	10	To the extent not deductible as taxes (e.g., assessment for streets and sidewalks that increase the value of the property versus one for maintenance or repair or for meeting interest charges).
Bad debts	Decrease	7	Only the specific charge-off method is permitted.
Capital additions	Increase	13	Certain items, at the taxpayer's election, can be capitalized or deducted (e.g., selected medical expenses).
Casualty	Decrease	7	For a casualty loss, the amount of the adjustment is the sum of the deductible loss and the insurance proceeds received. For a casualty gain, the amount of the adjustment is the insurance proceeds received reduced by the recognized gain.
Condemnation	Decrease	13	Same as for Casualty.
Cost recovery	Decrease	8	§ 168 is applicable to tangible assets placed in service after 1980 whose useful life is expressed in terms of years; includes additional first-year (bonus) depreciation.
Depletion	Decrease	8	Use the greater of cost or percentage depletion. Percentage depletion can still be deducted when the basis is zero.
Depreciation	Decrease	8	§ 167 is applicable to tangible assets placed in service before 1981 and to tangible assets not depreciated in terms of years.
Easement	Decrease	13	If the taxpayer does not retain any use of the land, all of the basis is allocable to the easement transaction. However, if only part of the land is affected by the easement, only part of the basis is allocable to the easement transaction.
Expensing under § 179	Decrease	8	Occurs only if the taxpayer elects § 179 treatment.
Improvements by lessee to lessor's property	Increase	1	Adjustment occurs only if the lessor is required to include the fair market value of the improvements in gross income under § 109.
Imputed interest	Decrease	16	Amount deducted is not part of the cost of the asset.
Medical capital expenditure permitted as a medical expense	Decrease	10	Adjustment is the amount of the deduction (the effect on basis is to increase it by the amount of the capital expenditure net of the deduction).
Real estate taxes: apportionment between the buyer and seller	Increase or decrease	10	To the extent the buyer pays the seller's pro rata share, the buyer's basis is increased. To the extent the seller pays the buyer's pro rata share, the buyer's basis is decreased.
Rebate from manufacturer	Decrease	5	Because the rebate is treated as an adjustment to the purchase price, it is not included in the buyer's gross income.
Stock dividend	Decrease	13	Adjustment occurs only if the stock dividend is nontaxable. Although the basis per share decreases, the total stock basis does not change.
Stock rights	Decrease	13	Adjustment to stock basis occurs only for nontaxable stock rights and only if the fair market value of the rights is at least 15% of the fair market value of the stock or, if less than 15%, the taxpayer elects to allocate the basis between the stock and the rights.
Theft	Decrease	7	Same as for Casualty.

LO.5

State and explain the rationale for nonrecognition (postponement) of gain or loss in certain property transactions.

13-3 NONTAXABLE EXCHANGES

A taxpayer who is going to replace a business asset (e.g., land and building) may decide to sell the old asset and purchase a new asset. In this case, any realized gain or loss on the asset sold is recognized and the basis of the new asset is its cost. Alternatively, the taxpayer may be able to trade the old asset (e.g., land and building) for a new asset (e.g., a large parcel of land on which the taxpayer will construct a new manufacturing plant) in an exchange that might qualify for nontaxable exchange treatment.

The tax law recognizes that nontaxable exchanges result in a change in the *form* but not in the *substance* of the taxpayer's relative economic position. Effectively, the replacement property received in the exchange is viewed as a continuation of the old investment.[62] In addition, a nontaxable exchange often does not provide the taxpayer with the *wherewithal to pay* the tax on any realized gain that would be recognized (i.e., the taxpayer does not have the cash that would have been received in a sale).

In a **nontaxable exchange**, realized gains or losses are not recognized. Instead, the recognition of gain or loss is *postponed* (deferred) until the property received in the nontaxable exchange is subsequently sold in a taxable transaction. This "deferral" is accomplished by assigning a carryover basis to the replacement property.

EXAMPLE

35

Debra completes a nontaxable exchange of property with an adjusted basis of $10,000 and a fair market value of $12,000 for property with a fair market value of $12,000.

Debra has a realized gain of $2,000 ($12,000 amount realized − $10,000 adjusted basis). Her recognized gain is $0. Her basis in the replacement property is a carryover basis of $10,000.

Assume that the replacement property is nondepreciable and that Debra subsequently sells it for $12,000. Her realized and recognized gain will be the $2,000 gain that was postponed (deferred) in the nontaxable transaction. If the replacement property is depreciable, the carryover basis of $10,000 is used in calculating depreciation.

In some nontaxable exchanges, only part of the property involved in the transaction qualifies for nonrecognition treatment. If the taxpayer receives cash or other nonqualifying property, part or all of the realized gain from the exchange is recognized, since the taxpayer has the wherewithal to pay tax. Here, the basis of the replacement property is adjusted to reflect any deferred gain (gain realized but not recognized).

It is important to distinguish between a nontaxable disposition, as the term is used in the statute, and a tax-free transaction. The term *nontaxable* refers to postponement of recognition via a carryover basis. In a *tax-free* transaction, the nonrecognition is permanent. Here, the basis of any property acquired does not depend on the basis of the property sold by the taxpayer. In this chapter, we discuss two nontaxable transactions (like-kind exchanges and involuntary conversions) and one tax-free transaction (sale of a personal residence).

LO.6

Apply the nonrecognition provisions and basis determination rules for like-kind exchanges.

13-4 LIKE-KIND EXCHANGES—§ 1031

Section 1031 requires nontaxable treatment if the following **like-kind exchange** requirements are satisfied:[63]

- The property is *like-kind* property (only *real property* qualifies).[64]
- The form of the transaction is an *exchange*.
- Both the property given up and the property received are either "used in a trade or business" *or* "held for investment."

---

[62]Reg. § 1.1002–1(c).

[63]§ 1031(a) and Reg. § 1.1031(a)–1(a).

[64]§ Prior to 2018, business and investment *personalty* also qualified for like-kind exchange treatment. Personalty includes machines, equipment, furniture and fixtures, trucks, and automobiles.

Business and investment personal property (i.e., non-real property), inventory, any property held for personal use, domestic property exchanged for foreign property, and partnership interests (both limited and general) do *not* qualify under the like-kind exchange rules. In addition, financial instruments (e.g., stock, bonds, or a note) do *not* qualify for like-kind exchange treatment even though they are held for investment.

If a taxpayer exchanges like-kind property *solely* for like-kind property, gain or loss realized is not recognized (it is deferred), and the basis and holding period from the old property attaches (carries over) to the new property.[65]

> **EXAMPLE 36**
>
> During the current year, Andy exchanged 40 acres of unimproved land in Illinois (fair market value $200,000, basis $70,000) for 10 acres of unimproved land in California (fair market value $200,000).
>
> Although Andy has a realized gain of $130,000 on this transaction ($200,000 amount realized − $70,000 basis), none of the gain is recognized; the transaction qualifies as a like-kind exchange. Andy's basis in the new property is $70,000. This carryover basis reflects the realized gain that is deferred ($200,000 California property fair market value − $130,000 gain deferred). The like-kind exchange rules acknowledge that Andy—after the exchange—would not have the wherewithal to pay tax if the realized gain were recognized.
>
> If Andy were to sell the California property for its market value, he would have a realized and recognized gain of $130,000.

The nonrecognition provision for like-kind exchanges is *mandatory* rather than elective. A taxpayer who wants to recognize a realized gain or loss will have to structure the transaction in a way that fails the like-kind exchange requirements. For example, a taxpayer may want to avoid like-kind treatment so that a realized loss can be recognized. Or a taxpayer might want to recognize a gain so that capital loss carryovers can be used. We discuss this more in the Tax Planning section of the chapter.

> **EXAMPLE 37**
>
> During the current year, Stephanie exchanged her rental condo in Vail, worth $250,000 (basis of $325,000), plus $80,000 of cash for a rental condo in Malibu worth $330,000. Although Stephanie has a realized loss of $75,000 on this transaction [$330,000 amount realized − ($325,000 basis + $80,000 cash)], none of the loss is recognized since the transaction qualifies as a like-kind exchange.
>
> Stephanie would likely be better off for tax purposes by selling her Vail condo (and recognizing the loss) and then buying the Malibu property.

The like-kind exchange rules are applied independently to each taxpayer in the exchange; one taxpayer may qualify for like-kind treatment, and the other may not.

13-4a Like-Kind Property

According to the Regulations, the term *like-kind* is intended to be interpreted very broadly.[66] *Real property* (or realty) includes rental buildings, office and store buildings, manufacturing plants, warehouses, and land. It is immaterial whether realty is improved or unimproved. As a result, unimproved land can be exchanged for an apartment house. Real property held primarily for sale (i.e., inventory) does *not* qualify as like-kind property.[67]

---

[65]Subject to certain exceptions, related parties can engage in tax-free like-kind exchanges, but a two-year holding period applies to both the relinquished property and the replacement property [§ 1031(f)].

[66]Reg. § 1.1031(a)–1(b).
[67]§ 1031(a)(2).

The like-kind exchange Regulations also indicate that if the exchange transaction involves multiple business assets (e.g., a television station for another television station), the determination of whether the assets qualify as like-kind property are not made at the business level.[68] Instead, the underlying assets must be evaluated, and only the real property that is part of the exchange would qualify for like-kind exchange treatment.

13-4b Exchange Requirement

The transaction must involve a direct exchange of property to qualify as a like-kind exchange. The sale of old property and the purchase of new property, even though like-kind, is not an exchange. However, if the two transactions are mutually dependent, the IRS may treat them as a like-kind exchange.[69]

Time Limitations

Like-kind exchanges of real estate can be complex. Further, it can be extremely difficult to coordinate a simultaneous transaction if the properties being exchanged are located in different counties or states. As a result, delayed (nonsimultaneous) exchanges are allowed, but there are time limits.

In a delayed like-kind exchange (often called a *Starker exchange*[70]), one party does not take immediate title to the new property because it has not yet been identified. The Code provides that the delayed swap—often made with the assistance of a qualified intermediary—will qualify as a like-kind exchange if the following requirements are satisfied (see Concept Summary 13.5):[71]

- *Identification period.* The new property must be identified within 45 days of the date when the old property was transferred to the qualified intermediary.
- *Exchange period.* The new property must be received:[72]
  - Within 180 days of the date when the old property was transferred to the qualified intermediary, or
  - If *earlier*, by the due date (including extensions) for the tax return covering the year of the transfer.

EXAMPLE 38

Phil owns a store in downtown Plano. Adjacent to his store is a commercial parking lot owned by Sally (fair market value of $175,000). Phil would like to acquire the parking lot, which would allow him to expand his store, but Sally does not want to sell the lot due to the large gain she would recognize (her basis in the lot is only $3,000).

Phil agrees to purchase any "like-kind" property worth $175,000 that is acceptable to Sally if Sally agrees to immediately transfer the parking lot to Phil. Sally agrees to the plan, and the commercial lot is transferred to Phil on October 1 of the current year.

Later that month, Sally identifies a townhouse worth $175,000 and directs Phil to buy it for her. Phil negotiates the sale, which closes on December 12, and transfers the property to Sally.

This is a like-kind exchange since the replacement property was identified within 45 days of the parking lot being transferred to Phil and the townhouse was transferred to Sally within 180 days of the original transfer date. In effect, Sally sold the parking lot to Phil for $175,000 and then reinvested the proceeds in another piece of real estate without having to pay tax on the realized gain. Her basis in the townhouse ($3,000) reflects the realized gain that is deferred.

---

[68]Reg. § 1.1031(j)–1.

[69]Rev.Rul. 61–119, 1961–1 C.B. 395.

[70]*T.J. Starker v. U.S.*, 79–2 USTC ¶9541, 44 AFTR 2d 79–5525, 602 F.2d 1341 (CA–9, 1979). This decision first allowed deferred like-kind exchanges.

[71]§ 1031(a)(3).

[72]In general, the IRS allows *no deviation* from either the identification period or the exchange period even when events outside the taxpayer's control preclude strict compliance. However, see Rev.Proc. 2010–14, 2010–12 I.R.B. 456. Here, the IRS allowed an exception where the qualified intermediary defaulted due to bankruptcy.

Concept Summary 13.5

Delayed § 1031 Exchange

13-4c **Boot**

It is unusual to find like-kind transactions where the value of the property given up is exactly equal to the value of the property received. In most situations, one party normally provides some other property (e.g., cash) to "even out" the exchange. When a taxpayer in a like-kind exchange gives or receives some property that is *not* like-kind property, gain or loss recognition may occur. Property that is not like-kind, including cash, is referred to as **boot** . Although the term *boot* does not appear in the Code, tax practitioners commonly use it rather than saying "property that is not like-kind property."

The *receipt* of boot will trigger recognition of gain if there is realized gain. The amount of the recognized gain is the *lesser* of the boot received or the realized gain (realized gain serves as the ceiling on recognition). If a taxpayer recognizes gain in a like-kind exchange, the character of the gain depends on the character of the asset given up (and depreciation recapture rules can apply; see text Section 14-10).

Implications of Boot Received

Emily and Fran exchange land, and the exchange qualifies as like kind. Because Emily's land (adjusted basis of $20,000) is worth $24,000 and Fran's land has a fair market value of $19,000, Fran also gives Emily cash of $5,000.

Emily's recognized gain is $4,000, the lesser of the realized gain ($24,000 amount realized − $20,000 adjusted basis) or the fair market value of the boot received ($5,000).

EXAMPLE 39

Assume the same facts as in the previous example, except that Fran's land is worth $21,000 (not $19,000). Under these circumstances, Fran gives Emily cash of $3,000 to make up the difference.

Emily's recognized gain is $3,000, the lesser of the realized gain of $4,000 ($24,000 amount realized − $20,000 adjusted basis) or the fair market value of the boot received of $3,000.

EXAMPLE 40

The receipt of boot does not result in recognition if there is realized loss.

Implications of Boot Received

Assume the same facts as in Example 39, except that the adjusted basis of Emily's land is $30,000. Emily's realized loss is $6,000 ($24,000 amount realized − $30,000 adjusted basis). The receipt of the boot of $5,000 does not trigger loss recognition; the recognized loss is $0.

The *giving* of boot usually does not trigger recognition. If the boot given is cash, no realized gain or loss is recognized.

Implications of Boot Given

Sarah and Gary exchange land in a like-kind exchange. Sarah receives land with a fair market value of $75,000 and transfers land worth $63,000 (adjusted basis of $45,000) and cash of $12,000.
    Sarah's realized gain is $18,000 ($75,000 amount realized − $45,000 adjusted basis − $12,000 cash). However, none of Sarah's realized gain is recognized.

If, however, the boot given is appreciated or depreciated property, gain or loss is recognized to the extent of the difference between the adjusted basis and the fair market value of the boot. For this purpose, *appreciated or depreciated property* is defined as property whose adjusted basis is not equal to the fair market value.

Implications of Boot Given

Assume the same facts as in the previous example, except that Sarah transfers land worth $30,000 (adjusted basis of $36,000) and boot worth $45,000 (adjusted basis of $27,000). Sarah's net gain on this exchange is $12,000 [$75,000 amount realized − adjusted basis of $63,000 ($36,000 + $27,000)]. But she is transferring two pieces of property: land (like-kind property) with a built-in realized loss of $6,000 ($30,000 fair market value − $36,000 adjusted basis) and non-like-kind property (boot) with a built-in realized gain of $18,000 ($45,000 fair market value − $27,000 adjusted basis).
    In this case, the $6,000 realized loss on the like-kind property is *deferred* (not recognized) and the $18,000 realized gain on the non-like-kind property is recognized. In other words, the realized loss on the like-kind property *cannot* be used to offset the realized gain on the boot given up as part of the transaction.

13-4d **Basis and Holding Period of Property Received**

The basis of property received in a like-kind exchange must be adjusted to reflect any postponed (deferred) gain or loss. The basis of *like-kind property* received in the exchange is the property's fair market value less postponed gain or plus postponed loss (this is often referred to as the "simplified method"). The basis of any *boot* received is the boot's fair market value.

Basis of Like-Kind Property Received

Jaime exchanges a building (used in his business) with an adjusted basis of $430,000 and a fair market value of $438,000 for land with a fair market value of $438,000. The exchange qualifies as like kind (an exchange of business real property for investment real property) and the $8,000 realized gain is deferred.

The basis of the land is $430,000 (land's fair market value of $438,000 − $8,000 postponed gain on the building). If the land later is sold for its fair market value of $438,000, the $8,000 postponed gain is recognized.

EXAMPLE 44

Assume the same facts as in the previous example, except that the building has an adjusted basis of $480,000 and a fair market value of only $380,000. Jaime receives land with a fair market value of $380,000, and the $100,000 realized loss is deferred.

The basis in the newly acquired land is $480,000 (fair market value of $380,000 + $100,000 postponed loss on the building). If the land later is sold for its fair market value of $380,000, the $100,000 postponed loss is recognized.

EXAMPLE 45

Code § 1031(d) provides an alternative approach for determining the basis of like-kind property received.

> Adjusted basis of like-kind property surrendered
> + Adjusted basis of boot given
> + Gain recognized
> − Fair market value of boot received
> − Loss recognized
> = *Basis of like-kind property received*

This approach is logical in terms of the recovery of capital doctrine. That is, the unrecovered cost or other basis is increased by additional cost (boot given) or decreased by cost recovered (boot received). Any gain recognized is included in the basis of the new property. The taxpayer has been taxed on this amount and now is entitled to recover it tax-free. Any loss recognized is deducted from the basis of the new property because the taxpayer has received a tax benefit on that amount.

The holding period of the property surrendered in the exchange carries over and *tacks on* to the holding period of the like-kind property received.[73] The holding period for boot received in a like-kind exchange begins with the date of the exchange. See text Section 14-4 for a discussion of the relevance of the holding period.

Depreciation recapture potential carries over to the property received in a like-kind exchange.[74] See text Section 14-11 for a discussion of this topic.

The following comprehensive examples illustrate the like-kind exchange rules.

Like-Kind Exchanges: Comprehensive Examples

Vicki exchanged a building used in her business for a parcel of unimproved land on which she plans to construct a new building. Her building has a fair market value of $1,200,000 and an adjusted basis of $400,000. The land she acquires has a fair market value of $900,000, and she will receive cash of $300,000 as part of the exchange. What is Vicki's realized and recognized gain or loss, and what is her basis in the land she receives [using both the § 1031(d) approach and the simplified method]?

EXAMPLE 46

continued

---

[73]§ 1223(1) and Reg. § 1.1223–1(a). The like-kind property surrendered must have been either a capital asset or § 1231 property.

[74]Reg. §§ 1.1245–2(a)(4) and 1.1250–2(d)(1).

Realized Gain (Loss)

	Amount realized ($900,000 + $300,000)	$1,200,000
−	Adjusted basis of building	(400,000)
=	Realized gain	$ 800,000

Boot Received

Cash	$ 300,000

Recognized Gain

Lesser of realized gain or boot received	$ 300,000

Basis of New Land [§ 1031(d)]

	Adjusted basis of property given up	$ 400,000
+	Adjusted basis of boot given	–0–
+	Gain recognized	300,000
−	Fair market value of boot received	(300,000)
−	Loss recognized	–0–
=	Basis of like-kind property received	$ 400,000

Basis of New Land (Simplified Method)

	Fair market value of property received	$ 900,000
−	Postponed gain ($800,000 − $300,000)	(500,000)
=	Basis of like-kind property received	$ 400,000

EXAMPLE 47

Assume the same facts as Example 46, except that Vicki's building has a fair market value of $300,000 and she provides $600,000 cash to the seller as part of the exchange.

Realized Gain (Loss)

	Amount realized (FMV of new land)	$ 900,000
−	Adjusted basis ($400,000 building + $600,000 cash)	(1,000,000)
=	Realized loss	($ 100,000)

Boot Received $ –0–

Recognized Loss $ –0–

Basis of New Land [§ 1031(d)]

	Adjusted basis of property given up	$ 400,000
+	Adjusted basis of boot given	600,000
+	Gain recognized	–0–
−	Fair market value of boot received	–0–
−	Loss recognized	–0–
=	Basis of like-kind property received	$ 1,000,000

Basis of New Land (Simplified Method)

	Fair market value of property received	$ 900,000
+	Postponed loss	100,000
=	Basis of like-kind property received	$ 1,000,000

If the taxpayer assumes a liability (or takes property subject to a liability) in the exchange, the amount of the liability is treated as boot given. For the taxpayer whose liability is assumed (or whose property is taken subject to the liability), the amount of the liability is treated as boot received.

Jill Rodriguez and Rick Thompson exchange real estate investments. Jill gives up property with an adjusted basis of $250,000 (fair market value of $420,000) that is subject to a mortgage of $80,000 (assumed by Rick). In return for this property, Jill receives property with a fair market value of $340,000 (Rick's adjusted basis in the property is $200,000). Jill's and Rick's realized and recognized gains and their basis in the like-kind property received are computed as follows:[75]

EXAMPLE 48

		Jill	Rick
Compute Realized Gain (Loss)			
	FMV of like-kind property received	$ 340,000	$ 420,000
+	FMV of other property received		
+	Cash received		
+	Debt relief	80,000	
−	Cash paid		
−	Debt assumed		(80,000)
=	Net consideration received	$ 420,000	$ 340,000
−	Adjusted basis of property given	(250,000)	(200,000)
=	Realized gain (loss)	$ 170,000	$ 140,000
Compute Boot Received			
	Debt relief	$ 80,000	$ –0–
+	Cash received		–0–
+	FMV of other property received		
=	Boot received	$ 80,000	$ –0–
Compute Recognized Gain			
	Lesser of realized gain or boot received	$ 80,000	$ –0–
Compute Basis for New Property (Other Than Cash)			
	Adjusted basis of property given	$ 250,000	$ 200,000
+	Boot given (cash paid, debt assumed)	–0–	80,000
+	Gain recognized	80,000	–0–
−	Boot received	(80,000)	–0–
=	Basis of new property	$ 250,000	$ 280,000

13-4e Reporting Considerations

Section 1031 transactions are reported on Form 8824 (Like-Kind Exchanges). Part III of Form 8824 (on the next page) is based on the information provided for Jill Rodriguez's exchange (Example 48).

This form must be filed even if the like-kind exchange transaction results in no recognized gain or loss. It is filed with the regular return for the tax year when the like-kind exchange occurs.

13-5 INVOLUNTARY CONVERSIONS—§ 1033

LO.7

Explain the nonrecognition provisions available on the involuntary conversion of property.

In most cases, taxpayers sell property (or exchange it) when they need to do so. There are times, however, when the taxpayer *involuntarily* (i.e., outside the taxpayer's control) disposes of property. When this happens, the taxpayer usually receives some sort of compensation (e.g., insurance proceeds or a condemnation award). Section 1033 provides that a taxpayer who experiences an involuntary conversion of property may postpone recognition of *gain* realized from the conversion. As a result, this provision provides relief to a taxpayer who has experienced an involuntary conversion and does not have the *wherewithal to pay* the tax on any gain realized as a result of the conversion.

---

[75]Example (2) of Reg. § 1.1031(d)–2 illustrates a special situation where both the buyer and the seller transfer liabilities that are assumed by the other party (or both parties acquire property that is subject to a liability).

Form 8824 (2019)   Page **2**

Name(s) shown on tax return. Do not enter name and social security number if shown on other side.	Your social security number
Jill Rodriguez (Example 48)	

Part III   Realized Gain or (Loss), Recognized Gain, and Basis of Like-Kind Property Received

Caution: If you transferred **and** received **(a)** more than one group of like-kind properties or **(b)** cash or other (not like-kind) property, see **Reporting of multi-asset exchanges** in the instructions.

Note: Complete lines 12 through 14 **only** if you gave up property that was not like-kind. Otherwise, go to line 15.

12	Fair market value (FMV) of other property given up	12	
13	Adjusted basis of other property given up	13	
14	Gain or (loss) recognized on other property given up. Subtract line 13 from line 12. Report the gain or (loss) in the same manner as if the exchange had been a sale	14	
	Caution: *If the property given up was used previously or partly as a home, see* **Property used as home** *in the instructions.*		
15	Cash received, FMV of other property received, plus net liabilities assumed by other party, reduced (but not below zero) by any exchange expenses you incurred. See instructions	15	80,000
16	FMV of like-kind property you received	16	340,000
17	Add lines 15 and 16	17	420,000
18	Adjusted basis of like-kind property you gave up, net amounts paid to other party, plus any exchange expenses **not** used on line 15. See instructions	18	250,000
19	**Realized gain or (loss).** Subtract line 18 from line 17	19	170,000
20	Enter the smaller of line 15 or line 19, but not less than zero	20	80,000
21	Ordinary income under recapture rules. Enter here and on Form 4797, line 16. See instructions . .	21	0
22	Subtract line 21 from line 20. If zero or less, enter -0-. If more than zero, enter here and on Schedule D or Form 4797, unless the installment method applies. See instructions	22	80,000
23	**Recognized gain.** Add lines 21 and 22	23	80,000
24	Deferred gain or (loss). Subtract line 23 from line 19. If a related party exchange, see instructions . .	24	90,000
25	**Basis of like-kind property received.** Subtract line 15 from the sum of lines 18 and 23	25	250,000

Realized gain is postponed to the extent the taxpayer *reinvests* the amount realized (e.g., insurance proceeds) in replacement property. The rules for nonrecognition of gain are as follows:

- If the amount reinvested in replacement property *equals or exceeds* the amount realized, realized gain is *not recognized*.

- If the amount reinvested in replacement property is *less than* the amount realized, realized gain *is recognized* to the extent of the deficiency.

Involuntary Conversions: General Rules

EXAMPLE 49

Jason operates a charter fishing business in Panama City, Florida, taking customers out in the Gulf of Mexico on daylong fishing trips. Unfortunately, his boat was completely destroyed when Hurricane Michael hit the Florida coast. His boat had a basis of $78,000 ($120,000 cost − $42,000 of accumulated depreciation). Fortunately, Jason had marine insurance (which included a replacement cost rider). He filed an insurance claim shortly after his boat was destroyed and received $175,000 in insurance proceeds three weeks later.

Jason has a realized gain of $97,000, computed as follows:

Amount realized (insurance proceeds)	$175,000
Less: Adjusted basis	(78,000)
Realized gain	$ 97,000

Jason can defer the entire realized gain, provided that he uses all of the insurance proceeds to purchase a new boat.

EXAMPLE 49

Refer to the facts of Example 49, and assume that Jason buys a new boat for $180,000. He uses the entire insurance settlement as part of the purchase.

In this case, Jason's $97,000 realized gain is deferred, and the basis of his new boat must reflect that deferral. As a result, his new boat's basis is $83,000 ($180,000 cost − $97,000 deferred gain).

Involuntary Conversions: General Rules

Continuing with the facts of Example 49, assume that Jason is able to negotiate an excellent price for his new boat. In fact, he is able to replace his old boat for only $168,000 and uses the $7,000 remaining from the insurance settlement to pay for other business expenses.

Jason recognizes a gain of $7,000, the difference between the $175,000 insurance settlement and the amount he paid for the new boat ($168,000; the amount of the insurance proceeds he reinvested in replacement property).

The balance of the realized gain is deferred, and the basis of his new boat must reflect that deferral. As a result, his new boat's basis is $78,000 ($168,000 cost − $90,000 deferred gain).

If an involuntary conversion results in a *loss*, § 1033 does not change the normal loss recognition rules. If a realized loss would otherwise be recognized, § 1033 does not change the result.

Refer to the facts of Example 49, but assume that Jason had only partial coverage on his boat and his insurance settlement is only $50,000. In this case, Jason has a loss of $28,000, computed as follows:

Amount realized (insurance proceeds)	$ 50,000
Less: Adjusted basis	(78,000)
Realized loss	($ 28,000)

No tax deferral applies; Jason's realized loss of $28,000 is recognized.

13-5a Involuntary Conversion Defined

An **involuntary conversion** results from the destruction (complete or partial), theft, seizure, condemnation, or sale or exchange under threat of condemnation (e.g., a city seizing property under its right of eminent domain) of the taxpayer's property.[76] A voluntary act (e.g., a taxpayer destroying the property by arson) is *not* an involuntary conversion.[77]

Government seizures are unique events, and as a result, a unique set of rules has developed. In general, the government entity must have made a decision to acquire the property for public use and the taxpayer must have reasonable grounds to believe the property will be taken.[78]

13-5b Computing the Amount Realized

The amount realized from an involuntary conversion typically includes any insurance proceeds received. In the case of the condemnation of property, the amount realized usually includes only the amount received as compensation for the property.[79]

Any amount received that is designated as severance damages by both the government and the taxpayer is *not* included in the amount realized. *Severance awards* usually occur when only a portion of the property is condemned (e.g., a strip of land is taken to build a highway). Severance damages are awarded because the value of the taxpayer's remaining property has declined as a result of the condemnation. In general, severance damages are a tax-free recovery of capital and reduce the basis of the property.

[76]§ 1033(a) and Reg. §§ 1.1033(a)–1(a) and –2(a).

[77]Rev.Rul. 82–74, 1982–1 C.B. 110.

[78]Rev.Rul. 63–221, 1963–2 C.B. 332 and *Joseph P. Balistrieri*, 38 TCM 526, T.C.Memo. 1979–115.

[79]*Pioneer Real Estate Co.*, 47 B.T.A. 886 (1942), *acq.* 1943 C.B. 18.

EXAMPLE

53

The government condemns a portion of Ron's farmland to upgrade a highway for driverless vehicles. Because the project denies his cattle access to a pond and some grazing land, Ron receives severance damages in addition to the condemnation proceeds for the land taken.

Ron must reduce the basis of the property by the amount of the severance damages. If the amount of the severance damages received exceeds the adjusted basis, Ron recognizes gain.

13-5c Replacement Property

The requirements for replacement property generally are more restrictive than those for like-kind property. The basic requirement is that the replacement property be *similar or related in service or use* to the involuntarily converted property.[80]

Different interpretations of the phrase *similar or related in service or use* apply depending on whether the involuntarily converted property is held by an *owner-user* (e.g., in a business or by an individual) or by an *owner-investor* (e.g., lessor). For an owner-investor, the *taxpayer use test* applies, and for an owner-user, the *functional use test* applies. In most cases, the functional use test is more restrictive than the taxpayer use test. In addition, a special rule applies in the case of involuntary conversions that result from condemnations.

Taxpayer Use Test

The taxpayer use test for owner-investors provides much more flexibility in terms of what qualifies as replacement property. Essentially, the properties must be used by the owner-investor in similar endeavors. For example, rental property held by an owner-investor qualifies if replaced with other rental property, regardless of the type of rental property involved. For example, the test is met if the owner-investor of a building being rented to a manufacturing business replaces the facility with a building rented to a business using the facility as a grocery warehouse.[81] The replacement of a rental residence with a personal residence does *not* meet the test.[82]

Functional Use Test

The functional use test applies to owner-users. Under this test, the taxpayer's use of the replacement property and of the involuntarily converted property must be the same. A manufacturer whose manufacturing plant is destroyed by fire must replace the plant with another facility of similar functional use. Replacing a manufacturing plant with an office building (both used in the same business) does *not* meet this test. The manufacturing plant would have to be replaced with another manufacturing plant. Replacing a rental residence with a personal residence also does not pass the test.

Special Rule for Condemnations

If business real property or investment real property is *condemned*, the broader replacement rules for like-kind exchanges can be used instead of the narrower involuntary conversion replacement rules. This gives the taxpayer substantially more flexibility in selecting replacement property. For example, improved real property can be replaced with unimproved real property.

---

[80]§ 1033(a) and Reg. § 1.1033(a)–1.

[81]*Loco Realty Co. v. Comm.*, 62–2 USTC ¶9657, 10 AFTR 2d 5359, 306 F.2d 207 (CA–8, 1962).

[82]Rev.Rul. 70–466, 1970–2 C.B. 165.

The rules concerning the nature of replacement property relative to involuntary conversions are illustrated in Concept Summary 13.6.

Concept Summary 13.6

Involuntary Conversions: Replacement Property Tests

Type of Property and User	Taxpayer Use Test	Functional Use Test	Special Rule for Condemnations*
An investor's rented shopping mall is destroyed by fire; the mall may be replaced with other rental properties (e.g., an apartment building).	X		
A manufacturing plant is destroyed by fire; replacement property must consist of another manufacturing plant that is functionally the same as the property converted.		X	
Personal residence of a taxpayer is condemned by a local government authority; replacement property must consist of another personal residence.		X	
Land used by a manufacturing company is condemned by a local government authority.			X
Apartment and land held by an investor are sold due to the threat or imminence of condemnation.			X

*Uses the like-kind exchange rules.

13-5d Time Limitation on Replacement

In general, the taxpayer must acquire replacement property within a two-year period after the close of the taxable year in which gain is realized.[83] Typically, gain is realized when insurance proceeds or damages are received.

EXAMPLE 54

Megan's warehouse is destroyed by fire on December 16, 2019. The adjusted basis is $325,000. Megan receives $400,000 from the insurance company on February 2, 2020. She is a calendar year and cash method taxpayer.

The latest date for replacement is December 31, 2022 (the end of the taxable year in which realized gain occurred plus two years). The critical date is not the date the involuntary conversion occurred, but rather the date of gain realization.

In the case of a condemnation of real property used in a trade or business or held for investment, a three-year period is substituted for the normal two-year period.

EXAMPLE 55

Assume the same facts as in the previous example, except that Megan's warehouse is condemned. Megan receives notification of the future condemnation on November 1, 2019. The condemnation occurs on December 16, 2019, with the condemnation proceeds being received on February 2, 2020.

The latest date for replacement is December 31, 2023 (the end of the taxable year in which realized gain occurred plus three years).

The *earliest date* for replacement typically is the date the involuntary conversion occurs. However, if the property is condemned, it is possible to replace the condemned property before this date. In this case, the earliest date is the date of the threat of condemnation of the property. This rule allows the taxpayer to make an orderly replacement of the condemned property.

---

[83]§§ 1033(a)(2)(B) and (g)(4) and Reg. § 1.1033(a)–2(c)(3). The two-year period is extended to a four-year period if the property is located in a Federally declared disaster area. The taxpayer can apply for an extension of this time period anytime before its expiration [Reg. § 1.1033(a)–2(c)(3)]. The period for filing the application for extension also can be extended if the taxpayer shows reasonable cause.

Assume the same facts as in Example 55. The earliest date that Megan can replace the warehouse is November 1, 2019, which is the date of an official notice regarding the condemnation of the warehouse.

13-5e **Nonrecognition of Gain**

Nonrecognition of gain can be either mandatory or elective, depending on whether the conversion is direct (into replacement property) or indirect (into money).

Direct Conversion

If the conversion is directly into replacement property rather than into money, non-recognition of realized gain is *mandatory*. In this case, the basis of the replacement property is the same as the adjusted basis of the converted property. Direct conversion is rare in practice and usually involves condemnations.

Lupe's property, with an adjusted basis of $20,000, is condemned by the state. Lupe receives property with a fair market value of $50,000 as compensation for the property taken.

Because the nonrecognition of realized gain is mandatory for direct conversions, Lupe's realized gain of $30,000 is not recognized and the basis of the replacement property is $20,000 (adjusted basis of the condemned property).

Conversion into Money

If the conversion is into money, the realized gain is recognized only to the extent the amount realized from the involuntary conversion exceeds the cost of the qualifying replacement property.[84] This is the usual case, and nonrecognition (postponement) is *elective*. If the election is not made, the realized gain is recognized.

The basis of the replacement property is the property's cost less any postponed (deferred) gain.[85] If the election to postpone gain is made, the holding period of the replacement property includes the holding period of the converted property.

Section 1033 applies *only to gains* and *not to losses*. Losses from involuntary conversions are recognized if the property is held for business or income-producing purposes. Certain personal casualty losses are recognized (the limitations are discussed in text Section 7-3), but condemnation losses related to personal use assets (e.g., a personal residence) are neither recognized nor postponed.

Return to the facts of *The Big Picture* on p. 13-1. Alice's building (used in her trade or business), with an adjusted basis of $50,000, is destroyed by fire on October 5, 2020. Alice is a calendar year taxpayer. On November 17, 2020, she receives an insurance reimbursement of $100,000 for the loss. Alice invests $80,000 in a new building. Alice uses the other $20,000 of insurance proceeds to pay off credit card debt.

- Alice has until December 31, 2022, to make the new investment and qualify for the nonrecognition election.

- Alice's realized gain is $50,000 ($100,000 insurance proceeds received − $50,000 adjusted basis of old building).

- Assuming that the replacement property qualifies as similar or related in service or use, Alice's recognized gain is $20,000. Because she reinvested $20,000 less than the insurance proceeds received ($100,000 proceeds − $80,000 reinvested), her realized gain is recognized to that extent.

- Alice's basis in the new building is $50,000. This is the building's cost of $80,000 less the postponed gain of $30,000 (realized gain of $50,000 − recognized gain of $20,000).

[84]§ 1033(a)(2)(A) and Reg. § 1.1033(a)–2(c)(1).   [85]§ 1033(b).

The Big Picture

Return to the facts of *The Big Picture* on p. 13-1. Assume the same facts as in the previous example, except that Alice receives only $45,000 of insurance proceeds. She has a realized and recognized loss of $5,000. The basis of the new building is the building's cost of $80,000.

EXAMPLE 59

If the destroyed building in Example 59 had been held for personal use, the recognized loss would have been subject to the casualty loss limitations.[86] Personal casualty losses are deductible only if they occur in a Federally declared disaster area. In that case, the loss of $5,000 would have been limited to the decline in fair market value of the property, and the amount of the loss would have been reduced first by $100 and then by 10 percent of adjusted gross income (see text Section 7-3d).

13-5f Reporting Considerations

In general, taxpayers are allowed to elect whether to defer any gain realized from an involuntary conversion. Normally, the election is made by not reporting any gain on the tax return. However, the tax return filed for the year of conversion must include detailed information related to the involuntary conversion.[87] This requirement usually is satisfied with a statement attached to the return detailing the involuntary conversion and the replacement property acquired.

What if the taxpayer intends to acquire qualifying replacement property but has not done so by the time the tax return is filed? The taxpayer should elect involuntary conversion treatment and report all the details of the transaction on a statement attached to the return. When the qualifying replacement property is acquired, the taxpayer attaches a statement to the tax return that contains relevant information on the replacement property.

An amended return must be filed if qualified replacement property is not acquired during the replacement time period. An amended return also is required if the cost of the replacement property is less than the amount realized from the involuntary conversion. In this case, the return would recognize the portion of the realized gain that no longer can be deferred.

13-6 SALE OF A RESIDENCE—§ 121

LO.8

Describe the provision for the permanent exclusion of gain on the sale of a personal residence.

A taxpayer's **personal residence** is a personal use asset. Therefore, a realized loss from the sale of a personal residence is not recognized.[88]

A realized gain from the sale of a personal residence is recognized. However, taxpayers meeting the **§ 121 exclusion** requirements are allowed to exclude up to $250,000 ($500,000 on certain joint returns) of realized gain on the sale of a principal residence.[89] Any gain in excess of this amount normally qualifies as a long-term capital gain (with preferential tax rates).

EXAMPLE 60

Tom and Eileen Atwood bought their home in 2011 for $525,000 and have used it as their principal residence since that time. In July 2020, they sell their home for $670,000. The Atwoods have a realized gain of $145,000 on the sale ($670,000 − $525,000), and the entire gain is excluded as a result of § 121.

What if the Atwoods sold their home for $500,000? In this case, since their home is a personal use asset, they would have a $25,000 realized loss that would not be recognized.

---

[86]§ 165(c)(3) and Reg. § 1.165–7.
[87]Reg. § 1.1033(a)–2(c)(2).
[88]§ 165(c).
[89]§ 121(b).

13-6a **Principal Residence**

Whether property is the taxpayer's principal residence "depends upon all of the facts and circumstances in each case." According to the Regulations, the most important factor is where the taxpayer spends most of his or her time.[90] A residence does not have to be a house. For example, a houseboat, a house trailer, or a motor home can qualify.[91] The principal residence includes the land on which a home sits (so any gain on the land also qualifies for exclusion). An adjacent lot can qualify if it is regularly used by the owner as part of the residential property.

EXAMPLE 61

Mitch graduates from college and moves to Boston, where he is employed. He decides to rent an apartment in Boston because of its proximity to his office. He purchases a beach condo in the Cape Cod area that he occupies most weekends. Mitch does not intend to live at the beach condo except on weekends. The apartment in Boston is his principal residence.

13-6b **Requirements for Exclusion Treatment**

To qualify for exclusion treatment, at the date of the sale, the residence must have been *owned* and *used* by the taxpayer as the principal residence for at least two years during the five-year period ending on the date of the sale of a taxpayer's principal residence.[92]

EXAMPLE 62

Melissa sells her principal residence on September 18, 2020. She had purchased it on July 5, 2018, and lived in it since then. The sale of Melissa's residence qualifies for the § 121 exclusion.

The ownership and use requirements are *two separate tests*. Although in most situations ownership and use overlap (as in Example 62), there is no requirement that they do for purposes of § 121. Further, the law does not require that the two-year periods be continuous.[93]

Ownership and Use Tests

EXAMPLE 63

Sarah purchased a home in San Diego in May 2005 and lived in it until she took a new job in Los Angeles on January 1, 2016. From January 2016 until she sold the house on July 31, 2020, she only used the home occasionally since she lived in an apartment near her job in downtown Los Angeles. Because the house was sold on July 31, 2020, the five-year window runs from August 1, 2015, to the date of sale.

In determining whether the § 121 exclusion is available, Sarah meets the ownership test because she owned the house for two of the five years prior to its sale. However, she fails the use test. During the five-year window, she used the house as her principal residence for only five months (from August 1, 2015, to December 31, 2015).

---

[90]Other factors include the address listed on a driver's license and/or voter registration card, the location of the taxpayer's employer, and the mailing address used for bills and correspondence. Regulation § 1.121–1(b)(2) includes the complete list of factors to be considered.

[91]Reg. § 1.121–1(b)(1); Reg. § 1.1034–1(c)(3)(i).

[92]§ 121(a). Section 121(d)(10) provides that exclusion treatment does not apply if the residence was acquired in a like-kind exchange within the prior five years of the sale of the residence.

[93]According to Reg. § 1.121–1(c)(1), taxpayers must document 730 days (365 × 2) of ownership and use during the five-year period that ends on the sale date.

Ownership and Use Tests

Charles lives in a townhouse that he rents from 2013 through January 17, 2017. On January 18, 2017, he purchases the townhouse. On February 1, 2018, due to a decline in health, Charles moves into his daughter's home. On May 25, 2020, while still living in his daughter's home, Charles sells his townhouse.

The § 121 exclusion applies because Charles *owned* the townhouse for at least two years out of the five years preceding the sale (from January 19, 2017, until May 25, 2020)[94] and he *used* the townhouse as his principal residence for at least two years during the five-year period preceding the sale [from May 25, 2015 (the beginning of the five-year window) until February 1, 2018].

In applying the use test, short absences (i.e., vacation or other seasonal absence) are counted as periods of use. In addition, short-term rental of the property is ignored.[95]

Aaron has owned and used his house as his principal residence since 2003. On January 31, 2017, Aaron moves to another state. Aaron rents his house to tenants from that date until April 18, 2019, when he sells it.

Aaron is eligible for the § 121 exclusion because he has owned and used the house as his principal residence for at least two of the five years preceding the sale.

The five-year window enables the taxpayer to qualify for the § 121 exclusion even though the property is not his or her principal residence at the date of the sale.

Benjamin sells his former principal residence on August 16, 2020. He had purchased it on April 1, 2012, and lived in it until July 1, 2019, when he converted it to rental property.

Even though the property is rental property on August 16, 2020, rather than Benjamin's principal residence, the sale qualifies for the § 121 exclusion.[96] During the five-year period from August 16, 2015, to August 16, 2020, Benjamin owned and used the property as his principal residence for at least two years.

In addition to the ownership and use requirements, § 121 can be used by a taxpayer only once every two years.[97] This rule restricts taxpayers who might be tempted to make liberal use of the § 121 exclusion as a means of speculating when the price of residential housing is rising. Without any time restriction on its use, § 121 would permit the exclusion of realized gain on multiple sales of principal residences.

Mike sells his principal residence (the first residence) in June 2019 for $150,000 (realized gain of $60,000). He then buys and sells the following (all of which qualify as principal residences):

	Date of Purchase	Date of Sale	Purchase/ Sales Price
Second residence	July 2019		$160,000
Second residence		April 2020	180,000
Third residence	May 2020		200,000

Because multiple sales have taken place within a period of two years, § 121 does not apply to the sale of the second residence. As a result, the realized gain of $20,000 [$180,000 (selling price) − $160,000 (purchase price)] must be recognized.

---

[94]As discussed in text Section 14-4a, holding period begins the day after acquisition date and includes the disposition date.

[95]Reg. § 1.121–1(c)(2)(i).

[96]However, any realized gain on the sale that is attributable to depreciation is not eligible for the § 121 exclusion. See Example 74.

[97]§ 121(b)(3) denies the application of the § 121 exclusion to sales occurring within two years of its last use.

13-6c Calculating the Exclusion

General Rule

The § 121 exclusion available on the sale of a principal residence is $250,000.[98] If the realized gain does not exceed $250,000, there is no recognized gain.

Realized gain is calculated in the normal manner. The *amount realized* is the selling price less any selling expenses (e.g., real estate broker commissions, advertising expenses, and legal fees). Repairs and maintenance costs to aid in selling the property are personal expenses and not deductible (and they do not increase the home's basis).

The § 121 Exclusion Amount

 EXAMPLE 68

Mandy, who is single, sells her personal residence (adjusted basis of $130,000) for $290,000. She has owned and lived in the residence for three years. Her selling expenses are $18,000. Three weeks prior to the sale, Mandy paid a carpenter and a painter $1,000 to make some repairs and paint two rooms. Her recognized gain is $0.

Amount realized ($290,000 − $18,000)	$ 272,000
Adjusted basis	(130,000)
Realized gain	$ 142,000
§ 121 exclusion	(142,000)
Recognized gain	$ –0–

Since the available § 121 exclusion of $250,000 exceeds Mandy's realized gain of $142,000, her recognized gain is $0.

EXAMPLE 69

Assume the same facts as in the previous example, but the selling price is $490,000. Since the realized gain of $342,000 exceeds the § 121 exclusion amount of $250,000, Mandy's recognized gain is $92,000 ($342,000 − $250,000).

Amount realized ($490,000 − $18,000)	$ 472,000
Adjusted basis	(130,000)
Realized gain	$ 342,000
§ 121 exclusion	(250,000)
Recognized gain	$ 92,000

Married Couples

If a married couple files a joint return, the $250,000 amount is increased to $500,000 if the following requirements are met:[99]

- Either spouse meets the at-least-two-years *ownership* requirement.
- Both spouses meet the at-least-two-years *use* requirement.
- Neither spouse sold a principal residence within the prior two years and used the § 121 exclusion.

A surviving spouse can use the $500,000 exclusion amount on the sale of a personal residence for the two years following the year of the deceased spouse's death. If the sale occurs in the year of death, however, a joint return must be filed by the surviving spouse.

---

[98]§ 121(b)(1).   [99]§ 121(b)(2).

Margaret sells her personal residence (adjusted basis of $150,000) for $650,000. She has owned and lived in the residence for six years. Her selling expenses are $40,000. Margaret is married to Ted, and they file a joint return. Ted has lived in the residence since they were married two and one-half years ago.

Amount realized ($650,000 − $40,000)	$ 610,000
Adjusted basis	(150,000)
Realized gain	$ 460,000
§ 121 exclusion	(460,000)
Recognized gain	$ −0−

Because the realized gain of $460,000 is less than the available § 121 exclusion amount of $500,000, no gain is recognized.

13-6d Exceptions to the Two-Year Rules

The two-year ownership and use requirements and the "only once every two years" rule could create a hardship for taxpayers in certain situations that are beyond their control. As a result, under the following special circumstances, the requirements are waived.[100]

- Change in place of employment,
- Health issues, or
- Unforeseen circumstances (as identified in the Regulations).

Treasury Department guidance on these three exceptions is discussed in the sections that follow.[101] Each of these exceptions provides a *partial* exclusion. The calculation of the partial exclusion is discussed after each of the exceptions is reviewed.

Change in Place of Employment

For this exception to apply, the taxpayer measures the distance (in miles) between (1) the taxpayer's *old residence* and *old job location* and (2) the taxpayer's *old residence* and *new job location*. The exception applies if (2) exceeds (1) by at least 50 miles. The location of the new residence does not matter for this purpose.

In addition, the house being sold must be used as the principal residence of the taxpayer when the employment change happens. The exception applies whether the taxpayer takes a job with a new employer; is transferred by the current employer; or, if self-employed, moves the proprietorship to a new location.

Assume the same facts as in Example 67, except that in March 2020, Mike's employer transfers him to a job in another state that is 400 miles away.

As a result, the sale of the second residence and the purchase of the third residence were due to relocation of employment. Consequently, the § 121 exclusion is partially available on the sale of the second residence.

Health Issues

The health exception uses either a general facts and circumstances approach or a safe harbor established in the Regulations. If a physician recommends a change of location due to health issues (or to obtain specialized care), the safe harbor is met. A sale that is merely beneficial to the general health or well-being of the individual will not qualify.

---

[100]§ 121(c)(2)(B).

[101]See Reg. § 1.121–3 and IRS Publication 523 (*Selling Your Home*) for further details and illustrations.

Unforeseen Circumstances

For the unforeseen circumstances exception to apply, the primary reason for the sale or exchange of the residence must be an event the taxpayer did not anticipate before purchasing and occupying the residence. The Regulations provide a safe harbor opportunity that applies in any of the following instances:

- Involuntary conversion of the residence.
- Natural or human-made disasters or acts of war or terrorism resulting in a casualty to the residence.
- Death of a qualified individual.
- Cessation of employment resulting in eligibility for unemployment compensation.
- Change in employment or self-employment that results in the taxpayer being unable to pay housing costs and reasonable basic living expenses for the taxpayer's household.
- Divorce or legal separation.
- Multiple births resulting from the same pregnancy.

If none of the listed opportunities applies, the taxpayer can use a general facts and circumstances approach to justify the exception

EXAMPLE 72

Debra and Raji are engaged and buy a house (sharing the mortgage payments) and live in it as their personal residence. Eighteen months after the purchase, they cancel their wedding plans, and Raji moves out of the house. Because Debra cannot afford to make the payments alone, they sell the house.

Although the sale does not fit under the safe harbor events, the broken engagement is an unforeseen event; it qualifies under the "facts and circumstances" provision.[102]

Partial § 121 Exclusion

A partial § 121 exclusion is available when one of the exceptions applies. Then the exclusion amount ($250,000 or $500,000) is multiplied by a fraction, the numerator of which is the number of qualifying months and the denominator of which is 24 months. The resulting amount is the excluded gain.[103]

EXAMPLE 73

On October 1, 2019, Rich and Audrey, who file a joint return and live in Chicago, sell their personal residence, which they have owned and lived in for eight years. The realized gain of $325,000 is excluded under § 121. They purchase another personal residence for $525,000 on October 2, 2019. Audrey's employer transfers her to the Denver office in August 2020. Rich and Audrey sell their Chicago residence on August 2, 2020, and they purchase a residence in Denver shortly thereafter. The realized gain on the sale is $300,000.

The $325,000 gain on the first Chicago residence is excluded under § 121. The sale of the second Chicago residence is within the two-year window of the prior sale, but because it resulted from a change in employment, Rich and Audrey can qualify for partial exclusion treatment.

Realized gain	$ 300,000
§ 121 exclusion:	
$\frac{10 \text{ months}}{24 \text{ months}} \times \$500,000$	(208,333)
Recognized gain	$ 91,667

---

[102]Reg. § 1.121–3(e)(4), Example (6).   [103]§ 121(c)(1).

Basis of New Residence

Because § 121 is an exclusion provision (rather than a deferral of gain provision), the basis of a new residence is its cost.[104]

Implications of Renting or Using a Residence as a Home Office

The residence does not have to be the taxpayer's principal residence at the date of sale to qualify for the § 121 exclusion. During part of the five-year window, it could have been rental property (e.g., either a vacation home or entirely rental property). Or the taxpayer might have used part of the principal residence as a qualifying home office.

In either of these circumstances, the taxpayer may have claimed deductions for the expenses attributable to the rental or business use. But what effect, if any, do such deductions have on a later sale of the residence? Will the sales proceeds still qualify for nonrecognition of gain treatment under § 121?

As long as the various § 121 requirements are met, an income exclusion will be available. However, if the taxpayer deducted depreciation, any realized gain is recognized to the extent of the depreciation deductions.[105]

On December 5, 2020, Amanda sells her principal residence, which qualifies for the § 121 exclusion. Her realized gain is $190,000. From January through November 2019, she was temporarily out of town on a job assignment in another city and rented the residence to a college student. For this period, she deducted MACRS cost recovery of $7,000.

Without the depreciation provision, Amanda could exclude the $190,000 realized gain. However, the depreciation taken requires her to recognize $7,000 of the realized gain.

EXAMPLE
74

13-7 TAX PLANNING

LO.9

Review and apply various tax planning opportunities related to selected property transactions.

13-7a Cost Identification and Documentation Considerations

When multiple assets are acquired in a single transaction, the contract price must be allocated for several reasons. First, some of the assets may be depreciable but others are not. Here, the buyer and the seller may have different tax perspectives that will need to be reconciled. The seller will likely prefer a high allocation for nondepreciable assets (see Chapter 14); the purchaser likely will prefer a high allocation for depreciable assets subject to cost recovery. Second, the seller must be able to characterize gains and losses appropriately as capital or ordinary. Allocating the price among the assets sold allows this to happen. For example, an allocation to goodwill or to a covenant not to compete (see Chapters 8 and 14) produces different tax consequences to the seller. Third, the buyer must identify the adjusted basis of each asset to be able to determine cost recovery, amortization, or depletion (if available), and to calculate the realized gain or loss if an asset is sold.

13-7b Selection of Property for Making Gifts

A donor can achieve several tax advantages by making gifts of appreciated property. The donor avoids income tax on the unrealized gain that would have occurred had the property been sold. And if the donee is in a lower tax bracket than the donor, there will be tax savings if the property is sold. Any increase in value after the gift also is taxed at a lower rate. Such gifts of appreciated property can be an effective tool in family tax planning.

Taxpayers generally should not make gifts of property that, if sold, would produce a realized loss because the donor does not receive an income tax deduction for the

---

[104]§ 1012. [105]§ 121(d)(6).

unrealized loss element. In addition, the donee receives no benefit from this unrealized loss upon the subsequent sale of the property because of the loss basis rule. If the donor anticipates that the donee will sell the property upon receiving it, the donor should sell the property and take the loss deduction, assuming that the loss is deductible. The donor can then give the proceeds from the sale to the donee.

13-7c Selection of Property to Pass at Death

A taxpayer generally should distribute appreciated property via his or her will. Doing so enables both the decedent and the heir to avoid income tax on the unrealized gain because the recipient takes the fair market value as his or her basis.

A taxpayer generally should not distribute property that, if sold, would produce a realized loss via his or her will because the decedent does not receive an income tax deduction for the unrealized loss. In addition, the heir will receive no benefit from this unrealized loss upon the subsequent sale of the property.

EXAMPLE 75

On the date of her death in 2020, Marta owned land held for investment purposes. The land had a basis of $130,000 and a fair market value of $100,000. If Marta had sold the property before her death, the recognized loss would have been $30,000.

If instead, Roger inherits the property and later sells it for $90,000, the recognized loss is $10,000 (the decline in value since Marta's death). In addition, regardless of the period of time Roger holds the property, the holding period is long term.

From an income tax perspective, it is better to transfer appreciated property as an inheritance rather than as a gift. Why? Because inherited property receives a step-up in basis but property received by gift has a carryover basis to the donee. However, in making this decision, the estate tax consequences of the inheritance should be weighed against the gift tax consequences of the gift.

13-7d Disallowed Losses

Taxpayers should avoid transactions that activate the related-party loss disallowance rules. Even with the ability of the related-party buyer to offset his or her realized gain by the related-party seller's disallowed loss, several inequities exist. First, any tax benefit associated with the disallowed loss is shifted to the related-party buyer (the related-party seller receives no tax benefit). Second, the tax benefit of this offset is delayed until the related-party buyer sells the property. Third, if the property does not appreciate during the time period the related-party buyer holds it, part or all of the disallowed loss is permanently lost. Fourth, the right of offset is available only to the original transferee (the related-party buyer). As a result, the disallowed loss is eliminated permanently if the original transferee transfers the property by gift or inheritance.

EXAMPLE 76

Tim sells property with an adjusted basis of $35,000 to Wes, his brother, for $25,000, the fair market value of the property. The $10,000 realized loss to Tim is disallowed by § 267.

If Wes subsequently sells the property to an unrelated party for $37,000, he has a recognized gain of $2,000 (realized gain of $12,000 reduced by disallowed loss of $10,000). Therefore, from the perspective of the family unit, the original $10,000 realized loss ultimately is recognized.

However, if Wes sells the property for $29,000, he has a recognized gain of $0 (realized gain of $4,000 reduced by disallowed loss of $4,000 necessary to offset the realized gain). From the perspective of the family unit, $6,000 of the realized loss of $10,000 is permanently lost ($10,000 realized loss − $4,000 offset permitted).

13-7e Like-Kind Exchanges

Because the like-kind exchange provisions are mandatory rather than elective, in certain instances, it may be preferable to avoid qualifying for § 1031 nonrecognition. For example, immediate recognition of gain (which also will result in a higher basis for the newly acquired asset) may be preferable if the taxpayer has unused capital loss carryovers. If so, the taxpayer can structure the transaction so that at least one of the § 1031 like-kind exchange requirements is not met.

Alicia sells land and a building (used in her business) with an adjusted basis of $300,000 for $400,000. She also acquires a new building and land for $900,000. Alicia has a $125,000 capital loss carryover.

If § 1031 applies, the $100,000 realized gain is not recognized and the basis of the new land and building is reduced by $100,000 (from $900,000 to $800,000). Assuming no other capital asset transactions, Alicia can deduct only $3,000 of her capital loss carryover.

If § 1031 does not apply, a $100,000 gain is recognized and can be used to offset her $125,000 capital loss carryover. In addition, the basis of the new land and building is $900,000 rather than $800,000 because the entire gain was recognized (allowing for a larger depreciation deduction on the new building).

The like-kind exchange rules also should be avoided when a realized loss exists (adjusted basis exceeds the fair market value).

Assume the same facts as in the previous example, except that the fair market value of the land and building is $250,000. If § 1031 applies, the $50,000 realized loss is not recognized.

To recognize the loss, Alicia should sell the old land and building and purchase the new one. The purchase and sale transactions should be with different taxpayers.

Tax planning for exchanges must consider the present value of tax deferrals and the possibility of future changes in tax rates. Taxpayers may prefer to pay no more than 20 percent today (the maximum tax rate on long-term capital gains) if they believe that tax rates will go up in the future. Although turning down a tax deferral may sound like a strange strategy, it fits the notion of "pay a tax today to avoid a higher tax tomorrow."

13-7f Involuntary Conversions

In certain cases, a taxpayer may prefer to recognize gain from an involuntary conversion, a possibility because involuntary conversion treatment generally is an elective provision.

Ahmad has a $40,000 realized gain from the involuntary conversion of an office building. He reinvests the entire proceeds of $450,000 in a new office building. He does not elect to postpone gain under § 1033, however, because a net operating loss carryforward offsets the gain.

Because Ahmad did not elect gain postponement, his basis in the replacement property is the property's cost of $450,000 rather than $410,000 ($450,000 reduced by the $40,000 realized gain).

13-7g **Sale of a Principal Residence**

Waiving the Exclusion

The § 121 exclusion automatically applies if the taxpayer is eligible (i.e., the taxpayer need not make an election). However, a taxpayer can waive the § 121 exclusion.[106]

EXAMPLE 80

George owns two personal residences that satisfy the two-year ownership and use test with respect to the five-year window. The Elm Street residence has appreciated by $25,000, and the Maple Street residence has appreciated by $230,000. He intends to sell both of them and move into a rental property. He sells the Elm Street residence in December 2020 and expects to sell the Maple Street residence early next year.

Unless George elects not to apply the § 121 exclusion to the sale of the Elm Street residence, he will exclude the $25,000 realized gain on that residence in 2020. In 2021, however, he recognizes a gain of $230,000 on the sale of the Maple Street residence.

If George elects to waive the exclusion on the Elm Street residence sale, he will report a recognized gain of $25,000 on this sale in 2020. But by using the § 121 exclusion in 2021, he will eliminate the recognized gain of $230,000 on the sale of the Maple Street residence.

Qualification for § 121 Exclusion

The key requirement for the § 121 exclusion is that the taxpayer must have *owned* and *used* the property as a principal residence for at least two years during the five-year window. As taxpayers advance in age, they frequently make decisions related to their personal residence(s).

- Sell the principal residence and buy a smaller residence or rent a principal residence.
- Sell vacation homes they own.
- Sell homes they are holding as rental property.

These properties may have experienced substantial appreciation while owned by the taxpayers. Proper planning can make it possible for multiple properties to qualify for the exclusion. Although this strategy may require taxpayers to be flexible about where they live, it can result in substantial tax savings.

EXAMPLE 81

Eleanor and David, residents of Virginia, are approaching retirement. They have substantial appreciation on their principal residence in Richmond and on a house they own in Virginia Beach (about two hours away). After retirement, they plan to move to Florida. They have owned and lived in the principal residence for 28 years and have owned the beach house for 9 years.

If they sell their principal residence, it qualifies for the § 121 exclusion. At retirement, they could move into their beach house for two years and make it eligible for the exclusion before they relocate to Florida.

If the beach house were close enough to things they needed to do in Richmond currently (e.g., work), they could sell the principal residence now and move into the beach house to start the running of the two-year use period. As noted previously, any realized gain on the beach house attributable to depreciation is not eligible for the § 121 exclusion. In addition, a reduction in the § 121 exclusion for prior use as a vacation home is required.[107]

---

[106]§ 121(f).

[107]Additional information and examples can be found on pp. 3–6 of IRS Publication 523 (*Selling Your Home*).

SALE OR GIFT OF INHERITED HOUSE AND OTHER PROPERTY TRANSACTIONS

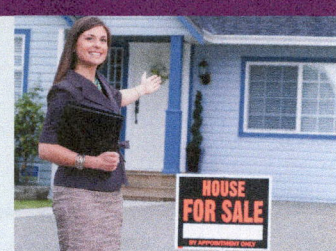

Gift of Inherited House

Based on an inquiry you made of Alice, this is the only gift she would make to Michael this year. She has made no prior gifts to any individual that exceeded the annual per donee exclusion amount (i.e., currently $15,000).

With this information, you inform Alice that no gift tax would be due on the gift of the house to Michael. However, she would use up $585,000 ($600,000 − $15,000) of her lifetime gift tax exemption of $11.58 million. Michael's basis for the house would be a carryover of Alice's basis of $475,000 (i.e., for inherited property, the fair market value at the date of the decedent's death).

Sale of Inherited House

You advise Alice that her adjusted basis for the house in calculating gain or loss on its sale is the $475,000 fair market value on the date of her grandmother's death. If Alice sells the house for $800,000, her projected selling expenses (i.e., real estate agent's commission, attorney's fees, other closing costs) would be $40,000 ($800,000 × 5%). She would have a recognized gain of $285,000 as calculated below. The house is a capital asset, and Alice's holding period is long term because she inherited the house. Thus, the gain would be classified as a long-term capital gain (i.e., subject to the 15 percent or 20 percent tax rate). So the Federal income tax due would be $42,750 ($285,000 × 15%) if the 15 percent rate applies.

Amount realized ($800,000 − $40,000)	$ 760,000
Less: Adjusted basis	(475,000)
Realized gain	$ 285,000
Recognized gain	$ 285,000

Other Issues

See Examples 12 and 13 for the tax consequences associated with Alice's questions regarding selling the boat. See Examples 30 and 31 for the tax consequences associated with Alice's questions regarding the wash sale of the stock.

See Examples 58 and 59 for Alice's tax consequences associated with the involuntary conversion.

What If?

Alice is leaning toward selling the house. However, she knows that her grandmother would not want her to have to pay income taxes on the sale. Alice inquires as to whether there is any way she could reduce the Federal income tax on the sale to $0.

You inform Alice of the exclusion provision under § 121 of the Code. She can qualify for this gain exclusion rule if she satisfies the at least two-out-of-five-years ownership and use requirements. This would necessitate her moving into the house for at least two years and occupying it as her principal residence.

From a tax planning perspective, what could Alice have done so that none of the $50,000 of realized gain in Example 58 from the involuntary conversion was recognized?

To have full postponement of the $50,000 realized gain, Alice would have to reinvest all of the $100,000 of insurance proceeds received in another qualifying building. Under this circumstance, the basis of a replacement building costing $100,000 would be a carryover basis of $50,000 ($100,000 cost − $50,000 deferred gain).

Key Terms

Adjusted basis, 13-5

Amount realized, 13-4

Boot, 13-25

Fair market value, 13-4

Goodwill, 13-11

Holding period, 13-13

Involuntary conversion, 13-31

Like-kind exchanges, 13-22

Nontaxable exchange, 13-22

Personal residence, 13-35

Realized gain, 13-3

Realized loss, 13-3

Recognized gain, 13-8

Recognized loss, 13-8

Section 121 exclusion, 13-35

Wash sale, 13-16

Discussion Questions

Critical Thinking   1.   **LO.1** Ivan invests in land, and Grace invests in taxable bonds. The land appreciates by $8,000 each year, and the bonds earn interest of $8,000 each year. After holding the land and bonds for five years, Ivan and Grace sell them. There is a $40,000 realized gain on the sale of the land and no realized gain or loss on the sale of the bonds. Are the tax consequences to Ivan and Grace the same for each of the five years? Explain.

2.   **LO.1, 2** Carol and Dave each purchase 100 shares of stock of Burgundy, Inc., a publicly owned corporation, in July for $10,000 each. Carol sells her stock on December 31 for $8,000. Because Burgundy's stock is listed on a national exchange, Dave can ascertain that his shares are worth $8,000 on December 31. Does the Federal income tax law treat the decline in value of the stock differently for Carol and Dave? Explain.

3.   **LO.1** If a taxpayer sells property for cash, the amount realized consists of the net proceeds from the sale. For each of the following, indicate the effect on the amount realized if:

a.   The property is sold on credit.

b.   A mortgage on the property is assumed by the buyer.

c.   A mortgage on the property is assumed by the seller.

d.   The buyer acquires the property subject to a mortgage of the seller.

e.   Stock that has a basis to the purchaser of $6,000 and a fair market value of $10,000 is received by the seller as part of the consideration.

Decision Making   4.   **LO.1** Taylor is negotiating to buy some land. Under the first option, Taylor will give Ella $150,000 and assume her mortgage on the land for $100,000. Under the second option, Taylor will give Ella $250,000 and she will immediately pay off the mortgage. Taylor wants his basis for the land to be as high as possible. Given this objective, which option should Taylor select? Explain.

5.   **LO.1** Marge owns land and a building (held for investment) with an adjusted basis of $75,000 and a fair market value of $250,000. The property is subject to a mortgage of $400,000. Because Marge is in arrears on the mortgage payments, the creditor is willing to accept the property in return for canceling the amount of the mortgage.

a.   How can the adjusted basis of the property be less than the amount of the mortgage?

b.   If the creditor's offer is accepted, what are the effects on the amount realized, the adjusted basis, and the realized gain or loss for Marge?

6. **LO.4** On July 16, 2020, Logan acquires land and a building for $500,000 to use in his sole proprietorship. Of the purchase price, $400,000 is allocated to the building, and $100,000 is allocated to the land. Cost recovery of $4,708 is deducted in 2020 for the building (nonresidential real estate).

    a. What is the adjusted basis for the land and the building at the acquisition date?

    b. What is the adjusted basis for the land and the building at the end of 2020?

7. **LO.1** Auralia owns stock in Orange Corporation and Blue Corporation. She receives a $10,000 distribution from both corporations. Information from Orange states that the $10,000 is a dividend. Blue states that the $10,000 is not a dividend. What could cause the instructions to differ as to the Federal income tax consequences?

8. **LO.2** Wanda is considering selling two personal use assets that she owns. One has appreciated in value by $20,000, and the other has declined in value by $17,000. Wanda believes that she should sell both assets in the same tax year so that the loss of $17,000 can offset the gain of $20,000.

    Decision Making

    a. Advise Wanda regarding the tax consequences of her plan.

    b. Could Wanda achieve better tax results by selling the assets in different tax years? Explain.

9. **LO.2** Ron sold his sailboat for a $5,000 loss in the current year because he was diagnosed with skin cancer. His spouse wants him to sell his Harley-Davidson motorcycle because her brother broke his leg while riding his motorcycle. Because Ron no longer has anyone to ride with, he is seriously considering his wife's advice.

    Critical Thinking

    Because the motorcycle is a classic model, Ron has received two offers. Each offer would result in a $5,000 gain. Joe would like to purchase the motorcycle before Christmas, and Jeff would like to purchase it after New Year's. Identify the relevant tax issues Ron faces in making his decision.

10. **LO.1, 2, 3, 9** Simon owns stock that has declined in value since acquired. He will either give the stock to his nephew, Fred, or sell it and give Fred the proceeds. If Fred receives the stock, he then would sell it to obtain the proceeds. Simon is in the 12% Federal income tax bracket, and Fred's bracket is 22%. In either case, the holding period for the stock will be short term.

    Critical Thinking

    Identify the tax issues relevant to Simon in deciding whether to give the stock or the sale proceeds to Fred.

11. **LO.3** Robin inherits 1,000 shares of Wal-Mart stock from her aunt Julieta in 2020. According to the information received from the executor of Julieta's estate, Robin's adjusted basis for the stock is $55,000. Albert, Robin's fiancé, receives 1,000 shares of Wal-Mart stock from his uncle Roberto as a gift in 2020. Roberto tells Albert that his adjusted basis for the Wal-Mart stock is $7,000. What could cause the substantial difference in the adjusted basis for Robin's and Albert's respective 1,000 shares of Wal-Mart stock?

12. **LO.3** Thelma inherited land from Sadie on June 7, 2020. The land appreciated in value by 100% during the six months Sadie owned it. The value has remained stable during the three months Thelma has owned it, and she expects it to continue to do so in the near future. Although she would like to sell the land now, Thelma has decided to postpone the sale for another three months. The delay is undertaken to enable the recognized gain to qualify for long-term capital gain treatment. Evaluate Thelma's understanding of the tax law.

13. **LO.4** Marilyn owns land that she acquired three years ago as an investment for $250,000. Because the land has not appreciated in value as she anticipated, she sells it to her brother, Amos, for its fair market value of $180,000. Amos sells the land two years later for $240,000.

   a.   Explain why Marilyn's realized loss of $70,000 ($180,000 amount realized − $250,000 adjusted basis) is disallowed at the time of the sale to her brother.

   b.   Explain why Amos records neither a recognized gain nor a recognized loss on his sale of the land.

   c.   How does the related-party disallowance rule affect the total gain or loss recognized by the family unit?

   d.   Which party wins and which party loses, in a Federal income tax sense?

   e.   How could Marilyn have avoided the loss disallowance on her sale of the land?

14. **LO.4, 5** Comment on the following transactions.

   a.   Mort owns 500 shares of Pear, Inc. stock with an adjusted basis of $22,000. On July 28, 2020, he sells 100 shares for $3,000. On August 16, 2020, he purchases another 100 shares for $3,400. Explain why Mort's realized loss of $1,400 ($3,000 − $4,400) on the July 28 sale is not recognized and his adjusted basis for the 100 shares purchased on August 16 is $4,800.

   b.   Explain how and why your answer in part (a) would change if Mort purchased the 100 shares on December 27, 2020, rather than on August 16, 2020.

15. **LO.6** Which of the following currently qualify as like-kind exchanges under § 1031?

   a.   Improved for unimproved real estate.

   b.   Rental house for personal residence.

   c.   Business land for rental house (held for investment).

   d.   Warehouse for office building (both used for business).

   e.   Truck for computer (both used in business).

   f.   Rental house for land (both held for investment).

   g.   Office furniture for office equipment (both used in business).

   h.   Unimproved land in Jackson, Mississippi, for unimproved land in Toledo, Spain.

   i.   General partnership interest for a general partnership interest.

Critical Thinking   16. **LO.6** Ross would like to dispose of some land he acquired five years ago because he believes it will not continue to appreciate. Its value has increased by $50,000 over the five-year period. He also intends to sell stock that has declined in value by $50,000 during the eight-month period he has owned it.

   Ross has four offers to acquire the stock and land. Identify the tax issues relevant to Ross in disposing of this land and stock.

   Buyer 1:   Exchange land.
   Buyer 2:   Purchase land for cash.
   Buyer 3:   Exchange stock.
   Buyer 4:   Purchase stock for cash.

17. **LO.6** Edith exchanges a building and land used in her business for land and stock of Teal, Inc. If Edith had sold her building and land, she would have had a realized gain. Explain why the new land will have a different holding period than the stock.

18. **LO.6** Mortgaged real estate may be received in a like-kind exchange. If the taxpayer's mortgage is assumed, what effect does the mortgage have on the recognition of realized gain? On the basis of the real estate received?

19. **LO.7** Sheila's appreciated property is involuntarily converted. She receives insurance proceeds equal to the fair market value of the property. What is the minimum amount Sheila must reinvest in qualifying property to defer recognition of realized gain?

20. **LO.7** Vera owns an office building that she leases to tenants. If the building is destroyed by a tornado, is the *functional use test* or the *taxpayer use test* applied as to replacement property? Explain the differences between the two tests.

21. **LO.7** Reba, a calendar year taxpayer, owns an office building that she uses in her business. The building is involuntarily converted on November 15, 2020. On January 5, 2021, Reba receives enough proceeds to produce a realized gain. What is the latest date she can replace the building and qualify for § 1033 postponement treatment if the conversion event is:

    a. A flood?

    b. A condemnation?

    c. A tornado?

22. **LO.7** Bob is notified by the city public housing authority on May 3, 2020, that his apartment building is going to be condemned as part of an urban renewal project. On June 1, 2020, Carol offers to buy the building from Bob. Bob sells the building to Carol on June 30, 2020. Condemnation occurs on September 1, 2020, and Carol receives the condemnation proceeds from the city. Both Bob and Carol are calendar year taxpayers.

    a. What is the earliest date on which Bob can dispose of the building and qualify for involuntary conversion treatment?

    b. Does the sale to Carol qualify as an involuntary conversion? Why or why not?

    c. What is the latest date on which Carol can acquire qualifying replacement property and qualify for postponement of the realized gain?

    d. What type of property will be qualifying replacement property?

23. **LO.7** A warehouse owned by Martha and used in her business (i.e., to store inven-   *Critical Thinking*
tory) is being condemned by the city to provide a right-of-way for a highway. The warehouse has appreciated by $180,000 based on Martha's estimate of its fair market value. In the negotiations, the city is offering $35,000 less than what Martha believes the property is worth.

    Alan, a real estate broker, has offered to purchase Martha's property for $20,000 more than the city's offer. Martha plans to invest the proceeds she will receive in an office building she will lease to various tenants.

    a. Identify the relevant tax issues for Martha.

    b. Would the answer in part (a) change if Martha's warehouse was property being held for investment rather than being used in her business? Explain.

24. **LO.8** To qualify for exclusion treatment on the sale of a principal residence, the residence must have been owned and used by the taxpayer for at least two years during the five-year period ending on the date of the sale. Are there any exceptions to this provision? Explain.

Computational Exercises

25. **LO.1** Sally owns real property for which the annual property taxes are $9,000. She sells the property to Kate on March 9, 2020, for $550,000. Kate pays the real property taxes for the entire year on October 1, 2020.

    a. How much of the property taxes can be deducted by Sally and how much by Kate?

    b. What effect does the property tax apportionment have on Kate's adjusted basis in the property?

    c. What effect does the apportionment have on Sally's amount realized from the sale?

    d. How would the answers in parts (b) and (c) differ if Sally paid the taxes?

26. **LO.1** Melba purchases land from Adrian. Melba gives Adrian $225,000 in cash and agrees to pay Adrian an additional $400,000 one year later plus interest at 5%.

    a.   What is Melba's adjusted basis for the land at the acquisition date?

    b.   What is Melba's adjusted basis for the land one year later?

27. **LO.1** On July 1, 2020, Katrina purchased tax-exempt bonds (face value of $75,000) for $82,000. The bonds mature in five years, and the annual interest rate is 3%.

    a.   How much interest income and/or interest expense must Katrina report in 2020, assuming that straight-line amortization is appropriate?

    b.   What is Katrina's adjusted basis for the bonds on January 1, 2021?

28. **LO.3** Luciana, a nonshareholder, purchases a condominium from her employer for $85,000. The fair market value of the condominium is $120,000. What is Luciana's basis in the condominium and the amount of any income as a result of this purchase?

29. **LO.3** Sebastian purchases two pieces of equipment for $100,000. Appraisals of the equipment indicate that the fair market value of the first piece of equipment is $72,000 and that of the second piece of equipment is $108,000. What is Sebastian's basis in these two assets?

30. **LO.3** Juliana purchased land three years ago for $50,000. She gave the land to Tom, her brother, in the current year, when the fair market value was $70,000. No gift tax is paid on the transfer. Tom subsequently sells the property for $63,000.

    a.   What is Tom's basis in the land, and what is his realized gain or loss on the sale?

    b.   Assume instead that the land has a fair market value of $45,000 and that Tom sold the land for $43,000. Now what is Tom's basis in the land, and what is his realized gain or loss on the sale?

31. **LO.4** Lisa sells business property with an adjusted basis of $130,000 to her son, Alfred, for its fair market value of $100,000.

    a.   What is Lisa's realized and recognized gain or loss?

    b.   What is Alfred's recognized gain or loss if he subsequently sells the property for $138,000? For $80,000?

32. **LO.4** Arianna's personal residence has an adjusted basis of $230,000 and a fair market value of $210,000. Arianna converts the personal residence to rental property. What is Arianna's gain basis? What is her loss basis?

33. **LO.4** Peyton sells an office building and the associated land on May 1 of the current year. Under the terms of the sales contract, Peyton is to receive $1,600,000 in cash. The purchaser is to assume Peyton's mortgage of $950,000 on the property. To enable the purchaser to obtain adequate financing, Peyton is to pay the $9,000 in points charged by the lender. The broker's commission on the sale is $75,000. What is Peyton's amount realized?

34. **LO.6, 9** Vijay owns land (adjusted basis of $40,000) that he uses in his business. He exchanges the land and $20,000 in cash for a different parcel of land worth $50,000. May Vijay avoid like-kind exchange treatment to recognize his realized loss of $10,000? Explain.

35. **LO.6** In June 2020, Sue exchanges a sport-utility vehicle (adjusted basis of $16,000; fair market value of $19,500) for cash of $2,000 and a pickup truck (fair market value of $17,500). Both vehicles are for business use. Sue believes that her basis for the truck is $17,500. Is Sue correct? Why or why not?

36. **LO.6** Logan and Jonathan exchange land, and the exchange qualifies as like kind under § 1031. Because Logan's land (adjusted basis of $85,000) is worth $100,000 and Jonathan's land has a fair market value of $80,000, Jonathan also gives Logan cash of $20,000.
    a. What is Logan's recognized gain?
    b. Assume instead that Jonathan's land is worth $90,000 and he gives Logan $10,000 cash. Now what is Logan's recognized gain?

37. **LO.7** On June 5, 2020, Brown, Inc., a calendar year taxpayer, receives cash of $750,000 from the county upon condemnation of its warehouse building (adjusted basis of $500,000 and fair market value of $750,000).
    a. What must Brown do to qualify for § 1033 postponement of gain treatment?
    b. How would your advice to Brown differ if the adjusted basis was $795,000?

38. **LO.7** Camilo's property, with an adjusted basis of $155,000, is condemned by the state. Camilo receives property with a fair market value of $180,000 as compensation for the property taken.
    a. What is Camilo's realized and recognized gain?
    b. What is the basis of the replacement property?

39. **LO.7** On February 24, 2020, Allison's building, with an adjusted basis of $1,300,000 (and used in her trade or business), is destroyed by fire. On March 31, 2020, she receives an insurance reimbursement of $1,650,000 for the loss. Allison invests $1,550,000 in a new building and buys stock with the balance of insurance proceeds. Allison is a calendar year taxpayer.
    a. By what date must Allison make the new investment to qualify for the nonrecognition election?
    b. Assuming that the replacement property qualifies as similar or related in service or use, what are Allison's realized gain, recognized gain, and basis in the replacement building?

40. **LO.8** Gary, who is single, sells his principal residence (owned and occupied by him for seven years) in November 2020 for a realized gain of $148,000. He had purchased a more expensive new residence eight months prior to the sale. He anticipates that he will occupy this new house as his principal residence for only about 18 additional months. He expects it to appreciate substantially while he owns it.
    Gary would like to recognize the realized gain on the 2020 sale to offset a large investment loss from the sale of stock. Can he recognize the realized gain of $148,000 on the sale of his principal residence in 2020? Explain.

41. **LO.8** Constanza, who is single, sells her current personal residence (adjusted basis of $165,000) for $450,000. She has owned and lived in the house for 30 years. Her selling expenses are $22,500. What is Constanza's realized and recognized gain?

42. **LO.8** On August 31, 2019, Harvey and Ling, who file a joint return and live in Charleston, South Carolina, sell their personal residence, which they have owned and lived in for 10 years. The realized gain of $292,000 was excluded under § 121. They purchased another personal residence in Charleston for $480,000 on September 1, 2019. However, in 2020, Harvey's employer transfers him to Houston, Texas. The couple sells the Charleston home on February 28, 2020, and purchases a new home in Houston. The realized gain on the second sale is $180,000. What is Harvey and Ling's recognized gain on the second sale?

Problems

43. **LO.1** Anne sold her home for $290,000 in 2020. Selling expenses were $17,400. She purchased it in 2014 for $200,000. During the period of ownership, Anne had done the following:

    • Deducted $50,500 office-in-home expenses, which included $4,500 in depreciation. (Refer to text Section 9-6a.)

    • Deducted a casualty loss in 2016 for residential trees destroyed by a hurricane (her county was declared a Federal disaster area). The total loss was $19,000 (after the $100 floor and the 10%-of-AGI floor), and Anne's insurance company reimbursed her for $13,500. (Refer to text Section 7-3.)

    • Paid street paving assessment of $7,000 and added sidewalks for $8,000.

    • Installed an elevator for medical reasons. The total cost was $20,000, and Anne deducted $13,000 as medical expenses. (Refer to text Section 10-1b.)

    What is Anne's realized gain?

44. **LO.1** Kareem bought a rental house in March 2015 for $300,000, of which $50,000 is allocated to the land and $250,000 to the building. Early in 2017, he had a tennis court built in the backyard at a cost of $7,500. Kareem has deducted $30,900 for depreciation on the house and $1,300 for depreciation on the court. In January 2020, he sells the house and tennis court for $330,000 cash.

    a. What is Kareem's realized gain or loss?

    b. If an original mortgage of $80,000 is still outstanding and the buyer assumes the mortgage in addition to the cash payment, what is Kareem's realized gain or loss?

    c. If the buyer takes the property subject to the $80,000 mortgage rather than assuming it, what is Kareem's realized gain or loss?

45. **LO.1** Norm is negotiating the sale of a tract of his land to Pat. Use the following classification scheme to classify each of the items contained in the proposed sales contract.

Legend	
DARN =	Decreases amount realized by Norm
IARN =	Increases amount realized by Norm
DABN =	Decreases adjusted basis to Norm
IABN =	Increases adjusted basis to Norm
DABP =	Decreases adjusted basis to Pat
IABP =	Increases adjusted basis to Pat

    a. Norm is to receive cash of $50,000.

    b. Norm is to receive Pat's note payable for $25,000, payable in three years.

    c. Pat assumes Norm's mortgage of $5,000 on the land.

    d. Pat agrees to pay the realtor's sales commission of $8,000.

    e. Pat agrees to pay the property taxes on the land for the entire year. If each party paid his or her respective share, Norm's share would be $1,000 and Pat's share would be $3,000.

    f. Pat pays legal fees of $500.

    g. Norm pays legal fees of $750.

46. **LO.1, 2** Liam owns a personal use boat that has a fair market value of $35,000 and an adjusted basis of $45,000. Liam's AGI is $100,000. Calculate the realized and recognized gain or loss if:

    a. Liam sells the boat for $35,000.

    b. Liam exchanges the boat for another boat worth $35,000.

c. The boat is stolen and Liam receives insurance proceeds of $35,000.

d. Would your answer in part (a) change if the fair market value and the selling price of the boat were $48,000? Explain.

47. **LO.1** Chee purchases Tan, Inc. bonds for $108,000 on January 2, 2020. The face value of the bonds is $100,000; the maturity date is December 31, 2024; and the annual interest rate is 5%. Chee will amortize the premium only if he is required to do so. Chee sells the bonds on July 1, 2022, for $106,000.

a. Determine the interest income Chee should report for 2020.

b. Calculate Chee's recognized gain or loss on the sale of the bonds in 2022.

48. **LO.1, 2** Which of the following results in a recognized gain or loss?

a. Kay sells her vacation cabin (adjusted basis of $100,000) for $150,000.

b. Hernan sells his personal residence (adjusted basis of $150,000) for $100,000.

c. Carl's personal residence (adjusted basis of $65,000) is condemned by the city. He receives condemnation proceeds of $55,000.

d. Olga's land is worth $40,000 at the end of the year. She had purchased the land six months earlier for $25,000.

e. Vera's personal vehicle (adjusted basis of $22,000) is stolen. She receives $23,000 from the insurance company and does not plan to replace the automobile.

f. Jerry sells used clothing (adjusted basis of $500) to a thrift store for $50.

49. **LO.1, 2** Yancy's personal residence is condemned as part of an urban renewal project. His adjusted basis for the residence is $480,000. He receives condemnation proceeds of $460,000 and invests the proceeds in stocks and bonds.

a. Calculate Yancy's realized and recognized gain or loss.

b. If the condemnation proceeds are $505,000, what are Yancy's realized and recognized gain or loss?

c. What are Yancy's realized and recognized gain or loss in part (a) if the house was rental property?

50. **LO.3** Buddy Morgan is a real estate agent for Coastal Estates, a residential real estate development. Because of his outstanding sales performance, Buddy is permitted to buy a lot for $300,000 that normally would sell for $500,000. Buddy is the only real estate agent for Coastal Estates who is permitted to do so.   Communications

a. Does Buddy recognize gross income from the transaction? Explain.

b. What is Buddy's adjusted basis for the land?

c. Write a letter to Buddy informing him of the income tax consequences of his acquisition of the lot. His address is 100 Tower Road, San Diego, CA 92182.

51. **LO.1, 2, 3** Karen Samuels (Social Security number 123-45-6789) makes the following purchases and sales of stock:

Transaction	Date	Number of Shares	Company	Price per Share
Purchase	1-1-2018	300	MDG	$ 75
Purchase	6-1-2018	150	GRU	300
Purchase	11-1-2018	60	MDG	70
Sale	12-3-2018	200	MDG	80
Purchase	3-1-2019	120	GRU	375
Sale	8-1-2019	90	GRU	330
Sale	1-1-2020	150	MDG	90
Sale	2-1-2020	75	GRU	500

Assuming that Karen is unable to identify the specific lots that are sold with the original purchase, determine the recognized gain or loss on each type of stock.

a. As of July 1, 2018.

b. As of December 31, 2018.

c. As of December 31, 2019.

d. As of July 1, 2020.

e. Form 8949 and Schedule D (Form 1040) are used to report sales of capital assets (which include stock sales). Go to the IRS website, and download the 2019 Form 8949 and Schedule D (Form 1040). Then complete the forms for part (c) of this problem, assuming that the brokerage firm did not report Karen's basis to the IRS [complete Schedule D (Form 1040) through line 16].

52. **LO.1, 2, 3** Kevin purchases 1,000 shares of Bluebird Corporation stock on October 3, 2020, for $300,000. On December 12, 2020, Kevin purchases an additional 750 shares of Bluebird stock for $210,000. According to market quotations, Bluebird stock is selling for $285 per share on December 31, 2020. Kevin sells 500 shares of Bluebird stock on March 1, 2021, for $162,500.

a. What is the adjusted basis of Kevin's Bluebird stock on December 31, 2020?

b. What is Kevin's recognized gain or loss from the sale of Bluebird stock on March 1, 2021, assuming that the shares sold are from the shares purchased on December 12, 2020?

c. What is Kevin's recognized gain or loss from the sale of Bluebird stock on March 1, 2021, assuming that Kevin cannot adequately identify the shares sold?

Communications   53. **LO.3** Rod Clooney purchases Sian Mitchell's sole proprietorship for $990,000 on August 15, 2020. The assets of the business are:

Asset	Agnes's Adjusted Basis	FMV
Accounts receivable	$ 70,000	$ 70,000
Inventory	90,000	100,000
Equipment	150,000	160,000
Furniture and fixtures	95,000	130,000
Building	190,000	250,000
Land	25,000	75,000
Total	$620,000	$785,000

a. Calculate Sian's realized and recognized gain.

b. Determine Rod's basis for each of the assets.

c. Write a letter to Rod informing him of the tax consequences of the purchase. His address is 300 Riverview Drive, Delaware, OH 43015.

54. **LO.1, 2, 3** Roberto has received various gifts over the years and has decided to dispose of several of these assets. What is the recognized gain or loss from each of the following transactions, assuming that no Federal gift tax was paid when the gifts were made?

a. In 1981, he received land worth $32,000. The donor's adjusted basis was $35,000. Roberto sells the land for $95,000 in 2020.

b. In 1986, he received stock in Gold Company. The donor's adjusted basis was $19,000. The fair market value on the date of the gift was $34,000. Roberto sells the stock for $40,000 in 2020.

c. In 1992, he received land worth $15,000. The donor's adjusted basis was $20,000. Roberto sells the land for $9,000 in 2020.

d. In 2013, he received stock worth $30,000. The donor's adjusted basis was $42,000. Roberto sells the stock for $38,000 in 2020.

e. Build a spreadsheet-based solution that provides the solution to parts (a) through (d) above and uses only the donor's basis, the fair market value at the time of the gift, and the selling price as inputs. You may want to use the IF and AND functions together.

55. **LO.1, 2, 3** Nicky receives a car from Sam as a gift. Sam paid $48,000 for the car. Sam had used it for business purposes and had deducted $10,000 for depreciation up to the time she gave the car to Nicky. The fair market value of the car is $33,000.

   a. Assuming that Nicky uses the car for business purposes, what is her basis for depreciation?

   b. Assume that Nicky deducts depreciation of $6,500 and then sells the car for $32,500. What is her recognized gain or loss?

   c. Assume that Nicky deducts depreciation of $6,500 and then sells the car for $20,000. What is her recognized gain or loss?

56. **LO.3** Margo receives a gift of real estate with an adjusted basis of $175,000 and a fair market value of $100,000. The donor paid gift tax of $15,000 on the transfer. If Margo later sells the property for $110,000, what is her recognized gain or loss?

57. **LO.3** On September 18, 2020, Gerald received land and a building from Luna as a gift. No gift tax was paid on the transfer. Luna's records show the following:

Asset	Adjusted Basis	FMV
Land	$100,000	$212,000
Building	80,000	100,000

   a. Determine Gerald's adjusted basis for the land and building.

   b. Assume instead that the fair market value of the land was $87,000 and that of the building was $65,000. Determine Gerald's adjusted basis for the land and building.

58. **LO.1, 2, 3, 9** Ira Cook is planning to make a charitable contribution to the Boy Scouts. He will contribute Crystal, Inc. stock worth $20,000. The stock has an adjusted basis of $15,000. A friend has suggested that Ira sell the stock and contribute the $20,000 in proceeds rather than contribute the stock.

Critical Thinking

Communications

   a. Should Ira follow the friend's advice? Why or why not?

   b. Assume that the fair market value is only $13,000. In this case, should Ira follow the friend's advice? Why or why not?

   c. Rather than make a charitable contribution to the Boy Scouts, Ira is going to make a gift to Nancy, his niece. Advise Ira regarding parts (a) and (b).

   d. Write a letter to Ira regarding whether in part (a) he should sell the stock and contribute the cash or contribute the stock. He has informed you that he purchased the stock six years ago. Ira's address is 500 Ireland Avenue, DeKalb, IL 60115.

59. **LO.3** As sole heir, Dazie receives all of Mary's property (adjusted basis of $11,400,000 and fair market value of $13,820,000). Six months after Mary's death, the fair market value is $13,835,000.

   a. Can the executor of Mary's estate elect the alternate valuation date and amount? Explain.

   b. What is Dazie's basis for the property?

   c. Assume instead that the fair market value six months after Mary's death is $13,800,000. Respond to parts (a) and (b).

60. **LO.3** Dan bought a hotel for $2,600,000 in January 2016. In May 2020, he died and left the hotel to Ed. While Dan owned the hotel, he deducted $289,000 of cost recovery. The fair market value in May 2020 was $2,800,000. The fair market value six months later was $2,850,000.

   a. What is the basis of the property to Ed?

   b. What is the basis of the property to Ed if the fair market value six months later was $2,500,000 (not $2,850,000) and the objective of the executor was to minimize the estate tax liability?

Communications   61. **LO.3** Helene and Pauline are twin sisters who live in Louisiana and Mississippi, respectively. Helene is married to Frank, and Pauline is married to Richard. Frank and Richard are killed in an auto accident in 2020 while returning from a sporting event.

   Helene and Frank jointly owned some farmland in Louisiana, a community property state (value of $940,000, cost of $450,000). Pauline and Richard jointly owned some farmland in Mississippi, a common law state (value of $940,000, cost of $450,000). Assume that all of Frank's and Richard's property passes to their surviving wives.

   a. Calculate Helene's basis in the land.

   b. Calculate Pauline's basis in the land.

   c. What causes the difference? Summarize your answer in a one-paragraph e-mail to your instructor.

Decision Making   62. **LO.3, 4** Sheila sells land to Elaine, her sister, for the fair market value of $40,000. Six months later when the land is worth $45,000, Elaine gives it to Jacob, her son. (No gift tax resulted.) Shortly thereafter, Jacob sells the land for $48,000.

   a. Assuming that Sheila's adjusted basis for the land is $24,000, what are Sheila's and Jacob's recognized gain or loss on the sales?

   b. Assuming that Sheila's adjusted basis for the land is $60,000, what are Sheila's and Jacob's recognized gain or loss on the sales?

63. **LO.1, 2, 3, 4** Louis owns three pieces of land with an adjusted basis as follows: parcel A, $75,000; parcel B, $125,000; and parcel C, $175,000. Louis sells parcel A to his uncle for $50,000, parcel B to his partner for $120,000, and parcel C to his mother for $150,000.

   a. What is the recognized gain or loss from the sale of each parcel?

   b. If Louis's uncle eventually sells his land for $90,000, what is his recognized gain or loss?

   c. If Louis's partner eventually sells his land for $130,000, what is his recognized gain or loss?

   d. If Louis's mother eventually sells her land for $165,000, what is her recognized gain or loss?

Decision Making   64. **LO.1, 2, 3, 4** Tyneka inherited 1,000 shares of Aqua, Inc. stock from Joe. Joe's basis was $35,000, and the fair market value on July 1, 2020 (the date of death), was $45,000. The shares were distributed to Tyneka on July 15, 2020. Tyneka sold the stock on July 30, 2021, for $33,000. After giving the matter more thought, she decides that Aqua is a good investment and purchases 1,000 shares for $30,000 on August 20, 2021.

   a. What is Tyneka's basis for the 1,000 shares purchased on August 20, 2021?

   b. Could Tyneka have obtained different tax consequences in part (a) if she had sold the 1,000 shares on December 27, 2020, and purchased the 1,000 shares on January 5, 2021? Explain.

65. **LO.1, 2, 4** Abby's home had a basis of $360,000 ($160,000 attributable to the land) and a fair market value of $340,000 ($155,000 attributable to the land) when she converted 70% of it to business use by opening a bed-and-breakfast. Four

years after the conversion, Abby sells the home for $500,000 ($165,000 attributable to the land).

a. Calculate Abby's basis for gain, loss, and cost recovery for the portion of her personal residence that was converted to business use.

b. Calculate the cost recovery deducted by Abby during the four-year period of business use, assuming that the bed-and-breakfast is opened on January 1 of year 1 and the house is sold on December 31 of year 4.

c. What is Abby's recognized gain or loss on the sale of the business use portion?

66. **LO.4** Surendra's personal residence originally cost $340,000 (ignoring the value of the land). After living in the house for five years, he converts it to rental property. At the date of conversion, the fair market value of the house is $320,000. As to the rental property, calculate Surendra's basis for:

Critical Thinking

Communications

a. Loss.

b. Depreciation.

c. Gain.

d. Could Surendra have obtained better tax results if he had sold his personal residence for $320,000 and then purchased another house for $320,000 to hold as rental property? Explain.

e. Summarize your answer to this problem in an e-mail to your instructor.

67. **LO.6** Katrina owns undeveloped land with an adjusted basis of $300,000. She exchanges it for other undeveloped land worth $750,000.

a. What are Katrina's realized and recognized gain or loss?

b. What is Katrina's basis in the undeveloped land she receives?

c. Would the answers in parts (a) and (b) change if Katrina exchanged the undeveloped land for land and a building? Explain.

68. **LO.6** Daniela Fletcher owns undeveloped land (adjusted basis of $80,000 and fair market value of $92,000) on the East Coast. On January 4, 2020, she exchanges it with Lisa Martin (an unrelated party) for undeveloped land on the West Coast and $3,000 cash. Lisa has an adjusted basis of $72,000 for her land, and its fair market value is $89,000. Because the real estate market on the East Coast is thriving, on September 1, 2021, Lisa sells the land she acquired for $120,000.

Critical Thinking

Communications

a. What are Daniela's recognized gain or loss and adjusted basis for the West Coast land on January 4, 2020?

b. What are Lisa's recognized gain or loss and adjusted basis for the East Coast land on January 4, 2020?

c. What is Lisa's recognized gain or loss from the September 1, 2021 sale?

d. What effect does Lisa's 2021 sale have on Daniela?

e. Write a letter to Daniela advising her of the Federal income tax consequences of this exchange. Her address is The Corral, El Paso, TX 79968.

69. **LO.6** Sarah exchanges a building and land (used in her business) for Tyler's land and building and some equipment (used in his business). The assets have the following characteristics:

	Adjusted Basis	Fair Market Value
Sarah's real property	$120,000	$300,000
Tyler's real property	60,000	220,000
Equipment	50,000	80,000

a. What are Sarah's recognized gain or loss and basis for the land and building and equipment acquired from Tyler?

b. What are Tyler's recognized gain or loss and basis for the land and building acquired from Sarah?

Critical Thinking   70.   **LO.6, 9** In two unrelated transactions, Laura exchanges property that qualifies for like-kind exchange treatment. In the first exchange, Laura gives up land purchased in May 2018 (adjusted basis of $20,000; fair market value of $17,000) in exchange for a different parcel of land (fair market value of $15,000) and $2,000 cash. In the second exchange, Laura receives a parking garage (to be used in her business) with a fair market value of $50,000 in exchange for a plot of land she had held for investment. The land was purchased in April 2012 for $12,000 and has a current fair market value of $48,000. In addition to transferring the land, Laura pays an additional $2,000 to the other party.

a.   What is Laura's adjusted basis for the new parcel of land?

b.   When does the holding period begin?

c.   What is Laura's adjusted basis for the parking garage?

d.   When does the holding period begin?

e.   How could Laura structure either of the transactions differently to produce better tax consequences?

71.   **LO.6** What is the basis of the new property in each of the following exchanges?

a.   Apartment building held for investment (adjusted basis of $145,000) for office building to be held for investment (fair market value of $225,000).

b.   Land and building used as a barbershop (adjusted basis of $190,000) for land and building used as a grocery store (fair market value of $350,000).

c.   Office building (adjusted basis of $45,000) for bulldozer (fair market value of $42,000), both held for business use.

d.   IBM common stock (adjusted basis of $20,000) for ExxonMobil common stock (fair market value of $28,000).

e.   Rental house (adjusted basis of $90,000) for mountain cabin to be held for rental use (fair market value of $225,000).

f.   General partnership interest (adjusted basis of $400,000) for a limited partnership interest (fair market value of $580,000).

72.   **LO.6** Suni owns land (adjusted basis of $90,000; fair market value of $125,000) that she uses in her business. She exchanges it for another parcel of land (worth $100,000) and stock (worth $25,000). Determine Suni's:

a.   Realized and recognized gain or loss on the exchange.

b.   Basis in the new land.

c.   Basis in the stock she received.

73.   **LO.6** Ed owns investment land with an adjusted basis of $35,000. Polly has offered to purchase the land from Ed for $175,000 for use in a real estate development. The amount offered by Polly is $10,000 in excess of what Ed perceives as the fair market value of the land. Ed would like to dispose of the land to Polly but does not want to incur the tax liability that would result. He identifies an office building with a fair market value of $175,000 that he would like to acquire. Polly purchases the office building and then exchanges the office building for Ed's land.

a.   Calculate Ed's realized and recognized gain on the exchange and his basis for the office building.

b.   Calculate Polly's realized and recognized gain on the exchange and her basis in the land.

Decision Making   74.   **LO.6** Steve owns real estate (adjusted basis of $12,000 and fair market value of $15,000), which he uses in his business. Steve sells the real estate for $15,000 to Aubry (a dealer) and then purchases a new parcel of land for $15,000 from Joan (also a dealer). The new parcel of land would normally qualify as like-kind property.

a.   What are Steve's realized and recognized gain on the sale of the land he sold to Aubry?

b.   What is Steve's basis for the land he purchased from Joan?

c.   What factors would motivate Steve to sell his land to Aubry and purchase the land from Joan rather than exchange one parcel of land for the other?

d.   Assume that the adjusted basis of Steve's original parcel of land is $15,000 and the fair market value of both parcels of land is $12,000. Respond to parts (a) through (c).

75. **LO.6, 9** Tom Howard and Frank Pérez are good friends (and former college roommates). Each owns investment property in the other's hometown (Tom lives in Kalamazoo, MI; Frank lives in Austin, TX). To make their lives easier, they decide to exchange the investment properties. Under the terms of the exchange, Frank will transfer realty (20 acres of unimproved land; adjusted basis of $52,000; fair market value of $80,000) and Tom will exchange realty (25 acres of unimproved land; adjusted basis of $60,000; fair market value of $92,000). Tom's property is subject to a mortgage of $12,000 that will be assumed by Frank.

Critical Thinking
Communications

a.   What are Frank's and Tom's recognized gains?

b.   What are their adjusted bases?

c.   As an alternative, Frank has proposed that rather than assuming the mortgage, he will transfer cash of $12,000 to Tom. Tom would use the cash to pay off the mortgage. In an e-mail, advise Tom on whether this alternative would be beneficial to him from a tax perspective.

d.   Assuming that Tom and Frank proceed with the original exchange [rather than the alternative in part (c)], complete Form 8824 (Parts I and III) for Tom. Assume that the exchange occurs on September 16, 2019 (Tom acquired his 25-acre parcel on February 15, 2011). Tom's Social Security number is 123-45-6789.

76. **LO.6** Determine the realized, recognized, and postponed gain or loss and the new basis for each of the following like-kind exchanges.

Critical Thinking
Communications

	Adjusted Basis of Old Asset	Boot Given	Fair Market Value of New Asset	Boot Received
a.	$ 7,000	$ –0–	$12,000	$4,000
b.	14,000	2,000	15,000	–0–
c.	3,000	7,000	8,000	500
d.	15,000	–0–	29,000	–0–
e.	10,000	–0–	11,000	1,000
f.	17,000	–0–	14,000	–0–

g.   Create a Microsoft Excel spreadsheet that—by entering the fair market value and basis of property given up and the fair market value of property received—will compute (1) realized gain or loss, (2) boot received, (3) boot given, (4) gain (loss) recognized, (5) gain (loss) deferred, and (6) the basis of like-kind property received. In separate tabs, the spreadsheet should apply the "simplified method" and the "§ 1031(d) method." Ignore the implications of debt and depreciation. Test your spreadsheet using the data in this problem. E-mail your spreadsheet to your instructor along with a brief summary of how you built the spreadsheet.

77. **LO.7** Hakeem's roadside vegetable stand (adjusted basis of $275,000) is destroyed by a tractor-trailer accident. He receives insurance proceeds of $240,000 ($300,000 fair market value − $60,000 coinsurance). Hakeem immediately uses the proceeds plus additional cash of $45,000 to build another roadside vegetable stand at the same location. What are the Federal income tax consequences to Hakeem?

78. **LO.7** Albert owns 100 acres of land on which he grows spruce trees. His adjusted basis for the land is $100,000. He receives condemnation proceeds of $10,000 when the city's new beltway takes 5 acres along the eastern boundary of his property.

He also receives a severance award of $6,000 associated with the possible harmful effects of exhaust fumes on his trees. Albert invests the $16,000 in a growth mutual fund. Determine the tax consequences to Albert of the:

a.   Condemnation proceeds.

b.   Severance award.

79. **LO.7** Mitchell, a calendar year taxpayer, is the sole proprietor of a fast-food restaurant. His adjusted basis for the building and the related land is $450,000. On March 12, 2020, state authorities notify Mitchell that his property is going to be condemned so that the highway can be widened. On June 20, Mitchell's property is officially condemned, and he receives an award of $625,000. Because Mitchell's business has been successful in the past, he would like to reopen the restaurant in a new location.

a.   What is the earliest date Mitchell can acquire a new restaurant and qualify for gain postponement?

b.   On June 30, Mitchell purchases land and a building for $610,000. Assuming that he elects the maximum postponement amount, what is his recognized gain?

c.   What is Mitchell's adjusted basis for the new land and building?

d.   If he does not elect § 1033, what are Mitchell's recognized gain and adjusted basis?

e.   Suppose he invests the $625,000 condemnation proceeds in the stock market on June 30. What is Mitchell's recognized gain?

80. **LO.7** Edith's warehouse (adjusted basis of $450,000) is destroyed by a hurricane in October 2020. Edith, a calendar year taxpayer, receives insurance proceeds of $525,000 in January 2021. Calculate Edith's realized gain or loss, recognized gain or loss, and basis for the replacement property if she:

a.   Acquires a new warehouse for $550,000 in January 2021.

b.   Acquires a new warehouse for $500,000 in January 2021.

c.   Does not acquire replacement property.

Critical Thinking   81. **LO.7** Cabel's warehouse, which has an adjusted basis of $380,000 and a fair market value of $490,000, is condemned by an agency of the Federal government to make way for a highway interchange. The initial condemnation offer is $425,000. After substantial negotiations, the agency agrees to transfer to Cabel a surplus warehouse that is worth $490,000. Cabel is a calendar year taxpayer. The condemnation and related asset transfer occur during September 2020.

a.   What are the recognized gain or loss and the basis of the replacement warehouse if Cabel's objective is to recognize as much gain as possible?

b.   Advise Cabel regarding what he needs to do by what date to achieve his objective.

82. **LO.7** What are the *maximum* postponed gain or loss and the basis for the replacement property for the following involuntary conversions?

	Property	Type of Conversion	Amount Realized	Adjusted Basis	Amount Reinvested
a.	Drugstore (business)	Casualty	$160,000	$130,000	$110,000
b.	Apartments (investment)	Condemned	100,000	125,000	175,000
c.	Grocery store (business)	Casualty	400,000	300,000	450,000
d.	Residence (personal)	Casualty*	16,000	18,000	17,000
e.	Vacant lot (investment)	Condemned	240,000	160,000	220,000
f.	Residence (personal)	Casualty*	20,000	18,000	19,000
g.	Residence (personal)	Condemned	18,000	20,000	26,000
h.	Apartments (investment)	Condemned	150,000	100,000	200,000

* Casualty occurred in a Federally declared disaster area.

83. **LO.7, 9** Wanda, a calendar year taxpayer, owned a building (adjusted basis of   Decision Making
    $250,000) in which she operated a bakery that was destroyed by fire in
    December 2020. She receives insurance proceeds of $290,000 for the building the
    following March. Wanda is considering two options regarding the investment of the
    insurance proceeds. First, she could purchase a local building (suitable for a bakery)
    that is for sale for $275,000. Second, she could buy a new home for $290,000 and
    go back to college and finish her degree.

    a. To minimize her tax liability, which of these alternatives should Wanda choose?
    b. What is the latest date on which Wanda can replace the involuntarily converted
        property to qualify for § 1033?
    c. What is the latest date on which Wanda can replace the involuntarily converted
        property to qualify for § 1033 if the involuntary conversion is a condemnation?

84. **LO.8, 9** Karl purchased his residence on January 2, 2019, for $260,000, after hav-   Critical Thinking
    ing lived in it during 2018 as a tenant under a lease with an option to buy
    clause. On August 1, 2020, Karl sells the residence for $315,000. On June 13, 2020,
    Karl purchases a new residence for $367,000.

    a. What is Karl's recognized gain? His basis for the new residence?
    b. Assume instead that Karl purchased his original residence on January 2, 2018
        (rather than January 2, 2019). What is Karl's recognized gain? His basis for the
        new residence?
    c. In part (a), what could Karl do to minimize his recognized gain?

85. **LO.8** Wesley, who is single, listed his personal residence with a real estate agent on
    March 3, 2020, at a price of $390,000. He rejected several offers in the $350,000
    range during the summer. Finally, on August 16, 2020, he and the purchaser signed
    a contract to sell for $363,000. The sale (i.e., closing) took place on September 7,
    2020. The closing statement showed the following disbursements:

Real estate agent's commission	$ 21,780
Appraisal fee	600
Exterminator's certificate	300
Recording fees	800
Mortgage to First Bank	305,000
Cash to seller	34,520

    Wesley's adjusted basis for the house is $200,000. He owned and occupied the
    house for seven years. On October 1, 2020, Wesley purchases another residence
    for $325,000.

    a. Calculate Wesley's recognized gain on the sale.
    b. What is Wesley's adjusted basis for the new residence?
    c. Assume instead that the selling price is $800,000. What is Wesley's recognized
        gain? His adjusted basis for the new residence?

86. **LO.8** Pedro, age 57, is the sole owner of his principal residence, which he has
    owned and occupied for 10 years. Maria, his spouse, has lived there with
    Pedro for the full 10 years. He sells the house for a realized gain of $340,000.

    a. Can Pedro use the § 121 exclusion if he and Maria file a joint return? If so, what
        are the available amount of the exclusion and the recognized gain?
    b. Can Pedro use the § 121 exclusion if he files a separate return? If so, what are
        the available amount of the exclusion and the recognized gain?
    c. Assume instead that the realized gain is $550,000 and a joint return is filed.
    d. Assume instead that the realized gain is $550,000 and separate returns are filed.
    e. Assume instead that Maria and Pedro have been married for only 18 months and
        that she has lived in his house only since their marriage. They file a joint return.

Communications   87.   **LO.8** Nell, Nina, and Nora Potter, who are sisters, sell their principal residence (owned as tenants in common) in which they have lived for the past 25 years. The youngest of the sisters is age 60. The selling price is $960,000, selling expenses and legal fees are $63,000, and the adjusted basis is $120,000 (the fair market value of the residence when inherited from their parents 25 years ago; they made no capital improvements during the time they held the residence). The sisters plan to move into rental housing and not acquire another residence. Nell has contacted you on behalf of the Potters regarding the tax consequences of the sale.

a.   Write a letter to Nell advising her of the tax consequences and how taxes can be minimized. Nell's address is 100 Oak Avenue, Billings, MT 59101.

b.   Prepare a memo discussing your approach to the situation for the tax files.

Critical Thinking   88.   **LO.8** Lloyd owns a beach house (four years) and a cabin in the mountains (six years). His adjusted basis is $300,000 in the beach house and $315,000 in the mountain cabin. Lloyd also rents a townhouse in the city where he is employed. During the year, he occupies each of the three residences as follows:

Townhouse	135 days
Beach house	155 days
Mountain cabin	75 days

The beach house is close enough to the city so that he can commute to work during the spring and summer. Although this level of occupancy may vary slightly from year to year, it is representative during the time period that Lloyd has owned the two residences.

Because Lloyd plans to retire in several years, he sells both the beach house and the mountain cabin. The mountain cabin is sold on March 3, 2020, for $540,000 (related selling expenses of $35,000). The beach house is sold on December 10, 2020, for $700,000 (related selling expenses of $42,000).

a.   Calculate Lloyd's least allowable recognized gain on the sale of the two residences.

b.   Assume instead that both residences satisfy the two-year ownership and use tests as Lloyd's principal residence. Because the mountain cabin is sold first, can Lloyd apply the § 121 exclusion to the sale of the beach house? Explain.

Critical Thinking   89.   **LO.8, 9** Missy, age 30, has owned her principal residence (adjusted basis of $225,000) for five years. During the first three years of ownership, she occupied it as her principal residence. During the past two years, she was in graduate school and rented the residence. After graduate school, Missy returned to the same location where she previously worked. At this point, she purchased another residence for $400,000 and listed her old residence for sale at $340,000. Due to a slow real estate market, 11 months later Missy finally receives an offer of $330,000.

a.   What is Missy's recognized gain if she immediately accepts the $330,000 offer (i.e., 11 months after the listing date)? Selling expenses are $20,000.

b.   What is Missy's recognized gain if she rejects the $330,000 offer and accepts another offer of $340,000 three months later (i.e., 14 months after the listing date)?

c.   Advise Missy on which offer she should accept (assume that she is in the 24% tax bracket).

Tax Return Problems

90. Alton Newman, age 67, is married and files a joint return with his wife, Clair, age 65. Alton and Clair are both retired, and during 2019, they received Social Security benefits of $10,000. Both Alton and Clair are covered by Medicare. Alton's Social Security number is 111-11-1119, and Clair's is 123-45-6786. They reside at 210 College Drive, Columbia, SC 29201.

Tax Forms Problem

Alton, who retired on January 1, 2019, receives benefits from a qualified pension plan of $2,750 a month for life. His total contributions to the plan (none of which were deductible) were $168,250. In January 2019, he received a bonus of $2,000 from his former employer for service performed in 2018. No income taxes were withheld on this bonus by his former employer (Amalgamated Industries, Inc.; EIN 12-3456789; 114 Main Street, Columbia, SC 29201). Although Amalgamated Industries, Inc., accrued the bonus in 2018, it was not paid until 2019.

Clair, who retired on December 31, 2018, started receiving benefits of $1,400 a month on January 1, 2019. Her contributions to the qualified pension plan (none of which were deductible) were $74,100.

On September 27, 2019, Alton and Clair received a pro rata 10% stock dividend on 600 shares of stock they owned. They had bought the stock on March 5, 2012, for $20 a share. On December 16, 2019, they sold the 60 dividend shares for $55 a share.

On October 10, 2019, Clair sold the car she had used in commuting to and from work for $17,000. She had paid $31,000 for the car in 2013.

On July 14, 2011, Alton and Clair received a gift of 1,000 shares of stock from their son, Thomas. Thomas's basis in the stock was $35 a share (fair market value at the date of gift was $25). No gift tax was paid on the transfer. Alton and Clair sold the stock on October 8, 2019, for $24 a share.

On May 1, 2019, Clair's mother died, and Clair inherited her personal residence. In February 2019, her mother had paid the property taxes for 2019 of $2,100. The residence had a fair market value of $235,000 and an adjusted basis to the mother of $160,000 on the date of her death. Clair listed the house with a real estate agent, who estimated it was worth $240,000 as of December 31, 2019.

Clair received rent income of $6,000 on a beach house she inherited three years ago from her uncle Charles. She had rented the property for one week during the July 4 weekend and one week during the Thanksgiving holiday. Charles's adjusted basis in the beach house was $150,000, and its fair market value on the date of his death was $240,000. Clair and Alton used the beach house for personal purposes for 56 days during the year. Expenses associated with the house were $3,700 for utilities, maintenance, and repairs; $2,200 for property taxes; and $800 for insurance. There are no mortgages on the property.

Clair and Alton paid estimated Federal income tax of $2,000 and had itemized deductions of $6,800 (excluding any itemized deductions associated with the beach house). They did not engage in any virtual currency transactions during the year. If they have overpaid their Federal income tax, they want the amount refunded. Both Clair and Alton want $3 to go to the Presidential Election Campaign Fund.

Compute their net tax payable or refund due for 2019, using the appropriate tax rate schedule (not the Tax Tables). If you use tax forms for your computations, you will need at a minimum Form 1040–SR and Schedule D. Suggested software: ProConnect Tax Online.

Tax Forms Problem

91. Devon Bishop, age 45, is single. He lives at 1507 Rose Lane, Albuquerque, NM 87131. His Social Security number is 111-11-1117. Devon did not engage in any virtual currency transactions during the year, and he does not want $3 to go to the Presidential Election Campaign Fund.

Devon's wife, Ariane, passed away in 2015. Devon's son, Tom, who is age 18, resides with Devon. Tom's Social Security number is 123-45-6788.

Devon owns a sole proprietorship for which he uses the accrual method of accounting and maintains no inventory; the business operates as Devon's Copy Shop, 422 E. Main Street, Albuquerque, NM 87131, IRS business activity code: 453990. His revenues and expenses for 2019 are as follows:

Sales revenue	$740,000
Cost of goods sold (based on purchases for the year)	405,000
Salary expense	88,000
Rent expense	30,000
Utilities	8,000
Telephone	6,500
Advertising	4,000
Bad debts	5,000
Depreciation*	21,000
Health insurance**	26,000
Accounting and legal fees	7,000
Supplies	1,000

*New office equipment ($21,000); Devon uses the immediate expense election.
**$18,000 for employees and $8,000 for Devon.

Other income received by Devon includes the following:

Dividend income (qualified dividends):	
Swan, Inc.	$10,000
Wren, Inc.	2,000
Interest income:	
First National Bank	11,000
Second City Bank	2,500
County of Santa Fe, NM bonds	17,000

During the year, Devon and his sole proprietorship were involved in the following property transactions. Stock transactions were reported to Devon on Form 1099–B; basis was not reported to the IRS.

a. Sold Blue, Inc. stock for $45,000 on March 12, 2019. He had purchased the stock on September 5, 2016, for $50,000.

b. Received an inheritance of $300,000 from his uncle, Henry. Devon used $200,000 to purchase Green, Inc. stock on May 15, 2019, and invested $100,000 in Gold, Inc. stock on May 30, 2019.

c. Received Orange, Inc. stock worth $9,500 as a gift from his aunt, Jane, on June 17, 2019. Her adjusted basis for the stock was $5,000. No gift taxes were paid on the transfer. Jane had purchased the stock on April 1, 2013. Devon sold the stock on July 1, 2019, for $22,000.

d. On July 15, 2019, Devon sold one-half of the Green, Inc. stock for $40,000.

e. Devon was notified on August 1, 2019, that Yellow, Inc. stock he purchased from a colleague on September 1, 2018, for $52,500 had become worthless. Although he understood that investing in Yellow was risky, Devon did not anticipate that the corporation would declare bankruptcy.

f. On August 15, 2019, Devon received a parcel of land in Phoenix worth $220,000 in exchange for a parcel of land he owned in Tucson. Because the Tucson parcel was worth $245,000, he also received $25,000 cash. Devon's adjusted basis for the Tucson parcel was $210,000. He originally purchased it on September 18, 2016.

g. On December 1, 2019, Devon sold the condominium in which he had been living for the past 20 years (1844 Lighthouse Lane, Albuquerque, NM 87131) and moved into a rented townhouse. The sales price was $480,000, selling expenses were $28,500, and repair expenses related to the sale were $9,400. Devon purchased the condominium for $180,000.

Devon's potential itemized deductions, exclusive of the aforementioned information, are as follows:

Medical expenses (before the 7.5%-of-AGI floor)	$ 9,500
Property taxes on residence	5,800
State income taxes	4,000
Charitable contributions	10,000
Mortgage interest on residence (First National Bank)	9,900
Sales taxes paid	5,000

During the year, Devon makes estimated Federal income tax payments of $35,000.

Compute Devon's lowest net tax payable or refund due for 2019 assuming that he makes any available elections that will reduce the tax. If you use tax forms for your computations, you will need Form 1040 and its Schedules 1, 2, 3, A, B, C, D, and SE and Forms 4562, 8824, 8949, and 8995. Suggested software: ProConnect Tax Online.

92. Tom and Alice Honeycutt, ages 45 and 46, respectively, live at 101 Glass Road, Delton, MI 49046. Tom is a county employee, and Alice is a self-employed accountant. Tom's Social Security number is 111-11-1111; Alice's Social Security number is 123-45-6789. The income and expenses associated with Alice's accounting practice for 2020 are as follows:

Tax Computation Problem

Critical Thinking

Communications

Revenues (cash receipts during 2020)	$185,000
Expenses	
Salaries	$ 45,000
Office supplies	3,200
Postage	2,900
Depreciation of equipment	42,000
Telephone	800
	$ 93,900

Because Alice is a cash method taxpayer, she does not record her receivables as revenue until she receives cash payment. At the beginning of 2020, her accounts receivable were $48,000, and the balance had decreased to $8,000 by the end of the year.

Alice used one room in their 10-room house as the office for her accounting practice (400 square feet out of a total square footage of 4,000). They paid the following expenses related to the house during 2020:

Utilities	$4,500
Insurance	2,100
Property taxes	5,200
Repairs	3,500

Tom and Alice purchased the house on September 1, 2019, for $400,000 (exclusive of land cost).

Tom and Alice have one child, Connor, age 18. Connor's Social Security number is 123-45-6788.

Tom received a salary of $50,000 during 2020. The appropriate amounts of Social Security tax and Medicare tax were withheld. In addition, $5,000 of Federal income taxes and $2,000 of state income taxes were withheld.

Tom and Alice's allowable itemized deductions during 2020, excluding any itemized deductions related to the house, were $20,600. They made estimated Federal income tax payments of $20,000.

Part 1—Tax Computation
Compute Tom and Alice's lowest net tax payable or refund due for 2020.

Part 2—Tax Planning
Tom and Alice own 30 acres of prime farmland that they inherited from Tom's father several years ago. At that time, the fair market value of the land was $150,000 (which became their basis in the land). The Honeycutts have been holding the land

as an investment. The property recently was appraised for $190,000, and there is an outstanding mortgage on the land of $28,000. They are considering trading this land for property in the mountains of southern Colorado. The Colorado property owner—who has significant land holdings in the area—has provided two options to Tom and Alice (in both cases, the Colorado property owner would assume the mortgage as part of the exchange).

1. 15 acres of property with a fair market value of $135,000 plus $27,000 of cash or
2. 10 acres of property with a fair market value of $160,000 plus $2,000 of cash

The Honeycutts have come to you for advice, believing either transaction to be a like-kind exchange that will allow them to defer any gain. Assume that Tom and Alice expect their 2021 taxable income to be about the same as in 2020 (with any net capital gain taxed at a 15% rate). Write a letter to Tom and Alice that contains your advice on the proposed transactions.

Research Problems

Note: Solutions to the Research Problems can be prepared by using the Thomson Reuters Checkpoint™ online tax research database, which accompanies this textbook. Solutions can also be prepared by using research materials found in a typical tax library.

Research Problem 1. Terry owns real estate with an adjusted basis of $600,000 and a fair market value of $1,100,000. The amount of the nonrecourse mortgage on the property is $2,500,000. Because of substantial past and projected future losses associated with the real estate development (occupancy rate of only 37% after three years), Terry deeds the property to the creditor.

a. What are the tax consequences to Terry?

b. Assume that the data are the same, except that the fair market value of the property is $2,525,000. Therefore, when Terry deeds the property to the creditor, she also receives $25,000 from the creditor. What are the tax consequences to Terry?

Communications **Research Problem 2.** Ruth Ames died on January 10, 2020. In filing the estate tax return, her executor, Melvin Sims, elects the primary valuation date and amount (fair market value on the date of death). On March 12, 2020, Melvin invests $30,000 of cash that Ruth had in her money market account in acquiring 1,000 shares of Orange, Inc. ($30 per share). On January 10, 2020, Orange was selling for $29 per share. The stock is distributed to a beneficiary, Annette Rust, on June 1, 2020, when it is selling for $33 per share.

Melvin wants you to determine the amount at which the Orange shares should appear on the estate tax return and the amount of Annette's adjusted basis for the stock. Write a letter to Melvin in which you respond to his inquiry, and prepare a memo for the tax files. His address is 100 Center Lane, Miami, FL 33124.

Research Problem 3. Randall owns an office building (adjusted basis of $250,000) that he has been renting to a group of physicians. During negotiations over a new seven-year lease, the physicians offer to purchase the building for $900,000. Randall accepts the offer with the stipulation that the sale be structured as a delayed § 1031 transaction. Consequently, the sales proceeds are paid to a qualified third-party intermediary on the closing date of September 30, 2020.

On October 2, 2020, Randall properly identifies an office building that he would like to acquire. Unfortunately, on November 10, 2020, the property Randall selected is withdrawn from the market. Working with the intermediary, on November 12, 2020, Randall identifies another office building that meets his requirements. The purchase of this property closes on December 15, 2020, and the title is transferred to Randall.

Randall treats the transaction as a like-kind exchange. Even though the original office building identified was not acquired, Randall concludes that in substance, he has satisfied the 45-day rule. He identified the acquired office building as soon as the negotiations ceased on his first choice. Should the IRS accept Randall's attempt to comply? Explain.

Use internet tax resources to address the following questions. Look for reliable websites and blogs of the IRS and other government agencies, media outlets, businesses, tax professionals, academics, think tanks, and political outlets.

Research Problem 4. How are transactions using Bitcoin (or another virtual currency) treated under U.S. tax law? Some background on Bitcoin can be found at **bitcoin .org/en/faq**. Locate the current IRS guidance on this question. In addition, locate the American Institute of CPAs Comment Letter on virtual currency (issued in May 2018). After reading these materials, provide a one-page written summary for your instructor.

Communications

Research Problem 5. How do U.S. individuals generate their income? Does it vary by size of income (AGI)? Go to the IRS tax statistics website (**irs.gov/statistics**), and download a recent tax year's information on "sources of income." Compare the following types of income by size of AGI: (1) wages, (2) capital gain distributions, (3) sales of capital assets, and (4) sales of property other than capital assets. Cluster the data into no more than six AGI categories. Present your findings in a visual (e.g., bar chart), and summarize your findings in a one-page memo to your instructor.

Data Analytics

Communications

Becker CPA Review Questions

1. Jasmin purchased 100 shares of Pinkstey Corporation (publicly traded company) on January 1 of year 1 for $5,000. The FMV of the shares at the end of year 1 was $6,000. On January 1 of year 4, Pinkstey Corporation declared a 2-for-1 stock split when the fair market value of the stock was $65 per share. On January 1 of year 5, Jasmin sold all of her Pinkstey Corporation stock when the fair market value was $40 per share. Which of the following statements is true?

    a. Jasmin reports $6,500 in gross income for the 2-for-1 stock split in year 4.

    b. Jasmin's basis in the Pinkstey Corporation stock at the end of year 4 is $65 per share.

    c. Jasmin has no taxable income for the Pinkstey Corporation stock in year 4.

    d. Jasmin owns 100 shares in Pinkstey Corporation stock at the end of year 4.

2. Alice gifted stock to her son, Bob, in year 5. Alice bought the stock in year 1 for $8,300. The value of the stock on the date of gift was $6,400. Bob sold the stock in year 7 for $15,800. What is Bob's recognized gain or loss on the sale in year 7?

    a. $0   c. $9,400 gain
    b. $7,500 gain   d. $15,800 gain

3. Jerry inherits an asset from his uncle, who purchased the asset five days before he died. Which of the following statements is correct?

    a. If Jerry sells the asset a few days after receiving it, any gain or loss on the sale will be short term.

    b. Jerry's basis in the asset is the carryover basis from his uncle.

    c. Jerry's basis is the FMV on the alternate valuation date or date it is distributed to him.

    d. Jerry's basis is the FMV on his uncle's date of death.

4. Which of the following statements is *not* correct?

   a. The basis of an asset that is purchased must be adjusted for depreciation allowable.

   b. The general rule for the basis of property acquired by gift is a carryover of basis from the donor.

   c. If an asset is acquired by gift and the FMV on the date of gift is lower than the donor's carryover basis, the recipient's basis cannot be determined until the asset is disposed of.

   d. The basis of property acquired from a decedent is always the FMV on the date of death.

5. Rick purchased 100 shares of XYZ stock on April 4, year 4, for $8,600. He sold 50 shares on February 8, year 5, for $3,000. He then bought another 50 shares of XYZ on March 1, year 5, for $3,200. How much loss will Rick realize in year 5?

   a. $0   c. $3,000
   b. $1,300   d. $5,600

6. Agnes sold 50 shares of ABC stock to her son, Steve, in year 4 for $42,000. She bought the stock eight years ago for $50,000. Steve sold the stock to an unrelated party in year 6 for $60,000. How much gain will Steve recognize from the sale in year 6?

   a. $0   c. $18,000
   b. $10,000   d. $60,000

7. On February 1 of the current year, Duffy learned that he was bequeathed 1,000 shares of common stock under his father's will. Duffy's father had paid $12,500 for the stock 20 years ago. Fair market value of the stock on February 1 of the current year, the date of his father's death, was $14,000 and had increased to $15,500 six months later. The executor of the estate elected the alternative valuation date for estate tax purposes. Duffy sold the stock for $14,500 on June 1 of the current year, the date that the executor distributed the stock to him. How much income should Duffy include in his current-year individual income tax return for the inheritance of the 1,000 shares of stock which he received from his father's estate, assuming the estate tax law in effect for 2011 and forward?

   a. $5,500   c. $2,500
   b. $4,000   d. $0

8. On January 25, year 10, Mother Hall gave her daughter, Nadyne, 500 shares of common stock of XYZ, Corp. The fair market value of the stock on January 25 was $2,000. Mother Hall had paid $4,000 for the stock three years earlier. Nadyne decided a month after receiving the stock that she doesn't want to hold it and sold it for $1,000, the fair market value at the time of the sale. How much income (loss) must Nadyne include in her tax return for year 10 in regards to the sale of the stock?

   a. $0   c. ($2,000)
   b. ($1,000)   d. ($3,000)

9. In early year 8, Alice sold Tom, her son, 20 shares of common stock for $20,000. Alice had paid $25,000 for the stock in year 2. In late year 8, Tom sold the stock to an unrelated third party for $35,000. How much gain must Tom report in his year 8 tax return for the sale of the stock?

   a. $0   c. $10,000
   b. $5,000   d. $15,000

10. Susie purchased her primary residence on March 15, year 4, for $550,000. She sold it on October 15, year 7, for $240,000. What amount of loss from the sale is recognized on her year 7 income tax return?

   a. $0
   b. $60,000
   c. $250,000
   d. $310,000

11. Chad owned an office building that was destroyed in a tornado. The adjusted basis of the building at the time was $890,000. After the deductible, Chad received an insurance check for $850,000. He used the $850,000 to purchase a new building that same year. How much is Chad's recognized loss, and what is his basis in the new building?

	Recognized Loss	New Basis
a.	$0	$850,000
b.	$0	$890,000
c.	$40,000	$850,000
d.	$40,000	$890,000

12. Chad owned an office building that was destroyed in a tornado. The adjusted basis of the building at the time was $890,000. After the deductible, Chad received an insurance check for $950,000. He used $900,000 of the insurance proceeds to purchase a new building that same year. How much is Chad's recognized gain, and what is his basis in the new building?

	Recognized Gain	New Basis
a.	$0	$890,000
b.	$0	$900,000
c.	$50,000	$890,000
d.	$60,000	$900,000

13. Marsha exchanged land in Florida with an FMV of $72,700 and an adjusted basis of $40,000 for land in Iowa with an FMV of $57,700. Marsha also assumed a $5,000 liability on the land received in the transaction and was relieved of a $20,000 liability on the land that was given up. What is Marsha's recognized gain on the transaction?

   a. $0
   b. $15,000
   c. $20,000
   d. $32,700

14. Marsha exchanged land in Florida with an FMV of $52,700 and an adjusted basis of $60,000 for land in Iowa with an FMV of $57,700. Marsha also paid $5,000 cash in the transaction. What is Marsha's basis in the land received?

   a. $55,000
   b. $57,700
   c. $60,000
   d. $65,000

CHAPTER 14

Property Transactions: Capital Gains and Losses, § 1231, and Recapture Provisions

LEARNING OBJECTIVES: *After completing Chapter 14, you should be able to:*

LO.1 Explain the general scheme of taxation for capital gains and losses.

LO.2 Distinguish capital assets from ordinary assets.

LO.3 State and explain the relevance of a sale or exchange to classification as a capital gain or loss and apply the special rules for the capital gain or loss treatment of the retirement of corporate obligations, options, patents, franchises, and lease cancellation payments.

LO.4 Determine whether the holding period for a capital asset is long term or short term.

LO.5 Describe the beneficial tax treatment for capital gains and the detrimental tax treatment for capital losses for noncorporate taxpayers.

LO.6 Describe the tax treatment for capital gains and the detrimental tax treatment for capital losses for corporate taxpayers.

LO.7 State and explain the rationale for and the nature and treatment of gains and losses from the disposition of business assets.

LO.8 Distinguish § 1231 assets from ordinary assets and capital assets and calculate the § 1231 gain or loss.

LO.9 Determine when § 1245 recapture applies and how it is computed.

LO.10 Determine when § 1250 recapture applies.

LO.11 State and explain considerations common to §§ 1245 and 1250.

LO.12 Recognize special recapture provisions that are part of the tax law.

LO.13 Describe the reporting procedures for §§ 1231, 1245, and 1250.

LO.14 Identify tax planning opportunities arising from the sale or exchange of capital assets and avoid pitfalls associated with the recapture provisions.

CHAPTER OUTLINE

14-1 **General Scheme of Taxation, 14-3**
14-2 **Capital Assets, 14-3**
    14-2a Definition of a Capital Asset (§ 1221), 14-4
    14-2b Effect of Judicial Action, 14-6
    14-2c Statutory Expansions, 14-7
14-3 **Sale or Exchange, 14-8**
    14-3a Worthless Securities and § 1244 Stock, 14-8
    14-3b Retirement of Corporate Obligations, 14-9
    14-3c Options, 14-9
    14-3d Patents, 14-11
    14-3e Franchises, Trademarks, and Trade Names (§ 1253), 14-12
    14-3f Lease Cancellation Payments, 14-14
14-4 **Holding Period, 14-15**
    14-4a General Rules, 14-15
    14-4b Special Holding Period Rules, 14-15
    14-4c Special Rules for Short Sales, 14-16
14-5 **Tax Treatment of Capital Gains and Losses of Noncorporate Taxpayers, 14-19**
    14-5a Capital Gain and Loss Netting Process, 14-19
    14-5b Qualified Dividend Income, 14-22
    14-5c Alternative Tax on Net Capital Gain and Qualified Dividend Income, 14-22
    14-5d Treatment of Net Capital Losses, 14-26
14-6 **Tax Treatment of Capital Gains and Losses of Corporate Taxpayers, 14-27**
14-7 **Overview of § 1231 and the Recapture Provisions, 14-28**
14-8 **Section 1231 Assets, 14-28**
    14-8a Relationship to Capital Assets, 14-28
    14-8b Property Included, 14-29
    14-8c Property Excluded, 14-30

    14-8d Section 1231 Assets Disposed of by Casualty or Theft, 14-30
    14-8e General Procedure for § 1231 Computation, 14-32
14-9 **Section 1245 Recapture, 14-35**
    14-9a Section 1245 Property, 14-37
    14-9b Observations on § 1245, 14-38
14-10 **Section 1250 Recapture, 14-38**
    14-10a Section 1250 Recapture Situations, 14-39
    14-10b Unrecaptured § 1250 Gain (Real Estate 25% Gain), 14-39
14-11 **Considerations Common to §§ 1245 and 1250, 14-41**
    14-11a Exceptions, 14-41
    14-11b Other Applications, 14-43
14-12 **Special Recapture Provisions, 14-44**
    14-12a Special Recapture for Corporations, 14-44
    14-12b Gain from Sale of Depreciable Property between Certain Related Parties, 14-45
    14-12c Intangible Drilling Costs, 14-45
14-13 **Reporting Procedures, 14-45**
14-14 **Tax Planning, 14-46**
    14-14a Importance of Capital Asset Status, 14-46
    14-14b Planning for Capital Asset Status, 14-46
    14-14c Effect of Capital Asset Status in Transactions Other Than Sales, 14-47
    14-14d Stock Sales, 14-48
    14-14e Maximizing Benefits, 14-48
    14-14f Year-End Planning, 14-48
    14-14g Timing of § 1231 Gain, 14-48
    14-14h Timing of Recapture, 14-49
    14-14i Postponing and Shifting Recapture, 14-49
    14-14j Avoiding Recapture, 14-50

MANAGING CAPITAL ASSET TRANSACTIONS

Maurice has come to you for tax advice regarding his investments. He inherited $750,000 from his uncle, Joe. A financial adviser suggested that he make the following investments, which he did nine months ago.

- $5,000 for 100 shares of Eagle Company stock.
- $50,000 for a 50 percent interest in a patent that Kevin, a college roommate who is an unemployed inventor, obtained for a special battery he developed to power green cars. To date, Kevin has been unable to market the battery to an auto manufacturer or supplier, but he has high hopes of doing so in the future.
- $95,000 to invest in a franchise from Orange, Inc.
- $200,000 in the stock of Purple, Inc., a publicly held bank that follows a policy of occasionally paying dividends. At one time, the stock appreciated to $300,000, but now it is worth only $210,000. Maurice is considering selling this stock.
- $50,000 in tax-exempt bonds. The interest rate on the bonds is only 3 percent. Maurice is considering moving this money into taxable bonds that pay 3.5 percent.
- $100,000 for a 10 percent ownership interest as a limited partner in a real estate development. Lots in the development are selling well.

Maurice read an article that discussed the beneficial tax rates for capital assets and dividends. He really liked the part about "costless" capital gains, although he did not understand it.

Maurice has retained his job as a toll booth supervisor at the municipal airport. His annual compensation is $35,000. He likes the job and has met some interesting people there.

Respond to Maurice's request for tax advice.

Read the chapter and formulate your response.

FRAMEWORK 1040   Tax Formula for Individuals

This chapter covers the boldfaced portions of the Tax Formula for Individuals that was introduced in Concept Summary 3.1 on p. 3-3. Below those portions are the sections of Form 1040 where the results are reported.

Income *(broadly defined)*	$ xx,xxx
Less: Exclusions	(x,xxx)
Gross income	**$ xx,xxx**

FORM 1040 (p. 1)

6	Capital gain or (loss). Attach Schedule D if required. If not required, check here ▶	☐

FORM 1040 (Schedule 1)

3	Business income or (loss). Attach Schedule C. . . . .
4	Other gains or (losses). Attach Form 4797 . . . .

Adjusted gross income	$ xx,xxx
Less: The greater of total itemized deductions *or* the standard deduction	(x,xxx)
Personal and dependency exemptions*	(x,xxx)
Deduction for qualified business income**	(x,xxx)
Taxable income	$ xx,xxx
Tax on taxable income *(see Tax Tables or Tax Rate Schedules)*	**$ x,xxx**

FORM 1040 (p. 2)

12a	**Tax** (see inst). Check if any from Form(s): **1** ☐ 8814 **2** ☐ 4972 **3** ☐ _____	

Less: Tax credits *(including income taxes withheld and prepaid)*	(xxx)
Tax due (or refund)	$ xxx

* Exemption deductions are not allowed from 2018 through 2025.
** Only applies from 2018 through 2025.

F ourteen years ago, a taxpayer purchased 100 shares of IBM stock for $17 a share. This year the taxpayer sells the shares for $141 a share. Should the $124 per-share gain receive any special tax treatment? The $124 gain has built up over 14 years, so it may not be fair to tax it the same as income that was all earned this year.

What if the stock had been purchased for $141 per share and sold for $17 a share? Should the $124 loss be fully deductible? The tax law has an intricate approach to answering these investment activity-related questions.

Property transactions involve the *disposition* of *assets*. The sale of the IBM stock was the disposition of an investment-related asset. As you study this chapter, keep in mind that how investment-related gains and losses are taxed can dramatically affect whether taxpayers make investments and which investments are made. Except for a brief discussion in Chapter 3, earlier chapters dwelt on how to determine the amount of gain or loss from a property disposition, but did not discuss the classification of gains and losses. This chapter will focus on that topic.

The tax law requires **capital gains** and **capital losses** to be separated from other types of gains and losses. There are two reasons for this treatment. First, long-term capital gains may be taxed at a lower rate than ordinary gains. Second, a net capital loss is subject to deduction limitations. For noncorporate taxpayers, a net capital loss is only deductible up to $3,000 per year. Any excess loss over the annual limit carries over and may be deductible in a future tax year.

For these reasons, capital gains and losses must be distinguished from other types of gains and losses. This chapter describes:

- The intricate rules needed to determine what *type* of gains and losses the taxpayer has,
- How those gains and losses are intermingled among themselves,
- How the result of that intermingling then is integrated with the other items on the taxpayer's tax return, and
- How those gains and losses are taxed as part of the taxpayer's taxable income.

14-1 GENERAL SCHEME OF TAXATION

LO.1

Explain the general scheme of taxation for capital gains and losses.

Recognized gains and losses must be properly *classified*. Proper classification depends on three characteristics:

- The tax *status* of the property (capital, § 1231, or ordinary).
- The manner of the property's *disposition* (sale, exchange, casualty, theft, or condemnation).
- The *holding period* of the property (*short-term*: one year or less; *long-term*: more than one year).

A major focus of this chapter is capital gains and losses. But in addition, § 1231 assets and ordinary gains and losses also are discussed.

14-2 CAPITAL ASSETS

LO.2

Distinguish capital assets from ordinary assets.

Personal use assets and investment assets are the most common capital assets owned by individual taxpayers. Personal use assets usually include things like a residence, furniture, clothing, recreational equipment, and automobiles. Investment assets usually include stocks, bonds, and mutual funds. Remember, however, that losses from the sale or exchange of personal use assets are not recognized.

The crux of capital asset determination hinges on whether the asset is held for personal use (capital asset), investment (capital asset), or business (ordinary asset). How a taxpayer uses the property typically answers this question.

EXAMPLE

1

David buys an expensive painting.

- If David purchased the painting for personal use (as a decoration in his home) and it is not of investment quality, it is a capital asset. However, any loss on its sale is not usable, whereas gain from its sale is taxable. Investment quality generally means that the painting is expected to appreciate in value.

- If the painting is used to decorate David's business office and is of investment quality, the painting is not depreciable and, therefore, is a capital asset.

- If David's business is buying and selling paintings, the painting is inventory and, therefore, an ordinary asset.

- If the painting is not of investment quality and the business did not purchase it for investment, the painting is an ordinary asset and it is depreciable even though it serves a decorative purpose in David's office. If David depreciates the painting, that is evidence that the painting is held for use in his business (and *not* being held for investment or as inventory). As a result, it is not a capital asset.

Since capital assets receive preferential tax treatment, taxpayers prefer capital gains rather than ordinary gains. So the definition of a capital asset is critically important. As discussed next, this definition has been the subject of many court cases and rulings.

14-2a **Definition of a Capital Asset (§ 1221)**

Capital assets are not directly defined in the Code. Instead, § 1221(a) defines what is *not* a capital asset. In general, a <mark>capital asset</mark> is property *other than* inventory, accounts and notes receivable, supplies, and most fixed assets of a business.

Specifically, the Code defines a capital asset as property held by the taxpayer (when it is connected with the taxpayer's business) that is *not* any of the following:

- Inventory or property held primarily for sale to customers in the ordinary course of a business.
- Accounts and notes receivable generated from the sale of goods or services in a business.
- Depreciable property or real estate used in a business.
- A patent, invention, model, or design (whether or not patented); a secret formula or process; certain copyrights; literary, musical, or artistic compositions; or letters, memoranda, or similar property created by or for the taxpayer.[1]
- Certain U.S. government publications.
- Supplies used in a business.

Often, the only business asset that is a capital asset is "self-generated" goodwill (purchased goodwill is a § 1231 asset). The following discussion provides further detail on each part of the capital asset definition.

Inventory

What constitutes inventory is determined by the taxpayer's business.

Inventory Determination

EXAMPLE 2

Green Company buys and sells used cars. Its cars are inventory. Its gains from the sale of the cars are ordinary income.

EXAMPLE 3

Soong sells her personal use automobile at a $500 gain. The automobile is a personal use asset and, therefore, a capital asset. The gain is a capital gain.

No asset is inherently capital or ordinary. If Soong (Example 3) sells her "capital asset" automobile to Green Company (Example 2), that same automobile loses its capital asset status, because the automobile is inventory to Green Company. Whether an asset is capital or ordinary, therefore, depends entirely on the relationship of the asset to the taxpayer who sold it. This classification dilemma is but one feature of capital asset treatment that makes this area so confusing and complicated.

Accounts and Notes Receivable

Accounts and notes receivable are often created as part of a business transaction. These assets may be collected by the creditor, be sold by the creditor, or become completely or partially worthless. Also, the creditor may be on the accrual or cash basis of accounting.

Collection of an *accrual basis* account or note receivable does not result in a gain or loss because the amount collected equals the receivable's basis. If sold, an ordinary gain or loss is generated if the receivable is sold for more or less than its basis (the receivable

---

[1]§§ 1221(a)(3) and 1221(b)(3).

is an ordinary asset). If the receivable is partially or wholly worthless, the creditor has a "bad debt," which may result in an ordinary deduction (see text Section 7-1).

Collection of a *cash basis* account or note receivable does not result in a gain or loss because the amount collected is ordinary income. In addition, a cash basis receivable has a zero basis since no revenue is recorded until the receivable is collected. If sold, an ordinary gain is generated (the receivable is an ordinary asset). There is no bad debt deduction for cash basis receivables because they have no basis. See text Section 14-3 for more details on "sale or exchange."

Oriole Company has accounts receivable of $100,000. Because Oriole needs working capital, it sells the receivables for $83,000 to a financial institution.

If Oriole is an *accrual basis taxpayer*, it has a $17,000 ordinary loss. Revenue of $100,000 would have been recorded and a $100,000 basis would have been established when the receivable was created.

If Oriole is a *cash basis taxpayer*, it has $83,000 of ordinary income because it would not have recorded any revenue earlier; as a result, the receivable has no tax basis.

EXAMPLE 4

Business Fixed Assets

Depreciable personal property and real estate (both depreciable and nondepreciable) used by a business are *not* capital assets. The tax law related to this property is very complex; most of these rules are discussed later in this chapter. Although business fixed assets are not capital assets, a long-term capital gain can sometimes result from their sale. The potential capital gain treatment for business fixed assets under § 1231 is also discussed later in this chapter. Another rule—real property subdivided for sale (§ 1237)—is discussed in text Section 14-2c.

Inventions and Processes

A patent, invention, model, or design (whether or not patented) and a secret formula or process are excluded from being a capital asset. These are *ordinary* assets. The assets may be held either by the taxpayer who created the property or by a taxpayer who received the asset from the taxpayer who created the property. As a result, gains or losses from the sale or exchange of these assets do *not* receive capital gain treatment. In limited circumstances, patents (even though they are not capital assets) may be *treated* as capital assets. Those special rules are discussed in text Section 14-3d.

Abigail invents a multifunctional case for a popular brand of cell phones. She has a manufacturer produce them for her and sells them via the internet. Her cost is $2.30 per case, and she sells each one for $10. To her surprise, she quickly achieves $45,000 in total sales. She has not capitalized any of the costs of developing the invention and has not patented it.

She sells all of her rights to the invention for $350,000 to a company that is in the business of producing cell phone cases. Her profit from sales of the cases is ordinary income because the cases are inventory. The $350,000 gain from selling the rights to the invention is an ordinary gain because the invention is not a capital asset.

EXAMPLE 5

Copyrights and Creative Works

Generally, the person whose efforts led to the copyright or creative work has an ordinary asset, not a capital asset. *Creative works* include the works of authors, composers, and artists. Also, the person for whom a letter, a memorandum, or another similar property was created has an ordinary asset. Finally, a person receiving a copyright, a creative work, a letter, a memorandum, or similar property by gift from the creator or the person for whom the work was created has an ordinary asset. A taxpayer may elect to treat the sale or exchange of a musical composition or a copyright of a musical work as the disposition of a capital asset.

Creative Works

EXAMPLE 6

Wanda is a part-time music composer. A music publisher purchases one of her songs for $5,000.
  Wanda has a $5,000 ordinary gain from the sale of an ordinary asset unless she elects to treat the gain as a capital gain.

EXAMPLE 7

Ed received a letter from the President of the United States in 1982. In the current year, Ed sells the letter to a collector for $300.
  Ed has a $300 ordinary gain from the sale of an ordinary asset (because the letter was created for Ed).

EXAMPLE 8

Isabella gives her son a song she composed. The son sells the song to a music publisher for $5,000.
  The son has a $5,000 ordinary gain from the sale of an ordinary asset unless he elects to treat the gain as a capital gain.
  If the son inherits the song from Isabella, his basis for the song is its fair market value at Isabella's death. In this situation, the song is a capital asset because the son's basis is not related to Isabella's basis for the song.

ETHICS & EQUITY   Sculpture as a Capital Asset

Cynthia is a successful sculptor who created a work that is now worth $400,000 and has no tax basis. Cynthia forms a corporation and contributes the sculpture to it in exchange for the corporation's shares. Fourteen months later, she sells all the stock for $400,000. She wants to treat the sale of the stock as a long-term capital gain. Evaluate the propriety of Cynthia's actions.

U.S. Government Publications

U.S. government publications received from the U.S. government (or its agencies) for a reduced price are *not* capital assets. This prevents a taxpayer from later donating the publications to charity and claiming a charitable contribution deduction equal to the fair market value of the publications. Normally, the charitable contribution of an ordinary asset provides a deduction equal to the asset's basis. If the taxpayer received the property at no cost, its basis is equal to zero. If this property is given to someone else, it retains its ordinary asset status (see text Section 10-4e for more about property contributions).

14-2b Effect of Judicial Action

Because the Code only lists categories of what are *not* capital assets, judicial interpretation is sometimes required to determine whether a specific item fits into one of those categories. The Supreme Court follows a literal interpretation of the categories. For instance, because corporate stock is not mentioned in § 1221, it is *usually* a capital asset. However, what if corporate stock is purchased for resale to customers? Then it is *inventory* (and not a capital asset) because inventory is one of the categories in § 1221.

Intent also matters. What happens when a taxpayer who does not normally acquire stock for resale to customers acquires stock but intends to resell it? The Supreme Court decided that because the stock was not acquired primarily for sale to customers (the taxpayer did not sell the stock to its regular customers), the stock was a capital asset.[2]

---

[2]*Arkansas Best v. Comm.*, 88–1 USTC ¶9210, 61 AFTR 2d 88–655, 108 S.Ct. 971 (USSC, 1988).

Because of the uncertainty associated with capital asset status, Congress has enacted several Code Sections to clarify its definition. These clarifications are discussed next.

14-2c Statutory Expansions

In several instances, Congress has clarified its general definition of what is *not* a capital asset.

Dealers in Securities

As a general rule, securities (stocks, bonds, and other financial instruments) held by a dealer are considered to be inventory and are, therefore, not subject to capital gain or loss treatment. A *dealer in securities* is a merchant (e.g., a brokerage firm) that regularly engages in the purchase and resale of securities to customers.

The dealer must identify any securities being held for investment. Generally, if a dealer clearly identifies certain securities as held for investment purposes by the close of business on the acquisition date, gain from the securities' sale will be capital gain. However, the gain will not be capital gain if the dealer ceases to hold the securities for investment prior to the sale. Losses are capital losses if at any time the securities have been clearly identified by the dealer as held for investment.

EXAMPLE 9

Tracy is a securities dealer. She purchases 100 shares of Swan stock. If Tracy takes no further action, the stock is inventory and an ordinary asset.

If she designates in her records that the stock is held for investment, the stock is a capital asset. Tracy must designate the investment purpose by the close of business on the acquisition date. If Tracy maintains her investment purpose and later sells the stock, the gain or loss is capital gain or loss.

If Tracy redesignates the stock as held for resale (inventory) and then sells it, any gain is ordinary, but any loss is capital loss.

Real Property Subdivided for Sale (§ 1237)

Substantial real property development activities may result in the owner being considered a dealer for tax purposes. If so, ordinary income will result from any lots sold. However, § 1237 allows real estate investors capital gain treatment if they engage *only* in *limited* development activities. To be eligible for § 1237 treatment, the following requirements must be met:

- The taxpayer may not be a corporation.
- The taxpayer may not be a real estate dealer.
- No substantial improvements may be made to the lots sold. *Substantial* generally means more than a 10 percent increase in the value of a lot. Shopping centers and other commercial or residential buildings are considered substantial improvements, while filling, draining, leveling, and clearing operations are not.
- The taxpayer must have held the lots sold for at least 5 years, except for inherited property. The substantial improvements test is less stringent if the property is held at least 10 years.

If these requirements are met, all gain is capital gain until the tax year in which the *sixth* lot is sold. Sales of contiguous lots to a single buyer in the same transaction count as the sale of one lot. Beginning with the tax year the *sixth* lot is sold, 5 percent of the revenue from lot sales is potential ordinary income. That potential ordinary income is offset by any selling expenses from the lot sales. As sales commissions often are at least 5 percent of the sales price, typically none of the gain is treated as ordinary income.

Section 1237 does not apply to losses. A loss from the sale of subdivided real property is an ordinary loss unless the property qualifies as a capital asset under § 1221. The following example illustrates the application of § 1237.

EXAMPLE 10

Jack owns a large tract of land and subdivides it for sale. Assume that Jack meets all of the requirements of § 1237 and during the tax year sells the first 10 lots to 10 different buyers for $10,000 each. Jack's basis in each lot sold is $3,000, and he incurs total selling expenses of $4,000 ($400 for each lot) on the sales. Jack's gain is computed as follows:

Selling price (10 × $10,000)	$100,000	
Less: Selling expenses (10 × $400)	(4,000)	
Amount realized		$ 96,000
Basis (10 × $3,000)		(30,000)
Realized and recognized gain		$ 66,000
Classification of recognized gain:		
Ordinary income		
Five percent of selling price (5% × $100,000)	$ 5,000	
Less: Selling expenses	(4,000)	
Ordinary gain		(1,000)
Capital gain		$ 65,000

A portion of the gain is given ordinary treatment because the *sixth* lot is sold in the current year.

Nonbusiness Bad Debts

A loan not made in the ordinary course of business is classified as a nonbusiness receivable. In the year the receivable becomes completely worthless, it is a *nonbusiness bad debt*, and the bad debt is treated as a short-term capital loss. Even if the receivable was outstanding for more than one year, the loss is still a short-term capital loss. Chapter 7 discusses nonbusiness bad debts more thoroughly (see text Section 7-1b).

LO.3

State and explain the relevance of a sale or exchange to classification as a capital gain or loss and apply the special rules for the capital gain or loss treatment of the retirement of corporate obligations, options, patents, franchises, and lease cancellation payments.

14-3 **SALE OR EXCHANGE**

Recognition of capital gain or loss usually requires a sale or exchange of a capital asset. The Code uses the term `sale or exchange`, but does not define it. Generally, a property *sale* involves the receipt of money by the seller and/or the assumption by the purchaser of the seller's liabilities. An *exchange* involves the transfer of property for other property. So an involuntary conversion (casualty, theft, or condemnation) is not a sale or exchange.

In several situations, Congress has created rules that specifically provide for sale or exchange treatment. For example, assume that the expiration of a right to personal property (other than stock) that would be a capital asset in the hands of the taxpayer results in a recognized gain or loss. This is a capital gain or loss.[3] Several of these special rules are discussed below, including worthless securities, the retirement of corporate obligations, options, patents, franchises, and lease cancellation payments.

14-3a **Worthless Securities and § 1244 Stock**

Occasionally, securities such as stock and, especially, bonds may become worthless due to the insolvency of their issuer. If such a security is a capital asset, the loss is deemed to have occurred as the result of a sale or exchange on the *last day* of the tax year.[4] This last-day rule may have the effect of converting what otherwise would have been a short-term capital loss into a long-term capital loss. Section 1244 allows an ordinary deduction on disposition of stock at a loss. The stock must be that of a small business corporation, and the ordinary deduction is limited to $50,000 ($100,000 for married taxpayers filing jointly) per year. See Chapter 7 (and text Sections 7-2a and 7-2b) for a more complete discussion of these rules.

[3] § 1234A.

[4] § 165(g)(1).

14-3b **Retirement of Corporate Obligations**

A debt obligation (e.g., a bond or note payable) may have a tax basis in excess of or less than its redemption value because it may have been acquired at a premium or discount. Consequently, the collection of the redemption value may result in a loss or gain. Generally, the collection of a debt obligation is *treated* as a sale or exchange.[5] Therefore, any loss or gain can be a capital loss or capital gain because a sale or exchange has taken place.

Fran acquires $1,000 of Osprey Corporation bonds for $980 in the open market. If the bonds are held to maturity, the $20 difference between Fran's collection of the $1,000 redemption value and her cost of $980 is treated as capital gain.

EXAMPLE 11

Original Issue Discount (§§ 1272–1288)

The benefit of the sale or exchange exception that allows a capital gain from the collection of certain obligations is reduced when the obligation has original issue discount. **Original issue discount (OID)** arises when the issue price of a debt obligation is less than the maturity value of the obligation. OID must generally be amortized over the life of the debt obligation using the effective interest method. The OID amortization increases the basis of the bond.

Most new publicly traded bond issues do not carry OID because the stated interest rate is set to make the market price on issue the same as the bond's face amount. In addition, even if the issue price is less than the face amount, the difference is not considered to be OID if the difference is less than one-fourth of 1 percent of the redemption price at maturity multiplied by the number of years to maturity.[6]

In the case where OID does exist, it may or may not have to be amortized, depending upon the date the obligation was issued. When OID is amortized, the amount of gain upon collection, sale, or exchange of the obligation is correspondingly reduced. The obligations covered by the OID amortization rules and the method of amortization are presented in §§ 1272–1275. Similar rules for other obligations can be found in §§ 1276–1288.

Jerry purchases $10,000 of newly issued White Corporation bonds for $6,000. The bonds have OID of $4,000. Jerry must amortize the discount over the life of the bonds. The OID amortization *increases* his interest income. (The bonds were selling at a discount because the market rate of interest was greater than the bonds' stated interest rate.) After Jerry has amortized $1,800 of OID, he sells the bonds for $8,000. Jerry has a capital gain of $200 [$8,000 − ($6,000 cost + $1,800 OID amortization)].

The OID amortization rules prevent him from converting ordinary interest income into capital gain. Without the OID amortization, Jerry would have capital gain of $2,000 ($8,000 − $6,000 cost).

EXAMPLE 12

14-3c **Options**

Frequently, a potential buyer of property wants some time to make the purchase decision, but wants to control the sale and/or the sale price in the meantime. **Options** are used to achieve these objectives. The potential purchaser (grantee) pays the property owner (grantor) for an option on the property. The grantee then becomes the option holder. The option, which usually sets a price at which the grantee can buy the property, expires after a specified period of time.

Exercise of Options by Grantee

If the option is exercised, the amount paid for the option is added to the optioned property's selling price. This increases the gain (or reduces the loss) to the grantor resulting from the sale of the property. The grantor's gain or loss is capital or ordinary depending on the tax status of the property. The grantee adds the cost of the option to the basis of the property purchased.

---

[5]§ 1271.

[6]§ 1273(a)(3).

Sale of an Option

A grantee may sell or exchange the option rather than exercise it or let it expire. Generally, the grantee's sale or exchange of the option results in capital gain or loss if the option property is (or would be) a capital asset to the grantee.[7]

Rosa wants to buy some vacant land for investment purposes. However, she cannot afford the full purchase price at the present time. Instead, Rosa (grantee) pays the landowner (grantor) $3,000 to obtain an option to buy the land for $100,000 anytime in the next two years. The option is a capital asset for Rosa because if she actually purchased the land, the land would be a capital asset.

Three months after purchasing the option, Rosa sells it for $7,000. She has a $4,000 ($7,000 − $3,000) short-term capital gain on this sale because she held the option for one year or less.

Failure to Exercise Options

If an option holder (grantee) fails to exercise the option, the lapse of the option is considered a sale or exchange on the option expiration date. As a result, the loss is a capital loss if the property subject to the option is (or would be) a capital asset in the hands of the grantee.

The grantor of an option on *stocks, securities, commodities, or commodity futures* receives short-term capital gain treatment upon the expiration of the option. Options on property *other than* stocks, securities, commodities, or commodity futures (for instance, vacant land) result in ordinary income to the grantor when the option expires.

For example, an individual investor who owns certain stock (a capital asset) may sell a call option, entitling the buyer of the option to acquire the stock at a specified price higher than the value at the date the option is granted. The writer of the call receives a premium (e.g., 10 percent) for writing the option. If the price of the stock does not increase during the option period, the option will expire unexercised. When the option expires, the grantor must recognize short-term capital gain (whereas the grantee recognizes a loss, the character of which depends on the underlying asset). These rules do not apply to options held for sale to customers (the inventory of a securities dealer).

The Big Picture

EXAMPLE 14

Return to the facts of *The Big Picture* on p. 14-1. On February 1, 2020, Maurice purchases 100 shares of Eagle Company stock for $5,000. On April 1, 2020, he writes a call option on the stock, giving the grantee the right to buy the stock for $6,000 during the following six-month period. Maurice (the grantor) receives a call premium of $500 for writing the call.

- If the call is exercised by the grantee on August 1, 2020, Maurice has $1,500 ($6,000 + $500 − $5,000) of short-term capital gain from the sale of the stock. The grantee has a $6,500 ($500 option premium + $6,000 purchase price) basis for the stock.

- Investors sometimes get nervous and want to "lock in" gains or losses.
  - ‣ Assume that Maurice, prior to exercise of the grantee's call, decides to sell his stock for $6,000 and enters into a closing transaction by purchasing a call on 100 shares of Eagle Company stock for $5,000.
  - ‣ Because the Eagle stock is selling for $6,000, Maurice must pay a call premium of $1,000.
  - ‣ He recognizes a $500 short-term capital loss [$500 (call premium received) − $1,000 (call premium paid)] on the closing transaction.

continued

---

[7]§ 1234(a) and Reg. § 1.1234–1(a)(1).

➤ On the actual sale of the Eagle stock, Maurice has a short-term capital gain of $1,000 [$6,000 (selling price) − $5,000 (cost)].

➤ The original grantee is not affected by Maurice's closing transaction. The original option is still in existence, and the grantee's tax consequences depend on what action the grantee takes—exercising the option, letting the option expire, or selling the option.

- Assume that the original option expired unexercised. Maurice has a $500 short-term capital gain equal to the call premium received for writing the option. This gain is not recognized until the option expires. The grantee has a loss from expiration of the option. The nature of the loss will depend upon whether the option was a capital asset or an ordinary asset.

Concept Summary 14.1 summarizes the consequences of various transactions involving options to both the grantor and grantee.

Concept Summary 14.1

Options: Consequences to the Grantor and Grantee

Event	Effect on	
	Grantor	**Grantee**
Option is granted.	Receives value and has a contract obligation (a liability).	Pays value and has a contract right (an asset).
Option is exercised.	Amount received for option increases proceeds from sale of the option property.	Amount paid for option becomes part of the basis of the option property purchased.
Option is sold or exchanged by grantee.	Result depends upon whether option later expires or is exercised (see above).	Could have gain or loss (capital gain or loss if option property would have been a capital asset for the grantee).
Option expires.	Has a short-term capital gain if the option property is stocks, securities, commodities, or commodity futures. Otherwise, gain is ordinary income.	Has a loss (capital loss if option property would have been a capital asset for the grantee).

14-3d Patents

Transfer of a **patent** is treated as the sale or exchange of a long-term capital asset when *all substantial rights* to the patent are transferred by a *holder*.[8] The transferor/holder may receive payment in virtually any form, including contingent payments based on the transferee/purchaser's productivity, use, or disposition of the patent. If the transfer meets these requirements, any gain or loss is *automatically a long-term* capital gain or loss. Whether the asset was a capital asset for the transferor, whether a sale or exchange occurred, and how long the transferor held the patent are not relevant.

Substantial Rights

To receive favorable capital gain treatment, *all substantial rights* to the patent must be transferred. The sale of a partial interest qualifies if the sale places no restrictions on the use of the patent by the purchaser. All substantial rights have not been transferred when the transfer is limited geographically within the issuing country or when the transfer is for a period less than the remaining life of the patent. All the facts and circumstances of the transaction, not just the language of the transfer document, are examined when making this determination.[9]

---

[8]§ 1235.   [9]Reg. § 1.1235–2(b)(1).

Example 15 illustrates the special treatment for patents.

The Big Picture

EXAMPLE 15

Return to the facts of *The Big Picture* on p. 14-1. Shortly after your conversation with Maurice, Green Battery Company offers to buy the patent developed by Kevin for $2,000,000 plus $0.50 for each battery sold. Kevin and Maurice agree to sell the patent.

As Maurice transferred all his remaining rights, he automatically has a long-term capital gain from both his 50% share of the lump-sum payment ($1,000,000) and the $0.50 per battery royalty to the extent those proceeds exceed his basis for the patent.

Whether Maurice gets long-term capital gain treatment depends upon whether Maurice is a *holder*. See the following discussion and Example 16.

Holder Defined

The *holder* of a patent must be an *individual*. Usually, this is the invention's creator or an individual who purchases the patent rights from the creator before the patented invention is put into production ("reduced to practice"). So if the creator's employer has all rights to an employee's inventions, the employer is *not* eligible for long-term capital gain treatment. The employer normally will have an ordinary asset because the patent was developed as part of its business.

The Big Picture

EXAMPLE 16

Return to the facts of *The Big Picture* on p. 14-1. Continuing with the facts of Example 15, Kevin is clearly a holder of the patent because he is the inventor and was not an employee when he invented the battery. When Maurice purchased a 50% interest in the patent nine months ago, he became a *holder* because the patent was not being used to manufacture batteries at the time of the purchase (i.e., it had not been "reduced to practice").

Since Maurice is also a holder, he will have an automatic long-term capital gain or loss if he transfers all substantial rights in his 50% interest to Green Battery Company. Maurice's basis for his share of the patent is $50,000, and the proceeds from Green Battery Company equal $1,000,000 plus $0.50 for each battery sold; Maurice has a long-term capital gain even though he has not held his interest in the patent for more than one year.

Compare the results here to those in Example 5. There, Abigail sold all substantial rights, but she had no patent and the invention had been "reduced to practice" because it was being manufactured and sold.

14-3e Franchises, Trademarks, and Trade Names (§ 1253)

A mode of operation, a widely recognized brand name (trade name), and a widely known business symbol (trademark) are all valuable assets. These assets may be licensed (commonly known as franchising) by their owner for use by other businesses. Many fast-food restaurants (such as McDonald's and Taco Bell) are franchises. The franchisee usually pays the owner (franchisor) an initial fee plus a contingent fee. The contingent fee is often based upon the franchisee's sales volume.

For Federal income tax purposes, a **franchise** is an agreement that gives the franchisee the right to distribute, sell, or provide goods, services, or facilities within a specified area.[10] A franchise transfer includes the grant of a franchise, a transfer by one franchisee to another person, or the renewal of a franchise.

Section 1253 provides that a transfer of a franchise, trademark, or trade name is not a transfer of a capital asset when the transferor retains any significant power, right, or continuing interest in the property transferred.

---

[10] § 1253(b)(1).

Significant Power, Right, or Continuing Interest

In most franchising operations, the transferor retains some powers or rights. As a result, the transaction is not a capital asset transfer. *Significant powers, rights, or continuing interests* include control over franchise assignment, quality of products and services, sale or advertising of products or services, the requirement that substantially all supplies and equipment be purchased from the transferor, and the right to terminate the franchise.

In the unusual case where the transferor does not retain any significant power, right, or continuing interest, a capital gain or loss may occur. For capital gain or loss treatment to be available, the asset transferred must qualify as a capital asset.

The Big Picture

EXAMPLE
17

Return to the facts of *The Big Picture* on p. 14-1. Maurice sells for $210,000 to Mauve, Inc., the franchise purchased from Orange, Inc., nine months ago. The $210,000 received by Maurice is not contingent, and all significant powers, rights, and continuing interests are transferred.

The $115,000 gain ($210,000 proceeds − $95,000 basis) is a short-term capital gain because Maurice has held the franchise for only nine months.

Franchise Payments

In most franchise settings, when the transferor retains significant power or rights, both contingent (e.g., based on sales) and noncontingent payments occur.

Noncontingent Payments Any noncontingent payments made by the franchisee to the franchisor are ordinary income to the franchisor. The franchisee capitalizes the payments and amortizes them over 15 years. If the franchise is sold, the amortization is subject to recapture under § 1245.[11]

EXAMPLE
18

Grey Company signs a 10-year franchise agreement with DOH Donuts. Grey (the franchisee) makes payments of $3,000 per year for the first 8 years of the franchise agreement—a total of $24,000. Grey cannot deduct $3,000 per year as the payments are made. Instead, Grey may amortize the $24,000 total over 15 years. As a result, Grey may deduct $1,600 per year for each of the 15 years of the amortization period.

The same result would occur if Grey made a $24,000 lump-sum payment at the beginning of the franchise period. Assuming that DOH Donuts (the franchisor) retains significant powers, rights, or a continuing interest, it will have ordinary income when it receives the payments from Grey.

Contingent Payments Any contingent franchise payments are ordinary income for the franchisor and an ordinary deduction for the franchisee. Contingent payments must meet the following requirements:

- The payments are made at least annually throughout the term of the transfer agreement.
- The payments are substantially equal in amount or are payable under a fixed formula.

EXAMPLE
19

TAK, a spicy chicken franchisor, transfers an eight-year franchise to Phyllis. TAK retains a significant power, right, or continuing interest. Phyllis, the franchisee, agrees to pay TAK 15% of sales. This contingent payment is ordinary income to TAK and a business deduction for Phyllis as the payments are made.

---

[11]The recapture rules are discussed later in this chapter.

Sports Franchises

Professional sports franchises (e.g., the Detroit Tigers) are subject to § 1253. Player contracts are usually one of the major assets acquired with a sports franchise. These contracts last only for the time stated in the contract. By being classified as § 197 intangibles, the player contracts and other intangible assets acquired in the purchase of the sports franchise are amortized over a statutory 15-year period.[12]

Concept Summary 14.2 reviews the effects of transactions involving franchises on both the franchisor and franchisee.

Concept Summary 14.2

Franchises: Consequences to the Franchisor and Franchisee

Event	Effect on	
	Franchisor	**Franchisee**
Franchisor Retains Significant Powers and Rights		
Noncontingent payment	Ordinary income.	Capitalized and amortized over 15 years as an ordinary deduction; if franchise is sold, amortization is subject to recapture under § 1245.
Contingent payment	Ordinary income.	Ordinary deduction.
Franchisor Does *Not* Retain Significant Powers and Rights		
Noncontingent payment	Ordinary income if franchise rights are an ordinary asset; capital gain if franchise rights are a capital asset (unlikely).	Capitalized and amortized over 15 years as an ordinary deduction; if the franchise is sold, amortization is subject to recapture under § 1245.
Contingent payment	Ordinary income.	Ordinary deduction.

14-3f Lease Cancellation Payments

The tax treatment of payments received for canceling a lease depends on whether the recipient is the `lessor` or the `lessee` and whether the lease is a capital asset.

Lessee Treatment

Lease cancellation payments received by a lessee are treated as an exchange.[13] The treatment of these payments depends on the underlying use of the property and how long the lease has existed.[14]

- If the property was used personally (e.g., an apartment used as a residence), the payment results in a capital gain (and long term if the lease existed for more than one year).

- If the property was used for business and the lease existed for one year or less, the payment results in ordinary income.

- If the property was used for business and the lease existed for more than one year, the payment results in a § 1231 gain.

---

[12]§ 197(a).

[13]§ 1241 and Reg. § 1.1241–1(a).

[14]Reg. § 1.1221–1(b) and PLR 200045019.

Mark owns an apartment building that he is going to convert into an office building. Vicki is one of the apartment tenants and receives $1,000 from Mark to cancel the lease.

Vicki has a capital gain of $1,000 (which is long term or short term depending upon how long she has held the lease). Mark has an ordinary deduction of $1,000.

Lessor Treatment

Payments received by a lessor for a lease cancellation are always ordinary income because they are considered to be in lieu of rental payments.[15]

Floyd owns an apartment building near a university campus. Hui-Fen is one of the tenants. Hui-Fen is graduating early and offers Floyd $800 to cancel the apartment lease. Floyd accepts the offer.

Floyd has ordinary income of $800. Hui-Fen has a nondeductible payment because the apartment was personal use property.

14-4 HOLDING PERIOD

Determine whether the holding period for a capital asset is long term or short term.

14-4a General Rules

Property must be held *more than one year* to qualify for long-term capital gain or loss treatment.[16] Property held for one year or less results in short-term capital gain or loss. To compute the holding period, start counting on the day *after* the property was acquired and include the day of disposition.

The Big Picture

Return to the facts of *The Big Picture* on p. 14-1. Assume that Maurice purchased the Purple stock on January 15, 2020. If he sells it on January 16, 2021, Maurice's holding period is more than one year, and therefore, long term.

If, instead, Maurice sells the stock on January 15, 2021, the holding period is exactly one year and the gain or loss is short term.

An asset's holding period is based on calendar months and fractions of calendar months (not the number of days). It does not matter that different months have different numbers of days.[17]

Leo purchases a capital asset on February 29, 2021. If Leo sells the asset on February 28, 2022, the holding period is one year and Leo will have a short-term capital gain or loss.

If Leo sells the asset on March 1, 2022, the holding period is more than one year and he will have a long-term capital gain or loss.

14-4b Special Holding Period Rules

There are several special holding period rules.[18] The application of these rules depends upon the type of asset and how it was acquired.

Nontaxable Exchanges

The holding period of property received in a like-kind exchange includes the holding period of the former asset if the property that has been exchanged is a capital asset or a § 1231 asset. In these settings, the holding period of the former property is *tacked on* to the holding period of the newly acquired property.

[15]Reg. § 1.61–8(b).
[16]§ 1222.
[17]Rev.Rul. 66–7, 1966–1 C.B. 188.
[18]§ 1223.

On April 22, 2020, Vern exchanges a business building he acquired on March 15, 2017, for another business building in a qualifying like-kind exchange.

    The holding period of the replacement building begins March 15, 2017, because the holding period of the building given up in the exchange *tacks* to the holding period of the replacement building.

Gifts

When a gift occurs, if the donor's basis carries over to the recipient, the donor's holding period is *tacked on* to the recipient's holding period. This will occur when the property's fair market value at the date of the gift is greater than the donor's adjusted basis. Transactions of this nature are discussed in Chapter 13.

Carryover Basis

Kareem acquires 100 shares of Robin Corporation stock for $1,000 on December 31, 2016. He transfers the shares by gift to Megan on December 31, 2019, when the stock is worth $2,000. Kareem's basis of $1,000 becomes the basis for determining gain or loss on a subsequent sale by Megan. Megan's holding period begins with the date the stock was acquired by Kareem.

Assume the same facts as in Example 25, except that the fair market value of the shares is only $800 on the date of the gift. The holding period begins on the date of the gift if Megan sells the stock for a loss. The value of the shares on the date of the gift is used in determining her basis for loss. If she sells the shares for $500 on April 1, 2020, Megan has a $300 recognized capital loss and the holding period is from December 31, 2019, to April 1, 2020 (as a result, the loss is short term).

Certain Disallowed Loss Transactions

Under several Code provisions, realized losses are disallowed. When a loss is disallowed, there is no carryover of holding period. Losses can be disallowed under § 267 (sale or exchange between related taxpayers) and § 262 (sale or exchange of personal use assets) as well as other Code Sections. Taxpayers who acquire property in a disallowed loss transaction will have a new holding period begin and will have a basis equal to the purchase price.

Janet sells her personal automobile at a loss. She may not deduct the loss because it arises from the sale of personal use property. Janet purchases a replacement automobile for more than the selling price of her former automobile. Janet has a basis equal to the cost of the replacement automobile, and her holding period begins when she acquires the replacement automobile.

Inherited Property

The holding period for inherited property is treated as long term no matter how long the property is actually held by the heir. The holding period of the decedent or the decedent's estate is not relevant for the heir's holding period.

Shonda inherits Blue Company stock from her father, who died in 2020. She receives the stock on April 1, 2020, and sells it on November 1, 2020. Even though Shonda did not hold the stock more than one year, she receives long-term capital gain or loss treatment on the sale.

14-4c   Special Rules for Short Sales

General

The Code provides special holding period rules for short sales.[19] A **short sale** occurs when a taxpayer sells borrowed property and repays the lender with substantially identical property either held on the date of the sale or purchased after the sale (even though they are not capital assets).

---

[19]§ 1233.

Short sales usually involve corporate stock. The seller's objective is to make a profit in anticipation of a decline in the stock's price. If the price declines, the seller in a short sale recognizes a profit equal to the difference between the sales price of the borrowed stock and the price paid for the replacement stock.

Chris does not own any shares of Brown Corporation. However, Chris sells 30 shares of Brown. The shares are borrowed from Chris's broker and must be replaced within 45 days. Chris has a short sale because he was short the shares he sold. He will close the short sale by purchasing Brown shares and delivering them to his broker.

If the original 30 shares were sold for $10,000 and Chris later purchased 30 shares for $8,000, he would have had a gain of $2,000. Chris's hunch that the price of Brown stock would decline was correct. Chris was able to profit from selling high and buying low.

If Chris had to purchase Brown shares for $13,000 to close the short sale, he would have a loss of $3,000. In this case, Chris would have sold low and bought high—not the result he wanted. Chris would be making a short sale against the box if he borrowed shares from his broker to sell and then closed the short sale by delivering other Brown shares he owned at the time he made the short sale.

Concept Summary 14.3 summarizes the short sale rules. These rules are intended to prevent the conversion of short-term capital gains into long-term capital gains and long-term capital losses into short-term capital losses.

In most settings, short sale gain or loss results in a capital gain or loss. The gain or loss is not recognized until the short sale is closed. Generally, the holding period of the short sale property is determined by how long the property used to close the short sale was held. However, when *substantially identical property* (e.g., other shares of the same stock) is held by the taxpayer, the holding period is determined as follows:

- The short sale *gain or loss* is *short term* when, on the short sale date, the substantially identical property has been held *short term* (i.e., for one year or less). (See Examples 30 and 31.)

- The short sale *gain* is *long term* when, on the short sale date, the substantially identical property has been held *long term* (i.e., for more than one year) and is used to close the short sale. If the long-term substantially identical property is not used to close the short sale, the short sale gain is *short term*. (See Example 32.)

- The short sale *loss* is *long term* when, on the short sale date, the substantially identical property has been held *long term* (i.e., for more than one year).

- The short sale *gain or loss* is *short term* if the substantially identical property is acquired *after* the short sale date and on or before the closing date. (See Example 33.)

Disposition Rules for Short Sales against the Box

A short sale against the box occurs when the stock is borrowed from a broker by a seller and the seller already owns substantially identical securities on the short sale date or acquires them before the closing date.[20] To remove the taxpayer's flexibility as to when the short sale gain must be reported, a constructive sale approach is used. If the taxpayer has not closed the short sale by delivering the short sale securities to the broker *before* January 31 of the year following the short sale, the short sale is deemed to have been closed on the *earlier* of two events:

- On the short sale date if the taxpayer owned substantially identical securities at that time.

- On the date during the year of the short sale that the taxpayer acquired substantially identical securities.[21]

---

[20]The "box" refers to the safe deposit box that stock owners routinely used to keep physical stock certificates safe. Although today shares of stock are typically held electronically (rather than physically), the terminology *short sale against the box* is still used.

[21]§ 1259.

Concept Summary 14.3

Short Sales of Securities

Has the taxpayer held substantially identical securities for the required long-term holding period at the date of the short sale?

Yes — To the extent of the number of shares sold short, any loss arising from the closing of the short sale is long-term loss regardless of the holding period of the securities used to close the short sale.

If the securities held for the required long-term holding period are used to close the short sale, any gain is long term.

No — Any gain or loss from the close of the short sale is short term.

And / And — For the number of shares sold short, the holding period of substantially identical securities not held long term at the short sale date or acquired after the short sale date and before the closing date begins with the earlier of the date of sale of those securities or the closing date of the short sale. This holding period rule applies in the order of the acquisition dates of the substantially identical property.

The basis of the shares in the deemed transfer of shares is used to compute the gain or loss on the short sale. As Examples 32 and 33 illustrate, when shares are *actually* transferred to the broker to close the short sale, there may be a gain or loss because the shares transferred will have a basis equal to the short sale date price and the value at the *actual* short sale closing date may be different from the short sale date price.

Illustrations

The following examples illustrate the treatment of short sales and short sales against the box.

Short Sales and Short Sales against the Box

EXAMPLE 30

On January 4, 2020, Donald purchases five shares of Osprey Corporation common stock for $100. On April 14, 2020, he engages in a short sale of five shares of the same stock for $150. On August 15, Donald closes the short sale by repaying the borrowed stock with the five shares purchased on January 4. Because his substantially identical shares were held short term as of the short sale date, Donald's $50 capital gain is short term.

EXAMPLE 31

Assume the same facts as in the previous example, except that Donald closes the short sale on January 28, 2021, by repaying the borrowed stock with five shares purchased on January 27, 2021, for $200. Because Donald's substantially identical property (purchased on January 4, 2020) was short-term property at the April 14, 2020 short sale date, his $50 capital loss ($200 cost of stock purchased on January 27, 2021, and a short sale selling price of $150) is short term.

Short Sales and Short Sales against the Box

On January 18, 2018, Rita purchases 200 shares of Owl Corporation stock for $1,000. On November 11, 2019, she sells short, for $1,300, 200 shares of Owl Corporation stock that she borrows from her broker. On February 10, 2020, Rita closes the short sale by delivering the 200 shares of Owl Corporation stock that she had acquired in 2018. On that date, Owl Corporation stock had a market price of $3 per share.

Because Rita owned substantially identical stock on the date of the short sale and did not close the short sale before January 31, 2020, she is *deemed* to have closed the short sale on November 11, 2019 (the date of the short sale). On her 2019 tax return, she reports a $300 long-term capital gain ($1,300 short sale price − $1,000 basis).

On February 10, 2020, Rita has a $700 short-term capital loss [$600 short sale closing date price (200 shares × $3 per share) − $1,300 basis] because the holding period of the shares used to close the short sale commences with the date of the short sale.

Assume the same facts as in Example 32, except that Rita did not own any Owl Corporation stock on the short sale date and acquired the 200 shares of Owl Corporation stock for $1,000 on December 12, 2020 (after the November 11, 2020 short sale date).

The *deemed* closing of the short sale is December 12, 2020, because Rita held substantially identical shares at the end of 2020 and did not close the short sale before January 31, 2021. Her 2020 short sale gain is a *short-term* gain of $300 ($1,300 short sale price − $1,000 basis), and she still has a short-term capital loss of $700 on February 10, 2021.

14-5 TAX TREATMENT OF CAPITAL GAINS AND LOSSES OF NONCORPORATE TAXPAYERS

LO.5

Describe the beneficial tax treatment for capital gains and the detrimental tax treatment for capital losses for noncorporate taxpayers.

All taxpayers net their capital gains and losses. Short-term gains and losses (if any) are netted against one another, and long-term gains and losses (if any) are netted against one another. The results will be net short-term gain or loss and net long-term gain or loss. If these two net positions are of opposite sign (one is a gain and one is a loss), they are netted against each other.

Six possibilities exist for the result after all possible netting has been completed.

1. A net long-term capital gain (NLTCG).
2. A net short-term capital gain (NSTCG).
3. Both NLTCG and NSTCG.
4. A net long-term capital loss (NLTCL).
5. A net short-term capital loss (NSTCL).
6. Both NLTCL and NSTCL.

Net long-term capital gains of noncorporate taxpayers are eligible for an alternative tax calculation that normally results in a lower tax liability. Neither NLTCLs nor NSTCLs are treated as ordinary losses. Treatment as an ordinary loss generally is preferable to capital loss treatment because ordinary losses are deductible in full while the deductibility of capital losses is subject to certain limitations. An individual taxpayer may deduct a maximum of $3,000 of net capital losses for a taxable year.[22]

14-5a Capital Gain and Loss Netting Process

Net short-term capital gain is not eligible for any special tax rate. It is taxed at the same rate as the taxpayer's other taxable income.

Net long-term capital gain is eligible for one or more of *five* alternative tax rates: 0 percent, 15 percent, 20 percent, 25 percent, and 28 percent. The 25 percent and 28 percent rates are used only in unique circumstances. The net long-term capital gain components are referred to as the *0%/15%/20% gain*, the *25% gain*, and the *28% gain*.

---

[22]§ 1211(b).

The *25% gain* is called the unrecaptured § 1250 gain and is related to gain from disposition of § 1231 assets (discussed later in this chapter). Here, the discussion focuses only on how the *25% gain* is taxed and not how it is determined. The *28% gain* relates to collectibles and qualified small business stock (§ 1202, see discussion in Chapter 18). The definition of collectibles is discussed later in this section. As discussed in text Section 14-5c, the 0%/15%/20% rates are applied at various ranges of taxable income based on the taxpayer's filing status (see also Exhibit 14.1).

When the long-term capital gain exceeds the short-term capital loss, a net capital gain (NCG) exists.[23] Net capital gain qualifies for beneficial alternative tax treatment (see the coverage later in the chapter).

Because there are both short- and long-term capital gains and losses and because the long-term capital gains may be taxed at various rates, an *ordering procedure* is required. The ordering procedure, which ensures that any long-term capital gain is taxed at the lowest preferential rate possible, includes the following steps:

Step 1. Group all gains and losses into four groups: short term, and 28%, 25%, and 0%/15%/20% long term.

Step 2. Net the gains and losses within each group.

Step 3. Offset the net 28% and net 25% amounts, if they are of opposite sign.

Step 4. Offset the results after step 3 against the 0%/15%/20% amount, if they are of opposite sign. If the 0%/15%/20% amount is a loss, offset it against the *highest-taxed gain first*. After this step, there is a net long-term capital gain or loss. If there is a net long-term capital gain, it may consist of only *28% gain*, only *25% gain*, only *0%/15%/20% gain*, or some combination of all of these gains. If there is a net long-term capital loss, it is simply a net long-term capital loss.

Step 5. Offset the net short-term amount against the long-term results of step 4, if they are of opposite sign. The netting rules offset net short-term capital loss against the *highest-taxed gain first*. So a net short-term capital loss first offsets any *28% gain*, then any *25% gain*, and finally any *0%/15%/20% gain*.

If the result of step 5 is *only* a short-term capital gain, the taxpayer is not eligible for a reduced tax rate. If the result of step 5 is a loss, the taxpayer may be eligible for a *capital loss deduction* (discussed later in this chapter). If there was no offsetting in step 5 because the short-term and step 4 results were both gains *or* if the result of the offsetting is a long-term gain, a net capital gain exists and the taxpayer may be eligible for a reduced tax rate. The net capital gain may consist of *28% gain*, *25% gain*, and/or *0%/15%/20% gain*.

As you might suspect, this *ordering procedure* can produce many different results. The following series of examples illustrates some of these outcomes.

Capital Gain and Loss Netting Process

EXAMPLE 34

This example shows how a *net short-term capital gain* may result from the netting process.

Step	Short Term	Long-Term Gains and Losses			Comment
		28%	25%	0%/15%/20%	
1	$13,000	$ 12,000		$ 3,000	
	(2,000)	(20,000)			
2	$11,000	($ 8,000)		$ 3,000	
3					No 28%/25% netting because no opposite sign.
4		3,000 →		(3,000)	Netted because of opposite sign.
		($ 5,000)		$ –0–	
5	(5,000) ←	5,000			The net short-term capital gain is taxed as ordinary income.
	$ 6,000	$ –0–			
	Net short-term capital gain				

Capital Gain and Loss Netting Process

This example shows how a *net long-term capital gain* may result from the netting process.

EXAMPLE 35

		Long-Term Gains and Losses			
Step	Short Term	28%	25%	0%/15%/20%	Comment
1	$ 3,000	$15,000	$4,000	$ 3,000	
	(5,000)	(7,000)		(8,000)	
2	($ 2,000)	$ 8,000	$4,000	($ 5,000)	
3					No 28%/25% netting because no opposite sign.
4		(5,000) ←		5,000	Netted because of opposite sign. Net 0%/15%/20% loss is netted against 28% gain first.
		$ 3,000			
				$ –0–	
5	2,000 →	(2,000)			The net short-term capital loss is netted against 28% gain first. The net long-term capital gain is $5,000 ($1,000 + $4,000).
	$ –0–	$ 1,000	$4,000		
		Net 28% gain	Net 25% gain		

This example shows how a *net long-term capital loss* may result from the netting process.

EXAMPLE 36

		Long-Term Gains and Losses			
Step	Short Term	28%	25%	0%/15%/20%	Comment
1	$ 3,000	$ 1,000		$ 3,000	
				(8,000)	
2	$ 3,000	$ 1,000		($ 5,000)	
3					No 28%/25% netting because no opposite sign.
4		(1,000) →		1,000	Netted because of opposite sign.
		$ –0–		($ 4,000)	
5	(3,000) →		→	3,000	The net short-term capital gain is netted against the net long-term capital loss, and the remaining loss is eligible for the capital loss deduction.
	$ –0–			($ 1,000)	
				Net long-term capital loss	

Use of Capital Loss Carryovers

A short-term capital loss carryover to the current year retains its character as short term and is combined with the short-term items of the current year. A net long-term capital loss carries over as a long-term capital loss and is combined with the current-year long-term items. The long-term loss carryover is first offset with *28% gain* of the current year, then *25% gain*, and then *0%/15%/20% gain* until it is absorbed.

EXAMPLE
37

In 2020, Abigail has a $4,000 short-term capital gain, a $36,000 28% long-term capital gain, and a $13,000 0%/15%/20% long-term capital gain. She also has a $3,000 short-term capital loss carry-over and a $2,000 long-term capital loss carryover from 2019.

As a result, in 2020, Abigail has a $1,000 net short-term capital gain ($4,000 − $3,000), a $34,000 net 28% long-term capital gain ($36,000 − $2,000), and a $13,000 net 0%/15%/20% long-term capital gain.

Definition of Collectibles

Capital assets that are collectibles, even though they are held long term, are not eligible for the *0%/15%/20%* alternative tax rate. Instead, a 28 percent alternative tax rate applies. For capital gain or loss purposes, **collectibles** include:[24]

- Any work of art.
- Any rug or antique.
- Any metal or gem.
- Any stamp.
- Any alcoholic beverage.
- Most coins.
- Any historical objects (documents, clothes, etc.).

14-5b Qualified Dividend Income

Dividends paid by domestic and certain foreign corporations are eligible to be taxed at the 0%/15%/20% long-term capital gain rates if they are **qualified dividend income (QDI)** (see the discussion of QDI in text Section 4-3b). Here, the discussion focuses on how the qualified dividend income is taxed.

The Big Picture

EXAMPLE
38

Return to the facts of *The Big Picture* on p. 14-1. After holding the Purple stock for 10 months, Maurice receives $350 of dividends. If Purple is a domestic or qualifying foreign corporation, these are qualified dividends eligible for the 0%/15%/20% tax rate.

After the net capital gain or loss has been determined, the QDI is added to the net long-term capital gain portion of the net capital gain and is taxed as 0%/15%/20% gain. If there is a net capital loss, the net capital loss is still deductible *for* AGI up to $3,000 per year with the remainder of the loss (if any) carrying forward. In this case, the QDI is still eligible to be treated as *0%/15%/20% gain* in the alternative tax calculation (it is *not* offset by the net capital loss).

EXAMPLE
39

Refer to Example 35, but assume that there is qualified dividend income (QDI) of $2,500 in addition to the items shown. The QDI is not netted against the capital gains and losses. Instead, the taxpayer has $1,000 of *28% gain*, $4,000 of *25% gain*, and $2,500 of QDI taxed at 0%/15%/20%.

Refer to Example 36, but assume that there is QDI of $2,500 in addition to the items shown. The QDI is not netted against the net capital loss. The taxpayer has $1,000 capital loss deduction and $2,500 of QDI taxed at 0%/15%/20%.

14-5c Alternative Tax on Net Capital Gain and Qualified Dividend Income

Code § 1 contains the rules that enable the *net capital gain* to be taxed at special rates (0, 15, 20, 25, and 28 percent). This calculation is referred to as the **alternative tax** on net capital gain.[25] The alternative tax applies only if taxable income includes some

---

[24]§ 408(m)(2) and Reg. § 1.408–10(b).

long-term capital gain (there is net capital gain) and/or qualified dividend income (QDI). Taxable income includes *all* of the net capital gain and/or QDI unless taxable income is less than the net capital gain and/or QDI. In addition, the net capital gain and/or QDI is taxed *last*, after other taxable income (including any short-term capital gain).

The *0%/15%/20%* rates are applied to any net capital gain and qualified dividend income based on the taxpayer's filing status and taxable income (see Exhibit 14.1). The taxable income ranges are adjusted for inflation each year.

Joan, a single taxpayer, has taxable income of $118,000, including a $10,000 net capital gain and $2,000 QDI. The last $12,000 of her $118,000 taxable income is the layer related to the net capital gain and/or QDI. The first $106,000 ($118,000 − $12,000) of her taxable income is her other taxable income and is not subject to any special tax rate, so it is taxed using the regular tax rates.

Because the net capital gain and/or QDI may be made up of various *rate layers*, it is important to know in what order those layers are taxed. (Review the five-step ordering procedure discussed in text Section 14-5a and the related examples.) For *each* of the layers, the taxpayer compares the regular tax rate on that layer of income and the alternative tax rate on that portion of the net capital gain and/or QDI.

The layers are taxed in the following order:

- Any *25% gain*,
- Any *28% gain*,
- The 0 percent portion of the *0%/15%/20% gain* and/or QDI,
- The 15 percent portion of the *0%/15%/20% gain* and/or QDI, and then
- The 20 percent portion of the *0%/15%/20% gain* and/or QDI.

EXHIBIT 14.1	**Alternative Tax Rates on Net Capital Gains (NCG)** **(Based on Filing Status and Taxable Income)**							

2020: FILING STATUS								
Single		**Married, Filing Jointly**		**Married, Filing Separately**		**Head of Household**		**NCG Tax Rate**
Taxable Income		**Taxable Income**		**Taxable Income**		**Taxable Income**		
Greater Than	No More Than	Greater Than	No More Than	Greater Than	No More Than	Greater Than	No More Than	
$ –0–	$ 40,000	$ –0–	$ 80,000	$ –0–	$ 40,000	$ –0–	$ 53,600	0%
40,000	441,450	80,000	496,600	40,000	248,300	53,600	469,050	15%
441,450		496,600		248,300		469,050		20%

2019: FILING STATUS								
Single		**Married, Filing Jointly**		**Married, Filing Separately**		**Head of Household**		**NCG Tax Rate**
Taxable Income		**Taxable Income**		**Taxable Income**		**Taxable Income**		
Greater Than	No More Than	Greater Than	No More Than	Greater Than	No More Than	Greater Than	No More Than	
$ –0–	$ 39,375	$ –0–	$ 78,750	$ –0–	$ 39,375	$ –0–	$ 52,750	0%
39,375	434,550	78,750	488,850	39,375	244,425	52,750	461,700	15%
434,550		488,850		244,425		461,700		20%

---

[25]§ 1(h). Note: Examples 41, 42, and 43 use the 2020 Tax Rate Schedules rather than the 2020 Tax Tables (which are not yet available) to calculate the tax on the non-long-term capital gain portion of taxable income. This approach is used to better illustrate the concepts under discussion. The actual tax on the non-long-term portion of taxable income would be calculated using the Tax Tables because that income is less than $100,000.

As a result of this layering:

- The taxpayer benefits from the 0 percent portion of the net capital gain and/or QDI if the taxpayer is still in the 10 percent or 12 percent regular tax bracket after taxing other taxable income and the 25 percent and 28 percent portions of the net capital gain. Depending on the taxpayer's filing status, however, a portion of income in the taxpayer's 12 percent tax bracket is subject to the 15 percent alternative tax rate. In 2020, the 0 percent alternative tax rate applies only through $80,000 of taxable income for married taxpayers filing jointly or surviving spouses, $40,000 for single taxpayers, $53,600 for heads of household, and $40,000 for married taxpayers filing separately. These "break points" for the alternative tax rates do not correspond with the normal tax bracket "break points" (see the 2020 Tax Rate Schedules in Appendix A). This means that in 2020, the last $250 (married, filing jointly and surviving spouses), $125 (single), $100 (heads of household), and $125 (married, filing separately) in the 12 percent bracket is subject to the 15 percent alternative rate. As the normal tax rate (12 percent) is less than the alternative tax rate (15 percent), this means that for these small ranges, any net capital gain or QDI will be taxed at 12 percent (rather than 15 percent).

- The taxpayer benefits from the 15 percent portion of the net capital gain and/or QDI if the taxpayer is in the 22 percent, 24 percent, and 32 percent brackets or a portion of the 35 percent regular rate bracket after taxing other taxable income and the 25 percent, 28 percent, and 0 percent portions of the net capital gain and/or QDI. In 2020, the 15 percent tax rate applies until taxable income exceeds $496,600 for married taxpayers filing jointly, $469,050 for heads of household, and $248,300 for married taxpayers filing separately.

- The taxpayer benefits from the 20 percent portion of the net capital gain and/or QDI when taxable income exceeds the maximum taxable income thresholds for the 15 percent alternative tax rate.

Concept Summary 14.4 summarizes the alternative tax computation.

Concept Summary 14.4

Income Layers for Alternative Tax on Capital Gain Computation

Compute tax on:	Other taxable income (including net short-term capital gain) using the regular tax rates.
Compute tax on:	Each of the layers below using the *lower* of the alternative tax rate or the regular tax rate for that layer (or portion of a layer) of taxable income.

+   25% long-term capital gain (unrecaptured § 1250 gain) portion of taxable income.

+   28% long-term capital gain.

+   0% long-term capital gain [portion of *0%/15%/20% gain* and/or qualified dividend income (QDI) that is taxed at 0%; available only if other taxable income plus 25% and 28% capital gain layers do not put the taxpayer above specified thresholds in the 12% regular tax bracket*; 0% rate is no longer available once income, including the portion of the gain and/or QDI taxed at 0%, puts the taxpayer above these thresholds].

+   15% long-term capital gain (portion of *0%/15%/20% gain* and/or QDI that is taxed at 15%; available only if other taxable income plus the 25%, 28%, and 0% layers put the taxpayer above the 12% regular tax bracket and only until other taxable income plus the 25%, 28%, 0%, and 15% layers put the taxpayer at or below specified thresholds in the 35% regular tax rate bracket)**.

+   20% long-term capital gain (portion of *0%/15%/20% gain* and/or QDI that is taxed at 20%; available when other taxable income plus the 25%, 28%, 0%, and 15% layers put the taxpayer above the specified thresholds in the 35% regular tax rate bracket).

=   Alternative tax on taxable income

*See Exhibit 14.1 for the taxable income ranges where the 0%/15%/20% rates apply. In 2020, the last $250 (married filing jointly and surviving spouse), $125 (single), $100 (heads of household), and $125 (married filing separately) of the 12% bracket is subject to the 15% alternative tax rate. As the normal tax rate of 12% is less than the alternative tax rate of 15%, any *0%/15%/20% gain* or QDI in these ranges will be taxed at 12%.

**See Exhibit 14.1 for the taxable income amounts where the 20% rate begins to apply.

Alternative Tax on Net Capital Gain

EXAMPLE 41

In Example 40, Joan had $118,000 taxable income. Now assume that Joan's $10,000 net capital gain is made up of $7,000 *25% gain* and $3,000 *0%/15%/20% gain*. In addition, she has $2,000 of QDI. Examination of the 2020 tax rates reveals that $106,000 ($118,000 − $12,000) of other taxable income for a single individual puts Joan at a marginal tax rate of 24%. Consequently, she uses the alternative tax on the $7,000 gain, the $3,000 gain, and the $2,000 QDI.

Her alternative tax liability for 2020 is $21,950:

	$19,520	(tax on $106,000 of other taxable income)
+	1,680	($7,000 × 0.24; 24% rate on *25% gain*)
+	450	($3,000 × 0.15; 15% rate on *0%/15%/20% gain*)
+	300	($2,000 × 0.15; 15% rate on QDI)
=	$21,950	Alternative tax liability

Since her marginal tax rate is still 24% after taxing the $106,000 other taxable income, she uses the 24% regular tax rate rather than the 25% alternative tax rate on the $7,000 *25% gain*. As the combination of the $106,000 other taxable income and her $7,000 *25% gain* puts her above the 12% regular tax bracket, none of the $3,000 *0%/15%/20% gain* or $2,000 QDI is taxed at 0%.

Her regular tax liability on $118,000 is $22,400. As a result, Joan saves $450 ($22,400 − $21,950) by using the alternative tax calculation. Because Joan's taxable income is $441,450 or less, none of her *0%/15%/20% gain* or QDI is taxed at the 20% alternative tax rate.

EXAMPLE 42

Assume that Joan, a single taxpayer, has 2020 taxable income of $25,000. Of this amount, $11,000 is net capital gain, $1,000 is QDI, and $13,000 is other taxable income. The $11,000 net capital gain is made up of $8,300 of *25% gain* and $2,700 of *0%/15%/20% gain*.

Her alternative tax liability for 2020 is $2,359:

	$1,363	(tax on $13,000 of other taxable income)
+	996	(tax on $8,300 *25% gain* at 12%)
+	0	(tax on $2,700 *0%/15%/20% gain* at 0%)
+	0	(tax on $1,000 QDI at 0%)
=	$2,359	Alternative tax liability

Because her marginal rate is still 12% after taxing the $13,000 of other taxable income, she uses the 12% regular tax rate rather than the 25% alternative tax rate on the $8,300 *25% gain*. After taxing the $13,000 and the $8,300, a total of $21,300 of the $25,000 taxable income has been taxed. Because her remaining taxable income ($3,700) remains in the 12% tax bracket (and her total taxable income does not exceed $40,000), she uses the 0% alternative rate for the $2,700 of *0%/15%/20% gain* and $1,000 QDI.

Joan's regular tax liability on $25,000 is $2,803. As a result, she saves $444 ($2,803 − $2,359) by using the alternative tax calculation.

The alternative tax computation allows the taxpayer to receive the *lower of* the regular tax or the alternative tax on *each layer* of net capital gain and/or QDI or *portion of each layer* of net capital gain and/or QDI.

EXAMPLE 43

Assume the same facts as in Example 42, except that Joan's 2020 taxable income is $42,000, consisting of $11,000 of net capital gain, $1,000 of QDI, and $30,000 of other taxable income.

Not all of the combined *0%/15%/20% gain* and QDI ($3,700; $2,700 + $1,000) is taxed at 0% because Joan's taxable income exceeds $40,000, taking her out of the 0% alternative tax. Consequently, the last $2,000 ($42,000 − $40,000) of the $3,700 is taxed at 12% and 15% rather than 0%.

continued

Her tax liability using the alternative tax computation is $4,695:

$3,403   (tax on $30,000 of other taxable income)
+   996   (tax on $8,300 *25% gain* at 12%)
+   0   (tax on $1,700 of the $3,700 combined *0%/15%/20% gain* and QDI at 0%)
+   15   (tax on $125 of the $3,700 combined *0%/15%/20% gain* and QDI at 12%)
+   281   (tax on $1,875 of the $3,700 combined *0%/15%/20% gain* and QDI at 15%)
= **$4,695**   Alternative tax liability

Joan's regular tax liability on $42,000 is $5,030. As a result, she saves $335 ($5,030 − $4,695) by using the alternative tax calculation.

14-5d Treatment of Net Capital Losses

Computation of Net Capital Loss

A **net capital loss (NCL)** results if capital losses exceed capital gains for the year. An NCL may be all long term, all short term, or part long and part short term.[26] The characterization of an NCL as long or short term is important in determining the capital loss deduction (discussed next).

EXAMPLE 44

Three different individuals have the following capital gains and losses during the year:

	Short Term			Long Term			Combined Short Term and Long Term	Description of Result
Taxpayer	STCG	STCL	Net Short Term	LTCG	LTCL	Net Long Term		
Paulina	$1,000	($ 500)	$ 500	$1,000	($2,800)	($1,800)	($1,300)	NLTCL
Carlos	1,000	(2,800)	(1,800)	1,000	(500)	500	(1,300)	NSTCL
Anibal	500	(1,200)	(700)	400	(1,200)	(800)	(1,500)	NSTCL ($700) NLTCL ($800)

Paulina's NCL of $1,300 is all long term. Carlos's NCL of $1,300 is all short term. Anibal's NCL is $1,500, $700 of which is short term and $800 of which is long term.

Capital Loss Deduction

A net capital loss is deductible *for* AGI, but limited to no more than $3,000 per tax year.[27] So although a net capital gain receives favorable tax treatment, there is *unfavorable* treatment for capital losses due to the $3,000 annual limitation. If the NCL includes both long- and short-term capital loss, the short-term capital loss is counted first toward the $3,000 annual limitation.

EXAMPLE 45

Burt has an NCL of $5,500, of which $2,000 is STCL and $3,500 is LTCL. Burt has a capital loss deduction of $3,000 ($2,000 of STCL and $1,000 of LTCL). He has an LTCL carryforward of $2,500 ($3,500 − $1,000).

Carryovers

Taxpayers are allowed to carry over unused capital losses indefinitely. The short-term capital loss (STCL) retains its character as STCL. Likewise, the long-term capital loss retains its character as LTCL.

[26]Section 1222(10) defines a net capital loss as the net loss after the capital loss deduction. However, that definition confuses the discussion of net capital loss. Therefore, net capital loss is used here to mean the result after netting capital gains and losses and before considering the capital loss deduction. The capital loss deduction is discussed later in this section.

[27]§ 1211(b)(1). Married taxpayers filing separate returns are limited to a $1,500 deduction per tax year. When a taxpayer has both a capital loss deduction and negative taxable income, a special computation of the capital loss carryover is required. See § 1212(b).

In 2020, Mark incurred $1,000 of STCL and $11,000 of LTCL. In 2021, Mark has a $400 LTCG.

EXAMPLE
46

- Mark's NCL for 2020 is $12,000. Mark deducts $3,000 ($1,000 STCL and $2,000 LTCL). He has $9,000 of LTCL carried forward to 2021.

- Mark combines the $9,000 LTCL carryforward with the $400 LTCG for 2021. He has an $8,600 NLTCL for 2021. Mark deducts $3,000 of LTCL in 2021 and carries forward $5,600 of LTCL to 2022.

Concept Summary 14.5 summarizes the rules for noncorporate taxpayers' treatment of capital gains and losses.

Concept Summary 14.5

Final Results of the Capital Gain and Loss Netting Process and How They Are Taxed

Result	Maximum Tax Rate	Comments
Net short-term capital loss	—	Eligible for capital loss deduction ($3,000 maximum per year).
Net long-term capital loss	—	Eligible for capital loss deduction ($3,000 maximum per year).
Net short-term capital loss *and* net long-term capital loss	—	Eligible for capital loss deduction ($3,000 maximum per year). Short-term capital losses are counted first toward the deduction.
Net short-term capital gain	10%–37%	Taxed as ordinary income.
Net long-term capital gain	0%–28%	The net long-term capital gain may have as many as five tax rate components: 25%, 28%, and 0%/15%/20%.
• The net long-term capital gain is the *last* portion of taxable income.		The components are taxed in the following order: 25%, 28%, 0%, 15%, 20%. They are taxed *after* the non-long-term capital gain portion of taxable income has been taxed. The 0%/15%/20% component may include qualified dividend income.
• Each net long-term capital gain component of taxable income is taxed at the *lower* of the regular tax on that component or the alternative tax.		The alternative tax on net long-term capital gain can never increase the tax on taxable income, but it can reduce the tax on taxable income.
Net short-term capital gain *and* net long-term capital gain	10%–37% on net short-term capital gain; 0%–28% on net long-term capital gain	The net short-term capital gain is taxed as ordinary income; the net long-term capital gain is taxed as discussed above for just net long-term capital gain.

14-6 TAX TREATMENT OF CAPITAL GAINS AND LOSSES OF CORPORATE TAXPAYERS

LO.6

Describe the tax treatment for capital gains and the detrimental tax treatment for capital losses for corporate taxpayers.

The treatment of a corporation's net capital gain or loss differs from the rules for individuals. Briefly, the differences are as follows:

- There is no NCG alternative tax rate.

- Capital losses offset only capital gains. No deduction of capital losses is permitted against other taxable income (whereas a $3,000 deduction is allowed to individuals).[28]

- Corporations may carry back net capital losses (whether long term or short term) as short-term capital losses for three years; if losses still remain after the carryback, the remaining losses may be carried forward five years.[29] Individuals may carry forward unused capital losses indefinitely, but there is no carryback.

---

[28] § 1211(a).   [29] § 1212(a)(1).

EXAMPLE
47

Sparrow Corporation has a $15,000 NLTCL for the current year and $57,000 of other taxable income. Sparrow may not offset the $15,000 NLTCL against its other income by taking a capital loss deduction.

The $15,000 NLTCL becomes a $15,000 STCL for carryback and carryover purposes. This amount may be offset against capital gains in the three-year carryback period or, if not absorbed there, offset capital gains in the five-year carryforward period. Any amount remaining after this carryforward period expires is permanently lost.

14-7 OVERVIEW OF § 1231 AND THE RECAPTURE PROVISIONS

Generic Manufacturing LLC (a limited liability company) sold machinery, office furniture, and unneeded production plants for $100 million last year. The company's disposition of these assets resulted in $60 million of gains and $13 million of losses. How are these gains and losses treated for tax purposes? Do any special tax rules apply? Could any of the gains and losses receive capital gain or loss treatment?

The remainder of this chapter answers these questions by explaining how to *classify* gains and losses from the disposition of assets that are used in the business rather than held for resale. Chapter 8 discussed how to *depreciate* such assets. Chapter 13 discussed how to determine the *adjusted basis* and the *amount* of gain or loss from their disposition.

A long-term capital gain was defined earlier in this chapter as the recognized gain from the sale or exchange of a capital asset held for the required long-term holding period.[30] Long-term capital assets are capital assets held more than one year.

The remainder of this chapter is concerned with classification under § 1231, a very complex Code Section, but one that impacts many transactions involving business assets. These transactions generally involve depreciable assets and land. Taxpayers that are affected by § 1231 are those involved in a business (sole proprietors, partnerships, corporations, and some trusts) and taxpayers owning rental property.

In general, § 1231 applies to the sale or exchange of business properties and to certain involuntary conversions. These properties are *not* capital assets because they are depreciable and/or real property used in business or for the production of income.[31] Nonetheless, these business properties may be held for long periods of time and may be sold at a gain.

Congress decided many years ago that § 1231 assets deserved limited capital gain-type treatment. Capital gain treatment sometimes gives too much tax advantage when assets are eligible for depreciation (or cost recovery). As a result, depreciation recapture rules were created to prevent capital gain treatment when gains are realized on § 1231 assets. This chapter also covers the recapture rules that treat a portion (or all) of the gain as ordinary income (even though the gain might otherwise qualify for long-term capital gain treatment).

14-8 SECTION 1231 ASSETS

LO.7

State and explain the rationale for and the nature and treatment of gains and losses from the disposition of business assets.

14-8a Relationship to Capital Assets

Because depreciable property and real property used in business are not capital assets, the recognized gains from the disposition of this property would appear to be ordinary income rather than capital gain. Due to § 1231, however, *net gain* from the

---

[30]§ 1222(3).   [31]§ 1221(a)(2).

disposition of this property is sometimes *treated* as *long-term capital gain*. In order for this to occur:

- A long-term holding period requirement must be met (held for *more than* a year);
- The disposition must generally be from a sale, exchange, or involuntary conversion; and
- Certain recapture provisions must be satisfied.

Section 1231 may also apply to involuntary conversions of capital assets even though such a disposition, which is not a sale or exchange, normally would not result in a capital gain.

If the disposition of depreciable property and real property used in business results in a *net loss*, § 1231 *treats* the *loss* as an *ordinary loss* rather than as a capital loss. Ordinary losses are fully deductible *for* adjusted gross income (AGI). Capital losses offset capital gains, and if any loss remains, the loss is deductible to the extent of $3,000 per year for individuals and currently is not deductible at all by regular corporations.

In general, § 1231 provides the *best* of both potential results: net gain may be treated as long-term capital gain, and net loss is treated as ordinary loss; note the results in Examples 48 and 49.

Section 1231 Treatment

Roberto sells a building at a $5,000 gain and equipment at a $3,000 loss. Both properties were § 1231 assets because they were used in Roberto's trade or business and held for the long-term holding period (more than one year).

Roberto's net gain is $2,000, and that net gain *may* (depending on various recapture rules discussed later in this chapter) be treated as a long-term capital gain under § 1231.

EXAMPLE 48

Samantha sells business equipment at a $10,000 loss and business land at a $2,000 gain.

Both properties were held for the long-term holding period and, therefore, are § 1231 assets. Samantha's net loss is $8,000, and that net § 1231 loss is an ordinary loss.

EXAMPLE 49

The rules regarding § 1231 treatment do *not* apply to *all* business property. Section 1231 has specific holding period requirements and, in general, requires that the property must be either depreciable property or real estate used in business. As a result, neither inventory nor receivables are § 1231 assets. Nor is § 1231 necessarily limited to business property. Transactions involving certain capital assets may fall into the § 1231 category.

As discussed earlier in this chapter, long-term capital gains receive beneficial tax treatment. Section 1231 requires netting of §1231 gains and losses . If the result is a gain, it may be treated as a long-term capital gain. The net gain is added to the "real" long-term capital gains (if any) and netted with capital losses (if any). As a result, the net § 1231 gain may eventually be eligible for beneficial capital gain treatment or help avoid the deduction limitations that apply to a net capital loss. If the § 1231 gain and loss netting results in a loss, it is an ordinary loss. Finally, § 1231 assets are treated the same as capital assets for purposes of the appreciated property charitable contribution provisions (refer to Chapter 10).

14-8b **Property Included**

Section 1231 property generally includes the following assets if they are held for more than one year:

- Depreciable or real property used in business or for the production of income (principally machinery and equipment, buildings, and land).
- Timber, coal, or domestic iron ore.

LO.8

Distinguish § 1231 assets from ordinary assets and capital assets and calculate the § 1231 gain or loss.

- Livestock held for draft, breeding, dairy, or sporting purposes.
- Unharvested crops on land used in business.
- Certain *purchased* intangible assets (such as patents and goodwill) that are eligible for amortization.

These assets are ordinary assets until they have been held for more than one year. Only then do they become § 1231 assets.

14-8c Property Excluded

Section 1231 property generally does *not* include the following:

- Property not held for the long-term holding period.[32]
- Nonpersonal use property where casualty losses exceed casualty gains for the taxable year. If a taxpayer has a net casualty loss, the individual casualty gains and losses are treated as ordinary gains and losses.
- Inventory and property held primarily for sale to customers.
- A patent, invention, model, or design (whether or not patented); a secret formula or process; certain copyrights; literary, musical, or artistic compositions; and certain U.S. government publications.
- Accounts receivable and notes receivable arising in the ordinary course of the trade or business.

14-8d Section 1231 Assets Disposed of by Casualty or Theft

When § 1231 assets are disposed of by casualty or theft, a special netting rule is applied. For simplicity, the term *casualty* is used to mean both casualty and theft dispositions. First, the casualty gains and losses from § 1231 assets *and* the casualty gains and losses from long-term nonpersonal use capital assets are determined.[33] A nonpersonal use capital asset might be art held as an investment or a baseball card collection held by a nondealer.

Next, the § 1231 asset casualty gains and losses and the nonpersonal use capital asset casualty gains and losses are netted together (see Concept Summary 14.6).

- If the result is a *net loss*, the § 1231 casualty gains and the nonpersonal use capital asset casualty gains are treated as ordinary gains, the § 1231 casualty losses are deductible *for* AGI, and the nonpersonal use capital asset casualty losses are deductible *from* AGI as miscellaneous itemized deductions (which are not deductible from 2018 through 2025).
- If the result of the netting is a *net gain*, the net gain is treated as a § 1231 gain.

As a result, a § 1231 asset disposed of by casualty may or may not get § 1231 treatment, depending on whether the netting process results in a gain or a loss. Also, a nonpersonal use capital asset disposed of by casualty may get § 1231 treatment or ordinary treatment, but will not get capital gain or loss treatment.

Casualties, thefts, and condemnations are *involuntary conversions*. Involuntary conversion gains may be deferred if conversion proceeds are reinvested; involuntary conversion losses are recognized currently (refer to Chapter 13) regardless of whether the conversion proceeds are reinvested. Thus, the special netting process discussed previously for casualties and thefts would not include gains that are not currently recognizable because the insurance proceeds are reinvested.

---

[32]Because the benefit of § 1231 is long-term capital gain treatment, the holding period must correspond to the more-than-one-year holding period that applies to capital assets. Livestock must be held at least 12 months (24 months in some cases). Unharvested crops do not have to be held for the required long-term holding period, but the land must be held for the long-term holding period.

[33]*Personal use property casualty* losses (unless they arise in a Federal disaster area) are not usable except to the extent they offset casualty gains. *Personal use property net casualty gains* are treated as long-term capital gains.

Concept Summary 14.6

Section 1231 Netting Procedure (Discussed in Section 14-8e)

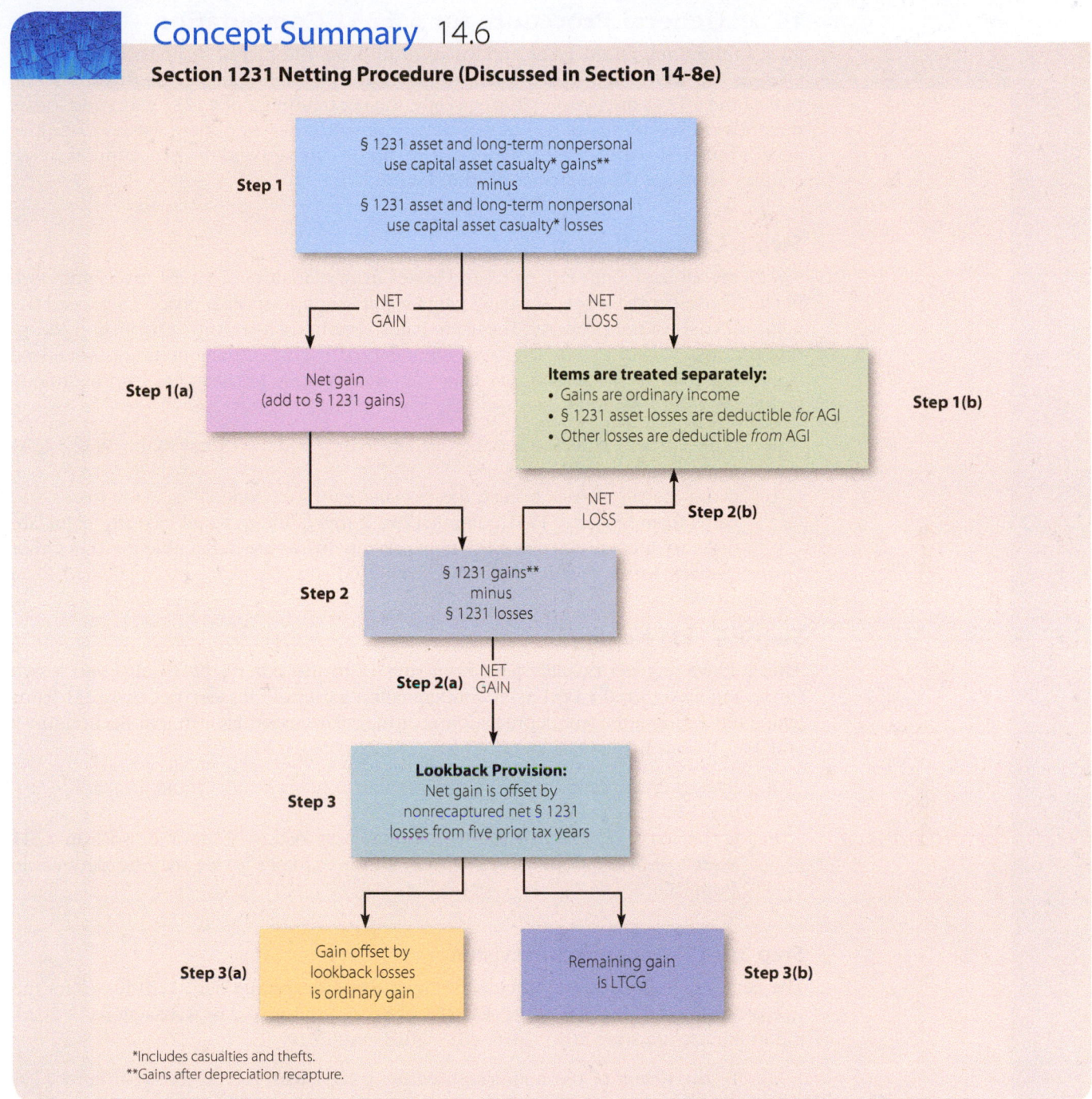

*Includes casualties and thefts.
**Gains after depreciation recapture.

The special netting process for casualties and thefts also does not include condemnation gains and losses. Consequently, a § 1231 asset disposed of by condemnation will receive § 1231 treatment. This variation between recognized casualty and condemnation gains and losses sheds considerable light on what § 1231 is all about. Section 1231 has no effect on whether *realized* gain or loss is recognized. Instead, § 1231 merely dictates how such *recognized* gain or loss is *classified* (ordinary, capital, or § 1231) under certain conditions.[34]

---

[34]*Personal use property condemnation* gains and losses are not subject to the § 1231 rules. The gains are capital gains (because personal use property is a capital asset), and the losses are nondeductible because they arise from the disposition of personal use property.

14-8e General Procedure for § 1231 Computation

Most of the time, § 1231 gains and losses result from the sale of business assets. However, as we have already discussed, disposition by casualty and/or theft can also be part of the § 1231 discussion. Consequently, the tax treatment of § 1231 gains and losses depends on the results of a complex *netting* procedure. When there are no casualties and/or thefts (the usual case), step 1 below can be skipped and the procedure is much simpler. Here are the steps that need to be followed:

Step 1: Casualty Netting

Net all recognized long-term gains and losses from casualties of § 1231 assets and non-personal use capital assets. Casualty gains result when insurance proceeds exceed the adjusted basis of the property. These are gains remaining after any depreciation recapture (discussed later in text Sections 14-9 and 14-10). This casualty netting is beneficial because if there is a net gain, the gain may receive long-term capital gain treatment. If there is a net loss, it receives ordinary loss treatment.

    a.   If the casualty gains exceed the casualty losses, add the excess to the other § 1231 gains for the taxable year.

    b.   If the casualty losses exceed the casualty gains, exclude all casualty losses and gains from further § 1231 computation. If this is the case, all casualty gains are ordinary income. Section 1231 asset casualty losses are deductible *for* AGI. Other casualty losses may be deductible *from* AGI.

Step 2: § 1231 Netting

After adding any net casualty gain from step 1a to the other § 1231 gains and losses (including recognized § 1231 asset condemnation gains and losses), net all § 1231 gains [gains remaining after any depreciation recapture (discussed later in text Sections 14-9 and 14-10)] and losses.

    a.   If the gains exceed the losses, the net gain is offset by the "lookback" nonrecaptured § 1231 losses (see step 3).

    b.   If the losses exceed the gains, all gains are ordinary income. Section 1231 asset losses are deductible *for* AGI. Other casualty losses may be deductible *from* AGI.

Step 3: § 1231 Lookback Provision

The net § 1231 gain from step 2a is offset by the nonrecaptured net § 1231 losses for the five preceding taxable years (the **§ 1231 lookback** provision). For transactions in 2020, the lookback years are 2015, 2016, 2017, 2018, and 2019.

    a.   To the extent of the nonrecaptured net § 1231 loss, the current-year net § 1231 gain is ordinary income. The *nonrecaptured* net § 1231 losses are those that have not already been used to offset net § 1231 gains.

    b.   Only the net § 1231 gain exceeding this net § 1231 loss carryforward is given long-term capital gain treatment.

Concept Summary 14.6 on p. 14-31 summarizes the § 1231 computational procedure. Examples 50 and 51 illustrate its application without the § 1231 lookback provision. Examples 52 and 53 illustrate its application with the § 1231 lookback provision.

Section 1231 Computations

During 2020, Ross had $125,000 of AGI before considering the following recognized gains and losses:

Capital Gains and Losses	
Long-term capital gain	$3,000
Long-term capital loss	(400)
Short-term capital gain	1,000
Short-term capital loss	(200)

Casualties	
Theft of diamond ring (owned four months)	($ 800)*
Fire damage to personal residence (owned 10 years)	(400)*
Gain from insurance recovery on fire loss to business building (owned two years)	200

§ 1231 Gains and Losses from Sale of Depreciable Business Assets Held Long Term	
Asset A	$ 300
Asset B	1,100
Asset C	(500)

Gains and Losses from Sale of Depreciable Business Assets Held Short Term	
Asset D	$ 200
Asset E	(300)

*As adjusted for the $100 floor on personal casualty losses.

Ross had no net § 1231 losses in tax years before 2020.

Ross's gains and losses receive the following tax treatment. [The gains on the business building and Assets A and B are *after* any depreciation recapture (discussed later in the chapter).]

- The diamond ring and the residence are personal use assets. Therefore, these casualties are not § 1231 transactions. The $800 (ring) plus $400 (residence) losses are not deductible because they are not Federal disaster area losses and there are no personal use property casualty gains to offset these losses.

- **Step 1:** Only the business building (a § 1231 asset) casualty gain remains. The netting of the § 1231 asset and nonpersonal use capital asset casualty gains and losses contains only one item—the $200 gain from the business building. Consequently, there is a net gain, and that gain is treated as a § 1231 gain (and added to the § 1231 gains).

- **Step 1(a):** The gains from § 1231 transactions (Assets A and B and the § 1231 asset casualty gain) exceed the losses (Asset C) by $1,100 ($1,600 − $500). This excess is a long-term capital gain and is added to Ross's other long-term capital gains.

- **Step 2:** Ross's net long-term capital gain is $3,700 ($3,000 + $1,100 from § 1231 transactions − $400 long-term capital loss). Ross's net short-term capital gain is $800 ($1,000 − $200). The result is capital gain net income of $4,500. The $3,700 net long-term capital gain portion is eligible for beneficial capital gain treatment [assume that all of the gain is *0%/15%/20% gain* (see the discussion earlier in this chapter)]. The $800 net short-term capital gain is subject to tax as ordinary income.[35]

continued

EXAMPLE
50

---

[35]Ross's taxable income (unless his itemized deductions are extremely large) will put him in at least the 24% bracket. Thus, the alternative tax computation will yield a lower tax. See Example 41.

- Ross treats the gain and loss from Assets D and E (depreciable business assets held for less than the long-term holding period) as ordinary gain and loss.

Results of the Gains and Losses on Ross's Tax Computation	
NLTCG	$ 3,700
NSTCG	800
Ordinary gain from sale of Asset D	200
Ordinary loss from sale of Asset E	(300)
AGI from other sources	125,000
AGI	$129,400

- Ross will have personal use property casualty losses of $1,200 [$800 (diamond ring) + $400 (personal residence)]. The $1,200 is not deductible because the losses are not Federal disaster area losses and there are no personal use property casualty gains to offset these losses.

EXAMPLE 51

Assume the same facts as in Example 50, except that the loss from Asset C was $1,700 instead of $500.

- The treatment of the casualty losses is the same as in Example 50.
- **Step 1(b):** The losses from § 1231 transactions now exceed the gains by $100 ($1,700 − $1,600). As a result, the gains from Assets A and B and the § 1231 asset casualty gain are ordinary income, and the loss from Asset C is a deduction *for* AGI (a business loss). The same result can be achieved by simply treating the $100 net loss as a deduction *for* AGI.
- Capital gain net income is $3,400 ($2,600 long term + $800 short term). The $2,600 net long-term capital gain portion is eligible for beneficial capital gain treatment, and the $800 net short-term capital gain is subject to tax as ordinary income.

Results of the Gains and Losses on Ross's Tax Computation	
NLTCG	$ 2,600
NSTCG	800
Net ordinary loss on Assets A, B, and C and § 1231 casualty gain	(100)
Ordinary gain from sale of Asset D	200
Ordinary loss from sale of Asset E	(300)
AGI from other sources	125,000
AGI	$128,200

- The $1,200 of personal casualty losses is not deductible because the losses are not Federal disaster area losses and there are no personal use property casualty gains to offset these losses.

EXAMPLE 52

Assume the same facts as in Example 50, except that Ross has a $700 nonrecaptured net § 1231 loss from 2019.

- The treatment of the casualty losses is the same as in Example 50.
- **Step 3(a):** The 2020 net § 1231 gain of $1,100 is treated as ordinary income to the extent of the 2018 nonrecaptured § 1231 loss of $700.
- **Step 3(b):** The remaining $400 net § 1231 gain is a long-term capital gain and is added to Ross's other long-term capital gains.

continued

- Ross's net long-term capital gain is $3,000 ($3,000 + $400 from § 1231 transactions − $400 long-term capital loss). Ross's net short-term capital gain is still $800 ($1,000 − $200). The result is capital gain net income of $3,800. The $3,000 net long-term capital gain portion is eligible for beneficial capital gain treatment, and the $800 net short-term capital gain is subject to tax as ordinary income.

Results of the Gains and Losses on Ross's Tax Computation	
NLTCG	$ 3,000
NSTCG	800
Ordinary gain from recapture of § 1231 losses	700
Ordinary gain from sale of Asset D	200
Ordinary loss from sale of Asset E	(300)
AGI from other sources	125,000
AGI	$129,400

- The $1,200 of personal casualty losses is not deductible because the losses are not Federal disaster area losses and there are no personal use property casualty gains to offset these losses.

Assume the same facts as in Example 50, except that Ross had a net § 1231 loss of $2,700 in 2018 and a net § 1231 gain of $300 in 2019.

- The treatment of the casualty losses is the same as in Example 50.

- **Step 3(a):** The 2017 net § 1231 loss of $2,700 will have carried over to 2018 and been offset against the 2018 net § 1231 gain of $300. Thus, the $300 gain will have been classified as ordinary income, and $2,400 of nonrecaptured 2017 net § 1231 loss will carry over to 2019. The 2019 net § 1231 gain of $1,100 will be offset against this loss, resulting in $1,100 of ordinary income. The nonrecaptured net § 1231 loss of $1,300 ($2,400 − $1,100) carries over to 2020.

- Capital gain net income is $3,400 ($2,600 net long-term capital gain + $800 net short-term capital gain). The $2,600 net long-term capital gain portion is eligible for beneficial capital gain treatment, and the $800 net short-term capital gain is subject to tax as ordinary income.

Results of the Gains and Losses on Ross's Tax Computation	
NLTCG	$ 2,600
NSTCG	800
Ordinary gain from recapture of § 1231 losses	1,100
Ordinary gain from sale of Asset D	200
Ordinary loss from sale of Asset E	(300)
AGI from other sources	125,000
AGI	$129,400

- The $1,200 of personal casualty losses is not deductible because the losses are not Federal disaster area losses and there are no personal use property casualty gains to offset these losses.

14-9 SECTION 1245 RECAPTURE

LO.9

Determine when § 1245 recapture applies and how it is computed.

Now that the basic rules of § 1231 have been introduced, it is time to add some additional complications. The Code contains two major *recapture* provisions—§§ 1245 and 1250.[36] These provisions cause *gain* to be treated *initially* as ordinary gain. Thus, what may appear to be a § 1231 gain is ordinary gain instead. This recapture phenomenon applies exclusively to § 1231 gains; § 1231 assets generating losses are unaffected by these recapture provisions.

---

[36]Due to the passage of time, § 1250 is largely ineffective, but is still important in certain situations.

These recapture provisions may also cause a gain in a nonpersonal use casualty to be *initially* ordinary gain rather than casualty gain. Classifying gains (and losses) properly is important; improper initial classification may lead to incorrect mixing and matching of gains and losses. We begin by discussing the § 1245 recapture rules; the § 1250 recapture rules are discussed in text Section 14-10.

Section 1245 requires taxpayers to treat all gain as ordinary gain unless the property is disposed of for more than its original cost. This result is accomplished by requiring that all gain be treated as ordinary gain to the extent of the depreciation taken on the property disposed of. The excess of the sales price over the original cost is § 1231 gain. Section 1245 applies *primarily* to non-real-estate property like machinery, trucks, and office furniture. Section 1245 does not apply if property is disposed of at a loss. Generally, the loss will be a § 1231 loss unless the form of the disposition is a casualty.

EXAMPLE 54

Alice purchased a $100,000 business machine and deducted $70,000 depreciation before selling it for $80,000. If it were not for § 1245, the $50,000 gain would be § 1231 gain ($80,000 amount realized − $30,000 adjusted basis). Section 1245 prevents this potentially favorable result by treating as ordinary income (not as § 1231 gain) any gain to the extent of depreciation taken. In this example, the entire $50,000 gain would be ordinary income.

If Alice had sold the machine for $120,000, she would have a gain of $90,000 ($120,000 amount realized − $30,000 adjusted basis). The § 1245 gain would be $70,000 (equal to the depreciation taken), and the § 1231 gain would be $20,000 (equal to the excess of the sales price over the original cost).

Section 1245 recapture provides, in general, that the portion of recognized gain from the sale or other disposition of § 1245 property that represents depreciation is *recaptured* as ordinary income.[37] As a result, in Example 54, $50,000 of the $70,000 depreciation taken is recaptured as ordinary income when the business equipment is sold for $80,000. Only $50,000 is recaptured rather than $70,000 because Alice is only required to recognize § 1245 recapture ordinary gain equal to the *lower* of the depreciation taken or the gain recognized.

The method of depreciation (e.g., accelerated or straight-line) does not matter. All depreciation taken is potentially subject to recapture. For this reason, § 1245 recapture is often referred to as *full recapture*. Any remaining gain after subtracting the amount recaptured as ordinary income will usually be § 1231 gain.

If the property is disposed of in a casualty event, however, the remaining gain will be casualty gain. If the business machine in Example 54 had been disposed of by casualty and the $80,000 received had been an insurance recovery, Alice would still have a gain of $50,000, and the gain would still be recaptured by § 1245 as ordinary gain. The § 1245 recapture rules apply before there is any casualty gain. Because all the $50,000 gain is recaptured, no casualty gain arises from the casualty.

The following examples illustrate the general application of § 1245.

Section 1245 Recapture Computations

EXAMPLE 55

In the current year, Gary sold for $13,000 a machine acquired several years ago for $12,000. He had taken $10,000 of depreciation on the machine.

- The recognized gain from the sale is $11,000. This is the amount realized of $13,000 less the adjusted basis of $2,000 ($12,000 cost − $10,000 depreciation taken).

- Depreciation taken is $10,000. Therefore, because § 1245 recapture gain is the lower of depreciation taken or gain recognized, $10,000 of the $11,000 recognized gain is ordinary income, and the remaining $1,000 gain is § 1231 gain.

- The § 1231 gain of $1,000 is also equal to the excess of the sales price over the original cost of the property ($13,000 − $12,000 = $1,000 $1231 gain).

---

[37]The term *depreciation* includes § 167 depreciation, § 168 cost recovery, § 179 immediate expensing, § 168(k) additional first-year depreciation, and § 197 amortization.

Section 1245 Recapture Computations

Assume the same facts as in the previous example, except that the asset is sold for $9,000 instead of $13,000.

- The recognized gain from the sale is $7,000. This is the amount realized of $9,000 less the adjusted basis of $2,000.

- Depreciation taken is $10,000. Therefore, because the $10,000 depreciation taken exceeds the recognized gain of $7,000, the entire $7,000 recognized gain is ordinary income.

- The § 1231 gain is zero. There is no § 1231 gain because the selling price ($9,000) does not exceed the original purchase price ($12,000).

EXAMPLE
56

Assume the same facts as in Example 55, except that the asset is sold for $1,500 instead of $13,000.

- The recognized loss from the sale is $500. This is the amount realized of $1,500 less the adjusted basis of $2,000.

- Because there is a loss, there is no depreciation recapture. All of the loss is § 1231 loss.

EXAMPLE
57

If § 1245 property is disposed of in a transaction other than a sale, exchange, or involuntary conversion, the maximum amount recaptured is the excess of the property's fair market value over its adjusted basis. See the discussion under Considerations Common to §§ 1245 and 1250 in text Section 14-11.

14-9a Section 1245 Property

Generally, §1245 property includes all depreciable personal property (e.g., machinery and equipment), including livestock. Buildings and their structural components generally are not § 1245 property. The following property is *also* subject to § 1245 treatment:

- Amortizable personal property such as goodwill, patents, copyrights, and leaseholds of § 1245 property.

- Professional baseball and football player contracts.

- Certain depreciable tangible real property (other than buildings and their structural components) employed as an integral part of certain activities such as manufacturing and production. For example, a natural gas storage tank where the gas is used in the manufacturing process is § 1245 property.

- Pollution control facilities, railroad grading and tunnel bores, on-the-job training, and child care facilities.

- Single-purpose agricultural and horticultural structures and petroleum storage facilities (e.g., a greenhouse or silo).

- Fifteen-year, 18-year, and 19-year nonresidential real estate for which accelerated cost recovery is used. This property, known as ACRS property, would have been placed in service after 1980 and before 1987.

Steve acquired nonresidential real estate on December 1, 1986, for $100,000. He used the required ACRS accelerated method to compute the cost recovery. He sells the asset on January 15, 2020, for $120,000. The amount and nature of Steve's gain are computed as follows:

EXAMPLE
58

Amount realized		$120,000
Adjusted basis		
Cost	$ 100,000	
Less cost recovery: 1986–2005	(100,000)	
2006–2020	(–0–)	
January 15, 2020 adjusted basis		(–0–)
Gain realized and recognized		$120,000

continued

> The gain of $120,000 is treated as ordinary income to the extent of *all* depreciation taken because the property is 19-year nonresidential real estate for which accelerated depreciation was used. As a result, Steve reports ordinary income of $100,000 and § 1231 gain of $20,000 ($120,000 − $100,000).

14-9b Observations on § 1245

- In most instances, the total depreciation taken will exceed the recognized gain. Therefore, the disposition of § 1245 property usually results in ordinary income rather than § 1231 gain. No § 1231 gain will occur unless the § 1245 property is disposed of for more than its original cost. Refer to Examples 55 and 56.

- Recapture applies to the total amount of depreciation allowed or allowable regardless of the depreciation method used.

- Recapture applies regardless of the holding period of the property. If the property is held for less than the long-term holding period, the entire recognized gain is ordinary income because § 1231 does not apply.

- Section 1245 does not apply to losses, which receive § 1231 treatment.

- Gains from the disposition of § 1245 assets may also be treated as passive activity gains (see Chapter 11).

LO.10

Determine when § 1250 recapture applies.

14-10 SECTION 1250 RECAPTURE

Generally, **§ 1250 property** is depreciable real property (principally buildings and their structural components) that is not subject to § 1245.[38] Intangible real property, such as leaseholds of § 1250 property, is also included.

Section 1250 recapture rarely applies because only the amount of *additional depreciation* (depreciation *in excess* of straight-line depreciation) is subject to recapture. Straight-line depreciation is not recaptured (except for property held one year or less). Because the straight-line depreciation method is required for depreciable real property placed in service after 1986, there will usually be *no § 1250 depreciation recapture* on such property. Finally, § 1250 does not apply if the real property is sold at a loss.

Although there is no depreciation recapture on § 1250 property, the gain from this property may be subject to a special 25 percent tax rate. See the discussion of Unrecaptured § 1250 Gain (Real Estate 25% Gain) in text Section 14-10b.

EXAMPLE 59

> Sanjay acquires a residential rental building on January 1, 2019, for $300,000. He receives an offer of $450,000 for the building in 2019 and sells it on December 23, 2020.
>
> - Sanjay takes $20,909 {($300,000 × 0.03485) + [$300,000 × 0.03636 × (11.5/12)] = $20,909} of total depreciation for 2019 and 2020, and the adjusted basis of the property is $279,091 ($300,000 − $20,909).
>
> - Sanjay's recognized gain is $170,909 ($450,000 − $279,091).
>
> - All of the gain is § 1231 gain.

---

[38]As noted previously, in one limited circumstance, § 1245 does apply to nonresidential real estate. If the nonresidential real estate was placed in service after 1980 and before 1987 and accelerated depreciation was used, the § 1245 recapture rules would apply (rather than the § 1250 recapture rules).

14-10a Section 1250 Recapture Situations

In addition to residential real estate acquired before 1987 and nonresidential real estate acquired before 1981, accelerated depreciation may be taken on other types of real property. The § 1250 recapture rules apply to the following property for which accelerated depreciation was used:

- Real property used predominantly outside the United States.
- Certain government-financed or low-income housing.[39]

Concept Summary 14.7 compares and contrasts the § 1245 and § 1250 depreciation recapture rules.

Concept Summary 14.7

Comparison of § 1245 and § 1250 Depreciation Recapture

	§ 1245	§ 1250
Property affected	All depreciable personal property, but also nonresidential real property acquired after December 31, 1980, and before January 1, 1987, for which accelerated cost recovery was used. Also includes miscellaneous items such as § 179 expense and § 197 amortization of intangibles such as goodwill, patents, and copyrights.	Nonresidential real property acquired after December 31, 1969, and before January 1, 1981, on which accelerated depreciation was taken. Residential rental real property acquired after December 31, 1975, and before January 1, 1987, on which accelerated depreciation was taken.
Depreciation recaptured	Potentially all depreciation taken. If the selling price is greater than or equal to the original cost, all depreciation is recaptured. If the selling price is between the adjusted basis and the original cost, only some depreciation is recaptured.	Normally, there is no depreciation recapture, but in the special situations listed above, there can be § 1250 depreciation recapture of additional depreciation (the excess of accelerated cost recovery over straight-line cost recovery or the excess of accelerated depreciation over straight-line depreciation).
Limit on recapture	Lower of depreciation taken or gain recognized.	Lower of additional depreciation or gain recognized.
Treatment of gain exceeding recapture gain	Usually § 1231 gain.	Usually § 1231 gain.
Treatment of loss	No depreciation recapture; loss is usually § 1231 loss.	No depreciation recapture; loss is usually § 1231 loss.

14-10b Unrecaptured § 1250 Gain (Real Estate 25% Gain)

Any unrecaptured § 1250 gain is subject to a 25 percent tax rate. This gain, which relates to the sale of depreciable real estate, is used in the alternative tax computation for net capital gain discussed earlier in this chapter. Unrecaptured § 1250 gain (*25% gain*) is some or all of the § 1231 gain that is treated as long-term capital gain.

The maximum amount of this *25% gain* is the depreciation taken on real property sold at a recognized gain. That maximum amount is computed in one or more of the following ways:

- The recognized gain from disposition is more than the depreciation taken. The *25% gain* is equal to the depreciation taken. Refer to Example 59. The depreciation taken was $20,909, but the recognized gain was $170,909. Consequently, *some* of the recognized gain is potential *25%* § 1231 gain.

---
[39]Described in § 1250(a)(1)(B).

- The recognized gain from disposition is less than or equal to the depreciation taken. In this case, the *25% gain* is all of the recognized gain. Refer to Example 59, but assume that the building sales price is $285,000. The recognized gain is $5,909 ($285,000 − $279,091), all of this gain is a § 1231 gain, and it is entirely a *25% § 1231 gain*.

- There is § 1245 depreciation recapture because the property is nonresidential real estate acquired in 1981–1986 on which accelerated depreciation was taken. No *25% § 1231 gain* will be left because § 1245 will recapture all of the depreciation or the recognized gain, whichever is less. Refer to Example 58. Depreciation of $100,000 was taken, but all of it was recaptured as ordinary income by § 1245. Thus, there is no remaining potential *25% § 1231 gain*. The entire $20,000 § 1231 gain in Example 58 is potential *0%/15%/20% gain*.

- Section 1231 loss from disposition of other § 1231 assets held long term reduces the gain from real estate.

- Section 1231 lookback losses convert some or all of the potential *25% § 1231 gain* to ordinary income.

Special 25% Gain Netting Rules

Where there is a § 1231 gain from real estate and that gain includes both potential *25% gain* and potential *0%/15%/20% gain*, any § 1231 loss from disposition of other § 1231 assets *first offsets* the *0%/15%/20%* portion of the § 1231 gain and then offsets the *25% gain* portion of the § 1231 gain. Also, any § 1231 lookback loss *first recharacterizes* the *25% gain* portion of the § 1231 gain and then recharacterizes the *0%/15%/20%* portion of the § 1231 gain as ordinary income.

Net § 1231 Gain Limitation

The amount of unrecaptured § 1250 gain may not exceed the net § 1231 gain that is eligible to be treated as long-term capital gain. The unrecaptured § 1250 gain is the *lesser of* the unrecaptured § 1250 gain or the net § 1231 gain that is treated as capital gain. Thus, if there is a net § 1231 gain but it is all converted to ordinary income by the five-year § 1231 lookback loss provision, there is no surviving § 1231 gain or unrecaptured § 1250 gain.

Refer to Example 52. There was $200 of § 1231 gain from the building fire that would also be potential *25% gain* if at least $200 of depreciation was taken. The net § 1231 gain was $1,100 including the $200 building gain. (The $500 loss from Asset C would offset the potential *0%/15%/20% § 1231 gain* and not the potential *25% gain*, so all of the potential *25% gain* of $200 is in the $1,100 net § 1231 gain.) However, the $700 of § 1231 lookback losses would *first* absorb the $200 building gain, so the $400 of § 1231 gain that is treated as long-term capital gain includes no *25% gain*.

Section 1250 Property for Purposes of the Unrecaptured § 1250 Gain

Section 1250 property includes any real property (other than § 1245 property) that is or has been depreciable. Land is *not* § 1250 property because it is not depreciable.

EXAMPLE 60

Bridget is a single taxpayer with 2020 taxable income of $120,000 composed of:

- $100,000 ordinary taxable income,

- $(3,000) short-term capital loss,

- $15,000 long-term capital gain from sale of stock, and

- $8,000 § 1231 gain that is all unrecaptured § 1250 gain (the actual unrecaptured gain was $11,000, but net § 1231 gain is only $8,000).

Bridget's net capital gain is $20,000 ($15,000 long-term capital gain + $8,000 unrecaptured § 1250 gain/net § 1231 gain − $3,000 short-term capital loss). The $3,000 short-term capital loss is

continued

offset against the $8,000 unrecaptured § 1250 gain, reducing that gain to $5,000 (see the discussion earlier in the chapter concerning netting of capital losses). Bridget's adjusted net capital gain is $15,000 ($20,000 net capital gain − $5,000 unrecaptured § 1250 gain).

Bridget's total tax (using the alternative tax calculation discussed earlier) is $21,530 [$18,080 (tax on $100,000 other taxable income) + $1,200 ($5,000 unrecaptured § 1250 gain × 24%) + $2,250 ($15,000 adjusted net capital gain × 15%)]. Bridget uses the regular 24% tax rate on the $5,000 unrecaptured § 1250 gain because it is less than the 25% alternative tax rate on the gain.

ETHICS & EQUITY The Sale of a "Cost-Segregated" Building

Many taxpayers have "cost-segregated" their buildings. This means that an engineering study is done to determine whether some of a building's cost can be segregated into tangible personal property (generally a 5-year or 7-year MACRS life with accelerated depreciation) rather than real property (a 27.5-year or 39-year MACRS life with straight-line depreciation). The faster depreciation for the tangible personal property yields significant tax savings.

A CPA is determining the gain or loss from disposition of an office building. A sale document details the selling price of the land and building. However, the building was cost-segregated and the CPA finds records of cost and related depreciation for the tangible personal property that was part of the cost segregation. No mention of this tangible personal property was made in the sale agreement, but the building and all of its contents were sold. What should the CPA do?

14-11 CONSIDERATIONS COMMON TO §§ 1245 AND 1250

LO.11

State and explain considerations common to §§ 1245 and 1250.

14-11a Exceptions

Gifts

Depreciation recapture potential carries over to the donee.[40]

EXAMPLE 61

Wade gives his daughter, Helen, § 1245 property with an adjusted basis of $1,000. The amount of recapture potential is $700. Helen uses the property in her business and claims further depreciation of $100 before selling it for $1,900.

Helen's recognized gain is $1,000 ($1,900 amount realized − $900 adjusted basis), of which $800 is recaptured as ordinary income ($100 depreciation taken by Helen + $700 recapture potential carried over from Wade). The remaining gain of $200 is § 1231 gain. Even if Helen used the property for personal purposes, the $700 recapture potential would still be carried over.

Death

Although not a very attractive tax planning approach, death eliminates all recapture potential.[41] Any depreciation recapture potential is eliminated when property passes from a decedent to an estate or heir.

EXAMPLE 62

Assume the same facts as in Example 61, except that Helen receives the property as a result of Wade's death. The $700 recapture potential from Wade is extinguished. Helen has a basis for the property equal to the property's fair market value at Wade's death (assume that the FMV is $1,700).

Helen will have a $300 gain when the property is sold because the selling price ($1,900) exceeds the property's adjusted basis of $1,600 ($1,700 original basis to Helen − $100 depreciation) by $300. Because of § 1245, $100 is ordinary income. The remaining gain of $200 is § 1231 gain.

---

[40]§§ 1245(b)(1) and 1250(d)(1) and Reg. §§ 1.1245–4(a)(1) and 1.1250–3(a)(1).   [41]§§ 1245(b)(2) and 1250(d)(2).

Charitable Transfers

If depreciable property is contributed to a charity, the contribution deduction (normally fair market value) must be reduced by any ordinary gain that would have resulted had the property been sold (e.g., from depreciation recapture).[42]

EXAMPLE 63

Kanisha donates to her church § 1245 property with a fair market value of $10,000 and an adjusted basis of $7,000. Assume that the amount of recapture potential is $2,000 (the amount of recapture that would occur if the property were sold).

Her charitable contribution deduction (subject to the limitations discussed in Chapter 10) is $8,000 ($10,000 fair market value − $2,000 recapture potential).

Certain Nontaxable Transactions

In certain transactions, the transferor's adjusted basis of property carries over to the transferee.[43] If this is the case, any depreciation recapture potential also carries over to the transferee.[44] Included in this category are the following transfers of property:

- Nontaxable incorporations under § 351 (see Chapter 18).
- Certain subsidiary liquidations under § 332 (see Chapter 20).
- Nontaxable contributions to a partnership under § 721 (see Chapter 21).
- Nontaxable reorganizations (see Chapter 20).

Gain may be recognized in these transactions if boot is received. If gain is recognized, it is treated as ordinary income to the extent of the recapture potential or recognized gain, whichever is lower.[45]

Like-Kind Exchanges (§ 1031) and Involuntary Conversions (§ 1033)

Realized gain is recognized to the extent of boot received in a like-kind exchange. Realized gain also will be recognized to the extent the proceeds from an involuntary conversion are not reinvested in similar property. Any recognized gain is subject to recapture as ordinary income under §§ 1245 and 1250. However, since only real property can be the subject of a like-kind exchange, § 1245 recapture is not likely because it generally only applies to tangible personal property. Section 1250 recapture is also not likely because it infrequently applies to dispositions of real property. On the other hand, unrecaptured § 1250 gain (25% gain) is likely to be present if depreciable real property was the subject of the exchange. The remaining recapture potential, if any, carries over to the property received in the exchange. Realized losses are not recognized in like-kind exchanges, but are recognized in involuntary conversions (see Chapter 13).

---

[42]§ 170(e)(1)(A) and Reg. § 1.170A–4(b)(1). In certain circumstances, § 1231 gain also reduces the amount of the charitable contribution. See § 170(e)(1)(B).

[43]§§ 1245(b)(3) and 1250(d)(3) and Reg. §§ 1.1245–4(c) and 1.1250–3(c).

[44]Reg. §§ 1.1245–2(a)(4) and –2(c)(2) and 1.1250–2(d)(1) and (3) and –3(c)(3).

[45]§§ 1245(b)(3) and 1250(d)(3) and Reg. §§ 1.1245–4(c) and 1.1250–3(c).

Sometimes, transactions *structured as exchanges* do not qualify as § 1031 like-kind exchanges. For example, exchanges of personalty do not qualify for like-kind treatment (see Chapter 13). Assume that Hazel exchanges equipment (fair market value $128,000, adjusted basis $74,960, and § 1245 depreciation recapture potential $375,040) by "trading it in" on replacement property. If the equipment received in the exchange was worth $150,000, Hazel would have to pay $22,000 of cash ($150,000 − value of the equipment given up in the exchange) to acquire the replacement property. In this situation, Hazel would not have a § 1031 like-kind exchange because this was not an exchange of real property.

Instead, her realized and recognized ordinary gain is $53,040 ($128,000 fair market value of the equipment given up − $74,960 adjusted basis of the equipment given up). All of the gain is recaptured by § 1245 because it is less than the $375,040 depreciation taken.

The remaining recapture potential of $322,000 ($375,040 − $53,040) is extinguished, and the basis of the replacement equipment is its fair market value, $150,000.

14-11b Other Applications

The §§ 1245 and 1250 recapture rules *override* all other Code Sections.[46] Special applications include installment sales and property dividends.

Installment Sales

Recapture gain is recognized in the year of the sale regardless of whether gain is otherwise recognized under the installment method.[47] All gain is ordinary income until the recapture potential is fully absorbed. Nonrecapture (§ 1231) gain is recognized under the installment method as cash is received.

Seth sells § 1245 property for $20,000, to be paid in 10 annual installments of $2,000 each plus interest at 6%. Seth realizes a $6,000 gain from the sale, of which $4,000 is attributable to depreciation taken.

If Seth uses the installment method, he recognizes the entire $4,000 of recapture gain as ordinary income in the year of the sale. The $2,000 of nonrecapture (§ 1231) gain will be recognized at the rate of $200 per year for 10 years.

Gain is also recognized on installment sales in the year of the sale in an amount equal to the § 179 (immediate expensing) deduction taken with respect to the property sold, because § 179 immediate expensing is depreciation subject to recapture.

Property Dividends

A corporation generally recognizes gain if it distributes appreciated property as a dividend. Recapture under §§ 1245 and 1250 applies to the extent of the *lower* of the recapture potential or the excess of the property's fair market value over the adjusted basis.[48]

Emerald Corporation distributes § 1245 property as a dividend to its shareholders. The amount of the recapture potential is $300, and the excess of the property's fair market value over the adjusted basis is $800. Emerald recognizes $300 of ordinary income and $500 of § 1231 gain.

Concept Summary 14.8 integrates the depreciation recapture rules with the § 1231 netting process. It is an expanded version of Concept Summary 14.6.

---

[46]§§ 1245(d) and 1250(i).

[47]§ 453(i). The installment method of reporting gains on the sale of property is discussed in Chapter 16.

[48]§ 311(b) and Reg. §§ 1.1245–1(c) and –6(b) and 1.1250–1(a)(4), –1(b)(4), and –1(c)(2).

Concept Summary 14.8

Depreciation Recapture and § 1231 Netting Procedure

```
┌──────────────────┐                    ┌──────────────────────┐                    ┌──────────────────┐
│ § 1231 asset and │                    │ § 1231 asset and long-│                    │ § 1231 asset and │
│   long-term      │   Remaining        │ term nonpersonal use  │                    │   long-term      │
│  nonpersonal     │   Gain             │ capital asset casualty*│                   │  nonpersonal     │
│ use capital asset│ ──────────────────▶│      gains            │◀──────────────────│ use capital asset│
│  casualty gains  │                    │       minus           │                    │  casualty losses │
└──────────────────┘                    │ § 1231 asset and long-│                    └──────────────────┘
         │                              │ term nonpersonal use  │
         │ Depreciation                 │ capital asset casualty*│
         │ Recapture              NET   │      losses           │  NET
         │                        GAIN  └──────────────────────┘  LOSS
         ▼                          │                        │
┌──────────────┐              ┌──────────────────┐    ┌────────────────────────────────┐
│   Ordinary   │              │     Net gain     │    │ Items are treated separately:  │
│    income    │              │ (add to § 1231   │    │ • Gains are ordinary income    │
└──────────────┘              │     gains)       │    │ • § 1231 asset losses are      │
         ▲                    └──────────────────┘    │   deductible for AGI           │
         │ Depreciation                 │             │ • Other losses are deductible  │
         │ Recapture              NET    │       NET   │   from AGI                     │
         │                        GAIN   │       LOSS  └────────────────────────────────┘
┌──────────────────┐         ┌──────────────────┐                  ┌──────────────────┐
│  § 1231 assets   │  Remaining│  § 1231 gains   │                  │  § 1231 assets   │
│  sold at a gain  │ ──────────▶│     minus       │◀─────────────────│  sold at a loss  │
└──────────────────┘  Gain    │  § 1231 losses   │                  └──────────────────┘
                              └──────────────────┘
                                       │
                                  NET GAIN
                                       ▼
                         ┌──────────────────────────┐
                         │   Lookback Provision:     │
                         │ Net gain is offset by     │
                         │ nonrecaptured net § 1231  │
                         │ losses from five prior    │
                         │       tax years           │
                         └──────────────────────────┘
                              │                │
                              ▼                ▼
                  ┌──────────────────┐  ┌──────────────────┐
                  │  Gain offset by  │  │  Remaining gain  │
                  │  lookback losses │  │    is LTCG       │
                  │ is ordinary gain │  └──────────────────┘
                  └──────────────────┘
```

*Includes casualties and thefts.

LO.12

Recognize special recapture provisions that are part of the tax law.

14-12 SPECIAL RECAPTURE PROVISIONS

14-12a Special Recapture for Corporations

Corporations selling depreciable real estate may have ordinary income in addition to that required by § 1250.[49] Under this provision, corporations selling depreciable real property are required to recapture as ordinary income the smaller of two amounts: (1) 20 percent of the recognized gain or (2) 20 percent of the depreciation taken. See Chapter 17 for further discussion.

---

[49]§ 291(a)(1).

14-12b   Gain from Sale of Depreciable Property between Certain Related Parties

If related parties sell or exchange property that is depreciable in the hands of the *transferee* (principally machinery, equipment, and buildings, but not land), any gain recognized by the *transferor* is ordinary income.[50] This rule applies to both direct and indirect sales or exchanges. A <mark>related party</mark> is defined as an individual and his or her controlled corporation or partnership or a taxpayer and any trust in which the taxpayer (or the taxpayer's spouse) is a beneficiary.

EXAMPLE 67

Isabella sells a personal use automobile (therefore nondepreciable) to her controlled corporation. The automobile, which was purchased two years ago, originally cost $5,000 and is sold for $7,000. The automobile is to be used in the corporation's business.

  If the related-party provision did not exist, Isabella would realize a $2,000 long-term capital gain. The income tax consequences would be favorable because Isabella's controlled corporation is entitled to depreciate the automobile based on the purchase price of $7,000. Under the related-party provision, Isabella's $2,000 gain is ordinary income.

14-12c   Intangible Drilling Costs

Taxpayers may elect to either *expense or capitalize* intangible drilling and development costs for oil, gas, or geothermal properties.[51] <mark>Intangible drilling and development costs (IDCs)</mark> include operator (one who holds a working or operating interest in any tract or parcel of land) expenditures for wages, fuel, repairs, hauling, and supplies. These expenditures must be incident to and necessary for the drilling of wells and preparation of wells for production. In most instances, taxpayers elect to expense IDCs to maximize tax deductions during drilling.

  Intangible drilling and development costs are subject to § 1254 recapture when the property is sold. Any gain realized on the disposition is recognized as ordinary income to the extent of IDCs expensed (but limited to the realized gain).

14-13   REPORTING PROCEDURES

LO.13

Describe the reporting procedures for §§ 1231, 1245, and 1250.

Noncapital gains and losses are reported on Form 4797 (Sales of Business Property). However, before Form 4797 is filled out, Part B of Form 4684 (Casualties and Thefts) must be completed to determine whether any casualties will enter into the § 1231 computation procedure. Recall that recognized gains from § 1231 asset casualties may be recaptured by § 1245 or § 1250. These gains will not appear on Form 4684. The § 1231 gains and nonpersonal use long-term capital gains are netted against § 1231 losses and nonpersonal use long-term capital losses on Form 4684 to determine if there is a net gain to transfer to Form 4797, Part I.

ETHICS & EQUITY   Incorrect Depreciation and Recognized Gain

  A staff accountant for a large international company is calculating the tax gain from a disposition of business equipment. The equipment was seven-year MACRS property and has been fully depreciated for tax purposes. The staff accountant notices that the equipment was used in Germany, not the United States, although it is listed as an asset of the U.S. company for which the staff accountant works. Because the property was used outside the United States, it should have been depreciated using straight-line over a nine-year life. Consequently, the tax depreciation has been overstated, and the tax basis should be greater than zero, causing a smaller gain. What should the staff accountant do?

---

[50]§ 1239.   [51]§ 263(c).

LO.14

Identify tax planning opportunities arising from the sale or exchange of capital assets and avoid pitfalls associated with the recapture provisions.

14-14 TAX PLANNING

14-14a Importance of Capital Asset Status

Why is capital asset status important? Because of the alternative tax on net capital gain. Individuals who receive income in the form of long-term capital gains or qualified dividend income have an advantage over taxpayers who cannot receive income in these forms.

If a net capital loss results, the maximum deduction is $3,000 per year. Consequently, capital gains and losses must be segregated from other types of gains and losses and must be reported separately on Schedule D of Form 1040.

14-14b Planning for Capital Asset Status

Capital asset status often is a question of objective evidence. Property that is not a capital asset to one person may qualify as a capital asset to another person.

EXAMPLE 68

Diane, a real estate dealer, transfers by gift a tract of land to Jeff, her son. The land was recorded as part of Diane's inventory (it was held for resale) and was therefore not a capital asset to her. Jeff, however, treats the land as an investment. The land is a capital asset in Jeff's hands, and any later taxable disposition of the property by him will yield a capital gain or loss.

With proper tax planning, even a dealer may obtain long-term capital gain treatment on the sale of property normally held for resale.

EXAMPLE 69

Jim, a real estate dealer, segregates Tract A from the real estate he regularly holds for resale and designates the property as being held for investment purposes. The property is not advertised for sale and is disposed of several years later. The negotiations for the subsequent sale were initiated by the purchaser and not by Jim. Under these circumstances, it would appear that any gain or loss from the sale of Tract A should be a capital gain or loss.[52]

When a business is being sold, one of the major decisions usually concerns whether a portion of the sales price is for goodwill. For the seller, goodwill generally represents the disposition of a capital asset. Goodwill has no basis and represents a residual portion of the selling price that cannot be allocated reasonably to the known assets. As a result, the amount of goodwill represents capital gain.

From a legal perspective, the buyer may prefer that the residual portion of the purchase price be allocated to a covenant not to compete (a promise that the seller will not compete against the buyer by conducting a business similar to the one the buyer has purchased). Both purchased goodwill and a covenant not to compete are § 197 intangibles. As a result, both must be capitalized and can be amortized over a 15-year statutory period.

To the seller, a covenant produces ordinary income. So, the seller would prefer that the residual portion of the selling price be allocated to goodwill—a capital asset. If the buyer does not need the legal protection provided by a covenant, the buyer is neutral regarding whether the residual amount is allocated to a covenant or to goodwill. Because the seller would receive a tax advantage from labeling the residual amount as goodwill, the buyer should factor this into the negotiation of the purchase price.

---

[52]*Toledo, Peoria & Western Railroad Co.*, 35 TCM 1663, T.C.Memo. 1976–366.

GLOBAL TAX ISSUES   **Capital Gain Treatment in the United States and Other Countries**

The United States currently requires a complex tax calculation when taxable income includes net long-term capital gain. However, the alternative tax on net long-term capital gain can generate tax savings even when the taxpayer is in the lowest regular tax bracket (10 percent) because there is an alternative tax rate of 0 percent. Many other countries also have an alternative tax rate on long-term capital gains. Consequently, even though the U.S. system is complex, it may be preferable because of the lower tax rates and because the lower rates are available to taxpayers in all tax brackets.

EXAMPLE 70

Marcia is buying Jack's dry cleaning proprietorship. An appraisal of the assets indicates that a reasonable purchase price would exceed the value of the known assets by $30,000. If the purchase contract does not specify the nature of the $30,000, the amount will be for goodwill and Jack will have a long-term capital gain of $30,000. Marcia will have a 15-year amortizable $30,000 asset.

If Marcia is paying the extra $30,000 to prevent Jack from operating another dry cleaning business in the area (a covenant not to compete), Jack will have $30,000 of ordinary income. Marcia will have a $30,000 deduction over the statutory 15-year amortization period rather than over the actual life of the covenant (e.g., 5 years).

14-14c Effect of Capital Asset Status in Transactions Other Than Sales

The nature of an asset (capital or ordinary) is important in determining the tax consequences that result when a sale or exchange occurs. It may, however, be just as significant in circumstances other than a taxable sale or exchange. When a capital asset is disposed of, the result is not always a capital gain or loss. Rather, in general, the disposition must be a sale or exchange. Collection of a debt instrument having a basis less than the face value results in a capital gain if the debt instrument is a capital asset. The collection is a sale or exchange. Sale of the debt shortly before the due date for collection will produce a capital gain.[53] If selling the debt in such circumstances could produce a capital gain but collecting could not, the consistency of what constitutes a capital gain or loss would be undermined. Another illustration of the sale or exchange principle involves a donation of certain appreciated property to a qualified charity. Recall that in certain circumstances, the measure of the charitable contribution is fair market value when the property, if sold, would have yielded a long-term capital gain (refer to the discussion of contributions of capital gain property in Chapter 10).

EXAMPLE 71

Sharon wants to donate a tract of unimproved land (basis of $40,000 and fair market value of $200,000) held for the required long-term holding period to State University (a qualified charitable organization). However, Sharon currently is under audit by the IRS for capital gains she reported on certain real estate transactions during an earlier tax year. Although Sharon is not a licensed real estate broker, the IRS agent conducting the audit is contending that she has achieved dealer status by virtue of the number and frequency of the real estate transactions she has conducted.

Under these circumstances, Sharon would be well advised to postpone the donation to State University until her status is clarified. If she has achieved dealer status, the unimproved land may be inventory (refer to Example 69 for another possible result) and Sharon's charitable contribution deduction would be limited to $40,000. If not and if the land is held as an investment, Sharon's deduction is $200,000 (the fair market value of the property).

---

[53]§ 1271(b).

14-14d Stock Sales

The following rules apply in determining the date of a stock sale:

- The date the sale is executed is the date of the sale. The execution date is the date the broker completes the transaction on the stock exchange.
- The settlement date is the date the cash or other property is paid to the seller of the stock. This date is *not* relevant in determining the date of sale.

EXAMPLE 72

Lupe, a cash basis taxpayer, sells stock that results in a gain. The sale was executed on December 29, 2019. The settlement date is January 2, 2020. The date of sale is December 29, 2019 (the execution date). The holding period for the stock sold ends with the execution date.

14-14e Maximizing Benefits

Ordinary losses generally are preferable to capital losses because of the limitations imposed on the deductibility of net capital losses and the requirement that capital losses be used to offset capital gains. The taxpayer may be able to convert what would otherwise have been capital loss to ordinary loss. For example, business (but not nonbusiness) bad debts, losses from the sale or exchange of small business investment company stock, and losses from the sale or exchange of small business corporation stock all result in ordinary losses.[54]

Although capital losses can be carried over indefinitely, *indefinite* becomes definite when a taxpayer dies. Any loss carryovers not used by the taxpayer are permanently lost. That is, no tax benefit can be derived from the carryovers subsequent to death.[55] Therefore, the potential benefit of carrying over capital losses diminishes when dealing with older taxpayers.

It is usually beneficial to spread gains over more than one taxable year. In some cases, this can be accomplished through the installment sales method of accounting.

14-14f Year-End Planning

The following general rules can be applied for timing the recognition of capital gains and losses near the end of a taxable year:

- If the taxpayer already has recognized more than $3,000 of capital loss, sell assets to generate capital gain equal to the excess of the capital loss over $3,000.

EXAMPLE 73

Kevin has already incurred a $7,000 STCL. Kevin should generate $4,000 of capital gain. The gain will be offset by $4,000 of the loss. The remaining loss of $3,000 can be deducted against ordinary income.

- If the taxpayer already has recognized capital gain, sell assets to generate capital loss equal to the capital gain. The gain will not be taxed, and the loss will be fully *deductible* against the gain.
- Generally, if the taxpayer has a choice between recognizing short-term capital gain or long-term capital gain, long-term capital gain should be recognized because it is subject to a lower tax rate.

14-14g Timing of § 1231 Gain

Although § 1245 recaptures much of the gain from the disposition of business property, sometimes § 1231 gain is still substantial. For instance, land held as a business asset will generate either § 1231 gain or § 1231 loss. If the taxpayer already has a capital loss for

---

[54]§§ 166(d), 1242, and 1244. Refer to the discussion in Chapter 7.   [55]Rev.Rul. 74–175, 1974–1 C.B. 52.

the year, the sale of land at a gain should be postponed so that the net § 1231 gain is not netted against the capital loss. The capital loss deduction will therefore be maximized for the current tax year, and the capital loss carryforward (if any) may be offset against the gain when the land is sold. If the taxpayer already has a § 1231 loss, § 1231 gains might be postponed to maximize the ordinary loss deduction this year. However, the carryforward of unrecaptured § 1231 losses will make the § 1231 gain next year an ordinary gain.

Section 1231 Planning

EXAMPLE 74

Mark has a $2,000 net STCL for 2020. He could sell business land held 27 months for a $3,000 § 1231 gain. He will have no other capital gains and losses or § 1231 gains and losses in 2020 or 2021. He has no nonrecaptured § 1231 losses from prior years. Mark is in the 24% tax bracket in 2019 and will be in the 22% bracket in 2021. If he sells the land in 2019, he will have a $1,000 net LTCG ($3,000 § 1231 gain − $2,000 STCL) and will pay a tax of $150 ($1,000 × 15%).

If Mark sells the land in 2021, he will have a 2020 tax savings of $480 ($2,000 capital loss deduction × 24% tax rate on ordinary income). In 2021, he will pay tax of $450 ($3,000 × 15%).

By postponing the sale by a year, Mark gets the use of $630 ($480 + $150) of tax savings until he has to pay $450 in 2021, for a net savings of $180 between the two years without considering the time value of money and other factors.

EXAMPLE 75

Beth has a $15,000 § 1231 loss in 2020. She could sell business equipment held 30 months for a $20,000 § 1231 gain and a $12,000 § 1245 gain. Beth is in the 24% tax bracket in 2020 and will be in the 22% bracket in 2021. She has no nonrecaptured § 1231 losses from prior years. If she sold the equipment in 2020, she would have a $5,000 net § 1231 gain and $12,000 of ordinary gain. Her tax would be $3,630 [($5,000 § 1231 gain × 15%) + ($12,000 ordinary gain × 24%)].

If Beth postponed the equipment sale until 2021, she would have a 2020 ordinary loss of $15,000 and tax savings of $3,600 ($15,000 × 24%). In 2021, she would have $5,000 of § 1231 gain (the 2020 § 1231 loss carries over and recaptures $15,000 of the 2021 § 1231 gain as ordinary income) and $27,000 of ordinary gain. Her tax would be $6,690 [($5,000 § 1231 gain × 15%) + ($27,000 ordinary gain × 22%)].

By postponing the sale of the § 1231 property until 2021, Beth gets the use of $7,230 ($3,600 + $3,630) of tax savings until she has to pay $6,690 in 2021, for a net savings of $540 between the two years without considering the time value of money and other factors.

14-14h Timing of Recapture

Because recapture is usually not triggered until the property is sold or disposed of, it may be possible to plan for recapture in low tax bracket or loss years. If a taxpayer has net operating loss (NOL) carryovers, the recognition of ordinary income from recapture may be advisable to absorb the loss carryovers.

EXAMPLE 76

Ahmad has a $15,000 NOL carryover. He owns a machine that he plans to sell in the early part of next year. The expected gain of $17,000 from the sale of the machine will be recaptured as ordinary income under § 1245. Ahmad sells the machine before the end of this year and uses the $15,000 NOL carryover to offset $15,000 of the ordinary income.

14-14i Postponing and Shifting Recapture

It is also possible to postpone recapture or to shift the burden of recapture to others. For example, recapture is postponed and shifted on the exchange of a § 1231 asset if the taxpayer exchanges the property for stock in a § 351 nontaxable incorporation. In this instance, the recapture potential is shifted to the corporation.

Recapture can be shifted to others through the gratuitous transfer of § 1245 or § 1250 property to family members. A subsequent sale of such property by the donee will trigger recapture to the donee rather than the donor (refer to Example 61). This procedure would be advisable only if the donee was in a lower income tax bracket compared with the donor.

14-14j Avoiding Recapture

The immediate expensing election (§ 179) and additional first-year (bonus) depreciation [§ 168(k)] are subject to § 1245 recapture. If the elections are not made, the § 1245 recapture potential will accumulate more slowly (refer to Chapter 8). Because using the immediate expense election and/or additional first-year depreciation deduction complicates depreciation and book accounting for the affected asset(s), not taking these deductions may make sense even though the time value of money might indicate that they should be taken.

REFOCUS ON THE BIG PICTURE

MANAGING CAPITAL ASSET TRANSACTIONS

You explain to Maurice that your area of expertise is tax, so you are providing tax advice and not investment advice. From an overall perspective, he is correct that certain capital gains and dividends are eligible for either a 0 percent, a 15 percent, or a 20 percent tax rate rather than the regular income tax rates that go as high as 37 percent. You then discuss the potential tax consequences of each of his investments.

- *Purple stock and Eagle stock*. To qualify for the beneficial tax rate, the holding period for the stock must be longer than one year. From a tax perspective, Maurice should retain his stock investments for at least an *additional* three months and a day. To be eligible for the "costless" capital gains as a single taxpayer (i.e., taxed at the 0 percent rate), his taxable income should not exceed $40,000 for 2020. The dividends received on the Purple stock are "qualified dividends" eligible for the 0%/15%/20% alternative tax rate.

- *Patent*. Because he is a "holder" of the patent, it will qualify for the beneficial capital gain rate regardless of the holding period if the patent should produce income in excess of his $50,000 investment. However, if he loses money on the investment, he will be able to deduct only $3,000 of the loss per year against his ordinary income (assuming that there are no offsetting capital gains). See Examples 15 and 16.

- *Tax-exempt bonds*. The after-tax return on the taxable bonds would be less than the 3 percent on the tax-exempt bonds. In addition, the interest on the taxable bonds would increase his taxable income, possibly moving it out of the desired 12 percent marginal tax rate into the 22 percent marginal tax rate.

- *Franchise rights*. The franchise rights purchased from Orange, Inc., probably require the payment of a franchise fee based upon the sales in the franchise business. Maurice should either start such a business or sell the franchise rights.

- *Partnership interest*. Whether Maurice receives capital or ordinary treatment associated with his partnership interest depends on whether he is reporting his share of profits or losses (ordinary income or ordinary loss) or is reporting recognized gain or loss from the sale of his partnership interest (capital gain or capital loss).

You conclude your tax advice to Maurice by telling him that whatever he does regarding his investments should make economic sense. There are no 100 percent tax rates. For example, disposing of the bank stock in the current market could be the wise thing to do.

Key Terms

Alternative tax, 14-22	Lessor, 14-14	Sale or exchange, 14-8
Capital asset, 14-4	Long-term nonpersonal use capital assets, 14-30	Section 1231 gains and losses, 14-29
Capital gains, 14-2		Section 1231 lookback, 14-32
Capital losses, 14-2	Net capital gain (NCG), 14-20	Section 1231 property, 14-29
Collectibles, 14-22	Net capital loss (NCL), 14-26	Section 1245 property, 14-37
Franchise, 14-12	Options, 14-9	Section 1245 recapture, 14-36
Holding period, 14-15	Original issue discount (OID), 14-9	Section 1250 property, 14-38
Intangible drilling and development costs (IDCs), 14-45	Patent, 14-11	Section 1250 recapture, 14-38
	Qualified dividend income (QDI), 14-22	Short sale, 14-16
Lessee, 14-14	Related party, 14-45	Unrecaptured § 1250 gain, 14-20

Discussion Questions

1. **LO.2, 4, 5** Sheila inherited 300 shares of stock, 100 shares of Magenta and 200 shares of Purple. She has a stockbroker sell the shares for her, uses the proceeds for personal expenses, and thinks nothing further about the transactions. What issues does she face when she prepares her Federal income tax return? *Critical Thinking*

2. **LO.2** An individual taxpayer sells some used assets at a garage sale. Why are none of the proceeds taxable in most situations? *Critical Thinking*

3. **LO.2, 4** Alison owns a painting that she received as a gift from her aunt 10 years ago. The aunt created the painting. Alison has displayed the painting in her home and has never attempted to sell it. Recently, a visitor noticed the painting and offered Alison $5,000 for it. If Alison decides to sell the painting, what tax issues does she face? *Critical Thinking*

4. **LO.2** Is a note receivable that arose in the ordinary course of the taxpayer's retail business a capital asset? Why or why not?

5. **LO.2** Anwar owns vacant land that he purchased many years ago as an investment. After getting approval to subdivide it into 35 lots, he made minimal improvements and then sold the entire property to a real estate developer. Anwar's recognized gain on the sale was $1,200,000. Is this transaction eligible for the "real property subdivided for sale" rules? Why or why not?

6. **LO.3** Hubert purchases all of the rights in a patent from the inventor who developed the patented product. After holding the patent for two years, Hubert sells all of the rights in the patent for a substantial gain. What issues does Hubert face if he wants to treat the gain as a long-term capital gain? *Critical Thinking*

7. **LO.3** Blue Corporation and Fuchsia Corporation are engaged in a contract negotiation over the use of Blue's trademarked name, DateSiteForSeniors. For a one-time payment of $45,000, Blue licensed Fuchsia to use the name DateSiteForSeniors, and the license requires that Fuchsia pay Blue a royalty every time a new customer signs up on Fuchsia's website. Blue is a developer of "website ideas" that it then licenses to other companies such as Fuchsia. Did Fuchsia purchase a franchise right from Blue, or did Fuchsia purchase the name DateSiteForSeniors from Blue?

8. **LO.4** At the date of a short sale, Sylvia has held substantially identical securities for more than 12 months. What is the nature of any gain or loss from the close of her short sale?

9. **LO.5** After netting all of her short-term and long-term capital gains and losses, Misty has a net short-term capital loss and a net long-term capital loss. Can she net these against each other? Why or why not?

10. **LO.2, 5** Charlie sells his antique farm tractor collection at a loss. He had acquired all of the tractors for his personal pleasure and sold all of them for less than he paid for them. What is the tax status of the tractors? Is his loss a 28% collectibles loss? Explain.

Critical Thinking

11. **LO.7, 8** Hakim's rental building (a § 1231 asset) was not insured when it was destroyed by a hurricane. His adjusted basis for the building was substantial but was less than he had paid for the building in 2015. The building was Hakim's only asset that was damaged by the hurricane. How should Hakim handle this situation?

12. **LO.8** An individual taxpayer had a net § 1231 loss in 2020. Could any of this loss be treated as a long-term capital loss? Why or why not?

Critical Thinking

13. **LO.8** Steven established a sole proprietorship in 2014. He sold § 1231 assets at a loss in 2018 and 2019. He had only sold § 1231 assets at a gain before 2018. In 2020, he could sell a § 1231 asset at a gain and would like to have the gain taxed as a long-term capital gain. What issue is Steven facing?

14. **LO.8** Review Examples 50 and 52 in the text. In both examples, the taxpayer's AGI is $129,400 even though in Example 52 there is $700 of nonrecaptured § 1231 loss from 2019. Explain why the two AGI amounts are the same.

15. **LO.8** A depreciable business dump truck has been owned for four years and is no longer useful to the taxpayer. What would have to be true for the disposition of the dump truck to generate at least some § 1231 loss?

16. **LO.7, 9** If depreciable equipment used in a business is sold at a recognized gain on July 10, 2020, and it was purchased on August 21, 2019, does § 1245 depreciation recapture apply to the asset? Explain.

Communications

17. **LO.9** A retailer's store is destroyed by a tornado but is insured for its replacement cost. Consequently, the retailer has a $40,000 gain after receiving the insurance proceeds. The store is not replaced because the retailer spends the insurance proceeds on additional inventory. What is the nature of the gain if the building originally cost $100,000 three years ago and had an adjusted basis of $82,000 at the time of its destruction? Prepare an e-mail to your supervisor, Sharon Regan, summarizing your answer. E-mail this response to your instructor.

18. **LO.10** In the current year, an individual taxpayer has net long-term capital gain from disposition of capital assets and has unrecaptured § 1250 gain. What would the circumstances have to be for the unrecaptured § 1250 gain to be taxed at 25%?

19. **LO.9, 11** Mary receives tangible personal property as a gift. The property was depreciated by the donor, and Mary will also depreciate it. At the date of the gift, the property was worth more than the donor's adjusted basis. What is the impact of these facts on Mary when she sells the property at a gain several years after she acquired it?

20. **LO.9, 11** Thomas receives tangible personal property as an inheritance from a decedent who died in 2020. The property was depreciated by the deceased, and Thomas will also depreciate it. At the date of the deceased's death, the property was worth more than the deceased's adjusted basis. What is the impact of these facts on Thomas when he sells the property at a gain several years after he acquired it?

21. **LO.9, 11** Dino contributes to charity some tangible personal property that he had used in his business and depreciated. At the date of the donation, the

property has a fair market value greater than its adjusted basis, but less than the original cost. What is the impact of these facts on Dino's charitable contribution?

22. **LO.9, 11** A corporation distributes a truck it has owned for three years to its sole shareholder. The shareholder will use the truck for personal use activity. The truck's fair market value at the time of the distribution is greater than its adjusted basis but less than its original cost. Does the corporation recognize a gain? If so, what is the character of the gain?

23. **LO.12** A corporation distributes a truck it has owned for three years to its sole shareholder. The shareholder will use the truck for business activity. The truck's fair market value at the time of the distribution is greater than its adjusted basis but less than its original cost. Does the corporation recognize a gain? If so, what is the character of the gain?

Computational Exercises

24. **LO.2** Dexter owns a large tract of land and subdivides it for sale. Assume that Dexter meets all of the requirements of § 1237 and during the tax year sells the first eight lots to eight different buyers for $22,000 each. Dexter's basis in each lot sold is $15,000, and he incurs total selling expenses of $900 on each sale. What is the amount of Dexter's capital gain and ordinary income? Formulate your answer by constructing a spreadsheet using a format similar to that found in Example 10.

25. **LO.3** Sheila purchases $50,000 of newly issued Gingo Corporation bonds for $45,000. The bonds have original issue discount (OID) of $5,000. After Sheila amortized $2,300 of OID and held the bonds for four years, she sold the bonds for $48,000. What is the amount and character of her gain or loss?

26. **LO.3** Olivia wants to buy some vacant land for investment purposes. She cannot afford the full purchase price. Instead, Olivia pays the landowner $8,000 to obtain an option to buy the land for $175,000 anytime in the next four years. Fourteen months after purchasing the option, Olivia sells the option for $10,000. What is the amount and character of Olivia's gain or loss?

27. **LO.3** On May 9, 2020, Glenna purchases 500 shares of Ignaz Company stock for $7,500. On June 30, 2020, she writes a call option on the stock, giving the grantee the right to buy the stock for $9,000 during the following 12-month period. Glenna receives a call premium of $750 for writing the call. The call is exercised by the grantee on December 15, 2020.
   a. What is the amount and character of Glenna's gain or loss?
   b. Assume that the original option expired unexercised. What is the amount and character of Glenna's gain or loss?

28. **LO.4** Shen purchased corporate stock for $20,000 on April 10, 2018. On July 14, 2020, when the stock was worth $12,000, Shen died and his son, Mijo, inherited the stock. Mijo sold the stock for $14,200 on November 12, 2020. What is the amount and character of Mijo's gain or loss?

29. **LO.5** Coline has the following capital gain and loss transactions for 2020.

Short-term capital gain	$ 5,000
Short-term capital loss	(2,100)
Long-term capital gain (28%)	6,000
Long-term capital gain (15%)	2,000
Long-term capital loss (28%)	(10,500)

After the capital gain and loss netting process, what is the amount and character of Coline's gain or loss?

30. **LO.5** Elliott has the following capital gain and loss transactions for 2020.

Short-term capital gain	$ 1,500
Short-term capital loss	(3,600)
Long-term capital gain (28%)	12,000
Long-term capital gain (25%)	4,800
Long-term capital gain (15%)	6,000
Long-term capital loss (28%)	(4,500)
Long-term capital loss (15%)	(9,000)

After the capital gain and loss netting process, what is the amount and character of Elliott's gain or loss?

31. **LO.7** Lena is a sole proprietor. In April of this year, she sold equipment purchased four years ago for $26,000 with an adjusted basis of $15,500 for $17,000. Later in the year, Lena sold another piece of equipment purchased two years ago with an adjusted basis of $8,200 for $5,500. What is the amount and character of Lena's gain or loss?

32. **LO.9** Renata Corporation purchased equipment in 2018 for $180,000 and has taken $83,000 of regular MACRS depreciation. Renata Corporation sells the equipment in 2020 for $110,000. What is the amount and character of Renata's gain or loss?

33. **LO.9** Jacob purchased business equipment for $56,000 in 2017 and has taken $35,000 of regular MACRS depreciation. Jacob sells the equipment in 2020 for $26,000. What is the amount and character of Jacob's gain or loss?

34. **LO.7, 8, 9** Shannon owns two items of business equipment. Both were purchased in 2016 for $100,000, both have a 7-year MACRS recovery period, and both have an adjusted basis of $37,490. Shannon is considering selling these assets in 2020. One of them is worth $60,000, and the other is worth $23,000. Because both items were used in her business, Shannon simply assumes that the loss on one will offset the gain from the other and that the net gain or loss will increase or reduce her business income. What is the amount and character of Shannon's gain or loss?

35. **LO.10** An apartment building was acquired in 2011. The depreciation taken on the building was $123,000, and the building was sold for a $34,000 gain. What is the maximum amount of *25% gain?*

36. **LO.10** Enzo is a single taxpayer with the following gains and losses for 2020:
   - $2,100 short-term capital loss.
   - $24,000 long-term capital gain from sale of stock.
   - $14,000 § 1231 gain that is all unrecaptured § 1250 gain.

   What is the amount and character of Enzo's gain or loss?

37. **LO.11** In a § 1031 like-kind exchange, Rafael exchanges a business building that originally cost $200,000. On the date of the exchange, the building given up has an adjusted basis of $85,000 and a fair market value of $110,000. Rafael pays $15,000 and receives a building with a fair market value of $125,000. What is the amount and character of Rafael's gain or loss?

Problems

38. **LO.2** During the year, Eugene had the four property transactions summarized on the next page. Eugene is a collector of antique glassware and occasionally sells a piece to get funds to buy another. What are the amount and nature of the gain or loss from each of these transactions?

Property	Date Acquired	Date Sold	Adjusted Basis	Sales Price
Antique vase	06/18/09	05/23/20	$37,000	$42,000
Blue Growth Fund (100 shares)	12/23/11	11/22/20	22,000	38,000
Orange bonds	02/12/12	04/11/20	34,000	42,000*
Green stock (100 shares)	02/14/20	11/23/20	11,000	13,000

*The sales price included $750 of accrued interest.

39. **LO.2, 5** Rennie owns a video game arcade. He buys vintage video games from estates, often at much less than the retail value of the property. He usually installs the vintage video games in a special section of his video game arcade that appeals to players of "classic" video games. Recently, Rennie sold a classic video game that a customer "just had to have." Rennie paid $11,250 for it, owned it for 14 months, and sold it for $18,000. Rennie had suspected that this particular classic video game would be of interest to collectors; so he had it refurbished, put it on display in his video arcade, and listed it for sale on the internet. No customers in the arcade had played it other than those testing it before considering it for purchase. Rennie would like the gain on the sale of the classic video game to be a long-term capital gain. Did he achieve that objective? Why or why not?

    Decision Making

    Critical Thinking

40. **LO.2** George is the owner of numerous classic automobiles. His intention is to hold the automobiles until they increase in value and then sell them. He rents the automobiles for use in various events (e.g., antique automobile shows) while he is holding them. In 2020, he sold a classic automobile for $1,500,000. He had held the automobile for five years, and it had a tax basis of $750,000.

  a. Was the automobile a capital asset? Why or why not?

  b. Assuming a rate of return of 7%, how much would he have had to invest five years ago (instead of putting $750,000 into the car) to have had $1,500,000 this year? See Appendix G for the present value factors.

41. **LO.2, 4** Barbella purchased a wedding ring for $15 at a yard sale in May. She thought the ring was costume jewelry, but it turned out to be a real diamond ring. She is not in the business of buying and selling anything. She researched the ring on the internet and discovered that it was worth at least $1,000. She sold it on an internet auction site for $1,100 in July. Was the ring a capital asset? What were the amount and nature of the gain or loss from its sale by Barbella? Prepare your answer in the form of an e-mail communication between you as a staff person of the Fuchsia CPA Firm LLP and your boss, Maria Hernandez, CPA. Assume that her e-mail address is *mhernandez@fuchsiacpas.com*. Maria referred the situation to you and is aware of the facts and the questions you should answer.

    Communications

42. **LO.2** Pebble Securities is a corporation that buys and sells financial assets. It purchases notes receivable from manufacturers that need cash immediately and cannot wait to collect the notes. Pebble pays about 88% of the face value of the receivables and then collects them. Because of the quality of the notes, Pebble collected less than it paid for some of the notes. Does Pebble have a capital loss when it collects the receivables for less than it paid for them? Explain.

43. **LO.2** Faith Godwin is a dealer in securities. She has spotted a fast-rising company and would like to buy and hold its stock for investment. The stock is currently selling for $2 per share, and Faith thinks it will climb to $40 a share within two years. Faith's coworkers have told her that there is "no way" she can get long-term capital gain treatment when she purchases stock because she is a securities dealer. Faith has asked you to calculate her potential gain and tell her whether her coworkers are right. Draft a letter to Faith, responding to her request. Her address is 200 Catamon Drive, Great Falls, MT 59406.

    Communications

44. **LO.2** Maria meets all of the requirements of § 1237 (subdivided realty). In 2020, she begins selling lots and sells four separate lots to four different purchasers. She also sells two contiguous lots to another purchaser. The sales price of each lot is $30,000. Maria's basis for each lot is $15,000. Selling expenses are $500 per lot.

    a. What are the realized and recognized gain?
    b. Explain the nature of the gain (i.e., ordinary income or capital gain).
    c. Would your answers change if, instead, the lots sold to the fifth purchaser were not contiguous? If so, how?

Decision Making
Critical Thinking

45. **LO.2, 3, 5** Melaney has had a bad year with her investments. She lent a friend $8,000; the friend did not repay the loan when it was due and then declared bankruptcy. The loan is totally uncollectible. Melaney also was notified by her broker that the Oak corporate bonds she owned became worthless on October 13, 2020. She had purchased the bonds for $22,000 on November 10, 2019. Melaney also had a $60,000 loss on the disposition of § 1244 corporate stock that she purchased several years ago. Melaney is single.

    a. What are the nature and amount of Melaney's losses?
    b. What is Melaney's AGI for 2020 assuming that she has $65,000 of ordinary gross income from sources other than those discussed?
    c. What are the nature and amount of Melaney's loss carryforwards?

46. **LO.2, 3** Benny purchased $400,000 of Peach Corporation face value bonds for $320,000 on November 13, 2019. The bonds had been issued with $80,000 of original issue discount because Peach was in financial difficulty in 2019. On December 3, 2020, Benny sold the bonds for $283,000 after amortizing $1,000 of the original issue discount. What are the nature and amount of Benny's gain or loss?

Decision Making
Critical Thinking

47. **LO.3** Fred is an investor in vacant land. When he thinks he has identified property that would be a good investment, he approaches the landowner, pays the landowner for a "right of first refusal" to purchase the land, records this right in the property records, and then waits to see if the land increases in value. The right of first refusal is valid for four years. Fourteen months ago, Fred paid a landowner $9,000 for a right of first refusal. The land was selected as the site of a new shopping center, and the landowner was offered $1,000,000 for the land. In its title search on the land, the buyer discovered Fred's right of first refusal and involved him in the purchase negotiations. Ultimately, the landowner paid Fred $220,000 to give up his right of first refusal; the landowner then sold the land to the buyer for $4,220,000. Fred has a marginal tax rate of 37%.

    a. What difference does it make whether Fred treats the right of first refusal as an option to purchase the land?
    b. What difference does it make whether Fred is a "dealer" in land?

48. **LO.3** Carla was the owner of vacant land that she was holding for investment. She paid $2,000,000 for the land in 2018. Raymond was an investor in vacant land. He thought Carla's land might be the site of an exit ramp from a new freeway. Raymond gave Carla $836,000 for an option on her land in 2019. The option was good for two years and gave Raymond the ability to purchase Carla's land for $4,765,000. The freeway was not approved by the government, and Raymond's option expired in 2020. Does Carla have $836,000 of long-term capital gain upon the expiration of the option? Explain.

49. **LO.3** Hilde purchased all of the rights to a patent on a new garden tool developed by a friend of hers who is an amateur inventor. The inventor obtained the patent rights, set up a manufacturing company to produce and sell the garden tool, and produced substantial quantities of the tool, but he then became discouraged when no large garden company would agree to distribute the tool for him. Hilde purchased the patent rights (but not the manufacturing company) for $120,000 on

October 24, 2019. Hilde had never engaged in such a transaction before, but she is a salesperson in the garden industry and thought she could succeed where her friend had failed. On June 27, 2020, she sold all patent rights to Garden Tool Company for $1,233,000. Garden Tool will manufacture the tool in its own factory and sell it to its customers. What is the nature of Hilde's gain from this transaction?

50. **LO.3, 4, 14** Mac, an inventor, obtained a patent on a chemical process to clean old aluminum siding so that it can be easily repainted. Mac has a $50,000 tax basis in the patent. Mac does not have the capital to begin manufacturing and selling this product, so he has done nothing with the patent since obtaining it two years ago. Now a group of individuals has approached him and offered two alternatives. Under one alternative, they will pay Mac $600,000 (payable evenly over the next 15 years) for the exclusive right to manufacture and sell the product. Under the other, they will form a business and contribute capital to it to begin manufacturing and selling the product; Mac will receive 20% of the company's shares of stock in exchange for all of his patent rights. Discuss which alternative is better for Mac.

Decision Making
Critical Thinking

51. **LO.3** Freys, Inc., sells a 12-year "stuffed potato" franchise to Reynaldo. The franchise contains many restrictions on how Reynaldo may operate his store. For instance, Reynaldo cannot use less than Grade 10 Idaho potatoes, must bake the potatoes at a constant 410 degrees, must dress store personnel in Freys-approved uniforms, and must have a Freys sign that meets detailed specifications on size, color, and construction. When the franchise contract is signed, Reynaldo makes a noncontingent $160,000 payment to Freys. During the same year, Reynaldo pays Freys $300,000—14% of Reynaldo's sales. How does Freys treat each of these payments? How does Reynaldo treat each of the payments?

52. **LO.3** Angie owns numerous strip malls. A major tenant of one of the strip malls wanted to cancel its lease because it was moving to another city. After lengthy negotiations, the tenant paid Angie $60,000 to cancel its obligations under the lease. If the tenant had fulfilled the lease terms, Angie would have received rent of $700,000. What factors should Angie consider to determine the amount and character of her income from these circumstances?

Critical Thinking

53. **LO.3** Consuela was a tenant in a campus apartment. She is a student at State University. Her lease began on August 1, 2020, and was due to expire on July 31, 2021. However, her landlord sold the building, and the new owner wanted to demolish it to build a retail building. Consuela's landlord paid her $1,000 to cancel the lease. Consuela received the $1,000 on November 30, 2020; moved out; and rented another apartment. How should Consuela treat the $1,000?

54. **LO.4** Roger inherited 100 shares of Periwinkle stock when his mother, Emily, died. Emily had acquired the stock for a total of $60,000 on November 15, 2016. She died on August 10, 2020, and the shares were worth a total of $55,000 at that time. Roger sold the shares for $36,000 on December 22, 2020. How much gain or loss does Roger recognize? What is the nature of that gain or loss?

55. **LO.4** Sarah received a gift of farmland from her father. The land was worth $4,000,000 at the date of the gift, had been farmed by her father for 40 years, and had a tax basis for her father of $30,000. Sarah never farmed the land and sold it eight months after receiving it from her father for $4,200,000. What is Sarah's holding period for the farmland? What is the nature of the gain from its disposition?

56. **LO.4** Dennis sells short 100 shares of ARC stock at $20 per share on January 15, 2020. He buys 200 shares of ARC stock on April 1, 2020, at $25 per share. On May 2, 2020, he closes the short sale by delivering 100 of the shares purchased on April 1.
   a. What are the amount and nature of Dennis's loss upon closing the short sale?
   b. When does the holding period for the remaining 100 shares begin?
   c. If Dennis sells (at $27 per share) the remaining 100 shares on January 20, 2021, what will be the nature of his gain or loss?

Communications   57. **LO.5** Elaine Case (single with no dependents) has the following transactions in 2020:

AGI (exclusive of capital gains and losses)	$540,000
Long-term capital gain	22,000
Long-term capital loss	(8,000)
Short-term capital gain	19,000
Short-term capital loss	(23,000)

What is Elaine's net capital gain or loss? Draft a letter to Elaine describing how the net capital gain or loss will be treated on her tax return. Note that Elaine's income from other sources puts her in the 37% tax bracket. Elaine's address is 300 Ireland Avenue, Shepherdstown, WV 25443.

Communications   58. **LO.3, 5** In 2020, Bertha Jarow had a $28,000 loss from the sale of a personal residence. She also purchased a patent on a rubber bonding process from an individual inventor for $7,000 (and resold it in two months for $18,000). The patent had not yet been reduced to practice. Bertha purchased the patent as an investment. In addition, she had the following capital gains and losses from stock transactions:

Long-term capital loss	($ 6,000)
Long-term capital loss carryover from 2019	(12,000)
Short-term capital gain	21,000
Short-term capital loss	(7,000)

What is Bertha's net capital gain or loss? Draft a letter to Bertha, explaining the tax treatment of the sale of her personal residence. Assume that Bertha's income from other sources puts her in the 24% bracket. Bertha's address is 1120 West Street, Ashland, OR 97520.

Critical Thinking   59. **LO.2, 4, 5, 14** Bridgette is known as the "doll lady." She started collecting dolls as a child, always received one or more dolls as gifts on her birthday, never sold any dolls, and eventually owned 600 dolls. She is retiring and moving to a small apartment and has decided to sell her collection. She lists the dolls on an internet auction site and, to her great surprise, receives an offer from another doll collector of $45,000 for the entire collection. Bridgette sells the entire collection, except for five dolls she purchased during the last year. She had owned all of the dolls sold for more than a year. What tax factors should Bridgette consider in deciding how to report the sale?

60. **LO.5** Phil and Susan Hammond are married taxpayers filing a joint return. The couple have two dependent children. Susan has wages of $34,000 in 2019. Phil does not work due to a disability, but he is a buyer and seller of stocks. He generally buys and holds for long-term gain, but occasionally gets in and out of a stock quickly. The couple's 2019 stock transactions are detailed below. In addition, they have $2,300 of qualifying dividends.

Item	Date Acquired	Date Sold	Cost	Sales Price
Blue stock (10 shares)	11/10/18	03/12/19	$ 3,000	$ 6,000
Purple stock (100 shares)	12/13/17	05/23/19	36,000	32,000
Beige stock (50 shares)	12/14/14	07/14/19	13,000	14,500
Red stock (100 shares)	06/29/18	05/18/19	26,000	27,000
Black stock (100 shares)	05/15/18	10/18/19	67,000	67,800
Gray stock (100 shares)	04/12/17	10/18/19	89,000	88,200

a.   What is Phil and Susan's AGI?

b.   Complete a Form 8949 for the Hammonds (Phil's Social Security number is 123-45-6789). Assume that the stock sale information was reported to the Hammonds on a Form 1099–B and that basis information was provided to the IRS.

61. **LO.5** Paul has the following long-term capital gains and losses for 2020: $62,000 28% gain, $21,000 28% loss, $18,000 25% gain, and $64,000 0%/15%/20% gain. He also has a $53,000 short-term loss and a $5,000 short-term gain. What is Paul's AGI from these transactions? If he has a net long-term capital gain, what is its makeup in terms of the alternative tax rates?

62. **LO.5** Helena has the following long-term capital gains and losses for 2020: $65,000 28% gain, $53,000 28% loss, $28,000 25% gain, and $24,000 0%/15%/20% loss. She also has a $33,000 short-term loss and a $65,000 short-term gain. What is Helena's AGI from these transactions? If she has a net long-term capital gain, what is its makeup in terms of the alternative tax rates?

63. **LO.5** For 2020, Ashley has gross income of $38,350 and a $5,000 long-term capital loss. She claims the standard deduction. Ashley is 35 years old and unmarried with two dependent children. How much of Ashley's $5,000 capital loss carries over to 2021?

64. **LO.5** Jane and Blair are married taxpayers filing jointly and have 2020 taxable income of $107,000. The taxable income includes $5,000 of gain from a capital asset held five years, $2,100 of gain from a capital asset held seven months, and $13,000 of gain from a capital asset held four years. All of the capital assets were stock in publicly traded corporations. Jane and Blair also have qualified dividend income of $3,000. What is the couple's tax on taxable income and the related tax savings from the alternative tax computation (if any)?

65. **LO.5** For 2020, Wilma has properly determined taxable income of $36,000, including $3,000 of unrecaptured § 1250 gain and $8,200 of 0%/15%/20% gain. Wilma qualifies for head-of-household filing status. Compute Wilma's tax liability and the tax savings from the alternative tax on net capital gain.

66. **LO.5** Asok's AGI for 2020 is $133,250. Included in this AGI is a $45,000 25% long-term capital gain and a $13,000 0%/15%/20% long-term capital gain. Asok is single and uses the standard deduction. Compute his taxable income, the tax liability, and the tax savings from the alternative tax on net capital gain.

67. **LO.6** Gray, Inc., a C corporation, has taxable income from operations of $1,452,000 for 2020. It also has a net long-term capital loss of $355,000 from the sale of a subsidiary's stock. The year 2020 is the first year in the last 10 years that Gray has not had at least $500,000 per year of net long-term capital gains. What is Gray's 2020 taxable income? What, if anything, can it do with any unused capital losses?

68. **LO.3, 14** Harriet, who is single, is the owner of a sole proprietorship. Two years ago, Harriet developed a process for preserving doughnuts that gives the doughnuts a much longer shelf life. The process is not patented or copyrighted, and only Harriet knows how it works. Harriet has been approached by a company that would like to buy the process. Harriet insists that she receive a long-term employment contract with the acquiring company as well as be paid for the rights to the process. The acquiring company offers Harriet a choice of two options: (1) $650,000 in cash for the process and a 10-year covenant not to compete at $65,000 per year or (2) $650,000 in cash for a 10-year covenant not to compete and $65,000 per year for 10 years in payment for the process. Which option should Harriet accept? What is the tax effect on the acquiring company of each approach?

Decision Making
Critical Thinking

69. **LO.8** A sculpture that Korliss Kane held for investment was destroyed in a flood. The sculpture was insured, and Korliss had a $60,000 gain from this casualty. He also had a $17,000 loss from an uninsured antique vase that was destroyed by the flood. The vase was also held for investment. Korliss had no other property transactions during

Communications

the year and has no nonrecaptured § 1231 losses from prior years. Both the sculpture and the vase had been held more than one year when the flood occurred (i.e., both are long-term nonpersonal use capital assets). Compute Korliss's net gain or loss, and identify how it would be treated. Also write a letter to Korliss, explaining the nature of the gain or loss. Korliss's address is 2367 Meridian Road, Hannibal, MO 63401.

70. **LO.8** Keshara has the following net § 1231 results for each of the years shown. What would be the nature of the net gains in 2019 and 2020?

Tax Year	Net § 1231 Loss	Net § 1231 Gain
2015	$18,000	
2016	33,000	
2017	42,000	
2018		$41,000
2019		30,000
2020		41,000

Decision Making
Critical Thinking

71. **LO.8, 14** Jinjie owns two parcels of business land (§ 1231 assets). One parcel can be sold at a loss of $60,000, and the other parcel can be sold at a gain of $70,000. Jinjie has no nonrecaptured § 1231 losses from prior years. The parcels could be sold at any time because potential purchasers are abundant. Jinjie has a $35,000 short-term capital loss carryover from a prior tax year and no capital assets that could be sold to generate long-term capital gains. Both land parcels have been held more than one year. What should Jinjie do based upon these facts? (Assume that tax rates are constant, and ignore the present value of future cash flow.)

72. **LO.7, 8, 9** Siena Industries (a sole proprietorship) sold three § 1231 assets during 2020. Data on these property dispositions are as follows:

Asset	Cost	Acquired	Accumulated Depreciation	Sold for	Sold on
Rack	$100,000	10/10/16	$62,000	$85,000	10/10/20
Forklift	35,000	10/16/17	23,000	5,000	10/10/20
Bin	87,000	03/12/19	34,000	60,000	10/10/20

   a. Determine the amount and the character of the recognized gain or loss from the disposition of each asset.

   b. Assuming that Siena has no nonrecaptured net § 1231 losses from prior years, analyze these transactions and determine the amount (if any) that will be treated as a long-term capital gain.

73. **LO.8, 9** Copper Industries (a sole proprietorship) sold three § 1231 assets during 2020. Data on these property dispositions are as follows:

Asset	Cost	Acquired	Accumulated Depreciation	Sold for	Sold on
Rack	$110,000	10/10/17	$70,000	$55,000	10/10/20
Forklift	45,000	10/16/16	21,000	15,000	10/10/20
Bin	97,000	03/12/19	31,000	60,000	10/10/20

   a. Determine the amount and the character of the recognized gain or loss from the disposition of each asset.

   b. Assuming that Copper has $6,000 nonrecaptured net § 1231 losses from prior years, analyze these transactions and determine the amount (if any) that will be treated as a long-term capital gain.

Communications

74. **LO.8, 9** On December 1, 2018, Lavender Manufacturing Company (a corporation) purchased another company's assets, including a patent. The patent was used

in Lavender's manufacturing operations; $49,500 was allocated to the patent, and it was amortized at the rate of $275 per month. On July 30, 2020, Lavender sold the patent for $95,000. Twenty months of amortization had been taken on the patent. What are the amount and nature of the gain Lavender recognizes on the disposition of the patent? Prepare your solution using Microsoft Excel (or a similar program). Write a letter to Lavender, discussing the treatment of the gain. Lavender's address is 6734 Grover Street, Boothbay Harbor, ME 04538. The letter should be addressed to Bill Cubit, Controller.

75. **LO.8, 10** On June 1, 2016, Skylark Enterprises, a calendar year LLC reporting as a sole proprietorship, acquired a retail store building for $500,000 (with $100,000 being allocated to the land). The store building was 39-year real property, and the straight-line cost recovery method was used. The property was sold on June 21, 2020, for $385,000.

a. Compute the cost recovery and adjusted basis for the building using Exhibit 8.8 from Chapter 8.

b. What are the amount and nature of Skylark's gain or loss from disposition of the property? What amount, if any, of the gain is unrecaptured § 1250 gain?

76. **LO.8, 9, 10** On May 2, 1990, Hannah Weather (Social Security number: 111-22-3333) acquired residential real estate for $450,000. Of the cost, $100,000 was allocated to the land and $350,000 to the building. On August 20, 2019, the building, which then had an adjusted basis of $0, was sold for $545,000 and the land for $200,000.

a. Determine the amount and character of the recognized gain from the sale of the building.

b. Determine the amount and character of the recognized gain from the sale of the land.

c. Complete a Form 4797 for these transactions. Assume that there are no § 1231 lookback losses.

77. **LO.8, 9, 10** Larry is the sole proprietor of a trampoline shop. During 2020, the following transactions occurred:

- Unimproved land adjacent to the store was condemned by the city on February 1. The condemnation proceeds were $15,000. The land, acquired in 1987, had an allocable basis of $40,000. Larry has additional parking across the street and plans to use the condemnation proceeds to build his inventory.

- A truck used to deliver trampolines was sold on January 2 for $3,500. The truck was purchased on January 2, 2016, for $6,000. On the date of sale, the adjusted basis was zero.

- Larry sold an antique rowing machine at an auction. Net proceeds were $4,900. The rowing machine was purchased as used equipment 17 years ago for $5,200 and is fully depreciated.

- Larry sold an apartment building for $300,000 on September 1. The rental property was purchased on September 1, 2017, for $150,000 and was being depreciated over a 27.5-year life using the straight-line method. At the date of sale, the adjusted basis was $124,783.

- Larry's personal yacht was stolen on September 5. The yacht had been purchased in August at a cost of $25,000. The fair market value immediately preceding the theft was $19,600. Larry was insured for 50% of the original cost, and he received $12,500 on December 1.

- Larry sold a Buick on May 1 for $9,600. The vehicle had been used exclusively for personal purposes. It was purchased on September 1, 2016, for $20,800.

- Larry's trampoline stretching machine (owned two years) was stolen on May 5, but the business's insurance company will not pay any of the machine's value because Larry failed to pay the insurance premium. The machine had a fair market value of $8,000 and an adjusted basis of $6,000 at the time of theft.

- Larry had AGI of $102,000 from sources other than those described above.
- Larry has no nonrecaptured § 1231 lookback losses.

a. For each transaction, what are the amount and nature of recognized gain or loss?

b. What is Larry's 2020 AGI?

Communications   78. **LO.8, 10** On January 1, 2011, Stephanie Bridges acquired depreciable real property for $50,000. She used straight-line depreciation to compute the asset's cost recovery. The asset was sold for $96,000 on January 3, 2020, when its adjusted basis was $38,000.

a. What are the amount and nature of the gain if the real property is residential?

b. Stephanie is curious about how the recapture rules differ for tangible personal property and for residential rental real estate acquired in 1987 and thereafter. Write a letter to Stephanie, explaining the differences. Her address is 2345 Westridge Street #23, Edna, KS 67342.

Decision Making   79. **LO.8, 9, 11, 14** Joanne is in the 24% tax bracket and owns depreciable business
Critical Thinking   equipment that she purchased several years ago for $135,000. She has taken $100,000 of depreciation on the equipment, and it is worth $55,000. Joanne's niece, Susan, is starting a new business and is short of cash. Susan has asked Joanne to gift the equipment to her so that Susan can use it in her business. Joanne no longer needs the equipment. Identify the alternatives available to Joanne if she wants to help Susan and the tax effects of those alternatives. (Assume that all alternatives involve the business equipment in one way or another, and ignore the gift tax.)

80. **LO.8, 9, 11** Anna received tangible personal property with a fair market value of $65,000 as a gift in 2018. The donor had purchased the property for $77,000 and had taken $77,000 of depreciation. Anna used the property in her business. Anna sells the property for $23,000 in 2020. What are the tax status of the property and the nature of the recognized gain when she sells the property?

81. **LO.8, 9, 11** Miguel receives tangible personal property as an inheritance in 2018. The property was depreciated by the deceased (Miguel's father), and Miguel will also depreciate it. At the date of the deceased's death, the property was worth $532,000. The deceased had purchased it for $900,000 and taken $523,000 of depreciation on the property. Miguel takes $223,000 of depreciation on the property before selling it for $482,000 in 2020. What are the tax status of the property and the nature of the recognized gain when Miguel sells the property?

82. **LO.11** David contributes to charity some tangible personal property that he had used in his business and depreciated. At the date of the donation, the property has a fair market value of $233,000 and an adjusted basis of zero; it was originally acquired for $400,000. What is the amount of David's charitable contribution?

83. **LO.8, 9, 11** Dedriea contributes to her wholly owned corporation some tangible personal property she had used in her sole proprietorship business and depreciated. She had acquired the property for $566,000 and had taken $431,000 of depreciation on it before contributing it to the corporation. At the date of the contribution, the property had a fair market value of $289,000. The corporation took $100,000 of depreciation on the property and then sold it for $88,000 in 2020. What are the tax status of the property to the corporation and the nature of the recognized gain or loss when the corporation sells the property?

84. **LO.8, 9, 12** Tan Corporation purchased depreciable tangible personal property for $100,000 in 2018 and immediately expensed the entire cost under § 179. In 2020, when the property was worth $80,000, Tan distributed it as a dividend to the corporation's sole shareholder. What was the tax status of this property for Tan? What is the nature of the recognized gain or loss from the distribution of the property?

85. **LO.7, 8, 10** Jasmine owned rental real estate that she sold to her tenant in an installment sale. Jasmine acquired the property in 2008 for $400,000; took $178,000 of depreciation on it; and sold it for $210,000, receiving $25,000 immediately and the balance (plus interest at a market rate) in equal payments of $18,500 for 10 years.

    a. What is the nature of the recognized gain or loss from this transaction?

    b. Assuming that the interest rate on the installment contract is 5%, what is the present value of the installment payments? See Appendix G for present value factors.

86. **LO.9** Jay sold three items of business equipment for a total of $300,000. None of the equipment was appraised to determine its value. Jay's cost and adjusted basis for the assets are shown below.

Decision Making
Critical Thinking

Asset	Cost	Adjusted Basis
Skidder	$230,000	$ 40,000
Driller	120,000	60,000
Platform	620,000	–0–
Total	$970,000	$100,000

Jay has been unable to establish the fair market values of the three assets. All he can determine is that combined they were worth $300,000 to the buyer in this arm's length transaction. How should Jay allocate the sales price and figure the gain or loss on the sale of the three assets?

Tax Return Problems

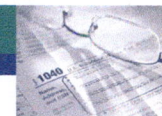

87. Ashley Panda lives at 1310 Meadow Lane, Wayne, OH 43466, and her Social Security number is 123-45-6777. Ashley is single and has a 20-year-old son, Bill. His Social Security number is 111-11-1112. Karl lives with Ashley, and she fully supports him. Bill spent 2019 traveling in Europe and was not a college student. He had gross income of $4,655 in 2019. Bill paid $4,000 of lodging expenses that Ashley reimbursed after they were fully documented. Ashley paid the $4,000 to Bill using a check from her sole proprietorship. That amount is not included in the items listed below. Ashley had substantial health problems during 2019, and many of her expenses were not reimbursed by her health insurance.

Tax Forms Problem

Ashley owns Panda Enterprises LLC (98-7654321), a data processing service that she reports as a sole proprietorship. Her business is located at 456 Hill Street, Wayne, OH 43466. The business activity code is 514210. Her 2019 Form 1040, Schedule C for Panda Enterprises shows revenues of $315,000, office expenses of $66,759, employee salary of $63,000, employee payroll taxes of $4,820, business meal expenses (before the 50% reduction) of $22,000, and rent expense of $34,000. The rent expense includes payments related to renting an office ($30,000) and payments related to renting various equipment ($4,000). There is no depreciation because all depreciable equipment owned has been fully depreciated in previous years. No fringe benefits are provided to the employee. Ashley personally purchases health insurance on herself and Bill. The premiums are $23,000 per year.

Ashley has an extensive stock portfolio and has prepared the following analysis:

Stock	Number of Shares	Date Purchased	Date Sold	Per-Share Cost	Per-Share Selling Price	Total Dividends
Beige	10	10/18/18	10/11/19	$80	$ 74	$30
Garland	30	10/11/12	10/11/19	43	157	70
Peach	15	3/10/19	8/11/19	62	33	45

Note: Ashley received a Form 1099–B from her stockbroker that included the adjusted basis and sales proceeds for each of her stock transactions. The per-share cost includes commissions, and the per-share selling price is net of commissions. Also, the dividends are the actual dividends received in 2019, and these are both ordinary dividends and qualified dividends.

Ashley had $800 of interest income from State of Ohio bonds and $600 of interest income on her Wayne Savings Bank account. She paid $25,000 of alimony to her former husband (divorce finalized in June 2017). His Social Security number is 123-45-6788.

Ashley itemizes her deductions and provides the following information, which may be relevant to her return:

Item	Amount	Comment
Unreimbursed medical expenses for Ashley	$9,748	Does not include health insurance premiums.
State income taxes paid	1,830	
Real property taxes on personal residence	3,230	
Interest paid on home mortgage (Form 1098)	8,137	The loan is secured by the residence and was incurred when the home was purchased.
Charitable contributions	1,399	$940 cash payments to Ashley's church and $459 cash payments made to homeless persons for whom she felt sorry. She can document all the expenditures.
Sales taxes	619	Amount per sales tax table.

Ashley paid $27,000 in estimated Federal income taxes, did not engage in any virtual currency transactions during the year, does not want any of her taxes to finance presidential elections, has no foreign bank accounts or trusts, and wants any refund to be applied against her 2020 taxes.

Compute Ashley's net tax payable or refund due for 2019. If you use tax forms for your computations, you will need Form 1040 and its Schedules 1, 2, 3, A, C, D, and SE and Form 8949. Ashley qualifies for the § 199A deduction for qualified business income. Be sure to include that in your calculations. Suggested software: ProConnect Tax Online.

Tax Forms Problem

88. Justin Stone was an employee of DataCare Services, Inc. His salary was $45,000 through November 10, 2019, when he was laid off. DataCare Services provided medical insurance for Justin and his family during his employment and agreed to continue this coverage through the end of 2019. He received $7,000 of unemployment compensation from November 11, 2019, through December 31, 2019. FICA withholdings were as follows: Social Security of $2,790 ($45,000 × 6.2%) and Medicare of $653 ($45,000 × 1.45%). Justin lives at 112 Green Road, Crown City, OH 45623. His Social Security number is 111-11-1118. Justin owned an apartment building until November 22, 2019, when he sold it for $200,000 (the apartment building's address is 4826 Orange Street, Crown City, OH 45623). For 2019, he had rent revenue of $33,000. He incurred and paid expenses as follows: $4,568 of repairs, $12,000 of mortgage interest, $10,000 of real estate taxes, and $1,000 of miscellaneous expenses. He purchased the building on January 2, 2013, for $125,000 (the related land was purchased for $10,000). The building generated an operating profit each year that Justin owned it. Justin received $13,000 in cash as a gift from his mother to help "tide him over" while he was unemployed. He also withdrew $10,000 from his checking account. He "invested" $300 in lottery tickets during the year but had no winnings.

Other information follows:

- On November 22, 2019, Justin sold for $3,500 equipment that had been used for repairing various items in the apartments. The equipment was purchased for $25,000 on July 10, 2012, and was fully depreciated prior to 2019.
- Justin has $3,000 of unrecaptured § 1231 losses from prior years.
- Justin is age 38; is single; is divorced; and has custody of his nine-year-old son, Flint.
- Justin provides more than 50% of Flint's support. Flint's Social Security number is 123-45-6788.
- Justin had $1,000 interest income from Blue Corporation bonds.
- Justin had $1,500 interest income from a State Bank certificate of deposit.

- Justin had a $2,000 0%/15%/20% long-term capital gain distribution from the Brown Stock Investment Fund.

- Justin had the following itemized deductions: $4,600 real estate taxes on his home; $8,900 mortgage interest on his home; $4,760 charitable contributions (all in cash, all properly documented, and no single contribution exceeding $25); $4,300 state income tax withholding during 2019; $2,000 state estimated income tax payments during 2019; $2,600 sales taxes paid.

- Justin does not own or use any virtual currency.

- Justin does not want to donate to the Presidential Election Campaign Fund.

- He had $10,000 of Federal income tax withholding during 2019 and made total Federal estimated income tax payments of $12,000 during 2019.

Compute Justin's 2019 net tax payable or refund due. Ignore the § 199A deduction for qualified business income (if applicable). If you use tax forms for your computations, you will need Form 1040 and its Schedules 1, 3, A, B, D, and E. You will also need Forms 4797 and 8582. Suggested software: ProConnect Tax Online.

See Appendix E for Comprehensive Tax Return Problems—Form 1040

Research Problems

Note: Solutions to the Research Problems can be prepared by using the Thomson Reuters Checkpoint™ online tax research database, which accompanies this textbook. Solutions can also be prepared by using research materials found in a typical tax library.

Research Problem 1. Siva Nathaniel owns various plots of land in Fulton County, Georgia. He acquired the land at various times during the last 20 years. About every fourth year, Siva subdivides into lots one of the properties he owns. He then has water, sewer, natural gas, and electricity hookups put in each lot and paves new streets. Siva has always treated his sales of such lots as sales of capital assets. His previous tax returns were prepared by an accountant whose practice you recently purchased. Has the proper tax treatment been used on the prior tax returns? Explain.

Partial list of research aids:
§§ 1221 and 1237 and *Jesse W. and Betty J. English*, 65 TCM 2160, T.C.Memo. 1993–111.

Research Problem 2. Clyde had worked for many years as the chief executive of Red Industries, Inc., and had been a major shareholder. Clyde and the company had a falling out, and Clyde was terminated. Clyde and Red executed a document under which Clyde's stock in Red would be redeemed and Clyde would agree not to compete against Red in its geographic service area. After extensive negotiations between the parties, Clyde agreed to surrender his Red stock in exchange for $600,000. Clyde's basis in his shares was $143,000, and he had held the shares for 17 years. The agreement made no explicit allocation of any of the $600,000 to Clyde's agreement not to compete against Red. How should Clyde treat the $600,000 payment on his 2020 tax return?

Research Problem 3. Your client, Alternate Fuel, Inc. (a regular corporation), owns three sandwich shops in the Philadelphia area. In 2017, the year Alternate Fuel incorporated, it acquired land on the outskirts of Philadelphia with the hope of someday farming the land to cultivate humanely harvested meat and grow organic fruits and vegetables to use in its sandwich shops. In 2019, Alternate Fuel drew up plans for the farm and began consulting with agricultural experts about the best locations for crops and the number of animals that could be sustained on the acreage. After reviewing those plans, Alternate Fuel's CEO decided that the plans are not currently financially feasible and would like to sell the land in 2020. The land has appreciated substantially in value, and the company could use the cash infusion. Given that the land has not been used in the business, will any gain realized be categorized as a § 1231 gain or as a long-term capital gain? Explain.

Research Problem 4. Your supervisor at your CPA firm has questioned whether the depreciation taken on a building under § 168(k) is subject to § 1250 depreciation recapture. Find a discussion in the Form 4797 instructions confirming that this depreciation is subject to § 1250 recapture.

Use internet tax resources to address the following questions. Look for reliable websites and blogs of the IRS and other government agencies, media outlets, businesses, tax professionals, academics, think tanks, and political outlets.

Research Problem 5. Perform a Google search to find information about capital gains tax rates worldwide (and across U.S. states). Try searching for "capital gains rate by country (state)." What jurisdiction has the highest capital gains tax rate? What U.S. states have high capital gains tax rates?

Data Analytics

Research Problem 6. Using the *IRS Tax Statistics* that can be found at **irs.gov/statistics**, based on adjusted gross income for the most recent year available, determine the amount of net long-term capital gain taxpayers reported. Use the search function to look for a table related to "capital gain."

Becker CPA Review Questions

Becker.

1. A gain on the sale of which of the following assets will *not* result in a capital gain?
   a. Stock in a public company
   b. A home used as a personal residence
   c. Goodwill of a corporation
   d. Inventory of a corporation

2. Conner purchased 300 shares of Zinco stock for $30,000 in year 1. On May 23, year 6, Conner sold all the stock to his daughter Alice for $20,000, its then fair market value. Conner realized no other gain or loss during year 6. On July 26, year 6, Alice sold the 300 shares of Zinco for $25,000. What was Alice's recognized gain or loss on her sale?

   a. $0   c. $5,000 short-term loss
   b. $5,000 long-term gain   d. $5,000 long-term loss

3. Brad and Angie are married and file a joint return. For year 14, they had income from wages in the amount of $100,000 and had the following capital transactions to report on their income tax return:

Carryover of capital losses from year 13	$200,000
Loss on sale of stock purchased in March year 14, sold on October 10, year 14, and repurchased on November 2, year 14	20,000
Gain on the sale of stock purchased 5 years ago and sold on March 14, year 14	15,000
Gain on the sale of their personal residence (all qualifications have been met for the maximum allowable gain exclusion)	675,000
Loss on the sale of their personal automobile	10,000
Gain on the sale of their personal furniture	5,000
Loss on the sale of investment property (land only)	150,000

What is the amount of capital loss carryover to year 15?

a. ($155,000)   c. ($132,000)
b. ($152,000)   d. ($125,000)

4. A piece of depreciable machinery is sold. It has been held for three years and quali-fies as § 1231 property. The selling price is greater than the adjusted basis, but less than the original purchase price. Which statement below is correct?

   a. All of the gain will be subject to § 1245 recapture.
   b. Only a portion of the gain will be subject to § 1245 recapture.
   c. None of the gain will be subject to § 1245 recapture.
   d. Section 1245 recapture will not apply because there is a loss on the sale.

5. Jerry uses a building for business purposes. The building was purchased on April 1, year 3, for $124,000. It was sold on October 3, year 6, for $200,000. Accumulated depreciation as of the date of sale was $14,000, $4,000 of which was in excess of straight line. How much of the gain in year 6 is recaptured as ordinary under § 1250?

   a. $4,000   c. $14,000
   b. $10,000   d. $100,000

6. Jerry uses a building for business purposes. The building was purchased on April 1, year 3, for $124,000. It was sold on October 3, year 6, for $200,000. Accumulated depreciation as of the date of sale was $14,000, $4,000 of which was in excess of straight line. How much of the gain in year 6 is unrecaptured § 1250 gain?

   a. $4,000   c. $14,000
   b. $10,000   d. $100,000

7. Wally, Inc., sold the following three personal property assets in year 6:

Asset	Purchase Date	Cost	Accumulated Depreciation	Selling Price
A	5/1/year 3	$5,000	$3,000	$2,300
B	8/13/year 4	1,200	500	2,000
C	2/18/year 4	3,800	1,800	1,500

What is Wally's net § 1231 gain or loss in year 6?

   a. $500 loss   c. $800 gain
   b. $300 gain   d. $1,600 gain

8. Wally, Inc., sold the following three personal property assets in year 6:

Asset	Purchase Date	Cost	Accumulated Depreciation	Selling Price
A	5/1/year 3	$5,000	$3,000	$1,300
B	8/13/year 4	1,200	500	1,100
C	2/18/year 4	3,800	1,800	1,500

What is Wally's net § 1231 gain or loss in year 6?

   a. $500 loss   c. $1,200 loss
   b. $700 loss   d. $1,200 gain

9. Wally, Inc., sold the following three personal property assets in year 6:

Asset	Purchase Date	Cost	Accumulated Depreciation	Selling Price
A	5/1/year 3	$5,000	$3,000	$2,300
B	8/13/year 4	1,200	500	2,000
C	2/18/year 6	3,800	1,800	1,500

What is Wally's net § 1231 gain or loss in year 6?

a. $500 loss   c. $800 gain

b. $300 gain   d. $1,600 gain

10. Wally, Inc., sold the following three personal property assets in year 6:

Asset	Purchase Date	Cost	Accumulated Depreciation	Selling Price
A	5/1/year 3	$5,000	$3,000	$2,300
B	8/13/year 4	1,200	500	2,000
C	2/18/year 6	3,800	1,800	1,500

What is Wally's § 1245 recapture in year 6?

a. $500 loss   c. $800 gain

b. $300 gain   d. $1,600 gain

11. Net § 1231 losses are:

a. Deducted as a capital loss against other capital gains and nothing against ordinary income.

b. Deducted as a capital loss against other capital gains and up to $3,000 against ordinary income.

c. Not allowed as a deduction.

d. Deducted as an ordinary loss.

12. Section 1245 recapture applies to which of the following?

a. Section 1231 real property sold at a gain with accumulated depreciation in excess of straight line.

b. Section 1231 personal property sold at a gain with accumulated depreciation.

c. Section 1231 real property sold at a gain with accumulated depreciation equal to straight-line depreciation.

d. Section 1231 personal property sold at a loss.

13. Section 1250 recapture applies to which of the following?

a. Section 1231 real property sold at a gain with accumulated depreciation in excess of straight line.

b. Section 1231 personal property sold at a gain with accumulated depreciation.

c. Section 1231 real property sold at a gain with accumulated depreciation equal to straight-line depreciation.

d. Section 1231 personal property sold at a loss.

SPECIAL TAX COMPUTATIONS AND ACCOUNTING PERIODS AND METHODS

CHAPTER **15**

The Deduction for Qualified Business Income for Noncorporate Taxpayers

CHAPTER **16**

Accounting Periods and Methods

Part 5 begins by discussing the distinctions between various taxpayer entities, including sole proprietorships, partnerships, and corporations. Then the deduction for qualified business income available to *noncorporate* taxpayers is explored. This part also provides a comprehensive examination of the accounting periods and accounting methods that were introduced in Part 2.

CHAPTER

15

The Deduction for Qualified Business Income for Noncorporate Taxpayers

LEARNING OBJECTIVES: *After completing Chapter 15, you should be able to:*

LO.1 Summarize the tax treatment of various forms of conducting a business.

LO.2 Explain the rationale for the deduction for qualified business income.

LO.3 Describe the types of taxpayers and activities that potentially generate a deduction for qualified business income.

LO.4 Determine a taxpayer's deduction for qualified business income.

LO.5 List and evaluate tax planning ideas for choice of entity and the deduction for qualified business income.

CHAPTER OUTLINE

15-1 Tax Treatment of Various Business Forms, 15-2
    15-1a Sole Proprietorships, 15-2
    15-1b Partnerships, 15-3
    15-1c Corporations, 15-3
    15-1d Limited Liability Companies, 15-7

15-2 The Tax Cuts and Jobs Act (TCJA) of 2017 and Entity Tax Rates, 15-8
    15-2a Challenges of Lowering Tax Rates, 15-8
    15-2b Lowering Tax Rates for Different Business Forms, 15-9

15-3 The Deduction for Qualified Business Income, 15-9
    15-3a General Rule, 15-10
    15-3b The Overall Limitation: Modified Taxable Income, 15-10
    15-3c Definition of Qualified Business Income, 15-10

    15-3d Definition of a Qualified Trade or Business, 15-11
    15-3e Limitations on the QBI Deduction, 15-12
    15-3f Limitation Based on Wages and Capital Investment, 15-14
    15-3g Limitation for "Specified Services" Businesses, 15-17
    15-3h Treatment of Losses, 15-21
    15-3i Coordination with Other Rules, 15-22
    15-3j Considerations for Partnerships and S Corporations, 15-22
    15-3k Other Issues, 15-22

15-4 Tax Planning, 15-23
    15-4a Corporate versus Noncorporate Forms of Business Organization, 15-23
    15-4b Optimizing the Deduction for Qualified Business Income, 15-24

ASPEN PHOTO/SHUTTERSTOCK.COM

ENTREPRENEURIAL PURSUITS

Amy plans to start at least two different business activities after she graduates from college. She will apply the knowledge gained in her business courses to use various forms of social media to promote her skills and experience as a volleyball player to help younger players develop their skills. She plans to generate income from advertising on her social media sites. She also will use her artistic and marketing talents to find work using several web platforms, like Upwork and Freelancer.

Based on what she has read on websites and heard from friends, Amy is wondering if she should form a corporation or a limited liability company for these pursuits or just be a sole proprietor. She is also curious whether, for tax and legal purposes, she has one business or two.

After reading this chapter, you can help Amy with her questions, including aiding her in better framing the questions should she decide to seek assistance from an attorney on business entity formation matters or a CPA for tax and accounting assistance.

Read the chapter and formulate your response.

For Federal income tax purposes, the distinctions among forms of business organization are important. This chapter begins by discussing the distinctions between sole proprietorships, partnerships, S corporations, and regular corporations. Limited liability companies, which generally are taxed as one of these entity forms, are also introduced.

A key piece of the TCJA of 2017 was to lower the corporate income tax rate from a progressive tax rate structure (with rates from 15 percent to 35 percent) to a flat tax of 21 percent. To also provide a tax reduction for businesses that do *not* operate as regular corporations, the TCJA of 2017 created a special deduction for noncorporate taxpayers with business income. These changes affect both tax liabilities and tax planning, including the form of business organization.

LO.1

Summarize the tax treatment of various forms of conducting a business.

15-1 TAX TREATMENT OF VARIOUS BUSINESS FORMS

Business operations can be conducted in a number of different forms including:

- Sole proprietorships.
- Partnerships.
- Trusts and estates.
- S corporations.
- Regular corporations.
- Limited liability companies.

15-1a Sole Proprietorships

A sole proprietorship is not a separate taxable entity. Rather, its operations are reported as part of the sole proprietor's individual income tax return. The owner of a sole proprietorship reports all business income and expenses of the proprietorship on Schedule C of Form 1040, with the net profit or loss from the proprietorship included in the taxable income of the individual proprietor. The proprietor reports all of the net profit from the business, regardless of any amounts actually withdrawn during the year.

Income and expenses of the proprietorship retain their character when reported by the proprietor. For example, ordinary income of the proprietorship is treated as ordinary income when reported by the proprietor, and capital gain is treated as capital gain. In addition, a deduction for qualified business income (§ 199A, discussed in text Section 15-3) is available for sole proprietors. In general, this deduction is 20 percent of proprietorship net income (or, if less, taxable income before the qualified business income deduction less any net capital gain) and is claimed on the proprietor's Form 1040 in determining taxable income.[1]

The Big Picture

EXAMPLE

1

Return to the facts of *The Big Picture* on p. 15-1. The easiest business entity for Amy to form is a sole proprietorship. She need not create any legal documents for the proprietorship, although she may need to obtain a business license in her county or city (and pay a tax or fee for it), including filing a statement of business purpose.

She should also set up accounting records (e.g., using QuickBooks) and make her accounting and tax record keeping simpler by having a separate bank account and credit card for business purposes (accounts that are *not* used for personal purchases).

---

[1]There are limitations on this deduction for higher-income taxpayers. This chapter includes a detailed discussion of the deduction for qualified business income. For treatment of the qualified business income deduction by partnerships and S corporations, see Chapters 21 and 22, respectively.

15-1b Partnerships

Partnerships are not subject to a Federal income tax. However, a partnership is required to file Form 1065, which reports the results of the partnership's activities. Business income and expense items are aggregated in computing the ordinary business income (loss) of the partnership on Form 1065. Any remaining income and expense items are reported separately to the partners.[2] Partnerships are discussed in detail in Chapter 21.

The partnership ordinary business income (loss) and the separately reported items are allocated to the partners according to the partnership's profit and loss sharing agreement. Each partner receives a Schedule K–1 that reports this information. Each partner then reports these items on his or her own tax return. In addition, individual partners can claim the deduction for qualified business income (to the extent available) on their individual tax return (Form 1040).

EXAMPLE 2

Sundra and Patel are equal partners in Canary Enterprises, a calendar year partnership. During the year, Canary Enterprises had $500,000 gross income and $350,000 operating expenses. In addition, the partnership sold land that had been held for investment purposes for a long-term capital gain of $60,000. During the year, Sundra withdrew $40,000 from the partnership, and Patel withdrew $45,000.

The partnership's Form 1065 reports ordinary business income of $150,000 ($500,000 income − $350,000 expenses) and long-term capital gain of $60,000 as a separately stated item.

Sundra and Patel each receive a Schedule K–1 reporting ordinary business income of $75,000 and separately stated long-term capital gain of $30,000. Each partner reports ordinary business income of $75,000 and long-term capital gain of $30,000 on his own return. Likewise, Sundra and Patel would claim any related deduction for qualified business income on their individual tax returns.

15-1c Corporations

Corporations are governed by Subchapter C or Subchapter S of the Internal Revenue Code. Those governed by Subchapter C are referred to as **C corporations** or **regular corporations**. Corporations governed by Subchapter S are referred to as **S corporations**.

S corporations, which generally do not pay Federal income tax, are similar to partnerships in that ordinary business income (loss) flows through to the shareholders to be reported on the shareholder's separate returns. Also like partnerships, certain items flow through from the S corporation to the shareholders and retain their separate character when reported on the shareholders' returns. In general, only individuals can be S corporation shareholders (no such limitation exists for partnerships). The S corporation ordinary business income (loss) and the separately reported items are allocated to the shareholders according to their stock ownership interests. In addition, S corporation shareholders can claim the deduction for qualified business income (to the extent available) on their individual tax return (Form 1040). S corporations are discussed in detail in Chapter 22.

Unlike proprietorships, partnerships, and S corporations, C corporations are subject to an entity-level Federal income tax. This results in what is known as *double taxation*. A C corporation reports its income and expenses on Form 1120 and then computes tax on its taxable income using a flat 21 percent rate.[3] When a corporation distributes its income, the corporation's shareholders report dividend income on their own tax returns; further, no corporate deduction is allowed for the dividends paid (discussed next). As a result, income that has already been taxed at the corporate level is also taxed at the shareholder level.

Taxation of Dividends

Double taxation stems, in part, from the fact that dividend distributions are not deductible by a C corporation. To avoid this, closely held corporation shareholders try to convert dividend distributions into tax-deductible expenses. A common way to do this

---

[2]Some examples of separately reported income items are interest income, dividend income, and long-term capital gain. Examples of separately reported expenses include charitable contributions and expenses related to investment income.

[3]For taxable years prior to 2018, corporations faced tax rates that varied from 15% to 39%. Corporations with taxable income of $18,333,333 or more paid a flat 35% tax rate.

is to increase compensation to shareholder-employees. However, the IRS scrutinizes compensation and other economic transactions (e.g., loans, leases, and sales) between shareholders and closely held corporations to ensure that payments are reasonable in amount.[4]

For individual shareholders, some of the double taxation effect is alleviated because dividends are generally taxed at lower tax rates. Qualified dividend income is taxed at a rate of 15 percent (20 percent for high-income taxpayers; 0 percent for lower-income taxpayers).[5] These rates also apply to long-term capital gains.[6]

Double Taxation Illustrated

Lavender Corporation has taxable income of $100,000 in 2020. It pays corporate tax of $21,000. This leaves $79,000, all of which is distributed as a dividend to Ashley, a 43-year-old single individual and the corporation's sole shareholder. Ashley has no income sources other than Lavender Corporation.

Ashley has taxable income of $66,600 ($79,000 − $12,400 standard deduction). She pays tax at the preferential rate applicable to qualified dividends received by individuals. Her tax is $3,986 [($40,000 × 0%) + ($125 × 12%) + ($26,475 × 15%)].

The combined tax on the corporation's net profit is $24,986 ($21,000 paid by the corporation + $3,986 paid by the shareholder).

Assume the same facts as in Example 3, except that the business is organized as a sole proprietorship. Ashley reports the $100,000 profit from the business on her tax return. Ashley pays self-employment taxes of $14,130 ($100,000 × 0.9235 × 15.3%); one-half of this amount ($7,065) is a deduction *for* AGI. She has taxable income of $64,428 {$100,000 − $7,065 SE tax deduction − $12,400 standard deduction − $16,107 deduction for qualified business income [($100,000 − $7,065 − $12,400) × 20%]} and pays tax of $9,964.

As a result, operating the business as a sole proprietorship results in an income tax *savings* of $15,022 in 2020 [$24,986 (from Example 3) − $9,964].

Comparison of Corporations and Other Forms of Doing Business

When comparing C corporations to other business forms, there are a number of factors to consider including:

- Tax rates,
- Character of business income,
- Business losses,
- Employment taxes, and
- State taxes.

Each of these is discussed below.

Tax Rates As noted earlier, a flat rate of 21 percent applies to corporate taxable income. The marginal rates for individuals range from 10 percent to 37 percent. In many cases, taxes will be greater in the corporate form (as in Example 3). However, the corporate form of doing business presents tax savings opportunities when the applicable corporate marginal rate is *lower* than the applicable individual marginal rate.

---

[4]See Chapter 19 for a discussion of constructive dividends.

[5]The 0% (20%) rate applies if taxable income, including the net capital gain, is below (above) specific thresholds based on filing status. In 2020, below $80,000 (or above $496,600) for married taxpayers filing a joint return; below $40,000 (or above $441,450) for single taxpayers.

[6]A 3.8% Medicare surtax applies to net investment income in excess of modified adjusted gross income of $200,000 ($250,000 if married filing jointly), thus increasing the double taxation of dividend income for high-income taxpayers.

Susanna, an individual taxpayer in the 37% marginal tax rate bracket, can generate $100,000 of additional taxable income in the current year. If the income is taxed to Susanna, the associated tax is $37,000 ($100,000 × 37%).

If, however, Susanna is able to shift the income to a newly created corporation, the corporate tax is $21,000 ($100,000 × 21%). As a result, by taking advantage of the lower corporate marginal tax rates, a tax *savings* of $16,000 ($37,000 − $21,000) is achieved.

Any attempt to take advantage of the difference between the corporate and individual marginal tax rates also must consider the effect of double taxation. When the preferential rate for dividend income is considered, however, tax savings opportunities still exist.

Assume in Example 5 that the corporation distributes all of its after-tax earnings to Susanna as a dividend. The dividend results in income tax of $15,800 [($100,000 − $21,000) × 20%] to Susanna.

As a result, even when the double taxation effect is considered, the combined tax burden of $36,800 ($21,000 paid by the corporation + $15,800 paid by the shareholder) represents an income tax *savings* of $200 when compared to the $37,000 of tax that results when the $100,000 of income is subject to Susanna's 37% marginal rate.

Examples 5 and 6 ignore other tax issues that also must be considered in selecting the proper form of doing business (e.g., the availability of the deduction for qualified business income), but they illustrate the tax savings that can be achieved by taking advantage of rate differentials.

Character of Business Income Unlike other forms of business, the tax attributes of income and expense items of a C corporation do not pass through the corporate entity to the shareholders. As a result, if the business is expected to generate tax-favored income (e.g., tax-exempt income or long-term capital gains), it may be better to choose a different business form.

Pass-Through of Losses C corporation losses are treated differently than losses of other business forms. A loss incurred by a proprietorship may be deductible by the owner, because all income and expense items are reported by the proprietor. Partnership and S corporation losses are passed through the entity and may be deductible by the partners or S corporation shareholders. C corporation losses, however, are retained at the corporate level. If losses are anticipated, it may be better to choose a business form other than a C corporation.

Franco plans to start a business this year. He expects that the business will incur operating losses for the first three years and then become highly profitable. Franco decides to operate as an S corporation during the loss period, because the losses will flow through and be deductible on his personal return. When the business becomes profitable, he intends to switch to C corporation status.

Employment Taxes The net income of a proprietorship is subject to the self-employment tax (15.3 percent), as are some partnership allocations of income to partners. Alternatively, wages paid to a shareholder-employee of a corporation (C or S) are subject to payroll taxes. The combined corporation-employee payroll tax burden must be compared with the self-employment tax in the proprietorship and partnership business forms. This analysis should include the benefit of the deduction available to a corporation for payroll taxes paid, as well as the deduction available to an individual for one-half of the self-employment taxes paid.

State Taxes At the entity level, state corporate income taxes and/or franchise taxes apply to corporations. Some states impose a franchise tax on all business forms (including partnerships and S corporations). If a business will be operating in multiple states, state taxes become more important (Chapter 24 discusses the taxation of multistate corporations). At the owner level, the income of sole proprietorships, S corporations, and partnerships (along with dividend distributions) is subject to state individual income taxation.

The tax attributes of the various forms of business entities are compared in Concept Summary 15.1.

Concept Summary 15.1

Tax Treatment of Business Forms Compared

	Sole Proprietorships	Partnerships	S Corporations	Regular (C) Corporations
Entity tax return	None	Form 1065	Form 1120S	Form 1120
Taxation of entity income	No separate entity-level income tax. Proprietorship's income and expenses are reported on owner's Form 1040 (Schedule C). Character of entity income and expenses retained at owner level. Proprietor eligible for deduction for qualified business income.	No separate entity-level income tax. Partnership's income and expenses are allocated and reported (on Schedule K–1) to partners who report these items on their returns (e.g., Form 1040 for individual partners). Character of entity income and expenses retained at partner level. Individual partners eligible for deduction for qualified business income.	Generally, no separate entity-level income tax. S corporation's income and expenses are allocated and reported (on Schedule K–1) to shareholders who report these items on their returns (e.g., Form 1040 for individual shareholders). Character of entity income and expenses retained at shareholder level. Shareholders eligible for deduction for qualified business income.	Corporate income tax applies. Flat rate of 21% on corporate taxable income.
Taxation of withdrawals/ distributions from entity	Withdrawals by owner are not subject to separate tax.	Distributions to partners are generally not subject to separate tax.	Distributions to shareholders are generally not subject to separate tax.	Character of entity income and expenses not retained at shareholder level. Instead, distributions to shareholders are generally taxed as dividend income. Preferential tax rates (0%/15%/20%) apply to qualified dividends.
Employment taxes	Schedule C income subject to self-employment tax.	Some partnership allocations subject to self-employment tax.	Compensation paid to shareholder/employees subject to payroll taxes. Shareholder's allocated portion of entity income not subject to self-employment tax.	Compensation paid to shareholder/employees subject to payroll taxes.

GLOBAL TAX ISSUES   U.S. Corporate Taxes and International Business Competitiveness

In a 2017 study, the Tax Foundation examined the impact of national tax systems on international business competitiveness. In its report, the Tax Foundation ranked the international tax competitiveness of the 35 members of the Organization for Economic Co-operation and Development (OECD) by examining each country's tax policies. The rankings were based on many tax policy factors, including corporate and individual tax rates, consumption taxes, payroll and property taxes, and international tax rules.

The United States ranked 30th out of the 35 OECD countries in overall international tax competitiveness, largely due to its comparative rankings on corporate taxes (35th) and international tax rules (33rd). Estonia claimed the top ranking in the report, followed by New Zealand, Switzerland, and Latvia.

One of the primary goals underlying the enactment of the TCJA of 2017 was to increase the international competitiveness of U.S. businesses. The reduction in the corporate tax rate to 21 percent was the centerpiece of that legislation. In the 2019 Tax Foundation rankings, the United States moved from 30th to 21st (primarily due to TCJA of 2017 changes). An interactive tool allows readers to explore their data in more depth (**tax-competition.org**). It will be interesting to see how the United States ranks in future studies on international tax competitiveness.

Source: taxfoundation.org/2019-international-index/.

Nontax Considerations

Nontax considerations may override tax considerations and lead owners to conclude that a business should be operated as a corporation. Here are some of the more important *nontax considerations*.

- Sole proprietors and general partners in partnerships face the danger of *unlimited liability*. That is, business creditors can file claims against the assets of the business *and* the personal assets of proprietors or general partners. State corporate law protects the personal assets of shareholders.

- The corporate form of business provides a vehicle for *raising capital* through widespread stock ownership. Most major businesses in the United States are operated as corporations.

- Shares of stock in a corporation are *freely transferable*; a partner's sale of his or her partnership interest must be approved by the other partners.

- A corporation continues to exist even when a shareholder dies. Death or withdrawal of a partner, on the other hand, may terminate the existing partnership and cause financial difficulties that result in dissolution of the entity. This *continuity of life* is a distinct advantage of the corporate form.

- Corporations have *centralized management*. All management responsibility is assigned to a board of directors, who appoint officers to carry out the corporation's business. Partnerships often have decentralized management, in which every partner has a right to participate in the organization's business decisions. Limited partnerships, though, may have centralized management.

15-1d Limited Liability Companies

The limited liability company (LLC) is a business form that blends some corporate form advantages into a flow-through entity. All 50 states and the District of Columbia have passed laws that allow LLCs, and thousands of companies have chosen LLC status. As with a corporation, operating as an LLC allows its owners (called "members") to avoid unlimited liability exposure, which is a primary *nontax* consideration in choosing a business form. The tax advantage of LLCs is that qualifying businesses may be treated as proprietorships or partnerships for tax purposes, thereby avoiding the problem of double taxation associated with regular corporations.[7]

---

[7]Some states allow an LLC to have centralized management, but not continuity of life or free transferability of interests. Other states allow LLCs to adopt any or all of the corporate characteristics of centralized management, continuity of life, and free transferability of interests.

Entity Classification

Can an organization that is *not* a corporation under state law still be treated as one for Federal income tax purposes? The tax law defines a corporation as including "associations, joint stock companies, and insurance companies."[8] Unfortunately, the Code contains no definition of what constitutes an *association*, and the issue became the subject of frequent litigation.

It was finally determined that an entity would be treated as a corporation if it had a majority of characteristics common to corporations.

- Continuity of life.
- Centralized management.
- Limited liability.
- Free transferability of interests.

These criteria did not resolve all of the problems that continued to arise over corporate classification. And when the states allowed the creation of LLCs, the IRS was deluged with inquiries regarding its tax status. The Code does not identify LLCs as a business form. And state LLC laws differed (e.g., some allowed centralized management, but others did not). So the question was how these entities would be treated under Federal tax law.

To ease this problem, the **Check-the-box Regulations** were issued by the Treasury Department.[9] The Regulations enable taxpayers to choose the tax status of a business entity without regard to its corporate (or noncorporate) characteristics. These rules simplified tax administration considerably and eliminated much of the litigation related to association (i.e., corporation) status.

Under the Check-the-box Regulations, an unincorporated entity with *more than one* owner is, by default, classified as a partnership. An unincorporated entity with *only one* owner is, by default, classified as a **disregarded entity** (or DRE). A DRE is treated as a sole proprietorship if it is owned by an individual or as a branch or a division of a corporate owner. If the entity wants to use its default status, it simply files the appropriate tax return. If it wants to use a different status or change its status, it does so by "checking a box" on Form 8832. Thus, an LLC (single or multi-member) can choose to be taxed as a C corporation and, if it otherwise qualifies, even elect S corporation status.[10] Although an LLC does not typically pay Federal income taxes, LLCs are required to report and pay employment and excise taxes.

15-2 THE TAX CUTS AND JOBS ACT (TCJA) OF 2017 AND ENTITY TAX RATES

A primary goal for tax reform in 2017 was to lower the Federal income tax rate for C corporations, improving the international competitiveness of U.S. corporations and attracting investment in the United States from non-U.S. multinational corporations. As described below, lowering corporate tax rates is a challenging task.

15-2a Challenges of Lowering Tax Rates

The Tax Reform Act of 1986 lowered the Federal corporate income tax rate from a maximum of 46 percent to 34 percent. This led many other industrialized countries also to lower their corporate tax rate. After many years, most of these countries had

---

[8]§ 7701(a)(3).

[9]Reg. §§ 301.7701–1 through –4, and –7.

[10]The "check-the-box" option is not available to entities that are incorporated under state law or to entities that are required to be taxed as corporations under Federal law (e.g., certain publicly traded partnerships). LLCs are not treated as being incorporated under state law, so they default to either partnership or DRE status.

lowered their rate below 34 percent, while the United States *raised* the top corporate rate to 35 percent. With U.S. companies facing increasing global competition, most members of Congress and U.S. Presidents favored lowering the corporate tax rate.

One obstacle to lowering the Federal corporate income tax rate is that most businesses in the United States operate as sole proprietorships, partnerships, or S corporations, rather than as C corporations. These non-C corporation entities are pass-through entities, where the business income is taxed to owners (rather than being subject to double taxation). In addition, the owners of these businesses are likely to recognize other forms of income. For example, a sole proprietor is likely to also have investment income and wages. As a result, determining how to tax the business income of pass-through entities in a manner comparable to that of a C corporation is challenging, as explained next. Text Section 15-3 then explains how Congress met this challenge with a special deduction for qualified business income for owners of pass-through entities.

15-2b Lowering Tax Rates for Different Business Forms

LO.2

Explain the rationale for the deduction for qualified business income.

There is more than one way to lower the tax rate on the business income that non-corporate taxpayers earn from their businesses. For example, similar to the lower income tax rates that apply to the net capital gains and qualified dividends received by noncorporate taxpayers, an alternative rate structure could be applied to business income. Or noncorporate taxpayers could be allowed a special deduction to reduce the income from their business activities, thereby lowering the tax base (and lowering the taxes due).

Challenges exist in both of these approaches, as well as in determining what rate is comparable to the corporate tax rate given the double taxation of corporate income. These challenges include entity differences (e.g., sole proprietors and partnerships do not pay wages to their owners, but S corporations generally do).

Congress chose to adopt a deduction against qualified business income (QBI), allowing up to a 20 percent deduction on the qualified business income of *noncorporate* taxpayers. As a result, this deduction is potentially available to individuals, trusts, and estates. Owners of partnerships and S corporations use relevant information provided to them from the entity (on their Schedule K–1 and related attachments) to calculate the deduction on their tax return (e.g., an individual's Form 1040).

The balance of this chapter explains the deduction for qualified business income. The QBI deduction includes numerous definitions, limitations, and special rules. Appreciating the purpose of the deduction—to reduce the tax on business income derived outside of the C corporate form—will help in understanding this provision.

15-3 THE DEDUCTION FOR QUALIFIED BUSINESS INCOME

LO.3

Describe the types of taxpayers and activities that potentially generate a deduction for qualified business income.

With the reduction in the corporate income tax rate to 21 percent in 2018, Congress needed to provide a means of reducing the taxes on businesses that operate in different business forms (e.g., sole proprietors, partnerships, and S corporations). Congress accomplished this with the creation of the **deduction for qualified business income** (§ 199A), which applies to *noncorporate taxpayers*.[11]

In general, the deduction for qualified business income is 20 percent of qualified business income. As you would suspect, however, the deduction is subject to a variety of limitations. We begin by discussing the general rules, defining key terms, and providing some basic examples. Then we turn our attention to the various limitations that apply to higher-income taxpayers and conclude with some other implications of the qualified business income deduction (**QBI deduction**).

---

[11]§ 199A(a).

LO.4

Determine a taxpayer's deduction for qualified business income.

15-3a General Rule

At its most basic level, § 199A permits an individual to deduct 20 percent of the qualified business income generated through a sole proprietorship, a partnership, or an
S corporation.[12] As will quickly become apparent, § 199A uses the word *qualified*
to modify many phrases. For example, to determine the "qualified business income
deduction," one has to understand the definition of a "qualified trade or business" and
"qualified business income." But let's begin with the basics. In general, the deduction
for qualified business income is the *lesser of*:[13]

1. 20 percent of qualified business income (QBI),[14] or
2. 20 percent of modified taxable income.[15]

Effectively, the QBI deduction—a *from* AGI deduction—is the last deduction taken
in determining taxable income.[16] Further, the deduction is available whether a taxpayer
uses the standard deduction or itemizes deductions.[17]

There are *three limitations* on the QBI deduction: an overall limitation (based on
modified taxable income), another that applies to high-income taxpayers, and a third
that applies to certain types of services businesses. The second and third limitations
only apply when taxable income before the QBI deduction exceeds, in 2020, $326,600
(married taxpayers filing a joint return) or $163,300 (single and head-of-household
taxpayers).[18]

15-3b The Overall Limitation: Modified Taxable Income

In all cases, the § 199A deduction may not exceed 20 percent of the taxpayer's modified
taxable income. Modified taxable income is taxable income *before* the deduction for
qualified business income[19] reduced by any net capital gain.[20] In computing modified
taxable income, the term *net capital gain* includes both a net capital gain [the excess
of a long-term capital gain over a short-term capital loss; § 1222(11)] plus any qualified
dividend income.[21]

15-3c Definition of Qualified Business Income

Qualified business income[22] is defined as the ordinary income less ordinary deductions a
taxpayer earns from a "qualified trade or business" conducted in the United States by the
taxpayer (e.g., from a sole proprietorship).[23] It also includes the distributive share of these
amounts from each partnership or S corporation interest held by the taxpayer.

In determining QBI, all deductions attributable to a trade or business are taken into
account.[24] Relevant deductions include the self-employment tax deduction [§ 164(f)], the
self-employed health insurance deduction [§ 162(l)], and any deduction for contributions
to qualified retirement plans [§ 404].[25] See Chapters 7 and 8.

---

[12]§§ 199A(a)(1)(A), (b)(1)(A), and (b)(2)(A).

[13]§ 199A(a)(1).

[14]If the taxpayer has more than one qualified trade or business, the qualified
business income deduction is determined for each business independently
[§ 199A(b)(1)(A)]. These are then combined [into the "combined qualified
business income amount" of § 199A(a)(1)(A)] and compared to the modified taxable income limitation.

[15]In addition, taxpayers are allowed a deduction for 20% of qualified
REIT dividends and 20% of qualified publicly traded partnership income
[§ 199A(b)(1)(B)].

[16]See TCJA § 11011(b), the last sentence of § 62(a), and § 63(b)(3).

[17]§ 63(d)(3).

[18]In 2020, married taxpayers filing separately (MFS) have a threshold amount
of $163,300 (Rev.Proc. 2019–44, 2019–47 I.R.B. 1093). We have not included

MFS in the text discussion. In 2019, the threshold amounts were $321,400
(married taxpayers filing a joint return), $160,725 (married taxpayers filing
separately), and $160,700 (single and head-of-household taxpayers).

[19]§ 199A(e)(1).

[20]§ 199A(a)(1)(B).

[21]§ 199A(a)(1)(B)(ii) and Reg. § 1.199A–1(b)(3); § 199A relies on the definition
of "net capital gain" in § 1(h).

[22]§ 199A(c).

[23]§ 199A(c)(3)(A). As a result, foreign trade or business income does not qualify for the deduction. Certain Puerto Rico activities qualify for the deduction.

[24]§ 199A(c)(3)(A).

[25]Reg. § 1.199A–3(b)(1)(vi).

EXAMPLE 8

Vicki Howard's sole proprietorship reports $54,000 of net income [on Schedule C (Form 1040)]. As a result, Vicki's self-employment tax liability is $7,630 ($54,000 × 0.9235 × 15.3%). She is allowed a *for AGI* deduction for one-half of her self-employment tax liability ($3,815; $7,630 × ½). Vicki's QBI is $50,185 ($54,000 − $3,815).

Qualified business income does not include certain types of investment income, such as:[26]

- Capital gains or capital losses (including any net § 1231 gain included in capital gain and loss computations),[27]
- Dividends,
- Interest income (unless "properly allocable" to a trade or business, such as lending), or
- Certain other investment items.

Nor does qualified business income include:[28]

- The "reasonable compensation" paid to the taxpayer with respect to any qualified trade or business, or
- Guaranteed payments made to a partner for services rendered.

15-3d Definition of a Qualified Trade or Business

For taxpayers who fall below critical taxable income thresholds established under § 199A (in 2020, $326,600 for married taxpayers filing jointly; $163,300 for single and head-of-household taxpayers), the scope of a **qualified trade or business** (QTB) is broad. In general, it includes any trade or business other than providing services as an employee.[29]

Basic QBI Deduction Computation

EXAMPLE 9

Sanjay, a married taxpayer, operates a candy store as a sole proprietor. The business has no employees (Sanjay provides all services to customers). During 2020, Sanjay's qualified business income is $210,000 [this is his Schedule C (Form 1040) net income reduced by his self-employment tax deduction]. Sanjay's AGI is $274,800, which includes wages earned by his spouse, but no other income. He and his spouse claim the standard deduction ($24,800). Sanjay's modified taxable income is $250,000 ($274,800 − $24,800).

Sanjay's QBI deduction is $42,000, the *lesser of:*

1. 20% of qualified business income ($42,000; $210,000 × 20%), or
2. 20% of modified taxable income ($50,000; $250,000 × 20%).

Sanjay's taxable income is $208,000 ($250,000 of taxable income before the QBI deduction less his $42,000 QBI deduction).

EXAMPLE 10

Assume that Abby is a single taxpayer who does not itemize deductions and operates a sole proprietorship. During 2020, her business generates $140,000 of business income, $40,000 of deductible business expenses (including her self-employment tax deduction), and $2,400 of interest income from her business deposits. She has no other sources of income. Abby's AGI is $102,400.

Abby has $100,000 of qualified business income ($140,000 − $40,000). The interest income does not qualify for the QBI deduction. Her modified taxable income is $90,000 ($102,400 AGI − $12,400 standard deduction).

Abby's QBI deduction is $18,000, the *lesser of:*

1. 20% of qualified business income ($20,000; $100,000 × 20%), or
2. 20% of modified taxable income ($18,000; $90,000 × 20%).

Abby's taxable income is $72,000 ($90,000 of taxable income before the QBI deduction less her $18,000 QBI deduction).

[26]§ 199A(c)(3)(B).
[27]Reg. § 1.199A–3(b)(2)(ii).

[28]§ 199A(c)(4).
[29]§ 199A(d)(1)(B).

Basic QBI Deduction Computation

EXAMPLE 11

Assume the same facts as in Example 10, except that Abby has no interest income, but $2,400 of qualified dividend income. Abby's AGI remains $102,400, and her taxable income before the QBI deduction remains $90,000 ($102,400 AGI − $12,400 standard deduction).

However, Abby's modified taxable income is now $87,600 [$90,000 taxable income before the QBI deduction less $2,400 of "net capital gain" (the qualified dividend income)].

Abby's QBI deduction is $17,520, the *lesser of*:

1. 20% of qualified business income ($20,000; $100,000 × 20%), or
2. 20% of modified taxable income ($17,520; $87,600 × 20%).

Abby's taxable income is $72,480 ($90,000 of taxable income before the QBI deduction less her $17,520 QBI deduction).

Taxpayers with Multiple Businesses

The deduction for qualified business income must be determined separately for each qualified trade or business.[30] These independent calculations are then aggregated (becoming the "combined qualified business income amount"). This combined amount is then compared to the overall modified taxable income limit.

15-3e Limitations on the QBI Deduction

The basic application of § 199A becomes more complex once a taxpayer reaches certain taxable income thresholds. These taxable income thresholds—determined without regard to the QBI deduction—are $326,600 for married taxpayers filing jointly and $163,300 for single and head-of-household taxpayers in 2020.[31]

Once these thresholds are reached, § 199A imposes two *independent* limitations.

1. The QBI deduction is capped based on the percentage of the W–2 wages paid by the business (i.e., wages paid to its employees) *or* based on a smaller percentage of W–2 wages paid by the business and a percentage of the cost of its depreciable property used to produce QBI.[32]

2. The QBI deduction generally is *not available* for income earned from "specified service" businesses.[33] "Specified service" businesses include doctors, dentists, lawyers, accountants, consultants, investment advisers, entertainers, and athletes (among others), but not engineers and architects.

These limitations, discussed in more detail below, are fully phased in once taxable income (before the QBI deduction) exceeds $426,600 for married taxpayers filing jointly and $213,300 for single and head-of-household taxpayers. Within the phase-in ranges ($100,000 for married taxpayers filing jointly; $50,000 for all other taxpayers), the limitations are each applied by comparing the amount of taxable income that exceeds the threshold amount to the appropriate phase-in range.[34]

Because the "specified services" limitation can be more complex (due to incorporating the "wages and capital investment" limitation after the "specified services" limitation), the wages and capital investment limitation is discussed first, followed by the "specified services" limitation.

Concept Summary 15.2 provides a flowchart to assist in applying these rules.

---

[30]§ 199A(b)(2).

[31]§ 199A(e)(2). The threshold amount for married taxpayers filing separately is the same as that for single and head-of-household taxpayers. The threshold amounts are indexed for inflation. In 2019, these amounts were $321,400 and $160,700.

[32]§ 199A(b)(2)(B).

[33]§ 199A(d)(2).

[34]§§ 199A(b)(3)(B) and (d)(3).

Concept Summary 15.2

An Overview of the 2020 Qualified Business Income Deduction

<u>How to Use the Concept Summary:</u> **First,** identify all qualified trades or businesses (QTB) of the taxpayer and the related qualified business income (QBI). **Then** for each QTB, move through the flowchart to determine the QBI amount for each QTB. Once this process is complete, combine all of the QBI amounts (this is the "combined qualified business income amount"). **Finally,** apply the *overall limitation* (based on modified taxable income). The QBI deduction is the *lesser of:*

1. The combined "qualified business income (QBI) amount," or
2. 20% of modified taxable income.*

* Modified taxable income is taxable income *before* the QBI deduction less any "net capital gain" (including any qualified dividend income).

Is taxable income before the QBI deduction *over* $163,300 (single/head of household) or $326,600 (married filing jointly)?
— *No* → **QBI Amount = 20% × QBI**

↓ *Yes*

Is the QTB a "specified service" business?

Yes ← → *No*

Yes branch:

Is taxable income before the QBI deduction *over* $213,300 (S/HH) or $426,600 (MFJ)?

No ↓   *Yes* → **No QBI Deduction Allowed**

Determine Applicable Percentage

100% less the following ratio:

MFJ: $\dfrac{\text{Taxable Income} - \$326,600}{\$100,000}$

S/HH: $\dfrac{\text{Taxable Income} - \$163,300}{\$50,000}$

↓

Determine Initial QBI Amount

20% × QBI × Applicable Percentage

↓

Wage/Capital Investment Limitation

(1) Calculate 50% of W–2 wages × Applicable Percentage

(2) Calculate 25% of W–2 wages *plus* 2.5% of Unadjusted basis of qualified property × Applicable Percentage

(3) Wage/Capital Investment Limitation is *greater of* (1) or (2)

↓

Is Initial QBI Amount *less than* Wage/Capital Investment Limitation?
— *No* → (to Determine Reduction Ratio)

↓ *Yes*

QBI Amount is Initial QBI Amount

No branch:

Determine Initial QBI Amount

20% × QBI

↓

Wage/Capital Investment Limitation

(1) Calculate 50% of W–2 wages

(2) Calculate 25% of W–2 wages *plus* 2.5% of Unadjusted basis of qualified property

(3) Wage/Capital Investment Limitation is *greater of* (1) or (2)

↓

Is taxable income before the QBI deduction *over* $213,300 (S/HH) or $426,600 (MFJ)?

No ↓   *Yes* →

Yes: **QBI Amount is *lesser of*:**
(1) Initial QBI Amount, or
(2) Wage/Capital Investment Limitation Amount

No: Is Initial QBI Amount *less than* Wage/Capital Investment Limitation?

Yes ↓   *No* →

QBI Amount is Initial QBI Amount

Determine Reduction Ratio

MFJ: $\dfrac{\text{Taxable Income} - \$326,600}{\$100,000}$

S/HH: $\dfrac{\text{Taxable Income} - \$163,300}{\$50,000}$

↓

Determine Reduction in Wage/Capital Investment Limitation

Difference between Initial QBI Amount and Wage/Capital Investment Limitation × Reduction Ratio

↓

Determine Final QBI Amount

Initial QBI Amount − Reduction in Wage/Capital Investment Limitation

15-3f Limitation Based on Wages and Capital Investment

The W–2 Wages/Capital Investment Limit , which does not apply to taxpayers below the taxable income thresholds mentioned previously and is phased in as a taxpayer's income exceeds those thresholds, limits the 20 percent QBI deduction to the *greater of*:

1. 50 percent of the "W–2 wages" paid by the QTB, or
2. 25 percent of the "W–2 wages" paid by the QTB *plus* 2.5 percent of the taxpayer's share of the unadjusted basis immediately after acquisition of all tangible depreciable property (including real estate) used in the QTB that has not been fully depreciated prior to the close of the taxable year.

W–2 Wages Limit

"W–2 wages" includes the total amount of wages subject to income tax withholding, compensation paid into qualified retirement accounts, and certain other forms of deferred compensation paid to the employees of the business.[35] For labor-intensive businesses, 50 percent of the W–2 wages paid by the business will likely be the relevant limit on the QBI deduction.

W–2 Wages/Capital Investment Limit

For capital-intensive businesses (e.g., real estate), an alternate limit exists. It begins with 25 percent of W–2 wages paid by the QTB and adds to this amount 2.5 percent of the unadjusted basis (immediately after acquisition) of "qualified property."

W–2 Wages Limit

EXAMPLE 12

Simone, a married taxpayer, operates a business as a sole proprietor. The business has one employee, who is paid $80,000 during 2020. Assume that the business has no significant assets. During 2020, Simone's qualified business income is $230,000, and her modified taxable income is $250,000 (this is also her taxable income before the QBI deduction).

Since Simone's taxable income before the QBI deduction is below the income threshold for married taxpayers filing a joint return ($326,600), the W–2/Capital Investment Limitation does not apply. As a result, Simone's QBI deduction is $46,000, the *lesser of*:

1. 20% of qualified business income ($46,000; $230,000 × 20%), or
2. 20% of modified taxable income ($50,000; $250,000 × 20%).

EXAMPLE 13

Assume the same facts as in Example 12, except that Simone's qualified business income is $500,000 and her modified taxable income is $600,000 (this is also her taxable income before the QBI deduction). Because Simone's taxable income before the QBI deduction exceeds $426,600, the W–2/Capital Investment Limitation fully applies. As a result, Simone's QBI deduction is $40,000, the *lesser of*:

1. 20% of qualified business income ($100,000; $500,000 × 20%), or
2. 50% of W–2 wages ($40,000; $80,000 × 50%).

And *no more than*:

3. 20% of modified taxable income ($120,000; $600,000 × 20%).

Qualified property includes depreciable tangible property—real or personal—that is used by the QTB during the year and whose "depreciable period" has not ended before the end of the taxable year.[36] Land and intangible assets are *not* qualified property. The "depreciable period" for "qualified property" under § 199A is a minimum of 10 years.[37]

---

[35] § 199A(b)(4).

[36] § 199A(b)(6)(A).

[37] § 199A(b)(6)(B).

EXAMPLE 14

Tom and Eileen are married and file a joint return for 2020. Their taxable income before the QBI deduction is $500,000 (this is also their modified taxable income). They have $400,000 in QBI from a restaurant they own (a two-member LLC that reports as a partnership). They employed four individuals (cook, bartender, and wait staff) during the year and paid them $150,000 in W–2 wages. They own the building in which the restaurant is located. They bought the building (and its furniture and fixtures) four years ago for $600,000, and the land was worth $100,000, so the unadjusted acquisition basis of the building (and its furniture and fixtures) is $500,000.

Since their taxable income before the QBI deduction exceeds the $426,600 threshold, the W–2 Wages/Capital Investment Limit comes into play. Their QBI deduction is $75,000, computed as follows:

1. 20% of qualified business income ($400,000 × 20%)		$ 80,000
2. But no more than the *greater of*:		
• 50% of W–2 wages ($150,000 × 50%), or		$ 75,000
• 25% of W–2 wages ($150,000 × 25%) *plus*	$37,500	
• 2.5% of the unadjusted basis of qualified property ($500,000 × 2.5%)	12,500	$ 50,000
And *no more than*:		
3. 20% of modified taxable income ($500,000 × 20%)		$100,000

Many owners of pass-through businesses, especially landlords, have no employees. As a result, the 25 percent of W–2 wages plus 2.5 percent of the unadjusted basis of qualified property is most likely to affect them.

EXAMPLE 15

Jiaxiu, a single taxpayer, owns a five-unit apartment building that he purchased five years ago. His unadjusted basis in the building (purchase price minus the value of the land) is $500,000. He has taxable income before the QBI deduction of $250,000 during 2020 (this is also his modified taxable income). He has no employees in his business, and his QBI is $220,000.

Since his taxable income before the QBI deduction exceeds the $213,300 threshold, the W–2 Wages/Capital Investment Limit comes into play. His QBI deduction is $12,500, computed as follows:

1. 20% of qualified business income ($220,000 × 20%)		$44,000
2. But no more than the *greater of*:		
• 50% of W–2 wages ($0 × 50%), or		$ –0–
• 25% of W–2 wages ($0 × 25%) *plus*	$ –0–	
• 2.5% of the unadjusted basis of qualified property ($500,000 × 2.5%)	12,500	$12,500
And *no more than*:		
3. 20% of modified taxable income ($250,000 × 20%)		$50,000

Phase-In of W–2 Wages/Capital Investment Limit

The W–2 Wages/Capital Investment Limit does not apply to taxpayers with taxable income before the QBI deduction less than the threshold amount ($326,600 for married taxpayers filing jointly; $163,300 for singles and heads of household). And if taxable income before the QBI deduction exceeds the threshold amount by more than $100,000 (married filing jointly) or $50,000 (all other taxpayers), the W–2 Wages/Capital Investment Limit must be used.

If, however, the taxpayer's taxable income before the QBI deduction is between these two amounts *and the W–2 Wages/Capital Investment portion of the QBI deduction is capping the deduction*, then the general 20 percent QBI amount is used, but reduced as follows:

1. Determine difference between the general 20 percent QBI deduction amount and the W–2 Wages/Capital Investment amount.[38]
2. Determine the Reduction Ratio:[39]

---

[38] This is the "excess amount" in § 199A(b)(3)(B)(iii).   [39] § 199A(b)(3)(B)(ii).

$$\text{Reduction Ratio} \ \Longrightarrow \ \frac{\text{Taxable income before the QBI deduction} \ - \ \text{Threshold amount}}{\$100,000 \text{ (married filing jointly); } \$50,000 \text{ (others)}}$$

3. Determine the Reduction in the W–2 Wages/Capital Investment Limit:

    Reduction = Difference [from (1)] × Reduction ratio [from (2)]

4. Determine QBI amount:

    20% QBI deduction − Reduction [from (3)]

EXAMPLE 16

Return to the facts of Example 14, but assume that Tom and Eileen's taxable income before the QBI deduction is $366,600 (this is also their modified taxable income), QBI is $320,000, and W–2 wages are $100,000. Their unadjusted property basis remains at $500,000. Tom and Eileen's initial calculation yields a qualified business income amount of $50,000, computed as follows:

1. 20% of qualified business income ($320,000 × 20%)		$64,000
2. But no more than the *greater of*:		
• 50% of W–2 wages ($100,000 × 50%), or		$50,000
• 25% of W–2 wages ($100,000 × 25%) *plus*	$25,000	
• 2.5% of the unadjusted basis of qualified property ($500,000 × 2.5%)	12,500	$37,500

And *no more than*:

3. 20% of modified taxable income ($366,600 × 20%)	$73,320

Since Tom and Eileen's taxable income before the QBI deduction exceeds $326,600 but is less than $426,600 and *the W–2 Wages/Capital Investment portion of the computation is capping the deduction*, the general 20% QBI amount is used, but reduced as follows:

1. Determine the difference between the general 20% QBI deduction amount and the W–2 Wages/Capital Investment amount:

General 20% QBI deduction amount	$64,000
Less: The W–2 Wages/Capital Investment Limit	(50,000)
Excess	$14,000

2. Determine the Reduction Ratio:

$$\text{Reduction Ratio} = \frac{\$40,000 \ (\$366,600 - \$326,600)}{\$100,000} = 40\%$$

3. Determine the Reduction in the W–2 Wages/Capital Investment Limit:

    Excess ($14,000) × Reduction ratio (40%) = $5,600

4. Determine Final QBI Amount:

General 20% QBI deduction amount	$64,000
Less: Reduction in the W–2 Wages/Capital Investment Limit	(5,600)
Final QBI amount	$58,400

Since the QBI amount ($58,400) is less than 20% of their modified taxable income ($73,320; $366,600 × 20%), they will be allowed a $58,400 deduction for qualified business income.

15-3g Limitation for "Specified Services" Businesses

For high-income taxpayers (in 2020, $426,600 for married taxpayers filing jointly; $213,300 for single and head-of-household taxpayers), § 199A excludes any "specified service trade or business" from the definition of a qualified trade or business.[40] A **specified service trade or business** includes those involving:[41]

- The performance of services in certain fields, including health, law, accounting, actuarial science, performing arts, consulting, athletics, financial services, and brokerage services;
- Services consisting of investing and investment management, trading or dealing in securities, partnership interests, or commodities; and
- Any trade or business where the business's principal asset is the reputation of one or more of its employees or owners.

Architects and engineers are specifically excluded from this definition.[42] A *de minimis* rule excludes from the "specified services" rule a business that derives a small amount of its gross receipts from specified service activities (i.e., services income is *less than 10 percent* of gross receipts earned by the business).[43]

According to the legislative history of the TCJA of 2017, the taxable income thresholds where the QBI deduction is phased out for "specified service" businesses were set by Congress "to deter high-income taxpayers from attempting to convert wages or other compensation for personal services to income eligible for the 20 percent deduction under the provision." However, the phaseout rules operate without regard to the taxpayer's specific motivation.

EXAMPLE 17

In Example 9, Sanjay operated a sole proprietorship that generated QBI of $210,000 and he was able to claim a QBI deduction of $42,000.

But if his spouse had a salary of $300,000 (instead of $64,000), Sanjay would not be able to claim a QBI deduction since their taxable income before the QBI deduction exceeds $426,600 [$210,000 (QBI) + $300,000 (spouse's wages) − $24,800 (standard deduction) = $485,200]. Sanjay did not attempt to "convert wages to . . . income eligible for the (QBI) deduction." The *income of his spouse* triggered the limitation.

Phase-In of the "Specified Services" Limit

In computing the qualified business income with respect to a "specified services" business, the taxpayer takes into account only the "applicable percentage" of QBI *and* the components of the W–2 Wages/Capital Investment Limit.[44]

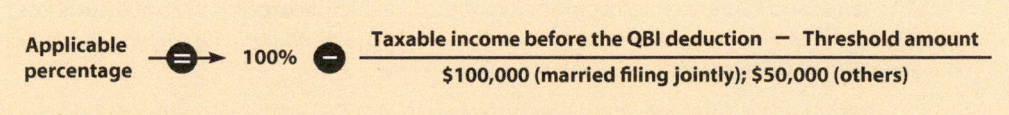

$$\text{Applicable percentage} = 100\% - \frac{\text{Taxable income before the QBI deduction} - \text{Threshold amount}}{\$100,000 \text{ (married filing jointly); } \$50,000 \text{ (others)}}$$

---

[40]§§ 199A(d)(1)(A) and (d)(2).

[41]§ 199A(d)(2); see also § 1202(e)(3)(A).

[42]§ 199A(d)(2)(A).

[43]The *de minimis* exception threshold is reduced to 5% for a business with greater than $25 million of gross receipts. Reg. § 1.199A–5(c)(1).

[44]§ 199A(d)(3)(B).

EXAMPLE 18

In 2020, a single taxpayer has modified taxable income of $193,300, of which $150,000 is attributable to an accounting sole proprietorship that pays wages of $100,000 to employees.

The taxpayer has an applicable percentage of 40%, computed as follows:

$$\text{Applicable percentage} = 100\% - \frac{\$193,300 - \$163,300}{\$50,000} = 40\%$$

In determining includible qualified business income, the taxpayer takes into account 40% of $150,000, or $60,000. In determining the includible W–2 wages, the taxpayer takes into account 40% of $100,000, or $40,000.

A second complication exists if a taxpayer has a "specified services" business with taxable income before the QBI deduction in the phaseout range. Here, in addition to the amount of QBI, W–2 wages, and unadjusted basis of property being subject to a limitation, the W–2 Wages/Capital Investment Limitation might also apply (provided the 20 percent QBI deduction is greater than the W–2 Wages/Capital Investment Limit). The following example illustrates the complexity.

"Specified Services" Limit

EXAMPLE 19

In 2020, Jenna and Paul have taxable income before the QBI deduction (and modified taxable income) of $366,600, and Jenna is a part-time financial adviser (a "specified service trade or business") with QBI of $75,000. Jenna pays $20,000 in wages to employees and has qualified business property of $90,000.

Normally, Jenna and Paul would be entitled to a QBI deduction of $15,000 ($75,000 × 20%). But since their taxable income exceeds the threshold for married taxpayers ($326,600), their QBI deduction is limited to $7,800, computed as follows:

1. Determine Applicable Percentage:

$$\text{Applicable percentage} = 100\% - \frac{\$40,000\,(\$366,600 - \$326,600)}{\$100,000} = 60\%$$

2. Determine QBI deduction:

a. 20% of qualified business income ($75,000 × 20%)		$15,000
× Applicable percentage		× 60%
		$ 9,000
b. But no more than the *greater of*:		
• 50% of W–2 wages ($20,000 × 50% × 60%), or		$ 6,000
• 25% of W–2 wages ($20,000 × 25% × 60%) *plus*	$3,000	
• 2.5% of the unadjusted basis of qualified property ($90,000 × 2.5% × 60%)	1,350	$ 4,350

Since Jenna and Paul's taxable income before the QBI deduction exceeds $326,600 but is less than $426,600 and *the W–2 Wages/Capital Investment portion of the computation is capping the deduction*, the general 20% QBI amount is used, but reduced as follows:

1. Determine the difference between the general 20% QBI deduction amount and the W–2 Wages/Capital Investment amount:

General 20% QBI deduction amount	$ 9,000
Less: The W–2 Wages/Capital Investment Limit	(6,000)
Excess	$ 3,000

2. Determine the Reduction Ratio:

$$\text{Reduction Ratio} = \frac{\$40,000\,(\$366,600 - \$326,600)}{\$100,000} = 40\%$$

continued

3. Determine the Reduction in the W–2 Wages/Capital Investment Limit:

$$\text{Excess (\$3,000)} \times \text{Reduction Ratio (40\%)} = \underline{\$1,200}$$

4. Determine Final QBI Amount:

General 20% QBI deduction amount	$ 9,000
Less: Reduction in the W–2 Wages/Capital Investment Limit	(1,200)
Final QBI amount	$ 7,800

Since the QBI amount ($7,800) is less than 20% of their modified taxable income ($73,320; $366,600 × 20%), they will be allowed a $7,800 deduction for qualified business income.

Assume the same facts as Example 19, except that Jenna and Paul's taxable income before the QBI deduction is $450,000.

Because their modified taxable income exceeds the $426,600 threshold for married taxpayers, and their only QBI is from a "specified services" business, Jenna and Paul are not allowed a QBI deduction.

Now assume the same facts as Example 19, except that Jenna's business is a flower and gift shop (*not* a "specified services" business). As before, Jenna and Paul have modified taxable income of $366,600 and Jenna has QBI of $75,000, pays $20,000 in wages to employees, and has qualified business property of $90,000. Their QBI deduction is $13,000, computed as follows:

1. 20% of qualified business income ($75,000 × 20%)		$15,000
2. But no more than the *greater of*:		
• 50% of W–2 wages ($20,000 × 50%), or		$10,000
• 25% of W–2 wages ($20,000 × 25%) *plus*	$5,000	
• 2.5% of the unadjusted basis of qualified property ($90,000 × 2.5%)	2,250	$ 7,250

And *no more than*:

3. 20% of modified taxable income ($366,600 × 20%)		$73,320

Since Jenna and Paul's modified taxable income exceeds $326,600 but is less than $426,600 and *the W–2 Wages/Capital Investment portion of the computation is capping the deduction*, the general 20% QBI amount is used, but reduced as follows:

1. Determine the difference between the general 20% QBI deduction amount and the W–2 Wages/Capital Investment amount:

General 20% QBI deduction amount	$15,000
Less: The W–2 Wages/Capital Investment Limit	(10,000)
Excess	$ 5,000

2. Determine the Reduction Ratio:

$$\text{Reduction Ratio} = \frac{\$40,000\ (\$366,600 - \$326,600)}{\$100,000} = 40\%$$

3. Determine the Reduction in the W–2 Wages/Capital Investment Limit:

$$\text{Excess (\$5,000)} \times \text{Reduction Ratio (40\%)} = \underline{\$2,000}$$

4. Determine Final QBI Amount:

General 20% QBI deduction amount	$15,000
Less: Reduction in the W–2 Wages/Capital Investment Limit	(2,000)
Final QBI amount	$13,000

Since the QBI amount ($13,000) is less than 20% of their modified taxable income ($73,320; $366,600 × 20%), they will be allowed a $13,000 deduction for qualified business income.

A comparison of Examples 19 and 21 demonstrates the implications (and disadvantages) of having a "specified services" business.

An even more complex setting is having multiple businesses—some "specified services" and others not. Here, a QBI deduction is determined for each business and then combined. This "combined qualified business income amount" is then compared to the overall modified taxable income limitation.

EXAMPLE 22

Chaz and Abby Klein are involved in two businesses during 2020. Chaz is a management consultant. Chaz's consulting business is an LLC (and a "specified services" business), which he reports as a sole proprietorship. The proprietorship generates qualified business income of $230,000, Chaz pays W–2 wages of $50,000 to an employee, and he has $100,000 of qualified property. Chaz and his wife, Abby, also own and operate rental properties. The couple report $146,400 of net income from their rental real estate (three rental properties that they manage). They pay no wages with respect to the rental properties, and they have $450,000 of qualified property. They have no other income or deductions (and will use the standard deduction).

Their modified taxable income is $351,600 (AGI of $376,400 less their $24,800 standard deduction); this is also taxable income before the QBI deduction. The maximum QBI deduction they can claim is $70,320 ($351,600 × 20%). Because their modified taxable income is more than $326,600 and less than $426,600, both of the QBI deduction limitations apply.

Consulting ("Specified Services") Business

1. Determine Applicable Percentage:

$$\text{Applicable percentage} = 100\% - \frac{\$25,000\ (\$351,600 - \$326,600)}{\$100,000} = 75\%$$

2. Determine QBI deduction:

a. 20% of qualified business income ($230,000 × 20%) $46,000
    × Applicable percentage   × 75%
                                         $34,500

b. But no more than the *greater of*:

- 50% of W–2 wages ($50,000 × 50% × 75%), or $18,750

- 25% of W–2 wages ($50,000 × 25% × 75%) *plus* $9,375
- 2.5% of the unadjusted basis of qualified
  property ($100,000 × 2.5% × 75%)   1,875 $11,250

Since their taxable income before the QBI deduction exceeds $326,600 but is less than $426,600 and *the W–2 Wages/Capital Investment portion of the computation is capping the deduction*, the general 20% QBI amount is used, but reduced as follows:

1. Determine the difference between the general 20% QBI deduction amount and the W–2 Wages/Capital Investment amount:

General 20% QBI deduction amount $34,500
Less: The W–2 Wages/Capital Investment Limit   (18,750)
    Excess $15,750

2. Determine the Reduction Ratio:

$$\text{Reduction Ratio} = \frac{\$25,000\ (\$351,600 - \$326,600)}{\$100,000} = 25\%$$

3. Determine the Reduction in the W–2 Wages/Capital Investment Limit:

Excess ($15,750) × Reduction Ratio (25%) = $3,938

4. Determine Final QBI Amount:

General 20% QBI deduction amount $34,500
Less: Reduction in the W–2 Wages/Capital Investment Limit   (3,938)
    Final QBI amount $30,562

continued

Rentals

1. General QBI Deduction Computation:

    a. 20% of qualified business income ($146,400 × 20%) $29,280

    b. But no more than the *greater of*:

    • 50% of W–2 wages ($0 × 50%), or $ –0–

    • 25% of W–2 wages ($0 × 25%) *plus* $ –0–

    • 2.5% of the unadjusted basis of qualified
       property ($450,000 × 2.5%)   11,250 $11,250

Since their taxable income before the QBI deduction exceeds $326,600 but is less than $426,600 and *the W–2 Wages/Capital Investment portion of the computation is capping the deduction*, the general 20% QBI amount is used, but reduced as follows:

1. Determine the difference between the general 20% QBI deduction amount and the W–2 Wages/Capital Investment amount:

    General 20% QBI deduction amount $29,280
    Less: The W–2 Wages/Capital Investment Limit   (11,250)
        Excess $18,030

2. Determine the Reduction Ratio:

$$\text{Reduction Ratio} = \frac{\$25,000\ (\$351,600 - \$326,600)}{\$100,000} = 25\%$$

3. Determine the Reduction in the W–2 Wages/Capital Investment Limit:

    Excess ($18,030) × Reduction Ratio (25%) = $4,508

4. Determine Final QBI Amount:

    General 20% QBI deduction amount $29,280
    Less: Reduction in the W–2 Wages/Capital Investment Limit   (4,508)
        Final QBI amount $24,772

So for Chaz and Abby, the "combined qualified income amount" is $55,334, computed as follows:

      QBI amount from consulting business $30,562
    + QBI amount from rental business   24,772
      Combined qualified business income amount $55,334

Since the combined QBI amount ($55,334) is *less than* 20% of their modified taxable income ($70,320; $351,600 × 20%), they will be allowed a $55,334 deduction for qualified business income. Their final taxable income is $296,266 ($351,600 − $55,334).

15-3h **Treatment of Losses**

If a taxpayer has a qualified business loss in one year, no QBI deduction is allowed, and the loss is carried over to the next year to reduce QBI (but not below zero).[45] Further, if a taxpayer has more than one QTB and the net results of all businesses create a loss, the net loss is carried forward to the following year.

EXAMPLE 23

A taxpayer has QBI of $20,000 from qualified business A and a qualified business loss of $50,000 from qualified business B in 2019. The taxpayer is not permitted a deduction for year 1 and has a carryover qualified business loss of $30,000 to 2020.

In 2020, the taxpayer has QBI of $20,000 from qualified business A and QBI of $50,000 from qualified business B. To determine the deduction for 2020, the taxpayer reduces the 20% deductible amount determined for the QBI of $70,000 from qualified businesses A and B by 20% of the $30,000 carryover qualified business loss.

The result is that the taxpayer has a QBI deduction in 2020 of $8,000 [($20,000 + $50,000) − $30,000 = $40,000 × 20% = $8,000].

[45]§ 199A(c)(2).

15-3i **Coordination with Other Rules**

The deduction for qualified business income operates along with other rules (e.g., how to determine business income). In other cases, Congress specified the treatment. For example, § 199A(f)(3) provides that the QBI deduction is allowed only for *income* taxes. As a result, the QBI deduction does not reduce the tax bases for self-employment taxes or the net investment income tax (NIIT).

Also, in computing an individual's alternative minimum taxable income (AMTI), qualified business income is not changed by any of the AMT's preferences or adjustments (like depreciation) that usually apply in determining AMTI.[46]

15-3j **Considerations for Partnerships and S Corporations**

Although the earlier examples involved sole proprietors, the same result would occur if the business income was instead generated by a partnership or an S corporation. These entities will need to report information to their owners (on the Schedule K–1) to enable the owners to compute their QBI deduction. The QBI deduction will vary among owners even if they share equally in the net earnings of the partnership or S corporation because the taxable income of owners will vary.

EXAMPLE 24

AB Partnership operates an accounting practice and is equally owned by two CPAs, Amy and Barbara. In 2020, partnership income is $340,000 and no guaranteed payments are made to the partners. Both Amy and Barbara are married and file jointly with their spouses. Amy's spouse has wage income of $80,000, and Barbara's spouse has wage income of $300,000. Assume that each couple has other income equal to their standard deduction amount.

The CPA practice is a "specified services" trade or business. Limitations on the QBI deduction will apply if the taxpayer's taxable income exceeds $326,600 if married filing jointly, and no deduction will be available if the couple's taxable income exceeds $426,600.

Amy and her spouse have taxable income of $250,000 ($170,000 partnership income + $80,000 of wage income). They may claim a QBI deduction. In contrast, Barbara and her spouse have taxable income of $470,000 ($170,000 partnership income + $300,000 of wage income). This couple may *not* claim a QBI deduction.

15-3k **Other Issues**

Employee Turned Independent Contractor

An employee of an employer who becomes an independent contractor while providing substantially the same services (either directly or indirectly through another entity) to the same employer is presumed, for a three-year period, still to be an employee.[47] The purpose of this rule is to prevent taxpayers from converting wages (non-QBI) into self-employment (or pass-through) income (QBI).

EXAMPLE 25

Corbin is an attorney employed as an associate with LegalEagles LLP (LE). Corbin and the other associates in LE have taxable income below the threshold amount. LE terminates its employment relationship with Corbin and its other associates, allowing Corbin and the other former associates to form a new partnership, LegalBeagles LLP (LB). LB then contracts to perform services to LE. Corbin continues to provide substantially the same services to LE and its clients through LB.

continued

---

[46]The alternative minimum tax is discussed in text Section 12–5d.

[47]This presumption may be overturned if it can be demonstrated—using common law and statutory rules—that the individual is *not* an employee. Reg. § 1.199A–5(d)(3).

The goal, obviously, is for Corbin (and the other associates) to convert wage income into pass-through income from LB that is eligible for the QBI deduction (even though LB is a "specified services" business, Corbin is below the taxable income threshold).

Because Corbin was formerly an employee of LE and continues to provide substantially the same services to LE, Corbin is presumed to be an employee of LE. Unless the presumption is rebutted, Corbin's distributive share of income from LB will be treated like wages for purposes of § 199A for a period of three years and will not be treated as qualified business income.

What if LB, instead, provides contractual services to a *different* law firm? Now the QBI deduction is available (again assuming that Corbin is below the taxable income threshold).

Determination of "W–2 Wages"

In general, the term *W–2 wages* includes the total amount of wages [as defined in § 3401(a)] plus the total amount of elective compensation deferrals (under § 457) plus the amount of designated Roth contributions (§ 402A).[48]

A business can take into account any W–2 wages paid by another business provided that the W–2 wages were paid to "common law employees or officers" of that business.[49] This means that a business using a professional employer organization (PEO) to manage parts of its business (e.g., human resources) or to lease employees can use an allocable portion of the PEO's W–2 wages in determining its total W–2 wages. The business that actually paid and reported the W–2 wages must then reduce its § 199A wages by the same amount.

Determination of Unadjusted Basis Immediately After Acquisition (UBIA)

UBIA generally will be the property's cost (under § 1012) when the property is placed in service. An addition or improvement to qualified property already placed in service is treated as *separate qualified property* on the date the addition or improvement is placed in service.[50] For purposes of the QBI deduction, property is not qualified property if it is acquired within 60 days of the end of the tax year and disposed of within 120 days without having been used in a trade or business for at least 45 days prior to disposition, unless the taxpayer demonstrates that the principal purpose of the acquisition and disposition was a purpose other than increasing the QBI deduction.[51]

15-4 TAX PLANNING

LO.5

List and evaluate tax planning ideas for choice of entity and the deduction for qualified business income.

15-4a Corporate versus Noncorporate Forms of Business Organization

The form of business organization is an important tax planning consideration. It affects the application of various tax rules including tax rates, deductions, tax accounting methods, and tax years. The decision on what form to use can change as a business grows. For example, in the early years of a business (when it is more likely to generate losses), a pass-through entity is usually desired so that individual owners can utilize the losses generated by the business. If instead the entity was a C corporation from the beginning, it would not be able to use the losses until later years when it generates taxable income.

---

[48]Reg. § 1.199A–2(b)(2). Notice 2018–64 (2018–34 I.R.B. 347) and Rev.Proc. 2019–11 (2019–9 I.R.B. 742) provide detailed guidance about calculating "W–2 wages" for purposes of the QBI deduction.

[49]Reg. § 1.199A–2(b)(2)(ii).

[50]Reg. § 1.199A–2(c)(1)(ii).

[51]Reg. § 1.199A–2(c)(1)(iv).

15-4b Optimizing the Deduction for Qualified Business Income

As noted in a few of the QBI deduction examples, some planning is possible to increase the deduction or perhaps to avoid losing the deduction.

- For taxpayers with taxable income above the pertinent thresholds, consider converting any contractor payments to employee wages to increase the 50 percent of W–2 wages limitation.

- For a married couple who does not reside in a community property state and has "specified services" business income above the thresholds that allow a QBI deduction, determine whether it might be better to file separate tax returns, enabling the spouse with QBI to qualify for the QBI deduction.

- Consider how businesses can be combined or separated, including perhaps placing one or more in separate legal entities, to increase the QBI deduction.

- Employees might consider whether they can become self-employed in their field (which would enable the QBI deduction). As part of this consideration, the employee will need to consider whether it is possible to generate greater income tax savings via the QBI deduction (and other business deductions). Also important will be considering the effect of self-employment taxes and the need to provide health insurance and other benefits, as well as potentially incurring additional business expenses.

REFOCUS ON THE BIG PICTURE

ENTREPRENEURIAL PURSUITS

The simplest entity for Amy to use is a sole proprietorship. If she generates losses, they can be used to offset other income she might have (e.g., if she also takes on a part-time job until her businesses generate sufficient income to enable Amy to support herself).

If the risks for her business, such as injury to customers, are minimal, she will likely find that forming an LLC or a corporation to reduce her personal risk is not warranted. The additional formation costs, continuing fees, and possible business taxes she might owe in her state of residence can be avoided. And Amy can purchase insurance to reduce the costs of any personal risk.

If Amy wants a more formal structure or a legal structure to reduce her personal risk, an S corporation should work well since it allows her income and losses to flow through to her individual tax return. As Amy's income grows, she might consider converting to a C corporation due to the 21 percent maximum rate, although she must also consider the effect of double taxation.

Amy must also consider the QBI deduction (assuming that she does not operate as a C corporation). Until her income reaches the thresholds for the specified service trade or business, she should obtain a deduction even though both of her pursuits might be a "specified services" business (i.e., consulting or where the principal business asset is Amy's reputation or skill).

Finally, Amy should consider state and local taxes. She will need to determine, for example, if a business license tax is owed at the local level and if she is considered to have one business or two.

Key Terms

C corporations, 15-3	Limited liability company (LLC), 15-7	Regular corporations, 15-3
Check-the-box Regulations, 15-8	Limited partnerships, 15-7	S corporations, 15-3
Deduction for qualified business income, 15-9	QBI deduction, 15-9	Specified service trade or business, 15-17
	Qualified business income, 15-10	W–2 Wages/Capital Investment Limit, 15-14
Disregarded entity, 15-8	Qualified trade or business, 15-11	

Discussion Questions

1. **LO.1** Jennifer and Jamie are starting a business and have asked you for advice about whether they should form a partnership, a corporation, or some other type of entity. Prepare a list of questions you would ask in helping them decide which type of entity they should choose. Explain your reasons for asking each of the questions.

2. **LO.1** Barbara owns 40% of the stock of Cassowary Corporation (a C corporation) and 40% of the stock of Emu Corporation (an S corporation). In the current year, each corporation has operating income of $120,000 and tax-exempt interest income of $8,000. Neither corporation pays any dividends during the year. Discuss how this information will be reported by the corporations and Barbara for the year.

3. **LO.1, 5** Art, an executive with Azure Corporation, plans to start a part-time business selling products on the internet. He will devote about 15 hours each week to running the business. Art's salary from Azure places him in the 35% tax bracket. He projects substantial losses from the new business in each of the first three years and expects sizable profits thereafter. Art plans to leave the profits in the business for several years, sell the business, and then retire. Would you advise Art to incorporate the business or operate it as a sole proprietorship? Why?

4. **LO.1** Can a sole proprietor form as a single member limited liability company (LLC)? If so, how would such an LLC be taxed?

5. **LO.1** In the current year, Juanita and Joseph form a two-member LLC and do not file Form 8832 (Entity Classification Election). As a result, the LLC will be treated as a partnership for Federal income tax purposes. Assess the validity of this statement.

6. **LO.2** Why did the TCJA of 2017 include a deduction for qualified business income?

7. **LO.3** Who can claim the qualified business income (QBI) deduction?

8. **LO.4** What are the general rules surrounding the QBI deduction? How is it computed?

9. **LO.3, 4** Define each of the following terms, and explain how each is used in determining the QBI deduction.
   a. Modified taxable income.
   b. Qualified business income.
   c. Qualified trade or business.
   d. "Specified services" business.

10. **LO.3, 4, 5** Jane and Ben are married and usually file a joint return. They live in a separate property state (rather than a community property state). Jane is a partner in a law firm and typically generates income of $162,000. Ben is a grade school teacher with wage income of $75,000. The couple has investment income that

is less than their standard deduction. With enactment of the deduction for qualified business income, the couple is wondering if they should continue to file as married filing jointly or instead use the married filing separately status. Why do they wonder this, and what advice would you offer them and why?

11. **LO.3, 4** Which of the following taxpayers may claim a deduction for qualified business income?

    a.   A driver for Uber or Lyft.

    b.   A veterinarian operating as an S corporation. In addition to veterinary services, revenues are also derived from the sale of pet food and supplies and from the boarding of animals.

    c.   A CPA operating as an LLC taxed as a sole proprietorship. The CPA is single and has taxable income of $150,000.

    d.   Same as part (c), except that the CPA has taxable income of $200,000.

    e.   A real estate salesperson.

    f.   A pet sitter/dog walker.

    g.   A sole proprietor software developer.

    h.   An individual wage earner who derives $60,000 of rental income from a duplex she owns.

12. **LO.2, 4** Why do you think the QBI deduction is limited to earnings from a business conducted in the United States and doesn't also include business income from a foreign business activity?

Computational Exercises

13. **LO.3, 4** In 2020, Meghann Carlson, a single taxpayer, has QBI of $110,000 and modified taxable income of $78,000 (this is also her taxable income before the QBI deduction). Given this information, what is Meghann's QBI deduction?

14. **LO.3, 4** Charlotte is a partner in, and sales manager for, CD Partners, a domestic business that is not a "specified services" business. During the tax year, she receives guaranteed payments of $250,000 from CD Partners for her services to the partnership as its sales manager. In addition, her distributive share of CD Partners' ordinary income (its only item of income or loss) was $175,000. What is Charlotte's qualified business income?

15. **LO.3, 4** Robert is the sole shareholder and CEO of ABC, Inc., an S corporation that is a qualified trade or business. During the current year, ABC has net income of $325,000 after deducting Robert's $100,000 salary. In addition to his compensation, ABC pays Robert dividends of $250,000.

    a.   What is Robert's qualified business income?

    b.   Would your answer to part (a) change if you determined that reasonable compensation for someone with Robert's experience and responsibilities is $200,000? Why or why not?

16. **LO.3, 4** Maria and Javier are the equal partners in MarJa, a partnership that is a qualfied trade or business. In the current year, MarJa had $350,000 of ordinary income after reporting $500,000 in guaranteed payments to Maria and Javier for their services to MarJa ($250,000 each).

    a.   What is Maria's and Javier's qualified business income?

    b.   How would your answer to part (a) change if MarJa had $550,000 of ordinary income after reporting $300,000 in guaranteed payments to Maria and Javier ($150,000 each)?

17. **LO.3, 4** Thad, a single taxpayer, has taxable income before the QBI deduction of $193,300. Thad, a CPA, operates an accounting practice as a single member LLC (which he reports as a sole proprietorship). During 2020, his proprietorship generates qualified business income of $150,000, W–2 wages of $125,000, and $10,000 of qualified property. What is Thad's qualified business income deduction?

18. **LO.3, 4** Jason and Paula are married. They file a joint return for 2020 on which they report taxable income before the QBI deduction of $200,000. Jason operates a sole proprietorship, and Paula is a partner in the PQRS Partnership. Both are a qualified trade or business, and neither is a "specified services" business. Jason's sole proprietorship generates $150,000 of qualified business income and W–2 wages of $45,000 and has qualified property of $50,000. Paula's partnership reports a loss for the year, and her allocable share of the loss is $40,000. The partnership reports no W–2 wages, and Paula's share of the partnership's qualified property is $20,000. What is their QBI deduction for the year?

19. **LO.3, 4** In 2020, Henry Jones works as a freelance driver, finding customers using various platforms like Uber and Grubhub. He is single and has no other sources of income. In 2020, Henry's qualified business income from driving is $61,200. Compute Henry's QBI deduction and his tax liability for 2020.

Problems

20. **LO.1** Ellie and Linda are equal owners in Otter Enterprises, a calendar year business. During the current year, Otter Enterprises has $320,000 of gross income and $210,000 of operating expenses. In addition, Otter has a long-term capital gain of $15,000 and makes distributions to Ellie and Linda of $25,000 each. Discuss the impact of this information on the taxable income of Otter, Ellie, and Linda if Otter is:
    a. A partnership.
    b. An S corporation.
    c. A C corporation.

21. **LO.1** Purple Company has $200,000 in net income for 2020 before deducting any compensation or other payment to its sole owner, Kirsten. Kirsten is single, and she claims the $12,400 standard deduction for 2020. Purple Company is Kirsten's only source of income. Ignoring any employment tax considerations, compute Kirsten's after-tax income if:
    a. Purple Company is a proprietorship and Kirsten withdraws $50,000 from the business during the year; Kirsten claims a $37,520 deduction for qualified business income.
    b. Purple Company is a C corporation and the corporation pays out all of its after-tax income as a dividend to Kirsten.
    c. Purple Company is a C corporation and the corporation pays Kirsten a salary of $158,000.

22. **LO.3, 4** Shelly has $200,000 of QBI from her local jewelry store (a sole proprietorship). Shelly's proprietorship paid $30,000 in W–2 wages and has $20,000 of qualified property. Shelly's spouse earned $74,800 of wages as an employee, they earned $20,000 of interest income during the year, and they will be filing jointly and using the standard deduction. What is their QBI deduction for 2020?

23. **LO.3, 4** Peter Samuels owns and manages his single member LLC that provides a wide variety of financial services to his clients. He is married and will file a joint tax return with his spouse, Amy. His LLC reports $300,000 of qualified business income, W–2 wages of $120,000, and assets with an unadjusted basis of $75,000. Their taxable income before the QBI deduction is $285,000 (this is also their modified taxable income). Determine their QBI deduction for 2020.

24. **LO.3, 4** Ashley (a single taxpayer) is the owner of ABC LLC. The LLC (which reports as a sole proprietorship) generates QBI of $900,000 and is not a "specified services" business. ABC paid total W–2 wages of $300,000, and the total unadjusted basis of property held by ABC is $30,000. Ashley's taxable income before the QBI deduction is $740,000 (this is also her modified taxable income). What is Ashley's QBI deduction for 2020?

25. **LO.3, 4** Donald (a married taxpayer filing jointly) owns a wide variety of commercial rental properties held in a single member LLC. Donald's LLC reports rental income of $1,500,000. The LLC pays no W–2 wages; rather, it pays a management fee to an S corporation Donald controls. The management company pays W–2 wages but reports no income (or loss). Donald's total unadjusted basis of the commercial rental property is $10,000,000. Donald's taxable income before the QBI deduction (and his modified taxable income) is $2,000,000. What is Donald's QBI deduction for 2020?

26. **LO.3, 4** Scott and Laura are married and will file a joint tax return. Laura has a sole proprietorship (not a "specified services" business) that generates qualified business income of $300,000. The proprietorship pays W–2 wages of $40,000 and holds property with an unadjusted basis of $10,000. Scott is employed by a local school district. Their taxable income before the QBI deduction is $386,600 (this is also their modified taxable income).

    a. Determine Scott and Laura's QBI deduction, taxable income, and tax liability for 2020.

    b. After providing you the original information in the problem, Scott finds out that he will be receiving a $6,000 bonus in December 2020 (increasing their taxable income before the QBI deduction by this amount). Redetermine Scott and Laura's QBI deduction, taxable income, and tax liability for 2020.

    c. What is the marginal tax rate on Scott's bonus?

27. **LO.3, 4** Stella Watters is a CPA and operates her own accounting firm (Watters CPA LLC). As a single member LLC, Stella reports her accounting firm operations as a sole proprietorship. Stella has QBI from her accounting firm of $540,000, she reports W–2 wages of $156,000, and the unadjusted basis of property used in the LLC is $425,000. Stella is married and will file a joint tax return with her spouse. Their taxable income before the QBI deduction is $475,000, and their modified taxable income is $448,000. Determine Stella's QBI deduction for 2020.

28. **LO.3, 4** Ben and Molly are married and will file jointly. Ben generates $300,000 of qualified business income from his single member LLC (a law firm). He reports his business as a sole proprietorship. Wages paid by the law firm amount to $40,000; the law firm has no significant property. Molly is employed as a tax manager by a local CPA firm. Their modified taxable income is $386,600 (this is also their taxable income before the deduction for qualified business income). Determine their QBI deduction for 2020.

29. **LO.3, 4** Tammy, a single taxpayer, has a part-time job at BigCo, a company in which she has no ownership interest. In addition, she owns and operates LittleCo, a sole proprietorship that is a qualified trade or business. Tammy is paid wages of $40,000 by BigCo and has $100,000 in qualified business income from LittleCo. She has no other items of income or loss and $25,000 of itemized deductions. What is her qualified business income deduction for 2020?

30. **LO.3, 4** Assume the same facts as in Problem 29, except that Tammy does not have a part-time job at BigCo. How does this affect her qualified business income deduction?

31. **LO.3, 4** Susan, a single taxpayer, owns and operates a bakery (as a sole proprietorship). The business is *not* a "specified services" business. In 2020, the business pays $100,000 in W–2 wages, has $150,000 of qualified property, and generates $350,000 of qualified business income. Susan has no other items of income or loss and will take the standard deduction. What is Susan's qualified business income deduction?

32. **LO.3, 4** Assume the same facts as in Problem 31, except that Susan's business generates $150,000 of qualified business income. What is Susan's QBI deduction?

33. **LO.3, 4** Assume the same facts as in Problem 31, except that Susan's business pays $60,000 of W–2 wages and generates $200,000 of qualified business income. Susan also has a part-time job earning wages of $11,100 and receives $3,300 of interest income. What is Susan's QBI deduction?

34. **LO.3, 4** Jennifer is a CPA and a single taxpayer using the standard deduction. In 2020, her CPA practice generates qualified business income of $162,400 and she has no other income or losses. Jennifer's taxable income before the QBI deduction is $150,000 ($162,400 – $12,400 standard deduction). Jennifer employs an administrative assistant in her practice and pays him $75,000 in wages. The unadjusted basis of depreciable assets employed in the practice totals $30,000.
    a. What is Jennifer's qualified business income deduction?
    b. Determine Jennifer's qualified business income deduction if her CPA practice generates qualified business income of $273,800.

35. **LO.3, 4** Elliot operates his clothing store as a single member LLC (which he reports as a sole proprietorship). In 2020, his proprietorship generates qualified business income of $280,000, he pays W–2 wages of $170,000, and he has qualified business property of $140,000. Elliot's wife, Julie, is an attorney who works for a local law firm and receives wages of $90,000. They will file a joint tax return and use the standard deduction. What is Elliot's qualified business income deduction?

36. **LO.3, 4** Assume the same facts as in Problem 35, except that the business is a "specified services" business (e.g., a consulting firm) owned equally by Elliot and Conrad (an unrelated individual) in a two-member LLC. Assume that each member's share of qualified business income, W–2 wages, and qualified business property is one-half of the information provided in Problem 35. Conrad's wife, Rachel, earned wages during the year of $350,000, and Conrad and Rachel have itemized deductions of $62,000.
    a. What is Elliot's qualified business income deduction?
    b. What is Conrad's qualified business income deduction?

Research Problems

Note: Solutions to the Research Problems can be prepared by using the Thomson Reuters Checkpoint™ online tax research database, which accompanies this textbook. Solutions can also be prepared by using research materials found in a typical tax library.

Research Problem 1. A client has asked you for guidance on selecting the best type of entity for her new business. Using the internet as your sole research source, prepare an outline detailing the advantages and disadvantages of the entity forms available to a sole owner. Include both tax and nontax issues in your analysis.

Research Problem 2. The deduction for qualified business income received considerable praise and criticism in the press from the time it was introduced in November 2017 to the present. Find reliable articles that explain at least two arguments for and against the QBI deduction. Explain whether you agree with these positions and why.

Research Problem 3. Some states automatically conform to any Federal tax changes, but others require special legislation to conform. Generally, states do not conform to rate changes because state income tax systems have their own rate structure (generally at rates well below the Federal tax rates). Find out if your state conformed to the deduction for qualified business income. Explain why the state did or did not conform. Do you agree? Explain.

Becker CPA Review Questions

Becker.

1. Which of the following is considered a specified service trade or business (SSTB) for purposes of the qualifying business income deduction?
   a. Accounting firm.
   c. Engineering firm.
   b. Manufacturing company.
   d. Architectural services.

2. What is the basic deduction calculation for the qualifying business income deduction?
   a. 30% × Qualifying business income (QBI).
   b. 20% × W–2 wages.
   c. 20% × Qualifying business income (QBI).
   d. 30% × W–2 wages.

3. Which of the following statements is true regarding taxpayers with taxable income below the taxable income limitations for the qualifying business income (QBI) deduction?
   a. QBI deduction is only allowed if a qualified trade or business (QTB).
   b. QBI deduction is a phased-out deduction if a specified service trade or business (SSTB).
   c. QBI deduction is limited to 50 percent of W–2 wages.
   d. A qualified trade or business (QTB) and specified trade or business (SSTB) are treated the same.

4. Which of the following is true about the qualifying business income (QBI) deduction for taxpayers with taxable income above the taxable income limitations?

    a. If the taxpayer is a specified service trade or business (SSTB), no QBI deduction is allowed.

    b. If the taxpayer is a qualified trade or business (QTB), W–2 wage and property limitations do not apply.

    c. If the taxpayer is a qualified trade or business (QTB), W–2 wage and property limitations are phased in.

    d. If the taxpayer is a specified service trade or business (SSTB), W–2 wage and property limitations apply.

5. Which of the following is the overall limitation to the qualifying business income (QBI) deduction?

    a. Lesser of 50 percent of combined QBI or 20 percent of the taxpayer's taxable income in excess of net capital gain.

    b. Lesser of combined QBI or 20 percent of the taxpayer's taxable income in excess of net capital gain.

    c. Lesser of 50 percent of W–2 wages or 25 percent of W–2 wages plus 2.5 percent of the unadjusted basis of qualified property.

    d. Taxable income limitations based on filing status.

6. Calculate the taxpayer's qualifying business income deduction for a qualified trade or business:

Filing status:	Single
Taxable income:	$100,000
Net capital gains:	$0
Qualified business income (QBI):	$30,000
W–2 wages:	$10,000

    a. $5,000   c. $20,000

    b. $70,000   d. $6,000

7. Calculate the taxpayer's 2020 qualifying business income deduction for a qualified trade or business:

Filing status:	Single
Taxable income:	$180,000
Net capital gains:	$0
Qualified business income (QBI):	$80,000
W–2 wages:	$20,000

    a. $16,000   c. $2,700

    b. $10,000   d. $13,996

LEARNING OBJECTIVES: *After completing Chapter 16, you should be able to:*

LO.1 Explain the relevance of the accounting period concept, accounting period options, and the limitations on their use.

LO.2 Apply the cash method, accrual method, and hybrid method of accounting.

LO.3 Explain the procedure for changing accounting methods.

LO.4 Determine when the installment method of accounting applies and its effect on taxable income.

LO.5 Recognize the methods of accounting for long-term contracts.

LO.6 Recognize when accounting for inventories must occur and the key tax accounting methods applicable to inventory.

LO.7 Identify tax planning opportunities related to accounting periods and accounting methods.

CHAPTER OUTLINE

16-1 Accounting Periods, 16-2
16-1a Specific Provisions for Partnerships, S Corporations, and Personal Service Corporations, 16-3
16-1b Selecting the Tax Year, 16-6
16-1c Changes in the Accounting Period, 16-6
16-1d Taxable Periods of Less Than One Year, 16-7
16-1e Mitigation of the Annual Accounting Period Concept, 16-8

16-2 Accounting Methods, 16-10
16-2a Permissible Methods, 16-10
16-2b Cash Receipts and Disbursements Method, 16-11
16-2c Accrual Method, 16-13
16-2d Hybrid Method, 16-16
16-2e Change of Method, 16-17

16-3 Special Accounting Methods, 16-19
16-3a Installment Method, 16-19
16-3b Long-Term Contracts, 16-27

16-4 Inventories, 16-30
16-4a Determining Inventory Cost, 16-31
16-4b The LIFO Election, 16-35
16-4c Special Inventory Methods Relating to Farming and Ranching, 16-36
16-4d Inventory of Small Taxpayers, 16-36

16-5 Tax Planning, 16-37
16-5a Taxable Year, 16-37
16-5b Cash Method of Accounting, 16-37
16-5c Installment Method, 16-37
16-5d Inventories, 16-38

ACCOUNTING PERIOD AND METHOD

Pearl, Inc. (a C corporation), Tweety, Inc. (an S corporation), and Belinda (an individual) are going to form a partnership (Silver Partnership). The ownership interests and tax years of the partners are as follows:

Partner	Partnership Interest	Tax Year Ends
Belinda	25%	December 31
Pearl, Inc.	35%	November 30
Tweety, Inc.	40%	June 30

The partnership expects to begin business on April 1, 2020. The partners have several issues they would like you to address.

- A potential conflict exists among the partners regarding when the tax year should end for Silver. Belinda and Pearl would like a year-end close to their own year-ends, and Tweety would like to have a June 30 year-end. Is this a decision Tweety can make because it owns more of the partnership than either of the other two partners? Is this a decision Belinda and Pearl can make because collectively they own more of the partnership than Tweety owns?

- Because Silver will begin business on April 1, 2020, will the first tax year be a "short" tax year? Will annualization of the net income of the partnership be required?

- How will the partners know when their share of Silver's net income or net loss should be reported on their respective income tax returns?

- Belinda is a cash basis taxpayer, and the other partners use the accrual method to report their incomes. What accounting method must be used to compute Belinda's share of the partnership income?

Read the chapter and formulate your response.

FRAMEWORK 1040 Tax Formula for Individuals

This chapter covers the boldfaced portions of the Tax Formula for Individuals that was introduced in Concept Summary 3.1 on p. 3-3. Below those portions are the sections of Form 1040 where the results are reported.

Income *(broadly defined)*	$ xx,xxx
Less: Exclusions	(x,xxx)
Gross income	**$xx,xxx**

FORM 1040 (Schedule 1)

3	Business income or (loss). Attach Schedule C.	

Less: Deductions *for* adjusted gross income	(x,xxx)
Adjusted gross income	$ xx,xxx
Less: The greater of total itemized deductions *or* the standard deduction	(x,xxx)
Personal and dependency exemptions*	(x,xxx)
Deduction for qualified business income**	(x,xxx)
Taxable income	$ xx,xxx
Tax on taxable income *(see Tax Tables or Tax Rate Schedules)*	$ x,xxx
Less: Tax credits *(including income taxes withheld and prepaid)*	(xxx)
Tax due (or refund)	$ xxx

* Exemption deductions are not allowed from 2018 through 2025.
** Only applies from 2018 through 2025.

Tax professionals must determine *when* items of income and expense are recognized as well as *whether* the items are includible in taxable income. Earlier chapters discussed the types of income subject to tax (gross income and exclusions) and allowable deductions (the *whether* issue).[1] This chapter focuses chiefly on the related issue of the periods in which income and deductions are reported (the *when* issue). Generally, a taxpayer's income and deductions must be assigned to identified 12-month periods—calendar years or fiscal years.

Income and deductions are placed within tax years through the use of tax accounting methods. The basic tax accounting methods are the cash receipts and disbursements method, the accrual method, and a hybrid method. Other special purpose methods, such as the installment method and the methods used for long-term construction contracts, are available for specific circumstances or types of transactions.

Over the long run, the accounting period and tax accounting methods used by a taxpayer will not affect the aggregate (or lifetime) amount of reported taxable income. However, taxable income for a given tax year may vary significantly due to the use of a particular accounting method. This chapter discusses the taxpayer's alternatives for accounting periods and accounting methods.

16-1 ACCOUNTING PERIODS

LO.1

Explain the relevance of the accounting period concept, accounting period options, and the limitations on their use.

Generally, an individual or a corporation that keeps adequate books and records may elect a **fiscal year**, a 12-month period ending on the *last day* of a month other than December, for the **accounting period**. Otherwise, a *calendar year* must be used.[2] Frequently, corporations can satisfy the record-keeping and other requirements and

---

[1]See Chapters 4, 5, and 6.   [2]§ 441(c) and Reg. § 1.441–1(b)(1)(ii).

elect to use a fiscal year.[3] Often, the fiscal year conforms to a natural business year (e.g., a summer resort's fiscal year may end on September 30, after the close of the season). Individuals seldom use a fiscal year because they do not maintain the necessary books and records to do so, and because common reporting forms they receive such as Forms W–2 and 1099 report income based on the calendar year.

Generally, a tax year may not exceed 12 calendar months. However, if certain requirements are met, a taxpayer may elect to use an annual period that varies from 52 to 53 weeks.[4] In that case, the year-end must be on the same day of the week (e.g., the Tuesday falling closest to September 30, or the last Tuesday in September). The day of the week selected for ending the tax year may depend upon business considerations. For example, a retail business that is not open on Sundays may end its tax year on a Sunday so that it can take an inventory without interrupting business operations.

EXAMPLE 1

Wade, Inc., is in the business of selling farm supplies. Its natural business year terminates at the end of October with the completion of harvesting. At the end of the fiscal year, Wade must take an inventory, which is most easily accomplished on a Friday. Therefore, Wade could adopt a 52- to 53-week tax year ending on the Friday closest to October 31.

If the company selects this approach, the year-end date may fall in the following month if that Friday is closer to October 31. The tax year ending in 2020 will contain 52 weeks beginning on Saturday, November 2, 2019, and ending on Friday, October 30, 2020. The tax year ending in 2021 will have 52 weeks beginning on Saturday, October 31, 2020, and ending on Friday, October 29, 2021.

16-1a Specific Provisions for Partnerships, S Corporations, and Personal Service Corporations

When a partner's tax year and the partnership's tax year differ, the partner may enjoy a deferral of income. This results because the partner reports his or her share of the partnership's income and deductions for the partnership's tax year ending within or with the partner's tax year.[5] For example, if the tax year of the partnership ends on January 31, a calendar year partner will not report partnership profits for the first 11 months of the partnership tax year until the following year. To minimize abuse of this arrangement, the tax law provides special tax year requirements.

In general, the partnership tax year must be the same as the tax year of the majority interest partners. The **majority interest partners** are the partners who together own a greater-than-50-percent interest in the partnership capital and profits. If there is no majority interest tax year, the partnership must adopt the same tax year as all of its principal partners. A **principal partner** is a partner with a 5 percent or more interest in the partnership capital or profits.[6]

EXAMPLE 2

The RST Partnership is owned equally by Rose Corporation, Sunflower Corporation, and Tom. The partners use the following tax years.

	Partner's Tax Year Ending
Rose Corporation	June 30
Sunflower Corporation	June 30
Tom	December 31

The partnership's tax year must end on June 30 because Rose Corporation and Sunflower Corporation together have a greater-than-50% interest in the partnership. If Sunflower Corporation's as well as Tom's year ended on December 31, the partnership would be required to adopt a calendar year.

---

[3]Reg. § 1.441–1(e)(2).
[4]§ 441(f).

[5]Reg. § 1.706–1(a).
[6]§§ 706(b)(1)(B) and 706(b)(3).

If all of the principal partners do not have the same tax year and no majority of partners have the same tax year, the partnership must use a year that results in the *least aggregate deferral* of income.[7] Under the <mark>least aggregate deferral method</mark>, the different tax years of the principal partners are tested to determine which produces the least aggregate taxable income deferral. This is calculated by first multiplying the combined percentages of the principal partners with the same tax year by the months of deferral for the test year. Once this is done for each set of principal partners with the same tax year, the resulting products are summed to produce the aggregate deferral. After the aggregate deferral is calculated for each of the test years, the test year with the smallest total (the least aggregate deferral) becomes the tax year for the partnership.

The Big Picture

EXAMPLE 3

Return to the facts of *The Big Picture* on p. 16-1. The partnership's tax year must end on November 30, because using that year-end results in the least aggregate deferral of partnership income as demonstrated below.

Test for Tax Year Ending December 31

	Partner's Year-End	1 Profit Percentage	2 Months Income Deferred	1 × 2 Aggregate Months of Deferral
Belinda	12/31	25%	0	0
Pearl, Inc.	11/30	35%	11	3.85
Tweety, Inc.	6/30	40%	6	2.40
				6.25

Test for Tax Year Ending November 30

	Partner's Year-End	Profit Percentage	Months Income Deferred	Aggregate Months of Deferral
Belinda	12/31	25%	1	0.25
Pearl, Inc.	11/30	35%	0	0
Tweety, Inc.	6/30	40%	7	2.80
				3.05

Test for Tax Year Ending June 30

	Partner's Year-End	Profit Percentage	Months Income Deferred	Aggregate Months of Deferral
Belinda	12/31	25%	6	1.50
Pearl, Inc.	11/30	35%	5	1.75
Tweety, Inc.	6/30	40%	0	0
				3.25

[7]Reg. § 1.706–1(b)(3).

Generally, S corporations must adopt a calendar year.[8] However, partnerships and S corporations may *elect* an otherwise *impermissible year* under either of the following conditions.

- A business purpose for the year can be demonstrated.[9]
- The partnership or S corporation makes a timely election to use a taxable year that results in a deferral of not more than three months' income, and the entity agrees to make required tax payments that relate to this deferral.[10]

Business Purpose

The only business purpose for a fiscal year the IRS has acknowledged is the need to conform the tax year to the natural business year of a company.[11] Generally, only seasonal businesses have a natural business year. For example, the natural business year for a retailer may end on January 31, after holiday sales returns have been processed and clearance sales have been completed.

Required Tax Payments

Under the required payments system, a tax payment is due from a fiscal year partnership or S corporation by May 15 of each tax year.[12] The amount due is computed by applying the highest individual tax rate plus 1 percentage point to an estimate of the deferral period income. The deferral period runs from the close of the fiscal year to the end of the required year. Estimated income for this period is based on the average monthly earnings for the previous fiscal year. The amount due is reduced by the amount of the required tax payment for the previous year.[13]

EXAMPLE 4

Brown, Inc., an S corporation, timely elected a fiscal year ending September 30. Bob is the only shareholder and is a calendar year taxpayer. The "required" tax year ends on December 31, 2020, the major shareholder's year-end, and the deferral period is the maximum of three months. For the fiscal year ending September 30, 2020, Brown earned $100,000. The required tax payment for the previous year was $5,000. The corporation must pay $4,500 by May 15, 2021.

$$(\$100,000 \times \tfrac{3}{12} \times 38\%^*) - \$5,000 = \$4,500$$

*Maximum individual tax rate of 37% + 1%.

ETHICS & EQUITY Who Benefits from the Change in Tax Year?

Ajit, a public accounting sole practitioner, has reached a breaking point. All of his clients use the calendar year to report income. Many of the clients are S corporations and partnerships. Ajit's workload the first four months of the year is so heavy that it is putting the quality of his work at risk.

Ajit is considering telling his clients that any new partnership or S corporation that is formed must timely elect, under the required tax payments system, to use a fiscal year ending September 30 (assuming that the required year would otherwise be a calendar year). Although the shareholders and partners would be subject to the required tax payments rule, Ajit will sell the plan to them by promising better service. Evaluate the plan proposed by Ajit.

---

[8]§§ 1378(a) and (b).

[9]§§ 706(b)(1)(C) and 1378(b)(2).

[10]§ 444. See Form 8716.

[11]Rev.Proc. 2006–46, 2006–2 C.B. 859. Also see the following discussion in text Section 16-1c.

[12]§ 444(c) and Reg. § 1.7519–2T(a)(4)(ii). No payment is required if the calculated amount is $500 or less. See Form 8752.

[13]§ 7519(b).

Personal Service Corporations

A <mark>personal service corporation (PSC)</mark> is a corporation whose shareholder-employees provide personal services (e.g., medical, dental, legal, accounting, engineering, actuarial, consulting, or performing arts). Generally, a PSC must use a calendar year.[14] However, a PSC can *elect* a fiscal year under either of the following conditions.

- A business purpose for the year can be demonstrated.
- The PSC year results in a deferral of not more than three months' income, the corporation pays the shareholder-employee's salary during the portion of the calendar year after the close of the fiscal year, and the salary for that period is at least proportionate to the shareholder-employee's salary received for the preceding fiscal year.[15]

Nancy's corporation paid her a salary of $120,000 during its tax year ending September 30, 2020. The corporation cannot satisfy the business purpose test for a fiscal year. The corporation can continue to use its non-calendar tax year for Federal income tax purposes, provided that Nancy receives at least $30,000 [(3 months/12 months) × $120,000] of salary during the period October 1 through December 31, 2020.

If the salary test is not satisfied, the PSC can retain the fiscal year, but the corporation's deduction for salary may be limited. Any amount not deductible is carried over to the next year.

16-1b Selecting the Tax Year

A taxpayer elects to use a calendar year or, if eligible, a fiscal year by the timely filing of the initial tax return. For all subsequent tax years, the taxpayer must use this same period unless approval for change is obtained from the IRS.[16]

16-1c Changes in the Accounting Period

A taxpayer must obtain consent from the IRS before changing its tax year.[17] This arrangement permits the IRS to issue administrative guidelines that must be met by taxpayers who want to change their accounting period. An application for permission to change tax years must be made on Form 1128, Application for Change in Accounting Period. Generally, the application must be filed by the due date (including extensions) for the short taxable period that results from the change.[18]

Beginning in 2020, Gold Corporation, a calendar year taxpayer, would like to switch to a tax year ending March 31. This change results in a short-period return encompassing January 1 to March 31, 2020. The extended due date for this short period return is January 15, 2021, which is also the due date for the Form 1128.

The IRS will not grant permission for the change unless the taxpayer can establish a substantial business purpose for the request. One substantial business purpose is to change to a tax year that coincides with the *natural business year* (the completion of an annual business cycle). The IRS applies an objective gross receipts test to determine

---

[14]§ 441(i).

[15]§§ 444 and 280H.

[16]Reg. §§ 1.441–1(b)(3) and 1.441–1(b)(4).

[17]§ 442. Under certain conditions, corporations are allowed to change tax years without obtaining IRS approval. See Reg. § 1.442–1(c)(1); Rev.Proc. 2006–45, 2006 C.B. 851, modified by Rev.Proc. 2007–64, 2007–2 C.B. 818.

[18]Reg. § 1.442–1(b)(1), Rev.Proc. 2006–45, 2006–2 C.B. 851, and Form 1128 instructions.

whether the entity has a natural business year. At least 25 percent of the entity's gross receipts for the 12-month period must be realized in the final two months of the 12-month period for three consecutive years.[19]

A Virginia Beach motel reported the following gross receipts.

	2018	2019	2020
July–August receipts	$ 300,000	$250,000	$ 325,000
September 1–August 31 receipts	1,000,000	900,000	1,250,000
Receipts for final 2 months divided by receipts for 12 months	30.0%	27.8%	26.0%

Because it satisfies the natural business year test, the motel can use a tax year ending August 31.

The IRS usually establishes certain conditions that the taxpayer must accept if the approval for change is to be granted. In particular, if a corporation has a capital loss for the short period, the IRS may require that the loss only be carried forward.[20] Recall that corporations otherwise carry back a capital loss for three years and then forward for five years (see text Section 14-6). Denying a carryback is intended to prevent abuse of the change in tax year rules.

Parrot Corporation, a manufacturer that is not an S corporation, changed from a calendar year to a fiscal year ending September 30. The short-period return for the nine months ending September 30, 2020, reflected a $60,000 long-term capital loss. The corporation incurred a $100,000 long-term capital gain in 2017. As a condition for granting approval, the IRS requires Parrot to carry it forward rather than carry it back to 2017.

16-1d Taxable Periods of Less Than One Year

A **short taxable year** (or **short period**) is a period of less than 12 calendar months. A taxpayer may have a short year for (1) the first income tax return, (2) the final income tax return, or (3) a change in the tax year. If the short period results from a change in the taxpayer's annual accounting period, the taxable income for the period is annualized in calculating tax liability for the short period. With a flat Federal corporate income tax rate though, annualization is not needed for C corporations. However, as shown in Example 9, annualization is required to calculate state income taxes if the state has a progressive tax rate structure. The calculations to determine the annualized tax for a short tax period resulting from change in accounting period follow.

1. Annualize the short-period income.

---

[19]Rev.Proc. 2006–46, 2006–2 C.B. 859; Rev.Rul. 87–57, 1987–2 C.B. 117; and Rev.Proc. 2002–39, 2002–1 C.B. 1046.

[20]Rev.Proc. 2002–39, 2002–1 C.B. 1046, modified by Rev.Proc. 2003–34, 2003–1 C.B. 856.

2.   Compute the tax on the annualized income.
3.   Convert the tax on the annualized income to a short-period tax.

| Tax on annualized income | X | $\dfrac{\text{Number of months in the short period}}{12}$ | = | Short-period tax |

EXAMPLE 9

Gray Corporation, a retailer that is not an S corporation, obtained permission to change from a calendar year to a fiscal year ending September 30, beginning in 2021. For the short period January 1 through September 30, 2021, the corporation's taxable income was $48,000. Gray does business in State X. The relevant tax rates in State X and the resulting short-period tax are:

Amount of Taxable Income	Tax Rates
$1–$50,000	5% of taxable income
Over $50,000	$2,500 plus 7% of taxable income in excess of $50,000

Calculation of Short-Period Tax

Annualized income
$48,000 \times \frac{12}{9} = \$64,000$

Tax on annualized income
$\$2,500 + 7\%(\$64,000 - \$50,000) = \$3,480$

Short-period tax
$\$3,480 \times \frac{9}{12} = \$2,610$ due to State X

Tax with annualizing	$ 2,610
Tax without annualizing (5% × $48,000)	(2,400)
State income tax increase due to annualizing	$ 210

Gray's Federal income tax for the short period is $10,080 (21% × $48,000). Because of the flat corporate rate, no annualization is required to compute Gray's Federal income tax liability for the short tax year.

Some tax rules also require annualization of short-period information. For example, for the average annual gross receipts test explained in text Section 16-2, the gross receipts of any prior short period must be annualized.

Often, the short year counts as a full year for purposes of the carryback and carry-forward rules for various losses and credits.[21]

16-1e Mitigation of the Annual Accounting Period Concept

Several provisions in the Code are designed to give the taxpayer relief from the seemingly harsh results that may occur due to the combined effects of an arbitrary accounting period and the progressive rate structure that applies to individuals. For example, under the NOL carryover rules, a loss in one year can be carried forward and applied against

---

[21]Reg. §§ 1.172–4(a)(2), 1.46–2(k), and 1.904–2(e). Certain farm losses can be carried back two years. If one of those carryback years is a short year, it counts as one of the carryback years.

taxable income in subsequent years.[22] In addition, the Code provides special relief provisions for casualty losses arising from a Federally declared disaster and for the reporting of insurance proceeds from destruction of crops.[23]

Farm Relief

Farmers and fishermen often are subject to fluctuations in income between years, some of which are due to the weather. Congress has provided these taxpayers with a special method of computing their tax on income from farming or fishing. In the high-income years, these taxpayers can elect to compute their tax on income from farming or fishing as though it were earned equally in the three previous years.[24] Thus, the tax on the farming or fishing income for the year is the sum of the additional tax that would have been due in the three previous years if one-third of the income had been earned in each of those years. This averaging system enables the taxpayer to avoid the higher marginal tax rates associated with a large amount of income received in one year.

The income pattern for farmers can also be disrupted by natural disasters that are covered by insurance. The disaster may occur and the **crop insurance proceeds** may be received in a year before the income from the crop would have been realized. Under these circumstances, the farmer can defer reporting the gross income from the insurance proceeds until the year following the disaster. Similar relief is available when livestock must be sold due to drought or other weather-related conditions.[25]

Restoration of Amounts Received under a Claim of Right

The court-made **claim of right doctrine** applies when the taxpayer receives property as income and treats it as his or her own but a dispute arises over the taxpayer's rights to the income.[26] According to the doctrine, the taxpayer must include the amount as income in the year of receipt. The rationale for the doctrine is that the Federal government cannot await the resolution of all disputes before exacting a tax. As a corollary to the doctrine, if the taxpayer later is required to repay the funds, a deduction generally is allowed in the year of repayment.[27]

EXAMPLE 10

In 2020, Pedro received a $5,000 bonus computed as a percentage of profits. In 2021, Pedro's employer determined that the 2020 profits had been computed incorrectly, and Pedro was to refund the $5,000 in 2021. Pedro must include the $5,000 in his 2020 gross income, but he can claim a $5,000 deduction in 2021.

In Example 10, the transactions were a wash; that is, the income and deduction were the same ($5,000). Suppose, however, that Pedro was in the 35 percent tax bracket in 2020 but in the 22 percent bracket in 2021. Without some relief provision, the mistake would be costly to Pedro. He paid a $1,750 tax in 2020 (35% × $5,000), but the deduction reduced his tax liability in 2021 by only $1,000 (22% × $5,000).

The Code does provide relief in such cases. Under § 1341, when income that has been taxed under the claim of right doctrine later must be repaid, the taxpayer can

---

[22]§ 172. Refer to text Section 7-6.

[23]§§ 165(i) and 451(d).

[24]§ 1301. The tax is calculated on Schedule J.

[25]§§ 451(f) and (g).

[26]*North American Consolidated Oil Co. v. Burnet,* 3 USTC ¶943, 11 AFTR 16, 52 S.Ct. 613 (USSC, 1932).

[27]*U.S. v. Lewis,* 51–1 USTC ¶9211, 40 AFTR 258, 71 S.Ct. 522 (USSC, 1951).

use the tax rate of the year that produces the greatest tax benefit. As a result, in Example 10, the repayment in 2021 would reduce Pedro's 2021 tax liability by $1,750 [the higher 2020 rate (35%) applied to the $5,000 deduction in 2021]. However, relief is provided only in cases where the tax is significantly different (i.e., when the deduction for the amount previously included in income exceeds $3,000).

ETHICS & EQUITY   Special Tax Relief

A taxpayer who reports gross income in one year but must repay the income in a subsequent year is granted special tax relief. If the taxpayer is in a lower marginal tax bracket in the year the income is repaid than in the year it was received, the deduction reduces the tax for the year of repayment by using the higher tax rate that applied to the income when it was received.

In contrast, if a taxpayer takes a deduction in one year and receives a refund of the amount giving rise to the deduction in a subsequent year, the refund is taxed at the marginal tax rate in the year of refund. This is true even though the taxpayer's marginal tax rate in the year of receipt is higher than that in the year of the deduction.

Should adjustments to income and adjustments to deductions receive the same tax relief? Or should neither situation be granted special relief? Discuss.

LO.2

Apply the cash method, accrual method, and hybrid method of accounting.

16-2 ACCOUNTING METHODS

16-2a Permissible Methods

Section 446 requires the taxpayer to compute taxable income using the method of accounting regularly employed in keeping the corresponding financial accounting records ("the books"), provided the method clearly reflects income. The Code recognizes the following as generally permissible **accounting methods**.

- The cash receipts and disbursements method.
- The accrual method.
- A hybrid method (a combination of cash and accrual).

The Regulations refer to these alternatives as *overall methods* and add that the term *method of accounting* includes not only the taxpayer's overall method of accounting but also the accounting treatment of any item.[28]

Generally, any of the three overall methods of accounting may be used if the method is consistently employed and clearly reflects income. However, certain taxpayers whose average annual gross receipts (computed over the three preceding years) exceed $26 million are required to use the accrual method.

In general, taxpayers that maintain inventory for sale to customers are required to use the accrual method of accounting for determining sales and cost of goods sold. However, taxpayers with average annual gross receipts of $26 million or less for the most recent three-year period can use the cash method to account for inventories, as long as inventories are not a material income-producing factor.[29] No more than 2 percent of all U.S. businesses report average gross receipts in excess of $26 million.

A taxpayer who has more than one trade or business may use a different method of accounting for each trade or business unless the taxpayer is required to use the accrual method. Furthermore, a taxpayer may use one method of accounting to determine

---

[28]Reg. § 1.446–1(a)(1).

[29]Reg. § 1.446–1(a)(4)(i), Reg. § 1.446–1(c)(2)(i), § 448, and § 471(c). Special methods are permitted for installment sales, long-term construction contracts, and farmers, as discussed in this chapter.

income from a trade or business and use another method to compute nonbusiness items of income and deductions.[30]

The Code grants the IRS broad powers to determine whether the taxpayer's accounting method *clearly reflects income*. Thus, if the method employed does not clearly reflect income, the IRS can prescribe the method to be used by the taxpayer.[31]

16-2b Cash Receipts and Disbursements Method

Most individuals and many businesses use the cash basis to report income and deductions. The popularity of this method can largely be attributed to its simplicity and flexibility.

Under the **cash method**, income is not recognized until the taxpayer actually receives, or constructively receives, cash or its equivalent (e.g., the receipt of accounts receivable does not trigger income until collected). Cash is constructively received if it is available to the taxpayer.[32] Generally, a cash equivalent is anything with a fair market value, including any goods or services received in a barter transaction and a note receivable from a customer.

The Big Picture

EXAMPLE 11

Return to the facts of *The Big Picture* on p. 4-1 in Chapter 4. Recall that Dr. Cliff Payne opened a dental practice as a sole proprietorship and does not accept credit cards. In the second year of business, he adopts a new policy of requiring that his patients either pay cash at the time the services are performed or give him a note receivable with interest at the market rate. Generally, the notes can be sold to the local banks for 95% of their face amount.

At the end of the second year, Dr. Payne holds $60,000 in notes receivable from patients. The notes receivable are a cash equivalent and have a fair market value of $57,000 ($60,000 × 95%). As a result, Dr. Payne must include $57,000 in his gross income for this year.

Deductions generally are permitted in the year of payment under the cash method. Thus, year-end accounts payable and accrued expenses are not deducted in the determination of taxable income.

In many cases, a taxpayer using the cash method can choose the year in which a deduction is claimed simply by postponing or accelerating the payment of expenses. For fixed assets, however, the cash basis taxpayer claims deductions through depreciation or amortization, as does an accrual basis taxpayer. In addition, prepaid expenses must be capitalized and amortized if the life of the asset extends substantially beyond the end of the tax year.[33]

The Regulations provide a **one-year rule for prepaid expenses** that permits the taxpayer to deduct expenditures for rights that do not extend beyond the earlier of (1) 12 months after the first date on which the taxpayer realizes the right or (2) the end of the tax year following the year of payment. Both cash basis and accrual basis taxpayers can use the one-year rule.[34]

Restrictions on Use of the Cash Method

The cash method could distort income from a merchandising or manufacturing operation, because the cost of goods sold would be a function of when payments for the goods were made rather than when they were sold. Thus, the Regulations require the accrual method to measure sales and cost of goods sold if inventories are material to the business. This targeted prohibition on the use of the cash method for taxpayers with inventories is intended to ensure that annual taxable income is clearly reflected.[35]

---

[30]§ 446(d) and Reg. § 1.446–1(c)(1)(iv)(b).

[31]§ 446(b), as limited by § 471(c)(1)(B).

[32]Reg. § 1.451–1(a). Refer to text Section 4-2c for a discussion of constructive receipt.

[33]Reg. § 1.461–1(a)(1).

[34]Reg. § 1.263(a)–4(f). Refer to text Section 6-2d for further discussion of the one-year rule.

[35]Reg. § 1.446–1(a)(4)(i).

The following taxpayers may not use the cash method (and must use the accrual method) for Federal income tax purposes regardless of whether inventories are material: (1) a corporation (other than an S corporation), (2) a partnership with a corporate partner (that is not an S corporation), and (3) a tax shelter. This accrual method requirement of § 448 has three exceptions, each of which allows the cash method to be used.

- A farming business (other than certain corporations).
- A *qualified personal service corporation* (a corporation that performs services in health, law, engineering, architecture, accounting, actuarial science, performing arts, or consulting and whose employees own substantially all of the stock) regardless of gross receipts level.
- A corporation, or a partnership with a corporate partner, whose average annual gross receipts for the prior three-year period do not exceed $26 million.

None of the exceptions apply to an entity that meets the definition of a tax shelter. A tax shelter must use the accrual method.[36]

Overall Accounting Method Rules

EXAMPLE 12

Stern and Stern, CPAs, is a C corporation owned by ten CPAs that provides accounting and tax services. Its average annual gross receipts are $30,000,000. Because this entity is a qualified personal service corporation and has no inventory, it may use the cash method of accounting.

EXAMPLE 13

Fit Corporation is a C corporation that operates several fitness centers. Its average annual gross receipts are $30,000,000. Fit must use the accrual method because it is a C corporation and its average annual gross receipts for the prior three-year period exceeded $26,000,000. If its average annual gross receipts in the prior three-year period were $26,000,000 or less, it could use the cash method.

If Fit were a sole proprietorship, a partnership without a C corporation partner, or an S corporation, it would be allowed to use the cash method regardless of its gross receipts level, because it is not subject to the required accrual method rule of § 448 and has no inventory.

Special Rules for Farmers

The tax accounting rules include several special rules and exceptions for farmers. Generally, farmers with average annual gross receipts in the prior three-year period of $26 million or less may use the cash method.

Farmers with average annual gross receipts greater than $26 million may be required to use the accrual method. However, exceptions exist based on the type of entity.[37] For example, a partnership without a corporate partner generally can use the cash method. In this regard, whether certain costs related to production of products must be capitalized depends on the type of product.[38]

Farmers who produce crops that take more than a year from planting to harvesting (e.g., pineapples) can elect to use the crop method to report the income. Under the **crop method**, the costs of raising the crop are capitalized as those costs are incurred and then deducted in the year the income from the crop is realized.[39] This method is analogous to the completed contract method, discussed in text Section 16-3b.

---

[36]§§ 448(a) and 448(b). For this purpose, the hybrid method of accounting is considered the same as the cash method. Also see § 447. *Tax shelter* is defined at § 448(d)(3).

[37]See §§ 447(c), 448(b), and 464.
[38]§ 263A(d).
[39]Reg. §§ 1.61–4 and 1.162–12(a).

Generally, a cash basis farmer must capitalize the purchase price of an animal whether it is acquired for sale or for breeding. However, costs to raise the animal generally can be deducted immediately.[40]

16-2c Accrual Method

The tax rules governing when an accrual method taxpayer reports income or claims deductions include an "all events test." The timing rules for deductions also include an "economic performance" requirement. These timing rules for income and deductions of accrual method taxpayers are explained below.

All Events Test for Income

Under the accrual method, an item generally is included in gross income for the year in which it is earned, regardless of when the income is collected. An item of income is earned when (1) all of the events have occurred to fix the taxpayer's right to receive the income and (2) the amount of income (the amount the taxpayer has a right to receive) can be determined with reasonable accuracy.[41] However, generally, the income cannot be deferred beyond the tax year in which it is included in the taxpayer's applicable financial statement.[42]

Andre Corporation, a calendar year taxpayer that uses the accrual basis of accounting, was to receive a bonus equal to 6% of Blue Corporation's net income for its fiscal year ending each June 30. For the fiscal year ending June 30, 2020, Blue reported net income of $240,000. For the six months ending December 31, 2020, its net income was $150,000.

Andre includes gross income of $14,400 (6% × $240,000) for 2020 because its right to the amount became fixed when Blue's tax year closed. However, Andre would not accrue income based on Blue's profits for the last six months of 2020, because its right to the income does not accrue until the close of Blue's tax year.

An accrual basis taxpayer's amount of income and the tax year the income is recognized are based on its right to receive the income. Thus, unlike the case of a cash basis taxpayer, the fair market value of a receivable is irrelevant.

Marcey Corporation, an accrual basis taxpayer, has provided services to clients and has the right to receive $60,000. The clients have signed notes receivable to Marcey that have a fair market value of $57,000. The corporation must include gross income of $60,000, the amount it has the right to receive, rather than the fair market value of the notes of $57,000.

If an accrual basis taxpayer receives advance payments for services, goods, or licensing of software, it should consider electing a special deferral method.[43] Under this special accounting method, in the year the advance payment is received, the taxpayer reports on its tax return the same amount reported on its financial statement. In the subsequent year, the balance of the advance payment is reported on the tax return regardless of how much is reported on the financial statement for that year (see text Section 4-2d).

[40]Reg. § 1.162–12(a).

[41]§ 451(b) and Reg. § 1.451–1(a). Refer to text Section 4-2 for further discussion of the accrual method.

[42]§ 451(b). *Applicable financial statement* is defined at § 451(b)(3) and generally is a statement prepared in accordance with generally accepted accounting principles and certified as such, or per international reporting standards, or is required by a regulatory or government body.

[43]Prior to the change to § 451(c) by the TCJA of 2017, the deferral method for advance payments for services, goods, and licensing of intellectual property was provided at Rev.Proc. 2004–34. Per Notice 2018–35, 2018–18 I.R.B. 522, taxpayers may continue to rely on Rev.Proc. 2004–34 until the IRS finalizes guidance under § 451(c).

EXAMPLE 16

Troy Corporation is an accrual method taxpayer that has properly adopted the deferral method of § 451(c). Troy sells computers and two-year service contracts on the computers. On November 1, 2020, Troy sold a 24-month service contract and received $240. For financial reporting purposes, Troy reports $20 of gross income for 2020, $120 for 2021, and $100 for 2022. For tax purposes, Troy reports $20 of income for 2020 (same as for financial reporting) and $220 of income for 2021 (the balance of the advance payment).

Prepaid rental income, prepaid interest income, warranty or guarantee contracts, insurance premiums, and payments with respect to certain financial instruments must be recognized in the year of receipt and may not be deferred.[44]

In a situation where the accrual method taxpayer's right to income is being contested and the income has not yet been collected, generally, no income is recognized until the dispute has been settled.[45] Before the settlement, "all of the events have not occurred that fix the right to receive the income."

All Events and Economic Performance Tests for Deductions

A three-part test is applied to determine when an accrual method taxpayer considers a liability as either an expense or a capital expenditure. The three parts are (1) the **all events test**, (2) whether the amount is determinable with reasonable accuracy, and (3) the **economic performance test**. The all events test is met when all events have occurred to establish the fact that a liability exists (that is, the taxpayer legally owes money to another party).[46]

As to when economic performance is met, that depends on the nature of the liability. For example, if an accrual method taxpayer owes money to another entity that provided services to it, economic performance is met as the services are provided. Concept Summary 16.1 lists common types of liabilities covered by the economic performance Regulations (Reg. § 1.461–4) and when economic performance is met for each liability.

Concept Summary 16.1

Accruals Under the Economic Performance Test

Event	Example	When Economic Performance Is Satisfied
The taxpayer's use of the owner's property	Rent	Ratably over the period used
Specific property provided to the taxpayer	A company's office supplies are purchased	When the taxpayer receives the supplies
Specific services provided to the taxpayer	The taxpayer contracts for repairs to be made to its equipment	When the repairs are made
Services to be provided for a specific time period	The taxpayer purchases a service contract, such as for cleaning services	Ratably over the contract period
Property or services provided by the taxpayer	A manufacturer provides a warranty on items sold to customers	When the manufacturer incurs costs in fixing the customer's item covered by the warranty
Rebates	Manufacturer rebates based on quantity of purchases	When the rebate is paid
Tort claims	Customers are awarded claims for harm caused by the taxpayer's product	When payment is made to the injured party; not eligible for the recurring item exception
State income tax	Taxes due when filing the return	When payment is made

---

[44]§ 451(c)(4)(B).

[45]*Burnet v. Sanford & Brooks Co.*, 2 USTC ¶636, 9 AFTR 603, 51 S.Ct. 150 (USSC, 1931).

[46]§ 461 and Reg. § 1.461–1(a)(2).

Economic Performance

An accrual basis calendar year taxpayer, JAB, Inc., promoted a boxing match held in the company's arena on December 31, 2020. CLN, Inc., was contracted to clean the arena for $5,000 but did not actually perform the work until January 1, 2021. JAB paid the $5,000 on January 3, 2021 (once CLN had completed its work).

Although financial accounting rules would require JAB to accrue the $5,000 cleaning expense in 2020 to match the revenues from the fight, the economic performance test was not satisfied until 2021, when CLN performed the service. Thus, JAB deducts the expense in 2021.

Agmax Corporation farms land owned by an individual. Agmax's contract to use the land is for three years, and at the end of three years, Agmax agreed to apply lime to the farmland. The contract term expired in 2020, and Agmax applied the lime in 2021. The all events test was satisfied at the end of 2020. However, Agmax did not provide the lime until 2021. Agmax was obligated to provide property (lime) and services. The deduction is not permitted until 2021, when Agmax incurs costs in fulfilling its obligation.[47]

The economic performance requirement is accelerated, allowing year-end accruals to be deducted, if all of the following conditions are met. This is known as the *recurring item exception*.

- The all events test is met, and the amount of the liability can be determined with reasonable accuracy.
- Economic performance occurs on or before the earlier of the date the taxpayer files the return (including extension) or 8½ months after the close of the taxable year.
- The item is recurring in nature.
- Either the item is not material or accruing it results in a better matching of revenues and expenses.

EXAMPLE 19

Green Corporation often sells goods that are on hand but cannot be shipped for another week. The all events test for the sale is satisfied; therefore, the revenue is recognized although the goods have not been shipped at year-end. Green Corporation is obligated to pay shipping costs. Although the company's obligation for shipping costs can be determined with reasonable accuracy, economic performance is not satisfied until Green (or its agent) actually delivers the goods. However, accruing shipping costs on sold items will better match expenses with revenues for the period. Therefore, the company should accrue the shipping costs on items sold but not shipped at year-end.

The economic performance test detailed in the Code does not address all possible accrued expenses. That is, in some cases, the taxpayer has a liability (owes money for something) even though no property or services were received. In these instances, economic performance generally is not satisfied until the liability is paid. The following liabilities illustrate cases in which payment is the only means of satisfying economic performance.[48]

1. Workers' compensation.
2. Torts.
3. Breach of contract.
4. Violation of law.
5. Rebates and refunds.
6. Awards, prizes, and jackpots.
7. Insurance, warranty, and service contracts.[49]
8. Taxes.

---

[47]Reg. § 1.461–4.
[48]Reg. §§ 1.461–4(g)(2)–(6) and 1.461–5(c).

[49]This item applies to contracts the taxpayer enters into for his or her own protection rather than the taxpayer's liability as insurer, warrantor, or service provider.

FINANCIAL DISCLOSURE INSIGHTS   **Tax Deferrals from Reserves**

The tax law generally applies the all events and economic performance tests in determining when an expense is deductible. Accordingly, the use of reserves for financial accounting purposes does not carry over to the tax return. When a business creates a reserve, for example, to account for warranty obligations to customers or vacation pay for employees, book expenses are allowed, but the corresponding tax deduction usually is delayed until an expenditure is actually incurred. The temporary book-tax difference typically creates or adds to a deferred tax asset on the entity's balance sheet.

On a GAAP balance sheet, all deferred tax assets are deemed to be noncurrent.

EXAMPLE 20

Yellow Corporation sold defective merchandise that injured a customer. Yellow admitted liability in 2020 but did not pay the claim until January 2021. The customer's tort claim cannot be deducted by Yellow until it is paid.

Items (5) through (8) above are eligible for the recurring item exception.

EXAMPLE 21

Pelican Corporation, a calendar year taxpayer, filed its 2020 state income tax return in March 2021 and its 2020 Federal return on September 15, 2021. At the time the state return was filed, Pelican was required to pay an additional $5,000. The state taxes are eligible for the recurring item exception. Thus, the $5,000 of state income taxes can be deducted on the corporation's 2020 Federal tax return. The deduction is allowed because all of the events had occurred to fix the liability as of the end of 2020, the payment was made by the earlier of the return filing date or 8½ months after the end of the tax year, the item is recurring in nature, and allowing the deduction in 2020 results in a better matching of revenues and expenses.

Reserves

Generally, the all events and economic performance tests prevent the income tax use of reserves (e.g., for product warranty expense) frequently used in financial accounting to match expenses with revenues. However, small banks can use a bad debt reserve.[50] In addition, an accrual basis taxpayer in a service business may be allowed to not accrue revenue that appears uncollectible based on experience. In effect, this approach indirectly allows a tax reserve.[51]

16-2d   Hybrid Method

A **hybrid method** of accounting involves the use of more than one overall method. For example, a taxpayer who uses the accrual basis to report sales and cost of goods sold but uses the cash basis to report other items of income and expense is employing a hybrid method. The Code permits the use of a hybrid tax accounting method provided the taxpayer's income is clearly reflected.[52] A taxpayer who uses the accrual method for business expenses must also use the accrual method for business income.

---

[50]§ 585.
[51]§ 448(d)(5).
[52]§ 446(c)(3).

The Loyal Pet Clinic boards animals, provides veterinarian services, and sells pet supplies and medicines (inventory). The clinic's gross receipts are approximately $4,000,000 per year, and 40% of the receipts are from sales of pet supplies. Under its hybrid method of accounting, the clinic uses the accrual method for the sales of supplies and medicines, because inventories are a material income-producing factor. The services income is reported using the cash method.

Businesses with average annual gross receipts in the prior three-year period of $26,000,000 or less are not required to use the accrual method. As a result, Loyal Pet Clinic should consider a change in its method from hybrid to cash and treat its inventory as deductible when purchased (and paid for) or as nonincidental supplies (further discussed in text Section 16-4).

EXAMPLE

22

16-2e Change of Method

LO.3

Explain the procedure for changing accounting methods.

The taxpayer, in effect, makes an election to use a particular accounting method when its initial tax return is filed using that method. Once chosen, the taxpayer must obtain the permission of the IRS later to change its accounting method. The request for change is made on Form 3115, Application for Change in Accounting Method. Generally, the form must be filed within the taxable year of the desired change.[53]

As previously mentioned, the term *accounting method* encompasses not only the overall accounting method used by the taxpayer (the cash or accrual method) but also the treatment of any material item of income or deduction.[54] For example, a change in the method of deducting property taxes from a cash basis to an accrual basis that results in a deduction for taxes in a different year constitutes a change in an accounting method. Another example of an accounting method change is a change involving the method or basis used in the valuation of inventories. However, a change in treatment resulting from a change in the underlying facts does not constitute a change in the taxpayer's method of accounting.[55] For example, a change in employment contracts so that an employee accrues one day of vacation pay for each month of service rather than 12 days of vacation pay for a full year of service is a change in the underlying facts and is not an accounting method change.

Correction of an Error

A change in accounting method is not the same as the *correction of an error*. The taxpayer can correct an error (by filing amended returns) without permission of the IRS, and the IRS simply adjusts the taxpayer's liability if an error is discovered on audit of the return. Some examples of errors are incorrect postings, errors in the calculation of tax liability or tax credits, deductions of business expense items that are actually personal, and omissions of income and deductions.[56] Unless the taxpayer or the IRS corrects the error within the statute of limitations (in general, three years after a tax return is filed), the taxpayer's total lifetime taxable income is overstated or understated by the amount of the error.

Change from an Incorrect Method

An *incorrect accounting method* is the consistent (for at least two tax returns) use of an incorrect rule to report an item of income or expense. The incorrect accounting method will not affect the taxpayer's total lifetime income (unlike the error). That is, an incorrect method has a self-balancing mechanism. For example, deducting freight on inventory in the year the goods are purchased rather than when the inventory is sold

---

[53]See Rev.Proc. 2015–13, 2015–5 I.R.B. 419, for the method change procedures and Rev.Proc. 2019–43, 2019–48 I.R.B. 1107, for the list of automatic method changes. Generally, for an automatic method change, Form 3115 is due when the tax return for the year of change is filed, including extension.

[54]Reg. § 1.446–1(a)(1).
[55]Reg. § 1.446–1(e)(2)(ii).
[56]Reg. § 1.446–1(e)(2)(ii)(b).

is an incorrect accounting method. The total cost of goods sold over the life of the business is not affected, but the year-to-year income is incorrect.[57]

If a taxpayer is employing an incorrect method of accounting, permission must be obtained from the IRS to change to a correct method. An incorrect method is not treated as a mechanical error that can be corrected by merely filing an amended tax return.

The tax return preparer as well as the taxpayer will be subject to penalties if the tax return is prepared using an incorrect method of accounting and permission for a change to a correct method has not been requested.[58]

Net Adjustments Due to Change in Method of Accounting

In the year of a change in accounting method, an adjustment is generally required in order to prevent the omission or duplication of income or expense items.

EXAMPLE 23

White, a C corporation, operates a web platform that allows bookkeepers and accountants to offer their services to companies and individuals who need such services. It operates similar to Uber, TaskRabbit, and similar freelancing platforms. Its gross receipts have increased significantly every year since it began operations in 2015. For 2020, White determines that its average annual gross receipts for the prior three years crossed the $26,000,000 threshold. As a result, White must change its accounting method from cash to accrual starting in 2020 (*the year of change*). It must also calculate a "net § 481(a) adjustment" to be sure that no income or expense is omitted from income or duplicated when it makes this method change. Relevant information to calculate this adjustment includes:

Accounts receivable at December 31, 2019	$1,100,000
Accounts payable at December 31, 2019	860,000

Because White used the cash method of accounting for tax purposes, the $1,100,000 of receivables was not yet reported in taxable income. Similarly, the $860,000 of payables has not yet been claimed as a deduction. When White changes from the cash method to the accrual method starting with its 2020 tax year, it will behave as if it was always using the accrual method. As a result, when it collects the $1,100,000 of receivables in 2020, White will not report it in gross income because, if White had always been using the accrual method, that income would have been reported earlier when earned. Similarly, when White pays the payables in 2020, it will not claim a deduction because if White had always used the accrual method, the payables would have been deducted earlier when incurred.

To avoid omission of the $1,100,000 of income, White has a positive "§ 481(a) adjustment" of $1,100,000 (meaning it increases White's taxable income). To avoid omission of the $860,000 of deductions, White has a negative "§ 481(a) adjustment" of $860,000. These amounts are combined to yield a "net positive § 481(a) adjustment" of $240,000.

Reporting the Net § 481(a) Adjustment

Required changes in tax accounting methods can result from an IRS examination. Generally, if the IRS finds that a taxpayer is using an incorrect method of accounting, a change is imposed, but on less favorable terms than if the taxpayer had corrected the erroneous method on its own. For example, the IRS may require the taxpayer to correct the method for the earliest year open under the statute of limitations and record any positive § 481 adjustment entirely in that year (rather than over four years allowed for a voluntary change in method). Additional tax and interest then may be due.[59]

---

[57]But see *Korn Industries v. U.S.*, 76–1 USTC ¶9354, 37 AFTR 2d 76–1228, 532 F.2d 1352 (Ct.Cls., 1976).

[58]§ 446(f).

[59]§ 481(b). Guidance on IRS-initiated method changes can be found in Rev.Proc. 2002–18, 2002–1 C.B. 678.

To encourage taxpayers to *voluntarily* change from incorrect methods (rather than wait for an IRS audit resulting in a required change) and to facilitate changes from one correct method to another, the IRS generally allows the taxpayer to spread a positive adjustment into future years. One-fourth of the adjustment is applied to the year of the change, and one-fourth of the adjustment is applied to each of the next three taxable years. A negative adjustment is deducted in the year of the change.[60]

White Corporation in Example 23 must add $60,000 ($\frac{1}{4}$ × $240,000 positive adjustment) to its 2020, 2021, 2022, and 2023 income.

EXAMPLE 24

ETHICS & EQUITY Change in Accounting Method

The IRS faces a difficult choice when it deals with taxpayers who use incorrect accounting methods. On the one hand, the taxpayer who has used an incorrect accounting method may be just as culpable as a person who has omitted income or taken an improper deduction. On the other hand, it often is difficult to discover that a taxpayer is using an incorrect accounting method.

Therefore, the IRS relies to some extent on self-reporting by taxpayers. The Service encourages voluntary changes in incorrect accounting methods by waiving penalties for an underpayment of prior years' taxes, thus permitting the taxpayer, in effect, to pay the related taxes over a four-year period. Is this equitable treatment?

16-3 SPECIAL ACCOUNTING METHODS

LO.4
Determine when the installment method of accounting applies and its effect on taxable income.

Generally, accrual basis taxpayers recognize gross income when goods are sold. Cash basis taxpayers generally recognize income from a sale on the collection of cash from the customer. The tax law provides special accounting methods for certain installment sales and long-term contracts. These special methods were enacted, in part, to ensure that the tax will be due when the taxpayer is best able to pay the tax.

16-3a Installment Method

Under the general rule for computing the gain or loss from the sale of property, the taxpayer recognizes the entire amount of gain or loss upon the sale or other disposition of the property.

Mark sells property to Pooja for $10,000 cash plus Pooja's note (fair market value and face amount of $90,000). Mark's basis for the property was $15,000. Gain or loss is computed under either the cash or accrual basis as follows.

EXAMPLE 25

Selling price	
Cash down payment	$ 10,000
Note receivable	90,000
	$100,000
Basis in the property	(15,000)
Realized gain	$ 85,000

---

[60]Rev.Proc. 2015–13, 2015–5 I.R.B. 419.

In Example 25, the general rule for recognizing gain or loss requires Mark to pay a substantial amount of tax on the gain in the year of sale even though he received only $10,000 cash. Congress enacted the installment sales provisions to prevent this sort of hardship by allowing the taxpayer to spread the gain from installment sales over the collection period, when the taxpayer perhaps is best able to pay the tax. The installment method is an important planning tool because of the tax deferral possibilities.

Eligibility and Calculations

The installment method applies to *gains* (but not losses) from the sale of property by a taxpayer who will receive at least one payment *after* the year of sale. However, the installment method cannot be used for:[61]

- Gains on property held for sale in the ordinary course of business.
- Depreciation recapture amounts.
- Gains on stocks or securities traded on an established market.

As an exception to the first item, the installment method may be used to report gains from sales of:[62]

- Time-share units (e.g., the right to use real property for two weeks each year).
- Residential lots (if the seller is not to make any improvements).
- Any property used or produced in the trade or business of farming.

The Nonelective Aspect

As a general rule, eligible sales *must* be reported by the installment method.[63] A special election is required to report the gain by any other method of accounting.

Computing the Gain for Each Year Payments Are Received

The gain reported on each sale is computed using the following formula.

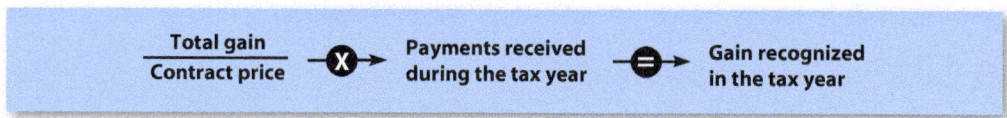

1. *Total gain* is the selling price reduced by selling expenses and the adjusted basis of the property. The selling price is the total consideration received by the seller, including notes receivable from the buyer and the seller's liabilities assumed by the buyer.
2. *Contract price* is the selling price less the seller's liabilities that are assumed by the buyer. Generally, the contract price is the amount, other than interest, the seller will receive from the purchaser.
3. *Payments received* are the collections on the contract price received in each tax year. This generally is equal to the cash received less the interest income collected for the period. If the buyer pays any of the seller's expenses, the seller regards the amount paid as a payment received.[64]

---

[61]§§ 453(b), (i), and (l).
[62]§ 453(l)(2).

[63]§ 453(a).
[64]The gain is reported on Form 6252.

Gonzalo, not a dealer, reports the following concerning a sale of investment land.

EXAMPLE 26

Sales price		
Cash down payment	$ 1,000	
Seller's mortgage assumed by the buyer	3,000	
Notes payable to the seller	13,000	$ 17,000
Selling expenses		(500)
Seller's basis		(10,000)
Total gain		$ 6,500

The contract price is $14,000 ($17,000 − $3,000). Assuming that the $1,000 is the only payment in the year of sale, the recognized gain in that year is:

$$\frac{\$6,500 \text{ (total gain)}}{\$14,000 \text{ (contract price)}} \times \$1,000 = \$464 \text{ (gain recognized in year of sale)}$$

If the sum of the seller's basis and selling expenses is less than the liabilities assumed by the buyer, the difference must be added to the contract price and to the payments (treated as *deemed payments*) received in the year of sale.[65] This adjustment to the contract price is required so that the ratio of total gain to contract price will not be greater than one. The adjustment also accelerates the reporting of income from the deemed payments.

Assume the same facts as in Example 26, except that Gonzalo's basis in the property is only $2,000. The total gain, therefore, is $14,500 [$17,000 − ($2,000 + $500)]. Payments in the year of sale are $1,500.

EXAMPLE 27

Down payment	$1,000
Excess of mortgage assumed over seller's basis and selling expenses [$3,000 − ($2,000 + $500)]	500
Total payments	$1,500

The contract price is $14,500 [$17,000 (selling price) − $3,000 (seller's mortgage assumed) + $500 (excess of mortgage assumed over seller's basis and selling expenses)]. The gain recognized in the year of sale is computed as follows.

$$\frac{\$14,500 \text{ (total gain)}}{\$14,500 \text{ (contract gain)}} \times \$1,500 \text{ total payments received} =$$

$1,500 gain recognized in year of sale

In subsequent years, all amounts that Gonzalo collects on the note principal ($13,000) constitute recognized gain ($13,000 × 100%).

As previously discussed, any depreciation recapture amounts generate gain recognized in the year of sale, and the installment sale gain is any remaining amount.

---

[65]Reg. § 15a.453–1(b)(3)(i).

Olaf sold equipment for $50,000 cash and a $75,000 note due in two years. Olaf's cost of the property was $90,000, and he had deducted depreciation of $65,000. Thus, the basis in the property was $25,000 ($90,000 − $65,000).

Olaf's realized gain is $100,000 ($125,000 − $25,000), and the $65,000 depreciation recapture gain must be recognized in the year of sale. Of the $35,000 remaining § 1231 gain, $14,000 must be recognized in the year of sale.

$$\frac{\text{§ 1231 gain}}{\text{Contract price}} \times \text{Payment received} = \frac{\$125,000 - \$25,000 - \$65,000}{\$125,000} \times \$50,000$$

$$= \frac{\$35,000}{\$125,000} \times \$50,000 = \$14,000$$

The remaining realized gain of $21,000 ($35,000 − $14,000) is recognized as the $75,000 note is collected.

Character of the Gain on Depreciable Real Estate

As discussed in text Section 14-10b, an individual's recognized gain from the sale of depreciable real estate may be subject to a 25 percent tax rate. The gain to the extent of straight-line depreciation taken is subject to the special rate and is referred to as "unrecaptured § 1250 gain." The recognized gain in excess of the depreciation is a § 1231 gain eligible for the 0%/15%/20% rate. Under the installment sale rules, when the sale results in both 25% gain and 0%/15%/20% gain, the 25% gain is reported first.

Continue with the facts in Example 28, but assume the asset sold was a building, and that the realized gain was $100,000, of which $40,000 was § 1250 ordinary income. The straight-line depreciation would have been $25,000 (total depreciation of $65,000 less excess depreciation of $40,000). As a result, the unrecaptured § 1250 gain is $25,000. Since the recognized installment gain in the year of sale of $24,000 was less than the unrecaptured § 1250 gain of $25,000, the $24,000 recognized gain in the year of sale is subject to the 25% tax rate.

Imputed Interest

If a deferred payment contract for the sale of property with a selling price greater than $3,000 does not contain a reasonable interest rate, a reasonable rate is imputed.[66] The imputing of interest effectively restates the selling price of the property to the sum of the payments at the date of the sale and the discounted present value of the future payments. The difference between the present value of a future payment and the payment's face amount is taxed as interest income, as discussed in the following paragraphs. Thus, the imputed interest rules prevent sellers of capital assets from increasing the selling price to reflect the equivalent of unstated interest on deferred payments and thereby converting ordinary (interest) income into long-term capital gains. The imputed interest rules also affect the timing of income recognition.

Generally, if the contract does not charge at least the Federal rate, interest will be imputed at that rate. The Federal rate is the interest rate the Federal government pays on new borrowing and is published monthly by the IRS.[67]

---

[66]§§ 483 and 1274.

[67]§ 1274(d)(1). There are three Federal rates: short-term (not over three years), midterm (over three years but not over nine years), and long-term (over nine years).

As a general rule, the buyer and seller must account for interest on the accrual basis with semiannual compounding.[68] The use of the accrual basis ensures that the seller's interest income and the buyer's interest expense are reported in the same tax year.

Peggy, a cash basis taxpayer, sold land on January 1, 2020, for $200,000 cash and $6,000,000 due on December 31, 2021, with 2% interest payable December 31, 2020, and December 31, 2021. At the time of the sale, the applicable Federal rate was 4% (compounded semiannually). Because Peggy did not charge interest at least equal to the Federal rate, interest is imputed at 4%.

Date	Payment	Present Value (at 4%) on 1/1/2020	Imputed Interest
12/31/2020	$ 120,000	$ 115,384	$ 4,616
12/31/2021	6,120,000	5,658,284	461,716
	$6,240,000	$5,773,668	$466,332

As a result, the selling price is restated to $5,973,668 ($200,000 + $5,773,668) rather than $6,200,000 ($200,000 + $6,000,000). Peggy will recognize interest income using the following amortization schedule.

	Beginning Balance	Interest (at 4%)*	Received	Ending Balance
2020	$5,773,668	$230,947	$ 120,000	$5,884,615
2021	5,884,615	235,385	6,120,000	–0–

*Compounded semiannually.

EXAMPLE
30

Congress has created several exceptions regarding the rate at which interest is imputed and the method of accounting for the interest income and expense. Additional rules and exceptions are summarized in Concept Summary 16.2.

Related-Party Sales of Nondepreciable Property

If the Code did not contain special rules, a taxpayer could make an installment sale of property to a related party (e.g., a family member) as part of a tax deferral plan. Then the purchasing family member could immediately sell the property to an unrelated party for cash with no recognized gain or loss (because the amount realized would equal the basis in the sold asset). The related-party purchaser would not pay the installment note to the selling family member until a later year. The net result would be that the family has the cash, but no taxable gain is recognized until the purchasing family member makes payments on the installment note.

Under special rules designed to address the scheme described above, the proceeds from the subsequent sale (the second sale) by the purchasing family member are treated as though they were used to pay the installment note due the selling family member (the first sale). As a result, the recognition of gain from the original sale between the related parties is accelerated.[69]

---

[68]§§ 1274(a), 1273(a), and 1272(a).

[69]§ 453(e).

Concept Summary 16.2

Interest on Installment Sales

	Imputed Interest Rate
General rule	Federal rate
Exceptions:	
• Principal not over a ceiling amount.[1]	Lesser of Federal rate or 9%
• Sale of land (with a calendar year ceiling of $500,000) between family members (the seller's spouse, brothers, sisters, ancestors, or lineal descendants).[2]	Lesser of Federal rate or 6%

	Method of Accounting for Interest	
	Seller's Interest Income	Buyer's Interest Expense
General rule[3]	Accrual	Accrual
Exceptions:		
• Total payments under the contract are $250,000 or less.[4]	Taxpayer's overall method	Taxpayer's overall method
• Sale of a farm (sales price of $1 million or less).[5]	Taxpayer's overall method	Taxpayer's overall method
• Sale of a principal residence.[6]	Taxpayer's overall method	Taxpayer's overall method
• Sale for a note with principal not over a ceiling amount, the seller is on the cash basis, the property sold is not inventory, and the buyer agrees to report expense by the cash method.[7]	Cash	Cash

[1] § 1274A(b). This amount is adjusted annually for inflation (see Rev.Proc. 2019–44, 2019–47 I.R.B. 1093). For 2020, the amount is $6,039,100.
[2] §§ 1274(c)(3)(F) and 483(e).
[3] §§ 1274(a) and 1272(a)(3).
[4] §§ 1274(c)(3)(C) and 483.
[5] §§ 1274(c)(3)(A) and 483.
[6] §§ 1274(c)(3)(B) and 483.
[7] § 1274A(c). This amount is adjusted annually for inflation (see Rev.Proc. 2019–44, 2019–47 I.R.B. 1093). For 2020, the amount is $4,313,600.

However, even with these special rules, Congress did not eliminate the benefits of all related-party installment sales.

- Related parties include only the first seller's brothers, sisters, ancestors, lineal descendants, controlled corporations, and partnerships, trusts, and estates in which the seller has an interest.[70]

- There is no acceleration if the second disposition occurs more than two years after the first sale.[71]

As a result, if the taxpayer can sell the property to an "unrelated" family member or a "patient" family member, the intrafamily installment sale still is a powerful tax planning tool.[72]

Related-Party Sales of Depreciable Property

The installment method cannot be used to report a gain on the sale of depreciable property to a controlled entity. The purpose of this rule is to prevent the seller from

---

[70] § 453(f)(1), cross-referencing §§ 267(b) and 318(a). Although spouses are related parties, the exclusion of gains between spouses (§ 1041) makes the second-disposition rules inapplicable when the first sale was between spouses.

[71] § 453(e)(2). But see § 453(e)(2)(B) for extensions of the two-year period.
[72] Other exceptions also can be applied in some circumstances. See §§ 453(e)(6) and (7).

deferring gain (until collections are received) while the related purchaser is enjoying a stepped-up basis for depreciation purposes.[73]

The prohibition on the use of the installment method applies to sales between the taxpayer and a partnership or corporation in which the taxpayer holds a more-than-50-percent interest. Constructive ownership rules are used in applying the ownership test (e.g., the taxpayer is considered to own stock owned by a spouse and certain other family members).[74] However, if the taxpayer can establish that tax avoidance was not a principal purpose of the transaction, the installment method can be used to report the gain.

EXAMPLE

31

Alan purchased an apartment building from his controlled corporation, Emerald Corporation. Alan was short of cash at the time of the purchase (December 2020) but was to collect a large cash payment in January 2021. The agreement required Alan to pay the entire arm's length price in January 2021. Alan had good business reasons for acquiring the building.

Emerald should be able to convince the IRS that tax avoidance was not a principal purpose for the installment sale, because of Alan's cash flow issues. Emerald will report all of the gain in the year following the year of sale, and Alan depreciates the building over 27.5 years (the cost recovery period for residential real estate).

Interest on Deferred Tax

The installment method allows the seller to defer the payment of taxes on the gain from the sale of property until payments are received from the buyer (borrower). Congress was concerned that this deferral in addition to the seller earning interest on the receivable was too significant of a benefit. To address this concern, sellers are required to pay interest on the deferred taxes if *both* of the following requirements are met.

- The installment obligation arises from the sale of property (other than farming property) for more than $150,000.
- The taxpayer's total installment obligations outstanding at the close of the tax year exceed $5 million.[75]

Disposition of Installment Obligations

Generally, a taxpayer must recognize the deferred profit from an installment sale when the obligation is transferred to another party or is otherwise relinquished. The rationale for accelerating the gain is that the deferral should continue for no longer than the taxpayer owns the installment obligation.[76]

The gift or cancellation of an installment note is treated as a taxable disposition by the donor. This discourages attempts to shift income among family members. The amount realized from the cancellation is the face amount of the note if the parties (obligor and obligee) are related to each other.[77]

---

[73]§ 453(g).

[74]§§ 1239(b) and (c).

[75]§ 453A and IRS Publication 537. This amount is not indexed for inflation.

[76]§ 453B(a).

[77]§ 453B(f)(2).

EXAMPLE 32

Liz cancels a note issued by Ting (Liz's daughter) that arose in connection with the sale of property. At the time of the cancellation, the note had a basis to Liz of $10,000, a face amount of $25,000, and a fair market value of $20,000. Presuming that the initial sale by Liz qualified as an installment sale, the cancellation results in gain of $15,000 ($25,000 − $10,000) to Liz.

Certain exceptions to the recognition of gain provisions are provided for transfers of installment obligations to the transferor's 80 percent controlled corporation, contributions of capital to a partnership, certain corporate liquidations, transfers due to the taxpayer's death, and transfers between spouses or incident to divorce.[78] In such situations, the deferred profit merely is shifted to the transferee, who is responsible for the payment of tax on the subsequent collections of the installment obligations. But in the case of a transfer of installment obligations to a partnership by a partner, the transferor partner is taxed on the income when the partnership collects on the installment receivables.

The Big Picture

EXAMPLE 33

Return to the facts of *The Big Picture* on p. 16-1. Assume that Belinda's capital contribution to the partnership in 2020 was an installment obligation with a basis of $40,000 and a face amount of $100,000. In 2021, the partnership collected the $100,000. The transfer in 2020 was not a taxable disposition, but in 2021 when the receivable is collected, Belinda recognizes a gain of $60,000.

Electing Out of the Installment Method

While the installment method is mandatory when it applies, a taxpayer can *elect not to use* it. The election is made by reporting the entire recognized gain on the seller's timely filed return.[79]

The election frequently is applied to year-end sales by taxpayers who expect to be in a higher tax bracket in the following year. Permission of the IRS is required to revoke an election not to use the installment method.[80]

EXAMPLE 34

On December 31, 2020, Kurt sold investment land to Jodie for $20,000 (fair market value). He had owned the land for seven years. Jodie will pay Kurt $20,000 in cash on January 4, 2021. Kurt is a cash basis taxpayer, and his basis in the land is $8,000. As a result, he realizes a $12,000 capital gain from the sale. Kurt has a large casualty loss that, when combined with his ordinary income, gives him a marginal tax rate of 12% in 2020. He expects his tax rate to increase to 35% in 2021.

The transaction constitutes an installment sale because a payment will be received in a tax year after the tax year of disposition. Jodie's promise to pay Kurt is an installment obligation, and under the Regulations, the value of the installment obligation is equal to the value of the property sold ($20,000). If Kurt elects out of the installment method, he will shift the $12,000 capital gain from the expected higher capital gains rate in 2021 of 15% to the 0% rate for long-term capital gains in 2020. The expected tax savings based on the rate differential may exceed the benefit of the tax deferral available with the installment method.

---

[78]§§ 453B(c), (d), and (g).
[79]§ 453(d) and Reg. § 15a.453–1(d).

[80]§ 453(d)(3) and Reg. § 15a.453–1(d)(4).

16-3b **Long-Term Contracts**

A long-term contract is a building, installation, construction, or manufacturing contract that is entered into but not completed within the same tax year.[81] However, a *manufacturing* contract is long term *only* if the contract is to manufacture (1) a unique item not normally carried in finished goods inventory or (2) items that normally require more than 12 calendar months to complete.[82] An item is *unique* if it is designed to meet the customer's needs and is not suitable for use by others. A contract to perform services (e.g., auditing or legal services) cannot qualify as a long-term contract.

LO.5

Recognize the methods of accounting for long-term contracts.

> **EXAMPLE**
> **35**
>
> Rocky, a calendar year taxpayer, entered into two contracts during the year.
>
> One contract was to construct a building foundation. Work was to begin in October 2020 and was to be completed by June 2021. The contract is long term because it will not be entered into and completed in the same tax year. The fact that the contract requires less than 12 calendar months to complete is not relevant because the contract is not for manufacturing.
>
> The second contract was for architectural services to be performed over two years. These services do not qualify for long-term contract treatment.

Generally, the taxpayer must accumulate all of the direct and indirect costs incurred under a contract. This means that the production costs must be accumulated and allocated to individual contracts. Furthermore, mixed services costs (costs that benefit contracts as well as the general administrative operations of the business) must be allocated between production and general administration on a rational basis. Exhibit 16.1 lists the types of costs that must be accumulated and allocated to contracts.[83]

> **EXAMPLE**
> **36**
>
> Falcon, Inc., uses detailed cost accumulation records to assign labor and materials to its contracts in progress. The total cost of fringe benefits is allocated to a contract on the following basis.
>
> $$\frac{\text{Labor on the contract}}{\text{Total salaries and labor}} \times \text{Total cost of fringe benefits}$$
>
> Similarly, storage and handling costs for materials are allocated to contracts on the following basis.
>
> $$\frac{\text{Contract materials}}{\text{Material purchases}} \times \text{Storage and handling costs}$$
>
> The cost of the personnel operations, a mixed services cost, is allocated between production and general administration based on the number of employees in each function. The personnel cost allocated to production is allocated to individual contracts on the basis of the formula used to allocate fringe benefits.

The accumulated costs are deducted when the revenue from the contract is recognized. Generally, two methods of accounting are used in varying circumstances to determine when the revenue from a contract is recognized.[84]

- The completed contract method.
- The percentage of completion method.

---

[81]Special rules apply when the Federal government is a party to the contract. §§ 460(c) and (d).

[82]§ 460(f) and Reg. § 1.460–2(a).

[83]Reg. §§ 1.460–5(b) and 1.263A–1(e).

[84]§ 460.

EXHIBIT 16.1	Contract Costs, Mixed Services Costs, and Current Expense Items for Contracts	

	Contracts Eligible for the Completed Contract Method	Other Contracts
Contract costs:		
Direct materials (a part of the finished product).	Capitalize	Capitalize
Indirect materials [consumed in production but not in the finished product (e.g., grease and oil for equipment)].	Capitalize	Capitalize
Storage, handling, and insurance on materials.	Expense	Capitalize
Direct labor (worked on the product).	Capitalize	Capitalize
Indirect labor [worked in the production process but not directly on the product (e.g., a construction supervisor)].	Capitalize	Capitalize
Fringe benefits for direct and indirect labor (e.g., vacation, sick pay, unemployment, and other insurance).	Capitalize	Capitalize
Pension costs for direct and indirect labor:		
Current cost.	Expense	Capitalize
Past service costs.	Expense	Capitalize
Depreciation on production facilities:		
For financial statements.	Capitalize	Capitalize
Tax depreciation in excess of financial statements.	Expense	Capitalize
Depreciation on idle facilities.	Expense	Expense
Property taxes, insurance, rent, and maintenance on production facilities.	Capitalize	Capitalize
Bidding expenses—successful.	Expense	Capitalize
Bidding expenses—unsuccessful.	Expense	Expense
Interest to finance real estate construction.	Capitalize	Capitalize
Interest to finance personal property:		
Production period of one year or less.	Expense	Expense
Production period exceeds one year, and costs exceed $1 million.*	Capitalize	Capitalize
Production period exceeds two years.*	Capitalize	Capitalize
Mixed services costs:		
Personnel operations.	Expense	Allocate
Data processing.	Expense	Allocate
Purchasing.	Expense	Allocate
Selling, general, and administrative expenses (including an allocated share of mixed services).	Expense	Expense
Losses.	Expense	Expense

*The production period does not include the aging period for beer, wine, and certain distilled spirits, for interest paid or accrued before 2020.

The *completed contract method may be used* for (1) home construction contracts (contracts in which at least 80 percent of the estimated costs are for dwelling units in buildings with four or fewer units) and (2) certain other real estate construction contracts. Other real estate contracts can qualify for the completed contract method if both of the following requirements are satisfied.

- The contract is expected to be completed within the two-year period beginning on the commencement date of the contract.
- The contract is performed by a taxpayer whose average annual gross receipts for the three taxable years preceding the taxable year in which the contract is entered into do not exceed $26 million.

The percentage of completion method must be used for all other contracts.

Completed Contract Method

Under the <mark>completed contract method</mark>, no revenue from the contract is recognized until the contract is completed and accepted. Generally, the contract is completed when it is accepted by the customer as finished, or when the customer begins using the subject of the contract.[85]

In some situations, the original contract price may be disputed, or the buyer may want additional work to be done on a long-term contract. If the disputed amount is substantial (it is not possible to determine whether a profit or loss will ultimately be realized on the contract), no amount of income or loss is recognized until the dispute is resolved. In all other cases, the profit or loss (reduced by the amount in dispute) is recognized in the current period upon completion of the contract. However, additional work may need to be performed with respect to the disputed contract. When the amount in dispute is less than the net profit on the contract before the estimated additional cost, the taxpayer must report in the year of completion the applicable profit, reduced by the estimated additional cost.[86]

EXAMPLE 37

Ted, a calendar year taxpayer using the completed contract method of accounting, constructed a building for Brad under a long-term contract. The gross contract price was $500,000. Ted finished construction in 2020 at a cost of $475,000. When Brad examined the building, he insisted that the building be repainted or that the contract price be reduced. The estimated cost of repainting is $10,000. Under the terms of the contract, Ted is assured a profit of at least $15,000 ($500,000 − $475,000 − $10,000) even if the dispute is ultimately resolved in Brad's favor. As a result, Ted must include $490,000 ($500,000 − $10,000) in gross income and is allowed deductions of $475,000 for 2020.

In 2021, Ted and Brad resolve the dispute, and Ted repaints certain portions of the building at a cost of $6,000. Ted must include $10,000 in 2021 gross income and may deduct the $6,000 expense in that year.

If the net profit less the estimated additional cost results in a loss, the loss is deferred until the dispute is resolved.

EXAMPLE 38

Assume the same facts as in the previous example, except that the estimated cost of repainting the building is $50,000. Because the resolution of the dispute completely in Brad's favor would mean a net loss on the contract for Ted ($500,000 − $475,000 − $50,000 = $25,000 loss), Ted does not recognize any income or loss until the year the dispute is resolved.

Percentage of Completion Method

Under the <mark>percentage of completion method</mark>, a portion of the gross contract price is included in income during each period as the work progresses. The revenue accrued each period (except for the final period) is:[87]

$$\frac{C}{T} \times P$$

Where C = Contract costs incurred during the period
T = Estimated total cost of the contract
P = Contract price

[85]Reg. § 1.460–1(c)(3).
[86]Reg. §§ 1.451–3(d)(2)(ii)–(vii), Example 2.
[87]§ 460(b)(1)(A).

All of the costs allocated to the contract during the period are deductible from the accrued revenue.[88] The revenue reported in the final period is any remaining revenue from the contract. Because T in this formula is an estimate that frequently differs from total actual costs (which are not known until the contract has been completed), the profit on a contract for a particular period may be overstated or understated (such that related income taxes may be overpaid or underpaid).

EXAMPLE 39

Tan, Inc., entered into a contract that was to take two years to complete, with an estimated cost of $2,250,000. The contract price was $3,000,000. Costs of the contract for 2019, the first year, totaled $1,350,000. The gross profit reported by the percentage of completion method for 2019 was $450,000 [($1,350,000/$2,250,000 × $3,000,000) − $1,350,000].

The contract was completed at the end of 2020 at a total cost of $2,700,000. In retrospect, the 2019 profit should have been $150,000 [($1,350,000/$2,700,000 × $3,000,000) − $1,350,000]. As a result, taxes were overpaid for 2019.

Under a *de minimis* rule, if less than 10 percent of the estimated contract costs have been incurred by the end of the taxable year, the taxpayer can elect to defer the recognition of income and the related costs until the taxable year in which the 10 percent threshold is met.[89]

Lookback Provision

In the year a contract is completed, a *lookback* provision requires the recalculation of annual profits reported on the contract under the percentage of completion method. Interest is paid to the taxpayer if taxes were overpaid, and interest is payable by the taxpayer if there was an underpayment.[90] For a corporate taxpayer, the lookback interest paid by the taxpayer is deductible, but for an individual taxpayer, it is nondeductible personal interest associated with a tax liability.

EXAMPLE 40

Assume that Tan, Inc., in Example 39, was in the 21% tax bracket in both years and the relevant interest rate was 5%. For 2019, the company paid excess taxes of $63,000 [($450,000 − $150,000) × 21%]. When the contract is completed at the end of 2020, Tan should receive interest of $3,150 ($63,000 × 5%) for one year on the tax overpayment.

LO.6

Recognize when accounting for inventories must occur and the key tax accounting methods applicable to inventory.

16-4 INVENTORIES

The use of inventories is necessary to clearly reflect income of any business engaged in the production, purchase, or sale of merchandise. Inventories might not be required for small taxpayers, defined for this purpose as those with average annual gross receipts for the prior three-year period of $26 million or less.[91] Generally, when a taxpayer is required to account for inventories for tax purposes, tax accounting and financial accounting for inventories are much the same.

- The use of inventories is necessary to clearly reflect the income of any business engaged in the production and sale or purchase and sale of goods.[92]
- The inventories should include all finished goods, goods in process, and raw materials and supplies that will become part of the product (including containers).

---

[88]Reg. § 1.451–3(c)(3).

[89]§ 460(b)(5).

[90]§§ 460(b)(2) and (6). The taxpayer can elect not to apply the lookback method in situations where the cumulative taxable income as of the close of each prior year is within 10% of the correct income for each prior year.

[91]Reg. § 1.471–1.

[92]§ 471(a) and Reg. §§ 1.471–1 and −2.

- Inventory rules must give effect to the *best accounting practice* of a particular trade or business, and the taxpayer's method should be consistently followed from year to year.
- All items included in inventory should be valued at either (1) cost or (2) the lower of cost or market value.

The reason for the similarities between tax and financial accounting for inventories is that § 471 establishes a two-prong test. Under this provision, "inventories shall be taken . . . on such basis . . . as conforming as nearly as may be to the *best accounting practice* in the trade or business and as most *clearly reflecting the income*." The best accounting practice is synonymous with generally accepted accounting principles (GAAP). However, the IRS determines whether an inventory method clearly reflects income.

In *Thor Power Tool Co. v. Comm.*, there was a conflict between the two tests.[93] The taxpayer's method of valuing obsolete parts was in conformity with GAAP. The IRS, however, successfully argued that the clear reflection of income test was not satisfied because the taxpayer's procedures for valuing its inventories were contrary to the Regulations. Under the taxpayer's method, inventories for parts in excess of estimated future sales were expensed, although the parts were kept on hand and their asking prices were not reduced. [Under Reg. § 1.471–4(b), inventories cannot be written down unless the selling prices also are reduced.] The taxpayer contended that conformity to GAAP creates a presumption that the method clearly reflects income.

The Supreme Court disagreed, concluding that the clear reflection of income test was *paramount*. Moreover, the Court indicated that the IRS position controls in determining whether the method of inventory clearly reflects income. As a result, the best accounting practice test was rendered meaningless by this decision: the taxpayer's method of inventory must strictly conform to the Regulations regardless of what GAAP may require.

16-4a Determining Inventory Cost

For merchandise purchased, cost is the invoice price less trade discounts plus freight and other handling charges.[94] Cash discounts approximating a fair interest rate can be deducted or capitalized at the taxpayer's option provided the method used is consistently applied.

Uniform Capitalization (UNICAP)

Section 263A provides that for inventory and property produced by the taxpayer, "(A) the direct cost of such property, and (B) such property's share of those indirect costs (including taxes) part or all of which are allocable to such property" must be capitalized. The application of the UNICAP rules is not required for taxpayers whose average annual gross receipts (computed over the three preceding years) are $26 million or less.

The UNICAP rules constitute a set of capitalization rules that apply to all types of businesses: contractors, manufacturers, farmers, wholesalers, and retailers.[95] Congress has labeled the system the **uniform capitalization (UNICAP) rules**, and many practitioners refer to the rules as a *super-full absorption costing system*.

---

[93]79-1 USTC ¶9139, 43 AFTR 2d 79–362, 99 S.Ct. 773 (USSC, 1979). See text Section 4-1d for the case's discussion of the differences between tax and financial accounting.

[94]Reg. § 1.471–3(b).

[95]H. Rep. 99–841, 99th Cong., 2nd Sess., 1986, pp. 302–309. See also Reg. § 1.263A–1(a).

To value inventory under the UNICAP rules, a *producer* must apply the following steps.[96]

- Classify all costs into three categories: (1) production, (2) general administration (nonproduction), and (3) mixed services [activities that benefit both category (1) and (2) activities, such as the legal and human resources departments].
- Allocate mixed services costs to production and general administration.[97]
- Allocate the production costs (that now include the mixed service costs allocated to production) between the cost of goods sold and the ending inventory.

Exhibit 16.1 (see the "Other Contracts" column) lists typical items that are included in the three classes of costs. The mixed services costs should be allocated to production on a rational basis. For example, the costs of operating the human resources department may be allocated between production and general administration (e.g., based on the number of applications processed or the number of employees). In lieu of allocating each mixed services cost, the taxpayer can elect a *simplified method* whereby the total of all mixed services costs is allocated to production in this manner.[98]

$$MSP = \frac{TP}{TC} \times TMS$$

Where MSP = Mixed services costs allocated to production
        TP = Total production costs other than interest and mixed services
        TC = Total costs other than interest; state, local, or foreign income taxes; and mixed services costs
     TMS = Total mixed services costs

Traditional cost accounting techniques (e.g., average cost per equivalent unit) can be used to allocate the costs between the cost of goods sold and the ending inventory. Alternatively, the producer can elect to allocate mixed services costs to production on the basis of labor charges only (production labor as a percentage of total labor costs).

The costs included in the inventory of *wholesalers and retailers* are comparable to those of the producer. However, many of these costs are captured in the price these taxpayers pay for the goods. The following additional costs are capitalized by these taxpayers.

- All storage costs for wholesalers.
- Off-site storage costs for retailers.
- Purchasing costs (e.g., buyers' wages or salaries).
- Handling, processing, assembly, and repackaging.
- The portion of mixed services costs allocable to these functions.
- Interest expense on loans related to production of inventory must be capitalized if (1) the estimated production period exceeds one year and the costs exceed $1 million or (2) the estimated production period exceeds two years.[99]

Mixed services costs are allocated to off-site storage, purchasing, and packaging on the basis of direct labor costs of these departments pro rata to total payroll.

The UNICAP rules may result in some costs being capitalized for tax purposes but not for financial accounting purposes. For example, a wholesaler's or manufacturer's storage costs generally are expensed for financial reporting purposes but are capitalized for tax purposes. The taxpayer may capitalize straight-line depreciation of production equipment for financial accounting purposes, but tax depreciation amounts are capitalized for UNICAP.

---

[96]Reg. § 1.263A–1(c).

[97]Producers with mixed services costs of $200,000 or less for the year are not required to allocate mixed services costs if the simplified method is used to allocate their production costs. Reg. § 1.263A–1(b)(12).

[98]Reg. § 1.263A–1(h)(5).

[99]§ 263A(f). The $1 million amount is not indexed for inflation.

Taxpayers with average annual gross receipts of $26 million or less (for the previous three years) are not required to apply the UNICAP rules, including the interest capitalization rules. Special rules exempt certain farming property as well as deductible research expenditures from UNICAP.[100]

Lower of Cost or Market

Except for those taxpayers who use the LIFO method, inventories may be valued at the <mark>lower of cost or market (replacement cost)</mark>.[101] Any write-down of damaged or shopworn merchandise and goods that otherwise are unsalable at normal prices is not considered to be an application of the lower of cost or market method. Such items are valued at bona fide selling price less direct cost of disposal.[102]

In the case of excess inventories (as in *Thor Power Tool Co.*, discussed previously), the goods can be written down only to the taxpayer's offering price. If the offering price on the goods is not reduced, the goods are valued at cost.

EXAMPLE 41

Cardinal Publishing Company invested $50,000 in printing 10,000 copies of a book. Although only 7,000 copies were sold in the first 3 years and none in the next 5 years, management is convinced that the book will become a classic in 20 years. Cardinal leaves the cover price the same as it was when the book was first distributed ($18 per copy). The remaining 3,000 books are valued at cost ($15,000). In this way, the tax law provides an incentive for the taxpayer to destroy or abandon its excess inventory and obtain an immediate deduction rather than wait for the event of future sales.

In applying the lower of cost or market method, *each* item included in the inventory must be valued at the lower of its cost or market value.[103]

EXAMPLE 42

Information related to a taxpayer's ending inventory follows. Under the lower of cost or market method, the inventory is valued at $7,500 rather than $9,500.

Item	Cost	Market	Lower of Cost or Market
A	$5,000	$ 4,000	$4,000
B	3,000	2,000	2,000
C	1,500	6,000	1,500
	$9,500	$12,000	$7,500

Inventory Shrinkage

The difference between the inventory per physical count and the company's records is referred to as *inventory shrinkage*. Inventory shrinkage is the result of accidents, theft, and errors in recording. Many companies take physical inventories at times other than the last day of the tax year and adjust their inventory per books to agree with the physical count. In addition, companies often adjust the ending inventory, to be used in deriving cost of goods sold, for the estimated shrinkage that has occurred between the date of the physical inventory and the last day of the tax year. The adjustment often is based on the historical relationship between inventory shrinkage and sales.[104]

---

[100]§§ 263A(d) and (e)(3).
[101]Reg. § 1.472–4.
[102]Reg. § 1.471–2(c).

[103]Reg. § 1.471–4(c).
[104]§ 471(b).

Determining Cost—Specific Identification, FIFO, and LIFO

In some cases, it is feasible to determine the cost of the particular item sold. For example, an automobile dealer can determine the specific cost of each automobile that has been sold. However, in most businesses, it is necessary to resort to a flow of goods assumption such as *first in, first out (FIFO), last in, first out (LIFO),* or an *average cost* method. A taxpayer may use any of these methods provided the method selected is consistently applied from year to year.

During a period of rising prices, LIFO generally produces a lower ending inventory valuation, resulting in a greater cost of goods sold than would be obtained under the FIFO method.

On January 1, 2020, the taxpayer opened a retail store to sell refrigerators. At least 10 refrigerators must be carried in inventory to satisfy customer demands. The initial investment in the 10 refrigerators is $5,000. During the year, 10 refrigerators were sold at $750 each and were replaced at a cost of $6,000 ($600 each). Gross profit under the LIFO and FIFO methods is computed as follows.

		FIFO		LIFO
Sales (10 × $750)		$ 7,500		$ 7,500
Beginning inventory	$ 5,000		$ 5,000	
Purchases	6,000		6,000	
	$11,000		$11,000	
Ending inventory				
10 × $600	(6,000)			
10 × $500			(5,000)	
Cost of goods sold		(5,000)		(6,000)
Gross profit		$ 2,500		$ 1,500

Dollar-Value LIFO

In the previous example, the taxpayer was buying and selling a single product, a particular model of a refrigerator. The taxpayer employed the specific goods LIFO technique. Under the specific goods approach, if the identical items are not on hand at the end of the period, the LIFO inventory is depleted and all of the deferred profit is recognized. Thus, taxpayers who frequently change the items carried in inventory might realize little benefit from LIFO. The dollar-value LIFO technique can address this problem.

Under **dollar-value LIFO**, each inventory item is assigned to a pool. A *pool* is a collection of similar items and is treated as a separate inventory. Determining whether items are similar involves considerable judgment. In general, however, the taxpayer would prefer broad pools so that when a particular item is sold out, it can be replaced with increases in other items in the same pool. Generally, all products manufactured at a particular plant can be treated as a pool.[105] An automobile dealer may have separate pools for new cars, lightweight trucks, heavy-duty trucks, and car and truck parts.

At the end of the period, ending inventory is valued at the current-year prices, and then at the LIFO base period (the year LIFO was adopted). The ratio of the ending inventory at current prices to the ending inventory at base period prices is the *LIFO index.* If the total current inventory at base period prices is greater than the base period inventory at base period prices, a LIFO layer must be added. The LIFO index is applied to the LIFO layer to convert it to current prices.

---

[105]See, generally, Reg. § 1.472–8.

Black Company adopted LIFO effective January 1, 2020. The base LIFO inventory (from December 31, 2019) was $1,000,000. On December 31, 2020, the inventory was $1,320,000 at end-of-2020 prices and $1,200,000 at end-of-2019 (the base period) prices. As a result, Black added a 2020 LIFO layer of $200,000 ($1,200,000 − $1,000,000). The layer must be converted to 2020 prices.

$$\text{LIFO index} = \$1,320,000/\$1,200,000 = 1.10$$

$$\text{2019 layer} \times \text{LIFO index} = \$200,000 \times 1.10 = \$220,000$$

Therefore, the 2020 ending inventory is $1,000,000 + $220,000 = $1,220,000.

The inventory on December 31, 2021, is $1,325,000 using 2020 prices and $1,250,000 using base period prices. The 2021 LIFO layer is $50,000 ($1,250,000 − $1,200,000), and the 2021 LIFO index is $1,325,000/$1,250,000 = 1.06. The LIFO inventory on December 31, 2021, is computed as follows.

	Base Period Cost	LIFO Index	LIFO Layers
Base inventory	$1,000,000	1.00	$1,000,000
2020 layer	200,000	1.10	220,000
2021 layer	50,000	1.06	53,000
	$1,250,000		$1,273,000

ETHICS & EQUITY Preserving the LIFO Reserve

Blanch Corporation has been using the dollar-value LIFO inventory method for 20 years. The company maintains one inventory pool that includes raw materials, goods in process, and finished goods. The LIFO deferral is several million dollars. At the end of the current year, the corporation's inventory of finished goods was almost depleted because the company's major competitor had to recall a substantial portion of its products.

Blanch's management is aware that if the inventory is not replenished, the corporation will recognize income that has been deferred for 20 years. Blanch's controller has suggested that the company buy sufficient raw materials to substitute for the depleted finished goods. This will require having on hand at the end of the year the raw materials required for the next 18 months, when ordinarily the company has only a three-month supply on hand. The controller argues that the cost of carrying the additional inventory is much less than the additional taxes that will be due if the inventories are allowed to decrease.

The operations manager has suggested that the company buy the raw materials before the end of the year and have the supplier store the materials. Furthermore, the supplier would act as Blanch's agent to sell the excess materials. This would minimize the actual investment in inventory. Do you think the corporation should follow either proposal? Explain.

16-4b The LIFO Election

A taxpayer may adopt LIFO by merely using the method in the tax return for the year of the change and attaching Form 970 (Application to Use LIFO Inventory Method) to the tax return (i.e., a taxpayer is assured IRS approval for the change). Once the election is made, it cannot be revoked. A prospective change from LIFO to any other inventory method can be made only if the consent of the IRS is obtained.[106]

The beginning inventory valuation for the first LIFO year is computed by the costing method used in the preceding year. As a result, the beginning LIFO inventory generally equals the closing inventory for the preceding year. Because lower of cost or market cannot be used in conjunction with LIFO, previous write-downs to market for items included in the beginning inventory must be restored to income. The amount the

---

[106]Reg. §§ 1.472–3(a) and 1.472–5.

inventories are written up is an adjustment due to a change in accounting method.[107] The taxpayer can spread the adjustment ratably over the year of the change and the two succeeding years.[108]

In 2019, Paul used the lower of cost or market FIFO inventory method. The FIFO cost of his ending inventory was $30,000, and the market value of the inventory was $24,000. As a result, the ending inventory for 2019 was $24,000.

Paul switched to LIFO in 2020 and was required to write up the beginning inventory to $30,000. Paul must add $2,000 ($6,000 ÷ 3) to his gross income in 2020, 2021, and 2022.

Once the LIFO election is made for tax purposes, the taxpayer's financial reports to owners and creditors also must be prepared on the basis of LIFO.[109] The *conformity* of financial reports to tax reporting is required by the Code and is strictly enforced by the IRS.

16-4c Special Inventory Methods Relating to Farming and Ranching

Farmers who do not use the cash method and therefore account for inventories may elect to use the **farm price method** or the **unit-livestock-price method** rather than one of the inventory methods discussed previously. Under the farm price method, the inventory is valued at its market price less disposition costs (e.g., transportation and selling expenses).[110] If the taxpayer uses the unit-livestock-price method, the animals are valued at a standard cost, which is based on the average cost of raising an animal with the characteristics of the animals included in the ending inventory.[111]

16-4d Inventory of Small Taxpayers

Small taxpayers, defined as those with average annual gross receipts of $26 million or less in the prior three-year period, may use the cash method of accounting, and they have three method choices in accounting for inventory.[112]

1. Treat inventory as nonincidental materials and supplies. Under this method, the taxpayer deducts the cost of the inventory when it is used (i.e., when it is sold to the customer). Because the taxpayer is using the cash method, it may only deduct the inventory if it has not only sold it but also paid for it.
2. If the taxpayer has an *applicable financial statement* (generally a certified GAAP financial statement), it may treat the inventory as it does in the financial statements.
3. If the taxpayer does not have an applicable financial statement, it may deduct the inventory in the same manner as it reports the inventory on its books and records—"prepared in accordance with the taxpayer's accounting procedures."

---

[107]Reg. § 1.472–2(c). In Rev.Rul. 76–282, 1976–2 C.B. 137, the IRS required the restoration of write-downs for damaged and shopworn goods when the taxpayer switched to LIFO.

[108]§ 472(d).

[109]§ 472(d).

[110]Reg. § 1.471–6(d).

[111]Reg. § 1.471–6(e). See also IRS Pub. 225 (*Farmers Tax Guide*), p. 7.

[112]§ 471(c).

EXAMPLE

46

Jain is a sole proprietor selling widgets online. Her gross receipts average $2,700,000 per year. She buys her goods on credit, usually paying the bills when received (about 30 days after purchase). Jain has adopted the cash method and treats her inventory as nonincidental supplies.

In 2020, Jain recorded beginning inventory of $30,000 (cost), purchases of $1,800,000, and ending inventory of $20,000 (cost). She had outstanding payables for inventory purchases of $50,000 (including for the ending inventory). Jain's records show that all of the beginning inventory was paid for in 2019 and sold in 2020.

The 2020 inventory deduction is:

Beginning inventory paid for in 2019 but not sold until 2020	$ 30,000
Inventory purchased during the year less $50,000 not paid by year-end (including the ending inventory)	1,750,000
Inventory deduction for 2020	$1,780,000

16-5 TAX PLANNING

LO.7

Identify tax planning opportunities related to accounting periods and accounting methods.

16-5a Taxable Year

Under the general rules for tax years, partnerships and S corporations frequently must use a calendar year. However, if the partnership or S corporation can demonstrate a business purpose for a fiscal year, it can use that year. The advantage to a fiscal year is that the calendar year partners and S corporation shareholders may be able to defer from tax the income earned from the close of the fiscal year until the end of the calendar year. Tax advisers for these entities should apply the IRS's gross receipts test to determine whether permission for the fiscal year will be granted.[113]

16-5b Cash Method of Accounting

The cash method of accounting gives the taxpayer considerable control over the recognition of expenses and some control over the recognition of income. This method can be used by proprietorships, partnerships without a C corporation partner, S corporations, qualified personal service corporations, small C corporations, and small partnerships with a C corporation partner (annual gross receipts of $26 million or less over the prior three-year period). Most farmers also can use the cash method.

16-5c Installment Method

Unlike the cash and accrual methods, the installment method often results in an interest-free loan (of deferred taxes) from the government. When eligible property is sold, the installment method is an important tax planning technique, under which the seller may defer gain and attain a higher interest rate than from alternative investments. These benefits must be weighed against the risks of nonpayment by the buyer. If the taxpayer expects to be in a higher tax bracket when the payments will be received, he or she can elect not to use the installment method.

Related Parties

Intrafamily installment sales can be a useful family tax planning tool. If the related party holds the property more than two years, a subsequent sale will not accelerate the gain from the first disposition. Patience and forethought are rewarded.

---

[113]Rev.Proc. 2006–46, 2006–2 C.B. 859.

Disposition of Installment Obligations

A disposition of an installment obligation can be a serious income tax matter. Gifts of the obligations accelerate income to the seller. In each instance where transfers of installment obligations are contemplated, the tax adviser should analyze thoroughly the related tax and nontax consequences.

16-5d Inventories

The ending inventory valuation can be minimized and thus taxable income reduced by using elective accounting methods: (1) purchase prices can be stated net of cash discounts, (2) the lower of cost or market method may be applied, and (3) the LIFO method can be adopted during periods of significantly rising prices.

REFOCUS ON THE BIG PICTURE

ACCOUNTING PERIOD AND METHOD

Selection of a Tax Year

An entity's tax form will govern the rules for determining the entity's tax year. Because Silver is a partnership, the Code's provisions for partnerships are applicable.

In this case, Tweety's 40 percent ownership interest in Silver is not sufficient to enable it to control the selection of the partnership's tax year. Likewise, Belinda and Pearl's collective controlling interest will not allow them to control the selection of the tax year for the partnership.

The partnership applies rules in the following sequence to determine its tax year-end.

- *Majority interest tax year.* The tax year of the partners who have a common year-end and collectively own a greater-than-50-percent interest in the partnership capital and profits.

- *Principal partners' tax year.* The tax year if all of the principal partners (5 percent or greater interest in capital or profits) use the same tax year.

- *Least aggregate deferral tax year.* The tax year of the principal partners (grouped by a common year-end) that produces the least aggregate deferral of income.

Alternatively, the partnership can select its tax year based on a business purpose for the tax year selected. However, this requires the approval of the IRS, which is unlikely to be granted. The only business purpose the IRS has acknowledged is the need to conform the tax year to the entity's natural business year.

Therefore, it appears that Silver will determine its tax year by using the least aggregate deferral method. Based on this method, Silver's tax year will end on November 30 (see the calculations in Example 3).

Short Tax Year

Silver will have a short tax year that begins on April 1, 2020, and ends on November 30, 2020, as determined by the least aggregate deferral method.

continued

Partnership's Accounting Method

If Silver Partnership's average annual gross receipts for the prior three-year period exceed $26 million, it must use the accrual method to compute its income because one of the partners is a C corporation. Even though Belinda is a cash basis taxpayer, her share of the partnership income is computed using the accrual method.

Key Terms

Accounting methods, 16-10	Economic performance test, 16-14	Majority interest partners, 16-3
Accounting period, 16-2	Farm price method, 16-36	One-year rule for prepaid expenses, 16-11
Accrual method, 16-13	Fiscal year, 16-2	Percentage of completion method, 16-29
All events test, 16-14	Hybrid method, 16-16	Personal service corporation (PSC), 16-6
Cash method, 16-11	Imputed interest, 16-22	Principal partner, 16-3
Claim of right doctrine, 16-9	Installment method, 16-20	Short period, 16-7
Completed contract method, 16-29	Least aggregate deferral method, 16-4	Short taxable year, 16-7
Crop insurance proceeds, 16-9	Long-term contract, 16-27	Uniform capitalization (UNICAP) rules, 16-31
Crop method, 16-12	Lower of cost or market (replacement cost), 16-33	Unit-livestock-price method, 16-36
Dollar-value LIFO, 16-34		

Discussion Questions

1. **LO.1** Would a calendar or fiscal year be more suitable for a ski lodge? Why?

2. **LO.1** Assume that a partnership is profitable and that its tax year ends on December 31 but one of the partners' tax year ends on September 30. Does the partner enjoy a tax benefit or detriment from the partnership's use of a December 31 tax year-end? Explain.

3. **LO.1** A law practice was incorporated on January 1, 2020, and expects to earn $25,000 per month before deducting attorney Shonda's salary. Shonda owns 100% of the stock in the practice. The corporation and Shonda both use the cash method of accounting. The corporation does not need to retain any of the earnings in the business; thus, the salary of Shonda (a calendar year taxpayer) is the corporation's net income before salary expense.

   Decision Making

   If the corporation could choose any tax year and pay Shonda's salary at the time that would be most tax efficient (but at least once every 12 months), what tax year should the corporation choose? When should the salary be paid each year? Be specific.

4. **LO.1** Art Funkel started his incorporated medical practice on June 1 of the current year. He immediately made an S election for the corporation. Art would like the corporation to adopt a tax year ending May 31 so that a full 12 months of income would be included in the first tax year. Can the corporation elect a fiscal year ending May 31? Explain.

Critical Thinking   5. **LO.1** Fred, a cash basis taxpayer, received a $15,000 bonus from his employer in 2020. The bonus was based on the company's profits for 2019. In 2021, the company discovered that its 2019 profits were computed incorrectly. As a result, Fred received an additional $10,000 with respect to 2019 profits. Fred's marginal tax rate in 2020 was 12%, and it was 35% in 2021.

Sue, also a cash basis taxpayer, received a $35,000 bonus in 2020 that was based on 2019 profits. In 2021, the company discovered that it had overstated its profits in 2020. As a result, Sue was required to repay $10,000 of her bonus in 2021. Sue was in the 35% marginal tax bracket in 2020 and in the 12% marginal bracket in 2021.

What special tax treatment is available to Fred and Sue as a result of their employer's errors?

6. **LO.2** Under what conditions would the cash method of accounting be advantageous over the accrual basis?

7. **LO.2** In December 2020, Nell, Inc., an accrual basis taxpayer, paid $12,000 for insurance premiums for the 2021 calendar year. How much of the premiums can Nell, Inc., deduct in 2020?

8. **LO.2** In 2020, the taxpayer became ineligible to use the cash method of accounting. At the beginning of the year, accounts receivable totaled $240,000, accounts payable for merchandise totaled $80,000, and inventory on hand totaled $320,000. What is the amount of the adjustment due to the change in accounting method?

9. **LO.2** Osprey Corporation, an accrual basis taxpayer, reported taxable income for 2020 and paid $40,000 on its estimated state income tax for the year. During 2020, the company received a $4,000 refund upon filing its 2019 state income tax return. The company filed its 2020 state income tax return in August 2021 and paid the $7,000 state income tax due for 2020. In December 2020, the company received a notice from the state tax commission that an additional $6,000 of income tax was due for 2018 because of an error on the return. The company acknowledged the error in December 2020 and paid the additional $6,000 in tax in February 2021. What is Osprey's 2020 Federal income tax deduction for state income taxes?

10. **LO.2** Compare the results of using cash and accrual methods of accounting for the following events.
    a. Purchased new equipment, paying $50,000 cash and giving a note payable for $30,000 due next year.
    b. Paid $3,600 for a three-year service contract on the new equipment.
    c. Collected $1,800 for services to be provided over the current and following years.
    d. Received a $3,000 note from a customer for services provided in the current year. The market value of the note was only $2,400.

Decision Making   11. **LO.2** Edgar uses the cash method to report the income from his software consulting business. A large publicly held corporation has offered to invest in Edgar's business as a limited partner. What tax accounting complications would be created if Edgar and the corporation became partners?

12. **LO.2** Samantha, an accrual basis taxpayer, subscribes to a service that updates a database used in her business. In December 2020, Samantha paid the $120,000 subscription for the period January 2020 through December 2021. What is Samantha's deduction for 2020?

13. **LO.2** Emerald Motors is an automobile dealer. The controller consults with you about the type of accounting used for a special offer to its new car customers. Emerald has offered to provide at no charge to the customer the first four recommended service visits (i.e., at 3,000, 6,000, 9,000, and 12,000 miles). It is a virtual certainty that all customers will exercise their rights to the service, and the cost of the services can be accurately estimated. The controller reasons that the estimated

cost should be accrued when the sale of an automobile is made so that all of the costs of the sale can be matched with the revenue. How would you respond to the controller?

14. **LO.4, 7** Irene has made Sara an offer on the purchase of a capital asset. Irene will pay (1) $200,000 cash or (2) $50,000 cash and a 6% installment note for $150,000 guaranteed by City Bank of New York. If Sara sells for $200,000 cash, she will invest the after-tax proceeds in certificates of deposit yielding 6% interest. Sara's cost of the asset is $25,000. Why would Sara prefer the installment sale?

Decision Making

15. **LO.4** Arnold gave land to his son, Bruce. Arnold's basis in the land was $100,000, and its fair market value at the date of the gift was $150,000. Bruce borrowed $130,000 from a bank; he used the funds to improve the property. He sold the property to Della for $360,000. Della paid Bruce $90,000 in cash, assumed his $120,000 mortgage, and agreed to pay $150,000 in two years. Bruce's selling expenses were $10,000. Della is going to pay adequate interest. What is Bruce's installment sale gain in the year of sale?

16. **LO.4** A seller and a buyer agree that the sales/purchase price for land is $1,500,000 down and two annual payments of $1,500,000 each to be made over the next two years. The buyer intends to construct a building on the land that will be used as the buyer's warehouse. It will be built over the next two years. The seller proposes that the contract should read that the total selling price is $4,300,000 and that the two deferred payments of $1,500,000 each include interest at 4%, which is the current Federal intermediate-term rate but is less than the current interest rate on commercial real estate. The land is a long-term capital asset to the seller. Why should the seller and not the buyer be more concerned about the stated interest rate?

Critical Thinking

17. **LO.4, 7** On June 1, 2018, Father sold land to Son for $300,000. Father reported the gain by the installment method, with the gain to be spread over five years. In May 2020, Son received an offer of $400,000 for the land, to be paid over three years. What would be the tax consequences of Son's sale? How could the tax consequences be improved?

Critical Thinking

18. **LO.4, 7** In December 2020, Carl Corporation sold land it held as an investment. The corporation received $50,000 in 2020 and a note payable (with adequate interest) for $150,000 to be paid in 2022. Carl Corporation's cost of the land was $80,000. The corporation has a $90,000 net capital loss carryover that will expire in 2020. Should Carl report the sale in 2020 or use the installment method to report the income as payments are received?

Decision Making

19. **LO.2, 5** What are the similarities between the crop method used for farming and the completed contract method used for long-term construction?

20. **LO.5** Nathan uses the percentage of completion method to report income from his real estate construction contracts. A contract was begun in 2020 and completed in 2021. In 2020, Nathan reported gross income from the partial completion of the contract. In 2021, however, costs had increased above the original estimate. The contract was completed with the actual profit on the contract being less than the income from the contract reported in 2020. What mechanism should be used to correct for the overpayment of tax in 2020? Be specific.

21. **LO.5** Neal uses the percentage of completion method to report his gross income from long-term contracts that were to begin in 2020. In 2021, he completes a contract for more than the estimate of total costs that was used in the prior year. What are the tax accounting implications of the incorrect estimate?

22. **LO.5** The Hawk Corporation builds yachts. The vessels it currently produces are practically identical and are completed in approximately 8 months. A customer has approached Hawk about constructing a larger yacht that would take approximately 15 months to complete. What are the tax implications of accepting the contract proposal?

Critical Thinking

Critical Thinking 23. **LO.6** Largo Company is an engineering consulting business that uses the accrual method of accounting for its services. Mango Company is a manufacturer of nuts and bolts that also uses the accrual method to account for its sales. Each company has a personnel department. How should the cost of personnel operations be treated by each of the two companies? *Hint:* Consider whether the UNICAP rules apply.

Critical Thinking 24. **LO.6** Amber Auto Parts adopted the dollar-value LIFO inventory method. The company has consistently used a retail price index when it should have used a producer's. As a result, its LIFO layers have been consistently undervalued. Why is the company's error exacerbated by the fact that the company uses the LIFO method instead of the FIFO method?

Critical Thinking 25. **LO.6** Opal, Inc., is about to make its first attempt to borrow from a local bank. The company uses LIFO for tax purposes, solely to defer taxes, and it believes that income computed using the FIFO method would better reflect its income. The company also uses the double-declining balance method of depreciation for tax purposes, even though the straight-line method better reflects the actual depreciation. The company would like to present its financial position in the most favorable light. Therefore, Opal's CEO intends to provide the bank with an income statement prepared using the FIFO inventory method and straight-line depreciation. What problems will presenting the income statement to the bank in this fashion cause for Opal?

Critical Thinking 26. **LO.6** Blue is a retailer that uses the FIFO inventory method. Blue always takes its physical inventory at the end of the last day of its tax year, December 31. This practice is very unpopular with its employees, who do not like working on New Year's Eve. The company is considering taking the inventory at the end of November and adjusting for sales and purchases in the last month of the year. However, the CFO has raised the issue that by taking the inventory at the end of November, loss from theft and breakage in December will not be taken into account until the physical inventory is taken in the following year. Is the CFO's concern valid? Explain.

Computational Exercises

27. **LO.2** Gaffney Corporation is a wholesale distributor of auto parts and uses the cash method of accounting. The company's sales have been about $20,000,000 per year for the last few years. However, Gaffney has the opportunity to acquire an unincorporated competitor with annual sales of $10,000,000. What would be the tax accounting implications of acquiring the competitor?

28. **LO.1** In 2020, Aurora received a $25,000 bonus computed as a percentage of profits. In 2021, Aurora's employer determined that the 2020 profits had been incorrectly computed, and Aurora had to refund the $8,000 in 2021. Assume that Aurora was in the 35% tax bracket in 2020 but in the 12% bracket in 2021.
    a. In 2020, how much is Aurora required to include in income?
    b. In 2021, what is the amount of the deduction Aurora can claim? What is the reduction in taxes for 2021 as a result of the deduction?

29. **LO.2** In 2020, Chaya Corporation, an accrual basis, calendar year taxpayer, provided services to clients and earned $25,000. The clients signed notes receivable to Chaya that have a fair market value of $22,000 at year-end. In addition, Chaya sold a 36-month service contract on June 1, 2020, and received payment in full of $12,000. How much gross income does Chaya report from these transactions in 2020?

30. **LO.3** For 2020, Essence Company, a calendar year taxpayer, will change from using the cash method for tax purposes to the accrual method. At the end of 2019, Essence showed the following items.

Accounts receivable	$200,000
Accounts payable	135,000
Bank loan	100,000

What is the § 481(a) adjustment for this change in accounting method? Be sure to state whether it is positive or negative.

31. **LO.4** On December 30, 2020, Whitney sold a piece of property for $85,000. Her basis in the property was $40,000, and she incurred $1,200 in selling expenses. The buyer paid $5,000 down with the balance payable in $10,000 installments over the next eight years. In addition, the buyer assumed a $15,000 mortgage on the property. Under the installment sales method, what is the total contract price, the total gain on the sale, and the amount of gain reported in 2020? Round any division to four decimal places, and use that amount in subsequent computations.

32. **LO.4** In 2020, Skylar sold an apartment building for $20,000 cash and a $300,000 note due in two years. Skylar's cost of the property was $250,000, and he had deducted depreciation of $150,000, $60,000 of which was in excess of what the straight-line amount would have been.
    a. Under the installment sales method, what is Skylar's total realized gain?
    b. In 2020, how much § 1250 gain does Skylar recognize? How much § 1231 gain does he recognize?

33. **LO.4** Mason canceled a note issued by Emma (Mason's niece) that arose in connection with the sale of property. At the time of the cancellation, the note had a basis to Mason of $30,000, a face amount of $55,000, and a fair market value of $42,000. Presuming that the initial sale by Mason qualified as an installment sale, how much gain does the cancellation result in for Mason?

34. **LO.5** Jebali Corporation, a calendar year taxpayer utilizing the completed contract method of accounting, constructed a building for Samson, Inc., under a long-term contract. The gross contract price was $2,300,000. Jebali finished construction in 2020 at a cost of $2,100,000. However, Samson insisted that Jebali redo the doorway; otherwise, the contract price would be reduced. The estimated cost of redoing the doorway is $80,000. In 2021, the dispute is settled and Jebali fixed the doorway at a cost of $65,000.
    a. How much must Jebali include in gross income for these items? What amount of deductions is Jebali allowed for 2020?
    b. In 2021, how much must Jebali include in gross income? What amount of expenses can Jebali deduct in that year?

35. **LO.5** Shumpert, Inc., entered into a contract that was to take two years to complete, with an estimated cost of $900,000. The contract price was $1,300,000. Costs of the contract for 2019, the first year, totaled $675,000.
    a. What was the gross profit reported by the percentage of completion method for 2019?
    b. After the contract was completed at the end of 2020 at a total cost of $950,000, what was the gross profit reported by the percentage of completion method for 2020?

36. **LO.6** The taxpayer's ending inventory is valued as follows. Under the lower of cost or market method, what is the value of the taxpayer's inventory?

Item	Cost	Market
Rakes	$8,100	$7,900
Shovels	$3,800	$4,300
Hoes	$6,000	$6,250

37. **LO.6** Shondee Corporation uses the lower of cost or market and FIFO inventory methods. At the end of 2019, the FIFO cost of the ending inventory was $181,000, and the market value of the inventory was $160,000. The corporation switched to LIFO in 2020. As a result, how much must Shondee add to its gross income for each of the years 2020, 2021, and 2022?

Problems

38. **LO.1** Red, White, and Blue are unrelated corporations engaged in real estate development. The three corporations formed a joint venture (treated as a partnership) to develop a tract of land. Assuming that the venture does not have a natural business year, what tax year must the joint venture adopt under the following circumstances?

		Tax Year Ending	Interest in Joint Venture
a.	Red	March 31	60%
	Blue	June 30	20%
	White	October 31	20%
b.	Red	October 31	30%
	White	September 30	40%
	Blue	January 31	30%

Decision Making   39. **LO.1, 7** The Cardinal Wholesale Company is an S corporation that began business on March 1, 2020. Robert, a calendar year taxpayer, owns 100% of the Cardinal stock. He has $400,000 taxable income from other sources each year. Robert will work approximately 30 hours a week for the corporation. Cardinal sells swimming pool supplies, and its natural business year ends in September. Approximately 80% of Cardinal's gross receipts occur in June through September.

a.   What tax year should Cardinal elect, assuming that Robert anticipates the company producing a net profit for all years?

b.   What tax year should Cardinal elect, assuming that it will lose $10,000 a month for the first 12 months and an average of $5,000 a month for the next 12 months? In the third year, the corporation will earn taxable income.

40. **LO.1** In 2019, Juan entered into a contract to write a book. The publisher advanced Juan $50,000, which was to be recovered out of future royalties. If the book was not completed by the end of 2020, however, Juan would be required to repay the publisher for the advance. Juan did not complete the book in 2020, and in accordance with the agreement, he repaid the $50,000 to the publisher in 2021. Juan is a cash basis taxpayer. What are the tax consequences to Juan of the repayment under the following assumptions?

a.   Juan's marginal tax rate was 15% in 2019 and 35% in 2021.

b.   Juan's marginal tax rate was 35% in 2019 and 12% in 2021.

41. **LO.2** Gold, Inc., is an accrual basis taxpayer. In 2020, an employee accidentally spilled hazardous chemicals on leased property. The chemicals destroyed trees on neighboring property, resulting in $30,000 of damages. In 2020, the owner of the property sued Gold, Inc., for the $30,000. Gold's attorney believes that it is liable and that the only issue is whether the neighbor will also seek punitive damages that could be as much as three times the actual damages. In addition, as a result of the spill, Gold was in violation of its lease and was therefore required to pay the landlord $15,000. However, the amount due for the lease violation is not payable until the termination of the lease in 2022. None of these costs were covered by insurance.

    Jeff Stuart, the president of Gold, Inc., is generally familiar with the accrual basis tax accounting rules and is concerned about when the company can deduct the amounts the company is required to pay as a result of this environmental disaster. Write Mr. Stuart a letter explaining these issues. Gold's address is 200 Elm Avenue, San Jose, CA 95192.

Communications

42. **LO.2** Compute Mary's income or deductions for 2020 using (1) the cash basis and (2) the accrual basis for each of the following.

a. In May 2020, Mary paid a license fee of $1,200 for the period June 1, 2020, through May 31, 2021.

b. In December 2020, Mary collected $10,000 for January 2021 rents. In January 2020, Mary collected $2,000 for December 2020 rents.

c. In June 2020, Mary paid $7,200 for an office equipment service contract for the period July 1, 2020, through December 31, 2021.

d. In June 2020, Mary purchased office furniture for $273,000. She paid $131,000 in cash and gave a $142,000 interest-bearing note for the balance. The office furniture has a MACRS cost recovery period of seven years. Mary did not make the § 179 election and elected not to take additional first-year depreciation.

43. **LO.2, 5** Which accounting method (cash or accrual) would you recommend for the following businesses?

a. A gift shop with average annual gross receipts of $900,000.

b. An accounting partnership with average annual gross receipts of $12,000,000.

c. A drywall subcontractor who works on residences and records annual gross receipts of $3,000,000.

d. An incorporated insurance agency with average annual gross receipts of $28,000,000.

e. A sole proprietor operating a retail clothing store with average annual gross receipts of $12,000,000.

f. A sole proprietor operating a widget manufacturing plant with average annual gross receipts of $27,000,000.

Critical Thinking

44. **LO.2** Blue Company, an architectural firm, has a bookkeeper who maintains a cash receipts and disbursements journal. At the end of the year (2020), the company hires you to convert the cash receipts and disbursements into accrual basis revenues and expenses. The total cash receipts are summarized as follows.

Decision Making

Cash sales	$150,000
Collections on accounts receivable	350,000
Bank loan	90,000
Total cash receipts	$590,000

    The accounts receivable from customers at the end of the year are $120,000. You note that the accounts receivable at the beginning of the year were $190,000. The cash sales included $30,000 of prepayments for services to be provided over the period January 1, 2020, through December 31, 2022.

a.   Compute the company's accrual basis gross income for 2020.

b.   Would you recommend that Blue use the cash method or the accrual method? Why?

c.   The company does not maintain an allowance for uncollectible accounts. Would you recommend that such an allowance be established for tax purposes? Explain.

45.   **LO.2** How do the all events and economic performance requirements apply to the following transactions by an accrual basis taxpayer?

a.   The company guarantees its products for six months. At the end of 2020, customers had made valid claims for $600,000 that were not paid until 2021. Also, the company estimates that another $400,000 in claims from 2020 sales will be filed and paid in 2021.

b.   The accrual basis taxpayer reported $200,000 in corporate taxable income for 2020. The state income tax rate was 6%. The corporation paid $7,000 in estimated state income taxes in 2020 and paid $2,000 on 2019 state income taxes when it filed its 2019 state income tax return in March 2020. The company filed its 2020 state income tax return in March 2021 and paid the remaining $5,000 of its 2020 state income tax liability.

c.   An employee was involved in an accident while making a sales call. The company paid the injured victim $15,000 in 2020 and agreed to pay the victim $15,000 a year for the next nine years.

46.   **LO.3** Ross Company is a C corporation providing property management services. Ross has used the cash method since inception because its gross receipts did not exceed $26,000,000. This year its average annual gross receipts for the prior three years crossed the $26,000,000 mark, requiring Ross to change from the cash method to the accrual method. At the end of its prior year, Ross had accounts receivable of $850,000 and accounts payable of $540,000.

a.   Compute and explain the adjustment to taxable income that Ross must make due to the change in accounting method.

b.   When must Ross include this adjustment in its income?

Decision Making   47.   **LO.2, 3** Raven Finance Company experiences bad debts of about 3% of its outstanding loans. At the end of the year, the company had outstanding receivables of $18,000,000. This balance included $2,000,000 of accrued interest receivable. Raven's loan loss reserve for the year was computed as follows.

Balance, January 1, 2020	$500,000
Accounts written off as uncollectible	
Loans made in 2020	(20,000)
Loans made in prior years	(40,000)
Collections on loans previously written off	15,000
Adjustment to required balance	85,000
Balance, December 31, 2020	$540,000

a.   Determine the effects of the above on Raven's taxable income for 2020.

b.   Assume that Raven has used the reserve method to compute its taxable income for the 10 years the company has been in existence. In 2020, you begin preparing Raven's tax return. What should be done on the return with regard to the reserve?

Communications   48.   **LO.2, 3, 6** Jeffrey Boyd, the president of Eagle Furniture Company (average annual gross receipts of $30,000,000), has prepared the company's financial statements and income tax returns for the past 15 years. In July 2021, however, he hires you to prepare the 2020 corporate income tax return because he has not studied taxes for over 20 years and suspects that the rules may have changed. Eagle uses the accrual method of accounting. Based on an initial examination of Eagle's trial balance and some account analyses, you have determined that the following items may require adjustments.

- The company uses the FIFO inventory method, as valued at cost. However, all freight expenses on incoming merchandise have been expensed for the 15 years the company has been in business.
- The company experiences inventory shrinkage (due to breakage and theft) of about 1% of sales each year. The shrinkage is not taken into account until the company takes a physical inventory each October, but the corporation's fiscal year ends January 31.
- The company has used an allowance for uncollectible accounts, which has a balance of $60,000. In the past, the company has been able to accurately predict its actual bad debt expense.
- The company sells a three-year service contract on its appliances. The company treats $\frac{1}{36}$ of the contract price as earned each month. At the beginning of the year, the company had $120,000 in its account for unearned revenues from the service contracts.
- The company deducts its state income tax in the year paid. Thus, the 2020 state income tax expense includes the estimated taxes paid in 2020 and the additional amount paid in 2020 on 2019 taxes.

Write a letter to Mr. Boyd, explaining what adjustments will be required and how they will be implemented. The address of Eagle Furniture Company is 1000 East Maryland Street, Evansville, IL 47722.

49. **LO.4, 7** Floyd, a cash basis taxpayer, has received an offer to purchase his land.   *Decision Making* The cash basis buyer will pay him either $100,000 at closing or $50,000 at closing and $56,000 two years after the date of closing. If Floyd recognizes the entire gain in the current year, his marginal tax rate will be 25% (combined Federal and state rates). However, if he spreads the gain over the two years, his combined marginal tax rate on the gain will be only 20%. Floyd does not consider the buyer a credit risk, and he understands that shifting the gain to next year with an installment sale will save taxes. Still, he realizes that the deferred payment will, in effect, earn only $6,000 for waiting two years for the other $50,000. Floyd believes he can earn a 10% before-tax rate of return on his after-tax cash. Floyd's adjusted basis for the land is $25,000, the buyer is also a cash basis taxpayer, and the short-term Federal rate is 4%. Floyd has asked you to evaluate the two alternatives on an after-tax basis.

50. **LO.4, 7** Ted purchased equipment and used materials to develop a patent. The   *Decision Making* development costs were deducted on prior returns. The bases and fair market values of the assets are presented below.

Assets	Fair Market Value		Basis
Equipment	$350,000	Cost	$ 350,000
		Less: Depreciation	(250,000)
Patent	250,000		–0–
	$600,000		$ 100,000

Sarah has made an offer to purchase the assets. Under one plan, she would pay $200,000 now and $400,000 plus interest at 5% (the Federal rate) in one year. Alternatively, Ted would incorporate the assets and then sell the stock to Sarah.

Incorporating the assets would not be a taxable event to Ted, and his basis in the stock would equal his basis in the assets of $100,000. The corporation's basis in the assets would also be $100,000, the same as Ted's basis for the stock. Because the corporation would have a basis in the assets of less than the fair market value (and therefore, there would be less depreciation and amortization than with an asset sale by Ted), Sarah would pay $200,000 in the current year but only $350,000, plus interest at 5%, in one year. Assume that Ted's combined Federal and state marginal tax rate is 35% and his combined capital gain tax rate is 20%.

a. What is Ted's gain in the year of sale from the installment sale of his assets?

b. Assuming that Ted's time value of money is 5%, would he prefer the sale of the assets or the sale of the stock? Why?

51. **LO.4** Kay, who is not a real estate dealer, sold an apartment house to Polly during the current year (2020). The closing statement for the sale is as follows.

Total selling price		$ 190,000
Add: Polly's share of property taxes (six months) paid by Kay		3,000
Less: Kay's 8% mortgage assumed by Polly	$55,000	
Polly's refundable binder ("earnest money") paid in 2019	1,000	
Polly's 8% installment note given to Kay	99,000	
Kay's real estate commissions and attorney's fees	8,000	(163,000)
Cash paid to Kay at closing		$ 30,000
Cash due from Polly = $30,000 + $8,000 expenses		$ 38,000

During 2020, Kay collected $9,000 in principal on the installment note and $2,000 of interest. Kay's basis in the property was $110,000 [$125,000 − $15,000 (depreciation)]. The Federal rate is 6%.

a. Compute the following.
1. Total gain.
2. Contract price.
3. Payments received in the year of sale.
4. Recognized gain in the year of sale and the character of such gain.

(*Hint:* Think about the manner in which the property taxes are handled before you begin your computations.)

b. Same as parts (a)(2) and (3), except that Kay's basis in the property was $35,000.

Critical Thinking

52. **LO.4** On June 30, 2020, Kelly sold property for $240,000 cash and a $960,000 note due on September 30, 2021. The note pays 6% interest, which is higher than the Federal rate. Kelly's cost of the property was $400,000. She is concerned that Congress may increase the tax rate that will apply when the note is collected. Kelly's after-tax rate of return on investments is 6%.

a. What can Kelly do to avoid the expected higher tax rate?

b. Assuming that Kelly's marginal combined Federal and state tax rate is 25% in 2020, how much would the tax rates need to increase to make the option identified in part (a) advisable?

Decision Making

53. **LO.4** On December 30, 2019, Maud sold land to her son, Charles, for $50,000 cash and a 7% installment note for $350,000, payable over 10 years. Maud's cost of the land was $150,000. In October 2021, after Charles had paid $60,000 on the principal of the note, he received an offer to sell the land for $500,000 cash. What advice can you provide Charles that will minimize the present value of the tax liability for himself and Maud?

54. **LO.4** George sold land to an unrelated party in 2019. His basis in the land was $45,000, and the selling price was $120,000—$30,000 payable at closing and $30,000 (plus 10% interest) due January 1, 2020, 2021, and 2022. What would be the tax consequences of the following? [Treat each part independently, and assume that (1) George did not elect out of the installment method and (2) the installment obligations have values equal to their face amounts. Ignore interest in your calculations.]

   a. In 2020, George borrowed $40,000 from the bank. The loan was partially secured by the installment notes, but George was personally liable for the loan.

   b. In 2020, George gave to his daughter the right to collect all future payments on the installment obligations.

   c. On December 31, 2020, George received the payment due on January 1, 2021. On December 15, 2021, George died, and the remaining installment obligation was transferred to his estate. The estate collected the amount due on January 1, 2022.

55. **LO.5** The Wren Construction Company reports its income by the completed contract method. At the end of 2020, the company completed a contract to construct a building at a total cost of $800,000. The contract price was $1,200,000, and the customer paid Wren $900,000. However, the customer refused to accept the work and would not pay anything else on the contract because she claimed that the roof did not meet specifications. Wren's engineers estimated that it would cost $140,000 to bring the roof up to the customer's standards. In 2021, the dispute was settled in the customer's favor; the roof was improved at a cost of $150,000, and the customer accepted the building and paid the remaining $300,000.

   a. What would be the effects of the above on Wren's taxable income for 2020 and 2021?

   b. Same as part (a), except that Wren had $1,100,000 of accumulated costs under the contract at the end of 2020.

56. **LO.5** Rust Company is a real estate construction company. Rust uses the completed contract method, and the contracts require 18 months to complete.   Communications

   a. Which of the following costs would be allocated to construction in progress by Rust?

      1. The payroll taxes on direct labor.
      2. The current services pension costs for employees whose wages are included in direct labor.
      3. Accelerated depreciation on equipment used on contracts.
      4. Freight charges on materials assigned to contracts.
      5. The past service costs for employees whose wages are included in direct labor.
      6. Bidding expenses for contracts awarded.

   b. Assume that Rust generally builds commercial buildings under contracts with the owners and reports the income using the completed contract method. The company is considering building a series of similar stores for a retail chain. The gross profit margin would be a low percentage, but the company's gross receipts would triple. Write a letter to your client, Rust Company, explaining the tax accounting implications of entering into these contracts. Rust's mailing address is PO Box 1000, Harrisonburg, VA 22807.

57. **LO.5** On March 31, 2018, Big Boats Company entered into a contract with Vacations Unlimited to produce a state-of-the-art cruise ship to be completed within three years. Big Boats estimated the total cost of building the ship at $300,000,000. The contract price was $400,000,000. The ship was completed on February 15, 2021.

   a.   What tax accounting method must Big Boats use for the contract? Why?

   b.   Using the financial data provided relating to the contract's performance, complete the following schedule.

Date	Total Costs Incurred to Date	Total Percentage of Contract Completed	Current-Year Revenue Accrued	Current-Year Costs Deductible
12/31/18	$ 90,000,000	_____	_____	_____
12/31/19	150,000,000	_____	_____	_____
12/31/20	270,000,000	_____	_____	_____
12/31/21	360,000,000	N/A	_____	_____

   c.   What are the consequences of the total cost of $360,000,000 exceeding the estimated total cost of $300,000,000?

58. **LO.5** Ostrich Company makes gasoline storage tanks. Everything produced is under contract (that is, the company does not produce any tanks until it gets a contract for a product). Ostrich makes three basic models. However, the tanks must be adapted to each individual customer's location and needs (e.g., the location of the valves and the quality of the materials and insulation). Discuss the following issues relative to Ostrich's operations.

   a.   An examining IRS agent contends that each of the company's contracts is to produce a "unique product." What difference does it make whether the product is unique or a "shelf item"?

   b.   Producing one of the tanks takes over one year from start to completion, and the total cost is in excess of $1,000,000. What costs must be capitalized for this contract that are not subject to capitalization for a contract with a shorter duration and lower cost?

   c.   What must Ostrich do with the costs of bidding on contracts?

   d.   Ostrich frequently makes several cost estimates for a contract, using various estimates of materials costs. These costs fluctuate almost daily. Assuming that Ostrich must use the percentage of completion method to report the income from the contract, what will be the consequence if the company uses the highest estimate of a contract's cost and the actual cost is closer to the lowest estimated cost?

Communications
Decision Making

59. **LO.5, 7** Swallow Company is a large real estate construction company that has made an S election. The company reports its income using the percentage of completion method. In 2021, the company completed a contract at a total cost of $4,800,000. The contract price was $7,200,000. At the end of 2020, the year the contract was begun, Swallow estimated that the total cost of the contract would be $5,400,000. Total accumulated cost on the contract at the end of 2020 was $1,800,000. The relevant tax rate is 35%, and the relevant Federal interest rate is 5%. Assume that all income tax returns were filed and taxes were paid on March 15 following the end of the calendar tax year.

   a.   Compute the gross profit on the contract for 2020 and 2021.

   b.   Compute the lookback interest due or receivable with the 2021 tax return.

c. Before bidding on a contract, Swallow generally makes three estimates of total contract costs: (1) optimistic, (2) pessimistic, and (3) most likely (based on a blending of optimistic and pessimistic assumptions). The company has asked you to write a letter explaining which of these estimates should be used for percentage of completion purposes. In writing your letter, you should consider the fact that Swallow is incorporated and has made an S election. Therefore, the income and deductions flow through to the shareholders who are all individuals in the 35% marginal tax bracket. The relevant Federal interest rate is 8%. Swallow's mailing address is 400 Front Avenue, Ashland, OR 97520.

60. **LO.6** Grouse Company is a furniture retailer whose average annual gross receipts for the three preceding years exceeded $26,000,000. In the current tax year, the company purchased merchandise with an invoice price of $15,000,000, less a 2% discount for early payment. However, the company had to borrow on a bank line of credit and paid $150,000 interest to take advantage of the discount for early payment. Freight on the merchandise purchased totaled $360,000. For September, Grouse agreed to pay the customer's freight on goods sold. The total cost of this freight-out was $70,000.

The company has three stores and operates a warehouse where it stores goods. The cost of operating the warehouse was $240,000. The $240,000 includes labor, depreciation, taxes, and insurance on the building. The cost of the purchasing operations totaled $420,000. The jurisdiction where the company operates imposes a tax on inventories on hand as of January 1. The inventory tax for this year is $24,000. The invoice cost of goods on hand at the end of the year is $3,000,000.

Compute Grouse's ending inventory using the FIFO method.

61. **LO.6, 7** Lavender Manufacturing Company began business in the current year. The   Decision Making
company uses the simplified method to allocate mixed services costs to production. The company's costs and expenses for the year were as follows.

Direct labor	$ 3,000,000
Direct materials	4,000,000
Factory supervision	800,000
Property tax on factory	100,000
Personnel department	400,000
Computer operations	250,000
General administration	550,000
Marketing	800,000
State income tax	200,000
	$10,100,000

a. Determine Lavender's total production costs for the year.

b. Assume that the hourly pay for direct labor is much lower than the hourly pay for employees in general administration and that the employee turnover is much higher for production employees than for general administration employees. How should these facts affect the company's decision to use the simplified mixed services method to allocate mixed services costs to production?

62. **LO.6** Silver Creek Ranch LLC is a small, family-owned cattle ranch that began   Critical Thinking
operations in the current year. The ranch grows hay that will be fed to its purebred cattle. It will take approximately three years to build up the herd and to begin producing a positive cash flow. The owners' other income will equal their deductions, so they will not be able to utilize farm losses for the first three years. The owners have asked you to discuss the Federal income tax accounting issues related to their cattle business.

63. **LO.3, 6** In 2020, Gail changed from the lower of cost or market FIFO method to the LIFO inventory method. The ending inventory for 2019 was:

Item	FIFO Cost	Replacement Cost	Lower of Cost or Market
A	$26,000	$15,000	$15,000
B	52,000	55,000	52,000
C	30,000	7,000	7,000
			$74,000

Item C was damaged goods, and the replacement cost used was actually the estimated selling price of the goods. The actual cost to replace item C was $32,000.

a. What is the correct beginning inventory for 2020 under the LIFO method?

b. What immediate tax consequences (if any) will result from the switch to LIFO?

Communications   64. **LO.4, 7** Your client, Bob Young, is negotiating a sale of investment real estate for $12,000,000. Bob believes that the buyer would pay cash of $8,000,000 and a note for $4,000,000 or $3,000,000 cash and a note for $9,000,000. The notes will pay interest at slightly above the market rate. Bob realizes that the second option involves more risks of collection, but he is willing to accept that risk if the tax benefits of the installment sale are substantial. Write a letter to Bob advising him of the tax consequences of choosing the lower down payment and larger note option, assuming that he has no other installment receivables. Bob's address is 200 Jerdone, Gettysburg, PA 17325.

65. **LO.2, 4** Ven Company is a retailer. In 2020, its before-tax net income for financial reporting purposes was $600,000. This included a $150,000 gain from the sale of land held for several years as a possible plant site. The cost of the land was $100,000, the contract price for the sale was $250,000, and the company collected $120,000 in the year of sale. The income per books also included $90,000 from a 24-month service contract entered into in July 2019 (the customer paid $180,000 in advance for this contract). The addition to the allowance for uncollectible accounts for the year was $70,000, and the actual accounts written off totaled $40,000.

Make the necessary adjustments to the before-tax net income per books to compute Ven's taxable income for the year.

Research Problems

Note: Solutions to the Research Problems can be prepared by using the Thomson Reuters Checkpoint™ online tax research database, which accompanies this textbook. Solutions can also be prepared by using research materials found in a typical tax library.

Research Problem 1. You recently obtained a new client that operates a chain of convenience stores that sell food and vehicle fuel. You notice that the company has a customer card program whereby customer purchases of fuel are entered on the card. For each gallon purchased, the customer is allowed a $0.05 discount per gallon purchased within the next three months. The client treats the $0.05 discount as "earned" by the customer (and deductible by the store) when the purchase is made, which gives the customer the right to the discount. The client justifies this as clearly reflecting the company's income because an obligation arises when the gasoline is purchased and the right to the future discount is earned. Is the client's accounting method correct? Explain.

Research Problem 2. Your client is a manufacturer. For several years, the company buried empty paint cans on its property. The paint was used in the production process. Recently, a state environmental agency informed the company that it was required to dig up the paint cans and decontaminate the land. The company spent a substantial amount for this environmental cleanup in the current year. An IRS agent contends that the cost must be added to the basis in the land because the cleanup improved the land. The company's CFO has asked you to determine whether any authority exists that would support a current deduction for these costs.

Research Problem 3. In 2020, your client, Clear Corporation, changed from the cash to the accrual method of accounting for its radio station. The company had a positive § 481 adjustment of $2,400,000 as a result of the change and began amortizing the adjustment in 2020. In 2021, Clear received an offer to purchase the assets of the radio station business (this would be considered a sale of a trade or business under § 1060). If the offer is accepted, Clear plans to purchase a satellite television business. Clear has asked you to explain the consequences of the sale of the radio station on the amortization of the § 481 adjustment.

Use internet tax resources to address the following questions. Look for reliable websites and blogs of the IRS and other government agencies, media outlets, businesses, tax professionals, academics, think tanks, and political outlets.

Research Problem 4. The U.S. tax system allows many businesses to use the cash method of accounting. Find another country that allows some businesses to use the cash method, and explain how that system compares to the U.S. system. E-mail your answer to your instructor, also noting the country and the references you used.

Communications

Research Problem 5. More than one president and others have called for repeal of the LIFO method for Federal income tax purposes. Conduct an internet search to find arguments for and against this proposal. Prepare a summary of these arguments. E-mail your document to your instructor. Provide citations for the items you found.

Communications

Becker CPA Review Question

Becker.

1. Paula has sales that qualify to be reported on the installment basis. In year 2, installment sales were $40,000 with a cost of $30,000. In year 3, installment sales were $50,000 with a cost of $25,000. Collections in year 2 were in the amount of $30,000. Collections in year 3 were $10,000 on the year 2 sales and $30,000 on the year 3 sales. How much deferred gross profit exists as of the end of year 2?

a. $2,500
b. $5,000
c. $7,500
d. $10,000

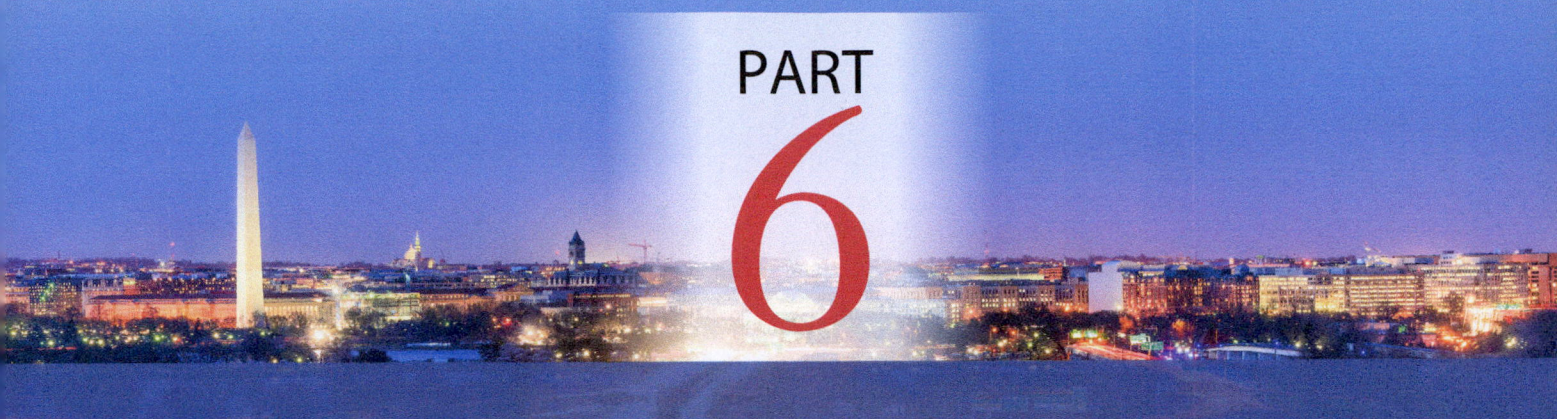

PART 6

CORPORATIONS

CHAPTER **17**

Corporations: Introduction and Operating Rules

CHAPTER **18**

Corporations: Organization and Capital Structure

CHAPTER **19**

Corporations: Distributions Not in Complete Liquidation

CHAPTER **20**

Corporations: Distributions in Complete Liquidation and an Overview of Reorganizations

A business must choose the legal and tax form in which it will operate. Part 6 of this text examines the effects of this choice, especially in context of the deduction for qualified business income. The discussion then turns to the operating rules that apply to C corporations and to the effects of various capital transactions on the entity and its shareholders. Part 6 also discusses the Federal income tax effects of changes in the corporation's capital structure.

CHAPTER

17

Corporations: Introduction and Operating Rules

LEARNING OBJECTIVES: *After completing Chapter 17, you should be able to:*

LO.1 Compare the taxation of individuals and corporations.

LO.2 List and apply the tax rules unique to corporations.

LO.3 Compute the corporate income tax.

LO.4 Explain the operation of the accumulated earnings and personal holding company taxes.

LO.5 Describe the reporting process for corporations.

LO.6 Determine the impact of tax return positions on corporate financial statements.

LO.7 Evaluate corporations as an entity form for minimizing income taxes on businesses.

CHAPTER OUTLINE

17-1 An Introduction to the Income Taxation of Corporations, 17-2
17-1a An Overview of Corporate versus Individual Income Tax Treatment, 17-2
17-1b Specific Provisions Compared, 17-3
17-1c Accounting Periods and Methods, 17-4
17-1d Capital Gains and Losses, 17-5
17-1e Recapture of Depreciation, 17-6
17-1f Business Interest Expense Limitation, 17-6
17-1g Passive Activity Losses, 17-8
17-1h Charitable Contributions, 17-9
17-1i Excessive Executive Compensation, 17-11
17-1j Net Operating Losses, 17-12
17-1k Deductions Available Only to Corporations, 17-12

17-2 Determining the Corporate Income Tax Liability, 17-18
17-2a Corporate Income Tax Rates, 17-18
17-2b Alternative Minimum Tax, 17-19
17-2c Restrictions on Corporate Accumulations, 17-19
17-2d Consolidated Returns, 17-20

17-3 Procedural Matters, 17-23
17-3a Filing Requirements for Corporations, 17-23
17-3b Estimated Tax Payments, 17-24
17-3c Schedule M–1—Reconciliation of Income (Loss) per Books with Income per Return, 17-24
17-3d Schedule M–2—Analysis of Unappropriated Retained Earnings per Books, 17-25
17-3e Schedule M–3—Net Income (Loss) Reconciliation for Corporations with Total Assets of $10 Million or More, 17-26
17-3f Income Taxes in the Financial Statements, 17-28

17-4 Tax Planning, 17-34
17-4a Corporate versus Noncorporate Forms of Business Organization, 17-34
17-4b Operating the Corporation, 17-35

RYAN MCVAY/PHOTODISC/GETTY IMAGES

A Half-Baked Idea?

Samantha Johnson owns Skylark Bakery. Currently, the bakery is operated as a sole proprietorship and generates an annual operating profit of $100,000. In addition, the bakery earns annual dividends of $5,000 from investing excess working capital in the stock of publicly traded corporations. These stock investments typically are held for a minimum of three to four months before funds are required for the business. As a result of earning income from other business ventures and investments, Samantha is in the 37 percent marginal tax bracket before considering bakery operations. In the past, Samantha has withdrawn $50,000 annually from the bakery, which she regards as reasonable payment for her services.

Samantha has asked you about the tax consequences of conducting the business as a regular (C) corporation. Based on the information given, what would be the annual income tax savings (or cost) of operating the bakery as a corporation? For purposes of this analysis, use the 2020 tax rates and ignore any employment tax or state tax considerations.

Read the chapter and formulate your response.

As discussed in Chapter 15, the distinctions among forms of business organizations are important. Chapter 17 begins a sequence of chapters focusing on corporations. Subchapter C of the Internal Revenue Code is devoted to the tax treatment of regular corporations (or C corporations). The chapter begins with an introduction to the income taxation of corporations, including the determination of taxable income. We then discuss calculating the tax liability of a corporation and special rules designed to prevent corporations and their shareholders from avoiding the double tax on dividend distributions. Finally, we discuss various procedural matters that a corporate taxpayer faces, including tax return filing requirements, estimated tax payments, reconciling book income to taxable income, and special disclosure schedules on the tax return.

LO.1

Compare the taxation of individuals and corporations.

17-1 AN INTRODUCTION TO THE INCOME TAXATION OF CORPORATIONS

When examining how corporations are treated under the Federal income tax law, a useful approach is to compare their treatment with that applicable to individual taxpayers. In addition, tax provisions that are unique to corporations must be addressed.

17-1a An Overview of Corporate versus Individual Income Tax Treatment

The corporate and individual tax formulas appear in Exhibit 17.1, and the following discussion highlights similarities and differences between the two formulas.

Similarities

Gross income of a corporation is determined in much the same manner as it is for individuals. As a result, gross income includes compensation for services rendered, business income, gains from selling property, interest, rents, royalties, and dividends. Although both individuals and corporations are entitled to exclusions from gross income, fewer exclusions are available to corporate taxpayers. Interest on municipal bonds and life insurance proceeds are exclusions that apply to both individual and corporate taxpayers.

Gains and losses from property transactions are handled similarly. For example, whether a gain or loss is capital or ordinary depends on the nature of the asset in the

EXHIBIT 17.1	Tax Formulas		
Corporations		**Individuals**	
Income (broadly defined)		Income (broadly defined)	
(Exclusions)		(Exclusions)	
Gross income		Gross income	
(Deductions except for NOL and DRD*)		(Deductions *for* AGI**)	
Taxable income before NOL and DRD		Adjusted gross income	
(Net operating loss deduction)		(Greater of itemized or standard deductions)	
(Dividends received deduction)		(Deduction for qualified business income)	
Taxable income		Taxable income	
Tax on taxable income		Tax on taxable income	
(Tax credits)		(Tax credits)	
Tax due (or refund)		Tax due (or refund)	

*NOL = net operating loss; DRD = dividends received deduction.
**AGI = adjusted gross income.

hands of the taxpayer. In defining what is *not* a capital asset, § 1221 makes no distinction between corporate and noncorporate taxpayers.

In the area of nontaxable exchanges, both corporations and individuals do not recognize gain or loss on a like-kind exchange and may defer realized gain on an involuntary conversion. The disallowance of losses on property sales to related parties (e.g., a corporation and a more-than-50% shareholder) and on wash sales of securities apply to both individual and corporate taxpayers. The exclusion of gain from the sale of a personal residence does not apply to corporations.

Business deductions are allowed for both corporations and individuals. Business deductions include interest (subject to the limitations discussed in text Section 17-1f), certain taxes, losses (including casualty and theft losses), bad debts, cost recovery, charitable contributions, net operating losses, research and experimental expenditures, and some other less common deductions. In the corporate form, there is no distinction between business and nonbusiness bad debts. Like individuals, corporations are not allowed an interest expense deduction if tax-exempt securities are purchased with borrowed funds. The same holds true for entertainment expenses, expenses contrary to public policy, certain accrued expenses between related parties, and lobbying expenses.

Some of the tax credits available to individuals, such as the foreign tax credit, can also be claimed by corporations. Not available to corporations are certain credits that are personal in nature, such as the child and dependent tax credits, the credit for elderly or disabled taxpayers, and the earned income credit.

Differences

The income taxation of corporations and individuals also differs significantly. Individuals are subject to a progressive tax rate structure; a flat tax rate applies to corporations. The corporate tax rate is discussed in more detail later in the chapter (see Examples 25 and 26). Further, individuals are subject to an alternative minimum tax while the corporate AMT was repealed by the Tax Cuts and Jobs Act (TCJA) of 2017.

All allowable corporate deductions are treated as business deductions. As a result, the determination of adjusted gross income (AGI), so essential for individual taxpayers, has no relevance to corporations. Taxable income is computed simply by subtracting all allowable deductions from gross income. Itemized deductions (and the related limitations), the standard deduction, and the deduction for qualified business income do not apply to corporations. In addition, individuals are subject to a limitation on "excess business losses" (which does not apply to corporations).[1]

17-1b Specific Provisions Compared

A comparison of the income taxation of individuals and corporations appears in Concept Summary 17.2 (located at the end of text Section 17-1). Some of the key differences include:

- Accounting periods and methods.
- Capital gains and losses.
- Recapture of depreciation.
- Business interest expense limitation.
- Passive activity losses.
- Charitable contributions.
- Executive compensation.
- Net operating losses.
- Special deductions available only to corporations.

---

[1]§ 461(l).

17-1c Accounting Periods and Methods

Accounting Periods

Corporations generally have the same choices of accounting periods as do individual taxpayers. A corporation may choose a calendar year or a fiscal year for reporting purposes, but corporations normally can have different tax years from those of their shareholders. Newly formed corporations (as new taxpayers) usually can choose an accounting period (IRS consent is not needed). **Personal service corporations (PSCs)** and S corporations, however, are restricted in the use of fiscal years. The rules applicable to S corporations are discussed in Chapter 22.

A PSC is a corporation:[2]

- Formed to provide "personal services" (services in the fields of health, law, engineering, architecture, accounting, actuarial science, performing arts, or consulting);
- Where the services are substantially performed by shareholder-employees; and
- Where more than 10 percent of the stock (in value) is held by shareholder-employees.

To limit deferral of income possibilities, PSCs must generally adopt a calendar year.[3] The exceptions that permit the use of a fiscal year are discussed in Chapter 16.

Accounting Methods

As a general rule, the cash method of accounting is unavailable to corporations.[4] However, several important exceptions apply in the case of the following types of corporations:

- S corporations.
- Corporations engaged in the trade or business of farming or timber.
- Qualified PSCs.
- Corporations with average annual gross receipts of $26 million or less for the most recent three-year period.

In general, entities that maintain inventory for sale to customers are required to use the accrual method of accounting for determining sales and cost of goods sold. However, entities with average annual gross receipts of $26 million or less for the most recent three-year period can use the cash method to account for inventories.[5] See Chapter 16 for additional discussion of this exception.

A corporation using the accrual method of accounting must observe a special rule in dealing with cash basis-related parties. If the corporation has an accrual outstanding at the end of any taxable year with a related party, it cannot claim a deduction until the related party reports the amount as income.[6] This rule is most often encountered when an accrual method corporation deals with a cash method individual who owns (directly or indirectly) more than 50 percent of the corporation's stock. However, in the case of a personal service corporation, *any* shareholder-employee is treated as a related party for purposes of this limitation.

The Big Picture

EXAMPLE 1

Return to the facts of *The Big Picture* on p. 17-1. Assume that Samantha incorporates her business as Skylark Bakery, Inc., a calendar year, accrual method C corporation. Samantha, a cash method taxpayer, owns 100% of the corporation's stock at the end of 2020. On December 31, 2020, Skylark Bakery has accrued a $10,000 bonus to Samantha. Samantha receives the bonus in 2021 and reports it on her 2021 tax return. Skylark Bakery cannot claim a deduction for the $10,000 until 2021.

---

[2]§ 448(d)(2)(A) and Reg. § 1.441–3(d)(1). Any stock held by an employee on any *one day* causes the employee to be a shareholder-employee.

[3]§ 441(i). In some cases, a PSC was able to retain the same year as its fiscal year ending in 1987. See § 444(b)(3).

[4]§ 448(a).

[5]Such an entity can account for inventory as non-incidental materials and supplies or as conforms to its financial accounting for inventories. The average annual gross receipts test was $25 million for taxable years beginning in 2018; the $25 million amount is adjusted for inflation each year and rounded to the nearest $1 million multiple.

[6]§ 267(a)(2).

Accrual basis taxpayers generally must recognize gross income no later than the tax year in which the income is included as income for financial statement purposes. In addition, accrual taxpayers can elect to defer income inclusion of advance payments for goods and services to the end of the tax year following the tax year of receipt.[7]

17-1d Capital Gains and Losses

Capital gains and losses result from the taxable sales or exchanges of capital assets.[8] These gains and losses are classified as long term or short term depending on the holding period. Each year, a taxpayer's short-term gains and losses are combined, and long-term gains and losses are combined. The result is a net short-term capital gain or loss and a net long-term capital gain or loss. If gains *and* losses result (e.g., net short-term capital gain and net long-term capital loss), these amounts are further netted against each other. If instead the results are *all* gains or *all* losses (e.g., net short-term capital loss and net long-term capital loss), no further combination is necessary.

Capital Gains

Individuals pay the required tax using a preferential rate of 0, 15, or 20 percent on net capital gains (i.e., excess of net long-term capital gain over net short-term capital loss).[9] Corporations, however, receive no favorable tax rate on long-term capital gains; this income is taxed at the normal corporate tax rate.

Capital Losses

Net capital losses of corporate and individual taxpayers receive different income tax treatment. Generally, individual taxpayers can deduct up to $3,000 of net capital losses against other income. Any remaining capital losses are carried forward to future years until absorbed by capital gains or by the $3,000 annual deduction. Loss carryovers retain their identity as either long term or short term.[10]

EXAMPLE 2

Robin, an individual, incurs a net long-term capital loss of $7,500 for calendar year 2020. Assuming adequate taxable income, Robin may deduct $3,000 of this loss on her 2020 return. The remaining $4,500 ($7,500 − $3,000) of the loss is carried forward to 2021 and years thereafter until completely deducted. The $4,500 will be carried forward as a long-term capital loss.

Unlike individuals, corporate taxpayers are not permitted to deduct any net capital losses against ordinary income. Capital losses, therefore, can be used only as an offset against capital gains. Corporations, however, carry back net capital losses three years, applying them first to the earliest year. Carryforwards then are allowed for a period of five years from the year of the loss. When carried back or forward, a long-term capital loss is treated as a short-term capital loss.[11]

EXAMPLE 3

Assume the same facts as in Example 2, except that Robin is a corporation. None of the $7,500 long-term capital loss incurred in 2020 can be deducted that year. Robin Corporation may, however, carry back the loss to 2017, 2018, and 2019 (in this order) and offset it against any capital gains recognized in these years.

If the carryback does not exhaust the loss, it may be carried forward to 2021, 2022, 2023, 2024, and 2025 (in this order). The long-term capital loss is treated as short term in any carryover year.

---

[7]This deferral applies only if the advance payment is similarly deferred for financial statement purposes. See Chapter 16 for a detailed discussion of accounting periods and methods.

[8]See Chapter 14 for a detailed discussion of capital gains and losses.

[9]In 2020, the 0% rate applies when taxable income does not exceed $80,000 (married, filing jointly), $53,600 (head of household), and $40,000 (single and married, filing separately). The 20% rate applies only when the taxpayer's taxable income exceeds $496,600 (married, filing jointly), $248,300 (married, filing separately), $469,050 (head of household), and $441,450 (single).

[10]§§ 1211(b) and 1212(b).

[11]§§ 1211(a) and 1212(a).

17-1e **Recapture of Depreciation**

The §§ 1245 and 1250 depreciation recapture rules apply to both individual and corporate taxpayers (see Chapter 14). However, corporations may have more depreciation recapture (ordinary income) on the disposition of § 1250 property than do individuals because of § 291 recapture.

Under § 291, a corporation has additional ordinary income equal to *20 percent* of the excess of (1) the amount of depreciation recapture that would be required *if* § 1245 applied to the disposition (i.e., § 1245 recapture potential) over (2) the amount of depreciation recapture computed under § 1250 (without regard to § 291). As a result, the § 1231 portion of the corporation's gain on the disposition is reduced by the additional recapture.

Under § 1250, recapture is limited to the excess of accelerated depreciation over straight-line depreciation. In general, only straight-line depreciation is allowed for real property placed in service after 1986; thus, there will usually be no § 1250 depreciation recapture. In contrast, all depreciation taken on § 1245 property is subject to recapture.

EXAMPLE 4

Red Corporation purchases nonresidential real property on May 1, 2005, for $800,000. Straight-line depreciation is taken in the amount of $316,239 before the property is sold on October 7, 2020, for $1,200,000.

First, determine the recognized gain:

Sales price		$1,200,000
Less: Adjusted basis—		
Cost of property	$ 800,000	
Less: Cost recovery	(316,239)	(483,761)
Recognized gain		$ 716,239

Second, determine the § 1245 recapture potential. This is the lesser of $716,239 (recognized gain) or $316,239 (cost recovery claimed).

Third, determine the normal § 1250 recapture amount:

Cost recovery taken	$ 316,239
Less: Straight-line cost recovery	(316,239)
§ 1250 ordinary income	$ −0−

Fourth, because the taxpayer is a corporation, determine the ordinary income recognized under § 291:

§ 1245 recapture potential	$ 316,239
Less: § 1250 recapture amount	(−0−)
Excess § 1245 recapture potential	$ 316,239
Apply § 291 percentage	× 20%
Additional ordinary income under § 291	$ 63,248

Red Corporation's recognized gain of $716,239 is accounted for as follows:

Ordinary income under § 1250	$ −0−
Ordinary income under § 291	63,248
§ 1231 gain	652,991
Total recognized gain	$ 716,239

17-1f **Business Interest Expense Limitation**

A limitation on the deduction for business interest applies to all taxpayers.[12] Business interest is interest paid or accrued on trade or business debt. Although the limitation applies to *any* business, the rules are most likely to affect large corporations and flow-through entities due to a small business exception.

---

[12]§ 163(j); the limitation applies to tax years beginning after 2017.

Under § 163(j), the deduction for business interest for any year is limited to the sum of:

1. The taxpayer's *business interest income* for the year,
2. 30 percent of the taxpayer's *adjusted taxable income* for the year, and
3. The taxpayer's *floor plan financing interest* for the year.

Any business interest deduction disallowed by reason of the limitation is treated as business interest paid or accrued in the succeeding tax year. The carryforward period is unlimited.

The business interest deduction limitation does not apply to certain small businesses. In general, the small business exception applies to taxpayers with average gross receipts for the prior three-year period of $26 million or less.[13]

Business Interest Income

"Business interest income" is the amount of interest income includible in gross income for the year that is related to a trade or business. Congress believes that a corporation typically will have neither investment interest income nor investment interest expense; instead, all interest income and interest expense of a corporation is assumed to be part of the corporation's trade or business.[14]

Adjusted Taxable Income

"Adjusted taxable income"[15] is taxable income computed without regard to any:

1. Nonbusiness income, gain, deduction, or loss;
2. Business interest or business interest income;
3. Net operating loss (NOL) deduction;
4. Deduction for qualified business income (§ 199A); and
5. Deduction allowable for depreciation, amortization, or depletion.[16]

The Treasury Department and the IRS are authorized to provide other adjustments to the computation of adjusted taxable income.[17] The 30 percent of adjusted taxable income amount cannot be less than zero.[18]

Floor Plan Financing Interest

Virtually all auto dealers acquire their inventory via debt (known as "floor plan" financing), with the debt being secured by the inventory. Interest on this debt ("floor plan financing interest") is deductible without limitation.

Business Interest Expense Limitation

In 2020, Tangerine Corporation, a calendar year C corporation, has $5,000,000 of adjusted taxable income, $75,000 of business interest income, zero floor plan financing interest, and $600,000 of business interest expense.

Tangerine's business interest deduction limitation is $1,575,000 [$75,000 (business interest income) + $1,500,000 (30% × $5,000,000 adjusted taxable income)]. As a result, Tangerine can deduct all $600,000 of its business interest expense.

EXAMPLE 5

Assume the same facts as in Example 5, except that Tangerine has $2,000,000 of business interest expense. Here, the deduction for business interest is limited to $1,575,000, and the disallowed amount of $425,000 ($2,000,000 − $1,575,000) is carried forward to next year and treated as business interest in that year.

If Tangerine satisfies the small business exception (i.e., had average gross receipts for the prior three-year period of $26,000,000 or less), the limitation on business interest does not apply and the entire $2,000,000 of business interest is deductible in the current year.

EXAMPLE 6

---

[13]§ 163(j)(3). The average annual gross receipts test was $25 million for taxable years beginning in 2018; the $25 million amount is adjusted for inflation each year and rounded to the nearest $1 million multiple.

[14]TCJA of 2017 Joint Explanatory Statement, p. 288. The Joint Explanatory Statement relies on the rationale that since § 163(d)—the investment interest expense limitation—does not apply to corporations, then any interest income and interest expense should be related to the corporation's trade or business activities (not investment activities).

[15]§ 163(j)(8)(A).

[16]The depreciation, amortization, and depletion adjustment only applies to taxable years beginning before January 1, 2022; § 163(j)(8)(A)(v).

[17]§ 163(j)(8)(B). See, for example, Prop.Reg. § 1.163(j)–1(b)(1).

[18]§ 163(j)(1), flush language.

Business Interest Expense Limitation

EXAMPLE 7

In 2020, Eagle Corporation, a calendar year C corporation, has ($1,000,000) of adjusted taxable income, $40,000 of business interest income, zero floor plan financing interest, and $100,000 of business interest expense.

Eagle's business interest deduction limitation is $40,000 [$40,000 (business interest income) + $0 (30% × adjusted taxable income amount, but not less than zero)]. As a result, Eagle's current-year deduction for business interest is limited to $40,000, and the disallowed amount of $60,000 ($100,000 − $40,000) is carried forward to next year and treated as business interest in that year.

If Eagle satisfies the small business exception (i.e., had average gross receipts for the prior three-year period of $26,000,000 or less), the limitation on business interest does not apply and the entire $100,000 of business interest is deductible in the current year.

Other Rules

Flow-Through Entities In the case of a partnership or an S corporation, the business interest deduction limitation applies at the entity level. The general carryforward rule for disallowed business interest does not apply to partnerships (or S corporations); rather, a partner (or S corporation shareholder) can deduct the disallowed interest under a special carryforward rule. A partner's (or S corporation shareholder's) adjusted taxable income is determined without regard to the partner's (or shareholder's) distributive share of the partnership's (or S corporation's) items of income, gain, deduction, or loss.[19]

Trade or Business The term *trade or business* does not include performing services as an employee.[20] As a result, an individual cannot include W–2 wages in adjusted taxable income for purposes of computing the interest deduction limitation. The term also does not include certain real property trades or businesses and certain farming businesses.

17-1g Passive Activity Losses

The passive activity loss rules apply to individual taxpayers, closely held C corporations, and personal service corporations (PSCs; see definition in text Section 17-1c).[21] These rules prevent taxpayers from incorporating to avoid the passive activity loss limitations (refer to Chapter 11). A corporation is *closely held* if, at any time during the last half of the taxable year, more than 50 percent of the value of the corporation's outstanding stock is owned, directly or indirectly, by five or fewer individuals.

PSCs generally cannot deduct passive activity losses against either active income or portfolio income. However, the application of the passive activity loss rules is not as harsh for closely held C corporations (that are not PSCs). They may offset passive activity losses against *net active income*, but not against portfolio income. The special rules applicable to PSCs are recapped in Concept Summary 17.1.

EXAMPLE 8

Brown, a closely held C corporation that is *not* a PSC, has $300,000 of passive activity losses from a rental activity, $200,000 of net active income, and $100,000 of portfolio income. The corporation may offset $200,000 of the $300,000 passive activity loss against the $200,000 of net active income but may not offset the remainder against the $100,000 of portfolio income.

If Brown is a PSC, then none of the $300,000 of passive activity losses is deductible in the current year.

---

[19]§ 163(j)(4).
[20]§ 163(j)(7).

[21]§ 469(a). For S corporations and partnerships, passive activity income or loss flows through to the owners, and the passive activity loss rules are applied at the owner level. For definitions, see § 469(j)(1) (closely held) and § 469(j)(2) (PSC).

Concept Summary 17.1

Special Rules Applicable to Personal Service Corporations (PSCs)

Item	PSC Treatment
Accounting periods	Calendar year is generally required. Fiscal year exceptions are available for a business purpose or under a § 444 election.
Accounting methods	Both cash and accrual methods are generally available. Any PSC shareholder-employee is treated as a related party for purposes of the accrued expenditure limitation.
Passive activity losses	Passive activity loss rules apply.

17-1h Charitable Contributions

Both corporate and individual taxpayers may deduct charitable contributions for the year in which the payment is made. However, an *accrual basis corporation* may claim the deduction in the year *preceding* payment if two requirements are met. First, the contribution must be authorized by the board of directors by the end of that year. Second, it must be paid on or before the due date of the corporation's tax return (i.e., the fifteenth day of the fourth month following the close of its taxable year).[22]

EXAMPLE 9

On December 28, 2020, Peach Company, a calendar year, accrual basis partnership, authorizes a $5,000 donation to the Atlanta Symphony Association (a qualified charitable organization). The donation is made on April 12, 2021.

If Peach Company is a corporation and the December 28, 2020 authorization was made by its board of directors, Peach may claim the $5,000 donation as a deduction for calendar year 2020.

However, if Peach Company is a partnership, the contribution cannot be deducted until 2021.[23]

Property Contributions

Generally, a charitable contribution of property results in a deduction equal to the property's fair market value at the date of the gift. As a result, a contribution of loss property (fair market value less than basis) should be avoided. Instead, the loss property should be sold (allowing the loss to be recognized) and the proceeds contributed to the charity.

EXAMPLE 10

Heron Corporation owns inventory with a basis of $10,000 and a fair market value of $8,000. A charitable contribution of the inventory results in a deductible amount of $8,000, the inventory's fair market value.

However, a sale of the inventory, for a recognized loss of $2,000 ($8,000 amount realized − $10,000 basis), and donation of the sale proceeds, for a charitable deduction of $8,000, results in a combined deduction of $10,000.

Fair market value also is the valuation amount for most charitable contributions of capital gain property. *Capital gain property* is property that, if sold, would result in long-term capital gain or § 1231 gain for the taxpayer.

---

[22]§ 170(a)(2).

[23]Each partner will report an allocable portion of the charitable contribution deduction as of December 31, 2020 (the end of the partnership's tax year). See Chapter 21.

EXAMPLE 11

During the current year, Mallard Corporation donates a parcel of land (a capital asset) to Oakland Community College. Mallard acquired the land five years ago for $60,000, and the fair market value on the date of the contribution is $100,000.

The corporation's charitable contribution deduction (subject to a percentage limitation discussed later) is measured by the asset's fair market value of $100,000, even though the $40,000 appreciation on the land has never been included in Mallard's income.

In two situations, a charitable contribution of capital gain property is measured by the basis of the property rather than fair market value. First, if the taxpayer contributes *tangible personal property* and the charitable organization puts the property to an *unrelated use*, the deduction is limited to the basis of the property. If the use is related to the charity's exempt purpose, the contribution deduction will be based on the property's fair market value. Second, the deduction for charitable contributions of capital gain property to certain private foundations is also limited to the basis of the property.

Contributions of Tangible Personal Property

EXAMPLE 12

During the current year, White Corporation donates a painting worth $200,000 to Western States Art Museum (a qualified organization), which exhibits the painting. White had acquired the painting in 2000 for $90,000. Because the museum put the painting to a related use, White is allowed to deduct $200,000, the fair market value of the painting.

EXAMPLE 13

Assume the same facts as in the previous example, except that White Corporation donates the painting to the American Cancer Society, which sells the painting and deposits the $200,000 proceeds in the organization's general fund.

Here, White's deduction is limited to the $90,000 basis because it contributed tangible personal property that was put to an unrelated use by the charitable organization.

As a general rule, the deduction for a contribution of ordinary income property also is limited to the *basis* of the property. *Ordinary income property* is appreciated property that, if sold, would not result in long-term capital gain (inventory and stock held for 12 months or less are common examples).[24] On certain contributions of inventory by *corporations*, however, the amount of the deduction is equal to the *lesser of* (1) the sum of the property's basis plus 50 percent of the appreciation on the property or (2) twice the property's basis. The following inventory contributions qualify for this increased contribution amount:

- A contribution of property to a charitable organization whose exempt purpose includes the care of the ill, the needy, or infants.

- A contribution of tangible personal research property constructed by the corporation to a qualified educational or scientific organization that uses the property for research or experimentation or for research training.[25]

EXAMPLE 14

Lark Corporation, a clothing retailer, donates children's clothing to the Salvation Army to be used to clothe homeless children. Lark's basis in the clothes is $2,000, and the fair market value is $3,000. Lark's deduction is $2,500 [$2,000 basis + 50%($3,000 − $2,000)].

If, instead, the fair market value is $7,000, Lark's deduction is limited to $4,000 (2 × $2,000 basis).

---

[24]In addition, § 1231 property (depreciable property used in a trade or business) is treated as ordinary income property to the extent of any depreciation recaptured under § 1245 or § 1250 (as adjusted under § 291).

[25]The property must be contributed within two years from the date of its construction by the donor, and its original use must begin with the donee. S corporations do not qualify for the increased contribution amount for inventory. These conditions are identified in §§ 170(e)(3) and (4).

Limitations Imposed on Charitable Contribution Deductions

Like individuals, corporations are subject to percentage limits on the charitable contribution deduction.[26] For any tax year, a corporate taxpayer's contribution deduction is limited to 10 percent of taxable income. For this purpose, taxable income is computed without regard to the charitable contribution deduction, any net operating loss carryback or capital loss carryback, and dividends received deduction.

Any contributions in excess of the 10 percent limitation may be carried forward to the five succeeding tax years. Any carryforward is combined with contributions in those years and then subject to the 10 percent limitation. The current year's contributions are always deducted first, with carryover amounts from previous years deducted in order of time.[27]

Annual Limitation and Carryover Rules Illustrated

EXAMPLE 15

During 2020, Orange Corporation (a calendar year taxpayer) had the following income and expenses:

Income from operations	$140,000
Expenses from operations	110,000
Dividends received	10,000
Charitable contributions made in May 2020	6,000

For purposes of the 10% limitation *only*, Orange Corporation's taxable income is $40,000 ($140,000 − $110,000 + $10,000). Consequently, the allowable charitable contribution deduction for 2020 is $4,000 (10% × $40,000). The $2,000 unused portion of the contribution can be carried forward to 2021, 2022, 2023, 2024, and 2025 (in that order) until exhausted.

EXAMPLE 16

Assume the same facts as in Example 15. In 2021, Orange Corporation has taxable income (for purposes of the 10% limitation) of $50,000 and makes a charitable contribution of $4,500. The maximum deduction allowed for 2021 is $5,000 (10% × $50,000).

The $5,000 deduction allowed is made up of the 2021 $4,500 contribution and $500 of the carryforward from 2020. Current-year contributions are always used first. The remaining $1,500 of the 2020 contribution may be carried over until it is used (or until the five-year carryfoward period ends).

17-1i **Excessive Executive Compensation**

A closely held corporation's deduction for shareholder-employee compensation is subject to the reasonableness standard of § 162(a)(1). A second limitation applies to *publicly held corporations*. In general, § 162(m) limits the deductible amount of a publicly held corporation's compensation to any covered employee to $1 million annually. Covered employees are the principal executive officer, the principal financial officer, and the three other most highly compensated officers.[28]

In general, the $1 million maximum applies to compensation, commissions based on individual performance, and performance-based compensation tied to overall company performance. Before 2018, the $1 million limit *excluded* commissions and performance-based compensation. Contracts in place on November 2, 2017, are grandfathered under pre-2018 law as long as there are no material changes to the contract. The limitation also

---

[26]The percentage limitations applicable to individuals and corporations are identified in § 170(b).

[27]The carryover rules relating to all taxpayers are in § 170(d).

[28]An individual is a covered employee if the individual holds one of the principal officer positions at any time during the taxable year. Further, an individual who is a covered employee for any tax year beginning after 2016 remains a covered employee for all future years, including years during which the individual is no longer employed by the corporation and years after the individual has died. For example, the limitation would apply to deferred compensation payments to a covered employee after the individual's departure from the corporation.

does not apply to retirement plan contributions or employer-provided benefits that are excludible from gross income by the employee (e.g., health care benefits).

EXAMPLE 17

Dora is the newly hired chief executive officer of White Corporation, a publicly traded corporation. For the current year, her compensation package consists of:

Cash compensation	$2,700,000
Taxable fringe benefits	200,000
Bonus tied to company performance	5,000,000
Nontaxable fringe benefits	100,000

White Corporation can deduct $1,100,000 of Dora's compensation package ($1,000,000 of the cash compensation, taxable fringe benefits, and bonus) plus the nontaxable fringe benefits of $100,000.

17-1j Net Operating Losses

As for individuals, the net operating loss (NOL) of a corporation generally may be carried forward indefinitely to offset taxable income for those future years. The NOL deduction for any carryover year is limited to 80 percent of taxable income (determined without regard to the NOL deduction) for both individuals and corporations.[29]

Unlike individual taxpayers, however, a corporation:[30]

- Does not adjust its tax loss for the year for any capital losses (since a corporation cannot deduct net capital losses),

- Does not make adjustments for any nonbusiness deductions (as individual taxpayers do), and

- Is allowed to include the dividends received deduction (discussed below) in computing its NOL.

EXAMPLE 18

In 2020, Green Corporation has gross income (including dividends) of $200,000 and deductions of $300,000 excluding the dividends received deduction. Green Corporation had received $100,000 of dividends from Fox, Inc., in which Green holds a 5% stock interest. Green has an NOL computed as follows:

Gross income (including dividends)		$ 200,000
Less: Business deductions	$300,000	
Dividends received deduction		
(50% × $100,000)*	50,000	(350,000)
Taxable income (or loss)		($ 150,000)

*See the discussion of the dividends received deduction beginning on the next page.

The NOL is carried forward to 2021 and future years until it is used up. In addition, the NOL can offset no more than 80% of taxable income (computed without regard to the NOL) in those years.

LO.2

List and apply the tax rules unique to corporations.

17-1k Deductions Available Only to Corporations

Certain deductions are specific to corporate taxpayers, including the dividends received deduction and the organizational expenditures deduction.

---

[29]These rules apply for NOLs arising in tax years ending after 2017. For NOLs arising in prior years, a 2-year carryback and 20-year carryforward apply, and there is no taxable income limitation on the deductibility of the NOL carryovers.

[30]The modifications required to arrive at the amount of NOL that can be carried forward are in § 172(d).

EXHIBIT 17.2	Dividends Received Deduction	

Percentage of Ownership by Corporate Shareholder	Deduction Percentage
Less than 20%	50%
20% or more (but less than 80%)	65%
80% or more*	100%

*The payor corporation must be a member of an affiliated group with the recipient corporation.

Dividends Received Deduction

The purpose of the <mark>dividends received deduction</mark> is to mitigate multiple taxation of corporate income. Without the deduction, dividend income paid to a corporation would be taxed to the recipient corporation, with no corresponding deduction to the distributing corporation. Later, when the recipient corporation distributed the income to its shareholders, the income would *again* be subject to taxation, with no corresponding deduction to the corporation. The dividends received deduction alleviates this inequity.

As Exhibit 17.2 illustrates, the amount of the dividends received deduction depends on the percentage of ownership (voting power and value) the recipient corporate shareholder holds in a *domestic corporation* making the dividend distribution.[31]

The dividends received deduction cannot exceed the taxable income limitation. This limitation is equal to the corporation's taxable income multiplied by the same percentage used to compute the deduction. As a result, if a corporate shareholder owns less than 20 percent of the stock in the distributing corporation, the dividends received deduction is limited to 50 percent of taxable income. For this purpose, taxable income is computed without regard to the NOL deduction, the dividends received deduction, and any capital loss carryback. However, the taxable income limitation does not apply if the corporation has an NOL for the current taxable year.[32]

The following steps are useful in applying these rules:

1. Multiply the dividends received by the deduction percentage.
2. Multiply the taxable income by the deduction percentage.
3. Limit the deduction to the lesser of Step 1 or Step 2, unless deducting the amount derived in Step 1 results in an NOL. If so, the amount derived in Step 1 is used. This sometimes is referred to as the *NOL rule*.

EXAMPLE 19

Red, White, and Blue corporations are three unrelated calendar year corporations. During the year, they report the following information:

	Red Corporation	White Corporation	Blue Corporation
Gross income from operations	$ 400,000	$ 320,000	$ 230,000
Expenses from operations	(340,000)	(340,000)	(340,000)
Dividends received from domestic corporations (less than 20% ownership)	200,000	200,000	200,000
Taxable income before the dividends received deduction	$ 260,000	$ 180,000	$ 90,000

continued

---

[31]§ 243(a). Dividends from foreign corporations generally do not qualify for a dividends received deduction. But see §§ 245 and 245A.

[32]Further, the limitation does not apply in the case of the 100% deduction available to members of an affiliated group. § 246(b).

In determining the dividends received deduction, use the three-step procedure described previously.

	Red Corporation	White Corporation	Blue Corporation
Step 1 (50% × $200,000)	$100,000	$100,000	$100,000
Step 2			
50% × $260,000 (taxable income)	$130,000		
50% × $180,000 (taxable income)		$ 90,000	
50% × $90,000 (taxable income)			$ 45,000
Step 3			
Lesser of Step 1 or Step 2	$100,000	$ 90,000	
Deduction results in an NOL (use Step 1)			$100,000

White Corporation is subject to the 50% of taxable income limitation (Step 2). The NOL rule does not apply because subtracting $100,000 (Step 1) from $180,000 (taxable income before the dividends received deduction) does not yield a negative figure. Blue Corporation qualifies for NOL rule treatment because subtracting $100,000 (Step 1) from $90,000 (taxable income before the dividends received deduction) yields a negative figure.

In summary, each corporation has a dividends received deduction for the year: $100,000 for Red Corporation, $90,000 for White Corporation, and $100,000 for Blue Corporation.

In those cases where the taxable income limitation applies, the taxpayer should consider the proper timing of income and deductions to bring the NOL rule into play. This can result in a significant increase in the amount of a corporation's dividends received deduction.

EXAMPLE 20

Pearl Corporation, a calendar year C corporation, has the following information for the year:

Gross income from operations	$ 200,000
Expenses from operations	(245,000)
Dividends received from domestic corporations (less than 20% ownership)	100,000
Taxable income before dividends received deduction	$ 55,000

Pearl's dividends received deduction is $27,500 [50% × $55,000 (taxable income limitation)].

If, however, Pearl incurs additional expenses of $5,001 (or defers $5,001 of income), its taxable income before the dividends received deduction will be reduced to $49,999. If this occurs, the NOL rule applies and Pearl's dividends received deduction is $50,000 [50% × $100,000 (dividends received)].

No dividends received deduction is allowed unless the corporation has held the stock for more than 45 days.[33] This restriction was enacted to close a tax loophole involving dividends on stock that is held only briefly. When stock is purchased shortly before a dividend record date and soon thereafter sold ex-dividend, a capital loss corresponding to the amount of the dividend often results (ignoring other market valuation changes). If the dividends received deduction was allowed in such cases, the capital loss resulting from the stock sale would exceed the taxable portion of the related dividend income.

---

[33]The stock must be held more than 45 days during the 91-day period beginning on the date that is 45 days before the ex-dividend date (or in the case of preferred stock, more than 90 days during the 181-day period beginning on the date that is 90 days before the ex-dividend date). § 246(c).

EXAMPLE
21

On October 1, 2020, Pink Corporation declares a $1-per-share dividend for shareholders of record as of November 1, 2020, and payable on December 1, 2020. Black Corporation purchases 10,000 shares of Pink stock on October 30, 2020, for $25,000 and sells those 10,000 shares ex-dividend on November 6, 2020, for $15,000. (It is assumed that there is no fluctuation in the market price of the Pink stock other than the dividend element.) The sale results in a short-term capital loss of $10,000 ($15,000 amount realized − $25,000 basis). On December 1, Black receives a $10,000 dividend from Pink.

Without the holding period restriction, Black Corporation would recognize a $10,000 capital loss deduction (subject to the capital loss limitation) but only $5,000 of income [$10,000 dividend − $5,000 dividends received deduction ($10,000 × 50%)], or a $5,000 net loss. However, because Black did not hold the Pink stock for more than 45 days, no dividends received deduction is allowed.

ETHICS & EQUITY Pushing the Envelope on Year-End Planning

As of December of the current year, Larson Corporation (a calendar year taxpayer) has gross income from operations of $497,000, expenses from operations of $596,000, and dividends received from domestic corporations (less than 20 percent ownership) of $200,000.

Currently, Larson does not expect any more income or expenses to be realized by year-end. However, Larson's tax department has suggested that the corporation incur another $1,001 of deductible expenditures before year-end. What is the motivation behind the tax department's recommendation, and is such year-end planning ethical?

Organizational Expenditures Deduction

Expenses incurred in connection with the organization of a corporation normally are capitalized. That they benefit the corporation during its existence seems clear. But how can they be amortized when most corporations possess unlimited life? If a useful life cannot be determined, no deduction is allowed. Section 248 was enacted to solve this problem.

Under § 248, a corporation may *elect* to amortize **organizational expenditures** over the 180-month period beginning with the month in which the corporation begins business.[34] Organizational expenditures include the following:

- Legal services related to organization (e.g., drafting the corporate charter, bylaws, minutes of organizational meetings, and terms of original stock certificates).
- Necessary accounting services.
- Expenses of temporary directors and of organizational meetings of directors or shareholders.
- Fees paid to the state of incorporation.

Expenses that *do not qualify* as organizational expenditures include those connected with issuing or selling shares of stock or other securities (e.g., commissions, professional fees, and printing costs) or with transferring assets to a corporation. These expenses must be capitalized.

The first $5,000 of organizational costs is immediately expensed, with any remaining costs amortized over a 180-month period. However, the $5,000 expensing amount is phased out on a dollar-for-dollar basis when these costs exceed $50,000.

---

[34]The month in which a corporation begins business may not be immediately apparent. Ordinarily, a corporation begins business when it starts the business operations for which it was organized. Reg. § 1.248–1(d). For a similar problem in the Subchapter S area, see Chapter 22.

Stork Corporation (a calendar year C corporation) began business on July 1 of the current year and incurred $52,000 of organizational expenditures. Stork wants to expense as much of these expenditures as possible, electing to amortize any amount it cannot expense. Stork's current-year deduction is $4,633, determined as follows:

Immediate expense [$5,000 − ($52,000 − $50,000)]	$3,000
Amortization [($52,000 − $3,000) ÷ 180] × 6 months in tax year	1,633
Total	$4,633

To qualify for the election, the expenditures must be *incurred* before the end of the tax year in which the corporation begins business. The corporation's method of accounting is of no consequence; an expense incurred by a cash basis corporation in its first tax year qualifies even though it is not paid until a subsequent year. However, this rule could prove to be an unfortunate trap for corporations formed late in the first taxable year. Consider the following example.

Thrush Corporation is formed in December 2020. Qualified organizational expenditures are incurred as follows: $62,000 in December 2020 and $30,000 in January 2021. If Thrush uses the calendar year for tax purposes, only $62,000 of the organizational expenditures can be written off over a period of 180 months.

Being aware of the rule and planning appropriately can solve this problem. One option is to make sure that all of the expenditures are incurred in December. Another option is to adopt a different year-end. If Thrush Corporation adopts a fiscal year that ends at or beyond January 31, all organizational expenditures will then have been incurred before the close of the first tax year. With either of these options, $92,000 ($62,000 + $30,000) of organizational expenditures can be amortized over 180 months.

A corporation is deemed to have made the election to amortize organizational expenditures for the taxable year in which it begins business. A corporation can elect to forgo the election by capitalizing organizational expenditures on its first tax return.

Black Corporation (an accrual method, calendar year C corporation) was formed and began operations on April 1, 2020. The following expenses were incurred during its first year of operations (April 1 through December 31, 2020):

Expenses of temporary directors and of organizational meetings	$15,500
Fee paid to the state of incorporation	2,000
Accounting services incident to organization	18,000
Legal services for drafting the corporate charter and bylaws	32,000
Expenses incident to the printing and sale of stock certificates	48,000

Black Corporation elects to amortize organizational costs under § 248. Because of the dollar cap (i.e., dollar-for-dollar reduction for amounts in excess of $50,000), none of the $5,000 expensing allowance is available. The monthly amortization is $375 [($15,500 + $2,000 + $18,000 + $32,000) ÷ 180 months], and $3,375 ($375 × 9 months) is deductible for tax year 2020.

Note that the $48,000 of expenses incident to the printing and sale of stock certificates does not qualify for the election. These expenses must be capitalized.

Organizational expenditures are different from *startup expenditures*.[35] Startup expenditures include various investigation expenses involved in entering a new business (e.g., travel, market surveys, financial audits, and legal fees) and operating expenses such as rent and payroll that are incurred by a corporation before it actually begins to produce any gross income. In general, startup expenditures must be capitalized. However, at the election of the taxpayer, startup expenditures are deductible in the same manner as

---

[35]§ 195. The deduction for startup expenditures is also available to noncorporate taxpayers.

organizational expenditures. So up to $5,000 can be immediately expensed (subject to the phaseout) and any remaining amounts amortized over a period of 180 months. The same rules that apply to the deemed election (and election to forgo the election) for organizational expenditures also apply to startup expenditures.

Concept Summary 17.2

Income Taxation of Individuals and Corporations Compared

	Individuals	Corporations
Computation of gross income	§ 61.	§ 61.
Computation of taxable income	§ 62 and §§ 63(b) through (g).	§ 63(a). Concept of AGI has no relevance.
Deductions	Trade or business (§ 162); nonbusiness (§ 212); deduction for qualified business income (§ 199A); reimbursed employee business expenses; some personal expenses (generally deductible as itemized deductions).	Trade or business (§ 162).
Charitable contributions	Limited in any tax year to 50% of AGI (60% of AGI for cash contributions); generally limited to 30% of AGI for capital gain property.	Limited in any tax year to 10% of taxable income computed without regard to the charitable contribution deduction, net operating loss carryback, capital loss carryback, and dividends received deduction.
	Excess charitable contributions carried over for five years.	Same as for individuals.
	Amount of deduction is the fair market value of capital gain property; ordinary income property is limited to adjusted basis; capital gain property is treated as ordinary income property if tangible personalty is donated to a nonuse charity or the donation is to certain private foundations.	Same as for individuals, but exceptions allowed for certain inventory and for research property where one-half of the appreciation also is allowed as a deduction.
	Time of deduction is the year in which payment is made.	Time of deduction is the year in which payment is made unless accrual basis taxpayer. Accrual basis corporation can take deduction in year preceding payment if contribution was authorized by board of directors by end of year and contribution is paid by fifteenth day of fourth month of following year.
Casualty losses	Personal casualty losses limited to losses attributable to a Federally declared disaster; $100 floor on losses; total personal casualty losses deductible only to extent losses exceed 10% of AGI.	Deductible in full.
Net operating loss	Adjusted for several items, including nonbusiness deductions over nonbusiness income.	Generally no adjustments.
	Indefinite carryforward; carryforward deduction limited to 80% of taxable income.	Same as for individuals.
Dividends received deduction	None.	50%, 65%, or 100% of dividends received depending on percentage of ownership by corporate shareholder.
Net capital gains	Taxed in full. Tax rate is 0%, 15%, or 20% on net capital gains.	Taxed in full. No preferential tax rate.
Capital losses	Only $3,000 of capital loss per year can offset ordinary income; unused loss is carried forward indefinitely to offset capital gains or ordinary income up to $3,000; short- and long-term carryovers retain their character.	Can offset only capital gains; unused loss is carried back three years and forward five; carryovers and carrybacks are characterized as short-term losses.

continued

	Individuals	Corporations
Passive activity losses	In general, passive activity losses cannot offset either active income or portfolio income.	Passive activity loss rules apply to closely held C corporations and personal service corporations. For personal service corporations, passive activity losses cannot offset either active income or portfolio income. For closely held C corporations, passive activity losses may offset active income but not portfolio income.
Tax rates	Progressive with seven rates (10%, 12%, 22%, 24%, 32%, 35%, and 37%).	Flat rate of 21%.
Alternative minimum tax	Applied at a graduated rate schedule of 26% and 28%. Exemption allowed depending on filing status (e.g., $113,400 for married filing jointly in 2020); phaseout begins when AMTI reaches a certain amount (e.g., $1,036,800 in 2020 for married filing jointly).	None.

Income Taxation of Individuals and Corporations Compared—(Continued)

Compute the corporate income tax.

17-2 DETERMINING THE CORPORATE INCOME TAX LIABILITY

17-2a Corporate Income Tax Rates

Corporate income tax rates have fluctuated over the years. The top corporate income tax rate was reduced from 46 percent to 34 percent in 1986, and then raised to a top rate of 35 percent a few years later (see Exhibit 17.3). This rate was the highest of all the developed countries in the world prior to the enactment of the TCJA of 2017. The TCJA of 2017 reduced the corporate tax rate to a flat rate of 21 percent for tax years beginning after 2017 (including for PSCs).[36]

EXAMPLE 25

Agile Corporation, a calendar year C corporation, has taxable income of $1,000,000. For 2020, Agile Corporation's tax liability is $210,000 ($1,000,000 × 21%).
  If, instead, the tax year is 2017, Agile's tax liability is $340,000 {$113,900 + [($1,000,000 − $335,000) × 34%]} (see Exhibit 17.3).

The Big Picture

EXAMPLE 26

Return to the facts of *The Big Picture* on p. 17-1. Assume that Samantha incorporates her business as Skylark Bakery, Inc., a calendar year C corporation. The corporation pays Samantha a salary of $50,000 for the current year. Therefore, Skylark Bakery has taxable income of $52,500 [$100,000 operating profit + $5,000 dividends − $50,000 salary deduction − $2,500 dividends received deduction ($5,000 × 50%)]. Its income tax liability is $11,025 ($52,500 × 21%).

[36]§ 11(b).

EXHIBIT 17.3	Corporate Income Tax Rates for Taxable Years Beginning Before 2018

Taxable Income		Tax Is:		
Over—	But Not Over—			Of the Amount Over—
$ 0	$ 50,000		15%	$ 0
50,000	75,000	$ 7,500 +	25%	50,000
75,000	100,000	13,750 +	34%	75,000
100,000	335,000	22,250 +	39%	100,000
335,000	10,000,000	113,900 +	34%	335,000
10,000,000	15,000,000	3,400,000 +	35%	10,000,000
15,000,000	18,333,333	5,150,000 +	38%	15,000,000
18,333,333	—		35%	0

Note: PSCs are taxed at a flat rate of 35%.

17-2b Alternative Minimum Tax

Prior to the enactment of the TCJA of 2017, corporations were subject to an alternative minimum tax (AMT) that was structured similarly to the individual AMT. However, the TCJA of 2017 repealed the corporate AMT for tax years beginning after 2017.

17-2c Restrictions on Corporate Accumulations

LO.4

Explain the operation of the accumulated earnings and personal holding company taxes.

Over the past several decades, there has been little difference between the top individual and corporate marginal tax rates. For instance, prior to the TCJA of 2017, there was less than a 5 percent difference between those rates (39.6 percent individual rate versus 35 percent corporate rate). This nominal differential in top rates limited the tax savings opportunities that could be achieved by individuals shifting income to a corporation. However, this landscape changed dramatically with the enactment of the corporate 21 percent flat tax rate. Consequently, a high-income individual now can achieve up to a 16 percent reduction in tax rate by shifting income to a corporation (37 percent individual rate versus 21 percent corporate rate). As a result, high-income individuals might consider the corporate entity form as a means to reduce their tax burdens.

The taxation of dividend distributions to shareholders will reduce the tax savings that can be achieved through the shifting of income to a corporation and the arbitraging of tax rates. However, what if the double taxation of corporate earnings could be deferred or possibly avoided entirely? Double taxation is deferred to the extent earnings are accumulated within the corporation instead of being distributed to shareholders. The present value of any tax liability on dividends is reduced the longer distributions are deferred. Also, a corporation's accumulation of earnings should cause its stock to appreciate in value. If a shareholder dies with such appreciated stock, all of the appreciation would avoid income taxation due to the step-up in basis under § 1014 (see Chapter 27). In addition, for most taxpayers, no estate tax would be assessed on the appreciated stock due to the high estate exclusion amount. Thus, double taxation could be avoided entirely by accumulating earnings within the corporation and a subsequent transfer of the stock by death.

Two provisions of the Code are designed to prevent corporations and their shareholders from avoiding the double tax on dividend distributions. Both provisions impose a penalty tax on undistributed income retained by the corporation. The rules underlying these provisions are complex and beyond the scope of this text. However, a brief description is provided as an introduction.

Accumulated Earnings Tax

The accumulated earnings tax (described in §§ 531–537) imposes a 20 percent tax on the current year's corporate earnings that have been accumulated without a reasonable business need. The burden of proving what constitutes a reasonable need is borne by the taxpayer. In determining accumulated income, businesses are allowed a $250,000 ($150,000 for service corporations) minimum credit. As a result, most corporations can accumulate $250,000 in earnings over a series of years without fear of an accumulated earnings tax. Beyond the minimum credit, earnings can be accumulated for reasonable needs of the business, such as expansion of the business, replacement of plant and equipment, working capital needs, product liability losses, debt retirement, self-insurance, and loans to suppliers and customers. Reasonable needs do *not* include loans to shareholders, investments in unrelated properties or businesses, and unrealistic hazards and contingencies. Finally, the accumulated earnings tax can be further reduced or eliminated by distributing dividends.

Personal Holding Company Tax

The personal holding company (PHC) tax (described in §§ 541–547) was enacted to discourage the sheltering of certain kinds of passive income in corporations owned by individuals with high marginal tax rates. Historically, the tax was aimed at "incorporated pocketbooks" that were frequently found in the entertainment and construction industries. For example, a taxpayer could shelter income from securities in a corporation, which would pay no dividends, and allow the corporation's stock to increase in value. Like the accumulated earnings tax, the PHC tax employs a 20 percent rate and is designed to force a corporation to distribute earnings to shareholders.

In any single year, the IRS cannot impose both the PHC tax and the accumulated earnings tax. Generally, a company is considered a PHC and may be subject to the tax if:

- More than 50 percent of the value of the outstanding stock is owned by five or fewer individuals at any time during the last half of the year, and
- A substantial portion (60 percent or more) of the corporation's income is comprised of passive types of income including dividends, interest, rents, royalties, or certain personal service income.

Similar to the accumulated earnings tax, the PHC tax can be further reduced or eliminated by distributing dividends.

17-2d Consolidated Returns

The privilege of filing a consolidated return is based on the concept that an affiliated group of corporations constitutes a single taxable entity despite the existence of technically separate businesses (e.g., a parent and its subsidiary). By filing a consolidated return, the corporation can eliminate intercompany profits and losses on the principle that its tax liability should be based on transactions with outsiders rather than on intragroup affairs.

Advantages and Disadvantages of Filing Consolidated Returns

The advantages of a consolidated return are summarized below.

- Losses of one group member can be used to shelter the income of other members. See Example 29.
- Taxation of intercompany dividends may be eliminated.
- Deductions may be optimized due to percentage limitations being modified as a result of the consolidation process. See Example 29.
- Recognition of income from certain intercompany transactions can be deferred. See Example 31.

Consolidation also eliminates any intercompany pricing problems among related corporations that might arise under § 482.[37]

---

[37]§ 482 (Allocation of Income and Deductions Among Taxpayers) is further discussed in Chapter 25 in regard to international situations.

Rust Corporation leases a building to Crimson Corporation for $6,000 a month. If the IRS determines that the market value is really $9,000 per month, a § 482 allocation would increase Rust Corporation's monthly rent income by $3,000. If, however, Rust and Crimson are members of an affiliated group that files a consolidated return, the § 482 adjustment would not be made. Increasing Rust Corporation's rent income by $3,000 is meaningless as it is offset by a $3,000 increase in Crimson Corporation's deduction for rent expense.

EXAMPLE

27

Consolidated returns also have a number of potential disadvantages.

- An election is binding on subsequent years and can be avoided only if the makeup of the affiliated group changes or the IRS consents to the revocation of consolidated return status.

- Recognition of losses from certain intercompany transactions is deferred.

- The requirement that all group members use the parent's tax year could create short tax years for the subsidiaries. This could cause a bunching of income and use up a full year for carryover purposes.

- Additional administrative compliance costs may be incurred as the consolidated tax return provisions are extensive and complex.

A further negative consideration is that the tax rules for filing a consolidated return may not mesh with those applicable for financial accounting purposes. For example, foreign corporations cannot be included in the consolidated tax return but should be considered when preparing financial statements. This variance in treatment may require explanatory reconciliation and will further add to the administrative burden.

Eligibility and the Election

The election to file a consolidated return is available only to an **affiliated group**.[38] An affiliated group exists when one corporation owns at least 80 percent of the voting power *and* stock value of another corporation. The stock ownership test must be met on every day of the tax year. Multiple tiers and chains of corporations are allowed as long as the group has an identifiable parent corporation (i.e., at least 80 percent of one corporation must be owned by another).

Members of an affiliated group need not file a consolidated return, and absent an election to consolidate, each corporation files its own Form 1120. If and when an election is made, all of the transactions for the group are combined and reported on one Form 1120. A Form 1122 (Authorization and Consent of Subsidiary Corporation to Be Included in a Consolidated Income Tax Return) should be attached to the first consolidated Form 1120 for every subsidiary included in the group. Each subsequent consolidated Form 1120 must include a Form 851 (Affiliation Schedule) that provides pertinent information as to the members of the group.

Computing Consolidated Taxable Income

Several categories of transactions do not enter into the determination of taxable income.

- Some intercompany transactions are disregarded. Examples would be dividends paid by one group member to another. See also the situation presented in Example 27.

- Gains and losses from certain intercompany sales are not recognized until the sold asset leaves the affiliated group (e.g., disposition of the property to an outside party). See Examples 31 and 32.

In computing the taxable income for any consolidated return year, several items are computed on a group basis. These include net capital (and § 1231) gain or loss, casualty gain or loss, charitable contributions, the dividends received deduction, and net operating loss. The importance of this grouping is illustrated below.

---

[38]§ 1504(a). Most of the tax rules governing consolidated returns are contained in the Regulations. The delegation of this rule-making authority is contained in § 1502.

FINANCIAL DISCLOSURE INSIGHTS   GAAP and Tax Treatment of Consolidations

Both U.S. financial accounting and tax rules use the term *consolidation*, but there is only a slight resemblance in the content of those rules. Here are some of the key similarities and differences between the book and tax treatment of conglomerates.

- GAAP consolidations for the most part are *mandatory* when specified ownership levels are met. Federal income tax consolidation is an *election* by the affiliates to join the parent's tax return.

- GAAP consolidations can include entities such as partnerships and non-U.S. entities. Federal income tax rules generally limit the consolidated return only to U.S. C corporations.

- Ownership levels required for a U.S. subsidiary to consolidate with a parent differ between the book and tax rules. For example, not only does GAAP set a lower maximum for consolidation (50 percent versus 80 percent) but consolidation may not be elective (see above). Furthermore, the categorization and treatment of minority interests may vary.

- Tax rules treat a merger or an acquisition of a target corporation by a parent as a nontaxable transaction, assuming that the requirements of a § 368 reorganization are met (see Chapter 20). Under GAAP, the transaction usually is reported as a purchase of the target's identifiable assets and liabilities.

- After a takeover occurs, book cost amounts are "stepped up" or "down" to fair market value and any excess purchase price is deemed to be goodwill. For Federal income tax purposes, if reorganization treatment is available, the target's basis in its assets carries over to the parent's accounts.

- Goodwill is treated differently under book and tax rules. Financial accounting goodwill cannot be amortized, but impairments to its value are reported as operating losses. Book income results if that impairment of the goodwill is reversed, for example, because the value of the goodwill has increased. For Federal income tax purposes, purchased goodwill is amortized over 15 years.

Computing Various Items on a Group Basis

EXAMPLE 28

Maize Corporation owns 100% of the stock of Ecru Corporation, and both use a calendar year for tax purposes. For 2020, they had the following transactions and filed *separate* returns:

	Maize	Ecru
Income from operations	$300,000	$170,000
Capital gain	50,000	
Capital loss of $45,000		(–0–)*
Charitable contribution of $40,000	(35,000)**	
Taxable income	$315,000	$170,000

*No deduction is allowed to a corporation for a net capital loss.

**The charitable deduction is limited to 10% of taxable income, as computed prior to the charitable contribution deduction. In this example, 10% × $350,000 ($300,000 + $50,000) = $35,000.

EXAMPLE 29

Assume the same facts as in Example 28, except that a consolidated return is filed for 2020. The results are:

Income from operations ($300,000 + $170,000)		$470,000
Capital transactions—		
Capital gain	$ 50,000	
Capital loss	(45,000)*	5,000
Charitable contribution		(40,000)**
Taxable income		$435,000

*A capital loss can be used to offset a capital gain.

**The 10% of taxable income limitation now becomes 10% × $475,000 = $47,500. As a result, the full charitable deduction is allowed.

One of the advantages of filing a consolidated return can be seen by comparing the results reached in Examples 28 and 29. Note that in Example 28, the combined taxable income is $485,000 ($315,000 + $170,000), while in Example 29, taxable income is $435,000, or $50,000 less ($485,000 – $435,000).

The consolidated return rules allow the group to make use of the losses of one (or more) of its members. Because this possibility could lead to major tax avoidance (e.g., a profitable corporation acquires a loss corporation to take advantage of its loss carryovers), multiple safeguards have been enacted by Congress to preclude (or curtail) such potential abuse.

One such safeguard protects against the use of losses and deductions that arose in a separate return year.[39]

For calendar year 2020, Kingfisher Corporation and Starling Corporation first elect to file a consolidated return. As of January 1, 2020, Starling owned land (held as an investment) with a basis of $300,000 and a fair market value of $280,000. During 2020, the land is sold for $270,000. On a consolidated return, only $10,000 of the loss can be claimed. The other $20,000 loss comes from a separate return year(s) and relates only to Starling Corporation. It cannot be used by the affiliated group.

EXAMPLE 30

A further safeguard limits the use of losses and deductions when ownership changes within the affiliated group have taken place.[40]

Deferral Treatment for Intercompany Sales

As noted previously, the deferral of certain intercompany sales can be advantageous (if gains are involved) or disadvantageous (if losses are involved). The realized gain or loss from the intercompany sale is not recognized but is deferred.

In 2020, Peach Corporation sells land (basis of $100,000) to Beige Corporation for its fair market value of $180,000. Both Peach and Beige are members of the same affiliated group that files a consolidated return for 2020. None of the $80,000 realized gain is recognized on this return.

EXAMPLE 31

The deferred gain or loss may be recognized in a later year when the property ultimately is sold to outsiders.

Assume the same facts as in Example 31. In 2022, Beige Corporation sells the land to an unrelated real estate developer for $210,000. A consolidated return for 2022 should report a recognized gain of $110,000 ($80,000 of which was previously deferred).

EXAMPLE 32

17-3 PROCEDURAL MATTERS

LO.5

Describe the reporting process for corporations.

This section covers various aspects of the corporate income tax return, including filing requirements, estimated tax payments, and special disclosure schedules on the return.

17-3a Filing Requirements for Corporations

A corporation must file a Federal income tax return whether it has taxable income or not. If a corporation began (or ceased) operations during a year, a short-period return (less than 12 months) must be filed for that year.[41]

The corporate income tax return is Form 1120. Corporations electing under Subchapter S (see Chapter 22) use Form 1120S. Forms 1120 and 1120S are reproduced in Appendix B. Corporations with assets of $10 million or more generally are required to file returns electronically.[42]

---

[39]Aside from the Regulations issued by the Treasury Department, the separate return limitation year (SRLY) safeguards can be invoked pursuant to § 269 (Acquisitions Made to Evade or Avoid Income Tax) and § 482 (Allocation of Income and Deductions Among Taxpayers).

[40]The major statutory weapons available to the IRS are § 381 (Carryovers in Certain Corporate Acquisitions) and § 382 (Limitation on Net Operating Loss Carryforwards and Certain Built-in Losses Following Ownership Change).

[41]§ 6012(a)(2) and Reg. § 1.6012–2(a). A corporation must file a return even though it has ceased to do business if it has valuable claims for which it will bring suit. A corporation is relieved of filing income tax returns only when it ceases to do business and retains no assets.

[42]Reg. §§ 1.6012–2(a)(3) (Form 1120), 1.6012–2(h) (Form 1120S), and 301.6011–5 (electronic filing).

A Form 1120 must be filed on or before the fifteenth day of the fourth month following the close of a corporation's tax year.[43] A regular corporation, other than a PSC, can use either a calendar year or a fiscal year to report its taxable income. A Form 1120S must be filed on or before the fifteenth day of the third month following the close of an S corporation's tax year.[44]

A corporation that needs more time to prepare and file its tax return can receive an automatic six-month extension of its tax return due date if it files Form 7004 (and pays the related tax liability) by the due date of its return.[45] The IRS may terminate an extension by mailing a 10-day notice to the corporation.

17-3b Estimated Tax Payments

A corporation must make estimated tax payments unless its tax liability can reasonably be expected to be less than $500. The required annual payment is the *lesser* of:

1. 100 percent of the corporation's tax for the current year, or
2. 100 percent of the tax for the preceding year (if that was a 12-month tax year, the return filed showed a tax liability, and the corporation involved is not a *large corporation*).

Estimated payments can be made in four installments due on or before the fifteenth day of the fourth month, the sixth month, the ninth month, and the twelfth month of the corporate taxable year.[46]

Failure to make the required estimated tax prepayments results in a nondeductible penalty being imposed on the corporation. The penalty is avoided, however, if any of various exceptions apply.

17-3c Schedule M–1—Reconciliation of Income (Loss) per Books with Income per Return

Schedule M–1 of Form 1120 is used to *reconcile* net income as computed for financial accounting purposes [i.e., using generally accepted accounting principles (GAAP)] with taxable income reported on the corporation's income tax return (commonly referred to as book-tax differences). Schedule M–1 is required of corporations with less than $10 million of total assets.

The starting point on Schedule M–1 is net income (or loss) per books. Additions and subtractions are entered for items that affect financial accounting net income and taxable income differently. The following items are entered as additions (see lines 2 through 5 of Schedule M–1):

- Federal income tax expense per books (deducted in computing net income per books but not deductible in computing taxable income).

- The excess of capital losses over capital gains (deducted for financial accounting purposes but not deductible by corporations for income tax purposes).

- Income that is reported in the current year for tax purposes but is not reported in computing net income per books (e.g., prepaid income).

- Various expenses that are deducted in computing net income per books but are not allowed in computing taxable income (e.g., charitable contributions in excess of the 10 percent ceiling applicable to corporations).

The following subtractions are entered on lines 7 and 8 of Schedule M–1:

- Income reported for financial accounting purposes but not included in taxable income (e.g., tax-exempt interest).

- Deductions taken on the tax return but not expensed in computing net income per books (e.g., tax depreciation in excess of financial accounting depreciation).

---

[43]§ 6072(a). A corporation with a June 30 year-end must file a Form 1120 by the fifteenth day of the *third* month following the close of its fiscal year through 2025 [P.L. 114–41, § 2006(a)(3)(B)]. If the due date falls on a Saturday, Sunday, or legal holiday, the due date is the next business day.

[44]§ 6072(b).

[45]Reg. § 1.6081–3. An extension of seven months applies for C corporations with a June 30 year-end through 2025 [§ 6081(b)].

[46]§ 6655. If the due date falls on Saturday, Sunday, or a legal holiday, the due date is the next business day. See § 6655(g)(2) for the definition of a *large corporation*.

The result is taxable income (before the NOL deduction and the dividends received deduction). Concept Summary 17.3 provides a conceptual diagram of Schedule M–1.

EXAMPLE 33

During the current year, Tern Corporation had the following transactions:

Net income per books (after tax)	$89,400
Taxable income	50,000
Federal income tax expense per books (21% × $50,000)	10,500
Interest income from tax-exempt bonds	5,000
Interest paid on a loan, the proceeds of which were used to purchase the tax-exempt bonds	500
Life insurance proceeds received as a result of the death of a key employee	50,000
Premiums paid on the key employee life insurance policy	2,600
Excess of capital losses over capital gains	2,000

For book and tax purposes, Tern determines depreciation under the straight-line method. Tern's Schedule M–1 for the current year follows:

Schedule M-1	**Reconciliation of Income (Loss) per Books With Income per Return**					
	Note: The corporation may be required to file Schedule M-3 (see instructions).					
1	Net income (loss) per books	89,400	7	Income recorded on books this year not included on this return (itemize):		
2	Federal income tax per books	10,500	a	Tax-exempt interest $ 5,000		
3	Excess of capital losses over capital gains	2,000	b	Other (itemize):		
4	Income subject to tax not recorded on books this year (itemize):			_Life insurance proceeds on key employee $50,000_	55,000	
			8	Deductions on this return not charged against book income this year (itemize):		
5	Expenses recorded on books this year not deducted on this return (itemize):		a	Depreciation . . $		
a	Depreciation . . . . $		b	Charitable contributions $		
b	Charitable contributions $		c	Other (itemize):		
c	Travel and entertainment $					
d	Other (itemize):					
	Prem.–life ins. $2,600; Int.–tax-exempt bonds $500	3,100	9	Add lines 7 and 8	55,000	
6	Add lines 1 through 5	105,000	10	Income—line 6 less line 9	50,000	

17-3d Schedule M–2—Analysis of Unappropriated Retained Earnings per Books

Schedule M–2 reconciles unappropriated retained earnings at the beginning of the year with unappropriated retained earnings at year-end. In general, this financial statement reconciliation is done by adding net income per books to the beginning balance of retained earnings and subtracting distributions made during the year. Other sources of increases or decreases in retained earnings are also listed on Schedule M–2.

EXAMPLE 34

Assume the same facts as in Example 33. Tern Corporation's beginning balance in unappropriated retained earnings is $125,000. During the year, Tern distributed a cash dividend of $30,000 to its shareholders. Based on this additional information, Tern's Schedule M–2 for the current year is constructed as follows:

Schedule M-2	**Analysis of Unappropriated Retained Earnings per Books**					
1	Balance at beginning of year	125,000	5	Distributions:	a Cash	30,000
2	Net income (loss) per books	89,400			b Stock	
3	Other increases (itemize):				c Property . . .	
			6	Other decreases (itemize):		
			7	Add lines 5 and 6		30,000
4	Add lines 1, 2, and 3	214,400	8	Balance at end of year (line 4 less line 7)		184,400

Corporations with less than $250,000 of gross receipts and less than $250,000 in assets do not have to complete Schedule L (balance sheet) and Schedules M–1 and M–2 of Form 1120. Similar rules apply to Form 1120S (used by S corporations). These rules are intended to ease the compliance burden on small business.

Concept Summary 17.3

Conceptual Diagram of Schedule M–1 (Form 1120)

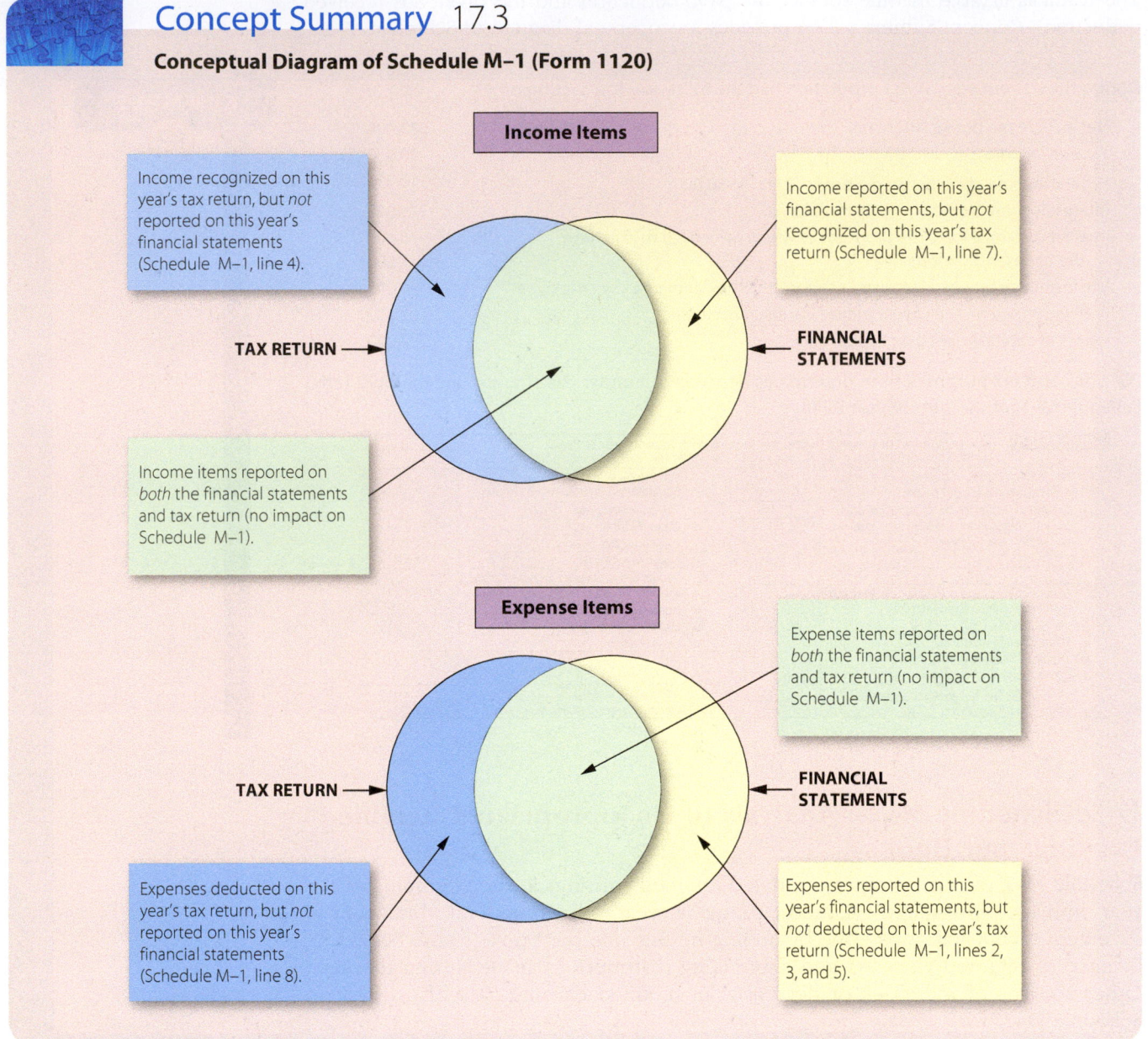

17-3e Schedule M–3—Net Income (Loss) Reconciliation for Corporations with Total Assets of $10 Million or More

Corporate taxpayers with total assets of $10 million or more are required to report much greater detail relative to differences between income (loss) reported for financial purposes and income (loss) reported for tax purposes. This expanded reconciliation of book and taxable income (loss) is reported on **Schedule M–3**.[47] Schedule M–3 is reproduced in Appendix B.

Schedule M–3 is a response, at least in part, to a variety of financial reporting scandals. One objective of Schedule M–3 is to create greater transparency between corporate financial statements and tax returns. Another objective is to identify corporations that engage in aggressive tax practices by requiring that transactions that create book-tax differences be disclosed on corporate tax returns.

---

[47]Corporations that are not required to file Schedule M–3 may do so voluntarily. Any corporation that files Schedule M–3 is not allowed to file Schedule M–1. Corporations (and partnerships) with $10 million to $50 million of total assets may elect to file Schedule M–1 in lieu of Schedule M–3, Parts II and III. Electing entities must still file Schedule M–3, Part I (lines 1–12). Entities with less than $10 million of assets that voluntarily file Schedule M–3 also may elect the reduced Schedule M–3 filing requirements.

Part I—Financial Information and Net Income (Loss) Reconciliation

Part I requires the following financial information about the corporation:

- The source of the financial net income (loss) amount used in the reconciliation— SEC Form 10–K, audited financial statements, prepared financial statements, or the corporation's books and records.

- Any restatements of the corporation's income statement for the filing period, as well as any restatements for the past five filing periods.

- Any required adjustments to the net income (loss) amount referred to previously (see Part I, lines 5 through 10).

The adjusted net income (loss) amount must be reconciled with the amount of taxable income reported on the corporation's Form 1120.

Because of Schedule M–3's complexity, our coverage is limited to some of the more important concepts underlying the schedule. A series of examples adapted from the instructions for Schedule M–3 are used to illustrate these concepts.

Southwest Sportsman's Corporation (SSC) sells hunting and fishing equipment. SSC has several stores in Texas, New Mexico, and Arizona. It also has a subsidiary in Mexico, which is organized as a Mexican corporation.

SSC, which does not file a Form 10–K with the SEC, reports income from its Mexican subsidiary on its audited financial statements, which show net income of $45,000,000 in the current year. The Mexican corporation, which is not consolidated by SSC for tax purposes (and, as a result, is not an includible corporation), had net income of $7,000,000.

SSC will enter $7,000,000 on Part I, line 5a, of Schedule M–3, resulting in "net income per income statement of includible corporations" of $38,000,000 (Part I, line 11).

A situation similar to that described in Example 35 could result in additional entries in Part I of Schedule M–3. For example, if SSC engaged in transactions with its non-includible Mexican subsidiary, an entry would be required on line 8 (adjustment to eliminations of transactions between includible corporations and nonincludible entities).

Part II—Reconciliation of Net Income (Loss) per Income Statement of Includible Corporations with Taxable Income per Return

Part II reconciles income and loss items of includible corporations (Part III reconciles expenses and deductions). As indicated in Example 35, corporations included in a financial reporting group may differ from corporations in a tax reporting group. Corporations may also be partners in a partnership, which is a flow-through entity. The following example illustrates the adjustments that are required in this situation.

Southwest Sportsman's Corporation also owns an interest in a U.S. partnership, Southwest Hunting Lodges (SHL). On its audited financial statements, SSC treats the difference between financial statement net income and taxable income from its investment in SHL as a permanent difference. During the year, SSC reported net income of $10,000,000 as its distributive share from SHL. (See Chapter 21 for a complete discussion of partnership taxation.) SSC's Schedule K–1 from SHL reports the following amounts:

Ordinary income	$5,000,000
Long-term capital gain	7,000,000
Charitable contributions	4,000,000
Section 179 expense	100,000

To adjust for the flow-through items from the partnership, SSC must report these items on Schedule M–3, Part II, line 9 [Income (loss) from U.S. partnerships]. The corporation reports $10,000,000 (book income) on line 9, column (a). SSC reports income per tax return of $7,900,000 ($5,000,000 + $7,000,000 − $4,000,000 − $100,000) in column (d) of line 9 and a permanent difference of $2,100,000 in column (c).

Part III—Reconciliation of Expense/Deduction Items

Part III lists 37 reconciling items relating to expenses and deductions. For these items, taxpayers must reconcile differences between income statement amounts (column a) and tax return amounts (column d), and then classify these differences as temporary (column b) or permanent (column c) differences. The totals of the reconciling items from Part III are transferred to Part II, line 27 and are included with other items required to reconcile financial statement net income (loss) to tax return net income (loss).

Book-Tax Differences Reconciled

EXAMPLE 37

Southwest Sportsman's Corporation acquired intellectual property in the current year and expensed amortization of $20,000 on its financial statements, which were prepared according to GAAP. For Federal income tax purposes, SSC deducted $30,000.

The corporation must report the amortization on line 28, Part III as follows: $20,000 book amortization in column (a), $10,000 temporary difference in column (b), and $30,000 tax return amortization in column (d).

EXAMPLE 38

In January of the current year, Southwest Sportsman's Corporation established an allowance for uncollectible accounts (bad debt reserve) of $35,000 on its books and increased the allowance by $65,000 during the year. As a result of a client's bankruptcy, SSC decreased the allowance by $25,000 later in the year. The corporation expensed the $100,000 of increases to the allowance on its income statement but was not allowed to deduct that amount on its tax return. On its tax return, the corporation was allowed to deduct the $25,000 actual loss sustained because of its client's bankruptcy.

These amounts must be reported on line 32, Part III as follows: $100,000 book bad debt expense in column (a), $75,000 temporary difference in column (b), and $25,000 tax return bad debt deduction in column (d).

Example 37 illustrates the Schedule M–3 reporting when book expenses are less than tax return deductions. Example 38 illustrates reporting procedures when book expenses are greater than tax return deductions. Both examples illustrate the reporting of temporary differences. The amounts from both examples are included in the totals derived in Part III and are carried to Part II, line 27. The reconciliation of book income and taxable income occurs in lines 26 through 30. The reconciled amount on Part II, line 30, column (a) must be equal to the net income per income statement of includible corporations on Part I, line 11. The reconciled amount on Part II, line 30, column (d) must be equal to the taxable income reported on Form 1120.

LO.6

Determine the impact of tax return positions on corporate financial statements.

17-3f Income Taxes in the Financial Statements

A review of the Schedule M–1 (or Schedule M–3) adjustments to Form 1120 (see text Sections 17-3c and 3e) reveals many differences in the tax and financial accounting treatment of various transactions. These differences can be *permanent* and appear on *either* the tax return or the financial statements but not on both. Permanent differences include interest income on municipal bonds, the dividends received deduction, and fines and penalties. Other differences are *temporary* and appear on *both* the tax return and the financial statements but in different reporting periods. Here, the variation is due to timing as to when (or how much of) the transaction is taken into account. Temporary differences include depreciation, depletion, unearned income, reserves for bad debts and product warranties, NOLs, and excess capital losses and charitable contributions.

Generally Accepted Accounting Principles and ASC 740

Accounting for income taxes under GAAP is governed by Accounting Standards Codification (ASC) 740. Consistent with most financial accounting principles, **ASC 740** emphasizes the balance sheet, taking a **balance sheet approach** to the accounting for income taxes. Specifically, it requires that the balance sheet reflect both a current liability related to all income taxes (Federal, state and local, and foreign) reflected on its tax returns for the year as well as a **deferred tax liability** or **deferred tax asset** for the future tax effects of items included in its current and prior financial statements but not in taxable income (i.e., temporary book-tax differences). That is, ASC 740 adopts a comprehensive inter-period allocation approach to income taxes, requiring that all income taxes that relate to the income reported in the current financial statements be reported in those same financial statements regardless of when they might be legally due under the tax law. The sum of the liabilities reflected on the current tax returns represents a corporation's **current tax expense** while the future tax effects related to its temporary book-tax differences lead to the recognition of either a **deferred tax expense** or **deferred tax benefit**.

EXAMPLE 39

In 2020, PanCo, Inc., earns $100,000 in pretax book income before considering a $30,000 gain realized on an installment sale. This gain represents a favorable, temporary book-tax difference. For financial reporting purposes, the entire $30,000 gain is recognized in current-year income. However, for tax purposes, the gain can be recognized over the periods in which the sales proceeds are collected. Assuming that the proceeds will be collected evenly over three years, beginning in 2020, PanCo will report the installment sale gain as follows.

	Book Income	Taxable Income
2020	$30,000	$10,000
2021	–0–	10,000
2022	–0–	10,000
	$30,000	$30,000

In 2020, PanCo will report $130,000 ($100,000 + $30,000 gain) of pretax book income. However, it will report only $110,000 ($100,000 + $10,000 gain) of taxable income and pay $23,100 ($110,000 × 21%) of income taxes for the year. Therefore, its financial statements will reflect a current tax liability, and current tax expense, of $23,100.

However, PanCo will also report a deferred tax liability, and deferred tax expense, of $4,200 ($20,000 deferred gain × 21%). The total tax expense reported in the financial statements, $27,300 ($23,100 current tax expense + $4,200 deferred tax expense), captures the total income tax that will be paid on the $130,000 of pretax book income even though some of that tax expense is not yet due.

Note that in Example 39, the total tax expense reported in the financial statements is equal to the tax related to pretax book income. This is the intended result of ASC 740, which requires the recognition of the deferred tax liability and related expense. Due to the recording of the deferred tax expense, temporary differences will never cause the tax expense reported on the books to differ from what might be expected based on pretax book income. Even with a temporary difference, the total tax expense on the financial statements reflects taxes on the entire pretax book income, although some of that tax is deferred.

However, the same is not true for permanent book-tax differences. As a result, if there are permanent book-tax differences, tax expense cannot be determined simply by multiplying pretax book income by the tax rate.

Referring back to Example 39, assume that PanCo's pretax book income included a $5,000 nondeductible fine. Its pretax book income would remain $130,000. However, its taxable income and related tax expense would be calculated as follows:

Pretax book income	$130,000
Book-tax permanent differences:	
Fines	5,000
Book-tax temporary differences:	
Gain deferred on installment sale	(20,000)
Taxable income	$115,000
Tax rate	× 21%
Current tax payable/expense	$ 24,150
Deferred tax expense (from Example 3)	4,200
Total tax expense	$ 28,350

Notice that in Example 40, total tax expense ($28,350) is greater than one might have expected based on pretax book income [$27,300 ($130,000 × 21%)]. This is due to the unfavorable, permanent book-tax difference ($5,000 × 21% = $1,050).

Capturing, Measuring, and Recording Tax Expense—The Provision Process

The process used to capture, measure, and record the tax expense reported in the financial statements, as well as the expense itself, is often referred to as the *tax provision*. As discussed previously, ASC 740 requires the reporting on the balance sheet of both a current tax liability (related to the liability reflected in a corporation's current tax returns) and a deferred asset or liability (related to the future tax consequences of items reported in the current or prior financial statements). However, while a corporation may have to issue its financial statements, including the tax provision, soon after year-end, its tax returns may not be filed until much later.[48] In this case, estimates of book-tax differences and the current and deferred tax liabilities must be made as part of the tax provision process before the tax return is filed.

Current Tax Expense

Determining current tax expense begins with estimating the current tax liabilities to be reflected on the corporation's tax returns. This includes three steps.

1.   Identifying (and adjusting pretax book income for) all permanent and temporary book-tax differences.
2.   Identifying (and adjusting pretax book income for) any tax carryovers that may impact current taxable income (e.g., capital losses, charitable contributions, NOLs).
3.   Identifying (and adjusting the current tax liability for) any tax credits that may be available but have no impact on either book or taxable income.

Exhibit 17.4 illustrates the process for determining current tax expense. Note that the book-tax differences captured in steps 1 and 2 above (with the exception of an NOL carryover) are the same items that are expected to appear in Schedule M–1 (see Example 33) or Schedule M–3 (reproduced in Appendix B) of the corporation's federal tax return when it is eventually filed.

Deferred Tax Expense

A deferred tax expense is the result of a deferred tax liability (a future tax liability related to transactions already reflected in the financial statements). Similarly, a deferred tax benefit is the result of a deferred tax asset (future tax savings related to transactions already reflected in the financial statements).

---

[48]Although the due date for a Federal corporate tax return is three and one-half months after year-end (April 15 for a calendar year corporation), many corporations request an extension of time to file the tax return (using Form 7004). This six-month extension request is automatically approved by the IRS. While the due date for filing the tax return is extended, any taxes due must be paid by the original due date of the return.

EXHIBIT 17.4	**Current Tax Expense (Simplified)**

Pretax book income
± Schedule M–1/M–3 adjustments
_____

Taxable income before NOLs
− NOL carryforwards
_____

Taxable income
× Applicable tax rate
_____

Current tax expense (provision) before tax credits
− Tax credits
_____

Current tax expense (provision)
_____

Deferred tax assets and liabilities can be generated in several ways. The most common way is the use of different accounting methods for financial reporting and taxable income in the current period, resulting in book-tax temporary differences. For most large corporations, the accrual method generally is required for both financial reporting and tax purposes. However, in several situations, the accrual method is applied differently in determining book and taxable income. Further, different accounting methods may be used for specific transactions (e.g., the installment method is available for tax purposes in certain situations).

Generally, a *deferred tax asset* is produced when:

- The recognition of revenue is accelerated for tax purposes relative to book (e.g., the recognition of unearned revenues for tax earlier than book), or

- The deductibility of an expense reported in the financial statements is deferred for tax purposes (e.g., an expense reported in the financial statements has not yet met the economic performance test for tax).

Generally, a *deferred tax liability* is produced when:

- The recognition of revenue is deferred for tax purposes relative to book (e.g., when installment sale treatment is available for tax purposes but not for book), or

- The deductibility of an expense reported in the financial statements is accelerated for tax purposes (e.g., the use of accelerated cost recovery methods for tax purposes).

Identifying and Measuring Deferred Tax Assets and Liabilities

As discussed above, an accounting method difference that causes current book and taxable income to differ will produce both a deferred tax asset or liability on the balance sheet and a deferred tax benefit or expense on the income statement. However, a deferred tax benefit or expense itself relates to the *future* tax consequences attributable to events reported in the current or prior financial statements, not the differences in current book and taxable income. As you will see, not all future tax benefits and expenses related to transactions already recorded in the financial statements are the result of accounting method differences. As a result, successfully identifying all deferred tax assets and liabilities requires more than the identification of current differences in book and taxable income.

A review of financial accounting principles may help at this point. Recall the basic accounting equation:

$$\text{Assets} = \text{Liabilities} + \text{Owners' Equity}$$

The equation suggests that income (which represents a change in owners' equity) must be accompanied by a similar change in assets or liabilities.

Imagine that we simultaneously maintain an accounting equation (or a set of double-entry books and records) for tax purposes using tax accounting methods rather than GAAP. In this system, assets and liabilities would be measured by their tax adjusted bases (AB) rather than their net book value (NBV). Any taxable income would similarly correspond to a change in the bases of assets and liabilities.[49] If the same accounting methods were used for financial reporting and tax purposes, assets, liabilities, and income would be the same in both equations (i.e., there would be no book-tax differences). However, the use of different methods results not only in book-tax differences in income, but also differences in the tax ABs and the NBVs of assets and liabilities. Since it is the use of assets and the incurrence of liabilities that produce future income, it is these differences in the current NBV and tax ABs of assets and liabilities that will cause differences in future financial reporting and taxable income and, therefore, related deferred tax assets and liabilities.

Deferred Tax Assets and Liabilities

EXAMPLE 41

Orange, Inc., acquired an asset during the current year. Book depreciation, using the straight-line method over the asset's useful life, is $100. However, MACRS produces a $500 cost recovery deduction for tax purposes. The impact of the asset's depreciation for book and tax purposes would be reflected in journal entries as follows:

Book		
Depreciation expense	$100	
Net book value (NBV) of asset		$100
Tax		
Cost recovery deduction	$500	
Tax adjusted basis (AB) of asset		$500
Difference between NBV and AB of asset		$400

The $400 difference in the current net book value and tax adjusted basis of the asset will result in future taxable income being $400 higher than future book income. This will lead to a tax liability higher than what would relate to future book income, creating a *deferred tax liability*.

EXAMPLE 42

Blue, Inc., sells products subject to a two-year warranty. Blue estimates that it will spend $10,000 to make repairs pursuant to warranties on products it sold in the current year. For book purposes, it accrues this $10,000 as a current-year expense. However, because there has been no economic performance, the estimated expenses are not currently deductible. This would be reflected in the financial and tax books as follows:

Book		
Warranty expense	$10,000	
Warranty liability (NBV)		$10,000
Tax		
Warranty expense	$ 0	
Warranty liability (AB)		$ 0
Difference between NBV and AB of liability		$10,000

The $10,000 difference in the net book value and tax adjusted basis of the liability reflects the $10,000 tax deduction available to Blue in the future for the expense reflected on the books currently. This future deduction represents a *deferred tax asset*.

Although accounting method differences produce NBV-AB differences (and, as a result, deferred tax assets and liabilities), not all deferred tax assets and liabilities are the result of accounting method differences. As a result, ASC 740 defines *temporary differences*, to which deferred tax assets and liabilities relate, as differences in the net book value and tax adjusted basis of a corporation's assets and liabilities (not differences

---

[49]Note that although we typically do not consider a liability to have a tax basis, the idea is to capture what would be on the balance sheet if the taxpayer were using a double-entry accounting system for tax purposes.

in current book and taxable income and expenses). Accordingly, the tax provision process requires the identification and measurement of these differences between net book value and tax adjusted basis. ASC 740 refers to temporary differences that lead to deferred tax assets as *deductible differences* while those that lead to deferred tax liabilities are referred to as *taxable differences*.

Of course, although the differences in the net book value and tax adjusted bases of a company's assets and liabilities lead to deferred tax assets and liabilities, these temporary differences do not accurately capture those deferred tax assets and liabilities. Rather, we are interested in the future tax consequences of these differences. As a result, these differences must be multiplied by the appropriate tax rate to capture a corporation's deferred tax assets and liabilities.

Examples 43 and 44 illustrate the determination of deferred tax expense.[50]

Deferred Tax Expense

EXAMPLE 43

PJ Enterprises began operations in 2020 and earned pretax book income of $500,000 in its first year of operations. In performing its 2020 tax provision, PJ noted the following temporary differences.

- In January 2020, PJ purchased equipment at a cost of $800,000. For book purposes, PJ depreciated the asset on a straight-line basis over ten years, resulting in $80,000 of depreciation expense in 2020. For tax purposes, PJ was able to use a combination of accelerated cost recovery methods and deducted $720,000 in 2020.

- PJ sells most of the goods it produces on account. At the end of 2020, it had established an allowance for uncollectible accounts of $30,000. For tax purposes, PJ must use the direct write-off method to account for uncollectible accounts, and no write-offs occurred during 2020.

PJ operates in a state with an income tax, making its combined Federal and state tax rate equal to 25%. No laws have been passed that will change the tax rates faced by PJ in the future. The provision for PJ's 2020 deferred tax expense was determined as follows.

Partial Balance Sheet (December 31, 2020)

	Net Book Value	Tax Adjusted Basis	Temporary Difference	Combined Tax Rate	Deferred Tax Asset/(Liability)
Accounts receivable (net of allowance for uncollectible accounts)	$100,000	$130,000	$ 30,000	25%	$ 7,500
Equipment	720,000	80,000	640,000	25%	(160,000)
Net deferred tax liability					($152,500)

At the end of 2020, PJ had a net deferred tax liability of $152,500, consisting of a $7,500 deferred tax asset (for the NBV–AB difference related to the accounts receivable) and a $160,000 deferred tax liability (for the NBV–AB difference related to the equipment). PJ made the following journal entry to record its 2020 deferred tax expense.

Deferred tax expense (income statement)	$152,500	
Deferred tax liability (balance sheet)		$152,500

EXAMPLE 44

PJ Enterprises, from Example 43, earned pretax book income of $600,000 in 2021. PJ continues to use the equipment it acquired in 2020 and to depreciate it on a straight-line basis over ten years. For tax purposes, PJ can recover $32,000 of the equipment's cost in 2021. At the end of 2021, it estimates that $45,000 of its accounts receivable will be uncollectible. The provision for PJ's 2021 deferred income tax expense is determined as follows.

continued

---

[50]For a more complete discussion of the impact of taxes in the financial statements, see *South-Western Federal Taxation: Corporations, Partnerships, Estates & Trusts* (2021 edition), Chapter 14.

Partial Balance Sheet (December 31, 2021)

	Net Book Value	Tax Adjusted Basis	Temporary Difference	Combined Tax Rate	Deferred Tax Asset/(Liability)
Accounts receivable (net of allowance for uncollectible accounts)	$150,000	$195,000	$ 45,000	25%	$ 11,250
Equipment	640,000	48,000	592,000	25%	(148,000)
Net deferred tax liability					($136,750)

At the end of 2021, PJ has a net deferred tax liability of $136,750, consisting of a $11,250 deferred tax asset (for the NBV–AB difference related to the accounts receivable) and a $148,000 deferred tax liability (for the NBV–AB difference related to the equipment).

PJ must reduce the $152,500 deferred tax liability recorded in 2020 to $136,750, with the $15,750 liability reduction representing a deferred tax benefit. PJ would make the following journal entry to record its 2020 deferred taxes.

Deferred tax liability (balance sheet)	$15,750	
Deferred tax benefit (income statement)		$15,750

After the above journal entry, PJ's 2021 balance sheet will reflect a deferred tax liability of $136,750.

LO.7

Evaluate corporations as an entity form for minimizing income taxes on businesses.

17-4 TAX PLANNING

17-4a Corporate versus Noncorporate Forms of Business Organization

The decision to use the corporate form in conducting a trade or business must be weighed carefully. Besides the nontax considerations of the corporate form (limited liability, continuity of life, free transferability of interests, centralized management), tax ramifications will play an important role in any such decision. Close attention should be paid to the following:

1. Operating as a regular corporate entity (C corporation) results in the imposition of the corporate income tax. Corporate taxable income will be taxed twice—once as earned by the corporation and again when distributed to the shareholders. Because dividends are not deductible, a closely held corporation may have a strong incentive to structure corporate distributions in a deductible form. With the preferential rates on qualified dividends, shareholders may save taxes by having the corporation pay dividends rather than salaries, rent, or interest, which could be taxed at an individual marginal rate as high as 37 percent. The decision should be made only after comparing the tax cost of the two alternatives. The 3.8 percent additional tax on net investment income (including dividend and net capital gain income) also must be considered in this analysis.

2. The differences in Federal income tax brackets between an individual and a corporation can be substantial. The potential for a 16 percent difference between the top individual rate and the corporate rate (i.e., 37 percent less 21 percent) presents opportunities for significant tax savings. However, several state and local governments impose higher taxes on corporations than on individuals. In these jurisdictions, the combined Federal, state, and local tax rates on the two types of taxpayers must be evaluated. In addition, the deduction for qualified business income must be considered in any tax savings determination. The savings associated with incorporating is enhanced to the extent double taxation of corporate earnings can be deferred or avoided completely. The TCJA of 2017 significantly increased the estate exemption ($11.58 million for 2020), thus creating greater opportunities for the complete avoidance of double taxation. This complete tax avoidance can be achieved by never distributing corporate earnings and obtaining a stepped-up basis for the corporate stock upon a shareholder's death. However, the accumulated earnings tax and the personal holding company tax may limit opportunities for

corporate accumulations and must be factored into any analysis. Consequently, the tax ramifications of incorporating can be determined *only* on a case-by-case basis.

3. Corporate-source income loses its identity as it passes through the corporation to the shareholders. Thus, preferential tax treatment of certain items by the corporation (e.g., interest on municipal bonds) does not carry over to the shareholders.

4. As noted in Chapter 19, it may be difficult for shareholders to recover some or all of their investment in the corporation without an ordinary income result. Most corporate distributions are treated as dividends to the extent of the corporation's earnings and profits. However, the preferential rate on qualified dividends reduces the impact of such a result.

5. Corporate losses cannot be passed through to the shareholders.[51]

6. The liquidation of a corporation will normally generate tax consequences to both the corporation and its shareholders (see Chapter 20).

7. The corporate form provides shareholders with the opportunity to be treated as employees for tax purposes if the shareholders render services to the corporation. Such status makes a number of attractive tax-sheltered fringe benefits available. They include, but are not limited to, group term life insurance and excludible meals and lodging. One of the most attractive benefits of incorporation is the ability of the business to provide accident and health insurance to its employees, including shareholder-employees. Such benefits are not included in the employee's gross income. Similar rules apply to other medical costs paid by the employer. These benefits are not available to partners, sole proprietors, and more-than-2% shareholder-employees of S corporations.

17-4b Operating the Corporation

Tax planning to reduce corporate income taxes should occur before the end of the tax year. Effective planning can cause income to be shifted to the next tax year and can produce large deductions by incurring expenses before year-end. Particular attention should be focused on the following.

Timing of Capital Gains and Losses

A corporation should consider offsetting gains on the sale of capital assets by selling some of the depreciated securities in the corporate portfolio. In addition, any already realized capital losses should be carefully monitored. Recall that corporate taxpayers are not permitted to claim any net capital losses as deductions against ordinary income. Capital losses can be used only as an offset against capital gains. Further, net capital losses can only be carried back three years and forward five. Gains from the sales of capital assets should be timed to offset any capital losses. The expiration of the carryover period for any net capital losses should be watched carefully so that sales of appreciated capital assets occur before that date.

Planning for the Business Interest Expense Limitation

Some business sectors (e.g., health care) are currently more exposed to the limitation than others due to a greater reliance on debt financing, but the limitation's reach is expected to expand significantly in 2022. Beginning in 2022, depreciation, amortization, and depletion will be deducted in arriving at "adjusted taxable income," thus reducing the allowable business interest deduction. The clearest path for reducing the limitation's impact is to pay down debt, such as issuing stock to replace debt. Other alternatives might include forgoing stock buybacks and/or dividends in favor of debt reduction and issuing new debt to replace existing higher interest rate debt.

Charitable Contributions

Recall that accrual basis corporations may claim a deduction for charitable contributions in the year preceding payment. The contribution must be authorized by the board of directors by the end of the tax year and paid on or before the fifteenth day of the fourth

---

[51]Points 1, 2, and 5 could be resolved by making a Subchapter S election (see Chapter 22), assuming that the corporation qualifies for the election. In part, the same can be said for point 3.

month of the following year. It might be useful to authorize a contribution even though it may not ultimately be made. A deduction cannot be thrown back to the previous year (even if paid within the three and a half months) if it has not been authorized.

The enhanced deduction amount for contributions of qualified inventory can produce significant tax savings. Gifts of inventory should be designed to take advantage of this provision whenever feasible. Effort should be taken to properly document the type of inventory donated and each recipient charitable organization, since the statutory provisions that allow for an enhanced deduction have very specific requirements for qualification. Further, a corporation's cost of goods sold must be reduced to reflect any charitable contribution of inventory.

Executive Compensation

A written binding contract in effect on November 2, 2017, is grandfathered under the old executive compensation rules, but only if the contract is not "materially modified" after such date. The renewal of a contract in effect on November 2, 2017, will be treated as a new contract that is not grandfathered. Since performance-based compensation is excluded from the $1 million limitation under prior law, material modifications of grandfathered contracts with such incentives should be avoided. For example, a material modification generally results if a contract is amended to increase or accelerate payment of an employee's compensation.[52]

Net Operating Losses

The 80 percent of taxable income limitation applies to NOLs arising after 2017. NOLs arising in earlier years and carried over to years after 2017 are not subject to the taxable income limitation.

EXAMPLE 45

In 2020, Ruby Corporation has a $10,000,000 carryover of an NOL that originated in 2017. Ruby has 2020 taxable income (before the NOL deduction) of $11,000,000. Since the $10,000,000 NOL carryover arose prior to 2018, the taxable income limitation does not apply and the full amount is deductible in 2020.

For a tax year in which the taxable income limitation is applicable, a corporation might consider taking steps to increase the deductible amount. These steps might include accelerating income into the current tax year or deferring deductions to a subsequent tax year.

Shareholder-Employee Payment of Corporate Expenses

In a closely held corporate setting, shareholder-employees often pay corporate expenses (e.g., office supplies) for which they are not reimbursed by the corporation. Prior to 2018, unreimbursed employee expenses were deductible by an employee (subject to certain limitations). However, from 2018 through 2025, miscellaneous itemized deductions (which includes unreimbursed employee expenses) are not deductible. To preserve the deduction of corporate expenses incurred by shareholder-employees, corporate policy should provide for the reimbursement of these items. The issue can be avoided entirely by having the corporation directly incur the related expenses (e.g., providing a corporate credit card to the shareholder-employee for corporate expenditures).

Avoiding the Accumulated Earnings Tax

The 21 percent flat corporate tax rate will encourage high-income individual taxpayers to shift income to C corporations to obtain a potential 16 percent reduction in their current tax rate (a maximum 37 percent individual tax rate). This tax savings is enhanced the longer dividend distributions can be deferred, thus increasing the possible imposition of the accumulated earnings tax (AET). However, $250,000 ($150,000 for service corporations) of earnings can be accumulated without imposition of the penalty tax.

Accumulations for reasonable needs of the business in excess of the minimum credit amount should be specific, definite, and feasible (see Reg. § 1.537 for further insight

---

[52]See Notice 2018–68, 2018–36 I.R.B. 418.

into what constitutes reasonable needs of the business). Dividends reduce the impact of the AET, and if the corporation lacks liquidity to make a distribution, a consent dividend (under § 565) should be considered (here, a dividend is deemed distributed by the corporation to the shareholder, then an equal amount is deemed contributed to the capital of the corporation by the shareholder). The lack of liquidity to make dividend distributions is not a defense against the imposition of the AET.

REFOCUS ON THE BIG PICTURE

COOKED TO PERFECTION

Conducting Skylark Bakery as a C corporation could save Samantha $8,475 ($38,000 − $29,525) in income taxes annually, computed as follows:

Bakery Operated as Sole Proprietorship	
Operating profit of $100,000:	
Tax on $100,000 × 37%	$37,000
Dividends of $5,000:	
Tax on $5,000 × 20%	1,000
Withdrawals of $50,000:	
No tax	–0–
Total income tax when operated as sole proprietorship	$38,000

Bakery Operated as Regular (C) Corporation	
Corporate taxable income of $52,500*:	
Tax on $52,500 × 21%	$11,025
Samantha's salary of $50,000:	
Tax on $50,000 × 37%	18,500
Total income tax when operated as C corporation	$29,525

*Computation of corporate taxable income:	
Operating profit	$100,000
Dividend income	5,000
Less: Salary to Samantha	(50,000)
Dividends received deduction (50%)	(2,500)
Taxable income	$ 52,500

Note: If available, the deduction for qualified business income would reduce Samantha's $100,000 proprietorship operating profit and, thereby, reduce the tax savings of incorporating.

The example illustrates the tax savings available when a high-income individual taxpayer takes advantage of the lower corporate tax rate. However, other issues such as employment tax considerations, the deduction for qualified business income, and the taxation of dividend distributions (i.e., additional Medicare tax on wages and tax on net investment income) also should be considered. Further, other potential entity options, such as the LLC and S corporation, also should be evaluated.

What If?

What if the bakery in the first year it becomes a corporation generates a $10,000 short-term capital loss (STCL) on the disposition of some of its stock investments? Regular corporations can only deduct capital losses against capital gains; thus, the $10,000 STCL would not be deductible currently by the corporation and, instead, would be carried forward for up to five years. If the bakery is operated as a sole proprietorship, Samantha would report the capital loss on her individual return. She could use the $10,000 STCL to offset any capital gains she may have and deduct up to $3,000 of the loss against ordinary income.

Key Terms

Accumulated earnings tax, 17-20

Affiliated group, 17-21

ASC 740, 17-29

Balance sheet approach, 17-29

C corporations, 17-2

Current tax expense, 17-29

Deferred tax asset, 17-29

Deferred tax benefit, 17-29

Deferred tax expense, 17-29

Deferred tax liability, 17-29

Dividends received deduction, 17-13

Generally accepted accounting principles (GAAP), 17-24

Organizational expenditures, 17-15

Passive activity loss, 17-8

Personal holding company (PHC) tax, 17-20

Personal service corporations (PSCs), 17-4

Reasonable needs of the business, 17-20

Regular corporations, 17-2

Schedule M–1, 17-24

Schedule M–3, 17-26

Discussion Questions

1. **LO.1** Janice is the sole owner of Catbird Company. In the current year, Catbird had operating income of $100,000, a long-term capital gain of $15,000, and a charitable contribution of $5,000. Janice withdrew $70,000 of profit from Catbird. How should Janice report this information on her individual tax return if Catbird Company is:

   a.   An LLC?

   b.   An S corporation?

   c.   A C corporation?

   Critical Thinking   2. **LO.1** Joel is the sole shareholder of Manatee Corporation, a C corporation. Because Manatee's sales have increased significantly over the last several years, Joel has determined that the corporation needs a new distribution warehouse. Joel has asked your advice as to whether (1) Manatee should purchase the warehouse or (2) he should purchase the warehouse and lease it to Manatee. What relevant tax issues will you discuss with Joel?

3. **LO.1** In the current year, Jeanette, an individual in the 24% marginal tax bracket, recognized a $20,000 long-term capital gain. Also in the current year, Parrot Corporation, a calendar year C corporation, recognized a $20,000 long-term capital gain. Neither taxpayer had any other property transactions in the year. What tax rates are applicable to these capital gains?

4. **LO.1** John (a sole proprietor) and Eagle Corporation (a C corporation) each recognize a long-term capital gain of $10,000 and a short-term capital loss of $18,000 on the sale of capital assets. Neither taxpayer had any other property transactions during the year. Describe the tax consequences of these gains and losses for John and for Eagle.

5. **LO.1** A taxpayer sells a warehouse for a recognized gain. Depreciation had been properly claimed on the property based on the straight-line method over a 39-year recovery period. Will the same amount of depreciation recapture result whether the taxpayer is an individual or a C corporation? Explain.

6. **LO.1** In general, what is the limitation on the deductibility of business interest expense? What happens to any business interest deduction disallowed under the limitation?

7. **LO.1** Osprey Corporation, a closely held corporation, has $100,000 of net active income, $25,000 of portfolio income, and a $120,000 loss from a passive activity.

   a.   How much of the passive activity loss can Osprey deduct in the current year if it is a PSC?

   b.   If it is not a PSC?

8. **LO.1** On December 28, 2020, the directors of Partridge Corporation, an accrual basis calendar year taxpayer, authorized a cash contribution of $10,000 to the American Cancer Association. The payment is made on April 13, 2021. Can Partridge deduct the charitable contribution in 2020? Explain.

9. **LO.1, 7** The board of directors of Orange Corporation, a calendar year taxpayer, is holding its year-end meeting on December 28, 2020. One topic on the board's agenda is the approval of a $25,000 gift to a qualified charitable organization. Orange has a $20,000 charitable contribution carryover to 2020 from a prior year. Identify the tax issues the board should consider regarding the proposed contribution. *Critical Thinking*

10. **LO.1, 2, 7** Gold Corporation, a calendar year C corporation, was formed in 2012 and has been profitable until the current year. In 2020, Gold incurs a net operating loss. Identify the issues that Gold Corporation should consider regarding its NOL. *Critical Thinking*

11. **LO.2** Marmot Corporation pays a dividend of $100,000 in the current year. Otter Corporation, a calendar year C corporation, owns 15% of Marmot's stock. Gerald, an individual taxpayer in the 24% marginal bracket, also owns 15% of Marmot's stock. Compare and contrast the treatment of the dividend by Otter Corporation and Gerald.

12. **LO.2** Determine whether the following expenditures by Cuckoo Corporation are organizational expenditures, startup expenditures, or neither.
    a. Legal expenses incurred for drafting the corporate charter and bylaws.
    b. Accounting fees incurred in organization.
    c. Expenses of temporary board of directors' organizational meetings.
    d. Employee salaries incurred during the training period before opening for business.
    e. Brokerage fees incurred in initial stock sales.

13. **LO.4** Omar, an individual in the 37% tax bracket, wants to shift some of his income to a new corporation in order to take advantage of the 21% corporate tax rate. Omar plans to avoid any tax on dividends by retaining all earnings within the corporation. Will Omar's plan work? Discuss.

14. **LO.5** When are C corporations required to make estimated tax payments? How are these payments calculated?

15. **LO.5** Schedule M–1 of Form 1120 is used to reconcile financial accounting net income with taxable income reported on the corporation's income tax return as follows: Net income per books + Additions − Subtractions = Taxable income. Classify the following items as additions or subtractions in the Schedule M–1 reconciliation.
    a. Life insurance proceeds received upon death of covered executive.
    b. Tax depreciation in excess of book depreciation.
    c. Federal income tax per books.
    d. Capital loss in excess of capital gain.
    e. Charitable contributions in excess of taxable income limitation.
    f. Premiums paid on life insurance policies covering executives (corporation is beneficiary).

16. **LO.5** In the current year, Woodpecker, Inc., a C corporation with $8,500,000 in assets, reported amortization of $40,000 on its financial statements and deducted amortization of $55,000 on its Federal tax return. Is Woodpecker required to file Schedule M–3? If a Schedule M–3 is filed by Woodpecker, how is the difference in amortization amounts treated on that schedule?

17. **LO.6** Marcellus Jackson, the CFO of Mac, Inc., notices that the tax liability reported on Mac's tax return is less than the tax expense reported on Mac's financial statements. Provide a letter to Jackson outlining why these two tax expense numbers differ. Mac's address is 482 Linden Road, Paris, KY 40362. *Communications*

18. **LO.6** Define the terms *temporary difference* and *permanent difference* as they pertain to the financial reporting of income tax expenses. Describe how these two book-tax differences affect the gap between book and taxable income. How are permanent and temporary differences alike? How are they different? *Critical Thinking*

Computational Exercises

19. **LO.1** Goose Corporation, a C corporation, incurs a net capital loss of $12,000 for 2020. It also has ordinary income of $10,000 in 2020. Goose had net capital gains of $2,500 in 2016 and $5,000 in 2019.

   a. Determine the amount, if any, of the net capital loss of $12,000 that is deductible in 2020.

   b. Determine the amount, if any, of the net capital loss of $12,000 that is carried forward to 2021.

20. **LO.1** Aqua Corporation purchases nonresidential real property on May 8, 2017, for $1,000,000. Straight-line cost recovery is taken in the amount of $89,765 before the property is sold on November 27, 2020, for $1,500,000.

   a. Compute the amount of Aqua's recognized gain on the sale of the realty.

   b. Determine the amount of the recognized gain that is treated as § 1231 gain and the amount that is treated as § 1250 recapture (ordinary income).

21. **LO.1** In the current year, Nighthawk Corporation, a calendar year C corporation, has $3,700,000 of adjusted taxable income, $125,000 of business interest income, zero floor plan financing interest, and $1,400,000 of business interest expense.

   a. Assume that Nighthawk has average gross receipts for the prior three-year period of $33,000,000. Determine Nighthawk's current-year deduction for business interest.

   b. Assume that Nighthawk has average gross receipts for the prior three-year period of $23,000,000. Determine Nighthawk's current-year deduction for business interest.

22. **LO.1** Hummingbird Corporation, a closely held C corporation that is not a PSC, has $40,000 of net active income, $15,000 of portfolio income, and a $45,000 loss from a passive activity. Compute Hummingbird's taxable income for the year.

23. **LO.1** Compute the charitable contribution deduction (ignoring the percentage limitation) for each of the following C corporations.

   a. Amber Corporation donated inventory of clothing (basis of $24,000, fair market value of $30,000) to a qualified charitable organization that operates homeless shelters.

   b. Brass Corporation donated stock held as an investment to Western College (a qualified organization). Brass acquired the stock three years ago for $18,000, and the fair market value on the date of the contribution is $32,000. Western College plans on selling the stock.

   c. Ruby Corporation donates a sculpture held as an investment and worth $130,000 to a local museum (a qualified organization), which exhibits the sculpture. Ruby acquired the sculpture four years ago for $55,000.

24. **LO.2** Crane and Loon corporations, two unrelated calendar year C corporations, have the following transactions for the current year:

	Crane	Loon
Gross income from operations	$180,000	$300,000
Expenses from operations	255,000	310,000
Dividends received from domestic corporations (15% ownership)	100,000	230,000

   a. Compute the dividends received deduction for Crane Corporation.

   b. Compute the dividends received deduction for Loon Corporation.

25. **LO.2** Cherry Corporation, a calendar year C corporation, is formed and begins business on April 1 of the current year. In connection with its formation, Cherry incurs organizational expenditures of $54,000. Determine Cherry Corporation's deduction for organizational expenditures for the current year.

26. **LO.3** Compute the current-year income tax liability for each of the following unrelated calendar year C corporations.
    a. Darter Corporation has taxable income of $68,000.
    b. Owl Corporation has taxable income of $10,800,000.
    c. Toucan Corporation, a personal service corporation, has taxable income of $170,000.

27. **LO.6** Prance, Inc., earns pretax book net income of $800,000 in 2019. Prance acquires a depreciable asset that year, and first-year tax depreciation exceeds book depreciation by $80,000. Prance reported no other temporary or permanent book-tax differences. The pertinent U.S. tax rate is 21%, and Prance earns an after-tax rate of return on capital of 8%. Compute Prance's current income tax expense for the year.

28. **LO.6** Using the facts of Problem 27, determine Prance's 2019 deferred tax expense and any deferred tax asset or liability.

Problems

29. **LO.1** In the current year, Riflebird Company had operating income of $220,000, operating expenses of $175,000, and a long-term capital loss of $10,000. How do Riflebird Company and Roger, the sole owner of Riflebird, report this information on their respective Federal income tax returns for the current year under the following assumptions?
    a. Riflebird Company is a proprietorship (Roger did not make any withdrawals from the business).
    b. Riflebird Company is a C corporation (no dividends were paid during the year).

30. **LO.1** In the current year, Azure Company has $350,000 of net operating income before deducting any compensation or other payment to its sole owner, Sasha. In addition, Azure has interest on municipal bonds of $25,000. Sasha has significant income from other sources and is in the 37% marginal tax bracket. Based on this information, determine the income tax consequences to Azure Company and to Sasha during the year for each of the following independent situations. (Ignore the deduction for qualified business income and the 3.8% Medicare surtax on net investment income.)
    a. Azure is a C corporation and pays no dividends or salary to Sasha.
    b. Azure is a C corporation and distributes $75,000 of dividends to Sasha.
    c. Azure is a C corporation and pays $75,000 of salary to Sasha.
    d. Azure is a sole proprietorship, and Sasha withdraws $0.
    e. Azure is a sole proprietorship, and Sasha withdraws $75,000.

31. **LO.1** In the current year, Wilson Enterprises, a calendar year taxpayer, suffers a casualty loss of $90,000. The casualty was attributable to a Federally declared disaster. How much of the casualty loss will be deductible by Wilson under the following circumstances?
    a. Wilson is an individual proprietor and has AGI of $225,000. The casualty loss was a personal loss, and the insurance recovered was $50,000.
    b. Wilson is a corporation, and the insurance recovered was $50,000.

32. **LO.3, 7** Benton Company (BC), a calendar year entity, has one owner, who is in the 37% Federal income tax bracket (any net capital gains or dividends would be taxed at a 20% rate). BC's gross income is $395,000, and its ordinary trade or business deductions are $245,000. Compute the Federal income tax liability on BC's income for the current year under the following assumptions. Ignore the standard deduction (or itemized deductions) and the deduction for qualified business income.

   a.   BC is operated as a proprietorship, and the owner withdraws $100,000 for personal use.

   b.   BC is operated as a corporation, pays out $100,000 as salary, and pays no dividends to its shareholder.

   c.   BC is operated as a corporation and pays out no salary or dividends to its shareholder.

   d.   BC is operated as a corporation, pays out $100,000 as salary to its shareholder, and pays out the remainder of its earnings as dividends.

   e.   Assume that Robert Benton of 1121 Monroe Street, Ironton, OH 45638 is the owner of BC, which was operated as a proprietorship. Robert is thinking about incorporating the business for next year and asks your advice. He expects about the same amounts of income and expenses and plans to take $100,000 per year out of the company whether he incorporates or not. Based on your analysis in parts (a) and (b), write a letter to Robert containing your recommendations.

33. **LO.1, 3** In the current year, Tanager Corporation (a calendar year C corporation) had operating income of $480,000 and operating expenses of $390,000. In addition, Tanager had a long-term capital gain of $55,000 and a short-term capital loss of $40,000.

   a.   Compute Tanager's taxable income and tax for the year.

   b.   Assume instead that Tanager's long-term capital gain was $15,000 (not $55,000). Compute Tanager's taxable income and tax for the year.

34. **LO.1** Virginia owns 100% of Goshawk Company. In the current year, Goshawk Company sells a capital asset (held for three years) at a loss of $40,000. In addition, Goshawk has a short-term capital gain of $18,000 and net operating income of $90,000 during the year. Virginia has no recognized capital gain (or loss) before considering her ownership in Goshawk. How much of the capital loss may be deducted for the year, and how much is carried back or forward if Goshawk is:

   a.   A proprietorship?

   b.   A C corporation?

35. **LO.1** During 2020, Gorilla Corporation, a calendar year C corporation, has net short-term capital gains of $15,000, net long-term capital losses of $105,000, and taxable income from other sources of $460,000. Prior years' transactions included the following:

2016 net short-term capital gains	$40,000
2017 net long-term capital gains	18,000
2018 net short-term capital gains	25,000
2019 net long-term capital gains	20,000

   a.   How are the capital gains and losses treated on Gorilla's 2020 tax return?

   b.   Determine the amount of the 2020 capital loss that is carried back to each of the previous years.

   c.   Compute the amount of capital loss carryforward, if any, and indicate the years to which the loss may be carried.

   d.   If Gorilla is a sole proprietorship rather than a corporation, how would the owner report these transactions on her 2020 tax return?

e. Assume that Gorilla Corporation's capital loss carryfoward in part (c) is $27,000 and that Gorilla will be able to use $11,000 of the carryover to offset capital gains in 2021 and the remaining $16,000 to offset capital gains in 2022. In present value terms, determine the tax savings of the $105,000 long-term capital loss recognized in 2020. Assume a discount rate of 5% (present value factors are in Appendix G). Further, assume that Gorilla Corporation's marginal income tax rate is 34% for all tax years prior to 2018. Create a spreadsheet using Microsoft Excel (or a similar software program) that summarizes your analysis.

36. **LO.1** Heron Company purchases commercial realty on November 13, 2002, for $650,000. Straight-line depreciation of $287,492 is claimed before the property is sold on February 22, 2020, for $850,000. What are the tax consequences of the sale of realty if Heron is:

a. A C corporation?

b. A sole proprietorship?

37. **LO.1** In the current year, Plum, Inc., a closely held C corporation, has $410,000 of net active income, $20,000 of portfolio income, and a $75,000 passive activity loss. What is Plum's taxable income for the current year under the following circumstances?

a. Plum is a personal service corporation.

b. Plum is not a personal service corporation.

38. **LO.1, 7** Joseph Thompson is president and sole shareholder of Jay Corporation (a cash method, calendar year C corporation). In December 2020, Joe asks your advice regarding a charitable contribution he plans to have the corporation make to the University of Maine, a qualified public charity. Joe is considering the following alternatives as charitable contributions in December 2020:

Decision Making
Critical Thinking
Communications

	Fair Market Value
(1) Cash donation	$200,000
(2) Unimproved land held for six years ($110,000 basis)	200,000
(3) Maize Corporation stock held for eight months ($140,000 basis)	200,000
(4) Brown Corporation stock held for nine years ($360,000 basis)	200,000

Joe has asked you to help him decide which of these potential contributions will be most advantageous taxwise. Jay's taxable income is $3,500,000 before considering the contribution. Rank the four alternatives, and write a letter to Joe communicating your advice. The corporation's address is 1442 Main Street, Freeport, ME 04032.

39. **LO.1, 7** In 2020, Gray Corporation, a calendar year C corporation, has a $75,000 charitable contribution carryover from a gift made in 2015. Gray is contemplating a gift of land to a qualified charity in either 2020 or 2021. Gray purchased the land as an investment five years ago for $100,000 (current fair market value is $250,000). Before considering any charitable deduction, Gray projects taxable income of $1,000,000 for 2020 and $1,200,000 for 2021. Should Gray make the gift of the land to charity in 2020 or in 2021? Provide support for your answer.

Decision Making
Critical Thinking

40. **LO.1, 7** Julieta Simms is the president and sole shareholder of Simms Corporation (a cash method, calendar year C corporation), 1121 Madison Street, Seattle, WA 98121. Julieta plans for the corporation to make a charitable contribution to the University of Washington, a qualified public charity. She will have the corporation donate Jaybird Corporation stock, held for five years, with a basis of $11,000 and a fair market value of $25,000. Julieta projects a $310,000 net profit for Simms Corporation in 2020 and a $100,000 net profit in 2021. Julieta calls you on December 10, 2020, and asks whether she should make the contribution in 2020 or 2021. Write a letter advising Julieta about the timing of the contribution.

Decision Making
Critical Thinking
Communications

41. **LO.1** Florence is the newly hired chief financial officer of Hazel Corporation, a publicly traded, calendar year C corporation. For the current year, her compensation package consists of:

Cash compensation	$1,500,000
Bonus tied to company performance	700,000
Taxable fringe benefits	250,000
Nontaxable fringe benefits	75,000

How much of Florence's compensation is deductible by Hazel Corporation?

42. **LO.1, 2** During the current year, Swallow Corporation, a calendar year C corporation, has the following transactions:

Income from operations	$660,000
Expenses from operations	760,000
Dividends received from Brown Corporation	240,000

a. Swallow Corporation owns 12% of Brown Corporation's stock. How much is Swallow's taxable income or NOL for the year?

b. Assume instead that Swallow Corporation owns 26% of Brown Corporation's stock. How much is Swallow's taxable income or NOL for the year?

43. **LO.2** In each of the following independent situations, determine the dividends received deduction for the calendar year C corporation. Assume that none of the corporate shareholders owns 20% or more of the stock in the corporations paying the dividends.

	Almond Corporation	Banana Corporation	Cherry Corporation
Income from operations	$ 700,000	$ 800,000	$ 900,000
Expenses from operations	(600,000)	(860,000)	(910,000)
Qualifying dividends	100,000	100,000	100,000

44. **LO.2** Gull Corporation, a cash method, calendar year C corporation, was formed and began business on November 1, 2020. Gull incurred the following expenses during its first year of operations (November 1, 2020–December 31, 2020):

Expenses of temporary directors and organizational meetings	$21,000
Fee paid to state of incorporation	3,000
Expenses for printing and sale of stock certificates	11,000
Legal services for drafting the corporate charter and bylaws (not paid until January 2021)	19,000

a. Assuming that Gull Corporation elects under § 248 to expense and amortize organizational expenditures, what amount may be deducted in 2020?

b. Assume the same facts as above, except that the amount paid for the legal services was $28,000 (instead of $19,000). What amount may be deducted as organizational expenditures in 2020?

45. **LO.2** Egret Corporation, a calendar year C corporation, was formed on March 6, 2020, and opened for business on July 1, 2020. After its formation but prior to opening for business, Egret incurred the following expenditures:

Accounting	$ 7,000
Advertising	14,500
Employee payroll	11,000
Rent	8,000
Utilities	1,000

What is the maximum amount of these expenditures that Egret can deduct in 2020?

46. **LO.3** In each of the following *independent* situations, determine the corporation's income tax liability. Assume that all corporations use a calendar year for tax purposes and that the tax year involved is 2020.

	Taxable Income
Purple Corporation	$ 65,000
Azul Corporation	290,000
Pink Corporation	12,350,000
Turquoise Corporation	19,000,000
Teal Corporation (a personal service corporation)	130,000

47. **LO.5** The following information for 2020 relates to Sparrow Corporation, a calendar year, accrual method taxpayer:

Net income per books (after-tax)	$205,050
Federal income tax expense per books	55,650
Tax-exempt interest income	4,500
MACRS depreciation in excess of straight-line depreciation used for financial statement purposes	7,200
Excess of capital loss over capital gains	9,400
Nondeductible meals and entertainment	5,500
Interest on loan to purchase tax-exempt bonds	1,100

Based on the above information, use Schedule M–1 of Form 1120, which is available on the IRS website, to determine Sparrow's taxable income for 2020.

48. **LO.5** Dove Corporation, a calendar year C corporation, had the following information for 2020:

Net income per books (after-tax)	$386,250
Taxable income	120,000
Federal income tax per books	25,200
Cash dividend distributions	150,000
Unappropriated retained earnings, as of January 1, 2020	796,010

Based on the above information, use Schedule M–2 of Form 1120 (see Example 34 in the text) to determine Dove's unappropriated retained earnings balance as of December 31, 2020.

49. **LO.5** In the current year, Pelican, Inc., a calendar year C corporation, incurs $10,000 of meals and entertainment expenses that it deducts in computing net income per the corporation's financial statements. All of the meals and entertainment expenditures are subject to the 100% disallowance rule applicable to such expenditures. How is this information reported on Schedule M–3?

50. **LO.5** In January 2020, Pelican, Inc., established an allowance for uncollectible accounts (bad debt reserve) of $70,000 on its books and increased the allowance by $120,000 during the year. As a result of a client's bankruptcy, Pelican, Inc., decreased the allowance by $60,000 in November 2020. Pelican, Inc., expensed the $190,000 of increases to the allowance on its 2020 income statement but was not allowed to deduct that amount on its tax return. On its 2020 tax return, the corporation was allowed to deduct the $60,000 actual loss sustained because of its client's bankruptcy. On its financial statements, Pelican, Inc., treated the $190,000 increase in the bad debt reserve as an expense that gave rise to a temporary difference. On its 2020 tax return, Pelican, Inc., took a $60,000 deduction for bad debt expense. How is this information reported on Schedule M–3?

See Appendix E for Comprehensive Tax Return Problems—Form 1120

Research Problems

the answer company™
THOMSON REUTERS®

Note: Solutions to the Research Problems can be prepared by using the Thomson Reuters Checkpoint™ online tax research database, which accompanies this textbook. Solutions can also be prepared by using research materials found in a typical tax library.

Research Problem 1. A personal service corporation (PSC) generally is limited to the calendar year for reporting purposes. One exception to this rule is when the PSC can demonstrate a business purpose for a fiscal year-end. Discuss the business purpose exception, including examples of when the standard is and is not satisfied. Support your research with proper citations of tax authority.

Partial list of research aids:
§ 441(i).
Reg. § 1.441–3.

Communications

Research Problem 2. A new client, Southwest Grocers, is a calendar year C corporation that owns and operates a chain of grocery stores. Southwest Grocers is interested in donating food inventory to one or more charitable organizations that will use the food as part of their exempt purpose (e.g., a food bank or homeless shelter). In some cases, the donated items may consist of dented canned food and fungible food items (e.g., baked goods) nearing their freshness expiration dates. Inedible food or food past its expiration date would not be included in any donation. Prepare an outline detailing the information you would provide to Southwest Grocers regarding charitable contributions of food inventory. Make sure to include support for the content of your outline.

Partial list of research aids:
§ 170(e)(3).
Reg. § 1.170A–4A.
Lucky Stores, Inc., 105 T.C. 420 (1995).

Communications

Research Problem 3. A new client, John Dobson, recently formed John's Premium Steakhouse, Inc., to operate a new restaurant. The restaurant will be a first-time business venture for John, who recently retired after 30 years of military service. John transferred cash to the corporation in exchange for 100% of its stock, and the corporation has leased a building and restaurant equipment. John has asked you for guidance on the tax treatment of various expenses (e.g., licensing, training, advertising) he expects the corporation to incur during the restaurant's preopening period. Research the tax treatment of startup expenditures, including the point at which a business begins for purposes of determining what expenses are included. Prepare a memo for the client files describing the results of your research.

Partial list of research aids:
§ 195.
Reg. § 1.195–1.

Use internet tax resources to address the following questions. Look for reliable websites and blogs of the IRS and other government agencies, media outlets, businesses, tax professionals, academics, think tanks, and political outlets.

Communications

Research Problem 4. A significant percentage of U.S. corporations are closely held corporations, with the stock of such corporations often owned predominantly or exclusively by family members. Using the internet as your sole research source, prepare an outline describing the tax implications and planning opportunities unique to family-owned, closely held corporations.

Data Analytics

Communications

Research Problem 5. Find the most recent *IRS Tax Statistics* (**irs.gov/statistics**) for the Corporation Income Tax Returns Complete Report. Based solely on this report, prepare an outline highlighting the top three industries based on corporate pretax profits reported (Figure B), the three most common corporate tax reporting year-ends (Figure D), and the three most common types of corporate returns filed (Figure E).

Becker.

1. In the current year, Acorn, Inc., had the following items of income and expense:

Sales	$500,000
Cost of sales	250,000
Dividends received	25,000

   The dividends were received from a corporation of which Acorn owns 30%. In Acorn's current-year corporate income tax return, what amount should be reported as income before special deductions?

   a. $525,000
   b. $505,000
   c. $275,000
   d. $250,000

2. Before the provision for Federal income tax, Karas Corporation had book income of $400,000 for the current year. The book income included $100,000 of dividends received from a 15% owned domestic corporation. What was Karas Corporation's taxable income for the current year?

   a. $300,000
   b. $335,000
   c. $350,000
   d. $400,000

3. In year 6, Garland Corp. contributed $40,000 to a qualified charitable organization. Garland's year 6 taxable income before the deduction for charitable contributions was $410,000. Included in that amount is a $20,000 dividends received deduction. Garland also had carryover contributions of $5,000 from the prior year. In year 6, what amount can Garland deduct as charitable contributions?

   a. $40,000
   b. $41,000
   c. $43,000
   d. $45,000

4. Tapper Corp., an accrual basis calendar year corporation, was organized on January 2, year 1. During year 1, revenue was exclusively from sales proceeds and interest income. The following information pertains to Tapper:

Taxable income before charitable contributions for the year ended December 31, year 1	$500,000
Tapper's matching contribution to employee-designated qualified universities made during year 1	10,000
Board of Directors' authorized contribution to a qualified charity (authorized December 1, year 1, made February 1, year 2)	30,000

   What is the maximum allowable deduction that Tapper may take as a charitable contribution on its tax return for the year ended December 31, year 1?

   a. $0
   b. $10,000
   c. $30,000
   d. $40,000

5. Campbell Corporation, an accrual basis calendar year corporation, had income of $450,000 for financial statement purposes in year 7. This amount included book depreciation of $50,000. The related tax depreciation was $65,000. Further, the financial statements reported $100,000 of municipal bond interest income, an expense of $2,000 for life insurance premiums on the corporation's president, charitable contributions of $5,000, excess capital losses over capital gains of $3,000, income tax penalties of $10,000, state income tax of $40,000, and Federal income tax expense of $175,000. What is the amount of Campbell's taxable income for year 7?

   a. $522,000
   b. $525,000
   c. $530,000
   d. $565,000

6. Hirsch, Incorporated, is a calendar year corporation that has had revenues of less than $500,000 since inception. In 2019, Hirsch had a net operating loss that was able to be used in full in 2020. For 2020, Hirsch expects to have taxable income of $100,000. How will Hirsch avoid a penalty for underpayment of estimated Federal taxes in 2020?

    a. Hirsch must pay 100% of the tax shown on its 2020 return via estimated taxes to avoid an underpayment penalty.

    b. Hirsch must pay the amount of taxes owed on its 2019 return via estimated taxes to avoid an underpayment penalty.

    c. Hirsch must pay 90% of the tax shown on its 2020 return via estimated taxes to avoid an underpayment penalty.

    d. Hirsch may pay the lower of the amount of taxes owed in 2019 or 100% of the tax shown on the return for 2020 via estimated taxes to avoid an underpayment penalty.

7. The dividends received deduction (DRD) is a tax deduction that may be taken by which of the following?

    a. An individual

    b. An S corporation

    c. A partnership

    d. A C corporation

8. Which of the following statements is *not* true for tax years beginning after 2017?

    a. Affiliated corporations that file consolidated returns can take a 100% dividends received deduction.

    b. The dividends received deduction for a small investment in an unrelated corporation is 50%.

    c. The dividends received deduction for a large investment in a corporation is 65%.

    d. There is no income limitation on the dividends received deduction.

9. Parent Corp. owns 40% of Sub Corp. In the current year, Parent has gross income of $43,000 and allowable deductions of $30,000 before considering any dividends received deduction (DRD). Included in the $43,000 gross income is $8,000 of dividends from Sub. What is the maximum DRD available to Parent?

    a. $4,000

    b. $5,200

    c. $8,000

    d. $8,450

10. Parent Corp. owns 15% of Sub Corp. Parent has gross income of $43,000 and allowable deductions of $40,000 before considering any dividends received deduction (DRD). Included in the $43,000 gross income is $8,000 in dividends from Sub. What is the maximum DRD available to Parent?

    a. $1,500

    b. $1,950

    c. $4,000

    d. $8,000

CHAPTER

18

Corporations: Organization and Capital Structure

LEARNING OBJECTIVES: *After completing Chapter 18, you should be able to:*

LO.1 Explain the tax consequences of incorporating a business.

LO.2 Describe the special rules that apply when a corporation assumes shareholder liabilities.

LO.3 Identify the basis issues relevant to the shareholder and the corporation.

LO.4 Explain the tax aspects of the capital structure of a corporation.

LO.5 Characterize the tax differences between debt and equity investments.

LO.6 Handle the tax treatment of shareholder debt and stock gains and losses.

LO.7 Identify tax planning opportunities associated with organizing and financing a corporation.

CHAPTER OUTLINE

18-1 Organization of and Transfers to Controlled Corporations, 18-2
18-1a Section 351 Rationale and General Rules, 18-2
18-1b Property Defined, 18-5
18-1c Stock Transferred, 18-6
18-1d Control of the Corporation, 18-6
18-1e Assumption of Liabilities—§ 357, 18-10
18-1f Basis Determination and Related Issues, 18-12

18-2 Capital Structure of a Corporation, 18-18
18-2a Capital Contributions, 18-18
18-2b Debt in the Capital Structure, 18-18

18-3 Investor Losses, 18-21
18-3a Stock and Security Losses, 18-21
18-3b Business versus Nonbusiness Bad Debts, 18-21
18-3c Section 1244 Stock, 18-23

18-4 Gain from Qualified Small Business Stock, 18-24

18-5 Tax Planning, 18-24
18-5a Working with § 351, 18-24
18-5b Selecting Assets to Transfer, 18-26
18-5c Debt in the Capital Structure, 18-26
18-5d Investor Losses, 18-27
18-5e Corporations versus Flow-Through Entities, 18-28

THE VEHICLE FOR BUSINESS GROWTH IS THE CORPORATE FORM

Emily has operated her startup venture as a sole proprietorship since launching the business two years ago. David, a friend from college, has been collaborating with Emily. Together they have developed an innovative software app. They were overjoyed that as soon as the app was introduced into the market, it was an immediate hit—and it has gained increasing recognition and market traction as sales continue to rise. After only a short period of success though, Emily becomes convinced that the upside potential for even more growth is significant. However, she realizes that a leap to that level of growth and market penetration can only be achieved with a large infusion of capital that she is unable to fund from her resources.

Fortunately, Emily's friend Ethan, who is a venture capitalist, is enthusiastic about making a large investment in the business in exchange for an equity stake. Ethan agrees that Emily's startup easily will enjoy remarkable success once it has the necessary additional resources. To integrate Ethan's capital into the venture, the sole proprietorship will be incorporated with Emily and Ethan each contributing assets in exchange for stock in newly formed Transformation, Inc. Emily also has asked David, an invaluable employee and a major contributor to the app's development, if he would be interested in becoming a shareholder in Transformation. He was given the option of transferring either property or services in exchange for stock. However, at this point, David is undecided about what he will do.

Emily will receive 200 shares of Transformation stock in exchange for transferring the following sole proprietorship assets to the new corporation:

	Adjusted Basis	Fair Market Value
Accounts receivable	$ –0–	$ 50,000
Building	100,000	400,000
Proprietary information—app	300,000	1,550,000
	$400,000	$2,000,000

Ethan will contribute $48,000,000 of cash for 4,800 shares of Transformation stock.

What will be the tax and nontax implications relating to the formation of Transformation, Inc.?

Read the chapter and formulate your response.

Chapter 17 dealt with four principal areas fundamental to working with corporations: (1) understanding the unique treatment that applies to entities treated as corporations for Federal income tax purposes, (2) recognizing specific income tax rules that apply only to corporations, (3) identifying filing and reporting procedures, and (4) considering special situations involving corporations.

Chapter 18 continues this approach and addresses issues involving corporate formations, capital structure, and special investor rules:

- The tax consequences to shareholders and the corporation when shareholders transfer property to form a new corporation.
- The tax results when shareholders transfer property to an already-existing corporation.
- The capital structure of a corporation, including equity and debt financing.
- The special tax treatment of corporate investor losses.
- The special treatment given to gain realized from the disposition of qualified small business stock.

LO.1

Explain the tax consequences of incorporating a business.

18-1   ORGANIZATION OF AND TRANSFERS TO CONTROLLED CORPORATIONS

Property transactions normally result in recognized gain or loss when taxpayers realize gain or loss. As a result, unless special provisions in the Code apply, a transfer of property to a corporation in exchange for stock is a taxable transaction. Realized gain or loss equals the difference between the fair market value of the stock received and the tax basis of the property transferred.

18-1a   Section 351 Rationale and General Rules

In contrast to the typical result of full gain or loss recognition, the Code permits nonrecognition of gain or loss in limited circumstances. For example, both § 1031 (like-kind exchanges) and § 351 (transfers of property to controlled corporations) postpone gain or loss recognition until a substantive change in the taxpayer's investment occurs (e.g., a sale of property or ownership shares to outsiders). Section 1031 provides for gain or loss deferral when a taxpayer exchanges certain property for "like-kind property." The rules accomplish this deferral by reducing the basis of the property received by the deferred gain or increasing the basis by the deferred loss. This substituted basis results in the taxpayer recognizing the gain or loss when the taxpayer sells the new property for cash or non-like-kind property.[1]

Similarly, Example 1 below illustrates that § 351 defers gain or loss when transferring property to a controlled corporation (defined in text Section 18-1d) in exchange for the corporation's own stock. There are at least three reasons for this tax deferral treatment. First, contributing property to a corporation leaves an owner's economic status unchanged; the contribution changes only the *form* of the investment. The investment in the business assets carries over to an investment in corporate stock. Second, when a shareholder receives only stock in the corporation, the shareholder lacks the cash to pay a tax on any realized gain. Thus, this approach is justified under the *wherewithal to pay concept* discussed in Chapter 1. As noted later, however, when the taxpayer receives property other than stock (i.e., cash or other "boot") from the corporation, the shareholder recognizes some or all of the realized gain. A third justification for the nonrecognition of gain or loss provisions under § 351 is that Congress believes tax rules should not impede a taxpayer's judgment about the best choice of entity form for conducting business.

---

[1]For a complete discussion of the rationale and rules pertaining to like-kind exchanges under § 1031, see Chapter 13.

GLOBAL TAX ISSUES   **Tax Reform Adds a New Wrinkle to the Choice of Organizational Form When Operating Overseas**

When the management of a corporation decides to expand its business by establishing a presence in a foreign market, the new business venture may take one of several organizational forms. As each form comes with its respective advantages and disadvantages, making the best choice can be difficult. And the choice is even more challenging now because a new set of rules applies to the taxation of international operations with the enactment of the Tax Cuts and Jobs Act (TCJA) of 2017.

One common approach is to conduct the foreign activity as a *branch* operation of the U.S. corporation. The foreign branch is not a separate legal entity, but a division of the U.S. corporation established overseas. As a result, the U.S. corporation includes in its financial results any gains and losses that the foreign branch produces.

Another common approach to foreign expansion is to organize the foreign operations as a *subsidiary* of the U.S. parent corporation. The subsidiary may be either a *domestic* subsidiary (i.e., organized in the United States) or a *foreign* subsidiary (organized under the laws of a foreign country).

One fundamental tax difference between these two approaches is that the gains and losses of a domestic subsidiary may be consolidated with the operations of the U.S. parent, but the operations of a foreign subsidiary cannot. Thus, the use of a domestic subsidiary to conduct foreign operations generally yields the same final result as the use of a branch. With both approaches, the financial statements of the U.S. parent reflect the results of its worldwide operations.

The TCJA of 2017 changed many of the tax rules associated with international operations and their impact on organizational forms. Now the United States uses a "territorial system" when taxing foreign earnings. These rules generally require U.S. corporations to pay U.S. tax only on their domestic income. Given the complexity of the organizational form decisions and the significance of the changes to international taxation rules in the TCJA of 2017, it will take time for tax professionals to determine the most tax-effective ways of structuring foreign operations of U.S. corporations. See Chapter 25 for additional discussion of the taxation of international operations.

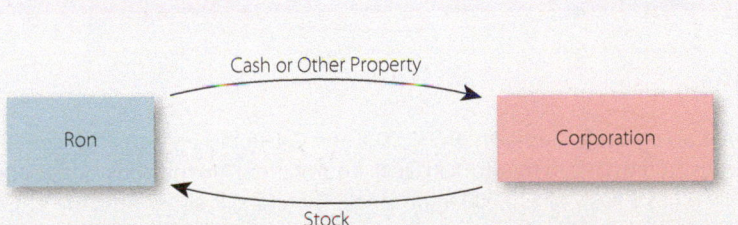

Ron is considering incorporating his sole proprietorship to obtain the limited liability of the corporate form. Ron realizes that if he incorporates, depending on state law, he will be personally liable only for the debts of the business that he has guaranteed.

If Ron incorporates his business, he will transfer the following assets to the corporation:

	Tax Basis	Fair Market Value
Cash	$ 10,000	$ 10,000
Furniture and fixtures	20,000	60,000
Land and building	240,000	300,000
	$270,000	$370,000

Ron will receive the corporation's stock worth $370,000 in exchange for the assets he transfers. Without the deferral provisions of § 351, Ron would recognize a taxable gain of $100,000 on the transfer ($370,000 value of the stock received − $270,000 basis of the assets transferred).

Under § 351, however, Ron recognizes no gain because his economic status has not really changed. Ron's ownership of stock in the corporation now represents his investment in the assets of his sole proprietorship. Ron will take a $270,000 basis in his stock and *not* a $370,000 cost basis. This adjustment to his stock basis results in a $100,000 gain *deferral* and not gain *exemption*. As a result, § 351 provides for tax neutrality on the incorporation decision because there is no tax cost of incorporating his business.

In a manner similar to a like-kind exchange, if a taxpayer transfers property to a corporation and receives "boot" (cash or property other than stock), the taxpayer recognizes gain (but not loss) to the extent of the lesser of the gain realized or the value of the boot received. Any gain recognized is classified (e.g., ordinary, capital) according to the type of assets transferred.[2] As discussed in more detail later, a substituted basis in the shareholder's stock accomplishes the deferral of gain or loss by reducing basis by the deferred gain or increasing basis by the deferred loss.[3] Following Example 2, Concept Summary 18.1 summarizes the major shareholder consequences of a taxable property transaction versus a tax-deferred transaction.

EXAMPLE

2

Amanda and Calvin form Quail Corporation. Amanda transfers equipment with an adjusted basis of $30,000, fair market value of $60,000, for 50% of the stock, worth $60,000. Calvin transfers equipment with an adjusted basis of $70,000, fair market value of $60,000, for the remaining 50% of the stock. The transfers qualify under § 351.

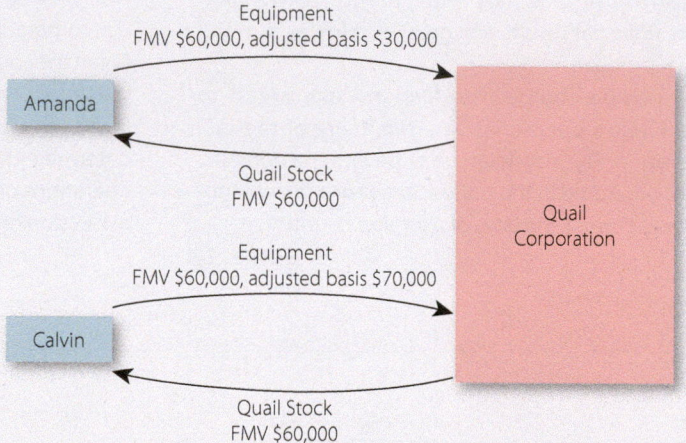

Amanda has an unrecognized gain of $30,000, and Calvin has an unrecognized loss of $10,000. Both have a substituted basis in the stock in Quail Corporation. Amanda has a basis of $30,000 in her stock, and Calvin has a basis of $70,000 in his stock. Therefore, if either Amanda or Calvin later disposes of the Quail stock in a taxable transaction (e.g., a sale), this deferred gain/loss will then be fully recognized—a $30,000 gain to Amanda and a $10,000 loss to Calvin.

Alternatively, if Amanda and Calvin each received Quail stock worth $50,000 and cash of $10,000, Amanda would recognize $10,000 of the $30,000 realized gain because she received boot of $10,000, while Calvin's receipt of boot would not trigger the recognition of a loss (i.e., recognition of loss never occurs in a § 351 transaction on the receipt of boot). Additional discussion of gain/loss recognition and the basis of stock received appears later in the chapter.

Section 351 is *mandatory* if a transaction satisfies the provision's requirements. As explained in the following sections, the three requirements for nonrecognition of gain or loss under § 351 are that (1) *property is transferred* (2) in exchange for *stock* and (3) the property transferors are in *control* of the corporation after the exchange. Therefore, if recognition of gain or loss is *desired*, the taxpayer must plan to fail to meet at least one of these requirements.

---

[2]§ 351(b) and Rev.Rul. 68–55, 1968–1 C.B. 140.

[3]§ 358(a). See the discussion preceding Example 22.

Concept Summary 18.1

Shareholder Consequences: Taxable Corporate Formation versus Tax-Deferred § 351 Transaction

18-1b **Property Defined**

The definition of property for § 351 purposes is broad. For example, along with plant and equipment, unrealized receivables of a cash basis taxpayer and installment notes are considered property.[4] Proprietary processes and formulas as well as proprietary information in the general nature of a patentable invention also qualify as property under § 351.[5]

Section 351 specifically excludes services from the definition of property. So a taxpayer must report as income the fair market value of stock and any other consideration as compensation for services.[6] Consequently, when a taxpayer receives stock as consideration for rendering services to the corporation, the income the taxpayer recognizes equals the fair market value of the stock received. This immediate taxation results in a fair market value stock basis for the taxpayer.

Ann and Bob form Olive Corporation with the transfer of the following consideration:

EXAMPLE 3

	Consideration Transferred		
	Basis to Transferor	Fair Market Value	Number of Shares Issued
From Ann:			
Personal services rendered to Olive Corporation	$ –0–	$20,000	200
From Bob:			
Installment note receivable	5,000	40,000	
Inventory	10,000	30,000	800
Proprietary process	–0–	10,000	

continued

---

[4]*Hempt Brothers, Inc. v. U.S.*, 74–1 USTC ¶9188, 33 AFTR 2d 74–570, 490 F.2d 1172 (CA–3, 1974), and Reg. § 1.453–9(c)(2).

[5]Rev.Rul. 64–56, 1964–1 C.B. 133; Rev.Rul. 71–564, 1971–2 C.B. 179.
[6]§§ 61 and 83.

The value of each share in Olive Corporation is $100.[7] Ann has income of $20,000 on the transfer because services do not qualify as "property." She has a basis of $20,000 in her 200 shares of Olive (i.e., Ann is treated as having bought some of the Olive stock by rendering services).

In contrast, Bob has no recognized gain on the receipt of stock because he transfers "property" and he has "control" of Olive after the transfer; see the discussion concerning control that follows. Bob has a substituted basis of $15,000 in the Olive stock.

18-1c Stock Transferred

Nonrecognition of gain occurs only when the shareholder receives stock. Stock includes common and most preferred shares. However, it does not include "nonqualified preferred stock," which possesses many of the attributes of debt. In addition, the Regulations state that the term *stock* does not include stock rights and stock warrants. Otherwise, the term *stock* generally needs no clarification.[8]

As a result, any corporate debt or securities (e.g., long-term debt such as bonds) received are treated as boot because they are not shares of stock. Therefore, a shareholder who receives corporate debt in exchange for the transfer of appreciated property to a controlled corporation recognizes gain if the shareholder realizes a gain on the contribution.

The Big Picture

EXAMPLE 4

Return to the facts of *The Big Picture* on p. 18-1. Assume that the proposed transaction involving Emily and Ethan qualifies under § 351, but Emily decides to receive some corporate debt along with the stock.

If she receives Transformation stock worth $1,900,000 and Transformation debt of $100,000 in exchange for the property transferred, Emily realizes gain of $1,600,000 [$2,000,000 (value of consideration received) − $400,000 (basis in the transferred property)]. However, because the transaction qualifies under § 351, only $100,000 of gain is recognized—the $100,000 of Transformation debt is treated as boot. The remaining realized gain of $1,500,000 is deferred.

18-1d Control of the Corporation

For the transaction to qualify as nontaxable under § 351, the property transferors must be in control of the corporation immediately after the exchange. That is, the person or persons transferring the property must have at least an 80 percent stock ownership in the corporation. More specifically, the property transferors must own stock possessing at least 80 percent of the total combined *voting power* of all classes of stock entitled to vote *and* at least 80 percent of the total *number of shares* of all other classes of stock.[9]

Control Immediately after the Transfer

Control after the exchange can apply to a single person or to several taxpayers if they are all parties in an integrated transaction. To satisfy the timing requirement, when more than one person is involved, the exchange does not necessarily require simultaneous exchanges by those persons. However, the rights of those transferring property to the corporation must be previously set out and determined. Also, the agreement to transfer property should be executed "with an expedition consistent with orderly procedure," and the transfers should occur close together in time.[10]

---

[7]The value of closely held stock normally is presumed to equal the value of the property transferred.

[8]§ 351(g). Examples of nonqualified preferred stock include preferred stock that is redeemable within 20 years of issuance and whose dividend rate is based on factors other than corporate performance. See also Reg. § 1.351–1(a)(1)(ii).

[9]§ 368(c). Nonqualified preferred stock is treated as stock, not boot, for purposes of this control test.

[10]Reg. § 1.351–1(a)(1).

The Point at Which Control Is Determined

EXAMPLE
5

Jack exchanges property with a basis of $60,000 and fair market value of $100,000 for 70% of the stock of Gray Corporation. The other 30% of the stock is owned by Jane, who acquired it several years ago. The fair market value of Jack's stock is $100,000.

Jack recognizes a taxable gain of $40,000 on the transfer because he does not control the corporation after his transfer and his transaction cannot be integrated with Jane's for purposes of the control requirement.

The Big Picture

EXAMPLE
6

Return to the facts of *The Big Picture* on p. 18-1. Assume that the proposed transaction involving Emily and Ethan occurs as described. However, in addition, David decides to contribute property to the new corporation in exchange for an equity interest.

As a result, Emily exchanges her property for 200 shares of Transformation, Inc. stock on January 7, 2019, David exchanges his property for 10 shares of Transformation stock on January 14, 2019, and Ethan exchanges his property for 4,800 shares in Transformation on March 5, 2019.

Because the three exchanges are part of a prearranged plan and the control test is met, the nonrecognition provisions of § 351 apply to all of the exchanges.

Once control has been achieved, it is not necessarily lost if, shortly after the transaction, stock received by shareholders is sold or given to persons who are not parties to the exchange.[11]

EXAMPLE
7

Naomi and Eric form Eagle Corporation. They transfer appreciated property to the corporation with each receiving 50 shares of Eagle stock. Shortly after the formation, Naomi gives 25 shares to her son.

Because Naomi was not committed to making the gift, she met the control test "immediately after the exchange." Therefore, Naomi and Eric meet the requirements of § 351, and neither recognizes gain on the exchange.

The following two examples show that a different result might occur if a plan for the ultimate disposition of the stock existed *before* the exchange. In other words, mere momentary control on the part of the transferor may not suffice if loss of control is required by a prearranged agreement.[12]

The Impact of a Preconceived Plan on the Control Requirement

EXAMPLE
8

Assume the same facts as in Example 7, except that Naomi immediately gives 25 shares to a business associate pursuant to a plan to satisfy an outstanding obligation.

In this case, the formation of Eagle would be taxable to Naomi and Eric because they jointly owned only 75% of the stock.

EXAMPLE
9

For many years, Paula operated a business as a sole proprietor employing Brooke as manager. To dissuade Brooke from quitting and going out on her own, Paula promised her a 30% interest in the business. To fulfill this promise, Paula transfers the business to newly formed Green Corporation in return for all of its stock. Immediately thereafter, Paula transfers 30% of the stock to Brooke.

Section 351 probably does not apply to Paula's transfer to Green Corporation because it appears that Paula was under an obligation to relinquish control. If this preexisting obligation exists, § 351

continued

---

[11] *Wilgard Realty Co. v. Comm.,* 42–1 USTC ¶9452, 29 AFTR 325, 127 F.2d 514 (CA–2, 1942).

[12] Rev.Rul. 54–96, 1954–1 C.B. 111.

> will not be available to Paula because, as the sole property transferor, she does not have 80% control of Green Corporation.
>
> However, if there is no obligation and the loss of control was voluntary on Paula's part, momentary control would suffice.[13]

Stock need not be issued to the property transferors in the same proportion as the relative value of the property transferred by each. However, when stock received is not proportionate to the value of the property transferred, the actual effect of the transactions must be properly characterized. For example, in such situations, one transferor may actually be making a gift to another transferor.

EXAMPLE 10

Noah and Shelia, father and daughter, form Oak Corporation. Noah transfers property worth $50,000 in exchange for 100 shares of stock, and Shelia transfers property worth $50,000 for 400 shares of stock.

The transfers qualify under § 351 because Noah and Shelia have control of the Oak stock immediately after the transfers of property. However, the implicit gift of 150 shares by Noah to Shelia must be recognized and appropriately characterized. As such, the value of the gift might be subject to the gift tax (see Chapter 27).

Transfers for Property and Services

Examples 5, 8, and 9 show that taxpayers can lose § 351 treatment if persons who do not transfer property own "too much" stock. Example 11 shows how a service contributor can cause a property contributor to fail the control test and thus have to recognize gain.

EXAMPLE 11

Sarah transfers property with a basis of $400,000 and fair market value of $1,000,000 to Garden, Inc., and receives 50% of its stock. Tiffany receives the other 50% of the stock for services rendered (worth $1,000,000).

Tiffany has ordinary income of $1,000,000 because she contributes only services. She must recognize compensation income for services rendered.

Sarah contributes property, but she receives only 50% of Garden's stock. Because Sarah does not own at least 80% of Garden's stock, she has a taxable gain of $600,000 [$1,000,000 (fair market value of the stock in Garden) − $400,000 (basis in the transferred property)].

As noted earlier, a person receiving stock in exchange for services and for property transferred is taxed on the stock value related to those services but not on the stock issued for property, assuming the property transferors control the corporation. In addition, such a person can still be treated as a "property transferor," and in this case, all stock received by the person transferring both property and services counts toward whether the transferors control the corporation.[14]

EXAMPLE 12

Assume the same facts as in Example 11, except that Tiffany transfers property worth $800,000 (basis of $260,000) in addition to services rendered to Garden, Inc. (valued at $200,000).

Now Tiffany becomes a part of the control group. Sarah and Tiffany, as property transferors, together receive 100% of the corporation's stock. Consequently, § 351 applies to the exchanges.

As a result, Sarah recognizes no gain. Tiffany does not recognize gain on the transfer of the property, but she recognizes ordinary income to the extent of the value of the shares issued for services rendered. Thus, Tiffany recognizes $200,000 of ordinary income currently.

---

[13]Compare *Fahs v. Florida Machine and Foundry Co.*, 48–2 USTC ¶9329, 36 AFTR 1161, 168 F.2d 957 (CA–5, 1948), with *John C. O'Connor*, 16 TCM 213, T.C.Memo. 1957–50, *aff'd* in 58-2 USTC ¶9913, 2 AFTR 2d 6011, 260 F.2d 358 (CA–6, 1958).

[14]Reg. § 1.351–1(a)(2), Ex. 3.

Transfers for Services and Nominal Property

Note that to be part of the group meeting the 80 percent control test, the person contributing services must transfer property having more than a "relatively small value" compared with the services performed. When the primary purpose of the transfer is to qualify the transaction under § 351 for concurrent transferors, the Regulations provide that stock issued for property whose value is relatively small compared with the value of the stock already owned (or to be received for services rendered) will not be treated as issued in return for property.[15]

Exactly when a taxpayer who renders services and transfers property is included in the control group is often subject to question. However, the IRS has stated that such a transferor can be included in the control group if the value of the property transferred is at least 10 percent of the value of the services provided. If the value of the property transferred is less than this amount, the IRS is likely to treat the property contributed as having a relatively small value and disregard it in applying the control test.[16]

Determining Control Group Membership When Services Are Rendered

EXAMPLE 13

Ava and Rick form Grouse Corporation. Ava transfers land worth $100,000 with a basis of $20,000. Rick transfers equipment worth $50,000 with an adjusted basis of $10,000 and provides services worth $50,000. Ava and Rick each receive 50% of the Grouse stock.

Because the value of the property Rick transfers is not small relative to the value of the services he renders, his stock in Grouse Corporation is counted in determining control under § 351; thus, Ava and Rick jointly own 100% of the stock in Grouse. In addition, all of Rick's stock, not just the shares received for the equipment, counts in determining control.

As a result, Ava does not recognize gain on the transfer of the land. Rick similarly does not recognize the gain on his equipment; however, he must recognize income of $50,000 on the transfer of services. Even though the transfer of the equipment qualifies Rick as a property contributor under § 351, his transfer of services for stock is still taxable compensation income.

EXAMPLE 14

Assume the same facts as in Example 13, except that the value of Rick's property is $2,000 and the value of his services is $98,000.

In this situation, the value of the property is small relative to the value of the services (and well below the 10% IRS threshold); therefore, Rick does not qualify as a property transferor. Consequently, the transaction is fully taxable to both Ava and Rick. In this situation, Ava, the sole property transferor, lacks at least 80% control of Grouse Corporation following the transfer.

As a result, she will fully recognize her realized gain. Further, because Rick is not treated as having transferred property, the § 351 deferral is not available to him. As a result, he will recognize income of $98,000 relating to the services provided along with any realized gain or loss on the transfer of the additional $2,000 of property.

Transfers to Existing Corporations

Once a corporation is operational, § 351 also applies to any later transfers of property for stock by either new or existing shareholders. That is, § 351 does not apply solely at the time of corporate formation.

EXAMPLE 15

Tyrone and Andrew formed Blue Corporation three years ago. Both Tyrone and Andrew transferred appreciated property to Blue in exchange for 50 shares each in the corporation. The original transfers qualified under § 351, and neither Tyrone nor Andrew recognizes gain or loss on the exchange. In the current year, Tyrone transfers property (worth $90,000, adjusted basis of $5,000) for 50 additional Blue shares.

Tyrone has a taxable gain of $85,000 on the transfer. The exchange does not qualify under § 351 because Tyrone does not have 80% control of Blue Corporation immediately after the transfer—he owns 100 shares of the 150 shares outstanding, or a 66⅔% interest.

---

[15]Reg. § 1.351–1(a)(1)(ii).   [16]Rev.Proc. 77–37, 1977–2 C.B. 568.

LO.2

Describe the special rules that apply when a corporation assumes shareholder liabilities.

18-1e Assumption of Liabilities—§ 357

It is not uncommon to form a corporation by transferring assets *and* liabilities of an unincorporated business. Generally, the party that enjoys the debt relief treats it as cash received equal to the debt relief. Without a provision to the contrary, the transfer of mortgaged property to a controlled corporation could trigger gain to the property transferor if the corporation took over the mortgage. Section 357(a) provides, however, that when the acquiring corporation assumes a liability in a § 351 transaction, the liability is not treated as boot received for gain recognition purposes. (However, liabilities assumed by the corporation are treated as boot in determining the basis of the stock received by the shareholder.) As a result, the basis of the stock received is reduced by the amount of the liabilities assumed by the corporation. See the more complete discussion of basis computations in text Section 18-1f.

The Big Picture

EXAMPLE 16

Return to the facts of *The Big Picture* on p. 18-1. Assume that you learn that David is not interested in becoming a stockholder in Transformation, Inc., and that Emily and Ethan will transfer their property for 100% of the stock. In addition, you learn that Emily's building is subject to a liability of $70,000 that Transformation assumes. Consequently, Emily receives her Transformation stock, is relieved of the $70,000 liability, and contributes property with an adjusted basis of $400,000 and fair market value of $2,000,000.

The exchange is tax-free to Emily under § 351 because § 357(a) precludes treating the debt relief as boot for determining recognized gain. However, the basis to Emily of the Transformation stock is $330,000 [$400,000 (basis of property transferred) − $70,000 (amount of the liability Transformation assumes)]. This basis reduction reflects the economic benefit that Emily enjoys by transferring her mortgage to the corporation.

The general rule of § 357(a) has two exceptions: (1) § 357(b) provides that if the principal purpose of the assumption of the liabilities is to avoid tax *or* if there is no bona fide business purpose behind the exchange, the liabilities are treated as boot for determining recognized gain and (2) § 357(c) provides that if the sum of the liabilities exceeds the adjusted basis of the properties transferred, the excess is taxable gain.

Exception (1): Tax Avoidance or No Bona Fide Business Purpose

Satisfying the bona fide business purpose under § 357(b) is not difficult if the liabilities are incurred in connection with the transferor's normal course of conducting a trade or business. But what if the shareholder borrows money shortly before transferring the property and uses the proceeds for personal purposes?[17] This type of situation is analogous to the corporation transferring both stock and cash to the shareholder, resulting in boot treatment for the liabilities assumed.

EXAMPLE 17

Dan transfers real estate with a basis of $140,000 and fair market value of $190,000 to a controlled corporation in return for stock in the corporation. However, shortly before the transfer, Dan mortgages the real estate and uses the $20,000 of proceeds to meet personal obligations.

In this case, the assumption of the mortgage lacks a bona fide business purpose. Consequently, § 357(b) treats the debt relief as boot received, and Dan has a taxable gain of $20,000 on the transfer.[18]

Amount realized:	
Stock	$ 170,000
Release of liability—treated as boot	20,000
Total amount realized	$ 190,000
Less: Basis of real estate	(140,000)
Realized gain	$ 50,000
Recognized gain	$ 20,000

---

[17]See, for example, *Campbell, Jr. v. Wheeler*, 65–1 USTC ¶9294, 15 AFTR 2d 578, 342 F.2d 837 (CA–5, 1965).

[18]§ 351(b).

The effect of the application of § 357(b) is to taint *all* liabilities transferred even if *some* are supported by a bona fide business purpose.

Tim, an accrual basis taxpayer, incorporates his sole proprietorship. Among the liabilities transferred to the new corporation are trade accounts payable of $100,000 and a credit card bill of $5,000. Tim had used the credit card to purchase an anniversary gift for his spouse.

Under these circumstances, *all* of the $105,000 of liabilities are treated as boot and trigger the recognition of gain to the extent gain is realized.

EXAMPLE 18

Exception (2): Liabilities in Excess of Basis

The second exception in § 357(c) provides that if the amount of a shareholder's liabilities assumed exceeds the total of the adjusted bases of the properties transferred by that shareholder, the excess is taxable gain. Without this provision, when there are liabilities in excess of basis in a property exchange, a taxpayer would have a negative basis in the stock received in the controlled corporation.[19] Section 357(c) precludes the negative basis possibility by treating the excess over basis as gain to the transferor.

Andre transfers land and equipment with adjusted bases of $350,000 and $50,000, respectively, to a newly formed corporation in exchange for 100% of the stock. The corporation assumes a $500,000 liability on the transferred land.

Without § 357(c), Andre's basis in the stock of the new corporation would be negative $100,000 [$400,000 (bases of properties transferred) + $0 (gain recognized) − $0 (boot received) − $500,000 (liability assumed)]. Section 357(c), however, requires Andre to recognize gain of $100,000 ($500,000 liability assumed − $400,000 total bases of assets transferred).

As a result, the stock has a zero basis in Andre's hands, determined as follows:

EXAMPLE 19

Bases in the properties transferred ($350,000 + $50,000)	$ 400,000
Plus: Gain recognized	100,000
Less: Boot received	–0–
Less: Liability assumed	(500,000)
Basis in the stock received	$ –0–

Consequently, Andre recognizes $100,000 of gain and avoids a negative stock basis.

The definition of liabilities under § 357(c) *excludes* obligations that would have been deductible to the transferor had those obligations been paid before the transfer. Therefore, accounts payable of a cash basis taxpayer are ignored when applying § 357(c) and in computing the shareholder's stock basis.

Tina, a cash basis taxpayer, incorporates her sole proprietorship. In return for all of the stock of the new corporation, she transfers the following items:

EXAMPLE 20

	Adjusted Basis	Fair Market Value
Cash	$10,000	$10,000
Unrealized accounts receivable (amounts due to Tina but not yet received by her)	–0–	40,000
Trade accounts payable	–0–	30,000
Note payable	5,000	5,000

continued

---

[19] *Jack L. Easson*, 33 T.C. 963 (1960), *rev'd* in 61–2 USTC ¶9654, 8 AFTR 2d 5448, 294 F.2d 653 (CA–9, 1961).

Because uncollected accounts receivable and unpaid trade accounts payable have a zero basis for cash basis taxpayers, they recognize no income until they collect the receivables and no deduction until they pay the accounts payable. The note payable has a basis because it was issued for consideration received.

In this situation, Tina disregards the accounts payable for determining her recognized gain and for determining her stock basis. Thus, for purposes of § 357(c), because the balance of the note payable does not exceed the basis of the assets transferred, Tina does not face the situation of liabilities in excess of basis (i.e., the note payable of $5,000 does not exceed the aggregate basis in the cash and accounts receivable of $10,000).

Conceivably, a situation could arise where both §§ 357(b) and (c) apply in the same transfer. In such a situation, § 357(b) predominates.[20] This could be significant because § 357(b) does not automatically create gain on the transfer, as does § 357(c), but merely converts the liability to boot. Thus, the realized gain limitation continues to apply to § 357(b) transactions.

EXAMPLE 21

Chris forms Robin Corporation by transferring land with a basis of $100,000 and a fair market value of $1,000,000. The land is subject to a mortgage of $300,000. One month before incorporating Robin, Chris borrows $200,000 for personal purposes and gives the lender a second mortgage on the land. Therefore, on the incorporation, Robin issues stock worth $500,000 to Chris and assumes the two mortgages on the land.

Section 357(c) seems to apply to the transfer, given that the mortgages on the property exceed the basis of the property. As a result, Chris would have a gain of $400,000 under § 357(c).

Section 357(b), however, also applies to the transfer because Chris borrowed $200,000 just prior to the transfer and used the loan proceeds for personal purposes. Thus, under § 357(b), Chris has boot of $500,000 in the amount of the liabilities, which triggers $500,000 of recognized gain. Note that *all* of the liabilities are treated as boot, not just the tainted $200,000 liability.

	§ 357(b) Result	§ 357(c) Result
Amount realized:		
Robin Corporation stock	$ 500,000	$ 500,000
Release of mortgage on land	300,000	300,000
Release of second mortgage—personal purposes	200,000	200,000
Total amount realized	$1,000,000	$1,000,000
Basis of land	(100,000)	(100,000)
Realized gain	$ 900,000	$ 900,000
Gain recognized under § 357(b) ($300,000 + $200,000)	$ 500,000	
Gain recognized under § 357(c)		
[($300,000 + $200,000) − $100,000]		$ 400,000

Unfortunately for Chris, the relatively more onerous rule of § 357(b) predominates over § 357(c), requiring the recognition of $500,000 of gain.

Concept Summary 18.2 summarizes the tax rules that apply when liabilities are transferred in property transactions, including the special rules that apply in § 351 transactions.

LO.3

Identify the basis issues relevant to the shareholder and the corporation.

18-1f **Basis Determination and Related Issues**

Recall that § 351(a) postpones gain or loss until the transferor-shareholder disposes of the stock in a taxable transaction. The postponement of shareholder gain or loss has a corollary effect on the basis of the stock received by the shareholder and the basis of the property received by the corporation. This procedure ensures that the corporation recognizes the gain or loss postponed under § 351 when it sells the contributed asset in a taxable transaction.

---

[20]§ 357(c)(2)(A).

Concept Summary 18.2

Tax Consequences of Liability Assumption

General rule: (§ 1001)	If Red Corporation takes property subject to Taxpayer's liability or assumes Taxpayer's liability, Taxpayer is treated as having received cash due to the debt relief. Therefore, if the liability is $20,000, Taxpayer is treated as receiving Red stock of $80,000 and cash of $20,000 in a fully taxable transaction. Gain realized and recognized is $60,000.
Special rule in a § 351 transaction: [§ 357(a)]	Assume the same facts as above, except that the transfer is a § 351 transaction. Taxpayer is not treated as receiving cash of $20,000 for gain recognition purposes (the debt relief is *not* treated as boot). Therefore, gain recognition is avoided. The debt relief will, however, reduce the Taxpayer's basis in Red Corporation stock.
Exception to § 351 transaction rule—Tax avoidance or no bona fide business purpose: [§ 357(b)]	Assume the same facts as above, except that the transfer is a § 351 transaction and the liability does not have a business purpose. Taxpayer is treated as receiving cash of $20,000 for gain recognition purposes (the debt relief *is* treated as boot). Therefore, $20,000 of the realized gain is recognized.
Exception to § 351 transaction rule—Liabilities in excess of basis: [§ 357(c)]	Assume the same facts as above, except that the transfer is a § 351 transaction, the liability is $45,000, the Red stock is worth $55,000, and § 357(b) does not apply. Taxpayer recognizes $5,000 of gain (excess of $45,000 liability over $40,000 property basis).

Basis of Stock to Shareholder

For a taxpayer transferring property to a corporation in a § 351 transaction, the shareholder's *stock* received in the transaction takes a *substituted basis*. Specifically, the stock's basis equals the taxpayer's basis in the property transferred plus any gain recognized on the exchange of property minus the fair value of boot received (see Exhibit 18.1). Recall that for computing basis, boot received always includes liabilities transferred by the shareholder to the corporation. Also note that if the shareholder receives *other property* (i.e., boot) along with the stock, that property takes a basis equal to its fair market value.[21] See the discussion below relating to an elective stock basis reduction that may be made when a shareholder contributes property with a net built-in loss.

EXHIBIT 18.1	Shareholder's Basis of Stock Received in Exchange for Property
Adjusted basis of property transferred	$xx,xxx
Plus: Gain recognized	xxx
Minus: Boot received (including any liabilities transferred)	(xxx)
Minus: Adjustment for loss property (if elected)	(xxx)
Equals: Basis of stock received	$xx,xxx

[21]§ 358(a). Recall from earlier discussions that the basis of stock received for services rendered equals its fair market value.

Basis of Property to Corporation

The basis of *property* received by the corporation generally is determined under a *carryover basis* rule. Because a shareholder's stock embeds unrecognized gain or loss into the stock basis, a similar *carryover* basis rule exists for computing the basis of the corporation's *property*. This rule provides that the property's basis to the corporation equals the basis in the hands of the transferor plus any gain recognized on the transfer by the transferor-shareholder.[22]

Examples 22 and 23 illustrate these basis rules.

Calculating Basis: Shareholder Stock and Corporate Property

EXAMPLE 22

Kesha and Ned form Brown Corporation. Kesha transfers land (basis of $30,000 and fair market value of $70,000); Ned invests cash ($60,000). They each receive 50 shares in Brown Corporation worth $60,000, but Kesha also receives $10,000 in cash from Brown.

The transfers of property, the realized and recognized gain on the transfers, and the basis of the stock in Brown Corporation to Kesha and Ned are as follows:

	A	B	C	D	E	F
	Basis of Property Transferred	FMV of Stock Received	Boot Received	Realized Gain (B + C − A)	Recognized Gain (Lesser of C or D)	Basis of Stock in Brown (A − C + E)
From Kesha:						
Land	$30,000	$60,000	$10,000	$40,000	$10,000	$30,000
From Ned:						
Cash	60,000	60,000	–0–	–0–	–0–	60,000

Brown Corporation has a basis of $40,000 in the land (Kesha's basis of $30,000 plus her recognized gain of $10,000).

EXAMPLE 23

Assume the same facts as in Example 22, except that Kesha's basis in the land is $68,000 (instead of $30,000). Because recognized gain cannot exceed realized gain, the transfer generates only $2,000 of gain to Kesha. The realized and recognized gain and the basis of the stock in Brown Corporation to Kesha are as follows:

	A	B	C	D	E	F
	Basis of Property Transferred	FMV of Stock Received	Boot Received	Realized Gain (B + C − A)	Recognized Gain (Lesser of C or D)	Basis of Stock in Brown (A − C + E)
Land	$68,000	$60,000	$10,000	$2,000	$2,000	$60,000

Brown's basis in the land is $70,000 ($68,000 basis to Kesha + $2,000 gain recognized by Kesha).

Exhibit 18.2 summarizes the basis calculation for property received by a corporation. Concept Summary 18.3 shows the shareholder and corporate consequences of a transfer of property to a corporation for stock, with and without the application of § 351. The facts applicable to shareholder Kesha's transfer in Example 22 are used to illustrate the differences between the transaction being tax-deferred and taxable.

EXHIBIT 18.2	Corporation's Basis in Property Received
Adjusted basis of property transferred	$xx,xxx
Plus: Gain recognized by transferor-shareholder	xxx
Minus: Adjustment for loss property (if required)	(xxx)
Equals: Basis of property to corporation	$xx,xxx

---

[22]§ 362(a).

Concept Summary 18.3

Tax Consequences to the Shareholders and Corporation: With and Without the Application of § 351 (Based on the Facts of Example 22)

Shareholder	With § 351			Without § 351		
	Gain/Loss Recognized	Stock Basis	Other Property Basis	Gain/Loss Recognized	Stock Basis	Other Property Basis
Kesha	Realized gain recognized to extent of boot received; loss not recognized.	Substituted (see Exhibit 18.1).	FMV	All realized gain or loss recognized.	FMV	FMV
	$10,000	$30,000	$10,000	$40,000	$60,000	$10,000

Corporation	With § 351		Without § 351	
	Gain/Loss Recognized	Property Basis	Gain/Loss Recognized	Property Basis
Brown	No gain or loss recognized on the transfer of corporate stock for property.	Carryover (see Exhibit 18.2).	No gain or loss recognized on the transfer of corporate stock for property.	FMV
	$0	$40,000	$0	$70,000

Note that the benefit to Kesha of deferring $30,000 of gain under § 351 comes with a cost: her stock basis is $30,000 (rather than $60,000), and the corporation's basis in the property received is $40,000 (rather than $70,000). In this sense, the deferred gain reduces the basis of the stock for Kesha ($30,000 stock basis = $60,000 FMV − $30,000 deferred gain) and the basis of the land for Brown Corporation ($40,000 land basis = $70,000 FMV − $30,000 deferred gain).

Basis Adjustment for Loss Property

Concept Summary 18.3 shows that when Kesha contributes property in a § 351 transaction, Kesha and the corporation reduce the basis of Kesha's stock and the basis of the contributed assets. This duplicates the gain potential for the two entities. Despite this, the government does not allow taxpayers to duplicate losses in a similar manner. Accordingly, when a taxpayer contributes **built-in loss property** to a corporation, the aggregate basis of the assets transferred by a shareholder can exceed their fair market value. When this built-in loss situation exists, an anti-loss duplication rule requires the basis in the loss properties to be stepped down by allocating the built-in loss proportionately among the assets.[23]

> **EXAMPLE 24**
>
> In a transaction qualifying under § 351, Charles transfers the following assets to Gold Corporation in exchange for all of its stock:
>
> | | Tax Basis | Fair Market Value | Built-In Gain/(Loss) |
> |---|---|---|---|
> | Equipment | $100,000 | $ 90,000 | ($10,000) |
> | Land | 200,000 | 230,000 | 30,000 |
> | Building | 150,000 | 100,000 | (50,000) |
> | | $450,000 | $420,000 | ($30,000) |
>
> Charles's stock basis is $450,000 [$450,000 (basis of the property transferred) + $0 (gain recognized) − $0 (boot received)]. However, Gold's basis for the loss assets transferred must be reduced by the amount of the net built-in loss ($30,000) in proportion to each asset's share of the loss.
>
> *continued*

---

[23]§ 362(e)(2). This adjustment is determined separately with respect to each property transferor. This adjustment also is required in the case of a contribution to capital by a shareholder.

	Unadjusted Tax Basis	Adjustment	Adjusted Tax Basis
Equipment	$100,000	($ 5,000)*	$ 95,000
Land	200,000		200,000
Building	150,000	(25,000)**	125,000
	$450,000	($30,000)	$420,000

* $\dfrac{\$10,000 \text{ (loss attributable to equipment)}}{\$60,000 \text{ (total built-in loss)}} \times \$30,000 \text{ (net built-in loss)}$

= $5,000 (adjustment to basis in equipment)

** $\dfrac{\$50,000 \text{ (loss attributable to building)}}{\$60,000 \text{ (total built-in loss)}} \times \$30,000 \text{ (net built-in loss)}$

= $25,000 (adjustment to basis in building)

Note the end result for Example 24:

- Charles still has a built-in loss in his stock basis. As a result, if he sells the Gold Corporation stock, he will recognize a loss of $30,000 [$420,000 (selling price based on presumed value of the stock) − $450,000 (basis in the stock)].

- Gold Corporation can no longer recognize a loss on the sale of *all* of its assets [$420,000 (selling price based on value of assets) − $420,000 (adjusted basis in assets) = $0 (gain or loss)].

In the event a corporation is subject to the built-in loss adjustment, an alternative approach is available. If *both* the shareholder and the corporation elect, the basis reduction can be made to the shareholder's stock rather than to the corporation's property.

EXAMPLE 25

Assume the same facts as in the previous example. If Charles and Gold elect, Charles can reduce his stock basis to $420,000 ($450,000 − $30,000). As a result, Gold's aggregate basis in the assets is $450,000.

If Charles has no intention of selling his stock, this election could be desirable since it benefits Gold by giving the corporation a higher depreciable basis in the equipment and building. In addition, reducing a capital loss or increasing a capital gain can impose lower tax costs on the shareholder than the adjustment to a corporation's asset bases.

Note the end result for Example 25:

- Charles has no built-in loss. As a result, if he sells the Gold Corporation stock, he will recognize no gain or loss [$420,000 (presumed value of the stock) − $420,000 (basis in the stock)].

- Gold Corporation has a built-in loss. As a result, if it sells *all* of its assets [$420,000 (selling price based on value of assets) − $450,000 (basis in assets)], it recognizes a loss of $30,000.

Consequently, as shown in the two previous examples, the built-in loss adjustment places the loss with *either* the shareholder or the corporation but not both.

Corporate Treatment When Issuing Stock for Services

A corporation's transfer of its stock for property is not a taxable exchange. A transfer of shares for services is also not a taxable transaction to a corporation.[24] But another issue arises: Can a corporation deduct as a business expense the fair market value of the stock it issues in consideration of services? Yes, unless the services are a capital expenditure.[25]

---

[24]Reg. § 1.1032–1(a).

[25]Rev.Rul. 62–217, 1962–2 C.B. 59, modified by Rev.Rul. 74–503, 1974–2 C.B. 117.

The Big Picture

EXAMPLE
26

Return to the facts of *The Big Picture* on p. 18-1. Emily transfers her $2,000,000 of property to Transformation, Inc., and receives 200 shares of stock, and Ethan transfers $48,000,000 of cash for 4,800 shares of stock. In the same transaction, David transfers property worth $800,000 (basis of $260,000) and agrees to serve as manager of the corporation for one year (services worth $200,000) for 100 shares of the stock.

Emily's, Ethan's, and David's transfers qualify under § 351. None of them is taxed on the transfer of his or her property. However, David has income of $200,000, the value of the stock received for the services he will render to Transformation, Inc.

Transformation has a basis of $260,000 in the property it acquired from David, and it may claim a compensation expense deduction under § 162 for $200,000. David's stock basis is $460,000 [$260,000 (basis of property transferred) + $200,000 (income recognized for services rendered)].

The Big Picture

EXAMPLE
27

Assume the same facts as in Example 26, except that David provides legal services (instead of management services) in organizing the corporation. The value of David's legal services is $200,000.

David has no gain on the transfer of the property but has income of $200,000 for the value of the stock received for the services rendered. Transformation, Inc., has a basis of $260,000 in the property it acquired from David and must capitalize the $200,000 as an organizational expenditure. David's stock basis is $460,000 [$260,000 (basis of property transferred) + $200,000 (income recognized for services rendered)].

Holding Period for Shareholder and Transferee Corporation

In a § 351 transfer, the shareholder's holding period for stock received in exchange for a capital asset or § 1231 property includes the holding period of the property transferred to the corporation. That is, the holding period of the property is "tacked on" to the holding period of the stock. The holding period for stock received for any other property (e.g., cash or inventory) begins on the day after the exchange.

The corporation's holding period for property acquired in a § 351 transfer is the holding period of the transferor-shareholder regardless of the character of the property in the transferor's hands. For instance, whether the property transferred is an ordinary asset (e.g., inventory), a § 1231 asset, or a capital asset, the corporation's holding period is the same as the transferor's.[26]

Recapture Considerations

Sales of depreciable assets with a value that exceeds their basis result in ordinary gain up to the accumulated depreciation deducted. The rest of the gain usually is § 1231 gain. Because § 351 defers the gain when a shareholder contributes depreciable property to a corporation, the depreciation recapture potential also transfers to the corporation.[27] That is, any recapture potential associated with the property carries over to the corporation. This rule prevents taxpayers from converting ordinary income into § 1231 gain by transferring the property to a controlled corporation.

EXAMPLE
28

Paul transfers equipment (adjusted basis of $30,000, original cost of $120,000, and fair market value of $100,000) to a controlled corporation in return for stock. If Paul had sold the equipment, it would have yielded a gain of $70,000, all of which would have been treated as ordinary income under the § 1245 depreciation recapture rules.

Because the transfer comes within § 351, Paul has no recognized gain and no depreciation to recapture. However, if the corporation later disposes of the equipment in a taxable transaction, it must take into account the § 1245 recapture potential originating with Paul.

So, for example, if the corporation were to sell the asset shortly after incorporation for $100,000, all of the $70,000 gain recognized would be given ordinary treatment because of the depreciation recapture rules.

---

[26]§§ 1223(1) and (2).

[27]§§ 1245(b)(3) and 1250(d)(3).

18-2 **CAPITAL STRUCTURE OF A CORPORATION**

When forming or expanding a corporation, the transaction can be financed with capital contributions or debt proceeds, or a combination of the two. Evaluating the relative tax and nontax advantages and disadvantages of these two basic elements in the capital structure of a corporation can help the corporation decide how to finance its activities.

18-2a **Capital Contributions**

Corporations recognize no gain or loss when they issue shares of stock (including treasury stock) for money or property.[28] This is also true for voluntary or required shareholder contributions of money or property when the corporation issues no shares in return. The contributions represent an additional price paid for the shares held by the shareholders and are treated as additions to the capital of the corporation.[29]

In addition, corporations sometimes receive assets from *nonshareholders*. If a civic or government entity contributes property to a corporation to induce the corporation to locate in a particular community, the contributions are not tax-free capital contributions. Instead, the corporation includes these contributions in the corporation's gross income and takes a fair market value basis in the assets.[30] However, a governmental tax abatement granted to a corporation for locating in the jurisdiction is not taxable. The abatement just reduces future payments and related deductions for state and local taxes and is therefore ignored when granted.

EXAMPLE 29

A city donates land worth $400,000 to Teal Corporation as an inducement for Teal to locate in the city. The city also agreed to reduce the standard real estate tax rate for Teal by 50% on newly constructed property in the city.

The receipt of the land produces $400,000 of gross income to Teal, and the land's basis to the corporation is $400,000. However, the real estate tax abatement is not taxable to Teal.

A corporation recognizes income if a nonshareholder (a customer or potential customer) contributes assets to a corporation, even if the corporation labels these as contributions to aid construction or other capital expenditures.[31] Further, a corporation must recognize income if a nonshareholder transfers property to a corporation in exchange for goods or services.

EXAMPLE 30

A cable television company charges its customers an initial fee to hook up to a new cable system installed in the area. These payments help to finance the total cost of constructing the cable company's infrastructure. Customers will also make monthly payments for the cable service.

The initial payments are used for capital expenditures, but they represent payments for services to be rendered by the cable company. As such, they are taxable income to the cable company and not contributions to capital.

The basis of property a shareholder transfers to a corporation as a `capital contribution` equals the basis of the shareholder's basis in the property on the contribution date. However, the corporation must reduce this basis if the entire contribution has a built-in loss on the contribution date. This reduction is the same as illustrated in Example 24.[32] The basis of property transferred to a corporation that is not a capital contribution (e.g., by a governmental entity) equals the property's fair market value.

18-2b **Debt in the Capital Structure**

Various tax and nontax characteristics of debt and equity are relevant when developing the capital structure of a corporation. The relative amounts of debt and equity are a strategic variable for the corporation.

---

[28]§ 1032.

[29]§ 118(a) and Reg. § 1.118–1.

[30]§ 118(b)(2). However, under the law in effect on and before December 22, 2017, such contributions *were* excluded from gross income.

[31]§ 118(b)(1).

[32]§§ 362(a) and 362(e).

Advantages of Debt

The advantages of issuing long-term debt instead of stock are numerous. Interest on debt is deductible by the corporation, but dividend payments are not. Further, loan repayments are not taxable to investors unless the repayments exceed basis. In contrast, property distributions from a corporation to its shareholders are not tax-free if the corporation has earnings and profits (see Chapter 19). The government taxes these distributions as dividends to the extent of the corporation's earnings and profits.

Another distinction between debt and equity relates to the taxation of dividend and interest income. Shareholders enjoy preferential tax treatment on dividend income but not on interest income, which is taxed at the shareholder's regular income tax rates.

EXAMPLE

31

Wade transfers cash of $100,000 to a newly formed corporation for 100% of its stock. In its initial year, the corporation has net income and "earnings and profits" of $40,000. If the corporation distributes $7,500 to Wade, the distribution is a taxable dividend to Wade with no corresponding deduction to the corporation.

Assume, instead, that Wade transfers to the corporation cash of $50,000 for stock and cash of $50,000 for a note of the same amount. The note is payable in equal annual installments of $5,000 and bears interest at the rate of 5%. At the end of the year, the corporation pays Wade interest of $2,500 ($50,000 × 5%) and a note repayment of $5,000. The interest payment is a deductible expense to the corporation and taxable to Wade. The $5,000 principal repayment on the note is neither deducted by the corporation nor taxed to Wade.

Based on current tax rates, the table below computes the after-tax impact to Wade and the corporation under each alternative. For both Wade and the corporation, the better outcome occurs when the distribution is comprised of a note repayment and interest. That is, the after-tax income to Wade is higher, and the after-tax cost to the corporation is lower, under the debt scenario.

	If the Distribution Is	
	$7,500 Dividend	**$5,000 Note Repayment and $2,500 Interest**
*After-tax benefit to Wade**		
[$7,500 × (1 − 15%)]	$6,375	
{$5,000 + [$2,500 × (1 − 35%)]}		$6,625
After-tax cost to corporation		
No deduction to corporation	$7,500	
{$5,000 + [$2,500 × (1 − 21%)]}		$6,975

*Assumes that Wade's dividend income is taxed at the 15% capital gains rate and that his interest income is taxed at the 35% ordinary income rate.

Reclassification of Debt as Equity (Thin Capitalization Problem)

In situations where the IRS concludes that a corporation is thinly capitalized, the IRS contends that debt is an equity interest and denies the corporation the tax advantages of debt financing. **Thin capitalization** occurs when shareholder debt is high relative to shareholder equity. If the debt instrument has too many features of stock, the government can treat it as stock for tax purposes. This will result in treating principal and interest payments as dividends. Now that individual rates are higher (up to 37 percent) than corporate rates (21 percent), however, the IRS may be less inclined to raise the thin capitalization issue because the conversion of interest income to dividend income would produce a tax benefit to individual investors.

Section 385 lists several factors that the IRS uses to determine whether a debtor-creditor relationship or a shareholder-corporation relationship exists. Also, the section authorizes the Treasury to prescribe Regulations that provide more definitive guidelines. For years, however, definitive Treasury Regulations have not been available to provide guidance in this area. As a result, taxpayers have had to rely on numerous judicial decisions to determine whether a true debtor-creditor relationship exists.

In late 2016, the Treasury Department released Final and Temporary Regulations under § 385, which target certain "earnings stripping" transactions and related-party loans.[33] However, portions of the Regulations apply only to debt instruments issued on or after January 1, 2018. According to some tax professionals, these rules have left other important questions unanswered. As a result, the long line of judicial decisions establishing key guidelines and principles are likely to have continuing relevance.

For the most part, the principles used to classify debt as equity are most relevant for closely held corporations because the holders of the debt are also shareholders. Consequently, the rules have often proved inadequate for dealing with such problems in large, publicly traded corporations.

Together, Congress and the courts have identified the following factors as important in distinguishing between debt and equity:

- Whether the debt instrument is in proper form. The IRS is more likely to treat a verbal, unwritten debt agreement as a contribution to capital than a loan evidenced by a properly written note.[34]

- Whether the debt instrument bears a reasonable rate of interest and has a definite maturity date. When a shareholder advance does not provide for interest, the return expected may appear to be a share of the profits or an increase in the value of the shares.[35] Likewise, a lender unrelated to the corporation will usually be unwilling to commit funds to the corporation without a definite due date.

- Whether the corporation repays the debt on a timely basis. A lender's failure to insist upon timely repayment or satisfactory renegotiation indicates that the return sought does not depend upon interest income and the repayment of principal.

- Whether payment is contingent upon earnings. A lender ordinarily will not advance funds that are likely to be repaid only if the venture is successful.

- Whether the debt is subordinated to other liabilities. Subordination tends to reduce a significant characteristic of the creditor-debtor relationship. Creditors should have the right to share with other general creditors in the event of the corporation's dissolution or liquidation. Subordination also weakens another basic attribute of creditor status—the power to demand payment at a fixed maturity date.[36]

- Whether holdings of debt and stock are proportionate to shares owned (e.g., each shareholder owns the same percentage of debt as stock). When debt and equity obligations are held in the same proportion, shareholders are, apart from tax considerations, indifferent as to whether corporate distributions are in the form of interest or dividends.

- Whether funds loaned to the corporation are used to finance initial operations or capital asset acquisitions. Funds used to finance initial operations or to acquire capital assets the corporation needs are generally obtained through equity investments.

- Whether the corporation has a high ratio of shareholder debt to shareholder equity. Thin capitalization indicates that the corporation lacks reserves to pay interest and principal on debt when corporate income is insufficient to meet current needs.[37] In determining a corporation's debt-equity ratio, courts look at the relation of the debt both to the book value of the corporation's assets and to their fair market value.[38]

Section 385 gives the IRS the authority to classify an instrument either as *wholly* debt or equity or as *part* debt and *part* equity. This flexible approach is important because some instruments cannot readily be classified either wholly as stock or wholly as debt. It may also provide an avenue for the IRS to address problems in publicly traded corporations.

---

[33]See Final and Temporary Reg. §§ 1.385–1 to –4T (T.D. 9790).

[34]*Estate of Mixon, Jr. v. U.S.,* 72–2 USTC ¶9537, 30 AFTR 2d 72–5094, 464 F.2d 394 (CA–5, 1972).

[35]*Slappey Drive Industrial Park v. U.S.,* 77–2 USTC ¶9696, 40 AFTR 2d 77–5940, 561 F.2d 572 (CA–5, 1977).

[36]*Fin Hay Realty Co. v. U.S.,* 68-2 USTC ¶9438, 22 AFTR 2d 5004, 398 F.2d 694 (CA–3, 1968).

[37]A court held that a debt-equity ratio of approximately 14.6:1 was not excessive. See *Tomlinson v. 1661 Corp.,* 67–1 USTC ¶9438, 19 AFTR 2d 1413, 377 F.2d 291 (CA–5, 1967). A 26:1 ratio was found acceptable in *Delta Plastics, Inc.,* 85 TCM 940, T.C.Memo. 2003–54.

[38]In *Bauer v. Comm.,* 84–2 USTC ¶9996, 55 AFTR 2d 85–433, 748 F.2d 1365 (CA–9, 1984), a debt-equity ratio of 92:1 resulted when book value was used. But the ratio ranged from 2:1 to 8:1 when equity included both paid-in capital and accumulated earnings.

18-3 INVESTOR LOSSES

LO.6
Handle the tax treatment of shareholder debt and stock gains and losses.

The tax law provides some special rules for recognizing gains and losses from investing in corporate stock and debt. This section describes some of these special rules for losses, and the next section describes some of the rules for gains.

18-3a Stock and Security Losses

If corporate stock and bonds are capital assets in the hands of investors, losses from their worthlessness are governed by § 165(g)(1). Under this provision, a capital loss materializes as of the last day of the taxable year in which the stock or bonds become worthless. Investors cannot deduct a mere decline in value because there is no realization event. The burden of proving complete worthlessness is on the taxpayer claiming the loss. One way to recognize partial worthlessness is to dispose of the stock or bonds in a taxable sale or exchange.[39] But even then, the **investor loss** is disallowed if the sale or exchange is to a related party as defined under § 267(b) (e.g., parents and children are related, but aunts, uncles, and cousins are not considered related).

Stock and bonds are usually held as investments and so are capital assets. However, when they are not capital assets, such as when they are held by a broker for resale to customers, worthlessness yields an ordinary loss.[40]

Under certain circumstances involving stock and bonds of affiliated corporations, an ordinary loss is allowed upon worthlessness.[41] A corporation is an affiliate of another corporation if the corporate shareholder owns at least 80 percent of the voting power of all classes of stock entitled to vote and 80 percent of each class of nonvoting stock. Further, to be considered affiliated, the worthless corporation must have derived more than 90 percent of its aggregate gross receipts for all taxable years from sources other than passive income. Passive income for this purpose includes items such as rents, royalties, dividends, and interest. The reason for this latter requirement is to prevent a corporation from creating a subsidiary corporation by contributing capital assets and then taking an ordinary loss instead of capital losses from the capital assets.

18-3b Business versus Nonbusiness Bad Debts

In addition to worthlessness of stock and bonds, the financial demise of a corporation can result in bad debt deductions to those who have extended credit to the corporation. These deductions can be either business bad debts or **nonbusiness bad debts**. The distinction between the two types of deductions is important for tax purposes in the following respects:

- Business bad debts result in ordinary losses, while nonbusiness bad debts result in short-term capital losses.[42] A business bad debt can also result in (or increase) a net operating loss, but a nonbusiness bad debt cannot.[43]

ETHICS & EQUITY Can a Loss Produce a Double Benefit?

In late 2008, Sally invested $100,000 in TechCo, a startup high-tech venture. Although she had great expectations of financial gain, TechCo's efforts were not well received in the market, and the value of its stock plummeted. Four years ago when TechCo declared bankruptcy, Sally wrote off her $100,000 stock investment as worthless securities.

To Sally's surprise, this year she receives $40,000 from the bankruptcy trustee as a final settlement for her TechCo stock.

Sally now realizes that she probably should not have claimed the loss four years ago because the stock was not *completely* worthless.

However, since the statute of limitations has passed, she does not plan to amend her tax return from four years ago. She also decides that the $40,000 is not income but is merely a recovery of some of her original investment. How do you react to Sally's plans?

---

[39]Reg. § 1.165–4(a).

[40]§ 165(a) and Reg. § 1.165–5(b).

[41]§ 165(g)(3).

[42]Compare § 166(a) with § 166(d)(1)(B).

[43]Note the modification required by § 172(d)(2).

- A deduction is allowed for the partial worthlessness of a business debt, but investors can deduct nonbusiness debts only when they become entirely worthless.[44]

- Because corporations do not engage in personal transactions, all of their bad debts qualify as business bad debts and are never given nonbusiness bad debt treatment.[45]

When is a debt business or nonbusiness? Because the Code sheds little light on this question, the distinction has been left to the courts.[46] In a leading decision, the Supreme Court somewhat clarified the picture when it held that if individual shareholders lend money to a corporation in their capacity as investors, any resulting bad debt is classified as nonbusiness.[47] Nevertheless, the Court did not preclude the possibility of a shareholder-creditor incurring a business bad debt.

If a loan is made in some capacity that qualifies as a trade or business, nonbusiness bad debt treatment is avoided. For example, if an employee who is also a shareholder makes a loan to preserve employment status, the loan qualifies for business bad debt treatment.[48] Shareholders also receive business bad debt treatment if they are in the trade or business of lending money or of buying, promoting, and selling corporations. If the shareholder has multiple motives for making the loan, according to the Supreme Court, the "dominant" or "primary" motive for making the loan controls the classification of the loss.[49]

> **EXAMPLE 32**
>
> Juwon owns 48% of the stock of Lark Corporation, which he acquired several years ago at a cost of $600,000. Juwon is also employed by the corporation at an annual salary of $240,000.
>
> At a time when Lark Corporation experienced financial problems, Juwon loaned it $300,000. Later, the corporation became bankrupt, and both Juwon's stock investment and his loan became worthless.
>
> Juwon's stock investment results in a long-term capital loss (assuming that § 1244 does not apply, as discussed below). But how is the bad debt classified? If Juwon can prove that his dominant or primary reason for making the loan was to protect his salary, a business bad debt deduction results. If not, it is likely that Juwon was trying to protect his stock investment, and nonbusiness bad debt treatment results.

Factors in resolving the matter of business versus nonbusiness bad debts include the following:

- A comparison of the amount of the stock investment with the trade or business benefit derived. In Example 32, the stock investment of $600,000 is compared with the annual salary of $240,000. In this regard, the salary should be considered as a recurring item and not viewed in isolation. A salary of $240,000 each year means a great deal to a person who has no other means of support and may have difficulty obtaining similar employment elsewhere.

- A comparison of the amount of the loan with the stock investment and the trade or business benefit derived.

- The percentage of stock ownership held by the shareholder. A minority shareholder, for example, is under more compulsion to lend the corporation money to protect a job than a person who controls corporate decision making.

In summary, without additional facts, it is impossible to conclude whether Juwon in Example 32 suffered a business or nonbusiness bad debt. Even with such facts, the guidelines are vague. Recall that a taxpayer's intent or motivation is at issue. For this reason, the problem is frequently the subject of litigation.[50]

---

[44]Compare § 166(a)(2) with § 166(d)(1)(A).

[45]§ 166(d)(1).

[46]For definitional purposes, § 166(d)(2) is almost as worthless as the debt it purports to describe.

[47]*Whipple v. Comm.*, 63–1 USTC ¶9466, 11 AFTR 2d 1454, 83 S.Ct. 1168 (USSC, 1963).

[48]*Trent v. Comm.*, 61–2 USTC ¶9506, 7 AFTR 2d 1599, 291 F.2d 669 (CA–2, 1961).

[49]*U.S. v. Generes*, 72–1 USTC ¶9259, 29 AFTR 2d 72–609, 92 S.Ct. 827 (USSC, 1972).

[50]See, for example, *Kelson v. U.S.*, 74–2 USTC ¶9714, 34 AFTR 2d 74–6007, 503 F.2d 1291 (CA–10, 1974), *Kenneth W. Graves*, 87 TCM 1409, T.C.Memo. 2004–140, and *Harry Robert Haury*, 104 TCM 121, T.C.Memo. 2012–215.

18-3c **Section 1244 Stock**

In an exception to the capital treatment that generally results, § 1244 permits ordinary loss treatment for losses on the sale or worthlessness of stock of so-called small business corporations. By placing shareholders on a more nearly equal basis with proprietors and partners in terms of the tax treatment of losses, the provision encourages investment of capital in small corporations. Gain on the sale of § 1244 stock remains capital. Consequently, the shareholder has nothing to lose and everything to gain by complying with § 1244.

Qualification for § 1244

The ordinary loss treatment for §1244 stock applies to the first $1 million of capitalized value of the corporation's stock. If more than $1 million of the corporation's stock is issued, the entity designates which of the shares qualify for § 1244 treatment.[51] In measuring the capitalization of the newly issued stock, property received in exchange for stock is valued at its adjusted basis, reduced by any liabilities assumed by the corporation or to which the property is subject. The fair market value of the property is not considered, presumably because determining fair market value is costly and sometimes difficult, especially for small businesses. The $1 million limitation is determined on the date the stock is issued. Consequently, even though a corporation fails to meet these requirements when the stock is disposed of later by the shareholder, the stock can still qualify as § 1244 stock if the requirements were met on the date the stock was issued.

Mechanics of the Loss Deduction

The ordinary loss deduction limit in any one year from the disposition of § 1244 stock is $50,000 (or $100,000 for spouses filing a joint return). Any loss sustained in the taxable year exceeding the limit is considered a capital loss.

Several years ago, Chao acquired § 1244 stock at a cost of $100,000. He sells the stock for $10,000 in the current year. He has an ordinary loss of $50,000 and a capital loss of $40,000. Alternatively, on a joint return, the entire $90,000 loss is ordinary.

EXAMPLE
33

Only the original holder of § 1244 stock, whether an individual or a partnership, qualifies for ordinary loss treatment. If the stock is sold or donated, it loses its § 1244 status.

Shareholders must apply a special basis reduction if they receive § 1244 stock for property with an adjusted basis above its fair market value immediately before the exchange. These shareholders must reduce their stock basis to the fair market value of the property on the date of the exchange when they compute the ordinary loss upon a later sale. This rule is another effort to prevent taxpayers from converting capital losses into ordinary losses. Note, however, that this rule applies even if shareholders contribute ordinary income property to the corporation.

Dana transfers property with a basis of $10,000 and a fair market value of $5,000 to a corporation in exchange for shares of § 1244 stock. Assuming that the transfer qualifies under § 351, the basis of the stock under the general rule is $10,000, the same as Dana's basis in the property.

However, for purposes of § 1244 and measuring the amount of ordinary loss, the stock basis is only $5,000. If the stock is later sold for $3,000, the total loss sustained is $7,000 ($3,000 − $10,000); however, only $2,000 of the loss is ordinary ($3,000 − $5,000). The remaining portion of the loss, $5,000, is a capital loss.

EXAMPLE
34

Recall the advantages of issuing some debt to shareholders in exchange for cash contributions to a corporation. A disadvantage of issuing debt is that it does not qualify under § 1244. If the debt become worthless, the taxpayer generally has a short-term capital loss rather than the ordinary loss for § 1244 stock.

---

[51]Reg. § 1.1244(c)–2(b)(2).

18-4 GAIN FROM QUALIFIED SMALL BUSINESS STOCK

To further encourage corporate formations by small businesses, § 1202 gives shareholders special tax relief for gains recognized on the sale or exchange of stock acquired in a ==qualified small business corporation==. The holder of ==qualified small business stock== excludes a portion of gain from the sale or exchange of such stock. The exclusion percentage varies, depending on when the shareholder acquired the qualified small business stock. For example, shareholders exlude 100 percent of the gain for qualified stock acquired after September 27, 2010, but can exclude only either 75 percent or 50 percent for earlier acquisitions of stock.[52]

To qualify for the exclusion, the taxpayer must have held the stock for more than five years and must have acquired the stock as part of an original issue.[53] Only noncorporate shareholders qualify for the exclusion.

A qualified small business corporation is a C corporation whose aggregate gross assets did not exceed $50 million on the date the stock was issued.[54] The corporation must use at least 80 percent of its assets in the active conduct of one or more qualified trades or businesses.

A shareholder can exclude gain up to the greater of (1) $10 million or (2) 10 times the shareholder's aggregate adjusted basis in the qualified stock disposed of during a taxable year.[55]

EXAMPLE 35

Star Corporation originally issued stock in January 2012 to Jenna and Hao for capital contributions of $3,000,000 each. Star manufactures pipe fittings and other plumbing materials that are much less prone to failure and require much less maintenance than standard fittings. All Star assets contribute to the production and distribution of its products. The corporation performed extremely well, rising in value to $100,000,000. Unfortunately, Hao resigned from the corporation after several heated and unpleasant arguments with Jenna over the future direction of the company. In the middle of the current year, Hao sold his investment in Star to a private equity investment firm for $50,000,000.

Hao's sale qualifies for a 100% § 1202 gain exclusion. Hao is an original individual investor, he has held the stock for over five years, Star's initial assets amounted to far less than $50,000,000, and Star uses all of its assets in a business. The results of the sale are:

- Realized gain = $50,000,000 amount realized − $3,000,000 basis = $47,000,000.
- § 1202 exclusion = greater of $10,000,000 or ($3,000,000 × 10) = $30,000,000.
- Long-term capital gain = $47,000,000 − $30,000,000 = $17,000,000.
- Hao's expected tax cost = $17,000,000 × 23.8% = $4,000,000 (rounded).

The tax rate applied to this gain equals the top 20% net long-term capital gain rate plus the 3.8% net investment income tax rate. Note that if § 1202 did not exist, Hao's expected tax liability would be $11,200,000 (rounded) ($47,000,000 × 23.8%). Thus, the § 1202 gain exclusion resulted in a tax savings to Hao of over $7,000,000.

LO.7

Identify tax planning opportunities associated with organizing and financing a corporation.

18-5 TAX PLANNING

With any provision in the tax law affording special treatment, taxpayers must consider whether they *qualify* or *could* qualify for the special treatment and whether they *should* take advantage of the treatment. Section 351 provides one such provision that requires careful planning.

18-5a Working with § 351

Effective tax planning with transfers of property to corporations requires a clear understanding of § 351 and its related Code provisions. The most important question in planning is simply this: Does the desired tax result come from complying with § 351 or from avoiding it? The following discussion reviews key requirements to meet as well as traps to avoid when planning a § 351 transaction.

---

[52]§ 1202(a).

[53]The stock must have been issued after August 10, 1993, which is the original effective date of § 1202.

[54]§ 1202(d). Its aggregate assets may not exceed this amount at any time between August 10, 1993, and the date the stock was issued.

[55]§ 1202(b). The amount is $5 million for married taxpayers filing separately.

Using § 351

If shareholders want § 351 tax deferral, they should ensure that the parties transferring property (which includes cash) receive control of the corporation. Simultaneous transfers are not necessary, but a long period of time between transfers can trigger problems if the transfers are not properly documented as part of a single plan. The parties should document and preserve written evidence of their intentions. Also, it is helpful to have some reasonable explanation for any delay in the transfers.

The control requirement can be especially difficult to meet for exchanges of property for stock of a mature corporation. In these situations, gain deferral might require a larger contribution of assets than the new shareholders can afford. This provides an incentive to convince existing shareholders to make an "accommodation transfer" so that their shares count toward the control requirement. However, the Regulations make clear that an existing shareholder's previously acquired shares do not count toward meeting the control test if (a) the primary purpose of the transfer is to qualify other transferors for § 351 treatment and (b) the value of the "new stock" received is relatively small compared to the value of stock already owned.[56] Therefore, if a transferring shareholder who does not meet the 80 percent control test desires tax-deferred treatment of § 351, then the other shareholders should contribute property that equals at least 10 percent of the fair market value of the stock already owned.[57]

Avoiding § 351

Although § 351 frequently benefits shareholders by deferring gain, in some situations, shareholders benefit from avoiding § 351. This can occur if the transferors prefer to recognize gain on the transfer of property if the tax cost from the gain is low. For example, they may be in low tax brackets, or they could have capital losses available to offset capital gains. The corporation will then have a fair market value basis in the transferred property at a low or no tax cost.

A transferor might also prefer to avoid § 351 to allow for immediate recognition of a loss. Recall that § 351 provides for the nonrecognition of both gains and losses. A transferor who wants to recognize loss has several alternatives:

- Sell the property to the corporation for its stock. The IRS could attempt to collapse the "sale," however, by taking the approach that the transfer really falls under § 351.[58] If the sale is disregarded, the transferor ends up with a realized but unrecognized loss.
- Sell the property to the corporation for other property or boot. Because the transferor receives no stock, § 351 is inapplicable.
- Transfer the property to the corporation in return for securities or nonqualified preferred stock. Recall that § 351 does not apply to a transferor who receives securities or nonqualified preferred stock. In both this and the previous alternatives, watch for the possible disallowance of the loss under the related-party rules.

The deferral provisions in § 351 effectively transfer gains and some losses from shareholders to the corporation. This can increase or decrease future corporate tax liabilities. That is, transferring a gain asset creates a deferred tax liability for the corporation, but transferring a loss asset creates a deferred tax asset. Shareholders could justifiably consider this in establishing the number of shares granted, even if the properties transferred have the same fair market value.

EXAMPLE 36

Iris and Lamont form Wren Corporation with the following investments: property by Iris (basis of $40,000 and fair market value of $50,000) and property by Lamont (basis of $60,000 and fair market value of $50,000). Each receives 50% of the Wren stock. Has Lamont acted wisely in settling for only 50% of the stock?

At first, it would appear so because Iris and Lamont each invested property of the same value ($50,000). But what about tax considerations? By applying the general carryover basis rules, the corporation now has a basis of $40,000 in Iris's property and $60,000 in Lamont's property. In essence, Iris transferred a possible $10,000 gain to the corporation, while Lamont transferred a $10,000 potential loss. Thus, an equitable allocation of the Wren stock would call for Lamont to receive a greater percentage interest than Iris would receive.

continued

---

[56]Reg. § 1.351–1(a)(1)(ii).
[57]Rev.Proc. 77–37, 1977–2 C.B. 568.

[58]*U.S. v. Hertwig*, 68–2 USTC ¶9495, 22 AFTR 2d 5249, 398 F.2d 452 (CA–5, 1968).

> This issue is further complicated by the special basis adjustment required when a shareholder such as Lamont contributes property with a built-in loss to a corporation. In this situation, if Wren is to take a carryover basis in Lamont's property, Lamont must reduce his stock basis by the $10,000 built-in loss. This reduced stock basis, of course, could lead to a greater tax burden on Lamont when he sells the Wren stock. This may suggest additional support for Lamont having a greater percentage interest than Iris has.

18-5b Selecting Assets to Transfer

To obtain an optimal result when planning to incorporate a business, the organizers must determine which assets and liabilities shareholders should transfer to the corporation. A transfer of assets that produce passive income (rents, royalties, dividends, and interest) can cause the corporation to be a personal holding company in a tax year when operating income is low. Thus, the corporation could be subject to the personal holding company penalty tax (imposed by § 541 and discussed in Chapter 17) in addition to the regular income tax.

Leasing property to the corporation sometimes is a more attractive alternative than transferring ownership. Leasing provides the taxpayer with the opportunity to withdraw money from the corporation in a deductible form instead of receiving a nondeductible dividend. If the property is given to a family member in a lower tax bracket, the lease income can be shifted as well. If the depreciation and other deductions available in connection with the property are larger than the lease income, the taxpayer would retain the property until the income exceeds the deductions.

When an existing cash basis business is incorporated, the business owner must consider whether to contribute the business's accounts receivable and accounts payable to the new corporation or keep them. This decision will determine whether the new corporation or the owner of the old unincorporated business will recognize the income from collecting the cash basis receivables. Paying cash basis accounts payable raises the corresponding issue of who will claim the deduction.

The Big Picture

EXAMPLE 37

Return to the facts of *The Big Picture* on p. 18-1. If Emily decides to retain the $50,000 of cash basis accounts receivable rather than transfer them to the newly formed Transformation, Inc., she will recognize $50,000 of ordinary income upon their collection.

Alternatively, if she contributes the receivables to Transformation as the facts suggest, the corporation will recognize the ordinary income when they are collected. However, a subsequent corporate distribution to Emily of the cash collected could be subject to double taxation as a dividend (see Chapter 19 for further discussion). Given the alternatives available, Emily needs to evaluate which approach is better for the parties involved.

Another way to shift income to other taxpayers is by the use of corporate debt. Shareholders who also own corporate debt can give the debt to family members in a lower tax bracket. This gift will shift the interest income without losing control of the corporation.

18-5c Debt in the Capital Structure

The advantages and disadvantages of debt as opposed to equity have previously been noted. To increase debt without incurring the thin capitalization problem, consider the following tax planning strategies:

- Preserve the formalities of the debt. This includes providing for written instruments, realistic interest rates, and specified due dates.
- If possible, have the corporation repay the debt when it comes due. If this is not possible, have the parties renegotiate the arrangement. Try to proceed as a nonshareholder creditor would. It is not unusual, for example, for bondholders of publicly held corporations to extend due dates when default occurs. The alternative is to foreclose and perhaps seriously impair the amount the creditors will recover.

- Avoid provisions in the debt instrument that make the debt convertible to equity in the event of default. These provisions are standard practice when nonshareholder creditors are involved. They serve no purpose if the shareholders are also the creditors and hold debt in proportion to ownership shares.

Gail, Cliff, and Ruth are equal shareholders in Magenta Corporation. Each transfers cash of $100,000 to Magenta in return for its bonds. The bond agreement provides that the holders will receive additional voting rights in the event Magenta Corporation defaults on its bonds.

The voting rights provision is worthless and merely raises the issue of thin capitalization. Gail, Cliff, and Ruth already control Magenta Corporation, so what purpose is served by increasing their voting rights? The parties probably used a boilerplate bond agreement that was designed for third-party lenders (e.g., banks and other financial institutions).

- Pro rata holding of debt is difficult to avoid. For example, if each of the shareholders owns one-third of the stock, each will want one-third of the debt. Nevertheless, some variation is possible.

Assume the same facts as Example 38, except that only Gail and Cliff acquire the bonds. Ruth leases property to Magenta Corporation at an annual rent that approximates the yield on the bonds.

Presuming the rent passes the arm's length test (i.e., what unrelated parties would charge), all parties reach the desired result. Gail and Cliff withdraw corporate profits in the form of interest income, and Ruth is provided for with rent income. Magenta Corporation can deduct both the interest and the rent payments.

- Try to keep the debt-equity ratio within reasonable proportions. A problem frequently arises when the parties form the corporation. Often, the amount invested in capital stock is the minimum required by state law. For example, if the state of incorporation permits a minimum of $1,000, limiting the investment to this amount does not provide much safety for later debt financing by the shareholders.

Emily, Josh, and Jun form Black Corporation with the following capital investments: cash of $200,000 from Emily, land worth $200,000 (basis of $20,000) from Josh, and a patent worth $200,000 (basis of $0) from Jun. To state that the equity of Black Corporation is $220,000 (the tax basis to the corporation) does not reflect reality. The equity account is more properly stated at $600,000 ($200,000 + $200,000 + $200,000).

- The nature of the business can have an effect on what is an acceptable debt-equity ratio. Capital-intensive industries (e.g., manufacturing and transportation) characteristically rely heavily on debt financing. Consequently, it is easier for shareholders to justify higher debt levels for corporations in these industries.

What if a corporation's efforts to avoid the thin capitalization problem fail and the IRS raises the issue in a tax audit? What steps should the shareholders take? They should hedge their position by filing a protective claim for refund, claiming dividend treatment on the previously reported interest income. In such an event, ordinary income would be converted to preferential dividend income treatment. Otherwise, the IRS could ultimately invoke the statute of limitations and achieve the best of all possible worlds—the shareholders would have been taxed on the interest income at the ordinary income rates, and the corporation would receive no deduction for what is now reclassified as a dividend. By filing the claim for refund, the shareholders have kept the statute of limitations from running until the thin capitalization issue is resolved at the corporate level.

18-5d Investor Losses

Section 1244 can provide beneficial treatment to qualifying taxpayers. However, careful planning may be necessary to avoid the risk of losing the attributes of the provision. Only the original holder of § 1244 stock is entitled to ordinary loss treatment. Shareholders lose the benefits of § 1244 if they transfer shares of stock to family members.

EXAMPLE 41

Norm incorporates his business by transferring property with a basis of $100,000 for 100 shares of stock. The stock qualifies as § 1244 stock. Norm later gives 50 shares each to his children, Susan and Paul. Eventually, the business fails, and the shares of stock become worthless.

If Norm had retained the stock, he would have had an ordinary loss deduction of $100,000 (assuming that he filed a joint return). Susan and Paul, however, have a capital loss of $50,000 each because the § 1244 attributes are lost as a result of the gift (i.e., neither Susan nor Paul was an original holder of the stock).

A similar result occurs with § 1202 small business stock. The exclusion of capital gain is available only to the original shareholder, not later holders of the stock.

18-5e Corporations versus Flow-Through Entities

Corporations have certain advantages over unincorporated businesses, such as easier capital formation, unlimited life, and limited liability. However, double taxation presents a potentially sizable tax disadvantage. The TCJA of 2017 changed the extent of this disadvantage in two ways. First, it reduced the corporate tax rate from 35 percent to 21 percent. Second, it created a new 20 percent deduction under § 199A for qualified business income of flow-through entities (see Chapter 15). The example below illustrates the effects of these offsetting changes.

EXAMPLE 42

Albert owns 100% of A Corporation, Betty is the sole proprietor of B Company, and Cai is the sole proprietor of C Company. Each business generated $500,000 of taxable income and before-tax cash flow. A Corporation and B Company produce a product, but C Company provides accounting services. A Corporation will distribute all of its after-tax income to Albert. All three owners face a 37% marginal tax rate on ordinary income. What is the after-tax cash flow and effective tax rate for each business?

B Company qualifies for the § 199A deduction, but C Company does not because it provides accounting services and its taxable income exceeds the threshold for that deduction. The table below compares the tax and cash flow consequences for each business.

	A Corporation	B Company	C Company
Taxable income and before-tax cash flow	$ 500,000	$ 500,000	$ 500,000
Corporate tax @ 21%	(105,000)	–0–	–0–
Cash available to owners	$ 395,000	$ 500,000	$ 500,000
§ 199A deduction @ 20%	–0–	(100,000)	–0–
Taxable income to owners	$ 395,000	$ 400,000	$ 500,000
Shareholder tax on dividend income @ 23.8%	($ 94,010)	$ –0–	$ –0–
Individual tax on ordinary income @ 37%	$ –0–	($ 148,000)	($ 185,000)
Before-tax cash flow	$ 500,000	$ 500,000	$ 500,000
Corporate tax	(105,000)	–0–	–0–
Shareholder tax on dividend income	(94,010)	–0–	–0–
Individual tax on ordinary income	–0–	(148,000)	(185,000)
After-tax cash flow	$ 300,990	$ 352,000	$ 315,000
Effective tax rate	39.8%	29.6%	37.0%

The effective tax rate equals the total tax paid divided by the before-tax cash flow. Note that the 20 percent § 199A qualified business income deduction results in a significantly higher after-tax cash flow for B Company than for the corporation. In contrast, the after-tax cash flow for C Company is only slightly higher than for the corporation. Thus, the § 199A deduction results in rough parity between qualifying flow-through entities and corporations. However, this conclusion results when the corporation distributes 100 percent of its after-tax earnings. Reducing and postponing dividend payments will increase corporate after-tax cash flows.

THE VEHICLE FOR BUSINESS GROWTH IS THE CORPORATE FORM

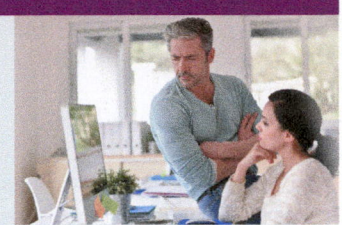

Emily and Ethan, the sole property transferors, must acquire at least 80 percent of the stock issued by Transformation, Inc., for the transaction to receive tax-deferred treatment under § 351. This stock ownership threshold is easily achieved under the facts as presented. Otherwise, Emily will recognize a tremendous amount of gain (up to $1,600,000). Because Ethan transfers cash, he will not recognize gain even if the transaction fails to qualify under § 351 (i.e., the fair market value and basis of the cash are identical). However, even if § 351 is available, any debt issued by the corporation is boot and will trigger gain recognition to Emily (see Example 4). Therefore, Emily must evaluate the cost of recognizing gain now versus the benefit of Transformation obtaining an interest deduction later.

If David decides to transfer property to Transformation in exchange for stock, § 351 also is available to him as long as his transfer is considered part of a prearranged plan that involves Emily, Ethan, and himself (see Example 6). In addition, if David's transaction involves transferring property *and* services in return for stock, § 351 shelters gain recognition only for the property—he will recognize ordinary income for the value of the services rendered (see Examples 26 and 27).

As a result of the incorporation, in addition to being able to raise significant capital with Ethan's equity investment, Emily also benefits from another significant corporate nontax advantage: state law protects her personal assets from unlimited liability exposure.

Another benefit of Transformation operating as a corporation is that Emily and Ethan could easily admit David as a shareholder later (assuming he does not participate at the time of incorporation). They could offer him outright stock ownership in exchange for services rendered or establish a stock incentive plan as a reward for his outstanding service and longevity with the business. Further, Emily and Ethan can use similar techniques to entice into the business new employees who may possess unique talents needed to support future expansion.

What If?

Can the § 351 transaction be modified to further reduce personal and business tax costs, both at the time of formation and in future years? Several strategies may be worth considering.

- Instead of having Transformation issue debt on formation (see Example 4), Emily might withhold certain assets. If the building is not transferred, for example, it can be leased to the corporation. The resulting rent payment would mitigate the double tax problem by producing a tax deduction for Transformation.

- An additional benefit results if Emily does not transfer the cash basis receivables to Transformation. This approach avoids an income tax at the corporate level and a further income tax when the receipts are distributed in the form of a dividend. Only Emily will pay tax on the receivables income if she retains those assets (see Example 37). Double taxation can be mitigated in certain situations with a modest amount of foresight.

- The Transformation case facts do not mention any accounts payable outstanding at the time of corporate formation. If they do exist, which is likely, it might be wise for Emily to transfer them to Transformation. The subsequent corporate payment of the liability produces a corporate deduction that will reduce any corporate income tax.

Key Terms

Built-in loss property, 18-15

Capital contribution, 18-18

Control, 18-6

Investor loss, 18-21

Liabilities in excess of basis, 18-11

Nonbusiness bad debts, 18-21

Property, 18-5

Qualified small business corporation, 18-24

Qualified small business stock, 18-24

Section 1244 stock, 18-23

Securities, 18-6

Thin capitalization, 18-19

Discussion Questions

1. **LO.1** In terms of justification and effect, § 351 (transfers to a controlled corporation) and § 1031 (like-kind exchanges) are much alike. Explain.

2. **LO.1, 2** Under what circumstances will a realized gain and/or loss be recognized on a § 351 transfer?

3. **LO.1** What does "property" include for purposes of § 351?

4. **LO.2** Can gain ever be recognized in a § 351 transfer if boot is not received? Explain.

5. **LO.1** Does the receipt of securities in exchange for the transfer of appreciated property to a controlled corporation cause recognition of gain? Explain.

6. **LO.1** What is the control requirement of § 351? Describe the effect of the following in satisfying this requirement:
   a. A shareholder renders only services to the corporation for stock.
   b. A shareholder renders services and transfers property to the corporation for stock.
   c. A shareholder has only momentary control after the transfer.
   d. A long period of time elapses between the transfers of property by different shareholders.

Critical Thinking 7. **LO.1** Nancy and her daughter, Kathleen, have been working together in a cattery called "The Perfect Cat." Nancy formed the business several years ago as a sole proprietorship, and it has been very successful. Assets currently have a fair market value of $450,000 and a basis of $180,000. On the advice of their tax accountant, Nancy decides to incorporate "The Perfect Cat." Because of Kathleen's participation, Nancy would like her to receive shares in the corporation. What are the relevant tax issues?

Decision Making 8. **LO.1, 2, 7** Four friends plan to form a corporation for purposes of constructing a shopping center. Charlie will be contributing the land for the project and wants more security than shareholder status provides. He is contemplating two possibilities: receive corporate bonds for his land or take out a mortgage on the land before transferring it to the corporation. Comment on the choices Charlie is considering. What alternatives can you suggest?

Critical Thinking

Critical Thinking 9. **LO.1** At a point when Robin Corporation has been in existence for six years, shareholder Ted transfers real estate (adjusted basis of $20,000 and fair market value of $100,000) to the corporation for additional stock. At the same time, Peggy, the other shareholder, acquires one share of stock for cash. After the two transfers, the percentages of stock ownership are as follows: 79% by Ted and 21% by Peggy.
   a. What were the parties trying to accomplish?
   b. Will it work? Explain.

10. **LO.2, 3** How does the transfer of mortgaged property to a controlled corporation affect the transferor-shareholder's basis in stock received? Assume that no gain is recognized on the transfer.

11. **LO.1, 2, 3** Discuss how each of the following affects the calculation of the basis of stock received by a shareholder in a § 351 transfer.
    a. The transfer of a liability to the corporation along with property.
    b. The basis in the property transferred to the corporation.
    c. Property that has been transferred to the corporation has built-in losses.
    d. The receipt of "other property" (i.e., boot) in addition to stock.

12. **LO.3** In a § 351 transfer, Grebe Corporation receives property in exchange for stock. Will Grebe's holding period for the property be the same as the shareholder's holding period for the stock? Explain.

13. **LO.3, 4** A corporation acquires property as a contribution to capital from a shareholder. Describe the rules pertaining to the property's basis.

14. **LO.5** In structuring the capitalization of a corporation, what are the advantages and disadvantages of utilizing debt rather than equity?

15. **LO.6** Hai, a single taxpayer, invested $75,000 in the stock of Penguin Corporation, which recently declared bankruptcy. Although distressed over the loss of her investment, Hai is relieved that she can claim a $75,000 ordinary (rather than capital) loss deduction. Comment on Hai's expectations.

16. **LO.6** Under what circumstances, if any, may a shareholder deduct a business bad debt on a loan made to the corporation?

17. **LO.1, 7** Keith's sole proprietorship holds assets that, if sold, would yield a gain   Critical Thinking
    of $100,000. It also owns assets that would yield a loss of $30,000. Keith incorporates his business using only the gain assets. Two days later, Keith sells the loss assets to the newly formed corporation. What is Keith trying to accomplish? Will he be successful? Explain.

18. **LO.1, 7** Sarah incorporates her small business but does not transfer the machinery   Critical Thinking
    and equipment the business uses to the corporation. Subsequently, the machinery and equipment are leased to the corporation for an annual rent. What tax reasons might Sarah have for not transferring the machinery and equipment to the corporation when the business was incorporated?

Computational Exercises

19. **LO.1, 3** Marie and Ethan form Roundtree Corporation with the transfer of the following. Marie performs personal services for the corporation with a fair market value of $80,000 in exchange for 400 shares of stock. Ethan contributes an installment note receivable (basis $25,000; fair market value $30,000), land (basis $50,000; fair market value $170,000), and inventory (basis $100,000; fair market value $120,000) in exchange for 1,600 shares. Determine Marie and Ethan's current income, gain, or loss; calculate the basis that each takes in the Roundtree stock.

20. **LO.1, 3** Grady exchanges qualified property, basis of $12,000 and fair market value of $18,000, for 60% of the stock of Eadie Corporation. The other 40% of the stock is owned by Pedro, who acquired it five years ago. Calculate Grady's current income, gain, or loss and the basis he takes in his shares of Eadie stock as a result of this transaction.

21. **LO.1, 2, 3** Jocelyn contributes land with a basis of $60,000 and fair market value of $90,000 and inventory with a basis of $5,000 and fair market value of $8,000 in exchange for 100% of Zion Corporation stock. The land is subject to a $15,000 mortgage. Determine Jocelyn's recognized gain or loss and the basis in the Zion stock received.

22. **LO.1, 2, 3** Diego transfers real estate with an adjusted basis of $260,000 and fair market value of $350,000 to a newly formed corporation in exchange for 100% of the stock. The corporation assumes the liability on the transferred real estate in the amount of $300,000. Determine Diego's recognized gain on the transfer and the basis for his stock.

23. **LO.1, 3** Yvonne and Simon form Ion Corporation. Yvonne transfers equipment (basis of $110,000 and fair market value of $165,000). Simon invests $130,000 of cash. They each receive 100 shares in Ion Corporation, worth $130,000, but Yvonne also receives $35,000 in cash from Ion. Calculate Ion Corporation's basis in the equipment. In addition, determine Yvonne and Simon's basis in the Ion stock.

24. **LO.5** Chaz transfers cash of $60,000 to a newly formed corporation for 100% of the stock. In its initial year, the corporation has net income of $15,000. The income is credited to its earnings and profits account. The corporation distributes $5,000 to Chaz.

    a. How do Chaz and the corporation treat the $5,000 distribution?

    b. Assume instead that Chaz transfers to the corporation cash of $30,000 for stock and cash of $30,000 for a note of the same amount. The note is payable in equal annual installments of $3,000 each (beginning at the end of the corporation's initial year of operations) and bears interest at the rate of 6%. At the end of the year, the corporation pays an amount to meet this obligation (i.e., the annual $3,000 principal payment plus the interest due). Determine the total amount of the payment and its tax treatment to Chaz and the corporation.

25. **LO.6** Several years ago, Minjun, who is single, acquired § 1244 stock in Blue Corporation at a cost of $60,000. He sells the Blue stock for $5,000 in the current year. Determine the amount and nature of Minjun's gain or loss recognized this year.

Problems

26. **LO.1, 3** Seth, Pete, Cara, and Jen form Kingfisher Corporation with the following consideration:

	Consideration Transferred		
	Basis to Transferor	Fair Market Value	Number of Shares Issued
From Seth—			
Inventory	$30,000	$96,000	30*
From Pete—			
Equipment ($30,000 of depreciation taken by Pete in prior years)	45,000	99,000	30**
From Cara—			
Proprietary process	15,000	90,000	30
From Jen—			
Cash	30,000	30,000	10

*Seth receives $6,000 in cash in addition to the 30 shares.
**Pete receives $9,000 in cash in addition to the 30 shares.

Assume that the value of each share of Kingfisher stock is $3,000. As to these transactions, provide the following information:

a. Seth's recognized gain or loss. Identify the nature of any such gain or loss.

b. Seth's basis in the Kingfisher Corporation stock.

c. Kingfisher Corporation's basis in the inventory.

d. Pete's recognized gain or loss. Identify the nature of any such gain or loss.

e. Pete's basis in the Kingfisher Corporation stock.

f. Kingfisher Corporation's basis in the equipment.

g. Cara's recognized gain or loss.

h. Cara's basis in the Kingfisher Corporation stock.

i. Kingfisher Corporation's basis in the proprietary process.

j. Jen's recognized gain or loss.

k. Jen's basis in the Kingfisher stock.

l. During discussions relating to the formation of Kingfisher, Seth mentions that he may be interested in either (1) just selling all of his inventory in the current year for its fair market value of $96,000 or (2) proceeding with his involvement in Kingfisher's formation as shown above but followed by a sale of his stock five years later for $90,000. What would be the tax cost of these alternative plans stated in present value terms? Referring to Appendix G, assume a discount rate of 6%. Further, assume Seth's marginal income tax rate is 35% and his capital gains rate is 15%.

m. Prepare your solution to part (l) using spreadsheet software such as Microsoft Excel.

27. **LO.1, 3** Tom and Gail form Owl Corporation with the following consideration:

	Consideration Transferred		
	Basis to Transferor	Fair Market Value	Number of Shares Issued
From Tom—			
Cash	$ 50,000	$ 50,000	
Installment note	240,000	350,000	40
From Gail—			
Inventory	60,000	50,000	
Equipment	125,000	250,000	
Patentable invention	15,000	300,000	60

The installment note has a face amount of $350,000 and was acquired last year from the sale of land held for investment purposes (adjusted basis of $240,000). As to these transactions, provide the following information:

a. Tom's recognized gain or loss.

b. Tom's basis in the Owl Corporation stock.

c. Owl Corporation's basis in the installment note.

d. Gail's recognized gain or loss.

e. Gail's basis in the Owl Corporation stock.

f. Owl Corporation's basis in the inventory, equipment, and patentable invention.

g. How would your answers to the preceding questions change if Tom received common stock and Gail received preferred stock?

h. How would your answers change if Gail was a partnership?

i. Gail is considering an alternative to the plan as presented above. She is considering selling the inventory to an unrelated third party for $50,000 in the current year instead of contributing it to Owl. After the sale, she will transfer the $50,000 sales proceeds along with the equipment and patentable invention to Owl for 60 shares of Owl stock. Whether or not she pursues the alternative, she plans to sell her Owl stock in six years for an anticipated sales price of $700,000. In present value terms and assuming she later sells her Owl stock, determine the tax cost of (1) contributing the property as originally planned or (2) pursuing the alternative she has identified. Referring to Appendix G, assume a discount rate of 6%. Further, assume Gail's marginal income tax rate is 32% and her capital gains rate is 15%.

j.   Prepare your solution to part (i) using spreadsheet software such as Microsoft Excel.

Decision Making   28.   **LO.1, 7** Luciana, Jon, and Clyde incorporate their respective businesses and form Starling Corporation. On March 1 of the current year, Luciana exchanges her property (basis of $50,000 and value of $150,000) for 150 shares in Starling Corporation. On April 15, Jon exchanges his property (basis of $70,000 and value of $500,000) for 500 shares in Starling. On May 10, Clyde transfers his property (basis of $90,000 and value of $350,000) for 350 shares in Starling.

a.   If the three exchanges are part of a prearranged plan, what gain will each of the parties recognize on the exchanges?

b.   Assume that Luciana and Jon exchanged their property for stock four years ago, while Clyde transfers his property for 350 shares in the current year. Clyde's transfer is not part of a prearranged plan with Luciana and Jon to incorporate their businesses. What gain will Clyde recognize on the transfer?

c.   Returning to the original facts, if the property that Clyde contributes has a basis of $490,000 (instead of $90,000), how might the parties otherwise structure the transaction?

Communications   29.   **LO.1** Troy Kennedy (1635 Maple Street, Syracuse, NY 13201) exchanges property (basis of $200,000 and fair market value of $850,000) for 75% of the stock of Red Corporation. The other 25% is owned by Sarah Mitchell, who acquired her stock several years ago. You represent Troy, who asks whether he must report gain on the transfer. Prepare a letter to Troy and a memorandum for the tax files documenting your response.

30.   **LO.1, 3** Dan Knight and Patricia Chen, who are good friends, form Crane Corporation. Dan transfers land (worth $200,000, basis of $60,000) for 50% of the stock in Crane. Patricia transfers machinery (worth $150,000, adjusted basis of $30,000) and provides services worth $50,000 for 50% of the stock.

a.   Will the transfers qualify under § 351? Explain.

b.   What are the tax consequences to Dan and Patricia?

c.   What is Crane Corporation's basis in the land and the machinery?

d.   Enter the results of this transaction to Patricia on her Form 1040 (use the most current form available). Assume Patricia is single, has no other income, and claims the standard deduction ($12,400 for 2020; $12,200 for 2019). Complete the Form 1040 to the taxable income line.

31.   **LO.1, 3** Ann and Bob form Robin Corporation. Ann transfers property worth $420,000 (basis of $150,000) for 70 shares in Robin Corporation. Bob receives 30 shares for property worth $165,000 (basis of $30,000) and for legal services (worth $15,000) in organizing the corporation.

a.   What gain or income, if any, will the parties recognize on the transfer?

b.   What basis do Ann and Bob have in the Robin Corporation stock?

c.   What is Robin Corporation's basis in the property and services it received from Ann and Bob?

32. **LO.1, 7** Rhonda owns 50% of the stock of Peach Corporation. She and the other 50% shareholder, Rachel, have decided that additional contributions of capital are needed if Peach is to remain successful in its competitive industry. The two shareholders have agreed that Rhonda will contribute assets having a value of $200,000 (adjusted basis of $15,000) in exchange for additional shares of stock. After the transaction, Rhonda will hold 75% of Peach Corporation and Rachel's interest will fall to 25%.

Decision Making
Communications

   a. What gain is realized on the transaction? How much of the gain will be recognized?

   b. Rhonda is not satisfied with the transaction as proposed. How will the consequences change if Rachel agrees to transfer $1,000 of cash in exchange for additional stock? In this case, Rhonda will own slightly less than 75% of Peach and Rachel's interest will be slightly more than 25%.

   c. If Rhonda still is not satisfied with the result, what should be done to avoid any gain recognition?

   d. Summarize your solution in an e-mail, and send it to your instructor.

33. **LO.1, 2, 3** Cynthia, a sole proprietor, was engaged in a service business and reported her income on the cash basis. In February of the current year, she incorporates her business as Dove Corporation and transfers the assets of the business to the corporation in return for all of the stock in addition to the corporation's assumption of her proprietorship's liabilities. All of the receivables and the unpaid trade payables are transferred to the newly formed corporation. The balance sheet of the corporation immediately after its formation is as follows:

Assets		
	Basis to Dove	**Fair Market Value**
Cash	$ 80,000	$ 80,000
Accounts receivable	–0–	240,000
Equipment (cost $180,000; depreciation previously claimed $60,000)	120,000	320,000
Building (straight-line depreciation)	160,000	400,000
Land	40,000	160,000
Total	$400,000	$1,200,000

Liabilities and Stockholders' Equity	
Liabilities:	
Accounts payable—trade	$ 120,000
Notes payable—bank	360,000
Stockholders' equity:	
Common stock	720,000
Total	$1,200,000

Discuss the tax consequences of the incorporation of the business to Cynthia and to Dove Corporation.

34. **LO.1, 2, 3** Allie forms Broadbill Corporation by transferring land (basis of $125,000, fair market value of $775,000), which is subject to a mortgage of $375,000. One month prior to incorporating Broadbill, Allie borrows $100,000 for personal reasons and gives the lender a second mortgage on the land. Broadbill Corporation issues stock worth $300,000 to Allie and assumes the mortgages on the land.

    a.   What are the tax consequences to Allie and to Broadbill Corporation?

    b.   How would the tax consequences to Allie differ if she had not borrowed the $100,000?

Decision Making   35. **LO.1, 3** Rafael transfers the following assets to Crane Corporation in exchange for all of its stock. (Assume that neither Rafael nor Crane plans to make any special tax elections at the time of incorporation.)

Assets	Rafael's Adjusted Basis	Fair Market Value
Inventory	$ 60,000	$100,000
Equipment	150,000	105,000
Shelving	80,000	65,000

    a.   What is Rafael's recognized gain or loss?

    b.   What is Rafael's basis in the stock?

    c.   What is Crane's basis in the inventory, equipment, and shelving?

    d.   If Rafael has no intentions of selling his Crane stock for at least 15 years, what action would you recommend that Rafael and Crane Corporation consider? How does this change the previous answers?

36. **LO.1, 3** Alice and Jane form Osprey Corporation. Alice transfers property, basis of $25,000 and value of $200,000, for 50 shares in Osprey Corporation. Jane transfers property, basis of $50,000 and value of $165,000, and agrees to serve as manager of Osprey for one year; in return, Jane receives 50 shares in Osprey. The value of Jane's services to Osprey is $35,000.

    a.   What gain or income do Alice and Jane recognize on the exchange?

    b.   What is Osprey Corporation's basis in the property transferred by Alice and Jane? How does Osprey treat the value of the services that Jane renders?

37. **LO.1, 3** Assume in Problem 36 that Jane receives the 50 shares of Osprey Corporation stock in consideration for the appreciated property and for the provision of accounting services in organizing the corporation. The value of Jane's services is $35,000.

    a.   What gain or income does Jane recognize?

    b.   What is Osprey Corporation's basis in the property transferred by Jane? How does Osprey treat the value of the services that Jane renders?

38. **LO.4** Red Corporation wants to set up a manufacturing facility in a midwestern state. After considerable negotiations with a small town in Ohio, Red accepts the following offer: land (fair market value of $3,000,000) and cash of $1,000,000.

    a.   How much income, if any, must Red Corporation recognize?

    b.   What basis will Red Corporation have in the land?

    c.   Assume that in addition to the facts given, the small town offers to reduce the established property tax rate by 40% on new assets acquired by Red during the two-year period after locating in the town. What are the Federal income tax consequences of the property tax abatement?

39. **LO.5, 6** Emily Patrick (36 Paradise Road, Northampton, MA 01060) formed Teal
    Corporation a number of years ago with an investment of $200,000 cash,
    for which she received $20,000 in stock and $180,000 in bonds bearing interest of
    8% and maturing in nine years. Several years later Emily lent the corporation an
    additional $50,000 on open account. In the current year, Teal Corporation becomes
    insolvent and is declared bankrupt. During the corporation's existence, Emily was
    paid an annual salary of $60,000. Write a letter to Emily in which you explain how
    she would treat her losses for tax purposes.   *Critical Thinking*

    Communications

40. **LO.5, 6** Stock in Jaybird Corporation (555 Industry Lane, Pueblo, CO 81001)
    is held equally by Vera, Wade, and Wes. Jaybird seeks additional capi-
    tal in the amount of $900,000 to construct a building. Vera, Wade, and Wes
    each propose to lend Jaybird Corporation $300,000, taking from Jaybird a
    $300,000 four-year note with interest payable annually at two points below
    the prime rate. Jaybird Corporation has current taxable income of $2,000,000.
    You represent Jaybird Corporation. Jaybird's president, Steve Ferguson, asks you
    how the payments on the notes might be treated for tax purposes. Prepare
    a letter to Ferguson and a memo for your tax files in which you document
    your conclusions.   *Critical Thinking*

    Communications

41. **LO.6** Sam Upchurch, a single taxpayer, acquired stock in Hummer Corporation that
    qualified as a small business corporation under § 1244 at a cost of $100,000
    three years ago. He sells the stock for $10,000 in the current tax year.   *Critical Thinking*

    a. How will the loss be treated for tax purposes?

    b. Assume instead that Sam sold the stock to his sister, Kara Upchurch, a few
        months after it was acquired for $100,000 (its fair market value). If Kara sells
        the Hummer stock for $60,000 in the current year, how should she treat the
        loss for tax purposes?

    c. Enter the results of this transacton to Kara on Form 1040, Schedule D (p. 1) (use
        the most current form available). Her Social Security number is 123-45-6789.
        Assume that relevant facts from the transaction initially had been shown on
        Form 8949 with Box F checked.

42. **LO.6, 7** Three years ago at a cost of $40,000, Paul Sanders acquired stock in a
    corporation that qualified as a small business corporation under § 1244.
    A few months after he acquired the stock, when it was still worth $40,000,
    he gave it to his brother, Mike Sanders. Mike, who is married and files a joint
    return, sells the stock for $25,000 in the current tax year. Mike asks you, his tax
    adviser, how the sale will be treated for tax purposes. Prepare a letter to your
    client and a memo for the file. Mike's address is 10 Hunt Wood Drive, Hadley,
    PA 16130.   *Communications*

43. **LO.6** Gigi transfers real estate (basis of $60,000 and fair market value of $40,000)
    to Monarch Corporation in exchange for shares of § 1244 stock. (Assume that
    the transfer qualifies under § 351.)   *Critical Thinking*

    a. What is the basis of the stock to Gigi? (Gigi and Monarch do not make an elec-
        tion to reduce her stock basis.)

    b. What is the basis of the stock to Gigi for purposes of § 1244?

    c. If Gigi sells the stock for $38,000 two years later, how will the loss be treated
        for tax purposes?

Decision Making 44. **LO.5, 7** Frank, Cora, and Mitch are equal shareholders in Purple Corporation. The corporation's assets have a tax basis of $50,000 and a fair market value of $600,000. In the current year, Frank and Cora each loan Purple Corporation $150,000. The notes to Frank and Cora bear interest of 8% per annum. Mitch leases equipment to Purple Corporation for an annual rental of $12,000. Discuss whether the shareholder loans from Frank and Cora might be reclassified as equity. Consider in your discussion whether Purple Corporation has an acceptable debt-equity ratio.

45. **LO.6, 7** Julio sold his corporation to a competitor, Exeter LLC, for $100,000,000. Julio incorporated his business seven years ago by investing $500,000 plus his proprietary know-how. There have been no other corporate shareholders. Compute Julio's after-tax cash flow from the sale, assuming he is in the 35% tax bracket and has no other property sales during the year.

46. **LO.7** Refer to Example 42 in text Section 18-5e. What will be the values of A Corporation, B Company, and C Company after three years? Assume that each business can reinvest its after-tax cash flow back into the business and that there is no unrealized appreciation of their assets. Use spreadsheet software such as Microsoft Excel to prepare your answer.

Research Problems

the answer company™
THOMSON REUTERS®

Note: Solutions to the Research Problems can be prepared by using the Thomson Reuters Checkpoint™ online tax research database, which accompanies this textbook. Solutions can also be prepared by using research materials found in a typical tax library.

Decision Making
Communications

Research Problem 1. Lynn Jones, along with Shawn, Walt, and Donna, are deciding whether they should organize a corporation and transfer their shares of stock in several corporations to this new corporation. All of their shares are listed on the New York Stock Exchange and are readily marketable. Lynn would transfer shares in Brown Corporation, Shawn would transfer stock in Rust Corporation, Walt would transfer stock in White Corporation, and Donna would transfer stock in several corporations. The stock would be held by the newly formed corporation for investment purposes. Lynn asks you, her tax adviser, whether she would have gain on the transfer of her substantially appreciated shares in Brown Corporation if she transferred the shares to a newly formed corporation. Your input will be critical as they make their decision. Prepare a letter to your client, Lynn Jones, and a memo for the firm's files. Lynn's address is 1540 Maxwell Avenue, Highland, KY 41099.

Research Problem 2. Tim is a real estate broker who specializes in commercial real estate. Although he usually buys and sells on behalf of others, he also maintains a portfolio of property of his own. He holds this property, mainly unimproved land, either as an investment or for sale to others.

In early 2016, Irene and Al contact Tim regarding a tract of land located just outside the city limits. Tim bought the property, which is known as the Moore farm, several years ago for $600,000. At that time, no one knew that it was located on a geological fault line. Irene, a well-known architect, and Al, a building contractor, want Tim to join them in developing the property for residential use. They are aware of the fault line but believe that they can circumvent the problem by using newly developed design and construction technology. Because of the geological flaw, however, they regard the Moore farm as being worth only $450,000. Their intent is to organize a corporation to build the housing project, and each party will receive stock commensurate to the property or services contributed.

After consulting his tax adviser, Tim agrees to join the venture if certain modifications to the proposed arrangement are made. The transfer of the land would be structured as a sale to the corporation. Instead of receiving stock, Tim would receive a note from the corporation. The note would be interest-bearing and be due in five years. The maturity value of the note would be $450,000—the amount that even Tim concedes is the fair market value of the Moore farm.

What income tax consequences ensue from Tim's suggested approach? Compare this result with what would happen if Tim merely transferred the Moore farm in return for stock in the new corporation.

Research Problem 3. Sarah is the sole owner of Bluegrass Corporation. The basis and value of her stock investment in Bluegrass are approximately $100,000. In addition, she manages Bluegrass's operations on a full-time basis and pays herself an annual salary of $40,000. Because of a recent downturn in business, she needs to put an additional $80,000 into her corporation to help meet short-term cash-flow needs (e.g., inventory costs, salaries, and administrative expenses). Sarah believes that the $80,000 transfer can be structured in one of three ways: as a capital contribution, as a loan made to protect her stock investment, or as a loan intended to protect her job. From a tax perspective, which alternative would be preferable in the event that Bluegrass's economic slide worsens and bankruptcy results? Explain your answer.

Partial list of research aids:
Kenneth W. Graves, 87 TCM 1409, T.C.Memo. 2004–140.

Use internet tax resources to address the following questions. Look for reliable websites and blogs of the IRS and other government agencies, media outlets, businesses, tax professionals, academics, think tanks, and political outlets.

Research Problem 4. Find an SEC offering that involves a corporation that originally was established as other than a C corporation (e.g., an S corporation). Describe the particular circumstances that justified the original non-C status and the rationale for subsequently converting to a C corporation.

Research Problem 5. Has § 1202, which relates to qualified small business stock, been widely used since its enactment? What leads you to this conclusion? What rationale did Congress provide as a justification for the provision's enactment? Do you believe that such rationale still is valid in today's environment?

Research Problem 6. Many newly created businesses are established using a tax status [Data Analytics] that avoids the double tax that applies to C corporations and their owners. Calculate the percentage of entities that filed income tax returns as C corporations (Form 1120), S corporations (Form 1120S), and partnerships and other flow-through entities (Form 706) for the most recent year for which data are available. Use data from the *IRS Tax Statistics* as the basis for your calculations. Compare your findings with comparable percentages for the third and fifth prior years. Using a spreadsheet software such as Microsoft Excel, create graphs that illustrate the results of your research. Be sure the graphs have proper labels and explanations.

Becker CPA Review Questions

Becker.

1. Gearty and Olinto organized The Worthington Corp., which issued voting common stock with a fair market value of $240,000. They each transferred property in exchange for stock as follows:

	Property	Adjusted Basis	Fair Market Value	Percentage of The Worthington Corp. Stock Acquired
Gearty	Building	$80,000	$164,000	60%
Olinto	Land	10,000	96,000	40%

The building was subject to a $20,000 mortgage that was assumed by The Worthington Corp. What was The Worthington Corp.'s basis in the building?

a. $60,000

b. $80,000

c. $144,000

d. $104,000

2. Angie and Brad form Cats Are Us, Inc. Angie contributes $120,000 cash for 60% of the stock. Brad contributes an asset with an FMV of $90,000 and an adjusted basis of $30,000 for 40% of the stock. Brad also receives $10,000 cash from the corporation. What is the corporation's basis in the asset received from Brad?

   a. $10,000   c. $40,000
   b. $30,000   d. $90,000

3. Gearty and Olinto organized The Worthington Corp., which issued voting common stock with a fair market value of $240,000. They each transferred property in exchange for stock as follows:

	Property	Adjusted Basis	Fair Market Value	Percentage of The Worthington Corp. Stock Acquired
Gearty	Building	$80,000	$164,000	60%
Olinto	Land	10,000	96,000	40%

   The building was subject to a $20,000 mortgage that was assumed by The Worthington Corp. What was Gearty's basis in The Worthington Corp. stock?

   a. $164,000   c. $60,000
   b. $80,000   d. $0

4. Gearty and Olinto organized The Worthington Corp., which issued voting common stock with a fair market value of $240,000. They each transferred property in exchange for stock as follows:

	Property	Adjusted Basis	Fair Market Value	Percentage of The Worthington Corp. Stock Acquired
Gearty	Building	$80,000	$164,000	60%
Olinto	Land	10,000	96,000	40%

   The building was subject to a $20,000 mortgage that was assumed by The Worthington Corp. What amount of gain did Gearty recognize on the exchange?

   a. $0   c. $84,000
   b. $20,000   d. $104,000

5. Ron, David, and Mary formed Widget, Inc. Ron and David each received 40% of the stock, and Mary received the remaining 20%. Ron contributed land with an FMV of $70,000 and an adjusted basis of $20,000. The corporation also assumed a $30,000 liability on the property. David contributed land with an FMV of $30,000 and an adjusted basis of $15,000. David also contributed $10,000 in cash. Mary received her stock for services rendered. She would normally bill $20,000 for these services. What is Ron's basis in the corporate stock received?

   a. $0   c. $40,000
   b. $20,000   d. $70,000

6. Ron, David, and Mary formed Widget, Inc. Ron and David each received 40% of the stock, and Mary received the remaining 20%. Ron contributed land with an FMV of $70,000 and an adjusted basis of $20,000. The corporation also assumed a $30,000 liability on the property. David contributed land with an FMV of $30,000 and an adjusted basis of $15,000. David also contributed $10,000 in cash. Mary received her stock for services rendered. She normally would bill $20,000 for these services. What is Mary's basis in the corporate stock received?

   a. $0   c. $15,000
   b. $10,000   d. $20,000

7. Ron, David, and Mary formed Widget, Inc. Ron and David each received 40% of the stock, and Mary received the remaining 20%. Ron contributed land with an FMV of $70,000 and an adjusted basis of $20,000. The corporation also assumed a $30,000 liability on the property. David contributed land with an FMV of $30,000 and an adjusted basis of $15,000. David also contributed $10,000 in cash. Mary received

her stock for services rendered. She normally would bill $20,000 for these services. What is Ron's taxable gain as a result of this transaction?

a. $0
c. $20,000
b. $10,000
d. $30,000

8. In year 1, Stone, a cash basis taxpayer, incorporated her CPA practice. No liabilities were transferred. The following assets were transferred to the corporation:

Cash (checking account)	$ 500
Computer equipment:	
Adjusted basis	30,000
Fair market value	34,000
Cost	40,000

Immediately after the transfer, Stone owned 100% of the corporation's stock. The corporation's total basis for the transferred assets is:

a. $30,000
c. $34,500
b. $30,500
d. $40,500

9. Adams, Beck, and Carr organized Flexo Corp. with authorized voting common stock of $100,000. Adams received 10% of the capital stock in payment for the organizational services that he rendered for the benefit of the newly formed corporation. Adams did not contribute property to Flexo and was under no obligation to be paid by Beck or Carr. Beck and Carr transferred property in exchange for stock as follows:

	Adjusted Basis	Fair Market Value	Percentage of Flexo Stock Acquired
Beck	$ 5,000	$20,000	20%
Carr	60,000	70,000	70%

What amount of gain did Carr recognize from this transaction?

a. $40,000
c. $10,000
b. $15,000
d. $0

10. Clark and Hunt organized Jet Corp. with authorized voting common stock of $400,000. Clark contributed $60,000 cash. Both Clark and Hunt transferred other property in exchange for Jet stock as follows:

	Adjusted Basis	Fair Market Value	Percentage of Jet Stock Acquired
Clark	$ 50,000	$100,000	40%
Hunt	120,000	240,000	60%

What was Clark's basis in Jet stock?

a. $0
c. $110,000
b. $100,000
d. $160,000

11. Ron, David, and Mary formed Widget, Inc. Ron and David each received 40% of the stock, and Mary received the remaining 20%. Ron contributed land with an FMV of $70,000 and an adjusted basis of $20,000. The corporation also assumed a $30,000 liability on the property. David contributed land with an FMV of $30,000 and an adjusted basis of $15,000. David also contributed $10,000 in cash. Mary received her stock for services rendered. She normally would bill $20,000 for these services. What is David's basis in the corporate stock received?

a. $0
c. $25,000
b. $10,000
d. $40,000

12. Which of the following is *not* a requirement about the exclusion of gain for small business stock?

a. The corporation must be a C corporation.
b. The stock must be issued after August 10, 1993.
c. As of the date of the stock issuance, the capital must be less than $50,000,000.
d. The stockholder does not have to be an original stockholder of the corporation.

CHAPTER

19

Corporations: Distributions Not in Complete Liquidation

LEARNING OBJECTIVES: *After completing Chapter 19, you should be able to:*

LO.1 Explain the role that earnings and profits play in determining the tax treatment of distributions.

LO.2 Compute a corporation's earnings and profits (E & P).

LO.3 Determine taxable dividends paid during the year by correctly allocating current and accumulated E & P to corporate distributions.

LO.4 Describe the tax treatment of dividends for individual shareholders.

LO.5 Evaluate the tax impact of property dividends by computing the shareholder's dividend income, basis in the property received, and the effect on the distributing corporation's E & P and taxable income.

LO.6 Recognize situations when constructive dividends exist and compute the tax resulting from such dividends.

LO.7 Determine the tax implications from receipt of stock dividends and stock rights and the shareholder's basis in the stock and stock rights received.

LO.8 Identify various stock redemptions that qualify for sale or exchange treatment.

LO.9 Determine the tax impact of stock redemptions on the distributing corporation.

LO.10 Identify planning opportunities available to minimize the tax impacts of corporate distributions, constructive dividends, and stock redemptions.

CHAPTER OUTLINE

19-1 Corporate Distributions—Overview, 19-2

19-2 Earnings and Profits (E & P), 19-3
19-2a Computation of E & P, 19-3
19-2b Summary of E & P Adjustments, 19-6
19-2c Current versus Accumulated E & P, 19-8
19-2d Allocating E & P to Distributions, 19-8

19-3 Dividends, 19-12
19-3a Rationale for Reduced Tax Rates on Dividends, 19-12
19-3b Qualified Dividends, 19-13
19-3c Property Dividends, 19-14
19-3d Constructive Dividends, 19-16
19-3e Stock Dividends and Stock Rights, 19-19

19-4 Stock Redemptions, 19-21
19-4a Overview, 19-21
19-4b Historical Background, 19-24

19-4c Stock Attribution Rules, 19-25
19-4d Not Essentially Equivalent Redemptions, 19-26
19-4e Disproportionate Redemptions, 19-27
19-4f Complete Termination Redemptions, 19-28
19-4g Redemptions to Pay Death Taxes, 19-28

19-5 Stock Redemptions—Effect on the Corporation, 19-29
19-5a Recognition of Gain or Loss, 19-29
19-5b Effect on Earnings and Profits, 19-30
19-5c Redemption Expenditures, 19-30

19-6 Other Corporate Distributions, 19-30

19-7 Tax Planning, 19-30
19-7a Corporate Distributions, 19-30
19-7b Planning for Qualified Dividends, 19-32
19-7c Constructive Dividends, 19-33
19-7d Stock Redemptions, 19-33

ALEXANDER RATHS/SHUTTERSTOCK.COM

TAXING CORPORATE DISTRIBUTIONS

Plainwell Ice Cream Corporation (Plainwell), a premium ice cream manufacturer, has had a very profitable year. To share its profits with its two equal shareholders, Waffle Cone Corporation and Luis, it distributes cash of $200,000 to Waffle Cone and real estate worth $300,000 (adjusted basis of $20,000) to Luis (a married taxpayer filing a joint return). The real estate is subject to a mortgage of $100,000, which Luis assumes. The distribution is made on December 31, Plainwell's year-end.

Plainwell has had both good and bad years in the past. More often than not, however, it has lost money. Despite this year's record profits, the GAAP-based balance sheet for Plainwell indicates a year-end deficit in retained earnings. Consequently, the distribution of cash and land is treated as a liquidating distribution for financial reporting purposes, resulting in a reduction of Plainwell's paid-in capital account.

The tax consequences of the distributions to Plainwell and its shareholders depend on a variety of factors that are not directly related to the financial reporting treatment. Identify these factors, and explain the tax effects of the distributions to both Plainwell Ice Cream Corporation and its two shareholders.

Read the chapter and formulate your response.

C hapter 18 examined the tax consequences of corporate formation. In Chapters 19 and 20, the focus shifts to the tax treatment of corporate distributions, a topic that plays a leading role in tax planning. The importance of corporate distributions comes from the variety of tax treatments that may apply.

From the *shareholder's perspective*, distributions received from the corporation may be treated as ordinary income, preferentially taxed dividend income, capital gain, or a nontaxable return of capital.

From the *corporation's perspective*, distributions made to shareholders are generally not deductible. However, a corporation may recognize losses in liquidating distributions (see Chapter 20), and gains may be recognized at the corporate level on distributions of appreciated property.

In the most common scenario, a corporate distribution is dividend income to the shareholder and provides no deduction to the corporation, resulting in a double tax (i.e., a tax is levied at both the corporate and shareholder levels). The effects of this double tax may be reduced by the corporate dividends received deduction and preferential tax rates on qualified dividends paid to individuals.

The tax treatment of corporate distributions can be affected by a number of items.

- The availability of earnings to be distributed.
- The basis of the shareholder's stock.
- The character of the property being distributed.
- Whether the distribution is a "qualified dividend."
- Whether the shareholder is an individual or another kind of taxpaying entity.
- Whether the shareholder gives up ownership in return for the distribution.
- Whether the distribution is nonliquidating or liquidating.

This chapter discusses the tax rules related to nonliquidating distributions of cash and other property. Distributions of stock and stock rights also are addressed along with the tax treatment of stock redemptions (a nonliquidating distribution where the shareholder gives up stock). Corporate liquidations are discussed in Chapter 20.

19-1 CORPORATE DISTRIBUTIONS—OVERVIEW

LO.1

Explain the role that earnings and profits play in determining the tax treatment of distributions.

When a distribution is made from corporate earnings and profits (E & P), the shareholder is deemed to receive a dividend, which is taxed either as ordinary income or as preferentially taxed dividend income.[1] Generally, corporate distributions are presumed to be paid out of E & P (discussed in text Section 19-2) and are treated as dividends *unless* the parties to the transaction can show otherwise. Distributions not treated as dividends (because of insufficient E & P) are treated as a nontaxable return of capital to the extent of the shareholder's stock basis, which is reduced accordingly. If the distribution exceeds the shareholder's basis, the excess is treated as a gain from the sale or exchange of the stock.[2]

EXAMPLE 1

At the beginning of the year, Amber Corporation (a calendar year taxpayer) has E & P of $15,000. The corporation generates no additional E & P during the year. On July 1, the corporation distributes $20,000 to its sole shareholder, Bonnie, whose stock basis is $4,000.

In this situation, Bonnie recognizes dividend income of $15,000 (the amount of E & P distributed). Of the remaining $5,000 distributed, $4,000 reduces her stock basis to zero and Bonnie recognizes a taxable gain of $1,000.

---

[1] §§ 301(c)(1), 316, and 1(h)(11).   [2] §§ 301(c)(2) and (3).

19-2 **EARNINGS AND PROFITS (E & P)**

The notion of earnings and profits (E & P) is similar in many respects to the accounting concept of retained earnings. Both are measures of the firm's accumulated capital. E & P includes both the accumulated E & P of the corporation since its incorporation date (or February 28, 1913, if later) and the current year's E & P. A difference exists, however, in the way these figures are calculated. The computation of retained earnings is based on financial accounting rules, while E & P is determined using rules specified in the tax law.

Congress has not provided a specific calculation of *earnings and profits* in the Internal Revenue Code. Rather, in § 312, it has provided adjustments that must be made to a corporation's taxable income to arrive at E & P. The Treasury Department (through Regulations), the IRS (through rulings), and the courts (through case law) have provided additional guidance. All these must be taken into account when calculating E & P.

E & P is a measure of the dividend-paying capacity of a corporation (i.e., a measure of economic income). As a result, when a corporation makes a distribution to a shareholder, E & P identifies the maximum amount of dividend income that shareholders must recognize. As a result, the effect of a specific transaction on E & P may often be determined by assessing whether the transaction increases or decreases the corporation's ability to pay a dividend.

19-2a **Computation of E & P**

The Code, Regulations, rulings, and court cases provide a series of adjustments to taxable income that result in a measure of the corporation's dividend-paying capacity (or economic income). Both cash basis and accrual basis corporations use the same approach when determining E & P.[3]

LO.2

Compute a corporation's earnings and profits (E & P).

Additions to Taxable Income

To determine current E & P, *all* excluded income items are added back to taxable income. These positive adjustments include tax-exempt interest, life insurance proceeds (in excess of cash surrender value), and Federal income tax refunds from tax paid in prior years.

The dividends received deduction (see Chapter 17) is also added back to taxable income to determine E & P since it does not impair a corporation's ability to pay dividends. Effectively, the dividends received deduction is a partial *exclusion* for a specific type of income (dividend income).

Subtractions from Taxable Income

When calculating current E & P, certain nondeductible expenses are subtracted from taxable income. These negative adjustments include the nondeductible portion of meals; entertainment expenses; related-party losses; expenses incurred to produce tax-exempt income; Federal income taxes paid; nondeductible key employee life insurance premiums (net of increases in cash surrender value); and nondeductible fines, penalties, and lobbying expenses.

E & P Calculations

Eagle Corporation paid $120,000 of Federal income taxes this year. Eagle also received $6,000 of tax-exempt interest on State of Pennsylvania bonds.

In calculating taxable income for Eagle, the $120,000 is not deductible and the $6,000 is not taxable. The Federal taxes are subtracted from taxable income to compute Eagle's E & P because this is an amount not available for distribution to shareholders. In contrast, the tax-exempt interest is added to taxable income to compute Eagle's E & P because it represents funds available for distribution.

EXAMPLE
2

---

[3]Section 312 describes many of the adjustments to taxable income necessary to determine E & P. Regulation § 1.312–6 addresses the effect of accounting methods on E & P.

E & P Calculations

EXAMPLE 3

Herron Corporation sells property with a basis of $10,000 to its sole shareholder for $8,000. Because of § 267 (disallowance of losses on sales between related parties), Herron cannot deduct the $2,000 loss when calculating its taxable income.

However, because the overall economic effect of the transaction is a decrease in its assets by $2,000, the loss reduces Herron's current E & P for the year of sale.

EXAMPLE 4

Crane Corporation pays a $10,000 premium on a key employee life insurance policy covering the life of its president. As a result of the payment, the cash surrender value of the policy is increased by $7,000.

Although none of the $10,000 premium is deductible for tax purposes, current E & P is reduced by $3,000 (i.e., amount of the premium payment net of the increase in the cash surrender value). The $7,000 increase in cash surrender value is not subtracted because it does not represent a decrease in Crane's ability to pay a dividend. Instead, it represents a shift in Crane's assets from cash to life insurance.

Timing Adjustments

Some E & P adjustments shift the effect of a transaction from the year of its inclusion in the computation of taxable income to the year in which it has an economic effect on the corporation. Charitable contributions, net operating losses, and capital losses all necessitate this kind of adjustment.

EXAMPLE 5

During 2020, Hawk Corporation makes charitable contributions, $12,000 of which cannot be deducted when calculating its taxable income for the year because of the 10% of taxable income limitation. Consequently, the $12,000 is carried forward to 2021 and fully deducted in that year.

The excess charitable contribution reduces Hawk's current E & P for 2020 by $12,000 and increases its current E & P for 2021 (when the deduction is allowed) by the same amount. The increase in E & P in 2021 is necessary because the charitable contribution carryover reduces the taxable income for that year (the starting point for computing E & P) but already has been taken into account in determining Hawk's E & P for 2020.

Gains and losses from property transactions generally affect the determination of E & P only to the extent they are recognized for tax purposes. As a result, gains and losses deferred under the like-kind exchange provision and gains deferred under the involuntary conversion provision do not affect E & P until recognized.

Accounting Method Adjustments

In addition to the above adjustments, accounting methods used for determining E & P generally are more conservative than those allowed for calculating taxable income. For example, the installment method is not permitted for E & P purposes.[4] As a result, an adjustment is required for the deferred gain from property sales made during the year under the installment method. All principal payments are treated as having been received in the year of sale.

EXAMPLE 6

In 2020, Cardinal Corporation, a cash basis calendar year taxpayer, sells unimproved real estate for $100,000; its basis in the land is $20,000. Under the terms of the sale, Cardinal will receive two payments, $60,000 in 2021 and $40,000 in 2022, along with interest of 4%. Cardinal Corporation does not elect out of the installment method.

continued

---

[4]§ 312(n)(5).

Because Cardinal's taxable income for 2020 will not reflect any of the gain from the sale, the corporation must make an $80,000 positive adjustment for 2020 (the deferred gain from the sale). Then negative adjustments of $48,000 in 2021 and $32,000 in 2022 will be required when the deferred gain is recognized under the installment method.

Treatment of the gain for regular tax and E & P purposes is summarized as follows:

Tax Year	Regular Tax Treatment	E & P Treatment	E & P Adjustment
2020	$ –0–	$80,000	$ 80,000
2021	48,000	–0–	(48,000)
2022	32,000	–0–	(32,000)

A similar analysis can be used for most of the timing and accounting method adjustments.

The alternative depreciation system (ADS) must be used for purposes of computing E & P.[5] This method requires straight-line depreciation with a half-year convention over a recovery period equal to the Asset Depreciation Range (ADR) midpoint life of an asset.[6] Also, ADS prohibits additional first-year (bonus) depreciation.[7] If MACRS cost recovery is used for income tax purposes, a positive or negative adjustment equal to the difference between MACRS and ADS must be made each year. Likewise, when assets are sold, an additional adjustment to taxable income is required to account for the difference in gain or loss between income tax basis and the E & P basis.[8] The adjustments arising from depreciation are illustrated in the following example.

EXAMPLE 7

On January 2, 2018, White Corporation paid $30,000 to purchase equipment with an ADR midpoint life of 10 years and a MACRS class life of 7 years. The equipment was depreciated under MACRS. The asset was sold on July 2, 2020, for $27,000. For purposes of determining taxable income and E & P, cost recovery claimed on the equipment is summarized below. Assume that White elected not to claim § 179 expense or additional first-year depreciation on the property.

Year	Cost Recovery Computation	MACRS	ADS	E & P Adjustment
2018	$30,000 × 14.29%	$ 4,287		
	$30,000 ÷ 10-year ADR recovery period × ½ (half-year for first year of service)		$1,500	$2,787
2019	$30,000 × 24.49%	7,347		
	$30,000 ÷ 10-year ADR recovery period		3,000	4,347
2020	$30,000 × 17.49% × ½ (half-year for year of disposal)	2,624		
	$30,000 ÷ 10-year ADR recovery period × ½ (half-year for year of disposal)		1,500	1,124
	Total cost recovery	$14,258	$6,000	$8,258

Each year, White Corporation will increase taxable income by the adjustment amount indicated previously to determine E & P. In addition, when computing E & P for 2020, White will reduce taxable income by $8,258 to account for the excess gain recognized for income tax purposes.

continued

---

[5]§ 312(k)(3)(A).

[6]See § 168(g)(2). The ADR midpoint lives for most assets are set out in Rev.Proc. 87–56, 1987–2 C.B. 674. The recovery period is 5 years for automobiles and light-duty trucks and 40 years for real property. For assets with no class life, the recovery period is 12 years.

[7]§ 168(k). In general, additional first-year depreciation (also called "bonus depreciation") is allowed for qualified property placed in service after 2011 and before 2027. No bonus depreciation is scheduled for tax years after 2026. Different rules applied between 2008 and 2011 and prior to 2005.
[8]§ 312(f)(1).

	Income Tax	E & P
Amount realized	$ 27,000	$ 27,000
Adjusted basis for income tax ($30,000 cost − $14,258 MACRS)	(15,742)	
Adjusted basis for E & P ($30,000 cost − $6,000 ADS)		(24,000)
Gain on sale	$ 11,258	$ 3,000
E & P adjustment ($3,000 − $11,258)	($ 8,258)	

In addition to more conservative depreciation methods, the E & P rules impose limitations on the deductibility of § 179 expense. Specifically, any § 179 expense must be deducted over a period of five years (20 percent per year).[9] As a result, in any year that § 179 is elected, 80 percent of the resulting expense must be added back to taxable income to determine current E & P. In each of the following four years, a subtraction from taxable income equal to 20 percent of the § 179 expense must be made.

EXAMPLE 8

On January 2, 2019, Blue Corporation placed in service a five-year depreciable asset. The acquisition price of the asset was $25,000, and Blue Corporation claimed a § 179 deduction for the full amount. Treatment of the § 179 deduction for regular tax and E & P purposes is summarized as follows:

Tax Year	Regular Tax Treatment	E & P Treatment	E & P Adjustment
2019	($25,000)	($5,000)	$20,000
2020	–0–	(5,000)	(5,000)
2021	–0–	(5,000)	(5,000)
2022	–0–	(5,000)	(5,000)
2023	–0–	(5,000)	(5,000)

The E & P rules also require specific accounting methods in various situations. For example:

- E & P requires cost depletion rather than percentage depletion.[10]
- When accounting for long-term contracts, E & P requires the percentage of completion method rather than the completed contract method.[11]
- E & P does not allow for the amortization of organizational expenses. As a result, any expense deducted when computing taxable income must be added back to determine E & P.[12]
- If a corporation is using the LIFO inventory method, E & P requires an adjustment for changes in the LIFO recapture amount (the excess of FIFO over LIFO inventory value) during the year. Increases in LIFO recapture are added to taxable income, and decreases are subtracted.[13]
- E & P requires that intangible drilling costs and mine exploration and development costs be amortized over a period of 60 months and 120 months, respectively.[14]

19-2b Summary of E & P Adjustments

Recall that E & P serves as a measure of a corporation's dividend-paying capacity. Concept Summary 19.1 summarizes the required adjustments to the corporation's taxable income to arrive at current E & P. Other items that affect E & P, such as property dividends and stock redemptions, are covered later in the chapter.

[9]§ 312(k)(3)(B).
[10]Reg. § 1.316–2(e).
[11]§ 312(n)(6).
[12]§ 312(n)(3).
[13]§ 312(n)(4).
[14]§ 312(n)(2).

Concept Summary 19.1

E & P Adjustments

Nature of the Transaction	Adjustment to Taxable Income to Determine Current E & P	
	Addition	**Subtraction**
Tax-exempt income	X	
Dividends received deduction	X	
Collection of proceeds from insurance policy on life of corporate employee (in excess of cash surrender value)	X	
Deferred gain on installment sale (all gain is added to E & P in year of sale)	X	
Future recognition of installment sale gross profit		X
Excess charitable contribution (over 10% limitation) and excess capital loss in year incurred		X
Deduction of charitable contribution, NOL, or capital loss carryovers in succeeding taxable years (increases E & P because deduction reduces taxable income while E & P was reduced in a prior year)	X	
Federal income taxes paid		X
Federal income tax refund	X	
Loss on sale between related parties		X
Nondeductible fines, penalties, entertainment, and lobbying expenses		X
Nondeductible portion of meal expenses		X
Payment of premiums on insurance policy on life of corporate employee (in excess of increase in cash surrender value of policy)		X
Realized gain (not recognized) on an involuntary conversion	No effect	
Realized gain or loss (not recognized) on a like-kind exchange	No effect	
Excess percentage depletion (only cost depletion can reduce E & P)	X	
Accelerated depreciation (E & P is reduced only by straight-line, units-of-production, or machine hours depreciation)	X	X
Additional first-year (bonus) depreciation	X	
Section 179 expense in year elected (80%)	X	
Section 179 expense in four years following election (20% each year)		X
Increase (decrease) in LIFO recapture amount	X	X
Intangible drilling costs deducted currently (reduce E & P in future years by amortizing costs over 60 months)	X	
Mine exploration and development costs (reduce E & P in future years by amortizing costs over 120 months)	X	

EXAMPLE 9

Crimson Corporation (a calendar year, accrual basis taxpayer) reports taxable income of $429,000 in 2020. In addition, it provides the following information:

Federal income tax liability paid	$ 90,090
Tax-exempt interest income	6,250
Meal expenses (total)	10,000
Entertainment expenses	3,000
Premiums paid on key employee life insurance*	8,500
Life insurance proceeds from key employee life insurance policy*	250,000
Excess of capital losses over capital gains	22,000
MACRS cost recovery deduction	82,000
E & P depreciation (straight-line depreciation using ADS)	64,000
Section 179 expense elected and deducted during 2017 for regular tax purposes	120,000
Dividends received from domestic corporations (less than 20% owned)	35,000

*Term policy; no cash surrender value.

continued

Crimson sold property on installment during 2018. The property was sold for $120,000 and had an $84,000 adjusted basis when sold. During 2020, Crimson received a $30,000 payment on the installment sale. Finally, assume that Crimson did not claim any § 179 expense or bonus depreciation in 2020. What is Crimson's current E & P?

Taxable income	$429,000
Federal income tax liability paid	(90,090)
Tax-exempt interest income	6,250
Disallowed portion of meal expenses	(5,000)
Entertainment expenses	(3,000)
Life insurance premiums paid	(8,500)
Proceeds from life insurance policy	250,000
Excess capital losses	(22,000)
Excess of MACRS cost recovery over E & P (ADS) depreciation	18,000**
Allowable portion of 2017 § 179 expenses (20% × $120,000)	(24,000)
Dividends received deduction (50% × $35,000)	17,500
Installment sale gain	(9,000)***
Current E & P	$559,160

**$82,000 − $64,000

***[($120,000 sales price − $84,000 adjusted basis) ÷ $120,000 sales price] × $30,000

How would your answer change if Crimson told you that the $82,000 MACRS cost recovery deduction was entirely a § 179 expense election?

For E & P purposes, the $82,000 § 179 expense must be deducted over five years (20% per year). So 80% of the $82,000 would be an addition to taxable income in 2020, and there would be no need to compute E & P depreciation on these items (so the $18,000 E & P depreciation add-back would be eliminated). As a result, Crimson's current E & P would be $606,760 ($559,160 + $65,600 − $18,000). Over each of the next four taxable years, Crimson would have a $16,400 current E & P deduction to account for the § 179 expense taken in 2020 for regular tax purposes ($82,000 × 20%).

19-2c Current versus Accumulated E & P

Accumulated E & P is the total of all previous years' current E & P (since February 28, 1913) reduced by distributions made from E & P in previous years. It is important to distinguish between **current E & P** and **accumulated E & P** because the taxability of corporate distributions depends upon how these two accounts are allocated to each distribution made during the year. A complex set of rules governs the allocation process.[15] These rules are described in the following section and summarized in Concept Summary 19.2.

19-2d Allocating E & P to Distributions

LO.3

Determine taxable dividends paid during the year by correctly allocating current and accumulated E & P to corporate distributions.

When a positive balance exists in both the current and accumulated E & P accounts, corporate distributions are deemed to be made first from current E & P and then from accumulated E & P. If there is only one distribution during the year and the distribution is less than total E & P (both current and accumulated), the distribution will be classified as a dividend.

When there are multiple distributions and total distributions exceed the amount of current E & P, it becomes necessary to allocate current and accumulated E & P to each distribution made during the year. First, current E & P is prorated among the distributions using the following formula:[16]

[15]Regulations relating to the source of a distribution are at Reg. § 1.316–2.   [16]Reg. § 1.316–2(b), (c) Example.

Concept Summary 19.2

Allocating E & P to Distributions

Current E & P at Time of Distribution	Accumulated E & P at Time of Distribution	Outcome	Illustration
Positive	Positive	Current E & P is applied first to distributions on a pro rata basis; then accumulated E & P is applied (as necessary) in chronological order beginning with the earliest distribution.	Example 10
		Unless the parties can show otherwise, it is presumed that current E & P covers all distributions.	Example 11
Positive	Deficit	Current and accumulated E & P are *not* netted. Distributions are dividends to the extent of current E & P. If the distribution exceeds the current E & P, the excess first reduces the stock basis to zero and then generates a taxable gain.	Example 12
Deficit	Positive	Current and accumulated E & P are netted. Any loss in current E & P is deemed to accrue ratably throughout the year unless the corporation can show otherwise.	
		(1) If net amount is *positive*: Distribution is a dividend to the extent of the balance. If the distribution exceeds the net E & P, the excess first reduces the stock basis to zero and then generates a taxable gain.	Example 13
		(2) If net amount is *negative*: Distribution is treated as a return of capital, first reducing the stock basis to zero, then generating taxable gain.	Example 14
Deficit	Deficit	Distribution is treated as a return of capital, first reducing the basis of the stock to zero, then generating taxable gain.	Example 15

Then accumulated E & P is applied in chronological order beginning with the earliest distribution (i.e., on a "first-come, first-served" basis).[17] As shown in the next example, this allocation is important if any shareholder sells stock during the year.

EXAMPLE
10

On January 1 of the current year, Black Corporation has accumulated E & P of $10,000. Current E & P for the year amounts to $30,000, earned evenly throughout the year. Megan and Matt are sole *equal* shareholders of Black from January 1 to July 31.

On August 1, Megan sells all of her stock to Sundra. Black makes two distributions to the shareholders during the year: $40,000 to Megan and Matt ($20,000 each) on July 1 and $40,000 to Matt and Sundra ($20,000 each) on December 1. Current and accumulated E & P are applied to the two distributions as follows:

	Source of Distribution		
	Current E & P	Accumulated E & P	Return of Capital
July 1 distribution ($40,000)	$15,000	$10,000	$15,000
December 1 distribution ($40,000)	15,000	–0–	25,000

Because 50% of the total distributions are made on July 1 and December 1, respectively, one-half of current E & P is applied to each of the two distributions. Accumulated E & P is applied in chronological order, so the entire amount attaches to the July 1 distribution. The tax consequences to the shareholders are presented on the next page.

continued

---
[17]Ibid.

	Shareholder		
	Megan	**Matt**	**Sundra**
July distribution ($40,000)			
Dividend income—			
From current E & P ($15,000)	$ 7,500	$ 7,500	$ –0–
From accumulated E & P ($10,000)	5,000	5,000	–0–
Return of capital ($15,000)	7,500	7,500	–0–
December distribution ($40,000)			
Dividend income—			
From current E & P ($15,000)	–0–	7,500	7,500
From accumulated E & P ($0)	–0–	–0–	–0–
Return of capital ($25,000)	–0–	12,500	12,500
Total distribution	$20,000	$40,000	$20,000
Total dividend income	$12,500	$20,000	$ 7,500
Nontaxable return of capital (assuming sufficient basis in the stock investment)	$ 7,500	$20,000	$12,500

Because the balance in the accumulated E & P account is exhausted when it is applied to the July 1 distribution, Megan has more dividend income than Sundra, even though both receive equal distributions during the year. In addition, each shareholder's basis is reduced by the nontaxable return of capital; any excess over basis results in taxable gain.

When the tax years of the corporation and its shareholders are not the same, it may be impossible to determine the amount of current E & P on a timely basis. For example, if shareholders use a calendar year and the corporation uses a fiscal year, then current E & P may not be known until after the shareholders' returns have been filed. To address this timing issue, the allocation rules presume that current E & P is sufficient to cover every distribution made during the year until the parties can show otherwise.

EXAMPLE 11

Green Corporation uses a June 30 fiscal year for tax purposes. Carol, Green's only shareholder, uses a calendar year. On July 1, 2020, Green Corporation has a zero balance in its accumulated E & P account. On August 1, 2020, Green distributes $10,000 to Carol. For fiscal year 2020–2021, the corporation determines that it has a $5,000 deficit in current E & P.

Because Carol cannot prove until June 30, 2021, that the corporation has a current E & P deficit for the 2020–2021 fiscal year, she must assume that current E & P is sufficient to cover the $10,000 distribution. As a result, the distribution will be dividend income to Carol and reported as such when she files her tax return for the 2020 calendar year. When Carol learns of the deficit, she can file an amended return for 2020 showing the $10,000 as a return of capital.

Additional difficulties arise when either the current or the accumulated E & P account has a deficit balance. When current E & P is positive and accumulated E & P has a deficit balance, accumulated E & P is *not* netted against current E & P. Instead, the distribution is deemed to be a taxable dividend to the extent of the positive current E & P balance.

The Big Picture

EXAMPLE 12

Return to the facts of *The Big Picture* on p. 19-1. Recall that Plainwell Ice Cream Corporation had a deficit in GAAP-based retained earnings at the start of the year and record profits during the current year. Assume that these financial results translate into an $800,000 deficit in accumulated E & P at the start of the year and current E & P of $600,000. In addition, for purposes of this example, assume that there is no mortgage on the real estate.

In this case, current E & P would exceed the total cash and property distributed to the shareholders. The distributions are treated as taxable dividends; they are deemed to be paid from current E & P even though Plainwell still has a deficit in accumulated E & P at the end of the year.

Alternatively, when a deficit exists in current E & P and a positive balance exists in accumulated E & P, the accounts are *netted* at the date of distribution. If the resulting balance is zero or negative, the distribution is a return of capital to the extent of basis; any excess over basis results in a taxable gain. If a positive balance results, the distribution is a dividend to the extent of the balance. A deficit in current E & P is deemed to accrue ratably throughout the year unless the parties can show otherwise.

Distributions with E & P Deficits

At the beginning of the current year, Gray Corporation (a calendar year taxpayer) has accumulated E & P of $10,000. During the year, the corporation incurs a $15,000 deficit in current E & P that accrues ratably. On July 1, Gray distributes $6,000 in cash to Jennifer, its sole shareholder. Jennifer has a $7,500 basis in her Gray Corporation stock.

EXAMPLE 13

To determine how much of the $6,000 cash distribution represents dividend income to Jennifer, the balances of both accumulated and current E & P as of July 1 are determined and netted. This is necessary because of the deficit in current E & P.

	Source of Distribution	
	Current E & P	Accumulated E & P
January 1		$10,000
July 1 (½ of $15,000 current E & P deficit)	($7,500)	2,500
Outcome: July 1 distribution of $6,000:		
Dividend: $2,500		
Return of capital: $3,500		

The balance in E & P just before the July 1 distribution is $2,500. As a result, of the $6,000 distribution, $2,500 is taxed as a dividend and $3,500 represents a return of capital. After the distribution, Jennifer's stock basis is $4,000 ($7,500 − $3,500).

Assume the same facts as Example 13, except that Gray Corporation's current E & P deficit amounts to $30,000 and Jennifer's stock basis is $5,000.

EXAMPLE 14

	Source of Distribution	
	Current E & P	Accumulated E & P
January 1		$10,000
July 1 (½ of $30,000 current E & P deficit)	($15,000)	(5,000)
Outcome: July 1 distribution of $6,000:		
Return of capital: $5,000		
Taxable gain: $1,000		

The balance in E & P just before the July 1 distribution is a deficit of $5,000. As a result, the distribution is first treated as a return of capital (to the extent of Jennifer's stock basis) and then as a taxable gain. Here, Jennifer's basis is reduced to zero and she has a taxable (capital) gain of $1,000.

Assume the same facts as Example 14, except that Gray Corporation began the year with an accumulated E & P deficit of $10,000.

EXAMPLE 15

Because Gray has deficits in both accumulated and current E & P, the outcome is the same as in Example 14: a $5,000 return of capital and a $1,000 taxable (capital) gain.

ETHICS & EQUITY Shifting E & P

Ten years ago, Spencer began a new business venture with Robert. Spencer owns 70 percent of the outstanding stock, and Robert owns 30 percent. The business has had some difficult times, but current prospects are favorable.

On November 15, Robert decides to quit the venture and plans to sell all of his stock to Spencer's sister, Heidi, a longtime employee of the business. Robert will sell his stock to Heidi after the company pays out the current-year shareholder distribution of about $100,000. Spencer is looking forward to working with his sister, but he now faces a terrible dilemma.

The corporation has a $300,000 deficit in accumulated E & P and only about $20,000 of current E & P to date.

Within the next two months, however, Spencer expects to sign a major deal with a large client. If Spencer signs the contract before the end of the year, the corporation will have a large increase in current E & P, causing the upcoming distribution to be fully taxable to Robert as a dividend.

Since a similar contract is not expected next year, most of next year's distribution will be treated as a tax-free return of capital for Heidi. Alternatively, if Spencer waits until January, both he and Robert will receive a nontaxable distribution this year. However, next year's annual distribution will be fully taxable to his sister as a dividend. What should Spencer do?

LO.4

Describe the tax treatment of dividends for individual shareholders.

19-3 DIVIDENDS

Distributions by a corporation from its E & P are treated as dividends. The tax treatment of dividends varies, depending on whether the shareholder receiving them is a corporation or an individual. All corporations treat dividends as ordinary income and are permitted a dividends received deduction (see Chapter 17). In contrast, individuals apply reduced tax rates on qualified dividend income received, while nonqualified dividends are taxed as ordinary income.

19-3a Rationale for Reduced Tax Rates on Dividends

The double tax on corporate income has always been controversial. Arguably, taxing dividends twice creates several undesirable economic distortions, including:

- An incentive to invest in noncorporate rather than corporate entities.

- An incentive for corporations to finance operations with debt rather than with equity because interest payments are deductible. Notably, this behavior increases the vulnerability of corporations in economic downturns because of higher leverage.

- An incentive for corporations to retain earnings and structure distributions of profits to avoid the double tax.

Collectively, these distortions raise the cost of capital for corporate investments. Estimates are that eliminating the double tax would increase capital stock in the corporate sector by as much as $500 billion.[18] In addition, some argue that elimination of the double tax would make the United States more competitive globally since a majority of our trading partners assess only one tax on corporate income.

Although many support a reduced or no tax rate on dividends, others contend that the double tax should remain in place because of the concentration of economic power held by publicly traded corporations. And many of the distortions noted previously can be avoided through the use of deductible payments by C corporations (e.g., by

---

[18]Integration of Individual and Corporate Tax Systems, Report of the Department of the Treasury (January 1992); "Eliminating Double Taxation Through Corporate Integration," Tax Foundation, February 23, 2015.

employing, renting property from, or borrowing money from shareholders) or by using other entity types (e.g., partnerships, limited liability companies, and S corporations). Those favoring retention of the double tax also note that the benefits of reduced tax rates on dividends flow disproportionately to the wealthy.[19]

Because of these differing opinions, the taxation of dividends in the United States has varied through the years. The reduced tax rate on <mark>qualified dividends</mark> for individuals reflects a compromise between the complete elimination of tax on dividends and the treatment of dividends as ordinary income.

19-3b Qualified Dividends

Qualified Dividends—Application and Effect

For most individual taxpayers, dividends that meet certain requirements (called "qualified dividends") are subject to a 15 percent tax rate. High-income taxpayers are subject to a 20 percent rate; a zero percent rate applies to lower-income taxpayers.[20]

Qualified Dividends—Requirements

To be taxed at the lower rates, dividends must be paid by either domestic or certain qualified foreign corporations. Qualified foreign corporations include those traded on a U.S. stock exchange or any corporation located in a country that (1) has a comprehensive income tax treaty with the United States, (2) has an information-sharing agreement with the United States, and (3) is approved by the Treasury.[21]

Two other requirements must be met for dividends to qualify for the favorable rates. First, dividends paid to shareholders who hold both long and short positions in the stock do not qualify. Second, the stock on which the dividend is paid must be held for more than 60 days during the 121-day period beginning 60 days before the ex-dividend date.[22] To allow for settlement delays, the ex-dividend date is typically two days before the date of record on a dividend. This holding period rule parallels the rule applied to corporations that claim the dividends received deduction.[23]

EXAMPLE 16

In June of the current year, Green Corporation announces that a dividend of $1.50 will be paid on each share of its common stock to shareholders of record on July 15. The ex-dividend date is July 13. Amy and Caleb, two unrelated shareholders, own 1,000 shares of the stock on the record date (July 15). Consequently, each receives $1,500 (1,000 shares × $1.50). Assume that Amy purchased her stock on January 15 of this year and that Caleb purchased his stock on July 1. Both shareholders sell their stock on July 20.

To qualify for the lower dividend rate, stock must be held for more than 60 days during the 121-day period beginning 60 days prior to July 13 (the ex-dividend date). In this case, the 121-day period runs from May 14 to September 11. The $1,500 Amy receives is subject to preferential tax treatment since she held the stock for more than 60 days during this 121-day period. The $1,500 Caleb receives, however, is not. Caleb did not meet the 60-day holding requirement, so his dividend will be taxed as ordinary income.

---

[19]The Urban Institute–Brookings Institution Tax Policy Center estimates that more than half of the benefits from the reduced tax rate on dividends go to the 0.2% of households with incomes over $1 million.

[20]See §§ 1(h)(1) and (11). In 2020, the 20% rate applies to married taxpayers filing jointly with taxable income greater than $496,600 ($441,450 for single taxpayers); the 0% rate applies to married taxpayers filing jointly with taxable income of $80,000 or less ($40,000 for single taxpayers). In 2019, these amounts were $488,850, $434,550, $78,750, and $39,375, respectively.

[21]In Notice 2011–64, 2011–37 I.R.B 231, the Treasury identified 57 qualifying countries (among those included on the list are the members of the European Union, the Russian Federation, Canada, and Mexico). Nonqualifying countries not on the list include most of the former Soviet republics (except Kazakhstan), Bermuda, and the Netherlands Antilles.

[22]§ 1(h)(11)(B)(iii)(I).

[23]See § 246(c) and the relevant discussion in Chapter 17.

LO.5

Evaluate the tax impact of property dividends by computing the shareholder's dividend income, basis in the property received, and the effect on the distributing corporation's E & P and taxable income.

19-3c **Property Dividends**

Although most corporate distributions are cash, a corporation may distribute a **property dividend** for various reasons. For example, the shareholders might want a particular property that is held by the corporation. Similarly, a corporation with low cash reserves may still want to distribute a dividend to its shareholders.

Property distributions have the same impact as cash distributions except for effects related to any difference between the basis and the fair market value of the distributed property. In most situations, distributed property is appreciated, so its sale would result in a gain to the corporation. Distributions of property with a basis that differs from fair market value raise several tax questions.

- *For the shareholder:*
  - ➤ What is the amount of the distribution?
  - ➤ What is the basis of the property in the shareholder's hands?
- *For the corporation:*
  - ➤ Is a gain or loss recognized as a result of the distribution?
  - ➤ What is the effect of the distribution on E & P?

Property Dividends—Effect on the Shareholder

When a corporation distributes property rather than cash to a shareholder, the amount distributed is measured by the fair market value of the property on the date of distribution.[24] As with a cash distribution, the portion of a property distribution covered by existing E & P is a dividend, with any excess treated as a return of capital until stock basis is recovered. If the fair market value of the property distributed exceeds *both* the corporation's E & P and the shareholder's stock basis, a taxable (capital) gain usually results.

If, as part of the distribution, the shareholder assumes a liability of the corporation or if the property the shareholder receives is subject to a liability (both immediately before and immediately after the distribution), the amount of the distribution is reduced by the liability, but not below zero. The basis of the distributed property for the shareholder is the fair market value of the property on the date of the distribution.

The Big Picture

EXAMPLE 17

Return to the facts of *The Big Picture* on p. 19-1. Plainwell Ice Cream Corporation distributed property with a $300,000 fair market value and $20,000 adjusted basis to Luis, one of its shareholders. The property was subject to a $100,000 mortgage, which Luis assumed.

As a result, Luis has a distribution of $200,000 [$300,000 (fair market value) − $100,000 (liability)] that is treated as a taxable dividend. The basis of the property to Luis is $300,000.

EXAMPLE 18

Red Corporation owns 10% of Tan Corporation. Tan has ample E & P to cover any distributions made during the year. One distribution made to Red Corporation consists of a vacant lot with an adjusted basis of $80,000 and a fair market value of $50,000. Red has a taxable dividend of $50,000 (before the dividends received deduction), and its basis in the lot is $50,000.

As discussed in the following section, distributing depreciated property is not wise from a tax perspective.

Property Dividends—Effect on the Corporation

All distributions of appreciated property generate gain recognition to the distributing corporation.[25] In effect, a corporation that distributes appreciated property is treated as if it had sold the property to the shareholder for its fair market value. However, the distributing corporation does *not* recognize loss on distributions of property.

---

[24]Section 301 describes the tax treatment of corporate distributions to shareholders.

[25]Section 311 describes how corporations are taxed on distributions.

Refer back to the facts of Example 18. Tan Corporation is not allowed to recognize the $30,000 loss on the property distribution. The $30,000 basis disappears ($50,000 fair market value less $80,000 adjusted basis).

As an alternative, Tan Corporation could sell the vacant lot for $50,000 and use the related $30,000 loss to reduce its taxes. Then Tan could distribute the $50,000 of sales proceeds to its shareholders. Either way, the shareholders end up with property worth $50,000. But by selling the vacant lot and distributing the cash, Tan Corporation benefits by being able to use the $30,000 loss.

EXAMPLE 19

The Big Picture

Return to the facts of *The Big Picture* on p. 19-1. Plainwell Ice Cream Corporation distributed property with a fair market value of $300,000 and an adjusted basis of $20,000 to Luis, one of its shareholders. As a result, Plainwell recognizes a $280,000 gain on the distribution.

EXAMPLE 20

If the distributed property is subject to a liability in excess of its basis or the shareholder assumes the liability, a special rule applies. For purposes of determining gain on the distribution, the fair market value of the property is treated as being at least the amount of the liability.[26]

Assume that the land in Example 18 is subject to a liability of $85,000. Tan Corporation recognizes a gain of $5,000 on the distribution ($85,000 liability − $80,000 basis of land). Red Corporation has no dividend income (the liability assumed exceeds the fair market value of the land), and its basis in the land is $85,000 (the land's deemed fair market value based on the liability assumed).

EXAMPLE 21

Corporate distributions reduce E & P by the amount of money distributed or by the *greater* of the fair market value or the adjusted basis of property distributed, less the amount of any liability on the property.[27] E & P is increased by gain recognized on appreciated property distributed as a property dividend.

Property Distributions—E & P Impacts

Crimson Corporation distributes property (basis of $10,000 and fair market value of $20,000) to Brenda, its shareholder. Crimson recognizes a $10,000 gain. Crimson's E & P is increased by the $10,000 gain and decreased by the $20,000 fair market value of the distribution. Brenda has dividend income of $20,000 (presuming sufficient E & P).

EXAMPLE 22

Assume the same facts as in Example 22, except that Crimson's adjusted basis of the property is $25,000. Because the loss is not recognized and the adjusted basis is greater than fair market value, E & P is reduced by $25,000, which is greater than the property's fair market value. Brenda reports dividend income of $20,000.

EXAMPLE 23

Assume the same facts as in Example 23, except that the property is subject to a liability of $6,000, which Brenda assumes. E & P is now reduced by $19,000 ($25,000 adjusted basis − $6,000 liability). Brenda has a dividend of $14,000 ($20,000 amount of the distribution − $6,000 liability), and her basis in the property is $20,000.

EXAMPLE 24

Under no circumstances can a distribution, whether cash or property, either generate a deficit in E & P or add to a deficit in E & P. Deficits can arise only through corporate operations.

[26]§ 311(b)(2).

[27]§§ 312(a), (b), and (c).

EXAMPLE 25

Teal Corporation has accumulated E & P of $10,000 at the beginning of the current tax year. During the year, it has current E & P of $15,000. At the end of the year, it distributes cash of $30,000 to Walter, its sole shareholder. Walter's basis in his Teal stock is $18,000.

Teal's E & P at the end of the year is reduced to zero in the following manner: first, the accumulated E & P of $10,000 is increased by current E & P of $15,000, and then this amount is reduced by $25,000 (the amount of the distribution treated as a dividend).

The remaining $5,000 of the distribution to Walter does not reduce E & P because a distribution cannot generate a deficit in E & P. Instead, the remaining $5,000 is a return of capital and reduces Walter's stock basis to $13,000 ($18,000 − $5,000).

The noncash property distribution rules are summarized in Concept Summary 19.3.

Concept Summary 19.3

Noncash Property Distributions

Appreciated Property	Depreciated Property
1. Regular Tax: Increase regular taxable income by regular tax gain (difference between FMV and regular tax adjusted basis).	1. Regular Tax: No impact on regular taxable income (regular tax loss not recognized).
2. Current E & P: Increase current earnings and profits by E & P gain (difference between FMV and E & P adjusted basis).	2. Current E & P: Generally, no change in current earnings and profits.
3. Shareholder(s): Determine impact of distribution on the shareholder(s).	3. Shareholder(s): Determine impact of distribution on the shareholder(s).
4. End-of-Year E & P: Decrease earnings and profits by the *fair market value* of property (net of liabilities assumed by the shareholder). As with cash distributions, property distributions cannot create an E & P deficit.	4. End-of-Year E & P: Decrease earnings and profits by the *E & P adjusted basis* of property (net of liabilities assumed by the shareholder). As with cash distributions, property distributions cannot create an E & P deficit.
Note: The Internal Revenue Code puts the corporation in the same position as if it had sold the property and distributed the cash.	Note: Earnings and profits will reflect the "loss" on the distribution of depreciated property (via the adjusted basis decrease to E & P), but the regular tax loss vanishes.

LO.6

Recognize situations when constructive dividends exist and compute the tax resulting from such dividends.

19-3d Constructive Dividends

An economic benefit provided by a corporation to a shareholder can be treated as a dividend for Federal income tax purposes even though it is not formally declared or identified as a dividend. **Constructive dividends** need not be issued pro rata to all shareholders nor satisfy the legal requirements of a dividend.[28]

For tax purposes, constructive distributions are treated the same as actual distributions.[29] As a result, the corporation providing the constructive dividend is not allowed a deduction, corporate shareholders can use the dividends received deduction (see Chapter 17), and noncorporate shareholders can apply the preferential tax rates (0, 15, or 20 percent) on qualified constructive dividends. The constructive distribution is taxable as a dividend only to the extent of the corporation's current and accumulated E & P; constructive distributions in excess of E & P are treated as a return of capital and then a taxable (capital) gain.

Constructive dividend situations usually arise in closely held corporations. Here, the dealings between the parties are less structured and may not be well documented. The constructive dividend often is intended to convert a nondeductible dividend into

---

[28]See *Lengsfield v. Comm.*, 57–1 USTC ¶9437, 50 AFTR 1683, 241 F.2d 508 (CA–5, 1957).

[29]*Simon v. Comm.*, 57–2 USTC ¶9989, 52 AFTR 698, 248 F.2d 869 (CA–8, 1957).

some type of corporate deduction.[30] Alternatively, the shareholders may be seeking benefits for themselves while avoiding the recognition of income.

Although some constructive dividends are disguised dividends, not all are deliberate attempts to avoid dividends; many are inadvertent. As a result, being aware of the most common types of constructive dividends is important; these are briefly summarized next.

Shareholder Use of Corporate-Owned Property

A constructive dividend can occur when a shareholder uses a corporation's property for personal purposes at no cost. Personal use of corporate-owned automobiles, airplanes, yachts, and facilities used for entertainment (e.g., a lake house that is used for entertaining clients) is commonplace in some closely held corporations. In these situations, the shareholder has dividend income equal to the fair rental value of the property for the period of its personal use.[31]

Bargain Sale of Corporate Property to a Shareholder

Shareholders often purchase property from a corporation at a cost below the fair market value. These bargain sales produce dividend income equal to the difference between the property's fair market value on the date of sale and the amount the shareholder paid for the property.[32]

Bargain Rental of Corporate Property

A bargain rental of corporate property by a shareholder also produces dividend income. Here, the measure of the constructive dividend is the excess of the property's fair rental value over the rent actually paid.

Payments for the Benefit of a Shareholder

If a corporation pays a shareholder's personal expenses (or obligations), these payments are treated as a constructive dividend. Forgiveness of shareholder debt by the corporation also results in a constructive dividend.[33] Excessive rentals paid by a corporation for the use of shareholder property are treated as constructive dividends.

Constructive Dividends—Shareholder Benefit

EXAMPLE 26

Libby, the president and sole shareholder of Taylor Corporation, is paid an annual salary of $400,000 by the corporation. She is always looking for ways to receive additional benefits from the corporation. However, Libby wants to avoid dividends (because of the effects of double taxation) and has no desire to increase her compensation because she is concerned that additional salary payments might cause the IRS to contend that her salary is unreasonable. (See the discussion of unreasonable compensation that follows.)

Libby has been considering donating $50,000 to her alma mater to establish scholarships for needy students. Taylor Corporation could make the contribution instead of Libby. The payment clearly benefits Libby, but the amount of the contribution is not taxed to her.[34] Taylor Corporation claims a charitable contribution deduction for the payment.

EXAMPLE 27

Assume in Example 26 that Libby has made an individual pledge to the university to provide $50,000 for scholarships for needy students. Taylor Corporation satisfies Libby's obligation by paying the $50,000 to the university. The $50,000 will be taxed to Libby.[35] In this context, the $50,000 payment to the university may be treated as indirect compensation to Libby.

In determining whether Libby's salary is unreasonable, both the *direct* salary payment of $400,000 and the *indirect* $50,000 payment are considered. Libby's total compensation package is $450,000. Libby may be eligible for a charitable contribution deduction of up to 50% of her adjusted gross income.

---

[30]Recall that dividend distributions do not provide the distributing corporation with an income tax deduction, although they do reduce E & P.

[31]See *Daniel L. Reeves*, 94 TCM 287, T.C.Memo. 2007–273.

[32]Reg. § 1.301–1(j).

[33]Reg. § 1.301–1(m).

[34]*Henry J. Knott*, 67 T.C. 681 (1977).

[35]*Schalk Chemical Co. v. Comm.*, 62–1 USTC ¶9496, 9 AFTR 2d 1579, 304 F.2d 48 (CA–9, 1962).

Unreasonable Compensation

A salary payment to a shareholder-employee that is determined to be ==unreasonable compensation== is frequently treated as a constructive dividend and, as a result, is not deductible by the corporation. Whether compensation is reasonable or not depends on all the facts and circumstances. In determining the reasonableness of salary payments, the following factors have been used by courts:[36]

- The employee's qualifications.
- A comparison of salaries with dividend distributions.
- The prevailing rates of compensation for comparable positions in comparable business concerns.
- The nature and scope of the employee's work.
- The size and complexity of the business.
- A comparison of salaries paid with both gross and net income.
- The taxpayer's salary policy toward all employees.
- For small corporations with a limited number of officers, the amount of compensation paid to the employee in question in previous years.
- Whether a shareholder, acting in the best interests of the corporation, would have agreed to the level of compensation paid.

The last factor above, known as the "reasonable investor test," has been used in different ways by different courts.[37] In some cases, the Seventh Circuit Court of Appeals has relied solely on the reasonable investor test in determining reasonableness. On the other hand, the Tenth Circuit Court of Appeals has largely ignored this factor. Other Federal circuits have used an approach that considers all of the factors in the list.[38]

Ultimately, this is a challenging area. Taxpayers, the IRS, and the courts apply these factors in different ways to support conclusions that often differ. Taxpayers should keep good records and be prepared to defend their conclusions.

Loans to Shareholders

Advances to shareholders that are not bona fide loans usually are reclassified as constructive dividends. As with the reasonableness of compensation, whether an advance qualifies as a bona fide loan depends on all the facts and circumstances. Factors considered in determining whether an advance is a bona fide loan include the following:[39]

- Whether the advance is on open account or is evidenced by a written instrument.
- Whether the shareholder furnished collateral or other security for the advance.
- How long the advance has been outstanding.
- Whether any repayments have been made, excluding dividend sources.
- The shareholder's ability to repay the advance.
- The shareholder's use of the funds (e.g., payment of routine bills versus nonrecurring, extraordinary expenses).
- The regularity of the advances.
- The dividend-paying history of the corporation.

Even when a corporation makes a bona fide loan to a shareholder, a constructive dividend may be triggered if the loan is interest-free (or carries a very low rate of

---

[36]All but the final factor in this list are identified in *Mayson Manufacturing Co. v. Comm.,* 49–2 USTC ¶9467, 38 AFTR 1028, 178 F.2d 115 (CA–6, 1949).

[37]For example, see *Alpha Medical, Inc. v. Comm.,* 99–1 USTC ¶50,461, 83 AFTR 2d 99–697, 172 F.3d 942 (CA–6, 1999).

[38]See *Vitamin Village, Inc.,* 94 TCM 277, T.C.Memo. 2007–272, for an example of a case that uses the reasonable investor test and other factors.

[39]*Fin Hay Realty Co. v. U.S.,* 68–2 USTC ¶9438, 22 AFTR 2d 5004, 398 F.2d 694 (CA–3, 1968). But see *Nariman Teymourian,* 90 TCM 352, T.C.Memo. 2005–302, for an example of how good planning can avoid constructive dividends in the shareholder loan context.

interest). In this case, the constructive dividend is equal to the amount of imputed (forgone) interest on the loan.[40] Imputed interest is the interest on the loan (calculated using the interest rate the Federal government applies to new borrowings, compounded semiannually), in excess of the interest actually charged on the loan.

When the imputed interest provision applies, the shareholder is deemed to have made an interest payment to the corporation equal to the amount of imputed interest and the corporation is deemed to have repaid the imputed interest to the shareholder through a constructive dividend. As a result, the corporation receives interest income and makes a nondeductible dividend payment, and the shareholder has taxable dividend income that might be offset with an interest deduction.

EXAMPLE 28

Mallard Corporation lends its principal shareholder, Henry, $100,000 on January 2 of the current year. The loan is interest-free and payable on demand. On December 31, the imputed interest rules are applied. Assuming that the Federal rate is 2%, compounded semiannually, the amount of imputed interest for the year is $2,010. This amount is deemed paid by Henry to Mallard in the form of interest. Mallard then is deemed to return the amount to Henry as a constructive dividend.

As a result, Henry has dividend income of $2,010, which might be offset with a deduction for the interest deemed paid to Mallard. Mallard has interest income of $2,010 for the interest received, with no offsetting deduction for the dividend payment.

Loans to a Corporation by Shareholders

Shareholder loans to a corporation may be reclassified as equity if the debt has too many features of stock. Any interest and principal payments made by the corporation to the shareholder are then treated as constructive dividends. This topic is covered more thoroughly in Chapter 18 (see text Section 18-2b and the discussion of "thin capitalization").

19-3e Stock Dividends and Stock Rights

Stock Dividends

In general, **stock dividends** are excluded from income on the theory that the ownership interest of the shareholder is unchanged as a result of the distribution.[41]

When a stock dividend is declared, the shareholder ends up with additional shares of stock but retains the same total stock basis. As a result, the shareholder's basis is reallocated across both the original shares and the new shares.[42] In total, the basis remains the same, but the *per-share* basis decreases.

LO.7

Determine the tax implications from receipt of stock dividends and stock rights and the shareholder's basis in the stock and stock rights received.

EXAMPLE 29

Green Corporation declares a 10% stock dividend when its stock is selling for $100 per share. As a result of the stock dividend, the per-share stock value declines to $90.91 (Green's market capitalization remains the same, but it is spread over 10% more shares). Jennifer owns 100 shares of Green and has a basis of $1,100 for those shares. Jennifer receives 10 shares as a result of the stock dividend. How does the stock dividend affect Jennifer?

1. The stock dividend does not generate gross income to Jennifer (and has no impact on Green Corporation's taxable income or E & P).
2. Before the stock dividend, Jennifer had 100 shares and a basis of $11 per share ($1,100/100).
3. After the stock dividend, Jennifer has the same total basis ($1,100), but it is now allocated over the original shares plus the shares received in the stock dividend.
4. Each share of Jennifer's stock now has a basis of $10 ($1,100/110 shares).

---

[40]See § 7872.

[41]§ 305(a); see *Eisner v. Macomber*, 1 USTC ¶32, 3 AFTR 3020, 40 S.Ct. 189 (USSC, 1920).

[42]§ 307(a).

Stock splits—a more common occurrence—are treated in the same way as a stock dividend. So a 4-for-1 stock split provides a shareholder with three additional shares for each share held before the split. Total basis of the original shares is reallocated across all shares after the split. This means that each share carries one-quarter the per-share basis of the original shares.

EXAMPLE 30

Assume the same information as in Example 29, except that Green Corporation declares a 4-for-1 stock split. After the split, Jennifer will own 400 shares, but her total basis remains $1,100. So her per-share basis is $2.75 ($1,100 ÷ 400 shares).

If the dividend stock is not identical to the underlying shares (e.g., a stock dividend of preferred on common), basis is determined by allocating the basis of the formerly held shares between the old and new stock according to the fair market value of each. The holding period includes the holding period of the formerly held stock.[43]

EXAMPLE 31

Gail bought 1,000 shares of common stock two years ago for $10,000. In the current tax year, she receives a nontaxable preferred stock dividend of 100 shares. The preferred stock has a fair market value of $1,000, and the common stock, on which the preferred is distributed, has a fair market value of $19,000.

After the receipt of the stock dividend, the basis of the common stock is $9,500 and the basis of the preferred is $500, computed as follows:

Fair market value of common	$19,000
Fair market value of preferred	1,000
	$20,000
Basis of common: 19/20 × $10,000	$ 9,500
Basis of preferred: 1/20 × $10,000	$ 500

Recognizing that some distributions of stock could affect ownership interests, Congress added rules that tax stock dividends in certain situations.[44] The § 305 rules are based on the proportionate interest concept. Under the general rule illustrated above, stock dividends are excluded from income if they are pro rata stock distributions paid on common stock.

If the stock dividend is a disproportionate distribution, the stock dividend is taxable. For example, a stock dividend where some common shareholders receive common stock and other common shareholders receive preferred stock would be a disproportionate distribution. The same is true if preferred shareholders received a common stock dividend.

If a stock dividend is determined to be taxable, the fair market value of the shares received is included in the shareholder's gross income. The shareholder's basis for the newly received shares is fair market value, and the holding period starts on the date of receipt. Since taxable stock dividends are rarely encountered in practice, we have chosen not to discuss the technical intricacies of § 305(b).

If stock dividends are not taxable, the corporation's E & P is not reduced.[45] If the stock dividends are taxable, the distributing corporation treats the distribution in the same manner as any other taxable property dividend.

Stock Rights

The rules for determining taxability of stock rights are identical to those for determining taxability of stock dividends. If the rights are taxable, the recipient has income equal to the fair market value of the rights. The fair market value then becomes the shareholder-distributee's basis in the rights.[46] If the rights are exercised, the holding period for the new stock begins on the date the rights (whether taxable or nontaxable) are exercised.

[43]§ 1223(5).
[44]§ 305(b); see "Stock Dividends," S.Rept. 91–552, 1969–3 C.B. 519.

[45]§ 312(d)(1).
[46]Reg. § 1.305–1(b).

The basis of the new stock is the basis of the rights plus the amount of any other consideration given.

If stock rights are not taxable and the value of the rights is less than 15 percent of the value of the old stock, the basis of the rights is zero. However, the shareholder may elect to have some of the basis in the formerly held stock allocated to the rights.[47] The election is made by attaching a statement to the shareholder's return for the year in which the rights are received.[48] If the fair market value of the rights is 15 percent or more of the value of the old stock and the rights are exercised or sold, the shareholder *must* allocate some of the basis in the formerly held stock to the rights.

> **EXAMPLE**
> **32**
>
> A corporation with common stock outstanding declares a nontaxable dividend payable in rights to subscribe to common stock. Each right entitles the holder to purchase one share of stock for $90. One right is issued for every two shares of stock owned. Fred owns 400 shares of stock purchased two years ago for $15,000. At the time of the distribution of the rights, the market value of the common stock is $100 per share, and the market value of the rights is $8 per right. Fred receives 200 rights. He exercises 100 rights and sells the remaining 100 rights three months later for $9 per right.
>
> Fred need not allocate the cost of the original stock to the rights because the value of the rights is less than 15% of the value of the stock ($1,600 ÷ $40,000 = 4%). If Fred does not allocate his original stock basis to the rights, the tax consequences are as follows:
>
> - Basis of the new stock is $9,000 [$90 (exercise price) × 100 (shares)]. The holding period of the new stock begins on the date the stock was purchased.
>
> - Sale of the rights produces long-term capital gain of $900 [$9 (sales price) × 100 (rights)]. The holding period of the rights starts with the date the original 400 shares of stock were acquired.
>
> If Fred elects to allocate basis to the rights, the tax consequences are as follows:
>
> - Basis of the stock is $14,423 [$40,000 (value of stock) ÷ $41,600 (value of rights and stock) × $15,000 (cost of stock)].
>
> - Basis of the rights is $577 [$1,600 (value of rights) ÷ $41,600 (value of rights and stock) × $15,000 (cost of stock)].
>
> - When Fred exercises the rights, his basis for the new stock will be $9,288.50 [$9,000 (cost) + $288.50 (basis for 100 rights)].
>
> - Sale of the rights would produce a long-term capital gain of $611.50 [$900 (sales price) − $288.50 (basis for the remaining 100 rights)].

19-4 STOCK REDEMPTIONS

LO.8

Identify various stock redemptions that qualify for sale or exchange treatment.

19-4a Overview

When a shareholder sells stock to an unrelated third party, the transaction typically is treated as a sale or exchange. Here, the amount realized is offset by the shareholder's stock basis and a capital gain (or loss) results. Effectively, the Code treats the proceeds as a return *of* the shareholder's stock investment.

The Big Picture

> **EXAMPLE**
> **33**
>
> Return to the facts of *The Big Picture* on p. 19-1. Assume that Luis sells some of his shares of Plainwell Ice Cream Corporation stock (stock basis, $80,000) to a third party for $1,200,000. If the transaction is treated as a sale or exchange (a return *of* the owner's stock investment), Luis has a long-term capital gain of $1,120,000 [$1,200,000 (amount realized) – $80,000 (stock basis)].

In a stock redemption, where a shareholder sells stock back to the *issuing corporation* for cash or other property, the transaction can have the *effect* of a dividend distribution (rather than a sale or exchange). This is particularly the case when the stock

---

[47]§ 307(b)(1).   [48]Reg. § 1.307–2.

of the corporation is closely held. For instance, consider a redemption of stock from a sole shareholder. Here, the shareholder's ownership interest is not affected by the stock redemption (the shareholder owns 100 percent of the corporation's outstanding shares before *and* after the transaction). If these redemptions were granted sale or exchange treatment, dividend distributions could be avoided entirely. Instead of formally distributing dividends, the corporation could redeem stock whenever corporate cash was desired by shareholders. Nontaxable stock dividends then could be used to replenish shares as needed.

The key distinction between a sale of stock to an unrelated third party and some stock redemptions is the effect of the transaction on the shareholder's ownership interest in the corporation. In a sale of stock to an unrelated third party, the shareholder's ownership interest in the corporation is reduced ("diminished"). In the case of many stock redemptions, however, there is little or no change to the shareholder's ownership interest. In general, if a shareholder's ownership interest is *not* reduced as a result of a stock redemption, the Code will treat the transaction as a dividend distribution (a return *from* the shareholder's stock investment).

However, the Code does allow sale or exchange treatment for *certain* kinds of stock redemptions. In these transactions, as a general rule, the shareholder's ownership interest is reduced as a result of the redemption. (The requirements for qualifying stock redemptions are provided later in this chapter.)

The Big Picture

EXAMPLE 34

Return to the facts of *The Big Picture* on p. 19-1 and the previous example. Assume that Plainwell Ice Cream Corporation redeems some of its shares from Luis (stock basis, $80,000) for $1,200,000.

If the redemption is treated as a sale or exchange (a return *of* the owner's stock investment), Luis has a long-term capital gain of $1,120,000 [$1,200,000 (amount realized) − $80,000 (stock basis)]. However, if the redemption is treated as a dividend distribution (a return *from* the owner's stock investment), Luis has $1,200,000 of dividend income (assuming adequate E & P).

Stock redemptions occur for a variety of reasons. Publicly traded corporations often reacquire their shares in order to increase shareholder value. For corporations where the stock is closely held, redemptions frequently occur to achieve shareholder objectives. For instance, a closely held corporation might use a redemption to acquire the stock of a deceased shareholder. Using corporate funds to purchase the stock from the decedent's estate means that the remaining shareholders do not need to use their own money to aquire the stock. Stock redemptions also occur as a result of property settlements when a divorce occurs. When spouses jointly own a controlling stock interest in a corporation, a divorce decree may require that the interest of one spouse be bought out. A redemption accomplishes this without using the other spouse's personal assets. Stock redemptions are also frequently incorporated into buy-sell agreements between shareholders. This allows a corporation to redeem (purchase) the stock of a shareholder who wants to end his or her ownership in the corporation.

Noncorporate shareholders generally prefer to have a stock redemption treated as a sale or exchange rather than as a dividend distribution. As Examples 35 and 36 illustrate, a stock redemption that qualifies for sale or exchange treatment is preferred because it results in *both* the tax-free recovery of the redeemed stock's basis and the ability to offset any capital gain by capital losses. In a nonqualified stock redemption, the *entire* distribution (assuming adequate E & P) is taxed as dividend income and cannot be offset by capital losses. For individual taxpayers, the tax rate for long-term capital gains and qualified dividend income is 0, 15, or 20 percent, depending on the taxpayer's taxable income.[49]

---

[49]A 3.8% additional tax on net investment income of certain high-income taxpayers applies to capital gains and dividend income.

GLOBAL TAX ISSUES   **Foreign Shareholders Prefer Sale or Exchange Treatment in Stock Redemptions**

As a general rule, foreign shareholders are subject to U.S. tax on dividend income from U.S. corporations but not on capital gains from the sale of U.S. stock.

In some situations, a nonresident alien is taxed on a capital gain from the disposition of stock in a U.S. corporation, but only if the stock was effectively connected with the conduct of a U.S. trade or business of the individual. Foreign corporations are similarly taxed on gains from the sale of U.S. stock investments.

Whether a stock redemption qualifies for sale or exchange treatment therefore takes on added significance for foreign shareholders. If one of the qualifying stock redemption rules can be satisfied, the foreign shareholder typically will avoid U.S. tax on the transaction. If, instead, dividend income is the result, a 30 percent withholding tax typically applies. For further details, see Chapter 25.

Qualifying and Nonqualified Redemptions Compared

Abby, an individual in the 32% income tax bracket, acquired stock in Quail Corporation four years ago for $80,000. In the current year, Quail Corporation (E & P of $1,000,000) redeems her shares for $170,000. If the redemption qualifies for sale or exchange treatment, Abby has a long-term capital gain of $90,000 [$170,000 (redemption amount) − $80,000 (basis)]. Her income tax liability on the $90,000 gain is $13,500 ($90,000 × 15%).

If the stock redemption does not qualify as a sale or exchange, the entire distribution is treated as a dividend and Abby's income tax liability is $25,500 ($170,000 × 15%). Thus, Abby saves $12,000 ($25,500 − $13,500) in income taxes if the transaction is a qualifying stock redemption.

EXAMPLE **35**

Assume in Example 35 that Abby has a capital loss carryover of $60,000 in the current tax year. If the transaction is a qualifying stock redemption, Abby can offset the entire $60,000 capital loss carryover against her $90,000 long-term capital gain. As a result, only $30,000 of the gain is taxed and her income tax liability is only $4,500 ($30,000 × 15%).

On the other hand, if the transaction does not qualify for sale or exchange treatment, the entire $170,000 is taxed as a dividend at 15%. In addition, assuming that she has no capital gains in the current year, Abby is able to deduct only $3,000 of the $60,000 capital loss carryover to offset her other ordinary income.

EXAMPLE **36**

In contrast, *corporate* shareholders normally receive more favorable tax treatment from a dividend distribution. As a result, most corporations would prefer a *nonqualifying* stock redemption. Corporate taxpayers typically report only a portion of a dividend distribution as taxable income because of the dividends received deduction (see Chapter 17). In addition, corporations do not have a preferential tax rate on dividend and long-term capital gain income. As a result, tax planning for stock redemptions must consider the different preferences of corporate and noncorporate shareholders.

Assume in Example 35 that Abby is a calendar year C corporation, that the stock represents a 40% ownership interest in Quail Corporation, and that in the current year Abby has corporate taxable income of $850,000 before the redemption transaction. If the transaction is a qualifying stock redemption, Abby has a long-term capital gain of $90,000 that is subject to tax at 21%, or $18,900.

On the other hand, if the $170,000 distribution is treated as a dividend, Abby has a dividends received deduction of $110,500 ($170,000 × 65%); so only $59,500 of the payment is taxed. Consequently, Abby's tax liability on the transaction is only $12,495 ($59,500 × 21%).

EXAMPLE **37**

When a qualifying stock redemption results in a *loss* to a shareholder rather than a gain, § 267 disallows loss recognition if the shareholder owns (directly or indirectly) more than 50 percent of the corporation's stock.

A shareholder's basis in any property received in a stock redemption, qualifying or nonqualified, generally will be the property's fair market value on the date of the redemption. The holding period of the property also begins on that date.

The Code establishes the criteria for determining whether a transaction is a qualifying stock redemption for tax purposes and thus receives sale or exchange treatment. Section 302(b) provides several types of qualifying stock redemptions. In addition, § 303 allows certain distributions of property to an estate in exchange for a deceased shareholder's stock to be treated as a qualifying stock redemption. Each of these types of qualifying redemptions is discussed later in this section.

19-4b Historical Background

Under prior law, the *dividend equivalency rule* was used to determine which stock redemptions qualified for sale or exchange treatment. Under that rule, if the facts and circumstances of a redemption indicated that it was essentially equivalent to a dividend, the redemption did not qualify for sale or exchange treatment. Instead, the amount received by the shareholder was taxed as dividend income to the extent of the corporation's E & P.

The uncertainty and subjectivity surrounding the dividend equivalency rule led Congress to enact several objective tests for determining the status of a redemption. Currently, the following types of stock redemptions qualify for sale or exchange treatment:

- Distributions not essentially equivalent to a dividend ("not essentially equivalent redemptions"; see text Section 19-4d).

- Distributions substantially disproportionate in terms of shareholder effect ("disproportionate redemptions"; see text Section 19-4e).

- Distributions in complete termination of a shareholder's interest ("complete termination redemptions"; see text Section 19-4f).

- Distributions to pay a shareholder's death taxes ("redemptions to pay death taxes"; see text Section 19-4g).

Concept Summary 19.4 summarizes the requirements for each of these qualifying stock redemptions.

Concept Summary 19.4

Summary of the Qualifying Stock Redemption Rules

Type of Redemption	Requirements to Qualify
Not essentially equivalent to a dividend [§ 302(b)(1)]	Meaningful reduction in the shareholder's voting interest. Reduction in the shareholder's right to share in earnings or assets upon liquidation also is considered. Stock attribution rules apply.
Substantially disproportionate [§ 302(b)(2)]	Shareholder's interest in the corporation, after the redemption, must be less than 80% of interest before the redemption and less than 50% of the total combined voting power of all classes of stock entitled to vote. Stock attribution rules apply.
Complete termination [§ 302(b)(3)]	Entire stock ownership terminated. In general, stock attribution rules apply. However, *family* attribution rules are waived when the former shareholder has no interest, other than as a creditor, in the corporation for at least 10 years after the redemption and files an agreement to notify the IRS of any prohibited interest acquired during the 10-year period. Shareholder must retain all necessary records during the 10-year period.
Redemption to pay death taxes [§ 303]	Value of the stock of one corporation in the gross estate exceeds 35% of the value of the adjusted gross estate. Redemption limited to the sum of death taxes and funeral and administration expenses. Generally tax-free because the estate's tax basis of stock is FMV on the date of the decedent's death and the value is unchanged at redemption. Stock attribution rules do not apply.

19-4c **Stock Attribution Rules**

As explained earlier, to qualify for sale or exchange treatment, a stock redemption generally must result in the reduction of the shareholder's ownership interest in the corporation. In determining whether a stock redemption has sufficiently reduced a shareholder's interest, the stock owned by certain related parties is attributed to the redeeming shareholder.[50]

Congress created stock attribution rules to serve this purpose. Under these rules, related parties are defined to include the following family members: spouses, children, grandchildren, and parents. Attribution also takes place *from* and *to* partnerships, estates, trusts, and corporations (50 percent or more ownership required in the case of regular corporations). Exhibit 19.1 summarizes the stock attribution rules.

EXHIBIT 19.1	Stock Attribution Rules
	Deemed or Constructive Ownership
Family	An individual is deemed to own the stock owned by his or her spouse, children, grandchildren, and parents (not siblings or grandparents).
Partnership	A partner is deemed to own the stock owned by a partnership to the extent of the partner's proportionate interest in the partnership.
	Stock owned by a partner is deemed to be owned in full by a partnership.
Estate or trust	A beneficiary or an heir is deemed to own the stock owned by an estate or a trust to the extent of the beneficiary's or heir's proportionate interest in the estate or trust.
	Stock owned by a beneficiary or an heir is deemed to be owned in full by an estate or a trust.
Corporation	Stock owned by a regular corporation is deemed to be owned proportionately by any shareholder owning 50% or more of the corporation's stock.
	Stock owned by a shareholder who owns 50% or more of a regular corporation is deemed to be owned in full by the corporation.

The Big Picture

EXAMPLE 38

Return to the facts of *The Big Picture* on p. 19-1. Assume instead that Luis owns 30% (rather than 50%) of the stock in Plainwell Ice Cream Corporation and his two children own 20% of the Plainwell stock. For purposes of the stock attribution rules, Luis is treated as owning 50% of the stock in Plainwell Ice Cream Corporation. He owns 30% directly and, because of the family attribution rules, 20% indirectly through his children.

EXAMPLE 39

Chris owns 40% of the stock in Gray Corporation. The other 60% is owned by a partnership in which Chris has a 20% interest. Chris is deemed to own 52% of Gray Corporation: 40% directly and, because of the partnership interest, 12% indirectly (20% × 60%).

As discussed later, the *family* attribution rules (refer to Example 38) can be waived in the case of some complete termination redemptions. In addition, the stock attribution rules do not apply to stock redemptions to pay death taxes.

When a redemption *fails* to satisfy any of the qualifying stock redemption rules, the basis of the redeemed shares does not disappear. Typically, the basis will attach to the basis of the redeeming shareholder's remaining shares in the corporation. If, however, the redeeming shareholder has terminated his or her direct stock ownership and the redemption is nonqualified due to the attribution rules, the basis of the redeemed shares will attach to the basis of the constructively owned stock.[51] In this manner, a nonqualified stock redemption can result in stock basis being shifted from one taxpayer (the redeeming shareholder) to another taxpayer (the shareholder related under the attribution rules).

---

[50]§ 318.

[51]Reg. § 1.302–2(c).

EXAMPLE

40

Fran and Floyd, a married couple, each own 50 shares in Grouse Corporation, representing 100% of the corporation's stock. All of the stock was purchased for $50,000. Both Fran and Floyd serve as directors of the corporation. The corporation redeems Floyd's 50 shares, but he continues to serve as director of the corporation. The redemption is treated as a dividend distribution (assuming adequate E & P) because Floyd constructively owns Fran's stock, or 100% of the Grouse stock outstanding. Floyd's $25,000 basis in the 50 shares redeemed attaches to Fran's stock; thus, Fran now has a basis of $50,000 in the 50 shares she owns in Grouse.

Concept Summary 19.5 reviews the major tax consequences of stock redemptions to shareholders.

Concept Summary 19.5

Tax Consequences of Stock Redemptions to Shareholders

Qualifying Stock Redemption?

Yes

1. **Sale or exchange treatment:**
   - Tax-free recovery of stock basis
   - Capital gain (loss)
   - 0/15/20% preferential tax rate for individual shareholder

2. **FMV basis for property received**

No

1. **Dividend treatment:**
   - Limited to E & P of distributing corporation
   - 0/15/20% preferential tax rate for individual shareholder
   - Dividends received deduction for corporate shareholder

2. **Basis of redeemed shares added to basis of shareholder's remaining shares**

3. **FMV basis for property received**

19-4d Not Essentially Equivalent Redemptions

Under § 302(b)(1), a redemption qualifies for sale or exchange treatment if it is "not essentially equivalent to a dividend." This is a continuation of the dividend equivalency rule. It was retained principally for redemptions of preferred stock because preferred shareholders often have no control over when corporations redeem preferred stock.[52] Like its predecessor, the not essentially equivalent redemption is a subjective test. Each case must be resolved based on all the facts and circumstances.[53]

Based upon the Supreme Court's decision in *U.S. v. Davis*,[54] a redemption will qualify as a not essentially equivalent redemption only when the shareholder's interest in the redeeming corporation has been meaningfully reduced. In determining whether the meaningful reduction test has been met, the stock attribution rules apply. A decrease in the redeeming shareholder's voting control appears to be the most significant indicator of a meaningful reduction,[55] but reductions in the rights of the shareholders to share in corporate earnings or to receive corporate assets upon liquidation also are considered.[56]

Meaningful Reduction Test

EXAMPLE

41

Pat owns 58% of the common stock of Falcon Corporation. As a result of a redemption of some of his stock, Pat's ownership interest in Falcon is reduced to 51%.

Because Pat continues to have voting control over Falcon after the redemption, the distribution is treated as essentially equivalent to a dividend. As a result, the entire amount of the distribution is treated as a dividend (assuming adequate E & P).

---

[52]See S.Rept. No. 1622, 83d Cong., 2d Sess., 44 (1954).

[53]Reg. § 1.302–2(b)(1).

[54]70–1 USTC ¶9289, 25 AFTR 2d 70–827, 90 S.Ct. 1041 (USSC, 1970).

[55]See, for example, *Jack Paparo*, 71 T.C. 692 (1979).

[56]See, for example, *Grabowski Trust*, 58 T.C. 650 (1972).

Maroon Corporation redeems 2% of its stock from Maria. Before the redemption, Maria owned 10% of Maroon Corporation. In this case, the redemption *may* qualify as a not essentially equivalent redemption. Maria experiences a reduction in her voting rights, her right to participate in current earnings and accumulated surplus, and her right to share in net assets upon liquidation.

EXAMPLE
42

19-4e Disproportionate Redemptions

A redemption qualifies for sale or exchange treatment under § 302(b)(2) as a <mark>disproportionate redemption</mark> if *both* of the following conditions are met:

- After the distribution, the shareholder owns *less than* 80 percent of the interest owned in the corporation before the redemption.

- After the distribution, the shareholder owns *less than* 50 percent of the total combined voting power of all classes of stock entitled to vote.

In determining a shareholder's ownership interest before and after a redemption, the attribution rules apply. Compare Examples 43 and 44.

Paulina, Carl, and Dan, unrelated individuals, own 30 shares, 30 shares, and 40 shares, respectively, in Wren Corporation. Wren has 100 shares outstanding and E & P of $200,000. The corporation redeems 20 shares of Dan's stock for $30,000. Dan paid $200 a share for the stock two years ago. Dan's ownership in Wren Corporation before and after the redemption is as follows:

EXAMPLE
43

	Total Shares	Dan's Ownership	Ownership Percentage	80% of Original Ownership
Before redemption	100	40	40% (40 ÷ 100)	32% (80% × 40%)
After redemption	80	20	25% (20 ÷ 80)*	

*Note that the denominator of the fraction is reduced after the redemption (from 100 to 80).

Dan's 25% ownership after the redemption meets both tests of § 302(b)(2). It is less than 80% of his original ownership and less than 50% of the total voting power. The distribution qualifies as a disproportionate redemption and receives sale or exchange treatment. As a result, Dan has a long-term capital gain of $26,000 [$30,000 − $4,000 (20 shares × $200)].

Assume in Example 43 that Carl and Dan are father and son. In this case, the redemption would *not* qualify for sale or exchange treatment because of the *attribution rules*. Dan is deemed to own Carl's stock before and after the redemption. Dan's ownership in Wren Corporation before and after the redemption is as follows:

EXAMPLE
44

	Total Shares	Dan's Direct Ownership	Carl's Ownership	Dan's Direct and Indirect Ownership	Ownership Percentage	80% of Original Ownership
Before redemption	100	40	30	70	70% (70 ÷ 100)	56% (80% × 70%)
After redemption	80	20	30	50	62.5% (50 ÷ 80)	

Dan's direct and indirect ownership of 62.5% fails to meet either of the tests of § 302(b)(2). After the redemption, Dan owns more than 80% of his original ownership and more than 50% of the voting stock. As a result, the redemption does not qualify for sale or exchange treatment and results in a dividend distribution of $30,000 to Dan. The basis in the 20 shares redeemed is added to Dan's basis in his remaining 20 shares.

A redemption that does not qualify as a disproportionate redemption may still qualify as a not essentially equivalent redemption if it meets the meaningful reduction test (see Example 42).

19-4f Complete Termination Redemptions

A redemption that terminates a shareholder's *entire* stock ownership in a corporation qualifies for sale or exchange treatment. The attribution rules generally apply in determining whether the shareholder's stock ownership has been terminated. However, the *family* attribution rules do not apply to a <mark>complete termination redemption</mark> if *both* of the following conditions are met:

- The former shareholder does not hold or acquire any interest, other than that of a creditor, in the corporation for at least 10 years after the redemption (including an interest as an officer, a director, or an employee). This is called a "prohibited interest."
- The former shareholder files a statement agreeing to notify the IRS within 30 days if a prohibited interest is aquired in the 10-year postredemption period and retains all records related to the redemption during this time period.

The acquisition of stock in the corporation by bequest or inheritance is not a prohibited interest. The required statement must be signed by the former shareholder and attached to the tax return for the year in which the redemption occurs.[57]

Family Attribution Waiver

EXAMPLE 45

Kevin owns 50% of the stock in Green Corporation, and the remaining interests in Green are held as follows: 40% by Wilma (Kevin's spouse) and 10% by Carmen (a key employee). Green redeems all of Kevin's stock for its fair market value. As a result, Wilma and Carmen are the only remaining shareholders, now owning 80% and 20%, respectively.

If the two requirements for the family attribution waiver are met, the transaction will qualify as a complete termination redemption and will result in sale or exchange treatment. If the waiver requirements are not satisfied, Kevin will be deemed to own Wilma's (his spouse's) stock and the entire distribution will be taxed as a dividend (assuming adequate E & P).

EXAMPLE 46

Assume in Example 45 that Kevin qualifies for the family attribution waiver for the redemption. In the year of the redemption, Kevin treats the transaction as a sale or exchange. However, if he purchases Carmen's stock seven years after the redemption, he has acquired a prohibited interest and the redemption distribution is reclassified as a dividend. Kevin must notify the IRS and will owe additional taxes due to this revised treatment.

19-4g Redemptions to Pay Death Taxes

Section 303 provides sale or exchange treatment to a redemption of stock included in, and representing a substantial part of, a decedent's gross estate. This provision provides an estate with liquidity to pay death-related expenses when a significant portion of the estate consists of stock in a closely held corporation.

Because closely held corporation stock is not easily marketable, a stock redemption usually represents the only way to dispose of the stock. The redemption might not satisfy any of the other qualifying stock redemption provisions because of the attribution rules (e.g., attribution to estate from beneficiaries). A <mark>redemption to pay death taxes</mark> provides sale or exchange treatment without regard to the attribution rules. However, this treatment is limited to the sum of the death taxes and funeral and administration expenses. A redemption in excess of these expenses may qualify for sale or exchange treatment under one of the § 302 provisions.

An estate's basis in property acquired from a decedent is generally the property's fair market value on the date of death.[58] Typically, there is little change in the fair market

---

[57]Reg. § 1.302–4(a).

[58]If available and elected, an alternate valuation date would apply. § 1014(a).

value of stock from the date of a decedent's death to the date of a redemption to pay death taxes. When the redemption price is the same as the estate's basis in the stock, a redemption to pay death taxes results in no gain (or loss) to the estate.

Section 303 applies only to a distribution made with respect to stock of a corporation that is included in the gross estate of a decedent and whose value *exceeds* 35 percent of the value of the adjusted gross estate.[59] (For definitions of *gross estate* and *adjusted gross estate*, see the Glossary in Appendix C.)

EXAMPLE 47

Juan's adjusted gross estate is $15,000,000. The death taxes and funeral and administration expenses of the estate total $1,440,000. Included in the gross estate is stock of Yellow Corporation, valued at $5,600,000. Juan had acquired the stock nine years ago at a cost of $600,000. Yellow redeems $1,440,000 of the stock from Juan's estate.

Because the value of the Yellow stock in Juan's estate exceeds the 35% threshold ($5,600,000 ÷ $15,000,000 = 37.3%), the redemption qualifies under § 303 as a sale or exchange to Juan's estate. Assuming that the value of the stock has remained unchanged since the date of Juan's death, there is no recognized gain (or loss) on the redemption [$1,440,000 (amount realized) − $1,440,000 (estate's stock basis)].

19-5 STOCK REDEMPTIONS—EFFECT ON THE CORPORATION

LO.9

Determine the tax impact of stock redemptions on the distributing corporation.

Thus far, the discussion of stock redemptions has focused on the tax consequences to the *shareholder*. There are also several tax issues surrounding the redeeming *corporation* that must be addressed:

- The recognition of gain or loss on property distributed pursuant to a redemption,
- The effect of a qualifying stock redemption on a corporation's E & P, and
- The deductibility of expenditures incurred in connection with a redemption.

These issues are discussed in the following paragraphs.

19-5a Recognition of Gain or Loss

Distributions in redemption of stock, qualifying or not, are nonliquidating distributions. Section 311 provides that corporations recognize *gain* on all nonliquidating distributions of appreciated property as if the property had been sold for its fair market value. When distributed property is subject to a corporate liability and that liability is greater than the property's fair market value, the liability amount is used to determine the recognized gain.

Losses are not recognized on nonliquidating distributions of property. Therefore, a corporation should avoid distributing loss property (fair market value less than basis) in a stock redemption. However, the corporation could sell the property in a taxable transaction, recognize a loss, and then distribute the proceeds.

EXAMPLE 48

To carry out a redemption, Blackbird Corporation distributes land (basis of $80,000, fair market value of $300,000) to a shareholder's estate. Blackbird has a recognized gain of $220,000 ($300,000 − $80,000). If the land is subject to a liability of $330,000, Blackbird has a recognized gain of $250,000 ($330,000 − $80,000). If the value of the property distributed was less than its adjusted basis, the realized loss would not be recognized.

---

[59]§ 303(b)(2)(A). For purposes of this test, the stock of two or more corporations in which the decedent held a 20% or more interest (by value) is treated as the stock of one corporation [§ 303(b)(2)(B)].

19-5b **Effect on Earnings and Profits**

In a qualifying stock redemption, the E & P of the distributing corporation is reduced by no more than the percentage of the corporation's stock redeemed.[60]

EXAMPLE 49

Navy Corporation has 100 shares of stock outstanding. In a qualifying stock redemption, Navy distributes $200,000 in exchange for 30 of its shares. At the time of the redemption, Navy has paid-in capital of $120,000 and E & P of $450,000. Navy's E & P is reduced by $135,000 (30% of the corporation's E & P). The remainder of the redemption price ($65,000) is a reduction of the Navy paid-in capital account.

If, instead, the 30 shares were redeemed for $80,000, E & P would be reduced by $80,000, the amount Navy paid to carry out the stock redemption.

19-5c **Redemption Expenditures**

In redeeming its shares, a corporation may incur certain expenses such as accounting, brokerage, legal, and loan fees. Section 162(k) specifically denies a deduction for redemption expenditures incurred in connection with a stock redemption. The disallowance does not apply to amounts otherwise deducted under § 163, such as interest from debt-financed redemptions.

19-6 **OTHER CORPORATE DISTRIBUTIONS**

Partial liquidations of a corporation, if in compliance with the statutory requirements of § 302(e), will result in sale or exchange treatment to noncorporate shareholders. Distributions of stock and securities of a controlled corporation to the shareholders of the parent corporation will be free of any tax consequences if they fall under § 355. Both of these types of corporate distributions are similar to stock redemptions and dividend distributions in some respects but are not discussed here because of their limited applicability.

See Concept Summary 19.6 for a listing of key points to consider when working with corporate distributions.

19-7 **TAX PLANNING**

LO.10

Identify planning opportunities available to minimize the tax impacts of corporate distributions, constructive dividends, and stock redemptions.

19-7a **Corporate Distributions**

The following points are especially important when planning for corporate distributions.

- Because E & P is the pool of funds from which dividends may be distributed, its computation is essential to corporate planning. However, many corporations do not calculate E & P on a regular basis. Some firms view the financial accounting concept of "retained earnings" as a surrogate; if there are sufficient retained earnings, they assume there is sufficient E & P. And in many instances, this is a fairly safe assumption. But if retained earnings is reduced (or low), the corporation may be at risk for making a distribution that is not a dividend for tax purposes (and, instead, a return of capital). Thus, an E & P account should be established and maintained.

- Accumulated E & P is the sum of all past years' current E & P. Because there is no statute of limitations on the computation of E & P, the IRS can redetermine a corporation's current E & P for a tax year long since passed. Any changes made will affect accumulated E & P and have a direct impact on the taxability of current distributions to shareholders.

- Distributions can be planned to avoid or minimize dividend exposure.

---

[60]§ 312(n)(7).

Concept Summary 19.6

Corporate Distributions

1. Without a special provision, corporate distributions are taxed as dividend income to the recipient shareholders to the extent of the distributing corporation's E & P accumulated since February 28, 1913, or to the extent of current E & P. Any excess is treated as a return of capital to the extent of the shareholder's basis in the stock and, thereafter, as capital gain.

2. Property distributions are considered dividends (taxed as noted in item 1) in the amount of their fair market value. The amount distributed is reduced by any liabilities on the property distributed. The shareholder's basis in the property is its fair market value.

3. Earnings and profits of a corporation are increased by corporate earnings for the taxable year computed in the same manner as the corporation computes its taxable income. As a general rule, the account is increased for all items of income, whether taxed or not, and reduced by all items of expense, whether deductible or not. Refer to Concept Summary 19.1 for a summary of the effect of certain transactions on taxable income in arriving at current E & P.

4. A corporation recognizes gain, but not loss, on distributions of property to its shareholders. E & P of the distributing corporation is reduced by the amount of money distributed or by the greater of the fair market value or the adjusted basis of property distributed less the amount of any liability applicable to the distributed property.

5. As a general rule, stock dividends or stock rights (representing stock in the distributing corporation) are not taxed, with certain exceptions.

6. Stock redemptions that qualify under § 302(b) are given sale or exchange treatment. This provision requires that such distributions be substantially disproportionate, complete terminations, or not essentially equivalent to a dividend. In determining whether a transaction is a not essentially equivalent redemption or a disproportionate redemption, the attribution rules apply. However, in a complete termination redemption, the family attribution rules may be waived if certain conditions are met.

7. If stock included in a decedent's estate represents more than 35% of the adjusted gross estate, § 303 provides automatic sale or exchange treatment on its redemption.

8. A corporation is taxed on the appreciation of property distributed in redemption of its stock.

9. In a qualifying stock redemption, the E & P account of the distributing corporation is reduced by an amount not in excess of the ratable share of its E & P that is attributable to the stock redeemed.

EXAMPLE
50

After several unprofitable years, Darter Corporation has a deficit in accumulated E & P of $100,000 as of January 1, 2020. Starting in 2020, Darter expects to generate annual E & P of $50,000 for the next four years and would like to distribute this amount to its shareholders. The corporation's cash position (for dividend purposes) will correspond to the current E & P generated. Consider the following two distribution schedules:

1. On December 31 of 2020, 2021, 2022, and 2023, Darter Corporation distributes cash of $50,000.
2. On December 31 of 2021 and 2023, Darter Corporation distributes cash of $100,000.

The two alternatives are illustrated as follows:

Year	Accumulated E & P (First of Year)	Current E & P	Distribution	Amount of Dividend
Alternative 1				
2020	($100,000)	$50,000	$50,000	$50,000
2021	(100,000)	50,000	50,000	50,000
2022	(100,000)	50,000	50,000	50,000
2023	(100,000)	50,000	50,000	50,000
Alternative 2				
2020	($100,000)	$50,000	$ –0–	$ –0–
2021	(50,000)	50,000	100,000	50,000
2022	(50,000)	50,000	–0–	–0–
2023	–0–	50,000	100,000	50,000

Alternative 1 produces $200,000 of dividend income because each $50,000 distribution is fully covered by current E & P. Alternative 2, however, produces only $100,000 of dividend income for the shareholders. The remaining $100,000 is a return of capital. Why?

continued

At the time Darter Corporation made its first distribution of $100,000 on December 31, 2021, it had a deficit of $50,000 in accumulated E & P (the original deficit of $100,000 is reduced by the $50,000 of current E & P from 2020). Consequently, the $100,000 distribution yields a $50,000 dividend (the current E & P for 2021), and $50,000 is treated as a return of capital.

As of January 1, 2022, Darter's accumulated E & P has a deficit balance of $50,000 because a distribution cannot increase a deficit in E & P. After adding the remaining $50,000 of current E & P from 2022, the balance on January 1, 2023, is zero. As a result, the second distribution of $100,000 made on December 31, 2023, also yields $50,000 of dividends (the current E & P for 2023) and a $50,000 return of capital.

19-7b Planning for Qualified Dividends

Retirement Plans

The reduced tax rates available to individual taxpayers on net capital gain and qualified dividend income are not available when stock is held in retirement accounts. Because income in § 401(k) plans and IRAs is not taxed when earned, the benefits of the lower tax rates on these forms of income are lost. Instead, distributions from these plans (other than Roth IRAs) are taxed at ordinary income tax rates.

Closely Held Corporations

Closely held corporations have considerable discretion regarding their dividend policies. In the past, the double tax result provided strong motivation to avoid the payment of dividends. Instead, the incentive was to bail out corporate profits in a manner that provided tax benefits to the corporation. As a result, liberal use was made of compensation, loan, and lease arrangements because salaries, interest, and rent are deductible. Under current law, however, shareholders might prefer dividends because salaries, interest, and rent are taxed at ordinary rates while dividends receive preferential treatment. As a result, the question becomes this: Should the *corporation* or the *shareholders* benefit? In general, the best strategy considers the tax consequences to *both parties*.

EXAMPLE 51

Consider a corporation paying tax at the 21% rate and an individual shareholder in the 32% tax bracket. A deductible $10,000 payment to the shareholder will *save* the corporation $2,100 in tax, resulting in an after-tax cost of $7,900. The shareholder will pay $3,200 in tax, resulting in after-tax income of $6,800. This creates a joint tax burden of $1,100 ($3,200 tax paid by the shareholder − $2,100 tax saved by the corporation).

If, instead, the corporation paid a $10,000 qualified dividend (subject to a 15% tax rate) to the shareholder, no tax savings would be realized by the corporation, resulting in an after-tax cost of $10,000. The shareholder would owe $1,500 in taxes, leaving $8,500 of income. Considering both the corporation and the shareholder, a dividend creates $400 more tax liability than a deductible payment; so the deductible payment is more tax-efficient.

In Example 51, when the deductible payment is made, the shareholder bears an increased tax burden of $1,700 ($3,200 tax due from the deductible payment − $1,500 tax due from the dividend) while the corporation saves $2,100 ($2,100 tax saved because of the deductible payment − $0 tax saved because of the dividend). Both parties can actually benefit if the corporation transferred part of its benefit to the shareholder through a larger deductible payment.

EXAMPLE 52

Assume the same facts as in Example 51, except that the corporation pays a $12,600 deductible payment to the shareholder. In this case, the corporation will save $2,646 ($12,600 × 21%) in tax, resulting in an after-tax cost of $9,954.

From the corporation's perspective, this is preferable to a $10,000 dividend because it costs $46 less after tax ($10,000 dividend cost − $9,954 after-tax cost of a $12,600 deductible payment). The shareholder will pay taxes of $4,032 on the deductible payment, resulting in after-tax income of $8,568. The shareholder will also prefer this payment to a $10,000 dividend because it generates $68 more after-tax income ($8,568 − $8,500 from a dividend).

As a result, if properly structured, deductible payments by the corporation to the shareholder can be preferable to dividends in many situations.

19-7c Constructive Dividends

Tax planning can be particularly effective in avoiding constructive dividend situations. Shareholders should try to structure their dealings with the corporation on an arm's length basis. For example, reasonable rent should be paid for the use of corporate property, and a fair price should be paid by a shareholder for its purchase. The parties should support the amount involved with appraisal data or market information obtained from reliable sources at or near the time of the transaction. In the case of loans to shareholders, the parties should provide for an adequate rate of interest and written evidence of the debt. Shareholders should also establish and follow a realistic repayment schedule.

If shareholders want to bail out corporate profits in a form deductible to the corporation, a balanced mix of the possible alternatives lessens the risk of constructive dividend treatment. Rent for the use of shareholder property, interest on amounts borrowed from shareholders, or salaries for services rendered by shareholders are all feasible substitutes for dividend distributions. Overdoing any one approach, however, may attract the attention of the IRS. Too much interest, for example, may mean that the corporation is thinly capitalized, and some of the debt may be reclassified as an equity investment.

Much can be done to protect against the disallowance of unreasonable compensation. Example 53 is an illustration, all too common in a family corporation, of what *not* to do.

EXAMPLE
53

Rebecca Cole wholly owns Eagle Corporation. Corporate employees and their annual salaries include Bob, Rebecca's husband ($120,000); Sam, Rebecca's son ($80,000); Rebecca ($640,000); and Tanuja, Rebecca's longtime friend who is unrelated to the Cole family ($320,000). The operation of Eagle Corporation is shared about equally between Rebecca and Tanuja.

Bob performed significant services for Eagle during its formative years, but now merely attends the annual meeting of the board of directors. Sam is a full-time student and occasionally signs papers for the corporation in his capacity as treasurer. Eagle Corporation has not distributed a dividend for 10 years although it has accumulated substantial E & P. Bob, Sam, and Rebecca run the risk of a finding of unreasonable compensation based on the following factors:

- Bob's salary is vulnerable unless proof is available that some or all of his $120,000 annual salary is payment for services rendered to the corporation in prior years and that he was underpaid for those years.[61]

- Sam's salary is also vulnerable; he does not appear to earn the $80,000 paid to him by the corporation. Neither Sam nor Bob is a shareholder, but each one's relationship to Rebecca is enough of a tie-in to raise the unreasonable compensation issue.

- Rebecca's salary could be challenged by the IRS. Why is Rebecca receiving $320,000 more than Tanuja when they share equally in the operation of the corporation?

- The fact that Eagle Corporation has not distributed dividends over the past 10 years, even though it is capable of doing so, also increases the likelihood of a constructive dividend.

19-7d Stock Redemptions

Stock redemptions offer several possibilities for tax planning.

- Stock redemptions are particularly well suited for purchasing the interest of a retiring or deceased shareholder. Rather than the remaining shareholders buying the stock of the retiring or deceased shareholder, corporate funds are used to redeem these shares. A life insurance policy held by the corporation on a shareholder's life can be used to fund a redemption. Upon the shareholder's death, the corporation receives tax-free life insurance proceeds that are used to redeem the stock

[61]See, for example, *R. J. Nicoll Co.*, 59 T.C. 37 (1972).

of the deceased shareholder. The ability to use the corporation's funds to buy out a shareholder's interest is also advantageous in property settlements between divorcing taxpayers.

- A third party who wants to purchase all of the stock of a corporation can utilize a stock redemption to finance some of the stock acquisition cost. This technique is referred to as a "bootstrap acquisition." The third party first purchases a small amount of stock from the shareholders. The corporation then redeems all of its outstanding stock except that of the third party. The third party becomes the sole shareholder of the corporation, but corporate funds finance most of the acquisition. Some leveraged buyouts (LBOs) are structured like a bootstrap acquisition.

- The timing and sequence of a redemption should be considered carefully, because a series of redemptions may have the effect of a dividend distribution. The following example illustrates this point.

EXAMPLE 54

Sparrow Corporation's stock is held by three unrelated shareholders: Alma (60 shares), Antonio (20 shares), and Ali (20 shares). The corporation redeems 24 of Alma's shares. Shortly thereafter, it redeems 5 of Antonio's shares. Does Alma's redemption qualify as a disproportionate redemption?

Taken in isolation, Alma's redemption satisfies the 80% and 50% tests. Yet, if the IRS takes into account the later redemption of Antonio's shares, Alma has not satisfied the 50% test; she still owns 36/71 of the corporation after the two redemptions. A greater time lag between the redemptions places Alma in a better position to argue against collapsing the two redemptions as parts of one integrated plan.

- For a family corporation in which all of the shareholders are related to each other, the only hope of achieving sale or exchange treatment may lie in the use of a complete termination redemption. Here, strict compliance with the requirements for the family attribution waiver is critical (e.g., the withdrawing shareholder does not acquire a prohibited interest in the corporation within 10 years).

- In a redemption to pay death taxes, the amount sheltered from dividend treatment is limited to the sum of death taxes and funeral and administration expenses. The estate tax exemption amount was nearly doubled by the Tax Cuts and Jobs Act (TCJA) of 2017 (after adjustment for inflation). This change will result in far fewer taxpayers incurring any Federal estate tax, further limiting the applicability of qualified redemption treatment under § 303. However, a redemption in excess of the limitation can qualify for sale or exchange treatment under one of the other qualifying stock redemption rules.

- A qualifying stock redemption financed by installment notes can provide tax benefits to both the corporation and the shareholder. For the corporation, the related interest expense is deductible (subject to the business interest expense limitation; see Chapter 17), while the shareholder can use the installment method to defer to the point of collection the gain that is attributable to the notes.

TAXING CORPORATE DISTRIBUTIONS

ALEXANDER RATHS/SHUTTERSTOCK.COM

A number of factors affect the tax treatment of Plainwell Ice Cream Corporation's distributions. The amount of current and accumulated E & P (which differ from the financial reporting concept of retained earnings) partially determines the tax effect on the shareholders. Given that Plainwell Ice Cream Corporation has had a highly profitable year (see Example 12), it is likely that there is sufficient current E & P to cover the distributions. If so, they are dividends to the shareholders rather than a return of capital. Waffle Cone Corporation receives $200,000 of dividend income that is offset by

continued

the dividends received deduction.* Luis has $200,000 of dividend income (i.e., $300,000 value of the land less the $100,000 mortgage). Assuming that Plainwell is a domestic corporation and that Luis has held his stock for the entire year, the land is a qualified dividend. As a result, the tax depends on Luis's taxable income.** Luis's basis in the land is its fair market value at distribution, or $300,000 (see Example 17).

From Plainwell Ice Cream Corporation's perspective, the distribution of appreciated property creates a deemed gain (see Example 20). As a result, a $280,000 gain results ($300,000 fair market value of the land less its adjusted basis of $20,000). Although the gain increases Plainwell's E & P, the distributions to the shareholders reduce it by $200,000 for the cash and $200,000 for the land ($300,000 fair market value reduced by the $100,000 mortgage).

What If?

What if current E & P balance is less than the cash and land distributed to the shareholders? Current E & P is applied pro rata to the cash and the land. Because the amounts received by the two shareholders are equal ($200,000 each), the current E & P applied is taxed as a dividend and is treated as previously described. To the extent the distributions are not covered by current E & P, accumulated E & P is then applied in a pro rata fashion (because both distributions were made on December 31). However, Plainwell probably has a deficit in accumulated E & P. As a result, the remaining amounts distributed to the two shareholders are first a tax-free recovery of stock basis, and any excess is taxed as a sale of the stock (likely classified as capital gain).

* Because both shareholders received equal distributions ($200,000), it would appear that each is a 50% shareholder. As a result, Waffle Cone's dividends would be offset by a 65% dividends received deduction.
** Because Luis is married filing jointly in 2020, there will be no tax on the dividend if his taxable income is $80,000 or less; a 20% tax if his taxable income is greater than $496,600; a 15% tax if his taxable income is between these two figures.

Accumulated E & P, 19-8	Earnings and profits (E & P), 19-3	Stock dividends, 19-19
Attribution, 19-25	Meaningful reduction test, 19-26	Stock redemption, 19-21
Complete termination redemption, 19-28	Not essentially equivalent redemption, 19-26	Stock rights, 19-20
Constructive dividends, 19-16	Property dividend, 19-14	Unreasonable compensation, 19-18
Current E & P, 19-8	Qualified dividends, 19-13	
Disproportionate redemption, 19-27	Redemption to pay death taxes, 19-28	

Discussion Questions

1. **LO.2** In determining Blue Corporation's current E & P for 2020, how should taxable income be adjusted as a result of the following transactions?
    a. A capital loss carryover from 2019, fully used in 2020.
    b. Nondeductible meal expenses in 2020.
    c. Interest on municipal bonds received in 2020.
    d. Nondeductible lobbying expenses in 2020.
    e. Loss on a sale between related parties in 2020.
    f. Federal income tax refund received in 2020.

2. **LO.3** Describe the effect of a distribution in a year when the distributing corporation has any of the following:
   a. A deficit in accumulated E & P and a positive amount in current E & P.
   b. A positive amount in accumulated E & P and a deficit in current E & P.
   c. A deficit in both current and accumulated E & P.
   d. A positive amount in both current and accumulated E & P.

3. **LO.3** A calendar year corporation has substantial accumulated E & P, but it expects to incur a deficit in current E & P for the year due to significant losses in the last half of the year. A cash distribution to its shareholders on January 1 should result in a return of capital. Comment on the validity of this statement.

4. **LO.4** Discuss the rationale for the reduced tax rates on dividends paid to individuals.

Critical Thinking 5. **LO.1, 2, 3, 4, 5** Orange Corporation distributes $200,000 in cash to each of its three shareholders: Sandy, Byron, and Fuchsia Corporation. What factors must be considered when determining how the distribution is treated for tax purposes by the shareholders?

Critical Thinking 6. **LO.5** Assume the same facts as in Question 5, except that noncash property is distributed. What factors must be considered when determining how the distribution is treated for tax purposes by Orange Corporation?

7. **LO.5** Orion Corporation's board of directors decides to distribute property to its shareholders rather than pay a cash dividend. Why might Orion's board make this decision?

Decision Making 8. **LO.5** Raven Corporation owns three machines that it uses in its business. It no longer needs two of these machines and is considering distributing them to its two shareholders as a property dividend. All three machines have a fair market value of $20,000 each. The basis of each machine is as follows: Machine A, $27,000; Machine B, $20,000; and Machine C, $12,000. The corporation has asked you for advice. What do you recommend?

Critical Thinking 9. **LO.5** Tangerine Corporation is considering a property distribution to its shareholders. If appreciated property is to be used, does it matter to Tangerine whether the property distributed is a long-term capital asset or property subject to depreciation recapture? Would your answer differ if the property distributed has a fair market value less than the adjusted basis? Explain.

Critical Thinking 10. **LO.6** Samantha is the president and sole shareholder of Toucan Corporation. She is paid an annual salary of $500,000, and her son, Aaron, the company's chief financial officer, is paid a salary of $290,000. Aaron works for Toucan on a part-time basis and spends most of his time training for triathlons. Toucan advances $85,000 to Samantha as an interest-free loan. What are the tax issues?

11. **LO.6** Whether compensation paid to a corporate employee is reasonable is a question of fact to be determined from the surrounding circumstances. How would the resolution of this problem be affected by each of the following factors?
    a. The employee owns no stock but is the mother-in-law of the sole shareholder.
    b. The shareholder-employee does not have a college degree.
    c. The shareholder-employee works 40 hours per week for another unrelated employer.
    d. The shareholder-employee was underpaid for services during the formative period of the corporation.
    e. The corporation has never paid a dividend.
    f. Year-end bonuses are paid to all employees, but officer-shareholders receive disproportionately larger bonuses.

12. **LO.6, 10** Pink Corporation has several employees. Their names and salaries are listed below.

Judy	$470,000
Holly (Judy's daughter)	100,000
Terry (Judy's son)	100,000
John (an unrelated third party)	320,000

Holly and Terry are the only shareholders of Pink Corporation. Judy and John share equally in the management of the company's operations. Holly and Terry are both full-time college students at a university 200 miles away. Pink has substantial E & P and has never distributed a dividend. Discuss any problems related to Pink's salary arrangement.

13. **LO.8, 9, 10** Chao, Louis, and Mari, unrelated individuals, own all of the shares   *Critical Thinking* of Cerise Corporation. All three shareholders have been active in the management of Cerise since its inception. In the current year, Chao wants to retire and sell all of her shares in the corporation. What issues should be considered in determining whether Chao should sell her stock to one of the other shareholders, to Cerise Corporation, or to a third party?

14. **LO.8** Corporate shareholders typically prefer dividend treatment on a stock redemption. Why?

15. **LO.8** Do the stock attribution rules apply to all stock redemptions? Explain.

16. **LO.8** Briefly discuss the requirements for a redemption to qualify as a not essentially equivalent redemption.

17. **LO.8** If a redemption is treated as a dividend ("nonqualified stock redemption"), what happens to the basis of the stock redeemed?

18. **LO.8, 9** Tammy and Barry formed Pheasant Corporation several years ago in a   *Critical Thinking* transaction that qualified under § 351. Both shareholders serve as officers and on the board of directors of Pheasant. In the current year, Pheasant Corporation redeemed all of Barry's shares in the corporation with a property distribution. What are the tax issues for Barry and Pheasant?

19. **LO.8** Explain the requirements for a redemption to pay death taxes. What are the tax consequences of a redemption to pay death taxes for the shareholder and the corporation?

20. **LO.8, 9** Angie and her daughter, Ann, who are the only shareholders of Bluebird   *Critical Thinking* Corporation, each paid $200,000 four years ago for their shares in Bluebird. Angie also owns 20% of the stock in Redbird Corporation. The Redbird stock is worth $1,000,000, and Angie's basis in the stock is $100,000. Angie dies in the current year leaving all of her property to her spouse, Gary, but Ann wants to be the sole shareholder of Bluebird Corporation. Bluebird has assets worth $8,000,000 (basis of $1,400,000) and E & P of $2,000,000. Angie's estate is worth approximately $16,000,000. Angie had made gifts during her lifetime to Ann. What are the tax issues for Angie's estate, Ann, and Bluebird?

Computational Exercises

21. **LO.1** At the beginning of the year, Myrna Corporation (a calendar year taxpayer) has E & P of $32,000. The corporation generates no additional E & P during the year. On December 31, the corporation distributes $50,000 to its sole shareholder, Abby, whose stock basis is $10,000. How is the distribution treated for tax purposes?

22. **LO.3** On January 1 of the current year, Rhondell Corporation has accumulated E & P of $13,000. Current E & P for the year is $84,000, earned evenly throughout the year. Elizabeth and Jonathan are sole equal shareholders of Rhondell from January 1 to April 30. On May 1, Elizabeth sells all of her stock to Marshall. Rhondell makes two distributions to shareholders during the year: a total of $42,000 ($21,000 to Elizabeth and $21,000 to Jonathan) on April 30 and a total of $58,000 ($29,000 to Jonathan and $29,000 to Marshall) on December 31.

    Determine the allocation of the distributions by completing the table below. Assume that the shareholders have sufficient basis in their stock for any amount that is treated as return of capital.

	From Current E & P	From Accumulated E & P	Treated as Return of Capital
April 30 distribution of $42,000	_____	_____	_____
December 31 distribution of $58,000	_____	_____	_____

Decision Making

23. **LO.4, 10** Rover Corporation would like to transfer excess cash to its sole shareholder, Aleshia, who is also an employee. Aleshia is in the 24% tax bracket, and Rover is subject to a 21% rate. Because Aleshia's contribution to the business is substantial, Rover believes that a $25,000 bonus in the current year is reasonable compensation and should be deductible by the corporation. However, Rover is considering paying Aleshia a $25,000 dividend because the tax rate on dividends is lower than the tax rate on compensation. Is Rover correct in believing that a dividend is the better choice? Why or why not?

24. **LO.5** Global Corporation distributed property with an $850,000 fair market value and a $415,000 adjusted basis to one of its shareholders. The property was subject to a $230,000 mortgage, which the shareholder assumed. Global has ample E & P to cover any distribution made during the year. What is the amount of the shareholder's dividend income on the distribution? What is the shareholder's basis in the property received?

25. **LO.5** Quinlan has ample E & P to cover any distributions made during the year. One distribution made to a shareholder consists of a property with an adjusted basis of $150,000 and a fair market value of $90,000. What are the tax consequences of this distribution to Quinlan?

26. **LO.6** Deerwood Corporation lends its principal shareholder, Lafayette, $500,000 on July 1 of the current year. The loan is interest-free and payable on demand. On December 31, the imputed interest rules are applied. Assume that the Federal rate is 3%, compounded semiannually. What are the tax consequences of this loan to Lafayette?

27. **LO.7** What are the tax consequences to Euclid from the following independent events?

    a. Euclid bought 500 shares of common stock five years ago for $50,000. This year, Euclid receives 20 shares of common stock as a nontaxable stock dividend. What is Euclid's basis per share after this event?

    b. Assume instead that Euclid received a nontaxable preferred stock dividend of 20 shares. The preferred stock has a fair market value of $5,000, and the common stock, on which the preferred is distributed, has a fair market value of $75,000.

28. **LO.8** During the current year, Gnatcatcher, Inc. (E & P of $1,000,000), distributed $200,000 each to Brandi and Yuen in redemption of some of their Gnatcatcher

stock. The two shareholders acquired their shares five years ago. Each shareholder is in the 32% tax bracket, and each had a $45,000 basis in her redeemed stock.

a. Assume that the distribution to Brandi is a qualifying stock redemption. Determine Brandi's tax liability on the distribution.

b. Assume that the distribution to Yuen is a nonqualified stock redemption. Determine Yuen's tax liability on the distribution.

29. **LO.8** Rosalie owns 50% of the outstanding stock of Salmon Corporation. In a qualifying stock redemption, Salmon distributes $80,000 to Rosalie in exchange for one-half of her shares, which have a basis of $100,000. Compute Rosalie's recognized loss, if any, on the redemption.

30. **LO.8** Derk owns 250 shares of stock in Rose Corporation. The remaining 750 shares of Rose are owned as follows: 150 by Derk's daughter, 200 by Derk's aunt, and 400 by a partnership in which Derk has an 80% interest. Determine the number of shares Derk owns (directly and indirectly) in Rose Corporation.

31. **LO.9** Caramel Corporation has 5,000 shares of stock outstanding. In a qualifying stock redemption, Caramel distributes $145,000 in exchange for 1,000 of its shares. At the time of the redemption, Caramel has paid-in capital of $800,000 and E & P of $300,000. Calculate the reduction to Caramel's E & P as a result of the distribution.

Problems

32. **LO.1, 4** At the start of the current year, Blue Corporation (a calendar year taxpayer) has accumulated E & P of $100,000. Blue's current E & P is $60,000, and at the end of the year, it distributes $200,000 ($100,000 each) to its equal shareholders, Pam and Jon. Pam's stock basis is $11,000; Jon's stock basis is $26,000. How is the distribution treated for tax purposes?

33. **LO.1, 2** Cardinal Corporation, a calendar year taxpayer, receives dividend income of $250,000 from a corporation in which it holds a 10% interest. Cardinal also receives interest income of $35,000 from municipal bonds. (The municipality used the proceeds from the bond issue to construct a library.) Cardinal borrowed funds to purchase the municipal bonds and pays $20,000 of interest on the loan. Excluding these three items, Cardinal's taxable income is $500,000. Cardinal has $150,000 of accumulated E & P at the end of the prior year, and it paid Federal income taxes of $131,250 during the year.

a. What is Cardinal Corporation's taxable income after these three items are taken into account?

b. What is Cardinal Corporation's accumulated E & P at the start of next year?

34. **LO.1, 2, 3** On September 30, Silver Corporation, a calendar year taxpayer, sold a parcel of land (basis of $400,000) for a $1,000,000 note. The note is payable in five installments, with the first payment due next year. Because Silver did not elect out of the installment method, none of the $600,000 gain is taxed this year.

Silver Corporation had a $300,000 deficit in accumulated E & P at the beginning of the year. Before considering the effect of the land sale, Silver had a deficit in current E & P of $50,000.

Javiera, the sole shareholder of Silver, has a basis of $200,000 in her stock. If Silver distributes $900,000 to Javiera on December 31, how much income must she report for tax purposes?

35. **LO.2** Sparrow Corporation (a calendar year, accrual basis taxpayer) had the following transactions in 2020, its second year of operation:

Taxable income	$330,000
Federal income tax liability paid	69,300
Tax-exempt interest income	5,000
Meals expense (total)	3,000
Premiums paid on key employee life insurance	3,500
Increase in cash surrender value attributable to life insurance premiums	700
Proceeds from key employee life insurance policy	130,000
Cash surrender value of life insurance policy at distribution	20,000
Excess of capital losses over capital gains	13,000
MACRS deduction	26,000
Straight-line depreciation using ADS lives	16,000
Section 179 expense elected during 2019	25,000
Dividends received from domestic corporations (less than 20% owned)	35,000

Sparrow uses the LIFO inventory method, and its LIFO recapture amount increased by $10,000 during 2020. In addition, Sparrow sold property on installment during 2019. The property was sold for $40,000 and had an adjusted basis at sale of $32,000. During 2020, Sparrow received a $15,000 payment on the installment sale. Finally, assume that no additional first-year depreciation was claimed. Compute Sparrow's current E & P.

Critical Thinking   36. **LO.1, 2** In each of the following independent situations, indicate the effect on taxable income and E & P, stating the amount of any increase (or decrease) in each as a result of the transaction. Assume that E & P has already been increased by taxable income.

	Transaction	Taxable Income Increase (Decrease)	E & P Increase (Decrease)
a.	Realized gain of $80,000 on involuntary conversion of building ($10,000 of gain is recognized).	_____	_____
b.	Mining exploration costs incurred on May 1 of current year; $24,000 is deductible from current-year taxable income.	_____	_____
c.	Sale of equipment to unrelated third party for $240,000; basis is $120,000 (no election out of installment method; no payments are received in current year).	_____	_____
d.	Dividends of $20,000 received from 5% owned corporation, together with dividends received deduction (assume that taxable income limit does not apply).	_____	_____
e.	Additional first-year (bonus) depreciation of $45,000 claimed in current year.	_____	_____
f.	Section 179 expense deduction of $25,000 in current year.	_____	_____
g.	Impact of current-year § 179 expense deduction in succeeding year.	_____	_____
h.	MACRS depreciation of $80,000. ADS depreciation would have been $90,000.	_____	_____
i.	Federal income taxes of $80,000 paid in current year.	_____	_____

37. **LO.1, 3** Black Corporation and Tom each own 50% of Tan Corporation's common stock. On January 1, Tan has a deficit in accumulated E & P of $200,000. Its current E & P is $90,000. During the year, Tan makes cash distributions of $40,000 each to Black and Tom.

   a.   How are the two shareholders taxed on the distribution?

   b.   What is Tan Corporation's accumulated E & P at the end of the year?

38. **LO.1, 3** Complete the following schedule for each case. Unless otherwise indicated, assume that the shareholders have ample basis in the stock investment.

	Accumulated E & P Beginning of Year	Current E & P	Cash Distributions (All on Last Day of Year)	Dividend Income	Return of Capital
a.	($200,000)	$ 70,000	$130,000	————	————
b.	150,000	(120,000)	210,000	————	————
c.	90,000	70,000	150,000	————	————
d.	120,000	(60,000)	130,000	————	————
e.	Same as part (d), except that the distribution of $130,000 is made on June 30 and the corporation uses the calendar year for tax purposes.			————	————

39. **LO.1, 3** Larry, the sole shareholder of Brown Corporation, sold his Brown stock to Ed on July 30 for $270,000. Larry's basis in the stock was $200,000 at the beginning of the year. Brown had accumulated E & P of $120,000 on January 1 and has current E & P of $240,000. During the year, Brown made the following distributions: $450,000 of cash to Larry on July 1 and $150,000 of cash to Ed on December 30. How will Larry and Ed be taxed on the distributions? How much gain will Larry recognize on the sale of his stock to Ed?

40. **LO.4** In November of the current year, Emerald Corporation declared a dividend of $2 per share (the shareholder record date is December 15). Assume that Emerald has sufficient current E & P to cover the dividend payment. If Judy purchases 500 shares of Emerald stock on December 5 and sells the stock on December 25, how is she taxed on the $1,000 dividend?

41. **LO.1, 5** Heather, an individual, owns all of the outstanding stock in Silver Corporation. Heather purchased her stock in Silver nine years ago, and her basis is $56,000. At the beginning of this year, the corporation has $76,000 of accumulated E & P and no current E & P (before considering the effect of the distributions as noted below). What are the tax consequences to Heather (amount and type of income and basis in property received) and Silver Corporation (gain or loss and effect on E & P) in each of the following situations?

    a. Silver distributes land to Heather. The land was held as an investment and has a fair market value of $54,000 and an adjusted basis of $42,000.

    b. Assume that Silver Corporation has no current or accumulated E & P prior to the distribution. How would your answer to part (a) change?

    c. Assume that the land distributed in part (a) is subject to a $46,000 mortgage (which Heather assumes). How would your answer change?

    d. Assume that the land has a fair market value of $54,000 and an adjusted basis of $62,000 on the date of the distribution. How would your answer to part (a) change?

    e. Instead of distributing land in part (a), assume that Silver decides to distribute equipment used in its business. The equipment has a $14,000 market value, a $1,200 adjusted basis for income tax purposes, and a $5,200 adjusted basis for E & P purposes. When the equipment was purchased four years ago, its original fair market value was $18,000.

42. **LO.1, 5** Lime Corporation, with E & P of $500,000, distributes land (worth $300,000, adjusted basis of $350,000) to Harry, its sole shareholder. The land is subject to a liability of $120,000, which Harry assumes. What are the tax consequences to Lime and to Harry?

Critical Thinking

43. **LO.1, 3** At the beginning of the year, Penguin Corporation (a calendar year taxpayer) has accumulated E & P of $55,000. During the year, Penguin incurs a $36,000 loss from operations that accrues ratably. On October 1, Penguin distributes $40,000 in cash to Holly, its sole shareholder. How is Holly taxed on the distribution?

Critical Thinking   44. **LO.1, 2, 3, 4, 5** Cerulean Corporation has two equal shareholders, Marco and Avery. Marco acquired his Cerulean stock three years ago by transferring property worth $700,000, basis of $300,000, for 70 shares of the stock. Avery acquired 70 shares in Cerulean Corporation two years ago by transferring property worth $660,000, basis of $110,000. Cerulean Corporation's accumulated E & P as of January 1 of the current year is $350,000. On March 1 of the current year, the corporation distributed to Marco property worth $120,000, basis to Cerulean of $50,000. It distributed cash of $220,000 to Avery. On July 1 of the current year, Avery sold her stock to Harpreet for $820,000. On December 1 of the current year, Cerulean distributed cash of $90,000 each to Harpreet and Marco. What are the tax issues?

45. **LO.5** Iris Corporation owns 30% of Fresia Corporation's stock. On November 15, Fresia Corporation, with current E & P of $320,000, distributes land (fair market value of $100,000; basis of $160,000) to Iris. The land is subject to a liability of $80,000, which Iris assumes.

     a.   How is Iris Corporation taxed on the distribution?

     b.   What is Fresia Corporation's E & P after the distribution?

Critical Thinking   46. **LO.2, 6** Parrot Corporation is a closely held company with accumulated E & P of $300,000 and current E & P of $350,000. Tom and Jerry are brothers; each owns a 50% share in Parrot, and they share management responsibilities equally. What are the tax consequences of each of the following independent transactions involving Parrot, Tom, and Jerry? How does each transaction affect Parrot's E & P?

     a.   Parrot sells an office building (adjusted basis of $350,000; fair market value of $300,000) to Tom for $275,000.

     b.   Parrot lends Jerry $250,000 on March 31 of this year. The loan is evidenced by a note and is payable on demand. No interest is charged on the loan (the current applicable Federal interest rate is 3%).

     c.   Parrot owns an airplane that it leases to others for a specified rental rate. Tom and Jerry also use the airplane for personal use and pay no rent. During the year, Tom used the airplane for 120 hours and Jerry used it for 160 hours. The rental value of the airplane is $350 per hour, and its maintenance costs average $80 per hour.

     d.   Tom leases equipment to Parrot for $20,000 per year. The same equipment can be leased from another company for $9,000 per year.

Communications   47. **LO.7** Jacob Corcoran bought 10,000 shares of Grebe Corporation stock two years ago for $24,000. Last year, Jacob received a nontaxable stock dividend of 2,000 shares in Grebe Corporation. In the current tax year, Jacob sold all of the stock received as a dividend for $18,000. Prepare a letter to Jacob and a memo for the file describing the tax consequences of the stock sale. Jacob's address is 925 Arapahoe Street, Boulder, CO 80304.

Decision Making

Critical Thinking

Communications

  48. **LO.4** Kristen, the president and sole shareholder of Egret Corporation, has earned a salary bonus of $30,000 for the current year. Because of the lower tax rates on qualifying dividends, Kristen is considering substituting a dividend for the bonus. Assume that the tax rates are 24% for Kristen and 21% for Egret Corporation.

     a.   How much better off would Kristen be if she were paid a dividend rather than salary?

     b.   How much better off would Egret Corporation be if it paid Kristen a salary rather than a dividend?

c.   If Egret Corporation paid Kristen a salary bonus of $35,000 instead of a $30,000 dividend, how would your answers to parts (a) and (b) change?

d.   What should Kristen do? Summarize your conclusion in a two- to three-paragraph e-mail to your instructor.

49. **LO.8** Julio Gonzales is in the 32% tax bracket. He acquired 2,000 shares of stock in Gray Corporation seven years ago at a cost of $50 per share. In the current year, Julio received a payment of $150,000 from Gray Corporation in exchange for 1,000 of his shares in Gray. Gray has E & P of $1,000,000. What income tax liability would Julio incur on the $150,000 payment in each of the following situations? Assume that Julio has no capital losses.

a.   The stock redemption qualifies for sale or exchange treatment.

b.   The stock redemption does not qualify for sale or exchange treatment.

c.   For part (b), prepare Julio's Schedule B (Form 1040) to reflect the tax reporting required of the transaction. Julio's Social Security number is 123-45-6789. Assume that Julio did not have an interest in or signature authority over any financial account in a foreign country; in addition, he did not have any relationship with a foreign trust.

50. **LO.8** How would your answer to parts (a) and (b) of Problem 49 differ if Julio were a corporate shareholder rather than an individual shareholder and the stock ownership in Gray Corporation represented a 25% interest?

51. **LO.8** Silver Corporation has 2,000 shares of common stock outstanding. Howard owns 600 shares, Howard's grandfather owns 300 shares, Howard's mother owns 300 shares, and Howard's son owns 100 shares. In addition, Maroon Corporation owns 500 shares. Howard owns 70% of the stock in Maroon Corporation.

a.   Applying the § 318 stock attribution rules, how many shares does Howard own in Silver Corporation?

b.   Assume that Howard owns only 40% of the stock in Maroon Corporation. How many shares does Howard own, directly and indirectly, in Silver Corporation?

c.   Assume the same facts as in part (a) above, but in addition, Howard owns a 25% interest in Yellow Partnership. Yellow owns 200 shares in Silver Corporation. How many shares does Howard own, directly and indirectly, in Silver Corporation?

52. **LO.8** Shonda owns 1,000 of the 1,500 shares outstanding in Rook Corporation (E & P of $1,000,000). Shonda paid $50 per share for the stock seven years ago. The remaining stock in Rook is owned by unrelated individuals. What are the tax consequences to Shonda in the following independent situations?

a.   Rook Corporation redeems 450 shares of Shonda's stock for $225,000.

b.   Rook Corporation redeems 600 shares of Shonda's stock for $300,000.

53. **LO.8, 9** Stork Corporation (E & P of $850,000) has 1,000 shares of common stock outstanding. The shares are owned by the following individuals: Lana Johnson, 400 shares; Lori Jones (Lana's mother), 200 shares; and Leo Jones (Lana's brother), 400 shares. Lana paid $200 per share for the Stork stock eight years ago. Lana is interested in reducing her stock ownership in Stork via a stock redemption for $1,000 per share, the fair market value of the stock. Stork Corporation would distribute cash for the entire redemption transaction. In late October, Lana inquired as to the minimum number of shares she would have to redeem to obtain favorable long-term capital gain treatment and the overall tax consequences of such a redemption to both her and Stork Corporation.

Communications

Critical Thinking

a.   Prepare a letter to Lana (1000 Main Street, St. Paul, MN 55166) and a memo for the file in which you explain your conclusions.

b.   Using Microsoft Excel (or a similar software program), create a spreadsheet template that computes the minimum shares that must be redeemed to qualify for a disproportionate redemption. For Microsoft Excel, use the Solver Add-in in your template.

54. **LO.8** Cyan Corporation (E & P of $700,000) has 4,000 shares of common stock outstanding. The shares are owned as follows: Angelica, 2,000 shares; Dean (Angelica's son), 1,500 shares; and Walter (Angelica's uncle), 500 shares. In the current year, Cyan redeems all of Angelica's shares. Determine whether the redemption can qualify for sale or exchange treatment under the complete termination redemption rules in each of the following independent circumstances.

    a. Angelica remains as a director of Cyan Corporation.

    b. Three years after the redemption, Angelica loans $100,000 to Cyan Corporation and receives in return a two-year note receivable.

    c. Dean replaces Angelica as president of Cyan Corporation.

    d. Six years after the redemption, Angelica receives 250 shares in Cyan as a gift from Walter.

55. **LO.8, 9** Robert and Lori (Robert's sister) own all of the stock in Swan Corporation (E & P of $1,000,000). Each owns 500 shares and has a basis of $85,000 in the shares. Robert wants to sell his stock for $600,000, the fair market value, but he will continue to be employed as an officer of Swan Corporation after the sale. Lori would like to purchase Robert's shares, becoming the sole shareholder in Swan, but Lori is short of funds. What are the tax consequences to Robert, Lori, and Swan Corporation under the following circumstances?

    a. Swan Corporation distributes cash of $600,000 to Lori, and she uses the cash to purchase Robert's shares.

    b. Swan Corporation redeems all of Robert's shares for $600,000.

56. **LO.8, 9** The gross estate of Raul, decedent, includes stock in Iris Corporation (E & P of $8,000,000) valued at $6,000,000. At the time of his death, Raul owned 60% of the Iris stock outstanding and he had a basis of $840,000 in the stock. The death taxes and funeral and administration expenses related to Raul's estate amount to $2,000,000, and the adjusted gross estate is $16,000,000. The remainder of the Iris stock is owned by Monica, Raul's daughter and sole heir of his estate. What are the tax consequences to Raul's estate if Iris Corporation distributes $6,000,000 to the estate in redemption of all of its stock in the corporation?

57. **LO.8, 9** Broadbill Corporation (E & P of $650,000) has 1,000 shares of common stock outstanding. The shares are owned by the following individuals: Tammy, 300 shares; Yvette, 400 shares; and Jeremy, 300 shares. Each of the shareholders paid $50 per share for the Broadbill stock four years ago. In the current year, Broadbill Corporation distributes $75,000 to Tammy in redemption of 150 of her shares. Determine the tax consequences of the redemption to Tammy and to Broadbill under the following independent circumstances.

    a. Tammy and Jeremy are grandmother and grandson.

    b. The three shareholders are siblings.

Communications 58. **LO.9** Crane Corporation has 2,000 shares of stock outstanding. It redeems 500 shares for $370,000 when it has paid-in capital of $300,000 and E & P of $1,200,000. The redemption qualifies for sale or exchange treatment for the shareholder. Crane incurred $13,000 of accounting and legal fees in connection with the redemption transaction and $18,500 of interest expense on debt incurred to finance the redemption. What is the effect of the distribution on Crane Corporation's E & P? Also, what is the proper tax treatment of the redemption expenditures? Prepare a letter to the president of Crane Corporation (506 Wall Street, Winona, MN 55987) and a memo for the file in which you explain your conclusions.

Research Problems

Note: Solutions to the Research Problems can be prepared by using the Thomson Reuters Checkpoint™ online tax research database, which accompanies this textbook. Solutions can also be prepared by using research materials found in a typical tax library.

Research Problem 1. Kenny Merinoff and his son, John, own all of the outstanding stock of Flamingo Corporation. Both John and Kenny are officers in the corporation and, together with John's uncle, Ira, comprise the entire board of directors. Flamingo uses the cash method of accounting and has a calendar year-end. In late 2012, the board of directors adopted the following legally enforceable resolution (agreed to in writing by each of the officers):

> Salary payments made to an officer of the corporation that shall be disallowed in whole or in part as a deductible expense for Federal income tax purposes shall be reimbursed by such officer to the corporation to the full extent of the disallowance. It shall be the duty of the board of directors to enforce payment of each such amount.

In 2018, Flamingo paid Kenny $800,000 in compensation. John received $650,000. On an audit in late 2019, the IRS found the compensation of both officers to be excessive. It disallowed deductions for $400,000 of the payment to Kenny and $350,000 of the payment to John. The IRS recharacterized the disallowed payments as constructive dividends. Complying with the resolution by the board of directors, both Kenny and John repaid the disallowed compensation to Flamingo Corporation in 2020. John and Kenny have asked you to determine how their repayments should be treated for tax purposes. John is still working as a highly compensated executive for Flamingo, while Kenny is retired and living off his savings. Prepare a memo for your firm's client files describing the results of your research.

Partial list of research aids:
§ 1341.
Vincent E. Oswald, 49 T.C. 645 (1968).

Communications

Research Problem 2. Emerald Corporation is required to change its method of accounting for Federal income tax purposes. The change will require an adjustment to income to be made over three tax periods. Jonas, the sole shareholder of Emerald Corporation, wants to better understand the implications of this adjustment for E & P purposes, because he anticipates a distribution from Emerald in the current year. Prepare a memo for your firm's client files describing the results of your research.

Partial list of research aids:
§ 481(a).
Rev.Proc. 97–27, 1997–1 C.B. 680.

Communications

Research Problem 3. Your firm has a new individual client, Carla Navarro, who has been assigned to you for preparation of the current year's tax return. Upon review of Carla's tax returns from prior years, you notice that she reported a large capital gain from a stock redemption in 2019. Upon further investigation, you determine that stock in the corporation was owned by some of Carla's family members at the time of the redemption and that the only way the redemption would have qualified for sale or exchange treatment would have been if Carla had availed herself of the family attribution waiver for a complete termination redemption. You establish that the redemption terminated Carla's direct stock ownership in the corporation, that she had no interest in the corporation since the redemption, and that she retained all records pertaining to the redemption. However, you cannot find any evidence that the notification agreement required of a family attribution waiver was properly filed. When asked about the missing agreement, Carla indicated that she knew nothing

Communications

Critical Thinking

Communications

about any required agreement and that if such an agreement was required, her previous CPA should have taken care of it. Your partner has asked you to research whether it is still possible to file an effective family attribution waiver agreement for Carla. In a memo for the tax file, summarize the results of your research.

Use internet tax resources to address the following questions. Look for reliable websites and blogs of the IRS and other government agencies, media outlets, businesses, tax professionals, academics, think tanks, and political outlets.

Data Analytics
Communications

Research Problem 4. Just how common are dividend distributions? Are dividends concentrated in the companies traded on the New York Stock Exchange, or do closely held corporations pay dividends in a similar manner? Did dividends decrease during the Great Recession of 2008 and 2009? Search for answers to these questions on the internet and/or in academic journal articles.

In addition, using data from the IRS Tax Statistics website (**irs.gov/statistics**), find and analyze corporate balance sheet data (overall and by size of total assets) to provide answers to the questions above. Summarize the data you find in a Microsoft Excel spreadsheet, and report your findings to your instructor in a three-paragraph e-mail.

Communications

Research Problem 5. Stock buy-back (redemption) programs are a frequent occurrence among publicly traded corporations. Using the internet as your sole research source, find at least six publicly traded corporations that announced stock buy-back programs in 2019. What are some of the reasons noted by these corporations for the buy-back programs? Summarize your findings in an e-mail and send it to your instructor.

Becker CPA Review Questions

Becker.

1. On January 1, year 5, Olinto Corp., an accrual basis, calendar year C corporation, had $35,000 in accumulated earnings and profits. For year 5, Olinto had current earnings and profits of $15,000 and made two $40,000 cash distributions to its shareholders, one in April and one in September of year 5. What amount of the year 5 distributions is classified as dividend income to Olinto's shareholders?

   a. $15,000   c. $50,000
   b. $35,000   d. $80,000

2. Fox Corp. owned 2,000 shares of Duffy Corp. stock that it bought in year 0 for $9 per share. In year 8, when the fair market value of the Duffy stock was $20 per share, Fox distributed this stock to a noncorporate shareholder. Fox's recognized gain on this distribution was:

   a. $40,000   c. $18,000
   b. $22,000   d. $0

3. Ridge Corp., a calendar year C corporation, made a nonliquidating cash distribution to its shareholders of $1,000,000 with respect to its stock. At that time, Ridge's current and accumulated earnings and profits totaled $750,000 and its total paid-in capital for tax purposes was $10,000,000. Ridge had no corporate shareholders. Ridge's cash distribution:

   I.   Was taxable as $750,000 in dividend income to its shareholders.
   II. Reduced its shareholders' adjusted bases in Ridge stock by $250,000.

   a. I only   c. Both I and II
   b. II only   d. Neither I nor II

4. Which of the following statements is *not* true?

   a. Affiliated corporations that file consolidated returns can take a 100% dividends received deduction.

   b. The dividends received deduction for a small investment in an unrelated corporation is 50%.

   c. The dividends received deduction for a large investment in a corporation is 65%.

   d. There is no income limitation on the dividends received deduction.

5. Jane is the sole shareholder of Buttons, Inc. Buttons has a deficit of $60,000 in accumulated earnings and profits (E & P) at the beginning of the current year. Current E & P is $35,000. If Buttons pays out a cash distribution to Jane during the current year of $50,000, how much is a taxable dividend to Jane?

   a. $0

   b. $35,000

   c. $50,000

   d. $85,000

6. Jane is the sole shareholder of Buttons, Inc. Buttons has accumulated earnings and profits (E & P) of $65,000 at the beginning of the current year. The current E & P is $35,000. Buttons pays out a property distribution to Jane during the current year with an FMV of $150,000 and an adjusted basis of $130,000. How much is a taxable dividend to Jane?

   a. $35,000

   b. $100,000

   c. $120,000

   d. $150,000

7. ABC Corp. paid two cash distributions during year 5. The first was $42,000, and the second was $33,000. Accumulated earnings and profits (E & P) at the end of year 4 were $80,000. Current E & P for year 5 is $30,000. How will the second distribution be allocated between current E & P and accumulated E & P?

	Current E & P	Accumulated E & P
a.	$13,200	$19,800
b.	$16,500	$16,500
c.	$19,800	$13,200
d.	$30,000	$30,000

8. ABC Corp. paid two cash distributions during year 5. The first was $42,000, and the second was $33,000. Accumulated earnings and profits (E & P) at the end of year 4 were $10,000. Current E & P for year 5 is $30,000. How will the first distribution be allocated between current E & P and accumulated E & P?

	Current E & P	Accumulated E & P
a.	$16,800	$25,200
b.	$16,800	$10,000
c.	$25,200	$16,800
d.	$30,000	$10,000

CHAPTER

20

Corporations: Distributions in Complete Liquidation and an Overview of Reorganizations

LEARNING OBJECTIVES: *After completing Chapter 20, you should be able to:*

LO.1 Determine the tax consequences of complete liquidations for both the corporation and its shareholders.

LO.2 Determine the tax consequences of subsidiary liquidations for both the parent and the subsidiary corporations.

LO.3 Explain the general requirements and tax consequences of corporate reorganizations.

LO.4 Identify tax planning opportunities available to minimize the tax impact in complete liquidations and corporate reorganizations.

CHAPTER OUTLINE

20-1 Liquidations—In General, 20-2
20-1a The Liquidation Process, 20-2
20-1b Liquidating and Nonliquidating Distributions Compared, 20-2

20-2 Liquidations—Effect on the Distributing Corporation, 20-3
20-2a The General Rule, 20-3
20-2b Antistuffing Rules, 20-4

20-3 Liquidations—Effect on the Shareholder, 20-8

20-4 Liquidations—Parent-Subsidiary Situations, 20-9
20-4a Minority Shareholder Interests, 20-10
20-4b Indebtedness of the Subsidiary to the Parent, 20-11
20-4c Basis of Property Received by the Parent Corporation—The General Rule, 20-12
20-4d Basis of Property Received by the Parent Corporation—§ 338 Election, 20-12

20-5 Corporate Reorganizations, 20-14
20-5a In General, 20-15
20-5b Summary of the Different Types of Reorganizations, 20-15
20-5c Summary of the Tax Consequences in a Tax-Free Reorganization, 20-15

20-6 Tax Planning, 20-19
20-6a Effect of a Liquidating Distribution on the Corporation, 20-19
20-6b Effect of a Liquidating Distribution on the Shareholder, 20-19
20-6c Parent-Subsidiary Liquidations, 20-20
20-6d Asset Purchase versus Stock Purchase, 20-20

THE OPTIONS FOR TRANSITIONING TO RETIREMENT

Mr. and Mrs. Albert Smithson have experienced great pride in Orange Corporation, the successful business that they built over their careers, but they believe the time has come for them to think seriously about retirement. They own all of the stock in Orange, a C corporation, and their stock investment has a basis of $200,000. The business, which pays Federal income tax at the 21 percent rate, owns net assets that are worth $4,000,000 and have a basis of $1,500,000.

Unfortunately, the Smithsons have no family members who are interested in carrying on the business, so they must resort to liquidating Orange Corporation. Their strategy, in general, is to convert the value of their business into a diversified portfolio of marketable securities and to live off the earnings generated by the portfolio during their retirement years. The Smithsons realize that such a plan will be taxable, so they would like to know the amount that will be available after all Federal taxes are paid. It is important that they have a realistic idea of the amount of the after-tax proceeds so that they can determine whether retiring at this point is even feasible. After working for their entire lives, they are eager to live comfortably off their retirement nest egg.

Read the chapter and formulate your response.

ike individuals, corporations sometimes can be personified as being in a particular stage of life. It may be early in a corporation's life, struggling for direction, or it could be later in life, thriving and enjoying continually higher levels of success. Alternatively, the corporation could be at a stage where its viability as a going concern does not seem feasible any longer, or the shareholders may believe the entity's future could be brighter if it were to reshape itself. This chapter discusses the tax implications if the shareholders decide to terminate the existence of the corporation by complete liquidation. In addition, corporate reorganizations are discussed, which essentially are business realignments where the business of the entity operates in a new form. In the case of a complete liquidation, both the shareholders and the corporation face tax consequences, unless a subsidiary corporation is liquidated by its parent. In contrast, a reorganization can produce tax-deferred treatment to both the shareholders and the corporations if the transaction takes one of several forms specified in the Code.

20-1 LIQUIDATIONS—IN GENERAL

LO.1

Determine the tax consequences of complete liquidations for both the corporation and its shareholders.

When a corporation makes a nonliquidating distribution (e.g., stock redemption), the entity continues as a going concern. With a complete liquidation, however, corporate existence terminates, as does each shareholder's ownership interest. A complete liquidation, like a qualifying stock redemption, produces sale or exchange treatment to the *shareholder*. However, the tax effects of a liquidation to the *corporation* vary somewhat from those of a redemption. Sale or exchange treatment is also the general rule for the liquidating corporation, although some losses are disallowed.

20-1a The Liquidation Process

A corporate liquidation occurs when a corporation ceases to be a going concern. The corporation continues solely to wind up affairs, pay debts, and distribute any remaining assets to its shareholders. A legal dissolution under state law is not required. Further, a corporation can retain a nominal amount of assets to pay remaining debts and/or preserve its legal status and still liquidate for tax purposes.[1]

Shareholders may decide to liquidate a corporation for one or more reasons, including:

- The corporate business has been unsuccessful.
- The shareholders want to acquire the corporation's assets.
- Another person or entity wants to purchase the corporation's assets. The purchaser may buy the shareholders' stock and then liquidate the corporation to acquire the assets. Alternatively, the purchaser may buy the assets directly from the corporation. After the assets are sold, the corporation distributes the sales proceeds to its shareholders and liquidates.

As one might expect, the different means used to liquidate a corporation produce varying tax results.

20-1b Liquidating and Nonliquidating Distributions Compared

As discussed in Chapter 19, a *nonliquidating* distribution of noncash property produces gain (but not loss) recognition to the distributing corporation. For the shareholder, the receipt of cash or other property produces dividend income to the extent of the corporation's E & P or, in the case of a qualifying stock redemption, results in sale or exchange treatment.

Like a qualifying stock redemption, a *liquidation* produces sale or exchange treatment for the shareholders. E & P has no impact on the gain or loss recognized.[2] However, in a liquidation, a corporation generally recognizes gain *and* loss on any assets distributed.

---

[1]Reg. § 1.332–2(c).   [2]§ 331.

EXAMPLE 1

Goose Corporation, with E & P of $40,000, makes a cash distribution of $50,000 to a shareholder. The shareholder's basis in the Goose stock is $20,000. If the distribution is not a qualifying stock redemption or in complete liquidation, the shareholder recognizes dividend income of $40,000 (the amount of Goose's E & P) and treats the remaining $10,000 of the distribution as a return of capital (i.e., stock basis is reduced to $10,000).

If the distribution is a qualifying stock redemption or is pursuant to a complete liquidation, the shareholder has a capital gain of $30,000 ($50,000 distribution − $20,000 stock basis). In the case of these distributions, Goose's E & P does not affect the shareholder's tax result.

In the event a corporate distribution results in a *loss* to the shareholder, another distinction exists between nonliquidating distributions and liquidations. Section 267 disallows recognition of losses between related parties in nonliquidating distributions but not in liquidating distributions.

EXAMPLE 2

The stock of Tern Corporation is owned equally by three sisters, Pam, Meghann, and Natalie. When Natalie's basis in her stock is $40,000, the corporation distributes $30,000 to her in cancellation of all of her shares.

If the distribution is a qualifying stock redemption, the $10,000 realized loss is not recognized because Natalie and Tern Corporation are related parties. Under § 267, Natalie is deemed to own more than 50% in value of the corporation's outstanding stock. Natalie's direct ownership is 33⅓%, but through her sisters, she owns indirectly another 66⅔% for a total of 100%.

Alternatively, if the distribution is pursuant to a complete liquidation, Natalie's $10,000 realized loss is recognized.

The rules governing the basis of property received from a corporation are identical for both nonliquidating and liquidating distributions. Under § 301(d), the basis of property received in a *nonliquidating distribution* is its fair market value on the date of distribution, while § 334(a) provides the same treatment for property received in a *liquidating distribution*.

Text Section 20-2 discusses the tax consequences of a complete liquidation first from the view of the distributing corporation, and text Section 20-3 discusses the shareholder impacts. Because the tax rules differ when a subsidiary corporation is liquidated, these rules are discussed separately in text Section 20-4.

20-2 LIQUIDATIONS—EFFECT ON THE DISTRIBUTING CORPORATION

A corporation generally recognizes gain or loss on the distribution of property in a complete liquidation, but there are several exceptions to this rule.

20-2a The General Rule

Under § 336(a), a corporation recognizes *gain or loss* on the distribution of property in a complete liquidation as if the property were sold at its fair market value. This treatment is consistent with the notion of double taxation that is inherent in operating a business as a C corporation—once at the corporate level and again at the shareholder level.

As in the case of a nonliquidating distribution, if distributed property is subject to a corporate liability that is greater than the fair market value of the property, the liability amount is used to calculate gain or loss.

EXAMPLE 3

As part of a complete liquidation, Warbler Corporation distributes to its shareholders land held as an investment (basis of $200,000, fair market value of $300,000).

If no liability is involved, Warbler has a gain of $100,000 on the distribution ($300,000 − $200,000). The same result occurs (a gain of $100,000) if the land is subject to a liability of $250,000.

If, instead, the liability were $350,000, Warbler's gain on the distribution would be $150,000 ($350,000 − $200,000).

Liquidation expenses incurred by a corporation are deductible as trade or business expenses under § 162. Examples include accounting and legal costs of drafting and implementing a plan of liquidation and the cost of revoking the corporation's charter. However, expenses related to the sale of property (e.g., brokerage commissions and legal costs incurred in title transfers) reduce the amount realized on the sale.

There are four exceptions to the general rule of gain and loss recognition by a liquidating corporation:

- *Losses* are not recognized on certain liquidating distributions to related-party shareholders.

- *Losses* are not recognized on certain sales and liquidating distributions of property that was contributed to the corporation with a built-in loss shortly before the adoption of a plan of liquidation.

- A subsidiary corporation does not recognize *gains or losses* on liquidating distributions to its parent corporation.

- A subsidiary corporation does not recognize *losses* on liquidating distributions to its minority shareholders.

The first two exceptions, referred to as the "antistuffing rules," are discussed in detail in text Section 20-2b and are summarized in Concept Summary 20.1. The last two exceptions, dealing with the liquidation of a subsidiary corporation, are discussed in text Section 20-4.

20-2b **Antistuffing Rules**

When property is transferred to a corporation in a § 351 transaction or as a contribution to capital, carryover basis rules generally apply (see Chapter 18). Usually, the transferee corporation takes a basis in the property equal to that of the transferor-shareholder, and the shareholder takes an equal basis in the stock received in the exchange (or adds this amount to existing stock basis in the case of a capital contribution). Without special limitations, a transfer of loss property (fair market value less than basis) in a carryover basis transaction would present opportunities for the duplication of losses.

The Big Picture

EXAMPLE

4

Return to the facts of *The Big Picture* on p. 20-1. Assume that Mr. and Mrs. Smithson transfer property (basis of $100,000, fair market value of $55,000) to Orange Corporation in exchange for additional stock. The exchange qualifies under § 351. Absent any exceptions to the contrary, the general rule of carryover basis would apply and Orange would take a carryover basis of $100,000 in the property while the Smithsons would take a $100,000 basis in the additional stock.

A sale or liquidating distribution of the property by Orange Corporation would produce a $45,000 loss [$55,000 (fair market value of property) − $100,000 (property basis)]. Similarly, a sale by the Smithsons of the stock acquired in the § 351 exchange would also generate a $45,000 loss [$55,000 (fair market value of stock) − $100,000 (stock basis)].

Congress addressed this loss duplication issue by enacting two loss limitation ("antistuffing") rules under § 336(d) that apply to corporations upon liquidation—loss property distributed to related parties and certain loss property distributed or sold that had been contributed with a built-in loss. The effect of these rules is to disallow some or all of a loss realized by a corporation in liquidating distributions (and, in some cases, sales) of certain property. Each of these rules is discussed below.

These two antistuffing rules limited the duplication of losses realized upon a corporation's liquidation, but loss duplication was still possible in other situations (e.g., if the corporation sold high-basis property in the normal course of business rather than in a liquidation).

As a result, Congress enacted § 362(e)(2), which requires a corporation to step down the basis of property acquired in a § 351 or contribution to capital transaction by the amount of any net built-in loss embodied in such property. The basis step-down is required when a shareholder transfers properties having an aggregate basis in excess of their aggregate fair market value ("net built-in loss"), and it is allocated proportionately among the properties having built-in losses. Alternatively, the transferor-shareholder can elect to reduce his or her stock basis by the amount of net built-in loss. (See Chapter 18 for a complete discussion of the basis step-down rules.)

Although the antistuffing rules of § 336(d) continue to apply in the case of liquidating distributions (and certain sales) of loss property, their bite has been lessened somewhat by the § 362(e)(2) basis step-down rules.

Related-Party Loss Limitation

Losses are disallowed on distributions to *related parties* in either of the following cases:

- The distribution is *not* pro rata, or
- The property distributed is *disqualified property*.[3]

A corporation and a shareholder are considered related if the shareholder owns (directly or indirectly) more than 50 percent in value of the corporation's stock.[4]

A *pro rata distribution* is a distribution where *each* shareholder receives his or her proportionate share of the corporate asset distributed. Examples 5 and 6 illustrate a non pro rata distribution. *Disqualified property* is property that is acquired by the liquidating corporation in a § 351 or contribution to capital transaction during the five-year period ending on the date of the distribution. The related-party loss limitation can apply even if the property was appreciated (fair market value greater than basis) when it was transferred to the corporation. See Examples 7 and 8.

Related-Party Loss Limitations

EXAMPLE 5

Bluebird Corporation stock is owned by Ana and Sanjay, who are unrelated. Ana owns 80% and Sanjay owns 20% of the stock in the corporation. Bluebird has the following assets (none of which was acquired in a § 351 or contribution to capital transaction); all are distributed in complete liquidation of the corporation.

	Adjusted Basis	Fair Market Value
Cash	$600,000	$600,000
Equipment	150,000	200,000
Building	400,000	200,000

Assume that Bluebird Corporation distributes the equipment to Sanjay and the cash and the building to Ana. Bluebird recognizes a gain of $50,000 on the distribution of the equipment. The loss of $200,000 on the building is disallowed because the property is distributed to a related party and the distribution is not pro rata (i.e., the building is not distributed 80% to Ana and 20% to Sanjay).

EXAMPLE 6

Assume in Example 5 that Bluebird Corporation distributes the cash and equipment to Ana and the building to Sanjay.

As in Example 5, Bluebird recognizes the $50,000 gain on the equipment. However, it now recognizes the $200,000 loss on the building because the property is not distributed to a related party (i.e., Sanjay does not own more than 50% of the stock in Bluebird Corporation).

[3]§ 336(d)(1).

[4]Section 267 provides the definition of a related party for purposes of this provision. The rules are similar to the stock attribution rules discussed in

Chapter 19; one exception, however, is that stock owned by a sibling is treated as owned by the taxpayer under § 267.

Related-Party Loss Limitations

EXAMPLE 7

Wren Corporation's stock is held equally by three brothers. Four years before Wren's liquidation, the shareholders transfer jointly owned property (basis of $150,000, fair market value of $200,000) to the corporation in return for stock in a § 351 transaction. When the property is worth $100,000, it is distributed pro rata to the brothers in a liquidating distribution.

Because disqualified property is involved and each brother owns directly and indirectly more than 50% of the stock (each owns 100% in this situation), Wren recognizes none of the $50,000 realized loss [$100,000 (fair market value) − $150,000 (basis)].

EXAMPLE 8

Assume in Example 7 that the property's fair market value is $100,000 at the time of the § 351 transfer and $75,000 at the time of the liquidating distribution to the brothers. As a result of the § 362(e)(2) basis step-down rules, Wren Corporation's basis in the property is $100,000 [$150,000 (basis to brothers) − $50,000 (net built-in loss of property transferred)].

In a liquidating distribution of the property to the brothers, Wren would realize a loss of $25,000 [$75,000 (fair market value of property at distribution) − $100,000 (Wren's stepped-down basis in property)]. However, because this is a distribution of disqualified property to related parties, none of the $25,000 loss is recognized by Wren.

Built-In Loss Limitation

A second loss limitation applies to sales, exchanges, or distributions of built-in loss property (fair market value less than basis) that is transferred to a corporation shortly before the corporation is liquidated. The *built-in loss limitation* applies when *both* of the following conditions are met:

- The property was acquired by the corporation in a § 351 (or contribution to capital) transaction.
- This acquisition was part of a plan whose principal purpose was to recognize a loss on that property by the liquidating corporation. A tax avoidance purpose is presumed in the case of transfers occurring *within two years* of a liquidation plan being adopted.

This disallowance rule applies only to the extent that a property's built-in loss at transfer is not eliminated by a § 362(e)(2) stepped-down basis. Some built-in losses on property transfers will avoid the basis step-down either because built-in gain properties were also transferred by the shareholder (see Example 9) or because the shareholder elected to step down the basis of his or her stock instead. Any loss related to a decline in a property's value *after* its transfer to the corporation is not subject to the built-in loss limitation.[5]

EXAMPLE 9

In the current year, Brown Corporation acquires two properties from a shareholder in a transaction that qualifies under § 351.

	Shareholder's Basis	Fair Market Value	Built-In Gain/(Loss)
Land	$100,000	$50,000	($50,000)
Securities	10,000	35,000	25,000
			($25,000)

The net built-in loss of $25,000 results in a stepped-down basis of $75,000 in the land for Brown Corporation [$100,000 (shareholder's basis) − $25,000 (step-down equal to net built-in loss)]. Later in the year, Brown adopts a plan of liquidation and distributes the land to an unrelated shareholder when the land is worth $30,000.

Of the $45,000 loss realized by Brown on the distribution [$30,000 (value of land on date of distribution) − $75,000 (basis in land)], $25,000 is disallowed by the built-in loss limitation [$50,000 (value of land when acquired by Brown) − $75,000 (stepped-down basis in land)] and $20,000 is recognized (equal to the decline in value occurring after acquisition by Brown).

[5]§ 336(d)(2).

The built-in loss limitation applies to a broader range of transactions than the related-party exception, which disallows losses only on certain *distributions* to related parties (i.e., more-than-50 percent shareholders). The built-in loss limitation can apply to distributions of property to any shareholder, including an unrelated party, and to a *sale or exchange* of property by a liquidating corporation. However, the limitation is narrower than the related-party exception in that it applies only to property that had a built-in loss upon its acquisition by the corporation (as adjusted by the basis step-down rules).

EXAMPLE 10

Assume in Example 9 that the land had a fair market value of $120,000 on the date Brown Corporation acquired it. Since there is no net built-in loss on the transfer, Brown will have a basis of $100,000 in the land. If the distribution is to an unrelated shareholder, Brown will recognize the entire $70,000 loss [$30,000 (fair market value on date of distribution) − $100,000 (basis)].

However, if the distribution is to a related party, Brown cannot recognize any of the loss under the related-party loss limitation because the property is disqualified property. When the distribution is to a related party, the loss is disallowed even though the entire decline in value occurred during the period the corporation held the property.

Property held by the corporation for more than two years prior to the liquidation is usually not subject to the built-in loss limitation. Further, the presumption of a tax avoidance purpose for property transferred to a corporation in the "two years prior to liquidation" window can be contested if there is a clear and substantial business purpose for the transfer. When there is a business reason for the transfer, the built-in loss limitation will not apply. Compare Examples 11 and 12.

Presumption of Tax Avoidance Purpose

EXAMPLE 11

Cardinal Corporation's stock is held by two unrelated individuals: 60% by Manuel and 40% by Jack. One year before Cardinal's liquidation, Manuel transfers land (basis of $150,000, fair market value of $100,000) and equipment (basis of $10,000, fair market value of $70,000) to the corporation as a contribution to capital. Since there is no net built-in loss on the transfer, Cardinal will have a basis of $150,000 in the land. There is no business reason for the transfer.

In liquidation, Cardinal distributes the land (now with a fair market value of $90,000) to Jack. Even though the distribution is to an unrelated party, the built-in loss of $50,000 is not recognized. However, Cardinal Corporation can recognize the loss of $10,000 ($90,000 − $100,000) that occurred while it held the land.

If, instead, the land is distributed to Manuel, a related party, the entire $60,000 loss is disallowed under the related-party loss limitation.

EXAMPLE 12

Assume in Example 11 that the land and equipment are transferred to Cardinal Corporation because a bank required the additional capital investment as a condition to making a loan to the corporation.

Because there is a business purpose for the transfer, all of the $60,000 loss is recognized if the land is distributed to Jack in liquidation.

If, instead, the land is distributed to Manuel, a related party, the entire loss is still disallowed under the related-party loss limitation.

Concept Summary 20.1

Summary of Antistuffing Loss Disallowance Rules

Related-Party Loss Limitation

Distribution of loss property to a related party *and* distribution is not pro rata *or* property is disqualified property.

- Related party if shareholder owns directly or indirectly *more than* 50% in value of the stock.
  - Section 267 attribution rules apply. Similar to § 318 attribution rules but includes stock owned by siblings.
- Distribution is pro rata if each shareholder receives proportional interest in property.
- Disqualified property is property acquired by the corporation within five years of the distribution date in a § 351 or contribution to capital transaction.

Limitation can apply even if a corporation acquired property by purchase or in a carryover basis transaction with no built-in loss (i.e., fair market greater than basis).

Limitation does not apply to *sales* of loss property.

Built-In Loss Limitation

Distribution, sale, or exchange of certain built-in loss property (fair market value less than basis).

- Property was acquired in a § 351 or contribution to capital transaction.
- Acquisition was part of a plan whose principal purpose was to recognize a loss on the property by the corporation upon liquidation.
  - Presumption of tax avoidance purpose if property was acquired within two years of the date of the plan of liquidation.
  - Clear and substantial business purpose for a transfer of property to a corporation can rebut the presumption.
  - Transfers occurring more than two years before liquidation are rarely subject to the loss limitation.

Loss limitation applies only to amount of the built-in loss at the time of transfer to a corporation (excess of corporation's basis in property over fair market value of property).

- Basis step-down rules will eliminate many built-in losses. However, loss limitation remains applicable where built-in loss is not entirely eliminated by the basis step-down (i.e., built-in gain property transferred with built-in loss property) or where the shareholder elected to step down basis of stock.

20-3 LIQUIDATIONS—EFFECT ON THE SHAREHOLDER

The tax consequences to the shareholders of a corporation in the process of liquidation are generally governed by § 331. The exception to this rule, § 332, applies in the liquidation of a subsidiary (discussed in text Section 20-4).

Section 331(a) requires sale or exchange treatment for the shareholders. As a result, the difference between the fair market value of the assets received from the corporation and the basis of the stock surrendered is the gain or loss recognized by the shareholder. The fair market value of property received subject to a corporate liability is reduced by the amount of the liability. Typically, the stock is a capital asset in the hands of the shareholder, and capital gain or loss results. The taxpayer must be able to document the basis of the stock. Without documentation, the stock is deemed to have a zero basis.[6] The basis of property received in a liquidation is the property's fair market value on the date of distribution.[7] If installment notes are distributed in liquidation, shareholders can use the installment method to defer to the point of collection the portion of their gain that is attributable to the notes.[8]

---

[6]See *John Calderazzo*, 34 TCM 1, T.C.Memo. 1975–1, and *Coloman v. Comm.*, 76–2 USTC ¶9581, 38 AFTR 2d 5523, 540 F.2d 427 (CA–9, 1976).

[7]§ 334(a).

[8]§ 453(h). Shareholders must allocate their stock basis between the notes and the other assets received in the liquidation. Upon distribution, the corporation generally recognizes gain (or loss) equal to the difference between the fair market value of the notes and the corporation's basis in the notes. § 453B(a).

Any taxes paid by a corporation as a result of liquidation gains will reduce the proceeds available to be distributed to the shareholders. This will reduce the amount realized by the shareholders, which will then reduce their gain (or increase the loss) recognized.

The Big Picture

EXAMPLE 13

Return to the facts of *The Big Picture* on p. 20-1. At the point when the Smithsons are contemplating retirement, their business, Orange Corporation, has net assets worth $4,000,000. This valuation is after the payment of all of Orange's corporate debts except for taxes it would pay on net gains recognized if it liquidates. Assuming that the Smithsons decide to liquidate the corporation and the taxes the corporation pays total $525,000, the amount realized by the Smithsons is $3,475,000 ($4,000,000 − $525,000).

The Big Picture

EXAMPLE 14

Return to the facts of *The Big Picture* on p. 20-1. Continuing with the preceding example, if Orange Corporation liquidates and the Smithsons receive a liquidating distribution of $3,475,000, they will recognize a capital gain of $3,275,000 ($3,475,000 amount realized − $200,000 stock basis). The basis of any property the Smithsons receive will be its fair market value.

ETHICS & EQUITY **Transferee Liability for Tax Deficiency of Liquidated Corporation**

In 2018, Loon Corporation distributed all of its remaining assets to two equal shareholders in a complete liquidation. The two shareholders, Gloria Martinez and Roger Stinson, each received a distribution of $250,000 for their stock in Loon.

In 2020, the IRS audited Loon Corporation and assessed additional income tax of $175,000 (plus penalties and interest)

against the corporation. Since Loon was defunct and without assets, the IRS then assessed the entire deficiency against Gloria Martinez based on transferee liability. The IRS did not attempt to collect any of the deficiency from Roger Stinson.

Is this an equitable solution to the collection of Loon's tax liability?

20-4 LIQUIDATIONS—PARENT-SUBSIDIARY SITUATIONS

LO.2

Determine the tax consequences of subsidiary liquidations for both the parent and the subsidiary corporations.

Section 332, an exception to the general rule of § 331, provides that a parent corporation does *not* recognize gain or loss on a liquidation of a subsidiary. In addition, the subsidiary corporation recognizes *neither gain nor loss* on liquidating distributions of property to its parent.[9]

There are three requirements for applying § 332:

- The parent must own at least 80 percent of the subsidiary's stock (both voting power and value).
- All of the subsidiary's property must be distributed in complete cancellation of all of its stock within the taxable year or within three years from the close of the tax year in which the first distribution occurred.
- The subsidiary must be solvent.[10]

---

[9]§ 337(a). This is an exception to the general rule of § 336.

[10]§ 332(b) and Reg. §§ 1.332–2(a) and (b).

If these requirements are met, nonrecognition of gains and losses is *mandatory*. However, if the subsidiary is insolvent, the parent corporation will have an ordinary loss deduction under § 165(g) equal to its basis in the subsidiary stock.

If the liquidation involves several distributions, the 80 percent test must be met on the date the plan of liquidation is adopted and maintained until the final liquidating distribution is received by the parent.[11] If the parent fails the 80 percent test at any time, the provisions for nonrecognition of gain or loss do not apply to any distribution.[12]

The parent-subsidiary rules are contrasted with other liquidation rules in Concept Summary 20.2.

Concept Summary 20.2

Summary of Liquidation Rules

Effect on the Shareholder	Basis of Property Received	Effect on the Corporation
§ 331—The general rule provides for gain or loss treatment on the difference between the FMV of property received and the basis of the stock in the corporation. Gain allocable to installment notes received can be deferred to the point of collection.	§ 334(a)—Basis of assets received by the shareholder will be the FMV on the date of distribution (except for installment obligations in which gain is deferred to the point of collection).	§ 336—Gain or loss is recognized for distributions in kind and for sales by the liquidating corporation. Losses are not recognized for distributions to related parties if the distribution is not pro rata or if disqualified property is distributed. Losses may be disallowed on sales and distributions of certain other property even if made to unrelated parties.
§ 332—In liquidation of a subsidiary, no gain or loss is recognized by the parent. Subsidiary must distribute all of its property within the taxable year or within three years from the close of the taxable year in which the first distribution occurs. Minority shareholders are taxed under the general rule of § 331.	§ 334(b)(1)—Property has the same basis that it had in the hands of the subsidiary. Parent's basis in the stock disappears. Carryover rules of § 381 apply. Minority shareholders get FMV basis under § 334(a).	§ 337—No gain or loss is recognized by the subsidiary on distributions to the parent. Gain (but not loss) is recognized on distributions to minority shareholders.
	§ 338—Subsidiary need not be liquidated. If subsidiary is liquidated, parent's basis in the assets is the new stepped-up (or -down) basis. Parent's basis in the stock disappears. Carryover rules of § 381 apply, but such amounts are likely to be nominal.	§ 338—Gain or loss is recognized by the subsidiary. Subsidiary is treated as a new corporation, and its basis in the assets is stepped up (or down) to reflect the parent's basis in the subsidiary stock plus subsidiary's liabilities. New basis is allocated among various asset classes.

20-4a **Minority Shareholder Interests**

In a § 332 parent-subsidiary liquidation, up to 20 percent of the subsidiary's stock can be owned by minority shareholders. In such liquidations, a distribution of property to a minority shareholder is treated in the same manner as a *nonliquidating* distribution. That is, the subsidiary corporation recognizes gain (but not loss) on the property distributed to the minority shareholder.[13]

---

[11]Establishing the date of the adoption of a plan of complete liquidation could be crucial in determining whether § 332 applies. See, for example, *George L. Riggs, Inc.*, 64 T.C. 474 (1975).

[12]§ 332(b)(3) and Reg. § 1.332–2(a).

[13]§§ 336(a) and (d)(3).

The stock of Tan Corporation is held by Mustard Corporation (80%) and by Arethia, an individual (20%). Tan Corporation is liquidated pursuant to a plan adopted earlier in the year. At the time of its liquidation, Tan has assets with a basis of $100,000 and fair market value of $500,000. Tan Corporation distributes the property pro rata to Mustard Corporation and to Arethia.

Tan must recognize a gain of $80,000 [($500,000 fair market value − $100,000 basis) × 20% minority interest]. The remaining gain of $320,000 is not recognized because it relates to property being distributed to Mustard, the parent corporation.

A minority shareholder is subject to the general rule requiring the recognition of gain or loss in a liquidation. As a result, the difference between the fair market value of the assets received and the basis of the minority shareholder's stock is the amount of gain or loss recognized. The basis of property received by the minority shareholder is the property's fair market value on the date of distribution.[14]

20-4b **Indebtedness of the Subsidiary to the Parent**

If a subsidiary transfers appreciated property to its parent to satisfy a debt, it must recognize gain on the transaction unless the subsidiary is liquidating and the conditions of § 332 apply. When § 332 applies, the subsidiary does not recognize gain or loss upon the transfer of property to the parent in satisfaction of indebtedness.[15]

Eagle Corporation owes $200,000 to its parent, Finch Corporation. It satisfies the obligation by transferring land (basis of $170,000, fair market value of $200,000) to Finch. Normally, Eagle would recognize a gain of $30,000 on the transaction. However, if the transfer relates to a liquidation under § 332, Eagle does not recognize a gain.

This nonrecognition provision does not apply to the parent corporation. The parent corporation recognizes gain or loss on the transfer of property in satisfaction of indebtedness even if the property is received during liquidation of the subsidiary.

Pelican Corporation owns bonds (basis of $95,000) of its subsidiary, Crow Corporation, that were acquired at a discount. Upon liquidation of Crow pursuant to § 332, Pelican receives a distribution of $100,000, the face amount of the bonds. The transaction has no tax effect on Crow. However, Pelican Corporation recognizes a gain of $5,000 [$100,000 (amount realized) − $95,000 (basis in bonds)].

GLOBAL TAX ISSUES **Basis Rules for Liquidations of Foreign Subsidiaries**

The basis of property acquired by a parent corporation in the liquidation of a subsidiary corporation is generally equal to the basis the subsidiary had in such property. However, legislation a number of years ago modified the basis rules regarding property acquired by a U.S. parent in certain § 332 liquidations of foreign subsidiaries.

In general, if the aggregate basis in a foreign subsidiary's assets exceeds their aggregate fair market value, the U.S. parent will take a fair market value basis in the property acquired. The purpose of this amendment is to deny the importation of built-in losses (excess of basis over fair market value). [See §§ 334(b)(1)(B) and 362(e)(1)(B).]

---

[14]§ 334(a).

[15]§ 337(b)(1).

20-4c Basis of Property Received by the Parent Corporation—The General Rule

Property received by the parent corporation in the complete liquidation of a subsidiary has the same basis it had in the hands of the subsidiary.[16] Unless the parent corporation makes a § 338 election (discussed in text Section 20-4d), this carryover basis in the assets generally will differ from the parent's basis in the stock of the subsidiary. Because the liquidation is a nontaxable exchange, the parent's gain or loss on the difference in basis is not recognized. Further, the parent's basis in the stock of the subsidiary disappears.

Basis Issues in Subsidiary Liquidations

EXAMPLE 18

Lark Corporation has a basis of $200,000 in the stock of Heron Corporation, a subsidiary in which it owns 85% of all classes of stock. Lark purchased the Heron stock 10 years ago. In the current year, Lark liquidates Heron and acquires assets with a fair market value of $800,000 and a tax basis to Heron of $500,000.

Lark Corporation takes a basis of $500,000 in the assets, with a potential gain on their sale of $300,000. Lark's $200,000 basis in Heron's stock disappears.

EXAMPLE 19

Indigo Corporation has a basis of $600,000 in the stock of Kackie Corporation, a wholly owned subsidiary acquired 10 years ago. It liquidates Kackie Corporation and receives assets with a fair market value of $400,000 and a tax basis to Kackie of $300,000.

Indigo Corporation takes a basis of $300,000 in the assets it acquires from Kackie. If it sells the assets for $400,000, it has a gain of $100,000 in spite of the fact that its basis in the Kackie stock was $600,000. Indigo's loss on its stock investment in Kackie will never be recognized.

In addition to the parent corporation taking the subsidiary's basis in its assets, the parent's holding period for the assets includes that of the subsidiary.[17] Further, the carryover rules of § 381 apply. As a result, the parent acquires other tax attributes of the subsidiary, including the subsidiary's net operating loss carryover, business credit carryover, capital loss carryover, and E & P.

20-4d Basis of Property Received by the Parent Corporation—§ 338 Election

As discussed previously, the liquidation of a subsidiary generally is a nontaxable transaction resulting in the nonrecognition of gain or loss for both the parent and the subsidiary corporations and the carryover of the subsidiary's asset bases (and other tax attributes). This treatment reflects the fact that such a liquidation often is merely a change in corporate structure and not a change in substance. This is particularly the case when the parent has owned the stock of the subsidiary since the subsidiary's inception. In these cases, the carried-over bases are comparable to what the parent would have if it, and not the subsidiary, had originally acquired the assets.

The carryover basis rule for § 332 liquidations can result in some inequities when the subsidiary has been in existence for some time prior to the parent's acquisition of the subsidiary's stock. The parent's basis in the stock of the subsidiary will reflect the fair market value of the subsidiary's assets (and goodwill) at the time of the stock purchase. As a result, the parent's basis in the stock of the subsidiary will usually be greater than the subsidiary's basis in its assets. In this case, a subsidiary liquidation under § 332 would result in the parent taking a basis in the subsidiary's assets that is less than the parent's basis in the stock of the subsidiary. This is the case even if the parent acquired the subsidiary stock solely to obtain the subsidiary's assets.

---

[16]§ 334(b)(1) and Reg. § 1.334–1(b). But see § 334(b)(1)(B) (exception for property acquired in some liquidations of foreign subsidiaries).

[17]§ 1223(2).

If the parent could treat the purchase of the subsidiary stock as a purchase of its assets, the parent could take a basis in the assets equal to the acquisition cost of the stock. In most cases, this would mean a higher asset basis and, as a result, larger depreciation deductions and lower gains upon disposition for the parent. To obtain this stock-basis-for-asset-basis result, taxpayers successfully devised stock purchase/subsidiary liquidation transactions that fell outside § 332.[18] Congress codified this treatment by enacting § 338, which permits the purchase of a controlling interest of stock to be treated as a purchase of the subsidiary's assets.

Requirements for Application

A corporation (the "parent") may *elect* the provisions of § 338 if it acquires at least 80 percent of the stock (both voting power and value) of another corporation (the "subsidiary") within a 12-month period ("*qualified stock purchase*"). The stock must be acquired in a *taxable* transaction (i.e., a transaction where § 351 and other nonrecognition provisions do not apply). An acquisition of stock by any member of an affiliated group that includes the parent corporation is considered to be an acquisition by the parent. The §338 election must be made by the fifteenth day of the ninth month beginning after the month in which a qualified stock purchase occurs. If made, the election is irrevocable.

Tax Consequences

If § 338 is elected, the subsidiary is treated as having sold its assets on the qualified stock purchase date for a value that is determined with reference to the parent's basis in the subsidiary stock plus any liabilities of the subsidiary ("aggregate deemed sales price").[19] The subsidiary is then treated as a new corporation that purchased those assets for a similarly computed amount ("adjusted grossed-up basis") on the day following the qualified stock purchase date.[20] The deemed sale results in gain (or loss) recognition by the subsidiary, and the deemed purchase results in a stepped-up (or -down) basis for the subsidiary's assets.[21] The subsidiary may, but need not, be liquidated. If the subsidiary is liquidated, the parent will obtain a carryover of the stepped-up (or -down) basis of the subsidiary's assets.

A Comparison of the General Rule and the § 338 Election

Under § 332, the liquidation of a subsidiary is tax-free to both the subsidiary (except for any minority interest) and the parent corporation. Under § 338, the subsidiary recognizes gain (or loss) on the deemed disposition of its assets, while the liquidation of the subsidiary remains tax-free to the parent. Although a carryover basis rule applies in both cases, the subsidiary's assets generally will have a stepped-up basis as a result of the § 338 election and a liquidation of the subsidiary will result in a carryover of the stepped-up basis to the parent. Regardless of whether a § 338 election is made, a liquidation of the subsidiary results in a carryover of its other tax attributes (e.g., E & P) to the parent. However, when the election is made, the subsidiary is treated as a new corporation as of the day following the qualified stock purchase date; as a result, any tax attributes acquired by the parent are likely to be nominal (or zero) in amount.

The holding period of the subsidiary's assets is determined with reference to the substance of the transaction. When the subsidiary is liquidated and there is no § 338 election, the subsidiary's historical holding period in its assets carries over to the parent. This is the typical carryover rule found in other nonrecognition provisions. A § 338 election, however, assumes a sale and repurchase of the subsidiary's assets. As a result of these deemed transactions, the holding period starts anew. If there is a § 338 election and the subsidiary is liquidated, the holding period of the property received by the parent begins on the date of the qualified stock purchase. Alternatively, if there is a § 338 election and the subsidiary is not liquidated, the holding period of the assets begins on the day *after* the qualified stock acquisition date. Exhibit 20.1 illustrates the consequences of a § 338 election to both the parent and subsidiary corporations.

---

[18]See, for example, *U.S. v. M.O.J. Corp.*, 60–1 USTC ¶9209, 5 AFTR 2d 535, 274 F.2d 713 (CA–5, 1960). See also *Kimbell-Diamond Milling Co.*, 14 T.C. 74 (1950), *aff'd* 51–1 USTC ¶9201, 40 AFTR 328, 187 F.2d 718 (CA–5, 1951), *cert. den.* 72 S.Ct. 50 (USSC, 1951) (IRS argued stock-for-asset basis).

[19]See §§ 338(a)(1) and (b) and Reg. § 1.338–4.

[20]See §§ 338(a)(2) and (b) and Reg. § 1.338–5.

[21]For the rules governing the allocation of the purchase price to the assets, see § 338(b)(5) and Reg. § 1.338–6.

EXHIBIT 20.1	Consequences of a Section 338 Election

Assume the following:

- Parent acquires 100% of Subsidiary's stock for $750,000 on August 5, 2020.

- Subsidiary (E & P of $400,000) has only one asset, land (fair market value of $1,000,000, basis of $504,000), no liabilities, and no loss or tax credit carryovers.

- Parent files a timely § 338 election, and both aggregate deemed sale price (ADSP) and adjusted grossed-up basis (AGUB) are $815,392.

Subsidiary Is Liquidated

Consequences to Subsidiary:
Deemed to have sold the land for ADSP of $815,392, which results in a recognized gain of $311,392 [$815,392 (ADSP) − $504,000 (basis)], and tax of $65,392 ($311,392 × 21%). The land's new basis is $815,392 (AGUB). No gain or loss recognized on distribution of land to Parent.

Consequences to Parent:
No gain or loss recognized on receipt of land from Subsidiary. Basis in land is $815,392; holding period for the land begins on August 5, 2020; and basis in Subsidiary stock disappears. Acquires Subsidiary's E & P, but that amount is $0 as a result of the § 338 election.

Subsidiary Is *Not* Liquidated

Consequences to Subsidiary:
Deemed to have sold the land for ADSP of $815,392, which results in a recognized gain of $311,392 [$815,392 (ADSP) − $504,000 (basis)], and tax of $65,392 ($311,392 × 21%). Treated as a new corporation (e.g., E & P of $0) as of August 6, 2020; land's new basis is $815,392 (AGUB); and holding period for the land begins on August 6, 2020.

Consequences to Parent:
No tax consequences. Basis in Subsidiary stock remains unchanged at $750,000.

Explain the general requirements and tax consequences of corporate reorganizations.

20-5 CORPORATE REORGANIZATIONS

A reorganization is a change in the legal or economic structure of a business entity. It may be a process of combining two or more corporations into one entity, but it may also be the spin-off or split-up of one large corporation into multiple separate entities. Corporations may engage in reorganizations to improve efficiency, consolidate management functions, or enhance operations. No matter the outcome, a reorganization can significantly change the structure and appearance of the business.

Corporate reorganizations can be very expensive and chaotic. Because the dollar value of most reorganizations is substantial, the tax implications can be significant. Shareholders and corporations generally avoid gain or loss recognition if they plan and execute a reorganization as one of seven major types identified in the Code. Gain is recognized when cash or property other than stock is received, or when debt is transferred in excess of the total adjusted basis of property transferred.

Tax planning is essential to minimizing tax liability in corporate reorganizations. When feasible, parties contemplating a corporate reorganization should obtain a letter ruling from the IRS to determine the anticipated income tax effect of the reorganization. Such a letter acts as insurance that the transaction qualifies for elimination or reduction of the possible current-period taxes for the corporations and their shareholders.[22]

---

[22]To expedite the letter ruling process, the IRS attempts to issue rulings within 10 weeks from the date of request. Rev.Proc. 2005–68, 2005–2 C.B. 694.

20-5a **In General**

Although the term <mark>reorganization</mark> is commonly associated with a corporation in financial difficulty, for tax purposes, the term refers to any corporate restructuring that may be tax-free under § 368. To qualify as a tax-free reorganization, a corporate restructuring must meet not only the specific requirements of the tax Code but also several general requirements. These requirements include the following:

1. There must be a *plan of reorganization*.
2. The reorganization must meet the *continuity of interest* and the *continuity of business enterprise* tests provided in the Regulations.
3. The judicial doctrine of having a *sound business purpose* must be met.
4. The court-imposed *step transaction* doctrine should not be applicable.

While all of these concepts are important, the initial and most important consideration is whether the reorganization qualifies for nonrecognition status under § 368, which is described next.

20-5b **Summary of the Different Types of Reorganizations**

The tax law specifies seven corporate restructurings or reorganizations that will qualify as nontaxable exchanges. If the transaction fails to qualify as a reorganization, it will not receive the special tax-favored treatment. Therefore, a corporation considering a business reorganization must determine in advance whether the proposed transaction specifically falls within one of these seven types.

The Code states, in § 368(a)(1), that the term *reorganization* applies to any of the following:

A. A statutory merger or consolidation.
B. The acquisition by a corporation of another using solely stock of each corporation (voting stock-for-stock exchange).
C. The acquisition by a corporation of substantially all of the property of another corporation in exchange for voting stock (voting stock-for-asset exchange).
D. The transfer of all or part of a corporation's assets to another corporation when the original corporation's shareholders are in control of the new corporation immediately after the transfer (divisive exchange: spin-off, split-off, or split-up).
E. A recapitalization.
F. A mere change in identity, form, or place of organization.
G. A transfer by a corporation of all or a part of its assets to another corporation in a bankruptcy or receivership proceeding.

These seven types of tax-free reorganizations typically are designated by their identifying letters: "Type A," "Type B," "Type C," etc. For the most part, excepting the recapitalization (E), the change in form (F), and the insolvent corporation (G) provisions, a tax-free reorganization is (1) a statutory merger or consolidation, (2) an exchange of stock for voting stock, (3) an exchange of assets for voting stock, or (4) a divisive reorganization (a so-called spin-off, split-off, or split-up).

20-5c **Summary of the Tax Consequences in a Tax-Free Reorganization**

The tax treatment for the parties involved in a tax-free reorganization almost parallels the treatment under the like-kind exchange provisions of § 1031 (see Chapter 13). However, the like-kind exchange provisions only apply to real estate and not to the exchange of stock or securities.[23]

---

[23]§ 1031(a)(2).

When an investor exchanges stock in one corporation for another, the exchange generally constitutes a taxable transaction. A qualifying reorganization avoids such treatment by creating a nontaxable exchange under § 368. As previously noted, this tax treatment mirrors the like-kind exchange rules for sales involving real property. The four-column template of Concept Summary 20.3 is useful in computing the gain or loss recognized and the basis in the new stock received in a corporate reorganization.

EXAMPLE 20

Castel holds 1,000 shares of Lotus stock that were purchased for $6,000 several years ago. In a merger of Lotus into Blossom, Inc., Castel exchanges these 1,000 Lotus shares for 500 Blossom shares. The Lotus stock and the Blossom stock both are valued at $10,000. Assuming that this exchange qualifies for tax-free treatment under § 368, Castel's recognized gain and basis in the Blossom stock are computed as follows:

Realized Gain	Recognized Gain	Postponed Gain	Basis in Blossom Stock
$10,000	$–0–	$4,000	$10,000
−6,000			−4,000
$ 4,000			$ 6,000

The exchange of Castel's stock has no tax consequences for Lotus or Blossom.

Concept Summary 20.3

Gain and Basis Rules for Nontaxable Exchanges

(1) Realized Gain/Loss	(2) Recognized Gain (Not Loss)	(3) Postponed Gain/Loss	(4) Basis of New Asset
Amount realized	Lesser of boot received or gain realized	Realized gain/loss (column 1)	FMV of asset (stock) received
− Basis of asset(s) surrendered		− Recognized gain (column 2)	− Postponed gain (column 3) or + Postponed loss (column 3)
Realized gain/loss	Recognized gain	Postponed gain/loss	Basis in new asset (stock)

Gain or Loss

Corporations meeting the requirements of § 368 do not recognize gains or losses on reorganizations. However, recognition, and therefore taxation, occurs when other property is transferred by the acquiring corporation in the reorganization. <mark>Other property</mark>, also called <mark>boot</mark>, is any asset other than stock or securities exchanged in the reorganization.[24] If boot is transferred, gain but not loss may be recognized.

In a qualifying reorganization, Acquiring exchanges $800,000 of stock and land valued at $200,000 (basis of $150,000) for all of Target's assets, which have a value of $1,000,000 and a basis of $600,000. Due to the boot (land) it used in the transfer, Acquiring recognizes a gain of $50,000 ($200,000 − $150,000) on the reorganization. If Target distributes the land to its shareholders, it does not recognize gain. If Target retains the land, however, it recognizes a gain to the extent of the boot received, $200,000.

EXAMPLE 21

Generally, the shareholders of corporations involved in a tax-free reorganization do not recognize gain or loss when exchanging their stock unless they receive boot in addition to stock. As demonstrated in Concept Summary 20.3, the gain recognized by the shareholder is the lesser of the boot received or the realized gain. This is analogous to the treatment of boot in a real estate like-kind exchange. The only instance when shareholders may recognize (deduct) losses in reorganizations is when they receive solely boot and no stock.

Kalla, the sole shareholder of Target in Example 21, has a basis of $700,000 in her stock. She exchanges her Target stock for the $800,000 of Acquiring stock plus the land ($200,000) transferred by Acquiring to Target. The recognized gain for Kalla is the lesser of boot received (land, $200,000) or realized gain ($300,000). Thus, Kalla incurs a recognized gain on the reorganization of $200,000.

EXAMPLE 22

Realized Gain	Recognized Gain	Postponed Gain	Basis in Acquiring Stock
$1,000,000*	$200,000	$300,000	$800,000
−700,000	Boot	−200,000	−100,000
$ 300,000		$100,000	$700,000

*$800,000 Acquiring stock + $200,000 land.

Once the recognized gain is computed, its tax character must be determined. The following are the possibilities for gain characterization:

- The gain is taxed as a dividend to the extent of the shareholder's proportionate share of earnings and profits (E & P). The remaining gain generally is capital gain.
- If the requirements of § 302(b) can be met, the transaction is treated similarly to a qualifying stock redemption, receiving capital gain treatment (see text Section 19-4).

Sam acquired his 5% interest in Target 15 years ago for $55,000. He exchanges his Target stock for $50,000 of cash and 2% of Acquiring's outstanding stock worth $100,000. At the time of the reorganization, Target's E & P is $60,000. Sam's recognized gain and basis in the Acquiring stock are computed as follows:

EXAMPLE 23

Realized Gain	Recognized Gain	Postponed Gain	Basis in Acquiring Stock
$150,000*	$50,000	$95,000	$100,000
−55,000	Boot	−50,000	−45,000
$ 95,000		$45,000	$ 55,000

*$100,000 Acquiring stock + $50,000 cash.

The first $3,000 ($60,000 Target E & P × 5% ownership) of the $50,000 gain recognized by Sam is taxed as a dividend, and the remaining $47,000 is treated as a long-term capital gain.

---

[24]§§ 361(a) and (b). In a Type A or Type C reorganization, gain will not be recognized due to the retention of other property because the target is liquidated under the reorganization rules (i.e., no property is retained by the target).

Debt security holders receive treatment similar to shareholders. They recognize gain only when the principal (face) amount of the securities received is greater than the principal (face) amount of the securities surrendered. For example, if securities are received and none are relinquished, the gain will be recognized.

The term *security* is not defined in the Code or the Regulations. Generally, however, debt instruments with terms longer than 10 years (e.g., bonds) are treated as securities, and those with terms of 5 years or less (e.g., notes) are not. An exception to this general rule occurs when the debt instrument issued by the acquiring corporation is exchanged for target securities having the same term and/or maturity date.[25]

EXAMPLE 24

Addison holds a security issued by Hibiscus with a principal value of the security of $10,000 and a maturity date of December 31, 2022. In connection with the merger of Hibiscus and Tea, Addison exchanges the Hibiscus security for a $10,000 Tea note that also matures on December 31, 2022. Even though the Tea notes do not have a term remaining of more than five years, they qualify for tax-free reorganization treatment because they have the same term as the Hibiscus security.

Assume, instead, that in exchange for the $10,000 security, Addison receives a note from Tea with a $15,000 principal value. Addison recognizes a $5,000 capital gain on the exchange. The basis in the Tea bond is $15,000 ($10,000 original basis + $5,000 gain recognized).

Basis

The assets transferred from the target corporation to the acquiring corporation retain their basis (called carryover basis). However, the acquiring corporation's carryover basis is increased by any gain recognized by the target corporation on the reorganization, as shown in Concept Summary 20.4.

EXAMPLE 25

Target exchanges its assets with a value of $5,000,000 and a basis of $3,000,000 for $4,500,000 of Acquiring stock and $500,000 of land. Assume that Target does not distribute the land to its shareholders. Target recognizes a $500,000 gain on the reorganization due to the boot (land) not being distributed. Acquiring's basis in the assets received from Target is $3,500,000 [$3,000,000 (Target's basis) + $500,000 (Target's gain recognized)].

Concept Summary 20.4

Basis to Acquiring Corporation of Property Received

Target's basis in property transferred	$xx,xxx
Plus: Gain recognized by Target on the transaction	x,xxx
Equals: Basis of property to Acquiring corporation	$xx,xxx

In a tax-free reorganization, the shareholder/bondholder generally starts with a tax basis in the stock and securities received that is equal to the basis of the stock and securities surrendered (called substituted basis). This basis is decreased by the fair market value of boot received and increased by the gain and/or dividend income recognized on the transaction.

Basis also may be computed using the Concept Summary 20.3 template. Using the template, the fair market value of the stock and securities received is reduced by the gain (or increased by the loss) postponed. This basis computation ensures that the postponed gain or loss is recognized when the new stock or securities are disposed of in a future taxable transaction.

[25]Rev.Rul. 2004–78, 2004–2 C.B. 108.

Basis Computations

All of Quinn's stock in Target is exchanged for stock in Acquiring plus $3,000 of cash. The exchange is pursuant to a tax-free reorganization. Quinn paid $10,000 for the stock in Target two years ago. The Acquiring stock received by Quinn has a fair market value of $12,000. Quinn has a realized gain of $5,000, which is recognized to the extent of the boot received, $3,000. The basis in the Acquiring stock is $10,000.

EXAMPLE 26

Realized Gain	Recognized Gain	Postponed Gain	Basis in Acquiring Stock
$15,000*	$3,000	$5,000	$12,000
−10,000	Boot	−3,000	−2,000
$ 5,000		$2,000	$10,000

*$12,000 Acquiring stock + $3,000 cash.

Assume the same facts as in Example 26, except that Quinn's basis in the Target stock was $16,000. Quinn realizes a loss of $1,000 on the exchange, none of which is recognized. The basis in the Acquiring stock is computed as follows:

EXAMPLE 27

Realized Gain	Recognized Loss	Postponed Loss	Basis in Acquiring Stock
$15,000*	$ −0−	($1,000)	$12,000
−16,000		−0−	+1,000
($ 1,000)		($1,000)	$13,000

*$12,000 Acquiring stock + $3,000 cash.

20-6 TAX PLANNING

LO.4

Identify tax planning opportunities available to minimize the tax impact in complete liquidations and corporate reorganizations.

20-6a Effect of a Liquidating Distribution on the Corporation

With the exception of parent-subsidiary liquidations, liquidating distributions are taxed at both the corporate level and the shareholder level. When a corporation liquidates, it generally can claim losses on assets that have declined in value. These assets should not be distributed in the form of a property dividend or stock redemption because losses are not recognized on nonliquidating distributions.

20-6b Effect of a Liquidating Distribution on the Shareholder

Shareholders faced with large prospective gains in a liquidation may consider shifting part or all of that gain to other taxpayers. One approach is to donate stock to charity. A charitable contribution of the stock produces a deduction equal to the stock's fair market value (see Chapter 10). Alternatively, the stock may be given to family members in the 10 or 12 percent marginal tax bracket. Here, some or all of the gain on liquidation could be taxed at the 0 percent preferential rate on long-term capital gains. However, there is a risk that the donor may be deemed to have made an anticipatory assignment of income. If so, the gain is still taxed to the donor. In addition, any gift tax issues on the stock transfer must be considered (see Chapter 27). Advance planning of stock transfers, therefore, is crucial in arriving at the desired tax result.

The installment sale rules might also provide some relief. Rather than distributing assets to its shareholders, a sale of the liquidating corporation's assets in exchange for installment notes should be considered. Shareholders receiving the notes in a liquidation can then report their gain on the installment method as payments on the notes are collected. Gain deferred under the installment method is subject to the tax rates applicable in each year of collection. Taxpayers may be able to reduce the tax consequences of an installment sale by directing collections to a year in which a lower rate applies to the capital gain.

20-6c Parent-Subsidiary Liquidations

The nonrecognition provision applicable to the liquidation of a subsidiary, § 332, is not elective. Nevertheless, some flexibility may be available.

- Whether § 332 applies depends on the 80 percent stock ownership test. A parent corporation may be able to avoid § 332 by reducing its stock ownership in the subsidiary below this percentage to allow for recognition of a loss. Alternatively, the opposite approach may be desirable to avoid gain recognition. A corporate shareholder possessing less than the required 80 percent ownership may want to acquire additional stock to qualify for § 332 treatment.

- Once § 332 becomes effective, less latitude is allowed in determining the parent's basis in the subsidiary's assets. Generally, the subsidiary's existing basis in its assets carries over to the parent. If a timely § 338 election is made, the subsidiary's basis in its assets is stepped up to reflect, in part, the parent's basis in the subsidiary stock. If the subsidiary also is liquidated, the parent obtains assets with the stepped-up basis.

- An election to have the § 338 rules apply should be carefully weighed since the election can be detrimental. The income tax liability on the subsidiary's recognized gain that results from the deemed sale of its assets is the cost under § 338 for obtaining the stepped-up basis. As a result, a § 338 election may be a viable option only when the subsidiary possesses loss and/or credit carryovers that can be used to offset the associated tax.

20-6d Asset Purchase versus Stock Purchase

The acquisition of a corporation's assets generally takes one of two forms. In one form, the acquirer purchases the stock of the target corporation from its shareholders and then the target (subsidiary) is liquidated. In the other form, the acquirer purchases the assets of the target corporation and then the target distributes the proceeds to its shareholders in liquidation. Nontax considerations may affect the form of acquisition, with each form having both favorable and unfavorable aspects.

An asset purchase requires that title be transferred and that creditors be notified. Further, an asset purchase may not be feasible if valuable nontransferable trademarks, contracts, or licenses are involved. Alternatively, an asset purchase may be preferable to a stock purchase if the target's shareholders refuse to sell their stock. In addition, an asset purchase avoids the transfer of liabilities (including unknown liabilities) generally inherent in stock acquisitions. An asset purchase also has the advantage of allowing the purchaser to avoid the acquisition of unwanted assets, whereas a stock purchase would involve all of a target's assets.

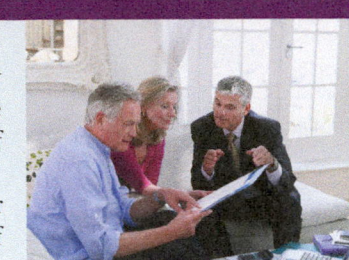

REFOCUS ON THE BIG PICTURE

THE TRANSITION TO RETIREMENT IS SUBJECT TO DOUBLE TAXATION

The Smithsons are wise to evaluate the affordability of their retirement plan *before* they sell or liquidate their business. Nonetheless, after payment of income tax at both the corporate and shareholder levels, they will net only $2,820,000 from the sale of their $4,000,000 business.

Specifically, in the event the corporation is able to sell the business assets for $4,000,000, the realized gain of $2,500,000 will give rise to Federal income tax of $525,000 ($2,500,000 × 21%). Following the payment of the corporate income tax, the net proceeds to the Smithsons will be $3,475,000. After offsetting the amount realized from the liquidation by their stock basis of $200,000, their capital gain of $3,275,000 will be subject to capital gains tax of $655,000 ($3,275,000 × 20%). Therefore, the net after-tax cash available for investment will be $2,820,000 ($3,475,000 proceeds − capital gains tax of $655,000). (To simplify this analysis, the 3.8 percent additional tax on net investment income is not considered.) Now the question for the Smithsons is whether this amount will likely be sufficient to fund the type of retirement they desire.

What If?

Instead of the complete liquidation transaction just described, the Smithsons should consider alternatives that could produce a better tax result such as the following:

- If the Smithsons are able to find a buyer who is interested in maintaining the business in the current corporate form, they should try to sell their *stock* in the business rather than selling the business assets in liquidation. If the buyer is willing to pay $4,000,000 for the corporation's stock, the Smithsons would recognize a capital gain of $3,800,000 and net $3,240,000 after tax ($4,000,000 proceeds − capital gains tax of $760,000). This approach would increase the net after-tax amount available to fund their retirement portfolio by $420,000 due to the fact that the corporate-level tax is avoided. Again, the 3.8 percent additional tax on net investment income is not considered in this analysis.

- Another approach would be to attempt to market the corporation as a potential takeover target in a tax-free reorganization. With this approach, the Smithsons would receive stock in the acquiring corporation without having to recognize *any* gain from the transaction. This strategy could enable the Smithsons to live off the subsequent dividend distributions made by the acquiring corporation. Further, if they needed additional cash flow to meet living expenses, they could sell shares of stock in the acquiring corporation as needed, and any resulting gain would be subject to the capital gains rates at that time. An obvious advantage of this approach is that gain from the disposition of their stock would be deferred until the stock in the acquiring corporation is sold in a taxable transaction. However, a disadvantage the Smithsons would need to evaluate is that they would not be able to build a diversified portfolio, given that their investment holdings would largely, if not completely, consist of the stock of the acquiring corporation.

Key Terms

Boot, 20-17

Corporate liquidation, 20-2

Other property, 20-17

Reorganization, 20-15

Section 338 election, 20-13

Discussion Questions

1. **LO.1** Under what circumstances are losses disallowed to a corporation in liquidation?

2. **LO.1** For purposes of the related-party loss limitation within the context of a complete liquidation of a corporation, what is the definition of *disqualified property?*

3. **LO.1** For the built-in loss limitation to apply, the property must have been acquired by the corporation as part of a plan whose principal purpose was to recognize a loss on the property by the liquidating corporation. Explain.

4. **LO.1** Explain the tax consequences to a shareholder of a corporation in the process of liquidation under the general rule of § 331.

5. **LO.2** Discuss the tax consequences to the parent corporation in a § 332 liquidation of a subsidiary.

6. **LO.2** In terms of the rules applying to a § 332 parent-subsidiary liquidation, comment on each of the following:
   a. The parent corporation's ownership interest in the subsidiary.
   b. The period of time in which the subsidiary must liquidate.
   c. The solvency of the subsidiary.

7. **LO.2** A subsidiary corporation is liquidated under § 332. Pursuant to its liquidation, the subsidiary distributed property to a minority shareholder. With respect to this distribution, what are the tax consequences to the subsidiary corporation and to the minority shareholder?

8. **LO.2** In general, what are the tax consequences of a § 338 election?

9. **LO.2** From the perspective of the parent corporation, contrast the tax consequences of a subsidiary liquidation under the general nonrecognition rules with a subsidiary liquidation that follows a § 338 election.

10. **LO.3** Explain why a private letter ruling from the IRS is like an insurance policy for a corporate reorganization.

11. **LO.3** How is the four-column template in Concept Summary 20.3 used to determine a shareholder's basis in the stock received in a corporate restructuring?

Computational Exercises

12. **LO.1** Sunset Corporation, with E & P of $400,000, makes a cash distribution of $120,000 to a shareholder. The shareholder's basis in the Sunset stock involved is $50,000.
    a. Determine the tax consequences to the shareholder if the distribution is a non-qualified stock redemption.
    b. Determine the tax consequences to the shareholder if the distribution is a qualifying stock redemption.
    c. Determine the tax consequences to the shareholder if the distribution is pursuant to a complete liquidation of Sunset.

13. **LO.1** Pursuant to a complete liquidation, Carrot Corporation distributes to its shareholders real estate held as an investment (basis of $650,000, fair market value of $880,000).
    a. Determine the gain or loss recognized by Carrot on the distribution if no liability is involved.

b. Determine the gain or loss recognized by Carrot on the distribution if the real estate is subject to a liability of $690,000.

c. Determine the gain or loss recognized by Carrot on the distribution if the real estate is subject to a liability of $885,000.

14. **LO.1** Osprey Corporation stock is owned by Pedro and Pittro, who are unrelated. Pedro and Pittro each own 50% of the stock in the corporation. Osprey has the following assets (none of which were acquired in a § 351 or contribution to capital transaction) that are distributed in complete liquidation of the corporation.

	Adjusted Basis	Fair Market Value
Cash	$300,000	$300,000
Land	200,000	440,000
Equipment	250,000	140,000

Assume that Osprey Corporation distributes the land to Pedro and the cash and equipment to Pittro.

a. Determine Osprey's recognized gain or loss on the distribution of land.

b. Determine Osprey's recognized gain or loss on the distribution of the equipment.

15. **LO.1** On January 7, 2020, Martin Corporation acquires two properties from a shareholder solely in exchange for stock in a transaction that qualifies under § 351. The shareholder's basis, the fair market value, and the built-in gain (loss) of each property are:

	Shareholder's Basis	Fair Market Value	Built-In Gain (Loss)
Property 1	$300,000	$375,000	$ 75,000
Property 2	525,000	400,000	(125,000)
Net built-in loss			($ 50,000)

Martin adopts a plan of liquidation later in the year and distributes Property 2 to a 30% shareholder when the property is worth $350,000.

a. Compute Martin's basis in Property 1 and in Property 2 as of January 7, 2020.

b. Compute Martin's realized and recognized loss on the liquidating distribution of Property 2.

16. **LO.1** Green Corporation's assets are valued at $920,000 after payment of all corporate debts, except for $134,000 of taxes payable on net gains it recognized on the liquidation. Bruno, an individual and the sole shareholder of Green, has a basis of $280,000 in his stock. Compute the gain or loss recognized by Bruno on the liquidation of Green Corporation.

17. **LO.2** The stock of Quail Corporation is held as follows: 85% by Pheasant Corporation and 15% by Gisela, an individual. Quail Corporation is liquidated in December of the current year pursuant to a plan adopted earlier in the year. At the time of its liquidation, Quail Corporation has assets with a basis of $730,000 and fair market value of $1,000,000. Quail Corporation distributes the property pro rata to Pheasant Corporation and to Gisela.

a. Compute Quail's recognized gain or loss on the distribution of property to Pheasant.

b. Compute Quail's recognized gain or loss on the distribution of property to Gisela.

18. **LO.2** Goose Corporation has a basis of $2,400,000 in the stock of Swift Corporation, a wholly owned subsidiary acquired 30 years ago. Goose liquidates Swift Corporation and receives assets that are worth $2,000,000 and have a basis to Swift of $1,700,000.

a. Determine Goose Corporation's recognized gain or loss on the liquidation.

b. Determine Goose Corporation's basis in the assets received in liquidation.

19. **LO.3** Rebecca holds 100 shares of Gotchas stock that she purchased for $1,000 several years ago. In a merger of Gotchas into Solis, Inc., Rebecca exchanges her 100 Gotchas shares for 1,000 Solis shares and $500. Gotchas is valued at $40 per share and Solis at $3.50 per share. Prepare your solution using spreadsheet software such as Microsoft Excel.

    a. What is Rebecca's realized and recognized gain/loss from the reorganization?

    b. What is Rebecca's basis in her Solis stock?

20. **LO.3** In a qualifying reorganization, Cato Corporation exchanges $1,200,000 worth of stock and property valued at $500,000 ($245,000 basis) for all of Firestar Corporation's assets, which have a value of $1,700,000 and a $500,000 basis. Firestar distributes the property received from Cato. The exchange meets the § 368 requirements.

    a. What is Cato's recognized gain/loss from the reorganization?

    b. What is Firestar's recognized gain/loss from the reorganization?

21. **LO.3** Townsend, the sole shareholder of Pruett Corporation, has a $480,000 basis in his stock. He exchanges his Pruett stock for $600,000 of Rogers Corporation voting common stock plus land with a fair market value of $100,000 and basis of $25,000. Pruett distributed the land to Townsend. This exchange qualifies under § 368.

    a. What is Townsend's recognized gain/loss from the reorganization? Prepare your solution using spreadsheet software such as Microsoft Excel.

    b. What is the gain/loss recognized by Pruett Corporation and Rogers Corporation on the reorganization?

    c. What is Townsend's basis in the Rogers stock and the land received?

22. **LO.3** Hosha exchanges all of her Leaf stock for Petal stock plus $5,000 cash. The exchange is pursuant to a tax-free reorganization. Hosha paid $25,000 for the Leaf stock five years ago. The Petal stock received by Hosha has an $18,000 fair market value.

    a. What is Hosha's realized and recognized gain/loss from the reorganization? Prepare your solution using spreadsheet software such as Microsoft Excel.

    b. What is Hosha's basis in the Petal stock she received?

Problems

23. **LO.1, 4** Dove Corporation (E & P of $800,000) has 1,000 shares of stock outstanding. The shares are owned as follows: Julia, 600 shares; Maxine (Julia's sister), 300 shares; and Janine (Julia's daughter), 100 shares. Dove Corporation owns land (basis of $300,000, fair market value of $260,000) that it purchased as an investment seven years ago. Dove distributes the land to Julia in exchange for all of her shares in the corporation. Julia had a basis of $275,000 in the shares. What are the tax consequences for both Dove Corporation and Julia if the distribution is:

    a. A qualifying stock redemption?

    b. A liquidating distribution?

24. **LO.1** Pursuant to a complete liquidation, Oriole Corporation distributes to its shareholders land held for three years as an investment (adjusted basis of $250,000, fair market value of $490,000). The land is subject to a liability of $520,000.

    a. What are the tax consequences to Oriole Corporation on the distribution of the land?

    b. If the land is, instead, subject to a liability of $400,000, what are the tax consequences to Oriole on the distribution?

25. **LO.1** The stock of Mulberry Corporation is owned by Archana (60%) and Anar (40%), who are mother and daughter. Pursuant to a plan of complete liquidation adopted earlier in the current year, Mulberry distributes land worth $575,000 to Anar (basis of $100,000 in Mulberry stock). The land was purchased by Mulberry

Corporation three years ago for $650,000, and it is distributed subject to a liability of $425,000. What amount of gain or loss is recognized by Mulberry Corporation and by Anar with respect to the distribution of the land?

26. **LO.1** Last year Lory Corporation, a land development company, acquired land and construction equipment from its sole shareholder in a § 351 transaction. At the time, the land had a basis of $790,000 and a fair market value of $650,000 and the equipment had a basis of $130,000 and a fair market value of $300,000. The assets were transferred to Lory Corporation for the purpose of developing the land and constructing a residential home community. However, the residential housing market suffered a steep decline in the current year, and as a result of financial difficulties, Lory Corporation was forced to sell its assets and liquidate. Pursuant to a plan of liquidation adopted during the year, Lory sold the land to an unrelated party for its current fair market value of $500,000. What amount of loss, if any, is recognized by Lory Corporation on the sale of the land?

27. **LO.1** Last year a shareholder transferred land (basis of $650,000, fair market value of $575,000) to Roadrunner Corporation in a § 351 transaction. This was the only property transferred to Roadrunner at that time. During the current year, Roadrunner Corporation adopted a plan of liquidation and distributed the land to Rhonda, a 15% shareholder. On the date of the distribution, the land had a fair market value of $400,000. Roadrunner Corporation never used the land for business purposes during the time it owned the property. What amount of loss may Roadrunner recognize on the distribution of the land?

28. **LO.1, 4** Last year Pink Corporation acquired land and securities in a § 351 tax-free   Decision Making
exchange. On the date of the transfer, the land had a basis of $720,000 and a fair market value of $1,000,000 and the securities had a basis of $110,000 and a fair market value of $250,000. Pink Corporation has two shareholders, Maria and Paul, who are unrelated. Maria owns 85% of the stock in the corporation, and Paul owns 15%. Pink adopts a plan of liquidation in the current year. On this date, the value of the land has decreased to $500,000. What is the effect of each of the following on Pink Corporation? Which option should be selected?
   a.   Distribute all of the land to Maria.
   b.   Distribute all of the land to Paul.
   c.   Distribute 85% of the land to Maria and 15% to Paul.
   d.   Distribute 50% of the land to Maria and 50% to Paul.
   e.   Sell the land and distribute the proceeds of $500,000 proportionately to Maria and to Paul.

29. **LO.1, 4** Assume in Problem 28 that the land had a fair market value of $630,000 on   Decision Making
the date of its transfer to the corporation. On the date of the liquidation, the land's fair market value has decreased to $500,000. How would your answer to Problem 28 change if:
   a.   All of the land is distributed to Maria?
   b.   All of the land is distributed to Paul?
   c.   The land is distributed 85% to Maria and 15% to Paul?
   d.   The land is distributed 50% to Maria and 50% to Paul?
   e.   The land is sold and the proceeds of $500,000 are distributed proportionately to Maria and to Paul?

30. **LO.1** Pursuant to a complete liquidation in the current year, Scarlet Corporation distributes to Jake land (basis of $425,000, fair market value of $390,000) that was purchased three years ago and held as an investment. The land is subject to a liability of $250,000. Jake, who owned 35% of the Scarlet Corporation shares outstanding, had a basis of $60,000 in the stock. What are the tax consequences of the liquidating distribution to Scarlet Corporation and to Jake?

31. **LO.2** The stock of Magenta Corporation is owned by Fuchsia Corporation (95%) and Marta (5%). Magenta is liquidated in the current year, pursuant to a plan of liquidation adopted earlier in the year. In the liquidation, Magenta distributes various assets worth $950,000 (basis of $620,000) to Fuchsia (basis of $700,000 in Magenta stock) and a parcel of land worth $50,000 (basis of $75,000) to Marta (basis of $30,000 in Magenta stock). Assuming that the § 338 election is not made, what are the tax consequences of the liquidation to Magenta, Fuchsia, and Marta?

32. **LO.2** The stock in Ivory Corporation is owned by Gold Corporation (80%) and Imelda (20%). Gold Corporation purchased its shares in Ivory nine years ago at a cost of $650,000, and Imelda purchased her shares in Ivory four years ago at a cost of $175,000. Ivory Corporation has the following assets that are distributed in complete liquidation:

	Adjusted Basis	Fair Market Value
Cash	$600,000	$600,000
Inventory	80,000	200,000
Equipment	350,000	200,000

   a. Assume that Ivory Corporation distributes the cash and inventory to Gold Corporation and the equipment to Imelda. What are the tax consequences of the distributions to Ivory Corporation, to Gold Corporation, and to Imelda?

   b. Assume that Ivory Corporation distributes the cash and equipment to Gold Corporation and the inventory to Imelda. What are the tax consequences of the distributions to Ivory Corporation, to Gold Corporation, and to Imelda?

33. **LO.2** Orange Corporation purchased bonds (basis of $350,000) of its wholly owned subsidiary, Green Corporation, at a discount. Upon liquidation of Green pursuant to § 332, Orange receives payment in the form of land worth $400,000, the face amount of the bonds. Green Corporation had a basis of $320,000 in the land. What are the tax consequences of this land transfer to Green Corporation and to Orange Corporation?

34. **LO.2** On July 15, 2019, Lilac Corporation purchased 25% of the Coffee Corporation stock outstanding. Lilac Corporation purchased an additional 40% of the stock in Coffee on March 24, 2020, and an additional 20% on May 5, 2020. On September 25, 2020, Lilac Corporation purchased the remaining 15% of Coffee Corporation stock outstanding. For purposes of the § 338 election, on what date does a qualified stock purchase occur? What is the due date for making the § 338 election?

35. **LO.2** On April 23, 2020, Auk Corporation acquires 100% of the outstanding stock of Amazon Corporation (E & P of $750,000) for $1,200,000. Amazon Corporation has assets with a fair market value of $1,400,000 (basis of $800,000), no liabilities, and no loss or tax credit carryovers. Auk Corporation files a timely § 338 election. Assume that both the aggregate deemed sale price (ADSP) and adjusted grossed-up basis (AGUB) are $1,306,329.

   a. What are the tax consequences of the § 338 election to Amazon Corporation and to Auk Corporation?

   b. Assume that Amazon Corporation is liquidated immediately following the § 338 election. What are the tax consequences of the liquidation to Amazon Corporation and to Auk Corporation?

36. **LO.3** Quail Corporation was created six years ago through contributions from Kasha ($900,000) and Frank ($100,000). In a transaction qualifying as a reorganization, Quail exchanges all of its assets currently valued at $1,800,000 (basis of $1,200,000) for 12,000 shares of Covey Corporation stock valued at $1,700,000 plus $100,000 in Covey bonds. Quail distributes the Covey stock and bonds proportionately to Frank and Kasha in exchange for their stock in Quail. Quail's current and accumulated E & P before the reorganization amounts to $70,000.

a.   How do Kasha and Frank treat this transaction for income tax purposes? What is Kasha's and Frank's basis in their Covey stock? Prepare your solution using spreadsheet software such as Microsoft Excel.

b.   How do Quail and Covey treat this transaction for income tax purposes? What is Covey's basis in the assets it receives from Quail?

37. **LO.3** Jed acquired 25% of the stock of Alpha (basis of $100,000) 12 years ago, and the other 75% was purchased by Zia (basis of $400,000) three years ago.

Alpha enters into a tax-free consolidation with Beta, in which Jed will receive an 8% interest in the new AlphaBeta (value $90,000) plus $36,000 cash and Zia will receive a 28% interest (value $315,000) plus land worth $63,000. Alpha's basis in the land is $35,000.

Before the reorganization or distributions to its shareholders, Alpha's value is $504,000 and Beta's value is $720,000.

a.   What is Jed's and Zia's recognized gain or loss on the reorganization? What is each shareholder's basis in his or her AlphaBeta stock? Prepare your solution using spreadsheet software such as Microsoft Excel.

b.   What is Alpha's and Beta's recognized gain or loss on the reorganization?

c.   Diagram the consolidation of Alpha and Beta corporations.

38. **LO.3** Target Corporation holds assets with a fair market value of $4,000,000 (adjusted basis of $2,200,000) and liabilities of $1,500,000. It transfers assets worth $3,700,000 to Acquiring Corporation in a "Type C" reorganization, in exchange for Acquiring voting stock and the assumption of $1,400,000 of Target's liabilities.

Target retained a building worth $300,000 (adjusted basis of $225,000). Target distributes the Acquiring voting stock and the building with an associated $100,000 mortgage to Wei, its sole shareholder, for all of her stock in Target. Wei's basis in her stock is $2,100,000.

a.   What is the value of the stock transferred from Acquiring to Target?

b.   What is the amount of gain (loss) recognized by Wei, Target, and Acquiring on the reorganization?

c.   What is Wei's basis in the stock and building she received? Prepare your solution using spreadsheet software such as Microsoft Excel.

Research Problems

Note: Solutions to the Research Problems can be prepared by using the Thomson Reuters Checkpoint™ online tax research database, which accompanies this textbook. Solutions can also be prepared by using research materials found in a typical tax library.

the answer company™
THOMSON REUTERS®

Research Problem 1. Shelly Zumaya (2220 East Hennepin Avenue, Minneapolis, MN 55413) is the president and sole shareholder of Kiwi Corporation (stock basis of $400,000). Incorporated in 2009, Kiwi Corporation's sole business has consisted of the purchase and resale of used farming equipment. In December 2018 , Kiwi transferred its entire inventory (basis of $1,200,000) to Shelly in a transaction described by the parties as a sale. According to Shelly and collaborated by the minutes of the board of directors, the inventory was sold to her for the sum of $2,000,000, the fair market value of the inventory. The terms of the sale provided that Shelly would pay Kiwi Corporation the $2,000,000 at some future date. This debt obligation was not evidenced by a promissory note, and to date, Shelly has made no payments (principal or interest) on the obligation. The inventory transfer was not reported on Kiwi's 2018 tax return as either a sale or a distribution. After the transfer of the inventory to Shelly, Kiwi Corporation had no remaining assets and ceased to conduct any business. Kiwi did not formally liquidate under state law. On an audit of Kiwi Corporation's 2018 tax

Communications

Critical Thinking

return, the IRS asserted that the transfer of inventory constituted a liquidation of Kiwi; as a result, the corporation recognized a gain on the liquidating distribution in the amount of $800,000 [$2,000,000 (fair market value) − $1,200,000 (inventory basis)]. Further, because Kiwi Corporation is devoid of assets, the IRS assessed the entire tax liability against Shelly, based on transferee liability. Finally, the IRS assessed a tax due from Shelly for her gain recognized in the purported liquidating distribution. Shelly has contacted you regarding the IRS's determination. Prepare a letter to Shelly Zumaya and a memo for the file, documenting your research.

Research Problem 2. Paloma purchased all of the outstanding Dove stock six years ago. Dove has prospered under Paloma's direction, and now Hawk Corporation is interested in acquiring Dove, but not directly. Hawk forms a new subsidiary, called Starling, whose purpose is to merge with Dove. Starling (the target) transfers its asset, Hawk stock, to Dove (acquiring) in exchange for all of the Dove stock. Dove distributes the Hawk stock to Paloma in exchange for her Dove stock. Starling distributes the Dove stock to its shareholder, Hawk, and then ceases to exist. Dove is now a wholly owned subsidiary of Hawk, and Paloma is a Hawk shareholder.

Hawk immediately liquidates Dove to acquire all of Dove's assets and liabilities. Hawk continues Dove's previous line of business. The end result is that Hawk has all of Dove's assets and liabilities and that Paloma is a shareholder of Hawk.

Explain whether this reverse triangular restructuring qualifies as a reorganization under § 368 or whether the step transaction doctrine causes it to be disqualified.

Use internet tax resources to address the following questions. Look for reliable websites and blogs of the IRS and other government agencies, media outlets, businesses, tax professionals, academics, think tanks, and political outlets.

Communications **Research Problem 3.** The requirements for effectively liquidating a corporate entity under state law vary from state to state. Using the internet as your sole research source, prepare an outline discussing how an entity incorporated in your home state is liquidated, including any reporting requirements associated with such liquidation.

Communications **Research Problem 4.** Although the requirements for a § 332 parent-subsidiary liquidation are fairly straightforward, some planning and reporting issues must be addressed to ensure the proper outcome. Using the internet as your sole research source, prepare an outline discussing the general requirements for a § 332 parent-subsidiary liquidation, including any associated planning and reporting considerations.

Data Analytics **Research Problem 5.** Corporate executives engage in reorganizations to improve
Critical Thinking shareholder value. If shareholder value increases, the reorganization often is deemed
Communications a success. If shareholder value falls, corporate executives may take the blame.

Pick a reorganization of a publicly traded company that occurred between three and seven years ago. Obtain the monthly stock price for the parent company for the three-year period before and the three-year period after the reorganization (six years total). Then, obtain the monthly stock price of an S&P 500 Index mutual fund, as well as the monthly stock price of a major competitor of your company over the same period.

Pick two performance metrics (e.g., return on assets, return on equity), and calculate those ratios for the merged company for the three years following the reorganization. Compare those performance metrics to the same metrics for the firm's major competitor for the same period.

Use Microsoft Excel, or a data visualization software package, to create no more than five of the most appropriate tables or charts that show how the reorganization added or diminished shareholder value. Place those charts into Microsoft PowerPoint along with two other slides that provide your arguments for or against the success of the merger. Your PowerPoint slides should be visually appealing, easy to interpret, and concise.

Research Problem 6. Browse the internet sites of several public accounting firms and find discussions comparing stock purchases with asset purchases when acquiring a business. Based solely on your findings, prepare an outline of the advantages and disadvantages of each form of acquisition.

Communications

Becker CPA Review Questions

Becker⁺

1. Krol Corp. distributed marketable securities in redemption of its stock in a complete liquidation. On the date of distribution, these securities had a basis of $100,000 and a fair market value of $150,000. What gain does Krol have as a result of the distribution?

    a. $0
    b. $50,000 capital gain

    c. $50,000 § 1231 gain
    d. $50,000 ordinary gain

2. A corporation was completely liquidated and dissolved during year 14. The filing fees, professional fees, and other expenditures incurred in connection with the liquidation and dissolution are:

    a. Deductible in full by the dissolved corporation.

    b. Deductible by the shareholders and *not* by the corporation.

    c. Treated as capital losses by the corporation.

    d. Not deductible either by the corporation or shareholders.

3. Generally, in a direct distribution of assets to the shareholders that results in a complete corporate liquidation:

    a. There is no taxable event.

    b. The corporation recognizes no gain or loss because it transfers the assets to the shareholders at the corporation's basis immediately before the distribution.

    c. The shareholders recognize dividend income in the amount of the fair market value of property received.

    d. The shareholders recognize gain or loss to the extent the fair market value of the distributed assets differs from the adjusted basis of the stock.

4. Olinto Corp., an accrual basis calendar year C corporation, had no corporate shareholders when it liquidated in year 12. In cancellation of all their Olinto Corp. stock, each Olinto Corp. shareholder received in year 12 a liquidating distribution of $12,000 cash and land with a corporate tax basis of $15,000 and a fair market value of $20,500. Before the distribution, each shareholder's tax basis in Olinto Corp. stock was $16,500. What amount of gain should each Olinto Corp. shareholder recognize on the liquidating distribution?

    a. $0
    b. $10,500

    c. $4,000
    d. $16,000

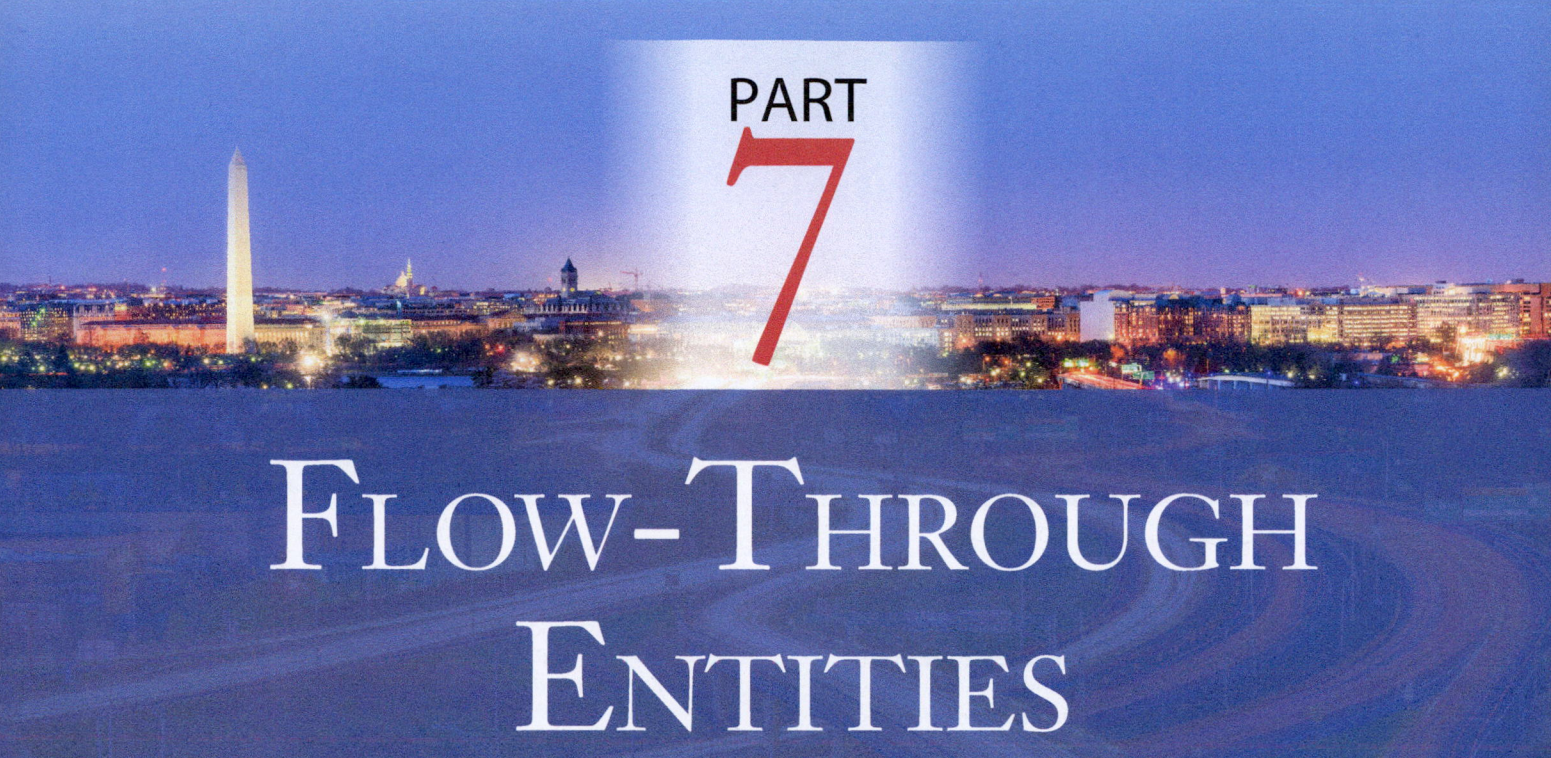

PART

7

FLOW-THROUGH ENTITIES

CHAPTER **21**
Partnerships

CHAPTER **22**
S Corporations

Unlike C corporations, some business entities are taxed under the conduit principle. Generally, this means the tax attributes of various transactions are retained as they flow through the entity directly to the owners. Usually, no Federal income tax is imposed at the entity level. Part 7 of this text discusses two types of flow-through entities—partnerships and corporations that make an S election. Similarities and differences in the taxing systems for the two types of entities are highlighted. By comparing the tax attributes of C corporations, S corporations, and partnerships, the owners are provided with the tools needed to choose the most appropriate tax and legal form for conducting a business.

CHAPTER

21 Partnerships

LEARNING OBJECTIVES: *After completing Chapter 21, you should be able to:*

LO.1 Distinguish among the various types of entities treated as partnerships for tax purposes.

LO.2 Describe the conceptual basis for partnership taxation and how partnership income is reported and taxed.

LO.3 Determine the tax effects (and special rules) when forming a partnership with cash and property contributions.

LO.4 Identify elections available to a partnership and specify the tax treatment of expenditures of a newly formed partnership.

LO.5 Specify the accounting methods and taxable years available to a partnership.

LO.6 Calculate a partnership's taxable income and separately stated items and describe how the partnership's income is reported on Form 1065.

LO.7 Describe the information provided on a partner's Schedule K–1 and how the partner reports that information.

LO.8 Outline and discuss the requirements for allocating income, gains, losses, deductions, and credits among the partners.

LO.9 Determine a partner's basis in the partnership interest.

LO.10 Explain how liabilities affect a partner's basis.

LO.11 Illustrate a partner's capital account rollforward and explain why the year-end balance might differ from the partner's year-end basis in the partnership interest.

LO.12 List and review the limitations on deducting partnership losses.

LO.13 Describe how a partner calculates self-employment tax and net investment income tax on partnership income.

LO.14 Define terms related to distributions from a partnership and determine the tax treatment of proportionate current distributions from a partnership to a partner and the tax treatment of proportionate distributions that liquidate a partnership.

LO.15 Calculate the selling partner's amount and character of gain or loss on the sale or exchange of a partnership interest.

LO.16 Describe the application of partnership provisions to limited liability companies (LLCs) and limited liability partnerships (LLPs).

LO.17 Identify tax planning opportunities related to partnerships and their partners.

CHAPTER OUTLINE

21-1 Overview of Partnership Taxation, 21-2
21-1a What Is a Partnership?, 21-2
21-1b Key Concepts in Taxation of Partnership Income, 21-4

21-2 Formation of a Partnership: Tax Effects, 21-6
21-2a Contributions to the Partnership, 21-6
21-2b Exceptions to the General Rule of § 721, 21-7
21-2c Other Issues Related to Contributed Property, 21-9
21-2d Tax Accounting Elections, 21-11
21-2e Initial Costs of a Partnership, 21-12
21-2f Method of Accounting, 21-12
21-2g Taxable Year of the Partnership, 21-13

21-3 Partnership Operations and Reporting, 21-15
21-3a Partnership Reporting, In General, 21-15
21-3b Measuring Partnership Income, 21-16
21-3c Form 1065 Example, 21-18

21-4 Partner Calculations and Reporting, 21-24
21-4a Partner Reporting of Partnership Income, 21-24
21-4b Partner Allocations, 21-26
21-4c Schedule K–1 Example, 21-28
21-4d Partner's Basis, 21-31
21-4e Effect of Partnership Liabilities on Partner's Basis, 21-31

21-4f Partner's Capital Account, 21-35
21-4g Loss Limitations, 21-36

21-5 Other Taxes on Partnership Income, 21-38
21-5a Self-Employment Tax, 21-38
21-5b Net Investment Income Tax, 21-39

21-6 Distributions from the Partnership, 21-40
21-6a Distributions in General, 21-40
21-6b Proportionate Current Distributions, 21-41
21-6c Proportionate Liquidating Distributions, 21-43

21-7 Sale of a Partnership Interest, 21-46
21-7a General Rules, 21-46
21-7b Hot Assets and Carried Interests, 21-48

21-8 Limited Liability Entities, 21-49
21-8a Limited Liability Companies, 21-49
21-8b Limited Liability Partnerships, 21-49

21-9 Tax Planning, 21-50
21-9a Choosing Partnership Taxation, 21-50
21-9b Formation and Operation of a Partnership, 21-51
21-9c Basis Considerations and Loss Deduction Limitations, 21-51
21-9d Transactions between Partners and Partnerships, 21-51
21-9e Drafting the Partnership Agreement, 21-52

RODERICK PAUL WALKER/ALAMY STOCK PHOTO

WHY USE A PARTNERSHIP, ANYWAY?

For 15 years, Maria has owned and operated a seaside bakery and café called The Beachsider. Each morning, customers line up on the boardwalk in front of the building and enjoy fresh coffee and croissants while waiting for a table. "The building is too small," Maria commented to her landlord, Kyle. "Is there any way we can expand?" The Beachsider occupies one of several buildings on three acres of a 10-acre parcel that Kyle inherited several years ago. The remaining seven acres are undeveloped.

Kyle and Maria talked to Josh, a real estate developer, and he proposed an expansion to The Beachsider and upgrades to the other buildings. The improvements would preserve the character of the original retail center, and the remaining acreage would be available for future expansion.

They liked his ideas, so Kyle, Maria, and Josh agreed to form a partnership to own and operate The Beachsider and to improve and lease the other buildings. Josh summarized the plan as follows: "Kyle and Maria will each contribute one-half of the capital we need. Kyle's real estate is valued at about $2,000,000. Maria's bakery equipment and the café furnishings are valued at about $500,000. The improvements will cost about $1,500,000 of cash, which Maria has agreed to contribute to the partnership."

Josh continued, "You have agreed that I do not need to contribute any capital to the partnership. I will oversee the construction, and when it is complete, I will vest in a 5 percent interest in the partnership's capital. On an ongoing basis, I will oversee the partnership's operations in exchange for a fixed salary and 20 percent of the partnership's ongoing profits. The construction should be completed in June of this year, and my capital interest is estimated to be valued at $200,000 at that time."

What are the tax consequences if the trio forms Beachside Properties as a partnership to own and operate the retail center? What issues might arise later in the life of the entity?

Read the chapter and formulate your response.

We'll talk about partnerships and S corporations in this and the next chapter. These entities are called *flow-through* or *pass-through* entities, because the entity's income, gains, losses, deductions, credits, and general tax information flow through and are taxed or attributed to the owners. As we'll discuss, a pass-through entity is flexible and has a single level of taxation. This combination can result in significant tax and business advantages over a C corporation.

This chapter addresses partnership formations, operations, and current distributions and, in addition, sales of partnership interests and partnership liquidating distributions. Chapter 22 discusses the taxation of S corporations.

21-1 OVERVIEW OF PARTNERSHIP TAXATION

Let's look at some of the general concepts that apply to all partnerships.

21-1a What Is a Partnership?

Partnerships are governed by Subchapter K of the Internal Revenue Code. A partnership is defined as an association formed by two or more persons to carry on a trade or business, with each contributing money, property, labor, or skill, and with all expecting to share in profits and losses. The entity must be unincorporated and cannot be otherwise classified as a corporation, trust, or estate.[1]

Types of Partnerships

You'll see several types of partnerships, each suited for different situations. Partnership entities are defined and formed under state law. They are typically distinguished based on the classification of the partners as **general partners** or **limited partners** and the types of business permitted to be conducted.

- General partners can participate in managing the entity. A general partner legally can be required to repay a partnership's "recourse" debt (described later).
- Limited partners are typically not permitted to participate in entity management, and they are not liable for partnership debts (except to the extent the partner owes unpaid contributions to the partnership).

Some of the more common types of entities treated as partnerships include the following.

- A **general partnership (GP)** consists of two or more general partners who may participate in management; there are no limited partners. General partnerships often are used for operating activities (e.g., product manufacturing or sales) and corporate joint ventures.
- A **limited partnership (LP)** is a partnership with at least one general partner and one or more limited partners.[2] These partnerships often have numerous limited partners and are used to raise capital for real estate development, oil and gas exploration, research and development, and various financial product investment vehicles. To reduce exposure to the entity's liabilities, the general partners are often entities that, themselves, have limited liability, such as a C corporation (or a limited liability company, discussed next).
- In a **limited liability company (LLC)**, the owners (termed "members") are a hybrid type of partner. With respect to the LLC's debts, members are treated as limited partners. However, LLC members generally participate in management of the LLC. Therefore, an LLC combines the corporate benefit of limited liability for the owners

---

[1]A "person" can be an individual, trust, estate, corporation, association, or another partnership. §§ 7701(a)(1) and (2).

[2]A limited liability limited partnership (LLLP) is an extension of the limited partnership form in which all partners, whether general or limited, are accorded limited liability. At this writing, about half of U.S. states permit formation of LLLPs or recognize LLLPs formed in another state. LLLPs are not discussed further in this chapter.

with the benefits of partnership taxation, including the single level of tax. A properly structured multi-owner[3] LLC is generally treated as a partnership for all Federal tax purposes.[4]

- In most states, a <mark>limited liability partnership (LLP)</mark> is treated similarly to a general partnership; however, an LLP partner is not personally liable for any malpractice committed by other partners. The LLP is currently the organizational form of choice for the large accounting firms.

A <mark>partnership agreement</mark> is signed by each partner. This document outlines the rights and obligations of the partners; the allocation of income, deductions, and cash flows; initial and future capital contribution requirements; conditions for terminating the partnership; and other matters. The governing agreement of an LLC is known as an <mark>operating agreement</mark>.

Concept Summary 21.1 summarizes characteristics of the various entities treated as partnerships.

Concept Summary 21.1

Comparison of Partnership Types

The following table summarizes information about the types of partnerships and limited liability entities discussed in this chapter.

Type of entity	Types of owners	Are owners liable for entity debts?	May owners participate in entity management?	Types of businesses operated by entity*
General partnership (GP)	General partners only	Yes, recourse to GP No, debt secured only by property	Yes	Operating businesses, and joint ventures formed by other operating businesses
Limited partnership (LP)	Limited partners plus at least one general partner**	Yes, for general partners No, for limited partners	Yes, for general partners No, for limited partners	Entities raising capital from investors
Limited liability company (LLC)	"Members" have some general and some limited characteristics	No	Yes, generally	Generally, operating businesses and nonprofessional service businesses
Limited liability partnership (LLP)	General partners with limited liability for malpractice committed by other partners	Yes, for general liabilities and partner's own malpractice	Yes	Professional service entities such as accounting and law firms

*In general; permitted business operations depend on state law.

**The general partner is often a C corporation or LLC, to minimize exposure to entity liabilities.

The Big Picture

EXAMPLE 1

Return to the facts of *The Big Picture* on p. 21-1. When Beachside Properties is formed, Kyle, Maria, and Josh must first decide which type of entity to form. They've narrowed the decision to a C corporation or a partnership. Assume that all three owners are single individuals in the highest tax brackets before considering Beachside's income.

If they form a C corporation, the entity will pay them modest salaries and distribute all of Beachside's remaining cash flows currently as dividends. The amounts paid as wages would be subject to a 37% tax (plus employment taxes, discussed near the end of the chapter). The C corporation's taxable income (after deducting wages) would be taxed at 21%. The remaining 79% of income can

continued

---

[3]Note that an LLC might have only one owner. Single-member LLCs (SMLLCs) are treated as sole proprietorships or disregarded entities rather than partnerships. SMLLCs are not discussed further in this chapter.

[4]In most of the examples in this chapter, the entities are structured as LLCs for state law purposes. Unless otherwise indicated, assume that these entities are treated as partnerships for Federal income tax purposes.

be distributed and would be taxed at 23.8% (20% tax rate on qualified dividends plus 3.8% net investment income tax) for a combined effective tax rate of about 39.8%.

If they form a partnership, the income will be subject to one 37% tax (again, plus employment taxes, discussed later). This single level of tax is less than the 39.8% combined effective rate that would apply to a C corporation's taxable income. In addition, to the extent the income is qualified business income (as described later in this chapter), the partners can deduct 20% of their shares of income, effectively lowering the tax rate to 29.6%.

As a result of the potential tax savings, Kyle, Maria, and Josh decided to form a partnership. They must next decide which type of partnership to utilize.

With a GP, Kyle, Maria, and Josh would each be jointly and severally liable for all entity debts. With an LP, one of the partners would be designated as a general partner and would be liable for all entity debts. Neither of these is ideal if there's a way all three owners can have limited liability.

An LLP is not considered because LLPs are typically reserved for service-providing entities, such as accounting firms.

With an LLC, each partner's losses will be limited to the partner's contributed capital. Therefore, Kyle, Maria, and Josh decide to form Beachside Properties as an LLC.

21-1b Key Concepts in Taxation of Partnership Income

LO.2

Describe the conceptual basis for partnership taxation and how partnership income is reported and taxed.

A partnership is not a taxable entity.[5] Rather, the taxable income or loss of the partnership flows through to the partners at the end of the partnership's tax year.[6]

Flow-Through Status of Entity

The partnership itself pays no Federal income tax.[7] Instead, the partners report their **distributive share** of the partnership's income or loss on their tax returns and pay any tax due.

A partnership files Form 1065, U.S. Return of Partnership Income. This return includes a **Schedule K–1** for each partner (with a copy provided to the partner) that shows that partner's share of partnership items. The partners use the Schedules K–1 in preparing their tax returns and paying tax on the entity's income. See text Sections 21-3c and 21-4a later in the chapter.

EXAMPLE 2

Adam contributes land with a basis and value of $60,000 in exchange for a 40% share of the profits and losses of the calendar year ABC LLC. In 2020, ABC generates $200,000 of ordinary taxable income and distributes cash of $5,000 to Adam. Adam is taxed on his $80,000 allocable share of income. He is not separately taxed on the $5,000 distribution.

The same result would arise if ABC reported a loss: 40% of the loss would be allocated to Adam, and he would deduct the loss, subject to the loss limitation rules discussed later.

Conceptual Framework for Partnership Taxation

The unique tax treatment of partners and partnerships can be traced to two legal concepts: the **aggregate (or conduit) concept** and the **entity concept**.

Aggregate (or Conduit) Concept   The aggregate concept treats the partnership as a channel through which income, credits, deductions, and other items flow to the

Just a platform

Total is reported and we use it to funnel it to the k-1's

---

[5] § 701.
[6] § 702.

[7] However, as discussed in text Section 21-3, the partnership may be required to pay employment taxes for its employees (not partners), interest under various "lookback rules" (e.g., for the percentage of completion method of accounting), or certain U.S. state franchise taxes or fees.

partners. The partnership is regarded as a collection of taxpayers joined in an agency relationship. For example, the income tax is imposed on the partners rather than the partnership.

Entity Concept The entity concept treats partners and partnerships as separate units and gives the partnership its own tax "personality." For example, the partnership must file an information return that summarizes its activities for the tax year.

It has it's own merit, own makes elections decisions it abides by.

Combined Concepts The "aggregate" concept governs most of the "general rules" for partnerships; the "entity" concept governs many of the exceptions to those general rules. Some rules are governed by both aggregate and entity concepts.

Inside and Outside Bases

Skip

The partnership basis rules are the key reason single taxation of partnership income is possible. A partnership has an <mark>inside basis</mark> for each asset it owns, and each partner has an <mark>outside basis</mark> in the partnership interest. In general, the partnership basis rules—an aggregate concept—ensure that the partnership's total inside basis in all assets equals the sum of the outside basis of all partners' partnership interests. In this chapter, you can assume that inside basis equals outside basis unless noted otherwise.

When income or gain flows through to a partner from the partnership, the partner's outside basis in the partnership interest is increased. When a deduction or loss flows through to a partner, the outside basis is reduced. These adjustments ensure that partnership items are taxed only once.

EXAMPLE 3

In Example 2, Adam's outside basis in the LLC interest is $60,000 after his contribution of land in exchange for the LLC interest. The LLC's inside basis in the land is also $60,000. When Adam reports his $80,000 share of the LLC's income, his outside basis is increased to $140,000.

If Adam sold his interest at the beginning of 2021 for its presumed value of $140,000, he would have no gain or loss. If, instead, there were no adjustments to basis, Adam's outside basis would be only $60,000, and he would be taxed on an $80,000 gain in addition to paying tax on his $80,000 share of ABC's income. Without the basis adjustment, the LLC's income would be subject to double taxation.

Partners' Ownership and Allocation of Partnership Items

Another "aggregate" concept is that each partner typically owns both a <mark>capital interest</mark> and a <mark>profits (loss) interest</mark> in the partnership. A capital interest is measured by a partner's <mark>capital sharing ratio</mark>, which is the partner's percentage ownership of the capital of the partnership. Generally, this is the share of capital the partner would receive if the entity was liquidated.

A profits (loss) interest is simply the partner's share of the partnership's current operating results. <mark>Profit and loss sharing ratios</mark> are usually specified in the partnership agreement and are used to determine each partner's allocation of the partnership's ordinary taxable income and loss items.[8]

A key advantage of partnerships is that these ratios and allocations can differ for a given partner, provided the <mark>capital account maintenance</mark> rules discussed later in the chapter are followed. These rules generally work to ensure that everything evens out over time—at the latest, by the time the partnership liquidates.

Later in the chapter, we will also discuss <mark>separately stated items</mark> (items that could differently affect two partners' tax situations) and <mark>special allocations</mark> (items that the partnership does not allocate using profit or loss interests).

---

[8]§ 704(a).

In Example 2, Adam contributed $60,000 of property in exchange for a 40% share of ABC LLC's profits. Assume that the other LLC members, Beth and Carl, only contributed capital of $20,000 each for their 30% share of profits, for a total of $100,000 of contributed capital. When the partnership is formed, Adam's capital sharing ratio is 60%, because he would be entitled to 60% of the partnership's $100,000 of capital if the partnership was liquidated immediately.

Adam's profit sharing ratio is 40% in Example 2. In addition, the LLC's operating agreement could easily allocate 30% of losses to Adam and provide a special allocation of 100% of depreciation deductions to him.

Because of the capital account maintenance rules, by the time the partnership liquidates, Adam will receive the capital he deserves. Each year, his capital sharing ratio will be adjusted to reflect his percentage ownership.

Determine the tax effects (and special rules) when forming a partnership with cash and property contributions.

21-2 FORMATION OF A PARTNERSHIP: TAX EFFECTS

When a partnership is formed, the partners contribute cash and other property in exchange for the partnership interest. This transaction has implications for both the partners and the partnership. Are any gains or losses recognized? What is the basis for each property and the basis of each partnership interest? How does the partnership recover (depreciate, deduct, amortize) the basis of contributed property? What issues must the partnership address in its initial year?

21-2a Contributions to the Partnership

Congress intended the partnership formation transaction to be tax-neutral so partnerships can be formed without (generally) prohibitive tax consequences.

Gain or Loss Recognition

As a general rule, neither the partner nor the partnership recognizes any realized gain or loss arising on contribution of property to a partnership. This applies upon formation of the entity or if the contribution occurs at some later date. The realized gain or loss is deferred, rather than forgiven.[9]

Alicia transfers assets to the Wren LLC on the day the entity is created, in exchange for a 60% profit and loss interest worth $60,000. She contributes cash of $40,000 and retail display fixtures (basis to her as a sole proprietor, $8,000; fair market value, $20,000). Alicia *realizes* a $12,000 gain [$60,000 fair market value of LLC interest − $48,000 basis ($40,000 cash + $8,000 basis in fixtures)].

Alicia *does not recognize* the $12,000 realized gain in the year of contribution. She received only a nonliquid LLC interest; she received no cash with which to pay any resulting tax liability.

Similarly, if Alicia's basis had been $25,000 in the contributed assets, § 721 would have disallowed the $5,000 realized loss [$60,000 − ($40,000 + $25,000)].

Basis Issues

When a partner makes a tax-deferred contribution of an asset to the capital of a partnership, any potential gain or loss recognition is merely postponed, instead of being permanently excluded.[10]

---

[9]§ 721.

[10]§ 723.

Partnership's Basis in Assets The partnership takes a *carryover basis* in the contributed assets it receives. This means that the partner's basis in the asset carries over to become the partnership's inside basis in the asset.

Partner's Basis in the Partnership Interest The partner takes a *substituted basis* in the partnership interest. This means that the partner's basis in the contributed assets transfers over to become the partner's outside basis in the partnership interest.

Holding Period

Partnership's Holding Period in Assets The partnership's holding period for the contributed assets includes the period during which the partner owned the asset.

Partner's Holding Period in the Partnership Interest The partner's holding period in the partnership interest depends on the type of contributed assets. To the extent a partner contributes capital and § 1231 assets, the partner's holding period in the partnership interest is the same as that partner's holding period for these assets. To the extent the partner contributes cash or noncapital/§ 1231 assets, the holding period in the partnership interest begins on the date the partnership interest is acquired.

> **EXAMPLE 6**
>
> Luis transfers a capital asset in exchange for a one-third interest in JKL LLC. The asset has an adjusted basis to Luis of $10,000 and a fair market value of $30,000. Luis has a $20,000 realized gain on the exchange ($30,000 − $10,000), but under § 721, he does not recognize any of the gain.
>
> Luis's outside basis for his LLC interest is a substituted basis of $10,000. This rule ensures that Luis's $20,000 deferred gain would be recognized on a subsequent sale at its $30,000 fair market value. Because Luis contributed a capital asset, his holding period "tacks" and becomes his holding period for the partnership interest.
>
> The LLC's inside basis for the contributed property is a carryover basis of $10,000. This basis ensures that Luis's $20,000 deferred gain would be recognized if the LLC sold the property for its $30,000 fair market value. Luis's holding period for the capital asset becomes the partnership's holding period for the asset.
>
> Note that if Luis had contributed cash for the interest, both his and the partnership's holding periods would begin on the date the cash was contributed.

21-2b Exceptions to the General Rule of § 721

In certain situations, the nonrecognition provisions do not apply. The most widely applicable situations are when:

- Appreciated stocks and securities are contributed to an investment partnership.
- The transaction is essentially a disguised sale or exchange of properties.
- The partnership interest is received in exchange for services rendered to the partnership by the partner.

Investment Partnership

If the transfer consists of appreciated stocks and securities and the partnership is an investment partnership, it is possible that the contributing partner will recognize the inherent realized gain at the time of the contribution.[11] This rule prevents investors from using the partnership form to diversify their investment portfolios on a tax-free basis.

---

[11]§ 721(b).

Disguised Sale or Exchange

If a transaction appears to be a sale or exchange of property rather than a contribution, it is deemed a disguised sale and § 721 cannot be used to defer a gain or loss. For example, if a partner contributes appreciated property to a partnership and soon thereafter receives a distribution of cash or other property from the partnership, the distribution could be viewed as a payment to purchase the contributed property.[12]

EXAMPLE 7

Kim's basis in her KLM partnership interest was $50,000. She transfers to the partnership a property with an adjusted basis of $20,000 (and a fair market value of $50,000), resulting in a basis of $70,000 in her partnership interest. Two weeks later, the partnership distributes $25,000 of cash to Kim (this is one-half of the value of the property Kim contributed). Under the general rule, the distribution would not be taxable to Kim but instead reduces her basis in the partnership interest to $45,000 ($70,000 basis − $25,000 cash distribution). However, the transaction appears to be a disguised purchase-sale transaction. Therefore, Kim must recognize gain of $15,000 on transfer of the property, and the partnership is deemed to have purchased the property for $25,000.

The partnership's basis in the property becomes $35,000 ($10,000 basis in 50% portion that is "contributed" property + $25,000 amount deemed paid for 50% portion that is "purchased" property).

Extensive Regulations outline situations in which the IRS may presume that a disguised sale has occurred. For example, a disguised sale is presumed to exist if both of the following occur.

- A contractual agreement requires a contribution by one partner to be followed within two years by a specified distribution from the partnership.

- The distribution is to be made without regard to partnership profits. In other words, the forthcoming distribution is not subject to significant "entrepreneurial risk."

If the distribution occurs more than two years after the property contribution, or if it is deemed "reasonable" in relation to the partner's invested capital, the distribution is *not* presumed to be a disguised sale.

Services

A partner may receive an interest in partnership capital or profits in exchange for services rendered to the partnership. In certain circumstances, special rules will apply.

Capital Interest Received in Exchange for Services When a partner receives a fully vested interest in partnership capital (i.e., unrestricted liquidation rights) in exchange for services, the value of the interest is generally taxable to the partner as ordinary compensation income. Services are not treated as "property" that can be transferred to a partnership on a tax-free basis. Generally, the partner's ordinary income equals the amount the partner would receive if the partnership was liquidated immediately following the contribution of services, less any amount the partner paid for the interest.[13]

The partnership may deduct any amount included in the service partner's income if the services are of a deductible nature.[14] Otherwise, they must be capitalized. Any deduction related to the service partners' interest is generally allocated to the other partners in the partnership.

---

[12]§ 707(a)(2)(B) and related Regulations and Proposed Regulations.

[13]§ 83(a); for treatment when there is a "substantial risk of forfeiture," also see Reg. § 1.83–3, Prop.Reg. § 1.83–3, and Notice 2005–43, 2005–1 C.B. 1221.

[14]§ 83(h).

Profits Interest Received in Exchange for Services Transfer of a partnership *profits* interest in exchange for services is generally taxed to the recipient partner as the profits are earned. The amount of the partnership's future profits cannot typically be determined, so there is no current value to the interest.[15]

If the future profits interest is classified as a <mark>carried interest</mark>, special rules apply. The effect of these rules is that, for certain types of interests received in exchange for services, future capital gain allocations can be recharacterized as ordinary income to the partner. The details of carried interests are beyond the scope of this chapter, but you should note that a carried interest does not arise to the extent the partner "pays" a fair value for a capital interest, either with contributed cash or other assets or through income recognition under § 83.

Dave receives his one-third capital and profits interest in BCD LLC (valued at $20,000) as compensation for tax planning services he provided before the LLC was formed.

Dave recognizes $20,000 of compensation income, and he takes a $20,000 basis in his LLC interest. The interest is not a carried interest because Dave "pays" for the capital interest by recognizing the value as compensation income.

The same result would occur if the LLC had paid Dave $20,000 for his services and he immediately contributed that amount to the entity for a one-third ownership interest. The LLC will probably treat the $20,000 as an organizational or startup cost, and amortization of that amount would be allocated to Bill and Carlos. Organizational and startup costs are discussed later in the chapter.

21-2c Other Issues Related to Contributed Property

When property is contributed to a partnership, other issues arise, including cost recovery, allocations related to the property, and subsequent dispositions of the property.

Depreciation Method and Period

If a partner contributes depreciable property, the partnership generally "steps into the shoes" of the contributing parter and continues to use the depreciation schedule and calculations the partner used.[16] The partnership may not claim a § 179 deduction with respect to contributed property.

Amortization of Intangible Assets

Similarly, if a partner contributes an existing intangible asset to the partnership, the partnership generally will "step into the shoes" of the partner in determining future amortization deductions. Section 197 intangible assets are amortized over 15 years and include purchased goodwill, going-concern value, information systems, customer- or supplier-related intangible assets, patents, licenses obtained from a governmental unit, franchises, trademarks, covenants not to compete, and other items. Other intangible assets (i.e., not addressed in § 197) are amortized over their useful life, if any.[17]

On January 1 of the current year, Jan contributed the assets of a sole proprietorship in exchange for a 50% interest in the JK LLC. One of the assets was a commercial property (depreciable over 39 years) that had been purchased seven years ago. For that property, JK will claim the year 8 depreciation and continue with the remainder of Jan's 39-year schedule.

A second property was a § 197 intangible asset that Jan had acquired three years earlier. That property was being amortized over 15 years. Again, JK will continue Jan's amortization schedule for years 4 to 15.

---

[15]For situations in which the future interest might be taxable, see Rev.Proc. 93–27, 1993–2 C.B. 343, as clarified by Rev.Proc. 2001–43, 2001–2 C.B. 191.

[16]§ 168(i)(7).

[17]Reg. § 1.167(a)–3.

Character of Gain or Loss on Disposition of Receivables, Inventory, and Built-In Loss Properties

When a partner contributes certain types of property to a partnership, the aggregate theory comes into play if the partnership later sells it. In three situations, the character of the partnership's gain or loss is not necessarily what you would expect.[18]

Ordinary Income Property If the partner contributes either of the following types of property, the partnership's later sale of the property results in ordinary income:

- Accounts receivable where the contributing partner has not yet recognized the related income (e.g., cash basis accounts receivable).
- Inventory (in the contributing partner's hands) that would have resulted in ordinary income if the partner had sold it, *if* the partnership sells the inventory *within five years of the contribution date.*

Capital Loss Property Similarly, if the partner contributes property with a "built-in" capital loss at the contribution date, the partnership's later sale of that property *within five years of the contribution date* results in a capital loss. The capital loss is limited to the "built-in" loss at the contribution date.

EXAMPLE 10

Deon contributed accounts receivable, inventory, and land to DR LLC as follows:

	Adjusted Basis	Fair Market Value
Receivables	$ –0–	$20,000
Inventory	25,000	50,000
Land (investment property to Deon)	12,000	9,000

Soon after formation, DR collects $20,000 cash for the receivables and sells the inventory for $50,000 cash. The LLC recognizes ordinary income of $20,000 for the receivables and $25,000 for the inventory, even if the property is not an ordinary trade receivable or inventory in the LLC's hands.

DR uses the land as a parking lot for a year (§ 1231 property) and then sells it for $7,000. The LLC's loss on the land is $5,000 ($7,000 selling price − $12,000 adjusted basis). DR classifies the $3,000 precontribution loss ($9,000 − $12,000) as a capital loss because it would have been a capital loss to Deon. The remaining $2,000 loss ($7,000 − $9,000) is a § 1231 loss based on DR's use of the land.

Allocations Related to Contributed Property

As discussed later in the chapter, special allocations must be made relative to contributed property that is appreciated or depreciated. The partnership's income and losses must be allocated to ensure that the inherent gain or loss is not shifted away from the contributing partner. So, in Example 10, the precontribution portion of the income, gains, and losses would be allocated to Deon.

The Big Picture

EXAMPLE 11

Return to the facts of *The Big Picture* on p. 21-1. Assume that Kyle's $2,000,000 of contributed real estate consists of land with a $600,000 basis and a fully depreciated building and fixtures ($0 basis). Maria has fully depreciated the $500,000 of bakery equipment and café furnishings that she contributed and so has a $0 basis in those assets.

When Beachside Properties LLC is formed, no tax arises for the LLC or for Kyle or Maria. Kyle does not recognize his $1,400,000 realized gain, nor does Maria recognize her $500,000 realized gain.

continued

---

[18]§ 724.

Kyle takes a substituted basis of $600,000 for his interest, and Maria takes a substituted basis of $1,500,000 ($1,500,000 of contributed cash + $0 basis in contributed property). Beachside Properties assumes a carryover basis of $600,000 for the real estate contributed by Kyle and $0 for the property contributed by Maria. If there had been a remaining depreciable basis for any of the contributed property, the LLC would have "stepped into the member's shoes" in calculating depreciation deductions. Any future income related to the precontribution gains will be allocated to the contributing member.

When Josh vests in his 5% *capital interest* in the LLC, the $200,000 value of the interest is taxable to him because he received it in exchange for services. Beachside Properties will capitalize this amount and allocate it to the building expansion and new fixtures. Josh's 20% interest in the *future profits* of the LLC will be taxed to him as profits are earned by the LLC.[19]

Concept Summary 21.2 reviews the rules that apply to partnership asset contributions and basis adjustments.

Concept Summary 21.2

Partnership Formation and Initial Basis Computations

1. Under the general rule of § 721, partners or partnerships do not recognize gain or loss when property is contributed in exchange for capital interests.

2. Partners take a substituted basis in their partnership interest (*outside basis*) equal to the basis of the property contributed to the partnership.

3. The partnership takes a carryover basis in assets received (*inside basis*) equal to the partner's basis in those assets.

4. The partner's holding period in the partnership interest begins when the interest is acquired (for cash or "other" property contributions) and/or on the date the contributed property was acquired (for contributions of capital or § 1231 property).

5. The partnership's holding period for contributed property includes the contributing partner's holding period.

6. The partnership "steps into the partner's shoes" in calculating depreciation and amortization of contributed property.

7. Rules prevent the recharacterization of ordinary income as capital gains for inventory and accounts receivable and prevent conversion of capital losses to ordinary losses.

8. The general rule of § 721 does not apply to partnership interests received upon formation of certain investment partnerships, as a disguised sale or exchange, or as a fully vested capital interest received in exchange for services.

 Start

21-2d Tax Accounting Elections

A newly formed partnership must make numerous tax accounting elections stating how certain transactions or tax attributes should be handled. In general, these elections must be made by the partnership rather than by the partners individually.[20] For example, as discussed later in the chapter, the partnership selects its taxable year and accounting method and elects the treatment of organizational and startup expenditures.

The partnership, rather than the partners, makes other elections and calculations under general tax accounting rules, including:

- Cost recovery methods and assumptions. Depreciation
- Section 179 deductions for certain tangible personal property. *If you meet certain criteria, you don't have to write it off acc. to IRS Depr. rules rather you can write the whole thing off.*
- Inventory method. *FIFO or LIFO*
- Calculation of the partnership's allowable business interest expense deduction.

---

[19]While beyond the scope of the text, note that the 15% difference between the "paid for" capital interest and the future services interest might be considered a "carried interest." As such, a portion of future capital gains allocated to Josh from the LLC might be recharacterized as ordinary income under the rules of § 1061.

[20]§ 703(b).

LO.4

Identify elections available to a partnership and specify the tax treatment of expenditures of a newly formed partnership.

- Calculation of all partnership tax credits except foreign tax credit.
- Cost or percentage depletion method, excluding oil and gas wells.
- Amounts and treatment of research and experimental expenditures.

Each partner is bound by the decisions made by the partnership relative to these items. If the partnership fails to make an election, a partner cannot make the election individually.

There are three rather narrow exceptions to this general rule. Each *partner* is separately required to make a specific election for the following tax issues:

- Whether to reduce the basis of depreciable property when first excluding income from discharge of indebtedness.
- Whether to claim cost or percentage depletion for oil and gas wells.
- Whether to take a deduction or credit for taxes paid to non-U.S. jurisdictions.

21-2e Initial Costs of a Partnership

In its initial stages, a partnership incurs expenses related to some or all of the following activities: forming the partnership (organizational costs), starting business operations (startup costs), admitting partners to the partnership, marketing and selling partnership units to prospective partners (syndication costs), and acquiring assets.

Organizational and Startup Costs

A partnership's organizational costs and startup costs parallel the rules illustrated in text Section 17-1k for corporations. Refer to Examples 22 to 24. Each type of cost is considered separately, so for each category, a partnership can deduct up to $5,000 immediately (subject to phaseout) with the excess amortized over 180 months, beginning with the month in which the partnership begins business.[21] This treatment is elected simply by deducting the proper amounts on the tax return.[22]

Syndication Costs

==Syndication costs== are capitalized, but no amortization election is available.[23] Syndication costs include expenditures incurred for promoting and marketing partnership interests such as brokerage fees, registration fees, certain legal fees, accounting fees related to the offering materials, and printing costs of the prospectus and other selling materials. As with organizational and startup costs, this parallels the corporate tax treatment of stock marketing, issuance, and brokerage costs.

Contra Equity

It's not an expense directly related to bring in rev. so it isn't an expense and isn't deductible. It's money spent to bring in partners. It's an Equity transaction.

Acquisition Costs of Depreciable Assets

As mentioned earlier, the partnership typically determines its depreciation deductions by "stepping into the shoes" of the contributing partner. If additional costs are incurred, though, the additional basis is treated as a new MACRS asset, placed in service on the date the partnership places the asset in service. For example, legal fees and transfer taxes incurred in transferring assets to a partnership must be capitalized. Cost recovery for these amounts commences when the partnership places the underlying property in service (not when the partner originally placed the asset in service).

LO.5

Specify the accounting methods and taxable years available to a partnership.

21-2f Method of Accounting

A newly formed partnership may adopt either the cash or accrual method of accounting or a hybrid of these two methods.

If a partnership uses the accrual method of accounting, its income must be reported no later than the date that income would be reported on the partnership's "applicable

---

[21]§§ 709(b) and 195(b)(1).
[22]Reg. §§ 1.709–1 and 1.195–1.

[23]§ 709(a).

financial statement" (e.g., an audited financial statement) or other similar financial statement.[24] This rule is designed to ensure that any advance payments (i.e., cash receipts) received by the taxpayer are reported in taxable income at least as quickly as they are reported in book income.

Two exceptions limit use of the cash method of accounting by partnerships.[25] The cash method may *not* be adopted by a partnership that: *[handwritten: They have to File an Accrual tax return]*

- Has one or more C corporation partners or
- Is a tax shelter.

As an "exception to the exception," a nontax shelter partnership with a C corporation partner may still elect to use the cash method if:

- The partnership meets the $26 million gross receipts test described below; *[handwritten: take 3 years of receipts and if the average is less than 26 million]*
- The C corporation partner(s) is a qualified personal service corporation, such as an incorporated attorney; or
- The partnership is engaged in the business of farming.

A partnership meets the $26 million gross receipts test if it has not received average annual gross receipts of more than $26 million for 2020. "Average annual gross receipts" is the average of gross receipts for the three tax years (or the number of prior years the partnership has been in existence, if fewer) ending with the tax period *prior to* the tax year in question. If the gross receipts test is not met, the partnership must change to the accrual method the next tax year. *[handwritten: created a limited partnership]*

A tax shelter is a partnership whose interests have been sold in a registered offering, a partnership in which more than 35 percent of the losses during the taxable year are allocated to limited partners, or a partnership with a significant purpose to avoid or evade Federal income tax.

[handwritten: got til here]

21-2g Taxable Year of the Partnership

Partnership taxable income (and any separately stated items) flows through to each partner at the end of the *partnership's* taxable year. A *partner's* taxable income, then, includes the distributive share of partnership income for any *partnership* taxable year that ends during the partner's tax year. A partnership must use either the ==required taxable year== or one of three alternate taxable years, as shown in Exhibit 21.1.

Deferral of Partnership Income

The required taxable year rules prevent excess deferral of tax on the partnership's income. How might deferral arise?

Suppose Partners A, B, and C use a calendar year. What if their partnership, ABC, could use a February 28 fiscal year-end? ABC's income through February 2020 (including income earned since March 2019) would not be taxed to Partners A, B, and C until December 31, 2020. This would allow taxation of ABC's income to be deferred 10 months.

Instead of this result, you'll see that the permitted year-end rules result in partnership income being taxed sooner rather than later. In our example, Partnership ABC would be required to use a calendar year or certain alternative permitted years.

Required Taxable Year

The partnership's required taxable year is determined under the first of three rules that applies.[26] The rules are evaluated in order. First, the partnership uses the tax year of the "majority partners" if partners owning more than 50 percent of partnership capital and profits have the same tax year.

---

[24]§§ 451(a) and (b).

[25]§ 448. For tax years beginning before 2018, a $5 million average annual gross receipts test applied. Consequently, a partnership might have been required to use the accrual method in prior years before being permitted

to change to the cash method in 2018. The $26 million threshold is indexed for inflation; it was $25 million for 2018.

[26]§ 706(b).

EXHIBIT 21.1	Permitted Taxable Years of Partnerships

Required Taxable Year

In Order, Partnership Must Use	Requirements
Majority partners' tax year	• More than 50% of capital *and* profits is owned by partners who have the same taxable year.
Principal partners' tax year	• All partners who own 5% or more of capital *or* profits are principal partners.
	• All principal partners must have the same tax year.
Year with smallest amount of income deferred	• "Least aggregate deferral rule" per IRS regulations.

Alternative Tax Years

Business purpose year	• Use an IRS-approved year-end for which there is a business purpose.
Three-month deferral year	• Use a year-end with not more than a 3-month deferral of income, compared to the required tax year, and pay an interest deposit on the deferred tax.
52–53 week fiscal year	• Use a year ending on a specific day of the week rather than the last day of a month.

If there are no "majority partners" (e.g., if there are two 50 percent partners with different tax years), we go to the second rule. Under this rule, the partnership uses the tax year of the "principal partners" if all partners who own 5 percent or more of capital or profits have the same tax year.

If no year-end can be determined under the first two rules, the partnership determines a year under the <mark>least aggregate deferral rule</mark> as outlined in the Regulations for § 706.

Alternative Tax Years

If the required tax year is undesirable to the entity, three alternative tax years may be available. (1) The taxpayer can establish a business purpose for a different taxable year.[27] (2) The taxpayer can elect a year-end with not more than a three-month deferral of income, relative to the required taxable year, under § 444. (3) The taxpayer can use a 52-53 week taxable year.[28] Details of these rules are beyond the scope of the text.

EXAMPLE 12

Crimson, Inc., and Indigo, Inc. (both are C corporations), are equal partners in the CI Partnership. Crimson uses the calendar year, and Indigo uses a fiscal year ending August 31. Neither Crimson nor Indigo is a majority partner as neither owns more than 50%. Although Crimson and Indigo are both principal partners (i.e., each owns at least 5%), they do not have the same tax year. Therefore, the general rules indicate that the partnership's required tax year must be determined by the "least aggregate deferral rule."

Assume the least aggregate deferral rule yields a required taxable year of August 31. In 2020, CI closes its books and files a Form 1065 as of August 31. Indigo reports its share of CI's income (from the Schedule K–1 received from CI) in its tax return for the year ending August 31, 2020. Crimson reports its share of CI's income in its 2020 calendar year return.

If August 31 is not a desirable year-end, CI can use a 52- to 53-week year ending around August 31; establish a business purpose tax year; or select May, June, or July as the taxable year under § 444.

---

[27]Rev.Proc. 2006–46, 2006–2 C.B. 859, § 5.07.   [28]§ 441(f).

21-3 PARTNERSHIP OPERATIONS AND REPORTING

LO.6

Calculate a partnership's taxable income and separately stated items and describe how the partnership's income is reported on Form 1065.

As a business entity, a partnership is just like any other enterprise. It produces and sells products and/or services, it owns property and pays employees, and it distributes profits to owners or holds those profits for reinvestment in the company. For income tax purposes, a partnership is a tax-reporting, rather than a taxpaying, entity.

21-3a Partnership Reporting, In General

The partnership prepares Form 1065 to report information from its operations. The partners receive a Schedule K–1 for use in preparing their returns.

Partnership Reporting and Form 1065

The partnership's Form 1065 organizes and reports the transactions of the entity for the tax year. Form 1065 is included in Appendix B, and all tax forms can be downloaded at **irs.gov**. Find a copy of Form 1065 and follow along. Form 1065 consists of five pages, and is organized as follows.

- Page 1 summarizes the partnership's ordinary income and loss from trade or business activities. Cost of goods sold (line 2) is calculated on Form 1125–A and carried to this page.[29]

- Pages 2 and 3 provide information about the partnership's activities and general information about the partners.

- Page 4 (Schedule K) summarizes the partnership's ordinary income or loss, separately stated items, and other information the partners need to prepare their returns. Schedule K, line 1, shows the ordinary income/loss from page 1.

- Page 5 provides several schedules, including a balance sheet (Schedule L), a reconciliation of book and "taxable" income (Schedule M–1), and a reconciliation of partners' beginning and ending capital (Schedule M–2).

Form 1065 is due by the fifteenth day of the third month following the end of the tax year. For a calendar year partnership, this deadline is March 15. The partnership may request (by the original due date) an automatic six-month extension of time for filing (to September 15 for a calendar year partnership). Note that these due dates are one month earlier than the due date and extended deadline for individual taxpayers.

Partner Reporting and Schedule K–1

Almost any type of entity can be a partner: individuals, corporations, trusts, estates, or another partnership, for example. Consequently, the partnership's income, deductions, credits, and alternative minimum tax (AMT) preferences and adjustments can ultimately be reported and taxed on any of a number of income tax returns [e.g., Forms 1040 (individuals), 1041 (fiduciaries, see Chapter 28), 1120 (C corporations), and 1120S (S corporations)].

These partners must be informed of their shares of partnership income, expenses, gains, losses, and other information they must report. Therefore, the partnership prepares a Schedule K–1 for each partner; one copy is filed with the Form 1065, and another copy is provided to the respective partner. Schedule K–1 is discussed in more detail in text Section 21-4.

---

[29]A "Tax and Payment" section is completed in unusual situations where the partnership is required to pay interest related to certain permitted tax deferral situations (e.g., where the taxpayer uses the percentage of completion method of accounting and must pay interest under the lookback rule).

Other Partnership Taxes

A partnership is subject to all taxes (other than income taxes) in the same manner as any other business. Thus, the partnership files returns and pays the outstanding amount of appropriate sales taxes and property taxes. For employees (not partners), the partnership files returns and pays Social Security, unemployment, and other payroll taxes. In some states, franchise taxes are assessed based on partnership net income or gross receipts, or capital or asset values.

21-3b Measuring Partnership Income

A partnership measures and reports two kinds of income: ordinary business income (Form 1065, page 1, shown on p. 21-19) and separately stated items (Form 1065, Schedule K, shown on p. 21-20).

Ordinary Business Income

A partnership's ordinary business income consists of any income or expenses that are not required to be separately stated. For example, the partnership's sales revenues, utilities, rent expense, and depreciation expense related to business assets are reported on Form 1065, page 1. As mentioned earlier, the partnership makes elections related to inventory, depreciation, research and experimentation expenses, and similar business-related amounts, so it makes sense that the partners don't need separate information about these calculations. The partnership also calculates and claims the allowable business interest expense deduction, but any disallowed interest expense is treated as a separately stated item, as discussed later.

Separately Stated Items

A separately stated item is any item with tax attributes that *might* affect any two partner's tax liabilities in different ways.[30] For example, charitable contributions are separately stated because partners need to compute their own deductions for charitable contributions. Other income and deduction items passed through separately include the following:

- Net short- and long-term capital gains or losses. (Note that the partnership reports both a net long-term and a net short-term gain or loss. The final short- and/or long-term netting is done at the partner level.)
- Section 1231 gains and losses.
- Portfolio income items (qualified and ordinary dividends, interest, and royalties).
- Expenses related to portfolio income.
- Disallowed business interest expense and related information.
- Immediately expensed tangible personal property (§ 179).
- Guaranteed payments, discussed later in this section.
- Passive activity items such as rental real estate income or loss.
- Intangible drilling and development costs.
- General business tax credits (the partnership calculates the credit and allocates the credit to the partners so they can apply their limitations).
- Taxes paid to non-U.S. countries and to U.S. possessions (the partners calculate this credit and determine any limitations).[31]

The reason for separately reporting the preceding items is rooted in the aggregate or conduit concept. These items affect various exclusions, deductions, and credits at the partner level and must pass through without loss of identity so that the proper tax for each partner may be determined.[32]

[30]§ 703(a)(1).
[31]§ 702(a).
[32]§ 702(b).

A partnership is not allowed to claim the following deductions:

- Net operating losses (NOLs).
- Depletion of oil and gas interests.
- Dividends received deduction.

Deductions taken by individuals, such as standard deductions, are not available to the partnership. If a partnership makes a payment on behalf of a partner, such as for alimony, medical expenses, or items that might constitute deductions to individuals, the partnership treats the payment as a distribution or guaranteed payment to the partner, and the partner then determines whether any deduction is permitted.

The Big Picture

EXAMPLE 13

Return to the facts of *The Big Picture* on p. 21-1. In its second year of operations, Beachside Properties LLC reports income and expenses from operating the café; rent income and expenses from leasing the other buildings; and contributions, distributions, and other information as follows.

Sales revenue	$2,000,000
Cost of sales	800,000
W–2 wages paid to employees	500,000
Cost recovery deductions (related to the Beachsider café business only)	91,984
Utilities, supplies, and other expenses	128,016
Taxes and licenses (including payroll taxes)	60,000
Guaranteed payments to LLC members	240,000
Charitable contributions	6,000
Short-term capital gain	12,000
Net income from rental real estate (net of all expenses, including $26,153 of depreciation on rental property)	300,000
Qualified dividends received	4,000
Tax-exempt income (bond interest)	2,100
Alternative minimum tax (AMT) adjustment (cost recovery)	18,224
Payment of medical expenses on behalf of Kyle *(distribution)*	4,000
Contribution of additional cash from Maria	110,000
Contribution of other property from Maria (basis $0)	50,000
Distribution of cash to Maria	30,000

Beachside will determine its ordinary income or loss for the year, along with its separately stated items. As discussed next, the guaranteed payments are either deducted or capitalized by the LLC; they are reported as ordinary income by the member who receives them. Beachside also reports any additional information the members might need to prepare their individual income tax returns.

The LLC cannot deduct the payment for Kyle's medical expenses. This payment is probably handled as a distribution to Kyle, who may report it as a medical expense on his Schedule A in determining his itemized deductions. Similarly, the LLC cannot deduct the distribution to Maria (distributions are discussed later in this chapter). The AMT adjustment is not a separate component of the LLC's income. However, it must be reported to Beachside's members so that they can properly calculate any AMT liability. Other information will also be passed through, including information for business interest deduction carryovers, qualified business income (the § 199A deduction), and self-employment and other taxes. These topics are discussed later.

Last year (the first year of operations), the LLC reported a $250,000 net loss from operations. Beachside could not deduct that loss; instead, it was passed through to the LLC members. Loss deduction limitations might have applied at the member level. These limitations are discussed later in the chapter.

Guaranteed Payments Paid by the Partnership

A <mark>guaranteed payment</mark> is a payment to a partner for services performed by the partner or for the use of the partner's capital. These payments resemble the salary or interest payments of other businesses.[33] The partnership either deducts or capitalizes the payment, depending on its nature. As discussed later, regardless of the partnership's treatment, the partner reports the payment as ordinary income.

Guaranteed payments are usually expressed as a fixed-dollar amount or as a percentage of capital the partner has invested in the partnership. By definition, a guaranteed payment cannot be calculated based on partnership income (e.g., as a percentage of annual income).

The Big Picture

EXAMPLE 14

Return to the facts of *The Big Picture* as revised in Example 13. Assume that Josh was elected as managing member of Beachside Properties LLC; he has the sole authority to contract for the LLC and works 1,000 hours per year in the business. Maria works 1,000 hours per year in the café. After transferring his land to Beachside, Kyle has generally not been involved in the LLC's operations. In addition, recall that the LLC uses capital contributed by Maria and Kyle ($2,000,000 each in year 1).

Josh and Maria both receive guaranteed payments of $5,000 per month for services to the LLC. In addition, Maria and Kyle both receive guaranteed payments of $5,000 per month for the LLC's use of their capital. The guaranteed payments total $240,000 for the year (12 months × $5,000 × 4 payments). Beachside may deduct these payments.

Deductible guaranteed payments, like other deductible expenses of a partnership, can create an ordinary loss for the entity.[34]

Partnership Interest Expense

A partnership's interest expense also is subject to special reporting rules: it must be allocated among the partnership's various activities, generally based on how and why the underlying debt arose. For example, some interest expense might relate to funds borrowed for investment purposes. In that case, it is classified as investment interest expense and must be separately stated on Schedule K, line 13b.

Special rules apply to business interest expense, as discussed in text Section 17-1f. For a partnership (or an S corporation), in the year the interest expense arises, the entity determines the amount that can be deducted.[35] If the entity is defined as a small business or if it is an electing business in certain fields (e.g., real estate or farming), the business interest expense limitation does not apply. For other businesses, the 30 percent limitation described in Chapter 17 applies. The entity deduction is an ordinary business deduction (i.e., not a separately stated item), and so would be deducted on page 1 of the partnership or S corporation return.

Any disallowed business interest expense is passed through to the partners (reducing their basis in the partnership interest) and can be used to offset the partnership's "excess taxable income" in future years.

21-3c **Form 1065 Example**

Let's look at an example. Pages 1, 4, and 5 of the Beachside Form 1065 for its second tax year are constructed on the following pages.

---

[33]§ 707(c).

[34]According to Rev.Rul. 2007–40, 2007–1 C.B. 1426, if the partnership distributes appreciated property to pay a guaranteed payment, the partnership recognizes any gain on the transfer.

[35]§ 163(j)(4).

Form **1065**	U.S. Return of Partnership Income	OMB No. 1545-0123

Department of the Treasury
Internal Revenue Service

For calendar year 2019, or tax year beginning _____, 2019, ending _____, 20 _____.

▶ Go to *www.irs.gov/Form1065* for instructions and the latest information.

2019

A Principal business activity *Restaurant/Commercial Rental*	Name of partnership *Beachside Properties LLC*	**D** Employer identification number *11-1111111*
B Principal product or service *Food service*	Number, street, and room or suite no. If a P.O. box, see instructions. *1600 Ocean Vista Way*	**E** Date business started *1/1/2018*
C Business code number *722110*	**Type or Print** City or town, state or province, country, and ZIP or foreign postal code *Surfside*	**F** Total assets (see instructions) *from schedule L* $ *3,218,100*

G Check applicable boxes: **(1)** ☐ Initial return   **(2)** ☐ Final return   **(3)** ☐ Name change   **(4)** ☐ Address change   **(5)** ☐ Amended return

H Check accounting method: **(1)** ☐ Cash   **(2)** ☒ Accrual   **(3)** ☐ Other (specify) ▶ _____

I Number of Schedules K-1. Attach one for each person who was a partner at any time during the tax year ▶ _____ *3*   *b/c 3 partners*

J Check if Schedules C and M-3 are attached   ▶ ☐

K Check if partnership: **(1)** ☐ Aggregated activities for section 465 at-risk purposes   **(2)** ☐ Grouped activities for section 469 passive activity purposes

Caution: Include **only** trade or business income and expenses on lines 1a through 22 below. See instructions for more information.

Income

1a	Gross receipts or sales	1a	2,000,000	
b	Returns and allowances	1b		
c	Balance. Subtract line 1b from line 1a		**1c**	2,000,000
2	Cost of goods sold (attach Form 1125-A)		**2**	800,000
3	Gross profit. Subtract line 2 from line 1c		**3**	1,200,000
4	Ordinary income (loss) from other partnerships, estates, and trusts (attach statement)		**4**	
5	Net farm profit (loss) (attach Schedule F (Form 1040 or 1040-SR))		**5**	
6	Net gain (loss) from Form 4797, Part II, line 17 (attach Form 4797)		**6**	
7	Other income (loss) (attach statement)		**7**	
8	**Total income (loss). Combine lines 3 through 7**		**8**	1,200,000

Deductions (see instructions for limitations)

9	Salaries and wages (other than to partners) (less employment credits)		**9**	500,000
10	Guaranteed payments to partners		**10**	240,000
11	Repairs and maintenance		**11**	
12	Bad debts		**12**	
13	Rent		**13**	
14	Taxes and licenses		**14**	60,000
15	Interest (see instructions)		**15**	
16a	Depreciation (if required, attach Form 4562)	16a	91,984	
b	Less depreciation reported on Form 1125-A and elsewhere on return	16b		**16c**	91,984
17	Depletion (**Do not deduct oil and gas depletion.**)		**17**	
18	Retirement plans, etc.		**18**	
19	Employee benefit programs		**19**	
20	Other deductions (attach statement)		**20**	128,016
21	**Total deductions.** Add the amounts shown in the far right column for lines 9 through 20		**21**	1,020,000
22	**Ordinary business income (loss).** Subtract line 21 from line 8		**22**	180,000

Tax and Payment

23	Interest due under the look-back method—completed long-term contracts (attach Form 8697)	**23**	
24	Interest due under the look-back method—income forecast method (attach Form 8866)	**24**	
25	BBA AAR imputed underpayment (see instructions)	**25**	
26	Other taxes (see instructions)	**26**	
27	**Total balance due.** Add lines 23 through 26	**27**	
28	Payment (see instructions)	**28**	
29	**Amount owed.** If line 28 is smaller than line 27, enter amount owed	**29**	
30	**Overpayment.** If line 28 is larger than line 27, enter overpayment	**30**	

Sign Here

Under penalties of perjury, I declare that I have examined this return, including accompanying schedules and statements, and to the best of my knowledge and belief, it is true, correct, and complete. Declaration of preparer (other than partner or limited liability company member) is based on all information of which preparer has any knowledge.

▶ _____ Signature of partner or limited liability company member   ▶ _____ Date

May the IRS discuss this return with the preparer shown below? See instructions. ☐ Yes ☐ No

Paid Preparer Use Only

Print/Type preparer's name	Preparer's signature	Date	Check ☐ if self-employed	PTIN
Firm's name ▶			Firm's EIN ▶	
Firm's address ▶			Phone no.	

For Paperwork Reduction Act Notice, see separate instructions.   Cat. No. 11390Z   Form **1065** (2019)

Form 1065 (2019) *Beachside Properties LLC*   *11-1111111*   Page **4**

Schedule K		Partners' Distributive Share Items			Total amount
Income (Loss)	**1**	Ordinary business income (loss) (page 1, line 22)		**1**	180,000
	2	Net rental real estate income (loss) (attach Form 8825)		**2**	300,000
	3a	Other gross rental income (loss)	**3a**		
	b	Expenses from other rental activities (attach statement)	**3b**		
	c	Other net rental income (loss). Subtract line 3b from line 3a		**3c**	0
	4	Guaranteed payments: **a** Services **4a** 120,000 **b** Capital **4b** 120,000			
		c Total. Add lines 4a and 4b		**4c**	240,000
	5	Interest income		**5**	
	6	Dividends and dividend equivalents: **a** Ordinary dividends		**6a**	4,000
		b Qualified dividends **6b** 4,000 **c** Dividend equivalents **6c**			
	7	Royalties		**7**	
	8	Net short-term capital gain (loss) (attach Schedule D (Form 1065))		**8**	12,000
	9a	Net long-term capital gain (loss) (attach Schedule D (Form 1065))		**9a**	
	b	Collectibles (28%) gain (loss)	**9b**		
	c	Unrecaptured section 1250 gain (attach statement)	**9c**		
	10	Net section 1231 gain (loss) (attach Form 4797)		**10**	
	11	Other income (loss) (see instructions) Type ▶		**11**	
Deductions	**12**	Section 179 deduction (attach Form 4562)		**12**	
	13a	Contributions		**13a**	6,000
	b	Investment interest expense		**13b**	
	c	Section 59(e)(2) expenditures: **(1)** Type ▶_____ **(2)** Amount ▶		**13c(2)**	
	d	Other deductions (see instructions) Type ▶		**13d**	
Self-Employ-ment	**14a**	Net earnings (loss) from self-employment		**14a**	150,000
	b	Gross farming or fishing income		**14b**	
	c	Gross nonfarm income		**14c**	720,000
Credits	**15a**	Low-income housing credit (section 42(j)(5))		**15a**	
	b	Low-income housing credit (other)		**15b**	
	c	Qualified rehabilitation expenditures (rental real estate) (attach Form 3468, if applicable) . .		**15c**	
	d	Other rental real estate credits (see instructions) Type ▶_____		**15d**	
	e	Other rental credits (see instructions) Type ▶_____		**15e**	
	f	Other credits (see instructions) Type ▶		**15f**	
Foreign Transactions	**16a**	Name of country or U.S. possession ▶_____			
	b	Gross income from all sources		**16b**	
	c	Gross income sourced at partner level		**16c**	
		Foreign gross income sourced at partnership level			
	d	Reserved for future use ▶_____ **e** Foreign branch category . . . . . ▶		**16e**	
	f	Passive category ▶_____ **g** General category ▶_____ **h** Other (attach statement) ▶		**16h**	
		Deductions allocated and apportioned at partner level			
	i	Interest expense ▶_____ **j** Other . . . . ▶		**16j**	
		Deductions allocated and apportioned at partnership level to foreign source income			
	k	Reserved for future use ▶_____ **l** Foreign branch category . . . . . ▶		**16l**	
	m	Passive category ▶_____ **n** General category ▶_____ **o** Other (attach statement) ▶		**16o**	
	p	Total foreign taxes (check one): ▶ Paid ☐ Accrued ☐		**16p**	
	q	Reduction in taxes available for credit (attach statement)		**16q**	
	r	Other foreign tax information (attach statement)			
Alternative Minimum Tax (AMT) Items	**17a**	Post-1986 depreciation adjustment		**17a**	18,224
	b	Adjusted gain or loss		**17b**	
	c	Depletion (other than oil and gas)		**17c**	
	d	Oil, gas, and geothermal properties—gross income		**17d**	
	e	Oil, gas, and geothermal properties—deductions		**17e**	
	f	Other AMT items (attach statement)		**17f**	
Other Information	**18a**	Tax-exempt interest income		**18a**	2,100
	b	Other tax-exempt income		**18b**	
	c	Nondeductible expenses		**18c**	
	19a	Distributions of cash and marketable securities		**19a**	34,000
	b	Distributions of other property		**19b**	
	20a	Investment income		**20a**	12,000
	b	Investment expenses		**20b**	
	c	Other items and amounts (attach statement)			*

* As shown in Example 24 later in the chapter, a supporting schedule will show the partnership's totals for additional information
related to the partners' qualified business income deduction.

Form **1065** (2019)

Form 1065 (2019)   *Beachside Properties LLC*   11-1111111   Page **5**

Analysis of Net Income (Loss)

1	Net income (loss). Combine Schedule K, lines 1 through 11. From the result, subtract the sum of Schedule K, lines 12 through 13d, and 16p					**1**	730,000	

2	Analysis by partner type:	(i) Corporate	(ii) Individual (active)	(iii) Individual (passive)	(iv) Partnership	(v) Exempt Organization	(vi) Nominee/Other
a	General partners						
b	Limited partners		486,000	244,000			

Schedule L — Balance Sheets per Books

		Beginning of tax year		End of tax year	
	Assets	(a)	(b)	(c)	(d)
1	Cash		97,503		123,740
2a	Trade notes and accounts receivable				
b	Less allowance for bad debts		0		0
3	Inventories		60,000		80,000
4	U.S. government obligations				
5	Tax-exempt securities		40,000		40,000
6	Other current assets (attach statement)				
7a	Loans to partners (or persons related to partners) .				
b	Mortgage and real estate loans				
8	Other investments (attach statement)		120,000		860,000
9a	Buildings and other depreciable assets	3,400,000		3,400,000	
b	Less accumulated depreciation	1,767,503	1,632,497	1,885,640	1,514,360
10a	Depletable assets				
b	Less accumulated depletion		0		0
11	Land (net of any amortization)		600,000		600,000
12a	Intangible assets (amortizable only)	10,000		10,000	
b	Less accumulated amortization	10,000	0	10,000	0
13	Other assets (attach statement)				
14	Total assets		2,550,000		3,218,100
	Liabilities and Capital				
15	Accounts payable				
16	Mortgages, notes, bonds payable in less than 1 year				
17	Other current liabilities (attach statement)				
18	All nonrecourse loans		500,000		600,000
19a	Loans from partners (or persons related to partners) .				
b	Mortgages, notes, bonds payable in 1 year or more .				
20	Other liabilities (attach statement)				
21	Partners' capital accounts		2,050,000		2,618,100
22	Total liabilities and capital		2,550,000		3,218,100

Schedule M-1 — Reconciliation of Income (Loss) per Books With Income (Loss) per Return

Note: The partnership may be required to file Schedule M-3. See instructions.

1	Net income (loss) per books	492,100	6	Income recorded on books this year not included on Schedule K, lines 1 through 11 (itemize):		
2	Income included on Schedule K, lines 1, 2, 3c, 5, 6a, 7, 8, 9a, 10, and 11, not recorded on books this year (itemize): _____	0	a	Tax-exempt interest $ _____ 2,100		2,100
3	Guaranteed payments (other than health insurance)	240,000	7	Deductions included on Schedule K, lines 1 through 13d, and 16p, not charged against book income this year (itemize):		
4	Expenses recorded on books this year not included on Schedule K, lines 1 through 13d, and 16p (itemize):		a	Depreciation $ _____		0
a	Depreciation $ _____		8	Add lines 6 and 7		2,100
b	Travel and entertainment $ _____	0	9	Income (loss) (Analysis of Net Income (Loss), line 1). Subtract line 8 from line 5		730,000
5	Add lines 1 through 4	732,100				

municipal bond is tax exempt

Schedule M-2 — Analysis of Partners' Capital Accounts

1	Balance at beginning of year . . .	2,050,000	6	Distributions: **a** Cash		34,000
2	Capital contributed: **a** Cash . . .	110,000		**b** Property		
	b Property . .		7	Other decreases (itemize): _____		
3	Net income (loss) per books	492,100				
4	Other increases (itemize): _____	0	8	Add lines 6 and 7		34,000
5	Add lines 1 through 4	2,652,100	9	Balance at end of year. Subtract line 8 from line 5		2,618,100

Form **1065** (2019)

Beachside's Form 1065

Beachside's Form 1065, page 1, includes general information, ordinary business income (loss), information related to certain (rare) taxes that might apply to the partnership, and signatures of officers and tax return preparers.

Schedule K includes "Partners' Distributive Share Items." The Schedule K shows subheadings down the left side of the form for the various types of information provided. These subheadings include separately stated income and deductions, and then additional information the partners would need related to self-employment taxes, tax credits, foreign taxes, alternative minimum taxes, and other information.

Form 1065, page 5, includes an "Analysis of Net Income (Loss)," a balance sheet, a reconciliation of book and tax income, and an analysis of partners' capital accounts.

The Big Picture

EXAMPLE 15

Continue with the facts of Examples 13 and 14, and refer to pages 1, 4, and 5 of Beachside's Form 1065 on the preceding pages. Beachside's ordinary income on Form 1065, page 1, is $180,000 after considering the sales revenue, cost of sales, guaranteed payments, and other operating expenses.

On Schedule K (Form 1065, page 4), Beachside's separately stated income and deduction items (lines 1 to 13a) include net income from rental real estate, guaranteed payments (reported as income by the members), qualified dividends received, short-term capital gain, and charitable contributions.

Beachside's real estate rental operations are reported separately from the bakery's income on a Form 8825 (not shown) and included with Beachside's tax return. Beachside's *deduction* for guaranteed payments is shown on Form 1065, page 1, and the amount the LLC members must report as *income* (from capital and services) is shown on Schedule K, line 4.

Other Items Reported on Schedule K

As mentioned, the partnership must report any information the partners might need to prepare a complete and accurate income tax return. Separately stated income and deductions are reported on Schedule K, lines 1 to 13. Other information is reported on Schedule K, beginning on line 13d, and includes:

- The partner's share of tax credits calculated at the partnership level.
- Information the partner uses to make various tax or credit calculations (e.g., foreign tax credit or deduction, self-employment tax, net investment income tax, alternative minimum tax).
- Information the partner needs for other calculations and limitations (e.g., information for the qualified business income (QBI) deduction or interest expense deductions discussed elsewhere in the chapter).
- Information the partner needs to calculate the basis in the partnership interest (e.g., cash and property distributions received and tax-exempt/nondeductible items).
- Any additional information (e.g., summary schedules for each partnership activity or state tax information) the partners might need in preparing their tax returns.

EXAMPLE 16

Continue with the information in Examples 13 to 15. In addition to the business income and separately stated items described in Example 17, the LLC also reports the following information that the LLC members will use in preparing their tax returns:

Additional Information (Schedule K)	
Net earnings (loss) from self-employment (line 14a)	$150,000
AMT adjustment—cost recovery (line 17a)	18,224
Tax-exempt income—bond interest (line 18a)	2,100
Distributions (line 19a)	34,000
Investment income (line 20a)	12,000
Other information for LLC member-level calculations	

Investment income on line 20a (used to calculate any allowable investment interest expense deduction) includes Beachside's short-term capital gains but does not include favorably taxed qualified dividends.

Other information for LLC member-level calculations is reported on supporting schedules and includes net investment income (for calculating the net investment income tax), excess taxable income (for calculating business interest expense carryover deductions), and information the members need for qualified business income calculations.

Reconciling Taxable Income

The partnership reconciles "book" income with income reported on the return. Refer to pages 4 and 5 of Beachside's Form 1065.

The partnership calculates "taxable income"—the net of the partnership's ordinary and separately stated income and expense amounts on Schedule K (generally, lines 1 to 13 less any foreign tax payments shown on line 16p). It reports that amount on line 1 of the Analysis of Net Income (Loss) (page 5 of Form 1065). Note that, because guaranteed payments are shown separately on Schedule K, line 4, the partnership's "taxable income" is calculated *before* the deduction for guaranteed payments.

Book income is reconciled to this "taxable income" on either Schedule M–1 or Schedule M–3. Schedule M–1 is found on page 5 of Form 1065. Schedule M–3 is a separate three-page form and is often required (in lieu of Schedule M–1) for larger partnerships. The Schedule M–1 or Schedule M–3 is completed similarly to the forms shown for a C corporation; see text Sections 17-3c and 17-3e.

EXAMPLE 17

Continue with the facts in Examples 13 to 16, and follow along on Beachside's Form 1065, page 5. To calculate Beachside's "taxable income" on the Analysis of Net Income (Loss) schedule, we combine the ordinary income of $180,000, the guaranteed payments of $240,000, and the four separately stated income and deduction amounts [lines 2, 6a, 8, and 13a (negative)] from Beachside's Schedule K. This net amount is $730,000 and is the amount to which the $492,100 (assumed) of book income is reconciled on Schedule M–1, line 9.

Reconciling Partners' Capital

Schedule M–2 reconciles partners' beginning and ending capital accounts, considering contributions to and distributions from the partnership as well as the partnership's income, gains, losses, and deductions. Schedule M–2 can be prepared using any of several methods, including the tax basis, generally accepted accounting principles (GAAP), or the "§ 704(b) book" method. The method used on Schedule M–2 should also be used in preparing the capital account reconciliation on the partners' Schedules K–1.

Financial Disclosure Insights   Financial Reporting for Partnerships

Partnerships might be required to prepare GAAP-basis financial statements so they can be provided to a lender, the Securities and Exchange Commission, or even financially savvy partners who want to see GAAP-basis information.

A partnership's financial statements look quite similar to GAAP-basis corporate financial statements, with two major exceptions. First, a partnership will prepare a "Statement of Changes in Partners' Capital" rather than a "Statement of Shareholders' Equity." Second, a partnership will *not* record a Federal income tax liability/tax provision, because the income taxes are paid by the partners.

In the statements themselves, calculations are made using financial reporting methods rather than tax methods. For example, GAAP methods are used to calculate depreciation expense recorded on the partnership's books; you won't see bonus depreciation or § 179 deductions.

A partnership's footnotes to the financial statements describe various *accounting* methods, but they don't typically describe any *tax* elections the partnership has made. A tax footnote will generally be included, but its main function is to describe that the partners pay the tax, so a tax provision is *not* recorded.

The tax footnote also explains whether any tax returns are under examination by the IRS or other tax authority (e.g., state tax agencies), and if any potential partnership-level tax liability might exist (e.g., if state franchise taxes are due, or if it is likely that a penalty might be assessed at the partnership level because the partnership made aggressive elections regarding certain tax matters).

A partnership's financial statements will also outline the rights and obligations of the general and limited (if any) partner groups, including any requirements the partners might face for guaranteeing entity debt.

If these GAAP-basis financial statements are available, the partnership generally will use the GAAP basis to prepare Form 1065 Schedule L (Balance Sheet per Books), Schedule M–2 (Analysis of Partners' Capital Accounts), and the Partner's Capital Account Analysis on the partners' Schedules K–1. An interested party would need to examine Schedule M–1 or Schedule M–3 to see the nature of any book-tax differences.

The Big Picture

EXAMPLE 18

Continue with Examples 13 to 17 and the Beachside Properties Form 1065 excerpts. Beachside prepares its Schedule L and Schedule M–2 using the same ("tax") method, so Beachside's beginning and ending capital accounts have the same balances on both Schedule L and Schedule M–2.

In addition to Beachside's book income, Schedule M–2 also reflects the $30,000 cash distribution to Maria, payment of medical expenses of $4,000 to Kyle, and a $110,000 cash contribution from Maria. Because this is tax method reporting, Maria's property contribution (valued at $50,000) is not shown: that property has a $0 basis to Maria, and, as such, has a $0 carryover basis to Beachside.

LO.7

Describe the information provided on a partner's Schedule K–1 and how the partner reports that information.

21-4 PARTNER CALCULATIONS AND REPORTING

Once partnership items are calculated on Schedule K, they are allocated among the partners on their Schedules K–1 and reported on their personal income tax returns.

21-4a Partner Reporting of Partnership Income

Schedule K summarizes the tax-related items for the entire partnership. Schedule K–1 summarizes the tax-related items for each partner after considering the allocation conventions outlined in the partnership agreement or required under the Code and Regulations. For each partnership item, the sum of the amounts allocated to all the partners on Schedules K–1 should equal the partnership's total amount per Schedule K.

We'll discuss the information on Maria's Schedule K–1 later in this section. For now, refer to the form on the next page and compare it to the partnership's Schedule K. As you can see, the lines in Part III of a partner's Schedule K–1 correspond to the same lines in the partnership's Schedule K, as shown on p. 21-20. In addition, the partners might need additional information not shown on the face of Schedule K–1.

651119

☐ Final K-1 ☐ Amended K-1	OMB No. 1545-0123

Schedule K-1 (Form 1065)

Department of the Treasury
Internal Revenue Service

2019

For calendar year 2019, or tax year

beginning   /   / 2019   ending   /   /

Partner's Share of Income, Deductions, Credits, etc.

▶ See back of form and separate instructions.

Part I   Information About the Partnership

A   Partnership's employer identification number
11-1111111

B   Partnership's name, address, city, state, and ZIP code
Beachside Properties LLC
1600 Ocean Vista Way
Surfside

C   IRS Center where partnership filed return ▶ *P.O. Box 409101, Ogden, UT 84409*

D   ☐ Check if this is a publicly traded partnership (PTP)

Part II   Information About the Partner

E   Partner's SSN or TIN (Do not use TIN of a disregarded entity. See inst.)
111-11-1111

F   Name, address, city, state, and ZIP code for partner entered in E. See instructions.
Maria LeClerc
1600 Ocean Vista Way
Surfside

G   ☐ General partner or LLC member-manager   ☒ Limited partner or other LLC member

H1   ☒ Domestic partner   ☐ Foreign partner

H2   ☐ If the partner is a disregarded entity (DE), enter the partner's:
   TIN _____ Name _____

I1   What type of entity is this partner?   *Active Individual*

I2   If this partner is a retirement plan (IRA/SEP/Keogh/etc.), check here ☐

J   Partner's share of profit, loss, and capital (see instructions):

	Beginning	Ending
Profit	40.000000 %	40.000000 %
Loss	40.000000 %	40.000000 %
Capital	47.500000 %	47.500000 %

Check if decrease is due to sale or exchange of partnership interest   ☐

K   Partner's share of liabilities:

	Beginning	Ending
Nonrecourse	$ 200,000	$ 240,000
Qualified nonrecourse financing	$	$
Recourse	$	$

☐ Check this box if Item K includes liability amounts from lower tier partnerships.

L   **Partner's Capital Account Analysis**

Beginning capital account	$ 1,400,000
Capital contributed during the year	$ 110,000
Current year net income (loss)	$ 214,840
Other increase (decrease) (attach explanation)	$
Withdrawals & distributions	$ (30,000)
Ending capital account	$ 1,694,840

M   Did the partner contribute property with a built-in gain or loss?
☒ Yes   ☐ No   If "Yes," attach statement. See instructions.

N   Partner's Share of Net Unrecognized Section 704(c) Gain or (Loss)
Beginning $ 500,000
Ending $ 550,000

Part III   Partner's Share of Current Year Income, Deductions, Credits, and Other Items

#	Item	Amount	#	Item	Amount
1	Ordinary business income (loss)	90,000	15	Credits	
2	Net rental real estate income (loss)	120,000		*(300,000 × .40)*	
3	Other net rental income (loss)		16	Foreign transactions	
4a	Guaranteed payments for services	60,000			
4b	Guaranteed payments for capital	60,000			
4c	Total guaranteed payments	120,000			
5	Interest income				
6a	Ordinary dividends	1,600			
6b	Qualified dividends	1,600			
6c	Dividend equivalents		17	Alternative minimum tax (AMT) items	
			A		7,290
7	Royalties				
8	Net short-term capital gain (loss)	4,800			
9a	Net long-term capital gain (loss)		18	Tax-exempt income and nondeductible expenses	
9b	Collectibles (28%) gain (loss)		A		840
9c	Unrecaptured section 1250 gain				
10	Net section 1231 gain (loss)				
			19	Distributions	
11	Other income (loss)		A		30,000
			20	Other information	
12	Section 179 deduction		A		4,800
			Z*	STMT (statement follows)	
13	Other deductions				
A		2,400		Section 199A income	210,000
				W–2 wages	200,000
				UBIA	600,000
14	Self-employment earnings (loss)				
A	*for services*	60,000			
C		480,000			

21 ☒ More than one activity for at-risk purposes*
22 ☒ More than one activity for passive activity purposes*

See attached statement for additional information.

For IRS Use Only

Other Schedule K–1 Information

Often, the person (or firm) that prepares a *partnership* return is different from the person (or firm) that prepares a given *partner's* tax return. Therefore, Schedule K–1 is designed to include any information the partner might need in preparing the tax return, including some information not summarized on Schedule K.

Line 20 is designated for "Other Information," and could include several lines of additional details. Page 2 of Schedule K–1 defines "Codes" that can be used to identify the type of information being provided. That page is not included, but you can download it at **irs.gov**.

Guaranteed Payments on Schedule K–1

A partner who receives guaranteed payments during a partnership year must include the payments in income as if they were received on the last day of the partnership year. Guaranteed payments are not "allocated" among the partners; instead, they are attributed to the partner who actually received the payment. Guaranteed payments are always taxable as ordinary income to the recipient partner.

The amount the partner receives is reported on Schedule K–1, line 4. The partner uses this information (in lieu of a Form W–2 or 1099) to report the income on the partner's tax return. A guaranteed payment often is subject to self-employment tax and, potentially, other additional taxes, as discussed later in the chapter.

21-4b Partner Allocations

LO.8

Outline and discuss the requirements for allocating income, gains, losses, deductions, and credits among the partners.

Once the partnership's overall information is determined (including any additional information the partners might need), the total amounts for each item must be allocated among the partners (or, in the case of guaranteed payments, attributed to the partner receiving the payment). These allocations must have economic effect and substantiality, and they must take into account any precontribution gains and losses.[36]

Economic Effect

Partnership allocations are made in accordance with the partnership agreement or an LLC's operating agreement. These allocations can be flexible. Profits, losses, and cash flows are not required to be allocated in accordance with capital ownership, as is the case under state law for most corporate entities. Partnership allocations have, at times, been used to manipulate the allocation of tax benefits among partners. Extensive Regulations[37] are designed to ensure that allocations do not result in undue tax revenue losses to the Treasury. The rules are complex, but the primary general rule—the economic effect test—can be easily understood.

The economic effect test has three general requirements.

- Section 704(b) book capital accounts must be maintained as described in the Regulations.[38] These capital accounts reflect contributions and distributions at their fair market values. An allocation of income or gain to a partner must increase the partner's capital account, and an allocation of deduction or loss must decrease the partner's capital account.

- When the partnership interest is liquidated, if a partner has a *positive* balance in the capital account, the partner must receive net assets with a fair market value equal to that positive balance.

- When the partnership interest is liquidated, if a partner has a *negative* balance in the capital account, the partner must "restore" that account, generally by contributing cash. Alternative tests (beyond the scope of this text) may also be used to meet this requirement.

---

[36]§§ 704(a), (b), and (c).
[37]Reg. § 1.704–1(b)(2)(i).

[38]§ 1.704–1(b)(2)(iv).

These capital account maintenance requirements are designed to ensure that a partner bears the economic burden of a loss or deduction allocation and receives the economic benefit of an income or gain allocation.

The Big Picture

EXAMPLE 19

Continue with Examples 13 to 15 and the Beachside Properties Form 1065 excerpts. Maria arrives at the bakery at 4 A.M. (or earlier) six days a week to make sure her cinnamon rolls and croissants are ready when the café opens at 7. Consequently, the other LLC members have agreed with Maria that she should be allocated the first $30,000 of gross revenues (and cash flows) from bakery operations each year, starting in year 2. All other revenues and expenses (including W–2 wages and depreciation expense) are allocated in the expected 40%/40%/20% ratios to Kyle, Maria, and Josh.

Beachside's Form 1065, page 1, for the LLC's second year of operations includes only the bakery's retail operations. To simplify the illustration, assume that the § 704(b) book income and taxable income are the same amount. Maria is entitled to the first $30,000 shown on that page. The remaining $150,000 of ordinary income and all other items of partnership income, gain, loss, or deduction are allocated based on the members' profit sharing percentages.

Assume *for this example only* that the bakery operations are the only item impacting the § 704(b) book capital accounts this year and that the initial § 704(b) book capital amounts are as follows:

	Maria	Kyle	Josh
Beginning § 704(b) book capital	$1,900,000	$1,900,000	$150,000
Special allocation of gross income	30,000	–0–	–0–
Allocation of remaining net income	60,000	60,000	30,000
Ending § 704(b) book capital	$1,990,000	$1,960,000	$180,000

This allocation will be respected as long as the members eventually (i.e., any time on or before liquidation) receive cash and property that reflects their ending § 704(b) book capital account values.

Substantiality

Partnership allocations must also have "substantial" effect.[39] In general, an allocation does not meet the "substantial" test unless it has economic consequences in addition to tax consequences that might benefit a subset of the partners. Allocations are not generally permitted if they are for tax reasons only or if an allocation in one tax year is required to be offset by an equal allocation in a future tax year.

The Big Picture

EXAMPLE 20

In Example 19, assume instead (for this example only) that the $30,000 special allocation of net income was awarded to Maria in year 2 simply to allow Maria to utilize her personal expiring net operating loss carryover and that an offsetting $30,000 special allocation of deductions would be made to Maria the following tax year.

Even though the LLC's allocations meet the "economic effect" tests, they would not be permitted because there is no substantial nontax economic reason for the allocations. The allocations over the two-year period are intended only to reduce the LLC members' combined income tax liability.

Precontribution Gain or Loss

For property contributed to a partnership, the difference between fair market value and basis at the contribution date is a **precontribution gain or loss**. The partnership keeps track of these gains and losses in its § 704(b) book accounting records. Allocated

---

[39]Reg. § 1.704–1(b)(2)(iii).

income, gain, loss, or deduction related to such property takes the precontribution amount into account.[40] Certain § 704(c) information must be reported on the partners' Schedules K–1.

An easy example occurs when a gain or loss is recognized when a nondepreciable contributed property is later sold by the partnership. The precontribution portion of the gain or loss is allocated to the contributing partner.

As you can imagine, allocations are more challenging when depreciable property is involved. Regulations (beyond the scope of this chapter) describe several permitted depreciation allocation methods.[41]

The Big Picture

EXAMPLE

21

Return to the facts of *The Big Picture* on p. 21-1. When Beachside Properties LLC was formed, Kyle contributed land (value of $800,000 and basis of $600,000) and buildings (value of $1,200,000 and basis of $0). Maria contributed $1,500,000 of cash, plus equipment and furnishings (value of $500,000 and basis of $0). For § 704(b) book capital account purposes, Beachside records the land and other properties at their fair market values. For tax purposes, the LLC takes carryover bases in the properties. The LLC must keep track of the differences between the basis in each property and the value at the contribution date. If any of this property is sold, the gain must be allocated to the contributing partner to the extent of any previously unrecognized built-in gain.

For example, if Beachside sells the land contributed by Kyle for $1,100,000, the gain would be calculated and allocated as follows:

	§ 704(b) Book	Tax
Amount realized	$1,100,000	$1,100,000
Less: Adjusted basis	800,000	600,000
Gain realized	$ 300,000	$ 500,000
Built-in gain to Kyle	–0–	200,000
Remaining gain (allocated proportionately)	$ 300,000	$ 300,000

For tax purposes, Kyle would recognize $320,000 of the gain [($300,000 × 40%) + $200,000 built-in gain], Maria would recognize $120,000 ($300,000 × 40%), and Josh would recognize $60,000 ($300,000 × 20%).

21-4c Schedule K–1 Example

Let's look in detail at Maria's Schedule K-1 from Beachside Properties on p. 21-25. Part I includes information about the partnership. Part II includes information about the partner, including the partner's profit, loss, and capital sharing percentages; share of partnership liabilities at the beginning and end of the year; and changes in the partner's capital account during the year.

Part III includes information the partners use in completing their tax return. As a parallel to Schedule K, you'll find that Schedule K–1, lines 1 to 13 reflect the partner's distributive share of the partnership's income and deductions, including any amounts specially allocated to that partner; lines 14 to 17 include information the partner needs to calculate other amounts (e.g., self-employment tax, alternative minimum tax, etc.); lines 18 and 19 help the partner calculate the outside basis in the partnership interest; and line 20 provides additional information the partner might need (e.g., information for the QBI deduction, discussed next).

---

[40]§§ 704(c)(1)(A) and (C).

[41]Reg. § 1.704–3.

The Big Picture

EXAMPLE 22

Continue with the Beachside Properties examples and the Form 1065 excerpts. Also refer to Maria's Schedule K–1 on p. 21-25. Maria, a 40% owner, will receive a Schedule K–1 from Beachside Properties. Part III, line 1, of Maria's Schedule K–1 reflects her $30,000 special allocation of ordinary income, plus her normal allocation of 40% of the remaining ordinary income, for a total of $90,000 (calculated in Example 19). She is also allocated 40% of all separately stated items.

On her Form 1040, Maria includes $90,000 of ordinary income, a $2,400 charitable contribution, a $4,800 short-term capital gain, $120,000 of passive rental income, and $1,600 of qualified dividend income. On the first page of Form 1040, Maria lists her $840 share of tax-exempt interest income. She must also report, as ordinary income, the $120,000 guaranteed payment she received.

Therefore, Maria's taxable income is increased by $336,400 from the LLC ($90,000 + $4,800 + $120,000 + $1,600 + $120,000), and she can deduct $2,400 if she itemizes deductions. As discussed next, she might also be able to claim a deduction related to her "qualified business income" from the LLC. In determining her AMT liability (if any), Maria takes into account a $7,290 positive adjustment.

Note that the specially allocated income simply increases Maria's amount on line 1 and decreases the amounts allocated to the other members. Kyle's and Josh's allocations on line 1 will be $60,000 and $30,000, respectively. The total remains $180,000, as shown on Form 1065, page 1, and Schedule K, line 1.

On her personal tax return, Maria combines the partnership's amounts with similar items from sources other than Beachside. For example, if Maria has a $3,000 long-term capital loss from a stock transaction, the overall net short-term capital gain calculated on Schedule D of her Form 1040 is $1,800 ($4,800 − $3,000).

For each LLC item, the sum of the allocated amounts on Josh's, Kyle's, and Maria's K–1s will equal the totals on Beachside Properties' Schedule K.

Qualified Business Income Skip

Under § 199A, a noncorporate taxpayer can deduct up to 20 percent of "the combined qualified business income amount" (the "QBI deduction"). The deduction is limited to the lesser of 20 percent of "qualified business income" (QBI), with additional limitations related to the taxpayer's modified taxable income, the entity's wages/capital investment, and based on whether or not the business is a "specified service trade or business" ("SSTB") (e.g., certain service-oriented businesses). There is no cash outflow related to this deduction; it just works to lower the noncorporate party's effective tax rate on this income. For more information on the QBI deduction, the wages/capital investment limitations, SSTBs, and specific calculations, see text Section 15-3. S corporation considerations are discussed in text Section 22-3b.

For a partner, QBI does not include guaranteed payments received for *services* provided to the partnership or payments from the partnership under § 707(a) for *services* unrelated to the partnership's business (e.g., payments by a restaurant LLC to a member for providing accounting services). In addition, the § 199A Regulations provide that guaranteed payments for the use of the partner's *capital* do not constitute QBI as it is more in the nature of investment income to the partner.[42]

The QBI deduction is calculated at the partner level. The partnership determines its QBI and reports, on Schedules K–1, any information the partners need to complete their tax returns.[43] The partner's QBI generally equals the share of business income on Schedule K–1 Part III, lines 1, 2, and (possibly) 3, reduced by business expenses on lines 12 and 13.

The partnership reports "Z* STMT" on line 20 of the Schedule K–1 and provides a supporting schedule with all information the partner needs to calculate the § 199A deduction. For example, the statement will report the partnership's QBI, W–2 wages, and the "unadjusted basis immediately after acquisition of qualified property" (termed UBIA in

---

[42]Reg. § 1.199A–3(b)(1)(ii).

[43]§ 199A(f)(1).

the Regulations). The W–2 wages and UBIA are allocated among the partners in the same manner as the related wage and depreciation deductions are allocated to the partners or shareholders. If the entity has multiple trades or businesses and/or income from SSTBs, additional schedules should be provided with allocated amounts for each business.[44]

The Big Picture

EXAMPLE 23

Continue with the Beachside Properties examples and the Form 1065 excerpts. Beachside has income from real estate and from a restaurant. Neither business is an SSTB. The income from the café is a qualified trade or business and Beachside has elected to treat the real estate rental activity as such. On Maria's Schedule K–1, Beachside reports ordinary business income of $90,000 (line 1, per Example 22) and net rental real estate income of $120,000 (line 2).

The LLC prepares a supporting schedule for code Z, which includes any information the partner might need to calculate the QBI deduction. Maria's QBI, calculated by the LLC, is $210,000. Per Example 13, the LLC pays W–2 wages of $500,000; guaranteed payments and other payments to partners are not included in this amount. Per Example 11, the property contributed by Kyle and Maria is either land (ineligible) or fully depreciated property. Immediately after formation, the LLC spent $1,500,000 on improvements, so this is the LLC's UBIA. The LLC allocates these amounts to Kyle, Maria, and Josh in the 40%/40%/20% proportions, respectively, in which the related wage expense and depreciation deductions are allocated. Maria's allocated amounts are $200,000 for W–2 wages and $600,000 for UBIA. These amounts are included in the code Z statement, but for convenience, we show the information directly on Maria's Schedule K–1. Additional information would be provided for the rental and sales activities.

In her personal QBI deduction calculation, Maria considers the $210,000 of QBI from the partnership, less her personal deductions related to this income, such as her self-employment tax deduction, and self-employed medical insurance deduction. (See text Section 15-3c.)

Concept Summary 21.3 reviews the tax-reporting rules for partnership items at both the partnership and partner levels.

Concept Summary 21.3

Tax Reporting of Partnership Items

Item	Partnership reports on Form 1065	Partner's share reported on Schedule K–1, Part III
1. Partnership ordinary income or loss.	Page 1, line 22. Schedule K, line 1.	Line 1. Special allocations, basis adjustments, and loss limitations may apply.
2. Guaranteed payments to partners for capital or services.	Page 1, line 10, if deductible; otherwise capitalized. All amounts on Schedule K, line 4, for partner reporting.	Line 4. Partner reports as ordinary income; no basis adjustment.
3. Separately stated income and deduction items such as portfolio income, capital gain and loss, and § 179 deductions.	Schedule K, lines 2, 3, and 5 to 13.	Lines 2, 3, and 5 to 13. Special allocations, basis adjustments, and loss limitations may apply.
4. Net earnings from self-employment.	Schedule K, line 14a.	Line 14, code A.
5. Additional information so partner can make various calculations (e.g., AMT, foreign tax credits, net investment income tax, and the partner's outside basis).	Schedule K, lines 15 to 20.	Lines 15 to 20. Each partner's share of each item is passed through and considered in various calculations.
6. Qualified business income.	Schedule K, line 20 supporting schedule.	Line 20, supporting statement(s) for code Z.

---

[44]See Reg. § 1.199A–6 for complete information related to computational and reporting rules.

Til here

21-4d **Partner's Basis** *outside Basis*

Each partner has an outside basis in the partnership interest. That basis is increased/ (decreased) over time for the partner's share of income/(deductions), contributions/ (distributions), and increases/(decreases) in the partner's share of partnership liabilities.

LO.9
Determine a partner's basis in the partnership interest.

Relevance of Partner's Basis

The partner's basis is important for determining the treatment of distributions from the partnership to the partner and establishing the deductibility of partnership losses. When a partnership interest is sold (or liquidated by the partnership), the partner's gain or loss is determined by reference to the adjusted basis of the partnership interest (see text Section 21-6). Generally, the total of the partners' outside bases equals the partnership's inside basis in its assets.

A partner's basis is not reflected anywhere on the Schedule K–1. Instead, each partner should maintain a personal record of the basis in the partnership interest. Under no circumstances can the partner's adjusted basis for the partnership interest be reduced below zero.

Adjustments to Basis

As discussed earlier, the partner's initial outside basis generally equals the partner's basis in contributed assets. This could be a cost basis (plus any amount recognized as income on contribution of services) or a basis determined under the gift or inheritance rules. After the partner is admitted to the partnership, the partner's basis is adjusted for numerous items. The following items *increase* a partner's adjusted basis:

- The partner's proportionate share of partnership income (including capital gains and tax-exempt income).
- The partner's proportionate share of any increase in partnership liabilities (as discussed in text Section 21-4e).
- Contributions of cash or property from the partner to the partnership after the partnership is formed.

The following items *decrease* the partner's adjusted basis in the partnership:

- The partner's proportionate share of partnership deductions and losses [including capital losses, foreign taxes, charitable contributions (including the allocable basis of donated property), and suspended business interest expense that will be available for future tax years].
- The partner's proportionate share of nondeductible expenses.
- The partner's proportionate share of any reduction in partnership liabilities (as discussed in text Section 21-4e).[45]
- Distributions of cash or property from the partnership to the partner after the partnership is formed.

As shown in Example 3 earlier in the chapter, increasing the adjusted basis for the partner's share of partnership taxable income is logical because the partner has already been taxed on the income. By increasing the partner's basis, the partner is not taxed again on the income when the interest is sold or a distribution is received from the partnership.

Using the same logic, tax-exempt income (or noncapitalizable, nondeductible expenditures) should increase (decrease) the partner's basis. If the income is exempt in the current period, it should not contribute to the recognition of gain when the partner either sells the interest or receives a distribution from the partnership.

21-4e **Effect of Partnership Liabilities on Partner's Basis**

All partnership debt is allocated among the partners and included in the partners' bases.[46] [In contrast, the liabilities of an S corporation are generally *not* included in the shareholder's bases (see text Section 22-3f).] Partnership debt includes any partnership

LO.10
Explain how liabilities affect a partner's basis.

---

[45]§§ 705 and 752.   [46]§ 752.

obligation that creates an asset; results in an expense to the partnership; or results in a nondeductible, noncapitalizable item at the partnership level. This definition includes certain contingent liabilities.[47] The definition also includes most debt that is considered a liability under financial accounting rules. However, partnership debt does not include accounts payable of a *cash basis* partnership.

Allocation of Partnership Liabilities—In General

An increase in a partner's share of partnership debt is treated as a cash contribution by the partner to the partnership and increases the partner's basis. A decrease in a partner's share of partnership debt is treated as a cash distribution from the partnership to the partner and decreases the partner's basis.

EXAMPLE 24

Jim and Becky contribute property to form the JB Partnership. Jim contributes cash of $30,000. Becky contributes land with an adjusted basis and fair market value of $45,000, subject to a liability of $15,000; the partnership assumes the debt (treated as a distribution to Becky). The partnership borrows $50,000 to finance construction of a building on the contributed land.

At the end of the first year, the accrual basis partnership owes $3,500 in trade accounts payable to various vendors. Disregard any operating activities and deductions related to these debts. *If Jim and Becky share equally in liabilities*, the partners' bases in their partnership interests are determined as follows:

Jim's Basis		Becky's Basis	
Contributed cash	$30,000	Basis in contributed land	$ 45,000
		Less: Debt assumed by partnership	(15,000)
Share of debt on land	7,500	Share of debt on land	7,500
Initial basis	$37,500	Initial basis	$ 37,500
Share of construction loan	25,000	Share of construction loan	25,000
Share of trade accounts payable (accrual basis)	1,750	Share of trade accounts payable (accrual basis)	1,750
Basis, end of first year	$64,250	Basis, end of first year	$ 64,250

Assume in the following year that the partnership pays off its accounts payable, debt on land, and construction loan. The partners' bases would be correspondingly decreased and (disregarding any other operating activities) would become $30,000 each at the end of that second year.

In the previous example, liabilities were allocated equally between the two partners. In addition, each partner contributed an asset with an identical $30,000 net basis (basis less related debt), so the partners' ending bases were the same.

However, it's not generally that simple. Look at Maria's Schedule K–1 on p. 21-25. In Part II, item K, you can see that partnership debt, at the beginning and end of the partnership's tax year, is allocated based on whether it is recourse, nonrecourse, or qualified nonrecourse financing.

Recourse debt is partnership debt for which the partnership or at least one of the partners is personally liable. This personal liability can exist, for example, through the operation of state law or through personal guarantees that a partner makes to the creditor. **Nonrecourse debt** is debt for which no partner is personally liable. Lenders of nonrecourse debt generally require that collateral be pledged against the loan.

---

[47]Reg. § 1.752–1(a)(4)(ii).

Upon default, the lender can claim only the collateral, not the partners' personal assets. Qualified nonrecourse financing is a subset of nonrecourse debt that applies for purposes of the at-risk limitation discussed later in the chapter. Qualified nonrecourse financing is generally bank debt (or similar third-party debt) on real estate.

In general (disregarding any personal guarantees of any partnership debt), recourse debt is allocated among *general partners only*, and nonrecourse debt is allocated among *all partners*. If any partner or LLC member personally guarantees a debt, it is treated as a recourse debt with respect to that partner. For an LLC, most debt will, by default, be treated as nonrecourse debt because the LLC members, by definition, have no liability for entity debts.

Recourse Debt Rules

Recourse debt is allocated based on each partner's "economic risk of loss." For a partnership in which all contributions and allocations have been proportionate to the capital contributions, recourse debt is allocated among the general partners in proportion to their *loss sharing* ratios. In more complex situations, the partner's economic risk of loss is determined under a constructive liquidation scenario outlined in the Regulations.[48]

Hill, Inc., and Dart, Inc., own the newly created HD Partnership, where both entities are treated as general partners. Assume that all contributions and allocations are equal (50%/50%). At the end of the year, HD has $40,000 of recourse accounts payable and a $100,000 personal property loan that is guaranteed by Dart.

Because recourse debt is allocated according to loss sharing ratios, each partner is allocated 50% of the accounts payable. Dart is allocated 100% of the debt it guaranteed. Hill's share of recourse debt is $20,000, and Dart's share is $120,000.

Nonrecourse Debt Rules

Nonrecourse debt (including qualified nonrecourse financing) is allocated among all the partners. For our purposes, it is allocated to the partners in accordance with their *profit sharing* ratios.[49]

In Example 25, assume instead that HD is an LLC instead of a general partnership. Also assume that 40% of profits are allocated to Hill and 60% are allocated to Dart. (Losses are still allocated equally.)

In an LLC, accounts payable are treated as nonrecourse debt and are allocated according to profit sharing ratios. Therefore, the $40,000 of accounts payable are allocated $16,000 (40%) to Hill and $24,000 (60%) to Dart. The debt guaranteed by Dart remains a recourse debt allocated 100% to Dart. Therefore, Hill's Schedule K–1 will show $16,000 of nonrecourse debt, and Dart's will show $24,000 of nonrecourse debt and $100,000 of recourse debt.

---

[48]See Reg. § 1.752–2 and related Regulations and Proposed Regulations. Under the constructive liquidation scenario, debts are allocated based on which partner would be required to pay the debt in the event of a hypothetical catastrophic event that left all of the partnership's assets worthless. The assumed losses are allocated among the partners, and the debt is allocated in proportion to the partners' negative capital accounts after this deemed allocation.

[49]Reg. § 1.752–3. This Regulation outlines a first stage allocation of minimum gain and a second stage allocation where liabilities on contributed property exceed the tax basis of the contributed property. These first two stages are beyond the scope of this text.

EXHIBIT 21.2	Partner's Basis in Partnership Interest

Basis is generally adjusted in the following order every tax year.

Initial basis or beginning basis for the taxable year.

+ Partner's contributions, including increases in the partner's share of partnership debt.

+ Partner's share of the partnership's:

- Taxable income items.
- Tax-exempt income items.
- Excess of depletion deductions over adjusted basis of property subject to depletion.

− Partner's distributions and withdrawals, including decreases in the partner's share of partnership debt.

− Partner's share of the partnership's:

- Separately stated foreign taxes, charitable contributions (limited to the basis of contributed property), and other deductions.
- Nondeductible items not chargeable to a capital account.
- Special depletion deduction for oil and gas wells.
- Other loss items.

The basis of a partner's interest can never be negative.

Exhibit 21.2 summarizes the rules for computing a partner's basis in a partnership interest and the order in which the rules are applied.

The Big Picture

EXAMPLE 27

Return to the facts of *The Big Picture* on p. 21-1. Example 22 described how the income and deduction items of Beachside Properties LLC are allocated to Maria on her Schedule K–1. But how is Maria's basis affected by those items?

Assume that at the beginning of that tax year (Beachside's second year of operations), Maria's basis in her LLC interest was $1,600,000, including a $200,000 share of the LLC's $500,000 of nonrecourse debt. At the end of the year, Beachside had $600,000 of debt, which was again treated as nonrecourse to all of the LLC members.

During the year, Maria contributes to the LLC cash of $110,000 and additional property (basis of $0 and fair market value of $50,000). Maria also received a cash distribution equal to her $30,000 special allocation of the LLC's gross income. Maria's share of Beachside's income, gain, and deductions is as described in Example 22 and on her Schedule K–1.

Maria's basis can be calculated using the ordering rules shown in Exhibit 21.2. The $120,000 guaranteed payment Maria received does not directly affect Maria's basis, even though it affects her taxable income. It's cash she received that is taxable as if it was salary or interest revenue to her.

The $840 of tax-exempt income increases Maria's basis, even though it is not taxed to Maria. Similarly, the charitable contribution reduces her basis even though it might not be deductible to her. Maria's QBI deduction does not affect her basis.

continued

At the end of the year, Maria's basis is as follows:

Beginning basis (including beginning liability share)	$1,600,000
Contributions, including increase in share of liabilities	
Share of net increase in LLC liabilities [40% × ($600,000 − $500,000)]	40,000
Cash contribution to LLC capital	110,000
Maria's basis in noncash capital contribution	–0–
Share of LLC income items	
Ordinary LLC income	90,000
LLC's net passive activity income from rental real estate	120,000
Tax-exempt income	840
Short-term capital gain	4,800
Qualified dividend income	1,600
Distributions and withdrawals	
Capital withdrawal (distribution related to special allocation of income)	(30,000)
Share of LLC deduction items	
Charitable contribution	(2,400)
Ending basis (including ending liability share)	$1,934,840

21-4f **Partner's Capital Account**

As mentioned earlier in the chapter, the partner's basis is not the same as the partner's capital account. Think of the capital account as an accounting calculation of the partner's ownership in the entity.

The partner's *capital account* is a measure of the partner's share of the net liquidation value of *all* partnership assets (partnership equity, or assets less liabilities). GAAP method and § 704(b) book capital also considers any previously untaxed appreciation or depreciation of the underlying property assets. A partner's *tax basis* measures the amount the partner can receive relative to the partnership interest without paying additional tax (e.g., as a cash distribution or if the partner were to sell the partnership interest).

The capital account analysis (sometimes called a "rollforward" or "reconciliation") is shown on the partner's Schedule K–1 (see text Section 21-4a). This calculation shows the change in the partner's capital account from the beginning to the end of the tax year.

This capital account analysis can be prepared using any of several methods, including the tax basis, GAAP, or the § 704(b) book method. The method selected is indicated on the Schedule K–1 and should be the same method that was used in preparing the partnership's Schedule M–2 (Analysis of Partners' Capital Accounts). The partnership might need to keep track of partners' capital using more than one method—for example, using both GAAP and the § 704(b) book method. For example, smaller partnerships with no external financial reporting requirements might calculate capital accounts on the tax basis. Larger partnerships with third-party reporting obligations (e.g., because of bank loans or SEC filing requirements) likely will calculate capital account information using GAAP. Any partnership with contributions or distributions of appreciated or depreciated property must maintain § 704(b) book capital accounts to ensure that liquidating distributions are in accordance with those capital accounts.

A partner's capital account can sometimes be negative. If this happens, additional information (beyond the scope of the text) must be reported to the IRS by the partnership.

The total of the partners' beginning and ending capital accounts of all Schedules K–1 should equal the beginning and ending balances shown on the partnership's Schedule M–2. These amounts should also generally equal the balances shown on the partnership's balance sheet (Schedule L) (or an explanation of the differences should be attached).

The partner's ending capital account balance is rarely the same amount as the partner's tax basis. For example, a partner's tax basis includes the partner's share of partnership liabilities; these liabilities are not included in a partner's capital. The partner's share of partnership liabilities is shown separately in Part II of Schedule K–1.

LO.11

Illustrate a partner's capital account rollforward and explain why the year-end balance might differ from the partner's year-end basis in the partnership interest.

Sometimes, the partner's ending tax basis in the partnership interest can be estimated by adding the partner's ending capital and the partner's share of liabilities. This would be accurate, for example, when the partner has been in the partnership since its inception and the capital account analysis is prepared on a tax basis.

The Big Picture

EXAMPLE 28

Maria's Schedule K–1 shows her capital account rollforward from the prior year to the current year. Her capital account was calculated on a tax basis, and the beginning capital account balance was $1,400,000. The reconciliation shows the $110,000 of cash Maria contributed, the $0 basis of other contributed property, and the $30,000 distribution related to the special allocation of cash to Maria.

The current-year increase (decrease) of $214,840 is the combination (additions and subtractions) of Maria's amounts shown on Schedule K–1, Part III, lines 1 to 13 (excluding the guaranteed payment), plus the tax-exempt income shown on line 18. (Note that the ordinary/qualified dividends are included only one time.)

Maria's ending tax-basis capital account on Schedule K–1 is $1,694,840. Her Schedule K–1 shows a $240,000 share of nonrecourse liabilities. While this will not always be the case, the sum of these amounts equals her ending tax basis of $1,934,840 as calculated in Example 27.

21-4g Loss Limitations

LO.12

List and review the limitations on deducting partnership losses.

Partnership losses flow through to the partners to be reported on their income tax returns. However, the loss deduction might be limited at the partner level. When limitations apply, all or a portion of the losses are suspended until a triggering event occurs. No time limit is imposed on such loss carryforwards.

The following different limitations might apply.

1. *Basis limitation* [§ 704(d)]. This limitation allows a loss deduction only to the extent of the partner's adjusted outside basis.
2. *At-risk limitation* (§ 465). Losses that are deductible under the basis limitation are deductible only to the extent the partner is at risk for the partnership interest.
3. *Passive activity loss limitation* (§ 469). Any losses that survive this second limitation may be subject to the passive activity loss rules.
4. *Excess business losses* [§ 461(l)]. If a loss passes the above three limitations, a noncorporate taxpayer must consider whether the excess business loss limitation applies.

The partner can only deduct losses that make it through all of the hurdles. Special rules apply to losses from real estate activities.

EXAMPLE 29

Megan is a 50% member in Green LLC, which does not invest in real estate. On January 1, 2020, Megan's adjusted basis for her LLC interest is $50,000, and her at-risk amount is $35,000. Her share of losses from Green for 2020 is $60,000, all of which is a passive activity loss. She owns another investment that produced $25,000 of passive activity income. She has no other passive or active losses. Megan can deduct $25,000 of Green's losses on her Form 1040 for 2020, calculated as follows:

Applicable Provision	Deductible Loss	Suspended Loss
§ 704(d) basis limitation	$50,000	$10,000
At-risk limitation	35,000	15,000
Passive activity loss limitation	25,000	10,000
Excess business loss limitation	25,000	–0–

Megan can deduct only $50,000 under the basis limitation. Of this $50,000, only $35,000 is deductible under the at-risk limitation. Under the passive activity loss limitation, passive activity losses can be deducted only against passive activity income. The net passive income/loss is $0, so the excess business loss limitation does not apply. Thus, Megan can deduct $25,000. This amount, plus the three suspended loss amounts, equals the original $60,000 loss.

Basis Limitation

For the first limitation, basis is determined at the end of the partnership's taxable year. It is adjusted for any partnership income and gain items and contributions and distributions made during the year, but it is determined *before considering any loss or deduction items for the year.* (In Exhibit 21.2, basis would be calculated through "partner's distributions and withdrawals.")

Losses that cannot be deducted because of this rule are suspended and carried forward (never back) for use against future increases in the partner's adjusted basis. Such increases might result from additional capital contributions, from sharing in additional partnership debt, or from future partnership income.

At-Risk Limitation

Under the at-risk rules, certain loss deductions are limited to amounts that are economically invested in the partnership. Limited losses are from business and income-producing activities allocated to individual partners and closely held C corporation partners. Suspended losses are carried forward until a partner has a sufficient amount at risk in the activity to absorb them.[50]

Invested amounts include cash, the adjusted basis of property contributed by the partner, and the partner's share of partnership earnings that have not been withdrawn.[51]

Recourse debt generally is included in the amount at risk, but nonrecourse debt is not. As an exception, qualified nonrecourse financing is deemed to be at risk.[52] In general terms, qualified nonrecourse financing is nonrecourse financing provided by a bank, retirement plan, or similar party or by a Federal, state, or local government for the purchase of real estate.

EXAMPLE 30

In Example 29, Megan's amount at risk was $35,000, and $15,000 was suspended under the at-risk limitation. Assume that this limitation applied because Megan's basis in her LLC interest included a $15,000 nonrecourse debt that could not be included in her amount at risk.

If, instead, the activity was a real estate activity and the debt was qualified nonrecourse financing, Megan's basis and at-risk amounts would have been the same ($50,000) and no additional loss deduction would have been suspended under the at-risk rules.

Passive Activity Loss Limitation

The third loss limitation is that passive activity losses can generally only be deducted to the extent they offset passive activity income.[53] These rules apply to partners who are individuals, estates, trusts, closely held C corporations, or personal service corporations.

Passive activity income (see Chapter 11) is income from a trade or business activity in which the partner does not materially participate on a regular, continuous, and substantial basis or income from rental activities.[54]

Material participation means that the partner should have substantial involvement in daily operations of the activity. By definition, a partner treated as a limited partner is typically considered *not* to materially participate in partnership activities.[55]

Rent income from real or personal property generally is passive activity income, regardless of the partner's level of participation. The primary exception is that rental real estate is not treated as a passive activity for a person who qualifies as a real estate professional.

As a special allowance, individuals can offset up to $25,000 of passive activity losses from rental real estate against active and portfolio income.[56] (This amount is phased out at a rate of $0.50 for every excess dollar, starting at $100,000 of modified adjusted gross income.) This deduction is available to those who actively (rather than materially) participate in rental real estate activities.

For additional information regarding loss limitations, the passive activity loss rules, and the rental real estate exception, refer to Chapter 11.

---

[50]§ 465(a)(2).
[51]§ 465(a).
[52]§ 465(b)(6).
[53]§ 469(a)(1).

[54]§§ 469(c)(1) and (2).
[55]§ 469(h)(2).
[56]§ 469(i).

Excess Business Losses of Noncorporate Taxpayers

If a noncorporate taxpayer has net losses that (1) pass the above three tests and (2) exceed a threshold amount, the excess loss is carried forward as part of the taxpayer's net operating loss carryover.[57] The threshold is $259,000 for single taxpayers and $518,000 for married taxpayers filing a joint tax return. These amounts are adjusted for inflation each year.

The limitation is applied at the partner or S corporation shareholder level. As examples, losses from farming, active business losses, or losses of a real estate professional might be subject to this rule.

Til here

21-5 OTHER TAXES ON PARTNERSHIP INCOME

LO.13

Describe how a partner calculates self-employment tax and net investment income tax on partnership income.

A partner is not treated as an employee for tax purposes. Thus, certain types of partnership income allocated to an individual taxpayer may be considered "net earnings from self-employment" [subject to self-employment (SE) tax] or "net investment income" [subject to the tax on net investment income (NII)].

21-5a Self-Employment Tax

Self-employed individuals may be liable for an SE tax, consisting of a 12.4 percent tax for old-age, survivors, and disability insurance (on up to $137,700 of SE income in 2020, less any wages on which the tax is withheld) and a 2.9 percent tax for hospital insurance (on all SE income).[58] An additional Medicare tax of 0.9 percent applies to SE income in excess of $250,000 for married taxpayers filing joint tax returns (or half that amount if a separate return is filed) or $200,000 for other taxpayers.[59] The taxpayer calculates the SE tax on Schedule SE and the additional Medicare tax on Form 8959.

SE Treatment of Distributive Shares versus Guaranteed Payments

With a total potential tax rate of 15.3 percent (or even 16.2 percent), it behooves the partners to pay careful attention to whether their income shares might be excluded from SE income.

---

[57]§§ 461(l)(1) and (4).

[58]§§ 1401(a) and (b)(1).

[59]§ 1401(b)(2).

Distributive Shares SE income includes a general partner's distributive share of income from a partnership's trade or business, whether or not that income is distributed (e.g., income reported on line 1 of Schedule K–1). It also includes the distributive share allocated to a "limited partner" that is in the nature of compensation for services performed for or on behalf of the partnership.[60] However, SE income does not include the distributive share allocated to a limited partner who merely is an investor in the entity.

Guaranteed Payments Because of the rules above, for both general and limited partners, any guaranteed payments for *services* are subject to the SE tax. Guaranteed payments for use of the partner's *capital* are not subject to the SE tax.

SE Treatment of General versus Limited Partners

Because of the rules above, for SE tax purposes, a taxpayer might take extra measures to be classified as a *limited* partner. As a result, this has been a contentious area for the IRS. According to Proposed Regulations dating from 1997, a partner or an LLC member will be treated as a *general* partner if:

- The partner has personal liability for partnership debts by virtue of status as a partner,
- The partner can enter into contractual relationships on behalf of the partnership, or
- The partner works more than 500 hours in the partnership's trade or business during the tax year.

The Big Picture

EXAMPLE 31

Return to the facts of *The Big Picture* in Examples 14 and 22. Beachside's Schedule K and Schedules K–1 were prepared in accordance with these Proposed Regulations, with the members' distributive shares and guaranteed payments being treated as follows:

	Distributive Share (Proposed Regulations)	Guaranteed Payments [§ 1402(a)(13)]
Kyle	$60,000—not SE income	$60,000—not SE income (capital)
Maria	$90,000—not SE income*	$60,000—SE income (services) and $60,000—not SE income (capital)
Josh	$30,000—SE income	$60,000—SE income (services)

*See Prop.Reg. § 1.1402(a)–2(i), Example (iii). Maria works more than 500 hours in the business, but because she has identical management rights and obligations as Kyle, her distributive share is not subject to SE tax.

21-5b Net Investment Income Tax

An individual taxpayer's "net investment income" (NII) is subject to an additional tax of 3.8 percent to the extent the taxpayer's modified adjusted gross income (MAGI) exceeds $250,000 for married taxpayers filing joint returns (or half that amount if a separate return is filed) or $200,000 for other taxpayers.[61] MAGI equals the taxpayer's adjusted gross income increased by any foreign earned income exclusion.[62] This tax is calculated on Form 8960.

Certain types of income allocated from a partnership are treated as NII, including dividends, interest, passive activity income, and gains from property not used in a trade or business. In addition, the partner's distributive share is considered NII if the partner is a "passive" investor, as defined under the passive activity loss rules. The tax also applies to "income on investment of working capital," which includes guaranteed payments for use of a partner's capital. Tax-exempt income is not subject to this tax.

---

[60]§§ 1402(a) and (a)(13). See also Prop.Reg. § 1.1402(a)–2(h).

[61]§ 1411; the dollar amounts are not adjusted for inflation.

[62]§ 911.

EXAMPLE
32

Refer to Maria's Schedule K–1 on p. 21-25. Maria's NII includes the $60,000 guaranteed payment she received in exchange for capital plus her distributive share of the partnership's qualified dividends ($1,600) and net short-term capital gains ($4,800). It does not include the $840 of tax-exempt interest income reported to her on line 18.

Maria will prepare Form 8960 to calculate her net investment income tax. Assuming that Maria has no net investment income from other sources and files as a single taxpayer, she will pay a tax of 3.8% on the lesser of $66,400 ($60,000 + $1,600 + $4,800) or the excess of her modified AGI over $200,000.

LO.14

Define terms related to distributions from a partnership and determine the tax treatment of proportionate current distributions from a partnership to a partner and the tax treatment of proportionate distributions that liquidate a partnership.

21-6 DISTRIBUTIONS FROM THE PARTNERSHIP

Distributions don't typically cause the partner to recognize income or gain. Instead, the partner's outside basis is reduced by the amount of cash received. The partnership's inside basis in assets is also reduced. This reflects the aggregate theory, which holds that the partner essentially owns a share of the partnership's underlying assets.

21-6a Distributions in General

First, consider a few definitions. A *distribution* is a payment from a partnership to a partner with respect to the partner's ownership interest in the partnership.

Not all payments from a partnership to a partner are treated as distributions. For example, as discussed in text Section 21-9d, a partnership may pay rent to a partner for use of the partner's property, make a guaranteed payment to a partner for services or for use of the partner's capital, or purchase property from a partner.

Current versus Liquidating Distributions

If a payment is treated as a distribution from the partnership to the partner, it falls into one of two categories:

- Current (or nonliquidating) distributions.
- Liquidating distributions.

These distributions may consist of cash or partnership property. Whether a distribution is a ==current distribution== or a ==liquidating distribution== depends solely on whether the partner remains a partner in the partnership after the distribution is made.

Liquidating Distributions A *liquidating distribution* occurs either (1) when a partnership itself liquidates and distributes all of its property to its partners or (2) when an ongoing partnership redeems the interest of one of its partners.

Current Distributions A *current distribution* (sometimes called a "nonliquidating distribution") is any distribution from a continuing partnership to a continuing partner—that is, any distribution that is not a liquidating distribution.

EXAMPLE
33

Kate buys a 25% interest in the KLM LLC by contributing $40,000 of cash. Her distributive share of the LLC's income that year is $25,000. Assume that the LLC distributes $65,000 ($25,000 share of profits + $40,000 initial capital contribution) to Kate on the last day of the LLC's tax year. Even though Kate's capital account and basis are reduced to $0, the distribution is a current distribution if Kate continues to be a member of the LLC. If the LLC liquidates or if Kate's interest is liquidated, it is a liquidating distribution.

Proportionate versus Disproportionate Distributions

Each distribution is also classified based on whether it is proportionate or disproportionate. In a ==proportionate distribution==, a partner receives the appropriate share of certain ordinary income-producing assets of the partnership. A ==disproportionate distribution==

occurs when the distribution increases or decreases the distributee partner's interest in these assets. The tax treatment of disproportionate distributions illustrates yet another effect of the aggregate theory: the partner is deemed to own a share of each of the partnership's underlying ordinary income-producing assets. These rules can be complex and are beyond the scope of this discussion.

21-6b Proportionate Current Distributions

In general, neither the partner nor the partnership recognizes gain or loss when a current distribution occurs.[63] The partner usually takes a carryover basis in the assets distributed.[64] The distributee partner's outside basis is reduced (but not below zero) by the amount of cash and the adjusted basis of property distributed.[65] As the following example illustrates, a distribution does not change a partner's overall economic position.

> **EXAMPLE 34**
>
> Payton owns a 25% interest in the SP LLC. On the last day of the current year, Payton's basis in the LLC interest is $40,000 and its fair market value is $70,000. On that date, the LLC distributes $25,000 of cash plus a parcel of land (adjusted basis to the LLC is $13,000; fair market value is $30,000). The distribution is not taxable to Payton or the LLC. Payton's $40,000 basis is reduced by the $25,000 cash and the LLC's $13,000 basis in the land. After the distribution, Payton's basis in the LLC interest is $2,000, the basis in the land is a carryover basis of $13,000, and Payton has $25,000 of cash—for a before and after total basis of $40,000. Similarly, the fair market value of Payton's remaining interest in the LLC interest is (arguably) reduced to $15,000 [$70,000 − ($25,000 cash + $30,000 value of land)].
>
> If Payton sells the land and remaining LLC interest on the first day of the next year (the day after the distribution), he realizes and recognizes gains of $17,000 ($30,000 − $13,000) on the land and $13,000 ($15,000 − $2,000) on the LLC interest. These gains total $30,000, which is the amount of the original deferred gain.

Partnership distributions are governed by the aggregate theory; C corporation distributions are governed by the entity theory. In a C corporation, a distribution from current or accumulated income (earnings and profits) is taxable as a dividend to the shareholder, and the corporation does not receive a deduction for the amount distributed. This results in corporate income being subject to double taxation. In a partnership, a partner pays tax when the share of income is earned by the partnership; this income is not taxed again when distributed, so only a single level of taxation occurs.

Cash Distributions

Gain and Loss Recognition A proportionate current distribution of cash is taxable to the partner to the extent the distributed cash exceeds the partner's outside basis.[66] In a current distribution, losses are not recognized by the partner.

> **EXAMPLE 35**
>
> Samantha's basis in her LLC interest is $50,000 on December 31, after accounting for the calendar year LLC's current-year operations. On that date, the LLC distributes $60,000 of cash to Samantha. She recognizes a $10,000 gain from this distribution ($60,000 cash received − $50,000 basis in her LLC interest). Most likely, this gain is taxed as a capital gain.[67]

---

[63]§§ 731(a) and (b).

[64]§ 732(a)(1).

[65]§ 733.

[66]§ 731(a)(1).

[67]§ 731(a). If the partnership holds any "hot assets," however, Samantha will probably recognize some ordinary income. See § 751(b) and the related discussion of ordinary income ("hot") assets later in this chapter.

Liability Reduction Treated as Cash Distribution Recall from earlier in the chapter that the reduction of a partner's share of partnership debt is treated as a distribution of cash from the partnership to the partner. A reduction of a partner's share of partnership debt, then, first reduces the partner's basis in the partnership. Any reduction of a share of debt in excess of a partner's basis in the partnership is taxable to the partner as a gain.

Return to the facts of Example 35, except that, rather than cash being distributed, assume that Samantha's $50,000 basis in her LLC interest included a $60,000 share of the LLC's liabilities. If the LLC repays all of its liabilities, Samantha is treated as receiving a $60,000 cash distribution. The first $50,000 reduces her basis to $0. The last $10,000 creates a taxable gain to Samantha of $10,000.

Marketable Security Distributions Treated as Cash A distribution of marketable securities can also be treated as a distribution of cash. Discussion of such distributions is beyond the scope of this chapter.

Property Distributions

In general, a distributee partner does not recognize gain from a property distribution, whether the distribution is current or liquidating. If the partnership's basis in the property is greater than the partner's basis in the partnership interest, the distributed asset takes the lower substituted basis. This ensures that the partner does not receive asset basis that is not "paid for."

Amanda holds a $50,000 basis in her LLC interest. The LLC distributes land that had a partnership basis of $60,000 and a fair market value of $100,000. Amanda does not recognize any gain on this distribution because it is a distribution of property, not cash. Amanda takes a substituted basis of $50,000 in the land. Her basis in her LLC interest is reduced by the basis she takes in the asset received, or $50,000. Therefore, Amanda has a $50,000 basis in the land and a $0 basis in her LLC interest, and she recognizes no gain on this distribution.

If Amanda later sells the land for its $100,000 value, she will recognize a $50,000 gain, which includes the partnership's $40,000 inherent gain at the distribution date, plus the $10,000 excess value of the land over Amanda's basis in the partnership interest.

Ordering Rules

When multiple properties are distributed, the assets are deemed distributed in the following order:

- Step 1. Cash is distributed first.
- Step 2. Unrealized receivables and inventory ("hot assets") are distributed second.
- Step 3. All other assets are distributed last.

Unrealized Receivables and Inventory Defined <mark>Unrealized receivables</mark> are generally cash basis receivables that will result in ordinary income when collected. In addition, for purposes of the distribution rules, unrealized receivables also include depreciation recapture income that would arise if the partnership sold its depreciable assets (regardless of whether the taxpayer uses the cash or accrual method).

<mark>Inventory</mark>, for purposes of these ordering rules, includes any partnership assets except cash, capital, or § 1231 assets. The definition is so broad that all accounts receivable are considered to be inventory, although only cash basis receivables are "unrealized receivables."

One often hears unrealized receivables and inventory referred to as <mark>hot assets</mark>. In general, the partnership rules work to ensure that each partner is accountable for his/her/its share of hot assets and the related built-in ordinary income. The basis of the hot assets distributed cannot be increased, and the partner must recognize his/her/its share of ordinary income when the distributed assets are sold.

Basis in Distributed Property and Partnership Interest In a current distribution, the partner cannot step up (increase) the basis in distributed property beyond the partnership's basis. However, a current distribution can result in a step down (reduction to the property's basis). These potential decreases to basis are determined at each step of the asset distribution. For example, after a cash distribution (step 1), the partner's basis in the interest is recomputed. Then we can determine the effect of a distribution of unrealized receivables or inventory (step 2). If the remaining outside basis at the end of any step is insufficient to cover the entire inside basis of the assets in the next step, the basis in the remaining assets (step 3) is stepped down to equal the partner's remaining basis in the partnership interest.[68]

Effect of Ordering Rules

EXAMPLE 38

Lindsey holds a $48,000 basis in her partnership interest. On October 10, Lindsey receives a distribution from the partnership of (1) cash of $12,000, (2) cash basis receivables (inside basis, $0; fair market value, $10,000), and (3) land (inside basis and fair market value, $60,000). Lindsey has realized gain of $34,000 [$12,000 + $10,000 + $60,000 (values) − $48,000 (basis)].

However, none of that gain is recognized yet. The cash distribution (step 1) is considered first. No gain arises because the cash does not exceed Lindsey's basis in the partnership interest before the distribution ($12,000 cash < $48,000 basis in partnership). It reduces her basis in the partnership interest to $36,000 ($48,000 − $12,000). The receivables (step 2) are distributed next, taking a $0 carryover basis to Lindsey. Her partnership basis remains $36,000. The land is distributed last (step 3). Lindsey's remaining $36,000 basis in the partnership interest is less than the partnership's basis in the land ($60,000), so Lindsey takes a substituted basis of $36,000 in the land and reduces the basis for her partnership interest to $0.

EXAMPLE 39

Assume the same facts as in Example 38, and assume that Lindsey sells the parcel of land early the following year for its fair market value of $60,000. She also collects $10,000 from the cash basis receivables. Now she recognizes all of the previously deferred $34,000 gain ($70,000 amount realized and collected − $36,000 basis for the land − $0 basis for the receivables).

In Examples 38 and 39, although Lindsey does not recognize any of the gain from the distribution, she has a zero outside basis for her partnership interest. If the partnership generates net losses in the following year, she will not be able to deduct them.

When more than one asset in a particular class is distributed, special rules may apply, as discussed in text Section 21-6c. Concept Summary 21.4 reviews the general rules that apply to proportionate current partnership distributions.

21-6c **Proportionate Liquidating Distributions**

Proportionate liquidating distributions consist of a single distribution or a series of distributions that result in the termination of the partner's entire interest in the partnership. This section examines the rules for liquidating distributions that arise when the partnership itself is liquidating.

No Partnership Level Gain or Loss

In a proportionate liquidating distribution where the partnership liquidates, the partnership does not recognize either gain or loss. In contrast, if a corporation distributes property in a complete liquidation, the corporation recognizes gain or loss as if it sold all of its property at fair market value. This is another example of how the aggregate theory applies to partnerships and the entity theory applies to corporations.

---

[68]§ 732.

Concept Summary 21.4

Proportionate Current Distributions (General Rules)

Gains and Losses

- Generally, neither the distributee partner nor the partnership recognizes any gain or loss on a proportionate current distribution of cash or property.

- Exception: Gain is recognized if *cash* (and deemed cash) distributions exceed the distributee partner's basis.

Basis in Partnership Interest and Property Received

- The partner's basis in the partnership interest is reduced by the partner's basis in distributed property.

- General rule: Partner's basis in distributed property equals partnership's basis before distribution (carryover basis).

- Exception: Where the partner's *outside* basis is less than the partnership's *inside* (property) basis, partner's *outside* basis is assigned to distributed property (substituted basis).

Other Issues

- If the partner recognizes gain on a *proportionate* current distribution, the gain is a capital gain.

- Neither the partner nor the partnership recognizes loss on a *proportionate* current distribution of cash or property.

Proportionate Current Distribution Inputs and Calculations

Input the following information and complete the Calculations chart to determine the partner's gain or loss and basis in distributed property on a proportionate current distribution:

Inputs

Line 1 below	Partner's outside basis before distribution	_____
Line 2 below	Step 1. Cash and deemed cash distributed	_____
Line 5 below	Step 2. Partnership's basis in distributed hot assets	_____
Line 8 below	Step 3. Partnership's basis in other distributed property	_____

Calculations

1. Partner's outside basis (input above).	_____
2. Step 1. Cash and deemed cash distributed (input above).	_____
3. **Gain recognized by partner (excess of line 2 over line 1, if any).**	_____
4. Partner's remaining outside basis (line 1 − line 2). If less than $0, enter $0.	_____
5. Step 2. Partnership's basis in distributed hot assets (input above).	_____
6. **Partner's basis in distributed hot assets (lesser of line 4 or line 5).**	_____
7. Partner's remaining outside basis (line 4 − line 6). Cannot be < $0.	_____
8. Step 3. Partnership's basis in other distributed property (input above).	_____
9. **Partner's basis in other distributed property (lesser of line 7 or line 8).**	_____
10. Partner's remaining outside basis (line 7 − line 9). Cannot be < $0.	_____

Gain Recognition and Ordering Rules

When a partnership liquidates, the liquidating distributions to a partner usually consist of an interest in several or all of the partnership's assets. The ordering rules parallel those for current distributions, except that the partner's *entire* basis in the partnership interest is allocated to the assets received in the liquidating distribution, *unless* the partner is required to recognize a loss (see the discussion that follows).

The general ordering and gain recognition rules for a proportionate liquidating distribution are summarized as follows. You should recognize the first two steps from the prior discussion of current distributions.

- Step 1. Cash is distributed first. As with a proportionate current distribution, the cash distribution results in a capital gain if the amount distributed exceeds the partner's basis in the partnership interest. The cash distributed (including "deemed cash," such as relief of the partner's share of partnership debt) reduces the liquidated partner's outside basis dollar for dollar, except that the partner's basis cannot be reduced below zero.

- Step 2. Unrealized receivables and inventory are distributed second. As with proportionate nonliquidating distributions, these assets take a basis equal to the lesser of the partnership's inside basis in those assets or the partner's remaining outside basis. The partner's outside basis is reduced by the amount of basis assigned to these ordinary income-producing assets.

- Step 3. Here's where proportionate liquidating and nonliquidating distributions differ: for a liquidating distribution, if the liquidating partner has any remaining outside basis, that basis is allocated to *all* the assets received in step 3.[69]

EXAMPLE 40

When Tara's basis in her LLC interest is $70,000, she receives cash of $15,000 (step 1), a proportionate share of inventory (basis to LLC, $20,000; fair market value, $30,000) (step 2), and land (basis to LLC, $8,000; fair market value, $12,000) (step 3). The distribution liquidates both the LLC and Tara's entire LLC interest. The partnership has no hot assets other than the inventory, so this is a proportionate distribution.

In this case, Tara recognizes no gain or loss. Tara's $70,000 basis is reduced to $55,000 by the $15,000 cash received (step 1). The inventory (step 2) takes a basis to Tara of $20,000 and reduces her basis in the LLC interest to $35,000. The land (step 3) absorbs Tara's remaining LLC basis of $35,000.

Multiple Properties in an Asset Class

When more than one asset in a particular class is distributed in either a proportionate current distribution or a proportionate liquidating distribution, special rules may apply. If a step-*down* is needed (i.e., the partner's remaining basis for the partnership interest is *less than* the partnership's basis for the distributed assets in the particular class), the partner's remaining basis for each distributed asset is proportionately reduced, so as to reduce the differences between each asset's basis and its fair market value.

If, however, in a liquidating distribution a step-*up* is needed (i.e., the partner's remaining basis for the partnership interest is *greater than* the partnership's basis for the distributed assets in the "other assets" class), the partner's basis for the assets in the class is determined such that the basis amounts ultimately are in proportion to the fair market values of the distributed assets in that class.

EXAMPLE 41

Assume the same facts as in Example 40, except that Tara receives two parcels of land instead of one. The LLC's basis for the parcels is $2,000 for Parcel 1 and $6,000 for Parcel 2. Each parcel has a fair market value of $6,000.

Tara again takes a $15,000 basis for the cash and a $20,000 carryover basis for the inventory. Now Tara has a $35,000 remaining basis that must be allocated to the two parcels of land (step 3). The partnership's inside basis for the land of $8,000 is stepped up by $27,000.

Without going through the detailed rules, the remaining $35,000 basis is allocated $17,500 to each parcel of land. The step-up allocation and ending basis follows the intuitive result because the properties' fair market values are equal.

Loss Recognition

The distributee partner recognizes a *loss* on a liquidating distribution only if both of the following are true:

- The partner receives *only* cash, unrealized receivables, or inventory. The word *only* is important. A distribution of any other property precludes recognition of the loss.

- The partner's outside basis exceeds the partnership's inside basis for the distributed cash and hot assets.

---

[69]§§ 731 and 732.

The basis of hot assets cannot be increased. Therefore, the step 2 assets take a carryover basis, and the partner claims a loss for any remaining basis in the partnership interest.[70]

Liquidating Distributions with Potential Losses

EXAMPLE 42

When Ramon's outside basis is $40,000, he receives a liquidating distribution of $7,000 cash and a proportionate share of inventory having a partnership basis of $3,000 and a fair market value of $10,000. Ramon is not allowed to "step up" the basis in the inventory, so it is allocated a $3,000 carryover basis. Ramon's unutilized outside basis is $30,000 ($40,000 − $7,000 − $3,000). Because he receives a liquidating distribution of *only* cash and inventory, he recognizes a capital loss of $30,000 on the liquidation.

EXAMPLE 43

Assume the same facts as in Example 42, except that in addition to the cash and inventory, Ramon receives an antique desk he used while working at the partnership. The desk originally was purchased at a flea market for $100. Later, it was discovered that the desk was valued at $2,000, but because the desk was held as a § 1231 asset rather than an investment, it was depreciable. By the time the partnership liquidated, the desk was fully depreciated, with a basis of $0 and potential depreciation recapture (a "hot asset" for distribution purposes) of $100.

The $100 of potential depreciation recapture (with a $0 basis) is added to the hot assets in step 2. Therefore, Ramon's step 2 assets include inventory (basis $3,000, value $10,000) and depreciation recapture (basis $0, value $100).

As with the last example, Ramon's basis is $30,000 after the step 2 allocation. Because the desk is not cash, an unrealized receivable, or inventory, he cannot recognize a loss. Therefore, Ramon's remaining basis in his partnership interest is allocated to the desk.

What can Ramon do with a $30,000 antique desk (valued at $2,000)? If he continues to use it in a trade or business, he can depreciate it. Once he has established his business use of the desk, he can sell it and recognize a large § 1231 loss, which would be treated as an ordinary loss if it is the only § 1231 loss of Ramon's tax year. (Because depreciation recapture is not recognized on a loss, the $100 of potential ordinary income from prior depreciation deductions simply disappears.)

If the antique desk, however, is held as an investment asset, it will generate a $28,000 capital loss if it is sold at its $2,000 value. With proper planning, no liquidated partner should be forced to recognize a capital loss instead of an ordinary loss.

If the withdrawing partner later sells distributed inventory, gain on the sale is ordinary income unless the sale occurs more than five years after the distribution.[71] The withdrawing partner's holding period for all other property received in a liquidating distribution includes the partnership's related holding period.

Start

LO.15

Calculate the selling partner's amount and character of gain or loss on the sale or exchange of a partnership interest.

21-7 **SALE OF A PARTNERSHIP INTEREST**

A partner can sell or exchange all or part of a partnership interest. For example, in *The Big Picture* at the beginning of the chapter, one alternative is for Kyle and Maria to sell their LLC interests directly to the new developer. A sale of a partnership interest to a third party is similar in concept to a sale of corporate stock. However, because both the entity and aggregate theories are at work, the partner might be required to split the gain or loss on disposition of the partnership interest into ordinary and capital gains or losses.

21-7a **General Rules**

Generally, the sale or exchange of a partnership interest results in gain or loss, measured by the difference between the amount realized and the selling partner's basis in the partnership interest.[72]

Outside Basis doesn't affect it's a Basis

---

[70]§ 731(a)(2).
[71]§ 735(a)(2).

[72]§ 741.

Liabilities

In computing the amount realized and the basis of the interest sold, the selling partner's share of partnership liabilities must be considered, as discussed in text Section 21-4e. The purchasing partner includes any assumed indebtedness as a part of the consideration paid for the partnership interest, just as the selling partner includes the share of liabilities in the basis in the partnership interest. The concern is that the liabilities will be incorrectly excluded from either the selling price or basis when they should be included in both amounts.[73]

EXAMPLE 44

Cole originally contributed $50,000 in cash for a one-third interest in the CDE LLC. During the time Cole was a member of the LLC, his share of the LLC's income was $90,000 and he withdrew $60,000 cash. Cole's capital account balance (determined using the tax method) is now $80,000, and the LLC's liabilities are $45,000, of which Cole's share is $15,000. Cole's outside basis is $95,000 ($80,000 capital account + $15,000 share of the LLC's debts).

Cole sells his LLC interest to Stephanie for $110,000 of cash, with Stephanie also assuming Cole's share of the LLC's liabilities. The total amount realized by Cole is $125,000 ($110,000 cash received + $15,000 of the LLC's debts transferred to Stephanie). Cole's gain on the sale is $30,000 ($125,000 amount realized − $95,000 outside basis).

Stephanie's adjusted basis for her LLC interest is the purchase price of $125,000 ($110,000 cash paid + $15,000 assumed LLC debt).

Income Allocation

When a partner sells an entire interest in the partnership:

- Income for the partnership interest for the tax year is allocated between the buying partner and the selling partner, and
- The partnership's tax year "closes" with respect to the selling partner.

The closing of the tax year causes the selling partner to report the share of income on the sale date rather than at the end of the partnership's tax year. There are several acceptable methods of determining the partner's share of income.[74]

The selling partner's basis is adjusted for the allocated income or loss before the partner calculates the gain or loss on the sale of the interest.

EXAMPLE 45

On September 30, 2020, Erica sells her 20% interest in Evergreen LLC to Jason for $25,000. Erica is a calendar year taxpayer. Evergreen owns no hot assets (see discussion below), and its tax year ends on June 30.

On January 1, 2020, Erica's basis in Evergreen is $5,000. Here's what happens to Erica in calendar year 2020. First, on June 30, 2020, Evergreen's fiscal tax year closes, and Erica is allocated $3,000 of the LLC's income for that year.

On July 1, 2020, Erica's basis in the LLC interest is $8,000 ($5,000 beginning basis + $3,000 fiscal year 2019–2020 allocation). Evergreen determines that Erica's share of LLC income is $10,000 for the additional period she owned the LLC interest (July 1 to September 30, 2020). Because the LLC's tax year closes with respect to Erica, she must also report that $10,000 of income on her 2020 tax return. Her basis in the LLC interest is increased to $18,000, and she recognizes a $7,000 capital gain on the sale ($25,000 − $18,000).

In her calendar year 2020 tax return, Erica reports income from two Schedules K–1 ($3,000 and $10,000), plus her gain on the sale ($7,000). This $20,000 of reported income accounts for the difference between her $5,000 basis at the beginning of the year and the $25,000 she received from Jason.

---

[73]§ 742.

[74]§ 706(d)(1) and related Regulations and 2015 Proposed Regulations.

21-7b **Hot Assets and Carried Interests**

Special rules apply if the partnership owns hot assets, or if the partnership interest is a "carried interest" (as defined in text Section 21-2b). If the partnership holds hot assets, the selling partner will incur both ordinary income (loss) and capital gain (loss) on the sale of the interest. In general, *hot assets* are *unrealized receivables* and *inventory*, which when collected or disposed of by the partnership, would cause it to recognize ordinary income or loss. When a partner sells the interest in a partnership, it is as if the partner sold the underlying share of the partnership's ordinary income (loss) assets. The primary purpose of this rule is to prevent a partner from converting ordinary income into capital gain through the sale of a partnership interest.[75] The partner's § 751 gain or loss is reported on the selling partner's Schedule K–1.

Unrealized Receivables

The term *unrealized receivables* generally includes the accounts receivable of a cash basis partnership and, for sale or exchange purposes, depreciation recapture potential.[76]

The cash basis Canary LLP owns only a $10,000 receivable for rendering health care advice. Its basis in the receivable is zero because no income has been recognized. This item is a hot asset because ordinary income is not generated until Canary collects on the account.

Jacob, a 50% partner, sells his interest to Mark for $5,000. If Jacob's basis in his partnership interest is $0, his total gain is $5,000. The entire gain is attributable to Jacob's 50% share of the unrealized receivable, so his gain is taxed as ordinary income.

Inventory

For a sale or exchange of a partnership interest, the term *inventory* includes all partnership property except money, capital assets, and § 1231 assets. Receivables of an accrual basis partnership are included in the definition of inventory, as they are not cash, capital assets, or § 1231 assets.[77] This definition also is broad enough to include all items considered to be unrealized receivables.

Jan sells her one-third interest in the JKL LLC to Matt for $20,000 cash when her basis was $15,000. The interest has an outside basis of $15,000. On the sale date, the LLC's balance sheet reflects the following:

	Adjusted Basis	FMV		Adjusted Basis	FMV
Cash	$10,000	$10,000	Jan, capital	$15,000	$20,000
Inventory	21,000	30,000	Kelly, capital	15,000	20,000
Capital assets	14,000	20,000	Luis, capital	15,000	20,000
Total	$45,000	$60,000	Total	$45,000	$60,000

The overall gain on the sale is $5,000 ($20,000 − $15,000). Jan's share of the appreciation in the inventory is $3,000 [($30,000 − $21,000) × ⅓]. Therefore, she recognizes $3,000 of ordinary income because of the inventory and $2,000 of capital gain from the rest of the sale.

[75]§ 751(a).

[76]§ 751(a)(1).

[77]§ 751(d).

Sale of Carried Interests

As a further exception, if the partnership interest being sold is classified as a "carried interest," any gain on the sale of that interest is treated as a short-term capital gain, unless the interest has been held for more than three years.[78] Carried interests were introduced in text Section 21-2b. Most carried interests are held by investors for more than three years, so this provision likely will be encountered only rarely.

21-8 LIMITED LIABILITY ENTITIES

LO.16

Describe the application of partnership provisions to limited liability companies (LLCs) and limited liability partnerships (LLPs).

21-8a Limited Liability Companies

The limited liability company, introduced in text Section 21-1a, combines partnership taxation with limited personal liability for all owners of the entity.

Taxation of LLCs

A properly structured LLC with two or more owners is generally taxed as a partnership. Because none of the LLC members are personally liable for any debts of the entity, the LLC is effectively treated as a limited partnership with no general partners. As described earlier in this chapter, this results in unusual application of partnership taxation rules in areas such as allocation of liabilities to the LLC members, inclusion or exclusion of debt for at-risk purposes, passive or active status of a member for passive activity loss purposes, and determination of a member's liability for self-employment tax.

Converting to an LLC

A partnership can convert to an LLC with few, if any, tax ramifications: the old elections of the partnership continue, and the partners retain their bases and ownership interests in the new entity. However, a C or S corporation that reorganizes as an LLC is treated as having liquidated prior to forming the new entity. The transaction is taxable to both the corporation and the shareholders.

Advantages of an LLC

An LLC offers certain advantages over a limited partnership, including the following:

- Generally, none of the owners of an LLC are personally liable for the entity's debts. General partners in a limited partnership have personal liability for partnership recourse debts.
- Limited partners cannot participate in the management of the partnership. All owners of an LLC have the legal right to participate in the entity's management.

Disadvantages of an LLC

The disadvantages of an LLC stem primarily from the lack of Final Regulations in certain areas. There is only a limited body of case law interpreting the various state statutes, so the application of some provisions is uncertain. An additional uncertainty for LLCs that operate in more than one jurisdiction is which state's law will prevail and how it will be applied.

21-8b Limited Liability Partnerships

A limited liability partnership (LLP) is similar to a general partnership. The differences between the two entities are small, but very significant. Recall that general partners are jointly and severally liable for all partnership debts. In some states, partners in a registered LLP are jointly and severally liable for contractual liabilities (i.e., they are treated as general partners for commercial debt). They are also always personally liable for their own malpractice or other torts. They are not, however, personally

---

[78]§ 1061(a).

liable for the malpractice and torts of their partners. As a result, the exposure of their personal assets to lawsuits filed against other partners and the partnership is considerably reduced.

LLPs are treated as partnerships under Federal income tax statutes. They are most similar to general partnerships. An LLP must have formal documents of organization and register with the state. Because the LLP is a general partnership in other respects, it does not have to pay any state franchise taxes on its operations—an important difference between LLPs and LLCs in states that impose franchise taxes on LLCs.

See Concept Summary 22.4 in Chapter 22 for a review of the various tax implications of LLCs and LLPs.

LO.17

Identify tax planning opportunities related to partnerships and their partners.

21-9 **TAX PLANNING**

21-9a **Choosing Partnership Taxation**

A partnership often provides tax advantages over a C or S corporation. Partnership income is subject to only a single level of taxation; for partners who are individual taxpayers the rate can be as high as 37 percent (or 40.8 percent if subject to the net investment income tax). Individual partners can deduct up to 20 percent of QBI passed through from a partnership; the maximum effective tax rate on this income is 29.6 percent. Corporate income, however, is taxed at the entity level (at 21 percent) and upon distribution to corporate owners as dividends (at up to 23.8 percent for qualified dividends paid to individual shareholders). Partnership income may be subject to high tax rates at the partner level, but (especially for QBI) this tax will generally be lower than the combined layers of tax on corporate income (about 40 percent).

Income tax rates, however, don't tell the full story. Self-employment tax or the net investment income tax might also apply. An active "general" partner might be subject to self-employment tax (up to 15.3 percent of income, plus additional Medicare tax of up to 0.9 percent) on the entire distributive share from the partnership, as well as on any guaranteed payments for services. A C or S corporation shareholder, however, will only be subject to employment taxes to the extent the shareholder receives wages from the entity. Distributions from a C corporation (dividends) might be subject to net investment income tax, but for partners or S corporation shareholders this tax only applies to distributive shares of the entity's actual investment income.

When selecting a legal form in which to conduct business, a complete analysis, then, must consider the expected types and amounts of income for both the entity and the owners, plans to distribute cash flows (i.e., present value considerations), differences between actual salaries or wages that might be paid versus the amounts a partner would be required to report as self-employment income, and whether additional taxes might apply.

The chief disadvantage of partnerships is that any general partners might be liable for entity debts (which only occurs with C or S corporations if the debt is guaranteed). However, if the partnership can operate as an LLC or LLP, the owners' liability is minimized. In addition, any general partners (for example in a GP or LP) could be structured as LLCs or corporate entities to minimize the general partners' liability.

For both C and S corporations, income or loss allocations or distributions are required to be proportionate to ownership interests. A partnership, though, may adjust its allocations of income and cash flow among the partners each year according to their needs, as long as the allocation meets the substantial economic effect and capital account maintenance rules discussed in the chapter.

For smaller business operations, a partnership enables several owners to combine their resources at low cost. It offers simple filing requirements, the taxation of income only once, and the ability to discontinue operations relatively inexpensively.

For larger businesses, a partnership offers a unique ability to raise capital with low filing and reporting costs compared to corporate stock or bond issuances.

Concept Summary 21.5 outlines considerations in choosing to use a C corporation, an S corporation, or a partnership as a means of doing business.

Concept Summary 21.5

Major Advantages and Disadvantages of the Partnership Form

The partnership form may be attractive when one or more of the following factors is present:

- The entity will generate net taxable losses and/or valuable tax credits, which will be of use to the owners (subject to loss limitation rules).
- The entity will have individual partners and will generate qualified business income, of which up to 20% can be deducted.
- The partners' distributive shares of income will be taxed at lower individual tax rates (e.g., 10%, 12%, 22%, etc.).
- Any individual partners will be passive or will have sufficient wages from other sources so self-employment taxes will be minimized
- The owners want to avoid complex corporate administrative and filing requirements.
- The owners want to make special allocations of certain income or deduction items.
- Other means by which to reduce the effects of corporate double taxation (e.g., compensation to owners, interest, and rental payments) have been exhausted. {Corporate double taxation can result in total Federal tax at rates up to 39.8% [21% corporate rate + tax on the remaining 79% of income at 20% capital gains rates + (potentially) 3.8% net investment income tax].}

- The owners anticipate liquidating the entity within a short period of time. Liquidation of a C or S corporation would generate entity-level recognized gains on appreciated property distributed.

The partnership form may be less attractive when one or more of the following factors is present:

- The tax paid by the individual owners of a partnership is greater than the tax the entity would pay if it were a C corporation. [An individual partner in a partnership could pay Federal tax at up to 40.8% if the income is not QBI (37% top rate plus 3.8% net investment income tax plus potential self-employment taxes).]
- The entity is generating net taxable income without distributing any cash to the owners. The owners may not have sufficient cash with which to pay the tax on the entity's earnings. (Federal tax on corporate income is only 21% until that income is distributed to the shareholders.)
- The entity is in a high-exposure business, and the owners want protection from personal liability. An LLC or LLP, however, would limit personal liability.
- The entity has already been formed as a corporation, and conversion to partnership status could result in significant liquidation taxes.

21-9b Formation and Operation of a Partnership

Potential partners should ensure that they will not be taxed on gains realized when transferring assets to create the entity. A partner can make a tax-deferred contribution of assets to the entity either at the inception of the partnership or later. This possibility is not available to less-than-controlling shareholders in a corporation.

Partnership allocation rules should be used to the partners' best advantage. Special allocations of income, expense, or credit items must satisfy certain requirements to be acceptable to the IRS.

21-9c Basis Considerations and Loss Deduction Limitations

If a partnership incurs a loss for the taxable year, careful planning will help ensure that the partners can claim the deduction.

A partner can contribute capital to the partnership before the end of the tax year to ensure there is adequate basis to absorb the loss. If economic conditions warrant, the partnership could incur additional debt. The partner's cash contribution or share of debt increases the partner's basis in the partnership interest. If the loss also meets the "at-risk," "passive activity," and "excess business loss" hurdles, the loss can be deducted.

In the following year, if the partnership is expected to report taxable income, the partner could withdraw cash or the partnership could pay off debt, without triggering gain recognition.

21-9d Transactions between Partners and Partnerships

If both a partner and a partnership are involved in a single transaction, pay attention to how the transaction is structured. Consider the impact of related-party rules, and restructure the transaction, if necessary, to avoid unanticipated adverse tax results.

Under § 707(a), certain transactions between a partner and the partnership are treated as if the partner were an outsider, dealing with the partnership at arm's length.[79] This includes loan transactions, rental payments, sales of property between the partner and the partnership, and payments for services when the services are short-term technical services the partner also provides for parties other than the partnership.

On the other hand, for some transactions, the partner and partnership are treated as related parties, and the tax treatment is adjusted accordingly. For example, § 707(b)(1) provides that no loss is recognized on a sale of property between a person and a partnership when the person owns, directly or indirectly, more than 50 percent of partnership capital or profits. (Note that the disallowed loss might not vanish entirely, however. If the transferee eventually sells the property at a gain, the disallowed loss reduces any gain on subsequent sale of the property.)

Similarly, under § 707(b)(2), gain is treated as ordinary income (rather than capital gain) if the sale or exchange is between a partnership and a more-than-50% partner, unless the property is a capital asset to both parties. Note that this provision recharacterizes the gain from capital gain to ordinary income, whereas the above provision disallows a realized loss.

One option is for the partner to consider leasing, rather than selling, property to a partnership. The partner recognizes rent income (which might be qualified business income, eligible for up to a 20 percent deduction), and the partnership has a rent expense. Alternatively, the partner can sell the property to an outside third party who leases the property to the partnership for a fair rental.

21-9e Drafting the Partnership Agreement

A partner's distributive share of income, gain, loss, deduction, or credit is determined in accordance with the partnership agreement. In addition, the partner's status as a limited or general partner is often determined by reference to the rights the partner has in managing the entity. While a formal agreement is not always required, an agreement that sets forth the obligations, rights, and powers of the partners would provide some certainty as to the tax consequences of the partners' actions.

REFOCUS ON THE BIG PICTURE

WHY USE A PARTNERSHIP, ANYWAY?

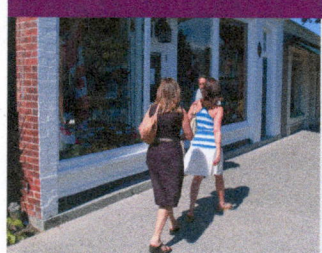

RODERICK PAUL WALKER/ALAMY STOCK PHOTO

After considering the various types of partnerships, Kyle, Maria, and Josh decided to form Beachside Properties as an LLC (see Example 1). On formation of the entity, there was no tax to the LLC or to any of its members (see Example 11). Beachside Properties computes its income as shown in Examples 13 and 15. Beachside determines additional information the three members will need (Example 16) and reconciles book and tax income and members' capital (Examples 17 and 18). Payments to the members for services or for the use of their capital are treated as guaranteed payments; the amounts are deducted by the LLC and reported as income by the LLC members (see Examples 14 and 22). The LLC members can claim a qualified business income deduction related to Beachside's operating income, rental income, and Kyle's and Maria's guaranteed payments for capital; the LLC will report additional information the members need to calculate their deduction limitations (see Example 23).

continued

---

[79]§ 707(a).

A portion of ordinary income was specially allocated to Maria under the substantial economic effect rules; precontribution gains will eventually be specially allocated under § 704(c); and the remaining income is allocated according to profit sharing ratios (Examples 19 to 22). The LLC's income affects the members' bases and capital accounts as shown in Examples 27 and 28.

An important consideration for the LLC members is whether their distributive shares and guaranteed payments will be treated as self-employment income or subject to net investment income tax (Examples 31 and 32).

What If?

What happens in the future when the LLC members decide to expand or renovate Beachside's facilities? At that time, the existing members can contribute additional funds, the LLC can obtain new members, or the entity can solicit third-party financing. An LLC is not subject to the 80 percent control requirement applicable to the formation of and subsequent transfers of property to a corporation. Therefore, new investors can contribute cash or other property in exchange for interests in the LLC—and the transaction will qualify for tax-deferred treatment.

Key Terms

Aggregate (or conduit) concept, 21-4	Hot assets, 21-42	Profits (loss) interest, 21-5
Capital account maintenance, 21-5	Inside basis, 21-5	Proportionate distribution, 21-40
Capital interest, 21-5	Inventory, 21-42	Qualified nonrecourse financing, 21-33
Capital sharing ratio, 21-5	Least aggregate deferral rule, 21-14	Recourse debt, 21-32
Carried interest, 21-9	Limited liability company (LLC), 21-2	Required taxable year, 21-13
Constructive liquidation scenario, 21-33	Limited liability partnership (LLP), 21-3	Schedule K–1, 21-4
Current distribution, 21-40	Limited partners, 21-2	Section 704(b) book capital accounts, 21-26
Disguised sale, 21-8	Limited partnership (LP), 21-2	Separately stated items, 21-5
Disproportionate distribution, 21-40	Liquidating distribution, 21-40	Special allocation, 21-5
Distributive share, 21-4	Nonrecourse debt, 21-32	Step down, 21-43
Economic effect test, 21-26	Operating agreement, 21-3	Step up, 21-43
Entity concept, 21-4	Outside basis, 21-5	Syndication costs, 21-12
General partners, 21-2	Partnership agreement, 21-3	Unrealized receivables, 21-42
General partnership (GP), 21-2	Precontribution gain or loss, 21-27	
Guaranteed payment, 21-18	Profit and loss sharing ratios, 21-5	

Discussion Questions

1. **LO.1** What is a partnership agreement? What types of provisions does it include?

2. **LO.1** What is the difference between a general partnership and a limited liability company? When might each type of entity be used? Why?

3. **LO.2, 4, 6, 7, 8** Describe how a partnership reports its income for tax purposes. *Critical Thinking* Who makes most elections related to partnership income and deductions? What two theories underlie most partnership tax rules? As an example, contrast the treatment of the business interest expense limitation with the qualified business income deduction.

4. **LO.3** Compare the provision for the nonrecognition of gain or loss on contributions to a partnership (i.e., § 721) with the similar provision related to corporate formation (i.e., § 351). What are the major differences and similarities?

Communications   5. **LO.4** If a partner contributes depreciable or amortizable property to the partnership, how is the basis of those properties recovered? In addition, what types of expenditures might a new partnership incur? How are those costs treated for Federal tax purposes? Create a chart describing the property or expenditure, the treatment, and the Code section requiring this treatment.

6. **LO.5** When can a partnership use the cash method of accounting?

7. **LO.6, 7, 13** What is a guaranteed payment? How is it reported on Form 1065 and its various schedules? How is it reported and taxed to the partner (including taxes other than income taxes)? Describe ways in which the tax treatment of a guaranteed payment for services differs from guaranteed payments for use of the partner's capital.

8. **LO.6, 7** What is the purpose of the qualified business income deduction under § 199A? How is the deduction calculated? What information does the partnership report?

9. **LO.8** What is the purpose of the three rules that implement the economic effect test?

10. **LO.9, 10** Discuss the adjustments that must be made to a partner's basis in the partnership interest. When are such adjustments made? Why?

11. **LO.11** What is a partner's capital account? What methods can be used to determine the capital account and when might these methods be used? Describe how a partner's ending capital account balance is determined.

12. **LO.13** When is partnership income subject to self-employment tax or the net investment income tax by an individual partner?

Communications   13. **LO.10, 12, 13, 17** Write an e-mail to a client describing situations in which the partnership entity form might be more advantageous (or disadvantageous) than operating as a C corporation. Use subheadings and bullet points to highlight your major thoughts.

Critical Thinking

14. **LO.14** What is the difference between the definition of a proportionate current distribution and a proportionate liquidating distribution? What is the significance of the word *proportionate*?

15. **LO.14** How does a proportionate current distribution of cash from a partnership to a partner compare with one from a Subchapter C corporation to a shareholder?

Computational Exercises

16. **LO.2** Enercio contributes $100,000 in exchange for a 40% interest in the calendar year ABC LLC, which is taxed as a partnership. This year, the LLC generates $80,000 of ordinary taxable income and has no separately stated income or expenses. Enercio withdrew $10,000 from the partnership during the year. Enercio is taxed on what amount of ABC's income? On how much of the $10,000 distribution will Enercio be taxed?

17. **LO.3** Henrietta transfers cash of $75,000 and equipment with a fair market value of $25,000 (basis to her as a sole proprietor, $10,000) in exchange for a 40% profit and loss interest worth $100,000 in a partnership.
    a. How much are Henrietta's realized and recognized gains?
    b. What is the amount of Henrietta's basis in her partnership interest?
    c. What is the partnership's basis in the contributed equipment?

18. **LO.3** On January 2 of the current year, Fenton and Myers form the FM LLC. Their contributions to the LLC are as follows:

	Adjusted Basis	Fair Market Value
From Fenton:		
Cash	$ 50,000	$ 50,000
Accounts receivable	–0–	90,000
Inventory	25,000	60,000
From Myers:		
Land	250,000	200,000

FM originally intended to hold the inventory as investment property. Myers held the land as long-term investment property, but FM will use it in its business as a § 1231 asset.

Within 30 days of formation, FM collects the receivables. Two years later, FM sells the inventory contributed by Fenton for $60,000 cash. After three years, FM sells the land for $200,000. How much income does FM recognize from these transactions, and what is its character? Why does this result apply?

19. **LO.7** This year, the Tastee Partnership reported income before guaranteed payments of $92,000. Stella owns a 90% profits interest and works 1,600 hours per year in the business. Euclid owns a 10% profits interest (with a basis of $30,000 at the beginning of the tax year) and performs no services for the partnership during the year. For services performed during the year, Stella receives a "salary" of $6,000 per month. Euclid withdrew $10,000 from the partnership during the year as a normal distribution of cash from Tastee (i.e., not for services).

    a. What is the amount of guaranteed payments made by the partnership this year?
    b. How much is the partnership's ordinary income after any permitted deduction for guaranteed payments?
    c. How much income will Stella report?
    d. How much income will Euclid report?

20. **LO.8** When Padgett Properties LLC was formed, Nova contributed land (value of $200,000 and basis of $50,000) and $100,000 cash, and Oscar contributed cash of $300,000. Both members received a 50% interest in LLC profits and capital.

    a. How is the land recorded for § 704(b) book capital account purposes?
    b. What is Padgett's tax basis in the land?
    c. If Padgett sells the land several years later for $300,000, how much tax gain will Nova and Oscar report?

21. **LO.12** Tobias is a 50% member in Solomon LLC, which does not invest in real estate. On January 1, Tobias's adjusted basis for his LLC interest is $130,000, and his at-risk amount is $105,000. His share of losses from Solomon for the current year is $150,000, all of which is passive. Tobias owns another investment that produced $90,000 of passive activity income during the year. (Assume that Tobias is a single taxpayer, there were no distributions or changes in liabilities during the year, and that the Solomon loss is Tobias's only loss for the year from any activity.)

    How much of Solomon's losses may Tobias deduct on his Form 1040? How much of the loss is suspended, and what Code provisions cause the suspensions?

22. **LO.12, 17** Heather sells land (adjusted basis, $75,000; fair market value, $85,000) to a partnership in which she controls an 80% capital interest. The partnership pays her only $50,000 for the land.

    a. How much loss does Heather realize and recognize?
    b. If the partnership later sells the land to a third party for $80,000, how much gain does that partnership realize and recognize?

23. **LO.14** Pablo has a $63,000 basis in his partnership interest. On May 9 of the current tax year, the partnership distributes to him, in a proportionate current distribution, cash of $25,000, cash basis receivables with an inside basis of $0 and a fair market value of $16,000, and land with a basis and fair market value to the partnership of $80,000.

   a.   How much is Pablo's realized and recognized gain on the distribution?

   b.   What is Pablo's basis in the receivables, land, and partnership interest following the distribution?

24. **LO.14** When Bruno's basis in his LLC interest is $150,000, he receives cash of $55,000, a proportionate share of inventory, and land in a distribution that liquidates both the LLC and his entire LLC interest. The inventory has a basis to the LLC of $45,000 and a fair market value of $48,000. The land's basis is $70,000, and the fair market value is $60,000. How much gain or loss does Bruno recognize, and what is his basis in the inventory and land received in the distribution?

25. **LO.15** Sweeney originally contributed $175,000 in cash for a one-fourth interest in the Gilbert LLC. During the several years that Sweeney was a member of the LLC, his share of the LLC's income was $90,000 and he withdrew $75,000 cash. The LLC's liabilities are $80,000, of which Sweeney's share is $20,000. The LLC has $40,000 of hot assets, of which Sweeney's share is $10,000.

   Sweeney sells his LLC interest to Jana for $225,000 cash, with Jana also assuming Sweeney's share of the LLC's liabilities.

   How much is Sweeney's gain on the sale, and what is its character? How much is Jana's adjusted basis for her LLC interest?

Problems

Critical Thinking 26. **LO.3, 17** Kenisha and Shawna form the equal KS LLC with a cash contribution of $360,000 from Kenisha and a property contribution (adjusted basis of $380,000, fair market value of $360,000) from Shawna.

   a.   How much gain or loss, if any, does Shawna realize on the transfer? Does Shawna recognize any gain or loss? If so, how much?

   b.   What is Kenisha's tax basis in her LLC interest? Section 704(b) book basis?

   c.   What is Shawna's tax basis in her LLC interest? Section 704(b) book basis?

   d.   What tax basis does the LLC take in the property transferred by Shawna?

   e.   Are there more effective ways to structure the formation? Explain.

Critical Thinking 27. **LO.3, 8** Liz and John formed the equal LJ Partnership on January 1 of the current year. Liz contributed $80,000 of cash and land with a fair market value of $90,000 and an adjusted basis of $75,000. John contributed equipment with a fair market value of $170,000 and an adjusted basis of $20,000. John had used the equipment in his sole proprietorship.

   a.   How much gain or loss will Liz, John, and the partnership realize?

   b.   How much gain or loss will Liz, John, and the partnership recognize?

   c.   What tax bases will Liz and John take in their partnership interests?

   d.   What § 704(b) book basis will Liz and John take in their partnership interests?

   e.   What bases will LJ take in the assets it receives?

   f.   Are there any differences between inside basis and outside basis? Explain.

   g.   How will the partnership depreciate any assets it receives from the partners?

   h.   Do additional considerations arise because of the difference between the basis and fair market values of the property John contributed?

28. **LO.3** Mike and Melissa want to form the equal MM Partnership. Melissa will contribute cash of $140,000. Mike has cash of $40,000 and land (fair market value of $100,000, adjusted basis of $136,000). Mike purchased the land several years ago as an investment (capital) asset. Mike and MM LLC are trying to decide between two alternatives.

    Critical Thinking
    Decision Making

    • In Alternative 1, Mike will contribute the land to the LLC. MM will use the property as a § 1231 asset (a parking lot) and then sell it in six years at an estimated $100,000 price. (Disregard any potential improvements to the land.)

    • In Alternative 2, Mike will sell the land immediately to a third party and contribute to MM the $100,000 cash proceeds from the sale. MM will use that cash to purchase similar land for $100,000 (also to be used as a parking lot).

    Use the following additional assumptions: (1) neither Mike nor MM will realize other capital or § 1231 gains or losses now or in the future, (2) Mike's marginal tax rate is 35%, (3) a reasonable annual discount rate is 3%, and (4) the tax treatment of capital and § 1231 gains and losses does not change in the foreseeable future.

    a. For each alternative, when would the $36,000 loss be recognized, to whom would the loss be allocated, what is the character of the loss, and over what time period can the loss be deducted?

    b. In these two alternatives, calculate Mike's tax savings each year from deducting his share of any loss allocated to him that year. Use the tables in Appendix G (or Microsoft Excel) to calculate the present value of these savings. Considering only tax savings, as Mike's tax adviser, would you recommend Alternative 1 or Alternative 2? Why? What other issues should Mike consider?

    c. How would the results in parts (a) and (b) change if MM were to sell the property in Alternative 1 after only four years? Answer conceptually; do not make calculations.

29. **LO.3, 17** During the current tax year, Dave and Stu formed the DS LLC with Dave contributing land with a basis of $360,000 and a fair market value of $600,000 at the contribution date. At the end of the year, the LLC distributes $300,000 of cash to Dave. The LLC made no distributions to Stu. Assume there were no other income or loss transactions for the year that would affect Dave's basis in his LLC interest.

    Decision Making

    a. Under general tax rules, how would the payment to Dave be treated?

    b. Under general tax rules, how much income or gain would Dave recognize as a result of the contribution and distribution?

    c. Under general tax rules, what basis would the LLC take in the land Dave contributed?

    d. What alternative treatment might the IRS try to impose?

    e. Under the alternative treatment, how much income or gain would Dave recognize?

    f. Under the alternative treatment, what basis would the LLC take in the land contributed by Dave?

30. **LO.5** Browne and Red, both C corporations, formed the BR Partnership on January 1, 2020. Neither Browne nor Red is a personal service corporation, and BR is not a tax shelter. BR's gross receipts were $22,000,000, $28,000,000, $34,000,000, and $36,000,000, respectively, for 2020 to 2023. Describe the methods of accounting available to BR in each tax year.

    Critical Thinking

31. **LO.5** Cerulean, Inc., Coral, Inc., and Crimson, Inc., form the Three Cs Partnership on January 1 of the current year. Cerulean is a 50% partner, and Crimson and Coral are 25% partners. For reporting purposes, Crimson uses a fiscal year with an October 31 year-end, Coral uses the calendar year, and Cerulean uses a fiscal year with a February 28/29 year-end. In general terms, how is the required taxable year

determined (no calculations required)? Explain. If the *required* taxable year is, say, October 31, what alternative tax years could the new partnership consider?

Decision Making   32. **LO.7** CL LLC is a manufacturing business and reported taxable income of $40,000,000 before interest expense, taxes, depreciation, and amortization ("tax EBITDA"), plus $1,500,000 of separately stated investment income. CL incurred interest expense of $1,000,000 in connection with this investment income and $14,000,000 in connection with its trade or business.

a.   How much interest expense can CL deduct?

b.   How is the interest expense reported on CL's Schedule K?

c.   What action, if any, is needed by the LLC members?

d.   How would your answers to parts (a) through (c) change if CL's tax EBITDA was $4,000,000 (plus $150,000 of investment income), its average annual gross receipts for all prior tax years was $10,000,000 or less, and the interest expense amounts were $100,000 (investment) and $1,400,000 (business)?

33. **LO.3, 7, 8** Phoebe and Parker are equal members in Phoenix Investors LLC. They are real estate investors who formed the LLC several years ago with equal cash contributions. Phoenix then purchased a parcel of land.

On January 1 of the current year, to acquire a one-third interest in the entity, Reece contributed to the LLC some land she had held for investment. Reece purchased the land five years ago for $75,000; its fair market value at the contribution date was $90,000. No special allocation agreements were in effect before or after Reece was admitted to the LLC. Phoenix holds all land for investment.

Immediately before Reece's property contribution, the balance sheet of Phoenix Investors LLC was as follows:

	Basis	FMV		Basis	FMV
Land	$30,000	$180,000	Phoebe, capital	$15,000	$ 90,000
			Parker, capital	15,000	90,000
	$30,000	$180,000		$30,000	$180,000

a.   At the contribution date, what is Reece's basis in her interest in the LLC?

b.   When does the LLC's holding period begin for the contributed land?

c.   On June 30 of the current year, the LLC sold the land contributed by Reece for $90,000. What is the LLC's recognized gain or loss? How is it allocated among the LLC members?

d.   Prepare a balance sheet reflecting basis and fair market value for the LLC immediately after the land sale described in part (c). No other transactions occurred during the year.

34. **LO.6, 7, 8, 11** Marcus and Madison are equal members of an LLC. On January 1 of the current year, to acquire a one-third interest in the entity, Nora contributed a parcel of land she had held for investment. (At this time, the entity will be renamed MMN LLC.) Nora had purchased the land for $120,000; its fair market value was $90,000 at the contribution date.

A few years later, the LLC sells Nora's land for $84,000. At the beginning of that year, Nora's capital account (determined using the tax basis) was $200,000 and Marcus and Madison's capital accounts (also calculated on the tax basis) were $170,000.

a.   What is the LLC's recognized gain or loss? How is it allocated among the LLC members?

b.   Use Microsoft Excel to prepare schedules that compute the partners' tax basis capital accounts immediately after the sale. Use variables to input the amount allocated to each LLC member and the total *not* specially allocated.

35. **LO.6, 7, 9, 10** Amy and Mitchell share equally in the profits, losses, and capital of the accrual basis AM Products LLC. The LLC does not need to report financial information to any third parties, so capital accounts are determined using tax rules (rather than GAAP). Amy is a managing member of the LLC (treated as a general partner) and is a U.S. person.

    At the beginning of the current year, Amy's *capital account* has a balance of $300,000, and the LLC has debts of $200,000 payable to unrelated parties. The debts are recourse to the LLC, but neither of the LLC members has personally guaranteed them. For basis purposes, all LLC debt is shared equally between the partners. The following information about AM's operations for the current year is obtained from the LLC's records.

Revenues	$1,400,000
Other operating expenses (e.g., utilities, repairs, rent, etc.)	500,000
W–2 wages to employees	200,000
Depreciation expense	300,000
Interest income	4,000
Long-term capital gain	6,000
Charitable contribution (cash)	4,000
Cash distribution to Amy	20,000
Unadjusted basis of partnership depreciable property immediately after acquisition	1,600,000

    Year-end LLC debt payable to unrelated parties is $140,000. All transactions are reflected in her beginning capital account and tax basis in the same manner. All AM Products' activities are eligible for the qualified business income deduction.

    a. Calculate Amy's tax basis in her LLC interest at the beginning and end of the tax year. Use her capital account as a starting point.
    b. What income, gains, losses, and deductions does Amy report on her income tax return?
    c. What other calculations is Amy required to make?
    d. Prepare Amy's tax-basis capital account rollforward from the beginning to the end of the tax year. How does her ending capital account differ from her ending tax basis in the LLC interets as calculated in part (a)?
    e. Using the information from parts (a) to (d), prepare Amy's Schedule K–1 as if you were the preparer of AM Products LLC's tax return. Provide all information that Amy needs to the extent you can. For Parts I and II (items A to F), omit any missing information (e.g., last names, addresses, EINs, etc.).

36. **LO.7, 8, 9, 11** Barney is a managing LLC member (treated as a general partner) of BG LLC and is allocated qualified business income (QBI) from BG of $800,000. (BG is not a "specified service trade or business.") Barney's Schedule K–1 reflects a $300,000 share of BG's W–2 wages and a $1,200,000 share of BG's UBIA (unadjusted basis immediately after acquisition). Assume also that Barney's taxable income excluding capital gains is $600,000 and that Barney has no income from REITs, publicly traded partnerships, or other qualified businesses. Refer to the QBI discussion in this chapter, the discussion in text Section 15-3, and the flowchart in Concept Summary 15.2.

    a. Calculate Barney's deduction under § 199A for qualified business income. Show your work and show how any limitations are calculated.
    b. How does Barney's § 199A deduction affect his (1) cash flow, (2) basis in the LLC interest, and (3) capital account?

37. **LO.7, 8, 9** The KL Partnership is owned equally by Kayla and Lisa. At the beginning of the year, Kayla's tax basis in her KL interest is $20,000 and Lisa's tax basis is $16,000. Partnership debt did not change from the beginning to the end of

Decision Making

the tax year. KL reported the following income and expenses for the current tax year:

Sales revenue	$150,000
Cost of sales	80,000
Distribution to Lisa	15,000
Depreciation expense	20,000
Utilities	14,000
Rent expense	18,000
Long-term capital gain	6,000
Payment to Mercy Hospital for Kayla's medical expenses	12,000

a.   Prepare a Microsoft Excel spreadsheet that could be used to accumulate KL's information to be reported on Form 1065, page 1 [Ordinary business income (loss)] and page 4 (Schedule K). Include calculations and subtotals to ensure the spreadsheet will update if the information changes. How much is the partnership's ordinary income on page 1? What information is shown on Schedule K?

b.   Use the information in part (a) to prepare Form 1065, pages 1 and 4 (Schedule K) for the KL Partnership. On page 1, omit items A to J at the top if the facts do not provide that information. For Schedule K, line 14, assume both partners are active in the partnership.

c.   Add columns to your spreadsheet to allocate amounts to Kayla and Lisa. (For this requirement, disregard the income from self-employment and information related to the qualified business income deduction.) Show the partners' allocation percentages at the top of their columns, and use those percentages in formulas to allocate any separately stated items that should be allocated. (Note that some items are directly assigned to a partner.) What information will be shown on Kayla's and Lisa's Schedules K–1, Part III? What items will Kayla and Lisa report on their Federal income tax returns?

d.   Expand your spreadsheet. Add rows for beginning basis and ending basis below Kayla's and Lisa's columns, and calculate each partner's ending basis in the partnership interest. How do you make this calculation? What is each partner's basis in her partnership interest at the end of the tax year?

e.   Consider the results if the partnership's revenues were $100,000 instead of $150,000. What happens if you update the revenues line on your spreadsheet? Are your new amounts correct for the Form 1065/Schedule K information, Schedule K–1 information, and partners' bases? Why or why not? What conclusions can you draw?

Critical Thinking   38.   **LO.3, 6, 7, 9, 10** Suzy contributed assets valued at $360,000 (basis of $200,000) in exchange for her 40% interest in Suz-Anna GP (a general partnership in which both partners are active owners). Anna contributed land and a building valued at $640,000 (basis of $380,000) in exchange for the remaining 60% interest. Anna's property was encumbered by qualified nonrecourse financing of $100,000, which was assumed by the partnership.

The partnership reports the following income and expenses for the current tax year:

Sales	$560,000
Utilities, salaries, depreciation, and other operating expenses	360,000
Short-term capital gain	10,000
Tax-exempt interest income	4,000
Charitable contributions (cash)	8,000
Distribution to Suzy	10,000
Distribution to Anna	20,000

During the current tax year, Suz-Anna refinanced the land and building (i.e., the original $100,000 debt was repaid and replaced with new debt). At the end of the year, Suz-Anna held recourse debt of $100,000 for partnership accounts payable (recourse to the partnership but not personally guaranteed by either of the partners) and qualified nonrecourse financing of $200,000.

a. What is Suzy's basis in Suz-Anna after formation of the partnership? Anna's basis?

b. What income and separately stated items does the partnership report on Suzy's Schedule K–1? What income, deduction, and taxes does Suzy report on her tax return? What additional information is needed?

c. Assume that all partnership debts are shared proportionately. At the end of the tax year, what are Suzy's basis and amount at risk in her partnership interest?

d. Assume that Suz-Anna prepares the capital account rollforward on the partners' Schedules K–1 on a tax basis. What are Suzy's capital account balances at the beginning and end of the tax year? What accounts for the difference between Suzy's ending capital account and her ending tax basis in the partnership interest?

e. Now think about what would happen if Suz-Anna was formed as an LLC instead of a general partnership. How would Suz-Anna's ending liabilities be treated? How would Suzy's basis and amount at risk be different?

39. **LO.7** Burgundy, Inc., and Violet are equal partners in the calendar year BV LLC. Burgundy uses a fiscal year ending April 30, and Violet uses a calendar year. Burgundy receives an annual guaranteed payment of $100,000 for use of capital contributed by Burgundy. BV's taxable income (after deducting the payment to Burgundy, Inc.) is $80,000 for 2020 and $90,000 for 2021.

a. What is the amount of income from the LLC that Burgundy must report for its tax year ending April 30, 2021?

b. What is the amount of income from the LLC that Violet must report for her tax year ending December 31, 2021?

c. Now assume that Burgundy, Inc.'s annual guaranteed payment is increased to $120,000 starting on January 1, 2021, and the LLC's taxable income for 2020 and 2021 (after deducting Burgundy's guaranteed payment) is the same (i.e., $80,000 and $90,000, respectively). What is the amount of income from the LLC that Burgundy, Inc., must report for its tax year ending April 30, 2021?

40. **LO.3, 7, 9, 12** Bryan and Cody each contributed $120,000 to the newly formed BC   Critical Thinking
Partnership in exchange for a 50% interest. The partnership used the available funds to acquire equipment costing $200,000 and to fund current operating expenses. The partnership agreement provides that depreciation will be allocated 80% to Bryan and 20% to Cody. All other items of income and loss will be allocated equally between the partners.

Upon liquidation of the partnership, property will be distributed to the partners in accordance with their § 704(b) book capital account balances. Any partner with a negative capital account must contribute cash in the amount of the negative balance to restore the capital account to $0.

In its first year, the partnership reported an ordinary loss (before depreciation) of $80,000 and depreciation expense of $36,000. In its second year, the partnership reported $40,000 of income from operations (before depreciation), and it reported depreciation expense of $57,600.

a. Calculate the partners' bases in their partnership interests at the end of the first and second tax years. Are any losses suspended? Explain.

b. Does the allocation provided in the partnership agreement have economic effect? Explain.

c. Now assume that on the first day of the third tax year, the partnership sells the equipment for $150,000. The gain on the sale is allocated equally to the partners. The partnership distributes all cash in accordance with the partners' capital account balances, and the partnership liquidates. How will partnership cash balances be distributed to the partners upon liquidation? (*Hint:* First, calculate the partners' bases in their partnership interests after reflecting any gain or loss on disposal of the equipment. Disregard any depreciation in year 3.) What observations can you make regarding the value of a deduction to each partner?

41. **LO.10** This year, Callie and Neil formed CN LLC. Callie contributed $300,000 of cash, and Neil contributed real estate valued at $450,000 (basis of $200,000). The property was subject to a recourse liability of $150,000 that was assumed by the LLC, but which is not guaranteed by either LLC member. Callie and Neil's profit sharing ratios are 40%/60%, respectively, but the loss sharing ratios are 50%/50%. Is the debt treated as a recourse debt or a nonrecourse debt to the LLC members? How is the debt allocated between Callie and Neil? What are Neil's and Callie's bases in the LLC interest immediately after the LLC was formed? Show your calculations.

Communications
Decision Making

42. **LO.3, 9, 10** Paul and Anna plan to form the PA LLC by the end of the current year to produce and sell specialty athletic apparel. Paul and Anna will both serve as member-managers of the LLC and will be active in its operations. The members will each contribute $80,000 of cash, and in addition, the LLC will borrow $440,000 from First State Bank. The $600,000 will be used to buy equipment and to lease a property they can use as a small manufacturing facility and a storefront.

The bank has stated that the debt must be guaranteed, and Anna has agreed to guarantee the entire amount. At the end of the year, the LLC also expects to have accounts payable of $40,000 for inventory and supplies.

The LLC's operating agreement provides that all LLC items will be allocated equally. The agreement also provides that capital accounts will be properly maintained and that each member must restore any deficit in the capital account upon the LLC's liquidation.

If the LLC claims 100% bonus depreciation, it will report a loss of about $580,000 in its first year, which the LLC members would like to deduct.

Paul and Anna would like to know how the debt ($440,000 loan and $40,000 of accounts payable) will be allocated, and how that allocation affects their ability to deduct the losses. Assume both Paul and Anna are single individual taxpayers. If limitations arise, can any adjustments be made to ensure the losses can be deducted? Consider all potential loss limitations and assume that neither Paul nor Anna will have business income or losses from other sources. Using the format (1) facts, (2) at issue, (3) conclusion and recommendations, and (4) law and analysis, draft a memo for the PA LLC tax planning file for your manager's review that describes how the debt will be shared between Paul and Anna for purposes of computing the adjusted basis of each LLC interest. Include any planning ideas that could be addressed to improve the results.

Critical Thinking

43. **LO.9, 10, 12, 17** The BCD Partnership plans to distribute cash of $20,000 to partner Brad at the end of the tax year. The partnership reported a loss for the year, and Brad's share of the loss is $10,000. At the beginning of the tax year, Brad's basis in his partnership interest, including his share of partnership liabilities, was $15,000. The partnership expects to report substantial income in future years.

a. What ordering rules are used to calculate Brad's ending basis in his partnership interest?

b. How much gain or loss will Brad report for the tax year?

c. Will the deduction for the $10,000 loss be suspended? Why or why not?

d. Could any planning opportunities be used to minimize any negative tax ramifications of the distribution? Explain.

44. **LO.14** When Teri's outside basis in the TMF Partnership is $80,000, the partnership distributes to her $30,000 of cash, an account receivable (fair market value of $60,000, inside basis to the partnership of $0), and a parcel of land (fair market value of $60,000, inside basis to the partnership of $80,000). Teri remains a partner in the partnership, and the distribution is proportionate to the partners.

    a. Use the format of Concept Summary 21.4 to create a spreadsheet to calculate the effects of the distribution. Set up an Input area for the amounts on lines 1, 2, 5, and 8. Code the formulas shown in the Calculations section of the concept summary to calculate the amounts in the remaining lines. You will use "sum," "min," and "max" formulas. Enter Teri's relevant facts in the input section of your spreadsheet.

    b. Based on the information in your spreadsheet, how much gain or loss will Teri recognize as a result of the distribution? Explain your answer.

    c. How much is Teri's basis in the land, account receivable, and TMF Partnership after the distribution? What can you conclude regarding Teri's basis in the assets and the fair market value she received?

    d. How would your answer to part (c) change if, instead, the partnership's basis in the land was $10,000 and its fair market value was $30,000 (and the cash and unrealized receivable distributions do not change)? Adjust the input section of your spreadsheet, and explain your findings.

45. **LO.14** Consider each of the following independent situations, and answer the following questions. For each fact pattern, indicate: **Decision Making**

    • Whether the partner recognizes gain or loss.
    • Whether the partnership recognizes gain or loss.
    • The partner's adjusted basis for the property distributed.
    • The partner's outside basis in the partnership after the distribution.

    In each case, assume the partnership owns no hot assets. Show your calculations in Microsoft Excel using a template similar to the format shown in Concept Summary 21.4. You will use "sum," "min," and "max" formulas.

    a. Kim receives $20,000 of cash in partial liquidation of her interest in the partnership. Kim's outside basis for her partnership interest immediately before the distribution is $3,000.

    b. Kourtni receives $40,000 of cash and land with an inside basis to the partnership of $30,000 (value of $50,000) in partial liquidation of her interest. Kourtni's outside basis for her partnership interest immediately before the distribution is $80,000.

    c. Assume the same facts as in part (b), except that Kourtni's outside basis for her partnership interest immediately before the distribution is $60,000.

    d. Klois receives $50,000 of cash and inventory with a basis of $30,000 and a fair market value of $50,000 in partial liquidation of her partnership interest. Her basis was $90,000 before the distribution.

46. **LO.14** At the beginning of the tax year, Melodie's basis in the MIP LLC was $60,000, including her $40,000 share of the LLC's liabilities. At the end of the year, MIP distributed to Melodie cash of $10,000 and inventory (basis of $6,000, fair market value of $10,000). In addition, MIP repaid all of its liabilities by the end of the year.

    a. If this is a proportionate current distribution, what is the tax effect of the distribution to Melodie and MIP? After the distribution, what is Melodie's basis in the inventory and in her MIP interest?

    b. Would your answers to part (a) change if this had been a proportionate liquidating distribution? Explain.

47. **LO.14** In each of the following independent liquidating distributions in which the partnership also liquidates, prepare a Microsoft Excel spreadsheet to determine the amount and character of any gain or loss to be recognized by each partner and the basis of each asset (other than cash) received. In each case, assume that distributions of hot assets are proportionate to the partners. Be sure to explain your rationale.

   a. Landon has a partnership basis of $40,000 and receives a distribution of $50,000 in cash.

   b. Mark has a partnership basis of $50,000 and receives $20,000 of cash and a capital asset with a basis to the partnership of $25,000 and a fair market value of $40,000.

   c. Neil has a partnership basis of $100,000 and receives $40,000 of cash, inventory with a basis to the partnership of $30,000, and a capital asset with a partnership basis of $20,000. The inventory and capital asset have fair market values of $20,000 and $30,000, respectively.

   d. Oscar has a partnership basis of $40,000 and receives a distribution of $10,000 of cash and an account receivable with a basis of $0 to the partnership (value is $15,000).

Communications

Critical Thinking

48. **LO.15** BDD Partnership is a service-oriented partnership that has three equal general partners. One of them, Barry Evans, sells his interest to another partner, Dale Allen, on December 31 (the last day of the current tax year), for $90,000 of cash and the assumption of Barry's share of partnership liabilities. (Liabilities are shared equally by the partners.)

Immediately before the sale (after reflecting operations for the year), the partnership's cash basis balance sheet is as shown below. Assume that the capital accounts *before* the sale reflect the partners' bases in their partnership interests, excluding liabilities. The payment exceeds the stated fair market value of the assets because of goodwill that is not recorded on the books.

	Basis	**FMV**		**Basis**	**FMV**
Cash	$120,000	$120,000	Note payable	$ 30,000	$ 30,000
Accounts receivable	–0–	90,000	Capital accounts		
Capital assets	30,000	75,000	Barry	40,000	85,000
			David	40,000	85,000
			Dale	40,000	85,000
Total	$150,000	$285,000	Total	$150,000	$285,000

   a. What is the total amount realized by Barry on the sale?

   b. How much, if any, ordinary income must Barry recognize on the sale?

   c. How much capital gain must Barry report?

   d. What is Dale's basis in the partnership interest acquired?

   e. Refer to Reg. § 1.751–1(a)(3). What information is the seller required to provide? Draft a statement that meets these requirements.

See Appendix E for Comprehensive Tax Return Problem—Form 1065

Research Problems

Note: Solutions to the Research Problems can be prepared by using the Thomson Reuters Checkpoint™ online tax research database, which accompanies this textbook. Solutions can also be prepared by using research materials found in a typical tax library.

Research Problem 1. Barry, an individual, and Aldrin, Inc., a domestic C corporation, have decided to form BA LLC. The new LLC will produce a product that Barry recently developed and patented. Barry and Aldrin, Inc., will each own a 50% capital and profits interest in the LLC. Barry is a calendar year U.S. taxpayer, while Aldrin, Inc., uses a July 1–June 30 fiscal year. The LLC does not have a "natural business year" and elects to be taxed as a partnership.

a.   Determine the taxable year of the LLC under the Code and Regulations.

b.   Two years after formation of the LLC, Barry sells half of his interest (25%) to Aldrin, Inc. Can the LLC retain the taxable year determined in part (a)? Why or why not?

Research Problem 2. Your clients, Grayson Investments, Inc. (Ana Marks, President), and Blake Caldwell, each contributed $200,000 of cash to form the Realty Management Partnership, a limited partnership. Grayson is the general partner, and Blake is the limited partner. The partnership used the $400,000 cash to make a down payment on a building. The rest of the building's $4,000,000 purchase price was financed with an interest-only nonrecourse loan of $3,600,000, which was obtained from an independent third-party bank.

  The partnership allocates all partnership items equally between the partners except for the MACRS deductions and building maintenance, which are allocated 70% to Blake and 30% to Grayson. The partnership wants to satisfy the "economic effect" requirements of Reg. §§ 1.704–1 and 1.704–2 and will reallocate MACRS, if necessary, to satisfy the requirements of the Regulations.

  Under the partnership agreement, liquidation distributions will be paid in proportion to the partners' positive capital account balances. Capital accounts are maintained as required in the Regulations. Grayson Investments has an unlimited obligation to restore its capital account, while Blake is subject to a qualified income offset provision.

  Assume that all partnership items, except for MACRS, will net to zero throughout the first three years of the partnership operations. Also assume that each year's MACRS deduction will be $200,000 (to simplify the calculations).

  Draft a letter to the partnership, evaluating the allocation of MACRS in each of the three years under Reg. §§ 1.704–1 and −2. The partnership's address is 53 East Marsh Ave., Smyrna, GA 30082. Do not address the "substantial" test.

Research Problem 3. Texas Land, Inc., wanted to acquire and develop 100 acres of property in west Texas at a cost of $10,000,000 ($4,000,000 to purchase the land from ABC, Inc., and $6,000,000 for development costs). However, Texas Land had only $2,000,000 of cash available for the land purchase, and no funds to put toward the development costs.

Critical Thinking

  Texas Land approached Gateway Savings & Loan, an S&L with significant tax losses but available cash. Gateway agreed to contribute the remaining $2,000,000 (for the land purchase) to a partnership (TG Partners) that would acquire and develop the property. Gateway would also make additional funds available for the development as needed. (Gateway's additional contributions would never total the remaining $6,000,000 cost because portions of the property were intended to be sold as they were completed, and those sales proceeds would fund future phases of the improvements.)

  In return, Gateway will receive a guaranteed payment of 10% of its capital each year, plus Gateway and Texas Land will share (50%/50%) any profits on the development and sale of the property. The parties also agreed that Texas Land would manage the property and oversee its development and would receive a fixed guaranteed payment related to those services. No partnership agreement was drafted or signed.

As it turned out, Texas Land located another party (DEF, Inc.) that wanted to purchase "the best" 30 acres of the property for $5,000,000. Texas Land and Gateway arranged that the closing on the 100-acre purchase from ABC would occur the same day as the closing on the 30-acre sale to DEF. The $5,000,000 sales proceeds were enough to pay the entire purchase price to ABC, with $1,000,000 left over to begin improvements on the remaining 70-acre parcel. That first $4,000,000 of sales proceeds essentially funded the $2,000,000 capital contributions for both Texas Land and Gateway, so neither partner needed to immediately contribute cash to TG Partners.

Even though neither Texas Land nor Gateway invested cash upon formation, they intend to carry on as if TG Partners was established and is the entity completing the development activities. However, they are concerned that the IRS might contend that no partnership was formed, and that the arrangement was simply designed to shift a tax liability (gain on the development) from Texas Land to Gateway, which has no current tax liability.

a. All of these events happened in the prior year and now it's February and TG Partners is your client. Review the rules of § 761. Under these rules, make your best case that TG Partners is, indeed, a partnership. (TG will operate on the calendar year.)

b. Consider the effect of the Check-the-box Regulations under Reg. § 301.7701 and your knowledge, in general, of partnership taxation. What can you do to ensure that partnership treatment is assured?

Use internet tax resources to address the following questions. Look for reliable websites and blogs of the IRS and other government agencies, media outlets, businesses, tax professionals, academics, think tanks, and political outlets.

Research Problem 4. Search for news or current reports related to partnerships, LLCs, or limited partnerships. What entities did you find that are taking advantage of the partnership entity form? In what industries do they operate? What are their gross receipts and asset holdings?

Communications
Data Analytics

Research Problem 5. The IRS Statistics on Income division accumulates information each year on the various types of businesses operating as partnerships. At **irs.gov/taxstats**, click "Partnerships," and then click "By Sector or Industry." Open the Microsoft Excel file for one of the tables (e.g., Table 1) for the most recent tax year available. For that year, sort and evaluate the data various ways to "dig deeper" into the various ways in which partnerships are used.

Write a memo to your instructor that describes some of the things you learned. For example, in which industries do you find the largest numbers of partnerships, the largest numbers of partners, and/or the largest concentration of gross and net assets? What conclusions can you draw? Support your findings with at least one graphic or chart prepared in Microsoft Excel.draw.

Becker CPA Review Questions

1. Gray is a 50% partner in Fabco Partnership. Gray's tax basis in Fabco on January 1, year 4, was $5,000. Fabco made no distributions to the partners during year 4 and recorded the following.

Ordinary income	$20,000
Tax-exempt income	8,000
Portfolio income	4,000

What is Gray's tax basis in Fabco on December 31, year 4?

a. $21,000   c. $12,000

b. $16,000   d. $10,000

2. Nick, Chris, Stacey, and Mike are each 25% partners in Liberty Partnership, a general partnership. During the current year, the partnership had revenues of $300,000 and nonseparately allocated business expenses of $100,000, including a guaranteed payment of $30,000 to Nick for services rendered. Also, during the current year, the partnership had interest income of $10,000 and charitable contributions of $16,000. With regard to activity in the partnership, what should Stacey report on her income tax return for the current year?

	Ordinary Income	Interest Income	Charitable Contributions
a.	$200,000	$10,000	$16,000
b.	$80,000	$2,500	$4,000
c.	$57,500	$2,500	$4,000
d.	$50,000	$2,500	$4,000

3. Duffy Associates is a partnership engaged in real estate development. Olinto, a civil engineer, billed Duffy $40,000 in the current year for consulting services rendered. In full settlement of this invoice, Olinto accepted a $15,000 cash payment plus the following.

	Fair Market Value	Carrying Amount on Duffy's Books
10% partnership interest in Duffy	$10,000	N/A
Automobile	7,000	$3,000

What amount should Olinto, a cash basis taxpayer, report on his current-year return as income for the services rendered to Duffy?

a. $15,000   c. $32,000

b. $28,000   d. $40,000

4. At partnership inception, Black acquires a 50% interest in Decorators Partnership by contributing property with an adjusted basis of $250,000. Black recognizes a gain if:

I. The fair market value of the contributed property exceeds its adjusted basis.
II. The property is encumbered by a mortgage with a balance of $100,000.

a. I only   c. Both I and II

b. II only   d. Neither I nor II

5. When a partner's share of partnership liabilities increases, that partner's basis in the partnership interest:

a. Increases by the partner's share of the liabilities.

b. Decreases by the partner's share of the liabilities.

c. Decreases, but not to less than zero.

d. Is not affected.

6. Peter, a 25% partner in Gold & Stein Partnership, received a $20,000 guaranteed payment in the current year for deductible services rendered to the partnership. Guaranteed payments were not made to any other partner. Gold & Stein's current-year partnership income consisted of:

Net business income before guaranteed payments	$80,000
Net long-term capital gains	10,000

What amount of income should Peter report from Gold & Stein Partnership on his current-year tax return? (Disregard the character of the income and just calculate the total increase to Peter's income.)

a. $37,500   c. $22,500

b. $27,500   d. $20,000

7. Hart's adjusted basis of his interest in a partnership was $30,000. He received a proportionate nonliquidating distribution of $24,000 cash plus a parcel of land with a fair market value and partnership basis of $9,000. Hart's basis for the land is:

a. $9,000   c. $3,000

b. $6,000   d. $0

8. Gearty's adjusted basis in Worthington Company, a partnership, was $18,000 at the time Gearty received the following proportionate nonliquidating distributions of partnership property:

Cash	$ 6,000
Land	
Adjusted basis	14,000
Fair market value	12,000
Inventory	
Adjusted basis	7,000
Fair market value	10,000

What is Gearty's tax basis in the land received from the partnership?

a. $0   c. $12,000

b. $5,000   d. $14,000

9. Desi's adjusted basis of her partnership interest was $40,000 immediately before she received a distribution in full liquidation of her Makris partnership interest. (The partnership had no hot assets and also liquidated.) The distribution consisted of $25,000 in cash and land with a fair market value of $30,000. Makris's basis in the land was $10,000 immediately prior to the distribution. During the year, Desi sold the land for $50,000. How will Desi report the liquidating distribution and the sale on her income tax return?

	Liquidating Distribution	Sale of the Land
a.	No gain or loss	$35,000 capital gain
b.	No gain or loss	$40,000 capital gain
c.	$15,000 gain	$20,000 capital gain
d.	$5,000 loss	$40,000 capital gain

10. On December 31 of the current year, after receipt of his share of partnership income, Fox sold his interest in a limited partnership for $50,000 of cash plus relief of all liabilities. On that date, the adjusted basis of Fox's partnership interest was $60,000, consisting of his capital account of $35,000 and his share of the partnership liabilities of $25,000. The partnership has no unrealized receivables or substantially appreciated inventory. What is Fox's gain or loss on the sale of his partnership interest?

a. Ordinary loss of $10,000   c. Capital loss of $10,000

b. Ordinary gain of $15,000   d. Capital gain of $15,000

CHAPTER

22

S Corporations

LEARNING OBJECTIVES: *After completing Chapter 22, you should be able to:*

LO.1 Explain the tax effects that S corporation status has on shareholders.

LO.2 Identify corporations that qualify for the S election.

LO.3 Explain how to make an S election.

LO.4 Explain how an S election can be terminated.

LO.5 Compute nonseparately stated income and identify separately stated items.

LO.6 Allocate income, deductions, and credits to shareholders.

LO.7 Determine how distributions to S corporation shareholders are taxed.

LO.8 Calculate a shareholder's basis in S corporation stock.

LO.9 Explain the tax effects that losses have on shareholders.

LO.10 Compute the built-in gains and passive investment income penalty taxes.

LO.11 Engage in tax planning for S corporations.

CHAPTER OUTLINE

22-1 Choice of Business Entity, 22-2
  22-1a An Overview of S Corporations, 22-2

22-2 Qualifying for S Corporation Status, 22-3
  22-2a Definition of a Small Business Corporation, 22-3
  22-2b Making the Election, 22-5
  22-2c Shareholder Consent, 22-6
  22-2d Loss of the Election, 22-7

22-3 Operational Rules, 22-9
  22-3a Computation of Taxable Income, 22-9
  22-3b Qualified Business Income Deduction, 22-12
  22-3c Allocation of Income and Loss, 22-12
  22-3d Tax Treatment of Distributions to Shareholders, 22-13

  22-3e Tax Treatment of Noncash Property Distributions by the Corporation, 22-18
  22-3f Shareholder's Basis in S Stock, 22-19
  22-3g Treatment of Losses, 22-21
  22-3h Tax on Pre-Election Built-In Gain, 22-23
  22-3i LIFO Recapture Tax, 22-24
  22-3j Passive Investment Income Penalty Tax, 22-24
  22-3k Other Operational Rules, 22-25

22-4 Tax Planning, 22-26
  22-4a When the Election Is Advisable, 22-26
  22-4b Making a Proper Election, 22-26
  22-4c Operation of the S Corporation, 22-27

22-5 Overall Comparison of Forms of Doing Business, 22-28

DEDUCTIBILITY OF LOSSES AND THE CHOICE OF BUSINESS ENTITY

Cane, Inc., has been a C corporation for a number of years, earning taxable income of less than $100,000 per year. Thus, the business has been subject to the lower C corporation tax rates, but due to competitors' sales of cheap imports from China, Cane's two owners, Smith and Jones, expect operating losses for the next two or three years. They hope to outsource some of the manufacturing to Vietnam and turn the company around. How can they deduct these anticipated future losses?

The corporation receives some tax-exempt income, generates a small amount of passive investment income, and holds some C corporation earnings and profits. Each owner draws a salary of $92,000. Cane has issued two classes of stock, voting and nonvoting common. Cane is located in Texarkana, Texas. Smith lives in Texas, and Jones lives in Arkansas. Both are married to nonresident aliens.

Should Smith and Jones elect to have Cane treated as an S corporation?

Read the chapter and formulate your response.

An individual establishing a business has a number of choices as to the form of business entity under which to operate. Chapters 17 through 20 outline many of the rules, advantages, and disadvantages of operating as a regular C corporation. Chapter 21 discusses the partnership entity and the limited liability company (LLC) and limited liability partnership (LLP) forms.

Another alternative, the S corporation, provides many of the benefits of partnership taxation and at the same time gives the owners limited liability protection from creditors. The S corporation rules, which are contained in Subchapter S of the Internal Revenue Code (§§ 1361–1379), were enacted to allow flexibility in the entity choice that businesspeople face. Thus, S status combines the legal environment of C corporations with taxation similar to that applying to partnerships. S corporation status is obtained through an election by a *qualifying* corporation with the consent of its shareholders. Exhibit 22.1 compares the number and operations of the various entity choices.

EXHIBIT 22.1	Comparison of Business Entities			
	Returns	**Receipts**	**Income**	**Assets**
Sole Proprietorships (non-farm) (2016)	25.5M	$1,422.2B	$328.2B	Unknown
Partnerships (2016)	3.715M[1]	6.98T	791.7B	$29T
C Corporations (2014)[2]	6.0M	31.6T	1.4T[3]	96T

[1]69.6% LLCs; 11.07% LPs.

[2]4.4M pass-through entities in 2014 and 1.6M Form 1120s.

[3]Income subject to Federal income tax.

LO.1

Explain the tax effects that S corporation status has on shareholders.

22-1 CHOICE OF BUSINESS ENTITY

S corporations (like C corporations) are organized under state law. Other than for income tax purposes, they are recognized as separate legal entities and generally provide shareholders with the same liability protection available to C corporations. For Federal income tax purposes, however, taxation of S corporations resembles that of partnerships. As with partnerships, the income, deductions, and tax credits of an S corporation flow through to shareholders annually, regardless of whether distributions of wealth (like cash) are made to the shareholders. Thus, income is taxed at the shareholder level and not at the corporate level. Payments to S shareholders by the corporation are distributed tax-free to the extent the distributed earnings were previously taxed.

Although the Federal tax treatment of S corporations and partnerships is similar, the two sets of computations are not identical. For instance, liabilities of the entity affect an owner's basis differently, and S corporations may incur a tax liability at the corporate level. Furthermore, an S corporation may not make a special allocation of tax items like a partnership can, and distributions of appreciated property are taxable for S corporations (see Concept Summary 22.2 later in this chapter).

As a general rule, where the S corporation provisions are silent, C corporation rules apply. For example, the liquidation of C and S corporations is taxed in the same way.

22-1a An Overview of S Corporations

S corporations can be advantageous even when the individual tax rate exceeds the corporate tax rate.

S Corporation Advantages

EXAMPLE 1

An S corporation earns $300,000 for the tax year. The marginal individual tax rate applicable to the entity's shareholders is 37% on ordinary income and 20% on dividends (ignoring the 3.8% investment income tax). The corporate tax rate is 21%, and the S corporation shareholders receive the full 20% qualified business income deduction (see text Section 22-3b). All after-tax income is distributed currently.

	C Corporation	S Corporation
Earnings	$300,000	$300,000
Less: Corporate tax	(63,000)	(–0–)
Available for distribution	$237,000	$300,000
Less: Tax at owner level	(47,400)	(88,800)
Available after-tax earnings	$189,600	$211,200

The S corporation generates an extra $21,600 of after-tax earnings ($211,200 − $189,600) when compared with a similar C corporation. The C corporation might be able to reduce this disadvantage by paying out its earnings as deductible compensation, rents, or interest expense. Tax at the owner level also can be deferred or avoided by not distributing after-tax earnings.

EXAMPLE 2

A new corporation elects S status and incurs a net operating loss (NOL) of $300,000. The shareholders may use their proportionate shares of the NOL to offset other taxable income in the current year, providing an immediate tax savings. In contrast, a newly formed C corporation is required to carry the NOL forward and does not receive any tax benefit in the current year. Hence, an S corporation can accelerate NOL deductions and thereby provide a greater present value for tax savings generated by the loss.

22-2 QUALIFYING FOR S CORPORATION STATUS

LO.2

Identify corporations that qualify for the S election.

22-2a Definition of a Small Business Corporation

To achieve S corporation status, a corporation *first* must qualify as a ==small business corporation==. If each of the following requirements is met, then the entity can elect S corporation status.

- Is a domestic corporation (incorporated and organized in the United States).
- Is an eligible corporation (see the following section for ineligible types).
- Issues only one class of stock.
- Is limited to a theoretical maximum of 100 shareholders.
- Has only individuals, estates, and certain trusts and exempt organizations as shareholders.
- Has no nonresident alien shareholders.

No maximum or minimum dollar sales or capitalization restrictions apply to small business corporations.

Ineligible Corporations

Small business corporation status is not permitted for non-U.S. corporations or for certain banks and insurance companies.

Any domestic corporation that is not an ineligible corporation can be a qualified Subchapter S corporation subsidiary (QSSS) if another S corporation holds 100 percent of its stock and elects to treat the subsidiary as a QSSS.[1] QSSSs are separate entities for legal purposes, but they are treated as a division of the parent for Federal income tax purposes.

One Class of Stock

A small business corporation may have only one class of stock issued and outstanding.[2] This restriction permits differences in voting rights, but not differences in distribution or liquidation rights.[3] Thus, two classes of common stock that are identical, except that one class is voting and the other is nonvoting, are treated as a single class of stock for S corporation purposes. In contrast, voting common stock and voting preferred stock (with a preference on dividends) are treated as two classes of stock. Authorized and unissued stock or treasury stock of another class do not count as a second class of stock. Likewise, unexercised stock options, phantom stock, stock appreciation rights, warrants, and convertible debentures usually do not constitute a second class of stock.[4]

The Big Picture

EXAMPLE 3

Return to the facts of *The Big Picture* on p. 22-1. Cane, Inc., could elect S status as long as the two classes of common stock are identical except for differences in voting rights. In this situation, one class of common stock is voting and the other class is nonvoting. This situation does not violate the one-class-of-stock rule.

You learn that both shareholders have binding employment contracts with Cane, Inc. The amount of compensation paid by the corporation to Jones under her contract is reasonable, but the amount paid to Smith under his contract is excessive, resulting in a constructive dividend. Smith's employment contract was not designed to circumvent the one-class-of-stock requirement.

Because employment contracts are not considered governing provisions, Cane still is treated as though it has only one class of stock if an S election is made.

Number of Shareholders

A small business corporation theoretically is limited to 100 shareholders. Several exceptions, though, allow the number of shareholders to exceed 100. For instance, if shares of stock are owned jointly by two individuals, they generally are treated as separate shareholders. But a group of family members may be treated as one shareholder for purposes of determining the number of shareholders. The term *members of the family* includes a "common ancestor, the lineal descendants of the common ancestor, and the spouses (or former spouses) of the lineal descendants or common ancestor."[5]

EXAMPLE 4

Fred and Wilma (husband and wife) jointly own 10 shares in Marlins, Inc., an S corporation, with the remaining 290 shares outstanding owned by 99 other unrelated shareholders. Fred and Wilma are divorced; pursuant to the property settlement approved by the court, the 10 shares held by Fred and Wilma are divided between them, five shares to each.

Before the divorce settlement, Marlins had 100 shareholders under the small business corporation rules. After the settlement, it still has 100 shareholders and continues to qualify as a small business corporation. A former spouse is treated as being in the same family as the individual to whom he or she was married.

---

[1]§ 1361(b)(3)(B).
[2]1361(b)(1)(D).
[3]§ 1361(c)(4).

[4]Reg. § 1.1361–1(l)(1).
[5]§§ 1361(c)(1)(A)(ii) and (B)(i).

Type of Shareholder Limitation

Small business corporation shareholders may be resident individuals, estates, certain trusts, and certain tax-exempt organizations.[6] Charitable organizations, employee benefit trusts exempt from taxation, and a one-person LLC also can qualify as shareholders of an S corporation. This limitation prevents partnerships, corporations, limited liability partnerships, most LLCs, and most IRAs and Roth IRAs from owning S corporation stock. Partnerships and corporate shareholders could circumvent the 100-shareholder limitation as illustrated in the following example.

Saul and 105 of his friends want to form an S corporation. Saul reasons that if he and his friends form a partnership, the partnership can then form an S corporation and act as a single shareholder, thereby avoiding the 100-shareholder rule. Saul's plan will not work because partnerships cannot own stock in a small business corporation.

EXAMPLE
5

Although partnerships and corporations cannot own S corporation stock, small business corporations can be partners in a partnership or shareholders in a corporation. This approach allows the 100-shareholder requirement to be bypassed in a limited sense. For example, if two small business corporations, both with 80 shareholders, form a partnership, then the shareholders of both corporations can enjoy the limited liability conferred by S corporation status and a single level of tax on partnership profits.

Nonresident Aliens

Nonresident aliens cannot own stock in a small business corporation.[7] That is, individuals who are not U.S. citizens *must live in the United States* to own S corporation stock. Therefore, shareholders with nonresident alien spouses in community property states[8] cannot own S corporation stock because the nonresident alien spouse would be treated as owning half of the community property.[9] Similarly, if a resident alien shareholder moves outside the United States, the S election is terminated.

The Big Picture

Return to the facts of *The Big Picture* on p. 22-1. Because Jones lives in Arkansas, a common law property state, the fact that she is married to a nonresident alien spouse would not affect an S election. However, because Smith lives in Texas, a community property state, his nonresident alien spouse would be treated as owning half of his community property stock, and an S election would not be allowed. To qualify for S status, Smith could move to Arkansas or his wife could move to Texas (becoming a resident alien).

EXAMPLE
6

22-2b Making the Election

To become an S corporation, the entity must file a valid election with the IRS. The election is made on Form 2553. For the election to be valid, it should be filed on a timely basis and all shareholders must consent.

LO.3

Explain how to make an S election.

---

[6]§ 1361(b)(1)(B). Foreign trusts, charitable remainder trusts, and charitable lead trusts cannot be S shareholders.

[7]§ 1362(b)(1)(C).

[8]Assets acquired by a married couple are generally considered community property in these states: Arizona, California, Idaho, Louisiana, Nevada, New Mexico, Texas, Washington, Wisconsin, and (if elected) Alaska.

[9]See *Ward v. U.S.*, 81–2 USTC ¶9674, 48 AFTR 2d 81–5942, 661 F.2d 226 (Ct.Cl., 1981), where the court found that the stock was owned as community property. Because the taxpayer-shareholder (a U.S. citizen) was married to a citizen and resident of Mexico, the nonresident alien prohibition was violated. If the taxpayer-shareholder had held the stock as separate property, the S election would have been valid.

For S corporation status to apply in the current tax year, the election must be filed either in the previous year or on or before the fifteenth day of the third month of the current year.

The Big Picture

EXAMPLE 7

Return to the facts of *The Big Picture* on p. 22-1. Suppose that in 2020, shareholders Smith and Jones decide to become an S corporation beginning January 1, 2021. Because the C corporation uses a calendar tax year, the S election can be made at any time in 2020 or by March 15, 2021. An election after March 15, 2021, is not effective until the 2022 calendar tax year.

Even if the 2½-month deadline is met, an S election is not valid unless the corporation qualifies as a small business corporation for the *entire* tax year. Otherwise, the election is not effective until the following tax year.

A corporation that does not yet exist cannot make an S corporation election.[10] Thus, for new corporations, a premature election may not be effective. A new corporation's 2½-month election period begins at the earliest occurrence of any of the following events.

- When the corporation has shareholders.
- When it acquires assets.
- When it begins doing business.[11]

EXAMPLE 8

Several individuals acquire assets on behalf of Rock Corporation on June 29, 2020, and they begin doing business on July 3, 2020. They subscribe to shares of stock; file articles of incorporation for Rock; and become shareholders on July 6, 2020. The S election must be filed no later than 2½ months after June 29, 2020 (i.e., on or before September 12), to be effective for 2020.

22-2c **Shareholder Consent**

A qualifying election requires the consent of all of the corporation's shareholders.[12] Consent must be in writing, and it generally must be filed by the election deadline. A consent extension is available only if Form 2553 is filed on a timely basis, reasonable cause is given, and the interests of the government are not jeopardized.[13]

EXAMPLE 9

Vern and Yvonne decide to convert their C corporation into a calendar year S corporation for 2020. At the end of February 2020 (before the election is filed), Yvonne travels to Ukraine and forgets to sign a consent to the election. Yvonne will not return to the United States until June, and she cannot be reached by fax or e-mail.

Vern files the S election on Form 2553 and requests an extension of time to file Yvonne's consent to the election. Vern indicates that there is a reasonable cause for the extension: a shareholder is out of the country. Because the government's interest is not jeopardized, the IRS probably will grant Yvonne an extension of time to file the consent. Vern must file the election on Form 2553 on or before March 15, 2020, for the election to be effective for the 2020 calendar year.

---

[10]See, for example, *T.H. Campbell & Bros., Inc.*, 34 TCM 695, T.C.Memo. 1975–149; Ltr.Rul. 8807070.

[11]Reg. § 1.1362–6(a)(2)(ii)(C). Also see, for example, *Nick A. Artukovich*, 61 T.C. 100 (1973).

[12]§ 1362(a)(2).

[13]Rev.Rul. 60–183, 1960–1 C.B. 625; *William Pestcoe*, 40 T.C. 195 (1963); Reg. § 1.1362–6(b)(3)(iii).

Both husband and wife must consent if they own their stock jointly (as joint tenants, tenants in common, tenants by the entirety, or community property), even though they count as one shareholder.

Three shareholders, Amy, Monty, and Dianne, incorporate in January and file Form 2553. Amy is married and lives in California. Monty is single, and Dianne is married; both live in South Carolina. Because Amy is married and lives in a community property state, her husband also must consent to the S election. South Carolina is not a community property state, so Dianne's husband need not consent.

For current-year S elections, persons who were shareholders during any part of the taxable year before the election date but were not shareholders when the election was made also must consent to the election.[14]

On January 15, 2020, the stock of Columbus Corporation (a calendar year C corporation) was held equally by three individual shareholders: Jim, Sally, and LuEllen. On that date, LuEllen sells her interest to Jim and Sally. On March 14, 2020, Columbus Corporation files Form 2553. Jim and Sally indicate their consent by signing the form. Columbus cannot become an S corporation until 2021 because LuEllen did not indicate consent. Had all three shareholders consented by signing Form 2553, S status would have taken effect as of January 1, 2020.

22-2d Loss of the Election

LO.4
Explain how an S election can be terminated.

An S election remains in force until it is revoked or lost. Election or consent forms are not required for future years. However, an S election can terminate if any of the following occurs.

- Shareholders owning a majority of shares (voting and nonvoting) voluntarily revoke the election.
- A new shareholder owning more than one-half of the stock affirmatively refuses to consent to the election.
- The corporation no longer qualifies as a small business corporation.
- The corporation fails the passive investment income test.

Voluntary Revocation

A **voluntary revocation** of the S election requires the consent of shareholders owning a majority of shares on the day the revocation is to be made.[15] A revocation filed up to and including the fifteenth day of the third month of the tax year is effective for the entire tax year, unless a later date is specified. Similarly, unless an effective date is specified, revocation made after the first 2½ months of the current tax year is effective for the following tax year.

The shareholders of Petunia Corporation, a calendar year S corporation, voluntarily revoke the S election on January 5 of the current year (not a leap year). They do not specify a future effective date in the revocation. If the revocation is properly executed and timely filed, Petunia will be a C corporation for the entire current tax year. If the election is not made until June, though, Petunia remains an S corporation for this year; it becomes a C corporation at the beginning of the next year.

[14]§ 1362(b)(2)(B)(ii). [15]§ 1362(d)(1).

A corporation can revoke its S status *prospectively* by specifying a future date when the revocation is to be effective. A revocation that designates a future effective date splits the corporation's tax year into a short S corporation year and a short C corporation year. The day on which the revocation occurs is treated as the first day of the C corporation year. The corporation allocates income or loss for the entire year on a pro rata basis, using the number of days in each short year.

Assume the same facts as in the preceding example, except that Petunia designates July 1 as the revocation date. Accordingly, June 30 is the last day of the S corporation's tax year. The C corporation's tax year runs from July 1 to December 31 of the current year. Income or loss for the 22-month period is allocated between the two short years (i.e., 184/365 to the C corporation year).

Rather than allocating on a pro rata basis, the corporation can elect to compute actual income or loss attributable to the two short years. This election requires the consent of everyone who was a shareholder at any time during the S corporation's short year and everyone who owns stock on the first day of the C corporation's year.[16]

Assume the same facts as in the preceding example, except that all of Petunia's shareholders consent to allocate the income or loss to the two short tax years based on its actual realization. Assume further that Petunia experiences a total loss of $102,000, of which $72,000 is incurred in the first half of the year. Because $72,000 of the loss occurs before July 1, this amount is allocated to the S corporation short year, and only $30,000 of the loss is allocated to the C corporation year.

Loss of Small Business Corporation Status

If an S corporation fails to qualify as a small business corporation at any time after the election has become effective, its status as an S corporation ends. The termination occurs on the day the corporation ceases to be a small business corporation.[17] Thus, if the corporation ever has more than 100 qualified shareholders, a second class of stock, a nonqualifying shareholder, or otherwise fails to meet the definition of a small business corporation, the S election is immediately terminated.

Peony Corporation has been a calendar year S corporation for three years. On August 13, one of its 100 shareholders sells *some* of her stock to an outsider. Peony now has 101 shareholders, and it ceases to be a small business corporation. For the tax year, Peony is an S corporation through August 12 and a C corporation from August 13 to December 31.

Passive Investment Income Limitation

The Code provides a passive investment income (PII) limitation for a few S corporations. If an S corporation holds C corporation E & P and it generates passive investment income in excess of 25 percent of its gross receipts for three consecutive tax years, the S election is terminated as of the beginning of the fourth year.[18]

For 2018, 2019, and 2020, Diapason Corporation, a calendar year S corporation, received passive investment income in excess of 25% of its gross receipts. If Diapason holds accumulated E & P from years in which it was a C corporation, its S election is terminated as of January 1, 2021.

---

[16]§ 1362(e)(3).

[17]§ 1362(d)(2)(B).

[18]§ 1362(d)(3)(A)(ii).

PII includes dividends, interest, rents, gains and losses from sales of capital assets, and royalties net of investment deductions. Rents are not considered PII if the corporation renders significant personal services to the occupant.

EXAMPLE

17

Violet Corporation owns and operates an apartment building. The corporation provides utilities for the building, maintains the lobby, and furnishes trash collection for tenants. These activities are not considered significant personal services, so any rent income earned by the corporation will be considered PII.

Alternatively, if Violet also furnishes maid services to its tenants (personal services beyond what normally would be expected from a landlord in an apartment building), the rent income would no longer be PII.

Reelection after Termination

After an S election has been terminated, the corporation must wait five years before reelecting S corporation status. The five-year waiting period is waived if:

- There is a more-than-50% change in ownership of the corporation after the first year for which the termination is applicable, or
- The event causing the termination was not reasonably within the control of the S corporation or its majority shareholders.

Conditions that a corporation must meet before S corporation status is available are illustrated in Exhibit 22.2.

22-3 OPERATIONAL RULES

S corporations are treated much like partnerships for tax purposes. With a few exceptions,[19] S corporations generally make tax accounting and other elections at the corporate level. Each year, the S corporation determines nonseparately stated income or loss and separately stated income, deductions, and credits. These items are taxed only once, at the shareholder level. All items are allocated to each shareholder based on average ownership of stock throughout the year. The *flow-through* of each item of income, deduction, and credit from the corporation to the shareholder is illustrated in Exhibit 22.3.

22-3a Computation of Taxable Income

LO.5

Compute nonseparately stated income and identify separately stated items.

An S corporation's taxable income or loss is determined in a manner similar to the tax rules that apply to partnerships, except that S corporations amortize organizational expenditures under the C corporation rules[20] and must recognize gains, *but not losses*, on distributions of appreciated property to shareholders.[21] Other provisions affecting only the computation of C corporation income, such as the dividends received deduction, do not extend to S corporations.[22] Finally, as with partnerships, certain deductions of individuals, such as the standard deduction, are not permitted.

In general, S corporation items are divided into (1) nonseparately stated income or loss and (2) separately stated income, losses, deductions, and credits that could affect the tax liability of any shareholder in a different manner, depending on other factors in the shareholder's tax situation.

---

[19]A few elections can be made at the shareholder level (e.g., the choice between a foreign tax deduction or credit). But shareholders cannot make these accounting method elections; only the entity can do so. *Caselli*, 115 TCM 1448, T.C. Memo. 2018–81.

[20]§§ 248 and 1363(b).
[21]§ 1363(b).
[22]§ 703(a)(2).

EXHIBIT 22.2   **Conditions Required to Elect S Corporation Status**

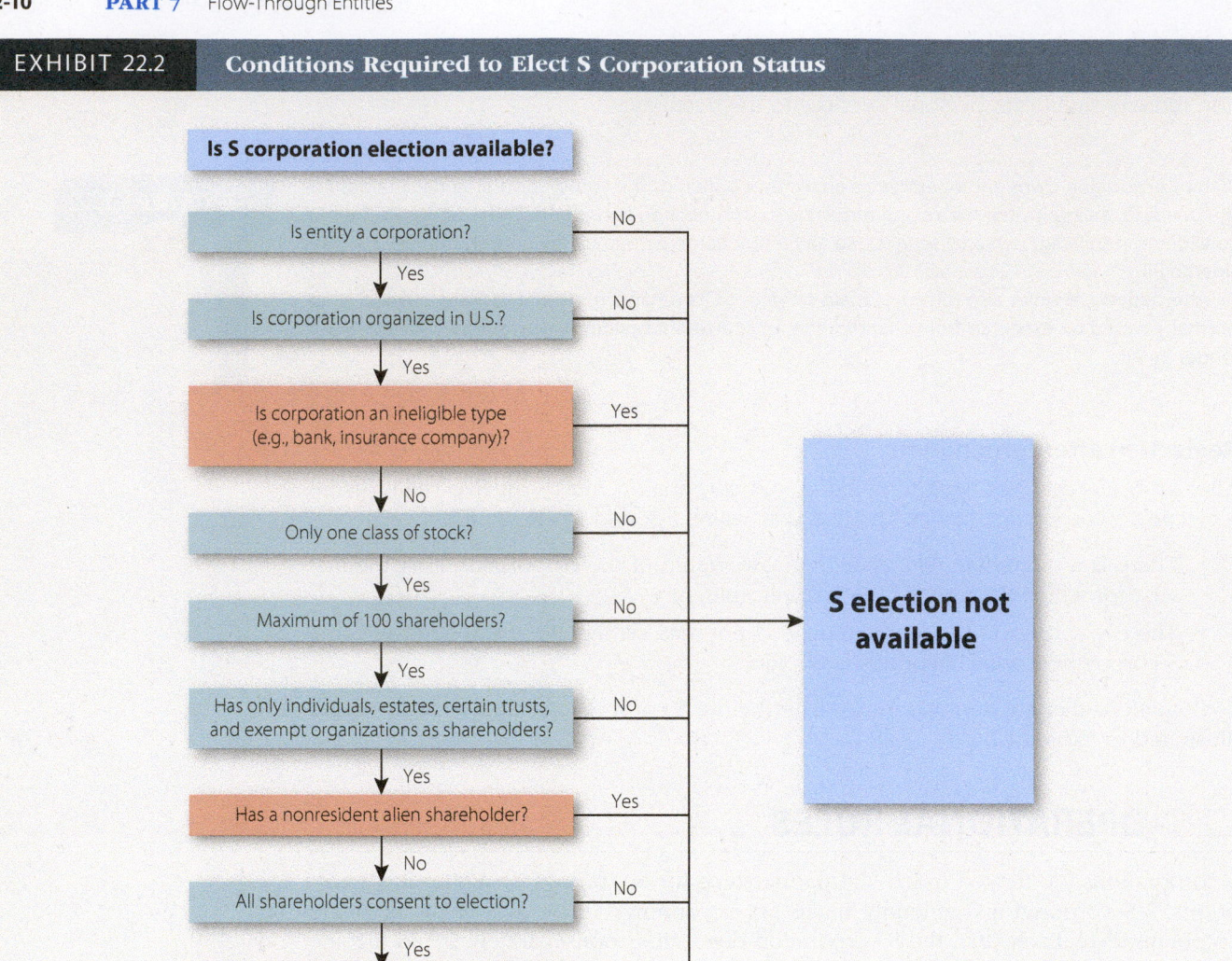

Nonseparate items are aggregated into an undifferentiated amount that constitutes S corporation ordinary income or loss. An S corporation's separately stated items are identical to those separately stated by partnerships. These items retain their tax attributes on the shareholder's return. Separately stated items are listed on Schedule K of the 1120S. They include the following.

- Tax-exempt income.
- Long-term and short-term capital gains and losses.
- § 1231 gains and losses.
- Charitable contributions (no grace period).
- Passive activity gains, losses, and credits.
- Data used to compute a § 199A deduction.
- § 179 deduction.

- Tax preferences and adjustments for the shareholders' potential alternative minimum tax.
- Depletion.
- Foreign income or loss.
- Recoveries of tax benefit items.
- Intangible drilling costs.
- Investment interest, income, and expenses.

EXHIBIT 22.3	Flow-Through of Separate Items (Selected) to S Corporation Shareholders

The following is the income statement for Jersey, Inc., an S corporation.

EXAMPLE

18

Sales		$40,000
Less cost of sales		(23,000)
Gross profit on sales		$17,000
Less: Interest expense	$1,200	
Charitable contributions	400	
Advertising expenses	1,500	
Other operating expenses	2,000	(5,100)
Book income from operations		$11,900
Add: Tax-exempt interest	$ 300	
Dividend income	200	
Long-term capital gain	500	1,000
Less: Short-term capital loss		(150)
Net income per books		$12,750

Jersey's ordinary income is calculated as follows, using net income for book purposes as the starting point.

Net income per books			$12,750
Separately stated items			
Deduct: Tax-exempt interest		$ 300	
Dividend income		200	
Long-term capital gain		500	(1,000)
Add:	Charitable contributions	$ 400	
	Short-term capital loss	150	550
Ordinary income			$12,300

The $12,300 of Jersey's ordinary income, as well as each of the five separately stated items, are divided among the shareholders based upon their stock ownership.

22-3b Qualified Business Income Deduction

To bring the taxation of flow-through entities such as S corporations closer to the C corporation 21 percent rate, shareholders of certain S corporations (and other qualified flow-through entities) may deduct up to 20 percent of certain qualified business income (QBI).[23] With the full 20 percent deduction, the pass-through top rate is 29.6 percent (0.80 × 0.37), ignoring payroll and other taxes. Income earned by a C corporation that is distributed after-tax as a dividend to the shareholders may be subject to a maximum Federal income tax rate of 39.8 percent [0.21 + (0.79 × 0.238)], which includes the 3.8 percent investment income tax rate.

The qualified business income deduction (QBID) is:

*Deduction limited for certain high-income service-type S corporations.
**Additional computations concerning the wage limit are discussed in text Section 15-3f.

This deduction has no effect on AAA or the shareholder's stock basis. If the S corporation is a specified service trade or business and the owner's income exceeds a maximum amount, the QBID is zero. See text Section 15-3g.

LO.6

Allocate income, deductions, and credits to shareholders.

22-3c Allocation of Income and Loss

Each shareholder is allocated a pro rata portion of nonseparately stated income or loss and all separately stated items. The pro rata allocation method assigns an equal amount of each of the S items to each day of the year. If a shareholder's stock holding changes during the year, this allocation assigns the shareholder a pro rata share of each item for *each* day the stock is owned. On the date of transfer, the transferor (and not the transferee) is considered to own the stock.[24]

The per-day allocation must be used, unless the shareholder disposes of his or her entire interest in the entity.[25]

---

[23]§ 199A. See also text Section 15-3.

[24]Reg. § 1.1377–1(a)(2)(ii).

[25]§§ 1366(a)(1) and 1377(a)(1).

Assume in the previous example that Pat, a shareholder, owned 10% of Jersey's stock for 100 days and 12% for the remaining 265 days of the tax year (not a leap year). Using the required per-day allocation method, Pat's share of the S corporation items is determined as follows.

EXAMPLE
19

	Schedule K Totals	Pat's Share 10%	Pat's Share 12%	Pat's Schedule K–1 Totals
Ordinary income	$12,300	$337	$1,072	$1,409
Tax-exempt interest	300	8	26	34
Dividend income	200	5	17	22
Long-term capital gain	500	14	44	58
Charitable contributions	400	11	35	46
Short-term capital loss	150	4	13	17

Pat's share of the Subchapter S ordinary income is the total of $12,300 \times [0.10 \times (100/365)]$ plus $12,300 \times [0.12 \times (265/365)]$, or $1,409. Each of the Schedule K–1 totals from the right column flows through to the appropriate lines on Pat's individual income tax return (Form 1040).

The Short-Year Election

If a shareholder's interest is completely terminated by a sale or by a disposition following death during the tax year, all shareholders holding stock during the year and the corporation may elect to treat the S taxable year as two taxable years. The first year ends on the date of the termination. Under this election, an interim closing of the books is undertaken, and the shareholders report their shares of the S corporation items as they occurred during the short tax year.[26]

The short-year election provides an opportunity to shift income, losses, and credits among shareholders. The election is desirable in circumstances where more loss can be allocated to taxpayers with higher marginal rates.

Alicia, the owner of all of the shares of an S corporation, transfers her stock to Cindy halfway through the tax year. There is a $100,000 NOL for the entire tax year, but $30,000 of the loss occurs during the first half of the year. Without a short-year election, $50,000 of the loss is allocated to Alicia, and $50,000 is allocated to Cindy. If the corporation makes the short-year election, Cindy is allocated $70,000 of the loss. Of course, the sales price of the stock would probably be increased to recognize the tax benefits being transferred from Alicia to Cindy.

EXAMPLE
20

22-3d Tax Treatment of Distributions to Shareholders

The amount of any actual distribution of wealth (like cash) to an S corporation shareholder is equal to the cash plus the fair market value of any other property distributed. How the distribution is taxed depends upon whether the S corporation has C corporation **accumulated earnings and profits (AEP)** (described in text Section 19-2).

No C Corporation AEP

If the S corporation never has been a C corporation or if it holds no C corporation AEP, the distribution is a tax-free recovery of capital to the extent that it does not exceed the shareholder's basis in the stock of the S corporation. When the amount of the

---

[26]§ 1377(a)(2).

distribution exceeds the basis of the stock, the excess is treated as a gain from the sale or exchange of property (capital gain in most cases). The vast majority of S corporations fall into this easy-to-apply category.

EXAMPLE 21

Twirl, Inc., a calendar year S corporation, has no AEP. During the year, Juan, an individual shareholder of the corporation, receives a cash distribution of $12,200 from Twirl. Juan's basis in his stock is $9,700. Juan recognizes a capital gain of $2,500, the excess of the distribution over the stock basis ($12,200 − $9,700). The remaining $9,700 is tax-free, but it reduces Juan's basis in his stock to zero.

C Corporation AEP Exists

S corporations that hold C corporation AEP treat distributions of pre-election (C corporation) and post-election (S corporation) earnings differently. This difference occurs when the entity previously was a C corporation, or when a C corporation was merged into it.

In this case, distributions of AEP are taxed as dividends, while distributions of previously taxed S corporation earnings are tax-free to the extent of the shareholder's basis in the stock.

Concept Summary 22.1 outlines the taxation of distributions in these circumstances. These rules are intended to prevent two problems that result when a profitable C corporation (i.e., one holding C corporation accumulated E & P) has been converted to an S corporation.

- Manipulation in the shareholders' favor could result because the AEP would not be taxed when an S distribution is made; S corporation shareholders are taxed on income, not on distributions.

- On the other hand, double taxation could occur if the rules acted to tax as dividend income any AEP that exists when a distribution is made to the S shareholders; S distributions usually are free of income tax.

The Accumulated Adjustments Account A special account is required to track undistributed earnings of an S corporation that have been taxed to shareholders previously. Distributions from this account, known as the **accumulated adjustments account (AAA)**, are tax-free. The AAA begins with a zero balance on the first day of an S corporation's first tax year. Essentially, the AAA is the cumulative total of undistributed nonseparately

Concept Summary 22.1

Classification Procedures for Distributions from an S Corporation

Where No Earnings and Profits Exist	Where Earnings and Profits Exist
	1. Distributions are tax-free to the extent of the AAA.*
	2. Distributions from AEP constitute dividend income.**
	3. Distributions are tax-free to the extent of the other adjustments account (OAA).*
1. Distributions are nontaxable to the extent of shareholder's basis of stock.*	4. Any residual distribution amount is nontaxable to the extent of shareholder's basis of stock.*
2. Excess is treated as gain from a sale or exchange of stock (capital gain in virtually all cases).	5. Excess is treated as gain from a sale or exchange of stock (capital gain in virtually all cases).

*The distribution reduces the stock basis. Once stock basis reaches zero, any distribution from the AAA is treated as a gain from the sale or exchange of stock. Thus, the shareholder's stock basis is an upper limit on what a shareholder may receive tax-free.

**The AAA bypass election is available to pay out AEP before reducing the AAA [§ 1368(e)(3)].

and separately stated items for S corporation tax years. Calculation of the AAA should be made by all S corporations, but the AAA is most important to those that have been C corporations. The AAA provides a mechanism to ensure that the earnings of an S corporation are taxed to shareholders only once.

The AAA is computed by making adjustments in the order specified in Exhibit 22.4. Its balance typically is determined at the end of each year, rather than at the time distributions are made. When more than one distribution occurs in the same year, a pro rata portion of each distribution is treated as having been made out of the AAA.

In calculating the amount in the AAA for purposes of determining the tax treatment of current-year distributions, the net negative adjustments (e.g., the excess of losses and deductions over income) for that tax year are ignored. Tax-exempt income and related expenses (e.g., insurance proceeds and premiums paid for life insurance) do not affect the AAA.

A shareholder has a proportionate interest in the AAA, regardless of the size of his or her stock basis.[27] However, because the AAA is a corporate account, no connection exists between the prior accumulated S corporation income and any specific shareholder.[28] Thus, the benefits of the AAA can be shifted from one shareholder to another shareholder. For example, when one S shareholder transfers stock to another shareholder, any AAA balance on the purchase date may be distributed tax-free to the purchaser. Similarly, issuing additional stock to a new shareholder in an S corporation with a positive balance in the AAA dilutes the account relative to the existing shareholders.

The AAA can have a negative balance. All losses decrease the AAA balance, even those in excess of the shareholder's stock basis. However, *distributions* may not make the AAA negative or increase a negative balance.

Distribution Ordering Rules A cash distribution from an S corporation with AEP comes first from the AAA.[29] Distributions from the AAA are tax-free. The remaining distribution is taxed as a dividend to the extent of AEP. After AEP is fully distributed, any residual amount is applied against the other adjustments account (OAA, discussed in the next section) and then the shareholder's remaining stock basis. The reduction in the shareholder's stock basis is a tax-free recovery of capital.[30] Any distributions once the stock basis reaches zero typically are taxed as capital gains.

EXHIBIT 22.4	Adjustments to the Corporate AAA

Increase by:

1. Schedule K income items other than tax-exempt income.
2. Nonseparately computed income.
3. Depletion in excess of basis in the property.

Decrease by:

4. Negative Schedule K adjustments other than distributions (e.g., losses and deductions).
5. Any portion of a distribution that is considered to be tax-free from the AAA (but not below zero).

Note: When the combination of items 1 through 4 results in a negative number, the AAA is adjusted first for the distribution and then for the adjustments in items 1 through 4.

---

[27]§ 1368(c).

[28]§ 1368(e)(1)(A).

[29]§§ 1368(c)(1) and (e)(1).

[30]§ 1368(c).

Ordering Rules for Distributions

Short, a calendar year S corporation, distributes $1,300 cash to its only shareholder, Otis, on December 31. Otis's basis in his stock is $1,400, Short's AAA balance is $500, and Short holds $750 AEP before the distribution.

According to the distribution ordering rules, the first $500 is a tax-free recovery of basis from the AAA. The next $750 is a taxable dividend distribution from AEP. The remaining $50 of cash is a tax-free recovery of basis. Immediately after the distribution, Short holds a zero balance in its AAA and AEP. Otis's stock basis now is $850.

	Corporate AAA	Corporate AEP	Otis's Stock Basis*
Balance before the distribution	$ 500	$ 750	$1,400
Distribution ($1,300)			
From AAA	(500)		(500)
From AEP		(750)	
From stock basis			(50)
Balance after the distribution	$ –0–	$ –0–	$ 850

*Details of basis adjustments are discussed later in the chapter.

Assume the same facts as in the preceding example. During the following year, Short reports zero ordinary income and distributes $1,000 to Otis. Of the distribution, $850 is a tax-free recovery of basis, and $150 is taxed to Otis as a capital gain.

With the consent of all of its shareholders, an S corporation can elect to have a distribution treated as if it were made from AEP rather than from the AAA. This mechanism is known as an AAA **bypass election**. This election may be desirable as a simple means by which to eliminate a small AEP balance and avoid related complications, such as those listed in Exhibit 22.5.

EXAMPLE 24

Collett, a calendar year S corporation, has AEP of $12,000 and a balance of $20,000 in the AAA. Collett Corporation may elect to distribute the AEP first, creating a $12,000 dividend for its shareholders, before using the AAA.

Other Aspects of the AAA

Schedule M–2. S corporations report changes in the AAA on Schedule M–2 of Form 1120S. Schedule M–2 contains a column labeled **other adjustments account (OAA)**. This account includes items that affect basis but not the AAA, such as tax-exempt

EXHIBIT 22.5	**Special Complications of Conversion of C Corporation to S Corporation**

- Positive accumulated earnings and profits (AEP) may cause distributions to be taxed as dividends.
- Positive AEP may trigger one or more corporate level taxes.
- Positive AEP with passive investment income exceeding 25 percent of gross income for three consecutive years causes loss of S status.
- Net operating loss from C years can only be used to reduce built-in gains.
- C corporation operating loss carryover period continues to run.
- S corporation may make a bypass election to distribute AEP before AAA.

income and any related nondeductible expenses. For example, life insurance proceeds received and insurance premiums paid are traced through the OAA. Distributions are made from the OAA after AEP and the AAA are depleted to zero. Distributions from the OAA generally are tax-free.

EXAMPLE 25

Sparrow, an S corporation, records the following items.

AAA, beginning of the year	$ 8,500
Ordinary income	25,000
Tax-exempt interest	4,000
Key employee life insurance proceeds received	5,000
Payroll penalty expense	2,000
Charitable contributions	3,000
Unreasonable compensation	5,000
Premiums on key employee life insurance	2,100
Distributions to shareholders	16,000

Sparrow's Schedule M–2 for the current year appears as follows.

Schedule M-2	**Analysis of Accumulated Adjustments Account, Shareholders' Undistributed Taxable Income Previously Taxed, Accumulated Earnings and Profits, and Other Adjustments Account** (see instructions)			
		(a) Accumulated adjustments account	**(b)** Shareholders' undistributed taxable income previously taxed	**(c)** Accumulated earnings and profits	**(d)** Other adjustments account
1	Balance at beginning of tax year	8,500			
2	Ordinary income from page 1, line 21	25,000			
3	Other additions				9,000**
4	Loss from page 1, line 21	( )	( )		
5	Other reductions	(10,000*)	( )		(2,100)
6	Combine lines 1 through 5	23,500			6,900
7	Distributions	16,000			
8	Balance at end of tax year. Subtract line 7 from line 6	7,500			6,900

* $2,000 (payroll penalty) + $3,000 (charitable contributions) + $5,000 (unreasonable compensation).
** $4,000 (tax-exempt interest) + $5,000 (life insurance proceeds).

Schedule M–3: Net Income or Loss Reconciliation. S corporations that have total assets on Schedule L at the end of the tax year that equal or exceed $10 million must file Schedule M–3 in lieu of Schedule M–1. Only a few large S corporations must file a Schedule M–3. The schedule provides detailed information about the entity's book-tax differences, and it can be used by the IRS to target specific items that will be subjected to an audit.

Effect of Terminating the S Election. Normally, distributions to shareholders from a C corporation are taxed as dividends to the extent of E & P. However, any distribution of *cash* by a corporation to shareholders during a one-year period[31] following S election termination receives a different treatment. Such a distribution is treated as a tax-free recovery of stock basis to the extent that it does not exceed the AAA.[32] To take advantage of post-termination benefits, an S corporation must know the amount of both the AAA and the OAA as of the date the election terminates.

EXAMPLE 26

Quinn, the sole shareholder of Roman, Inc., a calendar year S corporation, elects during 2020 to terminate the S election, effective January 1, 2021. As of the end of 2020, Roman holds an AAA of $1,300. Quinn can receive a nontaxable distribution of cash during a post-termination period of approximately one year to the extent of Roman's AAA. Although a cash distribution of $1,300 during 2021 would be nontaxable to Quinn, it would reduce the basis of his stock.

---

[31]The period is approximately one year in length. The post-termination transition period is discussed later in the chapter.

[32]§§ 1371(e) and 1377(b).

LO.7

Determine how distributions to S corporation shareholders are taxed.

22-3e **Tax Treatment of Noncash Property Distributions by the Corporation**

An S corporation recognizes a gain on any distribution of appreciated property in the same manner as if the asset were sold to the shareholder at its fair market value.[33] The corporate gain is passed through to the shareholders. The character of the gain—capital gain or ordinary income—depends upon the type of asset being distributed. There is an important reason for this gain recognition rule. Without it, property might be distributed tax-free (other than for certain recapture items) and later sold without income recognition to the shareholder because the shareholder's basis in the property equals its fair market value.

The S corporation does not recognize a loss when distributing assets that are worth less than their basis. As with gain property, the shareholder's basis is equal to the asset's fair market value. Thus, the potential loss is postponed until the shareholder sells the stock of the S corporation. Because loss property receives a step-down in basis without any loss recognition by the S corporation, distributions of loss property should be avoided. See Concept Summary 22.2.

Concept Summary 22.2

Consequences of Noncash Distributions

	Appreciated Property	Depreciated Property
S corporation	Realized gain is recognized by the corporation, which passes it through to the shareholders. Such gain increases a shareholder's stock basis, generating a basis in the property equal to FMV. On the distribution, the shareholder's stock basis is reduced by the FMV of the property (but not below zero).	Realized loss is not recognized. The shareholder takes an FMV basis in the property.
C corporation	Realized gain is recognized under § 311(b) and increases E & P (net of tax). The shareholder reports a taxable dividend to the extent of corporate E & P equal to the property's FMV. The shareholder takes an asset basis equal to its FMV.	Realized loss is not recognized. The shareholder takes an FMV basis in the property.
Partnership	No gain to the partnership or partner. The partner takes a carryover basis in the asset, but the asset basis is limited to the partner's basis in the partnership.	Realized loss is not recognized. The partner takes a carryover basis in the asset, but the asset basis is limited to the partner's basis in the partnership.

Noncash Distributions

EXAMPLE

27

Turnip, Inc., an S corporation for 10 years, distributes a tract of land held as an investment to Chang, its majority shareholder. The land was purchased for $22,000 many years ago and currently is worth $82,000. Turnip recognizes a capital gain of $60,000, which increases the AAA by $60,000. The gain appears on Turnip's Schedule K, and a proportionate share of it passes through to the shareholders' tax returns. Then the property distribution reduces the AAA by $82,000 (the fair market value). The tax consequences are the same for appreciated property, whether it is distributed to the shareholders and they dispose of it or the corporation sells the property and distributes the proceeds to the shareholders.

If the land had been purchased for $82,000 and was currently worth $22,000, Chang would take a $22,000 basis in the land. The $60,000 realized loss is not recognized at the corporate level. The loss does reduce Turnip's AAA, though not an attractive result for Turnip shareholders.

---

[33]§ 311(b).

Noncash Distributions

Assume the same facts as in the previous example, except that Turnip is a C corporation ($1,000,000 E & P balance) or a partnership. The partner's basis in the partnership interest is $100,000.

EXAMPLE

28

	Appreciated Property		
	S Corporation	C Corporation	Partnership
Entity gain/loss	$60,000	$60,000	$ –0–
Owner's gain/loss/dividend	60,000	82,000	–0–
Owner's basis in land	82,000	82,000	22,000
	Property That Has Declined in Value		
	S Corporation	C Corporation	Partnership
Entity gain/loss	$ –0–	$ –0–	$ –0–
Owner's gain/loss/dividend	–0–	22,000	–0–
Owner's basis in land	22,000	22,000	82,000

22-3f Shareholder's Basis in S Stock

LO.8

Calculate a shareholder's basis in S corporation stock.

The calculation of the initial tax basis of stock in an S corporation is similar to that for the basis of stock in a C corporation and depends upon the manner in which the shares are acquired (e.g., gift, inheritance, purchase, or exchange under § 351). Once the initial tax basis is determined, various transactions during the life of the corporation affect the shareholder's basis in the stock. Although each shareholder is required to compute his or her own basis in the S shares, neither Form 1120S nor Schedule K–1 provides a place for deriving this amount.

A shareholder's basis is increased by stock purchases and capital contributions. Operations during the year cause the following upward adjustments to basis.

- Nonseparately computed income.
- Separately stated income items (e.g., nontaxable income).
- Depletion in excess of basis in the property.

Basis then is reduced by distributions not reported as income by the shareholder (e.g., an AAA distribution). Next, the following items reduce basis (*but not below zero*).

- Nondeductible expenses of the corporation (e.g., fines, penalties, and illegal kickbacks).
- Nonseparately computed loss.
- Separately stated loss and deduction items.

As for partnerships, basis first is increased by income items; then it is decreased by distributions and finally by losses. In most cases, this *losses last* rule is advantageous to the S shareholder.

EXAMPLE

29

In its first year of operation, Iris, Inc., a calendar year S corporation in Clemson, South Carolina, earns income of $2,000. On February 2 in its second year of operation, Iris distributes $2,000 to Marty, its sole shareholder. During the remainder of the second year, the corporation incurs a $2,000 loss.

Before accounting for the entity's operating results, Marty's stock basis is zero. Under the S corporation ordering rules, the $2,000 distribution is tax-free AAA to Marty, and the $2,000 loss is suspended until Marty generates additional stock basis (e.g., from capital contributions or future entity profits).

A shareholder's basis in S stock never can be reduced below zero. Once stock basis reaches zero, any additional basis reductions from losses or deductions, but *not* distributions, decrease (but not below zero) the shareholder's basis in loans made to the S corporation. Any excess of losses or deductions over both bases is *suspended* until there are subsequent bases.

Once the basis of any debt is reduced, it later is increased (up to the original amount) by the subsequent *net* increase resulting from *all* positive and negative basis adjustments. The debt basis is adjusted back to the original amount by any "net increase" before any increase is made in the stock basis.[34] "Net increase" for a year is computed after taking distributions (other than those from AEP) into consideration.

A distribution in excess of stock basis does not reduce any debt basis. If a loss and a distribution occur in the same year, the loss reduces the stock basis last, *after* the distribution.

Stacey, a sole shareholder, has a $7,000 stock basis and a $2,000 basis in a loan that she made to Romulus, a calendar year S corporation with no AEP. At the beginning of the tax year, the corporation's AAA and OAA balances are zero. Ordinary income for the year is $8,200, during which Romulus received $2,000 of tax-exempt interest income.

Cash of $17,300 is distributed to Stacey on November 15. Stacey recognizes only a $100 capital gain.

	Corporate AAA	Corporate OAA	Stacey's Stock Basis	Stacey's Loan Basis
Beginning balance	$ –0–	$ –0–	$ 7,000	$2,000
Ordinary income	8,200		8,200	
Tax-exempt income		2,000	2,000	
Subtotal	$ 8,200	$ 2,000	$17,200	$2,000
Distribution ($17,300)				
From AAA	(8,200)		(8,200)	
From OAA		(2,000)	(2,000)	
From stock basis			(7,000)	
Ending balance	$ –0–	$ –0–	$ –0–	$2,000
Distribution in excess of basis = Capital gain			$ 100	

Pass-through losses can reduce loan basis, but distributions do not. Stock basis cannot be reduced below zero, so the $100 excess distribution does not reduce Stacey's loan basis.

The basis rules for an S corporation are similar to the rules for determining a partner's interest basis in a partnership. However, a partner's basis in the partnership interest includes the partner's direct investment plus a *ratable share* of any partnership liabilities.[35] If a partnership borrows from a partner, the partner receives a basis increase as if the partnership had borrowed from an unrelated third party.[36] In contrast, except for loans from the shareholder to the corporation, corporate borrowing has no effect on S corporation shareholder basis.

The fact that a shareholder has guaranteed a loan made to the corporation by a third party has no effect on the shareholder's loan basis, unless payments actually have been made as a result of that guarantee.[37]

[34]§ 1367(b)(2); Reg. § 1.1367–2(e).
[35]§ 752(a).
[36]Reg. § 1.752–1(e).

[37]See, for example, *Estate of Leavitt*, 90 T.C. 206 (1988), *aff'd* 89–1 USTC ¶9332, 63 AFTR 2d 89–1437, 875 F.2d 420 (CA–4, 1989); *Selfe v. U.S.*, 86–1 USTC ¶9115, 57 AFTR 2d 86–464, 778 F.2d 769 (CA–11, 1985); *James K. Calcutt*, 91 T.C. 14 (1988).

If a loan's basis has been reduced and is not restored, income is recognized when the S corporation repays the shareholder. If the corporation issued a note as evidence of the debt, repayment constitutes an amount received in exchange for a capital asset and the amount that exceeds the shareholder's basis is entitled to capital gain treatment.[38] However, if the loan is made on open account, the repayment constitutes ordinary income to the extent that it exceeds the shareholder's basis in the loan.[39] Each repayment is prorated between the gain portion and the repayment of the debt.[40] Thus, a written note should be given to ensure capital gain treatment for the income that results from a loan's repayment.

Effects of Debt

EXAMPLE
31

Sammy is a 57% owner of Falcon, an S corporation in Brooklyn, New York. At the beginning of the year, his stock basis is zero. Sammy's basis in a $12,000 loan made to Falcon and evidenced by Falcon's note has been reduced to $0 by prior losses. At the end of the year, he receives a $13,000 distribution. During the year, his net share of corporate taxable income is $11,000. Because there is no "net increase" (i.e., his share of income is less than the amount of the distribution), Sammy's debt basis is not restored. Instead, his share of income increases his stock basis to $11,000. Therefore, on receipt of the $13,000 distribution, $11,000 is a tax-free recovery of his stock basis, and $2,000 is a capital gain.[41]

EXAMPLE
32

Assume in the previous example that the distribution that Sammy receives is only $8,000. Because the "net increase" is $3,000 ($11,000 income share in excess of $8,000 distribution), the debt basis is restored by $3,000. Accordingly, the remaining income share not used to increase debt basis ($8,000) is used to increase Sammy's stock basis to $8,000. Therefore, on receipt of the $8,000 distribution, all $8,000 is tax-free, reducing the stock basis back to zero.

22-3g Treatment of Losses

Net Operating Loss

LO.9

Explain the tax effects that losses have on shareholders.

One major advantage of an S election is the ability to pass through any net operating loss of the corporation directly to the shareholders. A shareholder can deduct an NOL for the year in which the S corporation's tax year ends. The corporation does not deduct the NOL. A shareholder's basis in the stock is reduced to the extent of any pass-through of the NOL, and the entity's AAA is reduced by the same deductible amount.[42]

The Big Picture

EXAMPLE
33

Return to the facts of *The Big Picture* on p. 22-1. If Smith and Jones make the S election for Cane, Inc., they each can pass through any NOLs to the extent of the current stock basis. If the new S corporation incurs an NOL of $84,000 for the tax year, both shareholders are entitled to deduct $42,000 against other income for the tax year in which Cane's tax year ends. Any NOL incurred before the S election is in effect does not flow through to the two shareholders as long as the S election is maintained.

---

[38]*Joe M. Smith*, 48 T.C. 872 (1967), *aff'd* and *rev'd* in 70–1 USTC ¶9327, 25 AFTR 2d 70–936, 424 F.2d 219 (CA–9, 1970); Rev.Rul. 64–162, 1964–1 C.B. 304.

[39]Reg. § 1.1367–2. Open account debt is treated as if it were evidenced by a note if the shareholder's principal balance exceeds $25,000 at the end of the tax year.

[40]Rev.Rul. 68–537, 1968–2 C.B. 372.
[41]§ 1367(b)(2)(B); Reg. § 1.1367–2(e).
[42]§§ 1368(a)(1)(A) and (e)(1)(A).

Deductions for an S corporation's loss pass-throughs (e.g., NOL, capital loss, and charitable contributions) cannot exceed a shareholder's adjusted basis in the stock *plus* the basis of any loans made by the shareholder to the corporation. If a taxpayer is unable to prove the tax basis, the loss pass-through can be denied.

Distributions made by an S corporation are taken into account *before* applying the loss limitations for the year.

EXAMPLE 34

Pylon, Inc., a calendar year S corporation, is partly owned by Doris, who has a beginning stock basis of $10,000. During the year, Doris's share of a long-term capital gain (LTCG) is $2,000, and her share of an ordinary loss is $9,000. If Doris receives a $6,000 distribution, her deductible loss is calculated as follows.

Beginning stock basis	$10,000
Add: LTCG	2,000
Subtotal	$12,000
Less: Distribution	(6,000)
Basis for loss limitation purposes	$ 6,000
Deductible loss	($ 6,000)
Suspended loss	($ 3,000)

Doris's stock now has a basis of zero.

A shareholder's share of an NOL may be greater than both stock basis and loan basis. A shareholder can carry forward a loss to the extent that the loss for the year exceeds basis. Any loss carried forward may be deducted *only* by the *same* shareholder if and when the basis in the stock or loans to the corporation is restored.[43]

EXAMPLE 35

Dana has a stock basis of $4,000 in an S corporation. He has loaned $2,000 to the corporation and has guaranteed another $4,000 loan made to the corporation by a local bank. Although his share of the S corporation's NOL for the current year is $9,500, Dana may deduct only $6,000 of the NOL on his individual tax return; the loan guarantee had no effect on Dana's stock or loan basis.

Dana may carry forward $3,500 of the NOL, to be deducted when the basis in his stock or loan to the corporation is restored. Dana has a zero basis in both the stock and the loan after the flow-through of the $6,000 NOL.

Any loss carryover due to insufficient basis remaining at the end of an approximately one-year post-termination transition period is *lost forever*. The post-termination period includes the 120-day period beginning on the date of any determination pursuant to an audit of a taxpayer that follows the termination of the S corporation's election and that adjusts a Subchapter S item.[44] Thus, if a shareholder has a loss carryover, he or she should increase the stock or loan basis and flow through the loss before disposing of the stock.

Net operating losses from C corporation years cannot be utilized at the corporate level (except with respect to built-in gains, discussed in text Section 22-3h), nor can they be passed through to the shareholders. When a corporation is expecting losses in the future, an S election should be made *before* the loss years.

At-Risk Rules

S corporation shareholders, like partners, are limited in the amount of loss they may deduct by their "at-risk" amounts; see text Section 21-3e. These rules apply to the shareholders, but not to the corporation. An amount at risk is determined separately for each shareholder.

---

[43]§ 1366(d).   [44]§ 1377(b)(1).

Shareholder Ricketts has a basis of $35,000 in his S corporation stock. His share of this year's S corporation loss is $40,000.

Ricketts takes a $15,000 nonrecourse loan from a local bank and lends the proceeds to the S corporation. Ricketts now has a stock basis of $35,000 and a loan basis of $15,000. However, due to the at-risk rules, he can deduct only $35,000 of S corporation losses, reducing his stock basis to $0.

EXAMPLE
36

Passive Activity Losses and Credits

S corporations are not directly subject to the passive activity limits, but corporate rental activities are inherently passive, and other activities of an S corporation may be passive unless the shareholder(s) materially participate(s) in operating the business. If the corporate activity involves rentals or the shareholders do not materially participate, any loss or credit that flows through is passive. The shareholders can apply such losses or credits only against income from other passive activities.

22-3h Tax on Pre-Election Built-In Gain

LO.10

Compute the built-in gains and passive investment income penalty taxes.

In almost all cases, an S corporation does *not* pay an income tax, because all items flow through to the shareholders. But a few S corporations are required to pay a built-in gains tax, LIFO recapture tax, general business credit recapture, or passive investment income tax.

Without the **built-in gains tax** (§ 1374), it would be possible to avoid the corporate double tax on a disposition of appreciated property by electing S corporation status.

The built-in gains tax generally applies to C corporations converting to S status. It is a *corporate-level* tax on any built-in gain recognized when the S corporation disposes of an asset in a taxable disposition within five calendar years after the date on which the S election took effect.[45] The holding period begins on the date of the S election.

General Rules

The base for the built-in gains tax includes any unrealized gain on appreciated assets (e.g., real estate, cash basis receivables, and goodwill) held by a corporation on the day it elects S status. The highest corporate tax rate (currently 21 percent) is applied to the unrealized gain when any of the assets are sold. Furthermore, the gain on the sale (net of the tax itself)[46] passes through as a taxable gain to shareholders.

Zinnia, Inc., a C corporation, owns a single asset with a basis of $100,000 and a fair market value of $500,000. Zinnia elects S corporation status. A corporate-level tax must be paid by Zinnia if it sells the asset after electing S status. Upon sale of the asset, the corporation owes a tax of $84,000 ($400,000 × 21%). The shareholders report a $316,000 taxable gain ($400,000 − $84,000). In this manner, the built-in gains tax effectively imposes a double tax on Zinnia and its shareholders.

EXAMPLE
37

The gain that is subject to the tax is limited to the *aggregate net* built-in gain of the corporation at the time it converted to S status. Thus, at the time of the S election, unrealized gains of the corporation are reduced by unrealized losses from the contributed assets. This net amount sets an upper limit on the tax base for the built-in gains tax.

Recognized built-in losses and built-in gains are netted each year to determine the built-in gains tax base. The tax base then is limited to the entity's taxable income for the year.[47]

An S corporation can offset built-in gains with NOLs or unexpired capital losses from C corporation years.

---

[45]§ 1374(d)(7)(B).

[46]§ 1366(f)(2).

[47]§§ 1374(c)(2), (d)(1), and (d)(2)(A).

EXAMPLE
38

The Big Picture

Return to the facts of *The Big Picture* on p. 22-1. If Cane, Inc., becomes an S corporation, a built-in gain may be recognized. Assuming that Cane reports a $50,000 built-in gain on conversion and that it holds a $20,000 NOL carryforward for C corporation years before the S election, the NOL carryforward is applied against the built-in gain. Cane's built-in gains tax applies only to $30,000.

22-3i LIFO Recapture Tax

To preclude deferral of gain recognition by a C corporation that is electing S status, any LIFO recapture amount at the time of the S election is subject to a corporate-level tax.

The taxable LIFO recapture amount equals the excess of the inventory's value under FIFO over the LIFO value. No tax refund is allowed if the LIFO value is higher than the FIFO value.

The resulting tax is payable in four equal installments, with the first payment due on or before the due date for the corporate return for the last C corporation year (without regard to any extensions). The remaining three installments are paid on or before the due dates of the succeeding corporate returns.

No interest is due if payments are made by the due dates, and no estimated taxes are due on the four tax installments. The basis of the LIFO inventory is adjusted to account for this LIFO recapture amount, but the AAA is not decreased by payment of the tax.

22-3j Passive Investment Income Penalty Tax

A tax is imposed on the excess passive income of S corporations that possess AEP from C corporation years. The tax rate is the highest corporate rate for the year (21 percent currently). The rate is applied to excess net passive income (ENPI), which is determined using the following formula, and illustrated in Example 39.

Passive investment income (PII) includes gross receipts derived from royalties, passive rents, dividends, interest, and annuities. Only the net gain from the disposition of capital assets is taken into account in computing PII gross receipts.[48] Net passive income is PII reduced by any deductions directly connected with the production of that income. Any PII tax reduces the gross income that flows through to the shareholders.

The excess net passive income cannot exceed the S corporation's taxable income for the year, calculated as if it were a C corporation.[49]

EXAMPLE
39

Barnhardt Corporation, an S corporation, generates gross receipts for the year totaling $264,000 (of which $110,000 is PII). Expenditures directly connected to the production of the PII total $30,000. Therefore, Barnhardt reports net PII of $80,000 ($110,000 − $30,000), and its PII for the tax year exceeds 25% of its gross receipts by $44,000 [$110,000 PII − (25% × $264,000)]. Excess net passive income (ENPI) is $32,000, calculated as follows.

$$\text{ENPI} = \frac{\$44,000}{\$110,000} \times \$80,000 = \$32,000$$

Barnhardt's PII tax is $6,720 ($32,000 × 21%).

---

[48]§§ 1362(d)(3)(B) and (C).   [49]§ 1375(b)(1)(B).

22-3k **Other Operational Rules**

Several other points may be made about the possible effects of various Code provisions on S corporations.

- An S corporation must make estimated tax payments with respect to tax exposure because of any recognized built-in gain and excess passive investment income.

- An S corporation is *not* subject to the 10 percent of taxable income limitation applicable to charitable contributions made by a C corporation.

- Any family member who renders services or furnishes capital to an S corporation must be paid reasonable compensation. Otherwise, the IRS can make adjustments to reflect the value of the services or capital.[50] This rule may make it more difficult for related parties to shift Subchapter S taxable income to children or other family members.

- The flow-through of S items does not create self-employment income to the shareholder, nor is it subject to the additional Medicare tax on upper-income taxpayers.[51] This treatment is attractive compared to the treatment of a proprietorship or a partnership whose income is taxed as self-employment income to the owners. Compensation for services rendered to an S corporation is, however, subject to FICA taxes for an employee-shareholder, but it is not considered wages for the QBID.

S Corporations and SE Income

EXAMPLE 40

Mickey and Dana each own one-third of a fast-food restaurant, and their 14-year-old son owns the other shares. Both parents work full-time in the restaurant operations, but the son works infrequently. Neither parent receives a salary this year, when the taxable income of the S corporation is $160,000. The IRS can require that reasonable compensation be paid to the parents to prevent the full one-third of the $160,000 from being taxed to the son. Otherwise, this would be an effective technique to shift earned income to a family member to reduce the total family tax burden. Furthermore, low or zero salaries can reduce FICA taxes.

EXAMPLE 41

Dave is a professor at a southeastern university, earning a salary of $180,000. He also generates consulting income of $80,000. If the consulting business is organized as an S corporation, Dave should withdraw a reasonable salary from the S corporation for his services. The S corporation pays payroll and withholding tax on the salary.

If the business is operated as a proprietorship, Dave is exempt from the Social Security portion of the self-employment tax because his university salary exceeds the annual FICA ceiling. Here, operating as a proprietorship offers a tax advantage over an S corporation.

- Some or all of the entity's income may be subject to a state-level income tax (e.g., a gross receipts tax or a "sting tax" on large S corporations in Massachusetts).

- An S corporation may issue § 1244 stock to its shareholders to obtain ordinary loss treatment. Review text Section 18-3c for the Federal income tax effects of such stock.

- The exclusion of gain on disposition of small business stock is *not* available for S stock.[52]

- Losses may be disallowed due to a lack of a profit motive. If the activities at the corporate level are not profit-motivated, the losses may be disallowed under the hobby loss rules.[53]

---

[50]§ 1366(e). In addition, beware of an IRS search for the "real owner" of the stock under Reg. § 1.1373–1(a)(2).

[51]Rev.Rul. 59–221, 1959–1 C.B. 225.

[52]§ 1202.

[53]§ 183; *Michael J. Houston*, 69 TCM 2360, T.C.Memo. 1995–159; *Mario G. De Mendoza, III*, 68 TCM 42, T.C.Memo. 1994–314.

- A penalty is imposed for failure to file (including extensions) timely S corporation returns. The penalty for returns filed in 2021 is $210 per month times the number of S corporation shareholders. The penalty is assessed against the corporation for a maximum of 12 months.[54]

- Partnership treatment applies for certain fringe benefits to more-than-2% shareholder-employees of S corporations. Thus, these shareholders are not entitled to exclude certain fringe benefits from gross income. A more-than-2% shareholder-employee is allowed an above-the-line (*for* AGI) deduction on Form 1040 for accident and health insurance premiums.[55]

Engage in tax planning for S corporations.

22-4 TAX PLANNING

22-4a When the Election Is Advisable

Effective tax planning with S corporations begins with the determination of whether the election is appropriate. In this context, one should consider the following factors.

- Are losses from the business anticipated? If so, the S election may be highly attractive because these losses pass through to the shareholders.

- What are the tax brackets of the shareholders? If the shareholders are in high individual income tax brackets, it may be desirable to avoid S corporation status and have profits taxed to the entity at the lower C corporation rate (21 percent). However, the income still is not in the owners' hands.

- When the shareholders are in low individual income tax brackets, the pass-through of corporate profits is attractive, and reducing the combined income tax becomes the paramount consideration.

- Does a C corporation hold an NOL carryforward? Such a loss cannot be used in an S year (except for purposes of the built-in gains tax).

- S corporations generally use a calendar tax year.[56]

Concept Summary 22.3

Making an S Election

Various considerations will affect a decision to make an S election.

- Avoid the S election if shareholders have high marginal income tax rates relative to the C corporation rate.

- If corporate losses are anticipated and there is unlikely to be corporate taxable income soon, S corporation status is advisable.

- If a C corporation holds an NOL carryover from prior years, the losses cannot be used in an S corporation year (except with respect to built-in gains).

- There may be tax advantages to the S shareholder who receives a flow-through of passive activity income.

- Tax-exempt income at the S level does not lose its special tax treatment for shareholders.

22-4b Making a Proper Election

Once the parties have decided the election is appropriate, it becomes essential to ensure that the election is made properly.

- Make sure that all shareholders timely file a proper consent. If any doubt exists concerning the shareholder status of an individual, it would be wise to have that

---

[54]§ 6699.

[55]§ 1372(a); Notice 2008–1, 2008–2 I.R.B. 251.

[56]Entity tax-year constraints parallel those pertaining to partnerships, as discussed in text Section 21-2g. But the least aggregate deferral method is not used by S corporations. Also see Chapter 16.

party issue a consent anyway.[57] Too few consents are fatal to the election; the same cannot be said for too many consents.

- Make sure the election is timely and properly filed. Either hand-carry the election to an IRS office or send it by certified or registered mail or use a commercial delivery service. The date used to determine timeliness is the postmark date, not the date the IRS receives the election. A copy of the election should become part of the corporation's permanent files.

- Ascertain when the election period begins to run for a newly formed corporation. An election made too soon (before the corporation is in existence) is ineffective.

- An S election can be lost in several ways, and a five-year waiting period generally is imposed before another S election is available, so the S election must be preserved once it is made.

22-4c Operation of the S Corporation

Accumulated Adjustments Account

Although the corporate-level accumulated adjustments account (AAA) is used primarily by an S corporation with Subchapter C accumulated earnings and profits (AEP), all S corporations should maintain an accurate record of the AAA. Because there is a grace period for distributing the AAA after termination of the S election, the parties must be in a position to determine the balance of the account.

The AAA bypass election may be used to eliminate a small E & P balance and pay a small current tax, but then to avoid future exposure to taxable dividend distributions and the entity-level taxes of the S corporation.

Salary Structure

The salary paid to a shareholder-employee of an S corporation can have varying tax consequences and should be considered carefully. Larger amounts might be advantageous if the maximum contribution allowed for the shareholder-employee under the corporation's retirement plan has not been reached. Smaller amounts may be beneficial if the parties are trying to shift taxable income to lower-bracket shareholders, reduce payroll taxes, curtail a reduction of Social Security benefits, or restrict losses that do not pass through because of the stock basis limitation.[58]

A strategy of decreasing compensation and correspondingly increasing distributions to shareholder-employees often results in substantial savings in employment taxes. This technique also increases the QBID for shareholders.

The Big Picture

EXAMPLE 42

Return to the facts of *The Big Picture* on p. 22-1. The two shareholders should consider reducing their $92,000 salary and instead receiving a larger undistributed share of the S corporation income. A shareholder's share of pass-through S corporation income is not treated as self-employment income, whereas traditional compensation is subject to the Social Security and Medicare taxes for the corporation and both employees.

---

[57]See *William B. Wilson,* 34 TCM 463, T.C.Memo. 1975–92.

[58]Rev.Rul. 74–44, 1974–1 C.B. 287; *Spicer Accounting, Inc. v. U.S.,* 91–1 USTC ¶50,103, 66 AFTR 2d 90–5806, 918 F.2d 90 (CA–9, 1990); *Radtke v. U.S.,* 90–1 USTC ¶50,113, 65 AFTR 2d 90–1155, 895 F.2d 1196 (CA–7, 1990); *Joseph M. Grey Public Accountant, P.C.,* 119 T.C. 121 (2002); *David E.*

Watson, PC, v. U.S., 2010–1 USTC ¶50,444, 105 AFTR 2d 2010–2624, 714 F.Supp.2d 954 (S.D. Iowa). The IRS uses salary surveys and other statistical methods to determine the appropriate compensation level. *McAlary Ltd.,* T.C. Summary Opinion 2013–62.

The IRS can require that reasonable compensation be paid to family members who render services or provide capital to the S corporation. The IRS also can adjust the items taken into account by family-member shareholders to reflect the value of services or capital they provided (refer to Example 40).

Deductions for various tax-free fringe benefits are denied to a more-than-2% shareholder-employee of an S corporation. Such benefits include group term life insurance, medical insurance, and meals and lodging furnished for the convenience of the employer. These items are treated as wages and are subject to most payroll taxes. The employee can deduct medical insurance premiums on his or her tax return.

The choice between a salary and pass-through income is not clear-cut.

- Although a salary is subject to payroll tax and pass-through income is not, pass-through income does not accrue Social Security benefits for its recipient.

- S corporation income distributions do not count as compensation for computing an employee's contribution formula for a qualified retirement plan.

- The IRS and the courts require an S shareholder to take a reasonable salary (see footnote 58).

- If a partner or proprietor reports salary income from other sources and the aggregate salaries exceed the annual FICA ceiling, a partnership or proprietorship entity may provide tax savings over an S corporation.

Loss Considerations

A net loss in excess of tax basis may be carried forward and deducted only by the same shareholder in succeeding years. Thus, before disposing of the stock, a shareholder should increase the basis of such stock/loan to flow through the loss. The next shareholder does not obtain the loss carryover.

Any unused loss carryover in existence upon the termination of the S election may be deducted only in the next tax year and is limited to the individual's *stock* basis (not loan basis) in the post-termination year.[59] The shareholder may want to purchase more stock to increase the tax basis to absorb the loss.

Avoiding the Passive Investment Income Tax

Too much passive investment income (PII) may cause an S corporation to incur a penalty tax on excessive passive investment income and/or terminate the S election. Several planning techniques can be used to avoid both of these unfavorable events. The corporation might reduce taxable income below the excess net passive income; similarly, PII might be accelerated into years in which there is an offsetting NOL.

The tax also can be avoided if the corporation generates needed gross receipts. By increasing gross receipts without increasing PII, the amount of PII in excess of 25 percent of gross receipts is reduced.

EXAMPLE 43

An S corporation has paid a passive investment income penalty tax for two consecutive years. In the next year, the corporation has a large amount of AAA. One planning technique to address this situation is to manufacture a large amount of gross receipts without increasing PII through an action such as a merger with a grocery store. If the gross receipts from the grocery store are substantial, the amount of the PII in excess of 25% of gross receipts is reduced.

22-5 OVERALL COMPARISON OF FORMS OF DOING BUSINESS

See Concept Summary 22.4 for a detailed comparison of the tax consequences of the following forms of doing business: sole proprietorship, partnership, limited liability company, S corporation, and C corporation.

---

[59]§ 1366(d)(3).

Concept Summary 22.4

**Tax Attributes of Different Forms of Business
(Assume That Partners and Shareholders Are All Individuals)**

	Sole Proprietorship	Partnership/Limited Liability Company*	S Corporation	Regular (C) Corporation**
Restrictions on type or number of owners	One owner. The owner must be an individual.	Must have at least two owners.	Only individuals, estates, certain trusts, and certain tax-exempt entities can be owners. Maximum number of shareholders limited to 100.***	None, except that some states require a minimum of two shareholders.
Incidence of tax	Sole proprietorship's income and deductions are reported on Schedule C of the individual's Form 1040. A separate Schedule C is prepared for each business.	Entity not subject to tax. Owners in their separate capacity subject to tax on their distributive share of income. Entity files Form 1065.	Except for certain built-in gains and passive investment income when earnings and profits are present from C corporation tax years, entity not subject to Federal income tax. S corporation files Form 1120S. Shareholders are subject to tax on income attributable to their stock ownership.	Income subject to double taxation. Entity subject to tax, and shareholder subject to tax on any corporate dividends received. Corporation files Form 1120.
Highest tax rate	37% at individual level.	37% at owner level.	37% at shareholder level.	21% at corporate level plus 0%/15%/20% on any corporate dividends at shareholder level (if qualified dividends; otherwise 37%). NIIT of 3.8% may apply to dividend income.
Qualified business income deduction (§ 199A)	Applicable.	Applicable. Eligible partners (noncorporate) need data from the entity to compute the deduction amount.	Applicable. Eligible shareholders need data from the entity to compute the deduction amount.	Deduction not applicable to C corporations.
Self-employment (SE) tax on owner	Schedule C income subject to SE tax. Owner not treated as employee.	Guaranteed payment for services and distributive share of net earnings of general partner subject to SE tax. Partners not treated as employees.	Not applicable. Payroll taxes owed on reasonable compensation paid to shareholder/employee; no SE tax on shareholder's distributive share of earnings.	Not applicable. Payroll taxes owed on wages of shareholder/employee.
Choice of tax year	Same tax year as owner.	Selection generally restricted to coincide with tax year of majority owners or principal owners or to tax year determined under the least aggregate deferral method.	Restricted to a calendar year unless IRS approves a different year for business purposes or other exceptions apply.	Unrestricted selection allowed at time of filing first tax return.
Return due date (normal and extended) for a calendar year entity	April 15 October 15	March 15 September 15	March 15 September 15	April 15 October 15

continued

Tax Attributes of Different Forms of Business—(Continued)

	Sole Proprietorship	Partnership/Limited Liability Company*	S Corporation	Regular (C) Corporation**
Timing of taxation	Based on owner's tax year.	Owners report their share of income in their tax year with or within which the entity's tax year ends. Owners in their separate capacities are subject to payment of estimated taxes.	Shareholders report their shares of income in their tax year with or within which the corporation's tax year ends. Shareholders may be subject to payment of estimated taxes.	Corporation subject to tax at close of its tax year. May be subject to payment of estimated taxes. Dividends will be subject to tax at the shareholder level in the tax year received.
Basis for allocating income to owners	Not applicable (only one owner).	Profit and loss sharing agreement. Cash basis items of cash basis entities are allocated on a daily basis. Other entity items are allocated after considering varying interests of owners.	Pro rata share based on stock ownership. Shareholder's pro rata share is determined on a daily basis, according to the number of shares of stock held on each day of the corporation's tax year.	Not applicable.
Contribution of property to the entity	Not a taxable transaction.	Generally not a taxable transaction.	Taxable transaction unless the § 351 requirements are satisfied.	Taxable transaction unless the § 351 requirements are satisfied.
Character of income taxed to owners	Retains source characteristics.	Conduit—retains source characteristics.	Conduit—retains source characteristics.	All source characteristics are lost when income is distributed to owners.
Basis for allocating a net operating loss to owners	Not applicable (only one owner).	Profit and loss sharing agreement. Cash basis items of cash basis entities are allocated on a daily basis. Other entity items are allocated after considering varying interests of owners.	Prorated among shareholders on a daily basis.	Not applicable.
Limitation on losses deductible by owners	Investment plus liabilities.	Owner's investment plus share of liabilities.	Shareholder's investment plus loans made by shareholder to corporation.	Not applicable.
Subject to at-risk rules	Yes, at the owner level. Indefinite carryover of excess loss.	Yes, at the owner level. Indefinite carryover of excess loss.	Yes, at the shareholder level. Indefinite carryover of excess loss.	Yes, for closely held corporations. Indefinite carryover of excess loss.
Subject to passive activity loss rules	Yes, at the owner level. Indefinite carryover of excess loss.	Yes, at the owner level. Indefinite carryover of excess loss.	Yes, at the shareholder level. Indefinite carryover of excess loss.	Yes, for closely held corporations and personal service corporations. Indefinite carryover of excess loss.
Subject to limitation on excess business losses	Yes, at the owner level.	Yes, at the owner level (unless partner is a corporation).	Yes, at the shareholder level.	No. Limitation does not apply to corporate taxpayers.
Tax consequences of earnings retained by entity	Taxed to owner when earned and increases his or her investment in the sole proprietorship.	Taxed to owners when earned and increases their respective interests in the entity.	Taxed to shareholders when earned and increases their respective bases in stock.	Taxed to corporation as earned and may be subject to penalty tax if accumulated unreasonably.
Nonliquidating distributions to owners	Not taxable.	Not taxable unless money received exceeds recipient owner's basis in entity interest. Existence of § 751 assets may cause recognition of ordinary income.	Generally not taxable unless the distribution exceeds the shareholder's AAA or stock basis. Existence of accumulated earnings and profits could cause some distributions to be dividends.	Taxable in year of receipt to extent of earnings and profits or if exceeds basis in stock.

continued

Tax Attributes of Different Forms of Business—(Continued)

	Sole Proprietorship	Partnership/Limited Liability Company*	S Corporation	Regular (C) Corporation**
Capital gains	Taxed at owner level with opportunity to use alternative tax rate.	Conduit—owners must account for their respective shares.	Conduit, with certain exceptions (a possible penalty tax)—shareholders must account for their respective shares.	Taxed at corporate level with a maximum 21% rate. No other benefits.
Capital losses	Only $3,000 of capital losses can be offset each tax year against ordinary income. Indefinite carryover.	Conduit—owners must account for their respective shares.	Conduit—shareholders must account for their respective shares.	Carried back three years and carried forward five years. Deductible only to the extent of capital gains.
§ 1231 gains and losses	Taxable or deductible at owner level. Five-year lookback rule for § 1231 losses.	Conduit—owners must account for their respective shares.	Conduit—shareholders must account for their respective shares.	Taxable or deductible at corporate level only. Five-year lookback rule for § 1231 losses.
Foreign tax credits	Available at owner level.	Conduit—passed through to owners.	Generally conduit—passed through to shareholders.	Available at corporate level only.
§ 1244 treatment of loss on sale of interest	Not applicable.	Not applicable.	Available.	Available.
Basis treatment of entity liabilities	Includible in interest basis.	Includible in interest basis.	Not includible in stock basis.	Not includible in stock basis.
Built-in gains	Not applicable.	Not applicable.	Possible corporate-level tax.	Not applicable.
Special allocations to owners	Not applicable (only one owner).	Available if supported by substantial economic effect.	Not available.	Not applicable.
Deductibility of fringe benefits for owners	None.	None.	None unless a 2%-or-less shareholder.	Available within antidiscrimination rules.
Effect of liquidation/ redemption/ reorganization on basis of entity assets	Not applicable.	Usually carried over from entity to owner unless a § 754 election is made, excessive cash is distributed, or more than 50% of the capital interests are transferred within 12 months.	Taxable step-up to fair market value.	Taxable step-up to fair market value.
Sale of ownership interest	Treated as the sale of individual assets. Classification of recognized gain or loss depends on the nature of the individual assets.	Treated as the sale of an entity interest. Recognized gain or loss is classified as capital under § 741, subject to ordinary income treatment under § 751.	Treated as the sale of corporate stock. Recognized gain is classified as capital gain. Recognized loss is classified as capital loss, subject to ordinary loss treatment under § 1244.	Treated as the sale of corporate stock. Recognized gain is classified as capital gain. Recognized loss is classified as capital loss, subject to ordinary loss treatment under § 1244. If stock qualifies as original issue qualified business stock under § 1202, gain is excluded if noncorporate owner held the stock over 5 years.

continued

Tax Attributes of Different Forms of Business—(Continued)

	Sole Proprietorship	Partnership/Limited Liability Company*	S Corporation	Regular (C) Corporation**
Distribution of appreciated property	Not taxable.	No recognition at the entity level.	Recognition at the corporate level to the extent of the appreciation. Conduit—amount of recognized gain is passed through to shareholders.	Taxable at the corporate level to the extent of the appreciation.
Splitting of income among family members	Not applicable (only one owner). Spouses running a business together can elect "qualified joint venture" status where earnings are split and identical Schedule Cs are filed for each spouse rather than a partnership return [§ 761(f)].	IRS will not recognize a family member as an owner unless certain requirements are met.	IRS can make adjustments to reflect adequate compensation for services.	Other than unreasonable compensation, IRS generally cannot make adjustments to reflect adequate compensation for services and capital.
Organizational costs	Startup expenditures are eligible for $5,000 limited expensing (subject to phaseout) and amortizing balance over 180 months.	Organizational costs are eligible for $5,000 limited expensing (subject to phaseout) and amortizing balance over 180 months.	Same as partnership.	Same as partnership.
Charitable contributions	Limitations apply at owner level.	Conduit—owners are subject to deduction limitations in their own capacities.	Conduit—shareholders are subject to deduction limitations in their own capacities.	Limited to 10% of taxable income before certain deductions.
Alternative minimum tax	Applies at owner level. AMT rates are 26% and 28%.	Applies at the owner level rather than at the entity level. AMT preferences and adjustments are passed through from the entity to the owners.	Applies at the shareholder level rather than at the corporate level. AMT preferences and adjustments are passed through from the S corporation to the shareholders.	C corporations are not subject to AMT.
Tax preference and adjustment items	Apply at owner level in determining AMT.	Conduit—passed through to owners who must account for such items in their separate capacities.	Conduit—passed through to shareholders who must account for such items in their separate capacities.	C corporations are not subject to AMT.

*Refer to Chapter 21 for additional details on partnerships and limited liability companies.
**Refer to Chapters 17 through 20 for additional details on regular (C) corporations.
***Spouses and family members are treated as one shareholder.

REFOCUS ON THE BIG PICTURE

DEDUCTIBILITY OF LOSSES AND THE CHOICE OF BUSINESS ENTITY

As long as Smith and Jones, the owners of Cane, Inc., maintain C corporation status, they cannot deduct on their individual tax returns any NOLs the business incurs. For the owners to deduct any future NOLs on their Forms 1040, Cane should be operated as a flow-through entity. The most logical alternative is to make an S election or to become a limited liability company.

An S election may be appropriate for Cane. Cane should make a timely election on Form 2553, and both shareholders must consent to the election. The owners should make the election on or before the fifteenth day of the third month of the current year to claim losses for the current year. Otherwise, the S election becomes effective only at the beginning of the next tax year.

Normally, an S corporation does not pay any income tax because all items (including NOLs) flow through to the shareholders. A C corporation making an S election may be required to pay a corporate-level built-in gains tax or a LIFO recapture tax.

An S corporation can issue both voting and nonvoting common stock, provided that all shares have the same economic rights to corporate income or loss.

Cane might sell off the bonds that generate its tax-exempt income, which will not be reflected in the AAA. Although it is reflected in stock basis, tax-exempt income (as part of the OAA) is distributed to the shareholders only after the S corporation has distributed all of its C corporation earnings and profits.

What If?

Nonresident aliens cannot own S stock, so if joint ownership of the shares is desired among all of the spouses, a change in the spouses' residency must occur. When Cane begins to turn a profit, the S election will be less attractive, and termination of the S election should be considered by the parties.

LISA S./SHUTTERSTOCK.COM

Key Terms

Accumulated adjustments account (AAA), 22-14

Accumulated earnings and profits (AEP), 22-13

Built-in gains tax, 22-23

Bypass election, 22-16

Other adjustments account (OAA), 22-16

Passive investment income (PII), 22-8

Qualified business income deduction (QBID), 22-12

S corporation, 22-2

Small business corporation, 22-3

Subchapter S, 22-2

Voluntary revocation, 22-7

Discussion Questions

1. **LO.1** Which of these taxes may be incurred by an S corporation?
   a. Corporate income tax.
   b. Tax on certain built-in gains.
   c. Property tax assessed by the county.

2. **LO.2** Which of the following are requirements to be an S corporation?
   a. Is limited to an absolute maximum of 100 shareholders.
   b. Has no resident alien shareholders.
   c. Has only one class of stock.
   d. Cannot have any earnings and profits (E & P).

3.   **LO.2** Which of the following can be shareholders of an S corporation?

    a.   Partnership.

    b.   Limited liability partnership.

    c.   Corporation.

    d.   One-member limited liability company.

4.   **LO.2** Joey lives in North Carolina, a common law state. He is a shareholder in an S corporation. If he marries a nonresident alien, will the S election terminate? Would your answer change if he lived in Louisiana? Explain.

Critical Thinking

Communications

5.   **LO.2** Bob Roman, the majority owner of an S corporation, approaches you for some tax planning help. He would like to exchange some real estate in a like-kind transaction under § 1031 for real estate that may have some environmental liabilities. Prepare a letter to Bob outlining your suggestion. Bob's address is 8411 Huron Boulevard, West Chester, PA 19382.

Critical Thinking

6.   **LO.2, 3** On March 5, 2020, the two 50% shareholders of a calendar year corporation decide to elect S status. One of the shareholders, Terry, purchased her stock from a previous shareholder (a nonresident alien) on January 18, 2020. Identify any potential problems for Terry and the corporation.

Communications

7.   **LO.4** Caleb Samford calls you and says that his two-person S corporation was involuntarily terminated in February 2019. He asks you if they can make a new S election now, in November 2020. Draft a memo for your firm's tax research file, outlining what you told Caleb.

8.   **LO.6** Using the categories in the following legend, classify each transaction as a plus (+) or minus (−) on Schedule M–2 of Form 1120S. An answer might look like one of these: +AAA or −OAA.

Legend
AAA = Accumulated adjustments account
OAA = Other adjustments account
NA = No direct effect on Schedule M–2

    a.   Receipt of tax-exempt interest income.

    b.   Administrative expenses.

    c.   Depreciation recapture income.

    d.   Nontaxable life insurance proceeds.

    e.   Expenses related to tax-exempt securities.

    f.   Charitable contributions.

    g.   Business gifts in excess of $25.

    h.   Nondeductible fines and penalties.

Critical Thinking

9.   **LO.6, 11** Collette's S corporation holds a small amount of accumulated earnings and profits (AEP), thereby requiring the use of a more complex set of distribution rules. Collette's accountant tells her that this AEP requires the maintenance of the AAA figure each year. Discuss the issues that arise with respect to distributions when an S corporation holds AEP.

Communications

10.   **LO.6, 8** Scott Tierney owns 21% of an S corporation. He is confused with respect to the amounts of the corporate AAA and his stock basis. Write a memo to Scott identifying the key differences between AAA and an S shareholder's stock basis.

11. **LO.8** For each of the following independent statements, indicate whether the transaction will increase (+), decrease (−), or have no effect (*NE*) on the basis of
a shareholder's stock in an S corporation.

    a. Expenses related to tax-exempt income.
    b. Short-term capital gain.
    c. Nonseparately computed loss.
    d. Section 1231 gain.
    e. Depletion *not* in excess of basis.
    f. Separately computed income.
    g. Nontaxable return-of-capital distribution by the corporation.
    h. Advertising expenses.
    i. Business gifts in excess of $25.
    j. Depreciation recapture income.
    k. Dividend income received by the S corporation.
    l. LIFO recapture tax paid.
    m. Collection of a bad debt previously deducted.
    n. Long-term capital loss.
    o. Cash distribution to shareholder out of AAA (with positive stock basis).

12. **LO.9** Sheila Jackson is a 50% shareholder in Washington, Inc., an S corporation.   **Critical Thinking**
This year, Jackson's share of the Washington loss is $100,000. Jackson reports
income from several other sources. Identify at least four tax issues related to the
effects of the S corporation loss on Jackson's tax return.

13. **LO.1, 11** One of your clients is considering electing S status. Texas, Inc., is a   **Decision Making**
six-year-old manufacturing company with two equal shareholders, both
of whom paid $30,000 for their stock. Going into 2020, Texas holds a $110,000
NOL carryforward. Estimated income is $40,000 for 2020 and $25,000 for each
of the next three years. Should Texas make an S election for 2020? Why or
why not?

Computational Exercises

14. **LO.10** Matulis, Inc., a calendar year C corporation, owns a single asset with a basis
of $325,000 and a fair market value of $800,000. Matulis holds a positive
E & P balance. The entity elects S corporation status for 2021 and then sells the
asset. Compute the corporate-level built-in gains tax that must be paid by Matulis.

15. **LO.10** TyroneCo, an S corporation with a positive E & P balance, reports gross
receipts for the year totaling $400,000 (of which $200,000 is PII). Expenditures directly connected to the production of the PII total $80,000. Compute Tyrone's
PII tax.

16. **LO.6** Dion, an S shareholder, owned 20% of MeadowBrook's stock for 292 days
and 25% for the remaining 73 days in the year. Using the per-day allocation
method, compute Dion's share of the following S corporation items.

	Schedule K Totals	Dion's Schedule K–1 Totals
Ordinary income	$60,000	_____
Tax-exempt interest	1,000	_____
Charitable contributions	3,400	_____

17. **LO.6** Noelle, the owner of all of the shares of ClockCo, an S corporation, transfers her stock to Grayson on April 1. ClockCo reports a $70,000 NOL for the entire tax year, but only $10,000 of the loss occurs during January–March. Without a short-year election, how much of the loss is allocated to Noelle and how much is allocated to Grayson? If the corporation makes the short-year election, how much of the loss is allocated to Grayson? The tax year is not a leap year.

18. **LO.6** Holbrook, a calendar year S corporation, distributes $15,000 cash to its only shareholder, Cody, on December 31. Cody's basis in his stock is $20,000, Holbrook's AAA balance is $8,000, and Holbrook holds $2,500 AEP before the distribution. Complete the chart below using spreadsheet software such as Microsoft Excel.

	Basis in Stock	Distribution from Account	Effect on Stock Basis
From AAA account	_____	_____	_____
From AEP account	_____	_____	_____
From Cody's stock basis	_____	_____	_____

19. **LO.7** Vogel, Inc., an S corporation for five years, distributes a tract of land held as an investment to Jamari, its majority shareholder. The land was purchased for $45,000 ten years ago and is currently worth $120,000.

    a. As a result of the distribution, what is Vogel's recognized capital gain? How much is reported as a distribution to shareholders?

    b. What is the net effect of the distribution on Vogel's AAA?

    c. Assume instead that the land had been purchased for $120,000 and was currently worth $45,000. How much would Vogel recognize as a loss? What would be the net effect on Vogel's AAA? What would be Jamari's basis in the land?

20. **LO.8** Jonas is a 60% owner of Ard, an S corporation. At the beginning of the year, his stock basis is zero. Jonas's basis in a $20,000 loan made to Ard and evidenced by Ard's note has been reduced to $0 by prior losses.

    During the year, Jonas's net share of Ard's taxable income is $10,000. At the end of the year, Ard makes a $15,000 cash distribution to Jonas. After these transactions, what is Jonas's basis in his stock, and what is his basis in the debt? What is Jonas's recognized capital gain?

21. **LO.9** Kaiwan, Inc., a calendar year S corporation, is partly owned by Sharrod, whose beginning stock basis is $32,000. During the year, Sharrod's share of a Kaiwan long-term capital gain (LTCG) is $5,000, and his share of an ordinary loss is $18,000. Sharrod then receives a $20,000 cash distribution. Compute the following.

    a. Sharrod's deductible loss.

    b. Sharrod's suspended loss.

    c. Sharrod's new basis in the Kaiwan stock.

Problems

22. **LO.5, 6** The profit and loss statement of Kitsch Ltd., an S corporation, shows $100,000 book income. Kitsch is owned equally by four shareholders. From supplemental data, you obtain the following information about items that are included in book income.

Selling expenses	($21,200)
Tax-exempt interest income	3,000
Dividends received	9,000
§ 1231 gain	7,000
Depreciation recapture income	11,000
Net income from passive real estate rentals	5,000
Long-term capital loss	(6,000)
Salary paid to owners (each)	(12,000)
Cost of goods sold	(91,000)

a. Compute Kitsch's nonseparately stated income or loss for the tax year.

b. What would be the share of this year's nonseparately stated income or loss items for James Billings, one of the Kitsch shareholders?

c. What is James Billings's share of tax-exempt interest income, if any? Is the income taxable to him this year?

23. **LO.5, 6** Zebra, Inc., a calendar year S corporation, incurred the following items this year. Sammy is a 40% Zebra shareholder throughout the year.

Sales	$100,000
Cost of goods sold	(40,000)
Depreciation expense (MACRS)	(10,000)
Administrative expenses	(5,000)
§ 1231 gain	21,000
Depreciation recapture income	25,000
Short-term capital loss from stock sale	(6,000)
Long-term capital loss from stock sale	(4,000)
Long-term capital gain from stock sale	15,000
Charitable contributions	(4,500)

a. Calculate Sammy's share of Zebra's nonseparately computed income or loss.

b. Calculate Sammy's share of any Zebra long-term capital gain, if any.

c. Calculate Sammy's share of charitable contributions, if any.

24. **LO.6, 8, 9** Mary is a shareholder in CarrollCo, a calendar year S corporation. At the beginning of the year, her stock basis is $10,000, her share of the AAA is $2,000, and her share of corporate AEP is $6,000.

At the end of the year, Mary receives from CarrollCo a $6,000 cash distribution. Mary's share of S corporation items includes a $2,000 long-term capital gain and a $10,000 ordinary loss. Determine the effects of these events on Mary's share of the entity's AAA, her stock basis, and CarrollCo's AEP using spreadsheet software such as Microsoft Excel.

25. **LO.6, 7** On January 1, Kinney, Inc., an S corporation, reports $4,000 of accumulated E & P and a balance of $10,000 in AAA. Kinney has two shareholders, Erin and Frank, each of whom owns 500 shares of Kinney's stock. Kinney's nonseparately stated ordinary income for the year is $5,000.

Kinney distributes $6,000 to each shareholder on July 1, and it distributes another $3,000 to each shareholder on December 21. How are the shareholders taxed on the distributions? Ignore the 20% QBI deduction.

26. **LO.5, 6, 7** McLin, Inc., is a calendar year S corporation. Its AAA balance is zero.   Critical Thinking

a. McLin holds $90,000 of AEP. Tobias, the sole shareholder, has an adjusted basis of $80,000 in his stock. Determine the tax aspects if a $90,000 salary is paid to Tobias. Ignore the 20% QBI deduction.

b. Same as part (a), except that McLin pays Tobias a $90,000 cash distribution from AEP.

27. **LO.6, 7, 8** Tiger, Inc., a calendar year S corporation, is owned equally by four shareholders: Ann, Becky, Chris, and David. Tiger owns investment land that was purchased for $160,000 four years ago. On September 14, when the land is worth $240,000, it is distributed to David. Assuming that David's basis in his S corporation stock is $270,000 on the distribution date, discuss any Federal income tax ramifications. Ignore the 20% QBI deduction.

Communications   28. **LO.6, 8, 9, 11** Spence, Inc., a calendar year S corporation, generates an ordinary loss of $110,000 and makes a distribution of $140,000 to its sole shareholder, Storm Nelson. Nelson's stock basis and AAA at the beginning of the year are $200,000. Write a memo to your senior manager, Ahmad McMullin, discussing the tax treatment of Spence's activities.

29. **LO.6** Lonergan, Inc., a calendar year S corporation in Athens, Georgia, had a balance in AAA of $200,000 and AEP of $110,000 on December 31, 2020. During 2021, Lonergan, Inc., distributes $140,000 to its shareholders, while sustaining an ordinary loss of $120,000. Calculate the balance in Lonergan's AAA and AEP accounts at the end of 2021.

30. **LO.6** If the beginning balance in Swan, Inc.'s OAA is $6,700 and the following transactions occur, what is Swan's ending OAA balance?

Depreciation recapture income	$ 21,600
Payroll tax penalty	(4,200)
Tax-exempt interest income	4,012
Nontaxable life insurance proceeds	100,000
Life insurance premiums paid (nondeductible)	(3,007)

31. **LO.6, 8** Cougar, Inc., is a calendar year S corporation. Cougar's Form 1120S shows nonseparately stated ordinary income of $80,000 for the year. Johnny owns 40% of the Cougar stock throughout the year. The following information is obtained from the corporate records.

Tax-exempt interest income	$ 3,000
Salary paid to Johnny	(52,000)
Charitable contributions	(6,000)
Dividends received from a non-U.S. corporation	5,000
Short-term capital loss	(6,000)
Depreciation recapture income	11,000
Refund of prior state income taxes	5,000
Cost of goods sold	(72,000)
Long-term capital loss	(7,000)
Administrative expenses	(18,000)
Long-term capital gain	14,000
Selling expenses	(11,000)
Johnny's beginning stock basis	32,000
Johnny's additional stock purchases	9,000
Beginning AAA	31,000
Johnny's loan to corporation	20,000

    a.   Compute Cougar's book income or loss.

    b.   Compute Johnny's ending stock basis.

    c.   Calculate Cougar's ending AAA balance.

32. **LO.6, 7, 8** Money, Inc., a calendar year S corporation in Denton, Texas, has two unrelated shareholders, each owning 50% of the stock. Both shareholders record a $400,000 stock basis as of January 1. At the beginning of the tax year, Money reports balances in AAA of $300,000 and AEP of $600,000. During the year, Money

generates operating income of $100,000. At the end of the year, Money distributes securities worth $1,000,000, with an adjusted basis of $800,000. Determine the Federal income tax effects of these transactions.

33. **LO.6, 7, 8** Assume the same facts as in Problem 32, except that the two shareholders consent to an AAA bypass election.

34. **LO.7, 8, 9** At the beginning of the tax year, Lizzie holds a $10,000 stock basis as the sole shareholder of Spike, Inc., an S corporation. During the year, Spike reports the following. Determine Lizzie's stock basis at the end of the year and the treatment of her cash distribution.

Net taxable income from sales	$ 25,000
Net short-term capital loss	(18,000)
Cash distribution to Lizzie, 12/31	15,000

35. **LO.7, 8, 9** Assume the same facts as in Problem 34, except that the cash distribution to Lizzie amounts to $40,000. Determine Lizzie's stock basis at the end of the year and the treatment of her cash distribution.

36. **LO.7, 8** Jeff, a 52% owner of an S corporation, has a stock basis of zero at the beginning of the year. Jeff's basis in a $10,000 loan made to the corporation and evidenced by a corporate note has been reduced to zero by pass-through losses. During the year, his net share of the corporate taxable income is $11,000. At the end of the year, Jeff receives a $15,000 cash distribution. Discuss the tax effects of the distribution.

37. **LO.7, 8** Assume the same facts as in Problem 36, except that there is no cash distribution, but the corporation repays the loan principal to Jeff. Discuss the tax effects.

38. **LO.9** Maple, Inc., is an S corporation with a single shareholder, Bob Maple. Bob believes that his stock basis in the entity is $50,000, but he has lost some of the records to substantiate this amount. Maple reports an ordinary loss for the year of $80,000. What are the Federal income tax aspects to consider?   *Critical Thinking*

39. **LO.6, 9** At the beginning of the year, Ann and Becky own equally all of the stock of Whitman, Inc., an S corporation. Whitman generates a $120,000 loss for the year (not a leap year). On the 219th day of the year, Ann sells her half of the Whitman stock to her son, Scott. How much of the $120,000 loss, if any, belongs to Scott?

40. **LO.6, 9** In Problem 39, how much of the Whitman loss belongs to Ann and Becky? Becky's stock basis is $41,300.

41. **LO.5, 6, 8, 9** A calendar year S corporation reports an ordinary loss of $80,000 and a capital loss of $20,000. Mei Freiberg owns 30% of the corporate stock and has a $24,000 basis in her stock. Determine the amounts of the ordinary loss and capital loss, if any, that flow through to Freiberg. Prepare a tax memo for the files, explaining your computations.   *Communications*

42. **LO.10** Whindy Corporation, an S corporation, reports a recognized built-in gain of $80,000 and a recognized built-in loss of $10,000 this year. Whindy holds an $8,000 unexpired NOL carryforward from a C corporation year. Whindy's ordinary income for the year is $65,000. Calculate any built-in gains tax.

43. **LO.10** Flint, an S corporation with substantial AEP, reports operating gross receipts of $410,000, taxable interest income of $390,000, operating expenses of $260,000, and deductions attributable to the interest of $150,000. Calculate any passive investment income penalty tax payable.

Critical Thinking   44. **LO.5, 6, 11** Bonnie and Clyde each own one-third of a fast-food restaurant, and their 13-year-old daughter owns all of the other shares. Both parents work full-time in the restaurant, but the daughter works infrequently. Neither Bonnie nor Clyde receives a salary during the year, when the ordinary income of the S corporation is $180,000.

An IRS agent estimates that reasonable salaries for Bonnie, Clyde, and the daughter are $30,000, $35,000, and $10,000, respectively. What adjustments would you expect the IRS to impose upon these taxpayers?

Critical Thinking   45. **LO.6, 10** Samuel Reese sold 1,000 shares of his stock in Maroon, Inc., an S corporation. He sold the stock for $15,700 after he had owned it for six years. Samuel had paid $141,250 for the stock, which was issued under § 1244. Samuel is married and is the owner of the 1,000 shares. Determine the appropriate treatment of any gain or loss on the stock sale.

Critical Thinking   46. **LO.7, 11** Blue is the owner of all of the shares of an S corporation, and Blue is considering receiving a salary of $110,000 from the business. She will pay the 7.65% FICA taxes on the salary, and the S corporation will pay the same amount of FICA tax. If Blue reduces her salary to $50,000 and takes an additional $60,000 as a cash distribution, how would her Federal income tax liabilities change?

Critical Thinking   47. **LO.1, 6, 8, 9, 11** Orange, Inc., a calendar year corporation, elects S corporation status for 2020. The company generated a $74,000 NOL in 2019 and another NOL of $43,000 in 2020. Orange recorded no other transactions for the year.

At all times in 2019 and 2020, the stock of the corporation is owned by the same four shareholders, each owning 25% of the stock. Pete, one of the shareholders, holds a $6,020 basis in the Orange stock at the beginning of 2020. Identify the Federal income tax issues that Pete faces.

48. **LO.6** Based upon the following facts about Aqua, Inc., a calendar year S corporation, prepare the entity's Schedule M-2.

AAA, beginning of the year	$ 9,400
Ordinary income	24,600
Tax-exempt income	3,000
Key employee life insurance proceeds received	4,900
Payroll penalty expense	2,200
Charitable contributions	3,000
Unreasonable compensation	4,000
Premiums on key employee life insurance	2,300
Distribution to shareholders	17,000

49. **LO.6, 8, 9** Liang, a calendar year S corporation, distributes $13,000 cash to its only shareholder, Aaron, on December 31. Aaron's basis in his stock is $15,000. Liang's AAA balance is $5,000; Liang holds a $7,500 AEP before this distribution. There is no OAA balance. Complete the following chart using spreadsheet software such as Microsoft Excel.

	Distribution from AAA	Distribution from AEP	Aaron's Stock Basis
Beginning balance	_____	_____	_____
Distribution ($13,000)	_____	_____	_____
From AAA	_____	_____	_____
From AEP	_____	_____	_____
From stock basis	_____	_____	_____
Ending balance	_____	_____	_____

50. **LO.6, 8, 9** Drop, Inc., a calendar year S corporation, distributes $16,000 cash to its only shareholder, Luetta, on December 31. Luetta's basis in her stock is $20,000. Drop's AAA balance is $9,000, and Drop holds $3,000 of AEP and $1,000

of OAA before the distribution. Complete the following chart using spreadsheet software such as Microsoft Excel.

	Distribution from Account	Effect on Stock Basis	Balance after Distribution
From AAA account	_____	_____	_____
From AEP account	_____	_____	_____
From OAA account	_____	_____	_____
From Luetta's stock basis	_____	_____	_____

See Appendix E for Comprehensive Tax Return Problem—Form 1120S

Research Problems

Note: Solutions to the Research Problems can be prepared by using the Thomson Reuters Checkpoint™ online tax research database, which accompanies this textbook. Solutions can also be prepared by using research materials found in a typical tax library.

Research Problem 1. You are advising an owner of a sports team who wants to use the 20% Qualified Business Income deduction for her flow-through entity. Explain whether the § 199A deduction is available for this sports owner.

Research Problem 2. Sean Moon is president, secretary, treasurer, sole director, and sole shareholder of Streetz, an S corporation real estate company. He manages all aspects of the company's operations, and he is the only person working at the company that holds a real estate broker's license. Sean works 12-hour days and takes few days off. Streetz's gross receipts and net income figures were reported as follows.

Year	Gross Receipts	Net Income
1	$376,453	$122,605
2	405,244	161,660
3	518,189	231,454

Sean and his wife, Kim, filed joint Federal income tax returns, but they did not report any wages or salaries on line 7 of their Forms 1040. During year 3, Sean transferred $240,000 from the S corporation to his personal account.

You are an expert witness for the IRS. Identify the items you would present to the U.S. Tax Court with respect to the amount of Sean's compensation that is subject to employment taxes and any other taxes due for year 3 (especially the Medicare net investment income tax). *Hint:* This is a reasonable compensation issue.

Use internet tax resources to address the following questions. Look for reliable websites and blogs of the IRS and other government agencies, media outlets, businesses, tax professionals, academics, think tanks, and political outlets.

Research Problem 3. Prepare a graph of the growth in the number of S elections since 1980, using increments of no more than five years. On the same graph, show the maximum Federal income tax rates for those years as they applied to individuals and to C corporations. Send your graph and other observations in an e-mail to your instructor with some explanatory comments as to what you found. You might use the IRS Data Book and other items at **irs.gov** Tax Stats.

Data Analytics

Communications

Research Problem 4. Summarize the corrective actions required for a corporation to obtain a letter ruling under the inadvertent defective election provision since 1997. There have been almost 100 such letter rulings, and they have been limited to curing the defects that existed at the time the corporation filed its original Form 2553. Send your findings as a research memo in an e-mail to your instructor.

Communications

Becker CPA Review Questions

Becker.

1. Village Corp., a calendar year corporation, began business in year 1. Village made a valid S corporation election on December 5, year 4, with the unanimous consent of its shareholders. The eligibility requirements for S status continued to be met throughout year 5. On what date did Village's S status become effective?

   a. January 1, year 4
   b. January 1, year 5
   c. December 5, year 4
   d. December 5, year 5

2. Fox Corp., an S corporation, had an ordinary loss of $36,500 for the year ended December 31, year 2. At January 1, year 2, Duffy owned 50% of Fox's stock. Duffy held the stock for 40 days in year 2 before selling the entire 50% interest to an unrelated third party. Duffy's basis for the stock was $10,000. Duffy was a full-time employee of Fox until the stock was sold. Duffy's share of Fox's loss was:

   a. $0
   b. $2,000
   c. $10,000
   d. $18,250

3. An S corporation has 30,000 shares of voting common stock and 20,000 shares of nonvoting common stock issued and outstanding. The S election can be revoked voluntarily with the consent of the shareholders holding, on the day of the revocation, the following number of outstanding shares.

	Shares of Voting Stock	Shares of Nonvoting Stock
a.	0	20,000
b.	7,500	5,000
c.	10,000	16,000
d.	20,000	0

4. The Haas Corp., a calendar year S corporation, has two equal shareholders. For the year ended December 31, year 6, Haas had net income of $60,000, which included $50,000 from operations and $10,000 from investment interest income. There were no other transactions that year. Each shareholder's basis in the stock of Haas will increase by:

   a. $50,000
   b. $30,000
   c. $25,000
   d. $0

5. Zinco Corp. was a calendar year S corporation. Zinco's S status terminated on April 1, year 6, when Case Corp. became a shareholder. During year 6 (365-day calendar year), Zinco had nonseparately computed income of $310,250. If no election was made by Zinco, what amount of the income, if any, was allocated to the S short year for year 6?

   a. $233,750
   b. $155,125
   c. $76,500
   d. $0

6. The Matthew Corporation, an S corporation, is equally owned by three shareholders—Emily, Alejandra, and Kristina. The corporation is on the calendar year basis for tax and financial purposes. On April 1 of the current year, Emily sold her one-third interest in the Matthew Corporation equally to the other two shareholders. For the current year, the corporation had nonseparately stated ordinary income of $900,000. For the current year, how much ordinary income should be allocated to Kristina on her Schedule K–1?

   a. $25,000
   b. $75,000
   c. $337,500
   d. $412,500

7. After a corporation's status as an S corporation is revoked or terminated, how many years is the corporation required to wait before making a new S election in the absence of IRS consent to an earlier election?

    a. 1

    b. 3

    c. 5

    d. 10

8. An S corporation may deduct:

    a. Charitable contributions within the percentage of income limitation applicable to corporations.

    b. Net operating loss carryovers.

    c. Foreign income taxes.

    d. Compensation of officers.

9. Melanie is the sole stockholder of Machine Inc., an S corporation. Her basis in the stock as of the end of year 4 is $43,400. During year 5, Machine reported a loss of $19,000. During year 5, Melanie received a distribution of $38,000 from Machine and loaned $11,000 directly to Machine. What is Melanie's total of stock and debt basis in Machine stock as of the end of year 5?

    a. $0

    b. $24,400

    c. $35,400

    d. $54,400

10. Melanie is the sole stockholder of Machine Inc., an S corporation. Her basis in the stock as of the end of year 4 is $43,400. During year 5, Machine reported a loss of $19,000. During year 5, Melanie received a distribution of $38,000 from Machine and loaned $11,000 directly to Machine. Assuming that this is not a passive activity, what is Melanie's deductible loss for year 5?

    a. $0

    b. $5,400

    c. $16,400

    d. $19,000

11. XYZ Inc., was a C corporation through the end of year 6. Starting at the beginning of year 7, XYZ Inc., elected S corporation status. At the end of year 6, XYZ had accumulated earnings and profits (E & P) of $53,700. At the end of year 7, XYZ had a balance of $32,000 in its accumulated adjustments account (AAA). During year 8, XYZ had ordinary income of $15,300 and made distributions of $100,000. What amount of the distribution will be a taxable dividend to the shareholders of XYZ at the end of year 8?

    a. $1,000

    b. $47,300

    c. $52,700

    d. $53,700

12. XYZ Inc., was a C corporation through the end of year 6. Starting at the beginning of year 7, XYZ elected S corporation status. At the end of year 6, XYZ had accumulated earnings and profits (E & P) of $53,700. At the end of year 7, XYZ had a balance of $32,000 in its accumulated adjustments account (AAA). During year 8, XYZ had ordinary income of $15,300 and made distributions of $100,000. What amount of the distribution will be a nontaxable distribution out of S corporation earnings to the shareholders of XYZ at the end of year 8?

    a. $1,000

    b. $47,300

    c. $52,700

    d. $53,700

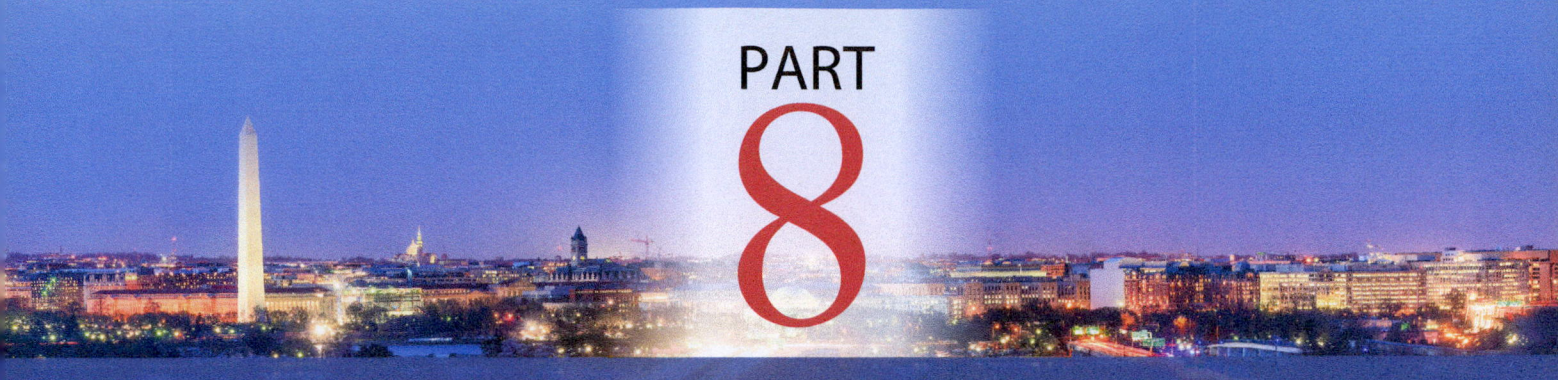

PART 8

ADVANCED TAX PRACTICE CONSIDERATIONS

CHAPTER 23
Exempt Entities

CHAPTER 24
Multistate Corporate Taxation

CHAPTER 25
Taxation of International Transactions

CHAPTER 26
Tax Practice and Ethics

In this part of the text, we discuss some of the more complex issues that regularly are addressed by the tax professional. When the taxpayer is exempt from Federal income taxation, disclosure and operating requirements often differ from those applicable to corporations. Many businesses operate in more than one U.S. state and must account for the taxable activities in each. This Part also discusses additional rules that apply when a U.S. taxpayer does business outside the United States. Finally, the conduct of a tax professional's practice is bound by ethical and operational constraints, exposing both the taxpayer and the tax professional to penalties, interest, and other sanctions.

Exempt Entities

LEARNING OBJECTIVES: *After completing Chapter 23, you should be able to:*

LO.1 Identify the different types of exempt organizations.

LO.2 List additional requirements for exempt status.

LO.3 Apply the tax consequences of exempt status, including certain restrictions on public charities and private foundations.

LO.4 Determine which exempt organizations are classified as private foundations.

LO.5 Recognize the taxes imposed on private foundations and calculate the related initial tax and additional tax amounts.

LO.6 Determine when an exempt organization is subject to the unrelated business income tax and calculate the amount of the tax.

LO.7 List the reports that exempt organizations must file with the IRS and the related due dates.

LO.8 Identify tax planning opportunities for exempt organizations.

CHAPTER OUTLINE

23-1 Types of Exempt Organizations, 23-3

23-2 Characteristics of Exempt Entities, 23-3
23-2a Serving the Common Good, 23-3
23-2b Not-for-Profit Entity, 23-3
23-2c Net Earnings and Members of the Organization, 23-3

23-3 Taxes on Exempt Entities, 23-5
23-3a Taxable Transactions, 23-5
23-3b Feeder Organizations, 23-8

23-4 Private Foundations, 23-8
23-4a Tax Consequences of Private Foundation Status, 23-8
23-4b Taxes Imposed on Private Foundations, 23-11

23-5 Unrelated Business Income Tax, 23-12
23-5a Unrelated Trade or Business, 23-13
23-5b Unrelated Business Taxable Income, 23-16

23-6 Reporting Requirements, 23-19
23-6a Obtaining Exempt Organization Status, 23-19
23-6b Annual Filing Requirements, 23-19
23-6c Disclosure Requirements, 23-21

23-7 Tax Planning, 23-21
23-7a General Considerations, 23-21
23-7b Maintaining Exempt Status, 23-21
23-7c Private Foundation Status, 23-22
23-7d Unrelated Business Income Tax, 23-22

EFFECT OF A FOR-PROFIT BUSINESS ON A TAX-EXEMPT ENTITY

Hopeful, Inc., is a tax-exempt organization under § 501(c)(3) that provides temporary lodging and psychological services for abused women and children. Its annual operating budget is $12 million. More than two decades ago, Betty Jones was a recipient of the services provided by Hopeful. Now Hopeful's administrator has been notified by the attorney for Betty's estate that her will transfers to Hopeful her share of the outstanding stock of Taste Good Ice Cream, a chain of 40 gourmet ice cream shops located in Virginia, North Carolina, and South Carolina. The business has been in existence for eight years and has produced substantially higher profits each year.

Hopeful's board is considering the following options regarding the bequest from Betty and has hired you to provide an analysis of the tax consequences of each option.

- Sell the stock of Taste Good Ice Cream and add the net proceeds to Hopeful's endowment.
- Continue to conduct the Taste Good Ice Cream business as a *division* of Hopeful.
- Continue to conduct the business as a *wholly owned subsidiary* of Hopeful.

With the second and the third options, the existing Taste Good management team will remain in place. After-tax profits not needed to expand the ice cream shop chain will be transferred to Hopeful, to be used in carrying out its exempt mission.

Read the chapter and formulate your response.

[handwritten margin note: If organizations are helping society, then the gov. helps them in return, they don't have to pay taxes]

T he Federal income tax falls on most individuals and business entities. But structures classified as <mark>exempt organizations</mark> may escape Federal income taxation. The House Report on the Revenue Act of 1938 explains:

> The exemption from taxation of money or property devoted to charitable and other purposes is based upon the theory that the Government is compensated for the loss of revenue by its relief from the financial burden which would otherwise have to be met by appropriations from public funds, and by the benefits resulting from the promotion of the general welfare.[1]

Subchapter F (Exempt Organizations) of the Code (§§ 501–530) provides the authority under which certain organizations are exempt from Federal income tax. Exempt status does not grant an absolute immunity from Federal taxation (e.g., Federal payroll taxes may apply to the entity). Two other broad categories of taxes can fall on otherwise exempt entities. First, the Federal income tax may fall on some of its operations.[2] Second, the organization may be subject to taxes that are designed to encourage or discourage certain of its activities.[3] Nonetheless, exemption from Federal income taxation is valuable for business and investment entities.

Benefits of Exempt Status

Governments support exempt entities in ways that far exceed the mere exemption from Federal income taxation. For instance, consider the most important of Federal tax benefits that accrue to a university sports team, in addition to its basic exemption from income taxes.

- *Charitable Contributions.* Donors can claim charitable contribution deductions for gifts to support the team and (to a limited extent) for assessments associated with obtaining and keeping "good seats" at games.
- *Interest Income Exclusion.* Bondholders do not pay Federal income tax on interest earned from purchases of university- or state-level debt that is used to build stadiums, workout facilities, and other permanent sports structures.
- *Business Deductions.* Businesses can claim advertising deductions for costs incurred to promote goods and services at sports facilities and in websites and publications.
- *Payroll Tax Exemption.* College athletes are not employees of the university, so all parties are exempt from payroll taxes, unemployment insurance, workers' compensation benefits, contributions to retirement plans, and the like.

The Exempt Economy

The tax-exempt sector is an important component of the U.S. economy. At least 1.5 million entities hold Federal income tax exempt status. These entities employ almost 15 million workers, representing about 9 percent of the nongovernment U.S. workforce and wages paid. Public charities control about $3.8 trillion in assets and account for over 5 percent of annual GDP.

About 40 percent of public charities are "small" (i.e., they hold assets of less than $500,000). Only about 11 percent of public charities hold more than $10 million of assets, but they account for 93 percent of the assets held and 87 percent of the revenue reported. About 3.5 percent of tax-exempt entities hold assets exceeding $50 million. The IRS audits fewer than 1 percent of these entities every tax year.

The Federal government gives up perhaps $100 billion per year in tax revenues by granting exempt status to these entities, due to the exemption from income tax and the charitable contribution deductions of donors to the organizations. Because most state and local governments also grant exemptions to public charities from income, sales, and property taxes, those jurisdictions suffer significant revenue losses when the entity is located or operates in the jurisdiction. Some local jurisdictions attempt to recoup some of this revenue by charging fees for specific services, like police protection and garbage collection, in lieu of tax assessments.

---

[1] See 1939–1 (Part 2) C.B. 742 for a reprint of H.R. No. 1860, 75th Congress, 3rd Session.

[2] See the subsequent discussion of Unrelated Business Income Tax (text Section 23-5).

[3] See the subsequent discussions of Taxable Transactions (text Section 23-3a) and Taxes Imposed on Private Foundations (text Section 23-4b).

A typical exempt organization uses a dual budgeting and reporting system.

- An *operating fund* is used to make expenditures in support of the entity's exempt purpose (e.g., providing hospital services or offering educational programs). Revenues are raised from donors, sales of goods and services, and contracts with governmental bodies or other exempt entities.
- An *endowment* holds long-term funds contributed by donors or accumulated from operating surpluses; these amounts are used to provide support for the organization's mission. Most endowments require that the principal of the endowment be invested for the entity's security and growth, and that the operating budget can spend only the current income earned by the endowment fund.

In addition to being exempt from Federal income tax, an exempt organization may:

- Be exempt from state income tax, state franchise tax, sales tax, or property tax, and
- Receive discounts on postage rates.

23-1 TYPES OF EXEMPT ORGANIZATIONS

LO.1
Identify the different types of exempt organizations.

An organization qualifies for exempt status *only* if it fits into one of the categories provided in the Code. Examples of qualifying exempt organizations and the specific statutory authority for their exempt status are listed in Exhibit 23.1.[4]

Not all exempt organizations are "charities" (i.e., qualifying their donors for tax deductions). For instance, one can claim a charitable contribution deduction for a gift to the Dallas Museum of Art, but not for a gift to the LPGA, the Teachers' Retirement Fund, or the Tempe Chamber of Commerce.

Generally, only contributions to § 501(c)(3) organizations (see Exhibit 23.1) qualify for a charitable contribution deduction. Payments to other exempt entities may be deductible as business expenses (e.g., advertising or membership dues).

23-2 CHARACTERISTICS OF EXEMPT ENTITIES

LO.2
List additional requirements for exempt status.

Many of the organizations that qualify for exempt status also must demonstrate the following characteristics.

- The organization serves some type of *common good*.[5]
- The organization is *not a for-profit* entity.[6]
- *Net earnings* do not benefit the members of the organization.[7]
- The organization can *influence legislation* to only a limited extent.[8] *(units okay)*

23-2a Serving the Common Good

The underlying rationale for all exempt organizations is that they serve some type of *common good*. If this test is interpreted broadly, the group being served is the general public (or a large subgroup of that population). If it is interpreted narrowly, the group being served may be a specific neighborhood or interest group.

23-2b Not-for-Profit Entity

The organization may not be organized or operated for the purpose of making a profit. For some types of exempt organizations, the *for-profit prohibition* appears in the statutory language. For other types, the prohibition is implied.

23-2c Net Earnings and Members of the Organization

How can the net earnings of a tax-exempt organization be used? One might think that the earnings should be used for the organization's exempt purpose. However, if the organization exists to help a specific group of members, such an open-ended

---

[4]Section 501(a) provides for exempt status for organizations described in §§ 401 and 501. The orientation of this chapter is toward organizations that conduct business activities. Therefore, the exempt organizations described in § 401 (i.e., qualified pension, profit sharing, and stock bonus trusts) are outside the scope of the chapter and are not discussed.

[5]See, for example, §§ 501(c)(3) and (4).

[6]See, for example, §§ 501(c)(3), (4), (6), (13), and (14).

[7]See, for example, §§ 501(c)(3), (6), (7), (9), (10), (11), and (19).

[8]§ 501(h).

EXHIBIT 23.1	Types of Exempt Organizations

Statutory Authority	Brief Description	Examples or Comments
§ 501(c)(1)	Federal and related agencies.	Commodity Credit Corporation, Federal Deposit Insurance Corporation, Federal Land Bank.
§ 501(c)(2)	Corporations holding title to property for and paying income to exempt organizations.	Corporation holding title to college fraternity house.
§ 501(c)(3)	Religious, charitable, educational, scientific, literary, etc., organizations.	Boy Scouts of America, Red Cross, Salvation Army, Episcopal Church, PTA, United Fund, University of Richmond.
§ 501(c)(4)	Civic leagues and employee unions.	Garden club, tenants' association promoting tenants' legal rights in entire community, League of Women Voters.
§ 501(c)(5)	Labor, agricultural, and horticultural organizations.	Teachers' association, organization formed to promote effective agricultural pest control, organization formed to test soil and to educate community members in soil treatment, garden club.
§ 501(c)(6)	Business leagues, chambers of commerce, real estate boards, etc.	Chambers of Commerce, American Plywood Association, National Hockey League (NHL), Ladies Professional Golfers Association (LPGA) Tour, medical association peer review board, organization promoting acceptance of women in business and professions.
§ 501(c)(7)	Social clubs.	Country club, rodeo and riding club, press club, bowling club, college fraternities.
§ 501(c)(8)	Fraternal beneficiary societies.	Lodges. Must provide for the payment of life, sickness, accident, or other benefits to members or their dependents.
§ 501(c)(9)	Voluntary employees' beneficiary associations.	Provide for the payment of life, sickness, accident, or other benefits to members, their dependents, or their designated beneficiaries.
§ 501(c)(10)	Domestic fraternal societies.	Lodges. Must not provide for the payment of life, sickness, accident, or other benefits and must devote any net earnings exclusively to religious, charitable, scientific, literary, educational, and fraternal purposes.
§ 501(c)(11)	Local teachers' retirement fund associations.	Can receive income only from (1) public taxation, (2) assessments on teaching salaries of members, and (3) income from investments.
§ 501(c)(12)	Local benevolent life insurance associations, mutual or cooperative telephone companies, etc.	Local cooperative telephone company, local mutual water company, local mutual electric company.
§ 501(c)(13)	Cemetery companies.	Must be operated exclusively for the benefit of lot owners who hold the lots for burial purposes.
§ 501(c)(14)	Credit unions.	Other than credit unions exempt under § 501(c)(1).
§ 501(c)(15)	Mutual insurance companies.	Mutual fire insurance company, mutual automobile insurance company.
§ 501(c)(16)	Corporations organized by farmers' cooperatives for financing crop operations.	Related farmers' cooperative must be exempt from tax under § 521.
§ 501(c)(19)	Armed forces members' posts or organizations.	Veterans of Foreign Wars (VFW), Reserve Officers Association.
§ 501(c)(20)	Group legal service plans.	Provided by a corporation for its employees.
§ 501(d)	Religious and apostolic organizations.	Communal organization. Members must include pro rata share of the net income of the organization in their gross income as dividends.
§ 501(e)	Cooperative hospital service organizations.	Centralized purchasing organization for exempt hospitals.
§ 501(f)	Cooperative service organization of educational institutions.	Organization formed to manage universities' endowment funds.
§ 529	Qualified tuition programs.	Prepaid tuition and educational savings programs.
§ 530	Coverdell education savings accounts.	Qualified education savings accounts.

interpretation could permit net earnings to benefit specific group members. As a result, the Code specifically prohibits certain types of exempt organizations from using their earnings in this way.

> . . . no part of the net earnings . . . inures to the benefit of any private shareholder or individual.[9]

In other instances, the definition of the exempt organization in the Code effectively prevents this kind of use.

> . . . the net earnings of which are devoted exclusively to religious, charitable, scientific, literary, educational, and fraternal purposes.[10]

Concept Summary 23.1 provides an overview of the consequences of tax-exempt status.

Concept Summary 23.1

Consequences of Exempt Status

General	Exempt from Federal income tax.
	Exempt from most state and local income, franchise, sales, and property taxes.
	Qualify for reductions in postage rates.
	Gifts to the organization often can be deducted by donor.
Exceptions	May be subject to Federal income tax associated with other activities, including the following.
	• Engaging in a taxable transaction (text Section 23-3a).
	• Being a feeder organization (text Section 23-3b).
	• Being a private foundation (text Section 23-4).
	• Generating unrelated business taxable income (text Section 23-5).

23-3 TAXES ON EXEMPT ENTITIES

Some exempt organizations still can incur Federal taxes.

- An exempt organization that engages in a *prohibited transaction* or is a so-called *feeder organization* is subject to tax.

- If the organization is classified as a *private foundation*, it may be partially subject to tax.

- An exempt organization can be subject to tax on its *unrelated business taxable income*.

L.O.3

Apply the tax consequences of exempt status, including certain restrictions on public charities and private foundations.

23-3a Taxable Transactions

Effects of Lobbying

A *public charity* (religious, charitable, educational, etc., organization)[11] cannot, as a "substantial" part of its activities, attempt to influence legislation (lobbying activities).[12] Such an organization that makes lobbying expenditures is subject to a 5 percent tax on the expenditures for the taxable year, and the entity's exempt status is jeopardized. A separate 5 percent tax also may be levied on the organization's management. This tax does not apply to private foundations.[13]

Public charities can engage in lobbying activities on a limited basis by making an affirmative election, the terms of which determine whether the lobbying activity is substantial.[14] Eligible for the election are most § 501(c)(3) organizations, but not churches.

If the election is made, some of the entity's lobbying expenditures are subject to a 25 percent tax. If the lobbying expenditures are excessive (i.e., they exceed a computed ceiling amount), the organization's exempt status may be in jeopardy.

---

[9]§ 501(c)(6).

[10]§ 501(c)(10).

[11]§ 501(c)(3). Public charities are discussed further in text Section 23-4a.

[12]§ 4912(a).

[13]§§ 4912(b), (c).

[14]§ 501(h).

EXHIBIT 23.2	Calculation of Lobbying Nontaxable Amount

Exempt Purpose Expenditures	Lobbying Nontaxable Amount Is
Not over $500,000	20% of exempt purpose expenditures*
Over $500,000 but not over $1 million	$100,000 + 15% of the excess of exempt purpose expenditures over $500,000
Over $1 million but not over $1.5 million	$175,000 + 10% of the excess of exempt purpose expenditures over $1 million
Over $1.5 million	$225,000 + 5% of the excess of exempt purpose expenditures over $1.5 million

*Exempt purpose expenditures generally are the amounts paid or incurred for the taxable year for the following uses: religious, charitable, scientific, literary, educational, fostering of national or international amateur sports competition, or the prevention of cruelty to children or animals.

Computing the Ceiling Two terms are key to the calculation of the ceiling amount: lobbying expenditures and grass roots expenditures. The same entity can incur both types of expenditures in the same tax year.

Lobbying expenditures influence legislation by communicating with any legislator, government official, or staff member who may participate in developing legislation (e.g., by taking a legislator out for a meal and discussing the desired outcome of the proposed law change). *Grass roots expenditures* influence legislation by attempting to affect the opinions of the general public, or a segment of that population (e.g., by printing and distributing posters and fliers promoting a position on a proposed law change).

A ceiling is computed for both lobbying expenditures and grass roots expenditures. Those amounts are derived as follows.

- 150% × Lobbying nontaxable amount = Lobbying expenditures ceiling.
- 150% × Grass roots nontaxable amount = Grass roots expenditures ceiling.

The *lobbying nontaxable amount* is the lesser of (1) $1 million or (2) the amount determined in Exhibit 23.2.[15] The *grass roots nontaxable amount* is 25 percent of the lobbying nontaxable amount.[16]

Determining the Tax An electing public charity is assessed a 25 percent tax on its excess lobbying expenditures.[17] Excess lobbying expenditures are the *greater* of the following amounts.[18]

- The excess of the lobbying expenditures for the taxable year over the lobbying nontaxable amount, or
- The excess of the grass roots expenditures for the taxable year over the grass roots nontaxable amount.

EXAMPLE 1

Tan, Inc., a qualifying § 501(c)(3) organization, makes a § 501(h) election. Its exempt purpose expenditures for the taxable year are $5,000,000, and during the year, it incurs lobbying expenditures of $525,000 and grass roots expenditures of $0.

Applying the table in Exhibit 23.2, the lobbying nontaxable amount is $400,000 [$225,000 + 5%($5,000,000 − $1,500,000)]. The ceiling on lobbying expenditures is $600,000 (150% × $400,000).

Tan's $525,000 of lobbying expenditures are under the ceiling of $600,000. However, the election results in a tax on the excess lobbying expenditures of $125,000 ($525,000 lobbying expenditures − $400,000 lobbying nontaxable amount). The resulting tax liability is $31,250 ($125,000 × 25%).

The entity computes its tax at the 25 percent rate even if the expenditures for the year exceed the ceiling, but the entity's exempt status is at risk if the ceiling amount is exceeded repeatedly. See Exhibit 23.3.

Intermediate Sanctions on Excess Benefit Transactions

When an individual who is related to a public charity receives inappropriate benefits from the charity, the Code applies intermediate sanctions, rather than revoking the

---

[15] § 4911(c)(2).
[16] § 4911(c)(4).
[17] § 4911(a)(1).
[18] § 4911(b).

EXHIBIT 23.3	Taxes on Lobbying Expenditures by Public Charities

- **Without § 501(h) election:** A 5% tax is assessed on all lobbying expenditures; exempt status is jeopardized.
- **With § 501(h) election:** Exempt status is not jeopardized unless the lobbying or grass roots expenditures ceiling is exceeded repeatedly.

Expenditures *below* lobbying/grass roots nontaxable amount ➡ No Tax

➡ Expenditures *between* lobbying/grass roots nontaxable amount and ceiling amount ➡ 25% tax

➡ Expenditures *above* lobbying/grass roots expenditures ceiling ➡ 25% tax on such lobbying expenditures; exempt status is jeopardized

entity's exempt status.[19] The intermediate sanctions consist of excise taxes imposed on disqualified persons (individuals who can exercise substantial influence over the affairs of the organization) who engage in *excess benefit transactions*.

In this case, a disqualified person engages in a non-fair-market-value transaction with the exempt organization (e.g., the purchase of property from the exempt entity at a large discount) or receives unreasonable compensation. The tax also can be assessed on exempt organization managers who participate in such a transaction, knowing that it is improper.

The excise tax on the disqualified person is 25 percent of the excess benefit. For the exempt organization management, the excise tax is 10 percent of the excess benefit (with a maximum of $20,000 for each excess benefit transaction), unless the participation is not willful and is due to reasonable cause. These excise taxes are referred to as first-level taxes.

A second-level tax applies to the disqualified person if the excess benefit transaction is not corrected (e.g., if the excess amount is *not* paid back to the charity) before the first-level tax is due. This excise tax is 200 percent of the excess benefit.

Excess Benefit Transactions

EXAMPLE 2

The compensation committee of an exempt organization is deciding what to pay its new president. A member of the organization's board of directors is on the committee and knows that the fair market value of the president's services is no more than $150,000. However, the board member votes to approve setting the new president's compensation at $250,000.

The board member will be subject to an excise tax of $10,000 (10% × $100,000 excess benefit), since he is an organization manager. In addition, the president will be subject to an excise tax of $25,000 (25% × $100,000 excess benefit) and would be required to repay the $100,000 excess benefit, plus interest, to the organization. If the president does not repay this amount, a second-level tax of $200,000 could be applied (200% × $100,000 excess benefit).

EXAMPLE 3

An exempt organization rents office space to a member of its board of directors for $100,000 per year. It later is determined that fair rental value is $140,000 per year.

The board member is subject to a first-level tax of $10,000 (25% × $40,000 excess benefit), and she must repay the $40,000 excess benefit, plus interest, to the organization. Failure to repay may result in a second-level tax of $80,000 (200% × $40,000 excess benefit).

If the board member participated in the decision to enter into the lease, she could be liable for an additional tax of $4,000 (10% × $40,000 excess benefit) as an organization manager.

---

[19]§ 4958.

Other Taxes on Certain Exempt Entities

Certain large private colleges and universities are subject to a 1.4 percent excise tax on their net investment income for the tax year. The tax is meant to encourage these institutions to use "excessive" endowment funds to increase student financial aid and to decrease tuition levels. The tax applies if the fair market value of the school's endowment fund divided by the number of tuition-paying full-time equivalent students at the school exceeds $500,000.[20] Fewer than 100 schools appear to be liable for this tax.

In addition, a 21 percent excise tax is applied to compensation paid to or vested for certain highly paid employees of exempt organizations. In general, the tax applies to compensation in excess of $1 million for the tax year and can be assessed only on the five highest-paid employees of the organization.[21] This tax might apply to a hospital administrator, a symphony conductor, or a university president or athletic department employee (e.g., the athletic director, football coach, or basketball coach).

23-3b Feeder Organizations

A **feeder organization** carries on a trade or business for the benefit of an exempt organization and remits its profits to the exempt organization. Feeder organizations are *not* exempt from Federal income tax.[22] This treatment prevents an entity, whose primary purpose is to conduct a profitable trade or business, from escaping taxation merely because its profits are given to one or more exempt organizations.

The Big Picture

EXAMPLE
4

Return to the facts of *The Big Picture* on p. 23-1. Recall that Hopeful, Inc., an exempt organization under § 501(c)(3) that provides temporary lodging and psychological services to abused women and children, is trying to decide what it should do with Taste Good Ice Cream, a chain of gourmet ice cream shops it has received as a bequest.

Assume that Hopeful decides to operate Taste Good as a *subsidiary*, with the profits going to Hopeful to support its tax-exempt mission. The subsidiary is a feeder organization, and its profits will be subject to the Federal income tax on corporations.

23-4 PRIVATE FOUNDATIONS

LO.4

Determine which exempt organizations are classified as private foundations.

23-4a Tax Consequences of Private Foundation Status

Certain exempt organizations are classified as **private foundations**. This classification produces two negative consequences. First, the classification may have an adverse effect on the contributions it receives, because the tax consequences for donors may not be as favorable as those given to other exempt organizations.[23] Second, the private foundation may be subject to Federal taxation. The reason for this less beneficial tax treatment is that private foundations seem to define *common good* more narrowly and are not seen as being supported sufficiently by, and operated for the good of, the public.

Definition of a Private Foundation

All § 501(c)(3) organizations are private foundations by default, unless one of the statutory exceptions applies. The following entities are *not* private foundations.[24]

1. Churches; educational institutions; hospitals and medical research organizations; and governmental units (favored activities category).

---

[20]§ 4968. There must be at least 500 such students, more than half of whom are located in the United States. "Tuition" includes payments made through scholarships and financial aid. Harvard University's endowment is about $41 billion, and its 2019 endowment tax is about $37.7 million. Yale University, Princeton University, and Stanford University each have endowments of about $25 billion.

[21]§ 4960. The $1 million amount is not indeed for inflation. Once an individual is a top-five paid employee, he or she is subject to the excise tax for the duration of employment with the organization. As a result, more than five individuals may be subject to the tax in a single year; § 4960(c)(2).

[22]§ 502(a).

[23]§ 170(e)(1)(B)(ii).

[24]§ 509(a).

2. Organizations that are broadly supported by the general public, by governmental units, or by organizations described in (1) above.
3. Entities organized and operated exclusively for the benefit of organizations described in (1) or (2) above (i.e., a supporting organization).

Public Charities

A *public charity* is either an organization listed in (1) above, or one that meets the "broadly supported" requirement in (2) above. To be a public charity and avoid private foundation status, *both* an *external support test* and an *internal support test* must be satisfied.[25]

The intent of the two tests is to grant the more favorable public charity status to those organizations that are responsive to the general public, rather than to the private interests of a limited number of donors or other persons.

Under the *external support test*, more than one-third of the organization's support each taxable year *normally* must come in the following forms.

- Gifts, grants, contributions, and membership fees.
- Gross receipts from admissions, sales of merchandise, performance of services, or the furnishing of facilities in an activity that is not an unrelated trade or business for purposes of the unrelated business income tax (discussed subsequently).
  - ▸ Gross receipts of this type from any person or governmental agency in excess of the greater of $5,000 or 1 percent of the organization's support for the taxable year are not counted in the numerator of the support fraction.

Amounts received from disqualified persons are not included in the numerator of the support fraction. For this purpose, disqualified persons include, among others:

- Substantial contributors whose cumulative gifts and bequests to the exempt entity exceed both 2 percent of aggregate contributions received by the entity and $5,000.
- Significant members of the governing body of the exempt entity, including officers, directors, trustees, and their families.

The *internal support test* limits the amount of support *normally* received from the sum of the following sources to one-third of the organization's support for the taxable year.

- Gross investment income (gross income from interest, dividends, rents, and royalties).
- Unrelated business taxable income (discussed subsequently) minus the related tax.

Support does not include *unusual grants* received or gain/loss from the sale of the entity's investment assets.

EXAMPLE 5

Lion, Inc., a § 501(c)(3) organization, received the following support during the taxable year. Lion wants to be classified as a public charity, not as a private foundation.

Governmental unit A for services rendered	$ 30,000
Governmental unit B for services rendered	20,000
General public for services rendered	20,000
Gross investment income	15,000
Contributions from individual substantial contributors (disqualified persons)	15,000
Total support	$100,000

The *internal support test* is satisfied for the taxable year.

continued

---

[25]§ 509(a)(2). An alternative means by which to qualify as a public charity, designed for organizations that operate largely using donations from third parties, is found at § 509(a)(1). The external and internal support tests generally must be met in each of the four preceding tax years. When these tests are met, public charity status is granted for the current year and for the subsequent year. Reg. §§ 1.509(a)–3(c) and 1.170A–9(e)(4)(i).

Internal Support Test	
Gross investment income	$15,000
Unrelated business taxable income	–0–
Total countable support	$15,000

$$\frac{\$15,000}{\$100,000} = 15\% \quad \textbf{Passes internal support test}$$

For purposes of the *external support test*, the support from A and B is counted only to the extent of $5,000 (greater of $5,000 or 1% of $100,000 support). The $15,000 received from disqualified persons is excluded from the numerator but is included in the denominator. As a result, Lion fails the test for the taxable year.

External Support Test	
Governmental unit A for services rendered	$ 5,000
Governmental unit B for services rendered	5,000
General public for services rendered	20,000
Total countable support	$30,000

$$\frac{\$30,000}{\$100,000} = 30\% \quad \textbf{Fails external support test}$$

Because Lion did not satisfy both tests, it does *not* qualify as an organization that is broadly supported. As a result, it is a private foundation.

Concept Summary 23.2 shows the classifications of exempt organizations and indicates the potential negative consequences of classification as a private foundation.

Concept Summary 23.2

Exempt Organizations: Classification

23-4b Taxes Imposed on Private Foundations

LO.5

Recognize the taxes imposed on private foundations and calculate the related initial tax and additional tax amounts.

There are about 100,000 private foundations that file annually with the IRS. These entities largely hold investment assets and make annual grants to third parties. Private foundations control about $750 billion in assets, but most of them are family-controlled organizations that hold no more than $10 million of investable assets.

Distributions of almost $90 million are made each tax year by private foundations of all sizes. Most of these distributions are made to other charitable entities. Foundation operating expenses generally amount to 10 percent of total grants made.

In general, a private foundation is exempt from Federal income tax. However, it may be subject to several Federal excise taxes.[26] Exhibit 23.4 includes additional information about these taxes.

These taxes restrict the permitted activities of private foundations. Two levels of tax may be imposed on the private foundation and the foundation manager: an initial tax and an additional tax. The initial taxes (first-level), with the exception of the tax based on investment income, are imposed because the private foundation engages in an undesirable activity (called a *prohibited transaction*). The additional taxes (second-level) are imposed only if these activities are not corrected within a statutory time period.[27]

Annually, about 1,700 private foundations incur an excise tax of this type. About $13 million in taxes are collected under these provisions; the largest amount of tax is collected for failing to distribute adequate amounts of the private foundation's income.

The tax on undistributed income will be used to illustrate how expensive these taxes can be (and why they should be avoided). Both an initial (first-level) tax and an additional (second-level) tax may be assessed. The initial (first-level) tax is 30 percent on the undistributed income for the taxable year that is not distributed by the end of the following taxable year. The tax applies on this undistributed income for each year until the tax is assessed by the IRS.

The additional (second-level) tax is 100 percent on the amount of the inadequate distribution. The additional tax is waived if the undistributed income is distributed within 90 days after the IRS mails a deficiency notice for the additional tax.

EXHIBIT 23.4	Taxes Imposed on Private Foundations					
			Private Foundation		**Foundation Manager**	
Type of Tax	**Code Section**	**Purpose**	**Initial Tax**	**Additional Tax**	**Initial Tax**	**Additional Tax**
On investment income	§ 4940	Audit fee to defray IRS expenses.	1.39%*			
On self-dealing	§ 4941	Engaging in transactions with disqualified persons.	10%**	200%**	5%†	50%†
On undistributed income	§ 4942	Failing to distribute adequate amount of income for exempt purposes, usually 5% of asset value.	30%	100%		
On excess business holdings	§ 4943	Investments that enable the private foundation to control unrelated businesses (usually by owning >20% of outstanding shares).	10%	200%		
On jeopardizing investments	§ 4944	Speculative investments that put the private foundation's assets at risk.	10%	25%	10%‡	5%†

*An exempt operating foundation [see §§ 4940(d)(2) and 4942(j)(3)] is not subject to the tax.
**Imposed on the disqualified person rather than the foundation.
†Subject to a statutory ceiling of $20,000.
‡Subject to a statutory ceiling of $10,000.

---

[26]§§ 4940–4945.   [27]§ 4961.

Undistributed income is the excess of the amount that should have been distributed over qualifying distributions made by the entity. The tax applies if the entity did not distribute its minimum investment return (i.e., typically 5 percent of the fair market value of the foundation's assets, net of any outstanding debt).[28] The undistributed amount is reduced by related salaries and administrative expenses, so the actual required distribution usually is less than 5 percent of asset value. The 5 percent rule was designed to provide a minimum amount that private foundations would distribute every year, but it acts more as a ceiling amount; most private foundations make distributions of 6 percent of their assets or less per year.

EXAMPLE 6

Gold, Inc., a private foundation, records undistributed income of $80,000 for the 2018 taxable year. It distributes $15,000 of this amount during 2019 and an additional $45,000 during 2020. An IRS deficiency notice is mailed to Gold on August 5, 2021. The initial tax is $25,500 [($65,000* × 30%) + ($20,000** × 30%)].

As of the date of the deficiency notice, Gold has made no additional distributions from the 2018 undistributed income. Therefore, because the remaining undistributed income of $20,000 has not been distributed by August 5, 2021, an additional tax of $20,000 ($20,000 × 100%) is imposed.

If Gold distributes the $20,000 of 2018 undistributed income within 90 days of the deficiency notice, the additional tax is waived. Without this distribution, however, the foundation will owe $45,500 in taxes ($25,500 + $20,000).

*$80,000 − $15,000.
**$80,000 − $15,000 − $45,000.

23-5 UNRELATED BUSINESS INCOME TAX

LO.6

Determine when an exempt organization is subject to the unrelated business income tax and calculate the amount of the tax.

Some entities that hold a Federal income tax exemption still are subject to a Federal income tax. We discussed the excise taxes that apply to private foundations in the previous section. In addition, an income tax on the business operations of an exempt organization may be incurred. About 210,000 exempt entities file a tax return with the IRS every year, and more than 10 percent of those report a tax liability on business income. Tax collections in a typical year equal about $600 million.

The **unrelated business income tax (UBIT)** is designed to treat charitable entities as if they were subject to the corporate income tax, chiefly because they compete with taxable enterprises. The corporate income tax rate is used for this purpose.[29]

In general, **unrelated business income (UBI)** is derived from activities not related to the exempt purpose of the exempt organization. The tax applies because the organization is engaging in substantial commercial activities.[30] Without this tax, taxable business entities would be at a competitive disadvantage. Thus, the UBIT is intended to neutralize the exempt entity's tax advantage.[31]

It is the source of the business profits that triggers the UBIT, not their use. UBI that is employed for the entity's exempt purpose still is subject to the tax.

The Big Picture

EXAMPLE 7

Return to the facts of *The Big Picture* on p. 23-1. Recall that Hopeful, Inc., an exempt organization under § 501(c)(3), has received Taste Good Ice Cream, a chain of gourmet ice cream shops, as a bequest.

Assume that Hopeful has decided to operate Taste Good as a *division*. Although the income from Taste Good's shops will be used to support Hopeful's exempt purpose, the net revenue constitutes unrelated business income; therefore, it is subject to the UBIT.

---

[28]§ 4942(e)(1).
[29]§ 511(a)(1).

[30]§ 512(a)(1).
[31]Reg. § 1.513–1(b).

The UBIT applies to all organizations that are exempt from Federal income tax under § 501(c), except Federal agencies. In addition, the tax applies to state colleges and universities.[32]

A materiality exception generally exempts an entity from being subject to the UBIT if such income is insignificant. This $1,000 "standard deduction" generally available to all exempt organizations is discussed later.

23-5a Unrelated Trade or Business

An exempt organization will be subject to the UBIT when all of the following conditions are met.[33]

- The organization conducts a trade or business.
- The trade or business is *not* substantially related to the exempt purpose of the organization.
- The trade or business is regularly carried on by the organization.

However, the Code specifically excludes the following activities from classification as an unrelated trade or business.

- A trade or business where the individuals performing substantially all of its work do so without compensation (e.g., an orphanage operates a retail store for sales to the general public, and all of the work is done by volunteers).
- The trade or business consists of selling merchandise, and substantially all of the merchandise has been received as contributions (e.g., thrift shops).
- For § 501(c)(3) organizations and for state colleges or universities, the trade or business is conducted primarily for the convenience of the organization's members, students, patients, officers, or employees (e.g., a college bookstore and a laundry operated by the college for laundering dormitory linens and students' clothing).
- For most employee unions, the trade or business consists of selling to members, at their usual place of employment, work-related clothing and equipment and items normally sold through vending machines, snack bars, or food-dispensing facilities.

Conducting a Trade or Business

Trade or business, for this purpose, is broadly defined. It includes any activity conducted for the production of income through the sale of merchandise or the performance of services. An activity need not generate a profit to be treated as a trade or business.[34]

EXAMPLE 8

Health, Inc., is an exempt hospital that operates a pharmacy. The pharmacy provides medicines and supplies to the patients in the hospital (i.e., it contributes to the conduct of the hospital's exempt purpose). In addition, the pharmacy sells medicines and supplies to the general public.
The activity of selling to the general public constitutes a trade or business for purposes of the UBIT.

An organization that has more than one unrelated trade or business must compute unrelated business taxable income separately for each of the activities. Losses from one unrelated trade or business cannot be used to offset income derived from a different activity.[35]

Not Substantially Related to the Exempt Purpose

Exempt organizations frequently conduct unrelated trades or businesses to provide income to help defray their costs. If the activity is related to its exempt purpose, it will escape the UBIT. To be related to the accomplishment of the exempt purpose, the business activities must contribute importantly to the exempt purpose.[36]

---

[32]§ 511(a)(2) and Reg. § 1.511–2(a)(2).

[33]§ 513(a) and Reg. § 1.513–2(a).

[34]Reg. § 1.513–1(b).

[35]§ 512(a)(6). The first unrelated trade or business is reported on the Form 990–T, and each additional business is reported on its own Schedule M (Form 990–T).

[36]Reg. § 1.513–1(d).

Is It an Unrelated Trade or Business?

Art, Inc., an exempt organization, operates a school for training children in the performing arts. As an essential part of that training, the children perform for the general public once a month. The children are paid for their performances, and Art receives income by charging admission to the performances.

The income from admissions is *not* income from an unrelated trade or business. The performances by the children contribute importantly to the accomplishment of the exempt purpose of providing training in the performing arts.

Assume the same facts as in Example 9, except that four performances are conducted each weekend of the year; each child must appear in three of the performances every week. Further, assume that this number of performances far exceeds that required for training the children.

Here, the income derived from admissions for any *excess* performances is income from an unrelated trade or business.

The trade or business may sell merchandise that has been produced as part of the accomplishment of the exempt purpose.[37] Income derived by the organization from use of its property for a nonexempt purpose is UBI.[38]

Unrelated Business Income

EXAMPLE 11

Help-Self, Inc., an exempt organization, conducts programs for the rehabilitation of the handicapped. One of the programs includes training in radio and television repair. Help-Self derives gross income by selling the repaired items.

The income is substantially related to the accomplishment of the exempt purpose (and, therefore, is not UBI).

EXAMPLE 12

Civil, Inc., an exempt organization, operates a museum. As part of the exempt purpose of the museum, educational lectures are given in the museum's theater during the operating hours of the museum. In the evening, when the museum is closed, the theater is leased to an individual who sells tickets and shows current movies to the general public. The lease income is UBI.

Corporate Sponsorship Payments The term *unrelated trade or business* does not include the soliciting and receiving of qualified sponsorship payments.[39] A qualified sponsorship payment must meet all of the following requirements.

- The trade or business making the payment expects no substantial benefit other than the use or acknowledgment of its name, logo, or product lines in connection with the activities of the exempt organization.

- The exempt organization does not advertise or endorse the payor's products or services.

- The payment does not include any amount that is contingent on the degree of public exposure that results (e.g., the level of attendance at one or more events, the number of website hits, or broadcast ratings).

---

[37]Reg. § 1.513–1(d)(4)(ii). If the merchandise is not sold in substantially the same state it was in at the completion of the exempt purpose (e.g., it has been converted into another product), the gross income subsequently derived from the sale of the merchandise *is* unrelated business income (UBI).

[38]Reg. § 1.513–1(d)(4)(iii) addresses the allocation of expenses to exempt and nonexempt activities.

[39]§ 513(i).

Sponsorship Payments

Pets, Inc., a manufacturer of cat food, contributes $25,000 to Feline Care, Inc., an exempt organization that cares for abandoned cats. In return for the contribution, Feline agrees to put Pets' corporate logo in its monthly newsletter to donors. The $25,000 payment is a qualified sponsorship payment and is not subject to the UBIT.

EXAMPLE 13

Assume the same facts as in Example 13, except that Feline agrees to endorse Pets' cat food in its monthly newsletter by stating that it feeds only Pets' cat food to its cats. The $25,000 payment is not a qualified sponsorship payment and is subject to the UBIT.

EXAMPLE 14

Bingo Games A *qualified bingo game* is not an unrelated trade or business if both of the following requirements are met.[40]

- The bingo game is legal under both state and local law.
- Commercial bingo games (conducted for a profit motive) ordinarily are not allowed in the pertinent jurisdiction.

Play, Inc., an exempt organization, conducts weekly bingo games. The state and municipality in which Play conducts the games allow exempt organizations to conduct bingo games, but they do not permit profit-oriented entities to do so.

Because both of the requirements for bingo games are satisfied, the bingo games conducted by Play are not an unrelated trade or business.

EXAMPLE 15

Distribution of Low-Cost Articles When a donor receives a product, like a briefcase, in exchange for a gift to a charity, it appears that a sale has occurred, and the entity has generated UBI. But where an exempt organization distributes low-cost items as an incidental part of its solicitation for charitable contributions, the activity is not considered an unrelated trade or business.

A low-cost article is an item that costs $11.20 or less in 2020 (indexed annually). Examples of such items are pens, stamps, stickers, stationery, and address labels. If more than one item is distributed to a person during the calendar year, the costs of the items are combined.[41]

Rental or Exchange of Membership Lists If an exempt organization sells or rents its donor or membership list (i.e., its mailing list) to other exempt organizations, the activity is *not* an unrelated trade or business.[42]

Regularly Carried on by the Organization

Requiring the activity to be one that is regularly carried on by the exempt organization ensures that only activities that are actually competing with taxable organizations are subject to the UBIT. The factors considered in applying the *regularly carried on* test include the frequency of the activity, the continuity of the activity, and the manner in which the activity is pursued.[43]

---

[40]§ 513(f).
[41]§ 513(h)(1)(A).

[42]§ 513(h)(1)(B).
[43]§ 512(a)(1) and Reg. § 1.513–1(c).

Activity Regularly Carried On

Silver, Inc., an exempt organization, owns land that is located next to the state fairgrounds. During the 10 days of the state fair, Silver uses the land as a parking lot and charges individuals attending the state fair for parking there. The activity is not regularly carried on.

Black, Inc., an exempt organization, has its offices in the downtown area. It owns a parking lot adjacent to its offices on which its employees park during the week. On Saturdays, it rents the spaces in the parking lot to individuals shopping or working in the downtown area. Black is conducting a business activity on a year-round basis, even though it is only for one day per week. Thus, an activity is regularly being carried on.

23-5b Unrelated Business Taxable Income

General Tax Model

A template for computing unrelated business taxable income (UBTI) appears in Exhibit 23.5. In computing UBTI, several adjustments are made to the entity's net UBI for the year, including the following.[44]

Positive adjustments—Add to UBI

1. A deduction is allowed for gifts to another charity, but it is limited to 10 percent of UBTI (without regard to the charitable contribution deduction). Amounts in excess of this limit are added back to UBI as a positive adjustment.

Brown, Inc., an exempt organization, records UBTI of $100,000 (before considering any charitable contributions). Total charitable contributions equal $13,000.

If $13,000 is deducted in calculating net unrelated business income, then $3,000 [$13,000 − 10%($100,000)] is a positive adjustment (i.e., an "add back" to reduce the deduction) in calculating UBTI.

2. Unrelated debt-financed income net of the unrelated debt-financed deductions (see subsequent discussion).

Negative adjustments—Subtract from UBI

1. Income from dividends, interest, and annuities, net of all directly related deductions.
2. Royalty income, regardless of whether it is measured by production, gross income, or taxable income from the property, net of all directly related deductions.

EXHIBIT 23.5	Tax Formula for Unrelated Business Taxable Income

Gross unrelated business income

− Deductions related to the business income

= Net unrelated business income (Net UBI)

± Adjustments (positive and negative)

− $1,000 "standard deduction"

= Unrelated business taxable income (UBTI)

---

[44]§ 512(b) and Reg. § 1.512(b)–1.

3. Rent income from real property and from certain personal property net of all directly related deductions.

- Personal property rents are included in the negative adjustment only if the personal property is leased with the real property. In addition, the personal property rent income must not exceed 10 percent of the gross rent income under the lease.

- None of rents are a negative adjustment if more than 50 percent of the rent income under the lease is derived from personal property.

Rentals as UBI

Beaver, Inc., an exempt organization, leases land and a building (realty) and computers (personalty) housed in the building. Under the lease, $46,000 of the rent is for the land and building and $4,000 is for the computers. Expenses incurred for the land and building are $10,000.

Here, the personal property rent ($4,000) does not exceed 10 percent of the gross rental income ($5,000; $50,000 × 10%). As a result, the net rent income from both the land and building of $36,000 ($46,000 − $10,000) and the income from the computers of $4,000 are negative adjustments in computing UBTI.

EXAMPLE 19

Assume the same facts as in Example 19, except that the rent income is $35,000 from the land and building and $15,000 from the computers.

Because the rent income from the computers exceeds $5,000 (10% × $50,000) and is not incidental, it is *not* a negative adjustment; it is a business activity and is included in UBTI. The $35,000 rent income from the real property remains a negative adjustment.

EXAMPLE 20

Assume the same facts as in Example 19, except that the rent income is $20,000 from the land and building and $30,000 from the computers.

Because more than 50% of the rent income under the lease is from the computers, neither the rent income from the land and building nor that from the computers is a negative adjustment.

EXAMPLE 21

4. Gains and losses from the sale, exchange, or other disposition of property *except for* inventory.

Beaver, the owner of the land, building, and computers in Example 19, sells these assets for $450,000. Their adjusted basis is $300,000.

Beaver's recognized gain of $150,000 is a negative adjustment.

EXAMPLE 22

In determining UBTI, a "standard deduction" of $1,000 is allowed.[45]

Petit Care, Inc., an exempt organization, reports net unrelated business income of $800. Because Petit claims a $1,000 "standard deduction," its UBTI is $0. Therefore, its income tax liability is $0.

EXAMPLE 23

After UBTI is determined, that amount is subject to tax using the Federal corporate income tax rate.[46]

Patient, Inc., an exempt organization, has UBTI of $500,000. Patient's income tax liability is $105,000 ($500,000 UBTI × 21% corporate tax rate).

EXAMPLE 24

Concept Summary 23.3 provides a summary of the UBIT rules.

---

[45]§ 512(b)(12).

[46]If the charity is organized as a trust, the rates under Subchapter J are used. See Exhibit 28.3 in Chapter 28.

Concept Summary 23.3

Unrelated Business Income Tax

Purpose	To tax the entity on unrelated business income as if it were subject to the corporate income tax.
Applicable tax rates	Corporate or trust tax rate.
Exempt organizations to which applicable	All organizations exempt under § 501(c), except Federal agencies.
Entities subject to the tax	The organization conducts a trade or business, the trade or business is not substantially related to the exempt purpose of the organization, and the trade or business is regularly carried on by the organization.
Exceptions to the tax	• Substantially all of the work is performed by volunteers.
	• Substantially all of the merchandise being sold has been received by gift.
	• For § 501(c)(3) organizations, the business is conducted primarily for the benefit of the organization's members, students, patients, officers, or employees.
	• For most employee unions, the trade or business consists of selling to members work-related clothing and equipment and items normally sold through vending machines, snack bars, or food-dispensing facilities.
	• Other items relating to bingo games, corporate sponsorships, list rentals, and the like.
$1,000 "standard deduction"	If gross income from an unrelated trade or business is less than $1,000, no tax results, and it is not necessary to file a return associated with the unrelated business income tax.

Unrelated Debt-Financed Income

In calculating UBTI (see Exhibit 23.5), unrelated debt-financed income is one of the positive adjustments. Examples of income from debt-financed property include rent income from real estate or tangible personal property (e.g., a church that owns and leases space in a leveraged office building), and gains from the disposition of debt-financed property.

Without this provision, a tax-exempt organization could use borrowed funds to acquire unrelated business or investment property and use the exempt earnings from the acquisition to pay for the property.

Definition of Debt-Financed Income   Debt-financed income is the gross income generated from debt-financed property. *Debt-financed property* is all property of the exempt organization that is held to produce income and on which there is acquisition indebtedness, *except* for the following.[47]

• Property where substantially all (at least 85 percent) of the use is devoted to the organization's exempt purpose.[48]

• Property whose gross income otherwise is treated as unrelated business income.

• Property whose gross income is from the following sources and otherwise is not treated as unrelated business income.

    ➤ Income from research performed for the United States or a Federal governmental agency, or a state or a political subdivision thereof.

    ➤ Income from research activities performed by a college, university, or hospital.

If the 85 percent test is not satisfied, only the portion of the property that is *not* used for the exempt purpose is debt-financed property.

EXAMPLE 25

Deer, Inc., an exempt organization, owns a five-story office building on which there is acquisition indebtedness. Three of the floors are used for Deer's exempt purpose. The two other floors are leased to Purple Corporation. In this case, the *substantially all* test is not satisfied. Therefore, 40% of the office building is debt-financed property, and 60% is not.

continued

---

[47]§ 514(b).

[48]Reg. § 1.514(b)–1(b)(1)(ii).

What if Deer used all but one-half of one floor for its exempt purpose (with Purple leasing the half floor)? Now the "substantially all" test is met, and the rent income is not a positive adjustment.

Certain land that is acquired by an exempt organization for later exempt use is excluded from debt-financed property if the following requirements are satisfied.[49]

- The principal purpose of acquiring the land is for use (substantially all) in achieving the organization's exempt purpose.

- This use will begin within 10 years of the acquisition date.

- At the date when the land is acquired, it is located in the *neighborhood* of other property of the organization for which substantially all of the use is for achieving the organization's exempt purpose.

If the exempt organization is a church, the 10-year period becomes a 15-year period, and the neighborhood requirement is waived.

Definition of Acquisition Indebtedness Acquisition indebtedness consists of amounts used to acquire or improve the debt-financed property.[50]

Red, Inc., an exempt organization, acquires land for $100,000. To finance the acquisition, Red mortgages the land and receives loan proceeds of $80,000. Red leases the land to Duck Corporation. The mortgage is acquisition indebtedness. Net profits from the leasing activities constitute UBTI for Red.

EXAMPLE

26

23-6 REPORTING REQUIREMENTS

LO.7

List the reports that exempt organizations must file with the IRS and the related due dates.

23-6a Obtaining Exempt Organization Status

Not all exempt organizations are required to obtain IRS approval to ensure their exempt status. Churches, and entities with typical annual gross receipts of up to $5,000, need not apply for exempt status.[51] The IRS approves about 80,000 applications for exempt status every year.

Even when not required to obtain IRS approval, most exempt organizations do apply for exempt status. Typically, an organization does not want to assume that it qualifies for exempt status and describe itself in that way to the public, only to have the IRS rule later that it does not qualify.

Organizations exempt under § 501(c)(3) use Form 1023 [Application for Recognition of Exemption under Section 501(c)(3)]; small organizations file Form 1023-EZ, which requires a smaller application fee.[52] Form 1024 [Application for Recognition of Exemption under Section 501(a)] is used by most other types of exempt organizations.

23-6b Annual Filing Requirements

Most exempt organizations are required to file an annual information return. The return is filed on Form 990 (Return of Organization Exempt from Income Tax). Religious groups and Federal agencies are exempt from filing a Form 990.[53]

---

[49]§ 514(b)(3).

[50]§ 514(c)(1). Educational organizations can exclude certain debt incurred for real property acquisitions from acquisition indebtedness.

[51]§ 508(c)(1).

[52]A small organization is defined as one that holds assets not in excess of $250,000, and its annual gross receipts for the last 3 years have not exceeded $50,000. More than one-half of all new applications for exempt status are received on Form 1023-EZ.

[53]§§ 6033(a)(1) and (3). For public charities, the form includes the names and addresses of significant donors. Other exempt entities can omit this information from the form, but they must keep the names and addresses in their private records. This data can facilitate a later IRS audit. See Rev. Proc. 2018–38, 2018–31 I.R.B. 280.

Small exempt organizations, whose annual gross receipts normally are $50,000 or less, must file a Form 990–N, known as the e-Postcard.[54] The e-Postcard is designed to be a simpler version of the full Form 990. Supporting organizations and private foundations cannot use the Form 990–N.

The Form 990–EZ, another abbreviated version of the Form 990, can be used by exempt organizations with gross receipts of less than $200,000 and total assets of less than $500,000.

Private foundations must file Form 990–PF (Return of Private Foundation). Form 990–PF requires more information than does Form 990. Form 4720 (Return of Certain Excise Taxes on Charities and Other Persons) is used to compute any excise tax liabilities of the private foundation. The return is filed with the private foundation's Form 990–PF.

The due date for Form 990 or Form 990–PF is the fifteenth day of the fifth month after the end of the taxable year. An automatic six-month extension of the filing deadline is available. A $20-per-day penalty is assessed when the entity fails to file a required return, subject to a $10,500 maximum amount; larger amounts apply to large charities.[55]

EXAMPLE 27

Green, Inc., a § 501(c)(3) organization, has a fiscal year that ends June 30, 2020. The due date for the annual return is November 15, 2020.

If Green were a calendar year entity, the due date for its 2020 return would be May 15, 2021, with an extension available to November 15, 2021.

Exempt organizations generating UBI file Form 990–T (Exempt Organization Business Income Tax Return). The return must be filed if the organization records gross income of at least $1,000 from an unrelated trade or business.

EXAMPLE 28

Here are some illustrations of the annual filing requirements faced by exempt organizations.

- During the year, the First Church of Kentwood receives parishioner contributions of $450,000. Of this amount, $125,000 is designated for the church building fund. None of its receipts constitute unrelated business income. First Church is not required to file an annual return (Form 990) because churches are exempt from doing so. In addition, it is not required to file Form 990–T.

- Colonial, Inc., is a private foundation. Gross receipts for the year total $800,000, of which 40% is from admission fees paid by members of the general public who visit Colonial's museum of eighteenth-century life. The balance is endowment income and contributions from the founding donor. Because Colonial is a private foundation, it files Form 990–PF.

- Orange, Inc., is an exempt organization and is not a private foundation. Gross receipts for the year are $20,000. None of this amount is unrelated business income. Orange is not required to file Form 990 because its annual gross receipts do not exceed $50,000. However, it must file an e-Postcard (Form 990–N).

- Restoration, Inc., is an exempt organization. Gross receipts for the year are $100,000. None of this amount is unrelated business income. Restoration files Form 990–EZ because of its level of gross receipts.

- During the year, the Second Church of Port Allen receives parishioner contributions of $300,000. In addition, the church has unrelated business income of $5,000. Second Church is not required to file Form 990 because churches are exempt from doing so. Form 990–T must be filed, however, because churches are not exempt from the UBIT, and Second Church's earnings exceed the $1,000 "standard deduction."

Form 990 is filed electronically. The entity's tax exemption is lost if the pertinent forms are not filed for three consecutive years. The IRS notifies the entity after the second consecutive year of non-filing.[56]

---

[54]Rev.Proc. 2011–15, 2011–3 I.R.B. 322.
[55]§ 6652(c).
[56]§ 6033(j).

23-6c Disclosure Requirements

Exempt entities must make copies of the following forms available to the general public.[57]

- Form 990.
- Form 1023 (or Form 1024).

Copies of the three most recent Forms 990 must be made available. Private foundations must make Form 990–PF available for public inspection.

If an individual requests the entity's tax form in person, the exempt entity must provide a copy immediately. If the request is received in writing or by e-mail, the copy must be provided within 30 days. The copy must be provided without charge, except for a reasonable fee for reproduction and mailing costs.

If the exempt entity has made the forms widely available to the general public, it is not required to fill individual requests.[58] Putting the forms on the organization's website meets this requirement. Individual requests can be disregarded if the exempt entity can show that the request is part of a harassment campaign.[59]

23-7 TAX PLANNING

LO.8

Identify tax planning opportunities for exempt organizations.

23-7a General Considerations

An organization is exempt from taxation only if it fits into one of the categories enumerated in the Code. Thus, particular attention must be given to the entity's qualification requirements. These requirements must continue to be satisfied to avoid termination of exempt status (in effect, they become maintenance requirements).

Organizations that want to engage in political activities beyond the elective lobbying limits cannot use the § 501(c)(3) classification. A § 501(c)(4) social welfare organization might be used instead. Such an entity can engage in partisan political work and promote specific candidates, as long as these activities do not reach 50 percent of its annual expenditures. Payments to a § 501(c)(4) entity are not deductible; the entity does not disclose the names of its donors.

23-7b Maintaining Exempt Status

To maintain exempt status, most organizations must satisfy both an organizational test and an operational test. The organizational test requires that the entity satisfy the statutory requirements for exempt status based on its legal structure. The operational test ensures that the entity satisfies the statutory requirements for exempt status through its mission and operations.

King Shipping Consum., Inc. (Zion Coptic Church, Inc.) illustrates that it is usually much easier to satisfy the organizational test than the operational test.[60] Zion's stated purpose was to engage in activities usually and normally associated with churches. Based on this, the IRS approved Zion's exempt status as a § 501(c)(3) organization.

Zion's real intent, however, was to smuggle illegal drugs into the country and to distribute them for profit. The church's justification for the drugs was that it used marijuana in its sacraments. During a four-month period, however, the police confiscated 33 tons of marijuana from church members. The IRS calculated that even assuming the maximum alleged church membership of several thousand, each member would have had to consume over 33 pounds of marijuana during the four-month period.

The court concluded that Zion's real purpose was to hide a large commercial drug smuggling operation. Because this activity was inconsistent with the religious purpose

---

[57]§ 6104(d), Reg. § 301.6104(d)–1, and T.D. 8818 (April 1999). One valuable source of Forms 990 and 990–PF and other relevant materials concerning exempt entities is **guidestar.org**.

[58]Reg. § 301.6104(d)-2.
[59]§ 6104(d)(4).
[60]58 TCM 574, T.C.Memo. 1989–593.

for exempt status, the court upheld the IRS's revocation of Zion's exempt status and the related tax assessment of approximately $1.6 million.

23-7c Private Foundation Status

Exempt organizations that can qualify as public charities receive more beneficial tax treatment than do those that qualify as private foundations. If possible, the organization should be structured to qualify as a public charity.

David has undeveloped land ($25,000 adjusted basis, $100,000 fair market value) that he is going to contribute to one of the following exempt organizations: Blue, Inc., a public charity, or Teal, Inc., a private foundation. David has owned the land for five years.

David asks the manager of each organization to describe the tax benefits of contributing the land to that organization. He tells them that he is in the 35% marginal income tax bracket.

Based on the data provided by the managers, David decides to contribute the land to Blue, Inc. He calculates the amount of the charitable contribution under each option as follows.[61]

Donee	David's Contribution Deduction	David's Tax Rate	Contribution Borne by U.S. Government
Blue	$100,000	35%	$35,000
Teal	25,000	35%	8,750

If the organization is a private foundation, care must be exercised to avoid the assessment of a tax liability on one of the prohibited transactions. This objective can best be achieved by establishing board-level and administrative controls that prevent the private foundation from engaging in transactions that trigger the imposition of the taxes. If an initial tax is assessed, corrective actions should be implemented to avoid the assessment of an additional tax.

23-7d Unrelated Business Income Tax

If the exempt organization conducts an unrelated trade or business, it may be subject to Federal income tax on the unrelated business income. Further, the unrelated trade or business could result in the loss of exempt status if the IRS determines that the activity is the primary purpose of the organization. In addition, land and buildings used to produce unrelated business income may be subject to state and local property taxes.

One approach that can be used to avoid the UBIT is for the organization to establish a taxable subsidiary to conduct the unrelated trade or business. With a subsidiary, the revenues and expenses of the exempt organization can be separated from those of the unrelated business. When the subsidiary remits its after-tax profits to the exempt organization in the form of dividends, the dividends will not be taxable to the exempt organization; dividends are eliminated from UBTI by a negative adjustment.

Another approach to avoiding the UBIT is to fail the definition of an unrelated trade or business. This is accomplished if:

- The activities do *not* constitute a trade or business.
- The activities are substantially related to the exempt purpose of the organization.
- The trade or business is *not* regularly carried on by the organization.

---

[61]Charitable contribution deductions for gifts of capital gain property made to private nonoperating foundations are limited to asset basis; § 170(e)(1)(B)(ii).

REFOCUS ON THE BIG PICTURE

EFFECT OF A FOR-PROFIT BUSINESS ON A TAX-EXEMPT ENTITY

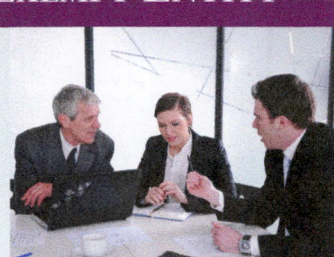

A § 501(c)(3) entity is exempt from Federal income tax only on the conduct of its charitable activities. However, if an exempt entity generates income from the conduct of a trade or business that is not related to the organization's exempt purpose, this income generally is subject to Federal income tax. These principles can be used in analyzing Hopeful's options for the ice cream business it inherited.

- *Sell the stock of Taste Good Ice Cream.* A sale of the Taste Good Ice Cream stock is unlikely to result in much realized gain because the fair market value probably has not changed very much in the limited time between the date of Betty's death and the present. In any case, this amount is not relevant because any realized gain on the sale of the stock is tax-exempt under § 501(c)(3).

- *Conduct the ice cream business as a division of Hopeful.* Under this option, the taxable income of the ice cream chain is classified as unrelated business income. Because the ice cream division is competing with for-profit entities, it is subject to the Federal income tax that applies to corporate entities. In essence, the tax is levied because the exempt organization is engaging in substantial commercial activities.

- *Conduct the ice cream business as a wholly owned subsidiary of Hopeful.* Under this option, the ice cream chain subsidiary is classified as a feeder organization (i.e., carries on a trade or business for the benefit of an exempt organization and remits its profits to that entity). As a result, the subsidiary pays Federal income tax on its profits.

What If?

Hopeful's board of directors must be careful that an acceptance of the Taste Good stock does not change the exempt status of the entity. If Hopeful owns "too much" of the Taste Good shares, Hopeful could lose its status as a § 501(c)(3) entity and be reclassified as a private foundation. Then an excise tax could apply if Hopeful is found to have "excess business holdings" in the form of the stock.

Key Terms

Debt-financed income, 23-18

Excess lobbying expenditures, 23-6

Exempt organizations, 23-2

Feeder organization, 23-8

Grass roots expenditures, 23-6

Intermediate sanctions, 23-6

Lobbying expenditures, 23-6

Private foundations, 23-8

Unrelated business income (UBI), 23-12

Unrelated business income tax (UBIT), 23-12

Discussion Questions

1. **LO.3** An exempt organization appropriately makes the § 501(h) election to lobby on a limited basis. The amount of its lobbying expenditures is less than its lobbying expenditures ceiling, yet it is subject to a tax at a 25% rate. Explain.

2. **LO.5** Although private foundations generally are exempt from Federal income tax, they may be subject to certain excise taxes. Identify these taxes, and discuss why they are imposed on private foundations.

3. **LO.5** Sunset, Inc., a § 501(c)(3) exempt organization that is classified as a private foundation, generates investment income of $500,000 for the current tax year. This amount represents 18% of Sunset's total income.

   a. What type of tax imposed on Sunset is associated with its investment income?

   b. Is the receipt of this investment income likely to result in Sunset losing its exempt status? Why or why not?

   c. Would your answers in parts (a) and (b) change if the $500,000 represented greater than 50% of Sunset's total income? Explain.

Critical Thinking   4. **LO.4, 5** Really Welcome, Inc., a tax-exempt organization, receives 30% of its support from disqualified persons. Another disqualified person has agreed to match this support if Really Welcome will appoint him to the organization's board of directors. What tax issues are relevant to Really Welcome as it makes this decision?

5. **LO.6** Winston recently became the treasurer of Homeless, Inc., a § 501(c)(3) organization that feeds individuals who are in challenging circumstances. One of the entity's directors has proposed that Homeless purchase and operate a fast-food franchise to raise additional revenue (a projected annual increase of 45%) for its charitable mission. Because the earnings generated by the fast-food franchise would be tax-exempt, substantial additional net revenues would be provided. How should Winston respond?

6. **LO.6** An exempt hospital operates a pharmacy that is staffed by a pharmacist 24 hours per day. The pharmacy serves only hospital patients. Is the pharmacy likely an unrelated trade or business? Explain.

Critical Thinking   7. **LO.6** An exempt organization is considering conducting bingo games on Thursday nights as a way of generating additional revenue to support its exempt purpose. Before doing so, however, the president of the organization asks you for advice regarding the effect on the organization's exempt status and whether the net income from the bingo games will be taxable. Identify the relevant tax issues.

8. **LO.6** Define the following with respect to unrelated business income computations.

   a. Debt-financed income.

   b. Debt-financed property.

   c. Acquisition indebtedness.

9. **LO.1, 7** Sofía is the treasurer of the Chestnut City Garden Club, a new entity in the community. A friend who is the treasurer of the garden club in a neighboring community tells Sofía that Chestnut need not file a request for exempt status with the IRS. Has Sofía received correct advice? Explain.

Critical Thinking   10. **LO.1, 7** Abby Wang recently became the treasurer of First Point Church. The church has existed for three years and never has filed any documents with the IRS. Identify any Federal income tax reporting responsibilities that Abby might have as church treasurer.

11. **LO.7** Wren, Inc., a private foundation, generated $46,000 of gross receipts this year.

   a. Must Wren file an annual information return? If so, what form should be used?

   b. Assume instead that Wren is a § 501(c)(3) organization that is not classified as a private foundation. How would your answer in part (a) change?

12. **LO.7** Shane is the treasurer for Jain Clinics, and Brittany is the treasurer for EmPowerMentors, both of which are § 501(c)(3) exempt organizations. Each year Jain files a Form 990, while EmPowerMentors files a Form 990–PF. Discuss the public disclosure requirements for each exempt entity.

Computational Exercises

13. **LO.3** Helpers, Inc., a qualifying § 501(c)(3) organization, incurs lobbying expenditures of $250,000 for the taxable year and grass roots expenditures of $0. Exempt purpose expenditures for the taxable year are $1,200,000. Helpers elects to make lobbying expenditures on a limited basis.

    a. What amount of lobbying expenditures is Helpers allowed to make tax-free under the terms of the election?

    b. What is its tax liability as a result of the election?

    c. Express your answer to part (b) as a Microsoft Excel formula.

14. **LO.3** Davis, an officer for a § 501(c)(3) organization, receives benefits in the form of an overly generous health insurance plan; these benefits are inappropriate in the context of a charitable entity of its type. The excess benefits are determined to be $35,000. Davis does not pay back the excess benefits to the organization before the first-level tax is due.

    a. Apply the rules for intermediate sanctions. What amount of first-level taxes are imposed on Davis? On the exempt organization management?

    b. What amount of second-level taxes are imposed on Davis?

15. **LO.5** Rejoice, Inc., a private foundation, has existed for 10 years. Rejoice held undistributed income of $160,000 at the end of its 2017 tax year. Of this amount, $90,000 was distributed in 2018, and $70,000 was distributed during the first quarter of 2019. The IRS mailed a deficiency notice to Rejoice on August 1, 2020, relating to the entity's undistributed income.

    a. What is Rejoice's initial tax on the 2017 undistributed taxable income for 2018? For 2019?

    b. Express the 2018 tax computation as a Microsoft Excel formula.

    c. What is Rejoice's additional tax for 2020 relative to the 2017 income?

Problems

16. **LO.1** Match the following exempt organizations with the statutory authority under which exempt status is granted. The statutory authority may apply to more than one exempt organization. Not all of the authority citations are used.

Exempt Organizations	Statutory Authority
Girl Scouts	§ 501(c)(1)
St. Óscar Romero Catholic Church	§ 501(c)(2)
American Red Cross	§ 501(c)(3)
Salvation Army	§ 501(c)(4)
United Fund	§ 501(c)(5)
Bill and Melinda Gates Foundation	§ 501(c)(6)
University of Richmond	§ 501(c)(7)
Association of Women Engineers	§ 501(c)(8)
Ladies PGA Tour	§ 501(c)(9)
Veterans of Foreign Wars (VFW)	§ 501(c)(10)
Dallas Rodeo Club	§ 501(c)(11)
Township School's Parent-Teacher Association (PTA)	§ 501(c)(12)
Toano Cemetery Association	§ 501(c)(13)
Alpha Chi Omega Sorority	§ 501(c)(14)
Green, Inc., Legal Services Plan	§ 501(c)(15)
National Press Club	§ 501(c)(16)
Federal Deposit Insurance Corporation (FDIC)	§ 501(c)(19)
League of Women Voters	§ 501(c)(20)
	§ 501(d)

17. **LO.1, 3** Wellness, Inc., a § 501(c)(3) organization, makes lobbying expenditures of $340,000 this year. Charitable expenditures were $600,000 for the first six months of the year and $950,000 for the last six months of the year. Determine the Federal income tax consequences to Wellness if:

    a. It does not make the § 501(h) lobbying election.

    b. It does make the § 501(h) lobbying election.

18. **LO.3** Wish, Inc., a § 501(c)(3) organization, pays unreasonable compensation to Renata, the treasurer of Wish. Renata's compensation is $600,000. Assume that reasonable compensation would be $500,000.

    a. Apply the rules for intermediate sanctions. Determine any tax consequences for Wish, Inc.

    b. Determine any tax consequences for Renata.

Decision Making 19. **LO.3, 6, 8** Roadrunner, Inc., is an exempt medical organization. Quail, Inc., a sporting goods retailer, is a wholly owned subsidiary of Roadrunner. Roadrunner inherited the Quail stock last year from a major benefactor. Quail's taxable income is $550,000. Quail remits all of its earnings, net of any taxes, to Roadrunner every year to support the exempt purpose of the parent.

Communications

    a. Is Quail subject to Federal income tax? If so, calculate the liability.

    b. Ling Zhao, the treasurer of Roadrunner, has contacted you regarding minimizing or eliminating Quail's Federal income tax liability. She would like to know if the tax consequences would be better if Quail were liquidated into Roadrunner. Write a letter to Ms. Zhao that contains your advice. Roadrunner's address is 500 Rouse Tower, Rochester, NY 14627.

20. **LO.3** Initiate, Inc., a § 501(c)(3) organization, receives the following revenues and incurs the following expenses.

Grant from Oprah Winfrey Foundation	$ 70,000
Charitable contributions received	625,000
Expenses in carrying out its exempt mission	500,000
Net income before taxes of Landscaping, Inc., a wholly owned for-profit subsidiary	400,000

Landscaping, Inc., remits all of its after-tax profits each year to Initiate. Calculate the amount of the Federal income tax, if any, for Initiate and for Landscaping.

Communications 21. **LO.4** Pigeon, Inc., a § 501(c)(3) organization, received support from the following sources.

Governmental unit A for services rendered	$ 6,300
Governmental unit B for services rendered	4,500
Fees from the general public for services rendered (Each payment was of $100)	75,000
Gross investment income	39,000
Contributions from disqualified persons	26,000
Contributions from other than disqualified persons (Each gift was of $50)	160,000
Total support	$310,800

    a. Does Pigeon satisfy the test for receiving broad public support? Why or why not?

    b. Is Pigeon a private foundation? Be specific in your answer.

    c. Elena Mariñez, Pigeon's treasurer, has asked you for advice on whether Pigeon is a private foundation. Write a letter to Elena in which you address the issue. Her address is 250 Bristol Road, Charlottesville, VA 22903.

22. **LO.5** Gray, Inc., a private foundation, reports the following items of income and deductions. Gray is not eligible for the 1% tax rate on net investment income.

Interest income	$ 29,000
Rent income	61,000
Dividend income	15,000
Royalty income	22,000
Unrelated business income	80,000
Rent expenses	(26,000)
Unrelated business expenses	(12,000)

   a. Calculate Gray's net investment income.
   b. Calculate Gray's tax on net investment income.

23. **LO.5, 8** Otis is the CEO of Rectify, Inc., a private foundation. Otis invests $500,000   Critical Thinking
   (80%) of the foundation's investment portfolio in high-risk derivatives. Previously, the $500,000 had been invested in corporate bonds with an AA rating that earned 4% per annum. If the derivatives investment works as Otis's investment adviser claims, the annual earnings could be as high as 20%.
   a. Determine whether Rectify is subject to any of the taxes imposed on private foundations.
   b. If so, calculate the amount of the initial tax.
   c. If so, calculate the amount of the additional tax if the act causing the imposition of the tax is not addressed within the correction period.
   d. Are Otis and the foundation better off financially if the prohibited transaction, if any, is addressed within the correction period? Explain.

24. **LO.5** The board of directors of White Pearl, Inc., a private foundation, consists of Charlyne, Beth, and Carlos. They vote unanimously to provide a $500,000 grant to Carlos. The grant is to be used for travel and education and does not qualify as a permitted grant to individuals (i.e., it is an act of self-dealing).
   a. Calculate the initial tax imposed on White Pearl.
   b. Calculate the initial tax imposed on the foundation manager (i.e., board of directors).
   c. Express the computation in part (b) as a Microsoft Excel formula.

25. **LO.6** The Open Museum is an exempt organization that operates a gift shop. The   Communications
   museum's annual operations budget is $3,200,000. Gift shop sales generate a profit of $900,000. Another $600,000 of investment income is generated by the museum's endowment fund.
      Both the gift shop and the endowment income are used to support the exempt purpose of the museum. The balance of $1,700,000 required for annual operations is provided through admission fees.
      Wayne Hsu, a new board member, does not understand why the museum is subject to tax at all, particularly because all of the entity's profits are used in carrying out the mission of the museum. The museum's address is 250 Oak Avenue, Peoria, IL 61625.
   a. Calculate the amount of unrelated business income.
   b. Assume instead that the investment income is reinvested in the endowment fund, rather than used to support annual operations. Calculate the amount of unrelated business income.
   c. As the museum treasurer, write a letter to Wayne explaining the reason for the tax consequences. Wayne's address is 45 Pine Avenue, Peoria, IL 61625.

26. **LO.6** Upward and Onward, Inc., a § 501(c)(3) organization that provides training programs for government assistance recipients, reports the following income and expenses from the sale of products associated with the training program. Calculate Upward and Onward's UBIT.

Gross income from sales	$425,000
Cost of goods sold	106,000
Advertising and selling expenses	26,000
Administrative expenses	112,500

   a. Assume that the sale of the training program products is substantially related to Upward and Onward's exempt purpose.

   b. Assume that the sale of the training program products is not substantially related to Upward and Onward's exempt purpose.

   c. Express the computation in part (b) as a Microsoft Excel formula.

Communications   27. **LO.6** Perch, Inc., an exempt organization, records unrelated business taxable income of $4,000,000.

   a. Calculate Perch's UBIT.

   b. Prepare an outline of a presentation you are going to give to the new members of Perch's board on why Perch is subject to the UBIT even though it is an exempt organization.

28. **LO.6** For each of the following organizations, determine its UBTI and any related UBIT.

   a. AIDS, Inc., an exempt charitable organization that provides support for individuals with AIDS, operates a retail medical supply store open to the general public. The net income of the store, before any Federal income taxes, is $305,000.

   b. St. Andrew Episcopal Church operates a retail gift shop. The inventory consists of the typical items sold by commercial gift shops in the city. The director of the gift shop estimates that 80% of the gift shop sales are to tourists and 20% are to church members. The net income of the gift shop, before the salaries of the three gift shop employees and any Federal income taxes, is $300,000. The salaries of the employees total $80,000.

   c. Innovation University, Inc., a private institution, has placed vending machines in the student dormitories and academic buildings on campus. In recognition of recent tuition increases, the university has adopted a policy of merely trying to recover its costs associated with the vending machine activity. For the current year, however, the net income of the activity, before any Federal income taxes, is $75,000.

29. **LO.6** For each of the following organizations, determine its UBTI and any related UBIT.

   a. Connect, Inc., an exempt organization, provides food for the homeless. It operates a thrift store that sells used clothing to the general public. The thrift shop is staffed solely by four salaried employees. All of the clothes it sells are received as contributions. The $100,000 profit generated for the year by the thrift shop is used in Connect's mission of providing food to the homeless.

   b. Small, Inc., an exempt organization, recorded gross unrelated business income of $900 and unrelated business expenses of $400.

   c. In Care, Inc., is a § 501(c)(3) exempt organization. It owns a convenience store and gas pumps, which it received as a bequest from a patron. The store/gas pumps entity is operated as StopBy, a C corporation. Because StopBy is profitable, In Care hires a manager and several employees to run the entity. For the current year, StopBy's profit is $640,000. All of this amount is distributed by StopBy to In Care to use in carrying out its exempt mission.

30. **LO.6** Harmony, Inc., an exempt organization, reports unrelated business income of $7,500 and unrelated business expenses of $4,000. Calculate Harmony's UBIT. Communications

31. **LO.6** Falcon Basketball League, an exempt organization, is a youth basketball league for children ages 12 through 14. The league has been in existence for 30 years. In the past, revenue for operations has been provided through community fund-raising and the sale of snacks at the games by the parents. Due to a projected revenue shortfall of approximately $5,000, the governing board has decided to charge admission to the basketball games of $1.00 for adults and $0.50 for children.

    a. Will the admission charge affect Falcon's exempt status? Explain.

    b. What are the tax consequences to Falcon of the net income from snack sales and the new admission fee?

    c. As the volunteer treasurer of the Falcon League, prepare a memo for the entity's board in which you explain the effect, if any, of the admission fee policy on Falcon's exempt status.

32. **LO.6** Forward, Inc., is an exempt organization that assists disabled individuals by training them in digital TV repair. Used digital TVs are donated to Forward, Inc., by both organizations and individuals. Some of the donated digital TVs are operational, but others are in disrepair. After being used in the training program, the digital TVs, all of which are now operational, are sold to the general public. Forward's revenues and expenses for the current period are reported as follows.

Contributions	$ 700,000
Revenues from digital TV sales	3,600,000
Administrative expenses	500,000
Materials and supplies for digital TV repairs	800,000
Utilities	25,000
Wages paid to disabled individuals in the training program (at minimum-wage rate)	1,200,000
Rent for building and equipment	250,000

    Any revenues not expended during the current period are deposited in a reserve fund to finance future activities.

    a. Is the digital TV repair and sales activity an unrelated trade or business? Explain.

    b. Calculate the net income of Forward, Inc., and the related Federal income tax liability, if any.

33. **LO.6** Save the Squirrels, Inc., a § 501(c)(3) organization that feeds the squirrels in municipal parks, receives a $250,000 contribution from Animal Feed, Inc., a for-profit entity that sells animal feed. In exchange for the contribution, Save the Squirrels will identify Animal Feed as a major supporter in its monthly newsletter. Determine Save the Squirrels's UBTI and any related UBIT under the following independent assumptions.

    a. Save the Squirrels receives no other similar payments.

    b. Save the Squirrels agrees to identify Animal Feed as a major supporter and to include a half-page advertisement for Animal Feed products in its monthly newsletter as a result of the contribution.

34. **LO.6** Faith Community Church is exempt from Federal income taxation under § 501(c)(3). To supplement its contribution revenue, it holds bingo games on Saturday nights. It holds all of the licenses and permits required to do so. Critical Thinking

    The net income from the bingo games is $90,000. Of these funds, $60,000 is used to support the ministry of the church. The balance of $30,000 is invested in Faith's endowment fund for church music.

Faith Community Church is located in a resort city where bingo games can be conducted by churches, charities, and for-profit entities.

a. Will conducting the bingo games affect the exempt status of Faith Community Church? Explain.

b. Calculate the Federal tax liability, if any, associated with the bingo games.

35. **LO.6** Fish, Inc., an exempt organization, reports unrelated business income of $500,000 (before any charitable contribution deduction). During the year, Fish makes charitable contributions to other organizations of $54,000, of which $38,000 is associated with the unrelated trade or business.

a. Calculate Fish's unrelated business taxable income (UBTI).

b. Express your computation in part (a) as a Microsoft Excel formula.

c. Assume instead that the charitable contributions are $41,000, of which $38,000 is associated with the unrelated trade or business. Calculate any UBTI.

36. **LO.6** Save, Inc., an exempt organization, sells the following assets during the tax year. Determine the effect of these transactions on Save's unrelated business taxable income.

Asset	Gain (Loss)	Use
Land and building	$100,000	In exempt purpose
Land	25,000	In exempt purpose
Equipment	(12,000)	Leased to a taxable entity
Automobile	(9,000)	Leased to a taxable entity

37. **LO.7** Seagull, Inc., a § 501(c)(3) exempt organization, uses a tax year that ends on October 31. Seagull's gross receipts are $600,000, and related expenses are $580,000.

a. Is Seagull required to file an annual Form 990?

b. If so, what is the due date?

38. **LO.7** Wong, Inc., a § 501(c)(3) organization, is a private foundation with a tax year that ends on May 31. Gross receipts for the fiscal year are $180,000, and the related expenses are $160,000.

a. Is the entity required to file an annual information return?

b. If so, what form is used?

c. If so, what is the due date?

d. How would your answers in parts (a), (b), and (c) change if Wong were an exempt organization that was not a private foundation?

Research Problems

the answer company™
THOMSON REUTERS®

Note: Solutions to the Research Problems can be prepared by using the Thomson Reuters Checkpoint™ online tax research database, which accompanies this textbook. Solutions can also be prepared by using research materials found in a typical tax library.

Communications   **Research Problem 1.** Wonderful Wilderness, Inc., is a tax-exempt organization. Its mission is to "make the world a greener place through education, research, exploration, and restoration."

Martín Morales, the chief financial officer, presents you with the following information. Wonderful Wilderness raises funds to support its mission in a variety of ways, including contributions and membership fees. As part of this effort, Wonderful Wilderness develops and maintains mailing lists of its members, donors, catalog purchasers, and other supporters.

Wonderful Wilderness holds exclusive ownership rights to its mailing lists. To acquire the names of additional prospective members and supporters, Wonderful Wilderness occasionally exchanges membership lists with other organizations. In addition, Wonderful Wilderness permits other tax-exempt organizations and commercial entities to pay a fee, identified in an annually updated schedule, to use its mailing lists on a one-time basis per transaction.

Martín is aware that the Federal income tax law applies a UBIT. He is also aware of the § 512(b)(2) provision that excludes royalties from the UBIT. An IRS agent has raised the issue that the revenue from the use of the mailing lists by other entities may be taxable as unrelated business income. Martín wants you to research this issue.

Write a letter to Martín that contains your findings, and prepare a memo for the tax research files. Wonderful Wilderness's address is 100 Wilderness Way, Pocatello, ID 83209.

Research Problem 2. Your client, Rich N. Ready, has come to you for advice. Rich is interested in many social welfare issues (e.g., access to higher education, prison reform, and abortion rights). He wants to use his wealth to educate the general public on these issues, as well as to influence related legislation. Further, he wants to assist the financing of campaigns for political candidates who reflect his views. `Communications`

Rich's friend Penny suggested that he organize a § 501(c)(4) organization, telling him not only that such organizations are tax-exempt but also that they need not disclose the names of their donors. Thus, Rich could participate in these activities anonymously. However, Rich read that such an organization must be operated exclusively for "the promotion of social welfare." This would seem to preclude the lobbying and political campaigning support that Rich desires.

Is a § 501(c)(4) organization appropriate for Rich's plans? Summarize your findings in an e-mail to your instructor; be specific in your answer(s).

Use internet tax resources to address the following questions. Look for reliable websites and blogs of the IRS and other government agencies, media outlets, businesses, tax professionals, academics, think tanks, and political outlets.

Research Problem 3. With respect to the constitutionality of a church to engage in political activities, submit to your instructor a two-page paper defining and tracing the history of the so-called *Johnson Amendment*. `Communications` `Critical Thinking`

Research Problem 4. Send your instructor a graph of the number of tax returns reporting UBI, and the UBIT collected from those returns, for the last 20 years. Use five-year intervals in your analysis. `Data Analytics`

Research Problem 5. Verify the exempt status of the symphony orchestra that performs closest to your home. Who are its three highest-paid associates? Send an e-mail to your instructor summarizing your results and explaining how you found this information. `Communications`

Research Problem 6. Use **guidestar.org** to obtain the following information on the Jamestown Yorktown Foundation, Inc., which is located in Williamsburg, Virginia. `Data Analytics`

- Locate the foundation's website.
- Under what paragraph of § 501(c) do you believe is the organization exempt from Federal income tax?
- Use the organization's Form 990 to determine the entity's total budget and the amount of compensation paid to officers and directors.

Becker CPA Review Questions

Becker.

1. Unrelated business income (UBI):

    a. includes unrelated income from an activity where all the work is performed by volunteers.

    b. is not created if the activity results in a loss.

    c. is 100% taxable on the exempt organization's tax return.

    d. excludes income from the research of a college or hospital.

2. Which of the following is a false statement?

    a. An annual information return (Form 990) stating gross income, receipts, contributions, and disbursements is required of many exempt organizations that are exempt from tax.

    b. For organizations that normally have less than $50,000 in annual gross receipts, a Form 990 or 990–EZ is not required; however, an "electronic postcard" (Form 990–N) is filed with the IRS and provides only limited information.

    c. An organization operated primarily for the purposes of carrying on a trade or business for profit can claim exemption from tax if all of its profits are payable to exempt organizations.

    d. If an organization fails to file the required return for three consecutive years, the tax-exempt status of the organization will be revoked.

CHAPTER

24

Multistate Corporate Taxation

LEARNING OBJECTIVES: *After completing Chapter 24, you should be able to:*

LO.1 Illustrate the computation of a multistate corporation's state income tax liability.

LO.2 Define nexus and explain its role in state income taxation.

LO.3 Distinguish between allocation and apportionment of a multistate corporation's taxable income.

LO.4 Describe the nature and treatment of business and nonbusiness income.

LO.5 Discuss the sales, payroll, and property apportionment factors.

LO.6 Apply the unitary method of state income taxation.

LO.7 Discuss the states' income tax treatment of S corporations, partnerships, and LLCs.

LO.8 Describe other commonly encountered state and local taxes on businesses.

LO.9 Recognize tax planning opportunities available to minimize a corporation's state and local tax liability.

CHAPTER OUTLINE

24-1 Corporate State Income Taxation, 24-2
24-1a Computing State Income Tax, 24-3
24-1b State Modifications, 24-3
24-1c The UDITPA and the Multistate Tax Commission, 24-6
24-1d Jurisdiction to Impose Tax: Nexus and Public Law 86–272, 24-6
24-1e Nexus in Today's Economy, 24-6

24-2 Apportionment and Allocation of Income, 24-8
24-2a The Apportionment Procedure, 24-9
24-2b Apportionable Income, 24-9
24-2c Apportionment Factors: Elements and Planning, 24-11
24-2d The Sales Factor, 24-13
24-2e The Payroll Factor, 24-14
24-2f The Property Factor, 24-16

24-3 The Unitary Theory, 24-18
24-3a What Is a Unitary Business? 24-19
24-3b Tax Effects of the Unitary Theory, 24-19
24-3c Consolidated and Combined Returns, 24-21

24-4 Taxation of S Corporations, 24-22
24-4a Eligibility, 24-22
24-4b State Tax Filing Requirements, 24-22

24-5 Taxation of Partnerships and LLCs, 24-23

24-6 Other State and Local Taxes, 24-23
24-6a State and Local Sales and Use Taxes, 24-23
24-6b Local Property Taxes, 24-25
24-6c Other Taxes, 24-26

24-7 Tax Planning, 24-28
24-7a Selecting the Optimal State in Which to Operate, 24-28
24-7b Restructuring Corporate Entities, 24-29
24-7c Subjecting the Corporation's Income to Apportionment, 24-31
24-7d Planning with Apportionment Factors, 24-32
24-7e Sales/Use Tax Compliance, 24-33
24-7f Capital Stock Taxation, 24-33

FOXY BURROW/SHUTTERSTOCK.COM

MAKING A MULTISTATE LOCATION DECISION

LocalCo has customers in most U.S. states. It does not employ a traditional sales force. Instead, it sells its products exclusively through internet solicitations and its elaborate website.

LocalCo has two product lines: smartphone accessories, which it manufactures in Alabama, and various sports-themed apparel items, all of which are produced in California. LocalCo has been quite profitable in the past, and it holds a sizable investment portfolio made up chiefly of U.S. Treasury securities. Banking, payroll, and other administrative operations are located in rural New York State, where the entity is incorporated. LocalCo's rank-and-file employees receive compensation packages that are below the national median, but its top 10 executives are highly paid.

In an effort to "go green," LocalCo wants to hold down its costs for shipping raw materials to its manufacturing facilities and for sending its sold goods to customers. As a result, it is considering the construction of a sizable new multifunction building. Ideally, the new facility would have access to both interstate highways and a reliable airport with excess capacity for freight operations.

How will LocalCo's expansion decision be affected by state and local tax considerations?

Read the chapter and formulate your response.

Although most of this text concentrates on the effects of the Federal income tax law upon the computation of a taxpayer's annual tax liability, a variety of tax bases apply to most business taxpayers. For instance, a multinational corporation may be subject to tax in a number of different countries (see Chapter 25). Furthermore, estimates are that at least 40 percent of the income tax dollars paid by business taxpayers go to state and local authorities.

U.S. state and local governments collect more than $3 trillion in taxes and fees each year; this comes to more than $9,000 per individual citizen. Individual income and sales/use taxes account for about one-fourth of state and local tax collections each. Local property taxes bring in about one-third of all revenues, and corporate income taxes bring in about 2.5 percent.

State/Local Taxes in Context

Businesses operate in a multistate environment for a variety of reasons. For the most part, nontax motivations drive such location decisions as where to build new plants or distribution centers or whether to move communications and data processing facilities and corporate headquarters. For instance, a business typically wants to be close to its largest markets and to operate in a positive private- and public-sector business climate, where it has access to well-trained and reasonably priced labor, suppliers and support operations, sources of natural resources, communication facilities, and transportation networks.

Many location decisions, though, are motivated by multistate tax considerations, such as the following.

- Tax credits and other incentives that encourage businesses to relocate, expand, or retain jobs in the area. Some of the incentives include *clawback* provisions, under which the tax savings granted must be returned to the state by the business if new job targets are not met or construction projects not completed.

- The compliance burdens created by each new level of tax compliance. For instance, how many tax returns must be filed by a three-shareholder S corporation operating in 15 states?

- The extent to which a local political climate encourages tax burdens on visitors and others who have no direct say in the reelection of local politicians.

This chapter reviews the basic tax concepts that are predominant among most states that impose a tax based on net income,[1] and it discusses the major areas in which tax planning can reduce a corporation's overall state tax burden. The chapter concludes with a review of other types of taxes used by the U.S. states, with a special focus on sales and use taxes.

24-1   CORPORATE STATE INCOME TAXATION

Forty-six states and the District of Columbia impose a tax based on a C corporation's taxable income. Because each state is free to create its own tax provisions, the taxpayer could be faced with 47 entirely different sets of state tax provisions.[2] All of the states require separate filing of tax returns (rather than linking their filings with other states and/or with the IRS).

---

[1]Some states refer to their tax on corporate income as a franchise tax, a business tax, a license tax, or a business profits tax.

[2]The District of Columbia operates in much the same manner as a state and imposes a tax based on income. Four states impose no corporate income tax at all: Nevada, South Dakota, Washington, and Wyoming. Corporations, however, are subject to a business and occupation tax in Washington. Several states base the tax on the entity's gross receipts, not on net income.

24-1a **Computing State Income Tax**

LO.1

Illustrate the computation of a multistate corporation's state income tax liability.

In more than 40 of the states that impose a corporate income tax, the starting point in computing the tax base is taxable income as reflected on the Federal corporate income tax return (Form 1120). Those states whose computation of state taxable income is not coupled to the Federal tax return have their own state-specific definitions of gross and taxable income. Nonetheless, even these states typically adopt most Federal income and deduction provisions.

Although Federal tax law plays a significant role in the computation of state taxable income, there is a wide disparity in both the methods used to determine a state's taxable income and the tax rates imposed on that income. Only a few states apply more than one or two tax rates to taxable income, so there is little progressivity to these tax systems.

State tax credits typically are designed to encourage increased hiring and investment in local facilities. Cities and states often use targeted tax credits to entice businesses to expand or relocate within their borders. For instance, a state might offer a $50,000 credit for each new job created by the taxpayer or a 15 percent credit for taxpayers who purchase automobiles that were assembled in the state.

Generally, the accounting period and methods used by a corporation for state tax purposes must be consistent with those used on the Federal tax return. States often apply different rules, however, in identifying the members of a group filing a consolidated return and the income of each group member that is subject to tax.

Virtually all of the states that levy an income tax require notification of the final settlement of a Federal income tax audit. In addition, some states share their audit results with other states. State authorities then adjust the originally calculated state tax liability to account for these out-of-state audit changes.

The formula used by a multistate corporation to determine its tax liability in a typical state is illustrated in Exhibit 24.1.

24-1b **State Modifications**

Federal taxable income generally is used as the starting point in computing the state's income tax base, but state adjustments or modifications often are made to Federal taxable income to:

- Reflect differences between state and Federal tax statutes.
- Remove income that a state is constitutionally prohibited from taxing.

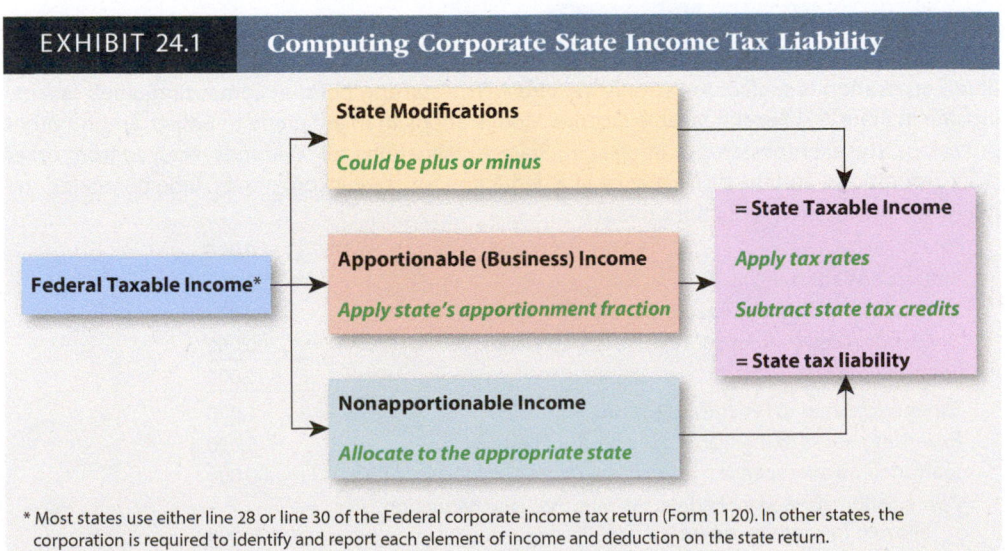

EXHIBIT 24.1   Computing Corporate State Income Tax Liability

* Most states use either line 28 or line 30 of the Federal corporate income tax return (Form 1120). In other states, the corporation is required to identify and report each element of income and deduction on the state return.

EXHIBIT 24.2	Common State Corporate Income Tax Modifications

Addition Modifications

- Interest income received on state and municipal obligations and any other interest income that is exempt from Federal income tax. For this purpose, some states exempt interest earned on their own obligations.
- Expenses deducted in computing Federal taxable income that are directly or indirectly related to U.S. obligations.
- Income-based franchise and income taxes imposed by any state and the District of Columbia that were deducted in computing Federal taxable income.
- The amount by which the Federal deductions for depreciation, amortization, or depletion exceed those permitted by the state.
- The amount by which the state gain or loss from the disposal of assets differs from the Federal gain or loss. Due to the difference in permitted depreciation methods and other adjustments, a corporation's assets may have different Federal and state tax bases. This adjustment is not necessary if the state and Federal basis provisions are identical.
- Adjustments required as a result of different elections being made for state and Federal purposes. Examples of such elections include the methods under which income from installment sales or long-term contracts is determined.
- Federal net operating loss deduction, if the starting point in the computation of taxable income is Federal taxable income after special deductions.

Subtraction Modifications

- Interest on U.S. obligations or obligations of Federal agencies to the extent included in Federal taxable income but exempt from state income taxes under U.S. law.
- Expenses that are directly or indirectly related to the state and municipal interest that is taxable for state purposes.
- Refunds of franchise and income taxes imposed by any state and the District of Columbia, to the extent included in Federal taxable income.
- The amount by which the state deductions for depreciation, amortization, or depletion exceed the deductions permitted for Federal tax purposes.
- Adjustments required as a result of different elections being made for state and Federal purposes, as above.
- Dividends received from other U.S. corporations, to the extent included in Federal taxable income.
- Net operating loss deduction as determined for state tax purposes.

Exhibit 24.2 lists the most frequently encountered state income tax modifications. In computing the taxable income for a given state, only some of these modifications may apply.

Computing State Taxable Income

EXAMPLE 1

Blue Corporation is subject to tax only in State A. The starting point in computing Blue's taxable income in State A is Federal taxable income. Modifications then are made to reflect, among other provisions, the exempt status of interest on State A obligations, all dividends received from other U.S. corporations, and the disallowance of a deduction for state income taxes. Blue generated the following income and deductions this year.

Sales	$1,500,000
Interest on Federal obligations	50,000
Interest on municipal obligations of State B	100,000
Dividends received from 30% owned U.S. corporations	200,000
Total income	$1,850,000
Expenses related to Federal obligations	$ 1,000
Expenses related to municipal obligations of State B	5,000
State income tax expense	50,000
Depreciation allowed for Federal tax purposes (the deduction allowed for state purposes is $300,000)	400,000
Other allowable deductions	1,000,000
Total deductions	$1,456,000

continued

Blue's taxable income for Federal and state purposes is computed as follows.

Federal Taxable Income	
Sales	$1,500,000
Interest on Federal obligations	50,000
Dividends received from U.S. corporations	200,000
Total income	$1,750,000
Expenses related to Federal obligations	$　1,000
State income tax expense	50,000
Depreciation	400,000
Other allowable deductions	1,000,000
Total deductions	$1,451,000
Taxable income before special deductions	$　299,000
Less: Dividends received deduction (65% × $200,000)	(130,000)
Federal taxable income	$　169,000

State A Taxable Income	
Federal taxable income	$169,000
Addition Modifications	
Interest on State B obligations	100,000
State income tax expense	50,000
Excess depreciation deduction allowed for Federal purposes ($400,000 − $300,000)	100,000
Expenses related to Federal obligations	1,000
Subtraction Modifications	
Expenses related to State B obligations	(5,000)
Dividends from other corporations, to extent included In Federal taxable income ($200,000 − $130,000)	(70,000)
Interest on Federal obligations	(50,000)
State A taxable income	$295,000

Continue with the facts of Example 1, except that the $100,000 of municipal bond interest (and related expenses) are associated with State A obligations. The computation of Federal taxable income is unaffected by this change. Because State A exempts interest on its own obligations from taxation, Blue's State A taxable income now is $200,000.

EXAMPLE 2

State A Taxable Income	
Federal taxable income	$169,000
Addition Modifications	
State income tax expense	50,000
Excess depreciation deduction allowed for Federal purposes ($400,000 − $300,000)	100,000
Expenses related to Federal obligations	1,000
Subtraction Modifications	
Dividends from other U.S. corporations, to extent included in Federal taxable income ($200,000 − $130,000)	(70,000)
Interest on Federal obligations	(50,000)
State A taxable income	$200,000

24-1c **The UDITPA and the Multistate Tax Commission**

The Multistate Tax Compact is a model law designed to promote uniformity in administering state income tax laws among the states. Part of the Compact includes the Uniform Division of Income for Tax Purposes Act (UDITPA), last revised in 2015, which relates to the assignment of income among the states for corporations that maintain operations in more than one state (multistate corporations). Many states have adopted the provisions of the UDITPA, either by adopting in full the Multistate Tax Compact or by modeling their laws after the provisions of the UDITPA.

The Multistate Tax Commission (MTC) is an agency created by the Multistate Tax Compact, made up of tax administrators from many of the states. The MTC writes regulations and other rules that interpret the UDITPA. When a new MTC rule or regulation is created, the member states propose its adoption to their respective legislatures. The majority of member states adopt the regulations with no exceptions or only minor changes.[3]

LO.2

Define nexus and explain its role in state income taxation.

24-1d **Jurisdiction to Impose Tax: Nexus and Public Law 86–272**

The state in which a business is incorporated (i.e., its state of *legal domicile*) has the jurisdiction to tax the corporation regardless of the volume of its business activity within the state. Whether a state can tax the income of a business that operates within its borders but is incorporated in a different state (i.e., the state in which the business has a *commercial domicile*) usually depends on the level of activity of the taxpayer in the state and on state law and principles of the U.S. Constitution.

The term nexus describes the degree of business activity that must be present before a taxing jurisdiction has the right to impose a tax on an out-of-state entity's income. Generally, each state defines nexus differently. Typically, sufficient nexus is present when a corporation derives income from sources within the state, owns or leases property in the state, employs personnel in the state, or has physical or financial capital there.

Public Law 86–272 (P.L. 86–272) limits the states' right to impose an income tax on certain interstate activities.[4] This Federal law prohibits a state from taxing a business whose only connection with the state is to solicit orders for sales of tangible personal property that is sent outside the state for approval or rejection. If approved, the orders must be filled and shipped by the business from a point outside the state.

Only the sales of tangible personal property are immune from taxation under this law, however. Leases, rentals, and other dispositions of tangible personal property are not protected activities. Moreover, dispositions of real property and intangible property, as well as sales of services, are not protected by P.L. 86–272.

Business activity that involves tangible personal property and consists merely of solicitation is immune from taxation. The statute does not define the term *solicitation*, but the Supreme Court has held that *solicitation of orders* includes any explicit verbal request for orders and any speech or conduct that implicitly invites an order.[5] The Court also created a *de minimis* rule, allowing immunity from nexus where a limited amount of solicitation occurs.

Exhibit 24.3 summarizes the activities the MTC has identified as being directly related to solicitation (protected activities) and activities unrelated to solicitation (which establish income tax nexus for the entity).

24-1e **Nexus in Today's Economy**

P.L. 86–272 was enacted by Congress in 1959. States and the MTC have issued regulations and interpretations of P.L. 86–272, but the law is not robust enough to account for

---

[3]Many of the states that are not members of the Multistate Tax Compact still model their laws after the UDITPA and the MTC regulations. See **www.mtc.gov** and **tinyurl.com/uditpa.**

[4]15 U.S.C. §§ 381–385.

[5]*Wisconsin Department of Revenue v. William Wrigley, Jr., Co.*, 505 U.S. 214 (1992).

EXHIBIT 24.3	Common Nexus Definitions under P.L. 86–272

General Rule P.L. 86–272 immunity from income tax nexus applies for sales of tangible personal property, where the seller's activities are ancillary to the order-solicitation process.

Activities That Usually Do Not Create Nexus

- Advertising campaigns.
- Carrying free samples only for display or distribution.
- Owning or furnishing automobiles, phones, and computers to salespersons.
- Passing inquiries or complaints on to the home office.
- Maintaining a sample or display room for two weeks or less during the year.
- Maintaining a website that presents information about items of tangible personal property that are for sale.

Activities Usually Sufficient to Establish Nexus

- Approving or rejecting orders.
- Making repairs or providing maintenance.
- Collecting delinquent accounts; investigating creditworthiness.
- Conducting installation or supervising installation.
- Conducting training classes, seminars, or lectures for persons other than sales personnel.
- Picking up or replacing damaged or returned property.
- Hiring, training, or supervising personnel other than sales employees.
- Providing shipping information and coordinating deliveries.
- Owning, leasing, maintaining, or otherwise using any of the following facilities or property in the state.

  - Real estate.
  - Parts department.
  - Employment office.
  - Meeting place for directors, officers, or employees.
  - Purchasing office.
  - Warehouse.
  - Call center.
  - Mobile retailing (e.g., trucks with driver-salespersons).

- Maintaining a website that offers for sale only items of tangible personal property, where an out-of-state customer interacts with the site (e.g., by placing an order or accepting cookies onto the remote computer).

many of today's economic transactions (e.g., sales of realty and intangible assets, net income from services, and e-commerce sales). As a result, many states contend that a broader definition of income tax nexus is needed. This alternative approach often is referred to as *economic nexus* because it is triggered by business and other activities, and not by more traditional legal connections or physical presence.

Several states, following an MTC model statute, automatically assign nexus to a taxpayer that exceeds at least one of the following thresholds for the tax year. As more states take this approach, the "factor presence nexus" standard may provide additional uniformity among the states as to measuring the taxpayer's business activities.

- $50,000 of property.
- $50,000 of payroll.
- $500,000 of sales.
- 25% of total property.
- 25% of total payroll.
- 25% of total sales.

Factor presence nexus standards provide a measure of the sales or solicitation activity in the state that indicates a "sufficient" economic presence to trigger income taxation there, even if the business has little or no physical presence in the state.

Concept Summary 24.1

Multistate Taxation

1. For a profitable business entity that operates in multiple U.S. states, at least 40 percent of the total tax expense may be made up of levies by state and local governments.

2. State and local tax incentives might be used to accomplish political goals or to provide incentives for businesses to remain in, or relocate to, the taxing jurisdiction.

3. A U.S. state can apply an income tax only on a business that has a sufficient presence ("nexus") with the state.

4. Multistate income tax planning involves the reduction of the overall state and local tax burden. This may be the result of being subject to tax in the fewest number of states or of reducing the tax burden in a particular state.

LO.3

Distinguish between allocation and apportionment of a multistate corporation's taxable income.

24-2 APPORTIONMENT AND ALLOCATION OF INCOME

A corporation that conducts business activities in more than one state must determine the portion of its net income that is subject to tax by each state. A corporation that has established sufficient nexus with another state generally must both **apportion** and **allocate** its income.

Apportionment is a means by which a corporation's taxable income is divided among the states in which it conducts business. Under an apportionment procedure, a corporation determines allowable income and deductions for the company as a whole and then apportions its income among the states in which it has nexus, according to an approved formula.

Allocation is a method under which specific components of a corporation's income, net of related expenses, are directly assigned to a certain state. Allocable income is assigned to a single state, whereas apportionable income is divided among several states. Nonapportionable (nonbusiness) income generally includes:

- Income or losses derived from the sale of nonbusiness real or tangible property, or

- Income or losses in the form of rentals and royalties from nonbusiness real or tangible personal property. Rentals and royalties constituting a business are apportioned.

Nonapportionable income is allocated to the state where the property that generated the income or loss is located.

EXAMPLE

3

Green Corporation conducts business in States N, O, P, and Q. Green's $900,000 taxable income consists of $800,000 apportionable income and $100,000 allocable income generated from transactions conducted in State Q. Green's sales, property, and payroll are evenly divided among the four states, and the states all employ an identical apportionment formula. As a result, $200,000 of Green's income is taxable in each of States N, O, and P. Green is subject to income tax on $300,000 of income in State Q.

Apportionable income	$800,000
Apportionment percentage (apportionable income is divided equally among the four states)	× 25%
Income apportioned to each state	$200,000

	State N	State O	State P	State Q
Income apportioned	$200,000	$200,000	$200,000	$200,000
Income allocated	–0–	–0–	–0–	100,000
Taxable income	$200,000	$200,000	$200,000	$300,000

24-2a **The Apportionment Procedure**

Apportionment assumes that the production of the taxpayer's income is linked to business activity, and the laws of each state define one or more factors believed to indicate the amount of corporate activity conducted within the state. However, apportionment often does not provide a uniform division of an organization's income based on its business activity, because each state is free to choose the type and number of factors it believes are indicative of the business activity conducted within its borders. As a result, a business may be subject to state income tax on more or less than 100 percent of its Federal taxable income.

An equally incongruous consequence of apportionment may occur when the operations in a state result in a loss.

EXAMPLE 4

Red Corporation's operations include two manufacturing facilities, one in State A and one in State B. The plant located in State A generated $500,000 of income, and the plant located in State B generated a loss of $200,000. Based on this information, Red's total taxable income is $300,000.

Applying the statutes of each state, Red determines that its apportionment factors for States A and B are 65% and 35%, respectively. As a result, Red's income is apportioned to the states as follows.

Income apportioned to State A : 65% × $300,000 = $195,000
Income apportioned to State B : 35% × $300,000 = $105,000

Red is subject to tax in State B on $105,000 of income, even though the operations conducted in that state resulted in a loss.

24-2b **Apportionable Income**

Apportionable income is assigned among the states by using an apportionment formula. In contrast, *nonapportionable income* is allocated to the state where the income-producing asset is located. For instance, income derived from the rental of nonbusiness real property generally is allocated to the state where the property is located.

LO.4

Describe the nature and treatment of business and nonbusiness income.

EXAMPLE 5

TNT Corporation, a manufacturer of explosive devices, is a multistate taxpayer that has nexus with States P and Q. During the taxable year, TNT's net sales of explosive devices were $900,000; $600,000 of these sales were made in State P, and $300,000 were made in State Q. The corporation also received $90,000 from the rental of nonbusiness real property located in State P. As a result, TNT's Federal taxable income is $990,000.

Applying the statutes of each state, TNT determines that its apportionment factors for States P and Q are 65% and 42%, respectively. TNT's taxable income for each state is determined as follows.

Income apportioned to State P	65% × $900,000	$585,000
Income allocated to State P		90,000
P taxable income		$ 675,000
Income apportioned to State Q	42% × $900,000 = Q taxable income	378,000
Aggregate state taxable income		$1,053,000

TNT's aggregate state taxable income exceeds its Federal taxable income. Tax rules in the two states differed, such that the apportionment factors totaled to more than 100%.

Apportionable income arises from the taxpayer's regular course of business or constitutes an integral part of the taxpayer's regular business.[6] In determining whether an

---

[6]MTC Reg. IV.1.(a).

item of income is apportionable (business) income, state courts have developed a variety of approaches to determine a taxpayer's "regular course of business."[7]

Nonapportionable income is "all income other than apportionable income."[8] Usually, nonapportionable income comprises passive and portfolio income, such as dividends, interest, rents, royalties, and certain capital gains. However, passive activity or portfolio income may be apportionable when the acquisition, management, and disposition of the underlying property constitute an integral part of the taxpayer's regular business operation.[9]

A few states fail to distinguish between apportionable and nonapportionable income. In these states, all of a corporation's income is deemed to be subject to apportionment.

Apportionable Income

Scarlet Corporation is subject to income tax in several states. Scarlet earned $2,500,000 from the sales of its products and $1,000,000 from the sale of assets that were unrelated to its regular business operations.

In the states that distinguish between business and nonbusiness income, $2,500,000 of Scarlet's income is apportioned to the state according to the state's apportionment formula. The gain on the sale of the nonbusiness assets is allocated to the state where the assets were located. In the states that subject a corporation's entire income to apportionment, $3,500,000 ($2,500,000 + $1,000,000) is apportioned among the states in which the taxpayer conducts business.

Gray Corporation owns and operates two manufacturing facilities, one in State A and the other in State B. Due to a temporary decline in sales, Gray has rented 10% of its State A facility to an unaffiliated corporation. Gray generated $100,000 net rent income and $900,000 income from manufacturing.

Both States A and B classify the rent income as allocable income. By applying the statutes of each state, Gray determines that its apportionment factors are 40% for State A and 60% for State B.

Income Subject to Tax in State A	
Taxable income	$1,000,000
Less: Allocable income	(100,000)
Apportionable income	$ 900,000
Times: Apportionment factor	× 40%
Income apportioned to State A	$ 360,000
Plus: Income allocated to State A	100,000
Income subject to tax in State A	$ 460,000

Income Subject to Tax in State B	
Taxable income	$1,000,000
Less: Allocable income	(100,000)
Apportionable income	$ 900,000
Times: Apportionment factor	× 60%
Income apportioned to State B	$ 540,000
Plus: Income allocated to State B	–0–
Income subject to tax in State B	$ 540,000

---

[7]*Atlantic Richfield Co. v. State of Colorado and Joseph F. Dolan*, 601 P.2d 628 (Colo.S.Ct., 1979); *Appeal of A. Epstein and Sons, Inc.* (Cal.State Bd. of Equalization, 1984).

[8]UDITPA § 1(e).
[9]MTC Reg. IV.1.(a)(5).

Apportionable Income

EXAMPLE 8

Continue with the facts of Example 7, but assume that B does not distinguish between apportionable and nonapportionable income. As a result, all of Gray's income is apportionable in State B.

Gray properly determines that its apportionment factors are 40% for State A and 58% for State B. In this situation, Gray's income that is subject to tax is greater than $1,000,000.

Income Subject to Tax in State A, computed in Example 7	$ 460,000
Income Subject to Tax in State B	
Apportionable income	$1,000,000
Times: Apportionment factor	× 58%
Income apportioned to State B	$ 580,000

24-2c **Apportionment Factors: Elements and Planning**

LO.5

Discuss the sales, payroll, and property apportionment factors.

Apportionable income is divided among the states by determining the appropriate apportionment percentage for each state that has a right to tax the entity. To determine the apportionment percentage for each state, a ratio is established for each of the factors included in the state's apportionment formula. Each ratio is calculated by comparing the level of a specific business activity within a state to the total corporate activity of that type. The ratios then are summed, averaged, and appropriately weighted to determine the taxpayer's apportionment percentage for a specific state.

The traditional three-factor formula equally weights sales, property, and payroll.[10] However, fewer than 10 states use an equal three-factor formula; in all other states, the sales factor receives more than a one-third weight.

The use of a higher-weighted sales factor tends to pull a larger percentage of an out-of-state corporation's income into the taxing jurisdiction of the state, because the corporation's major activity within the state—the sales of its goods and services—is weighted more heavily than are its payroll and property activities. Overweighting the sales factor, accordingly, provides income tax relief for corporations that are headquartered in the state. Those corporations generally own significantly more property and incur more payroll costs (factors that are given less weight in the apportionment formula) within the state than do out-of-state corporations.

EXAMPLE 9

Luna Corporation realized $500,000 of taxable income from the sales of its products in States A and B. Luna's activities in both states establish nexus for income tax purposes. Luna's sales, payroll, and property in the states include the following.

	State A	State B	Total
Sales	$1,250,000	$750,000	$2,000,000
Property	2,500,000	–0–	2,500,000
Payroll	1,500,000	–0–	1,500,000

If State B uses an equally weighted three-factor apportionment formula, $62,500 of Luna's taxable income is apportioned to State B.

continued

[10]Certain industries, such as financial services institutions, insurance companies, air and motor carriers, pipeline companies, and communications providers, typically are required to use apportionment formulas with different factors and weightings.

Sales ($750,000/$2,000,000)	=		37.5%
Property ($0/$2,500,000)	=		–0–
Payroll ($0/$1,500,000)	=		–0–
Sum of apportionment factors			37.5%
Average	÷		3
Apportionment factor for State B			12.5%
Taxable income	×		$500,000
Income apportioned to State B			$ 62,500

If State B uses a double-weighted sales factor in its three-factor apportionment formula, $93,750 of Luna's taxable income is apportioned to State B.

Sales ($750,000/$2,000,000)	=	37.5% × 2	=		75%
Property ($0/$2,500,000)	=				–0–
Payroll ($0/$1,500,000)	=				–0–
Sum of apportionment factors					75%
Average			÷		4
Apportionment factor for State B					18.75%
Taxable income			×		$500,000
Income apportioned to State B					$ 93,750

When a state uses a double-weighted sales factor, typically a larger percentage of an out-of-state corporation's income is subject to tax in the state. Here, an additional $31,250 ($93,750 − $62,500) of Luna's income is subject to tax in State B.

A single-factor apportionment formula consisting solely of a sales factor is even more detrimental to an out-of-state corporation than an apportionment factor that double-weights the sales factor. About 25 states use or allow a sales-factor-only apportionment formula.

Continue with the facts of Example 9. If State B uses a sales-factor-only apportionment formula, Luna's income apportionable to State B becomes $187,500.

Sales ($750,000/$2,000,000)	=		37.5%
Sum of apportionment factors			37.5%
Average	÷		1
Apportionment factor for State B			37.5%
Taxable income	×		$500,000
Income apportioned to State B			$187,500

Concept Summary 24.2

Apportionable Income

1. In most states, an apportionment procedure is used to assign the income of a multistate taxpayer to the various states in which business is conducted. Generally, nonapportionable income is allocated, rather than apportioned, directly to the state in which the nonbusiness income-generating assets are located.

2. Variations in state apportionment factors and formulas offer planning opportunities for businesses, in that more or less than 100% of the taxpayer's income may be subjected to state income tax.

3. A few states employ an equally weighted three-factor apportionment formula. In some states, the sales factor is doubled, and in other states, only the sales factor is used in apportioning multistate taxable income. Generally, the greater the relative weight assigned to the sales factor, the greater the tax burden on out-of-state taxpayers.

24-2d The Sales Factor

The **sales factor** is a fraction whose numerator is the corporation's total receipts in the state during the tax period. The denominator is the corporation's total receipts generated everywhere during the tax period. Gross receipts for this purpose generally are determined net of returns, allowances, and discounts.

Because the sales factor is a component in the formula used to apportion a corporation's business income to a state, only receipts that generate apportionable income are includible in the fraction. The sales factor generally includes business income from the sale of inventory or services, interest, dividends, rentals, royalties, sales of assets, and other business income. Income on Federal obligations, however, is not included in the sales factor.

These rules work best when the object of the sale is tangible property. Different rules may be needed when the taxpayer sells services, conducting work in one state for a customer in another. UDITPA sources service transactions to the location where the taxpayer incurred costs in conducting its work. About 20 states, though, have adopted *market-sourcing* rules, where a sale of services is sourced to the customer's state or states. The states do not apply uniform rules in this area, so aggregate state taxable income from service transactions may be greater or less than the corresponding Federal taxable income amount.

When the sale involves capital assets, some states require that the gross proceeds, rather than the net gain or loss, be included in the fraction. Most states allow incidental or occasional asset sales and sales of certain intangible assets to be excluded from gross receipts.[11]

In determining the numerator of the sales factor, most states follow the UDITPA's "ultimate destination concept," under which tangible asset sales are assumed to take place at the point of delivery, not at the location at which the shipment originates.

EXAMPLE 11

Olive Corporation, whose only manufacturing plant is located in State A, sells its products to residents of State A through its local retail store. Olive also ships its products to customers in States B and C. The products that are sold to residents of State A are assigned to State A, and the products that are delivered to States B and C are assigned to States B and C, respectively, even though all goods are manufactured in and shipped from State A.

Several exceptions exist concerning the ultimate destination concept. The most important of these exceptions include the following.

- Because the U.S. government is present in every state, sales to the Federal government are assigned to the sales factor numerator of the state from which the sale occurs.

- **Dock sales** occur where a purchaser uses its owned or rented vehicles, or a common carrier with which it has made arrangements, to take delivery of the product at the seller's shipping dock. In most states, if the seller makes dock sales to a purchaser that has an out-of-state location to which it returns with the product, the sale is assigned to the purchaser's state.

- Out-of-state sales that are not subject to tax in the destination state are pulled back into the origination state if that state has adopted a **throwback rule**. About half of the states apply this exception to the destination test. States that adopt a throwback rule attempt to make sure that a sale does not escape income taxation because it is made to a customer in a state in which the seller is not taxable. Such a case would place the sale in neither state's sales factor numerator (i.e., it could be called a "nowhere sale").

  Throwback sales are treated as in-state receipts of the origination state, and the actual destination of the product is disregarded. Consequently, when the seller is

---

[11]MTC Reg. IV.18.(c).

immune from tax in the destination state under P.L. 86–272, the sales are considered to be in-state receipts of the origination state if that state has a throwback provision.

Braun Corporation's entire operations are located in State A. Seventy percent ($700,000) of Braun's sales are made in State A, and the remaining 30% ($300,000) are made in State B. Braun's solicitation of sales in State B is limited to mailing a monthly catalog to its customers in that state. However, Braun employees do pick up and replace damaged merchandise in State B.

Under State A's rules, the pickup and replacement of damaged goods establishes nexus with State B. Braun's activities in State B are sufficient (as determined by State A's law) to subject Braun to a positive tax, based on its income. As a result, Braun is permitted to apportion its income between States A and B (70% and 30%, respectively). However, State B's definition of activities necessary to create nexus is less strict than that imposed by State A; in State B, the mere pickup and replacement of damaged goods does not establish income tax nexus.

Braun's taxable income is $900,000. Both States A and B impose a 10% corporate income tax and include only the sales factor in their apportionment formulas. If State A has not adopted a throwback rule, Braun's effective state income tax rate is 7%.

	Apportionment Factors	Taxable Income	Tax Rate	Tax
State A	70%	$900,000	10%	$63,000
State B	*	900,000	10%	–0–
Total tax liability				$63,000
Effective state income tax rate: $63,000/$900,000				7%

*As determined under State B's laws, Braun's income is not apportionable to State B, because of insufficient nexus.

If State A has adopted a throwback rule, Braun does not benefit from its lack of nexus with State B, because the sales in State B are considered to be in-state receipts of State A. As a result, Braun's effective tax rate is 10%.

	Apportionment Factors	Taxable Income	Tax Rate	Tax
State A	100%	$900,000	10%	$90,000
State B	–0–	900,000	10%	–0–
Total tax liability				$90,000
Effective state income tax rate: $90,000/$900,000				10%
Tax increase due to throwback provision ($90,000 − $63,000)				$27,000

24-2e The Payroll Factor

The **payroll factor** is determined by comparing the compensation paid for services rendered within a state to the total compensation paid by the corporation. Generally, the payroll factor is a fraction whose numerator is the total amount a corporation paid or accrued for compensation in a state during the tax period. The denominator is the total amount paid or accrued by the corporation for compensation during the tax period.

For purposes of the payroll factor, compensation includes wages, salaries, commissions, and any other form of remuneration paid or accrued to employees for personal services. Compensation also may include the value of board, rent, housing, lodging, and other benefits or services furnished to employees by the taxpayer in return for personal services, if these amounts constitute Federal gross income.

Payments made to an independent contractor or any other person who is not properly classifiable as an employee generally are excluded from the numerator and denominator of the payroll factor. A few states, including Delaware, New York, and North Carolina, exclude from the payroll factor the compensation paid to corporate officers. Most states exclude from the payroll factor any compensation made to corporate directors.

More than half of the states provide that earnings paid to a cash or deferred compensation plan, excluded from Federal gross income under § 401(k), are to be included in the numerator and the denominator of the payroll factor. As a result, the total compensation that is included in the denominator of a corporation's payroll factor may vary among the states in which the corporation's income is apportioned.

EXAMPLE
13

Mice Corporation's sales office and manufacturing plant are located in State A. Mice also maintains a manufacturing plant and sales office in State C. For purposes of apportionment, State A defines payroll as all compensation paid to employees, including contributions to § 401(k) deferred compensation plans. Under the statutes of State C, neither compensation paid to officers nor contributions to § 401(k) plans are included in the payroll factor. Mice incurred the following personnel costs.

	State A	State C	Total
Wages and salaries for employees other than officers	$350,000	$250,000	$600,000
Salaries for officers	150,000	100,000	250,000
Contributions to § 401(k) plans	30,000	20,000	50,000
Total	$530,000	$370,000	$900,000

The payroll factor for State A is computed as follows.

$$\frac{\$530,000}{\$900,000} = 58.89\%$$

Because State C excludes from the payroll factor any compensation paid to officers and contributions to § 401(k) plans, State C's factor is computed as follows.

$$\frac{\$250,000}{\$600,000} = 41.67\%$$

The aggregate of Mice's payroll factors is 100.56% (58.89% + 41.67%).

Typically, the compensation of an employee is not split between two or more states during the year unless he or she is transferred or changes positions during the year. Instead, each employee's entire compensation is assigned to only one state. Under the UDITPA, compensation is treated as being paid in the state (i.e., it is included in the numerator of the payroll factor) in which the services primarily are performed.

When an employee's services are performed in more than one state, his or her entire compensation is attributed to the employee's base of operations or, if there is no base of operations in any state in which some part of the service is performed, to the place from which the services are directed or controlled. When no services are performed in the state that serves as the base of operations or the place from which the services are directed, the employee's compensation is attributed to his or her state of residency.[12]

EXAMPLE
14

Geese Corporation has its headquarters and a manufacturing plant in State A. Reggie, a resident of State Y, works at the State A manufacturing plant. His compensation is included in the numerator of State A's payroll factor, because the service is performed entirely in State A. None of Reggie's compensation is included in the payroll factor of State Y, Reggie's "home" state.

Only compensation that is related to the production of apportionable income is included in the payroll factor.

[12]UDITPA § 14.

EXAMPLE 15

Dog Corporation, a manufacturer of automobile parts, is subject to tax in States X and Y. Dog incurred the following payroll costs.

	State X	State Y	Total
Wages and salaries for officers and personnel of manufacturing facilities	$450,000	$350,000	$800,000
Wages and salaries for personnel involved in nonapportionable rental activities	50,000	–0–	50,000

Dog's payroll factors are computed as follows.

Payroll factor for State X : $450,000/$800,000 = 56.25%

Payroll factor for State Y : $350,000/$800,000 = 43.75%

24-2f The Property Factor

The property factor generally is a fraction whose numerator is the average value of the corporation's real property and its tangible personal property owned and used or rented and used in the state during the taxable year. The denominator is the average value of all of the corporation's real property and its tangible personal property owned or rented and used during the taxable year, wherever it is located. In this manner, a state's property factor reflects the extent of total property usage by the taxpayer in the state.

For this purpose, property includes land, buildings, machinery, inventory, equipment, and other real and tangible personal property.[13] Other types of property that may be included in the factor are offshore property, outer space property (satellites), and partnership property.

In the case of property that is in transit between locations of the taxpayer or between a buyer and seller, the assets are included in the numerator of the destination state. With respect to mobile or movable property such as construction equipment, trucks, and leased equipment, which is both in- and outside the state during the tax period, the numerator of a state's property factor generally is determined on the basis of the total time the property was within the state.

Property owned by the corporation typically is valued at its average original or historical cost plus the cost of additions and improvements, but without adjusting for depreciation. Some states allow property to be included at net book value or adjusted tax basis. The value of the property usually is determined by averaging the values at the beginning and end of the tax period. Alternatively, some states allow or require the amount to be calculated on a monthly basis if annual computation results in substantial distortions.

EXAMPLE 16

Blond Corporation, a calendar year taxpayer, owns property in States A and B. Both States A and B require that the average value of assets be included in the property factor. State A requires that the property be valued at its historical cost, and State B requires that the property be included in the property factor at its net book value.

Account Balances at January 1			
	State A	State B	Total
Inventories	$ 150,000	$100,000	$ 250,000
Building and machinery (cost)	200,000	400,000	600,000
Accumulated depreciation for building and machinery	(150,000)	(50,000)	(200,000)
Land	50,000	100,000	150,000
Total	$ 250,000	$550,000	$ 800,000

continued

---

[13]MTC Reg. IV.10.(a).

Account Balances at December 31			
	State A	**State B**	**Total**
Inventories	$ 250,000	$ 200,000	$ 450,000
Building and machinery (cost)	200,000	400,000	600,000
Accumulated depreciation for building and machinery	(175,000)	(100,000)	(275,000)
Land	50,000	100,000	150,000
Total	$ 325,000	$ 600,000	$ 925,000

State A Property Factor			
Historical Cost	**January 1**	**December 31**	**Average**
Property in State A	$ 400,000*	$ 500,000**	$ 450,000
Total property	1,000,000[†]	1,200,000[‡]	1,100,000

*$150,000 + $200,000 + $50,000.
**$250,000 + $200,000 + $50,000.
[†]$250,000 + $600,000 + $150,000.
[‡]$450,000 + $600,000 + $150,000.

$$\text{Property factor for State A: } \frac{\$450,000}{\$1,100,000} = 40.91\%$$

State B Property Factor			
Net Book Value	**January 1**	**December 31**	**Average**
Property in State B	$550,000	$600,000	$575,000
Total property	800,000	925,000	862,500

$$\text{Property factor for State B: } \frac{\$575,000}{\$862,500} = 66.67\%$$

Due to the variations in the property factor rules, the aggregate of Blond's property factors equals 107.58% (40.91% + 66.67%).

Leased property, when included in the property factor, is valued at eight times its annual rental. Annual rentals may include payments such as real estate taxes and insurance made by the lessee in lieu of rent.

FINANCIAL DISCLOSURE INSIGHTS **State/Local Taxes and the Tax Expense**

In applying GAAP principles for a business entity, state and local tax expenses are found in several places in the taxpayer's financial reports. In the tax footnote, the state/local tax costs often are reported in dollar and/or percentage terms, in both current and deferred components. The following are examples of state/local tax expenses that were reported in a recent year.

	Current State/ Local Tax Expenses ($ million)	Deferred State/ Local Tax Expenses ($ million)
Eli Lilly	$ 10	$ 3
Wal-Mart	405	(12)
Amazon	208	(31)
Ford Motor	(6)	12

EXAMPLE 17

Jasper Corporation is subject to tax in States D and G. Both states require that leased or rented property be included in the property factor at eight times the annual rental costs and that the average historical cost be used for other assets. Information regarding Jasper's property and rental expenses follows.

Average Historical Cost	
Property located in State D	$ 750,000
Property located in State G	450,000
Total property	$1,200,000

Lease and Rental Expenses	
State D	$ 50,000
State G	150,000
Total	$200,000

Property factor for State D

$$\frac{\$750,000 + 8(\$50,000)}{\$1,200,000 + 8(\$200,000)} = \frac{\$1,150,000}{\$2,800,000} = 41.07\%$$

Property factor for State G

$$\frac{\$450,000 + 8(\$150,000)}{\$1,200,000 + 8(\$200,000)} = \frac{\$1,650,000}{\$2,800,000} = 58.93\%$$

Only property that is used in the production of apportionable income is includible in the numerator and denominator of the property factor. In this regard, idle property, property under construction, and property that is used in producing nonapportionable income generally are excluded.

LO.6

Apply the unitary method of state income taxation.

24-3 THE UNITARY THEORY

When two affiliated corporations are subject to tax in different states, each entity must file a return and report its income in the state in which it conducts business. Each entity reports its income separately from that of its affiliated corporations. In an effort to minimize overall state income tax, multistate entities have attempted to separate the parts of the business that are carried on in the various states.

EXAMPLE 18

Arts Corporation owns a chain of retail stores located in several states. To enable each store to file and report the income earned only in that state, each store was organized as a separate subsidiary in the state in which it did business. In this manner, each store is separately subject to tax only in the state in which it is located.

Most states attempt to assign as much of an entity's income to in-state sources as possible, so the unitary theory for computing state taxable income is attractive to them. Under this method, a corporation is required to file a combined return that includes the results from all of the operations of the related corporations, not just from those that transacted business in the state. In this manner, the unitary method allows a state to apply the apportionment formula to a firm's nationwide or worldwide unitary income. To include the activities of the corporation's subsidiaries in the apportionment formula, the state must determine that the subsidiaries' activities are an integral part of a unitary business and, as a result, are subject to apportionment.

24-3a What Is a Unitary Business?

A unitary business operates as a unit and cannot be segregated into independently operating divisions. The operations are integrated, and each division depends on or contributes to the operation of the business as a whole. It is not necessary that each unit operating within a state contribute to the activities of all divisions outside the state.

The unitary theory ignores the separate legal existence of the entities and focuses instead on practical business realities. As a result, the separate entities are treated as a single business for state income tax purposes, and the apportionment formula is applied to the combined income of the unitary business.

What Is a Unitary Business?

EXAMPLE 19

Continue with the facts of Example 18. Arts manufactured no goods, but it housed the central management, purchasing, distribution, advertising, and administrative departments. Each of the subsidiaries carried on a purely intrastate business, and they paid for the goods and services received at the parent company's cost plus overhead.

Arts and the subsidiaries constitute a unitary business due to their unitary operations (purchasing, distribution, advertising, and administrative functions). As a result, in states that have adopted the unitary method, the income and apportionment factors of the entire unitary group are combined and apportioned to the states in which at least one member of the group has nexus.

EXAMPLE 20

Crafts Corporation organized its departments as separate corporations on the basis of function: mining copper ore, refining the ore, and fabricating the refined copper into consumer products. Even though the various steps in the process are operated substantially independently of each other with only general supervision from Crafts' executive offices, Crafts is engaged in a single unitary business. Its various divisions are part of a large, vertically structured enterprise in which each business segment needs the products or raw materials provided by another. The flow of products among the affiliates also provides evidence of functional integration, which generally requires some form of central decision or policy making, another characteristic of a unitary business.

More than half of the states require or allow unitary reporting. Notice that the application of the unitary theory is based on a series of subjective observations about the organization and operation of the taxpayer's businesses, while the availability of Federal affiliated group status (see text Section 17-2d) is based on objective, mechanical ownership tests.

24-3b Tax Effects of the Unitary Theory

Use of the unitary approach by a state eliminates several of the planning techniques that could be used to shift income between corporate segments to avoid or minimize state taxes. In addition, the unitary approach usually results in a larger portion of the corporation's income being taxable in states where the compensation, property values, and sales prices are high relative to other states. This occurs because the larger in-state costs (numerators in the apportionment formula) include in the tax base a larger portion of the taxable income within the state's taxing jurisdiction. This has an adverse effect on the corporation's overall state tax burden if the states in which the larger portions are allocated impose a high tax rate relative to the other states in which the business is conducted.

The presence of a unitary business is favorable when losses of unprofitable affiliates may be offset against the earnings of profitable affiliates. It also is favorable when income earned in a high-tax state may be shifted to low-tax states due to the use of combined apportionment factors.

Effects of Unitary Computations

EXAMPLE 21

Rita Corporation owns two subsidiaries, Brown and Tan. Brown, located in State K, generated taxable income of $700,000. During this same period, Tan, located in State M, generated a loss of $400,000. If the subsidiaries are independent corporations, Brown is required to pay State K tax on $700,000 of income.

However, if the corporations constitute a unitary business, the incomes, as well as the apportionment factors, of the two entities are combined. As a result, the combined income of $300,000 ($700,000 − $400,000) is apportioned to unitary States K and M.

EXAMPLE 22

Eve Corporation, a wholly owned subsidiary of Dan Corporation, generated $1,000,000 of taxable income. Eve's activities and sales are restricted to State P, which imposes a 10% income tax. Dan's income for the taxable period is $1,500,000. Dan's activities and sales are restricted to State Q, which imposes a 5% income tax. Both states use a three-factor apportionment formula that equally weights sales, payroll, and property. Sales, payroll, and average property for each of the corporations are as follows.

	Eve Corporation	Dan Corporation	Total
Sales	$3,000,000	$7,000,000	$10,000,000
Payroll	2,000,000	3,500,000	5,500,000
Property	2,500,000	4,500,000	7,000,000

If the corporations are independent entities, the overall state income tax liability is $175,000.

State P (10% × $1,000,000)	=	$100,000
State Q (5% × $1,500,000)	=	75,000
Total state income tax		$175,000

If the corporations are members of a unitary business, the income and apportionment factors are combined in determining the income tax liability in unitary States P and Q. As a result of the combined reporting, the overall state income tax liability is reduced.

State P Income Tax

Total apportionable income			$2,500,000	
Apportionment formula				
Sales ($3,000,000/$10,000,000)	=	30.00%		
Payroll ($2,000,000/$5,500,000)	=	36.36%		
Property ($2,500,000/$7,000,000)	=	35.71%		
Total		102.07%		
Average (102.07% ÷ 3)			× 34.02%	
State P taxable income			$ 850,500	
Tax rate			× 10%	
State P tax liability				$85,050

State Q Income Tax

Total apportionable income			$2,500,000	
Apportionment formula				
Sales ($7,000,000/$10,000,000)	=	70.00%		
Payroll ($3,500,000/$5,500,000)	=	63.64%		
Property ($4,500,000/$7,000,000)	=	64.29%		
Total		197.93%		
Average (197.93% ÷ 3)			× 65.98%	
State Q taxable income			$1,649,500	
Tax rate			× 5%	
State Q tax liability				$82,475

continued

Total State Income Tax

Total state income tax if nonunitary	$ 175,000
Total state income tax if unitary ($85,050 + $82,475)	(167,525)
Tax reduction from unitary combined reporting	$ 7,475

The results of unitary reporting would have been detrimental if State Q had imposed a higher rate of tax than State P, because a larger percentage of the corporation's income is attributable to State Q when the apportionment factors are combined.

24-3c Consolidated and Combined Returns

As discussed in Chapter 17, an affiliated group of corporations may file a consolidated Federal return if all members of the group consent. Once such a return has been filed, the group must continue to file on a consolidated basis as long as it remains in existence, or until permission to file separate returns has been obtained. The consolidated return essentially treats the controlled corporations as a single taxable entity. As a result, the affiliated group pays only one tax, based on the combined income of its members after certain adjustments (e.g., net operating losses) and eliminations (e.g., intercompany dividends and inventory profits).

Several states permit affiliated corporations to file a consolidated return if such a return has been filed for Federal purposes. The filing of a consolidated return is mandatory in only a few states.

Usually, only corporations that are subject to tax in the state can be included in a consolidated return, unless specific requirements are met or the state permits the inclusion of corporations that do not have in-state nexus.

Do not confuse elective consolidated returns with required combined returns in unitary states. A combined return is filed in every unitary state in which one or more of the affiliates have nexus. A consolidated return often includes an election for affiliates to join in a return-filing group as initiated by the taxpayers; most states apply rules similar to those presented in text Section 17-2d.

GLOBAL TAX ISSUES   Water's Edge Is Not a Day at the Beach

As a result of pressure from the business community, the Federal government, and foreign countries, most of the states that impose an income tax on a unitary business's worldwide operations permit a multinational business to elect water's edge unitary reporting as an alternative to worldwide unitary filing.

The water's edge provision permits a multinational corporation to elect to limit the reach of the state's taxing jurisdiction over out-of-state affiliates to activities occurring within the boundaries of the United States. The decision to make a water's edge election may have a substantial effect on the apportionment computations and the tax liability of a multinational corporation. A water's edge election usually cannot be revoked for a number of years without permission from the appropriate tax authority.

Corporations making this election may be assessed an additional tax or fee for the privilege of excluding out-of-state entities from the combined report.

Concept Summary 24.3

Using Apportionment Formulas

1. The sales factor is based on the ultimate destination concept for sales of tangible personal property. Other rules apply when a sale of services is involved and when other exceptions are available.

2. The payroll factor generally includes compensation that is included in Federal gross income, but some states include excludible fringe benefits. An employee's compensation usually is not divided among states.

3. The property factor generally is derived using the average undepreciated historical costs for the assets and eight times the rental value of the assets.

4. The unitary theory may require the taxpayer to include worldwide activities and holdings in the apportionment factors. A *water's edge election* can limit these amounts to U.S. transactions.

5. When the unitary theory applies, a combined return is filed. This is different from the consolidated return that an affiliated group of corporations would file for Federal income tax purposes.

LO.7

Discuss the states' income tax treatment of S corporations, partnerships, and LLCs.

24-4 TAXATION OF S CORPORATIONS

The majority of the states that impose a corporate income tax apply special provisions, similar to the Federal law, that govern the taxation of S corporations. Only a few states—including New York and Tennessee—and the District of Columbia do not provide pass-through (no corporate-level tax) treatment for Federal S corporations.

In the non-S election states, a Federal S corporation generally is subject to tax in the same manner as a C corporation. As a result, if a multistate S corporation operates in any of these states, it is subject to state income tax and does not realize one of the primary benefits of S status—the avoidance of double taxation. Other potential tax-related benefits of the S election, such as the immediate deduction of net operating losses, may not be allowed.

EXAMPLE 23

Horizon, Inc., an S corporation, has established nexus in States A and B. State A recognizes S corporation status; State B does not. Horizon generated $600,000 of ordinary business income and $100,000 of dividends that were received from corporations in which Horizon owns 5% of the stock. Horizon's State B apportionment percentage is 50%.

For State B tax purposes, Horizon first computes its income as though it were a C corporation. It then apportions the resulting income to State B. Assuming that State B has adopted the Federal provisions governing the dividends received deduction, Horizon's income, determined as though it were a C corporation, is $650,000 {$600,000 + [(100% − 50%) × $100,000]}. Accordingly, Horizon may be subject to State B corporate income tax on $325,000 ($650,000 × 50% apportionment percentage) of taxable income.

24-4a Eligibility

All of the states that recognize S status permit a corporation to be treated as an S corporation for state purposes only if the corporation has a valid Federal S election in place. Generally, the filing of a Federal S election is sufficient to render the corporation an S corporation for state tax purposes. In most states, an entity that is an S corporation for Federal tax purposes automatically is treated as an S corporation for state tax purposes. New Jersey requires a separate state-level S election, and Pennsylvania allows the entity to *elect out* of its S status for state purposes.

24-4b State Tax Filing Requirements

About half of the states require the corporation to withhold taxes on the nonresident shareholders' portions of the entity's income.

Maple, an S corporation, is subject to income tax only in Vermont. On the last day of its taxable year, 40% of Maple's stock is held by nonresident shareholders. Maple withholds Vermont income tax for its nonresident shareholders.

EXAMPLE
24

In an effort to decrease compliance burdens and simplify the filing process for nonresident shareholders of S corporations, several states allow an S corporation to file a single income tax return and pay the resulting tax on behalf of some or all of its nonresident shareholders. State requirements for the filing of a "block" or **composite return** vary substantially.

24-5 TAXATION OF PARTNERSHIPS AND LLCS

Most states apply income tax provisions to partnerships, limited liability companies (LLCs), and limited liability partnerships (LLPs) in a manner that parallels Federal treatment. For income tax purposes, the entity is a tax-reporting, not a taxpaying, entity. Income, loss, and credit items are allocated and apportioned among the partners according to the terms of the partnership agreement and state income tax law.

Some states require that the entity make estimated tax payments on behalf of out-of-state partners. This approach helps to ensure that nonresident partners file appropriate forms and pay any resulting tax to the state. As is the case with S corporations, some states allow composite returns to be filed relative to out-of-state partners.

A few states impose a minimum income tax on flow-through entities, including S corporations, LLCs, and partnerships. Such a tax might be computed, for instance, as the greater of $800 or 1.5 percent of net revenues.

24-6 OTHER STATE AND LOCAL TAXES

LO.8
Describe other commonly encountered state and local taxes on businesses.

24-6a State and Local Sales and Use Taxes

Forty-five states and the District of Columbia impose a sales tax on retail sales of tangible personal property for use or consumption. In many of these states, in-state localities, including cities, towns, school districts, and counties, also have the power to levy a sales tax; likely 10,000 such taxing jurisdictions exist in the United States. A sales tax is imposed directly on the purchaser who acquires the asset at retail; the tax is measured by the price of the sale. The vendor or retailer merely acts as a collection agent for the government.

A use tax is designed to complement the sales tax. A use tax arises when the product in a taxable sale is sold in or shipped to another jurisdiction, one with which the seller has no sales tax nexus. The resulting use tax is payable to the customer's state and is the obligation of the purchaser. Rarely, the purchaser remits this tax to his or her state. More often, the seller collects the tax and remits it to the customer's state. See Exhibit 24.4.

The use tax has two purposes: to prevent consumers from evading sales tax by purchasing goods outside the state for in-state use, and to provide an equitable sales environment between in-state and out-of-state retailers.

Generally, sales of tangible personal property are subject to tax. In several states, selected services and digital goods also are subject to tax.

Each jurisdiction that applies a sales/use tax defines its own tax base (i.e., which items are taxable and to whom). For a multistate business, complying with the thousands of sets of sales/use tax statutes and regulations can be a difficult burden. In an effort to ease this confusion, state and local government officials in about half of the states developed the Streamlined Sales Tax Project (SSTP). Members working in conjunction with the SSTP wrote a model law for taxing jurisdictions to adopt, thereby allowing for a more uniform application of the rules and for a more efficient exchange of information among revenue agencies. However, little interest has been shown in having identical sales/use tax rates among all the taxing jurisdictions.

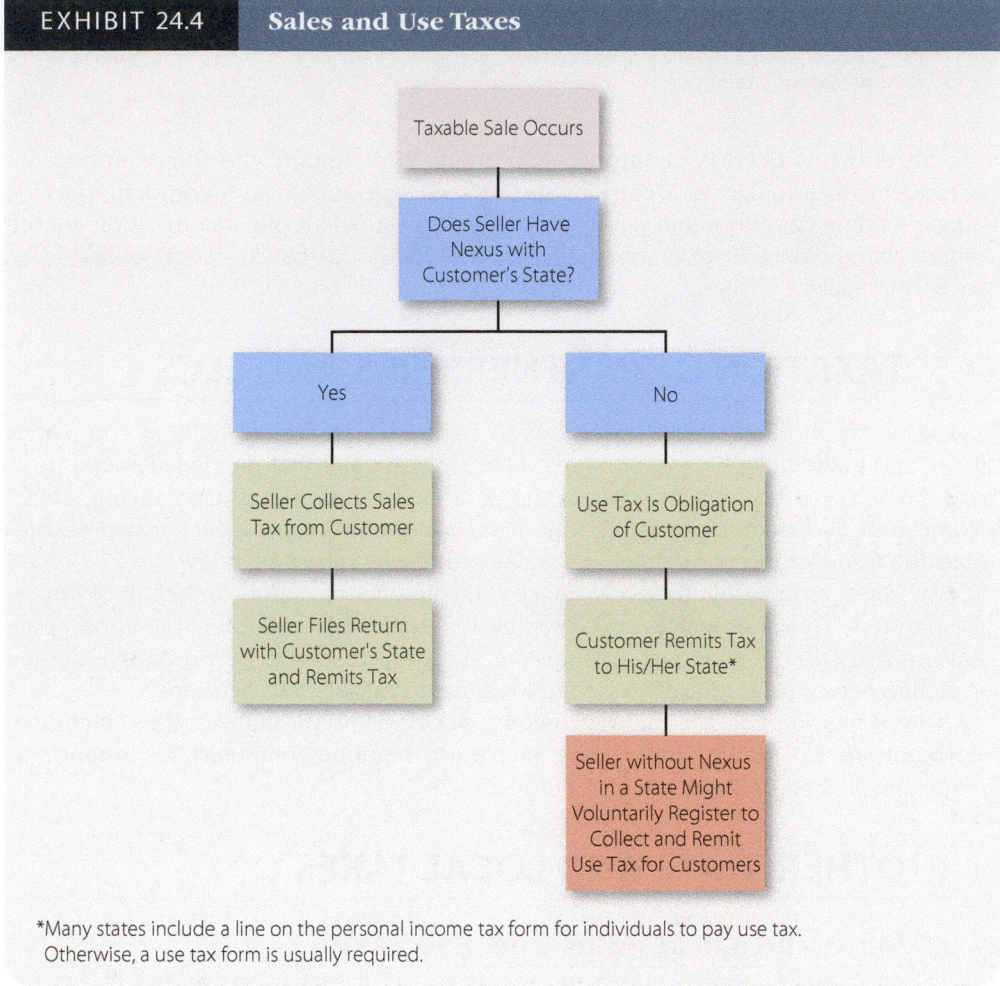

| EXHIBIT 24.4 | Sales and Use Taxes |

*Many states include a line on the personal income tax form for individuals to pay use tax. Otherwise, a use tax form is usually required.

To date, the most commonly adopted SSTP rules are those defining which products and services are subject to sales/use tax. For instance, SSTP rules set out the items of clothing that would be subject to tax, but each jurisdiction decides on its own whether to include clothing in the tax base and whether to allow "back-to-school" clothing amnesties (or holidays) during specific weeks of the year.

Sales/Use Tax Exemptions

A majority of the states exempt sales of certain items from the sales/use tax base. The most common exemptions and exclusions include the following.

- *Sales for resale* are exempt because the purchaser is not the ultimate user of the sold property. For instance, meat purchased by a grocer and a garment purchased by a retailer are not subject to sales/use tax under the resale rule.

- *Casual or occasional sales* that occur infrequently are exempt from the sales/use tax base chiefly for administrative convenience. Most states exclude rummage sales, the transfer of an entire business, and the like under this rule.

- Most *purchases by exempt organizations* are excluded from taxable sales. Charities, governments and their agencies, and other organizations qualifying for Federal income tax exemption (see text Section 23-2) are relieved of sales/use tax liabilities in all of the states.

- *Sales of necessities* such as groceries and medical prescriptions and equipment. Restaurant and other prepared meals typically are subject to tax, though.

- *Sales of targeted items* can be exempt to improve the equity of the sales/use tax system or support particular industries. Special exemptions for sales of farm, industrial, and computing equipment are allowed by several states.

- *Economic development concerns* A state or local government might waive the tax for a period of time to encourage a business to move to or remain in the jurisdiction.
- Certain *sales to manufacturers, producers, and processors* also may be exempt. Exemptions usually include one or more of the following.
  - Containers and other packing, packaging, and shipping materials actually used to transfer merchandise to customers of the purchaser.
  - Machines and specific processing equipment and repair parts or replacements exclusively and directly used in manufacturing tangible personal property.

Sales/Use Tax Nexus

Rules governing nexus for sales/use taxes are different from those used for income taxes. The regular solicitation of sales by independent brokers establishes sufficient nexus to require a nonresident seller to register and collect the use tax, even though the seller does not have regular employees, agents, and an office or other place of business in the state.[14] As a result, a corporation may be required to collect sales and use taxes in a state even though it is immune from the imposition of an income tax.

The states have a great degree of freedom to define sales/use tax nexus in their jurisdictions.[15] Nexus definitions for this purpose range from having a physical presence in the state to having customers in the jurisdiction (e.g., where the seller's only contact with the jurisdiction is through online sales).[16]

One common economic nexus rule, adopted by most of the states, makes the seller taxable in the state for the year if at least $100,000 in sales or 200 sales transactions are found. Sales/use tax nexus also is established in most states for a seller who uses affiliated vendors to take orders and process sales (e.g., Amazon is such a *marketplace facilitator* and must collect the sales/use tax with respect to sales made by its affiliates).

Sales/Use Tax on Services

Some states have added specific service transactions to their sales/use tax base. The services most commonly subjected to tax include transactions involving hotels and restaurants, hair and beauty salons, entertainment events, cable and satellite television subscriptions, and lawn care. To date, extension of the tax base for legal/accounting, medical, education, and advertising services largely has been blocked in most legislatures by the providers of these services.

Revenue shortfalls at the state and local levels and shifts in the general economy to the sales of services and goods other than tangible personal property, however, have led some legislatures to expand the sales/use tax base to include a broader array of consumption. For instance, some states tax the transfer of digital goods, such as downloads of songs, books, software, and games.

24-6b **Local Property Taxes**

Property taxes, a major source of revenue at the city and county levels, often are designated as *ad valorem* taxes because they are based on the value of property that is located in the state on a specific date. Generally, that date fixes taxable ownership, situs (location), and the valuation of the property.

Property taxes can take the form of either real property taxes or personal property taxes. States apply different tax rates and means of assessment to the two classes of property.

Although a personal property tax may be imposed on both intangible and tangible property, most states limit the tax to tangible property. The distinction between the various items of personal property is important because special rates, computations, or exemptions may apply. For instance, inventory constitutes tangible personal property, but it is exempt from property taxation in most states.

---

[14]*Scripto, Inc., v. Carson*, 362 U.S. 207 (1960).

[15]These privileges were confirmed in *South Dakota v. Wayfair, Inc.*, 138 S.Ct. 2080 (2018).

[16]Most taxing jurisdictions establish a *de minimis* rule, providing relief for sellers with only a limited amount of sales in the state.

24-6c **Other Taxes**

States may impose a variety of other state and local taxes on corporations, including incorporation or entrance fees or taxes, gross receipt taxes, stock transfer taxes, realty transfer and mortgage recording taxes, license taxes, and franchise taxes based on net worth or capital stock outstanding.

Administrative Taxes

An *incorporation tax* is an excise tax for the corporate privilege conferred on the business. At the time the business is incorporated, the state generally imposes a fee or tax for the privilege of conducting business as a corporation within the state. Similarly, an out-of-state corporation usually must pay an entrance fee or tax before it can transact business in a state other than its state of incorporation.

A *license tax* is an excise tax on the privilege of engaging in a certain business, occupation, or profession. A jurisdiction may impose business, occupational, or professional license taxes as a means of generating revenue or regulating the activities of the business, occupation, or profession for the public welfare.

Taxes on nonresident visitors to a state are common, since the one who pays the tax lives somewhere else and cannot vote against it. Examples are taxes on hotel rooms (such as a *transient occupancy tax*), rental cars, and other transient arrangements, like house sharing or swapping.

Stock and realty transfer and mortgage recording taxes are nonrecurring taxes that are imposed at the time of recording or transfer. *Stock transfer taxes* are imposed on the transfer of shares or certificates of stock of domestic and foreign corporations. The tax typically is based on the number of shares transferred and the par or market value of the stock.

The base of the *realty transfer tax* usually is measured by the consideration paid or to be paid for the realty. The *mortgage recording tax* may be based on the actual consideration given, the value of the property, or the debt to be secured by the instrument.

Collections of Unclaimed Property

All of the U.S. states enforce rules that allow them to take possession of certain unclaimed property. In essence, this procedure acts like a tax on businesses with large consumer operations.

Unclaimed property might take the form of an unused gift card or a paycheck the employee has not yet cashed. On the balance sheet, these amounts are reported as payables by the business. After a stated period of time passes (usually 5 or more years) and an effort is made to contact the holder of the business's obligation, the value of the property reverts to the state. These rights of the states often are referred to as *escheat* laws.

Because unclaimed property rules are not enacted as a taxing statute, the usual nexus and apportionment tests do not apply. Instead, the property is taken by the state in which the business is incorporated.[17]

Capital Stock and Franchise Taxes

Typically, a *capital stock tax* is an excise tax imposed on a domestic corporation for the privilege of existing as a corporation or imposed on an out-of-state corporation, either for the privilege of doing business or for the actual transaction of business within the state. This annual tax usually is based on the book value of the corporation's net worth, including capital, surplus, and retained earnings.

The majority of capital stock taxes are apportioned if the corporation does business or maintains an office in another state. In some states, however, the tax is levied on the entire authorized or issued capital stock of a domestic corporation, even though the corporation may be engaged in business in other states.

---

[17]*Texas v. New Jersey,* 379 U.S. 674 (1965).

State Franchise Tax on Net Worth

The balance sheet of Bull, a domestic corporation of State A, at the end of its taxable year is as follows.

EXAMPLE
25

Cash	$ 100,000
Equipment (net of $50,000 accumulated depreciation)	150,000
Building (net of $75,000 accumulated depreciation)	225,000
Land	125,000
Total assets	$ 600,000
Accounts payable and other short-term liabilities	$ 100,000
Long-term liabilities	200,000
Capital stock	50,000
Paid-in capital in excess of par value	50,000
Retained earnings	200,000
Total liabilities and equity	$ 600,000

State A imposes a 2% franchise tax based on the entire net worth of a domestic corporation. Bull is subject to a franchise tax in State A of $6,000 ($600,000 assets − $300,000 liabilities = $300,000 net worth × 2% rate).

Continue with the facts of Example 25, except that State A subjects a domestic corporation to tax only on the capital that is employed in the state. Bull properly determines that its State A apportionment percentage is 20%. In this case, Bull's State A franchise tax liability is $1,200 ($300,000 net worth × 20% apportionment percentage = $60,000 capital employed in State A × 2% rate).

EXAMPLE
26

ETHICS & EQUITY **Encouraging Economic Development through Tax Concessions**

The tax professional occasionally is in a position to negotiate with a state or city taxing jurisdiction to garner tax relief for a client as an incentive to locate a plant or distribution center in that geographic area. In times when construction budgets are high and interstate competition is fierce to attract or retain businesses that are making location decisions, such tax concessions can be significant.

For instance, to encourage a business to build a large distribution center in the area, community leaders might be agreeable to (1) paying for roads, sewer, water, and other improvements after issuing bonds, (2) reducing property taxes by 50 percent for the first 10 years of the center's operations, or (3) offering interest rate discounts or cash grants for the construction of new facilities. For corporate taxpayers, cash incentive payments received from a government or civic group constitute gross income.[18]

An incentive-granting community provides the concessions even though the influx of new workers may place a strain on public school facilities and likely necessitate improvements in traffic patterns and other infrastructure.

Consider the position of a large employer that has been located in the area for more than 50 years. By how much should it be willing to absorb the tax increases that result when economic development concessions are used to attract new, perhaps temporary, businesses to the area? Should the employer challenge the constitutionality of the grant of such sizable tax breaks to some, but not all, business taxpayers in the jurisdiction?

What should be the rate of "impact fees" assessed on new developments? Does your analysis change if the new business competes with the longtime resident for sales? For employees? For political power?

---

[18]§ 118(b)(2). See also CCA 20085201F.

LO.9

Recognize tax planning opportunities available to minimize a corporation's state and local tax liability.

24-7 TAX PLANNING

The inconsistencies in the tax laws and rates among the states not only complicate state tax planning but also provide the nucleus of pertinent planning opportunities. Although several income tax planning devices are available to a corporation that does business in only one state, most planning techniques are directed toward corporations that do business or maintain property in more than one state. All suggested tax planning strategies should be reviewed in light of practical business considerations and the additional administrative and other costs that may be incurred, because simply minimizing state taxes may not be prudent from a business perspective.

24-7a Selecting the Optimal State in Which to Operate

Because the states employ different definitions of the amount and type of activity necessary to establish nexus, a company has some latitude in selecting the states by which it will be taxed. When a corporation has only a limited connection with a high-tax state, it may abandon that activity by electing an alternative means of accomplishing the same result. For example, if providing a sales representative with a company-owned iPad constitutes nexus in an undesired state, the company could eliminate its connection with that state by reimbursing sales personnel for equipment expenses, instead of providing a company communications device. Similarly, when nexus is caused by conducting customer training sessions or seminars in the state, the corporation could conduct the meetings in another way. This can be done by sending the personnel to a nearby state in which nexus clearly has been established or in which the activity would not constitute nexus, or by meeting electronically.

In addition, when sufficient activity originates from the repair and maintenance of the corporation's products or the activities performed by the sales representatives within the state, the organization could incorporate the service or sales divisions. This would invalidate a nonunitary state's right to tax the parent corporation's income; only the income of the service or sales divisions would be subject to tax. However, this technique is successful only if the incorporated division is a *bona fide* business operation. Therefore, the pricing of any sales or services between the new subsidiary and the parent corporation must be at arm's length, and the operations of the new corporation preferably should result in a profit.

Although planning techniques often are employed to disconnect a corporation's activities from an undesirable state, they also can be utilized to create nexus in a desirable state. For example, when the presence of a company-owned computer creates nexus in a desirable state, the corporation could provide its sales representatives in that state with company-owned equipment, rather than reimbursing or providing increased compensation for equipment costs.

Establishing nexus in a state is advantageous, for instance, when that state has a lower tax rate than the state in which the income currently is taxed or when losses or credits become available to reduce tax liabilities in the state.

EXAMPLE

27

Bird Corporation generates $500,000 of taxable income from selling goods; specifically, 40% of its product is sold in State A and 60% in State B. Both states levy a corporate income tax and include only the sales factor in their apportionment formulas. The tax rate in State A is 10%; State B's rate is only 3%. Bird's manufacturing operation is located in State A; therefore, the corporation's income is subject to tax in that state. Currently, Bird is immune from tax under P.L. 86–272 in State B. Because State A has adopted a throwback provision, Bird incurs $50,000 of state income taxes.

	Apportionment Formula	Net Income	Tax Rate	Tax
State A	100/100	$500,000	10%	$50,000
State B	0/100	500,000	3%	–0–
Total tax liability				$50,000

continued

Because State B imposes a lower tax rate than State A does, Bird substantially reduces its state tax liability if sufficient nexus is created with State B.

	Apportionment Formula	Net Income	Tax Rate	Tax
State A	40/100	$500,000	10%	$20,000
State B	60/100	500,000	3%	9,000
Total tax liability				$29,000

24-7b Restructuring Corporate Entities

One of the major objectives of state tax planning is to design the proper mix of corporate entities. An optimal mix of entities often generates the lowest combined state income tax for the corporation. The goal of designing a good corporate combination often is to situate the highly profitable entities in states that impose a low (or no) income tax.

Matching Tax Rates and Corporate Income

When the corporation must operate in a high-tax state, divisions that generate losses also should be located there. Alternatively, unprofitable or less profitable operations can be merged into profitable operations to reduce the overall income subject to tax in the state. An ideal candidate for this type of merger may be a research and development subsidiary that is only marginally profitable but is vital to the parent corporation's strategic goals, and that may attract research credits and incentives for the taxpayer. By using simulation models, a variety of different combinations can be tested to determine the optimal corporate structure.

Unitary Operations

By identifying the states that have adopted the unitary method and the criteria under which a particular state defines a unitary business, a taxpayer may reduce its overall state tax by restructuring its corporate relationships to create or guard against a unitary relationship. For instance, an independent business enterprise can be made unitary by exercising day-to-day operational control and by centralizing functions such as marketing, financing, accounting, and legal services.

The Big Picture

EXAMPLE
28

Return to the facts of *The Big Picture* on p. 24-1. Assume that LocalCo already operates in both unitary and nonunitary states. Application of unitary corporate income tax rules can make tax planning more difficult. Subjecting certain LocalCo activities to the unitary theory could either increase or decrease the combined corporate income tax liability of the affiliates, depending especially on the apportionment formulas applied in the unitary states.

LocalCo needs to make projections of the profitability of its operations in the new multifunction building. Then LocalCo should determine the income tax effects of expanding its operations into several target states, including both unitary and nonunitary jurisdictions, and compare how the unitary rules (and all associated compliance costs) affect its after-tax profits.

Passive Investment Companies

The creation of a **passive investment company** is another restructuring technique utilized to minimize a nonunitary corporation's state tax burden. Nonbusiness or passive/portfolio income generally is allocated to the state in which the income-producing asset is located, rather than being apportioned among the states in which the corporation does business. Therefore, significant tax savings may be realized when nonbusiness assets are located in a state that either does not levy an income tax or provides favorable tax treatment for passive/portfolio income.

The corporation need not be domiciled in the state to benefit from these favorable provisions. Instead, the tax savings can be realized by forming a passive investment subsidiary to hold the intangible assets and handle the corporation's investment activities.

The passive investment subsidiary technique usually produces the desired result in any no-tax state. Delaware, however, often is selected for this purpose due to its other corporate statutory provisions and favorable political, business, and legal climate.

Delaware does not impose an income tax upon a corporation whose only activity within the state is the maintenance and management of intangible investments and the collection and distribution of income from such investments or from tangible property physically located in another state. Consequently, trademarks, patents, stock, and other intangible property can be transferred to a Delaware corporation whose activity is limited to collecting such income. The assets can be transferred to the subsidiary without incurring a current Federal income tax on the exchange (see text Section 18-1).

However, to receive the desired preferential state tax treatment, the holding company's activities within the state must be sufficient to establish income tax nexus in the state. The passive investment company should avoid performing any activity outside the state that may result in establishing nexus with another state. In addition, the formation of the subsidiary must be properly implemented to ensure the legal substance of the operation. The passive investment company must have a physical office, and it must function as an independent operation.

Because the subsidiary's activities are confined to Delaware (or some other no- or low-tax state) and its operations generate only passive/portfolio income, its income will not be taxed in any nonunitary state. Moreover, most states exclude dividends from taxation or otherwise treat them favorably; therefore, the earnings of a passive investment subsidiary can be distributed as a dividend to the parent at a minimal tax cost. If the state in which the parent is located does not levy the full income tax on dividends received, the entire measure of passive/portfolio income may escape taxation.

EXAMPLE 29

Purple Corporation generates $800,000 of taxable income; $600,000 is income from its manufacturing operations, and $200,000 is dividend income from passive investments. All of Purple's sales are made and assets are kept in State A, which imposes a 10% corporate income tax and permits a 100% deduction for dividends received from subsidiaries. The corporation is not subject to tax in any other state. Consequently, Purple incurs $80,000 of income tax (tax base $800,000 × tax rate 10%).

If Purple creates a passive investment subsidiary in State B, which does not impose an income tax upon a corporation whose only activity within the state is the maintenance and management of passive investments, Purple's tax liability is reduced by $20,000 (a 25% decrease). Because such income is nonapportionable (allocated for state tax purposes to the state in which it is located), the income earned from its passive investments is not subject to tax in State A.

	State A (Purple Corporation)	State B (Passive Investment Company)
Taxable income	$600,000	$200,000
Tax rate	× 10%	× –0–*
Tax liability	$ 60,000	$ –0–
Tax liability without restructuring		$ 80,000
Tax liability with restructuring		(60,000)
Tax reduction due to use of subsidiary		$ 20,000

*B does not impose an income tax on a passive investment corporation.

The income earned by the subsidiary from its passive investments can be distributed to Purple as a dividend without incurring a tax liability because State A allows a 100% deduction for dividends that are received from subsidiary corporations.

These desired results, however, will not be fully available in states that view the entire corporate operation as being unitary. Because those states require combined reporting, the income earned by the passive investment subsidiary is included in the corporation's apportionable or allocable income. Other states may levy gross receipts taxes or restrict interest and dividend deductions, or legislatively include in the income tax base any income resulting from credit card usage by customers or the use of intangible or digital assets in the state,[19] to limit the effectiveness of the passive investment subsidiary.

24-7c Subjecting the Corporation's Income to Apportionment

When a multistate organization is domiciled in a high-tax state, some of its apportionable income is eliminated from the tax base in that state. In light of the high tax rate, this may result in significant tax savings. Apportioning income will be especially effective where the income that is attributed to the other states is not subject to income tax. The income removed from the taxing jurisdiction of the domicile state entirely escapes state income taxation when the state to which the income is attributed (1) does not levy a corporate income tax, (2) requires a higher level of activity necessary to subject an out-of-state company to taxation than that adopted by the state of domicile, or (3) is prohibited under P.L. 86–272 from taxing the income (assuming that the domicile state has not adopted a throwback provision). As a result, the right to apportion income may provide substantial benefits because the out-of-state sales are excluded from the numerator of the sales factor and may not be taxed in another state.

However, to acquire the right to apportion its income, the organization must have sufficient activities in or contacts with one or more other states. Whether the type and amount of activities and/or contacts are considered adequate is determined by the other state's nexus rules. Therefore, a corporation should analyze its current activities in and contacts with other states to determine which, if any, activities or contacts could be redirected so that the corporation gains the right to apportion its income.

The Big Picture

EXAMPLE 30

Return to the facts of *The Big Picture* on p. 24-1. Most corporate taxpayers consist of a parent corporation and perhaps one or more existing subsidiaries. Given its expansion plans, LocalCo has the opportunity to determine "from scratch" in which states it wants to create nexus for the operations in the multifunction building.

The tax professional needs to offer advice to LocalCo's board of directors as to where the building might be situated and how the operations of any related sales and administrative personnel might be structured in an effort to provide optimal tax consequences. Nexus issues to be considered include the following.

- Is income tax nexus created with the target state?

- Is sales/use tax nexus created with the target state?

- How are the income tax apportionment factors affected by the expansion plans (e.g., whether the target state uses a property factor in the apportionment formula and, if so, how it is weighted)?

- Would a building such as that planned by LocalCo receive any special computational treatment for the target state's property factor (e.g., in averaging the building's costs or applying accumulated depreciation)?

---

[19]These laws often are rooted in *Geoffrey, Inc. v. South Carolina Tax Commission*, 437 SE2d 13 (SC S.Ct., 1993).

ETHICS & EQUITY   Can You Be a Nowhere Adviser?

The intent of much of today's multistate income tax planning is to create so-called *nowhere sales*, such that the income from the transaction is not subject to tax in any state. Suppose, for instance, that a sale is made from Georgia (a state with no throwback rule) into Nevada (the place of ultimate destination, but a state with no income tax). No state-level income tax liability is generated.

Is it ethical for a tax adviser to suggest such a strategy? Could you ethically propose the establishment of a sales office in a nonthrowback state, thereby avoiding state income tax on a transaction that is fully taxable under Federal rules?

24-7d Planning with Apportionment Factors

Sales Factor

Working with the sales factor often yields the greatest planning opportunities for a multistate corporation. In-state receipts include sales to purchasers with a destination point in that state; sales delivered to out-of-state purchasers are included in the numerator of the sales factor of the destination state. However, to be permitted to exclude out-of-state sales from the sales factor of the origination state, the seller generally must substantiate the shipment of goods to an out-of-state location. Therefore, the destinations of sales that a corporation makes and the means by which the goods are shipped must be carefully reviewed.

The corporation's overall state tax possibly can be reduced by establishing a better record-keeping system or by affecting the numerator of the sales factor by changing the delivery location or method.

For example, a corporation may substantially reduce its state income tax if the delivery location of its sales is changed from a state in which the company is taxed to one in which it is not. This technique may not benefit the corporation if the state in which the sales originate has adopted the throwback rule.

Property Factor

Because most fixed assets are physically stationary in nature, the property factor is not so easily manipulated in the short term. Nonetheless, significant tax savings can be realized by establishing a leasing subsidiary in a low- or no-tax state. If the property is located in a state that does not include leased assets in the property factor, the establishment of a subsidiary from which to lease the property eliminates the assets from the property factor in the parent's state.

Permanently idle property generally is excluded from the property factor. As a result, a corporation should identify and remove such assets from the property factor to ensure that the factor is not distorted.

EXAMPLE 31

The property factor valuations of Quake Corporation's holdings are as follows.

	State A	Total
Equipment (average historical cost)	$1,200,000	$2,000,000
Accumulated depreciation (average)	800,000	1,000,000

Twenty percent of the equipment in State A is fully depreciated and is idle. Assuming that State A includes property in the factor at historical cost, Quake's property factor is 54.55% [($1,200,000 − $240,000 idle property)/($2,000,000 − $240,000)]. If the idle property is not removed from the property factor, Quake's property factor in State A is incorrectly computed as 60% ($1,200,000/$2,000,000).

Payroll Factor

The payroll factor provides income tax planning potential where several corporate employees spend substantial periods of time outside their state of employment or the corporation is able to relocate highly paid employees to low- or no-tax states.

Because the commissions paid to independent contractors are excluded from the payroll factor, the taxpayer may reduce its payroll factor in a high-tax state.

> Yellow Corporation's total payroll costs are $1,400,000. Of this amount, $1,000,000 was attributable to State A, a high-tax state. Yellow's payroll factor in State A is 71.43% ($1,000,000/$1,400,000).
>
> Assuming that $200,000 of the State A compensation had been paid to sales representatives and that Yellow replaced its sales force with independent contractors, Yellow's payroll factor in State A would be reduced to 66.67% [($1,000,000 − $200,000)/($1,400,000 − $200,000)].

EXAMPLE 32

24-7e Sales/Use Tax Compliance

A seller conceivably must deal with thousands of different sales/use taxing jurisdictions, each with its own forms and filing deadlines, rates of applicable tax, and definitions of what is taxable or exempt. Examples of issues on which jurisdictions may disagree, presenting compliance problems for sellers, include the following.

- Are snack foods exempt groceries or taxable candy?
- Are therapeutic stockings exempt medical supplies or taxable clothing?
- Which types of software are subject to tax?

24-7f Capital Stock Taxation

Capital stock tax liabilities can be significant for capital-intensive taxpayers to the extent they reinvest a large portion of retained earnings (the tax base) in productive assets. If all nontax factors are equal, a taxpayer with sizable exposure to a capital stock tax should consider the following techniques.

- Funding expansion with debt rather than retained earnings.
- Funding subsidiary operations with debt rather than direct capital contributions.
- Regularly paying dividends to parent companies that are domiciled in tax-favored states such as Delaware and Nevada.

REFOCUS ON THE BIG PICTURE

MAKING A MULTISTATE LOCATION DECISION

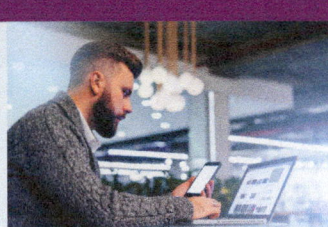

LocalCo holds a competitive advantage with the states and localities in negotiating where its new facility should be located. Politicians like to attract new facilities to their jurisdictions as a way to create construction jobs and to expand the income and sales/use tax base. LocalCo's top management should work with the governors and development executives of the states that are final candidates for the location of the proposed new building. LocalCo's agenda for these negotiations should include the following items.

- Many states offer targeted tax incentives to attract and retain "clean" businesses such as LocalCo. These incentives might include property tax abatements, research and investment credits, and tax waivers for the state and local income and payroll taxes on new jobs. The company should determine whether it qualifies for any existing incentives, and how to structure such incentives so as to avoid any

continued

FOXY BURROW/SHUTTERSTOCK.COM

inclusion in the gross income of the business. Government incentives such as tax abatements and infrastructure improvements are to be preferred for this purpose over upfront cash transfers.

- Currently, LocalCo's manufacturing operations are split between a low-tax state (Alabama) and a high-tax state (California). Under a relocation plan that does not jeopardize LocalCo's customer base, nexus might be eliminated with California and shifted to a low-tax jurisdiction. Nevada is a good candidate, given its proximity to the current sportswear location. But economic nexus thresholds might prevent this technique from working effectively.

- California applies the unitary theory of income taxation. LocalCo should determine whether unitary rules increase or decrease its total tax burden.

- Corporate headquarters currently are located in New York, another high-tax jurisdiction. If the new facility is located in a corporation-favorable, low-tax state, the company should consider moving its headquarters there.

- Relocating the corporate headquarters also could benefit the entity's highly paid executives. The individual income and sales/use tax burden of employees should be a factor in LocalCo's decision.

- States often assess special taxes on trucking and airport functions and might apply different income tax apportionment formulas to these operations. LocalCo's tax department and its outside advisers should research these features of the various relevant tax systems to avoid any unexpected surprises.

What If?

If LocalCo did not have a history of strong profitability, some of these state and local tax recommendations might be different. In that case, the company would consider issues such as how a state allows loss and credit carryovers. In addition, if there is no state income tax liability to pay, income tax credits and deductions would be less attractive, so the negotiations might focus on property and payroll taxes instead.

LocalCo's tax plans might be exposed to tax law changes that will work to its detriment. Its locations include some of the most aggressive legislatures and taxing agencies in the country, so the taxpayer must watch for changes in those states' rules concerning nexus, income sourcing, apportionment, and incentives. Tax planning ideas that work currently might be undone by the adoption of gross receipts taxes, a unitary approach, market-based income sourcing, or economic income and sales/use nexus provisions.

Key Terms

Allocate, 24-8	Nexus, 24-6	Throwback rule, 24-13
Apportion, 24-8	Passive investment company, 24-29	UDITPA, 24-6
Combined return, 24-18	Payroll factor, 24-14	Unclaimed property, 24-26
Composite return, 24-23	Property factor, 24-16	Unitary theory, 24-18
Dock sales, 24-13	Public Law 86–272, 24-6	Water's edge, 24-21
Multistate Tax Commission (MTC), 24-6	Sales factor, 24-13	

Discussion Questions

1. **LO.1** You are working with the top management of one of your clients in select-   *Critical Thinking*
   ing the U.S. location for a new manufacturing operation. Craft a plan for the   *Communications*
   CEO to use in discussions with the economic development representatives of several candidate states. In no more than three PowerPoint slides, list some of the tax
   incentives the CEO should request from a particular state during the negotiations.
   Be both creative and aggressive in the requests.

2. **LO.1** Complete the following chart by indicating whether each item is true or false.
   Explain your answers by referencing the overlap of rules appearing in Federal
   and most state income tax laws.

Item	True or False
a. Most of the states start with Federal taxable income in computing state taxable income.	_____
b. The states use a wide variety of rules to compute corporate taxable income; thus, there is no "typical" state income tax computation.	_____
c. Aggregate state taxable incomes always equal Federal taxable income; tax rules merely split the income among the states.	_____
d. The corporate income tax systems of most states can be described as applying progressive rate structures.	_____
e. A typical state income tax credit would equal 10% of the costs incurred to purchase and install solar energy panels for an existing factory.	_____

3. **LO.2** In no more than three PowerPoint slides, list some general guidelines   *Communications*
   that a taxpayer can use to determine whether it has an obligation to file an
   income tax return with a particular state. (Include the terms *nexus* and *domicile* in
   your answer.)

4. **LO.2** Josie is a sales representative for Talk2Me, a communications retailer based
   in Fort Smith, Arkansas. Josie's sales territory is Oklahoma, and she regularly
   takes day trips to Tulsa to meet with customers.
      During a typical sales call, Josie takes the customers' current orders for phones,
   cases, and attachments and, using an app on her wireless phone, sends the orders
   to headquarters in Fort Smith for immediate action. Approved orders are shipped
   from the Little Rock warehouse.
      Are Josie's sales subject to the Oklahoma corporate income tax? Explain.

5. **LO.2** Continue with the facts of Question 4. CheapPhones, one of Josie's customers
   who is facing tight cash-flow problems, wants to return about 100 defective
   cell phones. Talk2Me tells Josie to bring the phones back to headquarters. Fear-
   ing that she will lose CheapPhones as a customer if she does not comply with the
   request, Josie says, "Let me save you the time and cost of packing and shipping the
   defective phones. Put them in the trunk of my car, and I'll take them back." Does
   Josie's action change the answer to Question 4? Why or why not?

6. **LO.3** Indicate whether each of the following items should be *allocated* or *apportioned* by the taxpayer in computing state corporate taxable income. Assume
   that the state follows the general rules of UDITPA.
   a. Profits from sales activities.
   b. Profits from consulting and other service activities.
   c. Losses from sales activities.
   d. Profits from managing the stock portfolio of a client.
   e. Profits from managing one's own stock portfolio.
   f. Gain on the sale of a plot of land held by a real estate developer.

g. Gain on the sale of a plot of land held by a manufacturer, on which it may expand its factory.

h. Rent income received by a manufacturer from the leasing of space to a supplier.

Critical Thinking 7. **LO.3** Regarding the apportionment formula used to compute state taxable income, does each of the following independent characterizations describe a taxpayer that likely is based in state or out of state? Explain.

a. The sales factor is positively correlated with the payroll, but not the property, factor.

b. The sales factor is much higher than the property and payroll factors.

c. The property and payroll factors are much higher than those for other nexus states.

d. The sales and payroll factors are low, but the property factor is very high.

e. The sales factor is remaining constant, but the payroll factor is decreasing.

Critical Thinking 8. **LO.5** The trend in state income taxation is to adopt an apportionment formula that places extra weight on the sales factor. Many states now use sales-factor-only apportionment. Explain why this development is attractive to the taxing states.

9. **LO.5** Megan is an accountant for KnoxCo. She is a telecommuter and works most days from her home in Tennessee. Twice a month, she travels to Georgia for a staff meeting at the employer's Atlanta headquarters. In which state's payroll factor should Megan's compensation be included if:

a. Megan is an employee and is covered by the qualified retirement plan of her Atlanta employer?

b. Megan works as an independent contractor for several clients, including the Atlanta-based firm?

c. Megan is an employee, and for one day each month, she provides accounting services for KnoxCo's Memphis rental properties?

Critical Thinking 10. **LO.5** Keystone, your tax consulting client, is considering an expansion program that would entail the construction of a new logistics center in State Q. List at least five questions you should ask in determining whether an asset that is owned by Keystone is to be included in State Q's property factor numerator.

11. **LO.6** The trend in state income taxation is for states to adopt a version of the unitary theory of multijurisdictional taxation in their statutes and regulations.

a. Explain why some states are attracted to the unitary theory and a combined reporting scheme of multistate income taxation.

b. Is the application of the unitary theory a help or a detriment to the taxpayer? Why?

Critical Thinking 12. **LO.6** State A enjoys a prosperous economy, with high real estate values and compensation levels. State B's economy has seen better days—property values are depressed, and unemployment is higher than in other states. Most consumer goods are priced at about 10% less in State B than in State A. Both States A and B apply unitary income taxation to businesses that operate within the state. Does unitary taxation distort the assignment of taxable income between States A and B? Explain.

13. **LO.7** Evaluate this statement: An S corporation can facilitate the meeting of its state income tax filing obligations by developing a common spreadsheet that allocates and apportions income among the states with which it has nexus. This spreadsheet is attached to each of the state returns to be filed. (*Hint:* Use the term *composite return* in your answer.)

Communications 14. **LO.8** Create a PowerPoint outline describing the major exemptions and exclusions from the sales/use tax base of most states. Use your slides to discuss this topic with your accounting students' club.

15. **LO.8** Your client, HillTop, is a retailer of women's clothing. It has increased sales during the holiday season by advertising gift cards for in-store and online use. HillTop has found that gift card holders who come into the store tend to purchase goods that total more than the amount of the gift card. Further, about one-third of the gift cards never are redeemed, thereby yielding cash to the company without a reduction of inventory. What are the tax issues confronting HillTop related to the gift cards?   **Critical Thinking**

16. **LO.2, 9** Your client, Ecru Limited, uses a small sales force to solicit sales of its wholesale restaurant supplies. Ecru is based in State W, and the sales representatives are assigned territories in States X, Y, and Z. Ecru owns no property and employs no other personnel outside of State W.   **Communications**

    As Ecru's tax adviser, you are to write a policy manual listing various "do's and don'ts" for the sales personnel so that Ecru does not create income tax nexus with States X, Y, and Z.

    To prepare for your assignment, write a memo for the tax research file, summarizing the rules as to the ability of a corporation to terminate or create income tax nexus. Make certain that you discuss the *Wrigley* case [505 U.S. 214 (1992)] in your analysis.

17. **LO.9** Your client, Royal Corporation, generates significant interest income from its working capital liquid investments. Write a memo for the tax research file, discussing the planning opportunities presented by establishing a passive investment company. Support your memo with a diagram of the resulting flow of assets and income.   **Communications**

18. **LO.2, 5, 9** As the director of the multistate tax planning department of a consulting firm, you are developing a brochure to highlight the services it can provide. Part of the brochure is a list of five or so key techniques that clients can use to reduce state income tax liabilities. Develop this list for the brochure. Consider only income tax consequences in your analysis.

Computational Exercises

19. **LO.3, 5** Castle Corporation conducts business in States 1, 2, and 3. Castle's $630,000 taxable income consists of $555,000 apportionable income and $75,000 allocable income generated from transactions conducted in State 3. Castle's sales, property, and payroll are evenly divided among the three states, and the states all employ a three-equal-factors apportionment formula. How much of Castle's income is taxable in:

    a. State 1?

    b. State 2?

    c. State 3?

    d. Express your computation as a Microsoft Excel formula that will provide the correct solution for all three states.

20. **LO.3** Fillon Corporation's operations include two manufacturing facilities, one in State A and one in State B. The plant located in State A generated $200,000 of income, and the plant located in State B generated a loss of $50,000. Therefore, Fillon's total taxable income is $150,000. By applying the statutes of each state, Fillon determines that its apportionment factors for States A and B are 70% and 30%, respectively.

    How much of Fillon's income is apportioned to:

    a. State A?

    b. State B?

21. **LO.3, 4** Legends Corporation owns and operates two manufacturing facilities, one in State A and the other in State B. Due to a temporary decline in sales, Legends has rented 25% of its State A facility to an unaffiliated corporation. Legends generated $200,000 net rent income and $1,400,000 income from manufacturing. Both states classify the rent income as allocable (nonapportionable) income. By applying the statutes of each state, Legends determines that its apportionment factors are 70% for State A and 30% for State B.

How much income is subject to tax in:

a. State A?

b. State B?

22. **LO.5** Beckett Corporation realized $800,000 of taxable income from the sales of its products in States A and B. Beckett's activities establish nexus for income tax purposes in both states. Beckett's sales, payroll, and property in the states include the following.

	State A	State B	Total
Sales	$960,000	$640,000	$1,600,000
Property	180,000	–0–	180,000
Payroll	220,000	–0–	220,000

State B uses a double-weighted sales factor in its three-factor apportionment formula. How much of Beckett's taxable income is apportioned to State B?

23. **LO.5** Roger Corporation operates in two states, as indicated below. This year's operations generated $400,000 of apportionable income.

	State A	State B	Total
Sales	$800,000	$200,000	$1,000,000
Property	300,000	300,000	600,000
Payroll	200,000	50,000	250,000

Compute Roger's State A taxable income assuming that State A apportions income based on a:

a. Three-factor formula, equally weighted.

b. Three-factor formula, with a double-weighted sales factor.

c. Sales factor only.

24. **LO.5** Isle Corporation's entire operations are located in State A. Of Isle's $600,000 sales, 60% are made in State A and 40% are made in State B. Isle's solicitation of sales in State B is limited to mailing a monthly catalog to its customers in that state. However, Isle's employees pick up and replace damaged merchandise in State B. The pickup and replacement of damaged goods establish nexus with State A.

However, State B's definition of activities necessary to create income-tax nexus is less strict than that imposed by State A; in State B, the mere pickup and replacement of damaged goods does not create nexus there. Isle's taxable income is $60,000. Both states impose a 10% corporate income tax and include only the sales factor in their apportionment formulas.

Determine Isle's effective state income tax rate if:

a. State A *has not* adopted a throwback rule.

b. State A *has* adopted a throwback rule.

c. Create a Microsoft Excel formula that will compute correctly the State A taxable income regardless of whether a throwback rule has been adopted.

25. **LO.5** Sante Fe Corporation's sales office and manufacturing plant are located in State A. Sante Fe also maintains a manufacturing plant and sales office in State B. For purposes of apportionment, State A defines payroll as all compensation paid to employees, including contributions to § 401(k) deferred compensation plans. Under the statutes of State B, neither compensation paid to officers nor contributions to § 401(k) plans are included in the payroll factor. Sante Fe incurred the following personnel costs.

	State A	State B	Total
Wages and salaries for employees other than officers	$ 60,000	$40,000	$100,000
Salaries for officers	40,000	20,000	60,000
Contributions to § 401(k) plans	20,000	10,000	30,000
Total	$120,000	$70,000	$190,000

What is the payroll factor for:

a. State A?

b. State B?

26. **LO.6** Vogel Corporation owns two subsidiaries, Song and Bird. Song, located in State A, generated taxable income of $500,000. During this same period, Bird, located in State B, generated a loss of $100,000.

a. Determine Song's taxable income in States A and B, assuming that the subsidiaries constitute independent corporations under the tax law.

b. How does your answer change if the corporations constitute a unitary business?

Problems

27. **LO.1** Use Exhibit 24.1 to compute Balboa Corporation's State F taxable income for the year.

Addition modifications	$29,000
Allocated income (total)	25,000
Allocated income (State F)	3,000
Allocated income (State G)	22,000
Apportionment percentage	40%
Credits	800
Federal taxable income	90,000
Subtraction modifications	15,000
Tax rate	5%

28. **LO.1, 4** Use Exhibit 24.1 to provide the required information for Warbler Corporation, whose Federal taxable income totals $10,000,000.

Warbler apportions 70% of its manufacturing income to State C. Warbler generates $4,000,000 of nonapportionable income each year, and 30% of that income is allocated to State C. Applying the state income tax modifications, Warbler's total business income from the manufacturing operation this year is $12,000,000.

a. How much of Warbler's manufacturing income does State C tax?

b. How much of Warbler's allocable income does State C tax?

c. Explain your results.

29. **LO.1** For each of the following items considered independently, indicate whether the circumstances call for an addition modification (*A*), a subtraction modification (*S*), or no modification (*N*) in computing state taxable income. Then indicate the amount of any modification. The starting point in computing State Q taxable income is the year's Federal taxable income before any deduction for net operating losses.

    a. Federal cost recovery = $10,000, and State Q cost recovery = $15,000.
    b. Federal cost recovery = $15,000, and State Q cost recovery = $10,000.
    c. Federal income taxes paid = $30,000.
    d. Refund received from last year's State Q income taxes = $3,000.
    e. Local property taxes, deducted on the Federal return as a business expense = $80,000.
    f. Interest income from holding U.S. Treasury bonds = $5,000.
    g. Interest income from holding State Q revenue anticipation bonds = $3,000.
    h. Interest income from State P school district bonds = $10,000.
    i. Change in the excess of FIFO inventory valuation over the Federal LIFO amount = $6,000. State Q does not allow the LIFO method.
    j. An asset was sold for $18,000; its purchase price was $20,000. Accumulated Federal cost recovery = $15,000, and accumulated State Q cost recovery = $8,000.
    k. Dividend income received from State R corporation = $30,000, subject to a Federal dividends received deduction of 70%.

30. **LO.1** Perk Corporation is subject to tax only in State A. Perk generated the following income and deductions.

Federal taxable income	$300,000
State A income tax expense	15,000
Refund of State A income tax	3,000
Depreciation allowed for Federal tax purposes	200,000
Depreciation allowed for state tax purposes	120,000

    Federal taxable income is the starting point in computing State A taxable income. State income taxes are not deductible for State A tax purposes. Determine Perk's State A taxable income.

31. **LO.1** Fallow Corporation is subject to tax only in State X. Fallow generated the following income and deductions. State income taxes are not deductible for State X income tax purposes.

Sales	$4,000,000
Cost of sales	2,800,000
State X income tax expense	200,000
Depreciation allowed for Federal tax purposes	400,000
Depreciation allowed for state tax purposes	250,000
Interest income on Federal obligations	40,000
Interest income on State X obligations	30,000
Expenses related to carrying State X obligations	2,000

    a. The starting point in computing the State X income tax base is Federal taxable income. Derive this amount.
    b. Determine Fallow's State X taxable income assuming that interest on State X obligations is exempt from State X income tax.
    c. Determine Fallow's State X taxable income assuming that interest on State X obligations is subject to State X income tax.

32. **LO.5** Dillman Corporation has nexus in States A and B. Dillman's activities for the year are summarized below.

	State A	State B	Total
Sales	$1,200,000	$ 400,000	$1,600,000
Property			
Average historical cost	500,000	300,000	800,000
Average accumulated depreciation	(300,000)	(100,000)	(400,000)
Payroll	2,500,000	500,000	3,000,000
Rent expense	–0–	35,000	35,000

Determine the apportionment factors for States A and B assuming that State A uses a three-factor apportionment formula under which sales, property (net depreciated basis), and payroll are equally weighted and State B employs a single-factor formula that consists solely of sales. State A has adopted the UDITPA with respect to the inclusion of rent payments in the property factor.

33. **LO.5** Assume the same facts as in Problem 32, except that State A uses a single-factor apportionment formula that consists solely of sales and State B uses a three-factor apportionment formula that equally weights sales, property (at historical cost), and payroll. State B does not include rent payments in the property factor.

34. **LO.5** Assume the same facts as in Problem 32, except that both states employ a three-factor formula, under which sales are double-weighted. The property factor in State A is computed using historical cost; this factor in State B is computed using the net depreciated basis. Neither State A nor State B includes rent payments in the property factor.

35. **LO.5, 9** State E applies a throwback rule to sales, but State F does not. State G   Critical Thinking
has not adopted an income tax to date. Clay Corporation, headquartered in State E, reported the following sales for the year. All of the goods were shipped from Clay's State E manufacturing facilities.

Customer	Customer's Location	This Year's Sales
ShellTell, Inc.	State E	$ 75,000,000
Tourists, Ltd.	State F	40,000,000
PageToo Corp.	State G	100,000,000
Total		$215,000,000

a. Determine Clay's sales factor in these states.
b. Comment on Clay's location strategy using only your tax computations.

36. **LO.5, 9** Quinn Corporation is subject to tax in States G, H, and I. Quinn's compen-   Critical Thinking
sation expense includes the following.

	State G	State H	State I	Total
Salaries and wages for nonofficers	$200,000	$400,000	$400,000	$1,000,000
Officers' salaries	–0–	–0–	500,000	500,000
Total				$1,500,000

Officers' salaries are included in the payroll factor for States G and I, but not for State H. Compute Quinn's payroll factors for States G, H, and I. Comment on your results.

37. **LO.5** Kim Corporation, a calendar year taxpayer, operates manufacturing facilities in States A and B. A summary of Kim's property holdings follows.

| | Beginning of Year | | |
	State A	State B	Total
Inventory	$ 300,000	$ 200,000	$ 500,000
Plant and equipment	2,500,000	1,500,000	4,000,000
Accumulated depreciation:			
plant and equipment	(1,000,000)	(600,000)	(1,600,000)
Land	600,000	1,000,000	1,600,000
Rental property*	900,000	300,000	1,200,000
Accumulated depreciation:			
rental property	(200,000)	(90,000)	(290,000)

| | End of Year | | |
	State A	State B	Total
Inventory	$ 400,000	$ 200,000	$ 600,000
Plant and equipment	2,800,000	1,200,000	4,000,000
Accumulated depreciation:			
plant and equipment	(1,200,000)	(650,000)	(1,850,000)
Land	600,000	1,200,000	1,800,000
Rental property*	1,000,000	300,000	1,300,000
Accumulated depreciation:			
rental property	(250,000)	(100,000)	(350,000)

*Unrelated to regular business operations.

Determine Kim's property factors for the two states. The statutes of both States A and B provide that average historical cost of business property is to be included in the property factor.

Decision Making

Communications

38. **LO.6, 9** True Corporation, a wholly owned subsidiary of Trumaine Corporation, generated a $400,000 taxable loss in its first year of operations. True's activities and sales are restricted to State A, which imposes an 8% income tax.

In the same year, Trumaine's taxable income is $1,000,000. Trumaine's activities and sales are restricted to State B, which imposes an 11% income tax. Both states use a three-factor apportionment formula that equally weights sales, payroll, and property, and both require a unitary group to file on a combined basis. Sales, payroll, and average property for each corporation are as follows.

	True Corporation	Trumaine Corporation	Total
Sales	$2,500,000	$4,000,000	$6,500,000
Property	1,000,000	2,500,000	3,500,000
Payroll	500,000	1,500,000	2,000,000

True and Trumaine have been found to be members of a unitary business.

a. Determine the overall state income tax for the unitary group.

b. Determine aggregate state income tax for the entities as if they were nonunitary.

c. Compare your results, and comment on the desirability of True's arrangement. Incorporate this analysis in a letter to Trumaine's board of directors. Corporate offices are located at 1234 Mulberry Lane, Birmingham, AL 35298.

39. **LO.6** Chang Corporation is part of a three-corporation unitary business. The group has a water's edge election in effect with respect to unitary State Q. State B does not apply the unitary concept with respect to its corporate income tax laws. Nor does Despina, a European country to which Saldez paid a $7,000,000 value added tax this year.

Saldez was organized in Despina and conducts all of its business there. Given the summary of operations that follows, determine Chang's and Elena's sales factors in States B and Q.

Corporation	Customer's Location	Sales
Chang	State B	$20,000,000
	State Q	60,000,000
Elena	State Q	70,000,000
Saldez	Despina	50,000,000

40. **LO.8** Using the following information from the books and records of Grande Corporation, determine Grande's total sales that are subject to State C's sales tax. Grande operates a retail general store.

Sales to State C consumers, general merchandise	$1,100,000
Sales to State C consumers, crutches and other medical supplies	245,000
Sales to consumers in State D, via mail order	80,000
Purchases from suppliers	55,000

41. **LO.8** Indicate for each transaction whether a sales (*S*) or use (*U*) tax applies or whether the transaction is nontaxable (*N*). Assume that the most common definitional rules apply in both states. All taxpayers are individuals.
   a. A resident of State A purchases an automobile in State A.
   b. A resident of State A purchases groceries in State A.
   c. A resident of State B purchases an automobile in State A.
   d. A charity purchases office supplies in State A.
   e. A State A resident purchases an item in State B that will be in the inventory of her business.

42. **LO.5, 9** Dread Corporation operates in a high-tax state. The firm asks you for advice on a plan to outsource administrative work done in its home state to independent contractors. This work now costs the company $750,000 in wages and benefits. Dread's total payroll for the year is $8,000,000, of which $6,000,000 is for work currently done in the home state.   *Decision Making*

43. **LO.2, 5, 9** Prepare a PowerPoint presentation (maximum of six slides) entitled "Planning Principles for Our Multistate Clients." The slides will be used to lead a 20-minute discussion with colleagues in the corporate tax department. Keep the outline general, but assume that your colleagues have clients among them operating in at least 15 states. Address only income tax issues.   *Critical Thinking*   *Communications*

Research Problems

Use internet tax resources to address the following questions. Look for reliable websites and blogs of the IRS and other government agencies, media outlets, businesses, tax professionals, academics, think tanks, and political outlets.

Research Problem 1. Pick two of the following provisions that currently do not exist in your state. If your state does not levy a sales/use tax or an income tax on corporations, review the rules of a neighboring state. Send an e-mail to your instructor, listing pro and con arguments for the state to adopt the provisions.   *Critical Thinking*   *Communications*
   a. Exempt "green" technology from the apportionment weight for the property factor.
   b. Subject song and movie downloads to the sales/use tax.
   c. Allow an income tax credit for 20% of the cost of in-state construction projects that are substantially completed within the next 18 months.

d. Establish income tax nexus using the factor presence nexus standards of the Multistate Tax Commission.

e. Add an income-tax "nexus team" to find the taxpayers operating in your state but based in Ohio, Illinois, or Arizona.

f. Adopt the definitions and other rules of the Streamlined Sales Tax Project.

g. Allow an income tax credit for 25% of the wages paid to newly hired employees and contractors who work in the tech and pharma industries.

h. Apply a tax on S corporations operating in the state equal to 2% of the entity's gross receipts.

i. Convert the corporate income tax to a tax on gross receipts, in an effort to tax the profits of passive investment companies owned by in-state parent entities.

j. Broaden the definition of sales/use tax nexus so as to force sellers or marketplace facilitators to remit the tax for online sales.

Communications

Research Problem 2. For your state and one of its neighbors, find the following income tax rules. Place your data in a chart, and e-mail your findings to your instructor.

a. To what extent does each state follow the rulings of the Multistate Tax Commission?

b. Does the state adopt pertinent changes to the Internal Revenue Code? If so, as of what date?

c. What is the highest income tax rate for corporations?

d. Is the tax effectiveness of a passive investment company limited in some way? Has the state adopted the *Geoffrey* approach (see footnote 19) to the taxation of income from intangibles? Explain.

e. Does the state apply entity-level income taxes for S corporations, partnerships, and LLCs? If so, what are the terms of those taxes?

Communications

Data Analytics

Research Problem 3. For your state and one of its neighbors, find the following sales/use tax rules. Place your data in a chart, and e-mail your findings to your instructor.

a. What are the dollar amounts for sales and the number of sales transactions that trigger economic nexus with the state?

b. Describe any exemptions from the sales/use tax base that are allowed for transactions involving groceries, school clothing and supplies, religious goods, and legal services.

c. What is the discount allowed, if any, when a vendor remits sales/use tax to the state in a timely manner?

d. Is manufacturing equipment exempt from the sales/use tax? Medical devices for a clinic? Medical devices for a consumer?

e. Can a vendor use an electronic funds transfer system to remit its sales/use tax collections? If so, when is it required to do so?

f. Has the state joined the Streamlined Sales Tax Project? If yes, what is the effective date?

Data Analytics

Communications

Research Problem 4. Identify three states considered to be in the same economic region as your own. For each of the three states, answer the following questions. Answers to most can be found at **taxadmin.org**.

• What is the overall tax burden per capita, and where does it rank among all states?

• What is the overall tax burden as a percentage of personal income, and where does it rank among all states?

• From what source(s) does it raise most of its revenues (e.g., sales/use tax, highway tolls)? In what proportions?

• What is the highest marginal tax rate on corporate income?

• What is its apportionment formula, including factors and weights?

Summarize your findings in a Microsoft Excel spreadsheet, and submit it to your instructor.

Research Problem 5. Read the "tax footnote" of five publicly traded U.S. corporations. Find the effective state/local income tax rates of each. Create a PowerPoint presentation (maximum of three slides) for your instructor, summarizing the search and reporting your findings.

Data Analytics

Communications

Becker CPA Review Questions

1. Olinto, Inc., has taxable income (before special deductions and the net operating loss deduction) of $92,000. Included in that amount is $12,000 of interest and dividend income. Forty percent of Olinto's property, payroll, and sales are in its home state. What amount of this taxable income will be taxed by Olinto, Inc.'s home state?

   a. $12,000
   b. $36,800

   c. $44,000
   d. $90,000

2. In which of the following cases will Federal law prohibit a state from imposing an income tax on net income?

   a. The business has a retail outlet store in the state.
   b. The business has its corporate headquarters in the state and generates sales from there.
   c. Orders are taken within the state and accepted at corporate headquarters outside of the state and shipped from a location outside of the state.
   d. Orders are taken within the state and accepted at corporate headquarters outside of the state and shipped from a location inside the state.

3. Which of the following activities will not trigger nexus in a state in which a company operates?

   a. Providing installation services with the purchase of tangible personal property.
   b. Acceptance of an order within the state.
   c. Delivery by a common carrier.
   d. Collection of delinquent accounts.

4. Which of the following statements best describes a multistate corporation's approach to the apportionment and allocation of its income?

   I. The corporation will allocate its nonbusiness income.
   II. The corporation will apportion its business income.

   a. I only.
   b. II only.

   c. Both I and II.
   d. Neither I nor II.

5. Reiki Inc. operates stores in Massachusetts and Vermont. Reiki's payroll, property, and sales by state are as follows.

State	Payroll	Property (Ending)	Property (Average)	Sales
Massachusetts	$200,000	$175,000	$195,000	$ 750,000
Vermont	350,000	225,000	200,000	900,000
Total	550,000	400,000	395,000	1,650,000

   What is Reiki's apportionment factor for Massachusetts (round to two decimal places)?

   a. 41.86%
   b. 44.12%

   c. 45.45%
   d. 43.73%

CHAPTER

25

Taxation of International Transactions

LEARNING OBJECTIVES: *After completing Chapter 25, you should be able to:*

LO.1 Explain the framework underlying the U.S. taxation of cross-border transactions.

LO.2 Describe the interaction between Internal Revenue Code provisions and tax treaties.

LO.3 Apply the rules for sourcing income and deductions into U.S. and foreign categories.

LO.4 Apply foreign currency exchange rules as they affect the tax consequences of international transactions.

LO.5 Work with the U.S. tax provisions affecting U.S. persons earning foreign-source income, including the rules relating to cross-border asset transfers, antideferral provisions, and the foreign tax credit.

LO.6 Apply the U.S. tax provisions concerning nonresident alien individuals and foreign corporations.

CHAPTER OUTLINE

25-1 Overview of International Taxation, 25-3

25-2 Tax Treaties, 25-5

25-3 Sourcing of Income and Deductions, 25-6
    25-3a Income Sourcing Rules, 25-6
    25-3b Allocation and Apportionment of
        Deductions, 25-9
    25-3c Transfer Pricing, 25-10

25-4 Foreign Currency Gain/Loss, 25-14

25-5 U.S. Persons with Offshore Income, 25-15
    25-5a Export Property, Licenses, Foreign
        Branches, 25-15
    25-5b Creating a Cross-Border Business Entity, 25-18
    25-5c Tax Havens, 25-19

    25-5d Offshore (Foreign) Corporations Controlled by U.S.
        Persons, 25-20
    25-5e Movement Toward a Territorial System, 25-23

**25-6 U.S. Taxation of Nonresident Aliens and Foreign
Corporations, 25-26**
    25-6a Nonresident Alien Individuals, 25-26
    25-6b Foreign Corporations, 25-28
    25-6c Foreign Investment in Real Property Tax Act, 25-28
    25-6d Expatriation to Avoid U.S. Taxation, 25-28

25-7 Tax Planning, 25-29
    25-7a The Foreign Tax Credit Limitation and Sourcing
        Provisions, 25-30
    25-7b Transfer Pricing, 25-30

MONKEY BUSINESS IMAGES/SHUTTERSTOCK.COM

GOING INTERNATIONAL

VoiceCo, a domestic corporation, designs, manufactures, and sells specialty microphones for use in theaters. All of its activities take place in Florida, although it ships products to customers all over the United States. When it receives inquiries about its products from potential non-U.S. customers, VoiceCo decides to test the overseas market and places ads in various trade journals that have an international focus. Soon it is taking orders from offshore customers.

VoiceCo is concerned about its potential worldwide income tax exposure. Although it has no assets or employees outside the United States, it now is involved in international commerce. Is VoiceCo subject to income taxes in any other countries? Must it pay U.S. income taxes on the profits from its overseas sales? What if VoiceCo pays taxes to other countries? Does it receive any benefit from these payments on its U.S. tax return?

Later, VoiceCo establishes a manufacturing plant in Ireland to meet the European demand for its products. VoiceCo incorporates the Irish operation as VoiceCo-Ireland, an Irish corporation. Ireland imposes only a 12.5 percent tax on VoiceCo-Ireland's profits. How does U.S. corporate income tax law affect these activities?

Read the chapter and formulate your response.

n today's global business environment, most large businesses are truly international in scope. Large U.S. corporations earn on average more than 20 percent of their profits overseas, with offshore sales by "all-American" companies Coca-Cola and Apple exceeding 60 percent of their totals for a typical year. "Offshore" companies like Honda and Toyota operate large manufacturing plants in the United States, with perhaps one-third of their total sales taking place in the United States.

Global trade is an integral part of the U.S. economy. In a recent year, U.S. exports and imports of goods and services totaled $2.5 trillion and $3.13 trillion, respectively. The largest dollar volume of U.S. exports consists of petroleum products, autos, and airplanes/spacecraft. The top U.S. export partners are Mexico, Canada, and China.

This international trade creates significant U.S. tax consequences for both U.S. and offshore entities. In the most recent year for which data are available, U.S. corporations reported $419 billion in foreign-source taxable income, paid $187 billion in income taxes to foreign governments, and claimed foreign tax credits of about $118 billion. U.S. corporations controlled by non-U.S. owners reported $172 billion in U.S. gross receipts.

Cross-border transactions create the need for special tax considerations for both the United States and its trading partners. Tax planning opportunities can arise as different countries raise revenue through income and other taxes, applying various tax bases and tax rates. Exhibit 25.1 includes data about the top statutory tax rates that various countries apply to corporate taxable income.

From a U.S. perspective, international tax laws should promote the global competitiveness of U.S. enterprises while protecting the tax revenue base of the United States. These two objectives sometimes conflict, however. The need to deal with both contributes to the complexity of the rules governing the U.S. taxation of cross-border transactions.

EXAMPLE 1

U.S. persons engage in activities outside the United States for many different reasons. Consider two U.S. corporations that have established sales subsidiaries in foreign countries. Dedalus, Inc., operates in Germany, a high-tax country, because customers demand local attention from sales agents. Mulligan, Inc., operates in the Cayman Islands, a low-tax country, simply to shift income outside the United States. U.S. tax law must fairly address both situations with the same law.

EXHIBIT 25.1	Top Statutory Corporate Income Tax Rates for Selected Countries, 2019
Bermuda	0.0%
Ireland	12.5%
United Kingdom	19.0%
Sweden	21.4%
United States	27.0%
Germany	30.0%
Mexico	30.0%
Japan	30.6%
France	31.0%
Worldwide average	23.0%

Note: Tax rates include additional taxes on corporate taxable income levied by states, cities, provinces, cantons, and other smaller jurisdictions. Deductions, exemptions, and credits can reduce an entity's effective tax rate below the top statutory rate.

U.S. multinational taxpayers—and tax professionals—must understand the Federal tax rules related to international business, so that these rules can be incorporated into their overall tax plans. Generally, this involves reducing the exposure to double taxation of business profits, locating cash and other assets where they will be the most productive, and decreasing the present value of income tax liabilities (e.g., by accelerating losses and deductions and deferring taxable income recognition).

25-1 OVERVIEW OF INTERNATIONAL TAXATION

LO.1

Explain the framework underlying the U.S. taxation of cross-border transactions.

U.S. international tax provisions are concerned primarily with two types of potential taxpayers: U.S. persons earning foreign-source income and non-U.S. persons earning U.S.-source income.[1] U.S. persons earning U.S.-source income are taxed using only the domestic provisions of the Internal Revenue Code. Non-U.S. persons earning foreign-source income are not within the taxing jurisdiction of the United States (unless this income is connected to a U.S. trade or business). Exhibit 25.2 illustrates this categorization.

Most countries in the developed world use a *territorial* taxing system, under which only the taxable income generated within the country's borders is subject to tax there, regardless of who the taxpayer is. By taxing all events for all taxpayers that occur within their borders and nothing else, most business income generated in those countries is subject to tax only at one time and in one place. For the most part, U.S. corporate income tax law applies a territorial system for transactions entered into by non-U.S. persons.

In addition, most countries have been cutting their business income tax rates over the last two decades. Taxes have become a significant device by which countries compete for business, capital, and jobs.

U.S. business income tax provisions apply a *worldwide* system for U.S. persons. Under these rules, a U.S. person is subject to the U.S. income tax for all taxable income, regardless of where it is generated. This means that an item of taxable income for a U.S. entity could be subject to income tax in the United States and, simultaneously, in the non-U.S. country where it arises. Strict worldwide taxation systems are rare today throughout the developed world.

This potential for the *double taxation* of business income for a U.S. person under a worldwide system is addressed in the Code in several ways under legacy law, the most important of which is the **foreign tax credit (FTC)**. A credit is allowed against the U.S. income tax for income taxes paid on income generated in another country, up to the amount of U.S. income tax that would result from the same income.[2]

The worldwide taxing system still undergirds the income taxation of cross-border transactions conducted by U.S. persons, but important provisions overlay these rules, especially for large entities. These include the means by which to:

- Move toward a territorial system of taxation for U.S. businesses.
- Provide incentives for U.S. businesses to locate jobs in the United States and repatriate foreign profits back to the United States.
- Prevent U.S. entities from shifting taxable income outside the United States into low-tax-rate countries.

The U.S. taxation of cross-border transactions can be organized in terms of "outbound" and "inbound" taxation. **Outbound taxation** refers to the U.S. taxation of foreign-source income earned by U.S. taxpayers. **Inbound taxation** refers to the U.S. taxation of U.S.-source income earned by non-U.S. taxpayers.

---

[1] The term *person* includes an individual, corporation, partnership, trust, estate, or association; § 7701(a)(1). The terms *domestic* and *foreign* are defined in §§ 7701(a)(4) and (5).

[2] A carryback or carryforward of an FTC arose when the foreign tax paid exceeded the amount of the corresponding Federal income tax liability for the tax year.

EXHIBIT 25.2	U.S. Taxation of Cross-Border Transactions

*Depends on local country tax law.
**Worldwide tax rules may apply.

GLOBAL TAX ISSUES   Tax Reform Can Make Strange Bedfellows

As governments around the world seek new revenues to balance budgets, pay down debts, and stabilize their economies, new levels of political cooperation can emerge. Age-old banking secrecy rules and tax laws that allow entities to shift taxable income into low-taxing jurisdictions all are under serious scrutiny. The Organization for Economic Cooperation and Development (OECD), a group of about 35 developed countries dedicated to expanding economic progress and world trade, has developed a plan to curtail income shifting (called "tax base erosion") that solely is meant to reduce taxes. The Group of 20, the largest economies in the world, has signed on to the principles

of stopping base erosion as part of international tax reform. U.S. tax law now includes some anti-income-shifting rules.

Public pressure on such notable U.S. entities as Apple, Amazon, Google, and Starbucks has forced compromises in the U.S. companies' aggressive interpretation of tax law and treaties so that reported taxable income amounts might more closely correspond to where its customers reside (i.e., where its profit is earned, say in Germany, rather than where its holding company might exist, like in Luxembourg).

As these efforts to increase the tax liabilities of multinational entities expand, tax planners will need to find effective techniques to manage the tax costs of their operations.

The Big Picture

EXAMPLE 2

Return to the facts of *The Big Picture* on p. 25-1. Assume that VoiceCo operates an unincorporated manufacturing branch in Singapore to take advantage of local materials and low labor costs. This branch income is taxed in the United States as part of VoiceCo's worldwide income, but it also is taxed in Singapore. Without the availability of a foreign tax credit to mitigate this double taxation, VoiceCo would suffer an excessive tax burden and could not compete in a global environment. VoiceCo should arrange its affairs so that the territorial rules of U.S. tax law apply and double taxation on that income is avoided.

The Big Picture

EXAMPLE 3

Return to the facts of *The Big Picture* on p. 25-1. VoiceCo's major competitor is a Swiss-based foreign corporation with operations in the United States. Although not a U.S. person, the Swiss competitor is taxed in the United States on its U.S.-source business income. If the Swiss competitor could operate free of U.S. tax, VoiceCo would face a serious competitive disadvantage.

25-2 TAX TREATIES

LO.2

Describe the interaction between Internal Revenue Code provisions and tax treaties.

The U.S. tax rules governing cross-border transactions are based on both the Internal Revenue Code and tax treaties. U.S. tax treaties are bilateral agreements between countries that provide tax relief for those persons covered by the treaties. Tax treaty provisions must be harmonized with the treatment otherwise called for under the Internal Revenue Code or foreign tax statutes.[3] If there is a conflict, preference is given to whichever is newer, the treaty or the law; this is known as the "later in time" rule.[4]

Almost 70 income tax treaties between the United States and other countries are in effect (see Exhibit 25.3). These treaties generally provide *taxing rights* related to the taxable income of residents of one treaty country who have income sourced in the other treaty country. For the most part, neither country is prohibited from taxing the income of its own residents. The treaties generally give one country primary taxing rights, and they require the other country to allow a credit for the taxes paid on the twice-taxed income.

EXAMPLE 4

ForCo, Ltd., a resident of a country with which the United States has an income tax treaty, earns income attributable to a permanent establishment (e.g., a place of business) in the United States.

Under the treaty, the United States has primary taxing rights related to this income. The other country can require that the income be included in gross income and can subject the income to its income tax, but it must allow a credit, an exemption, or some other offset for the taxes paid to the United States on the income.

Treaty language usually allows the country of the taxpayer's residence to levy a tax first. Alternatively, treaties allow a tax if there is a *permanent establishment* in a treaty country to which the income is attributable. Generally, a permanent establishment is a branch, an office, a factory, a workshop, a warehouse, or another fixed place of business.

When a U.S. person makes a payment of income to a non-U.S. party, the U.S. payor usually withholds Federal income tax (and reduces the amount of the payment). This helps ensure that the non-U.S. party will pay the tax due. Most U.S. income tax treaties reduce the withholding tax rate on certain items of investment income, such as interest and dividends. Exhibit 25.4 summarizes the treaty-based withholding rates for selected countries. Lacking a treaty provision, the withholding rate likely would be 30 percent.

The United States has developed a Model Income Tax Convention as the starting point for negotiating income tax treaties with other countries.[5]

---

[3]§ 7852(d)(1).
[4]§ *Cook v. U.S.*, 288 U.S. 102 (1933).

[5]Treasury Department Model Income Tax Convention (November 17, 2016). See **tinyurl.com/16model**.

EXHIBIT 25.3	U.S. Income Tax Treaties in Force as of 2019		
Armenia	France	Lithuania	South Africa
Australia	Georgia	Luxembourg	Spain
Austria	Germany	Malta	Sri Lanka
Azerbaijan	Greece	Mexico	Sweden
Bangladesh	Hungary	Moldova	Switzerland
Barbados	Iceland	Morocco	Tajikistan
Belarus	India	Netherlands	Thailand
Belgium	Indonesia	New Zealand	Trinidad
Bulgaria	Ireland	Norway	Tunisia
Canada	Israel	Pakistan	Turkey
China	Italy	Philippines	Turkmenistan
Cyprus	Jamaica	Poland	Ukraine
Czech Republic	Japan	Portugal	United Kingdom
Denmark	Kazakhstan	Romania	Uzbekistan
Egypt	Korea	Russia	Venezuela
Estonia	Kyrgyzstan	Slovak Republic	
Finland	Latvia	Slovenia	

EXHIBIT 25.4	Selected Tax Treaty Withholding Rates, Income Paid by U.S. Entity		
	Interest	Dividends (in General)	Dividends Paid by U.S. Subsidiary to a Foreign Parent Corporation
Australia	10%	15%	5%
Canada	0%	15%	5%
China	10%	10%	10%
Ireland	0%	15%	5%
Japan	10%	10%	5%
Mexico	15%	10%	5%
Philippines	15%	25%	20%
United Kingdom	0%	15%	5%
Non-treaty countries	30%	30%	30%

Apply the rules for sourcing income and deductions into U.S. and foreign categories.

25-3 SOURCING OF INCOME AND DEDUCTIONS

The *sourcing* of income and deductions inside and outside the United States has a direct bearing on a number of tax provisions affecting both U.S. and offshore taxpayers. For example, non-U.S. taxpayers generally are taxed only on U.S.-source income, and U.S. taxpayers apply the sourcing rules in making several income, credit, and deduction computations.

25-3a Income Sourcing Rules

The determination of the source of income depends on the type of income realized (e.g., income from the sale of property versus income for the use of property).[6] An item is determined to be either "U.S.-source" or "foreign-source" under the following rules.

---

[6]Rules pertaining to the sourcing of income are found in §§ 861 through 865.

Interest

Interest income received from the U.S. government, from the District of Columbia, and from noncorporate U.S. residents or domestic corporations is U.S.-source income.

There are a few exceptions to this rule. Certain interest received from a U.S. corporation that earned 80 percent or more of its active business income from offshore sources over the prior three-year period is treated as foreign-source income. Interest received on amounts deposited with an overseas branch of a U.S. corporation also is treated as foreign-source income if the branch is engaged in the commercial banking business.

John holds a bond issued by Alpha, a domestic corporation. For the immediately preceding three tax years, 82% of Alpha's gross income has been active foreign business income. The interest income that John receives for the current tax year from Alpha is foreign-source income.

Dividends

Dividends received from domestic corporations typically are U.S.-source income. Typically, dividends paid by a non-U.S. corporation constitute foreign-source income. However, if an offshore corporation earned 25 percent or more of its gross income from income effectively connected with a U.S. trade or business during the three-year period immediately preceding the year of the dividend payment, that percentage of the dividend is treated as U.S.-source income.

Ann receives dividend income from the following corporations during the current tax year.

Amount	Corporation	Effectively Connected U.S. Income for Past Three Years	U.S.-Source Income
$500	Green, domestic	85%	$500
600	Brown, domestic	13%	600
300	Orange, foreign	92%	276

Because Green Corporation and Brown Corporation are domestic corporations, the dividends they pay are U.S.-source income. Orange Corporation is a non-U.S. corporation that earned 92% of its business income over the prior three years from income effectively connected with a U.S. trade or business. Because Orange meets the 25% threshold, 92% of its dividend is U.S. source.

Personal Services Income

The source of income from personal services is determined by the location in which the services are performed (inside or outside the United States). A limited *commercial traveler* exception is available. Under this exception, personal services income must meet *all* of the following requirements to avoid being classified as U.S.-source income.

- The services must be performed by a nonresident alien who is in the United States for 90 days or less during the taxable year.
- The compensation may not exceed $3,000 in total for the services performed in the United States.
- The services must be performed on behalf of:
  - A nonresident alien, non-U.S. partnership, or non-U.S. corporation that is not engaged in a U.S. trade or business, or
  - An office or place of business maintained in a country outside the United States by an individual who is a citizen or resident of the United States, a domestic partnership, or a domestic corporation.

EXAMPLE

7

Mark, a nonresident alien, is an engineer employed by a foreign oil company. He spent four weeks in the United States arranging the purchase of field equipment for his company. His salary for the four weeks was $3,500.

Even though the oil company is not engaged in a U.S. trade or business and Mark was in the United States for less than 90 days during the taxable year, the income is U.S.-source income because it exceeds $3,000.

Rents and Royalties

Income received for the use of tangible property is sourced to the country in which the property is located. The source of income received for the use of intangible property (e.g., patents, copyrights, processes, and formulas) is the country where the property is used.

Sale or Exchange of Property

Generally, the location of *real property* determines the source of any income derived from the sale of that property (usually, via a sale of the property). Income from the disposition of U.S. real property interests is U.S.-source income.

The source of income from the sale of *personal property* (assets other than real property) depends on several factors, including the following.

- Whether the property was produced by the seller.
- What type of property was sold (e.g., inventory or a capital asset).
- Where the residence of the seller was.

Generally, income, gain, or profit from the sale of personal property is sourced according to the residence of the seller. Income from the sale of *purchased* inventory, however, is sourced in the country where the sale takes place.[7]

When the seller has *produced* the inventory, the income is sourced to the country where the assets were produced.

Income from the sale of personal property other than inventory is sourced at the residence of the seller unless one of the following exceptions applies.

- Gain on the sale of depreciable personal property is sourced according to prior depreciation deductions to the extent of the deductions. Any excess gain is sourced the same as the sale of inventory.
- Gain on the sale of intangibles is sourced according to prior amortization deductions to the extent of the deductions.
- Gain attributable to an office or a fixed place of business maintained outside the United States by a U.S. resident is foreign-source income.
- Income or gain attributable to an office or a fixed place of business maintained in the United States by a nonresident is U.S.-source income.

Losses are sourced depending on the nature of the property. Different rules exist for the disposition of stock versus other personal property.[8]

Transportation and Communication Income

Income from transportation beginning *and* ending in the United States is U.S.-source income. Fifty percent of the income from transportation beginning *or* ending in the United States is U.S.-source income, unless the U.S. point is only an intermediate stop.

---

[7]§§ 861(a)(6) and 865. The sale is deemed to take place where title passes. Reg. § 1.861–7(c). There has been considerable conflict in this area. See, for example, *Liggett Group, Inc.*, 58 TCM 1167, T.C.Memo. 1990–18.

[8]See Reg. § 1.861–8(e)(7) and Reg. § 1.865–1(a)(1). See Reg. §§ 1.865–2(a)(1) and (2) regarding the source of losses on the disposition of stock.

Income from space and ocean activities conducted outside the jurisdiction of any country is sourced according to the residence of the person conducting the activity.

International communication income derived by a U.S. person is one-half U.S.-source when transmission is between the United States and another country. International communication income derived by non-U.S. persons is foreign-source income unless it is attributable to an office or another fixed place of business in the United States. In that case, it is U.S.-source income.

Software Income

Income from the sale or license of software is sourced depending on how the income is classified. A transfer of software is classified as either the transfer of a copyright (e.g., the right to the computer program itself) or the transfer of a copyrighted article (the right to use a copy of the computer program).[9] If the transfer is considered a transfer of a copyright, the income is sourced using the royalty income rules. If the transfer is considered a transfer of a copyrighted article, the income is treated as resulting from a sale of the article and is sourced based on the personal property sales rules.[10]

25-3b **Allocation and Apportionment of Deductions**

The United States levies a tax on *taxable income* (gross income minus deductions). Deductions and losses, therefore, also must be *allocated* and *apportioned* between U.S.- and foreign-source gross income to determine U.S.- and foreign-source taxable income. Deductions directly related to an activity or property are *allocated* to classes of income. Then these deductions are *apportioned* between U.S.- and foreign-source on a reasonable basis.[11]

EXAMPLE 8

Ace, Inc., a domestic corporation, reports $2,000,000 of gross income and $50,000 of expenses related to real estate sales and rental activities. The expenses can be *allocated* and then *apportioned* using gross income as a basis in the following way.

	Gross Income		Expense Allocation	Expense Apportionment	
	Foreign	U.S.		Foreign	U.S.
Sales	$1,000,000	$500,000	$37,500*	$25,000	$12,500**
Rentals	400,000	100,000	12,500	10,000	2,500***
Totals			$50,000	$35,000	$15,000

*$50,000 × ($1,500,000/$2,000,000).   ***$12,500 × ($100,000/$500,000).
**$37,500 × ($500,000/$1,500,000).

If, instead, Ace could show that $45,000 of the expenses were directly related to sales income, the $45,000 would be allocated specifically to that class of gross income, with the remainder allocated and apportioned ratably based on gross income.

Interest expense is allocated and apportioned based on the theory that borrowed money can be raised and spent in any country without being earmarked to any specific location or use (i.e., it is *fungible*). With limited exceptions, interest expense is attributable to all of the activities and property of the taxpayer, regardless of the specific

---

[9]Reg. § 1.861–18.   [11]Reg. § 1.861–8.

[10]Reg. §§ 1.861–18(f)(1) and (2).

purpose for incurring the debt on which interest is paid. Taxpayers allocate and apportion interest expense on the basis of the tax book value of the leveraged assets.[12]

The Big Picture

EXAMPLE 9

Return to the facts of *The Big Picture* on p. 25-1. Assume that VoiceCo generates U.S.-source and foreign-source gross income for the current year. VoiceCo's assets (measured at tax book value) are as follows.

Assets generating U.S.-source income	$18,000,000
Assets generating foreign-source income	5,000,000
	$23,000,000

VoiceCo incurs interest expense of $800,000 for the current year. Interest expense is apportioned to foreign-source income as follows.

$$\frac{\$5{,}000{,}000 \text{ (foreign assets)}}{\$23{,}000{,}000 \text{ (total assets)}} \times \$800{,}000 = \$173{,}913$$

Different rules apply to research and development (R&D) expenditures, certain costs of day-to-day management, legal and accounting fees and expenses, income taxes, and losses. Although U.S. companies incur about 90 percent of their R&D expenditures at U.S. facilities, several billion dollars are spent on offshore R&D each year. If the R&D relates to offshore product sales, a portion of a U.S. company's R&D expense is treated as foreign source.

Concept Summary 25.1

The Sourcing Rules

The Code and Regulations include rules that designate income and deduction items as U.S.-source or foreign-source. These rules are important for several purposes.

- A U.S. taxpayer uses U.S.- and foreign-source amounts in computing various income, credits, and deductions.

- A non-U.S. taxpayer is subject to U.S. Federal income taxes only on U.S.-source taxable income.

- An expatriate from the United States (e.g., an employee of a U.S. business entity who temporarily is stationed overseas) can claim a foreign earned income exclusion only on foreign-source income (§ 911; not otherwise discussed in this chapter).

25-3c **Transfer Pricing**

Income Shifting

A **transfer pricing** arrangement sets the internal prices at which goods and services are sold between related parties (e.g., a parent corporation and its subsidiary). Transfer pricing also can refer to the use of charges, such as fees for management services and database access, that are assessed on one related party by another. In this way, net profits can be shifted from one entity to a different entity, thereby achieving a tax advantage. For instance, an entity in a high-tax country might pay a management fee to its parent in a low-tax country. Doing so creates a valuable deduction in a high-tax jurisdiction, with the related income (the management fee received) subject to a lower tax rate.

---

[12]Reg. § 1.861–9T. Reg. § 1.861–10T(b) describes circumstances in which interest expense can be directly allocated to specific debt. This exception to the fungibility concept is limited to cases in which specific property is purchased or improved with nonrecourse debt.

The IRS uses § 482 to counter a taxpayer's improper use of transfer pricing to manipulate taxable income amounts within a group of entities. This provision gives the IRS the power to reallocate gross income, deductions, credits, or allowances between or among organizations, trades, or businesses owned or controlled directly or indirectly by the same interests. This can be done whenever the IRS determines that reallocation is necessary to prevent the evasion of taxes, or to reflect income more clearly.

Section 482 is a "one-edged sword" available only to the IRS. A taxpayer generally cannot invoke § 482 to reallocate income and expenses.[13]

ETHICS & EQUITY The Costs of Good Tax Planning

High Tech Tops (HTT), a C corporation based in California, manufactures resilient cases and covers for laptops, smartphones, and tablets. Its sales and profits have more than doubled in each of the last five years (i.e., the company is growth-oriented and recession-proof). Its employees and contractors make above-average wages, so they make important contributions to the local individual income, sales, and property tax collections.

But the Federal and state corporate income tax is another story. Using legal and effective transfer pricing techniques, HTT shifts most of its operating profits to low-tax subsidiaries in Ireland and Singapore. Most of the firm's executives, engineers, and designers are based in the United States, but almost all of the sales operations are run from overseas. HTT's customers live around the world, but its tax liabilities are concentrated in the low-tax jurisdictions.

You are the president of State University, across town from HTT's headquarters. The company sends hundreds of its employees to take graduate and professional courses on your campus, and several of the corporate leaders are frequent guest speakers and adjunct lecturers in classes.

Still, the state income tax the company avoids through its transfer pricing plans would fund millions of dollars of campus growth and improvements for State University.

Should you become involved in the politics of the matter and lobby at your statehouse for tighter rules on transfer pricing? Such an action might result in tax increases that would improve your university's situation, but it also might force HTT to consider moving its headquarters to another location.

EXAMPLE 10

Consider the transaction depicted in Exhibit 25.5. A U.S. corporation manufactures and sells inventory to an unrelated foreign customer. The sales price for the inventory is $1,000, and the related cost of goods sold (COGS) is $600. All of the resulting profit of $400 is taxed to the U.S. corporation, resulting in an $84 U.S. income tax liability ($400 × 21%). If the U.S. corporation has no business presence in the foreign jurisdiction and is merely selling to a customer located there, the foreign government is unlikely to impose any local income tax on the U.S. corporation. Consequently, the total tax burden imposed on the inventory sale is $84.

Suppose instead that the U.S. corporation attempts to reduce its total tax expense by channeling the inventory sale through a subsidiary in the same country as the foreign customer. In this case, because the U.S. corporation controls the foreign subsidiary, it chooses an intercompany sales price (the transfer price) that effectively moves a portion of the profits from the United States to the non-U.S. country.

By selling the inventory it manufactured to its 100%-owned foreign subsidiary for $700, the U.S. corporation reports only $100 of profits and an associated U.S. tax liability of $21. The subsidiary then sells the inventory to the ultimate customer for $1,000 and, with a $700 COGS, earns a $300 profit. In this example, the non-U.S. country imposes only a 10% tax on corporate profits, resulting in an income tax there of $30 ($300 × 10%). By using a related offshore entity in a lower-tax jurisdiction, the U.S. corporation has lowered its overall tax liability on the sale from $84 (all U.S.) to $51 ($21 U.S. and $30 foreign).

continued

---

[13]Reg. § 1.482–1(a)(3).

Will the IRS agree to $700 as the appropriate transfer price in considering whether to apply § 482? The IRS may question why the subsidiary deserved to earn $300 of the total $400 profit related to the manufacture and sale of the inventory. In general, the U.S. corporation must document the functions performed by its subsidiary, the assets it owns that assist in producing the income, or the risks it takes (e.g., credit risk) to justify its profit assignment.

If the IRS does not consider the $300 profit earned by the subsidiary to be appropriate, it will use § 482 to adjust the transfer price upward. If the IRS determines that the transfer price should have been, for example, $990, then the U.S. corporation reports a $390 profit (with $82 of U.S. income tax) and the non-U.S. corporation earns a $10 profit (with $1 of the other country's income tax). With this change in transfer price, the U.S. corporation reduces its tax liability, but only by $1 [$84 − ($82 + $1)].

EXHIBIT 25.5	**Transfer Pricing Example**

Sale Without Using Related Party

U.S. Corporation

Sales revenue	$1,000
COGS	(600)
Profit	$ 400
Tax @ 21%	$ 84

Worldwide Tax Cost	
U.S. tax	$ 84
Foreign tax	0
Total tax	$ 84

Sale Using Related Party

U.S. Corporation

Sales revenue	$ 700
COGS	(600)
Profit	$ 100
Tax @ 21%	$ 21

Foreign Subsidiary

Sales revenue	$1,000
COGS	(700)
Profit	$ 300
Tax @ 10%	$ 30

Worldwide Tax Cost	
U.S. tax	$ 21
Foreign tax	30
Total tax	$ 51

The IRS imposes an accuracy-related penalty of 20 percent when it makes a net transfer price adjustment in a taxable year that exceeds the lesser of $5 million or 10 percent of the taxpayer's gross receipts, or when the transfer price is overstated by 200 percent or more. The penalty is doubled for "gross misstatements" of taxable income due to transfer pricing arrangements.[14]

Preemptive Transfer Pricing Arrangements

As an aid to reducing pricing disputes, the IRS initiated the Advance Pricing Agreement (APA) program, where the taxpayer can propose a transfer pricing method for certain future cross-border transactions.[15] The taxpayer provides relevant data, which then are

---

[14]§§ 6662(e)(1)(B) and (h)(2)(A)(ii).

[15]Rev.Proc. 2015–41, 2015–35 I.R.B. 263. The IRS offers an application template based on this document.

evaluated by the IRS. If accepted, the APA provides a safe-harbor transfer pricing result for the taxpayer, preempting most later IRS adjustments.

APAs can be complex in their application, and they may take three or four years to negotiate fully. About 300 APAs have been executed over the past three years, and another 500 are pending. About 65 percent of the APAs affect transfer pricing between the United States and Japan, Canada, and India. About half of the APAs involve taxpayers in the manufacturing industries. Most APAs are effective for five years.

Additional Tax for Base Erosion

The Code provides another sanction for large C corporations that appear to shift "too much" taxable income to other countries where a lower income tax rate may be available. The *base erosion anti-abuse* provision applies to U.S. and non-U.S. corporations with average annual gross receipts of at least $500 million for the prior three tax years.

An alternative tax computation applies to the entity when "excessive" deductions result from payments made to a related (25 percent ownership) non-U.S. person. If these base erosion items total at least 3 percent of total deductible expenses for the year, the entity pays a Federal corporate income tax equal to the *greater of* the corporation's regular tax liability, or:

10% → **X** → **Taxable income (after adding back the base erosion items)**[16]

The base erosion anti-abuse tax (BEAT) is similar in nature to provisions adopted in the last decade by other developed countries that want to keep the income tax base indicative of where multinational profits are earned. The BEAT provisions effectively act as a minimum tax to keep a taxpayer from unduly reducing its U.S. taxable income to zero (or close to it), by using income-shifting deductions and other devices with a related party.

Base erosion items do not include those related to cost of goods sold or those where a withholding tax already applies.

EXAMPLE 11

ReichCo, a non-U.S. conglomerate, generates $3 billion in gross receipts annually. Its U.S. subsidiary, GiantCo, accounts for $750 million of the annual gross receipts (and its average annual gross receipts for the last three years is $685 million).

GiantCo generates U.S. taxable income of $120 million ($750 million gross receipts − $630 million total deductions). Included in the total deductions is a $250 million management fee that it pays to ReichCo. GiantCo reports no U.S. tax credits. The corporate income tax rate in ReichCo's country is 15%.

GiantCo is subject to the base erosion tax.

- Its average annual gross receipts for the last three years are at least $500 million.

- Base erosion items are at least 3% of deductible items for the year ($250 million base erosion items ÷ $630 million total deductions = 40%).

Now determine whether a base erosion tax is due. GiantCo pays the *greater of*:

- Regular U.S. income tax: $25.2 million = 21% × $120 million taxable income, or

- The base erosion tax: $37 million = 10% × $370 million modified taxable income ($120 million taxable income + $250 million base erosion items).

Apparently tempted by the low tax rate of its parent ReichCo, GiantCo has shifted "too much" income to the non-U.S. country with its deductible management fee. It incurs the base erosion anti-abuse tax for the tax year. GiantCo pays its regular U.S. corporate income tax of $25.2 million, plus the anti-abuse tax equal to the excess amount of $11.8 million, for a total of $37 million. GiantCo's U.S. income tax liability has increased by about one-half due to the anti-abuse tax.

---

[16]§ 59A. The 10% tax rate becomes 12.5% after 2025. The BEAT rate is not used for book purposes in deriving the deferred tax accounts.

LO.4

Apply foreign currency exchange rules as they affect the tax consequences of international transactions.

25-4 FOREIGN CURRENCY GAIN/LOSS

An exchange rate provides the relative value of a foreign currency to the U.S. dollar. Changes in this rate affect the dollar value of overseas property held by the taxpayer, the dollar value of non-U.S. debts, and the dollar amount of gain or loss on a transaction denominated in a foreign currency.[17] Almost every international tax issue requires consideration of currency exchange implications.

EXAMPLE

12

Dress, Inc., a domestic corporation, purchases merchandise for resale from Fiesta, Inc., a non-U.S. corporation, for 50,000K (a foreign currency). On the date of purchase, 1K is equal to $1 U.S. (1K:$1). At this time, the account payable is $50,000.

On the date of payment by Dress (the foreign exchange date), the exchange rate is 1.25K:$1. In other words, the foreign currency has been devalued in relation to the U.S. dollar, and Dress will pay Fiesta 50,000K, which will cost Dress only $40,000. Dress must record the purchase of the merchandise at $50,000 and recognize a foreign currency gain of $10,000 ($50,000 − $40,000).

The foreign currency exchange rates, however, have no effect on the transactions of a U.S. person who arranges all international transactions in U.S. dollars.

EXAMPLE

13

Sellers, Inc., a domestic corporation, purchases goods from Rose, Ltd., a foreign corporation, and pays for these goods in U.S. dollars. Rose then exchanges the U.S. dollars for the currency of the country in which it operates. Sellers has no foreign exchange considerations with which to contend.

If, instead, Rose required Sellers to pay for the goods in a foreign currency, Sellers would have to exchange U.S. dollars to obtain the foreign currency to make payment. If the exchange rate changed from the date of purchase to the date of payment, Sellers would have a foreign currency gain or loss on the currency exchange.

In recent years, U.S. currency abroad has amounted to more than 50 percent of the U.S. currency in circulation. Taxpayers may find it necessary to translate amounts denominated in foreign currency into U.S. dollars for any of the following purposes.

- Purchase of goods, services, and property.
- Sale of goods, services, and property.
- Collection of foreign receivables.
- Payment of foreign payables.
- Foreign tax credit calculations.

The IRS maintains that transactions involving virtual currencies and cryptocurrencies do not create foreign currency gain or loss.[18]

The Code generally adopts the **functional currency** approach. For book and tax purposes, the currency of the economic environment in which the non-U.S. entity operates generally is used as the monetary unit to measure gains and losses.[19]

All income tax determinations are made in the taxpayer's functional currency.[19] A taxpayer's default functional currency is the U.S. dollar. In most cases, a **qualified business unit (QBU)** operating in another country uses that country's currency as its functional currency. A QBU is a separate and clearly identified unit of a taxpayer's trade or business (e.g., a foreign branch).[20]

---

[17]§ 988(b).

[18]Notice 2014–21, 2014–16 I.R.B. 938.

[19]§ 985. These rules are similar to those of ASC 830.

[20]Reg. § 1.989(a)–1(b). An individual is not a QBU; however, a trade or business conducted by an individual may be a QBU.

25-5 U.S. PERSONS WITH OFFSHORE INCOME

LO.5

Work with the U.S. tax provisions affecting U.S. persons earning foreign-source income, including the rules relating to cross-border asset transfers, antideferral provisions, and the foreign tax credit.

U.S. taxpayers often "internationalize" gradually over time. A U.S. business may operate on a strictly domestic basis for several years, then explore offshore markets by exporting its products abroad, and later license its products to an overseas manufacturer or enter into a joint venture with a non-U.S. partner. If its forays into these markets are successful, the U.S. business may create a foreign branch and then a subsidiary, moving a portion of its operations abroad by establishing a sales or manufacturing facility.

Exhibit 25.6 shows a typical timeline for "going global." Both U.S. and offshore entities generally move into international markets in this manner. Each step in this process generates increasingly significant international income tax consequences.

The Big Picture

EXAMPLE

14

Return to the facts of *The Big Picture* on p. 25-1. It appears that VoiceCo has moved along the Global Activities Timeline (see Exhibit 25.6), in that it is making export sales, and it has a manufacturing plant in Ireland.

25-5a Export Property, Licenses, Foreign Branches

The easiest way for a U.S. business to engage in global commerce is simply to sell U.S.-produced goods and services abroad. These sales can be conducted with little or no foreign presence and allow the business to explore offshore markets without making costly financial commitments to overseas operations. Under the worldwide provisions of the U.S. tax law, a U.S. person immediately includes gross income from export sales.

Whether foreign taxes must be paid on this export income depends on the laws of the non-U.S. jurisdiction and whether the U.S. taxpayer is deemed to have a business presence there (i.e., a "permanent establishment"). In many cases, this export income is not taxed by the receiving country.

Fees from licensing arrangements generally are recognized by the U.S. taxpayer when earned or collected; these usually entail royalties and profit sharing payments.

A U.S. person's *foreign branch* typically is an offshore office or other operating facility owned by the U.S. business (and not a corporation, partnership, or other legal entity in the other country). Profits and losses from branch operations are recognized immediately (i.e., the operating results flow through to the U.S. parent's tax return in the same tax year). Branch operating losses generally produce an immediate deduction, and branch profits are taxed in the year earned. This often means that entities that generate current operating losses should remain branches of the U.S. parent. On the other hand, a profitable foreign branch can create a cash-flow problem if the U.S. tax liability is due before the cash related to those profits is repatriated to the U.S. parent.

Foreign Tax Credit

Income and loss from the export, licensing, and branch operations of a U.S. person are taxed under the worldwide system of business taxation. If the non-U.S. country also imposes an income tax on such income, the possibility of double taxation arises. Problems associated with double taxation include the stacking of tax rates for the various countries

EXHIBIT 25.6   **Global Activities Timeline**

TIME

Domestic operations only | Export | License to non-U.S. person | Foreign branch | Separate foreign entity upon each other, resulting in high effective tax rates on the dual-taxed income, and the lack of harmonization of the tax rules of the various countries to the taxpayer's detriment.

Concerns involving double taxation most often are addressed through language in applicable tax treaties, ideally assigning taxable income to only one of the countries involved, and through tax credits and exemptions in the taxpayer's home country. The United States long has allowed a foreign tax credit (FTC) for this purpose, typically for use when the dual-taxed transaction occurs in a non-treaty country.[21] The FTC is an annual taxpayer election; lacking an FTC election, the tax payments are claimed as deductions against gross income.

The FTC is allowed against the taxpayer's regular tax liability, such that only the non-U.S. tax obligation is paid on the dual-taxed income. The FTC is limited, though, to the U.S. tax that would be incurred on the income amount. As a result, the credit equals the *lesser of* (1) the foreign tax actually paid or (2) the corresponding U.S. income tax amount,[22] using the sourcing rules discussed in text Section 25-3, computed using the following formula.

$$\frac{\text{Foreign-source taxable income}}{\text{Total (worldwide) taxable income}} \quad \times \quad \text{U.S. tax before FTC}$$

Where a foreign tax payment is not allowed as a current-year credit under the *lesser of* rule, the disallowed amount is allowed in another tax year as a carryover. FTCs are carried back 1 year and forward 10 years. FTC carryovers tend to occur when the effective tax rate that applies to the dual-taxed income is lower in the United States than it is in the other country.

EXAMPLE

15

BlueCo, a U.S. corporation, manufactures and sells most of its products in the United States. It also conducts some business in the European Union through various branches. During the current year, BlueCo reports taxable income of $700,000, of which $500,000 is U.S.-source and $200,000 is foreign-source. Foreign income taxes paid amounted to $45,000. BlueCo's U.S. income tax liability before any foreign tax credit (FTC) is $147,000. What is its allowable FTC?

(1)	Foreign taxes paid	$45,000
(2)	U.S. tax associated with dual-taxed income	
	$\dfrac{\$200,000 \text{ (Foreign-source TI)}}{\$700,000 \text{ (Total TI)}} \times \$147,000 \text{ (U.S. tax)}$	$42,000
(3)	FTC allowed [lesser of (1) or (2)]	$42,000
(4)	FTC carryforward [(1) − (2), but not below $0]	$ 3,000

A separate FTC is computed for each of four types of taxable income. These FTC "baskets" were devised so that a taxpayer could not claim credits against a high-taxed type of income (like business profits) from foreign taxes paid concerning a low-taxed type of income (like portfolio interest, perhaps under treaty language). The taxpayer's FTC for the year is the sum of the separately computed amounts; there might be a carryforward in one basket and none in another, but the FTCs cannot be combined among baskets. The FTC baskets separately treat the following types of income.

- Portfolio income, like dividends and capital gains.
- Income from foreign branches.
- Certain intangible income (see text Section 25-5e).
- Active, business income not already assigned to a basket.

---

[21] The credit is allowed via § 27, but the qualifications and calculation procedure for the FTC are contained in §§ 901–908. Although taxpayers can claim a deduction for the foreign taxes paid, instead of a credit, in most instances, the credit is advantageous since it is a direct offset against the tax liability.

[22] § 904.

To qualify for the FTC, the foreign levy must resemble a tax on net income, like the Federal income tax. For instance, it cannot be a tax on gross receipts, on the right to extract minerals, or on property values.[23] However, these tax payments can be deducted by the taxpayer. A tax is available for the FTC when it is paid or accrued, according to the taxpayer's method of tax accounting. Concept Summary 25.2 summarizes the FTC rules.

Concept Summary 25.2

The Foreign Tax Credit

The foreign tax credit (FTC) is related to the worldwide system of income taxation that applies under U.S. income tax law to many cross-border transactions. The credit works to eliminate the exposure of a taxpayer to the double taxation of income that is generated in another country. In effect, foreign income taxes are used to reduce the Federal income tax liability, in a form of "revenue sharing" by the governments involved.

- The FTC is available to C corporations and individuals.
- The FTC is an annual taxpayer election. If the FTC is not used for foreign taxes, a deduction may be claimed.
- The FTC is allowed for taxes paid by the taxpayer directly or through a foreign withholding procedure.
- An FTC is allowed only for income taxes on net taxable income that are levied by the host country. Other forms of fees or non-income taxes can be claimed by the taxpayer as a deduction.

- The taxpayer's taxable income and foreign tax payments are split among four income "baskets" (i.e., among portfolio, intangible, foreign branch, and other business income).
- The FTC then is allowed in each income basket.
  - The FTC for the year in each basket equals the lesser of (1) the foreign taxes paid or accrued or (2) the share of the U.S. tax liability that corresponds to the foreign-source income of the taxpayer as a percentage of worldwide taxable income.
  - In this way, if the taxpayer is operating in a jurisdiction that applies an income tax rate that is higher than that of the United States, the credit cannot be used to offset income tax that relates to other types of income.
- If foreign taxes were paid but are not allowed for the current tax year because of this "lesser of" limitation, the credit is carried back 1 year and then forward 10 years.

Special Tax Rate for Intangible Income

The U.S. tax law provides an incentive for domestic C corporations to generate taxable income overseas in the form of intangible income, with most personnel and activities still in the United States.[24] A lower tax rate (effectively 13.125 percent) applies to income from intangible assets that the U.S. entity employs overseas. The lower tax rate is meant to encourage U.S. C corporations to conduct international business that leverages U.S. expertise (especially in technology fields) in operations around the world, by keeping the activity within (or moving it back to) the United States.

---

[23]§ 904(c).

[24]§ 250. The provision creates the computational amount known as foreign-derived intangible income (FDII).

The special tax rate is derived after allowing deductions against foreign-source income in excess of a normalized return on the entity's tangible assets. The details of those computations are not discussed here.[25] The special tax rate does not apply to income that otherwise is taxed under Subpart F of the Code (see text Section 25-5d). The base for the lower tax rate is limited to the entity's foreign-source taxable income for the year.

25-5b Creating a Cross-Border Business Entity

As part of "going international," a U.S. taxpayer may decide to transfer assets outside the United States and form a legal entity with which to conduct business overseas. This may take the form of a cash investment or a transfer of assets of a U.S. entity. After the transfer, the U.S. investor has created the equivalent of a new corporation.

In situations where potential taxable income is transferred to a corporation outside the U.S. taxing jurisdiction, the exchange may trigger an income tax. The tax result of transferring property to a non-U.S. corporation depends on the nature of the exchange, the assets involved, the income potential of the property, and the character of the property in the hands of the transferor or transferee. Exhibit 25.7 summarizes the taxation of cross-border asset transfers.

As discussed in Chapters 18 and 20, when assets are exchanged for corporate stock in a domestic transaction, realized gain or loss may be deferred. When assets are transferred to non-U.S. corporations, however, the assets leave the U.S. taxing jurisdiction and any deferred gains would never be subject to U.S. Federal income tax. Therefore, gain deferral is generally not allowed on transfers to non-U.S. corporations.[26]

EXAMPLE 16

Amelia, Inc., a domestic corporation, incorporates its profitable Irish manufacturing branch as a new wholly owned foreign corporation, St. George, Ltd., to engage in manufacturing activities in Ireland. The branch assets always have been used in Ireland. Amelia realizes the following gains and losses on the transfer of the assets to the new corporation.

Asset	Tax Basis	Market Value	Built-In Gain/Loss
Raw materials inventory	$100	$ 400	$ 300
Accounts receivable	200	250	50
Land	450	925	475
Equipment, furniture, and fixtures	150	50	(100)
Total	$900	$1,625	$ 725

Although the realized gains and losses would be deferred under § 351 in a purely domestic event, Amelia's realized gains are taxable because the assets are leaving the U.S. taxing jurisdiction. All of the realized gains are recognized by Amelia when the transfer occurs. Gain is recognized on an asset-by-asset basis with no offset for losses on other assets.

Intangible assets often qualify for a gain deferral when they are transferred.[27] The gain is treated as received by the transferor over the life of the intangible; only then does it constitute ordinary income. For this purpose, intangible assets include goodwill and the value of the entity's workforce in place.

---

[25]§ 250(b)(2)(A).

[26]§ 367.

[27]§§ 367(d) and 936(h)(3)(B).

| EXHIBIT 25.7 | Taxation of Cross-Border Asset Transfers |

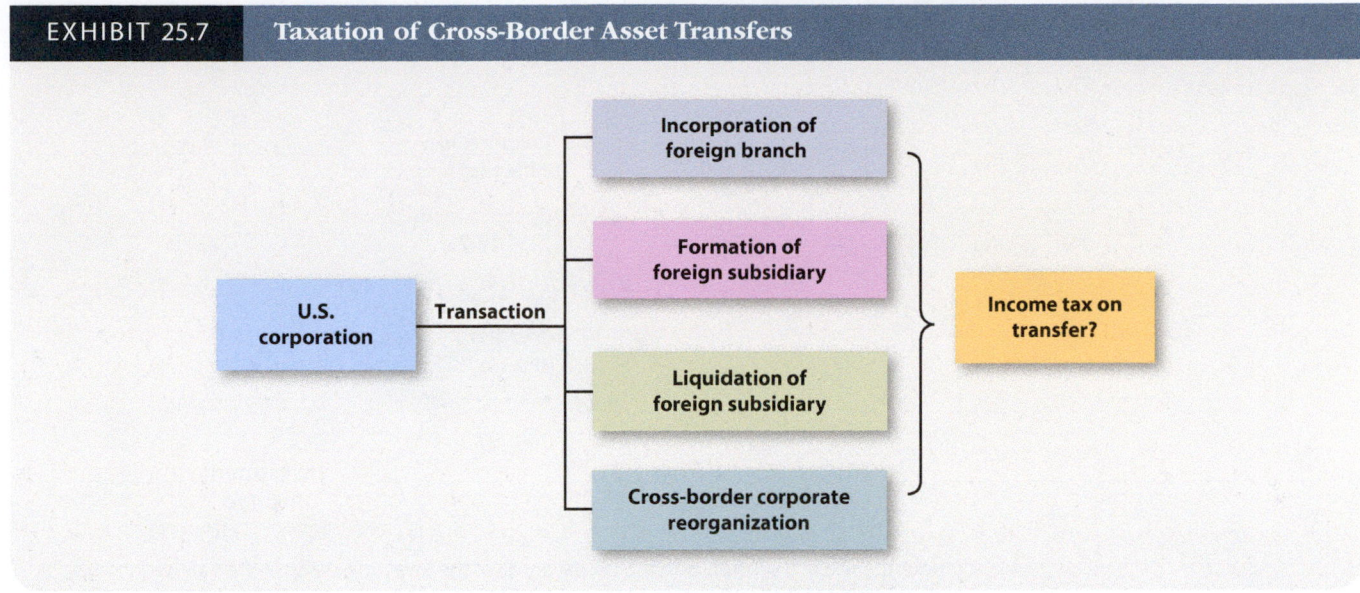

25-5c **Tax Havens**

Many outbound transfers of assets to foreign corporations are to countries with tax rates higher than or equal to the U.S. rate; tax avoidance is not the motive for these transfers. Some U.S. corporations, however, make their offshore investment in (or through) a tax haven. A **tax haven** is a country where either locally sourced income or residents are subject to zero or low levels of local income taxation. The Bahamas, Ireland, the Netherlands, the Cayman Islands, and Bermuda, among other countries, are seen as tax havens. U.S. corporations shift sizable amounts of taxable income annually to these countries.

A tax haven usually has adopted rules that allow taxpayers to establish residency with a minimal presence. Tax haven countries also may have in effect provisions limiting the exchange of financial and commercial information.[28]

Exhibit 25.8 illustrates this use of a tax haven by a U.S. corporation. The U.S. corporation uses a foreign subsidiary in a low- or no-tax country to earn either investment income or a portion of income from business activities (as illustrated previously in the transfer pricing discussion). Because the foreign subsidiary cannot be consolidated with the domestic parent under U.S. tax law and is not itself engaged in any U.S. trade or business, the subsidiary is not subject to U.S. taxation. Without the application of the transfer pricing rules, the base-erosion tax, or the Subpart F rules (discussed in text Section 25-5d), the subsidiary's income escapes U.S. taxation.

A tax haven also can, in effect, be created by an income tax treaty. For example, under an income tax treaty between Country A and Country B, residents of Country A are subject to a withholding tax of only 5 percent on dividend and interest income sourced in Country B. The United States and Country A have a similar treaty. The United States does not have a treaty with Country B, and the withholding tax is 30 percent. A U.S. corporation can create a foreign subsidiary in Country A and use that subsidiary to make investments in Country B.

---

[28]§ 894(c) contains additional limitations on the use of treaty benefits.

EXHIBIT 25.8   Use of a Tax Haven Corporation

Without the use of a subsidiary in the tax haven, all of the investment and shifted active income would be taxed at the U.S. tax rate of 21 percent. This tax can be reduced or eliminated by shifting some of the taxpayer's assets and operations to the tax haven country.

This practice often is referred to as treaty shopping. If the Country B investment income had been earned directly by the U.S. corporation, it would have been subject to a 30 percent withholding tax. As a result of investing through the foreign subsidiary created in Country A, the U.S. parent corporation pays only 10 percent in foreign taxes on the income earned (i.e., 5 percent to Country B and 5 percent to Country A).

25-5d Offshore (Foreign) Corporations Controlled by U.S. Persons

To minimize current tax liability, taxpayers often shift an income-generating activity to an entity that is not within the U.S. taxing jurisdiction. When a foreign corporation is used in this manner, offshore taxable income may be subject to lower income tax rates, and they may attract certain treaty benefits. U.S. tax law extends a worldwide approach to some of this income, treating such items on a pass-through basis that triggers immediate U.S. income taxation, even though a separate foreign corporation, and not just a branch, is used.

Controlled Foreign Corporations

An elaborate antideferral system is in place that attempts to keep U.S. taxpayers from sheltering current taxable income by using foreign subsidiaries. Subpart F of the Code provides that certain types of income generated by controlled foreign corporations (CFCs) are included in current-year gross income by the U.S. shareholders, without regard to actual distributions.[29] Subpart F and CFC rules thus create an immediate "flow-through" of taxable income from the foreign subsidiary to its U.S. shareholders.

About 90,000 CFCs exist, largely in the United Kingdom, Canada, China, Mexico, Germany, and the Netherlands.

A controlled foreign corporation (CFC) is any non-U.S. corporation in which more than 50 percent of (1) the total combined voting power of all classes of stock entitled to vote or (2) the total value of the stock of the corporation is owned by U.S. shareholders on any day during the taxable year of the foreign corporation. The offshore subsidiaries of most multinational U.S. parent corporations are CFCs.

---

[29]§§ 951 through 964.

For this purpose, a U.S. shareholder is defined as a U.S. person who owns, or is considered to own, 10 percent or more of the total combined voting power of all classes of voting stock of the non-U.S. corporation. Stock owned directly, indirectly, and constructively is counted.

When Subpart F applies, U.S. shareholders include in gross income their pro rata share of Subpart F income. The taxpayer includes a proportionate share of gross income in the year in which the CFC's taxable year ends.

Subpart F Constructive Dividends

Gray, Inc., a calendar year corporation, is a CFC for the entire tax year. Chance Company, a U.S. corporation, owns 60% of Gray's one class of stock for the entire year. Subpart F income is $100,000, and no distributions have been made during the year.

Chance, a calendar year taxpayer, includes $60,000 in gross income as a constructive dividend from Gray for the tax year.

Groth, Inc., is a CFC until July 1 of the calendar tax year (not a leap year) and earns $100,000 of Subpart F income. Terry, a U.S. citizen, owns 30% of its one class of stock for the entire year.

Terry includes $14,877 [$100,000 × 30% × (181 days/365 days)] in gross income as a constructive dividend from Groth for the tax year.

Subpart F Income Only certain income earned by the CFC triggers immediate U.S. taxation as a constructive dividend. This Subpart F income can be characterized as income with little or no economic connection with the CFC's country of incorporation. Subpart F income typically includes foreign base company income (FBCI), such as:

- Foreign personal holding company income.
- Foreign base company sales income.
- Foreign base company services income.

Foreign personal holding company (FPHC) income commonly includes:

- Dividends, interest, royalties, rents, and annuities.
- Excess gains over losses from the sale or exchange of property that gives rise to FPHC income.
- Excess of foreign currency gains over foreign currency losses (other than amounts directly related to the business needs of the CFC).

Foreign base company (FBC) sales income is income derived by a CFC where the CFC has very little connection with the process that generates the income, and a related party is involved. If the CFC earns income from the sale of property to customers outside the CFC's country of incorporation and either the supplier or the customer is related to the CFC, this typically constitutes FBC sales income. FBC sales income usually involves three different countries in the arrangement, as illustrated in Concept Summary 25.3.

Ulysses, Ltd., is a CFC organized in the United Kingdom and owned 100% by Joyce, Inc., a U.S. corporation. Ulysses purchases finished inventory from Joyce and sells the inventory to customers in Hong Kong. This sales income constitutes FBC sales income.

Concept Summary 25.3
Subpart F Income and a CFC

An exception applies to property that is manufactured, produced, grown, or extracted in the country in which the CFC was organized or created and to property sold for use, consumption, or disposition within that country. In both of these situations, fewer than three countries are involved, and the CFC has participated in the economic process that generates the income. No Subpart F income is created.

EXAMPLE 20

If Ulysses, from Example 19, purchases raw materials from Joyce and performs substantial manufacturing activity in the United Kingdom before selling the inventory to customers in Hong Kong, the income is not FBC sales income.

Even without the manufacturing activity, sales to customers within the United Kingdom would not produce FBC sales income.

FBC services income is income derived from the performance of services for or on behalf of a related person and performed outside the country in which the CFC was created or organized. Income from services performed in connection with the sale of property by a CFC that has manufactured, produced, grown, or extracted such property is *not* FBC services income.

Subpart F Income Exceptions Potentially large amounts of offshore profits (e.g., active trade or business income not involving related persons) escape the definition of Subpart F income, resulting in no immediate U.S. income taxation. Other exceptions also apply to the Subpart F rules.

- A *de minimis* rule provides that if the total amount of a foreign corporation's FBCI for the taxable year is less than the smaller of 5 percent of the CFC's gross income or $1 million, *none* of its gross income is treated as FBCI for the tax year.

- A *full inclusion* rule applies if a foreign corporation's FBCI exceeds 70 percent of total gross income. In this case, *all* of the corporation's gross income for the tax year is treated as Subpart F income.

- FBCI subject to high foreign taxes is not included under Subpart F. The taxpayer must establish that the income was taxed by the other country at an effective rate of more than 90 percent of the Federal corporate income tax rate. For example, the other country's effective income tax rate must be greater than 18.9 percent (90% × 21%, where 21 percent is the current U.S. corporate rate).

Subpart F Income

USP, Inc., is the sole U.S. shareholder of Gaelic, Inc., a CFC. During the taxable year, Gaelic reports gross income of $12,000,000 and FBCI of $521,000.

Since Gaelic's FBCI is less than the smaller of (1) 5% of gross income ($600,000; $12,000,000 × 5%) or (2) $1,000,000, the *de minimis* rule applies and *none* of Gaelic's gross income is treated as FBCI for the year.

EXAMPLE 21

Assume the same facts as in the previous example, except that Gaelic's FBCI is $8,500,000. Here, FBCI is 70.8% of gross income ($8,500,000 ÷ $12,000,000).

Under the *full inclusion* rule, *all* of Gaelic's gross income is treated as Subpart F income.

EXAMPLE 22

Other Tax Consequences of Being a CFC The Subpart F and CFC rules create an immediate flow-through of taxable income, regardless of distributions received by the taxpayer. This works in a manner similar to that of the income taxation of partnerships, S corporations, and similar entities (see Chapters 21 and 22). A foreign tax credit is allowed with respect to a Subpart F income inclusion.[30]

A U.S. shareholder's basis in CFC stock is increased by constructive dividends and decreased by subsequent distributions of previously taxed income.[31] The various constructive dividend possibilities for CFC income appear in Concept Summary 25.4.

CFC Tax Consequences

Singh, a U.S. shareholder in the CFC Bombay United, records a $100,000 constructive dividend from the entity as foreign base company services income under Subpart F rules. Singh's basis in the Bombay United stock increases correspondingly by $100,000.

EXAMPLE 23

Continue with the facts of Example 23. When Bombay United makes a $40,000 cash distribution to Singh from the prior constructive dividend, Singh's basis in the Bombay United stock is reduced by $40,000. The payment does not constitute gross income.

EXAMPLE 24

25-5e Movement Toward a Territorial System

U.S. income tax law generally applies a worldwide system with respect to the cross-border activities of U.S. persons, but most of the rest of the developed world uses a territorial approach. Congress believes that moving toward a territorial system will increase the competitiveness of U.S. businesses in the global marketplace, and it has taken steps to adopt some territorial aspects within current law, although the worldwide system still undergirds the taxation of outbound transactions.

Prior law promoted a "defer until repatriation" strategy by U.S. taxpayers: unless Subpart F or some other rule applied, gross income from overseas operations was not recognized by a U.S. entity until the profits were paid back into the United States in the form of dividend payments from a CFC to its domestic parent. Over time, about $3 trillion in unrepatriated profits had been accumulated offshore by U.S. taxpayers, especially in the tech and pharma industries; this unrepatriated cash represented about $1 trillion in deferred U.S. income tax collections. Congress used parts of the TCJA of 2017 to encourage the repatriation of these funds.

---

[30]§ 960.   [31]§ 961.

Concept Summary 25.4

Income of a CFC That Is Included in Gross Income of a U.S. Shareholder, Selected

*Plus all other income when foreign base company exceeds 70% of gross income.

Effective in 2018, many C corporations are allowed a limited version of territorial taxation, while also being encouraged to repatriate any profits accumulated from past tax years. A dividends received deduction (DRD) of 100 percent is allowed for amounts paid to a U.S.-parent C corporation from the earnings and profits (E & P) of a non-U.S., "10%-owned" subsidiary.[32] This rule fully exempts from U.S. taxation the foreign-source profits that underlie the dividend payment (thereby resembling a territorial taxing system), and it encourages the return of cash accumulations to the U.S. economy (perhaps in large amounts).

EXAMPLE 25

OffCo, a 100%-owned Nigerian subsidiary of the U.S. C corporation BossCo, earned a current-year profit of $10,000,000, and it immediately paid all of this amount to its parent in the form of a dividend. The income did not represent Subpart F income for BossCo.

BossCo reports zero gross income for OffCo's current activities; its income from the dividend received is fully offset by the 100% DRD.

The DRD is allowed even if the foreign affiliate is not a CFC of the U.S. parent. Subpart F pass-through constructive dividends do not qualify for the DRD. To qualify for the DRD, the U.S. parent must have owned the stock of the offshore affiliate for at least one year; this requirement may present problems when the entities were involved in recent merger or takeover activity.

In addition, any recognized gain on the sale or other disposition of stock of a 10%-owned CFC by a U.S. shareholder is treated as dividend income and triggers the DRD, to the extent of the transferor's share of unrepatriated, untaxed E & P of the corporation.[33] No foreign tax credit is allowed relative to dividends taxed under this provision.

---

[32]§ 245A; "10%-owned" means owning 10% or more of the voting stock of the foreign corporation.

[33]§ 1248.

One-Time 2017 Transition Tax The adoption of the U.S. version of territorial taxation, allowing significant amounts of offshore profits to fully escape Federal income taxation, came at a potentially steep price for some entities. Included in the 2017 Subpart F income of C corporations was the U.S. parent's share of the untaxed, unrepatriated post-1986 E & P of its 10%-owned foreign subsidiaries, measured typically as of the end of 2017.[34] This E & P triggered significant tax obligations for many U.S. entities, affecting both book and taxable income amounts.

This E & P was subjected to a tax rate of 15.5 percent (8 percent if the E & P was distributed in a form other than cash).[35] The tax was payable immediately, or by election the payment could be spread out over eight years.[36] No foreign tax credit was allowed against the one-time tax liability.[37]

EXAMPLE 26

HomeCo, a U.S. C corporation, ran its overseas operations through AwayCo, a 100%-owned subsidiary based in a low-tax country with which the United States does not hold a tax treaty. E & P accumulated within AwayCo amounted to $50,000,000 in cash, which remained unrepatriated, deferring the U.S. income taxation on those profits.

HomeCo's 2017 Subpart F income included this $50,000,000, and HomeCo incurred a one-time transition tax of $7,750,000 ($50,000,000 × 15.5% tax rate). HomeCo properly elected to pay this obligation over eight years.

Special rules apply to shareholders who are pass-through entities (e.g., S corporations and partnerships).[38]

Additional Tax on Intangible Income In the context of the adoption of a form of territorial taxation, Congress feared that U.S. CFCs would transfer portable types of income overseas to avoid Federal income taxation permanently and in full. To counter these possibilities, a tax applies at an effective rate of 10.5 percent on the shareholders of a CFC, where the entity generates intangible income that is foreign-sourced (called global intangible low-taxed income, or GILTI).[39]

Income taxed under this provision is not classified as Subpart F income, although it is taxed in a similar manner (i.e., immediately when earned).[40] Generally, the tax on GILTI is zero if the effective income tax rate in the host country is at least 13.125 percent.

The tax does not apply to income that is effectively connected to a U.S. business, nor to items already taxed under Subpart F. The base for the 10.5 percent tax is computed to allow for a normal return on the CFC's tangible assets; those calculations are not discussed here.[41] The foreign tax credit is allowed against this tax, but only to the extent of 80 percent of the foreign taxes paid, only within the FTC basket for GILTI, and without any carryover allowed to another tax year.

EXAMPLE 27

HornCo, a U.S. C corporation, conducts its overseas operations through its Algerian CFC, OtterCo. OtterCo's intangible income for the tax year totaled $5,000,000, on which it paid $200,000 Algeria income tax. These items did not constitute Subpart F income, and they were not effectively connected to HornCo's U.S. businesses.

HornCo includes the $5,000,000 intangible income in its own gross income for the year, and its shareholders are liable for a tax of $525,000 ($5,000,000 × 10.5%). Against this amount, HornCo shareholders can claim an aggregate foreign tax credit of $160,000 ($200,000 foreign tax paid × 80% maximum credit), with no carryover of the remaining $40,000 foreign tax paid.

---

[34]§ 965(a).
[35]§ 965(c).
[36]§ 965(h).
[37]§ 965(g).

[38]§§ 965(f) and (i).
[39]§ 951A.
[40]§ 951A(f).
[41]§§ 951A(b)–(d).

LO.6

Apply the U.S. tax provisions concerning nonresident alien individuals and foreign corporations.

25-6 U.S. TAXATION OF NONRESIDENT ALIENS AND FOREIGN CORPORATIONS

Generally, only the U.S.-source income of nonresident alien individuals and foreign corporations is subject to U.S. taxation. This reflects the reach of the U.S. tax jurisdiction. The constraint, however, does not prevent the United States from also taxing the foreign-source income of nonresident alien individuals and non-U.S. corporations when that income is effectively connected with the conduct of a U.S. trade or business, in the manner of territorial taxation.[42]

25-6a Nonresident Alien Individuals

A **nonresident alien (NRA)** individual is not a citizen or resident of the United States. For example, Prince William is an NRA because he is not a citizen or resident of the United States. Citizenship is determined under the immigration and naturalization laws of the United States.[43] Usually, citizenship statutes are broken down into two categories: nationality at birth or through naturalization.

Residency

An individual is a resident of the United States for income tax purposes if he or she meets either the green card test or the substantial presence test.[44] If either of these tests is met for the calendar year, the individual is deemed a U.S. resident for the year.

A non-U.S. person issued a green card is considered a U.S. resident on the first day he or she is physically present in the United States after issuance. The green card is Immigration Form I–551. Newly issued cards no longer are green, but the form still is referred to as the "green card." Status as a U.S. resident remains in effect until the green card has been revoked or the individual has abandoned lawful permanent resident status.

The *substantial presence* test is applied to an alien without a green card. It is a mathematical test involving physical presence in the United States. An individual who is physically present in the United States for at least 183 days during the calendar year is a U.S. resident for income tax purposes.

This 183-day requirement also can be met over a three-year period that includes the two immediately preceding years and the current year, as long as the individual is present in the United States at least 31 days during the current year.[45] For this purpose, each day of the current calendar year is counted as a full day, each day of the first preceding year as one-third day, and each day of the second preceding year as one-sixth day. A nominal presence of 10 days or less can be ignored in determining whether the substantial presence test is met.

EXAMPLE 28

Li, who is not a U.S. citizen, was present in the United States for 90 days in 2018, 180 days in 2019, and 110 days in 2020. For Federal income tax purposes, Li is a U.S. resident for 2020, because she was physically present for 185 days [(90 days × ⅙) + (180 days × ⅓) + (110 days × 1)] during the three-year period.

When counting days of physical presence in the United States, there are several exceptions. Commuters from Mexico and Canada who are employed in the United States but return home each day do not count those work days as days of physical presence. The same is true for individuals who are prevented from leaving the United States by medical conditions that arose while the individuals were in the United States.

---

[42]§§ 871, 881, and 882.

[43]Title 8, Aliens and Nationality, *United States Code.*

[44]§ 7701(b).

[45]§ 7701(b)(3)(A).

Some individuals are exempt altogether from the substantial presence test, including foreign government-related individuals (e.g., diplomats), qualified teachers, trainees and students, and certain professional athletes.

Nonresident Aliens Not Engaged in a U.S. Trade or Business

Certain U.S.-source income that is *not* effectively connected with the conduct of a U.S. trade or business is subject to a flat 30 percent tax. This income includes dividends, certain interest, rents, royalties, certain compensation, premiums, annuities, and other similar income. This tax generally requires the payors of the income to withhold 30 percent of gross amounts.[46] The withholding procedures work to eliminate the problems of ensuring payment by nonresidents and determining allowable deductions as well as, in most instances, the filing of tax returns by nonresidents.

Interest received from certain portfolio debt investments, even though U.S. sourced, is exempt from taxation when earned by non-U.S. persons. Interest earned on bank deposits also is exempt as long as it is not effectively connected with the conduct of a U.S. trade or business. These rules encourage offshore investors to purchase U.S. Treasury bonds and notes, and to deposit U.S. currency in domestic bank accounts.

Capital gains *not* effectively connected with the conduct of a U.S. trade or business are exempt from this tax, as long as the NRA was not present in the United States for 183 days or more during the taxable year. If an NRA has not established a taxable year, the calendar year is used. NRAs are not permitted to carry forward capital losses.[47]

Nonresident Aliens Engaged in a U.S. Trade or Business

Two important definitions determine the U.S. tax consequences to NRAs with U.S.-source income: "the conduct of a U.S. trade or business " and " effectively connected income ." Specifically, for an NRA's noninvestment income to be subject to U.S. taxation, the NRA must be considered engaged in a U.S. trade or business and must earn income effectively connected with that business.

General criteria for determining whether a U.S. trade or business exists include the location of production activities, management, distribution activities, and other business functions. Trading in commodities and securities ordinarily does not constitute a trade or business. Dealers, however, need to avoid maintaining a U.S. trading office and trading for their own accounts.

The Code does not explicitly define a U.S. trade or business, but case law looks for activities carried on in the United States that are regular, substantial, and continuous.[48] Once an NRA is considered engaged in a U.S. trade or business, all U.S.-source income other than investment and capital gain income is considered effectively connected to that trade or business and is therefore subject to U.S. taxation.

EXAMPLE 29

Vito, an NRA, produces wine for export. During the current year, Vito earns $500,000 from exporting wine to unrelated wholesalers in the United States. The title to the wine passes to the U.S. wholesalers in New York. Vito has no offices or employees in the United States. The income from wine sales is U.S.-source income, but because Vito is not engaged in a U.S. trade or business, the income is not subject to taxation in the United States.

Vito begins operating a hot dog cart in New York City. This activity constitutes a U.S. trade or business. Consequently, all U.S.-source income other than investment or capital gain income is taxed in the United States as income effectively connected with a U.S. trade or business. As a result, both the hot dog cart profits and the $500,000 in wine income are subject to U.S. income tax.

---

[46]§§ 871 and 1441. Tax treaty provisions can change these rates. See Exhibit 25.4.

[47]§ 871(a)(2).

[48]See, for example, *Higgins v. Comm.*, 41–1 USTC ¶9233, 25 AFTR 1160, 61 S.Ct. 475 (1941) and *Continental Trading, Inc. v. Comm.*, 59–1 USTC ¶9316, 3 AFTR 2d 923, 265 F.2d 40 (CA–9, 1959).

Effectively connected income is taxed at the same rates that apply to U.S. citizens and residents, and deductions for expenses attributable to that income are allowed. NRAs with income effectively connected with the conduct of a U.S. trade or business also are subject to the alternative minimum tax.

25-6b Foreign Corporations

A corporation created or organized in the United States is a domestic corporation. A foreign corporation is one that is not domestic. Although McDonald's is a global corporation, it is considered a domestic corporation for U.S. tax purposes, solely because it was organized in the United States.

Foreign corporations are taxed very much like NRAs. Capital gain income is exempt from tax, and a flat 30 percent tax rate is applied to U.S.-source investment income items if they are not effectively connected with a U.S. trade or business. Foreign corporations conducting a trade or business in the United States are subject to Federal income taxation on any U.S.-source income effectively connected with the trade or business.

25-6c Foreign Investment in Real Property Tax Act

At one time, NRAs and foreign corporations could avoid U.S. taxation on gains from the sale of U.S. real estate if the gains were treated as capital gains and were not effectively connected with the conduct of a U.S. trade or business. In the mid-1970s, midwestern farmers pressured Congress to eliminate what they saw as a tax advantage that would allow nonresidents to bid up the price of farmland. This and other concerns about foreign ownership of U.S. real estate led to the enactment of the **Foreign Investment in Real Property Tax Act (FIRPTA)**.

Under FIRPTA, gains and losses realized by NRAs and foreign corporations from the sale or other disposition of U.S. real property interests (USRPIs) are treated as effectively connected with the conduct of a U.S. trade or business, even when those individuals or corporations are not actually so engaged. Any direct interest in real property situated in the United States and any interest in a domestic corporation (other than solely as a creditor) are U.S. real property interests.

NRA individuals must pay a tax equal to the *lesser of*:

- The applicable tax on their alternative minimum taxable income, or
- Regular U.S. rates on the net U.S. real property gain for the taxable year.[49]

Any purchaser acquiring a USRPI from a foreign person must withhold 10 percent of the amount realized on the disposition.[50]

25-6d Expatriation to Avoid U.S. Taxation

U.S. taxation of U.S.-source income is required of individuals who relinquished their U.S. citizenship within 10 years of deriving that income if they gave up their citizenship to avoid U.S. taxation. Furthermore, NRAs who lost U.S. citizenship within a 10-year period immediately preceding the close of the tax year must pay taxes on their U.S.-source income as though they were still U.S. citizens. This provision applies only if the expatriation had as one of its principal purposes the avoidance of U.S. taxes. Individuals are presumed to have a tax avoidance purpose if they meet either of the following criteria.[51]

---

[49]§ 897.
[50]§ 1445.

[51]§ 877(a)(2). The dollar amounts are adjusted for inflation each year.

- Average annual net income tax for the five taxable years ending before the date of loss of U.S. citizenship is more than $171,000 for 2020.

- Net worth as of that date is at least $2 million.

These provisions also apply to "long-term lawful permanent residents" who cease to be taxed as U.S. residents. A long-term permanent resident is an individual (other than a citizen of the United States) who is a lawful permanent resident of the United States in at least 8 taxable years during the previous 15-year period. An exception applies to certain individuals with dual citizenship.

The United States continues to treat individuals as U.S. citizens or residents until the taxpayers provide required information and an expatriation notice. Expatriates who are subject to the 10-year rule outlined previously must file an information disclosure statement annually. If an expatriate is physically present in the United States for more than 30 days during a calendar year during the 10-year period, the individual is taxed as a U.S. citizen or resident.[52] These expatriation rules, taken as a whole, make it difficult to give up U.S. citizenship or residency simply to avoid U.S. taxation.

25-7 TAX PLANNING

Tax planning techniques for the multinational taxpayer are effective when they combine opportunities presented by Federal income tax law, the tax provisions and economic incentives offered by the overseas jurisdictions in which business is conducted, income-shifting devices, and the use of tax treaties and tax havens.

Return to the timeline of Exhibit 25.6, and consider the decision to operate a multinational business entity as a branch and when to convert the structure of the business to an overseas subsidiary. Exhibit 25.9 identifies the major advantages and disadvantages for each of these decisions from a Federal income tax standpoint.

Additional tax planning opportunities and considerations are discussed below.

EXHIBIT 25.9	Foreign Branch vs. Separate Overseas Entity: Tax Considerations	
U.S. Income Tax Considerations	**Operate as a Branch of the U.S. Corporation**	**Operate Through a Separate Overseas Entity (e.g., Subsidiary)**
Advantages	• Current U.S. deduction for foreign losses (i.e., flow-through treatment) • If permanent establishment tests are met, treaty benefits are available • Income taxes paid to other jurisdictions may qualify for foreign tax credit, thereby reducing exposure to double taxation • Lower tax rate on certain intangible income	• Exemption for U.S. income taxation on profits repatriated as dividends (except for GILTI and Subpart F income) • Availability of income shifting by transfer pricing strategies (e.g., by paying management fees or setting internal pricing levels) • Liability protection for U.S. net assets from overseas operations
Disadvantages	• Current profits are subject to immediate U.S. taxation (i.e., flow-through treatment, even without cash repatriations) • Local tax and financial incentives may not be available (i.e., to an "outside" entity)	• Exposure to taxes on intangible income • Subpart F rules might accelerate recognition of gross income from offshore profits • IRS might use § 482 powers to reallocate income/deductions to the United States

---

[52]§ 877(g)(1).

25-7a **The Foreign Tax Credit Limitation and Sourcing Provisions**

The FTC limitation is partially based on the amount of foreign-source taxable income in the numerator of the limitation formula. Consequently, the sourcing of income is extremely important. Generally, in this regard, the U.S. taxpayer benefits when the sourcing rules work to:

- Generate *income* items that are *foreign-source*, to maximize net foreign-source income (the numerator of the FTC fraction). Alternatively, a branch or flow-through entity might want overseas income to be U.S.-source, to increase its 20 percent deduction for qualified business income.[53]

- Realize *deduction* items as *U.S.-source*, to minimize any reduction in net foreign-source income (the numerator of the FTC fraction).

Income that is taxed by an overseas tax jurisdiction benefits from the FTC only to the extent that it is classified as foreign-source income under U.S. tax law. As a result, elements that affect the sourcing of income, such as the place of title passage, should be considered carefully before a transaction is undertaken.

It further may be possible for a U.S. corporation to alleviate the problem of excess foreign taxes by using the following techniques.

- Generate "same basket" foreign-source income that is subject to a tax rate lower than the U.S. tax rate.

- Reduce, by relocating operations, highly taxed foreign-source income in favor of foreign-source income that is taxed at a lower rate.

- Deduct foreign taxes for years when the deduction benefit would exceed the FTC benefit.

EXAMPLE 30

Donohoe, Inc., a U.S. corporation, reports total U.S. taxable income of $100,000, classified as follows.

	Total	U.S.-Source Income	Foreign-Source Income—Active Basket
Gross income	$150,000	$100,000	$ 50,000
Deductions	(50,000)	(40,000)	(10,000)
Taxable income	$100,000	$ 60,000	$ 40,000

U.S. income tax before the FTC is $21,000, and Donohoe's FTC limitation is $8,400 [($40,000 ÷ $100,000) × $21,000]. If, through planning and analysis, Donohoe is able to convert $5,000 of the deductions related to foreign-source income to U.S. source, the total taxable income would remain the same, but the FTC limitation would increase to $9,450 [($45,000 ÷ $100,000) × $21,000].

25-7b **Transfer Pricing**

U.S. multinational companies earn income across many different jurisdictions and operate through several different types of entities (e.g., subsidiary corporations, joint ventures, and partnerships). With proper planning and documentation, a U.S. corporation can organize its intercompany payments for goods and services, interest on debt, and royalties for use of intangible property in such a way as to minimize its worldwide tax burden. For example, a U.S. multinational may choose to borrow in high-tax jurisdictions (where the interest deduction will be more valuable) and earn royalty income in low-tax jurisdictions (where the income escapes heavy taxation). The anti-base-erosion tax might restrict these arrangements.

---

[53]§ 199A. See Chapter 15.

GOING INTERNATIONAL

Now you can address the questions about VoiceCo's activities that were posed at the beginning of the chapter. Simply selling assets overseas may not trigger any host country income tax consequences, but such income is taxed currently to VoiceCo in the United States. When VoiceCo sets up an Irish corporation as a manufacturer, it can avoid deemed dividends under Subpart F.

VoiceCo must file Form 5471 to report the activities of its foreign subsidiary. If VoiceCo receives dividends from such a subsidiary, it can claim exemption from U.S. taxation.

What If?

Suppose that although VoiceCo's European sales become a substantial part of its total revenues, it decides not to create a foreign subsidiary. Instead, because shipping costs are high and customers demand quick turnaround on product orders, VoiceCo decides to license its design and manufacturing process to a local European musical instruments company for sales in Europe. The European company pays VoiceCo a royalty equal to 25 percent of the sales price on all of its sales of microphones based on VoiceCo's design. The royalty income is foreign-source, because the underlying intangible property is exploited outside the United States.

The European country imposes a 5 percent withholding tax on all royalty payments to VoiceCo. The royalties are part of its worldwide income and so are currently taxed to VoiceCo in the United States. Will VoiceCo receive a foreign tax credit for the withholding tax?

MONKEY BUSINESS IMAGES/SHUTTERSTOCK.COM

Key Terms

Controlled foreign corporation (CFC), 25-20

Effectively connected income, 25-27

Foreign Investment in Real Property Tax Act (FIRPTA), 25-28

Foreign tax credit (FTC), 25-3

Functional currency, 25-14

Inbound taxation, 25-3

Nonresident alien (NRA), 25-26

Outbound taxation, 25-3

Qualified business unit (QBU), 25-14

Subpart F income, 25-21

Tax haven, 25-19

Tax treaties, 25-5

Transfer pricing, 25-10

Treaty shopping, 25-20

U.S. shareholder, 25-21

U.S. trade or business, 25-27

Discussion Questions

1. **LO.1** "U.S. persons are taxed on their worldwide income." Explain.

2. **LO.1, 5** Liang Corporation, a U.S. entity, owns 100% of ForCo, a non-U.S. corporation not engaged in a U.S. trade or business. Is Liang subject to any U.S. income tax on her dealings with ForCo? Explain.

Critical Thinking   3.   **LO.5** Randall operates his distribution business in several countries. He wants to move some equipment to a new corporation with an office in South Africa. This equipment includes assets with a large acquisition price and accumulated MACRS depreciation. The assets to be transferred would generate a $1,000,000 realized gain if sold. Advise Randall on the tax effects of his proposed asset transfer.

Communications   4.   **LO.5** Joy Marcus owns several income-producing assets, including a stock portfolio and a small consulting services proprietorship. She wants to start up a new corporation in the country Molto, where the income tax rates are about one-third of those in the United States, and transfer all of her assets and operations there.

How tax-effective is Joy's plan in shifting the income from her activities when they are placed in the Molto corporation? Write a memo for the tax research file highlighting the Federal income tax rules that apply.

5.   **LO.5** Five unrelated U.S. individuals own all of the shares of Popping, a corporation organized and operating fully in the country Vivace. Mariam, one of the shareholders, asks you whether the income from Popping will be taxed to her immediately as earned; she believes the entity is classified as "a controlled foreign corporation (CFC)." Explain how the Federal income tax law applies to the profits earned by Popping. Use the correct Federal income tax terminology in your comments.

6.   **LO.5** QuinnCo could not claim all of the income taxes it paid to Japan as a foreign tax credit (FTC) this year. What computational limit probably kept QuinnCo from taking its full FTC? Explain.

Critical Thinking   7.   **LO.5** Molly, Inc., a domestic corporation, generates income from the receipt of royalty income from patents that it owns. Molly wants to avoid U.S. income tax on these royalties, so it has its 100%-owned subsidiary, based in Nigeria, hold the patents and collect the royalties.

What U.S. income tax issues must be considered in assessing this arrangement by Molly, Inc.?

8.   **LO.5** HiramCo, a U.S. entity, wholly owns corporations that operate manufacturing businesses in both Mexico and Costa Rica, and it holds its investment portfolio in Sweden. How many foreign tax credit computations must HiramCo make? Be specific, and use the term *basket* in your answer.

Communications   9.   **LO.1, 6** Write a memo for the tax research file on the difference between "inbound" and "outbound" activities in the context of U.S. taxation of international income.

Communications   10.   **LO.1, 3, 5** Draft a short speech that you will give to your university's Business Club. The title of your talk is "What Is Worldwide Taxation and How Can I Avoid It?" Be certain to include the term *territorial taxing system* in your presentation.

Computational Exercises

11.   **LO.3** Shonda receives dividend income from the following foreign and domestic corporations in the current tax year.

Corporation	Dividends Received	Percentage of U.S. Income for Past 3 Years
Silver (foreign)	$1,500	35%
Bronze (domestic)	1,000	20%
Copper (domestic)	2,000	80%

Determine the amount of U.S.-source income for each corporation.

12. **LO.5** Cordeio, Inc., is a CFC for the entire tax year (not a leap year). Yancy Company, a U.S. corporation, owns 75% of Cordeio's one class of stock for the entire year. Cordeio's Subpart F income is $450,000, and no distributions have been made during the year. Both entities use the calendar tax year.

    a. What amount does Yancy include in gross income as a constructive dividend for the tax year?

    b. Assume that Cordeio is a CFC until March 1 of the calendar tax year. What amount does Yancy include in gross income as a constructive dividend for the tax year?

    c. Express your answer to part (b) as a Microsoft Excel formula.

13. **LO.5** Enders, Inc., a domestic corporation that invests in foreign securities, reports total taxable income for the tax year of $290,000, consisting of $208,800 in U.S.-source business profits and $81,200 of Subpart F income from foreign sources. Income taxes of $24,000 were withheld by foreign tax authorities. Enders's U.S. tax before the FTC is $60,900.

    a. Compute Enders's FTC for the tax year.

    b. Express your answer as a Microsoft Excel formula.

14. **LO.5** By the end of 2017, Klein, a domestic corporation, had accumulated $10,000,000 in cash from the overseas operations of its Liberia subsidiary. Klein made no distributions of this accumulated E & P during 2017. Compute the one-time transition tax liability that was incurred by Klein.

15. **LO.6** Velocity, Inc., a non-U.S. corporation, earned $500,000 U.S.-source income from royalties that it collected and $400,000 interest from its investment in U.S. Treasury bonds. Compute Velocity's U.S. income tax on these amounts.

Problems

16. **LO.3, 5** BlueCo, a domestic corporation, incorporates GreenCo, a new wholly owned entity, in Germany. Under both German and U.S. legal principles, this entity is a corporation. BlueCo faces a 21% U.S. tax rate.

    GreenCo earns $1,500,000 in net profits from its German manufacturing activities and makes no dividend distributions to BlueCo. How much U.S. income tax must BlueCo pay for the current year as a result of GreenCo's earnings, assuming that it triggers no constructive dividend under Subpart F?

17. **LO.3** Emma, a U.S. resident, received the following income items for the current tax year. Identify the sourcing of each item as either U.S. or foreign.

    a. $600 interest from a savings account at a Florida bank.

    b. $5,000 dividend from U.S. Flower Company, a U.S. corporation that operates solely in the eastern United States.

    c. $7,000 dividend from Stern Corporation, a U.S. corporation that generated total gross income of $4,000,000 from the active conduct of a foreign trade or business for the immediately preceding three tax years. Stern's total gross income for the same period was $5,000,000.

    d. $10,000 dividend from International Consolidated, Inc., a foreign corporation that reported gross income of $4,000,000 effectively connected with the conduct of a U.S. trade or business for the immediately preceding three tax years. International's total gross income for the same period was $12,000,000.

    e. $5,000 interest on Warren Corporation bonds. Warren is a U.S. corporation that derived $6,000,000 of its gross income for the immediately preceding three tax years from operation of an active foreign business. Warren's total gross income for this same period was $7,200,000.

Communications   18. **LO.3** Gloria Martinez, an NRA, is a professional golfer. She played in seven tournaments in the United States in the current year and earned $250,000 in prizes from these tournaments. She deposited the winnings in a bank account she opened in Mexico City after her first tournament win.

       Gloria played a total of 30 tournaments for the year and earned $800,000 in total prize money. She spent 40 days in the United States, 60 days in England, 20 days in Scotland, and the rest of the time in South America. Write a letter to Gloria explaining how much U.S.-source income she will generate, if any, from her participation in these tournaments and whether any of her winnings are subject to U.S. taxation. Gloria's address is AV Rio Branco, 149-4#, Rio de Janeiro, RJ 20180, Brazil.

19. **LO.3** Determine whether the sourcing of income for the following transactions is U.S. or foreign.

    a.   Suarez, an NRA, sells stock in Home Depot, a U.S. corporation, through a broker in San Antonio.

    b.   Chris sells stock in IBM, a U.S. corporation, to her brother, Rich. Both Chris and Rich are NRAs, and the sale takes place outside the United States.

    c.   Crows, Inc., sells inventory produced in the United States to customers in Europe. Title passes in the international waters of the Atlantic Ocean.

    d.   Doubles, Inc., a U.S. corporation, manufactures equipment in Malaysia and sells the equipment to customers in the United States.

20. **LO.3** Chock, a U.S. corporation, purchases inventory for resale from distributors within the United States and resells this inventory at a $1,000,000 profit to customers outside the United States. Title to the goods passes outside the United States. What is the sourcing of Chock's inventory sales income?

21. **LO.3** Willa, a U.S. corporation, owns the rights to a patent related to a medical device. Willa licenses the rights to use the patent to IrishCo, which uses the patent in its manufacturing facility located in Ireland. What is the sourcing of the $1,000,000 royalty income received by Willa from IrishCo for the use of the patent?

22. **LO.3** USCo incurred $100,000 in interest expense for the current year. The tax book value of USCo's assets generating foreign-source income is $5,000,000. The tax book value of USCo's assets generating U.S.-source income is $45,000,000. How much of the interest expense is allocated and apportioned to foreign-source income?

Critical Thinking   23. **LO.3** LearCo, a non-U.S. conglomerate, generates $4,000,000,000 in gross receipts annually. Its U.S. subsidiary, KingCo, accounts for $750,000,000 of the annual gross receipts; KingCo's average annual gross receipts for the last three years is $820,000,000. KingCo generates U.S. taxable income of $180,000,000, after deducting a $350,000,000 management fee that it pays to LearCo. KingCo reports no U.S. tax credits. The corporate income tax rate in LearCo's country is 14%. What are the tax implications (if any) of this arrangement?

24. **LO.4** Honk, Inc., a U.S. corporation, purchases weight-lifting equipment for resale from HiDisu, a Japanese corporation, for 60,000,000 yen. On the date of purchase, 110 yen is equal to $1 U.S. (¥110:$1). The purchase is made on December 15, 2020, with payment due in 90 days. Honk is a calendar year taxpayer. On December 31, 2020, the foreign exchange rate is ¥112:$1.

       On February 2, 2021, the invoice is paid when the exchange rate is ¥115:$1. What amount of foreign currency gain or loss, if any, must Honk recognize for 2020 as a result of this transaction? For 2021?

Critical Thinking   25. **LO.5** Packard, Inc., a domestic corporation, operates a branch in Mexico. Over the
Communications   last 10 years, this branch has generated $30,000,000 in losses. For the last 3 years, however, the branch has been profitable and has earned enough income

to offset the prior losses in full. Most of the assets are fully depreciated, and a net gain would be recognized if the assets were sold.

Packard's CFO believes that Packard should incorporate the branch now, so that this potential gain can be transferred to a foreign corporation, deferring the realized gain on the transfer under § 351. Draft a memo to Akiko Henderson, the CFO, addressing the tax issues involved in the proposed transaction.

26. **LO.5** USCo owns 65% of the voting stock of LandCo, a Country X corporation. Terra, an unrelated Country Y corporation, owns the other 35% of LandCo. LandCo owns 100% of the voting stock of OceanCo, a Country Z corporation. Assuming that USCo is a U.S. shareholder, do LandCo and OceanCo meet the definition of a CFC? Explain.

27. **LO.5** Hart Enterprises, a U.S. corporation, owns 100% of OK, Ltd., an Irish corporation. OK's gross income for the year is $10,000,000. Determine OK's Subpart F income (before any expenses) from the transactions that it reported this year.

   a. OK received $600,000 from sales of products purchased from Hart and sold to customers outside Ireland.

   b. OK received $1,000,000 from sales of products purchased from Hart and sold to customers in Ireland.

   c. OK received $400,000 from sales of products purchased from unrelated suppliers and sold to customers in Germany.

   d. OK purchased raw materials from Hart, used these materials to manufacture finished goods, and sold these goods to customers in Italy. OK earned $300,000 from these sales.

   e. OK received $100,000 for the performance of warranty services on behalf of Hart. These services were performed in Japan for customers located in Japan.

   f. OK received $50,000 in dividend income from investments in Canada and Mexico.

28. **LO.5** Brandy, a U.S. corporation, operates a manufacturing branch in Chad, which does not have an income tax treaty with the United States. Brandy's worldwide Federal taxable income is $30,000,000; it is subject to a 21% marginal tax rate. Profits and taxes in Chad for the current year are summarized as follows. Compute Brandy's foreign tax credit associated with its operations in Chad.

Income Item	Chad Income This Year	Chad Tax Rate	Chad Tax Paid
Manufacturing profits	$2,500,000	20%	$500,000
Dividend	300,000	5%	15,000

29. **LO.5** Weather, Inc., a domestic corporation, operates in both Fredonia and the United States. This year, the business generated taxable income of $600,000 from foreign sources and $900,000 from U.S. sources. All of Weather's foreign-source income is in the general limitation basket. Weather's total taxable income is $1,500,000. Weather pays Fredonia taxes of $228,000. What is Weather's FTC for the tax year? Assume a 21% U.S. income tax rate.

30. **LO.5** Blunt, Inc., a U.S. corporation, earned $600,000 in total taxable income, including $80,000 in foreign-source taxable income from its German branch's manufacturing operations and $30,000 in foreign-source taxable income from its Swiss branch's engineering services operations. Blunt paid $20,000 in German income taxes and $1,800 in Swiss income taxes. Compute Blunt's U.S. tax liability after any available FTCs. Blunt's Federal income tax rate is 21%.

31. **LO.5** Dunne, Inc., a U.S. corporation, earned $500,000 in total taxable income, including $50,000 in foreign-source taxable income from its branch manufacturing operations in Brazil and $20,000 in foreign-source income from interest earned on bonds issued by Dutch corporations. Dunne paid $25,000 in Brazilian income taxes and $3,000 in Dutch income taxes. Compute Dunne's U.S. tax liability after any available FTCs. Dunne's U.S. tax rate is 21%.

32. **LO.5** ABC, Inc., a domestic corporation, reports $50,000,000 of taxable income, including $15,000,000 of foreign-source taxable income from services rendered, on which ABC paid $2,500,000 in foreign income taxes. The U.S. tax rate is 21%. What is ABC's foreign tax credit?

Critical Thinking 33. **LO.1, 5** Indeco, a U.S. C corporation, operates Grange, a sales branch in Staccato. Indeco's U.S. marginal income tax rate is 21%; it is 15% for Staccato. Grange's pretax profit for the year is $1,000,000. There is no income tax treaty between the United States and Staccato. Staccato's currency is the U.S. dollar. Compute Indeco's combined U.S. and foreign income tax on the Grange profits under each of the following assumptions.

	U.S. Income Tax	Staccato Income Tax	Combined Tax Liability
a. U.S. income tax law allows no deduction or credit for foreign income taxes paid.	_____	_____	_____
b. U.S. income tax law allows only a deduction for foreign income taxes paid.	_____	_____	_____
c. U.S. income tax law allows only an exclusion of foreign branch profits.	_____	_____	_____
d. U.S. income tax law allows only a credit for the full amount of foreign income taxes paid.	_____	_____	_____
e. U.S. income tax law allows only a credit for the full amount of foreign income taxes paid. The applicable Staccato tax rate is now 30%.	_____	_____	_____
f. U.S. income tax law allows only a credit for the full amount of foreign income taxes paid, but limited currently to the corresponding tax on this income at U.S. rates. The applicable Staccato tax rate is now 30%.	_____	_____	_____

Critical Thinking 34. **LO.5** Night, Inc., a domestic corporation, earned $300,000 from offshore manufacturing activities on which it paid $36,000 of foreign income taxes. Night's foreign sales income is taxed at a 50% income tax rate. What amount of foreign sales income can Night earn without generating any excess FTCs for the current year? Assume a 21% U.S. tax rate.

Communications 35. **LO.3, 4, 5** You are the head tax accountant for Venture Company, a U.S. corporation. The board of directors is considering expansion overseas and asks you to present a summary of the U.S. tax consequences of investing overseas through an offshore subsidiary. Prepare a detailed outline of the presentation you will make to the board.

36. **LO.2, 6** IrishCo, a manufacturing corporation resident in Ireland, distributes products through a U.S. office. Current-year taxable income from such sales in the United States is $12,000,000. IrishCo's U.S. office deposits working capital funds in short-term certificates of deposit with U.S. banks. Current-year interest income from these deposits is $150,000.

IrishCo also invests in U.S. securities traded on the New York Stock Exchange. This investing is done by the home office. For the current year, IrishCo records realized capital gains of $300,000 and dividend income of $50,000 from these stock investments.

a. Compute IrishCo's U.S. tax liability, assuming that the U.S.-Ireland income tax treaty reduces withholding on dividends to 15% and on interest to 5%.

b. Express your solution as a Microsoft Excel command.

37. **LO.6** Clario, S.A., a Peruvian corporation, manufactures furniture in Peru. It sells the furniture to independent distributors in the United States. Because title to the furniture passes to the purchasers in the United States, Clario reports $2,000,000 in U.S.-source income. Clario has no employees or operations in the United States related to its furniture business.

As a separate line of business, Clario buys and sells antique toys. Clario has a single employee operating a booth on weekends at a flea market in Waldo, Florida. The antique toy business generated $85,000 in net profits from U.S. sources during the current year.

What is Clario's effectively connected income for the current year?

38. **LO.6** Martinho is a citizen of Brazil and lives there year-round. He has invested in a plot of Illinois farmland with a tax basis to him of $1,000,000. Martinho has no other business or investment activities in the United States. He is not subject to the alternative minimum tax.

a. Upon sale of the land for $1,500,000 to Emma, an Illinois individual, what are the Federal income tax consequences to Martinho?

b. What are the Federal income tax withholding requirements with respect to Martinho's sale? Who pays the withheld amount to the U.S. Treasury?

39. **LO.6** Sarah Liu is single, an attorney, and a U.S. citizen. Sarah's net worth is $5,000,000. Sarah recently attended a seminar where she heard that she could give up her U.S. citizenship, move to Bermuda (where she would pay no income tax), and operate a law practice long distance via the internet with no U.S. tax consequences. Write a letter informing Sarah of the tax consequences of the proposed actions. Her address is 1005 NE Farwell Street, Gainesville, GA 32612.

Critical Thinking

Communications

Research Problems

Note: Solutions to the Research Problems can be prepared by using the Thomson Reuters Checkpoint™ online tax research database, which accompanies this textbook. Solutions can also be prepared by using research materials found in a typical tax library.

the answer company™
THOMSON REUTERS®

Research Problem 1. Jerry Jeff Keen, the CFO of Boots Unlimited, a Texas corporation, has come to you regarding a potential restructuring of business operations. Boots has long manufactured its western boots in plants in Texas and Oklahoma. Recently, Boots has explored the possibility of setting up a manufacturing subsidiary in Ireland, where manufacturing profits are taxed at 12.5%. Jerry Jeff sees this as a great idea, given that the alternative is to continue all manufacturing in the United States, where profits are taxed at 21%.

Boots plans to continue all of the cutting, sizing, and hand tooling of leather in its U.S. plants. This material will be shipped to Ireland for final assembly, with the finished product shipped to retail outlets all over Europe and Asia.

Communications

Critical Thinking

Your initial concern is whether the income generated by the Irish subsidiary will be considered foreign base company income. Address this issue in a research memo, along with any planning suggestions.

Partial list of research aids:
§ 954(d).
Reg. § 1.954–3(a).
Bausch & Lomb, 71 TCM 2031, T.C.Memo. 1996–57.

Research Problem 2. Polly Ling is a successful professional golfer. She is a resident of a country that does not have a tax treaty with the United States. Ling plays matches around the world, about one-half of which are in the United States. Ling's reputation is without blemish; in fact, she is known as being exceedingly honest and upright, and many articles discuss how she is a role model for young golfers due to her tenacious and successful playing style and her favorable character traits. Every year, she reports the most penalty strokes on herself among the participants in women's matches, and this is seen as reinforcing her image as an honest and respectful competitor.

This combination of quality play and laudable reputation has brought many riches to Ling. She comes to you with several Federal income tax questions. She knows that as a non-U.S. resident, any of her winnings from tournament play that occur in the United States are subject to U.S. income taxation. But what about each of the following items? How does U.S. tax law affect Ling? Apply the sourcing rules in this regard, and determine whether the graduated U.S. Federal income Tax Rate Schedules apply.

- Endorsement income from YourGolf for wearing clothing during matches with its logo prominently displayed. Ling must play in at least 10 tournaments per year that are televised around the world. She also must participate in photo sessions and in blogs and tweets associated with the tournaments. Payment to Ling is structured as a flat fee, with bonuses paid if she finishes in the top five competitors for each match. This is known as an *on-court endorsement*.

- Endorsement income from GolfZone for letting the company use her likeness in a video game that simulates golf tournaments among known golfers and other players that the (usually middle-aged men and women) gamers identify. In this way, the gamer seems to be playing against Ling on famous golf courses. Two-thirds of all dollar sales of the game licenses are to U.S. customers.

- Endorsement income from Eliteness for appearing in print and internet ads that feature Ling wearing the company's high-end watches. One-fifth of all dollar sales of the watches are to U.S. customers. The latter two items are known as *off-court endorsements*.

Partial list of research aids:
Goosen, 136 T.C. (2011).

Use internet tax resources to address the following questions. Look for reliable websites and blogs of the IRS and other government agencies, media outlets, businesses, tax professionals, academics, think tanks, and political outlets.

Data Analytics

Communications

Research Problem 3. Locate data on the size of the international economy, including data on international trade, foreign direct investment by U.S. firms, and investment in the United States by foreign firms. Useful web locations include **census.gov** and **bea.gov**. Prepare an analysis of the data for a three-year period using spreadsheet and graphing software, and e-mail the results to your instructor.

Communications

Research Problem 4. Choose 10 countries, one of which is the United States. Create a table showing whether each country applies a worldwide or territorial approach to international income taxation. Then list the country's top income tax rate on business profits. Send a copy of this table to your instructor.

Communications

Research Problem 5. At **crsreports.congress.gov**, find a 2018 report that analyzes the 2017 tax law changes concerning international corporate taxation. In no more than one page each, summarize an important tax issue that:
a. Existed under legacy income tax law.
b. Arose after the 2017 tax reform provisions were adopted.

Becker CPA Review Questions

1. A binding contract between the IRS and the taxpayer with which the IRS agrees not to seek a transfer pricing adjustment for a covered transaction if the taxpayer files its return consistent with the agreed transfer pricing method is called a(n):

   a. Section 482 study

   b. Advance Pricing Agreement Program

   c. Request for competent authority

   d. Controlled transaction analysis agreement

2. Bangle Supplies, Inc. (a U.S. corporation), is a wholesale distributor of office supplies. In year 3, Bangle sells office supplies to Go Green Ltd. (a Canada corporation). Bangle ships $300,000 in office supplies to Go Green's headquarters in Quebec, Canada, and $250,000 in office supplies to Go Green's warehouse in Detroit, Michigan (with title passing upon delivery). In addition, Go Green pays Bangle $35,000 to provide environmental consulting services at its headquarters in Quebec. What is Bangle's U.S.-source and foreign-source income in year 3?

   a. U.S. source, $585,000; foreign source, $0

   b. U.S. source, $250,000; foreign source, $335,000

   c. U.S. source, $0; foreign source, $585,000

   d. U.S. source, $285,000; foreign source, $300,000

3. DomCo (a domestic corporation) owns 100% of ForCo (a foreign corporation), which operates outside of the United States. Which of the following statements is correct?

   a. ForCo is not considered a controlled foreign corporation (CFC).

   b. ForCo's Subpart F income will generally be treated as deemed dividend subject to immediate recognition by DomCo.

   c. ForCo's income will be subject to current taxation in the United States because ForCo is a foreign subsidiary.

   d. ForCo is considered a foreign branch of DomCo.

4. Which of the following is not a category of income for foreign tax credit limitation purposes?

   a. General category income

   b. Foreign-derived intangible income

   c. Passive category income

   d. Foreign branch income

5. The base erosion and anti-abuse tax (BEAT) may apply to corporations:

   a. Taxed as S corporations.

   b. With any deductible payments to non-U.S. persons.

   c. With net assets of $500 million or more in any of the three preceding tax years.

   d. With average annual gross receipts of $500 million or more for the three preceding tax years.

6. In which of the following situations will a foreign person not be treated as a U.S. resident?

   a. An individual who holds a permanent resident visa ("green card") and is present in the United States for more than 30 days during the current year

   b. An individual who holds a permanent resident visa ("green card") and is present in the United States for less than 30 days during the current year

   c. An individual who is present in the United States for 30 days during the current year and 350 days in each of the two preceding tax years

   d. An individual who is present in the United States for 40 days during the current year and 300 days in each of the two preceding tax years

CHAPTER

26

Tax Practice and Ethics

LEARNING OBJECTIVES: *After completing Chapter 26, you should be able to:*

LO.1 Illustrate the organization and structure of the IRS.

LO.2 Identify the various administrative pronouncements issued by the IRS and explain how they can be used in tax practice.

LO.3 Describe the audit process, including how tax returns are selected for audit and the various types of audits.

LO.4 Explain the taxpayer appeal process, including various settlement options available.

LO.5 Determine the amount of interest on a deficiency or a refund and when it is due.

LO.6 List and explain the various penalties that can be imposed on acts of noncompliance by taxpayers and return preparers.

LO.7 Recognize and apply the rules governing the statute of limitations on assessments and on refunds.

LO.8 Summarize the legal and ethical guidelines that apply to those engaged in tax practice.

CHAPTER OUTLINE

26-1 Tax Administration, 26-2
26-1a Organizational Structure of the IRS, 26-3
26-1b IRS Procedure—Letter Rulings, 26-4
26-1c IRS Procedure—Other Issuances, 26-4
26-1d Administrative Powers of the IRS, 26-5
26-1e The Audit Process, 26-6
26-1f The Taxpayer Appeal Process, 26-9
26-1g Offers in Compromise and Closing Agreements, 26-10
26-1h Interest, 26-12
26-1i Taxpayer Penalties, 26-13
26-1j Statute of Limitations, 26-21

26-2 The Tax Profession and Tax Ethics, 26-22
26-2a The Tax Professional, 26-22
26-2b Regulating Tax Preparers, 26-23

26-2c IRS Rules Governing Tax Practice, 26-23
26-2d Preparer Penalties, 26-24
26-2e Privileged Communications, 26-26
26-2f AICPA Statements on Standards for Tax Services, 26-27

26-3 Tax Planning, 26-30
26-3a Strategies in Seeking a Letter Ruling, 26-30
26-3b Considerations in Handling an IRS Audit, 26-30
26-3c Statute of Limitations, 26-31
26-3d Litigation Considerations, 26-32
26-3e Penalties, 26-32
26-3f Privileged Communications, 26-33

A Tax Adviser's Dilemma

Campbell Corporation is preparing its Form 1120 for the tax year. The corporation develops and manufactures a number of high-tech products, including a line of GPS applications that are downloaded onto tablets and phones. Campbell's research department needs to work with the U.S. government on this line of software because of the potential for security breaches when the software is used in sensitive parts of the world. Other efforts of the research department include traditional software architecture and development. Projections show that the GPS products will be highly profitable, with sales concentrated among various commercial and governmental communications providers around the world.

Some of the research department's work on the GPS products clearly qualifies for the Federal income tax credit for incremental research expenditures, but for some other items, the availability of the credit is not so certain. Because the Regulations related to Campbell's situation are unclear or because of the innovative aspects of the products under development, the law is silent as to whether Campbell can claim the credit.

You are Campbell's tax adviser. This situation presents you with several levels of difficulty. How aggressive should you advise Campbell to be in reporting items on the Form 1120 that qualify for the research credit? Will an overly aggressive position on the credit trigger a tax preparer penalty for your tax consulting firm? What level of diligence should you exercise in advising Campbell as to whether specific expenditures qualify for the credit, given that your expertise with GPS software is limited to using the unit in your personal auto?

Read the chapter and formulate your response.

F ew events arouse so much fear in the typical individual taxpayer or corporate tax department as the receipt of a letter from the Internal Revenue Service (IRS) notifying the taxpayer that prior years' tax returns are the subject of an audit. Almost immediately, calls are made to the tax adviser. Advice is sought as to what to reveal (or not reveal) in the course of the audit, how to delay or avoid the audit, and how friendly one should be with the auditor during the audit process.

The tax professional can render valuable services to the taxpayer in an audit context, thereby ensuring that tax payments for the disputed years are neither under- nor over-reported, as part of an ongoing tax practice. In this regard, the adviser must appreciate the following, each of which is addressed in this chapter.

- The elements of the Treasury's tax administration process and opportunities for appeal within the structure of the IRS.

- The extent of the negative sanctions that can be brought to bear against taxpayers whose returns are found to have been inaccurate.

- The ethical and professional constraints on the advice tax advisers can give and the actions they can take on behalf of their clients within the context of an adversarial relationship with the IRS.

26-1 TAX ADMINISTRATION

The Treasury has delegated the administration and enforcement of the tax laws to its subsidiary agency, the IRS. In this process, the IRS carries out duties concerning taxpayer service, tax compliance, and tax law enforcement. The IRS is responsible for providing adequate information, in the form of publications and forms with instructions, to taxpayers so that they can comply with the laws in an appropriate manner. The IRS collects current and delinquent tax payments. It carries out assessment and collection procedures under the restrictions of due process and other constitutional guarantees. The IRS also is responsible for several Affordable Care Act provisions.

The IRS employs more than 70,000 individuals, about two-thirds of whom are women; fewer than 3 percent of the staff is under age 30. The total agency budget is about $11.5 billion. In meeting its responsibilities, the IRS conducts audits of selected tax returns. About 0.6 percent of all individual tax returns are subjected to audit in a given tax year. However, certain types of both taxpayers and income—including, for instance, high-income individuals, cash-oriented businesses, real estate transactions, and estate- and gift-taxable transfers—are subject to much higher probabilities of audit, about 7 percent for individuals with $10 million or more of income.

The audit rate for corporations with at least $5 million in assets is about 10 percent, but only about 1 percent for businesses with less than $1 million in assets. In the past few years, the IRS has seen hiring freezes and personnel cuts in its audit and enforcement activities, and in the training of its staff, but it is targeting narrower issues that are projected to produce more revenue for the time spent. As a result, audit rates for large corporations have decreased, although the dollars collected from such audits continue to increase.

In recent years, Congress and the IRS have found ways to improve reporting by taxpayers, such as through information returns and document matching. For instance, when a taxpayer engages in a like-kind exchange or sells a personal residence, various parties to the transaction are required to report the nature and magnitude of the transaction to the IRS. Later, the Treasury's computers determine whether the transaction has been reported properly by comparing the information reported by the third parties with the events included on the relevant taxpayers' returns for the year.

In addition, the IRS has been placing increasing pressure on the community of tax advisers. IRS penalties may be assessed on those who have prepared the appropriate return when the IRS's interpretation of applicable law conflicts with that of the preparer.

Taxes Collected and the Tax Gap

The IRS processes almost 200 million income tax returns every year, of which about 88 percent are filed electronically (i.e., known as <mark>e-filing</mark>). About 60 percent of e-filed returns are submitted by tax professionals, and 40 percent are prepared by the taxpayers themselves.

The agency collects about $3.5 trillion in annual tax revenues and pays refunds to about 122 million individual taxpayers every year. The average Form 1040 refund is about $2,800.

As directed by Congress, the IRS estimates the size of the Federal income "tax gap"—the difference between how much tax *is* collected and how much *should be* collected.

According to the most recent analysis, the tax gap is a net amount of about $380 billion in income and employment taxes annually. More specifically, the underpayments total about $440 billion per year but are offset by $60 billion obtained through related IRS enforcement efforts (e.g., audits and collection procedures).

The IRS maintains that 86 percent of taxpayers report the "correct" amount of tax under the existing system of voluntary compliance, after accounting for audits. The main sources of the tax gap are:

- Underreporting net taxable income (80 percent of the tax gap).
- Underpayment of tax (11 percent of the tax gap).
- Nonfiling (9 percent of the tax gap).

26-1a **Organizational Structure of the IRS**

The structure of the IRS is illustrated in Exhibit 26.1. The IRS Commissioner, a Presidential appointee who serves a five-year renewable term, is the executive officer of the agency. The IRS is organized into four major operating divisions based on the type of tax returns to be processed. Administrative functions, such as those relating to personnel and computer issues, are organized on a shared-services model managed from the national office. Broader functions, such as litigation, investigations, and taxpayer relations, are managed at the national level as well. Congress has called for a reorganization of the agency's structure to improve customer service, train IRS employees to be effective in dealing with taxpayers, and improve its data processing and security functions.

LO.1

Illustrate the organization and structure of the IRS.

EXHIBIT 26.1   IRS National Office Organization

Commissioner — Chief Counsel

Shared Services
- Information
- Compliance Analytics
- Facilities, Finances, Operations
- Human Capital
- Privacy, Disclosure
- Procurement

Research, Analysis, Statistics

National Taxpayer Advocate

Independent Office of Appeals

Communication & Liaison

Operating Divisions
Wage and Investment
Small Business and Self-Employed
Large Business and International
Tax-Exempt/Government Entities

Other Functions
Professional Responsibility
Whistleblower
Online Services
Return Preparers
Criminal Investigation

Equity, Diversity, and Inclusion

The Chief Counsel, another Presidential appointee, is the head legal officer of the IRS. The Chief Counsel's office provides legal advice to the IRS and guidance to the public on matters pertaining to the administration and enforcement of the tax laws. For instance, the Chief Counsel's duties include establishing uniform nationwide interpretive positions on the law, drafting tax guide material for taxpayers and IRS personnel, issuing technical rulings to taxpayers, and providing advice and technical assistance to IRS personnel. The Chief Counsel represents the IRS in all litigation before the Tax Court.

The National Taxpayer Advocate is appointed by the Secretary of the Treasury and reports to the IRS Commissioner.[1] The Advocate's office includes about 1,800 employees who work with taxpayers when normal IRS channels have not brought about a satisfactory result; the Advocate works to ensure the fair treatment of the taxpayer and the exercise of applicable taxpayer rights. This independent office represents taxpayers who have experienced a delay of more than 30 days in resolving a matter and have experienced economic harm as a result. The Advocate issues an annual report to Congress,[2] identifying structural problems in Federal tax administration and offering proposed legislative and other solutions for them.

LO.2

Identify the various administrative pronouncements issued by the IRS and explain how they can be used in tax practice.

26-1b IRS Procedure—Letter Rulings

When a tax issue is controversial or a transaction involves considerable tax dollars, the taxpayer often wants to obtain either assurance or direction from the IRS as to the treatment of the event. The **letter ruling** process is an effective means of dealing directly with the IRS while in the planning stages of a large or otherwise important transaction.

Rulings issued by the National Office provide a written statement of the position of the IRS concerning the tax consequences of a course of action contemplated by the taxpayer. Letter rulings do not have the force and effect of law, but they do provide guidance and support for taxpayers in similar transactions. The IRS issues rulings only on uncompleted, actual (rather than hypothetical) transactions or on transactions that have been completed before the filing of the tax return for the year in question.

In certain circumstances, the IRS will not issue a ruling. It ordinarily will not rule in cases that essentially involve a question of fact.[3] For example, no ruling will be issued to determine whether compensation paid to employees is reasonable in amount and therefore allowable as a deduction.

A letter ruling represents the current opinion of the IRS on the tax consequences of a transaction with a given set of facts. IRS rulings are not unchangeable. They can be declared obsolete or superseded by new rulings in response to tax law changes.

A ruling may be relied upon only by the taxpayer who requested and received it. It must be attached to the tax return for the year in question.

Letter rulings benefit both the IRS and the taxpayer. They not only help promote a uniform application of the tax laws but also may reduce the potential for litigation or disputes with IRS agents. In addition, they make the IRS aware of significant transactions being consummated by taxpayers. A fee of $30,000 is charged for processing most ruling requests; the fee is reduced to $2,800 if the taxpayer's gross income is less than $250,000.

26-1c IRS Procedure—Other Issuances

In addition to issuing unpublished letter rulings and published rulings and procedures, the IRS issues determination letters and technical advice memoranda.

A **determination letter** relates to a completed transaction when the issue involved is covered by judicial or statutory authority, Regulations, or rulings. Determination letters are issued for various estate, gift, income, excise, and employment tax matters.

EXAMPLE 1

A group of physicians plans to form an entity to construct and operate a hospital. The determination letter procedure is appropriate to ascertain whether the group is subject to the Federal income tax or is tax-exempt.

---

[1]§ 7803(c).

[2]See **irs.gov/advocate/reports-to-congress**.

[3]Rev.Proc. 2020–1, 2020–1 I.R.B. 1.

ETHICS & EQUITY Tax Compliance Costs

By one estimate, the cost of compliance with Federal tax laws exceeds *$400 billion* per year. Roughly, this means that compliance costs act as an additional tax of almost *40 cents* for every tax dollar collected. This amount exceeds the gross domestic product of 36 U.S. states.

In this estimate, the following items were counted as costs of tax compliance.[4]

- The value of taxpayers' time spent record keeping, filing, planning, and otherwise complying with the tax laws.

- Tax collection costs (chiefly wages and benefits) of IRS employees.
- Expenditures made to professional tax preparers, consultants, and other preparers.

Comment on the appropriateness of Congress and the Treasury passing along to taxpayers the costs of its revenue collection operation.

A **technical advice memorandum (TAM)** is issued by the National Office to IRS personnel in response to a specific request by an agent, Appellate Conferee, or IRS executive. The taxpayer may request a TAM if an issue in dispute is not treated by the law or precedent and/or published rulings or Regulations. Technical advice requests arise from the audit or appeals process, whereas letter ruling requests typically are issued as part of the filing of an original tax return (i.e., before any IRS audit).

26-1d Administrative Powers of the IRS

Examination of Records

The IRS can examine the taxpayer's books and records as part of the process of determining the correct amount of tax due. The IRS also can require the persons responsible for the return to appear and to produce any necessary books and records.[5] Taxpayers are required to maintain certain record-keeping procedures and retain the records necessary to facilitate the audit.

Burden of Proof

If the taxpayer meets the record-keeping requirement and substantiates income and deductions properly, the IRS bears the burden of proof in establishing a tax deficiency during litigation. The taxpayer must have cooperated with the IRS regarding reasonable requests for information, documents, meetings, and interviews. For individual taxpayers, the IRS's burden of proof extends to penalties and interest amounts that it assesses in a court proceeding with the taxpayer.[6]

Assessment and Demand

The Code permits the IRS to assess a deficiency and to demand payment for the tax. However, no assessment or effort to collect the tax may be made until 90 days after a statutory notice of a deficiency (a *90-day letter*) is issued. The taxpayer then has 90 days to file a petition to the U.S. Tax Court, effectively preventing the deficiency from being assessed or collected pending the outcome of the case.[7]

Following assessment of the tax, the IRS issues a notice and demand for payment. The taxpayer can be given as little as 10 days to pay the tax after the demand for payment is issued. If the IRS believes the assessment or collection of a deficiency is in jeopardy, it may assess the deficiency and demand immediate payment.[8]

---

[4] **taxfoundation.org/compliance-costs-irs-regulations**.
[5] § 7602.
[6] §§ 7491(a)(1), (a)(2)(B), and (c).

[7] §§ 6212 and 6213.
[8] § 6861. A jeopardy assessment is appropriate, for instance, when the IRS fears that the taxpayer will flee the country or destroy valuable property.

Collection

If the taxpayer neglects or refuses to pay the tax after receiving the demand for payment, a lien in favor of the IRS is placed on all property (realty and personalty, tangible and intangible) belonging to the taxpayer.

The levy power of the IRS is very broad. It allows the IRS to garnish (*attach*) wages and salary and to seize and sell all nonexempt property by any means. After a notice period, the IRS can make successive seizures on any property owned by the taxpayer until the levy is satisfied.[9] A taxpayer's principal residence is exempt from the levy process, unless the disputed tax, interest, and penalty exceed $5,000 and a U.S. District Court judge approves of the seizure.[10]

26-1e **The Audit Process**

LO.3

Describe the audit process, including how tax returns are selected for audit and the various types of audits.

Selection of Returns for Audit

The IRS utilizes mathematical formulas to select tax returns that are most likely to contain errors and yield substantial amounts of additional tax revenues upon audit. The IRS does not disclose all of its audit selection techniques. However, some observations can be made regarding the probability of a return's selection for audit.

- Certain groups of taxpayers are subject to audit more frequently than others. These groups include individuals with gross income in excess of $200,000, self-employed individuals with substantial business income and deductions, and cash businesses where the potential for tax evasion is high.

EXAMPLE 2

Tracey owns and operates a liquor store. Because nearly all of her sales are for cash, Tracey might be a prime candidate for an audit by the IRS. Cash transactions are easier to conceal from the tax authorities than are those made by credit card or by using a payment "app" where funds are transferred between accounts of the seller and customer.

- If a taxpayer has been audited in a past year and the audit led to the assessment of a substantial deficiency, the IRS often will audit a subsequent tax return.

- An audit might materialize if information returns (e.g., Form W–2 and Form 1099) are not in substantial agreement with the income reported on the taxpayer's return. Obvious discrepancies do not necessitate formal audits and usually can be handled by correspondence with the taxpayer.

EXAMPLE 3

The IRS audits Phil's Form 1040 and finds that his dividend income increased sharply. The auditor wonders how Phil financed this stock purchase: there were no corresponding stock sales on his return that would create cash with which to make the acquisition.

Upon further inquiry, the auditor learns that the dividend yielding stock was a gift to Phil from his mother, Julie. Accordingly, the IRS investigates whether Julie filed a Federal gift tax return for the year of the stock transfer.

- If an individual's itemized deductions are in excess of norms established for various income levels, the probability of an audit increases. Certain deductions (e.g., casualty and theft losses, business use of the home, and tax-sheltered investments) are more likely to be scrutinized, because the IRS realizes that many taxpayers determine the amount of the deduction incorrectly or may not be entitled to the deduction at all.

- Information often is obtained by the IRS from outside sources, including other government agencies, news items, and informants.

---

[9]The taxpayer can keep certain personal and business property and a minimal amount of his or her income as a subsistence allowance, even if a lien is outstanding. § 6334(a).

[10]§§ 6334(a)(13)(A) and (e)(1).

EXAMPLE 4

After 15 years of employment, Betty is discharged by her employer, Dr. Franklin. Shortly thereafter, the IRS receives a letter from Betty stating that Franklin keeps two sets of books, one of which substantially understates his cash receipts.

The statistical models used by the IRS to select individual tax returns for audit come from random audits of a small number of taxpayers, who are required to document every entry they made on the Form 1040. The latest round of these National Research Program (NRP) audits resulted in the construction of new Discriminant Function (DIF) scores that project the amount of revenue the IRS will gain from pursuing tax returns with various statistical profiles. The higher the DIF score, the better the return to the IRS from pursuing the audit, and the higher the probability of selection for an examination.

These data-seeking audits are controversial and have led to taxpayer complaints to Congress about the stress they create.[11] The IRS believes that by constantly updating the NRP data through a diligent review of randomly selected tax returns, changes in tax avoidance behaviors will be detected and fewer routine audits will be required.

Many individual taxpayers mistakenly assume that if they do not hear from the IRS within a few weeks after filing their return or if they receive a refund check, no audit will be forthcoming. As a practical matter, most individual returns are examined about two years from the date of filing. If a return is not audited within this time period, it generally remains unaudited. All large corporations, however, are subject to annual audits.

About 10 percent of all completed audits of individual returns result in a "no change" recommendation for the taxpayer. A "no change" recommendation results for less than 40 percent of all partnership/LLC and S corporation audits, and for about 45 percent of audits of large corporations.

ETHICS & EQUITY Can the IRS Pretend to Be Your Friend?

Should IRS agents be allowed to identify audit subjects by reading the society page of the newspaper, looking for indicators of wealth? What if the agency subscribes to Facebook and seeks comments from its "friends" as to income windfalls and stock market dealings? In the past, some state and local taxing agencies have used social networking sites for audit selection purposes. State and local revenue agents have used the sites to find self-employed individuals who advertise their business and report about upcoming income-producing events. The sites also have been used to determine whether a taxpayer who has requested an extension of time to pay a delinquent tax actually is strapped for cash.

Some state tax officials claim that looking for a taxpayer's self-declarations on a website is a much more efficient way to find income understatements than searching through most other sources of nonstatistical data. Should taxing agencies be using Google, Facebook, and other public-domain online sources of taxpayer information to help find nonfilers and identify tax returns for audit?

Role of Informants

The IRS can pay awards to persons who provide information that leads to the detection and punishment of those who violate the tax laws. The awards are paid at the discretion of the IRS. Payments usually do not exceed 15 percent of the taxes, fines, and penalties recovered as a result of the information provided.[12]

About 200 informant awards are paid in the typical year. For fiscal year 2018, the IRS collected about $200 million in underpaid taxes from the informants' program, and it paid awards of over $10 million (i.e., at approximately a 5 percent rate).

Another IRS office, through the **Whistleblower Program**, offers special awards to informants who provide information concerning businesses or high-income (gross income exceeds $200,000) individuals when more than $2 million of tax, penalty, interest, and

---

[11]On average, the total annual NRP audit sample consists of 13,000 returns. Some of these returns are analyzed without contacting the taxpayer, and other taxpayers are contacted only by mail with queries about one or two items. Only a few returns are subjected to "line-by-line" review. Most of the returns are reviewed for a period of three tax years.

[12]§ 7623 and Reg. § 301.7623–1.

other fines is at stake. Some informants claim that hundreds of millions of dollars of tax, penalty, and interest are due from allegedly noncompliant taxpayers.

A whistleblower award can reach 30 percent of the amount collected by the Treasury and traceable to the whistleblower's information. The award can be reduced if the whistleblower participated in the original understatement of tax. About 12,000 claims are initiated every year, and the IRS annually pays awards to about 40 whistleblowers.

A final decision on a whistleblower case might not be made until five to seven years after the date the claim is filed. The award itself constitutes gross income when it is received. Legal fees for the whistleblower tend to be about 30 percent of the award; such fees may be deductible by the informant.

The whistleblower awards are paid out of the taxes recovered under the informant and whistleblower programs. To claim an award of this sort, an informant files Form 211 with the IRS. Federal income taxes are withheld from the whistleblower award.

Verification and Audit Procedures

The filed tax return is reviewed for mathematical accuracy when the IRS receives it. A check is also made for deductions, exclusions, etc., that are clearly erroneous. One obvious error would be the failure to comply with the AGI limitation on the deduction for medical expenses.

About 0.3 percent of all individual returns show a math error. When a math or clerical error occurs, the IRS sends the taxpayer revised computations and a bill or refund as appropriate, usually within one year of the filing date.

Taxpayers usually are able to settle routine tax disputes (e.g., queries involving the documentation of deductions) through a by-mail-only *correspondence audit* with the IRS, without the necessity of a formal meeting. The taxpayer receives a letter from the IRS wherein the tax is recomputed upward (e.g., because the amount of reported wages does not match that on Form W–2). The taxpayer then complies by paying the additional tax or objects by providing information and documentation showing that the reported amount was correct. About 75 percent of all Form 1040 audits are handled in this way.

Office audits are rare today; they are conducted in an office of the IRS. In most instances, the taxpayer is required to substantiate a deduction, a credit, or an item of income that appears on the return. The taxpayer presents documentation in the form of canceled checks, invoices, etc., for the items in question.

The *field audit* procedure commonly is used for corporate returns and for returns of individuals engaged in business or professional activities. This type of audit generally involves a more complete examination of a taxpayer's transactions.

A field audit is conducted by IRS agents at the office or home of the taxpayer or at the office of the taxpayer's representative. The agent's work may be facilitated by a review of certain tax workpapers and discussions with the taxpayer's representative about items appearing on the tax return.

Prior to or at the initial interview, the IRS must provide the taxpayer with an explanation of the audit process that is the subject of the interview and describe the taxpayer's rights under that process. If the taxpayer clearly states at any time during the interview the desire to consult with an attorney, a CPA, or an enrolled agent or any other person permitted to represent the taxpayer before the IRS, then the IRS representative must suspend the interview.[13]

Any officer or employee of the IRS must, upon advance request, allow a taxpayer to make an audio recording of any in-person interview with the officer or employee concerning the determination and collection of any tax.[14]

Settlement with the Revenue Agent

Following an audit, the IRS agent may either accept the return as filed or recommend certain adjustments. The Revenue Agent's Report (RAR) is reviewed within the IRS. In most instances, the agent's proposed adjustments are approved.

---

[13]§ 7521(b).   [14]§ 7521(a).

Agents must adhere strictly to IRS policy as reflected in published rulings, Regulations, and other releases. The agent cannot settle an unresolved issue based upon the probability of winning the case in court. Usually, issues involving factual questions can be settled at the agent level, and it may be advantageous for both the taxpayer and the IRS to reach agreement at the earliest point in the settlement process. For example, it may be best for the taxpayer to reach agreement at the agent level and avoid any further opportunity for the IRS to raise new issues.

If agreement is reached on the proposed deficiency, the taxpayer signs Form 870. One advantage to the taxpayer of signing Form 870 at this point is that interest stops accumulating on the deficiency 30 days after the form is filed.[15] When this form is signed, the taxpayer effectively waives the right to receive a statutory notice of deficiency (90-day letter) and to subsequently petition the Tax Court. In addition, it is no longer possible for the taxpayer later to go to the IRS Independent Office of Appeals.

26-1f The Taxpayer Appeal Process

If agreement cannot be reached at the agent level, the taxpayer receives a copy of the Revenue Agent's Report and a 30-day letter. The taxpayer has 30 days to request an administrative appeal. If an appeal is not requested, a 90-day letter is issued. Exhibit 26.2 illustrates the taxpayer's alternatives when a disagreement with the IRS persists.

LO.4

Explain the taxpayer appeal process, including various settlement options available.

EXHIBIT 26.2   Income Tax Appeal Procedure

If the taxpayer does not respond within 30 days or requests an immediate notice of deficiency

Appeals Conference (if previously bypassed)

Correspondence Start Here

IRS Response

Disagreement with Findings → Disagreement with Response → **Choice of Action** → Request for Appeals Conference (written protest when required)

Examination or Inquiry of Tax Return → Interview Start Here → Disagreement with Findings → Preliminary Notice (30-day letter)

Appeals Conference → Notice of Deficiency (90-day letter) → **Choice of Action**

Petition to Tax Court — Do Not Pay Tax → Tax Court*

If the taxpayer does not respond within 30 days or requests an immediate notice of deficiency

Pay Tax → File Claim for Refund → Consideration of Claim for Refund → Request for Appeals Conference (written protest when required) → Formal Notice (disallowance of claim)

Preliminary Notice

Appeals Conference

U.S. District Court or Court of Federal Claims*

At any stage, the taxpayer can:
- Agree and arrange to pay the amount due.
- Ask for a notice of deficiency so that a petition can be filed with the Tax Court.
- Pay the tax and file a claim for refund.

*Further appeals to the courts may be possible. There is no appeal from the Tax Court's Small Cases Division.

---

[15]§ 6601(c).

A taxpayer must make an appropriate request to the Independent Office of Appeals. The request must be accompanied by a written protest, except when:

- The proposed tax deficiency does not exceed $10,000 for any of the tax periods involved in the audit, and
- The deficiency resulted from a correspondence or office audit (i.e., not as a result of a field audit).

The Appeals Office is authorized to settle all tax disputes based on the hazards of litigation (the chances of winning in court). Because the Appeals Office has final settlement authority until a 90-day letter has been issued, the taxpayer may be able to negotiate a settlement. In addition, an overall favorable settlement may be reached by "trading" disputed issues.

EXAMPLE 5

At the time Terri is audited, the corporation that she controls had advances outstanding to her in the amount of $80,000. The IRS field agent held that these advances were constructive dividends to her (refer to the discussion in text Section 19-3d). Some facts point toward this result (e.g., the corporation is closely held, Terri has made no repayments, and the loan balance has increased over several years). Other facts, however, appear to indicate that these advances are bona fide loans (e.g., a written instrument provides for interest, Terri has the independent means of repayment, and the corporation has a good dividend-paying record).

Terri's representative assesses the hazards of litigation as being 50% for each side. As a result, if Terri chooses to take the issue to court, she would have an even chance of winning or losing her case. Based on this assessment, both sides agree to treat $40,000 of the advance as a dividend and $40,000 as a bona fide loan. The agreement enables Terri to avoid $40,000 of dividend income (the loan portion) and saves her the cost of litigating the issue.

So by going to the Appeals Office, Terri obtained a satisfactory settlement otherwise unobtainable from the agent.

The economic costs of a settlement offer from the Appeals Office should be weighed against the costs of litigation and the probability of winning the case. The taxpayer also should consider the effects of the settlement upon the tax liability for future periods in addition to the years under audit. If the taxpayer litigates the tax dispute, personal information may become public in a published court decision or in related media releases.

Taxpayers who file a petition with the U.S. Tax Court have the option of having the case heard before the more informal Small Cases Division if the amount of tax in dispute does not exceed $50,000.[16] If the Small Cases Division is used, neither party may appeal the decision.

26-1g Offers in Compromise and Closing Agreements

The IRS can negotiate a compromise if the taxpayer's ability to pay the tax is doubtful. If the taxpayer is financially unable to pay the total amount of the tax, a Form 656 (Offer in Compromise) is filed. An **offer in compromise** is appropriate in the following circumstances.[17]

- There is doubt as to the taxpayer's liability for the tax (i.e., disputed issues still exist).
- There is doubt as to the collectibility of the tax (i.e., the taxpayer's net worth and earnings capacity are low).
- Payment of the disputed amount would constitute an economic hardship for the taxpayer (e.g., the taxpayer is incapable of earning a living because of a long-term illness or disability, or liquidation of the taxpayer's assets to pay the amount due would leave the taxpayer unable to meet basic living expenses).

---

[16]§ 7463(a).   [17]§ 7122 and Reg. § 301.7122–1(b).

ETHICS & EQUITY Our Taxing System of Self-Assessment

The United States is a large country of diverse taxpayers and businesses. Perhaps the only way the massive dollar amounts of Federal income taxes can be collected on a timely basis is through a *self-assessment* process, whereby the taxpayer is charged with disclosing a full picture of the tax year's results and the corresponding computation of taxable income. But a system of self-assessment depends heavily on the honesty and integrity of the taxpayers and their ability to know and comply with the pertinent tax rules.

A recent survey of taxpayer attitudes by the IRS revealed the results shown to the right.

Given the results of this survey, do you think the current self-assessment system is satisfactory? If not, should Congress create additional enforcement procedures to ensure taxpayer compliance? What sort of new reporting rules might be useful?

Why Do You Report and Pay Your Taxes Honestly? (more than one answer allowed)

Taxpayer Responses	Taxpayers for Whom This Reason Is Key (Percent)
My own personal integrity	93%
A third party reported my information to the IRS (e.g., through a Form W–2 or Form 1099), so I must match that amount in my tax form	66%
Fear of an audit	63%
My neighbors report and pay their taxes honestly, so I will too	40%

What Is an Acceptable Amount by Which to Cheat on Your Income Taxes?

	Taxpayers Responding (Percent)
Not at all	85%
A little here and a little there	10%
As much as possible	3%
Other answers	2%

Source: *2018 IRS Comprehensive Taxpayer Attitude Survey* at **irs.gov/pub/irs-pdf/p5296.pdf**.

The IRS investigates the offer by evaluating the taxpayer's financial ability to pay the tax. In some instances, the compromise settlement includes an agreement for final settlement of the tax through payments of a specified percentage of the taxpayer's future earnings. This settlement procedure usually entails lengthy negotiations with the IRS, but the presumption is that the IRS will be able to settle with the taxpayer.

To settle their obligation, taxpayers can select either a "lump-sum" option (payments over no more than 5 months with 20 percent down) or a "periodic payment" option (equal payments over no more than 24 months). Either option requires a $186 filing fee. Low-income individuals generally receive a waiver of the fee and of the 20 percent down payment required under the lump-sum option.[18]

Every year, the IRS accepts about 25,000 offers in compromise out of about 60,000 applications, involving more than $250 million in unpaid taxes, interest, and penalties.

The IRS can agree to allow taxes to be paid on an installment basis if that arrangement facilitates the tax collection. An individual who has filed timely tax returns for five years is guaranteed the right to use an installment agreement when the amount in dispute does not exceed $10,000. The taxpayer uses Form 9465 to initiate an installment plan. If the tax owed does not exceed $50,000, a taxpayer can use an online application for an installment agreement.

A user fee is assessed with the application for the installment plan. The fee is between $31 and $225, depending on the taxpayer's income level and the form of payment (e.g., credit card, e-check, or funds transfer).

[18]Reg. § 300.3(b)(1)(ii). "Low-income" is defined as less than 250% of the Federal poverty level. A preliminary check as to the taxpayer's qualifications for an offer in compromise, and the construction of an initial application, is found at **irs.treasury.gov/oic_pre_qualifier/**.

The IRS provides an annual statement accounting for the status of the agreement. The agreement may later be modified or terminated because of (1) inadequate information, (2) subsequent change in financial condition, or (3) failure to pay an installment when due or to provide requested information.[19]

A <mark>closing agreement</mark> is binding on both the taxpayer and the IRS except upon a subsequent showing of fraud, malfeasance, or misrepresentation of a material fact.[20] The closing agreement may be used when disputed issues carry over to future years. It also may be employed to dispose of a dispute involving a specific issue for a prior year or a proposed transaction involving future years. If, for example, the IRS is willing to make substantial concessions in the valuation of assets for estate tax purposes, it may require a closing agreement from the recipient of the property to establish the income tax basis of the assets.

26-1h Interest

LO.5

Determine the amount of interest on a deficiency or a refund and when it is due.

Determination of the Interest Rate

Congress sets the interest rates applicable to Federal tax underpayments (deficiencies) and overpayments (refunds) close to the rates available in financial markets. The Code provides for the rates to be determined quarterly.[21] As a result, the rates that are determined during March are effective for the following April through June.

For tax purposes, interest is based on the Federal short-term rates published periodically by the IRS in Revenue Rulings. They are based on the average market yield on outstanding marketable obligations of the United States with remaining maturity of three years or less.

For noncorporate taxpayers, the interest rate applicable to *both* overpayments and underpayments is 5 percent for the first quarter of 2020. For most corporate taxpayers, the rate is 4 percent for overpayments and 5 percent for underpayments. Corporations with large overpayments or underpayments are subject to different rates. IRS interest is compounded daily. Tables for determining the daily compounded amount are available from the IRS and online.[22]

IRS Deficiency Assessments

Interest usually accrues from the unextended due date of the return until 30 days after the taxpayer agrees to the deficiency by signing Form 870. If the taxpayer does not pay the amount shown on the IRS's notice and demand (final tax bill) within 30 days, interest again accrues on the deficiency.

Refund of Taxpayer's Overpayments

If an overpayment is refunded to the taxpayer within 45 days after the date the return is filed or is due, no interest is allowed. When the taxpayer files an amended return or makes a claim for refund of a prior year's tax (e.g., when net operating loss carrybacks result in refunds of a prior year's tax payments), however, interest is authorized from the original due date of the return through the date when the amended return is filed. In general, taxpayers applying for refunds receive interest as follows.

- When a return is filed after the due date, interest on any overpayment accrues from the date of filing. However, no interest is due if the IRS makes the refund within 45 days of the date of filing.

IRS Interest Payments

EXAMPLE 6

Naomi, a calendar year taxpayer, files her 2020 return on December 1, 2021. The return reflects an overwithholding of $2,500. On June 8, 2022, Naomi receives a refund of her 2020 overpayment. Interest on the refund began to accrue on December 1, 2021 (not April 15, 2021).

---

[19]§ 6159.

[20]§ 7121(b).

[21]§ 6621.

[22]§ 6622. See, e.g., Rev.Rul. 2019–28, 2019–52 I.R.B. 1401.

IRS Interest Payments

Assume the same facts as in Example 6, except that the refund is paid to Naomi on January 5, 2022 (rather than June 8, 2022). No interest is payable by the IRS, because the refund was made within 45 days of the filing of the return.

EXAMPLE 7

- In no event will interest accrue on an overpayment unless the return that is filed is in "processible form." Generally, this means that the return must be signed[23] and contain enough information in a readable format to enable the IRS to identify the taxpayer and to determine the tax (and overpayment) involved.

- In the case of a carryback (e.g., capital loss or tax credit), interest on any refund begins to accrue on the due date of the return (disregarding extensions) for the year in which the carryback arises. Even then, however, no interest accrues until a return is filed or, if the return has been filed, if the IRS pays the refund within 45 days.

Top Corporation, a calendar year taxpayer, incurs a net capital loss during 2019 that it can carry back to tax year 2017 and obtain a refund. On December 28, 2020, Top files a claim for refund. The earliest that interest begins to accrue in this situation is April 15, 2020, the due date of the Form 1120, but because the return was not filed until December 28, 2020, the later date controls. If the IRS pays the refund within 45 days of December 28, 2020, no interest need be paid.

EXAMPLE 8

Concept Summary 26.1

Working with the IRS

1. The Internal Revenue Service (IRS) enforces the tax laws of the United States. Its size and form of organization reflect its various responsibilities relative to taxpayer interaction, litigation, and collection, as well as its internal functions.

2. The IRS issues various pronouncements in communicating its position on certain tax issues. These pronouncements promote the uniform enforcement of the tax law among taxpayers and among the internal divisions of the IRS. Taxpayers should seek such rulings and memoranda when the nature or magnitude of a pending transaction requires a high degree of certainty in the planning process.

3. IRS audits can take several forms. Taxpayers are selected for audit based on the probable net dollar return to the Treasury

from the process. Offers in compromise and closing agreements can be a useful means of completing an audit without resorting to litigation.

4. Certain IRS personnel are empowered to consider the hazards of litigation in developing a settlement with the taxpayer during the audit process.

5. The IRS pays interest to taxpayers on overpaid taxes, starting essentially 45 days after the due date of the return, in amounts tied to the Federal short-term rate. Interest paid to the IRS on underpayments is similarly based on the Federal rate, starting essentially on the due date of the return. Interest for both purposes is compounded daily.

26-1i Taxpayer Penalties

 LO.6

List and explain the various penalties that can be imposed on acts of noncompliance by taxpayers and return preparers.

Congress has enacted a comprehensive array of penalties for improper actions by taxpayers. In the typical year, about 40 million penalties are assessed, totaling about $17 billion in payments.

Tax penalties may involve both criminal and civil offenses. Criminal tax penalties are imposed only after the usual criminal process in which the taxpayer is entitled to the same constitutional guarantees as nontax criminal defendants. Normally, a criminal penalty

---

[23]Both taxpayers must sign on a Form 1040 joint return. *Reifler*, 106 TCM 554, T.C.Memo. 2015–199.

provides for fines and imprisonment. Civil tax penalties are collected in the same manner as other taxes and usually provide only for monetary fines. Criminal and civil penalties are not mutually exclusive; both types of sanctions may be imposed on a taxpayer.

The Code characterizes tax penalties as additions to tax; as a result, the taxpayer cannot subsequently deduct them.

Ad valorem penalties are additions to tax that are based upon a percentage of the owed tax. *Assessable penalties*, on the other hand, typically include a flat dollar amount.

Failure to File and Failure to Pay

For a *failure to file a tax return* by the due date (including extensions), a penalty of 5 percent per month (up to a maximum of 25 percent) is imposed on the amount of tax shown as due on the return, with a minimum penalty amount of $435.[24] If the failure to file is attributable to fraud, the penalty becomes 15 percent per month, to a maximum of 75 percent of the tax.[25]

For a *failure to pay the tax due* as shown on the return, a penalty of 0.5 percent per month (up to a maximum of 25 percent) is imposed on the amount of the tax. The penalty is doubled if the taxpayer fails to pay the tax after receiving a deficiency assessment.

In all of these cases, a fraction of a month counts as a full month. These penalties relate to the net amount of the tax due.

Obtaining an extension for filing a tax return does not by itself extend the date by which the taxes due must be paid. As a result, most applications requesting an extension of time to file a tax return are accompanied by the taxpayer's payment of a good faith estimate of the taxes that will be owed when the return is ultimately filed (i.e., by the extended due date). If the taxpayer does not make a good faith estimate and payment, the extension itself may be voided by the IRS (e.g., when the return is filed by the extended due date with a much larger amount due than had been estimated).

EXAMPLE 9

Conchita uses an automatic six-month extension for the filing of her Federal income tax return. As a result, the return is due on October 15, not on April 15. Conchita's application for the extension includes a $5,000 check, the amount that she estimates her return will show as owing for the year when she files it in October.

During any month in which both the failure to file penalty and the failure to pay penalty apply, the failure to file penalty is reduced by the amount of the failure to pay penalty.

EXAMPLE 10

Jason files his tax return 10 days after the due date. Along with the return, he remits a check for $5,000, which is the balance of the tax he owes. Disregarding any interest liabilities, Jason's total penalties are as follows.

Failure to pay penalty (0.5% × $5,000)		$ 25
Failure to file penalty (5% × $5,000)	$250	
Less: Failure to pay penalty for the same period	(25)	
Failure to file penalty		225
Total penalties		$250

The penalties for one full month are imposed even though Jason was delinquent by only 10 days. Unlike the method used to compute interest, any part of a month is treated as a whole month.

---

[24]§ 6651(a). The minimum penalty cannot exceed the amount of tax due on the return. As a result, if no tax is due, the penalty is zero. The penalty is waived if the tax is paid within 60 days of the due date of the return.

[25]§ 6651(f).

These penalties can be avoided if the taxpayer shows that the failure to file and/or failure to pay was due to reasonable cause and not due to willful neglect. The Code is silent as to what constitutes reasonable cause, and the Regulations do little to clarify this important concept.[26] Reasonable cause for failure to pay is presumed under the automatic six-month extension (Form 4868) when the additional tax due is not more than 10 percent of the tax liability shown on the return. In addition, the courts have ruled on some aspects of reasonable cause.

- Reasonable cause was found where the taxpayer worked with a competent tax adviser in good faith, the facts were fully disclosed to the adviser, and the taxpayer actually relied on the adviser's judgment in filing the return.[27] No reasonable cause was found, however, where the taxpayer delegated the filing task to another, even when that person was an accountant or an attorney.[28]

- Among the reasons not qualifying as reasonable cause were lack of information on the due date of the return,[29] illness that did not incapacitate a taxpayer from completing a return,[30] refusal of the taxpayer's spouse to cooperate for a joint return,[31] and ignorance or misunderstanding of the tax law.[32]

Accuracy-Related Penalties

Major civil penalties relating to the accuracy of tax return data, including misstatements stemming from taxpayer negligence and improper valuation of income and deductions, are coordinated under the umbrella term accuracy-related penalties.[33] This consolidation of related penalties into a single levy eliminates the possibility that multiple penalties will apply to a single understatement of tax.

The accuracy-related penalties each amount to 20 percent of the portion of the tax underpayment that is attributable to one or more of the following infractions.

- Negligence or disregard of rules and Regulations.
- Substantial understatement of tax liability.
- Substantial valuation overstatement.
- Substantial valuation understatement.

The penalties apply only where the taxpayer fails to show a *reasonable basis* for the position taken on the return.[34]

Negligence

For purposes of this accuracy-related penalty, negligence includes any failure to make a reasonable attempt to comply with the provisions of the tax law. The penalty also applies to any disregard (whether careless, reckless, or intentional) of rules and Regulations.[35] The penalty can be avoided upon a showing of reasonable cause and the fact that the taxpayer acted in good faith.[36]

---

[26] Reg. § 301.6651–1(c)(1) likens reasonable cause to the exercise of "ordinary business care and prudence" on the part of the taxpayer.

[27] *Neonatology Assoc., PC*, 115 T.C. 43 (2000).

[28] *U.S. v. Boyle*, 85–1 USTC ¶13,602, 55 AFTR 2d 85–1535, 105 S.Ct. 687 (USSC, 1985). This rule appears to apply to electronic as well as paper-based return filings, to employment as well as income taxes, and to returns where the tax preparer himself or herself commits a fraudulent act. *Brandon R. Ballantyne*, 99 TCM 1523, T.C.Memo. 2010–125; *McNair Eye Center, Inc.*, 99 TCM 1345, T.C.Memo. 2010–81. Knowledgeable taxpayers such as a tax attorney are held to a higher standard in determining negligence. *Pelton & Gunther P.C.*, 78 TCM 578, T.C.Memo. 1999–339. A taxpayer might be negligent if, when a complicated tax issue is involved, a tax expert is *not* consulted. *Zmuda v. Comm.*, 84-1 USTC ¶9,442, 53 AFTR 2d 84–1269, 731 F.2d 1417 (CA–9, 1984).

[29] *Beck Chemical Equipment Co.*, 27 T.C. 840 (1957).

[30] *Alex and Tonya Oria*, 94 TCM 170, T.C.Memo. 2007–276 and *Babetta Schmidt*, 28 T.C. 367 (1957). Compare *Estate of Kirchner*, 46 B.T.A. 578 (1942).

[31] *Electric and Neon, Inc.*, 56 T.C. 1324 (1971).

[32] *Stevens Brothers Foundation, Inc.*, 39 T.C. 93 (1965).

[33] § 6662.

[34] Reg. § 1.6662–3(b)(3). Most tax professionals measure this standard as a 20% probability of prevailing in court.

[35] § 6662(c). There can be no intentional disregard of the rules where the underlying law is unclear, complex, or subject to disagreement. *Simonsen*, 150 TC No. 8 (2018) and *Lansdown v. Comm.*, 96–1 USTC ¶50,025, 77 AFTR 2d 96–491, 73 F.3d 373 (CA–10, 1996).

[36] § 6664(c)(1).

The negligence penalty applies to *all* taxes, except when fraud is involved. A negligence penalty may be assessed when the taxpayer fails to report gross income, overstates deductions, or fails to keep adequate records. When the taxpayer takes a nonnegligent position on the return that is contrary to a judicial precedent or published pronouncement of the IRS, the penalty is waived if the taxpayer has a reasonable basis for the interpretation and has disclosed the disputed position on Form 8275.

Substantial Understatement of Tax Liability

The understatement penalty is designed to strike at middle- and high-income taxpayers who fail to apply the law correctly or take overly aggressive tax return filing positions.[37]

A substantial understatement of a tax liability transpires when the understatement exceeds the larger of 10 percent of the tax due or $5,000. For a C corporation, a substantial understatement is the lesser of the following.[38]

- 10 percent of the tax due, but at least $10,000.
- $10 million.

The understatement to which the penalty applies is the difference between the amount of tax required to be paid and the amount of tax actually shown on the return. The penalty is avoided under any of the following circumstances.[39]

- The taxpayer has **substantial authority** for the treatment. Substantial authority exists when it is perhaps 40 percent likely that a court would find in favor of the taxpayer's position. This conclusion might be reached with an examination of pertinent statutory, administrative, and judicial tax law.
- There is a *reasonable basis* for the tax return position, which is adequately disclosed in the return by attaching Form 8275 or as otherwise allowed by the IRS.[40]

Penalty for Overvaluation

The overvaluation penalty is meant to deter taxpayers from inflating values (or basis), usually of charitable contributions of property, to reduce income taxes.[41]

- The penalty applies only when the valuation used by the taxpayer is 150 percent or more of the correct valuation.
- The penalty is 20 percent of the additional tax that would have been paid had the correct valuation been used.
- The penalty is doubled if the valuation error is overstated by 200 percent or more (i.e., the valuation is *grossly* misstated).
- Finally, the penalty applies only when the resulting income tax underpayment exceeds $5,000 ($10,000 for C corporations).

EXAMPLE 11

Gretchen (a calendar year taxpayer) purchased a painting for $10,000. When the painting is worth $18,000 (as later determined by the IRS), Gretchen donates it to an art museum. Based on the appraisal of a cousin who is an amateur artist, she deducts $40,000 for the donation. Because Gretchen was in the 32% tax bracket, overstating the deduction by $22,000 results in a tax underpayment of $7,040.

Gretchen's penalty for overvaluation is $2,816, or *double* the regular penalty of $1,408 (20% × $7,040 underpayment) because the $40,000 deduction constitutes a gross overvaluation.

---

[37]§ 6662(b)(2).

[38]§ 6662(d)(1). For noncorporate taxpayers claiming the qualified business income deduction of § 199A, 5% is substituted for 10%. § 6662(d)(1)(C).

[39]§ 6662(d)(2)(B). Substantial authority is measured as of either the last day of the tax year to which the return relates or the date the return was filed. Reg. § 1.6662–4(d)(3)(iv)(C).

[40]See, for example, Rev.Proc. 2016–13, 2016–4 I.R.B. 290 and Rev.Proc. 2019–9, 2019–2 I.R.B. 292.

[41]§§ 6662(b)(3), (e), and (h).

The substantial valuation overstatement penalty is avoided if the taxpayer can show reasonable cause and good faith. However, when the overvaluation involves *charitable deduction property*, the taxpayer must substantiate both of the following.

- The claimed value of the property is based on a qualified appraisal made by a qualified appraiser.
- The taxpayer made a good faith investigation of the value of the contributed property.[42]

Based on these criteria, Gretchen in Example 11 would find it difficult to avoid the penalty. A cousin who is an amateur artist does not meet the definition of a qualified appraiser. Likewise, Gretchen apparently has not made her own good faith investigation of the value of the contributed property.

Penalty for Undervaluation

When attempting to minimize the income tax, it is to the benefit of taxpayers to *overvalue* deductions. When attempting to minimize transfer taxes (estate and gift taxes), however, executors and donors may be inclined to *undervalue* the assets transferred. A lower valuation reduces estate and gift taxes. An accuracy-related penalty is imposed for substantial estate or gift tax valuation understatements.[43] As with other accuracy-related penalties, reasonable cause and good faith on the part of the taxpayer can result in a waiver of the penalty.

- The penalty is 20 percent of the additional transfer tax that would have been due had the correct valuation been used on Form 706 (estate and generation-skipping tax return) or Form 709 (gift and generation-skipping tax return).
- The penalty applies only if the value of the property claimed on the return is 65 percent or less than the amount determined to be correct. The penalty is doubled if the reported valuation error is *gross* (reported value is 40 percent or less than the correct determination).
- The penalty applies only to an additional transfer tax liability in excess of $5,000.

Appraiser's Penalty

When a valuation penalty arises because of the taxpayer's reliance on an appraisal, a further penalty can apply.[44] If the appraiser knew or reasonably should have known that the appraisal would be used as part of a tax or refund computation and that the appraised value more likely than not was improper, then the appraiser pays a penalty equal to the lesser of:

- 10 percent of the tax understatement, but at least $1,000, or
- 125 percent of the gross income received by the appraiser from the engagement (e.g., the appraisal fee collected).

Penalty for Improper Refund Claim

Whenever a taxpayer files a claim for a tax refund and the refund claim later is found to exceed the final amount allowed by the IRS or a court, a penalty of 20 percent of the disallowed refund results.[45] The penalty is waived if the taxpayer can show a *reasonable cause* for the refund claim (i.e., probably a one-third chance that a court would allow the refund). This penalty is meant to discourage the taxpayer from overstating the amount of the refund requested from the IRS. It does not apply to claims for the earned income tax credit.

---

[42]§§ 6664(c)(2) and (3).

[43]§§ 6662(b)(5), (g), and (h).

[44]§ 6695A.

[45]§ 6676.

Civil Fraud Penalty

A 75 percent civil penalty is imposed on any underpayment resulting from <mark>fraud</mark> by the taxpayer who has filed a return.[46] For this penalty, the burden of proof *is on the IRS* to show that the taxpayer acted with a specific intent to evade a tax.

Once the IRS initially has established that fraud occurred, the taxpayer then bears the burden of proof to show by a preponderance of the evidence the portion of the underpayment that is not attributable to fraud.

Although the Code and Regulations do not provide any assistance in ascertaining what constitutes civil fraud, fraud can be described as actual, intentional wrongdoing, usually occurring over several tax years. Fraud has been found in cases of manipulations of the books, substantial omissions from income, and erroneous deductions.[47]

EXAMPLE 12

Frank underpaid his income tax by $90,000. The IRS can prove that $60,000 of the underpayment was due to fraud. The civil fraud penalty is $45,000 (75% × $60,000).

Failure to Pay Estimated Taxes

A penalty is imposed for a failure to pay estimated income taxes. The penalty applies to individuals and corporations and is based on the rate of interest in effect for deficiency assessments.[48] The penalty also applies to trusts and certain estates that are required to make estimated tax payments. The penalty is not imposed if the tax due for the year (less amounts withheld and credits) is less than $500 for corporations, $1,000 for all others. For employees, an equal part of withholding is deemed paid on each due date.

Quarterly payments are made on or before the fifteenth day of the fourth month (April 15 for a calendar year taxpayer), sixth month, ninth month, and the first month of the following year. Corporations must make the last quarterly payment by the twelfth month of the same year. Generally, the payment is one-fourth of the tax expected to be due.

ETHICS & EQUITY   First-Time Tax Violators Can Get Off with Just a Warning

Tax penalties can be a harsh wake-up call when a taxpayer understates a tax liability, and there appears to be "no mercy" when a penalty is applied. Often, a tax penalty arises when the taxpayer has undergone a change in life/business circumstances (e.g., as the consequence of a divorce, retirement, or merger). The taxpayer may not have prepared adequately for the resulting tax increase and a penalty results, but the taxpayer's legitimate response might be "I didn't mean to do it; I just didn't know the rules."

The Federal income tax law does allow a measure of mercy, though. A procedure exists under which the taxpayer can apply for an abatement (waiver) of a tax penalty if all of the following circumstances are met.

- The penalty relates to a single tax year.
- The taxpayer shows *reasonable cause* for the understatement of tax.
- The taxpayer otherwise is current as to tax filings and payment compliance.
- The taxpayer has not been assessed any other penalties of a significant amount on similar tax returns within the last three years.

An IRS oversight study estimates that only 10 percent of eligible taxpayers know about the first-time abatement (FTA) penalty waiver.[49] This likely is because guidelines for the program are difficult to find at **irs.gov**. Comment on how the IRS benefits from this penalty waiver.

---

[46]§ 6663. As noted later in the chapter, underpayments traceable to fraudulent acts are not subject to a statute of limitations.

[47]*Dogget v. Comm.*, 60–1 USTC ¶9342, 5 AFTR 2d 1034, 275 F.2d 823 (CA–4, 1960); *Harvey Brodsky*, 21 TCM 578, T.C.Memo. 1962–105; and *Lash v. Comm.*, 57–2 USTC ¶9725, 51 AFTR 492, 245 F.2d 20 (CA–1, 1957).

[48]§§ 6655 (corporations) and 6654 (other taxpayers). Other computations can avoid the penalty. See §§ 6654(d)(2) and (k), 6655(e) and (i).

[49]**tinyurl.com/first-time-abate**. The IRS estimates that almost 2 million FTA waivers will occur every year, abating about $850 million in penalties.

An individual's underpayment of estimated tax is the difference between the estimates that were paid and the least of:

- 90 percent of the current-year tax,
- 100 percent of the prior-year tax (the tax year must have been a full 12 months, and a return must have been filed), and
- 90 percent of the tax that would be due on an annualized income computation for the period running through the end of the quarter.

If the taxpayer's prior-year AGI exceeds $150,000, the 100 percent requirement becomes 110 percent.

A corporation's underpayment of estimated tax is the difference between the estimates that were paid and the least of:

- The current-year tax,
- The prior-year tax, and
- The tax on an annualized income computation using one of three methods of computation sanctioned by the Code.

For the prior-year alternative, (1) the prior tax year must have been a full 12 months, (2) a nonzero tax amount must have been generated for that year, and (3) large corporations (taxable income of $1 million or more in any of the three immediately preceding tax years) can use the alternative only for the first installment of a year.

In computing the penalty, Form 2210 (Underpayment of Estimated Tax by Individuals) or Form 2220 (Underpayment of Estimated Tax by Corporations) is used.

False Information with Respect to Withholding

Withholding from wages is an important element of the Federal income tax system, which is based on a pay-as-you-go approach. One way employees might hope to avoid this withholding would be to falsify the information provided to the employer on Form W–4 (Employee Withholding Allowance Certificate). For example, by overstating the number of exemptions, income tax withholdings could be reduced or completely eliminated.

To encourage compliance, a civil penalty of $500 applies when a taxpayer claims withholding allowances based on false information. The criminal penalty for willfully failing to supply information or for willfully supplying false or fraudulent information in connection with wage withholding is an additional fine of up to $1,000 and/or up to one year of imprisonment.[50]

Failure to Make Deposits of Taxes and Overstatements of Deposits

When a business is not doing well or cash-flow problems develop, employers have a great temptation to "borrow" from Uncle Sam. One way this can be done is to fail to pay to the IRS the amounts that have been withheld from the wages of employees for FICA and income tax purposes. The IRS can apply a number of weapons to discourage the practice.

- A penalty of up to 15 percent of any underdeposited amount not paid, unless the employer can show that the failure is due to reasonable cause and not to willful neglect.[51]
- Various criminal penalties.[52]
- A 100 percent penalty if the employer's actions are willful.[53] The penalty is based on the amount of the tax evaded (i.e., not collected or not accounted for or paid over). Because the penalty is assessable against the "responsible person" of the

---

[50]§§ 6682 and 7205.
[51]§ 6656.

[52]See, for example, § 7202 (willful failure to collect or pay over a tax).
[53]§ 6672.

business, more than one party may be vulnerable (e.g., the president and treasurer of a corporation, the third-party payroll service of the entity). Although the IRS may assess the penalty against several persons, it cannot collect more than 100 percent of the tax that is due.

In addition to these penalties, the actual tax due must be remitted. For instance, an employer remains liable for the employees' income and payroll taxes that should have been paid.

Failure to Provide Information Regarding Tax Shelters

The IRS has identified over two dozen transactions that it regards as improper in determining one's tax liability, usually because the transaction lacks economic substance beyond the resulting tax reduction. These arrangements are termed "reportable transactions" or "tax shelters," and they often involve leveraged financing and accelerated interest and cost recovery deductions.

A tax shelter organizer must inform the IRS of the arrangement before any sales are made to investors.[54] A penalty of $50,000 is assessed if the required information is not filed with the IRS, using Form 8886. The disclosure includes a description of the shelter and the tax benefits that are being used to attract investors.

Criminal Penalties

In addition to civil fraud penalties, the Code contains numerous criminal sanctions that carry various monetary fines and/or imprisonment. The IRS annually attains about 2,000 convictions. About 15 percent of the cases involve identity theft. More than 80 percent of criminal tax convictions result in incarceration, home confinement, or electronic monitoring.

The difference between civil and criminal fraud often is one of degree. Code § 7201, dealing with attempts to evade or defeat a tax, contains the following language.

> Any person who *willfully* attempts in any manner to evade or defeat any tax imposed by this title or the payment thereof shall, in addition to other penalties provided by law, be guilty of a felony and, upon conviction thereof, shall be fined not more than $100,000 ($500,000 in the case of a corporation), or imprisoned not more than five years, or both, together with the costs of prosecution. [Emphasis added.]

As to the burden of proof, the IRS must show that the taxpayer was guilty of willful evasion "beyond the shadow of any reasonable doubt." So to avoid a criminal tax penalty, the taxpayer needs to create a degree of reasonable doubt as to guilt. To do so, the taxpayer might assert that he or she was confused or ignorant about the application of the tax law or relied on the erroneous advice of a competent tax adviser. Another defense against a criminal tax penalty is the lack of capacity to plan and carry out tax evasion (e.g., mental limitations or other medical disorder).

Violations of the Federal criminal code in the context of filing tax returns also may arise from other crimes that are not provided for in the Internal Revenue Code. Examples include:

- Making a false claim against the Federal government.
- Participating in a conspiracy to evade Federal taxes (i.e., in addition to the tax understatement).
- Making a false statement to the Federal government or filing a false document (i.e., perjury).

---

[54]§ 6111. The penalty amount increases if the failure to disclose relates to a listed transaction or is intentional by the taxpayer.

26-1j Statute of Limitations

LO.7

Recognize and apply the rules governing the statute of limitations on assessments and on refunds.

A statute of limitations defines the period of time during which one party may pursue against another party a cause of action or other suit allowed under the governing law. Failure to satisfy any requirement provides the other party with an absolute defense should the statute be invoked. Inequity would result if no limits were placed on such suits. Permitting an extended period of time to elapse between the initiation of a claim and its pursuit could place the defense at a serious disadvantage. Witnesses may have died or disappeared; records or other evidence may have been discarded or destroyed.

Assessment and the Statute of Limitations

In general, any tax that is imposed must be assessed within three years of the later of (a) the filing date of the return or (b) the unextended due date of the return.[55] Some exceptions to this three-year limitation exist.

- If no return is filed or a fraudulent return is filed, assessments can be made at any time. The statute of limitations, in effect, never expires in these cases.

- If a taxpayer omits an amount of gross income in excess of 25 percent of the gross income stated on the return, the statute of limitations is increased to six years. The courts have interpreted this rule as including only items affecting income and not the omission of items affecting deductions, operating losses, or cost of sales.[56] *Gross income* here includes capital gains, but not reduced by capital losses. It also includes any gross income that results from an overstatement of tax basis (e.g., in an asset sale).[57]

EXAMPLE 13

During 2016, Jerry recorded the following income transactions (all of which were duly reported on his timely filed return).

Gross receipts		$ 480,000
Cost of sales		(400,000)
Net business income		$ 80,000
Capital gains and losses		
Capital gain	$ 36,000	
Capital loss	(12,000)	24,000
Total income		$ 104,000

Jerry retains your services in 2021 as a tax consultant. It seems that he inadvertently omitted some income on his 2016 return, and he wants to know if he is "safe" under the statute of limitations. The three-year statute of limitations has expired, but the six-year statute of limitations still applies, putting Jerry in a vulnerable position only if he omitted more than $129,000 on his 2016 return [($480,000 + $36,000) × 25%].

- The statute of limitations may be extended for a fixed period of time by mutual consent of the IRS and the taxpayer. This extension covers a definite period and is made by signing Form 872. The extension frequently is requested by the IRS when the lapse of the statutory period is imminent and the audit has not been completed. This practice often is applied to audits of corporate taxpayers and explains why many corporations have more than three "open years."

The statute also is suspended when the taxpayer is "financially disabled"; that is, the taxpayer has been rendered unable to manage his or her financial affairs by a physical or mental impairment that is likely to last for a year or more or to cause the taxpayer's death.[58]

---

[55]§§ 6501(a) and (b)(1).

[56]*The Colony, Inc. v. Comm.*, 58–2 USTC ¶9593, 1 AFTR 2d 1894, 78 S.Ct. 1033 (USSC, 1958).

[57]§ 6501(e)(1)(B)(ii).

[58]§§ 6501(c)(4) and 6511(h).

Refund Claims and the Statute of Limitations

The IRS accepts refund claims on Form 1040–X for individuals and Form 1120–X for corporations. About 3.5 million amended returns are filed every year. Amended returns cannot be e-filed. If the refund claim does not meet certain procedural requirements, the IRS may reject the claim with no consideration of its merit.

- A separate claim must be filed for each taxable period.
- The grounds for the claim must be stated in sufficient detail.
- The statement of facts must be sufficient to permit the IRS to evaluate the merits of the claim.

The refund claim must be filed within three years of the filing of the tax return or within two years following the payment of the tax if this period expires on a later date.[59]

EXAMPLE 14

On March 10, 2018, Louise filed her 2017 income tax return reflecting a tax of $10,500. On July 11, 2019, she filed an amended 2017 return showing an additional $3,000 of tax that was then paid. On May 19, 2021, she filed a claim for refund of $4,500.

Assuming that Louise is correct in claiming a refund, how much tax can she recover? Because the claim was not filed within the three-year statute of limitations period, Louise is limited to $3,000, the amount she actually paid during the last two years.

Special rules are available for claims relating to bad debts and worthless securities. A seven-year period of limitations applies in lieu of the normal three-year rule.[60] The extended period is provided in recognition of the inherent difficulty of identifying the exact year in which a bad debt or security becomes worthless.

26-2 THE TAX PROFESSION AND TAX ETHICS

LO.8

Summarize the legal and ethical guidelines that apply to those engaged in tax practice.

Society and its governments expect taxpayers to comply with the letter and the spirit of the tax laws. Tax audits and penalties encourage a high degree of technical tax conformity, but the proper functioning of a voluntary tax compliance system also depends on the ethics of the taxpayer and the tax adviser.

The Treasury and various professional organizations have issued ethical guidelines that are relevant to the tax profession. Professional licensing agencies also are likely to require tax professionals to receive training in ethics to obtain initial certification and to remain in good standing over time.

26-2a The Tax Professional

Who is a tax professional? What services does a tax professional perform? A number of different groups apply constraints on the way a tax professional conducts his or her practice.

Generally, practice before the IRS is limited to CPAs, attorneys, and persons who have been enrolled to practice before the IRS [**enrolled agents (EAs)**]. In most cases, EAs are admitted to practice only if they pass an examination administered by the IRS. CPAs and attorneys are not required to take this examination and are automatically admitted to practice if they are in good standing with the appropriate licensing board regulating their profession.

Persons other than CPAs, attorneys, and EAs may be allowed to practice before the IRS in limited situations. **Circular 230** ("Regulations Governing Practice before the Internal Revenue Service") issued by the Treasury Department permits certain notable exceptions.

---

[59]§§ 6511(a) and 6513(a).   [60]§ 6511(d)(1).

- A taxpayer always may represent himself or herself. A person also may represent a member of the immediate family if no compensation is received for such services.

- Full-time employees may represent their employers.

- Corporations may be represented by any of their officers.

- Partnerships may be represented by any of the partners.

- Trusts, receiverships, guardianships, or estates may be represented by their trustees, receivers, guardians, or administrators or executors, respectively.

- A taxpayer may be represented by the individual or entity who prepared the return for the year in question. Preparers who are not a CPA, an EA, or an attorney can represent a taxpayer in an audit only if they prepared and signed the return and completed a voluntary IRS continuing education program.

All nonattorney tax professionals should avoid becoming engaged in activities that constitute the *unauthorized practice of law*. If they engage in this practice (e.g., by drafting legal documents for a third party), action could be instituted against them in the appropriate state court by the local or state bar association or state Attorney General's office. What actions constitute the unauthorized practice of law are often specified by state statute or case law.

26-2b **Regulating Tax Preparers**

There are no minimum education or experience requirements for those who are paid to file Federal tax returns for others. But the IRS does require that all paid tax return preparers, including CPAs and attorneys, obtain a Preparer Tax Identification Number (PTIN) before they assist taxpayers with returns for a new filing season. A PTIN holder must confirm to the IRS that he or she has a system in place with which to protect taxpayer data from security breaches, reflecting that tax professionals can be targeted by identity thieves and others who want access to confidential client data.

The IRS may use PTIN data to identify preparers who commit a pattern of errors or who participate in fraudulent actions. With more than 700,000 paid preparers at work in any filing season,[61] the IRS uses an outside consultant to manage the registration process.

26-2c **IRS Rules Governing Tax Practice**

Circular 230 prescribes the rules governing practice before the IRS. Following are some of the most important rules imposed on CPAs, attorneys, EAs, and a few others specified in Circular 230.

- A requirement that the tax practitioner be competent in the matters involved in the engagement with the taxpayer (i.e., the practitioner can show appropriate levels of knowledge, skill, thoroughness, and preparation for the assigned tasks).

- A prohibition against willful or reckless behavior in signing a return that includes a position that could subject the practitioner to the preparer penalty such as because the position lacks a reasonable basis (see text Section 26-2d).

The Big Picture

EXAMPLE
15

Return to the facts of *The Big Picture* on p. 26-1. Campbell has developed a testing program to be used by its in-house engineers before a new GPS app is released to the public; Campbell wants to claim the research credit for that program. Based on their tax research on this issue, the members of your firm's tax department have severe doubts about taking the credit for this program. Your firm's position is that there is a one-in-six chance that the courts would allow Campbell's credit.

Claiming the credit fails the standard of Circular 230 because there is no reasonable basis (roughly 20% probability of prevailing if challenged by the government) for the position.

---

[61]Included in this number are about 210,000 CPAs, 55,000 EAs, and 30,000 attorneys.

- A requirement to inform clients of penalties likely to apply to return positions and of ways such penalties can be avoided.

- A requirement to make known to a client any error or omission the client may have made on any return or other document submitted to the IRS.

- A duty to submit, in a timely fashion, records or information lawfully requested by the IRS.

- An obligation to exercise *due diligence* and to use the *best practices* of the tax profession in preparing, reviewing, and filing tax returns accurately.

Your niece, Selma, plans to start a tax return preparation service. She seeks advice on what procedures and practices to establish in order to develop and maintain a successful business. As a starting point, Selma should set up a standardized procedure for receiving, processing, and reviewing client tax returns. A key to achieving a high-quality product would be an appropriate choice of tax accounting software. She should be sure that all client data are kept confidential and that the electronic files holding such data are secure and properly backed up.

Any employees who are hired should be technically competent and properly trained as to office procedure. All hires should be subject to a background check and be made aware that they are expected to participate in continuing education covering developments in tax law changes. In addition, Selma should formulate adequate disclaiming language so that e-mail and text recipients do not assume that the content represents technical advice upon which they can rely.

- A restriction against unreasonably delaying the prompt disposition of any matter before the IRS.

- A restriction against charging the client a contingent fee for preparing an original return. Such a fee can be charged when the tax professional deals with an audited return and when assisting the taxpayer in filing certain refund claims.

- A restriction against charging the client "an unconscionable fee" for representation before the IRS.

- A restriction against representing clients with conflicting interests.

In a firm that prepares tax returns for compensation, personnel supervisors must ensure that the work of staff members complies with Circular 230 rules. This usually entails education programs and other means by which the current Circular 230 rules are conveyed to all affected employees.

Circular 230 is administered by the IRS Office of Professional Responsibility (OPR). Among other duties, the OPR carries out disciplinary hearings and issues penalties, such as fines and licensing restrictions and retractions, relative to tax preparers. Information about Circular 230 violations is published in the Internal Revenue Bulletin. A Circular 230 violation could lead to the loss or suspension of a CPA's license at the state level as well.

26-2d **Preparer Penalties**

The Code provides penalties to discourage improper actions by tax professionals. **Tax preparer** penalties are assessed on any person who prepares for compensation, or engages employees to prepare, a substantial portion of any Federal tax return or refund claim.[62] The following individuals are exempt from the preparer penalties:[63]

- An IRS employee.

- A volunteer who prepares tax returns in a government assistance effort such as Tax Counseling for the Elderly (TCE) or the Volunteer Income Tax Assistance (VITA) program.

---

[62]§ 7701(a)(36); Reg. § 301.7701–15(a).

[63]Reg. § 301.7701–15(f).

- An employee preparing a return for the employer.
- A fiduciary preparing a return for a trust or an estate.
- An individual who provides only data processing, reproduction, or similar assistance in preparing a return.

The preparer penalties can compound quickly in a tax practice that has many professionals. Some of the most important tax preparer penalties include the following.

1. A penalty for understatements due to taking an <mark>unreasonable position</mark> on a tax return.[64] The penalty is imposed if the tax position:

    - Is not disclosed on the return and there was no *substantial authority* (i.e., a greater than 40 percent chance) that the tax position would be sustained by its merits on a final court review, or

    - Is disclosed on the return and there was not a *reasonable basis* (i.e., at least a 20 percent chance of success) for the position.

    The penalty is computed as the greater of $1,000 or one-half of the income of the practitioner that is attributable to the return or claim that violated the conduct standard. The penalty can be avoided by showing reasonable cause and by showing that the preparer acted in good faith.

EXAMPLE 17

Josie is the tax return preparer for Hal's Form 1040. The return includes a deduction that has a 60% chance of being sustained on its merits even though it is contrary to an applicable tax Regulation. If a court denies the deduction, Josie is not assessed a penalty for taking an unreasonable position on the tax return.

Now assume that Hal's deduction has a 30% chance of being sustained on its merits. If a court denies the deduction, Josie is assessed the penalty (unless the disputed position was disclosed on the return with a Form 8275–R). The amount of the penalty is the greater of $1,000 or one-half of Josie's fees for preparing Hal's Form 1040.

What if Hal's deduction has a 15% chance of being sustained on its merits? If a court denies the deduction, Josie is assessed a penalty for taking an unreasonable tax return position (even if the disputed position was disclosed on the return with a Form 8275–R). The amount of the penalty is the greater of $1,000 or one-half of Josie's fees for preparing Hal's Form 1040.

2. A penalty for willful and reckless conduct.[65] The penalty applies if any part of the understatement of a taxpayer's liability on a return or claim for refund is due to:

    - The preparer's willful attempt to understate the taxpayer's tax liability in any manner.

    - Any reckless or intentional disregard of IRS rules or Regulations by the preparer.

    The penalty is computed as the greater of $5,000 or 75 percent of the income of the practitioner that is attributable to the return or claim that violated the conduct standard. Adequate disclosure can avoid the penalty. If both this penalty and the unreasonable position penalty (see item 1) apply to the same return, the reckless conduct penalty is reduced by the amount of the penalty for unreasonable positions.

3. A $1,000 ($10,000 for the tax returns of corporations) penalty per return or document is imposed against persons who aid in the preparation of returns or other documents they know (or have reason to believe) would result in an understatement of the tax liability of another person.[66] As a result, this penalty also applies to those other than the preparer of the actual tax return (e.g., advisers, attorneys, corporate officers and executives, and tax shelter promoters). Administrative assistance in the return preparation process does not incur the penalty.

---

[64]§ 6694(a). For the most part, these standards match those that apply to the taxpayer penalties of § 6662(d). Stricter disclosure standards apply for tax shelter items and reportable transactions. § 6662A.

[65]§ 6694(b).

[66]§ 6701.

If this penalty applies, neither the unreasonable position penalty (item 1) nor the willful and reckless conduct penalty (item 2) is assessed.

4. A $250 penalty for each third-party disclosure or improper use of tax return data, up to a $10,000 annual maximum per practitioner.[67] These amounts become $1,000 and $50,000 when criminal identity theft of a taxpayer's data is involved.

5. A $50 penalty is assessed against the preparer for failure to sign a return or furnish the preparer's PTIN.[68]

6. A $50 penalty is assessed if the preparer fails to furnish a copy of the return or claim for refund to the taxpayer, and if the preparer fails to keeps its own copy thereof.

7. A $540 penalty may be assessed if a preparer endorses or otherwise negotiates a check for refund of tax issued to the taxpayer.

8. A $540 penalty for each instance of failure to be diligent in determining the taxpayer's eligibility for the earned income tax credit, child tax credit, other dependent credit, American Opportunity tax credit, or head-of-household filing status.

Other parts of the Code provide additional constraints to govern all parties engaged in rendering tax returns for the general public.

- A person who holds himself or herself out to the general public as possessing tax expertise could be liable to the client if services are performed in a negligent manner. At a minimum, the practitioner is liable for any interest and penalties the client incurs because of the practitioner's failure to exercise due professional care.

- If a practitioner agrees to perform a service (e.g., prepare a tax return) and subsequently fails to do so, the aggrieved party may be in a position to obtain damages for breach of contract.

- All persons who prepare tax returns or refund claims for a fee must sign as preparer of the return.[69] Failure to comply with this requirement could result in a penalty assessment against the preparer.

- Various penalties apply concerning the deliberate filing of false or fraudulent returns. These felonies apply to a tax practitioner who either was aware of the situation or actually perpetrated the false information or the fraud.[70]

- A criminal penalty applies to tax practitioners who recklessly disclose to third parties information they have received from clients in connection with the preparation of tax returns or the rendering of tax advice.[71] The penalty is $1,000 per violation, or $100,000 if identity theft is involved, or potential imprisonment.

EXAMPLE 18

Sarah operates a tax return preparation service. Her brother-in-law, Butch, has just taken a job as a life insurance salesperson. To help Butch find contacts, Sarah furnishes him with a list of the names and addresses of all of her clients who report AGI of $50,000 or more. Sarah is subject to the $1,000 reckless disclosure penalty.

26-2e Privileged Communications

Communications between an attorney and a client long have been protected from disclosure to other parties (such as the IRS and the courts). A similar privilege of

---

[67]§ 6713.

[68]§ 6695. The penalty amounts for the rest of this list are adjusted annually for inflation. Items 5. and 6. cannot exceed $27,000 per year for the preparer or firm. See § 6695(h) and Rev.Proc. 2019–44, 2019–47 I.R.B. 1093.

[69]Reg. § 1.6065–1(b)(1). Rev.Rul. 84–3, 1984–1 C.B. 264, contains a series of examples illustrating when a person is deemed to be a preparer of the return.

[70]§ 7206.

[71]§ 7216.

confidentiality extends to tax advice between a taxpayer and a Federally authorized tax practitioner (attorney, CPA, EA). The privilege is not available for matters involving criminal charges or questions brought by other agencies, such as the Securities and Exchange Commission. Nor is it allowed in matters involving promoting or participating in tax shelters.[72]

A taxpayer likely will want to protect documents such as the tax adviser's research memo detailing the strengths and weaknesses of a tax return position or a conversation about an appeals strategy. The confidentiality privilege should be interpreted in the following manner.

- The privilege for CPAs and EAs applies only to tax advice. Only attorneys can exercise the privilege concerning advice rendered as a business consultant, an estate/financial planner, etc.

- The privilege is not available for tax accrual workpapers prepared as part of an independent financial audit.

- Generally, there is no privilege as to taxpayer information that is intended to be disclosed on a tax return.

26-2f AICPA Statements on Standards for Tax Services

Tax practitioners who are CPAs, attorneys, or EAs must abide by the codes or canons of professional ethics applicable to their respective professions. The various codes and canons have much in common with and parallel the standards of conduct set forth in Circular 230.[73]

The AICPA has issued a series of Statements on Standards for Tax Services (SSTSs). The Statements are enforceable standards of professional practice for AICPA members working in state or Federal tax practice. The SSTSs comprise part of the AICPA's Code of Professional Conduct. Together with the provisions of Circular 230 and the penalty provisions of the Code, the SSTSs make up a set of guidelines for the conduct of the tax practitioner who is also a CPA. Other sources of professional ethics are issued by state bar associations and CPA societies, the American Bar Association, and the associations of enrolled agents.

Statement No. 1: Tax Return Positions

Under certain circumstances, a CPA may take a position that is contrary to that taken by the IRS. To do so, however, the CPA must have a good faith belief that the position has a realistic possibility (i.e., probably a one-in-three chance) of being sustained administratively or judicially on its merits if challenged. If the taxing authority (e.g., a state revenue statute) uses a lower standard than that of a *realistic possibility*, this higher standard still applies. But where the taxing authority applies a higher standard, such as one of *substantial authority*, that standard is in effect.

The client should be fully advised of the risks involved and the penalties that may result if the position taken on the tax return is not successful. The client also should be informed that disclosure on the return may avoid some or all of these penalties.

In no case, though, should the CPA exploit the audit lottery. That is, the CPA should not take a questionable position based on the probabilities that the client's return will not be chosen by the IRS for audit. Furthermore, the CPA should not "load" the return with questionable items in the hope that they might aid the client in a later settlement negotiation with the IRS.

---

[72]§ 7525.

[73]For an additional discussion of tax ethics, see Sawyers and Gill, *Federal Tax Research*, 11th ed. (Cengage Learning, 2018), especially Chapters 1 and 14.

The Big Picture

EXAMPLE 19

Return to the facts of *The Big Picture* on p. 26-1. Campbell's new marketing program solicits the opinions of a virtual focus group to test ideas for new products. Based on your tax research, you believe that because the program relies on innovative algorithms that use online contacts to carry out the focus group activities, the program might qualify for the Federal income tax research credit even though it involves marketing research that is excluded from the credit under § 41(d)(4). Still, you believe that there is only a 30% chance the courts would allow the credit.

You meet with Seung Watkins, Campbell's tax director, to convey the results of your research. Watkins agrees that the research credit would be turned down by an IRS auditor, but she says that Campbell never has been audited and that it is not likely to be audited as long as its legal structure and income levels do not significantly change. Watkins believes that Campbell's corporate officers will sign off on the credit, given both the firm's weak cash position and the low chances that the item will be discovered.

As a CPA, you must inform Campbell that claiming the credit for this activity is a position that lacks substantial authority. The 30% chance of being upheld indicates that it may have a reasonable basis, though. In that case, the position needs to be disclosed on the return to avoid a taxpayer penalty.

Whether the credit is claimed is the decision of your client, the taxpayer. But if Campbell wants to claim the credit without the required additional disclosures, you must terminate your engagement with Campbell, under the SSTS and other AICPA provisions.

Statement No. 2: Questions on Returns

A CPA should make a reasonable effort to obtain from the client and provide appropriate answers to all questions on a tax return before signing as preparer. Reasonable grounds may exist for omitting an answer.

- The information is not readily available, and the answer is not significant in amount in computing the tax.
- The meaning of the question as it applies to a particular situation is genuinely uncertain.
- The answer to the question is voluminous.

The fact that an answer to a question could prove disadvantageous to the client does not justify omitting the answer.

Statement No. 3: Procedural Aspects of Preparing Returns

In preparing a return, a CPA may in good faith rely without verification on information furnished by the client or by third parties. However, the CPA should make reasonable inquiries if the information appears to be incorrect, incomplete, or inconsistent. In this regard, the CPA should refer to the client's returns for prior years whenever appropriate.

EXAMPLE 20

While preparing Sunni's income tax return, you review her prior year's income tax return. In comparing the dividend income reported on the Schedule B for the two years, you note a significant decrease from last year's amounts. Further investigation reveals that the variation is due to a stock sale this year that was unknown to you until now. As a result, the review of the prior year's return has unearthed a transaction that should be reported on this year's return.

If the Code or Regulations require certain types of verification (as is the case with travel and entertainment expenses), the CPA must advise the client of these rules. In addition, the CPA must determine whether the client has complied with the verification requirements.

Statement No. 4: Estimates

A CPA may prepare a tax return using estimates received from a taxpayer if it is impracticable to obtain exact data. The estimates must be reasonable under the facts and circumstances as known to the CPA. When estimates are used, they should avoid the impression of greater accuracy than exists.

Statement No. 5: Recognition of Administrative Proceeding or Court Decision

As facts may vary from year to year, so may the position taken by a CPA. In these situations, the CPA is not bound by an administrative or judicial proceeding for a prior year.

As part of a prior year's audit of Ramon Corporation's income tax return, the IRS disallowed $78,000 of the $600,000 salary paid to its president and sole shareholder on the grounds that it is unreasonable. You are the CPA who has been engaged to prepare Ramon's income tax return for the current year. Again this year, the corporation paid its president a salary of $600,000 and chose to deduct this amount. Because you are not bound for this year's return by what the IRS deemed reasonable for the prior tax year, the full $600,000 can be claimed as a salary deduction, assuming that you and Ramon both believe that the entire salary represents reasonable compensation.

Statement No. 6: Knowledge of Error

A CPA should advise a client promptly upon learning of an error in a previously filed return or upon learning of a client's failure to file a required return, where the error has a significant (material in amount) effect on the tax liability. The advice can be oral or written and should include a recommendation of the corrective measures, if any, to be taken. The error or other omission should not be disclosed to the IRS without the client's consent.

If the past error is material in amount and is not corrected by the client, the CPA may be unable to prepare the current year's tax return. The CPA must consider the cumulative effects of the error on the taxpayer's liabilities for all tax years, including those in the future.

In preparing a client's year 2 income tax return, you discover that final inventory for year 1 was materially understated. First, you should advise the client to file an amended return for year 1 reflecting the correct amount in final inventory. Second, if the client refuses to make this adjustment, you should consider whether the error will preclude you from preparing a substantially correct return for year 2. Because this probably is the case (last year's closing inventory becomes this year's beginning inventory), you should withdraw from the engagement.

If the client corrects the error, you may proceed with the preparation of the year 2 tax return. You must assure yourself that the error is not repeated on the return that you are preparing.

Statement No. 7: Advice to Clients

In providing tax advice to a client, the CPA must use judgment to ensure that the advice reflects professional competence and appropriately serves the client's needs. No standard format or guidelines can cover all situations and circumstances involving written or oral advice by the CPA.

The CPA may communicate with the client when subsequent developments affect previous advice on significant matters. However, the CPA need not initiate the communication unless he or she has agreed to do so in the engagement letter with the client.

Concept Summary 26.2

Tax Profession and Ethics

1. The Treasury assesses penalties when the taxpayer fails to file a required tax return or pay a tax. Penalties also are assessed when an inaccurate return is filed due to negligence or other disregard of tax rules. Tax preparers are subject to penalties for assisting a taxpayer in filing an inaccurate return, failing to follow IRS rules in an appropriate manner, or mishandling taxpayer data or funds.

2. Statutes of limitations place outer boundaries on the timing and amounts of proposed amendments to completed tax returns that can be made by the taxpayer or the IRS.

3. Tax practitioners must operate under constraints imposed on them by codes of ethics or pertinent professional societies and by Treasury Circular 230. These rules also define the parties who can represent others in an IRS proceeding.

4. A limited privilege of confidentiality exists between the taxpayer and tax preparer who also is a CPA, an EA, or an attorney.

26-3 TAX PLANNING

26-3a Strategies in Seeking a Letter Ruling

In some cases, it may not be necessary or desirable to request an advance ruling from the IRS. For example, it generally is not desirable to request a ruling if the tax results are doubtful and the company is committed to completing the transaction in any event. If a ruling is requested and negotiations with the IRS indicate that an adverse determination will be forthcoming, it usually is possible to have the ruling request withdrawn. In determining the advisability of a ruling request, the taxpayer should consider the potential exposure of other items in the tax returns of all "open years."

26-3b Considerations in Handling an IRS Audit

As a general rule, a taxpayer should attempt to settle disputes at the earliest possible stage of the administrative appeal process. It usually is possible to limit the scope of the examination by furnishing pertinent information requested by the agent. Extraneous information or fortuitous comments may result in the opening of new issues and should be avoided. Agents usually appreciate prompt and efficient responses to inquiries, because their performance may in part be judged by their ability to close or settle assigned cases.

To the extent possible, it is advisable to conduct the investigation of field audits in the practitioner's office, not the client's office. This permits greater control over the audit investigation and facilitates the agent's review and prompt closure of the case.

Many practitioners believe that it is generally not advisable to have clients present at the scheduled conferences with the agent, because the client may give emotional or gratuitous comments that impair prompt settlement. If the client is not present, however, he or she should be advised of the status of negotiations. The client makes the final decision on any proposed settlement.

Preparing for the Audit

The tax professional must prepare thoroughly for the audit or Appeals proceeding. Practitioners often cite the following steps as critical to such preparations. Carrying out a level of due diligence in preparing for the proceeding is part of the tax professional's responsibility in representing the client.

- Make certain that both sides agree on the issues to be resolved in the audit. The goal here is to limit the IRS agent's list of open issues.

- Identify all of the facts underlying the issues in dispute, including those favorable to the IRS. Gather evidence to support the taxpayer's position, and evaluate the evidence supporting the other side.

- Conduct research with current tax law authorities as they bear on the facts and open issues, within the parameters of the audit that you and the IRS have agreed to. The IRS agent is bound only by U.S. Supreme Court cases and IRS pronouncements. Determine the degree of discretion that the IRS is likely to have in disposing of the case.

- Prepare a list of points supporting and contradicting the taxpayer's case. Include both minor points bearing little weight and core principles. Short research memos also will be useful in the discussion with the agent. Points favoring the taxpayer should be mentioned during the discussion and "entered into the record."

- Prepare tax and interest computations showing the effects of points that are in dispute so that the consequences of closing or compromising an issue can readily be determined.

- Determine a "litigation point" (i.e., at which the taxpayer will withdraw from further audit negotiation and pursue the case in the courts). This position should be based on the dollars of tax, interest, and penalty involved; the chances of prevailing in various trial-level courts; and other strategies discussed with the taxpayer. One must have an "end game" strategy for the audit, and thorough tax research is critical in developing that position in this context.

Documentation Issues

The tax practitioner's workpapers should include all research memoranda, and a list of resolved and unresolved issues should be continually updated during the course of the IRS audit. Occasionally, agents request access to excessive amounts of accounting data to engage in a so-called fishing expedition. Providing blanket access to working papers should be avoided. Workpapers should be reviewed carefully to minimize opportunities for the agent to raise new issues not otherwise apparent. It generally is advisable to provide the agent with copies of specific workpapers only upon request.

In unusual situations, a Special Agent may appear to gather evidence in the investigation of possible criminal fraud. When this occurs, the tax professional should be advised to seek separate legal counsel to determine the extent of his or her cooperation in providing information to the agent. If the taxpayer receives a Revenue Agent's Report, it generally indicates that the IRS has decided not to initiate criminal proceedings. The IRS usually does not take any action on a tax deficiency until any related criminal matter has been resolved.

26-3c **Statute of Limitations**

The IRS requests an extension of the statute of limitations when it finds that there is insufficient time to complete an audit or appellate review. The taxpayer is not compelled to agree to the extension request and may be averse to giving the IRS more time. But adverse consequences can result if the taxpayer denies the IRS request.

Although the statute of limitations governing Thornton's tax return is scheduled to expire in 15 days, the IRS has requested an extension for another 60 days. It wants to complete a more thorough investigation into a disputed $500,000 deduction. If Thornton refuses to agree to the extension, the IRS likely will disallow the entire deduction and issue a 90-day letter. However, if Thornton agrees to the extension, all or part of the deduction may be salvaged.

EXAMPLE
23

A disadvantage of extending the statute is that the IRS sometimes can raise new issues during the extension period. Moreover, any extension of the statute further extends the period for which the return is subject to audit in subsequent years. However, the taxpayer can take the following protective measures as a condition to agreeing to the extension.

- Shorten the extension period requested before signing the Form 872. This will reduce the chance that the IRS will find and investigate new issues.

- Restrict the scope of the issues covered by the extension (e.g., extend the period only as to the computation of cost of goods sold).

26-3d **Litigation Considerations**

During the process of settlement with the IRS, the taxpayer must assess the economic consequences of possible litigation. Specifically, the probability of winning in court should be weighed against the costs of litigating the dispute (legal, support, and court costs). In some instances, taxpayers become overly emotional and do not adequately consider the economic and psychological costs of litigation, nor do they consider the public nature of documents and other materials involved in litigation.

In selecting a proper tax forum, consideration should be given to the decisions of the various courts in related cases. The Tax Court follows the decisions of U.S. Courts of Appeals if the court is one to which the taxpayer may appeal.[74] For example, if an individual is in the jurisdiction of the Fifth Circuit Court of Appeals and that court has issued a favorable opinion on the same issue that currently confronts the taxpayer, the Tax Court will follow this opinion in deciding the taxpayer's case, even if previous Tax Court decisions have been adverse.

If the issue involves a question in which some special consideration is needed, strategy may dictate the choice of the Court of Federal Claims, which is seen by some observers as on occasion giving greater weight to equity considerations than to strict legal precedent, or of a Federal District Court, where a jury trial is available.

26-3e **Penalties**

The failure to file and failure to pay penalties are not a threat for most individual taxpayers. Those penalties are computed as a percentage of the unpaid tax liability; because most taxpayers receive a refund on the Form 1040, the penalty as computed would be zero.

The penalty for failure to pay estimated taxes can become quite severe. Often trapped by the provision are employed taxpayers with outside income. They may forget about the outside income and assume that the amount withheld from wages and salaries is adequate to cover their liability, and a penalty may be triggered.

To avoid tax preparer penalties, the tax professional must carry out a number of quality control measures within the context of his or her firm.

- Adopt a "tone at the top" that stresses ethical tax practice, emphasizing at all times the importance of integrity and objectivity in the context of client advocacy. Stress the importance of all employees to stay current with the requirements of Circular 230 and the tax preparer penalty rules.

- Establish and follow ethical guidelines with respect to all forms of client communication and documentation, including tax returns and written, spoken, and electronic tax advice.

- Prepare an engagement letter to lay out the responsibilities of all parties in complying with the tax law when taking on a new client, or whenever the scope of the work to be performed for a client changes. The firm should use the engagement

---

[74]*Jack E. Golsen*, 54 T.C. 742 (1970). See text Sections 2-1c and 2-3d.

letter to make certain that the client provides all documents needed to avoid penalties and compute the tax liability correctly, and to establish the high levels of tax ethics that will be met in the engagement. The client should be aware of, and participate in, this dedication to ethical behavior.

- Conduct annual reviews to ascertain that all tax preparers in the firm are current as to their PTIN registration and CPA or other licenses and certifications held. Emphasize the importance of data security and confidentiality, and of other aspects of the firm's best practices to all who handle tax return data.

- Monitor the compliance of all members of the firm with its established ethical guidelines. Use a peer review process periodically to confirm that the system is working as designed and to bring third-party suggestions into the process.

26-3f Privileged Communications

The CPA needs to exercise care to ensure that the privilege of confidentiality will apply to his or her tax work. Taking the following steps can help.

- Segregate the time spent and documents produced in rendering services for tax compliance from that devoted to tax advice. Doing this will protect the privilege from being waived as to the tax advice.

- Explain the extent of the privilege to the client—specify what will and will not be protected from the IRS in a dispute.

- Do not inadvertently waive the privilege, for example, by telling "too much" to the IRS or to a third party who is not protected by the privilege.

REFOCUS ON THE BIG PICTURE

A TAX ADVISER'S DILEMMA

Your work with Campbell Corporation and its incremental research credit may prove troublesome. To avoid the taxpayer and tax preparer penalties, substantial authority must exist for claiming the credit, but the tax cases and Regulations do not appear to provide much guidance with respect to research expenditures of this sort. How does one craft a tax return position when the tax law largely is silent as to the particulars of the facts of the taxpayer's situation? How much risk of incurring a tax penalty are the taxpayer and your firm willing to assume in deciding how and whether to report these expenditures?

Beyond the monetary effects of claiming the credit, you and the client must consider the publicity aspects of taking this issue to court: Does Campbell want to be the "test case" in the Tax Court on this matter? What would be the effects on your consulting firm if a preparer penalty or even loss of professional certification were to result? If the credit is to be claimed, what degree of "disclosure" does the law require?

At a minimum, your firm and Campbell's tax department must conduct thorough research of analogous situations in the law in which the incremental research credit was and was not allowed for the taxpayer. Due diligence in this regard would require that you examine how other software applications and similar technological innovations, probably having nothing to do with GPS software and national security concerns, were treated for tax credit purposes. Constrained only by the budget dollars that Campbell is willing to dedicate to this task, your research is likely to be both interesting and frustrating, as no "on point" resolution is likely to be found prior to a later audit of the Form 1120 and its disclosures.

continued

What If?

The risk profiles of the tax adviser and a client seldom are identical. What position should your firm take if Campbell's tax department decides to claim the full incremental research credit for an item on which the tax law is silent or unclear, but your firm recommends that a special disclosure be made on the return concerning the item? A disclosure of this sort would protect the parties from later assessment of tax penalties, but Campbell believes that drawing attention to the credit item would increase the likelihood of a targeted audit of the expenditures by the IRS.

Although you are certain that tax fraud is not a problem on the Campbell return, you are concerned about the ramifications of Campbell's desire to omit the recommended disclosure. Your firm might decide to leave the Campbell engagement altogether if it is especially sensitive to exposure to penalties, or if it is not certain that your tax research has established and documented that there is substantial authority or a reasonable basis for the tax return position. Charges of a lack of appropriate competence or due diligence by your firm might be brought by the IRS, the firm's professional ethics or certification bodies, or the issuer of its malpractice insurance. Clearly, none of these results is attractive to your firm.

Key Terms

30-day letter, 26-9	Enrolled agents (EAs), 26-22	Statute of limitations, 26-21
90-day letter, 26-9	Fraud, 26-18	Substantial authority, 26-16
Accuracy-related penalties, 26-15	Letter ruling, 26-4	Tax preparer, 26-24
Circular 230, 26-22	Negligence, 26-15	Technical advice memorandum
Closing agreement, 26-12	Offer in compromise, 26-10	(TAM), 26-5
Determination letter, 26-4	Reasonable cause, 26-15	Unreasonable position, 26-25
E-filing, 26-3	Revenue Agent's Report (RAR), 26-8	Whistleblower Program, 26-7

Discussion Questions

1. **LO.1** As a tax professional with a diverse group of clients and tax issues, why is it important that you understand how the IRS is organized and how its personnel are deployed?

2. **LO.1, 8** Your tax client Chen asks whether it is likely that her Form 1040 will be audited this year. You suspect that Chen might modify the information she reports on her return based on your answer. Address Chen's question, and provide her with a justification to comply fully with the tax law's reporting requirements.

Critical Thinking

3. **LO.1** Recently, a politician was interviewed about fiscal policy, and she mentioned reducing the "tax gap." Explain what this term means. What are some of the pertinent political and economic issues relative to the tax gap?

4. **LO.1** Review Exhibit 26.1, and identify the following.

    a.   The title of the IRS's chief executive officer.

    b.   The title of the "IRS's attorney."

    c.   The names of the four major operating divisions of the IRS.

    d.   The placement in the IRS organization of the Appeals and Criminal Investigation functions.

    e.   Initiatives of the IRS to become a more modern, well-managed organization.

5. **LO.3** During an interview with an IRS official on *Dateline*, the interviewer asks,   Critical Thinking
"So how do you decide which Forms 1040 get audited and which do not?"
How should the IRS official respond, taking into account that only some of the audit
selection process is public information?

6. **LO.3** On June 10, Ming states, "I filed my Form 1040 on April 5 and haven't heard from
the IRS since then, so I know I will not be audited!" Evaluate Ming's assumption.

7. **LO.3** You overhear Matheus say, "I am so glad to be divorced from my cheating
wife Larissa. She keeps two sets of books in her coding business, and I wish
the IRS would find out about it." Is Matheus a candidate for the informant award
program that is operated by the IRS? Explain how the program works and how an
award might be paid to Matheus.

8. **LO.6** Which of the valuation penalties is likely to arise when an aggressive taxpayer
reports:
   a. A charitable contribution?
   b. A business deduction?
   c. A decedent's taxable estate?

9. **LO.4, 5** Indicate whether each of the following statements is true or false.
   a. The government never pays a taxpayer interest on an overpayment of tax.
   b. The IRS can compromise on the amount of tax liability if there is doubt as to
   the taxpayer's ability to pay.
   c. The IRS is required to accept an application for an installment plan that delays
   the payment of the taxpayer's $6,000 outstanding tax liability.
   d. The offer in compromise program attempts to allow upper-income taxpayers
   additional time in which to pay delinquent tax amounts.

10. **LO.4, 6** In each of the following cases, distinguish between the terms.
    a. Offer in compromise and closing agreement.
    b. Failure to file and failure to pay.
    c. 90-day letter and 30-day letter.
    d. Negligence and fraud.
    e. Criminal and civil tax fraud.

11. **LO.7** Discuss the concept of statutes of limitations in the context of the Federal   Critical Thinking
income tax law.
    a. Who benefits when the statute applies—the government, the taxpayer, or both?
    b. What happens when the statute is scheduled to expire within two weeks but
    the IRS audit will not be completed by then?

12. **LO.8** Give the Circular 230 position concerning each of the following situations
sometimes encountered in the tax profession.
    a. Taking an aggressive pro-taxpayer position on a tax return.
    b. Not having a quality review process for a return completed by a partner of the
    tax firm.
    c. Purposely delaying compliance with a document request received from the IRS.
    d. Not keeping up with changes in the tax law.
    e. Charging $4,500 to complete a simple Form 1040 with no supporting schedules.
    f. When representing a taxpayer in a Federal income tax audit, charging a fee
    equal to one-third of the reduction of the tax proposed by the IRS agent.
    g. Representing both the husband and wife when negotiating tax matters pertinent
    to their divorce.
    h. Advertising on the Web for new tax clients and including *Se habla español* in
    the text of the ads.

13. **LO.8** Indicate whether each of the following parties could be subject to the tax preparer penalties.

    a.   Tom prepared Sally's return for $250.

    b.   Theresa prepared her grandmother's return for no charge.

    c.   Georgia prepared her church's return for $500 (she would have charged an unrelated party $3,000 for the same work).

    d.   Geoff prepared returns for low-income taxpayers under his college's VITA program.

    e.   Hildy prepared the return of her corporate employer.

    f.   Heejeo, an administrative assistant for an accounting firm, processed a client's return through TurboTax.

Communications   14. **LO.8** Using no more than five PowerPoint slides, create a presentation for your Advanced Accounting class, listing at least three of the Statements on Standards for Tax Services that apply to CPAs. For each standard you choose, provide a short explanation of its content.

Computational Exercises

15. **LO.6** Alexi files her tax return 20 days after the due date. Along with the return, she remits a check for $3,000, which is the balance of the tax she owes. Disregarding any interest liabilities, compute Alexi's total penalties for this period.

16. **LO.6** Marcella (a calendar year taxpayer) purchased a sculpture for $5,000. When the sculpture is worth $12,000 (as later determined by the IRS), Marcella donates it to the Peoria Museum of Art, a public charity. Based on the appraisal of a friend, Marcella deducts $38,000 for the donation. Because Marcella was in the 24% marginal Federal income tax bracket, overstating the deduction by $26,000 results in a tax underpayment of $6,240.

    a.   Compute Marcella's overvaluation penalty.

    b.   Construct a Microsoft Excel formula that will compute the penalty for all non-corporate taxpayers.

17. **LO.6** Rivera underpaid her income tax by $45,000. The IRS can prove that $40,000 of the underpayment was due to fraud.

    a.   Determine Rivera's civil fraud penalty.

    b.   Rivera pays the penalty five years after committing the fraudulent act. Her after-tax rate of return on available cash is 9%. What is the present value of Rivera's penalty? See text Appendix G.

18. **LO.7** On June 15, 2020, Sheridan filed his 2019 income tax return, paying a tax of $10,500. On October 5, 2021, he filed an amended 2019 return showing an additional $6,400 of tax, which he paid with the amended return. On August 22, 2023, he filed a claim for a refund of $7,000. How much Federal income tax can Sheridan recover on the amended return?

Problems

19. **LO.5** Gordon paid the $10,000 balance of his Federal income tax three months late. Ignore daily compounding of interest. Determine the interest rate that applies relative to this amount for the first quarter of 2020, assuming that:

    a. Gordon is an individual.

    b. Gordon is a calendar year C corporation.

    c. The $10,000 is not a tax that is due, but is a refund payable by the IRS to Gordon (an individual).

    d. The $10,000 is not a tax that is due, but is a refund payable by the IRS to Gordon (a calendar year C corporation).

20. **LO.6** Rita forgot to pay her Federal income tax on time. When she actually filed, she reported a balance due. Compute Rita's failure to file penalty in each of the following cases.

    a. Two months late, $1,000 additional tax due.

    b. Five months late, $3,000 additional tax due.

    c. Eight months late, $4,000 additional tax due.

    d. Two and a half months late, $3,000 additional tax due.

    e. Five months late due to fraud by Rita, $4,000 additional tax due.

    f. Ten months late due to fraud by Rita, $15,000 additional tax due.

21. **LO.6** Wade filed his Federal income tax return on time but did not remit the balance due. Compute Wade's failure to pay penalty in each of the following cases. The IRS has not issued a deficiency notice.

    a. Four months late, $3,000 additional tax due.

    b. Ten months late, $4,000 additional tax due.

    c. Five years late, $5,000 additional tax due.

22. **LO.6** Compute the failure to pay and failure to file penalties for John, who filed his 2019 income tax return on December 20, 2020, paying the $10,000 amount due at that time. On April 1, 2020, John received a six-month extension of time in which to file his return. He has no reasonable cause for failing to file his return by October 15 or for failing to pay the tax that was due on April 15. John's failure to comply with the tax laws was not fraudulent.

23. **LO.6** Olivia, a calendar year taxpayer, does not file her 2019 Form 1040 until December 12, 2020. At this point, she pays the $40,000 balance due on her 2019 tax liability of $70,000. Olivia did not apply for and obtain any extension of time for filing the 2019 return. When questioned by the IRS on her delinquency, Olivia asserts: "If I was too busy to file my regular tax return, I was too busy to request an extension."

    a. Is Olivia liable for any penalties for failure to file and for failure to pay?

    b. If so, compute the penalty amounts.

24. **LO.6** Maureen, a calendar year individual taxpayer, files her 2018 return on November 4, 2020. She did not obtain an extension for filing her return, and the return reflects additional income tax due of $15,000.

    a. What are Maureen's penalties for failure to file and to pay?

    b. Would your answer to part (a) change if Maureen, before the due date of the return, had retained a CPA to prepare and e-file the return, and it was the CPA's negligence that caused the delay? Explain.

25. **LO.6** Blair underpaid her taxes by $250,000. A portion of the underpayment was shown to be attributable to Blair's negligence ($100,000). A court found that the rest of the deficiency constituted civil fraud ($150,000).

    a. Compute the total fraud and negligence penalties incurred.

    b. Construct a Microsoft Excel formula that will compute the penalties incurred in part (a).

    c. Blair pays the penalties four years after committing the improper acts. Her after-tax rate of return on available cash is 7%. What is the present value of Blair's penalty obligations? See text Appendix G.

26. **LO.6** Compute the overvaluation penalty for each of the following independent cases involving the fair market value of charitable contribution property.

	Taxpayer	Corrected IRS Value	Reported Valuation	Applicable Tax Rate
a.	Individual	$ 40,000	$ 50,000	35%
b.	C corporation	30,000	50,000	21
c.	S corporation	40,000	50,000	35
d.	Individual	150,000	200,000	35
e.	Individual	150,000	250,000	35
f.	C corporation	150,000	750,000	21

27. **LO.6** Compute the undervaluation penalty for each of the following independent cases involving the value of a closely held business in the decedent's gross estate. In each case, assume a marginal Federal estate tax rate of 40%.

	Reported Value	Corrected IRS Valuation
a.	$ 20,000	$ 25,000
b.	100,000	150,000
c.	150,000	250,000
d.	150,000	500,000

28. **LO.6** Singh, a qualified appraiser of fine art and other collectibles, was advising Colleen when she was determining the amount of the charitable contribution deduction for a gift of a sculpture to a museum. Singh sanctioned a $900,000 appraisal, even though he knew the market value of the piece was only $300,000. Colleen assured Singh that she had never been audited by the IRS and that the risk of the government questioning his appraisal was negligible.

    But Colleen was wrong, and her return was audited. The IRS used its own appraisers to set the value of the sculpture at $400,000. Colleen is in the 32% Federal income tax bracket. Singh's fee for preparing the appraisal was $20,000.

    a. Compute the penalty the IRS can assess against Singh. (Do not consider the valuation penalty as to Colleen's return.)

    b. What is the penalty if Singh's appraisal fee was $7,500 (not $20,000)?

    c. Construct a Microsoft Excel formula that would generate the correct answer for parts (a) and (b).

29. **LO.6** Eggers Corporation filed an amended Form 1120, claiming an additional $400,000 deduction for payments to a contractor for a prior tax year. The amended return was based on the entity's interpretation of a Regulation that defined deductible advance payment expenditures. The nature of Eggers's activity with the contractor did not exactly fit the language of the Regulation. Nevertheless, because so much tax was at stake, Eggers's tax department decided to claim the deduction.

    Eggers's tax department estimated that there was only a 15% chance that Eggers's interpretation would stand up to a Tax Court review.

a. What is the amount of tax penalty that Eggers is risking by taking this position?

b. What would be the result if there was a 45% chance that Eggers's interpretation of the Regulation was correct?

c. Construct a Microsoft Excel formula that would generate the correct answer for parts (a) and (b).

30. **LO.6** Kaitlin donated a painting to the local art museum. Because she is subject to a 35% marginal tax rate, she is looking for a large charitable contribution deduction for the year. She engaged Vargas (who was referred to her by the museum) to provide an appraisal of the painting before she filed her Form 1040 for the year. Kaitlin told Vargas, "Be kind to me on this appraisal, and I'll send several more clients to you in the future." Kaitlin paid Vargas a $45,000 fee for his services.

Vargas completed his appraisal and determined that the painting was worth $500,000 under current market conditions. Still, in light of Kaitlin's promise of future business, Vargas sent Kaitlin an official appraisal reporting a $900,000 value for the artwork. Vargas had never compromised his integrity, but this time the temptation was too much.

Kaitlin used the appraisal to claim a $900,000 deduction for her charitable gift. Kaitlin will incur a valuation penalty now that her Form 1040 has been audited and the IRS has determined that the correct amount of the deduction is $500,000.

a. Compute any appraiser's penalty to which Vargas might be exposed.

b. Express the computation of this penalty as a Microsoft Excel formula.

31. **LO.6** Trudy's AGI last year was $200,000. Her Federal income tax came to $65,000, paid through both withholding and estimated payments. This year, her AGI will be $300,000, with a projected tax liability of $50,000, all to be paid through estimates. Trudy wants to pay the least amount of tax that does not incur a penalty.

a. Ignore the annualized income method. Compute Trudy's quarterly estimated tax payment schedule for this year.

b. Assume instead that Trudy's AGI last year was $100,000 and resulted in a Federal income tax of $20,000. Determine her quarterly estimated tax payment schedule for this year.

32. **LO.6** Kold Services Corporation estimates that its 2021 taxable income will be $500,000. Given the 21% Federal corporate income tax rate, it will incur a $105,000 liability. For each of the following independent cases, compute Kold's 2021 minimum quarterly estimated tax payments that will avoid an underpayment penalty.

a. For 2020, taxable income was ($200,000). As a result, Kold generated a zero 2020 liability.

b. For 2020, taxable income was $450,000, and tax liability was $94,500.

c. For 2019, taxable income was $2,000,000, and tax liability was $680,000. For 2020, taxable income was $400,000, and tax liability was $84,000.

33. **LO.6** Leake Company, owned equally by Jacquie (chair of the board of directors) and Jeff (company president), is in very difficult financial straits. Last month, Jeff used the $300,000 withheld from employee paychecks for Federal payroll and income taxes to pay a creditor who threatened to cut off all supplies. To keep the company afloat, Jeff used these government funds willfully for the operations of the business, but even that effort was not enough. The company missed the next two payrolls, and today other creditors took action to shut down Leake altogether.

How much will the IRS assess in taxes and penalties in this matter and from whom? How can you as a tax professional best offer service to Jacquie, Jeff, and Leake? Address these matters in a memo for the tax research file.

Critical Thinking

Communications

34. **LO.7** Linn filed her 2020 Form 1040 on April 4, 2021. What is the date on which the applicable statute of limitations expires in each of the following independent situations?

a. Linn incurred a bad debt loss that she failed to claim.

b. Linn inadvertently omitted one-third of the correct gross income.

c. Same as part (b), except that the omission was deliberate.

d. Linn innocently overstated her deductions by a large amount.

e. No return was filed by Linn.

Critical Thinking   35. **LO.7** Loraine (a calendar year taxpayer) reported the following transactions, all of which were properly included in a timely filed return.

Gross receipts		$ 975,000
Cost of sales		(850,000)
Gross profit		$ 125,000
Capital gain	$ 40,000	
Capital loss	(25,000)	15,000
Total income		$ 140,000

a. Presuming the absence of fraud, how much of an omission from gross income would trigger the six-year statute of limitations?

b. Would it matter if cost of sales had been inadvertently overstated by $150,000?

c. How does the situation change in the context of fraud by Loraine?

Critical Thinking   36. **LO.5, 7** On April 3, 2019, Luis filed his 2018 income tax return, which showed a tax due of $75,000. On June 1, 2021, he filed an amended return for 2018 that showed an additional tax of $10,000. Luis paid the additional amount. On May 18, 2022, Luis filed a claim for a 2018 refund of $25,000.

a. If Luis's claim for a refund is correct in amount, how much tax will he recover?

b. What is the period that government-paid interest runs with respect to Luis's claim for a refund?

c. How would you have advised him differently?

37. **LO.8** Rod's Federal income tax returns (Form 1040) for the indicated years were prepared by the following persons.

Year	Preparer
1	Rod
2	Ann
3	Salma

Ann is Rod's next-door neighbor and owns and operates a pharmacy. Salma is a licensed CPA and is engaged in private practice. In the event Rod is audited and all three returns are examined, who may represent him before the IRS at the agent level?

38. **LO.8** Christie is the preparer of the Form 1120 for Yostern Corporation. On the return, Yostern claimed a deduction that the IRS later disallowed on audit. Compute the tax preparer penalty that could be assessed against Christie in each of the following independent situations.

	Form 8275 Disclosure on the Return of the Disputed Deduction?	Tax Reduction Resulting from the Deduction	Probability That the Courts Would Approve the Deduction	Christie's Fee to Complete Yostern's Return
a.	No	$40,000	65%	$7,000
b.	No	40,000	35	7,000
c.	No	40,000	35	1,500
d.	Yes	40,000	35	7,000
e.	Yes	40,000	15	4,000

39. **LO.8** Discuss which penalties, if any, might be imposed on the tax adviser in each of the following independent circumstances. In this regard, assume that the tax adviser:

    a. Suggested to the client various means by which to generate excludible income.

    b. Suggested to the client various means by which to conceal cash receipts from gross income.

    c. Suggested to the client means by which to improve her cash flow by delaying for six months or more the deposit of the employees' share of Federal employment taxes.

    d. Failed, because of pressing time conflicts, to conduct the usual review of the client's tax return. The IRS later discovered that the return included fraudulent data.

    e. Failed, because of pressing time conflicts, to conduct the usual review of the client's tax return. The IRS later discovered a math error in the computation of the business mileage deduction.

40. **LO.8** Compute the preparer penalty the IRS could assess on Gerry in each of the following independent cases.

    a. On March 21, the copy machine was not working, so Gerry gave original returns to her 20 clients to file, that day without providing any duplicates for them. Copies for Gerry's records and for use in preparing state tax returns had been made on March 20.

    b. Because Gerry extended her vacation a few days, she missed the Annual Tax Update seminar that she usually attends. As a result, she was unaware that Congress had changed a law affecting limited partnerships. The change affected the transactions of 25 of Gerry's clients, all of whom understated their tax as a result.

    c. Gerry heard that the IRS was increasing its audits of corporations that hold assets in a foreign trust. As a result, Gerry instructed Hulan, the intern who prepared the initial drafts of the returns for five corporate clients, to leave blank the question about such trusts. Not wanting to lose her position, Hulan, a senior accounting major at State University, complied with Gerry's instructions.

41. **LO.8** You are the chair of the Ethics Committee of your state's CPA Licensing Commission. Interpret controlling AICPA authority in addressing the following assertions by your membership.   *Decision Making*

    a. When a CPA has reasonable grounds for not answering an applicable question on a client's return, a brief explanation of the reason for the omission should not be provided, because it would flag the return for audit by the IRS.

    b. If a CPA discovers during an IRS audit that the client has a material error in the return under examination, he should immediately withdraw from the engagement.

    c. If the client tells you that she paid $500 for office supplies but has lost the receipts, you should deduct an odd amount on her return (e.g., $499), because an even amount ($500) would indicate to the IRS that her deduction was based on an estimate.

    d. If a CPA knows that the client has a material error in a prior year's return, he should not, without the client's consent, disclose the error to the IRS.

    e. If a CPA's client will not correct a material error in a prior year's return, the CPA should not prepare the current year's return for the client.

Research Problems

the answer company™
THOMSON REUTERS®

Note: Solutions to the Research Problems can be prepared by using the Thomson Reuters Checkpoint™ online tax research database, which accompanies this textbook. Solutions can also be prepared by using research materials found in a typical tax library.

Communications

Critical Thinking

Research Problem 1. Lopez always had taken his Form 1040 data to the franchise tax preparers in a local mall, but this year, his friend Cheryl asked to prepare his return. Cheryl quoted a reasonable fee, and Lopez reasoned that, with finances especially tight in Cheryl's household, she could use the money.

Lopez delivered his Forms W–2, 1099, and other documentation and said, "I'll pick up the finished return from you on Monday." Cheryl completed the return by that deadline, and without signing and reviewing the forms, Lopez allowed Cheryl to e-file it that day. The arrangement was that Cheryl would receive the refund through a special bank account and write Lopez a check for that amount, minus her fee. When the refund came through about three weeks later, Cheryl wrote Lopez a check for $2,400, and all parties were satisfied. Lopez gladly used Cheryl to e-file the next year's return using the same procedures.

To his surprise, Lopez received a letter from the IRS about 18 months later. The auditor had found that the return Cheryl had e-filed vastly overstated deductions and wrongly calculated the earned income tax credit. According to the audit report, the refund issued was $4,500—Cheryl had pocketed the difference. As a result, the corrected tax liability meant that Lopez now owed $7,000 in tax, before considering interest and penalties.

Lopez contends that he relied on Cheryl's expertise in the tax law and e-filing procedures. Consequently, there was reasonable cause for the underpayment of tax, and the IRS should waive the understatement and negligence penalties. The IRS has expressed sympathy for Lopez's position, but it maintains that the penalty should stand. What do you think? Summarize your findings in a memo for the tax research file.

Communications

Research Problem 2. Blanche Creek (111 Elm Avenue, Plymouth, IN 46563) has engaged your firm because she has been charged with failure to file her 2019 Federal Form 1040. Blanche maintains that the "reasonable cause" exception should apply. During the entire tax filing season in 2020, she was under a great deal of stress at work and in her personal life. As a result, Blanche developed a sleep disorder, which was treated through a combination of pills and counseling.

Your firm ultimately prepared the 2019 tax return for Blanche, but it was filed far beyond the due date. Blanche is willing to pay the delinquent tax and related interest. However, she believes that the failure to pay penalty is unfair, because she was ill. Consequently, she could not be expected to keep to the usual deadlines for filing.

Write a letter to Blanche concerning these matters.

Use internet tax resources to address the following questions. Look for reliable websites and blogs of the IRS and other government agencies, media outlets, businesses, tax professionals, academics, think tanks, and political outlets.

Communications

Research Problem 3. Make a list of the individuals currently serving in the following tax-related positions. Identify the website address where you found this information. Send this list to your instructor.

a.   IRS Commissioner.

b.   IRS Chief Counsel.

c.   Heads of the four major operating divisions of the IRS.

d.   Heads of the IRS Appeals and Criminal Investigation divisions.

e.   Chair of the House Ways and Means Committee.

f.   Chair of the Senate Finance Committee.

g.   President of the Tax Foundation.

h.   Chair of the AICPA Tax Executive Committee.

Research Problem 4. Taxpayers generally "go to jail" on tax charges only when criminal activities have been involved. Find information about the criminal tax prosecutions the Treasury undertakes. Compare data for the last year of information available from the IRS and for five years prior to that.

Data Analytics
Communications

How many criminal tax charges are initiated in a year? How much time does a criminal tax case take from the filing of charges to disposition by the IRS or a court? What issues tend to be the focus of a criminal tax prosecution? How much additional tax, interest, and penalty revenue does the Treasury collect due to its criminal prosecutions? Summarize your findings for your classmates in no more than four PowerPoint slides.

Research Problem 5. Find a website that lists suggestions on how to deal with an IRS auditor during the first meeting with him or her. You might start at **irs.gov** by reading Publication 556. Then find at least three sites offered by tax professionals with different credentials and certifications. Summarize and evaluate each of the key points in an e-mail to your instructor.

Communications

Research Problem 6. Find a report issued by the Treasury Inspector General for Tax Administration, an IRS oversight group. Using information from this report, construct a chart for a specific tax year, showing the audit rate for high-income tax returns, broken down by income ranges such as $200,000 to $400,000 of total positive income, $400,000 to $600,000, and so on. Indicate in your chart how many Forms 1040 were filed in each income range for the tax year and how many of those were audited by the IRS.

Data Analytics
Communications

Research Problem 7. From the website for the National Tax Advocate at **irs.gov**, list the items that make up the Taxpayer Bill of Rights. Put that list into a PowerPoint file. Then choose any three of the rights and list specific applications of those rights, as suggested by the Advocate, each on one additional slide. E-mail the file to your instructor.

Communications

Research Problem 8. Security breaches occur with regularity in today's world, and the IRS offers tips with which a tax professional can safeguard a client's data. Find the documents (a) IRS Data Security Resource Guide for Tax Professionals and (b) Safeguarding Taxpayer Data. In a two-page memo, highlight the IRS's suggestions to better secure the data that a tax firm deals with. Identify some of the indicators that tax data may have been breached, including signs of phishing activity that may have occurred. List five specific internal controls that a tax firm can adopt to strengthen its data security. Submit your memo to your instructor.

Communications

Becker CPA Review Questions

1. A taxpayer presented her tax return preparer, Dev Powell, with documentation supporting income she had earned as an independent contractor. Although Powell knew that the taxpayer's income should be reported on the taxpayer's Form 1040 (U.S. individual income tax return), he intentionally did not report the income on the taxpayer's tax return. Powell understated the taxpayer's liability because he believed keeping the tax liability low would help retain the taxpayer as a client. In this situation, Powell may be subject to which of the following penalties?

    a. Understatement of taxpayer's liability due to failure to follow substantial authority by the tax return preparer.

    b. Failure to file correct information returns by a tax return preparer.

    c. Wrongful disclosure or use of tax return information by the tax return preparer.

    d. Understatement of taxpayer's liability due to willful or reckless conduct of the tax return preparer.

Becker.

2. Treasury Department Circular 230 provides guidance for doing which of the following activities?

   a. Practicing before the IRS.

   b. Practicing before the U.S. Tax Court.

   c. Presenting before state boards of accountancy.

   d. Reporting income taxes in financial statements.

3. Which of the following is *not* required conduct for a preparer of an income tax return, under AICPA Tax Standards?

   a. Abide by the tax Code and legally minimize the taxpayer's tax liability.

   b. Verify that the information the client provides is correct.

   c. Notify the client if the preparer becomes aware of an error in a tax return.

   d. Inform the taxpayer about how to correct the situation of the taxpayer's failure to file an income tax return.

PART

9

FAMILY TAX PLANNING

CHAPTER **27**

The Federal Gift and Estate Taxes

CHAPTER **28**

Income Taxation of Trusts and Estates

Family tax planning has as its objective the minimization of the present value of income and transfer taxes imposed on the family unit. Carrying out this objective requires a familiarity with the rules applicable to transfers by gift and at death. Entities often created as a result of these transfers (trusts and estates) are subject to unique income tax rules, as discussed in this part of the text.

CHAPTER

27

The Federal Gift and Estate Taxes

LEARNING OBJECTIVES: *After completing Chapter 27, you should be able to:*

LO.1 Explain the nature of the Federal asset transfer taxes.

LO.2 Describe and analyze the Federal gift tax formula.

LO.3 Describe and analyze the Federal estate tax formula.

LO.4 Illustrate the operation of the Federal gift tax.

LO.5 Calculate the Federal gift tax.

LO.6 Identify the components of the gross estate.

LO.7 Describe the components of the taxable estate.

LO.8 Calculate the Federal estate tax liability.

LO.9 Review and demonstrate the role of the generation-skipping transfer tax.

LO.10 Recognize strategies to minimize Federal gift and estate taxes.

CHAPTER OUTLINE

27-1 Transfer Taxes—In General, 27-2
27-1a Nature of the Taxes, 27-2
27-1b Valuation for Federal Transfer Tax Purposes, 27-5
27-1c Key Property Concepts, 27-6

27-2 The Federal Gift Tax, 27-7
27-2a General Considerations, 27-7
27-2b Transfers Subject to the Gift Tax, 27-9
27-2c Annual Gift Tax Exclusion, 27-10
27-2d Deductions, 27-11
27-2e Computing the Federal Gift Tax, 27-11
27-2f Procedural Matters, 27-12

27-3 The Federal Estate Tax, 27-13
27-3a Gross Estate, 27-13
27-3b Taxable Estate, 27-19
27-3c Estate Tax Credits, 27-22
27-3d Procedural Matters, 27-23

27-4 The Generation-Skipping Transfer Tax, 27-24
27-4a Inter-Generational Transfers, 27-24
27-4b The Tax on Generation-Skipping Transfers, 27-24

27-5 Tax Planning, 27-25
27-5a The Federal Gift Tax, 27-25
27-5b The Federal Estate Tax, 27-26

WILL SANDERS/STONE/GETTY IMAGES

AN EVENTFUL AND FINAL YEAR

Over his lifetime, Peter Hood started and purchased numerous automobile dealerships that he eventually transferred to a newly formed entity, Hood Corporation. Upon his death in a previous year, the stock in Hood Corporation passed in equal shares to Peter's surviving spouse, Martha, and their adult children, John and Helen.

For John Hood, 2020 proved to be an eventful and final tax year. Among the major happenings were the following:

- In January, John's divorce from his first wife, Hannah, became final.
- In February, he married Ashley, the manager of one of the Hood car dealerships.
- He made various gifts to family members.
- In July, John's mother, Martha, died of a heart condition, and John served as executor of her estate.
- In late November, he was seriously injured in a car accident (caused by another motorist).
- In early December, John carried out some pre-death estate and tax planning.
- John died of his injuries in mid-December.

What are some of the tax problems (i.e., income, gift, and estate taxes) that might be encountered as a result of these events?

Read the chapter and formulate your response.

U ntil now, this text has dealt primarily with various applications of the Federal income tax. We now add to the discussion the Federal excise taxes on an individual's right to transfer property to another party. The Federal gift, estate, and generation-skipping taxes constitute the central focus of this chapter.

27-1 TRANSFER TAXES—IN GENERAL

LO.1

Explain the nature of the Federal asset transfer taxes.

For about 100 years, Congress has applied a gift and estate tax on the right of individuals (rather than the government) to determine who will receive their assets as the result of a legal transfer of title during life or at death. The chief purposes of these taxes are to keep wealthy families from retaining "too much" over the generations such that competition in the marketplace would become unfair and to increase the chances that wealthy individuals pay a "fair share" of taxes to the government to support annual Federal expenditures.

In the typical year, fewer than 3 million U.S. individuals die. At the same time, only about 5,000 estates file a Federal estate tax return showing an estate tax liability. About half of these returns are filed for residents of New York, Florida, Illinois, and California. Likewise, about 3,000 Federal gift tax returns are filed each year showing a gift tax liability. Total collections of Federal estate and gift tax revenues amount to $25 to $30 billion per year.

27-1a Nature of the Taxes

The Code imposes a tax on the gratuitous transfer of property. If the transfer occurs during the owner's life (e.g., by a cash transfer or the use of a trust), it is subject to the Federal gift tax. If the property passes by virtue of the death of the owner (e.g., under the terms of a will or life insurance policy), the Federal estate tax applies. If the recipient (i.e., the donee, heir, or beneficiary) of the transfer is two or more generations younger than the person making the transfer, the generation-skipping transfer tax also applies.[1]

A **unified transfer tax** applies to all gratuitous transfers of assets by an individual, regardless of how or when the transfers are made.

The gift, estate, and generation-skipping transfer taxes operate as a single, cumulative tax over the course of one's lifetime. In general, planning techniques relative to transfer taxes attempt to avoid or defer the payment of any gift tax liabilities during lifetime; such lifetime payments essentially act as a prepayment of the estate tax on a given asset, and to avoid the payment of the tax on generation-skipping transfers, which acts as a tax penalty on aggressive family wealth transfers.

Persons Subject to the Tax

The Federal gift tax is imposed on the right of one person (the donor) to transfer property to another (the donee) for less than full and adequate consideration. The tax is payable by the donor.[2] If the donor fails to pay the tax when due, the donee may be held liable for the tax to the extent of the value of the property received.[3]

Upon the death of an individual, the Federal estate tax is imposed on the taxable estate.[4] The executor (or administrator) of the estate pays any estate tax that may be due.

The Federal gift, estate, and generation-skipping taxes apply to a resident or citizen of the United States, regardless of where the transferred property is located. Someone

---

[1]The estate tax was enacted in 1916. Because the estate tax could be avoided by making transfers just prior to dying (i.e., "deathbed gifts"), a gift tax was added in 1932.

[2]§ 2502(c).

[3]§ 6324(b). Known as the doctrine of transferee liability, this rule also operates to enable the IRS to enforce the collection of other taxes (e.g., income tax and estate tax).

[4]§ 2001(a). Subchapter A (§§ 2001 through 2058) covers the estate tax treatment of those who are either residents or citizens. Subchapter B (§§ 2101 through 2108) covers the estate tax applicable to NRAs; in those cases, different exemption and exclusion amounts apply.

GLOBAL TAX ISSUES   **U.S. Transfer Taxes and NRAs**

For individuals who are neither residents nor citizens of the United States (i.e., nonresident aliens, or NRAs), the Federal gift tax applies only to gifts of property situated within the United States. Exempted, however, are gifts of intangibles, such as stocks and bonds.

For decedents who are NRAs, the Federal estate tax is imposed on the value of property located within the United States. Unlike the gift tax, however, the estate tax applies to stock in U.S. corporations.

who is not a U.S. citizen or resident is subject to the taxes only if the transferred property is located in the United States.[5]

Types of Tax at Death

Taxes payable by virtue of a person's death fall into two categories: estate and inheritance. The U.S. government, some states, and several other countries impose estate taxes. Inheritance taxes are imposed by some states and other countries. A few states and countries use both types of taxes.

The Federal estate tax differs in several respects from the typical *inheritance tax*. First, the Federal estate tax is levied on the decedent's taxable estate. It is a tax on the right to pass property at death. Inheritance taxes apply to the right to receive property at death and are therefore levied on the heirs. Second, the relationship of the heirs to the decedent usually has a direct bearing on the amount of the inheritance tax. In general, the more closely related the parties, the larger the exemptions and the lower the applicable rates. Except for transfers to surviving spouses that may result in a marital deduction, the relationship of the heirs to the decedent has no effect on the Federal estate tax.

Formula for the Gift Tax

The Federal gift tax is reported annually on Form 709. Like the income tax, which uses taxable income (and not gross income) as a tax base, the gift tax usually does not apply to the full amount of the gift. Deductions and the annual exclusion may be allowed to arrive at the taxable gift.[6] Concept Summary 27.1 outlines the formula for the gift tax and its chief deductions and exclusions. For this discussion, we assume that the gift tax is applied at a flat 40 percent rate on the taxable gifts for the year.[7]

LO.2

Describe and analyze the Federal gift tax formula.

Concept Summary 27.1

Gift Tax Formula

Sum of fair market values of transfers that are subject to the Federal gift tax; this includes any "gift splitting" with a spouse		$xxx,xxx
Claim the annual exclusion ($15,000 per donee) as available	$xx,xxx	
Determine the charitable and marital deductions	xx,xxx	(xx,xxx)
Taxable gifts for the current period		$ xx,xxx
This year's gift tax, 40% of taxable gifts		$ x,xxx
Subtract: Unified transfer tax credit		(xxx)
Gift tax due		$ xxx

---

[5]§§ 2001(a), 2511(a), and 2801.

[6]§ 2503(a).

[7]The flat rate assumption is made throughout Chapters 27 and 28 to simplify the tax computations. The § 2001 Tax Rate Schedule for gifts and estates is reproduced on the inside back cover of this text. It shows some progressivity for taxable amounts under $1 million.

Because Congress did not intend for the gift tax to apply to smaller transfers, it provided for an annual exclusion, which reduces the taxable gift to zero when a small amount is involved. The exclusion amount periodically is adjusted for *significant* inflation. For 2018 through 2020, the exclusion is $15,000.[8]

Formula for the Federal Estate Tax

LO.3

Describe and analyze the Federal estate tax formula.

When a decedent transfers property as a result of death, the Federal estate tax can apply. As a simplifying assumption, a flat 40 percent tax rate applies to the taxable estate—the fair market value of property owned or controlled by the decedent at the date of death, minus various deductions. The unified transfer tax credit applies against this tax. There are more deductions allowed against the estate tax than can be used in computing the gift tax, as illustrated in Concept Summary 27.2. The gross estate is determined by using the fair market value of the property on the date of the decedent's death (or on the alternate valuation date if applicable).

Concept Summary 27.2

Estate Tax Formula

Gross estate, sum of fair market values of property owned and controlled on the date of death		$xxx,xxx
Subtract:		
Expenses, indebtedness, and taxes	$xx,xxx	
Losses	xx,xxx	
Charitable bequests	xx,xxx	
Marital deduction	xx,xxx	
State-level estate or inheritance taxes	xx,xxx	(xx,xxx)
Taxable estate		$ xx,xxx
Estate tax, 40% of taxable estate		$ xx,xxx
Subtract:		
Unified transfer tax credit, minus amount used against lifetime gifts	$ x,xxx	
Other tax credits (e.g., for non-U.S. taxes paid at death)	x,xxx	(x,xxx)
Estate tax due		$ x,xxx

The tax on generation-skipping transfers (GSTT)[9] acts as a penalty for passing assets to certain younger individuals. It applies to both lifetime and deathtime transfers, and the GSTT is added to the gift or estate tax that is computed above. Such a transfer thus can become quite expensive from a Federal transfer tax standpoint.

The chief purpose of the GSTT is to prevent families from transferring assets to much younger members, so as to reduce the present value of the transfer tax on the older generation's asset accumulations. The GSTT aims to apply a transfer tax to the family assets at least once every other generation.

The Unified Transfer Tax Credit

The purpose of the **unified transfer tax credit** is to allow donors and decedents to transfer specified amounts of wealth without being subject to current gift, estate, and generation-skipping transfer taxes. The unified credit offsets tax, computed using the applicable estate and gift tax rates, on a specified amount of transfers, referred to as the applicable exclusion amount.

Exhibit 27.1 shows the exclusion amount applicable to taxable asset transfers for the past several years. The exclusion amount is subject to annual indexation from its statutory amount of $10 million.[10]

---

[8]§ 2503(b)(2).
[9]§ 2601.
[10]§ 2010.

EXHIBIT 27.1	Unified Transfer Tax Exclusion Amount
Year of Transfer	**Exclusion Amount**
2018	$11,180,000
2019	11,400,000
2020	11,580,000

The **exclusion amount** (also termed the **exemption equivalent amount** and the **bypass amount**) is the amount of the transfer that will pass free of the gift or estate tax by virtue of the credit. Because the Federal transfer taxes are unified and cumulative in effect, these amounts are available to an individual only once during his or her lifetime.

Unified Transfer Tax Credit

In 2020, Janet makes a taxable gift of $6,000,000, the first taxable gift that she ever has made. Janet does not owe any Federal gift tax for the year.[11]

EXAMPLE 1

In 2020, Sanjay makes a taxable gift of $2,000,000. In prior years, Sanjay's taxable gifts totaled $10,000,000. The exclusion amount applies to Sanjay in a cumulative manner, such that his life-time taxable gifts amount to $12,000,000, and a Federal gift tax is due for 2020 on $420,000 ($12,000,000 − $11,580,000).

EXAMPLE 2

In 2020, Dulcea dies reporting a taxable estate of $2,000,000. In prior years, Dulcea's taxable gifts totaled $10,000,000. The exclusion amount applies to Dulcea in a cumulative manner, such that her lifetime and at-death taxable asset transfers amount to $12,000,000, and a Federal estate tax is due on $420,000 ($12,000,000 − $11,580,000).

EXAMPLE 3

27-1b Valuation for Federal Transfer Tax Purposes

The value of the property on the date of its transfer generally determines the amount that is subject to the Federal gift, GST, or estate tax. For this purpose, fair market value is used. Under certain conditions, however, an executor can elect to value estate assets on the **alternate valuation date**. The election is made by the executor of the estate and is irrevocable. There is no alternate valuation date election available for the gift tax.

The alternate valuation date election was designed as a relief provision to ease the economic hardship that could result when estate assets decline in value between the date of death and the payment of the estate tax liability. If the election is made, all assets of the estate are valued six months after death *or* on the date of disposition if this occurs earlier.[12] The election covers *all* assets in the gross estate and cannot be applied to only a portion of the property.

Roberto's gross estate consists of the following property:

	Value on Date of Death	**Value Six Months Later**
Land	$14,800,000	$14,840,000
Stock in Brown Corporation	900,000	700,000
Stock in Green Corporation	500,000	460,000
Total	$16,200,000	$16,000,000

EXAMPLE 4

If Roberto's executor elects the alternate valuation date, the estate must be valued at $16,000,000. It is not permissible to value the land at its date of death value ($14,800,000) and choose the alternate valuation date for the rest of the gross estate, so as to reduce the tax base.

---

[11]§ 2001(c).

[12]§ 2032(a)(1).

To be allowed, the election of the alternate valuation date must decrease the value of the gross estate *and* decrease the estate tax liability. The reason for this last requirement is that the income tax basis of property acquired from a decedent will be the value used for estate tax purposes. Without a special limitation, the alternate valuation date could be elected solely to add to income tax basis, at a zero estate tax cost.

Al's gross estate consists of assets with a date of death value of $16,000,000 and an alternate valuation date value of $16,100,000. Under Al's will, all of his property passes outright to Jean (Al's wife). Because of the marital deduction (see text Section 27-3b), no estate tax results regardless of which value is used. But if the alternate valuation date could be elected (which it cannot, because the tax liability is zero with and without the election), Jean would take a stepped-up income tax basis of $16,100,000 in the property acquired from Al, without incurring any Federal transfer tax liability.

27-1c Key Property Concepts

Separate and Joint Asset Ownership

Most property is owned by one individual, who holds title to the asset and perhaps to a liability associated with it. When that individual passes the title to the asset to another party, during lifetime or at death, a gift or bequest may occur, and a Federal transfer tax may apply.

Now assume that Dan and Vicky jointly own equal interests in a tract of land. Such ownership can fall into any of four categories, originating in common law statutes of the states: joint tenancy, tenancy by the entirety, tenancy in common, or community property. Estate tax consequences that arise when jointly owned property like this transfers on account of death are discussed in text Section 27-3a. During lifetime, one of the joint owners can make a gift of his or her "share" of the property, and a gift tax may apply at that time.

If Dan and Vicky hold ownership as ==joint tenants== or ==tenants by the entirety==, the right of survivorship exists. This means that the tenant(s) who survive receive full ownership of the property. Thus, if Dan predeceases Vicky, the land belongs entirely to Vicky. None of the land passes to Dan's heirs or is subject to provisions in Dan's will or other documents. A tenancy by the entirety is a joint tenancy between only a married couple.[13]

If Dan and Vicky hold ownership as ==tenants in common== or as community property, death does not defeat an owner's interest. Thus, if Dan predeceases Vicky, Dan's half interest in the land passes to his estate or heirs, as determined under his will or other arrangements. Vicky continues to own her share outright.

==Community property== interests arise from the marital relationship. Under this system, all property acquired after marriage, except by gift or inheritance, by spouses residing in a community property state becomes part of the community assets. The following states operate under the community property system: Arizona, California, Idaho, Louisiana, Nevada, New Mexico, Texas, Washington, Wisconsin, and (by election of the spouses) Alaska. All other states follow the common law system of ascertaining a spouse's rights to property acquired after marriage.

Marisol owns a building in an equal joint tenancy with Jada. While both individuals are living, Marisol can make a gift of her half of the property to Willie. But if Marisol dies and Jada survives, Marisol's one-half interest in the building passes to Jada automatically under state law, in the form of the

continued

---

[13]Some state laws do not use the term *tenancy by the entirety* but, nevertheless, recognize a joint tenancy between spouses.

survivorship feature of the joint tenancy. At that point, Marisol no longer can pass her half of the building to Willie, and a clause in Marisol's will that transfers a half interest to Willie is invalid.

If Marisol and Jada own the building as tenants in common or as community property, Marisol can pass her half of the asset to Willie as a lifetime gift or as a bequest at death. No right of survivorship exists under state property law.

27-2 THE FEDERAL GIFT TAX

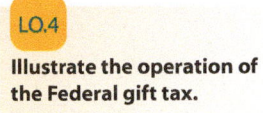

Illustrate the operation of the Federal gift tax.

27-2a General Considerations

In working with the gift tax, one first determines whether a gift has in fact taken place. In the typical situation, a gift occurs when one party takes ownership of an asset without providing full and adequate consideration to the other party.

Motivated by respect and admiration, Julie transfers some shares of stock to Pattie and receives nothing in return. Julie has made a gift to Pattie in the amount of the fair market value of the stock. Julie is the *donor*, and Pattie is the *donee*.

Similarly, if the stock is worth $50,000 and Pattie pays Julie $12,000 to take ownership of it, Julie has made a $38,000 gift to Pattie.

EXAMPLE

7

Requirements for a Gift

For a gift to be complete under state law, the following elements typically must be present:

- A donor competent to make the gift.
- A donee capable of receiving and possessing the property.
- Donative intent on behalf of the donor.
- Actual or constructive delivery of the property to the donee or the donee's representative.
- Acceptance of the gift by the donee.

Incomplete Transfers

The Federal gift tax does not apply to transfers that are incomplete. Thus, if the transferor retains the right to reclaim the property or has not really parted with the possession of the property, a taxable event has not taken place.

Business versus Personal Setting

In a business setting, full and adequate consideration for an exchange is apt to exist; thus, gifts in a business setting are rare. If the parties are acting in a personal setting, a gift is usually the result. Valuable consideration (such as would preclude a gift result) does not include a payment or transfer based on "love and affection … promise of marriage, etc."[14] Consequently, property settlements in consideration of marriage (i.e., pre- or antenuptial agreements) are regarded as gifts.

ETHICS & EQUITY **It's the Thought That Counts**

Joe (age 86) and Nicole (age 22) are married. Two days later, they exchange wedding gifts. Joe's gift to Nicole is stock in IBM (valued at $2 million), and Nicole's gift to Joe is a bottle of cologne (value of $32). What tax goals are they trying to accomplish? Will their plan work?

---

[14]Reg. § 25.2512–8.

Do not conclude that the presence of *some* consideration is enough to preclude Federal gift tax consequences. Again, the answer may rest on whether the transfer occurred in a business setting.

EXAMPLE 8

Peter sells Bob some real estate for $40,000. Unknown to Peter, the property contains valuable mineral deposits and is really worth $200,000. Peter may have made a bad business deal, but he has not made a gift of $160,000 to Bob.

Excluded Transfers

Transfers to political organizations are exempt from the application of the Federal gift tax.[15] This provision includes gifts to political parties, candidates, committees, and the like.

The Federal gift tax does not apply to tuition payments made to an educational organization (e.g., a college) on another's behalf. Nor does it apply to amounts paid on another's behalf for medical care.[16] In this regard, the law is realistic because it is unlikely that most donors would make such transfers when motivated solely by tax planning concerns. The payments, however, must be made directly to the provider (e.g., college, doctor, or hospital). There is no requirement that the student or patient qualify as a relative or dependent of the person making the payment.

The Big Picture

EXAMPLE 9

Return to the facts of *The Big Picture* on p. 27-1. After Peter died, his widow, Martha, continued to live in the family home and refused to move in with either of her children (John or Helen). As Martha's health and mental condition deteriorated, her children did everything possible to keep the family housekeeper from quitting. In fact, Helen paid for the housekeeper's gallbladder operation, and John paid the college tuition of her oldest son.

Neither Helen nor John has made gifts to the housekeeper or her son that are subject to taxation. Gifts would have occurred, however, if Helen and John had reimbursed the housekeeper for the amounts involved, instead of paying the providers (i.e., physician, hospital, and college) directly.

Satisfying an obligation of support is not subject to the gift tax. Thus, no gift takes place when parents pay for their children's elementary education, because one of the state-level obligations of parents is to educate their children. What constitutes an obligation of support is determined by applicable state law. In many states, for example, adult children may have an obligation of support with respect to providing for indigent parents, or a wealthy parent may have an obligation to support the law school tuition of a child. Similarly, payment of alimony or child support to an ex-spouse satisfies a legal obligation and does not constitute a gift to the recipient.

Lifetime versus Deathtime Transfers

One must distinguish between lifetime (*inter vivos*) and deathtime (testamentary) transfers.

EXAMPLE 10

Dudley buys a 12-month certificate of deposit (CD) from State Bank and lists ownership as follows: "Dudley, payable on proof of death to Faye." Nine months later, Dudley dies. When the CD matures, Faye collects the proceeds from State Bank. No gift takes place when Dudley invests in the CD; Faye has received a mere expectancy (i.e., to obtain ownership of the CD upon Dudley's death). At any time before his death, Dudley may withdraw the funds or delete Faye's name from the account, thereby cutting off her expectancy. Furthermore, no gift occurs upon Dudley's death; the CD passes to Faye as "payable on death," and it constitutes a deathtime bequest instead.

---

[15] § 2501(a)(5).   [16] § 2503(e).

A payable on death (POD) designation is a form of ownership frequently used in a family setting when investments are involved (e.g., stocks and bonds and savings accounts). The POD designation is simpler to use than a will or trust arrangement in the case of bank accounts and securities.

27-2b Transfers Subject to the Gift Tax

Property Settlements in Divorce

Transfers of property interests made under the terms of a written agreement between spouses in settlement of their marital or property rights are deemed to be for adequate consideration.[17] The transfers are exempt from the Federal gift tax if a final decree of divorce is obtained within the three-year period beginning on the date one year before the parties entered into the agreement. Likewise excluded are child support arrangements. Such an agreement need not be approved by the divorce decree.

The Big Picture

EXAMPLE 11

Return to the facts of *The Big Picture* on p. 27-1. Recall that John and Hannah's divorce became final in January. After extended but amicable negotiations, in September, John and Hannah agreed on a property settlement. In return for the receipt of $200,000 and title to their home, Hannah released all of her marital rights. Shortly thereafter, John made the transfer. The property settlement resulted in no gift tax consequences to John.

Disclaimers

A disclaimer is a refusal by a person to accept property that is designated to pass to him or her. The effect of the disclaimer is to pass the property to someone else, for instance, under the terms of the will. Assume that Julio dies and passes an asset to Maria. Maria does not want the asset, so she disclaims it back to Julio's estate, and the will directs that the asset now passes to Eva. If the disclaimer is executed properly, Maria *has not* made a gift of her own to Eva, and no gift tax is due from Maria.

The Big Picture

EXAMPLE 12

Return to the facts of *The Big Picture* on p. 27-1. Recall that Martha died of a heart condition in July. Under her will, her estate passes in equal parts to her son and daughter or, if they disclaim, to their children. Helen disclaims her share of the inheritance, and the assets pass to her children.

Why might Helen disclaim her inheritance and have the property pass directly from Martha to the children? By doing so, an extra transfer tax may be avoided. If the disclaimer does not take place (Helen accepts the inheritance) and the property eventually passes to the children (either by gift or at death), the later transfer is subject to the application of either the gift tax or the estate tax.

The Federal gift tax can also be avoided in cases of a partial disclaimer of assets.

The Big Picture

EXAMPLE 13

Assume the same facts as in Example 12. John's share of his inheritance from Martha also includes the family hunting lodge. Except for the hunting lodge, John disclaims his share of the inheritance, and the remaining assets pass to his children.

---

[17]§ 2516.

To be effective, the disclaimer must be in writing and timely made. Generally, this means that a statement must be executed no later than nine months after the right to the property arose. Furthermore, the person making the disclaimer must not have accepted any benefits or interest in the property during the nine-month period.

Other Transfers Subject to Gift Tax

Other transfers that may carry gift tax consequences (e.g., the creation of joint ownership) are discussed and illustrated in connection with the Federal estate tax.

Income Tax Considerations

Generally, a donor incurs no Federal income tax consequences on making a gift. A donee recognizes no income on the receipt of a gift.[18] A donee's income tax basis in the property received depends on a number of factors (e.g., donor's basis, fair market value of the asset on the transfer date) and is discussed in Chapter 13.

27-2c Annual Gift Tax Exclusion

The first $15,000 of gifts made to any one person during any calendar year is excluded in determining the total amount of taxable gifts for the year.[19] The ==annual exclusion== applies to all gifts of a *present interest* made during the calendar year, in the order in which they are made until the amount of the exclusion per donee is exhausted. For a gift in trust, each beneficiary of the trust is treated as a separate person for purposes of the exclusion.

Laura makes the following cash gifts: $8,000 to Rita and $18,000 to Maureen. Laura may claim an annual exclusion of $8,000 with respect to the gift to Rita and $15,000 with respect to the gift to Maureen.

A ==future interest== is defined as an interest that will come into being (as to use, possession, or enjoyment) at some future date. Examples of future interests include rights such as remainder interests that are commonly encountered when property is transferred to a trust.[20] A *present interest* is an unrestricted right to the immediate use, possession, or enjoyment of property or of the income.

By a lifetime gift, Ron transfers property to a trust with a life estate (income payable annually) to June and remainder (the trust's underlying assets) upon June's death to Albert. Ron made two gifts when the trust was created: one to June of a life estate and one to Albert of a remainder interest. The life estate is a present interest and qualifies for the annual exclusion. Albert's remainder is a future interest and does not qualify for the exclusion.

If a possibility exists that the income beneficiary may not receive the immediate enjoyment of the property, the transfer is of a future interest.

Assume the same facts as in Example 15, except that the income from the trust need not be payable annually to June. It may, at the trustee's discretion, be accumulated and added to the underlying trust assets. Because June's right to receive the income from the trust is conditioned on the trustee's discretion, it is not a present interest. No annual exclusion is allowed.

The mere possibility of diversion is enough. It would not matter if the trustee never exercised the discretion to accumulate and did, in fact, distribute the trust income to June annually.

---

[18]Both gifts and inheritances are excluded from the recipient's gross income under § 103. See Chapter 5.

[19]§ 2503(b).

[20]Trust terms are explained and trust arrangements are illustrated in text Exhibit 28.2.

Contributions to Qualified Tuition Programs

For income tax purposes, § 529 plans possess attributes that reflect the best of all possible worlds. Although no up-front Federal income tax deduction is allowed, income earned by the fund accumulates free of income tax and distributions are not taxed if they are used for educational purposes. A special provision allows a donor to enjoy a gift tax advantage by using five years of annual exclusions (e.g., for a large one-time gift), but only once in a five-year period. Moreover, these college plans are not included in the gross estate of the transferor.[21]

EXAMPLE 17

Trevor and Audrey would like to start building a college education fund for their 10-year-old grand-daughter Loni. Trevor contributes $150,000 to the designated carrier of their state's § 529 plan. By electing to split the gift and using five annual exclusions [2 (number of donors) × $15,000 (annual exclusion) × 5 years = $150,000], no taxable gift results. (The gift-splitting election is discussed in detail later in text Section 27-2e.) Making the five-year election precludes Trevor and Audrey from using an annual exclusion on gifts to Loni for the next four years.

27-2d Deductions

In arriving at taxable gifts, a deduction is allowed for transfers to certain qualified charitable organizations. On transfers between spouses, a marital deduction may be available. Because both the charitable and marital deductions also apply in determining the Federal estate tax, they are discussed later in the chapter.

27-2e Computing the Federal Gift Tax

LO.5
Calculate the Federal gift tax.

The Unified Transfer Tax

Generally, the gift tax rate is a flat 40 percent for most transfers made by U.S. citizens and residents.[22]

The Election to Split Gifts by Married Persons

To understand the reason for the gift-splitting election, consider the following situations.

Effect of Splitting Gifts

EXAMPLE 18

Kong and Margaret are husband and wife who reside in Michigan, a common law property state. Kong has been the only breadwinner in the family, and Margaret has no significant property of her own. Neither has made any prior taxable gifts. Kong makes a gift to Gita of $16,015,000. Presuming that the election to split gifts did not exist, Kong's gift tax is computed as follows:

Amount of gift	$16,015,000
Subtract: Annual exclusion	(15,000)
Taxable gift	$16,000,000
Taxable gift after exemption equivalent ($16,000,000 − $11,580,000)	$ 4,420,000
Gift tax due at assumed 40% rate	$ 1,768,000

[21]§ 529(c)(4).   [22]§ 2001(c)(2)(B). Cf. footnote 7.

Effect of Splitting Gifts

EXAMPLE 19

Assume the same facts as in Example 18, except that Kong and Margaret have always resided in California, a community property state. Even though Kong is the sole breadwinner, income from personal services generally is community property. Consequently, the gift to Gita probably involves community property. If this is the case, the gift tax is computed as follows:

	Kong	Margaret
Amount of gift	$8,007,500	$8,007,500
Subtract: Annual exclusion	(15,000)	(15,000)
Taxable gift	$7,992,500	$7,992,500
Taxable gift after exemption equivalent	$ –0–	$ –0–
Gift tax due	$ –0–	$ –0–

As the results of Examples 18 and 19 indicate, married donors residing in community property jurisdictions could possess a significant Federal gift tax advantage over those residing in common law states. To rectify this inequity, when a gift-splitting election is made, a gift made by a person to someone other than his or her spouse may be considered as having been made one-half by each spouse.[23]

Returning to Example 18, Kong and Margaret could treat the gift passing to Gita as being made one-half by each of them, even though all of the property belonged to Kong. As a result, the parties are able to achieve the same tax consequence as in Example 19. There is no such thing as a "joint return" for Federal gift tax purposes, but the gift-splitting election achieves the same result; both spouses must file a gift tax return making the election and assigning the "two halves" of the gift separately.

To split gifts, the spouses must be legally married to each other at the time of the gift. A gift-splitting election means that all gifts made in that calendar year are split between them. In addition, both must be citizens or residents of the United States on the date of the gift.

27-2f Procedural Matters

The Federal Gift Tax Return

For transfers by gift, a Form 709 (U.S. Gift Tax Return) must be filed whenever the gifts for any one calendar year exceed the annual exclusion or involve a gift of a future interest. The Form 709 also must be filed when the election to split gifts is made by the nonowner spouse (see Example 21). A Form 709 need not be filed, however, for transfers between spouses that are offset by the unlimited marital deduction, regardless of the amount of the transfer.[24]

When Must a Form 709 Be Filed?

EXAMPLE 20

This year, Larry makes five gifts, each in the amount of $15,000, to his five children. If the gifts do not involve future interests, a Form 709 need not be filed to report the transfers.

EXAMPLE 21

Esther makes a gift of $30,000 cash of her separate property to her daughter. To double the amount of the annual exclusion allowed, Jerry (Esther's husband) is willing to split the gift. To make the gift-splitting election, a Form 709 must be filed, even though no gift tax will be due as a result of the transfer.

---

[23]§ 2513.

[24]§ 6019(a)(2).

If a gift tax return is due, it must be filed on or before the fifteenth day of April following the year of the gift.[25] As with other Federal taxes, when the due date falls on Saturday, Sunday, or a legal holiday, the date for filing the return is the next business day. If sufficient reason is shown, the IRS is authorized to grant reasonable extensions of time for filing the return.[26]

Concept Summary 27.3

Federal Gift Tax Provisions

1. The Federal gift tax applies to all gratuitous transfers of property made by U.S. citizens or residents. In this regard, it does not matter where the property is located.

2. A gratuitous transfer is one not supported by full and adequate consideration. If the parties are acting in a business setting, such consideration usually exists. If purported sales are between family members, a gift element may be suspected.

3. Property settlements can escape the gift tax if a divorce occurs within a prescribed period of time.

4. A disclaimer is a refusal by a person to accept property designated to pass to that person. The effect of a disclaimer is to pass the property to someone else. If certain conditions are satisfied, the issuance of a disclaimer will not subject to the Federal gift tax the party making the disclaimer.

5. The donor is allowed an annual exclusion for a gift of a present interest to a donee.

6. The election to split a gift enables a married couple to be treated as two donors. The election doubles the annual exclusion and makes the nonowner spouse's exemption equivalent available to the owner spouse.

7. The Federal gift tax generally applies at a flat 40% rate on cumulative taxable gifts in excess of the exemption equivalent amount.

8. Taxable gifts are reported on Form 709. The return is due on April 15 following the year of the gift.

27-3 THE FEDERAL ESTATE TAX

The following discussion of the estate tax applies the formula that appeared earlier in the chapter in Concept Summary 27.2. The key components in the formula are the gross estate, the taxable estate, and the credits allowed against the tentative tax. This formula can be summarized as follows:

Gross estate − Deductions allowed = Taxable estate − Exemption equivalent × 40% tax rate − Tax credits* = Estate tax due

* Other than unified transfer tax credit

27-3a Gross Estate

Simply stated, the **gross estate** includes all property subject to the Federal estate tax. This includes the net assets owned and controlled by the decedent as of the date of death.

In contrast to the gross estate, one's **probate estate** is determined by state (rather than Federal) law. The probate estate consists of all of a decedent's property subject to disposition by the executor or administrator of the estate under the terms of the will. The administration is supervised by a local court (usually called a probate court). An executor is the decedent's personal representative appointed under the decedent's will. When a decedent dies without a will or fails to name an executor in the will (or that person refuses to serve), the local probate court appoints an administrator.

The probate estate frequently is smaller than the gross estate. It contains only property owned by the decedent at the time of death and passing to heirs under a will or under

LO.6

Identify the components of the gross estate.

---

[25]§ 6075(b)(1).

[26]§ 6081. Under § 6075(b)(2), an extension of time granted to a calendar year taxpayer for filing an income tax return automatically extends the due date of a gift tax return.

state law. Certain items like the proceeds of many life insurance policies and distributions from retirement plans are controlled by contracts outside of the will; they become part of the gross estate, as controlled by the decedent, but are not included in the probate estate.

All states provide for an order of distribution in the event someone dies *intestate* (i.e., without a will). After the surviving spouse receives some or all of the estate, the preference is usually in the following order: down to lineal descendants (e.g., children and grandchildren), then up to lineal ascendants (e.g., parents and grandparents), and out to collateral relations (e.g., brothers, sisters, aunts, and uncles).

Property Owned by the Decedent

Property owned by the decedent at the time of death is included in the gross estate. The nature of the property or the use to which it was put during the decedent-owner's lifetime has no significance as far as the estate tax is concerned. Thus, personal effects (such as clothing), stocks, bonds, mutual funds, furniture, jewelry, bank accounts, and certificates of deposit are included in the deceased's gross estate. No distinction is made between tangible and intangible, depreciable and nondepreciable, or business and personal assets.

Property Owned at Death

EXAMPLE 22

Rani dies owning some City of Denver bonds. The fair market value of the bonds plus any interest accrued to the date of Rani's death is included in her gross estate. Although interest on municipal bonds usually is not taxable under the Federal income tax, it is property owned by Rani at the time of death and is subject to the estate tax. Any interest accrued after death is not part of the gross estate.

EXAMPLE 23

Sharon dies on April 7, when she owns stock in Robin Corporation and in Wren Corporation. On March 2, both corporations had authorized a cash dividend payable on May 4. Robin's dividend is payable to shareholders of record as of April 2. Wren's date of record is April 9. Sharon's gross estate includes the following: the stock in Robin, the stock in Wren, and the dividend on the Robin stock. It does not include the dividend on the Wren stock because Sharon dies before the April 9 date of record.

EXAMPLE 24

Ray dies holding some promissory notes issued to him by his son. In his will, Ray forgives these notes, relieving the son of the obligation to make any payments. The fair market value of these notes is included in Ray's gross estate.

The Big Picture

EXAMPLE 25

Return to the facts of *The Big Picture* on p. 27-1. At the time of his death, John was the president of Hood Corporation. John's estate receives a distribution from Hood's qualified pension plan of $1,100,000 consisting of the following:

Hood's contributions	$450,000
John's after-tax contributions	350,000
Income earned by the plan over the years	300,000

John's estate also receives $150,000 from Hawk Insurance Company. The payment represents the maturity value of term life insurance from a group plan that Hood maintains for its employees. As to these amounts, John's gross estate includes $1,250,000 ($1,100,000 + $150,000). For income tax purposes, however, $750,000 ($450,000 + $300,000) is subject to tax and $500,000 ($350,000 + $150,000) is not.

In most cases, retirement plan benefits are subject to estate tax. Besides the conventional qualified pension and profit sharing plans involved in Example 25, retirement plans include those under § 401(k), § 403(b) for employees of tax-exempt organizations, § 457 for government employees, various plans for self-employed persons, and IRAs—both traditional and Roth.

In addition to the items noted previously, the gross estate includes many other assets that can be of significant value. Examples include:

- Real estate holdings.
- Present value of future royalty rights (e.g., patents, copyrights, and mineral interests).
- Interests in a business (e.g., sole proprietorship and partnership).
- Collectibles (e.g., works of art and coin collections).
- Unmatured insurance policies on the lives of others.
- Present value of settlements receivable from pending and potential lawsuits.
- Certain transfers that occur in the three years before death, or are made during lifetime but are effective only at death.[27]

Revocable Transfers

The gross estate includes the value of property interests transferred by the decedent if the enjoyment of the property transferred was subject, at the date of the decedent's death, to any power of the decedent to *alter, amend, revoke, or terminate* the transfer (i.e., it is more like a promise to pay). Transfers of this sort typically occur because the donor is not able or ready to part with the asset without qualifications (e.g., due to reservations about future events or about how the donee will use the transferred asset).

Joint Interests

The *Federal estate tax treatment* of tenancies in common or of community property follows the logical approach of taxing only the portion of the property included in the deceased owner's probate estate.

EXAMPLE
26

Homer, Wilma, and Thelma acquire a tract of land with ownership listed as tenants in common, each party furnishing $200,000 of the $600,000 purchase price. When the property is worth $900,000, Homer dies. If Homer's undivided interest in the property is 33⅓%, the gross estate *and* probate estate each include $300,000. This one-third interest is also the same amount that passes to Homer's heirs.

Unless the parties have provided otherwise, each tenant is deemed to own an interest equal to the portion of the original consideration he or she furnished. The parties in Example 26 could have provided that Homer would receive an undivided one-half interest in the property although he contributed only one-third of the purchase price. In that case, Wilma and Thelma have made a gift to Homer when the tenancy was created, and Homer's gross estate and probate estate each include $450,000.

For certain joint tenancies, the tax consequences are different. All of the property is included in the deceased co-owner's gross estate unless it can be proved that the

---

[27]§§ 2035–2037 and 2041.

surviving co-owners contributed to the cost of the property.[28] If a contribution can be shown, the amount to be *excluded* is calculated by the following formula:

$$\frac{\text{Surviving co-owner's initial contribution}}{\text{Total initial cost of the property}} \quad \times \quad \text{Fair market value of the property at death}$$

In computing a survivor's contribution, any funds received as a gift *from the deceased co-owner* and applied to the cost of the property are counted as zero.

EXAMPLE 27

Keith and Steve (father and son) acquire a tract of land with ownership listed as joint tenancy with right of survivorship. Keith furnished $400,000 and Steve $200,000 of the $600,000 purchase price. Of the $200,000 provided by Steve, $100,000 had previously been received as a gift from Keith. When the property is worth $900,000, Keith dies. Because only $100,000 of Steve's contribution can be counted (the other $100,000 was received as a gift from Keith), Steve has furnished only one-sixth ($100,000/$600,000) of the cost. Thus, Keith's gross estate must include five-sixths of $900,000, or $750,000.

This result presumes that Steve can prove that he did in fact make the $100,000 contribution. In the absence of such proof, the full value of the property is included in Keith's gross estate. Keith's death makes Steve the immediate owner of the property by virtue of the right of survivorship.

If the co-owners receive the property as a gift or bequest *from another*, each donee owner is deemed to have contributed to the cost (or value on date of death) of his or her own interest.

EXAMPLE 28

The Big Picture

Return to the facts of *The Big Picture* on p. 27-1. During his lifetime, Peter Hood purchased timberland, listing title as follows: "John and Helen Hood as equal tenants in common." John's basis in the property is one-half of Peter's cost. Upon John's death, one-half of the value of the timberland is included in his gross estate.

EXAMPLE 29

The Big Picture

Return to the facts of *The Big Picture* on p. 27-1. In her will, Martha leaves the Hood family residence to her children (John and Helen) as joint tenants with right of survivorship. John's income tax basis in the residence is one-half of the value on Martha's death. Upon John's later death, one-half of the value at that time is included in his gross estate. Under the right of survivorship, outright ownership of the residence goes to Helen and none of the property passes to John's heirs.

To simplify the joint ownership rules for *married persons*, an automatic inclusion rule applies upon the death of the first joint-owner spouse to die. Regardless of the amount contributed by each spouse, one-half of the value of the property is included in the gross estate of the spouse who dies first. The special rule eliminates the need to trace the source of contributions and recognizes that any inclusion in the gross estate likely is neutralized by the marital deduction.

---

[28]§ 2040(a).

The Big Picture

Return to the facts of *The Big Picture* on p. 27-1. Recall that after his divorce from Hannah, John married Ashley. Because Hannah kept John's prior home as part of the property settlement (see Example 11), he purchased a new residence. He listed title to the property as "John and Ashley Hood, tenancy by the entirety with right of survivorship." Upon John's death, only one-half of the value of the property is included in his gross estate.

If Ashley had died first, one-half of the value of the residence would have been included in her gross estate, even though she made no contribution to its cost.

Whether a *gift* results when property is transferred into some form of joint ownership depends on the consideration furnished by each of the contributing parties for the ownership interest acquired.

Joint Ownership and the Gift Tax

EXAMPLE 31

Brenda and Sarah purchase real estate as tenants in common. Of the $800,000 purchase price, Brenda furnishes $600,000, and Sarah furnishes $200,000. If they are equal owners in the property, Brenda has made a gift to Sarah of $200,000.

EXAMPLE 32

Martha purchases real estate for $900,000, the title to the property being listed as follows: "Martha, Sylvia, and Dan as joint tenants with the right of survivorship." If under state law Martha, Sylvia, and Dan are deemed to be equal owners in the property, Martha is treated as having made gifts of $300,000 to Sylvia and $300,000 to Dan.

Several important exceptions exist to the general rule that the creation of a joint ownership with disproportionate interests resulting from unequal consideration triggers gift treatment. First, if the transfer involves a joint bank account, there is no gift at the time of the contribution. If a gift occurs, it is when the noncontributing party withdraws the funds provided by the other joint tenant. Second, the same rule applies to the purchase of U.S. savings bonds.[29] Again, any gift tax consequences are postponed until the noncontributing party appropriates some or all of the proceeds for his or her individual use.

Life Insurance

Life insurance includes whole life policies, term insurance, group life insurance, and travel and accident insurance.[30]

Life insurance on the life of another owned by a decedent at the time of death is included in the gross estate as an asset owned by the decedent. The amount includible is the replacement value of the policy.[31] Under these circumstances, inclusion of the face amount of the policy is inappropriate; the policy has not yet matured.

At the time of his death, Luigi owned a life insurance policy on the life of Benito, face amount of $500,000 and replacement value of $50,000, with Sofia as the designated beneficiary. Because the policy had not matured at Luigi's death, only $50,000 (the policy's replacement value) is included in Luigi's gross estate.

---

[29]Reg. § 25.2511–1(h)(4).

[30]Reg. § 20.2042–1(a)(1). As to travel and accident insurance, see *Comm. v. Estate of Noel*, 65–1 USTC ¶12,311, 15 AFTR 2d 1397, 85 S.Ct. 1238 (USSC, 1965). As to employer-sponsored group term life insurance, see Example 25.

[31]Reg. § 20.2031–8(a)(1).

The gross estate includes life insurance on the decedent's life if:

- The policy's proceeds are receivable by the estate, or
- The decedent possessed any of the incidents of ownership in the policy.

Proceeds of insurance on the life of the decedent not receivable by the estate are includible if the decedent at death possessed any of the incidents of ownership in the policy. In this connection, *incidents of ownership* means not only the ownership of the policy but also the right of the insured or his or her estate to the economic benefits of the policy. Thus, it includes the power to change beneficiaries, pledge the policy for a loan, or surrender or cancel the policy.[32]

EXAMPLE 34

At the time of death, Broderick was the insured under a policy (face amount of $1,000,000) owned by Gregory, with Demi as the designated beneficiary. Broderick took out the policy five years ago and immediately transferred it as a gift to Gregory. Under the assignment, Broderick transferred all rights in the policy except the right to change beneficiaries.

Broderick died without having exercised this right, and the policy proceeds are paid to Demi. Broderick's retention of an incident of ownership in the policy (i.e., the right to change beneficiaries) causes $1,000,000 to be included in his gross estate, even though he never exercised the right.

Merely purchasing a life insurance contract and designating someone else as the beneficiary thereunder does not constitute a *gift*. As long as the purchaser still owns the policy, nothing yet has passed to the beneficiary, and the beneficiary can be changed. But consider the following possibility.

EXAMPLE 35

Kurt purchases an insurance policy on his own life and transfers the policy to Olga. Kurt retains no control over the policy (such as the power to change beneficiaries). In these circumstances, Kurt has made a gift to Olga. Furthermore, if Kurt continues to pay the premiums on the transferred policy, each payment constitutes a separate gift.

Under certain conditions, the death of the insured may constitute a gift to the beneficiary of part or all of the proceeds. This occurs when the owner of the policy is not the insured.

EXAMPLE 36

Miguel owns an insurance policy on the life of Frank, with Tracy as the designated beneficiary. Up until the time of Frank's death, Miguel retained the right to change the beneficiary of the policy. The proceeds paid to Tracy by the insurance company by reason of Frank's death constitute a gift from Miguel to Tracy.[33]

Concept Summary 27.4

Federal Estate Tax Provisions—Gross Estate

1. The starting point for applying the Federal estate tax is to determine which assets are subject to tax. Such assets comprise a decedent's gross estate.

2. The gross estate includes all assets owned by the decedent, regardless of where they are located.

3. Upon the death of a joint tenant, the full value of the property is included in the gross estate unless the survivor(s) made a contribution toward the cost of the property. Spouses include half of the value of the property in the gross estate of the first tenant to die.

4. The creation of joint ownership is subject to the gift tax when a tenant receives a lesser interest in the property than is warranted by the consideration furnished.

5. If the decedent is the insured, life insurance proceeds are included in the gross estate if either of two conditions is satisfied. First, the proceeds are paid to the estate. Second, the decedent possessed incidents of ownership (e.g., the right to change beneficiaries) over the policy.

---

[32]Reg. § 20.2042–1(c)(2).

[33]*Goodman v. Comm.*, 46–1 USTC ¶10,275, 34 AFTR 1534, 156 F.2d 218 (CA–2, 1946).

27-3b Taxable Estate

After the gross estate has been determined, the next step is to compute the taxable estate. The **taxable estate** is the gross estate minus a number of important deductions.

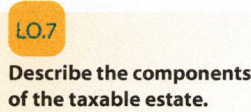

LO.7

Describe the components of the taxable estate.

Expenses, Indebtedness, and Taxes

A deduction is allowed for funeral expenses; expenses incurred in administering property; claims against the estate; and unpaid mortgages and other charges against property, whose value is included in the gross estate (without reduction for the mortgage or other indebtedness).

Expenses incurred in administering community property are deductible only in proportion to the deceased spouse's interest in the community.[34] Administration expenses include commissions of the executor or administrator, attorney's fees of the estate, accountant's fees, court costs, and certain selling expenses for disposition of estate property.

Claims against the estate include property taxes accrued before the decedent's death, unpaid income taxes on income received by the decedent before he or she died, and unpaid gift taxes on gifts made by the decedent before death.

The decedent's unpaid pledge or subscription in favor of a public, charitable, religious, or educational organization is deductible to the extent that it would have constituted an allowable deduction had it been a bequest.[35]

Deductible funeral expenses include the cost of interment or inurnment, the burial plot or vault, a gravestone, perpetual care of the grave site, and the transportation expense of the person bringing the body to the place of burial. No deduction is allowed for cemetery lots the decedent acquired before death, but the lots are not included in the decedent's gross estate as an asset of the decedent.

Losses

An estate tax deduction is allowed for losses from a casualty or theft incurred during the period when the estate is being settled. Any anticipated insurance recovery is taken into account in arriving at the amount of the deductible loss. Unlike the income tax, however, the deduction is not limited by a floor (e.g., $100) or a percentage amount (10 percent of adjusted gross income).

As is true of certain administration expenses, a casualty or theft loss of estate property can be claimed as an income tax deduction on the fiduciary return of the estate (Form 1041; see text Section 28-3d). But a double deduction prohibition applies, and claiming the income tax deduction eliminates any estate tax deduction.[36]

Transfers to Charity

A transfer tax deduction is allowed for the value of property in the decedent's gross estate that is transferred by the decedent through testamentary disposition to (or for the use of) any of the following:

- Federal, state, and local governments and agencies.
- Any corporation or association organized and operated exclusively for religious, charitable, scientific, literary, or educational purposes.
- Various veterans' organizations.

---

[34]*U.S. v. Stapf*, 63–2 USTC ¶12,192, 12 AFTR 2d 6326, 84 S.Ct. 248 (USSC, 1963).

[35]§ 2053(c)(1)(A) and Reg. § 20.2053–5.

[36]§§ 642(g) and 2054.

The organizations just described are identical to those that qualify for the Federal gift tax deduction. With the following exceptions, they are also the same organizations that qualify a donor for an income tax deduction.[37]

- Certain nonprofit cemetery associations qualify for income tax but not estate and gift tax purposes.
- Non-U.S. charities may qualify under the estate and gift tax but not under the income tax.

No deduction is allowed unless the charitable bequest is specified by a provision in the decedent's will or the transfer was made before death and the property is subsequently included in the gross estate. Generally, a deduction does not materialize when an individual dies without a will.

The amount of the bequest to charity must be mandatory and cannot be left to someone else's discretion. It is, however, permissible to allow another person, such as the executor of the estate, to choose which charity will receive the specified donation.

The Big Picture

EXAMPLE 37

Return to the facts of *The Big Picture* on p. 27-1. After John's accident, he was in the intensive care unit at a local hospital. Although physically incapacitated, he was mentally alert. In early December, he reviewed his financial affairs with his attorney and CPA and executed a new will. His prior will, drawn up several years ago, contained a bequest to the Hood Scholarship Foundation (HSF), an organization created by Peter (John's father) to provide financial assistance to community college students. HSF never applied for a tax exemption as a charity.

John's new will kept the bequest, but only if the IRS approved HSF as a charity. John's CPA arranged to have all of John's medical expenses (e.g., hospital and physicians) paid as incurred. He also advised John to make a substantial payment on his property taxes and state income taxes.

Marital Deduction

The **marital deduction** allows spouses to arrange their financial affairs without Federal gift or estate tax consequences. Assets can pass between them without any immediate gift or estate tax liability, with a deduction allowed to offset an otherwise taxable gift or estate amount. Used well, the marital deduction can be seen as a means by which to reduce the present value of the couple's transfer tax liability: the gift or bequest places the asset into the hands of (perhaps) a younger or healthier spouse, such that the Federal transfer tax on the asset is deferred until a later date.

The marital deduction is available to same-sex couples who are married. Registered domestic partnerships, civil unions, and similar formal relationships *are not* marriages, so no marital deduction can be claimed.

Passing Requirement The marital deduction is allowed only for property that is included in the deceased spouse's gross estate and that passes or has passed to the surviving spouse.[38]

The Big Picture

EXAMPLE 38

Return to the facts of *The Big Picture* on p. 27-1 and Example 37. In reviewing John's prior will, the parties discovered that one of the main beneficiaries was Hannah, John's first wife. The new will substituted Ashley (John's present wife) for Hannah, thereby preserving the marital deduction.

---

[37]§§ 170, 2055, and 2522.

[38]§§ 2056 and 2523.

Property that passes from the decedent to the surviving spouse includes any interest received as, for example, (1) the decedent's heir or donee, (2) the decedent's surviving tenant by the entirety or joint tenant, or (3) the beneficiary of insurance on the life of the decedent.

At the time of his death in the current year, Tao owned an insurance policy on his own life (face amount of $500,000) with Ella (his wife) as the designated beneficiary. Tao and Ella also owned real estate (worth $600,000) as tenants by the entirety (Tao had furnished all of the purchase price). As to these transfers, $800,000 ($500,000 + $300,000) is included in Tao's gross estate, and this amount represents the property that passes to Ella for purposes of the marital deduction, under the terms of the insurance contract and the state law survivorship feature.

Disclaimers can affect the amount passing to the surviving spouse. If, for example, the surviving spouse receives the remainder of the estate after all other obligations have been met, a disclaimer by another heir increases the amount passing to the surviving spouse. This, in turn, increases the amount of the marital deduction allowed.

When a property interest passing to the surviving spouse is subject to a mortgage or other debt, only the net value of the interest after reduction by the amount of the debt qualifies for the marital deduction.

In his will, Jacob leaves real estate (fair market value of $500,000) to Rachel, his wife. If the real estate is subject to a mortgage of $100,000 (upon which Jacob was personally liable), the marital deduction is limited to $400,000 ($500,000 – $100,000). The $100,000 mortgage is deductible as an obligation of the decedent (Jacob).

Terminable Interest Limitation Certain interests in property passing from the deceased spouse to the surviving spouse are referred to as ==terminable interests==. Such an interest will terminate or fail after the passage of time, upon the happening of some contingency, or upon the failure of some event to occur. Examples are life estates, annuities, receivables for terms of years, and patents. A terminable interest does not qualify for the marital deduction.[39]

The marital deduction is intended to merely postpone the transfer tax upon the death of the first spouse and to shift any such tax to the surviving spouse. Thus, it is appropriate that the marital deduction is not available where the surviving spouse can enjoy the property and still pass it to another with zero Federal estate tax consequences.

Olivia's gross estate includes an installment note receivable with payments scheduled to occur for 5 more years, as of the date of her death. Under Olivia's will, the note passes to her husband Josh, whose life expectancy is 17 years. The note is a terminable interest, and no marital deduction is allowed in computing Olivia's taxable estate. Because no asset will be placed in Josh's gross estate as to the note, the marital deduction for Olivia's estate is disallowed.

Consistent with the objective of the terminable interest rule, the marital deduction is allowed for transfers of ==qualified terminable interest property (QTIP)==. This is defined as property that passes from one spouse to another by gift or at death and for which the transferee-spouse has a qualifying income interest for life.

- The person is entitled for life to all of the income from the property (or a specific portion of it), payable at annual or more frequent intervals.
- No person has a power to appoint any part of the property to any person other than the surviving spouse during his or her life.[40]

---

[39]§§ 2056(b)(1) and 2523(b)(1).　　　　　　[40]§§ 2523(f) and 2056(b)(7).

If these conditions are met, an election can be made to claim a marital deduction as to the QTIP. The election is irrevocable.[41]

If the election is made, a transfer tax is imposed on the QTIP when the surviving spouse disposes of it by gift or upon death. If the later transfer occurs during the surviving spouse's life, the gift tax applies, measured by the fair market value of the property as of that time.[42] If no lifetime disposition takes place, the fair market value of the property on the date of death (or alternate valuation date) is included in the gross estate of the second spouse to die.[43]

In this manner, the QTIP election "plays fair" with the transferred income interest: a marital deduction is claimed on the first death, and the asset is included in the gross estate of the second death.

EXAMPLE
42

Clyde dies and provides in his will that certain assets (fair market value of $2,100,000) are to be transferred to a trust under which Lily (Clyde's wife) receives the income of the trust for her life, with the remainder passing to their children upon Lily's death. Presuming that all of the preceding requirements are satisfied and Clyde's executor so elects, his estate receives a marital deduction of $2,100,000.

Lily dies when the trust assets are worth $6,400,000. This amount is included in her gross estate.

State Taxes at Death

About a dozen states, and a number of cities, counties, and similar jurisdictions, levy taxes when property passes to another party because of the death of a decedent. These taxes can be assessed at marginal rates of almost 20 percent, and the applicable exemption amounts typically are less than that for the Federal estate tax. A deduction is allowed against the taxable estate for estate and inheritance taxes paid to such jurisdictions.[44]

The deduction for taxes paid to a state at death mitigates the effect of subjecting property to multiple taxes payable because of a death.

LO.8

Calculate the Federal estate tax liability.

27-3c **Estate Tax Credits**

Several credits, in addition to the unified transfer tax credit, are allowed in computing the Federal estate tax liability.

Credit for Tax on Prior Transfers

Suppose that Floyd owns some property that he passes at death to Sarah. Shortly thereafter, Sarah dies and passes the property to Juan. Assuming that both estates are subject to the Federal estate tax, the successive deaths result in an expensive and undesirable double taxation of the same asset.

To mitigate the multiple taxation that might result from successive unanticipated deaths, a credit is allowed for Federal estate tax paid on prior, overlapping transfers.[45] Here, Sarah's estate may be able to claim as a credit some of the taxes paid by Floyd's estate.

The credit is limited to the lesser of the following:

1. The amount of the Federal estate tax attributable to the transferred property in the transferor's estate.
2. The amount of the Federal estate tax attributable to the transferred property in the decedent's estate.

---

[41]§ 2056(b)(7)(B)(v).
[42]§§ 2519 and 2511.
[43]§ 2044.

[44]§ 2058.
[45]§ 2013.

GLOBAL TAX ISSUES Treaty Relief Is Not Abundant!

One means of mitigating double taxation at the international level is to take advantage of treaty provisions. A treaty will determine which country has primary taxing rights, and this may depend on such factors as the domicile of the decedent or the nature of the property involved (e.g., personalty or realty). Unfortunately, the United States has estate tax conventions with only these countries: Austria*, Belgium, Canada, Denmark*, Finland, France*, Germany*, Greece, Ireland, Italy, Japan*, the Netherlands, Norway, the Republic of South Africa, Sweden*, Switzerland, and the United Kingdom*. In contrast, almost 70 countries have income tax treaties with the United States. Thus, treaty relief in the estate tax area is not as widespread as with income tax situations.

*Indicates the existence of a gift tax treaty as well. The United States has a gift tax treaty with Australia, but no estate tax treaty.

The credit is allowed when the property is subjected to Federal estate taxation "too soon" after it was taxed at the first death. Exhibit 27.2 shows the relationship between the credit allowed and the time interval between the two deaths.

Time Interval between Successive Deaths

Under Floyd's will, Sarah inherits property. One year later, Sarah dies. Assume that the estate tax attributable to the inclusion of the property in Floyd's gross estate was $160,000 and that the estate tax attributable to the inclusion of the property in Sarah's gross estate is $120,000. Under these circumstances, Sarah's estate claims a credit against the estate tax of $120,000 (refer to limitation 2).

EXAMPLE 43

Assume the same facts as in Example 43, except that Sarah dies three years after Floyd. The credit now is 80% of $120,000, or $96,000 (see Exhibit 27.2).

EXAMPLE 44

Credit for Foreign Taxes Paid at Death

A credit is allowed against the estate tax for any estate, inheritance, legacy, or succession tax paid to another country.[46] The credit is allowed for taxes also paid to possessions or political subdivisions of foreign countries, and to U.S. possessions (e.g., Puerto Rico and Guam).

27-3d Procedural Matters

A Federal estate tax return, if required, is due nine months after the date of the decedent's death.[47] The time limit applies to all estates regardless of the nationality or

EXHIBIT 27.2	Credit for Tax on Prior Transfers
Interval between Deaths	**Credit Allowed**
Within 2 years	100%
Within 3 to 4 years	80%
Within 5 to 6 years	60%
Within 7 to 8 years	40%
Within 9 to 10 years	20%

---

[46]§ 2014. [47]§ 6075(a).

residence of the decedent. Frequently, an executor will request and obtain from the IRS an extension of time for filing Form 706 (estate tax return).[48] An *automatic* six-month extension of time to file the estate tax return can be claimed.

Concept Summary 27.5

Federal Estate Tax Provisions—Taxable Estate and Procedural Matters

1. In computing the taxable estate, certain deductions are allowed.

2. Deductions are permitted for various administration expenses (e.g., executor's commissions), professional fees (e.g., appraisal, accounting, and legal), debts of the decedent, certain unpaid taxes, and funeral expenses.

3. Casualty and theft losses occurring during the settlement of the estate and not compensated for by insurance can be deducted.

4. Charitable transfers are deductible if the designated organization holds qualified status with the IRS at the time of death.

5. Transfers to a surviving spouse yield a marital deduction if they do not violate the terminable interest rule. The terminable interest rule can be avoided by making a QTIP election.

6. A deduction is allowed for certain state and local taxes paid on account of a death.

7. If required, a Federal estate tax return (Form 706) must be filed within nine months of the date of the decedent's death. An extension for filing beyond this date is available.

LO.9

Review and demonstrate the role of the generation-skipping transfer tax.

27-4 THE GENERATION-SKIPPING TRANSFER TAX

To discourage families from deferring Federal gift and estate taxes by transferring assets to very young beneficiaries, the tax law imposes an additional generation-skipping transfer tax (GSTT). The tax is added to any gift or estate tax that may be due. The GSTT attempts to collect a Federal transfer tax from a family at least once *every other* generation, by blood or marriage.

27-4a Inter-Generational Transfers

Previously, it was possible to bypass a generation or more of Federal gift and estate taxes by structuring the transaction carefully.

Types of Generation-Skipping Transfers

Under his will, Edward creates a trust, life estate to Stephen (Edward's son) and remainder to Ava (Edward's granddaughter) upon Stephen's death. Edward is subject to the Federal estate tax, but no tax results upon Stephen's death. The result is that the property in trust skips a generation of transfer taxes.

Elena gives assets directly to Rodrigo (her grandson). The gift would circumvent any transfer taxes that would have resulted had the assets been channeled through Rodrigo's parents.

27-4b The Tax on Generation-Skipping Transfers

The GSTT is designed to preclude the avoidance of either the estate tax or the gift tax by making transfers that bypass the next lower generation. In the typical family setting, this involves transfers from grandparents to grandchildren.

The GSTT is triggered by any of these three events: a taxable *termination* occurs, a taxable *distribution* takes place, or a *direct skip* is made.[49] Example 45 illustrates a termination event. Upon Stephen's death, the fair market value of the trust property that passes to Ava is subject to the GSTT (imposed on the trust). The GSTT will have the effect of reducing the amount Ava receives from the trust.

[48]§ 6081.

[49]§ 2611.

Example 46 illustrates a lifetime version of the direct skip event.[50] In this situation, the GSTT is imposed upon Elena when the gift is made to Rodrigo, because the gift skips over the generation of Rodrigo's parents.

The GSTT rate is the highest rate under the gift and estate tax schedules (i.e., 40 percent). The GSTT base is reduced by the same exemption equivalent amount that is available against the Federal estate and gift tax (see Exhibit 27.1).[51] For a donor who is married, the election to split the gift (as under § 2513) can double the amount of the GSTT exemption.[52]

The tax base also is reduced by the annual gift tax exclusion and the charitable and marital deductions. The GSTT does not apply to gifts made for political, medical, and educational purposes, if the corresponding gift tax exemption applies. A credit is allowed for certain state-level GSTT paid.

Generations are assigned by birth or marriage. For other parties, a generation is 25 years long. The GSTT computation is made on a schedule that is part of Form 706 or 709 (i.e., the estate or gift tax return to which it relates).

EXAMPLE 47

Mother Anna (age 60) and son Barry (age 40) are in two successive GSTT generations. Father Carl (age 60) and daughter Denny (age 15) are in two successive generations.

Spouses E'Toin (age 60) and Fantasia (age 58) are in the same generation. Spouses Gerardo (age 60) and Hermosa (age 20) are in the same generation.

Unrelated individuals Ishu (age 60) and Jiva (age 50) are in the same generation. Unrelated individuals Kong (age 60) and Lian (age 12) are two generations apart.

27-5 TAX PLANNING

27-5a The Federal Gift Tax

LO.10

Recognize strategies to minimize Federal gift and estate taxes.

For gifts that generate a tax, consideration must be given to the present value to the donor of the gift taxes paid. Because the donor loses the use of these funds, the expected interval between a gift (the imposition of the gift tax) and death (the imposition of the estate tax) may make the gift less attractive from an economic standpoint. On the plus side, however, are the estate tax savings that result from any gift tax paid. Because these funds are no longer in the gross estate of the donor (except for certain gifts within three years of death), the estate tax thereon is avoided.

Gifts possess distinct advantages over transfers made at death. First, and often most important, income from the property is generally shifted to the donee. If the donee is in a lower bracket than the donor, the family unit will save on income taxes. Second, the proper spacing of gifts can further cut down the Federal gift tax by maximizing the number of annual exclusions available. Third, many states impose some type of tax at death, but only a relatively few impose a gift tax. Thus, a gift may completely avoid a state transfer tax.

In minimizing gift tax liability in lifetime asset transfers, the optimum use of the annual exclusion can have significant results. Because a new annual exclusion is available each year, spacing gifts over multiple years increases the amount that can be transferred free of gift tax.

EXAMPLE 48

Starting in 2013, Cora makes gifts in the amount of the annual exclusion to each of her five grandchildren. Taking into account the changes in the amount of the annual exclusion allowed, Cora will have transferred $575,000 through 2020 with no Federal gift tax consequences.

Years		Amount of Exclusion
2018–2020	$15,000 (annual exclusion) × 5 (number of donees) × 3 (number of years)	$225,000
2013–2017	$14,000 (annual exclusion) × 5 (number of donees) × 5 (number of years)	350,000

---

[50]§ 2612(c)(1).
[51]§ 2631(c).

[52]§ 2652(a)(2).

For married donors, the election to split gifts can double the amount of a tax-free transfer; see text Section 27-2e. Referring to Example 48, if Cora is married and her husband Julio makes the gift-splitting election for each year, $1.15 million [$575,000 (amount allowed Cora) × 2 (number of donors)] can be transferred with no gift tax consequences.

27-5b The Federal Estate Tax

Controlling the Amount of the Gross Estate

Presuming that an estate tax problem is anticipated, the starting point for planning purposes is to reduce the size of the potential gross estate. Aside from initiating a program of lifetime giving, as described next several other possibilities exist.

Proper Handling of Estate Tax Deductions

Estate taxes can be saved either by reducing the size of the gross estate or by increasing the total allowable deductions. Thus, the lower the taxable estate, the less the amount of estate tax generated. Planning with deductions includes:

- Making proper use of the marital deduction.
- Working effectively with the charitable deduction.
- Taking advantage of the bypass amount.
- Optimizing other deductions and losses allowed (discussed in text Section 27-3b).

Approach to the Marital Deduction

When planning for the estate tax marital deduction, both tax and nontax factors have to be taken into account. Taking into account the present value of taxes deferred, taxpayers should try to postpone estate taxation as long as possible. Usually, by maximizing the marital deduction on the death of the first spouse to die, not only are taxes saved, but the surviving spouse is enabled to trim his or her future estate by entering into a program of lifetime gifts. By making optimum use of the annual gift tax exclusion, considerable amounts can be shifted without incurring *any* transfer tax.

Effectively Working with the Charitable Deduction

As a general guide to obtain overall tax savings, contributions to charities during a taxpayer's life are preferred over a charitable bequest (a transfer via a will). For example, an individual who gave $200,000 to a qualified charity during his or her life could secure an income tax deduction, use the gift tax deduction to avoid any gift tax, and reduce the gross estate by the amount of the gift. On the other hand, if the $200,000 is transferred by will after the donor's death to the charity, no individual income tax deduction is available, and the amount of the transfer is includible in the decedent's gross estate (although later deducted for estate tax purposes). In short, the lifetime contribution provides a double tax benefit (income tax deduction plus reduced estate taxes) at no gift tax cost.

On occasion, a charitable bequest depends on the issuance of a disclaimer by a noncharitable heir.[53] Usually this involves special types of property or collections where the decedent allows a noncharitable heir to choose whether to receive the property or allow it to transfer to the charity.

---

[53]As noted earlier in this chapter, a disclaimer is a refusal to accept the property. If the disclaimer is timely made, the property is not treated as having passed through the person issuing the disclaimer and a gift tax is avoided.

Use of Disclaimers in Charitable Bequests

Megan specified in her will that her valuable art collection is to pass to her son or, if the son refuses, to a designated and qualified art museum. At the time the will was drawn, Megan knew that her son was not interested in owning the collection. If, after Megan's death, the son issues a timely disclaimer, the collection will pass to the designated museum, and Megan's estate is allowed a charitable deduction for its estate tax value.

EXAMPLE 49

Paresh's will specifies that one-half of his disposable estate is to pass to his wife and the remainder of his property to a designated and qualified charitable organization. If the wife issues a timely disclaimer after Paresh's death, all of the property passes to the charity and qualifies for the charitable deduction.

EXAMPLE 50

Did the son in Example 49 act wisely if he issued the disclaimer in favor of the museum? Although the disclaimer will provide Megan's estate with a deduction for the value of the art collection, consider the income tax deduction alternative. If the son accepts the bequest, he can still dispose of the collection (and fulfill his mother's philanthropic objectives) through a donation to the museum. At the same time, he obtains an income tax deduction of his own. Whether this will save taxes for the family unit depends on a comparison of Megan's estate tax bracket with the estimated income tax bracket of the son.

The use of a disclaimer in Example 50 would be sheer folly. It would not reduce Paresh's estate tax; it would merely substitute a charitable deduction for the marital deduction. Whether or not the wife issues a disclaimer, no estate taxes will be due. The wife should accept her bequest and, if she is so inclined, make lifetime gifts of it to a qualified charity. In so doing, she could generate an income tax deduction for herself.

Taking Advantage of the Bypass Amount

The bypass amount, also known as the exclusion amount or the exemption equivalent amount, is the amount that can pass free of a transfer tax due to the unified transfer tax credit. Generally, this amount of property should be transferred to children or other parties for whom the transfer does not produce an estate or gift tax deduction. The bypass amount increased significantly as a result of 2017 tax law changes.

Year	Bypass Amount
2017	$ 5,490,000
2018	11,180,000
2019	11,400,000
2020	11,580,000

Spousal Transfers In the past, a bypass amount frequently was wasted when the first spouse died. Human nature often compels a spouse to leave all of his or her assets to the survivor.

Ethan and Hope are married, and each has a net worth of $3,500,000. Upon Ethan's prior death in 2009, his will passed his entire net worth to Hope; this often is called an "I Love You" will. Although Ethan avoided any Federal estate tax due to the marital deduction, he wasted his bypass amount and concentrated additional assets in Hope's potential estate.

EXAMPLE 51

Under current Federal estate tax law, the bypass amount is "portable," meaning that a **deceased spouse's unused exclusion (DSUE)** amount is available to the surviving spouse.[54] This provision effectively treats a married couple as a single unit for estate tax purposes; lifetime transfers between spouses are not necessary to make use of the combined bypass amounts.

---

[54]§ 2010(c).

EXAMPLE 52

Assume the same facts as in Example 51, except that Ethan dies in 2017 with a net worth of $5,490,000, all of which he passes to Hope. Presuming a proper election was made on his return, Ethan's DSUE amount transfers to his wife. Should Hope die in 2020, her exclusion amount would be $17,070,000 [$5,490,000 (Ethan's DSUE amount) + $11,580,000 (her own exclusion amount)].

If a surviving spouse is predeceased by more than one spouse, the DSUE amount that is available for the surviving spouse is limited to the unused exclusion of the *last* surviving spouse.

Proper Handling of Other Deductions and Losses under §§ 2053 and 2054

Many estate-related deductions and losses may be claimed either as estate tax deductions or as income tax deductions of the estate on the fiduciary return (Form 1041), but a choice must be made.[55] The deduction for income tax purposes is not allowed unless the estate tax deduction is waived. It is possible for these deductions to be divided between the two returns.

REFOCUS ON THE BIG PICTURE

AN EVENTFUL AND FINAL YEAR

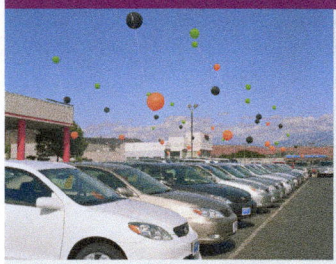

As to their divorce, John was able to carry out a property settlement with Hannah without incurring any gift tax consequences (see Example 11). Both Helen and John acted wisely when they chose to disclaim most of their inheritance from their mother. By making the disclaimers, they were able to pass the property to their children without a transfer tax being imposed (see Examples 12 and 13).

John's retirement plan benefits and the proceeds paid under his life insurance policy are included in his gross estate (see Example 25).

John's pre-death planning was highly advantageous in several respects.

- By drawing up a new will, the charitable and marital deductions were retained (see Examples 37 and 38).

- By prepaying state and local property and income taxes and staying current on medical expenses, John improved his Federal income tax position (see Example 37). He also avoided any estate taxes on the amounts used to pay these expenses.

WILL SANDERS/STONE/GETTY IMAGES

Key Terms

Alternate valuation date, 27-5	Exemption equivalent amount, 27-5	Taxable estate, 27-19
Annual exclusion, 27-10	Future interest, 27-10	Taxable gift, 27-3
Bypass amount, 27-5	Gross estate, 27-13	Tenants by the entirety, 27-6
Community property, 27-6	Joint tenants, 27-6	Tenants in common, 27-6
Deceased spouse's unused exclusion (DSUE), 27-27	Marital deduction, 27-20	Terminable interests, 27-21
Disclaimer, 27-9	Probate estate, 27-13	Unified transfer tax, 27-2
Exclusion amount, 27-5	Qualified terminable interest property (QTIP), 27-21	Unified transfer tax credit, 27-4

---

[55]§ 642(g) and Reg. § 20.2053–1(d).

Discussion Questions

1. **LO.1** How does the Federal unified transfer tax differ from an income tax?

2. **LO.1** Kim, a wealthy Korean national, is advised by his physicians to have an operation performed at the Mayo Clinic in Minnesota. Kim is hesitant to come to
   the United States because of the possible tax consequences. If the procedure is not
   successful, Kim does not want his wealth to be subject to the Federal estate tax. Are
   Kim's concerns justified? Explain.   *Critical Thinking*

3. **LO.1** Felipe will incur a $1,000,000 Federal transfer tax when he passes a plot of
   land to Barbara, an unrelated friend. Felipe's after-tax rate of return on his
   real estate investments is 3%. Compute the present value of the transfer tax if:
   a. Felipe transfers the land to Barbara as a lifetime taxable gift today.
   b. Felipe transfers the land to Barbara through his will after his death 20 years
      from now, as a gross estate asset.

4. **LO.1, 2, 3, 4** In no more than three PowerPoint slides, indicate how the time value   *Communications*
   of money affects the application of the Federal unified transfer taxes.
   Prepare your slides for a 45-minute presentation at your school's homecoming seminar, primarily attended by wealthy alumni.

5. **LO.2, 4, 5** Regarding the formula for the Federal gift tax (see Concept Summary 27.1),   *Critical Thinking*
   comment on the following observations.
   a. The annual exclusion is adjusted each year for inflation.
   b. The charitable and marital deductions play an important role.
   c. Some gratuitous transfers might not be subject to the gift tax.

6. **LO.3, 6** Regarding the formula for the Federal estate tax (see Concept Summary 27.2),
   comment on the following.
   a. The gross estate includes only property interests owned by the decedent at the
      time of death.
   b. The gross estate is not the same as the probate estate.
   c. Taxable estate × Applicable unified transfer tax rate = Estate tax due.

7. **LO.3** As to the alternate valuation date for asset transfers at death, comment on the
   following.
   a. The justification for the election.
   b. The main heir prefers the date of death value.
   c. An estate asset is sold seven months after the decedent's death.
   d. Effect of the election on the income tax basis in the property received by the heir.

8. **LO.4, 6** At a local bank, Jack purchases for $100,000 a five-year CD listing title as   *Critical Thinking*
   follows: "Meredith, payable on death to Briana." Four years later, Meredith
   dies. Briana, Meredith's daughter, then redeems the CD when it matures. Discuss
   the transfer tax consequences if Meredith is:
   a. Jack's wife.
   b. Jack's ex-wife.
   c. Jack's girlfriend.

Critical Thinking 9. **LO.4** Derek dies intestate (i.e., without a will) and is survived by a daughter, Ruth, and a grandson, Ted (Ruth's son). Derek's assets include a large portfolio of stocks and bonds and a beach house. Ruth has considerable wealth of her own; Ted just finished college and is unemployed. Under applicable state law, children have first priority as to bequests, and then grandchildren.

    a. To minimize future transfer taxes, what action might Ruth take? *Hint*: Use the term *disclaimer* in your answer, and consider the time value of money in your analysis.

    b. What if Ruth wants only the beach house?

10. **LO.4** Qualified tuition programs under § 529 enjoy significant tax advantages. Describe these advantages with regard to the Federal:

    a. Income tax.

    b. Gift tax.

    c. Estate tax.

11. **LO.5** Regarding the gift-splitting election, comment on the following.

    a. What it is designed to accomplish.

    b. How the election is made.

12. **LO.5** In connection with the filing of a Federal gift tax return, comment on the following.

    a. No Federal gift tax is due.

    b. The gift is between spouses.

    c. The donor obtained from the IRS an extension of time for filing his or her Federal income tax return.

13. **LO.4, 6** In each of the following independent situations, indicate whether the transfer is subject to the Federal gift tax.

    a. Asa contributes to his mayor's reelection campaign fund. The mayor has promised to get some of Asa's property rezoned from residential to commercial use.

    b. Mary Ann inherits her father's collection of guns and mounted animals. Five months later, she disclaims any interest in the mounted animals.

    c. Same as part (b). Ten months later, Mary Ann disclaims any interest in the guns.

    d. Haydon pays an orthodontist for the dental work performed on Michele, his cousin.

    e. Florence purchases a U.S. savings bond listing herself and Taylor (her daughter) as joint owners.

    f. Same as part (e). One year later, Taylor predeceases Florence.

    g. Same as part (e). One year later, Florence predeceases Taylor.

14. **LO.6** At the time of Emile's death, he was a joint tenant with Colette in a parcel of real estate. With regard to the inclusion of the realty in Emile's gross estate, comment on the following *independent* assumptions:

    a. Emile and Colette received the property as a gift from Douglas.

    b. Colette provided the entire purchase price of the property.

    c. Colette's contribution was received as a gift from Emile.

    d. Emile's contribution was derived from income generated by property he received as a gift from Colette.

15. **LO.6** With regard to "life insurance" in the context of the Federal estate tax, comment on the following.
    a. What the term includes (i.e., types of policies).
    b. The meaning of "incidents of ownership."
    c. When a gift occurs upon maturity of the policy.
    d. The tax consequences when the owner of the policy predeceases the insured and the beneficiary.

16. **LO.7** Bernice dies and, under a valid will, passes real estate to her surviving husband. The real estate is subject to a mortgage. For estate tax purposes, how is any marital deduction determined? Can Bernice's estate deduct the mortgage in computing the taxable estate? Explain.

17. **LO.8** Three unmarried and childless sisters live together. All are of advanced age and in poor health, and each owns a significant amount of wealth. Each has a will that passes her property to her surviving sister(s) or, if no survivor, to their church. Within a period of two years and on different dates, all three sisters die. Discuss the Federal estate tax consequences of these deaths.

Critical Thinking

Computational Exercises

18. **LO.3** Elizabeth made taxable gifts of $3,000,000 in 2019 and $14,000,000 in 2020. She paid no gift tax on the 2019 transfer. On what amount is the Federal gift tax computed for the 2020 gift?

19. **LO.3** Included in Mary's gross estate are the following assets:

	Fair Market Value	
	Date of Death	**Six Months Later**
Stock in Orange Corporation	$13,000,000	$13,100,000
Stock in Crimson Corporation	6,100,000	5,900,000

   a. How much is included in her gross estate if the alternate valuation date is elected?
   b. Instead, what if all of Mary's assets pass to her surviving husband?
   c. Express your answer in part (a) as a Microsoft Excel formula.

20. **LO.4** During the year, Rajeev makes the following transfers:
    - $1,000 to his mayor's reelection campaign.
    - $21,000 to his aunt, Ava, to reimburse her for what she paid the hospital for her gallbladder operation.
    - $18,000 paid directly to the surgeon who performed Ava's gallbladder operation.
    - $22,000 to purchase a used car for his son to use at college.

    Which of these transfers are subject to the Federal gift tax? (Include the total amount, and disregard the annual exclusion.)

21. **LO.4** In 2013 and with $200,000, Alice purchases a CD at State Bank listing title as follows: "Alice, payable on proof of death to Clark." Alice dies in 2020, and Clark (Alice's nephew) redeems the CD (now worth $205,000). Disregarding the annual exclusion, what is Alice's gift to Clark in:
    a. 2013?
    b. 2020?

Critical Thinking

22. **LO.5** Christian wants to transfer as much as possible to his four adult married children (including spouses) and eight minor grandchildren without using any unified transfer tax credit.

   a.   What amount should Christian transfer to accomplish his tax goal?

   b.   What if Christian's wife, Mia, joins in the gifts?

   c.   Express your computations for parts (a) and (b) as Microsoft Excel commands.

23. **LO.5** Noah and Sophia want to make a maximum contribution to their state's qualified tuition program (§ 529 plan) on behalf of their minor granddaughter, Amanda, without exceeding the annual Federal gift tax exclusion.

   a.   How much can they transfer to the plan for Amanda without incurring a current Federal gift tax?

   b.   Express your answer as a Microsoft Excel command.

24. **LO.6, 7** At his death, Andrew was a participant in his employer's contributory qualified pension plan. His account reflects the following:

Employer's contribution	$1,000,000
Andrew's contribution	800,000
Income earned and accumulated by the plan	500,000

   a.   As to this plan, how much is included in Andrew's gross estate?

   b.   If the account balance is paid to Andrew's surviving wife, how much qualifies for the marital deduction?

25. **LO.6** Mason buys real estate for $1,500,000 and lists ownership as follows: "Mason and Dana, joint tenants with the right of survivorship." Mason dies first, when the real estate is valued at $2,000,000. How much is included in Mason's gross estate if Mason and Dana are:

   a.   Brother and sister?

   b.   Husband and wife?

26. **LO.6** Matthew owns an insurance policy (face amount of $500,000) on the life of Emily, with Uma listed as the designated beneficiary. If Emily dies first and the $500,000 is paid to Uma, how much as to this policy is included in:

   a.   Matthew's gross estate?

   b.   Emily's gross estate?

27. **LO.7** Donald dies this year, and under his will, a trust is created in the amount of $6,000,000 with the following provisions: life estate to Cindy (Donald's wife) and remainder to their children. His will also passes land (cost basis of $1,000,000 and fair market value of $3,000,000) to the Salvation Army for the site of a new homeless housing project.

   a.   If a QTIP election is made, how much will these transactions reduce Donald's gross estate to arrive at the taxable estate?

   b.   If a QTIP election is not made?

28. **LO.8** Under Emma's will, Addison inherits property that generates an estate tax of $800,000. Three years later, Addison dies and the property generates an estate tax of $700,000.

   a.   What is the credit for estate tax on prior transfers claimed by Addison's estate?

   b.   Express your answer as a Microsoft Excel formula.

29. **LO.9** With $5,000,000, Paul's will creates a trust with the following provisions: life estate to Jacob (Paul's son) and remainder to Anastasia (Paul's granddaughter and Jacob's daughter). Jacob dies when the value of the trust is $8,000,000.

   a.   Does a generation-skipping transfer result?

   b.   If so, when and in what amount?

30. **LO.10** During 2020, Vasu wants to take advantage of the annual exclusion and make gifts to his 6 married children (including their spouses) and his 12 minor grandchildren.
    a. How much property can Vasu give away this year without creating a taxable gift?
    b. How does your answer change if Vasu's wife, Coleen, elects to join in making the gifts?

Problems

31. **LO.3** In each of the following independent situations, indicate whether the alternate valuation date can be elected. Explain why or why not.

	Value of Gross Estate		Estate Tax Liability	
Decedent	Date of Death	Six Months Later	Date of Death	Six Months Later
Jayden	$16,000,000	$15,900,000	$5,040,000	$5,039,000
Isabella	16,100,000	16,000,000	5,065,000	5,060,000
Liam	16,100,000	16,000,000	5,000,000	5,010,000
Lily	16,500,000	16,400,000	5,005,000	5,004,000

32. **LO.4, 6** Carl made the following transfers during the current year. What are Carl's taxable gifts for the current year?
    • Transferred $900,000 in cash and securities to a revocable trust, life estate to himself and remainder interest to his three adult children by a former wife.
    • In consideration of their upcoming marriage, gave Maria a $90,000 convertible.
    • Purchased a $100,000 certificate of deposit listing title as "Carl, payable on proof of death to Maria."
    • Established a joint checking account with his now-wife, Maria, in December of the current year with $30,000 of funds he inherited from his parents. In January of the following year, Maria withdrew $18,000 of the funds.
    • Purchased for $80,000 a paid-up insurance policy on his life (maturity value of $500,000). Carl designated Maria as the beneficiary.
    • Paid $23,400 to a college for his niece Mindy's tuition and $11,000 for her room and board. Mindy is not Carl's dependent.
    • Gave his aunt Betty $52,000 for her heart bypass operation. Betty is not Carl's dependent.

33. **LO.4, 7** In May 2019, Dudley and Eva enter into a property settlement preparatory to the dissolution of their marriage. Under the agreement, Dudley is to pay Eva $6,000,000 in full satisfaction of her marital rights. Of this amount, Dudley pays $2,500,000 immediately, and the balance is due one year later. The parties are divorced in July. Dudley dies in December, and his estate pays Eva the remaining $3,500,000 in May 2020. Discuss the Federal estate and gift tax ramifications of these transactions to the parties involved. *Critical Thinking*

34. **LO.4** Jesse dies intestate (i.e., without a will) in May year 1. Jesse's major asset is a tract of land. Under applicable state law, Jesse's property will pass to Lorena, who is his only child. In December year 1, Lorena disclaims one-half of the property. In June year 2, Lorena disclaims the other half interest. Under state law, Lorena's disclaimer results in the property passing to Arnold (Lorena's only child). *Critical Thinking*

    The value of the land (in its entirety) is as follows: $2,000,000 in May year 1, $2,100,000 in December year 1, and $2,200,000 in June year 2. Discuss the transfer tax ramifications of these transactions.

35. **LO.5** Using property she inherited, Lei makes a 2020 gift of $16,200,000 to her adult daughter, Doris. Neither Lei nor her husband, Greg, has made any prior taxable gifts. Assuming that a flat 40% tax rate applies, determine the Federal gift tax liability if:

   a. The election to split gifts is not made.

   b. The election to split gifts is made.

   c. What are the tax savings from making the election?

36. **LO.6, 7** At the time of his death this year on September 4, Kenneth owned the following assets, among others:

	Fair Market Value
City of Boston bonds	$2,500,000
Stock in Brown Corporation	900,000
Promissory note issued by Brad (Kenneth's son)	600,000

In October, the executor of Kenneth's estate received the following: $120,000 interest on the City of Boston bonds ($10,000 accrued since September 4) and a $7,000 cash dividend on the Brown stock (date of record was September 5). The declaration date on the dividend was August 12.

The $600,000 loan was made to Brad in late 2015, and he used the money to create a very successful business. The note was forgiven by Kenneth in his will.

What are the estate tax consequences of these transactions?

37. **LO.6** At the time of her death on September 4, Alicia held the following assets:

	Fair Market Value
Bonds of Emerald Tool Corporation	$ 900,000
Stock in Drab Corporation	1,100,000
Insurance policy (face amount of $400,000) on the life of her father, Mitch	80,000*
Traditional IRAs	300,000

*Cash surrender value.

Alicia also held a lifetime income interest in a trust (fair market value of trust assets $2,000,000) created by her late husband Bert. (The executor of Bert's estate had made a QTIP election.)

In October, Alicia's estate received an interest payment of $11,500 ($6,000 accrued before September 4) paid by Emerald and a cash dividend of $9,000 from Drab. The Drab dividend was declared on August 19 and was payable to date of record shareholders on September 3.

Although Mitch survives Alicia, she is the designated beneficiary of the insurance policy. The IRAs are distributed to Alicia's children.

What amount is included in Alicia's gross estate for these items?

38. **LO.6** Assume the same facts as in Problem 37 with the following modifications. What amount is included in Alicia's gross estate for these items?

   • Mitch is killed in a rockslide while mountain climbing in November, and the insurer pays Alicia's estate $400,000 before the end of the year.

   • Bert's executor did not make a QTIP election.

   • Alicia's IRAs were the Roth type (not traditional).

   • The record date for the Drab Corporation dividend is September 5 (not September 3).

   • On November 7, Alicia's estate receives from the IRS an $8,000 income tax refund, a receivable amount at her death relating to the taxes she paid for the preceding calendar year.

39. **LO.6, 7** At the time of Mateo's death, he was involved in the following transactions:

    - Mateo was a participant in his employer's contributory qualified pension plan. The plan balance of $2,000,000 is paid to Olivia, Mateo's daughter and beneficiary. The distribution consists of the following:

Employer contributions	$900,000
Mateo's after-tax contributions	600,000
Income earned and accumulated by the plan	500,000

    - Mateo was covered by his employer's group term life insurance plan for employees. The $200,000 proceeds are paid to Olivia, the designated beneficiary.

    a. What are the Federal estate tax consequences of these events?
    b. The income tax consequences?
    c. Would the answer to part (a) change if Olivia was Mateo's surviving spouse (not his daughter)? Explain.

40. **LO.6** At the time of his death on July 9, Aiden held rights in the following real estate: *Critical Thinking*

	Fair Market Value (on July 9)
Apartment building	$2,100,000
Tree farm	1,500,000
Pastureland	750,000
Residence	900,000

    The apartment building was purchased by Chloe, Aiden's mother, and is owned in a joint tenancy with her. The tree farm and pastureland were gifts from Chloe to Aiden and his two sisters. The tree farm is held in joint tenancy, and the pastureland is owned as tenants in common. Aiden purchased the residence and owns it with his wife as tenants by the entirety. How much is included in Aiden's gross estate based on the following assumptions?

    a. Aiden dies first and is survived by Chloe, his sisters, and his wife.
    b. Aiden dies after Chloe, but before his sisters and his wife.
    c. Aiden dies after Chloe and his sisters, but before his wife.
    d. Aiden dies last (i.e., he survives Chloe, his sisters, and his wife).

41. **LO.4, 6** Gordon purchased real estate for $900,000 and listed title to the property as "Gordon and Fawn, joint tenants with right of survivorship." Gordon predeceases Fawn when the real estate is worth $2,900,000. Gordon and Fawn are brother and sister.

    a. Did a gift occur when the real estate was purchased? Explain.
    b. What, if any, are the estate tax consequences upon Gordon's death?
    c. Under part (b), would your answer change if it was Fawn (not Gordon) who died? Explain.

42. **LO.4, 6, 7** Assume the same facts as in Problem 41, except that Gordon and Fawn are husband and wife (not brother and sister).

    a. What are the gift tax consequences when the real estate was purchased?
    b. What are the estate tax consequences upon Gordon's death?
    c. Under part (b), would your answer change if it was Fawn (not Gordon) who died? Explain.

43. **LO.5, 6, 7** In each of the *independent* situations below, determine the Federal estate and gift tax consequences of what has occurred. (In all cases, assume that Gene and Mary are married and that Tanisha is their daughter.)

    a. Mary purchases an insurance policy on Gene's life and designates Tanisha as the beneficiary. Mary dies first, and under her will, the policy passes to Gene.

    b. Gene purchases an insurance policy on Mary's life and designates Tanisha as the beneficiary. Tanisha dies first one year later.

    c. Assume the same facts as in part (b). Two years later, Mary dies. Because Gene has not designated a new beneficiary, the insurance proceeds are paid to him.

    d. Gene purchases an insurance policy on his life and designates Mary as the beneficiary. Gene dies first, and the policy proceeds are paid to Mary.

44. **LO.7** While vacationing in Florida in November, Sally was seriously injured in an automobile accident. Sally died several days later. Apply the Federal estate tax rules to each of these items.

    a. Bruce, Sally's son and executor, incurred $6,200 in travel expenses in flying to Florida, retrieving the body, and returning it to Frankfort, Kentucky, for burial.

    b. Sally had pledged $50,000 to the building fund of her church. Bruce paid this pledge from the assets of the estate.

    c. Prior to her death, Sally had promised to give her nephew, Gary, $20,000 when he passed the bar exam. Gary passed the exam late in the year, and Bruce kept Sally's promise by paying him $20,000 from estate assets.

    d. At the scene of the accident and before the ambulance arrived, someone took Sally's jewelry (i.e., Rolex watch and wedding ring) and money. The property (valued at $33,000) was not insured and was never recovered.

    e. As a result of the accident, Sally's auto was totally destroyed. The auto had a basis of $52,000 and a fair market value of $28,000. In January of the next year, the insurance company pays Sally's estate $27,000.

45. **LO.6, 7** Tavon dies and is survived by his wife, Marge. Under Tavon's will, all of his otherwise uncommitted assets pass to Marge. For each of the following property interests, determine the marital deduction allowed to Tavon's estate.

    a. Timberland worth $1,200,000 owned by Tavon, Marge, and Amber (Marge's sister) as equal tenants in common. Amber furnished the original purchase price.

    b. Residence of Tavon and Marge worth $900,000 owned by them as tenants by the entirety with right of survivorship. Tavon provided the original purchase price.

    c. Insurance policy on Tavon's life (maturity value of $1,000,000) owned by Marge and payable to her as the beneficiary.

    d. Insurance policy on Tavon's life (maturity value of $500,000) owned by Tavon with Marge as the designated beneficiary.

    e. Distribution from a qualified pension plan of $1,600,000 (Tavon matched his employer's contribution of $500,000) with Marge as the designated beneficiary.

46. **LO.8** Under Rowena's will, Mandy (Rowena's sister) inherits her property. One year later, Mandy dies. Based on the following independent assumptions, what is Mandy's credit for the tax on prior transfers?

    a. The estate tax attributable to the inclusion of the property in Rowena's gross estate is $700,000, and the estate tax attributable to the inclusion of the property in Mandy's gross estate is $800,000.

    b. The estate tax attributable to the inclusion of the property in Rowena's gross estate is $1,200,000, and the estate tax attributable to the inclusion of the property in Mandy's gross estate is $1,100,000.

c.   Express your computations for parts (a) and (b) as Microsoft Excel commands.

d.   Would your answers to parts (a) and (b) change if Mandy died seven years (rather than one year) after Rowena?

See Appendix E for Comprehensive Tax Return Problems—Form 709

Research Problems

Note: Solutions to the Research Problems can be prepared by using the Thomson Reuters Checkpoint™ online tax research database, which accompanies this textbook. Solutions can also be prepared by using research materials found in a typical tax library.

the answer company™
THOMSON REUTERS®

Research Problem 1. Grace Lang was employed as a waitress at the Pancake House in Grand Bay, Alabama. While working the morning shift on March 7, 2012, one of Grace's customers left her a Florida lottery ticket as a tip. When Grace discovered that she had won part of the Florida Lotto jackpot, the following steps were taken.

• Upon advice of her father and legal counsel, the Lang Corporation was formed and immediately made an S election.

• Grace received 49% of the stock in Lang, and the 51% balance was distributed to family members.

• Grace had the Florida gaming authorities designate the Lang Corporation as the recipient of the prize money—approximately $10,000,000 payable over 30 years.

• Grace's coworkers at the Pancake House filed suit against Grace based on an agreement they had to share any lottery winnings equally. The Alabama courts eventually decided that such an agreement did exist but that it was not enforceable. (Alabama law does not permit enforcement of contracts involving illegal activities—gambling is illegal in Alabama.)

In 2020, the IRS determined that Grace had made taxable gifts in 2012 when she shifted some of the lottery winnings to family members. She made the gifts by having 51% of the Lang Corporation stock issued to them. (Because Lang is an S corporation, gross income from the lottery passes through to the shareholders.)

Grace disputed the gift tax assessment by contending that her actions were required by the Lang family agreement. Under this agreement, it was understood that each member would take care of the others in the event he or she came into a "substantial amount" of money. Because Grace was bound by the Lang family agreement, she was compelled to relinquish any right to 51% of the Lang stock. Thus, the satisfaction of an obligation is not a gift. Since no gift occurred, the imposition of the gift tax is not appropriate.

Who should prevail?

Partial list of research aids:
Estate of Emerson Winkler, 36 TCM 1657, T.C.Memo. 1997–4.
Tonda Lynn Dickerson, 103 TCM 1280, T.C.Memo. 2012–60.

Research Problem 2. Before her death, Lucy entered into the following transactions. Discuss the estate and income tax ramifications of each of these transactions.

a.   Lucy borrowed $600,000 from her brother, Irwin, so that Lucy could start a business. The loan was on open account, and no interest or due date was provided for. Under applicable state law, collection on the loan was barred by the statute of limitations before Lucy died. Because the family thought that Irwin should recover his funds, the executor of the estate paid him $600,000.

b. Lucy promised her sister, Ida, a bequest of $500,000 if Ida would move in with her and care for her during an illness (which eventually proved to be terminal). Lucy never kept her promise; her will was silent on any bequest to Ida. After Lucy's death, Ida sued the estate and eventually recovered $600,000 for breach of contract.

Partial list of research aids:
§ 2053.
Reg. §§ 20.2053–4(d)(4) and (7).
Estate of Allie W. Pittard, 69 T.C. 391 (1977).
Joseph F. Kenefic, 36 TCM 1226, T.C.Memo. 1977–310.
Hibernia Bank v. U.S., 78–2 USTC ¶13,261, 42 AFTR 2d 78–6510, 581 F.2d 741 (CA–9, 1978).

Use internet tax resources to address the following questions. Look for reliable websites and blogs of the IRS and other government agencies, media outlets, businesses, tax professionals, academics, think tanks, and political outlets.

Communications   **Research Problem 3.** What type of transfer tax, if any, does your home state impose? What about the state(s) contiguous to your home state? (For Alaska, use Washington; for Hawaii, use California.) Make a chart relating your findings, and send it to your instructor.

Data Analytics
Communications   **Research Problem 4.** Make a graph showing the number of Forms 706 and 709 that have been filed for every third year starting with 2005. On the same graph, indicate the revenue collected by the Treasury from these taxes for each year.

Data Analytics
Communications   **Research Problem 5.** Consider the Deceased Spouse Unused Exclusion amount. For the last three years, on one graph, show the number of returns that included such an amount, and the dollar amount of such exclusions claimed. Comment on the size of the estate that tends to use the DSUE provision. Send your results to your instructor.

Research Problem 6. Perkins is a single individual. In 2019, she made a $13,000,000 taxable gift to her brother. Perkins never has been married and has made no prior taxable gifts. Compute Perkins's Federal gift tax liability, using the Form 709 and instructions at **irs.gov**.

Becker CPA Review Questions

Becker.   1. Fred and Amy Kehl, both U.S. citizens, are married. All of their real and personal property is owned by them as tenants by the entirety or as joint tenants with right of survivorship. The gross estate of the first spouse to die:
   a. Includes 50% of the value of all property owned by the couple, regardless of which spouse furnished the original consideration.
   b. Includes only the property that had been acquired with the funds of the deceased spouse.
   c. Does not include any of the value of the property held as joint tenancy with right of survivorship (or tenancy by the entirety) because of the unlimited marital deduction.
   d. Includes one-third of the value of all real estate owned by the Kehls as the dower right in the case of the wife or courtesy right in the case of the husband.

2. Which of the following requires filing a gift tax return if the transfer exceeds the available annual gift tax exclusion?

    a. Medical expenses paid directly to a physician on behalf of an individual unrelated to the donor.

    b. Tuition paid directly to an accredited university on behalf of an individual unrelated to the donor.

    c. Payments for college books, supplies, and dormitory fees on behalf of an individual unrelated to the donor.

    d. Campaign expenses paid to a political organization.

3. Steve and Kay Briar, U.S. citizens, were married for the entire calendar year. During 2020, Steve gave a $32,000 cash gift to his sister. The Briars made no other gifts in the year. They each signed a timely election to treat the $32,000 gift as made one-half by each spouse. Disregarding the applicable credit and estate tax consequences, what amount of the current-year gift is taxable to the Briars?

    a. $32,000   c. $2,000
    b. $30,000   d. $0

4. During the current year, Diane Stevens made two gifts to her son Greg. The first gift was ABC stock with a value at the date of the gift of $25,000. Diane's basis in ABC was $2,000. The second gift, in the same year, was XYZ stock with a value of $23,000 at the date of the gift and a basis to Diane of $24,000. For gift tax purposes, what is the value of the gifts made by Diane to Greg, before applying any annual gift tax exclusions?

	Value of ABC Stock	**Value of XYZ Stock**
a.	$25,000	$24,000
b.	$25,000	$23,000
c.	$23,000	$0
d.	$2,000	$0

5. Larry plans to gift his daughter $25,000 during the current taxable year. Further, provided she graduates from a four-year accredited college, he will also gift her $100,000. Which of the following is correct with regard to these gifts during the current year, assuming the cash is given to his daughter in the current year and she does not graduate from a four-year accredited college in the current year?

	$25,000	**$100,000**
a.	Completed Gift	Incomplete Gift
b.	Completed Gift	Completed Gift
c.	Incomplete Gift	Incomplete Gift
d.	Incomplete Gift	Completed Gift

6. Which of the following statements about the estate tax is *not* correct?

    a. The estate tax return, Form 706, is due nine months after the date of death.

    b. The alternate valuation date for an estate, if elected, is six months after the date of death.

    c. The estate may not deduct outstanding debts of the decedent.

    d. An estate is allowed an unlimited marital deduction.

7. Bob died in year 3. His gross estate consisted of assets with a fair market value of $13,500,000. In his will, Bob leaves $1,000,000 to his wife, $500,000 to his only daughter, and $250,000 to his favorite charity. Prior to Bob's death, he was involved in a lawsuit when one of his tenants slipped and fell at one of the rental properties owned by Bob. After his death, the personal representative settled the lawsuit for $750,000. The expenses to close Bob's estate were $50,000. In year 3, the Federal estate exclusion amount is $11,000,000. What amount, if any, does Bob's estate exceed the $11,000,000 exclusion amount?

    a. $450,000   c. $1,200,000
    b. $500,000   d. $0

8. David Collins died during the current year. The personal representative of David's estate identified the following assets:

Stocks in David's name only	$2,000,000
Investment property in a trust that David has the right to revoke	1,500,000
Primary home owned jointly with his wife (wife did not contribute to the purchase)	1,000,000
Insurance policy owned by and insuring David with the proceeds payable to his daughter	800,000
Vacation home owned jointly with his son (son did not contribute to the purchase)	500,000
Cash placed in an irrevocable trust by David eight years ago with David's friend as trustee	600,000

    What is the value of David's gross estate for estate tax purposes?

    a. $3,500,000   c. $5,300,000
    b. $4,250,000   d. $6,400,000

CHAPTER

28

Income Taxation of Trusts and Estates

LEARNING OBJECTIVES: *After completing Chapter 28, you should be able to:*

 LO.1 Use working definitions with respect to trusts, estates, beneficiaries, and other parties.

 LO.2 Identify the steps in determining the accounting and taxable income of a trust or an estate and the related taxable income of the beneficiaries.

 LO.3 Illustrate the uses and implications of distributable net income.

 LO.4 Apply the fiduciary income tax rules in a manner that minimizes the income taxation of trusts and estates and still accomplishes the intended objectives of the grantor or decedent.

CHAPTER OUTLINE

28-1   An Overview of Fiduciary Taxation, 28-2
   28-1a What Is a Trust? 28-2
   28-1b What Is an Estate? 28-5

28-2   Nature of Trust and Estate Taxation, 28-5
   28-2a Tax Accounting Periods and Methods, 28-6
   28-2b Tax Rates and Personal Exemption, 28-6
   28-2c Alternative Minimum Tax, 28-7
   28-2d Additional Tax on Net Investment Income, 28-8

28-3   Taxable Income of Trusts and Estates, 28-8
   28-3a Entity Accounting Income, 28-8
   28-3b Gross Income, 28-11
   28-3c Ordinary Deductions, 28-13
   28-3d Deductions for Losses, 28-15
   28-3e Charitable Contributions, 28-15
   28-3f Deduction for Distributions to Beneficiaries, 28-16
   28-3g Tax Credits, 28-19

28-4   Taxation of Beneficiaries, 28-20
   28-4a Distributions by Simple Trusts, 28-20
   28-4b Distributions by Estates and Complex Trusts, 28-20
   28-4c Character of Income, 28-22

28-5   Procedural Matters, 28-23

28-6   Tax Planning, 28-24
   28-6a A Trust or an Estate as an Income-Shifting Device, 28-24
   28-6b Income Tax Planning for Estates, 28-24
   28-6c Distributions of In-Kind Property, 28-25
   28-6d Additional Taxes on Capital Gains and Net Investment Income, 28-26

THE BIG PICTURE

SETTING UP A TRUST TO PROTECT A FAMILY

Anna Jiang is the main breadwinner in her family, which includes her husband Tom, a social worker, and two children, Bobby, age 6, and Sally, age 8. Anna has accumulated about $2 million in after-tax investment accounts, largely made up of growth stocks that do not regularly pay dividends; she inherited most of these securities when her grandmother died about five years ago. Anna has addressed the problem of probate costs through joint property ownership, life insurance policies, and beneficiary arrangements for her retirement plans. She and Tom update their wills every five years or so.

Because there is a history of Alzheimer's disease in her family, Anna Jiang wants to make certain that, if she becomes unable to work and cannot manage her financial assets, Tom and the children will have adequate cash flow from the investment assets. In addition, one of Anna's colleagues at the office suggests that Anna should set up a trust to take care of her family in case a medical problem ever arises.

Read the chapter and formulate your response.

Taxpayers create trusts for a variety of reasons. Some trusts are established primarily for tax purposes, but most are designed to accomplish a broader financial goal or to provide for the orderly management of assets in case of an emergency. Because a trust is a separate tax entity, its gross income and deductions must be measured and an annual tax return must be filed. Similarly, when an individual dies, a legal entity is created in the form of his or her estate. This chapter examines the rules related to the income taxation of trusts and estates.

28-1 AN OVERVIEW OF FIDUCIARY TAXATION

When a trust or estate is involved, a taxpayer has put a third party into a fiduciary relationship, where the third party (i.e., the trustee or executor) is required to act on the behalf (and for the benefit) of the taxpayer who assigned the duties to them. The fiduciary essentially acts in the place of the decedent or the creator of the trust, for instance, in making investment decisions and meeting financial obligations.

The income taxation of trusts and estates is governed by Subchapter J of Chapter 1 of the Internal Revenue Code, §§ 641 through 692. Certain similarities are apparent between Subchapter J and the income taxation of individuals (e.g., the definitions of gross income and deductible expenditures), partnerships and limited liability entities (e.g., the pass-through principle), and S corporations (e.g., the pass-through principle and the trust or estate as a separate taxable entity). Trusts also involve several important new concepts, however, including the determination of *distributable net income* and the *tier system* of distributions to beneficiaries.

Exhibit 28.1 lists some of the more common reasons that might prompt an individual to create a trust, and Exhibit 28.2 illustrates the structure of a typical trust and estate.

28-1a What Is a Trust?

The Code does not contain a definition of a trust; instead, trusts are defined and governed by state law. However, the term usually refers to an arrangement created by a will or by an *inter vivos* (lifetime) declaration through which trustees take title to property for the purpose of protecting or conserving it for the beneficiaries.[1] Usually, trust operations are controlled by the trust document and by the fiduciary laws of the state in which the trust documents are executed.

LO.1

Use working definitions with respect to trusts, estates, beneficiaries, and other parties.

EXHIBIT 28.1	Common Motivations for Creating a Trust
Type of Trust	**Financial and Other Goals**
Life insurance trust	Holds life insurance policies on the insured, removes the proceeds of the policies from the gross estate (if an irrevocable trust), and safeguards against receipt of the proceeds by a young or inexperienced beneficiary.
"Living" (revocable) trust	Manages assets, reduces probate costs, provides privacy for asset disposition, protects against medical or other emergencies, and provides relief from the necessity of day-to-day management of the underlying assets. No estate tax savings.
Trust for minors	Provides funds for a college education or other needs of the minor and transfers accumulated income without permanently parting with the underlying assets.
Divorce trust	Manages the assets of an ex-spouse and ensures that they are distributed in a timely fashion to specified beneficiaries (e.g., as alimony or child support).

[1]Reg. § 301.7701–4(a).

EXHIBIT 28.2	Structure of a Typical Trust and Estate

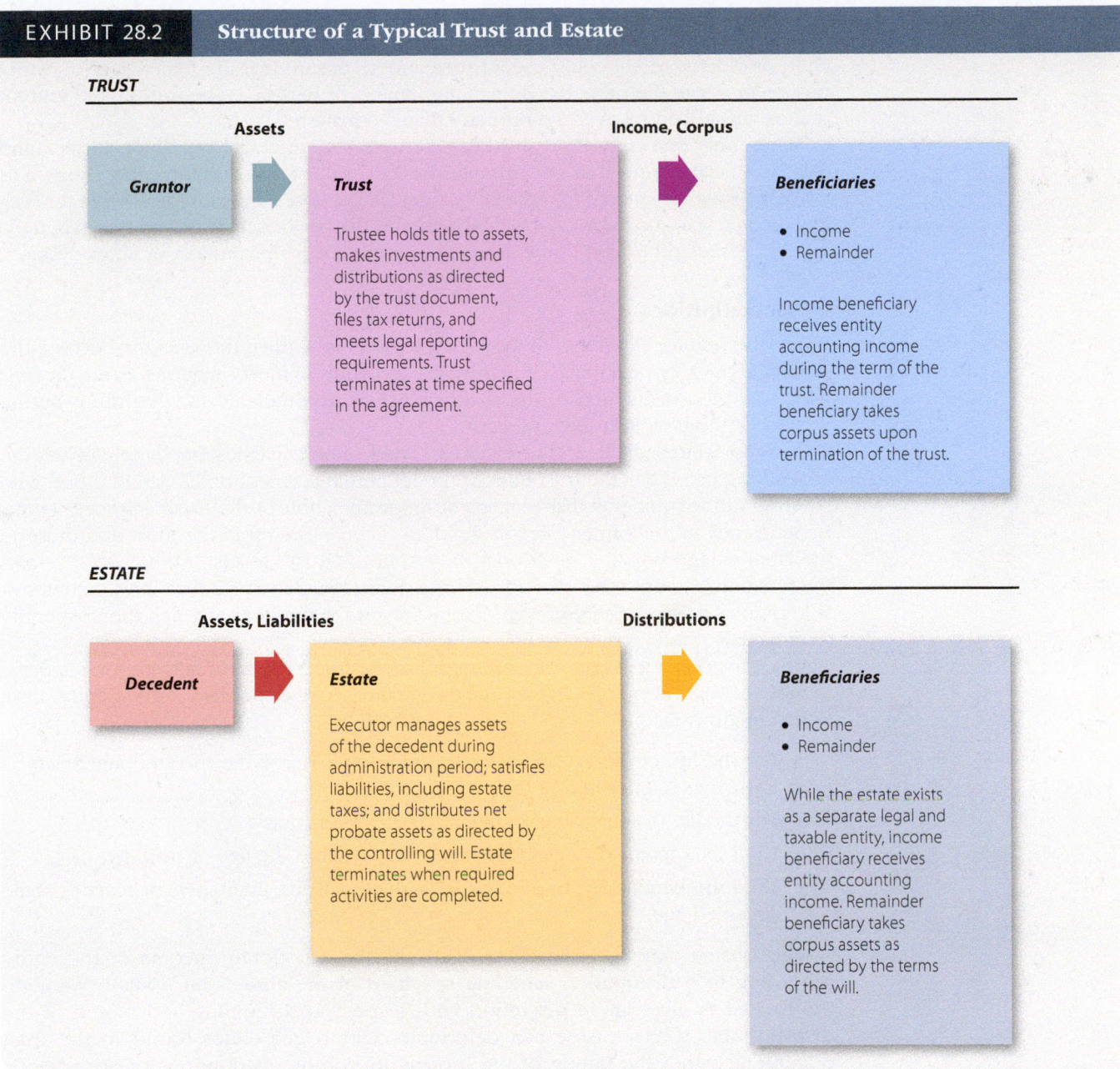

Typically, the creation of a trust involves at least three parties.

1. The **grantor** (sometimes referred to as the settlor or donor) transfers selected assets to the trust entity.
2. The trustee, who usually is either an individual or a corporation, is charged with the fiduciary duties associated with the trust.
3. The beneficiary is designated to receive income or property from the trust.

In some situations, fewer than three persons may be involved, as specified by the trust agreement. For instance, an elderly individual who no longer can manage his or her own property (e.g., because of ill health) may create a trust under which he or she is both the grantor and the beneficiary. In this case, a family member or corporate trustee is charged with the management of the grantor's assets.

In another situation, the grantor might designate himself or herself as the trustee of the trust assets. For example, someone who wants to transfer selected assets to a minor child or elderly parent could use a trust entity to ensure that the beneficiary does not misuse or waste the property. By naming himself or herself as the trustee, the grantor retains virtual control over the property that is transferred.

When only one party is involved (when the same individual is grantor, trustee, and sole beneficiary of the trust), Subchapter J rules do not apply and the entity (known as a grantor trust) is ignored for Federal income tax purposes; the grantor is liable for Federal income taxes on the entity's taxable income. This might occur, for instance, when the grantor desires protection of the assets and/or income from creditors or an ex-spouse.

Other Definitions

When the grantor transfers title of selected assets to a trust, those assets become the corpus (body), or principal, of the trust. Trust corpus, in most situations, earns *income*, which may be distributed to the beneficiaries or accumulated for the future by the trustee, as the trust instrument directs.

In a typical trust, the grantor creates two types of beneficiaries: one who receives the accounting income of the trust (a concept defined in text Section 28-3a), and one who receives the trust corpus that remains at the termination of the trust as a legal entity. Beneficiaries in the former category hold an *income interest* in the trust, and those in the latter category hold a *remainder interest* in the trust's assets. If the grantor retains the remainder interest (e.g., for a trust for a minor beneficiary's education), the interest is known as a reversionary interest (corpus reverts to the grantor when the trust entity terminates).

The trust document establishes the term of the trust. The term may be for a specific number of years (*term certain*) or until the occurrence of a specified event. For instance, a trust might exist:

- For the life of the income beneficiary, in which case the income beneficiary is known as a *life tenant* in the trust corpus;
- For the life of some other individual (e.g., one's spouse);
- Until the income or remainder beneficiary reaches the age of majority; or
- Until the beneficiary, or another individual, marries, graduates, or reaches some specified age.

The trustee may be required to distribute the accounting income of the entity according to a distribution schedule specified in the agreement. Usually, though, the trustee is given more discretion with respect to the timing and nature of the distributions. If the trustee can determine, within guidelines found in the trust document, either the timing of the income or corpus distributions or the specific beneficiaries who will receive them (from among those identified in the agreement), the trust is called a discretionary or sprinkling trust. Here, the trustee can "sprinkle" the distributions among the various beneficiaries. As discussed in Chapter 27, family-wide income taxes can be reduced by directing income to those who are subject to lower marginal tax rates. Thus, by giving the trustee a sprinkling power, the income tax liability of the family unit can be manipulated by applying the terms of the trust agreement.

For purposes of certain provisions of Subchapter J, a trust is classified as either a simple trust or a complex trust. A simple trust:

- Is required to distribute its entire accounting income to designated beneficiaries every year,
- Has no beneficiaries that are qualifying charitable organizations, and
- Makes no distributions of trust corpus during the year.

A complex trust is any trust that is not a simple trust.[2] These criteria are applied to the trust every year. Thus, every trust is classified as a complex trust in the year in which it terminates (because it distributes all of its corpus during that year).

28-1b What Is an Estate?

An estate is created upon the death of every individual. The entity is charged with collecting and conserving all of the individual's assets, satisfying all liabilities, and distributing the remaining assets to the heirs identified by state law or the will.

Typically, the creation of an estate involves at least three parties: the decedent, all of whose probate assets are transferred to the estate for disposition; the executor, who is appointed under the decedent's valid will (or the administrator, if no valid will exists); and the beneficiaries of the estate, who are to receive assets or income from the entity, as the decedent has indicated in the will. Refer to Exhibit 28.2 for an illustration of these relationships.

An estate's operations are controlled by the probate laws of the decedent's state of residence and by the terms of the will as interpreted by the probate court. If the decedent did not execute a valid will, state law dictates who will carry out the executor's duties and which beneficiaries will receive which of the decedent's net assets.

An estate is a separate legal and taxable entity. The termination date of the estate is somewhat discretionary, since it occurs when all of the assets and income of the decedent have been distributed, all estate and decedent liabilities have been satisfied, and all other business of the entity is completed. Thus, there may be an incentive to use the estate as part of an income-shifting strategy (e.g., where the income beneficiaries are subject to low marginal tax rates).

Maria dies, and her estate holds a high-yield investment portfolio. Paulo, the income beneficiary, is subject to a 15% marginal state and Federal income tax rate, and Julia, the remainder beneficiary, is subject to a 30% marginal rate. The tax adviser might suggest that Maria's estate delay its final distribution of assets by a year or more to take advantage of the income tax reduction that is available from Paulo's low rates, before the entity terminates.

EXAMPLE 1

If an estate's existence is unduly prolonged, however, the IRS can terminate it for Federal income tax purposes after the expiration of a reasonable period for completing the duties of administration.[3]

28-2 NATURE OF TRUST AND ESTATE TAXATION

Subchapter J produces a significant amount of income tax revenue. More than 3.1 million Forms 1041 are filed every year, and these returns reflect the following approximate aggregate amounts.

- Gross income of over $140 billion.
- Taxable income of about $70 billion.
- Tax liability of almost $24 billion.

For most fiduciaries, almost 70 percent of income is in the form of capital gains and dividends. The remaining income tends to be interest, rents, and royalties, in addition to pass-through amounts from partnerships and other fiduciaries.

In general, the taxable income of a trust or an estate is taxed to the entity or to its beneficiaries to the extent that each has received the accounting income of the entity. Thus, the Federal income tax law creates a modified pass-through principle relative to the income taxation of trusts, estates, and their beneficiaries. Whoever receives the accounting income of the entity, or some portion of it, is liable for the income tax that results.

---

[2]Reg. § 1.651(a)–1. [3]Reg. § 1.641(b)–3(a).

EXAMPLE 2

Adam receives 80% of the accounting income of the Zero Trust. The trustee accumulated the other 20% of the income at her discretion under the trust agreement and added it to trust corpus. Adam is liable for income tax only on the amount of the distribution, and Zero is liable for the income tax on the accumulated portion of the income.

Concept Summary 28.1 summarizes the major similarities and differences between the taxation of trusts and estates and that of other **pass-through entities**—partnerships, limited liability entities, and S corporations.

Concept Summary 28.1

Tax Characteristics of Major Pass-Through Entities

Tax Treatment	Subchapter K (Partnerships, LLCs)	Subchapter S (S Corporations)	Subchapter J (Trusts, Estates)
Controlling documents	Partnership agreement, LLC operating agreement.	Corporate charter and bylaws.	Trust document or will, state fiduciary or probate law.
Taxing structure	Pure pass-through, only one level of Federal income tax.	Chiefly pass-through, usually one level of Federal income tax.	Modified pass-through, Federal income tax falls on the recipient(s) of entity accounting income.
Entity-level Federal income tax?	Never.	Rarely. See text Sections 22-3h, 22-3i, and 22-3j.	Yes, if the entity retains any net taxable income amounts.
Form for reporting income and expense pass-through	Schedules K and K–1, Form 1065.	Schedules K and K–1, Form 1120S.	Schedules K and K–1, Form 1041.
Subject to entity-level AMT?	No, but preferences and adjustments pass through to owners.	No, but preferences and adjustments pass through to owners.	Yes, if the entity retains any AMT-related accounting income amounts.
Subject to entity-level NIIT?	No, but amounts and types of income are reported to owners.	No, but amounts and types of income are reported to shareholders.	Yes, on income items retained by the entity (i.e., not distributed to beneficiaries).

28-2a Tax Accounting Periods and Methods

An estate or a trust may use many of the tax accounting methods available to individuals. The method of accounting used by the grantor of a trust or the decedent of an estate need not carry over to the entity.

An estate has the same options for choosing a tax year as any new taxpayer. Thus, the estate of a calendar year decedent dying on March 3 can select any fiscal year or report on a calendar year basis. To eliminate the possibility of deferring the taxation of fiduciary-source income simply by using a fiscal tax year, virtually all trusts (other than tax-exempt trusts) are required to use a calendar tax year.[4]

28-2b Tax Rates and Personal Exemption

Congress's desire to stop trusts from being used as income-shifting devices has made the fiduciary entity the highest-taxed taxpayer in the Code. The entity reaches the 37 percent marginal Federal income tax rate in 2020 once taxable income exceeds $12,950, so the grantor's ability to shift income in a tax-effective manner is nearly eliminated. Exhibit 28.3, which lists the 2020 Federal income taxes paid by various entities on taxable income of $50,000, shows how different the applicable marginal tax

EXHIBIT 28.3	Comparative Tax Liabilities		
Filing Status/Entity	**Taxable Income**	**Marginal Income Tax Rate (%)**	**2020 Federal Income Tax Liability**
Single	$50,000	22	$ 6,790
Married, filing jointly	50,000	12	5,605
C corporation	50,000	21	10,500
Trust or estate	50,000	37	16,838

rates are, and how expensive the taxes on an accumulation of income within an estate or a trust can be. Given the current tax rates for individuals, proper income shifting usually will move assets *out of* the estate or trust and into the hands of the lower-bracket grantor or beneficiary.

A fiduciary's dividend income and net long-term capital gain are taxed at a nominal rate of no more than 20 percent. In addition to the regular income tax, an estate or a trust may be subject to the alternative minimum tax and the additional tax on net investment income (discussed in text Sections 28-2c and 28-2d). Estimated tax payments must take into account any liabilities for these taxes.

Both trusts and estates are allowed a personal exemption in computing the fiduciary tax liability. All estates are allowed a personal exemption of $600. The exemption available to a trust depends upon the type of trust involved. A trust that is required to distribute all of its income currently is allowed an exemption of $300. All other trusts are allowed an exemption of $100 per year.[5]

The classification of trusts as to the appropriate personal exemption is similar but not identical to the distinction between simple and complex trusts. The classification as a simple trust is more stringent.

EXAMPLE 3

Three trusts appear to operate in a similar fashion, but they are subject to different Subchapter J classifications and exemptions.

Trust Alpha is required to distribute all of its current accounting income to Susan. Thus, it is allowed a $300 personal exemption. No corpus distributions or charitable contributions are made during the year. Accordingly, Alpha is a simple trust.

Trust Beta is required to distribute all of its current accounting income; it is allowed a $300 personal exemption. The beneficiaries of these distributions are specified in the trust instrument: one-half of accounting income is to be distributed to Tyrone, and one-half is to be distributed to State University, a qualifying charitable organization. Because Beta has made a charitable distribution for the tax year, it is a complex trust.

The trustee of Trust Gamma can, at her discretion, distribute the current-year accounting income or corpus of the trust to Dr. Chapman. Because the trustee is not required to distribute current accounting income, only a $100 personal exemption is allowed. During the current year, the trustee distributed all of the accounting income of the entity to Dr. Chapman, but made no corpus or charitable distributions. Nonetheless, because it lacks the current-year income distribution requirement, Gamma is a complex trust.

28-2c **Alternative Minimum Tax**

The alternative minimum tax (AMT) may apply to a trust or an estate in any tax year. Given the nature and magnitude of the modifications that determine the AMT base, however, most trusts and estates are unlikely to incur the tax.

---

[5]§ 642(b). Fiduciary exemption amounts are not indexed for inflation.

In general, derivation of the AMT base for the entity follows the rules that apply to individual taxpayers. A brief discussion of the computation and payment of the AMT is provided in Chapter 12.

The fiduciary's AMT is computed using Schedule I of Form 1041. Two full pages of the Form 1041 are dedicated to the computation of taxable income and other items when the AMT applies to the trust or estate. A minimum tax credit might be available in future years through these computations.

The entity claims a $25,400 annual AMT exemption. The exemption phases out at a rate of one-fourth of the amount by which AMTI exceeds $84,800. These amounts are indexed annually.

A 26 percent AMT rate is applied to AMTI, increasing to 28 percent when AMTI in excess of the exemption reaches $197,900.

28-2d **Additional Tax on Net Investment Income**

Trusts and estates that are subject to the highest Federal income tax rate for the tax year must pay an additional tax to support the Medicare system, using Form 8960. This tax is 3.8 percent of the lesser of (A) the undistributed net investment income (NII) of the trust or (B) the excess (if any) of adjusted gross income (AGI) over $12,950 for 2020 ($12,750 for 2019).[6]

NII includes gross income (less deductions) from interest, dividends, royalties, rents, and passive activities. NII also includes net recognized gains from the disposition of assets producing such income (e.g., capital gains). NII items make up about 90 percent of income items for many investment-oriented fiduciary entities. The NII tax (NIIT) is in addition to the entity's ordinary income tax (maximum rate 37 percent) and net capital gains tax (maximum rate 20 percent).

EXAMPLE
4

The Zeta Trust reports $20,000 of net investment income (NII) and $30,000 in net profits from an active business operation for 2020. Zeta retains all of the business profits but, under the terms of the trust agreement, distributes $5,000 cash from the NII to its sole beneficiary Victoria. Zeta's liability under the additional tax on NII is $570 (3.8% × $15,000 undistributed NII). Undistributed NII is less than the excess of Zeta's AGI over $12,950.

LO.2

Identify the steps in determining the accounting and taxable income of a trust or an estate and the related taxable income of the beneficiaries.

28-3 **TAXABLE INCOME OF TRUSTS AND ESTATES**

Generally, the taxable income of an estate or a trust is computed similarly to that for an individual. Fiduciary income tax rules, however, include several important exceptions and provisions that make it necessary to use a systematic approach to calculate the taxable income of these entities. Exhibit 28.4 illustrates the procedure implied by the Code, and Exhibit 28.5 presents a systematic computation method followed in this chapter.

28-3a **Entity Accounting Income**

Step 1 in determining the taxable income of a trust or an estate is to compute the entity's accounting income for the period. Although this prerequisite is not apparent from a cursory reading of Subchapter J, a closer look at the Code reveals a number of references to the *income* of the entity.[7] Wherever the term *income* is used in this part of the Code without some modifier (e.g., *gross* income or *taxable* income), the statute is referring to the accounting income of the trust or estate for the tax year.

A definition of entity accounting income is critical to understanding the computation of fiduciary taxable income. Usually, entity accounting income is the amount the income beneficiary of the trust or estate is eligible to receive from the entity. More importantly, the calculation of accounting income is virtually under the control of the grantor or decedent (through a properly drafted trust agreement or will). If the document has been drafted at arm's length, a court will enforce a fiduciary's good faith efforts to carry out the specified computation of accounting income.

---

[6]This dollar amount is indexed annually. The "AGI" of a trust is similar to the AGI of an individual with a few variations, such as a deduction for certain administrative expenses. See § 67(e).

[7]For example, see §§ 651(a)(1), 652(a), and 661(a)(1).

| EXHIBIT 28.4 | Accounting Income, Distributable Net Income, and Taxable Income of the Entity and Its Beneficiaries—The Five-Step Procedure |

Step 1
Determine the accounting income of the entity

Step 2
Compute entity taxable income before the distribution deduction

Step 3
Determine distributable net income (DNI) and the distribution deduction

Step 4
Compute entity taxable income (step 2 less the deduction determined in step 3)

Step 5
Allocate DNI and its character to the beneficiaries. Use the tier system, if necessary.

| EXHIBIT 28.5 | Computational Template Applying the Five-Step Procedure |

Item	Totals	Accounting Income	Taxable Income	Distributable Net Income/Distribution Deduction
Income	_____	_____	_____	
Income	_____	_____	_____	
Expense	_____	_____	_____	
Expense	_____	_____	_____	
Personal exemption			_____	
Accounting income/taxable income before the distribution deduction		_____	_____	_____
		Step 1	*Step 2*	
Personal exemption				_____
Corpus capital gain/loss				_____
Net tax-exempt income				_____
Distributable net income				_____
Distribution deduction			_____ *Step 3*	
Entity taxable income			_____ *Step 4*	

Beneficiary taxable income is addressed in **step 5**.

Entity accounting income generally is defined by state laws that are derived from the Uniform Principal and Income Act (latest major revision, 1997). Most states have adopted some form of the Uniform Act, which essentially constitutes generally accepted accounting principles (GAAP) in the fiduciary tax setting.

When specific items of income and expenditure are allocated either to the income beneficiaries or to corpus, the desires of the grantor or decedent are put into effect. Exhibit 28.6 shows typical assignments of revenue and expenditure items to fiduciary income or corpus. Examples 5 through 7 illustrate that the amounts received by beneficiaries can vary widely due to changes in these allocations under the terms of the trust agreement.

Where the controlling document is silent as to whether an item should be assigned to income or corpus, state fiduciary law prevails. These allocations are an important determinant of the benefits received from the entity by its beneficiaries and the timing of those benefits.

Entity Accounting Income

EXAMPLE 5

The Arnold Trust is a simple trust. Mrs. Bennett is its sole beneficiary. In the current year, the trust earns $20,000 in taxable interest and $15,000 in tax-exempt interest. In addition, the trust recognizes an $8,000 long-term capital gain. The trustee assesses a fee of $11,000 for the year.

If the trust agreement allocates fees and capital gains to corpus, trust accounting income is $35,000 and Mrs. Bennett receives that amount. Thus, the income beneficiary receives no immediate benefit from the trust's capital gain, and she bears none of the financial burden of the fiduciary's fees.

Interest income	$35,000
Long-term capital gain	+ –0–*
Fiduciary's fees	– –0–*
Trust accounting income	$35,000

*Allocable to corpus.

EXAMPLE 6

Assume the same facts as in Example 5, except that the trust agreement allocates the fiduciary's fees to income. The trust accounting income is $24,000, and Mrs. Bennett receives that amount.

Interest income	$35,000
Long-term capital gain	+ –0–*
Fiduciary's fees	−11,000
Trust accounting income	$24,000

*Allocable to corpus.

EXAMPLE 7

Assume the same facts as in Example 5, except that the trust agreement allocates to income all capital gains and losses and one-half of the trustee's commissions. The trust accounting income is $37,500, and Mrs. Bennett receives that amount.

Interest income	$35,000
Long-term capital gain	+8,000
Fiduciary's fees	−5,500*
Trust accounting income	$37,500

*One-half allocable to corpus.

EXHIBIT 28.6	Common Allocations of Items to Income or Corpus

Allocable to Income	Allocable to Corpus
Ordinary and operating net income from trust assets	Depreciation on business assets
	Casualty gain/loss on income-producing assets
Interest, dividend, rent, and royalty income	Insurance recoveries on income-producing assets
Stock dividends	Capital gain/loss on investment assets
One-half of fiduciary fees/commissions	Adjustments due to stock splits
	One-half of fiduciary fees/commissions

28-3b Gross Income

The gross income of an estate or a trust is similar to that of an individual. In determining the gain or loss to be recognized by an estate or a trust upon the sale or other taxable disposition of assets, the rules for basis determination are similar to those applicable to other taxpayers. Thus, an estate's basis for property received from a decedent is stepped up or stepped down to the gross estate valuation (refer to Chapters 13 and 27 for a more detailed discussion). Property received as a gift during the donor's lifetime (e.g., in irrevocable trust arrangements) usually takes the donor's basis. Property purchased by the trust from a third party is assigned a basis equal to the purchase price.

Noncash Property Distributions

In general, the fiduciary entity does not recognize gain or loss upon its distribution of property to a beneficiary under the provisions of the will or trust document. The distributed property has the same basis to the beneficiary of the distribution as it did to the estate or trust. Moreover, the distribution absorbs distributable net income (DNI) and qualifies for a distribution deduction (both of which are explained in text Sections 28-3f and 28-4) to the extent of the lesser of the distributed asset's basis to the beneficiary or the asset's fair market value as of the distribution date.[8]

The Big Picture

EXAMPLE 8

Return to the facts of *The Big Picture* on p. 28-1. Assume that Anna has established the Jiang Family Trust. The trust distributes a painting (basis of $40,000 and fair market value of $90,000) to beneficiary Sally. Sally's basis in the painting is $40,000. The distribution absorbs $40,000 of the Jiang Family Trust's DNI, and the trust claims a $40,000 distribution deduction relative to the transaction.

A trustee or an executor can elect for the entity to recognize gain or loss with respect to all of its in-kind property distributions for the year. If the election is made, the beneficiary's basis in the asset is equal to the asset's fair market value as of the distribution date. The distribution absorbs DNI and qualifies for a distribution deduction to the extent of the asset's fair market value. However, the related-party rules can restrict an estate's or trust's deduction for such losses. Generally, related parties include a trust, its trustee, its grantor, and its beneficiaries, as well as an estate, its executor, and its beneficiaries.

Distributing Property

EXAMPLE 9

The Green Estate distributes an antique piano, basis to Green of $10,000 and fair market value of $15,000, to beneficiary Kyle. The executor elects that Green recognize the related $5,000 gain on the distribution. Accordingly, Kyle's basis in the piano is $15,000 ($10,000 basis to Green + $5,000 gain recognized). The election likely increased the Federal income tax paid related to the gain: Green almost certainly is subject to a higher marginal income tax rate than is Kyle. Without the election, Green would not recognize any gain, and Kyle's basis in the piano would be $10,000.

[8]§ 643(e).

Distributing Property

EXAMPLE 10

Assume the same facts as in Example 9, except that Green's basis in the piano is $18,000. The executor elects that Green be assigned the related $3,000 loss on the distribution. Accordingly, Kyle's basis in the piano is $15,000 ($18,000 − $3,000). Without the election, Kyle's basis in the piano would be $18,000.

The estate cannot deduct this loss, however. Because an estate and its beneficiaries are related parties, realized losses cannot be recognized immediately.[9] Instead, the disallowed loss can be recognized if Kyle later sells the piano to an unrelated party.

Income in Respect of a Decedent

The gross income of a trust or an estate includes **income in respect of a decedent (IRD)** that the entity received.[10] For a cash basis decedent, IRD includes accrued salary, interest, rent, and other income items that were not constructively received before death. For both cash and accrual basis decedents, IRD includes, for instance, death benefits from qualified retirement plans and deferred compensation contracts.

The tax consequences of IRD can be summarized as follows.

- The fair market value of the right to IRD on the appropriate valuation date is included in the decedent's gross estate. Thus, it is subject to the Federal estate tax.[11]

- The decedent's basis in the property carries over to the recipient (the estate or heirs). There is no step-up or step-down in the basis of IRD items.

- The recipient of the income recognizes gain or loss, measured by the difference between the amount realized and the adjusted basis of the IRD in the hands of the decedent. The character of the gain or loss matches the treatment that it would have received had it been realized by the decedent before death. Thus, if the decedent would have realized capital gain, the recipient must do likewise.

- Expenses related to the IRD (such as interest, taxes, and depletion) that were not deducted on the final income tax return of the decedent may be claimed by the recipient of the IRD. These items are known as **deductions in respect of a decedent**. Typically, such deductions also include fiduciary fees, commissions paid to dispose of estate assets, and state income taxes payable. They are deductible on the estate tax return *and* on the IRD recipient's income tax return, *for* or *from* adjusted gross income (AGI) as would have been the case for the decedent.

Working with IRD

EXAMPLE 11

Amanda died on July 13 of the current year. On August 2, the estate received a check (before withholdings) for $1,200 from Amanda's former employer; this was Amanda's compensation for the last pay period of her life. On November 23, the estate received a $45,000 distribution from the qualified profit sharing plan of Amanda's employer, the full amount to which Amanda was entitled under the plan. Both Amanda and the estate are calendar year, cash basis taxpayers.

The last salary payment and the profit sharing plan distribution constitute IRD to the estate. Amanda had earned these items during her lifetime, and the estate was to receive each of them after Amanda's death. Consequently, the gross estate includes $46,200 with respect to these two items. However, the income tax basis to the estate for these items is not stepped up (from zero to $1,200 and $45,000, respectively) upon distribution to the estate.

In addition, the estate must report gross income of $46,200 for the current tax year with respect to the IRD items [$1,200 + $45,000 (amounts realized) − $0 (adjusted bases)].

---

[9]§ 267(b)(13).

[10]See § 691 and the Regulations thereunder. The concept of IRD was introduced in Chapter 27.

[11]To mitigate the effect of double taxation (imposition of both the estate tax and the income tax), § 691(c) allows the recipient an income tax deduction for the incremental estate tax attributable to the net IRD.

Working with IRD

EXAMPLE 12

Assume the same facts as in Example 11. Amanda's last paycheck was reduced by $165 for state income taxes that were withheld by the employer. The $165 tax payment is a deduction in respect of a decedent and is allowed as a deduction on *both* Amanda's estate tax return *and* the estate's income tax return.

Including the IRD in both the taxpayer's gross estate and the gross income of the estate may seem harsh. Nevertheless, the tax consequences of IRD are similar to the treatment that applies to all of a taxpayer's earned income. The item is subject to income tax upon receipt, and to the extent it is not consumed by the taxpayer before death, it is included in the gross estate.

ETHICS & EQUITY To Whom Can I Trust My Pet?

Humane societies encourage the general public to care for their own pets and to adopt those who need owners. It is not uncommon to find provisions in a will to establish a trust or an endowment to care for the pets that the deceased leaves behind. After all, over 65 percent of all individuals live with a pet and about $70 billion is spent each year in caring for these companions.

Boilerplate legal language is available to establish a pet-assistance trust. The trust should provide a guaranteed distribution for pet care, including the costs of pet sitters, kennels, and veterinary fees. A few states (e.g., Kentucky and Minnesota) do not recognize such trusts, however.

When decedents establish permanent funds to provide for a favorite pet, the surviving (human) family members may not be so enthused. In a few cases, the survivors challenge the terms of the will or trust, often requesting that a judge downsize the principal amount involved or reduce the specified annual distributions. In this way, the human heirs benefit from any adjustment that is made.

How would you advise a client who wants to establish a well-funded trust to care for Fifi when the family members have income and asset needs of their own?

28-3c Ordinary Deductions

As a general rule, the taxable income of an estate or a trust is similar to that of an individual.[12] Deductions are allowed for ordinary and necessary expenses paid or incurred in carrying on a trade or business; for the production or collection of income; for the management, conservation, or maintenance of property; and in connection with the determination, collection, or refund of any tax.

Reasonable administration expenses, including fiduciary fees, tax preparation costs, appraisal fees, investment advisory fees for services beyond what an individual investor would need, and legal costs in connection with the duties of administration, also can be deductible. Business interest deductions are deductible up to 30 percent of related taxable income. State and local taxes not related to a business are deductible up to $10,000.[13]

Expenses attributable to the production or collection of tax-exempt income are not deductible.[14] The amount of the disallowed deduction is found by using a formula based on the composition of the income elements of entity accounting income for the year of the deduction. The deductibility of the fees is determined strictly by the usual Federal income tax rules, and the allocation of expenditures to income and to corpus is controlled by the trust agreement or will or by state law.

EXAMPLE 13

The Silver Trust operates a business and invests idle cash in marketable securities. Its sales proceeds for the current year are $180,000. Expenses for wages, cost of sales, and office administration are $80,000. Interest income recognized is $20,000 from taxable bonds and $50,000 from tax-exempt bonds. The trustee claims a $35,000 fee for its activities. According to the trust agreement, $30,000 of this amount is allocated to the income beneficiaries, and $5,000 is allocated to corpus. Entity accounting income is computed as follows.

continued

---

[12]§ 641(b).

[13]§§ 162, 163(j), 164(b)(6)(B), and 212. Reg. § 1.67–4(b).

[14]§ 265.

Sales proceeds	$180,000
Business expenses	(80,000)
Interest income (from all sources)	70,000
Fiduciary's fees, as allocated	(30,000)
Trust accounting income	$140,000

In computing the trust's taxable income, the sales proceeds are included in gross income under § 61. The costs associated with the business are deductible in full under § 162. The taxable interest income is included in Silver's gross income under § 61, but the tax-exempt interest is excluded under § 103. The fiduciary's fees are deductible by Silver under § 212, but a portion of the deduction is lost because § 265 prohibits deductions for expenses incurred in the generation of tax-exempt income.

As shown below, 50/250 of the fees of $35,000 can be traced to tax-exempt income, so $7,000 of the fees is nondeductible. For purposes of the computation, only the income elements of the year's trust accounting income are included in the denominator. Moreover, the allocation of portions of the fees to income and to corpus is irrelevant in the calculation. The disallowed deduction for fiduciary's fees is computed in the following manner.

$$\$35,000^{*}(\text{total fees paid}) \times \frac{\$50,000^{**}\ (\textit{tax-exempt}\ \text{income elements of trust accounting income})}{\$250,000^{**}\ (\textit{all}\ \text{income elements of trust accounting income})}$$

$$= \$7,000\ (\text{amount disallowed})$$

*All fees, and not just those that are allocated to income, are deductible by the trust under § 212.
**The numerator and denominator of this fraction are *not* reduced by expense items allocable to income (e.g., cost of sales).

Silver is a complex trust and makes no distributions to beneficiaries for the year. Silver's taxable income for the year is computed as follows.

Sales proceeds	$180,000
Deductible expenses	(80,000)
Taxable interest income	20,000
Fiduciary's fees, as reduced	(28,000)
Personal exemption	(100)
Taxable income	$ 91,900

Amounts deductible as administration expenses or losses for estate tax purposes cannot be claimed by the estate for income tax purposes unless the estate waives the estate tax deduction. Although these expenses cannot be deducted twice, they may be allocated as the fiduciary sees fit between Forms 706 and 1041; they need not be claimed in their entirety on either return.[15]

Trusts and estates are allowed cost recovery deductions. Such deductions are assigned proportionately among the recipients of the entity accounting income.[16]

Cost Recovery Deductions

EXAMPLE 14

Lisa and Martin are the equal income beneficiaries of the Needle Trust. Under the terms of the trust agreement, the trustee has complete discretion as to the timing of the distributions from Needle's current accounting income. The trust agreement allocates all depreciation expense to income. In the current year, the trustee distributes 40% of the current trust accounting income to Lisa and 40% to Martin; thus, 20% of the income is accumulated. The depreciation deduction allowable to Needle is $100,000. This deduction is allocated among the trust and its beneficiaries on the basis of the distribution of current accounting income: Lisa and Martin each claim a $40,000 deduction, and the trust can deduct $20,000.

EXAMPLE 15

Assume the same facts as in Example 14, except that the trust agreement allocates all depreciation expense to corpus. There is no change in the tax result; Lisa and Martin both still claim a $40,000 depreciation deduction, and Needle retains its $20,000 deduction. The Code assigns the depreciation deduction proportionately to the recipients of entity accounting income. Allocation of depreciation to income or to corpus is irrelevant in determining which party can properly claim the deduction.

---

[15]Reg. § 1.642(g)–2.   [16]§§ 167(h) and 611(b)(3) and (4).

If the entity operates a trade or business, the income beneficiaries of a fiduciary entity may qualify for the 20 percent deduction for qualified business income (QBI); see text Section 15-3. The trust or estate will report to the beneficiaries all information necessary for those parties to compute the deduction, such as QBI and W–2 wages. Such items are allocated to the beneficiaries proportionate to the amount of distributable net income (see text Section 28-3f) that they receive.[17] This means that the entity will claim its own QBI deduction if it retains some of the DNI for the tax year.

28-3d Deductions for Losses

An estate or a trust is allowed an income tax deduction for casualty or theft losses related to its assets that are not reimbursed by insurance or other arrangements. Such losses may also be deductible on a Federal estate tax return.[18] An estate is not allowed an income tax deduction unless the estate tax deduction is waived.

The net operating loss (NOL) deduction is available for estates and trusts (i.e., where trade or business income is generated). No more than 80 percent of entity taxable income can be offset by the NOL; see text Section 17-1j. The net capital losses of an estate or a trust can be claimed by the fiduciary. The tax treatment of these losses is the same as for individual taxpayers.

Fiduciary entities are subject to the passive activity loss limitations; passive activity losses can be deducted by the trust or estate only against income from passive activities. Excess business losses are not currently deductible to the extent they exceed $259,000 (in 2020).

28-3e Charitable Contributions

An estate or a complex trust is allowed a deduction for contributions from the gross income of the current tax year to charitable organizations under certain conditions.[19]

- The contribution is made pursuant to the will or trust instrument, and its amount is determinable using the language of that document.

- The recipient is a qualified organization. For this purpose, qualified organizations include the same charities for which individual and corporate donors are allowed deductions, except that estates and trusts also are permitted a deduction for contributions to certain foreign charitable organizations.

- Generally, the contribution is claimed in the tax year it is paid, but a fiduciary can treat amounts paid in the year immediately following as a deduction for the preceding year. Under this rule, estates and complex trusts may receive more favorable treatment than do individuals or C corporations.

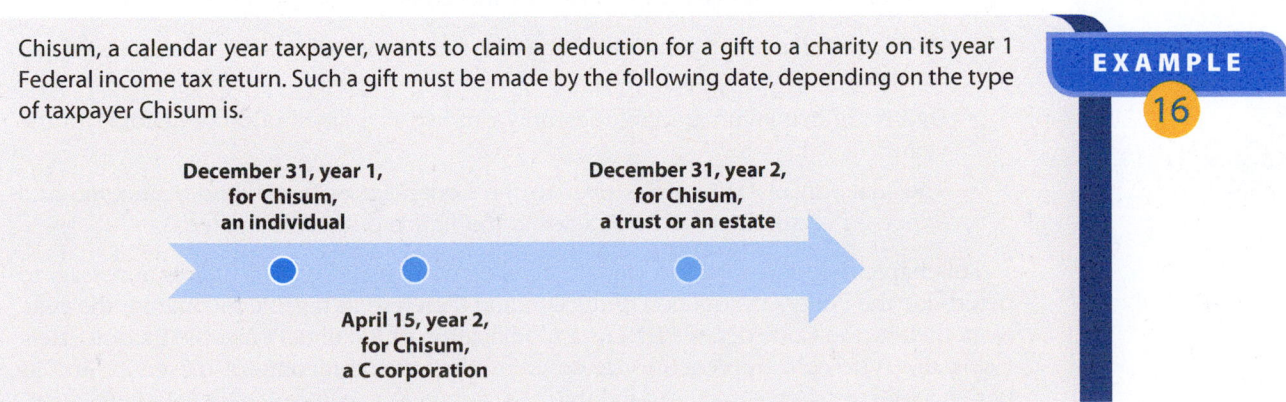

EXAMPLE 16

Chisum, a calendar year taxpayer, wants to claim a deduction for a gift to a charity on its year 1 Federal income tax return. Such a gift must be made by the following date, depending on the type of taxpayer Chisum is.

December 31, year 1, for Chisum, an individual

December 31, year 2, for Chisum, a trust or an estate

April 15, year 2, for Chisum, a C corporation

Unlike the charitable contribution deductions of individuals and corporations, the deductions of estates and complex trusts are not limited in amount (e.g., to a percentage of taxable or adjusted gross income). Nonetheless, the deduction is limited to amounts that have been included in the gross income of the entity.

---

[17]Reg. § 1.199A–6(d).

[18]§ 2054.

[19]§ 642(c)(1) and Reg. §§ 1.642(c)–1 and –3. But see *Green v. U.S.*,121 AFTR 2d 2018–427, 2018–1 USTC ¶50,126, 880 F.3d 519 (CA–10).

The deduction for a gift of a noncash asset is limited to that asset's basis to the fiduciary. A contribution is deemed to be made proportionately from each of the income elements of entity accounting income. However, if the will or trust agreement requires that the contribution be made from a specific type of income, or from income from a specified asset, the allocation of the contribution to taxable and tax-exempt income is not required.

The Big Picture

EXAMPLE 17

Return to the facts of *The Big Picture* on p. 28-1. Again assume that Anna has established the Jiang Family Trust. The trust reports gross rent income of $80,000, expenses attributable to the rents of $60,000, and tax-exempt interest from state bonds of $20,000. Under the trust agreement, the trustee is to pay 30% of the annual trust accounting income to the United Way, a qualifying organization. Accordingly, the trustee pays $12,000 to the charity (i.e., 30% × $40,000). The charitable contribution deduction allowed is $9,600 [($80,000/$100,000) × $12,000], even if the payment to the charity is not made until the following tax year.

The Big Picture

EXAMPLE 18

Assume the same facts as in Example 17, except that the trust instrument also requires that the contribution be paid from the net rent income. The agreement controls, and the allocation formula need not be applied. The entire $12,000 is allowed as a charitable deduction.

LO.3

Illustrate the uses and implications of distributable net income.

28-3f Deduction for Distributions to Beneficiaries

The modified pass-through approach of Subchapter J is embodied in the deduction allowed to trusts and estates for the distributions made to beneficiaries during the year. Some portion of any distribution that a beneficiary receives from a trust may be subject to income tax on the beneficiary's own return. At the same time, the distributing entity is allowed a deduction for some or all of the distribution.

A good analogy is to the taxability of corporate profits distributed to employees as taxable wages. The corporation is allowed a deduction for the payment, but the employee receives gross income in the form of compensation.

Distributable Net Income

A critical value that is used in computing the amount of the entity's distribution deduction is **distributable net income (DNI)**. As it is defined in Subchapter J, DNI serves several functions. Concept Summary 28.2 illustrates these critical roles of DNI.

- DNI is the maximum amount of the distribution on which the beneficiaries can be taxed.[20]
- DNI is the maximum amount the entity can use as a distribution deduction for the year.[21]
- The makeup of DNI carries over to the beneficiaries (the items of income and expenses retain their DNI character in the hands of the distributees).[22]

Subchapter J defines DNI in a circular manner, however. The DNI value is necessary to determine the entity's distribution deduction and therefore its taxable income for the year. Nonetheless, the Code defines DNI as a modification of the entity's taxable income itself. Using the systematic approach to determining the taxable income of the entity and its beneficiaries, as shown earlier in Exhibit 28.4, compute *taxable income before the distribution deduction*, modify that amount to determine DNI and the distribution deduction, return to the calculation of *taxable income*, and apply the deduction that has resulted.

[20]§§ 652(a) and 662(a).
[21]§§ 651(b) and 661(c).
[22]§§ 652(b) and 662(b).

Concept Summary 28.2

Uses of the DNI Amount

Taxable income before the distribution deduction (step 2) includes all of the entity's items of gross income, deductions, gains, losses, and exemptions for the year.

Therefore, to compute this amount, (1) determine the appropriate personal exemption for the year and (2) account for all of the other gross income and deductions of the entity.

Step 3 in Exhibit 28.4 is the determination of *distributable net income*, computed by making the following adjustments to the entity's *taxable income before the distribution deduction*.[23]

- Add back the entity's personal exemption.
- Add back *net* tax-exempt interest; reduce the total tax-exempt interest by charitable contributions and by related expenses that are not deductible.
- Add back the entity's net capital losses.
- Subtract any net capital gains allocable to corpus. The only net capital gains included in DNI are those attributable to income beneficiaries or to charitable contributions.[24]

Distribution Deduction

DNI includes the net tax-exempt interest income of the entity, so that amount must be removed from DNI in computing the distribution deduction. Moreover, for estates and complex trusts, DNI and the distribution amount may not be the same; the amount actually distributed during the year may include discretionary distributions of income and distributions of corpus permissible under the will or trust instrument.

The distribution deduction for estates and complex trusts is computed as the lesser of (1) the deductible portion of DNI or (2) the taxable amount actually distributed to the beneficiaries during the year. For a simple trust, however, full distribution is always assumed, relative to both the entity and its beneficiaries, in a manner similar to the pass-through entities.

DNI and the distribution deduction are computed on the entity's Form 1041. The beneficiaries' Schedules K–1 report the allocations of income, deduction, and credit items to them.

---

[23]These and other (less common) adjustments are detailed in § 643.   [24]§ 643(a)(3).

DNI and Distribution Deduction

EXAMPLE 19

The Zinc Trust is a simple trust. Because of severe liquidity problems, its year 1 accounting income is not distributed to its sole beneficiary, Mark, until early in year 2. Zinc still is allowed a full distribution deduction for, and Mark still is taxed upon, the entity's year 1 income in year 1.

EXAMPLE 20

The Pork Trust is required to distribute its current accounting income annually to its sole income beneficiary, Barbosa. Capital gains and losses and all other expenses are allocable to corpus. In the current year, Pork incurs the following items.

Dividend income	$25,000
Taxable interest income	15,000
Tax-exempt interest income	20,000
Net long-term capital gain	10,000
Fiduciary fees	6,000

Item	Totals	Accounting Income	Taxable Income	Distributable Net Income/ Distribution Deduction
Dividend income	$25,000	$25,000	$ 25,000	
Taxable interest income	15,000	15,000	15,000	
Tax-exempt interest income	20,000	20,000		
Net long-term capital gain	10,000		10,000	
Fiduciary fees	6,000		(4,000)	
Personal exemption			(300)	
Accounting income/taxable income before the distribution deduction		$60,000	$ 45,700	$ 45,700
		Step 1	*Step 2*	
Personal exemption				300
Corpus capital gain/loss				(10,000)
Net tax-exempt income				18,000
Distributable net income				$ 54,000
Distribution deduction		*Step 3*	(36,000)	
Entity taxable income		*Step 4*	$ 9,700	

Step 1. Trust accounting income is $60,000; this includes the tax-exempt interest income, but not the fees or the capital gains, pursuant to the trust document. Barbosa receives $60,000 from the trust for the current year.

Step 2. Taxable income before the distribution deduction is computed as directed by the Code. The tax-exempt interest is excluded under § 103. Only a portion of the fees is deductible {[($60,000 − $20,000)/$60,000] × $6,000 = $4,000} because some of the fees ($6,000 − $4,000) are traceable to the tax-exempt income. The trust claims a $300 personal exemption, because it is required to distribute its annual trust accounting income.

Step 3. DNI and the distribution deduction reflect the required adjustments. The distribution deduction is the lesser of the distributed amount ($60,000) or the deductible portion of DNI [$54,000 − $18,000 (net tax-exempt income)].

Step 4. Finally, return to the computation of the taxable income of the Pork Trust. A simple test should be applied at this point to ensure that the proper figure for the trust's taxable income has been determined. On what is Pork to be taxed? Pork has distributed to Barbosa $60,000, which is all of its gross income except the $10,000 net long-term capital gain. The $300 personal exemption reduces Pork's taxable income to $9,700.

DNI and Distribution Deduction

The Quick Trust is required to distribute all of its current accounting income equally to its two beneficiaries, Faith Gonzalez and the Universal Church, a qualifying charitable organization. Capital gains and losses and depreciation expenses are allocable to income. Fiduciary fees are allocable to corpus. In the current year, Quick incurs various items as indicated.

EXAMPLE
21

Item	Totals	Accounting Income	Taxable Income	Distributable Net Income/ Distribution Deduction
Rent income	$100,000	$100,000	$100,000	
Expenses—rent income	30,000	(30,000)	(30,000)	
Depreciation—rent income	15,000	(15,000)		
Net long-term capital gain	20,000	20,000	20,000	
Charitable contribution			(37,500)	
Fiduciary fees	18,000		(18,000)	
Personal exemption			(300)	
Accounting income/taxable income before the distribution deduction		$ 75,000	$ 34,200	$34,200
		Step 1	*Step 2*	
Personal exemption				300
Corpus capital gain/loss				
Net tax-exempt income				
Distributable net income				$34,500
Distribution deduction		*Step 3*	(34,500)	
Entity taxable income		*Step 4*	($ 300)	

Step 1. Trust accounting income of $75,000 reflects the indicated allocations of items to income and to corpus. Each income beneficiary receives $37,500.

Step 2. In the absence of tax-exempt income, a deduction is allowed for the full amount of the fiduciary's fees. Quick is a complex trust, but because it is required to distribute its full accounting income annually, a $300 exemption is allowed. Properly, the trust does not deduct any depreciation for the rental property. The depreciation deduction is available only to the recipients of the entity's accounting income for the period. Thus, the deduction is split equally between Faith and the church. The deduction probably is of no direct value to the church, a tax-exempt organization. The trust's charitable contribution deduction is based on the $37,500 the charity actually received (one-half of trust accounting income).

Step 3. Because there is no tax-exempt income, the only adjustment needed to compute DNI is to add back the trust's personal exemption. Subchapter J requires no adjustment for the charitable contribution. DNI is computed only from the perspective of Faith, who also received $37,500 from the trust.

Step 4. Perform the simple test (referred to in the previous example) to ensure that the proper taxable income for the Quick Trust has been computed. All of the trust's gross income has been distributed to Faith and the charity. As is the case with most trusts that distribute all of their accounting income, the Quick Trust "wastes" the personal exemption.

28-3g **Tax Credits**

Available tax credits are apportioned between the estate or trust and the beneficiaries on the basis of the entity accounting income allocable to each.

Concept Summary 28.3 outlines the principles underlying the Federal taxation of estates and trusts.

Concept Summary 28.3

Principles of Fiduciary Income Taxation

1. Estates and trusts are temporary entities created to locate, maintain, and distribute assets and to satisfy liabilities according to the wishes of the decedent or grantor as expressed in the will or trust document.

2. Generally, the estate or trust acts as a conduit of the taxable income that it receives. To the extent the income is distributed by the entity, it is taxed to the beneficiary. Taxable income retained by the entity is taxed to the entity itself.

3. The entity's accounting income first must be determined. Accounting conventions that are stated in the controlling document or, lacking such provisions, in state law allocate specific items of receipt and expenditure either to income or to corpus. Income beneficiaries typically receive payments from the entity equal to the accounting income.

4. The taxable income of the entity is computed using the template in Exhibit 28.4. The entity usually recognizes income in respect of a decedent.

5. Deductions for fiduciary's fees and for charitable contributions may be reduced if the entity received any tax-exempt income during the year.

6. Business deductions are allowed, including the QBI and NOL deductions, if the entity operates a trade or business. Deductions may be limited for business losses, business interest, passive activity losses, and state and local taxes. Cost recovery deductions are assigned proportionately to the recipients of accounting income.

7. Upon election, realized gain or loss on assets that are properly distributed in kind can be recognized by the entity.

28-4 TAXATION OF BENEFICIARIES

The beneficiaries of an estate or a trust receive taxable income from the entity under the modified pass-through principle of fiduciary income taxation. Distributable net income determines the maximum amount that can be taxed to the beneficiaries for any tax year. The constitution of DNI also carries over to the beneficiaries (e.g., net long-term capital gains and dividends retain their character when they are distributed from the entity to the beneficiary).

A beneficiary includes in gross income an amount based upon the DNI of the trust for any taxable year or years of the entity ending with or within his or her taxable year.[25] These amounts are reported to the beneficiary on the Form 1041, Schedule K–1.

28-4a Distributions by Simple Trusts

The amount taxable to the beneficiaries of a trust is limited by the trust's DNI. However, because DNI includes net tax-exempt income, the amount included in the gross income of the beneficiaries could be less than DNI. When there is more than one income beneficiary, the elements of DNI are apportioned ratably according to the amount required to be distributed currently to each.

EXAMPLE 22

A simple trust has ordinary income of $40,000, a long-term capital gain of $15,000 (allocable to corpus), and a trustee administrative expense of $4,000 (payable from corpus). The two income beneficiaries, Allie and Bart, are entitled to the trust's annual accounting income, based on shares of 75% and 25%, respectively.

Although Allie receives $30,000 as her share (75% × trust accounting income of $40,000), she is allocated DNI of only $27,000 (75% × $36,000). Likewise, Bart is entitled to receive $10,000 (25% × $40,000), but he is allocated DNI of only $9,000 (25% × $36,000). The $15,000 capital gain is taxed to the trust.

28-4b Distributions by Estates and Complex Trusts

Typically, an estate or a complex trust makes only discretionary distributions. In those cases, the DNI is apportioned ratably according to the distributed amounts as seen in Example 23.

A computational problem arises with estates and complex trusts when more than one beneficiary receives a distribution from the entity and the controlling document does not require a distribution of the entire accounting income of the entity.

---

[25]§§ 652(c) and 662(c).

The trustee of the Wilson Trust has the discretion to distribute the income or corpus of the trust in any proportion between the two beneficiaries of the trust, Wong and Washington. Under the trust instrument, Wong must receive $15,000 from the trust every year. In the current year, the trust's accounting income is $50,000, and its DNI is $40,000. The trustee pays $15,000 to Wong and $25,000 to Washington.

How is Wilson's DNI to be divided between Wong and Washington? Several arbitrary methods of allocating DNI between the beneficiaries could be devised. Subchapter J resolves the problem by creating a two-tier system to govern the taxation of beneficiaries in such situations.[26] The tier system determines which distributions will be included in the gross income of the beneficiaries in full, which will be included in part, and which will not be included at all.

First and Second Tiers

Income that is required to be distributed currently, whether or not it is distributed, is categorized as a *first-tier distribution*. All other discretionary amounts paid, credited, or distributed are *second-tier distributions*.[27] A formula is used to allocate DNI among the appropriate beneficiaries when only first-tier distributions are made and those amounts exceed DNI.

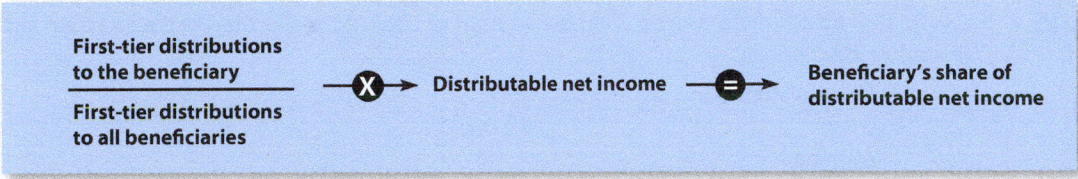

When both first-tier and second-tier distributions are made and the first-tier distributions exceed DNI, the above formula is applied to the first-tier distributions. In this case, none of the second-tier distributions are taxed, because all of the DNI has been allocated to the first-tier beneficiaries.

If both first-tier and second-tier distributions are made and the first-tier distributions do not exceed DNI, but the total of both first-tier and second-tier distributions does exceed DNI, the second-tier beneficiaries recognize income as shown below.

The trustee of the Gray Trust is required annually to distribute $10,000 each to Harriet and Wally, the two beneficiaries of the entity. In addition, the trustee can distribute other amounts of trust income or corpus at its sole discretion. In the current year, the trust reports accounting income of $60,000 and DNI of $50,000. However, the trustee distributes only the required $10,000 each to Harriet and to Wally. The balance of the income is accumulated and added to trust corpus.

In this case, only first-tier distributions have been made, but the total amount of the distributions does not exceed DNI for the year. Although DNI is the maximum amount included by the beneficiaries for the year, they can include no more in gross income than is distributed by the entity. Thus, both Harriet and Wally may be subject to tax on $10,000 as their proportionate shares of DNI.

---

[26]§§ 662(a)(1) and (2).   [27]Reg. §§ 1.662(a)−2 and −3.

Distributing DNI

EXAMPLE 25

Assume the same facts as in Example 24, except that DNI is $12,000. Harriet and Wally each receive $10,000, but they cannot be taxed in total on more than DNI. Each is taxed on $6,000 [DNI $12,000 × ($10,000/$20,000 of the first-tier distributions)].

EXAMPLE 26

Return to the facts in Example 23. Wong receives a first-tier distribution of $15,000. Now assume that second-tier distributions include $20,000 to Wong and $25,000 to Washington. Wilson's DNI is $40,000. Total distributions exceed the amount of DNI. The DNI is allocated between Wong and Washington as follows.

(1) **First-tier distributions**
    To Wong $15,000 DNI
    To Washington   –0–
    Remaining DNI = $25,000
(2) **Second-tier distributions**
    To Wong $11,111 DNI [(20/45) × $25,000]
    To Washington $13,889 DNI [(25/45) × $25,000]

EXAMPLE 27

Assume the same facts as in Example 26, except that accounting income is $80,000 and DNI is $70,000. Total distributions are less than the amount of DNI. DNI is allocated between Wong and Washington as follows.

(1) **First-tier distributions**
    To Wong $15,000 DNI
    To Washington   –0–
    Remaining DNI = $55,000
(2) **Second-tier distributions**
    To Wong $20,000 DNI
    To Washington $25,000 DNI

28-4c **Character of Income**

Consistent with the modified pass-through principle of Subchapter J, various classes of income (e.g., dividends, passive activity or portfolio gain and loss, AMT adjustments and preferences, tax-exempt interest) retain the same character for the beneficiaries that they had when they were received by the entity. If there are multiple beneficiaries *and* if all of the DNI is distributed, a problem arises in allocating the various classes of income among the beneficiaries.

Distributions are treated as consisting of the same proportion as the items that enter into the computation of DNI.

If the entity distributes only a part of its DNI, the amount of a specific class of DNI that is deemed distributed first must be determined.[28]

---
[28]Reg. § 1.662(b)–1.

DNI Flow-Throughs

The Baron Trust has DNI of $40,000, including the following: $10,000 of taxable interest, $10,000 of tax-exempt interest, and $20,000 of passive activity income. The trustee distributes, at her discretion, $8,000 to Mai and $12,000 to Nancy.

Beneficiary	Amount Received	Income Type		
		Taxable Interest	**Tax-Exempt Interest**	**Passive Activity Income**
Mai	$ 8,000	$2,000*	$2,000	$4,000
Nancy	12,000	3,000	3,000	6,000

*$8,000 distribution/$40,000 total DNI × $10,000 taxable interest in DNI.

EXAMPLE 28

Continue with the facts of Example 28. The character of the income that flows through to Mai and Nancy is effective for all other tax purposes. For instance, the $4,000 passive activity income that is allocated to Mai is available for offset against passive activity losses that she incurred from limited partnerships and rental activities for the year. Similarly, the $3,000 taxable interest income allocated to Nancy can be used to increase the amount of investment interest expense deductible by her in the year of the flow-through, and it may be subject to the net investment income tax. The interest is treated as if it had been received directly by the taxpayer.

EXAMPLE 29

Special Allocations

Under limited circumstances, the parties may modify the character-of-income allocation method set forth above. A modification is permitted only to the extent the allocation is required in the trust instrument and only to the extent it has an economic effect independent of the cash-flow and income tax consequences of the allocation.[29]

Return to the facts in Example 28. Assume that the beneficiaries are elderly individuals who have pooled their investment portfolios to avail themselves of the trustee's professional asset management skills. Suppose the trustee has the discretion to allocate different classes of income to different beneficiaries and she designates $10,000 of Nancy's $12,000 distribution as being from the tax-exempt income. Such a designation *would not be recognized* for tax purposes, and the allocation method of Example 28 must be used.

Suppose, however, the trust instrument stipulated that Nancy was to receive all of the income from the tax-exempt securities, because Nancy alone contributed the exempt securities to trust corpus. Under this provision, the $10,000 of the nontaxable interest is paid to Nancy. This allocation *is recognized*, and $10,000 of Nancy's distribution is tax-exempt.

EXAMPLE 30

28-5 PROCEDURAL MATTERS

The fiduciary is required to file a Form 1041 (U.S. Income Tax Return for Estates and Trusts) in the following situations.[30]

- For an estate that has gross income of $600 or more for the year.
- For a trust that either has any taxable income or, if there is no taxable income, has gross income of $600 or more.

The fiduciary return (and any related tax liability) is due no later than the fifteenth day of the fourth month following the close of the entity's taxable year. A filing extension

---

[29]Reg. § 1.652(b)–2(b). This is similar to the § 704(b)(2) requirement for partnerships. See text Section 21-4b.

[30]§§ 6012(a)(3) and (4).

is available to the last day of the ninth month after the end of the tax year. For calendar year entities, these dates are April 15 and September 30.

Many fiduciary entities recognize capital gains during the year, through sales of assets that are part of corpus. In that event, a Schedule D is filed with the Form 1041, and the fiduciary entity or its beneficiaries can qualify for the lower tax rates on long-term capital gains.

The pass-through of income and deduction items to the beneficiary is accomplished through Schedule K–1 to Form 1041. This form is similar in format and function to the Schedule K–1 for partners and S corporation shareholders (see Chapters 21 and 22). Because the typical fiduciary entity records only a few transactions during the year, the Schedule K–1 for Form 1041 is less detailed than those for Forms 1065 and 1120S.

Trusts and estates must make estimated Federal income tax payments using the same quarterly schedule that applies to individual taxpayers. This requirement applies to estates and grantor trusts only for tax years that end two or more years after the date of the decedent's death.[31]

Fiduciary entities also must determine filing requirements that must be met for each of the U.S. states. These matters may turn on the location of the entity, the trustee/executor, and the beneficiaries.

28-6 TAX PLANNING

LO.4

Apply the fiduciary income tax rules in a manner that minimizes the income taxation of trusts and estates and still accomplishes the intended objectives of the grantor or decedent.

Many of the tax planning possibilities for estates and trusts were discussed in Chapter 27. However, several specific tax planning possibilities are available to help minimize the present value of any income tax liabilities on estates and trusts and their beneficiaries.

28-6a A Trust or an Estate as an Income-Shifting Device

Opportunities to use fiduciary entities for effective income shifting from one individual to another are limited, because the kiddie tax might apply to the amounts received by the beneficiary, and the fiduciary is likely to be subject to a marginal tax rate that is equal to or higher than that of the grantor/decedent. Other strategies still should be considered by the parties.

- Trust corpus should be invested in growth assets that are low on yield but high on appreciation, so that the trustee can determine the timing of the gain and somewhat control the effective tax rate that applies.

- Trust corpus should be invested in tax-exempt securities such as municipal bonds and mutual funds that invest in them to eliminate the tax costs associated with the investment. If this approach is taken, a trust might be unnecessary—the parent should simply retain full control over the assets and invest in the tax-exempt securities in his or her own account.

- The grantor should retain high-yield assets, rather than contribute them to a fiduciary entity (i.e., where the tax cost is too high).

- Use of trust vehicles should be reserved for cases where professional management of the assets is necessary for portfolio growth and the additional tax costs can be justified.

28-6b Income Tax Planning for Estates

As a separate taxable entity, an estate can select its own tax year and accounting methods. The executor of an estate should consider selecting a fiscal year because this will determine when beneficiaries must include income distributions from the estate in their own tax returns. Beneficiaries must include the income for their tax year with or within which the estate's tax year ends. Proper selection of the estate's tax year can result in a smoothing out of income and a reduction of the income taxes for all parties involved.

---

[31]§ 6654(l)(2)(A).

The timing and amounts of income distributions to the beneficiaries present important tax planning opportunities. If the executor can make discretionary income distributions, he or she should evaluate the relative marginal income tax rates of the estate and its beneficiaries. By timing the distributions properly, the overall income tax liability can be minimized. Care should be taken, however, to time the distributions in light of the estate's DNI.

Distribution Strategies

For several years before his death on March 7, Don had entered into annual deferred compensation agreements with his employer. These agreements collectively called for the payment of $200,000 six months after Don's retirement or death. To provide a maximum 12-month period within which to generate deductions to offset this large item of income in respect of a decedent, the executor or administrator of the estate should elect a fiscal year ending August 31. The election is made simply by filing the estate's first tax return for the short period of March 7 to August 31.

EXAMPLE 31

Carol, the sole beneficiary of an estate, is a calendar year, cash basis taxpayer. If the estate elects a fiscal year ending January 31, all distributions during the period of February 1 to December 31, 2020, are reported on Carol's tax return for calendar year 2021 (due April 15, 2022). Thus, assuming that estimated tax requirements otherwise have been met, any income taxes that result from a $50,000 distribution made by the estate on February 20, 2020, may be deferred until April 15, 2022.

EXAMPLE 32

Assume the same facts as in Example 32. If the estate is closed on December 15, 2021, the DNI for both the fiscal year ending January 31, 2021, and the final tax year ending December 15, 2021, is included in Carol's tax return for the same calendar year. To avoid the effect of this bunching of income, the estate should not be closed until early in calendar year 2022.

EXAMPLE 33

In general, those beneficiaries who are subject to high income tax rates should be made beneficiaries of second-tier (but not IRD) distributions of the estate. Most likely, these individuals will have less need for an additional steady stream of (taxable) income while their income tax savings can be relatively large. Moreover, a special allocation of tax-favored types of income and expenses should be considered. For example, tax-exempt income can be directed more easily to beneficiaries in higher income tax brackets.

Review Examples 26 and 27 carefully. Note, for instance, the flexibility that is available to the executor or administrator in timing the second-tier distributions of income and corpus of the estate. To illustrate, if Washington is subject to a high tax rate, distributions to him should be minimized except in years when DNI is low. In this manner, Washington's exposure to gross income from the distributions can be controlled so that most of the distributions he receives will be free of income tax.

EXAMPLE 34

28-6c Distributions of In-Kind Property

The ability of the trustee or executor to elect to recognize the realized gain or loss relative to a distributed noncash asset allows the gain or loss to be allocated to the optimal taxpayer.

EXAMPLE 35

The Yorba Linda Estate distributed some inventory, basis of $40,000 and fair market value of $41,500, to beneficiary Larry. Yorba Linda is subject to a 24% marginal income tax rate, and Larry is subject to a 35% marginal rate. The executor of Yorba Linda should elect that the entity recognize the related $1,500 realized gain, thereby subjecting the gain to the estate's lower marginal tax rate.

Tax without election, at Larry's 35% rate	$525
Tax with election, at estate's 24% rate	360

ETHICS & EQUITY Who Should Be a Trustee?

Often, grantors choose a family member to be the trustee of the family savings, the children's education fund, or whatever other assets are placed into management by the trust. The relative chosen is often the most trusted but not always the one with the business skills. However, as the financial world has become more complex, with stock market fluctuations, increased fiduciary standards, and potential conflicts of interest, some question the wisdom of using a family member as the trustee.

Using a trust company or other financial institution as a trustee usually results in more stable (if lower) investment returns, eliminating both the highs and the lows of the stock market cycle. Institutions also can bring other advantages.

- They do not die, run away, become mentally or physically incapacitated, or otherwise unexpectedly become unqualified for the position.
- They are not easily swayed by emotional appeals; nor do they react to family jealousies.

- They are prohibited by law from acting under a conflict of interest, such as might exist between family members when the related trustee is also a trust beneficiary.

On the negative side, human trustees often waive or discount their fiduciary fee, but institutions do not. Especially for trusts with a small corpus, institutional trustees can be prohibitively expensive.

How would you advise a client to address this delicate issue? Compromise solutions might be to:

- Appoint co-trustees. Aunt Grace or Uncle Roberto can provide the personal touch and ensure that trust decisions recognize family needs, and the trust company maximizes investment returns and furnishes professional management.

- Keep the family trustee but hire professionals at an hourly rate, to provide advice only when needed. This approach avoids the fees based on asset values that trust companies usually charge.

28-6d Additional Taxes on Capital Gains and Net Investment Income

Aggressive income shifting among a fiduciary entity and its beneficiaries may be prompted by the fiduciary's exposure to the liabilities for additional Federal income taxes on capital gains and net investment income (NII). These additional taxes apply only to "high-income" taxpayers, but the income level at which the tax applies is much lower for fiduciaries than it is for individuals.

Thus, investment income and capital gains might best be distributed to individual beneficiaries, removing the items from the NII of the fiduciary, perhaps without creating an additional tax liability for the beneficiary.

The tax also can be reduced if the fiduciary invests in securities that produce tax-exempt or tax-deferred income or meets the material participation requirement for otherwise passive activities. In addition, the tax liability can be minimized if the entity invests in assets that produce a low yield (like growth stocks or funds) and if it arranges its portfolio to produce a low turnover rate.

SETTING UP A TRUST TO PROTECT A FAMILY

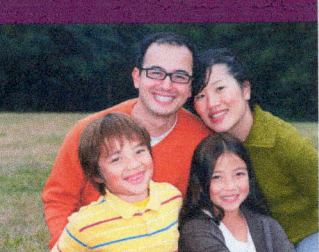

Anna Jiang and her family should consider the creation of one or more trusts to provide security in case Anna is incapacitated by medical problems and unable to manage the family's finances. Some suggestions for the family might be:

- Anna transfers some or all of the $2 million in assets to the Jiang Family Trust, with quarterly income payable to Tom and the children. Recipients would be designated by the trustee, but all of the entity's accounting income must be distributed. In this way, the income could be directed to the beneficiary most in need (e.g., to pay for education expenses or to start a new business). The children could be named first-tier beneficiaries, with Tom as a second-tier income beneficiary.

- While Anna is still healthy and earning a regular salary, the trustee could accumulate the accounting income and allow the corpus to grow. Alternatively, the trustee could make gifts to charity or fund education plans for Bobby and Sally.

- Anna should provide clear instructions to the trustee as to her preferences on how the trust corpus should be invested and specify which of Tom's and the children's expenses should and should not be covered.

- The children should be named as remainder beneficiaries of the Jiang Family Trust. In case the trust corpus exceeds the estate tax bypass amount, other remainder beneficiaries could be named to avoid any generation-skipping tax (see Chapter 27).

- Amendments to the trust document should be considered whenever Tom and Anna update their wills.

What If?

If Anna remains healthy, the Jiang Family Trust might be terminated when the children reach the age of majority, as their need for financial support will have diminished. However, if Tom is unable or unwilling to take over management of the assets, the trust should continue. In this event, the trustee should be chosen from family members or business associates who know Anna and Tom well and are familiar with the couple's objectives. Then the trustee might shift the focus to funding long-term care for the couple, making charitable gifts, or financing the education needs of grandchildren.

Key Terms

Complex trust, 28-4

Corpus, 28-4

Deductions in respect of a decedent, 28-12

Distributable net income (DNI), 28-16

Entity accounting income, 28-8

Fiduciary, 28-2

Grantor, 28-3

Grantor trust, 28-4

Income in respect of a decedent (IRD), 28-12

Pass-through entities, 28-6

Reversionary interest, 28-4

Simple trust, 28-4

Sprinkling trust, 28-4

Discussion Questions

Communications   1.   **LO.1** A local bank has asked you to speak at its Building Personal Wealth Conference on the topic of "What Should Your Trust Do for You?" Develop at least four PowerPoint slides, each one listing a function that a trust might be able to accomplish for an individual who has more than a modest level of financial resources.

2.   **LO.1** In general terms, describe how the following entities are subject to the Federal income tax. (Answer only for the entity, not for its owners, beneficiaries, etc.)
   a.   C corporations (Subchapter C).
   b.   Partnerships (Subchapter K).
   c.   S corporations (Subchapter S).
   d.   Trusts and estates (Subchapter J).

3.   **LO.1** Create a fact pattern that illustrates each of the following tax situations. Be specific.
   a.   A simple trust.
   b.   A complex trust with a $300 personal exemption.
   c.   A complex trust with a $100 personal exemption.

Communications   4.   **LO.2** Your college's accounting group has asked you to give a 10-minute speech titled "Trusts, Estates, and the QBI Deduction." The audience will be students who have completed at least one course concerning Federal income taxation. Develop a brief outline for your remarks, and e-mail it to your instructor.

5.   **LO.2** Using Exhibit 28.4 as a guide, describe the computation of a fiduciary entity's accounting income, taxable income, and distributable net income.

6.   **LO.2** The Liu Trust is short of cash. It is required to distribute $100,000 to Yang every year, and that payment is due in six weeks. In its asset corpus, Liu holds a number of investments that are valued at $100,000. One of them is a plot of land with a tax basis to the trust of $80,000. What are the Federal income tax consequences if Liu distributes this land to Yang? *Hint:* You should consider a trustee election in your answer.

Critical Thinking   7.   **LO.2** In its first tax year, the Vasquez Estate generated $50,000 of taxable interest income and $30,000 of tax-exempt interest income. It paid fiduciary fees of $8,000. The estate is subject to a 40% marginal estate tax rate and a 37% marginal income tax rate. How much should the executor assign as an estate tax deduction for the payment of the fees?

8.   **LO.2** The Sterling Trust owns a business and generated $100,000 in depreciation deductions for the tax year. Mona is one of the income beneficiaries of the entity.
   a.   Given the following information, compute Mona's deduction, if any, for the Sterling depreciation.
   b.   Express your solution as a Microsoft Excel command.

Sterling's taxable income from the business	$ 800,000
Sterling's gross income from the business	4,000,000
Mona's share of trust accounting income	500,000
Total trust accounting income	2,500,000
Mona's share of distributable net income	1,200,000
Total distributable net income	1,600,000

9. **LO.2** In year 1, the Helpful Trust agreed to make a $50,000 cash contribution to Local Soup Kitchen, a charitable organization. Helpful's board agreed to the gift at a November year 1 meeting, but the check was not issued until February 20, year 2 (i.e., during the next tax year).
   a. For which tax year can the trust claim a charitable contribution deduction?
   b. Would the answer to part (a) change if the check was issued on May 1, year 2? If so, how?

10. **LO.3** One of the key concepts in fiduciary income taxation is that of *distributable net income* (DNI). List the major functions of DNI on one PowerPoint slide, with no more than five bullets, to present to your classmates as part of the discussion of this chapter of the text. Just review the uses of DNI in Subchapter J, and do not discuss its computation.   Communications

11. **LO.3, 4** Comment on the following items relative to tax planning strategies of a fiduciary entity.   Decision Making
   a. To reduce taxes for a typical family, should income be shifted *to* a trust or *from* a trust? Why?
   b. From a tax planning standpoint, who should invest in tax-exempt bonds, the trust or its beneficiaries?
   c. To reduce overall taxes, should a high-income, wealthy beneficiary be assigned to the first or second tier of trust distributions? Why?
   d. To minimize taxes, how should a trust treat the distribution of an in-kind asset? Why?

Computational Exercises

12. **LO.1** Compute the Federal income tax liability for the Valerio Trust. The entity reports the following transactions for the 2020 tax year. The trustee accumulates all accounting income for the year.

Operating income from a business	$ 500,000
Dividend income, all from U.S. corporations (20% tax rate)	30,000
Interest income, City of San Antonio bonds	40,000
Fiduciary fees, deductible portion	(15,000)
Net rental losses, passive activity	(100,000)

13. **LO.1** The Wes Trust reports $100,000 of AMT income before the annual exemption. The entity's AMT for 2020 is:
   a. $19,604.
   b. $20,384.
   c. $26,000.
   d. $28,000.

14. **LO.1** For 2020, the Guess Trust retains all of its income items, which include only $100,000 of net investment income and $140,000 of profits from an active business operation. Guess incurs an additional tax on net investment income (NIIT) of:
   a. $9,120.
   b. $5,320.
   c. $3,800.
   d. $0.

15. **LO.2** The Bildge Trust is a simple trust. Crawford is its sole beneficiary. In the current year, the trust earns $3,200 in taxable interest and $8,000 in tax-exempt interest. In addition, the trust recognizes a $2,500 long-term capital gain. The trustee charges a fee of $1,800 for the year.

   a. Compute trust accounting income, where the trust agreement allocates fees and capital gains to corpus.

   b. Same as part (a), except that fees are allocated to income.

   c. Construct a Microsoft Excel formula that will generate the correct answer to both parts (a) and (b).

16. **LO.2** The Hosta Trust reports gross rent income of $72,000, expenses attributable to the rents of $55,000, and tax-exempt interest from state bonds of $18,000. Under the trust agreement, the trustee is to pay 20% of the annual trust accounting income to the American Red Cross, a qualifying charitable organization.

   a. Compute Hosta's charitable contribution deduction.

   b. Express the solution as a Microsoft Excel command.

Problems

17. **LO.1** Complete the following chart, indicating the comparative attributes of the typical simple trust and complex trust by answering yes/no or explaining the differences between the entities where appropriate.

Attribute	Simple Trust	Complex Trust
Trust could incur its own tax liability for the year		
Trust generally distributes all of the DNI		
Trust can deduct its charitable contributions in the year of, or the year after, payment		
Maximum tax rate on net long-term capital gains = 20%		
Trust can adopt the FIFO method for its inventory assets; the grantor had been using lower of cost or market		
Trust can use a tax year other than the calendar year		
Amount of personal exemption		

Decision Making   18. **LO.2** The Polozzi Trust will incur the following items in the next tax year, its first year of existence.

Interest income	$ 25,000
Rent income	100,000
Cost recovery deductions for the rental activity	35,000
Capital gain income	40,000
Fiduciary and tax preparation fees	7,000

Betty, the grantor of the trust, is working with you on the language in the trust instrument relative to the derivation of annual accounting income for the entity. She will name Shirley as the sole income beneficiary and Benny as the remainder beneficiary.

a. Suggest language to Betty that will maximize the annual income distribution to Shirley.

b. Suggest language to Betty that will minimize the annual distribution to Shirley and maximize the accumulation on Benny's behalf.

19. **LO.2** Complete the chart below, indicating the Calvet Trust's entity accounting income for each of the alternatives. For this purpose, use the following information.

Interest income, taxable	$300,000
Interest income, tax-exempt	30,000
Interest income, tax-exempt but AMT preference item	20,000
Long-term capital gain	40,000
Trustee fee	10,000

Trust Agreement Provisions	Trust Accounting Income
Fees and capital gains allocable to corpus	_____
Capital gains allocable to corpus, one-half of fees allocable to income	_____
Capital gains allocable to income, silent concerning allocation of fees	_____
Fees and exempt income allocable to corpus, silent concerning allocation of capital gain/loss	_____

20. **LO.1, 2, 3** Complete the following chart, indicating the comparative attributes of the typical trust and estate by answering yes/no or explaining the differences between the entities where appropriate.

Attribute	Estate	Trust
Separate income tax entity	_____	_____
Controlling document	_____	_____
Can have both income and remainder beneficiaries	_____	_____
Computes entity accounting income before determining entity taxable income	_____	_____
Termination date is determinable from controlling document	_____	_____
Document identifies both income and remainder beneficiaries	_____	_____
Generally must use calendar tax year	_____	_____

21. **LO.2** Sanchez incurred the following items.

Business income, exclusive of the following items	$80,000
Tax-exempt interest income	40,000
Payment to charity from 2020 Sanchez gross income, paid 3/1/21	20,000

Complete the following chart, indicating the charitable contributions deduction under the various assumptions. See also text Section 17-1h.

Assumption	2020 Deduction for Contribution
Sanchez is a cash basis individual.	_____
Sanchez is an accrual basis corporation.	_____
Sanchez is a trust.	_____

22. **LO.2, 3** The Allwardt Trust is a simple trust that correctly uses the calendar year for tax purposes. Its income beneficiaries (Lucy and Ethel) are entitled to the trust's annual accounting income in shares of one-half each.

For the current tax year, Allwardt reports the following.

Ordinary income	$100,000
Long-term capital gains, allocable to corpus	30,000
Legal and accounting fees, allocable to corpus	5,000

Use the format of Exhibit 28.5 to address the following items.

a. How much income is each beneficiary entitled to receive?
b. What is the trust's DNI?
c. What is the trust's taxable income?
d. How much gross income is reported by each of the beneficiaries?

23. **LO.2, 3** The Allwardt Trust is a simple trust that correctly uses the calendar year for tax purposes. Its income beneficiaries (Lucy and Ethel) are entitled to the trust's annual accounting income in shares of one-half each.

For the current tax year, Allwardt reports the following.

Ordinary income	$100,000
Long-term capital gains, allocable to income	30,000
Legal and accounting fees, allocable to corpus	5,000

a. How much income is each beneficiary entitled to receive?
b. What is the trust's DNI?
c. What is the trust's taxable income?
d. How much gross income is reported by each of the beneficiaries?

24. **LO.3** The Kilp Sisters Trust is required to distribute $60,000 annually equally to its two income beneficiaries, Clare and Renee. If trust income is not sufficient to pay these amounts, the trustee can invade corpus to the extent necessary.

During the current year, the trust generates only taxable interest income and records DNI of $160,000; the trustee distributes $30,000 to Clare and $150,000 to Renee.

a. Are these distributions first-tier or second-tier distributions?
b. How much of the $150,000 distributed to Renee is included in her gross income?
c. How much of the $30,000 distributed to Clare is included in her gross income?

25. **LO.3** The Dolce Estate reports the following items for the current tax year.

Dividend income	$ 50,000
Taxable interest income	8,000
Passive activity income	30,000
Tax-exempt interest income	12,000
Distributable net income	$100,000

Dolce's two noncharitable income beneficiaries, Brenda and Dev, receive cash distributions of $20,000 each. How much of each class of income is deemed to have been distributed to Brenda? To Dev?

26. **LO.2, 3** The trustee of the Pieper Trust can distribute any amount of accounting income and corpus to the trust's beneficiaries, Lydia and Avi. This year, the trust incurred the following.

Taxable interest income	$40,000
Tax-exempt interest income	20,000
Long-term capital gains—allocable to corpus	80,000
Legal and accounting fees—allocable to corpus	9,000

The trustee distributed $26,000 to Lydia and $13,000 to Avi.

a. What is Pieper's trust accounting income?

b. What is Pieper's DNI?

c. What is Pieper's taxable income?

d. What amounts are taxed to each of the beneficiaries?

27. **LO.2** Each of the following items was incurred by José, the cash basis, calendar year decedent. Under the terms of the will, Dora took immediate ownership in all of José's assets, except the dividend-paying stock. The estate received José's final paycheck.

Applying the rules for income and deductions in respect of a decedent, indicate on which return each item should be reported: Dora's income tax return (Form 1040), the estate's first income tax return (Form 1041), or the estate's estate tax return (Form 706). More than one alternative may apply in some cases.

Item Incurred	Form(s) Reported on
a. Wages, last paycheck	_____
b. State income tax withheld on last paycheck	_____
c. Capital gain portion of installment payment received	_____
d. Ordinary income portion of installment payment received	_____
e. Dividend income, record date was two days prior to José's death	_____
f. Unrealized appreciation on a mutual fund investment	_____
g. Apartment building, rents accrued but not collected as of death	_____
h. Apartment building, property tax accrued and assessed but not paid as of death	_____

See Appendix E for Comprehensive Tax Return Problem—Form 1041

Research Problems

Note: Solutions to the Research Problems can be prepared by using the Thomson Reuters Checkpoint™ online tax research database, which accompanies this textbook. Solutions can also be prepared by using research materials found in a typical tax library.

the answer company™
THOMSON REUTERS®

Research Problem 1. Winder Ltd. is an S corporation that is wholly owned by Juan Plowright. Because several of Juan's ancestors have had Alzheimer's disease, Juan is transferring many of his assets to trusts, and he is funding living wills in anticipation of future medical issues.

Juan wants to transfer his Winder stock to a trust, but he wants to keep control over its operations for as long as possible. Thus, he wants to retain a right to revoke the trust, until such time as the trustee (a Winder executive who is on good terms with Juan) and a medical professional determine that Juan no longer is competent. You have explained to Juan that this entity is a grantor trust and that there are no income-shifting or transfer-tax-saving aspects in using such a trust.

The pertinent tax issues to be addressed include:

Critical Thinking

Communications

- Does the grantor trust terminate Winder's status as an S corporation?
- Will Winder's S election survive Juan's death? Under the terms of Juan's will, the S shares will be held by his estate and not be distributed to his niece Beatriz until she reaches age 25.

All parties are residents of New Mexico. Cite and summarize your findings in an outline for a talk that you will deliver next week to your school's Accounting Club. Assume that Club members are knowledgeable about the taxation of S corporations and their shareholders (e.g., from Chapter 22).

Research Problem 2. For three generations, the Dexter family has sent its children to Private University, preparing them for successful professional careers. The Edna Dexter Trust was established in the 1950s by LaKeisha's late grandmother and has accumulated a sizable corpus. It makes distributions to Edna's descendants rarely, and then only when they need large capital amounts. For example, two years ago, the trust distributed $500,000 to DuJuan Dexter to aid him in starting a practice in retirement and elder law. In most years, the trust's income is donated to a single charity.

Under the terms of the trust, Bigby Dexter, LaKeisha's uncle and legal guardian, can specify the trust beneficiaries and the amounts to be distributed to them. He also can replace the trustee and designate the charity that will receive the year's contribution. Accordingly, the trust falls under the grantor trust rules, and Bigby reports the trust's transactions on his own Form 1040.

LaKeisha wants to attend the prestigious local Academy High School, which will require a four-year expenditure for tuition and fees of $150,000, payable in advance. She approaches the Dexter trustee and requests a current-year distribution of this amount, payable directly to the Academy. Under the laws of the state, the parent or guardian must provide a child with a public school education (no tuition charge) until age 16.

If the payment to the Academy is made, how is it treated under the Subchapter J rules: as a charitable contribution to the Academy, as a corpus distribution to LaKeisha, or in some other manner? Be specific.

Use internet tax resources to address the following questions. Look for reliable websites and blogs of the IRS and other government agencies, media outlets, businesses, tax professionals, academics, think tanks, and political outlets.

Data Analytics

Communications

Research Problem 3. How many estates filed a Form 1041 last year? Simple trusts? Complex trusts? Grantor trusts? How much Federal income tax has been collected on Forms 1041 over the last three tax years? Summarize your findings in a series of graphs to share with your classmates.

Communications

Research Problem 4. Under the income tax laws of your state applicable to fiduciaries, how are the following items allocated among the entity and the beneficiaries? Put your findings in a PowerPoint presentation for your classmates. *Hint:* Use an online tax research service to find this information.

- Capital gain.
- Cost recovery.
- Fiduciary fees.
- Exempt interest income.
- QBI deduction.
- General business credits.

Communications

Research Problem 5. Find the website of a law firm that seems to specialize in fiduciary entities, preferably a firm located in your state. Ask the firm to quote you a fee for (1) establishing a simple trust and (2) filing the annual Form 1041. Summarize your findings and your communications with the firm in an e-mail to your instructor.

Becker CPA Review Questions

1. On January 1, year 1, Olinto created a $650,000 trust that provided his mother with a lifetime income interest starting on January 1, year 1, with the remainder interest to go to his son. Olinto expressly retained the power to revoke both the income interest and the remainder interest at any time. Who is taxed on the trust's year 1 income?

    a.   Olinto's mother
    b.   Olinto's son
    c.   Olinto
    d.   The trust

2. A distribution from estate income *currently* required was made to the estate's sole beneficiary during its calendar year. The maximum amount of the distribution to be included in the beneficiary's gross income is limited to the estate's:

    a.   Capital gain income.
    b.   Ordinary gross income.
    c.   Distributable net income.
    d.   Net investment income.

3. Lyon, a cash basis taxpayer, died on January 15 of the current year. During the current year, the estate executor made the required periodic distribution of $9,000 from estate income to Lyon's sole heir. The following information pertains to the estate's income and disbursements for the year. For the current calendar year, what was the estate's distributable net income (DNI)?

Estate Income	
Taxable interest	$20,000
Net long-term capital gains allocable to corpus	10,000

Estate Disbursements	
Administrative expenses attributable to taxable income	$5,000

    a. $15,000
    b. $20,000
    c. $25,000
    d. $30,000

4. Reinus, a cash basis taxpayer, died on February 3. During the year, the estate's executor made a distribution of $12,000 from estate income to Reinus's sole heir and adopted a calendar year to determine the estate's taxable income. The following additional information pertains to the estate's income and disbursements for the year. For the calendar year, what was the estate's distributable net income (DNI)?

Estate Income	
Taxable interest	$85,000
Net long-term capital gains allocable to corpus	10,000

Estate Disbursements	
Administrative expenses attributable to taxable income	$24,000
Charitable contributions from gross income to a public charity, made under the terms of the will	19,000

    a. $39,000
    b. $42,000
    c. $58,000
    d. $65,000

5. A distribution to an estate's sole beneficiary for the calendar year equaled $15,000, the amount currently required to be distributed by the will. The estate's records showed the following. What amount of the distribution was taxable to the beneficiary?

Estate Income	
Taxable interest	$40,000

Estate Disbursements	
Expenses attributable to taxable interest	$34,000

a. $40,000 c. $6,000

b. $15,000 d. $0

6. Peyton Trust, which is a simple trust, distributed $45,000 to its sole beneficiary, Brooke, in the current year. Further, it had the following items of income and expense for the current year.

Interest income from municipal bonds	$10,000
Gross income from rental properties	30,000
Operating expenses for the rental properties	5,000
Trust fees allocable to the rental properties	2,000

What is Peyton's income distribution deduction for the current year?

a. $23,000 c. $40,000

b. $33,000 d. $45,000

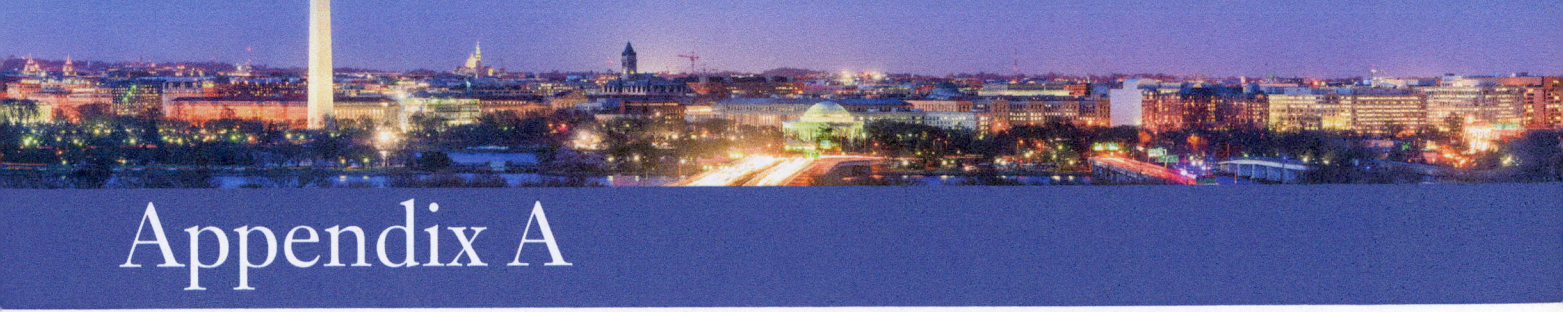

Appendix A

Tax Rate Schedules and Tables

2019	Income Tax Rate Schedules—Individuals	A-2
2020	Income Tax Rate Schedules—Individuals	A-2
2019	Tax Tables—Individuals	A-3
2019	Sales Tax Tables	A-15
2020	Income Tax Rates—Estates and Trusts	A-22
2019	Income Tax Rates—Estates and Trusts	A-22
	Income Tax Rates—C Corporations, 2018 and after	A-22
	Unified Transfer Tax Rates (For Gifts Made and for Deaths after 2012)	A-22

(The 2020 Tax Tables and 2020 Sales Tax Tables can be accessed at the IRS website when released: **irs.gov**)

2019 Tax Rate Schedules

Single—Schedule X

If taxable income is: Over—	But not over—	The tax is:	of the amount over—
$ 0	$ 9,700	.........10%	$ 0
9,700	39,475	$ 970.00 + 12%	9,700
39,475	84,200	4,543.00 + 22%	39,475
84,200	160,725	14,382.50 + 24%	84,200
160,725	204,100	32,748.50 + 32%	160,725
204,100	510,300	46,628.50 + 35%	204,100
510,300	....	153,798.50 + 37%	510,300

Head of household—Schedule Z

If taxable income is: Over—	But not over—	The tax is:	of the amount over—
$ 0	$ 13,850	.........10%	$ 0
13,850	52,850	$ 1,385.00 + 12%	13,850
52,850	84,200	6,065.00 + 22%	52,850
84,200	160,700	12,962.00 + 24%	84,200
160,700	204,100	31,322.00 + 32%	160,700
204,100	510,300	45,210.00 + 35%	204,100
510,300	....	152,380.00 + 37%	510,300

Married filing jointly or Qualifying widow(er)—Schedule Y–1

If taxable income is: Over—	But not over—	The tax is:	of the amount over—
$ 0	$ 19,400	.........10%	$ 0
19,400	78,950	$ 1,940.00 + 12%	19,400
78,950	168,400	9,086.00 + 22%	78,950
168,400	321,450	28,765.00 + 24%	168,400
321,450	408,200	65,497.00 + 32%	321,450
408,200	612,350	93,257.00 + 35%	408,200
612,350	....	164,709.50 + 37%	612,350

Married filing separately—Schedule Y–2

If taxable income is: Over—	But not over—	The tax is:	of the amount over—
$ 0	$ 9,700	.........10%	$ 0
9,700	39,475	$ 970.00 + 12%	9,700
39,475	84,200	4,543.00 + 22%	39,475
84,200	160,725	14,382.50 + 24%	84,200
160,725	204,100	32,748.50 + 32%	160,725
204,100	306,175	46,628.50 + 35%	204,100
306,175	....	82,354.75 + 37%	306,175

2020 Tax Rate Schedules

Single—Schedule X

If taxable income is: Over—	But not over—	The tax is:	of the amount over—
$ 0	$ 9,875	.........10%	$ 0
9,875	40,125	$ 987.50 + 12%	9,875
40,125	85,525	4,617.50 + 22%	40,125
85,525	163,300	14,605.50 + 24%	85,525
163,300	207,350	33,271.50 + 32%	163,300
207,350	518,400	47,367.50 + 35%	207,350
518,400	....	156,235.00 + 37%	518,400

Head of household—Schedule Z

If taxable income is: Over—	But not over—	The tax is:	of the amount over—
$ 0	$ 14,100	.........10%	$ 0
14,100	53,700	$ 1,410.00 + 12%	14,100
53,700	85,500	6,162.00 + 22%	53,700
85,500	163,300	13,158.00 + 24%	85,500
163,300	207,350	31,830.00 + 32%	163,300
207,350	518,400	45,926.00 + 35%	207,350
518,400	....	154,793.50 + 37%	518,400

Married filing jointly or Qualifying widow(er)—Schedule Y–1

If taxable income is: Over—	But not over—	The tax is:	of the amount over—
$ 0	$ 19,750	.........10%	$ 0
19,750	80,250	$ 1,975.00 + 12%	19,750
80,250	171,050	9,235.00 + 22%	80,250
171,050	326,600	29,211.00 + 24%	171,050
326,600	414,700	66,543.00 + 32%	326,600
414,700	622,050	94,735.00 + 35%	414,700
622,050	....	167,307.50 + 37%	622,050

Married filing separately—Schedule Y–2

If taxable income is: Over—	But not over—	The tax is:	of the amount over—
$ 0	$ 9,875	.........10%	$ 0
9,875	40,125	$ 987.50 + 12%	9,875
40,125	85,525	4,617.50 + 22%	40,125
85,525	163,300	14,605.50 + 24%	85,525
163,300	207,350	33,271.50 + 32%	163,300
207,350	311,025	47,367.50 + 35%	207,350
311,025	....	83,653.75 + 37%	311,025

2019 Tax Table

See the instructions for line 12a to see if you must use the Tax Table below to figure your tax.

Example. Mr. and Mrs. Brown are filing a joint return. Their taxable income on Form 1040, line 11b, is $25,300. First, they find the $25,300–25,350 taxable income line. Next, they find the column for married filing jointly and read down the column. The amount shown where the taxable income line and filing status column meet is $2,651. This is the tax amount they should enter in the entry space on Form 1040, line 12a.

Sample Table

At Least	But Less Than	Single	Married filing jointly*	Married filing separately	Head of a household
			Your tax is—		
25,200	25,250	2,833	2,639	2,833	2,750
25,250	25,300	2,839	2,645	2,839	2,756
25,300	25,350	2,845	(2,651)	2,845	2,762
25,350	25,400	2,851	2,657	2,851	2,768

If line 11b (taxable income) is— At least	But less than	Single	Married filing jointly *	Married filing separately	Head of a household
			Your tax is—		
0	5	0	0	0	0
5	15	1	1	1	1
15	25	2	2	2	2
25	50	4	4	4	4
50	75	6	6	6	6
75	100	9	9	9	9
100	125	11	11	11	11
125	150	14	14	14	14
150	175	16	16	16	16
175	200	19	19	19	19
200	225	21	21	21	21
225	250	24	24	24	24
250	275	26	26	26	26
275	300	29	29	29	29
300	325	31	31	31	31
325	350	34	34	34	34
350	375	36	36	36	36
375	400	39	39	39	39
400	425	41	41	41	41
425	450	44	44	44	44
450	475	46	46	46	46
475	500	49	49	49	49
500	525	51	51	51	51
525	550	54	54	54	54
550	575	56	56	56	56
575	600	59	59	59	59
600	625	61	61	61	61
625	650	64	64	64	64
650	675	66	66	66	66
675	700	69	69	69	69
700	725	71	71	71	71
725	750	74	74	74	74
750	775	76	76	76	76
775	800	79	79	79	79
800	825	81	81	81	81
825	850	84	84	84	84
850	875	86	86	86	86
875	900	89	89	89	89
900	925	91	91	91	91
925	950	94	94	94	94
950	975	96	96	96	96
975	1,000	99	99	99	99

1,000

At least	But less than	Single	Married filing jointly *	Married filing separately	Head of a household
			Your tax is—		
1,000	1,025	101	101	101	101
1,025	1,050	104	104	104	104
1,050	1,075	106	106	106	106
1,075	1,100	109	109	109	109
1,100	1,125	111	111	111	111
1,125	1,150	114	114	114	114
1,150	1,175	116	116	116	116
1,175	1,200	119	119	119	119
1,200	1,225	121	121	121	121
1,225	1,250	124	124	124	124
1,250	1,275	126	126	126	126
1,275	1,300	129	129	129	129
1,300	1,325	131	131	131	131
1,325	1,350	134	134	134	134
1,350	1,375	136	136	136	136
1,375	1,400	139	139	139	139
1,400	1,425	141	141	141	141
1,425	1,450	144	144	144	144
1,450	1,475	146	146	146	146
1,475	1,500	149	149	149	149
1,500	1,525	151	151	151	151
1,525	1,550	154	154	154	154
1,550	1,575	156	156	156	156
1,575	1,600	159	159	159	159
1,600	1,625	161	161	161	161
1,625	1,650	164	164	164	164
1,650	1,675	166	166	166	166
1,675	1,700	169	169	169	169
1,700	1,725	171	171	171	171
1,725	1,750	174	174	174	174
1,750	1,775	176	176	176	176
1,775	1,800	179	179	179	179
1,800	1,825	181	181	181	181
1,825	1,850	184	184	184	184
1,850	1,875	186	186	186	186
1,875	1,900	189	189	189	189
1,900	1,925	191	191	191	191
1,925	1,950	194	194	194	194
1,950	1,975	196	196	196	196
1,975	2,000	199	199	199	199

2,000

At least	But less than	Single	Married filing jointly *	Married filing separately	Head of a household
			Your tax is—		
2,000	2,025	201	201	201	201
2,025	2,050	204	204	204	204
2,050	2,075	206	206	206	206
2,075	2,100	209	209	209	209
2,100	2,125	211	211	211	211
2,125	2,150	214	214	214	214
2,150	2,175	216	216	216	216
2,175	2,200	219	219	219	219
2,200	2,225	221	221	221	221
2,225	2,250	224	224	224	224
2,250	2,275	226	226	226	226
2,275	2,300	229	229	229	229
2,300	2,325	231	231	231	231
2,325	2,350	234	234	234	234
2,350	2,375	236	236	236	236
2,375	2,400	239	239	239	239
2,400	2,425	241	241	241	241
2,425	2,450	244	244	244	244
2,450	2,475	246	246	246	246
2,475	2,500	249	249	249	249
2,500	2,525	251	251	251	251
2,525	2,550	254	254	254	254
2,550	2,575	256	256	256	256
2,575	2,600	259	259	259	259
2,600	2,625	261	261	261	261
2,625	2,650	264	264	264	264
2,650	2,675	266	266	266	266
2,675	2,700	269	269	269	269
2,700	2,725	271	271	271	271
2,725	2,750	274	274	274	274
2,750	2,775	276	276	276	276
2,775	2,800	279	279	279	279
2,800	2,825	281	281	281	281
2,825	2,850	284	284	284	284
2,850	2,875	286	286	286	286
2,875	2,900	289	289	289	289
2,900	2,925	291	291	291	291
2,925	2,950	294	294	294	294
2,950	2,975	296	296	296	296
2,975	3,000	299	299	299	299

(Continued)

* This column must also be used by a qualifying widow(er).

If line 11b (taxable income) is—		And you are—				If line 11b (taxable income) is—		And you are—				If line 11b (taxable income) is—		And you are—			
At least	But less than	Single	Married filing jointly *	Married filing separately	Head of a household	At least	But less than	Single	Married filing jointly *	Married filing separately	Head of a household	At least	But less than	Single	Married filing jointly *	Married filing separately	Head of a household
		Your tax is—						Your tax is—						Your tax is—			
3,000						**6,000**						**9,000**					
3,000	3,050	303	303	303	303	6,000	6,050	603	603	603	603	9,000	9,050	903	903	903	903
3,050	3,100	308	308	308	308	6,050	6,100	608	608	608	608	9,050	9,100	908	908	908	908
3,100	3,150	313	313	313	313	6,100	6,150	613	613	613	613	9,100	9,150	913	913	913	913
3,150	3,200	318	318	318	318	6,150	6,200	618	618	618	618	9,150	9,200	918	918	918	918
3,200	3,250	323	323	323	323	6,200	6,250	623	623	623	623	9,200	9,250	923	923	923	923
3,250	3,300	328	328	328	328	6,250	6,300	628	628	628	628	9,250	9,300	928	928	928	928
3,300	3,350	333	333	333	333	6,300	6,350	633	633	633	633	9,300	9,350	933	933	933	933
3,350	3,400	338	338	338	338	6,350	6,400	638	638	638	638	9,350	9,400	938	938	938	938
3,400	3,450	343	343	343	343	6,400	6,450	643	643	643	643	9,400	9,450	943	943	943	943
3,450	3,500	348	348	348	348	6,450	6,500	648	648	648	648	9,450	9,500	948	948	948	948
3,500	3,550	353	353	353	353	6,500	6,550	653	653	653	653	9,500	9,550	953	953	953	953
3,550	3,600	358	358	358	358	6,550	6,600	658	658	658	658	9,550	9,600	958	958	958	958
3,600	3,650	363	363	363	363	6,600	6,650	663	663	663	663	9,600	9,650	963	963	963	963
3,650	3,700	368	368	368	368	6,650	6,700	668	668	668	668	9,650	9,700	968	968	968	968
3,700	3,750	373	373	373	373	6,700	6,750	673	673	673	673	9,700	9,750	973	973	973	973
3,750	3,800	378	378	378	378	6,750	6,800	678	678	678	678	9,750	9,800	979	978	979	978
3,800	3,850	383	383	383	383	6,800	6,850	683	683	683	683	9,800	9,850	985	983	985	983
3,850	3,900	388	388	388	388	6,850	6,900	688	688	688	688	9,850	9,900	991	988	991	988
3,900	3,950	393	393	393	393	6,900	6,950	693	693	693	693	9,900	9,950	997	993	997	993
3,950	4,000	398	398	398	398	6,950	7,000	698	698	698	698	9,950	10,000	1,003	998	1,003	998
4,000						**7,000**						**10,000**					
4,000	4,050	403	403	403	403	7,000	7,050	703	703	703	703	10,000	10,050	1,009	1,003	1,009	1,003
4,050	4,100	408	408	408	408	7,050	7,100	708	708	708	708	10,050	10,100	1,015	1,008	1,015	1,008
4,100	4,150	413	413	413	413	7,100	7,150	713	713	713	713	10,100	10,150	1,021	1,013	1,021	1,013
4,150	4,200	418	418	418	418	7,150	7,200	718	718	718	718	10,150	10,200	1,027	1,018	1,027	1,018
4,200	4,250	423	423	423	423	7,200	7,250	723	723	723	723	10,200	10,250	1,033	1,023	1,033	1,023
4,250	4,300	428	428	428	428	7,250	7,300	728	728	728	728	10,250	10,300	1,039	1,028	1,039	1,028
4,300	4,350	433	433	433	433	7,300	7,350	733	733	733	733	10,300	10,350	1,045	1,033	1,045	1,033
4,350	4,400	438	438	438	438	7,350	7,400	738	738	738	738	10,350	10,400	1,051	1,038	1,051	1,038
4,400	4,450	443	443	443	443	7,400	7,450	743	743	743	743	10,400	10,450	1,057	1,043	1,057	1,043
4,450	4,500	448	448	448	448	7,450	7,500	748	748	748	748	10,450	10,500	1,063	1,048	1,063	1,048
4,500	4,550	453	453	453	453	7,500	7,550	753	753	753	753	10,500	10,550	1,069	1,053	1,069	1,053
4,550	4,600	458	458	458	458	7,550	7,600	758	758	758	758	10,550	10,600	1,075	1,058	1,075	1,058
4,600	4,650	463	463	463	463	7,600	7,650	763	763	763	763	10,600	10,650	1,081	1,063	1,081	1,063
4,650	4,700	468	468	468	468	7,650	7,700	768	768	768	768	10,650	10,700	1,087	1,068	1,087	1,068
4,700	4,750	473	473	473	473	7,700	7,750	773	773	773	773	10,700	10,750	1,093	1,073	1,093	1,073
4,750	4,800	478	478	478	478	7,750	7,800	778	778	778	778	10,750	10,800	1,099	1,078	1,099	1,078
4,800	4,850	483	483	483	483	7,800	7,850	783	783	783	783	10,800	10,850	1,105	1,083	1,105	1,083
4,850	4,900	488	488	488	488	7,850	7,900	788	788	788	788	10,850	10,900	1,111	1,088	1,111	1,088
4,900	4,950	493	493	493	493	7,900	7,950	793	793	793	793	10,900	10,950	1,117	1,093	1,117	1,093
4,950	5,000	498	498	498	498	7,950	8,000	798	798	798	798	10,950	11,000	1,123	1,098	1,123	1,098
5,000						**8,000**						**11,000**					
5,000	5,050	503	503	503	503	8,000	8,050	803	803	803	803	11,000	11,050	1,129	1,103	1,129	1,103
5,050	5,100	508	508	508	508	8,050	8,100	808	808	808	808	11,050	11,100	1,135	1,108	1,135	1,108
5,100	5,150	513	513	513	513	8,100	8,150	813	813	813	813	11,100	11,150	1,141	1,113	1,141	1,113
5,150	5,200	518	518	518	518	8,150	8,200	818	818	818	818	11,150	11,200	1,147	1,118	1,147	1,118
5,200	5,250	523	523	523	523	8,200	8,250	823	823	823	823	11,200	11,250	1,153	1,123	1,153	1,123
5,250	5,300	528	528	528	528	8,250	8,300	828	828	828	828	11,250	11,300	1,159	1,128	1,159	1,128
5,300	5,350	533	533	533	533	8,300	8,350	833	833	833	833	11,300	11,350	1,165	1,133	1,165	1,133
5,350	5,400	538	538	538	538	8,350	8,400	838	838	838	838	11,350	11,400	1,171	1,138	1,171	1,138
5,400	5,450	543	543	543	543	8,400	8,450	843	843	843	843	11,400	11,450	1,177	1,143	1,177	1,143
5,450	5,500	548	548	548	548	8,450	8,500	848	848	848	848	11,450	11,500	1,183	1,148	1,183	1,148
5,500	5,550	553	553	553	553	8,500	8,550	853	853	853	853	11,500	11,550	1,189	1,153	1,189	1,153
5,550	5,600	558	558	558	558	8,550	8,600	858	858	858	858	11,550	11,600	1,195	1,158	1,195	1,158
5,600	5,650	563	563	563	563	8,600	8,650	863	863	863	863	11,600	11,650	1,201	1,163	1,201	1,163
5,650	5,700	568	568	568	568	8,650	8,700	868	868	868	868	11,650	11,700	1,207	1,168	1,207	1,168
5,700	5,750	573	573	573	573	8,700	8,750	873	873	873	873	11,700	11,750	1,213	1,173	1,213	1,173
5,750	5,800	578	578	578	578	8,750	8,800	878	878	878	878	11,750	11,800	1,219	1,178	1,219	1,178
5,800	5,850	583	583	583	583	8,800	8,850	883	883	883	883	11,800	11,850	1,225	1,183	1,225	1,183
5,850	5,900	588	588	588	588	8,850	8,900	888	888	888	888	11,850	11,900	1,231	1,188	1,231	1,188
5,900	5,950	593	593	593	593	8,900	8,950	893	893	893	893	11,900	11,950	1,237	1,193	1,237	1,193
5,950	6,000	598	598	598	598	8,950	9,000	898	898	898	898	11,950	12,000	1,243	1,198	1,243	1,198

(Continued)

* This column must also be used by a qualifying widow(er).

2019 Tax Table — *Continued*

12,000

If line 11b (taxable income) is—		And you are—			
At least	But less than	Single	Married filing jointly *	Married filing separately	Head of a household
		Your tax is—			
12,000	12,050	1,249	1,203	1,249	1,203
12,050	12,100	1,255	1,208	1,255	1,208
12,100	12,150	1,261	1,213	1,261	1,213
12,150	12,200	1,267	1,218	1,267	1,218
12,200	12,250	1,273	1,223	1,273	1,223
12,250	12,300	1,279	1,228	1,279	1,228
12,300	12,350	1,285	1,233	1,285	1,233
12,350	12,400	1,291	1,238	1,291	1,238
12,400	12,450	1,297	1,243	1,297	1,243
12,450	12,500	1,303	1,248	1,303	1,248
12,500	12,550	1,309	1,253	1,309	1,253
12,550	12,600	1,315	1,258	1,315	1,258
12,600	12,650	1,321	1,263	1,321	1,263
12,650	12,700	1,327	1,268	1,327	1,268
12,700	12,750	1,333	1,273	1,333	1,273
12,750	12,800	1,339	1,278	1,339	1,278
12,800	12,850	1,345	1,283	1,345	1,283
12,850	12,900	1,351	1,288	1,351	1,288
12,900	12,950	1,357	1,293	1,357	1,293
12,950	13,000	1,363	1,298	1,363	1,298

13,000

At least	But less than	Single	Married filing jointly *	Married filing separately	Head of a household
13,000	13,050	1,369	1,303	1,369	1,303
13,050	13,100	1,375	1,308	1,375	1,308
13,100	13,150	1,381	1,313	1,381	1,313
13,150	13,200	1,387	1,318	1,387	1,318
13,200	13,250	1,393	1,323	1,393	1,323
13,250	13,300	1,399	1,328	1,399	1,328
13,300	13,350	1,405	1,333	1,405	1,333
13,350	13,400	1,411	1,338	1,411	1,338
13,400	13,450	1,417	1,343	1,417	1,343
13,450	13,500	1,423	1,348	1,423	1,348
13,500	13,550	1,429	1,353	1,429	1,353
13,550	13,600	1,435	1,358	1,435	1,358
13,600	13,650	1,441	1,363	1,441	1,363
13,650	13,700	1,447	1,368	1,447	1,368
13,700	13,750	1,453	1,373	1,453	1,373
13,750	13,800	1,459	1,378	1,459	1,378
13,800	13,850	1,465	1,383	1,465	1,383
13,850	13,900	1,471	1,388	1,471	1,388
13,900	13,950	1,477	1,393	1,477	1,394
13,950	14,000	1,483	1,398	1,483	1,400

14,000

At least	But less than	Single	Married filing jointly *	Married filing separately	Head of a household
14,000	14,050	1,489	1,403	1,489	1,406
14,050	14,100	1,495	1,408	1,495	1,412
14,100	14,150	1,501	1,413	1,501	1,418
14,150	14,200	1,507	1,418	1,507	1,424
14,200	14,250	1,513	1,423	1,513	1,430
14,250	14,300	1,519	1,428	1,519	1,436
14,300	14,350	1,525	1,433	1,525	1,442
14,350	14,400	1,531	1,438	1,531	1,448
14,400	14,450	1,537	1,443	1,537	1,454
14,450	14,500	1,543	1,448	1,543	1,460
14,500	14,550	1,549	1,453	1,549	1,466
14,550	14,600	1,555	1,458	1,555	1,472
14,600	14,650	1,561	1,463	1,561	1,478
14,650	14,700	1,567	1,468	1,567	1,484
14,700	14,750	1,573	1,473	1,573	1,490
14,750	14,800	1,579	1,478	1,579	1,496
14,800	14,850	1,585	1,483	1,585	1,502
14,850	14,900	1,591	1,488	1,591	1,508
14,900	14,950	1,597	1,493	1,597	1,514
14,950	15,000	1,603	1,498	1,603	1,520

15,000

At least	But less than	Single	Married filing jointly *	Married filing separately	Head of a household
15,000	15,050	1,609	1,503	1,609	1,526
15,050	15,100	1,615	1,508	1,615	1,532
15,100	15,150	1,621	1,513	1,621	1,538
15,150	15,200	1,627	1,518	1,627	1,544
15,200	15,250	1,633	1,523	1,633	1,550
15,250	15,300	1,639	1,528	1,639	1,556
15,300	15,350	1,645	1,533	1,645	1,562
15,350	15,400	1,651	1,538	1,651	1,568
15,400	15,450	1,657	1,543	1,657	1,574
15,450	15,500	1,663	1,548	1,663	1,580
15,500	15,550	1,669	1,553	1,669	1,586
15,550	15,600	1,675	1,558	1,675	1,592
15,600	15,650	1,681	1,563	1,681	1,598
15,650	15,700	1,687	1,568	1,687	1,604
15,700	15,750	1,693	1,573	1,693	1,610
15,750	15,800	1,699	1,578	1,699	1,616
15,800	15,850	1,705	1,583	1,705	1,622
15,850	15,900	1,711	1,588	1,711	1,628
15,900	15,950	1,717	1,593	1,717	1,634
15,950	16,000	1,723	1,598	1,723	1,640

16,000

At least	But less than	Single	Married filing jointly *	Married filing separately	Head of a household
16,000	16,050	1,729	1,603	1,729	1,646
16,050	16,100	1,735	1,608	1,735	1,652
16,100	16,150	1,741	1,613	1,741	1,658
16,150	16,200	1,747	1,618	1,747	1,664
16,200	16,250	1,753	1,623	1,753	1,670
16,250	16,300	1,759	1,628	1,759	1,676
16,300	16,350	1,765	1,633	1,765	1,682
16,350	16,400	1,771	1,638	1,771	1,688
16,400	16,450	1,777	1,643	1,777	1,694
16,450	16,500	1,783	1,648	1,783	1,700
16,500	16,550	1,789	1,653	1,789	1,706
16,550	16,600	1,795	1,658	1,795	1,712
16,600	16,650	1,801	1,663	1,801	1,718
16,650	16,700	1,807	1,668	1,807	1,724
16,700	16,750	1,813	1,673	1,813	1,730
16,750	16,800	1,819	1,678	1,819	1,736
16,800	16,850	1,825	1,683	1,825	1,742
16,850	16,900	1,831	1,688	1,831	1,748
16,900	16,950	1,837	1,693	1,837	1,754
16,950	17,000	1,843	1,698	1,843	1,760

17,000

At least	But less than	Single	Married filing jointly *	Married filing separately	Head of a household
17,000	17,050	1,849	1,703	1,849	1,766
17,050	17,100	1,855	1,708	1,855	1,772
17,100	17,150	1,861	1,713	1,861	1,778
17,150	17,200	1,867	1,718	1,867	1,784
17,200	17,250	1,873	1,723	1,873	1,790
17,250	17,300	1,879	1,728	1,879	1,796
17,300	17,350	1,885	1,733	1,885	1,802
17,350	17,400	1,891	1,738	1,891	1,808
17,400	17,450	1,897	1,743	1,897	1,814
17,450	17,500	1,903	1,748	1,903	1,820
17,500	17,550	1,909	1,753	1,909	1,826
17,550	17,600	1,915	1,758	1,915	1,832
17,600	17,650	1,921	1,763	1,921	1,838
17,650	17,700	1,927	1,768	1,927	1,844
17,700	17,750	1,933	1,773	1,933	1,850
17,750	17,800	1,939	1,778	1,939	1,856
17,800	17,850	1,945	1,783	1,945	1,862
17,850	17,900	1,951	1,788	1,951	1,868
17,900	17,950	1,957	1,793	1,957	1,874
17,950	18,000	1,963	1,798	1,963	1,880

18,000

At least	But less than	Single	Married filing jointly *	Married filing separately	Head of a household
18,000	18,050	1,969	1,803	1,969	1,886
18,050	18,100	1,975	1,808	1,975	1,892
18,100	18,150	1,981	1,813	1,981	1,898
18,150	18,200	1,987	1,818	1,987	1,904
18,200	18,250	1,993	1,823	1,993	1,910
18,250	18,300	1,999	1,828	1,999	1,916
18,300	18,350	2,005	1,833	2,005	1,922
18,350	18,400	2,011	1,838	2,011	1,928
18,400	18,450	2,017	1,843	2,017	1,934
18,450	18,500	2,023	1,848	2,023	1,940
18,500	18,550	2,029	1,853	2,029	1,946
18,550	18,600	2,035	1,858	2,035	1,952
18,600	18,650	2,041	1,863	2,041	1,958
18,650	18,700	2,047	1,868	2,047	1,964
18,700	18,750	2,053	1,873	2,053	1,970
18,750	18,800	2,059	1,878	2,059	1,976
18,800	18,850	2,065	1,883	2,065	1,982
18,850	18,900	2,071	1,888	2,071	1,988
18,900	18,950	2,077	1,893	2,077	1,994
18,950	19,000	2,083	1,898	2,083	2,000

19,000

At least	But less than	Single	Married filing jointly *	Married filing separately	Head of a household
19,000	19,050	2,089	1,903	2,089	2,006
19,050	19,100	2,095	1,908	2,095	2,012
19,100	19,150	2,101	1,913	2,101	2,018
19,150	19,200	2,107	1,918	2,107	2,024
19,200	19,250	2,113	1,923	2,113	2,030
19,250	19,300	2,119	1,928	2,119	2,036
19,300	19,350	2,125	1,933	2,125	2,042
19,350	19,400	2,131	1,938	2,131	2,048
19,400	19,450	2,137	1,943	2,137	2,054
19,450	19,500	2,143	1,949	2,143	2,060
19,500	19,550	2,149	1,955	2,149	2,066
19,550	19,600	2,155	1,961	2,155	2,072
19,600	19,650	2,161	1,967	2,161	2,078
19,650	19,700	2,167	1,973	2,167	2,084
19,700	19,750	2,173	1,979	2,173	2,090
19,750	19,800	2,179	1,985	2,179	2,096
19,800	19,850	2,185	1,991	2,185	2,102
19,850	19,900	2,191	1,997	2,191	2,108
19,900	19,950	2,197	2,003	2,197	2,114
19,950	20,000	2,203	2,009	2,203	2,120

20,000

At least	But less than	Single	Married filing jointly *	Married filing separately	Head of a household
20,000	20,050	2,209	2,015	2,209	2,126
20,050	20,100	2,215	2,021	2,215	2,132
20,100	20,150	2,221	2,027	2,221	2,138
20,150	20,200	2,227	2,033	2,227	2,144
20,200	20,250	2,233	2,039	2,233	2,150
20,250	20,300	2,239	2,045	2,239	2,156
20,300	20,350	2,245	2,051	2,245	2,162
20,350	20,400	2,251	2,057	2,251	2,168
20,400	20,450	2,257	2,063	2,257	2,174
20,450	20,500	2,263	2,069	2,263	2,180
20,500	20,550	2,269	2,075	2,269	2,186
20,550	20,600	2,275	2,081	2,275	2,192
20,600	20,650	2,281	2,087	2,281	2,198
20,650	20,700	2,287	2,093	2,287	2,204
20,700	20,750	2,293	2,099	2,293	2,210
20,750	20,800	2,299	2,105	2,299	2,216
20,800	20,850	2,305	2,111	2,305	2,222
20,850	20,900	2,311	2,117	2,311	2,228
20,900	20,950	2,317	2,123	2,317	2,234
20,950	21,000	2,323	2,129	2,323	2,240

(Continued)

* This column must also be used by a qualifying widow(er).

2019 Tax Table — *Continued*

Headers for all tables below:

If line 11b (taxable income) is — **At least** / **But less than**; And you are — **Single** / **Married filing jointly*** / **Married filing separately** / **Head of a household**. Your tax is —

21,000

At least	But less than	Single	Married filing jointly*	Married filing separately	Head of a household
21,000	21,050	2,329	2,135	2,329	2,246
21,050	21,100	2,335	2,141	2,335	2,252
21,100	21,150	2,341	2,147	2,341	2,258
21,150	21,200	2,347	2,153	2,347	2,264
21,200	21,250	2,353	2,159	2,353	2,270
21,250	21,300	2,359	2,165	2,359	2,276
21,300	21,350	2,365	2,171	2,365	2,282
21,350	21,400	2,371	2,177	2,371	2,288
21,400	21,450	2,377	2,183	2,377	2,294
21,450	21,500	2,383	2,189	2,383	2,300
21,500	21,550	2,389	2,195	2,389	2,306
21,550	21,600	2,395	2,201	2,395	2,312
21,600	21,650	2,401	2,207	2,401	2,318
21,650	21,700	2,407	2,213	2,407	2,324
21,700	21,750	2,413	2,219	2,413	2,330
21,750	21,800	2,419	2,225	2,419	2,336
21,800	21,850	2,425	2,231	2,425	2,342
21,850	21,900	2,431	2,237	2,431	2,348
21,900	21,950	2,437	2,243	2,437	2,354
21,950	22,000	2,443	2,249	2,443	2,360

22,000

At least	But less than	Single	Married filing jointly*	Married filing separately	Head of a household
22,000	22,050	2,449	2,255	2,449	2,366
22,050	22,100	2,455	2,261	2,455	2,372
22,100	22,150	2,461	2,267	2,461	2,378
22,150	22,200	2,467	2,273	2,467	2,384
22,200	22,250	2,473	2,279	2,473	2,390
22,250	22,300	2,479	2,285	2,479	2,396
22,300	22,350	2,485	2,291	2,485	2,402
22,350	22,400	2,491	2,297	2,491	2,408
22,400	22,450	2,497	2,303	2,497	2,414
22,450	22,500	2,503	2,309	2,503	2,420
22,500	22,550	2,509	2,315	2,509	2,426
22,550	22,600	2,515	2,321	2,515	2,432
22,600	22,650	2,521	2,327	2,521	2,438
22,650	22,700	2,527	2,333	2,527	2,444
22,700	22,750	2,533	2,339	2,533	2,450
22,750	22,800	2,539	2,345	2,539	2,456
22,800	22,850	2,545	2,351	2,545	2,462
22,850	22,900	2,551	2,357	2,551	2,468
22,900	22,950	2,557	2,363	2,557	2,474
22,950	23,000	2,563	2,369	2,563	2,480

23,000

At least	But less than	Single	Married filing jointly*	Married filing separately	Head of a household
23,000	23,050	2,569	2,375	2,569	2,486
23,050	23,100	2,575	2,381	2,575	2,492
23,100	23,150	2,581	2,387	2,581	2,498
23,150	23,200	2,587	2,393	2,587	2,504
23,200	23,250	2,593	2,399	2,593	2,510
23,250	23,300	2,599	2,405	2,599	2,516
23,300	23,350	2,605	2,411	2,605	2,522
23,350	23,400	2,611	2,417	2,611	2,528
23,400	23,450	2,617	2,423	2,617	2,534
23,450	23,500	2,623	2,429	2,623	2,540
23,500	23,550	2,629	2,435	2,629	2,546
23,550	23,600	2,635	2,441	2,635	2,552
23,600	23,650	2,641	2,447	2,641	2,558
23,650	23,700	2,647	2,453	2,647	2,564
23,700	23,750	2,653	2,459	2,653	2,570
23,750	23,800	2,659	2,465	2,659	2,576
23,800	23,850	2,665	2,471	2,665	2,582
23,850	23,900	2,671	2,477	2,671	2,588
23,900	23,950	2,677	2,483	2,677	2,594
23,950	24,000	2,683	2,489	2,683	2,600

24,000

At least	But less than	Single	Married filing jointly*	Married filing separately	Head of a household
24,000	24,050	2,689	2,495	2,689	2,606
24,050	24,100	2,695	2,501	2,695	2,612
24,100	24,150	2,701	2,507	2,701	2,618
24,150	24,200	2,707	2,513	2,707	2,624
24,200	24,250	2,713	2,519	2,713	2,630
24,250	24,300	2,719	2,525	2,719	2,636
24,300	24,350	2,725	2,531	2,725	2,642
24,350	24,400	2,731	2,537	2,731	2,648
24,400	24,450	2,737	2,543	2,737	2,654
24,450	24,500	2,743	2,549	2,743	2,660
24,500	24,550	2,749	2,555	2,749	2,666
24,550	24,600	2,755	2,561	2,755	2,672
24,600	24,650	2,761	2,567	2,761	2,678
24,650	24,700	2,767	2,573	2,767	2,684
24,700	24,750	2,773	2,579	2,773	2,690
24,750	24,800	2,779	2,585	2,779	2,696
24,800	24,850	2,785	2,591	2,785	2,702
24,850	24,900	2,791	2,597	2,791	2,708
24,900	24,950	2,797	2,603	2,797	2,714
24,950	25,000	2,803	2,609	2,803	2,720

25,000

At least	But less than	Single	Married filing jointly*	Married filing separately	Head of a household
25,000	25,050	2,809	2,615	2,809	2,726
25,050	25,100	2,815	2,621	2,815	2,732
25,100	25,150	2,821	2,627	2,821	2,738
25,150	25,200	2,827	2,633	2,827	2,744
25,200	25,250	2,833	2,639	2,833	2,750
25,250	25,300	2,839	2,645	2,839	2,756
25,300	25,350	2,845	2,651	2,845	2,762
25,350	25,400	2,851	2,657	2,851	2,768
25,400	25,450	2,857	2,663	2,857	2,774
25,450	25,500	2,863	2,669	2,863	2,780
25,500	25,550	2,869	2,675	2,869	2,786
25,550	25,600	2,875	2,681	2,875	2,792
25,600	25,650	2,881	2,687	2,881	2,798
25,650	25,700	2,887	2,693	2,887	2,804
25,700	25,750	2,893	2,699	2,893	2,810
25,750	25,800	2,899	2,705	2,899	2,816
25,800	25,850	2,905	2,711	2,905	2,822
25,850	25,900	2,911	2,717	2,911	2,828
25,900	25,950	2,917	2,723	2,917	2,834
25,950	26,000	2,923	2,729	2,923	2,840

26,000

At least	But less than	Single	Married filing jointly*	Married filing separately	Head of a household
26,000	26,050	2,929	2,735	2,929	2,846
26,050	26,100	2,935	2,741	2,935	2,852
26,100	26,150	2,941	2,747	2,941	2,858
26,150	26,200	2,947	2,753	2,947	2,864
26,200	26,250	2,953	2,759	2,953	2,870
26,250	26,300	2,959	2,765	2,959	2,876
26,300	26,350	2,965	2,771	2,965	2,882
26,350	26,400	2,971	2,777	2,971	2,888
26,400	26,450	2,977	2,783	2,977	2,894
26,450	26,500	2,983	2,789	2,983	2,900
26,500	26,550	2,989	2,795	2,989	2,906
26,550	26,600	2,995	2,801	2,995	2,912
26,600	26,650	3,001	2,807	3,001	2,918
26,650	26,700	3,007	2,813	3,007	2,924
26,700	26,750	3,013	2,819	3,013	2,930
26,750	26,800	3,019	2,825	3,019	2,936
26,800	26,850	3,025	2,831	3,025	2,942
26,850	26,900	3,031	2,837	3,031	2,948
26,900	26,950	3,037	2,843	3,037	2,954
26,950	27,000	3,043	2,849	3,043	2,960

27,000

At least	But less than	Single	Married filing jointly*	Married filing separately	Head of a household
27,000	27,050	3,049	2,855	3,049	2,966
27,050	27,100	3,055	2,861	3,055	2,972
27,100	27,150	3,061	2,867	3,061	2,978
27,150	27,200	3,067	2,873	3,067	2,984
27,200	27,250	3,073	2,879	3,073	2,990
27,250	27,300	3,079	2,885	3,079	2,996
27,300	27,350	3,085	2,891	3,085	3,002
27,350	27,400	3,091	2,897	3,091	3,008
27,400	27,450	3,097	2,903	3,097	3,014
27,450	27,500	3,103	2,909	3,103	3,020
27,500	27,550	3,109	2,915	3,109	3,026
27,550	27,600	3,115	2,921	3,115	3,032
27,600	27,650	3,121	2,927	3,121	3,038
27,650	27,700	3,127	2,933	3,127	3,044
27,700	27,750	3,133	2,939	3,133	3,050
27,750	27,800	3,139	2,945	3,139	3,056
27,800	27,850	3,145	2,951	3,145	3,062
27,850	27,900	3,151	2,957	3,151	3,068
27,900	27,950	3,157	2,963	3,157	3,074
27,950	28,000	3,163	2,969	3,163	3,080

28,000

At least	But less than	Single	Married filing jointly*	Married filing separately	Head of a household
28,000	28,050	3,169	2,975	3,169	3,086
28,050	28,100	3,175	2,981	3,175	3,092
28,100	28,150	3,181	2,987	3,181	3,098
28,150	28,200	3,187	2,993	3,187	3,104
28,200	28,250	3,193	2,999	3,193	3,110
28,250	28,300	3,199	3,005	3,199	3,116
28,300	28,350	3,205	3,011	3,205	3,122
28,350	28,400	3,211	3,017	3,211	3,128
28,400	28,450	3,217	3,023	3,217	3,134
28,450	28,500	3,223	3,029	3,223	3,140
28,500	28,550	3,229	3,035	3,229	3,146
28,550	28,600	3,235	3,041	3,235	3,152
28,600	28,650	3,241	3,047	3,241	3,158
28,650	28,700	3,247	3,053	3,247	3,164
28,700	28,750	3,253	3,059	3,253	3,170
28,750	28,800	3,259	3,065	3,259	3,176
28,800	28,850	3,265	3,071	3,265	3,182
28,850	28,900	3,271	3,077	3,271	3,188
28,900	28,950	3,277	3,083	3,277	3,194
28,950	29,000	3,283	3,089	3,283	3,200

29,000

At least	But less than	Single	Married filing jointly*	Married filing separately	Head of a household
29,000	29,050	3,289	3,095	3,289	3,206
29,050	29,100	3,295	3,101	3,295	3,212
29,100	29,150	3,301	3,107	3,301	3,218
29,150	29,200	3,307	3,113	3,307	3,224
29,200	29,250	3,313	3,119	3,313	3,230
29,250	29,300	3,319	3,125	3,319	3,236
29,300	29,350	3,325	3,131	3,325	3,242
29,350	29,400	3,331	3,137	3,331	3,248
29,400	29,450	3,337	3,143	3,337	3,254
29,450	29,500	3,343	3,149	3,343	3,260
29,500	29,550	3,349	3,155	3,349	3,266
29,550	29,600	3,355	3,161	3,355	3,272
29,600	29,650	3,361	3,167	3,361	3,278
29,650	29,700	3,367	3,173	3,367	3,284
29,700	29,750	3,373	3,179	3,373	3,290
29,750	29,800	3,379	3,185	3,379	3,296
29,800	29,850	3,385	3,191	3,385	3,302
29,850	29,900	3,391	3,197	3,391	3,308
29,900	29,950	3,397	3,203	3,397	3,314
29,950	30,000	3,403	3,209	3,403	3,320

(Continued)

* This column must also be used by a qualifying widow(er).

2019 Tax Table — *Continued*

Column headers for all tables below:

If line 11b (taxable income) is— At least	But less than	Single	Married filing jointly *	Married filing separately	Head of a household

Your tax is—

30,000

At least	But less than	Single	MFJ *	MFS	HoH
30,000	30,050	3,409	3,215	3,409	3,326
30,050	30,100	3,415	3,221	3,415	3,332
30,100	30,150	3,421	3,227	3,421	3,338
30,150	30,200	3,427	3,233	3,427	3,344
30,200	30,250	3,433	3,239	3,433	3,350
30,250	30,300	3,439	3,245	3,439	3,356
30,300	30,350	3,445	3,251	3,445	3,362
30,350	30,400	3,451	3,257	3,451	3,368
30,400	30,450	3,457	3,263	3,457	3,374
30,450	30,500	3,463	3,269	3,463	3,380
30,500	30,550	3,469	3,275	3,469	3,386
30,550	30,600	3,475	3,281	3,475	3,392
30,600	30,650	3,481	3,287	3,481	3,398
30,650	30,700	3,487	3,293	3,487	3,404
30,700	30,750	3,493	3,299	3,493	3,410
30,750	30,800	3,499	3,305	3,499	3,416
30,800	30,850	3,505	3,311	3,505	3,422
30,850	30,900	3,511	3,317	3,511	3,428
30,900	30,950	3,517	3,323	3,517	3,434
30,950	31,000	3,523	3,329	3,523	3,440

31,000

At least	But less than	Single	MFJ *	MFS	HoH
31,000	31,050	3,529	3,335	3,529	3,446
31,050	31,100	3,535	3,341	3,535	3,452
31,100	31,150	3,541	3,347	3,541	3,458
31,150	31,200	3,547	3,353	3,547	3,464
31,200	31,250	3,553	3,359	3,553	3,470
31,250	31,300	3,559	3,365	3,559	3,476
31,300	31,350	3,565	3,371	3,565	3,482
31,350	31,400	3,571	3,377	3,571	3,488
31,400	31,450	3,577	3,383	3,577	3,494
31,450	31,500	3,583	3,389	3,583	3,500
31,500	31,550	3,589	3,395	3,589	3,506
31,550	31,600	3,595	3,401	3,595	3,512
31,600	31,650	3,601	3,407	3,601	3,518
31,650	31,700	3,607	3,413	3,607	3,524
31,700	31,750	3,613	3,419	3,613	3,530
31,750	31,800	3,619	3,425	3,619	3,536
31,800	31,850	3,625	3,431	3,625	3,542
31,850	31,900	3,631	3,437	3,631	3,548
31,900	31,950	3,637	3,443	3,637	3,554
31,950	32,000	3,643	3,449	3,643	3,560

32,000

At least	But less than	Single	MFJ *	MFS	HoH
32,000	32,050	3,649	3,455	3,649	3,566
32,050	32,100	3,655	3,461	3,655	3,572
32,100	32,150	3,661	3,467	3,661	3,578
32,150	32,200	3,667	3,473	3,667	3,584
32,200	32,250	3,673	3,479	3,673	3,590
32,250	32,300	3,679	3,485	3,679	3,596
32,300	32,350	3,685	3,491	3,685	3,602
32,350	32,400	3,691	3,497	3,691	3,608
32,400	32,450	3,697	3,503	3,697	3,614
32,450	32,500	3,703	3,509	3,703	3,620
32,500	32,550	3,709	3,515	3,709	3,626
32,550	32,600	3,715	3,521	3,715	3,632
32,600	32,650	3,721	3,527	3,721	3,638
32,650	32,700	3,727	3,533	3,727	3,644
32,700	32,750	3,733	3,539	3,733	3,650
32,750	32,800	3,739	3,545	3,739	3,656
32,800	32,850	3,745	3,551	3,745	3,662
32,850	32,900	3,751	3,557	3,751	3,668
32,900	32,950	3,757	3,563	3,757	3,674
32,950	33,000	3,763	3,569	3,763	3,680

33,000

At least	But less than	Single	MFJ *	MFS	HoH
33,000	33,050	3,769	3,575	3,769	3,686
33,050	33,100	3,775	3,581	3,775	3,692
33,100	33,150	3,781	3,587	3,781	3,698
33,150	33,200	3,787	3,593	3,787	3,704
33,200	33,250	3,793	3,599	3,793	3,710
33,250	33,300	3,799	3,605	3,799	3,716
33,300	33,350	3,805	3,611	3,805	3,722
33,350	33,400	3,811	3,617	3,811	3,728
33,400	33,450	3,817	3,623	3,817	3,734
33,450	33,500	3,823	3,629	3,823	3,740
33,500	33,550	3,829	3,635	3,829	3,746
33,550	33,600	3,835	3,641	3,835	3,752
33,600	33,650	3,841	3,647	3,841	3,758
33,650	33,700	3,847	3,653	3,847	3,764
33,700	33,750	3,853	3,659	3,853	3,770
33,750	33,800	3,859	3,665	3,859	3,776
33,800	33,850	3,865	3,671	3,865	3,782
33,850	33,900	3,871	3,677	3,871	3,788
33,900	33,950	3,877	3,683	3,877	3,794
33,950	34,000	3,883	3,689	3,883	3,800

34,000

At least	But less than	Single	MFJ *	MFS	HoH
34,000	34,050	3,889	3,695	3,889	3,806
34,050	34,100	3,895	3,701	3,895	3,812
34,100	34,150	3,901	3,707	3,901	3,818
34,150	34,200	3,907	3,713	3,907	3,824
34,200	34,250	3,913	3,719	3,913	3,830
34,250	34,300	3,919	3,725	3,919	3,836
34,300	34,350	3,925	3,731	3,925	3,842
34,350	34,400	3,931	3,737	3,931	3,848
34,400	34,450	3,937	3,743	3,937	3,854
34,450	34,500	3,943	3,749	3,943	3,860
34,500	34,550	3,949	3,755	3,949	3,866
34,550	34,600	3,955	3,761	3,955	3,872
34,600	34,650	3,961	3,767	3,961	3,878
34,650	34,700	3,967	3,773	3,967	3,884
34,700	34,750	3,973	3,779	3,973	3,890
34,750	34,800	3,979	3,785	3,979	3,896
34,800	34,850	3,985	3,791	3,985	3,902
34,850	34,900	3,991	3,797	3,991	3,908
34,900	34,950	3,997	3,803	3,997	3,914
34,950	35,000	4,003	3,809	4,003	3,920

35,000

At least	But less than	Single	MFJ *	MFS	HoH
35,000	35,050	4,009	3,815	4,009	3,926
35,050	35,100	4,015	3,821	4,015	3,932
35,100	35,150	4,021	3,827	4,021	3,938
35,150	35,200	4,027	3,833	4,027	3,944
35,200	35,250	4,033	3,839	4,033	3,950
35,250	35,300	4,039	3,845	4,039	3,956
35,300	35,350	4,045	3,851	4,045	3,962
35,350	35,400	4,051	3,857	4,051	3,968
35,400	35,450	4,057	3,863	4,057	3,974
35,450	35,500	4,063	3,869	4,063	3,980
35,500	35,550	4,069	3,875	4,069	3,986
35,550	35,600	4,075	3,881	4,075	3,992
35,600	35,650	4,081	3,887	4,081	3,998
35,650	35,700	4,087	3,893	4,087	4,004
35,700	35,750	4,093	3,899	4,093	4,010
35,750	35,800	4,099	3,905	4,099	4,016
35,800	35,850	4,105	3,911	4,105	4,022
35,850	35,900	4,111	3,917	4,111	4,028
35,900	35,950	4,117	3,923	4,117	4,034
35,950	36,000	4,123	3,929	4,123	4,040

36,000

At least	But less than	Single	MFJ *	MFS	HoH
36,000	36,050	4,129	3,935	4,129	4,046
36,050	36,100	4,135	3,941	4,135	4,052
36,100	36,150	4,141	3,947	4,141	4,058
36,150	36,200	4,147	3,953	4,147	4,064
36,200	36,250	4,153	3,959	4,153	4,070
36,250	36,300	4,159	3,965	4,159	4,076
36,300	36,350	4,165	3,971	4,165	4,082
36,350	36,400	4,171	3,977	4,171	4,088
36,400	36,450	4,177	3,983	4,177	4,094
36,450	36,500	4,183	3,989	4,183	4,100
36,500	36,550	4,189	3,995	4,189	4,106
36,550	36,600	4,195	4,001	4,195	4,112
36,600	36,650	4,201	4,007	4,201	4,118
36,650	36,700	4,207	4,013	4,207	4,124
36,700	36,750	4,213	4,019	4,213	4,130
36,750	36,800	4,219	4,025	4,219	4,136
36,800	36,850	4,225	4,031	4,225	4,142
36,850	36,900	4,231	4,037	4,231	4,148
36,900	36,950	4,237	4,043	4,237	4,154
36,950	37,000	4,243	4,049	4,243	4,160

37,000

At least	But less than	Single	MFJ *	MFS	HoH
37,000	37,050	4,249	4,055	4,249	4,166
37,050	37,100	4,255	4,061	4,255	4,172
37,100	37,150	4,261	4,067	4,261	4,178
37,150	37,200	4,267	4,073	4,267	4,184
37,200	37,250	4,273	4,079	4,273	4,190
37,250	37,300	4,279	4,085	4,279	4,196
37,300	37,350	4,285	4,091	4,285	4,202
37,350	37,400	4,291	4,097	4,291	4,208
37,400	37,450	4,297	4,103	4,297	4,214
37,450	37,500	4,303	4,109	4,303	4,220
37,500	37,550	4,309	4,115	4,309	4,226
37,550	37,600	4,315	4,121	4,315	4,232
37,600	37,650	4,321	4,127	4,321	4,238
37,650	37,700	4,327	4,133	4,327	4,244
37,700	37,750	4,333	4,139	4,333	4,250
37,750	37,800	4,339	4,145	4,339	4,256
37,800	37,850	4,345	4,151	4,345	4,262
37,850	37,900	4,351	4,157	4,351	4,268
37,900	37,950	4,357	4,163	4,357	4,274
37,950	38,000	4,363	4,169	4,363	4,280

38,000

At least	But less than	Single	MFJ *	MFS	HoH
38,000	38,050	4,369	4,175	4,369	4,286
38,050	38,100	4,375	4,181	4,375	4,292
38,100	38,150	4,381	4,187	4,381	4,298
38,150	38,200	4,387	4,193	4,387	4,304
38,200	38,250	4,393	4,199	4,393	4,310
38,250	38,300	4,399	4,205	4,399	4,316
38,300	38,350	4,405	4,211	4,405	4,322
38,350	38,400	4,411	4,217	4,411	4,328
38,400	38,450	4,417	4,223	4,417	4,334
38,450	38,500	4,423	4,229	4,423	4,340
38,500	38,550	4,429	4,235	4,429	4,346
38,550	38,600	4,435	4,241	4,435	4,352
38,600	38,650	4,441	4,247	4,441	4,358
38,650	38,700	4,447	4,253	4,447	4,364
38,700	38,750	4,453	4,259	4,453	4,370
38,750	38,800	4,459	4,265	4,459	4,376
38,800	38,850	4,465	4,271	4,465	4,382
38,850	38,900	4,471	4,277	4,471	4,388
38,900	38,950	4,477	4,283	4,477	4,394
38,950	39,000	4,483	4,289	4,483	4,400

(Continued)

* This column must also be used by a qualifying widow(er).

2019 Tax Table — *Continued*

39,000

At least	But less than	Single	Married filing jointly *	Married filing separately	Head of a household
39,000	39,050	4,489	4,295	4,489	4,406
39,050	39,100	4,495	4,301	4,495	4,412
39,100	39,150	4,501	4,307	4,501	4,418
39,150	39,200	4,507	4,313	4,507	4,424
39,200	39,250	4,513	4,319	4,513	4,430
39,250	39,300	4,519	4,325	4,519	4,436
39,300	39,350	4,525	4,331	4,525	4,442
39,350	39,400	4,531	4,337	4,531	4,448
39,400	39,450	4,537	4,343	4,537	4,454
39,450	39,500	4,543	4,349	4,543	4,460
39,500	39,550	4,554	4,355	4,554	4,466
39,550	39,600	4,565	4,361	4,565	4,472
39,600	39,650	4,576	4,367	4,576	4,478
39,650	39,700	4,587	4,373	4,587	4,484
39,700	39,750	4,598	4,379	4,598	4,490
39,750	39,800	4,609	4,385	4,609	4,496
39,800	39,850	4,620	4,391	4,620	4,502
39,850	39,900	4,631	4,397	4,631	4,508
39,900	39,950	4,642	4,403	4,642	4,514
39,950	40,000	4,653	4,409	4,653	4,520

40,000

At least	But less than	Single	Married filing jointly *	Married filing separately	Head of a household
40,000	40,050	4,664	4,415	4,664	4,526
40,050	40,100	4,675	4,421	4,675	4,532
40,100	40,150	4,686	4,427	4,686	4,538
40,150	40,200	4,697	4,433	4,697	4,544
40,200	40,250	4,708	4,439	4,708	4,550
40,250	40,300	4,719	4,445	4,719	4,556
40,300	40,350	4,730	4,451	4,730	4,562
40,350	40,400	4,741	4,457	4,741	4,568
40,400	40,450	4,752	4,463	4,752	4,574
40,450	40,500	4,763	4,469	4,763	4,580
40,500	40,550	4,774	4,475	4,774	4,586
40,550	40,600	4,785	4,481	4,785	4,592
40,600	40,650	4,796	4,487	4,796	4,598
40,650	40,700	4,807	4,493	4,807	4,604
40,700	40,750	4,818	4,499	4,818	4,610
40,750	40,800	4,829	4,505	4,829	4,616
40,800	40,850	4,840	4,511	4,840	4,622
40,850	40,900	4,851	4,517	4,851	4,628
40,900	40,950	4,862	4,523	4,862	4,634
40,950	41,000	4,873	4,529	4,873	4,640

41,000

At least	But less than	Single	Married filing jointly *	Married filing separately	Head of a household
41,000	41,050	4,884	4,535	4,884	4,646
41,050	41,100	4,895	4,541	4,895	4,652
41,100	41,150	4,906	4,547	4,906	4,658
41,150	41,200	4,917	4,553	4,917	4,664
41,200	41,250	4,928	4,559	4,928	4,670
41,250	41,300	4,939	4,565	4,939	4,676
41,300	41,350	4,950	4,571	4,950	4,682
41,350	41,400	4,961	4,577	4,961	4,688
41,400	41,450	4,972	4,583	4,972	4,694
41,450	41,500	4,983	4,589	4,983	4,700
41,500	41,550	4,994	4,595	4,994	4,706
41,550	41,600	5,005	4,601	5,005	4,712
41,600	41,650	5,016	4,607	5,016	4,718
41,650	41,700	5,027	4,613	5,027	4,724
41,700	41,750	5,038	4,619	5,038	4,730
41,750	41,800	5,049	4,625	5,049	4,736
41,800	41,850	5,060	4,631	5,060	4,742
41,850	41,900	5,071	4,637	5,071	4,748
41,900	41,950	5,082	4,643	5,082	4,754
41,950	42,000	5,093	4,649	5,093	4,760

42,000

At least	But less than	Single	Married filing jointly *	Married filing separately	Head of a household
42,000	42,050	5,104	4,655	5,104	4,766
42,050	42,100	5,115	4,661	5,115	4,772
42,100	42,150	5,126	4,667	5,126	4,778
42,150	42,200	5,137	4,673	5,137	4,784
42,200	42,250	5,148	4,679	5,148	4,790
42,250	42,300	5,159	4,685	5,159	4,796
42,300	42,350	5,170	4,691	5,170	4,802
42,350	42,400	5,181	4,697	5,181	4,808
42,400	42,450	5,192	4,703	5,192	4,814
42,450	42,500	5,203	4,709	5,203	4,820
42,500	42,550	5,214	4,715	5,214	4,826
42,550	42,600	5,225	4,721	5,225	4,832
42,600	42,650	5,236	4,727	5,236	4,838
42,650	42,700	5,247	4,733	5,247	4,844
42,700	42,750	5,258	4,739	5,258	4,850
42,750	42,800	5,269	4,745	5,269	4,856
42,800	42,850	5,280	4,751	5,280	4,862
42,850	42,900	5,291	4,757	5,291	4,868
42,900	42,950	5,302	4,763	5,302	4,874
42,950	43,000	5,313	4,769	5,313	4,880

43,000

At least	But less than	Single	Married filing jointly *	Married filing separately	Head of a household
43,000	43,050	5,324	4,775	5,324	4,886
43,050	43,100	5,335	4,781	5,335	4,892
43,100	43,150	5,346	4,787	5,346	4,898
43,150	43,200	5,357	4,793	5,357	4,904
43,200	43,250	5,368	4,799	5,368	4,910
43,250	43,300	5,379	4,805	5,379	4,916
43,300	43,350	5,390	4,811	5,390	4,922
43,350	43,400	5,401	4,817	5,401	4,928
43,400	43,450	5,412	4,823	5,412	4,934
43,450	43,500	5,423	4,829	5,423	4,940
43,500	43,550	5,434	4,835	5,434	4,946
43,550	43,600	5,445	4,841	5,445	4,952
43,600	43,650	5,456	4,847	5,456	4,958
43,650	43,700	5,467	4,853	5,467	4,964
43,700	43,750	5,478	4,859	5,478	4,970
43,750	43,800	5,489	4,865	5,489	4,976
43,800	43,850	5,500	4,871	5,500	4,982
43,850	43,900	5,511	4,877	5,511	4,988
43,900	43,950	5,522	4,883	5,522	4,994
43,950	44,000	5,533	4,889	5,533	5,000

44,000

At least	But less than	Single	Married filing jointly *	Married filing separately	Head of a household
44,000	44,050	5,544	4,895	5,544	5,006
44,050	44,100	5,555	4,901	5,555	5,012
44,100	44,150	5,566	4,907	5,566	5,018
44,150	44,200	5,577	4,913	5,577	5,024
44,200	44,250	5,588	4,919	5,588	5,030
44,250	44,300	5,599	4,925	5,599	5,036
44,300	44,350	5,610	4,931	5,610	5,042
44,350	44,400	5,621	4,937	5,621	5,048
44,400	44,450	5,632	4,943	5,632	5,054
44,450	44,500	5,643	4,949	5,643	5,060
44,500	44,550	5,654	4,955	5,654	5,066
44,550	44,600	5,665	4,961	5,665	5,072
44,600	44,650	5,676	4,967	5,676	5,078
44,650	44,700	5,687	4,973	5,687	5,084
44,700	44,750	5,698	4,979	5,698	5,090
44,750	44,800	5,709	4,985	5,709	5,096
44,800	44,850	5,720	4,991	5,720	5,102
44,850	44,900	5,731	4,997	5,731	5,108
44,900	44,950	5,742	5,003	5,742	5,114
44,950	45,000	5,753	5,009	5,753	5,120

45,000

At least	But less than	Single	Married filing jointly *	Married filing separately	Head of a household
45,000	45,050	5,764	5,015	5,764	5,126
45,050	45,100	5,775	5,021	5,775	5,132
45,100	45,150	5,786	5,027	5,786	5,138
45,150	45,200	5,797	5,033	5,797	5,144
45,200	45,250	5,808	5,039	5,808	5,150
45,250	45,300	5,819	5,045	5,819	5,156
45,300	45,350	5,830	5,051	5,830	5,162
45,350	45,400	5,841	5,057	5,841	5,168
45,400	45,450	5,852	5,063	5,852	5,174
45,450	45,500	5,863	5,069	5,863	5,180
45,500	45,550	5,874	5,075	5,874	5,186
45,550	45,600	5,885	5,081	5,885	5,192
45,600	45,650	5,896	5,087	5,896	5,198
45,650	45,700	5,907	5,093	5,907	5,204
45,700	45,750	5,918	5,099	5,918	5,210
45,750	45,800	5,929	5,105	5,929	5,216
45,800	45,850	5,940	5,111	5,940	5,222
45,850	45,900	5,951	5,117	5,951	5,228
45,900	45,950	5,962	5,123	5,962	5,234
45,950	46,000	5,973	5,129	5,973	5,240

46,000

At least	But less than	Single	Married filing jointly *	Married filing separately	Head of a household
46,000	46,050	5,984	5,135	5,984	5,246
46,050	46,100	5,995	5,141	5,995	5,252
46,100	46,150	6,006	5,147	6,006	5,258
46,150	46,200	6,017	5,153	6,017	5,264
46,200	46,250	6,028	5,159	6,028	5,270
46,250	46,300	6,039	5,165	6,039	5,276
46,300	46,350	6,050	5,171	6,050	5,282
46,350	46,400	6,061	5,177	6,061	5,288
46,400	46,450	6,072	5,183	6,072	5,294
46,450	46,500	6,083	5,189	6,083	5,300
46,500	46,550	6,094	5,195	6,094	5,306
46,550	46,600	6,105	5,201	6,105	5,312
46,600	46,650	6,116	5,207	6,116	5,318
46,650	46,700	6,127	5,213	6,127	5,324
46,700	46,750	6,138	5,219	6,138	5,330
46,750	46,800	6,149	5,225	6,149	5,336
46,800	46,850	6,160	5,231	6,160	5,342
46,850	46,900	6,171	5,237	6,171	5,348
46,900	46,950	6,182	5,243	6,182	5,354
46,950	47,000	6,193	5,249	6,193	5,360

47,000

At least	But less than	Single	Married filing jointly *	Married filing separately	Head of a household
47,000	47,050	6,204	5,255	6,204	5,366
47,050	47,100	6,215	5,261	6,215	5,372
47,100	47,150	6,226	5,267	6,226	5,378
47,150	47,200	6,237	5,273	6,237	5,384
47,200	47,250	6,248	5,279	6,248	5,390
47,250	47,300	6,259	5,285	6,259	5,396
47,300	47,350	6,270	5,291	6,270	5,402
47,350	47,400	6,281	5,297	6,281	5,408
47,400	47,450	6,292	5,303	6,292	5,414
47,450	47,500	6,303	5,309	6,303	5,420
47,500	47,550	6,314	5,315	6,314	5,426
47,550	47,600	6,325	5,321	6,325	5,432
47,600	47,650	6,336	5,327	6,336	5,438
47,650	47,700	6,347	5,333	6,347	5,444
47,700	47,750	6,358	5,339	6,358	5,450
47,750	47,800	6,369	5,345	6,369	5,456
47,800	47,850	6,380	5,351	6,380	5,462
47,850	47,900	6,391	5,357	6,391	5,468
47,900	47,950	6,402	5,363	6,402	5,474
47,950	48,000	6,413	5,369	6,413	5,480

(Continued)

* This column must also be used by a qualifying widow(er).

2019 Tax Table — *Continued*

Columns for each block: At least | But less than | Single | Married filing jointly * | Married filing separately | Head of a household

(*) This column must also be used by a qualifying widow(er).

48,000

At least	But less than	Single	MFJ	MFS	HOH
48,000	48,050	6,424	5,375	6,424	5,486
48,050	48,100	6,435	5,381	6,435	5,492
48,100	48,150	6,446	5,387	6,446	5,498
48,150	48,200	6,457	5,393	6,457	5,504
48,200	48,250	6,468	5,399	6,468	5,510
48,250	48,300	6,479	5,405	6,479	5,516
48,300	48,350	6,490	5,411	6,490	5,522
48,350	48,400	6,501	5,417	6,501	5,528
48,400	48,450	6,512	5,423	6,512	5,534
48,450	48,500	6,523	5,429	6,523	5,540
48,500	48,550	6,534	5,435	6,534	5,546
48,550	48,600	6,545	5,441	6,545	5,552
48,600	48,650	6,556	5,447	6,556	5,558
48,650	48,700	6,567	5,453	6,567	5,564
48,700	48,750	6,578	5,459	6,578	5,570
48,750	48,800	6,589	5,465	6,589	5,576
48,800	48,850	6,600	5,471	6,600	5,582
48,850	48,900	6,611	5,477	6,611	5,588
48,900	48,950	6,622	5,483	6,622	5,594
48,950	49,000	6,633	5,489	6,633	5,600

49,000

At least	But less than	Single	MFJ	MFS	HOH
49,000	49,050	6,644	5,495	6,644	5,606
49,050	49,100	6,655	5,501	6,655	5,612
49,100	49,150	6,666	5,507	6,666	5,618
49,150	49,200	6,677	5,513	6,677	5,624
49,200	49,250	6,688	5,519	6,688	5,630
49,250	49,300	6,699	5,525	6,699	5,636
49,300	49,350	6,710	5,531	6,710	5,642
49,350	49,400	6,721	5,537	6,721	5,648
49,400	49,450	6,732	5,543	6,732	5,654
49,450	49,500	6,743	5,549	6,743	5,660
49,500	49,550	6,754	5,555	6,754	5,666
49,550	49,600	6,765	5,561	6,765	5,672
49,600	49,650	6,776	5,567	6,776	5,678
49,650	49,700	6,787	5,573	6,787	5,684
49,700	49,750	6,798	5,579	6,798	5,690
49,750	49,800	6,809	5,585	6,809	5,696
49,800	49,850	6,820	5,591	6,820	5,702
49,850	49,900	6,831	5,597	6,831	5,708
49,900	49,950	6,842	5,603	6,842	5,714
49,950	50,000	6,853	5,609	6,853	5,720

50,000

At least	But less than	Single	MFJ	MFS	HOH
50,000	50,050	6,864	5,615	6,864	5,726
50,050	50,100	6,875	5,621	6,875	5,732
50,100	50,150	6,886	5,627	6,886	5,738
50,150	50,200	6,897	5,633	6,897	5,744
50,200	50,250	6,908	5,639	6,908	5,750
50,250	50,300	6,919	5,645	6,919	5,756
50,300	50,350	6,930	5,651	6,930	5,762
50,350	50,400	6,941	5,657	6,941	5,768
50,400	50,450	6,952	5,663	6,952	5,774
50,450	50,500	6,963	5,669	6,963	5,780
50,500	50,550	6,974	5,675	6,974	5,786
50,550	50,600	6,985	5,681	6,985	5,792
50,600	50,650	6,996	5,687	6,996	5,798
50,650	50,700	7,007	5,693	7,007	5,804
50,700	50,750	7,018	5,699	7,018	5,810
50,750	50,800	7,029	5,705	7,029	5,816
50,800	50,850	7,040	5,711	7,040	5,822
50,850	50,900	7,051	5,717	7,051	5,828
50,900	50,950	7,062	5,723	7,062	5,834
50,950	51,000	7,073	5,729	7,073	5,840

51,000

At least	But less than	Single	MFJ	MFS	HOH
51,000	51,050	7,084	5,735	7,084	5,846
51,050	51,100	7,095	5,741	7,095	5,852
51,100	51,150	7,106	5,747	7,106	5,858
51,150	51,200	7,117	5,753	7,117	5,864
51,200	51,250	7,128	5,759	7,128	5,870
51,250	51,300	7,139	5,765	7,139	5,876
51,300	51,350	7,150	5,771	7,150	5,882
51,350	51,400	7,161	5,777	7,161	5,888
51,400	51,450	7,172	5,783	7,172	5,894
51,450	51,500	7,183	5,789	7,183	5,900
51,500	51,550	7,194	5,795	7,194	5,906
51,550	51,600	7,205	5,801	7,205	5,912
51,600	51,650	7,216	5,807	7,216	5,918
51,650	51,700	7,227	5,813	7,227	5,924
51,700	51,750	7,238	5,819	7,238	5,930
51,750	51,800	7,249	5,825	7,249	5,936
51,800	51,850	7,260	5,831	7,260	5,942
51,850	51,900	7,271	5,837	7,271	5,948
51,900	51,950	7,282	5,843	7,282	5,954
51,950	52,000	7,293	5,849	7,293	5,960

52,000

At least	But less than	Single	MFJ	MFS	HOH
52,000	52,050	7,304	5,855	7,304	5,966
52,050	52,100	7,315	5,861	7,315	5,972
52,100	52,150	7,326	5,867	7,326	5,978
52,150	52,200	7,337	5,873	7,337	5,984
52,200	52,250	7,348	5,879	7,348	5,990
52,250	52,300	7,359	5,885	7,359	5,996
52,300	52,350	7,370	5,891	7,370	6,002
52,350	52,400	7,381	5,897	7,381	6,008
52,400	52,450	7,392	5,903	7,392	6,014
52,450	52,500	7,403	5,909	7,403	6,020
52,500	52,550	7,414	5,915	7,414	6,026
52,550	52,600	7,425	5,921	7,425	6,032
52,600	52,650	7,436	5,927	7,436	6,038
52,650	52,700	7,447	5,933	7,447	6,044
52,700	52,750	7,458	5,939	7,458	6,050
52,750	52,800	7,469	5,945	7,469	6,056
52,800	52,850	7,480	5,951	7,480	6,062
52,850	52,900	7,491	5,957	7,491	6,071
52,900	52,950	7,502	5,963	7,502	6,082
52,950	53,000	7,513	5,969	7,513	6,093

53,000

At least	But less than	Single	MFJ	MFS	HOH
53,000	53,050	7,524	5,975	7,524	6,104
53,050	53,100	7,535	5,981	7,535	6,115
53,100	53,150	7,546	5,987	7,546	6,126
53,150	53,200	7,557	5,993	7,557	6,137
53,200	53,250	7,568	5,999	7,568	6,148
53,250	53,300	7,579	6,005	7,579	6,159
53,300	53,350	7,590	6,011	7,590	6,170
53,350	53,400	7,601	6,017	7,601	6,181
53,400	53,450	7,612	6,023	7,612	6,192
53,450	53,500	7,623	6,029	7,623	6,203
53,500	53,550	7,634	6,035	7,634	6,214
53,550	53,600	7,645	6,041	7,645	6,225
53,600	53,650	7,656	6,047	7,656	6,236
53,650	53,700	7,667	6,053	7,667	6,247
53,700	53,750	7,678	6,059	7,678	6,258
53,750	53,800	7,689	6,065	7,689	6,269
53,800	53,850	7,700	6,071	7,700	6,280
53,850	53,900	7,711	6,077	7,711	6,291
53,900	53,950	7,722	6,083	7,722	6,302
53,950	54,000	7,733	6,089	7,733	6,313

54,000

At least	But less than	Single	MFJ	MFS	HOH
54,000	54,050	7,744	6,095	7,744	6,324
54,050	54,100	7,755	6,101	7,755	6,335
54,100	54,150	7,766	6,107	7,766	6,346
54,150	54,200	7,777	6,113	7,777	6,357
54,200	54,250	7,788	6,119	7,788	6,368
54,250	54,300	7,799	6,125	7,799	6,379
54,300	54,350	7,810	6,131	7,810	6,390
54,350	54,400	7,821	6,137	7,821	6,401
54,400	54,450	7,832	6,143	7,832	6,412
54,450	54,500	7,843	6,149	7,843	6,423
54,500	54,550	7,854	6,155	7,854	6,434
54,550	54,600	7,865	6,161	7,865	6,445
54,600	54,650	7,876	6,167	7,876	6,456
54,650	54,700	7,887	6,173	7,887	6,467
54,700	54,750	7,898	6,179	7,898	6,478
54,750	54,800	7,909	6,185	7,909	6,489
54,800	54,850	7,920	6,191	7,920	6,500
54,850	54,900	7,931	6,197	7,931	6,511
54,900	54,950	7,942	6,203	7,942	6,522
54,950	55,000	7,953	6,209	7,953	6,533

55,000

At least	But less than	Single	MFJ	MFS	HOH
55,000	55,050	7,964	6,215	7,964	6,544
55,050	55,100	7,975	6,221	7,975	6,555
55,100	55,150	7,986	6,227	7,986	6,566
55,150	55,200	7,997	6,233	7,997	6,577
55,200	55,250	8,008	6,239	8,008	6,588
55,250	55,300	8,019	6,245	8,019	6,599
55,300	55,350	8,030	6,251	8,030	6,610
55,350	55,400	8,041	6,257	8,041	6,621
55,400	55,450	8,052	6,263	8,052	6,632
55,450	55,500	8,063	6,269	8,063	6,643
55,500	55,550	8,074	6,275	8,074	6,654
55,550	55,600	8,085	6,281	8,085	6,665
55,600	55,650	8,096	6,287	8,096	6,676
55,650	55,700	8,107	6,293	8,107	6,687
55,700	55,750	8,118	6,299	8,118	6,698
55,750	55,800	8,129	6,305	8,129	6,709
55,800	55,850	8,140	6,311	8,140	6,720
55,850	55,900	8,151	6,317	8,151	6,731
55,900	55,950	8,162	6,323	8,162	6,742
55,950	56,000	8,173	6,329	8,173	6,753

56,000

At least	But less than	Single	MFJ	MFS	HOH
56,000	56,050	8,184	6,335	8,184	6,764
56,050	56,100	8,195	6,341	8,195	6,775
56,100	56,150	8,206	6,347	8,206	6,786
56,150	56,200	8,217	6,353	8,217	6,797
56,200	56,250	8,228	6,359	8,228	6,808
56,250	56,300	8,239	6,365	8,239	6,819
56,300	56,350	8,250	6,371	8,250	6,830
56,350	56,400	8,261	6,377	8,261	6,841
56,400	56,450	8,272	6,383	8,272	6,852
56,450	56,500	8,283	6,389	8,283	6,863
56,500	56,550	8,294	6,395	8,294	6,874
56,550	56,600	8,305	6,401	8,305	6,885
56,600	56,650	8,316	6,407	8,316	6,896
56,650	56,700	8,327	6,413	8,327	6,907
56,700	56,750	8,338	6,419	8,338	6,918
56,750	56,800	8,349	6,425	8,349	6,929
56,800	56,850	8,360	6,431	8,360	6,940
56,850	56,900	8,371	6,437	8,371	6,951
56,900	56,950	8,382	6,443	8,382	6,962
56,950	57,000	8,393	6,449	8,393	6,973

(Continued)

* This column must also be used by a qualifying widow(er).

57,000

At least	But less than	Single	Married filing jointly *	Married filing separately	Head of a household
57,000	57,050	8,404	6,455	8,404	6,984
57,050	57,100	8,415	6,461	8,415	6,995
57,100	57,150	8,426	6,467	8,426	7,006
57,150	57,200	8,437	6,473	8,437	7,017
57,200	57,250	8,448	6,479	8,448	7,028
57,250	57,300	8,459	6,485	8,459	7,039
57,300	57,350	8,470	6,491	8,470	7,050
57,350	57,400	8,481	6,497	8,481	7,061
57,400	57,450	8,492	6,503	8,492	7,072
57,450	57,500	8,503	6,509	8,503	7,083
57,500	57,550	8,514	6,515	8,514	7,094
57,550	57,600	8,525	6,521	8,525	7,105
57,600	57,650	8,536	6,527	8,536	7,116
57,650	57,700	8,547	6,533	8,547	7,127
57,700	57,750	8,558	6,539	8,558	7,138
57,750	57,800	8,569	6,545	8,569	7,149
57,800	57,850	8,580	6,551	8,580	7,160
57,850	57,900	8,591	6,557	8,591	7,171
57,900	57,950	8,602	6,563	8,602	7,182
57,950	58,000	8,613	6,569	8,613	7,193

58,000

At least	But less than	Single	Married filing jointly *	Married filing separately	Head of a household
58,000	58,050	8,624	6,575	8,624	7,204
58,050	58,100	8,635	6,581	8,635	7,215
58,100	58,150	8,646	6,587	8,646	7,226
58,150	58,200	8,657	6,593	8,657	7,237
58,200	58,250	8,668	6,599	8,668	7,248
58,250	58,300	8,679	6,605	8,679	7,259
58,300	58,350	8,690	6,611	8,690	7,270
58,350	58,400	8,701	6,617	8,701	7,281
58,400	58,450	8,712	6,623	8,712	7,292
58,450	58,500	8,723	6,629	8,723	7,303
58,500	58,550	8,734	6,635	8,734	7,314
58,550	58,600	8,745	6,641	8,745	7,325
58,600	58,650	8,756	6,647	8,756	7,336
58,650	58,700	8,767	6,653	8,767	7,347
58,700	58,750	8,778	6,659	8,778	7,358
58,750	58,800	8,789	6,665	8,789	7,369
58,800	58,850	8,800	6,671	8,800	7,380
58,850	58,900	8,811	6,677	8,811	7,391
58,900	58,950	8,822	6,683	8,822	7,402
58,950	59,000	8,833	6,689	8,833	7,413

59,000

At least	But less than	Single	Married filing jointly *	Married filing separately	Head of a household
59,000	59,050	8,844	6,695	8,844	7,424
59,050	59,100	8,855	6,701	8,855	7,435
59,100	59,150	8,866	6,707	8,866	7,446
59,150	59,200	8,877	6,713	8,877	7,457
59,200	59,250	8,888	6,719	8,888	7,468
59,250	59,300	8,899	6,725	8,899	7,479
59,300	59,350	8,910	6,731	8,910	7,490
59,350	59,400	8,921	6,737	8,921	7,501
59,400	59,450	8,932	6,743	8,932	7,512
59,450	59,500	8,943	6,749	8,943	7,523
59,500	59,550	8,954	6,755	8,954	7,534
59,550	59,600	8,965	6,761	8,965	7,545
59,600	59,650	8,976	6,767	8,976	7,556
59,650	59,700	8,987	6,773	8,987	7,567
59,700	59,750	8,998	6,779	8,998	7,578
59,750	59,800	9,009	6,785	9,009	7,589
59,800	59,850	9,020	6,791	9,020	7,600
59,850	59,900	9,031	6,797	9,031	7,611
59,900	59,950	9,042	6,803	9,042	7,622
59,950	60,000	9,053	6,809	9,053	7,633

60,000

At least	But less than	Single	Married filing jointly *	Married filing separately	Head of a household
60,000	60,050	9,064	6,815	9,064	7,644
60,050	60,100	9,075	6,821	9,075	7,655
60,100	60,150	9,086	6,827	9,086	7,666
60,150	60,200	9,097	6,833	9,097	7,677
60,200	60,250	9,108	6,839	9,108	7,688
60,250	60,300	9,119	6,845	9,119	7,699
60,300	60,350	9,130	6,851	9,130	7,710
60,350	60,400	9,141	6,857	9,141	7,721
60,400	60,450	9,152	6,863	9,152	7,732
60,450	60,500	9,163	6,869	9,163	7,743
60,500	60,550	9,174	6,875	9,174	7,754
60,550	60,600	9,185	6,881	9,185	7,765
60,600	60,650	9,196	6,887	9,196	7,776
60,650	60,700	9,207	6,893	9,207	7,787
60,700	60,750	9,218	6,899	9,218	7,798
60,750	60,800	9,229	6,905	9,229	7,809
60,800	60,850	9,240	6,911	9,240	7,820
60,850	60,900	9,251	6,917	9,251	7,831
60,900	60,950	9,262	6,923	9,262	7,842
60,950	61,000	9,273	6,929	9,273	7,853

61,000

At least	But less than	Single	Married filing jointly *	Married filing separately	Head of a household
61,000	61,050	9,284	6,935	9,284	7,864
61,050	61,100	9,295	6,941	9,295	7,875
61,100	61,150	9,306	6,947	9,306	7,886
61,150	61,200	9,317	6,953	9,317	7,897
61,200	61,250	9,328	6,959	9,328	7,908
61,250	61,300	9,339	6,965	9,339	7,919
61,300	61,350	9,350	6,971	9,350	7,930
61,350	61,400	9,361	6,977	9,361	7,941
61,400	61,450	9,372	6,983	9,372	7,952
61,450	61,500	9,383	6,989	9,383	7,963
61,500	61,550	9,394	6,995	9,394	7,974
61,550	61,600	9,405	7,001	9,405	7,985
61,600	61,650	9,416	7,007	9,416	7,996
61,650	61,700	9,427	7,013	9,427	8,007
61,700	61,750	9,438	7,019	9,438	8,018
61,750	61,800	9,449	7,025	9,449	8,029
61,800	61,850	9,460	7,031	9,460	8,040
61,850	61,900	9,471	7,037	9,471	8,051
61,900	61,950	9,482	7,043	9,482	8,062
61,950	62,000	9,493	7,049	9,493	8,073

62,000

At least	But less than	Single	Married filing jointly *	Married filing separately	Head of a household
62,000	62,050	9,504	7,055	9,504	8,084
62,050	62,100	9,515	7,061	9,515	8,095
62,100	62,150	9,526	7,067	9,526	8,106
62,150	62,200	9,537	7,073	9,537	8,117
62,200	62,250	9,548	7,079	9,548	8,128
62,250	62,300	9,559	7,085	9,559	8,139
62,300	62,350	9,570	7,091	9,570	8,150
62,350	62,400	9,581	7,097	9,581	8,161
62,400	62,450	9,592	7,103	9,592	8,172
62,450	62,500	9,603	7,109	9,603	8,183
62,500	62,550	9,614	7,115	9,614	8,194
62,550	62,600	9,625	7,121	9,625	8,205
62,600	62,650	9,636	7,127	9,636	8,216
62,650	62,700	9,647	7,133	9,647	8,227
62,700	62,750	9,658	7,139	9,658	8,238
62,750	62,800	9,669	7,145	9,669	8,249
62,800	62,850	9,680	7,151	9,680	8,260
62,850	62,900	9,691	7,157	9,691	8,271
62,900	62,950	9,702	7,163	9,702	8,282
62,950	63,000	9,713	7,169	9,713	8,293

63,000

At least	But less than	Single	Married filing jointly *	Married filing separately	Head of a household
63,000	63,050	9,724	7,175	9,724	8,304
63,050	63,100	9,735	7,181	9,735	8,315
63,100	63,150	9,746	7,187	9,746	8,326
63,150	63,200	9,757	7,193	9,757	8,337
63,200	63,250	9,768	7,199	9,768	8,348
63,250	63,300	9,779	7,205	9,779	8,359
63,300	63,350	9,790	7,211	9,790	8,370
63,350	63,400	9,801	7,217	9,801	8,381
63,400	63,450	9,812	7,223	9,812	8,392
63,450	63,500	9,823	7,229	9,823	8,403
63,500	63,550	9,834	7,235	9,834	8,414
63,550	63,600	9,845	7,241	9,845	8,425
63,600	63,650	9,856	7,247	9,856	8,436
63,650	63,700	9,867	7,253	9,867	8,447
63,700	63,750	9,878	7,259	9,878	8,458
63,750	63,800	9,889	7,265	9,889	8,469
63,800	63,850	9,900	7,271	9,900	8,480
63,850	63,900	9,911	7,277	9,911	8,491
63,900	63,950	9,922	7,283	9,922	8,502
63,950	64,000	9,933	7,289	9,933	8,513

64,000

At least	But less than	Single	Married filing jointly *	Married filing separately	Head of a household
64,000	64,050	9,944	7,295	9,944	8,524
64,050	64,100	9,955	7,301	9,955	8,535
64,100	64,150	9,966	7,307	9,966	8,546
64,150	64,200	9,977	7,313	9,977	8,557
64,200	64,250	9,988	7,319	9,988	8,568
64,250	64,300	9,999	7,325	9,999	8,579
64,300	64,350	10,010	7,331	10,010	8,590
64,350	64,400	10,021	7,337	10,021	8,601
64,400	64,450	10,032	7,343	10,032	8,612
64,450	64,500	10,043	7,349	10,043	8,623
64,500	64,550	10,054	7,355	10,054	8,634
64,550	64,600	10,065	7,361	10,065	8,645
64,600	64,650	10,076	7,367	10,076	8,656
64,650	64,700	10,087	7,373	10,087	8,667
64,700	64,750	10,098	7,379	10,098	8,678
64,750	64,800	10,109	7,385	10,109	8,689
64,800	64,850	10,120	7,391	10,120	8,700
64,850	64,900	10,131	7,397	10,131	8,711
64,900	64,950	10,142	7,403	10,142	8,722
64,950	65,000	10,153	7,409	10,153	8,733

65,000

At least	But less than	Single	Married filing jointly *	Married filing separately	Head of a household
65,000	65,050	10,164	7,415	10,164	8,744
65,050	65,100	10,175	7,421	10,175	8,755
65,100	65,150	10,186	7,427	10,186	8,766
65,150	65,200	10,197	7,433	10,197	8,777
65,200	65,250	10,208	7,439	10,208	8,788
65,250	65,300	10,219	7,445	10,219	8,799
65,300	65,350	10,230	7,451	10,230	8,810
65,350	65,400	10,241	7,457	10,241	8,821
65,400	65,450	10,252	7,463	10,252	8,832
65,450	65,500	10,263	7,469	10,263	8,843
65,500	65,550	10,274	7,475	10,274	8,854
65,550	65,600	10,285	7,481	10,285	8,865
65,600	65,650	10,296	7,487	10,296	8,876
65,650	65,700	10,307	7,493	10,307	8,887
65,700	65,750	10,318	7,499	10,318	8,898
65,750	65,800	10,329	7,505	10,329	8,909
65,800	65,850	10,340	7,511	10,340	8,920
65,850	65,900	10,351	7,517	10,351	8,931
65,900	65,950	10,362	7,523	10,362	8,942
65,950	66,000	10,373	7,529	10,373	8,953

(Continued)

* This column must also be used by a qualifying widow(er).

2019 Tax Table — *Continued*

If line 11b (taxable income) is— At least	But less than	Single	Married filing jointly *	Married filing separately	Head of a household
66,000					
66,000	66,050	10,384	7,535	10,384	8,964
66,050	66,100	10,395	7,541	10,395	8,975
66,100	66,150	10,406	7,547	10,406	8,986
66,150	66,200	10,417	7,553	10,417	8,997
66,200	66,250	10,428	7,559	10,428	9,008
66,250	66,300	10,439	7,565	10,439	9,019
66,300	66,350	10,450	7,571	10,450	9,030
66,350	66,400	10,461	7,577	10,461	9,041
66,400	66,450	10,472	7,583	10,472	9,052
66,450	66,500	10,483	7,589	10,483	9,063
66,500	66,550	10,494	7,595	10,494	9,074
66,550	66,600	10,505	7,601	10,505	9,085
66,600	66,650	10,516	7,607	10,516	9,096
66,650	66,700	10,527	7,613	10,527	9,107
66,700	66,750	10,538	7,619	10,538	9,118
66,750	66,800	10,549	7,625	10,549	9,129
66,800	66,850	10,560	7,631	10,560	9,140
66,850	66,900	10,571	7,637	10,571	9,151
66,900	66,950	10,582	7,643	10,582	9,162
66,950	67,000	10,593	7,649	10,593	9,173
67,000					
67,000	67,050	10,604	7,655	10,604	9,184
67,050	67,100	10,615	7,661	10,615	9,195
67,100	67,150	10,626	7,667	10,626	9,206
67,150	67,200	10,637	7,673	10,637	9,217
67,200	67,250	10,648	7,679	10,648	9,228
67,250	67,300	10,659	7,685	10,659	9,239
67,300	67,350	10,670	7,691	10,670	9,250
67,350	67,400	10,681	7,697	10,681	9,261
67,400	67,450	10,692	7,703	10,692	9,272
67,450	67,500	10,703	7,709	10,703	9,283
67,500	67,550	10,714	7,715	10,714	9,294
67,550	67,600	10,725	7,721	10,725	9,305
67,600	67,650	10,736	7,727	10,736	9,316
67,650	67,700	10,747	7,733	10,747	9,327
67,700	67,750	10,758	7,739	10,758	9,338
67,750	67,800	10,769	7,745	10,769	9,349
67,800	67,850	10,780	7,751	10,780	9,360
67,850	67,900	10,791	7,757	10,791	9,371
67,900	67,950	10,802	7,763	10,802	9,382
67,950	68,000	10,813	7,769	10,813	9,393
68,000					
68,000	68,050	10,824	7,775	10,824	9,404
68,050	68,100	10,835	7,781	10,835	9,415
68,100	68,150	10,846	7,787	10,846	9,426
68,150	68,200	10,857	7,793	10,857	9,437
68,200	68,250	10,868	7,799	10,868	9,448
68,250	68,300	10,879	7,805	10,879	9,459
68,300	68,350	10,890	7,811	10,890	9,470
68,350	68,400	10,901	7,817	10,901	9,481
68,400	68,450	10,912	7,823	10,912	9,492
68,450	68,500	10,923	7,829	10,923	9,503
68,500	68,550	10,934	7,835	10,934	9,514
68,550	68,600	10,945	7,841	10,945	9,525
68,600	68,650	10,956	7,847	10,956	9,536
68,650	68,700	10,967	7,853	10,967	9,547
68,700	68,750	10,978	7,859	10,978	9,558
68,750	68,800	10,989	7,865	10,989	9,569
68,800	68,850	11,000	7,871	11,000	9,580
68,850	68,900	11,011	7,877	11,011	9,591
68,900	68,950	11,022	7,883	11,022	9,602
68,950	69,000	11,033	7,889	11,033	9,613

If line 11b (taxable income) is— At least	But less than	Single	Married filing jointly *	Married filing separately	Head of a household
69,000					
69,000	69,050	11,044	7,895	11,044	9,624
69,050	69,100	11,055	7,901	11,055	9,635
69,100	69,150	11,066	7,907	11,066	9,646
69,150	69,200	11,077	7,913	11,077	9,657
69,200	69,250	11,088	7,919	11,088	9,668
69,250	69,300	11,099	7,925	11,099	9,679
69,300	69,350	11,110	7,931	11,110	9,690
69,350	69,400	11,121	7,937	11,121	9,701
69,400	69,450	11,132	7,943	11,132	9,712
69,450	69,500	11,143	7,949	11,143	9,723
69,500	69,550	11,154	7,955	11,154	9,734
69,550	69,600	11,165	7,961	11,165	9,745
69,600	69,650	11,176	7,967	11,176	9,756
69,650	69,700	11,187	7,973	11,187	9,767
69,700	69,750	11,198	7,979	11,198	9,778
69,750	69,800	11,209	7,985	11,209	9,789
69,800	69,850	11,220	7,991	11,220	9,800
69,850	69,900	11,231	7,997	11,231	9,811
69,900	69,950	11,242	8,003	11,242	9,822
69,950	70,000	11,253	8,009	11,253	9,833
70,000					
70,000	70,050	11,264	8,015	11,264	9,844
70,050	70,100	11,275	8,021	11,275	9,855
70,100	70,150	11,286	8,027	11,286	9,866
70,150	70,200	11,297	8,033	11,297	9,877
70,200	70,250	11,308	8,039	11,308	9,888
70,250	70,300	11,319	8,045	11,319	9,899
70,300	70,350	11,330	8,051	11,330	9,910
70,350	70,400	11,341	8,057	11,341	9,921
70,400	70,450	11,352	8,063	11,352	9,932
70,450	70,500	11,363	8,069	11,363	9,943
70,500	70,550	11,374	8,075	11,374	9,954
70,550	70,600	11,385	8,081	11,385	9,965
70,600	70,650	11,396	8,087	11,396	9,976
70,650	70,700	11,407	8,093	11,407	9,987
70,700	70,750	11,418	8,099	11,418	9,998
70,750	70,800	11,429	8,105	11,429	10,009
70,800	70,850	11,440	8,111	11,440	10,020
70,850	70,900	11,451	8,117	11,451	10,031
70,900	70,950	11,462	8,123	11,462	10,042
70,950	71,000	11,473	8,129	11,473	10,053
71,000					
71,000	71,050	11,484	8,135	11,484	10,064
71,050	71,100	11,495	8,141	11,495	10,075
71,100	71,150	11,506	8,147	11,506	10,086
71,150	71,200	11,517	8,153	11,517	10,097
71,200	71,250	11,528	8,159	11,528	10,108
71,250	71,300	11,539	8,165	11,539	10,119
71,300	71,350	11,550	8,171	11,550	10,130
71,350	71,400	11,561	8,177	11,561	10,141
71,400	71,450	11,572	8,183	11,572	10,152
71,450	71,500	11,583	8,189	11,583	10,163
71,500	71,550	11,594	8,195	11,594	10,174
71,550	71,600	11,605	8,201	11,605	10,185
71,600	71,650	11,616	8,207	11,616	10,196
71,650	71,700	11,627	8,213	11,627	10,207
71,700	71,750	11,638	8,219	11,638	10,218
71,750	71,800	11,649	8,225	11,649	10,229
71,800	71,850	11,660	8,231	11,660	10,240
71,850	71,900	11,671	8,237	11,671	10,251
71,900	71,950	11,682	8,243	11,682	10,262
71,950	72,000	11,693	8,249	11,693	10,273

If line 11b (taxable income) is— At least	But less than	Single	Married filing jointly *	Married filing separately	Head of a household
72,000					
72,000	72,050	11,704	8,255	11,704	10,284
72,050	72,100	11,715	8,261	11,715	10,295
72,100	72,150	11,726	8,267	11,726	10,306
72,150	72,200	11,737	8,273	11,737	10,317
72,200	72,250	11,748	8,279	11,748	10,328
72,250	72,300	11,759	8,285	11,759	10,339
72,300	72,350	11,770	8,291	11,770	10,350
72,350	72,400	11,781	8,297	11,781	10,361
72,400	72,450	11,792	8,303	11,792	10,372
72,450	72,500	11,803	8,309	11,803	10,383
72,500	72,550	11,814	8,315	11,814	10,394
72,550	72,600	11,825	8,321	11,825	10,405
72,600	72,650	11,836	8,327	11,836	10,416
72,650	72,700	11,847	8,333	11,847	10,427
72,700	72,750	11,858	8,339	11,858	10,438
72,750	72,800	11,869	8,345	11,869	10,449
72,800	72,850	11,880	8,351	11,880	10,460
72,850	72,900	11,891	8,357	11,891	10,471
72,900	72,950	11,902	8,363	11,902	10,482
72,950	73,000	11,913	8,369	11,913	10,493
73,000					
73,000	73,050	11,924	8,375	11,924	10,504
73,050	73,100	11,935	8,381	11,935	10,515
73,100	73,150	11,946	8,387	11,946	10,526
73,150	73,200	11,957	8,393	11,957	10,537
73,200	73,250	11,968	8,399	11,968	10,548
73,250	73,300	11,979	8,405	11,979	10,559
73,300	73,350	11,990	8,411	11,990	10,570
73,350	73,400	12,001	8,417	12,001	10,581
73,400	73,450	12,012	8,423	12,012	10,592
73,450	73,500	12,023	8,429	12,023	10,603
73,500	73,550	12,034	8,435	12,034	10,614
73,550	73,600	12,045	8,441	12,045	10,625
73,600	73,650	12,056	8,447	12,056	10,636
73,650	73,700	12,067	8,453	12,067	10,647
73,700	73,750	12,078	8,459	12,078	10,658
73,750	73,800	12,089	8,465	12,089	10,669
73,800	73,850	12,100	8,471	12,100	10,680
73,850	73,900	12,111	8,477	12,111	10,691
73,900	73,950	12,122	8,483	12,122	10,702
73,950	74,000	12,133	8,489	12,133	10,713
74,000					
74,000	74,050	12,144	8,495	12,144	10,724
74,050	74,100	12,155	8,501	12,155	10,735
74,100	74,150	12,166	8,507	12,166	10,746
74,150	74,200	12,177	8,513	12,177	10,757
74,200	74,250	12,188	8,519	12,188	10,768
74,250	74,300	12,199	8,525	12,199	10,779
74,300	74,350	12,210	8,531	12,210	10,790
74,350	74,400	12,221	8,537	12,221	10,801
74,400	74,450	12,232	8,543	12,232	10,812
74,450	74,500	12,243	8,549	12,243	10,823
74,500	74,550	12,254	8,555	12,254	10,834
74,550	74,600	12,265	8,561	12,265	10,845
74,600	74,650	12,276	8,567	12,276	10,856
74,650	74,700	12,287	8,573	12,287	10,867
74,700	74,750	12,298	8,579	12,298	10,878
74,750	74,800	12,309	8,585	12,309	10,889
74,800	74,850	12,320	8,591	12,320	10,900
74,850	74,900	12,331	8,597	12,331	10,911
74,900	74,950	12,342	8,603	12,342	10,922
74,950	75,000	12,353	8,609	12,353	10,933

(Continued)

* This column must also be used by a qualifying widow(er).

2019 Tax Table — *Continued*

If line 11b (taxable income) is—		And you are—			
At least	But less than	Single	Married filing jointly *	Married filing separately	Head of a household
		Your tax is—			

75,000

At least	But less than	Single	MFJ*	MFS	HoH
75,000	75,050	12,364	8,615	12,364	10,944
75,050	75,100	12,375	8,621	12,375	10,955
75,100	75,150	12,386	8,627	12,386	10,966
75,150	75,200	12,397	8,633	12,397	10,977
75,200	75,250	12,408	8,639	12,408	10,988
75,250	75,300	12,419	8,645	12,419	10,999
75,300	75,350	12,430	8,651	12,430	11,010
75,350	75,400	12,441	8,657	12,441	11,021
75,400	75,450	12,452	8,663	12,452	11,032
75,450	75,500	12,463	8,669	12,463	11,043
75,500	75,550	12,474	8,675	12,474	11,054
75,550	75,600	12,485	8,681	12,485	11,065
75,600	75,650	12,496	8,687	12,496	11,076
75,650	75,700	12,507	8,693	12,507	11,087
75,700	75,750	12,518	8,699	12,518	11,098
75,750	75,800	12,529	8,705	12,529	11,109
75,800	75,850	12,540	8,711	12,540	11,120
75,850	75,900	12,551	8,717	12,551	11,131
75,900	75,950	12,562	8,723	12,562	11,142
75,950	76,000	12,573	8,729	12,573	11,153

76,000

At least	But less than	Single	MFJ*	MFS	HoH
76,000	76,050	12,584	8,735	12,584	11,164
76,050	76,100	12,595	8,741	12,595	11,175
76,100	76,150	12,606	8,747	12,606	11,186
76,150	76,200	12,617	8,753	12,617	11,197
76,200	76,250	12,628	8,759	12,628	11,208
76,250	76,300	12,639	8,765	12,639	11,219
76,300	76,350	12,650	8,771	12,650	11,230
76,350	76,400	12,661	8,777	12,661	11,241
76,400	76,450	12,672	8,783	12,672	11,252
76,450	76,500	12,683	8,789	12,683	11,263
76,500	76,550	12,694	8,795	12,694	11,274
76,550	76,600	12,705	8,801	12,705	11,285
76,600	76,650	12,716	8,807	12,716	11,296
76,650	76,700	12,727	8,813	12,727	11,307
76,700	76,750	12,738	8,819	12,738	11,318
76,750	76,800	12,749	8,825	12,749	11,329
76,800	76,850	12,760	8,831	12,760	11,340
76,850	76,900	12,771	8,837	12,771	11,351
76,900	76,950	12,782	8,843	12,782	11,362
76,950	77,000	12,793	8,849	12,793	11,373

77,000

At least	But less than	Single	MFJ*	MFS	HoH
77,000	77,050	12,804	8,855	12,804	11,384
77,050	77,100	12,815	8,861	12,815	11,395
77,100	77,150	12,826	8,867	12,826	11,406
77,150	77,200	12,837	8,873	12,837	11,417
77,200	77,250	12,848	8,879	12,848	11,428
77,250	77,300	12,859	8,885	12,859	11,439
77,300	77,350	12,870	8,891	12,870	11,450
77,350	77,400	12,881	8,897	12,881	11,461
77,400	77,450	12,892	8,903	12,892	11,472
77,450	77,500	12,903	8,909	12,903	11,483
77,500	77,550	12,914	8,915	12,914	11,494
77,550	77,600	12,925	8,921	12,925	11,505
77,600	77,650	12,936	8,927	12,936	11,516
77,650	77,700	12,947	8,933	12,947	11,527
77,700	77,750	12,958	8,939	12,958	11,538
77,750	77,800	12,969	8,945	12,969	11,549
77,800	77,850	12,980	8,951	12,980	11,560
77,850	77,900	12,991	8,957	12,991	11,571
77,900	77,950	13,002	8,963	13,002	11,582
77,950	78,000	13,013	8,969	13,013	11,593

78,000

At least	But less than	Single	MFJ*	MFS	HoH
78,000	78,050	13,024	8,975	13,024	11,604
78,050	78,100	13,035	8,981	13,035	11,615
78,100	78,150	13,046	8,987	13,046	11,626
78,150	78,200	13,057	8,993	13,057	11,637
78,200	78,250	13,068	8,999	13,068	11,648
78,250	78,300	13,079	9,005	13,079	11,659
78,300	78,350	13,090	9,011	13,090	11,670
78,350	78,400	13,101	9,017	13,101	11,681
78,400	78,450	13,112	9,023	13,112	11,692
78,450	78,500	13,123	9,029	13,123	11,703
78,500	78,550	13,134	9,035	13,134	11,714
78,550	78,600	13,145	9,041	13,145	11,725
78,600	78,650	13,156	9,047	13,156	11,736
78,650	78,700	13,167	9,053	13,167	11,747
78,700	78,750	13,178	9,059	13,178	11,758
78,750	78,800	13,189	9,065	13,189	11,769
78,800	78,850	13,200	9,071	13,200	11,780
78,850	78,900	13,211	9,077	13,211	11,791
78,900	78,950	13,222	9,083	13,222	11,802
78,950	79,000	13,233	9,092	13,233	11,813

79,000

At least	But less than	Single	MFJ*	MFS	HoH
79,000	79,050	13,244	9,103	13,244	11,824
79,050	79,100	13,255	9,114	13,255	11,835
79,100	79,150	13,266	9,125	13,266	11,846
79,150	79,200	13,277	9,136	13,277	11,857
79,200	79,250	13,288	9,147	13,288	11,868
79,250	79,300	13,299	9,158	13,299	11,879
79,300	79,350	13,310	9,169	13,310	11,890
79,350	79,400	13,321	9,180	13,321	11,901
79,400	79,450	13,332	9,191	13,332	11,912
79,450	79,500	13,343	9,202	13,343	11,923
79,500	79,550	13,354	9,213	13,354	11,934
79,550	79,600	13,365	9,224	13,365	11,945
79,600	79,650	13,376	9,235	13,376	11,956
79,650	79,700	13,387	9,246	13,387	11,967
79,700	79,750	13,398	9,257	13,398	11,978
79,750	79,800	13,409	9,268	13,409	11,989
79,800	79,850	13,420	9,279	13,420	12,000
79,850	79,900	13,431	9,290	13,431	12,011
79,900	79,950	13,442	9,301	13,442	12,022
79,950	80,000	13,453	9,312	13,453	12,033

80,000

At least	But less than	Single	MFJ*	MFS	HoH
80,000	80,050	13,464	9,323	13,464	12,044
80,050	80,100	13,475	9,334	13,475	12,055
80,100	80,150	13,486	9,345	13,486	12,066
80,150	80,200	13,497	9,356	13,497	12,077
80,200	80,250	13,508	9,367	13,508	12,088
80,250	80,300	13,519	9,378	13,519	12,099
80,300	80,350	13,530	9,389	13,530	12,110
80,350	80,400	13,541	9,400	13,541	12,121
80,400	80,450	13,552	9,411	13,552	12,132
80,450	80,500	13,563	9,422	13,563	12,143
80,500	80,550	13,574	9,433	13,574	12,154
80,550	80,600	13,585	9,444	13,585	12,165
80,600	80,650	13,596	9,455	13,596	12,176
80,650	80,700	13,607	9,466	13,607	12,187
80,700	80,750	13,618	9,477	13,618	12,198
80,750	80,800	13,629	9,488	13,629	12,209
80,800	80,850	13,640	9,499	13,640	12,220
80,850	80,900	13,651	9,510	13,651	12,231
80,900	80,950	13,662	9,521	13,662	12,242
80,950	81,000	13,673	9,532	13,673	12,253

81,000

At least	But less than	Single	MFJ*	MFS	HoH
81,000	81,050	13,684	9,543	13,684	12,264
81,050	81,100	13,695	9,554	13,695	12,275
81,100	81,150	13,706	9,565	13,706	12,286
81,150	81,200	13,717	9,576	13,717	12,297
81,200	81,250	13,728	9,587	13,728	12,308
81,250	81,300	13,739	9,598	13,739	12,319
81,300	81,350	13,750	9,609	13,750	12,330
81,350	81,400	13,761	9,620	13,761	12,341
81,400	81,450	13,772	9,631	13,772	12,352
81,450	81,500	13,783	9,642	13,783	12,363
81,500	81,550	13,794	9,653	13,794	12,374
81,550	81,600	13,805	9,664	13,805	12,385
81,600	81,650	13,816	9,675	13,816	12,396
81,650	81,700	13,827	9,686	13,827	12,407
81,700	81,750	13,838	9,697	13,838	12,418
81,750	81,800	13,849	9,708	13,849	12,429
81,800	81,850	13,860	9,719	13,860	12,440
81,850	81,900	13,871	9,730	13,871	12,451
81,900	81,950	13,882	9,741	13,882	12,462
81,950	82,000	13,893	9,752	13,893	12,473

82,000

At least	But less than	Single	MFJ*	MFS	HoH
82,000	82,050	13,904	9,763	13,904	12,484
82,050	82,100	13,915	9,774	13,915	12,495
82,100	82,150	13,926	9,785	13,926	12,506
82,150	82,200	13,937	9,796	13,937	12,517
82,200	82,250	13,948	9,807	13,948	12,528
82,250	82,300	13,959	9,818	13,959	12,539
82,300	82,350	13,970	9,829	13,970	12,550
82,350	82,400	13,981	9,840	13,981	12,561
82,400	82,450	13,992	9,851	13,992	12,572
82,450	82,500	14,003	9,862	14,003	12,583
82,500	82,550	14,014	9,873	14,014	12,594
82,550	82,600	14,025	9,884	14,025	12,605
82,600	82,650	14,036	9,895	14,036	12,616
82,650	82,700	14,047	9,906	14,047	12,627
82,700	82,750	14,058	9,917	14,058	12,638
82,750	82,800	14,069	9,928	14,069	12,649
82,800	82,850	14,080	9,939	14,080	12,660
82,850	82,900	14,091	9,950	14,091	12,671
82,900	82,950	14,102	9,961	14,102	12,682
82,950	83,000	14,113	9,972	14,113	12,693

83,000

At least	But less than	Single	MFJ*	MFS	HoH
83,000	83,050	14,124	9,983	14,124	12,704
83,050	83,100	14,135	9,994	14,135	12,715
83,100	83,150	14,146	10,005	14,146	12,726
83,150	83,200	14,157	10,016	14,157	12,737
83,200	83,250	14,168	10,027	14,168	12,748
83,250	83,300	14,179	10,038	14,179	12,759
83,300	83,350	14,190	10,049	14,190	12,770
83,350	83,400	14,201	10,060	14,201	12,781
83,400	83,450	14,212	10,071	14,212	12,792
83,450	83,500	14,223	10,082	14,223	12,803
83,500	83,550	14,234	10,093	14,234	12,814
83,550	83,600	14,245	10,104	14,245	12,825
83,600	83,650	14,256	10,115	14,256	12,836
83,650	83,700	14,267	10,126	14,267	12,847
83,700	83,750	14,278	10,137	14,278	12,858
83,750	83,800	14,289	10,148	14,289	12,869
83,800	83,850	14,300	10,159	14,300	12,880
83,850	83,900	14,311	10,170	14,311	12,891
83,900	83,950	14,322	10,181	14,322	12,902
83,950	84,000	14,333	10,192	14,333	12,913

(Continued)

* This column must also be used by a qualifying widow(er).

84,000

At least	But less than	Single	Married filing jointly *	Married filing separately	Head of a household
84,000	84,050	14,344	10,203	14,344	12,924
84,050	84,100	14,355	10,214	14,355	12,935
84,100	84,150	14,366	10,225	14,366	12,946
84,150	84,200	14,377	10,236	14,377	12,957
84,200	84,250	14,389	10,247	14,389	12,968
84,250	84,300	14,401	10,258	14,401	12,980
84,300	84,350	14,413	10,269	14,413	12,992
84,350	84,400	14,425	10,280	14,425	13,004
84,400	84,450	14,437	10,291	14,437	13,016
84,450	84,500	14,449	10,302	14,449	13,028
84,500	84,550	14,461	10,313	14,461	13,040
84,550	84,600	14,473	10,324	14,473	13,052
84,600	84,650	14,485	10,335	14,485	13,064
84,650	84,700	14,497	10,346	14,497	13,076
84,700	84,750	14,509	10,357	14,509	13,088
84,750	84,800	14,521	10,368	14,521	13,100
84,800	84,850	14,533	10,379	14,533	13,112
84,850	84,900	14,545	10,390	14,545	13,124
84,900	84,950	14,557	10,401	14,557	13,136
84,950	85,000	14,569	10,412	14,569	13,148

85,000

At least	But less than	Single	Married filing jointly *	Married filing separately	Head of a household
85,000	85,050	14,581	10,423	14,581	13,160
85,050	85,100	14,593	10,434	14,593	13,172
85,100	85,150	14,605	10,445	14,605	13,184
85,150	85,200	14,617	10,456	14,617	13,196
85,200	85,250	14,629	10,467	14,629	13,208
85,250	85,300	14,641	10,478	14,641	13,220
85,300	85,350	14,653	10,489	14,653	13,232
85,350	85,400	14,665	10,500	14,665	13,244
85,400	85,450	14,677	10,511	14,677	13,256
85,450	85,500	14,689	10,522	14,689	13,268
85,500	85,550	14,701	10,533	14,701	13,280
85,550	85,600	14,713	10,544	14,713	13,292
85,600	85,650	14,725	10,555	14,725	13,304
85,650	85,700	14,737	10,566	14,737	13,316
85,700	85,750	14,749	10,577	14,749	13,328
85,750	85,800	14,761	10,588	14,761	13,340
85,800	85,850	14,773	10,599	14,773	13,352
85,850	85,900	14,785	10,610	14,785	13,364
85,900	85,950	14,797	10,621	14,797	13,376
85,950	86,000	14,809	10,632	14,809	13,388

86,000

At least	But less than	Single	Married filing jointly *	Married filing separately	Head of a household
86,000	86,050	14,821	10,643	14,821	13,400
86,050	86,100	14,833	10,654	14,833	13,412
86,100	86,150	14,845	10,665	14,845	13,424
86,150	86,200	14,857	10,676	14,857	13,436
86,200	86,250	14,869	10,687	14,869	13,448
86,250	86,300	14,881	10,698	14,881	13,460
86,300	86,350	14,893	10,709	14,893	13,472
86,350	86,400	14,905	10,720	14,905	13,484
86,400	86,450	14,917	10,731	14,917	13,496
86,450	86,500	14,929	10,742	14,929	13,508
86,500	86,550	14,941	10,753	14,941	13,520
86,550	86,600	14,953	10,764	14,953	13,532
86,600	86,650	14,965	10,775	14,965	13,544
86,650	86,700	14,977	10,786	14,977	13,556
86,700	86,750	14,989	10,797	14,989	13,568
86,750	86,800	15,001	10,808	15,001	13,580
86,800	86,850	15,013	10,819	15,013	13,592
86,850	86,900	15,025	10,830	15,025	13,604
86,900	86,950	15,037	10,841	15,037	13,616
86,950	87,000	15,049	10,852	15,049	13,628

87,000

At least	But less than	Single	Married filing jointly *	Married filing separately	Head of a household
87,000	87,050	15,061	10,863	15,061	13,640
87,050	87,100	15,073	10,874	15,073	13,652
87,100	87,150	15,085	10,885	15,085	13,664
87,150	87,200	15,097	10,896	15,097	13,676
87,200	87,250	15,109	10,907	15,109	13,688
87,250	87,300	15,121	10,918	15,121	13,700
87,300	87,350	15,133	10,929	15,133	13,712
87,350	87,400	15,145	10,940	15,145	13,724
87,400	87,450	15,157	10,951	15,157	13,736
87,450	87,500	15,169	10,962	15,169	13,748
87,500	87,550	15,181	10,973	15,181	13,760
87,550	87,600	15,193	10,984	15,193	13,772
87,600	87,650	15,205	10,995	15,205	13,784
87,650	87,700	15,217	11,006	15,217	13,796
87,700	87,750	15,229	11,017	15,229	13,808
87,750	87,800	15,241	11,028	15,241	13,820
87,800	87,850	15,253	11,039	15,253	13,832
87,850	87,900	15,265	11,050	15,265	13,844
87,900	87,950	15,277	11,061	15,277	13,856
87,950	88,000	15,289	11,072	15,289	13,868

88,000

At least	But less than	Single	Married filing jointly *	Married filing separately	Head of a household
88,000	88,050	15,301	11,083	15,301	13,880
88,050	88,100	15,313	11,094	15,313	13,892
88,100	88,150	15,325	11,105	15,325	13,904
88,150	88,200	15,337	11,116	15,337	13,916
88,200	88,250	15,349	11,127	15,349	13,928
88,250	88,300	15,361	11,138	15,361	13,940
88,300	88,350	15,373	11,149	15,373	13,952
88,350	88,400	15,385	11,160	15,385	13,964
88,400	88,450	15,397	11,171	15,397	13,976
88,450	88,500	15,409	11,182	15,409	13,988
88,500	88,550	15,421	11,193	15,421	14,000
88,550	88,600	15,433	11,204	15,433	14,012
88,600	88,650	15,445	11,215	15,445	14,024
88,650	88,700	15,457	11,226	15,457	14,036
88,700	88,750	15,469	11,237	15,469	14,048
88,750	88,800	15,481	11,248	15,481	14,060
88,800	88,850	15,493	11,259	15,493	14,072
88,850	88,900	15,505	11,270	15,505	14,084
88,900	88,950	15,517	11,281	15,517	14,096
88,950	89,000	15,529	11,292	15,529	14,108

89,000

At least	But less than	Single	Married filing jointly *	Married filing separately	Head of a household
89,000	89,050	15,541	11,303	15,541	14,120
89,050	89,100	15,553	11,314	15,553	14,132
89,100	89,150	15,565	11,325	15,565	14,144
89,150	89,200	15,577	11,336	15,577	14,156
89,200	89,250	15,589	11,347	15,589	14,168
89,250	89,300	15,601	11,358	15,601	14,180
89,300	89,350	15,613	11,369	15,613	14,192
89,350	89,400	15,625	11,380	15,625	14,204
89,400	89,450	15,637	11,391	15,637	14,216
89,450	89,500	15,649	11,402	15,649	14,228
89,500	89,550	15,661	11,413	15,661	14,240
89,550	89,600	15,673	11,424	15,673	14,252
89,600	89,650	15,685	11,435	15,685	14,264
89,650	89,700	15,697	11,446	15,697	14,276
89,700	89,750	15,709	11,457	15,709	14,288
89,750	89,800	15,721	11,468	15,721	14,300
89,800	89,850	15,733	11,479	15,733	14,312
89,850	89,900	15,745	11,490	15,745	14,324
89,900	89,950	15,757	11,501	15,757	14,336
89,950	90,000	15,769	11,512	15,769	14,348

90,000

At least	But less than	Single	Married filing jointly *	Married filing separately	Head of a household
90,000	90,050	15,781	11,523	15,781	14,360
90,050	90,100	15,793	11,534	15,793	14,372
90,100	90,150	15,805	11,545	15,805	14,384
90,150	90,200	15,817	11,556	15,817	14,396
90,200	90,250	15,829	11,567	15,829	14,408
90,250	90,300	15,841	11,578	15,841	14,420
90,300	90,350	15,853	11,589	15,853	14,432
90,350	90,400	15,865	11,600	15,865	14,444
90,400	90,450	15,877	11,611	15,877	14,456
90,450	90,500	15,889	11,622	15,889	14,468
90,500	90,550	15,901	11,633	15,901	14,480
90,550	90,600	15,913	11,644	15,913	14,492
90,600	90,650	15,925	11,655	15,925	14,504
90,650	90,700	15,937	11,666	15,937	14,516
90,700	90,750	15,949	11,677	15,949	14,528
90,750	90,800	15,961	11,688	15,961	14,540
90,800	90,850	15,973	11,699	15,973	14,552
90,850	90,900	15,985	11,710	15,985	14,564
90,900	90,950	15,997	11,721	15,997	14,576
90,950	91,000	16,009	11,732	16,009	14,588

91,000

At least	But less than	Single	Married filing jointly *	Married filing separately	Head of a household
91,000	91,050	16,021	11,743	16,021	14,600
91,050	91,100	16,033	11,754	16,033	14,612
91,100	91,150	16,045	11,765	16,045	14,624
91,150	91,200	16,057	11,776	16,057	14,636
91,200	91,250	16,069	11,787	16,069	14,648
91,250	91,300	16,081	11,798	16,081	14,660
91,300	91,350	16,093	11,809	16,093	14,672
91,350	91,400	16,105	11,820	16,105	14,684
91,400	91,450	16,117	11,831	16,117	14,696
91,450	91,500	16,129	11,842	16,129	14,708
91,500	91,550	16,141	11,853	16,141	14,720
91,550	91,600	16,153	11,864	16,153	14,732
91,600	91,650	16,165	11,875	16,165	14,744
91,650	91,700	16,177	11,886	16,177	14,756
91,700	91,750	16,189	11,897	16,189	14,768
91,750	91,800	16,201	11,908	16,201	14,780
91,800	91,850	16,213	11,919	16,213	14,792
91,850	91,900	16,225	11,930	16,225	14,804
91,900	91,950	16,237	11,941	16,237	14,816
91,950	92,000	16,249	11,952	16,249	14,828

92,000

At least	But less than	Single	Married filing jointly *	Married filing separately	Head of a household
92,000	92,050	16,261	11,963	16,261	14,840
92,050	92,100	16,273	11,974	16,273	14,852
92,100	92,150	16,285	11,985	16,285	14,864
92,150	92,200	16,297	11,996	16,297	14,876
92,200	92,250	16,309	12,007	16,309	14,888
92,250	92,300	16,321	12,018	16,321	14,900
92,300	92,350	16,333	12,029	16,333	14,912
92,350	92,400	16,345	12,040	16,345	14,924
92,400	92,450	16,357	12,051	16,357	14,936
92,450	92,500	16,369	12,062	16,369	14,948
92,500	92,550	16,381	12,073	16,381	14,960
92,550	92,600	16,393	12,084	16,393	14,972
92,600	92,650	16,405	12,095	16,405	14,984
92,650	92,700	16,417	12,106	16,417	14,996
92,700	92,750	16,429	12,117	16,429	15,008
92,750	92,800	16,441	12,128	16,441	15,020
92,800	92,850	16,453	12,139	16,453	15,032
92,850	92,900	16,465	12,150	16,465	15,044
92,900	92,950	16,477	12,161	16,477	15,056
92,950	93,000	16,489	12,172	16,489	15,068

(Continued)

* This column must also be used by a qualifying widow(er).

2019 Tax Table — *Continued*

If line 11b (taxable income) is—		And you are—			
At least	But less than	Single	Married filing jointly *	Married filing separately	Head of a household
		Your tax is—			

93,000

At least	But less than	Single	MFJ	MFS	HoH
93,000	93,050	16,501	12,183	16,501	15,080
93,050	93,100	16,513	12,194	16,513	15,092
93,100	93,150	16,525	12,205	16,525	15,104
93,150	93,200	16,537	12,216	16,537	15,116
93,200	93,250	16,549	12,227	16,549	15,128
93,250	93,300	16,561	12,238	16,561	15,140
93,300	93,350	16,573	12,249	16,573	15,152
93,350	93,400	16,585	12,260	16,585	15,164
93,400	93,450	16,597	12,271	16,597	15,176
93,450	93,500	16,609	12,282	16,609	15,188
93,500	93,550	16,621	12,293	16,621	15,200
93,550	93,600	16,633	12,304	16,633	15,212
93,600	93,650	16,645	12,315	16,645	15,224
93,650	93,700	16,657	12,326	16,657	15,236
93,700	93,750	16,669	12,337	16,669	15,248
93,750	93,800	16,681	12,348	16,681	15,260
93,800	93,850	16,693	12,359	16,693	15,272
93,850	93,900	16,705	12,370	16,705	15,284
93,900	93,950	16,717	12,381	16,717	15,296
93,950	94,000	16,729	12,392	16,729	15,308

94,000

At least	But less than	Single	MFJ	MFS	HoH
94,000	94,050	16,741	12,403	16,741	15,320
94,050	94,100	16,753	12,414	16,753	15,332
94,100	94,150	16,765	12,425	16,765	15,344
94,150	94,200	16,777	12,436	16,777	15,356
94,200	94,250	16,789	12,447	16,789	15,368
94,250	94,300	16,801	12,458	16,801	15,380
94,300	94,350	16,813	12,469	16,813	15,392
94,350	94,400	16,825	12,480	16,825	15,404
94,400	94,450	16,837	12,491	16,837	15,416
94,450	94,500	16,849	12,502	16,849	15,428
94,500	94,550	16,861	12,513	16,861	15,440
94,550	94,600	16,873	12,524	16,873	15,452
94,600	94,650	16,885	12,535	16,885	15,464
94,650	94,700	16,897	12,546	16,897	15,476
94,700	94,750	16,909	12,557	16,909	15,488
94,750	94,800	16,921	12,568	16,921	15,500
94,800	94,850	16,933	12,579	16,933	15,512
94,850	94,900	16,945	12,590	16,945	15,524
94,900	94,950	16,957	12,601	16,957	15,536
94,950	95,000	16,969	12,612	16,969	15,548

95,000

At least	But less than	Single	MFJ	MFS	HoH
95,000	95,050	16,981	12,623	16,981	15,560
95,050	95,100	16,993	12,634	16,993	15,572
95,100	95,150	17,005	12,645	17,005	15,584
95,150	95,200	17,017	12,656	17,017	15,596
95,200	95,250	17,029	12,667	17,029	15,608
95,250	95,300	17,041	12,678	17,041	15,620
95,300	95,350	17,053	12,689	17,053	15,632
95,350	95,400	17,065	12,700	17,065	15,644
95,400	95,450	17,077	12,711	17,077	15,656
95,450	95,500	17,089	12,722	17,089	15,668
95,500	95,550	17,101	12,733	17,101	15,680
95,550	95,600	17,113	12,744	17,113	15,692
95,600	95,650	17,125	12,755	17,125	15,704
95,650	95,700	17,137	12,766	17,137	15,716
95,700	95,750	17,149	12,777	17,149	15,728
95,750	95,800	17,161	12,788	17,161	15,740
95,800	95,850	17,173	12,799	17,173	15,752
95,850	95,900	17,185	12,810	17,185	15,764
95,900	95,950	17,197	12,821	17,197	15,776
95,950	96,000	17,209	12,832	17,209	15,788

96,000

At least	But less than	Single	MFJ	MFS	HoH
96,000	96,050	17,221	12,843	17,221	15,800
96,050	96,100	17,233	12,854	17,233	15,812
96,100	96,150	17,245	12,865	17,245	15,824
96,150	96,200	17,257	12,876	17,257	15,836
96,200	96,250	17,269	12,887	17,269	15,848
96,250	96,300	17,281	12,898	17,281	15,860
96,300	96,350	17,293	12,909	17,293	15,872
96,350	96,400	17,305	12,920	17,305	15,884
96,400	96,450	17,317	12,931	17,317	15,896
96,450	96,500	17,329	12,942	17,329	15,908
96,500	96,550	17,341	12,953	17,341	15,920
96,550	96,600	17,353	12,964	17,353	15,932
96,600	96,650	17,365	12,975	17,365	15,944
96,650	96,700	17,377	12,986	17,377	15,956
96,700	96,750	17,389	12,997	17,389	15,968
96,750	96,800	17,401	13,008	17,401	15,980
96,800	96,850	17,413	13,019	17,413	15,992
96,850	96,900	17,425	13,030	17,425	16,004
96,900	96,950	17,437	13,041	17,437	16,016
96,950	97,000	17,449	13,052	17,449	16,028

97,000

At least	But less than	Single	MFJ	MFS	HoH
97,000	97,050	17,461	13,063	17,461	16,040
97,050	97,100	17,473	13,074	17,473	16,052
97,100	97,150	17,485	13,085	17,485	16,064
97,150	97,200	17,497	13,096	17,497	16,076
97,200	97,250	17,509	13,107	17,509	16,088
97,250	97,300	17,521	13,118	17,521	16,100
97,300	97,350	17,533	13,129	17,533	16,112
97,350	97,400	17,545	13,140	17,545	16,124
97,400	97,450	17,557	13,151	17,557	16,136
97,450	97,500	17,569	13,162	17,569	16,148
97,500	97,550	17,581	13,173	17,581	16,160
97,550	97,600	17,593	13,184	17,593	16,172
97,600	97,650	17,605	13,195	17,605	16,184
97,650	97,700	17,617	13,206	17,617	16,196
97,700	97,750	17,629	13,217	17,629	16,208
97,750	97,800	17,641	13,228	17,641	16,220
97,800	97,850	17,653	13,239	17,653	16,232
97,850	97,900	17,665	13,250	17,665	16,244
97,900	97,950	17,677	13,261	17,677	16,256
97,950	98,000	17,689	13,272	17,689	16,268

98,000

At least	But less than	Single	MFJ	MFS	HoH
98,000	98,050	17,701	13,283	17,701	16,280
98,050	98,100	17,713	13,294	17,713	16,292
98,100	98,150	17,725	13,305	17,725	16,304
98,150	98,200	17,737	13,316	17,737	16,316
98,200	98,250	17,749	13,327	17,749	16,328
98,250	98,300	17,761	13,338	17,761	16,340
98,300	98,350	17,773	13,349	17,773	16,352
98,350	98,400	17,785	13,360	17,785	16,364
98,400	98,450	17,797	13,371	17,797	16,376
98,450	98,500	17,809	13,382	17,809	16,388
98,500	98,550	17,821	13,393	17,821	16,400
98,550	98,600	17,833	13,404	17,833	16,412
98,600	98,650	17,845	13,415	17,845	16,424
98,650	98,700	17,857	13,426	17,857	16,436
98,700	98,750	17,869	13,437	17,869	16,448
98,750	98,800	17,881	13,448	17,881	16,460
98,800	98,850	17,893	13,459	17,893	16,472
98,850	98,900	17,905	13,470	17,905	16,484
98,900	98,950	17,917	13,481	17,917	16,496
98,950	99,000	17,929	13,492	17,929	16,508

99,000

At least	But less than	Single	MFJ	MFS	HoH
99,000	99,050	17,941	13,503	17,941	16,520
99,050	99,100	17,953	13,514	17,953	16,532
99,100	99,150	17,965	13,525	17,965	16,544
99,150	99,200	17,977	13,536	17,977	16,556
99,200	99,250	17,989	13,547	17,989	16,568
99,250	99,300	18,001	13,558	18,001	16,580
99,300	99,350	18,013	13,569	18,013	16,592
99,350	99,400	18,025	13,580	18,025	16,604
99,400	99,450	18,037	13,591	18,037	16,616
99,450	99,500	18,049	13,602	18,049	16,628
99,500	99,550	18,061	13,613	18,061	16,640
99,550	99,600	18,073	13,624	18,073	16,652
99,600	99,650	18,085	13,635	18,085	16,664
99,650	99,700	18,097	13,646	18,097	16,676
99,700	99,750	18,109	13,657	18,109	16,688
99,750	99,800	18,121	13,668	18,121	16,700
99,800	99,850	18,133	13,679	18,133	16,712
99,850	99,900	18,145	13,690	18,145	16,724
99,900	99,950	18,157	13,701	18,157	16,736
99,950	100,000	18,169	13,712	18,169	16,748

$100,000 or over use the Tax Computation Worksheet

* This column must also be used by a qualifying widow(er).

2019 OPTIONAL SALES TAX TABLES

When Used

The election to deduct state and local general sales taxes requires that the taxpayer give up any deduction for state and local income taxes. Whether this is advisable or not depends on a comparison of the amounts involved. In making the choice, however, the outcome could be influenced by the additional sales tax incurred due to certain "big ticket" purchases that were made. For example, a taxpayer who chose to deduct state and local income taxes for 2018 might well prefer the sales tax deduction in 2019 if a new boat was purchased or home improvements were made during the year. To make the sales tax election, the taxpayer must enter the amount on Schedule A, line 5a, and check the related box.

If the sales tax election is made, the amount of the deduction can be determined by use of the *actual expense method* or *the optional sales tax tables* issued by the IRS. The actual expense method can be used only when the taxpayer has actual receipts to support the deduction claimed. In the absence of receipts (the usual case with most taxpayers), the optional sales tax tables must be used. Sales taxes related to the purchase of items used in a taxpayer's trade or business are determined separately, with this amount deducted on Schedule C (Form 1040).

Adjustments Necessary

The optional sales tax tables are based on a number of assumptions that require adjustments to be made. As the starting point for the use of the tables is AGI, nontaxable receipts have not been included. Examples of receipts that should be added include: tax-exempt interest, veterans' benefits, nontaxable combat pay, public assistance payments, workers' compensation, nontaxable Social Security, and other retirement benefits. They do not include any large nontaxable items that are not likely to be spent. For example, a $100,000 inheritance should not be added if it was invested in a certificate of deposit.

The tables represent the sales tax on the average (and recurring) expenditures based on level of income by family size and do not include exceptional purchases. Therefore, add to the table amount any sales taxes on major purchases (such as motor vehicles, aircraft, boats, and home building materials, etc.).

When the optional sales tax tables are used, special adjustments may be needed when a taxpayer has lived in more than one taxing jurisdiction (e.g., state, county, city) during the year. The adjustments involve apportionment of taxes based on days involved and are illustrated in Instructions for Schedule A (Form 1040), pages A-3 to A-7.

Local Sales Taxes

Local sales taxes (i.e., those imposed by counties, cities, transit authorities) may or may not require a separate determination. In those states where they are not imposed, no further computations are necessary. This is also the case where the local taxes are uniform and are incorporated into the state sales tax table. In other situations, another step is necessary to arrive at the optional sales tax table deduction. Depending on where the taxpayer lives, one of two procedures needs to be used. In one procedure, the local sales tax is arrived at by using the **state table** amount—see Example 1 and the related worksheet. In the other procedure, special **local tables** issued by the IRS for specified state and local jurisdictions are modified (if necessary) and used—see Example 2 and the related worksheet.

Use Illustrated

EXAMPLE 1 The Archers file a joint return for 2019 reflecting AGI of $88,000 and have three dependents. They have tax-exempt interest of $3,000, and during the year they incurred sales tax of $1,650 on the purchase of an automobile for their dependent teenage son. They live in Bellaire, Texas, where the general sales tax rates are 6.25% for state and 2% for local. Since the IRS *has not issued* optional local sales tax tables for Texas, use the Worksheet below to arrive at the Archers' general sales tax deduction of $3,167.

Sales Tax Deduction Worksheet
(To be used when *no* IRS Optional Local Sales Tax Table Available)

Adjusted Gross Income (AGI) as listed on line 8b of Form 1040		$88,000
Add nontaxable items		3,000
Table income to be used for purposes of line 1 below		$91,000
1. Use table income to determine table amount—go to state of residence and find applicable range of table income and family size column for *state* sales tax		$ 1,149
2a. Enter local general sales tax rate	2.00	
2b. Enter state general sales tax rate	6.25	
2c. Divide 2a by 2b	0.32	
2d. Multiply line 1 by line 2c for the local sales tax		368
3. Enter general sales tax on large purchases		1,650
4. Deduction for general sales tax (add lines 1 + 2d + 3) and report on line 5a of Schedule A of Form 1040		$ 3,167

EXAMPLE 2 The Hardys file a joint return for 2019, reporting AGI of $42,000 and have two dependents. They received $30,000 in nontaxable pension benefits. Although the Hardys do not keep sales tax receipts, they can prove that they paid $1,185 in sales tax on the purchase of a new boat in 2019. The Hardys are residents of Georgia and live in a jurisdiction that imposes a 2% local sales tax. Since the IRS *has issued* optional local sales tax tables for Georgia, use the Worksheet below to arrive at the Hardys' general sales tax deduction of $2,117.

Sales Tax Deduction Worksheet
(To be used for Alaska, Arizona, Arkansas, Colorado, Georgia, Illinois, Louisiana, Mississippi, Missouri, New York, North Carolina, South Carolina, Tennessee, Utah, and Virginia)

Adjusted Gross Income (AGI) as listed on line 8b of Form 1040		$42,000
Add nontaxable income		30,000
Table income to be used for purposes of line 1 below		$72,000
1. Use the table income to determine *state* sales tax amount—go to table for state of residence and find applicable income range and family size column		$ 582
2a. Enter local general sales tax rate	2.0	
2b. Enter IRS *local* sales tax table amount (based on a 1% tax rate)	$175	
2c. Multiply line 2b by 2a for the local sales tax		350
3. Enter general sales tax on large purchases		1,185
4. Deduction for general sales tax (add lines 1 + 2c + 3) and report on line 5a of Schedule A of Form 1040		$ 2,117

2019 Optional State Sales Tax Tables

Block 1 — Alabama (1, 4.0000%), Arizona (2, 5.6000%), Arkansas (2, 6.5000%)

Income At least	But less than	Alabama 1	2	3	4	5	Over 5	Arizona 1	2	3	4	5	Over 5	Arkansas 1	2	3	4	5	Over 5
$0	$20,000	261	301	327	348	366	390	261	285	301	312	322	336	327	353	370	382	392	406
$20,000	$30,000	378	433	471	500	524	558	403	438	461	478	493	512	511	551	576	596	611	632
$30,000	$40,000	439	501	544	577	605	644	478	519	545	566	583	606	610	657	687	709	728	753
$40,000	$50,000	490	559	606	643	673	716	543	589	619	642	661	687	696	749	783	809	829	858
$50,000	$60,000	536	610	661	700	733	780	602	652	685	710	731	759	774	833	870	898	921	952
$60,000	$70,000	577	656	710	752	787	837	656	709	745	772	794	825	845	908	949	980	1004	1038
$70,000	$80,000	614	698	755	800	837	889	705	762	800	829	853	886	911	979	1022	1055	1082	1118
$80,000	$90,000	649	737	797	844	883	937	751	812	852	882	908	942	972	1044	1091	1126	1154	1193
$90,000	$100,000	682	773	836	885	925	982	795	858	900	933	959	996	1030	1107	1156	1192	1222	1263
$100,000	$120,000	725	822	888	939	982	1042	853	921	965	1000	1028	1067	1108	1190	1242	1282	1313	1357
$120,000	$140,000	782	884	955	1009	1055	1119	929	1002	1050	1087	1118	1160	1210	1299	1356	1398	1433	1480
$140,000	$160,000	834	943	1017	1075	1123	1191	1001	1078	1130	1169	1202	1247	1306	1401	1462	1508	1545	1596
$160,000	$180,000	882	996	1074	1134	1185	1256	1067	1149	1203	1245	1279	1327	1395	1496	1560	1609	1649	1703
$180,000	$200,000	928	1046	1127	1191	1243	1318	1130	1216	1273	1317	1353	1403	1479	1586	1654	1705	1747	1804
$200,000	$225,000	975	1098	1183	1249	1304	1382	1195	1286	1346	1392	1430	1482	1567	1680	1752	1806	1850	1910
$225,000	$250,000	1026	1154	1242	1311	1369	1450	1266	1361	1424	1473	1513	1568	1662	1781	1857	1915	1961	2025
$250,000	$275,000	1074	1207	1298	1370	1429	1513	1333	1432	1498	1549	1591	1648	1753	1877	1957	2018	2066	2133
$275,000	$300,000	1119	1257	1351	1425	1487	1574	1397	1500	1569	1622	1665	1726	1839	1969	2053	2116	2167	2237
$300,000	or more	1388	1551	1664	1752	1826	1930	1781	1908	1993	2058	2111	2186	2359	2522	2627	2707	2771	2858

Block 2 — California (3, 7.2500%), Colorado (2, 2.9000%), Connecticut (4, 6.3500%)

Income At least	But less than	California 1	2	3	4	5	Over 5	Colorado 1	2	3	4	5	Over 5	Connecticut 1	2	3	4	5	Over 5
$0	$20,000	328	352	367	379	389	402	135	148	156	162	167	174	299	323	338	349	358	370
$20,000	$30,000	504	538	561	578	592	611	206	225	236	246	253	263	466	503	527	544	558	577
$30,000	$40,000	597	637	663	683	699	721	244	265	279	289	298	310	556	600	627	648	665	687
$40,000	$50,000	678	722	751	773	791	816	277	300	316	327	337	350	633	683	715	738	757	783
$50,000	$60,000	750	799	831	855	875	902	306	332	348	361	372	386	703	759	794	820	841	869
$60,000	$70,000	816	869	903	929	950	979	333	360	378	392	403	419	767	827	865	894	917	948
$70,000	$80,000	877	933	969	997	1019	1050	357	386	406	420	432	449	826	891	932	962	987	1021
$80,000	$90,000	935	993	1031	1061	1084	1117	380	411	431	447	460	477	881	950	994	1027	1053	1088
$90,000	$100,000	988	1050	1090	1120	1145	1180	402	434	455	472	485	504	932	1006	1052	1087	1115	1152
$100,000	$120,000	1060	1125	1168	1200	1227	1263	431	465	488	505	519	539	1002	1081	1131	1168	1198	1238
$120,000	$140,000	1154	1224	1270	1305	1333	1373	469	505	530	548	564	585	1093	1179	1233	1273	1306	1350
$140,000	$160,000	1242	1316	1365	1402	1433	1475	504	543	569	589	605	628	1178	1270	1329	1372	1407	1455
$160,000	$180,000	1324	1402	1453	1493	1525	1569	537	578	605	626	643	667	1256	1355	1417	1464	1501	1552
$180,000	$200,000	1401	1483	1537	1578	1612	1658	568	611	639	661	679	704	1331	1436	1502	1551	1590	1644
$200,000	$225,000	1482	1568	1624	1667	1703	1751	600	645	675	698	717	743	1409	1520	1590	1642	1684	1741
$225,000	$250,000	1569	1659	1718	1763	1800	1852	635	682	714	738	758	785	1493	1610	1684	1739	1784	1844
$250,000	$275,000	1651	1745	1807	1854	1893	1946	668	717	750	775	796	825	1573	1696	1774	1832	1879	1942
$275,000	$300,000	1730	1827	1892	1941	1981	2037	699	751	785	811	833	863	1649	1778	1860	1921	1969	2036
$300,000	or more	2201	2320	2399	2459	2508	2576	888	950	992	1024	1051	1088	2104	2269	2373	2450	2512	2597

Block 3 — District of Columbia (4, 6.0000%), Florida (1, 6.0000%), Georgia (2, 4.0000%)

Income At least	But less than	D.C. 1	2	3	4	5	Over 5	Florida 1	2	3	4	5	Over 5	Georgia 1	2	3	4	5	Over 5
$0	$20,000	214	223	229	234	238	243	289	314	330	342	352	366	187	202	212	220	226	235
$20,000	$30,000	334	348	357	364	370	377	446	483	508	526	541	562	287	310	325	336	346	358
$30,000	$40,000	399	415	426	434	440	449	529	573	602	623	641	665	341	367	384	398	409	423
$40,000	$50,000	455	473	485	494	501	511	602	651	683	707	727	755	387	417	436	451	463	480
$50,000	$60,000	506	526	539	549	556	567	667	721	756	783	805	835	429	461	482	499	512	530
$60,000	$70,000	552	574	588	598	607	618	726	785	823	852	875	908	467	501	524	542	556	576
$70,000	$80,000	594	618	633	644	653	665	781	843	884	915	940	975	502	539	563	582	597	618
$80,000	$90,000	634	659	675	687	697	710	832	898	942	974	1001	1038	534	574	600	619	635	658
$90,000	$100,000	672	698	715	727	738	751	880	950	996	1030	1058	1097	565	607	634	654	671	695
$100,000	$120,000	723	750	768	782	792	807	944	1019	1068	1105	1135	1176	607	650	679	701	719	744
$120,000	$140,000	789	819	838	853	864	880	1029	1109	1162	1202	1235	1280	661	708	739	763	782	809
$140,000	$160,000	851	883	904	919	932	949	1107	1194	1250	1293	1328	1376	711	761	795	820	841	869
$160,000	$180,000	909	942	964	981	994	1012	1180	1272	1332	1377	1414	1465	758	811	846	873	895	925
$180,000	$200,000	964	999	1022	1039	1053	1072	1249	1346	1409	1457	1496	1549	803	858	895	923	946	978
$200,000	$225,000	1021	1058	1082	1100	1115	1135	1322	1423	1490	1540	1581	1638	849	908	946	976	1000	1034
$225,000	$250,000	1082	1122	1147	1166	1182	1203	1399	1506	1576	1629	1673	1732	899	960	1001	1032	1058	1093
$250,000	$275,000	1141	1182	1208	1228	1245	1267	1473	1585	1658	1714	1759	1822	946	1011	1053	1085	1112	1149
$275,000	$300,000	1197	1240	1267	1288	1305	1328	1543	1660	1737	1795	1842	1908	992	1058	1103	1137	1164	1203
$300,000	or more	1533	1586	1620	1646	1667	1696	1964	2109	2205	2277	2336	2418	1263	1345	1399	1441	1475	1523

Block 4 — Hawaii (1,6 — 4.0000%), Idaho (1, 6.0000%), Illinois (2, 6.2500%)

Income At least	But less than	Hawaii 1	2	3	4	5	Over 5	Idaho 1	2	3	4	5	Over 5	Illinois 1	2	3	4	5	Over 5
$0	$20,000	290	334	363	385	404	430	393	453	493	524	551	587	268	296	316	331	344	362
$20,000	$30,000	436	500	542	575	603	641	575	659	716	760	797	849	416	453	479	501	518	544
$30,000	$40,000	512	586	636	674	706	750	669	765	830	881	923	982	497	537	567	591	611	640
$40,000	$50,000	578	661	716	759	795	844	750	855	927	983	1030	1095	568	611	643	669	692	723
$50,000	$60,000	637	727	788	835	874	928	821	936	1014	1074	1125	1196	634	678	713	740	764	798
$60,000	$70,000	690	787	853	903	945	1004	885	1008	1091	1156	1210	1286	694	740	776	805	830	866
$70,000	$80,000	739	843	912	966	1011	1073	944	1074	1162	1231	1288	1368	750	797	835	865	891	929
$80,000	$90,000	784	894	968	1025	1072	1138	999	1135	1228	1300	1360	1444	804	852	890	922	949	988
$90,000	$100,000	827	943	1020	1080	1129	1199	1051	1193	1289	1365	1428	1516	855	903	942	975	1003	1044
$100,000	$120,000	884	1007	1089	1153	1206	1279	1119	1269	1371	1451	1517	1610	924	972	1013	1047	1076	1119
$120,000	$140,000	959	1091	1180	1248	1305	1384	1208	1368	1477	1562	1633	1733	1015	1064	1105	1141	1172	1217
$140,000	$160,000	1028	1169	1263	1337	1397	1482	1291	1460	1575	1666	1741	1846	1102	1150	1193	1230	1262	1309
$160,000	$180,000	1092	1241	1341	1418	1482	1572	1367	1544	1666	1760	1839	1950	1184	1231	1275	1312	1345	1394
$180,000	$200,000	1153	1309	1414	1495	1563	1657	1438	1624	1751	1850	1932	2048	1263	1309	1353	1391	1425	1476
$200,000	$225,000	1216	1380	1490	1576	1646	1745	1513	1707	1839	1943	2029	2150	1347	1391	1435	1474	1509	1561
$225,000	$250,000	1284	1456	1572	1662	1736	1839	1593	1795	1934	2042	2132	2258	1438	1480	1524	1564	1600	1654
$250,000	$275,000	1348	1528	1649	1743	1820	1929	1668	1879	2022	2135	2228	2360	1525	1565	1609	1650	1686	1741
$275,000	$300,000	1409	1596	1722	1820	1901	2014	1740	1958	2107	2224	2321	2457	1610	1648	1692	1732	1770	1825
$300,000	or more	1772	2003	2158	2278	2378	2517	2166	2427	2606	2746	2863	3027	2138	2155	2195	2236	2275	2337

2019 Optional State Sales Tax Tables (Continued)

Indiana (Family Size 4, 7.0000%) — Iowa (Family Size 1, 6.0000%) — Kansas (Family Size 1, 6.5000%)

Income At least	But less than	Indiana 1	2	3	4	5	Over 5	Iowa 1	2	3	4	5	Over 5	Kansas 1	2	3	4	5	Over 5
$0	$20,000	350	383	404	420	433	451	304	332	350	363	374	388	443	518	568	607	640	686
$20,000	$30,000	528	577	608	632	651	677	470	513	540	560	577	599	636	741	812	867	913	977
$30,000	$40,000	620	678	714	742	764	795	558	608	641	665	684	711	734	854	935	998	1050	1124
$40,000	$50,000	700	765	806	837	862	896	634	691	728	755	777	808	817	950	1039	1109	1167	1248
$50,000	$60,000	772	842	887	921	949	987	703	766	806	837	861	894	890	1034	1131	1206	1269	1357
$60,000	$70,000	836	912	961	998	1028	1068	765	834	878	910	937	973	956	1109	1213	1294	1361	1455
$70,000	$80,000	896	977	1029	1068	1100	1143	822	896	943	979	1007	1046	1016	1178	1288	1373	1444	1544
$80,000	$90,000	951	1037	1092	1134	1167	1213	876	955	1005	1042	1073	1114	1071	1242	1357	1447	1521	1626
$90,000	$100,000	1003	1093	1151	1195	1230	1279	927	1010	1063	1102	1135	1178	1123	1301	1422	1516	1593	1703
$100,000	$120,000	1072	1169	1230	1277	1314	1366	994	1083	1140	1183	1217	1264	1192	1380	1507	1606	1688	1804
$120,000	$140,000	1162	1266	1333	1383	1424	1479	1082	1179	1241	1287	1325	1376	1280	1481	1617	1723	1811	1934
$140,000	$160,000	1246	1357	1429	1482	1525	1585	1165	1269	1335	1385	1425	1480	1362	1575	1719	1831	1924	2055
$160,000	$180,000	1324	1441	1517	1573	1619	1682	1241	1352	1423	1475	1518	1577	1437	1661	1812	1930	2028	2165
$180,000	$200,000	1397	1521	1600	1660	1708	1774	1313	1430	1505	1561	1606	1668	1507	1741	1900	2023	2125	2268
$200,000	$225,000	1473	1603	1687	1749	1800	1870	1389	1513	1592	1651	1699	1764	1580	1825	1990	2119	2225	2375
$225,000	$250,000	1555	1692	1779	1845	1899	1972	1470	1601	1684	1747	1797	1866	1658	1914	2087	2221	2332	2489
$250,000	$275,000	1632	1775	1867	1936	1992	2069	1546	1684	1772	1838	1891	1963	1731	1997	2177	2317	2433	2596
$275,000	$300,000	1705	1855	1951	2023	2081	2161	1620	1764	1856	1925	1980	2056	1800	2076	2263	2408	2528	2697
$300,000	or more	2141	2326	2445	2534	2607	2706	2057	2239	2356	2443	2513	2609	2206	2539	2763	2938	3083	3287

Kentucky (Family Size 4, 6.0000%) — Louisiana (Family Size 2, 4.4500%) — Maine (Family Size 4, 5.5000%)

Income At least	But less than	Kentucky 1	2	3	4	5	Over 5	Louisiana 1	2	3	4	5	Over 5	Maine 1	2	3	4	5	Over 5
$0	$20,000	290	314	329	341	350	363	217	234	245	253	260	269	212	231	243	253	261	272
$20,000	$30,000	455	490	514	531	546	566	335	361	377	390	400	414	316	342	360	373	385	400
$30,000	$40,000	543	585	613	633	650	674	398	428	447	462	474	490	371	400	420	436	449	466
$40,000	$50,000	620	668	699	722	742	768	453	487	508	525	538	556	418	450	472	489	503	523
$50,000	$60,000	690	742	777	803	824	853	502	539	563	581	596	616	460	495	519	537	552	573
$60,000	$70,000	754	810	847	875	898	930	547	587	613	632	648	670	498	536	561	580	596	619
$70,000	$80,000	813	873	913	943	968	1002	588	631	658	679	696	719	534	573	599	620	637	661
$80,000	$90,000	868	932	974	1006	1033	1069	627	672	701	723	741	766	567	608	635	657	675	699
$90,000	$100,000	920	988	1032	1066	1094	1132	663	711	742	765	784	810	598	640	669	691	710	736
$100,000	$120,000	990	1063	1110	1146	1176	1216	712	763	795	820	841	868	639	684	714	738	757	784
$120,000	$140,000	1082	1160	1212	1251	1283	1327	775	830	866	893	915	945	693	740	773	798	818	847
$140,000	$160,000	1168	1252	1307	1349	1383	1431	835	894	932	961	984	1016	743	793	827	853	875	906
$160,000	$180,000	1248	1337	1395	1440	1477	1527	890	952	993	1023	1048	1082	790	842	877	905	928	960
$180,000	$200,000	1324	1418	1480	1527	1565	1618	942	1008	1050	1083	1109	1145	834	888	925	954	978	1011
$200,000	$225,000	1403	1502	1567	1617	1658	1714	996	1066	1111	1145	1172	1210	880	936	975	1005	1029	1064
$225,000	$250,000	1489	1593	1662	1715	1757	1816	1055	1128	1176	1211	1240	1280	930	988	1028	1059	1085	1121
$250,000	$275,000	1570	1680	1752	1807	1852	1914	1111	1187	1237	1274	1305	1347	977	1037	1078	1110	1137	1175
$275,000	$300,000	1648	1763	1838	1895	1942	2007	1164	1244	1296	1335	1367	1410	1022	1083	1126	1159	1187	1226
$300,000	or more	2116	2260	2354	2426	2485	2566	1481	1581	1646	1695	1734	1789	1289	1361	1412	1451	1484	1530

Maryland (Family Size 4, 6.0000%) — Massachusetts (Family Size 4, 6.2500%) — Michigan (Family Size 4, 6.0000%)

Income At least	But less than	Maryland 1	2	3	4	5	Over 5	Massachusetts 1	2	3	4	5	Over 5	Michigan 1	2	3	4	5	Over 5
$0	$20,000	232	259	278	294	307	325	255	274	286	295	302	312	276	299	314	326	335	348
$20,000	$30,000	359	395	421	442	460	485	385	411	428	441	452	466	423	456	479	495	509	528
$30,000	$40,000	429	468	497	521	541	570	454	483	503	517	529	546	501	540	565	585	601	623
$40,000	$50,000	491	532	564	590	612	643	513	545	567	583	597	615	568	612	640	662	680	705
$50,000	$60,000	548	591	624	652	675	709	566	601	624	642	657	677	629	676	708	732	751	778
$60,000	$70,000	600	644	679	708	733	769	613	651	676	695	711	732	684	735	769	795	816	845
$70,000	$80,000	649	694	731	761	787	825	658	698	724	744	761	783	735	789	825	853	875	906
$80,000	$90,000	696	741	779	810	837	877	699	741	769	790	807	831	782	840	878	907	930	963
$90,000	$100,000	740	786	824	857	885	926	738	782	811	833	851	876	827	888	927	958	983	1017
$100,000	$120,000	800	847	886	919	949	991	789	836	866	890	909	935	887	951	993	1026	1052	1089
$120,000	$140,000	880	927	967	1002	1033	1077	857	907	939	964	985	1013	966	1034	1080	1115	1143	1182
$140,000	$160,000	956	1002	1044	1080	1111	1158	920	973	1007	1034	1055	1085	1039	1112	1160	1198	1228	1270
$160,000	$180,000	1028	1073	1115	1152	1185	1234	979	1033	1070	1098	1120	1152	1107	1184	1235	1274	1306	1351
$180,000	$200,000	1097	1141	1184	1222	1255	1305	1034	1091	1129	1158	1182	1215	1171	1252	1306	1347	1381	1427
$200,000	$225,000	1171	1213	1256	1294	1329	1381	1092	1151	1191	1221	1246	1280	1239	1323	1380	1423	1458	1507
$225,000	$250,000	1251	1291	1334	1373	1409	1462	1154	1216	1257	1289	1315	1351	1311	1400	1459	1504	1541	1593
$250,000	$275,000	1328	1366	1409	1449	1485	1539	1212	1277	1320	1353	1380	1417	1380	1472	1534	1581	1620	1674
$275,000	$300,000	1402	1438	1481	1521	1558	1613	1268	1335	1380	1414	1442	1481	1445	1542	1606	1655	1695	1751
$300,000	or more	1869	1886	1924	1965	2003	2064	1603	1683	1736	1777	1811	1857	1838	1956	2034	2094	2144	2212

Minnesota (Family Size 1, 6.8750%) — Mississippi (Family Size 2, 7.0000%) — Missouri (Family Size 2, 4.2250%)

Income At least	But less than	Minnesota 1	2	3	4	5	Over 5	Mississippi 1	2	3	4	5	Over 5	Missouri 1	2	3	4	5	Over 5
$0	$20,000	298	317	328	337	344	353	484	557	607	644	676	719	208	230	244	255	264	276
$20,000	$30,000	466	495	513	527	538	552	704	810	880	934	979	1041	319	351	372	388	401	420
$30,000	$40,000	555	590	612	628	641	658	817	938	1019	1082	1133	1205	378	415	440	459	474	495
$40,000	$50,000	634	673	698	716	731	751	913	1048	1138	1207	1264	1344	430	471	498	519	537	561
$50,000	$60,000	704	748	775	796	812	834	998	1144	1242	1318	1380	1467	476	521	551	574	593	619
$60,000	$70,000	768	816	846	868	886	910	1074	1231	1336	1417	1484	1577	517	566	599	623	644	672
$70,000	$80,000	827	879	911	935	954	980	1144	1311	1422	1508	1579	1678	556	608	643	669	691	721
$80,000	$90,000	883	938	972	998	1018	1046	1208	1384	1502	1592	1667	1771	592	647	684	712	735	767
$90,000	$100,000	935	993	1030	1057	1078	1108	1269	1453	1576	1670	1749	1858	626	684	722	752	776	810
$100,000	$120,000	1005	1067	1107	1136	1159	1190	1349	1544	1674	1775	1857	1973	672	733	774	805	831	867
$120,000	$140,000	1097	1165	1207	1239	1264	1299	1453	1662	1801	1909	1998	2122	731	797	842	875	903	942
$140,000	$160,000	1182	1256	1302	1336	1363	1400	1548	1771	1919	2033	2128	2259	787	857	904	941	970	1012
$160,000	$180,000	1262	1340	1389	1426	1455	1494	1636	1871	2027	2147	2247	2385	839	913	963	1001	1033	1076
$180,000	$200,000	1337	1420	1472	1511	1542	1583	1719	1965	2128	2255	2359	2504	888	966	1018	1058	1091	1137
$200,000	$225,000	1416	1504	1559	1600	1633	1677	1805	2062	2234	2366	2475	2627	939	1021	1076	1118	1153	1201
$225,000	$250,000	1501	1594	1653	1696	1730	1777	1897	2166	2346	2484	2598	2758	994	1080	1138	1182	1219	1270
$250,000	$275,000	1582	1680	1741	1786	1823	1872	1983	2264	2451	2595	2715	2881	1046	1136	1196	1243	1281	1334
$275,000	$300,000	1659	1761	1826	1873	1912	1963	2065	2357	2551	2701	2825	2998	1096	1189	1252	1301	1341	1396
$300,000	or more	2120	2250	2332	2393	2442	2508	2546	2901	3138	3320	3471	3681	1394	1509	1587	1646	1696	1764

2019 Optional State Sales Tax Tables *(Continued)*

Nebraska (Family Size 1, 5.5000%) · Nevada (Family Size 5, 6.8500%) · New Jersey (Family Size 4, 6.6250%)

Income At least	But less than	Nebraska 1	2	3	4	5	Over 5	Nevada 1	2	3	4	5	Over 5	New Jersey 1	2	3	4	5	Over 5
$0	$20,000	274	300	316	328	338	352	320	344	360	372	381	395	274	288	297	305	310	318
$20,000	$30,000	423	462	487	505	520	541	488	523	546	564	578	597	440	460	474	484	493	505
$30,000	$40,000	501	547	577	599	617	641	577	618	645	665	681	704	530	554	570	582	592	606
$40,000	$50,000	569	622	655	680	700	728	655	700	730	752	770	795	611	637	655	668	680	695
$50,000	$60,000	630	688	725	753	775	805	724	773	806	830	850	878	684	712	732	747	759	776
$60,000	$70,000	686	748	788	818	843	876	787	840	875	901	922	952	751	781	802	818	831	850
$70,000	$80,000	737	804	847	879	905	941	845	902	938	966	989	1021	813	845	868	885	899	919
$80,000	$90,000	785	856	902	936	964	1002	900	959	998	1027	1052	1085	872	906	929	947	962	983
$90,000	$100,000	830	905	953	990	1019	1059	951	1013	1054	1085	1110	1145	928	963	988	1007	1022	1044
$100,000	$120,000	890	971	1022	1061	1092	1135	1020	1085	1129	1161	1188	1225	1003	1041	1067	1087	1103	1126
$120,000	$140,000	968	1056	1112	1154	1188	1235	1109	1180	1226	1261	1290	1330	1103	1143	1170	1192	1210	1235
$140,000	$160,000	1041	1136	1196	1241	1278	1328	1193	1268	1317	1355	1385	1428	1197	1239	1268	1291	1310	1336
$160,000	$180,000	1109	1209	1274	1322	1361	1414	1270	1349	1401	1441	1473	1518	1284	1328	1359	1383	1403	1431
$180,000	$200,000	1173	1279	1347	1398	1439	1495	1344	1426	1481	1523	1557	1603	1368	1414	1446	1471	1492	1522
$200,000	$225,000	1240	1352	1424	1477	1521	1580	1420	1507	1564	1608	1643	1693	1456	1504	1538	1564	1586	1617
$225,000	$250,000	1312	1430	1506	1563	1609	1671	1503	1594	1654	1699	1737	1788	1552	1601	1636	1664	1687	1719
$250,000	$275,000	1380	1504	1584	1644	1692	1758	1581	1676	1738	1786	1825	1879	1643	1694	1731	1759	1783	1817
$275,000	$300,000	1445	1575	1658	1721	1771	1840	1656	1754	1819	1869	1909	1965	1731	1784	1821	1851	1876	1911
$300,000	or more	1832	1996	2101	2180	2244	2331	2103	2222	2301	2362	2411	2480	2265	2326	2371	2407	2437	2479

New Mexico (Family Size 1, 5.1250%) · New York (Family Size 2, 4.0000%) · North Carolina (Family Size 2, 4.7500%)

Income At least	But less than	New Mexico 1	2	3	4	5	Over 5	New York 1	2	3	4	5	Over 5	North Carolina 1	2	3	4	5	Over 5
$0	$20,000	280	302	315	325	333	345	169	179	185	190	194	200	261	294	316	333	347	366
$20,000	$30,000	443	476	497	512	525	542	269	283	293	300	306	315	390	438	469	494	514	542
$30,000	$40,000	530	569	594	613	628	648	323	340	351	360	367	377	458	512	549	577	600	632
$40,000	$50,000	607	651	680	701	718	741	372	390	403	412	420	431	516	576	617	648	674	710
$50,000	$60,000	676	725	757	780	799	825	415	436	449	460	468	480	567	634	678	712	740	779
$60,000	$70,000	739	793	827	852	873	901	455	477	492	503	512	525	614	685	733	769	800	842
$70,000	$80,000	798	856	892	919	942	972	493	516	531	543	553	567	657	732	783	822	854	899
$80,000	$90,000	853	914	953	982	1006	1038	528	552	568	581	592	606	697	777	830	871	905	952
$90,000	$100,000	905	970	1011	1042	1067	1101	561	587	604	617	628	643	734	818	874	917	952	1002
$100,000	$120,000	975	1044	1088	1122	1148	1185	606	633	651	665	677	693	784	873	932	978	1016	1068
$120,000	$140,000	1066	1142	1190	1226	1255	1295	666	694	713	728	741	758	849	944	1008	1057	1098	1154
$140,000	$160,000	1152	1234	1285	1324	1355	1398	722	751	772	788	801	820	910	1011	1079	1131	1174	1234
$160,000	$180,000	1232	1319	1374	1415	1448	1494	774	805	827	843	857	877	966	1072	1144	1199	1244	1308
$180,000	$200,000	1308	1400	1458	1502	1537	1585	824	856	879	896	911	932	1019	1130	1205	1263	1311	1377
$200,000	$225,000	1388	1484	1546	1592	1630	1680	876	910	934	952	967	989	1074	1191	1269	1330	1380	1449
$225,000	$250,000	1473	1576	1641	1690	1729	1783	933	968	993	1012	1028	1051	1132	1255	1337	1401	1453	1527
$250,000	$275,000	1555	1663	1731	1783	1824	1881	987	1023	1049	1069	1086	1109	1188	1316	1402	1468	1523	1599
$275,000	$300,000	1633	1746	1818	1871	1915	1974	1039	1077	1103	1124	1141	1166	1241	1374	1463	1532	1589	1669
$300,000	or more	2103	2246	2337	2405	2460	2536	1356	1400	1431	1456	1477	1507	1556	1718	1827	1911	1981	2078

North Dakota (Family Size 1, 5.0000%) · Ohio (Family Size 1, 5.7500%) · Oklahoma (Family Size 1, 4.5000%)

Income At least	But less than	North Dakota 1	2	3	4	5	Over 5	Ohio 1	2	3	4	5	Over 5	Oklahoma 1	2	3	4	5	Over 5
$0	$20,000	228	250	266	278	287	301	276	292	303	312	318	328	284	326	355	377	396	422
$20,000	$30,000	346	378	399	416	431	450	435	459	474	487	496	510	417	476	517	549	575	613
$30,000	$40,000	408	444	469	489	505	528	521	548	567	581	592	608	487	554	600	637	667	710
$40,000	$50,000	462	502	530	552	570	595	596	627	647	663	676	693	546	620	672	712	745	793
$50,000	$60,000	510	554	584	608	627	655	665	698	720	737	751	770	599	679	735	778	815	866
$60,000	$70,000	554	601	633	658	679	709	727	763	787	805	820	841	647	732	791	838	877	932
$70,000	$80,000	594	644	678	705	727	758	786	823	849	868	884	906	691	781	844	893	934	992
$80,000	$90,000	632	684	720	748	772	805	841	880	907	927	944	967	732	826	892	944	987	1048
$90,000	$100,000	668	722	760	789	814	848	893	934	961	983	1000	1025	770	869	937	991	1036	1100
$100,000	$120,000	716	773	812	843	869	906	963	1006	1035	1058	1076	1102	821	925	997	1054	1102	1170
$120,000	$140,000	778	839	881	914	942	981	1055	1101	1132	1156	1176	1204	887	998	1075	1136	1187	1259
$140,000	$160,000	836	900	945	980	1010	1052	1141	1190	1223	1249	1270	1299	949	1066	1148	1212	1266	1343
$160,000	$180,000	890	957	1004	1041	1073	1116	1222	1273	1308	1335	1357	1388	1006	1129	1214	1282	1339	1419
$180,000	$200,000	942	1011	1061	1099	1132	1178	1299	1352	1388	1417	1440	1472	1060	1188	1277	1348	1407	1491
$200,000	$225,000	995	1068	1119	1160	1193	1241	1380	1435	1473	1502	1527	1561	1116	1249	1342	1416	1478	1565
$225,000	$250,000	1053	1128	1182	1224	1260	1310	1468	1525	1564	1595	1621	1656	1176	1315	1412	1489	1554	1645
$250,000	$275,000	1107	1186	1241	1285	1322	1374	1551	1610	1651	1683	1710	1747	1233	1377	1478	1558	1625	1720
$275,000	$300,000	1160	1241	1298	1344	1382	1436	1631	1692	1735	1768	1795	1834	1287	1436	1541	1623	1693	1792
$300,000	or more	1472	1568	1636	1691	1737	1802	2117	2189	2239	2278	2311	2358	1609	1785	1910	2009	2093	2211

Pennsylvania (Family Size 1, 6.0000%) · Rhode Island (Family Size 4, 7.0000%) · South Carolina (Family Size 2, 6.0000%)

Income At least	But less than	Pennsylvania 1	2	3	4	5	Over 5	Rhode Island 1	2	3	4	5	Over 5	South Carolina 1	2	3	4	5	Over 5
$0	$20,000	251	269	281	289	296	306	316	344	363	376	388	403	292	318	334	346	356	369
$20,000	$30,000	381	407	424	436	446	460	468	510	536	556	572	594	443	481	505	523	537	557
$30,000	$40,000	449	479	499	513	525	541	547	595	625	648	667	693	522	566	594	616	633	656
$40,000	$50,000	508	542	563	579	592	610	615	668	702	728	748	777	590	640	672	695	715	741
$50,000	$60,000	561	597	621	639	653	673	675	733	770	798	821	852	651	706	741	767	788	817
$60,000	$70,000	609	648	673	692	708	729	729	791	831	861	886	919	706	765	803	831	854	885
$70,000	$80,000	653	695	721	742	758	780	779	845	887	919	945	981	757	820	861	891	915	948
$80,000	$90,000	694	738	766	788	805	829	825	895	939	973	1001	1038	805	872	914	946	972	1007
$90,000	$100,000	733	779	808	831	849	874	868	941	988	1024	1052	1092	849	920	964	998	1025	1062
$100,000	$120,000	784	833	865	888	908	934	926	1003	1053	1091	1121	1163	909	984	1031	1067	1096	1136
$120,000	$140,000	852	904	938	964	984	1013	1000	1084	1137	1178	1211	1255	986	1067	1119	1157	1189	1231
$140,000	$160,000	914	970	1006	1033	1056	1086	1070	1158	1215	1258	1293	1341	1058	1145	1200	1241	1275	1320
$160,000	$180,000	972	1031	1069	1098	1121	1153	1133	1227	1287	1333	1369	1420	1124	1216	1275	1319	1354	1403
$180,000	$200,000	1027	1089	1129	1159	1184	1217	1194	1292	1355	1403	1441	1494	1187	1284	1346	1392	1429	1480
$200,000	$225,000	1084	1149	1191	1223	1248	1284	1256	1359	1425	1475	1516	1571	1253	1355	1420	1468	1508	1561
$225,000	$250,000	1146	1214	1258	1291	1318	1355	1323	1431	1501	1553	1595	1654	1323	1431	1499	1550	1592	1648
$250,000	$275,000	1204	1275	1321	1355	1384	1422	1386	1499	1571	1626	1670	1731	1390	1502	1574	1627	1671	1730
$275,000	$300,000	1259	1333	1381	1417	1446	1487	1446	1563	1639	1696	1742	1805	1453	1570	1645	1701	1746	1808
$300,000	or more	1589	1680	1738	1782	1818	1868	1800	1944	2036	2106	2162	2240	1829	1975	2068	2138	2194	2271

2019 Optional State Sales Tax Tables *(Continued)*

Income At least	But less than	South Dakota 1 — 4.5000%						Tennessee 2 — 7.0000%						Texas 1 — 6.2500%					
		1	2	3	4	5	Over 5	1	2	3	4	5	Over 5	1	2	3	4	5	Over 5
$0	$20,000	306	350	379	402	421	447	408	459	493	520	542	572	307	335	352	365	376	390
$20,000	$30,000	462	527	570	604	631	670	611	686	736	774	806	850	476	518	545	565	582	604
$30,000	$40,000	544	619	670	709	741	786	717	804	862	906	943	994	566	616	648	671	691	717
$40,000	$50,000	615	699	756	799	835	886	809	905	970	1019	1060	1117	644	700	737	764	785	815
$50,000	$60,000	678	770	832	880	920	975	890	996	1066	1120	1165	1227	714	776	816	846	871	904
$60,000	$70,000	735	835	902	953	996	1056	964	1077	1153	1211	1259	1326	777	845	889	921	948	984
$70,000	$80,000	788	894	966	1021	1066	1130	1032	1152	1233	1295	1346	1417	836	909	956	991	1019	1058
$80,000	$90,000	837	950	1025	1083	1131	1199	1095	1222	1307	1373	1427	1502	891	969	1019	1056	1086	1127
$90,000	$100,000	884	1002	1081	1142	1193	1263	1154	1288	1377	1445	1502	1581	942	1025	1078	1117	1149	1192
$100,000	$120,000	945	1071	1156	1221	1274	1349	1233	1375	1470	1543	1603	1687	1011	1100	1156	1199	1233	1279
$120,000	$140,000	1026	1162	1252	1323	1381	1462	1336	1488	1590	1669	1733	1824	1101	1198	1259	1305	1342	1393
$140,000	$160,000	1101	1246	1343	1418	1479	1566	1432	1594	1702	1786	1855	1951	1186	1290	1356	1405	1445	1499
$160,000	$180,000	1171	1324	1426	1505	1571	1662	1520	1691	1806	1894	1967	2068	1264	1374	1445	1497	1540	1598
$180,000	$200,000	1236	1397	1505	1588	1657	1753	1604	1783	1903	1996	2072	2179	1338	1455	1529	1585	1630	1691
$200,000	$225,000	1305	1474	1587	1675	1747	1848	1691	1879	2005	2102	2182	2294	1415	1539	1617	1676	1724	1789
$225,000	$250,000	1378	1556	1675	1767	1843	1949	1784	1982	2114	2216	2300	2417	1498	1629	1712	1774	1825	1893
$250,000	$275,000	1448	1634	1758	1854	1934	2045	1872	2078	2216	2323	2411	2533	1577	1714	1802	1867	1920	1992
$275,000	$300,000	1514	1708	1838	1938	2021	2136	1956	2171	2314	2425	2516	2644	1652	1796	1887	1956	2011	2087
$300,000	or more	1910	2148	2309	2432	2535	2678	2454	2717	2893	3029	3141	3297	2100	2283	2399	2486	2556	2652

Income At least	But less than	Utah 2,7 — 4.8130%						Vermont 1 — 6.0000%						Virginia 2 — 4.3000%					
		1	2	3	4	5	Over 5	1	2	3	4	5	Over 5	1	2	3	4	5	Over 5
$0	$20,000	285	320	343	361	376	396	195	205	211	216	219	224	207	230	245	257	267	281
$20,000	$30,000	427	478	512	538	559	589	293	307	316	323	328	335	318	349	371	388	402	422
$30,000	$40,000	501	560	600	630	655	689	344	360	371	378	384	392	377	413	438	457	473	496
$40,000	$50,000	565	631	675	709	737	775	388	406	417	426	433	442	429	469	496	517	535	560
$50,000	$60,000	622	694	742	779	810	852	427	447	459	468	476	486	476	519	548	571	590	618
$60,000	$70,000	674	751	803	843	875	921	462	483	497	507	515	526	519	564	596	620	641	670
$70,000	$80,000	721	804	859	901	936	984	494	517	532	542	551	562	560	607	640	666	687	718
$80,000	$90,000	766	853	911	955	992	1043	525	549	564	575	584	596	597	646	681	708	731	763
$90,000	$100,000	807	899	959	1006	1045	1098	553	578	594	606	615	628	633	684	720	748	772	806
$100,000	$120,000	863	960	1024	1074	1115	1172	591	618	634	647	657	670	681	734	772	802	827	862
$120,000	$140,000	935	1039	1108	1162	1206	1267	640	669	687	700	711	725	744	801	841	872	899	937
$140,000	$160,000	1002	1113	1187	1244	1290	1356	686	716	736	750	761	777	804	863	905	938	966	1006
$160,000	$180,000	1064	1181	1259	1319	1368	1437	728	760	780	796	808	824	860	921	964	999	1029	1071
$180,000	$200,000	1122	1245	1327	1390	1442	1515	768	802	823	839	851	868	913	976	1021	1058	1088	1132
$200,000	$225,000	1183	1312	1398	1464	1519	1595	809	845	867	884	897	915	969	1034	1081	1119	1151	1196
$225,000	$250,000	1248	1384	1474	1544	1601	1681	853	891	914	932	946	964	1029	1096	1145	1184	1218	1265
$250,000	$275,000	1310	1451	1546	1618	1678	1761	895	934	959	977	992	1011	1087	1156	1206	1247	1281	1330
$275,000	$300,000	1369	1516	1614	1690	1752	1839	935	976	1002	1020	1035	1056	1142	1213	1265	1307	1342	1393
$300,000	or more	1718	1898	2019	2111	2188	2294	1172	1222	1253	1276	1295	1320	1480	1559	1619	1668	1709	1769

Income At least	But less than	Washington 1 — 6.5000%						West Virginia 1 — 6.0000%						Wisconsin 1 — 5.0000%					
		1	2	3	4	5	Over 5	1	2	3	4	5	Over 5	1	2	3	4	5	Over 5
$0	$20,000	313	337	354	366	377	391	285	310	327	340	350	364	244	263	276	285	292	303
$20,000	$30,000	493	529	553	572	587	608	457	497	523	543	559	581	383	413	432	446	457	473
$30,000	$40,000	591	633	661	683	700	725	550	599	630	654	673	699	458	493	515	532	545	564
$40,000	$50,000	677	724	755	779	799	827	632	688	723	751	773	803	524	563	588	607	622	643
$50,000	$60,000	755	806	840	866	888	918	707	769	808	838	863	897	583	626	654	675	692	715
$60,000	$70,000	826	881	918	946	970	1002	775	842	886	919	946	982	636	684	714	737	755	780
$70,000	$80,000	893	951	990	1020	1045	1080	839	911	958	994	1023	1062	686	737	769	794	814	841
$80,000	$90,000	955	1016	1058	1090	1116	1153	899	976	1026	1064	1095	1137	733	787	822	848	869	897
$90,000	$100,000	1014	1078	1122	1155	1183	1221	955	1037	1090	1130	1163	1208	777	834	871	898	920	951
$100,000	$120,000	1094	1162	1208	1243	1273	1314	1031	1119	1177	1220	1255	1303	837	898	937	966	990	1022
$120,000	$140,000	1198	1271	1320	1359	1390	1435	1131	1228	1290	1337	1376	1428	914	980	1023	1055	1081	1116
$140,000	$160,000	1297	1374	1427	1467	1501	1548	1225	1329	1397	1448	1489	1546	987	1058	1104	1138	1166	1204
$160,000	$180,000	1389	1470	1525	1568	1604	1654	1313	1424	1496	1550	1595	1656	1055	1130	1179	1215	1245	1285
$180,000	$200,000	1477	1561	1619	1664	1702	1754	1396	1514	1590	1648	1695	1760	1119	1199	1250	1289	1320	1362
$200,000	$225,000	1569	1657	1718	1765	1804	1859	1484	1609	1690	1751	1801	1869	1187	1271	1325	1366	1398	1443
$225,000	$250,000	1669	1761	1825	1874	1915	1973	1579	1711	1797	1862	1915	1987	1259	1348	1405	1448	1483	1531
$250,000	$275,000	1763	1860	1926	1977	2020	2080	1669	1808	1899	1967	2023	2099	1328	1422	1482	1527	1563	1613
$275,000	$300,000	1855	1954	2023	2077	2121	2184	1755	1901	1996	2068	2127	2207	1394	1492	1555	1602	1640	1692
$300,000	or more	2409	2528	2611	2676	2730	2806	2277	2465	2587	2679	2754	2857	1792	1915	1994	2053	2101	2167

Income At least	But less than	Wyoming 1 — 4.0000%					
		1	2	3	4	5	Over 5
$0	$20,000	195	210	219	226	232	240
$20,000	$30,000	300	322	337	348	357	369
$30,000	$40,000	356	382	399	412	422	437
$40,000	$50,000	405	434	453	468	479	495
$50,000	$60,000	449	481	502	518	530	548
$60,000	$70,000	488	523	546	563	577	596
$70,000	$80,000	525	562	587	605	620	640
$80,000	$90,000	559	599	625	644	660	681
$90,000	$100,000	592	633	660	681	697	720
$100,000	$120,000	635	679	708	730	748	772
$120,000	$140,000	691	739	771	794	813	840
$140,000	$160,000	744	796	829	854	875	903
$160,000	$180,000	793	848	883	910	931	961
$180,000	$200,000	839	897	934	962	985	1017
$200,000	$225,000	888	948	988	1017	1041	1074
$225,000	$250,000	940	1004	1045	1076	1102	1136
$250,000	$275,000	989	1056	1099	1132	1159	1195
$275,000	$300,000	1036	1106	1151	1185	1213	1251
$300,000	or more	1318	1405	1461	1504	1538	1586

Note: Residents of **Alaska** do not have a state sales tax, but should follow the instructions on the next page to determine their local sales tax amount.
1.   Use the Ratio Method to determine your local sales tax deduction. Your state sales tax rate is provided next to the state name.
2.   Follow the instructions on the next page to determine your local sales tax deduction.
3.   The California table includes the 1.25% uniform local sales tax rate in addition to the 6.00% state sales tax rate for a total of 7.25%. Some California localities impose a larger local sales tax. Taxpayers who reside in those jurisdictions should use the Ratio Method to determine their local sales tax deduction. The denominator of the correct ratio is 7.25%, and the numerator is the total sales tax rate minus 7.25%.
4.   This state does not have a local general sales tax, so the amount in the state table is the only amount to be deducted.
5.   The Nevada table includes the 2.25% uniform local sales tax rate in addition to the 4.60% state sales tax rate for a total of 6.85%. Some Nevada localities impose a larger local sales tax. Taxpayers who reside in those jurisdictions should use the Ratio Method to determine their local sales tax deduction. The denominator of the correct ratio is 6.85%, and the numerator is the total sales tax rate minus 6.85%.
6.   The 4.0% rate for Hawaii is actually an excise tax but is treated as a sales tax for purpose of this deduction.
7.   The rate increased during 2019 so the given rate is an average for the year.

Which Optional Local Sales Tax Table Should I Use?

IF you live in the state of...	AND you live in...	THEN use Local Table...
Alaska	Juneau, Kenai, Ketchikan, Kodiak, Sitka, Wasilla, or any locality that imposes a local sales tax	C
Arizona	Glendale, Mesa, Peoria, Phoenix, Tucson	A
	Chandler, Gilbert, Scottsdale, Tempe, Yuma, or any other locality that imposes a local sales tax	B
Arkansas	Any locality that imposes a local sales tax	C
Colorado	Adams County, Arapahoe County, Aurora, Boulder County, Centennial, Colorado Springs, Denver City, El Paso County, Lakewood, Larimer County, Pueblo City, Pueblo County, or any other locality that imposes a local sales tax	A
	Arvada, Boulder, Fort Collins, Greeley, Jefferson County, Longmont, Thornton, or Westminster.	B
Georgia	Any locality that imposes a local sales tax	B
Illinois	Arlington Heights, Bloomington, Champaign, Chicago, Cicero, Decatur, Evanston, Joliet, Palatine, Peoria, Schaumburg, Skokie, Springfield, or any other locality that imposes a local sales tax	A
	Aurora, Elgin, Waukegan	B
Louisiana	East Baton Rouge Parish	B
	Ascension Parish, Bossier Parish, Caddo Parish, Calcasieu Parish, Iberia Parish, Jefferson Parish, Lafayette Parish, Lafourche Parish, Livingston Parish, Orleans Parish, Ouachita Parish, Rapides Parish, St. Bernard Parish, St. Landry Parish, St Tammany Parish, Tangipahoa Parish, Terrebonne Parish, or any other locality that imposes a local sales tax	C
Mississippi	City of Jackson only	A
	City of Tupelo only	C
Missouri	Any locality that imposes a local sales tax	B
New York	Counties: Chautauqua, Chenango, Columbia, Delaware, Greene, Hamilton, Tioga, Wayne Cities: New York, Norwich (Chenango County)	A
	Counties: Albany, Allegany, Broome, Cattaraugus, Cayuga, Chemung, Clinton, Cortland, Dutchess, Erie, Essex, Franklin, Fulton, Genesee, Herkimer, Jefferson, Lewis, Livingston, Madison, Monroe, Montgomery, Nassau, Niagara, Oneida, Onondaga, Ontario, Orange, Orleans, Oswego, Otsego, Putnam, Rensselaer, Rockland, St. Lawrence, Saratoga, Schenectady, Schoharie, Schuyler, Seneca, Steuben, Suffolk, Sullivan, Tompkins, Ulster, Warren, Washington, Westchester, Wyoming, or Yates. Cities: Auburn, Glens Falls, Gloversville, Ithaca, Johnstown, Mount Vernon, New Rochelle, Olean, Oneida (Madison County), Oswego, Rome, Salamanca, Saratoga Springs, Utica, White Plains, Yonkers	B
	Any other locality that imposes a local sales tax	D*
North Carolina	Any locality that imposes a local sales tax	A
South Carolina	Aiken County, Anderson County, Georgetown County, Greenwood County, Horry County, Lexington County, Myrtle Beach, Newberry County, Orangeburg County, Spartanburg County, and York County	A
	Allendale County, Bamberg County, Barnwell County, Calhoun County, Charleston County, Cherokee County, Chester County, Chesterfield County, Colleton County, Darlington County, Dillon County, Florence County, Hampton County, Jasper County, Kershaw County, Lancaster County, Lee County, Marion County, Marlboro County, McCormick County, Saluda County, Sumter County, and Williamsburg County	B
	Abbeville County, Berkeley County, Clarendon County, Dorchester County, Edgefield County, Fairfield County, Laurens County, Pickens County, Richland County, Union County, or any other locality that imposes a local sales tax	C
Tennessee	Any locality that imposes a local sales tax	C
Utah	Any locality that imposes a local sales tax	A
Virginia	Any locality that imposes a local sales tax	C

* Note: Local Table D is just 25% of the NY State table.

2019 Optional Local Sales Tax Tables

Note. The numbers provided in this table are the base local general sales taxes, figured using a local sales tax rate of 1 percent.

Income		Family Size						Family Size						Family Size						Family Size					
At least	But less than	1	2	3	4	5	Over 5	1	2	3	4	5	Over 5	1	2	3	4	5	Over 5	1	2	3	4	5	Over 5
		Local Table A						Local Table B						Local Table C						Local Table D					
$0	$20,000	43	47	50	52	53	55	56	63	68	72	76	80	68	78	84	89	93	99	42	45	46	48	49	50
$20,000	$30,000	67	72	76	79	81	84	83	93	101	106	111	118	100	114	123	130	136	145	67	71	73	75	77	79
$30,000	$40,000	80	86	90	93	96	100	97	109	117	124	129	137	116	132	143	151	158	168	81	85	88	90	92	94
$40,000	$50,000	91	98	102	106	109	113	109	122	132	139	145	153	130	148	160	169	177	188	93	98	101	103	105	108
$50,000	$60,000	101	108	113	117	120	125	120	134	144	152	159	168	143	162	175	185	193	205	104	109	112	115	117	120
$60,000	$70,000	110	118	123	127	131	135	129	145	156	164	171	181	154	175	189	199	208	221	114	119	123	126	128	131
$70,000	$80,000	119	127	132	137	140	145	138	155	167	175	183	193	164	186	201	212	222	235	123	129	133	136	138	142
$80,000	$90,000	127	135	141	146	149	155	147	164	176	186	193	204	174	197	213	225	235	249	132	138	142	145	148	152
$90,000	$100,000	134	143	149	154	158	163	154	173	186	195	203	215	183	207	223	236	246	261	140	147	151	154	157	161
$100,000	$120,000	144	154	160	165	169	175	165	184	198	208	217	229	195	220	238	251	262	278	152	158	163	166	169	173
$120,000	$140,000	158	168	174	180	184	190	179	199	214	225	234	247	210	238	256	271	282	299	167	174	178	182	185	190
$140,000	$160,000	170	181	188	193	198	205	191	213	228	240	250	263	225	254	273	289	301	319	181	188	193	197	200	205
$160,000	$180,000	182	193	200	206	211	218	203	226	242	254	265	279	238	269	289	305	319	337	194	201	207	211	214	219
$180,000	$200,000	193	204	212	218	223	231	214	238	255	268	278	294	251	283	304	321	335	354	206	214	220	224	228	233
$200,000	$225,000	205	216	224	231	236	244	226	251	268	282	293	309	264	297	320	337	352	372	219	228	234	238	242	247
$225,000	$250,000	217	229	238	245	250	258	238	265	283	297	308	325	278	313	336	355	370	391	233	242	248	253	257	263
$250,000	$275,000	229	242	250	257	263	272	250	277	296	311	323	340	291	327	352	371	387	409	247	256	262	267	272	277
$275,000	$300,000	241	253	263	270	276	285	261	290	309	324	337	355	303	341	367	387	403	426	260	269	276	281	285	292
$300,000	or more	310	325	336	344	351	362	328	362	386	404	419	441	377	423	454	478	498	526	339	350	358	364	369	377

Income Tax Rates—Estates and Trusts

Tax Year 2020

Taxable Income		The Tax Is:	
Over—	But not Over—		Of the Amount Over—
$ 0	$ 2,600	10%	$ 0
2,600	9,450	$ 260.00 + 24%	2,600
9,450	12,950	1,904.00 + 35%	9,450
12,950	....	3,129.00 + 37%	12,950

Tax Year 2019

Taxable Income		The Tax Is:	
Over—	But not Over—		Of the Amount Over—
$ 0	$ 2,600	10%	$ 0
2,600	9,300	$ 260.00 + 24%	2,600
9,300	12,750	1,868.00 + 35%	9,300
12,750	....	3,075.50 + 37%	12,750

Income Tax Rates—C Corporations, 2018 and after

For all income levels, the tax rate is 21%.

Unified Transfer Tax Rates

For Gifts Made and for Deaths after 2012

If the Amount with Respect to Which the Tentative Tax to Be Computed Is:	The Tentative Tax Is:
Not over $10,000	18 percent of such amount.
Over $10,000 but not over $20,000	$1,800, plus 20 percent of the excess of such amount over $10,000.
Over $20,000 but not over $40,000	$3,800, plus 22 percent of the excess of such amount over $20,000.
Over $40,000 but not over $60,000	$8,200, plus 24 percent of the excess of such amount over $40,000.
Over $60,000 but not over $80,000	$13,000, plus 26 percent of the excess of such amount over $60,000.
Over $80,000 but not over $100,000	$18,200, plus 28 percent of the excess of such amount over $80,000.
Over $100,000 but not over $150,000	$23,800, plus 30 percent of the excess of such amount over $100,000.
Over $150,000 but not over $250,000	$38,800, plus 32 percent of the excess of such amount over $150,000.
Over $250,000 but not over $500,000	$70,800, plus 34 percent of the excess of such amount over $250,000.
Over $500,000 but not over $750,000	$155,800, plus 37 percent of the excess of such amount over $500,000.
Over $750,000 but not over $1,000,000	$248,300, plus 39 percent of the excess of such amount over $750,000.
Over $1,000,000	$345,800, plus 40 percent of the excess of such amount over $1,000,000.

Appendix B

Tax Forms

(All Federal tax forms can be found at the IRS website: **irs.gov/forms-instructions**.)

Form 709	United States Gift (and Generation-Skipping Transfer) Tax Return (page 1)	B-3
Form 1040	U.S. Individual Income Tax Return (pages 1 and 2)	B-4
Schedule 1	Additional Income and Adjustments to Income	B-6
Schedule 2	Additional Taxes	B-7
Schedule 3	Additional Credits and Payments	B-7
Schedule A	Itemized Deductions	B-8
Schedule B	Interest and Ordinary Dividends	B-9
Schedule C	Profit or Loss from Business	B-10
Schedule D	Capital Gains and Losses	B-12
Schedule E	Supplemental Income and Loss	B-14
Schedule SE	Self-Employment Tax	B-16
Form 1041	U.S. Income Tax Return for Estates and Trusts	B-18
Schedule K–1	Beneficiary's Share of Income, Deductions, Credits, etc.	B-21
Form 1065	U.S. Return of Partnership Income	B-23
Schedule K–1	Partner's Share of Income, Deductions, Credits, etc.	B-28
Form 1120	U.S. Corporation Income Tax Return	B-30
Schedule M–3	Net Income (Loss) Reconciliation for Corporations With Total Assets of $10 Million or More	B-36

Form 1120-S   U.S. Income Tax Return for an
                     S Corporation   B-39

Schedule K–1   Shareholder's Share of Income, Deductions,
                     Credits, etc.   B-44

Form 4797   Sales of Business Property   B-46

Form 8949   Sales and Other Dispositions of Capital
                     Assets   B-48

Form 8960   Net Investment Income Tax—
                     Individuals, Estates, and Trusts   B-50

Form 8995   Qualified Business Income Deduction
                     Simplified Computation   B-51

Form 8995-A   Qualified Business Income Deduction   B-52

Form **709**

Department of the Treasury
Internal Revenue Service

United States Gift (and Generation-Skipping Transfer) Tax Return

▶ Go to *www.irs.gov/Form709* for instructions and the latest information.

(For gifts made during calendar year 2019)

▶ **See instructions.**

OMB No. 1545-0020

2019

Part 1—General Information

1 Donor's first name and middle initial	2 Donor's last name	3 Donor's social security number
4 Address (number, street, and apartment number)		5 Legal residence (domicile)
6 City or town, state or province, country, and ZIP or foreign postal code		7 Citizenship (see instructions)

		Yes	No
8	If the donor died during the year, check here ▶ ☐ and enter date of death _____ , _____ .		
9	If you extended the time to file this Form 709, check here ▶ ☐		
10	Enter the total number of donees listed on Schedule A. Count each person only once ▶		
11a	Have you (the donor) previously filed a Form 709 (or 709-A) for any other year? If "No," skip line 11b		
b	Has your address changed since you last filed Form 709 (or 709-A)?		
12	**Gifts by husband or wife to third parties.** Do you consent to have the gifts (including generation-skipping transfers) made by you and by your spouse to third parties during the calendar year considered as made one-half by each of you? (See instructions.) (If the answer is "Yes," the following information must be furnished and your spouse must sign the consent shown below. **If the answer is "No," skip lines 13–18.**)		

13 Name of consenting spouse	14 SSN		

		Yes	No
15	Were you married to one another during the entire calendar year? See instructions		
16	If line 15 is "No," check whether ☐ married ☐ divorced or ☐ widowed/deceased, and give date. See instructions ▶		
17	Will a gift tax return for this year be filed by your spouse? If "Yes," mail both returns in the same envelope		
18	**Consent of Spouse.** I consent to have the gifts (and generation-skipping transfers) made by me and by my spouse to third parties during the calendar year considered as made one-half by each of us. We are both aware of the joint and several liability for tax created by the execution of this consent.		

Consenting spouse's signature ▶   Date ▶

19	Have you applied a DSUE amount received from a predeceased spouse to a gift or gifts reported on this or a previous Form 709? If "Yes," complete Schedule C		

Part 2—Tax Computation

1	Enter the amount from Schedule A, Part 4, line 11	1	
2	Enter the amount from Schedule B, line 3	2	
3	Total taxable gifts. Add lines 1 and 2	3	
4	Tax computed on amount on line 3 (see *Table for Computing Gift Tax* in instructions)	4	
5	Tax computed on amount on line 2 (see *Table for Computing Gift Tax* in instructions)	5	
6	Balance. Subtract line 5 from line 4	6	
7	Applicable credit amount. If donor has DSUE amount from predeceased spouse(s) or Restored Exclusion Amount, enter amount from Schedule C, line 5; otherwise, see instructions	7	
8	Enter the applicable credit against tax allowable for all prior periods (from Sch. B, line 1, col. C) . . .	8	
9	Balance. Subtract line 8 from line 7. Do not enter less than zero	9	
10	Enter 20% (0.20) of the amount allowed as a specific exemption for gifts made after September 8, 1976, and before January 1, 1977. See instructions	10	
11	Balance. Subtract line 10 from line 9. Do not enter less than zero	11	
12	Applicable credit. Enter the smaller of line 6 or line 11	12	
13	Credit for foreign gift taxes (see instructions)	13	
14	Total credits. Add lines 12 and 13	14	
15	Balance. Subtract line 14 from line 6. Do not enter less than zero	15	
16	Generation-skipping transfer taxes (from Schedule D, Part 3, col. G, total)	16	
17	Total tax. Add lines 15 and 16	17	
18	Gift and generation-skipping transfer taxes prepaid with extension of time to file	18	
19	If line 18 is less than line 17, enter **balance due.** See instructions	19	
20	If line 18 is greater than line 17, enter **amount to be refunded**	20	

Attach check or money order here.

Sign Here

Under penalties of perjury, I declare that I have examined this return, including any accompanying schedules and statements, and to the best of my knowledge and belief, it is true, correct, and complete. Declaration of preparer (other than donor) is based on all information of which preparer has any knowledge.

May the IRS discuss this return with the preparer shown below? See instructions. ☐ Yes ☐ No

▶

Signature of donor   Date

Paid Preparer Use Only

Print/Type preparer's name	Preparer's signature	Date	Check ☐ if self-employed	PTIN
Firm's name ▶			Firm's EIN ▶	
Firm's address ▶			Phone no.	

For Disclosure, Privacy Act, and Paperwork Reduction Act Notice, see the instructions for this form.   Cat. No. 16783M   Form **709** (2019)

Form **1040**   Department of the Treasury—Internal Revenue Service   (99)
U.S. Individual Income Tax Return   **2019**   OMB No. 1545-0074   IRS Use Only—Do not write or staple in this space.

Filing Status
Check only one box.

☐ Single   ☐ Married filing jointly   ☐ Married filing separately (MFS)   ☐ Head of household (HOH)   ☐ Qualifying widow(er) (QW)

If you checked the MFS box, enter the name of spouse. If you checked the HOH or QW box, enter the child's name if the qualifying person is a child but not your dependent. ▶

Your first name and middle initial	Last name	Your social security number

If joint return, spouse's first name and middle initial	Last name	Spouse's social security number

Home address (number and street). If you have a P.O. box, see instructions.	Apt. no.	**Presidential Election Campaign**

Check here if you, or your spouse if filing jointly, want $3 to go to this fund. Checking a box below will not change your tax or refund.   ☐ You   ☐ Spouse

City, town or post office, state, and ZIP code. If you have a foreign address, also complete spaces below (see instructions).

Foreign country name	Foreign province/state/county	Foreign postal code

If more than four dependents, see instructions and ✓ here ▶ ☐

Standard Deduction

Someone can claim: ☐ You as a dependent   ☐ Your spouse as a dependent

☐ Spouse itemizes on a separate return or you were a dual-status alien

Age/Blindness   **You:** ☐ Were born before January 2, 1955   ☐ Are blind   **Spouse:** ☐ Was born before January 2, 1955   ☐ Is blind

Dependents (see instructions):

(1) First name Last name	(2) Social security number	(3) Relationship to you	(4) ✓ if qualifies for (see instructions):	
			Child tax credit	Credit for other dependents
			☐	☐
			☐	☐
			☐	☐
			☐	☐

Standard Deduction for—
- Single or Married filing separately, $12,200
- Married filing jointly or Qualifying widow(er), $24,400
- Head of household, $18,350
- If you checked any box under *Standard Deduction,* see instructions.

1	Wages, salaries, tips, etc. Attach Form(s) W-2	**1**	
2a	Tax-exempt interest	**2a**	**b** Taxable interest. Attach Sch. B if required	**2b**
3a	Qualified dividends	**3a**	**b** Ordinary dividends. Attach Sch. B if required	**3b**
4a	IRA distributions	**4a**	**b** Taxable amount	**4b**
c	Pensions and annuities . . .	**4c**	**d** Taxable amount	**4d**
5a	Social security benefits . . .	**5a**	**b** Taxable amount	**5b**
6	Capital gain or (loss). Attach Schedule D if required. If not required, check here . . . . . . ▶ ☐	**6**	
7a	Other income from Schedule 1, line 9	**7a**	
b	Add lines 1, 2b, 3b, 4b, 4d, 5b, 6, and 7a. This is your **total income** . . . . ▶	**7b**	
8a	Adjustments to income from Schedule 1, line 22	**8a**	
b	Subtract line 8a from line 7b. This is your **adjusted gross income** . . . . ▶	**8b**	
9	Standard deduction or itemized deductions (from Schedule A)	**9**	
10	Qualified business income deduction. Attach Form 8995 or Form 8995-A . . .	**10**	
11a	Add lines 9 and 10	**11a**	
b	**Taxable income.** Subtract line 11a from line 8b. If zero or less, enter -0-	**11b**	

For Disclosure, Privacy Act, and Paperwork Reduction Act Notice, see separate instructions.   Cat. No. 11320B   Form **1040** (2019)

Form 1040 (2019)   Page **2**

	12a	**Tax** (see inst.) Check if any from Form(s): **1** ☐ 8814 **2** ☐ 4972 **3** ☐ ____	12a	
	b	Add Schedule 2, line 3, and line 12a and enter the total . . . . ▶	12b	
	13a	Child tax credit or credit for other dependents	13a	
	b	Add Schedule 3, line 7, and line 13a and enter the total . . . . ▶	13b	
	14	Subtract line 13b from line 12b. If zero or less, enter -0-	14	
	15	Other taxes, including self-employment tax, from Schedule 2, line 10	15	
	16	Add lines 14 and 15. This is your **total tax** . . . . ▶	16	
	17	Federal income tax withheld from Forms W-2 and 1099	17	
• If you have a qualifying child, attach Sch. EIC. • If you have nontaxable combat pay, see instructions.	18	Other payments and refundable credits:		
	a	Earned income credit (EIC)	18a	
	b	Additional child tax credit. Attach Schedule 8812	18b	
	c	American opportunity credit from Form 8863, line 8	18c	
	d	Schedule 3, line 14	18d	
	e	Add lines 18a through 18d. These are your **total other payments and refundable credits** . . . . . ▶	18e	
	19	Add lines 17 and 18e. These are your **total payments** . . . . ▶	19	
Refund	20	If line 19 is more than line 16, subtract line 16 from line 19. This is the amount you **overpaid**	20	
Direct deposit? See instructions.	21a	Amount of line 20 you want **refunded to you**. If Form 8888 is attached, check here . . . . . . ▶ ☐	21a	
▶ b	Routing number ⬚⬚⬚⬚⬚⬚⬚⬚⬚ ▶ c Type: ☐ Checking ☐ Savings			
▶ d	Account number ⬚⬚⬚⬚⬚⬚⬚⬚⬚⬚⬚⬚⬚⬚⬚⬚⬚			
	22	Amount of line 20 you want **applied to your 2020 estimated tax** . . . . ▶	22	
Amount You Owe	23	**Amount you owe.** Subtract line 19 from line 16. For details on how to pay, see instructions . . . . . ▶	23	
	24	Estimated tax penalty (see instructions) . . . . ▶	24	

Third Party Designee
(Other than paid preparer)

Do you want to allow another person (other than your paid preparer) to discuss this return with the IRS? See instructions.   ☐ **Yes.** Complete below.   ☐ **No**

| Designee's name ▶ | Phone no. ▶ | Personal identification number (PIN) ▶ ⬚⬚⬚⬚⬚ |

Sign Here

Joint return? See instructions. Keep a copy for your records.

Under penalties of perjury, I declare that I have examined this return and accompanying schedules and statements, and to the best of my knowledge and belief, they are true, correct, and complete. Declaration of preparer (other than taxpayer) is based on all information of which preparer has any knowledge.

Your signature	Date	Your occupation	If the IRS sent you an Identity Protection PIN, enter it here (see inst.) ⬚⬚⬚⬚⬚⬚
Spouse's signature. If a joint return, **both** must sign.	Date	Spouse's occupation	If the IRS sent your spouse an Identity Protection PIN, enter it here (see inst.) ⬚⬚⬚⬚⬚⬚
Phone no.	Email address		

Paid Preparer Use Only

Preparer's name	Preparer's signature	Date	PTIN	Check if: ☐ 3rd Party Designee ☐ Self-employed
Firm's name ▶		Phone no.		
Firm's address ▶		Firm's EIN ▶		

Go to *www.irs.gov/Form1040* for instructions and the latest information.   Form **1040** (2019)

SCHEDULE 1
(Form 1040 or 1040-SR)

Department of the Treasury
Internal Revenue Service

Additional Income and Adjustments to Income

► **Attach to Form 1040 or 1040-SR.**
► Go to *www.irs.gov/Form1040* for instructions and the latest information.

OMB No. 1545-0074

20**19**

Attachment
Sequence No. **01**

Name(s) shown on Form 1040 or 1040-SR

Your social security number

At any time during 2019, did you receive, sell, send, exchange, or otherwise acquire any financial interest in any virtual currency? . . . .   ☐ **Yes** ☐ **No**

Part I	Additional Income		
1	Taxable refunds, credits, or offsets of state and local income taxes	**1**	
2a	Alimony received	**2a**	
b	Date of original divorce or separation agreement (see instructions) ► ------------------		
3	Business income or (loss). Attach Schedule C	**3**	
4	Other gains or (losses). Attach Form 4797	**4**	
5	Rental real estate, royalties, partnerships, S corporations, trusts, etc. Attach Schedule E	**5**	
6	Farm income or (loss). Attach Schedule F	**6**	
7	Unemployment compensation	**7**	
8	Other income. List type and amount ► --		
	--	**8**	
9	Combine lines 1 through 8. Enter here and on Form 1040 or 1040-SR, line 7a	**9**	

Part II	Adjustments to Income		
10	Educator expenses	**10**	
11	Certain business expenses of reservists, performing artists, and fee-basis government officials. Attach Form 2106	**11**	
12	Health savings account deduction. Attach Form 8889	**12**	
13	Moving expenses for members of the Armed Forces. Attach Form 3903	**13**	
14	Deductible part of self-employment tax. Attach Schedule SE	**14**	
15	Self-employed SEP, SIMPLE, and qualified plans	**15**	
16	Self-employed health insurance deduction	**16**	
17	Penalty on early withdrawal of savings	**17**	
18a	Alimony paid	**18a**	
b	Recipient's SSN . . . . ► ___ | ___ | ___		
c	Date of original divorce or separation agreement (see instructions) ► ------------------		
19	IRA deduction	**19**	
20	Student loan interest deduction	**20**	
21	Tuition and fees. Attach Form 8917	**21**	
22	Add lines 10 through 21. These are your **adjustments to income.** Enter here and on Form 1040 or 1040-SR, line 8a	**22**	

For Paperwork Reduction Act Notice, see your tax return instructions.   Cat. No. 71479F   **Schedule 1 (Form 1040 or 1040-SR) 2019**

SCHEDULE 2
(Form 1040 or 1040-SR)

Department of the Treasury
Internal Revenue Service

Additional Taxes

▶ **Attach to Form 1040 or 1040-SR.**
▶ **Go to** *www.irs.gov/Form1040* **for instructions and the latest information.**

OMB No. 1545-0074

2019

Attachment
Sequence No. **02**

Name(s) shown on Form 1040 or 1040-SR | Your social security number

Part I	**Tax**		
1	Alternative minimum tax. Attach Form 6251	1	
2	Excess advance premium tax credit repayment. Attach Form 8962 . . .	2	
3	Add lines 1 and 2. Enter here and include on Form 1040 or 1040-SR, line 12b	3	
Part II	**Other Taxes**		
4	Self-employment tax. Attach Schedule SE	4	
5	Unreported social security and Medicare tax from Form: a ☐ 4137 b ☐ 8919	5	
6	Additional tax on IRAs, other qualified retirement plans, and other tax-favored accounts. Attach Form 5329 if required	6	
7a	Household employment taxes. Attach Schedule H	7a	
b	Repayment of first-time homebuyer credit from Form 5405. Attach Form 5405 if required	7b	
8	Taxes from: a ☐ Form 8959 b ☐ Form 8960		
	c ☐ Instructions; enter code(s)	8	
9	Section 965 net tax liability installment from Form 965-A **9**		
10	Add lines 4 through 8. These are your **total other taxes.** Enter here and on Form 1040 or 1040-SR, line 15	10	

For Paperwork Reduction Act Notice, see your tax return instructions.   Cat. No. 71478U   Schedule 2 (Form 1040 or 1040-SR) 2019

SCHEDULE 3
(Form 1040 or 1040-SR)

Department of the Treasury
Internal Revenue Service

Additional Credits and Payments

▶ **Attach to Form 1040 or 1040-SR.**
▶ **Go to** *www.irs.gov/Form1040* **for instructions and the latest information.**

OMB No. 1545-0074

2019

Attachment
Sequence No. **03**

Name(s) shown on Form 1040 or 1040-SR | Your social security number

Part I	**Nonrefundable Credits**		
1	Foreign tax credit. Attach Form 1116 if required	1	
2	Credit for child and dependent care expenses. Attach Form 2441	2	
3	Education credits from Form 8863, line 19	3	
4	Retirement savings contributions credit. Attach Form 8880	4	
5	Residential energy credits. Attach Form 5695	5	
6	Other credits from Form: a ☐ 3800 b ☐ 8801 c ☐ _____	6	
7	Add lines 1 through 6. Enter here and include on Form 1040 or 1040-SR, line 13b	7	
Part II	**Other Payments and Refundable Credits**		
8	2019 estimated tax payments and amount applied from 2018 return	8	
9	Net premium tax credit. Attach Form 8962	9	
10	Amount paid with request for extension to file (see instructions)	10	
11	Excess social security and tier 1 RRTA tax withheld	11	
12	Credit for federal tax on fuels. Attach Form 4136	12	
13	Credits from Form: a ☐ 2439 b ☐ Reserved c ☐ 8885 d ☐ _____	13	
14	Add lines 8 through 13. Enter here and on Form 1040 or 1040-SR, line 18d	14	

For Paperwork Reduction Act Notice, see your tax return instructions.   Cat. No. 71480G   Schedule 3 (Form 1040 or 1040-SR) 2019

SCHEDULE A
(Form 1040 or 1040-SR)

(Rev. January 2020)

Department of the Treasury
Internal Revenue Service (99)

Itemized Deductions

▶ Go to *www.irs.gov/ScheduleA* for instructions and the latest information.

▶ Attach to Form 1040 or 1040-SR.

Caution: If you are claiming a net qualified disaster loss on Form 4684, see the instructions for line 16.

OMB No. 1545-0074

2019

Attachment
Sequence No. **07**

Name(s) shown on Form 1040 or 1040-SR | Your social security number

Medical and Dental Expenses		
	Caution: Do not include expenses reimbursed or paid by others.	
1	Medical and dental expenses (see instructions)	**1**
2	Enter amount from Form 1040 or 1040-SR, line 8b **2**	
3	Multiply line 2 by 7.5% (0.075)	**3**
4	Subtract line 3 from line 1. If line 3 is more than line 1, enter -0-	**4**

Taxes You Paid		
5	State and local taxes.	
a	State and local income taxes or general sales taxes. You may include either income taxes or general sales taxes on line 5a, but not both. If you elect to include general sales taxes instead of income taxes, check this box . . . . ▶ ☐	**5a**
b	State and local real estate taxes (see instructions)	**5b**
c	State and local personal property taxes	**5c**
d	Add lines 5a through 5c	**5d**
e	Enter the smaller of line 5d or $10,000 ($5,000 if married filing separately)	**5e**
6	Other taxes. List type and amount ▶ _____ _____	**6**
7	Add lines 5e and 6	**7**

Interest You Paid		
Caution: Your mortgage interest deduction may be limited (see instructions).	8	Home mortgage interest and points. If you didn't use all of your home mortgage loan(s) to buy, build, or improve your home, see instructions and check this box . . . . ▶ ☐	
	a	Home mortgage interest and points reported to you on Form 1098. See instructions if limited	**8a**
	b	Home mortgage interest not reported to you on Form 1098. See instructions if limited. If paid to the person from whom you bought the home, see instructions and show that person's name, identifying no., and address . . . . ▶ _____ _____	**8b**
	c	Points not reported to you on Form 1098. See instructions for special rules	**8c**
	d	Mortgage insurance premiums (see instructions)	**8d**
	e	Add lines 8a through 8d	**8e**
	9	Investment interest. Attach Form 4952 if required. See instructions .	**9**
	10	Add lines 8e and 9	**10**

Gifts to Charity		
Caution: If you made a gift and got a benefit for it, see instructions.	11	Gifts by cash or check. If you made any gift of $250 or more, see instructions	**11**
	12	Other than by cash or check. If you made any gift of $250 or more, see instructions. You **must** attach Form 8283 if over $500. . . .	**12**
	13	Carryover from prior year	**13**
	14	Add lines 11 through 13	**14**

Casualty and Theft Losses	15	Casualty and theft loss(es) from a federally declared disaster (other than net qualified disaster losses). Attach Form 4684 and enter the amount from line 18 of that form. See instructions	**15**

Other Itemized Deductions	16	Other—from list in instructions. List type and amount ▶ _____ _____	**16**

Total Itemized Deductions	17	Add the amounts in the far right column for lines 4 through 16. Also, enter this amount on Form 1040 or 1040-SR, line 9	**17**
	18	If you elect to itemize deductions even though they are less than your standard deduction, check this box . . . . ▶ ☐	

For Paperwork Reduction Act Notice, see the Instructions for Forms 1040 and 1040-SR.   Cat. No. 17145C   **Schedule A (Form 1040 or 1040-SR) 2019**

SCHEDULE B	**Interest and Ordinary Dividends**	OMB No. 1545-0074

SCHEDULE B
(Form 1040 or 1040-SR)

Department of the Treasury
Internal Revenue Service (99)

Interest and Ordinary Dividends

▶ Go to *www.irs.gov/ScheduleB* for instructions and the latest information.
▶ Attach to Form 1040 or 1040-SR.

OMB No. 1545-0074

2019

Attachment
Sequence No. **08**

Name(s) shown on return

Your social security number

Part I

Interest

(See instructions and the instructions for Forms 1040 and 1040-SR, line 2b.)

Note: If you received a Form 1099-INT, Form 1099-OID, or substitute statement from a brokerage firm, list the firm's name as the payer and enter the total interest shown on that form.

1 List name of payer. If any interest is from a seller-financed mortgage and the buyer used the property as a personal residence, see the instructions and list this interest first. Also, show that buyer's social security number and address ▶

	Amount
1	

2 Add the amounts on line 1 . . . .   **2**

3 Excludable interest on series EE and I U.S. savings bonds issued after 1989. Attach Form 8815 . . . .   **3**

4 Subtract line 3 from line 2. Enter the result here and on Form 1040 or 1040-SR, line 2b . . . . ▶   **4**

Note: If line 4 is over $1,500, you must complete Part III.

Part II

Ordinary Dividends

(See instructions and the instructions for Forms 1040 and 1040-SR, line 3b.)

Note: If you received a Form 1099-DIV or substitute statement from a brokerage firm, list the firm's name as the payer and enter the ordinary dividends shown on that form.

5 List name of payer ▶

	Amount
5	

6 Add the amounts on line 5. Enter the total here and on Form 1040 or 1040-SR, line 3b . . . . ▶   **6**

Note: If line 6 is over $1,500, you must complete Part III.

Part III

Foreign Accounts and Trusts

Caution: If required, failure to file FinCEN Form 114 may result in substantial penalties. See instructions.

You must complete this part if you **(a)** had over $1,500 of taxable interest or ordinary dividends; **(b)** had a foreign account; or **(c)** received a distribution from, or were a grantor of, or a transferor to, a foreign trust.

		Yes	No
7a	At any time during 2019, did you have a financial interest in or signature authority over a financial account (such as a bank account, securities account, or brokerage account) located in a foreign country? See instructions		
	If "Yes," are you required to file FinCEN Form 114, Report of Foreign Bank and Financial Accounts (FBAR), to report that financial interest or signature authority? See FinCEN Form 114 and its instructions for filing requirements and exceptions to those requirements		
b	If you are required to file FinCEN Form 114, enter the name of the foreign country where the financial account is located ▶		
8	During 2019, did you receive a distribution from, or were you the grantor of, or transferor to, a foreign trust? If "Yes," you may have to file Form 3520. See instructions		

For Paperwork Reduction Act Notice, see your tax return instructions.   Cat. No. 17146N   **Schedule B (Form 1040 or 1040-SR) 2019**

SCHEDULE C
(Form 1040 or 1040-SR)

Department of the Treasury
Internal Revenue Service (99)

Profit or Loss From Business
(Sole Proprietorship)

► Go to *www.irs.gov/ScheduleC* for instructions and the latest information.

► **Attach to Form 1040, 1040-SR, 1040-NR, or 1041; partnerships generally must file Form 1065.**

OMB No. 1545-0074

2019

Attachment
Sequence No. **09**

Name of proprietor | Social security number (SSN)

A Principal business or profession, including product or service (see instructions)

B Enter code from instructions ►

C Business name. If no separate business name, leave blank.

D Employer ID number (EIN) (see instr.)

E Business address (including suite or room no.) ► _____
City, town or post office, state, and ZIP code

F Accounting method: **(1)** ☐ Cash **(2)** ☐ Accrual **(3)** ☐ Other (specify) ► _____

G Did you "materially participate" in the operation of this business during 2019? If "No," see instructions for limit on losses   ☐ Yes ☐ No

H If you started or acquired this business during 2019, check here . . . . ► ☐

I Did you make any payments in 2019 that would require you to file Form(s) 1099? (see instructions) . . . . ☐ Yes ☐ No

J If "Yes," did you or will you file required Forms 1099? . . . . ☐ Yes ☐ No

Part I   Income

1	Gross receipts or sales. See instructions for line 1 and check the box if this income was reported to you on Form W-2 and the "Statutory employee" box on that form was checked . . . . ► ☐	**1**	
2	Returns and allowances	**2**	
3	Subtract line 2 from line 1	**3**	
4	Cost of goods sold (from line 42)	**4**	
5	**Gross profit.** Subtract line 4 from line 3	**5**	
6	Other income, including federal and state gasoline or fuel tax credit or refund (see instructions)	**6**	
7	**Gross income.** Add lines 5 and 6 . . . . ►	**7**	

Part II   Expenses. Enter expenses for business use of your home **only** on line 30.

8	Advertising	**8**		18	Office expense (see instructions)	**18**	
9	Car and truck expenses (see instructions)	**9**		19	Pension and profit-sharing plans .	**19**	
10	Commissions and fees .	**10**		20	Rent or lease (see instructions):		
11	Contract labor (see instructions)	**11**		a	Vehicles, machinery, and equipment	**20a**	
12	Depletion	**12**		b	Other business property . . .	**20b**	
13	Depreciation and section 179 expense deduction (not included in Part III) (see instructions)	**13**		21	Repairs and maintenance . . .	**21**	
				22	Supplies (not included in Part III) .	**22**	
				23	Taxes and licenses	**23**	
				24	Travel and meals:		
14	Employee benefit programs (other than on line 19) . .	**14**		a	Travel	**24a**	
15	Insurance (other than health)	**15**		b	Deductible meals (see instructions)	**24b**	
16	Interest (see instructions):			25	Utilities	**25**	
a	Mortgage (paid to banks, etc.)	**16a**		26	Wages (less employment credits) .	**26**	
b	Other	**16b**		27a	Other expenses (from line 48) . .	**27a**	
17	Legal and professional services	**17**		b	**Reserved for future use** . . .	**27b**	

28	**Total expenses** before expenses for business use of home. Add lines 8 through 27a . . . . . ►	**28**	
29	Tentative profit or (loss). Subtract line 28 from line 7	**29**	
30	Expenses for business use of your home. Do not report these expenses elsewhere. Attach Form 8829 unless using the simplified method (see instructions). **Simplified method filers only:** enter the total square footage of: (a) your home: _____ and (b) the part of your home used for business: _____ . Use the Simplified Method Worksheet in the instructions to figure the amount to enter on line 30	**30**	
31	**Net profit or (loss).** Subtract line 30 from line 29.		
	• If a profit, enter on both **Schedule 1 (Form 1040 or 1040-SR), line 3** (or **Form 1040-NR, line 13**) and on **Schedule SE, line 2.** (If you checked the box on line 1, see instructions). Estates and trusts, enter on **Form 1041, line 3.**	**31**	
	• If a loss, you **must** go to line 32.		
32	If you have a loss, check the box that describes your investment in this activity (see instructions).		
	• If you checked 32a, enter the loss on both **Schedule 1 (Form 1040 or 1040-SR), line 3** (or **Form 1040-NR, line 13**) and on **Schedule SE, line 2.** (If you checked the box on line 1, see the line 31 instructions). Estates and trusts, enter on **Form 1041, line 3.**	**32a** ☐ All investment is at risk. **32b** ☐ Some investment is not at risk.	
	• If you checked 32b, you **must** attach **Form 6198.** Your loss may be limited.		

For Paperwork Reduction Act Notice, see the separate instructions.   Cat. No. 11334P   Schedule C (Form 1040 or 1040-SR) 2019

Part III	Cost of Goods Sold (see instructions)

33 Method(s) used to
value closing inventory: **a** ☐ Cost **b** ☐ Lower of cost or market **c** ☐ Other (attach explanation)

34 Was there any change in determining quantities, costs, or valuations between opening and closing inventory?
If "Yes," attach explanation . . . . ☐ Yes ☐ No

35	Inventory at beginning of year. If different from last year's closing inventory, attach explanation . . .	**35**	
36	Purchases less cost of items withdrawn for personal use	**36**	
37	Cost of labor. Do not include any amounts paid to yourself	**37**	
38	Materials and supplies	**38**	
39	Other costs	**39**	
40	Add lines 35 through 39	**40**	
41	Inventory at end of year	**41**	
42	**Cost of goods sold.** Subtract line 41 from line 40. Enter the result here and on line 4	**42**	

Part IV	Information on Your Vehicle. Complete this part **only** if you are claiming car or truck expenses on line 9 and are not required to file Form 4562 for this business. See the instructions for line 13 to find out if you must file Form 4562.

43 When did you place your vehicle in service for business purposes? (month, day, year) ▶ _____ / _____ / _____

44 Of the total number of miles you drove your vehicle during 2019, enter the number of miles you used your vehicle for:

a Business _____ **b** Commuting (see instructions) _____ **c** Other _____

45 Was your vehicle available for personal use during off-duty hours? . . . . ☐ Yes ☐ No

46 Do you (or your spouse) have another vehicle available for personal use?. . . . . ☐ Yes ☐ No

47a Do you have evidence to support your deduction? . . . . ☐ Yes ☐ No

b If "Yes," is the evidence written? . . . . ☐ Yes ☐ No

Part V	Other Expenses. List below business expenses not included on lines 8–26 or line 30.

--	
--	
--	
--	
--	
--	
--	
48 Total other expenses. Enter here and on line 27a	**48**

SCHEDULE D		Capital Gains and Losses	OMB No. 1545-0074

SCHEDULE D
(Form 1040 or 1040-SR)

Department of the Treasury
Internal Revenue Service (99)

Capital Gains and Losses

► **Attach to Form 1040, 1040-SR, or 1040-NR.**
► **Go to www.irs.gov/ScheduleD for instructions and the latest information.**
► **Use Form 8949 to list your transactions for lines 1b, 2, 3, 8b, 9, and 10.**

OMB No. 1545-0074

2019

Attachment
Sequence No. **12**

Name(s) shown on return

Your social security number

Did you dispose of any investment(s) in a qualified opportunity fund during the tax year? ☐ Yes ☐ No
If "Yes," attach Form 8949 and see its instructions for additional requirements for reporting your gain or loss.

Part I   Short-Term Capital Gains and Losses—Generally Assets Held One Year or Less (see instructions)

See instructions for how to figure the amounts to enter on the lines below. This form may be easier to complete if you round off cents to whole dollars.	**(d)** Proceeds (sales price)	**(e)** Cost (or other basis)	**(g)** Adjustments to gain or loss from Form(s) 8949, Part I, line 2, column (g)	**(h) Gain or (loss)** Subtract column (e) from column (d) and combine the result with column (g)
1a Totals for all short-term transactions reported on Form 1099-B for which basis was reported to the IRS and for which you have no adjustments (see instructions). However, if you choose to report all these transactions on Form 8949, leave this line blank and go to line 1b .				
1b Totals for all transactions reported on Form(s) 8949 with **Box A** checked				
2 Totals for all transactions reported on Form(s) 8949 with **Box B** checked				
3 Totals for all transactions reported on Form(s) 8949 with **Box C** checked				

4 Short-term gain from Form 6252 and short-term gain or (loss) from Forms 4684, 6781, and 8824 . .	**4**	
5 Net short-term gain or (loss) from partnerships, S corporations, estates, and trusts from Schedule(s) K-1	**5**	
6 Short-term capital loss carryover. Enter the amount, if any, from line 8 of your **Capital Loss Carryover Worksheet** in the instructions	**6** ( )
7 **Net short-term capital gain or (loss).** Combine lines 1a through 6 in column (h). If you have any long-term capital gains or losses, go to Part II below. Otherwise, go to Part III on the back	**7**	

Part II   Long-Term Capital Gains and Losses—Generally Assets Held More Than One Year (see instructions)

See instructions for how to figure the amounts to enter on the lines below. This form may be easier to complete if you round off cents to whole dollars.	**(d)** Proceeds (sales price)	**(e)** Cost (or other basis)	**(g)** Adjustments to gain or loss from Form(s) 8949, Part II, line 2, column (g)	**(h) Gain or (loss)** Subtract column (e) from column (d) and combine the result with column (g)
8a Totals for all long-term transactions reported on Form 1099-B for which basis was reported to the IRS and for which you have no adjustments (see instructions). However, if you choose to report all these transactions on Form 8949, leave this line blank and go to line 8b .				
8b Totals for all transactions reported on Form(s) 8949 with **Box D** checked				
9 Totals for all transactions reported on Form(s) 8949 with **Box E** checked				
10 Totals for all transactions reported on Form(s) 8949 with **Box F** checked.				

11 Gain from Form 4797, Part I; long-term gain from Forms 2439 and 6252; and long-term gain or (loss) from Forms 4684, 6781, and 8824	**11**	
12 Net long-term gain or (loss) from partnerships, S corporations, estates, and trusts from Schedule(s) K-1	**12**	
13 Capital gain distributions. See the instructions	**13**	
14 Long-term capital loss carryover. Enter the amount, if any, from line 13 of your **Capital Loss Carryover Worksheet** in the instructions	**14** ( )
15 **Net long-term capital gain or (loss).** Combine lines 8a through 14 in column (h). Then go to Part III on the back	**15**	

For Paperwork Reduction Act Notice, see your tax return instructions.   Cat. No. 11338H   **Schedule D (Form 1040 or 1040-SR) 2019**

Part III	**Summary**

16   Combine lines 7 and 15 and enter the result **16**

- If line 16 is a **gain,** enter the amount from line 16 on Form 1040 or 1040-SR, line 6; or Form 1040-NR, line 14. Then go to line 17 below.
- If line 16 is a **loss,** skip lines 17 through 20 below. Then go to line 21. Also be sure to complete line 22.
- If line 16 is **zero,** skip lines 17 through 21 below and enter -0- on Form 1040 or 1040-SR, line 6; or Form 1040-NR, line 14. Then go to line 22.

17   Are lines 15 and 16 **both** gains?
☐ **Yes.** Go to line 18.
☐ **No.** Skip lines 18 through 21, and go to line 22.

18   If you are required to complete the **28% Rate Gain Worksheet** (see instructions), enter the amount, if any, from line 7 of that worksheet   . . . . ▶   **18**

19   If you are required to complete the **Unrecaptured Section 1250 Gain Worksheet** (see instructions), enter the amount, if any, from line 18 of that worksheet   . . . . ▶   **19**

20   Are lines 18 and 19 **both** zero or blank?
☐ **Yes.** Complete the **Qualified Dividends and Capital Gain Tax Worksheet** in the instructions for Forms 1040 and 1040-SR, line 12a (or in the instructions for Form 1040-NR, line 42). **Don't** complete lines 21 and 22 below.

☐ **No.** Complete the **Schedule D Tax Worksheet** in the instructions. **Don't** complete lines 21 and 22 below.

21   If line 16 is a loss, enter here and on Form 1040 or 1040-SR, line 6; or Form 1040-NR, line 14, the **smaller** of:

- The loss on line 16; or   } . . . .   **21** (   )
- ($3,000), or if married filing separately, ($1,500)

Note: When figuring which amount is smaller, treat both amounts as positive numbers.

22   Do you have qualified dividends on Form 1040 or 1040-SR, line 3a; or Form 1040-NR, line 10b?

☐ **Yes.** Complete the **Qualified Dividends and Capital Gain Tax Worksheet** in the instructions for Forms 1040 and 1040-SR, line 12a (or in the instructions for Form 1040-NR, line 42).

☐ **No.** Complete the rest of Form 1040, 1040-SR, or 1040-NR.

SCHEDULE E	**Supplemental Income and Loss**	OMB No. 1545-0074
(Form 1040 or 1040-SR)	(From rental real estate, royalties, partnerships, S corporations, estates, trusts, REMICs, etc.)	**2019**
Department of the Treasury Internal Revenue Service (99)	► **Attach to Form 1040, 1040-SR, 1040-NR, or 1041.** ► **Go to www.irs.gov/ScheduleE for instructions and the latest information.**	Attachment Sequence No. **13**

Name(s) shown on return	Your social security number

Part I **Income or Loss From Rental Real Estate and Royalties** Note: If you are in the business of renting personal property, use **Schedule C** (see instructions). If you are an individual, report farm rental income or loss from **Form 4835** on page 2, line 40.

A Did you make any payments in 2019 that would require you to file Form(s) 1099? (see instructions) . . . . . ☐ Yes ☐ No

B If "Yes," did you or will you file required Forms 1099? . . . . ☐ Yes ☐ No

1a	Physical address of each property (street, city, state, ZIP code)					
A						
B						
C						

1b	Type of Property (from list below)	2	For each rental real estate property listed above, report the number of fair rental and personal use days. Check the **QJV** box only if you meet the requirements to file as a qualified joint venture. See instructions.		Fair Rental Days	Personal Use Days	QJV
A				A			☐
B				B			☐
C				C			☐

Type of Property:

1 Single Family Residence   3 Vacation/Short-Term Rental 5 Land   7 Self-Rental

2 Multi-Family Residence   4 Commercial   6 Royalties   8 Other (describe)

Income:		Properties:		A	B	C
3	Rents received	3				
4	Royalties received	4				
Expenses:						
5	Advertising	5				
6	Auto and travel (see instructions)	6				
7	Cleaning and maintenance	7				
8	Commissions.	8				
9	Insurance	9				
10	Legal and other professional fees	10				
11	Management fees	11				
12	Mortgage interest paid to banks, etc. (see instructions)	12				
13	Other interest.	13				
14	Repairs.	14				
15	Supplies	15				
16	Taxes	16				
17	Utilities	17				
18	Depreciation expense or depletion	18				
19	Other (list) ► --	19				
20	Total expenses. Add lines 5 through 19	20				
21	Subtract line 20 from line 3 (rents) and/or 4 (royalties). If result is a (loss), see instructions to find out if you must file **Form 6198**	21				
22	Deductible rental real estate loss after limitation, if any, on **Form 8582** (see instructions)	22	( )	( )	( )	( )

23a	Total of all amounts reported on line 3 for all rental properties	23a	
b	Total of all amounts reported on line 4 for all royalty properties	23b	
c	Total of all amounts reported on line 12 for all properties	23c	
d	Total of all amounts reported on line 18 for all properties	23d	
e	Total of all amounts reported on line 20 for all properties	23e	

24	**Income.** Add positive amounts shown on line 21. **Do not** include any losses	24	
25	**Losses.** Add royalty losses from line 21 and rental real estate losses from line 22. Enter total losses here .	25	( )
26	**Total rental real estate and royalty income or (loss).** Combine lines 24 and 25. Enter the result here. If Parts II, III, IV, and line 40 on page 2 do not apply to you, also enter this amount on Schedule 1 (Form 1040 or 1040-SR), line 5, or Form 1040-NR, line 18. Otherwise, include this amount in the total on line 41 on page 2	26	

For Paperwork Reduction Act Notice, see the separate instructions.   Cat. No. 11344L   **Schedule E (Form 1040 or 1040-SR) 2019**

Schedule E (Form 1040 or 1040-SR) 2019   Attachment Sequence No. **13**   Page **2**

Name(s) shown on return. Do not enter name and social security number if shown on other side.	Your social security number

Caution: The IRS compares amounts reported on your tax return with amounts shown on Schedule(s) K-1.

Part II   **Income or Loss From Partnerships and S Corporations** — **Note:** If you report a loss, receive a distribution, dispose of stock, or receive a loan repayment from an S corporation, you **must** check the box in column **(e)** on line 28 and attach the required basis computation. If you report a loss from an at-risk activity for which **any** amount is **not** at risk, you **must** check the box in column **(f)** on line 28 and attach **Form 6198** (see instructions).

27   Are you reporting any loss not allowed in a prior year due to the at-risk or basis limitations, a prior year unallowed loss from a passive activity (if that loss was not reported on Form 8582), or unreimbursed partnership expenses? If you answered "Yes," see instructions before completing this section . . . . ☐ **Yes**   ☐ **No**

28	(a) Name	(b) Enter P for partnership; S for S corporation	(c) Check if foreign partnership	(d) Employer identification number	(e) Check if basis computation is required	(f) Check if any amount is not at risk
A			☐		☐	☐
B			☐		☐	☐
C			☐		☐	☐
D			☐		☐	☐

	Passive Income and Loss		Nonpassive Income and Loss		
	(g) Passive loss allowed (attach **Form 8582** if required)	(h) Passive income from **Schedule K-1**	(i) Nonpassive loss allowed (see **Schedule K-1**)	(j) Section 179 expense deduction from **Form 4562**	(k) Nonpassive income from **Schedule K-1**
A					
B					
C					
D					
29a Totals					
b Totals					

30	Add columns (h) and (k) of line 29a.	30	
31	Add columns (g), (i), and (j) of line 29b.	31	( )
32	**Total partnership and S corporation income or (loss).** Combine lines 30 and 31	32	

Part III   **Income or Loss From Estates and Trusts**

33	(a) Name	(b) Employer identification number
A		
B		

	Passive Income and Loss		Nonpassive Income and Loss	
	(c) Passive deduction or loss allowed (attach **Form 8582** if required)	(d) Passive income from **Schedule K-1**	(e) Deduction or loss from **Schedule K-1**	(f) Other income from **Schedule K-1**
A				
B				
34a Totals				
b Totals				

35	Add columns (d) and (f) of line 34a	35	
36	Add columns (c) and (e) of line 34b	36	( )
37	**Total estate and trust income or (loss).** Combine lines 35 and 36	37	

Part IV   **Income or Loss From Real Estate Mortgage Investment Conduits (REMICs)—Residual Holder**

38	(a) Name	(b) Employer identification number	(c) Excess inclusion from **Schedules Q,** line 2c (see instructions)	(d) Taxable income (net loss) from **Schedules Q,** line 1b	(e) Income from **Schedules Q,** line 3b

39	Combine columns (d) and (e) only. Enter the result here and include in the total on line 41 below	39	

Part V   **Summary**

40	Net farm rental income or (loss) from **Form 4835.** Also, complete line 42 below	40	
41	Total income or (loss). Combine lines 26, 32, 37, 39, and 40. Enter the result here and on Schedule 1 (Form 1040 or 1040-SR), line 5, or Form 1040-NR, line 18 ▶	41	

42   **Reconciliation of farming and fishing income.** Enter your **gross** farming and fishing income reported on Form 4835, line 7; Schedule K-1 (Form 1065), box 14, code B; Schedule K-1 (Form 1120-S), box 17, code AC; and Schedule K-1 (Form 1041), box 14, code F (see instructions) . | **42** | |

43   **Reconciliation for real estate professionals.** If you were a real estate professional (see instructions), enter the net income or (loss) you reported anywhere on Form 1040, Form 1040-SR, or Form 1040-NR from all rental real estate activities in which you materially participated under the passive activity loss rules . . . . . | **43** | |

Schedule E (Form 1040 or 1040-SR) 2019

SCHEDULE SE
(Form 1040 or 1040-SR)

Department of the Treasury
Internal Revenue Service (99)

Self-Employment Tax

▶ Go to *www.irs.gov/ScheduleSE* for instructions and the latest information.
▶ **Attach to Form 1040, 1040-SR, or 1040-NR.**

OMB No. 1545-0074

20**19**

Attachment
Sequence No. **17**

Name of person with self-employment income (as shown on Form 1040, 1040-SR, or 1040-NR)	Social security number of person with **self-employment** income ▶

Before you begin: To determine if you must file Schedule SE, see the instructions.

May I Use Short Schedule SE or Must I Use Long Schedule SE?

Note: Use this flowchart **only if** you must file Schedule SE. If unsure, see *Who Must File Schedule SE* in the instructions.

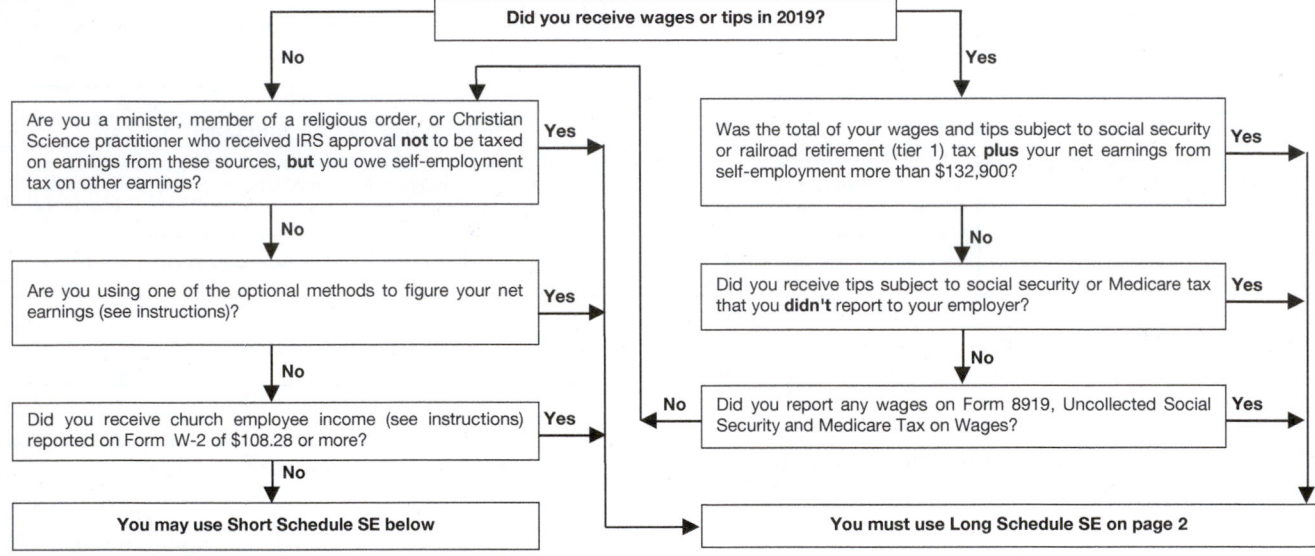

Section A—Short Schedule SE. Caution: Read above to see if you can use Short Schedule SE.

1a	Net farm profit or (loss) from Schedule F, line 34, and farm partnerships, Schedule K-1 (Form 1065), box 14, code A	**1a**
b	If you received social security retirement or disability benefits, enter the amount of Conservation Reserve Program payments included on Schedule F, line 4b, or listed on Schedule K-1 (Form 1065), box 20, code AH	**1b** ( )
2	Net profit or (loss) from Schedule C, line 31; and Schedule K-1 (Form 1065), box 14, code A (other than farming). Ministers and members of religious orders, see instructions for types of income to report on this line. See instructions for other income to report	**2**
3	Combine lines 1a, 1b, and 2	**3**
4	Multiply line 3 by 92.35% (0.9235). If less than $400, you don't owe self-employment tax; **don't** file this schedule unless you have an amount on line 1b . . . . ▶	**4**
	Note: If line 4 is less than $400 due to Conservation Reserve Program payments on line 1b, see instructions.	
5	**Self-employment tax.** If the amount on line 4 is:	
	• $132,900 or less, multiply line 4 by 15.3% (0.153). Enter the result here and on **Schedule 2 (Form 1040 or 1040-SR), line 4,** or **Form 1040-NR, line 55.**	
	• More than $132,900, multiply line 4 by 2.9% (0.029). Then, add $16,479.60 to the result. Enter the total here and on **Schedule 2 (Form 1040 or 1040-SR), line 4,** or **Form 1040-NR, line 55** .	**5**
6	**Deduction for one-half of self-employment tax.** Multiply line 5 by 50% (0.50). Enter the result here and on **Schedule 1 (Form 1040 or 1040-SR), line 14,** or **Form 1040-NR, line 27**	**6**	

For Paperwork Reduction Act Notice, see your tax return instructions.   Cat. No. 11358Z   Schedule SE (Form 1040 or 1040-SR) 2019

Schedule SE (Form 1040 or 1040-SR) 2019   Attachment Sequence No. **17**   Page **2**

Name of person with self-employment income (as shown on Form 1040, 1040-SR, or 1040-NR)	Social security number of person with **self-employment** income ▶

Section B—Long Schedule SE

Part I   Self-Employment Tax

Note: If your only income subject to self-employment tax is **church employee income,** see instructions. Also see instructions for the definition of church employee income.

A   If you are a minister, member of a religious order, or Christian Science practitioner **and** you filed Form 4361, but you had $400 or more of **other** net earnings from self-employment, check here and continue with Part I . . . . ▶ ☐

1a   Net farm profit or (loss) from Schedule F, line 34, and farm partnerships, Schedule K-1 (Form 1065), box 14, code A. **Note:** Skip lines 1a and 1b if you use the farm optional method (see instructions) . | **1a** |

b   If you received social security retirement or disability benefits, enter the amount of Conservation Reserve Program payments included on Schedule F, line 4b, or listed on Schedule K-1 (Form 1065), box 20, code AH | **1b** |( )

2   Net profit or (loss) from Schedule C, line 31; and Schedule K-1 (Form 1065), box 14, code A (other than farming). Ministers and members of religious orders, see instructions for types of income to report on this line. See instructions for other income to report. **Note:** Skip this line if you use the nonfarm optional method (see instructions) . . . . | **2** |

3   Combine lines 1a, 1b, and 2 . . . . | **3** |

4a   If line 3 is more than zero, multiply line 3 by 92.35% (0.9235). Otherwise, enter amount from line 3 . | **4a** |
    Note: If line 4a is less than $400 due to Conservation Reserve Program payments on line 1b, see instructions.

b   If you elect one or both of the optional methods, enter the total of lines 15 and 17 here . . . . . | **4b** |

c   Combine lines 4a and 4b. If less than $400, **stop;** you don't owe self-employment tax. **Exception:** If less than $400 and you had **church employee income,** enter -0- and continue . . . . ▶ | **4c** |

5a   Enter your **church employee income** from Form W-2. See instructions for definition of church employee income . . . . | **5a** |

b   Multiply line 5a by 92.35% (0.9235). If less than $100, enter -0- . . . . | **5b** |

6   Add lines 4c and 5b . . . . | **6** |

7   Maximum amount of combined wages and self-employment earnings subject to social security tax or the 6.2% portion of the 7.65% railroad retirement (tier 1) tax for 2019 . . . . | **7** | 132,900

8a   Total social security wages and tips (total of boxes 3 and 7 on Form(s) W-2) and railroad retirement (tier 1) compensation. If $132,900 or more, skip lines 8b through 10, and go to line 11 . . . . | **8a** |

b   Unreported tips subject to social security tax (from Form 4137, line 10) . . | **8b** |

c   Wages subject to social security tax (from Form 8919, line 10) . . . . . | **8c** |

d   Add lines 8a, 8b, and 8c . . . . | **8d** |

9   Subtract line 8d from line 7. If zero or less, enter -0- here and on line 10 and go to line 11 . . . ▶ | **9** |

10   Multiply the **smaller** of line 6 or line 9 by 12.4% (0.124) . . . . | **10** |

11   Multiply line 6 by 2.9% (0.029) . . . . | **11** |

12   **Self-employment tax.** Add lines 10 and 11. Enter here and on **Schedule 2 (Form 1040 or 1040-SR), line 4, or Form 1040-NR, line 55** . . . . | **12** |

13   **Deduction for one-half of self-employment tax.**
    Multiply line 12 by 50% (0.50). Enter the result here and on **Schedule 1 (Form 1040 or 1040-SR), line 14,** or **Form 1040-NR, line 27** . . . . | **13** |

Part II   Optional Methods To Figure Net Earnings   (see instructions)

Farm Optional Method. You may use this method **only** if **(a)** your gross farm income[1] wasn't more than $8,160, **or (b)** your net farm profits[2] were less than $5,891.

14   Maximum income for optional methods . . . . | **14** | 5,440

15   Enter the **smaller** of: two-thirds (⅔) of gross farm income[1] (not less than zero) or $5,440. Also include this amount on line 4b above . . . . | **15** |

Nonfarm Optional Method. You may use this method **only** if **(a)** your net nonfarm profits[3] were less than $5,891 and also less than 72.189% of your gross nonfarm income,[4] **and (b)** you had net earnings from self-employment of at least $400 in 2 of the prior 3 years. **Caution:** You may use this method no more than five times.

16   Subtract line 15 from line 14 . . . . | **16** |

17   Enter the **smaller** of: two-thirds (⅔) of gross nonfarm income[4] (not less than zero) **or** the amount on line 16. Also include this amount on line 4b above . . . . | **17** |

[1] From Sch. F, line 9, and Sch. K-1 (Form 1065), box 14, code B.
[2] From Sch. F, line 34, and Sch. K-1 (Form 1065), box 14, code A—minus the amount you would have entered on line 1b had you not used the optional method.

[3] From Sch. C, line 31; and Sch. K-1 (Form 1065), box 14, code A.
[4] From Sch. C, line 7; and Sch. K-1 (Form 1065), box 14, code C.

Schedule SE (Form 1040 or 1040-SR) 2019

Form **1041**

Department of the Treasury—Internal Revenue Service
U.S. Income Tax Return for Estates and Trusts
▶ Go to *www.irs.gov/Form1041* for instructions and the latest information.

2019 | OMB No. 1545-0092

A Check all that apply:
- ☐ Decedent's estate
- ☐ Simple trust
- ☐ Complex trust
- ☐ Qualified disability trust
- ☐ ESBT (S portion only)
- ☐ Grantor type trust
- ☐ Bankruptcy estate—Ch. 7
- ☐ Bankruptcy estate—Ch. 11
- ☐ Pooled income fund

For calendar year 2019 or fiscal year beginning _____ , 2019, and ending _____ , 20 ___

Name of estate or trust (If a grantor type trust, see the instructions.)

Name and title of fiduciary

Number, street, and room or suite no. (If a P.O. box, see the instructions.)

City or town, state or province, country, and ZIP or foreign postal code

C Employer identification number

D Date entity created

E Nonexempt charitable and split-interest trusts, check applicable box(es). See instructions.
- ☐ Described in sec. 4947(a)(1). Check here if not a private foundation . . ▶ ☐
- ☐ Described in sec. 4947(a)(2)

B Number of Schedules K-1 attached (see instructions) ▶

F Check applicable boxes:
- ☐ Initial return
- ☐ Final return
- ☐ Amended return
- ☐ Net operating loss carryback
- ☐ Change in trust's name
- ☐ Change in fiduciary
- ☐ Change in fiduciary's name
- ☐ Change in fiduciary's address

G Check here if the estate or filing trust made a section 645 election . . . . ▶ ☐ Trust TIN ▶

Income

1	Interest income	**1**
2a	Total ordinary dividends	**2a**
b	Qualified dividends allocable to: **(1)** Beneficiaries _____ **(2)** Estate or trust _____	
3	Business income or (loss). Attach Schedule C (Form 1040 or 1040-SR) . . .	**3**
4	Capital gain or (loss). Attach Schedule D (Form 1041)	**4**
5	Rents, royalties, partnerships, other estates and trusts, etc. Attach Schedule E (Form 1040 or 1040-SR)	**5**
6	Farm income or (loss). Attach Schedule F (Form 1040 or 1040-SR)	**6**
7	Ordinary gain or (loss). Attach Form 4797	**7**
8	Other income. List type and amount _____	**8**
9	**Total income.** Combine lines 1, 2a, and 3 through 8 . . . . . . ▶	**9**

Deductions

10	Interest. Check if Form 4952 is attached ▶ ☐	**10**
11	Taxes	**11**
12	Fiduciary fees. If only a portion is deductible under section 67(e), see instructions	**12**
13	Charitable deduction (from Schedule A, line 7)	**13**
14	Attorney, accountant, and return preparer fees. If only a portion is deductible under section 67(e), see instructions	**14**
15a	Other deductions (attach schedule). See instructions for deductions allowable under section 67(e)	**15a**
b	Net operating loss deduction. See instructions	**15b**
16	Add lines 10 through 15b . . . . ▶	**16**
17	Adjusted total income or (loss). Subtract line 16 from line 9 . . . . . **17**	
18	Income distribution deduction (from Schedule B, line 15). Attach Schedules K-1 (Form 1041) . .	**18**
19	Estate tax deduction including certain generation-skipping taxes (attach computation)	**19**
20	Qualified business income deduction. Attach Form 8995 or 8995-A	**20**
21	Exemption	**21**
22	Add lines 18 through 21 . . . . ▶	**22**

Tax and Payments

23	Taxable income. Subtract line 22 from line 17. If a loss, see instructions	**23**
24	**Total tax** (from Schedule G, Part I, line 9)	**24**
25	2019 net 965 tax liability paid from Form 965-A, Part II, column (k), line 3	**25**
26	**Total payments** (from Schedule G, Part II, line 17)	**26**
27	Estimated tax penalty. See instructions	**27**
28	**Tax due.** If line 26 is smaller than the total of lines 24, 25, and 27, enter amount owed	**28**
29	**Overpayment.** If line 26 is larger than the total of lines 24, 25, and 27, enter amount overpaid . .	**29**
30	Amount of line 29 to be: **a** Credited to 2020 ▶ _____ ; **b** Refunded . . . . . ▶	**30**

Sign Here

Under penalties of perjury, I declare that I have examined this return, including accompanying schedules and statements, and to the best of my knowledge and belief, it is true, correct, and complete. Declaration of preparer (other than taxpayer) is based on all information of which preparer has any knowledge.

▶ _____ Signature of fiduciary or officer representing fiduciary   Date   ▶ _____ EIN of fiduciary if a financial institution

May the IRS discuss this return with the preparer shown below? See Instr. ☐ Yes ☐ No

Paid Preparer Use Only

Print/Type preparer's name	Preparer's signature	Date	Check ☐ if self-employed	PTIN
Firm's name ▶			Firm's EIN ▶	
Firm's address ▶			Phone no.	

For Paperwork Reduction Act Notice, see the separate instructions.   Cat. No. 11370H   Form **1041** (2019)

Form 1041 (2019)   Page **2**

Schedule A	**Charitable Deduction.** Don't complete for a simple trust or a pooled income fund.		
1	Amounts paid or permanently set aside for charitable purposes from gross income. See instructions	**1**	
2	Tax-exempt income allocable to charitable contributions. See instructions	**2**	
3	Subtract line 2 from line 1	**3**	
4	Capital gains for the tax year allocated to corpus and paid or permanently set aside for charitable purposes	**4**	
5	Add lines 3 and 4	**5**	
6	Section 1202 exclusion allocable to capital gains paid or permanently set aside for charitable purposes. See instructions	**6**	
7	**Charitable deduction.** Subtract line 6 from line 5. Enter here and on page 1, line 13	**7**	

Schedule B	**Income Distribution Deduction**		
1	Adjusted total income. See instructions	**1**	
2	Adjusted tax-exempt interest	**2**	
3	Total net gain from Schedule D (Form 1041), line 19, column (1). See instructions	**3**	
4	Enter amount from Schedule A, line 4 (minus any allocable section 1202 exclusion)	**4**	
5	Capital gains for the tax year included on Schedule A, line 1. See instructions	**5**	
6	Enter any gain from page 1, line 4, as a negative number. If page 1, line 4, is a loss, enter the loss as a positive number	**6**	
7	**Distributable net income.** Combine lines 1 through 6. If zero or less, enter -0-	**7**	
8	If a complex trust, enter accounting income for the tax year as determined under the governing instrument and applicable local law	**8**	
9	Income required to be distributed currently	**9**	
10	Other amounts paid, credited, or otherwise required to be distributed	**10**	
11	Total distributions. Add lines 9 and 10. If greater than line 8, see instructions	**11**	
12	Enter the amount of tax-exempt income included on line 11	**12**	
13	Tentative income distribution deduction. Subtract line 12 from line 11	**13**	
14	Tentative income distribution deduction. Subtract line 2 from line 7. If zero or less, enter -0-	**14**	
15	**Income distribution deduction.** Enter the smaller of line 13 or line 14 here and on page 1, line 18	**15**	

Schedule G	**Tax Computation and Payments** (see instructions)			

Part I — Tax Computation

1	**Tax:**			
a	Tax on taxable income. See instructions	**1a**		
b	Tax on lump-sum distributions. Attach Form 4972	**1b**		
c	Alternative minimum tax (from Schedule I (Form 1041), line 54)	**1c**		
d	**Total.** Add lines 1a through 1c		**1d**	
2a	Foreign tax credit. Attach Form 1116	**2a**		
b	General business credit. Attach Form 3800	**2b**		
c	Credit for prior year minimum tax. Attach Form 8801	**2c**		
d	Bond credits. Attach Form 8912	**2d**		
e	**Total credits.** Add lines 2a through 2d		**2e**	
3	Subtract line 2e from line 1d. If zero or less, enter -0-		**3**	
4	Tax on the ESBT portion of the trust (from ESBT Tax Worksheet, line 17). See instructions		**4**	
5	Net investment income tax from Form 8960, line 21		**5**	
6	Recapture taxes. Check if from: ☐ Form 4255 ☐ Form 8611		**6**	
7	Household employment taxes. Attach Schedule H (Form 1040 or 1040-SR)		**7**	
8	Other taxes and amounts due		**8**	
9	**Total tax.** Add lines 3 through 8. Enter here and on page 1, line 24		**9**	

Part II — Payments

10	2019 estimated tax payments and amount applied from 2018 return	**10**	
11	Estimated tax payments allocated to beneficiaries (from Form 1041-T)	**11**	
12	Subtract line 11 from line 10	**12**	
13	Tax paid with Form 7004. See instructions	**13**	
14	Federal income tax withheld. If any is from Form(s) 1099, check here ▶ ☐	**14**	
15	2019 net 965 tax liability from Form 965-A, Part I, column (f), line 3	**15**	
16	Other payments: **a** Form 2439 _____ ; **b** Form 4136 _____ ; Total ▶	**16c**	
17	**Total payments.** Add lines 12 through 15 and 16c. Enter here and on page 1, line 26 ▶	**17**	

Form **1041** (2019)

Form 1041 (2019)   Page **3**

Other Information	**Yes**	**No**
1 Did the estate or trust receive tax-exempt income? If "Yes," attach a computation of the allocation of expenses. Enter the amount of tax-exempt interest income and exempt-interest dividends . . . ▶ \$ _____		
2 Did the estate or trust receive all or any part of the earnings (salary, wages, and other compensation) of any individual by reason of a contract assignment or similar arrangement?		
3 At any time during calendar year 2019, did the estate or trust have an interest in or a signature or other authority over a bank, securities, or other financial account in a foreign country?		
See the instructions for exceptions and filing requirements for FinCEN Form 114. If "Yes," enter the name of the foreign country ▶ _____		
4 During the tax year, did the estate or trust receive a distribution from, or was it the grantor of, or transferor to, a foreign trust? If "Yes," the estate or trust may have to file Form 3520. See instructions		
5 Did the estate or trust receive, or pay, any qualified residence interest on seller-provided financing? If "Yes," see the instructions for the required attachment		
6 If this is an estate or a complex trust making the section 663(b) election, check here. See instructions . . ▶ ☐		
7 To make a section 643(e)(3) election, attach Schedule D (Form 1041), and check here. See instructions . . ▶ ☐		
8 If the decedent's estate has been open for more than 2 years, attach an explanation for the delay in closing the estate, and check here . . . . ▶ ☐		
9 Are any present or future trust beneficiaries skip persons? See instructions		
10 Was the trust a specified domestic entity required to file Form 8938 for the tax year (see the Instructions for Form 8938)?		
11a Did the estate or trust distribute S corporation stock for which it made a section 965(i) election?		
b If "Yes," did each beneficiary enter into an agreement to be liable for the net tax liability? See instructions . . .		
12 Did the estate or trust make a section 965(i) election for S corporation stock held on the last day of the tax year? See instructions		
13 **ESBTs only.** Does the ESBT have a nonresident alien grantor? If "Yes," see instructions		
14 **ESBTs only.** Did the S portion of the trust claim a qualified business income deduction? If "Yes," see instructions		

Form **1041** (2019)

661117

☐ Final K-1	☐ Amended K-1 OMB No. 1545-0092

Schedule K-1
(Form 1041)

2019

Department of the Treasury
Internal Revenue Service

For calendar year 2019, or tax year

beginning ___ / ___ / 2019   ending ___ / ___ / ___

Beneficiary's Share of Income, Deductions, Credits, etc.

▶ **See back of form and instructions.**

Part I	**Information About the Estate or Trust**

A Estate's or trust's employer identification number

B Estate's or trust's name

C Fiduciary's name, address, city, state, and ZIP code

D ☐ Check if Form 1041-T was filed and enter the date it was filed

_____

E ☐ Check if this is the final Form 1041 for the estate or trust

Part II	**Information About the Beneficiary**

F Beneficiary's identifying number

G Beneficiary's name, address, city, state, and ZIP code

H ☐ Domestic beneficiary   ☐ Foreign beneficiary

Part III	**Beneficiary's Share of Current Year Income, Deductions, Credits, and Other Items**

1	Interest income	**11**	Final year deductions
2a	Ordinary dividends		
2b	Qualified dividends		
3	Net short-term capital gain		
4a	Net long-term capital gain		
4b	28% rate gain	**12**	Alternative minimum tax adjustment
4c	Unrecaptured section 1250 gain		
5	Other portfolio and nonbusiness income		
6	Ordinary business income		
7	Net rental real estate income		
		13	Credits and credit recapture
8	Other rental income		
9	Directly apportioned deductions		
		14	Other information
10	Estate tax deduction		

*See attached statement for additional information.

Note: A statement must be attached showing the beneficiary's share of income and directly apportioned deductions from each business, rental real estate, and other rental activity.

For IRS Use Only

For Paperwork Reduction Act Notice, see the Instructions for Form 1041.   www.irs.gov/Form1041   Cat. No. 11380D   **Schedule K-1 (Form 1041) 2019**

This list identifies the codes used on Schedule K-1 for beneficiaries and provides summarized reporting information for beneficiaries who file Form 1040 or 1040-SR. For detailed reporting and filing information, see the Instructions for Schedule K-1 (Form 1041) for a Beneficiary Filing Form 1040 or 1040-SR and the instructions for your income tax return.

Report on

1. Interest income — Form 1040 or 1040-SR, line 2b
2a. Ordinary dividends — Form 1040 or 1040-SR, line 3b
2b. Qualified dividends — Form 1040 or 1040-SR, line 3a
3. Net short-term capital gain — Schedule D, line 5
4a. Net long-term capital gain — Schedule D, line 12
4b. 28% rate gain — 28% Rate Gain Worksheet, line 4 (Schedule D Instructions)
4c. Unrecaptured section 1250 gain — Unrecaptured Section 1250 Gain Worksheet, line 11 (Schedule D Instructions)
5. Other portfolio and nonbusiness income — Schedule E, line 33, column (f)
6. Ordinary business income — Schedule E, line 33, column (d) or (f)
7. Net rental real estate income — Schedule E, line 33, column (d) or (f)
8. Other rental income — Schedule E, line 33, column (d) or (f)
9. Directly apportioned deductions

Code
A Depreciation — Form 8582 or Schedule E, line 33, column (c) or (e)
B Depletion — Form 8582 or Schedule E, line 33, column (c) or (e)
C Amortization — Form 8582 or Schedule E, line 33, column (c) or (e)
10. Estate tax deduction — Schedule A, line 16
11. Final year deductions
A Excess deductions — See the beneficiary's instructions
B Short-term capital loss carryover — Schedule D, line 5
C Long-term capital loss carryover — Schedule D, line 12; line 5 of the wksht. for Sch. D, line 18; and line 16 of the wksht. for Sch. D, line 19
D Net operating loss carryover — regular tax — Form 1040 or 1040-SR, Schedule 1, line 8
E Net operating loss carryover — minimum tax — Form 6251, line 2f
12. Alternative minimum tax (AMT) items
A Adjustment for minimum tax purposes — Form 6251, line 2j
B AMT adjustment attributable to qualified dividends
C AMT adjustment attributable to net short-term capital gain
D AMT adjustment attributable to net long-term capital gain
E AMT adjustment attributable to unrecaptured section 1250 gain — See the beneficiary's instructions and the Instructions for Form 6251
F AMT adjustment attributable to 28% rate gain
G Accelerated depreciation
H Depletion
I Amortization
J Exclusion items — 2020 Form 8801

13. Credits and credit recapture
Code — *Report on*
A Credit for estimated taxes — Form 1040 or 1040-SR, Schedule 3, line 8
B Credit for backup withholding — Form 1040 or 1040-SR, line 17
C Low-income housing credit
D Rehabilitation credit and energy credit
E Other qualifying investment credit
F Work opportunity credit
G Credit for small employer health insurance premiums
H Biofuel producer credit
I Credit for increasing research activities
J Renewable electricity, refined coal, and Indian coal production credit
K Empowerment zone employment credit — See the beneficiary's instructions
L Indian employment credit
M Orphan drug credit
N Credit for employer-provided child care and facilities
O Biodiesel and renewable diesel fuels credit
P Credit to holders of tax credit bonds
Q Credit for employer differential wage payments
R Recapture of credits
Z Other credits
14. Other information
A Tax-exempt interest — Form 1040 or 1040-SR, line 2a
B Foreign taxes — Form 1040 or 1040-SR, Schedule 3, line 1 or Sch. A, line 6
C Reserved
D Reserved
E Net investment income — Form 4952, line 4a
F Gross farm and fishing income — Schedule E, line 42
G Foreign trading gross receipts (IRC 942(a)) — See the Instructions for Form 8873
H Adjustment for section 1411 net investment income or deductions — Form 8960, line 7 (also see the beneficiary's instructions)
I Section 199A information — See the beneficiary's instructions
Z Other information — See the beneficiary's instructions

Note: If you are a beneficiary who does not file a Form 1040 or 1040-SR, see instructions for the type of income tax return you are filing.

Form **1065**

Department of the Treasury
Internal Revenue Service

U.S. Return of Partnership Income

For calendar year 2019, or tax year beginning _____, 2019, ending _____, 20_____.

▶ Go to *www.irs.gov/Form1065* for instructions and the latest information.

OMB No. 1545-0123

2019

A Principal business activity	**Type or Print** — Name of partnership	**D** Employer identification number
B Principal product or service	Number, street, and room or suite no. If a P.O. box, see instructions.	**E** Date business started
C Business code number	City or town, state or province, country, and ZIP or foreign postal code	**F** Total assets (see instructions) $

G Check applicable boxes: **(1)** ☐ Initial return **(2)** ☐ Final return **(3)** ☐ Name change **(4)** ☐ Address change **(5)** ☐ Amended return

H Check accounting method: **(1)** ☐ Cash **(2)** ☐ Accrual **(3)** ☐ Other (specify) ▶ _____

I Number of Schedules K-1. Attach one for each person who was a partner at any time during the tax year ▶ _____

J Check if Schedules C and M-3 are attached . . . . ▶ ☐

K Check if partnership: **(1)** ☐ Aggregated activities for section 465 at-risk purposes **(2)** ☐ Grouped activities for section 469 passive activity purposes

Caution: Include **only** trade or business income and expenses on lines 1a through 22 below. See instructions for more information.

Income

1a	Gross receipts or sales	1a	
b	Returns and allowances	1b	
c	Balance. Subtract line 1b from line 1a		1c
2	Cost of goods sold (attach Form 1125-A)		2
3	Gross profit. Subtract line 2 from line 1c		3
4	Ordinary income (loss) from other partnerships, estates, and trusts (attach statement)		4
5	Net farm profit (loss) (attach Schedule F (Form 1040 or 1040-SR))		5
6	Net gain (loss) from Form 4797, Part II, line 17 (attach Form 4797)		6
7	Other income (loss) (attach statement)		7
8	**Total income (loss).** Combine lines 3 through 7		8

Deductions (see instructions for limitations)

9	Salaries and wages (other than to partners) (less employment credits)		9
10	Guaranteed payments to partners		10
11	Repairs and maintenance		11
12	Bad debts		12
13	Rent		13
14	Taxes and licenses		14
15	Interest (see instructions)		15
16a	Depreciation (if required, attach Form 4562)	16a	
b	Less depreciation reported on Form 1125-A and elsewhere on return .	16b	16c
17	Depletion **(Do not deduct oil and gas depletion.)**		17
18	Retirement plans, etc.		18
19	Employee benefit programs		19
20	Other deductions (attach statement)		20
21	**Total deductions.** Add the amounts shown in the far right column for lines 9 through 20 . . .		21
22	**Ordinary business income (loss).** Subtract line 21 from line 8		22

Tax and Payment

23	Interest due under the look-back method—completed long-term contracts (attach Form 8697) .	23
24	Interest due under the look-back method—income forecast method (attach Form 8866) . . .	24
25	BBA AAR imputed underpayment (see instructions)	25
26	Other taxes (see instructions)	26
27	**Total balance due.** Add lines 23 through 26	27
28	Payment (see instructions)	28
29	**Amount owed.** If line 28 is smaller than line 27, enter amount owed	29
30	**Overpayment.** If line 28 is larger than line 27, enter overpayment	30

Sign Here

Under penalties of perjury, I declare that I have examined this return, including accompanying schedules and statements, and to the best of my knowledge and belief, it is true, correct, and complete. Declaration of preparer (other than partner or limited liability company member) is based on all information of which preparer has any knowledge.

▶ _____   ▶ _____
Signature of partner or limited liability company member   Date

May the IRS discuss this return with the preparer shown below? See instructions. ☐ Yes ☐ No

Paid Preparer Use Only

Print/Type preparer's name	Preparer's signature	Date	Check ☐ if self-employed	PTIN
Firm's name ▶			Firm's EIN ▶	
Firm's address ▶			Phone no.	

For Paperwork Reduction Act Notice, see separate instructions.   Cat. No. 11390Z   Form **1065** (2019)

Form 1065 (2019)   Page **2**

Schedule B	**Other Information**		

		Yes	No
1	What type of entity is filing this return? Check the applicable box:		
a	☐ Domestic general partnership **b** ☐ Domestic limited partnership		
c	☐ Domestic limited liability company **d** ☐ Domestic limited liability partnership		
e	☐ Foreign partnership **f** ☐ Other ▶		
2	At the end of the tax year:		
a	Did any foreign or domestic corporation, partnership (including any entity treated as a partnership), trust, or tax-exempt organization, or any foreign government own, directly or indirectly, an interest of 50% or more in the profit, loss, or capital of the partnership? For rules of constructive ownership, see instructions. If "Yes," attach Schedule B-1, Information on Partners Owning 50% or More of the Partnership		
b	Did any individual or estate own, directly or indirectly, an interest of 50% or more in the profit, loss, or capital of the partnership? For rules of constructive ownership, see instructions. If "Yes," attach Schedule B-1, Information on Partners Owning 50% or More of the Partnership		
3	At the end of the tax year, did the partnership:		
a	Own directly 20% or more, or own, directly or indirectly, 50% or more of the total voting power of all classes of stock entitled to vote of any foreign or domestic corporation? For rules of constructive ownership, see instructions. If "Yes," complete (i) through (iv) below		

(i) Name of Corporation	(ii) Employer Identification Number (if any)	(iii) Country of Incorporation	(iv) Percentage Owned in Voting Stock

		Yes	No
b	Own directly an interest of 20% or more, or own, directly or indirectly, an interest of 50% or more in the profit, loss, or capital in any foreign or domestic partnership (including an entity treated as a partnership) or in the beneficial interest of a trust? For rules of constructive ownership, see instructions. If "Yes," complete (i) through (v) below . .		

(i) Name of Entity	(ii) Employer Identification Number (if any)	(iii) Type of Entity	(iv) Country of Organization	(v) Maximum Percentage Owned in Profit, Loss, or Capital

		Yes	No
4	Does the partnership satisfy **all four** of the following conditions?		
a	The partnership's total receipts for the tax year were less than $250,000.		
b	The partnership's total assets at the end of the tax year were less than $1 million.		
c	Schedules K-1 are filed with the return and furnished to the partners on or before the due date (including extensions) for the partnership return.		
d	The partnership is not filing and is not required to file Schedule M-3		
	If "Yes," the partnership is not required to complete Schedules L, M-1, and M-2; item F on page 1 of Form 1065; or item L on Schedule K-1.		
5	Is this partnership a publicly traded partnership, as defined in section 469(k)(2)?		
6	During the tax year, did the partnership have any debt that was canceled, was forgiven, or had the terms modified so as to reduce the principal amount of the debt?		
7	Has this partnership filed, or is it required to file, Form 8918, Material Advisor Disclosure Statement, to provide information on any reportable transaction?		
8	At any time during calendar year 2019, did the partnership have an interest in or a signature or other authority over a financial account in a foreign country (such as a bank account, securities account, or other financial account)? See instructions for exceptions and filing requirements for FinCEN Form 114, Report of Foreign Bank and Financial Accounts (FBAR). If "Yes," enter the name of the foreign country ▶		
9	At any time during the tax year, did the partnership receive a distribution from, or was it the grantor of, or transferor to, a foreign trust? If "Yes," the partnership may have to file Form 3520, Annual Return To Report Transactions With Foreign Trusts and Receipt of Certain Foreign Gifts. See instructions		
10a	Is the partnership making, or had it previously made (and not revoked), a section 754 election?		
	See instructions for details regarding a section 754 election.		
b	Did the partnership make for this tax year an optional basis adjustment under section 743(b) or 734(b)? If "Yes," attach a statement showing the computation and allocation of the basis adjustment. See instructions		

Form **1065** (2019)

Form 1065 (2019)   Page **3**

Schedule B	**Other Information** (continued)	Yes	No
c	Is the partnership required to adjust the basis of partnership assets under section 743(b) or 734(b) because of a substantial built-in loss (as defined under section 743(d)) or substantial basis reduction (as defined under section 734(d))? If "Yes," attach a statement showing the computation and allocation of the basis adjustment. See instructions		
11	Check this box if, during the current or prior tax year, the partnership distributed any property received in a like-kind exchange or contributed such property to another entity (other than disregarded entities wholly owned by the partnership throughout the tax year) . . . . ▶ ☐		
12	At any time during the tax year, did the partnership distribute to any partner a tenancy-in-common or other undivided interest in partnership property?		
13	If the partnership is required to file Form 8858, Information Return of U.S. Persons With Respect To Foreign Disregarded Entities (FDEs) and Foreign Branches (FBs), enter the number of Forms 8858 attached. See instructions . . . . ▶		
14	Does the partnership have any foreign partners? If "Yes," enter the number of Forms 8805, Foreign Partner's Information Statement of Section 1446 Withholding Tax, filed for this partnership . . . ▶		
15	Enter the number of Forms 8865, Return of U.S. Persons With Respect to Certain Foreign Partnerships, attached to this return . . . . ▶		
16a	Did you make any payments in 2019 that would require you to file Form(s) 1099? See instructions		
b	If "Yes," did you or will you file required Form(s) 1099?		
17	Enter the number of Forms 5471, Information Return of U.S. Persons With Respect To Certain Foreign Corporations, attached to this return . . . . ▶		
18	Enter the number of partners that are foreign governments under section 892 . . . . ▶		
19	During the partnership's tax year, did the partnership make any payments that would require it to file Form 1042 and 1042-S under chapter 3 (sections 1441 through 1464) or chapter 4 (sections 1471 through 1474)?		
20	Was the partnership a specified domestic entity required to file Form 8938 for the tax year? See the Instructions for Form 8938		
21	Is the partnership a section 721(c) partnership, as defined in Regulations section 1.721(c)-1T(b)(14)?		
22	During the tax year, did the partnership pay or accrue any interest or royalty for which the deduction is not allowed under section 267A? See instructions		
	If "Yes," enter the total amount of the disallowed deductions . . . . ▶ $		
23	Did the partnership have an election under section 163(j) for any real property trade or business or any farming business in effect during the tax year? See instructions		
24	Does the partnership satisfy one or more of the following? See instructions		
a	The partnership owns a pass-through entity with current, or prior year carryover, excess business interest expense.		
b	The partnership's aggregate average annual gross receipts (determined under section 448(c)) for the 3 tax years preceding the current tax year are more than $26 million and the partnership has business interest.		
c	The partnership is a tax shelter (see instructions) and the partnership has business interest expense.		
	If "Yes" to any, complete and attach Form 8990.		
25	Is the partnership electing out of the centralized partnership audit regime under section 6221(b)? See instructions. If "Yes," the partnership must complete Schedule B-2 (Form 1065). Enter the total from Schedule B-2, Part III, line 3 . . . . ▶ _____		
	If "No," complete Designation of Partnership Representative below.		

Designation of Partnership Representative (see instructions)

Enter below the information for the partnership representative (PR) for the tax year covered by this return.

Name of PR ▶

U.S. address of PR ▶	U.S. phone number of ▶ PR

If the PR is an entity, name of the designated individual for the PR ▶

U.S. address of designated individual ▶	U.S. phone number of ▶ designated individual

26	Is the partnership attaching Form 8996 to certify as a Qualified Opportunity Fund?		
	If "Yes," enter the amount from Form 8996, line 14 . . . . ▶ $		
27	Enter the number of foreign partners subject to section 864(c)(8) as a result of transferring all or a portion of an interest in the partnership or of receiving a distribution from the partnership . . . . . ▶		
28	At any time during the tax year, were there any transfers between the partnership and its partners subject to the disclosure requirements of Regulations section 1.707-8?		

Form **1065** (2019)

Form 1065 (2019)   Page **4**

Schedule K		Partners' Distributive Share Items	Total amount

Income (Loss)

1	Ordinary business income (loss) (page 1, line 22)	**1**	
2	Net rental real estate income (loss) (attach Form 8825)	**2**	
3a	Other gross rental income (loss) **3a**		
b	Expenses from other rental activities (attach statement) **3b**		
c	Other net rental income (loss). Subtract line 3b from line 3a	**3c**	
4	Guaranteed payments: **a** Services **4a** **b** Capital **4b**		
	c Total. Add lines 4a and 4b	**4c**	
5	Interest income	**5**	
6	Dividends and dividend equivalents: **a** Ordinary dividends	**6a**	
	b Qualified dividends **6b** **c** Dividend equivalents **6c**		
7	Royalties	**7**	
8	Net short-term capital gain (loss) (attach Schedule D (Form 1065))	**8**	
9a	Net long-term capital gain (loss) (attach Schedule D (Form 1065))	**9a**	
b	Collectibles (28%) gain (loss) **9b**		
c	Unrecaptured section 1250 gain (attach statement) **9c**		
10	Net section 1231 gain (loss) (attach Form 4797)	**10**	
11	Other income (loss) (see instructions) Type ▶	**11**	

Deductions

12	Section 179 deduction (attach Form 4562)	**12**	
13a	Contributions	**13a**	
b	Investment interest expense	**13b**	
c	Section 59(e)(2) expenditures: **(1)** Type ▶ _____ **(2)** Amount ▶	**13c(2)**	
d	Other deductions (see instructions) Type ▶	**13d**	

Self-Employment

14a	Net earnings (loss) from self-employment	**14a**	
b	Gross farming or fishing income	**14b**	
c	Gross nonfarm income	**14c**	

Credits

15a	Low-income housing credit (section 42(j)(5))	**15a**	
b	Low-income housing credit (other)	**15b**	
c	Qualified rehabilitation expenditures (rental real estate) (attach Form 3468, if applicable) . .	**15c**	
d	Other rental real estate credits (see instructions) Type ▶	**15d**	
e	Other rental credits (see instructions) Type ▶	**15e**	
f	Other credits (see instructions) Type ▶	**15f**	

Foreign Transactions

16a	Name of country or U.S. possession ▶		
b	Gross income from all sources	**16b**	
c	Gross income sourced at partner level	**16c**	
	Foreign gross income sourced at partnership level		
d	Reserved for future use ▶ **e** Foreign branch category . . . . . ▶	**16e**	
f	Passive category ▶ _____ **g** General category ▶ _____ **h** Other (attach statement) ▶	**16h**	
	Deductions allocated and apportioned at partner level		
i	Interest expense ▶ _____ **j** Other . . . . ▶	**16j**	
	Deductions allocated and apportioned at partnership level to foreign source income		
k	Reserved for future use ▶ **l** Foreign branch category . . . . . ▶	**16l**	
m	Passive category ▶ _____ **n** General category ▶ _____ **o** Other (attach statement) ▶	**16o**	
p	Total foreign taxes (check one): ▶ Paid ☐ Accrued ☐	**16p**	
q	Reduction in taxes available for credit (attach statement)	**16q**	
r	Other foreign tax information (attach statement)		

Alternative Minimum Tax (AMT) Items

17a	Post-1986 depreciation adjustment	**17a**	
b	Adjusted gain or loss	**17b**	
c	Depletion (other than oil and gas)	**17c**	
d	Oil, gas, and geothermal properties—gross income	**17d**	
e	Oil, gas, and geothermal properties—deductions	**17e**	
f	Other AMT items (attach statement)	**17f**	

Other Information

18a	Tax-exempt interest income	**18a**	
b	Other tax-exempt income	**18b**	
c	Nondeductible expenses	**18c**	
19a	Distributions of cash and marketable securities	**19a**	
b	Distributions of other property	**19b**	
20a	Investment income	**20a**	
b	Investment expenses	**20b**	
c	Other items and amounts (attach statement)		

Form **1065** (2019)

Form 1065 (2019)   Page **5**

Analysis of Net Income (Loss)

1	Net income (loss). Combine Schedule K, lines 1 through 11. From the result, subtract the sum of Schedule K, lines 12 through 13d, and 16p **1**						

2	Analysis by partner type:	**(i)** Corporate	**(ii)** Individual (active)	**(iii)** Individual (passive)	**(iv)** Partnership	**(v)** Exempt Organization	**(vi)** Nominee/Other
a	General partners						
b	Limited partners						

Schedule L   Balance Sheets per Books

		Beginning of tax year		End of tax year	
	Assets	**(a)**	**(b)**	**(c)**	**(d)**
1	Cash				
2a	Trade notes and accounts receivable				
b	Less allowance for bad debts				
3	Inventories				
4	U.S. government obligations				
5	Tax-exempt securities				
6	Other current assets (attach statement)				
7a	Loans to partners (or persons related to partners) .				
b	Mortgage and real estate loans				
8	Other investments (attach statement)				
9a	Buildings and other depreciable assets				
b	Less accumulated depreciation				
10a	Depletable assets				
b	Less accumulated depletion				
11	Land (net of any amortization)				
12a	Intangible assets (amortizable only)				
b	Less accumulated amortization				
13	Other assets (attach statement)				
14	Total assets				
	Liabilities and Capital				
15	Accounts payable				
16	Mortgages, notes, bonds payable in less than 1 year				
17	Other current liabilities (attach statement)				
18	All nonrecourse loans				
19a	Loans from partners (or persons related to partners) .				
b	Mortgages, notes, bonds payable in 1 year or more .				
20	Other liabilities (attach statement)				
21	Partners' capital accounts				
22	Total liabilities and capital				

Schedule M-1   Reconciliation of Income (Loss) per Books With Income (Loss) per Return

Note: The partnership may be required to file Schedule M-3. See instructions.

1	Net income (loss) per books		**6**	Income recorded on books this year not included on Schedule K, lines 1 through 11 (itemize):	
2	Income included on Schedule K, lines 1, 2, 3c, 5, 6a, 7, 8, 9a, 10, and 11, not recorded on books this year (itemize): _____		**a**	Tax-exempt interest $_____	
3	Guaranteed payments (other than health insurance)		**7**	Deductions included on Schedule K, lines 1 through 13d, and 16p, not charged against book income this year (itemize):	
4	Expenses recorded on books this year not included on Schedule K, lines 1 through 13d, and 16p (itemize):		**a**	Depreciation $_____	
a	Depreciation $_____		**8**	Add lines 6 and 7	
b	Travel and entertainment $_____		**9**	Income (loss) (Analysis of Net Income (Loss), line 1). Subtract line 8 from line 5	
5	Add lines 1 through 4				

Schedule M-2   Analysis of Partners' Capital Accounts

1	Balance at beginning of year . . .		**6**	Distributions: **a** Cash	
2	Capital contributed: **a** Cash . . .			**b** Property	
	b Property . .		**7**	Other decreases (itemize): _____	
3	Net income (loss) per books				
4	Other increases (itemize): _____		**8**	Add lines 6 and 7	
5	Add lines 1 through 4		**9**	Balance at end of year. Subtract line 8 from line 5	

Form **1065** (2019)

651119

☐ Final K-1   ☐ Amended K-1   OMB No. 1545-0123

Schedule K-1
(Form 1065)
Department of the Treasury
Internal Revenue Service

2019

For calendar year 2019, or tax year

beginning   /   / 2019   ending   /   /

Partner's Share of Income, Deductions,
Credits, etc.   ▶ See back of form and separate instructions.

Part I	**Information About the Partnership**

A Partnership's employer identification number

B Partnership's name, address, city, state, and ZIP code

C IRS Center where partnership filed return ▶

D ☐ Check if this is a publicly traded partnership (PTP)

Part II	**Information About the Partner**

E Partner's SSN or TIN (Do not use TIN of a disregarded entity. See inst.)

F Name, address, city, state, and ZIP code for partner entered in E. See instructions.

G ☐ General partner or LLC member-manager   ☐ Limited partner or other LLC member

H1 ☐ Domestic partner   ☐ Foreign partner

H2 ☐ If the partner is a disregarded entity (DE), enter the partner's:
TIN _____ Name _____

I1 What type of entity is this partner? _____

I2 If this partner is a retirement plan (IRA/SEP/Keogh/etc.), check here ☐

J Partner's share of profit, loss, and capital (see instructions):

	Beginning	**Ending**
Profit	%	%
Loss	%	%
Capital	%	%

Check if decrease is due to sale or exchange of partnership interest . . ☐

K Partner's share of liabilities:

	Beginning	**Ending**
Nonrecourse . . .	$	$
Qualified nonrecourse financing . . .	$	$
Recourse . . .	$	$

☐ Check this box if Item K includes liability amounts from lower tier partnerships.

L   **Partner's Capital Account Analysis**

Beginning capital account . . . $ _____
Capital contributed during the year . . $ _____
Current year net income (loss) . . . $ _____
Other increase (decrease) (attach explanation) $ _____
Withdrawals & distributions . . . $ (_____)
Ending capital account . . . . $ _____

M Did the partner contribute property with a built-in gain or loss?
☐ Yes   ☐ No   If "Yes," attach statement. See instructions.

N   **Partner's Share of Net Unrecognized Section 704(c) Gain or (Loss)**
Beginning . . . . $ _____
Ending . . . . $ _____

Part III	**Partner's Share of Current Year Income, Deductions, Credits, and Other Items**

1	Ordinary business income (loss)	15	Credits
2	Net rental real estate income (loss)		
3	Other net rental income (loss)	16	Foreign transactions
4a	Guaranteed payments for services		
4b	Guaranteed payments for capital		
4c	Total guaranteed payments		
5	Interest income		
6a	Ordinary dividends		
6b	Qualified dividends		
6c	Dividend equivalents	17	Alternative minimum tax (AMT) items
7	Royalties		
8	Net short-term capital gain (loss)		
9a	Net long-term capital gain (loss)	18	Tax-exempt income and nondeductible expenses
9b	Collectibles (28%) gain (loss)		
9c	Unrecaptured section 1250 gain		
10	Net section 1231 gain (loss)		
		19	Distributions
11	Other income (loss)		
		20	Other information
12	Section 179 deduction		
13	Other deductions		
14	Self-employment earnings (loss)		

21 ☐ More than one activity for at-risk purposes*
22 ☐ More than one activity for passive activity purposes*
*See attached statement for additional information.

For IRS Use Only

For Paperwork Reduction Act Notice, see Instructions for Form 1065.   www.irs.gov/Form1065   Cat. No. 11394R   **Schedule K-1 (Form 1065) 2019**

This list identifies the codes used on Schedule K-1 for all partners and provides summarized reporting information for partners who file Form 1040 or 1040-SR. For detailed reporting and filing information, see the separate Partner's Instructions for Schedule K-1 and the instructions for your income tax return.

1. Ordinary business income (loss). Determine whether the income (loss) is passive or nonpassive and enter on your return as follows.

	Report on
Passive loss	See the Partner's Instructions
Passive income	Schedule E, line 28, column (h)
Nonpassive loss	See the Partner's Instructions
Nonpassive income	Schedule E, line 28, column (k)

2. Net rental real estate income (loss) — See the Partner's Instructions

3. Other net rental income (loss)
Net income	Schedule E, line 28, column (h)
Net loss	See the Partner's Instructions

4a. Guaranteed payment Services — See the Partner's Instructions
4b. Guaranteed payment Capital — See the Partner's Instructions
4c. Guaranteed payment Total — See the Partner's Instructions
5. Interest income — Form 1040 or 1040-SR, line 2b
6a. Ordinary dividends — Form 1040 or 1040-SR, line 3b
6b. Qualified dividends — Form 1040 or 1040-SR, line 3a
6c. Dividend equivalents — See the Partner's Instructions
7. Royalties — Schedule E, line 4
8. Net short-term capital gain (loss) — Schedule D, line 5
9a. Net long-term capital gain (loss) — Schedule D, line 12
9b. Collectibles (28%) gain (loss) — 28% Rate Gain Worksheet, line 4 (Schedule D instructions)
9c. Unrecaptured section 1250 gain — See the Partner's Instructions
10. Net section 1231 gain (loss) — See the Partner's Instructions

11. Other income (loss)
Code
A	Other portfolio income (loss)	See the Partner's Instructions
B	Involuntary conversions	See the Partner's Instructions
C	Sec. 1256 contracts & straddles	Form 6781, line 1
D	Mining exploration costs recapture	See Pub. 535
E	Cancellation of debt	
F	Section 743(b) positive adjustments	
G	Section 965(a) inclusion	
H	Income under subpart F (other than inclusions under sections 951A and 965)	See the Partner's Instructions
I	Other income (loss)	

12. Section 179 deduction — See the Partner's Instructions

13. Other deductions
A	Cash contributions (60%)	
B	Cash contributions (30%)	
C	Noncash contributions (50%)	
D	Noncash contributions (30%)	See the Partner's Instructions
E	Capital gain property to a 50% organization (30%)	
F	Capital gain property (20%)	
G	Contributions (100%)	
H	Investment interest expense	Form 4952, line 1
I	Deductions—royalty income	Schedule E, line 19
J	Section 59(e)(2) expenditures	See the Partner's Instructions
K	Excess business interest expense	See the Partner's Instructions
L	Deductions—portfolio (other)	Schedule A, line 16
M	Amounts paid for medical insurance	Schedule A, line 1, or Schedule 1 (Form 1040 or 1040-SR), line 16
N	Educational assistance benefits	See the Partner's Instructions
O	Dependent care benefits	Form 2441, line 12
P	Preproductive period expenses	See the Partner's Instructions
Q	Commercial revitalization deduction from rental real estate activities	See Form 8582 instructions
R	Pensions and IRAs	See the Partner's Instructions
S	Reforestation expense deduction	See the Partner's Instructions
T	through **U**	Reserved for future use
V	Section 743(b) negative adjustments	
W	Other deductions	See the Partner's Instructions
X	Section 965(c) deduction	

14. Self-employment earnings (loss)
Note: If you have a section 179 deduction or any partner-level deductions, see the Partner's Instructions before completing Schedule SE.
A	Net earnings (loss) from self-employment	Schedule SE, Section A or B
B	Gross farming or fishing income	See the Partner's Instructions
C	Gross non-farm income	See the Partner's Instructions

15. Credits
A	Low-income housing credit (section 42(j)(5)) from pre-2008 buildings	
B	Low-income housing credit (other) from pre-2008 buildings	
C	Low-income housing credit (section 42(j)(5)) from post-2007 buildings	See the Partner's Instructions
D	Low-income housing credit (other) from post-2007 buildings	
E	Qualified rehabilitation expenditures (rental real estate)	
F	Other rental real estate credits	
G	Other rental credits	

Code		*Report on*
H	Undistributed capital gains credit	Schedule 3 (Form 1040 or 1040-SR), line 13, box a
I	Biofuel producer credit	See the Partner's Instructions
J	Work opportunity credit	
K	Disabled access credit	
L	Empowerment zone employment credit	
M	Credit for increasing research activities	See the Partner's Instructions
N	Credit for employer social security and Medicare taxes	
O	Backup withholding	
P	Other credits	

16. Foreign transactions
A	Name of country or U.S. possession	
B	Gross income from all sources	Form 1116, Part I
C	Gross income sourced at partner level	

Foreign gross income sourced at partnership level
D	Reserved for future use	
E	Foreign branch category	
F	Passive category	Form 1116, Part I
G	General category	
H	Other	

Deductions allocated and apportioned at partner level
I	Interest expense	Form 1116, Part I
J	Other	Form 1116, Part I

Deductions allocated and apportioned at partnership level to foreign source income
K	Reserved for future use	
L	Foreign branch category	
M	Passive category	Form 1116, Part I
N	General category	
O	Other	

Other information
P	Total foreign taxes paid	Form 1116, Part II
Q	Total foreign taxes accrued	Form 1116, Part II
R	Reduction in taxes available for credit	Form 1116, line 12
S	Foreign trading gross receipts	Form 8873
T	Extraterritorial income exclusion	Form 8873
U	through **V**	Reserved for future use
W	Section 965 information	See the Partner's Instructions
X	Other foreign transactions	

17. Alternative minimum tax (AMT) items
A	Post-1986 depreciation adjustment	
B	Adjusted gain or loss	See the Partner's Instructions and the Instructions for Form 6251
C	Depletion (other than oil & gas)	
D	Oil, gas, & geothermal—gross income	
E	Oil, gas, & geothermal—deductions	
F	Other AMT items	

18. Tax-exempt income and nondeductible expenses
A	Tax-exempt interest income	Form 1040 or 1040-SR, line 2a
B	Other tax-exempt income	See the Partner's Instructions
C	Nondeductible expenses	See the Partner's Instructions

19. Distributions
A	Cash and marketable securities	
B	Distribution subject to section 737	See the Partner's Instructions
C	Other property	

20. Other information
A	Investment income	Form 4952, line 4a
B	Investment expenses	Form 4952, line 5
C	Fuel tax credit information	Form 4136
D	Qualified rehabilitation expenditures (other than rental real estate)	
E	Basis of energy property	See the Partner's Instructions
F	through **G**	
H	Recapture of investment credit	See Form 4255
I	Recapture of other credits	See the Partner's Instructions
J	Look-back interest—completed long-term contracts	See Form 8697
K	Look-back interest—income forecast method	See Form 8866
L	Dispositions of property with section 179 deductions	
M	Recapture of section 179 deduction	
N	Interest expense for corporate partners	
O	through **Y**	
Z	Section 199A information	
AA	Section 704(c) information	
AB	Section 751 gain (loss)	See the Partner's Instructions
AC	Section 1(h)(5) gain (loss)	
AD	Deemed section 1250 unrecaptured gain	
AE	Excess taxable income	
AF	Excess business interest income	
AG	Gross receipts for section 59A(e)	
AH	Other information	

Form **1120**
Department of the Treasury
Internal Revenue Service

U.S. Corporation Income Tax Return

For calendar year 2019 or tax year beginning _____, 2019, ending _____, 20 _____

▶ Go to *www.irs.gov/Form1120* for instructions and the latest information.

OMB No. 1545-0123

2019

A Check if:

1a Consolidated return (attach Form 851) ☐
b Life/nonlife consolidated return . . ☐
2 Personal holding co. (attach Sch. PH) . . ☐
3 Personal service corp. (see instructions) . ☐
4 Schedule M-3 attached ☐

TYPE OR PRINT

Name

Number, street, and room or suite no. If a P.O. box, see instructions.

City or town, state or province, country, and ZIP or foreign postal code

B Employer identification number

C Date incorporated

D Total assets (see instructions)
$

E Check if: **(1)** ☐ Initial return   **(2)** ☐ Final return   **(3)** ☐ Name change   **(4)** ☐ Address change

Income

1a	Gross receipts or sales	**1a**
b	Returns and allowances	**1b**
c	Balance. Subtract line 1b from line 1a	**1c**
2	Cost of goods sold (attach Form 1125-A)	**2**
3	Gross profit. Subtract line 2 from line 1c	**3**
4	Dividends and inclusions (Schedule C, line 23)	**4**
5	Interest	**5**
6	Gross rents	**6**
7	Gross royalties	**7**
8	Capital gain net income (attach Schedule D (Form 1120))	**8**
9	Net gain or (loss) from Form 4797, Part II, line 17 (attach Form 4797)	**9**
10	Other income (see instructions—attach statement)	**10**
11	**Total income.** Add lines 3 through 10 . . . . ▶	**11**

Deductions (See instructions for limitations on deductions.)

12	Compensation of officers (see instructions—attach Form 1125-E) . . . . ▶	**12**
13	Salaries and wages (less employment credits)	**13**
14	Repairs and maintenance	**14**
15	Bad debts	**15**
16	Rents	**16**
17	Taxes and licenses	**17**
18	Interest (see instructions)	**18**
19	Charitable contributions	**19**
20	Depreciation from Form 4562 not claimed on Form 1125-A or elsewhere on return (attach Form 4562) . . .	**20**
21	Depletion	**21**
22	Advertising	**22**
23	Pension, profit-sharing, etc., plans	**23**
24	Employee benefit programs	**24**
25	Reserved for future use	**25**
26	Other deductions (attach statement)	**26**
27	**Total deductions.** Add lines 12 through 26 . . . . ▶	**27**
28	Taxable income before net operating loss deduction and special deductions. Subtract line 27 from line 11. .	**28**
29a	Net operating loss deduction (see instructions) **29a**	
b	Special deductions (Schedule C, line 24) **29b**	
c	Add lines 29a and 29b	**29c**

Tax, Refundable Credits, and Payments

30	**Taxable income.** Subtract line 29c from line 28. See instructions	**30**
31	Total tax (Schedule J, Part I, line 11)	**31**
32	2019 net 965 tax liability paid (Schedule J, Part II, line 12)	**32**
33	Total payments, credits, and section 965 net tax liability (Schedule J, Part III, line 23)	**33**
34	Estimated tax penalty. See instructions. Check if Form 2220 is attached . . . . . ▶ ☐	**34**
35	**Amount owed.** If line 33 is smaller than the total of lines 31, 32, and 34, enter amount owed	**35**
36	**Overpayment.** If line 33 is larger than the total of lines 31, 32, and 34, enter amount overpaid	**36**
37	Enter amount from line 36 you want: **Credited to 2020 estimated tax** ▶ **Refunded** ▶	**37**

Sign Here

Under penalties of perjury, I declare that I have examined this return, including accompanying schedules and statements, and to the best of my knowledge and belief, it is true, correct, and complete. Declaration of preparer (other than taxpayer) is based on all information of which preparer has any knowledge.

▶ _____   _____   ▶ _____
Signature of officer   Date   Title

May the IRS discuss this return with the preparer shown below? See instructions. ☐ **Yes** ☐ **No**

Paid Preparer Use Only

Print/Type preparer's name	Preparer's signature	Date	Check ☐ if self-employed	PTIN

Firm's name ▶   Firm's EIN ▶

Firm's address ▶   Phone no.

For Paperwork Reduction Act Notice, see separate instructions.   Cat. No. 11450Q   Form **1120** (2019)

Form 1120 (2019)   Page **2**

Schedule C	**Dividends, Inclusions, and Special Deductions** (see instructions)	(a) Dividends and inclusions	(b) %	(c) Special deductions (a) × (b)
1	Dividends from less-than-20%-owned domestic corporations (other than debt-financed stock)		50	
2	Dividends from 20%-or-more-owned domestic corporations (other than debt-financed stock)		65	
3	Dividends on certain debt-financed stock of domestic and foreign corporations . .		see instructions	
4	Dividends on certain preferred stock of less-than-20%-owned public utilities . . .		23.3	
5	Dividends on certain preferred stock of 20%-or-more-owned public utilities		26.7	
6	Dividends from less-than-20%-owned foreign corporations and certain FSCs . . .		50	
7	Dividends from 20%-or-more-owned foreign corporations and certain FSCs . . .		65	
8	Dividends from wholly owned foreign subsidiaries		100	
9	**Subtotal.** Add lines 1 through 8. See instructions for limitations		see instructions	
10	Dividends from domestic corporations received by a small business investment company operating under the Small Business Investment Act of 1958		100	
11	Dividends from affiliated group members		100	
12	Dividends from certain FSCs		100	
13	Foreign-source portion of dividends received from a specified 10%-owned foreign corporation (excluding hybrid dividends) (see instructions)		100	
14	Dividends from foreign corporations not included on line 3, 6, 7, 8, 11, 12, or 13 (including any hybrid dividends)			
15	Section 965(a) inclusion		see instructions	
16a	Subpart F inclusions derived from the sale by a controlled foreign corporation (CFC) of the stock of a lower-tier foreign corporation treated as a dividend (attach Form(s) 5471) (see instructions)		100	
b	Subpart F inclusions derived from hybrid dividends of tiered corporations (attach Form(s) 5471) (see instructions)			
c	Other inclusions from CFCs under subpart F not included on line 15, 16a, 16b, or 17 (attach Form(s) 5471) (see instructions).			
17	Global Intangible Low-Taxed Income (GILTI) (attach Form(s) 5471 and Form 8992) . .			
18	Gross-up for foreign taxes deemed paid			
19	IC-DISC and former DISC dividends not included on line 1, 2, or 3			
20	Other dividends			
21	Deduction for dividends paid on certain preferred stock of public utilities			
22	Section 250 deduction (attach Form 8993)			
23	**Total dividends and inclusions.** Add column (a), lines 9 through 20. Enter here and on page 1, line 4			
24	**Total special deductions.** Add column (c), lines 9 through 22. Enter here and on page 1, line 29b			

Form **1120** (2019)

	Schedule J	Tax Computation and Payment (see instructions)		

Part I–Tax Computation

1	Check if the corporation is a member of a controlled group (attach Schedule O (Form 1120)). See instructions ▶ ☐		
2	Income tax. See instructions	2	
3	Base erosion minimum tax amount (attach Form 8991)	3	
4	Add lines 2 and 3	4	
5a	Foreign tax credit (attach Form 1118)	5a	
b	Credit from Form 8834 (see instructions)	5b	
c	General business credit (attach Form 3800)	5c	
d	Credit for prior year minimum tax (attach Form 8827)	5d	
e	Bond credits from Form 8912	5e	
6	**Total credits.** Add lines 5a through 5e	6	
7	Subtract line 6 from line 4	7	
8	Personal holding company tax (attach Schedule PH (Form 1120))	8	
9a	Recapture of investment credit (attach Form 4255)	9a	
b	Recapture of low-income housing credit (attach Form 8611)	9b	
c	Interest due under the look-back method—completed long-term contracts (attach Form 8697)	9c	
d	Interest due under the look-back method—income forecast method (attach Form 8866)	9d	
e	Alternative tax on qualifying shipping activities (attach Form 8902)	9e	
f	Other (see instructions—attach statement)	9f	
10	**Total.** Add lines 9a through 9f	10	
11	**Total tax.** Add lines 7, 8, and 10. Enter here and on page 1, line 31	11	

Part II–Section 965 Payments (see instructions)

12	2019 net 965 tax liability paid from Form 965-B, Part II, column (k), line 3. Enter here and on page 1, line 32 . .	12	

Part III–Payments, Refundable Credits, and Section 965 Net Tax Liability

13	2018 overpayment credited to 2019	13	
14	2019 estimated tax payments	14	
15	2019 refund applied for on Form 4466	15	( )
16	Combine lines 13, 14, and 15	16	
17	Tax deposited with Form 7004	17	
18	Withholding (see instructions)	18	
19	**Total payments.** Add lines 16, 17, and 18	19	
20	Refundable credits from:		
a	Form 2439	20a	
b	Form 4136	20b	
c	Form 8827, line 5c	20c	
d	Other (attach statement—see instructions)	20d	
21	**Total credits.** Add lines 20a through 20d	21	
22	2019 net 965 tax liability from Form 965-B, Part I, column (d), line 3. See instructions	22	
23	**Total payments, credits, and section 965 net tax liability.** Add lines 19, 21, and 22. Enter here and on page 1, line 33	23	

Form **1120** (2019)

Form 1120 (2019)   Page **4**

Schedule K	**Other Information** (see instructions)	Yes	No

1 Check accounting method: **a** ☐ Cash **b** ☐ Accrual **c** ☐ Other (specify) ▶ _____

2 See the instructions and enter the:

a Business activity code no. ▶ _____

b Business activity ▶ _____

c Product or service ▶ _____

3 Is the corporation a subsidiary in an affiliated group or a parent–subsidiary controlled group? . . . .

If "Yes," enter name and EIN of the parent corporation ▶ _____

4 At the end of the tax year:

a Did any foreign or domestic corporation, partnership (including any entity treated as a partnership), trust, or tax-exempt organization own directly 20% or more, or own, directly or indirectly, 50% or more of the total voting power of all classes of the corporation's stock entitled to vote? If "Yes," complete Part I of Schedule G (Form 1120) (attach Schedule G) . . . . . .

b Did any individual or estate own directly 20% or more, or own, directly or indirectly, 50% or more of the total voting power of all classes of the corporation's stock entitled to vote? If "Yes," complete Part II of Schedule G (Form 1120) (attach Schedule G) .

5 At the end of the tax year, did the corporation:

a Own directly 20% or more, or own, directly or indirectly, 50% or more of the total voting power of all classes of stock entitled to vote of any foreign or domestic corporation not included on **Form 851**, Affiliations Schedule? For rules of constructive ownership, see instructions. If "Yes," complete (i) through (iv) below.

(i) Name of Corporation	**(ii)** Employer Identification Number (if any)	**(iii)** Country of Incorporation	**(iv)** Percentage Owned in Voting Stock

b Own directly an interest of 20% or more, or own, directly or indirectly, an interest of 50% or more in any foreign or domestic partnership (including an entity treated as a partnership) or in the beneficial interest of a trust? For rules of constructive ownership, see instructions. If "Yes," complete (i) through (iv) below.

(i) Name of Entity	**(ii)** Employer Identification Number (if any)	**(iii)** Country of Organization	**(iv)** Maximum Percentage Owned in Profit, Loss, or Capital

6 During this tax year, did the corporation pay dividends (other than stock dividends and distributions in exchange for stock) in excess of the corporation's current and accumulated earnings and profits? See sections 301 and 316 . . . .

If "Yes," file **Form 5452**, Corporate Report of Nondividend Distributions. See the instructions for Form 5452.

If this is a consolidated return, answer here for the parent corporation and on Form 851 for each subsidiary.

7 At any time during the tax year, did one foreign person own, directly or indirectly, at least 25% of the total voting power of all classes of the corporation's stock entitled to vote or at least 25% of the total value of all classes of the corporation's stock? .

For rules of attribution, see section 318. If "Yes," enter:

(a) Percentage owned ▶ _____ and **(b)** Owner's country ▶ _____

(c) The corporation may have to file **Form 5472**, Information Return of a 25% Foreign-Owned U.S. Corporation or a Foreign Corporation Engaged in a U.S. Trade or Business. Enter the number of Forms 5472 attached ▶ _____

8 Check this box if the corporation issued publicly offered debt instruments with original issue discount . . . . . ▶ ☐

If checked, the corporation may have to file **Form 8281**, Information Return for Publicly Offered Original Issue Discount Instruments.

9 Enter the amount of tax-exempt interest received or accrued during the tax year ▶ $ _____

10 Enter the number of shareholders at the end of the tax year (if 100 or fewer) ▶ _____

11 If the corporation has an NOL for the tax year and is electing to forego the carryback period, check here (see instructions) ▶ ☐

If the corporation is filing a consolidated return, the statement required by Regulations section 1.1502-21(b)(3) must be attached or the election will not be valid.

12 Enter the available NOL carryover from prior tax years (do not reduce it by any deduction reported on page 1, line 29a.) . . . . ▶ $ _____

Form **1120** (2019)

Schedule K	Other Information *(continued from page 4)*		

		Yes	No
13	Are the corporation's total receipts (page 1, line 1a, plus lines 4 through 10) for the tax year **and** its total assets at the end of the tax year less than $250,000?		
	If "Yes," the corporation is not required to complete Schedules L, M-1, and M-2. Instead, enter the total amount of cash distributions and the book value of property distributions (other than cash) made during the tax year ▶ $_____		
14	Is the corporation required to file Schedule UTP (Form 1120), Uncertain Tax Position Statement? See instructions		
	If "Yes," complete and attach Schedule UTP.		
15a	Did the corporation make any payments in 2019 that would require it to file Form(s) 1099?		
b	If "Yes," did or will the corporation file required Form(s) 1099?		
16	During this tax year, did the corporation have an 80%-or-more change in ownership, including a change due to redemption of its own stock?		
17	During or subsequent to this tax year, but before the filing of this return, did the corporation dispose of more than 65% (by value) of its assets in a taxable, non-taxable, or tax deferred transaction?		
18	Did the corporation receive assets in a section 351 transfer in which any of the transferred assets had a fair market basis or fair market value of more than $1 million?		
19	During the corporation's tax year, did the corporation make any payments that would require it to file Forms 1042 and 1042-S under chapter 3 (sections 1441 through 1464) or chapter 4 (sections 1471 through 1474) of the Code?		
20	Is the corporation operating on a cooperative basis?		
21	During the tax year, did the corporation pay or accrue any interest or royalty for which the deduction is not allowed under section 267A? See instructions		
	If "Yes," enter the total amount of the disallowed deductions ▶ $_____		
22	Does the corporation have gross receipts of at least $500 million in any of the 3 preceding tax years? (See sections 59A(e)(2) and (3))		
	If "Yes," complete and attach Form 8991.		
23	Did the corporation have an election under section 163(j) for any real property trade or business or any farming business in effect during the tax year? See instructions		
24	Does the corporation satisfy one or more of the following? See instructions		
a	The corporation owns a pass-through entity with current, or prior year carryover, excess business interest expense.		
b	The corporation's aggregate average annual gross receipts (determined under section 448(c)) for the 3 tax years preceding the current tax year are more than $26 million and the corporation has business interest expense.		
c	The corporation is a tax shelter and the corporation has business interest expense.		
	If "Yes," to any, complete and attach Form 8990.		
25	Is the corporation attaching Form 8996 to certify as a Qualified Opportunity Fund?		
	If "Yes," enter amount from Form 8996, line 14 . . . . . ▶ $		

Form **1120** (2019)

Form 1120 (2019) Page **6**

Schedule L — Balance Sheets per Books

	Assets	Beginning of tax year (a)	(b)	End of tax year (c)	(d)
1	Cash				
2a	Trade notes and accounts receivable				
b	Less allowance for bad debts	( )		( )	
3	Inventories				
4	U.S. government obligations				
5	Tax-exempt securities (see instructions)				
6	Other current assets (attach statement)				
7	Loans to shareholders				
8	Mortgage and real estate loans				
9	Other investments (attach statement)				
10a	Buildings and other depreciable assets				
b	Less accumulated depreciation	( )		( )	
11a	Depletable assets				
b	Less accumulated depletion	( )		( )	
12	Land (net of any amortization)				
13a	Intangible assets (amortizable only)				
b	Less accumulated amortization	( )		( )	
14	Other assets (attach statement)				
15	Total assets				
	Liabilities and Shareholders' Equity				
16	Accounts payable				
17	Mortgages, notes, bonds payable in less than 1 year				
18	Other current liabilities (attach statement)				
19	Loans from shareholders				
20	Mortgages, notes, bonds payable in 1 year or more				
21	Other liabilities (attach statement)				
22	Capital stock: **a** Preferred stock				
	b Common stock				
23	Additional paid-in capital				
24	Retained earnings—Appropriated (attach statement)				
25	Retained earnings—Unappropriated				
26	Adjustments to shareholders' equity (attach statement)				
27	Less cost of treasury stock		( )		( )
28	Total liabilities and shareholders' equity				

Schedule M-1 — Reconciliation of Income (Loss) per Books With Income per Return

Note: The corporation may be required to file Schedule M-3. See instructions.

1	Net income (loss) per books		7	Income recorded on books this year not included on this return (itemize):	
2	Federal income tax per books				
3	Excess of capital losses over capital gains			Tax-exempt interest $ _____	
4	Income subject to tax not recorded on books this year (itemize): _____			_____	
	_____		8	Deductions on this return not charged against book income this year (itemize):	
5	Expenses recorded on books this year not deducted on this return (itemize):		**a**	Depreciation . . $ _____	
a	Depreciation . . . . $ _____		**b**	Charitable contributions $ _____	
b	Charitable contributions . $ _____			_____	
c	Travel and entertainment . $ _____			_____	
	_____		9	Add lines 7 and 8	
6	Add lines 1 through 5		10	Income (page 1, line 28)—line 6 less line 9	

Schedule M-2 — Analysis of Unappropriated Retained Earnings per Books (Line 25, Schedule L)

1	Balance at beginning of year		5	Distributions: **a** Cash	
2	Net income (loss) per books			**b** Stock	
3	Other increases (itemize): _____			**c** Property	
	_____		6	Other decreases (itemize): _____	
	_____		7	Add lines 5 and 6	
4	Add lines 1, 2, and 3		8	Balance at end of year (line 4 less line 7)	

Form **1120** (2019)

SCHEDULE M-3 (Form 1120) (Rev. December 2019) Department of the Treasury Internal Revenue Service	**Net Income (Loss) Reconciliation for Corporations With Total Assets of $10 Million or More** ▶ Attach to Form 1120 or 1120-C. ▶ Go to *www.irs.gov/Form1120* for instructions and the latest information.	OMB No. 1545-0123

Name of corporation (common parent, if consolidated return)	Employer identification number

Check applicable box(es):   (1) ☐ Non-consolidated return   (2) ☐ Consolidated return (Form 1120 only)

(3) ☐ Mixed 1120/L/PC group   (4) ☐ Dormant subsidiaries schedule attached

Part I   **Financial Information and Net Income (Loss) Reconciliation** (see instructions)

1a Did the corporation file SEC Form 10-K for its income statement period ending with or within this tax year?
  ☐ **Yes.** Skip lines 1b and 1c and complete lines 2a through 11 with respect to that SEC Form 10-K.
  ☐ **No.** Go to line 1b. See instructions if multiple non-tax-basis income statements are prepared.
 b Did the corporation prepare a certified audited non-tax-basis income statement for that period?
  ☐ **Yes.** Skip line 1c and complete lines 2a through 11 with respect to that income statement.
  ☐ **No.** Go to line 1c.
 c Did the corporation prepare a non-tax-basis income statement for that period?
  ☐ **Yes.** Complete lines 2a through 11 with respect to that income statement.
  ☐ **No.** Skip lines 2a through 3c and enter the corporation's net income (loss) per its books and records on line 4a.
2a Enter the income statement period: Beginning   MM/DD/YYYY   Ending   MM/DD/YYYY
 b Has the corporation's income statement been restated for the income statement period on line 2a?
  ☐ **Yes.** (If "Yes," attach an explanation and the amount of each item restated.)
  ☐ **No.**
 c Has the corporation's income statement been restated for any of the five income statement periods immediately preceding the period on line 2a?
  ☐ **Yes.** (If "Yes," attach an explanation and the amount of each item restated.)
  ☐ **No.**
3a Is any of the corporation's voting common stock publicly traded?
  ☐ **Yes.**
  ☐ **No.** If "No," go to line 4a.
 b Enter the symbol of the corporation's primary U.S. publicly traded voting common stock . . . .
 c Enter the nine-digit CUSIP number of the corporation's primary publicly traded voting common stock . . . .

4a	Worldwide consolidated net income (loss) from income statement source identified in Part I, line 1 .	**4a**	
b	Indicate accounting standard used for line 4a (see instructions):		
	(1) ☐ GAAP (2) ☐ IFRS (3) ☐ Statutory (4) ☐ Tax-basis (5) ☐ Other (specify) _____		
5a	Net income from nonincludible foreign entities (attach statement)	**5a**	( )
b	Net loss from nonincludible foreign entities (attach statement and enter as a positive amount) . . .	**5b**	
6a	Net income from nonincludible U.S. entities (attach statement)	**6a**	( )
b	Net loss from nonincludible U.S. entities (attach statement and enter as a positive amount)	**6b**	
7a	Net income (loss) of other includible foreign disregarded entities (attach statement)	**7a**	
b	Net income (loss) of other includible U.S. disregarded entities (attach statement)	**7b**	
c	Net income (loss) of other includible entities (attach statement)	**7c**	
8	Adjustment to eliminations of transactions between includible entities and nonincludible entities (attach statement)	**8**	
9	Adjustment to reconcile income statement period to tax year (attach statement)	**9**	
10a	Intercompany dividend adjustments to reconcile to line 11 (attach statement)	**10a**	
b	Other statutory accounting adjustments to reconcile to line 11 (attach statement)	**10b**	
c	Other adjustments to reconcile to amount on line 11 (attach statement)	**10c**	
11	**Net income (loss) per income statement of includible corporations.** Combine lines 4 through 10 .	**11**	

Note: Part I, line 11, must equal Part II, line 30, column (a), or Schedule M-1, line 1 (see instructions).

12 Enter the total amount (not just the corporation's share) of the assets and liabilities of all entities included or removed on the following lines.

		Total Assets	Total Liabilities
a	Included on Part I, line 4 . . . . ▶		
b	Removed on Part I, line 5 . . . . . . ▶		
c	Removed on Part I, line 6 . . . . . . ▶		
d	Included on Part I, line 7 . . . . . . ▶		

For Paperwork Reduction Act Notice, see the Instructions for Form 1120.   Cat. No. 37961C   Schedule M-3 (Form 1120) (Rev. 12-2019)

Schedule M-3 (Form 1120) (Rev. 12-2019)   Page **2**

Name of corporation (common parent, if consolidated return)	Employer identification number

Check applicable box(es): **(1)** ☐ Consolidated group   **(2)** ☐ Parent corp   **(3)** ☐ Consolidated eliminations   **(4)** ☐ Subsidiary corp   **(5)** ☐ Mixed 1120/L/PC group

Check if a sub-consolidated: **(6)** ☐ 1120 group   **(7)** ☐ 1120 eliminations

Name of subsidiary (if consolidated return)	Employer identification number

Part II **Reconciliation of Net Income (Loss) per Income Statement of Includible Corporations With Taxable Income per Return** (see instructions)

Income (Loss) Items (Attach statements for lines 1 through 12)	(a) Income (Loss) per Income Statement	(b) Temporary Difference	(c) Permanent Difference	(d) Income (Loss) per Tax Return
1 Income (loss) from equity method foreign corporations				
2 Gross foreign dividends not previously taxed				
3 Subpart F, QEF, and similar income inclusions				
4 Gross-up for foreign taxes deemed paid				
5 Gross foreign distributions previously taxed				
6 Income (loss) from equity method U.S. corporations				
7 U.S. dividends not eliminated in tax consolidation				
8 Minority interest for includible corporations				
9 Income (loss) from U.S. partnerships				
10 Income (loss) from foreign partnerships				
11 Income (loss) from other pass-through entities				
12 Items relating to reportable transactions				
13 Interest income (see instructions)				
14 Total accrual to cash adjustment				
15 Hedging transactions				
16 Mark-to-market income (loss)				
17 Cost of goods sold (see instructions)	( )			( )
18 Sale versus lease (for sellers and/or lessors)				
19 Section 481(a) adjustments				
20 Unearned/deferred revenue				
21 Income recognition from long-term contracts				
22 Original issue discount and other imputed interest				
23a Income statement gain/loss on sale, exchange, abandonment, worthlessness, or other disposition of assets other than inventory and pass-through entities				
b Gross capital gains from Schedule D, excluding amounts from pass-through entities				
c Gross capital losses from Schedule D, excluding amounts from pass-through entities, abandonment losses, and worthless stock losses				
d Net gain/loss reported on Form 4797, line 17, excluding amounts from pass-through entities, abandonment losses, and worthless stock losses				
e Abandonment losses				
f Worthless stock losses (attach statement)				
g Other gain/loss on disposition of assets other than inventory				
24 Capital loss limitation and carryforward used				
25 Other income (loss) items with differences (attach statement)				
26 **Total income (loss) items.** Combine lines 1 through 25				
27 **Total expense/deduction items** (from Part III, line 39)				
28 Other items with no differences				
29a Mixed groups, see instructions. All others, combine lines 26 through 28				
b PC insurance subgroup reconciliation totals				
c Life insurance subgroup reconciliation totals				
30 **Reconciliation totals.** Combine lines 29a through 29c				

Note: Line 30, column (a), must equal Part I, line 11, and column (d) must equal Form 1120, page 1, line 28.

Schedule M-3 (Form 1120) (Rev. 12-2019)

Schedule M-3 (Form 1120) (Rev. 12-2019)   Page **3**

Name of corporation (common parent, if consolidated return)	Employer identification number

Check applicable box(es): **(1)** ☐ Consolidated group   **(2)** ☐ Parent corp   **(3)** ☐ Consolidated eliminations   **(4)** ☐ Subsidiary corp   **(5)** ☐ Mixed 1120/L/PC group

Check if a sub-consolidated: **(6)** ☐ 1120 group   **(7)** ☐ 1120 eliminations

Name of subsidiary (if consolidated return)	Employer identification number

Part III **Reconciliation of Net Income (Loss) per Income Statement of Includible Corporations With Taxable Income per Return—Expense/Deduction Items** (see instructions)

Expense/Deduction Items	(a) Expense per Income Statement	(b) Temporary Difference	(c) Permanent Difference	(d) Deduction per Tax Return
1 U.S. current income tax expense				
2 U.S. deferred income tax expense				
3 State and local current income tax expense				
4 State and local deferred income tax expense				
5 Foreign current income tax expense (other than foreign withholding taxes)				
6 Foreign deferred income tax expense				
7 Foreign withholding taxes				
8 Interest expense (see instructions)				
9 Stock option expense				
10 Other equity-based compensation				
11 Meals and entertainment				
12 Fines and penalties				
13 Judgments, damages, awards, and similar costs				
14 Parachute payments				
15 Compensation with section 162(m) limitation				
16 Pension and profit-sharing				
17 Other post-retirement benefits				
18 Deferred compensation				
19 Charitable contribution of cash and tangible property				
20 Charitable contribution of intangible property				
21 Charitable contribution limitation/carryforward				
22 Domestic production activities deduction (see instructions)				
23 Current year acquisition or reorganization investment banking fees				
24 Current year acquisition or reorganization legal and accounting fees				
25 Current year acquisition/reorganization other costs				
26 Amortization/impairment of goodwill				
27 Amortization of acquisition, reorganization, and start-up costs				
28 Other amortization or impairment write-offs				
29 Reserved				
30 Depletion				
31 Depreciation				
32 Bad debt expense				
33 Corporate owned life insurance premiums				
34 Purchase versus lease (for purchasers and/or lessees)				
35 Research and development costs				
36 Section 118 exclusion (attach statement)				
37 Section 162(r)—FDIC premiums paid by certain large financial institutions (see instructions)				
38 Other expense/deduction items with differences (attach statement)				
39 **Total expense/deduction items.** Combine lines 1 through 38. Enter here and on Part II, line 27, reporting positive amounts as negative and negative amounts as positive				

Form **1120-S**

Department of the Treasury
Internal Revenue Service

U.S. Income Tax Return for an S Corporation

▶ Do not file this form unless the corporation has filed or
is attaching Form 2553 to elect to be an S corporation.
▶ Go to *www.irs.gov/Form1120S* for instructions and the latest information.

OMB No. 1545-0123

2019

For calendar year 2019 or tax year beginning _____, 2019, ending _____, 20____

A S election effective date	**D** Employer identification number
B Business activity code number (see instructions)	**E** Date incorporated
C Check if Sch. M-3 attached ☐	**F** Total assets (see instructions) $

TYPE OR PRINT

Name

Number, street, and room or suite no. If a P.O. box, see instructions.

City or town, state or province, country, and ZIP or foreign postal code

G Is the corporation electing to be an S corporation beginning with this tax year? ☐ Yes ☐ No   If "Yes," attach Form 2553 if not already filed

H Check if: **(1)** ☐ Final return **(2)** ☐ Name change **(3)** ☐ Address change **(4)** ☐ Amended return **(5)** ☐ S election termination or revocation

I Enter the number of shareholders who were shareholders during any part of the tax year . . . . ▶ _____

J Check if corporation: **(1)** ☐ Aggregated activities for section 465 at-risk purposes **(2)** ☐ Grouped activities for section 469 passive activity purposes

Caution: Include **only** trade or business income and expenses on lines 1a through 21. See the instructions for more information.

Income

1a	Gross receipts or sales	1a	
b	Returns and allowances	1b	
c	Balance. Subtract line 1b from line 1a		1c
2	Cost of goods sold (attach Form 1125-A)		2
3	Gross profit. Subtract line 2 from line 1c		3
4	Net gain (loss) from Form 4797, line 17 (attach Form 4797)		4
5	Other income (loss) (see instructions—attach statement)		5
6	**Total income (loss).** Add lines 3 through 5 ▶		6

Deductions (see instructions for limitations)

7	Compensation of officers (see instructions—attach Form 1125-E)	7
8	Salaries and wages (less employment credits)	8
9	Repairs and maintenance	9
10	Bad debts	10
11	Rents	11
12	Taxes and licenses	12
13	Interest (see instructions)	13
14	Depreciation not claimed on Form 1125-A or elsewhere on return (attach Form 4562)	14
15	Depletion **(Do not deduct oil and gas depletion.)**	15
16	Advertising	16
17	Pension, profit-sharing, etc., plans	17
18	Employee benefit programs	18
19	Other deductions (attach statement)	19
20	**Total deductions.** Add lines 7 through 19 ▶	20
21	**Ordinary business income (loss).** Subtract line 20 from line 6	21

Tax and Payments

22a	Excess net passive income or LIFO recapture tax (see instructions)	22a	
b	Tax from Schedule D (Form 1120-S)	22b	
c	Add lines 22a and 22b (see instructions for additional taxes)		22c
23a	2019 estimated tax payments and 2018 overpayment credited to 2019	23a	
b	Tax deposited with Form 7004	23b	
c	Credit for federal tax paid on fuels (attach Form 4136)	23c	
d	Reserved for future use	23d	
e	Add lines 23a through 23d		23e
24	Estimated tax penalty (see instructions). Check if Form 2220 is attached ▶ ☐		24
25	**Amount owed.** If line 23e is smaller than the total of lines 22c and 24, enter amount owed		25
26	**Overpayment.** If line 23e is larger than the total of lines 22c and 24, enter amount overpaid		26
27	Enter amount from line 26: **Credited to 2020 estimated tax** ▶ **Refunded** ▶		27

Sign Here

Under penalties of perjury, I declare that I have examined this return, including accompanying schedules and statements, and to the best of my knowledge and belief, it is true, correct, and complete. Declaration of preparer (other than taxpayer) is based on all information of which preparer has any knowledge.

▶ _____   _____ ▶ _____
Signature of officer   Date   Title

May the IRS discuss this return with the preparer shown below? See instructions. ☐ Yes ☐ No

Paid Preparer Use Only

Print/Type preparer's name	Preparer's signature	Date	Check ☐ if self-employed	PTIN
Firm's name ▶			Firm's EIN ▶	
Firm's address ▶			Phone no.	

For Paperwork Reduction Act Notice, see separate instructions.   Cat. No. 11510H   Form **1120-S** (2019)

Form 1120-S (2019)   Page **2**

Schedule B	**Other Information** (see instructions)		

		Yes	No
1	Check accounting method: **a** ☐ Cash **b** ☐ Accrual		
	c ☐ Other (specify) ▶ _____		
2	See the instructions and enter the:		
	a Business activity ▶ _____ **b** Product or service ▶ _____		
3	At any time during the tax year, was any shareholder of the corporation a disregarded entity, a trust, an estate, or a nominee or similar person? If "Yes," attach Schedule B-1, Information on Certain Shareholders of an S Corporation . .		
4	At the end of the tax year, did the corporation:		
a	Own directly 20% or more, or own, directly or indirectly, 50% or more of the total stock issued and outstanding of any foreign or domestic corporation? For rules of constructive ownership, see instructions. If "Yes," complete (i) through (v) below		

(i) Name of Corporation	**(ii)** Employer Identification Number (if any)	**(iii)** Country of Incorporation	**(iv)** Percentage of Stock Owned	**(v)** If Percentage in (iv) Is 100%, Enter the Date (if any) a Qualified Subchapter S Subsidiary Election Was Made

		Yes	No
b	Own directly an interest of 20% or more, or own, directly or indirectly, an interest of 50% or more in the profit, loss, or capital in any foreign or domestic partnership (including an entity treated as a partnership) or in the beneficial interest of a trust? For rules of constructive ownership, see instructions. If "Yes," complete (i) through (v) below		

(i) Name of Entity	**(ii)** Employer Identification Number (if any)	**(iii)** Type of Entity	**(iv)** Country of Organization	**(v)** Maximum Percentage Owned in Profit, Loss, or Capital

		Yes	No
5a	At the end of the tax year, did the corporation have any outstanding shares of restricted stock?		
	If "Yes," complete lines (i) and (ii) below.		
	(i) Total shares of restricted stock . . . . ▶ _____		
	(ii) Total shares of non-restricted stock . . . . ▶ _____		
b	At the end of the tax year, did the corporation have any outstanding stock options, warrants, or similar instruments? .		
	If "Yes," complete lines (i) and (ii) below.		
	(i) Total shares of stock outstanding at the end of the tax year . ▶ _____		
	(ii) Total shares of stock outstanding if all instruments were executed ▶ _____		
6	Has this corporation filed, or is it required to file, **Form 8918,** Material Advisor Disclosure Statement, to provide information on any reportable transaction?		
7	Check this box if the corporation issued publicly offered debt instruments with original issue discount . . . . ▶ ☐		
	If checked, the corporation may have to file **Form 8281,** Information Return for Publicly Offered Original Issue Discount Instruments.		
8	If the corporation **(a)** was a C corporation before it elected to be an S corporation **or** the corporation acquired an asset with a basis determined by reference to the basis of the asset (or the basis of any other property) in the hands of a C corporation **and (b)** has net unrealized built-in gain in excess of the net recognized built-in gain from prior years, enter the net unrealized built-in gain reduced by net recognized built-in gain from prior years. See instructions . . . . . . ▶ $ _____		
9	Did the corporation have an election under section 163(j) for any real property trade or business or any farming business in effect during the tax year? See instructions		
10	Does the corporation satisfy one or more of the following? See instructions		
a	The corporation owns a pass-through entity with current, or prior year carryover, excess business interest expense.		
b	The corporation's aggregate average annual gross receipts (determined under section 448(c)) for the 3 tax years preceding the current tax year are more than $26 million and the corporation has business interest expense.		
c	The corporation is a tax shelter and the corporation has business interest expense.		
	If "Yes," complete and attach Form 8990.		
11	Does the corporation satisfy **both** of the following conditions?		
a	The corporation's total receipts (see instructions) for the tax year were less than $250,000.		
b	The corporation's total assets at the end of the tax year were less than $250,000.		
	If "Yes," the corporation is not required to complete Schedules L and M-1.		

Form **1120-S** (2019)

Form 1120-S (2019)   Page **3**

Schedule B	**Other Information** (see instructions) *(continued)*	Yes	No

12 During the tax year, did the corporation have any non-shareholder debt that was canceled, was forgiven, or had the terms modified so as to reduce the principal amount of the debt? . . . .

    If "Yes," enter the amount of principal reduction . . . . ▶ $ _____

13 During the tax year, was a qualified subchapter S subsidiary election terminated or revoked? If "Yes," see instructions .

14a Did the corporation make any payments in 2019 that would require it to file Form(s) 1099? . . . .

  b If "Yes," did the corporation file or will it file required Form(s) 1099? . . . .

15 Is the corporation attaching Form 8996 to certify as a Qualified Opportunity Fund? . . . .

    If "Yes," enter the amount from Form 8996, line 14 . . . . ▶ $ _____

Schedule K	**Shareholders' Pro Rata Share Items**		Total amount

Income (Loss)

1	Ordinary business income (loss) (page 1, line 21)	**1**	
2	Net rental real estate income (loss) (attach Form 8825)	**2**	
3a	Other gross rental income (loss)	**3a**	
b	Expenses from other rental activities (attach statement)	**3b**	
c	Other net rental income (loss). Subtract line 3b from line 3a	**3c**	
4	Interest income	**4**	
5	Dividends: **a** Ordinary dividends	**5a**	
	b Qualified dividends	**5b**	
6	Royalties	**6**	
7	Net short-term capital gain (loss) (attach Schedule D (Form 1120-S)) . . .	**7**	
8a	Net long-term capital gain (loss) (attach Schedule D (Form 1120-S)) . . .	**8a**	
b	Collectibles (28%) gain (loss)	**8b**	
c	Unrecaptured section 1250 gain (attach statement)	**8c**	
9	Net section 1231 gain (loss) (attach Form 4797)	**9**	
10	Other income (loss) (see instructions) . . . Type ▶	**10**	

Deductions

11	Section 179 deduction (attach Form 4562)	**11**	
12a	Charitable contributions	**12a**	
b	Investment interest expense	**12b**	
c	Section 59(e)(2) expenditures **(1)** Type ▶ _____ **(2)** Amount ▶	**12c(2)**	
d	Other deductions (see instructions) . . . . Type ▶	**12d**	

Credits

13a	Low-income housing credit (section 42(j)(5))	**13a**	
b	Low-income housing credit (other)	**13b**	
c	Qualified rehabilitation expenditures (rental real estate) (attach Form 3468, if applicable) . .	**13c**	
d	Other rental real estate credits (see instructions) Type ▶ _____	**13d**	
e	Other rental credits (see instructions) . . . Type ▶ _____	**13e**	
f	Biofuel producer credit (attach Form 6478)	**13f**	
g	Other credits (see instructions) . . . . . . Type ▶	**13g**	

Foreign Transactions

14a	Name of country or U.S. possession ▶ _____		
b	Gross income from all sources	**14b**	
c	Gross income sourced at shareholder level	**14c**	
	Foreign gross income sourced at corporate level		
d	Reserved for future use	**14d**	
e	Foreign branch category	**14e**	
f	Passive category	**14f**	
g	General category	**14g**	
h	Other (attach statement)	**14h**	
	Deductions allocated and apportioned at shareholder level		
i	Interest expense	**14i**	
j	Other	**14j**	
	Deductions allocated and apportioned at corporate level to foreign source income		
k	Reserved for future use	**14k**	
l	Foreign branch category	**14l**	
m	Passive category	**14m**	
n	General category	**14n**	
o	Other (attach statement)	**14o**	
	Other information		
p	Total foreign taxes (check one): ☐ Paid ☐ Accrued . . . . ▶	**14p**	
q	Reduction in taxes available for credit (attach statement)	**14q**	
r	Other foreign tax information (attach statement)		

Form **1120-S** (2019)

Form 1120-S (2019)   Page **4**

Schedule K		Shareholders' Pro Rata Share Items *(continued)*			Total amount

	15a	Post-1986 depreciation adjustment	15a	
Alternative Minimum Tax (AMT) Items	b	Adjusted gain or loss	15b	
	c	Depletion (other than oil and gas)	15c	
	d	Oil, gas, and geothermal properties—gross income	15d	
	e	Oil, gas, and geothermal properties—deductions	15e	
	f	Other AMT items (attach statement)	15f	
Items Affecting Shareholder Basis	16a	Tax-exempt interest income	16a	
	b	Other tax-exempt income	16b	
	c	Nondeductible expenses	16c	
	d	Distributions (attach statement if required) (see instructions)	16d	
	e	Repayment of loans from shareholders	16e	
Other Information	17a	Investment income	17a	
	b	Investment expenses	17b	
	c	Dividend distributions paid from accumulated earnings and profits	17c	
	d	Other items and amounts (attach statement)		
Reconciliation	18	**Income (loss) reconciliation.** Combine the amounts on lines 1 through 10 in the far right column. From the result, subtract the sum of the amounts on lines 11 through 12d and 14p .	18	

Schedule L		Balance Sheets per Books	Beginning of tax year		End of tax year	
		Assets	(a)	(b)	(c)	(d)
1		Cash				
2a		Trade notes and accounts receivable . . .				
b		Less allowance for bad debts	( )		( )	
3		Inventories				
4		U.S. government obligations				
5		Tax-exempt securities (see instructions) . .				
6		Other current assets (attach statement) . . .				
7		Loans to shareholders				
8		Mortgage and real estate loans				
9		Other investments (attach statement) . . .				
10a		Buildings and other depreciable assets . . .				
b		Less accumulated depreciation	( )		( )	
11a		Depletable assets				
b		Less accumulated depletion	( )		( )	
12		Land (net of any amortization)				
13a		Intangible assets (amortizable only)				
b		Less accumulated amortization	( )		( )	
14		Other assets (attach statement)				
15		Total assets				
		Liabilities and Shareholders' Equity				
16		Accounts payable				
17		Mortgages, notes, bonds payable in less than 1 year				
18		Other current liabilities (attach statement) . .				
19		Loans from shareholders				
20		Mortgages, notes, bonds payable in 1 year or more				
21		Other liabilities (attach statement)				
22		Capital stock				
23		Additional paid-in capital				
24		Retained earnings				
25		Adjustments to shareholders' equity (attach statement)				
26		Less cost of treasury stock		( )		( )
27		Total liabilities and shareholders' equity . .				

Form **1120-S** (2019)

Schedule M-1 Reconciliation of Income (Loss) per Books With Income (Loss) per Return

Note: The corporation may be required to file Schedule M-3. See instructions.

1	Net income (loss) per books	
2	Income included on Schedule K, lines 1, 2, 3c, 4, 5a, 6, 7, 8a, 9, and 10, not recorded on books this year (itemize) _____	
3	Expenses recorded on books this year not included on Schedule K, lines 1 through 12 and 14p (itemize):	
a	Depreciation $ _____	
b	Travel and entertainment $ _____	
4	Add lines 1 through 3	

5	Income recorded on books this year not included on Schedule K, lines 1 through 10 (itemize):	
a	Tax-exempt interest $ _____	
6	Deductions included on Schedule K, lines 1 through 12 and 14p, not charged against book income this year (itemize):	
a	Depreciation $ _____	
7	Add lines 5 and 6	
8	Income (loss) (Schedule K, line 18). Subtract line 7 from line 4	

Schedule M-2 Analysis of Accumulated Adjustments Account, Shareholders' Undistributed Taxable Income Previously Taxed, Accumulated Earnings and Profits, and Other Adjustments Account (see instructions)

		(a) Accumulated adjustments account	(b) Shareholders' undistributed taxable income previously taxed	(c) Accumulated earnings and profits	(d) Other adjustments account
1	Balance at beginning of tax year				
2	Ordinary income from page 1, line 21 . . .				
3	Other additions				
4	Loss from page 1, line 21	( )			
5	Other reductions	( )			( )
6	Combine lines 1 through 5				
7	Distributions				
8	Balance at end of tax year. Subtract line 7 from line 6				

Form **1120-S** (2019)

671119

| | Final K-1 | | Amended K-1 | OMB No. 1545-0123 |

Schedule K-1
(Form 1120-S)
Department of the Treasury
Internal Revenue Service

2019

For calendar year 2019, or tax year

beginning / / 2019   ending / /

Shareholder's Share of Income, Deductions, Credits, etc.
▶ See back of form and separate instructions.

Part I	Information About the Corporation

A Corporation's employer identification number

B Corporation's name, address, city, state, and ZIP code

C IRS Center where corporation filed return

Part II	Information About the Shareholder

D Shareholder's identifying number

E Shareholder's name, address, city, state, and ZIP code

F Shareholder's percentage of stock
ownership for tax year . . . . _____ %

For IRS Use Only

Part III	Shareholder's Share of Current Year Income, Deductions, Credits, and Other Items

#	Item	#	Item
1	Ordinary business income (loss)	13	Credits
2	Net rental real estate income (loss)		
3	Other net rental income (loss)		
4	Interest income		
5a	Ordinary dividends		
5b	Qualified dividends	14	Foreign transactions
6	Royalties		
7	Net short-term capital gain (loss)		
8a	Net long-term capital gain (loss)		
8b	Collectibles (28%) gain (loss)		
8c	Unrecaptured section 1250 gain		
9	Net section 1231 gain (loss)		
10	Other income (loss)	15	Alternative minimum tax (AMT) items
11	Section 179 deduction	16	Items affecting shareholder basis
12	Other deductions		
		17	Other information

18		More than one activity for at-risk purposes*
19		More than one activity for passive activity purposes*

* See attached statement for additional information.

For Paperwork Reduction Act Notice, see the Instructions for Form 1120-S.   www.irs.gov/Form1120S   Cat. No. 11520D   **Schedule K-1 (Form 1120-S) 2019**

This list identifies the codes used on Schedule K-1 for all shareholders and provides summarized reporting information for shareholders who file Form 1040 or 1040-SR. For detailed reporting and filing information, see the separate Shareholder's Instructions for Schedule K-1 and the instructions for your income tax return.

1. **Ordinary business income (loss).** Determine whether the income (loss) is passive or nonpassive and enter on your return as follows:

	Report on
Passive loss	See the Shareholder's Instructions
Passive income	Schedule E, line 28, column (h)
Nonpassive loss	See the Shareholder's Instructions
Nonpassive income	Schedule E, line 28, column (k)

2. **Net rental real estate income (loss)** See the Shareholder's Instructions
3. **Other net rental income (loss)**
    - Net income Schedule E, line 28, column (h)
    - Net loss See the Shareholder's Instructions
4. **Interest income** Form 1040 or 1040-SR, line 2b
5a. **Ordinary dividends** Form 1040 or 1040-SR, line 3b
5b. **Qualified dividends** Form 1040 or 1040-SR, line 3a
6. **Royalties** Schedule E, line 4
7. **Net short-term capital gain (loss)** Schedule D, line 5
8a. **Net long-term capital gain (loss)** Schedule D, line 12
8b. **Collectibles (28%) gain (loss)** 28% Rate Gain Worksheet, line 4 (Schedule D instructions)
8c. **Unrecaptured section 1250 gain** See the Shareholder's Instructions
9. **Net section 1231 gain (loss)** See the Shareholder's Instructions
10. **Other income (loss)**
    - *Code*
    - A Other portfolio income (loss) See the Shareholder's Instructions
    - B Involuntary conversions See the Shareholder's Instructions
    - C Sec. 1256 contracts & straddles Form 6781, line 1
    - D Mining exploration costs recapture See Pub. 535
    - E Reserved for future use
    - F Section 965(a) inclusion
    - G Income under subpart F (other than inclusions under sections 951A and 965) See the Shareholder's Instructions
    - H Other income (loss)
11. **Section 179 deduction** See the Shareholder's Instructions
12. **Other deductions**
    - A Cash contributions (60%)
    - B Cash contributions (30%)
    - C Noncash contributions (50%)
    - D Noncash contributions (30%)
    - E Capital gain property to a 50% organization (30%) See the Shareholder's Instructions
    - F Capital gain property (20%)
    - G Contributions (100%)
    - H Investment interest expense Form 4952, line 1
    - I Deductions—royalty income Schedule E, line 19
    - J Section 59(e)(2) expenditures See the Shareholder's Instructions
    - K Section 965(c) deduction See the Shareholder's Instructions
    - L Deductions—portfolio (other) Schedule A, line 16
    - M Preproductive period expenses See the Shareholder's Instructions
    - N Commercial revitalization deduction from rental real estate activities See Form 8582 instructions
    - O Reforestation expense deduction See the Shareholder's Instructions
    - P through R Reserved for future use
    - S Other deductions See the Shareholder's Instructions
13. **Credits**
    - A Low-income housing credit (section 42(j)(5)) from pre-2008 buildings
    - B Low-income housing credit (other) from pre-2008 buildings
    - C Low-income housing credit (section 42(j)(5)) from post-2007 buildings
    - D Low-income housing credit (other) from post-2007 buildings See the Shareholder's Instructions
    - E Qualified rehabilitation expenditures (rental real estate)
    - F Other rental real estate credits
    - G Other rental credits
    - H Undistributed capital gains credit Schedule 3 (Form 1040 or 1040-SR), line 13, box a
    - I Biofuel producer credit
    - J Work opportunity credit
    - K Disabled access credit See the Shareholder's Instructions
    - L Empowerment zone employment credit
    - M Credit for increasing research activities

Code	Report on
N Credit for employer social security and Medicare taxes	
O Backup withholding	See the Shareholder's Instructions
P Other credits	

14. **Foreign transactions**
    - A Name of country or U.S. possession
    - B Gross income from all sources Form 1116, Part I
    - C Gross income sourced at shareholder level
    - *Foreign gross income sourced at corporate level*
    - D Reserved for future use
    - E Foreign branch category
    - F Passive category Form 1116, Part I
    - G General category
    - H Other
    - *Deductions allocated and apportioned at shareholder level*
    - I Interest expense Form 1116, Part I
    - J Other Form 1116, Part I
    - *Deductions allocated and apportioned at corporate level to foreign source income*
    - K Reserved for future use
    - L Foreign branch category
    - M Passive category Form 1116, Part I
    - N General category
    - O Other
    - *Other information*
    - P Total foreign taxes paid Form 1116, Part II
    - Q Total foreign taxes accrued Form 1116, Part II
    - R Reduction in taxes available for credit Form 1116, line 12
    - S Foreign trading gross receipts Form 8873
    - T Extraterritorial income exclusion Form 8873
    - U Section 965 information See the Shareholder's Instructions
    - V Other foreign transactions See the Shareholder's Instructions
15. **Alternative minimum tax (AMT) items**
    - A Post-1986 depreciation adjustment
    - B Adjusted gain or loss
    - C Depletion (other than oil & gas) See the Shareholder's Instructions and the Instructions for Form 6251
    - D Oil, gas, & geothermal—gross income
    - E Oil, gas, & geothermal—deductions
    - F Other AMT items
16. **Items affecting shareholder basis**
    - A Tax-exempt interest income Form 1040 or 1040-SR, line 2a
    - B Other tax-exempt income
    - C Nondeductible expenses
    - D Distributions See the Shareholder's Instructions
    - E Repayment of loans from shareholders
17. **Other information**
    - A Investment income Form 4952, line 4a
    - B Investment expenses Form 4952, line 5
    - C Qualified rehabilitation expenditures (other than rental real estate) See the Shareholder's Instructions
    - D Basis of energy property See the Shareholder's Instructions
    - E Recapture of low-income housing credit (section 42(j)(5)) Form 8611, line 8
    - F Recapture of low-income housing credit (other) Form 8611, line 8
    - G Recapture of investment credit See Form 4255
    - H Recapture of other credits See the Shareholder's Instructions
    - I Look-back interest—completed long-term contracts See Form 8697
    - J Look-back interest—income forecast method See Form 8866
    - K Dispositions of property with section 179 deductions
    - L Recapture of section 179 deduction See the Shareholder's Instructions
    - M through U
    - V Section 199A information
    - W through Z Reserved for future use
    - AA Excess taxable income
    - AB Excess business interest income See the Shareholder's Instructions
    - AC Other information

Form **4797**	**Sales of Business Property**	OMB No. 1545-0184
	(Also Involuntary Conversions and Recapture Amounts Under Sections 179 and 280F(b)(2))	**2019**
Department of the Treasury Internal Revenue Service	▶ Attach to your tax return. ▶ Go to *www.irs.gov/Form4797* for instructions and the latest information.	Attachment Sequence No. **27**

Name(s) shown on return	Identifying number

1 Enter the gross proceeds from sales or exchanges reported to you for 2019 on Form(s) 1099-B or 1099-S (or substitute statement) that you are including on line 2, 10, or 20. See instructions **1**

Part I   Sales or Exchanges of Property Used in a Trade or Business and Involuntary Conversions From Other Than Casualty or Theft—Most Property Held More Than 1 Year (see instructions)

2	(a) Description of property	(b) Date acquired (mo., day, yr.)	(c) Date sold (mo., day, yr.)	(d) Gross sales price	(e) Depreciation allowed or allowable since acquisition	(f) Cost or other basis, plus improvements and expense of sale	(g) Gain or (loss) Subtract (f) from the sum of (d) and (e)

3 Gain, if any, from Form 4684, line 39 . . . . **3**

4 Section 1231 gain from installment sales from Form 6252, line 26 or 37 . . . . **4**

5 Section 1231 gain or (loss) from like-kind exchanges from Form 8824 . . . . **5**

6 Gain, if any, from line 32, from other than casualty or theft **6**

7 Combine lines 2 through 6. Enter the gain or (loss) here and on the appropriate line as follows **7**

Partnerships and S corporations. Report the gain or (loss) following the instructions for Form 1065, Schedule K, line 10, or Form 1120-S, Schedule K, line 9. Skip lines 8, 9, 11, and 12 below.

Individuals, partners, S corporation shareholders, and all others. If line 7 is zero or a loss, enter the amount from line 7 on line 11 below and skip lines 8 and 9. If line 7 is a gain and you didn't have any prior year section 1231 losses, or they were recaptured in an earlier year, enter the gain from line 7 as a long-term capital gain on the Schedule D filed with your return and skip lines 8, 9, 11, and 12 below.

8 Nonrecaptured net section 1231 losses from prior years. See instructions **8**

9 Subtract line 8 from line 7. If zero or less, enter -0-. If line 9 is zero, enter the gain from line 7 on line 12 below. If line 9 is more than zero, enter the amount from line 8 on line 12 below and enter the gain from line 9 as a long-term capital gain on the Schedule D filed with your return. See instructions **9**

Part II   Ordinary Gains and Losses (see instructions)

10 Ordinary gains and losses not included on lines 11 through 16 (include property held 1 year or less):

11 Loss, if any, from line 7 . . . . **11** ( )

12 Gain, if any, from line 7 or amount from line 8, if applicable **12**

13 Gain, if any, from line 31 . . . . **13**

14 Net gain or (loss) from Form 4684, lines 31 and 38a **14**

15 Ordinary gain from installment sales from Form 6252, line 25 or 36 . . . . **15**

16 Ordinary gain or (loss) from like-kind exchanges from Form 8824 . . . . **16**

17 Combine lines 10 through 16 . . . . **17**

18 For all except individual returns, enter the amount from line 17 on the appropriate line of your return and skip lines a and b below. For individual returns, complete lines a and b below.

a If the loss on line 11 includes a loss from Form 4684, line 35, column (b)(ii), enter that part of the loss here. Enter the loss from income-producing property on Schedule A (Form 1040 or Form 1040-SR), line 16. (Do not include any loss on property used as an employee.) Identify as from "Form 4797, line 18a." See instructions **18a**

b Redetermine the gain or (loss) on line 17 excluding the loss, if any, on line 18a. Enter here and on Schedule 1 (Form 1040 or Form 1040-SR), Part I, line 4 . . . . **18b**

For Paperwork Reduction Act Notice, see separate instructions.   Cat. No. 13086I   Form **4797** (2019)

Form 4797 (2019) Page **2**

Part III Gain From Disposition of Property Under Sections 1245, 1250, 1252, 1254, and 1255 (see instructions)

19	(a) Description of section 1245, 1250, 1252, 1254, or 1255 property:		(b) Date acquired (mo., day, yr.)	(c) Date sold (mo., day, yr.)
A				
B				
C				
D				

	These columns relate to the properties on lines 19A through 19D. ▶		Property A	Property B	Property C	Property D
20	Gross sales price (**Note:** *See line 1 before completing.*) .	**20**				
21	Cost or other basis plus expense of sale	**21**				
22	Depreciation (or depletion) allowed or allowable. . .	**22**				
23	Adjusted basis. Subtract line 22 from line 21. . . .	**23**				
24	Total gain. Subtract line 23 from line 20	**24**				
25	**If section 1245 property:**					
a	Depreciation allowed or allowable from line 22 . . .	**25a**				
b	Enter the **smaller** of line 24 or 25a.	**25b**				
26	**If section 1250 property:** If straight line depreciation was used, enter -0- on line 26g, except for a corporation subject to section 291.					
a	Additional depreciation after 1975. See instructions .	**26a**				
b	Applicable percentage multiplied by the **smaller** of line 24 or line 26a. See instructions.	**26b**				
c	Subtract line 26a from line 24. If residential rental property **or** line 24 isn't more than line 26a, skip lines 26d and 26e	**26c**				
d	Additional depreciation after 1969 and before 1976. .	**26d**				
e	Enter the **smaller** of line 26c or 26d	**26e**				
f	Section 291 amount (corporations only)	**26f**				
g	Add lines 26b, 26e, and 26f	**26g**				
27	**If section 1252 property:** Skip this section if you didn't dispose of farmland or if this form is being completed for a partnership.					
a	Soil, water, and land clearing expenses	**27a**				
b	Line 27a multiplied by applicable percentage. See instructions	**27b**				
c	Enter the **smaller** of line 24 or 27b	**27c**				
28	**If section 1254 property:**					
a	Intangible drilling and development costs, expenditures for development of mines and other natural deposits, mining exploration costs, and depletion. See instructions	**28a**				
b	Enter the **smaller** of line 24 or 28a.	**28b**				
29	**If section 1255 property:**					
a	Applicable percentage of payments excluded from income under section 126. See instructions	**29a**				
b	Enter the **smaller** of line 24 or 29a. See instructions .	**29b**				

Summary of Part III Gains. Complete property columns A through D through line 29b before going to line 30.

30	Total gains for all properties. Add property columns A through D, line 24	**30**	
31	Add property columns A through D, lines 25b, 26g, 27c, 28b, and 29b. Enter here and on line 13	**31**	
32	Subtract line 31 from line 30. Enter the portion from casualty or theft on Form 4684, line 33. Enter the portion from other than casualty or theft on Form 4797, line 6	**32**	

Part IV Recapture Amounts Under Sections 179 and 280F(b)(2) When Business Use Drops to 50% or Less (see instructions)

			(a) Section 179	(b) Section 280F(b)(2)
33	Section 179 expense deduction or depreciation allowable in prior years.	**33**		
34	Recomputed depreciation. See instructions	**34**		
35	Recapture amount. Subtract line 34 from line 33. See the instructions for where to report . .	**35**		

Form **4797** (2019)

Form **8949**

Department of the Treasury
Internal Revenue Service

Sales and Other Dispositions of Capital Assets

▶ Go to *www.irs.gov/Form8949* for instructions and the latest information.
▶ File with your Schedule D to list your transactions for lines 1b, 2, 3, 8b, 9, and 10 of Schedule D.

OMB No. 1545-0074

2019

Attachment
Sequence No. **12A**

Name(s) shown on return	Social security number or taxpayer identification number

Before you check Box A, B, or C below, see whether you received any Form(s) 1099-B or substitute statement(s) from your broker. A substitute statement will have the same information as Form 1099-B. Either will show whether your basis (usually your cost) was reported to the IRS by your broker and may even tell you which box to check.

Part I **Short-Term.** Transactions involving capital assets you held 1 year or less are generally short-term (see instructions). For long-term transactions, see page 2.

Note: You may aggregate all short-term transactions reported on Form(s) 1099-B showing basis was reported to the IRS and for which no adjustments or codes are required. Enter the totals directly on Schedule D, line 1a; you aren't required to report these transactions on Form 8949 (see instructions).

You *must* check Box A, B, *or* C below. **Check only one box.** If more than one box applies for your short-term transactions, complete a separate Form 8949, page 1, for each applicable box. If you have more short-term transactions than will fit on this page for one or more of the boxes, complete as many forms with the same box checked as you need.

☐ **(A)** Short-term transactions reported on Form(s) 1099-B showing basis was reported to the IRS (see **Note** above)
☐ **(B)** Short-term transactions reported on Form(s) 1099-B showing basis **wasn't** reported to the IRS
☐ **(C)** Short-term transactions not reported to you on Form 1099-B

1 (a) Description of property (Example: 100 sh. XYZ Co.)	(b) Date acquired (Mo., day, yr.)	(c) Date sold or disposed of (Mo., day, yr.)	(d) Proceeds (sales price) (see instructions)	(e) Cost or other basis. See the **Note** below and see *Column (e)* in the separate instructions	Adjustment, if any, to gain or loss. If you enter an amount in column (g), enter a code in column (f). See the separate instructions.		(h) Gain or (loss). Subtract column (e) from column (d) and combine the result with column (g)
					(f) Code(s) from instructions	(g) Amount of adjustment	
2 Totals. Add the amounts in columns (d), (e), (g), and (h) (subtract negative amounts). Enter each total here and include on your Schedule D, **line 1b** (if **Box A** above is checked), **line 2** (if **Box B** above is checked), or **line 3** (if **Box C** above is checked) ▶							

Note: If you checked Box A above but the basis reported to the IRS was incorrect, enter in column (e) the basis as reported to the IRS, and enter an adjustment in column (g) to correct the basis. See *Column (g)* in the separate instructions for how to figure the amount of the adjustment.

For Paperwork Reduction Act Notice, see your tax return instructions.   Cat. No. 37768Z   Form **8949** (2019)

Form 8949 (2019)   Attachment Sequence No. **12A**   Page **2**

Name(s) shown on return. Name and SSN or taxpayer identification no. not required if shown on other side	Social security number or taxpayer identification number

Before you check Box D, E, or F below, see whether you received any Form(s) 1099-B or substitute statement(s) from your broker. A substitute statement will have the same information as Form 1099-B. Either will show whether your basis (usually your cost) was reported to the IRS by your broker and may even tell you which box to check.

Part II   **Long-Term.** Transactions involving capital assets you held more than 1 year are generally long-term (see instructions). For short-term transactions, see page 1.

Note: You may aggregate all long-term transactions reported on Form(s) 1099-B showing basis was reported to the IRS and for which no adjustments or codes are required. Enter the totals directly on Schedule D, line 8a; you aren't required to report these transactions on Form 8949 (see instructions).

You *must* check Box D, E, *or* F below. Check only one box. If more than one box applies for your long-term transactions, complete a separate Form 8949, page 2, for each applicable box. If you have more long-term transactions than will fit on this page for one or more of the boxes, complete as many forms with the same box checked as you need.

- ☐ **(D)** Long-term transactions reported on Form(s) 1099-B showing basis was reported to the IRS (see **Note** above)
- ☐ **(E)** Long-term transactions reported on Form(s) 1099-B showing basis **wasn't** reported to the IRS
- ☐ **(F)** Long-term transactions not reported to you on Form 1099-B

1 (a) Description of property (Example: 100 sh. XYZ Co.)	(b) Date acquired (Mo., day, yr.)	(c) Date sold or disposed of (Mo., day, yr.)	(d) Proceeds (sales price) (see instructions)	(e) Cost or other basis. See the **Note** below and see *Column (e)* in the separate instructions	(f) Code(s) from instructions	(g) Amount of adjustment	(h) Gain or (loss). Subtract column (e) from column (d) and combine the result with column (g)
2 Totals. Add the amounts in columns (d), (e), (g), and (h) (subtract negative amounts). Enter each total here and include on your Schedule D, **line 8b** (if **Box D** above is checked), **line 9** (if **Box E** above is checked), or **line 10** (if **Box F** above is checked) ▶							

Note: If you checked Box D above but the basis reported to the IRS was incorrect, enter in column (e) the basis as reported to the IRS, and enter an adjustment in column (g) to correct the basis. See *Column (g)* in the separate instructions for how to figure the amount of the adjustment.

Form **8949** (2019)

Form **8960**

Department of the Treasury
Internal Revenue Service (99)

Net Investment Income Tax—
Individuals, Estates, and Trusts

▶ Attach to your tax return.
▶ Go to *www.irs.gov/Form8960* for instructions and the latest information.

OMB No. 1545-2227

2019

Attachment
Sequence No. **72**

Name(s) shown on your tax return

Your social security number or EIN

Part I	Investment Income	☐ Section 6013(g) election (see instructions)
		☐ Section 6013(h) election (see instructions)
		☐ Regulations section 1.1411-10(g) election (see instructions)

1	Taxable interest (see instructions)			**1**	
2	Ordinary dividends (see instructions)			**2**	
3	Annuities (see instructions)			**3**	
4a	Rental real estate, royalties, partnerships, S corporations, trusts, etc. (see instructions)	**4a**			
b	Adjustment for net income or loss derived in the ordinary course of a non-section 1411 trade or business (see instructions)	**4b**			
c	Combine lines 4a and 4b			**4c**	
5a	Net gain or loss from disposition of property (see instructions)	**5a**			
b	Net gain or loss from disposition of property that is not subject to net investment income tax (see instructions)	**5b**			
c	Adjustment from disposition of partnership interest or S corporation stock (see instructions)	**5c**			
d	Combine lines 5a through 5c			**5d**	
6	Adjustments to investment income for certain CFCs and PFICs (see instructions)			**6**	
7	Other modifications to investment income (see instructions)			**7**	
8	Total investment income. Combine lines 1, 2, 3, 4c, 5d, 6, and 7			**8**	

Part II	Investment Expenses Allocable to Investment Income and Modifications

9a	Investment interest expenses (see instructions)	**9a**			
b	State, local, and foreign income tax (see instructions)	**9b**			
c	Miscellaneous investment expenses (see instructions)	**9c**			
d	Add lines 9a, 9b, and 9c			**9d**	
10	Additional modifications (see instructions)			**10**	
11	Total deductions and modifications. Add lines 9d and 10			**11**	

Part III	Tax Computation

12	Net investment income. Subtract Part II, line 11, from Part I, line 8. Individuals, complete lines 13–17. Estates and trusts, complete lines 18a–21. If zero or less, enter -0-			**12**	
	Individuals:				
13	Modified adjusted gross income (see instructions)	**13**			
14	Threshold based on filing status (see instructions)	**14**			
15	Subtract line 14 from line 13. If zero or less, enter -0-	**15**			
16	Enter the smaller of line 12 or line 15			**16**	
17	Net investment income tax for individuals. Multiply line 16 by 3.8% (0.038). **Enter here and include on your tax return** (see instructions)			**17**	
	Estates and Trusts:				
18a	Net investment income (line 12 above)	**18a**			
b	Deductions for distributions of net investment income and deductions under section 642(c) (see instructions)	**18b**			
c	Undistributed net investment income. Subtract line 18b from 18a (see instructions). If zero or less, enter -0-	**18c**			
19a	Adjusted gross income (see instructions)	**19a**			
b	Highest tax bracket for estates and trusts for the year (see instructions) . .	**19b**			
c	Subtract line 19b from line 19a. If zero or less, enter -0-	**19c**			
20	Enter the smaller of line 18c or line 19c			**20**	
21	Net investment income tax for estates and trusts. Multiply line 20 by 3.8% (0.038). **Enter here and include on your tax return** (see instructions)			**21**	

For Paperwork Reduction Act Notice, see your tax return instructions.   Cat. No. 59474M   Form **8960** (2019)

Form **8995**

Department of the Treasury
Internal Revenue Service

Qualified Business Income Deduction
Simplified Computation

▶ **Attach to your tax return.**

▶ **Go to** *www.irs.gov/Form8995* **for instructions and the latest information.**

OMB No. 1545-0123

2019

Attachment
Sequence No. **55**

Name(s) shown on return

Your taxpayer identification number

1	(a) Trade, business, or aggregation name	(b) Taxpayer identification number	(c) Qualified business income or (loss)
i			
ii			
iii			
iv			
v			

2	Total qualified business income or (loss). Combine lines 1i through 1v, column (c)	**2**		
3	Qualified business net (loss) carryforward from the prior year	**3**	( )	
4	Total qualified business income. Combine lines 2 and 3. If zero or less, enter -0-	**4**		
5	Qualified business income component. Multiply line 4 by 20% (0.20)			**5**	
6	Qualified REIT dividends and publicly traded partnership (PTP) income or (loss) (see instructions)	**6**		
7	Qualified REIT dividends and qualified PTP (loss) carryforward from the prior year	**7**	( )	
8	Total qualified REIT dividends and PTP income. Combine lines 6 and 7. If zero or less, enter -0-	**8**		
9	REIT and PTP component. Multiply line 8 by 20% (0.20)			**9**	
10	Qualified business income deduction before the income limitation. Add lines 5 and 9			**10**	
11	Taxable income before qualified business income deduction	**11**		
12	Net capital gain (see instructions)	**12**		
13	Subtract line 12 from line 11. If zero or less, enter -0-	**13**		
14	Income limitation. Multiply line 13 by 20% (0.20)			**14**	
15	Qualified business income deduction. Enter the lesser of line 10 or line 14. Also enter this amount on the applicable line of your return . . . . ▶			**15**	
16	Total qualified business (loss) carryforward. Combine lines 2 and 3. If greater than zero, enter -0- . .			**16**	( )
17	Total qualified REIT dividends and PTP (loss) carryforward. Combine lines 6 and 7. If greater than zero, enter -0-			**17**	( )

For Privacy Act and Paperwork Reduction Act Notice, see instructions.   Cat. No. 37806C   Form **8995** (2019)

Form **8995-A**

Department of the Treasury
Internal Revenue Service

Qualified Business Income Deduction

► **Attach to your tax return.**

► **Go to www.irs.gov/Form8995A for instructions and the latest information.**

OMB No. 1545-0123

2019

Attachment
Sequence No. **55A**

Name(s) shown on return

Your taxpayer identification number

Part I — Trade, Business, or Aggregation Information

Complete Schedules A, B, and/or C (Form 8995-A), as applicable, before starting Part I. Attach additional worksheets when needed. See instructions.

1	(a) Trade, business, or aggregation name	(b) Check if specified service	(c) Check if aggregation	(d) Taxpayer identification number	(e) Check if patron
A		☐	☐		☐
B		☐	☐		☐
C		☐	☐		☐

Part II — Determine Your Adjusted Qualified Business Income

			A	B	C
2	Qualified business income from the trade, business, or aggregation. See instructions	2			
3	Multiply line 2 by 20% (0.20). If your taxable income is $160,700 or less ($160,725 if married filing separately; $321,400 if married filing jointly), skip lines 4 through 12 and enter the amount from line 3 on line 13	3			
4	Allocable share of W-2 wages from the trade, business, or aggregation	4			
5	Multiply line 4 by 50% (0.50)	5			
6	Multiply line 4 by 25% (0.25)	6			
7	Allocable share of the unadjusted basis immediately after acquisition (UBIA) of all qualified property	7			
8	Multiply line 7 by 2.5% (0.025)	8			
9	Add lines 6 and 8	9			
10	Enter the greater of line 5 or line 9	10			
11	W-2 wage and qualified property limitation. Enter the smaller of line 3 or line 10	11			
12	Phased-in reduction. Enter the amount from line 26, if any. See instructions	12			
13	Qualified business income deduction before patron reduction. Enter the greater of line 11 or line 12	13			
14	Patron reduction. Enter the amount from Schedule D (Form 8995-A), line 6, if any. See instructions	14			
15	Qualified business income component. Subtract line 14 from line 13	15			
16	Total qualified business income component. Add all amounts reported on line 15 ▶	16			

For Privacy Act and Paperwork Reduction Act Notice, see separate instructions.   Cat. No. 71661B   Form **8995-A** (2019)

Part III Phased-in Reduction

Complete Part III only if your taxable income is more than $160,700 but not $210,700 ($160,725 and $210,725 if married filing separately; $321,400 and $421,400 if married filing jointly) and line 10 is less than line 3. Otherwise, skip Part III.

			A	B	C
17	Enter the amounts from line 3	17			
18	Enter the amounts from line 10	18			
19	Subtract line 18 from line 17	19			
20	Taxable income before qualified business income deduction	20			
21	Threshold. Enter $160,700 ($160,725 if married filing separately; $321,400 if married filing jointly)	21			
22	Subtract line 21 from line 20	22			
23	Phase-in range. Enter $50,000 ($100,000 if married filing jointly)	23			
24	Phase-in percentage. Divide line 22 by line 23	24	%		
25	Total phase-in reduction. Multiply line 19 by line 24	25			
26	Qualified business income after phase-in reduction. Subtract line 25 from line 17. Enter this amount here and on line 12, for the corresponding trade or business	26			

Part IV Determine Your Qualified Business Income Deduction

27	Total qualified business income component from all qualified trades, businesses, or aggregations. Enter the amount from line 16	27	
28	Qualified REIT dividends and publicly traded partnership (PTP) income or (loss). See instructions	28	
29	Qualified REIT dividends and PTP (loss) carryforward from prior years . . .	29	( )
30	Total qualified REIT dividends and PTP income. Combine lines 28 and 29. If less than zero, enter -0-	30	
31	REIT and PTP component. Multiply line 30 by 20% (0.20)	31	
32	Qualified business income deduction before the income limitation. Add lines 27 and 31 . . . . . ▶	32	
33	Taxable income before qualified business income deduction	33	
34	Net capital gain. See instructions	34	
35	Subtract line 34 from line 33. If zero or less, enter -0-	35	
36	Income limitation. Multiply line 35 by 20% (0.20)	36	
37	Qualified business income deduction before the domestic production activities deduction (DPAD) under section 199A(g). Enter the smaller of line 32 or line 36 . . . . ▶	37	
38	DPAD under section 199A(g) allocated from an agricultural or horticultural cooperative. Don't enter more than line 33 minus line 37	38	
39	Total qualified business income deduction. Add lines 37 and 38 . . . . ▶	39	
40	Total qualified REIT dividends and PTP (loss) carryforward. Combine lines 28 and 29. If zero or greater, enter -0-	40	( )

Appendix C

Glossary

The key terms in this glossary have been defined to reflect their conventional use in the field of taxation. The definitions may therefore be incomplete for other purposes.

A

AAA bypass election. In the context of a distribution by an S corporation, an election made by the entity to designate that the distribution is first from accumulated earnings and profits (AEP) and only then from the accumulated adjustments account (AAA).

Abandoned spouse. The abandoned spouse provision enables a married taxpayer with a dependent child whose spouse did not live in the taxpayer's home during the last six months of the tax year to file as a head of household rather than as married filing separately.

Accelerated cost recovery system (ACRS). A method in which the cost of tangible property is recovered (depreciated) over a prescribed period of time. This depreciation approach disregards salvage value, imposes a period of cost recovery that depends upon the classification of the asset into one of various recovery periods, and prescribes the applicable percentage of cost that can be deducted each year. A modified system is currently the default cost recovery method; it is referred to as MACRS. § 168.

Accelerated death benefits. The amount received from a life insurance policy by the insured who is terminally ill or chronically ill. Any realized gain may be excluded from the gross income of the insured if the policy is surrendered to the insurer or is sold to a licensed viatical settlement provider. § 101(g).

Acceleration rule. Treatment of an intercompany transaction on a consolidated return, when a sold asset leaves the group.

Accident and health benefits. Employee fringe benefits provided by employers through the payment of health and accident insurance premiums or the establishment of employer-funded medical reimbursement plans. Employers generally are entitled to a deduction for such payments, whereas employees generally exclude such fringe benefits from gross income. §§ 105 and 106.

Accident and health insurance benefits. See *accident and health benefits*.

Accountable plan. A type of expense reimbursement plan that requires an employee to render an adequate accounting to the employer and return any excess reimbursement or allowance. If the expense qualifies, it will be treated as a deduction *for* AGI.

Accounting income. The accountant's concept of income is generally based upon the realization principle. Financial accounting income may differ from taxable income (e.g., accelerated depreciation might be used for Federal income tax and straight-line depreciation for financial accounting purposes). Differences are included in a reconciliation of taxable and accounting income on Schedule M–1 or Schedule M–3 of Form 1120 for corporations.

Accounting method. The method under which income and expenses are determined for tax purposes. Important accounting methods include the cash basis and the accrual basis. Special methods are available for the reporting of gain on installment sales, recognition of income on construction projects (the completed contract and percentage of completion methods), and the valuation of inventories (last-in, first-out and first-in, first-out). §§ 446–474.

Accounting period. The period of time, usually a year, used by a taxpayer for the determination of tax liability. Unless a fiscal year is chosen, taxpayers must determine and pay their income tax liability by using the calendar year (January 1 through December 31) as the period of measurement. An example of a fiscal year is July 1 through June 30. A change in accounting period (e.g., from a calendar year to a fiscal year) generally requires the consent of the IRS. Usually, taxpayers are free to select either an initial calendar or a fiscal year without the consent of the IRS. §§ 441–444.

Accrual method. A method of accounting that recognizes expenses as incurred and income as earned. In contrast to the cash basis of accounting, expenses need not be paid to be deductible, nor need income be received to be taxable. § 446(c)(2).

Accumulated adjustments account (AAA). An account that aggregates an S corporation's post-1982 income, loss, and deductions for the tax year (including nontaxable income and nondeductible losses and expenses). After the year-end income and expense adjustments are made, the account is reduced by distributions made during the tax year.

Accumulated E & P. See *accumulated earnings and profits (AEP)*.

Accumulated earnings and profits (AEP). Net undistributed tax-basis earnings of a corporation aggregated from March 1, 1913, to the end of the prior tax year. Used to determine the amount of dividend income associated with a distribution to shareholders. § 316 and Reg. § 1.316–2.

Accumulated earnings tax. A special 20 percent tax imposed on C corporations that accumulate (rather than distribute) their earnings beyond the reasonable needs of the business. The accumulated earnings tax and related interest are imposed on accumulated taxable income in addition to the corporate income tax. §§ 531–537.

Accuracy-related penalties. Major civil taxpayer penalties relating to the accuracy of tax return data, including misstatements stemming from taxpayer negligence and improper valuation of income and deductions, are coordinated under this umbrella term. The penalty usually equals 20 percent of the understated tax liability.

Acquiescence. Agreement by the IRS on the results reached in certain judicial decisions; sometimes abbreviated *Acq.* or *A*.

Acquisition indebtedness. Debt incurred in acquiring, constructing, or substantially improving a qualified residence of the taxpayer. The interest on such loans is deductible as qualified residence interest. However, interest on such debt is deductible only on the portion of the indebtedness that does not exceed $750,000 ($1,000,000 for debt incurred before December 15, 2017). § 163(h)(3).

Active income. Wages, salary, commissions, bonuses, profits from a trade or business in which the taxpayer is a material participant, gain on the sale or other disposition of assets used in an active trade or business, and income from intangible property if the taxpayer's personal efforts significantly contributed to the creation of the property. The passive activity loss rules require classification of income and losses into three categories with active income being one of them.

Ad valorem taxes. A tax imposed on the value of property. The most common ad valorem tax is that imposed by states, counties, and cities on real estate. Ad valorem taxes can be imposed on personal property as well.

Additional first-year depreciation. In general, this provision provides for an additional cost recovery deduction of 100 percent for qualified property acquired and placed in service after September 27, 2017, and before January 1, 2027. (The bonus depreciation percentage is reduced by 20 percent for each tax year after 2022.) Qualified property includes most types of new and used property other than buildings. The taxpayer can elect to forgo this bonus depreciation. Different rules applied between 2008 and September 28, 2017.

Adjusted basis. The cost or other basis of property reduced by depreciation allowed or allowable and increased by capital improvements. Other special adjustments are provided in § 1016 and the related Regulations.

Adjusted gross estate. Used in determining eligibility for deferred payments of Federal estate tax. The gross estate less the sum allowable as deductions under § 2053 (expenses, indebtedness, and taxes) and § 2054 (casualty and theft losses during the administration of the estate). § 6166(b)(6).

Adjustments. In calculating AMTI, certain adjustments are added to or deducted from taxable income. These adjustments generally reflect timing differences. § 56.

Adoption expenses credit. A provision intended to assist taxpayers who incur nonrecurring costs directly associated with the adoption process, such as legal costs, social service review costs, and transportation costs. Up to $14,300 of costs incurred to adopt an eligible child qualify for the credit (unique rules apply when adopting a special needs child). A taxpayer may claim the credit in the year qualifying expenses are paid or incurred if the expenses are paid during or after the year in which the adoption is finalized. For qualifying expenses paid or incurred in a tax year prior to the year the adoption is finalized, the credit must be claimed in the tax year following the tax year during which the expenses are paid or incurred. § 23.

Affiliated group. A parent-subsidiary group of corporations that is eligible to elect to file on a consolidated basis. Eighty percent ownership of the voting power and value of all of the corporations must be achieved every day of the tax year, and an identifiable parent corporation must exist (i.e., it must own at least 80 percent of another group member without applying attribution rules).

Aggregate (or conduit) concept. A perspective taken towards a venture that regards the venture as an aggregation of its owners joined together in an agency relationship rather than as a separate entity. For tax purposes, this results in the income of the venture being taxable directly to its owners. For example, items of income and expense, capital gains and losses, tax credits, etc., realized by a partnership pass through the partnership (a conduit) and are subject to taxation at the partner level. Also, in an S corporation, certain items pass through and are reported on the returns of the shareholders. See also *entity concept*.

Alimony and separate maintenance payments. Alimony deductions result from the payment of a legal obligation arising from the termination of a marital relationship. Payments designated as alimony generally are included in the gross income of the recipient and are deductible *for* AGI by the payor. For divorce or separation instruments executed after December 31, 2018, alimony is neither gross income for the recipient nor deductible by the payor.

Alimony recapture. The amount of alimony that previously has been included in the gross income of the recipient and deducted by the payor that now is deducted by the recipient and included in the gross income of the payor as the result of front-loading. Alimony recapture is applicable for divorce or separation agreements executed before 2019. § 71(f).

All events test. As applied to the recognition of income, the all events test requires that income of an accrual basis taxpayer be recognized when (1) all events have occurred that fix the taxpayer's right to receive the income and (2) the amount can be determined with reasonable accuracy. The TCJA of 2017 added a rule at § 451(b) requiring an accrual method taxpayer to include amounts in income no later than for financial reporting purposes other than for special rules such as the installment method. As applied to the recognition of expenses, the all events test prevents the recognition of a deduction by an accrual basis taxpayer until all the events have occurred that fix the taxpayer's related obligation. This can be contrasted with GAAP under which a fixed or legal obligation is not required before an expense is recognized. Reg. §§ 1.446–1(c)(1)(ii) and 1.461–1(a)(2).

Allocate. The assignment of income for various tax purposes. A multistate corporation's nonbusiness income usually is allocated to the state where the nonbusiness assets are located; it is not apportioned with the rest of the entity's income. The income and expense items of an estate or a trust are allocated between income and corpus components. Specific items of income, expense, gain, loss, and credit can be allocated to specific partners if a substantial economic nontax purpose for the allocation is established.

Alternate valuation date. Property passing from a decedent by death may be valued for estate tax purposes as of the date of death or the alternate valuation date. The alternate valuation date is six months after the date of death or the date the property is disposed of by the estate, whichever comes first. To use the alternate valuation date, the executor or administrator of the estate must make an affirmative election. The election applies to all of the estate's assets. Election of the alternate valuation date is not available unless it decreases the amount of the gross estate and reduces the estate tax liability.

Alternative depreciation system (ADS). A cost recovery system in which the cost or other initial basis of an asset is recovered using the straight-line method over recovery periods similar to those used in MACRS. The alternative system must be used in certain instances and can be elected in other instances. § 168(g).

Alternative minimum tax (AMT). The AMT is a surtax, calculated as a percentage of alternative minimum taxable income (AMTI). AMTI generally starts with the taxpayer's taxable income, prior to any standard deduction taken. To this amount, the taxpayer (1) adds designated preference items (e.g., tax-exempt interest income on private activity bonds), (2) makes other specified adjustments (e.g., to reflect a slower cost recovery method), (3) adjusts certain AMT itemized deductions for individuals (e.g., interest incurred on housing), and (4) subtracts an exemption amount. The taxpayer must pay the greater of the resulting AMT or the regular income tax (reduced by all allowable tax credits). AMT preferences and adjustments are assigned to partners, LLC members, and S corporation shareholders. The AMT does not apply to C corporations for tax years beginning after 2017.

Alternative minimum tax credit. AMT liability can result from timing differences that give rise to positive adjustments in calculating AMTI. To provide equity for the taxpayer when these timing differences reverse, the regular tax liability may be reduced by a tax credit for a prior year's minimum tax liability attributable to timing differences. § 53.

Alternative minimum taxable income (AMTI). The base (prior to deducting the exemption amount) for computing a taxpayer's alternative minimum tax. This consists of the taxable income for the year modified for AMT adjustments and AMT preferences. § 55(b)(2).

Alternative tax. An option that is allowed in computing the tax on net capital gain. For noncorporate taxpayers, the rate is usually 15 percent (but is 25 percent for unrecaptured § 1250 gain and 28 percent for collectibles). However, the alternative tax rate is 0 percent (rather than 15 percent) for lower-income taxpayers (e.g., taxable income of $80,000 or less for married persons filing jointly). Certain high-income taxpayers (e.g., taxable income of more than $496,600 for married persons filing jointly) have an alternative tax rate of 20 percent. § 1(h).

Alternative tax NOL deduction (ATNOLD). In calculating the AMT, the taxpayer is allowed to deduct NOL carryovers following the regular tax NOL carryover provisions. The AMT NOL amount is referred to as the ATNOLD. The regular income tax NOL is modified for AMT adjustments and preferences to produce the ATNOLD. § 56(d).

American Opportunity credit. This credit applies for qualifying expenses for the first four years of postsecondary education. Qualified expenses include tuition and related expenses and books and other course materials. Room and board are ineligible for the credit. The maximum credit available per student is $2,500 (100 percent of the first $2,000 of qualified expenses and 25 percent of the next $2,000 of qualified expenses). Eligible students include the taxpayer, taxpayer's spouse, and taxpayer's dependents. To qualify for the credit, a student must take at least one-half of the full-time course load for at least one academic term at a qualifying educational institution. The credit is phased out for higher-income taxpayers. § 25A.

Amortization. The tax deduction for the cost or other basis of an intangible asset over the asset's estimated useful life. Examples of amortizable intangibles include patents, copyrights, and leasehold interests. Most purchased intangible assets (e.g., goodwill) can be amortized for income tax purposes over a 15-year period.

Amount realized. The amount received by a taxpayer upon the sale or exchange of property. Amount realized is the sum of the cash and the fair market value of any property or services received by the taxpayer plus any related debt assumed by the buyer. Determining the amount realized is the starting point for arriving at realized gain or loss. § 1001(b).

Annual exclusion. In computing the taxable gifts for the year, each donor excludes the first $15,000 (for 2020) of a gift to each donee. Usually, the annual exclusion is not available for gifts of future interests. § 2503(b).

Annuity. A fixed sum of money payable to a person at specified times for a specified period of time or for life. If the party making the payment (i.e., the obligor) is regularly engaged in this type of business (e.g., an insurance company), the arrangement is classified as a commercial annuity. A so-called private annuity involves an obligor that is not regularly engaged in selling annuities (e.g., a charity or family member).

Apportion. The assignment of the business income of a multistate corporation to specific states for income taxation. Usually, the apportionment procedure accounts for the property, payroll, and sales activity levels of the various states, and a proportionate assignment of the entity's total income is made using a statutory apportionment formula. Most states exclude nonbusiness income from the apportionment procedure; they allocate nonbusiness income to the states where the nonbusiness assets are located.

Appreciated inventory. In partnership taxation, appreciated inventory is a hot asset, and a partner's share of its ordinary income potential must be allocated. If a partner sells an interest in the partnership, ordinary income is recognized to the extent of the partner's share in the partnership's inventory and unrealized receivables. The definition of "inventory" here is broad enough to include any accounts receivable, including unrealized receivables.

Arm's length. See *arm's length price*.

Arm's length price. The standard under which unrelated parties would determine an exchange price for a transaction. Suppose, for example, Cardinal Corporation sells property to its sole shareholder for $10,000. In testing whether the $10,000 is an "arm's length" price, one would ascertain the price that would have been negotiated between the corporation and an unrelated party in a bargained exchange.

ASC 740. Under Generally Accepted Accounting Principles, the rules for the financial reporting of the tax expense of an enterprise. Permanent differences affect the enterprise's effective tax rate. Temporary differences create a deferred tax asset or a deferred tax liability on the balance sheet.

ASC 740-10. An interpretation by the Financial Accounting Standards Board. When an uncertain tax return position exists, this interpretation is used to determine the financial reporting treatment, if any, for the taxpayer. If it is more likely than not (i.e., a greater than 50 percent probability) that the uncertain return position will be sustained (e.g., by the courts) on its technical merits, it must be reported on the financial statements. The amount to be reported then is computed based on the probabilities of the outcome of the technical review and the amounts at which the dispute would be resolved. If the more-likely-than-not test is failed, no current financial disclosure of the results of the return position is required.

Asset Depreciation Range (ADR) system. A system of estimated useful lives for categories of tangible assets prescribed by the IRS. The system provides a range for each category that extends from 20 percent above to 20 percent below the guideline class lives prescribed by the IRS.

Asset use test. In the context of a corporate reorganization, a means by which to determine if the continuity of business enterprise requirement is met. The acquiring corporation must continue to use the target entity's assets in the acquiror's business going forward; if this is not the case, the requirement is failed.

Assignment of income. A taxpayer attempts to avoid the recognition of income by assigning to another the property that generates the income. Such a procedure will not avoid income recognition by the taxpayer making the assignment if the income was earned at the point of the transfer. In this case, the income is taxed to the person who earns it.

At-risk limitation. Generally, a taxpayer can deduct losses related to a trade or business, S corporation, partnership, or investment asset only to the extent of the at-risk amount. The taxpayer has an amount at risk in a business or investment venture to the extent that personal assets have been subjected to the risks of the business. Typically, the taxpayer's at-risk amount includes (1) the amount of money or other property that the investor contributed to the venture for the investment, (2) the amount of any of the entity's liabilities for which the taxpayer personally is liable and that relate to the investment, and (3) an allocable share of nonrecourse debts incurred by the venture from third parties in arm's length transactions for real estate investments.

Attribution. Under certain circumstances, the tax law applies attribution (constructive ownership) rules to assign to one taxpayer the ownership interest of another taxpayer. If, for example, the stock of Gold Corporation is held 60 percent by Marsha and 40 percent by Sidney, Marsha may be deemed to own 100 percent of Gold Corporation if Marsha and Sidney are mother and child. In that case, the stock owned by Sidney is attributed to Marsha. Stated differently, Marsha has a 60 percent direct and a 40 percent indirect interest in Gold Corporation. It can also be said that Marsha is the constructive owner of Sidney's interest.

Automatic mileage method. Automobile expenses are generally deductible only to the extent the automobile is used in business or for the production of income. Personal commuting expenses are not deductible. The taxpayer may deduct actual expenses (including depreciation and insurance), or the standard (automatic) mileage rate may be used (57.5 cents per mile for 2020 and 58 cents per mile for 2019). Automobile expenses incurred for medical purposes are deductible to the extent of actual out-of-pocket expenses or at the rate of 17 cents per mile for 2020 and 20 cents per mile for 2019. For charitable activities, the rate is 14 cents per mile.

B

Bad debt. A deduction is permitted if a business account receivable subsequently becomes partially or completely worthless, providing the income arising from the debt previously was included in income. Available methods are the specific charge-off method and the reserve method. However, except for certain financial institutions, TRA of 1986 repealed the use of the reserve method for 1987 and thereafter. If the reserve method is used, partially or totally worthless accounts are charged to the reserve. A nonbusiness bad debt deduction is allowed as a short-term capital loss if the loan did not arise in connection with the creditor's trade or business activities. Loans between related parties (family members) generally are classified as nonbusiness. § 166.

Balance sheet approach. The process under ASC 740 (SFAS 109) by which an entity's deferred tax expense or deferred tax benefit is determined as a result of the reporting period's changes in the balance sheet's deferred tax asset and deferred tax liability accounts.

Basis in partnership interest. The acquisition cost of the partner's ownership interest in the partnership. Includes purchase price and associated debt acquired from other partners and in the course of the entity's trade or business.

Benchmarking. The tax professional's use of two or more entities' effective tax rates and deferred tax balance sheet accounts. Used chiefly to compare the effectiveness of the entities' tax planning techniques and to suggest future tax-motivated courses of action.

Blockage rule. A factor to be considered in valuing a large block of corporate stock. Application of this rule generally justifies a discount in the asset's fair market value, because the disposition of a large amount of stock at any one time may depress the value of the shares in the marketplace.

Boot. Cash or property of a type not included in the definition of a tax-deferred exchange. The receipt of boot causes an otherwise tax-deferred transfer to become immediately taxable to the extent of the lesser of the fair market value of the boot or the realized gain on the transfer. For example, see transfers to controlled corporations under § 351(b), reorganizations under § 368, and like-kind exchanges under § 1031(b).

Built-in gains tax. A penalty tax designed to discourage a shift of the incidence of taxation on unrealized gains from a C corporation to its shareholders, via an S election. Under this provision, any recognized gain during the first five years of S status generates a corporate-level tax on a base not to exceed the aggregate untaxed built-in gains brought into the S corporation upon its election from C corporation taxable years.

Built-in loss property. Property contributed to a corporation under § 351 or as a contribution to capital that has a basis in excess of its fair market value. An adjustment is necessary to step down the basis of the property to its fair market value. The adjustment prevents the corporation and the contributing shareholder from obtaining a double tax benefit. The corporation allocates the adjustment proportionately among the assets with the built-in loss. As an alternative to the corporate adjustment, the shareholder may elect to reduce the basis in the stock.

Business bad debt. A tax deduction allowed for obligations obtained in connection with a trade or business that have become either partially or completely worthless. In contrast to nonbusiness bad debts, business bad debts are deductible as business expenses. § 166.

Business purpose. A justifiable business reason for carrying out a transaction. Mere tax avoidance is not an acceptable business purpose. The presence of a business purpose is crucial in the area of corporate reorganizations and certain liquidations.

Buy-sell agreement. An arrangement, particularly appropriate in the case of a closely held corporation or a partnership, whereby the surviving owners (shareholders or partners) or the entity agrees to purchase the interest of a withdrawing owner. The buy-sell agreement provides for an orderly disposition of an interest in a business and may aid in setting the value of the interest for estate tax purposes.

Bypass amount. The amount that can be transferred by gift or at death free of any unified transfer tax. For 2020, the bypass amount is $11.58 million for estate tax and $11.58 million for gift tax.

Bypass election. In the context of a distribution by an S corporation, an election made by the entity to designate that the distribution is first from accumulated earnings and profits and only then from the accumulated adjustments account (AAA).

C

C corporation. A separate taxable entity subject to the rules of Subchapter C of the Code. This business form may create a double taxation effect relative to its shareholders. The entity is subject to the regular corporate tax and a number of penalty taxes at the Federal level.

Cafeteria benefit plans. See *cafeteria plan.*

Cafeteria plan. An employee benefit plan under which an employee is allowed to select from among a variety of employer-provided fringe benefits. Some of the benefits may be taxable, and some may be statutory nontaxable benefits (e.g., health and accident insurance and group term life insurance). The employee is taxed only on the taxable benefits selected. A cafeteria benefit plan is also referred to as a flexible benefit plan. § 125.

Capital account. The financial accounting analog of a partner's tax basis in the entity.

Capital account maintenance. Under the § 704(b) Regulations, partnership allocations will be respected only if capital accounts are maintained in accordance with those regulations. These so-called "§ 704(b) book capital accounts" are properly maintained if they reflect the partner's contributions and distributions of cash; increases and decreases for the fair market value of contributed/distributed property; and adjustments for the partner's share of income, gains, losses, and deductions. Certain other adjustments are also required. See also *economic effect test* and *Section 704(b) book capital accounts.*

Capital asset. Broadly speaking, all assets are capital except those specifically excluded from that definition by the Code. Major categories of noncapital assets include property held for resale in the normal course of business (inventory), trade accounts and notes receivable, and depreciable property and real estate used in a trade or business (§ 1231 assets). § 1221.

Capital contribution. Various means by which a shareholder makes additional funds available to the corporation (placed at the risk of the business), sometimes without the receipt of additional stock. If no stock is received, the contributions are added to the basis of the shareholder's existing stock investment and do not generate gross income to the corporation. § 118.

Capital gains. The gain from the sale or exchange of a capital asset.

Capital gain property. Property contributed to a charitable organization that if sold rather than contributed, would have resulted in long-term capital gain to the donor.

Capital interest. Usually, the percentage of the entity's net assets that a partner would receive on liquidation. Typically determined by the partner's capital sharing ratio.

Capital losses. The loss from the sale or exchange of a capital asset.

Capital sharing ratio. A partner's percentage ownership of the entity's capital.

Carbon tax. A tax on fossil fuels to help reduce greenhouse gas emissions.

Carried interest. A "partnership interest held in connection with performance of services," as defined under § 1061. Long-term capital gains from such an interest are reclassified as short-term capital gains (with potential ordinary income treatment) unless the underlying asset that triggered the gain had more than a three-year holding period. This provision only applies to income and gains arising from managing portfolio investments on behalf of third-party investors, including publicly traded securities, commodities, certain real estate, or options to buy/sell such assets. Section 1061 was enacted in the TCJA of 2017 in an effort to curtail an industry practice that resulted in fund managers receiving partnership profits interests in exchange for services: these "profits partners" received long-term capital gain allocations from the fund, rather than ordinary income for the services provided in managing the fund's assets. In addition to § 1061, the IRS has, from time to time, announced that it might issue regulations (under its general "anti-abuse" authority) to expand the scope of the carried interest rules.

Cash balance plan. A hybrid form of pension plan similar in some aspects to a defined benefit plan. Such a plan is funded by the employer, and the employer bears the investment risks and rewards. But like defined contribution plans, a cash balance plan establishes allocations to individual employee accounts, and the payout for an employee depends on investment performance.

Cash method. See *cash receipts method*.

Cash receipts method. A method of accounting that reflects deductions as paid and income as received in any one tax year. However, deductions for prepaid expenses that benefit more than one tax year (e.g., prepaid rent and prepaid interest) usually are spread over the period benefited rather than deducted in the year paid. § 446(c)(1).

Casualty loss. A casualty is defined as "the complete or partial destruction of property resulting from an identifiable event of a sudden, unexpected or unusual nature" (e.g., floods, storms, fires, auto accidents). Individuals may deduct a casualty loss only if the loss is incurred in a trade or business or in a transaction entered into for profit or arises from fire, storm, shipwreck, or other casualty or from theft. Individuals usually deduct personal casualty losses as itemized deductions subject to a $100 nondeductible amount and to an annual floor equal to 10 percent of adjusted gross income that applies after the $100 per casualty floor has been applied. Special rules are provided for the netting of certain casualty gains and losses. For tax years beginning after 2017 (and before 2026), personal casualty losses are limited to those sustained in an area designated as a disaster area by the President of the United States.

Charitable contribution. Contributions made to qualified nonprofit organizations. Taxpayers, regardless of their accounting method, are generally allowed to deduct (subject to various restrictions and limitations) contributions in the year of payment. Accrual basis corporations may accrue contributions at year-end if payment is properly authorized before the end of the year and payment is made within three and one-half months after the end of the year. § 170.

Check-the-box Regulations. By using the check-the-box rules prudently, an entity can select the most attractive tax results offered by the Code, without being bound by legal forms. By default, an unincorporated entity with more than one owner is taxed as a partnership; an unincorporated entity with one owner is a disregarded entity, taxed as a sole proprietorship or corporate division. No action is necessary by the taxpayer if the legal form or default status is desired. Form 8832 is used to "check a box" and change the tax status. Not available if the entity is incorporated under state law.

Child tax credit. A tax credit based solely on the number of qualifying children under age 17. The maximum credit available is $2,000 per qualifying child. (In addition, a $500 nonrefundable credit is available for qualifying dependents other than qualifying children.) A qualifying child must be claimed as a dependent on a parent's tax return and have a Social Security number to qualify for the credit. Taxpayers who qualify for the child tax credit may also qualify for a supplemental credit. The supplemental credit is treated as a component of the earned income credit and is therefore refundable. The credit is phased out for higher-income taxpayers. § 24. See also *dependent tax credit*.

Circuit Court of Appeals. Any of 13 Federal courts that consider tax matters appealed from the U.S. Tax Court, a U.S. District Court, or the U.S. Court of Federal Claims. Appeal from a U.S. Court of Appeals is to the U.S. Supreme Court by Certiorari.

Circular 230. A portion of the Federal tax Regulations that describes the levels of conduct at which a tax preparer must operate. Circular 230 dictates, for instance, that a tax preparer may not charge an unconscionable fee or delay the execution of a tax audit with inappropriate delays. Circular 230 requires that there be a reasonable basis for a tax return position and that no frivolous returns be filed.

Citator. A tax research resource that presents the judicial history of a court case and traces the subsequent references to the case. When these references include the citing cases' evaluations of the cited case's precedents, the research can obtain some measure of the efficacy and reliability of the original holding.

Claim of right doctrine. A judicially imposed doctrine applicable to both cash and accrual basis taxpayers that holds that an amount is includible in income upon actual or constructive receipt if the taxpayer has an unrestricted claim to the payment. For the tax treatment of amounts repaid when previously included in income under the claim of right doctrine, see § 1341.

Closely held C corporation. A regular corporation (i.e., the S election is not in effect) for which more than 50 percent of the value of its outstanding stock is owned, directly or indirectly, by five or fewer individuals at any time during the tax year. The term is relevant in identifying C corporations that are subject to the passive activity loss provisions. § 469.

Closely held corporation. A corporation where stock ownership is not widely dispersed. Rather, a few shareholders are in control of corporate policy and are in a position to benefit personally from that policy.

Closing agreement. In a tax dispute, the parties sign a closing agreement to spell out the terms under which the matters are settled. The agreement is binding on both the Service and the taxpayer.

Collectibles. A special type of capital asset, the gain from which is taxed at a maximum rate of 28 percent if the holding period is more than one year. Examples include art, rugs, antiques, gems, metals, stamps, some coins and bullion, and alcoholic beverages held for investment.

Combined return. In multistate taxation, a group of unitary corporations may elect or be required to file an income tax return that includes operating results for all of the affiliates, not just those with nexus in the state. Thus, apportionment data is reported for the group's worldwide or water's-edge operations.

Community property. Arizona, California, Idaho, Louisiana, Nevada, New Mexico, Texas, Washington, and Wisconsin have community property systems. Alaska residents can elect community property status for assets. The rest of the states are common law property jurisdictions. The difference between common law and community property systems centers around the property rights possessed by married persons. In a common law system, each spouse owns whatever he or she earns. Under a community property system, one-half of the earnings of each spouse is considered owned by the other spouse. Assume, for example, that Jeff and Alice are husband and wife and that their only income is the $50,000 annual salary Jeff receives. If they live in New York (a common law state), the $50,000 salary belongs to Jeff. If, however, they live in Texas (a community property state), the $50,000 salary is owned one-half each by Jeff and Alice.

Compensatory damages. Damages received or paid by the taxpayer can be classified as compensatory damages or as punitive damages. Compensatory damages are paid to compensate one for harm caused by another. Compensatory damages received on account of physical injuries are excludible from the recipient's gross income.

Complete termination redemption. Sale or exchange treatment is available relative to this type of redemption. The shareholder must retire all of his or her outstanding shares in the corporation (ignoring family attribution rules) and cannot hold an interest, other than that of a creditor, for the 10 years following the redemption. § 302(b)(3).

Completed contract method. A method of reporting gain or loss on certain long-term contracts. Under this method of accounting, all gross income and expenses are recognized in the tax year in which the contract is completed. Reg. § 1.451–3.

Complex trust. Not a simple trust. Such trusts may have charitable beneficiaries, accumulate income, and distribute corpus. §§ 661–663.

Composite return. In multistate taxation, an S corporation may be allowed to file a single income tax return that assigns pass-through items to resident and nonresident shareholders. The composite or "block" return allows the entity to remit any tax that is attributable to the nonresident shareholders.

Conduit concept. A perspective taken toward a venture that regards the venture as an aggregation of its owners joined together in an agency relationship rather than as a separate entity. For tax purposes, this results in the income of the venture being taxable directly to its owners. For example, items of income and expense, capital gains and losses, tax credits, etc., realized by a partnership pass through the partnership (a conduit) and are subject to taxation at the partner level. Also, in an S corporation, certain items pass through and are reported on the returns of the shareholders.

Conduit perspective. See *conduit concept*.

Consolidated returns. A procedure whereby certain affiliated corporations may file a single return, combine the tax transactions of each corporation, and arrive at a single income tax liability for the group. The election to file a consolidated return usually is binding on future years. §§ 1501–1505 and related Regulations.

Consolidation. The combination of two or more corporations into a newly created corporation. Thus, Black Corporation and White Corporation combine to form Gray Corporation. A consolidation may qualify as a nontaxable reorganization if certain conditions are satisfied. §§ 354 and 368(a)(1)(A).

Constructive dividends. A taxable benefit derived by a shareholder from his or her corporation that is not actually initiated by the board of directors as a dividend. Examples include unreasonable compensation, excessive rent payments, bargain purchases of corporate property, and shareholder use of corporate property. Constructive dividends generally are found in closely held corporations.

Constructive liquidation scenario. The means by which recourse debt is shared among partners in basis determination.

Constructive receipt. If income is unqualifiedly available although not physically in the taxpayer's possession, it still is subject to the income tax. An example is accrued interest on a savings account. Under the constructive receipt concept, the interest is taxed to a depositor in the year available, rather than the year actually withdrawn. The fact that the depositor uses the cash basis of accounting for tax purposes is irrelevant. See Reg. § 1.451–2.

Continuity of business enterprise. In a tax-favored reorganization, the acquiring corporation must continue the historic business of the target or use a significant portion of the target's assets in the new business.

Continuity of interest. In a tax-favored reorganization, a shareholder or corporation that has substantially the same investment after an exchange as before should not be taxed on the transaction. Specifically, the target shareholders must acquire an equity interest in the acquiring corporation equal in value to at least 40 percent of all the outstanding stock of the target entity.

Control. Holding a specified level of stock ownership in a corporation. For § 351, the new shareholder(s) must hold at least 80 percent of the total combined voting power of all voting classes of stock and at least 80 percent of the shares of all nonvoting classes. Other tax provisions require different levels of control to bring about desired effects, such as 50 or 100 percent.

Controlled foreign corporation (CFC). A non-U.S. corporation in which more than 50 percent of the total combined voting power of all classes of stock entitled to vote or the total value of the stock of the corporation is owned by U.S. shareholders on any day during the taxable year of the foreign corporation. For purposes of this definition, a U.S. shareholder is any U.S. person who owns, or is considered to own, 10 percent or more of the total combined voting power of all classes of voting stock of the foreign corporation. Stock owned directly, indirectly, and constructively is used in this measure. See *U.S. shareholder*.

Controlled group. Controlled groups include parent-subsidiary groups, brother-sister groups, combined groups, and certain insurance companies. Controlled groups are required to share certain elements of tax calculations (e.g., $250,000 accumulated earnings credit) or tax credits (e.g., research credit). §§ 1561 and 1563.

Corporate liquidation. Occurs when a corporation distributes its net assets to its shareholders and ceases to be a going concern. Generally, a shareholder recognizes capital gain or loss upon the liquidation of the entity, regardless of the corporation's balance in its earnings and profits account. The liquidating corporation recognizes gain and loss on assets that it sells during the liquidation period and on assets that it distributes to shareholders in kind.

Corpus. The body or principal of a trust. Suppose, for example, Grant transfers an apartment building into a trust, income payable to Ruth for life, remainder to Shawn upon Ruth's death. Corpus of the trust is the apartment building.

Correspondence audit. An audit conducted by the IRS by the U.S. mail. Typically, the IRS writes to the taxpayer requesting the verification of a particular deduction or exemption. The remittance of copies of records or other support is requested of the taxpayer.

Cost depletion. Depletion that is calculated based on the adjusted basis of the asset. The adjusted basis is divided by the expected recoverable units to determine the depletion per unit. The depletion per unit is multiplied by the units sold during the tax year to calculate cost depletion.

Cost recovery. The system by which taxpayers are allowed to recover their investment in an asset by reducing their taxable income by the asset's cost or initial basis. Cost recovery methods include MACRS, § 179 expense, additional first-year depreciation, amortization, and depletion. §§ 168, 179, and 613.

Court of original jurisdiction. The Federal courts are divided into courts of original jurisdiction and appellate courts. A dispute between a taxpayer and the IRS is first considered by a court of original jurisdiction (i.e., a trial court). The four Federal courts of original jurisdiction are the U.S. Tax Court, the U.S. District Court, the U.S. Court of Federal Claims, and the Small Cases Division of the U.S. Tax Court.

Coverdell education savings account (§ 530 plan). Coverdell education savings account exempts from tax the earnings on amounts placed in a qualified account for the education expenses of a named beneficiary. Contributions are limited to $2,000 per year per beneficiary, and the proceeds can be withdrawn without tax provided the funds are used to pay qualified educational expenses for primary, secondary, or higher education. (There is an annual $10,000 per student limitation on distributions for tuition expenses for primary and secondary education.) Qualified educational expenses also include certain homeschooling expenses. The account is named for the late Senator Paul Coverdell (R-GA), who sponsored the legislation in Congress. § 530.

Credit for certain retirement plan contributions. A nonrefundable credit is available based on eligible contributions of up to $2,000 to certain qualified retirement plans, such as traditional and Roth IRAs and § 401(k) plans. The benefit provided by this credit is in addition to any deduction or exclusion that otherwise is available resulting from the qualifying contribution. The amount of the credit depends on the taxpayer's AGI and filing status. § 25B.

Credit for child and dependent care expenses. A tax credit ranging from 20 percent to 35 percent of employment-related expenses (child and dependent care expenses) for amounts of up to $6,000 is available to individuals who are employed (or deemed to be employed) and maintain a household for a dependent child under age 13, disabled spouse, or disabled dependent. § 21.

Credit for employer-provided child care. A nonrefundable credit is available to employers who provide child care facilities to their employees during normal working hours. The credit, limited to $150,000, is comprised of two components. The portion of the credit for qualified child care expenses is equal to 25 percent of these expenses, while the portion of the credit for qualified child care resource and referral services is equal to 10 percent of these expenses. Any qualifying expenses otherwise deductible by the taxpayer must be reduced by the amount of the credit. In addition, the taxpayer's basis for any property used for qualifying purposes is reduced by the amount of the credit. § 45F.

Credit for employer-provided family and medical leave. A nonrefundable credit is available to employers who pay wages to employees while they are on family and medical leave. The credit is equal to 12.5 percent of wages paid to qualifying employees (limited to 12 weeks per employee per year). Employers must pay a minimum of 50 percent of the wages normally paid; if wages paid during the leave *exceed* 50 percent of normal wages, the credit is increased by 0.25 percent for each percentage point above 50 percent to a maximum of 25 percent of wages paid. The credit does not apply to wages paid in taxable years beginning after 2020. § 45S.

Credit for small employer pension plan startup costs. A nonrefundable credit available to small businesses based on administrative costs associated with establishing and maintaining certain qualified plans. While such qualifying costs generally are deductible as ordinary and necessary business expenses, the availability of the credit is intended to lower the costs of starting a qualified retirement program and therefore encourage qualifying businesses to establish retirement plans for their employees. The credit is available for eligible employers at the rate of 50 percent of qualified startup costs. The maximum credit is $500 (based on a maximum $1,000 of qualifying expenses). § 45E.

Crop insurance proceeds. The proceeds received when an insured crop is destroyed. Section 451(d) permits the farmer to defer reporting the income from the insurance proceeds until the tax year following the taxable year of the destruction.

Crop method. A method of accounting for agricultural crops that are planted in one year but harvested in a subsequent year. Under this method, the costs of raising the crop are accumulated as inventory and are deducted when the income from the crop is realized.

Cross-purchase buy-sell agreement. Under this arrangement, the surviving owners of the business agree to buy out the withdrawing owner. Assume, for example, Ron and Sara are equal shareholders in Tip Corporation. Under a cross-purchase buy-sell agreement, Ron and Sara would contract to purchase the other's interest, should that person decide to withdraw from the business.

Current distribution. A payment made by a partnership to a partner when the partnership's legal existence does not cease thereafter. The partner usually assigns a basis in the distributed property that is equal to the lesser of the partner's basis in the partnership interest or the basis of the distributed asset to the partnership. The partner first assigns basis to any cash that he or she receives in the distribution. A cash distribution in excess of the partner's basis triggers a gain. The partner's remaining basis, if any, is assigned to the noncash assets according to their relative bases to the partnership.

Current E & P. Net tax-basis earnings of a corporation aggregated during the current tax year. A corporate distribution is deemed to be first from the entity's current earnings and profits and then from accumulated earnings and profits. Shareholders recognize dividend income to the extent of the earnings and profits of the corporation. A dividend results to the extent of current earnings and profits, even if there is a larger negative balance in accumulated earnings and profits.

Current tax expense. Under ASC 740 (SFAS 109), the book tax expense that relates to the current reporting period's net income and is actually payable (or creditable) to the appropriate governmental agencies for the current period. Also known as "cash tax" or "tax payable."

D

De minimis **fringe.** Benefits provided to employees that are too insignificant to warrant the time and effort required to account for the benefits received by each employee and the value of those benefits. Such amounts are excludible from the employee's gross income. § 132.

De minimis **fringe benefits.** See *de minimis fringe.*

Death benefits. A payment made by an employer to the beneficiary or beneficiaries of a deceased employee on account of the death of the employee.

Debt-financed income. Included in computations of the unrelated business income of an exempt organization, the gross income generated from debt-financed property.

Deceased spouse's unused exclusion (DSUE). In computing the Federal estate tax, the decedent uses the exclusion amount to shelter an amount of the gross estate from taxation. When the first spouse to die fails to use a portion of his/her exclusion amount, the unused portion is "portable" and becomes available to the surviving spouse. The surviving spouse can use the DSUE only of his/her last spouse to predecease.

Deduction for qualified business income. A deduction allowed for noncorporate taxpayers based on the qualified business income of a qualified trade or business. In general, the deduction is limited to the lesser of 20 percent of qualified business income, or 20 percent of taxable income before the qualified business income deduction less any net capital gain. There are *three limitations* on the deduction— an overall limitation (based on modified taxable income), another that applies to high-income taxpayers, and a third that applies to certain types of services businesses. § 199A.

Deduction for qualified tuition and related expenses. Taxpayers are allowed a deduction of up to $4,000 for higher education expenses. Certain taxpayers are not eligible for the deduction: those whose gross AGI exceeds a specified amount and those who can be claimed as a dependent by another taxpayer. These expenses are classified as a deduction *for* AGI, and they need not be employment-related. § 222.

Deductions *for* **adjusted gross income.** The Federal income tax is not imposed upon gross income. Rather, it is imposed upon taxable income. Congressionally identified deductions for individual taxpayers are subtracted either from gross income to arrive at adjusted gross income or from adjusted gross income to arrive at the tax base, taxable income.

Deductions *from* **adjusted gross income.** See *deductions for adjusted gross income.*

Deductions in respect of a decedent. Deductions accrued at the moment of death but not recognizable on the final income tax return of a decedent because of the method of accounting used. Such items are allowed as deductions on the estate tax return and on the income tax return of the estate (Form 1041) or the heir (Form 1040). An example of a deduction in respect of a decedent is interest expense accrued to the date of death by a cash basis debtor.

Deferred compensation. Compensation that will be taxed when received or upon the removal of certain restrictions on receipt and not when earned. Contributions by an employer to a qualified pension or profit sharing plan on behalf of an employee are an example. The contributions will not be taxed to the employee until the funds are made available or distributed to the employee (e.g., upon retirement).

Deferred tax asset. Under ASC 740, an asset recorded on the balance sheet to reflect the future tax benefits related to a transaction or activity which has already been reflected in the financial statements. A deferred tax asset is often the result of the deferral of a deduction or the acceleration of income for tax purposes relative to Generally Accepted Accounting Principles.

Deferred tax benefit. Under ASC 740, a reduction in the book tax expense that relates to the current reporting period's net income but will not be realized until a future reporting period. Creates or adds to the entity's deferred tax asset balance sheet account. For instance, the carryforward of a net operating loss is a deferred tax benefit.

Deferred tax expense. Under ASC 740, a book tax expense that relates to the current reporting period's net income but will not be realized until a future reporting period. Creates or adds to the entity's deferred tax liability balance sheet account. For instance, a deferred tax expense is created when tax depreciation deductions for the period are "accelerated" and exceed the corresponding book depreciation expense.

Deferred tax liability. Under ASC 740, a liability recorded on the balance sheet to reflect the future tax costs of a transaction or activity which has already been reflected in the financial statements. A deferred tax liability is often the result of the deferral of the recognition of income or the acceleration of a deduction for tax purposes relative to Generally Accepted Accounting Principles.

Defined benefit plan. Qualified plans can be dichotomized into defined benefit plans and defined contribution plans. Under a defined benefit plan, a formula defines the benefits employees are to receive. The formula usually includes years of service, employee compensation, and some stated percentage. The employer must make annual contributions based on actuarial computations that will be sufficient to pay the vested retirement benefits.

Defined contribution pension plan. Qualified plans can be dichotomized into defined benefit plans and defined contribution plans. Under a defined contribution plan, a separate account is maintained for each covered employee. The employee's benefits under the plan are based solely on (1) the amount contributed and (2) income from the fund that accrues to the employee's account. The plan defines the amount the employer is required to contribute (e.g., a flat dollar amount, an amount based on a special formula, or an amount equal to a certain percentage of compensation).

Dependency exemptions. See *personal and dependency exemptions.*

Dependent tax credit. For 2018 through 2025, the TCJA of 2017 replaced the dependency exemption with a $500 nonrefundable credit. This credit can be claimed for dependents who are not a qualifying child or under the age of 17. The dependent must be a citizen or resident of the United States.

Depletion. The process by which the cost or other basis of a natural resource (e.g., an oil or gas interest) is recovered upon extraction and sale of the resource. The two ways to determine the depletion allowance are the cost and percentage (or statutory) methods. Under cost depletion, each unit of production sold is assigned a portion of the cost or other basis of the interest. This is determined by dividing the cost or other basis by the total units expected to be recovered. Under percentage (or statutory) depletion, the tax law provides a special percentage factor for different types of minerals and other natural resources. This percentage is multiplied by the gross income from the interest to arrive at the depletion allowance. §§ 613 and 613A.

Depreciation. The system by which a taxpayer allocates for financial reporting purposes the cost of an asset to periods benefited by the asset.

Determination letter. Upon the request of a taxpayer, the IRS will comment on the tax status of a completed transaction. Determination letters frequently are used to determine whether a retirement or profit sharing plan qualifies under the Code and to determine the tax-exempt status of certain nonprofit organizations.

Disabled access credit. A tax credit designed to encourage small businesses to make their facilities more accessible to disabled individuals. The credit is equal to 50 percent of the eligible expenditures that exceed $250 but do not exceed $10,250. Thus, the maximum amount for the credit is $5,000. The adjusted basis for depreciation is reduced by the amount of the credit. To qualify, the facility must have been placed in service before November 6, 1990. § 44.

Disaster area losses. A casualty sustained in an area designated as a disaster area by the President of the United States. In such an event, the disaster loss may be treated as having occurred in the taxable year immediately preceding the year in which the disaster actually occurred. Thus, immediate tax benefits are provided to victims of a disaster. § 165(i).

Disclaimer. Rejections, refusals, or renunciations of claims, powers, or property. Section 2518 sets forth the conditions required to avoid gift tax consequences as the result of a disclaimer.

Disguised sale. When a partner contributes property to the entity and soon thereafter receives a distribution from the partnership, the transactions are collapsed and the distribution is seen as a purchase of the asset by the partnership. § 707(a)(2)(B).

Disproportionate distribution. A distribution from a partnership to one or more of its partners in which at least one partner's interest in partnership hot assets is increased or decreased. For example, a distribution of cash to one partner and hot assets to another changes both partners' interest in hot assets and is disproportionate. The intent of rules for taxation of disproportionate distributions is to ensure that each partner eventually recognizes his or her proportionate share of partnership ordinary income.

Disproportionate redemption. Sale or exchange treatment is available relative to this type of redemption. After the exchange, the shareholder owns less than 80 percent of his or her pre-redemption interest in the corporation and only a minority interest in the entity. § 302(b)(2).

Disregarded entity. The Federal income tax treatment of business income usually follows the legal form of the taxpayer (i.e., an individual's sole proprietorship is reported on the Form 1040); a C corporation's taxable income is computed on Form 1120. The check-the-box Regulations are used if the unincorporated taxpayer wants to use a different tax regime. Under these rules, a disregarded entity is taxed as an individual or a corporate division; other tax regimes are not available. For instance, a one-member limited liability company is a disregarded entity.

Distributable net income (DNI). The measure that determines the nature and amount of the distributions from estates and trusts that the beneficiaries must include in income. DNI also limits the amount that estates and trusts can claim as a deduction for such distributions. § 643(a).

Distributive share. In partnership or S corporation taxation, the distributive share is the amount of income, gain, deduction, loss, or credit allocated to a given partner or shareholder. The distributive share is the amount reported on a given line of the owner's Schedule K–1. For example, a partner's distributive share of ordinary income is the amount of income shown on that partner's Schedule K–1, Part III, line 1. For S corporations, the distributive share must be determined based on the shareholder's ownership percentage. For partnerships, the distributive share is generally determined in accordance with the partnership agreement. For both types of entities, amounts can be prorated if the ownership interest is transferred during the tax year.

Dividend. A nondeductible distribution to the shareholders of a corporation. A dividend constitutes gross income to the recipient if it is paid from the current or accumulated earnings and profits of the corporation.

Dividends received deduction. A deduction allowed a shareholder that is a corporation for dividends received from a domestic corporation. The deduction usually is 50 percent of the dividends received, but it could be 65 or 100 percent depending upon the ownership percentage held by the recipient corporation. §§ 243–246.

Divisive reorganization. A "Type D" spin-off, split-off, or split-up reorganization in which the original corporation divides its active business (in existence for at least five years) assets among two or more corporations. The stock received by the original corporation shareholders must be at least 80 percent of the other corporations.

Dock sales. A purchaser uses its owned or rented vehicles to take possession of the product at the seller's shipping dock. In most states, the sale is apportioned to the operating state of the purchaser, rather than the seller. See also *apportion* and *sales factor*.

Dollar-value LIFO. An inventory technique that focuses on the dollars invested in the inventory rather than the particular items on hand each period. Each inventory item is assigned to a pool. A pool is a collection of similar items and is treated as a separate inventory. At the end of the period, each pool is valued in terms of prices at the time LIFO was adopted (base period prices), whether or not the particular items were actually on hand in the year LIFO was adopted, to compare with current prices to determine if there has been an increase or decrease in inventories.

E

Earned income credit. A tax credit designed to provide assistance to certain low-income individuals who generally have a qualifying child. This is a refundable credit. To receive the most beneficial treatment, the taxpayer must have qualifying children. However, it is possible to qualify for the credit without having a child. See the text chapter on credits for the computation procedure required in order to determine the amount of the credit allowed.

Earnings and profits (E & P). Measures the economic capacity of a corporation to make a distribution to shareholders that is not a return of capital. Such a distribution results in dividend income to the shareholders to the extent of the corporation's current and accumulated earnings and profits.

Economic effect test. Requirements that must be met before a special allocation may be used by a partnership. The premise behind the test is that each partner who receives an allocation of income or loss from a partnership bears the economic benefit or burden of the allocation.

Economic income. The change in the taxpayer's net worth, as measured in terms of market values, plus the value of the assets the taxpayer consumed during the year. Because of the impracticality of this income model, it is not used for tax purposes.

Economic performance test. One of the requirements that must be satisfied for an accrual basis taxpayer to deduct an expense. Economic performance occurs when property or services are provided to the taxpayer, or in the case in which the taxpayer is required to provide property or services, whenever the property or services are actually provided by the taxpayer.

Education expenses. Employees may deduct education expenses that are incurred either (1) to maintain or improve existing job-related skills or (2) to meet the express requirements of the employer or the requirements imposed by law to retain employment status. The expenses are not deductible if the education is required to meet the minimum educational standards for the taxpayer's job or if the education qualifies the individual for a new trade or business. Reg. § 1.162–5.

Educational savings bonds. U.S. Series EE bonds whose proceeds are used for qualified higher educational expenses for the taxpayer, the taxpayer's spouse, or a dependent. The interest may be excluded from gross income, provided the taxpayer's adjusted gross income does not exceed certain amounts. § 135.

Effective tax rate. The financial statements for an entity include several footnotes, one of which reconciles the expected (statutory) income tax rate (e.g., 21 percent for a C corporation) with the effective tax rate (i.e., total tax expense as a percentage of book income). The reconciliation often is done in dollar and/or percentage terms.

Effectively connected income. Income of a nonresident alien or foreign corporation that is attributable to the operation of a U.S. trade or business under either the asset-use or the business-activities test.

E-file. The electronic filing of a tax return. The filing is either direct or indirect. In direct filing, the taxpayer goes online using a computer and tax return preparation software. Indirect filing occurs when a taxpayer utilizes an authorized IRS e-file provider. The provider often is the *tax preparer*.

E-filing. See *e-file*.

Employment taxes. Taxes that an employer must pay on account of its employees. Employment taxes include FICA (Federal Insurance Contributions Act) and FUTA (Federal Unemployment Tax Act) taxes. Employment taxes are paid to the IRS in addition to income tax withholdings at specified intervals. Such taxes can be levied on the employees, the employer, or both.

Energy credits. See *energy tax credits*.

Energy tax credits. Various tax credits are available to those who invest in certain energy property. The purpose of the credit is to create incentives for conservation and to develop alternative energy sources.

Enrolled agents (EAs). A tax practitioner who has gained admission to practice before the IRS by passing an IRS examination and maintaining a required level of continuing professional education.

Entertainment expenses. Expenses that are deductible only if they are directly related to or associated with a trade or business. Various restrictions and documentation requirements have been imposed upon the deductibility of entertainment expenses to prevent abuses by taxpayers. The TCJA of 2017 repealed the deduction for entertainment expenses paid or incurred after 2017. § 274.

Entity accounting income. Entity accounting income is not identical to the taxable income of a trust or estate, nor is it determined in the same manner as the entity's financial accounting income would be. The trust document or will determines whether certain income, expenses, gains, or losses are allocated to the corpus of the entity or to the entity's income beneficiaries. Only the items that are allocated to the income beneficiaries are included in entity accounting income.

Entity buy-sell agreement. An arrangement whereby the entity is to purchase a withdrawing owner's interest. When the entity is a corporation, the agreement generally involves a stock redemption on the part of the withdrawing shareholder. See also *buy-sell agreement* and *cross-purchase buy-sell agreement*.

Entity concept. A perspective taken toward a venture that regards the venture as an entity separate and distinct from its owners. For tax purposes, this results in the venture being directly responsible for the tax on the income it generates. The entity perspective taken toward C corporations results in the double taxation of income distributed to the corporation's owners.

Entity perspective. See *entity concept*.

Estate tax. A tax imposed on the right to transfer property by death. Thus, an estate tax is levied on the decedent's estate and not on the heir receiving the property.

Estimated tax. The amount of tax (including alternative minimum tax and self-employment tax) a taxpayer expects to owe for the year after subtracting tax credits and income tax withheld. The estimated tax must be paid in installments at designated intervals (e.g., for a calendar year individual taxpayer, by April 15, June 15, September 15, and January 15 of the following year).

Excess business loss. The excess of aggregate deductions of the taxpayer attributable to trades or businesses of the taxpayer over the sum of aggregate gross income or gain of the taxpayer plus a threshold amount. In 2020, the threshold amount is $259,000 ($518,000 in the case of a married taxpayer filing a joint return). The threshold amount is adjusted for inflation each year. This loss limitation applies to taxpayers other than C corporations and applies after the passive activity loss limitation of § 469. § 461(l).

Excess lobbying expenditures. An excise tax is applied on otherwise tax-exempt organizations with respect to the excess of total lobbying expenditures over grass roots lobbying expenditures for the year.

Excess loss account. When a subsidiary has generated more historical losses than its parent has invested in the entity, the parent's basis in the subsidiary is zero, and the parent records additional losses in an excess loss account. This treatment allows the parent to continue to deduct losses of the subsidiary, even where no basis reduction is possible, while avoiding the need to show a negative stock basis on various financial records. If the subsidiary stock is sold while an excess loss account exists, capital gain income usually is recognized to the extent of the balance in the account.

Excise taxes. A tax on the manufacture, sale, or use of goods; on the carrying on of an occupation or activity; or on the transfer of property. Thus, the Federal estate and gift taxes are, theoretically, excise taxes.

Exclusion amount. The value of assets that is exempt from transfer tax due to the credit allowed for gifts or transfers by death. For gifts and deaths in 2020, the exclusion amount is $11.58 million. An exclusion amount unused by a deceased spouse may be used by the surviving spouse. See also *exemption equivalent amount.*

Exempt organizations. An organization that is either partially or completely exempt from Federal income taxation. § 501.

Exemption amount. An amount deducted from alternative minimum taxable income (AMTI) to determine the alternative minimum tax base. The exemption amount is phased out when AMTI exceeds specified threshold amounts. § 55(d).

Exemption equivalent. The maximum value of assets that can be transferred to another party without incurring any Federal gift or estate tax. See also *exemption equivalent amount.*

Exemption equivalent amount. The nontaxable amount (in 2020, $11.58 million for gift tax and estate tax) that is the equivalent of the unified transfer tax credit allowed.

F

Fair market value. The amount at which property would change hands between a willing buyer and a willing seller, neither being under any compulsion to buy or to sell and both having reasonable knowledge of the relevant facts. Reg. §§ 1.1001–1(a) and 20.2031–1(b).

Farm price method. A method of accounting for agricultural crops. The inventory of crops is valued at its market price less the estimated cost of disposition (e.g., freight and selling expense).

Feeder organization. An entity that carries on a trade or business for the benefit of an exempt organization. However, such a relationship does not result in the feeder organization itself being tax-exempt. § 502.

FICA tax. An abbreviation that stands for Federal Insurance Contributions Act, commonly referred to as the Social Security tax. The FICA tax is comprised of the Social Security tax (old age, survivors, and disability insurance) and the Medicare tax (hospital insurance) and is imposed on both employers and employees. The employer is responsible for withholding from the employee's wages the Social Security tax at a rate of 6.2 percent on a maximum wage base and the Medicare tax at a rate of 1.45 percent (no maximum wage base). The maximum Social Security wage base for 2020 is $137,700 and for 2019 is $132,900.

Fiduciary. One who holds a legal obligation to act on another's behalf. A *trustee* and an *executor* take fiduciary relationships relative to the *grantor* and the *decedent*, respectively. The fiduciary is assigned specific duties by the principal party (e.g., to file tax returns, manage assets, satisfy debt and other obligations, and to make investment decisions). The fiduciary often possesses specialized knowledge and experience. A fiduciary must avoid conflicts of interest in which the principal's goals are compromised in some way.

Field audit. An audit conducted by the IRS on the business premises of the taxpayer or in the office of the tax practitioner representing the taxpayer.

Filing status. Individual taxpayers are placed in one of five filing statuses each year (single, married filing jointly, married filing separately, surviving spouse, or head of household). Marital status and household support are key determinants. Filing status is used to determine the taxpayer's filing requirements, standard deduction, eligibility for certain deductions and credits, and tax liability.

Final Regulations. The U.S. Treasury Department Regulations (abbreviated Reg.) represent the position of the IRS as to how the Internal Revenue Code is to be interpreted. Their purpose is to provide taxpayers and IRS personnel with rules of general and specific application to the various provisions of the tax law. Regulations are published in the *Federal Register* and in all tax services.

Financial Accounting Standards Board (FASB). See *Generally Accepted Accounting Principles (GAAP).*

Financial transaction tax. A tax imposed on some type of financial transaction, such as stock sales.

Fiscal year. A 12-month period ending on the last day of a month other than December. In certain circumstances, a taxpayer is permitted to elect a fiscal year instead of being required to use a calendar year.

Flat tax. A form of consumption tax designed to alleviate the regressivity of a value added tax (VAT). It is imposed on individuals and businesses at the same single (flat) rate.

Flexible spending plans. An employee benefit plan that allows the employee to take a reduction in salary in exchange for the employer paying benefits that can be provided by the employer without the employee being required to recognize income (e.g., medical and child care benefits). Contributions to a flexible spending plan are limited to $2,750 for 2020. § 125(i).

Flow-through entity. The entity is a tax reporter rather than a taxpayer. The owners are subject to tax. Examples are partnerships, S corporations, and limited liability companies.

Foreign earned income exclusion. The Code allows exclusions for earned income generated outside the United States to alleviate any tax base and rate disparities among countries. In addition, the exclusion is allowed for housing expenditures incurred by the taxpayer's employer with respect to the non-U.S. assignment, and self-employed individuals can deduct foreign housing expenses incurred in a trade or business. The exclusion is limited to $107,600 per year for 2020 ($105,900 in 2019). § 911.

Foreign Investment in Real Property Tax Act (FIRPTA). Under the Foreign Investment in Real Property Tax Act, gains or losses realized by nonresident aliens and non-U.S. corporations on the disposition of U.S. real estate creates U.S. source income and are subject to U.S. income tax.

Foreign tax credit (FTC). A U.S. citizen or resident who incurs or pays income taxes to a foreign country on income subject to U.S. tax may be able to claim some of these taxes as a credit against the U.S. income tax. §§ 27 and 901–905.

Franchise. An agreement that gives the transferee the right to distribute, sell, or provide goods, services, or facilities within a specified area. The cost of obtaining a franchise may be amortized over a statutory period of 15 years. In general, the franchisor's gain on the sale of franchise rights is an ordinary gain because the franchisor retains a significant power, right, or continuing interest in the subject of the franchise. §§ 197 and 1253.

Franchise tax. A tax levied on the right to do business in a state as a corporation. Although income considerations may come into play, the tax usually is based on the capitalization of the corporation.

Fraud. Tax fraud falls into two categories: civil and criminal. Under civil fraud, the IRS may impose as a penalty an amount equal to as much as 75 percent of the underpayment [§ 6651(f)]. Fines and/or imprisonment are prescribed for conviction of various types of criminal tax fraud (§§ 7201–7207). Both civil and criminal fraud involve a specific intent on the part of the taxpayer to evade the tax; mere negligence is not enough. Criminal fraud requires the additional element of willfulness (i.e., done deliberately and with evil purpose). In practice, it becomes difficult to distinguish between the degree of intent necessary to support criminal, rather than civil, fraud. In either situation, the IRS has the burden of proof to show the taxpayer committed fraud.

Fringe benefits. Compensation or other benefit received by an employee that is not in the form of cash. Some fringe benefits (e.g., accident and health plans, group term life insurance) may be excluded from the employee's gross income and therefore are not subject to the Federal income tax.

Fruit and tree metaphor. The courts have held that an individual who earns income from property or services cannot assign that income to another. For example, a father cannot assign his earnings from commissions to his child and escape income tax on those amounts.

Functional currency. The currency of the economic environment in which the taxpayer carries on most of its activities and in which the taxpayer transacts most of its business.

FUTA tax. An employment tax levied on employers. Jointly administered by the Federal and state governments, the tax provides funding for unemployment benefits. FUTA applies at a rate of 6.0 percent on the first $7,000 of covered wages paid during the year for each employee. The Federal government allows a credit for FUTA paid (or allowed under a merit rating system) to the state. The credit cannot exceed 5.4 percent of the covered wages.

Future interest. An interest that will come into being at some future time. It is distinguished from a present interest, which already exists. Assume that Dan transfers securities to a newly created trust. Under the terms of the trust instrument, income from the securities is to be paid each year to Wilma for her life, with the securities passing to Sam upon Wilma's death. Wilma has a present interest in the trust because she is entitled to current income distributions. Sam has a future interest because he must wait for Wilma's death to benefit from the trust. The annual exclusion of $15,000 (in 2020) is not allowed for a gift of a future interest. § 2503(b).

G

General business credit. The summation of various nonrefundable business credits, including the tax credit for rehabilitation expenditures, business energy credit, work opportunity credit, research activities credit, low-income housing credit, and disabled access credit. The amount of general business credit that can be used to reduce the tax liability is limited to the taxpayer's net income tax reduced by the greater of (1) the tentative minimum tax or (2) 25 percent of the net regular tax liability that exceeds $25,000. Unused general business credits can be carried back one year and forward 20 years. § 38.

General partners. A partner who is fully liable in an individual capacity for the debts owed by the partnership to third parties. A general partner's liability is not limited to the investment in the partnership. See also *limited partners*.

General partnership (GP). A partnership that is owned by general partners (only). Creditors of a general partnership can collect amounts owed them from both the partnership assets and the assets of the partners individually.

Generally Accepted Accounting Principles (GAAP). Guidelines relating to how to construct the financial statements of enterprises doing business in the United States. Promulgated chiefly by the Financial Accounting Standards Board (FASB).

Gift tax. A tax imposed on the transfer of property by gift. The tax is imposed upon the donor of a gift and is based on the fair market value of the property on the date of the gift.

Golden parachute payments. A severance payment to employees that meets the following requirements: (1) the payment is contingent on a change of ownership of a corporation through a stock or asset acquisition and (2) the aggregate present value of the payment equals or exceeds three times the employee's average annual compensation. To the extent the severance payment meets these conditions, a deduction is disallowed to the employer for the excess of the payment over a statutory base amount (a five-year average of compensation if the taxpayer was an employee for the entire five-year period). In addition, a 20 percent excise tax is imposed on the employee who receives the excess severance pay. §§ 280G and 4999.

Goodwill. The reputation and other unidentifiable intangible assets of a company. For accounting purposes, goodwill has no basis unless it is purchased. In the purchase of a business, goodwill generally is the difference between the purchase price and the fair market value of the assets acquired. The intangible asset goodwill can be amortized for tax purposes over a 15-year period. § 197 and Reg. § 1.167(a)–3.

Grantor. A transferor of property. The creator of a trust is usually referred to as the grantor of the entity.

Grantor trust. A trust under which the grantor retains control over the income or corpus (or both) to such an extent that he or she is treated as the owner of the property and its income for income tax purposes. Income from a grantor trust is taxable to the grantor and not to the beneficiary who receives it. §§ 671–679.

Grass roots expenditures. Exempt organizations are prohibited from engaging in political activities, but spending incurred to influence the opinions of the general public relative to specific legislation is permitted by the law.

Gross estate. The property owned or previously transferred by a decedent that is subject to the Federal estate tax. The gross estate can be distinguished from the probate estate, which is property actually subject to administration by the administrator or executor of an estate. §§ 2031–2046.

Gross income. Income subject to the Federal income tax. Gross income does not include all economic income. That is, certain exclusions are allowed (e.g., interest on municipal bonds). For a manufacturing or merchandising business, gross income usually means gross profit (gross sales or gross receipts less cost of goods sold). § 61 and Reg. § 1.61–3(a).

Group term life insurance. Life insurance coverage provided by an employer for a group of employees. Such insurance is renewable on a year-to-year basis, and typically no cash surrender value is built up. The premiums paid by the employer on the insurance are not taxed to the employees on coverage of up to $50,000 per person. § 79 and Reg. § 1.79–1(b).

Guaranteed payments. Payments made by a partnership to a partner for services rendered or for the use of capital to the extent the payments are determined without regard to the income of the partnership. The payments are treated as though they were made to a nonpartner and thus are deducted by the entity. A guaranteed payment might be subject to self-employment tax (guaranteed payment for services) or net-investment income tax (guaranteed payment for capital). Guaranteed payments are not eligible for the qualified business income deduction.

H

Half-year convention. A cost recovery convention that assumes that property is placed in service at mid-year and thus provides for a half-year's cost recovery for that year.

Head of household. An unmarried individual who maintains a household for another and satisfies certain conditions set forth in § 2(b). This status enables the taxpayer to use a set of income tax rates that are lower than those applicable to other unmarried individuals but higher than those applicable to surviving spouses and married persons filing a joint return.

Health Savings Account (HSA). A medical savings account created in legislation enacted in December 2003 that is designed to replace and expand Archer Medical Savings Accounts.

Highly compensated employee. The employee group is generally divided into two categories for fringe benefit (including pension and profit sharing plans) purposes. These are (1) highly compensated employees and (2) non-highly compensated employees. For most fringe benefits, if the fringe benefit plan discriminates in favor of highly compensated employees, it will not be a qualified plan with respect, at a minimum, to the highly compensated employees.

Historic business test. In a corporate reorganization, a means by which to determine if the continuity of business enterprise requirement is met. The acquiring corporation must continue to operate the target entity's existing business(es) going forward; if this is not the case, the requirement is failed.

Hobby losses. Losses from an activity not engaged in for profit. The Code restricts the amount of losses that an individual can deduct for hobby activities so that these transactions cannot be used to offset income from other sources. The TCJA of 2017 suspended the deduction of hobby expenses for tax years after 2017 (and through 2025). § 183.

Holding period. The period of time during which property has been held for income tax purposes. The holding period is significant in determining whether gain or loss from the sale or exchange of a capital asset is long or short term. § 1223.

Home equity loans. Loans that utilize the personal residence of the taxpayer as security. The interest on such loans is deductible as qualified residence interest. However, interest is deductible only on the portion of the loan that does not exceed the lesser of (1) the fair market value of the residence, reduced by the acquisition indebtedness, or (2) $100,000 ($50,000 for married persons filing separate returns). A major benefit of a home equity loan is that there are no tracing rules regarding the use of the loan proceeds. The TCJA of 2017 suspended the deduction of interest on home equity indebtedness for tax years after 2017 (and through 2025). § 163(h)(3).

Hot assets. Unrealized receivables and substantially appreciated inventory under § 751. When hot assets are present, the sale of a partnership interest or the disproportionate distribution of the assets can cause ordinary income to be recognized.

Hybrid method. A combination of the accrual and cash methods of accounting. That is, the taxpayer may account for some items of income on the accrual method (e.g., sales and cost of goods sold) and other items (e.g., interest income) on the cash method.

I

Imputed interest. For certain long-term sales of property, under §§ 483 and 1274 the IRS can convert some of the gain from the sale into interest income if the contract does not provide for a minimum rate of interest to be paid by the purchaser. The seller recognizes less long-term capital gain and more ordinary income (interest income). Imputed interest rules also apply on certain below-market loans under § 7872.

Inbound taxation. U.S. tax effects when a non-U.S. person begins an investment or business activity in the United States.

Incentive stock options (ISOs). A type of stock option that receives favorable tax treatment. If various qualification requirements can be satisfied, stock option grants do not create taxable income for the recipient. However, the spread (the excess of the fair market value at the date of exercise over the option price) is an adjustment item for purposes of the alternative minimum tax (AMT). The gain on disposition of the stock resulting from the exercise of the stock option will be classified as long-term capital gain if certain holding period requirements are met (the employee must not dispose of the stock within two years after the option is granted or within one year after acquiring the stock). § 422.

Income. For tax purposes, an increase in wealth that has been realized.

Income in respect of a decedent (IRD). Income earned by a decedent at the time of death but not reportable on the final income tax return because of the method of accounting that appropriately is utilized. Such income is included in the gross estate and is taxed to the eventual recipient (either the estate or heirs). The recipient is, however, allowed an income tax deduction for the estate tax attributable to the income. § 691.

Income tax provision. Under ASC 740, a synonym for the book tax expense of an entity for the financial reporting period. Following the "matching principle," all book tax expense that relates to the net income for the reporting period is reported on that period's financial statements, including not only the current tax expense but also any deferred tax expense and deferred tax benefit.

Income tax treaties. See *tax treaties.*

Independent contractor. A self-employed person as distinguished from one who is employed as an employee.

Indexation. A procedure whereby adjustments are made by the IRS to key tax components (e.g., standard deduction, tax brackets, personal and dependency exemptions) to reflect inflation. The adjustments usually are made annually and are based on the change in the consumer price index.

Individual Retirement Accounts (IRAs). A type of retirement plan to which an individual with earned income can contribute a statutory maximum of $6,000 in 2020. IRAs can be classified as traditional IRAs or Roth IRAs. With a traditional IRA, an individual can contribute and deduct a maximum of $6,000 per tax year in 2020. The deduction is a deduction *for* AGI. However, if the individual is an active participant in another qualified retirement plan, the deduction is phased out proportionally between certain AGI ranges (note that the phaseout limits the amount of the deduction and not the amount of the contribution). With a Roth IRA, an individual can contribute a maximum of $6,000 per tax year in 2020. No deduction is permitted. However, if a five-year holding period requirement is satisfied and if the distribution is a qualified distribution, the taxpayer can make tax-free withdrawals from a Roth IRA. The maximum annual contribution is phased out proportionally between certain AGI ranges. §§ 219 and 408A.

Inheritance tax. A tax imposed on the right to receive property from a decedent. Thus, theoretically, an inheritance tax is imposed on the heir. The Federal estate tax is imposed on the estate.

Inside basis. A partnership's basis in the assets it owns.

Installment method. A method of accounting enabling certain taxpayers to spread the recognition of gain on the sale of property over the collection period. Under this procedure, the seller arrives at the gain to be recognized by computing the gross profit percentage from the sale (the gain divided by the contract price) and applying it to each payment received. § 453.

Intangible drilling and development costs (IDCs). Taxpayers may elect to expense or capitalize (subject to amortization) intangible drilling and development costs. However, ordinary income recapture provisions apply to oil and gas properties on a sale or other disposition if the expense method is elected. §§ 263(c) and 1254(a).

Intermediate sanctions. The IRS can assess excise taxes on disqualified persons and organization management associated with so-called public charities engaging in excess benefit transactions. An excess benefit transaction is one in which a disqualified person engages in a non-fair market value transaction with the exempt organization or receives unreasonable compensation. Prior to the enactment of intermediate sanctions, the only option available to the IRS was to revoke the organization's exempt status.

International Accounting Standards Board (IASB). The body that promulgates International Financial Reporting Standards (IFRS). Based in London, representing accounting standard setting bodies in over 100 countries, the IASB develops accounting standards that can serve as the basis for harmonizing conflicting reporting standards among nations.

International Financial Reporting Standards (IFRS). Produced by the International Accounting Standards Board (IASB), guidelines developed since 2001 as to revenue recognition, accounting for business combinations, and a conceptual framework for financial reporting. IFRS provisions are designed so that they can be used by all entities, regardless of where they are based or conduct business. IFRS have gained widespread acceptance throughout the world, and the SEC is considering how to require U.S. entities to use IFRS in addition to, or in lieu of, the accounting rules of the Financial Accounting Standards Board.

Interpretive Regulations. A Regulation issued by the Treasury Department that purports to explain the meaning of a particular Code Section. An interpretive Regulation is given less deference than a legislative Regulation.

Inventory. Under § 1221(a)(1), a taxpayer's stock in trade or property held for resale. For partnership tax purposes, inventory is defined in § 751(d) as inventory (per the above definition) or any partnership asset other than capital or § 1231 assets. See also *appreciated inventory*.

Investment income. Consisting of virtually the same elements as portfolio income, a measure by which to justify a deduction for interest on investment indebtedness.

Investment interest. Payment for the use of funds used to acquire assets that produce investment income. The deduction for investment interest is limited to net investment income for the tax year.

Investor loss. Losses on stock and securities. If stocks and bonds are capital assets in the hands of the holder, a capital loss materializes as of the last day of the taxable year in which the stocks or bonds become worthless. Under certain circumstances involving stocks and bonds of affiliated corporations, an ordinary loss is permitted upon worthlessness.

Involuntary conversion. The loss or destruction of property through theft, casualty, or condemnation. Gain realized on an involuntary conversion can, at the taxpayer's election, be deferred for Federal income tax purposes if the owner reinvests the proceeds within a prescribed period of time in property that is similar or related in service or use. § 1033.

Itemized deductions. Personal expenditures allowed by the Code as deductions from adjusted gross income. Examples include certain medical expenses, interest on home mortgages, state income taxes, and charitable contributions. Itemized deductions are reported on Schedule A of Form 1040.

J

Joint tenants. Two or more persons having undivided ownership of property with the right of survivorship. Right of survivorship gives the surviving owner full ownership of the property. Suppose Bob and Tami are joint tenants of a tract of land. Upon Bob's death, Tami becomes the sole owner of the property. For the estate tax consequences upon the death of a joint tenant, see § 2040.

K

Keogh plans. Retirement plans available to self-employed taxpayers. They are also referred to as H.R. 10 plans. Under such plans, a taxpayer may deduct each year up to 100 percent of net earnings from self-employment or $57,000 for 2020, whichever is less. If the plan is a profit sharing plan, the percentage is 25 percent.

Kiddie tax. Passive income, such as interest and dividends, that is recognized by a child under age 19 (or under age 24 if a full-time student) is taxed according to the brackets applicable to the child's parent(s), generally to the extent the income exceeds $2,200 for 2020. The additional tax is assessed regardless of the source of the income or the income's underlying property. § 1(g).

L

Least aggregate deferral method. An algorithm set forth in the Regulations to determine the tax year for a partnership or limited liability entity with owners whose tax years differ. The tax year selected is the one that produces the least aggregate deferral of income for the owners.

Least aggregate deferral rule. See *least aggregate deferral method*.

Legislative Regulations. Some Code Sections give the Secretary of the Treasury or his delegate the authority to prescribe Regulations to carry out the details of administration or to otherwise complete the operating rules. Regulations issued pursuant to this type of authority truly possess the force and effect of law. In effect, Congress is almost delegating its legislative powers to the Treasury Department.

Lessee. One who rents property from another. In the case of real estate, the lessee is also known as the tenant.

Lessor. One who rents property to another. In the case of real estate, the lessor is also known as the landlord.

Letter ruling. The written response of the IRS to a taxpayer's request for interpretation of the revenue laws with respect to a proposed transaction (e.g., concerning the tax-free status of a reorganization). Not to be relied on as precedent by other than the party who requested the ruling.

Liabilities in excess of basis. On the contribution of capital to a corporation, an investor recognizes gain on the exchange to the extent contributed assets carry liabilities with a face amount in excess of the tax basis of the contributed assets. This rule keeps the investor from holding the investment asset received with a negative basis. § 357(c).

Life insurance proceeds. A specified sum (the face value or maturity value of the policy) paid to the designated beneficiary of the policy by the life insurance company upon the death of the insured.

Lifetime learning credit. A tax credit for qualifying expenses for taxpayers pursuing education beyond the first two years of postsecondary education. Individuals who are completing their last two years of undergraduate studies, pursuing graduate or professional degrees, or otherwise seeking new job skills or maintaining existing job skills are all eligible for the credit. Eligible individuals include the taxpayer, taxpayer's spouse, and taxpayer's dependents. The maximum credit is 20 percent of the first $10,000 of qualifying expenses and is computed per taxpayer. The credit is phased out for higher-income taxpayers. § 25A.

Like-kind exchanges. An exchange of real property held for productive use in a trade or business or for investment for other investment or trade or business real property. Unless non-like-kind property (boot) is received, the exchange is fully tax-deferred. § 1031.

Limited liability company (LLC). A legal entity in which all owners are protected from the entity's debts but which may lack other characteristics of a corporation (i.e., centralized management, unlimited life, free transferability of interests). LLCs generally are treated as partnerships (or disregarded entities if they have only one owner) for tax purposes.

Limited liability partnership (LLP). A legal entity allowed by many of the states, where a general partnership registers with the state as an LLP. All partners are at risk with respect to any contractual liabilities of the entity as well as any liabilities arising from their own malpractice or torts or those of their subordinates. However, all partners are protected from any liabilities resulting from the malpractice or torts of other partners.

Limited partners. A partner whose liability to third-party creditors of the partnership is limited to the amounts invested in the partnership. See also *general partners* and *limited partnership (LP)*.

Limited partnership (LP). A partnership in which some of the partners are limited partners. At least one of the partners in a limited partnership must be a general partner.

Liquidating distribution. A distribution by a partnership that is in complete liquidation of the entity's trade or business activities or in complete liquidation of a partner's interest in the partnership. A liquidating distribution is generally a tax-deferred transaction if it is proportionate with respect to the partnership's hot assets. In a proportionate liquidating distribution, the partnership recognizes no gain or loss. The partner only recognizes gain if the distributed cash (and cash equivalents, such as debt relief or certain marketable securities) exceeds the partner's basis in the partnership. The partner recognizes a loss if *only* cash and hot assets are distributed and their combined inside (partnership) basis is less than the partner's basis in the partnership interest. In any case where no gain or loss is recognized, the partner's basis in the partnership interest is fully assigned to the basis of the assets received in the distribution.

Listed property. Property that includes (1) any passenger automobile; (2) any other property used as a means of transportation; (3) any property of a type generally used for purposes of entertainment, recreation, or amusement; and (4) any other property of a type specified in the Regulations. If listed property is predominantly used for business, the taxpayer is allowed to use the statutory percentage method of cost recovery. Otherwise, the straight-line cost recovery method must be used. § 280F.

Lobbying expenditures. An expenditure made for the purpose of influencing legislation. Such payments can result in the loss of the exempt status of, and the imposition of Federal income tax on, an exempt organization. Lobby expenditures are not deductible.

Long-term care insurance. Insurance that helps pay the cost of care when the insured is unable to care for himself or herself. Such insurance is generally thought of as insurance against the cost of an aged person entering a nursing home. The employer can provide the insurance, and the premiums may be excluded from the employee's gross income. § 7702B.

Long-term contract. A building, installation, construction, or manufacturing contract that is entered into but not completed within the same tax year. A manufacturing contract is a long-term contract only if the contract is to manufacture (1) a unique item not normally carried in finished goods inventory or (2) items that normally require more than 12 calendar months to complete. The two available methods to account for long-term contracts are the percentage of completion method and the completed contract method. The completed contract method can be used only in limited circumstances. § 460.

Long-term nonpersonal use capital assets. Includes investment property with a long-term holding period. Such property disposed of by casualty or theft may receive § 1231 treatment.

Long-term tax-exempt rate. Used in deriving the yearly limitation on net operating loss and other tax benefits that carry over from the target to the acquiring when there is a more than 50-percentage-point ownership change (by value). The highest of the Federal long-term interest rates in effect for any of the last three months. § 382.

Lower of cost or market (replacement cost). An elective inventory method, whereby the taxpayer may value inventories at the lower of the taxpayer's actual cost or the current replacement cost of the goods. This method cannot be used in conjunction with the LIFO inventory method.

Low-income housing credit. Beneficial treatment to owners of low-income housing is provided in the form of a tax credit. The calculated credit is claimed in the year the building is placed in service and in the following nine years. § 42.

Lump-sum distribution. Payment of the entire amount due at one time rather than in installments. Such distributions often occur from qualified pension or profit sharing plans upon the retirement or death of a covered employee. The recipient of a lump-sum distribution may recognize both long-term capital gain and ordinary income upon the receipt of the distribution. The ordinary income portion may be subject to a special 10-year income averaging provision. § 402(e).

M

Majority interest partners. Partners who have more than a 50 percent interest in partnership profits and capital, counting only those partners who have the same taxable year. The term is of significance in determining the appropriate taxable year of a partnership. § 706(b).

Marital deduction. A deduction allowed against the taxable estate or taxable gifts upon the transfer of property from one spouse to another.

Marriage penalty. The additional tax liability that results for a married couple when compared with what their tax liability would be if they were not married and filed separate returns.

Matching rule. Treatment of an intercompany transaction on a consolidated return, when a sold asset remains within the group.

Material participation. If an individual taxpayer materially participates in a nonrental trade or business activity, any loss from that activity is treated as an active loss that can be offset against active income. Material participation is achieved by meeting any one of seven tests provided in the Regulations. § 469(h).

Meaningful reduction test. A decrease in the shareholder's voting control. Used to determine whether a stock redemption qualifies for sale or exchange treatment.

Medical expenses. Medical expenses of an individual, a spouse, and dependents are allowed as an itemized deduction to the extent such amounts (less insurance reimbursements) exceed 7.5 percent of adjusted gross income. § 213.

Merger. The absorption of one corporation by another with the corporation being absorbed losing its legal identity. Flow Corporation is merged into Jobs Corporation, and the shareholders of Flow receive stock in Jobs in exchange for their stock in Flow. After the merger, Flow ceases to exist as a separate legal entity. If a merger meets certain conditions, it is not currently taxable to the parties involved. § 368(a)(1).

Mid-month convention. A cost recovery convention that assumes that property is placed in service in the middle of the month that it is actually placed in service.

Mid-quarter convention. A cost recovery convention that assumes that property placed in service during the year is placed in service at the middle of the quarter in which it is actually placed in service. The mid-quarter convention applies if more than 40 percent of the value of property (other than eligible real estate) is placed in service during the last quarter of the year.

Miscellaneous itemized deductions. A special category of itemized deductions that includes expenses such as professional dues, tax return preparation fees, job-hunting costs, unreimbursed employee business expenses, and certain investment expenses. Such expenses are deductible only to the extent they exceed 2 percent of adjusted gross income. The TCJA of 2017 suspended the deduction for these items for tax years after 2017 (and through 2025). § 67.

Modified accelerated cost recovery system (MACRS). A method in which the cost of tangible property is recovered over a prescribed period of time. Enacted by the Economic Recovery Tax Act (ERTA) of 1981 and substantially modified by the Tax Reform Act (TRA) of 1986, the method disregards salvage value, imposes a period of cost recovery that depends upon the classification of the asset into one of various recovery periods, and prescribes the applicable percentage of cost that can be deducted each year. § 168.

Multiple support agreement. To qualify for a dependency exemption, the support test must be satisfied. This requires that over 50 percent of the support of the potential dependent be provided by the taxpayer. Where no one person provides more than 50 percent of the support, a multiple support agreement enables a taxpayer to still qualify for the dependency exemption. Any person who contributed more than 10 percent of the support is entitled to claim the exemption if each person in the group who contributed more than 10 percent files a written consent (Form 2120). Each person who is a party to the multiple support agreement must meet all of the other requirements for claiming the dependency exemption. § 152(c).

Multistate Tax Commission (MTC). A regulatory body of the states that develops operating rules and regulations for the implementation of the UDITPA and other provisions that assign the total taxable income of a multistate corporation to specific states.

N

National sales tax. Intended as a replacement for the current Federal income tax. Unlike a value added tax (VAT), which is levied on the manufacturer, it would be imposed on the consumer upon the final sale of goods and services. To reduce regressivity, individuals would receive a rebate to offset a portion of the tax.

Negligence. Failure to exercise the reasonable or ordinary degree of care of a prudent person in a situation that results in harm or damage to another. A penalty is assessed on taxpayers who exhibit negligence or intentional disregard of rules and Regulations with respect to the underpayment of certain taxes.

Net capital gain (NCG). The excess of the net long-term capital gain for the tax year over the net short-term capital loss. The net capital gain of an individual taxpayer is eligible for the alternative tax. § 1222(11).

Net capital loss (NCL). The excess of the losses from sales or exchanges of capital assets over the gains from sales or exchanges of such assets. Up to $3,000 per year of the net capital loss may be deductible by noncorporate taxpayers against ordinary income. The excess net capital loss carries over to future tax years. For corporate taxpayers, the net capital loss cannot be offset against ordinary income, but it can be carried back three years and forward five years to offset net capital gains. §§ 1211, 1212, and 1221(10).

Net investment income. The excess of investment income over investment expenses. Investment expenses are those deductible expenses directly connected with the production of investment income. Investment expenses do not include investment interest. The deduction for investment interest for the tax year is limited to net investment income. § 163(d).

Net operating loss (NOL). To mitigate the effect of the annual accounting period concept, § 172 allows taxpayers to use an excess loss of one year as a deduction for certain past or future years. In this regard, a carryback period of 2 (or more) years and a carryforward period of 20 years are allowed for NOLs generated before 2018. There is no carryback period and an indefinite carryforward period for NOLs arising in tax years beginning after 2017, and such NOLs are subject to an 80 percent of taxable income limitation in any carryforward year.

Nexus. The degree of activity that must be present before a taxing jurisdiction has the right to impose a tax on an out-of-state entity. The rules for income tax nexus are not the same as for sales tax nexus.

Ninety-day (90-day) letter. This notice is sent to a taxpayer upon request, upon the expiration of the 30-day letter, or upon exhaustion by the taxpayer of his or her administrative remedies before the IRS. The notice gives the taxpayer 90 days in which to file a petition with the U.S. Tax Court. If a petition is not filed, the IRS will demand payment of the assessed deficiency. §§ 6211–6216.

No-additional-cost service. Services the employer may provide the employee at no additional cost to the employer. Generally, the benefit is the ability to utilize the employer's excess capacity (e.g., vacant seats on an airliner). Such amounts are excludible from the recipient's gross income.

Nonaccountable plan. An expense reimbursement plan that does not have an accountability feature. The result is that employee expenses are not deductible.

Nonacquiescence. Disagreement by the IRS on the result reached in certain judicial decisions. *Nonacq.* or *NA.*

Nonbusiness bad debt. A bad debt loss that is not incurred in connection with a creditor's trade or business. The loss is classified as a short-term capital loss and is allowed only in the year the debt becomes entirely worthless. In addition to family loans, many investor losses are nonbusiness bad debts. § 166(d).

Nonqualified deferred compensation (NQDC). Compensation arrangements that are frequently offered to executives. Such plans may include stock options or annuities upon separation, for example. Often, an executive may defer the recognition of taxable income. The employer, however, does not receive a tax deduction until the employee is required to include the compensation in income.

Nonqualified stock option (NQSO). A type of stock option that does not satisfy the statutory requirements of an incentive stock option. If the NQSO has a readily ascertainable fair market value (e.g., the option is traded on an established exchange), the value of the option must be included in the employee's gross income at the date of the grant. Otherwise, the employee does not recognize income at the grant date. Instead, ordinary income is recognized in the year of exercise of the option.

Nonrecourse debt. Debt secured by the property that it is used to purchase. The purchaser of the property is not personally liable for the debt upon default. Rather, the creditor's recourse is to repossess the related property. Nonrecourse debt generally does not increase the purchaser's at-risk amount.

Nonrefundable credits. A credit that is not paid if it exceeds the taxpayer's tax liability. Some nonrefundable credits qualify for carryback and carryover treatment.

Nonresident alien (NRA). An individual who is neither a citizen nor a resident of the United States. Citizenship is determined under the immigration and naturalization laws of the United States. Residency is determined under § 7701(b) of the Internal Revenue Code.

Nontaxable exchange. A transaction in which realized gains or losses are not recognized. The recognition of gain or loss is postponed (deferred) until the property received in the nontaxable exchange is subsequently disposed of in a taxable transaction. Examples are § 1031 like-kind exchanges and § 1033 involuntary conversions.

Not essentially equivalent redemption. Sale or exchange treatment is given to this type of redemption. Although various safe-harbor tests are failed, the nature of the redemption is such that dividend treatment is avoided, because it represents a meaningful reduction in the shareholder's interest in the corporation. § 302(b)(1).

Notices. A Notice is issued by the National Office of the IRS as official guidance when such information is needed before the time it takes to issue a Final Regulation. Such guidance is typically transitional until final guidance is issued. A Notice is published in an *Internal Revenue Bulletin* (I.R.B.).

O

Occupational fee. A tax imposed on various trades or businesses. A license fee that enables a taxpayer to engage in a particular occupation.

Occupational taxes. See *occupational fee.*

Offer in compromise. A settlement agreement offered by the IRS in a tax dispute, especially where there is doubt as to the collectibility of the full deficiency. Offers in compromise can include installment payment schedules as well as reductions in the tax and penalties owed by the taxpayer.

Office audit. An audit conducted by the IRS in the agent's office.

Office in the home expenses. Employment and business-related expenses attributable to the use of a residence (e.g., den or office) are allowed only if the portion of the residence is exclusively used on a regular basis as a principal place of business of the taxpayer or as a place of business that is used by patients, clients, or customers. In computing the office in the home expenses, a taxpayer can use either the regular method or simplified method. As a general rule, the regular method requires more effort and recordkeeping but results in a larger deduction. Office in home expenses incurred by an employee are not deductible. § 280A.

One-year rule for prepaid expenses. Taxpayers who use the cash method are required to use the accrual method for deducting certain prepaid expenses (i.e., must capitalize the item and can deduct only when used). If a prepayment will not be consumed or expire by the end of the tax year following the year of payment, the prepayment must be capitalized and prorated over the benefit period. Conversely, if the prepayment will be consumed by the end of the tax year following the year of payment, it can be expensed when paid. To obtain the current deduction under the one-year rule, the payment must be a required payment rather than a voluntary payment.

Operating agreement. The governing document of a limited liability company. This document is similar in structure, function, and purpose to a partnership agreement.

Optional adjustment election. See *Section 754 election.*

Options. The sale or exchange of an option to buy or sell property results in capital gain or loss if the property is a capital asset. Generally, the closing of an option transaction results in short-term capital gain or loss to the writer of the call and the purchaser of the call option. § 1234.

Ordinary and necessary. Two tests for the deductibility of expenses incurred or paid in connection with a trade or business; for the production or collection of income; for the management, conservation, or maintenance of property held for the production of income; or in connection with the determination, collection, or refund of any tax. An expense is ordinary if it is common and accepted in the general industry or type of activity in which the taxpayer is engaged. An expense is necessary if it is appropriate and helpful in furthering the taxpayer's business or income-producing activity. §§ 162(a) and 212.

Ordinary income property. Property contributed to a charitable organization that, if sold rather than contributed, would have resulted in other than long-term capital gain to the donor (i.e., ordinary income property and short-term capital gain property). Examples are inventory and capital assets held for less than the long-term holding period. A contribution of ordinary income property must generally be valued at its fair market value less the gain, if any, that would have been realized if sold.

Organizational costs. See *organizational expenditures.*

Organizational expenditures. Expenditures related to the creation of a corporation or partnership. Common organizational expenditures include legal and accounting fees and state incorporation payments. Organizational expenditures exclude those incurred to obtain capital (underwriting fees) or assets (subject to cost recovery). Such expenditures incurred by the end of the entity's first year are eligible for a $5,000 limited expensing (subject to phaseout) and an amortization of the balance over 180 months. §§ 248 and 709(b).

Original issue discount (OID). The difference between the issue price of a debt obligation (e.g., a corporate bond) and the maturity value of the obligation when the issue price is less than the maturity value. OID represents interest and must be amortized over the life of the debt obligation using the effective interest method. The difference is not considered to be original issue discount for tax purposes when it is less than one-fourth of 1 percent of the redemption price at maturity multiplied by the number of years to maturity. §§ 1272 and 1273(a)(3).

Other adjustments account (OAA). Used in the context of a distribution from an S corporation. The net accumulation of the entity's exempt income (e.g., municipal bond interest), net of related nondeductible expenses.

Other property. In a corporate reorganization, any property in the exchange that is not stock or securities, such as cash or land. This amount constitutes boot. This treatment is similar to that in a like-kind exchange.

Outbound taxation. U.S. tax effects when a U.S. person begins an investment or business activity outside the United States.

Outside basis. A partner's basis in his or her partnership interest.

Ownership change. An event that triggers a § 382 limitation for the acquiring corporation.

P

Parent-subsidiary controlled group. A controlled or affiliated group of corporations where at least one corporation is at least 80 percent owned by one or more of the others. The affiliated group definition is more difficult to meet.

Partial liquidation. A stock redemption where noncorporate shareholders are permitted sale or exchange treatment. In certain cases, an active business must have existed for at least five years. Only a portion of the outstanding stock in the entity is retired. §§ 302(b)(4) and (e).

Partnership. For income tax purposes, a partnership includes a syndicate, group, pool, or joint venture as well as ordinary partnerships. In an ordinary partnership, two or more parties combine capital and/or services to carry on a business for profit as co-owners. § 7701(a)(2).

Partnership agreement. The governing document of a partnership. A partnership agreement should describe the rights and obligations of the partners; the allocation of entity income, deductions, and cash flows; initial and future capital contribution requirements; conditions for terminating the partnership; and other matters.

Passive activity loss. Any loss from (1) activities in which the taxpayer does not materially participate or (2) rental activities (subject to certain exceptions). Net passive activity losses cannot be used to offset income from nonpassive activity sources. Rather, they are suspended until the taxpayer either generates net passive activity income (and a deduction of such losses is allowed) or disposes of the underlying property (at which time the loss deductions are allowed in full). One relief provision allows landlords who actively participate in the rental activities to deduct up to $25,000 of passive activity losses annually. However, a phaseout of the $25,000 amount commences when the landlord's AGI exceeds $100,000. Another relief provision applies for material participation in a real estate trade or business.

Passive investment company. A means by which a multistate corporation can reduce the overall effective tax rate by isolating investment income in a low- or no-tax state.

Passive investment income (PII). Gross receipts from royalties, certain rents, dividends, interest, annuities, and gains from the sale or exchange of stock and securities. When earnings and profits (E & P) also exists, if the passive investment income of an S corporation exceeds 25 percent of the corporation's gross receipts for three consecutive years, S status is lost.

Pass-through entities. A form of business structure for which the income and other tax items are attributed directly to the owners and generally no separate tax is levied upon the entity itself. Examples include sole proprietorships, partnerships, and S corporations. Also referred to as a flow-through entity.

Patent. An intangible asset that may be amortized over a statutory 15-year period as a § 197 intangible. The sale of a patent usually results in favorable long-term capital gain treatment. §§ 197 and 1235.

Payroll factor. The proportion of a multistate corporation's total payroll that is traceable to a specific state. Used in determining the taxable income that is to be apportioned to that state.

Pension plan. A type of deferred compensation arrangement that provides for systematic payments of definitely determinable retirement benefits to employees who meet the requirements set forth in the plan.

Percentage depletion. Depletion based on a statutory percentage applied to the gross income from the property. The taxpayer deducts the greater of cost depletion or percentage depletion. § 613.

Percentage of completion method. A method of reporting gain or loss on certain long-term contracts. Under this method of accounting, the gross contract price is included in income as the contract is completed. Reg. § 1.451–3.

Permanent differences. Under ASC 740, tax-related items that appear in the entity's financial statements or its tax return but not both. For instance, interest income from a municipal bond is a permanent book-tax difference.

Permanent establishment (PE). A level of business activity, as defined under an income tax treaty, that subjects the taxpayer to taxation in a country other than that in which the taxpayer is based. Often evidenced by the presence of a plant, an office, or other fixed place of business. Inventory storage and temporary activities do not rise to the level of a PE. PE is the treaty's equivalent to nexus.

Personal and dependency exemptions. The tax law provides an exemption for each individual taxpayer and an additional exemption for the taxpayer's spouse if a joint return is filed. An individual may also claim a dependency exemption for each dependent, provided certain tests are met. The TCJA of 2017 suspended the deduction for exemptions for tax years after 2017 (and through 2025).

Personal exemptions. See *personal and dependency exemptions.*

Personal holding company (PHC) tax. A penalty tax imposed on certain closely held corporations with excessive investment income. Assessed at a 20 percent tax rate on personal holding company income, reduced by dividends paid and other adjustments. § 541.

Personal residence. If a residence has been owned and used by the taxpayer as the principal residence for at least two years during the five-year period ending on the date of sale, up to $250,000 of realized gain is excluded from gross income. For a married couple filing a joint return, the $250,000 is increased to $500,000 if either spouse satisfies the ownership requirement and both spouses satisfy the use requirement. § 121.

Personal service corporation (PSC). A corporation whose principal activity is the performance of personal services (e.g., health, law, engineering, architecture, accounting, actuarial science, performing arts, or consulting) and where such services are substantially performed by the employee-owners.

Personalty. All property that is not attached to real estate (realty) and is movable. Examples of personalty are machinery, automobiles, clothing, household furnishings, and personal effects.

Points. Loan origination fees that may be deductible as interest by a buyer of property. A seller of property who pays points reduces the selling price by the amount of the points paid for the buyer. While the seller is not permitted to deduct this amount as interest, the buyer may do so.

Portfolio income. Income from interest, dividends, rentals, royalties, capital gains, or other investment sources. Net passive activity losses cannot be used to offset net portfolio income.

Precedents. A previously decided court decision that is recognized as authority for the disposition of future decisions.

Precontribution gain or loss. Partnerships allow for a variety of special allocations of gain or loss among the partners, but gain or loss that is "built in" on an asset contributed to the partnership is assigned specifically to the contributing partner. § 704(c)(1)(A).

Preferences. In calculating alternative minimum taxable income (AMTI), preference items are added to the taxable income starting point of the AMT calculation. AMT preferences are amounts allowed in the calculation of regular taxable income but not allowed in the calculation of AMTI. For instance, interest income from certain state and local bonds (i.e., private activity bonds) is an AMT preference item.

Preferred stock bailout. A process where a shareholder used the issuance and sale, or later redemption, of a preferred stock dividend to obtain long-term capital gains, without any loss of voting control over the corporation. In effect, the shareholder received corporate profits without suffering the consequences of dividend income treatment. This procedure led Congress to enact § 306, which, if applicable, converts the prior long-term capital gain on the sale or redemption of the tainted stock to dividend income.

Premium Tax Credit (PTC). A tax credit that is refundable and available in advance of filing a return for the year. The PTC serves to reduce the cost of health coverage obtained on the Marketplace (Exchange). A PTC is available to individuals who purchase coverage on the Exchange and have household income equal to or greater than 100 percent of the Federal poverty line (FPL) and no greater than 400 percent of the FPL. Also, an individual must not have been able to obtain affordable coverage from his or her employer. If obtained in advance, the PTC is given to the insurance provider to lower the monthly premium cost to the individual. The PTC is reconciled on Form 8962 (Premium Tax Credit) filed with Form 1040 or 1040-A (not Form 1040-EZ). Individuals who obtain insurance through the Marketplace receive Form 1095-A (Health Insurance Marketplace Statement) by January 31 of the following year. This form provides information necessary to claim or reconcile the PTC, including the monthly cost of premiums and the amount of PTC received in advance each month. § 36B.

Principal partner. A partner with a 5 percent or greater interest in partnership capital or profits. § 706(b)(3).

Private activity bonds. Interest on state and local bonds is excludible from gross income. Certain such bonds are labeled private activity bonds. Although the interest on such bonds is excludible for regular income tax purposes, it is treated as a tax preference in calculating the AMT. §§ 57(a)(5) and 103.

Private foundations. An exempt organization that is subject to additional statutory restrictions on its activities and on contributions made to it, because it is not sufficiently supported by the public. Excise taxes may be levied on certain prohibited transactions, and the Code places more stringent restrictions on the deductibility of contributions to private foundations. § 509.

Probate costs. The costs incurred in administering a decedent's estate.

Probate estate. The property of a decedent that is subject to administration by the executor or administrator of an estate.

Procedural Regulations. A Regulation issued by the Treasury Department that is a housekeeping-type instruction indicating information that taxpayers should provide the IRS as well as information about the internal management and conduct of the IRS itself.

Profit and loss sharing ratios. Specified in the partnership agreement and used to determine each partner's allocation of ordinary taxable income and separately stated items. Profits and losses can be shared in different ratios. The ratios can be changed by amending the partnership agreement or by using a special allocation. § 704(a).

Profit sharing plan. A deferred compensation plan established and maintained by an employer to provide for employee participation in the company's profits. Contributions are paid from the employer's current or accumulated profits to a trustee. Separate accounts are maintained for each participant employee. The plan must provide a definite, predetermined formula for allocating the contributions among the participants. It also must include a definite, predetermined formula for distributing the accumulated funds after a fixed number of years, on the attainment of a stated age, or on the occurrence of certain events such as illness, layoff, or retirement.

Profits (loss) interest. The extent of a partner's entitlement to an allocation of the partnership's operating results. This interest is measured by the profit and loss sharing ratios.

Property. Assets defined in the broadest legal sense. Property includes the unrealized receivables of a cash basis taxpayer, but not services rendered. § 351.

Property dividend. Generally treated in the same manner as a cash distribution, measured by the fair market value of the property on the date of distribution. Distribution of appreciated property causes the distributing C or S corporation to recognize gain. The distributing corporation does not recognize loss on property that has depreciated in value.

Property factor. The proportion of a multistate corporation's total property that is traceable to a specific state. Used in determining the taxable income that is to be apportioned to that state.

Proportionate distribution. A distribution in which the partners' interests in hot assets does not change. This can happen, for instance, when no hot assets are distributed (e.g., a proportionate cash distribution) or when each partner in a partnership receives a pro rata share of hot assets being distributed. For example, a distribution of $10,000 of hot assets equally to two 50 percent partners is a proportionate distribution.

Proposed Regulations. A Regulation issued by the Treasury Department in proposed, rather than final, form. The interval between the proposal of a Regulation and its finalization permits taxpayers and other interested parties to comment on the propriety of the proposal.

Proprietorship. A business entity for which there is a single owner. The net profit of the entity is reported on the owner's Federal income tax return (Schedule C of Form 1040).

Public Law 86–272. A congressional limit on the ability of the state to force a multistate corporation to assign taxable income to that state. Under P.L. 86–272, where orders for tangible personal property are both filled and delivered outside the state, the entity must establish more than the mere solicitation of such orders before any income can be apportioned to the state.

Punitive damages. Damages received or paid by the taxpayer can be classified as compensatory damages or as punitive damages. Punitive damages are those awarded to punish the defendant for gross negligence or the intentional infliction of harm. Such damages are includible in gross income. § 104.

Q

QBI deduction. See *deduction for qualified business income.*

Qualified ABLE program. A state program that allows funds to be set aside for the benefit of an individual who became disabled or blind before age 26. Cash may be put into the fund annually up to the annual gift tax exclusion amount. Distributions to the designated beneficiary are not taxable provided they do not exceed qualified disability expenses for the year. § 529A.

Qualified business income (QBI). For purposes of the qualified business income deduction, it is the ordinary income less ordinary deductions a taxpayer earns from a qualified trade or business conducted in the United States by the taxpayer. Includes the distributive share of these amounts from each partnership or S corporation interest held by the taxpayer. Does not include certain types of investment income (e.g., capital gains or losses and dividends), "reasonable compensation" paid to a taxpayer with respect to any qualified trade or business, or guaranteed payments made to a partner for services rendered. § 199A(c).

Qualified business income deduction (QBID). See *deduction for qualified business income.*

Qualified business unit (QBU). A subsidiary, branch, or other business entity that conducts business using a currency other than the U.S. dollar.

Qualified dividend income (QDI). See *qualified dividends.*

Qualified dividends. Distributions made by domestic (and certain non-U.S.) corporations to noncorporate shareholders that are subject to tax at the same rates as those applicable to net long-term capital gains (i.e., 0 percent, 15 percent, or 20 percent). The 20 percent rate applies to certain high-income taxpayers. The dividend must be paid out of earnings and profits, and the shareholders must meet certain holding period requirements as to the stock. §§ 1(h)(1) and (11).

Qualified employee discount. Discounts offered employees on merchandise or services that the employer ordinarily sells or provides to customers. The discounts must be generally available to all employees. In the case of property, the discount cannot exceed the employer's gross profit (the sales price cannot be less than the employer's cost). In the case of services, the discounts cannot exceed 20 percent of the normal sales price. § 132.

Qualified improvement property. Any improvement to an interior portion of nonresidential real property made after the property is placed in service, including leasehold improvements.

Qualified joint venture. At the election of the taxpayers, certain joint ventures between spouses can avoid partnership classification. Known as a qualified joint venture, the spouses generally report their share of the business activities from the venture as sole proprietors (using two Schedule C forms). This would be reported on Schedule E if the venture relates to a rental property. § 761(f).

Qualified nonrecourse financing. Debt issued on realty by a bank, retirement plan, or governmental agency. Included in the at-risk amount by the investor. § 465(b)(6).

Qualified real property business indebtedness. Indebtedness that was incurred or assumed by the taxpayer in connection with real property used in a trade or business and is secured by such real property. The taxpayer must not be a C corporation. For qualified real property business indebtedness, the taxpayer may elect to exclude some or all of the income realized from cancellation of debt on qualified real property. If the election is made, the basis of the property must be reduced by the amount excluded. The amount excluded cannot be greater than the excess of the principal amount of the outstanding debt over the fair market value (net of any other debt outstanding on the property) of the property securing the debt. § 108(c).

Qualified residence interest. A term relevant in determining the amount of interest expense the individual taxpayer may deduct as an itemized deduction for what otherwise would be disallowed as a component of personal interest (consumer interest). Qualified residence interest consists of interest paid on qualified residences (principal residence and one other residence) of the taxpayer. Debt that qualifies as qualified residence interest is limited to $1,000,000 of debt to acquire, construct, or substantially improve qualified residences (acquisition indebtedness). For acquisition indebtedness incurred after December 15, 2017, the limit is reduced to $750,000. § 163(h)(3).

Qualified small business corporation. For purposes of computing an exclusion upon the sale of *qualified small business stock*, a C corporation that has aggregate gross assets not exceeding $50 million and that is conducting an active trade or business. § 1202.

Qualified small business stock. Stock in a qualified small business corporation, purchased as part of an original issue after August 10, 1993. The shareholder may exclude from gross income 100 (or 50 or 75) percent of the realized gain on the sale of the stock if he or she held the stock for more than five years. The exclusion percentage depends on when the stock was acquired. § 1202.

Qualified terminable interest property (QTIP). Generally, the marital deduction (for gift and estate tax purposes) is not available if the interest transferred will terminate upon the death of the transferee spouse and pass to someone else. Thus, if Jim (the husband) places property in trust, life estate to Mary (the wife), and remainder to their children upon Mary's death, this is a terminable interest that will not provide Jim (or Jim's estate) with a marital deduction. If, however, the transfer in trust is treated as qualified terminable interest property (the QTIP election is made), the terminable interest restriction is waived and the marital deduction becomes available. In exchange for this deduction, the surviving spouse's gross estate must include the value of the QTIP election assets, even though he or she has no control over the ultimate disposition of the asset. Terminable interest property qualifies for this election if the donee (or heir) is the only beneficiary of the asset during his or her lifetime and receives income distributions relative to the property at least annually. For gifts, the donor spouse is the one who makes the QTIP election. For property transferred by death, the executor of the estate of the deceased spouse makes the election. §§ 2056(b)(7) and 2523(f).

Qualified trade or business. Used in determining the deduction for qualified business income (§ 199A). In general, it includes any trade or business other than providing services as an employee. In addition, a "specified services trade or business" is not a qualified trade or business. § 199A(d)(1)(B).

Qualified transportation fringes. Transportation benefits provided by the employer to the employee. If these benefits are reimbursed by the employer, they are excludible from gross income by the employee, but not deductible by the employer after 2017. Such benefits include (1) transportation in a commuter highway vehicle between the employee's residence and the place of employment, (2) a transit pass, and (3) qualified parking. Qualified transportation fringes are excludible from the employee's gross income to the extent categories (1) and (2) above do not exceed $270 per month in 2020 and category (3) does not exceed $270 per month in 2020. These amounts are indexed annually for inflation. § 132.

Qualified tuition program (§ 529 plan). A program that allows college tuition to be prepaid for a beneficiary. When amounts in the plan are used, nothing is included in gross income provided they are used for qualified higher education expenses. § 529.

Qualifying child. An individual who, as to the taxpayer, satisfies the relationship, abode, and age tests. To be claimed as a dependent, such individual must also meet the citizenship and joint return tests and not be self-supporting. §§ 152(a)(1) and (c).

Qualifying relative. An individual who, as to the taxpayer, satisfies the relationship, gross income, support, citizenship, and joint return tests. Such an individual can be claimed as a dependent of the taxpayer. §§ 152(a)(2) and (d).

R

Rate reconciliation. Under Generally Accepted Accounting Principles, a footnote to the financial statements often includes a table that accounts for differences in the statutory income tax rate that applies to the entity (e.g., 21 percent) and the higher or lower effective tax rate that the entity realized for the reporting period. The rate reconciliation includes only permanent differences between the book tax expense and the entity's income tax provision. The rate reconciliation table often is expressed in dollar and/or percentage terms.

Realized gain. See *realized gain or loss.*

Realized gain or loss. The difference between the amount realized upon the sale or other disposition of property and the adjusted basis of the property. § 1001.

Realized loss. See *realized gain or loss.*

Realty. Real estate.

Reasonable cause. Relief from taxpayer and preparer penalties often is allowed where reasonable cause is found for the taxpayer's actions. For example, reasonable cause for the late filing of a tax return might be a flood that damaged the taxpayer's record-keeping systems and made a timely completion of the return difficult.

Reasonable needs of the business. A means of avoiding the penalty tax on an unreasonable accumulation of earnings. In determining the base for this tax (accumulated taxable income), § 535 allows a deduction for "such part of earnings and profits for the taxable year as are retained for the reasonable needs of the business." § 537.

Reasonableness. See *reasonableness requirement.*

Reasonableness requirement. The Code includes a reasonableness requirement with respect to the deduction of salaries and other compensation for services. The courts have expanded this requirement to all business expenses, ruling that an expense must be reasonable in order to be ordinary and necessary. What constitutes reasonableness is a question of fact. If an expense is unreasonable, the amount that is classified as unreasonable is not allowed as a deduction. The question of reasonableness generally arises with respect to closely held corporations where there is no separation of ownership and management. § 162(a)(1).

Recapitalization. A "Type E" reorganization, constituting a major change in the character and amount of outstanding equity of a corporation. Tax-free exchanges are stock for stock, bonds for bonds, and bonds for stock. For example, common stock exchanged for preferred stock can qualify as a tax-free "Type E" reorganization.

Recognized gain. See *recognized gain or loss.*

Recognized gain or loss. The portion of realized gain or loss subject to income taxation.

Recognized loss. See *recognized gain or loss.*

Recourse debt. Debt for which the lender may both foreclose on the property and assess a guarantor for any payments due under the loan. A lender also may make a claim against the assets of any general partner in a partnership to which debt is issued, without regard to whether the partner has guaranteed the debt.

Recovery of capital doctrine. When a taxable sale or exchange occurs, the seller may be permitted to recover his or her investment (or other adjusted basis) in the property before gain or loss is recognized.

Redemption to pay death taxes. Sale or exchange treatment is available relative to this type of stock redemption, to the extent of the proceeds up to the total amount paid by the estate or heir for estate/inheritance taxes and administration expenses. The stock value must exceed 35 percent of the value of the decedent's adjusted gross estate. In meeting this test, shareholdings in corporations where the decedent held at least 20 percent of the outstanding shares are combined. § 303.

Refundable credits. A credit that is paid to the taxpayer even if the amount of the credit (or credits) exceeds the taxpayer's tax liability.

Regular corporations. See *C corporation.*

Rehabilitation expenditures credit. A credit that is based on expenditures incurred to rehabilitate industrial and commercial buildings and certified historic structures. The credit is intended to discourage businesses from moving from older, economically distressed areas to newer locations and to encourage the preservation of historic structures. § 47.

Related party. Various Code Sections define related parties and often include a variety of persons within this (usually detrimental) category. Generally, related parties are accorded different tax treatment from that applicable to other taxpayers who enter into similar transactions. For instance, realized losses that are generated between related parties are not recognized in the year of the loss. However, these deferred losses can be used to offset recognized gains that occur upon the subsequent sale of the asset to a nonrelated party. Other uses of a related-party definition include the conversion of gain upon the sale of a depreciable asset into all ordinary income (§ 1239) and the identification of constructive ownership of stock relative to corporate distributions, redemptions, liquidations, reorganizations, and compensation.

Related-party transactions. The tax law places restrictions upon the recognition of gains and losses between related parties because of the potential for abuse. For example, restrictions are placed on the deduction of losses from the sale or exchange of property between related parties. In addition, under certain circumstances, related-party gains that would otherwise be classified as capital gain are classified as ordinary income. §§ 267, 707(b), and 1239.

Rental activity. Any activity where payments are received principally for the use of tangible property is a rental activity. Temporary Regulations provide that in certain circumstances, activities involving rentals of real and personal property are not to be treated as rental activities. The Temporary Regulations list six exceptions.

Reorganization. Any corporate restructuring, including when one corporation acquires another, a single corporation divides into two or more entities, a corporation makes a substantial change in its capital structure, a corporation undertakes a change in its legal name or domicile, or a corporation goes through a bankruptcy proceeding and continues to exist. The exchange of stock and other securities in a corporate reorganization can be effected favorably for tax purposes if certain statutory requirements are followed strictly. Tax consequences include the nonrecognition of any gain that is realized by the shareholders except to the extent of boot received. § 368.

Report of Foreign Bank and Financial Accounts (FBAR). FinCEN Form 114, Report of Foreign Bank and Financial Accounts (FBAR), must be filed by individuals and some businesses if they have foreign bank, brokerage or similar accounts where at any time during the calendar year the aggregate balance exceeds $10,000. The form is filed electronically with the U.S. Department of the Treasury and is due by April 15 with an automatic extension to October 15. Significant penalties apply for failure to file the FBAR. The form is not attached to the income tax return (it is separately filed), but any interest earned by the foreign accounts is generally included in the account holder's U.S. taxable income.

Required taxable year. A partnership or limited liability company must use a required tax year as its tax accounting period, or one of three allowable alternative tax year-ends. If there is a common tax year used by owners holding a majority of the entity's capital or profits interests or if the same year end is used by all "principal partners" (partners who hold 5 percent or more of the capital or profits interests), then that tax year-end is used by the entity. If neither of the first tests results in an allowable year-end (e.g., because there is no majority partner or because the principal partners do not have the same tax year), then the partnership uses the least aggregate deferral method to determine its tax year.

Research activities credit. A tax credit whose purpose is to encourage research and development. It consists of three components: the incremental research activities credit, the basic research credit, and the energy credit. The incremental research activities credit is equal to 20 percent of the excess qualified research expenditures over the base amount. The basic research credit is equal to 20 percent of the excess of basic research payments over the base amount. § 41.

Research and experimental expenditures. Costs incurred to develop a product or process for which there exists uncertainty regarding its viability. The Code provides three alternatives for the tax treatment of research and experimentation expenditures. They may be expensed in the year paid or incurred, deferred subject to amortization, or capitalized. If the taxpayer does not elect to expense such costs or to defer them subject to amortization (over 60 months), the expenditures must be capitalized. § 174. In general, research and experimentation expenditures paid or incurred after 2021 must be capitalized and amortized over a five-year period. Some of these expenditures may also qualify the taxpayer for the credit for increasing research activities. § 41.

Reserve method. A method of accounting whereby an allowance is permitted for estimated uncollectible accounts. Actual write-offs are charged to the reserve, and recoveries of amounts previously written off are credited to the reserve. The Code permits only certain financial institutions to use the reserve method. § 166.

Residential rental real estate. Buildings for which at least 80 percent of the gross rents are from dwelling units (e.g., an apartment building). This type of building is distinguished from nonresidential (commercial or industrial) buildings in applying the recapture of depreciation provisions. The term also is relevant in distinguishing between buildings that are eligible for a 27.5-year life versus a 39-year life for MACRS purposes. Generally, residential buildings receive preferential treatment.

Revenue Agent's Report (RAR). A Revenue Agent's Report (RAR) reflects any adjustments made by the agent as a result of an audit of the taxpayer. The RAR is mailed to the taxpayer along with the 30-day letter, which outlines the appellate procedures available to the taxpayer.

Revenue neutrality. A description that characterizes tax legislation when it neither increases nor decreases the total revenue collected by the taxing jurisdiction. Thus, any tax revenue losses are offset by tax revenue gains.

Revenue Procedures. A matter of procedural importance to both taxpayers and the IRS concerning the administration of the tax laws is issued as a Revenue Procedure (abbreviated Rev.Proc.). A Revenue Procedure is published in an *Internal Revenue Bulletin* (I.R.B.).

Revenue Rulings. A Revenue Ruling (abbreviated Rev.Rul.) is issued by the National Office of the IRS to express an official interpretation of the tax law as applied to specific transactions. It is more limited in application than a Regulation. A Revenue Ruling is published in an *Internal Revenue Bulletin* (I.R.B.).

Reversionary interest. The trust property that reverts to the grantor after the expiration of an intervening income interest. Assume that Phil places real estate in trust with income to Junior for 11 years and that upon the expiration of this term, the property returns to Phil. Under these circumstances, Phil holds a reversionary interest in the property. A reversionary interest is the same as a remainder interest, except that, in the latter case, the property passes to someone other than the original owner (e.g., the grantor of a trust) upon the expiration of the intervening interest.

Roth IRA. See *Individual Retirement Accounts (IRAs)*.

S

S corporation. The designation for a corporation that elects to be taxed similarly to a partnership. See also *Subchapter S*.

Sale or exchange. A requirement for the recognition of capital gain or loss. Generally, the seller of property must receive money or relief from debt to have sold the property. An exchange involves the transfer of property for other property. Thus, collection of a debt is neither a sale nor an exchange. The term *sale or exchange* is not defined by the Code.

Sales factor. The proportion of a multistate corporation's total sales that is traceable to a specific state. Used in determining the taxable income that is to be apportioned to that state.

Sales tax. A state- or local-level tax on the retail sale of specified property. Generally, the purchaser pays the tax, but the seller collects it, as an agent for the government. Various taxing jurisdictions allow exemptions for purchases of specific items, including certain food, services, and manufacturing equipment. If the purchaser and seller are in different states, a use tax usually applies.

Salvage value. The estimated amount a taxpayer will receive upon the disposition of an asset used in the taxpayer's trade or business. Salvage value is relevant in calculating depreciation under § 167, but is not relevant in calculating cost recovery under § 168.

Schedule K–1. A tax information form prepared for each partner in a partnership, each shareholder of an S corporation, and some beneficiaries of certain trusts. The Schedule K–1 reports the owner's share of the entity's ordinary income or loss from operations as well as the owner's share of separately stated items.

Schedule M–1. On the Form 1120, a reconciliation of book net income with Federal taxable income. Accounts for temporary and permanent differences in the two computations, such as depreciation differences, exempt income, and nondeductible items. On Forms 1120S and 1065, the Schedule M–1 reconciles book income with the owners' aggregate taxable income.

Schedule M–3. An *expanded* reconciliation of book net income with Federal taxable income (see *Schedule M–1*). Required of C and S corporations and partnerships/LLCs with total assets of $10 million or more.

Scholarship. Scholarships are generally excluded from the gross income of the recipient unless the payments are a disguised form of compensation for services rendered. However, the Code imposes restrictions on the exclusion. The recipient must be a degree candidate. The excluded amount is limited to amounts used for tuition, fees, books, supplies, and equipment required for courses of instruction. Amounts received for room and board are not eligible for the exclusion. § 117.

Section 121 exclusion. If a residence has been owned and used by the taxpayer as the principal residence for at least two years during the five-year period ending on the date of sale, up to $250,000 of realized gain is excluded from gross income. For a married couple filing a joint return, the $250,000 is increased to $500,000 if either spouse satisfies the ownership requirement and both spouses satisfy the use requirement.

Section 179 expensing. The ability to deduct the cost of qualified property in the year the property is placed in service rather than over the asset's useful life or cost recovery period. The annual ceiling on the deduction is $1,040,000 in 2020 ($1,020,000 in 2019). However, the deduction is reduced dollar for dollar when § 179 property placed in service during the taxable year exceeds $2,590,000 ($2,550,000 in 2019). In addition, the amount expensed under § 179 cannot exceed the aggregate amount of taxable income derived from the conduct of any trade or business by the taxpayer.

Section 179 expensing election. See *Section 179 expensing*.

Section 338 election. When a corporation acquires at least 80 percent of a subsidiary within a 12-month period, it can elect to treat the acquisition of such stock as an asset purchase. The acquiring corporation's basis in the subsidiary's assets then is the cost of the stock. The subsidiary is deemed to have sold its assets for an amount equal to the grossed-up basis in its stock.

Section 382 limitation. When one corporation acquires another, the acquiring corporation's ability to use the loss and credit carryovers of the target may be limited by this anti-abuse provision. For instance, the maximum NOL deduction available to the acquiring is the value of the target when acquired times the long-term tax-exempt interest rate on that date.

Section 401(k) plan. A cash or deferred arrangement plan that allows participants to elect to receive up to $19,500 in 2020 in cash (taxed currently) or to have a contribution

made on their behalf to a qualified retirement plan (excludible from gross income). The plan may be in the form of a salary reduction agreement between the participant and the employer.

Section 704(b) book capital accounts. Capital accounts calculated as described under Reg. § 1.704–1(b)(2)(iv). All partnerships must maintain § 704(b) book capital accounts for the partners with the intent that final liquidating distributions are in accordance with these capital account balances. Partnership allocations will not be accepted unless they are properly reflected in the partners' § 704(b) book capital accounts. These capital accounts are a hybrid of book and tax accounting methods. They reflect contributions and distributions of property at their fair market values, but the capital accounts are otherwise generally increased by the partnership's tax-basis income and decreased by tax-basis deductions (as reported on the partner's Schedule K–1). Liabilities are only reflected in these capital accounts to the extent the partnership assumes a partner's liability [reduces that partner's § 704(b) book capital account] or a partner assumes a partnership liability [increases that partner's § 704(b) book capital account]. See also *capital account maintenance* and *economic effect test*.

Section 754 election. An election that may be made by a partnership to adjust the basis of partnership assets to reflect a purchasing partner's outside basis in interest or to reflect a gain, loss, or basis adjustment of a partner receiving a distribution from a partnership. The intent of the election is to maintain the equivalence between outside and inside basis for that partner. Once the election is made, the partnership must make basis adjustments for all future transactions, unless the IRS consents to revoke the election.

Section 1231 gains and losses. If the combined gains and losses from the taxable dispositions of § 1231 assets plus the net gain from business involuntary conversions (of both § 1231 assets and long-term capital assets) is a gain, the gains and losses are treated as long-term capital gains and losses. In arriving at § 1231 gains, however, the depreciation recapture provisions (e.g., § 1245) are applied first to produce ordinary income. If the net result of the combination is a loss, the gains and losses from § 1231 assets are treated as ordinary gains and losses. § 1231(a).

Section 1231 lookback. For gain to be classified as § 1231 gain, the gain must survive the § 1231 lookback. To the extent of nonrecaptured § 1231 losses for the five prior tax years, the gain is classified as ordinary income. § 1231(c).

Section 1231 property. Depreciable assets and real estate used in trade or business and held for the required long-term holding period. § 1231(b).

Section 1244 stock. Stock issued under § 1244 by qualifying small business corporations. If § 1244 stock becomes worthless, the shareholders may claim an ordinary loss rather than the usual capital loss, within statutory limitations.

Section 1245 property. Property that is subject to the recapture of depreciation under § 1245. For a definition of § 1245 property, see § 1245(a)(3).

Section 1245 recapture. Upon a taxable disposition of § 1245 property, all depreciation claimed on the property is recaptured as ordinary income (but not to exceed any recognized gain from the disposition).

Section 1250 property. Real estate that is subject to the recapture of depreciation under § 1250. For a definition of § 1250 property, see § 1250(c).

Section 1250 recapture. Upon a taxable disposition of § 1250 property, accelerated depreciation or cost recovery claimed on the property may be recaptured as ordinary income.

Securities. Stock, debt, and other financial assets. To the extent securities other than the stock of the transferee corporation are received in a § 351 exchange, the new shareholder recognizes a gain. For purposes of corporate reorganizations, securities are generally debt with terms longer than 10 years. To the extent stock and securities are transferred in a corporate reorganization under § 368, no gain or loss is recognized.

Self-employment tax. A tax of 12.4 percent is levied on individuals with net earnings from self-employment (up to $137,700 in 2020) to provide Social Security benefits (i.e., the old age, survivors, and disability insurance portion) for such individuals. In addition, a tax of 2.9 percent is levied on individuals with net earnings from self-employment (with no statutory ceiling) to provide Medicare benefits (i.e., the hospital insurance portion) for such individuals. If a self-employed individual also receives wages from an employer that are subject to FICA, the self-employment tax will be reduced. A partial deduction is allowed in calculating the self-employment tax. Individuals with net earnings of $400 or more from self-employment are subject to this tax. §§ 1401 and 1402.

Separate foreign tax credit income categories. The foreign tax credit of a taxpayer is computed for each of several types of income sources, as specified by the Code to limit the results of tax planning. FTC income "baskets" include general and passive. The FTC for the year is the sum of the credits as computed within all of the taxpayer's separate FTC baskets used for the tax year.

Separate return limitation year (SRLY). A series of rules limits the amount of an acquired corporation's net operating loss carryforwards that can be used by the acquiror. Generally, a consolidated return can include the acquiree's net operating loss carryforward only to the extent of the lesser of the subsidiary's (1) current-year or (2) cumulative positive contribution to consolidated taxable income.

Separately stated items. Any item of a partnership or an S corporation that might be taxed differently to any two owners of the entity. These amounts are not included in the ordinary income of the entity, but are instead reported separately to the owners; tax consequences are determined at the owner level.

Severance taxes. A tax imposed upon the extraction of natural resources.

Short period. See *short taxable year*.

Short sale. A sale that occurs when a taxpayer sells borrowed property (usually stock) and repays the lender with substantially identical property either held on the date of the short sale or purchased after the sale. No gain or loss is recognized until the short sale is closed, and such gain or loss is generally short term. § 1233.

Short taxable year. A tax year that is less than 12 months. A short taxable year may occur in the initial reporting period, in the final tax year, or when the taxpayer changes tax years. Special income tax computations may be required.

Significant participation activity. Seven tests determine whether an individual has achieved material participation in an activity, one of which is based on more than 500 hours of participation in significant participation activities. A significant participation activity is one in which the individual's participation exceeds 100 hours during the year. Temp.Reg. § 1.469–5T.

Simple trust. Trusts that are not complex trusts. Such trusts may not have a charitable beneficiary, accumulate income, or distribute corpus.

Simplified employee pension (SEP) plans. An employer may make contributions to an employee's IRA in amounts not exceeding the lesser of 15 percent of compensation or $57,000 per individual in 2020. These employer-sponsored simplified employee pensions are permitted only if the contributions are nondiscriminatory and are made on behalf of all employees who have attained age 21 and have worked for the employer during at least three of the five preceding calendar years. § 219(b).

Small business corporation. A corporation that satisfies the definition of § 1361(b), § 1244(c), or both. Satisfaction of § 1361(b) permits an S election, and satisfaction of § 1244 enables the shareholders of the corporation to claim an ordinary loss on the worthlessness of stock.

Small business stock (§ 1244 stock). See *Section 1244 stock*.

Small Cases Division. A division within the U.S. Tax Court where jurisdiction is limited to claims of $50,000 or less. There is no appeal from this court.

Solicitation of orders. A level of activity brought about by the taxpayer within a specific state. Under Public Law 86-272, certain types of solicitation activities do not create nexus with the state. Exceeding mere solicitation, though, creates nexus.

Special allocation. Any amount for which an agreement exists among the partners of a partnership outlining the method used for spreading the item among the partners.

Special use value. Permits the executor of an estate to value, for estate tax purposes, real estate used in a farming activity or in connection with a closely held business at its current use value rather than at its most suitable or optimal use value. Under this option, a farm is valued for farming purposes even though, for example, the property might have a higher potential value as a shopping center. For the executor of an estate to elect special use valuation, the conditions of § 2032A must be satisfied.

Specific charge-off method. A method of accounting for bad debts in which a deduction is permitted only when an account becomes partially or completely worthless.

Specified service trade or business. For purposes of the deduction for qualified business income, a specified service trade or business includes those involving the performance of services in certain fields, including health, law, accounting, actuarial science, performing arts, consulting, athletics, financial services, and brokerage services; services consisting of investing and investment management, trading or dealing in securities, partnership interests, or commodities; and any trade or business where the business's principal asset is the reputation of one or more of its employees or owners. § 199A(d)(2).

Spin-off. A type of reorganization where, for example, Apple Corporation transfers some assets to Core Corporation in exchange for Core stock representing control. Apple then distributes the Core stock to its shareholders.

Split-off. A type of reorganization where, for example, Apple Corporation transfers some assets to Core Corporation in exchange for Core stock representing control. Apple then distributes the Core stock to its shareholders in exchange for some of their Apple stock. Not all shareholders need to exchange stock.

Split-up. A type of reorganization where, for example, Firefly Corporation transfers some assets to Fire Corporation and the remainder to Fly Corporation. In return, Firefly receives enough Fire and Fly stock representing control of each corporation. Firefly then distributes the Fire and Fly stock to its shareholders in return for all of their Firefly stock. Firefly then liquidates, and its shareholders now have control of Fire and Fly.

Sprinkling trust. When a trustee has the discretion to either distribute or accumulate the entity accounting income of the trust and to distribute it among the trust's income beneficiaries in varying magnitudes. The trustee can "sprinkle" the income of the trust.

Standard deduction. The individual taxpayer can either itemize deductions or take the standard deduction. The amount of the standard deduction depends on the taxpayer's filing status (single, head of household, married filing jointly, surviving spouse, or married filing separately). For 2020, the amount of the standard deduction ranges from $12,400 (for single) to $24,800 (for married, filing jointly). Additional standard deductions of either $1,300 (for married taxpayers) or $1,650 (for single taxpayers) are available if the taxpayer is blind or age 65 or over. Limitations exist on the amount of the standard deduction of a taxpayer who is another taxpayer's dependent. The standard deduction amounts are adjusted for inflation each year. § 63(c).

Startup expenditures. Expenditures paid or incurred prior to the beginning of the business that would have been deductible as an ordinary and necessary business expense if business operations had begun. Examples of such expenditures include advertising; salaries and wages; travel and other expenses incurred in lining up prospective distributors, suppliers, or customers; and salaries and fees to executives, consultants, and professional service providers. A taxpayer will immediately expense the first $5,000 (subject to phaseout) of startup expenditures and amortize the balance over a period of 180 months, unless the taxpayer elects not to do so.

Statute of limitations. Provisions of the law that specify the maximum period of time in which action may be taken concerning a past event. Code §§ 6501–6504 contain the limitation periods applicable to the IRS for additional assessments, and §§ 6511–6515 relate to refund claims by taxpayers.

Statutory employees. Statutory employees are considered self-employed independent contractors for purposes of reporting income and expenses on their tax returns. Generally, a statutory employee must meet three tests:

- It is understood from a service contract that the services will be performed by the person.

- The person does not have a substantial investment in facilities (other than transportation used to perform the services).

- The services involve a continuing relationship with the person for whom they are performed.

For further information on statutory employees, see Circular E, *Employer's Tax Guide* (IRS Publication 15).

Step down. See *step-down in basis*.

Step transaction. Disregarding one or more transactions to arrive at the final result. Assume, for example, Beta Corporation creates Alpha Corporation by transferring assets desired by Beta's sole shareholder, Carl. Carl then causes Alpha to liquidate to obtain the assets. Under these circumstances, the IRS may contend that the creation and liquidation of Alpha be disregarded. What really happened was a dividend distribution from Beta to Carl.

Step up. See *step-up in basis*.

Step-down in basis. A reduction in the tax basis of property. See also *step-up in basis*.

Step-up in basis. An increase in the income tax basis of property. In an estate context, a step-up in basis occurs when a decedent dies owning appreciated property. Since the estate or heir acquires a basis in the property equal to the property's fair market value on the date of death (or alternate valuation date if available and elected), any appreciation is not subject to the income tax. Thus, a step-up in basis is the result, with no immediate income tax consequences. In the partnership context, a step-up arises when a § 754 election is in effect and when one of several transactions arises: (1) a partner purchases a partnership interest for an amount that exceeds the partner's share of the partnership's inside basis, (2) the partner recognizes a gain on a distribution of cash from the partnership, or (3) the partnership takes a basis in a partnership property that is less than the partnership's basis in that asset. In the opposite situations (e.g., loss recognition), a step-down can arise. See also *step-down in basis*.

Stock bonus plan. A type of deferred compensation plan in which the employer establishes and maintains the plan and contributes employer stock to the plan for the benefit of employees. The contributions need not be dependent on the employer's profits. Any benefits of the plan are distributable in the form of employer stock, except that distributable fractional shares may be paid in cash.

Stock dividend. Not taxable if pro rata distributions of stock or stock rights on common stock. Section 305 governs the taxability of stock dividends and sets out five exceptions to the general rule that stock dividends are nontaxable.

Stock option. The right to purchase a stated number of shares of stock from a corporation at a certain price within a specified period of time. §§ 421 and 422.

Stock redemption. A corporation buys back its own stock from a specified shareholder. Typically, the corporation recognizes any realized gain on the noncash assets that it uses to effect a redemption, and the shareholder obtains a capital gain or loss upon receipt of the purchase price.

Stock rights. Assets that convey to the holder the power to purchase corporate stock at a specified price, often for a limited period of time. Stock rights received may be taxed as a distribution of earnings and profits. After the right is exercised, the basis of the acquired share includes the investor's purchase price or gross income, if any, to obtain the right. Disposition of the right also can be taxable.

Subchapter S. Sections 1361–1379 of the Internal Revenue Code. An elective provision permitting certain small business corporations (§ 1361) and their shareholders (§ 1362) to elect to be treated for income tax purposes in accordance with the operating rules of §§ 1363–1379. S corporations usually avoid the corporate income tax, and corporate losses can be claimed by the shareholders.

Subpart F income. Certain types of income earned by a controlled foreign corporation that are included in U.S. gross income by U.S. shareholders of such an entity as they are generated, not when they are repatriated.

Substance over form. A standard used when one must ascertain the true reality of what has occurred. Suppose, for example, a father sells stock to his daughter for $1,000. If the stock is really worth $50,000 at the time of the transfer, the substance of the transaction is probably a gift to her of $49,000.

Substantial authority. Taxpayer and tax preparer understatement penalties are waived where substantial authority existed for the disputed position taken on the return.

Substantial basis reduction. Arises when the partnership makes a distribution to a partner and the distributee partner recognizes a loss (or has a basis increase for the distributed assets) of at least $250,000. (The second situation would arise when the basis of the assets the partner receives must be stepped up to absorb all remaining partnership interest basis.) If there is a substantial basis reduction, the partnership is required to make a downward adjustment to the basis of its assets, even if the partnership does not have a § 754 election in effect. This adjustment is treated as a § 754 adjustment related to a distribution and so is allocated to the basis of all remaining partnership assets (except for cash). See also *substantial built-in loss* and *§ 754 election*.

Substantial built-in loss. Arises when a partner sells a partnership interest and the selling partner recognizes a loss on the sale of at least $250,000. In addition, a substantial built-in loss arises if the selling partner would be allocated more than a $250,000 loss if all partnership assets were sold (after considering special allocations). If there is a substantial built-in loss, the partnership is required to make a downward adjustment in the basis of its assets, even if the partnership does not have a § 754 election in effect. This adjustment is treated as a § 754 adjustment related to a sale of a partnership interest and so is allocated to the purchasing partner. See also *substantial basis reduction* and *§ 754 election*.

Sunset provision. A provision attached to new tax legislation that will cause such legislation to expire at a specified date. Sunset provisions are attached to tax cut bills for long-term budgetary reasons to make their effect temporary. Once the sunset provision comes into play, the tax cut is rescinded and former law is reinstated. An example of a sunset provision is contained in the Tax Relief Reconciliation Act of 2001 that related to the estate tax. After the estate tax was phased out in 2010, a sunset provision called for the reinstatement of the estate tax as of January 1, 2011.

Surviving spouse. When a husband or wife predeceases the other spouse, the survivor is known as a surviving spouse. Under certain conditions, a surviving spouse may be entitled to use the income tax rates in § 1(a) (those applicable to married persons filing a joint return) for the two years after the year of death of his or her spouse. § 2(a).

Syndication costs. Incurred in promoting and marketing partnership interests for sale to investors. Examples include legal and accounting fees, printing costs for prospectus and placement documents, and state registration fees. These items are capitalized by the partnership as incurred, with no amortization thereof allowed.

T

Tax avoidance. The minimization of one's tax liability by taking advantage of legally available tax planning opportunities. Tax avoidance can be contrasted with tax evasion, which entails the reduction of tax liability by illegal means.

Tax benefit rule. A provision that limits the recognition of income from the recovery of an expense or a loss properly deducted in a prior tax year to the amount of the deduction that generated a tax saving. Assume that last year Gary had medical expenses of $4,000 and adjusted gross income of $30,000. Because of the AGI limitation, Gary could deduct only $1,000 of these expenses [$4,000 − (10% × $30,000)]. If this year Gary is reimbursed in full by his insurance company for the $4,000 of expenses, the tax benefit rule limits the amount of income from the reimbursement to $1,000 (the amount previously deducted with a tax saving).

Tax credits. Amounts that directly reduce a taxpayer's tax liability. The tax benefit received from a tax credit is not dependent on the taxpayer's marginal tax rate, whereas the benefit of a tax deduction or exclusion is dependent on the taxpayer's tax bracket.

Tax evasion. The reduction of taxes by the use of subterfuge or fraud or other nonlegal means. For example, a cash basis taxpayer tries to increase his or her charitable contribution deduction by prepaying next year's church pledge with a pre-dated check issued in the following year.

Tax haven. A country in which either locally sourced income or residents of the country are subject to a low rate of taxation.

Tax preparer. One who prepares tax returns for compensation. A tax preparer must register with the IRS and receive a special ID number to practice before the IRS and represent taxpayers before the agency in tax audit actions. The conduct of a tax preparer is regulated under Circular 230. Tax preparers also are subject to penalties for inappropriate conduct when working in the tax profession.

Tax Rate Schedules. Rate schedules that are used by upper-income taxpayers and those not permitted to use the tax table. Separate rate schedules are provided for married individuals filing jointly, heads of households, single taxpayers, estates and trusts, and married individuals filing separate returns. § 1.

Tax research. The method used to determine the best available solution to a situation that possesses tax consequences. Both tax and nontax factors are considered.

Tax shelters. The typical tax shelter generated large losses in the early years of the activity. Investors would offset these losses against other types of income and therefore avoid paying income taxes on this income. These tax shelter investments could then be sold after a few years and produce capital gain income, which is taxed at a lower rate compared to ordinary income. The passive activity loss rules and the at-risk rules now limit tax shelter deductions.

Tax Table. A table that is provided for taxpayers with less than $100,000 of taxable income. Separate columns are provided for single taxpayers, married taxpayers filing jointly, heads of households, and married taxpayers filing separately. § 3.

Tax treaties. An agreement between the U.S. Department of State and another country designed to alleviate double taxation of income and asset transfers, and to share administrative information useful to tax agencies in both countries. The United States has income tax treaties with almost 70 countries and transfer tax treaties with about 20.

Taxable estate. The taxable estate is the gross estate of a decedent reduced by the deductions allowed by §§ 2053–2057 (e.g., administration expenses, marital and charitable deductions). The taxable estate is subject to the unified transfer tax at death. § 2051.

Taxable gift. The amount of a gift that is subject to the unified transfer tax. Thus, a taxable gift has been adjusted by the annual exclusion and other appropriate deductions (e.g., marital and charitable). § 2053.

Taxable year. The annual period over which income is measured for income tax purposes. Most individuals use a calendar year, but many businesses use a fiscal year based on the natural business year. Certain entities, including S corporations, have a required taxable year. §§ 441, 706, and 1378.

Technical Advice Memoranda (TAM). TAMs are issued by the IRS in response to questions raised by IRS field personnel during audits. They deal with completed rather than proposed transactions and are often requested for questions related to exempt organizations and employee plans.

Temporary differences. Under ASC 740 (SFAS 109), tax-related items that appear in the entity's financial statements and its tax return, but in different time periods. For instance, doubtful accounts receivable often create a temporary book-tax difference, as a bad debt reserve is used to compute an expense for financial reporting purposes, but a bad debt often is deductible only under the specific write-off rule for tax purposes, and the difference observed for the current period creates a temporary difference.

Temporary Regulations. A Regulation issued by the Treasury Department in temporary form. When speed is critical, the Treasury Department issues Temporary Regulations that take effect immediately. These Regulations have the same authoritative value as Final Regulations and may be cited as precedent for three years. Temporary Regulations are also issued as proposed Regulations.

Tenants by the entirety. Essentially, a joint tenancy between husband and wife.

Tenants in common. A form of ownership where each tenant (owner) holds an undivided interest in property. Unlike a joint tenancy or a tenancy by the entirety, the interest of a tenant in common does not terminate upon that individual's death (there is no right of survivorship). Assume that Tim and Cindy acquire real estate as equal tenants in common. Upon Tim's death, his one-half interest in the property passes to his estate or heirs, not automatically to Cindy.

Terminable interests. An interest in property that terminates upon the death of the holder or upon the occurrence of some other specified event. The transfer of a terminable interest by one spouse to the other may not qualify for the marital deduction. §§ 2056(b) and 2523(b).

Theft losses. A loss from larceny, embezzlement, or robbery. It does not include misplacement of items.

Thin capitalization. When debt owed by a corporation to the shareholders becomes too large in relation to the corporation's capital structure (i.e., stock and shareholder equity), the IRS may contend that the corporation is thinly capitalized. In effect, some or all of the debt is reclassified as equity. The immediate result is to disallow any interest deduction to the corporation on the reclassified debt. To the extent of the corporation's earnings and profits, interest payments and loan repayments on the reclassified debt are treated as dividends to the shareholders.

Thirty-day (30-day) letter. A letter that accompanies an RAR (Revenue Agent's Report) issued as a result of an IRS audit of a taxpayer (or the rejection of a taxpayer's claim for refund). The letter outlines the taxpayer's appeal procedure before the IRS. If the taxpayer does not request any such procedures within the 30-day period, the IRS issues a statutory notice of deficiency (the 90-day letter).

Throwback rule. If there is no income tax in the state to which a sale otherwise would be apportioned, the sale essentially is exempt from state income tax, even though the seller is domiciled in a state that levies an income tax. Nonetheless, if the seller's state has adopted a throwback rule, the sale is attributed to the seller's state and the transaction is subjected to a state-level tax.

Traditional IRA. See *Individual Retirement Accounts (IRAs)*.

Transfer pricing. The process of setting internal prices for transfers of goods and services among related taxpayers. For example, what price should be used when Subsidiary purchases management services from Parent? The IRS can adjust transfer prices when it can show that the taxpayers were attempting to avoid tax by, for example, shifting losses, deductions, or credits from low-tax to high-tax entities or jurisdictions.

Transportation expenses. Expenses that include the cost of transporting the self-employed taxpayer (or employee) from one place to another in the course of business when the taxpayer is not in travel status. For tax years beginning after 2017 and before 2026, only reimbursed transportation expenses are deductible by employees. Commuting expenses are not deductible.

Travel expenses. Expenses that include meals (generally subject to a 50 percent disallowance) and lodging and transportation expenses while away from home in the pursuit of a trade or business (including that of an employee). For tax years beginning after 2017 and before 2026, only reimbursed travel expenses are deductible by employees.

Treaty shopping. An international investor attempts to use the favorable aspects of a tax treaty to his or her advantage, often elevating the form of the transaction over its substance (e.g., by establishing only a nominal presence in the country offering the favorable treaty terms).

U

UDITPA. The Uniform Division of Income for Tax Purposes Act has been adopted in some form by many of the states. The Act develops criteria by which the total taxable income of a multistate corporation can be assigned to specific states.

Unclaimed property. A U.S. state may have the right to acquire property that has been made available to an individual or legal entity for a fixed period of time, where the claimant has not taken possession of the property after a notice period. Examples of such property that a state could acquire are an uncashed payroll check or an unused gift card.

Unearned income. Income received but not yet earned. Normally, such income is taxed when received, even for accrual basis taxpayers.

Unified transfer tax. Rates applicable to transfers by gift and death made after 1976. § 2001(c).

Unified transfer tax credit. A credit allowed against any unified transfer tax. §§ 2010 and 2505.

Uniform capitalization (UNICAP) rules. Under § 263A, the Regulations provide a set of rules that all taxpayers (regardless of the particular industry) can use to determine the items of cost (and means of allocating those costs) that must be capitalized with respect to the production of tangible property. Small businesses, defined as those with average annual gross receipts in the prior three-year period of $25 million or less, that are not a tax shelter, are not required to use the UNICAP rules.

Unitary approach. See *unitary theory*.

Unitary theory. Sales, property, and payroll of related corporations are combined for nexus and apportionment purposes, and the worldwide income of the unitary entity is apportioned to the state. Subsidiaries and other affiliated corporations found to be part of the corporation's unitary business (because they are subject to overlapping ownership, operation, or management) are included in the apportionment procedure. This approach can be limited if a water's-edge election is in effect.

Unit-livestock-price method. A method of accounting for the cost of livestock. The livestock are valued using a standard cost of raising an animal with the characteristics of the animals on hand to the same age as those animals.

Unrealized receivables. Amounts earned by a cash basis taxpayer but not yet received. Because of the method of accounting used by the taxpayer, these amounts have a zero income tax basis. When unrealized receivables are distributed to a partner, they generally convert a transaction from nontaxable to taxable or an otherwise capital gain to ordinary income (i.e., as a "hot asset").

Unreasonable compensation. A deduction is allowed for "reasonable" salaries or other compensation for personal services actually rendered. The issue of unreasonable compensation usually is limited to closely held corporations, where the motivation is to pay out profits in some form that is deductible to the corporation. To the extent compensation is "excessive" ("unreasonable"), the distribution could be treated as a dividend, such that no deduction is allowed.

Unreasonable position. A tax preparer penalty is assessed regarding the understatement of a client's tax liability due to a tax return position that is found to be too aggressive. The penalty is avoided if there is substantial authority for the position or if the position is disclosed adequately on the tax return. The penalty equals the greater of $1,000 or one-half of the tax preparer's fee that is traceable to the aggressive position.

Unrecaptured § 1250 gain. Gain from the sale of depreciable real estate held more than one year. The gain is equal to or less than the depreciation taken on such property and is reduced by § 1245 and § 1250 gain.

Unrelated business income (UBI). Income recognized by an exempt organization that is generated from activities not related to the exempt purpose of the entity. For instance, the gift shop located in a hospital may generate unrelated business income. §§ 511 and 512.

Unrelated business income tax (UBIT). Levied on the unrelated business income of an exempt organization.

U.S. Court of Federal Claims. A trial court (court of original jurisdiction) that decides litigation involving Federal tax matters. Appeal from this court is to the Court of Appeals for the Federal Circuit.

U.S. District Court. A trial court for purposes of litigating Federal tax matters. This court allows a jury trial.

U.S. shareholder. For purposes of classification of an entity as a controlled foreign corporation, a U.S. person who owns, or is considered to own, 10 percent or more of the total combined voting power of all classes of voting stock of a foreign corporation. Stock owned directly, indirectly, and constructively is counted for this purpose.

U.S. Supreme Court. The highest appellate court or the court of last resort in the Federal court system and in most states. Only a small number of tax decisions of the U.S. Courts of Appeal are reviewed by the U.S. Supreme Court under its certiorari procedure. The Supreme Court usually grants certiorari to resolve a conflict among the Courts of Appeal (e.g., two or more appellate courts have assumed opposing positions on a particular issue) or when the tax issue is extremely important (e.g., due to the size of the revenue loss to the Federal government).

U.S. Tax Court. One of four trial courts of original jurisdiction that decides litigation involving Federal income, death, or gift taxes. The only trial court where the taxpayer must not first pay the deficiency assessed by the IRS. The Tax Court does not have jurisdiction over a case unless a statutory notice of deficiency (90-day letter) has been issued by the IRS and the taxpayer files the petition for hearing within the time prescribed.

U.S. trade or business. A set of activities that is carried on in a regular, continuous, and substantial manner. A non-U.S. taxpayer is subject to U.S. tax on the taxable income that is effectively connected with a U.S. trade or business.

Use tax. A use tax is designed to complement the sales tax. The use tax has two purposes: to prevent consumers from evading sales tax by purchasing goods outside the state for in-state use, and to provide an equitable taxing environment between in-state and out-of-state retailers. Purchasers of taxable goods or services who were not charged sales tax because the seller did not have *nexus* with the purchaser's state may owe use tax on the purchase.

V

Vacation homes. The Code places restrictions upon taxpayers who rent their residences or vacation homes for part of the tax year. The restrictions may result in a scaling down of expense deductions for the taxpayers. § 280A.

Valuation allowance. Under ASC 740 (SFAS 109), a tax-related item is reported for book purposes only when it is more likely than not that the item actually will be realized. When the "more likely than not" test is failed, a contra-asset account is created to offset some or all of the related deferred tax asset. For instance, if the entity projects that it will not be able to use all of its net operating loss carryforward due to a lack of future taxable income, a valuation allowance is created to reduce the net deferred tax asset that corresponds to the carryforward. If income projections later change and it appears that the carryforward will be used, the valuation allowance is reversed or "released." Creation of a valuation allowance usually increases the current tax expense and thereby reduces current book income, and its release often increases book income in the later reporting period.

Value added tax (VAT). A national sales tax that taxes the increment in value as goods move through the production process. A VAT is much used in the majority of countries but has not yet been incorporated as part of the U.S. Federal tax structure.

Vesting requirements. A qualified deferred compensation arrangement must satisfy a vesting requirement. Under this provision, an employee's right to accrued plan benefits derived from employer contributions must be nonforfeitable in accordance with one of two vesting time period schedules (or two required alternate vesting schedules for certain employer matching contributions).

Voluntary revocation. The owners of a majority of shares in an S corporation elect to terminate the S status of the entity as of a specified date. The day on which the revocation is effective is the first day of the corporation's C tax year.

W

W–2 Wages/Capital Investment Limit. A limitation on the deduction for qualified business income that caps the deduction at the greater of (1) 50 percent of the wages paid by a qualified trade or business or (2) 25 percent of the wages paid by the qualified trade or business plus 2.5 percent of the taxpayer's share of the unadjusted basis of property used in the business that has not been fully depreciated prior to the close of the taxable year. § 199A(b)(2)(B).

Wash sale. A loss from the sale of stock or securities that is disallowed because the taxpayer, within 30 days before or after the sale, has acquired stock or securities substantially identical to those sold. § 1091.

Waters' edge. A limitation on the worldwide scope of the unitary theory. If a corporate waters'-edge election is in effect, the state can consider in the apportionment procedure only the activities that occur within the boundaries of the United States.

Waters'-edge election. See *waters' edge.*

Wherewithal to pay. This concept recognizes the inequity of taxing a transaction when the taxpayer lacks the means with which to pay the tax. Under it, there is a correlation between the imposition of the tax and the ability to pay the tax. It is particularly suited to situations in which the taxpayer's economic position has not changed significantly as a result of the transaction.

Whistleblower Program. An IRS initiative that offers special rewards to informants who provide evidence regarding tax evasion activities of businesses or high-income individuals. More than $2 million of tax, interest, and penalty must be at stake. The reward can reach 30 percent of the tax recovery that is attributable to the whistleblower's information.

Work opportunity tax credit. Employers are allowed a tax credit equal to 40 percent of the first $6,000 of wages (per eligible employee) for the first year of employment. Eligible employees include certain hard-to-employ individuals (e.g., qualified ex-felons, high-risk youth, food stamp recipients, and veterans). The employer's deduction for wages is reduced by the amount of the credit taken. For qualified summer youth employees, the 40 percent rate is applied to the first $3,000 of qualified wages. The credit does not apply to any amount paid to an individual who begins work for the employer after 2020. §§ 51 and 52.

Working condition fringes. A type of fringe benefit received by the employee that is excludible from the employee's gross income. It consists of property or services provided (paid or reimbursed) by the employer for which the employee could take a tax deduction if the employee had paid for them. § 132.

Worthless securities. A loss (usually capital) is allowed for a security that becomes worthless during the year. The loss is deemed to have occurred on the last day of the year. Special rules apply to securities of affiliated companies and small business stock. § 165.

Writ of Certiorari. Appeal from a U.S. Court of Appeals to the U.S. Supreme Court is by Writ of Certiorari. The Supreme Court need not accept the appeal and usually does not (*cert. den.*) unless a conflict exists among the lower courts that must be resolved or a constitutional issue is involved.

Appendix D-1

Table of Code Sections Cited

I.R.C. Sec.	This Work Page	I.R.C. Sec.	This Work Page
1	2-6, 3-17, 14-22	24(h)	3-15
1-5	2-5	24(h)(3)	3-15
1(e)	24-10	24(h)(4)	3-15
1(g)	12-17	24(h)(4)(7)	3-15
1(g)(2)	3-26	24(h)(4)(B)	3-16
1(h)	14-23	25A	9-37, 12-20
1(h)(1)	3-29, 19-13	25A(c)	12-17
1(h)(11)	4-14, 19-2	25(A)(c)	9-17
1(h)(11)(B)(iii)(I)	19-13	25A(d)	12-17
1(i)	3-24	25A(f)	9-16
1(j)	4-14	25A(i)	9-16
1(j)(4)(B)	3-26	25A(i)(1)	12-17
1(j)(4)(D)	3-26	25B	12-20
2	2-6, 2-7, 3-17	25B(a) through (d)	12-18
2(a)	3-19	25B(e)	12-19
2(a)(1)(A)	2-5, 2-6	27	25-16
2(b)	3-19	31	12-20
2(b)(1)(B)	3-19	32	12-12, 12-20
2(b)(3)(B)	3-19	32(a)(2)(B)	12-12
5	1-7	32(c)(1)(A)(ii)	12-12
7	2-2	38	12-21
8	2-2	38(b)	12-5
10	2-2	38(c)	12-5
11-12	2-5	39(a)(1)	12-5
12(d)	2-6	41	7-16, 12-8, 12-21
14	24-15	41(b)(3)(A)	12-8
21	12-14	41(b)(3)(D)	12-8
21(d)	12-15	41(c)(4)	12-8
22	12-20	41(c)(5)	12-8
23	5-15	41(d)	12-8
24	12-20	41(d)(4)	26-28
24(b)	3-16	42	12-9, 12-21
24(c)	3-15	42(j)(5)	21-20

I.R.C. Sec.	This Work Page
44	12-10, 12-21
45E	12-10, 12-21
45E(c)(1)	12-10
45E(d)(1)	12-10
45F	12-11
45F(d)	12-11
45S	12-11
47	12-6, 12-21
48(c)(1)	6-10
50(c)	12-6
51	12-7, 12-22
51(d)	12-7
55	12-25, 12-34
59A	25-13
59(e)	7-19
59(e)(2)	21-21
61	2-27, 4-2, 4-3, 4-19, 17-17, 18-5, 28-14
61(a)	2-38, 3-3, 4-3
61(a)(3)	13-8
61(a)(12)	5-29
62	3-5, 3-6, 6-3, 17-17
62(a)(1)	6-31, 7-15
62(a)(2)(A)	6-31
62(a)(2)(B)	6-31
62(a)(2)(D)	6-31, 9-17
62(a)(3)	6-31
62(a)(4)	6-31, 7-15
62(a)(15)	6-31
62(a)(18)	6-31
62(b)	9-33
63(a)	17-17
63(b) through (g)	17-17
63(c)	10-2
63(c)(1)	3-7
63(c)(5)	3-8
63(c)(6)	3-8
63(d)	10-2
63(d)(3)	15-10
66	4-18
67(b)(3)	7-15
67(g)	9-35
71	4-19
71-91	4-19
71(c)(2)	4-20
71(c)(3)	4-20
72(b)	4-26
72(d)	4-26
72(t)	9-17
72(t)(2)	9-29
72(t)(2)(B)	9-29
72(t)(2)(D)	9-29
72(t)(2)(E)	9-29
72(t)(2)(F)	9-29
73	4-13

I.R.C. Sec.	This Work Page
74	4-27, 5-22
74(b)	4-27
74(c)	4-27
74(d)	4-27
79	5-20, 5-22
83	18-5, 21-9
83(a)	4-10, 21-8
83(h)	21-8
85	4-28
86	4-28
101 through 140	5-2
101(a)	5-4
101(g)	5-5
102	5-3
102(a)	13-12
102(c)	5-3
103	6-29, 27-10, 28-14, 28-18
103(a)	5-23
104	2-38, 5-2
104(a)(1)	5-10
104(a)(2)	5-9
104(a)(3)	5-10
105	5-11, 5-21
105(a)	5-11
105(b)	5-11
105(c)	5-11
105(h)	5-11
106	5-11, 5-22
106(d)	5-12
107	5-14
108	5-29
108(a)	5-30
108(b)	5-30
108(c)	5-30
108(e)	5-30
108(e)(5)	5-30
108(e)(6)	5-30
108(f)	5-30
108(g)	5-30
109	1-34
111	5-27
111(a)	5-27
117	4-27, 5-2, 9-17
117(a)	5-7
117(b)	5-7
117(d)	5-7, 9-17
118(a)	18-18
118(b)(1)	18-18
118(b)(2)	18-18, 24-27
119	5-13, 5-22
119(a)	5-13
119(d)	5-14
121	5-2, 10-15, 13-35, 13-36, 13-37, 13-38, 13-39, 13-40, 13-41, 13-44, 13-45

I.R.C. Sec.	This Work Page
121(a)	13-36
121(b)	13-35
121(b)(1)	13-38
121(b)(2)	13-38
121(b)(3)	13-37
121(c)(1)	13-40
121(c)(2)(B)	13-39
121(d)(6)	13-41
121(d)(10)	13-36
121(f)	13-44
125	5-16
127	5-15, 5-22, 9-17
129	5-15, 5-22
132	5-17, 5-22
132(j)(1)	5-20
132(j)(4)	5-15
132(m)(2)	5-20
134	5-14
135	5-25, 5-42, 9-17
137	5-15
139	5-2, 5-3
139F	5-10
151(b)	3-9
151(c)	3-9
152(b)(2)	3-14
152(b)(3)	3-15
152(c)	3-10
152(c)(4)	3-11
152(d)	3-11
152(d)(2)(H)	3-12
152(d)(3)	3-13
152(e)(1)	3-14
152(e)(2)	3-14
152(e)(5)	3-14
152(f)(1)	3-20
152(f)(1)(A)(ii)	3-10
152(f)(2)	3-10
152(f)(3)	3-12
152(f)(5)	3-10
152(f)(6)	3-10
162	6-3, 6-4, 6-15, 6-17, 6-31, 9-17, 11-23, 17-17, 18-17, 20-4, 28-13, 28-14
162(a)	6-4, 6-31, 6-46, 9-10
162(a)(1)	6-5, 17-11
162(a)(2)	6-31
162(c)	2-23, 6-13
162(e)	6-16, 6-33
162(f)	6-14, 6-33, 9-8
162(f)(1)	6-13
162(g)	6-13
162(k)	19-30
162(l)	10-7
162(m)	6-16, 17-11
162(q)	6-30

I.R.C. Sec.	This Work Page
163	6-31, 19-30
163(a)	6-31
163(d)	6-31
163(d)(1)	11-22
163(d)(2)	11-23
163(d)(4)(B)	11-22
163(h)	6-31
163(h)(3)	10-15
163(h)(3)(E)(i)	10-16
163(h)(3)(E)(ii)	10-16
163(h)(3)(F)	10-14
163(j)	6-31, 8-23, 17-6
163(j)(1)	17-7
163(j)(3)	17-7
163(j)(4)	17-8, 21-18
163(j)(7)	17-8
163(j)(8)(A)	17-7
163(j)(8)(A)(v)	17-7
163(j)(8)(B)	17-7
164	6-31, 12-13
164(a)(1)	6-31
164(a)(2)	6-31
164(a)(3)	6-31
164(b)(6)	10-11
164(f)	9-31, 12-23
165	6-6
165(a)	13-8, 18-21
165(c)	7-7, 13-35
165(c)(1)	6-31, 11-2
165(c)(2)	11-2
165(c)(3)	6-31, 13-35
165(g)	7-5, 20-10
165(g)(1)	11-23, 14-8, 18-21
165(g)(3)	18-21
165(h)	7-10
165(h)(2)(B)	7-13
165(h)(3)	7-12
165(h)(4)(E)	7-9
165(h)(5)	7-12
165(h)(5)(B)	7-12
165(i)	7-8, 16-9
165(i)(5)	7-7
165(k)	7-8
166	6-31
166(a)	18-21
166(a)(2)	18-22
166(d)	14-48
166(d)(1)	18-22
166(d)(1)(A)	18-22
166(d)(1)(B)	18-21
166(d)(2)	18-22
167	13-21, 14-36
167(h)	28-14
168	8-2, 13-21, 14-36

I.R.C. Sec.	This Work Page
168(b)	8-5, 8-8, 8-9
168(b)(5)	8-8
168(c)	8-9
168(d)(1)	8-10
168(d)(3)	8-7
168(d)(4)(A)	8-6
168(e)	8-5
168(e)(3)	8-23
168(e)(6)	8-8
168(f)(1)	8-26
168(g)	8-23
168(g)(2)	19-5
168(g)(3)(B)	8-23
168(k)	8-15, 14-36, 19-5
168(k)(2)(E)(ii)(I)	8-15
168(k)(2)(F)(i)	8-19
170	6-31, 27-20
170(a)(2)	17-9
170(b)	17-11
170(b)(1)(C)(iii)	10-24
170(c)	10-20
170(d)	17-11
170(e)(1)(A)	14-42
170(e)(1)(B)	14-42
170(e)(1)(B)(i)	10-23
170(e)(1)(B)(ii)	10-24, 23-8, 23-22
170(e)(3)	17-10
170(e)(4)	17-10
170(f)	10-21
170(i)	10-19
170(j)	10-19
170(l)	10-19
171(c)	13-7
172	7-19, 16-9
172(a)	7-20
172(b)(1)(B)(i)	7-20
172(d)	17-12
172(d)(2)	18-21
172(d)(8)	7-20
174	12-8
174(a)(2)	7-17
174(b)(2)	7-16
179	1-27, 6-12, 8-20, 9-37, 13-21, 14-36, 14-39, 14-43, 14-62, 16-46, 17-27, 19-5, 19-6, 19-7, 19-8, 21-9, 21-11, 21-16, 21-20, 21-24, 22-10
183	6-19, 22-25
183(b)(2)	11-23
183(d)	6-19
195	6-17, 8-28, 8-43, 17-16, 17-46
195(a)	8-25
195(b)	6-18, 8-25
195(b)(1)	21-12
195(b)(1)(A)	8-25
195(b)(1)(B)	8-25
195(c)	8-28
195(c)(1)(A)	8-28
195(c)(1)(B)	8-28
195(d)	8-25
197	6-28, 8-25, 8-39, 14-14, 21-9
197(a)	8-25, 14-14
199A	6-7, 6-31, 14-64, 14-65, 15-11, 15-12, 15-14, 15-17, 15-23, 17-7, 17-17, 21-17, 21-29, 21-30, 21-59, 22-10, 22-12, 22-29, 25-30
199A(a)	6-7
199A(a)(1)	15-10
199A(a)(1)(A)	15-10
199A(a)(1)(B)	15-10
199A(a)(1)(B)(ii)	15-10
199A(b)(1)(A)	15-10
199A(b)(2)	15-12
199A(b)(2)(B)	15-12
199A(b)(3)(B)	15-12
199A(b)(3)(B)(ii)	15-15
199A(b)(3)(B)(iii)	15-15
199A(b)(4)	15-14
199A(b)(6)(A)	15-14
199A(b)(6)(B)	15-14
199A(c)	6-7, 15-10
199A(c)(2)	7-20, 15-21
199A(c)(3)(A)	15-10
199A(c)(3)(B)	15-11
199A(c)(4)	15-11
199A(d)(1)	6-8
199A(d)(1)(A)	15-17
199A(d)(1)(B)	15-11
199A(d)(2)	15-12, 15-17
199A(d)(3)(B)	15-17
199A(e)(1)	15-10
199A(e)(2)	15-12
199A(f)(1)	21-29
199A(f)(3)	15-22
211	2-25
212	6-29, 17-17, 28-13, 28-14
212(1)	2-5
212(2)	11-23
212(3)	10-5
213	6-31
213(a)	6-25
213(d)(1)(A)	10-3
213(d)(2)	10-6
213(d)(9)(A)	10-4
213(d)(10)	5-12
215	4-19
217	5-19
217(k)	9-22
219(b)(1)	9-26

I.R.C. Sec.	This Work Page
219(c)	9-26
219(c)(2)	9-26
219(f)(3)	9-29
219(g)	9-26
219(g)(4)	9-26
219(g)(7)	9-27
221	9-17, 10-14
221(b)(2)(C)	10-14
222	6-31, 9-17, 12-28
222(b)(2)(C)	9-16
222(c)	9-16
222(d)	9-16
223	5-12, 5-22, 10-8
223(b)	5-12
223(b)(2)	10-9
223(c)(2)	10-8
223(d)	5-12, 10-9
223(f)	10-9
241	2-5
243(a)	17-13
245	17-13
245A	17-13, 25-24
246(b)	17-13
246(c)	17-14, 19-13
248	17-15, 22-9
250	25-17
250(b)(2)(A)	25-18
262	6-31, 10-2, 10-27, 14-16
263(a)(1)	6-26
263(c)	14-45
263A	8-26
263A(d)	16-12
263A(i)	4-8
265	6-29, 28-13, 28-14
265(a)(2)	10-16
267	2-23, 13-42, 14-16, 20-3, 20-5, 20-8
267(a)(1)	6-29, 13-9
267(a)(2)	17-4
267(b)	16-24, 18-21
267(b)(13)	28-12
267(d)	13-16
269	17-23
269A(b)(2)	11-10
274	8-23, 9-22
274(a)(1)(A)	6-31
274(a)(4)	5-19, 6-30
274(b)(1)	9-24
274(c)	9-13
274(d)	8-23, 9-14
274(e)	9-22
274(h)(1)	9-11
274(i)	8-23
274(j)	4-7
274(k)	9-23

I.R.C. Sec.	This Work Page
274(m)(2)	9-12
274(m)(3)	9-12
274(n)	6-31, 9-22
275	10-10
276	6-15
280A	6-21, 11-23
280A through 280H	2-5
280A(c)(1)	9-18
280A(d)	6-23
280A(g)	6-22
280C(c)	12-8
280E	6-15
280F	8-18
280F(a)(1)	8-19
280F(b)(1)	8-21
280F(b)(2)	8-21
280F(b)(3)	8-19
280F(d)(1)	8-20
280F(d)(4)(A)	8-18
280F(d)(5)	8-19
291	17-6, 17-10
291(a)(1)	14-44
301	19-14
301(c)	5-24
301(c)(1)	19-2
301(c)(2)	19-2
301(c)(3)	19-2
301(d)	20-3
302	19-28
302(b)	20-17
302(b)(1)	19-24, 19-26
302(b)(2)	19-24, 19-27
302(b)(3)	19-24
302(e)	19-30
303	19-24, 19-28, 19-29, 19-31, 19-34
303(b)(2)(A)	19-29
303(b)(2)(B)	19-29
305	19-20
305(a)	5-25, 13-11
305(b)	5-25
307(a)	13-11, 19-19
307(b)(1)	19-21
311	19-14, 19-29
311(b)	14-43, 22-18
311(b)(2)	19-15
312	19-3
312(a)	19-15
312(b)	19-15
312(c)	19-15
312(d)(1)	19-20
312(f)(1)	19-5
312(k)(3)(A)	19-5
312(k)(3)(B)	19-6
312(n)(2)	19-6

I.R.C. Sec.	This Work Page
312(n)(3)	19-6
312(n)(4)	19-6
312(n)(5)	19-4
312(n)(6)	19-6
312(n)(7)	19-30
316	19-2
316(a)	5-24
318	2-23, 19-25, 20-8
318(a)	16-24
331	20-8, 20-9, 20-10
331(a)	20-8
332	14-42, 20-8, 20-9, 20-10, 20-11, 20-12, 20-13, 20-20, 20-22
332(b)	20-9
332(b)(3)	20-10
334(a)	20-3, 20-8, 20-10, 20-11
334(b)(1)	20-10, 20-12
334(b)(1)(B)	20-11, 20-12
336	20-9, 20-10
336(a)	20-3, 20-10
336(d)	20-4, 20-5, 20-6
336(d)(1)	20-5
336(d)(2)	20-6
337	20-10
337(a)	20-9
337(b)(1)	20-11
338	20-10, 20-12, 20-13, 20-14, 20-20, 20-26
338(a)(1)	20-13
338(a)(2)	20-13
338(b)(5)	20-13
351	14-42, 18-2, 18-3, 18-4, 18-5, 18-6, 18-7, 18-8, 18-10, 18-12, 18-13, 18-14, 18-15, 18-17, 18-23, 18-24, 18-25, 18-29, 20-4, 20-5, 20-6, 20-8, 20-13, 20-23, 20-25, 21-54, 22-19, 22-30, 25-18, 25-35
351(a)	18-12
351(b)	18-4
351(g)	18-6
355	19-30
357(a)	18-10
357(b)	18-10
357(c)	18-10, 18-11
357(c)(2)(A)	18-12
358(a)	18-13
361(a)	20-17
361(b)	20-17
362(a)	18-14, 18-18
362(e)	18-18
362(e)(1)(B)	20-11
362(e)(2)	18-15, 20-4
367	25-18
367(d)	25-18
368	17-22, 20-15, 20-16, 20-17, 20-24, 20-28

I.R.C. Sec.	This Work Page
368(a)(1)	20-15
368(c)	18-6
381	17-23, 20-10, 20-12
381-385	24-6
382	17-23
385	18-19, 18-20
401	23-3
401(a)(9)	9-27
401(c)(2)	9-31
401(c)(2)(A)(v)	9-31
401(k)	9-31, 13-14, 24-15, 27-15
402(g)(1)	9-25
402(g)(4)	9-25
403(b)	27-15
404(h)(1)(B)	9-29
408	9-32
408(d)(1)	9-29
408(m)(2)	14-22
408(o)	9-27
408(p)	9-32
408(p)(2)(E)(i)	9-32
408A	9-27
408A(c)(3)(B)	9-30
408A(c)(4)	9-30
415(b)(1)	9-31
415(c)(1)	9-31
441	4-6
441(c)	16-2
441(f)	16-3
441(i)	4-6, 16-6, 17-4, 17-46
442	16-6
444	16-6, 17-9, 21-14
444(b)(3)	17-4
444(c)	16-5
446	16-10
446(a)	6-10
446(b)	4-7, 6-10, 16-11
446(c)(3)	16-16
446(d)	16-11
446(e)	4-7, 6-10
446(f)	16-18
447	16-12
447(c)	16-12
448	4-8, 6-10, 16-10, 16-12, 21-13
448(a)	16-12, 17-4
448(b)	16-12
448(c)	4-8, 6-30
448(c)(1)	6-10
448(d)(2)(A)	11-10, 17-4
448(d)(3)	16-12
448(d)(5)	16-16
451(a)	21-13
451(b)	4-8, 16-13
451(b)(3)	16-13

I.R.C. Sec.	This Work Page
451(c)	4-12, 16-13
451(c)(4)(B)	16-14
451(d)	16-9
451(f)	16-9
451(g)	16-9
453	4-7
453(a)	16-20
453(b)	16-20
453(d)	16-26
453(d)(3)	16-26
453(e)	16-23
453(e)(2)	16-24
453(e)(2)(B)	16-24
453(e)(6)	16-24
453(e)(7)	16-24
453(f)(1)	16-24
453(g)	16-25
453(h)	20-8
453(i)	14-43, 16-20
453(j)	16-20
453(l)(2)	16-20
453A	16-25
453B(a)	16-25, 20-8
453B(c)	16-26
453B(d)	16-26
453B(f)(2)	16-25
453B(g)	16-26
454(a)	4-11
457	27-15
460	4-7, 16-27
460(b)(1)(A)	16-29
460(b)(2)	16-30
460(b)(5)	16-30
460(b)(6)	16-30
460(f)	16-27
461	16-14
461(g)(1)	10-17
461(g)(2)	10-16
461(h)	6-10
461(h)(3)(A)	6-11
461(l)	7-17, 21-36
461(l)(1)	21-38
461(l)(3)	7-17
461(l)(3)(A)(i)	7-18
461(l)(4)(A)	7-18
461(l)(5)	7-19
461(l)(6)	7-19
464	16-12, 16-21
465	11-37, 21-36
465(a)	21-37
465(a)(2)	21-37
465(b)(1)	11-4
465(b)(6)	11-4, 21-37
465(e)	11-5

I.R.C. Sec.	This Work Page
469	7-19, 11-5, 21-37
469(a)	11-9, 17-8
469(a)(1)	21-37
469(b)	11-8
469(c)(1)	21-37
469(c)(2)	11-15, 21-37
469(c)(7)	11-17
469(c)(7)(B)	11-18
469(d)(2)	11-8
469(f)	11-9
469(g)(2)	11-20
469(g)(3)	11-21
469(h)(2)	11-14, 21-37
469(h)(5)	11-14
469(i)	11-18, 21-37
469(i)(3)(F)	11-18
469(i)(6)	11-18
469(j)(1)	17-8
469(j)(2)	11-10, 17-8
469(j)(5)	11-19
469(j)(6)	11-21
469(j)(8)	11-15
471(c)	4-6, 4-8, 16-36
471(c)(1)(B)	16-11
474	2-33
481	16-18
481(a)	16-19, 19-45
481(b)	16-18
482	17-20, 17-21, 17-23
483	16-22
483(e)	16-24
501	10-20, 23-3
501-530	23-2
501(a)	23-3
501(c)	23-31
501(c)(1)	23-4, 23-25
501(c)(2)	23-4, 23-25
501(c)(3)	23-3, 23-4, 23-5, 23-8, 23-9, 23-12, 23-13, 23-18, 23-19, 23-20, 23-21, 23-23, 23-24, 23-25, 23-26
501(c)(4)	23-4, 23-21, 23-25, 23-31
501(c)(5)	23-4, 23-25
501(c)(6)	23-4, 23-5, 23-25
501(c)(7)	23-4, 23-25
501(c)(8)	23-4, 23-25
501(c)(9)	23-4, 23-25
501(c)(10)	23-4, 23-25
501(c)(11)	23-4, 23-25
501(c)(12)	23-4, 23-25
501(c)(13)	23-4, 23-25
501(c)(14)	23-4, 23-25
501(c)(15)	23-4, 23-25
501(c)(16)	23-4, 23-25
501(c)(19)	23-4, 23-25

I.R.C. Sec.	This Work Page
501(c)(20)	23-4, 23-25
501(d)	23-4, 23-25
501(e)	23-4
501(f)	23-4
501(h)	23-3, 23-5, 23-6, 23-7, 23-23, 23-26
502(a)	23-8
508(c)(1)	23-19
509(a)	23-8
509(a)(1)	23-8
509(a)(2)	23-9
511(a)(1)	23-12
511(a)(2)	23-13
512(a)(1)	23-15
512(a)(6)	23-13
512(b)	23-16
512(b)(2)	23-31
512(b)(12)	23-17
513(a)	23-13
513(f)	23-15
513(h)(1)(A)	23-15
513(h)(1)(B)	23-15
513(i)	23-14
514(b)	23-18
514(b)(3)	23-19
514(c)(1)	23-19
529	5-26, 5-27, 5-35, 9-17, 23-4, 27-11, 27-30
529(c)(4)	27-11
529A	5-27
530	5-26, 5-27, 9-17, 23-4
531–537	17-20
541	18-26
565	17-37
585	16-16
611(a)	8-29
611(b)(3)	28-14
611(b)(4)	28-14
612	8-29
613(a)	8-30
613A	8-30
641	28-2
641 through 692	28-2
641(b)	28-13
642(b)	28-7
642(c)(1)	28-15
642(g)	27-19
643	28-17
643(a)(3)	28-17
643(e)	28-11
645	28-6
651(a)(1)	28-8
651(b)	28-16
652(a)	4-16
652(b)	28-16
652(c)	28-20

I.R.C. Sec.	This Work Page
661(a)(1)	28-8
661(c)	28-16
662(a)	4-16
662(a)(1)	28-21
662(a)(2)	28-21
662(b)	28-16
662(c)	28-20
691	5-4, 28-12
691(a)(3)	13-15
691(c)	28-12
692	28-2
701	21-4
702	21-4
702(b)	21-16
703(a)(1)	21-16
703(a)(2)	22-9
703(b)	21-11
704(a)	21-5, 21-26
704(b)	21-23, 21-26, 21-27, 21-28, 21-34, 21-35, 21-61
704(b)(2)	28-23
704(c)	21-28, 21-53
704(c)(1)(A)	21-28
704(c)(1)(C)	21-28
704(d)	21-36
705	21-31
706	4-6, 21-14
706(a)	4-16
706(b)	21-13
706(b)(1)(B)	16-3
706(b)(1)(C)	16-5
706(b)(3)	16-3
706(d)(1)	21-47
707	13-16
707(a)	21-29, 21-52
707(a)(2)(B)	21-8
707(b)(2)	21-52
707(c)	21-18
709(a)	21-12
709(b)	21-12
721	14-42, 21-7, 21-8, 21-11, 21-54
721(b)	21-7
723	21-6
724	21-10
731	21-45
731(a)	21-41
731(a)(1)	21-41
731(a)(2)	21-46
731(b)	21-41
732	21-43
732(a)(1)	21-41
733	21-41
735(a)(2)	21-46
741	21-46, 22-31

I.R.C. Sec.	This Work Page
742	5-24, 21-47
751	22-31
751(a)	21-48
751(a)(1)	21-48
751(b)	21-41
751(d)	21-48
752	21-31
752(a)	22-20
754	22-31
861 through 865	25-6
861(a)(6)	25-8
865	25-8
871	25-26
871(a)(2)	25-27
877(a)(2)	25-28
877(g)(1)	25-29
877A	4-3
881	25-26
882	25-26
897	25-28
901-908	25-16
904	12-14, 25-16
904(c)	12-14, 25-17
911	9-34, 21-39, 25-10
911(a)	5-21
911(d)	5-22
936(h)(3)(B)	25-18
951 through 964	25-20
951A	25-25
951A(b)-(d)	25-25
951A(f)	25-25
952	25-24
954	25-24
954(d)	25-38
960	25-23
965(a)	25-25
965(c)	25-25
965(g)	25-25
965(h)	25-25
965(i)	25-25
985	25-14
988(b)	25-14
1001	18-13
1001(a)	13-3
1001(b)	13-4
1001(c)	13-8
1011	13-13
1011(a)	13-5
1012	13-10, 13-41
1014	17-19
1014(a)	13-14, 19-28
1014(b)(6)	13-15
1014(c)	13-15
1015(a)	13-12

I.R.C. Sec.	This Work Page
1015(d)(6)	13-13
1016(a)	31-5
1016(a)(2)	13-5
1016(a)(4)	13-6
1016(a)(5)	13-7
1017	5-29
1022	13-14
1031	13-22, 13-29, 13-43, 13-48, 13-66, 14-42, 14-43, 14-54, 18-2, 20-15, 22-34
1031(a)	13-22
1031(a)(2)	13-23, 20-15
1031(a)(3)	13-24
1031(d)	13-27, 13-28, 13-59
1031(f)	13-23
1032	18-18
1033	13-29, 13-31, 13-34, 13-43, 13-49, 13-51, 13-60, 14-42
1033(a)	13-31, 13-32
1033(a)(2)(A)	13-34
1033(a)(2)(B)	13-33
1033(b)	13-34
1033(g)(4)	13-33
1041	4-19, 16-24
1060	16-53
1061	21-11
1061(a)	21-49
1091(a)	13-17
1091(b)	13-18
1091(d)	13-17
1202	14-20, 18-24, 22-25
1202(a)	18-24
1202(b)	18-24
1202(d)	18-24
1202(e)(3)(A)	15-17
1211	11-23
1211(a)	14-27, 17-5
1211(b)	7-6, 14-19, 17-5
1211(b)(1)	14-26
1212	11-23
1212(a)	17-5
1212(a)(1)	14-27
1212(b)	14-26, 17-5
1221	14-4, 14-6, 14-7, 14-65, 17-3
1221(a)	14-4
1221(a)(2)	14-28
1221(a)(3)	14-4
1222(1)	2-5
1222(3)	14-28
1222(10)	14-26
1222(11)	14-20
1223	14-15
1223(1)	13-27, 18-17
1223(2)	13-13, 18-17, 20-12
1223(3)	13-17

I.R.C. Sec.	This Work Page
1223(5)	13-12, 19-20
1231	10-23, 13-11, 13-27, 14-3, 14-4, 14-5, 14-14, 14-15, 14-20, 14-28, 14-29, 14-30, 14-31, 14-32, 14-33, 14-34, 14-35, 14-36, 14-37, 14-38, 14-39, 14-40, 14-41, 14-42, 14-43, 14-44, 14-45, 14-47, 14-48, 14-49, 14-52, 14-60, 14-61, 14-62, 14-64, 14-66, 14-67, 14-68, 15-11, 16-22, 16-43, 17-6, 17-9, 17-10, 17-21, 17-40, 18-17, 21-7, 21-10, 21-11, 21-16, 21-42, 21-46, 21-48, 21-55, 21-57, 22-10, 22-31
1233	14-16
1234(a)	14-10
1234A	14-8
1235	14-11
1237	14-5, 14-7, 14-8, 14-56
1239	14-45
1239(b)	16-25
1239(c)	16-25
1241	14-14
1242	14-48
1244	2-29, 7-1, 7-6, 7-21, 7-22, 11-23, 14-8, 14-48, 18-22, 18-23, 18-27, 18-28, 18-32, 22-25, 22-31, 22-40
1244(c)(3)	7-6
1245	14-48, 17-6, 17-10, 18-17
1245(b)(1)	14-41
1245(b)(2)	14-42
1245(b)(3)	14-42, 18-17
1245(d)	14-43
1248	25-24
1250	14-20, 14-24, 14-35, 14-36, 14-37, 14-38, 14-39, 14-40, 14-41, 14-42, 14-43, 14-44, 14-45, 14-50, 14-52, 14-59, 14-61, 16-22, 16-43, 17-6, 17-10, 21-20, 21-25
1250(a)(1)(B)	14-39
1250(d)(1)	14-41
1250(d)(2)	14-41
1250(d)(3)	14-42, 18-17
1250(i)	14-43
1253	14-12, 14-14
1253(b)(1)	14-12
1254	14-45
1259	14-17
1271	14-9
1271(b)	14-47
1272-1275	14-9
1272-1288	14-9
1272(a)	16-23
1272(a)(2)	4-11
1272(a)(3)	4-10, 16-24
1273(a)	4-10, 16-23
1273(a)(3)	14-9
1274	16-22
1274(a)	16-23, 16-24
1274(c)(3)(A)	16-24
1274(c)(3)(C)	16-24
1274(c)(3)(F)	16-24
1274(d)	4-21
1274(d)(1)	16-22
1274A(b)	16-24
1274A(c)	16-24
1276-1288	14-9
1301	16-9
1341	16-9, 19-45
1361-1379	22-2
1361(a)	4-16
1361(b)(1)(B)	22-5
1361(b)(1)(D)	22-4
1361(b)(3)(B)	22-4
1361(c)(1)(A)(ii)	22-4
1361(c)(1)(B)(i)	22-4
1361(c)(4)	22-4
1362(a)(2)	22-6
1362(b)(1)(C)	22-5
1362(b)(2)(B)(ii)	22-7
1362(d)(1)	22-7
1362(d)(2)(B)	22-8
1362(d)(3)(A)(ii)	22-8
1362(d)(3)(B)	22-24
1362(d)(3)(C)	22-24
1362(e)(3)	22-8
1363(b)	22-9
1366	4-16
1366(a)(1)	22-12
1366(d)	22-22
1366(d)(3)	22-28
1366(e)	22-25
1366(f)(2)	22-23
1367(b)(2)	22-20
1367(b)(2)(B)	22-21
1368(a)(1)(A)	22-21
1368(c)	22-15
1368(c)(1)	22-15
1368(e)(1)	22-15
1368(e)(1)(A)	22-15
1368(e)(3)	22-14
1371(e)	22-17
1372(a)	22-26
1374	22-23
1374(c)(2)	22-23
1374(d)(1)	22-23
1374(d)(2)(A)	22-23
1374(d)(7)(B)	22-23
1375(b)(1)(B)	22-24
1377(a)(1)	22-12
1377(a)(2)	22-13

I.R.C. Sec.	This Work Page
1377(b)	22-17
1377(b)(1)	22-22
1378	4-6
1378(a)	16-5
1378(b)	16-5
1378(b)(2)	16-5
1402(a)	7-20, 9-31, 21-39
1402(a)(12)	12-23
1402(a)(13)	21-39
1411	11-26, 12-24, 21-39
1411(b)	12-24
1411(c)	12-25
1441	25-27
1441(b)	21-38
1445	25-28
1445(a)	21-38
1445(e)	21-38
1446(a)	21-38
1502	17-21
1504(a)	17-21
2001	27-2
2001 through 2058	27-2
2001(a)	27-2
2001(c)	27-5
2001(c)(2)(B)	27-11
2006(a)(3)(B)	17-24
2010	27-27
2010(c)	27-27
2013	27-22
2014	27-23
2032(a)(1)	13-14, 27-5
2032(c)	13-14
2040(a)	27-16
2040(b)	13-15
2041	27-15
2044	27-22
2053	27-28
2053(c)(1)(A)	27-19
2054	27-19, 28-15
2055	27-20
2056	27-20
2056(b)(1)	27-21
2056(b)(7)	27-21
2058	27-22
2101 through 2108	27-2
2501(a)(5)	27-8
2502(c)	27-2
2503(a)	27-3
2503(b)	27-10
2503(b)(2)	27-4
2503(e)	27-8
2511	27-22
2511(a)	27-3
2513	27-12
2516	27-9

I.R.C. Sec.	This Work Page
2519	27-22
2522	27-20
2523	27-20
2523(b)(1)	27-21
2601	27-4
2611	27-24
2612(c)(1)	27-25
2631(c)	27-25
2652(a)(2)	27-25
2801	27-3
3101(b)(2)	12-24
3121(d)(3)	9-5
3402	3-25
3508	9-5
4064	1-11
4911(a)(1)	23-6
4911(b)	23-6
4911(c)(2)	23-6
4911(c)(4)	23-6
4912(a)	23-5
4912(b)	23-5
4912(c)	23-5
4940	23-11
4940-4945	23-11
4940(d)(2)	23-11
4941	23-11
4942	23-11
4942(j)(3)	23-11
4943	23-11
4944	23-11
4958	23-7
4960	23-8
4960(c)(2)	23-8
4961	23-11
4968	23-8
4980D	5-11
6012(a)(1)	3-21
6012(a)(2)	17-23
6012(a)(3)	28-23
6012(a)(4)	28-23
6017	12-23
6019(a)(2)	27-12
6033(a)(1)	23-19
6033(a)(3)	23-19
6050Y	5-5
6072(a)	3-23, 17-24
6072(b)	17-24
6075(a)	27-23
6075(b)(1)	27-13
6075(b)(2)	27-13
6081	27-13
6081(b)	17-24
6104(d)	23-21
6104(d)(4)	23-21
6110	2-8

I.R.C. Sec.	This Work Page	I.R.C. Sec.	This Work Page
6110(k)(3)	2-9	6682	26-19
6111	26-20	6694(a)	26-25
6159	26-12	6694(b)	26-25
6212	26-5	6695	26-26
6213	26-5	6695(h)	26-26
6324(b)	27-2	6695A	26-17
6334(a)	26-6	6699	22-26
6334(a)(13)(A)	26-6	6701	26-25
6334(e)(1)	26-6	6713	26-26
6501(a)	26-21	6861	26-5
6501(b)(1)	26-21	7121(b)	26-12
6501(c)(4)	26-21	7122	26-10
6501(e)(1)(B)(ii)	26-21	7201	26-20
6511(a)	26-22	7202	26-19
6511(d)(1)	26-22	7205	26-19
6511(h)	26-21	7206	26-26
6513(a)	26-22	7216	26-26
6601(c)	26-9	7463(a)	26-10
6621	26-12	7482(a)	2-13
6622	26-12	7482(c)	2-13
6651(a)	26-14	7491(a)(1)	26-5
6651(f)	26-14	7491(a)(2)(B)	26-5
6654	3-25, 26-18	7491(C)	26-5
6654(c)(1)	12-23	7502(f)	3-23
6654(e)(1)	12-23	7519(b)	16-5
6654(k)	26-18	7521(a)	26-8
6654(l)(2)(A)	28-24	7521(b)	26-8
6655	17-24, 26-18	7525	26-27
6655(e)	26-18	7602	26-5
6655(g)(2)	17-24	7623	26-7
6655(i)	26-18	7701(a)(1)	21-2, 25-3
6656	26-19	7701(a)(2)	21-2
6662	2-25	7701(a)(3)	15-8
6662(a)	2-24	7701(a)(4)	25-3
6662(b)(1)	2-24	7701(a)(5)	25-3
6662(b)(2)	26-16	7701(a)(36)	26-24
6662(b)(3)	26-16	7701(b)	25-26
6662(b)(5)	26-17	7701(b)(3)(A)	25-26
6662(c)	2-24, 26-15	7702B	5-12, 10-4
6662(d)	26-16	7703(b)	3-20
6662(d)(1)	26-16	7803(c)	26-4
6662(d)(1)(C)	26-16	7805	2-6
6662(d)(2)(B)	26-16	7805(a)	2-7
6662(e)	26-16	7805(e)	2-7
6662(e)(1)(B)	25-12	7852(d)	2-17
6662(e)(1)(B)(ii)	26-21	7852(d)(1)	25-5
6662(g)	26-17	7872	19-19
6662(h)	26-17	7872(a)(1)	4-21
6662A	26-25	7872(b)(2)	4-21
6663	26-18	7872(c)	4-22
6664(c)(1)	26-15	7872(c)(2)	4-23
6664(c)(2)	26-17	7872(c)(3)	4-23
6664(c)(3)	26-17	7872(d)	4-23
6672	26-19	7872(f)(2)	4-21
6676	26-17	9831(d)	5-11

Appendix D-2

Table of Regulations Cited

Temporary Treasury Regulations

Temp.Reg. Sec.	This Work Page
1.101-7T	5-6
1.163-8T	10-15, 10-18, 10-44
1.163-8T(c)	11-37
1.274-5T(c)(3)	9-33
1.280F-6T(e)	8-19
1.385-1 to -4T	18-20
1.469-1T(e)(3)	11-15
1.469-5T(a)	11-13
1.469-5T(e)(3)(ii)	11-14
1.469-5T(f)(3)	11-14
1.861-9T	25-10
1.861-10T(b)	25-10
1.956-2T	2-34
1.7519-2T(a)(4)(ii)	16-5

Proposed Treasury Regulations

Prop.Reg. Sec.	This Work Page
1.2	2-7
1.83-3	21-8
1.117-6(b)(2)	5-8
1.163(j)-1(b)(1)	17-7
1.199A-5(c)(1)	6-8
1.280A-3(c)	6-23
1.280A-3(d)(4)	6-24
1.469-5	11-14
1.1402(a)-2(h)	21-39
1.1402(a)-2(i)	21-39

Treasury Regulations

Reg. Sec.	This Work Page
1.41-1	12-8
1.41-7	12-8

Treasury Regulations

Reg. Sec.	This Work Page
1.46-2(k)	16-8
1.61-1(a)	4-5, 4-6
1.61-2(d)(2)(i)	13-10
1.61-3	4-3
1.61-3(a)	6-15
1.61-4	16-12
1.61-6(a)	13-8, 13-10
1.61-8(b)	14-15
1.61-9(c)	4-15
1.61-14	4-4
1.61-14(a)	2-25, 2-26, 2-27
1.62-2	10-31
1.67-4(b)	28-13
1.72-7(c)(1)	5-6
1.79-3	5-21
1.79-3(d)(2)	5-20
1.83-3	21-8
1.107-1	5-14
1.117-2(a)	5-7
1.118-1	18-18
1.119-1(f)	5-14
1.121-1(b)(1)	13-36
1.121-1(c)(1)	13-36
1.121-1(c)(2)(i)	13-37
1.121-3	13-39
1.121-3(e)(4)	13-40
1.132-1(b)	5-17
1.132-2	5-17
1.152-1(a)	3-45
1.152-1(c)	3-45
1.162-2(b)(1)	9-12
1.162-3(a)(1)	6-26
1.162-5(b)(2)	9-14
1.162-5(b)(2)(iii)	9-14
1.162-5(b)(3)	9-14

Treasury Regulations

Reg. Sec.	This Work Page
1.162-5(b)(3)(ii)	9-15
1.162-8	6-6
1.162-12(a)	16-12, 16-13
1.162-17(b)(4)	9-33
1.162-21(b)	6-46
1.163-10(a)(2)	2-34
1.163(d)-1	11-26
1.164-4(a)	10-12
1.165-1	7-29
1.165-1(a)	13-8
1.165-1(d)(2)	7-8
1.165-1(d)(2)(i)	7-8
1.165-4(a)	18-21
1.165-5(b)	18-21
1.165-7	13-35
1.165-7(a)(2)(ii)	7-10
1.165-8(a)(2)	7-8
1.165-8(d)	7-8
1.165-9(b)(2)	13-19
1.166-1(e)	7-2
1.166-5(d)	7-4
1.167(a)-3	21-9
1.167(g)-1	13-13, 13-19
1.168(d)-1(b)(4)	8-13
1.170A-1(h)(3)	10-19
1.170A-4A	17-46
1.170A-4(b)(1)	14-42
1.170A-4(b)(3)(ii)(b)	10-23
1.170A-9(e)(4)(i)	23-9
1.170A-13(c)(2)	10-43
1.172-4(a)(2)	16-8
1.174-2(a)(1)	7-16
1.174-2(a)(2)	7-16
1.174-2(a)(3)	7-16
1.179-1(e)	8-14
1.183-1(b)(1)	6-21
1.183-2(b)(1) through (9)	6-19
1.195-1	17-46, 21-12
1.199A-1(b)(3)	15-10
1.199A-2(b)(2)	15-23
1.199A-2(b)(2)(ii)	15-23
1.199A-2(c)(1)(ii)	15-23
1.199A-2(c)(1)(iv)	15-23
1.199A-3(b)(1)(ii)	21-29
1.199A-3(b)(1)(vi)	15-10
1.199A-3(b)(2)(ii)	15-11
1.199A-5(c)(1)	15-17
1.199A-5(d)(3)	15-17
1.199A-6	21-30
1.199A-6(d)	28-15
1.212-1(f)	9-14

Reg. Sec.	This Work Page
1.212-1(g)	6-4
1.213-1(e)(1)(iii)	10-5
1.213-1(e)(1)(v)	10-4
1.213-1(e)(1)(v)(a)	10-4
1.248-1(d)	17-15
1.263(a)-1(f)(1)	6-27
1.263(a)-3(e)(1)	6-26
1.263(a)-3(e)(6)	6-27
1.263(a)-3(h)(1)	6-27
1.263(a)-3(i)(1)	6-27
1.263(a)-4(f)	6-12, 16-11
1.263(a)-4(f)(6)	6-12
1.263A-1(a)	16-31
1.263A-1(b)(12)	16-32
1.263A-1(e)	16-27
1.263A-1(h)(5)	16-32
1.267(d)-1(a)	13-16
1.267(d)-1(c)(3)	13-16
1.274-4	9-13
1.280F-7(a)	8-22
1.301-1(j)	13-10, 19-17
1.301-1(m)	19-17
1.302-2(b)(1)	19-26
1.302-2(c)	19-25
1.302-4(a)	19-28
1.305-1(b)	19-20
1.307-1(a)	13-12
1.307-2	19-21
1.316-2	19-8
1.316-2(b)	19-8
1.316-2(c)	19-8
1.316-2(e)	19-6
1.332-2(a)	20-9, 20-10
1.332-2(b)	20-9
1.332-2(c)	20-2
1.334-1(b)	20-12
1.338-4	20-13
1.338-5	20-13
1.338-6	20-13
1.351-1(a)(1)	18-6
1.351-1(a)(1)(ii)	18-6, 18-9, 18-25
1.351-1(a)(2)	18-8
1.401(k)-1(a)(6)(ii)	9-31
1.408-10(b)	14-22
1.441-1(b)(1)(ii)	16-2
1.441-1(b)(3)	16-6
1.441-1(b)(4)	16-6
1.441-1(e)(2)	16-3
1.441-3	17-46
1.441-3(d)(1)	17-4
1.442-1(b)(1)	16-6

Treasury Regulations

Reg. Sec.	This Work Page
1.442-1(c)(1)	16-6
1.446-1(a)(1)	16-10, 16-17
1.446-1(a)(2)	6-10
1.446-1(a)(3)	4-7
1.446-1(a)(4)(i)	16-10, 16-11
1.446-1(c)(1)(i)	4-7
1.446-1(c)(1)(iv)(b)	16-11
1.446-1(c)(2)	4-8
1.446-1(c)(2)(i)	4-6, 16-10
1.446-1(e)(2)(ii)	16-17
1.446-1(e)(2)(ii)(b)	16-17
1.451-1(a)	16-11, 16-13
1.451-2(a)	4-9
1.451-3(c)(3)	16-30
1.451-3(d)(2)(ii)-(vii)	16-29
1.453-9(c)(2)	18-5
1.460-1(c)(3)	16-29
1.460-2(a)	16-27
1.460-5(b)	16-27
1.461-1(a)	6-10
1.461-1(a)(1)	16-11
1.461-1(a)(2)	16-14
1.461-4	16-13, 16-15
1.461-4(g)(2)-(6)	16-15
1.461-5(c)	16-15
1.469-4	11-11
1.469-4(c)(3)	11-11
1.469-4(d)	11-12
1.469-4(f)	11-12
1.469-9	11-18
1.471-1	16-30
1.471-2	16-30
1.471-2(c)	16-33
1.471-3(b)	16-31
1.471-4(b)	16-31
1.471-4(c)	16-33
1.471-6(d)	16-36
1.471-6(e)	16-36
1.472-2(c)	16-36
1.472-3(a)	16-35
1.472-4	16-33
1.472-5	16-35
1.472-8	16-34
1.482-1(a)(3)	25-11
1.509(a)-3(c)	23-9
1.511-2(a)(2)	23-13
1.512(b)-1	23-16
1.513-1(b)	23-12, 23-13
1.513-1(c)	23-15
1.513-1(d)	23-13
1.513-1(d)(4)(ii)	23-14

Treasury Regulations

Reg. Sec.	This Work Page
1.513-1(d)(4)(iii)	23-14
1.513-2(a)	23-13
1.514(b)-1(b)(1)(ii)	23-18
1.537	17-36
1.641(b)-3(a)	28-5
1.642(c)-1	28-15
1.642(c)-3	28-15
1.642(g)-2	28-14
1.651(a)-1	28-5
1.652(b)-2(b)	28-23
1.662(a)-2	28-21
1.662(a)-3	28-21
1.662(b)-1	28-22
1.704-1	21-65
1.704-1(b)(2)(i)	21-26
1.704-1(b)(2)(iii)	21-27
1.704-2	21-65
1.704-3	21-28
1.706-1(a)	16-3
1.706-1(a)(1)	4-16
1.706-1(b)(3)	16-4
1.709-1	21-12
1.737-1(b)	13-4
1.751-1(a)(3)	21-64
1.752-1(a)(4)(ii)	21-32
1.752-1(e)	22-20
1.752-2	21-33
1.752-3	21-33
1.861-7(c)	25-8
1.861-8	25-9
1.861-8(e)(7)	25-8
1.861-18	25-9
1.861-18(f)(1)	25-9
1.861-18(f)(2)	25-9
1.865-1(a)(1)	25-8
1.865-(2)(a)(1)	25-8
1.865-(2)(a)(2)	25-8
1.871-2(b)	5-22
1.904-2(e)	16-8
1.904-2(g)	12-14
1.954-3(a)	25-38
1.989(a)-1(b)	25-14
1.1001-1(a)	13-3
1.1001-1(b)	13-4
1.1001-2(a)	5-29
1.1002-1(a)	13-8
1.1002-1(c)	13-22
1.1011-1	13-5, 13-13
1.1012-1(a)	13-10
1.1012-1(c)(1)	13-10
1.1015-1(a)(1)	13-12

Treasury Regulations

Reg. Sec.	This Work Page
1.1015-1(a)(3)	13-12
1.1015-5(c)(2)	13-13
1.1015-5(c)(5)	13-13
1.1016-1	13-5
1.1016-3(a)(1)(i)	13-5
1.1016-5(a)	13-6
1.1016-5(b)	13-7
1.1016-6(a)	13-6
1.1031(a)-(1)(a)	13-22
1.1031(a)-1(b)	13-23
1.1031(d)-2	13-29
1.1031(j)-1	13-24
1.1032-1(a)	18-16
1.1033(a)-1	13-32
1.1033(a)-1(a)	13-31
1.1033(a)-2(a)	13-31
1.1033(a)-2(c)(1)	13-34
1.1033(a)-2(c)(2)	13-35
1.1033(a)-2(c)(3)	13-33
1.1034-1(c)(3)(i)	13-36
1.1091-1(a)	13-17, 13-19
1.1091-1(c)	13-18
1.1091-1(f)	13-17
1.1091-2(a)	13-17
1.1221-1(b)	14-14
1.1223-1(a)	13-27
1.1223-1(b)	13-13
1.1223-1(d)	13-17
1.1223-1(e)	13-12
1.1234-1(a)(1)	14-10
1.1235-2(b)(1)	14-11
1.1241-1(a)	14-14
1.1244(c)-2(b)(2)	18-23
1.1245-1(c)	14-43
1.1245-2(a)(4)	13-27, 14-42
1.1245-2(c)(2)	14-42
1.1245-4(a)(1)	14-41
1.1245-4(c)	14-42
1.1245-6(b)	14-43
1.1250-1(a)(4)	14-43
1.1250-1(b)(4)	14-43
1.1250-1(c)(2)	14-43
1.1250-2(d)(1)	13-27, 14-42
1.1250-2(d)(3)	14-42
1.1250-3(a)(1)	14-41
1.1250-3(c)	14-42

Treasury Regulations

Reg. Sec.	This Work Page
1.1250-3(c)(3)	14-42
1.1361-1(l)(1)	22-4
1.1362-6(a)(2)(ii)(C)	22-6
1.1362-6(b)(3)(iii)	22-6
1.1367-2	22-21
1.1367-2(e)	22-20, 22-21
1.1373-1(a)(2)	22-25
1.1377-1(a)(2)(ii)	22-12
1.6012-2(a)	17-23
1.6012-2(a)(3)	17-23
1.6065-1(b)(1)	26-26
1.6081-3	17-24
1.6081-4	3-23
1.6661-3(b)(2)	2-25
1.6662-3(b)(3)	26-15
1.6662-4(d)(3)(iv)(C)	26-16
15a.453-1(b)(3)(i)	16-21
15a.453-1(d)	16-26
15a.453-1(d)(4)	16-26
20.2031-1(b)	13-4
20.2031-8(a)(1)	27-17
20.2042-1(a)(1)	27-17
20.2042-1(c)(2)	27-18
20.2053-1(d)	27-28
20.2053-4(d)(4)	27-38
20.2053-4(d)(7)	27-38
20.2053-5	27-19
25.2511-1(h)(4)	27-17
25.2512-3(a)	13-4
25.2512-8	27-7
31.3401(c)-(1)(b)	9-3
300.3(b)(1)(ii)	26-11
301.6104(d)-1	23-21
301.6104(d)-2	23-21
301.6114-1	2-17
301.6651-1(c)(1)	26-15
301.6712-1	2-17
301.7122-1(b)	26-10
301.7623-1	26-7
301.7701	21-66
301.7701-1 through -4	15-8
301.7701-1 through -7	15-8
301.7701-4(a)	28-2
301.7701-15(a)	26-24
301.7701-15(f)	26-24
301.7701(b)(7)	2-17

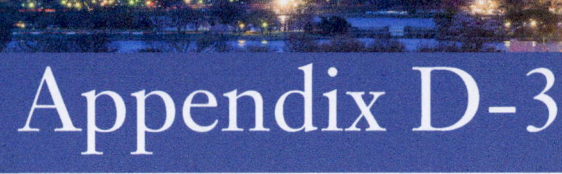

Appendix D-3

Table of Revenue Procedures and Revenue Rulings Cited

Revenue Procedures

Rev. Proc.	This Work Page
76-282	16-36
77-37	18-9, 18-25
87-1	2-24
87-54	4-27
87-56	8-5, 19-5
87-57	8-33, 8-34, 8-35, 16-7
93-27	21-9
94-27	10-16
97-27	19-45
2001-43	21-9
2002-18	16-18
2002-39	16-7
2003-34	16-7
2004-34	16-13
2005-68	20-14
2006-45	16-6
2006-46	16-5, 16-7, 16-37, 21-14
2007-64	16-6
2010-14	9-24
2011-15	23-20
2013-13	9-20
2015-13	16-17, 16-19
2015-14	6-27
2015-41	25-12
2016-13	26-16
2018-30	5-12
2018-38	23-19
2018-39	5-27
2019-9	26-16
2019-11	15-23
2019-12	10-19

Revenue Procedures

Rev. Proc.	This Work Page
2019-25	10-9
2019-26	8-19
2019-43	16-17
2019-44	15-10, 16-24, 26-26
2019-49	9-6
2020-1	26-4

Revenue Rulings

Rev. Rul.	This Work Page
54-96	18-7
56-60	13-14
56-406	13-17
57-374	4-27
57-418	6-17
58-25	10-10
59-86	13-13
59-221	22-25
60-183	22-6
61-119	13-24
61-146	5-11
62-102	5-4
62-217	18-16
63-221	13-31
63-232	7-7
64-56	18-5
64-162	22-21
66-7	14-15
68-55	18-4
68-291	13-7

Revenue Rulings

Rev. Rul.	This Work Page
68-537	22-21
68-662	6-14
69-188	10-16
69-292	9-14
70-466	13-32
71-190	10-13
71-564	18-5
72-312	4-14
72-592	7-7
73-529	9-11
74-44	22-27
74-78	9-14
74-175	14-48
74-503	18-16
75-168	9-10
75-448	5-8
77-263	5-7
77-282	3-13
77-318	5-44
77-414	13-7
78-39	6-10
78-340	10-4
79-379	4-16

Revenue Rulings

Rev. Rul.	This Work Page
80	5-13
80-52	4-9
80-335	6-10
81-191	10-10
81-288	10-10
82-74	13-31
82-196	5-11
82-208	10-13
84-3	26-26
84-31	4-8
87-22	10-16
87-106	10-5
92-29	10-31
2004-78	20-18
2007-40	21-18
2012-15	2-34
2015-13	3-23
2019-13	2-8
2019-24	3-46
2019-28	1-24, 26-12
2020-1	2-7
2020-3	2-8

Appendix E

Practice Set Assignments— Comprehensive Tax Return Problems

PROBLEM 1—INDIVIDUALS (FORM 1040)

Matthew B. (age 42) and Courtney S. (age 41) Mumford are married and live at 11426 W. Antelope Drive, Sioux Falls, SD 57107. Matthew is the manager for The Pour House, a popular bar and grill in Sioux Falls. Courtney is a self-employed architect. They are calendar year, cash basis taxpayers.

1. Matthew's annual salary from The Pour House is $98,000. He also earns an annual bonus. The amount is determined in late December based on performance during the year and is paid in January of the following year. Matthew's 2018 bonus was $6,000 (received in 2019), and his 2019 bonus was $7,000 (received in 2020). Matthew participates in his employer's group health insurance plan to which he contributed $7,200 in 2019 for medical coverage. These contributions are made with after-tax dollars. The health plan covers Matthew, Courtney, and their two dependent children. The Pour House does not provide any retirement benefits, but it has established a § 401(k) plan to enable its employees to save for retirement. Matthew contributed $19,000 to the plan in 2019. Matthew commutes to and from work 6 days a week (a roundtrip of 18 miles) in the family SUV. During 2019, Matthew drove the SUV a total of 12,700 miles.

2. Courtney is a licensed architect who works part time as an architectural consultant. Her professional activity code is 541310. Her major clients are real estate developers (both residential and commercial) for whom she prepares structural designs and construction plans. She also advises on building code requirements regarding the renovation and remodeling of existing structures. Courtney does some of her work at client locations and the remainder in her office at home (see item 3 below).

    Courtney collected $72,000 in consulting fees during 2019. This total includes a $3,000 payment for work she performed in 2018 and does not include $5,000 she billed in December for work performed in late 2019. In addition, Courtney has a $6,400 unpaid invoice for work done in 2017. This client was convicted of arson in August 2016 and is now serving a 5-year sentence in a state prison.

Courtney feels certain that she will never collect the $6,400 she is owed. Her business expenses for 2019 are as follows:

Drafting supplies	$4,800
Reproduction materials (e.g., molds, models, photos, blueprints, copies)	3,200
On-site work clothing (e.g., hip boots, safety glasses, safety helmet)	860
Professional license fee	400
Subscriptions to professional journals	250
Dues to professional organizations	240

In addition, Courtney drove the family Acura (purchased on June 7, 2018) 940 miles on her job assignments. She uses the standard mileage method to deduct business costs related to the Acura. During 2019, Courtney drove the car a total of 10,000 miles.

3. When the Mumfords purchased their home on February 2, 2017, they set aside 300 square feet (out of a total of 2,400 square feet) of living space for Courtney's office. The Mumfords do not use the simplified method for computing the home office deduction. As of January 1, 2019, the home had an adjusted basis of $240,000 ($40,000 of which is attributable to the land) for purposes of line 37 of Form 8829. The fair market value of the property was $282,000. Relevant information concerning the residence for all of 2019 appears below.

Homeowner's insurance	$3,200
Repairs and maintenance	1,800
Utilities	6,200
Painting (office area only)	1,250

The cost of Courtney's office furniture and equipment was previously deducted under § 179 in the years these assets were acquired. On June 29, 2019, she purchased a fireproof file cabinet for $800 to safeguard the blueprints of her structural designs and construction plans. Whenever possible, Courtney prefers to avoid depreciating capital expenditures over time.

4. One of Courtney's clients was interested in building a shopping center on a tract of land she owned in Lincoln County. Courtney inherited the property from her uncle when he died on June 6, 1999. At that time, the land was valued at $40,000. It has since been rezoned for commercial use and has a current value of $200,000. On February 10, 2019, Courtney exchanged the Lincoln parcel for a similar tract in Minnehaha County worth $190,000 and cash of $10,000.

5. On September 2, 2019, Courtney sold a tract of land in McCook County to a farmer who owned the adjoining property. The land was inherited from the same uncle who died in 1999 and was valued at $30,000 on June 6, 1999. Under the terms of the sale, Courtney received cash of $20,000 and a note receivable to be paid in four equal installments at 1-year intervals from the date of sale. Each note calls for the payment of $25,000 plus simple interest of 8%. To the extent allowed by law, Courtney wants to defer recognition of gain for as long as possible.

6. In early 2018, Matthew learned that one of the restaurant's best servers, Mindy Smith, was suffering domestic abuse at the hands of her husband Billy. When Billy started to abuse their 5-year-old daughter as well, Mindy decided it was time to leave. Before they left on April 14, 2018, Matthew loaned Mindy $5,500 to help her relocate with her daughter. Matthew had her sign an interest-free note due in 1 year. Matthew never heard from Mindy again. In late 2019, Matthew learned that Billy tracked Mindy and their daughter down and killed both of them before committing suicide. Given these tragic circumstances, Matthew has no expectation that the loan will ever be repaid.

7. On August 5, 2017, Matthew purchased 1,000 shares of Farmers' Markets America (FMA) common stock for $16 a share as part of its initial public offering. The corporation was formed to establish and operate farmers' markets in mid-size cities throughout the United States. Although some market locations were profitable, the venture as a whole proved to be a failure. In November 2019, FMA's remaining assets were seized by its creditors, and FMA stock became worthless.

8. In addition to the items previously noted, the Mumfords had the following receipts for 2019:

Interest income from:		
General Motors corporate bonds	$1,900	
City of Sioux Falls, SD bonds	1,400	
Castle Bank certificate of deposit	210	$ 3,510
Qualified dividends from MG&E Inc.		3,100
Refund from HomeStuff		430
Loan repayment by Sarah Mumford-Caine		4,500
Cash gifts from Courtney's parents		32,000
2018 Federal income tax refund		290

In December 2018, the Mumfords made a major purchase of household items (e.g., appliances, furniture, etc.) at HomeStuff. They called the manager when they realized they did not receive the advertised sale price. Consequently, the store corrected the mistake and sent a $430 refund to the Mumfords in January 2019.

Four years ago, Matthew lent his sister Sarah $4,000 to help pay for a honeymoon trip following her wedding to John Caine. Matthew was pleasantly surprised when Sarah paid him back (plus interest of $500) on December 20, 2019.

On March 20 of each year, Courtney's parents send a generous gift of cash as a birthday present. Just as she has done for the past 7 years, Courtney immediately invested the cash in her children's § 529 college savings plans.

9. The Mumfords had the following expenditures for 2019:

Courtney's contribution to her traditional IRA		$ 6,000
Net gambling loss		1,000
Life insurance premiums		2,700
Medical and dental expenses not covered by insurance		16,612
Taxes:		
Ad valorem taxes on personal residence	$4,100	
State and local sales taxes from receipts	2,800	6,900
Interest on home mortgage reported on Form 1098		4,000
Cash contributions:		
Feeding South Dakota (EIN 36-3293534)	$1,750	
South Dakota governor's election campaign fund	300	2,050

The $1,000 net gambling loss for 2019 is the difference between the Mumfords' gambling winnings of $1,200 and losses of $2,200. The life insurance premiums relate to the universal life insurance policies that Matthew and Courtney own. The first beneficiary on both policies is the other spouse, with the second beneficiaries being the children. Included in the medical expenses are $1,200 incurred in 2018, which were paid in early February 2019. While South Dakota does not impose income taxes on individuals, it does impose sales taxes. The Mumfords can substantiate the $2,800 in sales taxes paid based on their purchase receipts for the year. The local sales tax rate in Sioux Falls is 2%. (*Hint*: Be sure to check to see if the Optional Sales Tax Tables provide the Mumfords with a greater deduction.) Courtney contributed to the governor's campaign fund because she thinks her influence was key in getting the Minnehaha County land rezoned for commercial use (see item 4 above).

10. The Mumfords maintain a household that includes their two children, Nickolas (age 16) and Kaleigh (age 19). Nickolas is a junior in high school and a talented wrestler. In hopes of competing at the state tournament, all of his free time is consumed with weight training and wrestling practices. Kaleigh graduated from high school on June 7, 2018, and is undecided about college. She is an accomplished vocalist and during 2019 earned $7,200 performing at various events (e.g., weddings, funerals). Kaleigh placed most of her earnings in a savings account for future use and kept only a small amount to spend on herself.

11. Matthew's Form W–2 from The Pour House shows $15,800 withheld for Federal income tax. The Mumfords also made estimated tax payments to the IRS totaling $5,000 for 2019.

12. Relevant Social Security numbers are noted below.

Name	Social Security Number
Matthew B. Mumford	123-45-6786
Courtney S. Mumford	123-45-6787
Kaleigh J. Mumford	123-45-6788
Nickolas W. Mumford	123-45-6798

Requirements

Prepare an income tax return (with all appropriate forms and schedules) for the Mumfords for 2019, using the following guidelines:

- The Mumfords choose to file a joint income tax return.
- The Mumfords do not wish to contribute to the Presidential Election Campaign Fund.
- The Mumfords do not own any foreign bank accounts or other investments. In addition, the Mumfords do not have any financial interests in virtual currencies.
- The Mumfords prefer to receive a refund of any overpaid taxes.
- The taxpayers are preparing their own return (i.e., no preparer is involved).
- For the past several years, the Mumfords have itemized their deductions *from* AGI.
- The taxpayers have the necessary substantiation (e.g., records, receipts) to support all transactions reported on their tax return.
- Make necessary assumptions for information not given in the problem but needed to complete the return.

PROBLEM 2—INDIVIDUALS (FORM 1040)

Sean B. (age 42) and Michelle R. (age 48) Atwell are married and live at 5944 Overhill Road, Mission Hills, MO 66208 (a suburb of Kansas City). Sean is employed as a chemist by HMT Pharmaceuticals, Inc., and Michelle is a self-employed doctor of anesthesiology. They are calendar year, cash basis taxpayers.

1. HMT Pharmaceuticals develops and produces injectable medicines used in chemotherapy treatments for cancer patients. Sean manages the Kansas City facility for an annual salary of $95,000. HMT makes contributions to a qualified defined contribution pension plan for all of its full-time employees. Although Sean also has the opportunity to make contributions to the plan, he chose not to do so in 2019. Sean participates in his employer's group health insurance plan to which he contributed $4,000 in 2019 for medical coverage. These contributions are made with pretax dollars, so his taxable salary is reduced to $91,000 for W–2 reporting.

The health plan covers Sean, Michelle, and their two dependent children. Because of the risk associated with Sean's work (i.e., processing of chemotherapy drugs), HMT provides all of its employees with $200,000 of group term life insurance coverage. An additional $180 of income is included in Sean's Form W–2 to report the taxable value of this insurance.

2. HMT generally reimburses Sean for expenses related to his work for the company. However, as a matter of policy, HMT does not reimburse for the following:

Monthly dinner meetings of the Midwestern Chemists Association (MCA)	$825
Dues to professional organizations	240
Subscriptions to professional journals	180
MIA correspondence study course	230

Sean attended 11 MCA dinner meetings in 2016. Each dinner involved the following costs: $40 (fee for speaker), $25 (price of meal), and $10 (parking). Sean goes to the meetings from work and returns home the same night. The MIA (Management Institute of America) charge was for an online home study course on ways to improve safety measures and avoid accidents in the industrial workplace.

3. Michelle Atwell is a board-certified doctor of anesthesiology. She provides anesthesiology services at a number of hospitals and surgical centers in the greater Kansas City area. Michelle is well respected by the surgeons with whom she works. She uses her home as her business address. She keeps her records there, dictates notes to patient files, participates in conference calls regarding upcoming surgeries and postoperative surgical care, answers work-related phone calls, and compiles and sends patient bills. Because Michelle does not maintain a specific area for exclusive business use, she does not claim a tax deduction for a home office. Michelle's receipts from her practice during 2019 were $185,000, $16,000 of which was for services performed in 2018. Not included in these amounts is $17,500 she received in January 2020 for services rendered in December 2019. Michelle's professional activity code is 621111.

Michelle had the following business expenses in 2019:

Medical clothing (e.g., lab coats, surgical scrubs)	$2,200
Medical malpractice insurance	9,500
State medical license fee	450
Dues to professional organizations	350
Subscriptions to professional journals	340

In addition, she drove the family Suburban (purchased on March 2, 2018) 2,900 miles in connection with her work. She uses the standard mileage method for computing deductible vehicle costs. Total mileage for the Suburban is 9,000 miles for the year.

4. Sean's widowed mother, Lucy, endured a number of different medical challenges in late 2018. On December 30, 2018, she suffered a massive stroke and died in the hospital on January 16, 2019. Some of Lucy's medical expenses were covered by Medicare, with the remainder being paid by the Atwells. On February 18, 2019, Sean paid $39,800 to the hospital, $28,000 of which was attributable to expenses incurred in 2018. At the same time, Sean also paid the funeral expenses of $16,000. Although Lucy lived in her own home prior to the stroke, Sean and Michelle have properly claimed her as a dependent for the past few years.

5. As Lucy's sole heir, Sean inherited her home and its furnishings (located at 5422 SW Sena Drive, Topeka, KS 66604). The costs and values involved are as follows:

	Cost Basis	FMV on 2/3/19
Lot	$ 10,000	$ 30,000
House	110,000	250,000
Furnishings	55,000	25,000

Because the home was located in an attractive rental area, Sean decided not to sell. Instead, he rented the property fully furnished on May 1, 2019. The terms of the lease (executed on April 30) provide for the following: 1-year lease at $2,500 per month (payable on the first of each month), last month's rent payable in advance, and damage deposit of $1,500. In total, Sean received $24,000 from the tenants in 2019 for their use of the property. Besides depreciation, his expenses were as follows:

Property taxes	$4,800
Insurance	3,900
Repairs	2,100
Real estate renter's location service	400

For MACRS depreciation purposes, Sean plans to use the straight-line method with the mid-month convention to compute the deduction for the realty and the 200% declining-balance method with a half-year convention for the personalty.

6. While walking the family dogs in late July, Sean was struck by a delivery van and seriously injured. After being hospitalized for a week, he was released—bruised and sore—but with no permanent injuries. The driver of the van was arrested and ticketed by the police for reckless operation of a vehicle and was later prosecuted for drug use. To prevent adverse publicity related to a lawsuit, the owner of the delivery service paid for Sean's medical expenses and sent him a check on August 16, 2019, for $90,000. The check was accompanied by a letter that stated: "This $90,000 is a settlement for physical injuries sustained by Sean Atwell." Sean was represented in the negotiations with the delivery company by his brother, a practicing attorney. He did not charge the Atwells for his services.

7. The Atwells had the following property transactions during 2019:

   a. On May 5, the City Council condemned unimproved land owned by Sean for the construction of a fire station. He purchased the land (two vacant lots at 3400 and 3402 Sycamore Lane) as an investment on May 25, 2012, for $14,000. In exchange for the lots, the city gave Sean a large unimproved lot at 440 Genoa Street that was valued at $20,000. All in all, he was satisfied with the exchange because the Genoa Street property is in a better neighborhood and has a greater potential for appreciation.

   b. On August 22, Sean sold a gun collection for $32,000 to an avid collector. The collection was a gift from Sean's father on December 25, 2014, when it was worth $22,000. His father bought the collection in 1997 for $14,000. Sean's sale of the collection was documented by a bill of sale, signed by both Sean and the buyer.

   c. On September 9, the Atwells sold 3,000 shares of Dove Pharmaceuticals for $2,000. The couple purchased the stock on December 4, 2018, for $25,000. The investment was motivated by the rumor that Dove was developing a new drug for infertility. On September 7, the FDA announced that it would not approve the drug due to adverse side effects, and the Dove stock price plummeted. The Atwells' broker provided them with a Form 1099–B, which reported the gross proceeds from the sale and their basis in the stock.

8. The Atwells have a long-term capital loss carryover of $1,500 from 2018.

9. In March 2019, the Atwells were audited by the Missouri Department of Revenue for tax years 2016 and 2017. The audit proposed no changes for the 2016 tax return. However, the Atwells were assessed $2,250 additional income tax for 2017 (no interest or penalties were assessed). The Atwells agreed with the assessment and paid the $2,250 immediately.

10. During 2019, Sean served on a jury for a civil case that was litigated at the county courthouse. As a result of the service, he was paid $700 and incurred unreimbursed parking expenses of $60. In conformance with company policy, Sean remitted the $700 of jury duty fees to HMT.

11. In addition to the items already noted, the Atwells had the following receipts in 2019:

Life insurance proceeds		$50,000
2018 Missouri state income tax refund		450
Proceeds from garage sale		2,600
Interest income:		
Kansas City general purpose bonds	$480	
CitiBank certificate of deposit	600	1,080

   The insurance proceeds were paid to Sean as the designated beneficiary of Lucy's life insurance policy. At the garage sale, the Atwells sold personal items (e.g., camper, furniture, hunting and fishing equipment) that belonged to Sean's father and mother (i.e., Lucy). Sean and Michelle estimated the items they sold originally cost $7,100. The garage sale proceeds were donated to the Alzheimers Research Association (EIN 23-7438025) in memory of Sean's father.

12. The Atwells had the following additional expenditures for 2019:

Dental bills not covered by insurance	$ 3,100
Ad valorem property taxes on personal residence	14,100
Interest on home mortgage reported on Form 1098	2,600
Contributions to Metropolitan Lutheran Ministry (EIN 43-0970991)	23,600

   As part of a program sponsored by their church (a qualified charity), the Atwells used the family Suburban to transport senior citizens to religious services for a total of 900 miles during 2019. The Suburban also was used for numerous visits to an orthodontist for both the Atwells' children for a total of 480 miles.

13. The Atwells' household includes two dependent children: Ethan (age 15) and Bella (age 14), both of whom are full-time students in high school. Relevant Social Security numbers appear below.

Name	Social Security Number
Sean B. Atwell	123-45-6758
Michelle R. Atwell	123-45-6768
Lucy E. Atwell	123-45-6787
Ethan M. Atwell	123-45-6788
Bella A. Atwell	123-45-6978

14. Sean's Form W–2 from HMT Pharmaceuticals reflects income tax withholding of $6,500 for Federal income taxes and $4,000 for state of Missouri income taxes. The Atwells made quarterly income tax payments totaling $33,000 for their Federal taxes and totaling $20,000 for their state taxes. They had their Federal income tax refund of $3,000 (for 2018) applied toward their 2019 income tax.

Requirements

Prepare an income tax return (with all appropriate forms and schedules) for the Atwells for 2019, using the following guidelines:

- The Atwells choose to file a joint income tax return.
- The Atwells do not wish to contribute to the Presidential Election Campaign Fund.
- The Atwells do not own any foreign bank accounts or other investments. In addition, the Atwells do not have any financial interests in virtual currencies.
- The Atwells prefer to receive a refund of any overpaid taxes.
- The taxpayers are preparing their own return (i.e., no preparer is involved).
- For the past several years, the Atwells have itemized their deductions *from* AGI instead of using the standard deduction. In addition, the Atwells have deducted state income taxes (not sales taxes) for the past several years.
- The taxpayers have the necessary substantiation (e.g., records, receipts) to support all transactions reported on their tax return.
- Make necessary assumptions for information not given in the problem but needed to complete the return.

PROBLEM 3—C CORPORATION (FORM 1120)

On November 1, 2008, Janet Morton and Kim Wong formed Pet Kingdom, Inc., to sell pets and pet supplies. Pertinent information regarding Pet Kingdom is summarized as follows:

- Pet Kingdom's business address is 1010 Northwest Parkway, Dallas, TX 75225; its telephone number is (214) 555-2211; and its e-mail address is petkingdom@pki.com. The employer identification number is 11-1111112, and the principal business activity code is 453910.
- Janet and Kim each own 50% of the common stock; Janet is president and Kim is vice president of the company. No other class of stock is authorized.
- Both Janet and Kim are full-time employees of Pet Kingdom. Janet's Social Security number is 123-45-6788, and Kim's Social Security number is 123-45-6787.
- Pet Kingdom is an accrual method, calendar year taxpayer. Inventories are determined using FIFO and the lower of cost or market method. Pet Kingdom uses the straight-line method of depreciation for book purposes and accelerated depreciation (MACRS) for tax purposes.
- During 2019, the corporation distributed cash dividends of $250,000.

Pet Kingdom's financial statements for 2019 are shown below.

Income Statement

Income		
Gross sales		$ 5,750,000
Sales returns and allowances		(200,000)
Net sales		$ 5,550,000
Cost of goods sold		(2,300,000)
Gross profit		$ 3,250,000
Dividends received from stock investments in less-than-20%-owned U.S. corporations		43,750
Interest income:		
State bonds	$ 15,000	
Certificates of deposit	20,000	35,000
Total income		$ 3,328,750

continued

Expenses		
Salaries—officers:		
Janet Morton	$262,500	
Kim Wong	262,500	$525,000
Salaries—clerical and sales		725,000
Taxes (state, local, and payroll)		238,000
Repairs and maintenance		140,000
Interest expense:		
Loan to purchase state bonds	$ 9,000 *cant deduct*	
Other business loans	207,000	216,000
Advertising		58,000
Rental expense		109,000
Depreciation*		106,000
Charitable contributions		38,000 *upto 10% of NI*
Employee benefit programs		60,000
Premiums on term life insurance policies on lives of Janet Morton and Kim Wong; Pet Kingdom is the designated beneficiary		40,000 *cant deduct*
Total expenses		(2,255,000)
Net income before taxes		$ 1,073,750
Federal income tax		(221,734)
Net income per books		$ 852,016

*Depreciation for tax purposes is $136,000. You are not provided enough detailed data to complete a Form 4562 (depreciation). If you solve this problem using Intuit ProConnect, enter the amount of depreciation on line 20 of Form 1120.

Balance Sheet

Assets	January 1, 2019	December 31, 2019
Cash	$ 1,200,000	$ 1,039,461
Trade notes and accounts receivable	2,062,500	2,147,000
Inventories	2,750,000	3,030,000
Stock investment *1,525,000*	1,125,000	1,125,000
State bonds	375,000	375,000
Certificates of deposit	400,000	400,000
Prepaid Federal tax	–0–	2,266
Buildings and other depreciable assets	5,455,000	5,455,000
Accumulated depreciation	(606,000)	(712,000)
Land	812,500	812,500
Other assets	140,000	128,500
Total assets	$13,714,000	$13,802,727

Liabilities and Equity	January 1, 2019	December 31, 2019
Accounts payable	$ 2,284,000	$ 1,840,711
Other current liabilities	175,000	155,000
Mortgages	4,625,000	4,575,000
Capital stock	2,500,000	2,500,000
Retained earnings	4,130,000	4,732,016
Total liabilities and equity	$13,714,000	$13,802,727

4,130,000 + 852,016 (N.I.) − 250,000 (Div)

During 2019, Pet Kingdom made estimated tax payments of $56,000 each quarter to the IRS. Prepare a Form 1120 for Pet Kingdom for tax year 2019. Suggested software: ProConnect Tax Online.

PROBLEM 4—C CORPORATION (FORM 1120)

intuit proconnect™

On February 12, 2005, Nancy Trout and Delores Lake formed Kingfisher Corporation to sell fishing tackle. Pertinent information regarding Kingfisher is summarized as follows:

- Kingfisher's business address is 1717 Main Street, Ely, MN 55731; its telephone number is (218) 555-2211; and its e-mail address is kingfisher@kf.com.
- The employer identification number is 11-1111113, and the principal business activity code is 451110.
- Nancy owns 50% of the common stock and is president of the company, and Delores owns 50% of the common stock and is vice president of the company. No other class of stock is authorized.
- Both Nancy and Delores are full-time employees of Kingfisher. Nancy's Social Security number is 123-45-6788, and Delores's Social Security number is 123-45-6787.
- Kingfisher is an accrual method, calendar year taxpayer. Inventories are determined using FIFO and the lower of cost or market method. Kingfisher uses the straight-line method of deprecation for book purposes and accelerated depreciation (MACRS) for tax purposes.
- During 2019, the corporation distributed cash dividends of $80,000.

Kingfisher's financial statements for 2019 are shown below and on the next page.

Income Statement

Income

Gross sales		$2,408,000
Sales returns and allowances		(80,000)
Net sales		$2,328,000
Cost of goods sold		(920,000)
Gross profit		$1,408,000
Dividends received from stock investments in less-than-20%-owned U.S. corporations		12,000
Interest income:		
State bonds	$ 14,000	
Certificates of deposit	10,000	24,000
Total income		$1,444,000

(handwritten annotations: "exclude" next to State bonds $14,000; "place half and other half deduct" next to 12,000)

Expenses

Salaries—officers:		
Nancy Trout	$160,000	
Delores Lake	160,000	$320,000
Salaries—clerical and sales		290,000
Taxes (state, local, and payroll)		85,000
Repairs and maintenance		56,000
Interest expense:		
Business loans	$ 12,000	
Loan to purchase state bonds	8,000	20,000
Advertising		6,000
Rental expense		68,000
Depreciation*		40,000
Charitable contributions		15,000
Employee benefit programs		24,000
Premiums on term life insurance policies on lives of Nancy Trout and Delores Lake; Kingfisher is the designated beneficiary	16,000	
Total expenses		(940,000)
Net income before taxes		$ 504,000
Federal income tax		(106,680)
Net income per books		$ 397,320

(handwritten annotations: "cant deduct" next to Loan to purchase state bonds 8,000; "cant deduct" next to 16,000)

*You are not provided enough detailed information to complete a Form 4562 (depreciation). If you solve this problem using Intuit ProConnect, enter the amount of deprecation on line 20 of Form 1120.

Balance Sheet

Assets	January 1, 2019	December 31, 2019
Cash	$ 380,000	$ 337,300
Trade notes and accounts receivable	308,400	480,280
Inventories	900,000	1,012,000
State bonds	160,000	160,000
Federal income tax refund	–0–	1,320
Certificates of deposit	140,000	140,000
Stock investments	300,000	300,000
Building and other depreciable assets	240,000	240,000
Accumulated depreciation	(88,800)	(128,800)
Land	20,000	20,000
Other assets	3,600	2,000
Total assets	$2,363,200	$2,564,100

other current assets

Liabilities and Equity	January 1, 2019	December 31, 2019
Accounts payable	$ 300,000	$ 233,880
Other current liabilities	80,300	40,000
Mortgages	210,000	200,000
Capital stock	500,000	500,000
Retained earnings	1,272,900	1,590,220
Total liabilities and equity	$2,363,200	$2,564,100

→ 1,272,900 + 397,320 (NI) – 80,000 (Div.)

During 2019, Kingfisher made estimated tax payments of $27,000 each quarter to the IRS. Prepare a Form 1120 for Kingfisher for tax year 2019. Suggested software: ProConnect Tax Online.

27,000 × 4 = 108,000 line 33

PROBLEM 5—PARTNERSHIP (FORM 1065)

Ryan Ross (111-11-1112), Oscar Omega (222-22-2223), Clark Carey (333-33-3334), and Kim Kardigan (444-44-4445) are equal active members in ROCK the Ages LLC. ROCK serves as agent and manager for prominent musicians in the Los Angeles area. The LLC's Federal ID number is 55-5555556. It uses the cash basis and the calendar year and began operations on January 1, 2007. Its current address is 6102 Wilshire Boulevard, Suite 2100, Los Angeles, CA 90036. ROCK was the force behind such music icons as "Stake" Malone, Burgundy Six, Elena Gomez, Tyler Quick, Queen Bey, and Bruno Mercury and has had a very profitable year. The following information was taken from the LLC's income statement for the current year.

Revenues	
Fees and commissions	$4,800,000
Taxable interest income from bank deposits	1,600
Tax-exempt interest	3,200
Net gain on stock sales	4,000
Total revenues	$4,808,800

continued

Expenses

Advertising and public relations	$ 380,000
Charitable contributions	28,000
Section 179 expense	20,000
Employee W–2 wages	1,000,000
Guaranteed payment (services), Ryan Ross, office manager	800,000
Guaranteed payment (services), other members	600,000
Business meals subject to 50% disallowance	200,000
Travel	320,000
Legal and accounting fees	132,000
Office rentals paid	80,000
Interest expense on operating line of credit	10,000
Insurance premiums	52,000
Office expense	200,000
Payroll taxes	92,000
Utilities	54,800
Total expenses	$3,968,800

Recently, ROCK has taken advantage of bonus depreciation and § 179 deductions and fully remodeled the premises and upgraded its leasehold improvements. This year, ROCK wrapped up its remodel with the purchase of $20,000 of office furniture for which it will claim a § 179 deduction. (For simplicity, assume that ROCK uses the same cost recovery methods for both tax and financial purposes.) There is no depreciation adjustment for alternative minimum tax purposes.

ROCK invests much of its excess cash in non-dividend-paying growth stocks and tax-exempt securities. During the year, the LLC sold two securities. On June 15, ROCK purchased 1,000 shares of Tech, Inc. stock for $100,000; it sold those shares on December 15 for $80,000. On March 15 of last year, ROCK purchased 2,000 shares of BioLabs, Inc. stock for $136,000; it sold those shares for $160,000 on December 15 of the current year. These transactions were reported to the IRS on Forms 1099–B; ROCK's basis in these shares *was* reported.

Net income per books is $840,000. On January 1, the members' capital accounts equaled $200,000 each. No additional capital contributions were made this year. In addition to their guaranteed payments, each member withdrew $250,000 cash during the year. All contributions and distributions have been in cash, so the LLC has no net unrecognized § 704(c) gain or loss. The LLC's balance sheet as of December 31 of this year is as follows.

	Beginning	Ending
Cash	$ 444,000	$?
Tax-exempt securities	120,000	120,000
Marketable securities	436,000	300,000
Leasehold improvements, furniture, and equipment	960,000	980,000
Accumulated depreciation	(960,000)	(980,000)
Total assets	$1,000,000	$?

continued

	Beginning	Ending
Operating line of credit	$ 200,000	$ 160,000
Capital, Ross	200,000	?
Capital, Omega	200,000	?
Capital, Carey	200,000	?
Capital, Kardigan	200,000	?
Total liabilities and capital	$1,000,000	$?

All debt is shared equally by the members. Each member has personally guaranteed the debt of the LLC. All members are active in LLC operations.

For our purposes, assume the LLC is not considered an SSTB, and ROCK's operations constitute one active trade or business for purposes of the passive activity and at-risk limitations. (Note that the § 179 deduction is a business-related expense.) The LLC's UBIA (unadjusted basis immediately after acquisition) equals the total original cost of all leasehold improvements, or $980,000.

The appropriate business code for the entity is 711410. For the Form 1065, page 5, Analysis of Net Income, put all partners' allocations in cell 2(b)(ii), per IRS instructions for an LLC.

a. Prepare a Form 1065, pages 1, 4, and 5, for ROCK the Ages LLC using tax-basis information for Schedules L and M–2. Provide any special information the LLC members might need, including net income from self-employment and information for the § 199A calculation. Attach additional statements if needed.

b. If you are using tax return preparation software, prepare Forms 4562, 8949, and Schedule D.

c. Prepare Schedule K–1 for Ryan Ross, 15520 W. Earlson Street, Pacific Palisades, CA 90272.

PROBLEM 6—S CORPORATION (FORM 1120S)

John Parsons (123-45-6781) and George Smith (123-45-6782) are 70% and 30% owners, respectively, of Premium, Inc. (11-1111120), a candy company located at 1005 16th Street, Cut and Shoot, TX 77303. Premium's S election was made on January 15, 2012, its date of incorporation. The following information was taken from the company's 2019 income statement.

Interest income	$ 100,000
Gross sales receipts	2,410,000
Beginning inventory	9,607
Direct labor	(203,102)
Direct materials purchased	(278,143)
Direct other costs	(249,356)
Ending inventory	3,467
Salaries and wages	(442,103)
Officers' salaries ($75,000 each to Parsons and Smith)	(150,000)
Repairs	(206,106)
Depreciation expense, tax and book	(15,254)
Interest expense	(35,222)
Rent expense (operating)	(40,000)
Taxes	(65,101)
Charitable contributions (cash)	(20,000)
Advertising expenses	(20,000)
Payroll penalties	(15,000)
Other deductions	(59,899)
Book income	704,574

A comparative balance sheet appears below.

	January 1, 2019	December 31, 2019
Cash	$ 47,840	$?
Accounts receivable	93,100	123,104
Inventories	9,607	3,467
Prepaid expenses	8,333	17,582
Building and equipment	138,203	185,348
Accumulated depreciation	(84,235)	(?)
Land	2,000	2,000
Total assets	$214,848	$844,422
Accounts payable	$ 42,500	$ 72,300
Notes payable (less than 1 year)	4,500	2,100
Notes payable (more than 1 year)	26,700	24,300
Capital stock	30,000	30,000
Retained earnings	111,148	?
Total liabilities and capital	$214,848	$844,422

Premium's accounting firm provides the following additional information.

Distributions to shareholders	$100,000
Beginning balance, Accumulated adjustments account	111,148
Ordinary business income for QBI	639,574
W–2 wages for QBI	795,205

Prepare Premium's Form 1120S and Schedule K–1s for John Parsons and George Smith, 5607 20th Street, Cut and Shoot, TX 77303. Do not complete the Forms 1125–A, 1125–E, and 4562. Suggested software: ProConnect Tax Online.

PROBLEM 7—GIFT TAX (FORM 709)

James A. and Ella R. Polk, ages 70 and 65, respectively, are retired physicians who live at 3319 Taylorcrest Street, Houston, Texas 77079. Their three adult children (Benjamin Polk, Michael Polk, and Olivia Turner) are mature and responsible persons.

The Polks have heard that some in Congress have proposed lowering the Federal gift tax exclusion to $3,000,000. Although this change likely will not occur, the Polks believe that they should take advantage of the more generous exclusion available under existing law. Thus, the Polks make transfers of many of their high-value investments. These and other gifts made during the year are summarized below.

	Donor	
Asset Transfer	**James**	**Ella**
Condominium located in Conroe (TX) acquired in 2009, cost $1,200,000, to Benjamin, Michael, and Olivia as equal tenants in common.	$1,900,000	$1,900,000
Office building, located in Round Rock (TX) built in 2011, cost $1,800,000, to Benjamin, Michael, and Olivia as equal tenants in common.	2,300,000	2,300,000
Vacation ranch in Bandera (TX) inherited by James from his father in 2006, value then $900,000, to Benjamin, Michael, and Olivia as equal joint tenants with right of survivorship.	2,600,000	–0–
Ella used her separate property to reimburse her father (Alan Roberts) for his heart bypass operation.	–0–	82,000

continued

	Donor	
Asset Transfer	**James**	**Ella**
Paid for daughter's (Olivia's) wedding to John Turner, a state-law obligation of support	$ 20,000	$ 20,000
James used his separate property to purchase a new automobile (BMW) as a graduation present (from medical school) for his favorite niece (Carol Polk)	42,000	–0–

Prepare 2019 gift tax returns (Form 709) for both of the Polks to compute the total taxable gifts (line 3) for James and Ella; stop with line 3 of page 1, but complete pages 2 and 3 of the return.

An election to split gifts is made. The Polks have made no taxable gifts in prior years. Relevant Social Security numbers are 123-45-6789 (James) and 123-45-6788 (Ella).

PROBLEM 8—TRUST (FORM 1041)

Compute the 2019 fiduciary income and Federal income tax for the Blue Trust. Prepare a spreadsheet solution to make your computations. Then complete a Form 1041 for the entity.

In addition, determine the amount and character of the income and expense items that each beneficiary must report for the year. Omit any alternative minimum tax computations. The year's activities of the trust include the following.

Dividend income, all U.S. stocks	$50,000
Taxable interest income	10,000
Tax-exempt interest income	15,000
Fiduciary's fees	4,000

The trust and Betty both use the calendar tax year. Under the terms of the trust instrument, fiduciary's fees are allocated to income. The trustee must distribute all of the entity's accounting income to Betty Blue by February 15 of the following year. The trustee followed this charge and made no other distributions during the year. Fiduciary's fees were assigned properly as an offset to taxable interest income.

The trust was created on July 8, 2000. There are no tax credits for the year, and none of the entity's income was derived from a personal services contract. The trust has no economic interest in any foreign trust. Its Federal identification number is 11-1111121.

The trustee, Hoover State Federal Bank, is located at 49599 Cold Harbor Boulevard, Mountain Brook, AL 35223. Betty lives at 67671 Crestline Road, Birmingham, AL 35212. Her Social Security number is 123-45-6788.

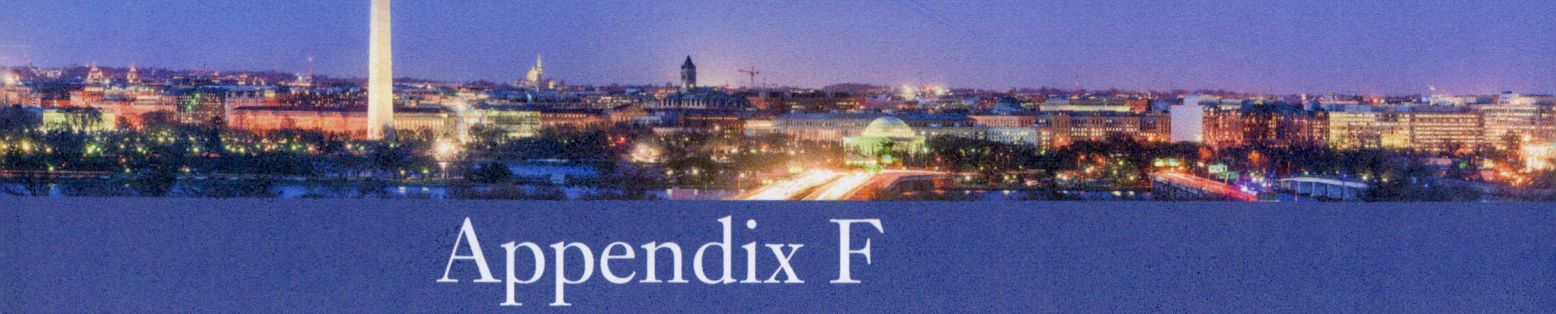

Appendix F

Tax Formulas

Tax Rate Schedules   F-2

Tax Formula for Individuals   F-3

Basic Standard Deduction Amounts   F-3

Amount of Each Additional Standard Deduction   F-3

Personal and Dependency Exemption   F-3

AMT Formula for Individuals   F-4

Income Tax Rates—Estates and Trusts   F-4

Income Tax Rates—C Corporations, 2018 and after   F-4

Unified Transfer Tax Rates (For Gifts Made and for
Deaths after 2012)   F-4

2019 Tax Rate Schedules

Single—Schedule X

If taxable income is: Over—	But not over—	The tax is:	of the amount over—
$ 0	$ 9,700	.........10%	$ 0
9,700	39,475	$ 970.00 + 12%	9,700
39,475	84,200	4,543.00 + 22%	39,475
84,200	160,725	14,382.50 + 24%	84,200
160,725	204,100	32,748.50 + 32%	160,725
204,100	510,300	46,628.50 + 35%	204,100
510,300	....	153,798.50 + 37%	510,300

Head of household—Schedule Z

If taxable income is: Over—	But not over—	The tax is:	of the amount over—
$ 0	$ 13,850	.........10%	$ 0
13,850	52,850	$ 1,385.00 + 12%	13,850
52,850	84,200	6,065.00 + 22%	52,850
84,200	160,700	12,962.00 + 24%	84,200
160,700	204,100	31,322.00 + 32%	160,700
204,100	510,300	45,210.00 + 35%	204,100
510,300	....	152,380.00 + 37%	510,300

Married filing jointly or Qualifying widow(er)—Schedule Y–1

If taxable income is: Over—	But not over—	The tax is:	of the amount over—
$ 0	$ 19,400	.........10%	$ 0
19,400	78,950	$ 1,940.00 + 12%	19,400
78,950	168,400	9,086.00 + 22%	78,950
168,400	321,450	28,765.00 + 24%	168,400
321,450	408,200	65,497.00 + 32%	321,450
408,200	612,350	93,257.00 + 35%	408,200
612,350	....	164,709.50 + 37%	612,350

Married filing separately—Schedule Y–2

If taxable income is: Over—	But not over—	The tax is:	of the amount over—
$ 0	$ 9,700	.........10%	$ 0
9,700	39,475	$ 970.00 + 12%	9,700
39,475	84,200	4,543.00 + 22%	39,475
84,200	160,725	14,382.50 + 24%	84,200
160,725	204,100	32,748.50 + 32%	160,725
204,100	306,175	46,628.50 + 35%	204,100
306,175	....	82,354.75 + 37%	306,175

2020 Tax Rate Schedules

Single—Schedule X

If taxable income is: Over—	But not over—	The tax is:	of the amount over—
$ 0	$ 9,875	.........10%	$ 0
9,875	40,125	$ 987.50 + 12%	9,875
40,125	85,525	4,617.50 + 22%	40,125
85,525	163,300	14,605.50 + 24%	85,525
163,300	207,350	33,271.50 + 32%	163,300
207,350	518,400	47,367.50 + 35%	207,350
518,400	....	156,235.00 + 37%	518,400

Head of household—Schedule Z

If taxable income is: Over—	But not over—	The tax is:	of the amount over—
$ 0	$ 14,100	.........10%	$ 0
14,100	53,700	$ 1,410.00 + 12%	14,100
53,700	85,500	6,162.00 + 22%	53,700
85,500	163,300	13,158.00 + 24%	85,500
163,300	207,350	31,830.00 + 32%	163,300
207,350	518,400	45,926.00 + 35%	207,350
518,400	....	154,793.50 + 37%	518,400

Married filing jointly or Qualifying widow(er)—Schedule Y–1

If taxable income is: Over—	But not over—	The tax is:	of the amount over—
$ 0	$ 19,750	.........10%	$ 0
19,750	80,250	$ 1,975.00 + 12%	19,750
80,250	171,050	9,235.00 + 22%	80,250
171,050	326,600	29,211.00 + 24%	171,050
326,600	414,700	66,543.00 + 32%	326,600
414,700	622,050	94,735.00 + 35%	414,700
622,050	....	167,307.50 + 37%	622,050

Married filing separately—Schedule Y–2

If taxable income is: Over—	But not over—	The tax is:	of the amount over—
$ 0	$ 9,875	.........10%	$ 0
9,875	40,125	$ 987.50 + 12%	9,875
40,125	85,525	4,617.50 + 22%	40,125
85,525	163,300	14,605.50 + 24%	85,525
163,300	207,350	33,271.50 + 32%	163,300
207,350	311,025	47,367.50 + 35%	207,350
311,025	....	83,653.75 + 37%	311,025

Tax Formula for Individuals

Income (broadly defined)..	$xx,xxx
Less: Exclusions...	(x,xxx)
Gross income...	$xx,xxx
Less: Deductions *for* adjusted gross income.......................................	(x,xxx)
Adjusted gross income..	$xx,xxx
Less: The greater of—	
Total itemized deductions	
or standard deduction......................................	(x,xxx)
Less: Personal and dependency exemptions*...	(x,xxx)
Deduction for qualified business income**......................	(x,xxx)
Taxable income..	$xx,xxx
Tax on taxable income...	$ x,xxx
Less: Tax credits (including Federal income tax	
withheld and prepaid)..	(xxx)
Tax due (or refund)..	$ xxx

*Exemption deductions are not allowed from 2018 through 2025.
**Only applies from 2018 through 2025.

Basic Standard Deduction Amounts

Filing Status	2019	2020
Single	$12,200	$12,400
Married, filing jointly	24,400	24,800
Surviving spouse	24,400	24,800
Head of household	18,350	18,650
Married, filing separately	12,200	12,400

Amount of Each Additional Standard Deduction

Filing Status	2019	2020
Single	$1,650	$1,650
Married, filing jointly	1,300	1,300
Surviving spouse	1,300	1,300
Head of household	1,650	1,650
Married, filing separately	1,300	1,300

Personal and Dependency Exemption*

2019	2020
$4,200	$4,300

*Note: Exemption deductions have been suspended from 2018 through 2025. However, the personal and dependency exemption amount is used for other purposes (including determining whether a "qualifying relative" is a taxpayer's dependent).

AMT Formula for Individuals

Taxable income (increased by any standard deduction taken)
Plus or minus: Adjustments
Plus: Preferences
Equals: Alternative minimum taxable income (AMTI)
Minus: Exemption
Equals: Alternative minimum tax (AMT) base
Multiplied by: 26% or 28% rate
Equals: Tentative minimum tax before foreign tax credit
Minus: AMT foreign tax credit
Equals: Tentative minimum tax (TMT)
Minus: Regular tax liability (less any foreign tax credit)
Equals: AMT (if TMT > regular tax liability)

Income Tax Rates—Estates and Trusts

Tax Year 2020

Taxable Income		The Tax Is:	Of the Amount
Over—	But not Over—		Over—
$ 0	$ 2,600	10%	$ 0
2,600	9,450	$ 260.00 + 24%	2,600
9,450	12,950	1,904.00 + 35%	9,450
12,950	....	3,129.00 + 37%	12,950

Income Tax Rates—C Corporations, 2018 and after

For all income levels, the tax rate is 21%.

Unified Transfer Tax Rates

For Gifts Made and for Deaths after 2012

If the Amount with Respect to Which the Tentative Tax to Be Computed Is:	The Tentative Tax Is:
Not over $10,000	18 percent of such amount.
Over $10,000 but not over $20,000	$1,800, plus 20 percent of the excess of such amount over $10,000.
Over $20,000 but not over $40,000	$3,800, plus 22 percent of the excess of such amount over $20,000.
Over $40,000 but not over $60,000	$8,200, plus 24 percent of the excess of such amount over $40,000.
Over $60,000 but not over $80,000	$13,000, plus 26 percent of the excess of such amount over $60,000.
Over $80,000 but not over $100,000	$18,200, plus 28 percent of the excess of such amount over $80,000.
Over $100,000 but not over $150,000	$23,800, plus 30 percent of the excess of such amount over $100,000.
Over $150,000 but not over $250,000	$38,800, plus 32 percent of the excess of such amount over $150,000.
Over $250,000 but not over $500,000	$70,800, plus 34 percent of the excess of such amount over $250,000.
Over $500,000 but not over $750,000	$155,800, plus 37 percent of the excess of such amount over $500,000.
Over $750,000 but not over $1,000,000	$248,300, plus 39 percent of the excess of such amount over $750,000.
Over $1,000,000	$345,800, plus 40 percent of the excess of such amount over $1,000,000.

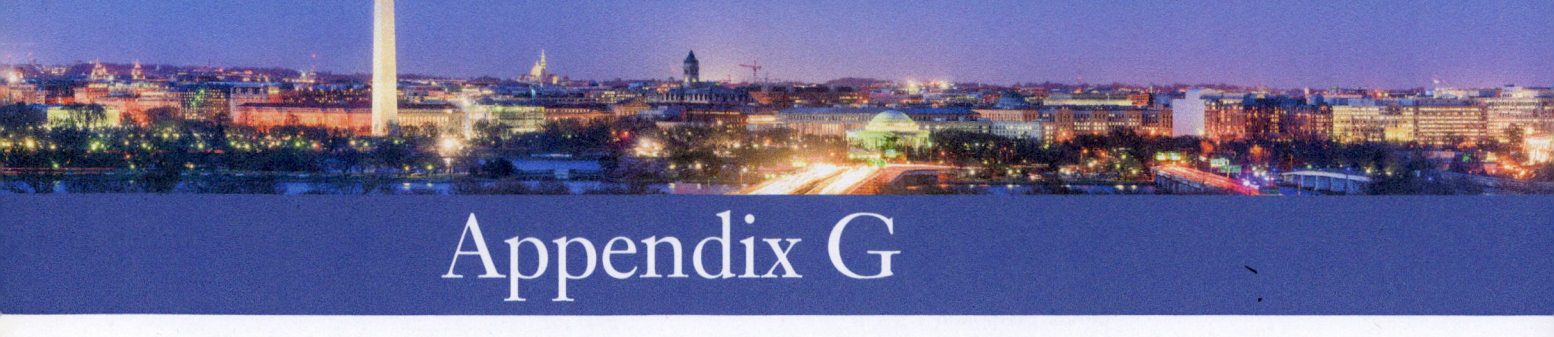

Appendix G

Present Value and Future Value Tables

Present Value of $1   G-2

Present Value of an Ordinary Annuity of $1   G-2

Future Value of $1   G-3

Future Value of an Ordinary Annuity of $1   G-3

Present Value of $1

N/R	1%	2%	3%	4%	5%	6%	7%	8%	9%	10%	11%	12%
1	0.9901	0.9804	0.9709	0.9615	0.9524	0.9434	0.9346	0.9259	0.9174	0.9091	0.9009	0.8929
2	0.9803	0.9612	0.9426	0.9246	0.9070	0.8900	0.8734	0.8573	0.8417	0.8264	0.8116	0.7972
3	0.9706	0.9423	0.9151	0.8890	0.8638	0.8396	0.8163	0.7938	0.7722	0.7513	0.7312	0.7118
4	0.9610	0.9238	0.8885	0.8548	0.8227	0.7921	0.7629	0.7350	0.7084	0.6830	0.6587	0.6355
5	0.9515	0.9057	0.8626	0.8219	0.7835	0.7473	0.7130	0.6806	0.6499	0.6209	0.5935	0.5674
6	0.9420	0.8880	0.8375	0.7903	0.7462	0.7050	0.6663	0.6302	0.5963	0.5645	0.5346	0.5066
7	0.9327	0.8706	0.8131	0.7599	0.7107	0.6651	0.6227	0.5835	0.5470	0.5132	0.4817	0.4523
8	0.9235	0.8535	0.7894	0.7307	0.6768	0.6274	0.5820	0.5403	0.5019	0.4665	0.4339	0.4039
9	0.9143	0.8368	0.7664	0.7026	0.6446	0.5919	0.5439	0.5002	0.4604	0.4241	0.3909	0.3606
10	0.9053	0.8203	0.7441	0.6756	0.6139	0.5584	0.5083	0.4632	0.4224	0.3855	0.3522	0.3220
11	0.8963	0.8043	0.7224	0.6496	0.5847	0.5268	0.4751	0.4289	0.3875	0.3505	0.3173	0.2875
12	0.8874	0.7885	0.7014	0.6246	0.5568	0.4970	0.4440	0.3971	0.3555	0.3186	0.2858	0.2567
13	0.8787	0.7730	0.6810	0.6006	0.5303	0.4688	0.4150	0.3677	0.3262	0.2897	0.2575	0.2292
14	0.8700	0.7579	0.6611	0.5775	0.5051	0.4423	0.3878	0.3405	0.2992	0.2633	0.2320	0.2046
15	0.8613	0.7430	0.6419	0.5553	0.4810	0.4173	0.3624	0.3152	0.2745	0.2394	0.2090	0.1827
16	0.8528	0.7284	0.6232	0.5339	0.4581	0.3936	0.3387	0.2919	0.2519	0.2176	0.1883	0.1631
17	0.8444	0.7142	0.6050	0.5134	0.4363	0.3714	0.3166	0.2703	0.2311	0.1978	0.1696	0.1456
18	0.8360	0.7002	0.5874	0.4936	0.4155	0.3503	0.2959	0.2502	0.2120	0.1799	0.1528	0.1300
19	0.8277	0.6864	0.5703	0.4746	0.3957	0.3305	0.2765	0.2317	0.1945	0.1635	0.1377	0.1161
20	0.8195	0.6730	0.5537	0.4564	0.3769	0.3118	0.2584	0.2145	0.1784	0.1486	0.1240	0.1037

Present Value of an Ordinary Annuity of $1

N/R	1%	2%	3%	4%	5%	6%	7%	8%	9%	10%	11%	12%
1	0.9901	0.9804	0.9709	0.9615	0.9524	0.9434	0.9346	0.9259	0.9174	0.9091	0.9009	0.8929
2	1.9704	1.9416	1.9135	1.8861	1.8594	1.8334	1.8080	1.7833	1.7591	1.7355	1.7125	1.6901
3	2.9410	2.8839	2.8286	2.7751	2.7232	2.6730	2.6243	2.5771	2.5313	2.4869	2.4437	2.4018
4	3.9020	3.8077	3.7171	3.6299	3.5460	3.4651	3.3872	3.3121	3.2397	3.1699	3.1024	3.0373
5	4.8534	4.7135	4.5797	4.4518	4.3295	4.2124	4.1002	3.9927	3.8897	3.7908	3.6959	3.6048
6	5.7955	5.6014	5.4172	5.2421	5.0757	4.9173	4.7665	4.6229	4.4859	4.3553	4.2305	4.1114
7	6.7282	6.4720	6.2303	6.0021	5.7864	5.5824	5.3893	5.2064	5.0330	4.8684	4.7122	4.5638
8	7.6517	7.3255	7.0197	6.7327	6.4632	6.2098	5.9713	5.7466	5.5348	5.3349	5.1461	4.9676
9	8.5660	8.1622	7.7861	7.4353	7.1078	6.8017	6.5152	6.2469	5.9952	5.7590	5.5370	5.3282
10	9.4713	8.9826	8.5302	8.1109	7.7217	7.3601	7.0236	6.7101	6.4177	6.1446	5.8892	5.6502
11	10.3676	9.7868	9.2526	8.7605	8.3064	7.8869	7.4987	7.1390	6.8052	6.4951	6.2065	5.9377
12	11.2551	10.5753	9.9540	9.3851	8.8633	8.3838	7.9427	7.5361	7.1607	6.8137	6.4924	6.1944
13	12.1337	11.3484	10.6350	9.9856	9.3936	8.8527	8.3577	7.9038	7.4869	7.1034	6.7499	6.4235
14	13.0037	12.1062	11.2961	10.5631	9.8986	9.2950	8.7455	8.2442	7.7862	7.3667	6.9819	6.6282
15	13.8651	12.8493	11.9379	11.1184	10.3797	9.7122	9.1079	8.5595	8.0607	7.6061	7.1909	6.8109
16	14.7179	13.5777	12.5611	11.6523	10.8378	10.1059	9.4466	8.8514	8.3126	7.8237	7.3792	6.9740
17	15.5623	14.2919	13.1661	12.1657	11.2741	10.4773	9.7632	9.1216	8.5436	8.0216	7.5488	7.1196
18	16.3983	14.9920	13.7535	12.6593	11.6896	10.8276	10.0591	9.3719	8.7556	8.2014	7.7016	7.2497
19	17.2260	15.6785	14.3238	13.1339	12.0853	11.1581	10.3356	9.6036	8.9501	8.3649	7.8393	7.3658
20	18.0456	16.3514	14.8775	13.5903	12.4622	11.4699	10.5940	9.8181	9.1285	8.5136	7.9633	7.4694

Future Value of $1

N/R	1%	2%	3%	4%	5%	6%	7%	8%	9%	10%	11%	12%
1	1.0100	1.0200	1.0300	1.0400	1.0500	1.0600	1.0700	1.0800	1.0900	1.1000	1.1100	1.1200
2	1.0201	1.0404	1.0609	1.0816	1.1025	1.1236	1.1449	1.1664	1.1881	1.2100	1.2321	1.2544
3	1.0303	1.0612	1.0927	1.1249	1.1576	1.1910	1.2250	1.2597	1.2950	1.3310	1.3676	1.4049
4	1.0406	1.0824	1.1255	1.1699	1.2155	1.2625	1.3108	1.3605	1.4116	1.4641	1.5181	1.5735
5	1.0510	1.1041	1.1593	1.2167	1.2763	1.3382	1.4026	1.4693	1.5386	1.6105	1.6851	1.7623
6	1.0615	1.1262	1.1941	1.2653	1.3401	1.4185	1.5007	1.5869	1.6771	1.7716	1.8704	1.9738
7	1.0721	1.1487	1.2299	1.3159	1.4071	1.5036	1.6058	1.7138	1.8280	1.9487	2.0762	2.2107
8	1.0829	1.1717	1.2668	1.3686	1.4775	1.5938	1.7182	1.8509	1.9926	2.1436	2.3045	2.4760
9	1.0937	1.1951	1.3048	1.4233	1.5513	1.6895	1.8385	1.9990	2.1719	2.3579	2.5580	2.7731
10	1.1046	1.2190	1.3439	1.4802	1.6289	1.7908	1.9672	2.1589	2.3674	2.5937	2.8394	3.1058
11	1.1157	1.2434	1.3842	1.5395	1.7103	1.8983	2.1049	2.3316	2.5804	2.8531	3.1518	3.4785
12	1.1268	1.2682	1.4258	1.6010	1.7959	2.0122	2.2522	2.5182	2.8127	3.1384	3.4985	3.8960
13	1.1381	1.2936	1.4685	1.6651	1.8856	2.1329	2.4098	2.7196	3.0658	3.4523	3.8833	4.3635
14	1.1495	1.3195	1.5126	1.7317	1.9799	2.2609	2.5785	2.9372	3.3417	3.7975	4.3104	4.8871
15	1.1610	1.3459	1.5580	1.8009	2.0789	2.3966	2.7590	3.1722	3.6425	4.1772	4.7846	5.4736
16	1.1726	1.3728	1.6047	1.8730	2.1829	2.5404	2.9522	3.4259	3.9703	4.5950	5.3109	6.1304
17	1.1843	1.4002	1.6528	1.9479	2.2920	2.6928	3.1588	3.7000	4.3276	5.0545	5.8951	6.8660
18	1.1961	1.4282	1.7024	2.0258	2.4066	2.8543	3.3799	3.9960	4.7171	5.5599	6.5436	7.6900
19	1.2081	1.4568	1.7535	2.1068	2.5270	3.0256	3.6165	4.3157	5.1417	6.1159	7.2633	8.6128
20	1.2202	1.4859	1.8061	2.1911	2.6533	3.2071	3.8697	4.6610	5.6044	6.7275	8.0623	9.6463

Future Value of an Ordinary Annuity of $1

N/R	1%	2%	3%	4%	5%	6%	7%	8%	9%	10%	11%	12%
1	1.0000	1.0000	1.0000	1.0000	1.0000	1.0000	1.0000	1.0000	1.0000	1.0000	1.0000	1.0000
2	2.0100	2.0200	2.0300	2.0400	2.0500	2.0600	2.0700	2.0800	2.0900	2.1000	2.1100	2.1200
3	3.0301	3.0604	3.0909	3.1216	3.1525	3.1836	3.2149	3.2464	3.2781	3.3100	3.3421	3.3744
4	4.0604	4.1216	4.1836	4.2465	4.3101	4.3746	4.4399	4.5061	4.5731	4.6410	4.7097	4.7793
5	5.1010	5.2040	5.3091	5.4163	5.5256	5.6371	5.7507	5.8666	5.9847	6.1051	6.2278	6.3528
6	6.1520	6.3081	6.4684	6.6330	6.8019	6.9753	7.1533	7.3359	7.5233	7.7156	7.9129	8.1152
7	7.2135	7.4343	7.6625	7.8983	8.1420	8.3938	8.6540	8.9228	9.2004	9.4872	9.7833	10.0890
8	8.2857	8.5830	8.8923	9.2142	9.5491	9.8975	10.2598	10.6366	11.0285	11.4359	11.8594	12.2997
9	9.3685	9.7546	10.1591	10.5828	11.0266	11.4913	11.9780	12.4876	13.0210	13.5795	14.1640	14.7757
10	10.4622	10.9497	11.4639	12.0061	12.5779	13.1808	13.8164	14.4866	15.1929	15.9374	16.7220	17.5487
11	11.5668	12.1687	12.8078	13.4864	14.2068	14.9716	15.7836	16.6455	17.5603	18.5312	19.5614	20.6546
12	12.6825	13.4121	14.1920	15.0258	15.9171	16.8699	17.8885	18.9771	20.1407	21.3843	22.7132	24.1331
13	13.8093	14.6803	15.6178	16.6268	17.7130	18.8821	20.1406	21.4953	22.9534	24.5227	26.2116	28.0291
14	14.9474	15.9739	17.0863	18.2919	19.5986	21.0151	22.5505	24.2149	26.0192	27.9750	30.0949	32.3926
15	16.0969	17.2934	18.5989	20.0236	21.5786	23.2760	25.1290	27.1521	29.3609	31.7725	34.4054	37.2797
16	17.2579	18.6393	20.1569	21.8245	23.6575	25.6725	27.8881	30.3243	33.0034	35.9497	39.1899	42.7533
17	18.4304	20.0121	21.7616	23.6975	25.8404	28.2129	30.8402	33.7502	36.9737	40.5447	44.5008	48.8837
18	19.6147	21.4123	23.4144	25.6454	28.1324	30.9057	33.9990	37.4502	41.3013	45.5992	50.3959	55.7497
19	20.8109	22.8406	25.1169	27.6712	30.5390	33.7600	37.3790	41.4463	46.0185	51.1591	56.9395	63.4397
20	22.0190	24.2974	26.8704	29.7781	33.0660	36.7856	40.9955	45.7620	51.1601	57.2750	64.2028	72.0524

Index

A

AAA. *See* Accumulated adjustments account
AAA bypass election, **22**:16
Abandoned spouse rules, **3**:20
ABLE (Achieving a Better Life Experience) plans, **5**:27
Above-the-line deductions, **3**:5
Accelerated cost recovery system (ACRS), **8**:2
   See also Modified accelerated cost recovery system
Accelerated death benefits, **5**:5
Accident and health benefits, **5**:11
   gross income exclusions for compensation from, **5**:10–11
Accident and health plans, employer-sponsored, **5**:11–12
   long-term care insurance benefits, **5**:12
   medical reimbursement plans, **5**:11–12
   See also Employee fringe benefits
Accountability to taxpayer, tax principles, **1**:8, **1**:9
Accountable plan, **9**:33–34
   deemed substantiation, **9**:34
   substantiation, **9**:33–34
Accounting income, **4**:4
   of entity and its beneficiaries, **28**:9
Accounting method, **4**:6–9, **6**:9, **16**:10–19
   change from an incorrect method, **16**:17–18
   change of method, **16**:17–19
   correction of an error, **16**:17
   disposition of installment obligations, **16**:25–26
   for trusts and estates, **28**:6
   income taxation of corporations, **17**:4–5
   long-term contracts, **16**:27–30
   net adjustments due to change in, **16**:18
   partnership, **21**:12–13
   permissible methods, **16**:10–11
   prescribed by the IRS, **16**:11
   reporting the net Section 481(a) adjustment, **16**:18–19
   special methods, **16**:19–30
   timing of expense recognition, **6**:9–10
   See also Accrual method; Cash receipts and disbursements method; Cash receipts method; Completed contract method; Hybrid method; Installment method; and Percentage of completion method
Accounting periods, **16**:2–10
   business purpose, **16**:5
   changes in, **16**:6–7
   for trusts and estates, **28**:6
   Form 1128, Application for Change in Accounting Period, **16**:6

income taxation of corporations, **17**:4
IRS requirements for changes in, **16**:6–7
mitigation of the annual accounting period concept, **16**:8–10
personal service corporations, **16**:6
required tax payments, **16**:5
selecting the tax year, **16**:6
specific provisions for partnerships, S corporations, and PSCs, **16**:3–6
taxable periods of less than one year, **16**:7–8
Accounts and notes receivable, definition of capital asset, **14**:4–5
Accrual basis account, collection of, **14**:4
Accrual basis corporations, charitable contributions, **17**:9
Accrual basis taxpayer, **17**:5
   exceptions applicable to, **4**:12
   special election for advance payments for goods and services, **4**:12
Accrual method, **4**:6, **4**:8, **16**:10, **16**:13–16
   all events and economic performance tests for deductions, **16**:14–16
   all events test for income, **16**:13–14
   income taxation of corporations, **17**:4
   requirement exceptions, **16**:12
   requirements, timing of expense recognition, **6**:10–11
   reserves, **16**:16
   taxpayers, special deferral rule for, **4**:12
Accruals under economic performance test, **16**:14
Accumulated adjustments account (AAA), **22**:14–15, **22**:27
   adjustments to corporate, **22**:15
Accumulated E & P (AEP), **19**:8, **22**:13
   allocating to distributions in chronological order, **19**:9
   dividends from, **5**:24
Accumulated earnings tax, **17**:20, **17**:36–37
Accuracy-related penalties, **2**:25, **26**:15
   for substantial estate or gift tax valuation understatements, **26**:17
   transfer pricing, **25**:12
Acquiescence ("A" or "Acq."), **2**:16
Acquisition indebtedness, **10**:15
   definition of, **23**:19
Acquisitions and negative consequences, **20**:16
ACRS. *See* Accelerated cost recovery system
Action on Decision, **2**:16, **2**:24
Active income, **11**:6
Active participant in a qualified plan, **9**:26
Active participation, real estate rental activities, **11**:18–20
Actual cost method, **9**:37
   computation of automobile expenses, **9**:7–9

Ad valorem penalties, **26**:14
Ad valorem taxes, **1**:10, **10**:11
   on personal property, **1**:10–11
   on real property, **1**:10
   other state and local taxes of a multistate corporation **24**:25
Additional depreciation, **14**:38
Additional first-year depreciation, **8**:10, **8**:14–15
   Section 1245 recapture and, **14**:50
Additional Medicare tax on
   unearned income, **12**:24–25
   wages, **12**:24
Additional standard deduction (age 65 or older or blind), **3**:7, **3**:21, **3**:22
   amounts, **3**:7
Additional tax for base erosion, transfer pricing, **25**:13
Additional tax on intangible income, territorial system, **25**:25
Additional tax on net investment income, **28**:8, **28**:26
   tax planning for effect of, **11**:26
Adjusted basis, **13**:5
Adjusted gross income (AGI), common deductions for, **6**:4
   See also Deductions for AGI; Deductions from AGI
Adjusted gross income thresholds
   and saver's credit rate, **12**:19
   education tax credits, **12**:17–18
Adjusted taxable income, business interest expense limitation and, **17**:7
Adjustments to basis, **13**:20, **13**:21
Administration proceeding, recognition of, SSTS No. 5, **26**:29
Administrative feasibility, influence of IRS, **1**:33
Administrative sources of the tax law, **2**:6–9
   assessing the validity of other, **2**:24
   letter rulings, **2**:8
   other administrative pronouncements, **2**:8–9
   Revenue Rulings and Revenue Procedures, **2**:7–8
   Treasury Department Regulations, **2**:6–7
Administrative taxes, **24**:26
Adoption assistance program, employee fringe benefits, **5**:15
Adoption expenses credit, **12**:20
Advance Pricing Agreement (APA), **25**:12
Affiliated group, **17**:21
Affiliation Schedule, Form 851, **17**:21
Affordable Care Act (ACA), **1**:17, **9**:36
   additional Medicare tax on unearned income, **12**:24–25
   additional Medicare tax on wages, **12**:24
   provisions, **10**:10, **12**:24–25, **26**:2

Age, additional standard deduction for 65 or older, **3**:7, **3**:22
Age test, qualifying child, **3**:10
Agent, income received by, **4**:16
Aggregate (or conduit) concept, **21**:4–5
AICPA. *See* American Institute of Certified Public Accountants
Alimony and separate maintenance payments, **4**:19–21
  child support, **4**:20
  front-loading, **4**:20
  inclusion in gross income, **4**:19–21
  property settlements, **4**:19
  requirements for alimony, **4**:19–20
Alimony recapture, **4**:20
All events test, **6**:10, **16**:14
  for deductions, **16**:14–16
  for income, **16**:13–14
Allocate, **24**:8
Allocation, **24**:8
  and apportionment of deductions, **25**:9–10
  of income and loss in S corporations, **22**:12–13
  of items to income or corpus, **28**:11
  parental tax, **3**:27
  related to contributed property, **21**:10–11
Allocation and apportionment of income of multistate corporations, **24**:8–18
  apportionable income, **24**:9–11
  apportionment factors: elements and planning, **24**:11–12
  apportionment procedure, **24**:9
  payroll factor, **24**:14–16
  property factor, **24**:16–18
  sales factor, **24**:13–14
Alternate valuation amount, **13**:14
Alternate valuation date, **13**:14, **27**:5–6
Alternative deprecation system (ADS), **8**:6, **8**:10, **8**:23–24
  computing E & P, **19**:5
  tables, **8**:35–36
Alternative minimum tax (AMT), **8**:23, **12**:25–27
  computing and paying, **12**:26–27
  corporate income tax liability, **17**:19
  income taxation of individuals and corporations compared, **17**:18
  liability, education tax credits and, **12**:17
  table, **8**:34
  tax base, **12**:26
  trusts and estates, **28**:7–8
Alternative minimum taxable income (AMTI)
  QBI and, **15**:22
  trusts and estates, **28**:7–8
Alternative tax, **14**:23
  on capital gain computation, income layers for, **14**:24
  on net capital gain and qualified dividend income, noncorporate taxpayers, **14**:22–27
  rates on net capital gains, **3**:30, **14**:23
American Federal Tax Reports (AFTR), **2**:16–17
American Institute of Certified Public Accountants (AICPA), **1**:8
  Code of Professional Conduct, **26**:27
  ethical guidelines, **1**:26
  statements on standards for tax services, **26**:27–29
American Opportunity credit, **9**:16, **9**:17, **9**:37, **12**:16–18, **12**:20
Americans with Disabilities Act, **12**:3

Amnesty programs, **1**:16
Amortizable bond premium as capital recovery, **13**:7
Amortizable Section 197 intangibles, **8**:25
Amortization, **8**:25–28, **8**:32
  of organizational expenditures under Section 248, **17**:15
Amount realized, **13**:4–5
  computing in involuntary conversions, **13**:31–32
  in Section 121 sale, **13**:38
Analysis of Net Income (Loss), **21**:15, **21**:21
Analysis of unappropriated retained earnings per books, Schedule M-2, **17**:25
Annotated, commercial tax services, **2**:18
Announcements, **2**:9
Annual accounting period concept, **1**:30–31
  mitigation of, **16**:8–10
Annual exclusion, **27**:10
  gift tax, **27**:3–4
  per donee, **1**:14–15
Annual gift tax exclusion, **27**:10–11
  contributions to qualified tuition programs, **27**:11
  GSTT tax base and, **27**:25
Annuity, **4**:24
  exclusion ratio, **4**:26
  expected return, **4**:25
  income from, **4**:24–26
  number of anticipated monthly payments under the simplified method, **4**:26
  one life–expected return multiples, **4**:25
  term certain, **4**:25
Anti-loss duplication rule, **18**:15
Antistuffing loss disallowance rules, summary of, **20**:8
Antistuffing rules, **20**:4–8
  built-in loss limitation, **20**:6–8
  related-party loss limitation, **20**:5–6
Antitrust law violations, **6**:13
APA. *See* Advance pricing agreement
Appeals, **2**:12
  Division of the IRS, **1**:23
  See also Courts
Appellate courts, **2**:12
  See also Courts
Apportion, **24**:8
Apportionable income, **24**:9–11, **24**:12
Apportionment, **24**:8
  factors, elements and planning, **24**:11–12, **24**:32–33
  formulas, using, **24**:22
  procedure, **24**:9
  tax planning for subjecting corporate income to, **24**:31
Appraiser's penalty, **26**:17
Appreciated property
  determining the deduction for contributions of, by individuals, **10**:25
  noncash distributions, **19**:16
Appropriate economic unit, **11**:11
Arm's length concept, **1**:33
ASC 740, **17**:29–30
Assessable penalties, **26**:14
Assessment and the statute of limitations, **26**:21
Asset Depreciation Range (ADR), **8**:5, **19**:5
Asset ownership, separate and joint, transfer taxes, **27**:6–7
Asset purchase vs. stock purchase, tax planning for, **20**:20

Asset transfers, taxation of cross-border, **25**:18
Assets
  capital, **14**:3–8
  choosing for immediate expensing, **8**:16–17
  classification and use of, **1**:10–11, **8**:3
  disposition of, **14**:2
  expenditures for intangible, **6**:28
  expenditures for tangible, **6**:27
  hot, sale of partnership interest, **21**:48–49
  in a lump-sum purchase, allocation of cost among multiple, **13**:10
  investment, **14**:3
  partnership acquisition costs of depreciable, **21**:12
  partnership's basis in, **21**:7
  partnership's holding period in, **21**:7
  personal use, **8**:3, **14**:3
  sale, exchange, or condemnation of personal use, **13**:9
  Section 1231, **14**:28–35
  tax planning for the selection of assets to transfer, **18**:26
  valuation of, **4**:4
Assignment of income, **4**:13
Association, entity classification, **15**:8
Assumption of liabilities, **18**:10–12
  liabilities in excess of basis, **18**:11–12
  tax avoidance or no bona fide business purpose, **18**:10–11
Athletic facilities, employee fringe benefits, **5**:15
Athletic scholarships, **5**:7
At-risk amount, calculation of, **11**:5
At-risk limitation, **11**:3, **11**:4–5
  and passive activity loss limitations, treatment of losses subject to, **11**:17
  and passive activity loss limits, interaction of, **11**:15–16
  partnerships, **21**:37
  Section 465, **21**:36
At-risk rules
  common investment loss limitation rules, **11**:24
  S corporation treatment of, **22**:22–23
Attribution, **19**:25
AUD (Auditing and Attestation), CPA examination, **2**:31
Audit preparation, **26**:30–31
Audit process, **1**:21–24, **26**:6–9
  correspondence audit, **26**:8
  field audit, **26**:8
  offers in compromise and closing agreements, **26**:10–12
  office audits, **26**:8
  role of informants, **26**:7–8
  selection of returns for, **1**:21–22, **26**:6–7
  settlement procedures, **1**:23–24
  settlement with the revenue agent, **26**:8–9
  taxpayer appeal process, **26**:9–10
  types of audits, **1**:22–23
  verification and audit procedures, **26**:8
  See also Internal Revenue Service (IRS); Tax administration
Auditing and Attestation (AUD), CPA examination, **2**:31
Automatic (standard) mileage method, **9**:6–7, **9**:37
Automobile expenses, computation of, **9**:6–9

Automobiles
  business and personal use of, **8**:18–23
  change from predominantly business use, **8**:21–22
  leased, **8**:22–23
  limits on cost recovery for, **8**:19–20
  not used predominantly in business, **8**:21
  passenger, **8**:19
  substantiation requirements, **8**:23
  used predominantly in business, **8**:19
Average cost method, **16**:34
Average tax rate, **3**:25
Awards, income from, **4**:27
Away-from-home requirement
  determining the tax home, **9**:10–11
  temporary assignments, **9**:10
  travel expenses, **9**:10–11

B

Bad debt deductions, **7**:5
Bad debts, **7**:2–5
  business vs. nonbusiness, **7**:4, **18**:21–22
  loans between related parties, **7**:5
  nonbusiness, **14**:8
  specific charge-off method, **7**:3–4
Balance sheet approach, **17**:29
Bankruptcy, **2**:12, **7**:3
  corporate reorganizations, **20**:15
Base erosion anti-abuse provision, **25**:13
Base erosion anti-abuse tax (BEAT), **25**:13
Basic research, defined, **12**:9
Basic standard deduction, **3**:7
  amounts, **3**:7
Basis
  adjusted, **13**:5
  adjustments to, **13**:21
  and gain rules for nontaxable exchanges, **20**:16
  carryover, **21**:7
  for depreciating the converted property, **13**:19
  substituted, **21**:7
  tax-free reorganizations, **20**:18–19
Basis considerations, **13**:10–21
  and loss deduction limitations, tax planning for partnerships, **21**:51
  conversion of property from personal use to business or income-producing use, **13**:19–20
  determination of cost basis, **13**:10–12
  disallowed losses, **13**:16–19
  gift basis, **13**:12–14
  inherited property, **13**:14–16
  summary of basis adjustments, **13**:20
Basis determination and related issues, **18**:12–17
  basis adjustment for loss property, **18**:15–16
  basis of property to corporation, **18**:14
  basis of stock to shareholders, **18**:13
  corporate treatment when issuing stock for services, **18**:16–17
  holding period for shareholder and transferee corporation, **18**:17
  recapture considerations, **18**:17
Basis in distributed property and partnership interest, **21**:43
Basis in partnership interest, partner's, **21**:34
Basis limitation [Section 704(d)], **21**:36
  partnerships, **21**:36–37

Basis of boot received in like-kind exchanges, **13**:26
Basis of property received
  by the parent corporation, parent-subsidiary liquidations, **20**:12–14
  in like-kind exchanges, **13**:26–29
  liquidations, **20**:3
Basis of stock to shareholders, **18**:13
Basis step-down rules, Section 362, **20**:4–5
Basis to acquiring corporation of property received, **20**:18
BEC (Business Environment and Concepts), CPA examination, **2**:31
Below-market loans
  effect of on the lender and borrower, **4**:22
  exceptions and limitations of imputed interest on, **4**:23–24
  exceptions to imputed interest rules for, **4**:24
  imputed interest on, **4**:21–24
Beneficiaries of estates and trusts, **4**:16
  deduction for distributions to, **28**:16–19
Beneficiaries, taxation of, **28**:20–23
  distributions by estates and complex trusts, **28**:20–22
  distributions by simple trusts, **28**:20
Beneficiary, **28**:3
Benefit received rule, **10**:18–19
Benefits of exempt status, **23**:2
Benefits, tax planning for maximizing, **14**:48
Bequests and inheritances, **5**:3
Best practices, **26**:24
Bingo games, unrelated trade or business of exempt entities, **23**:15
Bitcoin, **3**:31–32
Blindness, additional standard deduction for, **3**:7, **3**:22
Bluebook, **2**:25
Board of Tax Appeals, **2**:15
Bonus depreciation, **1**:16, **8**:10, **8**:14–15
  and Section 179, using effectively, **8**:15–18
  Section 1245 recapture and, **14**:50
Book income, reconciling taxable income, **21**:23
Book-tax differences and overseas operations, **25**:7
Boot, **13**:25–26, **18**:2–4, **18**:13, **20**:17
  given as appreciated or depreciated property, **13**:26
  giving of, **13**:26
  receipt of, **13**:25
Bracket creep, **1**:31
Branch operation of U.S. corporation, **18**:3
Bribes
  and kickbacks, **6**:13
  Section 162 exclusion, **6**:5
Built-in gains tax, **22**:23
  general rules, **22**:23–24
Built-in loss limitation, liquidation antistuffing rules, **20**:6–8
Built-in loss property, **18**:15
  character of gain or loss on disposition of, **21**:10
Business
  costs of investigating, **6**:18
  overall comparison of forms of, **22**:28–32
Business and personal use of automobiles and other listed property, **8**:18–23
  change from predominantly business use, **8**:21–22
  leased automobiles, **8**:22–23
  limits on cost recovery for automobiles, **8**:19–20

not used predominantly in business, **8**:21
  special limitation for support-utility vehicles (SUVs), **8**:20–21
  substantiation requirements, **8**:23
  used predominantly in business, **8**:19
Business bad debt, **7**:2, **7**:4, **18**:21–22
Business deductions, **23**:2
Business entities
  choice of, **22**:2–3
  comparison of, **22**:2
  tax attributes of the different forms, **22**:29–32
Business Environment and Concepts (BEC), CPA examination, **2**:31
Business expenses
  entertainment and meal expenses, **9**:22–24
  miscellaneous employee expenses, **9**:24–25
  moving expenses, **9**:22
  office in the home, **9**:18–21
  other, **9**:18–25
  Schedule C, **6**:8
Business fixed assets, definition of capital asset, **14**:4, **14**:5
Business forms
  lowering tax rates for different, **15**:9
  tax treatment of various forms of, **15**:2–8
  See also Business entity; C corporations; Closely held corporations; Corporations; Estates; Limited liability company (LLC); Partnerships; Personal service corporations; Regular corporations; S corporations; Sole proprietorships; Trusts
Business gifts, deductibility restrictions for, **9**:24
Business income, character of, comparison of corporations and other forms of doing business, **15**:5
Business income limitations, Section 179 expensing deduction limitations, **8**:12, **8**:13
Business interest expense limitation, **17**:6–8, **17**:35
Business interest income, business interest expense limitation and, **17**:7
Business losses, **6**:6–7
  pass-through of, comparison of corporations and other forms of doing business, **15**:5
Business meals, deductibility restrictions for, **9**:23
Business organization, tax planning for corporate vs. noncorporate, **15**:23, **17**:34–35
Business supplies, definition of capital asset, **14**:4
Business year, natural, **16**:6
Business-related tax credits, **12**:6–12
  credit for employer-provided child care, **12**:11
  credit for employer-provided family and medical leave, **12**:11–12
  credit for increasing research activities, **12**:8–9
  credit for small employer pension plan startup costs, **12**:10–11
  disabled access credit, **12**:10
  low-income housing credit, **12**:9–10
  tax credit for rehabilitation expenditures, **12**:6
  work opportunity tax credit, **12**:7
Bypass amount, **27**:5, **27**:27–28
  spousal transfers, **27**:27–28
Bypass election, **22**:16

C

C corporations, **15**:3–7, **17**:2
  comparison of business entities, **22**:2
  consequences of noncash distributions, **22**:18
  Form 1120, **15**:3, **17**:23
  See also Corporations; Closely held corporations; Personal service corporations; Regular corporations; S corporations
Cafeteria plan, **5**:15–16
Calendar year, **4**:6, **16**:2
  personal service corporations, **16**:6
  PSC, **17**:4
  S corporations, **16**:5
Canons (or principles) of taxation, **1**:8
Capital
  raising of, **15**:7
  recovery of, **4**:17
Capital account maintenance, **21**:5
Capital account, partner's, **21**:35–36
Capital additions, **13**:5
Capital asset, **3**:29, **14**:3–8
  definition of, **14**:4–6
  effect of judicial action, **14**:6–7
  long-term nonpersonal use, **14**:30
  relationship to Section 1231 assets, **14**:28–29
  status, tax planning for, **14**:46–47
  statutory expansions, **14**:7–8
Capital contribution, **18**:18
Capital doctrine, recovery of, **4**:3
Capital expenditures
  capitalization vs. expense, **6**:27–28
  disallowance of deductions for, **6**:26–28
  for medical purposes, **10**:4–5
Capital gain computation, income layers for alternative tax, **14**:24
Capital gain property, **10**:23–24
  charitable contributions, **17**:9
Capital gain treatment in the U.S. and other countries, **14**:47
Capital gains, **14**:2
  from property transactions, **3**:29–32
  income taxation of corporations, **17**:5
  netting process, **14**:19–22, **14**:27
  tax planning for additional taxes on, **28**:26
  tax planning for the timing of, **17**:35
  tax treatment of corporate taxpayers, **14**:27–28
  tax treatment of noncorporate taxpayers, **14**:19–27
  See also Long-term capital gain; Net capital gain; Net long-term capital gain; Net short-term capital gain
Capital interest, **21**:5
  received in exchange for services, **21**:8
Capital investment
  limit on QBI deduction based on wages and, **6**:7–8
  QBI deduction limitation based on, **15**:14–16
Capital loss carryovers, use of, **14**:21–22
Capital loss deduction, **14**:20, **14**:26
Capital loss netting process
  final results and how they are taxed, **14**:27
  use of capital loss carryovers, **14**:21–22
Capital loss property, **21**:10
Capital losses, **14**:2
  common investment loss limitation rules, **11**:24

from property transactions, **3**:29–32
income taxation of corporations, **17**:5
income taxation of individuals and corporations compared, **17**:17
netting process, **14**:19–22
tax planning for the timing of, **17**:35
tax treatment of corporate taxpayers, **14**:27–28
tax treatment of noncorporate taxpayers, **14**:19–27
worthless securities as, **7**:6
  See also Long-term capital loss; Net capital loss; Net long-term capital loss; Net short-term capital loss; Short-term capital loss
Capital recoveries, **13**:5–7
Capital sharing ratio, **21**:5
Capital stock tax, **24**:26–27
Capital stock taxation of a multistate corporation, tax planning for, **24**:33
Capitalization vs. expense, **6**:27–28
Carbon tax, **1**:21
Carried interest, **21**:9
  sale of, **21**:49
  sale of partnership interest, **21**:48–49
Carryover basis, **13**:12, **20**:18, **21**:7
Carryover basis rule
  basis of property to corporation, **18**:14
  for Section 332 liquidations, **20**:12
  Section 351 transaction, **20**:4
Cash basis account, collection of, **14**:5
Cash basis taxpayers, special rules applicable to, **4**:9–12
  amounts received under an obligation to repay, **4**:12
  constructive receipt, **4**:9–10
  original issue discount, **4**:10–11
  Series E and Series EE bonds, **4**:11
Cash distributions
  gain and loss recognition, **21**:41
  liability reduction treated as, **21**:42
  marketable security distributions treated as, **21**:42
  proportionate current distributions in partnerships, **21**:41–42
Cash management, relevance of taxation to accounting and finance professionals, **1**:3
Cash method, **16**:11, **16**:37
  income taxation of corporations, **17**:4
  restrictions on use of, **16**:11–12
  timing of expense recognition, **6**:10
  See also Cash receipts and disbursements method
Cash receipts and disbursements method, **4**:6, **16**:10, **16**:11–13
  special rules for farmers, **16**:12–13
  See also Cash method
Cash receipts method, **4**:7–8
Casualty gains and losses, **7**:14
Casualty loss, **7**:7, **7**:14, **7**:21
  as capital recovery, **13**:6
  Form 4684, Casualties and Thefts, **14**:45
  income taxation of individuals and corporations compared, **17**:17
  personal casualty gains and losses, **7**:12–14
  when to deduct, **7**:8–9
  See also Theft losses
Casualty netting, **14**:32
Catchup contribution, HSAs, **10**:9
CCH IntelliConnect, **2**:18
Ceiling amount, Section 179 expensing deduction limitations, **8**:11–12

Centralized management, **15**:7
Certainty, tax principles, **1**:8, **1**:9
Certiorari, **2**:25
CFC. *See* Controlled foreign corporations
Change in form, not in substance, **13**:22
Change in identity, form, or place of organization, corporate reorganizations, **20**:15
Charitable contribution deduction
  capital gain property, **10**:23–24
  contribution carryovers, **10**:25–26
  fifty percent ceiling, **10**:24
  limitations on, **10**:22–26
  ordinary income property, **10**:22–23
  tax planning for ensuring, **10**:29–31
  temporary sixty percent ceiling, **10**:24
  thirty percent ceiling, **10**:24–25
  twenty percent ceiling, **10**:25
Charitable contributions, **10**:18–26, **23**:2
  benefit received rule, **10**:18–19
  criteria for a gift, **10**:18–20
  defined, **10**:18
  documentation and substantiation requirements for, **10**:21
  Form 8283, Noncash Charitable Contributions, **10**:21
  in exchange for state and local tax credits, **10**:19
  income taxation of corporations, **17**:9–11
  income taxation of individuals and corporations compared, **17**:17
  limitations imposed on deductions of, **17**:11
  nondeductible items, **10**:19–20
  of services, **10**:19
  of trusts and estates, **28**:15–16
  property contributions, **17**:9–10
  qualified organizations, **10**:20
  record-keeping and valuation requirements, **10**:21–22
  Section 162 exclusion, **6**:5
  social considerations, **1**:29
  tax planning for, **17**:35–36
  time of deduction, **10**:20
  valuation requirement for, **10**:22
Charitable deduction
  GSTT tax base and, **27**:25
  property, penalty for overvaluation of, **26**:17
  tax planning for, **27**:26–27
Charitable transfers, recapture potential of, **14**:42
Charity
  act of affection or, **5**:4
  taxable estate transfers to, **27**:19–20
Checkpoint, **2**:8, **2**:18
Check-the-box Regulations, **15**:8
Chief Counsel, **26**:4
Chief Counsel Notices (CC), **2**:9
Chief executive officer (CEO), **6**:16
Chief financial officer (CFO), **6**:16
Child and dependent care expenses
  calculation of, **12**:15–16
  earned income ceiling, **12**:15
  eligibility for, **12**:15
  eligible employment-related expenses, **12**:15
  employee fringe benefits, **5**:15
  tax credit for, **12**:2, **12**:14–16
Child care, credit for employer-provided, **12**:11
Child care resource and referral services, **12**:11
Child support, **4**:20

Child tax credit, **3**:15–17, **12**:14
  phaseout, **3**:16
  refundable portion of, **3**:17
Children
  of divorced or separated parents, **3**:14
  personal services of, **4**:13
  unearned income of dependent, **3**:26–28, **3**:33
  See also Kiddie tax
Chronically ill, accelerated death benefits and, **5**:5
Chronological order, allocating accumulated E & P to distributions, **19**:9
Circuit Court of Appeals, **2**:12
  See also Courts
Circular 230, **26**:22, **26**:23–24, **26**:27
Citations, judicial, **2**:14–17
Citator, **2**:25
Citizenship test, determining dependents, **3**:15
Civil fraud penalty, **1**:25, **26**:18
Civil penalties, legal expenses incurred in defense of, **6**:13–14
Civil tax penalties, **26**:13–14
Civil union, filing status, **3**:19
Claim for refund, **1**:24
Claim of right doctrine, **4**:8, **16**:9
  deduction for repayment of amounts under, **10**:27
  restoration of amounts received under, **16**:9–10
Class lives, cost recovery periods for personalty and realty, **8**:4
Clawback, credit for employer-provided child care, **12**:11
Client letter, **2**:28
Clients, advice to, SSTS No. 7, **26**:29
Closely held C corporations, passive activity loss rules, **17**:8
Closely held corporation, **11**:10
  tax planning for qualified dividends, **19**:32–33
Closing agreement, **26**:12
Code of Professional Conduct, **1**:26
Collectibles, **3**:29, **14**:22
Collections of unclaimed property, **24**:26
Combined return, **24**:18
  unitary theory, **24**:21
Commerce Clearing House (CCH), **2**:15–16
Commercial traveler exception, **25**:7
Commissioner of Internal Revenue, **1**:21
Committee Reports, **2**:4
Common law employees, **9**:3
  or officers, determination of W-2 wages, **15**:23
Common law property system, **4**:17
Common law states
  gift-splitting election, **27**:12
  married taxpayers, **3**:18
  survivor's share of property, **13**:15
Common law system, **1**:32
  transfer taxes and, **27**:6
Communication income, income sourcing rules, **25**:8–9
Community property, **4**:17–18, **27**:6
  federal estate tax treatment, **27**:15–17
  jurisdictions, gift-splitting election, **27**:12
  survivor's share of, **13**:15
  system, **1**:32
Community property states
  income in, **4**:17–18
  married taxpayers, **3**:18
  spouses living apart, **4**:18

Commuter highway vehicle, **5**:19
Commuting expenses, **9**:6
  See also Travel expenses
Compensation
  excessive executive, **6**:16–17
  factors for determining reasonableness of, **19**:18
  reasonable investor test, **19**:18
  unreasonable, **19**:18
Compensation for injuries and sickness, **5**:8–11
  accident and health insurance benefits, **5**:10–11
  damages, **5**:8–10
  workers' compensation, **5**:10
  wrongful incarceration, **5**:10
Compensation-related loans
  effect of on lender and borrower, **4**:22
  exemption for, **4**:23
  imputed interest on below-market, **4**:22
Compensatory damages, **5**:9
Complete termination redemption, **19**:28
  summary of qualifying rules, **19**:24
Completed contract method, **4**:7, **16**:27–28, **16**:29
Complex trust, **28**:4
  distributions by, **28**:20–22
Compliance, relevance of taxation to accounting and finance professionals, **1**:3
Composite return, **24**:23
Conduit concept. *See* Aggregate concept
Conformity of financial reports, LIFO election, **16**:36
Congress, intent of, **2**:4
Consent to Extend the Time to Assess Tax, Form 872, **26**:21
Consistency, tax planning, **2**:30
Consolidated returns, **17**:20–23
  advantages and disadvantages of, **17**:20–21
  computing consolidated taxable income, **17**:21–23
  deferral treatment for intercompany sales, **17**:23
  eligibility and the election, **17**:21
  Form 1122, Consolidated Income Tax Return, Authorization and Consent of Subsidiary Corporation to be Included in, **17**:21
  unitary theory, **24**:21
Consolidation or merger, corporate reorganizations, **20**:15
Consolidations, GAAP and tax treatment of, **17**:22
Constructive dividends, **19**:16–19, **19**:33
  bargain rental of corporate property, **19**:17
  bargain sale of corporate property to a shareholder, **19**:17
  loans to a corporation by shareholders, **19**:19
  loans to shareholders, **19**:18–19
  payments for the benefit of a shareholder, **19**:17
  shareholder use of corporate-owned property, **19**:17
  unreasonable compensation, **19**:18
Constructive liquidation scenario, **21**:33
Constructive ownership provisions, **6**:28
Constructive ownership rules, **16**:25
Constructive receipt, **4**:9–10, **16**:11
Consumer interest, **10**:14
Consumption tax, **1**:20

Content Specification Outline (CSO), CPA examination, **2**:31
Contingent payments, franchises, **14**:13
Continuity of business enterprise test, reorganization, **20**:15
Continuity of interest test, reorganization, **20**:15
Continuity of life, **15**:7
Contract costs, **16**:28
Contract price, installment method computing of, **16**:20
Contracts, current expense items for, **16**:28
Contributed property
  allocations related to, **21**:10–11
  amortization of intangible assets, **21**:9
  character of gain or loss on disposition of receivables, inventory, and built-in loss properties, **21**:10
  depreciation method and period, **21**:9
  other issues relative to, **21**:9–11
Contributions
  and distributions, tax treatment of HSA, **10**:9
  for IRAs, timing of, **9**:29
  to the partnership, **21**:6–7
Control, **18**:6
Controlled corporations
  assumption of liabilities—Section 357, **18**:10–12
  basis determination and related issues, **18**:12–17
  control immediately after the transfer, **18**:6–8
  control of the corporation, **18**:6–9
  organization of and transfers to, **18**:2–17
  property defined, **18**:5–6
  Section 351 rationale and general rules, **18**:2–4
  stock transferred, **18**:6
  transfers for property and services, **18**:8
  transfers for services and nominal property, **18**:9
  transfers to existing corporations, **18**:9
  transfers to under Section 351, **18**:2–4
Controlled foreign corporation (CFC), **25**:20–23
  other tax consequences of, **25**:23
  Subpart F income, **25**:21–22
  Subpart F income exceptions, **25**:22–23
Controversy, relevance of taxation to accounting and finance professionals, **1**:3
Convenience of payment, tax principles, **1**:8, **1**:9
Conventions
  cost recovery periods for personalty and realty, **8**:4
  travel expenses restrictions on, **9**:11–12
Conversion approach, tax planning, **2**:29–30
Conversions, IRAs rollovers and, **9**:30
Copyrights, **8**:25
  and creative works, definition of capital asset, **14**:4, **14**:5–6
Corporate accumulations, restrictions on, **17**:19–20
Corporate distributions, **19**:2, **19**:30–32
  as capital recovery, **13**:6
  other, **19**:30
  Subchapter C, Corporate Distributions and Adjustments, **2**:5
  to shareholders, **5**:24–25
Corporate entities, multistate tax planning for restructuring, **24**:29–31

Corporate income, matching tax rates and, **24**:29

Corporate income tax, **1**:2, **1**:5

Corporate income tax liability
alternative minimum tax, **17**:19
consolidated returns, **17**:20–23
corporate income tax rates, **17**:18–19
determining, **17**:18–23
restrictions on corporate accumulations, **17**:19–20

Corporate income tax rates, **17**:18–19
for selected countries (2019), **25**:2
for taxable years beginning before 2018, **17**:19

Corporate liquidation, **20**:2
See also Liquidations

Corporate reorganizations, **20**:14–19

Corporate sponsorship payments of unrelated trade or business of exempt entities, **23**:14–15

Corporate state income tax liability, computing, **24**:3

Corporate state income tax modifications, common, **24**:4

Corporate state income taxation, **24**:2–8
computing state income tax, **24**:3
jurisdiction to impose tax: nexus and Public Law 86-272, **24**:6
nexus in today's economy, **24**:6–7
state modifications, **24**:3–5
UDITPA and Multistate Tax Commission, **24**:6

Corporate stock, as capital asset or inventory, **14**:6

Corporate taxpayers, tax treatment of capital gains and losses, **14**:27–28

Corporate treatment when issuing stock for services, **18**:16–17

Corporate vs. noncorporate forms of business organization, tax planning for, **15**:23, **17**:34–35

Corporate-level tax, **22**:23

Corporations
and other forms of doing business, comparison of, **15**:4–6
basis in property received, **18**:14
basis of property to, **18**:14
branch operations of, **18**:3
estimated tax payments, **17**:24
filing requirements for, **17**:23–24
multinational, **24**:2
nontax considerations, **15**:7
procedural matters, **17**:23–34
property dividends effect on, **19**:14–16
qualified small business, **18**:24
retirement of obligation, original issue discount, **14**:9
retirement of obligations, **14**:9
Schedule M-1, **17**:24–25
Schedule M-2, **17**:25
Schedule M-3, **17**:26–28
special recapture for, **14**:44
stock attribution rules, **19**:25
Subchapter C, **2**:5
subsidiary of U.S. parent, **18**:3
tax consequences with and without the application of Section 351, **18**:15
tax planning for liquidating distributions effect on, **20**:19
tax planning for operations of, **17**:35–37
tax treatment of, **15**:3–7
vs. flow-through entities, tax planning for, **18**:28

See also C corporations; Closely held corporations; Personal service corporations; Regular corporations; S corporations

Corporations, capital structure of, **18**:18–20
capital contributions, **18**:18
debt in the capital structure, **18**:18–20

Corporations, income taxation of, **17**:2–18
accounting periods and methods, **17**:4–5
business interest expense limitation, **17**:6–8
capital gains and losses, **17**:5
charitable contributions, **17**:9–11
corporate vs. individual income tax treatment, **17**:2–3
deductions available only to corporations, **17**:12–17
excessive executive compensation, **17**:11–12
net operating losses, **17**:12
passive activity losses, **17**:8–9
recapture of depreciation, **17**:6
specific provisions compared, **17**:3

Corporation-shareholder loans
effect of on lender and borrower, **4**:22
exceptions to imputed interest rules, **4**:24
exemption for, **4**:23
imputed interest on below-market, **4**:22

Corpus, **28**:4
common allocations of items to income or, **28**:11

Correspondence audit, **1**:22, **26**:8

Cosmetic surgery, deductible medical expenses, **10**:4

Cost basis
allocation problems, **13**:10–12
determination of, **13**:10–12
identification problems, **13**:10

Cost depletion, **8**:29–30

Cost identification and documentation considerations, tax planning for, **13**:41

Cost of repairs, **7**:9

Cost recovery, **8**:2, **8**:31
recapture, **8**:21
reporting procedures, **8**:24–25
tables, **8**:32–36
See also Accelerated cost recovery system (ACRS); Modified accelerated cost recovery system (MACRS)

Cost recovery allowances, as capital recovery, **13**:5–6

Cost recovery and depreciation, **8**:2–4
cost recovery allowed or allowable, **8**:3–4
cost recovery basis for personal use assets converted to business or income-producing use, **8**:4
nature of property, **8**:2–3
placed in service requirement, **8**:3

Cost recovery periods: MACRS personalty (and certain realty), **8**:5

Costs of investigating a business, **6**:18

Court decisions, recognition of, SSTS No. 5, **26**:29

Courts
appellate courts, **2**:12
Circuit Court of Appeals, **2**:12
Court of original jurisdiction, **2**:10, **2**:11–12
Federal Courts of Appeals, **2**:13
influence of, on the tax law, **1**:33–34
trial, **2**:10, **2**:11–12
U.S. Court of Appeals, **2**:12, **2**:13–14, **2**:15
judicial citations of, **2**:16–17

U.S. Court of Federal Claims, **2**:10, **2**:11–12, **2**:13–14, **2**:15
judicial citations of, **2**:16–17
jurisdiction of, **2**:11
U.S. District Court, **2**:10, **2**:11–12, **2**:15
judicial citations of, **2**:16–17
jurisdiction of, **2**:11
U.S. Supreme Court, **2**:13, **2**:15
judicial citations of, **2**:17
U.S. Tax Court, **2**:10, **2**:11–12, **2**:13–14, **2**:15
judicial citations of, **2**:14–16
jurisdiction of, **2**:11
Small Cases Division of, **2**:10, **2**:15

Covenants not to compete, **8**:25

Coverdell Education Savings Accounts (Section 530 plan), **5**:26–27
tax consequences of, **9**:17

CPA examination
aicpa.org/becomeacpa/cpaexam.html, **2**:33
taxation on, **2**:31–33

Credits
carryovers of passive activity, **11**:8–9
credit for basic research credit, **12**:9
credit for certain retirement plan contributions, **12**:18–19, **12**:20
credit for child and dependent care expenses, **12**:14–16, **12**:20, **12**:27
credit for employer-provided child care, **12**:11
credit for employer-provided family and medical leave, **12**:11–12, **12**:22
credit for foreign taxes paid at death, **27**:23
credit for increasing research activities, **12**:21
credit for incremental research activities, **12**:8–9
credit for small employer pension plan startup costs, **12**:10–11, **12**:21
credit for tax on prior transfers, **27**:22–23
passive activity, **11**:8
See also Education tax credits; Energy credits; Tax credits

Criminal fraud penalty, **1**:25

Criminal penalties, **26**:20
legal expenses incurred in defense of, **6**:13–14

Criminal tax penalties, **26**:13–14

Crop insurance proceeds, **16**:9

Crop method, **16**:12

Cross-border asset transfers, taxation of, **25**:18

Cross-border business entity, U.S. persons with offshore income, **25**:18–19

Cross-border transactions, **25**:2
tax treaties, **25**:5–6
U.S. taxation of, **25**:3–4

CSO (Content Specification Outline), CPA examination, **2**:31

Cumulative effect of Federal gift tax, **1**:14

Current distribution, **21**:40
in partnerships, proportionate, **21**:41–43

Current E & P, **19**:8
allocating to distributions on pro rata basis, **19**:8
dividends from, **5**:24

Current participation tests, **11**:13, **11**:14

Current tax expense, **17**:29, **17**:30, **17**:31

Current Tax Payment Act, **1**:6

Customs duties, **1**:4
federal, **1**:18

D

Daily Tax Reports, **2**:8
Damages, **5**:8–10
  compensatory, **5**:9
  personal injury, **5**:8–10
  punitive, **5**:9
  taxation of, **5**:9
Data analysis, relevance of taxation to accounting and finance professionals, **1**:3
De minimis exception, lobbying expenses, **6**:16
De minimis fringe, **5**:17, **5**:18
De minimis fringe benefit, **5**:20
  subsidized eating facilities and, **9**:22
De minimis rule
  allowing immunity from nexus, **24**:7
  percentage of completion method of accounting, **16**:30
  specified services businesses, **15**:17
  Subpart F income exceptions, **25**:22
De minimis safe harbor election, **6**:27
Dealers in securities, **14**:7
Death
  disposition of passive activity at, **11**:20
  recapture potential of, **14**:41
  tax planning for selection of property to pass at, **13**:42
Death benefits, **5**:4
  accelerated, **5**:5
Death tax, **1**:13
  types of, **27**:3
Debt
  distinguish from equity, **18**:19
  income from discharge of, **5**:29–30
  recourse and nonrecourse, **21**:32
  See also Bad debts; Business bad debt; Nonbusiness bad debt
Debt in the capital structure, **18**:18–20, **18**:26–27
  advantages of, **18**:19
  reclassification of debt as equity (thin capitalization problem), **18**:19–20
Debt security holders, **20**:18
Debt-financed income, definition of, **23**:18–19
Debt-financed property, **23**:18
Deceased spouse's unused exclusion (DSUE), **27**:27
Decedent, unrecovered investment in an annuity contract, **10**:27
Deduction criteria for Section 162 and Section 212, **6**:5–6
Deduction for distributions to beneficiaries of trusts and estates, **28**:16–19
Deduction for qualified business income (QBI), **15**:9–23, **15**:24
  considerations for partnerships and S corporations, **15**:22
  coordination with other rules, **15**:22
  definition of qualified business income, **15**:10-11
  definition of qualified trade or business, **15**:11–12
  fiduciary entity, **28**:15
  general rule, **15**:10
  limitation for specified services businesses, **15**:17–21
  limitations based on wages and capital investment, **15**:14–16
  limitations on QBI deduction, **15**:12
  other issues, **15**:22–23

overall limitation: modified taxable income, **15**:10
  treatment of losses, **15**:21
Deduction for qualified tuition and related expenses, **9**:14, **9**:16–17, **9**:37
Deduction limitations, Section 179 expensing, **8**:11–13
Deductions
  additional standard (age 65 or older or blind), **3**:7, **3**:21, **3**:22
  all events and economic performance tests for, **16**:14–16
  allocation and apportionment of, **25**:9–10
  authority for, **6**:3–5
  available only to corporations, **17**:12–17
  basic standard, **3**:7, **3**:22
  business and nonbusiness losses, **6**:6–7
  classification of, **6**:2–9
  deduction for qualified business income, **6**:7–8
  disallowance possibilities, **6**:13–30
  Federal gift tax, **27**:11
  income taxation of individuals and corporations compared, **17**:17
  individuals not eligible for the standard, **3**:8
  itemized, **3**:6, **6**:3, **9**:35
  limitations imposed on charitable contributions, **10**:22–26, **17**:11
  miscellaneous itemized, **10**:27
  ordinary, taxable income of trusts and estates, **28**:13–15
  personal expenses, **6**:6
  reporting procedures, **6**:8–9
  sourcing of, **25**:6–13
  standard, **3**:6–8, **3**:21
  tax planning for proper handling of estate tax, **27**:26
  timing of expense recognition, **6**:9–12
  timing of payments to maximize, **10**:26
Deductions and losses
  accrual method requirements, **6**:10–11
  cash method requirements, **6**:10
  importance of taxpayer's method of accounting, **6**:9–10
  prepaid expenses—12-month rule, **6**:12
  time value of tax deductions, **6**:12
  under Sections 2053 and 2054, tax planning for proper handling of other, **27**:28
Deductions for adjusted gross income (AGI), **3**:5, **6**:2, **7**:2
  common, **6**:4
  expenses of self-employed individuals, **9**:3
  home office expenses, **9**:19
  interest on qualified student loans, **10**:14
  medical insurance premiums of the self-employed, **10**:7
  ordinary losses, **14**:29
  reimbursed employee expenses under an accountable plan, **9**:33
  reporting procedures, **6**:8–9
Deductions for losses, of trusts and estates, **28**:15
Deductions from adjusted gross income, **3**:6, **6**:2, **7**:2
  employee business expenses, **9**:3
  itemized deductions, **10**:2
  reimbursed employee expenses under a nonaccountable plan, **9**:33
  reporting procedures, **6**:8–9
  unreimbursed employee expenses, **9**:33
Deductions in respect of a decedent, **28**:12

Deemed payments, installment method, **16**:21
Deemed substantiation, accountable plan, **9**:34
Deemed to be long term, holding period of inherited property, **13**:16
Defendant, **2**:11
Deferral and amortization method
  research and experimental expenditures, **7**:16–17
  taxable years beginning after December 31, 2021, **7**:17
  taxable years beginning before January 1, 2022, **7**:16–17
Deferral of income, tax planning, **2**:29–30
Deferral treatment for intercompany sales, **17**:23
Deferred tax asset, **17**:29
  identifying and measuring, **17**:31–34
Deferred tax benefit, **17**:29
Deferred tax expense, **17**:29, **17**:30–31
Deferred tax, interest on, **16**:25
Deferred tax liability, **17**:29
  identifying and measuring, **17**:31–34
Deficiency, payment of, **2**:11–12
Defined benefit Keogh plan, **9**:31
Defined contribution plan, **9**:25
  Keogh plan, **9**:31
Delayed Section 1031 exchange, **13**:25
Demonstration Cites and Metropolitan Development Act of 1966, **5**:19
Department of the Treasury, **1**:21
Dependency exemptions, **3**:9
Dependent care expenses, tax credit for child and, **12**:2
Dependent children, unearned income of, **3**:26–28
Dependent tax credit, **3**:15–17, **12**:14
  nonrefundable, **3**:17
  phaseout, **3**:16
Dependents, **3**:9–17
  child and dependent tax credits, **3**:15–17
  child care expenses, **12**:14–16, **12**:27
  citizenship test, **3**:15
  comparison of categories for, **3**:15
  filing requirements for, **3**:21–22
  joint return test, **3**:14
  limitations on standard deduction for individuals who can be claimed as, **3**:8
  medical expenses incurred for, **6**:25, **10**:5
  other rules for determining, **3**:14–15
  qualifying child, **3**:9–11
  qualifying relative, **3**:11–14
  tests to identify, **3**:15
Depletion, **8**:28–31
  cost depletion method, **8**:29–30
  intangible drilling and development costs (IDC), **8**:29
  percentage depletion method, **8**:30–31
Deposits, penalty for overstatements of, **26**:19–20
Depreciated property, noncash distributions, **19**:16
Depreciation, **8**:2
  additional, **14**:38
  additional first-year, **8**:10, **8**:14–15
  as capital recovery, **13**:5–6
  Form 4562, Depreciation and Amortization, **8**:24, **8**:26
  gift basis for **13**:13–14
  recapture of, **17**:6
  tax and book, **8**:6

Depreciation and cost recovery, **8**:2–4
  contributed property, **21**:9
  cost recovery allowed or allowable, **8**:3–4
  cost recovery basis for personal use assets converted to business or income-producing use, **8**:4
  nature of property, **8**:2–3
  placed in service requirement, **8**:3
Depreciation recapture
  and Section 1231 netting procedure, **14**:44
  comparison of Section 1245 and Section 1250, **14**:39
  in other countries, **14**:42
Determination letters, **2**:9, **2**:25, **26**:4
DIF score. *See* Discriminant Index Formula (DIF) score
Direct skip, GSTT, **27**:24
Direct tax, **1**:2
Disabled access credit, **12**:3, **12**:10, **12**:21
Disallowance possibilities
  deductions for capital expenditures, **6**:26–28
  excessive executive compensation, **6**:16–17
  expenditures incurred for taxpayer's benefit or taxpayer's obligation, **6**:25
  expenses and interest relating to tax-exempt income, **6**:29–30
  hobby losses, **6**:18–21
  investigation of a business, **6**:17–18
  other disallowances, **6**:30
  personal expenditures, **6**:26
  political contributions and lobbying activities, **6**:15–16
  public policy limitation, **6**:13–15
  rental of vacation homes, **6**:21–25
  substantiation requirements, **6**:29
  transactions between related parties, **6**:28–29
Disallowed losses, **13**:16–19, **13**:42
  holding period of certain transactions, **14**:16
  related taxpayers, **13**:16
  wash sales, **13**:16–19
Disaster area losses, **7**:8–9
Discharge of indebtedness, income from, **5**:29–30
Disclaimers, **27**:9–10
Disclosure requirements for exempt organizations, **23**:21
Discriminant Index Formula (DIF) score, **1**:22
Discriminant Inventory Function (DIF) score, **26**:7
Discrimination awards, **5**:9
Disguised sale, **21**:8
Disinterested generosity test, **10**:18
Disposition of installment obligations, tax planning for, **16**:38
Disproportionate distribution, **21**:40–41
Disproportionate redemptions, **19**:27
Disqualified property, **20**:5
Disregarded entity (DRE), **15**:8
Distributable net income (DNI), **28**:11, **28**:16–17
  amount, uses of, **28**:17
  of entity and its beneficiaries, **28**:9
  of a trust, **28**:2
Distribution deduction, beneficiaries of trusts and estates, **28**:17–19
Distribution defined, **21**:40
Distribution in general, partnerships, **21**:40–41

Distribution ordering rules, S corporations, **22**:15–16
Distributions
  allocating E & P to, **19**:8–11
  and contributions, tax treatment of HSA, **10**:9
  by estates and complex trusts, **28**:20–22
  by simple trusts, **28**:20
  consequences of noncash, **22**:18
  corporate, **19**:2
  current vs. liquidating, **21**:40
  from an S corporation, classification procedures for, **22**:14
  from the partnership, **21**:40–46
  liquidating and nonliquidating compared, **20**:2–3
  of in-kind property, tax planning for, **28**:25–26
  pro rata, **20**:5
  proportionate current (general rules), **21**:44
  proportionate vs. disproportionate, **21**:40–41
  taxation of income and, **4**:17
  to shareholders, **5**:24–25
Distributive share, **21**:4
  SE treatment of partnership income, **21**:39
District courts, **2**:11–12, **2**:13–14
  jurisdiction of, **2**:11
Dividend equivalency rule, **19**:24
Dividends, **5**:24, **19**:12–21
  constructive, **19**:16–19
  income from, **4**:14–15
  income sourcing rules, **25**:7
  property, **19**:14–16
  qualified, **19**:13
  rationale for reduced tax rates on, **19**:12–13
  recapture potential of property, **14**:43
  stock dividends and stock rights, **19**:19–21
  taxation of, **15**:3–4
Dividends received deduction (DRD), **17**:13–15, **25**:24
  income taxation of individuals and corporations compared, **17**:17
Divisive exchange, corporate reorganizations, **20**:15
Divorce
  property settlements in, federal gift tax **27**:9
  support test for children of divorced or separated parents, **3**:14
  tax issues, **4**:19–21
Divorce agreements and decrees, tax treatment of payments and transfers pursuant to, **4**:21
Divorce trust, **28**:2
Divorced parents with children, special rule for medical expenses of noncustodial parent, **10**:5
Dock sales, sales factor, **24**:13
Documentation
  and cost identification considerations, tax planning for, **13**:41
  and substantiation requirements for charitable contributions, **10**:21
  issues, handling an IRS audit, **26**:31
Dollar-value LIFO, **16**:34–35
Domestic corporation, **17**:13
  defined, **25**:28
Domestic domicile, **24**:6
Domestic partners, filing status, **3**:19

Domestic subsidiary, **18**:3
Domestic travel for business and pleasure, **9**:12–13
Donor, **28**:3
Double declining balance method, classification of property, **8**:5–6
Double taxation, **25**:3
  C corporations, **15**:3
Drug dealers, deduction of expenses, **6**:15
Dual basis rules, **13**:13
Due diligence, **26**:24

E

Earned income, **3**:8, **9**:31
Earned income ceiling, child and dependent care expenses, **12**:15
Earned income credit, **12**:3, **12**:12–13, **12**:20
  computing, **12**:12–13
  eligibility requirements, **12**:12
  qualifying child, **12**:12
  social considerations, **1**:29
  workers without children, **12**:12
Earnings and profits (E & P), **19**:3–12
  accounting method adjustments, **19**:4–6
  accumulated and current, **5**:24, **19**:8
  additions to taxable income, **19**:3
  allocating E & P to distributions, **19**:8–11
  computation of, **19**:3–6
  liquidations and, **20**:2
  stock redemptions effect on, **19**:30
  subtractions from taxable income, **19**:3–4
  summary of adjustments, **19**:6–8
  timing adjustments, **19**:4
Easements as capital recovery, **13**:7
Economic concept of income, **4**:4
Economic considerations
  control of the economy, **1**:27–28
  encouragement of certain activities, **1**:28
  encouragement of certain industries, **1**:28
  encouragement of small business, **1**:28
  tax law, **1**:34
Economic effect, partner allocations, **21**:26–27
Economic effect test, **21**:26
Economic growth and efficiency, tax principles, **1**:8, **1**:9
Economic income, **4**:4
Economic nexus, **24**:7
  rule, **24**:25
Economic performance test, **6**:10, **16**:14
  accruals under, **16**:14
  for deductions, **16**:14–16
  recurring item exception, **16**:15
Economy in collection, tax principles, **1**:8
Education
  tax consequences of provisions dealing with, **9**:17
  travel expenses restrictions on, **9**:12
Education expenses, **9**:14–17, **9**:37
  allowable, **9**:15
  condition for deducting regular, **9**:15
  deduction for qualified tuition and related expenses, **9**:16–17
  general requirements, **9**:14
  legal requirements to keep a job, **9**:14
  maintaining or improving existing skills, **9**:15
  other provisions dealing with education, **9**:17

Education savings programs
  Coverdell Education Savings Accounts, **5**:27
  qualified tuition program, **5**:26–27
  Section 529 and Section 530 plans, **5**:26–27
Education tax credits, **12**:16–18, **12**:20
  eligible individuals, **12**:17
  income limitations and refundability, **12**:17–18
  maximum credit, **12**:17
  restrictions on double tax benefit, **12**:18
  social considerations, **1**:29
Educational assistance plans
  employee fringe benefits, **5**:15
  tax consequences of, **9**:17
Educational savings bonds, **5**:25–26
  tax consequences of, **9**:17
Educator expenses
  deductibility of, **9**:24–25
  tax consequences of, **9**:17
Effective rate, tax planning, **3**:33
Effectively connected income, **25**:27
E-file, **3**:22–23
E-filing, **26**:3
Eighty percent control test, **18**:9
Eighty percent stock ownership requirement, **17**:21, **18**:6
Eighty-five percent test, debt-financed property, **23**:18
Elderly or disabled credit, **12**:20
  considerations, **1**:29
Election to expense assets (Section 179), **8**:10–14
  and the mid-quarter convention, **8**:13–14
  conversion to personal use, **8**:14
  deduction limitations, **8**:11–13
  effect on basis, **8**:13
Election to split gifts by married persons, **27**:11–12
Electronic (online) tax services, **2**:19
  noncommercial, **2**:19–20
Eligible expenditures, **12**:10
Eligible small business, **12**:10
Employee achievement awards, **4**:27
Employee casualty/theft losses, **7**:15
Employee death benefits, **5**:4
Employee expenses
  accountable plans, **9**:33–34
  classification of, **9**:33–34
  miscellaneous, **9**:24–25
Employee fringe benefits, **5**:14–21, **5**:22, **5**:30–31
  cafeteria plans, **5**:15–16
  de minimis fringes, **5**:18
  flexible spending plans, **5**:16
  general classes of excluded benefits, **5**:16–20
  group term life insurance, **5**:20–21
  no-additional-cost service, **5**:17
  nondiscrimination provisions, **5**:20
  qualified employee discounts, **5**:17–18
  qualified military base realignment and closure fringes, **5**:19
  qualified moving expense reimbursements, **5**:19
  qualified retirement planning services, **5**:19
  qualified transportation fringes, **5**:19
  specific benefits, **5**:15
  Tax Cuts and Jobs Act (TCJA) of 2017, **5**:20
  working condition fringes, **5**:18
  See also Accident and health plans

Employee or independent contractor status, Form SS-8, **9**:5
Employee turned independent contractor, QBI deduction, **15**:22–23
Employee vs. independent contractor, **9**:2–5
Employee-employer relationship, **9**:3
Employees
  and self-employed-related expenses—in general, **9**:5
  common law, **9**:3
  employer payments to, **5**:3–4
  Form W-4, Employee Withholding Allowance Certificate, **26**:19
  of educational institutions, housing exclusions, **5**:14
  personal services of, **4**:13
  statutory, **9**:5
Employer
  contributions to qualified pension or profit sharing plans, social considerations, **1**:28
  payments by, **12**:22
  payments to employees, **5**:3–4
  tax credit for providing child care expenses, social considerations, **1**:29
Employer-employee loans, exceptions to imputed interest rules, **4**:24
Employer-provided accident and health plans, social considerations, **1**:28
Employer-provided child care, credit for, **12**:11, **12**:21
Employer-provided group term life insurance, social considerations, **1**:28
Employer-sponsored accident and health plans, **5**:11–12
  long-term care insurance benefits, **5**:12
  medical reimbursement plans, **5**:11–12
Employment status, tax planning for, **9**:36
Employment taxes, **1**:17–18, **12**:19
  comparison of corporations and other forms of doing business, **15**:5
Employment-related expenses, child and dependent care expenses, **12**:15
En banc decision, **2**:11, **2**:25
Endowment, exempt organization, **23**:3
Energy credits, **12**:21
Energy research credit, **12**:9
Energy tax credits, **12**:18
  economic considerations, **1**:28
  See also Tax credits
Enrolled agents (EAs), **26**:22
Entertainment expenses, **9**:22–24
  and meal expenses, TCJA and, **9**:22
Entities, flow-through or pass-through, **21**:2
Entity accounting income, **28**:8–11
Entity classification
  election, Form, 8832, **15**:8
  limited liability companies, **15**:8
Entity concept, **21**:4–5
Entity, tax planning for the choice of, **2**:29–30
Entity tax rates
  challenges of lowering, **15**:8–9
  lowering for different business forms, **15**:9
  TCJA and, **15**:8–9
Equity
  distinguish debt from, **18**:19
  reclassification of debt as, **18**:19–20
  tax principles, **1**:8
Equity and fairness
  equity considerations, **1**:29
  tax principles, **1**:8, **1**:9

Equity considerations
  alleviating the effect of multiple taxation, **1**:30
  coping with inflation, **1**:31
  mitigating effect of the annual accounting period concept, **1**:30–31
  tax law, **1**:34
  wherewithal to pay concept, **1**:30
Error, knowledge of, SSTS No. 6, **26**:29
Escheat laws, **24**:26
Estate
  and trust, income taxation of, **28**:2–26
  as income-shifting device, **28**:24
  beneficiaries of, **4**:16
  definition of, **28**:5
  distributions by, **28**:20–22
  Form 1041, **28**:23
  income from, **4**:16–17
  income tax planning for, **28**:24–25
  procedural matters, **28**:23–24
  stock attribution rules, **19**:25
  structure of, **28**:3
  tax characteristics of, **28**:6
  taxation of beneficiaries, **28**:20–23
Estate tax, **1**:13, **27**:3
  Form 706, Estate and generation-skipping transfer tax return, **26**:17
  formula, **27**:4
  See also Federal estate tax
Estate tax credits
  credit for foreign taxes paid at death, **27**:23
  credit for tax on prior transfers, **27**:22–23
  See also Tax credits
Estate, taxable income of, **28**:8–20
  charitable contributions, **28**:15–16
  deduction for distributions to beneficiaries, **28**:16–19
  deductions for losses, **28**:15
  entity accounting income, **28**:8–11
  gross income, **28**:11–13
  ordinary deductions, **28**:13–15
  tax credits, **28**:19
Estate taxation
  additional tax on net investment income, **28**:8
  alternative minimum tax, **28**:7–8
  nature of, **28**:5–8
  tax accounting periods and methods, **28**:6
  tax rates and personal exemption, **28**:6–7
Estimated tax, **12**:23
  Form 1040-ES, **12**:23
  payments for corporations, **17**:24
  payments, failure to pay, **26**:18–19
  underpayment of by corporations, Form 2220, **26**:19
  underpayment of by individuals, Form 2210, **26**:19
Estimates, SSTS No. 4, **26**:29
Ethical guidelines, AICPAs, **1**:26
Excess benefit transactions, intermediate sanctions on, **23**:6–7
Excess business loss, **7**:17–19
  defined, 7:17–18
  from partnerships or S corporations, **7**:18–19
  limitation and Section 469 passive activity loss rules, **7**:19
  of noncorporate taxpayers, **21**:38
  other rules, **7**:19
  rules, **7**:18
  Section 461(l), **21**:36
Excess cost recovery, **8**:21
Excess lobbying expenditures, **23**:6
Excess net passive income (ENPI), **22**:24

Excessive executive compensation, **6**:16–17, **17**:11–12
Exchange, exceptions to Section 721, **21**:8
Exchange period, like kind exchanges, **13**:24
Exchange requirement, like-kind exchanges, **13**:24–25
Excise taxes, **1**:2, **1**:5, **1**:11
  federal, **1**:11
  state and local, **1**:11
Exclusion amount, **4**:24–26, **27**:5
  tax planning for taking advantage of, **27**:27–28
Exclusion treatment, life insurance proceeds transferred for valuable consideration, **5**:6
Exclusions from income, **3**:3
Executive compensation, tax planning for, **6**:33, **7**:36
Exempt economy, **23**:2–3
Exempt entities
  annual filing requirements, **23**:19–20
  characteristics of, **23**:3–5
  disclosure requirements, **23**:21
  feeder organizations, **23**:8
  obtaining exempt organization status, **23**:19
  private foundations, **23**:8–12
  reporting requirements, **23**:19–21
  tax planning for, **23**:21–22
  taxable transactions, **23**:5–8
  taxes on, **23**:5–8
  types of exempt organizations, **23**:3
  unrelated business income tax, **23**:12–19
Exempt entities characteristics
  net earnings and members of the organization, **23**:3–5
  not-for-profit entity, **23**:3
  serving the common good, **23**:3
Exempt organizations, **23**:2
  classification, **23**:10
  types of, **23**:3, **23**:4
Exempt status
  benefits of, **23**:2
  consequences of, **23**:5
  tax planning for maintaining, **23**:21–22
Exemption equivalent amount, **27**:5, **27**:27–28
Exemptions, **3**:9
  sales/use tax, **24**:24–25
Expatriation to avoid U.S. taxation, **25**:28–29
Expenditures incurred for taxpayer's benefit or taxpayer's obligation, disallowance possibilities, **6**:25
Expense method, research and experimental expenditures, **7**:16
Expense/deduction items, reconciliation of, Schedule M-3, Part III, **17**:28
Expenses
  classification of, **6**:31
  classification of deductible, **6**:2–9
  deemed to be contrary to public policy, social considerations, **1**:29
  employee and self-employed-related, **9**:5
  Form 8829, Expenses for Business Use of Your Home, **9**:19
  indebtedness, and taxes, taxable estate, **27**:19
Export property, U.S. business engaging in global commerce, **25**:15–18
External support test for public charity, **23**:9–10

Factor presence nexus, **24**:7
Facts and circumstances approach, health issues, **13**:39
Facts and circumstances test, **11**:13, **11**:14
Failure to file penalties, **1**:25
Failure to pay penalties, **1**:25
Fair market value, **13**:4
  valuation requirement for charitable contributions, **10**:22
Fair tax, **1**:20
Family attribution rules, complete termination redemption and, **19**:28
Family, stock attribution rules, **19**:25
FAR (Financial Accounting and Reporting), CPA examination, **2**:31
Farm price method, **16**:36
Farm relief, annual accounting period concept, **16**:9
Farmers, special rules for, **16**:12–13
Farming and ranching, special inventory methods relating to, **16**:36
Farming expenses, Schedule F, **6**:9
  Section 212 expenses, **6**:4
Federal Claims Reporter (Fed.Cl.), **2**:17
Federal Courts of Appeals, **2**:13
  See also Courts
Federal customs duties, **1**:18
Federal estate tax, **1**:11, **1**:13, **27**:13–24, **27**:26–28
  estate tax credits, **27**:22–23
  Form 706, **27**:24
  formula for, **27**:4
  gross estate, **27**:13–18
  on income in respect of a decedent, **10**:27
  procedural matters, **27**:23–24
  taxable estate, **27**:19–22
Federal gift tax, **1**:14–15, **27**:7–13, **27**:25–26
  annual gift tax exclusion, **27**:10–11
  business vs. personal setting, **27**:7–8
  deductions, **27**:11
  disclaimers, **27**:9–10
  election to split gifts by married persons, **27**:11–12
  excluded transfers, **27**:8
  Form 709, U.S. Gift Tax Return, **27**:3, **27**:12–13
  formula for, **27**:3–4
  general considerations, **27**:7–9
  income tax considerations, **27**:10
  incomplete transfers, **27**:7
  lifetime vs. death transfers, **27**:8–9
  other transfers subject to, **27**:10
  procedural matters, **27**:12–13
  property settlements in divorce, **27**:9
  provisions, **27**:13
  requirements for a gift, **27**:7
  transfers subject to, **27**:9–10
  unified transfer tax, **27**:11
Federal income taxes, **1**:15–16
Federal Insurance Contribution Act. *See* FICA
Federal judicial system, **2**:10
  trial courts, **2**:12
Federal Register, **2**:7
Federal Supplement Second Series (F.Supp.2d), **2**:16–17
Federal Tax Articles, **2**:18
Federal Tax Coordinator 2d, **2**:18, **2**:19
Federal tax law, understanding, **1**:27–34

Federal tax revenues (estimated) fiscal year 2020, **1**:6
Federal Third Series (F.3d), **2**:17
Federal Unemployment Tax Act. *See* FUTA
Feeder organization, **23**:5, **23**:8
Fees, occupational, **1**:19
FICA, **1**:17
FICA tax, **1**:17–18
  amount of, **12**:22
Fiduciary, **28**:2
Fiduciary taxation
  overview of, **28**:2–5
  principles of, **28**:20
Field audit, **1**:23, **26**:8
Field Service Advice Memoranda (FSAs), **2**:9
FIFO (first in, first out) method, **16**:34
  applied to carrybacks, carryovers, and utilization of general business credits, **12**:5
FIFO presumption, identification problems, **13**:10
Fifty percent organizations, **10**:24
50% rule exceptions, entertainment and meal expenses, **9**:22–23
Filing requirements
  e-filing, **3**:22–23
  for corporations, **17**:23–24
  for dependents, **3**:21–22
  for exempt organizations, **23**:19–20
  mode of payment, **3**:24
  selecting the proper form, **3**:22
  when and where to file, **3**:23–24
Filing status, **3**:17–20
  abandoned spouse rules, **3**:20
  civil union, **3**:19
  domestic partners, **3**:19
  head of household, **3**:19–20
  married taxpayers, **3**:18–19
  same-sex couples, **3**:19
  single taxpayers, **3**:18
  surviving spouse, **3**:19
Filing the return, **3**:17, **3**:21–24
  filing status, **3**:17–20
Final Regulations, **2**:7
Financial Accounting and Reporting (FAR), CPA examination, **2**:31
Financial accounting income vs. taxable income, **4**:4–5
Financial Accounting Standards Board (FASB), **2**:26
  Accounting Standards Codification (ASC) 740, *Income Taxes*, **1**:3
Financial information and net income (loss) reconciliation, Schedule M-3, Part I, **17**:27
Financial reporting
  for partnerships, **21**:24
  relevance of taxation to accounting and finance professionals, **1**:3
Financial statements
  GAAP-basis, **21**:24
  income taxes on, **17**:28–34
Financial transaction tax, **1**:21
Fines and penalties paid to a government for violation of law, **6**:13
Fines, Section 162 exclusion, **6**:5
First-tier distribution, **28**:21–22
Fiscal year, **4**:6, **16**:2
  PSC election of, **16**:6, **17**:4
Fixture, **1**:10
Flat tax, **1**:20
Flexible benefit plans, **5**:16
Flexible spending plans, **5**:16

Floor plan financing interest, business interest expense limitation and, **17**:7–8

Flow-through entities, **21**:2
business interest expense limitation and, **17**:8
vs. corporations, tax planning for, **18**:28

Foreign base company income (FBCI), **25**:21
sales income, **25**:21
services income, **25**:22

Foreign branches
U.S. business engaging in global commerce, **25**:15–18
vs. separate overseas entity, tax considerations for, **25**:29

Foreign corporations
definition of, **25**:28
expatriation to avoid U.S. taxation, **25**:28–29
Foreign Investment in Real Property Tax Act (FIRPTA), **25**:28
U.S. taxation of, **25**:28

Foreign Corrupt Practices Act (FCPA) of 1977, **6**:13, **6**:14

Foreign currency transactions, international taxation of, **25**:14

Foreign earned income, **5**:21–23

Foreign earned income exclusion, **5**:21
benefits are questioned, **5**:23

Foreign income. *See* Income; Offshore income

Foreign Investment in Real Property Tax Act (FIRPTA), **25**:28

Foreign personal holding company (FPHC) income, **25**:21

Foreign shareholders prefer sale or exchange treatment in stock redemptions, **19**:23

Foreign subsidiary, **18**:3
basis rules for liquidations of, **20**:11

Foreign tax credit (FTC), **12**:13–14, **12**:21, **13**:3, **25**:3, **25**:15–17
carryover provision, **12**:4
computation of, **12**:14
income sourcing in cyberspace, **12**:13
limitation and sourcing provisions, tax planning for, **25**:30

Foreign taxes paid at death, credit for, **27**:23

Foreign travel for business and pleasure, **9**:13

Foreign-source income, **25**:6

Form 10-K, SEC, **17**:27

Form 461, Limitation on Business Losses, **7**:19

Form 656, Offer in Compromise, **26**:10

Form 706, estate tax return, **26**:17, **27**:24

Form 709, U.S. Gift Tax Return, **26**:17, **27**:12–13

Form 851, Affiliation Schedule, **17**:21

Form 870, Waiver of Restrictions on Assessment and Collection of Deficiency in Tax, **26**:9

Form 872, Consent to Extend the Time to Assess Tax, **26**:21

Form 970, Application to Use LIFO Inventory Method, **16**:35

Form 990, Return of Organization Exempt from Income Tax, **23**:19–20

Form 990-EZ, **23**:20

Form 990-N (e-Postcard), **23**:20

Form 990-PF, Return of Private Foundation, **23**:20

Form 990–T, Exempt Organization Business Income Tax Return, **23**:20

Form 1023, Application for Recognition of Exemption under Section 501(c)(3), **23**:19

Form 1023-EZ, **23**:19

Form 1024, Application for Recognition of Exemption under Section 501(a), **23**:19

Form 1040, **1**:5, **3**:22, **6**:9, **21**:15
Schedule 1, **3**:22
Schedule 2, **3**:22
Schedule A, qualified residence interest indebtedness, **10**:17
Schedule C, Profit or Loss from Business, **8**:24, **8**:27, **9**:3, **10**:17, **15**:2
Schedule E, interest expenses related to rents or royalties, **10**:17

Form 1040-ES, Estimated Tax for Individuals, **3**:25, **12**:23

Form 1040SR, seniors, **3**:22

Form 1040X, amended return, **3**:24, **26**:22

Form 1041, U.S. Income Tax Return for Estates and Trusts, **21**:15, **28**:23

Form 1065, U.S. Return of Partnership Income, **4**:16, **15**:3, **21**:6, **21**:19–21
example, **21**:18–24

Form 1090-MISC (Miscellaneous Income), **9**:37

Form 1098-T, Tuition Statement, **9**:16

Form 1099-Q, Payments from Qualified Education Programs, **5**:26

Form 1120, C corporations, **15**:3, **17**:23, **21**:15

Form 1120S, S corporations, **17**:23, **21**:15

Form 1120X, tax refund for corporations, **26**:22

Form 1122, Authorization and Consent of Subsidiary Corporation to be Included in a Consolidated Income Tax Return, **17**:21

Form 1128, Application for Change in Accounting Period, **16**:6

Form 2120, Multiple Support Declaration, **3**:14

Form 2210, Underpayment of Estimated Tax by Individuals, **26**:19

Form 2220, Underpayment of Estimated Tax by Corporations, **26**:19

Form 2441, Credit for Child and Dependent Care Expenses, **12**:14

Form 2553, S corporation status, **22**:5

Form 3115, Application for Change in Accounting Method, **16**:17

Form 4562, Depreciation and Amortization, **8**:24, **8**:26

Form 4684, Casualties and Thefts, **14**:45

Form 4720, Return of Certain Excise Taxes on Charities and Other Persons, **23**:20

Form 4797, Sales of Business Property, **14**:45

Form 4868, Application for Automatic Extension of Time to File U.S. Individual Income Tax Return, **3**:23, **26**:15

Form 4952, Investment Interest Deduction, **11**:23

Form 5329, Additional Taxes on Qualified Plans (Including IRAs) and Other Tax-Favored Accounts), **5**:26

Form 6251, Alternative minimum tax (AMT), **12**:26

Form 7004, six-month extension, **17**:24

Form 8275, **26**:16

Form 8283, Noncash Charitable Contributions, **10**:21

Form 8332, Release of Claim to Exemption for Child of Divorced or Separated Parents, **3**:14

Form 8814, Parents' Election to Report Child's Interest and Dividends, **3**:28

Form 8824, Like-Kind Exchanges, **13**:29, **13**:30

Form 8829, Expenses for Business Use of Your Home, **9**:19

Form 8832, Entity Classification Election, **15**:8

Form 8917, Tuition and Fees Deduction, **9**:16

Form 8952, Application for Voluntary Classification Settlement Program (VCSP), **9**:37

Form 8959, additional Medicare tax, **21**:38

Form 8960, Net Investment Income Tax–Individuals, Estates, and Trusts, **21**:39, **28**:8

Form 9465, installment plan, **26**:11

Form of receipt, realization, **4**:5–6

Form SS-8, Determination of Worker Status for Purposes of Federal Employment Taxes and Income Tax Withholding, **9**:5

Form W-2, Wage and Tax Statement, **3**:25

Form W-4, Employee Withholding Allowance Certificate, **26**:19

For-profit prohibition, **23**:3

Foundations, private operating and private nonoperating **10**:23–24

Franchise payments, **14**:13

Franchise tax, **1**:5, **1**:19, **24**:26–27

Franchisee, **14**:12

Franchises, **8**:25, **14**:12–14
consequences to the franchisor and franchisee, **14**:14
contingent payments, **14**:13
noncontingent payments, **14**:13
significant power, right, or continuing interest, **14**:13
sports franchises, **14**:14

Franchising, **14**:12

Franchisor, **14**:12

Fraud, **1**:25, **26**:18

Fraudulent returns, **1**:24

Fringe benefits, **5**:14
See also Employee fringe benefits

Front-loading, alimony and separate maintenance payments, **4**:20

Fruit and tree metaphor, **4**:13

Full inclusion rule, Subpart F income exceptions, **25**:22

Full recapture, **14**:36

Functional currency, **25**:14

Functional use test, replacement property, **13**:32

FUTA, **1**:17
tax, **1**:18

Future interest, **27**:10

G

GAAP. *See* Generally accepted accounting principles

GAAP-basis financial statements, **21**:24

Gain
and basis rules for nontaxable exchanges, **20**:16

Gain *(continued)*
  determination of, **13**:2–9
  precontribution, **21**:27–28
  realized, **13**:2–8, **13**:9
  recognized, **13**:8–9
  Section 1231, **14**:29
  tax-free reorganizations, **20**:17–18
Gain basis
  for converted property, **13**:19
  of donee, **13**:13
  rules, holding period for property
    acquired by gift, **13**:13
Gain from qualified small business stock,
  18:24
Gain from sale of depreciable property
  between certain related parties,
  14:45
Gain, nonrecognition of, **13**:9
  in involuntary conversions, **13**:34–35
  sale, exchange, or condemnation of
    personal use assets, **13**:9
  under Section 351 and Section 1031,
    18:2–4
Gain on disposition of receivables,
  inventory, and built-in loss
  properties, character of, **21**:10
Gain or loss, no partnership level of, **21**:43
Gain recognition
  cash distributions, **21**:41
  for proportionate liquidating distributions
    from partnerships, **21**:44–45
  on contributions to the partnership,
    21:6
  stock redemptions, **19**:29
Gains from property transactions—in
  general, **3**:28–29
Gambling losses, miscellaneous deductions,
  10:27
General business credit, **12**:5, **12**:21
  treatment of unused, **12**:5–6
General Counsel Memoranda (GCMs), **2**:9,
  2:25
General partners, **21**:2
  material participation, **11**:14
  vs. limited partners, SE treatment of,
    21:39
General partnership (GP), **21**:2
  comparison of partnership types, **21**:3
General sales taxes, **1**:12
Generally accepted accounting principles
  (GAAP), **16**:31, **17**:24, **17**:29–30,
  28:10
  and tax treatment of consolidations, **17**:22
  partner's capital account analysis, **21**:35
  reconciling partner's capital, **21**:23–24
  sources of, **2**:26
Generation-skipping transfer tax (GSTT),
  27:4, **27**:24–25
  Form 709, gift and generation-skipping
    transfer tax return, **26**:17
  inter-generational transfers, **27**:24
  tax on generation-skipping transfers,
    27:24–25
Gift basis, **13**:12–14
  adjustment for gift tax, **13**:13
  basis for depreciation, **13**:13–14
  holding period, **13**:13
  rules, **13**:12–13
Gift loans
  effect of on lender and borrower, **4**:22
  exceptions to imputed interest rules, **4**:23
  imputed interest on below-market, **4**:22
Gift or loan, related parties, **7**:5
Gift splitting, **1**:14–15

Gift tax, **1**:14–15
  formula, **27**:3
Gifts
  criteria for, **10**:18–20
  disposition of passive activity by, **11**:21
  election to split by married persons,
    27:11–12
  recapture potential of, **14**:41
  requirements for, **27**:7
  Section 162 exclusion, **6**:5
  special holding period rules, **14**:16
  tax planning for the selection of property
    for making, **13**:41–42
  taxable, **27**:3
Gifts and inheritances, **5**:3–4
  employee death benefits, **5**:4
  employer payments to employees,
    5:3–4
  legislative intent, **5**:3
Global activities timeline, **25**:15
Global business environment, **25**:2
Global intangible low-taxed income
  (GILTI), **25**:25
Global tax issues
  basis rules for liquidations of foreign
    subsidiaries, **20**:11
  benefits of foreign earned income
    exclusion are questioned, **5**:23
  capital gain treatment in the U.S. and
    other countries, **14**:47
  choice of organizational form when
    operating overseas, **18**:3
  choose the charity wisely, **10**:22
  citizenship is not tax-free, **3**:5
  depreciation recapture in other countries,
    14:42
  foreign shareholders prefer sale or
    exchange treatment in stock
    redemptions, **19**:23
  from "all sources" is a broad definition,
    4:3
  outsourcing of tax return preparation,
    1:26
  overseas gun sales result in large fines,
    6:14
  sourcing income in cyberspace,
    calculating the foreign tax credit,
    12:13
  tax reform can make strange bedfellows,
    25:4
  tracking down tax dollars, **3**:23
  treaty relief, **27**:23
  U.S. corporate taxes and international
    business competitiveness, **15**:7
  U.S. transfer taxes and NRAs, **27**:3
  value added tax, **1**:21
  water's edge, **24**:21
  withholding requirements for non-U.S.
    partners, **21**:38
Global tax system, foreign earned income,
  5:21–23
Global trade, **25**:2
Going-concern value, **8**:25
Golsen rule, **2**:14
Goodwill, **8**:25, **13**:11
  self-generated, **14**:4
Government revenues, tax principles, **1**:8,
  1:9
Grantor, **28**:3
Grantor trust, **28**:4
Grass roots expenditures, **23**:5
Grass roots nontaxable amount, **23**:6
Gray areas, **2**:2, **2**:12
Green card test, **25**:26

Gross estate, **1**:13, **27**:13–18, **27**:26
Gross income, **3**:3–4, **4**:3–6, **4**:29–32
  computation of, income taxation of
    individuals and corporations
    compared, **17**:17
  economic and accounting concepts, **4**:4
  financial accounting income vs. taxable
    income, **4**:4–5
  form of receipt, **4**:5–6
  IRS definition, **3**:3
  items specifically excluded from, life
    insurance proceeds, **5**:4–6
  items specifically included in, **4**:19–29
  leased automobile inclusion amount,
    8:22
  of trusts and estates, **28**:11–13
  partial list of exclusions from, **3**:3
  partial list of items, **3**:4
  recovery of capital doctrine, **4**:3
  sources of and to whom they are taxed,
    4:13–18
  tax planning for minimizing income
    included in, **4**:30
  test, qualifying relative, **3**:12–13
  timing of income recognition, **4**:6–12
  See also Income
Gross income exclusions
  compensation for injuries and sickness,
    5:8–11
  corporate distributions to shareholders,
    5:24–25
  education savings programs (Section 529
    and Section 530 plans), **5**:26–27
  educational savings bonds, **5**:25–26
  employee fringe benefits, **5**:14–21
  employer-sponsored accident and health
    plans, **5**:11–12
  foreign earned income, **5**:21–23
  gifts and inheritances, **5**:3–4
  income from discharge of indebtedness,
    5:29–30
  interest on certain state and local
    government obligations, **5**:23–24
  meals and lodging, **5**:13–14
  qualified ABLE programs (Section 529A
    plans), **5**:27
  scholarships, **5**:7–8
  statutory authority, **5**:2–3
  tax benefit rule, **5**:27–28
Gross receipts test, **21**:13
Group term life insurance, **5**:20–21
  protection, uniform premiums for, **5**:21
Guaranteed payments, **21**:18
  on Schedule K-1, partner reporting of
    partnership income, **21**:26
  SE treatment of partnership income,
    21:39
*Guiding Principles of Good Tax Policy:
  A Framework for Evaluating Tax
  Proposals,* **1**:8
  application of, **1**:9

H

H.R. 10 plans. *See* Keogh plans
Half-year convention, **8**:6
Hall-Rabushka proposal, **1**:20
Handicapped person, impairment-related
  work expenses, **10**:27
Hazard of litigation, **1**:23
Head-of-household, **3**:19–20
Health insurance. *See* Employer-sponsored
  accident and health plans

Health Savings Account (HSA), **5**:12, **10**:8–9
  deductible amount, **10**:9
  high-deductible plans, **10**:8
  tax treatment of HSA contributions and
    distributions, **10**:9
Hobbies, common activities classified as,
  6:20
Hobbies/business, common questions from
  IRS concerning losses with, **6**:20
Hobby losses, **6**:18–21, **6**:32
  common investment loss limitation rules,
    11:24
  determining the amount of the deduction,
    6:20–21
  general rules, **6**:19
  presumptive rule of Section 183, **6**:19
  Schedule C, **6**:19
Holding period, **13**:13, **14**:15–19
  certain disallowed loss transactions,
    14:16
  contributions to the partnership, **21**:7
  for shareholder and transferee
    corporation, **18**:17
  general rules, **14**:15
  gifts, **14**:16
  inherited property, **14**:16
  nontaxable exchanges, **14**:15–16
  of the buyer, related taxpayers, **13**:16
  of new stock or securities, wash sales,
    13:17
  of nontaxable stock dividends, **13**:12
  short sales, special rules for, **14**:16–19
  special rules, **14**:15–16
Holding period of property, **14**:3
  acquired by gift, **13**:13
  received in like-kind exchanges,
    13:26–29
Home equity loans, **10**:15
Home for the aged, deductible medical
  expenses, **10**:4
Home office expense, **9**:18–21
Home-related capital expenditures for a
  physically handicapped individual,
  10:5
Hospital insurance, **1**:17
Hot assets, **21**:42
  sale of partnership interest, **21**:48–49
Hotel occupancy tax, **1**:11
House of Representatives, **2**:3–4
House Ways and Means Committee,
  2:3–4
Housekeeping-type instructions, **2**:24
Housing exclusions, other, **5**:14
Hybrid method, **4**:7, **4**:9, **16**:10, **16**:16–17

I

Identification period, like kind exchanges,
  13:24
Illegal business, deduction of expenses
  relating to, **6**:14–15
Immediate expensing (Section 179), **8**:10
  Section 1245 recapture and, **14**:50
  See also Section 179 expensing
Immigration Form I-551, **25**:26
Imputed interest, **4**:21, **16**:22–23
  exceptions and limitations of, **4**:23–24
  on below-market loans, **4**:21–24
  rules for below-market loans, exceptions
    to, **4**:24
Inbound taxation, **25**:3
Incidents of ownership, life insurance,
  27:18

Income, **3**:2–3, **4**:4
  active, **11**:6
  additional Medicare tax on unearned,
    12:24–25
  all events test for, **16**:13–14
  apportionable and nonapportionable,
    24:9–11, **24**:12
  assignment of, **4**:13
  character of for taxation of beneficiaries
    of trusts and estates, **28**:22–23
  common allocations of items to corpus
    or, **28**:11
  debt-financed, **23**:18–19
  deferral of partnership, **21**:13
  dependent children's unearned, **3**:26–28
  distributable net (DNI), **28**:16–17
  economic and accounting concepts of
    gross, **4**:4
  effectively connected, **25**:27
  entity accounting, **28**:8–11
  exclusions from, **3**:3
  expenses and interest relating to tax-
    exempt, **6**:29–30
  foreign base company (FBCI), **25**:21
  foreign-source, **25**:6
  gross, **4**:3–6
  investment, **11**:22
  least aggregate deferral method of, **16**:4
  measuring partnership, **21**:16–18
  multistate corporation's allocation and
    apportionment of, **24**:8–18
  net investment, **11**:22
  passive activity, **11**:6
  portfolio, **11**:6
  recovery of capital doctrine of gross, **4**:3
  S corporation allocation of, **22**:12–13
  S corporation computation of taxable,
    22:9–11
  Schedule M-1—reconciliation, **17**:24–25
  sourcing of, **25**:6–13
  Subpart F, **25**:21–22
  tax planning the deferral of, **2**:29–30
  tax planning the shifting of, **2**:29–30, **4**:32
  U.S.-source, **25**:6
  unearned, **4**:12
  See also Foreign income; Gross income;
    Offshore income
Income allocation in sale of partnership
  interest, **21**:47
Income and distributions, taxation of,
  4:17
Income earned from foreign bank and
  financial accounts and FBAR rules,
  4:29
Income from discharge of indebtedness,
  5:29–30
Income in community property states,
  4:17–18
Income in respect of a decedent (IRD), **5**:4,
  13:14–15, **28**:12–13
  Federal estate tax on, **10**:27
  gross income of trusts and estates,
    28:12–13
Income layers for alternative tax on capital
  gain computation, **14**:24
Income levels when Form 1040 must be
  filed, **3**:21
Income of a CFC included in gross income
  of a U.S. shareholder, **25**:24
Income of private foundations,
  undistributed, **23**:12
Income received by an agent, **4**:16
Income recognition, timing of, **4**:6–12
  accounting methods, **4**:6–9

  exceptions applicable to accrual basis
    taxpayers, **4**:12
  special rules applicable to cash basis
    taxpayers, **4**:9–12
  taxable year, **4**:6
Income shifting, transfer pricing, **25**:10–12
Income sources, **4**:13–18
  from partnerships, S corporations, trusts,
    and estates, **4**:16–17
  from property, **4**:13–15
  in community property states, **4**:17–18
  personal services, **4**:13
  received by an agent, **4**:16
Income sourcing in cyberspace, foreign tax
  credit, **12**:13
Income sourcing rules, **25**:6–13
  dividends, **25**:7
  interest, **25**:7
  personal services income, **25**:7–8
  rents and royalties, **25**:8
  sale or exchange of property, **25**:8
  software income, **25**:9
  transportation and communication
    income, **25**:8–9
Income tax, **1**:2, **1**:4, **1**:6, **1**:15–17
  appeal procedure, **26**:9
  corporate state, **24**:2–8
  deduction, tax credit and, **12**:3
  federal, **1**:15–16
  formula for individuals, **1**:15
  history of, **1**:4–6
  local, **1**:17, **10**:13
  rates, corporate, **17**:18–19
  state, **1**:16–17, **10**:13
  treatment, corporate vs. individual, **17**:2–3
Income taxation of individuals and
  corporations compared, **17**:17–18
Income taxes on financial statements,
  17:28–34
  GAAP principles, **17**:29–30
Income-shifting device, tax planning for a
  trust or an estate as, **28**:24
Income-splitting option, **3**:18
Incorporation tax, **24**:26
Indebtedness, income from discharge of,
  5:29–30
Independent contractor, **9**:2
  or employee status, Form SS-8, **9**:5
  vs. employee, **9**:2–5
  See also Self-employed individual
Index to Federal Tax Articles, **2**:18
Indexation, **1**:31
Indirect tax, **1**:2
Individual Retirement Accounts (IRAs), **9**:25,
  9:26–30, **9**:31
  comparison of, **9**:30
  deductions, phaseout of an active
    participant in 2020, **9**:27
  economic considerations, **1**:28
  rollovers and conversions, **9**:30
  Roth, **9**:27–28
  spousal, **9**:28–29
  tax consequences of early distributions
    from, **9**:17
  taxation of benefits, **9**:29
  timing of contributions, **9**:29
Individual Tax Identification Number
  (ITIN), **3**:23
Individuals and taxes, **1**:5
Inflation, **1**:31
Information matching, **1**:22
Information security, tax principles,
  1:8, **1**:9
Inheritance tax, **1**:13, **27**:3

Inheritances, tax planning for selection of property for, **13**:42
  See also Gifts and inheritances
Inherited property
  basis of, **13**:14–16
  holding period of, **13**:16
  income in respect of a decedent (IRD), **13**:14–15
  special holding period rules, **14**:16
  survivor's share of property, **13**:15
Inside basis, **21**:5
Installment method, **1**:31, **4**:7, **16**:19–26, **16**:37–38
  character of gain on depreciable real estate, **16**:22
  computing the gain for each year payments are received, **16**:20–22
  electing out of, **16**:26
  eligibility and calculations, **16**:20
  imputed interest, **16**:22–23
  interest on deferred tax, **16**:25
  nonelective aspect, **16**:20
  related-party sales of depreciable property, **16**:24–25
  related-party sales of nondepreciable property, **16**:23–24
Installment obligations, disposition of, **16**:25–26, **16**:38
Installment plan, Form 9465, **26**:11
Installment sale of a passive activity, **11**:21
Installment sales
  interest on, **16**:24
  recapture potential of, **14**:43
Insurance benefits, accident and health, **5**:10–11
Insurance, medical premiums of the self-employed, deductibility of, **10**:7
Intangible assets, amortization of, **8**:25
  contributed property, **21**:9
Intangible assets, expenditures for, **6**:28
Intangible drilling and development costs (IDC), **8**:29, **14**:45
Intangible income
  special tax rate for, **25**:17–18
  territorial system additional tax on, **25**:25
Intent of Congress, **2**:4
Inter vivos (lifetime), **28**:2
  gifts, **5**:3
  transfers, federal gift tax, **27**:8–9
Intercompany sales, deferral treatment for, **17**:23
Interest, **10**:14–18
  allowed and disallowed items, **10**:14–16
  as business expenses, Schedule C of Form 1040, **10**:7
  carried, **21**:9
  classification of interest expense, **10**:17
  consumer, **10**:14
  deductibility of personal, student loan, mortgage, and investment, **10**:18
  defined by Supreme Court, **10**:14
  imputed, **4**:21, **16**:22–23
  income from, **4**:14
  income sourcing rules, **25**:7
  investment, **10**:16, **11**:21
  IRS deficiency assessments, **26**:12
  personal, **10**:14
  prepaid, **10**:17
  prepayment penalty, **10**:16
  qualified residence interest, **10**:14–16
  restrictions on deductibility and timing considerations, **10**:17
  tax administration, **26**:12–13

tax-exempt securities, **10**:16
taxpayer's obligation, **10**:17
time of deduction, **10**:17
Interest expense
  allocation and apportionment of, **25**:9–10
  related to rents or royalties, Form 1040, Schedule E, **10**:17
Interest income exclusion, **23**:2
Interest on
  certain state and local government obligations, gross income exclusions, **5**:23–24
  deferred tax, **16**:25
  installment sales, **16**:24
  qualified student loans, **9**:17, **10**:14
  refund of taxpayer's overpayments, **26**:12–13
Interest paid for services, **10**:16
Interest rates, on taxes and tax refunds, **1**:24–25
Inter-generational transfers, GSTT, **27**:24
Intermediate sanctions, **23**:6
  on excess benefit transactions, **23**:6–7
Internal Legal Memoranda (ILMs), **2**:9
Internal Revenue Bulletin (I.R.B.), **2**:7, **2**:8, **2**:9, **2**:16, **7**:21
Internal Revenue Code, **8**:2
  arrangement of, **2**:5
  citing of, **2**:5–6
  interpreting, **2**:23
  of 1939, **1**:5, **2**:2
  of 1954, **1**:5, **2**:2
  of 1986, **1**:5, **2**:2, **2**:3–4, **2**:5
  origin of, **2**:2
Internal Revenue Service (IRS), **1**:2, **1**:21, **26**:2–33
  administrative powers of, **26**:5–6
  Appeals Division, **1**:23
  assessment by, **1**:24
  audit process, **26**:6–9, **26**:30–31
  audit types and rates (all returns), **1**:23
  Commissioner, **26**:3–4
  common questions concerning losses with hobbies/business, **6**:20
  home page, **2**:20
  influence of, **1**:32–33, **1**:34
  IRS Letter Rulings Reports, **2**:8
  national office organization, **26**:3
  offers in compromise and closing agreements, **26**:10–12
  organizational structure of, **26**:3–4
  procedure, other issuances, **26**:4–5
  rules governing tax practice, **26**:23–24
  taxpayer appeal process, **26**:9–10
  website, irs.gov, **2**:8
  working with, **26**:13
  See also Audit process; Tax administration
Internal support test for public charity, **23**:9–10
International business competitiveness, U.S. corporate taxes and, **15**:7
International Financial Reporting Standards (IFRS), **2**:26
International tax laws, **25**:2
International taxation
  foreign currency transactions, **25**:14
  overview of, **25**:3–5
  sourcing of income and deductions, **25**:6–13
  tax planning for, **25**:29–30
  tax treaties, **25**:5–6
  U.S. persons with offshore income, **25**:15–25

U.S. taxation of foreign corporations, **25**:26–29
U.S. taxation of nonresident aliens, **25**:26–29
International trade, **25**:2
Interpretive Regulations, **2**:24
Inventions
  and processes, definition of capital asset, **14**:5
  economic considerations, **1**:28
Inventory, **16**:30–37, **16**:38, **21**:42
  best accounting practice, **16**:31
  character of gain or loss on disposition of, **21**:10
  clear reflection of income test, **16**:31
  corporate stock as, **14**:6
  definition of capital asset, **14**:4
  determining inventory cost, **16**:31–35
  hot assets, **21**:48
  LIFO election, **16**:35–36
  small taxpayers, **16**:36–37
  special inventory methods relating to farming and ranching, **16**:36
Inventory cost
  dollar-value LIFO, **16**:34–35
  inventory shrinkage, **16**:33
  lower of cost or market, **16**:33
  specific identification, FIFO, and LIFO, **16**:34
  uniform capitalization (UNICAP), **16**:31–33
Investigation expenses, **6**:17
Investigation of a business, expenses incurred in, **6**:17–18
Investment assets, **14**:3
Investment earnings from the reinvestment of life insurance proceeds, **5**:6
Investment income, **11**:22
  and expenses, **11**:22
  net, **11**:22
  of certain children, **3**:26
  tax on, **1**:18
  tax planning for, **5**:31
Investment interest, **10**:16, **11**:21
  common investment loss limitation rules, **11**:24
  deductibility of, **10**:18
  Form 4952, Investment Interest Deduction, **11**:23
  limitation, **11**:21–23, **11**:26
Investment loss limitation rules, **11**:24
Investment losses, other, **11**:23–24
Investment partnership, exceptions to Section 721, **21**:7
Investor loss, **18**:21–23, **18**:27–28
  business vs. nonbusiness bad debts, **18**:21–22
  Section 1244 stock, **18**:23
  stock and security losses, **18**:21
Involuntary conversions, **14**:30
  computing the amount realized, **13**:31–32
  defined, **13**:31
  nonrecognition of gain, **13**:34–35
  recapture potential of, **14**:42–43
  replacement property, **13**:32–33
  reporting considerations, **13**:35
  Section 1033, **13**:29–35
  tax planning for, **13**:44
  time limitation on replacement, **13**:33–34
IRA. *See* Individual retirement accounts
IRs (News Releases), **2**:9
IRS. *See* Internal Revenue Service

Itemized deductions, **3**:6, **6**:3, **7**:2
limitations on, **9**:35
other, **10**:27
partial list of, **3**:6

J

Job-related education expenses, tax consequences of, **9**:17
Joint Conference Committee, **2**:4
example of compromise in, **2**:4
Joint interests, federal estate tax, **27**:15–17
Joint ownership rules for married persons, **27**:16–17
Joint return, married taxpayers, **3**:18
Joint return test, determining dependents **3**:14
Joint tenants, **27**:6
Jointly owned property, **4**:18
Judicial citations, **2**:14–17
U.S. District Court, Court of Federal Claims, and Court of Appeals, **2**:16–17
U.S. Supreme Court, **2**:17
U.S. Tax Court, **2**:14–16
Judicial concepts relating to tax, **1**:33–34
Judicial influence on statutory provisions, **1**:34
Judicial sources of tax law, **2**:10–17
appellate courts, **2**:12
appellate process, **2**:13–14
assessing the validity of, **2**:24–25
judicial citations, **2**:14–17
judicial process in general, **2**:10–11
trial courts, **2**:11–12
Jury trial, **2**:11

K

Keogh (H.R. 10) plans, **9**:25, **9**:31
contribution limitations, **9**:31
economic considerations, **1**:28
Kickbacks, Section 162 exclusion, **6**:5
Kiddie tax, **3**:26–28, **3**:33

L

Later in time rule, **25**:5
Lease cancellation payments, **14**:14–15
lessee treatment, **14**:14–15
lessor treatment, **14**:15
Least aggregate deferral method, **16**:4
Least aggregate deferral rule, **21**:14
Legal domicile, **24**:6
Legal expenses incurred in defense of civil or criminal penalties, **6**:13–14
Legal foundation, tax system, **1**:6–7
Legislative process, **2**:3–4
Legislative Regulations, **2**:24
Lessee, **14**:14
treatment, **14**:14–15
Lessor, **14**:14
treatment, **14**:15
Letter rulings, **2**:8, **2**:25, **26**:4, **26**:30
Liabilities
assumption of in controlled corporations, **18**:10–12
definition under Section 357, **18**:11–12
Liabilities in excess of basis, **18**:11–12
Liabilities in sale of partnership interest, **21**:47

Liability assumption, tax consequences of, **18**:13
Liability reduction treated as cash distribution, **21**:42
License tax, **24**:26
Licenses, U.S. business engaging in global commerce, **25**:15–18
Life insurance
federal estate tax, **27**:17–18
trust, **28**:2
Life insurance proceeds, **5**:4–6, **5**:30
accelerated death benefits, **5**:5
general rule, **5**:4–5
transfer for valuable consideration, **5**:6
Life tenant, **28**:4
Lifetime learning credit, **9**:16, **12**:16–18, **12**:20
tax consequences of, **9**:17
under Section 25A, **9**:37
LIFO, dollar-value, **16**:34–35
LIFO election, **16**:35–36
LIFO index, **16**:34
LIFO (last in, first out) method, **16**:34
Form 970, Application to Use LIFO Inventory Method, **16**:35
LIFO recapture tax, **22**:24
Like-kind exchanges, **13**:22–29, **13**:43
basis and holding period of property received, **13**:26–29
boot, **13**:25–26
exchange period, **13**:24
exchange requirement, **13**:24–25
Form 8824, Like-Kind Exchanges, **13**:29, **13**:30
identification period, **13**:24
in controlled corporations, **18**:2–4
like-kind property, **13**:23–24
recapture potential of, **14**:42–43
reporting considerations, **13**:29
time limitations, **13**:24–25
Like-kind property, **13**:23–24
Limitations based on wages and capital investment, **15**:14–16
Limitations on QBI deduction, **15**:12
Limited liability company (LLC), **15**:7–8, **21**:2–3, **21**:49
advantages of, **21**:49
comparison of partnership types, **21**:3
converting to, **21**:49
disadvantages of, **21**:49
entity classification, **15**:8
multistate corporate taxation of, **24**:23
tax attributes of, **22**:29–32
tax characteristics of, **28**:6
taxation of, **21**:49
Limited liability entities, **21**:49–50
Limited liability partnership (LLP), **21**:3, **21**:49–50
comparison of partnership types, **21**:3
multistate corporate taxation of, **24**:23
Limited partners, **21**:2
material participation, **11**:14
vs. general partners, treatment of, **21**:39
Limited partnership (LP), **15**:7, **21**:2
comparison of partnership types, **21**:3
Liquidating distribution, **21**:40
effect on corporation, tax planning for, **20**:19
effect on shareholder, tax planning for, **20**:19–20
proportionate, **21**:43–46
Liquidations
antistuffing rules, **20**:4–8

effect on the distributing corporation, **20**:3–8
effect on the shareholder, **20**:8–9
in general, **20**:2–3
liquidating and nonliquidating distributions compared, **20**:2–3
of foreign subsidiaries, basis rules for, **20**:11
parent-subsidiary situations, **20**:9–13
process of, **20**:2
summary of rules, **20**:10
Listed property, **8**:18
business and personal use of, **8**:18–23
change from predominantly business use, **8**:21–22
not used predominantly in business, **8**:21
substantiation requirements, **8**:23
used predominantly in business, **8**:19
Litigation considerations in tax planning, **26**:32
Living (revocable) trust, **28**:2
LLC. *See* Limited liability company
Loans
below-market, effect of on lender and borrower, **4**:22
between individuals, exceptions to imputed interest rules, **4**:24
between related parties, **7**:5
exceptions and limitations of imputed interest on below-market, **4**:23–24
home equity, **10**:15
imputed interest on below-market, **4**:21–24
Lobbying activities, **6**:15–16
Lobbying expenditures, **23**:5
taxes on by public charities, **23**:7
Lobbying nontaxable amount, **23**:6
Local taxes
and the tax expense, **24**:17
overall limit on deductibility of, **10**:11
Lodging for medical treatment, deductible medical expenses, **10**:6
Long-term capital gain, **14**:29
Long-term capital loss (LTCL), **14**:26
Long-term care insurance, employer-sponsored, **5**:12
Long-term contracts, **16**:27–30
completed contract method, **16**:29
lookback provisions, **16**:30
percentage of completion method, **16**:29–30
Long-term nonpersonal use capital assets, **14**:30
Lookback provision
long-term contracts, **16**:30
Section 1231, **14**:32–35
Loss
amount of, **7**:9–10
business and nonbusiness, **6**:6–7
business vs. nonbusiness bad debts, **18**:21–22
carryovers of suspended passive activity, **11**:7–8
common questions from IRS concerning hobbies/business, **6**:20
deductions for, of trusts and estates, **28**:15
determination of, **13**:2–9
disallowed, **13**:16–19, **13**:42
duplication of, **20**:4
impact of suspended passive activity, **11**:6–7
in related-party transactions, **6**:29
investor, **18**:21–23, **18**:27–28

Loss *(continued)*
  measuring the amount of, **7**:9–11
  net, **14**:29
  no partnership level gain or, **21**:43
  nonrecognition of, sale, exchange, or
    condemnation of personal use
    assets, **13**:9
  nonrecognition under Section 351 and
    Section 1031, **18**:2–4
  ordinary, **7**:6, **14**:29
  other investment, **11**:23–24
  precontribution, **21**:27–28
  realized, **13**:2–8, **13**:9
  recognized, **13**:8–9
  S corporation allocation of, **22**:12–13
  S corporation treatment of, **22**:21–23
  Section 1231, **14**:29
  Section 1244 stock, **18**:23
  stock and security, **18**:21
  taxable estate, **27**:19
  tax-free reorganizations, **20**:17–18
  timing of expense recognition, **6**:9–12
  treatment of QBI, **15**:21
  See also Capital losses; Net capital loss;
    Realized loss; Recognized loss
Loss basis of donee, **13**:13
Loss basis rules, holding period for
    property acquired by gift, **13**:13
Loss considerations of S corporations, tax
    planning for, **22**:28
Loss deduction, mechanics of, **18**:24
Loss limitation, liquidation antistuffing rules
    for built-in, **20**:6–8
Loss limitations in partnerships, **21**:36–38
  at-risk limitation, **21**:37
  basis limitation, **21**:37
  excess business losses of noncorporate
    taxpayers, **21**:38
  passive activity loss limitation, **21**:37
Loss of the election
  loss of small business corporation status,
    22:8
  passive investment income limitation, **22**:8–9
  reelection after termination, **22**:9
  S corporation status, **22**:7–9
  voluntary revocation, **22**:7–8
Loss on disposition of receivables,
    inventory, and built-in loss
    properties, character of, **21**:10
Loss on personal use assets, original basis
    for, **13**:19
Loss recognition
  cash distributions, **21**:41
  on contributions to the partnership, **21**:6
  proportionate liquidating distributions,
    21:45–46
  stock redemptions, **19**:29
Loss sharing ratios, partnership liabilities,
    21:33
Loss to shareholder, liquidations, **20**:3
Losses from property transactions—in
    general, **3**:28–29
Losses of individuals, **7**:7–15
  events that are not casualties, **7**:7
  measuring the amount of loss, **7**:9–11
  personal casualty gains and losses,
    7:12–14
  statutory framework for deducting, **7**:14–15
  theft losses, **7**:8
  when to deduct casualty losses, **7**:8–9
Losses subject to at-risk and passive activity
    loss limitations, treatment of, **11**:17
Lower of cost or market (replacement cost),
    16:33

Low-income housing credit, **12**:9–10, **12**:21
Lump-sum option, offers in compromise
    and closing agreements, **26**:11
Lump-sum purchase, allocation problems
    with, **13**:10

M

MACRS. *See* Modified accelerated cost
    recovery system
MACRS: class lives, methods, and
    conventions, **8**:4
Majority interest partners, **16**:3
Manufacturing contract, **16**:27
Marginal tax rate, **3**:25, **3**:32
Marital deduction, **1**:13, **1**:14–15, **27**:20–22,
    27:26
  GSTT tax base and, **27**:25
  passing requirement for property,
    27:20–21
  terminable interest limitation, **27**:21–22
Marital status for filing status purposes, **3**:18
Marketable security distributions treated as
    cash, **21**:42
Marketplace facilitator, **24**:25
Market-sourcing rules, sales factor, **24**:13
Married couples, calculating the Section 121
    exclusion, 13:38–39
Mass tax, **1**:6
Material participation, **11**:12–14, **11**:18
  current participation tests, **11**:14
  facts and circumstances tests, **11**:14
  in a real property rental trade or
    business, **11**:17–18
  limited partners, **11**:14
  participation defined, **11**:14
  prior participation tests, **11**:14
  Section 469, **11**:13
  tests to determine, **11**:14
Meal expenses, **9**:22–24
Meals and lodging, **5**:13–14
  for medical treatment, deductible medical
    expenses, **10**:6
  for the convenience of the employer,
    5:14
  furnished by the employer, **5**:13
  general rules for exclusion, **5**:13–14
  on the employer's business premises,
    5:13
  other housing exclusions, **5**:14
  required as a condition of employment,
    5:14
Meaningful reduction test, **19**:26
Mechanics of the loss deduction, **18**:24
Medical care, defined, **10**:3–4
Medical deductions, tax planning for
    maximizing, **10**:29
Medical expenses, **10**:3–10
  Affordable Care Act provisions, **10**:10
  amounts paid for medical insurance
    premiums, **10**:6–7
  capital expenditures for medical
    purposes, **10**:4–5
  defined, **10**:3–4
  examples of deductible and
    nondeductible, **10**:3
  for a dependent, **6**:25
  health savings accounts, **10**:8–9
  incurred for spouse and dependents,
    10:5
  permanent capital improvement as,
    10:5
  reimbursements, **10**:7–8

  transportation, meal, and lodging
    expenses for medical treatment,
    10:6
  year of deduction, **10**:7
Medical reimbursement plans, employer-
    sponsored, **5**:11–12
Medicare
  additional
    taxes on unearned income,
    12:24–25
    additional taxes on wages, **12**:24
  tax, **1**:17, **12**:22
Membership lists, rental or exchange of in
    exempt entities, **23**:15
Memorandum decisions, **2**:14–16, **2**:25
Mergers or consolidation, corporate
    reorganizations, **20**:15
Mertens Law of Federal Income Taxation,
    2:19
Methods, cost recovery periods for
    personalty and realty, **8**:4
Mid-month convention, **8**:10
Mid-quarter convention, **8**:7–8
  Section 179 and, **8**:13–14
Military personnel, housing exclusions, **5**:14
Millionaires provision, **6**:16
Minimum tax gap, tax principles, **1**:8, **1**:9
Ministers of the gospel, housing exclusions,
    5:14
Minority shareholder interests, parent-
    subsidiary liquidation, **20**:10–11
Minors, trust for, **28**:2
Miscellaneous employee expenses, TCJA
    and, **9**:24
Miscellaneous itemized deductions, **10**:27
  not subject to the 2%-of-AGI floor, **9**:35
  subject to the 2%-of-AGI floor, **9**:35
  TCJA and, **9**:5, **9**:33
Mixed services costs, **16**:28
Model Income Tax Convention, **25**:5
Modified accelerated cost recovery system
    (MACRS), **8**:2
  additional first-year depreciation, **8**:14–15
  alternative depreciation system (ADS),
    8:23–24
  business and personal use of automobiles
    and other listed property, **8**:18–23
  computing E & P, **19**:5
  conventions (by property type), **8**:6
  deductions, deferring to future years,
    8:15–16
  election to expense assets (Section 179),
    8:10–14
  general rules, **8**:4–10
  personalty (and certain realty): recovery
    periods and methods, **8**:5–9
  realty: recovery periods and methods,
    8:9–10
  special rules, **8**:10–24
  statutory percentage method, **9**:37
  tables, **8**:33–35
  using Section 179 and bonus depreciation
    effectively, **8**:15–18
  See also Accelerated cost recovery system
    (ACRS)
Modified adjusted gross income (MAGI),
    1:18, **4**:28, **5**:25
Modified taxable income, overall limitation
    of QBI deduction, **15**:10
Monitoring legislation, lobbying expenses,
    6:16
More-than-50 percent business usage test,
    8:19
Mortgage interest, deductibility of, **10**:18
Mortgage recording tax, **24**:26

Moving expenses, **9**:22
   TCJA and, **9**:22
Multinational corporation, **24**:2
Multiple assets in a lump-sum purchase, allocation of cost among, **13**:10
Multiple losses, measuring the amount of loss, **7**:10–11
Multiple properties in an asset class, proportionate liquidating distributions, **21**:45
Multiple support agreement, **3**:13–14
   Form 2120, Multiple Support Declaration, **3**:14
Multistate businesses, state/local taxes in context, **24**:2
Multistate corporate taxation
   allocation and apportionment of income, **24**:8–18
   corporate state income taxation, **24**:2–8
   other state and local taxes, **24**:23–27
   S corporations, **24**:22–23
   tax planning for, **24**:28–33
   taxation of partnerships and LLCs, **24**:23
   unitary theory, **24**:18–21
Multistate Tax Commission (MTC), **24**:6
Multistate tax considerations, **24**:2
Multistate taxation, **24**:8

N

National Research Program (NRP), **26**:7
National sales tax, **1**:20
National Taxpayer Advocate, **26**:4
Natural business year, **16**:3, **16**:6
Natural resources, **8**:28
Negligence, **26**:15–16
   penalty, **1**:25
Net active income, **17**:8
Net capital gain (NCG), **14**:20, **15**:10
   alternative tax on, **14**:22–27
   alternative tax rates on, **3**:30, **14**:23
   determination of, **3**:30–31
   income taxation of individuals and corporations compared, **17**:17
   taxation of, **3**:29–30
Net capital loss (NCL), **14**:26
   capital loss deduction, **14**:26
   carryovers, **14**:26–27
   computation of, **14**:26
   treatment of, **3**:31, **14**:26–27
Net earnings from self-employment, **12**:23
Net gain, **14**:28–29
Net income (loss), reconciliation of, Schedule M-3, **17**:26–28
Net income tax, **12**:5
Net investment income (NII), **11**:22, **12**:25, **21**:39–40
   additional tax on, **28**:8, **28**:26
   effect of additional tax on, **11**:26
Net investment income tax (NIIT)
   Form 8960, **28**:8
   QBI deduction and, **15**:22
   partnership income, **21**:39–40
Net long-term capital gain (NLTCG), **3**:30, **14**:19
Net long-term capital loss (NLTCL), **14**:19
Net loss, **14**:29
Net operating losses (NOL), **7**:19–20, **17**:36
   and deduction for qualified business income, **7**:20
   and self-employment taxes, **7**:20
   carryforward only, **7**:20
   deduction limit, **7**:20

deduction, trusts and estates, **28**:15
   income taxation of corporations, **17**:12
   NOL rule, **17**:13
   S corporation treatment of, **22**:21–22
Net regular tax liability, **12**:5
Net Section 481(a) adjustment, reporting of, **16**:18–19
Net Section 1231 gain limitation, **14**:40
Net short-term capital gain (NSTCG), **14**:19
Net short-term capital loss (NSTCL), **3**:30, **14**:19
Net taxes payable, computation of, **3**:25–26
Net unearned income of a dependent child, **3**:26
Netting process
   capital gain and loss, **14**:19–22
   use of capital loss carryovers, **14**:21–22
Neutrality, tax principles, **1**:8, **1**:9
Nexus, **24**:6
   and Public Law 86-272, jurisdiction to impose tax, **24**:6
   common definitions under P.L. 86-272, **24**:7
   in today's economy, **24**:6–7
   sales/use tax, **24**:25
90-day letter, **26**:5, **26**:9
No-additional-cost service, **5**:17
NOL. See Net operating loss
Nonaccountable plans, **9**:34
   failure to comply with accountable plan requirements, **9**:34
   unreimbursed employee expenses, **9**:34
Nonacquiescence ("NA" or "Nonacq."), **2**:16
Nonapportionable income, **24**:9–11
Nonbusiness bad debt, **7**:2, **7**:4, **14**:8, **18**:21–19
Nonbusiness losses, **6**:6–7
Noncash distributions, consequences of, **22**:18
Noncash property distributions, **19**:16
   by the corporation, tax treatment of, **22**:18–19
   taxable income of trusts and estates, **28**:11–12
Noncommercial electronic (online) tax services, **2**:19–20
Noncontingent payments, franchises, **14**:13
Noncorporate taxpayers
   alternative tax on net capital gain and qualified dividend income, **14**:22–27
   capital gain and loss netting process, **14**:19–22
   excess business losses of, **21**:38
   qualified dividend income, **14**:22
   tax treatment of capital gains and losses of, **14**:19–22
   treatment of net capital losses, **14**:26–27
Noncustodial parent, deductibility of medical expenses, **10**:5
Nondeductible contributions, IRAs, **9**:27
Nondeductible items, charitable contributions, **10**:19–20
Nondiscrimination provisions, employee fringe benefits, **5**:20
Nonliquidating distribution. See Current distribution
Nonliquidating property distribution, **20**:2
Nonoperating private foundations, **10**:23–24
Nonparental source income, net unearned income, **3**:26
Nonrecognition of gain
   conversion into money, **13**:34–35
   direct conversion, **13**:34
   or loss, **13**:9

Nonrecourse debt, **21**:32
   rules, **21**:33–35
Nonrecourse financing, **11**:3
   qualified, **11**:4
Nonrefundable credits, **12**:4
Nonresident alien (NRA), **25**:26–28
   individuals engaged in a U.S. trade or business, U.S. taxation of, **25**:27–28
   individuals not engaged in a U.S. trade or business, U.S. taxation of, **25**:27
   residency, U.S. taxation of, **25**:26–27
   small business corporation, **22**:5
   U.S. transfer taxes and, **27**:3
Nonresidential real estate, **8**:9
Nontaxable exchange, **13**:22
   gain and basis rules for, **20**:16
   special holding period rules, **14**:15–16
Nontaxable stock dividends, **13**:11–12
   holding period of, **13**:12
Nontaxable transactions, recapture exceptions, **14**:42
Not essentially equivalent redemption, **19**:26–27
   summary of qualifying rules, **19**:24
Notices, **2**:9
Nowhere sale, sales factor, **24**:14
Number of shares, **18**:6
Nursing home care, deductible medical expenses, **10**:4

O

ObamaCare. See Affordable Care Act
Obligation to repay, amounts received under, **4**:12
Obligations, retirement of corporate, **14**:9
Occupational fees, **1**:19
Offer in Compromise, **26**:10
Office audit, **1**:23, **26**:8
Office in the home expenses, **9**:18–21
Office of Professional Responsibility (OPR), **26**:24
Offset, right of, **13**:16
Offshore (foreign) corporations controlled by U.S. persons, **25**:20–23
Offshore income, U.S. persons with, **25**:15–25
Old age, survivors, and disability insurance, **1**:17
One other residence, **10**:15
$100-per-event and 10%-of-AGI floors, personal use loss reductions, **7**:10
One-year rule for prepaid expenses, **16**:11
Online tax services, **2**:19
   noncommercial, **2**:19–20
Operating agreement, **21**:3
Operating fund, exempt organization, **23**:2
Options, **14**:9–11
   consequences to grantor an grantee, **14**:11
   exercise of by grantee, **14**:9
   failure to exercise, **14**:10–11
   sale of, **14**:10
Ordering procedure, **14**:20
Ordering rules for proportionate current distribution from partnerships, **21**:42–43
Ordering rules for proportionate liquidating distributions from partnerships, **21**:44–45
Ordinary and necessary, **6**:5

Ordinary business income, measuring partnership income, **21**:16
Ordinary deductions, taxable income of trusts and estates, **28**:13–15
Ordinary income property, **10**:22–23, **21**:10
    as charitable contribution, **17**:10
Ordinary loss, **7**:6, **14**:29
Organization for Economic Cooperation and Development (OECD), **1**:21, **15**:7, **25**:4
Organizational costs, partnerships, **21**:12
Organizational expenditures, **17**:15
    deduction, **17**:15–17
Organizational form, choice of when operating overseas, **18**:3
Original issue discount (OID), **14**:9, **4**:10–11
Other adjustments account (OAA), **22**:15, **22**:16
Other property, **20**:17
Outbound taxation, **25**:3
Out-of-the-home expenses, child and dependent care expenses, **12**:15
Outside basis, **21**:5
Outsourcing of tax return preparation, **1**:26
Overseas operations and book-tax differences, **25**:17
Overvaluation, penalty for, **26**:16–17
Owner-investor, replacement property, **13**:32
Ownership and use requirements, sale of a residence exclusion treatment, **13**:36–37
Owner-user, replacement property, **13**:32

P

P.L. 86-272, **24**:6–7
    common nexus definitions under, **24**:7
Parent-subsidiary situations
    basis of property received by the parent corporation, **20**:12–14
    indebtedness of the subsidiary to the parent, **20**:11
    liquidations, **20**:9–13, **20**:20
    minority shareholder interests, **20**:10–11
Partner calculations and reporting, **21**:24–38
    effect of partnership liabilities on partner's basis, **21**:31–35
    loss limitations, **21**:36–38
    of partnership income, **21**:24–26
    partner allocations and reporting, **21**:26–28
    partner's capital account, **21**:35–36
    Schedule K-1, **21**:15, **21**:26, **21**:28–30
Partner's basis in partnership interest, **21**:35
Partner's capital, Form 1065 example of reconciling, **21**:23–24
Partners, Subchapter K, **2**:5
Partnership, **4**:16
    advantages and disadvantages of, **21**:51
    alternative tax years, **21**:14
    comparison of business entities, **15**:6, **22**:2
    consequences of noncash distributions, **22**:18
    contributions to, **21**:6–7
    deferral of partnership income, **21**:13
    definition of, **21**:2–4
    financial reporting for, **21**:24
    flow-through status of entity, **21**:4
    Form 1065, **15**:3, **21**:6

formation and operation of, **21**:6–14, **21**:51
    guaranteed payments paid by, **21**:18
    impermissible year election, **16**:5
    income from, **4**:16–17
    initial costs of, **21**:12
    losses from, excess business losses, **7**:18–19
    measuring partnership income, **21**:16–18
    multistate corporate taxation of, **24**:23
    other taxes, **21**:16
    permitted taxable years, **21**:14
    QBI deduction considerations for, **15**:22
    required taxable year, **21**:13–14
    Schedule K-1, **15**:3
    specific provisions for, **16**:3–6
    stock attribution rules, **19**:25
    Subchapter K, **2**:5
    tax attributes of, **22**:29–32
    tax characteristics of, **28**:6
    tax treatment of, **15**:3, **15**:6
    taxable year of, **21**:13–14
    transactions between partners and partnerships, **21**:51–52
    types of, **21**:2–4
    See also Business forms
Partnership agreement, **21**:3, **21**:52
Partnership distributions, **21**:40–46
Partnership formation and initial basis computation, **21**:11
Partnership income
    measuring, **21**:16–18
    net investment income tax, **21**:39–40
    ordinary business income, **21**:16
    other taxes on, **21**:38–40
    partner reporting of, **21**:24–26
    self-employment tax, **21**:38–39
    separately stated items, **21**:16–17
Partnership interest
    basis in distributed property and, **21**:43
    expense, **21**:18
    partner's basis in, **21**:7, **21**:34
    partner's holding period in, **21**:7
    sale of, **21**:46–49
Partnership items, tax reporting of, **21**:30
Partnership liabilities
    allocation of, **21**:32–33
    effect of on partner's basis, **21**:31–35
    nonrecourse debt rules, **21**:33–35
    recourse debt rules, **21**:33
Partnership operations and reporting, **21**:15–24
Partnership reporting
    Form 1065, **21**:15
    in general, **21**:15–16
Partnership taxation
    conceptual framework for, **21**:4–5
    definition of partnership, **21**:2–4
    inside and outside basis, **21**:5
    key concepts in taxation of income, **21**:4–6
    overview of, **21**:2–6
    partner's ownership and allocation of items, **21**:5–6
    tax planning for, **21**:50–51
Passenger automobiles, **8**:19
Passive activities
    identification of an activity, **11**:11–12
    material participation, **11**:12–14
    regrouping of activities, **11**:12
    rental activities defined, **11**:15
    rules for determining, **11**:10–15
    special grouping rules for rental activities, **11**:12

Passive activity credits, **11**:8
    carryovers of, **11**:8–9
Passive activity income and losses
    carryovers of passive activity credits, **11**:8–9
    carryovers of suspended passive activity losses, **11**:7–8
    classification and impact of, **11**:5–9
    impact of suspended passive activity losses, **11**:6–7
    passive activity changes to active, **11**:9
    passive activity credits, **11**:8
Passive activity loss, **11**:3, **17**:8, **11**:24–25
    and credits, S corporation treatment of, **22**:23
    carryovers of suspended, **11**:7–8
    impact of suspended, **11**:6–7
    income taxation of corporations, **17**:8–9
    income taxation of individuals and corporations compared, **17**:18
Passive activity loss limitation (Section 469), **21**:36
    common investment loss limitation rules, **11**:24
    fiduciary entity, **28**:15
    partnerships, **21**:37
    treatment of losses subject to at-risk and, **11**:17
Passive activity loss limits, **11**:5–21
    classification and impact of passive activity income and losses, **11**:5–9
    dispositions of passive interests, **11**:20–21
    entire interest in an activity, **11**:6
    interaction of the at-risk and passive activity loss limits, **11**:15–16
    rules for determining passive activities, **11**:10–15
    special passive activity rules for real estate activities, **11**:16–20
    taxpayers subject to passive activity loss rules, **11**:9–10
Passive activity loss rules
    closely held C corporations, **11**:10
    key issues and answers, **11**:22
    personal service corporations, **11**:9–10
    Section 469, **11**:5–9
    taxpayers subject to, **11**:9–10
Passive activity rules
    material participation in a real property rental trade or business, **11**:17–18
    real estate rental activities with active participation, **11**:18–20
Passive interests, dispositions of, **11**:20–21
Passive investment company, **24**:29–31
Passive investment income (PII), **22**:8, **22**:24
    penalty tax, S corporations, **22**:24, **22**:28
Pass-through entities, **21**:2, **28**:6
Patent, **8**:25, **14**:11–12
    economic considerations, **1**:28
    holder defined, **14**:12
    invention, model or design, definition of capital asset, **14**:4
    substantial rights, **14**:11–12
Payable on death (POD) designation, **27**:9
Pay-as-you-go tax income tax system, **1**:6, **1**:33
Payments received, installment method computing of, **16**:20
Payments, timing of to maximize deductions, **10**:26
Payroll factor, **24**:14–16, **24**:33
Payroll tax exemption, **23**:2

Penalties imposed on tax return preparers, **1**:26–27, **26**:24–26
Penalties of taxpayers, **26**:13–20, **26**:32–33
  accuracy-related, **25**:12, **26**:15
  ad valorem penalties, **26**:14
  appraiser's penalty, **26**:17
  assessable penalties, **26**:14
  civil fraud penalty, **1**:25, **26**:18
  civil tax penalties, **26**:13–14
  criminal fraud penalty, **1**:25
  criminal tax penalties, **26**:13–14, **26**:20
  failure to file and failure to pay, **1**:25, **26**:14–15
  failure to make deposits of taxes and overstatement of deposits, **26**:19–20
  failure to pay estimated taxes, **26**:18–19
  failure to provide information regarding tax shelters, **26**:20
  false information with respect to withholding, **26**:19
  for "gross misstatements," transfer pricing, **25**:12
  for improper refund claim, **26**:17
  for lack of compliance, **1**:25
  negligence penalty, **1**:25, **26**:15–16
  overvaluation, **26**:16–17
  penalty for improper refund claim, **26**:17
  Section 162 exclusion, **6**:5
  substantial understatement of tax liability, **26**:16
  undervaluation, **26**:17
Per diem allowance, deemed substantiation, **9**:34
Percentage depletion, **8**:29, **8**:30–31
  rates, selected, **8**:30
Percentage of completion method, **4**:7, **16**:27–28, **16**:29–30
Periodic payment option, offers in compromise and closing agreements, **26**:11
Permanent establishment, **25**:5, **25**:15
Personal casualty gains and losses, **7**:12–14
Personal casualty/theft losses, **7**:15
Personal exemption, **3**:9
Personal expenditures
  deduction of, **10**:2
  disallowance of, **6**:26
Personal expenses, deductions of, **6**:6
Personal holding company (PHC) tax, **17**:20
Personal injury, damages for, **5**:8–10
Personal interest, **10**:14
  deductibility of, **10**:18
Personal residence, **13**:35
Personal service corporations (PSC), **11**:9–10, **16**:6, **17**:4
  accounting period for, **16**:6, **17**:4
  calendar year, **16**:6
  fiscal year election, **16**:6
  passive activity loss rules, **17**:8
  special rules applicable to, **17**:9
  specific provisions for, **16**:3–6
Personal services, **4**:13
  income, income sourcing rules, **25**:7–8
  of a child, **4**:13
  of an employee, **4**:13
Personal use assets, **8**:3, **14**:3
  converted to business or income-producing use, cost recovery basis for, **8**:4
  original basis for loss on, **13**:19
  sale, exchange, or condemnation of, **13**:9
Personal use loss reductions, measuring the amount of loss, **7**:10
Personal use property, **8**:3

conversion to business or income-producing use, **13**:19–20
Personalty, **1**:10–11, **8**:2–3
Personalty: recovery periods and methods, **8**:5–9
  classification of property, **8**:5–6
  mid-quarter convention, **8**:7–8
  qualified improvement property, **8**:8
  straight-line election, **8**:8–9
  tangible, **10**:23
Petitioner, **2**:11
Piggyback approach to state income taxation, **1**:16
Plaintiff, **2**:11
Plan of reorganization, **20**:15
Planning, relevance of taxation to accounting and finance professionals, **1**:3
Points, **10**:16
Political considerations
  political expediency situations, **1**:31–32
  special interest legislation, **1**:31
  state and local government influences, **1**:32
  tax law, **1**:34
Political contributions, **6**:15–16
Pollution control facilities, economic considerations, **1**:28
Pool, **16**:34
Portfolio income, **11**:6
Practical Tax Expert, **2**:19
Precedential authority, doctrine of, **2**:10
Precedents, **2**:13
Precontribution gain or loss, **21**:27–28
Preferential tax treatment, **1**:31
Prepaid expenses, 12-month rule, **6**:12
Prepaid interest, **10**:17
Preparation blueprints, CPA examination, **2**:31
Preparer Tax Identification Number (PTIN), **26**:23
Prepayment penalty, **10**:16
Present interest, federal gift tax, **27**:10
Preserving formalities, tax planning, **2**:29–30
Principal partner, **16**:3
Principal residence, **10**:15, **13**:36
  sale of, tax planning for, **13**:44
Principles of fiduciary taxation, **28**:20
Prior participation tests, **11**:13, **11**:14
Private foundations, **23**:5, **23**:8–12, **23**:22
  definition of, **23**:8–9
  public charities, **23**:9–10
  tax consequences of status, **23**:8–10
  taxes imposed on, **23**:11–12
Private nonoperating foundations, **10**:23–24
Private operating foundations, **10**:23–24
Privileged communications, **26**:26–27, **26**:33
Prizes and awards, income from, **4**:27
Pro forma exemption amounts, **3**:9
Pro rata basis, allocating current E & P to distributions, **19**:8
Pro rata distribution, **20**:5
Probate estate, **27**:13
Procedural Regulations, **2**:24
Production of income casualty/theft losses, **7**:15
Professional employer organization (PEO), determination of W-2 wages, **15**:23
Profit and loss sharing ratios, **21**:5
Profit sharing ratios, nonrecourse debt rules, **21**:33

Profits (loss) interest, **21**:5
Profits interest received in exchange for services, **21**:9
Progressive taxes, **1**:7
Prohibited transaction, **23**:5
  exemptions, **2**:9
  private foundations, **23**:11
Property, **18**:5
  adjusted basis of disposed, **13**:5
  amount realized from a sale or other disposition of, **13**:4–5
  bargain purchase of, **13**:10
  bargain rental of corporate property by a shareholder, **19**:17
  bargain sale of corporate to a shareholder, **19**:17
  basis adjustment for loss, **18**:15–16
  boot given as appreciated or depreciated, **13**:26
  built-in loss, **18**:15
  business and personal use of listed, **8**:18–23
  capital gain, **10**:23–24
  capital loss, **21**:10
  collections of unclaimed, **24**:26
  debt-financed, **23**:18
  defined under Section 351, **18**:5
  disqualified, **20**:5
  excluded Section 1231, **14**:30
  fair market value of, **13**:4
  Form 4797, Sales of Business Property, **14**:45
  gain basis for converted, **13**:19
  holding periods of, **14**:3, **14**:16
  included Section 1231, **14**:29–30
  income from, **4**:13–15
  involuntary conversion of, **13**:29–35
  jointly owned, **4**:18
  key concepts for transfer taxes, **27**:6–7
  like-kind, **13**:23–24
  MACRS classification of, **8**:5–6
  manner of disposition, **14**:3
  marital deduction passing requirement of, **27**:20–21
  ordinary income, **10**:22–23, **21**:10
  personal use, **8**:3
  qualified for additional first-year depreciation, **8**:15
  replacement, **13**:32–33
  sale or exchange of, income sourcing rules, **25**:8
  sales of depreciable between related-parties, **16**:24–25
  sales of nondepreciable between related-parties, **16**:23–24
  Section 1245, **14**:37–38
  Section 1250, **14**:38
  separate and joint asset ownership, **27**:6–7
  shareholder use of corporate-owned, **19**:17
  shareholder's basis of stock received in exchange for, **18**:13
  substantially identical, **14**:17
  tax status of, **14**:3
  transfers of to controlled corporations, **18**:2–4
Property (ad valorem) taxes
  on personal, **1**:10–11
  on real, **1**:10
  other state and local taxes of a multistate corporation, **24**:25
Property acquired by gift, holding period for, **13**:13

Property acquired from a decedent, **13**:14–16

Property contributions, charitable contributions, **17**:9–10

Property distributions
by the corporation, tax treatment of noncash, **22**:18–19
noncash, **19**:16
noncash, gross income of trusts and estates, **28**:11–12
proportionate current distribution from partnership, **21**:42

Property dividends, **19**:14–16
effect on the corporation, **19**:14–16
effect on the shareholder, **19**:14
recapture potential of, **14**:43

Property factor, **24**:16–18, **24**:32

Property owned by the decedent, federal estate tax, **27**:14–15

Property placed in service maximum, Section 179 expensing deduction limitations, **8**:11–12

Property put to unrelated use, **10**:23
charitable contributions, **17**:10

Property received
basis to acquiring corporation of, **20**:18
corporation's basis in, **18**:14

Property settlements
divorce decree, **4**:19
in divorce, federal gift tax **27**:9

Property taxes, **1**:21:10–11, **10**:11–13
apportionment between seller and purchaser, **10**:12–13
assessments for local benefits, **10**:12

Property transactions
capital gains and losses, **3**:29–32
gains and losses from, **3**:28–29
tax planning for, **13**:41–44

Proportionate current distributions
general rules, **21**:44
partnerships, **21**:41–43

Proportionate distribution, **21**:40–41

Proportionate liquidating distributions
gain recognition and ordering rules, **21**:44–45
loss recognition, **21**:45–46
multiple properties in an asset class, **21**:45
no partnership level gain or loss, **21**:43
partnerships, **21**:43–46

Proposed Regulations, **2**:7

Provision process, capturing, measuring, and recording tax expense, **17**:30

Provisional income, Social Security benefits, **4**:28

Public charities, **10**:24, **23**:5, **23**:9–10
taxes on lobbying expenditures by, **23**:7

Public Law 86-272, **24**:6
and nexus, jurisdiction to impose tax, **24**:6

Public policy limitation, **6**:13–15
expenses relating to an illegal business, **6**:14–15
justification for denying deductions, **6**:13
legal expenses incurred in defense of civil or criminal penalties, **6**:13–14

Publicly held corporations, excessive executive compensation and, **17**:11

Publicly traded corporations, stock redemptions, **19**:22

Punitive damages, **5**:9

Q

QBI deduction, **15**:9
overview of 2020, **15**:13
under Section 199A, **21**:29–30
See also Qualified business income deduction (QBID),

Qualified ABLE program, **5**:27

Qualified business income (QBI), **6**:7, **15**:9
definition of, **15**:10–11
fiduciary entity deduction for, **28**:15
NOLs and deduction for, **7**:20
sole proprietorship deduction for, **15**:2
2020 limitations, **6**:8

Qualified business income deduction (QBID), **22**:12
See also QBI deduction

Qualified business unit (QBU), **25**:14

Qualified child care expenses, **12**:11

Qualified disaster, gross income exclusions under Section 139, **5**:2–3

Qualified dividend income (QDI), **14**:22, **15**:4
alternative tax on, **14**:22–27

Qualified dividends, **19**:13, **19**:32–33
application and effect, **19**:13
requirements, **19**:13

Qualified domestic organization, **10**:18

Qualified employee discount, **5**:17–18

Qualified higher education expenses, **5**:25

Qualified improvement property, **8**:8

Qualified military base realignment and closure fringes, **5**:17, **5**:19

Qualified moving expense reimbursements, **5**:17, **5**:19

Qualified nonrecourse financing, **11**:4, **21**:33

Qualified organizations, charitable contributions, **10**:20

Qualified parking, **5**:19

Qualified property, additional first-year depreciation, **8**:15

Qualified real property business indebtedness, **5**:29

Qualified residence, **10**:15

Qualified residence interest, **10**:14–16
indebtedness, Schedule A, Form 1040, **10**:17

Qualified retirement planning services, **5**:17, **5**:19

Qualified retirement plans, **9**:25

Qualified small business corporation, **18**:24

Qualified small business stock, **18**:24

Qualified stock purchase, **20**:13

Qualified subchapter S corporation subsidiary (QSSS), **22**:4

Qualified terminable interest property (QTIP), **27**:21

Qualified trade or business (QTB), **6**:8, **15**:9, **15**:11
definition of, **15**:11–12
taxpayers with multiple businesses, **15**:12

Qualified transportation fringes, **5**:17, **5**:19

Qualified tuition and related expenses, **9**:16
tax consequences of, **9**:17

Qualified tuition deduction, limitations for, **9**:16

Qualified tuition program (Section 529 plan), **5**:26–27
Federal gift tax and contributions to, **27**:11
tax consequences of, **9**:17

Qualified tuition reduction plan, tax consequences of, **9**:17

Qualifying child, **3**:9–11
age test, **3**:10
relationship test, **3**:10
residence test, **3**:10
support test, **3**:10–11
tiebreaker rules, **3**:11

Qualifying relative, **3**:11–14
gross income test, **3**:12–13
relationship test, **3**:12
support test, **3**:13–14

R

Real estate activities, special passive activity rules for, **11**:16–20

Real estate, character of gain on depreciable, **16**:22

Real property
like-kind property, **13**:23
rental trade or business, material participation in, **11**:17–18

Realistic possibility, **26**:27

Realization principle, **4**:4, **4**:5

Realized gain, **3**:28–29, **13**:2–8, **13**:9
additional complexities, **13**:7–8
adjusted basis, **13**:5
amount realized, **13**:4–5
capital additions, **13**:5
capital recoveries, **13**:5–7
computation of, **13**:3
sale or other disposition, **13**:2–3

Realized loss, **3**:28–29, **13**:2–8, **13**:9
additional complexities, **13**:7–8
adjusted basis, **13**:5
amount realized, **13**:4–5
capital additions, **13**:5
capital recoveries, **13**:5–7
computation of, **13**:3
sale or other disposition, **13**:2–3

Realty, **1**:10, **8**:2–3
recovery periods and methods, **8**:9–10
transfer tax, **24**:26

Reasonable basis, **26**:16, **26**:25

Reasonable cause, **26**:15

Reasonable investor test, **19**:18

Reasonable needs of the business, **17**:20

Reasonable prospect of full recovery, **7**:8

Reasonableness, **6**:5

Recapitalization, corporate reorganizations, **20**:15

Recapture
alimony, **4**:20
avoiding, tax planning for, **14**:50
postponing and shifting of, tax planning for, **14**:49–50
Section 1245, **14**:35–38
Section 1250, **14**:38–41
special provisions, **14**:44–45
timing of, tax planning for, **14**:49

Recapture considerations, basis determination and related issues, **18**:17

Recapture exceptions
certain nontaxable transactions, **14**:42
charitable transfers, **14**:42
death, **14**:41
gifts, **14**:41
like-kind exchanges and involuntary conversions, **14**:42–43

Recapture of depreciation, corporations, **17**:6

Recapture provisions
  gain from sale of depreciable property between certain related parties, **14**:45
  intangible drilling costs, **14**:45
  overview of Section 1231 and, **14**:28
  special recapture for corporations, **14**:44
Receivables, character of gain or loss on disposition of, **21**:10
Receivership, corporate reorganizations, **20**:15
Recognized gain, **3**:28–29, **13**:8–9
Recognized loss, **3**:28–29, **13**:8–9
Reconciliation
  financial information and net income (loss), Schedule M-3, Part I, **17**:27
  for corporations with total assets of $10 million or more, Schedule M-3—net income (loss), **17**:26–28
  of expense/deduction items, Schedule M-3, Part III, **17**:28
  of income (loss) per books with income per return, Schedule M-1, **17**:24–25
  of net income (loss) per income statement of includible corporations with taxable income per return, Schedule M-3, Part II, **17**:27
  partner's capital account analysis, **21**:35
Record-keeping requirements for charitable contributions, **10**:21–22
Record-keeping/documentation requirements, entertainment and meal expenses, **9**:24
Recourse debt, **21**:32
  rules, **21**:33
Recovery of capital doctrine, **4**:3, **4**:17
Recurring items, **6**:11
  exception, **16**:15
Redemption expenditures, **19**:30
Redemption to pay death taxes, **19**:28–29
  summary of qualifying rules, **19**:24
Refund claims and the statute of limitations, **26**:22
Refund, computation of, **3**:25–26
Refundable credits, **12**:3
  and nonrefundable credits, partial listing of, **12**:4
Refunds, limitations on, **1**:24
REG (Regulation), CPA examination, **2**:31
Regular (actual expense) method, **9**:18
Regular corporations, **15**:3–7, **17**:2
  tax attributes of, **22**:29–32
  tax treatment of business forms compared, **15**:6
  See also C corporations; Corporations; Closely held corporations; Personal service corporations; S corporations
Regular decisions, **2**:14–16, **2**:25
Regular method, office in the home expense, **9**:19
Regularly carried on test, unrelated trade or business of exempt entities, **23**:15-16
Regulation (REG), CPA examination, **2**:31-33
Regulations. *See* Treasury Department Regulations
Regulations Governing Practice before the Internal Revenue Service, Circular 230, **26**:22
Rehabilitation expenditures credit, **12**:6, **12**:21
Related party, **14**:45
  definition of, **6**:28
  disallowed losses between, **13**:16

installment sales, tax planning for, **16**:37
loans, **7**:5
loss limitation, liquidation antistuffing rules, **20**:5–6, **20**:8
recapture on gain from sale of depreciable property between, **14**:45
sales of depreciable property between, **16**:24–25
sales of nondepreciable property between, **16**:23–24
Related-party transactions, **6**:28–29
  losses, **6**:29
  relationships and constructive ownership, **6**:28
Relationship test
  qualifying child, **3**:10
  qualifying relative, **3**:12
Rent and royalty
  income sourcing rules, **25**:8
  partnership and fiduciary deductions, Schedule E, **6**:8
  Section 212 expenses, Schedule E, **6**:4
Rental activity, **11**:15
Rental car "surcharge", **1**:11
Rental of vacation homes, **6**:21–25
Rental real estate activities with active participation, passive activity rules, **11**:18–20
Reorganization, **20**:15
  continuity of business enterprise test, **20**:15
  continuity of interest test, **20**:15
  plan of, **20**:15
  sound business purpose, **20**:15
  step transaction doctrine, **20**:15
  summary of tax consequences in tax-free reorganizations, **20**:15–19
  See also Tax-free reorganizations
Repairs, cost of, **7**:9
Replacement property, **13**:32–33
  functional use test, **13**:32
  special rule for condemnations, **13**:32–33
  taxpayer use test, **13**:32
Report of Foreign Bank and Financial Accounts (FBAR), **4**:29
Required taxable year, **21**:13
Research activities credit, **12**:8–9
  credit for basic research, **12**:9
  credit for incremental research activities, **12**:8–9
  energy research credit, **12**:9
Research and development (R&D) expenditures
  allocation and apportionment of, **25**:10
  economic considerations, **1**:28
Research and experimental expenditures, **7**:15–17
  deferral and amortization method, **7**:16–17
  expense method, **7**:16
Research expenditures, **12**:8
Research Institute of America (RIA), **2**:15–16
Reserve method, **7**:3
Reserves, **6**:11, **16**:16
  tax deferrals from, **16**:16
Residence. *See* Personal residence
Residence test, qualifying child, **3**:10
Residency, **25**:26–27
Residential rental real estate, **8**:9
Respondent, **2**:11
Retained earnings, Schedule M-2, **17**:25
Retirement accounts, contributions to, **9**:25–26

Retirement plan benefits, estate tax and, **27**:15
Retirement plans
  for self-employed individuals, **9**:31–32
  simplified method for annuity distributions from, **4**:26
  tax planning for qualified dividends, **19**:32
Revenue acts, **1**:5
  of 1913, **1**:5
  of 1916, **1**:13
  of 1938, House report on, **23**:2
  of 1948, **1**:32
Revenue Agent's Report (RAR), **1**:23, **26**:8
Revenue, IRS as protector of, **1**:32–33
Revenue neutrality, **1**:27
Revenue Procedures, **2**:6, **2**:7–8
Revenue Rulings, **2**:6, **2**:7–8, **2**:24
Reversionary interest, **28**:4
Revocable transfers, **27**:15
Right of offset, **6**:29, **13**:16
Right of survivorship, **27**:6
Rollforward, partner's capital account analysis, **21**:35
Rollovers and conversions, IRAs, **9**:30
Roth IRA, **9**:27–28
  vs. traditional IRA, **9**:30

S

S corporation shareholders, flow-through of separate items of income and loss, **22**:11
S corporation status
  conditions required to elect, **22**:10
  Form 2553, **22**:5
S corporation(s), **4**:16, **15**:3, **22**:2, **22**:27–28
  calendar year, **16**:5
  classification procedures for distributions from, **22**:14
  consequences of noncash distributions, **22**:18
  Form 1120S, **17**:23
  impermissible year election, **16**:5
  income from, **4**:16–17
  losses from, excess business losses, **7**:18–19
  multistate corporate taxation of, **24**:22–23
  operational rules, **22**:9–26
  overview of, **22**:2–3
  QBI deduction considerations for, **15**:22
  qualifying status, **22**:3–9
  special complications of conversion of C corporation to, **22**:16
  specific provisions for, **16**:3–6
  Subchapter S, **2**:5
  tax attributes of, **22**:29–32
  tax characteristics of, **28**:6
  tax treatment of business forms compared, **15**:6
  See also C corporations; Corporations; Closely held corporations; Personal service corporations; Regular corporations
S election, tax planning for, **22**:26–27
Safe harbor, health issues, **13**:39
Salary structure of S corporations, tax planning for, **22**:27–28
Sale of a partnership interest, **21**:46–49
  general rules, **21**:46–47
  hot assets and carried interests, **21**:48–49
  income allocation, **21**:47
  liabilities, **21**:47

Sale of a residence
  calculating the Section 121 exclusion, **13**:38–39
  exceptions to the two-years rules, **13**:39–41
  principal residence, **13**:36
  requirements for exclusion treatment, **13**:36–37
  Section 121, **13**:35–41
Sale or exchange, **14**:8–15
  franchises, trademarks, and trade names (Section 1253), **14**:12–14
  lease cancellation payments, **14**:14–15
  options, **14**:9–11
  patents, **14**:11–12
  retirement of corporate obligations, **14**:9
  worthless securities and Section 1244 stock, **14**:8
Sales factor, **24**:13–14, **24**:32
Sales tax, **1**:2, **1**:12
  and use tax, **24**:24
  deductibility of state and local, **10**:13
  holiday, **1**:12
  national, **1**:20
  state and local, of a multistate corporation, **24**:23–25
Sales/use tax
  compliance, multistate tax planning with, **24**:33
  exemptions, **24**:24–25
  nexus, **24**:25
  on services, **24**:25
SALT deduction, **5**:28
Same-sex couples, filing status, **3**:19
Saver's credit, **12**:8
  rate and AGI thresholds (2020), **12**:19
Saving Incentive Match for employees (SIMPLE) plans, **9**:25, **9**:31, **9**:32
Schedule 1, Additional Income and Adjustments to Income, **3**:32
  Form 1040, **3**:22
Schedule 2, Form 1040, **3**:22
Schedule A, Itemized Deductions (Form 1040), **3**:22, **10**:28
  comprehensive example of, **10**:27–28
  qualified residence interest indebtedness, **10**:17
Schedule C, Form 1040, Profit or Loss from Business, **3**:22, **6**:4, **6**:8, **6**:19, **8**:24, **8**:27, **9**:3, **10**:17, **15**:2
Schedule E, rent, royalty, partnership and fiduciary deductions, **6**:4, **6**:8, **10**:17
Schedule F, farming expenses, **6**:4, **6**:9
Schedule K, Partners Distributive Share Items, **21**:20, **21**:22–23
  Form 1120S, separately stated items, **22**:10
Schedule K-1, **21**:4, **21**:15
  example, **21**:28–30
  partnerships, **15**:3, **21**:25, **21**:26
Schedule L, Balance Sheets per Books, **21**:15, **21**:21
Schedule M-1, Reconciliation of Income (Loss) per Books With Income (Loss) per Return, , **17**:24–25, **21**:15, **21**:21
  conceptual diagram of, **17**:26
Schedule M-2, **22**:16–17
  Analysis of Partners' Capital Accounts, 21:15, **21**:21, **21**:35
  Analysis of Unappropriated Retained Earnings per Books, **17**:25
Schedule M-3, Net Income or Loss Reconciliation, **17**:26–28, **22**:17

Part I, financial information and net income (loss) reconciliation, **17**:27
Part II, reconciliation of net income (loss) per income statement of includible corporations with taxable income per return, **17**:27
Part III, reconciliation of expense/deduction items, **17**:28
Schedule SE (Form 1040), self-employment tax, **3**:22, **21**:38
Scholarships, **5**:7–8
  general information, **5**:7–8
  tax consequences of, **9**:17
  timing issues, **5**:8
Second-tier distributions, **28**:21–22
Section 61 definition of gross income, **4**:3
Section 62, deductions for adjusted gross income, **6**:3
Section 111 tax benefit rule, **5**:27
Section 121 exclusion, **13**:35, **13**:37, **13**:44
Section 121—sale of a residence, **13**:35–41
Section 132, exclusion treatment, **5**:17
Section 139, Disaster Relief Payment, **5**:2
Section 139F, wrongful incarceration, **5**:10
Section 162, trade or business expenses, **6**:4–5, **6**:5–6
Section 179 expensing, **8**:11, **19**:6, **9**:37, **14**:50
  and bonus depreciation, using effectively, **8**:15–18
  Election to Expense Certain Depreciable Business Assets, **8**:10–14
Section 183 presumptive rule, **6**:19
Section 197 intangibles, **6**:28, **21**:9
Section 199A, deduction for qualified business income, **15**:9–23
Section 212 expenses, **6**:4, **6**:5–6
Section 248, election to amortize organization expenditures, **17**:15
Section 262, sale or exchange of personal use assets, **14**:16
Section 267, sale or exchange between related taxpayers, **14**:16, **19**:23
Section 291, recapture rules, **17**:6
Section 331, liquidations effect on shareholder, **20**:8–9
Section 332, parent-subsidiary liquidations, **20**:9–13
Section 336, antistuffing rules, **20**:4–5
Section 338 election, **20**:12–14
Section 351, transfers of property to controlled corporations, **18**:2–4, **18**:5, **18**:15, **18**:17, **18**:24–26
  liquidation property transfers, **20**:4
Section 357, assumption of liabilities under, **18**:10–12
Section 362, basis step-down rules, **20**:4–5
Section 368, corporate reorganizations, **20**:15
Section 401(k) plans, **9**:25–26
Section 446, permissible accounting methods, **16**:10–11
Section 469, passive activity loss rules, **7**:19, **11**:5–9, **11**:13
Section 482, IRS's one-edged sword, **25**:11
Section 501, organizations exempt under, **23**:5, **23**:8–9, **23**:19
Section 529 plans (Qualified Tuition Program), **5**:26–27, **27**:11
Section 529A plans, **5**:27
Section 530 plans (Coverdell Education Savings Accounts), **5**:26–27
Section 530 relief, **9**:36

Section 704(b) book capital accounts, **21**:23–24, **21**:26, **21**:35
Section 721 exceptions, gain or loss on partnership contributions, **21**:7–9
Section 1031—like-kind exchanges, **13**:22–29, **14**:42–43, **18**:2–4
Section 1033, Involuntary Conversions, **13**:29–35, **14**:42–43
Section 1221, definition of capital asset, **14**:4–6
Section 1231 assets, **14**:28–35
Section 1231 gains and losses, **14**:29, **14**:48–49
Section 1231 lookback provision, **14**:32–35
Section 1231 netting procedure, **14**:31, **14**:32, **14**:44
Section 1231 property, **14**:29–30
Section 1231, reporting procedures, **14**:45
Section 1237, real property subdivided for sale, **14**:7–8
Section 1244 stock, **7**:6, **7**:21, **18**:23, **18**:24
  sale or exchange of, **14**:8
Section 1245 property, **14**:37–38
Section 1245 recapture, **14**:35–38, **14**:39, **14**:41–43, **14**:43–44, **17**:6
Section 1245 reporting procedures, **14**:45
Section 1250 property, **14**:38, **14**:40–41
Section 1250 recapture, **14**:38–41, **14**:41–43, **14**:43–44, **17**:6
Section 1250 reporting procedures, **14**:45
Section 1253, sale or exchange, franchises, trademarks, and trade names, **14**:12–14
Section 1374, built-in gains tax, **22**:23
Section 2053, tax planning for proper handling of other deductions and losses under, **27**:28
Section 2054, tax planning for proper handling of other deductions and losses under, **27**:28
Section 2513, gift-splitting election, **27**:25
Securities, **18**:6
  dealers in, **14**:7
  short sales of, **14**:18
  tax-exempt, **10**:16
  worthless, **7**:6, **14**:8
Securities and Exchange Commission, **6**:14, **26**:27
Security losses, **18**:21
Self-employed individual
  deductibility of medical insurance premiums, **10**:7
  estimated tax, **12**:23
  Form 1040, Schedule C, Profit or Loss From Business, **9**:3
  Form 1040-ES, **3**:25
  payments by, **12**:22–23
  self-employment tax, **12**:23
  See also Independent contractor
Self-employed individual retirement plans, **9**:31–32
  Keogh (H.R. 10) plans, **9**:31
  savings incentive match plan for employees (SIMPLE plans), **9**:32
  simplified employee pension plan (SEPs), **9**:32
  Solo Section 401 (k) plans, **9**:31–32
Self-employment
  income, **1**:18
  net earnings from, **12**:23
  treatment of distributive shares vs. guaranteed payments in partnership income, **21**:38–39

Self-employment tax, **1**:18, **12**:23
    NOLs and, **7**:20
    partnerships, **21**:38–39
    QBI deduction and, **15**:22
    SE treatment of general vs. limited
        partners, **21**:39
Senate, **2**:3–4
Senate Finance Committee, **2**:3–4
SEP. *See* Simplified employee pension plan
Separate home for parent, head of
        household status, **3**:19
Separate qualified property, determination
        of UBIA, **15**:23
Separate returns, married individuals, **3**:18
Separately stated items, **21**:5
    measuring partnership income, **21**:16–17
    Schedule K of Form 1120S, **22**:10
Series E bonds, **4**:11
Series EE bonds, **3**:33, **4**:11, **4**:32, **5**:25, **5**:31
Service requirement for depreciation, **8**:3
Services
    contribution of, **10**:19
    corporate treatment when issuing stock
        for, **18**:16–17
    defined under Section 351, **18**:5
    interest paid for, **10**:16
    sales/use tax on, **24**:25
    Section 721 exceptions, **21**:8–9
Settlor, **28**:3
Severance awards, **13**:31
Severance taxes, **1**:12
Shareholder
    bargain rental of corporate property by,
        19:17
    bargain sale of corporate property to,
        19:17
    basis of stock to, **18**:13
    corporate distributions to, **5**:24–25
    flow-through of separate items of income
        and loss to S corporation, **22**:11
    income of a CFC that is included in gross
        income of a U.S., **25**:24
    liquidations effect on, **20**:8–9, **20**:19–20
    loans to, **19**:18–19
    loans to a corporation by, **19**:19
    payments for the benefit of, **19**:17
    property dividends effect on, **19**:14
    small business corporation number of,
        22:4
    tax consequences of stock redemptions
        to, **19**:26
    tax consequences with and without the
        application of Section 351, **18**:15
Shareholder consent, S corporation status,
        22:6–7
Shareholder consequences, taxable
        corporate formation vs. tax-deferred
        Section 351 transaction, **18**:5
Shareholder distributions, tax treatment of
        in S corporation, **22**:13–17
    accumulated adjustments account (AAA),
        22:14–15
    C corporation AEP exists, **22**:14–17
    distribution ordering rules, **22**:15–16
    effect of terminating the S election, **22**:17
    no C corporation AEP, **22**:13–14
    other aspects of the AAA, **22**:16–17
    Schedule M-2, **22**:16–17
    Schedule M-3, Net Income or Loss
        Reconciliation, **22**:17
Shareholder limitation, small business
        corporation type of, **22**:5
Shareholder use of corporate-owned
        property, **19**:17

Shareholder's basis
    in S stock, S corporation, **22**:19–21
    of stock received in exchange for
        property, **18**:13
Shareholder-employee payment of
        corporate expenses, tax planning
        for, **17**:36
Shares of stock, freely transferable, **15**:7
Shifting income, tax planning, **2**:29–30
Short period, **16**:7
Short sale, **14**:16
    of securities, **14**:18
    special rules for, **14**:16–19
Short sales against the box
    disposition rules, **14**:17–18
    illustrations of treatment, **14**:18–19
Short taxable year, **16**:7
Short-term capital loss (STCL), **7**:2, **14**:26
Short-year election, **22**:13
Significant participation activity, **11**:14
Significant power, right, or continuing
        interest, **14**:13
SIMPLE plans. *See* Savings incentive match
        plan for employees
Simple trust, **28**:4
    distributions by, **28**:20
Simplicity, tax principles, **1**:8, **1**:9
Simplified Employee Pension (SEP) plans,
        9:25, **9**:31, **9**:32
Simplified method, **9**:18, **16**:32
    basis of like-kind property received,
        13:26
    office in the home expense, **9**:20–21
Simplifying America's Tax System (SATS)
        proposal, **1**:20–21
Sixteenth Amendment, ratification of, **1**:5
Skill Specification Outline (SSO), CPA
        examination, **2**:31
Small business corporation, **4**:16, **7**:6,
        18:23, **22**:3–5
    definition of, **22**:3–5
    ineligible corporations, **22**:3–4
    nonresident aliens, **22**:5
    number of shareholders, **22**:4
    one class of stock, **22**:4
    type of shareholder limitation, **22**:5
Small business, encouragement of, **1**:28
Small business stock (Section 1244 stock),
        7:6, **7**:21
    common investment loss limitation rules,
        11:24
Small Cases Division of the U.S. Tax Court,
        2:10, **2**:15
Smith, Adam, **1**:8
Social considerations, tax law, **1**:34
Social Security benefits, **4**:28–29
    provisional income, **4**:28
Social Security tax (old age, survivors and
        disability insurance), **1**:17, **12**:22
Software income, income sourcing rules,
        25:9
Sole proprietors, reporting procedures, **8**:24
    Schedule C, Section 212 expenses, **6**:4
Sole proprietorships
    business entities, **22**:2
    Schedule C of Form 1040, **15**:2
    tax attributes of, **22**:29–32
    tax treatment of, **15**:2, **15**:6
    See also Business forms
Solicitation of orders, **24**:6
Solo Section 401(k) plans, **9**:25, **9**:31–32
Sound business purpose, reorganization,
        20:15
Sourcing rules, **25**:10

Special allocation, **21**:5
Specific charge-off method, **7**:3–4
    tax treatment of bad debts using, **7**:4
Specific identification method, **16**:34
    identification problems, **13**:10
Specified service trade or business (SSTB),
        15:17
    qualified business income, **21**:29–30
Specified services businesses, QBI limitation
        for, **15**:17–21
Specified services limit, phase-in of,
        15:17–21
Specified services limitation, QBI deduction,
        15:12
Spin-off, corporate reorganizations, **20**:15
Split-off, corporate reorganizations, **20**:15
Split-up, corporate reorganizations, **20**:15
Sports franchises, **14**:14
Spousal IRAs, **9**:28–29
Spouses
    abandoned spouse rules, **3**:20
    living apart, **4**:18
    medical expenses incurred for, **10**:5
    surviving spouse status, **3**:19
Sprinkling trust, **28**:4
SSO (Skill Specification Outline), CPA
        examination, **2**:31
Standard deduction, **3**:6–8, **3**:21, **3**:32
    individuals not eligible for, **3**:8
    limitations for individuals who can be
        claimed as dependents, **3**:8
Standard Federal Tax Reporter, **2**:18
Standard mileage method, **9**:6–7
Stare decisis, doctrine of, **2**:10
Starker exchange, **13**:24
Startup costs, partnerships, **21**:12
Startup expenditures, **6**:17, **8**:25–28,
        17:16–17
State corporate income tax modifications,
        common, **24**:4
State income taxation
    decoupling from selected Federal tax
        changes, **1**:16
    piggyback approach to, **1**:16
State taxes
    and local excise taxes, **1**:11
    and local sales and use taxes of multistate
        corporations, **24**:23–25, **24**:26–27
    and the tax expense, **24**:17
    comparison of corporations and other
        forms of doing business, **15**:6
    death taxes, **1**:13, **27**:22
    income taxes, **1**:16–17
    overall limit on deductibility of, **10**:11
State/local taxes in context, multistate
        businesses, **24**:2
Statements on Standards for Tax Services
        (SSTSs), **1**:26, **26**:27–29
Statute of limitations, **1**:24, **26**:21–22
    assessment and, **26**:21
    assessment by the IRS, **1**:24
    limitations on refunds, **1**:24
    refund claims and, **26**:22
    tax planning considerations, **26**:31–32
Statutory authority, **5**:2–3
Statutory employees, **9**:5
Statutory expansions, **14**:7–8
    dealers in securities, **14**:7
    nonbusiness bad debts, **14**:8
    real property subdivided for sale (Section
        1237), **14**:7–8
Statutory (nominal) rates, **3**:25
Statutory notice of a deficiency (90-day
        letter), **26**:5

Statutory sources of the tax law, **2**:2–6
   arrangement of the Internal Revenue
      Code, **2**:5
   citing the code, **2**:5–6
   legislative process, **2**:3–4
   origin of the internal revenue code, **2**:2
Stealth taxes, **1**:31
Step down, **21**:43
Step transaction doctrine, reorganization,
   20:15
Step up, **21**:43
Stock
   qualified small business, **18**:24
   S corporation shareholder's basis in,
      22:19–21
Stock attribution rules, **19**:25–26
Stock corporate treatment when issuing for
   services, **18**:16–17
Stock dividends, **5**:25, **19**:19–20
   holding period of nontaxable, **13**:12
   nontaxable, **13**:11–12
Stock losses, **18**:21
Stock ownership test, **17**:21
Stock purchase vs. asset purchase, tax
   planning for, **20**:20
Stock received in exchange for property,
   shareholder's basis of **18**:13
Stock redemptions, **19**:21–29, **19**:33–34
   complete termination redemptions, **19**:28
   corporate shareholders, **19**:23
   disproportionate redemptions, **19**:27
   effect on earnings and profits, **19**:30
   effect on the corporation, **19**:29–30
   foreign shareholders prefer sale or
      exchange treatment, **19**:23
   historical background, **19**:24
   noncorporate shareholders, **19**:22
   not essentially equivalent redemptions,
      19:26–27
   recognition of gain or loss, **19**:29
   redemption expenditures, **19**:30
   redemptions to pay death taxes, **19**:28–29
   stock attribution rules, **19**:25–26
   summary of qualifying rules, **19**:24
   tax consequences to shareholders, **19**:26
Stock rights, **19**:20–21
Stock sales, tax planning for, **14**:48
Stock splits, **19**:20
Stock transfer taxes, **24**:26
Stock transferred, controlled corporations,
   18:6
Stock value test, **17**:21
Straight-line cost recovery under MACRS
   (personalty vs. realty), **8**:9
Straight-line depreciation election, **8**:6, **8**:8–9
Straight-line method, **8**:18
   classification of property, **8**:5–6
Streamlined Sales Tax Project (SSTP), **24**:23
Student loan interest
   deductibility of, **10**:18
   deductions for AGI, **10**:14
   tax consequences of, **9**:17
Subchapter C, Corporate Distributions and
   Adjustments, **2**:5
Subchapter F (exempt organizations) of the
   Code (Sections 501–530), **23**:2
Subchapter K, Partners and Partnerships,
   2:5
Subchapter S, Tax Treatment of S
   Corporations and Their Shareholders,
   2:5, **22**:2
Subpart F income, **25**:21–22
   and a CFC, **25**:22
   exceptions, **25**:22–23

Substantial authority, **26**:16, **26**:25, **26**:27
Substantial limitations or restrictions, **4**:9
Substantial presence test, **25**:26
Substantial restrictions, **4**:9–10
Substantial rights, patents, **14**:11–12
Substantiality, **21**:27
Substantially disproportionate redemption,
   summary of qualifying rules, **19**:24
Substantially identical property, **14**:17
Substantially rehabilitated, **12**:6
Substantiation
   accountable plan, **9**:33–34
   requirements, **6**:29, **8**:23
Substituted basis, **18**:13, **20**:18, **21**:7
Sunset provision, **1**:27
Super-full absorption costing system, **16**:31
Support test
   children of divorced or separated parents,
      3:14
   multiple support agreement, **3**:13–14
   qualifying child, **3**:10–11
   qualifying relative, **3**:13–14
   special rule for noncustodial parent, **3**:14
Supreme Court
   certiorari, **2**:25
   definition of interest, **10**:14
   See also U.S. Supreme Court
Supreme Court Reporter (S.Ct.), **2**:17
Surviving spouse, **3**:19
Suspended passive activity losses
   carryovers of, **11**:7–8
   fully taxable disposition, **11**:7
   impact of, **11**:6–7
Syndication costs, **21**:12

T

Tables (MACRS, AMT, and ADS), **8**:32–36
Tangible assets, expenditures for, **6**:27
Tangible personal property, charitable
   contributions, **17**:10
Tangible personalty, **10**:23
Tariffs, **1**:4, **1**:18
Tax accounting elections, partnerships,
   21:11–12
Tax administration, **1**:21–27, **26**:2–22
   administrative powers of the IRS,
      26:5–6
   audit process, **1**:21–24, **26**:6–9
   interest, **1**:24–25, **26**:12–13
   Internal Revenue Service, **1**:21
   IRS procedures—letter rulings, **26**:4
   offers in compromise and closing
      agreements, **26**:10–12
   organizational structure of the IRS,
      26:3–4
   statute of limitations, **1**:24, **26**:21–22
   tax practice, **1**:25–27
   tax principles, **1**:8, **1**:9
   taxpayer appeal process, **26**:9–10
   taxpayer penalties, **26**:13–20
   See also Audit process; Internal Revenue
      Service (IRS)
Tax and book depreciation, **8**:6
Tax attributes of different forms of business,
   22:29–32
Tax avoidance, **2**:29–30
Tax base, **1**:7
   erosion, global tax issues, **25**:4
Tax basis
   partner's capital account analysis, **21**:35
   reconciling partner's capital, **21**:23–24
Tax benefit rule, **5**:27–28, **10**:7

Tax bills, legislative process for, **2**:3
Tax computations, **3**:24–28
   unearned income of dependent children,
      3:26–28
Tax consequences
   of liability assumption, **18**:13
   of provisions dealing with education,
      9:17
   of stock redemptions to shareholders,
      19:26
   to shareholders and corporation, with
      and without the application of
      Section 351, **18**:15
Tax conventions, **2**:17
Tax Counseling for the Elderly (TCE), **26**:24
Tax Court, **2**:15
   appellate precedents and, **2**:13–14
   See also Courts
Tax Court of the United States Reports (T.C.),
   2:14–15
Tax credits, **12**:2, **12**:3–6, **12**:20–22
   adoption expenses credit, **12**:20
   American Opportunity credit, **12**:20
   child and dependent care expenses, **12**:2,
      12:14–16, **12**:20
   credit for certain retirement plan
      contributions, **12**:18–19, **12**:20
   credit for employer-provided family and
      medical leave, **12**:22
   credit for increasing research activities,
      12:21
   credit for small employer pension plan
      startup costs, **12**:21
   disabled access credit, **12**:3, **12**:21
   distinguished from tax deductions, **3**:26
   earned income credit, **12**:3, **12**:12–13,
      12:20
   education tax credit, **12**:16–18, **12**:20
   elderly or disabled credit, **12**:20
   employer-provided child care, **12**:21
   energy credits, **12**:18, **12**:21
   foreign tax credit (FTC), **12**:4, **12**:13–14,
      12:21, **13**:3, **25**:30
   general business credit, **12**:5–6, **12**:21
   lifetime learning credit, **12**:20
   low-income housing credit, **12**:21
   other, **12**:12–19
   refundable vs. nonrefundable, **12**:3–5
   rehabilitation expenditures credit, **12**:21
   specific business-related, **12**:6–12
   tax withheld on wages, **12**:20
   taxable income of trust and estates, **28**:19
   unified transfer, **27**:4–5
   work opportunity tax credit, **12**:22
Tax Cuts and Jobs Act (TCJA) of 2017, **1**:20
   and entity tax rates, **15**:8–9
   bonus depreciation and, **8**:14–15
   child tax credit, **2**:4
   corporate AMT, **17**:3, **17**:19
   corporate income tax rates, **15**:2, **17**:18
   CPA exam, **2**:33
   deductibility of miscellaneous itemized
      deductions, **9**:5
   employee fringe benefits, **5**:20
   entertainment and meal expenses, **9**:22
   estate tax exemption amount and, **19**:34
   international competitiveness, **15**:7
   international operations, **18**:3
   miscellaneous employee expenses and,
      9:24
   miscellaneous itemized deductions, **9**:33
   moving expenses, **9**:22
   noncorporate taxpayers with business
      income, **15**:2

nondisclosure agreement, **1**:29
qualified moving expense reimbursements and, **5**:19
qualified transportation fringes and, **5**:19
rollovers from Section 539 account to ABLE account, **5**:27
specified services businesses and QBI deduction, **15**:17
Tax deductions
distinguished from tax credits, **3**:26
time value of, **6**:12
Tax deferrals
from reserves, **16**:16
tax planning for, **4**:30–32
Tax determination, unearned income of dependent children, **3**:27
Tax evasion, **2**:30
Tax file memorandum, **2**:27
Tax formula, **3**:2–9, **17**:2
application of, **3**:9
basic, **1**:7
components of, **3**:2–6
deductions for AGI, **3**:5
deductions from AGI, **3**:6
exclusions, **3**:3
for individuals, **3**:2, **3**:3
for UBTI, **23**:16
gross income, **3**:3–4
income (broadly defined), **3**:2–3
standard deduction, **3**:6–8
tax base, **1**:7
tax rates, **1**:7
Tax Foundation, **15**:7
Tax gap, taxes collected and the, **26**:3
Tax haven, **25**:19–20
corporation, use of, **25**:20
U.S. persons with offshore income, **25**:19–20
Tax home, determining, **9**:10–11
Tax law
assessing the validity of other administrative sources of, **2**:24
courts influence of, **1**:33–34
economic considerations, **1**:27–28, **1**:34
equity considerations, **1**:29–31, **1**:34
IRS influence of, **1**:32–33, **1**:34
judicial sources of, **2**:10–17, **2**:24–25
legislative process, **2**:3–4
political considerations, **1**:31–32, **1**:34
primary sources of, **2**:25
revenue needs, **1**:27
secondary sources of, **2**:25
social considerations, **1**:28–29, **1**:34
statutory sources of, **2**:2–6
tax planning, **2**:28–31
tax research, **2**:20–28
tax research tools, **2**:18–20
understanding the Federal, **1**:27–34
Tax law sources, **2**:2–18
administrative, **2**:6–9
assessing the validity of other, **2**:25
judicial, **2**:10–17
other, **2**:17–18
statutory, **2**:2–6
Tax liabilities
comparative, **28**:7
substantial understatement of, **26**:16
Tax loopholes, **1**:32
Tax Management Portfolios, **2**:19
Tax model for unrelated business taxable income (UBTI), **23**:16–18
negative adjustments, **23**:16–17
positive adjustments, **23**:16

Tax Notes, **2**:8
Tax on generation-skipping transfers, **27**:24–25
Tax on investment income, **1**:18
Tax on pre-election built-in gain, **22**:23–24
Tax on prior transfers, credit for, **27**:22–23
Tax payments, **12**:19–27
Affordable Care Act (ACA) provisions, **12**:24–25
alternative minimum tax, **12**:25–27
by employers, **12**:22
by self-employed persons, **12**:22–23
Tax periodicals, **2**:18
Tax planning
amortization, **8**:32
asset purchase vs. stock purchase, **20**:20
cash method of accounting, **16**:37
casualty losses, **7**:21
components of, **2**:29–30
constructive dividends, **19**:33
corporate distributions, **19**:30–32
corporate operations, **17**:35–37
corporate vs. noncorporate forms of business organization, **15**:23, **17**:34–35
corporations vs. flow-through entities, **18**:28
cost identification and documentation considerations, **13**:41
cost recovery, **8**:31
credit for child and dependent care expenses, **12**:27
debt in the capital structure, **18**:26–27
education expenses, **9**:37
effect of additional tax on net investment income, **11**:26
employee fringe benefits, **5**:30–31
employment status, **9**:36
ensuring charitable contribution deduction, **10**:29–31
executive compensation, **6**:33
exempt entities,, **23**:21–22
Federal estate tax, **27**:26–28
Federal gift tax, **27**:25–26
follow-up procedures, **2**:30
for maximizing benefits, **14**:48
for operation of S corporation, **22**:27–28
for privileged communications, **26**:33
for stock sales, **14**:48
for year-end planning, **14**:48
foreign tax credit limitation and sourcing provisions, **25**:30
handling an IRS audit, **26**:30–31
hobby losses, **6**:32
implications of misclassifying workers, **9**:36–37
installment method of accounting, **16**:37–38
international taxation, **25**:29–30
inventories, **16**:38
investment income, **5**:31
investment interest limitation, **11**:26
investor losses, **18**:27–28
life insurance, **5**:30
liquidating distributions effect on corporation, **20**:19
liquidating distributions effect on shareholder, **20**:19–20
litigation considerations, **26**:32
maximizing medical deductions, **10**:29
multistate corporations, **24**:28–33
nontax considerations, **2**:29

optimizing the deduction for qualified business income, **15**:24
parent-subsidiary liquidations, **20**:20
partnership taxation, **21**:50–51
penalties, **26**:32–33
qualified dividends, **19**:32–33
S election, **22**:26–27
selecting assets to transfer, **18**:26
selection of property to pass at death, **13**:42
shifting income to other taxpayers, **4**:32
small business stock losses, **7**:21
standard deduction, **3**:32
statute of limitations, **26**:31–32
stock redemptions, **19**:33–34
strategies for letter rulings, **26**:30
tax avoidance and tax evasion, **2**:30
tax deferral, **4**:30–32
tax rate differentials, **3**:32–33
taxable year, **16**:37
to avoid nondeductible treatment, **10**:31
transfer pricing, **25**:30
transportation and travel expenses, **9**:37
trust and estate as income shifting device, **28**:24
unearned income of children, **3**:33
using passive activity losses, **11**:24–25
vacation homes, **6**:30–32
working with Section 351, **18**:24–26
Tax planning considerations
avoiding recapture, **14**:50
capital asset status, **14**:46–47
disallowed losses, **13**:42
involuntary conversions, **13**:44
like-kind exchanges, **13**:43
postponing and shifting recapture, **14**:49–50
property transactions, **13**:41–44
sale of a principal residence, **13**:44
selection of property for making gifts, **13**:41–42
timing of recapture, **14**:49
timing of Section 1231 gain, **14**:48–49
Tax policy considerations, **13**:3
Tax practice, **1**:25–27
ethical guidelines, **1**:26
IRS rules governing, **26**:23–24
statutory penalties imposed on tax return preparers, **1**:26–27
Tax preparer, **26**:24
penalties, **26**:24–26
regulating of, **26**:23
Tax principles, **1**:8
Tax profession and tax ethics, **26**:22–30
AICPA statements on standards for tax services, **26**:27–29
preparer penalties, **26**:24–26
privileged communications, **26**:26–27
Tax professional, **26**:22–23
unauthorized practice of law, **26**:23
Tax provision, **17**:30
current tax expense, **17**:30
Tax rate differentials, tax planning, **3**:32–33
Tax rate schedule for single taxpayers (2020), **3**:24
Tax rate schedule method, **3**:24–25
Tax rates, **1**:7, **3**:24
and personal exemption, for trusts and estates, **28**:6–7
comparison of corporations and other forms of doing business, **15**:4–5, **17**:18
on dividends, rational for reduced, **19**:12–13

Tax Reform Act (TRA) of 1986, **1**:20, **2**:2, **15**:8
Tax reform can make strange bedfellows, global tax issues, **25**:4
Tax reporting of partnership items, **21**:30
Tax research, **2**:20–28
  arriving at the solution or at alternative solutions, **2**:25–26
  assessing the validity of the tax law sources, **2**:23–25
  communicating tax research, **2**:26–28
  identifying the problem, **2**:22
  locating the appropriate tax law sources, **2**:23
  refining the problem, **2**:22
Tax research process, **2**:22
Tax research tools, **2**:18–20
  commercial tax services, **2**:18–19
  noncommercial electronic (online) tax services, **2**:19–20
  using electronic (online) tax services, **2**:19
Tax return
  procedural aspects of preparing, SSTS No. 3, **26**:28
  questions on, SSTS No. 2, **26**:28
Tax return positions, SSTS No. 1, **26**:27
Tax return preparation, outsourcing of, **1**:26
Tax return preparers, statutory penalties imposed on, **1**:26–27
Tax services
  commercial, **2**:18–19
  statements on standards for, **1**:26
Tax shelters, **11**:2, **21**:13
  penalty for failure to provide information regarding, **26**:20
  problem, **11**:2–4
Tax system design, **1**:6–8
Tax table, **3**:24
Tax treaties, **2**:17, **25**:5–6
  in force as of 2019, U.S. income, **25**:6
  taxing rights, **25**:5
  withholding rates, **25**:6
Tax treatment of
  bad debts using specific charge-off method, **7**:4
  business forms compared, **15**:6
  capital gains and losses of noncorporate taxpayers, **14**:19–27
  payments and transfers pursuant to divorce agreements and decrees, **4**:21
  S Corporations and Their Shareholders, Subchapter S, **2**:5
Taxable distribution, GSTT, **27**:24
Taxable estate, **1**:13, **27**:19–22
  expenses, indebtedness, and taxes, **27**:19
  losses, **27**:19
  marital deduction, **27**:20–22
  state death taxes, **27**:22
  transfers to charity, **27**:19–20
Taxable gift, **27**:3
Taxable income, **1**:7
  allocation and apportionment of deductions, **25**:9–10
  computation of E & P with additions to, **19**:3
  computation of E & P with subtractions from, **19**:3–4
  computing consolidated, **17**:21–23
  Form 1065 example of reconciling, **21**:23

income taxation of individuals and corporations compared, **17**:17
  of entity and its beneficiaries, **28**:9
  of trusts and estates, **28**:8–20
  S corporation computation of, **22**:9–11
  vs. financial accounting income, **4**:4–5
Taxable termination, GSTT, **27**:24
Taxable transactions
  computing the ceiling, **23**:5–6
  determining the tax, **23**:6
  effects of lobbying, **23**:5–6
  intermediate sanctions on excess benefit transactions, **23**:6–7
  other taxes on certain exempt entities, **23**:8
  taxes on exempt entities, **23**:5–8
Taxable year, **4**:6, **16**:37
  of the partnership, **21**:13–14
Taxation
  alleviating the effect of multiple, **1**:30
  approaching study of, **1**:2–4
  defined, **1**:2
  general scheme of, **14**:3
  history of U.S., **1**:4–6
  in our lives, **1**:2–3
  of benefits for IRAs, **9**:29
  of income and distributions, **4**:17
  of virtual currency, **3**:31–32
  on the CPA examination, **2**:31–33
  relevance of to accounting and finance professionals, **1**:3–4
  territorial system, **3**:5
  worldwide system, **3**:5
  See also International taxation
TaxCenter, **2**:19
Taxes, **10**:10–13
  ad valorem, **1**:10
  additional Medicare tax on unearned income, **12**:24–25
  additional Medicare tax on wages, **12**:24
  administrative, **24**:26
  capital stock and franchise, **24**:26–27
  carbon, **1**:21
  consumption, **1**:20
  deductibility as, **10**:10–11
  deductible and nondeductible, **10**:11
  direct or indirect, **1**:2
  distinguished from fees, **10**:10
  employment, **1**:17–18, **12**:19
  estate, **1**:13
  estimated, **12**:23
  excise, **1**:2, **1**:5, **1**:11
  fair, **1**:20
  FICA, **1**:17–18
  financial transaction, **1**:21
  flat, **1**:20
  franchise, **1**:5, **1**:19, **24**:26–27
  FUTA, **1**:18
  gift taxes, **1**:14–15
  income, **1**:2, **1**:4, **1**:5, **1**:6, **1**:15–17, **10**:13
  individuals and, **1**:5
  inheritance, **1**:13
  interest on deferred, **16**:25
  major types of, **1**:8–21
  mass, **1**:6
  Medicare, **1**:17
  national sales, **1**:20
  other U.S., **1**:18–19
  partnership income, **21**:38–40
  penalty for failure to make deposits of, **26**:19–20
  progressive, **1**:7, **1**:29
  property, **1**:2, **1**:10–11, **10**:11–13
  proposed U.S. taxes, **1**:20–21

regressive or progressive, **1**:29
  sales, **1**:2, **1**:12, **10**:13, **24**:24
  self-employment, **12**:23
  severance, **1**:12
  Social Security, **1**:17
  state and local, **1**:19, **10**:10, **10**:11
  stealth, **1**:31
  transaction taxes, **1**:11–12
  transfer, **27**:2–7
  types of at death, **1**:13, **27**:3
  use, **1**:12, **24**:24
  value added, **1**:20–21
Taxes and tax expense, state/local, **24**:17
Taxes collected and the tax gap, **26**:3
Taxes imposed on private foundations, **23**:11–12
Taxes in U.S, overview of, **1**:19
Taxes on exempt entities, **23**:5–8
  taxable transactions, **23**:5–8
Taxes on lobbying expenditures by public charities, **23**:7
Tax-exempt income, expenses and interest relating to, **6**:29–30
Tax-exempt securities, **10**:16
Tax-free reorganizations
  basis, **20**:18–19
  gain or loss, **20**:17–18
  summary of tax consequences, **20**:15–19
Tax-free transaction, **13**:22
Taxpayer use test, replacement property, **13**:32
Taxpayers subject to passive activity loss rules, **11**:9–10
Taxpayers with multiple businesses, qualified trade or business (QTB), **15**:12
Tax-related websites, **2**:21
Technical Advice Memoranda (TAMs), **2**:9, **26**:5
Technical Expedited Advice Memorandums (TEAMs), **2**:9
Temporary assignments, travel expenses, **9**:10
Temporary Regulations, **2**:7
Tenants by the entirety, **27**:6
Tenants in common, **27**:6
  federal estate tax treatment, **27**:15–17
Tentative minimum tax, **12**:5
Term certain, **28**:4
Terminable interests, **27**:21
  limitation, taxable estate, **27**:21–22
Terminally ill, accelerated death benefits and, **5**:5
Territorial system approach to taxation, **3**:5
  additional tax on intangible income, **25**:25
  one-time 2017 transition tax, **25**:25
  taxing foreign earnings, **18**:3
  U.S. persons with offshore income, **25**:23–25
  U.S. taxpayers, **25**:3
Test based on facts and circumstances, **11**:13
Testamentary (death) transfers, federal gift tax, **27**:8–9
Tests based on current participation, **11**:13
Tests based on prior participation, **11**:13
Theft losses, **7**:8
  as capital recovery, **13**:6
  Form 4684, Casualties and Thefts, **14**:45
  See also Casualty loss
Thin capitalization, **18**:19–20

30-day letter, **26**:9
Throwback rule, sales factor, **24**:13–14
Tiebreaker rules, qualifying child, **3**:11
Tier system of distributions, trusts, **28**:2
Time value of tax deductions, **6**:12
Timing of expense recognition
    accrual method requirements, **6**:10–11
    cash method requirements, **6**:10
    deductions and losses, **6**:9–12
    importance of taxpayer's method of
        accounting, **6**:9–10
    prepaid expenses—12-month rule,
        6:12
    time value of tax deductions, **6**:12
Timing of income recognition, **4**:6–12
Topical, commercial tax services, **2**:18
Total gain, installment method computing
    of, **16**:20
Trade names, **14**:12–14
Trade or business
    business interest expense limitation and,
        17:8
    casualty/theft losses, **7**:15
    conducting, **23**:13
    expenses, Section 162, **6**:4–5
Trademarks, **8**:25, **14**:12–14
Traditional IRA vs. Roth IRA, **9**:30
Transaction taxes, **1**:11–12
Transactions between related parties,
    6:28–29
Transfer for valuable consideration, life
    insurance proceeds, **5**:6
Transfer pricing, **25**:10–13, **25**:30
    arrangements, preemptive, **25**:12–13
    example, **25**:12
    income shifting, **25**:10–12
Transfer taxes, **27**:2–7
    formula for the federal estate tax, **27**:4
    formula for the gift tax, **27**:3–4
    key property concepts, separate and joint
        asset ownership, **27**:6–7
    nature of, **27**:2–5
    persons subject to, **27**:2–3
    types of tax at death, **27**:3
    unified transfer tax credit, **27**:4–5
    valuation for federal transfer tax
        purposes, **27**:5–6
Transient occupancy tax (TOT), **1**:11, **24**:26
Transition tax, territorial system one-time
    2017, **25**:25
Transparency and visibility, tax principles,
    1:8, **1**:9
Transportation expenses, **9**:5–9, **9**:37
    commuting expenses, **9**:6
    computation of automobile expenses,
        9:6–9
    qualified expenses, **9**:5–6
Transportation for medical treatment,
    deductible medical expenses, **10**:6
Transportation income, income sourcing
    rules, **25**:8–9
Travel expenses, **9**:9–14, **9**:37
    away-from-home requirement, **9**:10–11
    combined business and pleasure travel,
        9:12–14
    definition of travel expenses, **9**:9–10
    domestic travel for business and pleasure,
        9:12–13
    foreign travel for business and pleasure,
        9:13
    record-keeping requirements, **9**:14
    restrictions on, **9**:11–12
Travel status, **9**:5
Treasury Decisions (TDs), **2**:7, **2**:8–9

Treasury Department Regulations, **2**:6–7,
    2:24
Treasury Regulations, assessing the validity
    of, **2**:23–24
Treaty relief, **27**:23
Treaty shopping, **25**:20
Trial courts, **2**:10, **2**:11–12
    See also Courts
Trust
    and estate, income taxation of, **28**:2–26
    as income-shifting device, **28**:24
    beneficiaries of, **4**:16, **28**:20–23
    complex, **28**:4, **28**:20–22
    definition of, **28**:2–5
    divorce trust, **28**:2
    for minors, **28**:2
    Form 1041, **28**:23
    grantor, **28**:4
    income from, **4**:16–17
    income interest in, **28**:4
    life insurance trust, **28**:2
    living (revocable) trust, **28**:2
    motivations for creating, **28**:2
    procedural matters, **28**:23–24
    remainder interest in, **28**:4
    simple, **28**:4
    sprinkling, **28**:4
    stock attribution rules, **19**:25
    structure of, **28**:3
    tax characteristics of, **28**:6
    taxable income of, **28**:8–20
Trust taxation
    additional tax on net investment income,
        28:8
    alternative minimum tax, **28**:7–8
    nature of, **28**:5–8
    tax accounting periods and methods, **28**:6
    tax rates and personal exemption, **28**:6–7
Trustee, **28**:3
Tuition expenses, deductible medical
    expenses, **10**:4
Tuition reduction plans for employee's
    spouse and dependents, **5**:7
25% gain netting rules, **14**:40
Two-year ownership rule exceptions
    basis of new residence, **13**:41
    change in place of employment, **13**:39
    health issues, **13**:39
    implications of renting or using a
        residence as a home office, **13**:41
    partial Section 121 exclusion, **13**:40
    sale of a residence, **13**:39–41
    unforeseen circumstances, **13**:40
Type A, mergers or consolidation, **20**:15
Type B, acquisition by voting stock-for-
    stock exchange, **20**:15
Type C, acquisition by voting stock-for-asset
    exchange, **20**:15
Type D, divisive exchange, **20**:15
Type E, recapitalization, **20**:15
Type F, change in identity, form, or place of
    organization, **20**:15
Type G, bankruptcy or receivership
    proceeding, **20**:15

U

U.S. corporate taxes and international
    business competitiveness, **15**:7
U.S. Court of Appeals, **2**:12, **2**:15
    See also Courts
U.S. Court of Federal Claims, **2**:10, **2**:15
    See also Courts

U.S. District Court, **2**:10, **2**:11–12, **2**:15
    judicial citations of, **2**:16–17
    See also Courts
U.S. government publications, definition of
    capital asset, **14**:4, **14**:6
U.S. income tax treaties in force as of 2019,
    25:6
U.S. persons with offshore income, **25**:15–25
    creating cross-border business entity,
        25:18–19
    export property, licenses, foreign
        branches, **25**:15–18
    movement toward a territorial system,
        25:23–25
    offshore (foreign) corporations controlled
        by U.S. persons, **25**:20–23
    tax havens, **25**:19–20
U.S. real property interest (USRPI), **25**:28
U.S. shareholder, **25**:21
U.S. Supreme Court, **2**:13, **2**:15
    appeals to, **2**:14
    judicial citations of, **2**:17
    See also Courts
U.S. Tax Cases (USTC), **2**:16–17
U.S. Tax Court, **2**:10, **2**:11–12
    judicial citations of, **2**:14–16
    jurisdiction of, **2**:11
    Small Cases Division, **2**:10
    website (ustaxcourt.gov), **2**:15
    See also Courts
U.S. taxation of cross-border transactions,
    25:3–4
U.S. trade or business, **25**:27
    U.S. taxation of nonresident aliens
        engaged in, **25**:27–28
    U.S. taxation of nonresident aliens not
        engaged in, **25**:27
U.S. transfer taxes and NRAs, **27**:3
U.S.-source income, **25**:6
UDITPA (Uniform Division of Income for
    Tax Purposes Act), **24**:6
Ultimate destination concept, sales factor,
    24:13
Unadjusted basis immediately after
    acquisition (UBIA)
    QBI deduction determination of, **15**:23
    qualified business income, **21**:29
Unclaimed property, **24**:26
    collections of, **24**:26
Understatement penalty, **26**:16
Undervaluation, penalty for, **26**:17
Undistributed income of private
    foundations, **23**:12
Unearned income, **1**:18, **3**:26, **4**:12
    additional Medicare tax on, **12**:24–25
Unearned income of dependent children,
    3:26–28, **3**:33
    election to claim certain unearned
        income on parent's return, **3**:27–28
    Form 8814, Parents' Election to Report
        Child's Interest and Dividends, **3**:28
    net unearned income, **3**:26
    other rules, **3**:28
    tax determination, **3**:27
Unemployment compensation, **4**:27–28
Unified transfer tax, **27**:2, **27**:11
    credit, **1**:13, **1**:14–15, **27**:4–5
    exclusion amount, **27**:5
    rate schedule, **1**:14
Uniform capitalization (UNICAP) rules,
    16:31–33
Uniform Gifts to Minors Act, **4**:32
Uniform Principal and Income Act, **28**:10
Unit of Property (UOP), **6**:26–27

Unitary business defined, **24**:19
Unitary operations, multistate tax planning for restructuring corporate entities, **24**:29
Unitary theory, **24**:18–21
  consolidated and combined returns, **24**:21
  tax effects of, **24**:19–21
  unitary business defined, **24**:19
United States Board of Tax Appeals Reports (B.T.A.), **2**:15
United States Reports, Lawyer's Edition (L.Ed.), **2**:17
United States Supreme Court Reports (U.S.), **2**:17
United States Tax Reporter, **2**:18
Unit-livestock-price method, **16**:36
Unlimited liability, sole proprietors and general partners, **15**:7
Unrealized receivables, **21**:42
  and inventory defined, **21**:42
  hot assets, **21**:48
Unreasonable compensation, **19**:18
Unreasonable position, **26**:25
Unrecaptured Section 1250 gain, **14**:20, **14**:39–41
  net Section 1231 gain limitation, **14**:40
  Section 1250 property for purposes of, **14**:40–41
  special 25% gain netting rules, **14**:40
Unreimbursed employee expenses, **9**:34
Unreimbursed employment-related expenses, child and dependent care expenses, **12**:15
Unrelated business income (UBI), **23**:12
Unrelated business income tax (UBIT), **23**:12–19, **23**:22
  unrelated business taxable income (UBTI), **23**:16–19
  unrelated debt-financed income, **23**:18–19
  unrelated trade or business, **23**:13–16
Unrelated business taxable income (UBTI), **23**:5, **23**:16–19
  general tax model, **23**:16–18
  tax formula for, **23**:16
Unrelated debt-financed income, **23**:18–19
  definition of acquisition indebtedness, **23**:19

Unrelated trade or business of exempt entities **23**:13–16
  conducting a trade or business, **23**:13
  not substantially related to the exempt purpose, **23**:13–15
  regularly carried on by the organization, **23**:15–16
Use or lose plans, **5**:16
Use tax, **1**:12
  and sales taxes, **24**:24
  state and local, of a multistate corporation, **24**:23–25

V

Vacation homes, **6**:21, **6**:30–32
  common investment loss limitation rules, **11**:24
  personal/rental use, **6**:23–25
  primarily personal use, **6**:22–23
  primarily rental use, **6**:23
  rental of, **6**:21–25
Valuation requirements for charitable contributions, **10**:22
Value added tax (VAT), **1**:20–21
Virtual currency, **3**:31–32
Visibility and transparency, tax principles, **1**:8, **1**:9
Voluntary Classification Settlement Program (VCSP), **9**:37
Voluntary revocation, **22**:7–8
Volunteer Income Tax Assistance (VITA) program, **26**:24
Voting power, **18**:6
  test, **17**:21
Voting stock-for-asset exchange, corporate reorganizations, **20**:15
Voting stock-for-stock exchange, corporate reorganizations, **20**:15

W

W-2 wages
  QBI deduction determination of, **15**:23
  qualified business income, **21**:29
W-2 wages limit, QBI deduction, **15**:14

W-2 wages/capital investment limit, **15**:14–15, **15**:18
  phase-in of, **15**:15–16
Wages
  additional Medicare tax on, **12**:24
  and capital investment limitation, QBI deduction, **6**:7–8, **15**:12
  Form W-2, Wage and Tax Statement, **3**:25
  QBI deduction limitation based on, **15**:14–16
Wash sale, **13**:16–19
  rules, **13**:18
Water's edge, **24**:21
Wealth of Nations, The, **1**:8
Websites, tax-related, **2**:21
Weight of authority, **2**:2
Westlaw, **2**:19
WestlawNext, **2**:19
Wherewithal to pay, **1**:30, **13**:22, **18**:2
Whistleblower program, **26**:7
Withholding, false information with respect to, **26**:19
Withholding requirements for non-U.S. partners, **21**:38
Work opportunity tax credit, **12**:7, **12**:22
Workers' compensation, **5**:10
Working condition fringes, **5**:17, **5**:18, **5**:20
Worldwide income tax base, **4**:3
Worldwide system approach to taxation, **3**:5
  for U.S. taxpayers, **25**:3
Worthless securities, **7**:6
  and Section 1244 stock, sale or exchange of, **14**:8
  common investment loss limitation rules, **11**:24
Writ of Certiorari, **2**:14
Wrongful incarceration, Section 139F, **5**:10

Y

Year of deduction, medical expenses, **10**:7
Year-end planning, tax planning for, **14**:48

Z

Zero-coupon bonds, **5**:31

CENGAGE | CNOW^{V2}

Make a better grade with CNOWv2
Here's how to make every study moment count

Multi-media study-tools such as videos, games, flashcards, crossword puzzles and more allow you to review and check your understanding of key concepts to help you prepare for quizzes and exams.

The *MindTap Reader* is fully optimized for the iPad, provides note-taking and highlighting capabilities and features an online text-to-speech application that vocalizes the content—offering a fun reading experience.

Flashcards—use the *MindTap Reader's* pre-made flashcards or make your own. Then print the cards and get to work.

CNOWv2 Users Achieve Higher Grades
(Student Grades, Scale = 0-100; N=246)

Treatment: 87
Control: 83

(X-axis: 80, 81, 82, 83, 84, 85, 86, 87, 88, 89, 90)

Legend: ■ Final Course Grades

Ask your instructor about *CNOWv2* for this course.
cengage.com/cnowv2

AMT Formula for Individuals

Taxable income (increased by any standard deduction taken)
Plus or minus: Adjustments
Plus: Preferences
Equals: Alternative minimum taxable income (AMTI)
Minus: Exemption
Equals: Alternative minimum tax (AMT) base
Multiplied by: 26% or 28% rate
Equals: Tentative minimum tax before foreign tax credit
Minus: AMT foreign tax credit
Equals: Tentative minimum tax (TMT)
Minus: Regular tax liability (less any foreign tax credit)
Equals: AMT (if TMT > regular tax liability)